The Bill James Handbook 2006

Baseball Info Solutions

www.baseballinfosolutions.com

Published by ACTA Sports

A Division of ACTA Publications

Cover by Tom A. Wright

Cover Photos by Scott Jordan Levy

First Edition: November 2005

Published by:
ACTA Sports, a division of ACTA Publications
5559 W. Howard Street, Skokie, IL 60077
(800) 397-2282
www.actasports.com www.actapublications.com

ISBN 0-87946-296-5

Printed in the United States of America

Acknowledgments

Obviously, baseball would be a different game today without Bill James. We all thank you for your continued innovation and creative thinking.

BIS has quickly become the best in the business due in large part to the efforts of its two top dogs, John Dewan and Steve Moyer. Thanks for your effort, patience, and knowledge in leading the company to success.

Damon Lichtenwalner has been with BIS from the get-go and without him the company simply would not function. The most common phrase heard in the office is, "I don't know…we'll have to ask Damon" and is an indicator as to how much everyone relies on his expertise.

The full time staff at BIS continues to grow each year. Andy Bausher is the resident pitch analysis expert and is now working through his fourth book. Matt Lorenzo has been a great asset to the company on the programming and operations side since joining the staff in 2004. Nate Birtwell has been deemed Steve's RHM and has had a hand in numerous projects while organizing a more coordinated operations effort for the season. Gary Read is filled with ideas and is always willing to go the extra mile. Todd Radcliffe trained our staff of helpers and performed countless hours of quality control on our data. Jim Swavely joined the staff prior to the season and has been a big help with programming issues. Pat Quinn has made the book process run more smoothly as we look to improve from year to year.

A special thanks goes out to Ryan Galla and Jon Vrecsics for their efforts during their time at BIS as well.

We tried something new this year and hired a group of interns to help collect our data. We hope that this group of young guys, looking to break into the baseball industry got as much out of the experience as we got out of them. Thank you to Dedan Brozino, Trevor Haley, Matt Halvorson, Jimmy Hartley, Brett Kelley, Rob Metzler, Thom Partridge, Tom Yost, and Zach Newberry.

Greg Pierce, Andrew Yankech, and the entire ACTA Sports staff are a tremendous help each year.

Thanks to our friends in the baseball industry: Greg Ambrosius, Jeff Barton, Matthew Berry, Jim Callis, Mike Canter, Frank Cooney, Doug Dennis, Jeff Erickson, Steve Goldstein, Steve Greenberg, Jason Grey, John Hunt, Peter Kreutzer, Josh Lewin, Gene McCaffrey, Bob Meyerhoff, Rob Neyer, Mat Olkin, David Pinto, Mike Phillips, Hal Richman, Ryan/Sanders Baseball, Peter Schoenke, Jon Sciambi, Ron Shandler, John Sickels, Sam Walker, Mark Watson, Rick Wolf, Trace Wood, and Todd Zola.

Many thanks to our remote helpers: Darin Brown, Sean Clennon, Brian Dewberry-Jones, David Dick, Joe Dimino, Robert Dudek, Durward Hamil, Don Masi, Al Melchior, John Menna, Gus Papadopoulos, Theo Papadopoulos, Daryl Ravani, Bob Routier, Kyle Schmidt, Wayne Sit, and John Wagner.

Last, but certainly not least, thanks to our best crew of local helpers yet: James Blas, Corey Brodhead, Mike Brodhead, Ryan Brodhead, Peter Daley, Kevin Drake, Pete Febbraro, Brian Frazier, Eric Holden, Dave Houck, Wes Koser, Chippy Lichtenwalner, Gino Pavan, Eric Schmitt, Mark Shive, Charlie Stivali, Brendan Van Ackeren, Dustin Webb, Mike Welsh, and Dan Zettlemoyer.

Dedication

Baseball is a game, meant to provide a few hours of refuge from the concerns of the world. But sometimes things happen that are so awful they cannot be ignored, even by the world of sports.

We dedicate this year's edition of *The Bill James Handbook* to the victims and survivors of hurricanes Katrina and Rita and pray that in the midst of the efforts to rebuild their communities the people of Louisiana, Mississippi, Alabama, and Texas will find time to take a few hours of enjoyment to watch or coach or play the great American pastime.

Gregory F. Augustine Pierce
President - ACTA Publications

Table of Contents

Introduction

As I type these words, the opening game of the 2005 playoffs – Padres @ Cardinals, Jake Peavy @ Chris Carpenter – Tuesday, October 4, 2005, is in the bottom of the seventh inning. It's the beginning of the end for baseball this year and the beginning of the end of the busy season (as if it's not busy during the offseason) here at Baseball Info Solutions.

And what a season it was. Derrek Lee and Andruw Jones finally put up the kinds of offensive seasons that were predicted for them as prospects. Bartolo Colon and Bob Wickman proved, as Billy Beane might say, one doesn't have to "sell jeans" to be a successful major league baseball player. The Astros, Indians and A's made torrid runs at playoff berths after terrible beginnings. The Orioles collapsed after 62 days in first place. Barry Bonds was almost nonexistent, then made a big splash when he finally showed up. How long of an Intro do you want?

In any case, I won't mention steroids, because you won't find any here. Instead you'll find all the Handbook features you look forward to every November, plus new Pitcher Projections, plus more Leader Boards than ever before, plus a brand new Baserunning section, and the obligatory "much, much more." To quote the recently-famous philosopher Napoleon, with the 2006 Bill James Handbook, "all your wildest dreams will come true."

Have fun.

Steve Moyer
President
Baseball Info Solutions

1

2005 Team Statistics

2005 American League Standings

Overall

EAST							CENTRAL							WEST						
Team	W-L	Pct	GB	D1	LD1	LLd	Team	W-L	Pct	GB	D1	LD1	LLd	Team	W-L	Pct	GB	D1	LD1	LLd
New York Yankees	95-67	.586	0.0	20	10/2	1.0	Chicago White Sox	99-63	.611	0.0	182	10/2	15.0	Los Angeles Angels	95-67	.586	0.0	170	10/2	8.5
Boston Red Sox*	95-67	.586	0.0	98	10/2	5.5	Cleveland Indians	93-69	.574	6.0	0	-	0.0	Oakland Athletics	88-74	.543	7.0	23	9/15	2.0
Toronto Blue Jays	80-82	.494	15.0	13	4/16	1.5	Minnesota Twins	83-79	.512	16.0	5	4/17	0.0	Texas Rangers	79-83	.488	16.0	11	6/7	1.0
Baltimore Orioles	74-88	.457	21.0	69	6/23	4.5	Detroit Tigers	71-91	.438	28.0	3	4/7	0.0	Seattle Mariners	69-93	.426	26.0	6	4/20	1.0
Tampa Bay Devil Rays	67-95	.414	28.0	2	4/9	0.0	Kansas City Royals	56-106	.346	43.0	0	-	0.0							

* Clinched Wild Card Birth on 10/1. Division Clinch Dates: Los Angeles 9/27, Chicago 9/29, New York 10/1.
D1 = Number of days a team had at least a share of first place of their division; LD1 = Last date the team had at least a share of first place; LLd = The largest number of games that a team led their division

East Division

Tm	AT		VERSUS							CONDITIONS				GAME			MONTHLY						ALL-STAR	
	Home	Road	East	Cent	West	NL	LHS	RHS		Day	Night	Grass	Turf	1-Rn	5+Rn	XInn	Apr	May	June	July	Aug	S/O	Pre	Post
NYY	53-28	42-39	41-33	18-13	25-14	11-7	30-23	65-44		33-22	62-45	83-58	12-9	27-16	29-20	4-4	10-14	17-10	12-14	17-9	19-10	20-10	46-40	49-27
Bos	54-27	41-40	39-35	22-13	22-13	12-6	29-22	66-45		30-19	65-48	87-54	8-13	27-15	28-22	6-2	12-11	16-12	17-9	14-13	18-9	18-13	49-38	46-29
Tor	43-38	37-44	38-36	15-19	19-17	8-10	23-24	57-58		22-35	58-47	30-39	50-43	16-31	25-14	4-6	13-12	15-12	12-15	13-12	13-15	14-16	44-44	36-38
Bal	36-45	38-43	36-37	13-22	17-19	8-10	25-30	49-58		23-30	51-58	62-78	12-10	14-25	17-30	2-6	16-7	15-13	12-15	8-18	11-17	12-18	47-40	27-48
TB	40-41	27-54	31-44	15-22	18-14	3-15	20-32	47-63		17-23	50-72	22-46	45-49	29-25	10-27	5-4	8-16	11-18	8-18	13-14	15-13	12-16	28-61	39-34

Central Division

Tm	AT		VERSUS							CONDITIONS				GAME			MONTHLY						ALL-STAR	
	Home	Road	East	Cent	West	NL	LHS	RHS		Day	Night	Grass	Turf	1-Rn	5+Rn	XInn	Apr	May	June	July	Aug	S/O	Pre	Post
CWS	47-34	52-29	20-13	52-22	15-22	12-6	23-20	76-43		37-20	62-43	89-58	10-5	35-19	21-16	11-8	17-7	18-10	17-10	15-11	12-16	19-12	57-29	42-34
Cle	43-38	50-31	19-17	40-35	19-14	15-3	26-24	67-45		24-29	69-40	84-62	9-7	22-36	34-14	6-8	9-14	16-11	17-10	13-16	19-8	19-10	47-41	46-28
Min	45-36	38-43	18-12	40-35	17-22	8-10	24-24	59-55		25-25	58-54	33-42	50-37	27-30	17-16	15-8	15-8	14-13	13-13	12-16	16-13	13-16	48-38	35-41
Det	39-42	32-49	19-19	29-46	14-17	9-9	21-21	50-70		26-31	45-60	65-80	6-11	22-26	20-25	8-3	11-11	12-15	13-13	14-15	13-13	8-24	42-44	29-47
KC	34-47	22-59	13-22	26-49	8-26	9-9	17-38	39-68		22-32	34-74	52-91	4-15	18-30	13-37	4-8	6-18	8-19	12-14	12-16	5-21	13-18	30-57	26-49

West Division

Tm	AT		VERSUS							CONDITIONS				GAME			MONTHLY						ALL-STAR	
	Home	Road	East	Cent	West	NL	LHS	RHS		Day	Night	Grass	Turf	1-Rn	5+Rn	XInn	Apr	May	June	July	Aug	S/O	Pre	Post
LAA	49-32	46-35	19-22	30-17	34-22	12-6	25-25	70-42		24-22	71-45	91-58	4-9	33-26	26-11	9-10	13-11	17-11	17-9	13-14	14-13	21-9	52-36	43-31
Oak	45-36	43-38	21-27	25-15	32-24	10-8	28-18	60-56		35-20	53-54	83-66	5-8	26-24	29-19	10-4	12-12	7-20	19-8	20-6	17-11	13-17	44-43	44-31
Tex	44-37	35-46	20-27	25-15	25-32	9-9	14-25	65-58		27-24	52-59	72-76	7-7	24-29	23-24	7-8	12-13	18-7	10-17	13-14	11-18	15-14	46-40	33-43
Sea	39-42	30-51	17-25	21-26	21-34	10-8	22-27	47-66		23-31	46-62	64-84	5-9	26-23	21-20	2-5	12-12	9-18	12-14	12-15	11-17	13-17	39-48	30-45

Team vs. Team Breakdown

	EAST					CENTRAL					WEST			
	NYY	Bos	Tor	Bal	TB	CWS	Cle	Min	Det	KC	LAA	Oak	Tex	Sea
New York Yankees	-	10	12	11	8	3	4	3	5	3	4	7	7	7
Boston Red Sox	9	-	7	10	13	4	4	4	6	4	6	6	7	3
Toronto Blue Jays	6	11	-	10	11	2	2	2	3	6	5	5	3	6
Baltimore Orioles	7	8	9	-	12	2	1	3	3	4	2	4	4	7
Tampa Bay Devil Rays	11	6	8	6	-	2	6	0	2	5	5	5	6	2
Chicago White Sox	3	3	4	6	4	-	14	11	14	13	4	2	3	6
Cleveland Indians	3	2	4	6	4	5	-	10	12	13	3	6	3	7
Minnesota Twins	3	2	4	3	6	7	9	-	11	13	4	4	3	6
Detroit Tigers	1	4	4	5	5	5	6	8	-	10	4	1	4	5
Kansas City Royals	3	2	3	2	3	5	6	6	9	-	2	2	2	2
Los Angeles Angels	6	4	1	4	4	6	5	6	6	7	-	10	15	9
Oakland Athletics	2	4	5	6	4	7	3	6	5	4	9	-	11	12
Texas Rangers	3	2	7	6	2	6	3	6	2	8	4	8	-	13
Seattle Mariners	3	3	4	3	4	3	3	4	4	7	9	6	6	-

2005 National League Standings

Overall

EAST

Team	W-L	Pct	GB	D1	LD1	LLd
Atlanta Braves	90-72	.556	0.0	101	10/2	7.0
Philadelphia Phillies	88-74	.543	2.0	3	4/6	1.0
New York Mets	83-79	.512	7.0	0	-	0.0
Florida Marlins	83-79	.512	7.0	33	6/3	1.5
Washington Nationals	81-81	.500	9.0	62	7/25	5.5

CENTRAL

Team	W-L	Pct	GB	D1	LD1	LLd
St Louis Cardinals	100-62	.617	0.0	171	10/2	16.0
Houston Astros*	89-73	.549	11.0	5	4/15	1.0
Milwaukee Brewers	81-81	.500	19.0	9	4/15	1.0
Chicago Cubs	79-83	.488	21.0	1	4/4	0.0
Cincinnati Reds	73-89	.451	27.0	4	4/7	0.5
Pittsburgh Pirates	67-95	.414	33.0	0	-	0.0

WEST

Team	W-L	Pct	GB	D1	LD1	LLd
San Diego Padres	82-80	.506	0.0	136	10/2	7.0
Arizona Diamondbacks	77-85	.475	5.0	11	8/1	0.5
San Francisco Giants	75-87	.463	7.0	3	4/11	0.0
Los Angeles Dodgers	71-91	.438	11.0	36	5/14	4.5
Colorado Rockies	67-95	.414	15.0	2	4/5	1.0

* Clinched Wild Card Birth on 10/1. Division Clinch Dates: St Louis 9/15, Atlanta 9/27, San Diego 9/28.
D1 = Number of days a team had at least a share of first place of their division; LD1 = Last date the team had at least a share of first place; LLd = The largest number of games that a team led their division

East Division

Tm	Home	Road	East	Cent	West	AL	LHS	RHS	Day	Night	Grass	Turf	1-Rn	5+Rn	XInn	Apr	May	June	July	Aug	S/O	Pre	Post
Atl	53-28	37-44	42-33	28-14	13-17	7-8	22-16	68-56	25-23	65-49	90-72	0-0	23-20	27-16	6-7	14-10	14-13	15-13	18-8	14-14	15-14	50-39	40-33
Phi	46-35	42-39	38-37	21-20	22-9	7-8	29-19	59-55	34-20	54-54	88-74	0-0	21-23	26-19	6-4	10-14	15-13	15-12	15-12	16-11	17-12	45-44	43-30
NYM	48-33	35-46	38-36	20-21	20-12	5-10	18-21	65-58	26-26	57-53	83-79	3-0	21-24	25-17	8-6	11-13	15-13	13-13	14-13	16-11	14-16	44-44	39-35
Fla	45-36	38-43	34-39	21-22	18-13	10-5	21-16	62-63	24-21	59-58	80-79	5-9	20-23	24-30	5-9	14-8	13-14	20-6	13-13	17-14	13-16	44-42	39-37
Was	41-40	40-41	34-41	19-20	16-14	12-6	23-23	58-58	25-30	56-51	80-79	1-2	30-31	13-18	6-11	13-11	14-14	20-6	9-18	13-15	12-17	52-36	29-45

Central Division

Tm	Home	Road	East	Cent	West	AL	LHS	RHS	Day	Night	Grass	Turf	1-Rn	5+Rn	XInn	Apr	May	June	July	Aug	S/O	Pre	Post
StL	50-31	50-31	18-14	51-29	21-14	10-5	32-20	68-42	33-26	67-36	96-60	4-2	21-25	31-13	5-3	15-7	18-11	16-11	17-9	19-11	15-13	56-32	44-30
Hou	53-28	36-45	20-16	43-36	19-13	7-8	25-24	64-49	22-23	67-50	89-73	0-0	25-21	24-14	4-4	9-13	10-19	16-9	22-7	13-14	19-11	44-43	45-30
Mil	46-35	35-46	18-18	38-41	17-15	8-7	27-20	54-61	30-27	51-54	77-76	4-5	21-21	18-14	3-8	10-13	14-14	12-15	16-12	13-14	16-13	42-46	39-35
ChC	38-43	41-40	11-23	43-36	19-15	6-9	24-27	55-56	41-44	38-39	79-83	0-0	26-20	18-22	5-5	12-11	14-13	14-13	13-15	10-18	16-13	43-44	36-39
Cin	42-39	31-50	16-19	33-46	17-16	7-8	24-29	49-60	27-22	46-67	73-89	0-0	21-18	27-29	5-2	10-13	11-18	9-16	17-11	15-12	11-19	35-53	38-36
Pit	34-47	33-48	14-19	30-50	18-19	5-7	19-27	48-68	21-31	46-64	67-95	0-0	15-28	22-32	4-8	8-14	15-13	11-16	10-18	11-17	12-17	39-48	28-47

West Division

Tm	Home	Road	East	Cent	West	AL	LHS	RHS	Day	Night	Grass	Turf	1-Rn	5+Rn	XInn	Apr	May	June	July	Aug	S/O	Pre	Post
SD	46-35	36-45	16-14	20-21	39-34	7-11	21-23	61-57	24-27	58-53	80-79	2-1	29-20	21-23	9-8	11-13	22-6	10-17	8-18	15-12	16-14	48-41	34-39
Ari	36-45	41-40	11-21	17-22	41-32	8-10	18-23	59-62	24-20	53-65	77-85	0-0	28-18	18-35	8-7	14-10	16-12	9-19	13-14	9-19	16-11	43-47	34-38
SF	37-44	38-43	11-19	20-21	38-35	6-12	24-20	51-67	22-30	53-57	73-86	2-1	27-25	13-24	4-7	12-11	11-16	10-17	12-15	14-14	16-14	37-50	38-37
LAD	40-41	31-50	13-18	20-19	33-41	5-13	16-22	55-69	20-25	51-66	71-91	0-0	20-23	18-24	7-5	15-8	11-17	12-15	10-17	14-14	10-19	40-48	31-43
Col	40-41	27-54	14-17	15-28	32-41	6-9	18-25	49-70	22-30	45-65	67-95	0-0	25-24	21-34	4-4	6-15	9-20	12-15	10-17	15-14	15-14	31-56	36-39

Team vs. Team Breakdown

	EAST					CENTRAL						WEST				
	Atl	Phi	Fla	NYM	Was	StL	Hou	Mil	ChC	Cin	Pit	SD	Ari	SF	LAD	Col
Atlanta Braves	-	9	10	13	10	3	5	3	6	7	4	1	3	4	3	2
Philadelphia Phillies	10	-	10	7	11	4	0	5	4	4	4	6	4	5	3	4
Florida Marlins	8	9	-	8	9	3	4	3	4	4	3	2	4	4	5	3
New York Mets	6	11	10	-	11	2	5	3	4	3	4	4	6	3	3	4
Washington Nationals	9	8	9	8	-	2	2	4	5	1	5	1	4	3	4	4
St Louis Cardinals	3	2	4	5	4	-	11	11	6	11	12	3	5	4	5	4
Houston Astros	1	6	3	5	5	5	-	10	7	12	9	4	3	3	4	5
Milwaukee Brewers	3	4	4	3	4	5	5	-	9	10	9	3	4	4	1	5
Chicago Cubs	1	2	5	2	1	10	9	7	-	6	11	4	2	5	4	4
Cincinnati Reds	3	3	2	3	5	5	4	6	9	-	9	4	3	4	2	3
Pittsburgh Pirates	3	3	4	3	1	4	7	7	5	7	-	3	4	2	2	7
San Diego Padres	5	0	4	2	5	4	3	4	3	2	4	-	9	12	7	11
Arizona Diamondbacks	3	3	2	1	2	2	3	2	5	2	3	10	-	7	13	11
San Francisco Giants	2	1	2	3	3	2	4	3	2	5	4	6	11	-	10	11
Los Angeles Dodgers	3	3	2	3	2	2	2	5	2	4	5	11	5	9	-	8
Colorado Rockies	4	2	3	3	2	4	1	1	3	3	3	7	7	7	11	-

American League Batting

Tm	G	AB	H	2B	3B	HR	(Hm	Rd)	TB	R	RBI	TBB	IBB	SO	HBP	SH	SF	ShO	SB	CS	SB%	GDP	LOB	Avg	OBP	Slg
Bos	162	5626	1579	339	21	199	(92	107)	2557	910	863	653	34	1044	47	14	63	5	45	12	.79	135	1249	.281	.357	.454
NYY	162	5624	1552	259	16	229	(126	103)	2530	886	847	637	41	989	73	28	43	2	84	27	.76	125	1264	.276	.355	.450
Tex	162	5716	1528	311	29	260	(153	107)	2677	865	834	495	20	1112	48	9	32	7	67	15	.82	123	1104	.267	.329	.468
Cle	162	5609	1522	337	30	207	(91	116)	2540	790	760	503	33	1093	54	39	50	11	62	36	.63	128	1148	.271	.334	.453
Tor	162	5581	1480	307	39	136	(76	60)	2273	775	735	486	18	955	89	21	56	14	72	35	.67	126	1118	.265	.331	.407
Oak	162	5627	1476	310	20	155	(71	84)	2291	772	739	537	22	819	52	19	40	12	31	22	.58	148	1170	.262	.330	.407
LAA	162	5624	1520	278	30	147	(71	76)	2299	761	726	447	51	848	29	43	39	6	161	57	.74	126	1086	.270	.325	.409
TB	162	5552	1519	289	40	157	(71	86)	2359	750	717	412	25	990	69	34	51	5	151	49	.76	133	1065	.274	.329	.425
CWS	162	5529	1450	253	23	200	(115	85)	2349	741	713	435	27	1002	79	53	49	7	137	67	.67	122	1032	.262	.322	.425
Bal	162	5551	1492	296	27	189	(93	96)	2409	729	700	447	31	902	54	40	42	5	83	37	.69	145	1103	.269	.327	.434
Det	162	5602	1521	283	45	168	(89	79)	2398	723	678	384	24	1038	53	44	52	10	66	28	.70	138	1077	.272	.321	.428
KC	162	5503	1445	289	34	126	(51	75)	2180	701	653	424	23	1008	63	46	50	10	53	33	.62	139	1062	.263	.320	.396
Sea	162	5507	1408	289	34	130	(63	67)	2155	699	657	466	50	986	48	37	37	5	102	47	.68	115	1076	.256	.317	.391
Min	162	5564	1441	269	32	134	(67	67)	2176	688	644	485	49	978	59	42	42	10	102	44	.70	155	1109	.259	.323	.391
AL	1134	78215	20933	4109	420	2437	(1229	1208)	33193	10790	10266	6811	448	13764	817	469	646	109	1216	509	.70	1858	15663	.268	.330	.424

American League Pitching

Tm	G	CG	Rel	IP	BFP	H	R	ER	HR	SH	SF	HB	TBB	IBB	SO	WP	Bk	W	L	Pct.	ShO	Sv-Op	Hld	OAvg	OOBP	OSlg	ERA
Cle	162	6	409	1452.2	6048	1363	642	582	157	36	41	41	413	20	1050	26	4	93	69	.574	10	51-66	74	.247	.302	.387	3.61
LAA	162	7	379	1464.1	6158	1419	643	598	158	39	35	48	443	24	1126	70	1	95	67	.586	11	54-71	55	.254	.312	.401	3.68
CWS	162	9	412	1475.2	6176	1392	645	592	167	45	35	52	459	42	1040	65	9	99	63	.611	10	54-73	79	.249	.310	.397	3.61
Oak	162	9	410	1450.1	6080	1315	658	594	154	32	38	60	504	42	1075	41	3	88	74	.543	12	38-56	47	.241	.311	.382	3.69
Min	162	9	396	1464.1	6072	1458	662	604	169	50	40	43	348	38	965	35	4	83	79	.512	8	44-60	52	.261	.307	.408	3.71
Tor	162	9	432	1447.0	6166	1475	705	653	185	31	43	68	444	29	958	39	5	80	82	.494	8	35-56	66	.264	.324	.418	4.06
Sea	162	6	433	1427.2	6172	1483	751	712	179	37	51	57	496	32	892	36	4	69	93	.426	7	39-59	73	.268	.332	.422	4.49
Det	162	7	425	1435.2	6139	1504	787	719	193	39	60	51	461	33	907	53	5	71	91	.438	2	37-57	56	.272	.330	.436	4.51
NYY	162	8	418	1430.2	6182	1495	789	718	164	27	49	84	463	25	985	37	6	95	67	.586	14	46-67	69	.269	.332	.422	4.52
Bal	162	2	474	1427.2	6242	1458	800	724	180	25	46	52	580	32	1052	70	11	74	88	.457	9	38-57	70	.263	.336	.416	4.56
Bos	162	6	442	1429.0	6227	1550	805	752	164	27	50	89	440	28	959	56	4	95	67	.586	8	38-57	59	.276	.335	.441	4.74
Tex	162	2	454	1440.0	6371	1589	858	794	159	45	44	60	522	31	932	44	4	79	83	.488	6	46-68	48	.279	.343	.428	4.96
KC	162	4	444	1413.1	6370	1640	935	862	178	34	49	74	580	33	924	69	9	56	106	.346	4	25-43	55	.291	.362	.463	5.49
TB	162	1	401	1421.2	6384	1570	936	851	194	47	59	64	615	41	949	53	5	67	95	.414	4	43-69	66	.280	.355	.455	5.39
AL	1134	85	5929	20180.0	86787	20711	10616	9755	2401	514	640	843	6768	450	13814	694	74	1144	1124	.504	113	588-859	869	.265	.328	.420	4.35

American League Fielding

Team	G	Inn	PO	Ast	OFAst	E	(Throw	Field)	TC	DP	GDP	SB	CS	SB%	CPkof	PPkof	PB	UER	UERA	FPct
Oakland	162	1450.1	4351	1649	25	88	34	54	6088	166	137	109	25	.81	0	4	5	62	0.38	.986
Seattle	162	1427.2	4283	1572	30	86	40	46	5941	145	119	89	43	.67	0	6	14	39	0.25	.986
Los Angeles	162	1464.1	4393	1520	27	87	45	42	6000	139	114	68	42	.62	3	2	13	45	0.28	.986
Chicago	162	1475.2	4427	1671	22	94	35	59	6192	167	143	103	25	.80	1	8	9	53	0.32	.985
Toronto	162	1447.0	4341	1754	30	95	47	48	6190	155	134	100	35	.74	2	6	6	52	0.32	.985
New York	162	1430.2	4292	1688	23	95	40	55	6075	151	127	125	50	.71	1	0	11	68	0.43	.984
Minnesota	162	1464.1	4393	1764	37	102	41	61	6259	171	141	44	36	.55	0	4	9	56	0.34	.984
Cleveland	162	1452.2	4358	1641	10	106	45	61	6105	156	136	103	33	.76	3	3	6	60	0.37	.983
Baltimore	162	1427.2	4283	1679	25	107	51	56	6069	154	126	115	34	.77	1	0	13	76	0.48	.982
Texas	162	1440.0	4320	1674	27	108	45	63	6102	149	126	69	26	.73	0	0	11	63	0.39	.982
Detroit	162	1435.2	4307	1789	22	110	59	51	6206	172	148	60	49	.55	7	2	4	66	0.41	.982
Boston	162	1429.0	4287	1622	34	109	51	58	6018	135	122	87	29	.75	1	4	13	52	0.33	.982
Kansas City	162	1413.1	4240	1644	34	125	51	74	6009	163	139	70	44	.61	3	6	5	62	0.39	.979
Tampa Bay	162	1421.2	4265	1445	29	124	53	71	5834	140	101	68	45	.60	3	1	13	83	0.53	.979
American League	1134	20180.0	60540	23112	375	1436	637	799	85088	2163	1813	1210	516	.70	25	46	132	837	0.37	.983

National League Batting

Tm	G	AB	H	2B	3B	HR	(Hm	Rd)	TB	R	RBI	TBB	IBB	SO	HBP	SH	SF	ShO	SB	CS	SB%	GDP	LOB	Avg	OBP	Slg
Cin	163	5565	1453	335	15	222	(126	96)	2484	820	784	611	42	1303	62	43	39	8	72	23	.76	116	1176	.261	.339	.446
Phi	162	5542	1494	282	35	167	(94	73)	2347	807	760	639	76	1083	56	62	46	9	83	36	.70	127	1251	.270	.348	.423
StL	162	5538	1494	287	26	170	(92	78)	2343	805	757	534	60	947	62	77	35	6	65	39	.63	131	1152	.270	.339	.423
Atl	162	5486	1453	308	37	184	(89	95)	2387	769	733	534	56	1084	45	75	46	6	92	32	.74	146	1114	.265	.333	.435
Col	162	5542	1477	280	34	150	(86	64)	2275	740	704	509	36	1103	64	88	34	10	65	32	.67	125	1197	.267	.333	.411
Mil	162	5448	1413	327	19	175	(91	84)	2303	726	689	531	55	1162	73	66	38	12	79	34	.70	137	1120	.259	.331	.423
NYM	162	5505	1421	279	32	175	(83	92)	2289	722	683	486	49	1075	48	69	38	11	153	40	.79	103	1122	.258	.322	.416
Fla	162	5502	1499	306	32	128	(57	71)	2253	717	678	512	61	918	67	82	50	8	96	38	.72	144	1181	.272	.339	.409
ChC	162	5584	1506	323	23	194	(99	95)	2457	703	670	419	49	920	55	69	37	8	65	39	.63	131	1133	.256	.332	.440
Ari	162	5550	1419	291	27	191	(97	94)	2337	696	670	606	51	1094	55	71	45	9	67	26	.72	132	1247	.256	.332	.421
Hou	163	5462	1400	281	32	161	(93	68)	2228	693	654	481	43	1037	72	82	42	17	115	44	.72	116	1136	.256	.322	.408
LAD	162	5433	1374	284	21	149	(80	69)	2147	685	653	541	30	1094	67	57	33	9	58	35	.62	139	1135	.253	.326	.395
SD	162	5502	1416	269	39	130	(54	76)	2153	684	655	600	41	977	49	72	48	9	99	44	.69	122	1220	.257	.333	.391
Pit	162	5573	1445	292	38	139	(59	80)	2230	680	656	471	38	1092	72	56	49	9	73	30	.71	130	1193	.259	.322	.400
SF	162	5462	1427	299	26	128	(64	64)	2162	649	617	431	26	901	49	91	44	7	71	35	.67	147	1093	.261	.319	.396
Was	162	5426	1367	311	32	117	(46	71)	2093	639	615	491	55	1090	89	91	45	11	45	45	.50	130	1137	.252	.322	.386
NL	1297	88120	23058	4754	468	2580	(1310	1270)	36488	11535	10982	8396	768	16880	980	1151	669	152	1349	560	.71	2052	18607	.262	.330	.414

National League Pitching

Tm	G	CG	Rel	IP	BFP	H	R	ER	HR	SH	SF	HB	TBB	IBB	SO	WP	Bk	W	L	Pct.	ShO	Sv-Op	Hld	OAvg	OOBP	OSlg	ERA
Hou	163	6	434	1443.0	6023	1336	609	563	155	61	33	59	440	29	1164	38	8	89	73	.549	11	45-58	66	.246	.308	.389	3.51
StL	162	15	436	1445.2	6047	1399	634	560	153	61	37	60	443	27	974	41	5	100	62	.617	14	48-65	86	.257	.318	.398	3.49
NYM	162	8	392	1435.2	6121	1390	648	599	135	83	34	56	491	43	1012	32	4	83	79	.512	11	38-59	49	.255	.321	.387	3.76
Was	162	4	470	1458.0	6286	1456	673	627	140	79	46	72	539	77	997	49	8	81	81	.500	9	51-69	69	.262	.333	.396	3.87
Atl	162	8	484	1443.2	6186	1487	674	639	145	61	28	32	520	52	929	42	5	90	72	.556	12	38-62	73	.268	.333	.406	3.98
Mil	162	7	395	1438.0	6208	1382	697	635	169	54	33	45	569	52	1173	66	8	81	81	.500	6	46-67	61	.251	.324	.408	3.97
ChC	162	8	457	1440.0	6185	1357	714	671	186	84	40	50	576	48	1256	57	7	79	83	.488	10	39-58	69	.250	.325	.407	4.19
Phi	162	4	442	1435.0	6119	1379	726	672	189	65	41	72	487	51	1159	36	9	88	74	.543	6	40-63	78	.253	.320	.426	4.21
SD	162	4	456	1455.1	6253	1452	726	668	146	46	45	46	503	45	1133	36	3	82	80	.506	8	45-65	70	.259	.322	.413	4.13
Fla	162	14	449	1442.1	6236	1459	732	666	116	80	42	65	563	57	1125	45	3	83	79	.512	15	42-60	55	.266	.339	.402	4.16
SF	162	4	511	1444.1	6280	1456	745	695	151	67	50	42	592	42	972	38	8	75	87	.463	8	46-74	89	.263	.336	.412	4.33
LAD	162	6	459	1427.1	6113	1434	755	695	182	90	39	64	471	34	1004	36	6	71	91	.438	9	40-59	66	.263	.327	.429	4.38
Pit	162	4	451	1436.0	6264	1456	769	706	162	68	57	65	612	65	958	53	4	67	95	.414	14	35-47	59	.267	.344	.424	4.42
Ari	162	6	458	1456.1	6402	1580	856	783	193	78	45	62	537	43	1038	58	5	77	85	.475	10	45-62	68	.278	.345	.455	4.84
Col	162	4	449	1418.2	6385	1600	862	808	175	66	55	84	604	54	981	53	6	67	95	.414	4	37-63	68	.287	.362	.457	5.13
Cin	163	2	491	1433.0	6397	1657	889	820	219	63	50	80	492	47	955	53	3	73	89	.451	1	31-47	63	.290	.352	.483	5.15
NL	1297	104	7244	23052.1	99505	23280	11709	10807	2616	1106	675	954	8439	766	16830	745	87	1286	1306	.496	148	666-978	1085	.264	.332	.418	4.22

National League Fielding

Team	G	Inn	PO	Ast	OFAst	E	(Throw	Field)	TC	DP	GDP	SB	CS	SB%	CPkof	PPkof	PB	UER	UERA	FPct
Atlanta	162	1443.2	4331	1801	41	86	(34	52)	6218	170	143	89	36	.71	2	2	8	35	0.22	.986
Houston	163	1443.0	4329	1697	26	89	(38	51)	6115	146	122	83	31	.63	3	4	6	45	0.28	.985
San Francisco	162	1444.1	4333	1630	18	90	(24	66)	6053	146	118	78	54	.59	0	1	5	47	0.29	.985
Philadelphia	162	1435.0	4305	1608	36	90	(41	49)	6003	132	111	82	26	.76	2	2	12	54	0.34	.985
Arizona	162	1456.1	4369	1792	18	94	(50	44)	6255	159	141	78	28	.74	0	4	11	68	0.42	.985
Washington	162	1458.0	4374	1546	30	92	(38	54)	6012	157	124	76	41	.65	4	4	7	46	0.28	.985
St Louis	162	1445.2	4337	1950	28	100	(40	60)	6387	196	181	32	33	.49	8	1	12	74	0.46	.984
Chicago	162	1440.0	4320	1657	22	101	(41	60)	6078	136	118	90	40	.69	1	8	6	43	0.27	.983
Florida	162	1442.1	4327	1660	26	103	(49	54)	6090	177	153	118	38	.76	1	4	9	61	0.38	.983
Los Angeles	162	1427.1	4282	1728	31	106	(41	65)	6116	142	119	130	34	.79	1	4	9	60	0.38	.983
Cincinnati	163	1433.0	4299	1587	31	104	(52	52)	5990	133	121	76	35	.68	0	5	9	65	0.41	.983
New York	162	1435.2	4307	1657	32	106	(42	64)	6070	146	127	107	25	.81	1	0	5	46	0.29	.983
San Diego	162	1455.1	4366	1523	21	109	(56	53)	5998	137	116	94	25	.79	4	2	12	58	0.36	.982
Pittsburgh	162	1436.0	4308	1799	22	117	(51	66)	6224	193	164	64	36	.64	1	3	16	61	0.38	.981
Colorado	162	1418.2	4256	1702	34	118	(66	52)	6076	158	131	102	37	.73	5	8	14	52	0.33	.981
Milwaukee	162	1438.0	4314	1483	24	119	(55	64)	5916	139	108	86	34	.72	0	12	8	61	0.38	.980
National League	1297	23052.1	69157	26820	440	1624	(718	906)	97601	2467	2097	1355	553	.71	33	64	149	876	0.34	.983

Team Efficiency Summary

Bill James

The Team Efficiency Summary (below) compares each team's individual player statistics to their team won-lost record, in three different ways. First, we compare the team's runs scored to their estimated runs created. If the team scores more runs than we would expect them to score, that's a "Hitting Efficiency" greater than 100. Second, we compare the team's expected Runs Allowed to their actual runs allowed, by a sort of runs created formula for pitchers. If the team allowed fewer runs than expected, that creates a "Pitching Efficiency" greater than 100. Third, we compare their expected wins by the Pythagorean method to their actual wins. If they win more games than would be expected, that creates a "Win Efficiency" greater than 100.

The final group of three columns, on the right, summarizes the team's overall performance versus expectations based on their statistics. The most interesting thing about this chart is that two teams which battled into the closing days of the season for a division title are on opposite ends of the chart. The Cleveland Indians, a team of young stars, should have won their division by a whopping 13 games.

2005 American League Team Efficiency Summary

	RC	Runs	Hit Eff	Exp RA	RA	Pit Eff	Exp Wins	Wins	Runs Eff	Eff Wins	Wins	Overall Eff
Chicago White Sox	739	741	100	658	645	102	92	99	107	90	99	110
Los Angeles Angels	738	761	103	669	643	104	95	95	101	89	95	107
Boston Red Sox	912	910	100	788	805	98	91	95	105	93	95	102
New York Yankees	906	886	98	744	789	94	90	95	105	97	95	98
Tampa Bay Devil Rays	762	750	98	893	936	95	63	67	106	68	67	98
Minnesota Twins	686	688	100	656	662	99	84	83	99	85	83	98
Kansas City Royals	679	701	103	915	935	98	58	56	96	58	56	97
Toronto Blue Jays	749	775	104	732	705	104	89	80	90	83	80	97
Seattle Mariners	673	699	104	750	751	100	75	69	92	72	69	95
Baltimore Orioles	759	729	96	781	800	98	73	74	101	79	74	94
Texas Rangers	855	865	101	810	858	94	82	79	97	85	79	93
Oakland Athletics	741	772	104	619	658	94	94	88	94	95	88	92
Detroit Tigers	745	723	97	767	787	98	74	71	96	79	71	90
Cleveland Indians	821	790	96	620	642	97	98	93	95	103	93	90

2005 National League Team Efficiency Summary

	RC	Runs	Hit Eff	Exp RA	RA	Pit Eff	Exp Wins	Wins	Runs Eff	Eff Wins	Wins	Overall Eff
Washington Nationals	657	639	97	706	673	105	77	81	105	75	81	108
St Louis Cardinals	786	805	102	649	634	102	100	100	100	96	100	104
Arizona Diamondbacks	769	696	90	831	856	97	64	77	119	75	77	103
Atlanta Braves	771	769	100	708	674	105	92	90	98	88	90	102
San Francisco Giants	668	649	97	730	745	98	70	75	107	74	75	102
Cincinnati Reds	829	820	99	916	889	103	74	73	98	73	73	100
Colorado Rockies	752	740	98	892	862	103	69	67	97	67	67	99
San Diego Padres	728	684	94	701	726	97	76	82	108	84	82	98
Milwaukee Brewers	740	726	98	720	697	103	84	81	96	83	81	97
Houston Astros	712	693	97	620	609	102	91	89	97	92	89	97
Florida Marlins	757	717	95	698	732	95	79	83	105	87	83	95
Los Angeles Dodgers	687	685	100	728	755	96	73	71	97	76	71	93
Philadelphia Phillies	838	807	96	701	726	97	90	88	98	95	88	92
Chicago Cubs	760	703	92	715	714	100	80	79	99	86	79	92
New York Mets	737	722	98	656	648	101	90	83	93	90	83	92
Pittsburgh Pirates	710	680	96	764	769	99	71	67	94	75	67	89

Career Register

The Career Register includes complete career statistics for every major league player through the 2005 season who played in 2005, plus a few bonus players.

As well as the usual Rocco Baldelli "missed all of last year but will be back this year" types, we've added four potential foreign imports: Kei Igawa is a top young Japanese lefty. His current Japanese team may not let him cross the ocean, but if they do, he has a great chance to make an impact. Akinori Iwamura is considered the best third baseman in Japan. He's also at the mercy of his current team, but, like Igawa, if he comes over he'll make headlines. Kenji Jojima is a top Japanese catcher and already plans to sign with a major league club for 2006. If you've already heard of any of these guys, it's probably Daisuke Matsuzaka, a top Japanese starter. He was in our book already last year, but wasn't able to come to the States for the 2005 season. As with Jojima, he's almost certain to appear in a major league uniform in 2006.

The reason you'll probably notice the Register teams being abbreviated this season is that the Register print size has been enlarged. We decided readability was more important than full team names.

Players who have appeared in fewer than three major league seasons have their full minor league statistics included. Major leaguers who spent time in the minors during the 2005 season have just their 2005 minor league numbers included, and indicated by an asterisk.

Players who led the league in a particular category will have that register total in boldface.

The Register also features Runs Created (RC) for hitters and Component ERA (ERC) for pitchers in addition to the traditional statistics. Developed by Bill James, Runs Created is a method of measuring every facet of a hitter's strength's and weaknesses, and combining those factors into one production number. Component ERC estimates what a pitcher's ERA should have been based upon his raw pitching statistics and gives us a good indication of whether or not a pitcher actually deserved his ERA. An explanation of Bill's most current formulas for both RC and ERC can be found in the Baseball Glossary at the end of the *Handbook.*

Just as a refresher:

Age is seasonal as of June 30, 2006

For pitchers BFP is batters facing pitcher; TBB is total walks (intentional and unintentional); Op is Save opportunities; Hld is holds.

For varying levels of Class-A ball we have used "A+" to denote High A and "A-" for Low A.

Brent Abernathy

Bats: R **Throws:** R **Pos:** 2B-17; LF-5; PH-3; PR-2; DH-1 **Ht:** 6'1" **Wt:** 191 **Born:** 9/23/1977 **Age:** 28

Year	Team	Lg	G	AB	H	2B	3B	HR	(Hm	Rd)	TB	R	RBI	RC	TBB	IBB	SO	HBP	SH	SF	SB	CS	SB%	GDP	Avg	OBP	Slg
2005	Roch*	AAA	57	215	70	13	0	6	(-	-)	101	35	25	40	21	0	20	3	7	3	7	3	.70	7	.326	.388	.470
2001	TB	AL	79	304	82	17	1	5	(3	2)	116	43	33	39	27	1	35	0	3	1	8	3	.73	3	.270	.328	.382
2002	TB	AL	117	463	112	18	4	2	(2	0)	144	46	40	48	25	0	46	6	8	2	10	4	.71	8	.242	.288	.311
2003	2 Tms	AL	12	34	2	0	0	0	(0	0)	2	3	0	0	1	0	3	0	2	0	1	0	1.00	2	.059	.086	.059
2005	MIN	AL	24	67	16	1	0	1	(1	0)	20	5	6	6	7	0	9	1	3	1	2	0	1.00	2	.239	.316	.299
03	TB	AL	2	7	0	0	0	0	(0	0)	0	1	0	0	0	0	0	0	0	0	1	0	1.00	2	.000	.000	.000
03	KC	AL	10	27	2	0	0	0	(0	0)	2	2	0	0	1	0	3	0	2	0	0	0	-	2	.074	.107	.074
4 ML YEARS			232	868	212	36	5	8	(6	2)	282	97	79	93	60	1	93	7	16	4	21	7	.75	15	.244	.297	.325

Bobby Abreu

Bats: L **Throws:** R **Pos:** RF-158; DH-3; PH-1 **Ht:** 6'0" **Wt:** 195 **Born:** 3/11/1974 **Age:** 32

Year	Team	Lg	G	AB	H	2B	3B	HR	(Hm	Rd)	TB	R	RBI	RC	TBB	IBB	SO	HBP	SH	SF	SB	CS	SB%	GDP	Avg	OBP	Slg
1996	HOU	NL	15	22	5	1	0	0	(0	0)	6	1	1	1	2	0	3	0	0	0	0	0	-	1	.227	.292	.273
1997	HOU	NL	59	188	47	10	2	3	(3	0)	70	22	26	25	21	0	48	1	0	0	7	2	.78	0	.250	.329	.372
1998	PHI	NL	151	497	155	29	6	17	(10	7)	247	68	74	101	84	14	133	0	4	4	19	10	.66	6	.312	.409	.497
1999	PHI	NL	152	546	183	35	11	20	(13	7)	300	118	93	131	109	8	113	3	0	4	27	9	.75	13	.335	.446	.549
2000	PHI	NL	154	576	182	42	10	25	(14	11)	319	103	79	130	100	9	116	1	0	3	28	8	.78	12	.316	.416	.554
2001	PHI	NL	162	588	170	48	4	31	(13	18)	319	118	110	125	106	11	137	1	0	9	36	14	.72	13	.289	.393	.543
2002	PHI	NL	157	572	176	50	6	20	(8	12)	298	102	85	112	104	9	117	3	0	6	31	12	.72	11	.308	.413	.521
2003	PHI	NL	158	577	173	35	1	20	(11	9)	270	99	101	120	109	13	126	2	0	7	22	9	.71	13	.300	.409	.468
2004	PHI	NL	159	574	173	47	1	30	(13	17)	312	118	105	139	127	10	116	5	0	7	40	5	.89	5	.301	.428	.544
2005	PHI	NL	162	588	168	37	1	24	(15	9)	279	104	102	116	117	15	134	6	0	8	31	9	.78	7	.286	.405	.474
10 ML YEARS			1329	4728	1432	334	42	190	(100	90)	2420	853	776	1000	879	89	1043	22	4	48	241	78	.76	81	.303	.411	.512

Jeremy Accardo

Pitches: R **Bats:** R **Pos:** RP-28 **Ht:** 6'2" **Wt:** 190 **Born:** 12/18/1981 **Age:** 24

Year	Team	Lg	G	GS	CG	GF	IP	BFP	H	R	ER	HR	SH	SF	HB	TBB	IBB	SO	WP	Bk	W	L	Pct	ShO	Sv-Op	Hld	ERC	ERA
2004	SnJos	A+	50	0	0	44	55.0	239	57	28	26	3	0	0	1	15	1	43	4	0	1	2	.333	0	27--	-	3.41	4.25
2004	Nrwich	AA	7	0	0	4	8.1	36	9	5	5	1	0	0	0	2	1	5	1	0	2	1	.667	0	1--	-	3.75	5.40
2005	Nrwich	AA	8	0	0	6	9.2	38	8	3	1	0	0	0	0	1	0	15	0	0	1	0	1.000	0	4--	-	1.57	0.93
2005	Fresno	AAA	25	0	0	11	32.1	132	25	7	7	0	1	0	0	10	1	30	2	0	2	0	1.000	0	3--	-	1.87	1.95
2005	SnJos	A+	2	0	0	2	2.0	8	1	0	0	0	0	0	1	1	0	3	0	0	0	0	-	0	1--	-	3.21	0.00
2005	SF	NL	28	0	0	7	29.2	124	26	13	13	2	1	1	1	9	1	16	1	0	1	5	.167	0	0-1	4	2.87	3.94

Jose Acevedo

Pitches: R **Bats:** R **Pos:** RP-31; SP-5 **Ht:** 6'0" **Wt:** 185 **Born:** 12/18/1977 **Age:** 28

Year	Team	Lg	G	GS	CG	GF	IP	BFP	H	R	ER	HR	SH	SF	HB	TBB	IBB	SO	WP	Bk	W	L	Pct	ShO	Sv-Op	Hld	ERC	ERA
2005	Lsvlle*	AAA	1	1	0	0	4.0	14	2	0	0	0	0	0	0	0	0	3	0	0	0	0	-	0	0--	-	0.54	0.00
2005	ColSpr*	AAA	4	4	0	0	13.2	60	17	5	5	3	0	1	1	2	0	11	0	0	1	2	.333	0	0--	-	5.59	3.29
2001	CIN	NL	18	18	0	0	96.0	417	101	61	58	17	6	3	3	34	2	68	4	0	5	7	.417	0	0-0	0	4.84	5.44
2002	CIN	NL	6	5	0	0	23.2	112	28	21	19	8	2	0	2	12	0	14	1	0	4	2	.667	0	0-0	0	7.81	7.23
2003	CIN	NL	5	4	1	1	27.0	103	17	8	8	3	1	2	1	6	1	23	1	0	2	0	1.000	0	0-0	0	1.75	2.67
2004	CIN	NL	39	27	0	3	157.2	704	188	108	104	30	3	7	5	45	8	117	3	1	5	12	.294	0	0-0	2	5.36	5.94
2005	COL	NL	36	5	0	7	64.0	292	86	48	46	13	2	5	1	16	3	31	0	1	2	4	.333	0	1-2	6	6.17	6.47
5 ML YEARS			104	59	1	11	368.1	1628	420	246	235	71	14	17	12	113	14	253	9	2	18	25	.419	0	1-2	8	5.20	5.74

Mike Adams

Pitches: R **Bats:** R **Pos:** RP-13 **Ht:** 6'5" **Wt:** 190 **Born:** 7/29/1978 **Age:** 27

Year	Team	Lg	G	GS	CG	GF	IP	BFP	H	R	ER	HR	SH	SF	HB	TBB	IBB	SO	WP	Bk	W	L	Pct	ShO	Sv-Op	Hld	ERC	ERA
2001	Ogden	R+	23	0	0	21	32.0	129	26	10	10	4	1	1	3	6	1	44	0	0	2	2	.500	0	12--	-	2.74	2.81
2002	Beloit	A	11	0	0	8	15.1	60	13	6	6	1	1	0	0	2	0	21	0	0	0	0	-	0	5--	-	2.09	3.52
2002	Hi Dsrt	A+	10	0	0	7	14.0	59	9	6	6	2	0	0	0	7	0	23	2	0	2	1	.667	0	5--	-	2.73	3.86
2002	Huntsvl	AA	13	0	0	7	18.2	81	14	11	11	3	1	0	1	12	0	17	1	0	1	0	1.000	0	1--	-	4.30	5.30
2003	Huntsvl	AA	45	2	0	34	74.1	318	58	30	26	6	4	0	2	33	1	83	3	2	3	7	.300	0	14--	-	2.93	3.15
2004	Indy	AAA	10	2	0	1	31.0	116	23	10	9	3	1	0	2	4	0	37	0	0	2	0	1.000	0	0--	-	2.08	2.61
2005	Nashv	AAA	26	0	0	11	36.0	155	35	23	23	3	2	3	0	12	0	45	2	0	3	4	.429	0	2--	-	3.47	5.75
2004	MIL	NL	46	0	0	13	53.0	225	50	21	20	5	5	2	2	14	2	39	2	0	2	3	.400	0	0-5	12	3.22	3.40
2005	MIL	NL	13	0	0	7	13.1	61	12	4	4	2	0	0	0	10	1	14	1	0	0	1	.000	0	1-2	2	5.12	2.70
2 ML YEARS			59	0	0	20	66.1	286	62	25	24	7	5	2	2	24	3	53	3	0	2	4	.333	0	1-7	14	3.58	3.26

Russ Adams

Bats: L **Throws:** R **Pos:** SS-132; PH-14; PR-2 **Ht:** 6'1" **Wt:** 180 **Born:** 8/30/1980 **Age:** 25

Year	Team	Lg	G	AB	H	2B	3B	HR	(Hm	Rd)	TB	R	RBI	RC	TBB	IBB	SO	HBP	SH	SF	SB	CS	SB%	GDP	Avg	OBP	Slg
2002	Auburn	A-	30	113	40	7	3	0	(-	-)	53	25	16	28	24	0	11	1	1	2	13	1	.93	1	.354	.464	.469
2002	Dnedin	A+	37	147	34	4	2	1	(-	-)	45	23	12	16	18	0	17	2	1	1	5	2	.71	1	.231	.321	.306
2003	Dnedin	A+	68	258	72	9	5	3	(-	-)	100	50	16	42	38	1	27	6	5	3	9	2	.82	5	.279	.380	.388
2003	NwHav	AA	65	271	75	10	4	4	(-	-)	105	42	26	39	30	1	37	0	4	0	8	1	.89	5	.277	.349	.387

Year	Team	Lg	G	AB	H	2B	3B	HR	(Hm	Rd)	TB	R	RBI	RC	TBB	IBB	SO	HBP	SH	SF	SB	CS	SB%	GDP	Avg	OBP	Slg
2004	Syrcse	AAA	122	483	139	37	3	5	(-	-)	197	58	54	70	45	1	62	5	2	5	6	2	.75	9	.288	.351	.408
2004	TOR	AL	22	72	22	2	1	4	(1	3)	38	10	10	11	5	0	5	1	0	0	1	0	1.00	3	.306	.359	.528
2005	TOR	AL	139	481	123	27	5	8	(5	3)	184	68	63	66	50	1	57	3	3	8	11	2	.85	5	.256	.325	.383
2 ML YEARS			161	553	145	29	6	12	(6	6)	222	78	73	77	55	1	62	4	3	8	12	2	.86	8	.262	.329	.401

Terry Adams

Pitches: R **Bats:** R **Pos:** RP-16 **Ht:** 6'3" **Wt:** 215 **Born:** 3/6/1973 **Age:** 33

Year	Team	Lg	G	GS	CG	GF	IP	BFP	H	R	ER	HR	SH	SF	HB	TBB	IBB	SO	WP	Bk	W	L	Pct	ShO	Sv-Op	Hld	ERC	ERA
2005	S-WB*	AAA	14	0	0	10	16.1	79	22	14	8	1	0	1	1	8	2	14	2	1	1	2	.333	0	0- -	-	6.13	4.41
1995	CHN	NL	18	0	0	7	18.0	86	22	15	13	0	0	0	0	10	1	15	1	0	1	1	.500	0	1-1	0	4.95	6.50
1996	CHN	NL	69	0	0	22	101.0	423	84	36	33	6	7	3	1	49	6	78	5	1	3	6	.333	0	4-8	11	3.20	2.94
1997	CHN	NL	74	0	0	39	74.0	341	91	43	38	3	1	2	1	40	6	64	6	0	2	9	.182	0	18-22	11	5.49	4.62
1998	CHN	NL	63	0	0	15	72.2	330	72	39	35	7	3	3	1	41	3	73	4	3	7	7	.500	0	1-7	13	4.55	4.33
1999	CHN	NL	52	0	0	38	65.0	277	60	33	29	9	1	3	0	28	2	57	6	0	6	3	.667	0	13-18	3	4.00	4.02
2000	LA	NL	66	0	0	18	84.1	369	80	42	33	6	3	0	0	39	0	56	5	0	6	9	.400	0	2-7	15	3.77	3.52
2001	LA	NL	43	22	0	10	166.1	708	172	84	80	9	6	0	3	54	1	141	7	2	12	8	.600	0	0-1	4	3.74	4.33
2002	PHI	NL	46	19	0	10	136.2	590	132	76	66	9	10	2	3	58	5	96	8	0	7	9	.438	0	0-1	12	3.77	4.35
2003	PHI	NL	66	0	0	16	68.0	284	68	22	20	1	3	2	2	23	4	51	4	0	1	4	.200	0	0-0	16	3.35	2.65
2004	2 Tms	NL	61	0	0	21	70.0	316	84	39	37	10	3	5	2	28	3	56	8	0	6	4	.600	0	3-6	3	5.63	4.76
2005	PHI	NL	16	0	0	5	13.1	77	25	19	19	3	1	0	4	10	2	4	0	0	0	2	.000	0	0-1	2	13.79	12.83
04	Tor	AL	42	0	0	20	43.0	197	49	20	19	4	3	2	1	22	2	35	6	0	4	4	.500	0	3-6	2	5.27	3.98
04	Bos	AL	19	0	0	1	27.0	119	35	19	18	6	0	3	1	6	1	21	2	0	2	0	1.000	0	0-0	1	6.16	6.00
11 ML YEARS			574	41	0	201	869.1	3801	890	448	403	63	38	20	17	380	33	691	54	6	51	62	.451	0	42-72	90	4.18	4.17

Jon Adkins

Pitches: R **Bats:** L **Pos:** RP-5 **Ht:** 6'0" **Wt:** 200 **Born:** 8/30/1977 **Age:** 28

Year	Team	Lg	G	GS	CG	GF	IP	BFP	H	R	ER	HR	SH	SF	HB	TBB	IBB	SO	WP	Bk	W	L	Pct	ShO	Sv-Op	Hld	ERC	ERA
2005	Charltt*	AAA	23	21	0	1	127.1	573	148	81	76	20	3	2	3	43	1	92	0	0	4	9	.308	0	0- -	-	5.17	5.37
2003	CHA	AL	4	0	0	2	9.1	42	8	5	5	1	1	1	1	7	0	3	0	0	0	0	-	0	0-0	1	5.27	4.82
2004	CHA	AL	50	0	0	19	62.0	271	75	35	32	13	3	1	1	20	3	44	1	0	2	3	.400	0	0-0	5	5.90	4.65
2005	CHA	AL	5	0	0	4	8.1	42	13	8	8	0	0	0	1	4	2	1	0	0	0	1	.000	0	0-0	0	6.94	8.64
3 ML YEARS			59	0	0	25	79.2	355	96	48	45	14	4	2	3	31	5	48	1	0	2	4	.333	0	0-0	5	5.96	5.08

Jeremy Affeldt

Pitches: L **Bats:** L **Pos:** RP-49 **Ht:** 6'4" **Wt:** 215 **Born:** 6/6/1979 **Age:** 27

Year	Team	Lg	G	GS	CG	GF	IP	BFP	H	R	ER	HR	SH	SF	HB	TBB	IBB	SO	WP	Bk	W	L	Pct	ShO	Sv-Op	Hld	ERC	ERA
2005	Omha*	AAA	9	0	0	3	8.1	40	9	7	6	1	1	0	0	6	0	9	2	0	0	1	.000	0	0- -	-	5.86	6.48
2002	KC	AL	34	7	0	4	77.2	353	85	41	40	8	2	1	3	37	4	67	5	2	3	4	.429	0	0-1	1	4.97	4.64
2003	KC	AL	36	18	0	4	126.0	533	126	58	55	12	2	5	5	38	1	98	2	1	7	6	.538	0	4-4	3	3.82	3.93
2004	KC	AL	38	8	0	26	76.1	344	91	49	42	6	4	4	3	32	2	49	4	3	3	4	.429	0	13-17	0	5.26	4.95
2005	KC	AL	49	0	0	13	49.2	232	56	35	29	3	0	1	0	29	2	39	5	0	0	2	.000	0	0-0	12	5.08	5.26
4 ML YEARS			157	33	0	48	329.2	1462	358	183	166	29	8	11	11	136	9	253	16	6	13	16	.448	0	17-22	16	4.61	4.53

Chris Aguila

Bats: R **Throws:** R **Pos:** LF-27; PH-22; RF-14; PR-9; CF-2 **Ht:** 5'11" **Wt:** 180 **Born:** 2/23/1979 **Age:** 27

Year	Team	Lg	G	AB	H	2B	3B	HR	(Hm	Rd)	TB	R	RBI	RC	TBB	IBB	SO	HBP	SH	SF	SB	CS	SB%	GDP	Avg	OBP	Slg
1997	Marlins	R	46	157	34	7	0	1	(-	-)	44	12	17	14	21	0	49	1	2	2	2	1	.67	3	.217	.309	.280
1998	Marlins	R	51	171	46	12	3	4	(-	-)	76	29	29	25	19	1	49	2	1	0	6	2	.75	4	.269	.349	.444
1999	Kane	A	122	430	105	21	7	15	(-	-)	185	74	78	58	40	2	127	9	3	2	14	4	.78	9	.244	.320	.430
2000	BrvdCt	A+	136	518	125	27	3	9	(-	-)	185	68	56	50	37	1	105	1	3	3	8	8	.50	11	.241	.292	.357
2001	BrvdCt	A+	73	272	75	15	3	10	(-	-)	126	44	34	39	21	2	54	2	0	4	8	4	.67	7	.276	.328	.463
2001	Portlnd	AA	64	241	62	16	1	4	(-	-)	92	25	29	26	18	1	50	3	3	4	5	7	.42	4	.257	.312	.382
2002	Portlnd	AA	130	429	126	28	4	6	(-	-)	180	62	46	66	48	0	101	4	5	2	14	8	.64	8	.294	.369	.420
2003	Marlins	R	1	4	3	0	0	1	(-	-)	6	1	2	2	0	0	1	0	0	0	0	0	-	0	.750	.750	1.500
2003	Carlina	AA	93	337	108	21	3	11	(-	-)	168	58	55	63	36	5	67	2	2	5	6	2	.75	6	.320	.384	.499
2004	Albq	AAA	97	330	103	23	2	11	(-	-)	163	61	56	60	37	0	82	2	2	5	8	3	.73	8	.312	.380	.494
2005	Albq	AAA	35	138	49	13	2	7	(-	-)	87	27	25	34	14	0	21	0	0	1	8	2	.80	3	.355	.412	.630
2004	FLA	NL	29	45	10	2	1	3	(1	2)	23	10	5	3	2	0	12	0	1	0	0	0	-	0	.222	.255	.511
2005	FLA	NL	65	78	19	3	0	0	(0	0)	22	11	4	4	3	0	19	0	0	0	0	1	.00	0	.244	.272	.282
2 ML YEARS			94	123	29	5	1	3	(1	2)	45	21	9	7	5	0	31	0	1	0	0	1	.00	0	.236	.266	.366

Kurt Ainsworth

Pitches: R **Bats:** R **Pos:** P **Ht:** 6'3" **Wt:** 192 **Born:** 9/9/1978 **Age:** 27

Year	Team	Lg	G	GS	CG	GF	IP	BFP	H	R	ER	HR	SH	SF	HB	TBB	IBB	SO	WP	Bk	W	L	Pct	ShO	Sv-Op	Hld	ERC	ERA
2001	SF	NL	2	0	0	2	2.0	12	3	3	3	1	0	0	1	2	0	3	0	0	0	0	-	0	0-0	0	16.26	13.50
2002	SF	NL	6	4	0	0	25.2	108	22	7	6	1	2	0	1	12	0	15	1	0	1	2	.333	0	0-0	0	3.34	2.10
2003	2 Tms		14	11	0	2	68.1	298	72	34	31	8	2	2	1	27	0	52	2	0	5	5	.500	0	0-0	0	4.55	4.08
2004	BAL	AL	7	7	0	0	30.2	151	39	34	33	6	2	2	5	20	0	20	4	0	0	1	.000	0	0-0	0	8.42	9.68

			HOW MUCH HE PITCHED						WHAT HE GAVE UP												THE RESULTS							
Year	Team	Lg	G	GS	CG	GF	IP	BFP	H	R	ER	HR	SH	SF	HB	TBB	IBB	SO	WP	Bk	W	L	Pct	ShO	Sv-Op	Hld	ERC	ERA
03	SF	NL	11	11	0	0	66.0	283	66	31	28	7	2	2	1	26	0	48	2	0	5	4	.556	0	0-0	0	4.19	3.82
03	Bal	AL	3	0	0	2	2.1	15	6	3	3	1	0	0	0	1	0	4	0	0	0	1	.000	0	0-0	0	16.91	11.57
	4 ML YEARS		29	22	0	4	126.2	569	136	78	73	16	6	4	8	61	0	90	7	0	6	8	.429	0	0-0	0	5.32	5.19

Manny Alexander

Bats: R **Throws:** R **Pos:** 2B-5; SS-4; PR-3; 1B-1; 3B-1; PH-1   **Ht:** 5'10" **Wt:** 180 **Born:** 3/20/1971 **Age:** 35

			BATTING																		BASERUNNING				AVERAGES		
Year	Team	Lg	G	AB	H	2B	3B	HR	(Hm	Rd)	TB	R	RBI	RC	TBB	IBB	SO	HBP	SH	SF	SB	CS	SB%	GDP	Avg	OBP	Slg
2005	Okla*	AAA	108	417	129	23	6	12	(-	-)	200	64	67	77	38	0	66	4	2	6	27	9	.75	8	.309	.368	.480
2005	Portlnd*	AAA	4	16	4	2	0	0	(-	-)	6	0	1	76	1	0	4	0	0	0	0	1	.00	0	.250	.294	.375
1992	BAL	AL	4	5	1	0	0	0	(0	0)	1	1	0	0	0	0	3	0	0	0	0	0	-	0	.200	.200	.200
1993	BAL	AL	3	0	0	0	0	0	(0	0)	0	1	0	0	0	0	0	0	0	0	0	0	-	-	-	-	-
1995	BAL	AL	94	242	57	9	1	3	(2	1)	77	35	23	24	20	0	30	2	4	0	11	4	.73	2	.236	.299	.318
1996	BAL	AL	54	68	7	0	0	0	(0	0)	7	6	4	0	3	0	27	0	2	0	3	3	.50	2	.103	.141	.103
1997	2 Tms	NL	87	248	66	12	4	3	(0	3)	95	37	22	30	17	3	54	3	3	1	13	1	.93	6	.266	.320	.383
1998	CHN	NL	108	264	60	10	1	5	(1	4)	87	34	25	23	18	1	66	1	5	1	4	1	.80	6	.227	.278	.330
1999	CHN	NL	90	177	48	11	2	0	(0	0)	63	17	15	20	10	0	38	0	1	1	4	0	1.00	1	.271	.309	.356
2000	BOS	AL	101	194	41	4	3	4	(1	3)	63	30	19	16	13	0	41	0	2	0	2	0	1.00	0	.211	.261	.325
2004	TEX	AL	21	21	5	2	0	0	(0	0)	7	3	3	3	1	0	7	0	0	0	0	0	-	0	.238	.273	.333
2005	SD	NL	10	18	2	1	0	0	(0	0)	3	0	0	1	2	1	5	1	0	0	0	0	-	0	.111	.238	.167
97	NYM	NL	54	149	37	9	3	2	(0	2)	58	26	15	18	9	1	38	1	1	1	11	0	1.00	3	.248	.294	.389
97	ChC	NL	33	99	29	3	1	1	(0	1)	37	11	7	12	8	2	16	2	2	0	2	1	.67	3	.293	.358	.374
	10 ML YEARS		572	1237	287	49	11	15	(4	11)	403	164	111	117	84	5	271	7	17	3	37	9	.80	17	.232	.284	.326

Antonio Alfonseca

Pitches: R **Bats:** R **Pos:** RP-33   **Ht:** 6'5" **Wt:** 250 **Born:** 4/16/1972 **Age:** 34

			HOW MUCH HE PITCHED						WHAT HE GAVE UP													THE RESULTS						
Year	Team	Lg	G	GS	CG	GF	IP	BFP	H	R	ER	HR	SH	SF	HB	TBB	IBB	SO	WP	Bk	W	L	Pct	ShO	Sv-Op	Hld	ERC	ERA
2005	Jupiter*	A+	3	1	0	0	3.0	12	3	1	1	0	0	0	0	0	4	0	0	0	0	0	-	0	0--	-	3.79	3.00
1997	FLA	NL	17	0	0	2	25.2	123	36	16	14	3	1	0	1	10	3	19	1	0	1	3	.250	0	0-2	6	6.41	4.91
1998	FLA	NL	58	0	0	27	70.2	316	75	32	32	10	7	6	3	33	9	46	1	0	4	6	.400	0	8-14	9	4.96	4.08
1999	FLA	NL	73	0	0	49	77.2	325	79	28	28	4	3	1	4	29	6	46	1	0	4	5	.444	0	21-25	5	3.96	3.24
2000	FLA	NL	68	0	0	62	70.0	311	82	35	33	7	3	1	1	24	3	47	0	2	5	6	.455	0	45-49	0	4.79	4.24
2001	FLA	NL	58	0	0	52	61.2	268	68	24	21	6	5	1	5	15	3	40	2	0	4	4	.500	0	28-34	0	4.24	3.06
2002	CHN	NL	66	0	0	55	74.1	330	73	34	33	5	4	3	3	36	3	61	1	0	2	5	.286	0	19-28	0	4.12	4.00
2003	CHN	NL	60	0	0	17	66.1	296	76	43	43	7	4	1	2	27	3	51	0	0	3	1	.750	0	0-4	9	5.05	5.83
2004	ATL	NL	79	0	0	11	73.2	313	71	24	21	5	6	1	0	28	5	45	5	0	6	4	.600	0	0-1	13	3.47	2.57
2005	FLA	NL	33	0	0	1	27.1	117	29	15	15	2	3	2	2	14	4	16	1	0	1	1	.500	0	0-2	8	5.01	4.94
	9 ML YEARS		512	0	0	276	547.1	2399	589	251	240	49	36	16	21	216	39	371	12	2	30	35	.462	0	121-159	44	4.47	3.95

Edgardo Alfonzo

Bats: R **Throws:** R **Pos:** 3B-97; PH-11; 2B-2   **Ht:** 5'11" **Wt:** 187 **Born:** 11/8/1973 **Age:** 32

			BATTING																		BASERUNNING				AVERAGES		
Year	Team	Lg	G	AB	H	2B	3B	HR	(Hm	Rd)	TB	R	RBI	RC	TBB	IBB	SO	HBP	SH	SF	SB	CS	SB%	GDP	Avg	OBP	Slg
2005	Fresno*	AAA	4	15	7	2	0	0	(-	-)	9	2	1	3	0	0	0	0	0	0	0	0	-	0	.467	.467	.600
1995	NYN	NL	101	335	93	13	5	4	(0	4)	128	26	41	37	12	1	37	1	4	4	1	1	.50	7	.278	.301	.382
1996	NYN	NL	123	368	96	15	2	4	(2	2)	127	36	40	38	25	2	56	0	9	5	2	0	1.00	8	.261	.304	.345
1997	NYN	NL	151	518	163	27	2	10	(4	6)	224	84	72	91	63	0	56	5	8	5	11	6	.65	4	.315	.391	.432
1998	NYN	NL	144	557	155	28	2	17	(8	9)	238	94	78	85	65	1	77	3	2	3	8	3	.73	11	.278	.355	.427
1999	NYN	NL	158	628	191	41	1	27	(11	16)	315	123	108	121	85	2	85	3	1	9	9	2	.82	14	.304	.385	.502
2000	NYN	NL	150	544	176	40	2	25	(13	12)	295	109	94	122	95	1	70	6	0	6	3	2	.60	12	.324	.425	.542
2001	NYN	NL	124	457	111	22	0	17	(6	11)	184	64	49	62	51	0	62	5	1	5	5	0	1.00	7	.243	.322	.403
2002	NYN	NL	135	490	151	26	0	16	(8	8)	225	78	56	90	62	8	55	7	0	3	6	0	1.00	5	.308	.391	.459
2003	SF	NL	142	514	133	25	2	13	(6	7)	201	56	81	76	58	5	44	4	3	7	5	2	.71	14	.259	.334	.391
2004	SF	NL	139	519	150	26	4	11	(8	3)	211	66	77	75	46	2	40	5	2	4	1	1	.50	16	.289	.350	.407
2005	SF	NL	109	368	102	17	1	2	(2	0)	127	36	43	45	27	1	34	2	1	4	2	0	1.00	11	.277	.327	.345
	11 ML YEARS		1476	5298	1521	280	18	146	(68	78)	2275	772	739	842	589	22	613	40	31	55	53	17	.76	109	.287	.359	.429

Chad Allen

Bats: R **Throws:** R **Pos:** DH-17; PH-7; PR-2; LF-1; RF-1   **Ht:** 6'1" **Wt:** 195 **Born:** 2/6/1975 **Age:** 31

			BATTING																		BASERUNNING				AVERAGES		
Year	Team	Lg	G	AB	H	2B	3B	HR	(Hm	Rd)	TB	R	RBI	RC	TBB	IBB	SO	HBP	SH	SF	SB	CS	SB%	GDP	Avg	OBP	Slg
2005	Okla*	AAA	45	200	69	12	0	8	(-	-)	105	34	33	39	10	2	31	0	0	1	9	2	.82	8	.345	.374	.525
2005	Memp*	AAA	25	86	25	6	0	3	(-	-)	40	11	13	52	7	0	14	0	0	2	1	2	.33	1	.291	.337	.465
1999	MIN	AL	137	481	133	21	3	10	(4	6)	190	69	46	61	37	1	89	2	1	2	14	7	.67	10	.277	.330	.395
2000	MIN	AL	15	50	15	3	0	0	(0	0)	18	2	7	6	3	0	14	1	0	1	0	2	.00	1	.300	.345	.360
2001	MIN	AL	57	175	46	13	2	4	(1	3)	75	20	20	23	19	1	37	0	0	1	1	2	.33	7	.263	.333	.429
2002	CLE	AL	5	10	1	1	0	0	(0	0)	2	0	0	0	0	0	2	0	1	0	0	0	-	1	.100	.100	.200
2003	FLA	NL	12	24	5	1	0	0	(0	0)	8	2	0	0	0	0	5	1	0	0	0	0	-	0	.208	.240	.333
2004	TEX	AL	20	58	14	4	1	0	(0	0)	20	4	6	2	2	0	13	0	2	1	0	1	.00	1	.241	.262	.345
2005	TEX	AL	21	53	15	1	1	0	(0	0)	18	5	5	7	2	0	13	0	1	0	0	1	.00	2	.283	.309	.340
	7 ML YEARS		267	851	229	44	8	14	(5	9)	331	102	84	99	63	2	173	4	5	5	15	13	.54	23	.269	.321	.389

Armando Almanza

Pitches: L Bats: L Pos: RP-6   Ht: 6'3" Wt: 240 Born: 10/26/1972 Age: 33

Year	Team	Lg	G	GS	CG	GF	IP	BFP	H	R	ER	HR	SH	SF	HB	TBB	IBB	SO	WP	Bk	W	L	Pct	ShO	Sv-Op Hld	ERC	ERA
2005	Tenn*	AA	6	0	0	5	7.1	35	9	5	4	1	1	0	0	4	0	7	1	0	1	0	1.000	0	1- -	6.16	4.91
2005	Tucsn*	AAA	15	0	0	1	15.0	64	12	6	3	2	0	0	0	7	0	19	2	0	1	0	1.000	0	1- -	3.40	1.80
2005	Memp*	AAA	10	0	0	0	10.0	45	13	7	7	2	0	0	2	2	0	9	5	0	0	0	-	0	0- -	6.80	6.30
2005	Fresno*	AAA	2	0	0	0	3.1	17	5	5	5	1	0	0	0	2	0	3	1	1	0	1	.000	0	0- -	9.61	13.50
1999	FLA	NL	14	0	0	2	15.2	64	8	4	3	1	1	1	1	9	1	20	0	1	0	1	.000	0	0-0 3	2.09	1.72
2000	FLA	NL	67	0	0	8	46.1	216	38	27	25	3	2	2	2	43	6	46	1	0	4	2	.667	0	0-4 13	4.79	4.86
2001	FLA	NL	52	0	0	8	41.0	178	34	24	22	8	1	3	0	26	1	45	2	0	2	2	.500	0	0-2 12	4.73	4.83
2002	FLA	NL	51	0	0	10	45.2	190	36	22	22	8	3	3	0	23	1	57	2	1	3	2	.600	0	2-4 12	3.85	4.34
2003	FLA	NL	51	0	0	15	50.1	230	59	37	34	10	1	3	2	25	2	49	2	1	4	5	.444	0	0-2 6	6.42	6.08
2004	ATL	NL	13	0	0	5	11.2	54	9	8	8	3	0	1	1	7	2	13	0	1	1	1	.500	0	0-0 4	4.48	6.17
2005	ARI	NL	6	0	0	1	4.0	19	5	1	1	1	0	0	0	3	0	2	1	0	0	0	-	0	0-1 2	8.64	2.25
7 ML YEARS			254	0	0	49	214.2	951	189	123	115	34	8	13	6	136	13	232	8	4	14	13	.519	0	2-13 48	4.79	4.82

Carlos Almanzar

Pitches: R Bats: R Pos: RP-6   Ht: 6'2" Wt: 200 Born: 11/6/1973 Age: 32

Year	Team	Lg	G	GS	CG	GF	IP	BFP	H	R	ER	HR	SH	SF	HB	TBB	IBB	SO	WP	Bk	W	L	Pct	ShO	Sv-Op Hld	ERC	ERA
1997	TOR	AL	4	0	0	2	3.1	12	1	1	1	1	0	0	0	1	0	4	0	0	0	1	.000	0	0-0 0	1.39	2.70
1998	TOR	AL	25	0	0	8	28.2	129	34	18	17	4	1	0	0	8	2	20	0	0	2	2	.500	0	0-3 1	4.85	5.34
1999	SD	NL	28	0	0	11	37.1	173	48	32	31	6	2	1	3	15	2	30	2	0	0	0	-	0	0-0 6	6.54	7.47
2000	SD	NL	62	0	0	11	69.2	308	73	35	34	12	2	3	4	25	2	56	2	0	4	5	.444	0	0-3 8	4.83	4.39
2001	NYA	AL	10	0	0	7	10.2	46	14	4	4	2	1	1	0	2	1	6	0	0	0	1	.000	0	0-2 0	5.63	3.38
2002	CIN	NL	8	1	0	4	11.2	45	6	4	3	0	0	2	0	5	1	7	1	0	1	0	1.000	0	0-0 0	1.26	2.31
2004	TEX	AL	67	0	0	18	72.2	298	66	32	30	8	2	3	4	19	4	44	1	0	7	3	.700	0	0-2 20	3.28	3.72
2005	TEX	AL	6	0	0	2	5.0	33	10	8	8	2	0	2	1	7	0	3	4	0	0	0	-	0	0-0 0	19.60	14.40
8 ML YEARS			210	1	0	63	239.0	1044	252	134	128	35	8	12	13	82	12	170	10	0	13	13	.500	0	0-10 29	4.61	4.82

Sandy Alomar Jr.

Bats: R Throws: R Pos: C-46; PH-2   Ht: 6'5" Wt: 235 Born: 6/18/1966 Age: 40

Year	Team	Lg	G	AB	H	2B	3B	HR	(Hm	Rd)	TB	R	RBI	RC	TBB	IBB	SO	HBP	SH	SF	SB	CS	SB%	GDP	Avg	OBP	Slg
1988	SD	NL	1	1	0	0	0	0	(0	0)	0	0	0	0	0	0	1	0	0	0	0	0	-	0	.000	.000	.000
1989	SD	NL	7	19	4	1	0	1	(1	0)	8	1	6	2	3	1	3	0	0	0	0	0	-	1	.211	.318	.421
1990	CLE	AL	132	445	129	26	2	9	(5	4)	186	60	66	60	25	2	46	2	5	6	4	1	.80	10	.290	.326	.418
1991	CLE	AL	51	184	40	9	0	0	(0	0)	49	10	7	10	8	1	24	4	2	1	0	4	.00	4	.217	.264	.266
1992	CLE	AL	89	299	75	16	0	2	(1	1)	97	22	26	26	13	3	32	5	3	0	3	3	.50	7	.251	.293	.324
1993	CLE	AL	64	215	58	7	1	6	(3	3)	85	24	32	28	11	0	28	6	1	4	3	1	.75	3	.270	.318	.395
1994	CLE	AL	80	292	84	15	1	14	(4	10)	143	44	43	48	25	2	31	2	0	1	8	4	.67	7	.288	.347	.490
1995	CLE	AL	66	203	61	6	0	10	(6	4)	97	32	35	30	7	0	26	3	4	1	3	1	.75	8	.300	.332	.478
1996	CLE	AL	127	418	110	23	0	11	(3	8)	166	53	50	44	19	0	42	3	2	2	1	0	1.00	20	.263	.299	.397
1997	CLE	AL	125	451	146	37	0	21	(9	12)	246	63	83	78	19	2	48	3	6	1	0	2	.00	16	.324	.354	.545
1998	CLE	AL	117	409	96	26	2	6	(3	3)	144	45	44	33	18	0	45	3	5	3	0	3	.00	15	.235	.270	.352
1999	CLE	AL	37	137	42	13	0	6	(4	2)	73	19	25	23	4	0	23	0	1	2	0	1	.00	1	.307	.322	.533
2000	CLE	AL	97	356	103	16	2	7	(5	2)	144	44	42	45	16	1	41	4	4	4	2	2	.50	9	.289	.324	.404
2001	CHA	AL	70	220	54	8	1	4	(1	3)	76	17	21	20	12	1	17	2	3	2	1	2	.33	6	.245	.288	.345
2002	2 Tms		89	283	79	14	1	7	(5	2)	116	29	37	30	9	0	33	1	1	2	0	0	-	11	.279	.302	.410
2003	CHA	AL	75	194	52	12	0	5	(3	2)	79	22	26	21	4	0	17	0	5	1	0	0	-	4	.268	.281	.407
2004	CHA	AL	50	146	35	4	0	2	(1	1)	45	15	14	12	11	2	13	2	3	2	0	0	-	4	.240	.298	.308
2005	TEX	AL	46	128	35	7	0	0	(0	0)	42	11	14	14	5	0	12	1	3	0	0	0	-	3	.273	.306	.328
02	CWS	AL	51	167	48	10	1	7	(5	2)	81	21	25	22	5	0	14	1	1	2	0	0	-	5	.287	.309	.485
02	Col	NL	38	116	31	4	0	0	(0	0)	35	8	12	8	4	0	19	0	0	0	0	0	-	6	.267	.292	.302
18 ML YEARS			1323	4400	1203	240	10	111	(52	59)	1796	511	571	524	209	15	482	41	48	32	25	24	.51	129	.273	.310	.408

Moises Alou

Bats: R Throws: R Pos: LF-74; RF-53; DH-3; PH-3   Ht: 6'3" Wt: 220 Born: 7/3/1966 Age: 39

Year	Team	Lg	G	AB	H	2B	3B	HR	(Hm	Rd)	TB	R	RBI	RC	TBB	IBB	SO	HBP	SH	SF	SB	CS	SB%	GDP	Avg	OBP	Slg
1990	2 Tms	NL	16	20	4	0	1	0	(0	0)	6	4	0	1	0	0	3	0	1	0	0	0	-	1	.200	.200	.300
1992	MON	NL	115	341	96	28	2	9	(6	3)	155	53	56	53	25	0	46	1	5	5	16	2	.89	5	.282	.328	.455
1993	MON	NL	136	482	138	29	6	18	(10	8)	233	70	85	79	38	9	53	5	3	7	17	6	.74	9	.286	.340	.483
1994	MON	NL	107	422	143	31	5	22	(9	13)	250	81	78	92	42	10	63	2	0	5	7	6	.54	7	.339	.397	.592
1995	MON	NL	93	344	94	22	0	14	(4	10)	158	48	58	52	29	6	56	9	0	4	4	3	.57	9	.273	.342	.459
1996	MON	NL	143	540	152	28	2	21	(14	7)	247	87	96	81	49	7	83	2	0	7	9	4	.69	15	.281	.339	.457
1997	FLA	NL	150	538	157	29	5	23	(12	11)	265	88	115	97	70	9	85	4	0	7	9	5	.64	13	.292	.373	.493
1998	HOU	NL	159	584	182	34	5	38	(17	21)	340	104	124	130	84	11	87	5	0	6	11	3	.79	14	.312	.399	.582
2000	HOU	NL	126	454	161	28	2	30	(17	13)	283	82	114	104	52	4	45	2	0	9	3	3	.50	21	.355	.416	.623
2001	HOU	NL	136	513	170	31	1	27	(15	12)	284	79	108	104	57	14	57	3	0	6	5	1	.83	18	.331	.396	.554
2002	CHN	NL	132	484	133	23	1	15	(7	8)	203	50	61	59	47	4	61	0	0	3	8	0	1.00	15	.275	.337	.419
2003	CHN	NL	151	565	158	35	1	22	(14	8)	261	83	91	94	63	7	67	7	0	3	3	1	.75	16	.280	.357	.462
2004	CHN	NL	155	601	176	36	3	39	(29	10)	335	106	106	110	68	2	80	0	0	6	3	0	1.00	12	.293	.361	.557
2005	SF	NL	123	427	137	21	3	19	(12	7)	221	67	63	74	56	1	43	3	0	4	5	1	.83	11	.321	.400	.518
90	Pit	NL	2	5	1	0	0	0	(0	0)	1	0	0	0	0	0	0	0	0	0	0	0	-	1	.200	.200	.200
90	Mon	NL	14	15	3	0	1	0	(0	0)	5	4	0	1	0	0	3	0	1	0	0	0	-	0	.200	.200	.333
14 ML YEARS			1742	6315	1901	375	37	297	(168	129)	3241	1002	1155	1134	680	84	829	43	9	74	100	35	.74	166	.301	.369	.513

Abe Alvarez

Pitches: L **Bats:** L **Pos:** RP-2 · **Ht:** 6'2" **Wt:** 190 **Born:** 10/17/1982 **Age:** 23

Year	Team	Lg	G	GS	CG	GF	IP	BFP	H	R	ER	HR	SH	SF	HB	TBB	IBB	SO	WP	Bk	W	L	Pct	ShO	Sv-Op	Hld	ERC	ERA
2003	Lowell	A-	9	9	0	0	19.0	68	9	2	0	0	0	1	0	2	1	19	0	0	0	0	-	0	0--	-	0.61	0.00
2004	Portlnd	AA	26	26	0	0	135.1	562	133	65	55	13	4	3	5	32	0	108	2	0	10	9	.526	0	0--	-	3.48	3.66
2005	Pwtckt	AAA	26	26	0	0	144.2	608	143	84	78	17	4	5	4	31	0	109	0	0	11	6	.647	0	0--	-	3.46	4.85
2004	BOS	AL	1	1	0	0	5.0	25	8	5	5	2	0	0	0	5	0	2	0	0	0	1	.000	0	0-0	0	15.00	9.00
2005	BOS	AL	2	0	0	1	2.1	13	6	4	4	1	0	0	0	0	0	1	0	0	0	0	-	0	0-0	0	15.72	15.43
	2 ML YEARS		3	1	0	1	7.1	38	14	9	9	3	0	0	0	5	0	3	0	0	0	1	.000	0	0-0	0	15.25	11.05

Wilson Alvarez

Pitches: L **Bats:** L **Pos:** RP-19; SP-2 · **Ht:** 6'1" **Wt:** 245 **Born:** 3/24/1970 **Age:** 36

Year	Team	Lg	G	GS	CG	GF	IP	BFP	H	R	ER	HR	SH	SF	HB	TBB	IBB	SO	WP	Bk	W	L	Pct	ShO	Sv-Op	Hld	ERC	ERA
2005	LsVgs*	AAA	4	4	0	0	7.2	29	4	2	2	1	1	0	0	2	0	9	0	0	0	1	.000	0	0--	-	1.46	2.35
1989	TEX	AL	1	1	0	0	0.0	5	3	3	3	2	0	0	0	2	0	0	0	0	0	1	.000	0	0-0	0	-	-
1991	CHA	AL	10	9	2	0	56.1	237	47	26	22	9	3	1	0	29	0	32	2	0	3	2	.600	1	0-0	0	4.09	3.51
1992	CHA	AL	34	9	0	4	100.1	455	103	64	58	12	3	4	6	65	2	66	2	0	5	3	.625	0	1-1	3	5.61	5.20
1993	CHA	AL	31	31	1	0	207.2	877	168	78	68	14	13	6	7	122	8	155	2	1	15	8	.652	1	0-0	0	3.69	2.95
1994	CHA	AL	24	24	2	0	161.2	682	147	72	62	16	6	3	0	62	1	108	3	0	12	8	.600	1	0-0	0	3.49	3.45
1995	CHA	AL	29	29	3	0	175.0	769	171	96	84	21	6	5	2	93	4	118	1	2	8	11	.421	0	0-0	0	4.66	4.32
1996	CHA	AL	35	35	0	0	217.1	946	216	106	102	21	5	2	4	97	3	181	2	0	15	10	.600	0	0-0	0	4.26	4.22
1997	2 Tms		33	33	2	0	212.0	896	180	97	82	18	10	6	4	91	4	179	5	1	13	11	.542	1	0-0	0	3.30	3.48
1998	TB	AL	25	25	0	0	142.2	624	130	78	75	18	1	2	9	68	0	107	4	0	6	14	.300	0	0-0	0	4.30	4.73
1999	TB	AL	28	28	1	0	160.0	703	159	92	75	22	3	3	6	79	1	128	3	0	9	9	.500	0	0-0	0	4.87	4.22
2002	TB	AL	23	10	0	3	75.0	339	80	47	44	13	2	3	4	36	3	56	2	0	2	3	.400	0	1-1	2	5.46	5.28
2003	LA	NL	21	12	1	2	95.0	377	80	27	25	5	2	1	5	23	1	82	1	0	6	2	.750	1	1-1	1	2.61	2.37
2004	LAN	NL	40	15	0	6	120.2	499	109	56	54	12	11	5	5	31	2	102	1	0	7	6	.538	0	1-2	2	3.13	4.03
2005	LAN	NL	21	2	0	3	24.0	109	31	15	15	7	2	2	0	7	0	16	0	0	1	4	.200	0	0-0	2	6.71	5.63
97	CWS	AL	22	22	2	0	145.2	613	126	61	49	9	6	5	3	55	1	110	4	0	9	8	.529	1	0-0	0	3.05	3.03
97	SF	NL	11	11	0	0	66.1	283	54	36	33	9	4	1	1	36	3	69	1	1	4	3	.571	0	0-0	0	3.86	4.48
	14 ML YEARS		355	263	12	18	1747.2	7518	1624	857	769	190	67	43	50	805	29	1330	28	4	102	92	.526	5	4-5	10	4.09	3.96

Chip Ambres

Bats: R **Throws:** R **Pos:** CF-24; LF-23; PH-10; PR-4; DH-2 · **Ht:** 6'1" **Wt:** 190 **Born:** 12/19/1979 **Age:** 26

Year	Team	Lg	G	AB	H	2B	3B	HR	(Hm	Rd)	TB	R	RBI	RC	TBB	IBB	SO	HBP	SH	SF	SB	CS	SB%	GDP	Avg	OBP	Slg
1999	Marlins	R	37	139	49	13	3	1	(-	-)	71	29	15	36	25	0	19	2	0	2	22	3	.88	0	.353	.452	.511
1999	Utica	A-	28	105	28	3	6	5	(-	-)	58	24	15	23	21	0	25	1	0	2	11	4	.73	1	.267	.388	.552
2000	Kane	A	84	320	74	16	3	7	(-	-)	117	46	28	46	52	0	72	3	3	2	26	8	.76	3	.231	.342	.366
2001	Kane	A	96	377	100	26	8	5	(-	-)	157	79	41	61	53	0	81	11	5	3	19	15	.56	7	.265	.369	.416
2002	Jupiter	A+	123	509	120	25	7	9	(-	-)	186	88	37	66	57	0	98	9	2	1	23	8	.74	6	.236	.323	.365
2003	Carlina	AA	127	380	98	23	8	10	(-	-)	167	75	55	67	72	1	81	2	0	3	9	6	.60	3	.258	.376	.439
2004	Carlina	AA	137	452	109	28	3	20	(-	-)	203	81	62	79	76	2	117	6	4	8	26	9	.74	7	.241	.352	.449
2005	Pwtckt	AAA	84	279	82	20	3	10	(-	-)	138	47	50	59	47	2	64	4	0	2	19	5	.79	7	.294	.401	.495
2005	KC	AL	53	145	35	8	0	4	(2	2)	55	25	9	13	16	1	32	2	3	1	3	2	.60	5	.241	.323	.379

Alfredo Amezaga

Bats: B **Throws:** R **Pos:** 3B-2; PH-2; SS-1; PR-1 · **Ht:** 5'10" **Wt:** 165 **Born:** 1/16/1978 **Age:** 28

Year	Team	Lg	G	AB	H	2B	3B	HR	(Hm	Rd)	TB	R	RBI	RC	TBB	IBB	SO	HBP	SH	SF	SB	CS	SB%	GDP	Avg	OBP	Slg
2005	Indy*	AAA	64	185	63	12	2	1	(-	-)	82	28	12	33	17	1	27	2	5	2	14	7	.67	1	.341	.398	.443
2002	ANA	AL	12	13	7	2	0	0	(0	0)	9	3	2	6	0	0	1	0	0	0	1	0	1.00	1	.538	.538	.692
2003	ANA	AL	37	105	22	3	2	2	(0	2)	35	15	7	7	9	0	23	1	5	0	2	2	.50	2	.210	.278	.333
2004	ANA	AL	73	93	15	2	0	2	(0	2)	23	12	11	5	3	0	24	3	6	0	3	2	.60	2	.161	.212	.247
2005	2 Tms	NL	5	6	1	0	0	0	(0	0)	1	2	0	0	1	0	0	0	0	0	1	0	1.00	0	.167	.286	.167
05	Col	NL	2	3	1	0	0	0	(0	0)	1	1	0	0	0	0	0	0	0	0	0	0	-	0	.333	.333	.333
05	Pit	NL	3	3	0	0	0	0	(0	0)	0	1	0	0	1	0	0	0	0	0	1	0	1.00	0	.000	.250	.000
	4 ML YEARS		127	217	45	7	2	4	(0	4)	68	32	20	18	13	0	48	4	11	0	7	4	.64	5	.207	.265	.313

Brian J Anderson

Pitches: L **Bats:** R **Pos:** SP-6 · **Ht:** 6'1" **Wt:** 183 **Born:** 4/26/1972 **Age:** 34

Year	Team	Lg	G	GS	CG	GF	IP	BFP	H	R	ER	HR	SH	SF	HB	TBB	IBB	SO	WP	Bk	W	L	Pct	ShO	Sv-Op	Hld	ERC	ERA
2005	Wichta*	AA	1	1	0	0	1.1	9	5	3	2	1	0	0	0	0	0	2	0	0	0	0	-	0	0--	-	29.54	13.50
2005	Omha*	AAA	1	1	0	0	4.1	17	3	3	3	1	0	0	0	1	0	2	0	0	0	0	-	0	0--	-	2.55	6.23
1993	CAL	AL	4	1	0	3	11.1	45	11	5	5	1	0	0	0	2	0	4	0	0	0	0	-	0	0-0	0	3.08	3.97
1994	CAL	AL	18	18	0	0	101.2	441	120	63	59	13	3	6	5	27	0	47	5	5	7	5	.583	0	0-0	0	5.05	5.22
1995	CAL	AL	18	17	1	0	99.2	433	110	66	65	24	5	5	3	30	2	45	1	3	6	8	.429	0	0-0	0	5.37	5.87
1996	CLE	AL	10	9	0	0	51.1	215	58	29	28	9	2	3	0	14	1	21	2	0	3	1	.750	0	0-0	1	4.96	4.91
1997	CLE	AL	8	8	0	0	48.0	199	55	28	25	7	0	5	0	11	0	22	1	0	4	2	.667	0	0-0	0	4.71	4.69
1998	ARI	NL	32	32	2	0	208.0	845	221	100	100	39	8	3	4	24	2	95	3	6	12	13	.480	1	0-0	0	3.99	4.33
1999	ARI	NL	31	19	2	1	130.0	549	144	69	66	18	4	0	1	28	3	75	0	2	8	2	.800	1	1-2	1	4.23	4.57
2000	ARI	NL	33	32	2	0	213.1	876	226	101	96	38	6	6	3	39	7	104	1	4	11	7	.611	0	0-0	0	4.15	4.05
2001	ARI	NL	29	22	1	1	133.1	571	156	93	77	25	7	4	1	30	2	55	2	1	4	9	.308	0	0-1	0	5.00	5.20
2002	ARI	NL	35	24	1	0	156.0	676	174	86	83	23	6	8	1	32	3	81	2	5	6	11	.353	0	0-0	1	4.28	4.79
2003	2 Tms	AL	32	31	2	0	197.2	821	212	110	83	27	4	12	4	43	3	87	3	1	14	11	.560	1	0-0	0	4.14	3.78

Year	Team	Lg	G	GS	CG	GF	IP	BFP	H	R	ER	HR	SH	SF	HB	TBB	IBB	SO	WP	Bk	W	L	Pct	ShO	Sv-Op	Hld	ERC	ERA
2004	KC	AL	35	26	2	2	166.0	745	217	123	104	33	5	7	1	53	4	70	2	0	6	12	.333	1	0-0	2	6.36	5.64
2005	KC	AL	6	6	0	0	30.2	133	39	24	23	7	0	1	0	4	1	17	0	1	1	2	.333	0	0-0	0	5.36	6.75
03	Cle	AL	25	24	0	0	148.0	623	162	88	61	21	3	10	4	32	3	72	2	1	9	10	.474	0	0-0	0	4.29	3.71
03	KC	AL	7	7	2	0	49.2	198	50	22	22	6	1	2	0	11	0	15	1	0	5	1	.833	1	0-0	0	3.72	3.99
13 ML YEARS			291	245	12	11	1547.0	6532	1743	897	814	264	50	60	23	337	28	723	22	28	82	83	.497	4	1-3	5	4.64	4.74

Brian Anderson

Bats: R **Throws:** R **Pos:** LF-9; CF-5; PH-3; PR-2; RF-1　　　　　**Ht:** 6'2" **Wt:** 205 **Born:** 3/11/1982 **Age:** 24

Year	Team	Lg	G	AB	H	2B	3B	HR	(Hm	Rd)	TB	R	RBI	RC	TBB	IBB	SO	HBP	SH	SF	SB	CS	SB%	GDP	Avg	OBP	Slg
2003	Gr Falls	R+	13	49	19	2	1	2	(-	-)	29	6	13	13	9	1	10	1	0	0	3	1	.75	1	.388	.492	.592
2004	WinSa	A+	69	254	81	22	4	8	(-	-)	135	43	46	51	29	5	44	3	0	1	10	1	.91	3	.319	.394	.531
2004	Brham	AA	48	185	50	9	3	4	(-	-)	77	26	27	26	19	3	30	3	1	1	3	2	.60	3	.270	.346	.416
2005	Charltt	AAA	118	448	132	24	3	16	(-	-)	210	71	57	77	44	0	115	4	1	4	4	2	.67	11	.295	.360	.469
2005	CHA	AL	13	34	6	1	0	2	(0	2)	13	3	3	2	0	0	12	0	1	0	1	0	1.00	2	.176	.176	.382

Garret Anderson

Bats: L **Throws:** L **Pos:** LF-106; DH-36　　　　　**Ht:** 6'3" **Wt:** 228 **Born:** 6/30/1972 **Age:** 34

Year	Team	Lg	G	AB	H	2B	3B	HR	(Hm	Rd)	TB	R	RBI	RC	TBB	IBB	SO	HBP	SH	SF	SB	CS	SB%	GDP	Avg	OBP	Slg
1994	CAL	AL	5	13	5	0	0	0	(0	0)	5	0	1	2	0	0	2	0	0	0	0	0	-	0	.385	.385	.385
1995	CAL	AL	106	374	120	19	1	16	(7	9)	189	50	69	63	19	4	65	1	2	4	6	2	.75	8	.321	.352	.505
1996	CAL	AL	150	607	173	33	2	12	(7	5)	246	79	72	68	27	5	84	0	5	3	7	9	.44	22	.285	.314	.405
1997	ANA	AL	154	624	189	36	3	8	(5	3)	255	76	92	80	30	6	70	2	1	5	10	4	.71	20	.303	.334	.409
1998	ANA	AL	156	622	183	41	7	15	(4	11)	283	62	79	88	29	8	80	1	3	3	8	3	.73	13	.294	.325	.455
1999	ANA	AL	157	620	188	36	2	21	(10	11)	291	88	80	92	34	8	81	0	0	6	3	4	.43	15	.303	.336	.469
2000	ANA	AL	159	647	185	40	3	35	(20	15)	336	92	117	95	24	5	87	0	1	9	7	6	.54	21	.286	.307	.519
2001	ANA	AL	161	672	194	39	2	28	(13	15)	321	83	123	97	27	4	100	0	0	5	13	6	.68	12	.289	.314	.478
2002	ANA	AL	158	638	195	56	3	29	(13	16)	344	93	123	108	30	11	80	0	0	10	6	4	.60	11	.306	.332	.539
2003	ANA	AL	159	638	201	49	4	29	(12	17)	345	80	116	114	31	10	83	0	0	4	6	3	.67	15	.315	.345	.541
2004	ANA	AL	112	442	133	20	1	14	(4	10)	197	57	75	70	29	6	75	1	0	3	2	1	.67	3	.301	.343	.446
2005	LAA	AL	142	575	163	34	1	17	(5	12)	250	68	96	82	23	8	84	0	0	5	1	1	.50	13	.283	.308	.435
12 ML YEARS			1619	6472	1929	403	29	224	(100	124)	3062	828	1043	959	303	75	891	5	12	57	69	43	.62	153	.298	.327	.473

Jason Anderson

Pitches: R **Bats:** L **Pos:** RP-3　　　　　**Ht:** 6'0" **Wt:** 170 **Born:** 6/9/1979 **Age:** 27

Year	Team	Lg	G	GS	CG	GF	IP	BFP	H	R	ER	HR	SH	SF	HB	TBB	IBB	SO	WP	Bk	W	L	Pct	ShO	Sv-Op	Hld	ERC	ERA
2005	Clmbs*	AAA	55	0	0	24	67.2	265	44	21	20	4	3	3	1	18	1	60	3	0	4	1	.800	0	10--	-	1.64	2.66
2003	2 Tms		28	0	0	14	31.1	147	33	19	17	5	0	4	3	19	5	16	3	0	1	0	1.000	0	0-0	0	5.74	4.88
2004	CLE	AL	1	0	0	0	1.0	8	1	5	5	1	0	0	0	4	1	1	0	0	0	0	-	0	0-0	0	28.92	45.00
2005	NYA	AL	3	0	0	1	5.2	27	4	5	5	0	0	0	0	7	1	2	0	0	1	0	1.000	0	0-0	0	4.51	7.94
03	NYY	AL	22	0	0	12	20.2	100	23	13	11	3	0	2	2	14	4	9	3	0	1	0	1.000	0	0-0	0	6.19	4.79
03	NYM	NL	6	0	0	2	10.2	47	10	6	6	2	0	2	1	5	1	7	0	0	0	0	-	0	0-0	0	4.86	5.06
3 ML YEARS			32	0	0	15	38.0	182	38	29	27	6	0	4	3	30	7	19	3	0	2	1	1.000	0	0-0	0	6.06	6.39

Marlon Anderson

Bats: L **Throws:** R **Pos:** PH-64; 1B-23; 2B-20; RF-14; LF-9; DH-2　　　　　**Ht:** 5'11" **Wt:** 200 **Born:** 1/6/1974 **Age:** 32

Year	Team	Lg	G	AB	H	2B	3B	HR	(Hm	Rd)	TB	R	RBI	RC	TBB	IBB	SO	HBP	SH	SF	SB	CS	SB%	GDP	Avg	OBP	Slg
1998	PHI	NL	17	43	14	3	0	1	(1	0)	20	4	4	7	1	0	6	0	0	1	2	0	1.00	1	.326	.333	.465
1999	PHI	NL	129	452	114	26	4	5	(4	1)	163	48	54	49	24	1	61	2	4	2	13	2	.87	6	.252	.292	.361
2000	PHI	NL	41	162	37	8	1	1	(1	0)	50	10	15	12	12	0	22	0	0	2	2	2	.50	5	.228	.282	.309
2001	PHI	NL	147	522	153	30	2	11	(7	4)	220	69	61	72	35	5	74	2	10	5	8	5	.62	12	.293	.337	.421
2002	PHI	NL	145	539	139	30	6	8	(4	4)	205	64	48	53	42	14	71	5	2	4	5	1	.83	16	.258	.315	.380
2003	TB	AL	145	482	130	27	3	6	(2	4)	181	59	67	70	41	5	60	3	4	5	19	3	.86	6	.270	.328	.376
2004	STL	NL	113	253	60	12	0	8	(2	6)	96	31	28	23	12	1	38	1	0	5	6	2	.75	5	.237	.269	.379
2005	NYN	NL	123	235	62	9	2	7	(3	4)	92	31	19	23	18	0	45	1	4	2	6	1	.86	2	.264	.316	.391
8 ML YEARS			860	2688	709	145	16	47	(24	23)	1027	316	296	309	185	26	377	14	24	24	61	16	.79	52	.264	.312	.382

Matt Anderson

Pitches: R **Bats:** R **Pos:** RP-12　　　　　**Ht:** 6'4" **Wt:** 190 **Born:** 8/17/1976 **Age:** 29

Year	Team	Lg	G	GS	CG	GF	IP	BFP	H	R	ER	HR	SH	SF	HB	TBB	IBB	SO	WP	Bk	W	L	Pct	ShO	Sv-Op	Hld	ERC	ERA
2005	ColSpr*	AAA	46	0	0	36	47.0	198	36	23	22	5	1	1	1	21	0	46	8	2	3	3	.500	0	9--	-	3.07	4.21
1998	DET	AL	42	0	0	10	44.0	194	38	16	16	3	6	3	2	31	4	44	2	0	5	1	.833	0	0-4	6	4.38	3.27
1999	DET	AL	37	0	0	9	38.0	180	33	27	24	8	0	2	1	35	1	32	3	0	5	1	.667	0	0-2	3	6.34	5.68
2000	DET	AL	69	0	0	27	74.1	324	61	44	39	8	2	6	3	45	4	71	4	0	3	2	.600	0	1-1	9	4.02	4.72
2001	DET	AL	62	0	0	41	56.0	239	56	33	30	2	1	2	0	18	4	52	9	1	3	1	.750	0	22-24	9	3.19	4.82
2002	DET	AL	12	0	0	10	11.0	58	17	13	11	1	1	2	0	8	1	8	1	0	0	1	.667	0	0-2	0	9.52	9.00
2003	DET	AL	23	0	0	10	23.1	105	25	17	14	5	2	1	1	9	1	13	1	0	0	1	.000	0	3-4	4	5.25	5.40
2005	COL	NL	12	0	0	6	10.0	62	19	14	14	3	1	1	2	11	0	4	0	0	0	0	-	0	0-0	2	16.08	12.60
7 ML YEARS			257	0	0	111	256.2	1162	249	167	148	30	13	17	11	157	15	224	20	1	15	7	.682	0	26-37	33	4.94	5.19

Robert Andino

Bats: R **Throws:** R **Pos:** SS-17; PH-1   **Ht:** 6'0" **Wt:** 170 **Born:** 4/25/1984 **Age:** 22

								BATTING													BASERUNNING				AVERAGES		
Year	Team	Lg	G	AB	H	2B	3B	HR	(Hm	Rd)	TB	R	RBI	RC	TBB	IBB	SO	HBP	SH	SF	SB	CS	SB%	GDP	Avg	OBP	Slg
2002	Marlins	R	9	27	7	0	0	0	(-	-)	7	2	2	3	5	0	6	0	0	1	3	0	1.00	1	.259	.364	.259
2002	Jmstwn	A-	9	36	6	1	1	0	(-	-)	9	2	3	1	1	0	9	0	0	0	1	0	1.00	2	.167	.189	.250
2003	Grnsbr	A	119	416	78	17	2	2	(-	-)	105	45	27	28	46	0	128	0	7	5	6	5	.55	6	.188	.266	.252
2004	Jupiter	A+	49	197	55	7	2	0	(-	-)	66	18	15	20	7	0	43	0	3	1	6	2	.75	3	.279	.302	.335
2004	Grnsbr	A	76	295	83	10	1	8	(-	-)	119	27	46	40	18	0	83	1	6	4	9	2	.82	5	.281	.321	.403
2005	Carlina	AA	127	516	139	30	0	5	(-	-)	184	63	48	64	37	0	111	6	8	4	22	7	.76	11	.269	.323	.357
2005	FLA	NL	17	44	7	4	0	0	(0	0)	11	4	1	1	5	1	8	0	1	0	1	0	1.00	2	.159	.245	.250

Greg Aquino

Pitches: R **Bats:** R **Pos:** RP-35   **Ht:** 6'1" **Wt:** 188 **Born:** 1/11/1978 **Age:** 28

				HOW MUCH HE PITCHED					WHAT HE GAVE UP										THE RESULTS						
Year	Team	Lg	G	GS	CG	GF	IP	BFP	H	R	ER	HR	SH	SF	HB	TBB	IBB	SO	WP	Bk	W	L	Pct	ShO	Sv-Op	Hld	ERC	ERA
1999	DBcks	R	13	2	0	4	19.0	89	17	11	8	0	0	1	2	13	0	20	2	0	1	2	.333	0	0- -	-	4.10	3.79
2000	Sbend	A	29	18	0	5	119.0	538	119	67	59	9	4	2	6	56	0	93	9	2	5	7	.417	0	0- -	-	4.26	4.46
2001	Lancst	A+	25	4	0	6	42.0	211	59	40	38	7	3	1	2	24	0	39	6	0	2	5	.286	0	0- -	-	7.86	8.14
2001	Yakima	A-	8	8	0	0	46.1	194	39	18	17	2	1	0	2	14	1	39	10	0	4	2	.667	0	0- -	-	2.57	3.30
2002	Yakima	A-	6	6	0	0	35.0	141	26	9	8	0	1	1	0	17	0	34	3	0	1	1	.500	0	0- -	-	2.46	2.06
2002	Lancst	A+	8	8	0	0	49.0	209	50	20	20	3	1	0	3	18	0	50	3	0	4	1	.800	0	0- -	-	4.12	3.67
2003	ElPaso	AA	20	20	0	0	106.2	458	115	43	41	5	3	0	4	38	1	91	7	3	7	3	.700	0	0- -	-	4.17	3.46
2004	Tucsn	AAA	21	2	0	7	29.2	141	33	25	21	2	0	0	4	18	0	19	2	0	1	3	.250	0	1- -	-	5.30	6.37
2005	Tucsn	AAA	6	0	0	4	8.2	30	4	1	1	0	0	0	0	0	0	7	0	0	0	1	1.000	0	0- -	-	0.46	1.04
2004	ARI	NL	34	0	0	26	35.1	147	24	15	12	4	2	2	2	17	2	26	4	0	0	2	.000	0	16-19	1	2.87	3.06
2005	ARI	NL	35	0	0	11	31.1	155	42	29	27	7	1	1	4	17	1	34	2	1	0	1	.000	0	1-3	3	8.22	7.76
	2 ML YEARS		69	0	0	37	66.2	302	66	44	39	11	3	3	6	34	3	60	6	1	0	3	.000	0	17-22	4	5.19	5.27

Danny Ardoin

Bats: R **Throws:** R **Pos:** C-80; PH-3   **Ht:** 6'0" **Wt:** 218 **Born:** 7/8/1974 **Age:** 31

								BATTING													BASERUNNING				AVERAGES		
Year	Team	Lg	G	AB	H	2B	3B	HR	(Hm	Rd)	TB	R	RBI	RC	TBB	IBB	SO	HBP	SH	SF	SB	CS	SB%	GDP	Avg	OBP	Slg
2005	ColSpr*	AAA	44	142	48	12	2	6	(-	-)	82	27	24	35	20	2	38	6	1	1	3	1	.75	7	.338	.438	.577
2000	MIN	AL	15	32	4	1	0	1	(0	1)	8	4	5	2	8	0	10	0	0	0	0	0	-	0	.125	.300	.250
2004	TEX	AL	6	8	1	0	0	0	(0	0)	1	1	1	1	3	0	2	0	0	0	0	0	-	0	.125	.364	.125
2005	COL	NL	80	210	48	10	0	6	(3	3)	76	28	22	21	20	2	69	9	7	2	1	1	.50	8	.229	.320	.362
	3 ML YEARS		101	250	53	11	0	7	(3	4)	85	33	28	24	31	2	81	9	7	2	1	1	.50	8	.212	.318	.340

Tony Armas Jr.

Pitches: R **Bats:** R **Pos:** SP-19   **Ht:** 6'4" **Wt:** 215 **Born:** 4/29/1978 **Age:** 28

				HOW MUCH HE PITCHED					WHAT HE GAVE UP										THE RESULTS						
Year	Team	Lg	G	GS	CG	GF	IP	BFP	H	R	ER	HR	SH	SF	HB	TBB	IBB	SO	WP	Bk	W	L	Pct	ShO	Sv-Op	Hld	ERC	ERA
2005	NewOr*	AAA	5	5	0	0	24.2	110	26	13	12	3	2	0	3	10	3	21	2	1	1	2	.333	0	0- -	-	4.87	4.38
1999	MON	NL	1	1	0	0	6.0	28	8	4	1	0	0	1	0	2	1	2	2	0	0	1	.000	0	0-0	0	4.53	1.50
2000	MON	NL	17	17	0	0	95.0	403	74	49	46	10	7	3	3	50	2	59	3	0	7	9	.438	0	0-0	0	3.49	4.36
2001	MON	NL	34	34	0	0	196.2	851	180	101	88	18	15	6	10	91	6	176	9	1	9	14	.391	0	0-0	0	3.95	4.03
2002	MON	NL	29	29	0	0	164.1	705	149	87	81	22	6	2	7	78	12	131	14	2	12	12	.500	0	0-0	0	4.19	4.44
2003	MON	NL	5	5	0	0	31.0	124	25	9	9	4	2	2	1	8	0	23	0	0	2	1	.667	0	0-0	0	2.84	2.61
2004	MON	NL	16	16	0	0	72.0	320	66	41	39	13	2	2	4	45	6	54	0	0	2	4	.333	0	0-0	0	5.26	4.88
2005	WAS	NL	19	19	0	0	101.1	451	100	57	56	16	4	1	5	54	4	59	6	2	7	7	.500	0	0-0	0	5.13	4.97
	7 ML YEARS		121	121	0	0	666.1	2882	602	348	320	83	36	17	30	328	31	504	34	5	39	48	.448	0	0-0	0	4.20	4.32

Bronson Arroyo

Pitches: R **Bats:** R **Pos:** SP-32; RP-3   **Ht:** 6'5" **Wt:** 194 **Born:** 2/24/1977 **Age:** 29

				HOW MUCH HE PITCHED					WHAT HE GAVE UP										THE RESULTS						
Year	Team	Lg	G	GS	CG	GF	IP	BFP	H	R	ER	HR	SH	SF	HB	TBB	IBB	SO	WP	Bk	W	L	Pct	ShO	Sv-Op	Hld	ERC	ERA
2000	PIT	NL	20	12	0	1	71.2	338	88	61	51	10	5	2	4	36	6	50	3	1	2	6	.250	0	0-0	0	6.18	6.40
2001	PIT	NL	24	13	1	1	88.1	390	99	54	50	12	4	6	4	34	6	39	4	1	5	7	.417	0	0-0	2	5.09	5.09
2002	PIT	NL	9	4	0	1	26.2	123	30	14	12	1	1	1	0	15	3	22	0	0	2	1	.667	0	0-0	1	4.71	4.05
2003	BOS	AL	6	0	0	0	17.1	66	10	5	4	0	0	0	1	4	2	14	0	0	0	0	-	0	1-1	0	1.14	2.08
2004	BOS	AL	32	29	0	0	178.2	764	171	99	80	17	5	4	20	47	3	142	5	0	10	9	.526	0	0-0	0	3.65	4.03
2005	BOS	AL	35	32	0	1	205.1	878	213	116	103	22	4	4	14	54	3	100	5	1	14	10	.583	0	0-0	0	4.04	4.51
	6 ML YEARS		126	90	1	6	588.0	2559	611	349	300	62	19	17	43	190	23	367	17	3	33	33	.500	0	1-1	3	4.24	4.59

Ezequiel Astacio

Pitches: R **Bats:** R **Pos:** SP-14; RP-8   **Ht:** 6'3" **Wt:** 150 **Born:** 11/4/1979 **Age:** 26

				HOW MUCH HE PITCHED					WHAT HE GAVE UP										THE RESULTS						
Year	Team	Lg	G	GS	CG	GF	IP	BFP	H	R	ER	HR	SH	SF	HB	TBB	IBB	SO	WP	Bk	W	L	Pct	ShO	Sv-Op	Hld	ERC	ERA
2001	Phillies	R	9	9	0	0	47.0	199	48	16	12	2	4	2	4	10	0	42	1	0	4	2	.667	0	0- -	-	3.40	2.30
2002	Lakwd	A	25	25	1	0	152.1	662	159	61	56	9	8	3	12	46	1	100	6	0	10	7	.588	0	0- -	-	3.92	3.31
2003	Clrwtr	A+	25	22	2	2	147.2	612	140	60	54	9	1	1	7	29	0	83	2	2	15	5	.750	1	0- -	-	2.92	3.29
2004	RdRck	AA	28	28	1	0	176.0	793	155	89	76	12	11	4	8	56	1	185	11	1	13	10	.565	0	0- -	-	3.04	3.89
2005	RdRck	AAA	13	12	0	1	65.2	262	53	25	22	6	2	1	8	12	0	57	0	0	4	4	.500	0	1- -	-	2.69	3.02
2005	HOU	NL	22	14	0	5	81.0	366	100	56	51	23	2	6	1	25	2	66	4	1	3	6	.333	0	0-0	0	6.38	5.67

Pedro Astacio

Pitches: R **Bats:** R **Pos:** SP-22; RP-2   **Ht:** 6'2" **Wt:** 210 **Born:** 11/28/1969 **Age:** 36

Year	Team	Lg	G	GS	CG	GF	IP	BFP	H	R	ER	HR	SH	SF	HB	TBB	IBB	SO	WP	Bk	W	L	Pct	ShO	Sv-Op	Hld	ERC	ERA
			HOW MUCH HE PITCHED						WHAT HE GAVE UP												THE RESULTS							
2005	Portlnd*	AAA	1	1	0	0	4.0	22	10	7	7	0	0	1	1	0	0	1	0	0	0	1	.000	0	0--	-	12.64	15.75
1992	LA	NL	11	11	4	0	82.0	341	80	23	18	1	3	2	2	20	4	43	1	0	5	5	.500	4	0-0	0	2.78	1.98
1993	LA	NL	31	31	3	0	186.1	777	165	80	74	14	7	8	5	68	5	122	8	9	14	9	.609	2	0-0	0	3.24	3.57
1994	LA	NL	23	23	3	0	149.0	625	142	77	71	18	6	5	4	47	4	108	4	0	6	8	.429	1	0-0	0	3.71	4.29
1995	LA	NL	48	11	1	7	104.0	436	103	53	49	12	5	3	4	29	5	80	5	0	7	8	.467	1	0-1	2	3.76	4.24
1996	LA	NL	35	32	0	0	211.2	885	207	86	81	18	11	5	9	67	9	130	6	2	9	8	.529	0	0-0	0	3.69	3.44
1997	2 Tms	NL	33	31	2	2	202.1	862	200	98	93	24	9	7	9	61	0	166	6	3	12	10	.545	1	0-0	0	3.92	4.14
1998	COL	NL	35	34	0	0	209.1	938	245	160	145	39	12	3	17	74	0	170	2	0	13	14	.481	0	0-0	0	5.91	6.23
1999	COL	NL	34	34	7	0	232.0	1008	258	140	130	38	6	10	11	75	6	210	5	0	17	11	.607	0	0-0	0	5.08	5.04
2000	COL	NL	32	32	3	0	196.1	875	217	119	115	32	7	4	15	77	5	193	8	0	12	9	.571	0	0-0	0	5.42	5.27
2001	2 Tms	NL	26	26	4	0	169.2	733	181	101	96	22	6	5	13	54	3	144	2	0	8	14	.364	1	0-0	0	4.68	5.09
2002	NYN	NL	31	31	3	0	191.2	828	192	106	102	32	8	7	16	63	5	152	1	2	12	11	.522	1	0-0	0	4.57	4.79
2003	NYN	NL	7	7	0	0	36.2	174	47	30	30	8	1	1	3	18	1	20	4	0	3	2	.600	0	0-0	0	7.42	7.36
2004	BOS	AL	5	1	0	1	8.2	43	13	10	10	2	0	0	0	5	0	6	1	0	0	0	-	0	0-0	0	9.09	10.38
2005	2 Tms		24	22	0	1	126.2	540	133	66	66	17	7	4	2	37	4	78	6	1	6	10	.375	0	0-0	0	4.19	4.69
97	LA	NL	26	24	2	2	153.2	654	151	75	70	15	9	5	4	47	0	115	4	3	7	9	.438	1	0-0	0	3.67	4.10
97	Col	NL	7	7	0	0	48.2	208	49	23	23	9	0	2	5	14	0	51	2	0	5	1	.833	0	0-0	0	4.72	4.25
01	Col	NL	22	22	4	0	141.0	617	151	91	86	21	5	4	10	50	3	125	2	0	6	13	.316	1	0-0	0	4.94	5.49
01	Hou	NL	4	4	0	0	28.2	116	30	10	10	1	1	1	3	4	0	19	0	0	2	1	.667	0	0-0	0	3.43	3.14
05	Tex	AL	12	12	0	0	67.0	288	79	45	45	13	3	2	1	11	1	45	3	1	2	8	.200	0	0-0	0	4.79	6.04
05	SD	NL	12	10	0	1	59.2	252	54	21	21	4	4	2	1	26	3	33	3	0	4	2	.667	0	0-0	0	3.49	3.17
14 ML YEARS			375	326	30	11	2106.1	9065	2183	1149	1080	277	88	64	110	695	51	1622	59	17	124	119	.510	11	0-1	2	4.42	4.61

Scott Atchison

Pitches: R **Bats:** R **Pos:** RP-6   **Ht:** 6'2" **Wt:** 180 **Born:** 3/29/1976 **Age:** 30

Year	Team	Lg	G	GS	CG	GF	IP	BFP	H	R	ER	HR	SH	SF	HB	TBB	IBB	SO	WP	Bk	W	L	Pct	ShO	Sv-Op	Hld	ERC	ERA
1999	Wisc	A	15	13	0	0	81.2	326	67	34	31	4	2	2	3	25	1	85	4	1	4	5	.444	0	0--	-	2.64	3.42
2000	Lancst	A+	19	19	1	0	97.2	436	117	58	40	10	2	4	4	21	0	77	2	0	5	5	.500	0	0--	-	4.52	3.69
2000	Tacom	AAA	5	5	0	0	26.0	103	22	11	11	3	0	0	0	6	0	18	0	0	1	1	.500	0	0--	-	2.76	3.81
2001	SnAnt	AA	24	24	1	0	136.0	596	171	84	64	11	8	5	12	28	0	83	6	0	9	10	.474	0	0--	-	5.07	4.24
2002	Tacom	AAA	27	21	0	3	124.1	528	123	68	64	13	3	5	9	31	0	112	1	0	5	10	.333	0	2--	-	3.72	4.63
2003	Tacom	AAA	39	7	0	10	108.2	474	114	57	52	8	7	2	3	37	2	83	2	0	6	9	.400	0	1--	-	3.96	4.31
2004	Tacom	AAA	40	1	0	16	69.1	304	71	35	32	8	2	2	2	26	2	76	5	0	5	3	.625	0	7--	-	4.23	4.15
2005	Ms	R	4	3	0	0	5.0	23	7	3	3	0	0	0	1	1	0	9	0	0	0	0	-	0	0--	-	5.74	5.40
2005	SnAnt	AA	5	0	0	3	6.0	23	3	0	0	0	0	0	0	2	0	8	0	0	0	0	-	0	0--	-	1.09	0.00
2005	Tacom	AAA	10	0	0	3	13.0	57	13	6	6	0	0	0	0	5	0	17	1	0	0	0	-	0	0--	-	3.23	4.15
2004	SEA	AL	25	0	0	8	30.2	133	29	12	12	4	2	1	0	14	2	36	2	0	2	3	.400	0	0-0	2	4.08	3.52
2005	SEA	AL	6	0	0	3	6.2	27	7	5	5	1	0	0	0	1	0	9	0	0	0	0	-	0	0-0	0	3.77	6.75
2 ML YEARS			31	0	0	10	37.1	160	36	17	17	5	2	1	0	15	2	45	2	0	2	3	.400	0	0-0	2	4.03	4.10

Garrett Atkins

Bats: R **Throws:** R **Pos:** 3B-136; PH-2   **Ht:** 6'3" **Wt:** 210 **Born:** 12/12/1979 **Age:** 26

Year	Team	Lg	G	AB	H	2B	3B	HR	(Hm	Rd)	TB	R	RBI	RC	TBB	IBB	SO	HBP	SH	SF	SB	CS	SB%	GDP	Avg	OBP	Slg
2005	ColSpr*	AAA	5	21	7	1	0	1	(-	-)	11	4	3	4	2	0	4	0	0	0	0	0	-	0	.333	.391	.524
2003	COL	NL	25	69	11	2	0	0	(0	0)	13	6	4	2	3	0	14	1	0	0	0	0	-	1	.159	.205	.188
2004	COL	NL	15	28	10	2	0	1	(1	0)	15	3	8	8	4	0	3	0	0	1	0	0	-	0	.357	.424	.536
2005	COL	NL	138	519	149	31	1	13	(9	4)	221	62	89	74	45	1	72	5	0	4	0	2	.00	18	.287	.347	.426
3 ML YEARS			178	616	170	35	1	14	(10	4)	249	71	101	84	52	1	89	6	0	5	0	2	.00	19	.276	.336	.404

Rich Aurilia

Bats: R **Throws:** R **Pos:** 2B-68; SS-30; 3B-18; PH-6   **Ht:** 6'1" **Wt:** 185 **Born:** 9/2/1971 **Age:** 34

Year	Team	Lg	G	AB	H	2B	3B	HR	(Hm	Rd)	TB	R	RBI	RC	TBB	IBB	SO	HBP	SH	SF	SB	CS	SB%	GDP	Avg	OBP	Slg
2005	Lsvlle*	AAA	3	1	1	1	0	0	(-	-)	2	2	1	1	2	0	1	0	0	0	0	0	-	0	.333	.600	.667
1995	SF	NL	9	19	9	3	0	2	(0	2)	18	4	4	7	1	0	2	0	0	1	1	0	1.00	1	.474	.476	.947
1996	SF	NL	105	318	76	7	1	3	(1	2)	94	27	26	29	25	2	52	1	6	2	4	1	.80	1	.239	.295	.296
1997	SF	NL	46	102	28	8	0	5	(1	4)	51	16	19	16	8	0	15	0	1	2	1	1	.50	3	.275	.321	.500
1998	SF	NL	122	413	110	27	2	9	(5	4)	168	54	49	54	31	3	62	2	5	3	3	3	.50	3	.266	.319	.407
1999	SF	NL	152	558	157	23	1	22	(9	13)	248	68	80	79	43	3	71	5	3	5	2	3	.40	16	.281	.336	.444
2000	SF	NL	141	509	138	24	2	20	(12	8)	226	67	79	74	54	2	90	0	4	4	1	2	.33	15	.271	.339	.444
2001	SF	NL	156	636	206	37	5	37	(15	22)	364	114	97	124	47	2	83	0	3	3	1	3	.25	14	.324	.369	.572
2002	SF	NL	133	538	138	35	2	15	(4	11)	222	76	61	61	37	0	90	4	3	7	1	3	.25	15	.257	.305	.413
2003	SF	NL	129	505	140	26	1	13	(6	7)	207	65	58	56	36	0	82	1	0	3	2	2	.50	18	.277	.325	.410
2004	2 Tms	NL	124	399	98	21	2	6	(3	3)	141	49	44	39	37	1	71	4	7	3	1	0	1.00	13	.246	.314	.353
2005	CIN	NL	114	426	120	23	2	14	(11	3)	189	61	68	70	37	2	67	1	1	3	2	0	1.00	8	.282	.338	.444
04	Sea	AL	73	261	63	13	0	4	(2	2)	88	27	28	25	22	1	43	2	6	1	1	0	1.00	11	.241	.304	.337
04	SD	NL	51	138	35	8	2	2	(1	1)	53	22	16	14	15	0	28	2	1	2	0	0	-	2	.254	.331	.384
11 ML YEARS			1231	4423	1220	234	18	146	(67	79)	1928	601	585	609	356	15	685	18	34	35	19	17	.53	107	.276	.330	.436

Brad Ausmus

Bats: R Throws: R Pos: C-134; 2B-1; SS-1; PH-1   Ht: 5'11" Wt: 200 Born: 4/14/1969 Age: 37

							BATTING														BASERUNNING				AVERAGES		
Year	Team	Lg	G	AB	H	2B	3B	HR	(Hm	Rd)	TB	R	RBI	RC	TBB	IBB	SO	HBP	SH	SF	SB	CS	SB%	GDP	Avg	OBP	Slg
1993	SD	NL	49	160	41	8	1	5	(4	1)	66	18	12	19	6	0	28	0	0	0	2	0	1.00	2	.256	.283	.413
1994	SD	NL	101	327	82	12	1	7	(6	1)	117	45	24	36	30	12	63	1	6	2	5	1	.83	8	.251	.314	.358
1995	SD	NL	103	328	96	16	4	5	(2	3)	135	44	34	49	31	3	56	2	4	4	16	5	.76	6	.293	.353	.412
1996	2 Tms		125	375	83	16	0	5	(2	3)	114	46	35	32	39	1	72	5	6	2	4	8	.33	8	.221	.302	.304
1997	HOU	NL	130	425	113	25	1	3	(1	3)	152	45	44	51	38	4	78	3	6	6	14	6	.70	8	.266	.326	.358
1998	HOU	NL	128	412	111	10	4	6	(2	4)	147	62	45	51	53	11	60	3	3	1	10	3	.77	18	.269	.356	.357
1999	DET	AL	127	458	126	25	6	9	(5	4)	190	62	54	69	51	0	71	14	3	1	12	9	.57	11	.275	.365	.415
2000	DET	AL	150	523	139	25	3	7	(3	4)	191	75	51	68	69	0	79	6	4	2	11	5	.69	19	.266	.357	.365
2001	HOU	NL	128	422	98	23	4	5	(4	1)	144	45	34	38	30	6	64	1	6	2	4	1	.80	13	.232	.284	.341
2002	HOU	NL	130	447	115	19	3	6	(4	2)	158	57	50	44	38	3	71	6	2	3	2	3	.40	30	.257	.322	.353
2003	HOU	NL	143	450	103	12	2	4	(1	3)	131	43	47	44	46	1	66	4	4	5	5	3	.63	8	.229	.303	.291
2004	HOU	NL	129	403	100	14	1	5	(2	3)	131	38	31	34	33	11	56	2	7	3	2	2	.50	13	.248	.306	.325
2005	HOU	NL	134	387	100	19	0	3	(2	1)	128	35	47	42	51	8	48	5	7	1	5	3	.63	17	.258	.351	.331
96	SD	NL	50	149	27	4	0	1	(0	1)	34	16	13	6	13	0	27	3	1	0	1	4	.20	4	.181	.261	.228
96	Det	AL	75	226	56	12	0	4	(2	2)	80	30	22	26	26	1	45	2	5	2	3	4	.43	4	.248	.328	.354
	13 ML YEARS		1577	5117	1307	224	30	71	(38	33)	1804	615	508	577	515	60	812	52	58	32	92	49	.65	161	.255	.328	.353

Luis Ayala

Pitches: R Bats: R Pos: RP-68   Ht: 6'2" Wt: 170 Born: 1/12/1978 Age: 28

			HOW MUCH HE PITCHED					WHAT HE GAVE UP										THE RESULTS						
Year	Team	Lg	G	GS	CG	GF	IP	BFP	H	R	ER	HR	SH	SF	HB	TBB	IBB	SO	WP	Bk	W	L	Pct	ShO	Sv-Op	Hld	ERC	ERA
2003	MON	NL	65	0	0	24	71.0	288	65	27	23	8	3	1	5	13	3	46	1	0	10	3	.769	0	5-8	19	3.11	2.92
2004	MON	NL	81	0	0	28	90.1	367	92	30	27	6	2	2	5	15	2	63	3	1	6	12	.333	0	2-7	21	3.32	2.69
2005	WAS	NL	68	0	0	18	71.0	293	75	23	21	7	8	3	6	14	4	40	0	0	8	7	.533	0	1-3	22	3.95	2.66
	3 ML YEARS		214	0	0	70	232.1	948	232	80	71	21	13	6	16	42	9	149	4	1	24	22	.522	0	8-18	62	3.44	2.75

Manny Aybar

Pitches: R Bats: R Pos: RP-22   Ht: 6'1" Wt: 177 Born: 5/4/1972 Age: 34

			HOW MUCH HE PITCHED					WHAT HE GAVE UP										THE RESULTS						
Year	Team	Lg	G	GS	CG	GF	IP	BFP	H	R	ER	HR	SH	SF	HB	TBB	IBB	SO	WP	Bk	W	L	Pct	ShO	Sv-Op	Hld	ERC	ERA
2005	Norfolk*	AAA	24	0	0	10	32.0	130	26	7	5	1	1	1	2	8	0	27	0	0	3	0	1.000	0	4--	-	2.33	1.41
1997	STL	NL	12	12	0	0	68.0	295	66	33	32	8	7	4	4	29	0	41	1	1	2	4	.333	0	0-0	0	4.40	4.24
1998	STL	NL	20	14	0	1	81.1	369	90	58	54	6	4	1	2	42	1	57	2	0	6	6	.500	0	0-0	0	5.04	5.98
1999	STL	NL	65	1	0	22	97.0	430	104	67	59	13	4	3	4	36	3	74	1	2	4	5	.444	0	3-5	12	4.68	5.47
2000	3 Tms	NL	54	0	0	20	79.1	349	74	42	38	11	5	4	2	35	3	45	7	1	2	2	.500	0	0-1	1	4.08	4.31
2001	CHN	NL	17	1	0	1	22.2	113	28	19	16	5	1	1	2	17	0	16	2	0	2	1	.667	0	0-0	2	8.38	6.35
2002	SF	NL	15	0	0	4	14.1	63	16	6	4	1	0	0	1	3	2	11	0	1	1	0	1.000	0	0-0	1	3.71	2.51
2003	SF	NL	3	0	0	1	3.0	16	4	2	2	1	0	1	0	3	0	2	0	0	0	0	-	0	0-0	0	10.72	6.00
2005	NYN	NL	22	0	0	4	25.1	114	31	17	17	4	1	2	1	7	1	27	0	0	0	0	-	0	0-1	2	5.31	6.04
00	Col	NL	1	0	0	0	1.2	10	5	3	3	1	0	0	0	0	0	0	0	0	0	1	.000	0	0-0	0	21.12	16.20
00	Cin	NL	32	0	0	10	50.1	226	51	31	27	7	4	3	2	22	2	31	7	1	1	1	.500	0	0-0	1	4.57	4.83
00	Fla	NL	21	0	0	10	27.1	113	18	8	8	3	1	1	0	13	1	14	0	0	1	0	1.000	0	0-1	0	2.53	2.63
	8 ML YEARS		208	28	0	53	391.0	1749	413	244	222	49	22	16	16	172	10	273	13	5	17	18	.486	0	3-7	18	4.82	5.11

Willy Aybar

Bats: B Throws: R Pos: 3B-20; 2B-6; PH-2   Ht: 6'0" Wt: 175 Born: 3/9/1983 Age: 23

							BATTING														BASERUNNING				AVERAGES		
Year	Team	Lg	G	AB	H	2B	3B	HR	(Hm	Rd)	TB	R	RBI	RC	TBB	IBB	SO	HBP	SH	SF	SB	CS	SB%	GDP	Avg	OBP	Slg
2000	Gr Falls	R+	70	266	70	15	1	4	(-	-)	99	39	49	37	36	2	45	0	6	2	5	5	.50	3	.263	.349	.372
2001	Wilmg	A	120	431	102	25	2	4	(-	-)	143	45	48	45	43	3	64	3	3	5	7	9	.44	4	.237	.307	.332
2001	VeroB	A+	2	7	2	0	0	0	(-	-)	2	0	0	0	1	0	2	0	0	0	0	0	-	0	.286	.375	.286
2002	VeroB	A+	108	372	80	18	2	11	(-	-)	135	56	65	52	69	4	54	3	2	4	15	8	.65	7	.215	.339	.363
2003	VeroB	A+	119	445	122	29	3	11	(-	-)	190	47	74	65	41	1	70	3	1	5	9	9	.50	3	.274	.336	.427
2004	Jaxnvl	AA	126	482	133	27	0	15	(-	-)	205	56	77	72	50	4	77	3	0	2	8	10	.44	11	.276	.346	.425
2005	LsVgs	AAA	108	401	119	26	4	5	(-	-)	168	47	60	61	40	0	56	1	1	7	1	6	.14	8	.297	.356	.419
2005	LAN	NL	26	86	28	8	0	1	(0	1)	39	12	10	21	18	0	11	1	0	0	3	1	.75	0	.326	.448	.453

Brandon Backe

Pitches: R Bats: R Pos: SP-25; RP-1   Ht: 6'0" Wt: 190 Born: 4/5/1978 Age: 28

			HOW MUCH HE PITCHED					WHAT HE GAVE UP										THE RESULTS						
Year	Team	Lg	G	GS	CG	GF	IP	BFP	H	R	ER	HR	SH	SF	HB	TBB	IBB	SO	WP	Bk	W	L	Pct	ShO	Sv-Op	Hld	ERC	ERA
2005	CpChr*	AA	2	2	0	0	8.0	29	4	2	2	1	0	0	0	1	0	11	1	0	0	1	.000	0	0--	-	1.09	2.25
2002	TB	AL	9	0	0	4	13.0	61	15	10	10	3	0	0	2	7	0	6	0	0	0	0	-	0	0-0	0	7.37	6.92
2003	TB	AL	28	0	0	8	44.2	192	40	28	27	6	2	1	2	25	1	36	3	0	1	1	.500	0	0-0	5	4.64	5.44
2004	HOU	NL	33	9	0	8	67.0	293	75	33	32	10	5	1	1	27	4	54	1	0	5	3	.625	0	0-0	3	5.18	4.30
2005	HOU	NL	26	25	1	0	149.1	653	151	82	79	19	7	1	4	67	1	97	5	2	10	8	.556	1	0-0	0	4.65	4.76
	4 ML YEARS		96	34	1	20	274.0	1199	281	153	148	38	14	3	9	126	6	193	9	2	16	12	.571	1	0-0	8	4.90	4.86

Carlos Baerga

Bats: B **Throws:** R **Pos:** PH-61; 3B-20; 1B-11; 2B-7; DH-1 **Ht:** 5'11" **Wt:** 215 **Born:** 11/4/1968 **Age:** 37

Year	Team	Lg	G	AB	H	2B	3B	HR	(Hm	Rd)	TB	R	RBI	RC	TBB	IBB	SO	HBP	SH	SF	SB	CS	SB%	GDP	Avg	OBP	Slg
1990	CLE	AL	108	312	81	17	2	7	(3	4)	123	46	47	36	16	2	57	4	1	5	0	2	.00	4	.260	.300	.394
1991	CLE	AL	158	593	171	28	2	11	(2	9)	236	80	69	81	48	5	74	6	4	3	3	2	.60	12	.288	.346	.398
1992	CLE	AL	161	657	205	32	1	20	(9	11)	299	92	105	103	35	10	76	13	2	9	10	2	.83	15	.312	.354	.455
1993	CLE	AL	154	624	200	28	6	21	(8	13)	303	105	114	104	34	7	68	6	3	13	15	4	.79	17	.321	.355	.486
1994	CLE	AL	103	442	139	32	2	19	(8	11)	232	81	80	74	10	1	45	6	3	8	8	2	.80	10	.314	.333	.525
1995	CLE	AL	135	557	175	28	2	15	(7	8)	252	87	90	87	35	6	31	3	0	5	11	2	.85	15	.314	.355	.452
1996	2 Tms		126	507	129	28	0	12	(5	7)	193	59	66	51	21	0	27	9	2	5	1	1	.50	23	.254	.293	.381
1997	NYN	NL	133	467	131	25	1	9	(4	5)	185	53	52	53	20	1	54	3	3	5	2	6	.25	13	.281	.311	.396
1998	NYN	NL	147	511	136	27	1	7	(3	4)	186	46	53	51	24	6	55	6	3	7	0	1	.00	21	.266	.303	.364
1999	2 Tms		55	137	33	1	0	3	(2	1)	43	10	10	12	10	1	24	2	2	1	2	1	.67	5	.241	.300	.314
2002	BOS	AL	73	182	52	11	0	2	(1	1)	69	17	19	18	7	1	20	2	1	2	6	0	1.00	6	.286	.316	.379
2003	ARI	NL	105	207	71	13	0	4	(4	0)	96	31	39	38	18	1	20	2	1	3	1	1	.50	6	.343	.396	.464
2004	ARI	NL	79	85	20	2	0	2	(0	2)	28	6	11	10	6	0	12	3	0	0	0	0	-	6	.235	.309	.329
2005	WAS	NL	93	158	40	7	0	2	(1	1)	53	18	19	17	7	0	17	8	1	0	0	0	-	4	.253	.318	.335
96	Cle	AL	100	424	113	25	0	10	(5	5)	168	54	55	47	16	0	25	7	2	4	1	1	.50	15	.267	.302	.396
96	NYM	AL	26	83	16	3	0	2	(0	2)	25	5	11	4	5	0	2	2	0	1	0	0	-	8	.193	.253	.301
99	SD	NL	33	80	20	1	0	2	(1	1)	27	6	5	9	6	0	14	2	1	0	1	0	1.00	1	.250	.318	.338
99	Cle	AL	22	57	13	0	0	1	(1	0)	16	4	5	3	4	1	10	0	1	1	1	1	.50	3	.228	.274	.281
14 ML YEARS			1630	5439	1583	279	17	134	(57	77)	2298	731	774	735	291	41	580	73	26	66	59	24	.71	158	.291	.332	.423

Danys Baez

Pitches: R **Bats:** R **Pos:** RP-67 **Ht:** 6'3" **Wt:** 225 **Born:** 9/10/1977 **Age:** 28

Year	Team	Lg	G	GS	CG	GF	IP	BFP	H	R	ER	HR	SH	SF	HB	TBB	IBB	SO	WP	Bk	W	L	Pct	ShO	Sv-Op	Hld	ERC	ERA
2001	CLE	AL	43	0	0	8	50.1	202	34	22	14	5	0	1	3	20	4	52	3	0	5	3	.625	0	0-1	14	2.51	2.50
2002	CLE	AL	39	26	1	9	165.1	726	160	84	81	14	2	8	9	82	5	130	6	1	10	11	.476	0	6-8	0	4.35	4.41
2003	CLE	AL	73	0	0	46	75.2	318	65	36	32	9	6	1	4	23	0	66	5	0	2	9	.182	0	25-35	5	3.22	3.81
2004	TB	AL	62	0	0	59	68.0	295	60	31	27	6	5	1	7	29	4	52	3	1	4	4	.500	0	30-33	1	3.73	3.57
2005	TB	AL	67	0	0	64	72.1	308	66	27	23	7	4	2	2	30	0	51	0	0	5	4	.556	0	41-49	5	3.74	2.86
5 ML YEARS			284	26	1	186	431.2	1849	385	200	177	41	17	13	25	184	13	351	17	2	26	31	.456	0	102-126	20	3.73	3.69

Jeff Bagwell

Bats: R **Throws:** R **Pos:** 1B-24; PH-15 **Ht:** 6'0" **Wt:** 215 **Born:** 5/27/1968 **Age:** 38

Year	Team	Lg	G	AB	H	2B	3B	HR	(Hm	Rd)	TB	R	RBI	RC	TBB	IBB	SO	HBP	SH	SF	SB	CS	SB%	GDP	Avg	OBP	Slg
2005	CpChr*	AA	3	9	2	0	0	0	(-	-)	2	1	1	1	3	0	3	0	0	0	0	0	-	1	.222	.417	.222
1991	HOU	NL	156	554	163	26	4	15	(6	9)	242	79	82	95	75	5	116	13	1	7	7	4	.64	12	.294	.387	.437
1992	HOU	NL	162	586	160	34	6	18	(8	10)	260	87	96	96	84	13	97	12	2	13	10	6	.63	17	.273	.368	.444
1993	HOU	NL	142	535	171	37	4	20	(9	11)	276	76	88	102	62	6	73	3	0	9	13	4	.76	20	.320	.388	.516
1994	HOU	NL	110	400	147	32	2	39	(23	16)	300	104	116	121	65	14	65	4	0	10	15	4	.79	12	.368	.451	**.750**
1995	HOU	NL	114	448	130	29	0	21	(10	11)	222	88	87	89	79	12	102	6	0	6	12	5	.71	9	.290	.399	.496
1996	HOU	NL	162	568	179	48	2	31	(16	15)	324	111	120	144	135	20	114	10	0	6	21	7	.75	15	.315	.451	.570
1997	HOU	NL	162	566	162	40	2	43	(22	21)	335	109	135	142	127	27	122	16	0	8	31	10	.76	10	.286	.425	.592
1998	HOU	NL	147	540	164	33	1	34	(20	14)	301	124	111	125	109	8	90	7	0	5	19	7	.73	14	.304	.424	.557
1999	HOU	NL	162	562	171	35	0	42	(12	30)	332	143	126	148	149	16	127	11	0	7	30	11	.73	18	.304	.454	.591
2000	HOU	NL	159	590	183	37	1	47	(28	19)	363	152	132	144	107	11	116	15	0	7	9	6	.60	19	.310	.424	.615
2001	HOU	NL	161	600	173	43	4	39	(21	18)	341	126	130	130	106	5	135	6	0	5	11	3	.79	20	.288	.397	.568
2002	HOU	NL	158	571	166	33	2	31	(16	15)	296	94	98	108	101	8	130	10	0	9	7	3	.70	16	.291	.401	.518
2003	HOU	NL	160	605	168	28	2	39	(22	17)	317	109	100	116	88	3	119	6	0	3	11	4	.73	25	.278	.373	.524
2004	HOU	NL	156	572	152	29	2	27	(18	9)	266	104	89	106	96	6	131	8	0	3	6	4	.60	12	.266	.377	.465
2005	HOU	NL	39	100	25	4	0	3	(3	0)	38	11	19	17	18	1	21	1	0	4	0	0	-	2	.250	.358	.380
15 ML YEARS			2150	7797	2314	488	32	449	(234	215)	4213	1517	1529	1683	1401	155	1558	128	3	102	202	78	.72	221	.297	.408	.540

Jeff Bajenaru

Pitches: R **Bats:** R **Pos:** RP-4 **Ht:** 6'1" **Wt:** 190 **Born:** 3/21/1978 **Age:** 28

Year	Team	Lg	G	GS	CG	GF	IP	BFP	H	R	ER	HR	SH	SF	HB	TBB	IBB	SO	WP	Bk	W	L	Pct	ShO	Sv-Op	Hld	ERC	ERA
2000	Bristol	R+	12	0	0	11	14.1	61	10	6	6	2	0	0	0	5	0	31	2	0	1	1	.500	0	5--	-	2.35	3.77
2000	WinSa	A+	10	0	0	7	12.1	52	7	6	6	1	0	3	2	5	0	15	4	0	2	0	1.000	0	2--	-	2.23	4.38
2001	WinSa	A+	35	0	0	0	40.1	21	32	16	15	3	0	0	1	21	2	51	3	1	2	4	.333	0	10--	-	30.58	3.35
2001	Brham	AA	2	0	0	28	4.1	174	4	0	0	0	4	0	0	3	0	5	1	0	0	0	-	0	0--	-	0.39	0.00
2003	Brham	AA	50	0	0	27	64.2	271	53	29	23	2	2	5	0	28	3	62	8	0	4	2	.667	0	14--	-	2.69	3.20
2004	Brham	AA	32	0	0	25	33.2	132	19	9	5	3	0	0	0	11	0	51	0	0	2	0	1.000	0	12--	-	1.58	1.34
2004	Charltt	AAA	16	0	0	15	20.0	76	12	6	4	2	0	0	1	3	0	16	1	0	1	2	.333	0	10--	-	1.46	1.80
2005	Charltt	AAA	61	0	0	48	70.1	285	45	14	11	4	5	0	0	29	5	88	1	1	4	6	.400	0	19--	-	1.88	1.41
2004	CHA	AL	9	0	0	4	8.1	44	15	10	10	1	0	1	0	6	1	8	0	0	0	1	.000	0	0-0	0	9.52	10.80
2005	CHA	AL	4	0	0	3	4.1	18	4	3	3	2	0	0	0	3	1	3	1	0	0	0	-	0	0-0	0	3.76	6.23
2 ML YEARS			13	0	0	7	12.2	62	19	13	13	2	1	0	0	6	1	11	1	0	0	1	.000	0	0-0	0	7.72	9.24

Jeff Baker

Bats: R Throws: R Pos: 3B-10; PH-2 — Ht: 6'2" Wt: 210 Born: 6/21/1981 Age: 25

								BATTING													BASERUNNING				AVERAGES		
Year	Team	Lg	G	AB	H	2B	3B	HR	(Hm	Rd)	TB	R	RBI	RC	TBB	IBB	SO	HBP	SH	SF	SB	CS	SB%	GDP	Avg	OBP	Slg
2003	Ashvlle	A	70	263	76	17	0	11	(-	-)	126	44	44	49	30	2	79	9	0	3	4	2	.67	2	.289	.377	.479
2004	Visalia	A+	73	271	88	23	1	11	(-	-)	146	60	64	64	47	0	73	6	0	1	1	0	1.00	5	.325	.434	.539
2004	Tulsa	AA	24	91	27	5	1	4	(-	-)	46	10	20	15	7	1	22	0	0	1	0	0	-	3	.297	.343	.505
2005	ColSpr	AAA	61	228	69	16	1	10	(-	-)	117	40	41	41	16	0	44	1	1	2	3	1	.75	7	.303	.348	.513
2005	COL	NL	12	38	8	4	0	1	(1	0)	15	6	4	4	5	0	12	0	0	0	0	0	-	1	.211	.302	.395

Scott Baker

Pitches: R Bats: R Pos: SP-9; RP-1 — Ht: 6'4" Wt: 221 Born: 9/19/1981 Age: 24

				HOW MUCH HE PITCHED						WHAT HE GAVE UP											THE RESULTS						
Year	Team	Lg	G	GS	CG	GF	IP	BFP	H	R	ER	HR	SH	SF	HB	TBB	IBB	SO	WP	Bk	W	L	Pct	ShO	Sv-Op	Hld	ERC	ERA
2003	QuadC	A	11	11	0	0	50.2	207	45	16	14	4	1	1	2	8	0	47	4	0	3	1	.750	0	0--	-	2.54	2.49
2004	FtMyrs	A+	7	7	0	0	45.0	181	40	13	12	1	0	0	6	6	0	37	1	0	4	2	.667	0	0--	-	2.01	2.40
2004	NwBrit	AA	10	10	2	0	70.1	276	44	23	19	2	0	0	6	13	2	72	0	0	5	3	.625	2	0--	-	1.39	2.43
2004	Roch	AAA	9	9	0	0	54.1	248	65	31	30	3	0	2	4	15	1	36	0	0	1	3	.250	0	0--	-	4.49	4.97
2005	Roch	AAA	22	22	1	0	134.2	554	123	50	45	15	4	4	7	26	1	107	4	0	5	8	.385	1	0--	-	3.05	3.01
2005	MIN	AL	10	9	0	0	53.2	217	48	21	20	5	2	2	0	14	0	32	0	0	3	3	.500	0	0-0	1	2.97	3.35

Paul Bako

Bats: L Throws: R Pos: C-13 — Ht: 6'2" Wt: 205 Born: 6/20/1972 Age: 34

								BATTING													BASERUNNING				AVERAGES		
Year	Team	Lg	G	AB	H	2B	3B	HR	(Hm	Rd)	TB	R	RBI	RC	TBB	IBB	SO	HBP	SH	SF	SB	CS	SB%	GDP	Avg	OBP	Slg
1998	DET	AL	96	305	83	12	1	3	(2	1)	106	23	30	34	23	4	82	0	1	4	1	1	.50	3	.272	.319	.348
1999	HOU	NL	73	215	55	14	1	2	(2	0)	77	16	17	26	26	3	57	0	3	3	1	1	.50	4	.256	.332	.358
2000	3 Tms	NL	81	221	50	10	1	2	(2	0)	68	18	20	20	27	10	64	1	1	1	0	0	-	6	.226	.312	.308
2001	ATL	NL	61	137	29	10	1	2	(0	2)	47	19	15	15	20	2	34	0	0	0	1	0	1.00	3	.212	.312	.343
2002	MIL	NL	87	234	55	8	1	4	(2	2)	77	24	20	20	20	3	46	0	3	0	0	2	.00	4	.235	.295	.329
2003	CHN	NL	70	188	43	13	3	0	(0	0)	62	19	17	21	22	3	47	1	1	1	0	1	.00	2	.229	.311	.330
2004	CHN	NL	49	138	28	8	0	1	(1	0)	39	13	10	11	15	3	29	2	1	1	1	0	1.00	4	.203	.288	.283
2005	LAN	NL	13	40	10	2	0	0	(0	0)	12	1	4	6	7	1	12	0	0	0	0	0	-	0	.250	.362	.300
00	Hou	NL	1	2	0	0	0	0	(0	0)	0	0	0	0	0	0	1	0	0	0	0	0	-	0	.000	.000	.000
00	Fla	NL	56	161	39	6	1	0	(0	0)	47	10	14	16	22	7	48	1	1	1	0	0	-	4	.242	.335	.292
00	Atl	NL	24	58	11	4	0	2	(2	0)	21	8	6	4	5	3	15	0	0	0	0	0	-	2	.190	.254	.362
	8 ML YEARS		530	1478	353	77	8	14	(9	5)	488	133	133	153	160	29	371	4	10	10	4	5	.44	26	.239	.313	.330

Rocco Baldelli

Bats: R Throws: R Pos: OF — Ht: 6'4" Wt: 187 Born: 9/25/1981 Age: 24

								BATTING													BASERUNNING				AVERAGES		
Year	Team	Lg	G	AB	H	2B	3B	HR	(Hm	Rd)	TB	R	RBI	RC	TBB	IBB	SO	HBP	SH	SF	SB	CS	SB%	GDP	Avg	OBP	Slg
2000	Princtn	R+	60	232	50	9	2	3	(-	-)	72	33	25	19	12	0	56	5	2	0	11	3	.79	3	.216	.269	.310
2001	CtnSC	A	113	406	101	23	6	8	(-	-)	160	58	55	48	23	0	89	11	5	6	25	9	.74	7	.249	.303	.394
2002	Bkrsfld	A+	77	312	104	19	1	14	(-	-)	167	63	51	62	18	2	63	7	4	1	21	6	.78	2	.333	.382	.535
2002	Orlndo	AA	17	70	26	3	1	2	(-	-)	37	10	13	15	5	0	11	2	0	3	3	2	.60	1	.371	.413	.529
2002	Drham	AAA	23	96	28	6	1	3	(-	-)	45	13	7	10	0	0	23	0	2	0	2	5	.29	1	.292	.292	.469
2003	TB	AL	156	637	184	32	8	11	(2	9)	265	89	78	77	30	4	128	8	3	6	27	10	.73	10	.289	.326	.416
2004	TB	AL	136	518	145	27	3	16	(6	10)	226	79	74	70	30	2	88	8	3	6	17	4	.81	12	.280	.326	.436
	2 ML YEARS		292	1155	329	59	11	27	(8	19)	491	168	152	147	60	6	216	16	6	12	44	14	.76	22	.285	.326	.425

James Baldwin

Pitches: R Bats: R Pos: RP-28 — Ht: 6'3" Wt: 235 Born: 7/15/1971 Age: 34

				HOW MUCH HE PITCHED						WHAT HE GAVE UP											THE RESULTS						
Year	Team	Lg	G	GS	CG	GF	IP	BFP	H	R	ER	HR	SH	SF	HB	TBB	IBB	SO	WP	Bk	W	L	Pct	ShO	Sv-Op	Hld	ERC	ERA
2005	Ottawa*	AAA	8	8	0	0	47.0	197	52	25	24	6	1	1	2	4	0	25	0	2	3	2	.600	0	0--	-	3.73	4.60
1995	CHA	AL	6	4	0	0	14.2	81	32	22	21	6	0	0	0	9	1	10	1	0	0	1	.000	0	0-0	0	16.49	12.89
1996	CHA	AL	28	28	0	0	169.0	719	168	88	83	24	2	2	4	57	3	127	12	1	11	6	.647	0	0-0	0	4.17	4.42
1997	CHA	AL	32	32	1	0	200.0	879	205	128	117	19	3	6	5	83	3	140	14	3	12	15	.444	0	0-0	0	4.28	5.27
1998	CHA	AL	37	24	1	3	159.0	712	176	103	94	18	3	5	10	60	2	108	5	1	13	6	.684	0	0-1	0	4.89	5.32
1999	CHA	AL	35	33	1	1	199.1	886	219	119	113	34	4	7	7	81	1	123	11	1	12	13	.480	0	0-0	0	5.33	5.10
2000	CHA	AL	29	28	2	0	178.0	758	185	96	92	34	6	5	8	59	3	116	4	1	14	7	.667	1	0-0	0	4.91	4.65
2001	2 Tms		29	28	2	0	175.0	764	191	95	86	25	7	7	7	63	1	95	7	0	10	11	.476	1	0-0	0	4.94	4.42
2002	SEA	AL	30	23	0	4	150.0	662	179	95	88	26	4	2	7	49	2	88	1	0	7	10	.412	0	0-0	0	5.70	5.28
2003	MIN	AL	10	0	0	3	15.0	69	21	10	9	6	0	2	0	4	1	7	0	0	0	1	.000	0	1-2	1	8.09	5.40
2004	NYN	NL	2	2	0	0	6.0	36	13	10	10	3	0	1	1	5	1	1	0	0	0	2	.000	0	0-0	0	18.95	15.00
2005	2 Tms	AL	28	0	0	13	56.2	238	54	28	24	8	1	5	3	16	1	29	2	1	0	2	.000	0	1-1	0	3.82	3.81
01	CWS	AL	17	16	2	0	95.2	431	109	56	49	15	3	5	4	38	0	42	4	0	7	5	.583	1	0-0	0	5.44	4.61
01	LA	NL	12	12	0	0	79.1	333	82	39	37	10	4	2	3	25	1	53	3	0	3	6	.333	0	0-0	0	4.35	4.20
05	Bal	AL	20	0	0	11	39.1	162	36	18	14	5	1	3	2	9	0	20	1	0	0	0	-	0	0-0	0	3.33	3.20
05	Tex	AL	8	0	0	2	17.1	76	18	10	10	3	0	2	1	7	1	9	1	1	0	2	.000	0	1-1	0	5.01	5.19
	11 ML YEARS		266	202	7	24	1322.2	5804	1443	794	737	203	31	41	52	486	19	844	57	8	79	74	.516	2	2-4	1	5.01	5.01

Grant Balfour

Pitches: R Bats: R Pos: P   Ht: 6'2" Wt: 185 Born: 12/30/1977 Age: 28

Year	Team	Lg	G	GS	CG	GF	IP	BFP	H	R	ER	HR	SH	SF	HB	TBB	IBB	SO	WP	Bk	W	L	Pct	ShO	Sv-Op	Hld	ERC	ERA
2001	MIN	AL	2	0	0	0	2.2	14	3	4	4	2	0	0	0	3	0	2	0	0	0	0	-	0	0-0	0	13.78	13.50
2003	MIN	AL	17	1	0	6	26.0	115	23	12	12	4	2	1	0	14	2	30	0	0	1	0	1.000	0	0-1	1	4.14	4.15
2004	MIN	AL	36	0	0	14	39.1	172	35	19	19	4	2	0	2	21	1	42	3	0	4	1	.800	0	0-1	4	4.16	4.35
	3 ML YEARS		55	1	0	20	68.0	301	61	35	35	10	4	1	2	38	3	74	3	0	5	1	.833	0	0-2	5	4.47	4.63

Rod Barajas

Bats: R Throws: R Pos: C-119; 1B-1   Ht: 6'2" Wt: 229 Born: 9/5/1975 Age: 30

Year	Team	Lg	G	AB	H	2B	3B	HR	(Hm	Rd)	TB	R	RBI	RC	TBB	IBB	SO	HBP	SH	SF	SB	CS	SB%	GDP	Avg	OBP	Slg
1999	ARI	NL	5	16	4	1	0	1	(1	0)	8	3	3	2	1	0	1	0	1	0	0	0	-	0	.250	.294	.500
2000	ARI	NL	5	13	3	0	0	1	(1	0)	6	1	3	1	0	0	4	0	0	0	0	0	-	0	.231	.231	.462
2001	ARI	NL	51	106	17	3	0	3	(2	1)	29	9	9	4	4	0	26	0	0	0	0	0	-	0	.160	.191	.274
2002	ARI	NL	70	154	36	10	0	3	(1	2)	55	12	23	15	10	4	25	3	2	3	1	0	1.00	4	.234	.288	.357
2003	ARI	NL	80	220	48	15	0	3	(3	0)	72	19	28	19	14	7	43	1	1	3	0	0	-	6	.218	.265	.327
2004	TEX	AL	108	358	89	26	1	15	(8	7)	162	50	58	43	13	0	63	3	8	7	0	1	.00	3	.249	.276	.453
2005	TEX	AL	120	410	104	24	0	21	(7	14)	191	53	60	56	26	0	70	6	4	3	0	0	-	6	.254	.306	.466
	7 ML YEARS		439	1277	301	79	1	47	(23	24)	523	147	184	140	68	11	232	13	16	16	1	1	.50	19	.236	.278	.410

Josh Bard

Bats: B Throws: R Pos: C-31; PH-5   Ht: 6'3" Wt: 215 Born: 3/20/1978 Age: 28

Year	Team	Lg	G	AB	H	2B	3B	HR	(Hm	Rd)	TB	R	RBI	RC	TBB	IBB	SO	HBP	SH	SF	SB	CS	SB%	GDP	Avg	OBP	Slg
2002	CLE	AL	24	90	20	5	0	3	(2	1)	34	9	12	7	4	0	13	0	1	0	0	0	-	6	.222	.255	.378
2003	CLE	AL	91	303	74	13	1	8	(5	3)	113	25	36	34	22	1	53	0	1	3	0	2	.00	9	.244	.293	.373
2004	CLE	AL	7	19	8	2	0	1	(1	0)	13	5	4	6	3	0	0	0	0	1	0	0	-	0	.421	.478	.684
2005	CLE	AL	34	83	16	4	0	1	(0	1)	23	6	9	8	9	0	11	0	1	2	0	0	-	2	.193	.266	.277
	4 ML YEARS		156	495	118	24	1	13	(8	5)	183	45	61	55	38	1	77	0	3	6	0	2	.00	17	.238	.289	.370

Clint Barmes

Bats: R Throws: R Pos: SS-80; PH-1   Ht: 6'0" Wt: 175 Born: 3/6/1979 Age: 27

Year	Team	Lg	G	AB	H	2B	3B	HR	(Hm	Rd)	TB	R	RBI	RC	TBB	IBB	SO	HBP	SH	SF	SB	CS	SB%	GDP	Avg	OBP	Slg
2005	Tulsa*	AA	8	34	11	1	0	0	(-	-)	12	6	0	4	1	0	3	0	0	0	1	0	1.00	2	.324	.343	.353
2003	COL	NL	12	25	8	2	0	0	(0	0)	10	2	2	3	0	0	10	2	0	1	0	0	-	0	.320	.357	.400
2004	COL	NL	20	71	20	3	1	2	(0	2)	31	14	10	12	3	0	10	1	2	0	0	1	.00	2	.282	.320	.437
2005	COL	NL	81	350	101	19	1	10	(7	3)	152	55	46	49	16	1	36	6	4	1	6	4	.60	4	.289	.330	.434
	3 ML YEARS		113	446	129	24	2	12	(7	5)	193	71	58	64	19	1	56	9	6	2	6	5	.55	6	.289	.330	.433

Michael Barrett

Bats: R Throws: R Pos: C-122; PH-15; DH-1   Ht: 6'2" Wt: 200 Born: 10/22/1976 Age: 29

Year	Team	Lg	G	AB	H	2B	3B	HR	(Hm	Rd)	TB	R	RBI	RC	TBB	IBB	SO	HBP	SH	SF	SB	CS	SB%	GDP	Avg	OBP	Slg
1998	MON	NL	8	23	7	2	0	1	(0	1)	12	3	2	5	3	0	6	1	0	0	0	0	-	0	.304	.407	.522
1999	MON	NL	126	433	127	32	3	8	(5	3)	189	53	52	59	32	4	39	3	0	1	0	2	.00	18	.293	.345	.436
2000	MON	NL	89	271	58	15	1	1	(0	1)	78	22	28	19	23	5	35	1	1	1	0	1	.00	7	.214	.277	.288
2001	MON	NL	132	472	118	33	2	6	(3	3)	173	42	38	46	25	2	54	2	4	3	2	1	.67	14	.250	.289	.367
2002	MON	NL	117	376	99	20	1	12	(4	8)	157	41	49	49	40	7	65	1	6	5	6	3	.67	14	.263	.332	.418
2003	MON	NL	70	226	47	9	2	10	(5	5)	90	33	30	25	21	7	37	2	2	1	0	0	-	6	.208	.280	.398
2004	CHN	NL	134	456	131	32	6	16	(9	7)	223	55	65	67	33	4	64	5	4	8	1	4	.20	13	.287	.337	.489
2005	CHN	NL	133	424	117	32	3	16	(9	7)	203	48	61	67	40	3	61	7	2	4	0	3	.00	7	.276	.345	.479
	8 ML YEARS		809	2681	704	175	18	70	(35	35)	1125	303	319	337	217	32	361	22	19	23	9	14	.39	79	.263	.320	.420

Jason Bartlett

Bats: R Throws: R Pos: SS-68; PR-7; DH-5   Ht: 6'0" Wt: 180 Born: 10/30/1979 Age: 26

Year	Team	Lg	G	AB	H	2B	3B	HR	(Hm	Rd)	TB	R	RBI	RC	TBB	IBB	SO	HBP	SH	SF	SB	CS	SB%	GDP	Avg	OBP	Slg
2001	Eugene	A-	68	267	80	12	4	3	(-	-)	109	49	37	42	28	0	47	4	2	3	12	4	.75	6	.300	.371	.408
2002	Lk Els	A+	75	308	77	14	4	1	(-	-)	102	57	33	37	32	0	53	5	1	2	24	5	.83	7	.250	.329	.331
2002	FtMyrs	A+	39	145	38	7	0	2	(-	-)	51	24	9	20	17	0	24	2	1	3	11	2	.85	1	.262	.341	.352
2003	NwBrit	AA	139	548	162	31	8	8	(-	-)	233	96	48	90	58	3	67	20	4	6	41	24	.63	7	.296	.380	.425
2004	Twins	R	5	14	5	1	0	0	(-	-)	6	1	1	2	3	0	3	1	0	0	0	0	-	0	.357	.400	.429
2004	Roch	AAA	67	269	89	15	7	3	(-	-)	127	54	29	55	33	1	37	7	2	2	7	3	.70	1	.331	.415	.472
2005	Roch	AAA	61	229	76	10	2	5	(-	-)	105	41	33	45	29	0	34	4	0	7	2	2	.50	3	.332	.405	.459
2004	MIN	AL	8	12	1	0	0	0	(0	0)	1	2	1	1	1	0	1	0	1	0	2	0	1.00	0	.083	.154	.083
2005	MIN	AL	74	224	54	10	1	3	(2	1)	75	33	16	22	21	0	37	4	2	1	4	0	1.00	6	.241	.316	.335
	2 ML YEARS		82	236	55	10	1	3	(2	1)	76	35	17	23	22	0	38	4	3	1	6	0	1.00	6	.233	.308	.322

Cliff Bartosh

Pitches: L Bats: L Pos: RP-19 Ht: 6'2" Wt: 180 Born: 9/5/1979 Age: 26

Year	Team	Lg	G	GS	CG	GF	IP	BFP	H	R	ER	HR	SH	SF	HB	TBB	IBB	SO	WP	Bk	W	L	Pct	ShO	Sv-Op	Hld	ERC	ERA
1998	Padres	R	13	5	0	0	44.0	190	43	23	17	2	1	2	4	16	0	43	4	0	3	2	.600	0	0--	-	3.79	3.48
1999	FtWyn	A	35	20	1	1	129.2	567	136	76	64	14	0	4	10	49	0	100	7	2	5	12	.294	1	0--	-	4.67	4.44
2000	FtWyn	A	50	4	0	18	77.0	335	50	40	26	6	2	3	5	44	3	94	8	2	8	4	.667	0	1--	-	2.77	3.04
2001	Lk Els	A+	38	0	0	25	45.2	194	42	17	8	2	2	1	2	12	5	66	7	2	6	2	.750	0	10--	-	2.67	1.58
2001	Mobile	AA	20	0	0	9	22.2	103	20	12	10	5	2	1	1	13	1	20	2	0	1	2	.333	0	2--	-	4.92	3.97
2002	Mobile	AA	62	0	0	42	70.2	298	54	28	25	4	4	4	2	32	5	70	5	0	2	4	.333	0	25--	-	2.69	3.18
2003	Portlnd	AAA	64	0	0	29	71.1	299	67	36	34	4	4	1	3	22	1	51	4	0	2	5	.286	0	10--	-	3.25	4.29
2004	Buffalo	AAA	28	0	0	16	35.1	144	26	11	11	3	0	0	4	8	2	46	2	0	0	3	.000	0	3--	-	2.26	2.80
2005	Iowa	AAA	22	0	0	7	28.1	141	40	18	16	3	3	0	1	16	2	26	3	0	1	2	.333	0	1--	-	7.20	5.08
2004	CLE	AL	34	0	0	2	19.1	91	22	10	10	4	0	0	0	11	0	25	0	1	1	0	1.000	0	0-2	3	6.28	4.66
2005	CHN	NL	19	0	0	7	19.2	91	23	13	12	7	2	1	2	11	0	15	0	0	0	2	.000	0	0-0	1	8.50	5.49
	2 ML YEARS		53	0	0	9	39.0	182	45	23	22	11	2	1	2	22	0	40	0	1	1	2	.333	0	0-2	4	7.36	5.08

Miguel Batista

Pitches: R Bats: R Pos: RP-71 Ht: 6'2" Wt: 195 Born: 2/19/1971 Age: 35

Year	Team	Lg	G	GS	CG	GF	IP	BFP	H	R	ER	HR	SH	SF	HB	TBB	IBB	SO	WP	Bk	W	L	Pct	ShO	Sv-Op	Hld	ERC	ERA
1992	PIT	NL	1	0	0	1	2.0	13	4	2	2	1	0	0	0	3	0	1	0	0	0	0	-	0	0-0	0	20.26	9.00
1996	FLA	NL	9	0	0	4	11.1	49	9	8	7	0	3	0	0	7	2	6	1	0	0	0	-	0	0-0	0	2.77	5.56
1997	CHN	NL	11	6	0	2	36.1	168	36	24	23	4	4	4	1	24	2	27	2	0	0	5	.000	0	0-0	0	5.09	5.70
1998	MON	NL	56	13	0	12	135.0	598	141	66	57	12	7	5	6	65	7	92	6	1	3	5	.375	0	0-0	3	4.70	3.80
1999	MON	NL	39	17	2	3	134.2	606	146	88	73	10	8	11	7	58	2	95	6	0	8	7	.533	1	1-1	0	4.62	4.88
2000	2 Tms		18	9	0	2	65.1	310	85	68	62	19	1	2	2	37	2	37	4	0	2	7	.222	0	0-2	0	8.37	8.54
2001	ARI	NL	48	18	0	6	139.1	581	113	57	52	13	9	3	10	60	2	90	6	0	11	8	.579	0	0-0	4	3.43	3.36
2002	ARI	NL	36	29	1	2	184.2	790	172	99	88	12	5	8	6	70	3	112	9	2	8	9	.471	0	0-0	2	3.45	4.29
2003	ARI	NL	36	29	2	5	193.1	822	197	85	76	13	10	6	8	60	3	142	7	0	10	9	.526	1	0-0	0	3.77	3.54
2004	TOR	AL	38	31	2	7	198.2	867	206	115	106	22	7	6	3	96	1	104	12	0	10	13	.435	1	5-5	0	4.84	4.80
2005	TOR	AL	71	0	0	62	74.2	331	80	39	34	9	2	2	2	27	5	54	3	0	5	8	.385	0	31-39	0	4.39	4.10
00	Mon	NL	4	0	0	0	8.1	49	19	14	13	2	1	1	2	3	0	7	0	0	0	1	.000	0	0-2	0	14.73	14.04
00	KC	AL	14	9	0	2	57.0	261	66	54	49	17	0	1	0	34	2	30	4	0	2	6	.250	0	0-0	0	7.50	7.74
	11 ML YEARS		363	152	7	106	1175.1	5135	1189	651	580	115	56	47	45	507	29	760	56	3	57	71	.445	3	37-47	9	4.38	4.44

Rick Bauer

Pitches: R Bats: R Pos: RP-5 Ht: 6'6" Wt: 212 Born: 1/10/1977 Age: 29

Year	Team	Lg	G	GS	CG	GF	IP	BFP	H	R	ER	HR	SH	SF	HB	TBB	IBB	SO	WP	Bk	W	L	Pct	ShO	Sv-Op	Hld	ERC	ERA
2005	Ottawa*	AAA	30	10	0	3	74.1	342	84	38	33	12	6	2	2	35	3	43	4	0	3	8	.273	0	1--	-	5.53	4.00
2001	BAL	AL	6	6	0	0	33.0	143	35	22	17	7	0	1	1	9	0	16	0	0	0	5	.000	0	0-0	0	4.74	4.64
2002	BAL	AL	56	1	0	15	83.2	358	84	41	37	12	2	2	4	36	4	45	4	0	6	7	.462	0	1-5	12	4.78	3.98
2003	BAL	AL	35	0	0	10	61.1	259	58	36	31	5	1	3	4	24	3	43	6	0	0	0	-	0	0-1	3	3.87	4.55
2004	BAL	AL	23	2	0	7	53.2	230	49	31	28	4	0	0	4	20	0	37	1	0	2	1	.667	0	0-1	0	3.59	4.70
2005	BAL	AL	5	0	0	2	8.1	40	13	9	9	2	0	0	0	4	0	5	0	0	0	0	-	0	0-0	0	9.38	9.72
	5 ML YEARS		125	9	0	34	240.0	1030	239	139	122	30	3	6	13	93	7	146	11	0	8	13	.381	0	1-7	15	4.41	4.58

Denny Bautista

Pitches: R Bats: R Pos: SP-7 Ht: 6'5" Wt: 170 Born: 8/23/1980 Age: 25

Year	Team	Lg	G	GS	CG	GF	IP	BFP	H	R	ER	HR	SH	SF	HB	TBB	IBB	SO	WP	Bk	W	L	Pct	ShO	Sv-Op	Hld	ERC	ERA
2000	Marlins	R	11	11	2	0	60.0	260	49	24	17	1	1	0	8	17	1	58	3	1	6	2	.750	0	0--	-	2.45	2.55
2000	Utica	A-	1	1	0	0	5.0	21	4	3	2	0	0	0	1	2	0	5	0	0	0	0	-	0	0--	-	3.13	3.60
2001	Kane	A	8	7	0	0	39.1	172	43	21	19	2	2	1	2	14	0	20	4	2	3	1	.750	0	0--	-	4.30	4.35
2001	Utica	A-	7	7	0	0	39.0	156	25	16	9	0	4	0	4	6	0	31	3	0	3	1	.750	0	0--	-	1.30	2.08
2002	Jupiter	A+	19	15	0	1	88.1	379	80	52	49	3	4	2	4	40	0	79	15	3	4	6	.400	0	0--	-	3.73	4.99
2003	Jupiter	A+	14	14	0	0	84.0	353	68	32	30	2	1	2	5	35	0	77	7	1	8	4	.667	0	0--	-	2.82	3.21
2003	Carlina	AA	11	11	0	0	53.1	239	45	33	22	5	3	1	1	35	0	61	8	0	4	5	.444	0	0--	-	4.17	3.71
2004	Bowie	AA	14	13	0	0	62.2	280	58	37	33	5	4	2	1	33	1	72	5	0	3	5	.375	0	0--	-	3.95	4.74
2004	Wichta	AA	12	12	2	0	81.2	341	68	32	23	3	4	3	4	32	0	73	10	1	4	3	.571	0	0--	-	2.92	2.53
2005	Omha	AAA	6	6	0	0	13.0	53	8	4	4	0	0	0	1	6	0	12	1	0	0	1	.000	0	0--	-	1.96	2.77
2004	2 Tms	AL	7	5	0	0	29.2	142	44	28	28	3	0	1	3	13	1	19	3	2	0	4	.000	0	0-0	0	7.76	8.49
2005	KC	AL	7	7	0	0	35.2	159	36	23	23	2	1	1	2	10	0	23	3	0	2	2	.500	0	0-0	0	4.31	5.80
04	Bal	AL	2	0	0	0	2.0	15	6	8	8	1	0	1	1	2	0	1	1	0	0	0	-	0	0-0	0	28.67	36.00
04	KC	AL	5	5	0	0	27.2	127	38	20	20	2	0	0	2	11	1	18	2	2	0	4	.000	0	0-0	0	6.50	6.51
	2 ML YEARS		14	12	0	0	65.1	301	80	51	51	5	1	2	5	30	1	42	6	2	2	6	.250	0	0-0	0	5.79	7.03

Jose Bautista

Bats: R Throws: R Pos: 3B-8; PH-3 Ht: 6'0" Wt: 192 Born: 10/19/1980 Age: 25

Year	Team	Lg	G	AB	H	2B	3B	HR	(Hm	Rd)	TB	R	RBI	RC	TBB	IBB	SO	HBP	SH	SF	SB	CS	SB%	GDP	Avg	OBP	Slg
2001	Wmspt	A-	62	220	63	10	3	5	(-	-)	94	43	30	35	21	0	41	6	0	0	8	1	.89	5	.286	.364	.427
2002	Hickory	A	129	438	132	26	3	14	(-	-)	206	72	57	82	67	3	104	8	5	2	3	2	.60	12	.301	.402	.470
2003	Pirates	R	7	23	8	1	0	1	(-	-)	12	5	3	5	4	1	7	0	0	1	0	0	-	0	.348	.429	.522
2003	Lynbrg	A+	51	165	40	14	2	4	(-	-)	70	28	20	24	27	0	48	3	0	0	1	5	.17	1	.242	.359	.424
2005	Altna	AA	117	445	126	27	1	23	(-	-)	224	63	90	83	48	2	101	9	2	2	7	3	.70	8	.283	.363	.503
2005	Indy	AAA	13	51	13	3	0	1	(-	-)	19	6	4	10	4	0	10	0	0	0	1	1	.50	2	.255	.309	.373

Year	Team	Lg	G	AB	H	2B	3B	HR	(Hm	Rd)	TB	R	RBI	RC	TBB	IBB	SO	HBP	SH	SF	SB	CS	SB%	GDP	Avg	OBP	Slg
2004	4 Tms		64	88	18	3	0	0	(0	0)	21	6	2	2	7	0	40	0	1	0	0	1	.00	1	.205	.263	.239
2005	PIT	NL	11	28	4	1	0	0	(0	0)	5	3	1	0	3	0	7	0	0	0	1	0	1.00	2	.143	.226	.179
04	Bal	AL	16	11	3	0	0	0	(0	0)	3	3	0	1	1	0	3	0	0	0	0	0	-	0	.273	.333	.273
04	TB	AL	12	12	2	0	0	0	(0	0)	2	1	1	0	3	0	7	0	0	0	0	1	.00	0	.167	.333	.167
04	KC	AL	13	25	5	1	0	0	(0	0)	6	1	1	0	1	0	12	0	0	0	0	0	-	0	.200	.231	.240
04	Pit	NL	23	40	8	2	0	0	(0	0)	10	1	0	1	2	0	18	0	1	0	0	0	-	1	.200	.238	.250
2 ML YEARS			75	116	22	4	0	0	(0	0)	26	9	3	2	10	0	47	0	1	0	1	1	.50	3	.190	.254	.224

Jason Bay

Bats: R **Throws:** R **Pos:** LF-146; CF-30   **Ht:** 6'2" **Wt:** 200 **Born:** 9/20/1978 **Age:** 27

Year	Team	Lg	G	AB	H	2B	3B	HR	(Hm	Rd)	TB	R	RBI	RC	TBB	IBB	SO	HBP	SH	SF	SB	CS	SB%	GDP	Avg	OBP	Slg
2003	2 Tms	NL	30	87	25	7	1	4	(2	2)	46	15	14	19	19	0	29	1	0	0	3	1	.75	0	.287	.421	.529
2004	PIT	NL	120	411	116	24	4	26	(15	11)	226	61	82	75	41	2	129	10	5	5	4	6	.40	9	.282	.358	.550
2005	PIT	NL	162	599	183	44	6	32	(9	23)	335	110	101	128	95	9	142	6	0	7	21	1	.95	12	.306	.402	.559
03	SD	NL	3	8	2	1	0	1	(0	1)	6	2	2	2	1	0	1	1	0	0	0	0	-	0	.250	.400	.750
03	Pit	NL	27	79	23	6	1	3	(2	1)	40	13	12	17	18	0	28	0	0	0	3	1	.75	0	.291	.423	.506
3 ML YEARS			312	1097	324	75	11	62	(26	36)	607	186	197	222	155	11	300	17	5	12	28	8	.78	21	.295	.387	.553

Jonah Bayliss

Pitches: R **Bats:** R **Pos:** RP-11   **Ht:** 6'2" **Wt:** 210 **Born:** 8/13/1980 **Age:** 25

Year	Team	Lg	G	GS	CG	GF	IP	BFP	H	R	ER	HR	SH	SF	HB	TBB	IBB	SO	WP	Bk	W	L	Pct	ShO	Sv-Op	Hld	ERC	ERA
2002	Spkane	A-	15	15	0	0	70.2	311	70	46	42	9	3	3	7	29	0	38	7	2	4	8	.333	0	0--	-	4.66	5.35
2003	Burlgtn	A	26	26	2	0	140.0	618	129	78	60	11	4	2	10	69	0	133	9	0	7	12	.368	1	0--	-	4.10	3.86
2004	Wilmg	A+	23	23	0	0	107.0	477	114	69	60	11	9	8	9	42	0	73	6	2	6	6	.500	0	0--	-	4.76	5.05
2005	Wichta	AA	30	0	0	15	57.0	240	43	19	18	5	0	1	2	26	0	63	5	0	1	2	.333	0	8--	-	2.99	2.84
2005	KC	AL	11	0	0	7	11.2	48	7	6	6	2	0	0	2	4	0	10	0	0	0	0	-	0	0-0	0	2.80	4.63

Yorman Bazardo

Pitches: R **Bats:** R **Pos:** RP-1   **Ht:** 6'2" **Wt:** 202 **Born:** 7/11/1984 **Age:** 21

Year	Team	Lg	G	GS	CG	GF	IP	BFP	H	R	ER	HR	SH	SF	HB	TBB	IBB	SO	WP	Bk	W	L	Pct	ShO	Sv-Op	Hld	ERC	ERA
2002	Jmstwn	A-	25	0	0	21	36.1	154	39	11	11	0	0	2	1	6	0	26	7	0	5	0	1.000	0	6--	-	2.95	2.72
2003	Grnsbr	A	21	21	4	0	130.0	548	132	56	45	8	3	4	9	26	0	70	4	2	9	8	.529	2	0--	-	3.38	3.12
2004	Jupiter	A+	25	25	2	0	154.1	654	161	78	56	3	9	13	10	30	0	95	9	1	5	9	.357	2	0--	-	3.20	3.27
2005	Carlina	AA	19	19	0	0	108.1	469	108	60	48	12	9	5	8	36	3	73	8	1	8	7	.533	0	0--	-	4.10	3.99
2005	SnAnt	AA	6	6	0	0	33.2	150	38	16	16	4	0	1	0	11	0	26	0	2	3	1	.750	0	0--	-	4.54	4.28
2005	FLA	NL	1	0	0	0	1.2	12	5	5	4	0	0	0	0	2	0	2	1	0	0	0	-	0	0-0	0	20.56	21.60

Colter Bean

Pitches: R **Bats:** L **Pos:** RP-1   **Ht:** 6'6" **Wt:** 255 **Born:** 1/16/1977 **Age:** 29

Year	Team	Lg	G	GS	CG	GF	IP	BFP	H	R	ER	HR	SH	SF	HB	TBB	IBB	SO	WP	Bk	W	L	Pct	ShO	Sv-Op	Hld	ERC	ERA
2000	StIslnd	A-	3	0	0	2	2.0	14	3	3	1	0	0	0	0	3	1	2	1	0	0	0	-	0	0--	-	8.06	4.50
2000	Grnsbr	A	18	0	0	9	25.2	109	21	16	14	1	0	0	1	11	0	35	4	0	1	0	1.000	0	0--	-	2.90	4.91
2001	Tampa	A+	32	0	0	10	49.1	193	27	9	8	0	0	0	3	18	2	77	2	0	7	1	.875	0	2--	-	1.39	1.46
2001	Nrwich	AA	1	0	0	1	1.0	5	1	1	1	0	0	0	0	1	0	0	0	0	1	0	1.000	0	0--	-	14.27	9.00
2002	Tampa	A+	46	0	0	25	54.2	219	34	17	12	2	3	2	5	21	2	78	1	0	2	2	.500	0	9--	-	1.98	1.98
2002	Nrwich	AA	12	0	0	4	10.2	52	14	8	8	1	1	1	2	6	0	9	0	0	0	2	.000	0	0--	-	7.49	6.75
2003	Trentn	AA	3	0	0	4	4.2	18	2	0	0	0	2	1	0	2	0	9	0	0	0	0	-	0	0--	-	1.08	0.00
2003	Clmbs	AAA	50	0	0	17	69.0	287	53	33	22	5	1	0	5	27	2	70	1	1	4	2	.667	0	4--	-	2.85	2.87
2004	Clmbs	AAA	53	0	0	12	82.2	332	61	24	21	3	0	0	8	23	0	109	2	1	9	3	.750	0	1--	-	2.24	2.29
2005	Clmbs	AAA	65	0	0	20	71.2	314	60	33	24	5	8	2	8	39	7	82	0	0	4	7	.364	0	0--	-	3.79	3.01
2005	NYA	AL	1	0	0	1	2.0	9	1	1	1	0	0	0	0	2	0	2	0	0	0	0	-	0	0-0	0	2.80	4.50

Josh Beckett

Pitches: R **Bats:** R **Pos:** SP-29   **Ht:** 6'5" **Wt:** 216 **Born:** 5/15/1980 **Age:** 26

Year	Team	Lg	G	GS	CG	GF	IP	BFP	H	R	ER	HR	SH	SF	HB	TBB	IBB	SO	WP	Bk	W	L	Pct	ShO	Sv-Op	Hld	ERC	ERA
2001	FLA	NL	4	4	0	0	24.0	99	14	9	4	3	0	0	1	11	0	24	1	0	2	2	.500	0	0-0	0	2.36	1.50
2002	FLA	NL	23	21	0	0	107.2	454	93	56	49	13	5	3	1	44	2	113	5	0	6	7	.462	0	0-0	0	3.50	4.10
2003	FLA	NL	24	23	0	1	142.0	601	132	54	48	9	5	1	2	56	4	152	6	1	9	8	.529	0	0-0	0	3.44	3.04
2004	FLA	NL	26	26	1	0	156.2	654	137	72	66	16	9	3	6	54	3	152	5	0	9	9	.500	1	0-0	0	3.32	3.79
2005	FLA	NL	29	29	2	0	178.2	729	153	75	67	14	8	2	7	58	2	166	5	0	15	8	.652	1	0-0	0	3.06	3.38
5 ML YEARS			106	103	3	1	609.0	2537	529	266	234	55	27	9	17	223	11	607	22	1	41	34	.547	2	0-0	0	3.26	3.46

Erik Bedard

Pitches: L Bats: L Pos: SP-24   **Ht: 6'1" Wt: 186 Born: 3/6/1979 Age: 27**

			HOW MUCH HE PITCHED						WHAT HE GAVE UP											THE RESULTS						
Year	Team	Lg	G	GS	CG	GF	IP	BFP	H	R	ER	HR	SH	SF	HB	TBB	IBB	SO	WP	Bk	W	L	Pct	ShO	Sv-Op Hld	ERC	ERA
2005	Dlmrva*	A	1	1	0	0	5.0	19	3	0	0	0	0	0	0	1	0	9	2	0	1	0	1.000	0	0- - -	1.11	0.00
2005	Bowie*	AA	1	1	0	0	2.0	9	2	2	2	0	0	0	0	1	0	4	0	0	0	1	.000	0	0- - -	3.63	9.00
2002	BAL	AL	2	0	0	0	0.2	4	2	1	1	0	0	0	0	0	0	1	0	0	0	0	-	0	0-0 0	14.52	13.50
2004	BAL	AL	27	26	0	0	137.1	633	149	83	70	13	0	4	7	71	1	121	7	2	6	10	.375	0	0-0 0	5.11	4.59
2005	BAL	AL	24	24	0	0	141.2	606	139	66	63	10	3	6	5	57	1	125	4	1	6	8	.429	0	0-0 0	3.95	4.00
	3 ML YEARS		53	50	0	0	279.2	1243	290	150	134	23	3	10	12	128	2	247	11	3	12	18	.400	0	0-0 0	4.53	4.31

Joe Beimel

Pitches: L Bats: L Pos: RP-7   **Ht: 6'3" Wt: 215 Born: 4/19/1977 Age: 29**

			HOW MUCH HE PITCHED						WHAT HE GAVE UP											THE RESULTS						
Year	Team	Lg	G	GS	CG	GF	IP	BFP	H	R	ER	HR	SH	SF	HB	TBB	IBB	SO	WP	Bk	W	L	Pct	ShO	Sv-Op Hld	ERC	ERA
2005	Drham*	AAA	48	0	0	14	52.2	237	58	28	23	3	2	1	1	21	1	36	4	0	1	2	.333	0	0- - -	4.28	3.93
2001	PIT	NL	42	15	0	9	115.1	511	131	72	67	12	3	1	6	49	4	58	3	0	7	11	.389	0	0-0 0	5.24	5.23
2002	PIT	NL	53	8	0	8	85.1	389	88	49	44	9	7	3	4	45	12	53	2	0	2	5	.286	0	0-1 5	4.68	4.64
2003	PIT	NL	69	0	0	11	62.1	276	69	35	35	7	3	5	4	33	6	42	0	1	1	3	.250	0	0-5 12	5.62	5.05
2004	MIN	AL	3	0	0	0	1.2	15	8	8	8	1	0	0	0	2	0	2	0	0	0	0	-	0	0-0 0	44.44	43.20
2005	TB	AL	7	0	0	3	11.0	51	15	4	4	1	0	0	0	4	1	3	1	0	0	0	-	0	0-0 0	5.80	3.27
	5 ML YEARS		174	23	0	31	275.2	1242	311	168	158	30	13	9	14	133	23	158	6	1	10	19	.345	0	0-6 17	5.34	5.16

Matt Belisle

Pitches: R Bats: B Pos: RP-55; SP-5   **Ht: 6'3" Wt: 195 Born: 6/6/1980 Age: 26**

			HOW MUCH HE PITCHED						WHAT HE GAVE UP											THE RESULTS						
Year	Team	Lg	G	GS	CG	GF	IP	BFP	H	R	ER	HR	SH	SF	HB	TBB	IBB	SO	WP	Bk	W	L	Pct	ShO	Sv-Op Hld	ERC	ERA
1999	Danvle	R+	14	14	0	0	71.1	329	86	50	37	3	0	2	8	23	0	60	6	2	2	5	.286	0	0- - -	4.86	4.67
2000	Macon	A	15	15	1	0	102.1	392	79	37	27	7	2	3	4	18	0	97	7	0	9	5	.643	0	0- - -	2.11	2.37
2000	MrtlBh	A+	12	12	0	0	78.2	319	72	32	30	5	3	5	2	11	0	71	9	1	3	4	.429	0	0- - -	2.49	3.43
2002	Grnville	AA	26	26	1	0	159.1	682	162	91	77	18	3	9	10	39	1	123	6	2	5	9	.357	0	0- - -	3.84	4.35
2003	Grnville	AA	21	21	1	0	125.1	532	128	59	49	5	8	5	4	42	2	94	3	2	6	8	.429	0	0- - -	3.74	3.52
2003	Rchmd	AAA	3	3	0	0	20.0	77	17	6	5	1	0	1	2	0	0	10	0	0	1	1	.500	0	0- - -	1.94	2.25
2003	Lsvlle	AAA	4	4	0	0	26.0	108	31	15	11	2	0	0	1	5	0	15	0	0	1	3	.250	0	0- - -	4.52	3.81
2004	Lsvlle	AAA	28	28	2	0	162.2	715	192	104	95	16	11	9	11	51	4	106	7	1	9	11	.450	1	0- - -	5.06	5.26
2003	CIN	NL	6	0	0	2	8.2	39	10	5	5	1	2	1	1	2	0	6	0	0	1	1	.500	0	0-1 0	4.73	5.19
2005	CIN	NL	60	5	0	17	85.2	382	101	49	42	11	4	2	6	26	6	59	3	0	4	8	.333	0	1-4 8	5.08	4.41
	2 ML YEARS		66	5	0	19	94.1	421	111	54	47	12	6	3	7	28	6	65	3	0	5	9	.357	0	1-5 8	5.05	4.48

David Bell

Bats: R Throws: R Pos: 3B-150; PH-1   **Ht: 5'10" Wt: 195 Born: 9/14/1972 Age: 33**

			BATTING																		BASERUNNING				AVERAGES		
Year	Team	Lg	G	AB	H	2B	3B	HR	(Hm	Rd)	TB	R	RBI	RC	TBB	IBB	SO	HBP	SH	SF	SB	CS	SB%	GDP	Avg	OBP	Slg
1995	2 Tms		41	146	36	7	2	2	(1	1)	53	13	19	14	4	0	25	2	0	1	1	2	.33	0	.247	.275	.363
1996	STL	NL	62	145	31	6	0	1	(1	0)	40	12	9	9	10	2	22	1	0	1	1	1	.50	3	.214	.268	.276
1997	STL	NL	66	142	30	7	2	1	(1	0)	44	9	12	11	10	2	28	0	2	1	1	0	1.00	1	.211	.261	.310
1998	3 Tms		132	429	117	30	2	10	(2	8)	181	48	49	53	27	4	65	2	1	5	0	4	.00	11	.273	.315	.422
1999	SEA	AL	157	597	160	31	2	21	(11	10)	258	92	78	87	58	0	90	2	3	7	7	4	.64	7	.268	.331	.432
2000	SEA	AL	133	454	112	24	2	11	(4	7)	173	57	47	54	42	0	66	6	6	4	2	3	.40	11	.247	.316	.381
2001	SEA	AL	135	470	122	28	0	15	(7	8)	195	62	64	58	28	1	59	3	5	4	2	1	.67	8	.260	.303	.415
2002	SF	NL	154	552	144	29	2	20	(7	13)	237	82	73	79	54	2	80	9	6	7	1	2	.33	18	.261	.333	.429
2003	PHI	NL	85	297	58	14	0	4	(1	3)	84	32	37	27	41	1	40	4	0	6	0	0	-	7	.195	.296	.283
2004	PHI	NL	143	533	155	33	1	18	(10	8)	244	67	77	87	57	4	75	6	2	5	1	1	.50	14	.291	.363	.458
2005	PHI	NL	150	557	138	31	1	10	(5	5)	201	53	61	55	47	6	69	5	4	4	0	1	.00	24	.248	.310	.361
95	Cle	AL	2	2	0	0	0	0	(0	0)	0	0	0	0	0	0	0	0	0	0	0	0	-	0	.000	.000	.000
95	StL	NL	39	144	36	7	2	2	(1	1)	53	13	19	14	4	0	25	2	0	1	1	2	.33	0	.250	.278	.368
98	StL	NL	4	9	2	1	0	0	(0	0)	3	0	0	1	0	0	3	0	0	0	0	0	-	0	.222	.222	.333
98	Cle	AL	107	340	89	21	2	10	(2	8)	144	37	41	41	22	4	54	2	1	5	0	4	.00	8	.262	.306	.424
98	Sea	AL	21	80	26	8	0	0	(0	0)	34	11	8	11	5	0	8	0	0	0	0	0	-	3	.325	.365	.425
	11 ML YEARS		1258	4322	1103	240	14	113	(50	63)	1710	527	526	534	378	22	619	40	29	45	16	19	.46	105	.255	.318	.396

Heath Bell

Pitches: R Bats: R Pos: RP-42   **Ht: 6'2" Wt: 244 Born: 9/29/1977 Age: 28**

			HOW MUCH HE PITCHED						WHAT HE GAVE UP											THE RESULTS						
Year	Team	Lg	G	GS	CG	GF	IP	BFP	H	R	ER	HR	SH	SF	HB	TBB	IBB	SO	WP	Bk	W	L	Pct	ShO	Sv-Op Hld	ERC	ERA
1998	Kngspt	R+	22	0	0	11	46.0	189	40	15	13	5	1	2	2	11	0	61	4	0	1	0	1.000	0	8- - -	2.96	2.54
1999	CptCty	A	55	0	0	48	62.1	251	47	23	18	3	2	0	0	17	0	68	3	1	1	7	.125	0	25- - -	1.99	2.60
2000	StLuci	A+	48	0	0	37	60.0	241	43	19	17	4	2	2	2	21	2	75	1	0	5	1	.833	0	23- - -	2.30	2.55
2001	Bnghtn	AA	43	0	0	22	61.1	285	82	44	41	13	1	4	5	19	3	55	4	0	3	1	.750	0	4- - -	6.81	6.02
2002	Bnghtn	AA	24	0	0	16	38.0	139	22	6	5	0	1	0	4	6	0	49	3	0	1	0	1.000	0	6- - -	1.00	1.18
2002	Norfolk	AAA	22	0	0	14	31.2	142	38	15	15	2	5	1	1	9	1	28	1	0	3	4	.429	0	5- - -	4.47	4.26
2003	Norfolk	AAA	40	0	0	25	49.2	206	54	26	26	4	4	1	2	8	0	54	4	0	2	3	.400	0	3- - -	3.70	4.71
2004	Bnghtn	AA	1	0	0	0	2.0	8	2	0	0	0	0	0	0	0	0	0	0	0	0	0	-	0	0- - -	1.95	0.00
2004	Norfolk	AAA	45	0	0	30	55.2	237	42	21	20	4	1	0	4	24	2	68	6	1	3	1	.750	0	16- - -	2.84	3.23
2005	Norfolk	AAA	13	2	0	8	26.2	100	15	5	5	1	1	1	0	5	0	29	1	0	1	0	1.000	0	6- - -	1.11	1.69
2004	NYN	NL	17	0	0	2	24.1	94	22	9	9	3	4	0	0	6	0	27	0	0	0	2	.000	0	0-1 1	3.86	3.33
2005	NYN	NL	42	0	0	12	46.2	206	56	30	29	5	1	0	1	13	3	43	0	1	1	3	.250	0	0-0 4	4.42	5.59
	2 ML YEARS		59	0	0	14	71.0	300	78	39	38	8	5	0	1	19	3	70	0	1	1	5	.167	0	0-1 5	4.25	4.82

Rob Bell

Pitches: R **Bats:** R **Pos:** RP-5; SP-3   **Ht:** 6'5" **Wt:** 225 **Born:** 1/17/1977 **Age:** 29

			HOW MUCH HE PITCHED						WHAT HE GAVE UP										THE RESULTS							
Year	Team	Lg	G	GS	CG	GF	IP	BFP	H	R	ER	HR	SH	SF	HB	TBB	IBB	SO	WP	Bk	W	L	Pct	ShO	Sv-Op Hld	ERC	ERA
2005	Drham*	AAA	22	2	0	5	44.1	217	64	39	38	12	6	2	1	20	2	26	4	0	1	3	.250	0	0- -	8.30	7.71
2000	CIN	NL	26	26	1	0	140.1	618	130	84	78	32	8	2	1	73	6	112	11	0	7	8	.467	0	0-0 0	4.98	5.00
2001	2 Tms		27	27	0	0	149.2	670	176	115	111	32	3	9	7	64	1	97	9	0	5	10	.333	0	0-0 0	6.40	6.67
2002	TEX	AL	17	15	0	0	94.0	425	113	69	65	16	1	6	1	35	0	70	7	0	4	3	.571	0	0-0 0	5.67	6.22
2003	TB	AL	19	18	0	0	101.0	441	103	64	62	15	2	2	5	39	1	44	0	0	5	4	.556	0	0-0 0	4.66	5.52
2004	TB	AL	24	19	1	3	123.0	529	121	71	61	16	2	2	5	41	0	57	10	0	8	8	.500	0	0-0 0	4.06	4.46
2005	TB	AL	8	3	0	4	25.0	129	41	25	23	7	0	1	2	12	0	13	3	0	1	1	.500	0	0-0 0	10.30	8.28
01	Cin	NL	9	9	0	0	44.1	188	46	28	27	9	0	1	3	17	1	33	1	0	0	5	.000	0	0-0 0	5.43	5.48
01	Tex	AL	18	18	0	0	105.1	482	130	87	84	23	3	8	4	47	0	64	8	0	5	5	.500	0	0-0 0	6.82	7.18
	6 ML YEARS		121	108	2	7	633.0	2812	684	428	400	118	16	22	21	264	8	393	40	0	30	34	.469	0	0-0 0	5.36	5.69

Mark Bellhorn

Bats: B **Throws:** R **Pos:** 2B-85; 3B-4; SS-3; PH-2; PR-1   **Ht:** 6'1" **Wt:** 205 **Born:** 8/23/1974 **Age:** 31

			BATTING																BASERUNNING				AVERAGES		
Year	Team	Lg	G	AB	H	2B	3B	HR	(Hm | Rd)	TB	R	RBI	RC	TBB	IBB	SO	HBP	SH	SF	SB	CS	SB%	GDP	Avg	OBP	Slg
2005	Pwtckt*	AAA	16	68	12	4	0	2	(- | -)	22	9	9	5	4	0	24	2	0	0	0	0	-	1	.176	.243	.324
1997	OAK	AL	68	224	51	9	1	6	(3 | 3)	80	33	19	29	32	0	70	0	5	0	7	1	.88	1	.228	.324	.357
1998	OAK	AL	11	12	1	1	0	0	(0 | 0)	2	1	1	1	3	0	4	1	0	0	2	0	1.00	0	.083	.313	.167
2000	OAK	AL	9	13	2	0	0	0	(0 | 0)	2	2	0	1	2	0	6	0	0	0	0	0	-	0	.154	.267	.154
2001	OAK	AL	38	74	10	1	2	1	(1 | 0)	18	11	4	3	7	0	37	0	1	0	0	0	-	1	.135	.210	.243
2002	CHN	NL	146	445	115	24	4	27	(15 | 12)	228	86	56	79	76	3	144	6	2	0	7	5	.58	6	.258	.374	.512
2003	2 Tms	NL	99	249	55	10	1	2	(1 | 1)	73	27	26	26	50	1	78	3	1	4	5	6	.45	3	.221	.353	.293
2004	BOS	AL	138	523	138	37	3	17	(11 | 6)	232	93	82	95	88	1	177	5	1	3	6	1	.86	8	.264	.373	.444
2005	2 Tms	AL	94	300	63	20	0	8	(3 | 5)	107	43	30	28	52	1	112	0	0	3	3	0	1.00	4	.210	.324	.357
03	ChC	NL	51	139	29	7	1	2	(1 | 1)	44	15	22	17	29	1	46	1	0	4	3	3	.50	2	.209	.341	.317
03	Col	NL	48	110	26	3	0	0	(0 | 0)	29	12	4	9	21	0	32	2	1	0	2	3	.40	1	.236	.368	.264
05	Bos	AL	85	283	61	20	0	7	(3 | 4)	102	41	28	28	49	1	109	0	0	3	3	0	1.00	4	.216	.328	.360
05	NYY	AL	9	17	2	0	0	1	(0 | 1)	5	2	2	0	3	0	3	0	0	0	0	0	-	0	.118	.250	.294
	8 ML YEARS		603	1840	435	102	11	61	(34 | 27)	742	296	218	262	310	6	628	15	10	10	30	13	.70	23	.236	.349	.403

Ronnie Belliard

Bats: R **Throws:** R **Pos:** 2B-141; PH-5; PR-1   **Ht:** 5'8" **Wt:** 197 **Born:** 4/7/1975 **Age:** 31

			BATTING																BASERUNNING				AVERAGES		
Year	Team	Lg	G	AB	H	2B	3B	HR	(Hm | Rd)	TB	R	RBI	RC	TBB	IBB	SO	HBP	SH	SF	SB	CS	SB%	GDP	Avg	OBP	Slg
1998	MIL	NL	8	5	1	0	0	0	(0 | 0)	1	1	0	0	0	0	0	0	0	0	0	0	-	0	.200	.200	.200
1999	MIL	NL	124	457	135	29	4	8	(5 | 3)	196	60	58	72	64	0	59	0	6	4	4	5	.44	16	.295	.379	.429
2000	MIL	NL	152	571	150	30	9	8	(4 | 4)	222	83	54	81	82	4	84	3	4	7	7	5	.58	12	.263	.354	.389
2001	MIL	NL	101	364	96	30	3	11	(7 | 4)	165	69	36	56	35	2	65	5	4	2	5	2	.71	5	.264	.335	.453
2002	MIL	NL	104	289	61	13	0	3	(0 | 3)	83	30	26	15	18	0	46	1	6	3	2	3	.40	8	.211	.257	.287
2003	COL	NL	116	447	124	31	2	8	(6 | 2)	183	73	50	71	49	0	71	2	6	1	7	2	.78	7	.277	.351	.409
2004	CLE	AL	152	599	169	48	1	12	(8 | 4)	255	78	70	87	60	5	98	2	0	7	3	2	.60	18	.282	.348	.426
2005	CLE	AL	145	536	152	36	1	17	(7 | 10)	241	71	78	71	35	0	72	1	8	7	2	2	.50	17	.284	.325	.450
	8 ML YEARS		902	3268	888	217	20	67	(33 | 34)	1346	465	372	453	343	11	495	14	34	26	30	21	.59	83	.272	.341	.412

Carlos Beltran

Bats: B **Throws:** R **Pos:** CF-150; PH-2   **Ht:** 6'1" **Wt:** 190 **Born:** 4/24/1977 **Age:** 29

			BATTING																BASERUNNING				AVERAGES		
Year	Team	Lg	G	AB	H	2B	3B	HR	(Hm | Rd)	TB	R	RBI	RC	TBB	IBB	SO	HBP	SH	SF	SB	CS	SB%	GDP	Avg	OBP	Slg
1998	KC	AL	14	58	16	5	3	0	(0 | 0)	27	12	7	9	3	0	12	1	0	1	3	0	1.00	2	.276	.317	.466
1999	KC	AL	156	663	194	27	7	22	(12 | 10)	301	112	108	100	46	2	123	4	0	10	27	8	.77	17	.293	.337	.454
2000	KC	AL	98	372	92	15	4	7	(4 | 3)	136	49	44	43	35	2	69	0	2	4	13	0	1.00	14	.247	.309	.366
2001	KC	AL	155	617	189	32	12	24	(7 | 17)	317	106	101	118	52	2	120	5	1	5	31	1	.97	7	.306	.362	.514
2002	KC	AL	162	637	174	44	7	29	(19 | 10)	319	114	105	117	71	1	135	4	3	7	35	7	.83	12	.273	.346	.501
2003	KC	AL	141	521	160	14	10	26	(10 | 16)	272	102	100	117	72	4	81	2	0	7	41	4	.91	5	.307	.389	.522
2004	2 Tms		159	599	160	36	9	38	(15 | 23)	328	121	104	124	92	10	101	7	3	7	42	3	.93	8	.267	.367	.548
2005	NYN	NL	151	582	155	34	2	16	(10 | 6)	241	83	78	88	56	5	96	2	4	6	17	6	.74	9	.266	.330	.414
04	KC	AL	69	266	74	19	2	15	(8 | 7)	142	51	51	57	37	7	44	2	1	3	14	3	.82	4	.278	.367	.534
04	Hou	NL	90	333	86	17	7	23	(7 | 16)	186	70	53	67	55	3	57	5	2	4	28	0	1.00	4	.258	.368	.559
	8 ML YEARS		1036	4049	1140	207	54	162	(73 | 89)	1941	699	647	716	427	26	737	25	13	47	209	29	.88	75	.282	.350	.479

Francis Beltran

Pitches: R **Bats:** R **Pos:** P   **Ht:** 6'5" **Wt:** 220 **Born:** 11/29/1979 **Age:** 26

			HOW MUCH HE PITCHED						WHAT HE GAVE UP										THE RESULTS							
Year	Team	Lg	G	GS	CG	GF	IP	BFP	H	R	ER	HR	SH	SF	HB	TBB	IBB	SO	WP	Bk	W	L	Pct	ShO	Sv-Op Hld	ERC	ERA
1997	Cubs	R	16	0	0	5	23.2	111	27	18	9	1	1	3	3	8	0	17	3	2	0	1	.000	0	1- -	4.49	3.42
1998	Cubs	R	12	5	0	3	35.2	165	49	23	22	1	4	2	2	14	1	26	1	1	1	1	.500	0	0- -	5.96	5.55
1999	Cubs	R	7	0	0	6	10.2	38	5	3	0	0	0	0	1	1	0	8	0	0	0	1	.000	0	2- -	0.78	0.00
1999	Eugene	A-	16	0	0	7	28.0	142	41	32	26	2	0	1	3	14	0	28	6	0	0	2	.000	0	0- -	7.34	8.36
2000	Lansng	A	16	0	0	11	17.2	97	24	22	19	0	0	3	4	19	0	16	4	0	1	1	.500	0	0- -	9.24	9.68
2000	Eugene	A-	25	0	0	13	43.2	180	28	16	13	1	1	1	1	20	2	52	6	0	2	2	.500	0	8- -	1.93	2.68
2001	Dytona	A+	21	18	0	0	95.1	424	93	62	53	10	1	4	9	40	1	72	4	0	6	9	.400	0	0- -	4.35	5.00
2002	WTenn	AA	39	0	0	35	41.2	171	28	14	12	2	3	1	2	19	2	43	3	2	2	2	.500	0	23- -	2.34	2.59
2003	Iowa	AAA	31	2	0	23	48.2	206	46	17	16	2	0	4	1	19	3	33	0	0	6	2	.750	0	4- -	3.34	2.96
2004	Edmtn	AAA	5	0	0	5	5.0	21	4	1	1	0	0	0	0	2	0	6	0	0	0	0	-	0	3- -	2.31	1.80

Year	Team	Lg	G	GS	CG	GF	IP	BFP	H	R	ER	HR	SH	SF	HB	TBB	IBB	SO	WP	Bk	W	L	Pct	ShO	Sv-Op	Hld	ERC	ERA
2004	Iowa	AAA	6	0	0	6	6.1	25	5	2	2	1	0	0	0	1	0	6	0	0	0	0	-	0	4--	-	2.37	2.84
2002	CHN	NL	11	0	0	4	12.0	65	14	11	10	2	3	1	0	16	1	11	2	0	0	0	-	0	0-0	0	9.45	7.50
2004	2 Tms	NL	45	0	0	13	49.1	221	47	31	30	11	4	2	2	27	1	48	2	0	2	2	.500	0	1-1	5	5.40	5.47
04	ChC	NL	34	0	0	10	35.0	152	27	19	18	8	3	1	0	22	0	40	1	0	2	2	.500	0	0-0	5	4.58	4.63
04	Mon	NL	11	0	0	3	14.1	69	20	12	12	3	1	1	2	5	1	8	1	0	0	0	-	0	1-1	0	7.56	7.53
	2 ML YEARS		56	0	0	17	61.1	286	61	42	40	13	7	3	2	43	2	59	4	0	2	2	.500	0	1-1	5	6.18	5.87

Adrian Beltre

Bats: R **Throws:** R **Pos:** 3B-155; DH-1   **Ht:** 5'11" **Wt:** 220 **Born:** 4/7/1979 **Age:** 27

Year	Team	Lg	G	AB	H	2B	3B	HR	(Hm	Rd)	TB	R	RBI	RC	TBB	IBB	SO	HBP	SH	SF	SB	CS	SB%	GDP	Avg	OBP	Slg
1998	LA	NL	77	195	42	9	0	7	(5	2)	72	18	22	20	14	0	37	3	2	0	3	1	.75	4	.215	.278	.369
1999	LA	NL	152	538	148	27	5	15	(6	9)	230	84	67	84	61	12	105	6	4	5	18	7	.72	4	.275	.352	.428
2000	LA	NL	138	510	148	30	2	20	(7	13)	242	71	85	85	56	2	80	2	3	4	12	5	.71	13	.290	.360	.475
2001	LA	NL	126	475	126	22	4	13	(4	9)	195	59	60	60	28	1	82	5	2	5	13	4	.76	9	.265	.310	.411
2002	LA	NL	159	587	151	26	5	21	(7	14)	250	70	75	74	37	4	96	4	1	6	7	5	.58	17	.257	.303	.426
2003	LA	NL	158	559	134	30	2	23	(13	10)	237	50	80	66	37	4	103	5	1	6	2	2	.50	13	.240	.290	.424
2004	LA	NL	156	598	200	32	0	48	(23	25)	376	104	121	120	53	9	87	2	0	4	7	2	.78	15	.334	.388	.629
2005	SEA	AL	156	603	154	36	1	19	(7	12)	249	69	87	75	38	6	108	5	0	4	3	1	.75	15	.255	.303	.413
	8 ML YEARS		1122	4065	1103	212	19	166	(72	94)	1851	525	597	584	324	38	698	32	13	34	65	27	.71	90	.271	.327	.455

Armando Benitez

Pitches: R **Bats:** R **Pos:** RP-30   **Ht:** 6'4" **Wt:** 229 **Born:** 11/3/1972 **Age:** 33

Year	Team	Lg	G	GS	CG	GF	IP	BFP	H	R	ER	HR	SH	SF	HB	TBB	IBB	SO	WP	Bk	W	L	Pct	ShO	Sv-Op	Hld	ERC	ERA
2005	SnJos*	A+	2	2	0	0	2.0	7	0	0	0	0	0	0	0	1	0	0	0	0	0	0	-	0	0--	-	0.27	0.00
1994	BAL	AL	3	0	0	1	10.0	42	8	1	1	0	0	0	1	4	0	14	0	0	0	0	-	0	0-0	0	2.71	0.90
1995	BAL	AL	44	0	0	18	47.2	221	37	33	30	8	2	3	5	37	2	56	3	1	1	5	.167	0	2-5	6	5.06	5.66
1996	BAL	AL	18	0	0	8	14.1	56	7	6	6	2	0	1	0	6	0	20	1	0	1	0	1.000	0	4-5	1	1.78	3.77
1997	BAL	AL	71	0	0	26	73.1	307	49	22	20	7	2	4	1	43	5	106	1	0	4	5	.444	0	9-10	20	2.92	2.45
1998	BAL	AL	71	0	0	54	68.1	289	48	29	29	10	3	2	4	39	2	87	0	0	5	6	.455	0	22-26	3	3.63	3.82
1999	NYN	NL	77	0	0	42	78.0	312	40	17	16	4	0	0	0	41	4	128	2	0	4	3	.571	0	22-28	17	1.69	1.85
2000	NYN	NL	76	0	0	68	76.0	304	39	24	22	10	2	1	0	38	2	106	0	0	4	4	.500	0	41-46	0	2.08	2.61
2001	NYN	NL	73	0	0	64	76.1	320	59	32	32	12	2	1	1	40	6	93	5	0	6	4	.600	0	43-46	0	3.67	3.77
2002	NYN	NL	62	0	0	52	67.1	275	46	20	17	8	3	2	3	25	0	79	1	0	1	0	1.000	0	33-37	0	2.55	2.27
2003	3 Tms	NL	69	0	0	49	73.0	313	59	27	24	6	0	1	0	41	3	75	3	1	4	4	.500	0	21-29	5	3.45	2.96
2004	FLA	NL	64	0	0	59	69.2	262	36	11	10	6	3	1	0	21	4	62	0	0	2	2	.500	0	47-51	0	1.36	1.29
2005	SF	NL	30	0	0	27	30.0	127	25	17	15	5	0	2	0	16	0	23	0	0	2	3	.400	0	19-23	0	4.20	4.50
03	NYM	NL	45	0	0	40	49.1	209	41	18	17	5	0	1	0	24	1	50	3	1	3	3	.500	0	21-28	0	3.46	3.10
03	NYY	AL	9	0	0	2	9.1	40	8	4	2	0	0	0	0	6	1	10	0	0	1	1	.500	0	0-0	4	3.40	1.93
03	Sea	AL	15	0	0	7	14.1	64	10	5	5	1	0	0	0	11	1	15	0	0	0	0	-	0	0-1	1	3.40	3.14
	12 ML YEARS		658	0	0	468	684.0	2828	453	239	222	78	17	18	15	351	28	849	16	2	34	36	.486	0	263-306	52	2.82	2.92

Gary Bennett

Bats: R **Throws:** R **Pos:** C-64; PH-7; PR-1   **Ht:** 6'0" **Wt:** 208 **Born:** 4/17/1972 **Age:** 34

Year	Team	Lg	G	AB	H	2B	3B	HR	(Hm	Rd)	TB	R	RBI	RC	TBB	IBB	SO	HBP	SH	SF	SB	CS	SB%	GDP	Avg	OBP	Slg
1995	PHI	NL	1	1	0	0	0	0	(0	0)	0	0	0	0	0	0	1	0	0	0	0	0	-	0	.000	.000	.000
1996	PHI	NL	6	16	4	0	0	0	(0	0)	4	0	1	1	2	1	6	0	0	0	0	0	-	0	.250	.333	.250
1998	PHI	NL	9	31	9	0	0	0	(0	0)	9	4	3	4	5	0	5	0	0	1	0	0	-	1	.290	.378	.290
1999	PHI	NL	36	88	24	4	0	1	(0	1)	31	7	21	7	4	0	11	0	0	2	0	0	-	7	.273	.298	.352
2000	PHI	NL	31	74	18	5	0	2	(0	2)	29	8	5	12	13	0	15	2	0	0	0	0	-	0	.243	.371	.392
2001	3 Tms	NL	46	131	32	6	1	2	(2	0)	46	15	10	15	12	4	24	1	2	2	0	0	-	1	.244	.308	.351
2002	COL	NL	90	291	77	10	2	4	(2	2)	103	26	26	29	15	2	45	6	2	0	1	3	.25	10	.265	.314	.354
2003	SD	NL	96	307	73	15	0	2	(1	1)	94	26	42	33	24	3	48	2	3	2	3	0	1.00	8	.238	.296	.306
2004	MIL	NL	75	219	49	14	0	3	(3	0)	72	18	20	15	22	3	32	2	0	3	1	0	1.00	9	.224	.297	.329
2005	WAS	NL	68	199	44	7	0	1	(1	0)	54	11	21	17	21	3	37	2	3	3	0	1	.00	7	.221	.298	.271
01	Phi	NL	26	75	16	3	1	1	(1	0)	24	8	6	7	9	1	19	0	1	0	0	0	-	1	.213	.294	.320
01	NYM	NL	1	1	1	0	0	0	(0	0)	1	0	0	0	0	0	0	0	0	0	0	0	-	0	1.000	1.000	1.000
01	Col	NL	19	55	15	3	0	1	(1	0)	21	7	4	7	3	3	5	1	1	1	0	0	-	0	.273	.317	.382
	10 ML YEARS		458	1357	330	61	3	15	(9	6)	442	115	149	133	118	16	224	15	10	13	5	4	.56	43	.243	.308	.326

Joaquin Benoit

Pitches: R **Bats:** R **Pos:** RP-23; SP-9   **Ht:** 6'3" **Wt:** 205 **Born:** 7/26/1977 **Age:** 28

Year	Team	Lg	G	GS	CG	GF	IP	BFP	H	R	ER	HR	SH	SF	HB	TBB	IBB	SO	WP	Bk	W	L	Pct	ShO	Sv-Op	Hld	ERC	ERA
2005	Rngrs*	R	1	1	0	0	2.0	7	0	0	0	0	0	0	0	1	0	4	0	0	0	0	-	0	0--	-	0.27	0.00
2005	Okla*	AAA	3	1	0	0	5.0	23	4	3	3	1	0	0	1	4	0	2	1	0	0	1	.000	0	0--	-	6.28	5.40
2001	TEX	AL	1	1	0	0	5.0	26	8	6	6	3	0	1	0	3	0	4	0	0	0	0	-	0	0-0	0	13.11	10.80
2002	TEX	AL	17	13	0	2	84.2	405	91	51	50	6	4	3	5	58	2	59	7	0	4	5	.444	0	1-1	0	5.52	5.31
2003	TEX	AL	25	17	0	1	105.0	462	99	67	64	23	1	4	3	51	0	87	3	1	8	5	.615	0	0-0	0	5.03	5.49
2004	TEX	AL	28	15	0	2	103.0	456	113	67	65	19	2	10	8	31	0	95	3	0	3	5	.375	0	0-0	0	5.10	5.68
2005	TEX	AL	32	9	0	6	87.0	369	69	39	36	9	2	1	2	38	0	78	1	0	4	4	.500	0	0-0	5	3.15	3.72
	5 ML YEARS		103	55	0	11	384.2	1718	380	230	221	60	9	19	18	181	2	323	14	1	19	19	.500	0	1-1	5	4.81	5.17

Kris Benson

Pitches: R **Bats:** R **Pos:** SP-28   **Ht:** 6'4" **Wt:** 200 **Born:** 11/7/1974 **Age:** 31

			HOW MUCH HE PITCHED						WHAT HE GAVE UP										THE RESULTS							
Year	Team	Lg	G	GS	CG	GF	IP	BFP	H	R	ER	HR	SH	SF	HB	TBB	IBB	SO	WP	Bk	W	L	Pct	ShO	Sv-Op Hld	ERC	ERA
2005	StLuci*	A+	1	1	0	0	3.0	9	0	0	0	0	0	0	1	0	0	4	0	0	0	0	-	0	0-- -	0.14	0.00
1999	PIT	NL	31	31	2	0	196.2	840	184	105	89	16	6	7	6	83	5	139	2	1	11	14	.440	1	0-0 0	3.78	4.07
2000	PIT	NL	32	32	2	0	217.2	936	206	104	93	24	7	6	10	86	5	184	5	0	10	12	.455	1	0-0 0	3.97	3.85
2002	PIT	NL	25	25	0	0	130.1	576	152	76	68	18	5	3	3	50	8	79	3	1	9	6	.600	0	0-0 0	5.31	4.70
2003	PIT	NL	18	18	0	0	105.0	475	127	67	58	14	3	4	1	36	4	68	7	0	5	9	.357	0	0-0 0	5.20	4.97
2004	2 Tms		31	31	1	0	200.1	854	202	106	96	15	8	6	10	61	8	134	5	0	12	12	.500	1	0-0 0	3.71	4.31
2005	NYN	NL	28	28	0	0	174.1	737	171	86	80	24	5	3	4	49	5	95	4	0	10	8	.556	0	0-0 0	3.78	4.13
04	Pit	NL	20	20	0	0	132.1	564	137	69	62	7	7	4	6	44	5	83	2	0	8	8	.500	0	0-0 0	3.84	4.22
04	NYM	NL	11	11	1	0	68.0	290	65	37	34	8	1	2	4	17	3	51	3	0	4	4	.500	1	0-0 0	3.45	4.50
	6 ML YEARS		165	165	5	0	1024.1	4418	1042	544	484	111	34	29	34	365	35	699	26	2	57	61	.483	2	0-0 0	4.14	4.25

Chad Bentz

Pitches: L **Bats:** R **Pos:** RP-4   **Ht:** 6'2" **Wt:** 215 **Born:** 5/5/1980 **Age:** 26

			HOW MUCH HE PITCHED						WHAT HE GAVE UP										THE RESULTS							
Year	Team	Lg	G	GS	CG	GF	IP	BFP	H	R	ER	HR	SH	SF	HB	TBB	IBB	SO	WP	Bk	W	L	Pct	ShO	Sv-Op Hld	ERC	ERA
2001	Vrmnt	A-	8	8	0	0	36.2	163	39	23	20	2	2	2	0	11	0	38	4	0	1	3	.250	0	0-- -	3.55	4.91
2002	BrvdCt	A+	23	0	0	16	29.2	136	30	14	12	1	3	1	2	14	2	34	2	0	1	0	1.000	0	5-- -	3.93	3.64
2003	Hrsbrg	AA	52	0	0	28	84.2	350	72	31	24	4	8	4	0	39	2	56	7	0	1	4	.200	0	16-- -	3.18	2.55
2004	Hrsbrg	AA	5	1	0	2	7.1	32	5	7	7	2	0	0	1	8	0	2	0	0	0	1	.000	0	1-- -	7.77	8.59
2004	Edmtn	AAA	5	0	0	0	5.0	23	5	2	2	1	0	0	0	3	0	2	0	0	0	0	-	0	0-- -	5.52	3.60
2005	Carlna	AA	7	0	0	2	7.0	31	6	3	1	0	0	0	0	4	0	5	0	0	1	0	1.000	0	0-- -	3.15	1.29
2005	Albq	AAA	31	0	0	8	33.2	151	36	20	15	4	2	0	1	14	0	32	2	0	0	1	.000	0	1-- -	4.71	4.01
2004	MON	NL	36	0	0	5	27.2	126	23	19	18	5	0	0	2	23	3	18	1	0	0	3	.000	0	0-0 5	5.66	5.86
2005	FLA	NL	4	0	0	0	2.0	14	8	7	7	2	0	0	0	0	0	0	0	0	0	0	-	0	0-0 2	34.98	31.50
	2 ML YEARS		40	0	0	5	29.2	140	31	26	25	7	0	0	2	23	3	18	1	0	0	3	.000	0	0-0 7	7.21	7.58

Jason Bergmann

Pitches: R **Bats:** R **Pos:** RP-14; SP-1   **Ht:** 6'4" **Wt:** 190 **Born:** 9/25/1981 **Age:** 24

			HOW MUCH HE PITCHED						WHAT HE GAVE UP										THE RESULTS							
Year	Team	Lg	G	GS	CG	GF	IP	BFP	H	R	ER	HR	SH	SF	HB	TBB	IBB	SO	WP	Bk	W	L	Pct	ShO	Sv-Op Hld	ERC	ERA
2003	Savann	A	23	22	1	0	109.0	488	108	57	52	8	1	2	11	53	0	82	10	0	6	11	.353	1	0-- -	4.56	4.29
2004	BrvdCt	A+	24	0	0	21	31.2	133	20	7	4	0	1	0	2	18	3	28	2	0	3	2	.600	0	8-- -	2.16	1.14
2004	Savann	A	13	13	0	0	65.0	296	67	43	35	6	3	7	7	34	0	58	6	1	3	7	.300	0	0-- -	5.12	4.85
2004	Hrsbrg	AA	2	0	0	1	4.0	21	7	5	4	3	0	0	0	2	1	3	1	0	0	2	.000	0	0-- -	14.59	9.00
2005	Hrsbrg	AA	21	0	0	8	37.0	154	27	7	5	3	0	0	2	16	1	37	2	0	2	0	1.000	0	5-- -	2.78	1.22
2005	NewOr	AAA	20	0	0	9	37.0	150	26	15	13	5	3	3	3	13	1	39	1	0	3	2	.600	0	2-- -	2.82	3.16
2005	WAS	NL	15	1	0	4	19.2	85	14	6	6	1	1	1	2	11	1	21	0	0	2	0	1.000	0	0-0 1	3.05	2.75

William Bergolla

Bats: R **Throws:** R **Pos:** 2B-9; PH-7; PR-2; SS-1   **Ht:** 6'0" **Wt:** 175 **Born:** 2/4/1983 **Age:** 23

			BATTING																		BASERUNNING				AVERAGES		
Year	Team	Lg	G	AB	H	2B	3B	HR	(Hm	Rd)	TB	R	RBI	RC	TBB	IBB	SO	HBP	SH	SF	SB	CS	SB%	GDP	Avg	OBP	Slg
2000	Reds	R	23	22	4	0	0	0	(-	-)	4	2	0	1	4	0	2	0	0	0	3	1	.75	0	.182	.308	.182
2001	Billings	R+	57	232	75	5	3	4	(-	-)	98	47	24	41	24	0	21	2	1	3	22	7	.76	1	.323	.387	.422
2002	Billings	R+	53	210	74	9	1	3	(-	-)	94	35	29	41	24	1	26	0	2	6	16	5	.76	2	.352	.408	.448
2002	Dayton	A	68	274	68	13	1	3	(-	-)	92	38	23	29	16	0	36	1	5	1	13	2	.87	6	.248	.291	.336
2003	Ptomc	A+	128	523	142	25	3	2	(-	-)	179	77	31	61	29	1	59	1	15	4	52	18	.74	13	.272	.309	.342
2004	Chatt	AA	116	466	132	26	1	4	(-	-)	172	79	38	67	40	1	63	3	15	2	36	6	.86	14	.283	.342	.369
2005	Lsvlle	AAA	98	400	117	23	5	2	(-	-)	156	59	38	54	19	0	39	1	6	2	16	3	.84	12	.293	.325	.390
2005	CIN	NL	17	38	5	0	0	0	(0	0)	5	3	1	0	0	0	10	0	0	0	0	0	-	1	.132	.132	.132

Lance Berkman

Bats: B **Throws:** L **Pos:** 1B-96; LF-39; RF-11; DH-3   **Ht:** 6'1" **Wt:** 220 **Born:** 2/10/1976 **Age:** 30

			BATTING																		BASERUNNING				AVERAGES		
Year	Team	Lg	G	AB	H	2B	3B	HR	(Hm	Rd)	TB	R	RBI	RC	TBB	IBB	SO	HBP	SH	SF	SB	CS	SB%	GDP	Avg	OBP	Slg
2005	RdRck*	AAA	4	14	4	1	0	0	(-	-)	5	2	1	2	3	1	4	0	0	0	0	0	-	0	.286	.412	.357
1999	HOU	NL	34	93	22	2	0	4	(2	2)	36	10	15	12	12	0	21	0	0	1	5	1	.83	2	.237	.321	.387
2000	HOU	NL	114	353	105	28	1	21	(10	11)	198	76	67	76	56	1	73	1	0	7	6	2	.75	6	.297	.388	.561
2001	HOU	NL	156	577	191	55	5	34	(13	21)	358	110	126	144	92	5	121	13	0	6	7	9	.44	8	.331	.430	.620
2002	HOU	NL	158	578	169	35	2	42	(20	22)	334	106	128	130	107	20	118	4	0	3	8	4	.67	10	.292	.405	.578
2003	HOU	NL	153	538	155	35	6	25	(11	14)	277	110	93	115	107	13	108	9	1	3	5	3	.63	10	.288	.412	.515
2004	HOU	NL	160	544	172	40	3	30	(8	22)	308	104	106	101	127	14	101	10	0	6	9	7	.56	11	.316	.450	.566
2005	HOU	NL	132	468	137	34	1	24	(13	11)	245	76	82	88	91	12	72	4	0	2	4	1	.80	18	.293	.411	.524
	7 ML YEARS		907	3151	951	229	18	180	(77	103)	1756	592	617	691	592	65	614	41	1	28	44	27	.62	65	.302	.416	.557

Adam Bernero

Pitches: R **Bats:** R **Pos:** RP-36   **Ht:** 6'4" **Wt:** 205 **Born:** 11/28/1976 **Age:** 29

			HOW MUCH HE PITCHED						WHAT HE GAVE UP										THE RESULTS							
Year	Team	Lg	G	GS	CG	GF	IP	BFP	H	R	ER	HR	SH	SF	HB	TBB	IBB	SO	WP	Bk	W	L	Pct	ShO	Sv-Op Hld	ERC	ERA
2005	Rchmd*	AAA	10	9	0	1	53.0	231	57	27	20	6	3	1	2	15	0	41	0	0	5	5	.500	0	0-- -	4.22	3.40
2000	DET	AL	12	4	0	4	34.1	141	33	18	16	3	2	3	1	13	1	20	1	0	0	1	.000	0	0-0 1	3.94	4.19
2001	DET	AL	5	0	0	4	12.1	56	13	13	10	4	0	1	4	4	0	8	1	0	0	0	-	0	0-0 0	5.79	7.30

Year	Team	Lg	G	GS	CG	GF	IP	BFP	H	R	ER	HR	SH	SF	HB	TBB	IBB	SO	WP	Bk	W	L	Pct	ShO	Sv-Op	Hld	ERC	ERA
2002	DET	AL	28	11	0	5	101.2	459	128	74	70	17	3	5	6	31	1	69	5	1	4	7	.364	0	0-0	0	5.95	6.20
2003	2 Tms		49	17	0	5	133.1	589	137	90	87	19	5	8	8	54	1	80	3	0	1	14	.067	0	0-2	5	4.77	5.87
2004	COL	NL	16	2	0	4	32.1	147	36	20	20	7	0	3	0	17	2	21	0	1	1		.500	0	0-1	1	6.03	5.57
2005	ATL	NL	36	0	0	12	47.0	216	61	35	34	5	2	3	4	12	3	37	1	0	4	3	.571	0	0-1	4	5.42	6.51
03	Det	AL	18	17	0	0	100.2	447	104	68	68	14	3	6	7	41	0	54	1	0	1	12	.077	0	0-0	0	4.83	6.08
03	Col	NL	31	0	0	5	32.2	142	33	22	19	5	2	2	1	13	1	26	2	0		2	.000	0	0-2	5	4.58	5.23
6 ML YEARS			146	34	0	34	361.0	1608	408	250	237	55	12	23	20	131	8	235	11	1	10	26	.278	0	0-4	11	5.25	5.91

Angel Berroa

Bats: R **Throws:** R **Pos:** SS-159 **Ht:** 6'0" **Wt:** 175 **Born:** 1/27/1978 **Age:** 28

							BATTING													BASERUNNING				AVERAGES		
Year	Team	Lg	G	AB	H	2B	3B	HR	(Hm | Rd)	TB	R	RBI	RC	TBB	IBB	SO	HBP	SH	SF	SB	CS	SB%	GDP	Avg	OBP	Slg
2001	KC	AL	15	53	16	2	0	0	(0 | 0)	18	8	4	6	3	0	10	0	0	0	2	0	1.00	2	.302	.339	.340
2002	KC	AL	20	75	17	7	1	0	(0 | 0)	26	8	5	8	7	1	10	1	0	0	3	0	1.00	1	.227	.301	.347
2003	KC	AL	158	567	163	28	7	17	(6 | 11)	256	92	73	82	29	3	100	18	13	8	21	5	.81	13	.287	.338	.451
2004	KC	AL	134	512	134	27	6	8	(3 | 5)	197	72	43	62	23	0	87	12	5	2	14	8	.64	10	.262	.308	.385
2005	KC	AL	159	608	164	21	5	11	(6 | 5)	228	68	55	68	18	3	108	14	10	2	7	5	.58	13	.270	.305	.375
5 ML YEARS			486	1815	494	85	19	36	(15 | 21)	725	248	180	226	80	7	315	45	28	12	47	18	.72	39	.272	.317	.399

Rafael Betancourt

Pitches: R **Bats:** R **Pos:** RP-54 **Ht:** 6'2" **Wt:** 176 **Born:** 4/29/1975 **Age:** 31

			HOW MUCH HE PITCHED						WHAT HE GAVE UP											THE RESULTS							
Year	Team	Lg	G	GS	CG	GF	IP	BFP	H	R	ER	HR	SH	SF	HB	TBB	IBB	SO	WP	Bk	W	L	Pct	ShO	Sv-Op	Hld	ERC	ERA
2003	CLE	AL	33	0	0	13	38.0	154	27	11	9	5	1	1	1	13	2	36	1	0	2	2	.500	0	1-3	4	2.54	2.13
2004	CLE	AL	68	0	0	21	66.2	286	71	32	29	7	1	2	0	18	6	76	5	1	5	6	.455	0	4-11	12	3.77	3.92
2005	CLE	AL	54	0	0	12	67.2	272	57	23	21	5	1	0	0	17	2	73	0	0	4	3	.571	0	1-3	10	2.49	2.79
3 ML YEARS			155	0	0	46	172.1	712	155	66	59	17	3	3	1	48	10	185	6	1	11	11	.500	0	6-17	26	2.98	3.08

Yuniesky Betancourt

Bats: R **Throws:** R **Pos:** SS-53; 2B-9; PR-1 **Ht:** 5'10" **Wt:** 190 **Born:** 1/31/1982 **Age:** 24

							BATTING													BASERUNNING				AVERAGES		
Year	Team	Lg	G	AB	H	2B	3B	HR	(Hm | Rd)	TB	R	RBI	RC	TBB	IBB	SO	HBP	SH	SF	SB	CS	SB%	GDP	Avg	OBP	Slg
2005	SnAnt	AA	52	227	62	10	3	5	(- | -)	93	23	20	28	9	1	18	1	0	2	12	7	.63	2	.273	.301	.410
2005	Tacom	AAA	49	183	54	9	6	2	(- | -)	81	13	30	26	6	0	14	2	2	1	7	5	.58	3	.295	.323	.443
2005	SEA	AL	60	211	54	11	5	1	(1 | 0)	78	24	15	21	11	0	24	2	2	2	1	3	.25	2	.256	.296	.370

Wilson Betemit

Bats: B **Throws:** R **Pos:** 3B-63; PH-26; SS-25; PR-11; 2B-1 **Ht:** 6'3" **Wt:** 190 **Born:** 7/28/1980 **Age:** 25

							BATTING													BASERUNNING				AVERAGES		
Year	Team	Lg	G	AB	H	2B	3B	HR	(Hm | Rd)	TB	R	RBI	RC	TBB	IBB	SO	HBP	SH	SF	SB	CS	SB%	GDP	Avg	OBP	Slg
2001	ATL	NL	8	3	0	0	0	0	(0 | 0)	0	1	0	0	2	0	3	0	0	0	1	0	1.00	0	.000	.400	.000
2004	ATL	NL	22	47	8	0	0	0	(0 | 0)	8	2	3	0	4	0	16	0	0	1	0	1	.00	0	.170	.231	.170
2005	ATL	NL	115	246	75	12	4	4	(0 | 4)	107	36	20	36	22	4	55	0	4	2	1	3	.25	5	.305	.359	.435
3 ML YEARS			145	296	83	12	4	4	(0 | 4)	115	39	23	36	28	4	74	0	4	3	2	4	.33	5	.280	.339	.389

Larry Bigbie

Bats: L **Throws:** R **Pos:** LF-57; CF-17; PH-12; RF-5; PR-2 **Ht:** 6'4" **Wt:** 190 **Born:** 11/4/1977 **Age:** 28

							BATTING													BASERUNNING				AVERAGES		
Year	Team	Lg	G	AB	H	2B	3B	HR	(Hm | Rd)	TB	R	RBI	RC	TBB	IBB	SO	HBP	SH	SF	SB	CS	SB%	GDP	Avg	OBP	Slg
2005	Ottawa*	AAA	4	17	5	2	0	1	(- | -)	10	3	2	2	0	0	6	0	0	0	0	0	-	1	.294	.294	.588
2005	ColSpr*	AAA	3	8	3	2	1	0	(- | -)	7	4	2	3	2	0	3	0	0	0	0	0	-	0	.375	.500	.875
2001	BAL	AL	47	131	30	6	0	2	(0 | 2)	42	15	11	14	17	1	42	0	1	0	4	1	.80	2	.229	.318	.321
2002	BAL	AL	16	34	6	1	0	0	(0 | 0)	7	1	3	1	1	0	11	0	0	1	1	0	1.00	1	.176	.194	.206
2003	BAL	AL	83	287	87	15	1	9	(4 | 5)	131	43	31	47	29	3	60	0	1	2	7	1	.88	2	.303	.365	.456
2004	BAL	AL	139	478	134	23	1	15	(8 | 7)	204	76	68	65	45	0	113	1	3	4	8	3	.73	7	.280	.341	.427
2005	2 Tms		90	272	65	10	2	5	(3 | 2)	94	27	23	28	24	1	67	1	5	2	5	3	.63	2	.239	.301	.346
05	Bal	AL	67	206	51	9	1	5	(3 | 2)	77	22	21	23	21	1	49	0	5	2	3	3	.50	2	.248	.314	.374
05	Col	NL	23	66	14	1	1	0	(0 | 0)	17	5	2	5	3	0	18	1	0	0	2	0	1.00	0	.212	.257	.258
5 ML YEARS			375	1202	322	55	4	31	(15 | 16)	478	162	136	155	116	5	293	2	10	9	25	8	.76	14	.268	.331	.398

Craig Biggio

Bats: R **Throws:** R **Pos:** 2B-141; PH-9; DH-5 **Ht:** 5'11" **Wt:** 185 **Born:** 12/14/1965 **Age:** 40

							BATTING													BASERUNNING				AVERAGES		
Year	Team	Lg	G	AB	H	2B	3B	HR	(Hm | Rd)	TB	R	RBI	RC	TBB	IBB	SO	HBP	SH	SF	SB	CS	SB%	GDP	Avg	OBP	Slg
1988	HOU	NL	50	123	26	6	1	3	(1 | 2)	43	14	5	11	7	2	29	0	1	0	6	1	.86	1	.211	.254	.350
1989	HOU	NL	134	443	114	21	2	13	(6 | 7)	178	64	60	64	49	8	64	6	6	5	21	3	.88	7	.257	.336	.402
1990	HOU	NL	150	555	153	24	2	4	(2 | 2)	193	53	42	68	53	1	79	3	9	1	25	11	.69	11	.276	.342	.348
1991	HOU	NL	149	546	161	23	4	4	(0 | 4)	204	79	46	79	53	3	71	2	5	3	19	6	.76	2	.295	.358	.374
1992	HOU	NL	162	613	170	32	3	6	(3 | 3)	226	96	39	95	94	9	95	7	5	2	38	15	.72	5	.277	.378	.369
1993	HOU	NL	155	610	175	41	5	21	(8 | 13)	289	98	64	105	77	7	93	10	4	5	15	17	.47	10	.287	.373	.474
1994	HOU	NL	114	437	139	44	5	6	(4 | 2)	211	88	56	94	62	1	58	8	2	2	39	4	.91	5	.318	.411	.483
1995	HOU	NL	141	553	167	30	2	22	(6 | 16)	267	123	77	116	80	1	85	22	11	7	33	8	.80	6	.302	.406	.483
1996	HOU	NL	162	605	174	24	4	15	(7 | 8)	251	113	75	105	75	0	72	27	8	8	25	7	.78	10	.288	.386	.415

Year	Team	Lg	G	AB	H	2B	3B	HR	(Hm	Rd)	TB	R	RBI	RC	TBB	IBB	SO	HBP	SH	SF	SB	CS	SB%	GDP	Avg	OBP	Slg
									BATTING												BASERUNNING				AVERAGES		
1997	HOU	NL	162	619	191	37	8	22	(7	15)	310	146	81	139	84	6	107	34	0	7	47	10	.82	0	.309	.415	.501
1998	HOU	NL	160	646	210	51	2	20	(10	10)	325	123	88	135	64	6	113	23	1	4	50	8	.86	10	.325	.403	.503
1999	HOU	NL	160	639	188	56	0	16	(10	6)	292	123	73	117	88	9	107	11	5	6	28	14	.67	5	.294	.386	.457
2000	HOU	NL	101	377	101	13	5	8	(2	6)	148	67	35	63	61	3	73	16	7	5	12	2	.86	10	.268	.388	.393
2001	HOU	NL	155	617	180	35	3	20	(10	10)	281	118	70	109	66	4	100	28	0	6	7	4	.64	11	.292	.382	.455
2002	HOU	NL	145	577	146	36	3	15	(7	8)	233	96	58	71	50	2	111	17	9	2	16	2	.89	15	.253	.330	.404
2003	HOU	NL	153	628	166	44	2	15	(6	9)	259	102	62	97	57	3	116	27	3	2	8	4	.67	4	.264	.350	.412
2004	HOU	NL	156	633	178	47	0	24	(13	11)	297	100	63	88	40	0	94	15	9	3	7	2	.78	8	.281	.337	.469
2005	HOU	NL	155	590	156	40	1	26	(19	7)	276	94	69	80	37	2	90	17	4	3	11	1	.92	10	.264	.325	.468
18 ML YEARS			2564	9811	2795	604	52	260	(121	139)	4283	1697	1063	1636	1097	67	1557	273	89	71	407	119	.77	130	.285	.370	.437

Travis Blackley

Pitches: L Bats: L Pos: P **Ht: 6'3" Wt: 190 Born: 11/4/1982 Age: 23**

Year	Team	Lg	G	GS	CG	GF	IP	BFP	H	R	ER	HR	SH	SF	HB	TBB	IBB	SO	WP	Bk	W	L	Pct	ShO	Sv-Op	Hld	ERC	ERA
					HOW MUCH HE PITCHED						WHAT HE GAVE UP												THE RESULTS				
2001	Everett	A-	14	14	0	0	78.2	319	60	34	29	7	2	2	1	29	0	90	3	0	6	1	.857	0	0--	-	2.70	3.32
2002	SnBrn	A+	21	20	1	1	121.1	505	102	52	47	11	4	0	7	44	0	152	11	2	5	9	.357	0	0--	-	3.25	3.49
2003	SnAnt	AA	27	27	0	0	162.1	658	125	55	47	11	5	4	6	62	0	144	9	2	17	3	.850	1	0--	-	2.77	2.61
2004	Tacom	AAA	19	18	2	0	110.1	455	100	49	47	14	6	1	3	47	0	80	9	3	8	6	.571	2	0--	-	4.12	3.83
2004	SEA	AL	6	6	0	0	26.0	134	35	31	29	9	1	1	1	22	0	16	3	1	1	3	.250	0	0-0	0	10.52	10.04

Casey Blake

Bats: R Throws: R Pos: RF-138; 3B-6; 1B-4; PH-4 **Ht: 6'2" Wt: 205 Born: 8/23/1973 Age: 32**

Year	Team	Lg	G	AB	H	2B	3B	HR	(Hm	Rd)	TB	R	RBI	RC	TBB	IBB	SO	HBP	SH	SF	SB	CS	SB%	GDP	Avg	OBP	Slg
									BATTING												BASERUNNING				AVERAGES		
1999	TOR	AL	14	39	10	2	0	1	(0	1)	15	6	1	4	2	0	7	0	0	0	0	0	-	1	.256	.293	.385
2000	MIN	AL	7	16	3	2	0	0	(0	0)	5	1	1	2	3	0	7	1	0	1	0	0	-	1	.188	.333	.313
2001	2 Tms	AL	19	37	9	1	0	1	(0	1)	13	3	4	5	4	1	12	0	0	0	3	0	1.00	0	.243	.317	.351
2002	MIN	AL	9	20	4	1	0	0	(0	0)	5	2	1	1	2	0	7	0	0	0	0	0	-	0	.200	.273	.250
2003	CLE	AL	152	557	143	35	0	17	(2	15)	229	80	67	68	38	1	109	10	8	8	7	9	.44	11	.257	.312	.411
2004	CLE	AL	152	587	159	36	3	28	(13	15)	285	93	88	88	68	2	139	9	1	3	5	8	.38	19	.271	.354	.486
2005	CLE	AL	147	523	126	32	1	23	(7	16)	229	72	58	53	43	3	116	10	2	5	4	5	.44	9	.241	.308	.438
01	Min	AL	13	22	7	1	0	0	(0	0)	8	1	2	4	3	1	8	0	0	0	1	0	1.00	0	.318	.400	.364
01	Bal	AL	6	15	2	0	0	1	(0	1)	5	2	2	1	1	0	4	0	0	0	2	0	1.00	0	.133	.188	.333
7 ML YEARS			500	1779	454	109	4	70	(22	48)	781	257	220	221	160	7	397	30	11	17	19	22	.46	41	.255	.324	.439

Hank Blalock

Bats: L Throws: R Pos: 3B-158; PH-3; DH-2 **Ht: 6'1" Wt: 195 Born: 11/21/1980 Age: 25**

Year	Team	Lg	G	AB	H	2B	3B	HR	(Hm	Rd)	TB	R	RBI	RC	TBB	IBB	SO	HBP	SH	SF	SB	CS	SB%	GDP	Avg	OBP	Slg
									BATTING												BASERUNNING				AVERAGES		
2002	TEX	AL	49	147	31	8	0	3	(2	1)	48	16	17	15	20	1	43	1	2	2	0	0	-	2	.211	.306	.327
2003	TEX	AL	143	567	170	38	4	29	(18	11)	296	89	90	90	44	1	97	1	0	3	2	3	.40	17	.300	.350	.522
2004	TEX	AL	159	624	172	38	3	32	(16	16)	312	107	110	119	75	7	149	6	0	8	2	2	.50	13	.276	.355	.500
2005	TEX	AL	161	647	170	34	0	25	(20	5)	279	80	92	86	51	1	132	3	0	4	1	0	1.00	16	.263	.318	.431
4 ML YEARS			512	1985	543	113	6	89	(56	33)	935	292	309	310	190	10	421	11	2	17	5	5	.50	48	.274	.338	.471

Andres Blanco

Bats: B Throws: R Pos: 2B-24; SS-7; PR-1 **Ht: 5'10" Wt: 150 Born: 4/11/1984 Age: 22**

Year	Team	Lg	G	AB	H	2B	3B	HR	(Hm	Rd)	TB	R	RBI	RC	TBB	IBB	SO	HBP	SH	SF	SB	CS	SB%	GDP	Avg	OBP	Slg
									BATTING												BASERUNNING				AVERAGES		
2002	Royals	R	52	193	48	8	0	0	(-	-)	56	27	14	20	15	0	29	4	6	1	16	4	.80	2	.249	.315	.290
2002	Wilmg	A+	5	13	4	1	0	0	(-	-)	5	2	0	1	1	0	4	0	2	0	0	0	-	0	.308	.357	.385
2003	Wilmg	A+	113	394	96	11	3	0	(-	-)	113	61	25	41	44	1	50	8	21	2	13	7	.65	9	.244	.330	.287
2004	Wichta	AA	93	324	80	10	2	0	(-	-)	94	34	21	25	18	2	44	7	8	2	7	6	.54	14	.247	.299	.290
2005	Royals	R	7	25	8	1	0	2	(-	-)	15	6	9	4	1	0	7	1	1	0	1	2	.33	0	.320	.370	.600
2005	Hi Dsrt	A+	3	10	5	1	0	0	(-	-)	6	0	3	1	0	0	1	0	0	0	1	2	.33	0	.500	.500	.600
2005	Wichta	AA	9	37	7	0	0	1	(-	-)	10	5	5	2	3	0	7	0	1	0	0	0	-	0	.189	.250	.270
2005	Omha	AAA	35	114	29	4	2	1	(-	-)	40	13	9	14	3	2	0	2	0	0	2	0	1.00	3	.254	.331	.351
2004	KC	AL	19	60	19	2	2	0	(0	0)	25	9	5	12	5	0	6	1	1	0	1	2	.33	0	.317	.379	.417
2005	KC	AL	26	79	17	0	1	0	(0	0)	19	6	5	3	0	0	5	1	4	2	0	1	.00	3	.215	.220	.241
2 ML YEARS			45	139	36	2	3	0	(0	0)	44	15	10	15	5	0	11	2	5	2	1	3	.25	3	.259	.291	.317

Henry Blanco

Bats: R Throws: R Pos: C-54; PR-1 **Ht: 5'11" Wt: 220 Born: 8/29/1971 Age: 34**

Year	Team	Lg	G	AB	H	2B	3B	HR	(Hm	Rd)	TB	R	RBI	RC	TBB	IBB	SO	HBP	SH	SF	SB	CS	SB%	GDP	Avg	OBP	Slg
									BATTING												BASERUNNING				AVERAGES		
1997	LA	NL	3	5	2	0	0	1	(0	1)	5	1	1	2	0	0	1	0	0	0	0	0	-	0	.400	.400	1.000
1999	COL	NL	88	263	61	12	3	6	(3	3)	97	30	28	32	34	1	38	1	3	2	1	1	.50	4	.232	.320	.369
2000	MIL	NL	93	284	67	24	0	7	(3	4)	112	29	31	33	36	6	60	0	0	4	0	3	.00	9	.236	.318	.394
2001	MIL	NL	104	314	66	18	3	6	(4	2)	108	33	31	30	34	6	72	2	5	2	3	1	.75	10	.210	.290	.344
2002	ATL	NL	81	221	45	9	1	6	(4	2)	74	17	22	15	20	5	51	1	2	5	0	2	.00	5	.204	.267	.335
2003	ATL	NL	55	151	30	8	0	1	(0	1)	41	11	13	13	10	2	21	1	3	1	0	0	-	3	.199	.252	.272
2004	MIN	AL	114	315	65	19	1	10	(4	6)	116	36	37	25	21	0	56	3	11	3	0	3	.00	8	.206	.260	.368
2005	CHN	NL	54	161	39	6	0	6	(2	4)	63	16	25	17	11	1	24	0	4	2	0	0	-	6	.242	.287	.391
8 ML YEARS			592	1714	375	96	8	43	(20	23)	616	173	188	167	166	21	323	8	28	19	4	10	.29	45	.219	.288	.359

Tony Blanco

Bats: R Throws: R Pos: PH-29; PR-12; LF-9; 3B-5; 1B-3; RF-2; DH-1   **Ht: 6'1" Wt: 175 Born: 11/10/1981 Age: 24**

					BATTING																**BASERUNNING**				**AVERAGES**			
Year	Team	Lg	G	AB	H	2B	3B	HR	(Hm	Rd)	TB	R	RBI	RC	TBB	IBB	SO	HBP	SH	SF	SB	CS	SB%	GDP	Avg	OBP	Slg
2000	RedSx	R	52	190	73	13	1	13	(-	-)	127	32	50	51	18	2	38	4	0	3	6	4	.60	3	.384	.442	.668
2000	Lowell	A-	9	28	4	1	0	0	(-	-)	5	1	0	0	2	0	12	1	0	0	1	0	1.00	6	.143	.226	.179
2001	Augsta	A	96	370	98	23	2	17	(-	-)	176	44	69	55	17	2	78	7	0	2	1	0	1.00	17	.265	.308	.476
2002	Srsota	A+	65	244	54	13	2	6	(-	-)	89	22	32	22	6	0	70	4	0	2	2	0	1.00	5	.221	.250	.365
2003	Ptomc	A+	69	241	64	17	2	10	(-	-)	115	33	49	41	26	2	62	4	0	7	0	0	-	5	.266	.338	.477
2004	Ptomc	A+	62	216	66	10	0	17	(-	-)	127	42	47	51	27	3	66	11	0	4	2	0	1.00	3	.306	.403	.588
2004	Chatt	AA	58	220	54	8	1	12	(-	-)	100	25	31	30	15	2	53	2	0	0	0	0	-	8	.245	.300	.455
2005	NewOr	AAA	16	64	18	4	0	2	(-	-)	28	7	14	8	2	0	13	0	0	2	1	0	1.00	0	.281	.294	.438
2005	WAS	NL	56	62	11	3	0	1	(0	1)	17	7	7	7	2	0	19	1	0	0	1	0	1.00	0	.177	.215	.274

Joe Blanton

Pitches: R Bats: R Pos: SP-33   **Ht: 6'3" Wt: 225 Born: 12/11/1980 Age: 25**

			HOW MUCH HE PITCHED						**WHAT HE GAVE UP**												**THE RESULTS**					
Year	Team	Lg	G	GS	CG	GF	IP	BFP	H	R	ER	HR	SH	SF	HB	TBB	IBB	SO	WP	Bk	W	L	Pct	ShO	Sv-Op	Hld	ERC	ERA
2002	Vancvr	A-	4	2	0	0	14.1	53	11	5	5	0	0	0	0	2	0	15	0	0	1	1	.500	0	0--	-	1.55	3.14
2002	Mdest	A	2	1	0	0	6.0	33	8	6	5	1	0	0	0	6	0	6	0	1	1	0	1.000	0	0--	-	8.82	7.50
2003	Kane	A	21	21	2	0	133.0	531	110	47	38	6	2	3	5	19	0	144	1	0	8	7	.533	2	0--	-	2.02	2.57
2003	Mdland	AA	7	5	1	2	35.2	129	21	6	5	1	1	0	0	7	0	30	0	0	3	1	.750	0	1--	-	1.22	1.26
2004	Scrmto	AAA	28	26	1	0	176.1	756	199	101	82	13	5	14	6	34	2	143	6	0	11	8	.579	0	0--	-	3.88	4.19
2004	OAK	AL	3	0	0	1	8.0	30	6	5	5	1	0	0	0	2	0	6	0	0	0	0	-	0	0-0	0	2.52	5.63
2005	OAK	AL	33	33	2	0	201.1	835	178	86	79	23	2	7	5	67	3	116	4	2	12	12	.500	0	0-0	0	3.37	3.53
	2 ML YEARS		36	33	2	1	209.1	865	184	91	84	24	2	7	5	69	3	122	4	2	12	12	.500	0	0-0	0	3.34	3.61

Willie Bloomquist

Bats: R Throws: R Pos: 2B-32; SS-24; CF-15; 3B-6; PR-5; PH-4; 1B-1; LF-1; DH-1   **Ht: 5'11" Wt: 180 Born: 11/27/1977 Age: 28**

						BATTING															**BASERUNNING**				**AVERAGES**		
Year	Team	Lg	G	AB	H	2B	3B	HR	(Hm	Rd)	TB	R	RBI	RC	TBB	IBB	SO	HBP	SH	SF	SB	CS	SB%	GDP	Avg	OBP	Slg
2002	SEA	AL	12	33	15	4	0	0	(0	0)	19	11	7	10	5	0	2	0	0	0	3	1	.75	0	.455	.526	.576
2003	SEA	AL	89	196	49	7	2	1	(1	0)	63	30	14	18	19	1	39	1	2	2	4	1	.80	6	.250	.317	.321
2004	SEA	AL	93	188	46	10	0	2	(0	2)	62	27	18	18	10	0	48	0	3	0	13	2	.87	2	.245	.283	.330
2005	SEA	AL	82	249	64	15	2	0	(0	0)	83	27	22	26	11	0	38	1	4	2	14	1	.93	5	.257	.289	.333
	4 ML YEARS		276	666	174	36	4	3	(1	2)	227	95	61	72	45	1	127	2	9	4	34	5	.87	13	.261	.308	.341

Geoff Blum

Bats: B Throws: R Pos: 3B-46; 2B-21; SS-20; PH-20; 1B-14; PR-1   **Ht: 6'3" Wt: 200 Born: 4/26/1973 Age: 33**

						BATTING															**BASERUNNING**				**AVERAGES**		
Year	Team	Lg	G	AB	H	2B	3B	HR	(Hm	Rd)	TB	R	RBI	RC	TBB	IBB	SO	HBP	SH	SF	SB	CS	SB%	GDP	Avg	OBP	Slg
2005	Lk Els*	A+	2	8	2	0	0	0	(-	-)	8	3	5	2	1	0	2	0	0	0	0	0	-	0	.250	.333	1.000
1999	MON	NL	45	133	32	7	2	8	(0	8)	67	21	18	22	17	3	25	0	3	0	1	0	1.00	3	.241	.327	.504
2000	MON	NL	124	343	97	20	2	11	(5	6)	154	40	45	50	26	2	60	3	3	4	1	4	.20	4	.283	.335	.449
2001	MON	NL	148	453	107	25	0	9	(6	3)	159	57	50	49	43	8	94	10	3	5	9	5	.64	12	.236	.313	.351
2002	HOU	NL	130	368	104	20	4	10	(6	4)	162	45	52	62	49	5	70	1	1	2	2	0	1.00	8	.283	.367	.440
2003	HOU	NL	123	420	110	19	0	10	(6	4)	159	51	52	40	20	1	50	2	2	5	0	0	-	15	.262	.295	.379
2004	TB		112	339	73	21	0	8	(2	6)	118	38	35	29	24	1	58	0	4	2	2	3	.40	4	.215	.266	.348
2005	2 Tms		109	319	73	15	2	6	(1	5)	110	32	25	27	28	0	43	3	0	1	3	3	.50	6	.229	.296	.345
05	SD	NL	78	224	54	13	1	5	(1	4)	84	26	22	23	24	0	28	3	0	1	2	2	.60	5	.241	.321	.375
05	CWS	AL	31	95	19	2	1	1	(0	1)	26	6	3	4	4	0	15	0	0	0	1	1	.50	1	.200	.232	.274
	7 ML YEARS		791	2375	596	127	10	62	(26	36)	929	284	277	279	207	20	400	19	16	19	18	15	.55	52	.251	.314	.391

Hiram Bocachica

Bats: R Throws: R Pos: RF-5; 3B-2; PH-2; PR-2; CF-1   **Ht: 5'11" Wt: 165 Born: 3/4/1976 Age: 30**

						BATTING															**BASERUNNING**				**AVERAGES**		
Year	Team	Lg	G	AB	H	2B	3B	HR	(Hm	Rd)	TB	R	RBI	RC	TBB	IBB	SO	HBP	SH	SF	SB	CS	SB%	GDP	Avg	OBP	Slg
2005	As*	R	4	12	1	1	0	0	(-	-)	2	1	1	0	0	0	3	0	0	0	0	0	-	0	.083	.083	.167
2005	Scrmto*	AAA	4	17	7	2	0	2	(-	-)	15	2	6	5	1	0	4	0	0	0	0	0	-	0	.412	.444	.882
2000	LA	NL	8	10	3	0	0	0	(0	0)	3	2	0	1	0	0	2	0	0	0	0	0	-	0	.300	.300	.300
2001	LA	NL	75	133	31	11	1	2	(2	0)	50	15	9	15	9	0	33	1	0	0	4	1	.80	0	.233	.287	.376
2002	2 Tms		83	168	37	7	0	8	(2	6)	68	26	17	13	10	0	41	0	1	0	3	3	.50	3	.220	.264	.405
2003	DET	AL	6	22	1	1	0	0	(0	0)	2	1	0	0	0	0	7	0	0	0	0	0	-	0	.045	.045	.091
2004	SEA	AL	50	90	22	5	0	3	(3	0)	36	9	6	9	12	0	27	1	3	1	5	4	.56	1	.244	.337	.400
2005	OAK	AL	9	19	2	0	0	0	(0	0)	2	2	0	0	0	0	7	0	0	0	0	0	-	0	.105	.105	.105
02	LA	NL	49	65	14	3	0	4	(1	3)	29	12	9	6	5	0	19	0	0	0	1	1	.50	1	.215	.271	.446
02	Det	AL	34	103	23	4	0	4	(1	3)	39	14	8	7	5	0	22	0	1	0	2	2	.50	2	.223	.259	.379
	6 ML YEARS		231	442	96	24	1	13	(7	6)	161	55	32	38	31	0	117	2	4	1	12	8	.60	5	.217	.271	.364

Jeremy Bonderman

Pitches: R Bats: R Pos: SP-29   **Ht: 6'2" Wt: 210 Born: 10/28/1982 Age: 23**

			HOW MUCH HE PITCHED						**WHAT HE GAVE UP**												**THE RESULTS**					
Year	Team	Lg	G	GS	CG	GF	IP	BFP	H	R	ER	HR	SH	SF	HB	TBB	IBB	SO	WP	Bk	W	L	Pct	ShO	Sv-Op	Hld	ERC	ERA
2003	DET	AL	33	28	0	0	162.0	727	193	118	100	23	3	6	4	58	2	108	12	2	6	19	.240	0	0-0	0	5.39	5.56

Year	Team	Lg	G	GS	CG	GF	IP	BFP	H	R	ER	HR	SH	SF	HB	TBB	IBB	SO	WP	Bk	W	L	Pct	ShO	Sv-Op	Hld	ERC	ERA
					HOW MUCH HE PITCHED						WHAT HE GAVE UP											THE RESULTS					
2004	DET	AL	33	32	2	0	184.0	793	168	101	100	24	10	5	10	73	5	168	7	0	11	13	.458	2	0-0	0	3.93	4.89
2005	DET	AL	29	29	4	0	189.0	801	199	101	96	21	3	3	4	57	0	145	5	1	14	13	.519	0	0-0	0	4.20	4.57
	3 ML YEARS		95	89	6	0	535.0	2321	560	320	296	68	16	14	18	188	7	421	24	3	31	45	.408	2	0-0	0	4.45	4.98

Barry Bonds

Bats: L Throws: L Pos: LF-13; PH-1 **Ht: 6'2" Wt: 228 Born: 7/24/1964 Age: 41**

						BATTING																BASERUNNING				AVERAGES		
Year	Team	Lg	G	AB	H	2B	3B	HR	(Hm	Rd)	TB	R	RBI	RC	TBB	IBB	SO	HBP	SH	SF	SB	CS	SB%	GDP	Avg	OBP	Slg
1986	PIT	NL	113	413	92	26	3	16	(9	7)	172	72	48	64	65	2	102	2	2	2	36	7	.84	4	.223	.330	.416
1987	PIT	NL	150	551	144	34	9	25	(12	13)	271	99	59	92	54	3	88	3	0	3	32	10	.76	4	.261	.329	.492
1988	PIT	NL	144	538	152	30	5	24	(14	10)	264	97	58	97	72	14	82	2	0	2	17	11	.61	3	.283	.368	.491
1989	PIT	NL	159	580	144	34	6	19	(7	12)	247	96	58	91	93	22	93	1	1	4	32	10	.76	9	.248	.351	.426
1990	PIT	NL	151	519	156	32	3	33	(14	19)	293	104	114	121	93	15	83	3	0	6	52	13	.80	8	.301	.406	.565
1991	PIT	NL	153	510	149	28	5	25	(12	13)	262	95	116	113	107	25	73	4	0	13	43	13	.77	8	.292	.410	.514
1992	PIT	NL	140	473	147	36	5	34	(15	19)	295	109	103	134	127	32	69	5	0	7	39	8	.83	9	.311	.456	.624
1993	SF	NL	159	539	181	38	4	46	(21	25)	365	129	123	155	126	43	79	2	0	7	29	12	.71	11	.336	.458	.677
1994	SF	NL	112	391	122	18	1	37	(15	22)	253	89	81	105	74	18	43	6	0	3	29	9	.76	3	.312	.426	.647
1995	SF	NL	144	506	149	30	7	33	(16	17)	292	109	104	125	120	22	83	5	0	4	31	10	.76	12	.294	.431	.577
1996	SF	NL	158	517	159	27	3	42	(23	19)	318	122	129	148	151	30	76	1	0	6	40	7	.85	11	.308	.461	.615
1997	SF	NL	159	532	155	26	5	40	(24	16)	311	123	101	140	145	34	87	8	0	5	37	8	.82	13	.291	.446	.585
1998	SF	NL	156	552	167	44	7	37	(21	16)	336	120	122	141	130	29	92	8	1	6	28	12	.70	15	.303	.438	.609
1999	SF	NL	102	355	93	20	2	34	(16	18)	219	91	83	85	73	9	62	3	0	3	15	2	.88	6	.262	.389	.617
2000	SF	NL	143	480	147	28	4	49	(25	24)	330	129	106	139	117	22	77	3	0	7	11	3	.79	6	.306	.440	.688
2001	SF	NL	153	476	156	32	2	73	(37	36)	411	129	137	191	177	35	93	9	0	2	13	3	.81	5	.328	.515	.863
2002	SF	NL	143	403	149	31	2	46	(19	27)	322	117	110	160	198	68	47	9	0	2	9	2	.82	3	.370	.582	.799
2003	SF	NL	130	390	133	22	1	45	(23	22)	292	111	90	129	148	61	58	10	0	2	7	0	1.00	7	.341	.529	.749
2004	SF	NL	147	373	135	27	3	45	(26	19)	303	129	101	171	232	120	41	9	0	3	6	1	.86	5	.362	.609	.812
2005	SF	NL	14	42	12	1	0	5	(2	3)	28	8	10	9	9	3	6	0	0	1	0	0	-	0	.286	.404	.667
	20 ML YEARS		2730	9140	2742	564	77	708	(351	357)	5584	2078	1853	2410	2311	607	1434	93	4	88	506	141	.78	143	.300	.442	.611

Chris Booker

Pitches: R Bats: R Pos: RP-3 **Ht: 6'3" Wt: 230 Born: 12/9/1976 Age: 29**

					HOW MUCH HE PITCHED						WHAT HE GAVE UP											THE RESULTS					
Year	Team	Lg	G	GS	CG	GF	IP	BFP	H	R	ER	HR	SH	SF	HB	TBB	IBB	SO	WP	Bk	W	L	Pct	ShO	Sv-Op	Hld	ERC	ERA
1995	Cubs	R	13	7	0	2	42.1	179	36	22	13	0	0	2	0	16	0	43	4	1	3	2	.600	0	1--	-	2.48	2.76
1996	Dytona	A+	1	1	0	0	2.1	11	1	1	0	0	0	0	0	3	0	2	1	0	0	0	-	0	0--	-	3.36	0.00
1996	Wmspt	A-	14	14	0	0	61.0	291	57	51	36	2	0	6	3	51	1	52	7	2	4	6	.400	0	0--	-	4.97	5.31
1997	Wmspt	A-	24	3	0	11	45.2	201	39	20	17	2	3	4	0	25	0	60	9	0	1	5	.167	0	1--	-	3.36	3.35
1998	Rckford	A	44	1	0	22	64.0	292	47	32	24	2	3	5	4	53	4	78	8	1	1	2	.333	0	4--	-	3.80	3.38
1999	Dytona	A+	42	0	0	29	73.0	328	72	45	32	6	2	3	3	37	1	68	5	0	2	5	.286	0	6--	-	4.36	3.95
2000	Dytona	A+	31	0	0	24	27.2	122	25	12	7	0	2	0	1	14	1	34	2	0	0	2	.000	0	10--	-	3.25	2.28
2000	WTenn	AA	12	0	0	3	14.2	66	10	8	6	1	0	0	0	12	0	21	0	0	1	0	1.000	0	0--	-	3.60	3.68
2001	WTenn	AA	45	0	0	13	52.0	231	39	29	25	7	5	3	1	36	2	76	7	0	2	6	.250	0	1--	-	4.01	4.33
2001	Chatt	AA	16	0	0	4	16.0	72	13	7	7	1	1	0	0	11	0	25	0	0	2	0	1.000	0	1--	-	3.78	3.94
2003	Reds	R	12	0	0	9	11.2	60	17	11	11	1	1	0	0	8	0	11	1	0	0	2	.000	0	2--	-	7.77	8.49
2003	Dayton	A	5	0	0	1	5.0	23	4	5	5	3	1	2	0	4	0	6	0	0	0	0	-	0	0--	-	8.23	9.00
2004	Chatt	AA	28	0	0	12	39.0	168	26	6	6	0	0	0	1	25	4	57	5	0	2	0	1.000	0	5--	-	2.39	1.38
2004	Lsvlle	AAA	7	0	0	2	12.0	56	10	6	6	2	0	0	0	10	0	9	4	0	0	1	.000	0	0--	-	5.24	4.50
2005	Lsvlle	AAA	59	0	0	48	65.0	268	45	20	18	2	0	3	1	28	1	91	3	0	8	4	.667	0	20--	-	2.15	2.49
2005	CIN	NL	3	0	0	1	2.0	15	6	8	7	2	0	0	0	4	0	2	0	0	0	0	-	0	0-0	0	40.92	31.50

Aaron Boone

Bats: R Throws: R Pos: 3B-142; DH-1; PR-1 **Ht: 6'2" Wt: 200 Born: 3/9/1973 Age: 33**

						BATTING																BASERUNNING				AVERAGES		
Year	Team	Lg	G	AB	H	2B	3B	HR	(Hm	Rd)	TB	R	RBI	RC	TBB	IBB	SO	HBP	SH	SF	SB	CS	SB%	GDP	Avg	OBP	Slg
1997	CIN	NL	16	49	12	1	0	0	(0	0)	13	5	5	3	2	0	5	0	1	0	1	0	1.00	1	.245	.264	.265
1998	CIN	NL	58	181	51	13	2	2	(2	0)	74	24	28	27	15	1	36	5	3	2	6	1	.86	3	.282	.350	.409
1999	CIN	NL	139	472	132	26	5	14	(7	7)	210	56	72	70	30	2	79	8	5	5	17	6	.74	6	.280	.330	.445
2000	CIN	NL	84	291	83	18	0	12	(5	7)	137	44	43	50	24	1	52	10	2	4	6	1	.86	5	.285	.356	.471
2001	CIN	NL	103	381	112	26	2	14	(10	4)	184	54	62	63	29	1	71	8	3	6	6	3	.67	9	.294	.351	.483
2002	CIN	NL	162	606	146	38	2	26	(14	12)	266	83	87	83	56	4	111	10	9	4	32	8	.80	9	.241	.314	.439
2003	2 Tms		160	592	158	32	3	24	(13	11)	268	92	96	89	46	2	104	8	6	2	23	3	.88	13	.267	.327	.453
2005	CLE	AL	143	511	124	19	1	16	(5	11)	193	61	60	52	35	3	92	9	4	6	9	3	.75	16	.243	.299	.378
03	Cin	NL	106	403	110	19	3	18	(10	8)	189	61	65	65	35	2	74	5	3	0	15	3	.83	6	.273	.339	.469
03	NYY	AL	54	189	48	13	0	6	(3	3)	79	31	31	24	11	0	30	3	3	2	8	0	1.00	7	.254	.302	.418
	8 ML YEARS		865	3083	818	173	15	108	(56	52)	1345	419	453	437	237	14	550	58	33	29	100	25	.80	62	.265	.327	.436

Bret Boone

Bats: R Throws: R Pos: 2B-88 **Ht: 5'10" Wt: 190 Born: 4/6/1969 Age: 37**

						BATTING																BASERUNNING				AVERAGES		
Year	Team	Lg	G	AB	H	2B	3B	HR	(Hm	Rd)	TB	R	RBI	RC	TBB	IBB	SO	HBP	SH	SF	SB	CS	SB%	GDP	Avg	OBP	Slg
1992	SEA	AL	33	129	25	4	0	4	(2	2)	41	15	15	7	4	0	34	1	1	0	1	1	.50	4	.194	.224	.318
1993	SEA	AL	76	271	68	12	2	12	(7	5)	120	31	38	35	17	1	52	4	6	4	2	3	.40	6	.251	.301	.443
1994	CIN	NL	108	381	122	25	2	12	(5	7)	187	59	68	65	24	1	74	8	5	6	3	4	.43	10	.320	.368	.491
1995	CIN	NL	138	513	137	34	2	15	(6	9)	220	63	68	70	41	0	84	6	5	5	5	1	.83	14	.267	.326	.429
1996	CIN	NL	142	520	121	21	3	12	(7	5)	184	56	69	50	31	0	100	3	5	9	3	2	.60	9	.233	.275	.354
1997	CIN	NL	139	443	99	25	1	7	(4	3)	147	40	46	42	45	4	101	4	4	5	5	5	.50	11	.223	.298	.332

			BATTING																			BASERUNNING				AVERAGES		
Year	Team	Lg	G	AB	H	2B	3B	HR	(Hm	Rd)	TB	R	RBI	RC	TBB	IBB	SO	HBP	SH	SF	SB	CS	SB%	GDP	Avg	OBP	Slg
1998	CIN	NL	157	583	155	38	1	24	(13	11)	267	76	95	80	48	3	104	4	9	4	6	4	.60	23	.266	.324	.458
1999	ATL	NL	152	608	153	38	1	20	(9	11)	253	102	63	77	47	0	112	5	4	2	14	9	.61	11	.252	.310	.416
2000	SD	NL	127	463	116	18	2	19	(8	11)	195	61	74	63	50	7	97	5	0	7	8	4	.67	11	.251	.326	.421
2001	SEA	AL	158	623	206	37	3	37	(19	18)	360	118	**141**	126	40	5	110	9	5	13	5	5	.50	11	.331	.372	.578
2002	SEA	AL	155	608	169	34	3	24	(13	11)	281	88	107	95	53	4	102	6	2	6	12	5	.71	11	.278	.339	.462
2003	SEA	AL	159	622	183	35	5	35	(16	19)	333	111	117	111	68	3	125	7	1	7	16	3	.84	17	.294	.366	.535
2004	SEA	AL	148	593	149	30	0	24	(12	12)	251	74	83	66	56	2	135	3	2	4	10	5	.67	18	.251	.337	.423
2005	2 Tms	AL	88	326	72	15	3	7	(2	5)	114	33	37	30	28	2	65	4	1	1	4	2	.67	12	.221	.290	.350
05	Sea	AL	74	273	63	15	3	7	(2	5)	105	30	34	28	24	2	52	3	1	1	4	2	.67	9	.231	.299	.385
05	Min	AL	14	53	9	0	0	0	(0	0)	9	3	3	2	4	0	13	1	0	0	0	0	-	3	.170	.241	.170
14 ML YEARS			1780	6683	1775	366	28	252	(123	129)	2953	927	1021	917	552	32	1295	69	55	73	94	53	.64	168	.266	.325	.442

Chris Bootcheck

Pitches: R Bats: R Pos: RP-3; SP-2

Ht: 6'5" Wt: 200 Born: 10/24/1978 Age: 27

			HOW MUCH HE PITCHED						WHAT HE GAVE UP												THE RESULTS							
Year	Team	Lg	G	GS	CG	GF	IP	BFP	H	R	ER	HR	SH	SF	HB	TBB	IBB	SO	WP	Bk	W	L	Pct	ShO	Sv-Op	Hld	ERC	ERA
2001	RCuca	A+	15	14	1	0	87.0	359	84	45	38	11	0	1	0	23	0	86	4	0	8	4	.667	0	0--	-	3.56	3.93
2001	Ark	AA	6	6	1	0	36.1	161	39	25	22	3	0	0	3	11	0	22	1	1	3	3	.500	0	0--	-	4.23	5.45
2002	Ark	AA	19	19	3	0	116.0	517	130	68	62	11	4	2	6	35	0	90	4	0	8	7	.533	0	0--	-	4.45	4.81
2002	Salt Lk	AAA	9	9	1	0	58.0	247	64	29	25	5	1	2	2	16	0	38	1	0	4	3	.571	1	0--	-	4.27	3.88
2003	Salt Lk	AAA	28	26	3	0	171.1	737	194	103	81	19	6	12	7	43	1	82	1	0	8	9	.471	0	0--	-	4.49	4.25
2004	Salt Lk	AAA	28	28	3	0	163.1	734	202	109	93	22	4	4	6	60	2	105	7	0	11	9	.550	1	0--	-	5.78	5.12
2005	Salt Lk	AAA	21	21	0	0	116.1	543	144	75	70	13	6	4	1	50	0	90	4	0	7	4	.636	0	0--	-	5.58	5.42
2003	ANA	AL	4	1	0	0	10.1	53	16	13	11	5	0	0	0	6	0	7	0	0	0	1	.000	0	0-0	0	11.53	9.58
2005	LAA	AL	5	2	0	1	18.2	80	19	7	7	1	0	1	0	4	1	8	1	0	0	1	.000	0	1-1	0	2.95	3.38
2 ML YEARS			9	3	0	3	29.0	133	35	20	18	6	0	1	0	10	1	15	1	0	0	2	.000	0	1-1	0	5.61	5.59

Joe Borchard

Bats: B Throws: R Pos: PH-4; RF-2; DH-2; PR-1

Ht: 6'5" Wt: 220 Born: 11/25/1978 Age: 27

			BATTING																			BASERUNNING				AVERAGES		
Year	Team	Lg	G	AB	H	2B	3B	HR	(Hm	Rd)	TB	R	RBI	RC	TBB	IBB	SO	HBP	SH	SF	SB	CS	SB%	GDP	Avg	OBP	Slg
2005	Charltt*	AAA	134	494	130	20	0	29	(-	-)	237	69	67	80	50	4	143	4	1	1	6	4	.60	19	.263	.335	.480
2002	CHA	AL	16	36	8	0	0	2	(0	2)	14	5	5	5	1	0	14	0	0	0	0	0	-	0	.222	.243	.389
2003	CHA	AL	16	49	9	1	0	1	(0	1)	13	5	5	2	5	0	18	0	0	3	0	1	.00	0	.184	.246	.265
2004	CHA	AL	63	201	35	4	1	9	(6	3)	68	26	20	13	19	1	57	1	1	0	1	0	1.00	4	.174	.249	.338
2005	CHA	AL	7	12	5	2	0	0	(0	0)	7	0	0	2	0	0	4	0	0	0	0	1	.00	0	.417	.417	.583
4 ML YEARS			102	298	57	7	1	12	(6	6)	102	36	30	22	25	1	93	1	1	3	1	2	.33	4	.191	.254	.342

Pat Borders

Bats: R Throws: R Pos: C-39

Ht: 6'2" Wt: 200 Born: 5/14/1963 Age: 43

			BATTING																			BASERUNNING				AVERAGES		
Year	Team	Lg	G	AB	H	2B	3B	HR	(Hm	Rd)	TB	R	RBI	RC	TBB	IBB	SO	HBP	SH	SF	SB	CS	SB%	GDP	Avg	OBP	Slg
2005	Nashv*	AAA	26	98	24	2	0	3	(-	-)	35	8	14	8	3	0	18	0	0	1	1	2	.33	6	.245	.265	.357
1988	TOR	AL	56	154	42	6	3	5	(2	3)	69	15	21	18	3	0	24	0	2	1	0	0	-	5	.273	.285	.448
1989	TOR	AL	94	241	62	11	1	3	(1	2)	84	22	29	22	11	2	45	1	1	2	2	1	.67	7	.257	.290	.349
1990	TOR	AL	125	346	99	24	2	15	(10	5)	172	36	49	48	18	2	57	0	1	3	0	1	.00	17	.286	.319	.497
1991	TOR	AL	105	291	71	17	0	5	(2	3)	103	22	36	26	11	1	45	1	6	3	0	0	-	8	.244	.271	.354
1992	TOR	AL	138	480	116	26	2	13	(7	6)	185	47	53	52	33	3	75	2	1	5	1	1	.50	11	.242	.290	.385
1993	TOR	AL	138	488	124	30	0	9	(6	3)	181	38	55	46	20	2	66	2	7	3	2	2	.50	18	.254	.285	.371
1994	TOR	AL	85	295	73	13	1	3	(3	0)	97	24	26	25	15	0	50	0	1	0	1	1	.50	7	.247	.284	.329
1995	2 Tms		63	178	37	8	1	4	(1	3)	59	15	13	14	9	2	29	0	0	0	0	0	-	3	.208	.246	.331
1996	3 Tms		76	220	61	7	0	5	(3	2)	83	15	18	23	9	0	43	0	5	0	0	2	.00	4	.277	.306	.377
1997	CLE	AL	55	159	47	7	1	4	(0	4)	68	17	15	21	9	0	27	2	0	0	0	2	.00	5	.296	.341	.428
1998	CLE	AL	54	160	38	6	0	0	(0	0)	44	12	6	11	10	0	40	2	2	1	0	2	.00	3	.238	.289	.275
1999	2 Tms	AL	12	34	9	0	1	1	(1	0)	14	3	6	4	1	0	5	0	0	0	0	1	.00	0	.265	.286	.412
2001	SEA	AL	5	6	3	0	0	0	(0	0)	3	1	0	1	0	0	1	0	1	0	0	0	-	0	.500	.500	.500
2002	SEA	AL	4	4	2	1	0	0	(0	0)	3	0	1	0	0	0	1	0	0	0	0	0	-	0	.500	.500	.750
2003	SEA	AL	12	14	2	1	0	0	(0	0)	3	1	1	1	1	0	5	0	0	0	0	0	-	0	.143	.200	.214
2004	2 Tms	AL	38	95	22	6	0	1	(0	1)	31	9	10	7	1	0	22	1	2	0	3	1	.75	2	.232	.247	.326
2005	SEA	AL	39	117	23	5	0	1	(0	1)	31	12	7	5	4	1	22	1	2	1	0	0	-	4	.197	.228	.265
95	KC	AL	52	143	33	8	1	4	(1	3)	55	14	13	14	7	1	22	0	0	0	0	0	-	1	.231	.267	.385
95	Hou	NL	11	35	4	0	0	0	(0	0)	4	1	0	0	2	1	7	0	0	0	0	0	-	2	.114	.162	.114
96	StL	NL	26	69	22	3	0	0	(0	0)	25	3	4	7	1	0	14	0	1	0	0	1	.00	1	.319	.329	.362
96	Cal	AL	19	57	13	3	0	2	(2	0)	22	6	8	5	3	0	11	0	1	0	0	1	.00	1	.228	.267	.386
96	CWS	AL	31	94	26	1	0	3	(1	2)	36	6	6	11	5	0	18	0	3	0	0	0	-	2	.277	.313	.383
99	Cle	AL	6	20	6	0	1	0	(0	0)	8	2	3	2	0	0	3	0	0	0	0	1	.00	0	.300	.300	.400
99	Tor	AL	6	14	3	0	0	1	(1	0)	6	1	3	2	1	0	2	0	0	0	0	0	-	0	.214	.267	.429
04	Sea	AL	19	53	10	2	0	1	(0	1)	15	6	5	1	1	0	12	0	1	0	1	1	.50	2	.189	.204	.283
04	Min	AL	19	42	12	4	0	0	(0	0)	16	3	5	6	0	0	10	1	1	0	2	0	1.00	0	.286	.302	.381
17 ML YEARS			1099	3282	831	168	12	69	(36	33)	1230	289	346	324	155	13	557	12	31	19	9	14	.39	94	.253	.288	.375

Joe Borowski

Pitches: R **Bats:** R **Pos:** RP-43   **Ht:** 6'2" **Wt:** 240 **Born:** 5/4/1971 **Age:** 35

Year	Team	Lg	G	GS	CG	GF	IP	BFP	H	R	ER	HR	SH	SF	HB	TBB	IBB	SO	WP	Bk	W	L	Pct	ShO	Sv-Op	Hld	ERC	ERA
2005	Iowa*	AAA	7	0	0	3	8.0	30	3	4	2	2	0	0	0	3	0	4	0	0	0	0	-	0	0--		1.67	2.25
1995	BAL	AL	6	0	0	3	7.1	30	5	1	1	0	0	0	0	4	0	3	0	0	0	0	-	0	0-0	0	2.32	1.23
1996	ATL	NL	22	0	0	8	26.0	121	33	15	14	4	5	0	1	13	4	15	1	0	2	4	.333	0	0-0	1	6.46	4.85
1997	2 Tms		21	0	0	9	26.0	123	29	13	12	2	1	0	0	20	5	8	0	0	2	3	.400	0	0-0	2	5.74	4.15
1998	NYA	AL	8	0	0	6	9.2	42	11	7	7	0	0	0	0	4	0	7	0	0	1	0	1.000	0	0-0	0	4.27	6.52
2001	CHN	NL	1	1	0	0	1.2	13	6	6	6	1	1	0	0	3	0	1	0	0	0	1	.000	0	0-0	0	39.91	32.40
2002	CHN	NL	73	0	0	25	95.2	391	84	31	29	10	5	3	1	29	6	97	1	0	4	4	.500	0	2-6	12	3.05	2.73
2003	CHN	NL	68	0	0	59	68.1	280	53	23	20	5	4	0	1	19	1	66	0	0	2	2	.500	0	33-37	1	2.26	2.63
2004	CHN	NL	22	0	0	19	21.1	106	27	19	19	3	1	1	0	15	2	17	0	0	2	4	.333	0	9-11	0	6.92	8.02
2005	2 Tms		43	0	0	7	46.1	184	38	23	23	8	1	0	0	12	1	27	1	0	1	5	.167	0	0-4	20	3.04	4.47
97	Atl	NL	20	0	0	8	24.0	111	27	11	10	2	1	0	0	16	4	6	0	0	2	2	.500	0	0-0	2	5.51	3.75
97	NYY	AL	1	0	0	1	2.0	12	2	2	2	0	0	0	0	4	1	2	0	0	0	1	.000	0	0-0	0	8.25	9.00
05	ChC	NL	11	0	0	3	11.0	47	12	8	8	5	0	0	0	1	0	11	0	0	0	0	-	0	0-0	1	5.36	6.55
05	TB	AL	32	0	0	4	35.1	137	26	15	15	3	1	0	0	11	1	16	1	0	1	5	.167	0	0-4	19	2.33	3.82
9 ML YEARS			264	1	0	136	302.1	1290	286	138	131	33	18	4	3	119	19	241	3	0	14	23	.378	0	44-58	36	3.75	3.90

Ricky Bottalico

Pitches: R **Bats:** L **Pos:** RP-40   **Ht:** 6'1" **Wt:** 215 **Born:** 8/26/1969 **Age:** 36

Year	Team	Lg	G	GS	CG	GF	IP	BFP	H	R	ER	HR	SH	SF	HB	TBB	IBB	SO	WP	Bk	W	L	Pct	ShO	Sv-Op	Hld	ERC	ERA
2005	Pwtckt*	AAA	6	0	0	1	8.1	34	5	4	4	1	0	2	0	4	0	6	1	0	0	0	-	0	0--		2.38	4.32
1994	PHI	NL	3	0	0	3	3.0	13	3	0	0	0	0	0	0	1	0	3	0	0	0	0	-	0	0-0	0	3.05	0.00
1995	PHI	NL	62	0	0	20	87.2	350	50	25	24	7	3	1	4	42	3	87	1	0	5	3	.625	0	1-5	20	2.17	2.46
1996	PHI	NL	61	0	0	56	67.2	269	47	24	24	6	4	2	2	23	2	74	3	0	4	5	.444	0	34-38	0	2.29	3.19
1997	PHI	NL	69	0	0	61	74.0	324	68	31	30	7	1	2	2	42	4	89	3	0	2	5	.286	0	34-41	0	4.29	3.65
1998	PHI	NL	39	0	0	28	43.1	206	54	31	31	7	1	2	1	25	5	27	2	0	1	5	.167	0	6-7	3	6.63	6.44
1999	STL	NL	68	0	0	40	73.1	347	83	45	40	8	3	0	3	49	1	66	6	0	3	7	.300	0	20-28	8	6.16	4.91
2000	KC	AL	62	0	0	50	72.2	319	65	40	39	12	3	1	2	41	3	56	5	1	9	6	.600	0	16-23	1	4.65	4.83
2001	PHI	NL	66	0	0	18	67.0	281	58	31	29	11	7	4	4	25	2	57	5	0	3	4	.429	0	3-7	22	3.88	3.90
2002	PHI	NL	30	0	0	6	27.1	128	33	16	14	2	1	2	2	13	2	24	2	0	0	3	.000	0	0-1	15	5.80	4.61
2003	ARI	NL	2	0	0	0	1.2	10	3	1	1	0	0	0	0	2	1	2	0	0	1	0	1.000	0	0-0	1	10.00	5.40
2004	NYN	NL	60	0	0	8	69.1	296	54	30	26	3	3	4	1	34	7	61	3	0	3	2	.600	0	0-4	12	2.87	3.38
2005	MIL	NL	40	0	0	11	41.2	188	43	24	21	7	1	2	3	19	0	29	7	0	2	2	.500	0	2-6	9	5.22	4.54
12 ML YEARS			562	0	0	301	628.2	2731	561	298	279	71	28	19	27	316	30	575	37	1	33	42	.440	0	116-160	91	4.06	3.99

Jason Botts

Bats: B **Throws:** R **Pos:** LF-7; DH-3; PR-1   **Ht:** 6'5" **Wt:** 250 **Born:** 7/26/1980 **Age:** 25

Year	Team	Lg	G	AB	H	2B	3B	HR	Hm	Rd	TB	R	RBI	RC	TBB	IBB	SO	HBP	SH	SF	SB	CS	SB%	GDP	Avg	OBP	Slg
2000	Rngrs	R	48	163	52	12	0	6	-	-	82	36	34	38	26	4	29	10	0	1	4	1	.80	5	.319	.440	.503
2001	Charltt	A+	4	12	2	1	0	0	-	-	3	1	0	1	4	0	4	0	0	0	0	0	-	0	.167	.375	.250
2001	Savann	A	114	392	121	24	2	9	-	-	176	63	50	77	53	4	88	20	0	1	13	7	.65	10	.309	.416	.449
2002	Charltt	A+	116	401	102	22	5	9	-	-	161	67	54	70	75	3	99	14	0	3	7	2	.78	4	.254	.387	.401
2003	Stckton	A+	76	283	89	14	2	9	-	-	134	58	61	58	45	1	59	1	0	1	12	3	.80	8	.314	.409	.473
2003	Frisco	AA	55	194	51	11	1	4	-	-	76	26	27	28	21	1	45	3	0	2	6	1	.86	6	.263	.341	.392
2004	Frisco	AA	132	476	141	25	3	24	-	-	244	85	92	100	76	4	125	10	1	4	7	4	.64	18	.296	.401	.513
2005	Okla	AAA	133	510	146	31	7	25	-	-	266	93	102	100	67	2	152	8	0	4	2	4	.33	13	.286	.375	.522
2005	TEX	AL	10	27	8	0	0	0	0	0	8	4	3	3	3	0	13	0	0	0	0	0	-	1	.296	.367	.296

Travis Bowyer

Pitches: R **Bats:** R **Pos:** RP-8   **Ht:** 6'3" **Wt:** 200 **Born:** 8/3/1981 **Age:** 24

Year	Team	Lg	G	GS	CG	GF	IP	BFP	H	R	ER	HR	SH	SF	HB	TBB	IBB	SO	WP	Bk	W	L	Pct	ShO	Sv-Op	Hld	ERC	ERA
1999	Twins	R	1	0	0	0	1.0	3	0	0	0	0	0	0	0	0	0	1	0	0	1	0	1.000	0	0--	-	0.00	0.00
2000	Twins	R	12	12	1	0	55.1	250	55	31	25	2	2	2	8	22	0	36	5	0	3	5	.375	0	0--	-	4.04	4.07
2001	Elizab	R+	9	8	0	0	38.1	173	38	30	26	3	1	3	3	20	0	34	7	0	2	5	.286	0	0--	-	4.63	6.10
2002	QuadC	A	39	9	0	12	91.2	395	74	28	22	2	7	3	3	46	0	90	11	0	4	4	.500	0	3--	-	2.96	2.16
2003	FtMyrs	A+	45	0	0	10	80.0	364	68	43	34	1	6	1	1	56	2	70	9	0	5	2	.714	0	1--	-	3.66	3.83
2004	FtMyrs	A+	17	0	0	3	29.2	124	18	6	1	0	0	1	0	17	2	32	3	0	3	0	1.000	0	2--	-	2.00	0.30
2004	NwBrit	AA	31	0	0	14	61.1	264	42	17	12	3	0	0	2	38	1	65	2	1	6	3	.667	0	3--	-	2.91	1.76
2005	Roch	AAA	59	0	0	41	74.1	314	51	23	23	4	2	0	2	40	0	96	3	2	4	2	.667	0	23--	-	2.68	2.78
2005	MIN	AL	8	0	0	5	9.2	42	10	6	6	3	0	1	1	3	0	12	1	0	0	1	.000	0	0-1	0	5.88	5.59

Blaine Boyer

Pitches: R **Bats:** R **Pos:** RP-43   **Ht:** 6'3" **Wt:** 215 **Born:** 7/11/1981 **Age:** 24

Year	Team	Lg	G	GS	CG	GF	IP	BFP	H	R	ER	HR	SH	SF	HB	TBB	IBB	SO	WP	Bk	W	L	Pct	ShO	Sv-Op	Hld	ERC	ERA
2000	Braves	R	11	5	0	2	32.1	140	24	16	9	0	4	0	3	19	0	27	3	2	1	3	.250	0	1--	-	3.02	2.51
2001	Danvle	R+	13	12	0	0	50.0	217	48	35	24	4	3	1	5	19	0	57	9	1	4	5	.444	0	0--	-	4.03	4.32
2002	Macon	A	43	0	0	22	70.1	302	52	30	24	0	6	3	5	39	3	73	8	2	5	9	.357	0	1--	-	2.74	3.07
2003	Rome	A	30	26	1	0	136.2	614	146	70	56	5	1	4	4	58	0	115	10	1	12	8	.600	0	0--	-	4.13	3.69
2004	MrtlBh	A+	28	28	0	0	154.0	649	138	63	51	4	15	6	7	49	0	95	7	0	10	10	.500	0	0--	-	2.85	2.98
2005	Missi	AA	14	8	0	2	48.1	225	62	28	27	4	3	3	2	18	3	40	0	0	2	4	.333	0	0--	-	5.45	5.03
2005	ATL	NL	43	0	0	5	37.2	157	32	13	13	1	1	1	2	17	0	33	2	0	4	2	.667	0	0-2	9	3.23	3.11

Chad Bradford

Pitches: R Bats: R Pos: RP-31　　　　　　　　　Ht: 6'5" Wt: 203 Born: 9/14/1974 Age: 31

Year	Team	Lg	G	GS	CG	GF	IP	BFP	H	R	ER	HR	SH	SF	HB	TBB	IBB	SO	WP	Bk	W	L	Pct	ShO	Sv-Op	Hld	ERC	ERA
2005	As*	R	3	3	0	0	3.0	12	3	0	0	0	0	0	0	0	0	2	0	0	0	0	-	0	0--	-	1.95	0.00
2005	Stcktn*	A+	3	0	0	0	2.1	11	3	1	1	0	0	0	0	1	0	1	0	0	0	0	-	0	0--	-	4.93	3.86
2005	Scrmto*	AAA	3	1	0	0	3.0	13	4	2	2	1	0	0	0	0	0	1	0	0	0	0	-	0	0--	-	5.82	6.00
1998	CHA	AL	29	0	0	8	30.2	125	27	16	11	0	0	0	0	7	0	11	1	1	2	1	.667	0	1-3	9	2.16	3.23
1999	CHA	AL	3	0	0	0	3.2	24	9	8	8	1	0	0	0	5	0	0	1	0	0	0	-	0	0-0	0	21.34	19.64
2000	CHA	AL	12	0	0	5	13.2	52	13	4	3	0	0	0	0	1	1	9	0	0	1	0	1.000	0	0-0	2	2.01	1.98
2001	OAK	AL	35	0	0	19	36.2	154	41	12	11	6	1	0	1	6	0	34	0	0	2	1	.667	0	1-4	4	4.36	2.70
2002	OAK	AL	75	0	0	14	75.1	311	73	29	26	2	2	2	5	14	5	56	0	1	4	2	.667	0	2-5	24	2.77	3.11
2003	OAK	AL	72	0	0	12	77.0	322	67	28	26	7	1	0	7	30	9	62	0	1	7	4	.636	0	2-5	23	3.50	3.04
2004	OAK	AL	68	0	0	16	59.0	251	51	32	29	5	3	1	5	24	9	34	0	0	5	7	.417	0	1-4	14	3.35	4.42
2005	BOS	AL	31	0	0	2	23.1	104	29	10	10	1	3	1	3	4	1	10	2	0	2	1	.667	0	0-1	8	4.54	3.86
8 ML YEARS			325	0	0	76	319.1	1343	310	139	124	22	10	4	21	91	25	216	4	3	23	16	.590	0	7-22	84	3.41	3.49

Milton Bradley

Bats: B Throws: R Pos: CF-73; PH-2　　　　　　　Ht: 6'0" Wt: 190 Born: 4/15/1978 Age: 28

Year	Team	Lg	G	AB	H	2B	3B	HR	(Hm	Rd)	TB	R	RBI	RC	TBB	IBB	SO	HBP	SH	SF	SB	CS	SB%	GDP	Avg	OBP	Slg
2005	LsVgs*	AAA	5	13	4	0	0	0	(-	-)	4	2	1	1	1	0	2	0	0	0	1	1	.50	0	.308	.357	.308
2000	MON	NL	42	154	34	8	1	2	(1	1)	50	20	15	14	14	0	32	1	1	1	2	1	.67	3	.221	.288	.325
2001	2 Tms		77	238	53	17	3	1	(0	1)	79	22	19	21	21	0	65	1	2	0	8	5	.62	7	.223	.288	.332
2002	CLE	AL	98	325	81	18	3	9	(4	5)	132	48	38	40	32	2	58	0	1	0	6	3	.67	12	.249	.317	.406
2003	CLE	AL	101	377	121	34	2	10	(4	6)	189	61	56	77	64	8	73	5	0	5	17	7	.71	10	.321	.421	.501
2004	LA	NL	141	516	138	24	0	19	(8	11)	219	72	67	70	71	3	123	6	3	1	15	11	.58	12	.267	.362	.424
2005	LAN	NL	75	283	82	14	1	13	(6	7)	137	49	38	40	25	1	47	2	4	1	6	1	.86	6	.290	.350	.484
01	Mon	NL	67	220	49	16	3	1	(0	1)	74	19	19	20	19	0	62	1	2	0	7	4	.64	5	.223	.288	.336
01	Cle	AL	10	18	4	1	0	0	(0	0)	5	3	0	1	2	0	3	0	0	0	1	1	.50	1	.222	.300	.278
6 ML YEARS			534	1893	509	115	10	54	(23	31)	806	272	233	262	227	14	398	15	11	8	54	28	.66	50	.269	.350	.426

Russell Branyan

Bats: L Throws: R Pos: 3B-59; PH-22; 1B-5; LF-3; DH-1　　Ht: 6'3" Wt: 195 Born: 12/19/1975 Age: 30

Year	Team	Lg	G	AB	H	2B	3B	HR	(Hm	Rd)	TB	R	RBI	RC	TBB	IBB	SO	HBP	SH	SF	SB	CS	SB%	GDP	Avg	OBP	Slg
2005	Nashv*	AAA	6	17	5	4	0	1	(-	-)	12	4	3	4	3	0	8	0	0	0	0	0	-	0	.294	.400	.706
1998	CLE	AL	1	4	0	0	0	0	(0	0)	0	0	0	0	0	0	2	0	0	0	0	0	-	0	.000	.000	.000
1999	CLE	AL	11	38	8	2	0	1	(0	1)	13	4	6	4	3	0	19	1	0	0	0	0	-	0	.211	.286	.342
2000	CLE	AL	67	193	46	7	2	16	(13	3)	105	32	38	34	22	1	76	4	0	1	0	0	-	2	.238	.327	.544
2001	CLE	AL	113	315	73	16	2	20	(11	9)	153	48	54	50	38	1	132	3	0	5	1	1	.50	2	.232	.316	.486
2002	2 Tms		134	378	86	13	1	24	(5	19)	173	50	56	49	51	3	151	2	0	4	4	3	.57	5	.228	.320	.458
2003	CIN	NL	74	176	38	12	0	9	(7	2)	77	22	26	23	27	0	69	1	0	1	0	0	-	1	.216	.322	.438
2004	MIL	NL	51	158	37	11	1	11	(8	3)	83	21	27	23	20	0	68	2	0	2	1	0	1.00	1	.234	.324	.525
2005	MIL	NL	85	202	52	11	0	12	(3	9)	99	23	31	38	39	10	80	0	1	0	1	0	1.00	3	.257	.378	.490
02	Cle	AL	50	161	33	4	0	8	(1	7)	61	16	17	14	17	0	65	1	0	2	1	2	.33	3	.205	.278	.379
02	Cin	NL	84	217	53	9	1	16	(4	12)	112	34	39	35	34	3	86	2	0	2	3	1	.75	2	.244	.349	.516
8 ML YEARS			536	1464	340	72	6	93	(47	46)	703	200	238	221	200	15	597	13	1	13	7	4	.64	14	.232	.327	.480

Dewon Brazelton

Pitches: R Bats: R Pos: RP-12; SP-8　　　　　　Ht: 6'4" Wt: 205 Born: 6/16/1980 Age: 26

Year	Team	Lg	G	GS	CG	GF	IP	BFP	H	R	ER	HR	SH	SF	HB	TBB	IBB	SO	WP	Bk	W	L	Pct	ShO	Sv-Op	Hld	ERC	ERA
2005	Mont*	AA	1	1	0	0	3.0	11	2	0	0	0	0	0	0	0	0	6	0	0	0	0	-	0	0--	-	0.91	0.00
2005	Drham*	AAA	5	5	0	0	29.0	130	29	17	12	3	1	3	1	14	0	26	1	0	2	2	.500	0	0--	-	4.49	3.72
2002	TB	AL	2	2	0	0	13.0	51	12	7	7	3	0	0	2	6	0	5	0	0	0	1	.000	0	0-0	0	6.29	4.85
2003	TB	AL	10	10	0	0	48.1	225	57	49	37	9	2	2	3	23	1	24	1	0	1	6	.143	0	0-0	0	6.29	6.89
2004	TB	AL	22	21	0	0	120.2	535	121	71	64	12	0	6	11	53	2	64	2	1	6	8	.429	0	0-0	0	4.58	4.77
2005	TB	AL	20	8	0	2	71.0	354	87	65	60	12	4	3	4	60	3	43	5	0	1	8	.111	0	0-1	1	8.13	7.61
4 ML YEARS			54	41	0	2	253.0	1165	277	192	168	36	6	11	20	142	6	136	8	1	8	23	.258	0	0-1	1	5.94	5.98

Yhency Brazoban

Pitches: R Bats: R Pos: RP-74　　　　　　　　Ht: 6'1" Wt: 170 Born: 6/11/1980 Age: 26

Year	Team	Lg	G	GS	CG	GF	IP	BFP	H	R	ER	HR	SH	SF	HB	TBB	IBB	SO	WP	Bk	W	L	Pct	ShO	Sv-Op	Hld	ERC	ERA
2002	Yanks	R	6	0	0	0	6.0	27	3	3	3	0	0	0	1	4	0	11	2	0	0	0	-	0	0--	-	2.17	4.50
2003	Yanks	R	3	0	0	0	3.0	15	5	3	2	0	1	0	0	1	1	5	0	0	0	0	-	0	0--	-	6.14	6.00
2003	Tampa	A+	24	0	0	22	28.2	124	27	13	9	0	0	1	1	12	2	34	2	0	0	2	.000	0	15--	-	3.12	2.83
2003	Trentn	AA	20	0	0	16	27.2	127	33	25	24	5	3	3	2	14	1	19	4	0	2	2	.500	0	3--	-	6.65	7.81
2004	Jaxnvl	AA	37	0	0	33	51.0	214	38	18	15	4	1	1	1	22	1	61	0	0	4	4	.500	0	13--	-	2.69	2.65
2004	LsVgs	AAA	10	0	0	7	12.1	52	14	3	3	1	0	0	0	1	0	17	0	0	2	0	1.000	0	1--	-	3.36	2.19
2004	LAN	NL	31	0	0	10	32.2	133	25	9	9	2	4	0	0	15	2	27	1	0	6	2	.750	0	0-0	5	2.76	2.48
2005	LAN	NL	74	0	0	44	72.2	317	70	46	43	11	7	2	5	32	4	61	1	0	4	10	.286	0	21-27	8	4.60	5.33
2 ML YEARS			105	0	0	54	105.1	450	95	55	52	13	11	2	5	47	6	88	2	0	10	12	.455	0	21-27	13	4.01	4.44

Craig Breslow

Pitches: L Bats: L Pos: RP-14   Ht: 6'1" Wt: 180 Born: 8/8/1980 Age: 25

Year	Team	Lg	G	GS	CG	GF	IP	BFP	H	R	ER	HR	SH	SF	HB	TBB	IBB	SO	WP	Bk	W	L	Pct	ShO	Sv-Op	Hld	ERC	ERA
2002	Ogden	R+	23	0	0	6	54.1	229	42	15	11	2	3	2	1	24	0	56	7	0	6	2	.750	0	2--	-	2.63	1.82
2003	Beloit	A	33	0	0	12	65.0	286	64	43	37	4	4	2	1	27	0	80	1	0	3	4	.429	0	2--	-	3.76	5.12
2004	Hi Dsrt	A+	23	0	0	9	41.1	202	54	39	33	5	0	0	2	24	0	41	4	0	1	3	.250	0	0--	-	6.95	7.19
2005	Mobile	AA	40	0	0	6	52.1	212	38	16	16	3	4	2	1	17	3	47	2	0	2	1	.667	0	0--	-	2.08	2.75
2005	Portlnd	AAA	7	0	0	6	9.0	39	11	4	4	1	1	1	0	1	0	9	0	0	0	1	.000	0	0--	-	4.14	4.00
2005	SD	NL	14	0	0	3	16.1	78	15	6	4	1	0	1	1	13	0	14	1	0	0	0	-	0	0-0	1	4.98	2.20

Eude Brito

Pitches: L Bats: L Pos: SP-5; RP-1   Ht: 5'11" Wt: 160 Born: 8/19/1978 Age: 27

Year	Team	Lg	G	GS	CG	GF	IP	BFP	H	R	ER	HR	SH	SF	HB	TBB	IBB	SO	WP	Bk	W	L	Pct	ShO	Sv-Op	Hld	ERC	ERA
1999	Phillies	R	12	3	0	3	28.2	144	39	22	16	0	2	2	0	19	0	23	4	1	0	1	.000	0	0--	-	6.29	5.02
2000	Phillies	R	9	7	0	1	49.2	206	38	20	14	1	0	1	3	19	0	42	10	0	3	5	.375	0	0--	-	2.46	2.54
2000	Batvia	A-	4	3	0	1	18.1	74	16	14	11	0	0	0	1	3	0	11	5	0	1	1	.500	0	0--	-	2.11	5.40
2001	Lakwd	A	44	0	0	20	69.1	275	53	28	21	7	5	0	2	14	2	58	3	2	4	3	.571	0	6--	-	2.18	2.73
2002	Clrwtr	A+	20	0	0	11	34.2	158	40	22	22	5	2	1	0	14	1	27	7	0	3	3	.500	0	0--	-	5.13	5.71
2002	Lakwd	A	11	0	0	9	17.2	73	14	5	5	1	2	0	0	6	0	11	0	0	1	1	.500	0	1--	-	2.43	2.55
2003	Clrwtr	A+	36	0	0	19	58.1	252	50	21	20	3	3	4	0	27	1	54	7	0	4	3	.571	0	6--	-	3.10	3.09
2004	Rdng	AA	43	7	1	15	97.2	430	95	56	48	10	3	5	4	42	2	84	7	3	8	6	.571	0	4--	-	4.13	4.42
2005	S-WB	AAA	28	15	0	3	98.1	431	97	59	53	13	2	5	8	39	0	76	3	3	6	2	.750	0	0--	-	4.53	4.85
2005	PHI	NL	6	5	0	0	22.0	94	20	9	9	2	0	1	2	11	1	15	0	1	1	2	.333	0	0-0	0	4.32	3.68

Doug Brocail

Pitches: R Bats: L Pos: RP-61   Ht: 6'5" Wt: 235 Born: 5/16/1967 Age: 39

Year	Team	Lg	G	GS	CG	GF	IP	BFP	H	R	ER	HR	SH	SF	HB	TBB	IBB	SO	WP	Bk	W	L	Pct	ShO	Sv-Op	Hld	ERC	ERA
1992	SD	NL	3	3	0	0	14.0	64	17	10	10	2	2	0	0	5	0	15	0	0	0	0	-	0	0-0	0	5.33	6.43
1993	SD	NL	24	24	0	0	128.1	571	143	75	65	16	10	8	4	42	4	70	4	1	4	13	.235	0	0-0	0	4.60	4.56
1994	SD	NL	12	0	0	4	17.0	78	21	13	11	1	1	1	2	5	3	11	1	1	0	0	-	0	0-1	0	4.79	5.82
1995	HOU	NL	36	7	0	12	77.1	339	87	40	36	10	1	1	4	22	2	39	1	1	6	4	.600	0	1-1	0	4.68	4.19
1996	HOU	NL	23	4	0	4	53.0	231	58	31	27	7	3	2	2	23	1	34	0	0	1	5	.167	0	0-0	1	5.26	4.58
1997	DET	AL	61	4	0	20	78.0	332	74	31	28	10	1	3	3	36	4	60	6	0	4	4	.429	0	2-9	16	4.42	3.23
1998	DET	AL	60	0	0	24	62.2	247	47	23	19	2	2	3	1	18	3	55	6	0	5	2	.714	0	0-1	11	1.99	2.73
1999	DET	AL	70	0	0	22	82.0	326	60	23	23	7	4	2	4	25	1	78	4	1	4	4	.500	0	2-4	23	2.43	2.52
2000	DET	AL	49	0	0	10	50.2	221	57	25	23	5	3	3	1	14	2	41	1	1	5	4	.556	0	0-5	19	4.25	4.09
2004	TEX	AL	43	0	0	14	52.1	232	54	29	24	2	4	2	5	20	1	43	2	1	4	1	.800	0	1-1	4	4.05	4.13
2005	TEX	AL	61	0	0	13	73.1	344	90	48	45	2	3	4	4	34	3	61	4	0	5	3	.625	0	1-4	5	5.15	5.52
11 ML YEARS			442	42	0	123	688.2	2985	708	348	311	64	34	29	30	244	24	507	29	6	37	40	.481	0	7-26	79	4.11	4.06

Frank Brooks

Pitches: L Bats: L Pos: RP-1   Ht: 6'1" Wt: 200 Born: 9/6/1978 Age: 27

Year	Team	Lg	G	GS	CG	GF	IP	BFP	H	R	ER	HR	SH	SF	HB	TBB	IBB	SO	WP	Bk	W	L	Pct	ShO	Sv-Op	Hld	ERC	ERA
1999	Batvia	A-	16	12	1	2	77.1	312	64	26	25	2	0	1	2	33	0	58	2	6	7	3	.700	1	0--	-	2.98	2.91
2000	Pmont	A	29	27	3	1	177.2	734	152	78	68	17	7	8	14	60	0	138	8	1	14	8	.636	2	0--	-	3.38	3.44
2001	Clrwtr	A+	37	15	0	5	112.2	504	113	70	59	18	1	5	9	58	2	92	9	0	5	10	.333	0	1--	-	5.33	4.71
2002	Clrwtr	A+	35	0	0	24	39.0	178	34	18	15	2	2	2	1	27	3	33	2	1	3	5	.375	0	7--	-	4.01	3.46
2002	Rdng	AA	17	1	0	9	29.0	122	29	11	10	1	1	0	0	12	0	23	0	0	1	1	.500	0	2--	-	3.77	3.10
2003	Altna	AA	1	0	0	1	2.1	10	3	2	2	1	2	3	0	0	0	4	0	0	0	0	-	0	0--	-	6.14	7.71
2003	Rdng	AA	34	0	0	19	58.2	224	40	16	15	5	2	3	0	13	1	71	2	0	3	4	.429	0	9--	-	1.75	2.30
2003	Nashv	AAA	16	0	0	4	28.1	113	22	9	8	2	1	0	0	11	2	22	1	0	2	0	1.000	0	0--	-	2.64	2.54
2004	Nashv	AAA	42	8	0	6	83.1	345	81	42	38	13	5	4	0	22	0	55	0	0	6	3	.667	0	2--	-	3.78	4.10
2005	LsVgs	AAA	1	0	0	0	1.2	8	2	2	0	0	0	0	0	1	0	0	0	0	0	0	-	0	0--	-	5.10	0.00
2005	Rchmd	AAA	54	0	0	15	56.0	238	46	27	17	4	2	7	0	24	2	49	3	1	3	4	.429	0	0--	-	2.91	2.73
2004	PIT	NL	11	1	0	3	17.1	73	13	10	9	5	0	0	0	9	2	18	0	1	0	1	.000	0	0-0	0	4.24	4.67
2005	ATL	NL	1	0	0	1	0.1	1	1	0	0	0	0	0	0	0	0	0	0	0	0	0	-	0	0-0	0	29.60	0.00
2 ML YEARS			12	1	0	4	17.2	74	14	10	9	5	0	0	0	9	2	18	0	1	0	1	.000	0	0-0	0	4.47	4.58

Ben Broussard

Bats: L Throws: L Pos: 1B-138; PH-16; DH-2   Ht: 6'2" Wt: 220 Born: 9/24/1976 Age: 29

Year	Team	Lg	G	AB	H	2B	3B	HR	(Hm	Rd)	TB	R	RBI	RC	TBB	IBB	SO	HBP	SH	SF	SB	CS	SB%	GDP	Avg	OBP	Slg
2002	CLE	AL	39	112	27	4	0	4	(2	2)	43	10	9	9	7	1	25	1	0	0	0	0	-	3	.241	.292	.384
2003	CLE	AL	116	386	96	21	3	16	(7	9)	171	53	55	53	32	2	75	5	3	3	5	2	.71	6	.249	.313	.443
2004	CLE	AL	139	418	115	28	5	17	(9	8)	204	57	82	79	52	3	95	5	1	2	4	2	.67	7	.275	.370	.488
2005	CLE	AL	142	466	119	30	5	19	(11	8)	216	59	68	60	32	5	98	4	0	3	2	2	.50	4	.255	.307	.464
4 ML YEARS			436	1382	357	83	13	56	(29	27)	634	179	214	201	123	11	293	22	4	8	11	6	.65	20	.258	.327	.459

Jim Brower

Pitches: R Bats: R Pos: RP-69   Ht: 6'3" Wt: 215 Born: 12/29/1972 Age: 33

Year	Team	Lg	G	GS	CG	GF	IP	BFP	H	R	ER	HR	SH	SF	HB	TBB	IBB	SO	WP	Bk	W	L	Pct	ShO	Sv-Op	Hld	ERC	ERA
2005	Rchmd*	AAA	4	0	0	3	4.0	15	1	1	1	0	0	1	0	2	0	1	0	0	0	1	.000	0	1- -	-	0.75	2.25
1999	CLE	AL	9	2	0	1	25.2	113	27	13	13	8	1	1	1	10	1	18	0	0	3	1	.750	0	0-0	0	5.96	4.56
2000	CLE	AL	17	11	0	1	62.0	293	80	45	43	11	1	0	2	31	1	32	3	0	2	3	.400	0	0-0	0	6.95	6.24
2001	CIN	NL	46	10	0	13	129.1	559	119	65	57	17	9	3	5	60	5	94	5	1	7	10	.412	0	1-2	2	4.21	3.97
2002	2 Tms	NL	52	0	0	23	80.1	344	77	40	39	7	2	1	4	32	2	57	1	0	3	2	.600	0	0-1	6	3.94	4.37
2003	SF	NL	51	5	0	13	100.0	411	90	48	44	8	5	4	1	39	2	65	4	0	8	5	.615	0	2-3	2	3.46	3.96
2004	SF	NL	89	0	0	21	93.0	401	90	42	34	6	11	2	4	36	2	63	10	0	7	7	.500	0	1-5	24	3.72	3.29
2005	2 Tms	NL	69	0	0	12	60.1	282	73	36	36	11	2	1	5	32	3	53	4	0	3	3	.500	0	1-3	12	6.86	5.37
02	Cin	NL	22	0	0	11	39.1	158	38	18	17	2	1	1	0	10	1	24	0	0	2	0	1.000	0	0-0	0	3.08	3.89
02	Mon	NL	30	0	0	12	41.0	186	39	22	22	5	1	0	4	22	1	33	1	0	1	2	.333	0	0-1	6	4.79	4.83
05	SF	NL	32	0	0	8	30.1	144	40	22	22	5	1	1	2	15	0	25	2	0	2	1	.667	0	1-3	5	7.24	6.53
05	Atl	NL	37	0	0	4	30.0	138	33	14	14	6	1	0	3	17	3	28	2	0	1	2	.333	0	0-0	7	6.47	4.20
7 ML YEARS			333	28	0	84	550.2	2403	556	289	266	68	31	12	22	240	16	382	27	1	33	31	.516	0	5-14	46	4.59	4.35

Emil Brown

Bats: R Throws: R Pos: RF-129; LF-11; DH-9; PH-3; PR-1   Ht: 6'2" Wt: 200 Born: 12/29/1974 Age: 31

				BATTING																			BASERUNNING				AVERAGES		
Year	Team	Lg	G	AB	H	2B	3B	HR	(Hm	Rd)	TB	R	RBI	RC	TBB	IBB	SO	HBP	SH	SF	SB	CS	SB%	GDP	Avg	OBP	Slg
1997	PIT	NL	66	95	17	2	1	2	(1	1)	27	16	6	9	10	1	32	7	0	0	5	1	.83	1	.179	.304	.284
1998	PIT	NL	13	39	10	1	0	0	(0	0)	11	2	3	3	1	0	11	1	0	0	0	0	-	0	.256	.293	.282
1999	PIT	NL	6	14	2	1	0	0	(0	0)	3	0	0	0	0	0	3	0	0	0	0	0	-	0	.143	.143	.214
2000	PIT	NL	50	119	26	5	0	3	(2	1)	40	13	16	11	11	0	34	3	1	1	3	1	.75	3	.218	.299	.336
2001	2 Tms	NL	74	137	26	4	1	3	(2	1)	41	21	13	12	16	1	49	2	0	0	12	4	.75	2	.190	.284	.299
2005	KC	AL	150	545	156	31	5	17	(8	9)	248	75	86	91	48	1	108	8	1	7	10	1	.91	14	.286	.349	.455
01	SD	NL	13	14	1	0	0	0	(0	0)	1	3	0	0	1	0	7	0	0	0	2	0	1.00	0	.071	.133	.071
01	Pit	NL	61	123	25	4	1	3	(2	1)	40	18	13	12	15	1	42	2	0	0	10	4	.71	2	.203	.300	.325
6 ML YEARS			359	949	237	44	7	25	(13	12)	370	127	124	126	86	3	237	21	2	8	30	7	.81	20	.250	.323	.390

Kevin Brown

Pitches: R Bats: R Pos: SP-13   Ht: 6'4" Wt: 200 Born: 3/14/1965 Age: 41

Year	Team	Lg	G	GS	CG	GF	IP	BFP	H	R	ER	HR	SH	SF	HB	TBB	IBB	SO	WP	Bk	W	L	Pct	ShO	Sv-Op	Hld	ERC	ERA
1986	TEX	AL	1	1	0	0	5.0	19	6	2	2	0	0	0	0	0	0	4	0	0	1	0	1.000	0	0-0	0	3.25	3.60
1988	TEX	AL	4	4	1	0	23.1	110	33	15	11	2	1	0	1	8	0	12	1	0	1	1	.500	0	0-0	0	6.33	4.24
1989	TEX	AL	28	28	7	0	191.0	798	167	81	71	10	3	6	4	70	2	104	7	2	12	9	.571	0	0-0	0	3.02	3.35
1990	TEX	AL	26	26	6	0	180.0	757	175	84	72	13	2	7	3	60	3	88	9	2	12	10	.545	2	0-0	0	3.54	3.60
1991	TEX	AL	33	33	0	0	210.2	934	233	116	103	17	6	4	13	90	5	96	12	3	9	12	.429	0	0-0	0	4.92	4.40
1992	TEX	AL	35	35	11	0	265.2	1108	262	117	98	11	7	8	10	76	2	173	8	2	21	11	.656	1	0-0	0	3.34	3.32
1993	TEX	AL	34	34	12	0	233.0	1001	228	105	93	14	5	3	15	74	5	142	8	1	15	12	.556	3	0-0	0	3.55	3.59
1994	TEX	AL	26	25	3	1	170.0	760	218	109	91	18	2	7	6	50	3	123	7	0	7	9	.438	0	0-0	0	5.49	4.82
1995	BAL	AL	26	26	3	0	172.1	706	155	73	69	10	5	2	9	48	1	117	3	0	10	9	.526	1	0-0	0	3.03	3.60
1996	FLA	NL	32	32	5	0	233.0	906	187	60	49	8	4	4	16	33	2	159	6	1	17	11	.607	3	0-0	0	2.00	1.89
1997	FLA	NL	33	33	6	0	237.1	976	214	77	71	10	5	1	14	66	7	205	7	1	16	8	.667	2	0-0	0	2.92	2.69
1998	SD	NL	36	35	7	0	257.0	1032	225	77	68	8	13	3	10	49	4	257	10	0	18	7	.720	3	0-0	0	2.35	2.38
1999	LA	NL	35	35	5	0	252.1	1018	210	99	84	19	7	1	7	59	1	221	4	1	18	9	.667	1	0-0	0	2.51	3.00
2000	LA	NL	33	33	5	0	230.0	921	181	76	66	21	13	4	9	47	1	216	4	0	13	6	.684	1	0-0	0	2.30	2.58
2001	LA	NL	20	19	1	0	115.2	465	94	41	34	8	5	0	2	38	2	104	3	1	10	4	.714	0	0-0	0	2.71	2.65
2002	LA	NL	17	10	0	0	63.2	278	68	36	34	9	2	0	5	23	1	58	2	0	3	4	.429	0	0-0	0	4.96	4.81
2003	LA	NL	32	32	0	0	211.0	856	184	67	56	11	12	2	5	56	2	185	5	1	14	9	.609	0	0-0	0	2.68	2.39
2004	NYA	AL	22	22	0	0	132.0	551	132	65	60	14	0	9	3	35	0	83	6	0	10	6	.625	0	0-0	0	3.71	4.09
2005	NYA	AL	13	13	0	0	73.1	346	107	57	53	5	3	3	7	19	1	50	6	0	4	7	.364	0	0-0	0	6.31	6.50
19 ML YEARS			486	476	72	1	3256.1	13542	3079	1357	1185	208	95	64	139	901	42	2397	108	15	211	144	.594	17	0-0	2	3.23	3.28

Jonathan Broxton

Pitches: R Bats: R Pos: RP-14   Ht: 6'4" Wt: 240 Born: 6/16/1984 Age: 22

Year	Team	Lg	G	GS	CG	GF	IP	BFP	H	R	ER	HR	SH	SF	HB	TBB	IBB	SO	WP	Bk	W	L	Pct	ShO	Sv-Op	Hld	ERC	ERA
2002	Gr Falls	R+	11	6	0	2	29.1	126	22	9	9	0	4	0	3	16	0	33	0	0	2	0	1.000	0	2- -	-	2.96	2.76
2003	SoGA	A	9	8	0	0	37.1	161	27	15	13	1	5	3	2	22	0	30	2	2	4	2	.667	0	0- -	-	2.96	3.13
2004	VeroB	A+	23	23	1	0	128.1	538	110	49	46	7	7	4	4	43	0	144	6	0	11	6	.647	1	0- -	-	2.84	3.23
2005	Jaxnvl	AA	33	13	0	15	96.2	400	79	36	34	4	3	2	1	31	0	107	7	0	5	3	.625	0	5- -	-	2.44	3.17
2005	LAN	NL	14	0	0	5	13.2	68	13	11	9	0	2	1	1	12	2	22	2	0	1	0	1.000	0	0-1	1	4.65	5.93

Brian Bruney

Pitches: R Bats: R Pos: RP-47   Ht: 6'3" Wt: 226 Born: 2/17/1982 Age: 24

Year	Team	Lg	G	GS	CG	GF	IP	BFP	H	R	ER	HR	SH	SF	HB	TBB	IBB	SO	WP	Bk	W	L	Pct	ShO	Sv-Op	Hld	ERC	ERA
2000	DBcks	R	20	2	0	11	25.0	131	21	23	18	2	0	1	6	29	0	24	5	1	4	1	.800	0	2- -	-	6.82	6.48
2001	Sbend	A	26	0	0	20	32.2	142	24	19	15	1	2	1	3	19	2	40	3	2	1	4	.200	0	8- -	-	3.05	4.13
2001	Yakima	A-	15	0	0	11	21.0	102	19	14	12	2	3	2	2	11	0	28	7	0	1	2	.333	0	1- -	-	3.93	5.14
2002	Sbend	A	37	0	0	28	48.1	203	37	15	9	1	5	3	2	17	4	54	2	1	4	3	.571	0	10- -	-	2.12	1.68
2002	ElPaso	AA	10	0	0	4	12.1	47	11	5	4	1	0	1	1	4	1	14	1	0	0	2	.000	0	0- -	-	3.66	2.92
2003	ElPaso	AA	28	0	0	25	31.1	140	29	17	9	1	1	1	1	13	2	28	0	1	0	2	.000	0	14- -	-	3.11	2.59
2003	Tucsn	AAA	32	0	0	29	32.0	139	24	12	10	0	2	3	2	18	0	32	2	0	3	1	.750	0	12- -	-	2.82	2.81

Year	Team	Lg	G	GS	CG	GF	IP	BFP	H	R	ER	HR	SH	SF	HB	TBB	IBB	SO	WP	Bk	W	L	Pct	ShO	Sv-Op	Hld	ERC	ERA
2004	Tucsn	AAA	31	0	0	14	38.0	156	18	8	6	1	0	0	2	20	1	42	1	1	2	0	1.000	0	5- -	-	1.56	1.42
2005	Tucsn	AAA	4	0	0	2	4.2	22	3	3	1	0	0	1	1	5	0	3	0	0	1	0	1.000	0	0- -	-	4.73	1.93
2004	ARI	NL	30	0	0	14	31.1	135	20	16	15	2	1	0	1	27	5	34	2	0	3	4	.429	0	0-1	3	3.54	4.31
2005	ARI	NL	47	0	0	21	46.0	230	56	39	38	6	2	1	5	35	2	51	2	0	1	3	.250	0	12-16	4	7.48	7.43
	2 ML YEARS		77	0	0	35	77.1	365	76	55	53	8	3	1	6	62	7	85	4	0	4	7	.364	0	12-17	7	5.80	6.17

Eric Bruntlett

Bats: R **Throws:** R **Pos:** 2B-28; PR-20; PH-17; CF-14; LF-11; SS-10; 3B-8; 1B-1; RF-1   **Ht:** 6'0" **Wt:** 200 **Born:** 3/29/1978 **Age:** 28

Year	Team	Lg	G	AB	H	2B	3B	HR	(Hm	Rd)	TB	R	RBI	RC	TBB	IBB	SO	HBP	SH	SF	SB	CS	SB%	GDP	Avg	OBP	Slg
2003	HOU	NL	31	54	14	3	0	1	(1	0)	20	3	4	5	0	0	10	0	1	1	0	0	-	1	.259	.255	.370
2004	HOU	NL	45	52	13	2	0	4	(3	1)	27	14	8	9	7	0	13	0	0	2	4	0	1.00	0	.250	.328	.519
2005	HOU	NL	91	109	24	5	2	4	(2	2)	45	19	14	12	10	0	25	1	1	0	7	2	.78	4	.220	.292	.413
	3 ML YEARS		167	215	51	10	2	9	(6	3)	92	36	26	26	17	0	48	1	2	3	11	2	.85	5	.237	.292	.428

Jaime Bubela

Bats: L **Throws:** R **Pos:** CF-6; PR-3; LF-1; PH-1   **Ht:** 6'1" **Wt:** 200 **Born:** 6/6/1978 **Age:** 28

Year	Team	Lg	G	AB	H	2B	3B	HR	(Hm	Rd)	TB	R	RBI	RC	TBB	IBB	SO	HBP	SH	SF	SB	CS	SB%	GDP	Avg	OBP	Slg
2000	Lancst	A+	9	29	4	1	0	0	(-	-)	5	6	2	2	5	0	12	1	1	0	4	0	1.00	1	.138	.286	.172
2000	Everett	A-	30	113	26	1	3	1	(-	-)	36	11	13	14	14	1	25	3	1	0	13	3	.81	0	.230	.331	.319
2001	Wisc	A	132	530	161	27	12	6	(-	-)	230	96	68	85	44	4	116	1	1	2	34	13	.72	5	.304	.357	.434
2002	SnBrn	A+	118	462	134	25	10	7	(-	-)	200	69	67	75	40	3	129	4	2	1	30	7	.81	7	.290	.351	.433
2003	SnAnt	AA	128	473	131	29	7	4	(-	-)	186	60	61	63	31	3	108	3	5	4	26	11	.70	4	.277	.323	.393
2004	Ms	R	16	67	23	3	1	2	(-	-)	34	12	12	12	4	0	9	0	0	1	2	1	.67	2	.343	.375	.507
2004	SnAnt	AA	46	166	37	3	0	2	(-	-)	46	13	15	11	8	0	42	2	2	0	2	2	.50	2	.223	.267	.277
2005	SnAnt	AA	130	520	152	20	5	9	(-	-)	209	84	57	78	34	4	118	5	4	2	40	6	.87	12	.292	.340	.402
2005	SEA	AL	11	19	2	0	0	0	(0	0)	2	3	0	0	1	0	4	0	0	0	1	0	1.00	1	.105	.150	.105

John Buck

Bats: R **Throws:** R **Pos:** C-117; PH-1   **Ht:** 6'3" **Wt:** 210 **Born:** 7/7/1980 **Age:** 25

Year	Team	Lg	G	AB	H	2B	3B	HR	(Hm	Rd)	TB	R	RBI	RC	TBB	IBB	SO	HBP	SH	SF	SB	CS	SB%	GDP	Avg	OBP	Slg
1998	Astros	R	36	126	36	9	0	3	(-	-)	54	24	15	19	13	0	22	2	1	0	2	2	.50	0	.286	.362	.429
1999	Auburn	A-	63	233	57	17	0	3	(-	-)	83	36	29	27	25	1	48	5	1	2	7	1	.88	7	.245	.328	.356
1999	Mich	A	4	10	1	1	0	0	(-	-)	2	1	0	0	2	0	3	0	0	0	0	0	-	0	.100	.250	.200
2000	Mich	A	109	390	110	33	0	10	(-	-)	173	57	71	63	55	6	81	5	0	5	2	4	.33	8	.282	.374	.444
2001	Lxngtn	A	122	443	122	24	1	22	(-	-)	214	72	73	69	37	0	84	12	2	4	4	9	.31	8	.275	.345	.483
2002	RdRck	AA	120	448	118	29	3	12	(-	-)	189	48	89	56	31	1	93	6	0	9	2	3	.40	11	.263	.314	.422
2003	NewOrl	AAA	78	274	70	18	2	2	(-	-)	98	32	39	26	14	0	53	4	1	0	1	0	1.00	11	.255	.301	.358
2004	NewOrl	AAA	65	227	68	11	0	12	(-	-)	115	31	35	37	21	2	39	4	1	1	0	1	.00	13	.300	.368	.507
2004	KC	AL	71	238	56	9	0	12	(6	6)	101	36	30	26	15	0	79	0	4	1	1	1	.50	8	.235	.280	.424
2005	KC	AL	118	401	97	21	1	12	(3	9)	156	40	47	43	23	2	94	3	1	2	2	2	.50	9	.242	.287	.389
	2 ML YEARS		189	639	153	30	1	24	(9	15)	257	76	77	69	38	2	173	3	5	3	3	3	.50	15	.239	.284	.402

Mark Buehrle

Pitches: L **Bats:** L **Pos:** SP-33   **Ht:** 6'2" **Wt:** 200 **Born:** 3/23/1979 **Age:** 27

Year	Team	Lg	G	GS	CG	GF	IP	BFP	H	R	ER	HR	SH	SF	HB	TBB	IBB	SO	WP	Bk	W	L	Pct	ShO	Sv-Op	Hld	ERC	ERA
2000	CHA	AL	28	3	0	6	51.1	225	55	27	24	5	1	0	3	19	1	37	0	0	4	1	.800	0	0-2	3	4.56	4.21
2001	CHA	AL	32	32	4	0	221.1	885	188	89	81	24	9	4	8	48	2	126	1	5	16	8	.667	2	0-0	0	2.79	3.29
2002	CHA	AL	34	34	5	0	239.0	984	236	102	95	25	9	3	3	61	7	134	6	1	19	12	.613	2	0-0	0	3.53	3.58
2003	CHA	AL	35	35	2	0	230.1	978	250	124	106	22	7	7	5	61	2	119	1	0	14	14	.500	0	0-0	0	4.10	4.14
2004	CHA	AL	35	35	4	0	245.1	1016	257	119	106	33	4	6	8	51	2	165	0	0	16	10	.615	1	0-0	0	4.00	3.89
2005	CHA	AL	33	33	3	0	236.2	971	240	99	82	20	7	4	4	40	4	149	2	2	16	8	.667	1	0-0	0	3.21	3.12
	6 ML YEARS		197	172	18	6	1224.0	5059	1226	560	494	129	37	24	31	280	18	730	10	8	85	53	.616	6	0-2	3	3.57	3.63

Ryan Bukvich

Pitches: R **Bats:** R **Pos:** RP-4   **Ht:** 6'3" **Wt:** 237 **Born:** 5/13/1978 **Age:** 28

Year	Team	Lg	G	GS	CG	GF	IP	BFP	H	R	ER	HR	SH	SF	HB	TBB	IBB	SO	WP	Bk	W	L	Pct	ShO	Sv-Op	Hld	ERC	ERA
2002	KC	AL	26	0	0	2	25.0	121	26	19	17	2	4	3	1	19	3	20	1	0	1	0	1.000	0	0-1	5	5.39	6.12
2003	KC	AL	9	0	0	2	10.1	52	12	11	11	2	1	1	0	9	0	8	1	0	1	0	1.000	0	0-0	0	7.65	9.58
2004	KC	AL	9	0	0	6	7.1	30	4	3	3	0	1	0	0	7	0	7	0	0	0	0	-	0	1-1	1	3.21	3.68
2005	TEX	AL	4	0	0	4	4.0	19	2	5	5	0	1	0	0	6	0	4	0	0	0	0	-	0	0-0	1	4.74	11.25
	4 ML YEARS		48	0	0	14	46.2	222	44	38	36	4	7	4	1	41	3	39	2	0	2	0	1.000	0	1-2	7	5.47	6.94

Jason Bulger

Pitches: R Bats: R Pos: RP-9   Ht: 6'4" Wt: 215 Born: 12/6/1978 Age: 27

		HOW MUCH HE PITCHED						WHAT HE GAVE UP												THE RESULTS						
Year	Team	Lg	G	GS	CG	GF	IP	BFP	H	R	ER	HR	SH	SF	HB	TBB	IBB	SO	WP	Bk	W	L	Pct	ShO	Sv-Op	Hld	ERC	ERA
2002	Lancst	A+	2	2	0	0	10.0	44	11	7	6	0	2	1	1	3	0	12	0	1	1	1	.500	0	0--	-	4.88	5.40
2002	Sbend	A	20	20	1	0	94.2	434	111	65	52	5	3	8	7	39	0	84	14	0	4	9	.308	0	0--	-	5.01	4.94
2003	Lancst	A+	4	4	0	0	17.1	80	23	13	13	3	7	6	3	5	0	20	0	0	2	1	.667	0	0--	-	6.98	6.75
2004	Lancst	A+	21	0	0	18	23.2	95	14	4	4	0	0	0	3	10	1	31	0	0	0	1	.000	0	11--	-	1.86	1.52
2004	ElPaso	AA	24	0	0	22	25.1	119	24	12	11	0	0	0	2	19	2	25	7	0	0	3	.000	0	8--	-	4.47	3.91
2005	Tucsn	AAA	56	0	0	18	56.0	245	50	28	22	3	3	3	2	27	1	55	3	1	3	6	.333	0	4--	-	3.53	3.54
2005	ARI	NL	9	0	0	5	10.0	48	14	6	6	1	1	0	0	5	1	9	0	0	1	0	1.000	0	0-0	0	6.68	5.40

Bryan Bullington

Pitches: R Bats: R Pos: RP-1   Ht: 6'4" Wt: 222 Born: 9/30/1980 Age: 25

		HOW MUCH HE PITCHED						WHAT HE GAVE UP												THE RESULTS						
Year	Team	Lg	G	GS	CG	GF	IP	BFP	H	R	ER	HR	SH	SF	HB	TBB	IBB	SO	WP	Bk	W	L	Pct	ShO	Sv-Op	Hld	ERC	ERA
2003	Lynbrg	A+	17	17	2	0	97.1	428	101	39	33	5	4	2	8	27	0	67	3	0	8	4	.667	1	0--	-	3.69	3.05
2003	Hickory	A	8	7	0	1	45.1	172	25	10	7	3	3	2	0	11	0	46	1	0	5	1	.833	0	0--	-	1.29	1.39
2004	Altna	AA	26	26	0	0	145.0	642	160	77	66	18	10	9	9	47	1	100	5	0	12	7	.632	0	0--	-	4.73	4.10
2005	Indy	AAA	18	18	1	0	109.1	458	104	48	41	11	10	2	4	26	1	82	0	0	9	5	.643	0	0--	-	3.28	3.38
2005	PIT	NL	1	0	0	0	1.1	7	1	2	2	0	0	1	0	1	0	1	0	0	0	0	-	0	0-0	0	5.91	13.50

Nate Bump

Pitches: R Bats: L Pos: RP-31   Ht: 6'2" Wt: 185 Born: 7/24/1976 Age: 29

		HOW MUCH HE PITCHED						WHAT HE GAVE UP												THE RESULTS						
Year	Team	Lg	G	GS	CG	GF	IP	BFP	H	R	ER	HR	SH	SF	HB	TBB	IBB	SO	WP	Bk	W	L	Pct	ShO	Sv-Op	Hld	ERC	ERA
2005	Albq*	AAA	1	1	0	0	5.0	19	4	1	1	0	0	0	0	0	0	6	0	0	1	0	1.000	0	0--	-	1.27	1.80
2003	FLA	NL	32	0	0	8	36.1	167	34	21	19	3	1	1	7	20	0	17	0	0	4	0	1.000	0	0-0	6	4.91	4.71
2004	FLA	NL	50	2	0	13	73.2	329	86	46	41	7	2	2	3	32	8	44	2	0	2	4	.333	0	1-4	5	5.20	5.01
2005	FLA	NL	31	0	0	2	38.0	165	43	18	17	5	2	0	2	12	1	18	0	0	0	3	.000	0	0-1	2	4.96	4.03
	3 ML YEARS		113	2	0	23	148.0	661	163	85	77	15	5	3	12	64	9	79	2	0	6	7	.462	0	1-5	13	5.07	4.68

Ambiorix Burgos

Pitches: R Bats: R Pos: RP-59   Ht: 6'3" Wt: 235 Born: 4/19/1984 Age: 22

		HOW MUCH HE PITCHED						WHAT HE GAVE UP												THE RESULTS						
Year	Team	Lg	G	GS	CG	GF	IP	BFP	H	R	ER	HR	SH	SF	HB	TBB	IBB	SO	WP	Bk	W	L	Pct	ShO	Sv-Op	Hld	ERC	ERA
2003	Royals	R	9	7	0	1	36.0	161	37	22	16	1	0	1	3	16	0	43	8	1	3	2	.600	0	0--	-	4.17	4.00
2003	Burlgtn	A	2	2	0	0	5.0	24	3	3	3	1	4	8	0	6	0	4	1	0	0	0	-	0	0--	-	5.62	5.40
2004	Burlgtn	A	27	26	0	0	133.2	585	109	70	65	13	6	5	13	75	1	172	13	4	7	11	.389	0	0--	-	4.03	4.38
2005	Wichta	AA	12	0	0	6	12.2	54	8	7	7	1	0	0	1	8	0	19	2	0	1	1	.500	0	1--	-	3.11	4.97
2005	KC	AL	59	0	0	17	63.1	278	60	29	28	6	2	1	5	31	1	65	8	2	3	5	.375	0	2-6	11	4.41	3.98

Chris Burke

Bats: R Throws: R Pos: LF-83; 2B-18; PH-15; CF-6; PR-3   Ht: 5'11" Wt: 180 Born: 3/11/1980 Age: 26

							BATTING															BASERUNNING				AVERAGES		
Year	Team	Lg	G	AB	H	2B	3B	HR	(Hm	Rd)	TB	R	RBI	RC	TBB	IBB	SO	HBP	SH	SF	SB	CS	SB%	GDP	Avg	OBP	Slg
2001	Mich	A	56	233	70	11	6	3	(-	-)	102	47	17	40	26	2	31	3	2	1	21	8	.72	3	.300	.376	.438
2002	RdRck	AA	136	481	127	19	8	3	(-	-)	171	66	37	56	39	3	61	10	5	3	16	15	.52	8	.264	.330	.356
2003	RdRck	AA	137	549	165	23	8	3	(-	-)	213	88	41	89	57	1	57	14	11	2	34	10	.77	8	.301	.379	.388
2004	NewOrl	AAA	123	483	152	33	6	16	(-	-)	245	93	52	96	55	2	76	13	4	5	37	14	.73	7	.315	.396	.507
2005	RdRck	AAA	22	90	28	6	2	2	(-	-)	44	15	11	18	8	0	13	2	2	0	9	0	1.00	3	.311	.380	.489
2004	HOU	NL	17	17	1	0	0	0	(0	0)	1	2	0	0	3	0	3	0	0	0	0	0	-	0	.059	.200	.059
2005	HOU	NL	108	318	79	19	2	5	(2	3)	117	49	26	35	23	0	62	6	9	3	11	6	.65	7	.248	.309	.368
	2 ML YEARS		125	335	80	19	2	5	(2	3)	118	51	26	35	26	0	65	6	9	3	11	6	.65	7	.239	.303	.352

Jamie Burke

Bats: R Throws: R Pos: 1B-1; PH-1   Ht: 6'0" Wt: 195 Born: 9/24/1971 Age: 34

							BATTING															BASERUNNING				AVERAGES		
Year	Team	Lg	G	AB	H	2B	3B	HR	(Hm	Rd)	TB	R	RBI	RC	TBB	IBB	SO	HBP	SH	SF	SB	CS	SB%	GDP	Avg	OBP	Slg
2005	Charltt*	AAA	102	358	95	22	1	10	(-	-)	149	50	53	55	36	0	53	13	3	4	1	3	.25	12	.265	.350	.416
2001	ANA	AL	9	5	1	0	0	0	(0	0)	1	1	0	0	0	0	2	0	0	0	0	0	-	0	.200	.200	.200
2003	CHA	AL	6	8	3	0	0	0	(0	0)	3	0	2	2	0	0	0	0	0	0	0	0	-	0	.375	.375	.375
2004	CHA	AL	57	120	40	9	0	0	(0	0)	49	22	15	21	10	0	13	1	1	1	0	0	-	3	.333	.386	.408
2005	CHA	AL	1	1	0	0	0	0	(0	0)	0	0	0	0	0	0	0	0	0	0	0	0	-	0	.000	.000	.000
	4 ML YEARS		73	134	44	9	0	0	(0	0)	53	23	17	23	10	0	15	1	1	1	0	0	-	3	.328	.377	.396

A.J. Burnett

Pitches: R Bats: R Pos: SP-32   Ht: 6'4" Wt: 229 Born: 1/3/1977 Age: 29

		HOW MUCH HE PITCHED						WHAT HE GAVE UP												THE RESULTS						
Year	Team	Lg	G	GS	CG	GF	IP	BFP	H	R	ER	HR	SH	SF	HB	TBB	IBB	SO	WP	Bk	W	L	Pct	ShO	Sv-Op	Hld	ERC	ERA
1999	FLA	NL	7	7	0	0	41.1	182	37	23	16	3	1	3	0	25	2	33	0	0	4	2	.667	0	0-0	0	4.00	3.48
2000	FLA	NL	13	13	0	0	82.2	364	80	46	44	8	6	3	2	44	3	57	2	0	3	7	.300	0	0-0	0	4.45	4.79
2001	FLA	NL	27	27	2	0	173.1	733	145	82	78	20	6	8	7	83	3	128	7	1	11	12	.478	1	0-0	0	3.76	4.05
2002	FLA	NL	31	29	7	0	204.1	844	153	84	75	12	9	4	9	90	5	203	14	0	12	9	.571	5	0-1	0	2.77	3.30
2003	FLA	NL	4	4	0	0	23.0	106	18	13	12	2	4	1	2	18	2	21	2	0	0	2	.000	0	0-0	0	4.36	4.70

Year	Team	Lg	G	GS	CG	GF	IP	BFP	H	R	ER	HR	SH	SF	HB	TBB	IBB	SO	WP	Bk	W	L	Pct	ShO	Sv-Op	Hld	ERC	ERA
2004	FLA	NL	20	19	1	0	120.0	490	102	50	49	9	3	3	4	38	0	113	7	0	7	6	.538	0	0-0	-	2.95	3.68
2005	FLA	NL	32	32	1	0	209.0	873	184	97	80	12	7	5	7	79	1	198	12	0	12	12	.500	2	0-0	-	3.20	3.44
	7 ML YEARS		134	131	14	0	853.2	3592	719	395	354	66	34	27	31	377	16	753	44	1	49	50	.495	8	0-1	0	3.36	3.73

Sean Burnett

Pitches: L **Bats:** L **Pos:** P **Ht:** 5'11" **Wt:** 190 **Born:** 9/17/1982 **Age:** 23

			HOW MUCH HE PITCHED						WHAT HE GAVE UP												THE RESULTS							
Year	Team	Lg	G	GS	CG	GF	IP	BFP	H	R	ER	HR	SH	SF	HB	TBB	IBB	SO	WP	Bk	W	L	Pct	ShO	Sv-Op	Hld	ERC	ERA
2000	Pirates	R	8	6	0	1	31.0	128	31	17	14	0	0	1	0	3	0	24	2	1	2	1	.667	0	0--	-	2.24	4.06
2001	Hickory	A	26	26	1	0	161.0	667	164	63	47	11	6	5	4	33	0	134	7	1	11	8	.579	0	0--	-	3.33	2.63
2002	Lynbrg	A+	26	26	2	0	155.1	605	118	46	31	4	5	5	1	33	0	96	3	1	13	4	.765	0	0--	-	1.78	1.80
2003	Altna	AA	27	27	2	0	159.2	649	158	60	57	2	8	9	7	29	1	86	10	0	14	6	.700	1	0--	-	2.83	3.21
2004	Nashv	AAA	10	10	0	0	47.0	205	58	29	28	5	2	3	2	17	2	25	1	0	1	5	.167	0	0--	-	5.66	5.36
2004	PIT	NL	13	13	1	0	71.2	318	86	41	40	9	2	1	1	28	2	30	2	0	5	5	.500	1	0-0	0	5.49	5.02

Jeromy Burnitz

Bats: L **Throws:** R **Pos:** RF-158; CF-3; PH-2 **Ht:** 6'0" **Wt:** 213 **Born:** 4/15/1969 **Age:** 37

			BATTING																			BASERUNNING				AVERAGES		
Year	Team	Lg	G	AB	H	2B	3B	HR	(Hm	Rd)	TB	R	RBI	RC	TBB	IBB	SO	HBP	SH	SF	SB	CS	SB%	GDP	Avg	OBP	Slg
1993	NYN	NL	86	263	64	10	6	13	(6	7)	125	49	38	42	38	4	66	1	2	2	3	6	.33	2	.243	.339	.475
1994	NYN	NL	45	143	34	4	0	3	(2	1)	47	26	15	17	23	0	45	1	1	0	1	1	.50	2	.238	.347	.329
1995	CLE	AL	9	7	4	1	0	0	(0	0)	5	4	0	2	0	0	0	0	0	0	0	0	-	0	.571	.571	.714
1996	2 Tms		94	200	53	14	0	9	(5	4)	94	38	40	37	33	2	47	4	0	2	4	1	.80	4	.265	.377	.470
1997	MIL	AL	153	494	139	37	8	27	(18	9)	273	85	85	100	75	8	111	5	3	0	20	13	.61	8	.281	.382	.553
1998	MIL	NL	161	609	160	28	1	38	(17	21)	304	92	125	102	70	7	158	4	1	7	7	4	.64	9	.263	.339	.499
1999	MIL	NL	130	467	126	33	2	33	(12	21)	262	87	103	104	91	7	124	16	0	6	7	3	.70	11	.270	.402	.561
2000	MIL	NL	161	564	131	29	2	31	(12	19)	257	91	98	94	99	10	121	14	0	9	6	4	.60	12	.232	.356	.456
2001	MIL	NL	154	562	141	32	4	34	(16	18)	283	104	100	97	80	9	150	5	0	4	0	4	.00	8	.251	.347	.504
2002	NYN	NL	154	479	103	15	0	19	(12	7)	175	65	54	48	58	5	135	10	1	2	10	7	.59	11	.215	.311	.365
2003	2 Tms		126	464	111	22	0	31	(10	21)	226	63	77	61	35	9	112	5	1	4	5	4	.56	5	.239	.299	.487
2004	COL	NL	150	540	153	30	4	37	(24	13)	302	94	110	99	58	7	124	5	0	3	5	6	.45	7	.283	.356	.559
2005	CHN	NL	160	605	156	31	2	24	(17	7)	263	84	87	79	57	3	109	3	1	5	5	4	.56	12	.258	.322	.435
96	Cle	AL	71	128	36	10	0	7	(4	3)	67	30	26	27	25	1	31	2	0	0	2	1	.67	3	.281	.406	.523
96	Mil	AL	23	72	17	4	0	2	(1	1)	27	8	14	10	8	1	16	2	0	2	2	0	1.00	1	.236	.321	.375
03	NYM	NL	65	234	64	18	0	18	(4	14)	136	38	45	41	21	6	55	4	0	1	4	2	.20	4	.274	.344	.581
03	LA	NL	61	230	47	4	0	13	(6	7)	90	25	32	20	14	3	57	1	0	1	4	0	1.00	1	.204	.252	.391
	13 ML YEARS		1583	5397	1375	286	29	299	(151	148)	2616	882	932	882	717	71	1302	73	9	41	73	57	.56	91	.255	.348	.485

Mike Burns

Pitches: R **Bats:** R **Pos:** RP-27 **Ht:** 6'1" **Wt:** 205 **Born:** 7/14/1978 **Age:** 27

			HOW MUCH HE PITCHED						WHAT HE GAVE UP												THE RESULTS							
Year	Team	Lg	G	GS	CG	GF	IP	BFP	H	R	ER	HR	SH	SF	HB	TBB	IBB	SO	WP	Bk	W	L	Pct	ShO	Sv-Op	Hld	ERC	ERA
2000	Mrtnsvl	R+	12	12	0	0	65.2	281	75	52	33	12	4	2	4	9	0	51	2	1	2	7	.222	0	0--	-	4.61	4.52
2001	Mich	A	29	21	1	3	132.0	554	131	67	58	10	4	5	13	27	0	108	0	1	7	7	.500	0	1--	-	3.50	3.95
2002	Mich	A	28	28	3	0	181.0	718	146	59	50	12	5	3	7	29	1	126	8	2	14	9	.609	2	0--	-	2.11	2.49
2003	RdRck	AA	38	14	0	9	105.2	476	129	80	72	15	4	3	4	30	3	89	4	0	2	13	.133	0	0--	-	5.22	6.13
2004	RdRck	AA	56	0	0	35	80.2	320	63	18	15	1	0	0	4	15	3	94	1	0	11	3	.786	0	9--	-	1.78	1.67
2005	RdRck	AAA	25	0	0	24	30.0	116	22	7	7	4	1	0	0	4	0	34	2	0	2	1	.667	0	13--	-	1.90	2.10
2005	HOU	NL	27	0	0	10	31.0	136	29	18	17	6	1	0	5	8	1	20	1	0	0	0	-	0	0-0	1	4.26	4.94

Pat Burrell

Bats: R **Throws:** R **Pos:** LF-153; PH-1 **Ht:** 6'4" **Wt:** 222 **Born:** 10/10/1976 **Age:** 29

			BATTING																			BASERUNNING				AVERAGES		
Year	Team	Lg	G	AB	H	2B	3B	HR	(Hm	Rd)	TB	R	RBI	RC	TBB	IBB	SO	HBP	SH	SF	SB	CS	SB%	GDP	Avg	OBP	Slg
2000	PHI	NL	111	408	106	27	1	18	(7	11)	189	57	79	69	63	2	139	1	0	2	0	0	-	5	.260	.359	.463
2001	PHI	NL	155	539	139	29	2	27	(10	17)	253	70	89	86	70	7	162	5	0	4	2	1	.67	12	.258	.346	.469
2002	PHI	NL	157	586	165	39	2	37	(18	19)	319	96	116	104	89	9	153	3	0	6	1	0	1.00	16	.282	.376	.544
2003	PHI	NL	146	522	109	31	4	21	(9	12)	211	57	64	57	72	2	142	4	0	1	0	0	-	18	.209	.309	.404
2004	PHI	NL	127	448	115	17	0	24	(14	10)	204	66	84	72	78	7	130	2	0	6	2	0	1.00	10	.257	.365	.455
2005	PHI	NL	154	562	158	27	1	32	(20	12)	283	78	117	109	99	6	160	3	0	5	0	0	-	12	.281	.389	.504
	6 ML YEARS		850	3065	792	170	10	159	(78	81)	1459	424	549	497	471	33	886	18	0	24	5	1	.83	73	.258	.358	.476

Sean Burroughs

Bats: L **Throws:** R **Pos:** 3B-78; PH-16; SS-1 **Ht:** 6'2" **Wt:** 200 **Born:** 9/12/1980 **Age:** 25

			BATTING																			BASERUNNING				AVERAGES		
Year	Team	Lg	G	AB	H	2B	3B	HR	(Hm	Rd)	TB	R	RBI	RC	TBB	IBB	SO	HBP	SH	SF	SB	CS	SB%	GDP	Avg	OBP	Slg
2005	Portlnd*	AAA	32	124	36	8	0	3	(-	-)	53	21	14	20	9	0	15	5	0	0	0	0	-	5	.290	.362	.427
2002	SD	NL	63	192	52	5	1	1	(0	1)	62	18	11	15	12	1	30	1	1	0	2	0	1.00	6	.271	.317	.323
2003	SD	NL	146	517	148	27	6	7	(2	5)	208	62	58	68	44	4	75	11	2	4	7	2	.78	13	.286	.352	.402
2004	SD	NL	130	523	156	23	3	2	(0	2)	191	76	47	70	31	4	52	9	1	0	5	4	.56	6	.298	.348	.365
2005	SD	NL	93	284	71	7	2	1	(1	0)	85	20	17	24	24	4	41	5	3	1	4	0	1.00	7	.250	.318	.299
	4 ML YEARS		432	1516	427	62	12	11	(3	8)	546	176	133	177	111	13	198	26	7	5	18	6	.75	32	.282	.340	.360

Dave Bush

Pitches: R **Bats:** R **Pos:** SP-24; RP-1   **Ht:** 6'2" **Wt:** 212 **Born:** 11/9/1979 **Age:** 26

			HOW MUCH HE PITCHED						WHAT HE GAVE UP													THE RESULTS						
Year	Team	Lg	G	GS	CG	GF	IP	BFP	H	R	ER	HR	SH	SF	HB	TBB	IBB	SO	WP	Bk	W	L	Pct	ShO	Sv-Op	Hld	ERC	ERA
2002	Auburn	A-	18	0	0	17	22.1	91	13	9	7	1	0	0	2	7	2	39	0	0	1	1	.500	0	10--	-	1.53	2.82
2002	Dnedin	A+	7	0	0	1	13.1	49	10	3	3	1	1	0	1	2	0	9	1	1	0	1	.000	0	0--	-	2.18	2.03
2003	Dnedin	A+	14	14	0	0	77.0	310	64	29	24	6	3	3	7	9	0	75	4	0	7	3	.700	0	0--	-	2.31	2.81
2003	NwHav	AA	14	14	1	0	81.0	333	73	26	25	4	3	2	4	19	1	73	2	0	7	3	.700	0	0--	-	2.76	2.78
2004	Syrcse	AAA	16	16	2	0	99.2	426	108	52	45	7	7	5	6	20	1	88	4	1	6	6	.500	1	0--	-	3.75	4.06
2005	Syrcse	AAA	9	9	0	0	55.0	239	65	28	27	6	2	1	2	9	0	40	1	0	2	2	.500	0	0--	-	4.30	4.42
2004	TOR	AL	16	16	0	0	97.2	412	95	47	40	11	4	4	6	25	2	64	3	0	5	4	.556	1	0-0	0	3.65	3.69
2005	TOR	AL	25	24	2	1	136.1	575	142	73	68	20	3	2	13	29	3	75	2	0	5	11	.313	0	0-0	0	4.28	4.49
2 ML YEARS			41	40	3	1	234.0	987	237	120	108	31	7	6	19	54	5	139	5	0	10	15	.400	1	0-0	0	4.01	4.15

Freddie Bynum

Bats: L **Throws:** R **Pos:** 2B-3; PH-2; PR-2; LF-1; CF-1   **Ht:** 6'1" **Wt:** 180 **Born:** 3/15/1980 **Age:** 26

			BATTING																	BASERUNNING				AVERAGES		
Year	Team	Lg	G	AB	H	2B	3B	HR	(Hm	Rd)	TB	R	RBI	RC	TBB	IBB	SO	HBP	SH	SF	SB	CS	SB%	GDP	Avg	OBP	Slg
2000	Vancvr	A-	72	281	72	10	1	1	(-	-)	87	52	26	32	31	0	58	5	3	0	22	12	.65	3	.256	.341	.310
2001	Mdest	A+	120	440	115	19	7	2	(-	-)	154	59	46	54	41	0	95	1	4	1	28	11	.72	8	.261	.325	.350
2002	Visalia	A+	135	539	165	26	5	3	(-	-)	210	83	56	87	64	1	116	7	15	3	41	21	.66	9	.306	.385	.390
2003	Mdland	AA	132	510	134	18	9	5	(-	-)	185	84	58	70	56	4	135	8	12	2	22	8	.73	6	.263	.344	.363
2004	Mdland	AA	65	265	71	13	4	1	(-	-)	95	38	22	34	24	0	56	2	5	1	18	7	.72	1	.268	.332	.358
2004	Scrmto	AAA	66	258	73	11	2	2	(-	-)	94	42	26	36	19	0	61	3	11	0	21	4	.84	8	.283	.339	.364
2005	Scrmto	AAA	102	378	105	16	9	2	(-	-)	145	56	40	55	38	1	83	3	7	2	23	7	.77	3	.278	.347	.384
2005	OAK	AL	7	7	2	1	0	0	(0	0)	3	0	1	1	0	0	3	0	0	0	0	0	-	0	.286	.286	.429

Marlon Byrd

Bats: R **Throws:** R **Pos:** LF-54; CF-16; PH-13; RF-4; DH-2; PR-2   **Ht:** 6'0" **Wt:** 225 **Born:** 8/30/1977 **Age:** 28

			BATTING																	BASERUNNING				AVERAGES		
Year	Team	Lg	G	AB	H	2B	3B	HR	(Hm	Rd)	TB	R	RBI	RC	TBB	IBB	SO	HBP	SH	SF	SB	CS	SB%	GDP	Avg	OBP	Slg
2005	S-WB*	AAA	5	19	7	1	0	3	(-	-)	17	4	5	5	0	0	3	0	0	0	0	0	-	0	.368	.368	.895
2005	NewOr*	AAA	21	81	33	6	0	5	(-	-)	54	19	11	23	9	0	7	2	0	0	4	1	.80	6	.407	.478	.667
2002	PHI	NL	10	35	8	2	0	1	(1	0)	13	2	1	0	1	0	8	0	0	0	0	2	.00	0	.229	.250	.371
2003	PHI	NL	135	495	150	28	4	7	(3	4)	207	86	45	72	44	3	94	7	4	3	11	1	.92	8	.303	.366	.418
2004	PHI	NL	106	346	79	13	2	5	(3	2)	111	48	33	35	22	1	68	7	2	1	2	2	.50	10	.228	.287	.321
2005	2 Tms		79	229	61	15	2	2	(0	2)	86	20	26	30	19	1	50	2	5	4	5	1	.83	5	.266	.323	.376
05	Phi	NL	5	13	4	0	0	0	(0	0)	4	0	0	2	1	0	3	1	0	0	0	0	-	0	.308	.400	.308
05	Was	NL	74	216	57	15	2	2	(0	2)	82	20	26	28	18	1	47	1	5	4	5	1	.83	5	.264	.318	.380
4 ML YEARS			330	1105	298	58	8	15	(7	8)	417	156	105	137	86	5	220	16	11	8	18	6	.75	23	.270	.329	.377

Paul Byrd

Pitches: R **Bats:** R **Pos:** SP-31   **Ht:** 6'1" **Wt:** 185 **Born:** 12/3/1970 **Age:** 35

			HOW MUCH HE PITCHED						WHAT HE GAVE UP													THE RESULTS						
Year	Team	Lg	G	GS	CG	GF	IP	BFP	H	R	ER	HR	SH	SF	HB	TBB	IBB	SO	WP	Bk	W	L	Pct	ShO	Sv-Op	Hld	ERC	ERA
1995	NYN	NL	17	0	0	6	22.0	91	18	6	5	1	0	2	1	7	1	26	1	2	2	0	1.000	0	0-0	3	2.53	2.05
1996	NYN	NL	38	0	0	14	46.2	204	48	22	22	7	1	1	0	21	4	31	3	0	1	2	.333	0	0-2	3	4.67	4.24
1997	ATL	NL	31	4	0	9	53.0	236	47	34	31	6	2	2	4	28	4	37	3	1	4	4	.500	0	0-0	1	4.15	5.26
1998	2 Tms		9	8	2	0	57.0	233	45	19	17	6	2	1	0	18	1	39	2	0	5	2	.714	0	0-0	0	2.62	2.68
1999	PHI	NL	32	32	1	0	199.2	872	205	119	102	34	5	6	17	70	2	106	11	3	15	11	.577	0	0-0	0	4.87	4.60
2000	PHI	NL	17	15	0	0	83.0	371	89	67	60	17	3	1	3	35	2	53	1	0	2	9	.182	0	0-0	0	5.42	6.51
2001	2 Tms		19	16	1	1	103.1	444	120	54	51	12	4	6	2	26	1	52	2	0	6	7	.462	0	0-0	0	4.62	4.44
2002	KC	AL	33	33	7	0	228.1	935	224	111	99	36	2	13	7	38	1	129	3	1	17	11	.607	2	0-0	0	3.55	3.90
2004	ATL	NL	19	19	0	0	114.1	482	123	57	50	18	3	3	3	19	0	79	1	0	8	7	.533	0	0-0	0	3.98	3.94
2005	LAA	AL	31	31	2	0	204.1	842	216	95	85	22	7	7	7	28	1	102	1	0	12	11	.522	0	0-0	0	3.56	3.74
98	Atl	NL	1	0	0	0	2.0	11	4	3	3	0	0	0	0	1	0	1	0	0	0	0	-	0	0-0	0	9.72	13.50
98	Phi	NL	8	8	2	0	55.0	222	41	16	14	6	2	1	0	17	1	38	2	0	5	2	.714	1	0-0	0	2.41	2.29
01	Phi	NL	3	1	0	1	10.0	45	10	9	9	1	2	2	1	4	0	3	1	0	0	1	.000	0	0-0	0	4.36	8.10
01	KC	AL	16	15	1	0	93.1	399	110	45	42	11	2	4	1	22	1	49	1	0	6	6	.500	0	0-0	0	4.65	4.05
10 ML YEARS			246	158	13	30	1111.2	4710	1135	584	522	159	29	42	43	290	17	654	28	7	72	64	.529	4	0-2	7	4.07	4.23

Tim Byrdak

Pitches: L **Bats:** L **Pos:** RP-41   **Ht:** 5'11" **Wt:** 190 **Born:** 10/31/1973 **Age:** 32

			HOW MUCH HE PITCHED						WHAT HE GAVE UP													THE RESULTS						
Year	Team	Lg	G	GS	CG	GF	IP	BFP	H	R	ER	HR	SH	SF	HB	TBB	IBB	SO	WP	Bk	W	L	Pct	ShO	Sv-Op	Hld	ERC	ERA
2005	Ottawa*	AAA	37	0	0	25	38.2	154	23	12	9	4	0	0	3	15	1	44	1	0	3	2	.600	0	11--	-	2.23	2.09
1998	KC	AL	3	0	0	0	1.2	9	5	1	1	1	0	0	0	0	0	0	0	0	0	0	-	0	0-0	0	23.52	5.40
1999	KC	AL	33	0	0	5	24.2	128	32	24	21	5	3	0	1	20	2	17	3	1	0	3	.000	0	1-4	10	8.29	7.66
2000	KC	AL	12	0	0	1	6.1	34	11	8	8	3	0	0	0	4	0	8	1	0	0	1	.000	0	0-2	3	13.14	11.37
2005	BAL	AL	41	0	0	3	26.2	131	27	14	12	1	2	1	1	21	1	31	5	0	0	1	.000	0	1-1	11	5.04	4.05
4 ML YEARS			89	0	0	9	59.1	302	75	47	42	10	5	1	2	45	3	57	9	1	0	5	.000	0	2-7	24	7.58	6.37

Eric Byrnes

Bats: R **Throws:** R **Pos:** LF-106; RF-13; CF-7; PH-5; DH-4; PR-3   **Ht:** 6'2" **Wt:** 210 **Born:** 2/16/1976 **Age:** 30

Year	Team	Lg	G	AB	H	2B	3B	HR	(Hm	Rd)	TB	R	RBI	RC	TBB	IBB	SO	HBP	SH	SF	SB	CS	SB%	GDP	Avg	OBP	Slg
2000	OAK	AL	10	10	3	0	0	0	(0	0)	3	5	0	1	0	0	1	1	0	0	2	1	.67	0	.300	.364	.300
2001	OAK	AL	19	38	9	1	0	3	(2	1)	19	9	5	7	4	0	6	1	0	0	1	0	1.00	0	.237	.326	.500
2002	OAK	AL	90	94	23	4	2	3	(2	1)	40	24	11	10	4	0	17	3	1	2	3	0	1.00	3	.245	.291	.426
2003	OAK	AL	121	414	109	27	9	12	(7	5)	190	64	51	68	42	4	71	2	0	2	10	2	.83	3	.263	.333	.459
2004	OAK	AL	143	569	161	39	3	20	(10	10)	266	91	73	87	46	0	111	12	0	5	17	1	.94	11	.283	.347	.467
2005	3 Tms		126	412	93	24	3	10	(5	5)	153	49	40	41	32	0	71	8	3	1	7	2	.78	7	.226	.294	.371
05	Oak	AL	59	192	51	15	2	7	(3	4)	91	30	24	29	14	0	27	7	1	1	2	2	.50	1	.266	.336	.474
05	Col	NL	15	53	10	2	0	0	(0	0)	12	2	5	4	7	0	11	0	0	0	2	0	1.00	1	.189	.283	.226
05	Bal	AL	52	167	32	7	1	3	(2	1)	50	17	11	8	11	0	33	1	2	0	3	0	1.00	5	.192	.246	.299
	6 ML YEARS		509	1537	398	95	17	48	(26	22)	671	242	180	214	128	4	277	27	4	10	40	6	.87	24	.259	.325	.437

Daniel Cabrera

Pitches: R **Bats:** R **Pos:** SP-29   **Ht:** 6'5" **Wt:** 230 **Born:** 5/28/1981 **Age:** 25

Year	Team	Lg	G	GS	CG	GF	IP	BFP	H	R	ER	HR	SH	SF	HB	TBB	IBB	SO	WP	Bk	W	L	Pct	ShO	Sv-Op	Hld	ERC	ERA
2001	Orioles	R	12	7	0	0	40.2	188	31	29	25	1	0	0	5	39	2	36	2	0	2	3	.400	0	0- -	-	4.79	5.53
2002	Bluefld	R+	12	12	0	0	60.1	253	52	25	22	0	1	1	4	25	0	69	2	2	5	2	.714	0	0- -	-	2.99	3.28
2003	Dlmrva	A	26	26	1	0	125.1	556	105	74	59	6	2	6	3	78	0	120	5	3	5	9	.357	0	0- -	-	3.70	4.24
2004	Bowie	AA	5	5	0	0	27.1	108	11	10	8	1	2	1	2	12	0	35	1	0	1	0	.000	0	0- -	-	1.29	2.63
2005	Bowie	AA	1	1	0	0	6.0	28	8	3	2	1	1	0	0	2	0	7	2	0	1	0	1.000	0	0- -	-	6.14	3.00
2004	BAL	AL	28	27	1	1	147.2	662	145	85	82	14	4	7	2	89	2	76	12	0	12	8	.600	1	1-1	0	4.79	5.00
2005	BAL	AL	29	29	0	0	161.1	716	144	92	81	14	2	3	11	87	2	157	9	1	10	13	.435	0	0-0	0	4.13	4.52
	2 ML YEARS		57	56	1	1	309.0	1378	289	177	163	28	6	10	13	176	4	233	21	1	22	21	.512	1	1-1	0	4.44	4.75

Fernando Cabrera

Pitches: R **Bats:** R **Pos:** RP-15   **Ht:** 6'4" **Wt:** 170 **Born:** 11/16/1981 **Age:** 24

Year	Team	Lg	G	GS	CG	GF	IP	BFP	H	R	ER	HR	SH	SF	HB	TBB	IBB	SO	WP	Bk	W	L	Pct	ShO	Sv-Op	Hld	ERC	ERA
2000	Burlgtn	R+	13	13	0	0	68.1	282	64	42	35	4	2	2	4	20	0	50	14	0	3	7	.300	0	0- -	-	3.33	4.61
2001	Clmbs	A	20	20	0	0	94.2	410	89	49	38	7	4	1	2	37	1	96	10	0	5	6	.455	0	0- -	-	3.53	3.61
2002	Kinston	A+	21	21	0	0	110.0	450	83	48	43	7	3	3	2	40	2	107	3	1	6	8	.429	0	0- -	-	2.44	3.52
2002	Akron	AA	7	4	0	1	27.0	118	26	16	16	1	0	0	3	12	0	29	0	0	1	2	.333	0	1- -	-	4.06	5.33
2003	Akron	AA	36	15	0	14	109.0	456	96	41	36	8	6	3	2	40	0	115	3	1	9	4	.692	0	5- -	-	3.20	2.97
2004	Buffalo	AAA	44	0	0	17	75.0	328	57	37	32	9	0	1	3	43	3	92	5	0	4	3	.571	0	5- -	-	3.58	3.84
2005	Buffalo	AAA	30	0	0	18	51.1	201	36	8	7	3	3	1	0	11	2	68	1	0	6	1	.857	0	3- -	-	1.62	1.23
2004	CLE	AL	4	0	0	2	5.1	20	3	3	2	0	0	1	0	1	0	6	0	0	0	0	-	0	0-0	0	0.99	3.38
2005	CLE	AL	15	0	0	6	30.2	124	24	7	5	1	0	0	1	11	1	29	1	1	2	1	.667	0	0-0	1	2.33	1.47
	2 ML YEARS		19	0	0	8	36.0	144	27	10	7	1	0	1	0	12	1	35	1	1	2	1	.667	0	0-0	1	2.06	1.75

Melky Cabrera

Bats: B **Throws:** L **Pos:** CF-6   **Ht:** 5'11" **Wt:** 170 **Born:** 8/11/1984 **Age:** 21

Year	Team	Lg	G	AB	H	2B	3B	HR	(Hm	Rd)	TB	R	RBI	RC	TBB	IBB	SO	HBP	SH	SF	SB	CS	SB%	GDP	Avg	OBP	Slg
2003	StsInd	A-	67	279	79	10	2	2	(-	-)	99	34	31	37	23	1	36	4	4	1	13	5	.72	6	.283	.345	.355
2004	Tampa	A+	85	333	96	20	3	8	(-	-)	146	48	51	51	23	1	59	5	0	3	3	1	.75	8	.288	.341	.438
2004	Btl Crk	A	42	171	57	16	3	0	(-	-)	79	35	16	31	15	0	23	0	0	2	7	2	.78	2	.333	.383	.462
2005	Trent	AA	106	426	117	22	3	10	(-	-)	175	57	60	60	28	2	72	4	1	5	11	2	.85	11	.275	.322	.411
2005	Clmbs	AAA	26	101	25	3	0	3	(-	-)	37	15	17	12	9	0	15	0	2	0	2	0	1.00	3	.248	.309	.366
2005	NYA	AL	6	19	4	0	0	0	(0	0)	4	1	0	0	0	0	2	0	0	0	0	0	-	0	.211	.211	.211

Miguel Cabrera

Bats: R **Throws:** R **Pos:** LF-134; 3B-30; PH-1   **Ht:** 6'2" **Wt:** 185 **Born:** 4/18/1983 **Age:** 23

Year	Team	Lg	G	AB	H	2B	3B	HR	(Hm	Rd)	TB	R	RBI	RC	TBB	IBB	SO	HBP	SH	SF	SB	CS	SB%	GDP	Avg	OBP	Slg
2003	FLA	NL	87	314	84	21	3	12	(7	5)	147	39	62	51	25	3	84	2	4	1	0	2	.00	12	.268	.325	.468
2004	FLA	NL	160	603	177	31	1	33	(14	19)	309	101	112	92	68	5	148	6	0	8	5	2	.71	20	.294	.366	.512
2005	FLA	NL	158	613	198	43	2	33	(11	22)	344	106	116	108	64	12	125	2	0	6	1	0	1.00	20	.323	.385	.561
	3 ML YEARS		405	1530	459	95	6	78	(32	46)	800	246	290	251	157	20	357	10	4	15	6	4	.60	52	.300	.366	.523

Orlando Cabrera

Bats: R **Throws:** R **Pos:** SS-141   **Ht:** 5'10" **Wt:** 185 **Born:** 11/2/1974 **Age:** 31

Year	Team	Lg	G	AB	H	2B	3B	HR	(Hm	Rd)	TB	R	RBI	RC	TBB	IBB	SO	HBP	SH	SF	SB	CS	SB%	GDP	Avg	OBP	Slg
1997	MON	NL	16	18	4	0	0	0	(0	0)	4	4	2	0	1	0	3	0	1	0	1	2	.33	1	.222	.263	.222
1998	MON	NL	79	261	73	16	5	3	(2	1)	108	44	22	34	18	1	27	0	5	1	6	2	.75	6	.280	.325	.414
1999	MON	NL	104	382	97	23	5	8	(6	2)	154	48	39	42	18	4	38	3	4	0	2	2	.50	9	.254	.293	.403
2000	MON	NL	125	422	100	25	1	13	(7	6)	166	47	55	43	25	3	28	1	3	3	4	4	.50	12	.237	.279	.393
2001	MON	NL	162	626	173	41	6	14	(7	7)	268	64	96	85	43	5	54	4	4	7	19	7	.73	15	.276	.324	.428
2002	MON	NL	153	563	148	43	1	7	(3	4)	214	64	56	61	48	4	53	2	9	4	25	7	.78	16	.263	.321	.380
2003	MON	NL	162	626	186	47	2	17	(8	9)	288	95	80	92	52	3	64	1	3	9	24	2	.92	18	.297	.347	.460
2004	2 Tms		161	618	163	38	3	10	(2	8)	237	74	62	67	39	0	54	3	3	10	16	4	.80	17	.264	.306	.383
2005	LAA	AL	141	540	139	28	3	8	(2	6)	197	70	57	60	38	4	50	3	4	2	21	2	.91	10	.257	.309	.365

Year	Team	Lg	G	AB	H	2B	3B	HR	(Hm	Rd)	TB	R	RBI	RC	TBB	IBB	SO	HBP	SH	SF	SB	CS	SB%	GDP	Avg	OBP	Slg
04	Mon	NL	103	390	96	19	2	4	(1	3)	131	41	31	37	28	0	31	2	2	3	12	3	.80	13	.246	.298	.336
04	Bos	AL	58	228	67	19	1	6	(1	5)	106	33	31	30	11	0	23	1	1	7	4	1	.80	4	.294	.320	.465
9 ML YEARS			1103	4056	1083	261	26	80	(37	43)	1636	510	469	485	282	24	371	17	36	36	118	32	.79	104	.267	.315	.403

Matt Cain

Pitches: R **Bats:** R **Pos:** SP-7   **Ht:** 6'3" **Wt:** 231 **Born:** 10/1/1984 **Age:** 21

			HOW MUCH HE PITCHED							WHAT HE GAVE UP										THE RESULTS						
Year	Team	Lg	G	GS	CG	GF	IP	BFP	H	R	ER	HR	SH	SF	HB	TBB	IBB	SO	WP	Bk	W	L	Pct	ShO	Sv-Op	Hld	ERC	ERA
2002	Giants	R	8	7	0	0	19.1	82	13	10	8	1	0	2	4	11	0	20	3	0	0	1	.000	0	0--	-	3.47	3.72
2003	Hgrstn	A	14	14	0	0	74.0	303	57	24	21	5	0	0	5	24	0	90	1	1	4	4	.500	0	0--	-	2.62	2.55
2004	SnJos	A+	13	13	0	0	72.2	293	58	25	15	5	0	4	4	17	0	89	0	0	7	1	.875	0	0--	-	2.40	1.86
2004	Nrwich	AA	15	15	0	0	86.0	371	73	44	32	7	1	7	3	40	0	72	4	0	6	4	.600	0	0--	-	3.46	3.35
2005	Fresno	AAA	26	26	1	0	145.2	628	118	77	71	22	3	4	5	73	0	176	6	0	10	5	.667	0	0--	-	3.86	4.39
2005	SF	NL	7	7	1	0	46.1	181	24	12	12	4	2	1	0	19	1	30	1	0	2	1	.667	0	0-0	0	1.61	2.33

Miguel Cairo

Bats: R **Throws:** R **Pos:** 2B-82; PH-12; 1B-8; 3B-3; LF-2; RF-1   **Ht:** 6'1" **Wt:** 200 **Born:** 5/4/1974 **Age:** 32

			BATTING																	BASERUNNING				AVERAGES		
Year	Team	Lg	G	AB	H	2B	3B	HR	(Hm	Rd)	TB	R	RBI	RC	TBB	IBB	SO	HBP	SH	SF	SB	CS	SB%	GDP	Avg	OBP	Slg
2005	Mets*	R	3	13	4	1	0	0	(-	-)	5	3	0	1	0	0	0	0	0	0	0	0	-	0	.308	.308	.385
2005	StLuci*	A+	1	4	1	0	0	0	(-	-)	1	0	0	0	0	0	1	0	0	0	0	0	-	0	.250	.250	.250
1996	TOR	AL	9	27	6	2	0	0	(0	0)	8	5	1	2	2	0	9	1	0	0	0	0	-	1	.222	.300	.296
1997	CHN	NL	16	29	7	1	0	0	(0	0)	8	7	1	3	2	0	3	1	0	0	0	0	-	0	.241	.313	.276
1998	TB	AL	150	515	138	26	5	5	(3	2)	189	49	46	58	24	0	44	6	11	2	19	8	.70	9	.268	.307	.367
1999	TB	AL	120	465	137	15	5	3	(1	2)	171	61	36	57	24	0	46	7	7	5	22	7	.76	13	.295	.335	.368
2000	TB	AL	119	375	98	18	2	1	(0	1)	123	49	34	42	29	0	34	2	6	5	28	7	.80	7	.261	.314	.328
2001	2 Tms		93	156	46	8	1	3	(2	1)	65	25	16	23	18	1	23	0	7	1	2	1	.67	4	.295	.366	.417
2002	STL	NL	108	184	46	9	2	2	(1	1)	65	28	23	19	13	2	36	3	6	2	1	1	.50	5	.250	.307	.353
2003	STL	NL	92	261	64	15	2	5	(2	3)	98	41	32	25	13	1	30	6	3	7	4	1	.80	6	.245	.289	.375
2004	NYA	NL	122	360	105	17	5	6	(4	2)	150	48	42	50	18	1	49	14	12	4	11	3	.79	7	.292	.346	.417
2005	NYN	NL	100	327	82	18	0	2	(1	1)	106	31	19	29	19	2	31	4	12	5	13	3	.81	5	.251	.296	.324
01	ChC	NL	66	123	35	3	1	2	(1	1)	46	20	9	17	16	1	21	0	7	1	2	1	.67	3	.285	.364	.374
01	StL	NL	27	33	11	5	0	1	(1	0)	19	5	7	6	2	0	2	0	0	0	0	0	-	1	.333	.371	.576
10 ML YEARS			929	2699	729	129	22	27	(14	13)	983	344	250	308	162	7	305	44	64	31	100	31	.76	57	.270	.318	.364

Kiko Calero

Pitches: R **Bats:** R **Pos:** RP-58   **Ht:** 6'1" **Wt:** 185 **Born:** 1/9/1975 **Age:** 31

			HOW MUCH HE PITCHED							WHAT HE GAVE UP										THE RESULTS						
Year	Team	Lg	G	GS	CG	GF	IP	BFP	H	R	ER	HR	SH	SF	HB	TBB	IBB	SO	WP	Bk	W	L	Pct	ShO	Sv-Op	Hld	ERC	ERA
2005	Scrmto*	AAA	2	2	0	0	2.0	10	4	2	2	0	0	0	0	0	0	2	0	0	0	0	-	0	0--	-	7.48	9.00
2003	STL	NL	26	1	0	7	38.1	162	29	12	12	5	1	3	1	20	2	51	3	1	1	1	.500	0	1-4	5	3.44	2.82
2004	STL	NL	41	0	0	4	45.1	168	27	14	14	5	4	0	1	10	1	47	1	0	3	1	.750	0	2-3	12	1.62	2.78
2005	OAK	AL	58	0	0	15	55.2	229	45	20	20	6	1	1	1	18	2	52	2	0	4	1	.800	0	1-2	12	2.80	3.23
3 ML YEARS			125	1	0	26	139.1	559	101	46	46	16	6	4	3	48	5	150	6	1	8	3	.727	0	4-9	25	2.56	2.97

Carmen Cali

Pitches: L **Bats:** L **Pos:** RP-6   **Ht:** 5'10" **Wt:** 185 **Born:** 11/4/1978 **Age:** 27

			HOW MUCH HE PITCHED							WHAT HE GAVE UP										THE RESULTS						
Year	Team	Lg	G	GS	CG	GF	IP	BFP	H	R	ER	HR	SH	SF	HB	TBB	IBB	SO	WP	Bk	W	L	Pct	ShO	Sv-Op	Hld	ERC	ERA
2000	NewJrs	A-	14	14	0	0	70.0	301	68	45	38	3	2	3	5	30	0	55	11	0	2	7	.222	0	0--	-	3.97	4.89
2001	Peoria	A	39	0	0	15	48.0	229	53	40	32	4	6	0	1	29	0	47	9	1	7	3	.700	0	1--	-	5.27	6.00
2001	Ptomc	A+	12	0	0	4	12.1	52	12	4	3	1	2	0	1	6	1	9	3	0	1	0	1.000	0	0--	-	4.56	2.19
2002	Ptomc	A+	29	0	0	6	35.0	154	31	18	16	1	2	0	6	21	2	24	2	0	2	2	.500	0	0--	-	4.39	4.11
2002	Peoria	A	24	0	0	5	35.1	156	36	17	7	0	2	1	0	14	0	27	1	0	1	1	.500	0	2--	-	3.36	1.78
2003	PlmBh	A+	62	0	0	23	70.1	321	72	49	39	2	7	4	6	32	6	70	2	0	2	1	.667	0	3--	-	3.97	4.99
2004	Tenn	AA	38	0	0	23	46.1	205	43	19	15	3	0	1	3	19	3	47	2	0	1	2	.333	0	14--	-	3.50	2.91
2004	Memp	AAA	17	0	0	7	20.0	81	17	6	6	4	0	0	0	4	0	20	2	0	1	1	.500	0	3--	-	3.06	2.70
2005	Memp	AAA	50	0	0	19	58.1	277	74	47	35	6	1	2	3	28	2	45	4	0	4	5	.444	0	2--	-	6.08	5.40
2004	STL	NL	10	0	0	2	7.1	40	13	7	7	1	0	1	0	6	1	8	1	0	0	0	-	0	0-0	0	10.96	8.59
2005	STL	NL	6	0	0	3	6.0	33	10	8	7	3	0	1	0	6	1	5	1	0	0	0	-	0	0-0	0	14.93	10.50
2 ML YEARS			16	0	0	5	13.1	73	23	15	14	4	0	2	0	12	2	13	2	0	0	0	-	0	0-0	0	12.73	9.45

Napoleon Calzado

Bats: R **Throws:** R **Pos:** PH-2; LF-1; CF-1; PR-1   **Ht:** 6'3" **Wt:** 201 **Born:** 2/9/1977 **Age:** 29

			BATTING																	BASERUNNING				AVERAGES		
Year	Team	Lg	G	AB	H	2B	3B	HR	(Hm	Rd)	TB	R	RBI	RC	TBB	IBB	SO	HBP	SH	SF	SB	CS	SB%	GDP	Avg	OBP	Slg
1998	Orioles	R	31	113	26	6	4	1	(-	-)	43	15	18	13	10	0	17	1	1	1	1	1	.50	2	.230	.296	.381
1999	Bluefld	R+	52	199	58	11	2	6	(-	-)	91	46	31	35	20	1	32	3	0	1	9	1	.90	2	.291	.363	.457
1999	Dlmrva	A	6	18	5	1	0	0	(-	-)	6	2	1	1	0	0	4	0	0	1	0	0	-	0	.278	.263	.333
2000	Dlmrva	A	131	503	140	20	6	7	(-	-)	193	81	83	68	31	0	68	11	4	8	29	12	.71	11	.278	.329	.384
2001	Frdrck	A+	121	464	133	20	2	5	(-	-)	172	50	41	57	16	2	52	6	5	4	34	14	.71	9	.287	.316	.371
2002	Bowie	AA	130	482	133	20	3	3	(-	-)	168	71	42	63	34	1	50	7	3	1	42	11	.79	12	.276	.332	.349
2003	Abrdn	A-	4	16	3	0	0	0	(-	-)	3	0	0	1	2	0	3	0	0	0	3	0	1.00	0	.188	.278	.188
2003	Bowie	AA	40	166	44	6	1	1	(-	-)	55	16	11	17	5	0	14	2	2	1	11	3	.79	4	.265	.293	.331
2003	Ottawa	AAA	51	196	61	7	4	0	(-	-)	76	30	15	29	14	0	30	2	0	0	9	3	.75	1	.311	.363	.388

Year	Team	Lg	G	AB	H	2B	3B	HR	(Hm	Rd)	TB	R	RBI	RC	TBB	IBB	SO	HBP	SH	SF	SB	CS	SB%	GDP	Avg	OBP	Slg
2004	Bowie	AA	4	15	4	1	0	0	(-	-)	5	2	0	2	1	0	1	0	0	0	2	0	1.00	0	.267	.313	.333
2004	Grnville	AA	119	449	161	28	7	8	(-	-)	227	68	59	88	22	1	59	8	2	4	18	8	.69	10	.359	.395	.506
2004	Rchmd	AAA	5	19	4	1	0	0	(-	-)	5	2	2	0	0	0	2	0	0	0	0	0	-	0	.211	.211	.263
2005	Ottawa	AAA	120	447	137	22	1	11	(-	-)	194	54	61	67	21	0	46	6	1	3	10	6	.63	13	.306	.344	.434
2005	BAL	AL	4	5	1	0	0	0	(0	0)	1	0	0	0	0	0	1	0	0	0	0	0	-	0	.200	.200	.200

Mike Cameron

Bats: R **Throws:** R **Pos:** RF-68; CF-10   **Ht:** 6'2" **Wt:** 195 **Born:** 1/8/1973 **Age:** 33

Year	Team	Lg	G	AB	H	2B	3B	HR	(Hm	Rd)	TB	R	RBI	RC	TBB	IBB	SO	HBP	SH	SF	SB	CS	SB%	GDP	Avg	OBP	Slg
2005	StLuci*	A+	4	10	3	2	0	0	(-	-)	5	3	0	3	3	0	3	2	0	0	0	0	-	0	.300	.533	.500
2005	Norfolk*	AAA	2	7	2	0	1	0	(-	-)	4	2	2	2	3	0	3	0	0	0	0	0	-	0	.286	.500	.571
1995	CHA	AL	28	38	7	2	0	1	(0	1)	12	4	2	3	3	0	15	0	3	0	0	0	-	0	.184	.244	.316
1996	CHA	AL	11	11	1	0	0	0	(0	0)	1	1	0	0	1	0	3	0	0	0	0	1	.00	0	.091	.167	.091
1997	CHA	AL	116	379	98	18	3	14	(10	4)	164	63	55	63	55	1	105	5	2	5	23	2	**.92**	6	.259	.356	.433
1998	CHA	AL	141	396	83	16	5	8	(5	3)	133	53	43	39	37	0	101	6	1	3	27	11	.71	6	.210	.285	.336
1999	CIN	NL	146	542	139	34	9	21	(12	9)	254	93	66	96	80	2	145	6	5	3	38	12	.76	4	.256	.357	.469
2000	SEA	AL	155	543	145	28	4	19	(5	14)	238	96	78	91	78	0	133	9	7	6	24	7	.77	10	.267	.365	.438
2001	SEA	AL	150	540	144	30	5	25	(7	18)	259	99	110	96	69	3	155	10	1	13	34	5	.87	13	.267	.353	.480
2002	SEA	AL	158	545	130	26	5	25	(7	18)	241	84	80	78	79	3	**176**	7	4	5	31	8	.79	8	.239	.340	.442
2003	SEA	AL	147	534	135	31	5	18	(11	7)	230	74	76	80	70	1	137	5	1	2	17	7	.71	13	.253	.344	.431
2004	NYN	NL	140	493	114	30	1	30	(11	19)	236	76	76	70	57	2	143	8	1	3	22	6	.79	5	.231	.319	.479
2005	NYN	NL	76	308	84	23	2	12	(7	5)	147	47	39	52	29	0	85	4	1	1	13	1	.93	5	.273	.342	.477
11 ML YEARS			1268	4329	1080	238	39	173	(75	98)	1915	690	625	668	558	12	1198	60	26	41	229	60	.79	72	.249	.340	.442

Shawn Camp

Pitches: R **Bats:** R **Pos:** RP-29   **Ht:** 6'1" **Wt:** 200 **Born:** 11/18/1975 **Age:** 30

Year	Team	Lg	G	GS	CG	GF	IP	BFP	H	R	ER	HR	SH	SF	HB	TBB	IBB	SO	WP	Bk	W	L	Pct	ShO	Sv-Op	Hld	ERC	ERA
1997	Idaho	R+	30	0	0	24	32.2	150	41	22	20	3	1	1	2	14	0	41	4	0	2	1	.667	0	12-	-	5.94	5.51
1998	Clinton	A	47	0	0	39	55.0	240	48	19	16	0	3	3	7	20	4	62	6	1	3	5	.375	0	13-	-	2.84	2.62
1999	RCuca	A+	53	0	0	28	66.0	285	68	37	29	4	4	4	1	25	3	78	7	1	1	5	.167	0	6-	-	3.87	3.95
2000	RCuca	A+	14	0	0	13	18.2	72	10	3	3	0	0	0	2	5	0	18	2	0	1	0	1.000	0	6-	-	1.29	1.45
2000	Mobile	AA	45	0	0	11	59.1	252	47	23	16	4	2	2	1	30	2	53	4	0	3	3	.500	0	1-	-	3.13	2.43
2001	Mobile	AA	35	1	0	16	48.2	204	46	24	24	2	5	2	6	15	1	55	2	0	6	2	.750	0	0-	-	3.54	4.44
2001	Portlnd	AAA	4	1	0	1	7.0	22	2	0	0	0	0	0	0	1	0	6	0	0	1	0	1.000	0	0-	-	0.37	0.00
2001	Altna	AA	8	3	0	1	23.1	103	25	14	11	3	0	2	3	8	1	19	1	1	4	0	1.000	0	0-	-	4.95	4.24
2001	Nashv	AAA	11	0	0	1	17.0	67	11	4	4	1	0	1	0	8	1	15	0	0	0	0	-	0	0-	-	2.24	2.12
2002	Nashv	AAA	39	0	0	15	58.1	234	50	22	21	5	3	1	6	15	3	59	0	1	4	1	.800	0	2-	-	3.10	3.24
2003	Altna	AA	18	0	0	3	29.0	127	26	14	14	2	2	0	4	11	0	35	2	0	0	2	.000	0	0-	-	3.68	4.34
2003	Nashv	AAA	33	1	0	9	43.1	193	50	26	24	2	2	1	2	15	2	36	4	0	1	0	1.000	0	0-	-	4.42	4.98
2004	Omha	AAA	15	0	0	7	22.0	99	26	14	13	2	0	0	1	6	0	21	1	0	1	1	.500	0	1-	-	4.60	5.32
2005	Omha	AAA	21	7	0	7	67.2	296	71	36	29	9	2	2	3	22	2	42	2	0	3	6	.333	0	1-	-	4.36	3.86
2004	KC	AL	42	0	0	12	66.2	286	74	37	29	10	2	3	5	16	1	51	2	1	2	2	.500	0	2-3	5	4.74	3.92
2005	KC	AL	29	0	0	7	49.0	228	69	40	35	4	0	3	4	13	3	28	3	0	1	4	.200	0	0-2	0	6.00	6.43
2 ML YEARS			71	0	0	19	115.2	514	143	77	64	14	2	6	9	29	4	79	5	1	3	6	.333	0	2-5	5	5.28	4.98

Jorge Campillo

Pitches: R **Bats:** R **Pos:** SP-1; RP-1   **Ht:** 6'1" **Wt:** 190 **Born:** 8/10/1978 **Age:** 27

Year	Team	Lg	G	GS	CG	GF	IP	BFP	H	R	ER	HR	SH	SF	HB	TBB	IBB	SO	WP	Bk	W	L	Pct	ShO	Sv-Op	Hld	ERC	ERA
2005	Ms	R	4	4	0	0	11.0	53	18	11	7	0	0	0	0	2	0	10	0	0	0	2	.000	0	0-	-	5.99	5.73
2005	Tacom	AAA	12	12	0	0	66.1	280	63	21	20	5	3	1	0	18	0	43	2	0	4	1	.800	0	0-	-	3.08	2.71
2005	SEA	AL	2	1	0	1	2.0	9	1	0	0	0	0	0	0	1	0	1	0	0	0	0	-	0	0-0	0	1.26	0.00

Robinson Cano

Bats: L **Throws:** R **Pos:** 2B-131; PH-2   **Ht:** 6'0" **Wt:** 170 **Born:** 10/22/1982 **Age:** 23

Year	Team	Lg	G	AB	H	2B	3B	HR	(Hm	Rd)	TB	R	RBI	RC	TBB	IBB	SO	HBP	SH	SF	SB	CS	SB%	GDP	Avg	OBP	Slg
2001	Yanks	R	57	200	46	14	2	3	(-	-)	73	37	34	28	28	0	27	3	0	2	11	2	.85	4	.230	.330	.365
2001	StlsInd	A-	2	8	2	0	0	0	(-	-)	2	0	2	0	0	0	2	0	0	0	0	0	-	0	.250	.250	.250
2002	StlsInd	A-	22	87	24	5	1	1	(-	-)	34	11	15	11	4	0	8	0	1	0	6	1	.86	1	.276	.308	.391
2002	Grnsbr	A	113	474	131	20	9	14	(-	-)	211	67	66	69	29	0	78	3	0	1	2	1	.67	8	.276	.321	.445
2003	Tampa	A+	90	366	101	16	3	5	(-	-)	138	50	50	44	17	1	49	4	0	3	1	1	.50	5	.276	.313	.377
2003	Trentn	AA	46	164	46	9	1	1	(-	-)	60	21	13	21	9	0	16	6	2	0	0	0	-	6	.280	.341	.366
2004	Trentn	AA	74	292	88	20	8	7	(-	-)	145	43	44	51	24	1	40	3	0	4	2	4	.33	8	.301	.356	.497
2004	Clmbs	AAA	61	216	56	9	2	6	(-	-)	87	22	30	28	18	1	27	1	3	2	0	1	.00	7	.259	.316	.403
2005	Clmbs	AAA	24	108	36	8	3	4	(-	-)	62	19	24	21	6	3	13	0	0	0	0	0	-	2	.333	.368	.574
2005	NYA	AL	132	522	155	34	4	14	(5	9)	239	78	62	59	16	1	68	3	7	3	1	3	.25	16	.297	.320	.458

Jorge Cantu

Bats: R Throws: R Pos: 2B-80; 3B-62; DH-13; PH-2   Ht: 6'1" Wt: 184 Born: 1/30/1982 Age: 24

									BATTING													BASERUNNING				AVERAGES		
Year	Team	Lg	G	AB	H	2B	3B	HR	(Hm	Rd)	TB	R	RBI	RC	TBB	IBB	SO	HBP	SH	SF	SB	CS	SB%	GDP	Avg	OBP	Slg
1999	HudVal	A-	72	281	73	17	2	1	(-	-)	97	33	33	28	20	0	59	2	4	1	3	4	.43	8	.260	.313	.345
2000	CtnSC	A	46	186	56	13	2	2	(-	-)	79	25	24	26	10	1	39	3	2	1	3	3	.50	3	.301	.345	.425
2000	StPtrb	A+	36	130	38	5	2	1	(-	-)	50	18	14	15	3	0	13	1	3	0	4	2	.67	3	.292	.313	.385
2001	Orlndo	AA	130	512	131	26	3	4	(-	-)	175	58	45	45	17	0	93	8	5	7	4	9	.31	13	.256	.287	.342
2002	Orlndo	AA	131	512	124	31	1	3	(-	-)	166	50	43	40	23	2	74	4	1	5	2	6	.25	13	.242	.278	.324
2003	Orlndo	AA	43	158	34	10	0	3	(-	-)	53	15	17	11	9	0	27	1	3	2	0	3	.00	3	.215	.259	.335
2003	Drhm	AAA	60	200	59	16	1	4	(-	-)	89	26	30	27	8	1	21	2	1	6	2	1	.67	5	.295	.319	.445
2004	Drhm	AAA	95	368	111	33	1	22	(-	-)	212	57	80	63	16	2	64	4	1	3	3	0	1.00	11	.302	.335	.576
2004	TB	AL	50	173	52	20	1	2	(0	2)	80	25	17	22	9	0	44	2	0	1	0	0	-	5	.301	.341	.462
2005	TB	AL	150	598	171	40	1	28	(16	12)	297	73	117	88	19	1	83	6	0	7	1	0	1.00	24	.286	.311	.497
	2 ML YEARS		200	771	223	60	2	30	(16	14)	377	98	134	110	28	1	127	8	0	8	1	0	1.00	29	.289	.318	.489

Jose Capellan

Pitches: R Bats: R Pos: RP-17   Ht: 6'4" Wt: 235 Born: 1/13/1981 Age: 25

			HOW MUCH HE PITCHED						WHAT HE GAVE UP										THE RESULTS						
Year	Team	Lg	G	GS	CG	GF	IP	BFP	H	R	ER	HR	SH	SF	HB	TBB	IBB	SO	WP	Bk	W	L	Pct	ShO	Sv-Op	Hld	ERC	ERA
2001	Danvle	A+	3	3	0	0	60.1	66	12	7	3	1	0	0	2	4	0	25	1	1	0	0	-	0	0--	-	0.59	0.45
2003	Braves	R	5	5	0	0	17.0	75	18	7	5	0	1	0	1	8	0	17	0	0	0	1	.000	0	0--	-	4.23	2.65
2003	Rome	A	14	12	1	0	47.1	194	43	23	20	2	3	2	0	19	0	32	2	1	1	2	.333	0	0--	-	3.30	3.80
2004	MrtlBh	A+	8	8	1	0	46.1	179	27	11	10	0	2	3	2	11	0	62	0	0	5	1	.833	1	0--	-	1.22	1.94
2004	Grnville	AA	9	8	0	1	50.1	205	53	15	14	1	2	1	0	19	0	53	1	1	5	1	.833	0	0--	-	3.98	2.50
2004	Rchmd	AA	7	7	0	0	43.0	172	33	13	12	0	3	1	0	15	1	37	3	0	4	2	.667	0	0--	-	2.05	2.51
2005	Nashv	AAA	36	12	0	18	90.2	402	88	42	39	4	2	5	3	42	2	76	2	0	5	3	.625	0	6--	-	3.78	3.87
2004	ATL	NL	3	2	0	0	8.0	42	14	10	10	2	1	1	0	5	0	4	0	0	0	1	.000	0	0-0	0	11.31	11.25
2005	MIL	NL	17	0	0	7	15.2	67	17	6	5	1	2	2	0	5	0	14	0	0	1	1	.500	0	0-0	3	4.01	2.87
	2 ML YEARS		20	2	0	7	23.2	109	31	16	15	3	3	3	0	10	0	18	0	0	1	2	.333	0	0-0	3	6.24	5.70

Matt Capps

Pitches: R Bats: R Pos: RP-4   Ht: 6'3" Wt: 238 Born: 9/3/1983 Age: 22

			HOW MUCH HE PITCHED						WHAT HE GAVE UP										THE RESULTS						
Year	Team	Lg	G	GS	CG	GF	IP	BFP	H	R	ER	HR	SH	SF	HB	TBB	IBB	SO	WP	Bk	W	L	Pct	ShO	Sv-Op	Hld	ERC	ERA
2002	Pirates	R	7	0	0	4	13.0	58	13	2	1	0	0	0	6	0	8	1	1	1	0	1.000	0	1--	-	3.50	0.69
2003	Pirates	R	10	10	1	0	62.2	237	40	16	13	1	0	1	5	9	0	54	1	0	5	1	.833	0	0--	-	1.35	1.87
2003	Lynbrg	A+	1	1	0	0	5.0	22	3	3	3	0	7	4	0	4	0	5	0	0	0	0	-	0	0--	-	2.64	5.40
2004	Wmsprt	A	11	11	0	0	65.0	283	84	43	35	7	3	1	2	4	1	33	1	0	3	5	.375	0	0--	-	4.45	4.85
2004	Hickory	A	12	8	0	1	42.0	224	82	55	47	8	0	1	5	16	0	27	0	0	2	3	.400	0	0--	-	11.55	10.07
2005	Hickory	A	35	0	0	27	53.2	213	47	15	15	0	4	2	2	5	2	39	2	0	3	4	.429	0	14--	-	1.79	2.52
2005	Altna	AA	17	0	0	12	20.0	82	21	8	6	2	0	0	0	1	0	26	0	1	0	2	.000	0	7--	-	2.93	2.70
2005	PIT	NL	4	0	0	0	4.0	16	5	2	2	0	0	0	1	0	0	3	0	0	0	0	-	0	0-0	0	4.62	4.50

Chris Capuano

Pitches: L Bats: L Pos: SP-35   Ht: 6'2" Wt: 219 Born: 8/19/1978 Age: 27

			HOW MUCH HE PITCHED						WHAT HE GAVE UP										THE RESULTS						
Year	Team	Lg	G	GS	CG	GF	IP	BFP	H	R	ER	HR	SH	SF	HB	TBB	IBB	SO	WP	Bk	W	L	Pct	ShO	Sv-Op	Hld	ERC	ERA
2003	ARI	NL	9	5	0	2	33.0	139	27	19	17	3	4	1	6	11	1	23	3	0	2	4	.333	0	0-0	1	3.45	4.64
2004	MIL	NL	17	17	0	0	88.1	385	91	55	49	18	4	1	5	37	1	80	3	1	6	8	.429	0	0-0	0	5.37	4.99
2005	MIL	NL	35	35	0	0	219.0	949	212	105	97	31	14	5	12	91	6	176	3	4	18	12	.600	0	0-0	0	4.44	3.99
	3 ML YEARS		61	57	0	2	340.1	1473	330	179	163	52	22	7	23	139	8	279	9	5	26	24	.520	0	0-0	1	4.58	4.31

Buddy Carlyle

Pitches: R Bats: L Pos: RP-10   Ht: 6'3" Wt: 185 Born: 12/21/1977 Age: 28

			HOW MUCH HE PITCHED						WHAT HE GAVE UP										THE RESULTS						
Year	Team	Lg	G	GS	CG	GF	IP	BFP	H	R	ER	HR	SH	SF	HB	TBB	IBB	SO	WP	Bk	W	L	Pct	ShO	Sv-Op	Hld	ERC	ERA
2005	Ddgrs*	R	1	1	0	0	3.0	12	3	1	1	0	0	0	0	0	0	1	0	0	0	0	-	0	0--	-	1.95	3.00
2005	LsVgs*	AAA	20	6	0	7	48.0	216	51	28	26	7	3	2	5	21	0	53	0	0	1	2	.333	0	2--	-	5.36	4.88
1999	SD	NL	7	7	0	0	37.2	162	36	28	25	7	1	2	2	17	0	29	1	0	1	3	.250	0	0-0	0	4.95	5.97
2000	SD	NL	4	0	0	2	3.0	18	6	7	7	0	0	0	0	3	0	2	0	0	0	0	-	0	0-0	0	12.01	21.00
2005	LAN	NL	10	0	0	2	14.0	62	16	13	13	4	2	0	1	4	0	13	0	0	0	0	-	0	0-1	0	6.07	8.36
	3 ML YEARS		21	7	0	4	54.2	242	58	48	45	11	3	2	3	24	0	44	1	0	1	3	.250	0	0-1	0	5.61	7.41

Chris Carpenter

Pitches: R Bats: R Pos: SP-33   Ht: 6'6" Wt: 215 Born: 4/27/1975 Age: 31

			HOW MUCH HE PITCHED						WHAT HE GAVE UP										THE RESULTS						
Year	Team	Lg	G	GS	CG	GF	IP	BFP	H	R	ER	HR	SH	SF	HB	TBB	IBB	SO	WP	Bk	W	L	Pct	ShO	Sv-Op	Hld	ERC	ERA
1997	TOR	AL	14	13	1	1	81.1	374	108	55	46	7	1	2	2	37	0	55	7	1	3	7	.300	1	0-0	0	6.38	5.09
1998	TOR	AL	33	24	1	4	175.0	742	177	97	85	18	4	5	5	61	1	136	5	0	12	7	.632	0	0-0	0	4.12	4.37
1999	TOR	AL	24	24	4	0	150.0	663	177	81	73	16	4	6	3	48	1	106	9	1	9	8	.529	0	0-0	0	4.90	4.38
2000	TOR	AL	34	27	2	1	175.1	795	204	130	122	30	3	1	5	83	1	113	3	0	10	12	.455	2	0-0	0	6.04	6.26
2001	TOR	AL	34	34	3	0	215.2	930	229	112	98	29	3	1	16	75	5	157	5	0	11	11	.500	2	0-0	0	4.82	4.09
2002	TOR	AL	13	13	1	0	73.1	327	89	45	43	11	4	4	1	27	0	45	3	0	4	5	.444	1	0-0	0	5.91	5.28

Year	Team	Lg	G	GS	CG	GF	IP	BFP	H	R	ER	HR	SH	SF	HB	TBB	IBB	SO	WP	Bk	W	L	Pct	ShO	Sv-Op	Hld	ERC	ERA
2004	STL	NL	28	28	1	0	182.0	746	169	75	70	24	6	3	8	38	2	152	4	0	15	5	.750	0	0-0	0	3.32	3.46
2005	STL	NL	33	33	7	0	241.2	953	204	82	76	18	7	7	3	51	0	213	5	0	21	5	.808	0	0-0	0	2.49	2.83
	8 ML YEARS		213	196	20	6	1294.1	5530	1357	677	613	153	29	29	46	420	10	977	41	2	85	60	.586	9	0-0	0	4.36	4.26

Giovanni Carrara

Pitches: R **Bats:** R **Pos:** RP-72 **Ht:** 6'2" **Wt:** 235 **Born:** 3/4/1968 **Age:** 38

Year	Team	Lg	G	GS	CG	GF	IP	BFP	H	R	ER	HR	SH	SF	HB	TBB	IBB	SO	WP	Bk	W	L	Pct	ShO	Sv-Op	Hld	ERC	ERA
1995	TOR	AL	12	7	1	2	48.2	229	64	46	39	10	1	2	1	25	1	27	1	0	2	4	.333	0	0-0	0	7.43	7.21
1996	2 Tms		19	5	0	4	38.0	188	54	36	34	11	1	0	2	25	3	23	1	0	1	1	.500	0	0-1	0	9.71	8.05
1997	CIN	NL	2	2	0	0	10.1	49	14	9	9	4	1	0	0	6	1	5	0	0	0	1	.000	0	0-0	0	9.47	7.84
2000	COL	NL	8	0	0	2	13.1	72	21	19	19	5	0	1	1	11	2	15	0	0	0	1	.000	0	0-1	0	12.21	12.83
2001	LA	NL	47	3	0	2	85.1	348	73	30	30	12	6	1	1	24	2	70	0	0	6	1	.857	0	0-3	9	3.10	3.16
2002	LA	NL	63	1	0	13	90.2	387	83	34	33	14	6	2	6	32	4	56	1	0	6	3	.667	0	1-6	14	3.97	3.28
2003	SEA	AL	23	0	0	7	29.0	137	40	22	22	6	1	0	2	14	0	13	0	0	2	0	1.000	0	0-0	4	8.10	6.83
2004	LA	NL	42	0	0	15	53.2	227	46	15	13	1	4	0	1	20	3	48	1	0	5	2	.714	0	2-3	6	2.60	2.18
2005	LAN	NL	72	0	0	18	75.2	326	65	35	33	6	9	5	6	38	5	56	4	0	7	4	.636	0	0-2	11	3.78	3.93
96	Tor	AL	11	0	0	3	15.0	76	23	19	19	5	0	0	2	12	2	10	1	0	0	1	.000	0	0-1	0	11.46	11.40
96	Cin	NL	8	5	0	1	23.0	112	31	17	15	6	1	0	2	13	1	13	0	0	1	0	1.000	0	0-0	0	8.62	5.87
	9 ML YEARS		288	18	1	63	444.2	1963	460	246	232	69	29	11	20	195	22	313	8	0	29	17	.630	0	3-16	44	4.94	4.70

D.J. Carrasco

Pitches: R **Bats:** R **Pos:** SP-20; RP-1 **Ht:** 6'2" **Wt:** 190 **Born:** 4/12/1977 **Age:** 29

Year	Team	Lg	G	GS	CG	GF	IP	BFP	H	R	ER	HR	SH	SF	HB	TBB	IBB	SO	WP	Bk	W	L	Pct	ShO	Sv-Op	Hld	ERC	ERA
2005	Omha*	AAA	11	3	0	5	27.2	118	24	9	7	1	4	3	1	11	1	21	2	0	3	2	.600	0	0--	-	3.27	2.28
2003	KC	AL	50	2	0	21	80.1	355	82	44	43	8	1	4	7	40	4	57	6	0	6	5	.545	0	2-5	6	4.94	4.82
2004	KC	AL	30	0	0	11	35.1	163	41	22	19	5	1	1	3	15	3	22	2	0	2	2	.500	0	0-3	4	5.56	4.84
2005	KC	AL	21	20	1	0	114.2	511	129	67	61	11	3	5	6	51	2	49	7	3	6	8	.429	0	0-0	0	5.20	4.79
	3 ML YEARS		101	22	1	32	230.1	1029	252	133	123	24	5	10	16	106	9	128	15	3	14	15	.483	0	2-8	10	5.17	4.81

Hector Carrasco

Pitches: R **Bats:** R **Pos:** RP-59; SP-5 **Ht:** 6'2" **Wt:** 220 **Born:** 10/22/1969 **Age:** 36

Year	Team	Lg	G	GS	CG	GF	IP	BFP	H	R	ER	HR	SH	SF	HB	TBB	IBB	SO	WP	Bk	W	L	Pct	ShO	Sv-Op	Hld	ERC	ERA
2005	NewOr*	AAA	6	0	0	6	8.0	30	4	1	0	0	1	0	1	2	0	10	0	0	1	0	1.000	0	4--	-	1.21	0.00
1994	CIN	NL	45	0	0	0	56.1	237	42	17	14	3	0	0	0	30	0	41	0	0	5	6	.455	0	6-0	0	2.89	2.24
1995	CIN	NL	64	0	0	0	87.1	391	86	45	40	1	0	0	0	46	0	64	0	0	2	7	.222	0	5-0	0	3.76	4.12
1996	CIN	NL	56	0	0	0	74.1	325	58	37	31	6	0	0	0	45	0	59	0	0	4	3	.571	0	0-0	0	3.46	3.75
1997	2 Tms		66	0	0	0	86.0	388	80	46	42	7	0	0	0	41	0	76	0	0	2	8	.200	0	0-0	0	3.66	4.40
1998	MIN	AL	63	0	0	0	61.2	287	75	30	30	4	0	0	0	31	0	46	0	0	4	2	.667	0	1-0	5	5.42	4.38
1999	MIN	AL	39	0	0	0	49.0	204	48	29	26	3	0	0	0	18	0	35	0	0	2	3	.400	0	1-0	0	3.66	4.78
2000	2 Tms		69	1	0	0	78.2	364	90	46	41	8	0	0	0	38	0	64	0	0	5	4	.556	0	1-0	0	5.13	4.69
2001	MIN	AL	56	0	0	0	73.2	317	77	40	38	8	0	0	0	30	0	70	0	0	4	3	.571	0	1-0	4	4.49	4.64
2003	BAL	AL	40	0	0	10	38.1	174	40	22	21	5	4	0	2	20	3	27	0	0	2	6	.250	0	1-3	8	5.09	4.93
2005	WAS	NL	64	5	0	13	88.1	358	59	23	20	6	4	4	6	38	7	75	6	1	5	4	.556	0	2-4	8	2.41	2.04
97	TB	AL	38	0	0	0	51.1	237	51	25	21	3	0	0	0	25	0	46	0	0	1	2	.333	0	0-0	0	3.84	3.68
97	KC	AL	28	0	0	0	34.2	151	29	21	21	4	0	0	0	16	0	30	0	0	1	6	.143	0	0-0	0	3.40	5.45
00	Min	AL	61	0	0	0	72.0	324	75	38	34	6	0	0	0	33	0	57	0	0	4	3	.571	0	1-0	0	4.31	4.25
00	Bos	AL	8	1	0	0	6.2	40	15	8	7	2	0	0	0	5	0	7	0	0	1	1	.500	0	0-0	0	15.94	9.45
	10 ML YEARS		562	6	0	23	693.2	3045	655	335	303	51	8	4	8	337	10	557	6	1	35	46	.432	0	18-7	16	3.89	3.93

Jamey Carroll

Bats: R **Throws:** R **Pos:** 2B-63; SS-41; PH-13; 3B-12; PR-4 **Ht:** 5'10" **Wt:** 175 **Born:** 2/18/1975 **Age:** 31

						BATTING													BASERUNNING				AVERAGES		
Year	Team	Lg	G	AB	H	2B	3B	HR	(Hm | Rd)	TB	R	RBI	RC	TBB	IBB	SO	HBP	SH	SF	SB	CS	SB%	GDP	Avg	OBP	Slg
2002	MON	NL	16	71	22	5	3	1	(1 | 0)	36	16	6	12	4	0	12	0	4	0	1	0	1.00	1	.310	.347	.507
2003	MON	NL	105	227	59	10	1	1	(1 | 0)	74	31	10	18	19	0	39	3	9	2	5	2	.71	10	.260	.323	.326
2004	MON	NL	102	218	63	14	2	0	(0 | 0)	81	36	16	28	32	1	21	1	2	3	5	1	.83	3	.289	.378	.372
2005	WAS	NL	113	303	76	8	1	0	(0 | 0)	86	44	22	38	34	1	55	5	13	3	3	4	.43	2	.251	.333	.284
	4 ML YEARS		336	819	220	37	7	2	(2 | 0)	277	127	54	96	89	2	127	9	28	8	14	7	.67	16	.269	.344	.338

Lance Carter

Pitches: R **Bats:** R **Pos:** RP-39 **Ht:** 6'1" **Wt:** 190 **Born:** 12/18/1974 **Age:** 31

Year	Team	Lg	G	GS	CG	GF	IP	BFP	H	R	ER	HR	SH	SF	HB	TBB	IBB	SO	WP	Bk	W	L	Pct	ShO	Sv-Op	Hld	ERC	ERA
2005	Drham*	AAA	8	7	0	0	35.0	157	40	24	20	8	0	2	0	12	0	30	2	0	1	5	.167	0	0--	-	5.48	5.14
1999	KC	AL	6	0	0	3	5.1	21	3	3	3	2	0	0	0	3	0	3	0	0	0	1	.000	0	0-0	0	4.22	5.06
2002	TB	AL	8	0	0	7	20.1	79	15	3	3	2	0	0	0	5	1	14	0	0	2	0	1.000	0	2-2	0	2.12	1.33
2003	TB	AL	62	0	0	55	79.0	328	72	39	38	12	1	6	4	19	6	47	0	0	7	5	.583	0	26-33	2	3.38	4.33
2004	TB	AL	56	0	0	27	80.1	336	77	32	31	12	1	5	1	23	2	36	1	0	3	3	.500	0	0-1	7	3.74	3.47
2005	TB	AL	39	0	0	18	57.0	239	61	31	31	9	1	3	1	15	1	22	0	0	1	2	.333	0	1-4	5	4.45	4.89
	5 ML YEARS		171	0	0	110	242.0	1003	228	108	106	37	3	14	6	65	10	122	1	0	13	11	.542	0	29-40	14	3.64	3.94

Marcos Carvajal

Pitches: R **Bats:** R **Pos:** RP-39   **Ht:** 6'4" **Wt:** 175 **Born:** 8/19/1984 **Age:** 21

				HOW MUCH HE PITCHED			WHAT HE GAVE UP											THE RESULTS							
Year	Team	Lg	G	GS	CG	GF	IP	BFP	H	R	ER	HR	SH	SF	HB	TBB	IBB	SO	WP	Bk	W	L	Pct	ShO	Sv-Op	Hld	ERC	ERA
2002	Ddgrs	R	13	5	0	3	42.0	171	30	12	8	0	0	1	4	15	0	35	1	0	3	2	.600	0	0--	-	2.15	1.71
2003	Ogden	R+	23	0	0	21	38.0	168	32	16	13	1	1	1	4	22	0	50	6	1	2	1	.667	0	0--	-	3.75	3.08
2004	Clmbs	A	36	0	0	21	72.0	301	50	19	15	2	3	4	5	35	0	72	7	0	4	2	.667	0	1--	-	2.55	1.88
2004	Jaxnvl	AA	1	0	0	0	3.0	13	2	0	0	0	0	0	0	2	0	2	1	0	0	0	-	0	0--	-	2.54	0.00
2005	COL	NL	39	0	0	11	53.0	229	52	30	30	8	2	2	3	21	0	47	4	0	0	2	.000	0	0-1	0	4.57	5.09

Raul Casanova

Bats: B **Throws:** R **Pos:** C-6; PH-1   **Ht:** 6'0" **Wt:** 216 **Born:** 8/23/1972 **Age:** 33

									BATTING												BASERUNNING				AVERAGES		
Year	Team	Lg	G	AB	H	2B	3B	HR	(Hm	Rd)	TB	R	RBI	RC	TBB	IBB	SO	HBP	SH	SF	SB	CS	SB%	GDP	Avg	OBP	Slg
2005	Charltt*	AAA	70	233	62	13	0	13			114	25	42	38	20	2	29	1	0	1	0	0	-	13	.266	.325	.489
1996	DET	AL	25	85	16	1	0	4	(1	3)	29	6	9	5	6	0	18	0	0	0	0	0	-	6	.188	.242	.341
1997	DET	AL	101	304	74	10	1	5	(5	0)	101	27	24	29	26	1	48	3	0	1	1	1	.50	10	.243	.308	.332
1998	DET	AL	16	42	6	2	0	1	(1	0)	11	4	3	3	5	0	10	1	0	0	0	0	-	0	.143	.250	.262
2000	MIL	NL	86	231	57	13	3	6	(4	2)	94	20	36	31	26	1	48	4	2	2	1	2	.33	5	.247	.331	.407
2001	MIL	NL	71	192	50	10	0	11	(7	4)	93	21	33	28	12	2	29	1	0	3	0	0	-	3	.260	.303	.484
2002	2 Tms		33	88	16	1	0	1	(0	1)	20	3	8	4	10	4	19	1	0	1	0	0	-	3	.182	.270	.227
2005	CHA	AL	6	5	1	0	0	0	(0	0)	1	0	0	1	0	0	1	0	0	0	0	0	-	0	.200	.200	.200
02	Mil	NL	31	87	16	1	0	1	(0	1)	20	3	8	4	10	4	18	1	0	1	0	0	-	3	.184	.273	.230
02	Bal	AL	2	1	0	0	0	0	(0	0)	0	0	0	0	0	0	1	0	0	0	0	0	-	0	.000	.000	.000
	7 ML YEARS		338	947	220	37	4	28	(18	10)	349	81	113	101	85	8	173	10	2	7	2	3	.40	27	.232	.300	.369

Sean Casey

Bats: L **Throws:** R **Pos:** 1B-134; PH-3; DH-1   **Ht:** 6'4" **Wt:** 225 **Born:** 7/2/1974 **Age:** 31

									BATTING												BASERUNNING				AVERAGES		
Year	Team	Lg	G	AB	H	2B	3B	HR	(Hm	Rd)	TB	R	RBI	RC	TBB	IBB	SO	HBP	SH	SF	SB	CS	SB%	GDP	Avg	OBP	Slg
1997	CLE	AL	6	10	2	0	0	0	(0	0)	2	1	1	1	1	0	2	1	0	0	0	0	-	0	.200	.333	.200
1998	CIN	NL	96	302	82	21	1	7	(3	4)	126	44	52	45	43	3	45	3	0	3	1	1	.50	11	.272	.365	.417
1999	CIN	NL	151	594	197	42	3	25	(11	14)	320	103	99	119	61	13	88	9	0	5	0	2	.00	15	.332	.399	.539
2000	CIN	NL	133	480	151	33	2	20	(9	11)	248	69	85	91	52	4	80	7	0	6	1	0	1.00	16	.315	.385	.517
2001	CIN	NL	145	533	165	40	0	13	(5	8)	244	69	89	86	43	8	63	9	0	3	3	1	.75	16	.310	.369	.458
2002	CIN	NL	120	425	111	25	0	6	(3	3)	154	56	42	45	43	6	47	5	0	3	2	1	.67	11	.261	.334	.362
2003	CIN	NL	147	573	167	19	3	14	(8	6)	234	71	80	84	51	4	58	2	0	1	4	0	1.00	19	.291	.350	.408
2004	CIN	NL	146	571	185	44	2	24	(9	15)	305	101	99	104	46	5	36	10	0	6	2	0	1.00	16	.324	.381	.534
2005	CIN	NL	137	529	165	32	0	9	(4	5)	224	75	58	72	48	3	48	5	0	5	2	0	1.00	27	.312	.371	.423
	9 ML YEARS		1081	4017	1225	256	11	118	(52	66)	1857	589	605	647	388	46	467	51	0	34	15	5	.75	131	.305	.371	.462

Kevin Cash

Bats: R **Throws:** R **Pos:** C-13; PH-1   **Ht:** 6'0" **Wt:** 185 **Born:** 12/6/1977 **Age:** 28

									BATTING												BASERUNNING				AVERAGES		
Year	Team	Lg	G	AB	H	2B	3B	HR	(Hm	Rd)	TB	R	RBI	RC	TBB	IBB	SO	HBP	SH	SF	SB	CS	SB%	GDP	Avg	OBP	Slg
2005	Drham*	AAA	42	147	43	10	0	9	(-	-)	80	25	27	28	12	0	42	3	1	2	0	0	-	1	.293	.354	.544
2002	TOR	AL	7	14	2	0	0	0	(0	0)	2	1	0	0	1	0	4	0	0	0	0	0	-	1	.143	.200	.143
2003	TOR	AL	34	106	15	3	0	1	(1	0)	21	10	8	0	4	0	22	1	5	1	0	0	-	6	.142	.179	.198
2004	TOR	AL	60	181	35	9	0	4	(2	2)	56	18	21	11	10	0	59	4	0	2	0	0	-	3	.193	.249	.309
2005	TB	AL	13	31	5	1	0	2	(1	1)	12	4	2	0	1	0	13	1	0	0	0	0	-	3	.161	.212	.387
	4 ML YEARS		114	332	57	13	0	7	(4	3)	91	33	31	11	16	0	98	6	5	3	0	0	-	13	.172	.221	.274

Scott Cassidy

Pitches: R **Bats:** R **Pos:** RP-11   **Ht:** 6'2" **Wt:** 175 **Born:** 10/3/1975 **Age:** 30

				HOW MUCH HE PITCHED					WHAT HE GAVE UP											THE RESULTS							
Year	Team	Lg	G	GS	CG	GF	IP	BFP	H	R	ER	HR	SH	SF	HB	TBB	IBB	SO	WP	Bk	W	L	Pct	ShO	Sv-Op	Hld	ERC	ERA
1998	MdHat	R+	15	14	0	0	81.1	325	71	31	22	4	2	3	5	14	0	82	2	0	8	1	.889	0	0--	-	2.50	2.43
1999	Hgrstn	A	27	27	1	0	170.2	694	151	78	62	13	2	1	21	30	0	178	3	2	13	7	.650	0	0--	-	2.95	3.27
2000	Dnedin	A+	14	13	1	1	88.0	342	53	15	13	4	3	2	3	34	2	89	4	0	9	3	.750	0	0--	-	1.82	1.33
2000	Tenn	AA	8	7	0	0	42.2	190	48	30	28	7	1	4	4	15	0	39	3	0	2	2	.500	0	0--	-	5.49	5.91
2001	Tenn	AA	16	15	4	0	96.2	394	78	45	37	10	3	0	7	27	0	81	1	0	6	6	.500	3	0--	-	2.90	3.44
2001	Syrcse	AAA	11	11	0	0	63.0	276	60	24	19	6	0	1	6	26	0	48	1	0	3	3	.500	0	0--	-	4.18	2.71
2002	Syrcse	AAA	3	2	0	1	9.0	33	8	4	4	2	0	0	0	0	0	4	1	0	1	0	1.000	0	0--	-	2.79	4.00
2003	Syrcse	AAA	57	0	0	21	80.2	354	75	31	29	3	0	0	3	46	7	75	5	0	3	4	.429	0	4--	-	3.92	3.24
2004	Pwtckt	AAA	28	12	0	3	80.2	345	72	34	31	10	4	3	3	38	0	72	1	0	5	3	.625	0	1--	-	4.11	3.46
2005	Pwtckt	AAA	26	3	0	6	60.0	257	54	31	27	5	4	4	2	23	2	66	0	0	6	3	.667	0	0--	-	3.38	4.05
2005	Portlnd	AAA	17	0	0	13	19.0	74	10	5	4	2	2	1	1	7	1	19	0	0	0	1	.000	0	11--	-	1.74	1.89
2002	TOR	AL	58	0	0	17	66.0	282	52	42	42	12	4	5	7	32	3	48	2	0	1	4	.200	0	0-7	7	4.17	5.73
2005	2 Tms		11	0	0	4	13.0	60	19	13	12	3	2	0	0	3	0	12	0	0	1	1	.500	0	0-0	1	7.11	8.31
05	Bos	AL	1	0	0	0	0.2	6	4	3	3	0	0	0	0	0	0	0	0	0	0	0	-	0	0-0	0	39.65	40.50
05	SD	NL	10	0	0	4	12.1	54	15	10	9	3	2	0	0	3	0	12	0	0	1	1	.500	0	0-0	1	5.71	6.57
	2 ML YEARS		69	0	0	21	79.0	342	71	55	54	15	6	5	7	35	3	60	2	0	2	5	.286	0	0-7	8	4.63	6.15

Vinny Castilla

Bats: R **Throws:** R **Pos:** 3B-138; PH-4   **Ht:** 6'1" **Wt:** 205 **Born:** 7/4/1967 **Age:** 38

Year	Team	Lg	G	AB	H	2B	3B	HR	(Hm	Rd)	TB	R	RBI	RC	TBB	IBB	SO	HBP	SH	SF	SB	CS	SB%	GDP	Avg	OBP	Slg
1991	ATL	NL	12	5	1	0	0	0	(0	0)	1	1	0	0	0	0	2	0	1	0	0	0	-	0	.200	.200	.200
1992	ATL	NL	9	16	4	1	0	0	(0	0)	5	1	1	2	1	1	4	1	0	0	0	0	-	0	.250	.333	.313
1993	COL	NL	105	337	86	9	7	9	(5	4)	136	36	30	34	13	4	45	2	0	5	2	5	.29	10	.255	.283	.404
1994	COL	NL	52	130	43	11	1	3	(1	2)	65	16	18	22	7	1	23	0	1	3	2	1	.67	3	.331	.357	.500
1995	COL	NL	139	527	163	34	2	32	(23	9)	297	82	90	94	30	2	87	4	4	6	2	8	.20	15	.309	.347	.564
1996	COL	NL	160	629	191	34	0	40	(27	13)	345	97	113	110	35	7	88	5	0	4	7	2	.78	20	.304	.343	.548
1997	COL	NL	159	612	186	25	2	40	(21	19)	335	94	113	110	44	9	108	8	0	4	2	4	.33	17	.304	.356	.547
1998	COL	NL	162	645	206	28	4	46	(26	20)	380	108	144	122	40	7	89	6	0	6	5	9	.36	24	.319	.362	.589
1999	COL	NL	158	615	169	24	1	33	(20	13)	294	83	102	93	53	7	75	1	0	5	2	3	.40	15	.275	.331	.478
2000	TB	AL	85	331	73	9	1	6	(2	4)	102	22	42	22	14	3	41	3	0	6	1	2	.33	9	.221	.254	.308
2001	2 Tms		146	538	140	34	1	25	(12	13)	251	69	91	70	35	3	108	4	0	4	1	4	.20	22	.260	.308	.467
2002	ATL	NL	143	543	126	23	2	12	(5	7)	189	56	61	36	22	4	69	7	0	6	4	1	.80	22	.232	.268	.348
2003	ATL	NL	147	542	150	28	3	22	(6	16)	250	65	76	70	26	3	86	3	1	6	1	2	.33	22	.277	.310	.461
2004	COL	NL	148	583	158	43	3	35	(14	21)	312	93	131	88	51	6	113	6	0	8	0	0	-	22	.271	.332	.535
2005	WAS	NL	142	494	125	36	1	12	(8	4)	199	53	66	52	43	7	82	7	1	4	4	2	.67	16	.253	.319	.403
01	TB	AL	24	93	20	6	0	2	(2	0)	32	7	9	7	3	0	22	1	0	0	0	0	-	3	.215	.247	.344
01	Hou	NL	122	445	120	28	1	23	(10	13)	219	62	82	63	32	3	86	3	0	4	1	4	.20	19	.270	.320	.492
15 ML YEARS			1767	6547	1821	339	28	315	(170	145)	3161	876	1078	925	414	64	1020	57	8	67	33	43	.43	217	.278	.324	.483

Alberto Castillo

Bats: R **Throws:** R **Pos:** C-35   **Ht:** 6'0" **Wt:** 200 **Born:** 2/10/1970 **Age:** 36

Year	Team	Lg	G	AB	H	2B	3B	HR	(Hm	Rd)	TB	R	RBI	RC	TBB	IBB	SO	HBP	SH	SF	SB	CS	SB%	GDP	Avg	OBP	Slg
2005	Scrmto*	AAA	4	13	1	0	0	0	(-	-)	1	2	0	0	1	0	4	0	0	0	0	0	-	0	.077	.143	.077
1995	NYN	NL	13	29	3	0	0	0	(0	0)	3	2	0	0	3	0	9	1	0	0	1	0	1.00	0	.103	.212	.103
1996	NYN	NL	6	11	4	0	0	0	(0	0)	4	1	0	1	0	0	4	0	0	0	0	0	-	0	.364	.364	.364
1997	NYN	NL	35	59	12	1	0	0	(0	0)	13	3	7	3	9	0	16	0	2	1	0	1	.00	3	.203	.304	.220
1998	NYN	NL	38	83	17	4	0	2	(0	2)	27	13	7	7	9	0	17	1	6	0	0	2	.00	1	.205	.290	.325
1999	STL	NL	93	255	67	8	0	4	(2	2)	87	21	31	29	24	1	48	2	5	4	0	0	-	6	.263	.326	.341
2000	TOR	AL	66	185	39	7	0	1	(1	0)	49	14	16	14	21	0	36	0	2	3	0	0	-	3	.211	.287	.265
2001	TOR	AL	66	131	26	4	0	1	(0	1)	33	9	4	7	7	0	30	3	5	0	1	1	.50	2	.198	.255	.252
2002	NYA	AL	15	37	5	1	1	0	(0	0)	8	3	4	1	1	0	12	0	3	0	0	0	-	0	.135	.158	.216
2003	SF	NL	11	15	3	1	0	1	(1	0)	7	2	4	2	0	0	5	0	0	0	0	0	-	0	.200	.200	.467
2004	KC	AL	29	89	24	6	0	1	(1	0)	33	12	11	10	14	0	10	0	1	1	0	2	.00	0	.270	.365	.371
2005	2 Tms		35	101	21	5	1	1	(1	0)	31	13	14	12	12	0	22	0	1	1	1	0	1.00	2	.208	.289	.307
05	KC	AL	34	100	21	5	1	1	(1	0)	31	13	14	12	12	0	21	0	1	1	1	0	1.00	2	.210	.292	.310
05	Oak	AL	1	1	0	0	0	0	(0	0)	0	0	0	0	0	0	1	0	0	0	0	0	-	0	.000	.000	.000
11 ML YEARS			407	995	221	37	2	11	(5	6)	295	93	98	86	100	1	209	7	25	10	3	6	.33	19	.222	.295	.296

Frank Castillo

Pitches: R **Bats:** R **Pos:** SP-1   **Ht:** 6'1" **Wt:** 198 **Born:** 4/1/1969 **Age:** 37

			HOW MUCH HE PITCHED						WHAT HE GAVE UP												THE RESULTS						
Year	Team	Lg	G	GS	CG	GF	IP	BFP	H	R	ER	HR	SH	SF	HB	TBB	IBB	SO	WP	Bk	W	L	Pct	ShO	Sv-Op Hld		ERC	ERA
2005	Albq*	AAA	27	24	0	0	143.1	649	161	102	88	20	7	4	10	58	3	80	4	0	9	11	.450	0	0- -	-	5.31	5.53
1991	CHN	NL	18	18	4	0	111.2	467	107	56	54	5	6	3	0	33	2	73	5	1	6	7	.462	0	0-0	0	3.04	4.35
1992	CHN	NL	33	33	0	0	205.1	856	179	91	79	19	11	5	6	63	6	135	11	0	10	11	.476	0	0-0	0	3.02	3.46
1993	CHN	NL	29	25	2	0	141.1	614	162	83	76	20	10	3	9	39	4	84	5	3	5	8	.385	0	0-0	0	4.98	4.84
1994	CHN	NL	4	4	1	0	23.0	96	25	13	11	3	1	0	0	5	0	19	0	0	2	1	.667	0	0-0	0	4.09	4.30
1995	CHN	NL	29	29	2	0	188.0	795	179	75	67	22	11	3	6	52	4	135	3	1	11	10	.524	2	0-0	0	3.49	3.21
1996	CHN	NL	33	33	1	0	182.1	789	209	112	107	28	4	5	8	46	4	139	2	1	7	16	.304	1	0-0	0	4.87	5.28
1997	2 Tms	NL	34	33	0	0	184.1	830	220	121	111	25	17	2	8	69	4	126	3	0	12	12	.500	0	0-0	0	5.51	5.42
1998	DET	AL	27	19	0	4	116.0	531	150	91	88	17	2	6	5	44	0	81	0	0	3	9	.250	0	1-1	0	6.32	6.83
2000	TOR	AL	25	24	0	1	138.0	576	112	58	55	18	5	2	5	56	0	104	0	0	10	5	.667	0	0-0	0	3.42	3.59
2001	BOS	AL	26	26	0	0	136.2	580	138	72	64	24	1	3	6	35	2	89	3	1	10	9	.526	0	0-0	0	3.68	4.21
2002	BOS	AL	36	23	0	2	163.1	711	174	101	92	19	1	11	7	58	6	112	1	2	6	15	.286	0	1-2	0	4.51	5.07
2004	BOS	AL	2	0	0	0	1.0	4	1	0	0	0	0	0	0	1	0	0	0	0	0	0	-	0	0-0	0	6.99	0.00
2005	FLA	NL	1	1	0	0	4.1	22	4	5	5	0	0	0	0	5	0	4	0	0	0	1	.000	0	0-0	0	5.62	10.38
97	ChC	NL	20	19	0	0	98.0	446	113	64	59	9	11	0	4	44	1	67	1	0	6	9	.400	0	0-0	0	5.23	5.42
97	Col	NL	14	14	0	0	86.1	384	107	57	52	16	6	2	4	25	3	59	2	0	6	3	.667	0	0-0	0	5.83	5.42
13 ML YEARS			297	268	10	9	1595.1	6871	1660	878	809	190	71	46	59	506	32	1101	33	9	82	104	.441	3	2-3	0	4.22	4.56

Jose Castillo

Bats: R **Throws:** R **Pos:** 2B-100; PR-1   **Ht:** 6'1" **Wt:** 200 **Born:** 3/19/1981 **Age:** 25

Year	Team	Lg	G	AB	H	2B	3B	HR	(Hm	Rd)	TB	R	RBI	RC	TBB	IBB	SO	HBP	SH	SF	SB	CS	SB%	GDP	Avg	OBP	Slg
1999	Pirates	R	47	173	46	9	0	4	(-	-)	67	27	30	22	11	1	23	3	3	3	8	0	1.00	4	.266	.316	.387
2000	Hickory	A	125	529	158	32	8	16	(-	-)	254	95	72	82	29	0	107	10	7	2	16	12	.57	10	.299	.346	.480
2001	Lynbrg	A+	125	485	119	20	7	7	(-	-)	174	57	49	48	21	2	94	9	4	2	23	10	.70	9	.245	.288	.359
2002	Lynbrg	A+	134	503	151	25	2	16	(-	-)	228	82	81	80	49	1	95	11	1	8	27	14	.66	18	.300	.370	.453
2003	Altna	AA	126	498	143	24	6	5	(-	-)	194	68	66	63	40	1	81	0	0	8	19	10	.66	18	.287	.339	.390
2005	Indy	AAA	4	13	5	1	0	2	(-	-)	12	2	2	4	2	0	1	0	0	0	0	0	-	0	.385	.467	.923
2004	PIT	NL	129	383	98	15	2	8	(3	5)	141	44	39	40	23	5	92	1	5	2	3	2	.60	12	.256	.298	.368
2005	PIT	NL	101	370	99	16	3	11	(2	9)	154	49	53	43	23	3	59	0	1	4	2	3	.40	11	.268	.307	.416
2 ML YEARS			230	753	197	31	5	19	(5	14)	295	93	92	83	46	8	151	1	6	6	5	5	.50	23	.262	.303	.392

49

Luis Castillo

Bats: B **Throws:** R **Pos:** 2B-120; PH-2   **Ht:** 5'11" **Wt:** 190 **Born:** 9/12/1975 **Age:** 30

Year	Team	Lg	G	AB	H	2B	3B	HR	(Hm	Rd)	TB	R	RBI	RC	TBB	IBB	SO	HBP	SH	SF	SB	CS	SB%	GDP	Avg	OBP	Slg
1996	FLA	NL	41	164	43	2	1	1	(0	1)	50	26	8	19	14	0	46	0	2	0	17	4	.81	0	.262	.320	.305
1997	FLA	NL	75	263	63	8	0	0	(0	0)	71	27	8	21	27	0	53	0	1	0	16	10	.62	6	.240	.310	.270
1998	FLA	NL	44	153	31	3	2	1	(0	1)	41	21	10	14	22	0	33	1	1	0	3	0	1.00	1	.203	.307	.268
1999	FLA	NL	128	487	147	23	4	0	(0	0)	178	76	28	78	67	0	85	0	6	3	50	17	.75	3	.302	.384	.366
2000	FLA	NL	136	539	180	17	3	2	(1	1)	209	101	17	95	78	0	86	0	9	0	62	22	.74	11	.334	.418	.388
2001	FLA	NL	134	537	141	16	10	2	(1	1)	183	76	45	67	67	0	90	1	4	3	33	16	.67	6	.263	.344	.341
2002	FLA	NL	146	606	185	18	5	2	(0	2)	219	86	39	84	55	4	76	2	4	1	48	15	.76	7	.305	.364	.361
2003	FLA	NL	152	595	187	19	6	6	(2	4)	236	99	39	87	63	0	60	2	15	1	21	19	.53	7	.314	.381	.397
2004	FLA	NL	150	564	164	12	7	2	(1	1)	196	91	47	84	75	2	68	1	5	4	21	4	.84	15	.291	.373	.348
2005	FLA	NL	122	439	132	12	4	4	(0	4)	164	72	30	61	65	1	32	1	18	1	10	7	.59	11	.301	.391	.374
10 ML YEARS			1128	4347	1273	130	42	20	(5	15)	1547	675	271	610	533	7	629	8	65	13	281	114	.71	67	.293	.370	.356

Bernie Castro

Bats: B **Throws:** R **Pos:** 2B-11; DH-9; PH-3; PR-2; LF-1   **Ht:** 5'10" **Wt:** 160 **Born:** 7/14/1979 **Age:** 26

Year	Team	Lg	G	AB	H	2B	3B	HR	(Hm	Rd)	TB	R	RBI	RC	TBB	IBB	SO	HBP	SH	SF	SB	CS	SB%	GDP	Avg	OBP	Slg
2000	Yanks	R	9	34	15	4	1	0	(-	-)	21	7	6	10	6	0	4	0	0	0	3	1	.75	1	.441	.525	.618
2001	StIsInd	A-	15	57	20	1	0	1	(-	-)	24	6	7	12	11	0	12	1	0	0	8	3	.73	0	.351	.464	.421
2001	Grnsbr	A	101	389	101	15	7	0	(-	-)	130	71	36	56	54	1	67	1	5	2	67	20	.77	5	.260	.350	.334
2002	Mobile	AA	109	419	109	13	3	0	(-	-)	128	61	32	52	52	1	67	3	2	1	53	20	.73	1	.260	.345	.305
2003	Portlnd	AAA	105	424	131	17	5	2	(-	-)	164	57	24	63	25	0	43	1	3	2	49	13	.79	5	.309	.347	.387
2004	Portlnd	AAA	90	308	81	8	1	0	(-	-)	91	38	20	30	22	2	30	0	2	2	17	9	.65	6	.263	.310	.295
2005	Ottawa	AAA	126	502	158	21	5	1	(-	-)	192	81	36	80	42	3	50	0	9	6	41	6	.87	5	.315	.364	.382
2005	BAL	AL	24	80	23	3	1	0	(0	0)	28	14	7	13	9	0	10	0	0	0	6	2	.75	0	.288	.360	.350

Juan Castro

Bats: R **Throws:** R **Pos:** SS-73; 3B-22; 2B-5; PR-3   **Ht:** 5'11" **Wt:** 195 **Born:** 6/20/1972 **Age:** 34

Year	Team	Lg	G	AB	H	2B	3B	HR	(Hm	Rd)	TB	R	RBI	RC	TBB	IBB	SO	HBP	SH	SF	SB	CS	SB%	GDP	Avg	OBP	Slg
1995	LA	NL	11	4	1	0	0	0	(0	0)	1	0	0	1	1	0	1	0	0	0	0	0	-	0	.250	.400	.250
1996	LA	NL	70	132	26	5	3	0	(0	0)	37	16	5	8	10	0	27	0	4	0	1	0	1.00	3	.197	.254	.280
1997	LA	NL	40	75	11	3	1	0	(0	0)	16	3	4	2	7	1	20	0	2	0	0	0	-	2	.147	.220	.213
1998	LA	NL	89	220	43	7	0	2	(0	2)	56	25	14	12	15	0	37	0	9	2	0	0	-	5	.195	.245	.255
1999	LA	NL	2	1	0	0	0	0	(0	0)	0	0	0	0	0	0	1	0	0	0	0	0	-	0	.000	.000	.000
2000	CIN	NL	82	224	54	12	2	4	(1	3)	82	20	23	20	14	1	33	0	4	2	0	2	.00	9	.241	.283	.366
2001	CIN	NL	96	242	54	10	0	3	(0	3)	73	27	13	16	13	2	50	0	4	2	0	0	-	9	.223	.261	.302
2002	CIN	NL	54	82	18	3	0	2	(0	2)	27	5	11	11	7	0	18	0	1	1					.220	.278	.329
2003	CIN	NL	113	320	81	14	1	9	(4	5)	124	28	33	36	18	1	58	0	7	3	2	3	.40	7	.253	.290	.388
2004	CIN	NL	111	299	73	21	2	5	(3	2)	113	36	26	26	14	1	51	0	2	1	1	0	1.00	11	.244	.277	.378
2005	MIN	AL	97	272	70	18	1	5	(2	3)	105	27	33	28	9	1	39	0	9	2	0	1	.00	8	.257	.279	.386
11 ML YEARS			765	1871	431	93	10	30	(10	20)	634	187	162	160	108	7	335	0	42	13	4	6	.40	54	.230	.271	.339

Ramon Castro

Bats: R **Throws:** R **Pos:** C-99; PH-1; PR-1   **Ht:** 6'3" **Wt:** 235 **Born:** 3/1/1976 **Age:** 30

Year	Team	Lg	G	AB	H	2B	3B	HR	(Hm	Rd)	TB	R	RBI	RC	TBB	IBB	SO	HBP	SH	SF	SB	CS	SB%	GDP	Avg	OBP	Slg
1999	FLA	NL	24	67	12	4	0	2	(0	2)	22	4	4	6	10	3	14	0	0	1	0	0	-	1	.179	.282	.328
2000	FLA	NL	50	138	33	4	0	2	(0	2)	43	10	14	14	16	7	36	1	0	2	0	0	-	1	.239	.318	.312
2001	FLA	NL	7	11	2	0	0	0	(0	0)	2	0	1	0	1	0	1	0	0	0	0	0	-	0	.182	.250	.182
2002	FLA	NL	54	101	24	4	0	6	(4	2)	46	11	18	14	14	3	24	0	1	3	0	0	-	4	.238	.322	.455
2003	FLA	NL	40	53	15	2	0	5	(4	1)	32	6	8	8	4	0	11	0	0	0	0	0	-	1	.283	.333	.604
2004	FLA	NL	32	96	13	3	0	3	(0	3)	25	9	8	4	11	2	30	1	0	3	0	0	-	1	.135	.231	.260
2005	NYN	NL	99	209	51	16	0	8	(5	3)	91	26	41	30	25	2	58	0	3	3	1	0	1.00	14	.244	.321	.435
7 ML YEARS			306	675	150	33	0	26	(13	13)	261	66	94	76	81	17	174	2	4	9	1	0	1.00	14	.222	.304	.387

Frank Catalanotto

Bats: L **Throws:** R **Pos:** LF-111; PH-17; DH-15   **Ht:** 5'11" **Wt:** 195 **Born:** 4/27/1974 **Age:** 32

Year	Team	Lg	G	AB	H	2B	3B	HR	(Hm	Rd)	TB	R	RBI	RC	TBB	IBB	SO	HBP	SH	SF	SB	CS	SB%	GDP	Avg	OBP	Slg
1997	DET	AL	13	26	8	2	0	0	(0	0)	10	2	3	4	3	0	7	0	0	0	0	0	-	0	.308	.379	.385
1998	DET	AL	89	213	60	13	2	6	(3	3)	95	23	25	30	12	1	39	4	0	5	3	2	.60	4	.282	.325	.446
1999	DET	AL	100	286	79	19	0	11	(6	5)	131	44	35	42	15	1	49	9	0	5	3	4	.43	5	.276	.327	.458
2000	TEX	AL	103	282	82	13	2	10	(6	4)	129	55	42	49	33	0	36	6	3	2	6	2	.75	5	.291	.375	.457
2001	TEX	AL	133	463	153	31	5	11	(4	7)	227	77	54	88	39	3	55	8	1	1	15	5	.75	5	.330	.391	.490
2002	TEX	AL	68	212	57	16	6	3	(2	1)	94	42	23	39	25	0	27	8	3	2	9	5	.64	3	.269	.346	.443
2003	TOR	AL	133	489	146	34	6	13	(7	6)	231	83	59	84	35	1	62	6	2	3	2	2	.50	9	.299	.351	.472
2004	TOR	AL	75	249	73	19	1	1	(1	0)	97	27	26	34	17	1	33	4	1	3	1	0	1.00	7	.293	.344	.390
2005	TOR	AL	130	419	126	29	5	8	(3	5)	189	56	59	80	37	0	53	10	4	5	3	2	.00	7	.301	.367	.451
9 ML YEARS			844	2639	784	176	27	63	(32	31)	1203	406	326	450	216	7	361	55	14	26	39	22	.64	47	.297	.359	.456

Roger Cedeno

Bats: B Throws: R Pos: PH-26; RF-10; LF-6   Ht: 6'1" Wt: 205 Born: 8/16/1974 Age: 31

Year	Team	Lg	G	AB	H	2B	3B	HR	(Hm	Rd)	TB	R	RBI	RC	TBB	IBB	SO	HBP	SH	SF	SB	CS	SB%	GDP	Avg	OBP	Slg
2005	Memp*	AAA	8	23	4	1	0	0	(-	-)	5	3	2	1	3	1	5	0	0	0	0	0	-	0	.174	.269	.217
1995	LA	NL	40	42	10	2	0	0	(0	0)	12	4	3	3	3	0	10	0	0	1	1	0	1.00	1	.238	.283	.286
1996	LA	NL	86	211	52	11	1	2	(0	2)	71	26	18	26	24	0	47	1	2	0	5	1	.83	0	.246	.326	.336
1997	LA	NL	80	194	53	10	2	3	(3	0)	76	31	17	31	25	2	44	3	3	2	9	1	.90	1	.273	.362	.392
1998	LA	NL	105	240	58	11	1	2	(2	0)	77	33	17	27	27	2	57	0	3	1	8	2	.80	1	.242	.317	.321
1999	NYN	NL	155	453	142	23	4	4	(4	0)	185	90	36	82	60	3	100	3	7	2	66	17	.80	5	.313	.396	.408
2000	HOU	NL	74	259	73	2	5	6	(3	3)	103	54	26	42	43	0	47	0	2	1	25	11	.69	6	.282	.383	.398
2001	DET	AL	131	523	153	14	11	6	(3	3)	207	79	48	76	36	1	83	2	6	5	55	15	.79	5	.293	.337	.396
2002	NYN	NL	149	511	133	19	2	7	(2	5)	177	65	41	60	42	1	92	2	5	2	25	4	.86	10	.260	.318	.346
2003	NYN	NL	148	484	129	25	4	7	(5	2)	183	70	37	52	38	3	86	1	2	2	14	9	.61	8	.267	.320	.378
2004	STL	NL	95	200	53	9	2	3	(0	3)	75	22	23	29	19	2	41	0	3	1	5	1	.83	5	.265	.327	.375
2005	STL	NL	37	57	9	1	0	0	(0	0)	10	4	8	0	2	0	6	1	0	1	0	2	.00	2	.158	.197	.175
	11 ML YEARS		1100	3174	865	127	32	40	(22	18)	1176	478	274	428	319	14	613	13	33	18	213	63	.77	44	.273	.340	.371

Ronny Cedeno

Bats: R Throws: R Pos: SS-29; PH-12; PR-3; 2B-1   Ht: 6'0" Wt: 180 Born: 2/2/1983 Age: 23

Year	Team	Lg	G	AB	H	2B	3B	HR	(Hm	Rd)	TB	R	RBI	RC	TBB	IBB	SO	HBP	SH	SF	SB	CS	SB%	GDP	Avg	OBP	Slg
2001	Cubs	R	52	206	72	13	4	1	(-	-)	96	36	17	38	13	0	32	5	3	2	17	10	.63	3	.350	.398	.466
2001	Lansng	A	17	56	11	4	1	1	(-	-)	20	9	2	3	2	0	18	1	0	0	0	2	.00	1	.196	.237	.357
2002	Boise	A-	29	110	24	5	2	0	(-	-)	33	17	6	10	9	0	25	0	2	1	8	2	.80	1	.218	.275	.300
2002	Lansng	A	98	376	80	17	4	2	(-	-)	111	44	31	29	22	0	74	8	8	3	14	10	.58	6	.213	.269	.295
2003	Dytona	A+	107	380	80	18	1	4	(-	-)	112	43	36	30	21	0	82	4	12	3	19	6	.76	5	.211	.257	.295
2004	WTenn	AA	116	384	107	19	5	6	(-	-)	154	39	48	51	24	3	74	8	8	8	10	10	.50	10	.279	.328	.401
2005	Iowa	AAA	65	245	87	14	1	8	(-	-)	127	42	36	51	20	2	31	1	7	2	11	3	.79	10	.355	.403	.518
2005	CHN	NL	41	80	24	3	0	1	(0	1)	30	13	6	11	5	1	11	2	2	0	1	0	1.00	4	.300	.356	.375

Matt Cepicky

Bats: L Throws: R Pos: LF-5; PH-5; RF-1   Ht: 6'2" Wt: 215 Born: 11/10/1977 Age: 28

Year	Team	Lg	G	AB	H	2B	3B	HR	(Hm	Rd)	TB	R	RBI	RC	TBB	IBB	SO	HBP	SH	SF	SB	CS	SB%	GDP	Avg	OBP	Slg
2005	NewOr*	AAA	99	342	92	23	3	14	(-	-)	163	52	68	58	43	3	85	1	1	4	1	3	.25	10	.269	.349	.477
2002	MON	NL	32	74	16	3	0	3	(2	1)	28	7	15	8	4	1	21	0	0	0	0	0	-	0	.216	.256	.378
2003	MON	NL	5	8	2	1	0	0	(0	0)	3	0	0	0	0	0	2	0	0	0	0	0	-	0	.250	.250	.375
2004	MON	NL	32	60	13	4	0	1	(1	0)	20	4	3	2	1	0	18	0	0	0	1	0	1.00	1	.217	.230	.333
2005	WAS	NL	11	25	6	3	0	0	(0	0)	9	1	3	1	1	0	8	0	0	0	0	1	.00	1	.240	.269	.360
	4 ML YEARS		80	167	37	11	0	4	(3	1)	60	12	21	11	6	1	49	0	0	0	1	1	.50	2	.222	.249	.359

Jaime Cerda

Pitches: L Bats: L Pos: RP-20   Ht: 6'0" Wt: 175 Born: 10/26/1978 Age: 27

Year	Team	Lg	G	GS	CG	GF	IP	BFP	H	R	ER	HR	SH	SF	HB	TBB	IBB	SO	WP	Bk	W	L	Pct	ShO	Sv-Op	Hld	ERC	ERA
2005	Omha*	AAA	35	0	0	11	49.2	218	48	33	29	6	0	2	1	21	1	47	6	0	4	1	.800	0	2- -	-	4.10	5.26
2002	NYN	NL	32	0	0	7	25.2	113	22	7	7	0	0	3	1	14	0	21	0	1	0	0	-	0	0-0	4	3.23	2.45
2003	NYN	NL	27	0	0	9	32.1	144	32	21	21	4	2	2	0	20	1	19	3	1	1	1	.500	0	0-1	2	5.08	5.85
2004	KC	AL	53	0	0	16	45.2	206	41	21	16	1	2	3	3	30	3	33	4	0	1	4	.200	0	2-3	12	4.04	3.15
2005	KC	AL	20	0	0	5	19.0	89	21	14	14	3	3	1	0	11	2	18	2	0	1	4	.200	0	0-1	3	5.54	6.63
	4 ML YEARS		132	0	0	33	122.2	552	116	63	58	8	7	9	4	75	6	91	9	2	3	9	.250	0	2-5	21	4.36	4.26

Gustavo Chacin

Pitches: L Bats: L Pos: SP-34   Ht: 5'11" Wt: 193 Born: 12/4/1980 Age: 25

Year	Team	Lg	G	GS	CG	GF	IP	BFP	H	R	ER	HR	SH	SF	HB	TBB	IBB	SO	WP	Bk	W	L	Pct	ShO	Sv-Op	Hld	ERC	ERA
1999	MdHat	R+	15	9	0	2	64.0	280	68	33	22	6	4	4	7	23	0	50	4	3	4	3	.571	0	1- -	-	4.73	3.09
2000	Dnedin	A+	25	21	0	1	127.2	584	138	69	57	14	1	2	3	64	0	77	9	0	9	5	.643	0	0- -	-	5.03	4.02
2000	Tenn	AA	2	2	0	0	5.0	31	7	7	7	1	0	0	1	6	0	5	0	1	0	2	.000	0	0- -	-	16.75	12.60
2001	Tenn	AA	25	23	1	0	140.1	588	138	66	62	17	2	3	7	39	0	86	5	0	11	8	.579	1	0- -	-	3.88	3.98
2002	Tenn	AA	35	13	1	8	119.2	542	131	73	62	12	6	5	8	59	0	68	4	1	6	5	.545	0	1- -	-	5.30	4.66
2003	NwHav	AA	46	2	0	9	69.1	314	78	39	32	1	3	4	2	29	1	55	7	3	3	4	.429	0	2- -	-	4.23	4.15
2004	Ham	AA	25	25	0	0	141.2	577	113	53	45	15	4	1	5	49	0	109	3	0	16	2	.889	0	0- -	-	2.99	2.86
2004	Syrcse	AAA	2	2	0	0	11.2	53	16	4	3	1	1	0	1	3	0	14	0	0	2	0	1.000	0	0- -	-	4.85	2.31
2004	TOR	AL	2	2	0	0	14.0	52	8	4	4	0	0	1	0	3	0	14	0	0	1	1	.500	0	0-0	0	1.24	2.57
2005	TOR	AL	34	34	0	0	203.0	872	213	93	84	20	8	10	8	70	3	121	3	0	13	9	.591	0	0-0	0	4.30	3.72
	2 ML YEARS		36	36	0	0	217.0	924	221	97	88	20	8	10	8	73	3	127	3	0	14	10	.583	0	0-0	0	4.06	3.65

Shawn Chacon

Pitches: R Bats: R Pos: SP-24; RP-3   Ht: 6'3" Wt: 212 Born: 12/23/1977 Age: 28

Year	Team	Lg	G	GS	CG	GF	IP	BFP	H	R	ER	HR	SH	SF	HB	TBB	IBB	SO	WP	Bk	W	L	Pct	ShO	Sv-Op	Hld	ERC	ERA
2005	ColSpr*	AAA	3	3	0	0	12.2	61	19	14	14	3	0	1	0	4	0	11	1	0	0	2	.000	0	0- -	-	7.69	9.95
2001	COL	NL	27	27	0	0	160.0	711	157	96	90	26	6	3	10	87	10	134	6	0	6	10	.375	0	0-0	0	5.22	5.06
2002	COL	NL	21	21	0	0	119.1	537	122	84	76	25	5	2	7	60	3	67	0	1	5	11	.313	0	0-0	0	5.63	5.73

			HOW MUCH HE PITCHED								WHAT HE GAVE UP												THE RESULTS						
Year	Team	Lg	G	GS	CG	GF	IP	BFP	H	R	ER	HR	SH	SF	HB	TBB	IBB	SO	WP	Bk	W	L	Pct	ShO	Sv-Op	Hld	ERC	ERA
2003	COL	NL	23	23	0	0	137.0	596	124	73	70	12	10	5	12	58	4	93	8	0	11	8	.579	0	0-0	0	3.82	4.60
2004	COL	NL	66	0	0	60	63.1	316	71	52	50	12	7	0	5	52	7	52	9	0	1	9	.100	0	35-44	0	7.30	7.11
2005	2 Tms		27	24	0	0	151.2	652	135	59	58	14	9	5	14	66	4	79	6	1	8	10	.444	0	0-0	1	3.89	3.44
05	Col	NL	13	12	0	0	72.2	322	69	33	33	7	9	4	8	36	4	39	3	0	1	7	.125	0	0-0	0	4.51	4.09
05	NYY	AL	14	12	0	0	79.0	330	66	26	25	7	0	1	6	30	0	40	3	1	7	3	.700	0	0-0	1	3.35	2.85
5 ML YEARS			164	95	0	60	631.1	2812	609	364	344	89	37	15	48	323	28	425	29	2	31	48	.392	0	35-44	1	4.85	4.90

Angel Chavez

Bats: R Throws: R Pos: 2B-5; SS-4; 3B-1; PH-1 **Ht: 6'1" Wt: 195 Born: 7/22/1981 Age: 24**

			BATTING																		BASERUNNING				AVERAGES		
Year	Team	Lg	G	AB	H	2B	3B	HR	(Hm	Rd)	TB	R	RBI	RC	TBB	IBB	SO	HBP	SH	SF	SB	CS	SB%	GDP	Avg	OBP	Slg
2000	Giants	R	7	29	8	0	1	1	(-	-)	13	2	7	3	1	0	5	0	1	0	1	1	.50	1	.276	.300	.448
2001	SnJos	A+	84	316	77	22	2	3	(-	-)	112	37	28	32	16	0	60	1	5	3	10	4	.71	9	.244	.280	.354
2001	Hgrstn	A	13	37	7	2	0	2	(-	-)	15	5	3	3	1	0	12	1	0	0	1	0	1.00	1	.189	.231	.405
2002	SnJos	A+	130	471	121	20	5	8	(-	-)	175	61	62	57	28	1	83	6	8	7	21	7	.75	12	.257	.303	.372
2003	SnJos	A+	120	478	134	23	6	10	(-	-)	199	69	58	64	22	0	60	4	2	6	20	11	.65	13	.280	.314	.416
2004	Giants	R	4	16	6	0	0	1	(-	-)	9	2	5	3	1	0	3	0	0	1	2	0	1.00	1	.375	.389	.563
2004	SnJos	A+	12	54	21	5	0	1	(-	-)	29	12	16	11	4	1	7	1	0	1	2	2	.50	1	.389	.433	.537
2004	Nrwich	AA	89	308	61	8	2	0	(-	-)	73	22	21	18	24	2	53	3	2	2	6	4	.60	10	.198	.261	.237
2005	SnJos	A+	30	120	34	2	1	5	(-	-)	53	22	19	17	5	0	21	0	1	0	4	0	1.00	7	.283	.310	.442
2005	Fresno	AAA	89	334	94	17	3	11	(-	-)	150	46	64	49	17	1	59	3	5	2	5	1	.83	6	.281	.320	.449
2005	SF	NL	10	19	5	1	0	0	(0	0)	6	1	1	2	0	0	3	0	1	0	0	0	-	0	.263	.263	.316

Endy Chavez

Bats: L Throws: L Pos: PH-49; CF-34; LF-20; PR-20; RF-5 **Ht: 6'0" Wt: 165 Born: 2/7/1978 Age: 28**

			BATTING																		BASERUNNING				AVERAGES		
Year	Team	Lg	G	AB	H	2B	3B	HR	(Hm	Rd)	TB	R	RBI	RC	TBB	IBB	SO	HBP	SH	SF	SB	CS	SB%	GDP	Avg	OBP	Slg
2005	NewOr*	AAA	23	87	22	4	0	1	(-	-)	29	11	4	11	10	1	7	0	4	0	6	1	.86	2	.253	.330	.333
2001	KC	AL	29	77	16	2	0	0	(0	0)	18	4	5	2	3	0	8	0	0	0	0	2	.00	3	.208	.238	.234
2002	MON	NL	36	125	37	8	5	1	(0	0)	58	20	9	14	5	0	16	0	7	1	3	5	.38	0	.296	.321	.464
2003	MON	NL	141	483	121	25	5	5	(4	1)	171	66	47	56	31	3	59	0	9	3	18	7	.72	7	.251	.294	.354
2004	MON	NL	132	502	139	20	6	5	(4	1)	186	65	34	56	30	0	40	1	12	2	32	7	.82	6	.277	.318	.371
2005	2 Tms	NL	98	116	25	4	3	0	(0	0)	35	19	11	8	7	0	14	0	7	0	2	2	.50	3	.216	.260	.302
05	Was	NL	7	9	2	1	0	0	(0	0)	3	2	1	1	3	0	1	0	0	0	0	1	.00	1	.222	.417	.333
05	Phi	NL	91	107	23	3	3	0	(0	0)	32	17	10	7	4	0	13	0	7	0	2	1	.67	2	.215	.243	.299
5 ML YEARS			436	1303	338	59	19	11	(8	3)	468	174	106	136	76	3	137	1	35	6	55	23	.71	19	.259	.299	.359

Eric Chavez

Bats: L Throws: R Pos: 3B-153; DH-6; PH-1 **Ht: 6'1" Wt: 206 Born: 12/7/1977 Age: 28**

			BATTING																		BASERUNNING				AVERAGES		
Year	Team	Lg	G	AB	H	2B	3B	HR	(Hm	Rd)	TB	R	RBI	RC	TBB	IBB	SO	HBP	SH	SF	SB	CS	SB%	GDP	Avg	OBP	Slg
1998	OAK	AL	16	45	14	4	1	0	(-	-)	20	6	6	7	3	1	5	0	0	0	1	1	.50	1	.311	.354	.444
1999	OAK	AL	115	356	88	21	2	13	(8	5)	152	47	50	50	46	4	56	0	0	0	1	1	.50	7	.247	.333	.427
2000	OAK	AL	153	501	139	23	4	26	(15	11)	248	89	86	86	62	8	94	1	0	5	2	2	.50	9	.277	.355	.495
2001	OAK	AL	151	552	159	43	0	32	(14	18)	298	91	114	99	41	9	99	4	0	7	8	2	.80	7	.288	.338	.540
2002	OAK	AL	153	585	161	31	3	34	(17	17)	300	87	109	103	65	13	119	1	0	2	8	3	.73	8	.275	.348	.513
2003	OAK	AL	156	588	166	39	5	29	(12	17)	302	94	101	97	62	10	89	1	0	3	8	3	.73	14	.282	.350	.514
2004	OAK	AL	125	475	131	20	0	29	(15	14)	238	87	77	84	95	10	99	3	0	4	6	3	.67	21	.276	.397	.501
2005	OAK	AL	160	625	168	40	1	27	(15	12)	291	92	101	95	58	4	129	2	0	9	6	0	1.00	9	.269	.329	.466
8 ML YEARS			1029	3727	1026	221	16	190	(96	94)	1849	593	644	621	432	59	690	12	0	30	40	15	.73	76	.275	.350	.496

Raul Chavez

Bats: R Throws: R Pos: C-36; PH-2 **Ht: 5'11" Wt: 210 Born: 3/18/1973 Age: 33**

			BATTING																		BASERUNNING				AVERAGES		
Year	Team	Lg	G	AB	H	2B	3B	HR	(Hm	Rd)	TB	R	RBI	RC	TBB	IBB	SO	HBP	SH	SF	SB	CS	SB%	GDP	Avg	OBP	Slg
2005	RdRck*	AAA	34	119	30	8	0	0	(-	-)	38	9	14	11	5	1	24	3	1	0	0	0	-	4	.252	.299	.319
1996	MON	NL	4	5	1	0	0	0	(0	0)	1	1	0	0	1	0	1	0	0	0	1	0	1.00	1	.200	.333	.200
1997	MON	NL	13	26	7	0	0	0	(0	0)	7	0	2	2	0	0	5	0	0	1	1	0	1.00	0	.269	.259	.269
1998	SEA	AL	1	1	0	0	0	0	(0	0)	0	0	0	0	0	0	0	0	0	0	0	0	-	0	.000	.000	.000
2000	HOU	NL	14	43	11	2	0	1	(0	1)	16	3	5	3	3	2	6	0	0	1	0	0	-	5	.256	.298	.372
2002	HOU	NL	2	4	1	1	0	0	(0	0)	2	1	0	1	1	0	0	1	0	0	0	0	-	0	.250	.500	.500
2003	HOU	NL	19	37	10	1	1	1	(0	1)	16	5	4	4	1	0	6	0	0	0	0	0	-	3	.270	.289	.432
2004	HOU	NL	64	162	34	8	0	0	(0	0)	42	9	23	10	10	3	38	0	4	0	0	1	.00	9	.210	.256	.259
2005	HOU	NL	37	99	17	3	0	2	(1	1)	26	6	6	2	4	0	18	1	0	1	1	0	1.00	5	.172	.210	.263
8 ML YEARS			154	377	81	15	1	4	(1	3)	110	25	40	22	20	5	74	2	4	3	3	1	.75	23	.215	.256	.292

Bruce Chen

Pitches: L Bats: L Pos: SP-32; RP-2 **Ht: 6'2" Wt: 210 Born: 6/19/1977 Age: 29**

			HOW MUCH HE PITCHED								WHAT HE GAVE UP												THE RESULTS						
Year	Team	Lg	G	GS	CG	GF	IP	BFP	H	R	ER	HR	SH	SF	HB	TBB	IBB	SO	WP	Bk	W	L	Pct	ShO	Sv-Op	Hld	ERC	ERA
1998	ATL	NL	4	4	0	0	20.1	91	23	9	9	3	1	0	1	9	1	17	0	0	2	0	1.000	0	0-0	0	5.55	3.98
1999	ATL	NL	16	7	0	3	51.0	214	38	32	31	11	1	1	2	27	3	45	0	0	2	2	.500	0	0-0	0	4.07	5.47
2000	2 Tms	NL	37	15	0	4	134.0	559	116	54	49	18	8	3	2	46	4	112	4	1	7	4	.636	0	0-0	0	3.35	3.29
2001	2 Tms	NL	27	27	0	0	146.0	634	146	90	79	29	4	7	1	59	4	126	5	0	7	7	.500	0	0-0	0	4.75	4.87
2002	3 Tms	NL	55	6	0	9	77.2	360	85	53	48	16	2	3	2	43	5	80	4	0	2	5	.286	0	0-0	4	5.99	5.56

HOW MUCH HE PITCHED						WHAT HE GAVE UP												THE RESULTS						
Year	Team	Lg	G	GS	CG	GF	IP	BFP	H	R	ER	HR	SH	SF	HB	TBB	IBB	SO	WP	Bk	W	L	Pct	ShO	Sv-Op	Hld	ERC	ERA
2003	2 Tms		16	2	0	4	24.1	110	26	16	15	6	3	3	2	10	1	20	0	0	0	1	.000	0	0-0	1	5.81	5.55
2004	BAL	AL	8	7	1	0	47.2	196	39	19	16	7	2	1	0	16	0	32	0	0	2	1	.667	0	0-0	0	3.13	3.02
2005	BAL	AL	34	32	1	0	197.1	832	187	94	84	33	3	3	9	63	0	133	2	1	13	10	.565	0	0-0	0	4.12	3.83
00	Atl	NL	22	0	0	4	39.2	176	35	15	11	4	3	2	1	19	2	32	0	1	4	0	1.000	0	0-0	0	3.62	2.50
00	Phi	NL	15	15	0	0	94.1	383	81	39	38	14	5	1	1	27	2	80	4	0	3	4	.429	0	0-0	0	3.22	3.63
01	Phi	NL	16	16	0	0	86.1	381	90	53	48	19	2	4	1	31	4	79	2	0	4	5	.444	0	0-0	0	4.87	5.00
01	NYM	NL	11	11	0	0	59.2	253	56	37	31	10	2	3	0	28	0	47	3	0	3	2	.600	0	0-0	0	4.58	4.68
02	NYM	NL	1	0	0	0	0.2	3	1	0	0	0	0	0	0	0	0	0	0	0	0	0	-	0	0-0	0	4.47	0.00
02	Mon	NL	15	5	0	4	37.1	179	47	29	29	9	0	0	1	23	3	43	3	0	2	3	.400	0	0-0	0	7.69	6.99
02	Cin	NL	39	1	0	5	39.2	178	37	24	19	7	2	3	1	20	2	37	1	0	0	2	.000	0	0-0	4	4.55	4.31
03	Hou	NL	11	0	0	2	12.0	60	14	8	8	2	3	2	2	8	1	8	0	0	0	0	-	0	0-0	1	7.11	6.00
03	Bos	AL	5	2	0	2	12.1	50	12	8	7	4	0	1	0	2	0	12	0	0	0	1	.000	0	0-0	0	4.40	5.11
	8 ML YEARS		197	100	2	20	698.1	2996	660	367	331	123	24	21	19	273	18	565	15	2	35	30	.538	0	0-0	5	4.32	4.27

Chin-Feng Chen

Bats: R Throws: R Pos: PH-4; LF-3; PR-2   Ht: 6'1" Wt: 189 Born: 10/27/1977 Age: 28

BATTING																				BASERUNNING				AVERAGES		
Year	Team	Lg	G	AB	H	2B	3B	HR	(Hm	Rd)	TB	R	RBI	RC	TBB	IBB	SO	HBP	SH	SF	SB	CS	SB%	GDP	Avg	OBP	Slg
2005	LsVgs*	AAA	87	317	88	20	2	15	(-	-)	157	59	63	56	38	0	82	2	1	5	3	3	.50	3	.278	.354	.495
2002	LA	NL	3	5	0	0	0	0	(0	0)	0	1	0	1	1	0	3	0	0	0	0	0	-	0	.000	.167	.000
2003	LA	NL	1	1	0	0	0	0	(0	0)	0	0	0	0	0	0	0	0	0	0	0	0	-	0	.000	.000	.000
2004	LA	NL	8	8	0	0	0	0	(0	0)	0	1	0	0	2	0	3	0	0	0	0	0	-	1	.000	.200	.000
2005	LAN	NL	7	8	2	0	0	0	(0	0)	2	1	2	1	0	0	4	0	0	0	0	0	-	0	.250	.250	.250
	4 ML YEARS		19	22	2	0	0	0	(0	0)	2	3	2	1	3	0	10	0	0	0	0	0	-	1	.091	.200	.091

Matt Childers

Pitches: R Bats: R Pos: RP-3   Ht: 6'5" Wt: 195 Born: 12/3/1978 Age: 27

HOW MUCH HE PITCHED									WHAT HE GAVE UP												THE RESULTS						
Year	Team	Lg	G	GS	CG	GF	IP	BFP	H	R	ER	HR	SH	SF	HB	TBB	IBB	SO	WP	Bk	W	L	Pct	ShO	Sv-Op	Hld	ERC	ERA
1997	Helena	R+	14	10	0	0	61.0	285	81	49	42	5	2	4	0	24	0	19	1	0	1	4	.200	0	1--	-	5.75	6.20
1998	Helena	R+	2	2	1	0	14.0	53	9	1	1	0	0	0	0	4	1	4	0	0	1	0	1.000	1	0--	-	1.39	0.64
1998	Beloit	A	14	12	3	0	67.0	303	89	55	38	5	3	2	4	20	0	49	2	0	3	7	.300	0	0--	-	5.71	5.10
1999	Beloit	A	20	19	0	0	100.0	448	129	72	66	9	1	5	5	30	1	52	0	2	3	10	.231	0	0--	-	5.54	5.94
2000	Beloit	A	12	12	1	0	73.0	300	64	33	22	4	0	0	1	17	0	47	2	1	8	2	.800	1	0--	-	2.52	2.71
2000	Mudvle	A+	15	15	0	0	85.1	388	103	59	45	10	2	2	3	32	0	43	3	2	3	9	.250	0	0--	-	5.41	4.75
2001	Hi Dsrt	A+	20	20	0	0	117.1	529	155	95	84	19	3	7	6	29	0	76	5	0	6	11	.353	0	0--	-	6.03	6.44
2001	Huntsvl	AA	7	7	0	0	39.1	172	41	19	15	3	1	1	5	12	0	21	3	0	2	2	.500	0	0--	-	4.27	3.43
2002	Huntsvl	AA	35	10	0	24	82.0	374	103	44	41	6	6	5	2	27	0	57	2	0	2	5	.286	0	12--	-	5.09	4.50
2002	Indy	AAA	3	0	0	1	5.0	18	1	0	0	0	0	0	0	2	0	4	0	0	0	0	-	0	0--	-	0.50	0.00
2003	Huntsvl	AA	36	1	0	20	73.2	316	67	32	24	3	2	3	5	24	0	44	2	0	1	0	1.000	0	8--	-	3.09	2.93
2003	Indy	AAA	11	0	0	4	19.0	75	15	2	1	1	2	0	0	6	2	19	0	1	3	0	1.000	0	0--	-	2.28	0.47
2004	Indy	AAA	35	10	0	12	98.0	422	100	55	53	8	6	6	6	27	3	65	2	0	5	5	.500	0	2--	-	3.72	4.87
2005	Rchmd	AAA	51	1	0	13	73.1	310	69	37	32	4	5	3	4	21	1	62	6	0	4	2	.667	0	2--	-	3.17	3.93
2002	MIL	NL	8	0	0	2	9.0	48	13	12	12	2	1	0	1	8	1	6	0	0	0	0	-	0	0-0	0	10.39	12.00
2005	ATL	NL	3	0	0	1	4.0	21	5	2	2	1	0	0	1	3	0	2	0	0	0	0	-	0	0-0	0	9.34	4.50
	2 ML YEARS		11	0	0	3	13.0	69	18	14	14	3	1	0	2	11	1	8	0	0	0	0	-	0	0-0	0	10.06	9.69

Randy Choate

Pitches: L Bats: L Pos: RP-8   Ht: 6'1" Wt: 180 Born: 9/5/1975 Age: 30

HOW MUCH HE PITCHED									WHAT HE GAVE UP												THE RESULTS						
Year	Team	Lg	G	GS	CG	GF	IP	BFP	H	R	ER	HR	SH	SF	HB	TBB	IBB	SO	WP	Bk	W	L	Pct	ShO	Sv-Op	Hld	ERC	ERA
2005	Tucsn*	AAA	47	0	0	16	40.0	186	44	22	15	4	2	0	2	22	1	20	2	0	1	1	.500	0	3--	-	5.35	3.38
2000	NYA	AL	22	0	0	6	17.0	75	14	10	9	3	0	1	1	8	0	12	1	0	0	1	.000	0	0-0	2	3.99	4.76
2001	NYA	AL	37	0	0	13	48.1	207	34	21	18	0	2	1	9	27	2	35	3	0	3	1	.750	0	0-0	3	3.03	3.35
2002	NYA	AL	18	0	0	11	22.1	101	18	18	15	1	0	0	3	15	0	17	4	0	0	0	-	0	0-0	0	4.13	6.04
2003	NYA	AL	5	0	0	2	3.2	16	7	3	3	0	0	0	0	1	0	0	0	0	0	0	-	0	0-0	0	9.72	7.36
2004	ARI	NL	74	0	0	17	50.2	232	52	26	26	1	0	4	5	28	11	49	1	1	2	4	.333	0	0-2	11	4.18	4.62
2005	ARI	NL	8	0	0	0	7.0	35	8	7	7	0	0	0	1	5	1	4	1	0	0	0	-	0	0-0	2	5.48	9.00
	6 ML YEARS		164	0	0	49	149.0	666	133	85	78	5	2	6	19	84	14	117	10	1	5	6	.455	0	0-2	18	3.95	4.71

Hee Seop Choi

Bats: L Throws: L Pos: 1B-83; PH-50   Ht: 6'5" Wt: 235 Born: 3/16/1979 Age: 27

BATTING																				BASERUNNING				AVERAGES		
Year	Team	Lg	G	AB	H	2B	3B	HR	(Hm	Rd)	TB	R	RBI	RC	TBB	IBB	SO	HBP	SH	SF	SB	CS	SB%	GDP	Avg	OBP	Slg
2002	CHN	NL	24	50	9	1	0	2	(1	1)	16	6	4	2	7	0	15	0	0	0	0	0	-	2	.180	.281	.320
2003	CHN	NL	80	202	44	17	0	8	(5	3)	85	31	28	28	37	1	71	4	2	2	1	1	.50	2	.218	.350	.421
2004	2 Tms	NL	126	343	86	21	1	15	(8	7)	154	53	46	58	63	6	96	4	2	4	1	0	1.00	6	.251	.370	.449
2005	LAN	NL	133	320	81	15	2	15	(9	6)	145	40	42	39	34	1	80	8	2	4	1	3	.25	10	.253	.336	.453
04	Fla	NL	95	281	76	16	1	15	(8	7)	139	48	40	54	52	4	78	3	2	2	1	0	1.00	4	.270	.388	.495
04	LA	NL	31	62	10	5	0	0	(0	0)	15	5	6	4	11	2	18	1	0	2	0	0	-	2	.161	.289	.242
	4 ML YEARS		363	915	220	54	3	40	(23	17)	400	130	120	127	141	8	262	16	6	8	3	4	.43	20	.240	.349	.437

Shin-Soo Choo

Bats: L Throws: L Pos: CF-5; PH-4; PR-1   Ht: 5'11" Wt: 178 Born: 7/13/1982 Age: 23

									BATTING													BASERUNNING				AVERAGES		
Year	Team	Lg	G	AB	H	2B	3B	HR	(Hm	Rd)	TB	R	RBI	RC	TBB	IBB	SO	HBP	SH	SF	SB	CS	SB%	GDP	Avg	OBP	Slg
2001	Ms	R	51	199	60	10	10	4	(-	-)	102	51	35	45	34	2	49	9	0	3	12	4	.75	1	.302	.420	.513
2001	Wisc	A	3	13	6	0	0	0	(-	-)	6	1	3	3	1	0	3	1	0	0	2	0	1.00	0	.462	.533	.462
2002	Wisc	A	119	420	127	24	8	6	(-	-)	185	69	48	81	70	5	98	13	3	1	34	21	.62	2	.302	.417	.440
2002	SnBrn	A+	11	39	12	5	1	1	(-	-)	22	14	9	11	9	1	9	2	1	0	3	0	1.00	0	.308	.460	.564
2003	InldEm	A+	110	412	118	18	13	9	(-	-)	189	62	55	71	44	1	84	9	2	4	18	10	.64	8	.286	.365	.459
2004	SnAnt	AA	132	517	163	17	7	15	(-	-)	239	89	84	97	56	4	97	2	1	3	39	9	.81	8	.315	.382	.462
2005	Tacom	AAA	115	429	121	21	5	11	(-	-)	185	73	54	75	69	0	97	1	2	1	20	10	.67	8	.282	.382	.431
2005	SEA	AL	10	18	1	0	0	0	(0	0)	1	1	1	0	3	0	4	0	0	0	0	0	-	0	.056	.190	.056

Jason Christiansen

Pitches: L Bats: R Pos: RP-68   Ht: 6'5" Wt: 241 Born: 9/21/1969 Age: 36

			HOW MUCH HE PITCHED						WHAT HE GAVE UP											THE RESULTS					
Year	Team	Lg	G	GS	CG	GF	IP	BFP	H	R	ER	HR	SH	SF	HB	TBB	IBB	SO	WP	Bk	W	L	Pct	ShO	Sv-Op	Hld	ERC	ERA
1995	PIT	NL	63	0	0	13	56.1	255	49	28	26	5	6	3	3	34	9	53	4	1	1	3	.250	0	0-4	12	3.89	4.15
1996	PIT	NL	33	0	0	9	44.1	205	56	34	33	7	2	3	1	19	2	38	1	1	3	3	.500	0	0-2	2	6.19	6.70
1997	PIT	NL	39	0	0	9	33.2	154	37	11	11	2	0	0	2	17	3	37	4	0	3	0	1.000	0	0-2	8	4.80	2.94
1998	PIT	NL	60	0	0	19	64.2	269	51	22	18	2	5	1	0	27	7	71	3	0	3	3	.500	0	6-10	15	2.39	2.51
1999	PIT	NL	39	0	0	17	37.2	158	26	17	17	2	2	1	2	22	4	35	0	0	2	3	.400	0	3-5	7	2.85	4.06
2000	2 Tms	NL	65	0	0	19	48.0	210	41	29	27	3	4	1	2	27	5	53	3	0	3	8	.273	0	1-4	22	3.60	5.06
2001	2 Tms	NL	55	0	0	11	36.1	149	29	13	13	5	1	3	1	15	1	31	4	0	2	1	.667	0	3-4	11	3.41	3.22
2002	SF	NL	6	0	0	1	5.0	21	6	3	3	1	0	0	0	2	0	1	0	0	0	1	.000	0	0-0	0	6.48	5.40
2003	SF	NL	40	0	0	7	26.0	115	25	15	15	3	0	0	1	11	0	22	2	0	0	0	-	0	0-1	7	4.11	5.19
2004	SF	NL	60	0	0	11	36.0	167	34	20	18	3	0	2	3	26	1	22	3	0	4	3	.571	0	3-6	8	5.19	4.50
2005	2 Tms	NL	68	0	0	11	45.2	208	55	28	26	4	1	4	0	17	2	21	0	0	6	1	.857	0	0-2	10	4.87	5.12
00	Pit	NL	44	0	0	17	38.0	164	28	22	21	2	3	1	0	25	4	41	3	0	2	8	.200	0	1-3	13	3.11	4.97
00	StL	NL	21	0	0	2	10.0	46	13	7	6	1	1	0	2	2	1	12	0	0	1	0	1.000	0	0-1	9	5.64	5.40
01	StL	NL	30	0	0	8	19.1	83	15	10	10	4	0	1	1	10	1	19	0	0	1	1	.500	0	3-3	4	4.12	4.66
01	SF	NL	25	0	0	3	17.0	66	14	3	3	1	1	2	0	5	0	12	4	0	1	0	1.000	0	0-1	7	2.62	1.59
05	SF	NL	56	0	0	10	42.0	188	48	27	25	4	1	4	0	15	2	17	0	0	6	1	.857	0	0-2	10	4.51	5.36
05	LAA	AL	12	0	0	1	3.2	20	7	1	1	0	0	0	0	2	0	4	0	0	0	0	-	0	0-0	0	9.31	2.45
11 ML YEARS			528	0	0	128	433.2	1911	409	220	207	37	21	18	15	217	34	384	27	2	27	26	.509	0	16-40	102	4.02	4.30

Vinnie Chulk

Pitches: R Bats: R Pos: RP-62   Ht: 6'2" Wt: 185 Born: 12/19/1978 Age: 27

			HOW MUCH HE PITCHED						WHAT HE GAVE UP											THE RESULTS					
Year	Team	Lg	G	GS	CG	GF	IP	BFP	H	R	ER	HR	SH	SF	HB	TBB	IBB	SO	WP	Bk	W	L	Pct	ShO	Sv-Op	Hld	ERC	ERA
2003	TOR	AL	3	0	0	2	5.1	25	6	3	3	0	0	0	0	3	0	2	0	0	0	0	-	0	0-1	0	4.53	5.06
2004	TOR	AL	47	0	0	10	56.0	248	59	30	29	6	1	1	1	27	1	44	2	0	1	3	.250	0	2-5	13	4.64	4.66
2005	TOR	AL	62	0	0	10	72.0	301	68	33	31	9	3	4	1	26	3	39	5	0	0	1	.000	0	0-1	13	3.83	3.88
3 ML YEARS			112	0	0	22	133.1	574	133	66	63	15	4	5	2	56	4	85	7	0	1	4	.200	0	2-7	26	4.28	4.25

Ryan Church

Bats: L Throws: L Pos: LF-51; PH-29; RF-21; CF-20; PR-3   Ht: 6'1" Wt: 190 Born: 10/14/1978 Age: 27

									BATTING													BASERUNNING				AVERAGES		
Year	Team	Lg	G	AB	H	2B	3B	HR	(Hm	Rd)	TB	R	RBI	RC	TBB	IBB	SO	HBP	SH	SF	SB	CS	SB%	GDP	Avg	OBP	Slg
2000	MhVlly	A-	73	272	81	16	5	10	(-	-)	137	51	65	54	38	3	49	8	0	3	11	4	.73	4	.298	.396	.504
2001	Clmbs	A	101	363	104	23	3	17	(-	-)	184	64	76	68	54	0	79	6	0	3	4	6	.40	6	.287	.385	.507
2001	Kinston	A+	24	83	20	7	0	5	(-	-)	42	16	15	16	18	2	23	1	0	1	1	0	1.00	1	.241	.379	.506
2002	Kinston	A+	53	181	59	12	1	10	(-	-)	103	30	30	41	31	6	51	4	0	1	4	4	.50	3	.326	.433	.569
2002	Akron	AA	71	291	86	17	4	12	(-	-)	147	39	51	44	12	2	58	2	0	3	1	0	1.00	4	.296	.325	.505
2003	Akron	AA	99	371	97	17	3	13	(-	-)	159	47	52	46	32	1	64	4	0	2	4	3	.57	17	.261	.325	.429
2004	Edmtn	AAA	98	347	119	29	8	17	(-	-)	215	74	78	85	51	7	62	4	1	5	0	1	.00	4	.343	.428	.620
2005	Hrsbrg	AA	4	18	5	1	0	0	(-	-)	6	2	0	1	0	0	5	0	0	0	0	0	-	0	.278	.278	.333
2004	MON	NL	30	63	11	1	0	1	(0	1)	15	6	6	2	7	1	16	0	1	0	0	0	-	3	.175	.257	.238
2005	WAS	NL	102	268	77	15	3	9	(5	4)	125	41	42	34	24	0	70	5	1	3	3	2	.60	6	.287	.353	.466
2 ML YEARS			132	331	88	16	3	10	(5	5)	140	47	48	36	31	1	86	5	2	3	3	2	.60	9	.266	.335	.423

Alex Cintron

Bats: B Throws: R Pos: PH-49; SS-39; 3B-32; 2B-23; PR-1   Ht: 6'2" Wt: 185 Born: 12/17/1978 Age: 27

									BATTING													BASERUNNING				AVERAGES		
Year	Team	Lg	G	AB	H	2B	3B	HR	(Hm	Rd)	TB	R	RBI	RC	TBB	IBB	SO	HBP	SH	SF	SB	CS	SB%	GDP	Avg	OBP	Slg
2001	ARI	NL	8	7	2	0	1	0	(0	0)	4	0	0	1	0	0	0	0	0	0	0	0	-	0	.286	.286	.571
2002	ARI	NL	38	75	16	6	0	0	(0	0)	22	11	4	5	12	2	13	0	3	0	0	0	-	2	.213	.322	.293
2003	ARI	NL	117	448	142	26	6	13	(6	7)	219	70	51	70	29	0	33	2	5	3	2	3	.40	7	.317	.359	.489
2004	ARI	NL	154	564	148	31	7	4	(1	3)	205	56	49	59	31	2	54	2	12	4	3	3	.50	11	.262	.301	.363
2005	ARI	NL	122	330	90	19	2	8	(5	3)	137	36	48	35	12	3	33	1	2	3	1	2	.33	8	.273	.298	.415
5 ML YEARS			439	1424	398	82	16	25	(12	13)	587	173	152	170	84	7	138	5	22	10	6	8	.43	28	.279	.320	.412

Jeff Cirillo

Bats: R **Throws:** R **Pos:** 3B-53; PH-31; 2B-3; 1B-1   **Ht:** 6'1" **Wt:** 190 **Born:** 9/23/1969 **Age:** 36

Year	Team	Lg	G	AB	H	2B	3B	HR	(Hm	Rd)	TB	R	RBI	RC	TBB	IBB	SO	HBP	SH	SF	SB	CS	SB%	GDP	Avg	OBP	Slg
2005	Nashv*	AAA	9	29	7	1	0	0	(-	-)	8	2	6	1	0	0	5	1	1	2	0	1	.00	1	.241	.250	.276
1994	MIL	AL	39	126	30	9	0	3	(1	2)	48	17	12	14	11	0	16	2	0	0	0	1	.00	4	.238	.309	.381
1995	MIL	AL	125	328	91	19	4	9	(6	3)	145	57	39	55	47	0	42	4	1	4	7	2	.78	8	.277	.371	.442
1996	MIL	AL	158	566	184	46	5	15	(6	9)	285	101	83	105	58	0	69	7	6	6	4	9	.31	14	.325	.391	.504
1997	MIL	AL	154	580	167	46	2	10	(6	4)	247	74	82	91	60	0	74	14	4	3	4	3	.57	13	.288	.367	.426
1998	MIL	NL	156	604	194	31	1	14	(6	8)	269	97	68	103	79	3	88	4	5	2	10	4	.71	26	.321	.402	.445
1999	MIL	NL	157	607	198	35	1	15	(6	9)	280	98	88	111	75	4	83	5	3	7	7	4	.64	15	.326	.401	.461
2000	COL	NL	157	598	195	53	2	11	(9	2)	285	111	115	108	67	4	72	6	1	12	3	4	.43	19	.326	.392	.477
2001	COL	NL	138	528	165	26	4	17	(9	8)	250	72	83	89	43	6	63	5	1	9	12	2	.86	15	.313	.364	.473
2002	SEA	AL	146	485	121	20	0	6	(2	4)	159	51	54	52	31	0	67	9	13	9	8	4	.67	12	.249	.301	.328
2003	SEA	AL	87	258	53	11	0	2	(1	1)	70	24	23	23	24	1	32	5	4	2	1	1	.50	6	.205	.284	.271
2004	SD	NL	33	75	16	3	0	1	(0	1)	22	12	7	6	5	0	14	0	0	1	0	0	-	0	.213	.259	.293
2005	SD	NL	77	185	52	15	0	4	(1	3)	79	29	23	30	23	0	22	4	7	0	4	2	.67	3	.281	.373	.427
	12 ML YEARS		1427	4940	1466	314	19	107	(53	54)	2139	743	677	787	523	18	642	65	45	55	60	36	.63	135	.297	.368	.433

Brady Clark

Bats: R **Throws:** R **Pos:** CF-145   **Ht:** 6'2" **Wt:** 195 **Born:** 4/18/1973 **Age:** 33

Year	Team	Lg	G	AB	H	2B	3B	HR	(Hm	Rd)	TB	R	RBI	RC	TBB	IBB	SO	HBP	SH	SF	SB	CS	SB%	GDP	Avg	OBP	Slg
2000	CIN	NL	11	11	3	1	0	0	(0	0)	4	1	2	1	0	0	2	0	0	0	0	0	-	0	.273	.273	.364
2001	CIN	NL	89	129	34	3	0	6	(4	2)	55	22	18	21	22	1	16	1	4	1	4	1	.80	6	.264	.373	.426
2002	2 Tms	NL	61	78	15	4	0	0	(0	0)	19	9	10	7	7	2	11	1	1	0	1	2	.33	2	.192	.267	.244
2003	MIL	NL	128	315	86	21	1	6	(5	1)	127	33	40	40	21	0	40	9	2	7	13	2	.87	12	.273	.330	.403
2004	MIL	NL	138	353	99	18	1	7	(1	6)	140	41	46	56	53	2	48	9	1	3	15	8	.65	9	.280	.385	.397
2005	MIL	NL	145	599	183	31	1	13	(8	5)	255	94	53	92	47	1	55	18	8	2	10	13	.43	13	.306	.372	.426
02	Cin	NL	51	66	10	3	0	0	(0	0)	13	6	9	5	6	2	9	1	1	0	1	2	.33	2	.152	.233	.197
02	NYM	NL	10	12	5	1	0	0	(0	0)	6	3	1	2	1	0	2	0	0	0	0	0	-	0	.417	.462	.500
	6 ML YEARS		572	1485	420	78	3	32	(18	14)	600	200	169	217	150	6	172	38	16	13	43	26	.62	42	.283	.361	.404

Doug Clark

Bats: L **Throws:** R **Pos:** PH-6; PR-2   **Ht:** 6'2" **Wt:** 207 **Born:** 3/5/1976 **Age:** 30

Year	Team	Lg	G	AB	H	2B	3B	HR	(Hm	Rd)	TB	R	RBI	RC	TBB	IBB	SO	HBP	SH	SF	SB	CS	SB%	GDP	Avg	OBP	Slg
1998	SlmKzr	A-	59	227	76	8	6	3	(-	-)	105	49	41	45	32	0	31	3	1	1	12	8	.60	1	.335	.422	.463
1999	Bkrsfld	A+	118	420	137	17	2	11	(-	-)	191	67	58	81	59	4	89	5	0	0	17	11	.61	5	.326	.415	.455
1999	Shreve	AA	15	50	11	3	0	1	(-	-)	17	6	6	4	4	0	9	0	0	0	0	0	-	2	.220	.278	.340
2000	Shreve	AA	131	492	134	20	7	10	(-	-)	198	68	75	70	43	5	102	5	1	7	12	4	.75	13	.272	.333	.402
2001	Shreve	AA	123	414	114	16	4	6	(-	-)	156	53	51	60	45	4	83	3	6	4	20	5	.80	8	.275	.348	.377
2002	Shreve	AA	44	138	36	6	1	2	(-	-)	50	13	13	17	19	4	35	0	2	1	5	7	.42	4	.261	.348	.362
2002	Fresno	AAA	70	212	57	9	1	5	(-	-)	83	24	19	28	15	2	52	5	1	1	3	3	.50	5	.269	.330	.392
2003	Nrwich	AA	113	396	119	23	4	4	(-	-)	162	47	49	63	45	1	67	2	1	4	8	5	.62	8	.301	.371	.409
2003	Fresno	AAA	13	21	5	0	0	0	(-	-)	5	4	0	1	2	0	3	0	0	0	0	1	.00	0	.238	.304	.238
2004	Nrwich	AA	140	537	157	23	13	10	(-	-)	236	82	71	87	44	1	103	3	1	2	33	8	.80	9	.292	.348	.439
2005	Fresno	AAA	127	472	149	30	5	13	(-	-)	228	81	59	85	35	1	87	5	3	3	29	12	.71	6	.316	.367	.483
2005	SF	NL	8	5	0	0	0	0	(0	0)	0	2	0	0	1	0	2	0	0	0	0	0	-	0	.000	.167	.000

Jermaine Clark

Bats: L **Throws:** R **Pos:** 2B-2; PR-2; LF-1; PH-1   **Ht:** 5'10" **Wt:** 175 **Born:** 9/29/1976 **Age:** 29

Year	Team	Lg	G	AB	H	2B	3B	HR	(Hm	Rd)	TB	R	RBI	RC	TBB	IBB	SO	HBP	SH	SF	SB	CS	SB%	GDP	Avg	OBP	Slg
2005	Scrmto*	AAA	70	256	64	13	4	5	(-	-)	100	32	28	39	41	0	33	2	2	4	14	8	.64	5	.250	.353	.391
2001	DET	AL	3	0	0	0	0	0	(0	0)	0	1	0	0	0	0	0	0	0	0	0	0	-	0	-	-	-
2003	2 Tms		25	48	8	2	0	0	(0	0)	10	2	7	5	6	0	5	0	1	2	2	2	.50	1	.167	.250	.208
2004	CIN	NL	14	30	4	1	0	0	(0	0)	5	4	2	2	1	0	8	2	1	0	1	0	1.00	0	.133	.212	.167
2005	OAK	AL	4	0	0	0	0	0	(0	0)	0	2	0	0	1	0	0	0	0	0	0	0	-	0	-	1.000	-
03	Tex	AL	24	46	8	2	0	0	(0	0)	10	2	6	5	6	0	4	0	1	1	2	1	.67	1	.174	.264	.217
03	SD	NL	1	2	0	0	0	0	(0	0)	0	0	1	0	0	0	1	0	0	1	0	1	.00	0	.000	.000	.000
	4 ML YEARS		46	78	12	3	0	0	(0	0)	15	9	9	7	8	0	13	2	2	2	3	2	.60	1	.154	.244	.192

Tony Clark

Bats: B **Throws:** R **Pos:** 1B-83; PH-48; DH-7   **Ht:** 6'7" **Wt:** 245 **Born:** 6/15/1972 **Age:** 34

Year	Team	Lg	G	AB	H	2B	3B	HR	(Hm	Rd)	TB	R	RBI	RC	TBB	IBB	SO	HBP	SH	SF	SB	CS	SB%	GDP	Avg	OBP	Slg
1995	DET	AL	27	101	24	5	1	3	(0	3)	40	10	11	11	8	0	30	0	0	0	0	0	-	2	.238	.294	.396
1996	DET	AL	100	376	94	14	0	27	(17	10)	189	56	72	55	29	1	127	0	0	6	0	1	.00	7	.250	.299	.503
1997	DET	AL	159	580	160	28	3	32	(18	14)	290	105	117	107	93	13	144	3	0	5	1	3	.25	11	.276	.376	.500
1998	DET	AL	157	602	175	37	0	34	(18	16)	314	84	103	107	63	5	128	3	0	5	3	3	.50	16	.291	.358	.522
1999	DET	AL	143	536	150	29	0	31	(12	19)	272	74	99	94	64	7	133	6	0	3	2	1	.67	14	.280	.361	.507
2000	DET	AL	60	208	57	14	0	13	(6	7)	110	32	37	35	24	2	51	0	0	0	0	0	-	10	.274	.349	.529
2001	DET	AL	126	428	123	29	3	16	(7	9)	206	67	75	74	62	10	108	1	0	6	0	1	.00	14	.287	.374	.481
2002	BOS	AL	90	275	57	12	1	3	(1	2)	80	25	29	19	21	0	57	1	0	1	0	0	-	11	.207	.265	.291
2003	NYN	NL	125	254	59	13	0	16	(9	7)	120	29	43	29	24	2	73	1	0	1	0	0	-	8	.232	.300	.472

Year	Team	Lg	G	AB	H	2B	3B	HR	(Hm	Rd)	TB	R	RBI	RC	TBB	IBB	SO	HBP	SH	SF	SB	CS	SB%	GDP	Avg	OBP	Slg
											BATTING										BASERUNNING				AVERAGES		
2004	NYA	AL	106	253	56	12	0	16	(5	11)	116	37	49	37	26	3	92	2	0	2	0	0	-	6	.221	.297	.458
2005	ARI	NL	130	349	106	22	2	30	(19	11)	222	47	87	71	37	6	88	1	0	6	0	0	-	10	.304	.366	.636
11 ML YEARS			1223	3962	1061	215	10	221	(112	109)	1959	566	722	639	451	49	1031	18	0	35	6	9	.40	109	.268	.343	.494

Brandon Claussen

Pitches: L **Bats:** R **Pos:** SP-29   **Ht:** 6'2" **Wt:** 175 **Born:** 5/1/1979 **Age:** 27

			HOW MUCH HE PITCHED						WHAT HE GAVE UP												THE RESULTS							
Year	Team	Lg	G	GS	CG	GF	IP	BFP	H	R	ER	HR	SH	SF	HB	TBB	IBB	SO	WP	Bk	W	L	Pct	ShO	Sv-Op	Hld	ERC	ERA
2003	NYA	AL	1	1	0	0	6.1	28	8	2	1	1	0	0	0	1	0	5	0	0	0	1	1.000	0	0-0	0	4.89	1.42
2004	CIN	NL	14	14	0	0	66.0	313	80	50	45	9	5	3	2	35	2	45	3	0	2	8	.200	0	0-0	0	6.11	6.14
2005	CIN	NL	29	29	0	0	166.2	731	178	89	78	24	8	6	7	57	5	121	2	1	10	11	.476	0	0-0	0	4.63	4.21
3 ML YEARS			44	44	0	0	239.0	1072	266	141	124	34	13	9	9	93	7	171	5	1	13	19	.406	0	0-0	0	5.04	4.67

Royce Clayton

Bats: R **Throws:** R **Pos:** SS-141; PH-3; PR-1   **Ht:** 6'0" **Wt:** 185 **Born:** 1/2/1970 **Age:** 36

			BATTING																		BASERUNNING				AVERAGES		
Year	Team	Lg	G	AB	H	2B	3B	HR	(Hm	Rd)	TB	R	RBI	RC	TBB	IBB	SO	HBP	SH	SF	SB	CS	SB%	GDP	Avg	OBP	Slg
1991	SF	NL	9	26	3	1	0	0	(0	0)	4	0	2	0	1	0	6	0	0	0	0	0	-	1	.115	.148	.154
1992	SF	NL	98	321	72	7	4	4	(3	1)	99	31	24	25	26	3	63	0	3	2	8	4	.67	11	.224	.281	.308
1993	SF	NL	153	549	155	21	5	6	(5	1)	204	54	70	64	38	2	91	5	8	7	11	10	.52	16	.282	.331	.372
1994	SF	NL	108	385	91	14	6	3	(1	2)	126	38	30	40	30	2	74	3	3	2	23	3	.88	7	.236	.295	.327
1995	SF	NL	138	509	124	29	3	5	(2	3)	174	56	58	53	38	1	109	3	4	3	24	9	.73	7	.244	.298	.342
1996	STL	NL	129	491	136	20	4	6	(6	0)	182	64	35	56	33	4	89	1	2	4	33	15	.69	13	.277	.321	.371
1997	STL	NL	154	576	153	39	5	9	(5	4)	229	75	61	67	33	4	109	3	2	5	30	10	.75	19	.266	.306	.398
1998	2 Tms		142	541	136	31	2	9	(2	7)	198	89	53	62	53	1	83	3	6	5	24	11	.69	10	.251	.319	.366
1999	TEX	AL	133	465	134	21	5	14	(6	8)	207	69	52	71	39	1	100	4	9	3	8	6	.57	6	.288	.346	.445
2000	TEX	AL	148	513	124	21	5	14	(9	5)	197	70	54	54	42	1	92	3	12	3	11	7	.61	21	.242	.301	.384
2001	CHA	AL	135	433	114	21	4	9	(6	3)	170	62	60	50	33	2	72	3	9	7	10	7	.59	16	.263	.315	.393
2002	CHA	AL	112	342	86	14	2	7	(4	3)	125	51	35	37	20	0	67	3	7	4	5	1	.83	7	.251	.295	.365
2003	MIL	NL	146	483	110	16	1	5	(5	6)	161	49	39	37	49	10	92	3	4	4	5	2	.71	25	.228	.301	.333
2004	COL	NL	146	574	160	36	4	8	(6	2)	228	95	54	75	48	0	125	4	24	2	10	5	.67	13	.279	.338	.397
2005	ARI	NL	143	522	141	28	4	2	(1	1)	183	59	44	55	38	0	105	1	10	2	13	3	.81	19	.270	.320	.351
98	StL	NL	90	355	83	19	1	4	(1	3)	116	59	29	37	40	1	51	2	3	2	19	6	.76	10	.234	.313	.327
98	Tex	AL	52	186	53	12	1	5	(1	4)	82	30	24	25	13	0	32	1	3	3	5	5	.50	6	.285	.330	.441
15 ML YEARS			1894	6730	1739	319	54	107	(61	46)	2487	862	671	746	521	31	1277	39	103	53	215	93	.70	197	.258	.313	.370

Roger Clemens

Pitches: R **Bats:** R **Pos:** SP-32   **Ht:** 6'4" **Wt:** 235 **Born:** 8/4/1962 **Age:** 43

			HOW MUCH HE PITCHED						WHAT HE GAVE UP												THE RESULTS							
Year	Team	Lg	G	GS	CG	GF	IP	BFP	H	R	ER	HR	SH	SF	HB	TBB	IBB	SO	WP	Bk	W	L	Pct	ShO	Sv-Op	Hld	ERC	ERA
1984	BOS	AL	21	20	5	0	133.1	575	146	67	64	13	2	3	2	29	3	126	4	0	9	4	.692	1	0-0	0	3.81	4.32
1985	BOS	AL	15	15	3	0	98.1	407	83	38	36	5	1	2	3	37	0	74	1	3	7	5	.583	1	0-0	0	2.96	3.29
1986	BOS	AL	33	33	10	0	254.0	997	179	77	70	21	4	6	4	67	0	238	11	3	24	4	.857	1	0-0	0	2.03	2.48
1987	BOS	AL	36	36	18	0	281.2	1157	248	100	93	19	6	4	9	83	4	256	4	3	20	9	.690	7	0-0	0	2.94	2.97
1988	BOS	AL	35	35	14	0	264.0	1063	217	93	86	17	6	3	6	62	4	291	4	0	18	12	.600	8	0-0	0	2.36	2.93
1989	BOS	AL	35	35	8	0	253.1	1044	215	101	88	20	9	5	6	93	5	230	7	0	17	11	.607	3	0-0	0	3.13	3.13
1990	BOS	AL	31	31	7	0	228.1	920	193	59	49	7	7	5	7	54	3	209	8	0	21	6	.778	4	0-0	0	2.33	1.93
1991	BOS	AL	35	35	13	0	271.1	1077	219	93	79	15	6	8	5	65	12	241	6	0	18	10	.643	4	0-0	0	2.23	2.62
1992	BOS	AL	32	32	11	0	246.2	989	203	80	66	11	5	5	9	62	5	208	3	0	18	11	.621	5	0-0	0	2.38	2.41
1993	BOS	AL	29	29	2	0	191.2	808	175	99	95	17	5	7	11	67	4	160	3	1	11	14	.440	1	0-0	0	3.53	4.46
1994	BOS	AL	24	24	3	0	170.2	692	124	62	54	15	2	5	4	71	1	168	4	0	9	7	.563	1	0-0	0	2.72	2.85
1995	BOS	AL	23	23	0	0	140.0	623	141	70	65	15	2	3	14	60	0	132	9	0	10	5	.667	0	0-0	0	4.67	4.18
1996	BOS	AL	34	34	6	0	242.2	1032	216	106	98	19	4	7	4	106	2	257	8	1	10	13	.435	2	0-0	0	3.52	3.63
1997	TOR	AL	34	34	9	0	264.0	1044	204	65	60	9	5	2	12	68	1	292	4	0	21	7	.750	3	0-0	0	2.17	2.05
1998	TOR	AL	33	33	5	0	234.2	961	169	78	69	11	8	2	7	88	0	271	6	0	20	6	.769	3	0-0	0	2.27	2.65
1999	NYA	AL	30	30	1	0	187.2	822	185	101	96	20	10	5	9	90	0	163	8	0	14	10	.583	1	0-0	0	4.59	4.60
2000	NYA	AL	32	32	1	0	204.1	878	184	96	84	26	1	2	10	84	0	188	2	1	13	8	.619	0	0-0	0	3.93	3.70
2001	NYA	AL	33	33	0	0	220.1	918	205	94	86	19	4	8	9	72	1	213	14	0	20	3	.870	0	0-0	0	3.43	3.51
2002	NYA	AL	29	29	0	0	180.0	768	172	94	87	18	5	5	7	63	6	192	14	0	13	6	.684	0	0-0	0	3.72	4.35
2003	NYA	AL	33	33	1	0	211.2	878	199	99	92	24	3	6	5	58	1	190	5	0	17	9	.654	1	0-0	0	3.44	3.91
2004	HOU	NL	33	33	0	0	214.1	878	169	76	71	15	8	7	6	79	5	218	5	0	18	4	.818	0	0-0	0	2.72	2.98
2005	HOU	NL	32	32	1	0	211.1	838	151	51	44	11	9	3	6	62	5	185	3	1	13	8	.619	0	0-0	0	1.96	1.87
22 ML YEARS			672	671	118	0	4704.1	19369	3997	1799	1632	347	112	99	150	1520	62	4502	133	20	341	172	.665	46	0-0	0	2.92	3.12

Matt Clement

Pitches: R **Bats:** R **Pos:** SP-32   **Ht:** 6'3" **Wt:** 213 **Born:** 8/12/1974 **Age:** 31

			HOW MUCH HE PITCHED						WHAT HE GAVE UP												THE RESULTS							
Year	Team	Lg	G	GS	CG	GF	IP	BFP	H	R	ER	HR	SH	SF	HB	TBB	IBB	SO	WP	Bk	W	L	Pct	ShO	Sv-Op	Hld	ERC	ERA
1998	SD	NL	4	2	0	0	13.2	62	15	8	7	0	2	0	2	7	1	13	2	0	1	0	1.000	0	0-0	0	4.14	4.61
1999	SD	NL	31	31	0	0	180.2	803	190	106	90	18	7	6	9	86	2	135	11	0	10	12	.455	0	0-0	0	4.89	4.48
2000	SD	NL	34	34	0	0	205.0	940	194	131	117	22	12	5	16	125	4	170	23	0	13	17	.433	0	0-0	0	4.87	5.14
2001	FLA	NL	31	31	0	0	169.1	760	172	102	95	15	14	3	15	85	2	134	15	0	9	10	.474	0	0-0	0	4.84	5.05
2002	CHN	NL	32	32	3	0	205.0	858	162	84	82	18	11	4	6	85	7	215	7	0	12	11	.522	2	0-0	0	2.96	3.60
2003	CHN	NL	32	32	2	0	201.2	851	169	100	92	22	10	2	14	79	2	171	13	0	14	12	.538	1	0-0	0	3.47	4.11
2004	CHN	NL	30	30	0	0	181.0	775	155	79	74	23	5	4	12	77	4	190	14	1	9	13	.409	0	0-0	0	3.78	3.68
2005	BOS	AL	32	32	1	0	191.0	830	192	102	97	18	2	6	16	68	1	146	13	0	13	6	.684	0	0-0	0	4.22	4.57
8 ML YEARS			226	224	6	0	1347.1	5879	1249	712	654	136	63	30	88	612	23	1174	98	1	82	81	.503	3	0-0	0	4.10	4.37

JD Closser

Bats: B Throws: R Pos: C-80; PH-21; PR-2   **Ht: 5'10" Wt: 176 Born: 1/15/1980 Age: 26**

										BATTING													BASERUNNING				AVERAGES		
Year	Team	Lg	G	AB	H	2B	3B	HR	(Hm	Rd)	TB	R	RBI	RC	TBB	IBB	SO	HBP	SH	SF	SB	CS	SB%	GDP	Avg	OBP	Slg
1998	DBcks	R	45	150	47	13	2	4	(-	-)	76	26	21	34	37	2	36	4	0	1	3	2	.60	3	.313	.453	.507
1998	Sbend	A	4	14	3	1	0	0	(-	-)	4	3	2	1	2	0	7	0	1	0	0	0	-	0	.214	.313	.286
1999	Sbend	A	52	174	42	8	0	3	(-	-)	59	29	27	24	34	0	37	1	0	3	0	1	.00	3	.241	.363	.339
1999	Msoula	R+	76	275	89	22	0	10	(-	-)	141	73	54	66	71	2	57	2	1	6	9	3	.75	8	.324	.458	.513
2000	Sbend	A	101	331	74	19	1	8	(-	-)	119	54	37	44	60	4	61	3	1	1	6	2	.75	7	.224	.347	.360
2001	Lancst	A+	128	468	136	26	6	21	(-	-)	237	85	87	85	65	4	106	2	1	4	6	7	.46	9	.291	.377	.506
2002	Carlina	AA	95	315	89	27	1	13	(-	-)	157	43	62	55	44	4	69	0	0	1	9	3	.75	7	.283	.369	.498
2003	Tulsa	AA	118	410	116	28	5	13	(-	-)	193	62	54	66	47	3	79	3	0	3	3	2	.60	10	.283	.359	.471
2004	ColSpr	AAA	83	298	89	19	1	7	(-	-)	131	53	54	52	41	0	47	2	4	3	0	2	.00	3	.299	.384	.440
2004	COL	NL	36	113	36	6	0	1	(0	1)	45	5	10	15	6	0	22	2	3	0	0	0	-	3	.319	.364	.398
2005	COL	NL	92	237	52	12	2	7	(2	5)	89	31	27	24	32	1	48	1	1	1	1	0	1.00	9	.219	.314	.376
	2 ML YEARS		128	350	88	18	2	8	(2	6)	134	36	37	39	38	1	70	3	4	1	1	0	1.00	12	.251	.329	.383

Todd Coffey

Pitches: R Bats: R Pos: RP-57   **Ht: 6'5" Wt: 230 Born: 9/9/1980 Age: 25**

			HOW MUCH HE PITCHED						WHAT HE GAVE UP											THE RESULTS						
Year	Team	Lg	G	GS	CG	GF	IP	BFP	H	R	ER	HR	SH	SF	HB	TBB	IBB	SO	WP	Bk	W	L	Pct	ShO	Sv-Op	Hld	ERC	ERA
1998	Billings	R+	3	2	0	1	12.0	50	13	4	4	1	2	0	2	1	0	8	0	0	0	0	-	0	0--	-	3.91	3.00
1999	Reds	R	5	2	0	0	16.0	71	9	12	6	1	0	1	1	14	0	14	2	2	1	1	.500	0	0--	-	3.41	3.38
2001	Billings	R+	14	2	0	6	33.1	149	34	21	13	2	1	1	4	15	0	33	2	0	2	2	.500	0	1--	-	4.28	3.51
2001	Reds	R	3	2	0	0	12.2	54	11	11	6	1	1	1	1	5	0	15	0	0	0	1	.000	0	0--	-	3.49	4.26
2002	Dayton	A	38	5	0	11	80.1	344	78	34	32	8	4	5	2	25	5	62	9	4	6	4	.600	0	2--	-	3.51	3.59
2003	Ptomc	A+	11	0	0	5	23.0	88	16	6	5	0	1	0	1	3	0	21	1	0	0	2	.000	0	2--	-	1.34	1.96
2003	Dayton	A	39	0	0	26	56.0	243	61	20	14	1	0	0	2	14	0	53	3	0	3	3	.500	0	9--	-	3.49	2.25
2004	Chatt	AA	40	0	0	34	45.1	176	36	13	12	3	1	0	0	4	1	53	1	1	4	1	.800	0	20--	-	1.67	2.38
2004	Lsvlle	AAA	15	0	0	11	13.2	58	15	8	8	1	0	0	1	2	0	11	1	0	1	0	1.000	0	4--	-	3.71	5.27
2005	Lsvlle	AAA	8	0	0	5	8.2	36	8	5	5	1	1	0	0	2	1	5	0	0	0	0	-	0	3--	-	2.88	5.19
2005	CIN	NL	57	0	0	14	58.0	265	84	33	29	5	3	2	5	11	2	26	1	0	4	1	.800	0	1-2	3	6.11	4.50

Jesus Colome

Pitches: R Bats: R Pos: RP-36   **Ht: 6'4" Wt: 205 Born: 12/23/1977 Age: 28**

			HOW MUCH HE PITCHED						WHAT HE GAVE UP											THE RESULTS						
Year	Team	Lg	G	GS	CG	GF	IP	BFP	H	R	ER	HR	SH	SF	HB	TBB	IBB	SO	WP	Bk	W	L	Pct	ShO	Sv-Op	Hld	ERC	ERA
2005	Mont*	AA	3	0	0	0	4.0	14	2	0	0	0	0	0	0	3	0	3	0	0	0	0	-	0	0--	-	0.54	0.00
2001	TB	AL	30	0	0	9	48.2	209	37	22	18	8	2	2	2	25	4	31	2	0	2	3	.400	0	0-0	6	3.62	3.33
2002	TB	AL	32	0	0	15	41.1	204	56	41	38	6	4	1	2	33	5	33	5	0	2	7	.222	0	0-5	3	8.57	8.27
2003	TB	AL	54	0	0	24	74.0	334	69	37	37	9	2	4	3	46	5	69	7	0	3	7	.300	0	2-8	11	4.76	4.50
2004	TB	AL	33	0	0	9	41.1	169	28	16	15	4	5	0	1	18	1	40	1	1	2	2	.500	0	3-4	8	2.54	3.27
2005	TB	AL	36	0	0	18	45.1	212	54	29	23	7	1	0	2	18	3	28	5	0	2	3	.400	0	0-1	2	5.46	4.57
	5 ML YEARS		185	0	0	75	250.2	1128	244	145	131	34	14	7	10	140	18	201	20	1	11	22	.333	0	5-18	30	4.83	4.70

Bartolo Colon

Pitches: R Bats: R Pos: SP-33   **Ht: 6'0" Wt: 235 Born: 5/24/1973 Age: 33**

			HOW MUCH HE PITCHED						WHAT HE GAVE UP											THE RESULTS						
Year	Team	Lg	G	GS	CG	GF	IP	BFP	H	R	ER	HR	SH	SF	HB	TBB	IBB	SO	WP	Bk	W	L	Pct	ShO	Sv-Op	Hld	ERC	ERA
1997	CLE	AL	19	17	1	0	94.0	427	107	66	59	12	4	1	3	45	1	66	5	0	4	7	.364	0	0-0	0	5.53	5.65
1998	CLE	AL	31	31	6	0	204.0	883	205	91	84	15	10	2	3	79	5	158	4	0	14	9	.609	2	0-0	0	3.87	3.71
1999	CLE	AL	32	32	1	0	205.0	858	185	97	90	24	5	4	7	76	5	161	4	0	18	5	.783	1	0-0	0	3.68	3.95
2000	CLE	AL	30	30	2	0	188.0	807	163	86	81	21	2	3	4	98	4	212	4	0	15	8	.652	1	0-0	0	3.97	3.88
2001	CLE	AL	34	34	1	0	222.1	947	220	106	101	26	8	4	2	90	2	201	4	1	14	12	.538	0	0-0	0	4.24	4.09
2002	2 Tms		33	33	8	0	233.1	966	219	85	76	20	19	6	2	70	5	149	4	0	20	8	.714	3	0-0	0	3.29	2.93
2003	CHA	AL	34	34	9	0	242.0	984	223	107	104	30	5	8	5	67	3	173	8	3	15	13	.536	0	0-0	0	3.47	3.87
2004	ANA	AL	34	34	0	0	208.1	897	215	122	116	38	5	8	3	71	1	158	1	0	18	12	.600	0	0-0	0	4.64	5.01
2005	LAA	AL	33	33	2	0	222.2	906	215	93	86	26	9	4	3	43	0	157	2	1	21	8	.724	0	0-0	0	3.28	3.48
02	Cle	AL	16	16	4	0	116.1	467	104	37	33	11	6	3	2	31	1	75	3	0	10	4	.714	2	0-0	0	3.09	2.55
02	Mon	NL	17	17	4	0	117.0	499	115	48	43	9	13	3	0	39	4	74	1	0	10	4	.714	1	0-0	0	3.48	3.31
	9 ML YEARS		280	278	30	0	1819.2	7675	1752	853	797	212	67	40	32	639	26	1435	36	5	139	82	.629	7	0-0	0	3.87	3.94

Roman Colon

Pitches: R Bats: R Pos: RP-28; SP-7   **Ht: 6'6" Wt: 225 Born: 8/13/1979 Age: 26**

			HOW MUCH HE PITCHED						WHAT HE GAVE UP											THE RESULTS						
Year	Team	Lg	G	GS	CG	GF	IP	BFP	H	R	ER	HR	SH	SF	HB	TBB	IBB	SO	WP	Bk	W	L	Pct	ShO	Sv-Op	Hld	ERC	ERA
1997	Braves	R	14	12	0	1	63.0	289	68	47	30	2	4	3	2	28	0	44	3	0	3	4	.429	0	0--	-	4.17	4.29
1998	Danvle	A+	13	13	0	0	73.1	336	92	59	47	7	1	0	2	28	0	53	11	0	1	7	.125	0	0--	-	5.53	5.77
1999	Jmstwn	A-	15	15	1	0	77.1	329	77	48	39	4	1	3	2	25	0	61	7	2	7	5	.583	0	0--	-	3.52	4.54
2001	Macon	A	23	21	0	1	128.0	543	136	69	51	9	5	7	3	26	0	91	16	4	7	7	.500	0	0--	-	3.50	3.59
2002	MrtlBh	A+	26	26	1	0	163.0	683	170	81	64	8	4	8	2	38	1	94	3	0	9	8	.529	0	0--	-	3.37	3.53
2003	Grnville	AA	39	12	1	8	107.0	448	104	48	40	9	9	3	4	33	3	58	3	0	11	3	.786	0	2--	-	3.60	3.36
2004	Grnville	AA	3	0	0	2	3.0	11	1	1	0	0	0	0	0	0	0	5	0	0	1	0	1.000	0	0--	-	0.69	0.00
2004	Rchmd	AAA	51	0	0	11	74.0	318	72	33	30	4	1	1	3	22	1	64	1	0	4	1	.800	0	0--	-	3.28	3.65
2005	Missi	AA	2	2	0	0	7.2	31	6	1	1	0	0	0	0	2	0	7	0	0	0	0	-	0	0--	-	1.81	1.17
2005	Rchmd	AAA	3	3	0	0	14.0	59	12	3	3	0	1	0	1	5	0	9	2	1	1	1	.500	0	0--	-	2.73	1.93
2004	ATL	NL	18	0	0	7	19.0	82	18	9	7	0	1	2	0	8	1	15	0	0	2	1	.667	0	0-1	1	3.05	3.32
2005	2 Tms		35	7	0	7	69.1	306	82	45	43	17	2	3	0	21	1	47	4	1	2	6	.250	0	0-1	2	5.75	5.58

Year	Team	Lg	G	GS	CG	GF	IP	BFP	H	R	ER	HR	SH	SF	HB	TBB	IBB	SO	WP	Bk	W	L	Pct	ShO	Sv-Op	Hld	ERC	ERA
05	Atl	NL	23	4	0	6	44.1	191	47	28	26	10	2	2	0	14	1	30	2	1	1	5	.167	0	0-0	2	4.90	5.28
05	Det	AL	12	3	0	1	25.0	115	35	17	17	7	0	1	0	7	0	17	2	0	1	1	.500	0	0-1	0	7.34	6.12
	2 ML YEARS		53	7	0	14	88.1	388	100	54	50	17	3	5	0	29	2	62	4	1	4	7	.364	0	0-2	3	5.14	5.09

Jeff Conine

Bats: R **Throws:** R **Pos:** 1B-45; PH-40; LF-37; RF-28; DH-3　　　　　　　　**Ht:** 6'1" **Wt:** 220 **Born:** 6/27/1966 **Age:** 40

							BATTING														BASERUNNING				AVERAGES		
Year	Team	Lg	G	AB	H	2B	3B	HR	(Hm | Rd)	TB	R	RBI	RC	TBB	IBB	SO	HBP	SH	SF	SB	CS	SB%	GDP	Avg	OBP	Slg
1990	KC	AL	9	20	5	2	0	0	(0 | 0)	7	3	2	2	2	0	5	0	0	0	0	0	-	1	.250	.318	.350
1992	KC	AL	28	91	23	5	2	0	(0 | 0)	32	10	9	10	8	1	23	0	0	0	0	0	-	1	.253	.313	.352
1993	FLA	NL	162	595	174	24	3	12	(5 | 7)	240	75	79	83	52	2	135	5	0	6	2	2	.50	14	.292	.351	.403
1994	FLA	NL	115	451	144	27	6	18	(8 | 10)	237	60	82	84	40	4	92	1	0	4	1	2	.33	8	.319	.373	.525
1995	FLA	NL	133	483	146	26	2	25	(13 | 12)	251	72	105	93	66	5	94	1	0	12	2	0	1.00	13	.302	.379	.520
1996	FLA	NL	157	597	175	32	2	26	(15 | 11)	289	84	95	99	62	1	121	4	0	7	1	4	.20	11	.293	.360	.484
1997	FLA	NL	151	405	98	13	1	17	(7 | 10)	164	46	61	55	57	3	89	2	0	2	2	0	1.00	11	.242	.337	.405
1998	KC	AL	93	309	79	26	0	8	(4 | 4)	129	30	43	40	26	1	68	2	0	6	3	0	1.00	8	.256	.312	.417
1999	BAL	AL	139	444	129	31	1	13	(6 | 7)	201	54	75	64	30	4	83	3	1	7	0	3	.00	12	.291	.335	.453
2000	BAL	AL	119	409	116	20	2	13	(6 | 7)	179	53	46	58	36	1	53	2	0	4	4	3	.57	12	.284	.341	.438
2001	BAL	AL	139	524	163	23	2	14	(5 | 9)	232	75	97	89	64	6	75	5	0	8	12	8	.60	12	.311	.386	.443
2002	BAL	AL	116	451	123	26	4	15	(12 | 3)	202	44	63	61	25	6	66	2	0	10	8	0	1.00	10	.273	.307	.448
2003	2 Tms		149	577	163	36	3	20	(11 | 9)	265	88	95	84	50	5	70	5	1	13	5	0	1.00	16	.282	.338	.459
2004	FLA	NL	140	521	146	35	1	14	(9 | 5)	225	55	83	78	48	3	78	2	2	6	5	5	.50	15	.280	.340	.432
2005	FLA	NL	131	335	102	20	2	3	(1 | 2)	135	42	33	46	38	2	58	3	2	6	2	0	1.00	12	.304	.374	.403
03	Bal	AL	124	493	143	33	3	15	(8 | 7)	227	75	80	73	37	5	60	5	0	12	5	0	1.00	14	.290	.338	.460
03	Fla	NL	25	84	20	3	0	5	(3 | 2)	38	13	15	11	13	0	10	0	1	1	0	0	-	2	.238	.337	.452
	15 ML YEARS		1781	6212	1786	346	31	198	(103 | 95)	2788	791	968	946	604	40	1067	37	6	91	47	27	.64	164	.288	.350	.449

Jose Contreras

Pitches: R **Bats:** R **Pos:** SP-32　　　　　　　　**Ht:** 6'4" **Wt:** 230 **Born:** 12/6/1971 **Age:** 34

			HOW MUCH HE PITCHED						WHAT HE GAVE UP												THE RESULTS					
Year	Team	Lg	G	GS	CG	GF	IP	BFP	H	R	ER	HR	SH	SF	HB	TBB	IBB	SO	WP	Bk	W	L	Pct	ShO	Sv-Op	Hld	ERC	ERA
2003	NYA	AL	18	9	0	2	71.0	293	52	27	26	4	0	1	5	30	1	72	2	0	7	2	.778	0	0-1	1	2.71	3.30
2004	2 Tms	AL	31	31	0	0	170.1	758	166	114	104	31	3	6	8	84	1	150	17	0	13	9	.591	0	0-0	0	5.05	5.50
2005	CHA	AL	32	32	1	0	204.2	857	177	91	82	23	7	2	9	75	2	154	20	2	15	7	.682	0	0-0	0	3.46	3.61
04	NYY	AL	18	18	0	0	95.2	425	93	66	60	22	1	4	6	42	1	82	10	0	8	5	.615	0	0-0	0	5.18	5.64
04	CWS	AL	13	13	0	0	74.2	333	73	48	44	9	2	2	2	42	0	68	7	0	5	4	.556	0	0-0	0	4.87	5.30
	3 ML YEARS		81	72	1	2	446.0	1908	395	232	212	58	10	9	22	189	4	376	39	2	35	18	.660	0	0-1	1	3.92	4.28

Aaron Cook

Pitches: R **Bats:** R **Pos:** SP-13　　　　　　　　**Ht:** 6'3" **Wt:** 175 **Born:** 2/8/1979 **Age:** 27

			HOW MUCH HE PITCHED						WHAT HE GAVE UP												THE RESULTS					
Year	Team	Lg	G	GS	CG	GF	IP	BFP	H	R	ER	HR	SH	SF	HB	TBB	IBB	SO	WP	Bk	W	L	Pct	ShO	Sv-Op	Hld	ERC	ERA
2005	Mdest*	A+	1	1	0	0	5.0	20	5	1	1	0	0	0	0	0	0	5	0	0	1	0	1.000	0	0- -	-	1.95	1.80
2005	Tri-Cit*	A-	2	2	0	0	7.0	22	1	0	0	0	0	0	0	0	0	0	0	0	0	0	-	0	0- -	-	0.05	0.00
2005	Tulsa*	AA	1	1	0	0	3.2	22	10	9	7	2	0	0	0	1	0	1	0	0	0	0	-	0	0- -	-	19.83	17.18
2005	ColSpr*	AAA	3	3	0	0	16.1	74	18	10	10	0	2	1	1	7	0	11	2	0	1	0	1.000	0	0- -	-	4.20	5.51
2002	COL	NL	9	5	0	1	35.2	154	41	18	18	4	0	0	2	13	0	14	0	0	2	1	.667	0	0-0	1	5.31	4.54
2003	COL	NL	43	16	1	4	124.0	579	160	89	83	4	6	8	8	57	7	43	10	0	4	6	.400	0	0-0	1	5.95	6.02
2004	COL	NL	16	16	1	0	96.2	433	112	47	46	7	5	1	7	39	5	40	6	1	6	4	.600	0	0-0	0	5.05	4.28
2005	COL	NL	13	13	2	0	83.1	357	101	38	34	8	1	3	2	16	2	24	3	0	7	2	.778	0	0-0	0	4.53	3.67
	4 ML YEARS		81	50	4	5	339.2	1523	414	192	181	27	10	10	19	125	14	121	19	1	19	13	.594	0	0-0	2	5.28	4.80

Brian Cooper

Pitches: R **Bats:** R **Pos:** RP-7; SP-1　　　　　　　　**Ht:** 6'1" **Wt:** 185 **Born:** 8/19/1974 **Age:** 31

			HOW MUCH HE PITCHED						WHAT HE GAVE UP												THE RESULTS					
Year	Team	Lg	G	GS	CG	GF	IP	BFP	H	R	ER	HR	SH	SF	HB	TBB	IBB	SO	WP	Bk	W	L	Pct	ShO	Sv-Op	Hld	ERC	ERA
2005	Fresno*	AAA	29	21	0	1	137.0	604	139	72	69	23	9	7	4	54	1	82	4	0	7	8	.467	0	0- -	-	4.65	4.53
1999	ANA	AL	5	5	0	0	27.2	124	23	15	15	3	0	1	0	18	0	15	0	0	1	1	.500	0	0-0	0	4.79	4.88
2000	ANA	AL	15	15	1	0	87.0	396	105	66	57	18	4	4	2	35	1	36	1	0	4	8	.333	1	0-0	0	6.17	5.90
2001	ANA	AL	7	1	0	5	13.2	55	10	5	4	2	0	1	0	4	0	7	0	0	0	1	.000	0	0-0	0	2.51	2.63
2002	TOR	AL	2	2	0	0	8.1	41	14	13	13	5	1	1	0	4	0	3	1	0	0	1	.000	0	0-0	0	13.71	14.04
2004	SF	NL	5	2	0	0	13.1	61	15	13	13	4	2	1	1	5	1	7	1	0	0	2	.000	0	0-0	0	6.25	8.78
2005	SF	NL	8	1	0	3	17.2	73	15	6	6	0	1	0	0	8	0	7	0	0	0	1	.000	0	0-0	0	2.85	3.06
	6 ML YEARS		42	26	1	8	167.2	750	182	118	108	32	8	8	7	74	2	75	3	0	5	14	.263	1	0-0	0	5.57	5.80

Alex Cora

Bats: L **Throws:** R **Pos:** 2B-50; SS-35; PH-11; PR-7; 3B-5; LF-1　　　　　　　　**Ht:** 6'0" **Wt:** 180 **Born:** 10/18/1975 **Age:** 30

							BATTING														BASERUNNING				AVERAGES		
Year	Team	Lg	G	AB	H	2B	3B	HR	(Hm	Rd)	TB	R	RBI	RC	TBB	IBB	SO	HBP	SH	SF	SB	CS	SB%	GDP	Avg	OBP	Slg
1998	LA	NL	29	33	4	0	1	0	(0	0)	6	1	0	1	2	0	8	1	2	0	0	0	-	1	.121	.194	.182
1999	LA	NL	11	30	5	1	0	0	(0	0)	6	2	3	0	0	0	4	1	0	0	0	0	-	1	.167	.194	.200
2000	LA	NL	109	353	84	18	6	4	(2	2)	126	39	32	38	26	4	53	7	6	2	4	1	.80	6	.238	.302	.357
2001	LA	NL	134	405	88	18	3	4	(2	2)	124	38	29	30	31	6	58	8	3	2	1	2	.00	16	.217	.285	.306
2002	LA	NL	115	258	75	14	4	5	(4	1)	112	37	28	46	26	4	38	7	2	1	7	2	.78	3	.291	.371	.434
2003	LA	NL	148	477	119	24	3	4	(3	1)	161	39	34	46	16	3	59	10	9	2	4	2	.67	5	.249	.287	.338

Year	Team	Lg	G	AB	H	2B	3B	HR	(Hm	Rd)	TB	R	RBI	RC	TBB	IBB	SO	HBP	SH	SF	SB	CS	SB%	GDP	Avg	OBP	Slg
2004	LA	NL	138	405	107	9	4	10	(4	6)	154	47	47	63	47	10	41	18	12	2	3	4	.43	9	.264	.364	.380
2005	2 Tms	AL	96	250	58	8	4	3	(1	2)	83	25	24	21	11	0	30	5	4	3	7	2	.78	6	.232	.275	.332
05	Cle	AL	49	146	30	5	2	1	(1	0)	42	11	8	9	5	0	18	4	1	1	6	0	1.00	3	.205	.250	.288
05	Bos	AL	47	104	28	3	2	2	(0	2)	41	14	16	12	6	0	12	1	3	2	1	2	.33	3	.269	.310	.394
8 ML YEARS			780	2211	540	92	25	30	(16	14)	772	228	197	245	159	27	291	57	38	11	25	13	.66	46	.244	.310	.349

Tim Corcoran

Pitches: R Bats: R Pos: RP-9; SP-1   Ht: 6'2" Wt: 205 Born: 4/15/1978 Age: 28

			HOW MUCH HE PITCHED						WHAT HE GAVE UP											THE RESULTS						
Year	Team	Lg	G	GS	CG	GF	IP	BFP	H	R	ER	HR	SH	SF	HB	TBB	IBB	SO	WP	Bk	W	L	Pct	ShO	Sv-Op	Hld	ERC	ERA
1997	Kngspt	R+	7	0	0	3	17.0	71	12	10	8	2	0	2	3	8	2	14	2	1	2	0	1.000	0	0--		3.44	4.24
1997	Mets	R	10	0	0	4	21.0	94	16	8	7	0	2	0	0	15	0	20	4	0	3	0	1.000	0	0--		3.15	3.00
1998	StLuci	A+	4	0	0	2	7.2	35	10	7	7	1	0	0	0	2	0	8	0	0	0	0	-	0	0--		5.37	8.22
1998	CptCty	A	20	1	0	10	48.1	203	43	21	14	4	1	1	5	15	0	38	3	0	2	3	.400	0	4--		3.43	2.61
1999	CptCty	A	40	3	0	10	75.0	328	62	43	37	5	4	3	9	41	0	89	8	1	0	3	.000	0	3--		3.93	4.44
2000	CptCty	A	31	0	0	13	53.1	233	46	28	24	7	0	0	4	27	2	58	11	0	3	5	.375	0	1--		4.16	4.05
2001	Frdrck	A+	33	0	0	25	50.1	207	37	16	15	4	5	1	2	19	3	42	5	0	6	5	.545	0	6--		2.51	2.68
2001	Bowie	AA	7	0	0	4	11.2	42	4	1	1	0	0	0	0	3	0	13	1	0	1	0	1.000	0	0--		0.59	0.77
2002	Bowie	AA	35	0	0	23	49.0	237	61	31	20	5	4	3	4	29	3	48	6	0	0	5	.000	0	1--		6.52	3.67
2003	Frdrck	A+	22	3	0	4	47.0	225	57	38	30	3	1	5	0	27	2	41	6	0	2	5	.286	0	0--		5.52	5.74
2003	Bowie	AA	26	2	0	14	44.0	188	37	22	20	1	1	0	2	19	2	33	1	0	4	1	.800	0	3--		2.87	4.09
2004	Mont	AA	6	2	0	3	16.1	66	14	5	5	2	0	0	1	3	0	12	0	0	1	0	1.000	0	0--		2.86	2.76
2004	Drham	AAA	33	0	0	9	50.2	231	46	22	22	4	1	3	2	33	1	40	2	0	3	3	.500	0	0--		4.43	3.91
2005	Drham	AAA	29	0	0	3	56.0	239	49	22	18	3	0	1	2	22	0	49	4	0	5	1	.833	0	0--		3.15	2.89
2005	TB	AL	10	1	0	4	22.2	97	19	15	15	1	0	0	1	12	0	13	2	0	0	0	-	0	0-0	0	3.49	5.96

Chad Cordero

Pitches: R Bats: R Pos: RP-74   Ht: 6'0" Wt: 195 Born: 3/18/1982 Age: 24

			HOW MUCH HE PITCHED						WHAT HE GAVE UP											THE RESULTS						
Year	Team	Lg	G	GS	CG	GF	IP	BFP	H	R	ER	HR	SH	SF	HB	TBB	IBB	SO	WP	Bk	W	L	Pct	ShO	Sv-Op	Hld	ERC	ERA
2003	MON	NL	12	0	0	4	11.0	40	4	2	2	1	1	0	0	3	1	12	1	0	1	0	1.000	0	1-1	1	0.86	1.64
2004	MON	NL	69	0	0	40	82.2	357	68	28	27	8	2	4	1	43	4	83	5	0	7	3	.700	0	14-18	8	3.47	2.94
2005	WAS	NL	74	0	0	62	74.1	300	55	24	15	9	2	1	2	17	2	61	0	0	2	4	.333	0	47-54	0	2.22	1.82
3 ML YEARS			155	0	0	106	168.0	697	127	54	44	18	5	5	3	63	7	156	6	0	10	7	.588	0	62-73	9	2.69	2.36

Francisco Cordero

Pitches: R Bats: R Pos: RP-69   Ht: 6'2" Wt: 200 Born: 5/11/1975 Age: 31

			HOW MUCH HE PITCHED						WHAT HE GAVE UP											THE RESULTS						
Year	Team	Lg	G	GS	CG	GF	IP	BFP	H	R	ER	HR	SH	SF	HB	TBB	IBB	SO	WP	Bk	W	L	Pct	ShO	Sv-Op	Hld	ERC	ERA
1999	DET	AL	20	0	0	4	19.0	91	19	7	7	2	2	4	0	18	2	19	1	0	2	2	.500	0	0-0	6	6.19	3.32
2000	TEX	AL	56	0	0	13	77.1	365	87	51	46	11	2	6	4	48	3	49	7	0	1	2	.333	0	0-3	4	6.15	5.35
2001	TEX	AL	3	0	0	2	2.1	12	3	1	1	0	0	0	0	2	1	1	1	0	0	1	.000	0	0-0	1	5.73	3.86
2002	TEX	AL	39	0	0	25	45.1	177	33	12	9	2	0	0	2	13	1	41	1	0	2	0	1.000	0	10-12	5	2.11	1.79
2003	TEX	AL	73	0	0	36	82.2	352	70	33	27	4	3	4	2	38	6	90	0	0	5	8	.385	0	15-25	18	3.08	2.94
2004	TEX	AL	67	0	0	63	71.2	304	60	19	17	1	5	1	1	32	2	79	3	2	3	4	.429	0	49-54	0	2.78	2.13
2005	TEX	AL	69	0	0	60	69.0	302	61	28	26	5	4	3	4	30	2	79	1	0	3	1	.750	0	37-45	0	3.47	3.39
7 ML YEARS			327	0	0	203	367.1	1603	333	151	133	25	16	18	13	181	17	358	13	2	16	18	.471	0	111-139	30	3.73	3.26

Wil Cordero

Bats: R Throws: R Pos: PH-15; 1B-12; DH-3   Ht: 6'2" Wt: 200 Born: 10/3/1971 Age: 34

			BATTING																		BASERUNNING				AVERAGES		
Year	Team	Lg	G	AB	H	2B	3B	HR	(Hm	Rd)	TB	R	RBI	RC	TBB	IBB	SO	HBP	SH	SF	SB	CS	SB%	GDP	Avg	OBP	Slg
2005	Ptomc*	A+	2	7	3	1	0	2	(-	-)	10	2	2	3	1	0	0	0	0	0	0	0	-	0	.429	.500	1.429
2005	Hrsbrg*	AA	2	8	4	2	0	0	(-	-)	6	0	1	2	0	0	1	0	0	0	0	0	-	0	.500	.500	.750
2005	Norfolk*	AAA	8	31	4	2	0	0	(-	-)	6	3	2	1	5	0	11	0	0	0	0	0	-	1	.129	.250	.194
1992	MON	NL	45	126	38	4	1	2	(1	1)	50	17	8	17	9	0	31	1	1	0	0	0	-	3	.302	.353	.397
1993	MON	NL	138	475	118	32	2	10	(8	2)	184	56	58	55	34	8	60	7	4	1	12	3	.80	12	.248	.308	.387
1994	MON	NL	110	415	122	30	6	15	(5	10)	203	65	63	74	41	3	62	6	2	3	16	3	.84	8	.294	.363	.489
1995	MON	NL	131	514	147	35	2	10	(2	8)	216	64	49	72	36	4	88	9	1	4	9	5	.64	11	.286	.341	.420
1996	BOS	AL	59	198	57	14	0	3	(2	1)	80	29	37	24	11	4	31	2	1	1	2	1	.67	8	.288	.330	.404
1997	BOS	AL	140	570	160	26	3	18	(11	7)	246	82	72	75	31	7	122	4	0	4	1	3	.25	11	.281	.320	.432
1998	CHA	AL	96	341	91	18	2	13	(5	8)	152	58	49	47	22	0	66	3	1	4	2	1	.67	7	.267	.314	.446
1999	CLE	AL	54	194	58	15	0	8	(3	5)	97	35	32	34	15	0	37	6	0	2	1	0	1.00	5	.299	.364	.500
2000	2 Tms		127	496	137	35	5	16	(8	8)	230	64	68	70	32	1	76	7	0	1	1	2	.33	18	.276	.328	.464
2001	CLE	AL	89	268	67	11	1	4	(2	2)	92	30	21	28	22	2	50	4	2	3	0	0	-	8	.250	.313	.343
2002	2 Tms		72	161	43	9	0	6	(2	4)	70	22	30	28	17	0	29	2	0	4	2	0	1.00	4	.267	.337	.435
2003	MON	NL	130	436	121	27	0	16	(8	8)	196	57	71	68	49	5	90	4	0	3	1	1	.50	11	.278	.354	.450
2004	FLA	NL	27	66	13	3	0	1	(0	1)	19	6	6	3	3	0	19	2	0	1	1	0	1.00	2	.197	.250	.288
2005	WAS	NL	29	51	6	2	0	0	(0	0)	8	2	2	2	3	1	14	0	0	2	0	0	-	0	.118	.161	.157
00	Pit	NL	89	348	98	24	3	16	(8	8)	176	46	51	55	25	1	58	4	0	1	1	2	.33	11	.282	.336	.506
00	Cle	AL	38	148	39	11	2	0	(0	0)	54	18	17	15	7	0	18	3	0	0	0	0	-	7	.264	.310	.365
02	Cle	AL	6	18	4	0	0	0	(0	0)	4	1	1	1	0	0	3	0	0	0	0	0	-	1	.222	.222	.222
02	Mon	NL	66	143	39	9	0	6	(2	4)	66	21	29	27	17	0	26	2	0	4	2	0	1.00	3	.273	.349	.462
14 ML YEARS			1247	4311	1178	261	19	122	(57	65)	1843	587	566	595	325	35	775	57	12	33	49	19	.72	110	.273	.330	.428

Lance Cormier

Pitches: R **Bats:** R **Pos:** RP-67 **Ht:** 6'1" **Wt:** 192 **Born:** 8/19/1980 **Age:** 25

			HOW MUCH HE PITCHED						WHAT HE GAVE UP										THE RESULTS					
Year	Team	Lg	G	GS	CG	GF	IP	BFP	H	R	ER	HR	SH	SF	HB	TBB	IBB	SO	WP	Bk	W	L	Pct	ShO	Sv-Op	Hld	ERC	ERA
2002	Yakima	A-	1	0	0	0	1.0	8	4	4	3	0	0	0	0	0	0	3	0	0	0	0	-	0	0- -	-	19.55	27.00
2002	Sbend	A	11	3	0	4	27.2	116	29	9	9	1	1	1	0	2	0	17	2	2	3	0	1.000	0	1- -	-	2.57	2.93
2003	Lancst	A+	15	15	0	0	94.1	390	102	55	40	6	5	3	2	16	1	59	4	1	6	5	.545	0	0- -	-	3.49	3.82
2003	ElPaso	AA	9	8	0	0	41.1	201	59	33	28	3	3	1	0	22	0	26	4	0	2	3	.400	0	0- -	-	6.95	6.10
2003	Tucsn	AAA	5	4	0	0	27.2	108	26	10	8	1	3	0	0	5	0	11	1	0	1	1	.500	0	0- -	-	2.64	2.60
2004	ElPaso	AA	10	8	0	0	63.0	259	66	19	16	3	8	2	2	17	0	58	3	1	2	3	.400	0	0- -	-	3.74	2.29
2004	Tucsn	AAA	8	8	2	0	50.1	212	50	17	15	0	1	1	2	17	1	37	3	0	3	3	.500	1	0- -	-	3.28	2.68
2005	Tucsn	AAA	1	1	0	0	3.2	22	6	6	6	1	0	1	0	5	0	5	1	0	1	0	1.000	0	0- -	-	14.10	14.73
2004	ARI	NL	17	5	0	3	45.1	218	62	42	41	13	2	3	2	25	2	24	2	1	1	4	.200	0	0-0	2	8.76	8.14
2005	ARI	NL	67	0	0	13	79.1	356	86	50	45	7	4	1	5	43	5	63	6	0	7	3	.700	0	0-1	13	5.30	5.11
	2 ML YEARS		84	5	0	16	124.2	574	148	92	86	20	6	4	7	68	7	87	8	1	8	7	.533	0	0-1	15	6.51	6.21

Rheal Cormier

Pitches: L **Bats:** L **Pos:** RP-57 **Ht:** 5'10" **Wt:** 187 **Born:** 4/23/1967 **Age:** 39

			HOW MUCH HE PITCHED						WHAT HE GAVE UP										THE RESULTS					
Year	Team	Lg	G	GS	CG	GF	IP	BFP	H	R	ER	HR	SH	SF	HB	TBB	IBB	SO	WP	Bk	W	L	Pct	ShO	Sv-Op	Hld	ERC	ERA
1991	STL	NL	11	10	2	1	67.2	281	74	35	31	5	1	3	2	8	1	38	2	1	4	5	.444	0	0-0	0	3.41	4.12
1992	STL	NL	31	30	3	1	186.0	772	194	83	76	15	11	3	5	33	2	117	4	2	10	10	.500	0	0-0	0	3.42	3.68
1993	STL	NL	38	21	1	4	145.1	619	163	80	70	18	10	4	4	27	3	75	6	0	7	6	.538	0	0-0	0	4.13	4.33
1994	STL	NL	7	7	0	0	39.2	169	40	24	24	6	1	2	3	7	0	26	2	0	3	2	.600	0	0-0	0	3.80	5.45
1995	BOS	AL	48	12	0	3	115.0	488	131	60	52	12	6	2	3	31	2	69	4	0	7	5	.583	0	0-2	9	4.56	4.07
1996	MON	NL	33	27	1	1	159.2	674	165	80	74	16	4	8	9	41	3	100	8	0	7	10	.412	1	0-0	0	3.93	4.17
1997	MON	NL	1	1	0	0	1.1	9	4	5	5	1	0	0	0	1	0	0	0	0	0	1	.000	0	0-0	0	27.46	33.75
1999	BOS	AL	60	0	0	7	63.1	275	61	34	26	4	1	3	5	18	2	39	1	0	2	0	1.000	0	0-3	15	3.33	3.69
2000	BOS	AL	64	0	0	12	68.1	293	74	40	35	7	5	2	0	17	2	43	1	0	3	3	.500	0	0-2	9	3.86	4.61
2001	PHI	NL	60	0	0	16	51.1	222	49	26	24	5	3	0	4	17	4	37	1	0	5	6	.455	0	1-6	12	3.67	4.21
2002	PHI	NL	54	0	0	7	60.0	268	61	38	35	6	0	2	4	32	6	49	4	0	5	6	.455	0	0-3	9	4.85	5.25
2003	PHI	NL	65	0	0	21	84.2	327	54	18	16	4	4	0	1	25	2	67	0	1	8	0	1.000	0	1-4	14	1.63	1.70
2004	PHI	NL	84	0	0	8	81.0	330	70	32	32	7	3	1	5	26	6	46	1	0	4	5	.444	0	0-7	28	3.16	3.56
2005	PHI	NL	57	0	0	10	47.1	211	56	33	31	9	2	2	2	16	1	34	3	0	4	2	.667	0	0-2	17	5.71	5.89
	14 ML YEARS		613	108	7	91	1170.2	4938	1196	588	531	115	51	32	47	299	34	740	37	4	69	61	.531	1	2-29	113	3.74	4.08

Kevin Correia

Pitches: R **Bats:** R **Pos:** SP-11; RP-5 **Ht:** 6'3" **Wt:** 200 **Born:** 8/24/1980 **Age:** 25

			HOW MUCH HE PITCHED						WHAT HE GAVE UP										THE RESULTS					
Year	Team	Lg	G	GS	CG	GF	IP	BFP	H	R	ER	HR	SH	SF	HB	TBB	IBB	SO	WP	Bk	W	L	Pct	ShO	Sv-Op	Hld	ERC	ERA
2005	SnJos*	A+	1	1	0	0	7.0	31	5	2	2	0	0	0	0	5	0	7	2	0	0	1	.000	0	0- -	-	2.92	2.57
2005	Fresno*	AAA	31	3	0	19	46.0	211	50	38	31	6	2	3	1	23	0	35	0	0	3	2	.600	0	7- -	-	5.20	6.07
2003	SF	NL	10	7	0	0	39.1	173	41	16	16	6	1	1	4	18	1	28	2	0	3	1	.750	0	0-0	0	5.46	3.66
2004	SF	NL	12	1	0	5	19.0	92	25	20	17	3	3	3	1	10	0	14	0	0	0	1	.000	0	0-0	0	7.12	8.05
2005	SF	NL	16	11	0	1	58.1	264	61	31	30	12	5	1	4	31	2	44	2	0	2	5	.286	0	0-0	0	5.94	4.63
	3 ML YEARS		38	19	0	7	116.2	529	127	67	63	21	9	5	9	59	3	86	4	0	5	7	.417	0	0-0	0	5.97	4.86

David Cortes

Pitches: R **Bats:** R **Pos:** RP-50 **Ht:** 5'11" **Wt:** 195 **Born:** 10/15/1973 **Age:** 32

			HOW MUCH HE PITCHED						WHAT HE GAVE UP										THE RESULTS					
Year	Team	Lg	G	GS	CG	GF	IP	BFP	H	R	ER	HR	SH	SF	HB	TBB	IBB	SO	WP	Bk	W	L	Pct	ShO	Sv-Op	Hld	ERC	ERA
2005	ColSpr*	AAA	12	0	0	6	15.2	69	15	9	7	3	0	2	0	7	0	15	0	0	1	0	1.000	0	1- -	-	4.57	4.02
1999	ATL	NL	4	0	0	0	3.2	18	3	3	2	0	0	0	0	4	0	2	0	0	0	0	-	0	0-0	0	4.78	4.91
2003	CLE	NL	2	0	0	2	3.0	18	8	5	4	1	0	1	0	0	0	1	0	0	0	0	-	0	0-0	0	14.61	12.00
2005	COL	NL	50	0	0	14	52.2	213	50	24	24	9	1	2	1	10	2	36	3	0	2	0	1.000	0	2-3	4	3.50	4.10
	3 ML YEARS		56	0	0	16	59.1	249	61	32	30	10	1	3	1	14	2	39	3	0	2	0	1.000	0	2-3	4	4.06	4.55

Fernando Cortez

Bats: L **Throws:** R **Pos:** PH-4; 2B-3; SS-2; 3B-1 **Ht:** 6'1" **Wt:** 175 **Born:** 8/10/1981 **Age:** 24

			BATTING																		BASERUNNING				AVERAGES		
Year	Team	Lg	G	AB	H	2B	3B	HR	(Hm	Rd)	TB	R	RBI	RC	TBB	IBB	SO	HBP	SH	SF	SB	CS	SB%	GDP	Avg	OBP	Slg
2001	HudVal	A-	55	234	65	14	3	1	(-	-)	88	36	25	30	15	1	26	3	3	2	6	3	.67	5	.278	.327	.376
2002	Charltt	A+	127	475	127	14	5	2	(-	-)	157	60	49	56	41	0	59	4	2	6	36	16	.69	9	.267	.327	.331
2003	Bkrsfld	A+	102	384	108	19	0	1	(-	-)	130	53	53	53	41	2	61	2	2	9	32	9	.78	7	.281	.346	.339
2003	Orlndo	AA	30	114	36	3	1	1	(-	-)	44	15	6	14	3	0	22	0	1	0	1	2	.33	2	.316	.333	.386
2004	Mont	AA	94	359	103	20	5	3	(-	-)	142	51	30	50	32	1	60	1	6	2	7	7	.50	3	.287	.345	.396
2005	Mont	AA	55	219	73	11	4	0	(-	-)	92	39	23	37	15	0	42	2	1	3	12	3	.80	3	.333	.377	.420
2005	Drham	AAA	58	238	54	8	2	2	(-	-)	72	26	26	21	10	0	38	3	3	1	13	1	.93	6	.227	.266	.303
2005	TB	AL	8	13	1	0	0	0	(0	0)	1	0	1	0	1	0	3	0	0	0	0	0	-	0	.077	.143	.077

Shane Costa

Bats: L Throws: R Pos: LF-20; DH-4; PH-4   Ht: 6'0" Wt: 220 Born: 12/12/1981 Age: 24

Year	Team	Lg	G	AB	H	2B	3B	HR	(Hm	Rd)	TB	R	RBI	RC	TBB	IBB	SO	HBP	SH	SF	SB	CS	SB%	GDP	Avg	OBP	Slg
2003	Royals	R	23	88	34	6	4	1	(-	-)	51	22	24	21	6	0	7	4	0	1	4	3	.57	2	.386	.444	.580
2003	Wilmg	A	3	7	1	1	0	0	(-	-)	2	1	0	1	2	0	1	1	0	0	0	0	-	0	.143	.400	.286
2004	Wilmg	A	121	443	136	20	4	7	(-	-)	185	69	59	71	32	1	43	11	0	6	9	3	.75	7	.307	.364	.418
2005	Wichta	AA	75	277	78	18	2	8	(-	-)	124	37	43	46	24	2	23	8	1	6	5	1	.83	10	.282	.349	.448
2005	Omha	AAA	4	16	3	1	0	0	(-	-)	4	1	1	0	0	0	1	0	0	0	0	0	-	0	.188	.188	.250
2005	KC	AL	27	81	19	2	0	2	(1	1)	27	13	7	7	5	0	11	1	1	0	0	0	-	3	.235	.287	.333

Humberto Cota

Bats: R Throws: R Pos: C-87; PH-6; PR-1   Ht: 6'0" Wt: 205 Born: 2/7/1979 Age: 27

Year	Team	Lg	G	AB	H	2B	3B	HR	(Hm	Rd)	TB	R	RBI	RC	TBB	IBB	SO	HBP	SH	SF	SB	CS	SB%	GDP	Avg	OBP	Slg
2005	Indy*	AAA	3	11	3	0	0	0	(-	-)	3	0	1	0	0	0	3	0	0	0	0	0	-	2	.273	.273	.273
2001	PIT	NL	7	9	2	0	0	0	(0	0)	2	0	1	0	0	0	5	0	0	0	0	0	-	0	.222	.222	.222
2002	PIT	NL	7	17	5	1	0	0	(0	0)	6	2	0	1	1	1	4	0	0	0	0	0	-	0	.294	.333	.353
2003	PIT	NL	10	16	4	1	0	0	(0	0)	5	1	1	0	1	0	5	0	0	0	0	0	-	0	.250	.294	.313
2004	PIT	NL	36	66	15	1	1	5	(3	2)	33	10	8	7	3	1	20	1	0	0	0	0	-	1	.227	.271	.500
2005	PIT	NL	93	297	72	20	1	7	(5	2)	115	29	43	30	17	2	80	2	1	3	0	0	-	8	.242	.285	.387
	5 ML YEARS		153	405	98	23	2	12	(8	4)	161	42	53	38	22	4	114	3	1	3	0	0	-	9	.242	.284	.398

Neal Cotts

Pitches: L Bats: L Pos: RP-69   Ht: 6'2" Wt: 200 Born: 3/25/1980 Age: 26

			HOW MUCH HE PITCHED						WHAT HE GAVE UP											THE RESULTS						
Year	Team	Lg	G	GS	CG	GF	IP	BFP	H	R	ER	HR	SH	SF	HB	TBB	IBB	SO	WP	Bk	W	L	Pct	ShO	Sv-Op Hld	ERC	ERA
2003	CHA	AL	4	4	0	0	13.1	69	15	12	12	1	1	0	0	17	0	10	0	0	1	1	.500	0	0-0 0	8.43	8.10
2004	CHA	AL	56	1	0	12	65.1	281	61	45	41	13	0	1	3	30	2	58	8	0	4	4	.500	0	0-2 4	4.84	5.65
2005	CHA	AL	69	0	0	10	60.1	248	38	16	13	1	0	3	4	29	5	58	3	0	4	0	1.000	0	0-2 13	2.03	1.94
	3 ML YEARS		129	5	0	22	139.0	598	114	73	66	15	1	4	7	76	7	126	11	0	9	5	.643	0	0-4 17	3.85	4.27

Craig Counsell

Bats: L Throws: R Pos: 2B-143; PH-8; SS-1   Ht: 6'0" Wt: 175 Born: 8/21/1970 Age: 35

Year	Team	Lg	G	AB	H	2B	3B	HR	(Hm	Rd)	TB	R	RBI	RC	TBB	IBB	SO	HBP	SH	SF	SB	CS	SB%	GDP	Avg	OBP	Slg
1995	COL	NL	3	1	0	0	0	0	(0	0)	0	0	0	0	1	0	0	0	0	0	0	0	-	0	.000	.500	.000
1997	2 Tms	NL	52	164	49	9	2	1	(1	0)	65	20	16	24	18	2	17	3	3	1	1	1	.50	5	.299	.376	.396
1998	FLA	NL	107	335	84	19	5	4	(2	2)	125	43	40	48	51	7	47	4	4	5	3	0	1.00	5	.251	.355	.373
1999	2 Tms	NL	87	174	38	7	0	0	(0	0)	45	24	11	12	14	0	24	0	5	2	1	0	1.00	2	.218	.274	.259
2000	ARI	NL	67	152	48	8	1	2	(0	2)	64	23	11	25	20	0	18	2	1	1	3	3	.50	4	.316	.400	.421
2001	ARI	NL	141	458	126	22	3	4	(4	0)	166	76	38	61	61	3	76	2	6	6	6	8	.43	9	.275	.359	.362
2002	ARI	NL	112	436	123	22	1	2	(0	2)	153	63	51	65	45	3	52	1	4	3	7	5	.58	10	.282	.348	.351
2003	ARI	NL	89	303	71	6	3	3	(3	0)	92	40	21	29	41	0	32	2	3	2	11	4	.73	4	.234	.328	.304
2004	MIL	NL	140	473	114	19	5	2	(1	1)	149	59	23	48	59	9	88	5	5	3	17	4	.81	5	.241	.330	.315
2005	ARI	NL	150	578	148	34	4	9	(5	4)	217	85	42	80	78	4	69	8	2	4	26	7	.79	8	.256	.350	.375
97	Col	NL	1	0	0	0	0	0	(0	0)	0	0	0	0	0	0	0	0	0	0	0	0	-	0	-	-	-
97	Fla	NL	51	164	49	9	2	1	(1	0)	65	20	16	24	18	2	17	3	3	1	1	1	.50	5	.299	.376	.396
99	Fla	NL	37	66	10	1	0	0	(0	0)	11	4	2	1	5	0	10	0	2	0	0	0	-	1	.152	.211	.167
99	LA	NL	50	108	28	6	0	0	(0	0)	34	20	9	11	9	0	14	0	3	2	1	0	1.00	1	.259	.311	.315
	10 ML YEARS		948	3074	801	146	24	27	(16	11)	1076	433	253	392	388	28	423	27	37	23	75	32	.70	52	.261	.346	.350

Jesse Crain

Pitches: R Bats: R Pos: RP-75   Ht: 6'1" Wt: 205 Born: 7/5/1981 Age: 24

			HOW MUCH HE PITCHED						WHAT HE GAVE UP											THE RESULTS						
Year	Team	Lg	G	GS	CG	GF	IP	BFP	H	R	ER	HR	SH	SF	HB	TBB	IBB	SO	WP	Bk	W	L	Pct	ShO	Sv-Op Hld	ERC	ERA
2002	QuadC	A	9	0	0	6	12.0	45	6	3	2	0	1	0	1	4	0	11	0	0	1	1	.500	0	1-- -	1.31	1.50
2002	Elizab	R+	9	0	0	6	15.2	61	4	2	1	0	2	1	1	7	3	18	0	0	2	1	.667	0	2-- -	0.62	0.57
2003	FtMyrs	A+	10	0	0	3	19.0	70	10	6	6	0	0	0	0	5	0	25	0	0	2	1	.667	0	0-- -	1.06	2.84
2003	NwBrit	AA	22	0	0	15	39.0	143	13	4	3	0	1	0	1	10	1	56	2	1	1	1	.500	0	9-- -	0.58	0.69
2003	Roch	AAA	23	0	0	20	26.0	113	24	10	9	0	3	1	1	10	1	33	2	0	3	1	.750	0	10-- -	2.91	3.12
2004	Roch	AAA	41	0	0	33	50.2	204	38	20	14	5	1	0	1	17	2	64	1	0	3	2	.600	0	19-- -	2.54	2.49
2004	MIN	AL	22	0	0	3	27.0	109	17	6	6	2	1	0	1	12	1	14	1	0	3	0	1.000	0	0-1 2	2.25	2.00
2005	MIN	AL	75	0	0	17	79.2	326	61	28	24	6	9	3	5	29	7	25	2	0	12	5	.706	0	1-4 11	2.66	2.71
	2 ML YEARS		97	0	0	20	106.2	435	78	34	30	8	10	3	6	41	8	39	3	0	15	5	.750	0	1-5 13	2.56	2.53

Carl Crawford

Bats: L Throws: L Pos: LF-147; CF-8; DH-1; PH-1; PR-1   Ht: 6'2" Wt: 219 Born: 8/5/1981 Age: 24

Year	Team	Lg	G	AB	H	2B	3B	HR	(Hm	Rd)	TB	R	RBI	RC	TBB	IBB	SO	HBP	SH	SF	SB	CS	SB%	GDP	Avg	OBP	Slg
2002	TB	AL	63	259	67	11	6	2	(1	1)	96	23	30	34	9	0	41	3	6	1	9	5	.64	0	.259	.290	.371
2003	TB	AL	151	630	177	18	9	5	(6	5)	228	80	54	80	26	4	102	1	3	1	55	10	.85	5	.281	.309	.362
2004	TB	AL	152	626	185	26	19	11	(6	5)	282	104	55	96	35	2	81	1	4	6	59	15	.80	2	.296	.331	.450
2005	TB	AL	156	644	194	33	15	15	(5	10)	302	101	81	102	27	1	84	5	5	6	46	8	.85	11	.301	.331	.469
	4 ML YEARS		522	2159	623	88	49	33	(17	16)	908	308	220	312	97	7	308	10	16	16	169	38	.82	18	.289	.320	.421

Joe Crede

Bats: R **Throws:** R **Pos:** 3B-130; PH-2; SS-1; DH-1   **Ht:** 6'2" **Wt:** 195 **Born:** 4/26/1978 **Age:** 28

												BATTING										BASERUNNING				AVERAGES		
Year	Team	Lg	G	AB	H	2B	3B	HR	(Hm	Rd)	TB	R	RBI	RC	TBB	IBB	SO	HBP	SH	SF	SB	CS	SB%	GDP	Avg	OBP	Slg
2000	CHA	AL	7	14	5	1	0	0	(0	0)	6	2	3	2	0	0	3	0	0	1	0	0	-	0	.357	.333	.429
2001	CHA	AL	17	50	11	1	1	0	(0	0)	14	1	7	4	3	0	11	1	0	1	1	0	1.00	1	.220	.273	.280
2002	CHA	AL	53	200	57	10	0	12	(7	5)	103	28	35	31	8	0	40	0	0	1	0	2	.00	1	.285	.311	.515
2003	CHA	AL	151	536	140	31	2	19	(11	8)	232	68	75	69	32	1	75	6	2	4	1	1	.50	10	.261	.308	.433
2004	CHA	AL	144	490	117	25	0	21	(12	9)	205	67	69	58	34	0	81	10	4	5	1	2	.33	13	.239	.299	.418
2005	CHA	AL	132	432	109	21	0	22	(12	10)	196	54	62	62	25	3	66	8	2	4	1	1	.50	7	.252	.303	.454
	6 ML YEARS		504	1722	439	89	3	74	(42	32)	756	220	251	226	102	4	276	25	8	16	4	6	.40	32	.255	.303	.439

Doug Creek

Pitches: L **Bats:** L **Pos:** RP-20   **Ht:** 6'0" **Wt:** 227 **Born:** 3/1/1969 **Age:** 37

			HOW MUCH HE PITCHED						WHAT HE GAVE UP												THE RESULTS					
Year	Team	Lg	G	GS	CG	GF	IP	BFP	H	R	ER	HR	SH	SF	HB	TBB	IBB	SO	WP	Bk	W	L	Pct	ShO	Sv-Op Hld	ERC	ERA
2005	Toledo*	AAA	28	1	0	4	27.1	124	28	14	14	2	0	2	2	14	4	32	2	0	2	2	.500	0	0- -	-	4.45	4.61
1995	STL	NL	6	0	0	1	6.2	24	2	0	0	0	0	0	0	3	0	10	0	0	0	0	-	0	0-0	0	0.83	0.00
1996	SF	NL	63	0	0	15	48.1	220	45	41	35	11	1	0	2	32	2	38	2	0	0	2	.000	0	0-1	7	5.80	6.52
1997	SF	NL	3	3	0	0	13.1	64	12	12	10	1	0	0	0	14	0	14	0	0	1	2	.333	0	0-0	0	5.94	6.75
1999	CHN	NL	3	0	0	2	6.0	32	6	7	7	0	1	0	1	8	1	6	1	0	0	0	-	0	0-0	0	8.01	10.50
2000	TB	AL	45	0	0	8	60.2	265	49	33	31	10	2	3	2	39	3	73	3	0	1	3	.250	0	1-3	2	4.50	4.60
2001	TB	AL	66	0	0	16	62.2	279	51	34	30	7	1	3	4	49	5	66	4	0	2	5	.286	0	0-3	15	4.84	4.31
2002	2 Tms	AL	52	0	0	17	55.2	262	57	37	36	10	1	1	7	35	2	56	4	0	3	2	.600	0	0-2	5	6.19	5.82
2003	TOR	AL	21	0	0	3	13.2	69	14	6	5	2	0	2	2	12	3	11	2	0	0	0	-	0	0-1	2	6.57	3.29
2005	DET	AL	20	0	0	8	22.1	101	27	18	17	7	1	1	0	7	0	18	0	0	0	0	-	0	0-0	1	6.38	6.85
02	TB	AL	29	0	0	6	37.1	172	39	27	26	8	0	0	3	21	1	37	2	0	2	1	.667	0	0-2	4	6.15	6.27
02	Sea	AL	23	0	0	11	18.1	90	18	10	10	2	1	1	4	14	1	19	2	0	1	1	.500	0	0-0	1	6.22	4.91
	9 ML YEARS		279	3	0	70	289.1	1316	263	188	171	49	6	11	17	199	16	292	16	0	7	14	.333	0	1-10	32	5.39	5.32

Coco Crisp

Bats: B **Throws:** R **Pos:** LF-138; CF-10; PR-1   **Ht:** 6'0" **Wt:** 185 **Born:** 11/1/1979 **Age:** 26

												BATTING										BASERUNNING				AVERAGES		
Year	Team	Lg	G	AB	H	2B	3B	HR	(Hm	Rd)	TB	R	RBI	RC	TBB	IBB	SO	HBP	SH	SF	SB	CS	SB%	GDP	Avg	OBP	Slg
2002	CLE	AL	32	127	33	9	2	1	(1	0)	49	16	9	19	11	0	19	0	3	2	4	1	.80	0	.260	.314	.386
2003	CLE	AL	99	414	110	16	6	3	(3	0)	146	55	27	48	23	1	51	0	7	3	15	9	.63	6	.266	.302	.353
2004	CLE	AL	139	491	146	24	2	15	(8	7)	219	78	71	72	36	4	69	0	9	2	20	13	.61	8	.297	.344	.446
2005	CLE	AL	145	594	178	42	4	16	(4	12)	276	86	69	92	44	1	81	0	**13**	5	15	6	.71	7	.300	.345	.465
	4 ML YEARS		415	1626	467	90	14	35	(16	19)	690	235	176	231	114	6	220	0	32	12	54	29	.65	19	.287	.332	.424

Bobby Crosby

Bats: R **Throws:** R **Pos:** SS-84   **Ht:** 6'3" **Wt:** 195 **Born:** 1/12/1980 **Age:** 26

												BATTING										BASERUNNING				AVERAGES		
Year	Team	Lg	G	AB	H	2B	3B	HR	(Hm	Rd)	TB	R	RBI	RC	TBB	IBB	SO	HBP	SH	SF	SB	CS	SB%	GDP	Avg	OBP	Slg
2005	Scrmto*	AAA	3	12	1	0	0	0	(-	-)	1	0	1	0	0	0	0	0	0	0	0	0	-	0	.083	.083	.083
2005	Stcktn*	A+	3	9	3	1	0	0	(-	-)	4	1	1	1	2	0	1	0	0	0	0	0	-	0	.333	.455	.444
2003	OAK	AL	11	12	0	0	0	0	(0	0)	0	1	0	0	1	0	5	1	0	0	0	0	-	0	.000	.143	.000
2004	OAK	AL	151	545	130	34	1	22	(11	11)	232	70	64	60	58	0	141	9	5	6	7	3	.70	20	.239	.319	.426
2005	OAK	AL	84	333	92	25	4	9	(3	6)	152	66	38	47	35	0	54	1	1	1	0	0	-	10	.276	.346	.456
	3 ML YEARS		246	890	222	59	5	31	(14	17)	384	137	102	107	94	0	200	11	6	7	7	3	.70	30	.249	.326	.431

Bubba Crosby

Bats: L **Throws:** L **Pos:** CF-41; RF-23; PR-19; LF-4; DH-2; PH-2   **Ht:** 5'11" **Wt:** 185 **Born:** 8/11/1976 **Age:** 29

												BATTING										BASERUNNING				AVERAGES		
Year	Team	Lg	G	AB	H	2B	3B	HR	(Hm	Rd)	TB	R	RBI	RC	TBB	IBB	SO	HBP	SH	SF	SB	CS	SB%	GDP	Avg	OBP	Slg
2005	Clmbs*	AAA	42	160	37	7	1	4	(-	-)	58	18	22	19	12	0	28	6	3	2	2	1	.67	2	.231	.306	.363
2003	LA	NL	9	12	1	0	0	0	(0	0)	1	0	1	0	0	0	3	0	0	0	0	0	-	0	.083	.083	.083
2004	NYA	AL	55	53	8	2	0	2	(2	0)	16	8	7	7	2	0	13	1	2	0	2	0	1.00	1	.151	.196	.302
2005	NYA	AL	76	98	27	0	1	1	(1	0)	32	15	6	9	4	0	14	0	1	0	4	1	.80	1	.276	.304	.327
	3 ML YEARS		140	163	36	2	1	3	(3	0)	49	23	14	16	6	0	30	1	3	0	6	1	.86	1	.221	.253	.301

Jim Crowell

Pitches: L **Bats:** R **Pos:** RP-4   **Ht:** 6'4" **Wt:** 225 **Born:** 5/14/1974 **Age:** 32

			HOW MUCH HE PITCHED						WHAT HE GAVE UP												THE RESULTS					
Year	Team	Lg	G	GS	CG	GF	IP	BFP	H	R	ER	HR	SH	SF	HB	TBB	IBB	SO	WP	Bk	W	L	Pct	ShO	Sv-Op Hld	ERC	ERA
2005	Albq*	AAA	55	0	0	28	60.2	250	54	19	18	6	6	0	3	14	2	44	3	0	1	4	.333	0	12- -	0	2.95	2.67
1997	CIN	NL	2	1	0	1	6.1	36	12	7	7	2	2	0	0	5	0	3	0	0	0	1	.000	0	0-	0	13.59	9.95
2004	PHI	NL	4	0	0	0	3.0	18	6	2	1	0	0	0	0	0	0	1	0	0	0	0	-	0	0-0	0	6.14	3.00
2005	FLA	NL	4	0	0	2	3.1	22	10	8	8	1	0	1	2	0	0	2	0	0	0	0	-	0	0-0	0	21.14	21.60
	3 ML YEARS		10	1	0	3	12.2	76	28	17	16	3	2	1	2	5	0	6	0	0	0	1	.000	0	0-0	0	13.35	11.37

Deivi Cruz

Bats: R **Throws:** R **Pos:** 2B-49; PH-26; SS-24; 3B-5; PR-1   **Ht:** 6'0" **Wt:** 184 **Born:** 11/6/1972 **Age:** 33

							BATTING														BASERUNNING				AVERAGES		
Year	Team	Lg	G	AB	H	2B	3B	HR	(Hm	Rd)	TB	R	RBI	RC	TBB	IBB	SO	HBP	SH	SF	SB	CS	SB%	GDP	Avg	OBP	Slg
1997	DET	AL	147	436	105	26	0	2	(0	2)	137	35	40	31	14	0	55	0	14	3	3	6	.33	9	.241	.263	.314
1998	DET	AL	135	454	118	22	3	5	(5	0)	161	52	45	42	13	0	55	3	5	2	3	4	.43	11	.260	.284	.355
1999	DET	AL	155	518	147	35	0	13	(9	4)	221	64	58	64	12	0	57	4	14	5	1	4	.20	10	.284	.302	.427
2000	DET	AL	156	583	176	46	5	10	(1	9)	262	68	82	74	13	2	43	4	8	7	1	4	.20	25	.302	.318	.449
2001	DET	AL	110	414	106	28	1	7	(2	5)	157	39	52	42	17	0	46	4	1	2	4	1	.80	13	.256	.291	.379
2002	SD	NL	151	514	135	28	2	7	(3	4)	188	49	47	40	22	2	58	3	3	5	2	3	.40	20	.263	.294	.366
2003	BAL	AL	152	548	137	24	2	14	(7	7)	207	61	65	55	13	1	49	2	7	2	1	2	.33	13	.250	.269	.378
2004	SF	NL	127	397	116	30	2	7	(2	5)	171	46	55	54	17	6	32	3	8	6	1	3	.25	12	.292	.322	.431
2005	2 Tms		101	260	69	11	1	5	(3	2)	97	28	20	25	11	1	34	1	3	0	0	1	.00	5	.265	.298	.373
05	SF	NL	81	209	56	10	1	5	(3	2)	83	26	19	21	10	1	31	0	2	0	0	1	.00	5	.268	.301	.397
05	Was	NL	20	51	13	1	0	0	(0	0)	14	2	1	4	1	0	3	1	1	0	0	0	-	0	.255	.283	.275
	9 ML YEARS		1234	4124	1109	250	16	70	(32	38)	1601	442	464	427	132	12	429	24	63	32	16	28	.36	118	.269	.293	.388

Jacob Cruz

Bats: L **Throws:** L **Pos:** PH-88; RF-12; LF-8; 1B-5; DH-1   **Ht:** 6'0" **Wt:** 210 **Born:** 1/28/1973 **Age:** 33

							BATTING														BASERUNNING				AVERAGES		
Year	Team	Lg	G	AB	H	2B	3B	HR	(Hm	Rd)	TB	R	RBI	RC	TBB	IBB	SO	HBP	SH	SF	SB	CS	SB%	GDP	Avg	OBP	Slg
1996	SF	NL	33	77	18	3	0	3	(3	0)	30	10	10	10	12	0	24	2	1	0	0	1	.00	2	.234	.352	.390
1997	SF	NL	16	25	4	1	0	0	(0	0)	5	3	3	1	3	0	4	0	0	1	0	0	-	3	.160	.241	.200
1998	2 Tms		4	4	0	0	0	0	(0	0)	0	0	0	0	0	0	3	0	0	0	0	0	-	0	.000	.000	.000
1999	CLE	AL	32	88	29	5	1	3	(3	0)	45	14	17	14	5	0	13	1	1	1	0	2	.00	4	.330	.368	.511
2000	CLE	AL	11	29	7	3	0	0	(0	0)	10	3	5	5	5	0	4	1	0	1	1	0	1.00	0	.241	.361	.345
2001	2 Tms		72	144	31	5	0	4	(2	2)	48	19	18	13	15	0	50	4	1	2	0	4	.00	4	.215	.303	.333
2002	DET	AL	35	88	24	3	1	2	(0	2)	35	12	6	11	13	0	20	3	1	2	3	1	.75	2	.273	.377	.398
2004	CIN	NL	96	147	33	8	0	3	(2	1)	50	22	28	20	16	2	43	4	0	0	0	0	-	5	.224	.317	.340
2005	CIN	NL	110	127	30	10	0	4	(3	1)	52	12	18	18	16	1	46	1	0	1	0	0	-	1	.236	.324	.409
98	SF	NL	3	3	0	0	0	0	(0	0)	0	0	0	0	0	0	2	0	0	0	0	0	-	0	.000	.000	.000
98	Cle	AL	1	1	0	0	0	0	(0	0)	0	0	0	0	0	0	1	0	0	0	0	0	-	0	.000	.000	.000
01	Cle	AL	28	68	15	4	0	3	(2	1)	28	12	11	7	5	0	23	3	0	0	0	2	.00	3	.221	.303	.412
01	Col	NL	44	76	16	1	0	1	(0	1)	20	7	7	6	10	0	27	1	1	2	0	2	.00	1	.211	.303	.263
	9 ML YEARS		409	729	176	38	2	19	(13	6)	275	95	105	92	85	3	207	16	4	8	4	8	.33	20	.241	.331	.377

Jose Cruz

Bats: B **Throws:** R **Pos:** RF-55; CF-53; PH-10; LF-4   **Ht:** 6'0" **Wt:** 210 **Born:** 4/19/1974 **Age:** 32

							BATTING														BASERUNNING				AVERAGES		
Year	Team	Lg	G	AB	H	2B	3B	HR	(Hm	Rd)	TB	R	RBI	RC	TBB	IBB	SO	HBP	SH	SF	SB	CS	SB%	GDP	Avg	OBP	Slg
2005	Tucsn*	AAA	1	3	1	1	0	0	(-	-)	2	1	0	0	0	0	1	0	0	0	0	0	-	0	.333	.333	.667
1997	2 Tms	AL	104	395	98	19	1	26	(11	15)	197	59	68	63	41	2	117	0	1	5	7	2	.78	5	.248	.315	.499
1998	TOR	AL	105	352	89	14	3	11	(4	7)	142	55	42	55	57	3	99	0	0	4	11	4	.73	0	.253	.354	.403
1999	TOR	AL	106	349	84	19	3	14	(8	6)	151	63	45	57	64	5	91	0	1	4	14	4	.78	6	.241	.358	.433
2000	TOR	AL	**162**	603	146	32	5	31	(15	16)	281	91	76	91	71	3	129	2	2	3	15	5	.75	11	.242	.323	.466
2001	TOR	AL	146	577	158	38	4	34	(15	19)	306	92	88	101	45	4	138	1	2	2	32	5	.86	8	.274	.326	.530
2002	TOR	AL	124	446	114	26	5	18	(11	7)	204	64	70	71	51	1	106	0	1	4	7	1	.88	8	.245	.317	.438
2003	SF	NL	158	539	135	26	1	20	(9	11)	223	90	69	71	102	6	121	0	2	7	5	8	.38	14	.250	.366	.414
2004	TB	AL	153	545	132	25	8	21	(13	8)	236	76	79	79	76	8	117	2	5	8	11	6	.65	6	.242	.333	.433
2005	3 Tms		115	370	93	24	2	18	(11	7)	175	46	50	55	66	3	101	0	0	1	10	2	.83	8	.251	.364	.473
97	Sea	AL	49	183	49	12	1	12	(7	5)	99	28	34	31	13	0	45	0	1	1	1	0	1.00	3	.268	.315	.541
97	Tor	AL	55	212	49	7	0	14	(4	10)	98	31	34	32	28	2	72	0	0	4	6	2	.75	2	.231	.316	.462
05	Ari	NL	64	202	43	9	0	12	(6	6)	88	23	28	25	42	2	54	0	0	1	0	1	.00	6	.213	.347	.436
05	Bos	AL	4	12	3	1	0	0	(0	0)	4	0	0	1	1	0	4	0	0	0	0	0	-	0	.250	.308	.333
05	LAD	NL	47	156	47	14	2	6	(5	1)	83	23	22	29	23	1	43	0	0	0	0	1	.00	4	.301	.391	.532
	9 ML YEARS		1173	4196	1049	223	32	193	(97	96)	1915	636	585	643	573	35	1019	5	14	34	102	37	.73	68	.250	.338	.456

Juan Cruz

Pitches: R **Bats:** R **Pos:** RP-28   **Ht:** 6'2" **Wt:** 165 **Born:** 10/15/1978 **Age:** 27

			HOW MUCH HE PITCHED						WHAT HE GAVE UP											THE RESULTS						
Year	Team	Lg	G	GS	CG	GF	IP	BFP	H	R	ER	HR	SH	SF	HB	TBB	IBB	SO	WP	Bk	W	L	Pct	ShO	Sv-Op	Hld	ERC	ERA
2005	Scrmto*	AAA	13	13	0	0	75.0	304	51	23	20	4	3	3	5	28	0	90	4	0	5	1	.833	0	0--	-	2.27	2.40
2001	CHN	NL	8	8	0	0	44.2	185	40	16	16	4	2	0	2	17	1	39	0	0	3	1	.750	0	0-0	0	3.59	3.22
2002	CHN	NL	45	9	0	14	97.1	431	84	56	43	11	7	8	8	59	4	81	1	0	3	11	.214	0	1-4	3	4.49	3.98
2003	CHN	NL	25	6	0	3	61.0	284	66	44	41	7	7	2	7	28	0	65	4	0	2	7	.222	0	0-1	1	5.23	6.05
2004	ATL	NL	50	0	0	22	72.0	300	59	24	22	7	4	1	2	30	1	70	1	0	6	2	.750	0	0-0	2	3.25	2.75
2005	OAK	AL	28	0	0	14	32.2	159	38	33	27	5	0	2	4	22	4	34	3	0	0	3	.000	0	0-0	0	6.87	7.44
	5 ML YEARS		156	23	0	53	307.2	1359	287	173	149	34	20	13	23	156	10	289	9	0	14	24	.368	0	1-5	6	4.44	4.36

Nelson Cruz

Bats: R **Throws:** R **Pos:** RF-6; LF-2   **Ht:** 6'3" **Wt:** 175 **Born:** 7/1/1980 **Age:** 25

							BATTING														BASERUNNING				AVERAGES		
Year	Team	Lg	G	AB	H	2B	3B	HR	(Hm	Rd)	TB	R	RBI	RC	TBB	IBB	SO	HBP	SH	SF	SB	CS	SB%	GDP	Avg	OBP	Slg
2001	As	R	23	88	22	3	1	3	(-	-)	36	11	16	10	4	0	29	0	1	0	6	3	.67	1	.250	.283	.409
2002	Vancvr	A-	63	214	59	14	0	4	(-	-)	85	23	25	29	9	0	58	4	4	1	12	1	.92	6	.276	.316	.397
2004	Mdest	A+	66	261	90	27	1	11	(-	-)	152	54	52	59	24	2	73	4	0	1	8	4	.67	2	.345	.407	.582
2004	Mdland	AA	67	262	82	14	2	14	(-	-)	142	51	45	52	26	0	69	1	0	0	8	3	.73	4	.313	.377	.542
2004	Scrmto	AAA	4	13	3	1	0	1	(-	-)	7	4	2	2	1	0	7	0	0	0	0	0	-	0	.231	.286	.538

						BATTING														BASERUNNING				AVERAGES		
Year	Team	Lg	G	AB	H	2B	3B	HR	(Hm	Rd)	TB	R	RBI	RC	TBB	IBB	SO	HBP	SH	SF	SB	CS	SB%	GDP	Avg	OBP	Slg
2005	Huntsvl	AA	68	248	76	19	0	16	(-	-)	143	45	54	55	31	0	71	4	0	3	10	3	.77	7	.306	.388	.577
2005	Nashv	AAA	60	208	56	13	0	11	(-	-)	102	33	27	40	30	2	62	8	0	0	9	4	.69	4	.269	.382	.490
2005	MIL	NL	8	5	1	1	0	0	(0	0)	2	1	0	1	2	0	0	0	0	0	0	0	-	0	.200	.429	.400

Mike Cuddyer

Bats: R **Throws:** R **Pos:** 3B-95; RF-20; 2B-11; 1B-8; PH-3; PR-2   **Ht:** 6'2" **Wt:** 190 **Born:** 3/27/1979 **Age:** 27

						BATTING														BASERUNNING				AVERAGES		
Year	Team	Lg	G	AB	H	2B	3B	HR	(Hm	Rd)	TB	R	RBI	RC	TBB	IBB	SO	HBP	SH	SF	SB	CS	SB%	GDP	Avg	OBP	Slg
2005	Roch*	AAA	3	9	1	0	0	0	(-	-)	1	1	0	1	3	0	1	0	0	0	2	0	1.00	0	.111	.333	.111
2001	MIN	AL	8	18	4	2	0	0	(0	0)	6	1	1	2	2	0	6	0	0	0	1	0	1.00	1	.222	.300	.333
2002	MIN	AL	41	112	29	7	0	4	(2	2)	48	12	13	14	8	0	30	1	1	1	2	0	1.00	3	.259	.311	.429
2003	MIN	AL	35	102	25	1	3	4	(1	3)	44	14	8	10	12	0	19	0	0	0	1	1	.50	1	.245	.325	.431
2004	MIN	AL	115	339	89	22	1	12	(8	4)	149	49	45	51	37	2	74	3	2	1	5	5	.50	8	.263	.339	.440
2005	MIN	AL	126	422	111	25	3	12	(8	4)	178	55	42	43	41	5	93	3	1	3	3	4	.43	19	.263	.330	.422
	5 ML YEARS		325	993	258	57	7	32	(19	13)	425	131	109	120	100	7	222	7	4	5	12	10	.55	37	.260	.330	.428

Midre Cummings

Bats: L **Throws:** R **Pos:** LF-1; PH-1   **Ht:** 6'0" **Wt:** 195 **Born:** 10/14/1971 **Age:** 34

						BATTING														BASERUNNING				AVERAGES		
Year	Team	Lg	G	AB	H	2B	3B	HR	(Hm	Rd)	TB	R	RBI	RC	TBB	IBB	SO	HBP	SH	SF	SB	CS	SB%	GDP	Avg	OBP	Slg
2005	Ottawa*	AAA	74	264	75	14	0	12	(-	-)	125	39	40	48	36	5	69	4	0	5	0	1	.00	3	.284	.372	.473
1993	PIT	NL	13	36	4	1	0	0	(0	0)	5	5	3	0	4	0	9	0	0	1	0	0	-	0	.111	.195	.139
1994	PIT	NL	24	86	21	4	0	1	(1	0)	28	11	12	8	4	0	18	1	0	1	0	0	-	0	.244	.283	.326
1995	PIT	NL	59	152	37	7	1	2	(1	1)	52	13	15	16	13	3	30	0	0	1	1	0	1.00	0	.243	.303	.342
1996	PIT	NL	24	85	19	3	1	3	(2	1)	33	11	7	7	0	0	16	0	1	1	0	0	-	0	.224	.221	.388
1997	2 Tms	NL	115	314	83	22	6	4	(3	1)	129	35	31	42	31	0	56	1	2	2	2	3	.40	3	.264	.330	.411
1998	BOS	AL	67	120	34	8	0	5	(4	1)	57	20	15	21	17	0	19	2	1	0	3	3	.50	2	.283	.381	.475
1999	MIN	AL	16	38	10	0	0	1	(1	0)	13	1	9	4	3	0	7	0	0	1	2	0	1.00	0	.263	.310	.342
2000	2 Tms	AL	98	206	57	10	0	4	(2	2)	79	29	24	25	17	1	28	3	1	0	0	0	-	5	.277	.341	.383
2001	ARI	NL	20	20	6	1	0	0	(0	0)	7	1	1	1	0	0	4	0	0	1	0	0	-	2	.300	.286	.350
2004	TB	AL	22	54	15	4	0	2	(2	0)	25	10	7	12	5	0	12	2	0	0	1	0	1.00	0	.278	.361	.463
2005	BAL	AL	2	2	0	0	0	0	(0	0)	0	0	0	0	0	0	1	0	0	0	0	0	-	0	.000	.000	.000
97	Pit	NL	52	106	20	6	2	3	(2	1)	39	11	8	9	8	0	26	1	1	0	0	0	-	0	.189	.252	.368
97	Phi	NL	63	208	63	16	4	1	(1	0)	90	24	23	33	23	0	30	0	1	2	2	3	.40	3	.303	.369	.433
00	Min	AL	77	181	50	10	0	4	(2	2)	72	28	22	22	11	1	25	3	1	0	0	0	-	4	.276	.328	.398
00	Bos	AL	21	25	7	0	0	0	(0	0)	7	1	2	3	6	0	3	0	0	0	0	0	-	1	.280	.419	.280
	11 ML YEARS		460	1113	286	60	8	22	(16	6)	428	136	124	136	94	4	200	9	5	7	9	6	.60	14	.257	.318	.385

Brian Dallimore

Bats: R **Throws:** R **Pos:** PH-4; 2B-2; SS-1   **Ht:** 6'1" **Wt:** 180 **Born:** 11/15/1973 **Age:** 32

						BATTING														BASERUNNING				AVERAGES		
Year	Team	Lg	G	AB	H	2B	3B	HR	(Hm	Rd)	TB	R	RBI	RC	TBB	IBB	SO	HBP	SH	SF	SB	CS	SB%	GDP	Avg	OBP	Slg
1996	Auburn	A-	74	290	77	17	3	5	(-	-)	115	50	30	37	18	0	38	10	0	4	7	5	.58	5	.266	.326	.397
1997	QuadC	A	130	492	128	23	3	6	(-	-)	175	80	48	59	38	0	76	20	6	5	24	8	.75	19	.260	.335	.356
1997	Kissim	A+	1	3	0	0	0	0	(-	-)	0	0	0	0	0	0	2	0	0	0	0	0	-	0	.000	.000	.000
1998	Kissim	A+	62	240	61	11	1	0	(-	-)	74	34	19	23	19	0	42	5	4	1	7	5	.58	6	.254	.321	.308
1999	Kissim	A+	19	74	20	2	0	0	(-	-)	22	12	5	8	4	0	10	3	1	1	2	1	.67	1	.270	.329	.297
1999	Jacksn	AA	70	251	67	13	1	5	(-	-)	97	38	19	31	16	0	44	10	2	1	13	3	.81	12	.267	.335	.386
2000	RdRck	AA	5	11	2	1	0	0	(-	-)	6	1	3	1	1	0	3	0	0	0	0	0	-	0	.182	.250	.545
2000	ElPaso	AA	107	356	99	16	1	4	(-	-)	129	50	53	43	25	3	55	6	3	5	17	3	.85	13	.278	.332	.362
2001	ElPaso	AA	127	517	169	38	6	8	(-	-)	243	74	67	86	30	1	56	13	12	1	11	13	.46	9	.327	.378	.470
2002	Tucsn	AAA	122	419	123	26	2	6	(-	-)	171	62	50	59	28	0	72	9	7	6	13	4	.76	10	.294	.346	.408
2003	Fresno	AAA	91	330	116	16	2	4	(-	-)	148	53	46	66	37	0	37	10	8	5	6	4	.60	6	.352	.427	.448
2004	Fresno	AAA	111	432	140	21	4	8	(-	-)	193	72	65	77	40	3	53	15	4	6	9	2	.82	13	.324	.396	.447
2005	Fresno	AAA	100	398	120	26	2	8	(-	-)	174	67	45	67	32	0	43	12	1	2	7	2	.78	14	.302	.369	.437
2004	SF	NL	20	43	12	2	0	1	(1	0)	17	8	7	6	4	0	7	1	0	1	0	1	.00	0	.279	.347	.395
2005	SF	NL	7	7	1	1	0	0	(0	0)	2	1	0	0	0	0	0	0	0	0	0	0	-	1	.143	.143	.286
	2 ML YEARS		27	50	13	3	0	1	(1	0)	19	9	7	6	4	0	7	1	0	1	0	1	.00	1	.260	.321	.380

Johnny Damon

Bats: L **Throws:** L **Pos:** CF-147; PH-2; DH-1; PR-1   **Ht:** 6'2" **Wt:** 190 **Born:** 11/5/1973 **Age:** 32

						BATTING														BASERUNNING				AVERAGES		
Year	Team	Lg	G	AB	H	2B	3B	HR	(Hm	Rd)	TB	R	RBI	RC	TBB	IBB	SO	HBP	SH	SF	SB	CS	SB%	GDP	Avg	OBP	Slg
1995	KC	AL	47	188	53	11	5	3	(1	2)	83	32	23	29	12	0	22	1	2	3	7	1	1.00	2	.282	.324	.441
1996	KC	AL	145	517	140	22	5	6	(3	3)	190	61	50	64	31	3	64	3	10	5	25	5	.83	4	.271	.313	.368
1997	KC	AL	146	472	130	12	8	8	(5	3)	182	70	48	63	42	2	70	3	6	1	16	10	.62	3	.275	.338	.386
1998	KC	AL	161	642	178	30	10	18	(11	7)	282	104	66	98	58	4	84	4	3	3	26	12	.68	4	.277	.339	.439
1999	KC	AL	145	583	179	39	9	14	(5	9)	278	101	77	108	67	5	50	3	3	4	36	6	.86	13	.307	.379	.477
2000	KC	AL	159	655	214	42	10	16	(10	6)	324	136	88	129	65	4	60	1	8	12	46	9	.84	7	.327	.382	.495
2001	OAK	AL	155	644	165	34	4	9	(5	4)	234	108	49	79	61	1	70	5	5	4	27	12	.69	7	.256	.324	.363
2002	BOS	AL	154	623	178	34	11	14	(5	9)	276	118	63	101	65	5	70	6	3	5	31	6	.84	4	.286	.356	.443
2003	BOS	AL	145	608	166	32	6	12	(5	7)	246	103	67	92	68	4	74	2	6	6	30	6	.83	5	.273	.345	.405
2004	BOS	AL	150	621	189	35	6	20	(9	11)	296	123	94	115	76	1	71	2	0	3	19	8	.70	8	.304	.380	.477
2005	BOS	AL	148	624	197	35	6	10	(3	7)	274	117	75	105	53	3	69	2	0	9	18	1	.95	5	.316	.366	.439
	11 ML YEARS		1555	6177	1789	326	80	130	(57	73)	2665	1073	700	983	598	32	704	32	46	55	281	75	.79	62	.290	.353	.431

Vic Darensbourg

Pitches: L Bats: L Pos: RP-22   Ht: 5'8" Wt: 170 Born: 11/13/1970 Age: 35

Year	Team	Lg	G	GS	CG	GF	IP	BFP	H	R	ER	HR	SH	SF	HB	TBB	IBB	SO	WP	Bk	W	L	Pct	ShO	Sv-Op	Hld	ERC	ERA
2005	Toledo*	AAA	44	0	0	15	30.2	120	17	3	1	0	1	1	2	11	1	30	0	0	2	0	1.000	0	7- -		1.41	0.29
1998	FLA	NL	59	0	0	10	71.0	287	52	5	29	5	3	3	0	30	6	74	4	0	0	1	.000	0	1-2	13	2.47	3.68
1999	FLA	NL	56	0	0	5	34.2	180	50	36	34	3	5	2	5	21	1	16	1	3	0	1	.000	0	0-1	10	7.90	8.83
2000	FLA	NL	56	0	0	17	62.0	274	61	32	28	7	3	6	2	28	1	59	1	0	5	3	.625	0	0-1	3	4.33	4.06
2001	FLA	NL	58	0	0	19	48.2	202	52	24	23	4	1	2	1	10	6	33	0	0	1	2	.333	0	1-3	11	3.52	4.25
2002	FLA	NL	42	0	0	13	48.1	233	61	34	33	10	2	3	2	26	4	33	0	0	1	2	.333	0	0-0	3	6.98	6.14
2003	2 Tms	NL	9	0	0	3	9.0	46	17	9	8	2	1	0	0	1	0	4	0	0	0	0	-	0	0-0	0	9.00	8.00
2004	2 Tms	NL	7	0	0	4	7.0	32	11	5	5	1	1	2	0	3	0	1	0	0	0	1	.000	0	0-0	0	8.67	6.43
2005	DET	AL	22	0	0	4	22.1	96	24	7	7	2	2	2	0	7	2	9	0	0	1	1	.500	0	0-0	1	3.93	2.82
03	Col	NL	3	0	0	2	2.1	12	4	1	0	0	0	0	0	0	0	0	0	0	0	0	-	0	0-0	0	5.18	0.00
03	Mon	NL	6	0	0	1	6.2	34	13	8	8	2	1	0	0	1	0	4	0	0	0	0	-	0	0-0	0	10.54	10.80
04	CWS	AL	2	0	0	2	1.1	4	1	0	0	0	0	0	0	1	0	0	0	0	0	0	-	0	0-0	0	5.10	0.00
04	NYM	NL	5	0	0	2	5.2	28	10	5	5	1	1	2	0	2	0	1	0	0	0	1	.000	0	0-0	0	9.47	7.94
	8 ML YEARS		309	0	0	75	303.0	1350	328	152	167	34	18	20	10	126	20	229	6	3	8	17	.320	0	2-7	41	4.69	4.96

Brian Daubach

Bats: L Throws: R Pos: PH-8; 1B-6; DH-2   Ht: 6'1" Wt: 233 Born: 2/11/1972 Age: 34

Year	Team	Lg	G	AB	H	2B	3B	HR	(Hm	Rd)	TB	R	RBI	RC	TBB	IBB	SO	HBP	SH	SF	SB	CS	SB%	GDP	Avg	OBP	Slg
2005	Norfolk*	AAA	99	345	112	29	1	16	(-	-)	191	63	62	81	62	8	68	1	1	3	1	2	.33	6	.325	.426	.554
1998	FLA	NL	10	15	3	1	0	0	(0	0)	4	0	3	1	1	0	5	1	0	0	0	0	-	0	.200	.294	.267
1999	BOS	AL	110	381	112	33	3	21	(11	10)	214	61	73	74	36	0	92	3	0	0	1	1	.50	5	.294	.360	.562
2000	BOS	AL	142	495	123	32	2	21	(10	11)	222	55	76	70	44	2	130	6	0	4	1	1	.50	6	.248	.315	.448
2001	BOS	AL	122	407	107	28	3	22	(11	11)	207	54	71	71	53	7	108	5	1	6	1	0	1.00	10	.263	.350	.509
2002	BOS	AL	137	444	118	24	2	20	(11	9)	206	62	78	76	51	4	126	7	0	4	2	1	.67	10	.266	.348	.464
2003	CHA	AL	95	183	42	11	0	6	(4	2)	71	26	21	25	34	1	54	1	0	1	1	0	1.00	3	.230	.352	.388
2004	BOS	AL	30	75	17	8	0	2	(1	1)	31	9	8	11	10	0	21	1	0	0	0	0	-	1	.227	.326	.413
2005	NYN	NL	15	25	3	2	0	1	(0	1)	8	4	3	2	7	1	5	1	0	1	0	0	-	2	.120	.324	.320
	8 ML YEARS		661	2025	525	139	10	93	(48	45)	963	271	333	330	236	15	541	25	1	16	5	3	.63	37	.259	.341	.476

Jeff DaVanon

Bats: B Throws: R Pos: DH-29; RF-26; CF-24; PH-20; LF-17; PR-12   Ht: 6'0" Wt: 185 Born: 12/8/1973 Age: 32

Year	Team	Lg	G	AB	H	2B	3B	HR	(Hm	Rd)	TB	R	RBI	RC	TBB	IBB	SO	HBP	SH	SF	SB	CS	SB%	GDP	Avg	OBP	Slg
1999	ANA	AL	7	20	4	0	1	1	(1	0)	9	4	4	2	2	0	7	0	0	0	1	0	.00	0	.200	.273	.450
2001	ANA	AL	40	88	17	2	1	5	(3	2)	36	7	9	9	11	0	29	0	0	1	1	3	.25	1	.193	.280	.409
2002	ANA	AL	16	30	5	3	0	1	(0	1)	11	3	4	4	2	0	6	0	1	0	1	0	1.00	0	.167	.219	.367
2003	ANA	AL	123	330	93	16	1	12	(3	9)	147	56	43	56	42	0	59	1	4	5	17	5	.77	6	.282	.360	.445
2004	ANA	AL	108	285	79	11	4	7	(4	3)	119	41	34	47	46	2	54	0	1	5	18	3	.86	2	.277	.372	.418
2005	LAA	AL	108	225	52	10	1	2	(1	1)	70	42	15	26	39	1	44	2	3	2	11	6	.65	6	.231	.347	.311
	6 ML YEARS		402	978	250	42	8	28	(12	16)	392	153	109	144	142	3	199	3	9	13	48	18	.73	15	.256	.348	.401

Kyle Davies

Pitches: R Bats: R Pos: SP-14; RP-7   Ht: 6'2" Wt: 205 Born: 9/9/1983 Age: 22

Year	Team	Lg	G	GS	CG	GF	IP	BFP	H	R	ER	HR	SH	SF	HB	TBB	IBB	SO	WP	Bk	W	L	Pct	ShO	Sv-Op	Hld	ERC	ERA
2001	Braves	R	12	9	1	0	56.0	223	47	17	14	2	1	4	5	8	0	53	2	0	4	1	.667	1	0- -		1.96	2.25
2001	Macon	A	1	1	0	0	6.0	21	2	0	0	0	0	0	0	1	0	7	1	0	1	0	1.000	0	0- -		0.45	0.00
2002	Danvle	R+	14	14	0	0	69.1	304	73	39	27	2	1	3	2	23	0	62	1	0	5	3	.625	0	0- -		3.64	3.50
2002	Macon	A	2	1	0	0	6.0	28	6	4	4	1	0	1	1	4	0	4	0	0	1	0	1.000	0	0- -		6.48	6.00
2003	Rome	A	27	27	1	0	146.1	620	128	52	47	9	1	2	6	53	0	148	7	0	8	8	.500	0	0- -		3.11	2.89
2004	MrtlBh	A+	14	14	0	0	75.1	313	55	24	22	3	2	3	4	32	0	95	7	0	9	2	.818	0	0- -		2.53	2.63
2004	Grnville	AA	11	10	0	0	62.0	248	40	18	16	9	3	0	2	22	0	73	3	0	4	0	1.000	0	0- -		2.44	2.32
2004	Rchmd	AAA	1	1	0	0	5.0	23	5	5	5	0	0	0	0	3	0	5	0	0	0	1	.000	0	0- -		3.99	9.00
2005	Rchmd	AAA	13	13	0	0	73.1	320	66	28	28	6	1	3	0	34	2	62	7	0	5	2	.714	0	0- -		3.52	3.44
2005	ATL	NL	21	14	0	2	87.2	403	98	51	48	8	3	0	1	49	5	62	4	0	7	6	.538	0	0-1	2	5.25	4.93

Doug Davis

Pitches: L Bats: R Pos: SP-35   Ht: 6'4" Wt: 190 Born: 9/21/1975 Age: 30

Year	Team	Lg	G	GS	CG	GF	IP	BFP	H	R	ER	HR	SH	SF	HB	TBB	IBB	SO	WP	Bk	W	L	Pct	ShO	Sv-Op	Hld	ERC	ERA
1999	TEX	AL	2	0	0	0	2.2	20	12	10	10	3	0	0	0	3	0	0	0	0	0	0	-	0	0-0	0	41.42	33.75
2000	TEX	AL	30	13	1	4	98.2	450	109	61	59	14	6	4	3	58	3	66	5	1	7	6	.538	0	0-3	2	5.93	5.38
2001	TEX	AL	30	30	1	0	186.0	828	220	103	92	24	4	6	3	69	1	115	7	2	11	10	.524	1	0-0	0	4.90	4.45
2002	TEX	AL	10	10	0	0	59.2	262	67	36	33	7	3	3	3	22	0	28	2	2	3	5	.375	1	0-0	0	5.05	4.98
2003	3 Tms	NL	21	20	1	0	109.1	491	123	55	49	16	6	2	1	51	1	62	7	0	7	8	.467	0	0-0	0	5.46	4.03
2004	MIL	NL	34	34	0	0	207.1	880	192	84	78	14	11	5	7	79	3	166	4	1	12	12	.500	0	0-0	0	3.49	3.39
2005	MIL	NL	35	35	2	0	222.2	946	196	103	95	26	12	2	4	93	5	208	3	2	11	11	.500	1	0-0	0	3.62	3.84
03	Tex	AL	1	1	0	0	3.0	17	4	4	4	2	0	0	0	4	0	2	0	0	0	0	-	0	0-0	0	15.81	12.00
03	Tor	AL	12	11	0	0	54.0	250	70	33	30	6	3	0	1	26	1	25	6	0	4	6	.400	0	0-0	0	6.39	5.00
03	Mil	NL	8	8	1	0	52.1	224	49	18	15	8	3	2	0	21	0	35	1	0	3	2	.600	0	0-0	0	4.06	2.58
	7 ML YEARS		162	142	6	4	886.1	3877	919	452	416	94	42	22	21	372	13	648	28	8	51	52	.495	2	0-3	2	4.49	4.22

J.J. Davis

Bats: R Throws: R Pos: LF-9; PH-5; RF-1; PR-1　　　　　　　　　　**Ht: 6'5" Wt: 250 Born: 10/25/1978 Age: 27**

						BATTING																	BASERUNNING				AVERAGES		
Year	Team	Lg	G	AB	H	2B	3B	HR	(Hm	Rd)	TB	R	RBI	RC	TBB	IBB	SO	HBP	SH	SF		SB	CS	SB%	GDP	Avg	OBP	Slg
2005	NewOr*	AAA	51	174	49	10	0	12	(-	-)	95	34	31	33	18	2	53	0	0	0		3	4	.43	4	.282	.359	.546
2005	ColSpr*	AAA	21	67	15	3	0	3	(-	-)	27	12	15	40	7	0	20	1	0	3		1	1	.50	2	.224	.295	.403
2002	PIT	NL	9	10	1	0	0	0	(0	0)	1	1	0	0	0	0	4	1	0	0		0	0	-	1	.100	.182	.100
2003	PIT	NL	19	35	7	0	0	1	(1	0)	10	1	4	2	3	0	13	0	0	0		0	1	.00	0	.200	.263	.286
2004	PIT	NL	25	35	5	1	0	0	(0	0)	6	4	3	2	4	0	10	0	0	1		2	0	1.00	0	.143	.225	.171
2005	WAS	NL	14	26	6	0	0	0	(0	0)	6	0	2	2	2	0	7	0	0	0		1	1	.50	2	.231	.286	.231
	4 ML YEARS		67	106	19	1	0	1	(1	0)	23	6	9	6	9	0	34	1	0	1		3	2	.60	3	.179	.248	.217

Jason Davis

Pitches: R Bats: R Pos: RP-7; SP-4　　　　　　　　　　**Ht: 6'6" Wt: 195 Born: 5/8/1980 Age: 26**

			HOW MUCH HE PITCHED						WHAT HE GAVE UP											THE RESULTS						
Year	Team	Lg	G	GS	CG	GF	IP	BFP	H	R	ER	HR	SH	SF	HB	TBB	IBB	SO	WP	Bk	W	L	Pct	ShO	Sv-Op	Hld	ERC	ERA
2005	Buffalo*		16	16	1	0	95.2	420	106	65	49	9	10	3	4	27	0	77	5	2	8	5	.615	0	0--	-	4.28	4.61
2002	CLE	AL	3	2	0	0	14.2	60	12	3	3	1	0	0	0	4	0	11	0	1	1	0	1.000	0	0-0	-	2.40	1.84
2003	CLE	AL	27	27	1	0	165.1	696	172	101	86	25	7	3	8	47	4	85	9	2	8	11	.421	0	0-0	-	4.44	4.68
2004	CLE	AL	26	19	0	2	114.1	540	148	81	70	13	7	2	4	51	1	72	7	1	2	7	.222	0	0-0	1	6.17	5.51
2005	CLE	AL	11	4	0	2	40.1	182	44	22	21	4	0	3	3	20	0	32	2	0	4	2	.667	0	0-0	0	5.34	4.69
	4 ML YEARS		67	52	1	4	334.2	1478	376	207	180	43	15	8	15	122	5	200	18	4	15	20	.429	0	0-0	1	5.03	4.84

Kane Davis

Pitches: R Bats: R Pos: RP-15　　　　　　　　　　**Ht: 6'3" Wt: 194 Born: 6/25/1975 Age: 31**

			HOW MUCH HE PITCHED						WHAT HE GAVE UP											THE RESULTS						
Year	Team	Lg	G	GS	CG	GF	IP	BFP	H	R	ER	HR	SH	SF	HB	TBB	IBB	SO	WP	Bk	W	L	Pct	ShO	Sv-Op	Hld	ERC	ERA
2005	Nashv*	AAA	45	0	0	17	62.2	260	49	18	17	5	2	3	0	23	0	81	0	0	4	2	.667	0	1--	-	2.61	2.44
2000	2 Tms		8	2	0	1	15.0	85	27	24	21	4	0	0	2	13	0	4	0	1	0	3	.000	0	0-0	0	13.77	12.60
2001	COL	NL	57	0	0	6	68.1	301	66	36	33	11	2	4	1	32	4	47	4	0	2	4	.333	0	0-5	9	4.50	4.35
2002	NYN	NL	16	0	0	5	14.0	70	15	11	11	2	2	1	1	11	2	24	1	0	1	1	.500	0	0-0	1	6.19	7.07
2005	MIL	NL	15	0	0	3	16.2	70	10	6	5	2	0	0	0	10	0	11	1	0	1	1	.500	0	0-2	2	2.78	2.70
00	Cle	AL	5	2	0	0	11.0	61	20	21	18	3	0	0	1	8	0	2	0	1	0	3	.000	0	0-0	0	12.94	14.73
00	Mil	NL	3	0	0	1	4.0	24	7	3	3	1	0	0	1	5	0	2	0	0	0	0	-	0	0-0	0	16.04	6.75
	4 ML YEARS		96	2	0	15	114.0	526	118	77	70	19	4	5	4	66	6	86	6	1	4	9	.308	0	0-7	12	5.48	5.53

Zach Day

Pitches: R Bats: R Pos: RP-9; SP-8　　　　　　　　　　**Ht: 6'4" Wt: 185 Born: 6/15/1978 Age: 28**

			HOW MUCH HE PITCHED						WHAT HE GAVE UP											THE RESULTS						
Year	Team	Lg	G	GS	CG	GF	IP	BFP	H	R	ER	HR	SH	SF	HB	TBB	IBB	SO	WP	Bk	W	L	Pct	ShO	Sv-Op	Hld	ERC	ERA
2005	Hrsbrg*	AA	3	3	0	0	13.0	85	14	4	4	1	2	0	0	1	0	10	1	0	1	0	1.000	0	0--	-	3.02	2.77
2005	ColSpr*	AAA	7	7	0	0	36.2	171	46	29	24	4	2	1	3	15	0	17	4	2	2	3	.400	0	0--	-	5.98	5.89
2002	MON	NL	19	2	0	5	37.1	153	28	18	15	3	1	1	1	15	2	25	1	0	4	1	.800	0	1-2	2	2.66	3.62
2003	MON	NL	23	23	1	0	131.1	580	132	64	61	8	2	5	10	59	3	61	13	0	9	8	.529	1	0-0	0	4.28	4.18
2004	MON	NL	19	19	1	0	116.2	496	117	53	51	13	4	1	4	45	7	61	5	0	5	10	.333	1	0-0	0	4.24	3.93
2005	2 Tms	NL	17	8	0	4	47.1	229	61	40	36	6	1	1	1	32	4	23	2	0	1	3	.250	0	0-1	0	7.17	6.85
05	Was	NL	12	5	0	4	36.0	170	41	29	27	4	1	1	1	25	3	16	1	0	1	2	.333	0	0-0	0	6.18	6.75
05	Col	NL	5	3	0	0	11.1	59	20	11	9	2	0	0	0	7	1	7	1	0	0	1	.000	0	0-1	0	10.55	7.15
	4 ML YEARS		78	52	2	9	332.2	1458	338	175	163	30	8	8	16	151	16	170	21	0	19	22	.463	2	1-3	2	4.46	4.41

Jorge de la Rosa

Pitches: L Bats: L Pos: RP-38　　　　　　　　　　**Ht: 6'1" Wt: 190 Born: 4/5/1981 Age: 25**

			HOW MUCH HE PITCHED						WHAT HE GAVE UP											THE RESULTS						
Year	Team	Lg	G	GS	CG	GF	IP	BFP	H	R	ER	HR	SH	SF	HB	TBB	IBB	SO	WP	Bk	W	L	Pct	ShO	Sv-Op	Hld	ERC	ERA
1998	DBcks	R	13	0	0	2	14.0	59	8	7	7	3	0	0	1	8	0	21	2	0	1	0	1.000	0	1--	-	3.39	4.50
1999	DBcks	R	8	0	0	6	14.0	56	12	5	5	1	0	0	0	3	0	17	2	1	0	0	-	0	2--	-	2.46	3.21
1999	Hi Dsrt	A+	2	0	0	2	3.0	12	1	0	0	0	0	0	0	2	0	3	0	0	0	0	-	0	0--	-	1.26	0.00
1999	Msoula	R+	13	0	0	6	14.2	75	22	17	13	2	0	0	0	9	0	14	4	0	0	1	.000	0	2--	-	8.19	7.98
2001	Srsota	A+	12	0	0	10	29.2	114	13	7	4	0	0	0	0	12	0	27	2	0	1	1	.000	0	0--	-	1.06	1.21
2001	Trentn	AA	29	0	0	4	37.0	187	56	35	24	4	1	1	4	20	1	27	6	0	1	3	.250	0	0--	-	8.31	5.84
2002	Srsota	A+	23	23	1	0	120.2	515	105	53	49	10	1	2	6	52	1	95	5	1	7	7	.500	1	0--	-	3.54	3.65
2002	Trentn	AA	4	4	0	0	18.0	82	17	12	11	0	0	0	2	9	0	15	3	0	1	2	.333	0	0--	-	3.73	5.50
2003	Portlnd	AA	22	20	0	0	99.2	413	87	39	31	6	2	2	5	36	0	102	8	1	6	3	.667	0	1--	-	3.21	2.80
2003	Pwtckt	AAA	5	5	0	0	24.0	110	27	14	10	0	1	0	0	12	0	17	2	1	1	2	.333	0	0--	-	4.34	3.75
2004	Indy	AAA	20	20	0	0	85.2	368	80	45	43	9	4	4	8	36	1	86	5	2	5	6	.455	0	0--	-	4.23	4.52
2004	MIL	NL	5	5	0	0	22.2	113	29	20	16	1	1	3	1	14	0	5	3	0	0	3	.000	0	0-0	0	6.12	6.35
2005	MIL	NL	38	0	0	13	42.1	208	48	23	21	1	2	2	0	38	4	42	6	0	2	2	.500	0	0-2	5	6.04	4.46
	2 ML YEARS		43	5	0	13	65.0	321	77	43	37	2	3	5	1	52	4	47	9	0	2	5	.286	0	0-2	5	6.08	5.12

Valerio de los Santos

Pitches: L Bats: L Pos: RP-27　　　　　　　　　　**Ht: 6'2" Wt: 206 Born: 10/6/1972 Age: 33**

			HOW MUCH HE PITCHED						WHAT HE GAVE UP											THE RESULTS						
Year	Team	Lg	G	GS	CG	GF	IP	BFP	H	R	ER	HR	SH	SF	HB	TBB	IBB	SO	WP	Bk	W	L	Pct	ShO	Sv-Op	Hld	ERC	ERA
2005	Jupiter*	A+	3	0	0	0	4.0	18	4	0	0	0	0	0	0	2	0	4	0	0	0	0	-	0	0--	-	3.63	0.00
2005	Albq*	AAA	6	0	0	2	5.1	24	7	1	1	0	0	0	1	1	0	6	1	0	0	0	-	0	1--	-	5.10	1.69
1998	MIL	NL	13	0	0	3	21.2	75	11	7	7	4	0	0	0	2	0	18	1	0	0	0	-	0	0-0	0	1.25	2.91

Year	Team	Lg	G	GS	CG	GF	IP	BFP	H	R	ER	HR	SH	SF	HB	TBB	IBB	SO	WP	Bk	W	L	Pct	ShO	Sv-Op	Hld	ERC	ERA
1999	MIL	NL	7	0	0	3	8.1	43	12	6	6	1	0	0	1	7	0	5	1	0	0	1	.000	0	0-0	1	9.65	6.48
2000	MIL	NL	66	2	0	15	73.2	320	72	43	42	15	2	1	1	33	7	70	3	1	2	3	.400	0	0-1	9	4.79	5.13
2001	MIL	NL	1	0	0	0	1.0	5	1	1	1	0	0	0	0	1	0	1	0	0	0	0	-	0	0-0	0	5.48	9.00
2002	MIL	NL	51	0	0	12	57.2	237	42	21	20	4	3	7	2	26	3	38	1	0	2	3	.400	0	0-0	7	2.70	3.12
2003	2 Tms	NL	51	0	0	6	52.0	228	45	31	26	8	7	4	5	25	0	39	2	0	4	3	.571	0	1-4	11	4.37	4.50
2004	TOR	AL	17	0	0	1	11.2	56	11	8	8	0	1	1	0	10	2	10	3	0	0	0	-	0	0-1	0	4.29	6.17
2005	FLA	NL	27	0	0	5	22.0	103	25	15	15	4	0	0	2	12	3	16	4	0	1	2	.333	0	0-1	1	6.23	6.14
03	Mil	NL	45	0	0	5	48.0	205	38	24	22	8	6	4	4	22	0	35	1	0	3	3	.500	0	1-4	11	3.92	4.13
03	Phi	NL	6	0	0	1	4.0	23	7	7	4	0	1	0	1	3	0	4	1	0	1	0	1.000	0	0-0	0	10.26	9.00
8 ML YEARS			233	2	0	45	248.0	1067	219	132	125	36	13	13	11	116	15	197	15	1	9	12	.429	0	1-7	28	4.09	4.54

Mike DeJean

Pitches: R Bats: R Pos: RP-66 **Ht: 6'4" Wt: 219 Born: 9/28/1970 Age: 35**

Year	Team	Lg	G	GS	CG	GF	IP	BFP	H	R	ER	HR	SH	SF	HB	TBB	IBB	SO	WP	Bk	W	L	Pct	ShO	Sv-Op	Hld	ERC	ERA
1997	COL	NL	55	0	0	15	67.2	295	74	34	30	4	3	1	3	24	2	38	2	0	5	0	1.000	0	2-4	13	4.29	3.99
1998	COL	NL	59	1	0	9	74.1	307	78	29	25	4	4	4	1	24	1	27	3	0	3	1	.750	0	2-3	11	3.92	3.03
1999	COL	NL	56	0	0	17	61.0	288	83	61	57	13	3	3	2	32	8	31	3	0	2	4	.333	0	0-4	9	7.77	8.41
2000	COL	NL	54	0	0	15	53.1	235	54	31	29	9	3	1	0	36	6	34	5	0	4	4	.500	0	0-4	7	5.22	4.89
2001	MIL	NL	75	0	0	19	84.1	371	75	31	26	4	1	4	9	39	7	68	8	0	4	2	.667	0	2-4	8	3.56	2.77
2002	MIL	NL	68	0	0	60	75.0	326	66	28	26	7	4	2	2	39	8	65	7	0	1	5	.167	0	27-30	0	3.74	3.12
2003	2 Tms	NL	76	0	0	45	82.2	365	86	46	43	13	1	3	2	39	7	71	3	0	5	8	.385	0	19-27	10	5.00	4.68
2004	2 Tms		54	0	0	20	61.0	288	70	34	31	2	4	2	8	33	8	60	4	0	0	5	.000	0	0-0	3	5.21	4.57
2005	2 Tms	NL	66	0	0	19	62.1	282	62	33	31	3	3	3	3	30	3	52	5	0	5	4	.556	0	0-3	20	3.98	4.48
03	Mil	NL	58	0	0	40	64.2	286	69	38	35	12	0	3	1	27	7	58	3	0	4	7	.364	0	18-26	5	5.02	4.87
03	StL	NL	18	0	0	5	18.0	79	17	8	8	1	1	0	1	12	0	13	0	0	1	1	.500	0	1-1	5	4.89	4.00
04	Bal	AL	37	0	0	12	39.2	197	49	29	27	2	2	2	6	28	6	36	2	0	0	5	.000	0	0-0	1	6.64	6.13
04	NYM	AL	17	0	0	8	21.1	91	21	5	4	0	2	0	2	5	2	24	2	0	0	0	-	0	0-0	2	2.85	1.69
05	NYM	NL	28	0	0	12	25.2	131	36	19	18	3	1	1	1	18	2	17	2	0	3	1	.750	0	0-0	2	7.84	6.31
05	Col	NL	38	0	0	7	36.2	151	26	14	13	0	2	2	2	12	1	35	3	0	2	3	.400	0	0-3	18	1.80	3.19
9 ML YEARS			563	1	0	219	621.2	2757	648	327	298	59	26	23	30	290	50	446	40	0	29	33	.468	0	52-79	81	4.62	4.31

David DeJesus

Bats: L Throws: L Pos: CF-119; PH-2; PR-2 **Ht: 5'11" Wt: 170 Born: 12/20/1979 Age: 26**

Year	Team	Lg	G	AB	H	2B	3B	HR	(Hm	Rd)	TB	R	RBI	RC	TBB	IBB	SO	HBP	SH	SF	SB	CS	SB%	GDP	Avg	OBP	Slg
2003	KC	AL	12	7	2	0	1	0	(0	0)	4	0	0	2	1	0	2	1	1	0	0	0	-	0	.286	.444	.571
2004	KC	AL	96	363	104	15	3	7	(2	5)	146	58	39	53	33	0	53	9	8	0	8	11	.42	7	.287	.360	.402
2005	KC	AL	122	461	135	31	6	9	(6	3)	205	69	56	77	42	1	76	9	5	6	5	5	.50	6	.293	.359	.445
3 ML YEARS			230	831	241	46	10	16	(8	8)	355	127	95	132	76	1	131	19	14	6	13	16	.45	13	.290	.361	.427

Manny Delcarmen

Pitches: R Bats: R Pos: RP-10 **Ht: 6'3" Wt: 195 Born: 2/16/1982 Age: 24**

Year	Team	Lg	G	GS	CG	GF	IP	BFP	H	R	ER	HR	SH	SF	HB	TBB	IBB	SO	WP	Bk	W	L	Pct	ShO	Sv-Op	Hld	ERC	ERA
2001	RedSx	R	11	8	0	2	46.0	192	35	16	13	0	2	1	7	19	0	62	2	0	4	2	.667	0	1--	-	2.78	2.54
2002	Augsta	A	26	24	0	1	136.0	588	124	77	62	15	6	1	14	56	0	136	3	1	7	8	.467	0	0--	-	4.12	4.10
2003	Srsota	A+	4	3	0	0	23.0	92	16	9	8	1	0	0	3	7	0	16	0	0	1	1	.500	0	0--	-	2.31	3.13
2004	Srsota	A+	19	18	0	1	73.0	323	84	43	38	10	4	3	4	20	1	76	1	0	3	6	.333	0	0--	-	4.85	4.68
2005	Portlnd	AA	31	0	0	8	39.0	168	31	23	14	3	3	0	0	20	1	49	6	0	4	4	.500	0	3--	-	3.12	3.23
2005	Pwtckt	AAA	15	0	0	10	21.0	93	17	3	3	0	0	0	1	13	1	23	1	1	3	1	.750	0	2--	-	3.19	1.29
2005	BOS	AL	10	0	0	2	9.0	41	8	3	3	0	0	0	1	7	0	9	0	0	0	0	-	0	0-0	0	4.68	3.00

Carlos Delgado

Bats: L Throws: R Pos: 1B-141; PH-3; DH-1 **Ht: 6'3" Wt: 230 Born: 6/25/1972 Age: 34**

Year	Team	Lg	G	AB	H	2B	3B	HR	(Hm	Rd)	TB	R	RBI	RC	TBB	IBB	SO	HBP	SH	SF	SB	CS	SB%	GDP	Avg	OBP	Slg
1993	TOR	AL	2	1	0	0	0	0	(0	0)	0	0	0	0	1	0	0	0	0	0	0	0	-	0	.000	.500	.000
1994	TOR	AL	43	130	28	2	0	9	(5	4)	57	17	24	20	25	4	46	3	0	1	1	1	.50	5	.215	.352	.438
1995	TOR	AL	37	91	15	3	0	3	(2	1)	27	7	11	5	6	0	26	0	0	2	0	0	-	1	.165	.212	.297
1996	TOR	AL	138	488	132	28	2	25	(12	13)	239	68	92	83	58	2	139	9	0	8	0	0	-	13	.270	.353	.490
1997	TOR	AL	153	519	136	42	3	30	(17	13)	274	79	91	94	64	9	133	8	0	4	0	3	.00	6	.262	.350	.528
1998	TOR	AL	142	530	155	43	1	38	(20	18)	314	94	115	117	73	13	139	11	0	6	3	0	1.00	3	.292	.385	.592
1999	TOR	AL	152	573	156	39	0	44	(17	**27**)	327	113	134	121	86	7	141	15	0	7	1	1	.50	11	.272	.377	.571
2000	TOR	AL	162	569	196	**57**	1	41	(**30**	11)	378	115	137	164	123	18	104	**15**	0	4	0	1	.00	12	.344	.470	.664
2001	TOR	AL	162	574	160	31	1	39	(13	**26**)	310	102	102	126	111	22	136	16	0	3	3	0	1.00	9	.279	.408	.540
2002	TOR	AL	143	505	140	34	2	33	(17	16)	277	103	108	117	102	18	126	13	0	8	1	0	1.00	8	.277	.406	.549
2003	TOR	AL	161	570	172	38	1	42	(18	14)	338	117	**145**	**146**	109	23	137	19	0	7	0	0	-	9	.302	.426	.593
2004	TOR	AL	128	458	123	26	0	32	(18	14)	245	74	99	88	69	12	115	13	0	11	0	1	.00	11	.269	.372	.535
2005	FLA	NL	144	521	157	41	3	33	(16	17)	303	81	115	110	72	20	121	17	0	6	0	0	-	16	.301	.399	.582
13 ML YEARS			1567	5529	1570	384	14	369	(191	178)	3089	970	1173	1191	899	148	1363	139	0	67	9	7	.56	109	.284	.393	.559

David Dellucci

Bats: L **Throws:** L **Pos:** DH-64; LF-47; PH-16; CF-3; RF-3   **Ht:** 5'11" **Wt:** 198 **Born:** 10/31/1973 **Age:** 32

								BATTING												BASERUNNING				AVERAGES		
Year	Team	Lg	G	AB	H	2B	3B	HR	(Hm | Rd)	TB	R	RBI	RC	TBB	IBB	SO	HBP	SH	SF	SB	CS	SB%	GDP	Avg	OBP	Slg
1997	BAL	AL	17	27	6	1	0	1	(0 | 1)	10	3	3	3	4	1	7	1	0	0	0	0	-	2	.222	.344	.370
1998	ARI	NL	124	416	108	19	12	5	(1 | 4)	166	43	51	51	33	2	103	3	0	1	3	5	.38	6	.260	.318	.399
1999	ARI	NL	63	109	43	7	1	1	(0 | 1)	55	27	15	24	11	0	24	3	0	0	2	0	1.00	3	.394	.463	.505
2000	ARI	NL	34	50	15	3	0	0	(0 | 0)	18	2	2	6	4	0	9	0	0	0	0	2	.00	1	.300	.352	.360
2001	ARI	NL	115	217	60	10	2	10	(5 | 5)	104	28	40	36	22	4	52	2	0	0	2	1	.67	2	.276	.349	.479
2002	ARI	NL	97	229	56	11	2	7	(2 | 5)	92	34	29	26	28	5	55	1	0	3	2	4	.33	7	.245	.326	.402
2003	2 Tms		91	216	49	12	3	3	(3 | 0)	76	26	23	23	23	1	58	5	2	2	12	0	1.00	6	.227	.313	.352
2004	TEX	AL	107	331	80	13	1	17	(9 | 8)	146	59	61	56	47	3	88	5	1	3	9	4	.69	4	.242	.342	.441
2005	TEX	AL	128	435	109	17	5	29	(14 | 15)	223	97	65	81	76	0	121	5	0	2	5	3	.63	7	.251	.367	.513
03	Ari	AL	70	165	40	11	3	2	(2 | 0)	63	18	19	21	19	1	45	3	1	2	9	0	1.00	4	.242	.328	.382
03	NYY	AL	21	51	9	1	0	1	(1 | 0)	13	8	4	2	4	0	13	2	1	0	3	0	1.00	2	.176	.263	.255
	9 ML YEARS		776	2030	526	93	26	73	(34 | 39)	890	319	289	306	248	16	517	25	3	11	35	19	.65	38	.259	.345	.438

Chris Demaria

Pitches: R **Bats:** B **Pos:** RP-8   **Ht:** 6'3" **Wt:** 210 **Born:** 9/28/1980 **Age:** 25

			HOW MUCH HE PITCHED						WHAT HE GAVE UP										THE RESULTS						
Year	Team	Lg	G	GS	CG	GF	IP	BFP	H	R	ER	HR	SH	SF	HB	TBB	IBB	SO	WP	Bk	W	L	Pct	ShO	Sv-Op	Hld	ERC	ERA
2002	Wmspt	A-	16	0	0	6	31.0	132	34	20	15	6	1	0	4	4	1	15	0	0	1	1	.500	0	1--	-	3.98	4.35
2003	Wmspt	A-	25	1	0	9	47.0	187	36	15	14	3	1	0	6	10	0	48	3	0	6	3	.667	0	3--	-	2.45	2.68
2004	Hickory	A	40	0	0	27	79.2	321	62	29	26	5	3	1	4	20	0	101	3	0	8	3	.727	0	10--	-	2.31	2.94
2005	Wichta	AA	10	0	0	6	15.1	60	12	3	3	3	1	0	0	2	0	19	1	0	0	1	.000	0	1--	-	2.43	1.76
2005	Hi Dsrt	A+	48	0	0	0	60.2	249	57	19	15	8	2	0	2	10	1	73	2	0	4	2	.667	0	19--	-	3.11	2.23
2005	KC	AL	8	0	0	5	9.0	44	14	10	9	3	0	0	0	5	0	11	1	0	1	0	1.000	0	0-0	0	10.57	9.00

Ryan Dempster

Pitches: R **Bats:** R **Pos:** RP-57; SP-6   **Ht:** 6'3" **Wt:** 215 **Born:** 5/3/1977 **Age:** 29

			HOW MUCH HE PITCHED						WHAT HE GAVE UP										THE RESULTS						
Year	Team	Lg	G	GS	CG	GF	IP	BFP	H	R	ER	HR	SH	SF	HB	TBB	IBB	SO	WP	Bk	W	L	Pct	ShO	Sv-Op	Hld	ERC	ERA
1998	FLA	NL	14	11	0	1	54.2	272	72	47	43	7	6	5	9	38	1	35	5	0	1	5	.167	0	0-1	0	8.14	7.08
1999	FLA	NL	25	25	0	0	147.0	666	146	77	77	21	3	6	6	93	2	126	8	0	7	8	.467	0	0-0	0	5.49	4.71
2000	FLA	NL	33	33	2	0	226.1	974	210	102	92	30	4	5	5	97	7	209	4	0	14	10	.583	1	0-0	0	4.04	3.66
2001	FLA	NL	34	34	2	0	211.1	954	218	123	116	21	15	7	10	112	5	171	5	0	15	12	.556	1	0-0	0	4.91	4.94
2002	2 Tms		33	33	4	0	209.0	915	228	127	125	28	9	6	10	93	2	153	2	0	10	13	.435	0	0-0	0	5.35	5.38
2003	CIN	NL	22	20	0	1	115.2	545	134	89	84	14	9	4	5	70	4	84	3	0	3	7	.300	0	0-0	0	6.11	6.54
2004	CHN	NL	23	0	0	8	20.2	93	16	9	9	1	1	0	2	13	0	18	1	0	1	1	.500	0	2-2	3	3.61	3.92
2005	CHN	NL	63	6	0	53	92.0	401	83	35	32	4	5	0	4	49	7	89	4	0	5	3	.625	0	33-35	0	3.69	3.13
02	Fla	NL	18	18	3	0	120.1	521	126	66	64	12	7	3	7	55	1	87	0	0	5	8	.385	0	0-0	0	4.95	4.79
02	Cin	NL	15	15	1	0	88.2	394	102	61	61	16	2	3	3	38	1	66	2	0	5	5	.500	0	0-0	0	5.90	6.19
	8 ML YEARS		247	162	8	63	1076.2	4820	1107	609	578	125	51	34	51	565	28	885	32	0	56	59	.487	2	35-38	3	5.03	4.83

Chris Denorfia

Bats: R **Throws:** R **Pos:** CF-10; PH-8; LF-2; RF-2   **Ht:** 6'1" **Wt:** 185 **Born:** 7/15/1980 **Age:** 25

								BATTING												BASERUNNING				AVERAGES		
Year	Team	Lg	G	AB	H	2B	3B	HR	(Hm	Rd)	TB	R	RBI	RC	TBB	IBB	SO	HBP	SH	SF	SB	CS	SB%	GDP	Avg	OBP	Slg
2002	Reds	R	57	200	68	9	2	0	(-	-)	81	38	19	38	31	0	23	0	0	2	18	8	.69	8	.340	.425	.405
2002	Dayton	A	3	10	0	0	0	0	(-	-)	0	2	0	0	0	0	3	0	0	0	0	0	-	1	.000	.000	.000
2002	Chatt	AA	3	7	3	2	1	0	(-	-)	7	0	0	3	2	0	1	0	0	0	0	0	-	0	.429	.556	1.000
2003	Ptomc	A+	128	470	111	10	5	4	(-	-)	143	60	39	51	54	0	106	3	11	3	20	7	.74	10	.236	.317	.304
2004	Ptomc	A+	75	269	84	18	4	11	(-	-)	143	52	51	60	48	0	66	1	1	2	10	6	.63	3	.312	.416	.532
2004	Chatt	AA	61	221	55	10	2	6	(-	-)	87	30	27	32	30	1	42	1	3	1	5	2	.71	1	.249	.340	.394
2005	Chatt	AA	46	188	62	15	3	7	(-	-)	106	40	26	39	17	1	38	2	2	0	4	3	.57	1	.330	.391	.564
2005	Lsvlle	AAA	91	323	100	12	6	13	(-	-)	163	50	61	65	41	1	54	4	3	3	8	3	.73	7	.310	.391	.505
2005	CIN	NL	18	38	10	3	0	1	(1	0)	16	8	2	3	6	0	9	0	0	0	1	0	1.00	1	.263	.364	.421

Jorge DePaula

Pitches: R **Bats:** R **Pos:** RP-3   **Ht:** 6'1" **Wt:** 160 **Born:** 11/10/1978 **Age:** 27

			HOW MUCH HE PITCHED						WHAT HE GAVE UP										THE RESULTS						
Year	Team	Lg	G	GS	CG	GF	IP	BFP	H	R	ER	HR	SH	SF	HB	TBB	IBB	SO	WP	Bk	W	L	Pct	ShO	Sv-Op	Hld	ERC	ERA
2003	NYA	AL	4	1	0	3	11.1	38	3	1	1	1	0	0	1	1	0	7	0	0	0	0	-	0	0-0	0	0.54	0.79
2004	NYA	AL	3	1	0	0	9.0	38	9	6	5	2	0	2	0	4	0	2	0	0	0	1	.000	0	0-0	0	5.32	5.00
2005	NYA	AL	3	0	0	2	6.2	30	8	6	6	2	0	0	0	3	0	3	0	0	0	0	-	0	0-0	0	7.11	8.10
	3 ML YEARS		10	2	0	5	27.0	106	20	13	12	5	0	2	1	8	0	12	0	0	0	1	.000	0	0-0	0	3.05	4.00

Mark DeRosa

Bats: R **Throws:** R **Pos:** RF-25; 2B-17; SS-16; 3B-5; PH-5; PR-3; DH-2; 1B-1   **Ht:** 6'1" **Wt:** 205 **Born:** 2/26/1975 **Age:** 31

								BATTING												BASERUNNING				AVERAGES		
Year	Team	Lg	G	AB	H	2B	3B	HR	(Hm	Rd)	TB	R	RBI	RC	TBB	IBB	SO	HBP	SH	SF	SB	CS	SB%	GDP	Avg	OBP	Slg
1998	ATL	NL	5	3	1	0	0	0	(0	0)	1	2	0	0	0	0	1	0	0	0	0	0	-	0	.333	.333	.333
1999	ATL	NL	7	8	0	0	0	0	(0	0)	0	0	0	0	0	0	2	0	0	0	0	0	-	0	.000	.000	.000
2000	ATL	NL	22	13	4	1	0	0	(0	0)	5	9	3	2	2	0	1	0	0	0	0	0	-	0	.308	.400	.385
2001	ATL	NL	66	164	47	8	0	3	(3	0)	64	27	20	22	12	6	19	5	1	2	2	1	.67	3	.287	.350	.390
2002	ATL	NL	72	212	63	9	2	5	(3	2)	91	24	23	27	12	3	24	3	2	3	2	3	.40	5	.297	.339	.429

Year	Team	Lg	G	AB	H	2B	3B	HR	(Hm	Rd)	TB	R	RBI	RC	TBB	IBB	SO	HBP	SH	SF	SB	CS	SB%	GDP	Avg	OBP	Slg
2003	ATL	NL	103	266	70	14	0	6	(3	3)	102	40	22	28	16	0	49	5	0	1	1	0	1.00	6	.263	.316	.383
2004	ATL	NL	118	309	74	16	0	3	(0	3)	99	33	31	24	23	3	53	3	4	6	1	3	.25	6	.239	.293	.320
2005	TEX	AL	66	148	36	5	0	8	(7	1)	65	26	20	20	16	0	35	2	0	0	1	0	1.00	5	.243	.325	.439
8 ML YEARS			459	1123	295	53	2	25	(16	9)	427	161	119	123	81	12	184	18	7	12	7	7	.50	25	.263	.319	.380

Elmer Dessens

Pitches: R **Bats:** R **Pos:** RP-21; SP-7   **Ht:** 6'0" **Wt:** 187 **Born:** 1/13/1972 **Age:** 34

			HOW MUCH HE PITCHED						WHAT HE GAVE UP											THE RESULTS						
Year	Team	Lg	G	GS	CG	GF	IP	BFP	H	R	ER	HR	SH	SF	HB	TBB	IBB	SO	WP	Bk	W	L	Pct	ShO	Sv-Op	Hld	ERC	ERA
2005	LsVgs*	AAA	3	3	0	0	8.0	32	6	3	3	1	1	0	0	2	0	6	0	0	0	0	-	0	0- -	-	2.33	3.38
1996	PIT	NL	15	3	0	1	25.0	112	40	23	23	2	3	1	0	4	0	13	0	0	0	2	.000	0	0-0	3	6.77	8.28
1997	PIT	NL	3	0	0	1	3.1	13	2	0	0	0	0	0	1	0	0	2	0	0	0	0	-	0	0-0	0	1.31	0.00
1998	PIT	NL	43	5	0	8	74.2	332	90	50	47	10	4	3	0	25	2	43	1	0	2	6	.250	0	0-1	6	5.19	5.67
2000	CIN	NL	40	16	1	6	147.1	640	170	73	70	10	12	7	3	43	7	85	4	0	11	5	.688	0	1-1	1	4.31	4.28
2001	CIN	NL	34	34	1	0	205.0	862	221	103	102	32	7	7	1	56	1	128	4	1	10	14	.417	1	0-0	0	4.49	4.48
2002	CIN	NL	30	30	0	0	178.0	737	173	70	60	24	7	1	7	49	8	93	3	1	7	8	.467	0	0-0	0	3.82	3.03
2003	ARI	NL	34	30	0	1	175.2	781	212	107	99	22	9	3	4	57	6	113	3	2	8	8	.500	0	0-0	0	5.19	5.07
2004	2 Tms	NL	50	10	0	9	105.0	468	123	61	52	15	4	3	1	31	4	73	2	0	2	6	.250	0	2-5	4	4.83	4.46
2005	LAN	NL	28	7	0	4	65.2	277	63	30	26	6	1	3	1	19	2	37	1	0	1	2	.333	0	0-0	1	3.35	3.56
04	Ari		38	9	0	7	85.1	386	107	54	45	11	4	3	1	23	4	55	2	0	1	6	.143	0	2-4	4	5.08	4.75
04	LA		12	1	0	2	19.2	82	16	7	7	4	0	0	0	8	0	18	0	0	1	0	1.000	0	0-1	0	3.74	3.20
9 ML YEARS			277	135	2	30	979.2	4222	1094	517	479	121	47	28	18	284	30	587	18	4	41	51	.446	1	3-7	15	4.51	4.40

Joey Devine

Pitches: R **Bats:** R **Pos:** RP-5   **Ht:** 5'11" **Wt:** 195 **Born:** 9/19/1983 **Age:** 22

			HOW MUCH HE PITCHED						WHAT HE GAVE UP											THE RESULTS						
Year	Team	Lg	G	GS	CG	GF	IP	BFP	H	R	ER	HR	SH	SF	HB	TBB	IBB	SO	WP	Bk	W	L	Pct	ShO	Sv-Op	Hld	ERC	ERA
2005	MrtlBh	A+	4	0	0	0	5.0	18	0	0	0	0	0	0	1	3	0	7	0	0	0	0	-	0	1- -	-	0.67	0.00
2005	Missi	AA	18	0	0	15	20.0	92	19	13	6	2	2	0	5	12	1	28	1	0	1	1	.500	0	5- -	5	5.62	2.70
2005	Rchmd	AAA	1	0	0	0	1.0	7	3	2	2	0	0	0	0	1	0	1	0	0	0	0	-	0	0- -	-	19.55	18.00
2005	ATL	NL	5	0	0	1	5.0	26	6	7	7	2	0	0	0	5	1	3	0	0	0	1	.000	0	0-0	1	9.97	12.60

Einar Diaz

Bats: R **Throws:** R **Pos:** C-50; PH-9; 1B-3; PR-2   **Ht:** 5'10" **Wt:** 190 **Born:** 12/28/1972 **Age:** 33

			BATTING																	BASERUNNING				AVERAGES		
Year	Team	Lg	G	AB	H	2B	3B	HR	(Hm	Rd)	TB	R	RBI	RC	TBB	IBB	SO	HBP	SH	SF	SB	CS	SB%	GDP	Avg	OBP	Slg
1996	CLE	AL	4	1	0	0	0	0	(0	0)	0	0	0	0	0	0	0	0	0	0	0	0	-	0	.000	.000	.000
1997	CLE	AL	5	7	1	1	0	0	(0	0)	2	1	1	0	0	0	2	0	0	0	0	0	-	0	.143	.143	.286
1998	CLE	AL	17	48	11	1	0	2	(1	1)	18	8	9	5	3	0	2	2	0	3	0	0	-	2	.229	.286	.375
1999	CLE	AL	119	392	110	21	1	3	(2	1)	142	43	32	46	23	0	41	5	6	1	11	4	.73	10	.281	.328	.362
2000	CLE	AL	75	250	68	14	2	4	(2	2)	98	29	25	30	11	0	29	8	6	0	4	2	.67	7	.272	.323	.392
2001	CLE	AL	134	437	121	34	1	4	(0	4)	169	54	56	53	17	0	44	16	8	0	1	2	.33	11	.277	.328	.387
2002	CLE	AL	102	320	66	19	0	2	(1	1)	91	34	16	14	17	1	27	6	6	2	0	1	.00	13	.206	.258	.284
2003	TEX	AL	101	334	86	14	1	4	(2	2)	114	30	35	31	9	0	32	10	4	4	3	1	.75	12	.257	.294	.341
2004	MON	NL	55	139	31	6	1	1	(1	0)	42	9	11	9	11	3	10	4	2	3	2	0	1.00	6	.223	.293	.302
2005	STL	NL	58	130	27	6	0	1	(1	0)	36	14	17	9	5	0	12	2	2	0	0	0	-	8	.208	.248	.277
10 ML YEARS			670	2058	521	116	6	21	(10	11)	712	222	202	197	96	4	199	53	34	13	21	10	.68	69	.253	.302	.346

Matt Diaz

Bats: R **Throws:** R **Pos:** LF-19; PH-9; DH-7; RF-2; PR-1   **Ht:** 6'1" **Wt:** 206 **Born:** 3/3/1978 **Age:** 28

			BATTING																	BASERUNNING				AVERAGES		
Year	Team	Lg	G	AB	H	2B	3B	HR	(Hm	Rd)	TB	R	RBI	RC	TBB	IBB	SO	HBP	SH	SF	SB	CS	SB%	GDP	Avg	OBP	Slg
2005	Royals*	R	3	13	6	2	0	0	(-	-)	8	2	2	2	0	0	2	0	0	0	0	1	.00	1	.462	.462	.615
2005	Wichta*	AA	7	26	7	0	0	1	(-	-)	10	6	6	3	3	0	5	0	0	1	1	0	1.00	1	.269	.333	.385
2005	Omha*	AAA	65	259	96	22	4	14	(-	-)	168	48	56	64	12	1	49	5	0	1	10	3	.77	14	.371	.408	.649
2003	TB	AL	4	9	1	0	0	0	(0	0)	1	2	0	0	1	0	3	0	0	0	0	0	-	0	.111	.200	.111
2004	TB	AL	10	21	4	1	1	1	(1	0)	10	3	3	2	1	0	6	2	0	0	0	0	-	0	.190	.292	.476
2005	KC	AL	34	89	25	4	2	1	(0	1)	36	7	9	11	4	0	15	2	1	1	0	1	.00	3	.281	.323	.404
3 ML YEARS			48	119	30	5	3	2	(1	1)	47	12	12	13	6	0	24	4	1	1	0	1	.00	3	.252	.308	.395

Victor Diaz

Bats: R **Throws:** R **Pos:** RF-78; PH-11; LF-3   **Ht:** 6'0" **Wt:** 200 **Born:** 12/10/1981 **Age:** 24

			BATTING																	BASERUNNING				AVERAGES		
Year	Team	Lg	G	AB	H	2B	3B	HR	(Hm	Rd)	TB	R	RBI	RC	TBB	IBB	SO	HBP	SH	SF	SB	CS	SB%	GDP	Avg	OBP	Slg
2001	Ddgrs	R	53	195	69	22	2	3	(-	-)	104	36	31	40	16	1	23	6	1	3	6	3	.67	3	.354	.414	.533
2002	SoGA	A	91	349	122	26	2	10	(-	-)	182	64	58	72	27	6	69	10	0	5	20	6	.77	4	.350	.407	.521
2002	Jaxnvl	AA	42	152	32	7	0	4	(-	-)	51	22	24	11	7	0	42	3	0	1	7	5	.58	5	.211	.258	.336
2003	Jaxnvl	AA	85	316	92	20	2	10	(-	-)	146	42	54	46	27	1	60	6	1	5	8	10	.44	10	.291	.353	.462
2003	Bnghtn	AA	45	175	62	11	0	6	(-	-)	91	29	23	32	8	0	32	1	1	2	7	5	.58	3	.354	.383	.520
2004	Norfolk	AAA	141	528	154	31	1	24	(-	-)	259	81	94	80	31	1	133	5	5	9	6	7	.46	12	.292	.332	.491
2005	Norfolk	AAA	42	170	51	11	0	10	(-	-)	92	30	34	32	14	1	47	0	0	0	6	2	.75	6	.300	.353	.541
2004	NYN	NL	15	51	15	3	0	3	(1	2)	27	8	8	6	1	0	15	1	0	0	0	0	-	3	.294	.321	.529
2005	NYN	NL	89	280	72	17	3	12	(4	8)	131	41	38	35	30	7	82	1	0	2	6	2	.75	13	.257	.329	.468
2 ML YEARS			104	331	87	20	3	15	(5	10)	158	49	46	41	31	7	97	2	0	2	6	2	.75	16	.263	.328	.477

R.A. Dickey

Pitches: R **Bats:** R **Pos:** RP-5; SP-4   **Ht:** 6'3" **Wt:** 205 **Born:** 10/29/1974 **Age:** 31

	HOW MUCH HE PITCHED						WHAT HE GAVE UP												THE RESULTS							
Year Team Lg	G	GS	CG	GF	IP	BFP	H	R	ER	HR	SH	SF	HB	TBB	IBB	SO	WP	Bk	W	L	Pct	ShO	Sv-Op	Hld	ERC	ERA
2005 Okla* AAA	19	17	1	0	121.2	556	152	88	81	12	5	0	8	39	0	81	9	2	10	6	.625	0	0--	-	5.41	5.99
2001 TEX AL	4	0	0	1	12.0	53	13	9	9	3	0	0	8	7	1	4	1	0	0	1	.000	0	0-0	-	6.57	6.75
2003 TEX AL	38	13	1	6	116.2	513	135	68	66	16	4	3	5	38	5	94	5	2	9	8	.529	1	1-1	3	5.09	5.09
2004 TEX AL	25	15	0	2	104.2	480	136	77	65	17	3	3	4	33	1	57	5	1	6	7	.462	0	1-1	0	6.06	5.59
2005 TEX AL	9	4	0	2	29.2	134	29	23	22	4	0	1	2	17	0	15	2	0	1	2	.333	0	0-0	0	5.18	6.67
4 ML YEARS	76	32	1	11	263.0	1180	313	177	162	40	7	7	11	95	7	170	13	3	16	18	.471	1	2-2	3	5.55	5.54

Mike DiFelice

Bats: R **Throws:** R **Pos:** C-11   **Ht:** 6'2" **Wt:** 205 **Born:** 5/28/1969 **Age:** 37

	BATTING																		BASERUNNING				AVERAGES		
Year Team Lg	G	AB	H	2B	3B	HR	(Hm	Rd)	TB	R	RBI	RC	TBB	IBB	SO	HBP	SH	SF	SB	CS	SB%	GDP	Avg	OBP	Slg
2005 Norfolk* AAA	81	300	74	17	0	14	(-	-)	133	31	52	46	36	2	72	5	2	0	1	2	.33	12	.247	.337	.443
1996 STL NL	4	7	2	1	0	0	(0	0)	3	0	2	1	0	0	1	0	0	0	0	0	-	0	.286	.286	.429
1997 STL NL	93	260	62	10	1	4	(1	3)	86	16	30	23	19	0	61	3	6	1	1	1	.50	11	.238	.297	.331
1998 TB AL	84	248	57	12	3	3	(1	2)	84	17	23	19	15	0	56	1	3	2	0	0	-	12	.230	.274	.339
1999 TB AL	51	179	55	11	0	6	(5	1)	84	21	27	29	8	0	23	3	0	1	0	0	-	1	.307	.346	.469
2000 TB AL	60	204	49	13	1	6	(4	2)	82	23	19	21	12	0	40	0	5	2	0	0	-	8	.240	.280	.402
2001 2 Tms	60	170	32	5	1	2	(0	2)	45	14	10	10	8	0	49	4	3	2	1	1	.50	3	.188	.239	.265
2002 STL NL	70	174	40	11	0	4	(3	1)	63	17	19	17	7	3	42	1	2	3	0	0	-	3	.230	.297	.362
2003 KC AL	62	189	48	16	1	3	(1	2)	75	29	25	26	9	0	30	4	1	2	1	0	1.00	6	.254	.299	.397
2004 2 Tms	17	25	3	0	1	0	(0	0)	5	3	2	1	3	0	4	0	0	0	0	0	-	3	.120	.214	.200
2005 NYN NL	17	17	2	0	0	0	(0	0)	2	0	0	0	2	0	5	0	0	0	0	0	-	0	.118	.211	.118
01 TB AL	48	149	31	5	1	2	(0	2)	44	13	9	10	8	0	39	3	2	2	1	1	.50	3	.208	.259	.295
01 Ari NL	12	21	1	0	0	0	(0	0)	1	1	1	0	0	0	10	1	1	0	0	0	-	0	.048	.091	.048
04 Det AL	13	22	3	0	1	0	(0	0)	5	3	2	1	3	0	3	0	0	0	0	0	-	3	.136	.240	.227
04 ChC NL	4	3	0	0	0	0	(0	0)	0	0	0	0	0	0	1	0	0	0	0	0	-	0	.000	.000	.000
10 ML YEARS	512	1473	350	79	8	28	(15	13)	529	140	157	147	93	3	311	16	20	13	3	2	.60	49	.238	.288	.359

Joe Dillon

Bats: R **Throws:** R **Pos:** PH-18; 2B-4; LF-3; 3B-2; 1B-1   **Ht:** 6'2" **Wt:** 215 **Born:** 8/2/1975 **Age:** 30

	BATTING																		BASERUNNING				AVERAGES		
Year Team Lg	G	AB	H	2B	3B	HR	(Hm	Rd)	TB	R	RBI	RC	TBB	IBB	SO	HBP	SH	SF	SB	CS	SB%	GDP	Avg	OBP	Slg
1997 Spkane A-	19	70	15	3	0	2	(-	-)	24	6	6	7	5	0	13	1	0	0	1	0	1.00	2	.214	.276	.343
1998 Lansng A	73	268	70	17	2	15	(-	-)	136	37	43	49	36	1	57	0	4	0	9	2	.82	5	.261	.349	.507
1999 Wilmg A	134	503	133	31	2	16	(-	-)	216	73	90	78	59	4	124	7	2	5	9	6	.60	12	.264	.347	.429
2000 Wichta AA	62	220	70	16	2	10	(-	-)	120	35	43	53	39	1	38	7	2	5	0	0	-	6	.318	.428	.545
2000 Omha AAA	45	149	42	11	2	1	(-	-)	60	19	11	23	17	0	26	2	0	0	1	0	1.00	6	.282	.363	.403
2001 Wichta AA	101	369	106	19	3	15	(-	-)	176	62	59	65	36	1	60	8	1	3	4	3	.57	10	.287	.361	.477
2002 NwBrit AA	103	344	90	20	2	9	(-	-)	141	47	50	57	54	3	62	6	0	4	3	1	.75	10	.262	.368	.410
2002 Edmtn AAA	6	18	3	1	0	0	(-	-)	4	5	0	1	2	0	2	0	0	0	1	0	1.00	1	.167	.250	.222
2004 Carlina AA	33	117	40	13	0	9	(-	-)	80	26	31	31	14	0	29	4	0	1	3	2	.60	1	.342	.426	.684
2004 Albq AAA	108	403	131	33	7	30	(-	-)	268	96	86	104	46	0	85	10	0	9	12	3	.80	7	.325	.400	.665
2005 Albq AAA	98	350	126	21	1	24	(-	-)	221	80	72	100	57	4	59	12	0	6	11	1	.92	7	.360	.459	.631
2005 FLA NL	27	36	6	1	0	1	(1	0)	10	6	1	0	1	0	8	1	1	0	0	0	-	3	.167	.211	.278

Lenny DiNardo

Pitches: L **Bats:** L **Pos:** RP-7; SP-1   **Ht:** 6'4" **Wt:** 195 **Born:** 9/19/1979 **Age:** 26

	HOW MUCH HE PITCHED						WHAT HE GAVE UP												THE RESULTS							
Year Team Lg	G	GS	CG	GF	IP	BFP	H	R	ER	HR	SH	SF	HB	TBB	IBB	SO	WP	Bk	W	L	Pct	ShO	Sv-Op	Hld	ERC	ERA
2001 Bklyn A-	9	5	0	0	36.0	148	26	10	8	0	0	2	0	17	0	40	4	0	1	2	.333	0	0--	-	2.35	2.00
2002 CptCty A	24	19	0	1	101.1	466	106	60	49	3	5	5	13	56	1	103	11	0	5	5	.500	0	1--	-	4.90	4.35
2003 StLuci A+	19	13	1	2	85.0	325	64	27	19	1	3	1	3	14	0	93	5	0	3	8	.273	0	1--	-	1.65	2.01
2003 Bnghtn AA	7	7	1	0	40.0	169	35	19	16	3	1	3	4	13	0	36	0	0	1	3	.250	0	0--	-	3.31	3.60
2004 RedSx R	2	1	0	0	3.0	11	3	0	0	0	0	0	0	0	0	5	0	0	0	0	-	0	0--	-	2.18	0.00
2004 Srsota A+	1	1	0	0	3.0	11	2	0	0	0	0	0	0	0	0	2	0	0	0	0	-	0	0--	-	0.91	0.00
2004 Portlnd AA	3	0	0	0	5.2	26	8	6	6	1	0	0	0	1	0	4	1	0	1	0	1.000	0	0--	-	6.00	9.53
2004 Pwtckt AAA	1	1	0	0	3.0	12	3	0	0	0	0	0	0	0	0	4	0	0	0	0	-	0	0--	-	1.95	0.00
2005 Pwtckt AAA	23	22	0	0	108.2	470	109	51	38	7	7	4	10	35	0	93	1	3	6	3	.667	0	0--	-	3.89	3.15
2004 BOS AL	22	0	0	6	27.2	130	34	17	13	1	1	1	2	12	1	21	0	0	0	0	-	0	0-0	0	5.17	4.23
2005 BOS AL	8	1	0	3	14.2	62	13	6	3	1	1	1	0	5	1	15	1	0	0	1	.000	0	0-0	0	2.86	1.84
2 ML YEARS	30	1	0	9	42.1	192	47	23	16	2	2	2	2	17	2	36	2	0	0	1	.000	0	0-0	0	4.33	3.40

Craig Dingman

Pitches: R **Bats:** R **Pos:** RP-34   **Ht:** 6'4" **Wt:** 215 **Born:** 3/12/1974 **Age:** 32

	HOW MUCH HE PITCHED						WHAT HE GAVE UP												THE RESULTS							
Year Team Lg	G	GS	CG	GF	IP	BFP	H	R	ER	HR	SH	SF	HB	TBB	IBB	SO	WP	Bk	W	L	Pct	ShO	Sv-Op	Hld	ERC	ERA
2005 Toledo* AAA	35	0	0	12	48.0	199	42	18	15	3	1	1	4	13	0	67	1	1	2	1	.667	0	4--	-	2.98	2.81
2000 NYA AL	10	0	0	4	11.0	51	18	8	8	1	0	0		3	0	8	0	0	0	0	-	0	0-0	0	-	6.55
2001 COL NL	7	0	0	0	7.1	37	11	11	11	4	1	0	0	3	2	2	0	0	0	0	-	0	1-1	0	-	13.50
2004 DET AL	24	0	0	5	29.1	141	33	22	22	3	1	2	4	22	3	16	1	0	2	2	.500	0	0-2	0	6.77	6.75
2005 DET AL	34	0	0	18	32.0	128	30	14	13	5	2	0	1	9	0	24	0	0	2	3	.400	0	4-5	4	3.95	3.66
4 ML YEARS	75	0	0	31	79.2	357	92	55	54	13	4	2	5	37	5	50	1	0	4	5	.444	0	5-8	4	6.02	6.10

Greg Dobbs

Bats: L Throws: R Pos: PH-26; DH-24; 1B-5; LF-4; 3B-2 Ht: 6'1" Wt: 205 Born: 7/2/1978 Age: 27

Year	Team	Lg	G	AB	H	2B	3B	HR	(Hm	Rd)	TB	R	RBI	RC	TBB	IBB	SO	HBP	SH	SF	SB	CS	SB%	GDP	Avg	OBP	Slg
2001	Everett	A-	65	249	80	17	2	6	(-	-)	119	37	41	47	30	3	39	2	1	2	5	3	.63	2	.321	.396	.478
2001	SnBrn	A+	3	13	5	1	0	1	(-	-)	9	2	3	3	0	0	4	0	0	1	0	0	-	0	.385	.357	.692
2002	Wisc	A	86	320	88	16	2	10	(-	-)	138	43	48	47	31	4	50	1	0	3	13	3	.81	6	.275	.338	.431
2002	SnAnt	AA	27	96	35	2	0	5	(-	-)	52	13	15	20	9	2	17	1	2	0	1	2	.33	2	.365	.425	.542
2003	SnAnt	AA	2	6	2	2	0	0	(-	-)	4	0	0	1	0	0	1	0	0	0	0	0	-	0	.333	.333	.667
2004	SnAnt	AA	51	203	66	14	4	5	(-	-)	103	25	34	35	11	2	23	5	0	1	5	4	.56	5	.325	.373	.507
2004	Tacom	AAA	67	255	69	9	2	8	(-	-)	106	28	31	26	5	2	36	1	0	1	4	3	.57	10	.271	.286	.416
2005	Tacom	AAA	50	190	61	9	0	3	(-	-)	79	27	22	30	14	2	22	1	1	2	5	2	.71	5	.321	.367	.416
2004	SEA	AL	18	53	12	1	0	1	(1	0)	16	4	9	5	1	0	14	1	0	1	0	0	-	0	.226	.250	.302
2005	SEA	AL	59	142	35	7	1	1	(0	1)	47	8	20	16	9	3	25	0	1	2	1	0	1.00	4	.246	.288	.331
	2 ML YEARS		77	195	47	8	1	2	(1	1)	63	12	29	21	10	3	39	1	1	3	1	0	1.00	4	.241	.278	.323

Scott Dohmann

Pitches: R Bats: R Pos: RP-32 Ht: 6'1" Wt: 180 Born: 2/13/1978 Age: 28

Year	Team	Lg	G	GS	CG	GF	IP	BFP	H	R	ER	HR	SH	SF	HB	TBB	IBB	SO	WP	Bk	W	L	Pct	ShO	Sv-Op	Hld	ERC	ERA
2000	Portlnd	A-	5	4	0	0	23.0	85	14	3	2	0	0	0	1	5	0	23	0	0	2	1	.667	0	0--	-	1.31	0.78
2000	Ashvlle	A	7	7	0	0	32.2	149	43	24	22	3	0	3	3	8	0	36	3	1	1	5	.167	0	0--	-	5.58	6.06
2001	Ashvlle	A	28	28	3	0	173.0	717	165	88	83	27	5	3	18	53	5	154	3	0	11	13	.458	1	0--	-	3.77	4.32
2002	Salem	A+	28	28	0	0	170.1	720	149	85	80	22	6	6	15	53	0	131	8	0	13	5	.722	0	0--	-	3.55	4.23
2003	Tulsa	AA	50	4	0	17	93.2	403	94	47	43	11	4	2	5	29	2	102	6	0	9	4	.692	0	4--	-	4.01	4.13
2004	ColSpr	AAA	18	0	0	6	22.0	94	22	5	4	1	1	0	0	7	1	31	2	0	1	0	1.000	0	2--	-	3.27	1.64
2005	ColSpr	AAA	34	0	0	10	39.0	174	41	19	19	5	0	3	3	16	1	53	3	1	2	1	.667	0	1--	-	4.86	4.38
2004	COL	NL	41	0	0	13	46.0	198	41	22	21	8	2	3	0	19	0	49	3	0	0	3	.000	0	0-4	4	3.94	4.11
2005	COL	NL	32	0	0	10	31.0	143	33	21	21	6	0	0	0	19	1	35	0	0	2	1	.667	0	0-3	7	5.94	6.10
	2 ML YEARS		73	0	0	23	77.0	341	74	43	42	14	2	3	0	38	1	84	3	0	2	4	.333	0	0-7	11	4.72	4.91

Juan Dominguez

Pitches: R Bats: R Pos: RP-12; SP-10 Ht: 6'2" Wt: 180 Born: 5/18/1980 Age: 26

Year	Team	Lg	G	GS	CG	GF	IP	BFP	H	R	ER	HR	SH	SF	HB	TBB	IBB	SO	WP	Bk	W	L	Pct	ShO	Sv-Op	Hld	ERC	ERA
2005	Frisco*	AA	15	2	0	5	37.2	152	30	14	11	4	0	1	1	9	1	31	4	0	2	0	1.000	0	2--	-	2.48	2.63
2005	Okla*	AAA	7	7	0	0	36.0	156	38	20	17	6	0	0	0	10	0	24	2	0	2	1	.667	0	0--	-	4.26	4.25
2003	TEX	AL	6	3	0	1	16.1	73	16	14	13	5	1	1	0	12	0	13	1	0	0	2	.000	0	0-0	0	7.22	7.16
2004	TEX	AL	4	4	0	0	23.0	98	25	11	10	2	1	1	2	5	0	14	0	2	1	2	.333	0	0-0	0	4.13	3.91
2005	TEX	AL	22	10	0	3	70.1	312	78	37	33	11	1	2	2	25	0	45	2	0	4	6	.400	0	0-1	0	5.00	4.22
	3 ML YEARS		32	17	0	4	109.2	483	119	62	56	18	3	4	4	42	0	72	3	2	5	10	.333	0	0-1	0	5.12	4.60

Andy Dominique

Bats: R Throws: R Pos: C-1; PH-1 Ht: 6'0" Wt: 220 Born: 10/30/1975 Age: 30

Year	Team	Lg	G	AB	H	2B	3B	HR	(Hm	Rd)	TB	R	RBI	RC	TBB	IBB	SO	HBP	SH	SF	SB	CS	SB%	GDP	Avg	OBP	Slg
1997	Batvia	A	72	277	77	17	0	14	(-	-)	136	52	48	47	26	0	60	10	0	5	4	1	.80	6	.278	.355	.491
1998	Pmont	A	133	514	145	38	0	24	(-	-)	255	82	102	90	61	4	97	12	0	4	0	2	.00	9	.282	.369	.496
1999	Clrwtr	A+	130	487	124	29	5	14	(-	-)	205	77	92	73	69	4	84	10	3	8	3	3	.50	13	.255	.354	.421
2000	Rdng	AA	104	327	78	27	0	13	(-	-)	144	46	50	44	35	0	56	8	3	4	0	1	.00	9	.239	.324	.440
2001	Rdng	AA	76	261	73	16	0	12	(-	-)	125	43	49	45	37	2	45	1	0	2	3	1	.75	6	.280	.369	.479
2001	S-WB	AAA	40	135	23	6	0	3	(-	-)	38	16	18	7	12	0	34	1	1	0	0	0	-	4	.170	.243	.281
2002	Clrwtr	A+	8	34	14	5	0	0	(-	-)	19	5	2	7	1	0	4	1	0	0	0	0	-	0	.412	.444	.559
2002	Trentn	AA	103	361	98	21	1	8	(-	-)	145	40	51	51	36	1	60	9	0	6	2	1	.67	9	.271	.347	.402
2003	Portlnd	AA	32	97	35	7	0	3	(-	-)	51	18	21	23	16	0	15	3	0	3	0	0	-	1	.361	.454	.526
2003	Pwtckt	AAA	79	289	88	18	0	13	(-	-)	145	42	57	49	22	0	45	7	1	3	2	1	.67	10	.304	.364	.502
2004	Pwtckt	AAA	111	419	112	28	0	15	(-	-)	185	54	69	65	55	1	87	8	0	4	0	2	.00	11	.267	.360	.442
2005	Syrcse	AAA	39	117	28	6	0	3	(-	-)	43	18	10	15	15	1	20	2	2	0	0	0	-	6	.239	.336	.368
2004	BOS	AL	7	11	2	0	0	0	(0	0)	2	0	1	0	0	0	3	0	0	0	0	0	-	0	.182	.182	.182
2005	TOR	AL	2	2	0	0	0	0	(0	0)	0	0	0	0	0	0	0	1	0	0	0	0	-	0	.000	.333	.000
	2 ML YEARS		9	13	2	0	0	0	(0	0)	2	0	1	0	0	0	3	1	0	0	0	0	-	0	.154	.214	.154

Brendan Donnelly

Pitches: R Bats: R Pos: RP-66 Ht: 6'3" Wt: 200 Born: 7/4/1971 Age: 34

Year	Team	Lg	G	GS	CG	GF	IP	BFP	H	R	ER	HR	SH	SF	HB	TBB	IBB	SO	WP	Bk	W	L	Pct	ShO	Sv-Op	Hld	ERC	ERA
2002	ANA	AL	46	0	0	11	49.2	199	32	13	12	2	3	1	2	19	3	54	1	0	1	1	.500	0	1-3	13	1.89	2.17
2003	ANA	AL	63	0	0	15	74.0	307	55	14	13	2	3	1	4	24	1	79	1	0	2	2	.500	0	3-5	29	2.12	1.58
2004	ANA	AL	40	0	0	10	42.0	172	34	14	14	5	2	2	1	15	0	56	0	0	5	2	.714	0	0-0	5	3.12	3.00
2005	LAA	AL	66	0	0	14	65.1	271	60	30	27	9	3	1	2	19	3	53	3	0	9	3	.750	0	0-5	16	3.52	3.72
	4 ML YEARS		215	0	0	50	231.0	949	181	71	66	18	11	5	9	77	7	242	5	0	17	8	.680	0	4-13	63	2.62	2.57

Octavio Dotel

Pitches: R **Bats:** R **Pos:** RP-15   **Ht:** 6'0" **Wt:** 200 **Born:** 11/25/1973 **Age:** 32

Year	Team	Lg	G	GS	CG	GF	IP	BFP	H	R	ER	HR	SH	SF	HB	TBB	IBB	SO	WP	Bk	W	L	Pct	ShO	Sv-Op	Hld	ERC	ERA
1999	NYN	NL	19	14	0	1	85.1	368	69	52	51	12	3	5	6	49	1	85	3	2	8	3	.727	0	0-0	0	4.30	5.38
2000	HOU	NL	50	16	0	25	125.0	563	127	80	75	26	7	8	7	61	3	142	6	0	3	7	.300	0	16-23	6	5.47	5.40
2001	HOU	NL	61	4	0	20	105.0	438	79	35	31	5	2	2	2	47	2	145	4	0	7	5	.583	0	2-4	14	2.62	2.66
2002	HOU	NL	83	0	0	22	97.1	376	58	21	20	7	3	7	4	27	2	118	2	0	6	4	.600	0	6-10	31	1.61	1.85
2003	HOU	NL	76	0	0	13	87.0	346	53	25	24	9	2	1	3	31	2	97	2	0	6	4	.600	0	4-6	33	2.02	2.48
2004	2 Tms		77	0	0	70	85.1	356	68	38	35	13	4	2	4	33	7	122	4	1	6	6	.500	0	36-45	0	3.31	3.69
2005	OAK	AL	15	0	0	13	15.1	65	10	6	6	2	0	0	0	11	2	16	1	0	1	2	.333	0	7-11	0	3.44	3.52
04	Hou	NL	32	0	0	29	34.2	146	27	15	12	4	2	1	1	15	4	50	3	1	0	4	.000	0	14-17	0	3.01	3.12
04	Oak	AL	45	0	0	41	50.2	210	41	23	23	9	2	1	3	18	3	72	1	0	6	2	.750	0	22-28	0	3.52	4.09
	7 ML YEARS		381	34	0	164	600.1	2512	464	257	242	74	21	25	26	259	19	725	22	3	37	31	.544	0	71-99	78	3.23	3.63

Sean Douglass

Pitches: R **Bats:** R **Pos:** SP-16; RP-2   **Ht:** 6'6" **Wt:** 198 **Born:** 4/28/1979 **Age:** 27

Year	Team	Lg	G	GS	CG	GF	IP	BFP	H	R	ER	HR	SH	SF	HB	TBB	IBB	SO	WP	Bk	W	L	Pct	ShO	Sv-Op	Hld	ERC	ERA
2005	Toledo*	AAA	14	14	0	0	81.2	333	61	26	26	5	2	3	3	27	1	76	2	0	9	1	.900	0	0--	-	2.35	2.87
2001	BAL	AL	4	4	0	0	20.1	94	21	12	12	3	0	1	1	11	0	17	1	1	2	1	.667	0	0-0	0	5.27	5.31
2002	BAL	AL	15	8	0	2	53.1	245	58	41	36	10	2	1	2	35	2	44	3	0	1	5	.000	0	0-0	0	6.56	6.08
2003	BAL	AL	3	0	0	0	8.0	44	14	12	12	2	0	0	1	6	0	3	0	0	0	0	-	0	0-0	0	12.56	13.50
2004	TOR	AL	14	3	0	4	38.2	179	37	27	27	6	0	2	2	28	4	36	2	0	0	2	.000	0	0-0	0	5.59	6.28
2005	DET	AL	18	16	0	1	87.1	374	92	57	54	13	1	5	2	33	2	55	2	0	5	5	.500	0	0-0	0	4.79	5.56
	5 ML YEARS		54	31	0	7	207.2	936	222	149	141	34	3	9	8	113	8	155	8	1	7	13	.350	0	0-0	0	5.70	6.11

Ryan Doumit

Bats: B **Throws:** R **Pos:** C-50; PH-17; DH-6; RF-3   **Ht:** 6'0" **Wt:** 200 **Born:** 4/3/1981 **Age:** 25

Year	Team	Lg	G	AB	H	2B	3B	HR	(Hm	Rd)	TB	R	RBI	RC	TBB	IBB	SO	HBP	SH	SF	SB	CS	SB%	GDP	Avg	OBP	Slg
1999	Bradtn	R	29	85	24	5	0	1	(-	-)	32	17	7	15	15	0	14	4	0	1	4	2	.67	0	.282	.410	.376
2000	Wmspt	A-	66	246	77	15	5	2	(-	-)	108	25	40	42	23	1	33	4	0	7	2	2	.50	7	.313	.371	.439
2001	Bradtn	R	7	17	4	2	0	0	(-	-)	6	2	3	2	2	1	0	0	0	0	0	0	-	0	.235	.316	.353
2001	Hickory	A	39	148	40	6	0	2	(-	-)	52	14	14	18	10	0	32	4	0	0	2	1	.67	2	.270	.333	.351
2001	Altna	AA	2	4	1	0	0	0	(-	-)	1	0	2	0	1	0	1	0	0	0	0	0	-	0	.250	.400	.250
2002	Hickory	A	68	258	83	14	1	6	(-	-)	117	46	47	44	18	0	40	8	2	5	3	5	.38	6	.322	.377	.453
2003	Lynbrg	A+	127	458	126	38	1	11	(-	-)	199	75	77	75	45	3	79	13	0	8	4	0	1.00	7	.275	.351	.434
2004	Altna	AA	67	221	58	20	0	10	(-	-)	108	31	34	38	21	2	49	8	1	4	0	1	.00	4	.262	.343	.489
2005	Indy	AAA	51	165	57	11	0	12	(-	-)	104	41	35	40	16	3	36	5	0	2	1	3	.25	3	.345	.415	.630
2005	PIT	NL	75	231	59	13	1	6	(4	2)	92	25	35	32	11	1	48	13	1	1	2	1	.67	5	.255	.324	.398

Scott Downs

Pitches: L **Bats:** L **Pos:** SP-13; RP-13   **Ht:** 6'2" **Wt:** 190 **Born:** 3/17/1976 **Age:** 30

Year	Team	Lg	G	GS	CG	GF	IP	BFP	H	R	ER	HR	SH	SF	HB	TBB	IBB	SO	WP	Bk	W	L	Pct	ShO	Sv-Op	Hld	ERC	ERA
2005	Syrcse*	AAA	7	7	0	0	39.1	166	45	21	21	5	0	0	0	3	0	35	0	0	2	3	.400	0	0--	-	3.68	4.81
2000	2 Tms		19	19	0	0	97.0	442	122	62	57	13	0	0	0	40	0	63	0	0	4	3	.571	0	0-0	0	5.92	5.29
2003	MON	NL	1	1	0	0	3.0	17	5	5	5	2	0	0	0	3	2	4	0	1	0	1	.000	0	0-0	0	15.01	15.00
2004	MON	NL	12	12	1	0	63.0	284	79	47	36	9	2	1	3	23	2	38	2	0	3	6	.333	1	0-0	0	5.97	5.14
2005	TOR	AL	26	13	0	0	94.0	400	93	49	45	12	0	1	5	34	0	75	3	0	4	3	.571	0	0-0	0	4.25	4.31
00	ChC	NL	18	18	0	0	94.0	426	117	59	54	13	0	0	0	37	0	63	0	0	4	3	.571	0	0-0	0	5.78	5.17
00	Mon	NL	1	1	0	0	3.0	16	5	3	3	0	0	0	0	3	0	0	0	0	0	0	-	0	0-0	0	10.34	9.00
	4 ML YEARS		58	45	1	0	257.0	1150	299	163	143	36	2	2	8	100	4	180	5	1	11	13	.458	1	0-0	0	5.39	5.01

Ryan Drese

Pitches: R **Bats:** R **Pos:** SP-23   **Ht:** 6'3" **Wt:** 220 **Born:** 4/5/1976 **Age:** 30

Year	Team	Lg	G	GS	CG	GF	IP	BFP	H	R	ER	HR	SH	SF	HB	TBB	IBB	SO	WP	Bk	W	L	Pct	ShO	Sv-Op	Hld	ERC	ERA
2001	CLE	AL	9	4	0	2	36.2	149	32	15	14	2	1	0	1	15	2	24	0	0	1	2	.333	0	0-0	0	3.27	3.44
2002	CLE	AL	26	26	1	0	137.1	635	176	104	100	15	3	9	6	62	1	102	11	0	10	9	.526	0	0-0	0	6.26	6.55
2003	TEX	AL	11	8	0	0	46.0	223	61	42	35	8	0	0	5	24	1	26	2	0	2	4	.333	0	0-0	1	7.60	6.85
2004	TEX	AL	34	33	2	1	207.2	897	233	104	100	17	6	5	11	58	6	98	1	0	14	10	.583	0	0-0	0	4.32	4.20
2005	2 Tms		23	23	1	0	129.1	583	162	90	83	8	4	5	8	46	2	46	4	0	7	12	.368	0	0-0	0	5.36	5.78
05	Tex	AL	12	12	1	0	69.2	317	96	52	50	5	2	1	3	24	1	20	1	0	4	6	.400	0	0-0	0	6.16	6.46
05	Was	NL	11	11	0	0	59.2	266	66	38	33	3	2	4	5	22	1	26	3	0	3	6	.333	0	0-0	1	4.48	4.98
	5 ML YEARS		103	94	4	3	557.0	2487	664	355	329	49	14	19	31	205	12	296	18	0	34	37	.479	0	0-0	1	5.21	5.32

J.D. Drew

Bats: L **Throws:** R **Pos:** RF-44; CF-30   **Ht:** 6'1" **Wt:** 195 **Born:** 11/20/1975 **Age:** 30

Year	Team	Lg	G	AB	H	2B	3B	HR	(Hm	Rd)	TB	R	RBI	RC	TBB	IBB	SO	HBP	SH	SF	SB	CS	SB%	GDP	Avg	OBP	Slg
1998	STL	NL	14	36	15	3	1	5	(4	1)	35	9	13	12	4	0	10	0	0	1	0	0	-	4	.417	.463	.972
1999	STL	NL	104	368	89	16	6	13	(5	8)	156	72	39	58	50	0	77	6	3	3	19	3	.86	4	.242	.340	.424
2000	STL	NL	135	407	120	17	2	18	(11	7)	195	73	57	80	67	4	99	6	5	1	17	9	.65	3	.295	.401	.479
2001	STL	NL	109	375	121	18	5	27	(15	12)	230	80	73	92	57	4	75	4	3	4	13	3	.81	6	.323	.414	.613

Year	Team	Lg	G	AB	H	2B	3B	HR	(Hm	Rd)	TB	R	RBI	RC	TBB	IBB	SO	HBP	SH	SF	SB	CS	SB%	GDP	Avg	OBP	Slg
2002	STL	NL	135	424	107	19	1	18	(9	9)	182	61	65	65	57	4	104	8	3	4	8	2	.80	4	.252	.349	.429
2003	STL	NL	100	287	83	13	3	15	(7	8)	147	60	42	58	36	0	48	3	2	0	2	2	.50	6	.289	.374	.512
2004	ATL	NL	145	518	158	28	8	31	(14	17)	295	118	93	121	118	2	116	5	1	3	12	3	.80	7	.305	.436	.569
2005	LAN	NL	72	252	72	12	1	15	(10	5)	131	48	36	49	51	3	50	5	0	3	1	1	.50	3	.286	.412	.520
8 ML YEARS			814	2667	765	126	27	142	(75	67)	1371	521	409	535	440	17	579	37	17	19	72	23	.76	37	.287	.393	.514

Travis Driskill

Pitches: R **Bats:** R **Pos:** RP-1   **Ht:** 6'0" **Wt:** 225 **Born:** 8/1/1971 **Age:** 34

Year	Team	Lg	G	GS	CG	GF	IP	BFP	H	R	ER	HR	SH	SF	HB	TBB	IBB	SO	WP	Bk	W	L	Pct	ShO	Sv-Op	Hld	ERC	ERA
2005	RdRck*	AAA	47	3	0	16	101.0	434	99	52	49	16	5	5	2	32	8	84	2	0	9	5	.643	0	4- -		3.92	4.37
2002	BAL	AL	29	19	0	6	132.2	589	150	78	73	21	2	2	8	48	1	78	6	0	8	8	.500	0	0-0	0	5.36	4.95
2003	BAL	AL	20	0	0	6	48.0	215	62	35	32	8	3	2	1	9	2	33	3	0	3	5	.375	0	1-1	0	5.30	6.00
2004	COL	NL	5	0	0	1	8.1	39	13	6	6	0	0	0	0	3	0	6	0	0	0	0	-	0	0-1	0	6.62	6.48
2005	HOU	NL	1	0	0	1	1.0	4	1	0	0	0	0	0	0	0	0	2	0	0	0	0	-	0	0-0	0	1.95	0.00
4 ML YEARS			55	19	0	14	190.0	847	226	119	111	29	5	4	9	60	3	119	9	0	11	13	.458	0	1-2	0	5.38	5.26

Jason Dubois

Bats: R **Throws:** R **Pos:** LF-41; PH-12; DH-10; RF-4   **Ht:** 6'5" **Wt:** 220 **Born:** 3/26/1979 **Age:** 27

Year	Team	Lg	G	AB	H	2B	3B	HR	(Hm	Rd)	TB	R	RBI	RC	TBB	IBB	SO	HBP	SH	SF	SB	CS	SB%	GDP	Avg	OBP	Slg
2001	Lansng	A	118	443	131	28	9	24	(-	-)	249	76	92	88	46	2	120	14	2	3	1	2	.33	8	.296	.377	.562
2002	Dytona	A+	99	361	116	25	1	20	(-	-)	203	64	85	82	57	0	95	9	0	4	6	2	.75	7	.321	.422	.562
2003	WTenn	AA	130	443	119	31	4	15	(-	-)	203	57	73	72	57	3	118	15	0	6	2	4	.33	12	.269	.367	.458
2004	Iowa	AAA	109	386	122	26	1	31	(-	-)	243	76	99	85	41	2	97	7	0	3	2	0	1.00	10	.316	.389	.630
2005	Iowa	AAA	4	17	9	1	0	1	(-	-)	13	4	6	5	1	0	3	0	0	0	0	0	-	0	.529	.556	.765
2005	Buffalo	AAA	13	53	15	3	0	4	(-	-)	30	7	10	9	3	0	14	1	0	0	1	1	.50	2	.283	.333	.566
2004	CHN	NL	20	23	5	0	1	1	(1	0)	10	2	5	4	1	0	7	0	0	1	0	0	-	0	.217	.240	.435
2005	2 Tms		66	187	44	12	0	9	(4	5)	83	21	24	19	12	1	74	3	0	0	1	0	.00	3	.235	.292	.444
05	ChC	NL	52	142	34	12	0	7	(3	4)	67	15	22	17	7	1	49	3	0	0	1	0	.00	3	.239	.289	.472
05	Cle	AL	14	45	10	0	0	2	(1	1)	16	6	2	2	5	0	25	0	0	0	0	0	-	0	.222	.300	.356
2 ML YEARS			86	210	49	12	1	10	(5	5)	93	23	29	23	13	1	81	3	0	1	1	0	.00	3	.233	.286	.443

Eric DuBose

Pitches: L **Bats:** L **Pos:** RP-12; SP-3   **Ht:** 6'3" **Wt:** 231 **Born:** 5/15/1976 **Age:** 30

Year	Team	Lg	G	GS	CG	GF	IP	BFP	H	R	ER	HR	SH	SF	HB	TBB	IBB	SO	WP	Bk	W	L	Pct	ShO	Sv-Op	Hld	ERC	ERA
2005	Bowie*	AA	21	20	0	0	122.0	508	113	52	44	10	6	5	4	29	0	114	5	1	8	10	.444	0	0- -		3.03	3.25
2005	Ottawa*	AAA	2	2	0	0	8.2	44	17	13	11	5	0	0	0	1	0	7	0	0	0	1	.000	0	0- -		12.93	11.42
2002	BAL	AL	4	0	0	2	6.0	25	7	2	2	1	0	0	1	1	0	4	0	0	0	0	-	0	0-0	0	5.59	3.00
2003	BAL	AL	17	10	1	3	73.2	305	60	33	31	6	2	3	5	25	2	44	0	1	3	6	.333	0	0-1	1	2.95	3.79
2004	BAL	AL	14	14	0	0	74.2	338	76	55	53	12	1	1	3	44	0	48	5	1	4	6	.400	0	0-0	0	5.60	6.39
2005	BAL	AL	15	3	0	2	29.1	135	28	21	18	4	0	0	1	19	0	17	1	0	2	3	.400	0	0-0	3	5.14	5.52
4 ML YEARS			50	27	1	7	183.2	803	171	111	104	23	3	4	10	89	2	113	6	2	9	15	.375	0	0-1	4	4.41	5.10

Justin Duchscherer

Pitches: R **Bats:** R **Pos:** RP-65   **Ht:** 6'3" **Wt:** 190 **Born:** 11/19/1977 **Age:** 28

Year	Team	Lg	G	GS	CG	GF	IP	BFP	H	R	ER	HR	SH	SF	HB	TBB	IBB	SO	WP	Bk	W	L	Pct	ShO	Sv-Op	Hld	ERC	ERA
2001	TEX	AL	5	2	0	0	14.2	76	24	20	20	5	0	0	0	4	0	11	0	0	1	1	.500	0	0-0	0	8.77	12.27
2003	OAK	AL	4	3	0	0	16.1	71	17	7	6	1	1	0	2	3	0	15	0	0	1	1	.500	0	0-0	0	3.58	3.31
2004	OAK	AL	53	0	0	18	96.1	398	85	37	35	13	7	1	5	32	6	59	1	1	7	6	.538	0	0-2	6	3.57	3.27
2005	OAK	AL	65	0	0	24	85.2	338	67	25	21	7	4	2	2	19	3	85	2	0	7	4	.636	0	5-7	10	2.23	2.21
4 ML YEARS			127	5	0	42	213.0	883	193	89	82	26	12	3	9	58	9	170	3	1	16	12	.571	0	5-9	16	3.32	3.46

Brandon Duckworth

Pitches: R **Bats:** R **Pos:** RP-5; SP-2   **Ht:** 6'2" **Wt:** 185 **Born:** 1/23/1976 **Age:** 30

Year	Team	Lg	G	GS	CG	GF	IP	BFP	H	R	ER	HR	SH	SF	HB	TBB	IBB	SO	WP	Bk	W	L	Pct	ShO	Sv-Op	Hld	ERC	ERA
2005	RdRck*	AAA	20	19	0	1	115.0	520	138	68	59	17	3	3	3	37	2	89	5	0	8	6	.571	0	0- -		5.25	4.62
2001	PHI	NL	11	11	0	0	69.0	289	57	29	27	2	7	3	6	29	5	40	2	0	3	2	.600	0	0-0	0	2.98	3.52
2002	PHI	NL	30	29	0	0	163.0	725	167	103	98	26	7	3	7	69	5	167	10	0	8	9	.471	0	0-0	0	4.80	5.41
2003	PHI	NL	24	18	0	2	93.0	424	98	58	51	12	9	1	10	44	3	68	5	0	4	7	.364	0	0-0	0	5.25	4.94
2004	HOU	NL	19	6	0	6	39.1	180	55	30	30	11	3	1	0	13	3	23	3	0	2	3	.333	0	0-0	0	7.56	6.86
2005	HOU	NL	7	2	0	1	16.1	82	24	20	20	4	0	1	5	7	1	10	0	0	0	1	.000	0	0-0	0	9.78	11.02
5 ML YEARS			91	66	0	9	380.2	1700	401	240	226	55	26	9	28	162	17	308	20	0	16	21	.432	0	0-0	0	5.02	5.34

Chris Duffy

Bats: L Throws: L Pos: CF-33; PH-9; RF-1

Ht: 5'10" Wt: 180 Born: 4/20/1980 Age: 26

								BATTING												BASERUNNING				AVERAGES		
Year	Team	Lg	G	AB	H	2B	3B	HR	(Hm | Rd)	TB	R	RBI	RC	TBB	IBB	SO	HBP	SH	SF	SB	CS	SB%	GDP	Avg	OBP	Slg
2001	Wmspt	A-	64	221	70	12	4	1	(- | -)	93	50	24	49	33	1	33	17	4	2	30	5	.86	0	.317	.440	.421
2002	Lynbrg	A+	132	539	162	27	5	10	(- | -)	229	85	52	85	33	1	101	12	10	3	22	7	.76	1	.301	.353	.425
2003	Altna	AA	137	494	135	23	6	1	(- | -)	173	84	42	69	44	6	78	20	8	3	34	12	.74	7	.273	.355	.350
2004	Altna	AA	113	453	140	23	6	8	(- | -)	199	84	41	80	33	2	77	17	6	0	30	8	.79	4	.309	.378	.439
2005	Indy	AAA	78	308	95	13	7	7	(- | -)	143	55	31	52	16	1	57	10	2	4	17	9	.65	4	.308	.358	.464
2005	PIT	NL	39	126	43	4	2	1	(0 | 1)	54	22	9	22	7	0	22	2	1	0	2	2	.50	1	.341	.385	.429

Zach Duke

Pitches: L Bats: L Pos: SP-14

Ht: 6'2" Wt: 212 Born: 4/19/1983 Age: 23

			HOW MUCH HE PITCHED						WHAT HE GAVE UP											THE RESULTS						
Year	Team	Lg	G	GS	CG	GF	IP	BFP	H	R	ER	HR	SH	SF	HB	TBB	IBB	SO	WP	Bk	W	L	Pct	ShO	Sv-Op	Hld	ERC	ERA
2002	Pirates	R	11	11	1	0	60.0	236	38	15	13	2	1	1	4	18	0	48	1	0	8	1	.889	1	0- -	-	1.71	1.95
2003	Hickory	A	26	26	1	0	141.2	595	124	66	49	7	0	1	5	46	0	113	2	2	8	7	.533	1	0- -	-	2.88	3.11
2004	Lynbrg	A+	17	17	1	0	97.0	384	73	24	15	3	8	2	5	20	1	106	1	0	10	5	.667	0	0- -	-	1.86	1.39
2004	Altna	AA	9	9	0	0	51.1	205	41	11	9	2	6	2	1	10	0	36	1	1	5	1	.833	0	0- -	-	1.97	1.58
2005	Indy	AAA	16	16	1	0	108.0	455	108	39	35	8	5	1	2	23	1	66	1	2	12	3	.800	0	0- -	-	3.18	2.92
2005	PIT	NL	14	14	0	0	84.2	341	79	20	17	3	3	1	2	23	2	58	1	0	8	2	.800	0	0-0	0	2.96	1.81

Chris Duncan

Bats: L Throws: R Pos: PH-9; 1B-2; RF-1

Ht: 6'5" Wt: 210 Born: 5/5/1981 Age: 25

								BATTING												BASERUNNING				AVERAGES		
Year	Team	Lg	G	AB	H	2B	3B	HR	(Hm	Rd)	TB	R	RBI	RC	TBB	IBB	SO	HBP	SH	SF	SB	CS	SB%	GDP	Avg	OBP	Slg
1999	JhsCty	R+	55	201	43	8	1	6	(-	-)	71	23	34	23	25	0	62	1	0	3	3	1	.75	4	.214	.300	.353
2000	Peoria	A	122	450	115	34	0	8	(-	-)	173	52	57	56	36	1	111	6	1	0	1	2	.33	11	.256	.319	.384
2001	Ptomc	A+	49	168	30	6	0	3	(-	-)	45	12	16	8	10	0	47	1	1	0	4	4	.50	5	.179	.229	.268
2001	Peoria	A	80	297	91	23	2	13	(-	-)	157	44	59	62	36	2	55	3	0	1	13	3	.81	10	.306	.386	.529
2002	Peoria	A	129	487	132	25	4	16	(-	-)	213	58	75	73	44	4	118	7	1	5	5	5	.50	8	.271	.337	.437
2003	PlmBh	A+	121	425	108	20	0	2	(-	-)	134	26	42	46	44	1	115	1	1	5	4	4	.50	12	.254	.322	.315
2003	Tenn	AA	10	25	5	1	0	1	(-	-)	9	1	3	1	0	0	6	0	0	0	0	0	-	1	.200	.200	.360
2004	Tenn	AA	120	387	112	23	0	16	(-	-)	183	57	65	75	64	8	94	3	0	1	8	4	.67	6	.289	.393	.473
2005	Memp	AAA	128	431	114	21	2	21	(-	-)	202	57	73	75	63	3	104	2	0	4	1	3	.25	14	.265	.358	.469
2005	STL	NL	9	10	2	1	0	1	(1	0)	6	2	3	2	0	0	5	0	0	0	0	0	-	1	.200	.200	.600

Adam Dunn

Bats: L Throws: R Pos: LF-133; 1B-33; PH-5

Ht: 6'6" Wt: 240 Born: 11/9/1979 Age: 26

								BATTING												BASERUNNING				AVERAGES		
Year	Team	Lg	G	AB	H	2B	3B	HR	(Hm	Rd)	TB	R	RBI	RC	TBB	IBB	SO	HBP	SH	SF	SB	CS	SB%	GDP	Avg	OBP	Slg
2001	CIN	NL	66	244	64	18	1	19	(8	11)	141	54	43	51	38	2	74	4	0	0	4	2	.67	4	.262	.371	.578
2002	CIN	NL	158	535	133	28	2	26	(13	13)	243	84	71	96	128	13	170	9	1	3	19	9	.68	8	.249	.400	.454
2003	CIN	NL	116	381	82	12	1	27	(16	11)	177	70	57	61	74	8	126	10	0	4	8	2	.80	4	.215	.354	.465
2004	CIN	NL	161	568	151	34	0	46	(25	21)	323	105	102	108	108	11	195	5	0	0	6	1	.86	8	.266	.388	.569
2005	CIN	NL	160	543	134	35	2	40	(26	14)	293	107	101	112	114	14	168	12	0	2	4	2	.67	6	.247	.387	.540
	5 ML YEARS		661	2271	564	127	6	158	(88	70)	1177	420	374	428	462	48	733	40	1	9	41	16	.72	30	.248	.383	.518

Erubiel Durazo

Bats: L Throws: L Pos: DH-39; PH-2; 1B-1

Ht: 6'3" Wt: 240 Born: 1/23/1975 Age: 31

								BATTING												BASERUNNING				AVERAGES		
Year	Team	Lg	G	AB	H	2B	3B	HR	(Hm	Rd)	TB	R	RBI	RC	TBB	IBB	SO	HBP	SH	SF	SB	CS	SB%	GDP	Avg	OBP	Slg
1999	ARI	NL	52	155	51	4	2	11	(4	7)	92	31	30	38	26	1	43	1	0	3	1	1	.50	1	.329	.422	.594
2000	ARI	NL	67	196	52	11	0	8	(3	5)	87	35	33	34	34	2	43	1	0	2	1	0	1.00	3	.265	.373	.444
2001	ARI	NL	92	175	47	11	0	12	(4	8)	94	34	38	34	28	1	49	2	0	2	0	0	-	2	.269	.372	.537
2002	ARI	NL	76	222	58	12	2	16	(11	5)	122	46	48	48	49	2	60	2	0	3	0	1	.00	1	.261	.395	.550
2003	OAK	AL	154	537	139	29	0	21	(10	11)	231	92	77	92	100	12	105	2	0	6	1	1	.50	11	.259	.374	.430
2004	OAK	AL	142	511	164	35	1	22	(12	10)	267	80	88	101	56	9	104	9	0	2	3	2	.60	7	.321	.396	.523
2005	OAK	AL	41	152	36	6	1	4	(3	1)	56	15	16	15	14	0	24	1	0	0	1	0	1.00	6	.237	.305	.368
	7 ML YEARS		624	1948	547	108	6	94	(47	47)	949	333	330	362	307	27	428	18	0	18	7	5	.58	30	.281	.381	.487

Ray Durham

Bats: B Throws: R Pos: 2B-133; PH-9; CF-1

Ht: 5'8" Wt: 180 Born: 11/30/1971 Age: 34

								BATTING												BASERUNNING				AVERAGES		
Year	Team	Lg	G	AB	H	2B	3B	HR	(Hm	Rd)	TB	R	RBI	RC	TBB	IBB	SO	HBP	SH	SF	SB	CS	SB%	GDP	Avg	OBP	Slg
1995	CHA	AL	125	471	121	27	6	7	(1	6)	181	68	51	57	31	2	83	6	5	4	18	5	.78	8	.257	.309	.384
1996	CHA	AL	156	557	153	33	5	10	(3	7)	226	79	65	87	58	4	95	10	7	7	30	4	.88	6	.275	.350	.406
1997	CHA	AL	155	634	172	27	5	11	(3	8)	242	106	53	83	61	0	96	6	2	8	33	16	.67	14	.271	.337	.382
1998	CHA	AL	158	635	181	35	8	19	(10	9)	289	126	67	110	73	3	105	6	6	3	36	9	.80	5	.285	.363	.455
1999	CHA	AL	153	612	181	30	8	13	(7	6)	266	109	60	103	73	1	105	4	3	2	34	11	.76	9	.296	.373	.435
2000	CHA	AL	151	614	172	35	9	17	(5	12)	276	121	75	100	75	0	105	7	5	8	25	13	.66	13	.280	.361	.450
2001	CHA	AL	152	611	163	42	10	20	(9	11)	285	104	65	97	64	3	110	4	6	6	23	10	.70	10	.267	.337	.466
2002	2 Tms	AL	150	564	163	34	6	15	(11	4)	254	114	70	96	73	1	93	7	10	5	26	7	.79	15	.289	.374	.450
2003	SF	NL	110	410	117	30	5	8	(3	5)	181	61	33	56	50	2	82	3	4	2	7	7	.50	4	.285	.366	.441
2004	SF	NL	120	471	133	28	8	17	(8	9)	228	95	65	83	57	3	60	6	4	4	10	4	.71	6	.282	.364	.484
2005	SF	NL	142	497	144	33	0	12	(6	6)	213	67	62	67	48	2	59	7	1	7	6	3	.67	19	.290	.356	.429

Year	Team	Lg	G	AB	H	2B	3B	HR	(Hm	Rd)	TB	R	RBI	RC	TBB	IBB	SO	HBP	SH	SF	SB	CS	SB%	GDP	Avg	OBP	Slg
02	CWS	AL	96	345	103	20	2	9	(6	3)	154	71	48	61	49	0	59	5	8	4	20	5	.80	13	.299	.390	.446
02	Oak	AL	54	219	60	14	4	6	(5	1)	100	43	22	35	24	1	34	2	2	1	6	2	.75	2	.274	.350	.457
11 ML YEARS			1572	6076	1700	354	70	149	(66	83)	2641	1050	666	939	663	21	993	66	53	56	248	89	.74	109	.280	.354	.435

Trent Durrington

Bats: R **Throws:** R **Pos:** PH-17; PR-10; 3B-1   **Ht:** 5'10" **Wt:** 188 **Born:** 8/27/1975 **Age:** 30

Year	Team	Lg	G	AB	H	2B	3B	HR	(Hm	Rd)	TB	R	RBI	RC	TBB	IBB	SO	HBP	SH	SF	SB	CS	SB%	GDP	Avg	OBP	Slg
2005	Nashv*	AAA	92	313	94	15	2	5	(-	-)	128	61	31	54	41	1	63	5	10	1	30	12	.71	6	.300	.389	.409
1999	ANA	AL	43	122	22	2	0	0	(0	0)	24	14	2	6	9	0	28	0	5	0	4	3	.57	1	.180	.237	.197
2000	ANA	AL	4	3	0	0	0	0	(0	0)	0	0	0	0	0	0	0	0	0	1	0	0	-	1	.000	.000	.000
2003	ANA	AL	12	14	2	0	0	0	(0	0)	2	5	1	0	3	0	0	0	0	0	1	1	.50	0	.143	.294	.143
2004	MIL	NL	53	82	19	2	3	2	(2	0)	33	13	4	8	4	0	23	0	1	0	4	0	1.00	1	.232	.267	.402
2005	MIL	NL	28	14	3	1	0	0	(0	0)	4	3	2	2	1	0	3	0	3	0	5	2	.71	0	.214	.267	.286
5 ML YEARS			140	235	46	5	3	2	(2	0)	63	35	9	16	17	0	54	0	9	0	14	6	.70	3	.196	.250	.268

Jermaine Dye

Bats: R **Throws:** R **Pos:** RF-140; PH-3; 1B-1; SS-1; DH-1; PR-1   **Ht:** 6'5" **Wt:** 220 **Born:** 1/28/1974 **Age:** 32

Year	Team	Lg	G	AB	H	2B	3B	HR	(Hm	Rd)	TB	R	RBI	RC	TBB	IBB	SO	HBP	SH	SF	SB	CS	SB%	GDP	Avg	OBP	Slg
1996	ATL	NL	98	292	82	16	0	12	(4	8)	134	32	37	36	8	0	67	3	0	3	1	4	.20	11	.281	.304	.459
1997	KC	AL	75	263	62	14	0	7	(3	4)	97	26	22	26	17	0	51	1	1	1	2	1	.67	6	.236	.284	.369
1998	KC	AL	60	214	50	5	1	5	(3	2)	72	24	23	17	11	2	46	1	0	4	2	2	.50	8	.234	.270	.336
1999	KC	AL	158	608	179	44	8	27	(15	12)	320	96	119	106	58	4	119	1	0	6	2	3	.40	17	.294	.354	.526
2000	KC	AL	157	601	193	41	2	33	(15	18)	337	107	118	125	69	6	99	3	0	6	0	1	.00	12	.321	.390	.561
2001	2 Tms	AL	158	599	169	31	1	26	(16	10)	280	91	106	99	57	6	112	7	1	11	9	1	.90	8	.282	.346	.467
2002	OAK	AL	131	488	123	27	1	24	(13	11)	224	74	86	70	52	2	108	10	0	5	2	0	1.00	15	.252	.333	.459
2003	OAK	AL	65	221	38	6	0	4	(3	1)	56	28	20	10	25	2	42	3	0	4	1	0	1.00	11	.172	.261	.253
2004	OAK	AL	137	532	141	29	4	23	(12	11)	247	87	80	69	49	4	128	4	0	5	4	2	.67	16	.265	.329	.464
2005	CHA	AL	145	529	145	29	2	31	(15	16)	271	74	86	80	39	3	99	9	0	2	11	4	.73	15	.274	.333	.512
01	KC	AL	97	367	100	14	0	13	(8	5)	153	50	47	54	30	3	68	6	1	6	7	1	.88	2	.272	.333	.417
01	Oak	AL	61	232	69	17	1	13	(8	5)	127	41	59	45	27	3	44	1	0	5	2	0	1.00	6	.297	.366	.547
10 ML YEARS			1184	4347	1182	242	19	192	(99	93)	2038	639	697	638	385	29	871	42	2	47	34	18	.65	119	.272	.334	.469

Damion Easley

Bats: R **Throws:** R **Pos:** 2B-46; SS-30; PH-23; 3B-10; PR-3   **Ht:** 5'11" **Wt:** 187 **Born:** 11/11/1969 **Age:** 36

Year	Team	Lg	G	AB	H	2B	3B	HR	(Hm	Rd)	TB	R	RBI	RC	TBB	IBB	SO	HBP	SH	SF	SB	CS	SB%	GDP	Avg	OBP	Slg
1992	CAL	AL	47	151	39	5	0	1	(1	0)	47	14	12	14	8	0	26	3	2	1	9	5	.64	2	.258	.307	.311
1993	CAL	AL	73	230	72	13	2	2	(0	2)	95	33	22	37	28	2	35	3	1	2	6	6	.50	5	.313	.392	.413
1994	CAL	AL	88	316	68	16	1	6	(4	2)	104	41	30	28	29	0	48	4	4	2	4	5	.44	8	.215	.288	.329
1995	CAL	AL	114	357	77	14	2	4	(1	3)	107	35	35	30	32	1	47	6	6	4	5	2	.71	11	.216	.288	.300
1996	2 Tms	AL	49	112	30	2	0	4	(1	3)	44	14	17	16	10	0	25	1	5	1	3	1	.75	0	.268	.331	.393
1997	DET	AL	151	527	139	37	3	22	(12	10)	248	97	72	88	68	3	102	16	4	5	28	13	.68	18	.264	.362	.471
1998	DET	AL	153	594	161	38	2	27	(19	8)	284	84	100	94	39	2	112	16	0	5	15	5	.75	8	.271	.332	.478
1999	DET	AL	151	549	146	30	1	20	(12	8)	238	83	65	82	51	2	124	19	2	6	11	3	.79	15	.266	.346	.434
2000	DET	AL	126	464	120	27	2	14	(7	7)	193	76	58	69	55	1	79	11	4	1	13	4	.76	11	.259	.350	.416
2001	DET	AL	154	585	146	27	7	11	(4	7)	220	77	65	72	52	3	90	13	4	4	10	5	.67	10	.250	.323	.376
2002	DET	AL	85	304	68	14	1	8	(4	4)	108	29	30	29	27	3	43	11	1	3	1	3	.25	4	.224	.307	.355
2003	TB	AL	36	107	20	3	1	1	(0	1)	28	8	7	3	2	0	18	0	1	0	0	0	-	3	.187	.202	.262
2004	FLA	NL	98	223	53	20	1	9	(5	4)	102	26	43	34	24	1	36	8	0	2	4	1	.80	6	.238	.331	.457
2005	FLA	NL	102	267	64	19	1	9	(5	4)	112	37	30	33	26	3	47	4	3	4	4	1	.80	6	.240	.312	.419
96	Cal	AL	28	45	7	1	0	2	(1	1)	14	4	7	4	6	0	12	0	3	0	0	0	-	0	.156	.255	.311
96	Det	AL	21	67	23	1	0	2	(0	2)	30	10	10	12	4	0	13	1	2	1	3	1	.75	0	.343	.384	.448
14 ML YEARS			1427	4786	1203	265	24	138	(73	65)	1930	654	586	629	451	21	832	115	37	37	113	54	.68	107	.251	.328	.403

Adam Eaton

Pitches: R **Bats:** R **Pos:** SP-22; RP-2   **Ht:** 6'2" **Wt:** 190 **Born:** 11/23/1977 **Age:** 28

			HOW MUCH HE PITCHED					WHAT HE GAVE UP											THE RESULTS							
Year	Team	Lg	G	GS	CG	GF	IP	BFP	H	R	ER	HR	SH	SF	HB	TBB	IBB	SO	WP	Bk	W	L	Pct	ShO	Sv-Op Hld	ERC	ERA
2005	Lk Els*	A+	1	1	0	0	3.0	12	1	0	0	0	0	0	0	2	0	2	0	0	0	0	-	0	0-- -	1.26	0.00
2005	Portlnd*	AAA	2	2	0	0	8.0	36	11	5	5	3	1	1	0	1	0	4	0	0	0	0	-	0	0-- -	7.01	5.63
2000	SD	NL	22	22	0	0	135.0	583	134	63	62	14	1	3	2	61	3	90	3	0	7	4	.636	0	0-0 0	4.34	4.13
2001	SD	NL	17	17	2	0	116.2	499	108	61	56	20	3	2	5	40	3	109	3	0	8	5	.615	0	0-0 0	4.01	4.32
2002	SD	NL	6	6	0	0	33.1	142	28	20	20	5	2	2	0	17	0	25	2	0	1	1	.500	0	0-0 0	4.28	5.40
2003	SD	NL	31	31	1	0	183.0	789	173	91	83	20	5	5	7	68	6	146	7	1	9	12	.429	0	0-0 0	3.78	4.08
2004	SD	NL	33	33	0	0	199.1	848	204	113	102	28	12	7	10	52	3	153	5	0	11	14	.440	0	0-0 0	4.10	4.61
2005	SD	NL	24	22	0	2	128.2	568	140	70	61	14	4	6	5	44	6	100	5	0	11	5	.688	0	0-0 0	4.44	4.27
6 ML YEARS			133	131	3	2	796.0	3429	787	418	384	101	27	25	31	282	21	623	25	1	47	41	.534	0	0-0 0	4.12	4.34

David Eckstein

Bats: R **Throws:** R **Pos:** SS-156; PH-2; PR-1   **Ht:** 5'8" **Wt:** 170 **Born:** 1/20/1975 **Age:** 31

Year	Team	Lg	G	AB	H	2B	3B	HR	(Hm	Rd)	TB	R	RBI	RC	TBB	IBB	SO	HBP	SH	SF	SB	CS	SB%	GDP	Avg	OBP	Slg
2001	ANA	AL	153	582	166	26	2	4	(3	1)	208	82	41	80	43	0	60	21	16	2	29	4	.88	11	.285	.355	.357
2002	ANA	AL	152	608	178	22	6	8	(3	5)	236	107	63	93	45	0	44	27	14	8	21	13	.62	7	.293	.363	.388
2003	ANA	AL	120	452	114	22	1	3	(1	2)	147	59	31	53	36	0	45	15	10	4	16	5	.76	9	.252	.325	.325
2004	ANA	AL	142	566	156	24	1	2	(2	0)	188	92	35	60	42	1	49	13	14	2	16	5	.76	11	.276	.339	.332
2005	STL	NL	158	630	185	26	7	8	(3	5)	249	90	61	103	58	0	44	13	8	4	11	8	.58	13	.294	.363	.395
	5 ML YEARS		725	2838	799	120	17	25	(12	13)	1028	430	231	389	224	1	242	89	62	20	93	35	.73	51	.282	.351	.362

Jim Edmonds

Bats: L **Throws:** L **Pos:** CF-139; PH-9   **Ht:** 6'1" **Wt:** 212 **Born:** 6/27/1970 **Age:** 36

Year	Team	Lg	G	AB	H	2B	3B	HR	(Hm	Rd)	TB	R	RBI	RC	TBB	IBB	SO	HBP	SH	SF	SB	CS	SB%	GDP	Avg	OBP	Slg
1993	CAL	AL	18	61	15	4	1	0	(0	0)	21	5	4	4	2	1	16	0	0	0	0	2	.00	1	.246	.270	.344
1994	CAL	AL	94	289	79	13	1	5	(3	2)	109	35	37	38	30	3	72	1	1	1	4	2	.67	3	.273	.343	.377
1995	CAL	AL	141	558	162	30	4	33	(16	17)	299	120	107	100	51	4	130	5	1	5	1	4	.20	10	.290	.352	.536
1996	CAL	AL	114	431	131	28	3	27	(17	10)	246	73	66	88	46	2	101	4	0	2	4	0	1.00	8	.304	.375	.571
1997	ANA	AL	133	502	146	27	0	26	(14	12)	251	82	80	90	60	5	80	4	0	5	5	7	.42	8	.291	.368	.500
1998	ANA	AL	154	599	184	42	1	25	(9	16)	303	115	91	104	57	7	114	1	1	1	7	5	.58	16	.307	.368	.506
1999	ANA	AL	55	204	51	17	2	5	(3	2)	87	34	23	30	28	0	45	0	0	1	5	4	.56	3	.250	.339	.426
2000	STL	NL	152	525	155	25	0	42	(22	20)	306	129	108	126	103	3	167	6	1	8	10	3	.77	5	.295	.411	.583
2001	STL	NL	150	500	152	38	1	30	(16	14)	282	95	110	113	93	12	136	4	1	10	5	5	.50	8	.304	.410	.564
2002	STL	NL	144	476	148	31	2	28	(17	11)	267	96	83	101	86	14	134	8	0	6	4	3	.57	9	.311	.420	.561
2003	STL	NL	137	447	123	32	2	39	(17	22)	276	89	89	87	77	6	127	4	1	2	1	3	.25	11	.275	.385	.617
2004	STL	NL	153	498	150	38	3	42	(24	18)	320	102	111	115	101	12	150	5	0	8	8	3	.73	4	.301	.418	.643
2005	STL	NL	142	467	123	37	1	29	(15	14)	249	88	89	95	91	10	139	4	1	4	5	5	.50	6	.263	.385	.533
	13 ML YEARS		1587	5557	1619	362	21	331	(173	158)	3016	1063	998	1091	825	79	1411	46	7	53	59	46	.56	92	.291	.384	.543

Mike Edwards

Bats: R **Throws:** R **Pos:** 3B-39; LF-32; PH-18; RF-3; PR-2; SS-1; DH-1   **Ht:** 6'1" **Wt:** 185 **Born:** 11/24/1976 **Age:** 29

Year	Team	Lg	G	AB	H	2B	3B	HR	(Hm	Rd)	TB	R	RBI	RC	TBB	IBB	SO	HBP	SH	SF	SB	CS	SB%	GDP	Avg	OBP	Slg
1995	Burlgtn	R+	43	130	22	2	0	0	(-	-)	24	20	5	6	17	0	35	2	0	0	5	2	.71	2	.169	.275	.185
1996	Burlgtn	R+	58	206	58	13	1	1	(-	-)	76	31	17	33	37	0	26	3	3	3	5	4	.56	4	.282	.394	.369
1997	Burlgtn	R+	60	236	68	16	2	4	(-	-)	100	50	41	40	38	1	53	1	0	2	10	5	.67	2	.288	.386	.424
1998	Clmbs	A	124	497	146	34	4	8	(-	-)	212	82	81	76	55	2	95	3	3	2	16	6	.73	13	.294	.366	.427
1999	Kinston	A+	133	456	132	25	4	16	(-	-)	213	76	89	91	93	6	117	9	0	9	8	3	.73	12	.289	.413	.467
2000	Akron	AA	136	481	142	25	2	11	(-	-)	204	72	63	82	68	2	86	5	3	3	7	3	.70	9	.295	.386	.424
2001	MhVlly	A-	20	71	26	5	0	6	(-	-)	49	19	24	20	12	0	7	1	0	0	0	1	.00	0	.366	.464	.690
2001	Akron	AA	29	111	37	7	3	6	(-	-)	68	21	24	24	13	1	28	0	0	0	0	0	-	1	.333	.403	.613
2001	Buffalo	AAA	3	9	2	0	0	0	(-	-)	2	1	1	0	1	0	3	0	0	0	0	0	-	1	.222	.300	.222
2002	Chatt	AA	119	424	130	19	2	11	(-	-)	186	57	60	65	41	1	57	10	6	5	9	11	.45	19	.307	.377	.439
2002	Lsvlle	AAA	15	57	23	5	1	2	(-	-)	36	7	8	14	6	0	9	0	0	0	0	0	-	1	.404	.460	.632
2003	Scrmto	AAA	125	436	130	23	4	14	(-	-)	203	78	95	76	60	0	78	6	1	4	5	2	.71	17	.298	.387	.466
2004	Scrmto	AAA	140	551	158	41	0	13	(-	-)	238	91	86	93	76	2	100	13	0	3	11	2	.85	14	.287	.384	.432
2005	LsVgs	AAA	32	118	33	6	0	4	(-	-)	51	18	21	19	11	0	21	3	0	1	3	1	.75	5	.280	.353	.432
2003	OAK	AL	4	4	1	0	0	0	(0	0)	1	0	0	1	2	0	1	0	0	0	0	0	-	0	.250	.500	.250
2005	LAN	NL	88	239	59	9	2	3	(1	2)	81	23	15	20	16	0	34	2	1	0	1	1	.50	6	.247	.300	.339
	2 ML YEARS		92	243	60	9	2	3	(1	2)	82	23	15	21	18	0	35	2	1	0	1	1	.50	6	.247	.304	.337

Joey Eischen

Pitches: L **Bats:** L **Pos:** RP-57   **Ht:** 6'0" **Wt:** 210 **Born:** 5/25/1970 **Age:** 36

Year	Team	Lg	G	GS	CG	GF	IP	BFP	H	R	ER	HR	SH	SF	HB	TBB	IBB	SO	WP	Bk	W	L	Pct	ShO	Sv-Op	Hld	ERC	ERA
2005	NewOr*	AAA	6	4	0	0	6.2	27	4	1	1	0	0	0	1	3	0	6	2	0	0	0	-	0	0--	-	2.12	1.35
1994	MON	NL	1	0	0	0	0.2	7	4	4	4	0	0	0	0	1	0	1	0	0	0	0	-	0	0-0	0	47.92	54.00
1995	LA	NL	17	0	0	8	20.1	95	19	9	7	1	0	0	2	11	1	15	1	0	0	0	-	0	0-0	1	3.97	3.10
1996	2 Tms		52	0	0	14	68.1	308	75	36	32	7	3	2	4	34	7	51	4	0	1	2	.333	0	0-2	2	5.15	4.21
1997	CIN	NL	1	0	0	0	1.1	7	2	2	1	0	0	0	0	1	0	2	1	0	0	0	-	0	0-0	0	7.52	6.75
2001	MON	NL	24	0	0	7	29.2	131	29	17	16	4	1	0	1	16	1	19	1	0	0	1	.000	0	0-2	2	4.89	4.85
2002	MON	NL	59	0	0	18	53.2	217	43	11	8	1	3	2	2	18	5	51	6	1	6	1	.857	0	2-3	11	2.31	1.34
2003	MON	NL	70	0	0	15	53.0	221	57	27	18	7	3	0	3	13	1	40	3	0	2	2	.500	0	1-4	15	4.44	3.06
2004	MON	NL	21	0	0	3	18.1	80	16	10	8	2	1	1	1	8	2	17	0	0	0	1	.000	0	0-1	2	3.53	3.93
2005	WAS	NL	57	0	0	14	36.1	169	34	14	13	1	6	2	6	19	7	30	5	1	2	1	.667	0	0-1	8	3.81	3.22
96	LA	NL	28	0	0	11	43.1	198	48	25	23	4	3	1	4	20	4	36	1	0	0	1	.000	0	0-0	1	5.07	4.78
96	Det	AL	24	0	0	3	25.0	110	27	11	9	3	0	1	0	14	3	15	3	0	1	1	.500	0	0-2	1	5.30	3.24
	9 ML YEARS		302	0	0	79	281.2	1235	279	130	107	23	17	20	120	24	226	21	2	11	8	.579	0	3-13	41	4.13	3.42

Scott Elarton

Pitches: R **Bats:** R **Pos:** SP-31   **Ht:** 6'8" **Wt:** 240 **Born:** 2/23/1976 **Age:** 30

Year	Team	Lg	G	GS	CG	GF	IP	BFP	H	R	ER	HR	SH	SF	HB	TBB	IBB	SO	WP	Bk	W	L	Pct	ShO	Sv-Op	Hld	ERC	ERA
1998	HOU	NL	28	2	0	7	57.0	227	40	21	21	5	1	1	4	20	0	56	1	0	2	1	.667	0	2-3	2	2.35	3.32
1999	HOU	NL	42	15	0	8	124.0	524	111	55	48	8	7	4	4	43	0	121	3	0	9	5	.643	0	1-4	5	3.16	3.48
2000	HOU	NL	30	30	2	0	192.2	855	198	117	103	29	5	7	6	84	1	131	8	0	17	7	.708	0	0-0	0	4.82	4.81
2001	2 Tms	NL	24	24	0	0	132.2	595	146	105	104	34	7	2	6	59	2	87	5	0	4	10	.286	0	0-0	0	6.21	7.06

Year	Team	Lg	G	GS	CG	GF	IP	BFP	H	R	ER	HR	SH	SF	HB	TBB	IBB	SO	WP	Bk	W	L	Pct	ShO	Sv-Op	Hld	ERC	ERA
2003	COL	NL	11	10	0	0	51.2	253	73	46	36	11	3	4	4	20	3	20	3	0	4	4	.500	0	0-0	0	7.79	6.27
2004	2 Tms		29	29	1	0	158.2	697	164	107	104	33	5	7	4	62	3	103	8	0	3	11	.214	1	0-0	0	5.04	5.90
2005	CLE	AL	31	31	1	0	181.2	774	189	100	93	32	3	10	6	48	1	103	4	1	11	9	.550	0	0-0	0	4.40	4.61
01	Hou	NL	20	20	0	0	109.2	499	126	88	87	26	7	2	6	49	1	76	5	0	4	8	.333	0	0-0	0	6.42	7.14
01	Col	NL	4	4	0	0	23.0	96	20	17	17	8	0	0	0	10	1	11	0	0		2	.000	0	0-0	0	5.18	6.65
04	Col	NL	8	8	0	0	41.1	199	57	45	45	8	2	3	0	20	1	23	5	0	0	6	.000	0	0-0	0	7.35	9.80
04	Cle	AL	21	21	1	0	117.1	498	107	62	59	25	3	4	4	42	2	80	3	0	3	5	.375	1	0-0	0	4.28	4.53
7 ML YEARS			195	141	4	15	898.1	3925	921	551	509	154	31	35	31	336	10	621	32	1	50	47	.515	1	3-7	7	4.72	5.10

Brad Eldred

Bats: R **Throws:** R **Pos:** 1B-50; PH-6   **Ht:** 6'5" **Wt:** 245 **Born:** 7/12/1980 **Age:** 25

Year	Team	Lg	G	AB	H	2B	3B	HR	(Hm	Rd)	TB	R	RBI	RC	TBB	IBB	SO	HBP	SH	SF	SB	CS	SB%	GDP	Avg	OBP	Slg
2002	Wmspt	AA	72	276	78	22	3	10	(-	-)	136	43	48	48	18	4	74	6	0	2	10	1	.91	4	.283	.338	.493
2003	Hickory	A	115	420	105	22	0	28	(-	-)	211	62	80	71	38	2	142	11	0	3	7	1	.88	5	.250	.326	.502
2004	Lynbrg	A+	91	335	104	22	1	21	(-	-)	191	54	77	75	35	3	97	15	0	3	5	2	.71	4	.310	.397	.570
2004	Altna	AA	39	147	41	9	0	17	(-	-)	101	24	16	32	6	0	51	5	0	0	0	0	-	3	.279	.329	.687
2005	Altna	AA	21	84	28	6	0	13	(-	-)	73	22	27	25	8	1	25	0	0	1	1	1	.50	0	.333	.387	.869
2005	Indy	AAA	54	195	55	13	1	15	(-	-)	115	31	48	39	14	1	57	3	0	2	4	0	1.00	3	.282	.336	.590
2005	PIT	NL	55	190	42	9	0	12	(4	8)	87	23	27	14	13	0	77	3	0	2	1	1	.50	5	.221	.279	.458

Cal Eldred

Pitches: R **Bats:** R **Pos:** RP-30; SP-1   **Ht:** 6'4" **Wt:** 235 **Born:** 11/24/1967 **Age:** 38

Year	Team	Lg	G	GS	CG	GF	IP	BFP	H	R	ER	HR	SH	SF	HB	TBB	IBB	SO	WP	Bk	W	L	Pct	ShO	Sv-Op	Hld	ERC	ERA
2005	Sprgfld*	AA	3	0	0	2	6.0	23	5	0	0	0	0	0	0	0	0	1	0	0	1	0	1.000	0	0--	1	1.37	0.00
1991	MIL	AL	3	3	0	0	16.0	73	20	9	8	2	0	0	0	6	0	10	0	0	2	0	1.000	0	0-0	0	5.57	4.50
1992	MIL	AL	14	14	2	0	100.1	394	76	21	20	4	1	0	2	23	0	62	3	0	11	2	.846	1	0-0	0	1.94	1.79
1993	MIL	AL	36	36	8	0	258.0	1087	232	120	115	32	5	12	10	91	5	180	2	0	16	16	.500	1	0-0	0	3.62	4.01
1994	MIL	AL	25	25	6	0	179.0	769	158	96	93	23	5	7	4	84	0	98	2	0	11	11	.500	0	0-0	0	3.97	4.68
1995	MIL	AL	4	4	0	0	23.2	104	24	10	9	4	1	0	1	10	0	18	1	1	1	1	.500	0	0-0	0	4.91	3.42
1996	MIL	AL	15	15	0	0	84.2	363	82	43	42	8	0	4	4	38	0	50	1	0	4	4	.500	0	0-0	0	4.33	4.46
1997	MIL	AL	34	34	1	0	202.0	885	207	118	112	31	4	6	9	89	0	122	5	0	13	15	.464	1	0-0	0	5.00	4.99
1998	MIL	NL	23	23	0	0	133.0	602	157	82	71	14	5	3	4	61	3	86	6	0	4	8	.333	0	0-0	0	5.54	4.80
1999	SF	NL	20	15	0	2	82.0	392	101	75	71	19	2	3	1	46	0	60	8	1	2	8	.200	0	0-0	0	7.13	7.79
2000	CHA	AL	20	20	2	0	112.0	492	103	61	57	12	3	2	5	59	0	97	4	0	10	2	.833	1	0-0	0	4.36	4.58
2001	CHA	AL	2	2	0	0	6.0	34	12	9	9	1	0	0	3	3	1	6	0	0	0	1	.000	0	0-0	0	14.25	13.50
2003	STL	NL	62	0	0	18	67.1	293	62	32	28	9	5	3	4	31	4	67	4	0	7	4	.636	0	8-14	11	4.25	3.74
2004	STL	NL	52	0	0	10	67.0	282	71	31	28	11	5	2	1	17	1	54	3	0	4	2	.667	0	1-3	9	4.34	3.76
2005	STL	NL	31	1	0	15	37.0	160	35	9	9	3	4	1	2	18	3	29	0	0	1	0	1.000	0	0-1	2	4.12	2.19
14 ML YEARS			341	192	19	45	1368.0	5930	1340	716	672	173	40	43	50	576	17	939	39	2	86	74	.538	4	9-18	22	4.37	4.42

Mark Ellis

Bats: R **Throws:** R **Pos:** 2B-115; SS-7; 1B-2; PH-2; PR-2; DH-1   **Ht:** 5'11" **Wt:** 180 **Born:** 6/6/1977 **Age:** 29

Year	Team	Lg	G	AB	H	2B	3B	HR	(Hm	Rd)	TB	R	RBI	RC	TBB	IBB	SO	HBP	SH	SF	SB	CS	SB%	GDP	Avg	OBP	Slg
2002	OAK	AL	98	345	94	16	4	6	(6	0)	136	58	35	55	44	1	54	4	8	3	4	2	.67	3	.272	.359	.394
2003	OAK	AL	154	553	137	31	5	9	(7	2)	205	78	52	69	48	4	94	7	9	5	6	2	.75	7	.248	.313	.371
2005	OAK	AL	122	434	137	21	5	13	(5	8)	207	76	52	78	44	1	51	4	4	0	1	3	.25	10	.316	.384	.477
3 ML YEARS			374	1332	368	68	14	28	(18	10)	548	212	139	202	136	6	199	15	21	8	11	7	.61	20	.276	.348	.411

Jason Ellison

Bats: R **Throws:** R **Pos:** CF-78; RF-32; LF-15; PH-13; PR-13   **Ht:** 5'10" **Wt:** 180 **Born:** 4/4/1978 **Age:** 28

Year	Team	Lg	G	AB	H	2B	3B	HR	(Hm	Rd)	TB	R	RBI	RC	TBB	IBB	SO	HBP	SH	SF	SB	CS	SB%	GDP	Avg	OBP	Slg
2005	Fresno*	AAA	8	38	9	2	0	0	(-	-)	11	5	3	3	2	0	9	1	0	0	0	0	-	0	.237	.293	.289
2003	SF	NL	7	10	1	0	0	0	(0	0)	1	1	0	0	0	0	1	0	0	0	0	0	-	0	.100	.100	.100
2004	SF	NL	13	4	2	0	0	1	(0	1)	5	4	3	3	0	0	1	0	0	0	2	0	1.00	0	.500	.500	1.250
2005	SF	NL	131	352	93	18	2	4	(2	2)	127	49	24	34	24	1	44	3	6	1	14	6	.70	7	.264	.316	.361
3 ML YEARS			151	366	96	18	2	5	(2	3)	133	54	27	37	24	1	46	3	6	1	16	6	.73	7	.262	.312	.363

Alan Embree

Pitches: L **Bats:** L **Pos:** RP-67   **Ht:** 6'2" **Wt:** 190 **Born:** 1/23/1970 **Age:** 36

Year	Team	Lg	G	GS	CG	GF	IP	BFP	H	R	ER	HR	SH	SF	HB	TBB	IBB	SO	WP	Bk	W	L	Pct	ShO	Sv-Op	Hld	ERC	ERA
1992	CLE	AL	4	4	0	0	18.0	81	19	14	14	3	0	1	0	8	0	12	1	1	0	2	.000	0	0-0	0	5.25	7.00
1995	CLE	AL	23	0	0	8	24.2	111	23	16	14	2	2	2	0	16	0	23	1	0	3	2	.600	0	1-1	6	4.51	5.11
1996	CLE	AL	24	0	0	2	31.0	141	30	26	22	10	1	3	0	21	3	33	3	0	1	1	.500	0	0-0	1	6.58	6.39
1997	ATL	NL	66	0	0	15	46.0	190	36	13	13	1	4	1	2	20	2	45	1	1	3	1	.750	0	0-0	16	2.66	2.54
1998	2 Tms	NL	55	0	0	16	53.2	237	56	32	25	7	4	1	1	23	0	43	3	0	4	2	.667	0	1-3	12	4.71	4.19
1999	SF	NL	68	0	0	13	58.2	244	42	22	22	6	3	2	3	26	2	53	3	0	3	2	.600	0	0-3	22	2.86	3.38
2000	SF	NL	63	0	0	21	60.0	263	62	34	33	4	4	5	3	25	2	49	1	0	3	5	.375	0	2-5	9	4.24	4.95
2001	2 Tms	NL	61	0	0	17	54.0	245	65	47	44	14	0	6	3	17	2	59	3	0	1	4	.200	0	0-3	9	6.20	7.33
2002	2 Tms	NL	68	0	0	20	62.0	251	47	19	14	6	1	2	1	20	3	81	1	0	4	6	.400	0	2-7	18	2.48	2.03
2003	BOS	AL	65	0	0	15	55.0	221	49	26	26	3	6	2	0	16	3	45	0	0	4	1	.800	0	1-2	14	3.01	4.25

			HOW MUCH HE PITCHED						WHAT HE GAVE UP												THE RESULTS						
Year	Team	Lg	G	GS	CG	GF	IP	BFP	H	R	ER	HR	SH	SF	HB	TBB	IBB	SO	WP	Bk	W	L	Pct	ShO	Sv-Op	Hld	ERC	ERA
2004	BOS	AL	71	0	0	11	52.1	217	49	28	24	7	2	2	1	11	1	37	0	0	2	2	.500	0	0-1	20	3.21	4.13
2005	2 Tms	AL	67	0	0	15	52.0	231	62	47	44	10	3	3	2	14	3	38	1	1	2	5	.286	0	1-3	10	5.34	7.62
98	Atl	NL	20	0	0	5	18.2	87	23	14	9	2	1	1	0	10	1	19	0	0	1	0	1.000	0	0-1	6	6.06	4.34
98	Ari	NL	35	0	0	11	35.0	150	33	18	16	5	3	0	1	13	0	24	3	0	3	2	.600	0	1-2	6	4.03	4.11
01	SF	NL	22	0	0	7	20.0	106	34	26	25	7	0	3	2	10	2	25	1	0	0	2	.000	0	0-1	0	11.29	11.25
01	CWS	AL	39	0	0	10	34.0	139	31	21	19	7	0	3	1	7	0	34	2	0	1	2	.333	0	0-2	9	3.61	5.03
02	SD	NL	36	0	0	13	28.2	118	23	7	3	2	0	0	0	9	2	38	1	0	3	4	.429	0	0-2	10	2.38	0.94
02	Bos	NL	32	0	0	13	33.1	133	24	12	11	4	1	2	1	11	1	43	0	0	1	2	.333	0	2-5	8	2.56	2.97
05	Bos	AL	43	0	0	11	37.2	163	42	33	32	8	1	2	1	11	2	30	1	0	1	4	.200	0	1-3	4	5.14	7.65
05	NYY	AL	24	0	0	4	14.1	68	20	14	12	2	2	1	1	3	1	8	0	1	1	1	.500	0	0-0	6	5.85	7.53
12 ML YEARS			635	4	0	153	567.1	2432	540	324	295	75	24	31	17	217	21	518	20	3	30	33	.476	0	8-28	137	4.01	4.68

Edwin Encarnacion

Bats: R **Throws:** R **Pos:** 3B-56; PH-13   **Ht:** 6'1" **Wt:** 195 **Born:** 1/7/1983 **Age:** 23

					BATTING																BASERUNNING				AVERAGES		
Year	Team	Lg	G	AB	H	2B	3B	HR	(Hm	Rd)	TB	R	RBI	RC	TBB	IBB	SO	HBP	SH	SF	SB	CS	SB%	GDP	Avg	OBP	Slg
2000	Rngrs	R	51	177	55	6	3	0	(-	-)	67	31	36	28	21	1	27	1	3	3	3	1	.75	7	.311	.381	.379
2001	Billings	R+	52	211	55	8	2	5	(-	-)	82	27	26	27	15	0	29	0	0	0	8	1	.89	6	.261	.307	.389
2001	Dayton	A	9	37	6	2	0	1	(-	-)	11	2	6	1	1	0	5	0	0	0	0	1	.00	1	.162	.184	.297
2001	Savann	A	45	170	52	9	2	4	(-	-)	77	23	25	27	12	0	34	2	1	2	3	3	.50	5	.306	.355	.453
2002	Dayton	A	136	517	146	32	4	17	(-	-)	237	80	73	84	40	2	108	7	0	6	25	7	.78	15	.282	.339	.458
2003	Ptomc	A+	58	215	69	15	1	6	(-	-)	104	40	29	42	24	1	32	1	1	3	7	1	.88	2	.321	.387	.484
2003	Chatt	AA	64	254	69	13	1	5	(-	-)	99	40	36	35	22	0	44	3	0	5	8	3	.73	3	.272	.331	.390
2004	Chatt	AA	120	469	132	35	1	13	(-	-)	208	73	76	78	53	3	79	0	1	3	17	3	.85	5	.281	.352	.443
2005	Lsvlle	AAA	78	290	91	23	0	15	(-	-)	159	44	54	62	33	1	53	4	0	3	7	2	.78	8	.314	.388	.548
2005	CIN	NL	69	211	49	16	0	9	(3	6)	92	25	31	24	20	2	60	3	0	0	3	0	1.00	8	.232	.308	.436

Juan Encarnacion

Bats: R **Throws:** R **Pos:** RF-135; CF-11; PH-4; PR-1   **Ht:** 6'3" **Wt:** 215 **Born:** 3/8/1976 **Age:** 30

					BATTING																BASERUNNING				AVERAGES		
Year	Team	Lg	G	AB	H	2B	3B	HR	(Hm	Rd)	TB	R	RBI	RC	TBB	IBB	SO	HBP	SH	SF	SB	CS	SB%	GDP	Avg	OBP	Slg
1997	DET	AL	11	33	7	1	1	1	(1	0)	13	3	5	4	3	0	12	2	0	0	3	1	.75	1	.212	.316	.394
1998	DET	AL	40	164	54	9	4	7	(4	3)	92	30	21	31	7	0	31	1	0	3	7	4	.64	2	.329	.354	.561
1999	DET	AL	132	509	130	30	6	19	(6	13)	229	62	74	64	14	1	113	9	4	2	33	12	.73	12	.255	.287	.450
2000	DET	AL	141	547	158	25	6	14	(4	10)	237	75	72	76	29	1	90	7	3	4	16	4	.80	15	.289	.330	.433
2001	DET	AL	120	417	101	19	7	12	(4	8)	170	52	52	48	25	1	93	6	5	4	9	5	.64	9	.242	.292	.408
2002	2 Tms	NL	152	584	158	22	5	24	(8	16)	262	77	85	74	46	0	113	4	3	7	21	9	.70	18	.271	.324	.449
2003	FLA	NL	156	601	162	37	6	19	(9	10)	268	80	94	76	37	0	82	4	5	6	19	8	.70	17	.270	.313	.446
2004	2 Tms	NL	135	484	114	30	2	16	(8	8)	196	63	62	60	38	2	86	7	1	2	5	4	.56	10	.236	.299	.405
2005	FLA	NL	141	506	145	27	3	16	(8	8)	226	59	76	79	41	2	104	9	4	3	6	5	.55	9	.287	.349	.447
02	Cin	NL	83	321	89	11	2	16	(6	10)	152	43	51	42	26	0	63	1	3	3	9	4	.69	7	.277	.330	.474
02	Fla	NL	69	263	69	11	3	8	(2	6)	110	34	34	32	20	0	50	3	0	4	12	5	.71	11	.262	.317	.418
04	LA	NL	86	324	76	18	1	13	(6	7)	135	42	43	38	21	0	53	4	0	1	3	3	.50	8	.235	.289	.417
04	Fla	NL	49	160	38	12	1	3	(2	1)	61	21	19	22	17	2	33	3	1	1	2	1	.67	2	.238	.320	.381
9 ML YEARS			1028	3845	1029	200	40	128	(52	76)	1693	501	541	512	240	7	724	49	25	31	119	52	.70	93	.268	.316	.440

Morgan Ensberg

Bats: R **Throws:** R **Pos:** 3B-148; PH-2   **Ht:** 6'2" **Wt:** 210 **Born:** 8/26/1975 **Age:** 30

					BATTING																BASERUNNING				AVERAGES		
Year	Team	Lg	G	AB	H	2B	3B	HR	(Hm	Rd)	TB	R	RBI	RC	TBB	IBB	SO	HBP	SH	SF	SB	CS	SB%	GDP	Avg	OBP	Slg
2000	HOU	NL	4	7	2	0	0	0	(0	0)	2	0	0	1	0	0	1	0	0	0	0	0	-	0	.286	.286	.286
2002	HOU	NL	49	132	32	7	2	3	(2	1)	52	14	19	13	18	0	25	3	0	0	2	0	1.00	8	.242	.346	.394
2003	HOU	NL	127	385	112	15	1	25	(16	9)	204	69	60	71	48	1	60	6	1	1	7	2	.78	10	.291	.377	.530
2004	HOU	NL	131	411	113	20	3	10	(9	1)	169	51	66	57	36	1	46	0	5	4	6	4	.60	17	.275	.330	.411
2005	HOU	NL	150	526	149	30	3	36	(20	16)	293	86	101	107	85	9	119	8	0	5	6	7	.46	12	.283	.388	.557
5 ML YEARS			461	1461	408	72	9	74	(47	27)	720	220	246	249	187	11	251	17	6	10	21	13	.62	47	.279	.365	.493

Scott Erickson

Pitches: R **Bats:** R **Pos:** RP-11; SP-8   **Ht:** 6'4" **Wt:** 230 **Born:** 2/2/1968 **Age:** 38

					HOW MUCH HE PITCHED						WHAT HE GAVE UP									THE RESULTS							
Year	Team	Lg	G	GS	CG	GF	IP	BFP	H	R	ER	HR	SH	SF	HB	TBB	IBB	SO	WP	Bk	W	L	Pct	ShO	Sv-Op	Hld	ERC	ERA
2005	LsVgs*	AAA	7	7	0	0	40.0	188	47	34	32	6	2	2	4	21	0	26	2	0	2	4	.333	0	0- -	1	6.43	7.20
1990	MIN	AL	19	17	1	0	113.0	485	108	49	36	9	5	2	5	51	4	53	3	0	8	4	.667	0	0-0	0	4.07	2.87
1991	MIN	AL	32	32	5	0	204.0	851	189	80	72	13	5	7	6	71	3	108	4	0	20	8	.714	3	0-0	0	3.36	3.18
1992	MIN	AL	32	32	5	0	212.0	888	197	86	80	18	9	7	8	83	3	101	6	1	13	12	.520	3	0-0	0	3.75	3.40
1993	MIN	AL	34	34	1	0	218.2	976	266	138	126	17	10	13	10	71	1	116	5	0	8	19	.296	0	0-0	0	5.05	5.19
1994	MIN	AL	23	23	2	0	144.0	654	173	95	87	15	3	4	9	59	0	104	10	0	8	11	.421	1	0-0	0	5.61	5.44
1995	2 Tms	AL	32	31	7	1	196.1	836	213	108	105	18	3	3	5	67	0	106	3	2	13	10	.565	2	0-0	0	4.48	4.81
1996	BAL	AL	34	34	6	0	222.1	968	262	137	124	21	5	5	11	66	4	100	1	0	13	12	.520	0	0-0	0	4.90	5.02
1997	BAL	AL	34	33	3	0	221.2	922	218	100	91	16	3	4	5	61	5	131	11	0	16	7	.696	2	0-0	0	3.40	3.69
1998	BAL	AL	36	36	11	0	251.1	1102	284	125	112	23	7	2	13	69	4	186	4	0	16	13	.552	2	0-0	0	4.40	4.01
1999	BAL	AL	34	34	6	0	230.1	995	244	127	123	27	7	6	11	99	4	106	10	0	15	12	.556	3	0-0	0	4.97	4.81
2000	BAL	AL	16	16	1	0	92.0	446	127	81	81	14	3	5	5	48	0	41	3	0	5	8	.385	0	0-0	0	7.50	7.87
2002	BAL	AL	29	28	3	0	160.2	719	192	109	99	20	3	7	8	68	2	74	5	0	5	12	.294	1	0-0	0	5.80	5.55
2004	2 Tms		6	6	0	0	27.0	136	38	22	22	7	0	3	3	20	0	9	2	0	1	4	.200	0	0-0	0	8.11	6.67
2005	LAN	NL	19	8	0	0	55.1	249	62	37	37	12	3	2	4	25	0	15	1	0	1	4	.200	0	0-0	0	6.26	6.02
95	Min	AL	15	15	0	0	87.2	390	102	61	58	11	2	1	4	32	0	45	1	0	4	6	.400	0	0-0	0	5.29	5.95

Year	Team	Lg	G	GS	CG	GF	IP	BFP	H	R	ER	HR	SH	SF	HB	TBB	IBB	SO	WP	Bk	W	L	Pct	ShO	Sv-Op	Hld	ERC	ERA
95	Bal	AL	17	16	7	1	108.2	446	111	47	47	7	1	2	1	35	0	61	2	2	9	4	.692	2	0-0	0	3.84	3.89
04	NYM	NL	2	2	0	0	8.0	42	15	9	7	1	0	0	0	4	0	3	1	0	0	1	.000	0	0-0	0	10.35	7.88
04	Tex	AL	4	4	0	0	19.0	94	23	13	13	2	0	3	0	16	0	6	1	0	1	3	.250	0	0-0	0	7.21	6.16
14 ML YEARS			380	364	51	8	2349.1	10227	2573	1294	1193	226	66	70	100	858	30	1250	68	3	142	136	.511	17	0-0	0	4.66	4.57

Darin Erstad

Bats: L **Throws:** L **Pos:** 1B-147; DH-5; PR-1   **Ht:** 6'2" **Wt:** 220 **Born:** 6/4/1974 **Age:** 32

Year	Team	Lg	G	AB	H	2B	3B	HR	(Hm	Rd)	TB	R	RBI	RC	TBB	IBB	SO	HBP	SH	SF	SB	CS	SB%	GDP	Avg	OBP	Slg
1996	CAL	AL	57	208	59	5	1	4	(1	3)	78	34	20	26	17	1	29	0	1	3	3	3	.50	3	.284	.333	.375
1997	ANA	AL	139	539	161	34	4	16	(8	8)	251	99	77	92	51	4	86	4	5	6	23	8	.74	5	.299	.360	.466
1998	ANA	AL	133	537	159	39	3	19	(9	10)	261	84	82	94	43	7	77	6	1	3	20	6	.77	2	.296	.353	.486
1999	ANA	AL	142	585	148	22	5	13	(7	6)	219	84	53	64	47	3	101	1	2	3	13	7	.65	16	.253	.308	.374
2000	ANA	AL	157	676	240	39	6	25	(11	14)	366	121	100	145	64	9	82	1	2	4	28	8	.78	8	.355	.409	.541
2001	ANA	AL	157	631	163	35	1	9	(3	6)	227	89	63	79	62	7	113	10	1	7	24	10	.71	8	.258	.331	.360
2002	ANA	AL	150	625	177	28	4	10	(2	8)	243	99	73	74	27	4	67	2	5	4	23	3	.88	9	.283	.313	.389
2003	ANA	AL	67	258	65	7	1	4	(1	3)	86	35	17	22	18	1	40	4	2	2	9	1	.90	8	.252	.309	.333
2004	ANA	AL	125	495	146	29	1	7	(3	4)	198	79	69	76	37	1	74	4	3	4	16	1	.94	9	.295	.346	.400
2005	LAA	AL	153	609	166	33	3	7	(4	3)	226	86	66	79	47	3	109	1	4	2	10	3	.77	8	.273	.325	.371
10 ML YEARS			1280	5163	1484	271	29	114	(49	65)	2155	810	620	751	413	40	778	33	26	38	169	50	.77	76	.287	.342	.417

Felix Escalona

Bats: R **Throws:** R **Pos:** SS-5; 3B-3; 1B-1; 2B-1; PR-1   **Ht:** 6'0" **Wt:** 196 **Born:** 3/12/1979 **Age:** 27

Year	Team	Lg	G	AB	H	2B	3B	HR	(Hm	Rd)	TB	R	RBI	RC	TBB	IBB	SO	HBP	SH	SF	SB	CS	SB%	GDP	Avg	OBP	Slg
2005	Clmbs*	AAA	91	307	84	14	1	7	(-	-)	121	42	45	49	28	3	58	18	10	5	5	0	1.00	3	.274	.363	.394
2002	TB	AL	59	157	34	8	2	0	(0	0)	46	17	9	12	3	0	44	7	3	1	7	2	.78	2	.217	.262	.293
2003	TB	AL	10	27	5	2	0	0	(0	0)	7	2	2	3	2	0	6	0	0	0	1	0	1.00	0	.185	.241	.259
2004	NYA	AL	5	8	0	0	0	0	(0	0)	0	1	0	0	0	0	2	1	0	0	0	0	-	0	.000	.111	.000
2005	NYA	AL	10	14	4	1	0	0	(0	0)	5	0	2	2	1	0	4	1	1	0	0	0	-	1	.286	.375	.357
4 ML YEARS			84	206	43	11	2	0	(0	0)	58	20	13	17	6	0	56	9	4	1	8	2	.80	3	.209	.261	.282

Alex Escobar

Bats: R **Throws:** R **Pos:** OF   **Ht:** 6'1" **Wt:** 180 **Born:** 9/6/1978 **Age:** 27

Year	Team	Lg	G	AB	H	2B	3B	HR	(Hm	Rd)	TB	R	RBI	RC	TBB	IBB	SO	HBP	SH	SF	SB	CS	SB%	GDP	Avg	OBP	Slg
2001	NYN	NL	18	50	10	1	0	3	(3	0)	20	3	8	5	3	0	19	0	0	0	1	0	1.00	1	.200	.245	.400
2003	CLE	AL	28	99	27	2	0	5	(4	1)	44	16	14	9	7	1	33	1	0	1	1	0	1.00	1	.273	.324	.444
2004	CLE	AL	46	152	32	8	2	1	(0	1)	47	20	12	17	23	0	42	1	3	0	1	1	.50	1	.211	.318	.309
3 ML YEARS			92	301	69	11	2	9	(7	2)	111	39	34	31	33	1	94	2	3	1	3	1	.75	2	.229	.309	.369

Kelvim Escobar

Pitches: R **Bats:** R **Pos:** RP-9; SP-7   **Ht:** 6'1" **Wt:** 210 **Born:** 4/11/1976 **Age:** 30

Year	Team	Lg	G	GS	CG	GF	IP	BFP	H	R	ER	HR	SH	SF	HB	TBB	IBB	SO	WP	Bk	W	L	Pct	ShO	Sv-Op	Hld	ERC	ERA
2005	RCuca*	A+	1	1	0	0	3.0	12	1	0	0	0	0	0	0	2	0	7	0	0	0	0	-	0	0--	-	1.26	0.00
2005	Salt Lk*	AAA	4	4	0	0	14.1	65	14	4	4	2	0	0	1	8	0	22	1	0	1	0	1.000	0	0--	-	5.12	2.51
1997	TOR	AL	27	0	0	23	31.0	139	28	12	10	1	2	0	0	19	2	36	0	0	3	2	.600	0	14-17	1	3.68	2.90
1998	TOR	AL	22	10	0	2	79.2	342	72	37	33	5	0	3	0	35	0	72	0	0	7	3	.700	0	0-1	5	3.41	3.73
1999	TOR	AL	33	30	1	2	174.0	795	203	118	110	19	2	8	10	81	2	129	6	1	14	11	.560	0	0-0	0	5.62	5.69
2000	TOR	AL	43	24	3	8	180.0	794	186	118	107	26	5	4	3	85	3	142	4	0	10	15	.400	1	2-3	3	4.94	5.35
2001	TOR	AL	59	11	1	15	126.0	517	93	51	49	8	2	5	3	52	5	121	2	0	6	8	.429	1	0-0	13	2.54	3.50
2002	TOR	AL	76	0	0	68	78.0	355	75	39	37	10	1	0	5	44	6	85	4	0	5	7	.417	0	38-46	0	4.77	4.27
2003	TOR	AL	41	26	1	12	180.1	797	189	94	86	15	5	5	9	78	3	159	9	0	13	9	.591	0	4-5	0	4.53	4.29
2004	ANA	AL	33	33	0	0	208.1	878	192	91	91	21	3	6	7	76	2	191	9	0	11	12	.478	0	0-0	0	3.65	3.93
2005	LAA	AL	16	7	0	2	59.2	242	45	21	20	4	2	0	2	21	1	63	4	0	3	2	.600	0	1-1	2	2.51	3.02
9 ML YEARS			350	141	6	132	1117.0	4859	1083	581	543	109	22	31	39	491	24	998	38	1	72	69	.511	3	59-73	24	4.15	4.38

Mike Esposito

Pitches: R **Bats:** R **Pos:** SP-3   **Ht:** 6'0" **Wt:** 190 **Born:** 9/27/1981 **Age:** 24

Year	Team	Lg	G	GS	CG	GF	IP	BFP	H	R	ER	HR	SH	SF	HB	TBB	IBB	SO	WP	Bk	W	L	Pct	ShO	Sv-Op	Hld	ERC	ERA
2003	Visalia	A+	27	27	1	0	161.0	716	173	83	67	14	7	2	5	55	0	116	10	2	12	6	.667	0	0--	-	4.19	3.75
2004	Tulsa	AA	24	24	1	0	143.1	603	138	57	53	12	5	3	4	35	1	90	8	0	10	6	.625	0	0--	-	3.21	3.33
2005	ColSpr	AAA	27	27	0	0	155.2	705	197	110	95	20	7	4	8	41	3	94	5	0	8	9	.471	0	0--	-	5.38	5.49
2005	COL	NL	3	3	0	0	14.2	73	21	11	11	3	1	0	0	9	1	5	0	0	0	2	.000	0	0-0	-	8.33	6.75

Shawn Estes

Pitches: L Bats: R Pos: SP-21   Ht: 6'2" Wt: 200 Born: 2/18/1973 Age: 33

			HOW MUCH HE PITCHED						WHAT HE GAVE UP										THE RESULTS							
Year	Team	Lg	G	GS	CG	GF	IP	BFP	H	R	ER	HR	SH	SF	HB	TBB	IBB	SO	WP	Bk	W	L	Pct	ShO	Sv-Op	Hld	ERC	ERA
2005	Tucsn*	AAA	2	2	0	0	11.0	42	5	2	2	1	0	0	0	4	0	9	1	0	0	0	-	0	0- -	-	1.35	1.64
1995	SF	NL	3	3	0	0	17.1	76	16	14	13	2	0	0	1	5	0	14	4	0	0	3	.000	0	0-0	0	3.37	6.75
1996	SF	NL	11	11	0	0	70.0	305	63	30	28	3	5	0	2	39	3	60	4	0	3	5	.375	0	0-0	0	3.78	3.60
1997	SF	NL	32	32	3	0	201.0	849	162	80	71	12	13	2	8	100	2	181	10	2	19	5	.792	2	0-0	0	3.28	3.18
1998	SF	NL	25	25	1	0	149.1	661	150	89	84	14	15	4	5	80	6	136	6	1	7	12	.368	1	0-0	0	4.71	5.06
1999	SF	NL	32	32	1	0	203.0	914	209	121	111	21	14	3	5	112	2	159	15	1	11	11	.500	1	0-0	0	4.96	4.92
2000	SF	NL	30	30	4	0	190.1	829	194	99	90	11	7	6	3	108	1	136	11	0	15	6	.714	2	0-0	0	4.75	4.26
2001	SF	NL	27	27	0	0	159.0	693	151	78	71	11	5	9	5	77	7	109	10	2	9	8	.529	0	0-0	0	3.96	4.02
2002	2 Tms	NL	29	29	1	0	160.2	713	171	94	91	13	7	6	9	83	9	109	3	1	5	12	.294	0	0-0	0	5.00	5.10
2003	CHN	NL	29	28	1	0	152.1	699	182	113	97	20	11	7	1	83	1	103	6	0	8	11	.421	1	0-0	0	6.15	5.73
2004	COL	NL	34	34	1	0	202.0	904	223	133	131	30	13	8	11	105	5	117	4	2	15	8	.652	0	0-0	0	5.86	5.84
2005	ARI	NL	21	21	2	0	123.2	535	132	70	66	15	10	4	4	45	0	63	4	0	7	8	.467	0	0-0	0	4.65	4.80
02	NYM	NL	23	23	1	0	132.2	580	133	70	67	12	7	4	5	66	9	92	2	1	4	9	.308	1	0-0	0	4.51	4.55
02	Cin	NL	6	6	0	0	28.0	133	38	24	24	1	0	2	4	17	0	17	1	0	1	3	.250	0	0-0	0	7.52	7.71
	11 ML YEARS		273	272	14	0	1628.2	7178	1653	921	853	152	100	49	54	837	36	1187	77	9	99	89	.527	8	0-0	0	4.72	4.71

Johnny Estrada

Bats: B Throws: R Pos: C-104; PH-3   Ht: 5'11" Wt: 209 Born: 6/27/1976 Age: 30

			BATTING																		BASERUNNING				AVERAGES		
Year	Team	Lg	G	AB	H	2B	3B	HR	(Hm	Rd)	TB	R	RBI	RC	TBB	IBB	SO	HBP	SH	SF	SB	CS	SB%	GDP	Avg	OBP	Slg
2001	PHI	NL	89	298	68	15	0	8	(7	1)	107	26	37	25	16	6	32	4	2	4	0	0	-	15	.228	.273	.359
2002	PHI	NL	10	17	2	1	0	0	(0	0)	3	0	2	0	2	1	2	0	0	0	0	0	-	0	.118	.211	.176
2003	ATL	NL	16	36	11	0	0	0	(0	0)	11	2	2	2	0	0	3	0	0	0	0	0	-	0	.306	.359	.306
2004	ATL	NL	134	462	145	36	0	9	(4	5)	208	56	76	78	39	7	66	11	1	4	0	0	-	18	.314	.378	.450
2005	ATL	NL	105	357	93	26	0	4	(2	2)	131	31	39	36	20	6	38	3	0	3	0	0	-	13	.261	.303	.367
	5 ML YEARS		354	1170	319	78	0	21	(13	8)	460	115	156	141	77	20	141	21	3	11	0	0	-	47	.273	.326	.393

Seth Etherton

Pitches: R Bats: R Pos: SP-3   Ht: 6'1" Wt: 200 Born: 10/17/1976 Age: 29

			HOW MUCH HE PITCHED						WHAT HE GAVE UP										THE RESULTS							
Year	Team	Lg	G	GS	CG	GF	IP	BFP	H	R	ER	HR	SH	SF	HB	TBB	IBB	SO	WP	Bk	W	L	Pct	ShO	Sv-Op	Hld	ERC	ERA
2005	Scrmto*	AAA	20	19	0	1	112.1	460	93	44	34	11	2	2	3	30	1	99	2	1	7	7	.500	0	0- -	-	2.70	2.72
2000	ANA	AL	11	11	0	0	60.1	270	68	38	37	16	0	0	0	22	0	32	0	0	5	1	.833	0	0-0	0	5.77	5.52
2003	CIN	NL	7	7	0	0	30.0	145	39	23	23	4	3	3	3	15	1	17	0	0	2	4	.333	0	0-0	0	6.85	6.90
2005	OAK	AL	3	3	0	0	17.2	74	16	13	13	4	0	1	0	5	0	10	1	1	1	1	.500	0	0-0	0	3.84	6.62
	3 ML YEARS		21	21	0	0	108.0	489	123	74	73	24	3	4	3	42	1	59	1	1	8	6	.571	0	0-0	0	5.76	6.08

Dana Eveland

Pitches: L Bats: L Pos: RP-27   Ht: 6'1" Wt: 220 Born: 10/29/1983 Age: 22

			HOW MUCH HE PITCHED						WHAT HE GAVE UP										THE RESULTS							
Year	Team	Lg	G	GS	CG	GF	IP	BFP	H	R	ER	HR	SH	SF	HB	TBB	IBB	SO	WP	Bk	W	L	Pct	ShO	Sv-Op	Hld	ERC	ERA
2003	Helena	R+	19	0	0	18	26.0	116	30	9	6	1	4	3	2	8	1	41	5	1	2	1	.667	0	14- -	-	4.33	2.08
2004	Beloit	A	22	16	1	4	117.1	484	108	48	37	8	4	5	4	24	0	119	2	0	9	6	.600	0	2- -	-	2.80	2.84
2004	Huntsvl	AA	4	4	0	0	23.2	98	23	9	6	0	5	1	1	4	0	14	1	0	2	0	.000	0	0- -	-	2.54	2.28
2005	Huntsvl	AA	18	18	0	0	109.0	461	96	42	33	4	4	2	4	38	1	98	7	2	10	4	.714	0	0- -	-	2.90	2.72
2005	MIL	NL	27	0	0	3	31.2	146	40	21	21	2	0	1	1	18	3	23	1	0	1	1	.500	0	1-2	7	6.16	5.97

Adam Everett

Bats: R Throws: R Pos: SS-150; PH-2; PR-2   Ht: 6'0" Wt: 156 Born: 2/5/1977 Age: 29

			BATTING																		BASERUNNING				AVERAGES		
Year	Team	Lg	G	AB	H	2B	3B	HR	(Hm	Rd)	TB	R	RBI	RC	TBB	IBB	SO	HBP	SH	SF	SB	CS	SB%	GDP	Avg	OBP	Slg
2001	HOU	NL	9	3	0	0	0	0	(0	0)	0	1	0	0	0	0	1	0	0	0	1	0	1.00	0	.000	.000	.000
2002	HOU	NL	40	88	17	3	0	0	(0	0)	20	11	4	6	12	1	19	1	2	0	3	0	1.00	1	.193	.297	.227
2003	HOU	NL	128	387	99	18	3	8	(5	3)	147	51	51	50	28	6	66	9	11	1	8	1	.89	7	.256	.320	.380
2004	HOU	NL	104	384	105	15	2	8	(5	3)	148	66	31	51	17	0	56	9	22	3	13	2	.87	4	.273	.317	.385
2005	HOU	NL	152	549	136	27	2	11	(7	4)	200	58	54	61	26	1	103	8	8	4	21	7	.75	5	.248	.290	.364
	5 ML YEARS		433	1411	357	63	7	27	(17	10)	515	187	140	168	83	8	245	27	43	8	46	10	.82	17	.253	.305	.365

Carl Everett

Bats: B Throws: R Pos: DH-107; LF-14; RF-8; PH-8   Ht: 6'0" Wt: 215 Born: 6/3/1971 Age: 35

			BATTING																		BASERUNNING				AVERAGES		
Year	Team	Lg	G	AB	H	2B	3B	HR	(Hm	Rd)	TB	R	RBI	RC	TBB	IBB	SO	HBP	SH	SF	SB	CS	SB%	GDP	Avg	OBP	Slg
1993	FLA	NL	11	19	2	0	0	0	(0	0)	2	0	0	0	1	0	9	0	0	0	1	0	1.00	0	.105	.150	.105
1994	FLA	NL	16	51	11	1	0	2	(2	0)	18	7	6	5	3	0	15	0	0	0	4	0	1.00	0	.216	.259	.353
1995	NYN	NL	79	289	75	13	1	12	(9	3)	126	48	54	41	39	2	67	2	1	0	2	5	.29	11	.260	.352	.436
1996	NYN	NL	101	192	46	8	1	1	(1	0)	59	29	16	21	21	2	53	4	1	1	6	0	1.00	4	.240	.326	.307
1997	NYN	NL	142	443	110	28	3	14	(11	3)	186	58	57	58	32	3	102	7	3	2	17	9	.65	7	.248	.308	.420
1998	HOU	NL	133	467	138	34	4	15	(4	11)	225	72	76	76	44	2	102	3	3	2	14	12	.54	11	.296	.359	.482
1999	HOU	NL	123	464	151	33	3	25	(11	14)	265	86	108	105	50	5	94	11	2	8	27	7	.79	5	.325	.398	.571
2000	BOS	AL	137	496	149	32	4	34	(17	17)	291	82	108	106	52	5	113	4	0	5	11	4	.73	4	.300	.373	.587
2001	BOS	AL	102	409	105	24	4	14	(6	8)	179	61	58	59	27	3	104	13	0	0	9	2	.82	3	.257	.323	.438
2002	TEX	AL	105	374	100	16	0	16	(11	5)	164	47	62	60	33	4	77	6	1	7	2	3	.40	7	.267	.333	.439

Year	Team	Lg	G	AB	H	2B	3B	HR	Hm	Rd	TB	R	RBI	RC	TBB	IBB	SO	HBP	SH	SF	SB	CS	SB%	GDP	Avg	OBP	Slg
2003	2 Tms	AL	147	526	151	27	3	28	(15	13)	268	93	92	102	53	6	84	15	4	4	8	4	.67	7	.287	.366	.510
2004	2 Tms	AL	82	281	73	17	1	7	(3	4)	113	29	35	37	16	3	45	10	0	3	1	0	1.00	1	.260	.319	.402
2005	CHA	AL	135	490	123	17	2	23	(15	8)	213	58	87	71	42	2	99	5	0	10	4	5	.44	11	.251	.311	.435
03	Tex	AL	74	270	74	13	3	18	(10	8)	147	53	51	57	31	2	48	5	4	3	4	1	.80	2	.274	.356	.544
03	CWS	AL	73	256	77	14	0	10	(5	5)	121	40	41	45	22	4	36	10	0	1	4	3	.57	5	.301	.377	.473
04	Mon	NL	39	127	32	10	0	2	(1	1)	48	8	14	13	8	2	19	5	0	1	0	0	-	8	.252	.319	.378
04	CWS	AL	43	154	41	7	1	5	(2	3)	65	21	21	24	8	1	26	5	0	2	1	0	1.00	3	.266	.320	.422
13 ML YEARS			1313	4501	1234	250	26	191	(106	85)	2109	670	759	741	413	37	964	84	15	39	106	51	.68	77	.274	.344	.469

Scott Eyre

Pitches: L Bats: L Pos: RP-86
Ht: 6'1" Wt: 210 Born: 5/30/1972 Age: 34

Year	Team	Lg	G	GS	CG	GF	IP	BFP	H	R	ER	HR	SH	SF	HB	TBB	IBB	SO	WP	Bk	W	L	Pct	ShO	Sv-Op	Hld	ERC	ERA
1997	CHA	AL	11	11	0	0	60.2	267	62	36	34	11	1	2	1	31	1	36	2	0	4	4	.500	0	0-0	0	5.37	5.04
1998	CHA	AL	33	17	0	10	107.0	491	114	78	64	24	2	3	2	64	0	73	7	0	3	8	.273	0	0-0	0	6.31	5.38
1999	CHA	AL	21	0	0	8	25.0	129	38	22	21	6	0	1	1	15	2	17	1	0	1	1	.500	0	0-0	1	9.23	7.56
2000	CHA	AL	13	1	0	3	19.0	93	29	15	14	3	0	2	1	12	0	16	0	0	1	1	.500	0	0-0	0	9.49	6.63
2001	TOR	AL	17	0	0	5	15.2	66	15	6	6	1	0	1	1	7	2	16	2	0	1	2	.333	0	2-3	3	3.96	3.45
2002	2 Tms		70	3	0	6	74.2	333	80	41	37	4	2	4	0	36	8	58	5	0	2	4	.333	0	0-1	18	4.26	4.46
2003	SF	NL	74	0	0	10	57.0	256	60	23	21	4	2	3	1	26	0	35	6	0	2	1	.667	0	1-3	20	4.37	3.32
2004	SF	NL	83	0	0	12	52.2	229	43	26	24	8	3	3	0	27	3	49	3	0	2	2	.500	0	1-5	23	3.67	4.10
2005	SF	NL	86	0	0	15	68.1	278	48	21	20	3	4	3	4	26	0	65	3	0	2	2	.500	0	0-2	32	2.31	2.63
02	Tor	AL	49	3	0	3	63.1	283	69	37	35	4	2	4	0	29	7	51	4	0	2	4	.333	0	0-1	12	4.32	4.97
02	SF	NL	21	0	0	3	11.1	50	11	4	2	0	0	0	0	7	1	7	1	0	0	0	-	0	0-0	6	3.91	1.59
9 ML YEARS			408	32	0	69	480.0	2142	489	268	241	64	14	22	11	244	16	365	29	0	18	25	.419	0	4-14	97	4.89	4.52

Brian Falkenborg

Pitches: R Bats: R Pos: RP-10
Ht: 6'6" Wt: 190 Born: 1/18/1978 Age: 28

Year	Team	Lg	G	GS	CG	GF	IP	BFP	H	R	ER	HR	SH	SF	HB	TBB	IBB	SO	WP	Bk	W	L	Pct	ShO	Sv-Op	Hld	ERC	ERA
2005	Portlnd*	AAA	28	0	0	2	36.0	165	35	25	21	2	0	1	2	21	1	26	0	0	3	4	.429	0	1-	-	4.39	5.25
2005	Memp*	AAA	13	0	0	6	16.0	63	10	3	3	1	0	0	1	5	0	14	0	0	1	0	1.000	0	5-	-	1.86	1.69
1999	BAL	AL	2	0	0	0	3.0	12	2	0	0	0	0	0	0	2	0	1	0	0	0	0	-	0	0-0	0	2.79	0.00
2004	LA	NL	6	0	0	1	14.1	73	19	14	12	2	2	0	3	9	0	11	1	0	1	0	1.000	0	0-0	0	8.19	7.53
2005	SD	NL	10	0	0	3	11.0	54	17	11	10	2	0	0	0	5	1	10	2	0	0	0	-	0	0-0	0	8.14	8.18
3 ML YEARS			18	0	0	4	28.1	139	38	25	22	4	2	0	3	16	1	22	3	0	1	0	1.000	0	0-0	0	7.55	6.99

Kyle Farnsworth

Pitches: R Bats: R Pos: RP-72
Ht: 6'4" Wt: 235 Born: 4/14/1976 Age: 30

Year	Team	Lg	G	GS	CG	GF	IP	BFP	H	R	ER	HR	SH	SF	HB	TBB	IBB	SO	WP	Bk	W	L	Pct	ShO	Sv-Op	Hld	ERC	ERA
1999	CHN	NL	27	21	1	1	130.0	579	140	80	73	28	6	2	3	52	1	70	7	1	5	9	.357	1	0-0	0	5.39	5.05
2000	CHN	NL	46	5	0	8	77.0	371	90	58	55	14	4	4	4	50	8	74	3	0	2	9	.182	0	1-6	6	6.72	6.43
2001	CHN	NL	76	0	0	24	82.0	339	65	26	25	8	2	2	1	29	2	107	2	2	4	6	.400	0	2-3	24	2.76	2.74
2002	CHN	NL	45	0	0	17	46.2	213	53	47	38	9	2	5	1	24	7	46	1	0	4	6	.400	0	1-7	6	5.89	7.33
2003	CHN	NL	77	0	0	13	76.1	312	53	31	28	6	4	1	0	36	1	92	6	0	3	2	.600	0	0-3	19	2.58	3.30
2004	CHN	NL	72	0	0	25	66.2	298	67	39	35	10	5	0	2	33	1	78	1	0	4	5	.444	0	0-4	18	4.91	4.73
2005	2 Tms		72	0	0	34	70.0	277	44	18	17	5	2	1	3	27	0	87	3	1	1	1	.500	0	16-18	19	2.12	2.19
05	Det	AL	46	0	0	16	42.2	174	29	12	11	1	1	1	1	20	0	55	2	0	1	1	.500	0	6-8	15	2.26	2.32
05	Atl	NL	26	0	0	18	27.1	103	15	6	6	4	1	0	2	7	0	32	1	1	0	0	-	0	10-10	4	1.86	1.98
7 ML YEARS			415	26	1	122	548.2	2389	512	299	271	80	25	15	14	251	20	554	23	4	23	38	.377	1	20-41	92	4.27	4.45

Sal Fasano

Bats: R Throws: R Pos: C-60; DH-3; PH-3; 1B-1
Ht: 6'2" Wt: 254 Born: 8/10/1971 Age: 34

Year	Team	Lg	G	AB	H	2B	3B	HR	Hm	Rd	TB	R	RBI	RC	TBB	IBB	SO	HBP	SH	SF	SB	CS	SB%	GDP	Avg	OBP	Slg
2005	Ottawa*	AAA	14	45	12	3	0	4	(-	-)	27	6	12	8	2	0	15	2	0	1	0	0	-	1	.267	.327	.600
1996	KC	AL	51	143	29	2	0	6	(1	5)	49	20	19	13	14	0	25	2	1	0	1	1	.50	3	.203	.283	.343
1997	KC	AL	13	38	8	2	0	1	(0	1)	13	4	1	2	1	0	12	0	0	0	0	0	-	1	.211	.231	.342
1998	KC	AL	74	216	49	10	0	8	(4	4)	83	21	31	26	10	1	56	16	3	2	1	0	1.00	4	.227	.307	.384
1999	KC	AL	23	60	14	2	0	5	(2	3)	31	11	16	16	7	0	17	7	0	1	0	1	.00	1	.233	.373	.517
2000	OAK	AL	52	126	27	6	0	7	(3	4)	54	21	19	16	14	0	47	3	0	1	0	0	-	3	.214	.306	.429
2001	3 Tms		39	85	17	5	0	3	(3	0)	31	12	9	10	5	0	31	4	2	0	0	0	-	3	.200	.277	.365
2002	ANA	AL	2	1	0	0	0	0	(0	0)	0	0	0	0	0	0	1	0	0	0	0	0	-	0	.000	.000	.000
2005	BAL	AL	64	160	40	3	0	11	(1	10)	76	25	20	17	9	0	41	5	0	0	0	0	-	5	.250	.310	.475
01	Oak	AL	11	21	1	0	0	0	(0	0)	1	2	0	0	1	0	12	1	0	0	0	0	-	1	.048	.130	.048
01	KC	AL	3	1	0	0	0	0	(0	0)	0	0	0	0	0	0	0	0	0	0	0	0	-	1	.000	.000	.000
01	Col	NL	25	63	16	5	0	3	(3	0)	30	10	9	10	4	0	19	3	2	0	0	0	-	1	.254	.329	.476
8 ML YEARS			318	829	184	30	0	41	(15	26)	337	114	115	96	60	1	230	37	6	4	2	2	.50	20	.222	.302	.407

Jeff Fassero

Pitches: L Bats: L Pos: RP-42; SP-6   Ht: 6'1" Wt: 200 Born: 1/5/1963 Age: 43

			HOW MUCH HE PITCHED						WHAT HE GAVE UP										THE RESULTS							
Year	Team	Lg	G	GS	CG	GF	IP	BFP	H	R	ER	HR	SH	SF	HB	TBB	IBB	SO	WP	Bk	W	L	Pct	ShO	Sv-Op	Hld	ERC	ERA
1991	MON	NL	51	0	0	30	55.1	223	39	17	15	1	6	0	1	17	1	42	4	0	2	5	.286	0	8-11	7	1.75	2.44
1992	MON	NL	70	0	0	22	85.2	368	81	35	27	1	5	2	2	34	6	63	7	1	8	7	.533	0	1-7	12	3.10	2.84
1993	MON	NL	56	15	1	10	149.2	616	119	50	38	7	7	4	0	54	0	140	5	0	12	5	.706	0	1-3	6	2.48	2.29
1994	MON	NL	21	21	1	0	138.2	569	119	54	46	13	7	2	1	40	4	119	6	0	8	6	.571	0	0-0	0	2.82	2.99
1995	MON	NL	30	30	1	0	189.0	833	207	102	91	15	19	7	2	74	3	164	7	1	13	14	.481	0	0-0	0	4.43	4.33
1996	MON	NL	34	34	5	0	231.2	967	217	95	85	20	16	5	3	55	3	222	5	2	15	11	.577	1	0-0	0	3.00	3.30
1997	SEA	AL	35	35	2	0	234.1	1010	226	100	94	21	7	10	3	84	6	189	13	2	16	9	.640	1	0-0	0	3.60	3.61
1998	SEA	AL	32	32	7	0	224.2	954	223	115	99	33	8	8	10	66	2	176	12	0	13	12	.520	0	0-0	0	4.10	3.97
1999	2 Tms	AL	37	27	0	2	156.1	751	208	135	125	35	2	7	4	83	3	114	9	0	5	14	.263	0	0-0	2	7.69	7.20
2000	BOS	AL	38	23	0	4	130.0	577	153	72	69	16	7	2	1	50	2	97	2	0	8	8	.500	0	0-0	5	5.25	4.78
2001	CHN	NL	82	0	0	30	73.2	308	66	31	28	6	1	2	1	23	5	79	3	0	4	4	.500	0	12-17	25	2.97	3.42
2002	2 Tms	NL	73	0	0	18	69.0	315	81	43	41	9	7	1	3	27	5	56	2	1	8	6	.571	0	0-3	13	5.25	5.35
2003	STL	NL	62	6	0	15	77.2	354	93	51	49	17	3	1	2	34	4	55	2	0	1	7	.125	0	3-6	11	6.34	5.68
2004	2 Tms	NL	41	12	0	2	112.0	508	136	73	68	9	5	7	4	44	5	60	4	1	3	8	.273	0	0-0	2	5.20	5.46
2005	SF	NL	48	6	0	11	91.0	384	92	48	41	7	7	3	0	31	1	60	3	0	4	7	.364	0	0-2	2	3.77	4.05
99	Sea	AL	30	24	0	1	139.0	669	188	123	114	34	1	6	4	73	3	101	7	0	4	14	.222	0	0-0	2	8.02	7.38
99	Tex	AL	7	3	0	1	17.1	82	20	12	11	1	1	1	0	10	0	13	2	0	1	0	1.000	0	0-0	0	5.21	5.71
02	ChC	NL	57	0	0	17	51.0	240	65	37	35	5	6	1	3	22	5	44	2	1	5	6	.455	0	0-1	6	5.79	6.18
02	StL	NL	16	0	0	1	18.0	75	16	6	6	4	1	0	0	5	0	12	0	0	3	0	1.000	0	0-2	7	3.91	3.00
04	Col	NL	40	12	0	2	111.0	505	136	73	68	9	5	7	4	44	5	59	4	1	3	8	.273	0	0-0	2	5.29	5.51
04	Ari	NL	1	0	0	0	1.0	3	0	0	0	0	0	0	0	0	0	1	0	0	0	0	-	0	0-0	0	0.00	0.00
15 ML YEARS			710	241	17	144	2018.2	8737	2060	1029	916	210	107	61	37	716	50	1636	84	8	120	123	.494	2	25-49	85	4.04	4.08

Scott Feldman

Pitches: R Bats: L Pos: RP-8   Ht: 6'5" Wt: 210 Born: 2/7/1983 Age: 23

			HOW MUCH HE PITCHED						WHAT HE GAVE UP										THE RESULTS							
Year	Team	Lg	G	GS	CG	GF	IP	BFP	H	R	ER	HR	SH	SF	HB	TBB	IBB	SO	WP	Bk	W	L	Pct	ShO	Sv-Op	Hld	ERC	ERA
2003	Rngrs	R	3	1	0	0	6.1	24	4	6	3	0	0	1	1	1	0	7	0	0	1	1	.500	0	0--	-	1.49	4.26
2004	Rngrs	R	4	3	0	0	7.0	24	2	0	0	0	0	1	0	1	0	5	0	0	0	0	-	0	0--	-	0.34	0.00
2005	Frisco	AA	46	0	0	34	61.0	249	43	18	16	3	3	0	0	23	8	41	5	0	1	2	.333	0	14--	-	1.93	2.36
2005	Bkrsfld	A+	6	0	0	0	9.0	34	5	2	0	0	0	0	0	2	0	11	1	0	0	0	-	0	3--	-	1.28	0.00
2005	TEX	AL	8	0	0	3	9.1	37	9	1	1	0	0	0	0	2	1	4	0	0	0	1	.000	0	0-0	1	2.48	0.96

Pedro Feliz

Bats: R Throws: R Pos: 3B-79; LF-75; 1B-15; PH-8   Ht: 6'1" Wt: 205 Born: 4/27/1975 Age: 31

			BATTING																		BASERUNNING				AVERAGES		
Year	Team	Lg	G	AB	H	2B	3B	HR	(Hm	Rd)	TB	R	RBI	RC	TBB	IBB	SO	HBP	SH	SF	SB	CS	SB%	GDP	Avg	OBP	Slg
2000	SF	NL	8	7	2	0	0	0	(0	0)	2	1	0	1	0	0	1	0	0	0	0	0	-	0	.286	.286	.286
2001	SF	NL	94	220	50	9	1	7	(3	4)	82	23	22	20	10	2	50	2	3	3	2	1	.67	5	.227	.264	.373
2002	SF	NL	67	146	37	4	1	2	(1	1)	49	14	13	12	6	1	27	0	0	1	0	0	-	2	.253	.281	.336
2003	SF	NL	95	235	58	9	3	16	(6	10)	121	31	48	34	10	0	53	1	1	2	2	2	.50	7	.247	.278	.515
2004	SF	NL	144	503	139	33	3	22	(11	11)	244	72	84	56	23	1	85	0	0	5	5	2	.71	18	.276	.305	.485
2005	SF	NL	156	569	142	30	4	20	(10	10)	240	69	81	58	38	1	102	1	1	6	0	2	.00	20	.250	.295	.422
6 ML YEARS			564	1680	428	85	12	67	(31	36)	738	210	248	181	87	5	318	4	5	17	9	7	.56	52	.255	.290	.439

Robert Fick

Bats: L Throws: R Pos: PH-34; 1B-29; C-28; RF-9; LF-4; DH-2; 3B-1   Ht: 6'1" Wt: 200 Born: 3/15/1974 Age: 32

			BATTING																		BASERUNNING				AVERAGES		
Year	Team	Lg	G	AB	H	2B	3B	HR	(Hm	Rd)	TB	R	RBI	RC	TBB	IBB	SO	HBP	SH	SF	SB	CS	SB%	GDP	Avg	OBP	Slg
2005	Portlnd*	AAA	10	32	12	1	0	3	(-	-)	22	5	11	11	10	1	3	1	0	1	1	0	1.00	1	.375	.523	.688
1998	DET	AL	7	22	8	1	0	3	(0	3)	18	6	7	6	2	0	7	0	0	0	1	0	1.00	1	.364	.417	.818
1999	DET	AL	15	41	9	0	0	3	(1	2)	18	6	10	6	7	0	6	0	0	1	1	0	1.00	1	.220	.327	.439
2000	DET	AL	66	163	41	7	2	3	(0	3)	61	18	22	21	22	2	39	1	0	2	2	1	.67	4	.252	.340	.374
2001	DET	AL	124	401	109	21	2	19	(8	11)	191	62	61	62	39	3	62	4	0	4	0	3	.00	10	.272	.339	.476
2002	DET	AL	148	556	150	36	2	17	(12	5)	241	66	63	70	46	4	90	7	0	5	0	1	.00	17	.270	.331	.433
2003	ATL	NL	126	409	110	26	1	11	(4	7)	171	52	80	68	42	4	47	2	0	7	1	0	1.00	9	.269	.335	.418
2004	2 Tms		89	226	45	5	2	6	(3	3)	72	14	26	22	22	2	36	3	0	2	0	0	-	0	.199	.277	.319
2005	SD	NL	93	230	61	10	2	3	(0	3)	84	25	30	29	26	2	33	1	1	2	0	2	.00	4	.265	.340	.365
04	TB	AL	76	214	43	5	2	6	(3	3)	70	12	26	21	20	2	32	2	0	2	0	0	-	0	.201	.273	.327
04	SD	NL	13	12	2	0	0	0	(0	0)	2	2	0	1	2	0	4	1	0	0	0	0	-	0	.167	.333	.167
8 ML YEARS			668	2048	533	106	11	65	(28	37)	856	249	299	284	206	17	320	18	1	23	5	7	.42	48	.260	.330	.418

Nate Field

Pitches: R Bats: R Pos: RP-7   Ht: 6'2" Wt: 200 Born: 12/11/1975 Age: 30

			HOW MUCH HE PITCHED						WHAT HE GAVE UP										THE RESULTS							
Year	Team	Lg	G	GS	CG	GF	IP	BFP	H	R	ER	HR	SH	SF	HB	TBB	IBB	SO	WP	Bk	W	L	Pct	ShO	Sv-Op	Hld	ERC	ERA
2005	Omha*	AAA	16	0	0	6	22.0	106	26	12	12	1	2	1	0	14	1	24	2	1	1	0	1.000	0	0--	-	5.42	4.91
2002	KC	AL	5	0	0	0	5.0	26	8	5	5	2	1	0	0	3	1	3	2	0	0	0	-	0	0-0	0	10.82	9.00
2003	KC	AL	19	0	0	7	21.2	97	19	10	10	3	0	1	1	14	1	19	0	0	1	1	.500	0	0-0	0	4.74	4.15
2004	KC	AL	43	0	0	23	44.1	191	40	25	21	5	1	2	2	19	2	30	2	0	2	3	.400	0	3-5	2	3.82	4.26
2005	KC	AL	7	0	0	3	6.2	35	13	7	7	1	0	0	0	5	2	4	1	0	0	0	-	0	0-0	1	12.38	9.45
4 ML YEARS			74	0	0	33	77.2	349	80	47	43	11	2	3	3	41	6	56	5	0	3	4	.429	0	3-5	5	5.10	4.98

Prince Fielder

Bats: L **Throws:** R **Pos:** PH-30; 1B-7; DH-4 **Ht:** 6'0" **Wt:** 260 **Born:** 5/9/1984 **Age:** 22

Year	Team	Lg	G	AB	H	2B	3B	HR	(Hm	Rd)	TB	R	RBI	RC	TBB	IBB	SO	HBP	SH	SF	SB	CS	SB%	GDP	Avg	OBP	Slg
2002	Ogden	R+	41	146	57	12	0	10	(-	-)	99	35	40	49	37	1	27	8	0	1	3	4	.43	2	.390	.531	.678
2002	Beloit	A	32	112	27	7	0	3	(-	-)	43	15	11	14	10	0	27	3	0	0	0	0	-	1	.241	.320	.384
2003	Beloit	A	137	502	157	22	2	27	(-	-)	264	81	112	110	71	16	80	15	0	6	2	1	.67	13	.313	.409	.526
2004	Huntsvl	AA	135	497	135	29	1	23	(-	-)	235	70	78	89	65	6	93	11	0	4	11	7	.61	11	.272	.366	.473
2005	Nashv	AAA	103	378	110	21	0	28	(-	-)	215	68	86	83	54	5	93	7	0	2	8	5	.62	11	.291	.388	.569
2005	MIL	NL	39	59	17	4	0	2	(2	0)	27	2	10	10	2	0	17	0	0	1	0	0	-	0	.288	.306	.458

Chone Figgins

Bats: B **Throws:** R **Pos:** 3B-56; CF-50; 2B-42; LF-15; RF-8; DH-7; SS-4; PH-1 **Ht:** 5'9" **Wt:** 155 **Born:** 1/22/1978 **Age:** 28

Year	Team	Lg	G	AB	H	2B	3B	HR	(Hm	Rd)	TB	R	RBI	RC	TBB	IBB	SO	HBP	SH	SF	SB	CS	SB%	GDP	Avg	OBP	Slg
2002	ANA	AL	15	12	2	1	0	0	(0	0)	3	6	1	0	0	0	5	0	0	0	2	1	.67	1	.167	.167	.250
2003	ANA	AL	71	240	71	9	4	0	(0	0)	88	34	27	39	20	0	38	0	6	4	13	7	.65	1	.296	.345	.367
2004	ANA	AL	148	577	171	22	17	5	(3	2)	242	83	60	93	49	0	94	0	10	4	34	13	.72	6	.296	.350	.419
2005	LAA	AL	158	642	186	25	10	8	(2	6)	255	113	57	94	64	1	101	0	9	5	62	17	.78	9	.290	.352	.397
	4 ML YEARS		392	1471	430	57	31	13	(5	8)	588	236	145	226	133	1	238	0	25	11	111	38	.74	17	.292	.349	.400

Steve Finley

Bats: L **Throws:** L **Pos:** CF-104; PH-7; DH-5 **Ht:** 6'2" **Wt:** 195 **Born:** 3/12/1965 **Age:** 41

Year	Team	Lg	G	AB	H	2B	3B	HR	(Hm	Rd)	TB	R	RBI	RC	TBB	IBB	SO	HBP	SH	SF	SB	CS	SB%	GDP	Avg	OBP	Slg
2005	RCuca*	A+	1	4	2	1	0	0	(-	-)	3	2	0	1	1	1	0	0	0	0	0	0	-	0	.500	.600	.750
1989	BAL	AL	81	217	54	5	2	2	(0	2)	69	35	25	23	15	1	30	1	6	2	17	3	.85	5	.249	.298	.318
1990	BAL	AL	142	464	119	16	4	3	(1	2)	152	46	37	47	32	3	53	2	10	5	22	9	.71	8	.256	.304	.328
1991	HOU	NL	159	596	170	28	10	8	(0	8)	242	84	54	80	42	5	65	2	10	6	34	18	.65	8	.285	.331	.406
1992	HOU	NL	162	607	177	29	13	5	(5	0)	247	84	55	93	58	6	63	3	16	2	44	9	.83	10	.292	.355	.407
1993	HOU	NL	142	545	145	15	13	8	(1	7)	210	69	44	64	28	1	65	3	6	3	19	6	.76	8	.266	.304	.385
1994	HOU	NL	94	373	103	16	5	11	(4	7)	162	64	33	54	28	0	52	2	13	1	13	7	.65	3	.276	.329	.434
1995	SD	NL	139	562	167	23	8	10	(4	6)	236	104	44	90	59	5	62	3	4	2	36	12	.75	4	.297	.366	.420
1996	SD	NL	161	655	195	45	9	30	(15	15)	348	126	95	117	56	5	87	4	1	5	22	8	.73	20	.298	.354	.531
1997	SD	NL	143	560	146	28	5	28	(5	23)	266	101	92	84	43	2	92	3	2	7	15	3	.83	10	.261	.313	.475
1998	SD	NL	159	619	154	40	6	14	(8	6)	248	92	67	76	45	0	103	3	3	4	12	3	.80	5	.249	.301	.401
1999	ARI	NL	156	590	156	32	10	34	(17	17)	310	100	103	105	63	7	94	3	2	5	8	4	.67	4	.264	.336	.525
2000	ARI	NL	152	539	151	27	5	35	(17	18)	293	100	96	104	65	7	87	8	2	9	12	6	.67	9	.280	.361	.544
2001	ARI	NL	140	495	136	27	4	14	(8	6)	213	66	73	71	47	9	67	1	2	3	11	7	.61	5	.275	.337	.430
2002	ARI	NL	150	505	145	24	4	25	(14	11)	252	82	89	94	65	7	73	3	1	3	16	4	.80	10	.287	.370	.499
2003	ARI	NL	147	516	148	24	10	22	(10	12)	258	82	70	85	57	4	94	6	0	3	15	8	.65	6	.287	.363	.500
2004	2 Tms	NL	162	628	170	28	1	36	(23	13)	308	92	94	86	61	1	82	1	9	7	9	7	.56	14	.271	.333	.490
2005	LAA	AL	112	406	90	20	3	12	(3	9)	152	41	54	39	26	3	71	3	1	4	8	4	.67	6	.222	.271	.374
04	Ari	NL	104	404	111	16	1	23	(14	9)	198	61	48	52	40	1	52	1	6	5	8	4	.67	9	.275	.338	.490
04	LA	NL	58	224	59	12	0	13	(9	4)	110	31	46	34	21	0	30	0	3	2	1	3	.25	5	.263	.324	.491
	17 ML YEARS		2401	8877	2426	425	112	297	(135	162)	3966	1368	1125	1312	790	66	1240	51	88	71	313	118	.73	144	.273	.334	.447

Jeff Fiorentino

Bats: L **Throws:** R **Pos:** CF-12; PH-1 **Ht:** 6'1" **Wt:** 188 **Born:** 4/14/1983 **Age:** 23

Year	Team	Lg	G	AB	H	2B	3B	HR	(Hm	Rd)	TB	R	RBI	RC	TBB	IBB	SO	HBP	SH	SF	SB	CS	SB%	GDP	Avg	OBP	Slg
2004	Dlmrva	A	49	179	54	15	2	10	(-	-)	103	40	36	38	20	1	50	3	0	1	2	2	.50	1	.302	.379	.575
2004	Abrdn	A-	14	46	16	7	1	2	(-	-)	31	9	12	14	9	3	4	2	0	0	3	1	.75	0	.348	.474	.674
2005	Frdrck	A+	103	413	118	18	4	22	(-	-)	210	70	66	73	34	2	90	4	4	0	12	6	.67	5	.286	.346	.508
2005	BAL	AL	13	44	11	2	0	1	(1	0)	16	7	5	2	2	0	10	0	0	1	1	0	1.00	0	.250	.277	.364

John Flaherty

Bats: R **Throws:** R **Pos:** C-45; 1B-1; PH-1 **Ht:** 6'1" **Wt:** 196 **Born:** 10/21/1967 **Age:** 38

Year	Team	Lg	G	AB	H	2B	3B	HR	(Hm	Rd)	TB	R	RBI	RC	TBB	IBB	SO	HBP	SH	SF	SB	CS	SB%	GDP	Avg	OBP	Slg
1992	BOS	AL	35	66	13	2	0	0	(0	0)	15	3	2	3	3	0	7	0	1	1	0	0	-	0	.197	.229	.227
1993	BOS	AL	13	25	3	2	0	0	(0	0)	5	3	2	1	2	0	6	1	1	0	0	0	-	0	.120	.214	.200
1994	DET	AL	34	40	6	1	0	0	(0	0)	7	2	4	0	1	0	11	0	2	1	0	1	.00	1	.150	.167	.175
1995	DET	AL	112	354	86	22	1	11	(6	5)	143	39	40	39	18	0	47	3	8	2	0	0	-	8	.243	.284	.404
1996	2 Tms	AL	119	416	118	24	0	13	(8	5)	181	40	64	53	17	2	61	3	4	4	3	3	.50	13	.284	.314	.435
1997	SD	NL	129	439	120	21	1	9	(4	5)	170	38	46	52	33	7	62	0	2	2	4	4	.50	11	.273	.323	.387
1998	TB	AL	91	304	63	11	0	3	(1	2)	83	21	24	17	22	0	46	1	4	3	0	5	.00	9	.207	.261	.273
1999	TB	AL	117	446	124	19	0	14	(3	11)	185	53	71	54	19	0	64	6	1	10	0	2	.00	14	.278	.310	.415
2000	TB	AL	109	394	103	15	0	10	(7	3)	148	36	39	41	20	2	57	0	2	2	1	0	1.00	11	.261	.296	.376
2001	TB	AL	78	248	59	17	1	4	(3	1)	90	20	29	22	10	1	33	1	5	1	1	0	1.00	9	.238	.269	.363
2002	TB	AL	76	281	73	20	0	4	(4	0)	105	27	33	32	15	0	50	1	2	4	2	2	.50	6	.260	.296	.374
2003	NYA	AL	40	105	28	8	0	4	(0	4)	48	16	14	12	4	1	19	1	5	1	0	0	-	6	.267	.297	.457
2004	NYA	AL	47	127	32	9	0	6	(6	0)	59	11	16	13	5	2	25	1	2	0	0	2	.00	5	.252	.286	.465
2005	NYA	AL	47	127	21	5	0	2	(0	2)	32	10	11	2	6	0	26	1	2	2	0	0	-	4	.165	.206	.252
96	Det	AL	47	152	38	12	0	4	(2	2)	62	18	23	17	8	1	25	1	3	1	1	0	1.00	5	.250	.290	.408
96	SD	NL	72	264	80	12	0	9	(6	3)	119	22	41	36	9	1	36	2	1	3	2	3	.40	8	.303	.327	.451
	14 ML YEARS		1047	3372	849	176	3	80	(42	38)	1271	319	395	341	175	15	514	19	41	33	10	19	.34	97	.252	.290	.377

Randy Flores

Pitches: L Bats: L Pos: RP-50 **Ht: 6'0" Wt: 180 Born: 7/31/1975 Age: 30**

Year	Team	Lg	G	GS	CG	GF	IP	BFP	H	R	ER	HR	SH	SF	HB	TBB	IBB	SO	WP	Bk	W	L	Pct	ShO	Sv-Op	Hld	ERC	ERA
2005	Memp*	AAA	6	0	0	1	7.0	29	16	8	6	5	1	1	2	1	0	0	6	0	0	1	0	1.000	0	0--	-	4.20	6.43
2002	2 Tms		28	2	0	9	29.0	140	40	26	24	7	2	2	3	16	3	14	4	0	0	2	.000	0	1-2	2	8.69	7.45
2004	STL	NL	9	1	0	3	14.0	57	13	3	3	0	1	1	3	3	1	7	0	0	1	0	1.000	0	0-0	0	3.15	1.93
2005	STL	NL	50	0	0	6	41.2	174	37	22	16	5	1	3	3	13	0	43	2	0	3	1	.750	0	1-3	11	3.55	3.46
02	Tex	AL	20	0	0	5	12.0	52	11	7	6	2	1	2	0	8	2	7	3	0	0	0	-	0	1-2	2	5.07	4.50
02	Col	NL	8	2	0	4	17.0	88	29	19	18	5	1	0	3	8	1	7	1	0	0	2	.000	0	0-0	0	11.52	9.53
	3 ML YEARS		87	3	0	18	84.2	371	90	51	43	12	4	6	9	32	4	64	6	0	4	3	.571	0	2-5	13	5.09	4.57

Ron Flores

Pitches: L Bats: L Pos: RP-11 **Ht: 5'11" Wt: 190 Born: 8/9/1979 Age: 26**

Year	Team	Lg	G	GS	CG	GF	IP	BFP	H	R	ER	HR	SH	SF	HB	TBB	IBB	SO	WP	Bk	W	L	Pct	ShO	Sv-Op	Hld	ERC	ERA
2000	Vancvr	A-	13	0	0	1	12.1	57	16	10	7	2	0	1	1	4	0	10	1	0	1	1	.500	0	0--	-	6.31	5.11
2001	Mdest	A+	47	0	0	23	66.0	280	53	24	21	4	6	2	1	29	7	71	3	0	5	2	.714	0	6--	-	2.75	2.86
2002	Visalia	A+	53	0	0	38	80.1	347	90	41	29	7	5	5	1	16	2	92	1	0	8	6	.571	0	11--	-	3.79	3.25
2003	Mdland	AA	39	0	0	17	59.1	237	44	19	19	6	3	4	1	15	3	66	4	0	3	2	.600	0	6--	-	2.17	2.88
2003	Scrmto	AAA	12	0	0	0	13.2	60	16	10	10	0	1	0	0	3	1	10	1	0	2	1	.667	0	0--	-	3.40	6.59
2004	Scrmto	AAA	55	0	0	13	54.0	241	60	27	23	5	0	1	0	19	4	55	3	0	4	3	.571	0	1--	-	4.23	3.83
2005	Scrmto	AAA	52	0	0	16	60.1	257	46	18	16	5	5	1	0	30	7	66	5	0	5	3	.625	0	3--	-	2.81	2.39
2005	OAK	AL	11	0	0	4	8.2	34	8	1	1	1	0	0	0	0	0	6	1	0	0	0	-	0	0-0	1	2.22	1.04

Cliff Floyd

Bats: L Throws: R Pos: LF-150; PH-2 **Ht: 6'4" Wt: 260 Born: 12/5/1972 Age: 33**

Year	Team	Lg	G	AB	H	2B	3B	HR	(Hm	Rd)	TB	R	RBI	RC	TBB	IBB	SO	HBP	SH	SF	SB	CS	SB%	GDP	Avg	OBP	Slg
1993	MON	NL	10	31	7	0	0	1	(0	1)	10	3	2	2	0	0	9	0	0	0	0	0	-	0	.226	.226	.323
1994	MON	NL	100	334	94	19	4	4	(2	2)	133	43	41	46	24	0	63	3	2	3	10	3	.77	3	.281	.332	.398
1995	MON	NL	29	69	9	1	0	1	(1	0)	13	6	8	2	7	0	22	1	0	0	3	0	1.00	1	.130	.221	.188
1996	MON	NL	117	227	55	15	4	6	(3	3)	96	29	26	35	30	1	52	5	1	3	7	1	.88	3	.242	.340	.423
1997	FLA	NL	61	137	32	9	1	6	(2	4)	61	23	19	23	24	0	33	2	1	1	6	2	.75	3	.234	.354	.445
1998	FLA	NL	153	588	166	45	3	22	(10	12)	283	85	90	92	47	7	112	3	0	3	27	14	.66	10	.282	.337	.481
1999	FLA	NL	69	251	76	19	1	11	(4	7)	130	37	49	45	30	5	47	2	0	2	5	6	.45	8	.303	.379	.518
2000	FLA	NL	121	420	126	30	0	22	(13	9)	222	75	91	88	50	5	82	8	0	9	24	3	.89	4	.300	.378	.529
2001	FLA	NL	149	555	176	44	4	31	(16	15)	321	123	103	121	59	19	106	10	0	5	18	3	.86	9	.317	.390	.578
2002	3 Tms		146	520	150	43	0	28	(13	15)	277	86	79	92	76	19	106	10	0	3	15	5	.75	6	.288	.388	.533
2003	NYN	NL	108	365	106	25	2	18	(10	8)	189	57	68	69	51	2	66	3	0	6	3	0	1.00	10	.290	.376	.518
2004	NYN	NL	113	396	103	26	0	18	(7	11)	183	55	63	64	47	6	103	11	0	3	11	4	.73	8	.260	.352	.462
2005	NYN	NL	150	550	150	22	2	34	(21	13)	278	85	98	99	63	13	98	11	0	2	12	2	.86	5	.273	.358	.505
02	Fla	NL	84	296	85	20	0	18	(7	11)	159	49	57	64	58	18	68	7	0	1	10	5	.67	0	.287	.414	.537
02	Mon	NL	15	53	11	2	0	3	(3	0)	22	7	4	2	3	1	10	1	0	0	1	0	1.00	0	.208	.263	.415
02	Bos	AL	47	171	54	21	0	7	(3	4)	96	30	18	26	15	0	28	2	0	2	4	0	1.00	6	.316	.374	.561
	13 ML YEARS		1326	4443	1250	298	21	202	(102	100)	2196	707	737	778	508	77	894	69	4	40	141	43	.77	70	.281	.361	.494

Gavin Floyd

Pitches: R Bats: R Pos: SP-4; RP-3 **Ht: 6'4" Wt: 212 Born: 1/27/1983 Age: 23**

Year	Team	Lg	G	GS	CG	GF	IP	BFP	H	R	ER	HR	SH	SF	HB	TBB	IBB	SO	WP	Bk	W	L	Pct	ShO	Sv-Op	Hld	ERC	ERA
2002	Lakwd	A	27	27	3	0	166.0	671	119	59	51	13	4	1	8	64	0	140	14	0	11	10	.524	0	0--	-	2.60	2.77
2003	Clrwtr	A+	24	20	1	0	138.0	577	128	61	46	9	4	3	7	45	0	115	6	0	7	8	.467	1	0--	-	3.39	3.00
2004	Rdng	AA	20	20	2	0	119.0	496	93	39	34	5	6	5	9	46	1	94	1	2	6	6	.500	1	0--	-	2.74	2.57
2004	S-WB	AAA	5	5	0	0	30.2	139	39	20	17	4	2	1	3	9	0	18	3	0	1	3	.250	0	0--	-	5.91	4.99
2005	S-WB	AAA	24	23	0	0	137.1	633	155	103	94	11	6	7	19	66	1	97	10	0	6	9	.400	0	0--	-	5.58	6.16
2004	PHI	NL	6	4	0	0	28.1	126	25	11	11	1	1	0	5	16	0	24	1	1	2	0	1.000	0	0-0	0	4.33	3.49
2005	PHI	NL	7	4	0	0	26.0	127	30	31	29	5	1	1	3	16	2	17	2	0	1	2	.333	0	0-0	0	6.82	10.04
	2 ML YEARS		13	8	0	0	54.1	253	55	42	40	6	2	1	8	32	2	41	3	1	3	2	.600	0	0-0	0	5.50	6.63

Josh Fogg

Pitches: R Bats: R Pos: SP-28; RP-6 **Ht: 6'0" Wt: 202 Born: 12/13/1976 Age: 29**

Year	Team	Lg	G	GS	CG	GF	IP	BFP	H	R	ER	HR	SH	SF	HB	TBB	IBB	SO	WP	Bk	W	L	Pct	ShO	Sv-Op	Hld	ERC	ERA
2001	CHA	AL	11	0	0	4	13.1	53	10	3	3	0	0	1	1	3	1	17	0	0	0	0	-	0	0-0	2	1.73	2.03
2002	PIT	NL	33	33	0	0	194.1	832	199	102	94	28	6	3	8	69	12	113	2	0	12	12	.500	0	0-0	0	4.46	4.35
2003	PIT	NL	26	26	1	0	142.0	625	166	90	83	22	6	4	9	40	0	71	2	0	10	9	.526	0	0-0	0	5.25	5.26
2004	PIT	NL	32	32	0	0	178.1	770	193	98	92	17	9	6	8	66	8	82	4	1	11	10	.524	0	0-0	0	4.59	4.64
2005	PIT	NL	34	28	0	1	169.1	742	196	106	95	27	4	6	6	53	11	85	2	1	6	11	.353	0	0-0	0	5.13	5.05
	5 ML YEARS		136	119	1	5	697.1	3022	764	399	367	94	25	20	32	231	32	368	10	2	39	42	.481	0	0-0	2	4.76	4.74

Mike Fontenot

Bats: L **Throws:** R **Pos:** PH-5; PR-2   **Ht:** 5'8" **Wt:** 160 **Born:** 6/9/1980 **Age:** 26

Year	Team	Lg	G	AB	H	2B	3B	HR	(Hm	Rd)	TB	R	RBI	RC	TBB	IBB	SO	HBP	SH	SF	SB	CS	SB%	GDP	Avg	OBP	Slg
2002	Frdrck	A+	122	481	127	16	4	8	(-	-)	175	61	53	61	42	1	117	10	9	5	13	9	.59	3	.264	.333	.364
2003	Bowie	AA	126	449	146	24	5	12	(-	-)	216	63	66	89	50	3	89	8	4	4	16	5	.76	6	.325	.399	.481
2004	Ottawa	AAA	136	524	146	30	10	8	(-	-)	220	73	49	80	48	0	111	9	4	5	14	7	.67	9	.279	.346	.420
2005	Iowa	AAA	111	379	103	22	10	6	(-	-)	163	60	39	66	59	3	77	6	3	2	3	2	.60	4	.272	.377	.430
2005	CHN	NL	7	2	0	0	0	0	(0	0)	0	4	0	1	2	0	0	1	0	0	0	0	-	0	.000	.600	.000

Jesse Foppert

Pitches: R **Bats:** R **Pos:** SP-2; RP-1   **Ht:** 6'6" **Wt:** 210 **Born:** 7/10/1980 **Age:** 25

Year	Team	Lg	G	GS	CG	GF	IP	BFP	H	R	ER	HR	SH	SF	HB	TBB	IBB	SO	WP	Bk	W	L	Pct	ShO	Sv-Op	Hld	ERC	ERA
2005	SnJos*	A+	3	3	0	0	8.2	37	5	2	2	0	0	0	0	6	0	9	0	0	0	1	1.000	0	0- -	1	2.20	2.08
2005	Fresno*	AAA	10	9	0	0	44.0	202	43	25	22	5	1	0	2	27	0	41	1	0	3	1	.750	0	0- -	-	5.02	4.50
2005	Tacom*	AAA	6	6	0	0	14.0	60	10	4	4	0	0	0	2	8	0	13	1	0	0	1	.000	0	0- -	-	3.03	2.57
2003	SF	NL	23	21	0	0	111.0	500	103	69	62	16	5	9	3	69	4	101	12	0	8	9	.471	0	0-0	1	4.89	5.03
2004	SF	NL	1	0	0	0	1.0	4	1	0	0	0	0	0	0	0	0	2	0	0	0	0	-	0	0-0	0	1.95	0.00
2005	SF	NL	3	2	0	0	10.1	53	11	7	6	2	0	2	1	13	0	6	0	1	0	0	-	0	0-0	0	9.72	5.23
	3 ML YEARS		27	23	0	0	122.1	557	115	76	68	18	5	11	4	82	4	109	12	1	8	9	.471	0	0-0	1	5.24	5.00

Lew Ford

Bats: R **Throws:** R **Pos:** CF-63; DH-44; LF-18; RF-16; PH-12   **Ht:** 6'0" **Wt:** 190 **Born:** 8/12/1976 **Age:** 29

Year	Team	Lg	G	AB	H	2B	3B	HR	(Hm	Rd)	TB	R	RBI	RC	TBB	IBB	SO	HBP	SH	SF	SB	CS	SB%	GDP	Avg	OBP	Slg
2003	MIN	AL	34	73	24	7	1	3	(2	1)	42	16	15	16	8	0	9	1	1	0	2	0	1.00	1	.329	.402	.575
2004	MIN	AL	154	569	170	31	4	15	(6	9)	254	89	72	101	67	3	75	13	2	7	20	2	.91	15	.299	.381	.446
2005	MIN	AL	147	522	138	30	4	7	(6	1)	197	70	53	70	45	2	85	16	2	5	13	6	.68	9	.264	.338	.377
	3 ML YEARS		335	1164	332	68	9	25	(14	11)	493	175	140	187	120	5	169	30	5	12	35	8	.81	25	.285	.363	.424

Casey Fossum

Pitches: L **Bats:** L **Pos:** SP-25; RP-11   **Ht:** 6'1" **Wt:** 165 **Born:** 1/6/1978 **Age:** 28

Year	Team	Lg	G	GS	CG	GF	IP	BFP	H	R	ER	HR	SH	SF	HB	TBB	IBB	SO	WP	Bk	W	L	Pct	ShO	Sv-Op	Hld	ERC	ERA
2001	BOS	AL	13	7	0	3	44.1	197	44	26	24	4	0	1	6	20	1	26	1	1	3	2	.600	0	0-0	0	4.70	4.87
2002	BOS	AL	43	12	0	13	106.2	461	113	56	41	12	2	4	4	30	0	101	3	0	5	4	.556	0	1-1	3	4.14	3.46
2003	BOS	AL	19	14	0	2	79.0	346	82	55	48	9	1	3	4	34	0	63	4	0	6	5	.545	0	1-1	0	4.77	5.47
2004	ARI	NL	27	27	0	0	142.0	652	171	111	105	31	8	4	10	63	5	117	4	2	4	15	.211	0	0-0	0	6.67	6.65
2005	TB	AL	36	25	0	1	162.2	725	170	100	89	21	3	5	18	60	3	128	8	1	8	12	.400	0	0-1	0	4.80	4.92
	5 ML YEARS		138	85	0	19	534.2	2381	580	348	307	77	14	17	42	207	9	435	20	4	26	38	.406	0	2-3	3	5.13	5.17

John Foster

Pitches: L **Bats:** L **Pos:** RP-62   **Ht:** 6'0" **Wt:** 200 **Born:** 5/17/1978 **Age:** 28

Year	Team	Lg	G	GS	CG	GF	IP	BFP	H	R	ER	HR	SH	SF	HB	TBB	IBB	SO	WP	Bk	W	L	Pct	ShO	Sv-Op	Hld	ERC	ERA
2005	Rchmd*	AAA	3	0	0	2	5.2	20	2	1	1	0	0	0	0	1	0	5	0	0	0	0	-	0	1- -	-	0.50	1.59
2002	ATL	NL	5	0	0	0	5.0	28	6	6	3	0	0	0	0	6	0	6	0	0	1	0	1.000	0	0-0	0	14.44	10.80
2003	MIL	NL	23	0	0	3	21.0	98	30	11	11	5	1	1	1	8	2	16	1	0	2	0	1.000	0	0-2	3	7.91	4.71
2005	ATL	NL	62	0	0	9	34.2	150	27	17	16	3	2	0	2	19	0	32	1	0	4	2	.667	0	1-2	12	3.53	4.15
	3 ML YEARS		90	0	0	12	60.2	276	63	34	33	11	3	1	4	33	2	54	2	0	7	2	.778	0	1-4	15	5.72	4.90

Keith Foulke

Pitches: R **Bats:** R **Pos:** RP-43   **Ht:** 6'0" **Wt:** 210 **Born:** 10/19/1972 **Age:** 33

Year	Team	Lg	G	GS	CG	GF	IP	BFP	H	R	ER	HR	SH	SF	HB	TBB	IBB	SO	WP	Bk	W	L	Pct	ShO	Sv-Op	Hld	ERC	ERA
2005	Lowell*	A-	3	0	0	0	3.2	20	8	4	3	0	0	0	0	1	0	5	0	0	0	0	-	0	0- -	-	9.93	7.36
1997	2 Tms		27	8	0	5	73.1	326	88	52	52	13	3	1	4	23	2	54	1	0	4	5	.444	0	3-6	5	5.68	6.38
1998	CHA	AL	54	0	0	18	65.1	267	51	31	30	9	2	2	4	20	3	57	3	1	3	2	.600	0	1-2	13	2.95	4.13
1999	CHA	AL	67	0	0	31	105.1	411	72	28	26	11	3	0	3	21	4	123	1	0	3	3	.500	0	9-13	22	1.80	2.22
2000	CHA	AL	72	0	0	58	88.0	350	66	31	29	9	5	2	2	22	2	91	1	0	3	1	.750	0	34-39	3	2.28	2.97
2001	CHA	AL	72	0	0	69	81.0	322	57	21	21	3	4	1	8	22	1	75	1	0	4	9	.308	0	42-45	0	2.06	2.33
2002	CHA	AL	65	0	0	35	77.2	306	65	26	25	7	2	0	2	13	2	58	1	0	2	4	.333	0	11-14	8	2.38	2.90
2003	OAK	AL	72	0	0	67	86.2	338	57	21	20	10	1	1	7	20	2	88	0	1	9	1	.900	0	43-48	0	2.07	2.08
2004	BOS	AL	72	0	0	61	83.0	333	63	22	20	8	2	4	6	15	5	79	3	0	5	3	.625	0	32-39	0	2.14	2.17
2005	BOS	AL	43	0	0	37	45.2	210	53	30	30	8	2	1	5	18	1	34	0	0	5	5	.500	0	15-19	1	5.93	5.91
97	SF	NL	11	8	0	0	44.2	209	60	41	41	9	2	0	4	18	1	33	1	0	1	5	.167	0	0-1	0	7.41	8.26
97	CWS	AL	16	0	0	5	28.2	117	28	11	11	4	1	0	0	5	1	21	0	0	3	0	1.000	0	3-5	5	3.27	3.45
	9 ML YEARS		544	8	0	381	706.0	2863	572	262	253	78	24	12	41	174	22	659	11	2	38	33	.535	0	190-225	52	2.73	3.23

Chad Fox

Pitches: R **Bats:** R **Pos:** RP-11 **Ht:** 6'3" **Wt:** 206 **Born:** 9/3/1970 **Age:** 35

			HOW MUCH HE PITCHED					WHAT HE GAVE UP								THE RESULTS					
Year	Team	Lg	G GS CG GF	IP	BFP	H R ER	HR SH SF HB	TBB IBB	SO WP Bk	W L	Pct	ShO	Sv-Op Hld	ERC	ERA
1997	ATL	NL	30 0 0 8	27.1	120	24 12 10	4 0 0 0	16 0	28 4 0	0 1	.000	0	0-1 7	4.44	3.29
1998	MIL	NL	49 0 0 12	57.0	242	56 27 25	4 6 0 1	20 0	64 5 0	1 4	.200	0	0-2 20	3.66	3.95
1999	MIL	NL	6 0 0 2	6.2	36	11 8 8	1 0 0 1	4 0	12 1 1	0 0	-	0	0-0 1	9.96	10.80
2001	MIL	NL	65 0 0 9	66.2	287	44 16 14	6 2 1 5	36 7	80 5 1	5 2	.714	0	2-4 20	2.75	1.89
2002	MIL	NL	3 0 0 0	4.2	25	6 3 3	0 1 0 0	5 1	3 0 0	1 0	1.000	0	0-0 0	7.03	5.79
2003	2 Tms		38 0 0 13	43.1	198	35 16 15	3 5 5 1	31 4	46 6 0	3 3	.500	0	3-5 7	3.80	3.12
2004	FLA	NL	12 0 0 1	10.2	49	9 8 8	1 0 0 1	8 0	17 1 0	0 1	.000	0	0-2 5	4.88	6.75
2005	CHN	NL	11 0 0 4	8.0	38	8 6 6	2 0 1 0	8 0	11 0 0	0 0	-	0	1-1 3	8.11	6.75
03	Bos	AL	17 0 0 10	18.0	93	19 10 9	2 2 1 1	17 2	19 1 0	1 2	.333	0	3-5 0	6.42	4.50
03	Fla	NL	21 0 0 3	25.1	105	16 6 6	1 3 4 0	14 2	27 5 0	2 1	.667	0	0-0 7	2.18	2.13
8 ML YEARS			214 0 0 49	224.1	995	193 96 89	21 14 7 9	128 12	261 22 2	10 11	.476	0	6-15 63	3.92	3.57

Jeff Francis

Pitches: L **Bats:** L **Pos:** SP-33 **Ht:** 6'5" **Wt:** 200 **Born:** 1/8/1981 **Age:** 25

			HOW MUCH HE PITCHED					WHAT HE GAVE UP								THE RESULTS					
Year	Team	Lg	G GS CG GF	IP	BFP	H R ER	HR SH SF HB	TBB IBB	SO WP Bk	W L	Pct	ShO	Sv-Op Hld	ERC	ERA
2002	TriCity	A-	4 3 0 0	10.2	40	5 0 0	0 0 0 1	4 0	16 0 0	0 0	-	0	0-- -	1.33	0.00
2002	Ashvlle	A	4 4 0 0	20.0	16	16 6 4	2 2 0 2	4 0	23 0 0	0 0	-	0	0-- -	15.60	1.80
2003	Visalia	A+	27 27 2 0	160.2	648	135 66 62	8 4 5 5	45 1	153 6 0	12 9	.571	2	0-- -	2.60	3.47
2004	Tulsa	AA	17 17 1 0	113.2	435	73 26 25	9 4 1 5	22 0	147 2 0	13 1	.929	1	0-- -	1.62	1.98
2004	ColSpr	AAA	7 7 0 0	41.0	165	35 16 13	3 0 1 4	7 0	49 2 0	3 2	.600	0	0-- -	2.66	2.85
2004	COL	NL	7 7 0 0	36.2	164	42 22 21	8 2 1 1	13 1	32 2 0	3 2	.600	0	0-0 0	5.62	5.15
2005	COL	NL	33 33 0 0	183.2	828	228 119 116	26 6 10 8	70 5	128 2 0	14 12	.538	0	0-0 0	5.94	5.68
2 ML YEARS			40 40 0 0	220.1	992	270 141 137	34 8 11 9	83 6	160 4 0	17 14	.548	0	0-0 0	5.89	5.60

Frank Francisco

Pitches: R **Bats:** R **Pos:** P **Ht:** 6'2" **Wt:** 180 **Born:** 9/11/1979 **Age:** 26

			HOW MUCH HE PITCHED					WHAT HE GAVE UP								THE RESULTS					
Year	Team	Lg	G GS CG GF	IP	BFP	H R ER	HR SH SF HB	TBB IBB	SO WP Bk	W L	Pct	ShO	Sv-Op Hld	ERC	ERA
1999	RedSx	R	12 7 0 1	53.1	253	58 39 27	3 1 1 4	35 0	48 7 3	2 4	.333	0	0-- -	5.52	4.56
2000	RedSx	R	1 0 0 0	1.0	7	2 3 2	0 0 0 0	2 0	1 1 0	0 0	-	0	0-- -	16.69	18.00
2001	Augsta	A	37 0 0 8	68.0	274	40 25 22	3 5 1 6	30 0	90 6 1	4 3	.571	0	2-- -	2.09	2.91
2002	Srsota	A+	16 10 0 2	53.0	217	33 19 15	1 3 5 4	27 0	58 4 0	1 5	.167	0	0-- -	2.28	2.55
2002	WinSa	A+	6 6 0 0	25.2	120	31 23 23	3 1 0 1	18 0	25 4 2	0 4	.000	0	0-- -	7.12	8.06
2002	Trentn	AA	9 0 0 1	16.0	77	10 13 10	0 1 0 2	16 1	18 3 0	2 2	.500	0	0-- -	3.67	5.63
2003	WinSa	A+	16 16 1 0	78.1	332	59 40 31	7 1 4 6	36 0	67 4 1	7 3	.700	1	0-- -	3.16	3.56
2003	Frisco	AA	7 6 0 0	35.1	167	43 33 33	5 0 4 4	18 1	22 0 0	2 3	.400	0	0-- -	6.58	8.41
2004	Frisco	AA	15 0 0 14	17.2	72	7 6 5	1 0 0 2	10 1	30 4 1	1 3	.250	0	6-- -	1.66	2.55
2005	Frisco	AA	4 3 0 0	3.1	16	4 6 3	0 2 2 0	2 0	3 1 1	0 1	.000	0	0-- -	5.10	8.10
2005	Okla	AAA	2 0 0 1	3.0	13	2 1 1	0 0 1 0	2 0	4 0 0	0 0	-	0	1-- -	2.54	3.00
2004	TEX	AL	45 0 0 7	51.1	216	36 19 19	4 2 1 3	28 2	60 4 1	5 1	.833	0	0-3 10	3.04	3.33

John Franco

Pitches: L **Bats:** L **Pos:** RP-31 **Ht:** 5'10" **Wt:** 185 **Born:** 9/17/1960 **Age:** 45

			HOW MUCH HE PITCHED					WHAT HE GAVE UP								THE RESULTS					
Year	Team	Lg	G GS CG GF	IP	BFP	H R ER	HR SH SF HB	TBB IBB	SO WP Bk	W L	Pct	ShO	Sv-Op Hld	ERC	ERA
1984	CIN	NL	54 0 0 30	79.1	335	74 24 23	3 4 4 2	36 4	55 2 0	6 2	.750	0	4-9 1	3.58	2.61
1985	CIN	NL	67 0 0 33	99.0	407	83 27 24	5 11 1 1	40 8	61 4 0	12 3	.800	0	12-15 11	2.86	2.18
1986	CIN	NL	74 0 0 52	101.0	429	90 40 33	7 8 3 2	44 12	84 4 2	6 6	.500	0	29-38 1	3.30	2.94
1987	CIN	NL	68 0 0 60	82.0	344	76 26 23	6 5 2 0	27 6	61 1 0	8 5	.615	0	32-41 0	3.10	2.52
1988	CIN	NL	70 0 0 61	86.0	336	60 18 15	3 5 1 0	27 3	46 1 2	6 6	.500	0	39-42 0	1.82	1.57
1989	CIN	NL	60 0 0 50	80.2	345	77 35 28	3 7 3 0	36 8	60 3 2	4 8	.333	0	32-39 0	3.42	3.12
1990	NYN	NL	55 0 0 48	67.2	287	66 22 19	4 3 1 0	21 2	56 7 2	5 3	.625	0	33-39 0	3.24	2.53
1991	NYN	NL	52 0 0 48	55.1	247	61 27 18	2 3 0 1	18 4	45 6 0	5 9	.357	0	30-35 0	3.73	2.93
1992	NYN	NL	31 0 0 30	33.0	128	24 6 6	1 0 2 0	11 2	20 0 0	6 2	.750	0	15-17 0	2.00	1.64
1993	NYN	NL	35 0 0 30	36.1	172	46 24 21	6 4 1 1	19 3	29 5 0	4 3	.571	0	10-17 0	6.62	5.20
1994	NYN	NL	47 0 0 43	50.0	216	47 20 15	2 2 1 1	19 0	42 1 0	1 4	.200	0	30-36 0	3.27	2.70
1995	NYN	NL	48 0 0 41	51.2	213	48 17 14	4 4 1 0	17 2	41 0 0	5 3	.625	0	29-36 0	3.26	2.44
1996	NYN	NL	51 0 0 44	54.0	235	54 15 11	2 6 0 0	21 0	48 2 0	4 3	.571	0	28-36 0	3.53	1.83
1997	NYN	NL	59 0 0 53	60.0	244	49 18 17	3 5 1 1	20 2	53 6 0	5 3	.625	0	36-42 0	2.57	2.55
1998	NYN	NL	61 0 0 54	64.2	289	66 28 26	4 4 5 4	29 7	59 2 0	0 8	.000	0	38-46 0	4.11	3.62
1999	NYN	NL	46 0 0 34	40.2	182	40 14 13	1 3 1 2	19 1	41 0 0	0 2	.000	0	19-21 1	3.77	2.88
2000	NYN	NL	62 0 0 14	55.2	239	46 24 21	6 3 0 2	26 6	56 2 0	5 4	.556	0	4-4 20	3.36	3.40
2001	NYN	NL	58 0 0 16	53.1	232	55 25 24	8 2 1 2	19 2	50 4 1	6 2	.750	0	2-7 17	4.50	4.05
2003	NYN	NL	38 0 0 13	34.1	148	35 11 10	5 1 1 1	13 2	16 2 0	0 3	.000	0	2-3 4	4.48	2.62
2004	NYN	NL	52 0 0 16	46.0	207	46 28 27	6 2 2 1	24 2	36 2 0	2 7	.222	0	0-1 11	4.74	5.28
2005	HOU	NL	31 0 0 4	15.0	77	23 13 12	0 0 0 1	9 2	16 0 0	0 1	.000	0	0-1 6	7.20	7.20
21 ML YEARS			1119 0 0 774	1245.2	5312	1166 466 400	81 82 31 22	495 78	975 54 9	90 87	.508	0	424-525 72	3.44	2.89

Julio Franco

Bats: R **Throws:** R **Pos:** 1B-62; PH-52; DH-4   **Ht:** 6'1" **Wt:** 188 **Born:** 8/23/1958 **Age:** 47

Year	Team	Lg	G	AB	H	2B	3B	HR	(Hm	Rd)	TB	R	RBI	RC	TBB	IBB	SO	HBP	SH	SF	SB	CS	SB%	GDP	Avg	OBP	Slg
1982	PHI	NL	16	29	8	1	0	0	(0	0)	9	3	3	2	2	1	4	0	1	0	0	2	.00	1	.276	.323	.310
1983	CLE	AL	149	560	153	24	8	8	(6	2)	217	68	80	62	27	1	50	2	3	6	32	12	.73	21	.273	.306	.388
1984	CLE	AL	160	**658**	188	22	5	3	(1	2)	229	82	79	72	43	1	68	6	1	10	19	10	.66	23	.286	.331	.348
1985	CLE	AL	160	636	183	33	4	6	(3	3)	242	97	90	78	54	2	74	4	0	9	13	9	.59	26	.288	.343	.381
1986	CLE	AL	149	599	183	30	5	10	(4	6)	253	80	74	76	32	1	66	0	0	5	10	7	.59	28	.306	.338	.422
1987	CLE	AL	128	495	158	24	3	8	(5	3)	212	86	52	81	57	2	56	3	0	5	32	9	.78	23	.319	.389	.428
1988	CLE	AL	152	613	186	23	6	10	(3	7)	251	88	54	89	56	4	72	2	1	4	25	11	.69	17	.303	.361	.409
1989	TEX	AL	150	548	173	31	5	13	(9	4)	253	80	92	93	66	11	69	1	0	6	21	3	.88	27	.316	.386	.462
1990	TEX	AL	157	582	172	27	1	11	(4	7)	234	96	69	94	82	3	83	2	2	2	31	10	.76	12	.296	.383	.402
1991	TEX	AL	146	589	201	27	3	15	(7	8)	279	108	78	113	65	8	78	3	0	2	36	9	.80	13	**.341**	.408	.474
1992	TEX	AL	35	107	25	7	0	2	(2	0)	38	19	8	12	15	2	17	0	1	0	1	1	.50	3	.234	.328	.355
1993	TEX	AL	144	532	154	31	3	14	(6	8)	233	85	84	83	62	4	95	1	5	7	9	3	.75	16	.289	.360	.438
1994	CHA	AL	112	433	138	19	2	20	(10	10)	221	72	98	87	62	4	75	5	0	5	8	1	.89	14	.319	.406	.510
1996	CLE	AL	112	432	139	20	1	14	(7	7)	203	72	76	79	61	2	82	3	0	3	8	8	.50	14	.322	.407	.470
1997	2 Tms	AL	120	430	116	16	1	7	(5	2)	155	68	44	58	69	4	116	1	1	4	15	6	.71	17	.270	.369	.360
1999	TB	AL	1	1	0	0	0	0	(0	0)	0	0	0	0	0	0	1	0	0	0	0	0	-	0	.000	.000	.000
2001	ATL	NL	25	90	27	4	0	3	(2	1)	40	13	11	14	10	1	20	1	0	0	0	0	-	3	.300	.376	.444
2002	ATL	NL	125	338	96	13	1	6	(3	3)	129	51	30	39	39	3	75	1	2	3	5	1	.83	13	.284	.357	.382
2003	ATL	NL	103	197	58	12	2	5	(1	4)	89	28	31	31	25	5	43	0	0	1	1	0	1.00	8	.294	.372	.452
2004	ATL	NL	125	320	99	18	3	6	(5	1)	141	37	57	57	36	4	68	1	1	3	4	2	.67	10	.309	.378	.441
2005	ATL	NL	108	233	64	12	1	9	(3	6)	105	30	42	36	27	1	57	1	1	3	4	0	1.00	10	.275	.348	.451
97	Cle	AL	78	289	82	13	1	3	(2	1)	106	46	25	37	38	2	75	0	1	0	8	5	.62	13	.284	.367	.367
97	Mil	AL	42	141	34	3	0	4	(3	1)	49	22	19	21	31	2	41	1	0	4	7	1	.88	4	.241	.373	.348
21 ML YEARS			2377	8422	2521	394	54	170	(86	84)	3533	1263	1152	1256	890	64	1269	37	19	78	273	105	.72	299	.299	.366	.419

Jeff Francoeur

Bats: R **Throws:** R **Pos:** RF-67; PH-2; PR-2   **Ht:** 6'4" **Wt:** 220 **Born:** 1/8/1984 **Age:** 22

Year	Team	Lg	G	AB	H	2B	3B	HR	(Hm	Rd)	TB	R	RBI	RC	TBB	IBB	SO	HBP	SH	SF	SB	CS	SB%	GDP	Avg	OBP	Slg
2002	Danvle	R+	38	147	48	12	1	8	(-	-)	86	31	31	32	15	0	34	3	0	2	8	5	.62	2	.327	.395	.585
2003	Rome	A	134	524	147	26	9	14	(-	-)	233	78	68	78	30	5	68	7	0	6	14	6	.70	21	.281	.325	.445
2004	MrtlBh	A+	87	331	97	26	0	15	(-	-)	168	56	52	58	22	3	69	7	0	4	10	6	.63	5	.293	.346	.508
2004	Grnville	AA	18	76	15	2	0	3	(-	-)	26	8	9	4	0	0	14	0	0	0	1	0	1.00	0	.197	.197	.342
2005	Missi	AA	84	335	92	28	2	13	(-	-)	163	40	62	54	21	6	76	5	0	6	13	4	.76	7	.275	.322	.487
2005	ATL	NL	70	257	77	20	1	14	(11	3)	141	41	45	50	11	3	58	4	0	2	3	2	.60	4	.300	.336	.549

Ryan Franklin

Pitches: R **Bats:** R **Pos:** SP-30; RP-2   **Ht:** 6'3" **Wt:** 165 **Born:** 3/5/1973 **Age:** 33

Year	Team	Lg	G	GS	CG	GF	IP	BFP	H	R	ER	HR	SH	SF	HB	TBB	IBB	SO	WP	Bk	W	L	Pct	ShO	Sv-Op	Hld	ERC	ERA
1999	SEA	AL	6	0	0	2	11.1	51	10	6	6	2	0	0	1	8	1	6	0	0	0	0	-	0	0-0	1	5.52	4.76
2001	SEA	AL	38	0	0	14	78.1	335	76	32	31	13	1	2	4	24	4	60	2	0	5	1	.833	0	0-1	5	4.08	3.56
2002	SEA	AL	41	12	0	10	118.2	495	117	62	53	14	5	5	5	22	1	65	0	0	7	5	.583	0	0-1	3	3.40	4.02
2003	SEA	AL	32	32	2	0	212.0	877	199	93	84	**34**	8	5	9	61	3	99	1	2	11	13	.458	1	0-0	0	3.90	3.57
2004	SEA	AL	32	32	2	0	200.1	870	224	116	109	33	2	**11**	10	61	1	104	0	3	4	16	.200	1	0-0	0	5.08	4.90
2005	SEA	AL	32	30	2	0	190.2	833	212	110	108	28	3	3	7	62	4	93	3	1	8	15	.348	1	0-0	0	4.88	5.10
6 ML YEARS			181	106	6	26	811.1	3461	838	419	391	124	19	26	36	238	14	427	6	6	35	50	.412	3	0-2	9	4.37	4.34

Wayne Franklin

Pitches: L **Bats:** L **Pos:** RP-13   **Ht:** 6'2" **Wt:** 205 **Born:** 3/9/1974 **Age:** 32

Year	Team	Lg	G	GS	CG	GF	IP	BFP	H	R	ER	HR	SH	SF	HB	TBB	IBB	SO	WP	Bk	W	L	Pct	ShO	Sv-Op	Hld	ERC	ERA
2005	Clmbs*	AAA	46	0	0	11	42.1	174	36	18	17	4	1	0	4	11	1	50	0	0	2	3	.400	0	1- -	3	3.04	3.61
2000	HOU	NL	25	0	0	4	21.1	103	24	14	13	2	0	2	4	12	1	21	0	1	0	0	-	0	0-0	8	6.01	5.48
2001	HOU	NL	11	0	0	3	12.0	60	17	9	9	4	0	0	0	9	0	9	0	0	0	0	-	0	0-0	1	10.43	6.75
2002	MIL	NL	4	4	0	0	24.0	103	16	8	7	1	1	0	0	17	1	17	0	0	2	1	.667	0	0-0	0	2.96	2.63
2003	MIL	NL	36	34	1	1	194.2	870	201	**129**	**119**	**36**	12	3	10	94	2	116	3	**4**	10	13	.435	1	0-0	0	5.43	5.50
2004	SF	NL	43	2	0	8	50.2	227	55	37	36	11	4	2	3	22	2	40	0	0	2	1	.667	0	0-1	5	5.77	6.39
2005	NYA	AL	13	0	0	2	12.2	57	11	12	9	1	1	1	1	8	0	10	0	0	0	0	1.000	0	0-3	3	4.37	6.39
6 ML YEARS			132	40	1	18	315.1	1420	324	209	193	55	18	8	18	162	6	213	3	5	14	16	.467	1	0-4	17	5.45	5.51

Jason Frasor

Pitches: R **Bats:** R **Pos:** RP-67   **Ht:** 5'10" **Wt:** 170 **Born:** 8/9/1977 **Age:** 28

Year	Team	Lg	G	GS	CG	GF	IP	BFP	H	R	ER	HR	SH	SF	HB	TBB	IBB	SO	WP	Bk	W	L	Pct	ShO	Sv-Op	Hld	ERC	ERA
1999	W Mich	A	4	4	0	0	24.0	9	17	10	7	2	0	0	2	9	0	33	0	3	2	1	.667	1	0- -	-	34.48	2.63
1999	Oneont	A-	12	11	0	0	58.2	22	36	16	11	3	0	1	1	22	0	69	3	2	3	3	.500	0	0- -	-	24.30	1.69
2000	W Mich	A	14	14	0	0	71.1	300	55	32	26	2	0	2	4	29	0	65	5	1	5	3	.625	0	0- -	-	2.58	3.28
2002	Lkland	A+	24	24	0	0	117.0	494	112	54	46	10	2	2	8	46	1	87	2	2	5	6	.455	0	0- -	-	4.07	3.54
2003	VeroB	A+	15	0	0	9	24.1	94	16	7	5	0	1	1	0	4	0	36	0	1	1	0	1.000	0	6- -	-	1.19	1.85
2003	Jaxnvl	AA	35	0	0	32	36.2	154	33	14	12	2	2	0	1	14	0	50	1	0	1	0	1.000	0	17- -	-	3.28	2.95
2004	Syrcse	AAA	3	0	0	2	4.0	18	1	1	1	0	0	0	0	5	0	6	0	0	0	0	-	0	0- -	-	2.38	2.25

Year	Team	Lg	G	GS	CG	GF	IP	BFP	H	R	ER	HR	SH	SF	HB	TBB	IBB	SO	WP	Bk	W	L	Pct	ShO	Sv-Op	Hld	ERC	ERA
2004	TOR	AL	63	0	0	37	68.1	299	64	31	31	4	3	3	2	36	3	54	4	2	4	6	.400	0	17-19	8	3.97	4.08
2005	TOR	AL	67	0	0	12	74.2	305	67	31	27	8	2	1	3	28	2	62	1	0	3	5	.375	0	1-3	15	3.72	3.25
	2 ML YEARS		130	0	0	49	143.0	604	131	62	58	12	5	4	5	64	5	116	5	2	7	11	.389	0	18-22	23	3.85	3.65

Ryan Freel

Bats: R **Throws:** R **Pos:** 2B-48; LF-25; CF-18; RF-13; 3B-10; PH-9; PR-2   **Ht:** 5'10" **Wt:** 178 **Born:** 3/8/1976 **Age:** 30

							BATTING															BASERUNNING				AVERAGES		
Year	Team	Lg	G	AB	H	2B	3B	HR	(Hm	Rd)	TB	R	RBI	RC	TBB	IBB	SO	HBP	SH	SF	SB	CS	SB%	GDP	Avg	OBP	Slg
2005	Chatt*	AA	5	17	3	0	0	0	(-	-)	3	3	1	0	3	0	5	0	0	1	0	1	.00	1	.176	.286	.176
2001	TOR	AL	9	22	6	1	0	0	(0	0)	7	1	3	3	1	0	4	1	0	0	2	1	.67	0	.273	.333	.318
2003	CIN	NL	43	137	39	6	1	4	(0	4)	59	23	12	17	9	1	13	4	2	1	9	4	.69	2	.285	.344	.431
2004	CIN	NL	143	505	140	21	8	3	(1	2)	186	74	28	73	67	0	88	12	8	0	37	10	.79	7	.277	.375	.368
2005	CIN	NL	103	369	100	19	3	4	(2	2)	137	69	21	55	51	0	59	8	3	0	36	10	.78	9	.271	.371	.371
	4 ML YEARS		298	1033	285	47	12	11	(3	8)	389	167	64	148	128	1	164	25	13	1	84	25	.77	18	.276	.369	.377

Choo Freeman

Bats: R **Throws:** R **Pos:** PR-9; CF-6; PH-4   **Ht:** 6'2" **Wt:** 200 **Born:** 10/20/1979 **Age:** 26

							BATTING															BASERUNNING				AVERAGES		
Year	Team	Lg	G	AB	H	2B	3B	HR	(Hm	Rd)	TB	R	RBI	RC	TBB	IBB	SO	HBP	SH	SF	SB	CS	SB%	GDP	Avg	OBP	Slg
1998	Rckies	R	40	147	47	3	6	1	(-	-)	65	35	24	29	15	0	25	4	0	3	14	1	.93	2	.320	.391	.442
1999	Ashvlle	A	131	485	133	22	4	14	(-	-)	205	82	66	71	39	1	132	7	1	2	16	4	.80	3	.274	.336	.423
2000	Salem	A+	127	429	114	18	7	5	(-	-)	161	73	54	53	37	0	104	4	1	5	16	8	.67	7	.266	.326	.375
2001	Salem	A+	132	517	124	16	5	8	(-	-)	174	63	42	52	31	1	108	9	8	5	19	7	.73	8	.240	.292	.337
2002	Carlina	AA	124	430	125	18	6	12	(-	-)	191	81	64	74	64	1	101	15	4	1	15	13	.54	15	.291	.400	.444
2003	ColSpr	AAA	103	327	83	9	4	7	(-	-)	121	44	36	36	23	1	71	7	4	2	2	8	.20	7	.254	.315	.370
2004	ColSpr	AAA	103	360	107	21	7	10	(-	-)	172	58	50	57	26	2	84	6	3	5	7	3	.70	11	.297	.350	.478
2005	ColSpr	AAA	97	354	99	10	6	10	(-	-)	151	46	59	52	29	2	78	2	1	4	4	3	.57	13	.280	.334	.427
2004	COL	NL	45	90	17	3	2	1	(0	1)	27	15	11	7	14	1	21	0	1	0	1	1	.50	1	.189	.298	.300
2005	COL	NL	18	22	6	1	1	0	(0	0)	9	6	0	2	0	0	5	0	0	0	0	0	-	0	.273	.273	.409
	2 ML YEARS		63	112	23	4	3	1	(0	1)	36	21	11	9	14	1	26	0	1	0	1	1	.50	5	.205	.294	.321

Alejandro Freire

Bats: R **Throws:** R **Pos:** 1B-16; DH-9; LF-1; PH-1   **Ht:** 6'2" **Wt:** 185 **Born:** 8/23/1974 **Age:** 31

							BATTING															BASERUNNING				AVERAGES		
Year	Team	Lg	G	AB	H	2B	3B	HR	(Hm	Rd)	TB	R	RBI	RC	TBB	IBB	SO	HBP	SH	SF	SB	CS	SB%	GDP	Avg	OBP	Slg
1994	Astros	R	29	83	25	4	0	1	(-	-)	32	8	13	12	5	0	17	3	2	2	5	1	.83	0	.301	.355	.386
1995	QuadC	A	125	417	127	23	1	15	(-	-)	197	71	65	78	50	1	83	6	2	7	9	5	.64	9	.305	.381	.472
1996	Kissim	A+	115	384	98	24	1	12	(-	-)	160	40	42	50	24	1	66	7	1	2	11	7	.61	11	.255	.309	.417
1997	Lkland	AA	130	477	154	30	2	24	(-	-)	260	85	92	104	50	1	84	12	0	7	13	4	.76	10	.323	.396	.545
1998	Jaxnvl	AA	129	494	136	30	0	16	(-	-)	214	79	78	76	33	4	83	17	1	9	3	1	.75	16	.275	.336	.433
1999	Lkland	A+	13	41	9	3	0	1	(-	-)	15	6	5	7	10	0	7	3	1	1	0	0	-	1	.220	.400	.366
1999	Jaxnvl	AA	66	243	72	20	0	10	(-	-)	122	45	43	46	23	0	44	6	0	4	2	0	1.00	8	.296	.366	.502
2000	Jaxnvl	AA	135	471	129	16	0	25	(-	-)	220	73	77	88	69	1	111	16	0	6	2	4	.33	13	.274	.381	.467
2001	Erie	AA	133	501	148	33	0	17	(-	-)	232	73	82	86	46	1	113	11	0	3	2	3	.40	17	.295	.365	.463
2002	Shreve	AA	55	177	50	9	0	10	(-	-)	89	24	32	32	19	1	38	4	0	1	0	2	.00	4	.282	.363	.503
2002	Fresno	AAA	45	145	39	7	1	3	(-	-)	57	12	7	21	14	0	28	5	0	0	0	0	-	3	.269	.354	.393
2003	Nrwich	AA	137	498	155	31	1	18	(-	-)	242	71	80	95	48	5	87	13	0	5	1	0	1.00	21	.311	.383	.486
2005	Bowie	AA	3	13	5	0	0	0	(-	-)	5	0	2	1	0	0	1	0	0	1	0	0	-	2	.385	.357	.385
2005	Ottawa	AAA	106	391	117	24	1	19	(-	-)	200	57	69	76	40	2	57	9	0	2	1	0	1.00	18	.299	.376	.512
2005	BAL	AL	25	65	16	3	0	1	(0	1)	22	7	4	5	6	0	17	1	0	0	0	0	-	4	.246	.319	.338

Brian Fuentes

Pitches: L **Bats:** L **Pos:** RP-78   **Ht:** 6'4" **Wt:** 220 **Born:** 8/9/1975 **Age:** 30

Year	Team	Lg	G	GS	CG	GF	IP	BFP	H	R	ER	HR	SH	SF	HB	TBB	IBB	SO	WP	Bk	W	L	Pct	ShO	Sv-Op	Hld	ERC	ERA
2001	SEA	AL	10	0	0	3	11.2	47	6	6	6	2	0	1	3	8	0	10	1	0	1	1	.500	0	0-1	1	4.39	4.63
2002	COL	NL	31	0	0	9	26.2	118	25	14	14	4	0	2	3	13	0	38	1	0	2	0	1.000	0	0-0	4	4.91	4.73
2003	COL	NL	75	0	0	23	75.1	320	64	24	23	7	0	3	6	34	2	82	2	1	3	3	.500	0	4-6	19	3.71	2.75
2004	COL	NL	47	0	0	12	44.2	201	46	30	28	5	7	0	4	19	6	48	3	0	2	4	.333	0	0-1	13	4.50	5.64
2005	COL	NL	78	0	0	55	74.1	321	59	25	24	6	5	1	10	34	4	91	8	0	2	5	.286	0	31-34	6	3.44	2.91
	5 ML YEARS		241	0	0	102	232.2	1007	200	99	95	24	12	7	26	108	12	269	15	1	10	13	.435	0	35-42	39	3.93	3.67

Aaron Fultz

Pitches: L **Bats:** L **Pos:** RP-62   **Ht:** 6'0" **Wt:** 200 **Born:** 9/4/1973 **Age:** 32

Year	Team	Lg	G	GS	CG	GF	IP	BFP	H	R	ER	HR	SH	SF	HB	TBB	IBB	SO	WP	Bk	W	L	Pct	ShO	Sv-Op	Hld	ERC	ERA
2000	SF	NL	58	0	0	18	69.1	299	67	38	36	8	7	6	3	28	0	62	0	2	5	2	.714	0	1-3	7	4.19	4.67
2001	SF	NL	66	0	0	17	71.0	300	70	40	36	9	3	4	1	21	3	67	1	0	3	1	.750	0	1-2	12	3.75	4.56
2002	SF	NL	43	0	0	12	41.1	185	47	22	22	4	2	1	3	19	3	31	1	0	2	2	.500	0	0-1	4	5.36	4.79
2003	TEX	AL	64	0	0	10	67.1	296	75	43	39	9	4	2	2	27	7	53	1	1	3	1	.250	0	0-0	19	4.99	5.21
2004	MIN	AL	55	0	0	16	50.0	216	50	28	28	5	1	4	1	23	2	37	3	0	3	3	.500	0	1-4	5	4.40	5.04
2005	PHI	NL	62	0	0	16	72.1	286	47	21	18	6	4	1	5	23	2	54	0	0	4	0	1.000	0	0-1	2	2.11	2.24
	6 ML YEARS		348	0	0	89	371.1	1582	356	192	179	41	21	18	15	141	17	304	6	3	18	11	.621	0	3-11	49	3.96	4.34

Rafael Furcal

Bats: B **Throws:** R **Pos:** SS-152; PH-1; PR-1   **Ht:** 5'10" **Wt:** 165 **Born:** 10/24/1977 **Age:** 28

Year	Team	Lg	G	AB	H	2B	3B	HR	(Hm	Rd)	TB	R	RBI	RC	TBB	IBB	SO	HBP	SH	SF	SB	CS	SB%	GDP	Avg	OBP	Slg
2000	ATL	NL	131	455	134	20	4	4	(1	3)	174	87	37	78	73	0	80	3	9	2	40	14	.74	2	.295	.394	.382
2001	ATL	NL	79	324	89	19	0	4	(3	1)	120	39	30	41	24	1	56	1	4	6	22	6	.79	5	.275	.321	.370
2002	ATL	NL	154	636	175	31	8	8	(4	4)	246	95	47	80	43	0	114	3	9	2	27	15	.64	8	.275	.323	.387
2003	ATL	NL	156	664	194	35	10	15	(4	11)	294	130	61	107	60	2	76	3	3	4	25	2	.93	1	.292	.352	.443
2004	ATL	NL	143	563	157	24	5	14	(5	9)	233	103	59	82	58	4	71	1	5	5	29	6	.83	9	.279	.344	.414
2005	ATL	NL	154	616	175	31	11	12	(9	3)	264	100	58	98	62	3	78	1	5	5	46	10	.82	11	.284	.348	.429
6 ML YEARS			817	3258	924	160	38	57	(26	31)	1331	554	292	486	320	10	475	12	35	24	189	53	.78	36	.284	.348	.409

J.J. Furmaniak

Bats: R **Throws:** R **Pos:** 2B-9; PH-3; SS-2   **Ht:** 6'3" **Wt:** 190 **Born:** 7/31/1979 **Age:** 26

Year	Team	Lg	G	AB	H	2B	3B	HR	(Hm	Rd)	TB	R	RBI	RC	TBB	IBB	SO	HBP	SH	SF	SB	CS	SB%	GDP	Avg	OBP	Slg
2000	Idaho	R+	62	245	84	18	2	5	(-	-)	121	72	38	57	44	1	48	5	0	4	10	3	.77	8	.343	.446	.494
2001	FtWyn	A	123	436	96	24	3	5	(-	-)	141	57	35	48	55	0	117	4	3	7	11	6	.65	10	.220	.309	.323
2002	Lk Els	A+	106	381	98	16	6	7	(-	-)	147	50	43	46	26	1	100	6	5	5	11	9	.55	8	.257	.311	.386
2003	Lk Els	A+	78	309	97	22	8	9	(-	-)	162	65	54	65	36	1	55	8	3	2	10	4	.71	5	.314	.397	.524
2003	Mobile	AA	31	103	27	4	1	3	(-	-)	42	10	11	14	8	0	27	4	1	1	0	0	-	0	.262	.336	.408
2004	Mobile	AA	14	51	10	4	0	1	(-	-)	17	10	8	5	7	0	15	1	0	0	1	0	1.00	1	.196	.305	.333
2004	Portlnd	AAA	120	425	125	24	4	17	(-	-)	208	71	73	73	33	2	86	6	2	7	8	5	.62	10	.294	.348	.489
2005	Portlnd	AAA	99	387	103	16	4	14	(-	-)	169	54	47	56	28	0	86	6	5	2	9	5	.64	8	.266	.324	.437
2005	Indy	AAA	36	139	40	5	3	2	(-	-)	57	12	21	18	4	0	32	2	1	1	5	3	.63	1	.288	.315	.410
2005	PIT	NL	13	26	5	1	1	0	(0	0)	8	3	1	2	4	0	4	0	0	0	0	0	-	0	.192	.300	.308

Eric Gagne

Pitches: R **Bats:** R **Pos:** RP-14   **Ht:** 6'2" **Wt:** 195 **Born:** 1/7/1976 **Age:** 30

			HOW MUCH HE PITCHED						WHAT HE GAVE UP										THE RESULTS							
Year	Team	Lg	G	GS	CG	GF	IP	BFP	H	R	ER	HR	SH	SF	HB	TBB	IBB	SO	WP	Bk	W	L	Pct	ShO	Sv-Op Hld	ERC	ERA
2005	LsVgs*	AAA	3	0	0	1	4.0	12	0	0	0	0	0	0	0	0	0	7	0	0	0	0	-	0	0-- -	0.00	0.00
1999	LA	NL	5	5	0	0	30.0	119	18	8	7	3	1	0	0	15	0	30	1	0	1	1	.500	0	0-0 0	2.42	2.10
2000	LA	NL	20	19	0	0	101.1	464	106	62	58	20	5	3	6	60	1	79	4	0	4	6	.400	0	0-0 0	5.97	5.15
2001	LA	NL	33	24	0	3	151.2	649	144	90	80	24	6	8	16	46	1	130	3	1	6	7	.462	0	0-0 0	4.22	4.75
2002	LA	NL	77	0	0	68	82.1	314	55	18	18	6	3	2	2	16	4	114	1	0	4	1	.800	0	52-56 1	1.60	1.97
2003	LA	NL	77	0	0	67	82.1	306	37	12	11	2	4	0	3	20	2	137	2	0	2	3	.400	0	55-55 0	0.93	1.20
2004	LA	NL	70	0	0	59	82.1	326	53	24	20	5	4	2	5	22	3	114	2	0	7	3	.700	0	45-47 0	1.72	2.19
2005	LAN	NL	14	0	0	13	13.1	53	10	4	4	2	0	0	0	3	0	22	3	0	1	0	1.000	0	8-8 0	2.38	2.70
7 ML YEARS			296	48	0	210	543.1	2231	423	218	198	62	23	15	29	182	11	626	16	1	25	21	.543	0	160-166 1	2.90	3.28

John Gall

Bats: R **Throws:** R **Pos:** PH-14; LF-10   **Ht:** 6'0" **Wt:** 195 **Born:** 4/2/1978 **Age:** 28

Year	Team	Lg	G	AB	H	2B	3B	HR	(Hm	Rd)	TB	R	RBI	RC	TBB	IBB	SO	HBP	SH	SF	SB	CS	SB%	GDP	Avg	OBP	Slg
2000	NewJrs	A-	71	259	62	10	0	4	(Hm	Rd)	78	28	27	27	25	0	37	1	0	4	16	5	.76	7	.239	.304	.301
2001	Ptomc	A+	84	319	101	25	0	4	(-	-)	138	44	33	50	24	4	40	3	0	1	5	6	.45	9	.317	.369	.433
2001	Peoria	A	57	205	62	23	0	4	(-	-)	97	27	44	35	16	1	18	4	0	7	0	3	.00	3	.302	.353	.473
2002	NwHav	AA	135	526	166	45	3	20	(-	-)	277	82	81	99	38	1	75	2	0	3	4	1	.80	26	.316	.362	.527
2003	Tenn	AA	12	52	17	1	0	3	(-	-)	27	6	12	9	3	0	4	0	0	1	0	1	.00	4	.327	.357	.519
2003	Memp	AAA	123	461	144	24	1	16	(-	-)	218	62	73	81	39	0	56	2	1	1	5	2	.71	13	.312	.368	.473
2004	Memp	AAA	135	506	148	34	0	22	(-	-)	248	77	84	89	48	2	68	1	0	8	1	1	.50	19	.292	.350	.490
2005	Memp	AAA	114	374	101	22	0	13	(-	-)	162	61	64	60	45	2	42	1	0	6	9	2	.82	12	.270	.345	.433
2005	STL	NL	22	37	10	3	0	2	(1	1)	19	5	10	6	1	0	8	0	0	1	0	0	-	0	.270	.282	.514

Mike Gallo

Pitches: L **Bats:** L **Pos:** RP-36   **Ht:** 6'0" **Wt:** 175 **Born:** 4/2/1977 **Age:** 29

			HOW MUCH HE PITCHED						WHAT HE GAVE UP										THE RESULTS							
Year	Team	Lg	G	GS	CG	GF	IP	BFP	H	R	ER	HR	SH	SF	HB	TBB	IBB	SO	WP	Bk	W	L	Pct	ShO	Sv-Op Hld	ERC	ERA
2005	RdRck*	AAA	37	1	0	6	54.1	239	56	29	22	2	5	5	1	20	4	33	1	0	4	2	.667	0	0-- -	3.55	3.64
2003	HOU	NL	32	0	0	6	30.0	121	28	10	10	3	2	3	1	10	2	16	0	0	1	0	1.000	0	0-1 6	3.66	3.00
2004	HOU	NL	69	0	0	5	49.1	223	55	27	26	12	1	6	20	7	34	3	0	2	0	1.000	0	0-1 4	6.16	4.74
2005	HOU	NL	36	0	0	5	20.1	87	18	6	6	1	2	1	2	10	2	12	0	0	0	1	.000	0	0-2 8	3.74	2.66
3 ML YEARS			137	0	0	16	99.2	431	101	43	42	16	6	5	9	40	11	62	3	0	3	1	.750	0	0-4 18	4.88	3.79

Eddy Garabito

Bats: B **Throws:** R **Pos:** PH-23; 2B-18; SS-2   **Ht:** 5'8" **Wt:** 188 **Born:** 12/2/1976 **Age:** 29

Year	Team	Lg	G	AB	H	2B	3B	HR	(Hm	Rd)	TB	R	RBI	RC	TBB	IBB	SO	HBP	SH	SF	SB	CS	SB%	GDP	Avg	OBP	Slg
1997	Bluefld	R+	2	4	0	0	0	0	(-	-)	0	0	0	0	0	0	0	3	2	7	0	0	-	5	.000	.214	.000
1997	Dlmrva	A	61	231	70	12	3	5	(-	-)	103	47	44	39	21	0	30	0	0	0	26	9	.74	6	.303	.361	.446
1998	Frdrck	A+	4	19	4	1	1	0	(-	-)	7	4	2	1	1	0	5	0	0	0	0	1	.00	1	.211	.250	.368
1998	Dlmrva	A	135	481	119	20	8	9	(-	-)	182	81	66	60	44	3	93	5	4	12	25	15	.63	9	.247	.310	.378
1999	Frdrck	A+	132	539	138	24	4	6	(-	-)	188	76	77	66	52	1	68	4	8	10	38	18	.68	7	.256	.321	.349
2000	Bowie	AA	116	482	121	21	3	6	(-	-)	166	72	52	55	27	1	55	5	8	7	22	0	1.00	7	.251	.294	.344
2000	Roch	AAA	9	35	3	1	0	0	(-	-)	4	3	0	0	2	0	10	0	0	0	1	0	1.00	0	.086	.135	.114

Year	Team	Lg	G	AB	H	2B	3B	HR	(Hm	Rd)	TB	R	RBI	RC	TBB	IBB	SO	HBP	SH	SF	SB	CS	SB%	GDP	Avg	OBP	Slg
2001	Roch	AAA	127	517	138	29	6	3	(-	-)	188	65	34	61	31	2	76	3	17	2	24	11	.69	7	.267	.311	.364
2002	Roch	AAA	110	434	112	20	4	4	(-	-)	152	52	32	47	24	1	48	4	8	4	11	8	.58	11	.258	.300	.350
2003	Ottawa	AAA	114	459	129	28	5	3	(-	-)	176	62	56	59	31	1	70	2	7	4	14	8	.64	8	.281	.327	.383
2004	Ottawa	AAA	124	450	134	27	5	6	(-	-)	189	52	37	69	40	3	48	4	3	2	19	12	.61	8	.298	.359	.420
2005	ColSpr	AAA	67	258	79	16	3	8	(-	-)	125	56	39	48	29	0	34	2	5	1	8	4	.67	6	.306	.379	.484
2005	COL	NL	42	88	27	5	0	1	(0	1)	35	15	8	14	8	0	12	3	3	0	3	2	.60	2	.307	.384	.398

Freddy Garcia

Pitches: R **Bats:** R **Pos:** SP-33   **Ht:** 6'4" **Wt:** 235 **Born:** 6/10/1976 **Age:** 30

					HOW MUCH HE PITCHED					WHAT HE GAVE UP												THE RESULTS						
Year	Team	Lg	G	GS	CG	GF	IP	BFP	H	R	ER	HR	SH	SF	HB	TBB	IBB	SO	WP	Bk	W	L	Pct	ShO	Sv-Op	Hld	ERC	ERA
1999	SEA	AL	33	33	2	0	201.1	888	205	96	91	18	3	6	10	90	4	170	12	3	17	8	.680	1	0-0	0	4.46	4.07
2000	SEA	AL	21	20	0	0	124.1	538	112	62	54	16	6	1	2	64	4	79	4	2	9	5	.643	0	0-0	0	4.20	3.91
2001	SEA	AL	34	34	4	0	**238.2**	971	199	88	81	16	8	5	5	69	6	163	3	1	18	6	.750	3	0-0	0	**2.61**	**3.05**
2002	SEA	AL	34	34	1	0	223.2	955	227	110	109	30	4	8	6	63	3	181	8	1	16	10	.615	0	0-0	0	3.98	4.39
2003	SEA	AL	33	33	1	0	201.1	862	196	109	101	31	2	8	11	71	2	144	11	0	12	14	.462	0	0-0	0	4.33	4.51
2004	2 Tms	AL	31	31	1	0	210.0	878	192	92	89	22	8	3	7	64	3	184	8	0	13	11	.542	0	0-0	0	3.37	3.81
2005	CHA	AL	33	33	2	0	228.0	943	225	102	98	26	5	5	3	60	2	146	**20**	1	14	8	.636	0	0-0	0	3.65	3.87
04	Sea	AL	15	15	1	0	107.0	446	96	39	38	8	4	1	2	32	1	82	5	0	4	7	.364	0	0-0	0	3.00	3.20
04	CWS	AL	16	16	0	0	103.0	432	96	53	51	14	4	2	5	32	2	102	3	0	9	4	.692	0	0-0	0	3.77	4.46
	7 ML YEARS		219	218	11	0	1427.1	6035	1356	659	623	159	36	36	44	481	24	1067	66	8	99	62	.615	4	0-0	0	3.73	3.93

Jairo Garcia

Pitches: R **Bats:** R **Pos:** RP-3   **Ht:** 6'0" **Wt:** 164 **Born:** 3/7/1983 **Age:** 23

					HOW MUCH HE PITCHED					WHAT HE GAVE UP												THE RESULTS						
Year	Team	Lg	G	GS	CG	GF	IP	BFP	H	R	ER	HR	SH	SF	HB	TBB	IBB	SO	WP	Bk	W	L	Pct	ShO	Sv-Op	Hld	ERC	ERA
2001	As	R	12	7	0	3	47.1	184	37	19	15	2	2	0	2	6	0	50	5	0	4	2	.667	0	0--	-	1.80	2.85
2002	As	R	13	8	0	1	59.0	242	56	24	16	5	5	3	3	17	0	66	4	1	2	1	.667	0	1--	-	3.56	2.44
2002	Vancvr	A-	3	3	0	0	12.1	59	15	11	10	1	0	1	1	7	0	16	1	1	0	3	.000	0	0--	-	6.18	7.30
2003	Kane	A	14	9	0	1	42.1	183	40	14	12	0	1	0	3	19	0	28	5	0	1	1	.000	0	0--	-	3.55	2.55
2004	Kane	A	25	0	0	24	30.0	117	16	2	1	0	0	0	4	6	2	49	3	0	1	0	1.000	0	16--	-	1.12	0.30
2004	Mdland	AA	13	0	0	9	18.0	80	10	3	3	0	0	0	1	15	0	32	2	0	2	0	1.000	0	2--	-	2.71	1.50
2004	Scrmto	AAA	11	0	0	10	13.2	60	10	6	6	1	0	0	0	9	1	21	0	0	1	2	.333	0	1--	-	3.21	3.95
2005	Mdland	AA	10	0	0	7	16.2	68	9	3	2	1	1	0	0	9	0	30	1	1	0	0	-	0	6--	-	1.95	1.08
2005	Scrmto	AAA	44	0	0	37	48.1	210	45	30	24	6	2	1	1	20	1	73	6	0	3	6	.333	0	20--	-	3.89	4.47
2004	OAK	AL	4	0	0	2	5.2	32	5	8	8	3	0	0	1	9	0	5	0	0	0	0	-	0	0-0	0	13.22	12.71
2005	OAK	AL	3	0	0	3	3.0	12	2	1	1	0	0	0	0	1	0	1	1	0	0	0	-	0	0-0	0	1.57	3.00
	2 ML YEARS		7	0	0	5	8.2	44	7	9	9	3	0	0	1	10	0	6	1	0	0	0	-	0	0-0	0	8.49	9.35

Jesse Garcia

Bats: R **Throws:** R **Pos:** SS-13; PH-3; 2B-2   **Ht:** 5'10" **Wt:** 171 **Born:** 9/24/1973 **Age:** 32

									BATTING												BASERUNNING				AVERAGES		
Year	Team	Lg	G	AB	H	2B	3B	HR	(Hm	Rd)	TB	R	RBI	RC	TBB	IBB	SO	HBP	SH	SF	SB	CS	SB%	GDP	Avg	OBP	Slg
2005	Mobile*	AA	7	31	6	2	0	1	(-	-)	11	4	3	2	0	0	4	1	1	1	1	1	.50	0	.194	.212	.355
2005	Portlnd*	AAA	63	210	42	7	2	3	(-	-)	62	18	26	13	6	0	34	0	3	2	6	1	.86	7	.200	.220	.295
1999	BAL	AL	17	29	6	0	0	2	(1	1)	12	6	2	3	2	0	3	0	3	0	0	0	-	1	.207	.258	.414
2000	BAL	AL	14	17	1	0	0	0	(0	0)	1	2	0	0	2	0	2	0	0	0	0	0	-	0	.059	.158	.059
2001	ATL	NL	22	5	1	0	0	0	(0	0)	1	3	0	0	0	0	1	0	1	0	6	2	.75	0	.200	.200	.200
2002	ATL	NL	39	61	12	1	0	0	(0	0)	13	6	5	4	0	0	14	0	0	0	0	1	.00	1	.197	.197	.213
2003	ATL	NL	13	10	4	0	1	0	(0	0)	6	6	2	3	0	0	1	0	0	0	0	1	.00	0	.400	.400	.600
2004	ATL	NL	50	115	29	4	1	1	(1	0)	38	14	10	10	1	0	16	1	1	1	1	2	.33	2	.252	.265	.330
2005	SD	NL	16	36	6	0	0	2	(0	2)	12	4	4	1	3	1	11	0	0	0	0	0	-	0	.167	.231	.333
	7 ML YEARS		171	273	59	5	2	5	(2	3)	83	41	23	21	8	1	48	1	5	0	7	6	.54	4	.216	.241	.304

Nomar Garciaparra

Bats: R **Throws:** R **Pos:** 3B-34; SS-26; PH-2   **Ht:** 6'0" **Wt:** 190 **Born:** 7/23/1973 **Age:** 32

									BATTING												BASERUNNING				AVERAGES		
Year	Team	Lg	G	AB	H	2B	3B	HR	(Hm	Rd)	TB	R	RBI	RC	TBB	IBB	SO	HBP	SH	SF	SB	CS	SB%	GDP	Avg	OBP	Slg
2005	Cubs*	R	2	5	1	0	0	0	(-	-)	1	0	0	0	0	0	1	0	0	0	0	0	-	0	.200	.200	.200
2005	Peoria*	A	2	5	1	0	0	0	(-	-)	1	1	2	0	2	0	0	0	0	0	0	0	-	0	.200	.429	.200
2005	WTenn*	AA	4	13	3	0	0	0	(-	-)	3	2	0	1	1	0	1	0	0	0	0	0	-	0	.231	.333	.231
1996	BOS	AL	24	87	21	2	3	4	(3	1)	41	11	16	13	4	0	14	0	1	1	5	0	1.00	0	.241	.272	.471
1997	BOS	AL	153	684	209	44	11	30	(11	19)	365	122	98	122	35	2	92	6	2	7	22	9	.71	9	.306	.342	.534
1998	BOS	AL	143	604	195	37	8	35	(17	18)	353	111	122	117	33	1	62	8	0	7	12	6	.67	20	.323	.362	.584
1999	BOS	AL	135	532	190	42	4	27	(14	13)	321	103	104	125	51	7	39	8	0	4	14	3	.82	11	**.357**	.418	.603
2000	BOS	AL	140	529	197	51	3	21	(7	14)	317	104	96	127	61	20	50	2	0	7	5	2	.71	8	**.372**	.434	.599
2001	BOS	AL	21	83	24	3	0	4	(3	1)	39	13	8	13	7	0	9	1	0	0	0	1	.00	1	.289	.352	.470
2002	BOS	AL	156	635	197	**56**	5	24	(10	14)	335	101	120	113	41	4	63	6	0	11	5	2	.71	17	.310	.352	.528
2003	BOS	AL	156	658	198	37	13	28	(18	10)	345	120	105	114	39	1	61	11	1	10	19	5	.79	10	.301	.345	.524
2004	2 Tms	AL	81	321	99	21	3	9	(6	3)	153	52	41	53	24	2	30	6	1	2	4	1	.80	10	.308	.365	.477
2005	CHN	NL	62	230	65	12	0	9	(5	4)	104	28	30	28	12	0	24	2	0	3	0	0	-	6	.283	.320	.452
04	Bos	AL	38	156	50	7	3	5	(3	2)	78	24	21	26	8	2	16	4	0	1	2	1	1.00	4	.321	.367	.500
04	ChC	NL	43	165	49	14	0	4	(3	1)	75	28	20	27	16	0	14	2	1	1	2	1	.67	6	.297	.364	.455
	10 ML YEARS		1071	4363	1395	305	50	191	(94	97)	2373	765	740	825	307	37	444	50	5	52	86	29	.75	92	.320	.367	.544

Lee Gardner

Pitches: R **Bats:** R **Pos:** RP-5   **Ht:** 6'0" **Wt:** 219 **Born:** 1/16/1975 **Age:** 31

			HOW MUCH HE PITCHED						WHAT HE GAVE UP											THE RESULTS						
Year	Team	Lg	G	GS	CG	GF	IP	BFP	H	R	ER	HR	SH	SF	HB	TBB	IBB	SO	WP	Bk	W	L	Pct	ShO	Sv-Op	Hld	ERC	ERA
1998	StPete	A+	3	0	0	1	4.0	15	3	0	0	0	0	0	0	1	0	2	0	0	0	0	-	0	0- -	-	1.79	0.00
1998	CtnSC	A	28	0	0	13	35.2	154	38	18	16	3	2	0	1	4	0	55	1	0	0	3	.000	0	3- -	-	3.14	4.04
1999	Orlndo	AA	1	0	0	0	2.0	9	3	2	2	0	0	0	0	1	0	1	0	0	0	0	-	0	0- -	-	7.26	9.00
1999	StPete	A+	20	0	0	13	23.0	96	20	7	5	1	1	1	2	5	0	22	0	0	2	0	1.000	0	7- -	-	2.60	1.96
2000	Orlndo	AA	36	0	0	24	45.0	186	34	19	17	0	4	3	2	14	1	48	6	0	3	2	.600	0	12- -	-	1.93	3.40
2000	Drham	AAA	21	0	0	9	18.2	75	12	7	7	1	1	0	0	9	1	8	1	0	1	0	1.000	0	5- -	-	2.18	3.38
2001	Orlndo	AA	1	0	0	0	1.2	4	0	0	0	0	0	0	0	0	0	0	0	0	0	0	-	0	0- -	-	0.00	0.00
2001	Drham	AAA	56	0	0	18	76.0	324	76	27	23	10	3	2	2	23	2	55	4	0	5	2	.714	0	2- -	-	3.95	2.72
2002	Drham	AAA	45	0	0	35	49.2	207	50	14	13	1	1	0	0	15	3	52	0	0	2	1	.667	0	25- -	-	3.14	2.36
2003	Drham	AAA	57	0	0	49	62.2	268	68	29	26	9	1	4	3	14	2	56	3	0	3	7	.300	0	30- -	-	4.28	3.73
2004	Fresno	AAA	57	0	0	16	70.2	313	79	40	35	8	1	2	1	22	3	42	5	0	7	4	.636	0	1- -	-	4.38	4.46
2005	Drham	AAA	48	0	0	44	52.0	227	56	25	19	8	4	0	2	15	0	35	1	0	4	3	.571	0	15- -	-	4.54	3.29
2002	TB	AL	12	0	0	3	13.1	65	12	11	6	3	1	2	3	8	0	8	0	0	1	1	.500	0	0-2	1	5.86	4.05
2005	TB	AL	5	0	0	2	7.1	37	12	9	4	2	0	1	0	2	0	4	0	0	0	0	-	0	0-0	0	8.45	4.91
	2 ML YEARS		17	0	0	5	20.2	102	24	20	10	5	1	3	3	10	0	12	0	0	1	1	.500	0	0-2	1	6.75	4.35

Ryan Garko

Bats: R **Throws:** R **Pos:** DH-1; PH-1   **Ht:** 6'2" **Wt:** 225 **Born:** 1/2/1981 **Age:** 25

						BATTING															BASERUNNING				AVERAGES		
Year	Team	Lg	G	AB	H	2B	3B	HR	(Hm	Rd)	TB	R	RBI	RC	TBB	IBB	SO	HBP	SH	SF	SB	CS	SB%	GDP	Avg	OBP	Slg
2003	MhVlly	A-	45	165	45	8	1	4	(-	-)	67	23	16	23	12	0	19	4	2	0	1	1	.50	5	.273	.337	.406
2004	Kinston	A+	65	238	78	17	1	16	(-	-)	145	44	57	60	26	3	34	15	0	1	4	1	.80	6	.328	.425	.609
2004	Akron	AA	43	172	57	15	0	6	(-	-)	90	29	38	35	14	0	28	6	0	2	1	0	1.00	3	.331	.397	.523
2004	Buffalo	AAA	6	24	9	1	0	0	(-	-)	10	3	7	4	2	0	4	0	0	2	0	0	-	0	.375	.393	.417
2005	Buffalo	AAA	127	452	137	25	3	19	(-	-)	225	75	77	87	44	2	92	18	2	5	1	3	.25	11	.303	.383	.498
2005	CLE	AL	1	1	0	0	0	0	(0	0)	0	0	0	0	0	0	1	0	0	0	0	0	-	0	.000	.000	.000

Jon Garland

Pitches: R **Bats:** R **Pos:** SP-32   **Ht:** 6'6" **Wt:** 205 **Born:** 9/27/1979 **Age:** 26

			HOW MUCH HE PITCHED						WHAT HE GAVE UP											THE RESULTS						
Year	Team	Lg	G	GS	CG	GF	IP	BFP	H	R	ER	HR	SH	SF	HB	TBB	IBB	SO	WP	Bk	W	L	Pct	ShO	Sv-Op	Hld	ERC	ERA
2000	CHA	AL	15	13	0	1	69.2	324	82	55	50	10	0	2	1	40	0	42	4	0	4	8	.333	0	0-0	1	6.26	6.46
2001	CHA	AL	35	16	0	8	117.0	510	123	59	48	16	2	5	4	55	2	61	3	0	6	7	.462	0	1-1	2	5.16	3.69
2002	CHA	AL	33	33	1	0	192.2	827	188	109	98	23	3	4	9	83	1	112	5	0	12	12	.500	1	0-0	0	4.46	4.58
2003	CHA	AL	32	32	0	0	191.2	813	188	103	96	28	4	8	4	74	1	108	8	0	12	13	.480	0	0-0	0	4.38	4.51
2004	CHA	AL	34	33	1	0	217.0	923	223	125	118	34	9	5	4	76	2	113	3	0	12	11	.522	0	0-0	0	4.56	4.89
2005	CHA	AL	32	32	3	0	221.0	901	212	92	86	26	**9**	8	7	47	3	115	2	0	18	10	.643	**3**	0-0	0	3.39	3.50
	6 ML YEARS		181	159	5	9	1009.0	4298	1016	543	496	137	27	32	29	375	9	551	25	0	64	61	.512	4	1-1	3	4.42	4.42

Dave Gassner

Pitches: L **Bats:** R **Pos:** SP-2   **Ht:** 6'2" **Wt:** 190 **Born:** 12/14/1978 **Age:** 27

			HOW MUCH HE PITCHED						WHAT HE GAVE UP											THE RESULTS						
Year	Team	Lg	G	GS	CG	GF	IP	BFP	H	R	ER	HR	SH	SF	HB	TBB	IBB	SO	WP	Bk	W	L	Pct	ShO	Sv-Op	Hld	ERC	ERA
2002	Dnedin	A+	23	21	2	0	146.2	609	143	64	56	17	5	4	4	26	1	104	4	1	11	6	.647	1	0- -	-	3.23	3.44
2002	Tenn	AA	4	4	0	0	25.1	105	22	8	7	1	0	0	1	7	1	14	1	1	1	2	.333	0	0- -	-	2.58	2.49
2002	Syrcse	AAA	1	1	0	0	5.0	24	7	3	3	0	0	0	0	2	0	1	0	0	0	1	.000	0	0- -	-	5.47	5.40
2003	NwHav	AA	35	19	1	4	145.1	603	139	54	45	10	1	5	4	28	1	92	2	1	10	4	.714	0	1- -	-	2.90	2.79
2003	Syrcse	AAA	1	1	0	0	5.0	21	5	1	1	0	2	6	0	1	0	4	0	0	1	0	1.000	0	0- -	-	2.60	1.80
2004	Roch	AAA	28	28	0	0	174.1	728	175	72	66	16	7	5	2	30	1	93	2	1	16	8	.667	0	0- -	-	3.14	3.41
2005	Roch	AAA	22	20	2	1	116.1	520	138	65	64	18	4	5	3	33	0	64	1	0	8	8	.500	0	0- -	-	5.09	4.95
2005	MIN	AL	2	2	0	0	7.2	34	9	7	5	1	0	1	0	1	0	2	0	0	1	0	1.000	0	0-0	0	3.95	5.87

Joey Gathright

Bats: L **Throws:** R **Pos:** CF-70; PR-7; PH-3; DH-1   **Ht:** 5'10" **Wt:** 170 **Born:** 4/27/1981 **Age:** 25

						BATTING															BASERUNNING				AVERAGES		
Year	Team	Lg	G	AB	H	2B	3B	HR	(Hm	Rd)	TB	R	RBI	RC	TBB	IBB	SO	HBP	SH	SF	SB	CS	SB%	GDP	Avg	OBP	Slg
2002	CtnSC	A	59	208	55	1	0	0	(-	-)	56	30	14	26	21	1	36	10	5	0	22	7	.76	1	.264	.360	.269
2003	Bkrsfld	A+	89	340	110	6	3	0	(-	-)	122	65	23	61	41	0	54	6	2	0	57	13	.81	3	.324	.406	.359
2003	Orlndo	AA	22	85	32	1	0	0	(-	-)	33	12	5	16	5	0	15	2	0	1	12	3	.80	0	.376	.419	.388
2004	Mont	AA	32	126	43	5	1	0	(-	-)	50	23	8	20	11	0	30	1	0	0	10	6	.63	1	.341	.399	.397
2004	Drham	AAA	60	236	77	9	1	0	(-	-)	88	34	8	35	19	0	46	3	2	0	33	13	.72	5	.326	.384	.373
2005	Drham	AAA	58	226	69	10	5	1	(-	-)	92	46	18	41	29	0	47	2	2	1	31	8	.79	0	.305	.388	.407
2004	TB	AL	19	52	13	0	0	0	(0	0)	13	11	1	4	2	0	14	3	0	0	6	1	.86	2	.250	.316	.250
2005	TB	AL	76	203	56	7	3	0	(0	0)	69	29	13	22	10	0	39	2	3	0	20	5	.80	5	.276	.316	.340
	2 ML YEARS		95	255	69	7	3	0	(0	0)	82	40	14	26	12	0	53	5	3	0	26	6	.81	7	.271	.316	.322

Chad Gaudin

Pitches: R **Bats:** R **Pos:** SP-3; RP-2   **Ht:** 5'11" **Wt:** 165 **Born:** 3/24/1983 **Age:** 23

			HOW MUCH HE PITCHED					WHAT HE GAVE UP										THE RESULTS							
Year	Team	Lg	G	GS	CG	GF	IP	BFP	H	R	ER	HR	SH	SF	HB	TBB	IBB	SO	WP	Bk	W	L	Pct	ShO	Sv-Op Hld	ERC	ERA
2005	Syrcse*	AAA	23	23	2	0	150.1	626	140	61	56	12	7	9	8	35	1	113	5	2	9	8	.529	2	0-- -	3.10	3.35
2003	TB	AL	15	3	0	5	40.0	173	37	18	16	4	0	2	1	16	0	23	1	0	2	0	1.000	0	0-0 0	3.70	3.60
2004	TB	AL	26	4	0	5	42.2	201	59	27	23	4	2	4	4	16	4	30	0	0	1	2	.333	0	0-1 5	6.46	4.85
2005	TOR	AL	5	3	0	0	13.0	74	31	19	19	6	0	1	1	6	0	12	0	0	1	3	.250	0	0-0 0	18.35	13.15
	3 ML YEARS		46	10	0	10	95.2	448	127	64	58	14	2	7	6	38	4	65	1	0	4	5	.444	0	0-1 5	6.57	5.46

Geoff Geary

Pitches: R **Bats:** R **Pos:** RP-40   **Ht:** 6'0" **Wt:** 175 **Born:** 8/26/1976 **Age:** 29

			HOW MUCH HE PITCHED					WHAT HE GAVE UP										THE RESULTS							
Year	Team	Lg	G	GS	CG	GF	IP	BFP	H	R	ER	HR	SH	SF	HB	TBB	IBB	SO	WP	Bk	W	L	Pct	ShO	Sv-Op Hld	ERC	ERA
2005	Rdng*	AA	1	0	0	0	2.0	6	0	0	0	0	0	0	0	0	0	2	0	0	0	0	-	0	0-- -	0.00	0.00
2005	S-WB*	AAA	10	0	0	3	16.2	67	15	5	5	0	0	0	0	2	0	14	1	0	1	2	.333	0	1-- -	1.89	2.70
2003	PHI	NL	5	0	0	2	6.0	28	8	3	3	0	1	0	0	3	0	3	0	0	0	0	-	0	0-0 0	5.70	4.50
2004	PHI	NL	33	0	0	16	44.2	200	52	29	27	8	1	2	3	16	3	30	2	1	0	1.000		0	0-0 0	5.63	5.44
2005	PHI	NL	40	0	0	12	58.0	247	54	29	24	5	2	4	1	21	4	42	3	0	2	1	.667	0	0-1 3	3.38	3.72
	3 ML YEARS		78	0	0	30	108.2	475	114	61	54	13	4	6	4	40	7	75	5	1	3	1	.750	0	0-1 3	4.39	4.47

Esteban German

Bats: R **Throws:** R **Pos:** PR-4; 2B-1; 3B-1   **Ht:** 5'9" **Wt:** 165 **Born:** 1/26/1978 **Age:** 28

			BATTING																			BASERUNNING				AVERAGES		
Year	Team	Lg	G	AB	H	2B	3B	HR	(Hm	Rd)	TB	R	RBI	RC	TBB	IBB	SO	HBP	SH	SF	SB	CS	SB%	GDP	Avg	OBP	Slg
2005	Okla*	AAA	117	489	153	27	6	5	(-	-)	207	103	68	94	65	0	74	7	1	3	43	6	.88	20	.313	.399	.423
2002	OAK	AL	9	35	7	0	0	0	(0	0)	7	4	0	2	4	0	11	1	0	0	1	0	1.00	0	.200	.300	.200
2003	OAK	AL	5	4	1	0	0	0	(0	0)	1	0	1	1	0	0	1	0	0	0	0	0	-	1	.250	.250	.250
2004	OAK	AL	31	60	15	1	1	0	(0	0)	18	9	7	8	4	0	13	0	1	0	0	1	.00	1	.250	.297	.300
2005	TEX	AL	5	4	3	1	0	0	(0	0)	4	3	1	2	0	0	1	0	0	0	2	0	1.00	0	.750	.750	1.000
	4 ML YEARS		50	103	26	2	1	0	(0	0)	30	16	9	13	8	0	26	1	1	0	3	1	.75	2	.252	.313	.291

Franklyn German

Pitches: R **Bats:** R **Pos:** RP-58   **Ht:** 6'4" **Wt:** 265 **Born:** 1/20/1980 **Age:** 26

			HOW MUCH HE PITCHED					WHAT HE GAVE UP										THE RESULTS							
Year	Team	Lg	G	GS	CG	GF	IP	BFP	H	R	ER	HR	SH	SF	HB	TBB	IBB	SO	WP	Bk	W	L	Pct	ShO	Sv-Op Hld	ERC	ERA
2002	DET	AL	7	0	0	1	6.2	25	3	0	0	0	2	0	1	2	1	6	0	0	1	0	1.000	0	1-1 1	1.09	0.00
2003	DET	AL	45	0	0	15	44.2	222	47	32	30	5	2	1	2	45	3	41	8	0	2	4	.333	0	5-7 4	7.06	6.04
2004	DET	AL	16	0	0	5	14.2	73	17	15	12	4	1	0	0	11	1	8	2	0	1	0	1.000	0	0-1 1	7.53	7.36
2005	DET	AL	58	0	0	19	59.0	270	63	26	24	7	2	5	7	34	4	38	4	1	4	0	1.000	0	1-3 4	5.80	3.66
	4 ML YEARS		126	0	0	40	125.0	590	130	73	66	16	7	6	10	92	9	93	14	1	8	4	.667	0	7-12 10	6.13	4.75

Jody Gerut

Bats: L **Throws:** L **Pos:** RF-26; LF-21; PH-13; DH-3; PR-1   **Ht:** 6'0" **Wt:** 190 **Born:** 9/18/1977 **Age:** 28

			BATTING																			BASERUNNING				AVERAGES		
Year	Team	Lg	G	AB	H	2B	3B	HR	(Hm	Rd)	TB	R	RBI	RC	TBB	IBB	SO	HBP	SH	SF	SB	CS	SB%	GDP	Avg	OBP	Slg
2005	Buffalo*	AAA	12	48	21	5	0	3	(-	-)	35	12	8	15	6	0	7	2	0	0	0	0	-	2	.438	.518	.729
2003	CLE	AL	127	480	134	33	2	22	(13	9)	237	66	75	73	35	4	70	7	1	2	4	5	.44	13	.279	.336	.494
2004	CLE	AL	134	481	121	31	5	11	(3	8)	195	72	51	60	54	4	59	7	3	3	13	6	.68	9	.252	.334	.405
2005	3 Tms		59	170	43	11	1	1	(1	0)	59	15	14	18	20	1	20	0	0	1	1	1	.50	4	.253	.330	.347
05	Cle	AL	44	138	38	9	1	1	(1	0)	52	12	12	17	18	1	14	0	0	1	1	1	.50	3	.275	.357	.377
05	ChC	NL	11	14	1	1	0	0	(0	0)	2	1	0	0	2	0	3	0	0	0	0	0	-	0	.071	.188	.143
05	Pit	NL	4	18	4	1	0	0	(0	0)	5	2	2	1	0	0	3	0	0	0	0	0	-	1	.222	.222	.278
	3 ML YEARS		320	1131	298	75	8	34	(17	17)	491	153	140	151	109	9	149	14	4	6	18	12	.60	26	.263	.334	.434

Jason Giambi

Bats: L **Throws:** R **Pos:** 1B-78; DH-59; PH-4   **Ht:** 6'3" **Wt:** 235 **Born:** 1/8/1971 **Age:** 35

			BATTING																			BASERUNNING				AVERAGES		
Year	Team	Lg	G	AB	H	2B	3B	HR	(Hm	Rd)	TB	R	RBI	RC	TBB	IBB	SO	HBP	SH	SF	SB	CS	SB%	GDP	Avg	OBP	Slg
1995	OAK	AL	54	176	45	7	0	6	(3	3)	70	27	25	27	28	0	31	3	1	2	2	1	.67	4	.256	.364	.398
1996	OAK	AL	140	536	156	40	1	20	(6	14)	258	84	79	88	51	3	95	5	1	5	0	1	.00	15	.291	.355	.481
1997	OAK	AL	142	519	152	41	2	20	(14	6)	257	66	81	91	55	3	89	6	0	8	0	1	.00	11	.293	.362	.495
1998	OAK	AL	153	562	166	28	0	27	(12	15)	275	92	110	103	81	7	102	5	0	9	2	2	.50	16	.295	.384	.489
1999	OAK	AL	158	575	181	36	1	33	(17	16)	318	115	123	132	105	6	106	7	0	8	1	1	.50	11	.315	.422	.553
2000	OAK	AL	152	510	170	29	1	43	(23	20)	330	108	137	152	137	6	96	9	0	8	2	0	1.00	9	.333	**.476**	.647
2001	OAK	AL	154	520	178	**47**	2	38	(27	11)	343	109	120	153	129	24	83	13	0	9	2	0	1.00	17	.342	**.477**	**.660**
2002	NYA	AL	155	560	176	34	1	41	(19	22)	335	120	122	139	109	9	112	15	0	5	2	2	.50	18	.314	.435	.598
2003	NYA	AL	156	535	134	25	0	41	(12	**29**)	282	97	107	120	129	9	**140**	21	0	5	2	1	.67	9	.250	.412	.527
2004	NYA	AL	80	264	55	9	0	12	(5	7)	100	33	40	42	47	1	62	8	0	3	0	1	.00	5	.208	.342	.379
2005	NYA	AL	139	417	113	14	0	32	(16	16)	223	74	87	102	**108**	5	109	19	0	1	0	0	-	7	.271	**.440**	.535
	11 ML YEARS		1483	5174	1526	310	8	313	(154	159)	2791	925	1031	1149	979	68	1025	111	2	63	13	10	.57	122	.295	.413	.539

Tony Giarratano

Bats: B **Throws:** R **Pos:** SS-13; PH-2   **Ht:** 6'0" **Wt:** 180 **Born:** 11/29/1982 **Age:** 23

Year	Team	Lg	G	AB	H	2B	3B	HR	(Hm	Rd)	TB	R	RBI	RC	TBB	IBB	SO	HBP	SH	SF	SB	CS	SB%	GDP	Avg	OBP	Slg
2004	W Mich	A	43	165	47	6	1	1	(-	-)	58	20	13	26	25	3	22	2	1	1	11	3	.79	4	.285	.383	.352
2004	Lkland	A+	53	202	76	11	0	5	(-	-)	102	30	25	41	16	0	38	1	6	2	14	8	.64	1	.376	.421	.505
2005	Erie	AA	89	346	92	22	3	3	(-	-)	129	40	32	46	32	0	75	5	3	3	12	5	.71	9	.266	.334	.373
2005	DET	AL	15	42	6	0	0	1	(0	1)	9	4	4	3	5	0	7	0	0	0	1	0	1.00	1	.143	.234	.214

Jay Gibbons

Bats: L **Throws:** L **Pos:** RF-71; DH-40; 1B-22; PH-10   **Ht:** 6'0" **Wt:** 200 **Born:** 3/2/1977 **Age:** 29

Year	Team	Lg	G	AB	H	2B	3B	HR	(Hm	Rd)	TB	R	RBI	RC	TBB	IBB	SO	HBP	SH	SF	SB	CS	SB%	GDP	Avg	OBP	Slg
2001	BAL	AL	73	225	53	10	0	15	(9	6)	108	27	36	31	17	0	39	4	0	0	0	1	.00	7	.236	.301	.480
2002	BAL	AL	136	490	121	29	1	28	(17	11)	236	71	69	71	45	3	66	2	0	4	1	3	.25	9	.247	.311	.482
2003	BAL	AL	160	625	173	39	2	23	(12	11)	285	80	100	94	49	11	89	3	0	5	0	1	.00	12	.277	.330	.456
2004	BAL	AL	97	346	85	14	1	10	(4	6)	131	36	47	38	29	0	64	1	1	3	1	1	.50	11	.246	.303	.379
2005	BAL	AL	139	488	135	33	3	26	(13	13)	252	72	79	73	28	3	56	1	0	1	0	0	-	15	.277	.317	.516
	5 ML YEARS		605	2174	567	125	7	102	(55	47)	1012	286	331	307	168	17	314	11	1	13	2	6	.25	54	.261	.315	.466

Geronimo Gil

Bats: R **Throws:** R **Pos:** C-62; PH-3   **Ht:** 6'2" **Wt:** 195 **Born:** 8/7/1975 **Age:** 30

Year	Team	Lg	G	AB	H	2B	3B	HR	(Hm	Rd)	TB	R	RBI	RC	TBB	IBB	SO	HBP	SH	SF	SB	CS	SB%	GDP	Avg	OBP	Slg
2005	Bowie*	AA	3	7	3	0	0	0	(-	-)	3	2	1	1	1	0	1	1	0	0	0	0	-	0	.429	.556	.429
2001	BAL	AL	17	58	17	2	0	0	(0	0)	19	3	6	7	5	0	7	2	1	0	0	0	-	1	.293	.369	.328
2002	BAL	AL	125	422	98	19	0	12	(5	7)	153	33	45	33	21	1	88	1	5	1	2	2	.50	17	.232	.270	.363
2003	BAL	AL	54	169	40	4	0	3	(2	1)	53	22	16	18	12	0	34	3	2	0	0	0	-	2	.237	.299	.314
2004	BAL	AL	12	32	9	2	0	0	(0	0)	11	1	4	5	3	1	5	0	0	0	0	0	-	0	.281	.343	.344
2005	BAL	AL	64	125	24	3	0	4	(1	3)	39	7	17	6	5	0	23	0	2	2	0	0	-	10	.192	.220	.312
	5 ML YEARS		272	806	188	30	0	19	(8	11)	275	66	88	69	46	2	157	6	10	3	2	2	.50	30	.233	.279	.341

Brian Giles

Bats: L **Throws:** L **Pos:** RF-143; CF-17; PH-3; LF-1   **Ht:** 5'10" **Wt:** 202 **Born:** 1/20/1971 **Age:** 35

Year	Team	Lg	G	AB	H	2B	3B	HR	(Hm	Rd)	TB	R	RBI	RC	TBB	IBB	SO	HBP	SH	SF	SB	CS	SB%	GDP	Avg	OBP	Slg
1995	CLE	AL	6	9	5	0	0	1	(0	1)	8	6	3	3	0	0	1	0	0	0	0	0	-	0	.556	.556	.889
1996	CLE	AL	51	121	43	14	1	5	(2	3)	74	26	27	29	19	4	13	0	0	3	3	0	1.00	6	.355	.434	.612
1997	CLE	AL	130	377	101	15	3	17	(7	10)	173	62	61	66	63	2	50	1	3	7	13	3	.81	10	.268	.368	.459
1998	CLE	AL	112	350	94	19	0	16	(10	6)	161	56	66	66	73	8	75	3	1	3	10	5	.67	7	.269	.396	.460
1999	PIT	NL	141	521	164	33	3	39	(24	15)	320	109	115	127	95	7	80	3	0	8	6	2	.75	14	.315	.418	.614
2000	PIT	NL	156	559	176	37	7	35	(16	19)	332	111	123	139	114	13	69	7	0	8	6	0	1.00	15	.315	.432	.594
2001	PIT	NL	160	576	178	37	7	37	(18	19)	340	116	95	131	90	14	67	4	0	4	13	6	.68	10	.309	.404	.590
2002	PIT	NL	153	497	148	37	5	38	(15	23)	309	95	103	128	135	24	74	7	0	5	15	6	.71	10	.298	.450	.622
2003	2 Tms	NL	134	492	147	34	6	20	(12	8)	253	93	88	102	105	12	58	8	0	4	4	3	.57	12	.299	.427	.514
2004	SD	NL	159	609	173	33	7	23	(10	13)	289	97	94	102	89	6	80	4	0	9	10	3	.77	12	.284	.374	.475
2005	SD	NL	158	545	164	38	8	15	(6	9)	263	92	83	112	**119**	9	64	2	0	8	13	5	.72	14	.301	.423	.483
03	Pit	NL	105	388	116	30	4	16	(10	6)	202	70	70	79	85	11	48	6	0	2	0	3	.00	8	.299	.430	.521
03	SD	NL	29	104	31	4	2	4	(2	2)	51	23	18	23	20	1	10	2	0	2	4	0	1.00	4	.298	.414	.490
	11 ML YEARS		1360	4656	1393	297	47	246	(120	126)	2522	863	858	1005	902	99	631	39	4	59	93	33	.74	110	.299	.413	.542

Marcus Giles

Bats: R **Throws:** R **Pos:** 2B-149; PH-3; 3B-1   **Ht:** 5'8" **Wt:** 180 **Born:** 5/18/1978 **Age:** 28

Year	Team	Lg	G	AB	H	2B	3B	HR	(Hm	Rd)	TB	R	RBI	RC	TBB	IBB	SO	HBP	SH	SF	SB	CS	SB%	GDP	Avg	OBP	Slg
2001	ATL	NL	68	244	64	10	2	9	(5	4)	105	36	31	33	28	0	37	0	1	0	2	5	.29	8	.262	.338	.430
2002	ATL	NL	68	213	49	10	1	8	(4	4)	85	27	23	22	25	3	41	2	1	1	1	1	.50	5	.230	.315	.399
2003	ATL	NL	145	551	174	49	2	21	(9	12)	290	101	69	101	59	2	80	11	10	4	14	4	.78	7	.316	.390	.526
2004	ATL	NL	102	379	118	22	2	8	(6	2)	168	61	48	67	36	0	70	9	3	7	17	4	.81	6	.311	.378	.443
2005	ATL	NL	152	577	168	45	4	15	(11	4)	266	104	63	96	64	1	108	5	4	4	16	3	.84	13	.291	.365	.461
	5 ML YEARS		535	1964	573	136	11	61	(35	26)	914	329	234	319	212	6	336	27	19	16	50	17	.75	39	.292	.366	.465

Keith Ginter

Bats: R **Throws:** R **Pos:** 2B-25; 3B-12; PH-11; DH-9; LF-2   **Ht:** 5'10" **Wt:** 190 **Born:** 5/5/1976 **Age:** 30

Year	Team	Lg	G	AB	H	2B	3B	HR	(Hm	Rd)	TB	R	RBI	RC	TBB	IBB	SO	HBP	SH	SF	SB	CS	SB%	GDP	Avg	OBP	Slg
2005	Scrmto*	AAA	14	57	19	8	0	3	(-	-)	36	9	12	13	4	0	11	1	1	0	0	0	-	0	.333	.387	.632
2000	HOU	NL	5	8	2	0	0	1	(1	0)	5	3	3	2	1	0	3	0	0	1	0	0	-	0	.250	.300	.625
2001	HOU	NL	1	1	0	0	0	0	(0	0)	0	0	0	0	0	0	0	0	0	0	0	0	-	0	.000	.000	.000
2002	2 Tms	NL	28	81	19	9	0	1	(1	0)	31	7	8	13	17	0	15	1	0	0	0	0	-	9	.235	.374	.383
2003	MIL	NL	127	358	92	15	2	14	(9	5)	153	51	44	52	37	1	87	17	0	3	1	1	.50	9	.257	.352	.427
2004	MIL	NL	113	386	101	23	2	19	(9	10)	185	47	60	57	37	2	100	6	4	4	8	1	.89	9	.262	.333	.479
2005	OAK	AL	51	137	22	5	0	3	(0	3)	36	12	25	9	13	0	25	1	2	3	0	0	-	5	.161	.234	.263
02	Hou	NL	7	5	1	1	0	0	(0	0)	2	1	0	1	2	0	1	1	0	0	0	0	-	0	.200	.500	.400
02	Mil	NL	21	76	18	8	0	1	(1	0)	29	6	8	12	15	0	14	0	0	0	0	0	-	0	.237	.363	.382
	6 ML YEARS		325	971	236	52	4	38	(20	18)	410	120	140	133	105	3	230	25	6	11	9	2	.82	23	.243	.329	.422

Matt Ginter

Pitches: R Bats: R Pos: RP-13; SP-1 Ht: 6'1" Wt: 220 Born: 12/24/1977 Age: 28

			HOW MUCH HE PITCHED						WHAT HE GAVE UP											THE RESULTS							
Year	Team	Lg	G	GS	CG	GF	IP	BFP	H	R	ER	HR	SH	SF	HB	TBB	IBB	SO	WP	Bk	W	L	Pct	ShO	Sv-Op	Hld	ERC	ERA
2005	Toledo*	AAA	17	10	0	1	68.2	288	72	35	33	9	2	0	3	10	0	49	2	1	4	3	.571	0	0- -	-	3.68	4.33
2000	CHA	AL	7	0	0	3	9.1	52	18	14	14	5	0	1	0	7	0	6	1	0	1	0	1.000	0	0-1	0	16.24	13.50
2001	CHA	AL	20	0	0	7	39.2	167	34	23	23	2	0	3	7	14	2	24	2	0	1	0	1.000	0	0-0	1	3.44	5.22
2002	CHA	AL	33	0	0	15	54.1	236	59	34	27	6	0	2	1	21	0	37	2	0	1	0	1.000	0	1-1	0	4.72	4.47
2003	CHA	AL	3	0	0	0	3.1	15	2	5	5	1	1	0	2	1	0	0	0	0	0	0	-	0	0-0	0	5.16	13.50
2004	NYN	NL	15	14	0	0	69.1	313	82	41	35	8	3	1	5	20	5	38	1	0	1	3	.250	0	0-0	0	4.87	4.54
2005	DET	AL	14	1	0	2	35.0	157	49	25	24	6	1	1	2	9	1	15	0	0	0	1	.000	0	0-0	0	6.81	6.17
	6 ML YEARS		92	15	0	27	211.0	940	244	142	128	28	5	8	17	72	8	120	6	0	4	4	.500	0	1-2	0	5.28	5.46

Charles Gipson

Bats: R Throws: R Pos: LF-7; PR-7; CF-5; RF-1; PH-1 Ht: 6'1" Wt: 195 Born: 12/16/1972 Age: 33

									BATTING											BASERUNNING				AVERAGES		
Year	Team	Lg	G	AB	H	2B	3B	HR	(Hm	Rd)	TB	R	RBI	RC	TBB	IBB	SO	HBP	SH	SF	SB	CS	SB%	GDP	Avg	OBP	Slg
2005	RdRck*	AAA	110	393	119	36	3	2	(-	-)	156	58	25	57	25	0	75	8	4	1	19	9	.68	3	.303	.356	.397
1998	SEA	AL	44	51	12	1	0	0	(0	0)	13	11	2	4	5	1	9	1	0	0	2	1	.67	1	.235	.316	.255
1999	SEA	AL	55	80	18	5	2	0	(0	0)	27	16	9	6	6	0	13	1	2	0	3	4	.43	2	.225	.287	.338
2000	SEA	AL	59	29	9	1	1	0	(0	0)	12	7	3	4	4	0	9	0	0	0	2	3	.40	0	.310	.394	.414
2001	SEA	AL	94	64	14	2	2	0	(0	0)	20	16	5	5	4	0	20	2	1	1	1	1	.50	2	.219	.282	.313
2002	SEA	AL	79	72	17	5	2	0	(0	0)	26	22	8	7	9	0	14	1	2	0	4	0	1.00	3	.236	.329	.361
2003	NYA	AL	18	10	2	0	0	0	(0	0)	2	3	2	1	1	0	2	0	1	0	2	1	.67	0	.200	.273	.200
2004	TB	AL	5	4	2	0	0	0	(0	0)	2	1	0	2	0	0	1	0	1	0	1	0	1.00	0	.500	.500	.500
2005	HOU	NL	19	11	2	1	0	0	(0	0)	3	2	1	1	1	0	3	0	2	0	1	1	.50	0	.182	.250	.273
	8 ML YEARS		373	321	76	15	7	0	(0	0)	105	78	30	30	30	1	71	5	9	1	16	11	.59	8	.237	.311	.327

Troy Glaus

Bats: R Throws: R Pos: 3B-145; PH-4; DH-1 Ht: 6'5" Wt: 245 Born: 8/3/1976 Age: 29

									BATTING											BASERUNNING				AVERAGES		
Year	Team	Lg	G	AB	H	2B	3B	HR	(Hm	Rd)	TB	R	RBI	RC	TBB	IBB	SO	HBP	SH	SF	SB	CS	SB%	GDP	Avg	OBP	Slg
1998	ANA	AL	48	165	36	9	0	1	(0	1)	48	19	23	13	15	0	51	0	0	2	1	0	1.00	3	.218	.280	.291
1999	ANA	AL	154	551	132	29	0	29	(12	17)	248	85	79	84	71	1	143	6	0	3	5	1	.83	9	.240	.331	.450
2000	ANA	AL	159	563	160	37	1	47	(24	23)	340	120	102	129	112	6	163	2	0	1	14	11	.56	14	.284	.404	.604
2001	ANA	AL	161	588	147	38	2	41	(22	19)	312	100	108	114	107	7	158	6	0	7	10	3	.77	16	.250	.367	.531
2002	ANA	AL	156	569	142	24	1	30	(13	17)	258	99	111	100	88	4	144	6	0	8	10	3	.77	12	.250	.352	.453
2003	ANA	AL	91	319	79	17	2	16	(9	7)	148	53	50	48	46	4	73	1	0	1	7	2	.78	8	.248	.343	.464
2004	ANA	AL	58	207	52	11	1	18	(9	9)	119	47	42	41	31	3	52	3	0	1	2	3	.40	6	.251	.355	.575
2005	ARI	NL	149	538	139	29	1	37	(20	17)	281	78	97	87	84	2	145	7	0	5	4	2	.67	7	.258	.363	.522
	8 ML YEARS		976	3500	887	194	8	219	(109	110)	1754	601	612	616	554	27	929	31	0	28	53	25	.68	75	.253	.358	.501

Tom Glavine

Pitches: L Bats: L Pos: SP-33 Ht: 6'0" Wt: 185 Born: 3/25/1966 Age: 40

					HOW MUCH HE PITCHED			WHAT HE GAVE UP												THE RESULTS							
Year	Team	Lg	G	GS	CG	GF	IP	BFP	H	R	ER	HR	SH	SF	HB	TBB	IBB	SO	WP	Bk	W	L	Pct	ShO	Sv-Op	Hld	ERC	ERA
1987	ATL	NL	9	9	0	0	50.1	238	55	34	31	5	2	3	3	33	4	20	1	1	2	4	.333	0	0-0	0	5.70	5.54
1988	ATL	NL	34	34	1	0	195.1	844	201	111	99	12	17	11	8	63	7	84	2	2	7	17	.292	0	0-0	0	3.74	4.56
1989	ATL	NL	29	29	6	0	186.0	766	172	88	76	20	11	4	2	40	3	90	2	0	14	8	.636	4	0-0	0	2.99	3.68
1990	ATL	NL	33	33	1	0	214.1	929	232	111	102	18	21	2	1	78	10	129	8	1	10	12	.455	0	0-0	0	4.24	4.28
1991	ATL	NL	34	34	9	0	246.2	989	201	83	70	17	7	6	2	69	6	192	10	2	20	11	.645	1	0-0	0	2.47	2.55
1992	ATL	NL	33	33	7	0	225.0	919	197	81	69	6	2	6	2	70	7	129	5	0	20	8	.714	5	0-0	0	2.61	2.76
1993	ATL	NL	36	36	4	0	239.1	1014	236	91	85	16	10	2	2	90	7	120	4	0	22	6	.786	2	0-0	0	3.70	3.20
1994	ATL	NL	25	25	2	0	165.1	731	173	76	73	10	9	6	1	70	10	140	8	1	13	9	.591	0	0-0	0	4.02	3.97
1995	ATL	NL	29	29	3	0	198.2	822	182	76	68	9	7	5	5	66	0	127	3	0	16	7	.696	1	0-0	0	3.14	3.08
1996	ATL	NL	36	36	1	0	235.1	994	222	91	78	14	15	2	6	85	7	181	4	0	15	10	.600	1	0-0	0	3.29	2.98
1997	ATL	NL	33	33	5	0	240.0	970	197	86	79	20	11	6	4	79	9	152	3	0	14	7	.667	2	0-0	0	2.80	2.96
1998	ATL	NL	33	33	4	0	229.1	934	202	67	63	13	6	2	2	74	2	157	3	0	20	6	.769	3	0-0	0	2.93	2.47
1999	ATL	NL	35	35	2	0	234.0	1023	259	115	107	18	22	10	4	83	14	138	2	0	14	11	.560	0	0-0	0	4.31	4.12
2000	ATL	NL	35	35	4	0	241.0	992	222	101	91	24	9	5	4	65	6	152	0	0	21	9	.700	2	0-0	0	3.19	3.40
2001	ATL	NL	35	35	1	0	219.1	929	213	92	87	24	5	8	2	97	10	116	2	0	16	7	.696	1	0-0	0	4.21	3.57
2002	ATL	NL	36	36	2	0	224.2	936	210	85	74	21	12	6	8	78	8	127	2	0	18	11	.621	1	0-0	0	3.61	2.96
2003	NYN	NL	32	32	0	0	183.1	791	205	94	92	21	7	4	4	66	7	82	2	0	9	14	.391	0	0-0	0	4.77	4.52
2004	NYN	NL	33	33	1	0	212.1	904	204	94	85	20	13	10	0	70	10	109	0	0	11	14	.440	1	0-0	0	3.43	3.60
2005	NYN	NL	33	33	2	0	211.1	901	227	88	83	12	19	3	3	61	5	105	1	0	13	13	.500	1	0-0	0	3.79	3.53
	19 ML YEARS		603	603	55	0	3951.2	16626	3810	1664	1512	300	205	101	55	1337	132	2350	62	7	275	184	.599	24	0-0	0	3.50	3.44

Ross Gload

Bats: L Throws: L Pos: 1B-24; PH-4; PR-4; LF-2; RF-1 Ht: 6'0" Wt: 185 Born: 4/5/1976 Age: 30

									BATTING											BASERUNNING				AVERAGES		
Year	Team	Lg	G	AB	H	2B	3B	HR	(Hm	Rd)	TB	R	RBI	RC	TBB	IBB	SO	HBP	SH	SF	SB	CS	SB%	GDP	Avg	OBP	Slg
2005	Charltt*	AAA	60	236	86	22	1	15	(-	-)	155	45	45	60	22	3	37	1	1	3	0	1	.00	2	.364	.416	.657
2000	CHN	NL	18	31	6	0	1	1	(0	1)	11	4	3	3	0	0	10	0	0	1	0	0	-	1	.194	.257	.355
2002	COL	NL	26	31	8	1	0	1	(1	0)	12	4	4	3	3	0	7	0	0	0	0	0	-	0	.258	.324	.387
2004	CHA	AL	110	234	75	16	0	7	(3	4)	112	28	44	41	20	1	37	2	1	3	0	3	.00	11	.321	.375	.479
2005	CHA	AL	28	42	7	2	0	0	(0	0)	9	2	5	2	2	0	9	0	0	0	0	0	-	1	.167	.205	.214
	4 ML YEARS		182	338	96	19	1	9	(4	5)	144	38	56	49	28	1	63	2	1	4	0	3	.00	13	.284	.339	.426

Gary Glover

Pitches: R Bats: R Pos: SP-11; RP-4　　　　Ht: 6'5" Wt: 205 Born: 12/3/1976 Age: 29

			HOW MUCH HE PITCHED						WHAT HE GAVE UP												THE RESULTS							
Year	Team	Lg	G	GS	CG	GF	IP	BFP	H	R	ER	HR	SH	SF	HB	TBB	IBB	SO	WP	Bk	W	L	Pct	ShO	Sv-Op	Hld	ERC	ERA
2005	Nashv*	AAA	17	16	1	1	92.0	396	91	39	31	9	3	3	1	29	1	75	5	0	6	4	.600	0	1--	-	3.62	3.03
1999	TOR	AL	1	0	0	1	1.0	3	0	0	0	0	0	0	0	1	0	0	0	0	0	0	-	0	0-0	0	1.26	0.00
2001	CHA	AL	46	11	0	10	100.1	429	98	61	55	16	2	2	4	32	3	63	4	0	5	5	.500	0	0-1	7	4.12	4.93
2002	CHA	AL	41	22	0	10	138.1	604	136	86	80	21	6	2	7	52	1	70	6	0	7	8	.467	0	1-1	2	4.39	5.20
2003	2 Tms	AL	42	0	0	15	62.2	279	77	33	33	6	0	5	3	22	3	37	2	0	2	0	1.000	0	0-0	1	5.37	4.74
2004	MIL	NL	4	3	0	0	18.0	82	18	9	7	2	2	2	2	8	1	8	1	0	2	1	.667	0	0-0	0	4.57	3.50
2005	MIL	NL	15	11	0	1	64.2	284	74	41	40	10	3	2	2	20	0	58	3	0	5	4	.556	0	0-0	0	5.06	5.57
03	CWS	AL	24	0	0	8	35.2	160	43	18	18	3	0	3	2	14	2	23	1	0	1	0	1.000	0	0-0	1	5.32	4.54
03	Ana	AL	18	0	0	7	27.0	119	34	15	15	3	0	2	1	8	1	14	1	0	1	0	1.000	0	0-0	0	5.44	5.00
6 ML YEARS			149	47	0	37	385.0	1681	403	230	215	55	13	13	18	135	8	236	16	0	21	18	.538	0	1-2	10	4.59	5.03

Ryan Glynn

Pitches: R Bats: R Pos: SP-3; RP-2　　　　Ht: 6'3" Wt: 200 Born: 11/1/1974 Age: 31

			HOW MUCH HE PITCHED						WHAT HE GAVE UP												THE RESULTS							
Year	Team	Lg	G	GS	CG	GF	IP	BFP	H	R	ER	HR	SH	SF	HB	TBB	IBB	SO	WP	Bk	W	L	Pct	ShO	Sv-Op	Hld	ERC	ERA
2005	Syrcse*	AAA	9	6	0	0	37.1	164	41	27	26	6	1	4	2	11	0	23	2	0	2	4	.333	0	0--	-	3.62	6.27
2005	Scrmto*	AAA	11	11	0	0	55.0	234	46	20	17	4	1	1	1	23	1	54	2	0	3	1	.750	0	0--	-	3.06	2.78
1999	TEX	AL	13	10	0	2	54.2	262	71	46	44	10	0	1	1	35	0	39	3	1	2	4	.333	0	0-0	0	7.77	7.24
2000	TEX	AL	16	16	0	0	88.2	412	107	65	55	15	3	0	3	41	2	33	3	0	5	7	.417	0	0-0	0	6.12	5.58
2001	TEX	AL	12	9	0	3	46.0	219	59	38	36	7	0	2	0	26	1	15	5	0	1	5	.167	0	0-0	0	6.81	7.04
2004	TOR	AL	6	2	0	0	20.0	89	19	9	9	4	1	1	3	8	1	14	0	0	1	0	1.000	0	0-0	0	4.99	4.05
2005	OAK	AL	5	3	0	2	17.0	82	24	16	13	5	0	0	0	7	0	15	0	0	0	4	.000	0	0-0	0	8.03	6.88
5 ML YEARS			52	40	0	7	226.1	1064	280	174	157	41	4	4	7	117	4	116	11	1	9	20	.310	0	0-0	0	6.69	6.24

Jimmy Gobble

Pitches: L Bats: L Pos: RP-24; SP-4　　　　Ht: 6'3" Wt: 190 Born: 7/19/1981 Age: 24

			HOW MUCH HE PITCHED						WHAT HE GAVE UP												THE RESULTS							
Year	Team	Lg	G	GS	CG	GF	IP	BFP	H	R	ER	HR	SH	SF	HB	TBB	IBB	SO	WP	Bk	W	L	Pct	ShO	Sv-Op	Hld	ERC	ERA
2005	Omha*	AAA	12	12	0	0	58.1	272	76	48	43	8	0	4	2	21	0	45	5	0	2	7	.222	0	0--	-	6.03	6.63
2003	KC	AL	9	9	0	0	52.2	230	56	32	27	8	1	3	4	15	0	31	1	0	4	5	.444	0	0-0	0	4.61	4.61
2004	KC	AL	25	24	1	0	148.0	638	157	94	88	24	4	7	3	43	0	49	4	0	9	8	.529	0	0-0	0	4.47	5.35
2005	KC	AL	28	4	0	11	53.2	249	64	34	34	9	3	1	1	30	4	38	2	0	1	1	.500	0	0-0	4	6.39	5.70
3 ML YEARS			62	37	1	11	254.1	1117	277	160	149	41	8	11	8	88	4	118	7	0	14	14	.500	0	0-0	4	4.89	5.27

Tyrell Godwin

Bats: L Throws: R Pos: PH-3　　　　Ht: 6'0" Wt: 200 Born: 7/10/1979 Age: 26

			BATTING																			BASERUNNING				AVERAGES		
Year	Team	Lg	G	AB	H	2B	3B	HR	(Hm	Rd)	TB	R	RBI	RC	TBB	IBB	SO	HBP	SH	SF		SB	CS	SB%	GDP	Avg	OBP	Slg
2001	Auburn	A-	33	117	43	8	2	2	(-	-)	61	26	15	28	19	0	27	2	0	0		9	5	.64	1	.368	.464	.521
2002	Auburn	A-	48	185	52	8	5	0	(-	-)	70	31	16	28	20	3	23	4	0	0		10	2	.83	2	.281	.364	.378
2003	Dnedin	A+	97	322	88	16	0	1	(-	-)	107	52	33	42	29	2	39	8	7	0		20	7	.74	6	.273	.344	.332
2003	NwHav	AA	33	123	38	6	3	1	(-	-)	53	20	13	18	3	0	27	1	1	1		6	1	.86	5	.309	.328	.431
2004	Ham	AA	133	521	132	21	7	6	(-	-)	185	85	40	68	52	0	110	5	4	2		42	12	.78	6	.253	.326	.355
2005	NewOr	AAA	129	499	160	22	6	9	(-	-)	221	83	48	87	50	2	77	5	6	1		22	12	.65	6	.321	.387	.443
2005	WAS	NL	3	3	0	0	0	0	(0	0)	0	0	0	0	0	0	1	0	0	0		0	0	-	0	.000	.000	.000

Jonny Gomes

Bats: R Throws: R Pos: DH-49; RF-36; LF-14; PH-4　　　　Ht: 6'1" Wt: 205 Born: 11/22/1980 Age: 25

			BATTING																			BASERUNNING				AVERAGES		
Year	Team	Lg	G	AB	H	2B	3B	HR	(Hm	Rd)	TB	R	RBI	RC	TBB	IBB	SO	HBP	SH	SF		SB	CS	SB%	GDP	Avg	OBP	Slg
2005	Drham*	AAA	45	162	52	13	0	14	(-	-)	107	34	46	47	30	2	44	8	0	2		7	1	.88	2	.321	.446	.660
2003	TB	AL	8	15	2	1	0	0	(0	0)	3	1	0	0	0	0	6	1	0	0		0	0	-	0	.133	.188	.200
2004	TB	AL	5	14	1	0	0	0	(0	0)	1	0	1	0	1	0	6	0	0	0		0	0	-	0	.071	.133	.071
2005	TB	AL	101	348	98	13	6	21	(11	10)	186	61	54	62	39	1	113	14	1	5		9	5	.64	6	.282	.372	.534
3 ML YEARS			114	377	101	14	6	21	(11	10)	190	62	55	62	40	1	125	15	1	5		9	5	.64	6	.268	.357	.504

Alexis Gomez

Bats: L Throws: L Pos: LF-6; CF-3; PH-2　　　　Ht: 6'2" Wt: 180 Born: 8/6/1978 Age: 27

			BATTING																			BASERUNNING				AVERAGES		
Year	Team	Lg	G	AB	H	2B	3B	HR	(Hm	Rd)	TB	R	RBI	RC	TBB	IBB	SO	HBP	SH	SF		SB	CS	SB%	GDP	Avg	OBP	Slg
2005	Toledo*	AAA	114	424	130	28	6	7	(-	-)	191	51	55	68	27	3	91	2	3	4		21	7	.75	7	.307	.348	.450
2002	KC	AL	5	10	2	0	0	0	(0	0)	2	0	0	0	0	0	2	0	0	0		0	0	-	0	.200	.200	.200
2004	KC	AL	13	29	8	1	0	0	(0	0)	9	1	4	3	2	0	8	0	0	0		0	0	-	1	.276	.323	.310
2005	DET	AL	9	16	3	0	0	0	(0	0)	3	2	1	1	2	0	2	0	0	0		0	0	-	0	.188	.278	.188
3 ML YEARS			27	55	13	1	0	0	(0	0)	14	3	5	4	4	0	12	0	0	0		0	0	-	1	.236	.288	.255

Chris Gomez

Bats: R **Throws:** R **Pos:** 1B-42; 2B-18; 3B-17; SS-10; PH-7; DH-6; PR-3   **Ht:** 6'1" **Wt:** 185 **Born:** 6/16/1971 **Age:** 35

Year	Team	Lg	G	AB	H	2B	3B	HR	(Hm	Rd)	TB	R	RBI	RC	TBB	IBB	SO	HBP	SH	SF	SB	CS	SB%	GDP	Avg	OBP	Slg
1993	DET	AL	46	128	32	7	1	0	(0	0)	41	11	11	12	9	0	17	1	3	0	2	2	.50	2	.250	.304	.320
1994	DET	AL	84	296	76	19	0	8	(5	3)	119	32	53	39	33	0	64	3	3	1	5	3	.63	8	.257	.336	.402
1995	DET	AL	123	431	96	20	2	11	(5	6)	153	49	50	43	41	0	96	3	3	4	4	1	.80	13	.223	.292	.355
1996	2 Tms		137	456	117	21	1	4	(2	2)	152	53	45	52	57	1	84	7	6	2	3	3	.50	16	.257	.347	.333
1997	SD	NL	150	522	132	19	2	5	(2	3)	170	62	54	52	53	1	114	5	3	3	5	8	.38	16	.253	.326	.326
1998	SD	NL	145	449	120	32	3	4	(3	1)	170	55	39	58	51	7	87	5	7	3	1	3	.25	11	.267	.346	.379
1999	SD	NL	76	234	59	8	1	1	(1	0)	72	20	15	23	27	3	49	1	2	1	1	2	.33	6	.252	.331	.308
2000	SD	NL	33	54	12	0	0	0	(0	0)	12	4	3	4	7	0	5	0	1	1	0	0	-	1	.222	.306	.222
2001	2 Tms		98	301	78	19	0	8	(5	3)	121	37	43	36	17	0	38	2	6	5	4	0	1.00	9	.259	.298	.402
2002	TB	AL	130	461	122	31	3	10	(2	8)	189	51	46	51	21	0	58	7	6	3	1	3	.25	8	.265	.305	.410
2003	MIN	AL	58	175	44	9	3	1	(0	1)	62	14	15	15	7	1	13	0	2	1	2	1	.67	10	.251	.279	.354
2004	TOR	AL	109	341	96	11	1	3	(1	2)	118	41	37	48	28	0	41	2	3	3	3	2	.60	4	.282	.337	.346
2005	BAL	AL	89	219	61	11	0	1	(0	1)	75	27	18	24	27	1	17	1	6	1	2	1	.67	14	.279	.349	.342
96	Det	AL	48	128	31	5	0	1	(1	0)	39	21	16	13	18	0	20	1	3	0	1	1	.50	5	.242	.340	.305
96	SD	NL	89	328	86	16	1	3	(1	2)	113	32	29	39	39	1	64	6	3	2	2	2	.50	11	.262	.349	.345
01	SD	NL	40	112	21	3	0	0	(0	0)	24	6	7	4	9	0	14	0	2	2	1	0	1.00	5	.188	.244	.214
01	TB	AL	58	189	57	16	0	8	(5	3)	97	31	36	32	8	0	24	2	4	3	3	0	1.00	4	.302	.332	.513
	13 ML YEARS		1278	4067	1045	207	17	56	(26	30)	1454	456	429	457	378	14	683	37	51	28	33	29	.53	118	.257	.324	.358

Adrian Gonzalez

Bats: L **Throws:** L **Pos:** DH-32; 1B-10; PH-2; RF-1; PR-1   **Ht:** 6'2" **Wt:** 220 **Born:** 5/8/1982 **Age:** 24

Year	Team	Lg	G	AB	H	2B	3B	HR	(Hm	Rd)	TB	R	RBI	RC	TBB	IBB	SO	HBP	SH	SF	SB	CS	SB%	GDP	Avg	OBP	Slg
2000	Marlins	R	53	193	57	10	1	0	(-	-)	69	24	30	30	32	3	35	2	0	2	0	0	-	6	.295	.397	.358
2000	Utica	A-	8	29	9	3	0	0	(-	-)	12	7	3	6	7	0	6	0	0	0	0	0	-	0	.310	.444	.414
2001	Kane	A	127	516	161	37	1	17	(-	-)	251	86	103	89	57	6	83	5	0	6	5	5	.50	17	.312	.382	.486
2002	Portlnd	AA	138	508	135	34	1	17	(-	-)	222	70	96	73	54	6	112	8	0	3	6	3	.67	13	.266	.344	.437
2003	Frisco	AA	45	173	49	6	2	3	(-	-)	68	16	17	21	11	2	27	1	0	2	0	0	-	2	.283	.326	.393
2003	Carlina	AA	36	137	42	9	1	1	(-	-)	56	15	16	19	14	0	25	0	0	1	1	1	.50	6	.307	.368	.409
2003	Albq	AAA	39	139	30	5	1	1	(-	-)	40	17	18	10	14	0	25	0	0	1	1	0	1.00	6	.216	.286	.288
2004	Okla	AAA	123	457	139	28	3	12	(-	-)	209	61	88	71	39	1	73	6	2	4	1	1	.50	17	.304	.364	.457
2005	Okla	AAA	84	328	111	17	1	18	(-	-)	184	61	65	72	32	3	44	4	0	4	0	0	-	13	.338	.399	.561
2004	TEX	AL	16	42	10	3	0	1	(1	0)	16	7	7	7	2	0	6	0	0	0	0	0	-	0	.238	.273	.381
2005	TEX	AL	43	150	34	7	1	6	(3	3)	61	17	17	13	10	2	37	0	0	2	0	0	-	3	.227	.272	.407
	2 ML YEARS		59	192	44	10	1	7	(4	3)	77	24	24	20	12	2	43	0	0	2	0	0	-	3	.229	.272	.401

Alex Gonzalez

Bats: R **Throws:** R **Pos:** SS-124; PR-5; PH-1   **Ht:** 6'0" **Wt:** 200 **Born:** 2/15/1977 **Age:** 29

Year	Team	Lg	G	AB	H	2B	3B	HR	(Hm	Rd)	TB	R	RBI	RC	TBB	IBB	SO	HBP	SH	SF	SB	CS	SB%	GDP	Avg	OBP	Slg
1998	FLA	NL	25	86	13	2	0	3	(1	2)	24	11	7	5	9	0	30	1	2	0	0	0	-	2	.151	.240	.279
1999	FLA	NL	136	560	155	28	8	14	(7	7)	241	81	59	69	15	0	113	12	1	3	3	5	.38	13	.277	.308	.430
2000	FLA	NL	109	385	77	17	4	7	(5	2)	123	35	42	26	13	0	77	2	5	2	7	1	.88	7	.200	.229	.319
2001	FLA	NL	145	515	129	36	1	9	(5	4)	194	57	48	56	30	6	107	10	3	3	2	2	.50	13	.250	.303	.377
2002	FLA	NL	42	151	34	7	1	2	(1	1)	49	15	18	14	12	1	32	4	3	2	3	1	.75	2	.225	.296	.325
2003	FLA	NL	150	528	135	33	6	18	(7	11)	234	52	77	67	33	13	106	13	3	5	0	4	.00	8	.256	.313	.443
2004	FLA	NL	159	561	130	30	3	23	(10	13)	235	67	79	58	27	9	126	4	3	4	3	1	.75	17	.232	.270	.419
2005	FLA	NL	130	435	115	30	0	5	(2	3)	160	45	45	47	31	10	81	5	4	3	5	3	.63	11	.264	.319	.368
	8 ML YEARS		896	3221	788	183	23	81	(41	40)	1260	363	375	342	170	39	672	51	24	22	23	17	.58	73	.245	.291	.391

Alex S Gonzalez

Bats: R **Throws:** R **Pos:** 3B-98; SS-12; PH-4   **Ht:** 6'0" **Wt:** 200 **Born:** 4/8/1973 **Age:** 33

Year	Team	Lg	G	AB	H	2B	3B	HR	(Hm	Rd)	TB	R	RBI	RC	TBB	IBB	SO	HBP	SH	SF	SB	CS	SB%	GDP	Avg	OBP	Slg
1994	TOR	AL	15	53	8	3	1	0	(0	0)	13	7	1	2	4	0	17	1	1	0	3	0	1.00	2	.151	.224	.245
1995	TOR	AL	111	367	89	19	4	10	(8	2)	146	51	42	47	44	1	114	1	9	4	4	4	.50	7	.243	.322	.398
1996	TOR	AL	147	527	124	30	5	14	(3	11)	206	64	64	61	45	0	127	5	7	3	16	6	.73	12	.235	.300	.391
1997	TOR	AL	126	426	102	23	2	12	(4	8)	165	46	35	50	34	1	94	5	11	2	15	6	.71	9	.239	.302	.387
1998	TOR	AL	158	568	136	28	1	13	(7	6)	205	70	51	56	28	1	121	6	13	3	21	9	.70	13	.239	.281	.361
1999	TOR	AL	38	154	45	13	0	2	(1	1)	64	22	12	23	16	0	23	3	0	0	4	2	.67	4	.292	.370	.416
2000	TOR	AL	141	527	133	31	2	15	(5	10)	213	68	69	64	43	0	113	4	16	1	4	4	.50	14	.252	.313	.404
2001	TOR	AL	154	636	161	25	5	17	(9	8)	247	79	76	72	43	0	149	7	7	10	18	11	.62	16	.253	.303	.388
2002	CHN	NL	142	513	127	27	5	18	(13	5)	218	58	61	59	46	7	136	3	4	2	5	3	.63	11	.248	.312	.425
2003	CHN	NL	152	536	122	37	0	20	(11	9)	219	71	59	57	47	1	123	6	8	4	3	3	.50	17	.228	.295	.409
2004	3 Tms		83	285	64	18	1	7	(2	5)	105	36	27	23	14	0	64	1	4	2	2	2	.50	7	.225	.263	.368
2005	TB	AL	109	349	94	20	1	9	(4	5)	143	47	38	37	26	1	74	3	2	3	2	1	.67	13	.269	.323	.410
04	ChC	NL	37	129	28	10	0	3	(0	3)	47	15	8	6	4	0	26	0	2	0	1	1	.50	6	.217	.241	.364
04	Mon	NL	35	133	32	7	0	4	(2	2)	51	19	16	14	8	0	32	1	2	0	1	1	.50	1	.241	.289	.383
04	SD	NL	11	23	4	1	1	0	(0	0)	7	2	3	3	2	0	6	0	0	2	0	0	-	0	.174	.240	.304
	12 ML YEARS		1376	4941	1205	274	27	137	(67	70)	1944	619	535	551	390	12	1155	45	82	32	97	48	.67	125	.244	.303	.393

Edgar Gonzalez

Pitches: R **Bats:** R **Pos:** RP-1   **Ht:** 6'0" **Wt:** 215 **Born:** 2/23/1983 **Age:** 23

			HOW MUCH HE PITCHED						WHAT HE GAVE UP												THE RESULTS							
Year	Team	Lg	G	GS	CG	GF	IP	BFP	H	R	ER	HR	SH	SF	HB	TBB	IBB	SO	WP	Bk	W	L	Pct	ShO	Sv-Op	Hld	ERC	ERA
2005	Tucsn*	AAA	28	24	0	1	167.0	724	185	94	81	20	10	8	7	38	0	116	2	0	11	6	.647	0	0- -	-	4.25	4.37
2003	ARI	NL	9	2	0	1	18.1	85	28	10	10	3	1	1	0	7	2	14	2	0	2	1	.667	0	0-1	0	7.81	4.91
2004	ARI	NL	10	10	0	0	46.1	228	72	49	48	15	5	1	5	18	4	31	3	1	0	9	.000	0	0-0	0	9.78	9.32
2005	ARI	NL	1	0	0	0	0.1	5	2	4	4	1	0	0	0	2	0	1	1	0	0	0	-	0	0-0	0	124.7	108.0
	3 ML YEARS		20	12	0	1	65.0	318	102	63	62	19	6	2	5	27	6	46	6	1	2	10	.167	0	0-1	0	9.65	8.58

Jeremi Gonzalez

Pitches: R **Bats:** R **Pos:** RP-25; SP-3   **Ht:** 6'0" **Wt:** 220 **Born:** 1/8/1975 **Age:** 31

			HOW MUCH HE PITCHED						WHAT HE GAVE UP												THE RESULTS							
Year	Team	Lg	G	GS	CG	GF	IP	BFP	H	R	ER	HR	SH	SF	HB	TBB	IBB	SO	WP	Bk	W	L	Pct	ShO	Sv-Op	Hld	ERC	ERA
2005	Pwtckt*	AAA	11	11	0	0	69.0	284	63	20	20	8	1	0	5	14	0	62	1	1	5	2	.714	0	0- -	-	3.23	2.61
1997	CHN	NL	23	23	1	0	144.0	613	126	73	68	16	4	5	2	69	5	93	1	1	11	9	.550	1	0-0	0	3.79	4.25
1998	CHN	NL	20	20	1	0	110.0	493	124	72	65	13	5	2	3	41	5	70	2	3	7	7	.500	1	0-0	0	4.80	5.32
2003	TB	AL	25	25	2	0	156.1	668	131	71	68	18	3	9	12	69	1	97	3	2	6	11	.353	0	0-0	0	3.74	3.91
2004	TB	AL	11	8	0	1	50.1	235	72	42	39	9	1	3	3	20	0	22	4	0	0	5	.000	0	0-0	0	7.77	6.97
2005	BOS	AL	28	3	0	7	56.0	244	64	39	38	7	0	4	2	16	2	28	1	1	2	1	.667	0	0-0	1	4.71	6.11
	5 ML YEARS		107	79	4	8	516.2	2253	517	297	278	63	13	23	22	215	13	310	11	7	26	33	.441	2	0-0	1	4.43	4.84

Juan Gonzalez

Bats: R **Throws:** R **Pos:** RF-1   **Ht:** 6'3" **Wt:** 220 **Born:** 10/16/1969 **Age:** 36

			BATTING																				BASERUNNING				AVERAGES		
Year	Team	Lg	G	AB	H	2B	3B	HR	(Hm	Rd)	TB	R	RBI	RC	TBB	IBB	SO	HBP	SH	SF	SB	CS	SB%	GDP	Avg	OBP	Slg
2005	Buffalo*	AAA	5	21	6	0	0	0	(-	-)	6	1	1	1	0	0	3	0	0	0	0	0	-	1	.286	.286	.286
1989	TEX	AL	24	60	9	3	0	1	(1	0)	15	6	7	2	6	0	17	0	2	0	0	0	-	1	.150	.227	.250
1990	TEX	AL	25	90	26	7	1	4	(3	1)	47	11	12	14	2	0	18	2	0	1	0	1	.00	2	.289	.316	.522
1991	TEX	AL	142	545	144	34	1	27	(7	20)	261	78	102	81	42	7	118	5	0	3	4	4	.50	10	.264	.321	.479
1992	TEX	AL	155	584	152	24	2	43	(19	24)	309	77	109	90	35	1	143	5	0	3	0	1	.00	16	.260	.304	.529
1993	TEX	AL	140	536	166	33	1	46	(24	22)	339	105	118	116	37	7	99	13	0	1	4	1	.80	12	.310	.368	.632
1994	TEX	AL	107	422	116	18	4	19	(6	13)	199	57	85	60	30	10	66	7	0	4	6	4	.60	18	.275	.330	.472
1995	TEX	AL	90	352	104	20	2	27	(15	12)	209	57	82	61	17	3	66	0	0	5	0	0	-	15	.295	.324	.594
1996	TEX	AL	134	541	170	33	2	47	(23	24)	348	89	144	119	45	12	82	3	0	3	2	0	1.00	10	.314	.368	.643
1997	TEX	AL	133	533	158	24	3	42	(18	24)	314	87	131	100	33	7	107	3	0	10	0	0	-	12	.296	.335	.589
1998	TEX	AL	154	606	193	50	2	45	(21	24)	382	110	157	128	46	9	126	6	0	11	2	1	.67	20	.318	.366	.630
1999	TEX	AL	144	562	183	36	1	39	(14	25)	338	114	128	121	51	7	105	4	0	12	3	3	.50	10	.326	.378	.601
2000	DET	AL	115	461	133	30	2	22	(8	14)	233	69	67	73	32	3	84	2	0	1	1	2	.33	13	.289	.337	.505
2001	CLE	AL	140	532	173	34	1	35	(22	13)	314	97	140	108	41	5	94	6	0	16	1	0	1.00	11	.325	.370	.590
2002	TEX	AL	70	277	78	21	1	8	(4	4)	125	38	35	38	17	1	56	1	0	1	2	0	1.00	11	.282	.324	.451
2003	TEX	AL	82	327	96	17	1	24	(11	13)	187	49	70	54	14	1	73	4	0	1	1	1	.50	10	.294	.329	.572
2004	KC	AL	33	127	35	4	1	5	(1	4)	56	17	17	18	9	1	19	1	0	1	0	1	.00	3	.276	.326	.441
2005	CLE	AL	1	1	0	0	0	0	(0	0)	0	0	0	0	0	0	0	0	0	0	0	0	-	0	.000	.000	.000
	17 ML YEARS		1689	6556	1936	388	25	434	(197	237)	3676	1061	1404	1183	457	74	1273	62	2	78	26	19	.58	184	.295	.343	.561

Luis Gonzalez

Bats: L **Throws:** R **Pos:** LF-152; PH-5   **Ht:** 6'2" **Wt:** 195 **Born:** 9/3/1967 **Age:** 38

			BATTING																				BASERUNNING				AVERAGES		
Year	Team	Lg	G	AB	H	2B	3B	HR	(Hm	Rd)	TB	R	RBI	RC	TBB	IBB	SO	HBP	SH	SF	SB	CS	SB%	GDP	Avg	OBP	Slg
1990	HOU	NL	12	21	4	2	0	0	(0	0)	6	1	0	2	2	1	5	0	0	0	0	0	-	0	.190	.261	.286
1991	HOU	NL	137	473	120	28	9	13	(4	9)	205	51	69	64	40	4	101	8	1	4	10	7	.59	9	.254	.320	.433
1992	HOU	NL	122	387	94	19	3	10	(4	6)	149	40	55	41	24	3	52	2	1	2	7	7	.50	6	.243	.289	.385
1993	HOU	NL	154	540	162	34	3	15	(8	7)	247	82	72	90	47	7	83	10	3	10	20	9	.69	9	.300	.361	.457
1994	HOU	NL	112	392	107	29	4	8	(3	5)	168	57	67	57	49	6	57	3	0	6	15	13	.54	10	.273	.353	.429
1995	2 Tms	NL	133	471	130	29	8	13	(6	7)	214	69	69	72	57	8	63	6	1	6	6	8	.43	16	.276	.357	.454
1996	CHN	NL	146	483	131	30	4	15	(6	9)	214	70	79	75	61	8	49	4	1	6	9	6	.60	13	.271	.354	.443
1997	HOU	NL	152	550	142	31	2	10	(4	6)	207	78	68	73	71	7	67	5	0	5	10	7	.59	12	.258	.345	.376
1998	DET	AL	154	547	146	35	5	23	(15	8)	260	84	71	89	57	7	62	8	0	8	12	7	.63	9	.267	.340	.475
1999	ARI	NL	153	614	206	45	4	26	(10	16)	337	112	111	129	66	6	63	7	1	5	9	5	.64	13	.336	.403	.549
2000	ARI	NL	162	618	192	47	2	31	(14	17)	336	106	114	128	78	6	85	12	2	12	2	4	.33	12	.311	.392	.544
2001	ARI	NL	162	609	198	36	7	57	(26	31)	419	128	142	164	100	24	83	14	0	5	1	1	.50	14	.325	.429	.688
2002	ARI	NL	148	524	151	19	3	28	(11	17)	260	90	103	114	97	8	76	5	0	7	9	2	.82	12	.288	.400	.496
2003	ARI	NL	156	579	176	46	4	26	(6	20)	308	92	104	113	94	17	67	3	0	3	5	3	.63	9	.304	.402	.532
2004	ARI	NL	105	379	98	28	5	17	(10	7)	187	69	48	62	68	11	58	2	0	2	2	2	.50	9	.259	.373	.493
2005	ARI	NL	155	579	157	37	0	24	(10	14)	266	90	79	87	78	12	90	10	0	4	1	8	.10	14	.271	.366	.459
	95 Hou	NL	56	209	54	10	4	6	(1	5)	90	35	35	26	18	3	30	3	1	3	1	3	.25	8	.258	.322	.431
	95 ChC	NL	77	262	76	19	4	7	(5	2)	124	34	34	46	39	5	33	3	0	3	5	5	.50	8	.290	.384	.473
	16 ML YEARS		2163	7766	2214	495	63	316	(137	179)	3783	1219	1251	1360	989	135	1061	100	10	85	121	82	.60	177	.285	.369	.487

Luis A Gonzalez

Bats: R **Throws:** R **Pos:** 2B-83; PH-22; SS-17; 3B-12; 1B-10; RF-7; LF-1; PR-1   **Ht:** 5'11" **Wt:** 170 **Born:** 6/26/1979 **Age:** 27

			BATTING																				BASERUNNING				AVERAGES		
Year	Team	Lg	G	AB	H	2B	3B	HR	(Hm	Rd)	TB	R	RBI	RC	TBB	IBB	SO	HBP	SH	SF	SB	CS	SB%	GDP	Avg	OBP	Slg
1998	Clmbs	A	101	320	87	14	1	3	(-	-)	112	48	32	41	28	0	63	8	0	1	10	3	.77	5	.272	.345	.350
1999	Clmbs	A	83	299	88	18	2	7	(-	-)	131	41	50	46	26	0	40	5	4	5	6	5	.55	5	.294	.355	.438
1999	Kinston	A+	1	1	0	0	0	0	(-	-)	0	0	0	0	0	0	0	0	0	0	0	0	-	0	.000	.000	.000
2000	Kinston	A+	79	284	70	11	0	2	(-	-)	87	32	33	27	21	0	54	6	12	2	6	6	.50	6	.246	.310	.306

Year	Team	Lg	G	AB	H	2B	3B	HR	(Hm	Rd)	TB	R	RBI	RC	TBB	IBB	SO	HBP	SH	SF	SB	CS	SB%	GDP	Avg	OBP	Slg
2001	Kinston	A+	52	183	59	14	0	5	(-	-)	88	31	19	33	14	0	36	8	1	2	3	5	.38	1	.322	.391	.481
2001	Akron	AA	52	199	60	12	2	5	(-	-)	91	41	17	28	7	0	26	2	0	2	2	3	.40	3	.302	.329	.457
2002	Akron	AA	73	263	70	10	3	6	(-	-)	104	42	24	32	12	0	37	5	5	6	4	0	1.00	6	.266	.304	.395
2002	Buffalo	AAA	6	19	2	0	0	0	(-	-)	2	0	1	0	1	0	4	1	0	0	0	0	-	1	.105	.190	.105
2003	Akron	AA	116	431	137	22	4	7	(-	-)	188	72	62	72	46	2	41	6	2	8	1	0	1.00	18	.318	.385	.436
2004	COL	NL	102	322	94	17	2	12	(4	8)	151	42	40	45	15	1	67	4	9	1	1	5	.17	5	.292	.330	.469
2005	COL	NL	128	404	118	25	0	9	(3	6)	170	51	44	49	20	0	63	6	8	3	3	4	.43	7	.292	.333	.421
2 ML YEARS			230	726	212	42	2	21	(7	14)	321	93	84	94	35	1	130	10	17	4	4	9	.31	12	.292	.332	.442

Mike Gonzalez

Pitches: L Bats: R Pos: RP-51　　　　　　　**Ht: 6'2" Wt: 213 Born: 5/23/1978 Age: 28**

			HOW MUCH HE PITCHED					WHAT HE GAVE UP										THE RESULTS						
Year	Team	Lg	G	GS	CG	GF	IP	BFP	H	R	ER	HR	SH	SF	HB	TBB	IBB	SO	WP	Bk	W	L	Pct	ShO	Sv-Op	Hld	ERC	ERA
2005	Indy*	AAA	2	0	0	0	3.1	10	0	0	0	1	0	0	0	0	0	5	0	0	0	0	-	0	0--	-	0.00	0.00
2003	PIT	NL	16	0	0	2	8.1	38	7	7	7	4	1	1	0	6	0	6	1	0	0	1	.000	0	0-0	3	7.18	7.56
2004	PIT	NL	47	0	0	12	43.1	169	32	7	6	2	3	0	1	6	0	55	4	0	3	1	.750	0	1-4	13	1.60	1.25
2005	PIT	NL	51	0	0	15	50.0	212	35	15	15	2	0	2	1	31	2	58	3	0	1	3	.250	0	3-3	15	2.90	2.70
3 ML YEARS			114	0	0	29	101.2	419	74	29	28	8	4	3	2	43	2	119	8	0	4	5	.444	0	4-7	31	2.61	2.48

Wiki Gonzalez

Bats: R Throws: R Pos: C-14　　　　　　　**Ht: 5'11" Wt: 203 Born: 5/17/1974 Age: 32**

			BATTING																	BASERUNNING				AVERAGES		
Year	Team	Lg	G	AB	H	2B	3B	HR	(Hm	Rd)	TB	R	RBI	RC	TBB	IBB	SO	HBP	SH	SF	SB	CS	SB%	GDP	Avg	OBP	Slg
2005	Tacom*	AAA	47	176	55	10	1	5	(-	-)	82	25	28	31	16	0	13	2	1	1	0	0	-	7	.313	.374	.466
1999	SD	NL	30	83	21	2	1	3	(1	2)	34	7	12	7	1	0	8	1	0	0	0	0	-	5	.253	.271	.410
2000	SD	NL	95	284	66	15	1	5	(1	4)	98	25	30	30	30	4	31	3	1	1	1	2	.33	5	.232	.311	.345
2001	SD	NL	64	160	44	6	0	8	(5	3)	74	16	27	25	11	1	28	4	0	1	2	0	1.00	3	.275	.335	.463
2002	SD	NL	56	164	36	8	1	1	(1	0)	49	16	20	18	27	3	24	1	0	2	0	0	-	10	.220	.330	.299
2003	SD	NL	24	65	13	5	0	0	(0	0)	18	1	10	6	5	1	13	1	1	1	0	0	-	3	.200	.264	.277
2005	SEA	AL	14	45	12	5	0	0	(0	0)	17	7	2	4	2	0	3	0	0	0	0	0	-	1	.267	.298	.378
6 ML YEARS			283	801	192	41	3	17	(8	9)	290	72	101	90	76	9	107	10	2	5	3	2	.60	27	.240	.312	.362

Andy Good

Pitches: R Bats: R Pos: RP-2　　　　　　　**Ht: 6'1" Wt: 209 Born: 9/19/1979 Age: 26**

			HOW MUCH HE PITCHED					WHAT HE GAVE UP										THE RESULTS						
Year	Team	Lg	G	GS	CG	GF	IP	BFP	H	R	ER	HR	SH	SF	HB	TBB	IBB	SO	WP	Bk	W	L	Pct	ShO	Sv-Op	Hld	ERC	ERA
2005	Toledo*	AAA	23	23	0	0	134.1	574	129	61	55	18	3	5	6	42	3	89	4	0	9	5	.643	0	0--	-	3.85	3.68
2003	ARI	NL	16	10	0	0	66.1	289	74	42	39	15	3	4	3	16	2	42	3	0	4	2	.667	0	0-0	1	5.06	5.29
2004	ARI	NL	17	2	0	3	40.2	177	43	25	24	8	1	2	3	13	0	26	2	0	1	2	.333	0	0-0	0	5.09	5.31
2005	DET	AL	2	0	0	2	5.0	20	4	3	3	1	0	0	0	1	0	7	0	0	0	0	-	0	0-0	0	2.80	5.40
3 ML YEARS			35	12	0	5	112.0	486	121	70	66	24	4	6	6	30	2	75	5	0	5	4	.556	0	0-0	1	4.96	5.30

Tom Gordon

Pitches: R Bats: R Pos: RP-79　　　　　　　**Ht: 5'10" Wt: 190 Born: 11/18/1967 Age: 38**

			HOW MUCH HE PITCHED					WHAT HE GAVE UP										THE RESULTS						
Year	Team	Lg	G	GS	CG	GF	IP	BFP	H	R	ER	HR	SH	SF	HB	TBB	IBB	SO	WP	Bk	W	L	Pct	ShO	Sv-Op	Hld	ERC	ERA
1988	KC	AL	5	2	0	0	15.2	67	16	9	9	1	0	0	0	7	0	18	0	0	0	2	.000	0	0-0	2	4.22	5.17
1989	KC	AL	49	16	1	16	163.0	677	122	67	66	10	4	4	1	86	4	153	12	0	17	9	.654	1	1-7	3	2.97	3.64
1990	KC	AL	32	32	6	0	195.1	858	192	99	81	17	8	2	3	99	1	175	11	0	12	11	.522	1	0-0	0	4.37	3.73
1991	KC	AL	45	14	1	11	158.0	684	129	76	68	16	5	3	4	87	6	167	5	0	9	14	.391	0	1-4	4	3.67	3.87
1992	KC	AL	40	11	0	13	117.2	516	116	60	60	9	2	6	4	55	4	98	5	2	6	10	.375	0	0-2	4	4.17	4.59
1993	KC	AL	48	14	2	18	155.2	651	125	65	62	11	6	6	1	77	5	143	17	0	12	6	.667	0	1-6	2	3.18	3.58
1994	KC	AL	24	24	0	0	155.1	675	136	79	75	15	3	8	3	87	3	126	12	1	11	7	.611	0	0-0	0	4.04	4.35
1995	KC	AL	31	31	2	0	189.0	843	204	110	93	12	7	11	4	89	4	119	9	0	12	12	.500	0	0-0	0	4.59	4.43
1996	BOS	AL	34	34	4	0	215.2	998	249	143	134	28	2	11	4	105	5	171	6	1	12	9	.571	1	0-0	0	5.50	5.59
1997	BOS	AL	42	25	2	16	182.2	774	155	85	76	10	3	4	3	78	1	159	5	0	6	10	.375	1	11-13	0	3.08	3.74
1998	BOS	AL	73	0	0	69	79.1	317	55	24	24	2	2	2	0	25	1	78	9	0	7	4	.636	0	46-47	0	1.72	2.72
1999	BOS	AL	21	0	0	15	17.2	82	17	11	11	2	0	0	1	12	2	24	0	0	2	0	.000	0	11-13	1	5.04	5.60
2001	CHN	NL	47	0	0	40	45.1	187	32	18	17	4	0	0	1	16	1	67	2	0	1	2	.333	0	27-31	0	2.27	3.38
2002	2 Tms		34	0	0	10	42.2	181	42	19	16	3	3	0	1	16	3	48	0	0	1	3	.250	0	0-6	6	3.71	3.38
2003	CHA	AL	66	0	0	35	74.0	310	57	29	26	4	4	3	4	31	3	91	5	0	7	6	.538	0	12-17	7	2.74	3.16
2004	NYA	AL	80	0	15	89.2	342	56	23	22	5	5	2	1	23	5	96	3	0	9	4	.692	0	4-10	36	1.50	2.21
2005	NYA	AL	79	0	0	17	80.2	324	59	25	23	8	1	3	0	29	4	69	1	1	5	4	.556	0	2-9	33	2.45	2.57
02	ChC	NL	19	0	0	7	23.2	104	27	12	9	1	1	0	1	10	1	31	0	0	1	1	.500	0	0-6	2	4.75	3.42
02	Hou	NL	15	0	0	3	19.0	77	15	7	7	2	2	0	0	6	2	17	0	0	0	2	.000	0	0-0	4	2.53	3.32
17 ML YEARS			750	203	18	275	1977.1	8486	1762	949	863	157	55	65	35	922	52	1802	102	5	127	115	.525	4	116-159	94	3.61	3.93

Tom Gorzelanny

Pitches: L Bats: L Pos: RP-2; SP-1　　　　　　　**Ht: 6'2" Wt: 205 Born: 7/12/1982 Age: 23**

			HOW MUCH HE PITCHED					WHAT HE GAVE UP										THE RESULTS						
Year	Team	Lg	G	GS	CG	GF	IP	BFP	H	R	ER	HR	SH	SF	HB	TBB	IBB	SO	WP	Bk	W	L	Pct	ShO	Sv-Op	Hld	ERC	ERA
2003	Wmspt	A-	8	8	0	0	30.1	134	23	6	6	1	1	0	1	19	0	61	1	0	1	2	.333	0	0--	-	3.18	1.78
2004	Lynbrg	A+	10	10	0	0	55.2	240	54	31	30	6	1	1	4	19	0	61	1	0	3	5	.375	0	0--	-	4.00	4.85

Year	Team	Lg	G	GS	CG	GF	IP	BFP	H	R	ER	HR	SH	SF	HB	TBB	IBB	SO	WP	Bk	W	L	Pct	ShO	Sv-Op	Hld	ERC	ERA
2004	Hickory	A	16	15	1	0	93.0	376	63	30	23	9	5	3	2	34	0	106	4	0	7	2	.778	0	0--	-	2.31	2.23
2005	Altna	AA	23	23	1	0	129.2	549	114	50	47	6	3	3	5	46	0	124	4	0	8	5	.615	1	0--	-	3.00	3.26
2005	PIT	NL	3	1	0	0	6.0	32	10	8	8	1	1	0	0	3	0	3	0	0	0	1	.000	0	0-0	0	8.76	12.00

Mike Gosling

Pitches: L **Bats:** L **Pos:** RP-8; SP-5 **Ht:** 6'2" **Wt:** 210 **Born:** 9/23/1980 **Age:** 25

Year	Team	Lg	G	GS	CG	GF	IP	BFP	H	R	ER	HR	SH	SF	HB	TBB	IBB	SO	WP	Bk	W	L	Pct	ShO	Sv-Op	Hld	ERC	ERA
2002	ElPaso	AA	27	27	2	0	166.2	705	149	66	58	7	8	6	4	62	4	115	9	1	14	5	.737	2	0--	-	3.03	3.13
2003	Tucsn	AAA	26	26	0	0	136.1	645	190	106	85	13	5	5	3	56	0	89	13	0	9	12	.429	0	0--	-	6.50	5.61
2004	Tucsn	AAA	24	21	0	0	128.1	581	160	101	83	16	5	8	3	53	0	67	12	0	9	5	.643	0	0--	-	5.94	5.82
2005	Tucsn	AAA	18	17	0	0	92.1	436	129	70	61	11	4	2	2	30	0	76	5	1	4	6	.400	0	0--	-	6.24	5.95
2004	ARI	NL	6	4	0	0	25.1	112	26	13	13	5	2	0	2	13	1	14	2	0	1	1	.500	0	0-0	0	5.83	4.62
2005	ARI	NL	13	5	0	5	32.1	154	40	20	16	2	2	0	0	19	2	14	0	0	0	3	.000	0	0-0	0	5.74	4.45
	2 ML YEARS		19	9	0	5	57.2	266	66	33	29	7	4	0	2	32	3	28	2	0	1	4	.200	0	0-0	0	5.79	4.53

Ruben Gotay

Bats: B **Throws:** R **Pos:** 2B-81; PH-8; DH-2; PR-1 **Ht:** 5'11" **Wt:** 160 **Born:** 12/25/1982 **Age:** 23

Year	Team	Lg	G	AB	H	2B	3B	HR	(Hm	Rd)	TB	R	RBI	RC	TBB	IBB	SO	HBP	SH	SF	SB	CS	SB%	GDP	Avg	OBP	Slg
2001	Royals	R	52	184	58	15	1	3	(-	-)	84	29	19	35	26	1	22	9	2	1	5	6	.45	2	.315	.423	.457
2002	Burlgtn	A	133	509	145	42	9	9	(-	-)	232	87	83	90	73	1	110	8	4	9	5	4	.56	5	.285	.377	.456
2003	Wilmg	A+	134	512	134	31	2	9	(-	-)	193	68	72	71	60	1	97	7	4	9	8	1	.89	7	.261	.343	.384
2004	Wichta	AA	106	404	117	22	6	9	(-	-)	178	71	68	66	51	0	60	6	9	5	9	10	.47	9	.290	.373	.441
2005	Wichta	AA	28	110	27	8	0	3	(-	-)	44	22	15	14	12	0	13	0	0	0	0	2	.00	2	.245	.320	.400
2004	KC	AL	44	152	41	7	3	1	(1	0)	57	17	16	17	9	0	36	2	1	2	0	1	.00	4	.270	.315	.375
2005	KC	AL	86	282	64	14	2	5	(2	3)	97	32	29	31	22	0	51	4	4	5	2	2	.50	3	.227	.288	.344
	2 ML YEARS		130	434	105	21	5	6	(3	3)	154	49	45	48	31	0	87	6	5	7	2	3	.40	7	.242	.297	.355

John Grabow

Pitches: L **Bats:** L **Pos:** RP-63 **Ht:** 6'3" **Wt:** 185 **Born:** 11/4/1978 **Age:** 27

Year	Team	Lg	G	GS	CG	GF	IP	BFP	H	R	ER	HR	SH	SF	HB	TBB	IBB	SO	WP	Bk	W	L	Pct	ShO	Sv-Op	Hld	ERC	ERA
2003	PIT	NL	5	0	0	1	5.0	22	6	3	2	0	0	0	0	0	0	9	0	0	0	0	-	0	0-0	0	2.73	3.60
2004	PIT	NL	68	0	0	10	61.2	286	81	39	35	8	6	1	0	28	7	64	5	0	2	5	.286	0	1-7	11	6.21	5.11
2005	PIT	NL	63	0	0	8	52.0	222	46	31	28	6	2	0	2	25	2	42	1	0	2	3	.400	0	0-1	14	4.04	4.85
	3 ML YEARS		136	0	0	19	118.2	530	133	73	65	14	8	1	2	53	9	115	6	0	4	8	.333	0	1-8	25	5.05	4.93

Jason Grabowski

Bats: L **Throws:** R **Pos:** PH-32; LF-28; RF-4; 1B-3; PR-3 **Ht:** 6'3" **Wt:** 200 **Born:** 5/24/1976 **Age:** 30

Year	Team	Lg	G	AB	H	2B	3B	HR	(Hm	Rd)	TB	R	RBI	RC	TBB	IBB	SO	HBP	SH	SF	SB	CS	SB%	GDP	Avg	OBP	Slg
2005	LsVgs*	AAA	52	181	56	16	1	6	(-	-)	92	37	33	38	30	1	26	1	0	0	0	0	-	5	.309	.410	.508
2002	OAK	AL	4	8	3	1	1	0	(0	0)	6	3	1	3	3	0	1	0	0	0	0	0	-	0	.375	.545	.750
2003	OAK	AL	8	8	0	0	0	0	(0	0)	0	0	0	0	1	0	5	0	0	0	0	0	-	0	.000	.111	.000
2004	LA	NL	113	173	38	7	0	7	(3	4)	66	18	20	21	19	0	50	0	0	0	0	0	-	4	.220	.297	.382
2005	LAN	NL	65	112	18	0	0	4	(2	2)	30	14	12	7	10	1	29	0	0	1	1	0	1.00	4	.161	.228	.268
	4 ML YEARS		190	301	59	8	1	11	(5	6)	102	35	33	31	33	1	85	0	0	1	1	0	1.00	8	.196	.275	.339

Tony Graffanino

Bats: R **Throws:** R **Pos:** 2B-73; 1B-22; 3B-17; PH-8; SS-1 **Ht:** 6'1" **Wt:** 190 **Born:** 6/6/1972 **Age:** 34

Year	Team	Lg	G	AB	H	2B	3B	HR	(Hm	Rd)	TB	R	RBI	RC	TBB	IBB	SO	HBP	SH	SF	SB	CS	SB%	GDP	Avg	OBP	Slg
1996	ATL	NL	22	46	8	1	1	0	(0	0)	11	7	2	3	4	0	13	1	0	1	0	0	-	0	.174	.250	.239
1997	ATL	NL	104	186	48	9	1	8	(5	3)	83	33	20	29	26	1	46	1	3	5	6	4	.60	3	.258	.344	.446
1998	ATL	NL	105	289	61	14	1	5	(3	2)	92	32	22	22	24	0	68	2	1	1	1	4	.20	7	.211	.275	.318
1999	TB	AL	39	130	41	9	4	2	(0	2)	64	20	19	23	9	0	22	1	2	0	3	2	.60	1	.315	.364	.492
2000	2 Tms	AL	70	168	46	6	1	2	(1	1)	60	33	17	23	22	0	27	2	1	1	7	4	.64	2	.274	.363	.357
2001	CHA	AL	74	145	44	9	0	2	(1	1)	59	23	15	22	16	0	29	1	4	3	4	1	.80	4	.303	.370	.407
2002	CHA	AL	70	229	60	12	4	6	(4	2)	98	35	31	35	22	1	38	2	4	2	2	1	.67	2	.262	.329	.428
2003	CHA	AL	90	250	65	15	3	7	(4	3)	107	51	23	36	24	1	37	3	3	1	8	0	1.00	1	.260	.331	.428
2004	KC	AL	75	278	73	11	0	3	(0	3)	93	37	26	35	27	0	38	3	4	2	10	2	.83	5	.263	.332	.335
2005	2 Tms	AL	110	379	117	17	3	7	(4	3)	161	66	38	58	31	2	51	4	2	1	7	2	.78	14	.309	.366	.425
00	TB	AL	13	20	6	1	0	0	(0	0)	7	8	1	2	1	0	2	1	0	0	0	0	-	1	.300	.364	.350
00	CWS	AL	57	148	40	5	1	2	(1	1)	53	25	16	21	21	0	25	1	1	1	7	4	.64	1	.270	.363	.358
05	KC	AL	59	191	57	5	2	3	(1	2)	75	29	18	32	22	1	28	2	2	0	3	1	.75	6	.298	.377	.393
05	Bos	AL	51	188	60	12	1	4	(3	1)	86	39	20	26	9	1	23	2	0	1	4	1	.80	8	.319	.355	.457
	10 ML YEARS		759	2100	563	103	18	42	(22	20)	828	339	213	286	205	5	369	20	24	17	48	20	.71	39	.268	.336	.394

Alex Graman

Pitches: L Bats: L Pos: RP-2 Ht: 6'4" Wt: 210 Born: 11/17/1977 Age: 28

Year	Team	Lg	G	GS	CG	GF	IP	BFP	H	R	ER	HR	SH	SF	HB	TBB	IBB	SO	WP	Bk	W	L	Pct	ShO	Sv-Op	Hld	ERC	ERA
1999	StlsInd	A-	14	14	0	0	81.1	324	74	30	27	7	3	1	1	16	0	85	1	1	6	3	.667	0	0--	-	2.84	2.99
2000	Tampa	A+	28	28	3	0	143.0	598	120	64	58	6	5	2	3	58	1	111	9	1	8	9	.471	1	0--	-	2.91	3.65
2000	Nrwich	AA	1	1	0	0	5.1	25	6	7	7	3	0	0	1	4	0	3	0	0	0	1	.000	0	0--	-	11.94	11.81
2001	Nrwich	AA	28	28	1	0	166.1	723	174	83	65	10	3	6	2	60	0	138	6	0	12	9	.571	0	0--	-	3.92	3.52
2002	Nrwich	AA	8	8	2	0	50.0	208	46	19	16	2	3	0	0	13	0	31	4	2	5	2	.714	0	0--	-	2.68	2.88
2002	Clmbs	AAA	20	20	1	0	124.0	545	141	74	64	11	5	3	3	37	3	98	10	2	6	9	.400	0	0--	-	4.38	4.65
2003	Clmbs	AAA	26	26	0	0	142.2	612	135	77	71	14	8	0	1	63	0	110	5	1	9	10	.474	0	0--	-	3.97	4.48
2004	Clmbs	AAA	24	22	1	0	131.0	550	115	56	49	12	10	5	3	53	0	129	7	0	11	6	.647	1	0--	-	3.48	3.37
2005	Clmbs	AAA	23	16	0	1	96.1	422	95	40	34	12	1	0	2	36	2	96	3	0	5	6	.455	0	1--	-	4.02	3.18
2005	Lsvlle	AAA	5	4	0	0	23.1	105	23	9	8	2	0	0	1	12	0	19	3	0	2	1	.667	0	0--	-	4.45	3.09
2004	NYA	AL	3	2	0	1	5.0	31	14	11	11	1	0	1	0	2	0	4	0	0	0	0	-	0	0-0	0	17.28	19.80
2005	NYA	AL	2	0	0	1	1.1	9	3	2	2	1	0	0	0	2	1	0	0	0	0	0	-	0	0-0	0	23.27	13.50
	2 ML YEARS		5	2	0	2	6.1	40	17	13	13	2	0	1	0	4	1	4	0	0	0	0	-	0	0-0	0	18.50	18.47

Curtis Granderson

Bats: L Throws: R Pos: CF-41; LF-20; PH-3 Ht: 6'1" Wt: 185 Born: 3/16/1981 Age: 25

Year	Team	Lg	G	AB	H	2B	3B	HR	(Hm	Rd)	TB	R	RBI	RC	TBB	IBB	SO	HBP	SH	SF	SB	CS	SB%	GDP	Avg	OBP	Slg
2002	Oneont	A-	52	212	73	15	4	3	(-	-)	105	45	34	44	20	0	35	7	0	1	9	2	.82	1	.344	.417	.495
2003	Lkland	A+	127	476	136	29	10	11	(-	-)	218	71	51	80	49	2	91	12	5	3	10	7	.59	5	.286	.365	.458
2004	Erie	AA	123	462	140	19	8	21	(-	-)	238	89	93	98	80	3	95	4	3	4	14	8	.64	1	.303	.407	.515
2005	Toledo	AAA	111	445	129	29	13	15	(-	-)	229	79	65	85	48	4	129	3	2	5	22	6	.79	7	.290	.359	.515
2004	DET	AL	9	25	6	1	1	0	(0	0)	9	2	0	2	3	0	8	0	0	0	0	0	-	1	.240	.321	.360
2005	DET	AL	47	162	44	6	3	8	(5	3)	80	18	20	26	10	0	43	0	0	2	1	1	.50	2	.272	.314	.494
	2 ML YEARS		56	187	50	7	4	8	(5	3)	89	20	20	28	13	0	51	0	0	2	1	1	.50	3	.267	.315	.476

Danny Graves

Pitches: R Bats: R Pos: RP-40 Ht: 6'0" Wt: 185 Born: 8/7/1973 Age: 32

Year	Team	Lg	G	GS	CG	GF	IP	BFP	H	R	ER	HR	SH	SF	HB	TBB	IBB	SO	WP	Bk	W	L	Pct	ShO	Sv-Op	Hld	ERC	ERA
2005	Norfolk*	AAA	5	0	0	1	6.0	40	15	12	12	2	0	0	0	7	0	4	0	0	0	1	.000	0	0--	-	20.53	18.00
1996	CLE	AL	15	0	0	5	29.2	129	29	18	15	2	0	1	0	10	0	22	1	0	2	0	1.000	0	0-1	0	3.37	4.55
1997	2 Tms		15	0	0	3	26.0	134	41	22	16	2	3	2	0	20	1	11	1	0	0	0	-	0	0-0	1	9.10	5.54
1998	CIN	NL	62	0	0	35	81.1	340	76	31	30	6	2	5	2	28	4	44	4	0	2	1	.667	0	8-8	6	3.38	3.32
1999	CIN	NL	75	0	0	56	111.0	454	90	42	38	10	5	2	2	49	4	69	3	0	8	7	.533	0	27-36	0	3.25	3.08
2000	CIN	NL	66	0	0	57	91.1	388	81	31	26	8	6	4	3	42	7	53	3	1	10	5	.667	0	30-35	0	3.64	2.56
2001	CIN	NL	66	0	0	54	80.1	337	83	41	37	7	3	2	4	18	6	49	2	1	6	5	.545	0	32-39	0	3.59	4.15
2002	CIN	NL	68	4	0	54	98.2	412	99	37	35	7	3	6	3	25	9	58	5	0	7	3	.700	0	32-39	0	3.33	3.19
2003	CIN	NL	30	26	2	3	169.0	741	204	108	100	30	6	3	7	41	6	60	2	0	4	15	.211	1	2-2	0	5.32	5.33
2004	CIN	NL	68	0	0	59	68.1	290	77	39	30	12	0	2	2	13	6	40	2	0	1	6	.143	0	41-50	0	4.47	3.95
2005	2 Tms		40	0	0	29	38.2	197	59	35	28	9	3	1	3	20	4	20	3	0	1	1	.500	0	10-12	1	8.99	6.52
97	Cle	AL	5	0	0	2	11.1	56	15	8	6	2	0	1	0	9	0	4	0	0	0	0	-	0	0-0	0	8.52	4.76
97	Cin	NL	10	0	0	1	14.2	78	26	14	10	0	3	1	0	11	1	7	1	0	0	0	-	0	0-0	1	9.52	6.14
05	Cin	NL	20	0	0	18	18.1	99	30	18	15	4	2	1	0	12	3	8	3	0	1	1	.500	0	10-12	0	9.50	7.36
05	NYM	NL	20	0	0	11	20.1	98	29	17	13	5	1	0	3	8	1	12	0	0	0	0	-	0	0-0	1	8.51	5.75
	10 ML YEARS		505	30	2	355	794.1	3422	839	404	355	93	31	28	26	266	47	426	26	2	41	43	.488	1	182-222	8	4.31	4.02

Andy Green

Bats: R Throws: R Pos: PH-9; 2B-5; SS-2; LF-2 Ht: 5'9" Wt: 180 Born: 7/7/1977 Age: 28

Year	Team	Lg	G	AB	H	2B	3B	HR	(Hm	Rd)	TB	R	RBI	RC	TBB	IBB	SO	HBP	SH	SF	SB	CS	SB%	GDP	Avg	OBP	Slg
2000	Sbend	A	3	9	0	0	0	0	(-	-)	0	1	0	0	0	0	1	2	0	0	0	0	-	0	.000	.182	.000
2000	Msoula	R+	23	83	19	2	1	0	(-	-)	23	10	16	9	12	0	9	2	1	5	8	3	.73	1	.229	.324	.277
2001	Sbend	A	128	477	143	18	6	5	(-	-)	188	76	59	81	59	1	50	7	11	8	51	15	.77	7	.300	.379	.394
2002	Tucsn	AAA	27	99	22	8	0	1	(-	-)	33	13	13	9	9	0	17	1	0	0	2	1	.67	2	.222	.294	.333
2002	Lancst	A+	102	401	124	36	4	6	(-	-)	186	74	50	74	60	0	59	5	6	5	15	10	.60	7	.309	.401	.464
2003	ElPaso	AA	126	490	148	38	2	2	(-	-)	196	70	51	74	38	1	51	13	11	3	17	9	.65	6	.302	.366	.400
2004	Tucsn	AAA	77	309	101	31	3	9	(-	-)	165	56	45	63	34	1	45	3	7	4	10	4	.71	3	.327	.394	.534
2005	Tucsn	AAA	135	530	182	46	13	19	(-	-)	311	125	80	126	68	1	82	6	2	3	9	6	.60	9	.343	.422	.587
2004	ARI	NL	46	109	22	2	1	1	(1	0)	29	13	4	7	5	0	17	1	3	1	1	1	.50	2	.202	.241	.266
2005	ARI	NL	17	31	7	1	0	0	(0	0)	8	5	2	3	7	0	3	0	0	1	0	0	-	1	.226	.359	.258
	2 ML YEARS		63	140	29	3	1	1	(1	0)	37	18	6	10	12	0	20	1	3	2	1	1	.50	3	.207	.271	.264

Nick Green

Bats: R Throws: R Pos: 2B-91; 3B-13; PH-6; PR-6; RF-1; DH-1 Ht: 6'0" Wt: 178 Born: 9/10/1978 Age: 27

Year	Team	Lg	G	AB	H	2B	3B	HR	(Hm	Rd)	TB	R	RBI	RC	TBB	IBB	SO	HBP	SH	SF	SB	CS	SB%	GDP	Avg	OBP	Slg
1999	Jmstwn	A-	73	273	81	15	0	11	(-	-)	129	52	41	47	26	0	66	4	0	3	14	4	.78	4	.297	.363	.473
1999	Macon	A	3	10	2	0	0	1	(-	-)	5	1	3	1	0	0	4	0	0	0	1	0	1.00	0	.200	.200	.500
2000	Macon	A	91	229	83	19	4	11	(-	-)	143	47	43	55	22	0	75	5	1	6	10	4	.71	4	.362	.420	.624
2000	MrtlBh	A+	27	91	22	6	0	1	(-	-)	31	13	6	11	10	0	23	3	1	0	3	2	.60	0	.242	.337	.341
2001	MrtlBh	A+	80	297	79	18	1	10	(-	-)	129	49	42	47	32	0	70	7	1	3	9	2	.82	2	.266	.348	.434
2001	Rchmd	AAA	2	5	1	0	0	0	(-	-)	1	0	1	0	0	0	3	0	0	0	0	0	-	0	.200	.200	.200
2002	Grnville	AA	94	355	85	16	2	15	(-	-)	150	49	50	45	36	3	92	4	0	3	2	5	.29	9	.239	.321	.423

Year	Team	Lg	G	AB	H	2B	3B	HR	(Hm	Rd)	TB	R	RBI	RC	TBB	IBB	SO	HBP	SH	SF	SB	CS	SB%	GDP	Avg	OBP	Slg
2003	Rchmd	AAA	124	399	99	26	1	11	(-	-)	160	40	51	46	26	1	79	7	2	4	7	5	.58	7	.248	.303	.401
2004	Rchmd	AAA	22	77	29	4	1	0	(-	-)	35	8	11	14	6	0	9	4	1	1	0	3	.00	3	.377	.443	.455
2004	ATL	NL	95	264	72	15	3	3	(3	0)	102	40	26	36	12	1	63	4	8	2	1	2	.33	1	.273	.312	.386
2005	TB	AL	111	318	76	15	2	5	(2	3)	110	53	29	38	33	0	86	11	10	3	3	1	.75	5	.239	.329	.346
2 ML YEARS			206	582	148	30	5	8	(5	3)	212	93	55	74	45	1	149	15	18	5	4	3	.57	5	.254	.321	.364

Shawn Green

Bats: L **Throws:** L **Pos:** RF-135; CF-41; PH-5; PR-1   **Ht:** 6'4" **Wt:** 200 **Born:** 11/10/1972 **Age:** 33

Year	Team	Lg	G	AB	H	2B	3B	HR	(Hm	Rd)	TB	R	RBI	RC	TBB	IBB	SO	HBP	SH	SF	SB	CS	SB%	GDP	Avg	OBP	Slg
1993	TOR	AL	3	6	0	0	0	0	(0	0)	0	0	0	0	0	0	1	0	0	0	0	0	-	0	.000	.000	.000
1994	TOR	AL	14	33	3	1	0	0	(0	0)	4	1	1	0	1	0	8	0	0	0	1	0	1.00	0	.091	.118	.121
1995	TOR	AL	121	379	109	31	4	15	(5	10)	193	52	54	61	20	3	68	3	0	3	1	2	.33	4	.288	.326	.509
1996	TOR	AL	132	422	118	32	3	11	(7	4)	189	52	45	64	33	3	75	8	0	2	5	1	.83	9	.280	.342	.448
1997	TOR	AL	135	429	123	22	4	16	(10	6)	201	57	53	70	36	4	99	1	1	4	14	3	.82	4	.287	.340	.469
1998	TOR	AL	158	630	175	33	4	35	(21	14)	321	106	100	108	50	2	142	5	1	3	35	12	.74	6	.278	.334	.510
1999	TOR	AL	153	614	190	45	0	42	(20	22)	361	134	123	132	66	4	117	11	0	5	20	7	.74	13	.309	.384	.588
2000	LA	NL	162	610	164	44	4	24	(15	9)	288	98	99	107	90	9	121	8	0	6	24	5	.83	18	.269	.367	.472
2001	LA	NL	161	619	184	31	4	49	(19	30)	370	121	125	134	72	10	107	5	0	5	20	4	.83	10	.297	.372	.598
2002	LA	NL	158	582	166	31	1	42	(18	24)	325	110	114	106	93	22	112	5	0	6	8	5	.62	26	.285	.385	.558
2003	LA	NL	160	611	171	49	2	19	(10	9)	281	84	85	92	68	2	112	6	0	4	6	2	.75	18	.280	.355	.460
2004	LA	NL	157	590	157	28	1	28	(16	12)	271	92	86	76	71	6	114	8	0	2	5	2	.71	17	.266	.352	.459
2005	ARI	NL	158	581	166	37	4	22	(12	10)	277	87	73	78	62	6	95	5	0	8	8	4	.67	18	.286	.355	.477
13 ML YEARS			1672	6106	1726	384	31	303	(153	150)	3081	994	958	1028	662	71	1171	65	2	49	147	47	.76	144	.283	.356	.505

Adam Greenberg

Bats: L **Throws:** L **Pos:** PH-1   **Ht:** 5'9" **Wt:** 180 **Born:** 2/21/1981 **Age:** 25

Year	Team	Lg	G	AB	H	2B	3B	HR	(Hm	Rd)	TB	R	RBI	RC	TBB	IBB	SO	HBP	SH	SF	SB	CS	SB%	GDP	Avg	OBP	Slg
2002	Lansng	A	35	116	26	7	2	1	(-	-)	40	20	11	15	15	2	22	4	4	1	2	1	.67	0	.224	.331	.345
2002	Dytona	A+	21	73	28	5	3	1	(-	-)	42	20	9	22	14	1	18	3	0	0	15	2	.88	0	.384	.500	.575
2003	Dytona	A+	72	271	81	11	5	3	(-	-)	111	42	27	47	38	0	46	2	2	2	26	9	.74	1	.299	.387	.410
2004	Dytona	A+	91	323	94	10	12	3	(-	-)	137	52	28	56	42	2	65	7	3	3	16	8	.67	4	.291	.381	.424
2004	WTenn	AA	32	112	31	7	2	3	(-	-)	51	22	10	20	14	1	30	3	2	2	3	0	1.00	1	.277	.366	.455
2004	Iowa	AAA	1	4	0	0	0	0	(-	-)	0	0	0	0	1	0	0	0	0	0	0	0	-	0	.000	.200	.000
2005	WTenn	AA	95	305	82	12	9	4	(-	-)	124	51	33	55	56	2	68	4	14	3	15	4	.79	1	.269	.386	.407
2005	CHN	NL	1	0	0	0	0	0	(0	0)	0	0	0	0	0	0	0	1	0	0	0	0	-	0	-	1.000	-

Khalil Greene

Bats: R **Throws:** R **Pos:** SS-121   **Ht:** 5'11" **Wt:** 210 **Born:** 10/21/1979 **Age:** 26

Year	Team	Lg	G	AB	H	2B	3B	HR	(Hm	Rd)	TB	R	RBI	RC	TBB	IBB	SO	HBP	SH	SF	SB	CS	SB%	GDP	Avg	OBP	Slg
2005	Lk Els*	A+	4	12	6	1	0	0	(-	-)	7	4	3	4	2	0	1	1	0	0	0	0	-	0	.500	.600	.583
2003	SD	NL	20	65	14	4	1	2	(0	2)	26	8	6	4	4	0	19	1	0	0	0	1	.00	3	.215	.271	.400
2004	SD	NL	139	484	132	31	4	15	(3	12)	216	67	65	73	53	10	94	8	1	8	4	2	.67	9	.273	.349	.446
2005	SD	NL	121	436	109	30	2	15	(6	9)	188	51	70	58	25	3	93	6	3	6	5	0	1.00	8	.250	.296	.431
3 ML YEARS			280	985	255	65	7	32	(9	23)	430	126	141	135	82	13	206	15	4	14	9	3	.75	20	.259	.321	.437

Todd Greene

Bats: R **Throws:** R **Pos:** C-33; PH-5   **Ht:** 5'10" **Wt:** 208 **Born:** 5/8/1971 **Age:** 35

Year	Team	Lg	G	AB	H	2B	3B	HR	(Hm	Rd)	TB	R	RBI	RC	TBB	IBB	SO	HBP	SH	SF	SB	CS	SB%	GDP	Avg	OBP	Slg
2005	ColSpr*	AAA	11	33	13	0	0	3	(-	-)	22	4	8	8	1	0	3	0	0	0	0	0	-	2	.394	.412	.667
1996	CAL	AL	29	79	15	1	0	2	(1	1)	22	9	9	4	4	0	11	1	0	0	2	0	1.00	4	.190	.238	.278
1997	ANA	AL	34	124	36	6	0	9	(5	4)	69	24	24	22	7	1	25	0	0	0	2	0	1.00	1	.290	.328	.556
1998	ANA	AL	29	71	18	4	0	1	(0	1)	25	3	7	7	2	0	20	0	0	0	0	0	-	0	.254	.274	.352
1999	ANA	AL	97	321	78	20	0	14	(7	7)	140	36	42	35	12	0	63	3	0	2	1	4	.20	8	.243	.275	.436
2000	TOR	AL	34	85	20	2	0	5	(2	3)	37	11	10	9	5	0	18	0	0	0	0	0	-	3	.235	.278	.435
2001	NYA	AL	35	96	20	4	0	1	(1	0)	27	9	11	5	3	0	21	1	0	0	0	0	-	3	.208	.240	.281
2002	TEX	AL	42	112	30	5	0	10	(6	4)	65	15	19	11	2	0	23	1	1	2	0	0	-	4	.268	.282	.580
2003	TEX	AL	62	205	47	10	1	10	(4	6)	89	25	20	14	2	0	47	2	0	1	0	0	-	2	.229	.243	.434
2004	COL	NL	75	195	55	14	0	10	(6	4)	99	23	35	28	13	4	38	0	0	1	0	0	-	9	.282	.325	.508
2005	COL	NL	38	126	32	4	0	7	(3	4)	57	10	23	19	7	0	21	1	0	0	0	0	-	5	.254	.299	.452
10 ML YEARS			475	1414	351	70	1	69	(35	34)	630	165	200	154	57	5	287	9	1	6	5	4	.56	40	.248	.281	.446

Kevin Gregg

Pitches: R **Bats:** R **Pos:** RP-31; SP-2   **Ht:** 6'6" **Wt:** 220 **Born:** 6/20/1978 **Age:** 28

	HOW MUCH HE PITCHED							WHAT HE GAVE UP											THE RESULTS					
Year	Team	Lg	G	GS	CG	GF	IP	BFP	H	R	ER	HR	SH	SF	HB	TBB	IBB	SO	WP	Bk	W	L	Pct	ShO	Sv-Op Hld	ERC	ERA
2005	Salt Lk*	AAA	7	6	0	0	34.2	150	36	15	15	2	0	1	2	10	0	36	3	0	3	1	.750	0	0- -	3.74	3.89
2003	ANA	AL	5	3	0	0	24.2	97	18	9	9	3	0	0	1	8	0	14	0	0	2	0	1.000	0	0-0	2.74	3.28
2004	ANA	AL	55	0	0	23	87.2	377	86	43	41	6	4	5	3	28	3	84	13	1	5	2	.714	0	1-2 3	3.47	4.21
2005	LAA	AL	33	2	0	9	64.1	289	70	37	36	8	1	1	3	29	2	52	5	0	1	2	.333	0	0-1 1	5.09	5.04
3 ML YEARS			93	5	0	32	176.2	763	174	89	86	17	5	6	7	65	5	150	18	1	8	4	.667	0	1-3 4	3.93	4.38

Zack Greinke

Pitches: R **Bats:** R **Pos:** SP-33   **Ht:** 6'2" **Wt:** 200 **Born:** 10/21/1983 **Age:** 22

			HOW MUCH HE PITCHED						WHAT HE GAVE UP												THE RESULTS							
Year	Team	Lg	G	GS	CG	GF	IP	BFP	H	R	ER	HR	SH	SF	HB	TBB	IBB	SO	WP	Bk	W	L	Pct	ShO	Sv-Op	Hld	ERC	ERA
2002	Royals	R	3	3	0	0	4.2	20	3	1	1	0	0	0	0	3	0	4	1	0	0	0	-	0	0- -	-	2.35	1.93
2002	Spkane	A-	2	2	0	0	4.2	23	9	4	4	0	0	0	0	0	0	5	1	0	0	0	-	0	0- -	-	7.03	7.71
2002	Wilmg	A+	1	0	0	0	2.0	6	1	0	0	0	0	0	0	0	0	0	0	0	0	0	-	0	0- -	-	0.63	0.00
2003	Wilmg	A+	14	14	3	0	87.0	330	56	16	11	5	1	0	2	13	0	78	1	0	11	1	.917	1	0- -	-	1.39	1.14
2003	Wichta	AA	9	9	0	0	53.0	214	58	20	19	5	0	3	3	5	2	34	0	0	4	3	.571	0	0- -	-	3.65	3.23
2004	Omha	AAA	6	6	0	0	28.2	119	25	8	8	2	3	1	2	6	0	23	2	1	1	1	.500	0	0- -	-	2.69	2.51
2004	KC	AL	24	24	0	0	145.0	599	143	64	64	26	3	2	8	26	3	100	1	1	8	11	.421	0	0-0	0	3.85	3.97
2005	KC	AL	33	33	2	0	183.0	829	233	125	118	23	4	4	13	53	0	114	4	2	5	17	.227	0	0-0	0	5.71	5.80
	2 ML YEARS		57	57	2	0	328.0	1428	376	189	182	49	7	6	21	79	3	214	5	3	13	28	.317	0	0-0	0	4.87	4.99

Seth Greisinger

Pitches: R **Bats:** R **Pos:** SP-1   **Ht:** 6'3" **Wt:** 200 **Born:** 7/29/1975 **Age:** 30

			HOW MUCH HE PITCHED						WHAT HE GAVE UP												THE RESULTS							
Year	Team	Lg	G	GS	CG	GF	IP	BFP	H	R	ER	HR	SH	SF	HB	TBB	IBB	SO	WP	Bk	W	L	Pct	ShO	Sv-Op	Hld	ERC	ERA
2005	Rchmd*	AAA	16	16	1	0	98.2	399	75	36	33	4	5	2	9	28	2	56	1	0	4	7	.364	0	0- -	-	2.34	3.01
1998	DET	AL	21	21	0	0	130.0	562	142	79	74	17	2	5	4	48	2	66	3	0	6	9	.400	0	0-0	0	4.89	5.12
2002	DET	AL	8	8	0	0	37.2	168	46	26	26	4	1	1	1	13	2	14	0	0	2	2	.500	0	0-0	0	5.23	6.21
2004	MIN	AL	12	9	0	1	51.0	233	68	40	35	12	1	2	2	15	1	36	1	0	2	5	.286	0	0-0	0	6.79	6.18
2005	ATL	NL	1	1	0	0	5.0	21	7	2	2	1	0	0	0	1	0	2	0	0	0	0	-	0	0-0	0	6.86	3.60
	4 ML YEARS		42	39	0	1	223.2	984	263	147	137	34	4	8	7	77	5	118	4	0	10	16	.385	0	0-0	0	5.41	5.51

Ben Grieve

Bats: L **Throws:** R **Pos:** PH-22; LF-1   **Ht:** 6'4" **Wt:** 216 **Born:** 5/4/1976 **Age:** 30

			BATTING																		BASERUNNING				AVERAGES		
Year	Team	Lg	G	AB	H	2B	3B	HR	(Hm	Rd)	TB	R	RBI	RC	TBB	IBB	SO	HBP	SH	SF	SB	CS	SB%	GDP	Avg	OBP	Slg
2005	Iowa*	AAA	86	293	78	19	1	14	(-	-)	141	44	51	54	48	4	59	1	0	0	0	0	-	9	.266	.371	.481
1997	OAK	AL	24	93	29	6	0	3	(3	0)	44	12	24	18	13	1	25	1	1	0	0	0	-	1	.312	.402	.473
1998	OAK	AL	155	583	168	41	2	18	(5	13)	267	94	89	101	85	3	123	9	0	1	2	2	.50	18	.288	.386	.458
1999	OAK	AL	148	486	129	21	0	28	(13	15)	234	80	86	81	63	2	108	8	0	1	4	0	1.00	17	.265	.358	.481
2000	OAK	AL	158	594	166	40	1	27	(13	14)	289	92	104	95	73	2	130	3	0	5	3	0	1.00	32	.279	.359	.487
2001	TB	AL	154	542	143	30	2	11	(5	6)	210	72	72	82	87	2	159	8	0	2	7	1	.88	13	.264	.372	.387
2002	TB	AL	136	482	121	30	0	19	(7	12)	208	62	64	68	69	5	121	8	0	2	8	2	.80	15	.251	.353	.432
2003	TB	AL	55	165	38	7	0	4	(2	2)	57	28	17	19	32	1	41	6	0	2	0	0	-	3	.230	.371	.345
2004	2 Tms	NL	123	250	65	17	0	8	(3	5)	106	30	35	39	39	5	70	2	0	3	0	0	-	4	.260	.361	.424
2005	CHN	NL	23	20	5	0	0	0	(0	0)	5	1	1	2	5	1	7	0	0	0	0	0	-	0	.250	.400	.250
04	Mil	NL	108	234	61	15	0	7	(3	4)	97	28	29	36	39	5	65	0	0	2	0	0	-	4	.261	.364	.415
04	ChC	NL	15	16	4	2	0	1	(0	1)	9	2	6	3	0	0	5	2	0	1	0	0	-	0	.250	.316	.563
	9 ML YEARS		976	3215	864	192	5	118	(51	67)	1420	471	492	505	466	22	784	45	1	16	24	5	.83	103	.269	.367	.442

Ken Griffey Jr.

Bats: L **Throws:** L **Pos:** CF-124; DH-2; PH-2   **Ht:** 6'3" **Wt:** 205 **Born:** 11/21/1969 **Age:** 36

			BATTING																		BASERUNNING				AVERAGES		
Year	Team	Lg	G	AB	H	2B	3B	HR	(Hm	Rd)	TB	R	RBI	RC	TBB	IBB	SO	HBP	SH	SF	SB	CS	SB%	GDP	Avg	OBP	Slg
1989	SEA	AL	127	455	120	23	0	16	(10	6)	191	61	61	64	44	8	83	2	1	4	16	7	.70	4	.264	.329	.420
1990	SEA	AL	155	597	179	28	7	22	(8	14)	287	91	80	101	63	12	81	2	0	4	16	11	.59	12	.300	.366	.481
1991	SEA	AL	154	548	179	42	1	22	(16	6)	289	76	100	112	71	21	82	1	4	9	18	6	.75	10	.327	.399	.527
1992	SEA	AL	142	565	174	39	4	27	(16	11)	302	83	103	102	44	15	67	5	0	3	10	5	.67	15	.308	.361	.535
1993	SEA	AL	156	582	180	38	3	45	(21	24)	359	113	109	137	96	25	91	6	0	7	17	9	.65	14	.309	.408	.617
1994	SEA	AL	111	433	140	24	4	40	(18	22)	292	94	90	107	56	19	73	2	0	2	11	3	.79	9	.323	.402	.674
1995	SEA	AL	72	260	67	7	0	17	(13	4)	125	52	42	49	52	6	53	0	0	2	4	2	.67	4	.258	.379	.481
1996	SEA	AL	140	545	165	26	2	49	(26	23)	342	125	140	131	78	13	104	7	1	7	16	1	.94	7	.303	.392	.628
1997	SEA	AL	157	608	185	34	3	56	(27	29)	393	125	147	142	76	23	121	8	0	12	15	4	.79	12	.304	.382	.646
1998	SEA	AL	161	633	180	33	3	56	(30	26)	387	120	146	136	76	11	121	7	0	4	20	5	.80	14	.284	.365	.611
1999	SEA	AL	160	606	173	26	3	48	(27	21)	349	123	134	132	91	17	108	7	0	2	24	7	.77	8	.285	.384	.576
2000	CIN	NL	145	520	141	22	3	40	(22	18)	289	100	118	111	94	17	117	9	0	8	6	4	.60	7	.271	.387	.556
2001	CIN	NL	111	364	104	20	2	22	(12	10)	194	57	65	69	44	6	72	4	1	4	2	0	1.00	8	.286	.365	.533
2002	CIN	NL	70	197	52	8	0	8	(4	4)	84	17	23	27	28	6	39	3	0	4	1	2	.33	6	.264	.358	.426
2003	CIN	NL	53	166	41	12	1	13	(5	8)	94	34	26	26	27	5	44	6	1	1	1	0	1.00	3	.247	.370	.566
2004	CIN	NL	83	300	76	18	0	20	(11	9)	154	49	60	56	44	3	67	2	0	2	1	0	1.00	8	.253	.351	.513
2005	CIN	NL	128	491	148	30	0	35	(15	20)	283	85	92	89	54	3	93	3	0	7	0	1	.00	9	.301	.369	.576
	17 ML YEARS		2125	7870	2304	430	36	536	(281	255)	4414	1405	1536	1591	1038	210	1416	74	8	82	178	67	.73	150	.293	.377	.561

John-Ford Griffin

Bats: L **Throws:** L **Pos:** DH-4; PH-4; PR-1   **Ht:** 6'0" **Wt:** 215 **Born:** 11/19/1979 **Age:** 26

			BATTING																		BASERUNNING				AVERAGES		
Year	Team	Lg	G	AB	H	2B	3B	HR	(Hm	Rd)	TB	R	RBI	RC	TBB	IBB	SO	HBP	SH	SF	SB	CS	SB%	GDP	Avg	OBP	Slg
2001	StIsInd	A-	66	238	74	17	1	5	(-	-)	108	46	43	48	40	0	41	3	1	2	10	4	.71	5	.311	.413	.454
2002	Tampa	A+	65	255	68	16	1	3	(-	-)	95	32	31	35	29	0	45	3	0	4	1	0	1.00	9	.267	.344	.373
2002	Mdland	AA	2	7	1	0	0	0	(-	-)	1	0	0	0	0	0	3	1	0	0	0	0	-	0	.143	.250	.143
2002	Nrwich	AA	18	67	22	3	0	5	(-	-)	40	17	10	15	8	1	13	0	0	0	0	1	.00	5	.328	.400	.597
2003	NwHav	AA	104	373	104	23	3	13	(-	-)	172	48	75	65	49	4	85	2	0	5	2	0	1.00	8	.279	.361	.461
2004	Ham	AA	129	467	116	28	1	22	(-	-)	212	66	81	73	56	2	128	4	0	1	1	1	.50	15	.248	.330	.454
2005	Syrcse	AAA	135	512	130	21	1	30	(-	-)	243	80	103	84	62	4	140	3	0	5	1	2	.33	10	.254	.335	.475
2005	TOR	AL	7	13	4	2	0	1	(1	0)	9	3	6	2	0	0	4	0	0	0	0	0	-	0	.308	.308	.692

Jason Grilli

Pitches: R Bats: R Pos: SP-2; RP-1   Ht: 6'5" Wt: 210 Born: 11/11/1976 Age: 29

Year	Team	Lg	G	GS	CG	GF	IP	BFP	H	R	ER	HR	SH	SF	HB	TBB	IBB	SO	WP	Bk	W	L	Pct	ShO	Sv-Op	Hld	ERC	ERA
2005	Toledo*	AAA	28	28	3	0	167.1	730	170	89	76	21	4	3	9	58	0	120	2	1	12	9	.571	2	0- -	-	4.31	4.09
2000	FLA	NL	1	1	0	0	6.2	35	11	4	4	0	2	0	2	2	0	3	0	0	1	0	1.000	0	0-0	0	7.84	5.40
2001	FLA	NL	6	5	0	1	26.2	115	30	18	18	6	1	0	2	11	0	17	0	0	2	2	.500	0	0-0	0	6.44	6.08
2004	CHA	AL	8	8	1	0	45.0	203	52	38	37	11	2	1	3	20	0	26	2	0	2	3	.400	0	0-0	0	6.67	7.40
2005	DET	AL	3	2	0	0	16.0	63	14	6	6	1	1	1	0	6	0	5	0	0	1	1	.500	0	0-0	0	3.27	3.38
	4 ML YEARS		18	16	1	1	94.1	416	107	66	65	18	6	2	7	39	0	51	2	0	6	6	.500	0	0-0	0	6.08	6.20

Jason Grimsley

Pitches: R Bats: R Pos: RP-22   Ht: 6'3" Wt: 205 Born: 8/7/1967 Age: 38

Year	Team	Lg	G	GS	CG	GF	IP	BFP	H	R	ER	HR	SH	SF	HB	TBB	IBB	SO	WP	Bk	W	L	Pct	ShO	Sv-Op	Hld	ERC	ERA
2005	Bowie*	AA	8	2	0	0	8.0	33	4	1	1	0	0	0	0	4	1	4	0	0	2	0	1.000	0	0- -	-	1.26	1.13
1989	PHI	NL	4	4	0	0	18.1	91	19	13	12	2	1	0	0	19	1	7	2	0	1	3	.250	0	0-0	0	6.86	5.89
1990	PHI	NL	11	11	0	0	57.1	255	47	21	21	1	2	1	2	43	0	41	6	1	3	2	.600	0	0-0	0	3.98	3.30
1991	PHI	NL	12	12	0	0	61.0	272	54	34	33	4	3	2	3	41	3	42	14	0	1	7	.125	0	0-0	0	4.39	4.87
1993	CLE	AL	10	6	0	1	42.1	194	52	26	25	3	1	0	1	20	1	27	2	0	3	4	.429	0	0-0	1	5.57	5.31
1994	CLE	AL	14	13	1	0	82.2	368	91	47	42	7	4	2	6	34	1	59	6	1	5	2	.714	0	0-0	0	4.89	4.57
1995	CLE	AL	15	2	0	2	34.0	165	37	24	23	4	1	2	2	32	1	25	7	0	0	0	-	0	1-1	0	7.37	6.09
1996	CAL	AL	35	20	2	4	130.1	620	150	110	99	14	4	5	13	74	5	82	11	0	5	7	.417	1	0-0	0	5.98	6.84
1999	NYA	AL	55	0	0	25	75.0	336	66	39	30	7	3	3	4	40	5	49	8	0	7	2	.778	0	1-4	8	3.87	3.60
2000	NYA	AL	63	4	0	18	96.1	428	100	58	54	10	2	6	5	42	1	53	16	0	3	2	.600	0	1-4	4	4.63	5.04
2001	KC	AL	73	0	0	24	80.1	327	71	32	27	8	2	1	2	28	5	61	4	0	1	5	.167	0	0-7	26	3.34	3.02
2002	KC	AL	70	0	0	26	71.1	310	64	32	31	4	1	0	1	37	8	59	8	0	4	7	.364	0	1-3	13	3.51	3.91
2003	KC	AL	76	0	0	5	75.0	346	88	47	43	6	6	5	5	36	5	58	4	0	2	6	.250	0	0-7	28	5.40	5.16
2004	2 Tms		73	0	0	7	63.0	285	61	36	27	4	3	1	3	35	6	39	6	0	5	7	.417	0	0-9	17	4.20	3.86
2005	BAL	AL	22	0	0	9	22.0	93	24	15	14	5	0	1	0	9	2	10	1	0	1	2	.333	0	0-3	5	5.67	5.73
04	KC	AL	32	0	0	4	26.2	118	24	11	10	1	1	0	1	15	3	18	4	0	3	3	.500	0	0-3	5	3.62	3.38
04	Bal	AL	41	0	0	3	36.1	167	37	25	17	3	2	1	2	20	3	21	2	0	2	4	.333	1	0-6	12	4.63	4.21
	14 ML YEARS		533	72	3	121	909.0	4090	924	534	481	79	33	29	47	490	44	612	95	2	41	56	.423	1	4-38	100	4.75	4.76

Marquis Grissom

Bats: R Throws: R Pos: CF-34; PH-7; LF-1; RF-1; PR-1   Ht: 5'11" Wt: 188 Born: 4/17/1967 Age: 39

Year	Team	Lg	G	AB	H	2B	3B	HR	(Hm	Rd)	TB	R	RBI	RC	TBB	IBB	SO	HBP	SH	SF	SB	CS	SB%	GDP	Avg	OBP	Slg
2005	Fresno*	AAA	4	15	3	0	0	1	(-	-)	6	4	2	1	0	0	3	0	0	0	0	0	-	0	.200	.200	.400
1989	MON	NL	26	74	19	2	0	1	(0	1)	24	16	2	10	12	0	21	0	1	0	1	0	1.00	1	.257	.360	.324
1990	MON	NL	98	288	74	14	2	3	(2	1)	101	42	29	37	27	2	40	0	4	1	22	2	.92	3	.257	.320	.351
1991	MON	NL	148	558	149	23	9	6	(3	3)	208	73	39	71	34	0	89	1	4	0	76	17	.82	8	.267	.310	.373
1992	MON	NL	159	653	180	39	6	14	(8	6)	273	99	66	96	42	6	81	5	3	4	78	13	.86	12	.276	.322	.418
1993	MON	NL	157	630	188	27	2	19	(9	10)	276	104	95	103	52	6	76	3	0	8	53	10	.84	9	.298	.351	.438
1994	MON	NL	110	475	137	25	4	11	(4	7)	203	96	45	73	41	4	66	1	0	4	36	6	.86	10	.288	.344	.427
1995	ATL	NL	139	551	142	23	3	12	(5	7)	207	80	42	68	47	4	61	3	1	4	29	9	.76	8	.258	.317	.376
1996	ATL	NL	158	671	207	32	10	23	(11	12)	328	106	74	111	41	6	73	3	4	4	28	11	.72	12	.308	.349	.489
1997	CLE	AL	144	558	146	27	6	12	(5	7)	221	74	66	69	43	1	89	6	6	9	22	13	.63	12	.262	.317	.396
1998	MIL	NL	142	542	147	28	1	10	(2	8)	207	57	60	59	24	2	78	2	2	2	13	8	.62	12	.271	.304	.382
1999	MIL	NL	154	603	161	27	1	20	(9	11)	250	92	83	81	49	4	109	0	4	5	24	6	.80	12	.267	.320	.415
2000	MIL	NL	146	595	145	18	2	14	(4	10)	209	67	62	59	39	2	99	0	2	4	20	10	.67	9	.244	.288	.351
2001	LA	NL	135	448	99	17	1	21	(9	12)	181	56	60	61	16	0	107	2	0	2	7	5	.58	12	.221	.250	.404
2002	LA	NL	111	343	95	21	4	17	(10	7)	175	57	60	54	22	2	68	2	0	4	5	1	.83	6	.277	.321	.510
2003	SF	NL	149	587	176	33	3	20	(10	10)	275	82	79	88	20	0	82	2	3	6	11	3	.79	14	.300	.322	.468
2004	SF	NL	145	562	157	26	2	22	(11	11)	253	78	90	72	37	5	83	1	2	4	3	1	.75	22	.279	.323	.450
2005	SF	NL	44	137	29	4	0	2	(1	1)	39	8	15	9	7	0	18	0	2	1	1	1	.50	9	.212	.248	.285
	17 ML YEARS		2165	8275	2251	386	56	227	(103	124)	3430	1187	967	1101	553	44	1240	31	38	62	429	116	.79	171	.272	.318	.415

Buddy Groom

Pitches: L Bats: L Pos: RP-47   Ht: 6'2" Wt: 207 Born: 7/10/1965 Age: 40

Year	Team	Lg	G	GS	CG	GF	IP	BFP	H	R	ER	HR	SH	SF	HB	TBB	IBB	SO	WP	Bk	W	L	Pct	ShO	Sv-Op	Hld	ERC	ERA
2005	Clmbs*	AAA	6	0	0	0	4.2	26	6	4	3	2	0	1	0	5	1	0	0	0	0	0	-	0	0- -	-	6.14	5.79
1992	DET	AL	12	7	0	3	38.2	177	48	28	25	4	3	2	0	22	4	15	0	1	0	5	.000	0	1-2	0	6.20	5.82
1993	DET	AL	19	3	0	8	36.2	170	48	25	25	4	2	4	2	13	5	15	2	1	0	2	.000	0	0-0	1	5.72	6.14
1994	DET	AL	40	0	0	10	32.0	139	31	14	14	4	0	3	2	13	2	27	0	0	1	1	.500	0	1-1	11	4.25	3.94
1995	2 Tms		37	4	0	11	55.2	274	81	47	46	8	2	4	2	32	4	35	3	0	2	5	.286	0	1-3	0	8.05	7.44
1996	OAK	AL	72	1	0	16	77.1	341	85	37	33	8	2	0	3	34	3	57	5	0	5	0	1.000	0	2-4	15	5.00	3.84
1997	OAK	AL	78	0	0	7	64.2	285	75	38	37	9	0	4	0	24	1	45	3	0	2	2	.500	0	3-5	12	5.18	5.15
1998	OAK	AL	75	0	0	13	57.1	251	62	30	27	4	1	3	1	20	1	36	1	0	3	1	.750	0	0-6	16	4.12	4.24
1999	OAK	AL	76	0	0	6	46.0	196	48	29	26	1	2	0	1	18	5	32	2	1	3	2	.600	0	0-3	27	3.71	5.09
2000	BAL	AL	70	0	0	14	59.1	260	63	37	32	5	5	5	0	21	2	44	1	0	6	3	.667	0	4-11	27	4.01	4.85
2001	BAL	AL	70	0	0	35	66.0	265	64	28	26	4	1	1	1	9	0	54	2	0	1	4	.200	0	11-13	16	2.75	3.55
2002	BAL	AL	70	0	0	17	62.0	239	44	11	11	4	0	1	2	12	3	48	0	0	3	2	.600	0	2-4	19	1.73	1.60
2003	BAL	AL	60	0	0	20	45.1	207	58	27	27	7	1	1	3	14	2	34	1	0	1	3	.250	0	1-3	16	5.93	5.36
2004	BAL	AL	60	0	0	22	52.2	236	67	30	28	6	0	2	1	16	1	32	0	1	4	1	.800	0	0-2	8	5.43	4.78
2005	2 Tms		47	0	0	13	41.0	186	51	22	22	5	1	2	3	12	3	20	0	0	1	1	.500	0	1-1	7	5.35	4.83
95	Det	AL	23	4	0	6	40.2	203	55	35	34	6	2	2	2	26	4	23	3	0	1	3	.250	0	1-3	0	7.54	7.52
95	Fla	NL	14	0	0	5	15.0	71	26	12	12	2	0	2	0	6	0	12	0	0	1	2	.333	0	0-0	0	9.52	7.20

			HOW MUCH HE PITCHED					WHAT HE GAVE UP											THE RESULTS					
Year	Team	Lg	G	GS	CG	GF	IP	BFP	H	R	ER	HR	SH	SF	HB	TBB	IBB	SO	WP	Bk	W	L	Pct	ShO	Sv-Op	Hld	ERC	ERA
05	NYY	AL	24	0	0	8	25.2	116	32	14	14	3	0	1	3	7	2	13	0	0	1	0	1.000	0	0-0	3	5.48	4.91
05	Ari	NL	23	0	0	5	15.1	70	19	8	8	2	1	1	0	5	1	7	0	0	0	1	.000	0	1-1	4	5.14	4.70
	14 ML YEARS		786	15	0	195	734.2	3226	825	403	379	73	19	30	21	260	36	494	20	4	31	32	.492	0	27-58	170	4.64	4.64

Gabe Gross

Bats: L **Throws:** R **Pos:** RF-20; LF-19; PH-6; DH-2　　　　　　**Ht:** 6'3" **Wt:** 209 **Born:** 10/21/1979 **Age:** 26

			BATTING																	BASERUNNING				AVERAGES		
Year	Team	Lg	G	AB	H	2B	3B	HR	(Hm	Rd)	TB	R	RBI	RC	TBB	IBB	SO	HBP	SH	SF	SB	CS	SB%	GDP	Avg	OBP	Slg
2001	Dnedin	A+	35	126	38	9	2	4	(-	-)	63	23	15	27	26	1	29	2	0	1	4	2	.67	2	.302	.426	.500
2001	Tenn	AA	11	41	10	1	0	3	(-	-)	20	8	11	7	6	1	12	3	0	1	0	1	.00	1	.244	.373	.488
2002	Tenn	AA	112	403	96	17	5	10	(-	-)	153	57	54	54	53	4	71	5	2	2	8	2	.80	4	.238	.333	.380
2003	NwHav	AA	84	310	99	23	3	7	(-	-)	149	52	51	62	52	1	53	5	2	2	3	2	.60	9	.319	.423	.481
2003	Syrcse	AAA	53	182	48	16	2	5	(-	-)	83	22	23	31	31	3	56	3	0	0	1	1	.50	2	.264	.380	.456
2004	Syrcse	AAA	103	377	111	29	2	9	(-	-)	171	52	54	63	53	2	81	1	0	2	4	5	.44	8	.294	.381	.454
2005	Syrcse	AAA	102	390	116	29	4	6	(-	-)	171	64	46	70	52	2	83	2	2	4	14	2	.88	5	.297	.379	.438
2004	TOR	AL	44	129	27	4	0	3	(2	1)	40	18	16	15	19	0	31	0	0	0	2	2	.50	1	.209	.311	.310
2005	TOR	AL	40	92	23	4	1	1	(1	0)	32	11	7	11	10	0	21	0	0	0	1	1	.50	0	.250	.324	.348
	2 ML YEARS		84	221	50	8	1	4	(3	1)	72	29	23	26	29	0	52	0	0	0	3	3	.50	1	.226	.316	.326

Mark Grudzielanek

Bats: R **Throws:** R **Pos:** 2B-137; PH-1　　　　　　**Ht:** 6'1" **Wt:** 185 **Born:** 6/30/1970 **Age:** 36

			BATTING																	BASERUNNING				AVERAGES		
Year	Team	Lg	G	AB	H	2B	3B	HR	(Hm	Rd)	TB	R	RBI	RC	TBB	IBB	SO	HBP	SH	SF	SB	CS	SB%	GDP	Avg	OBP	Slg
1995	MON	NL	78	269	66	12	2	1	(1	0)	85	27	20	24	14	4	47	7	3	0	8	3	.73	7	.245	.300	.316
1996	MON	NL	153	657	201	34	4	6	(5	1)	261	99	49	90	26	3	83	9	1	3	33	7	.83	10	.306	.340	.397
1997	MON	NL	156	649	177	54	3	4	(1	3)	249	76	51	75	23	0	76	10	3	3	25	9	.74	13	.273	.307	.384
1998	2 Tms	NL	156	589	160	21	1	10	(5	5)	213	62	62	64	26	2	73	11	8	7	18	5	.78	18	.272	.311	.362
1999	LA	NL	123	488	159	23	5	7	(4	3)	213	72	46	76	31	1	65	10	2	3	6	6	.50	13	.326	.376	.436
2000	LA	NL	148	617	172	35	6	7	(4	3)	240	101	49	80	45	0	81	9	2	3	12	3	.80	16	.279	.335	.389
2001	LA	NL	133	539	146	21	3	13	(8	5)	212	83	55	66	28	0	83	11	3	5	4	4	.50	9	.271	.317	.393
2002	LA	NL	150	536	145	23	0	9	(5	4)	195	56	50	53	22	4	89	3	1	4	4	1	.80	17	.271	.301	.364
2003	CHN	NL	121	481	151	38	1	3	(2	1)	200	73	38	71	30	0	64	11	7	2	6	2	.75	12	.314	.366	.416
2004	CHN	NL	81	257	79	12	1	6	(3	3)	111	32	23	35	15	0	32	1	4	1	1	1	.50	7	.307	.347	.432
2005	STL	NL	137	528	155	30	3	8	(3	5)	215	64	59	68	26	3	81	7	0	2	8	6	.57	14	.294	.334	.407
98	Mon	NL	105	396	109	15	1	8	(3	5)	150	51	41	47	21	1	50	9	5	4	11	5	.69	11	.275	.323	.379
98	LA	NL	51	193	51	6	0	2	(2	0)	63	11	21	17	5	1	23	2	3	3	7	0	1.00	7	.264	.286	.326
	11 ML YEARS		1436	5610	1611	303	29	74	(41	33)	2194	745	502	702	286	17	774	89	34	33	125	47	.73	136	.287	.330	.391

Kevin Gryboski

Pitches: R **Bats:** R **Pos:** RP-42　　　　　　**Ht:** 6'5" **Wt:** 235 **Born:** 11/15/1973 **Age:** 32

			HOW MUCH HE PITCHED						WHAT HE GAVE UP												THE RESULTS					
Year	Team	Lg	G	GS	CG	GF	IP	BFP	H	R	ER	HR	SH	SF	HB	TBB	IBB	SO	WP	Bk	W	L	Pct	ShO	Sv-Op	Hld	ERC	ERA
2005	Rome*	A	1	1	0	0	1.0	4	1	0	0	0	0	0	0	0	0	0	0	0	0	0	-	0	0--	1	1.95	0.00
2005	Okla*	AAA	9	0	0	4	10.1	51	14	7	6	2	1	0	1	6	1	5	1	0	0	2	.000	0	0--	-	8.01	5.23
2002	ATL	NL	57	0	0	10	51.2	238	50	20	20	6	1	0	5	37	5	33	2	0	2	1	.667	0	0-2	11	5.58	3.48
2003	ATL	NL	64	0	0	9	44.1	191	44	22	19	3	4	0	2	23	6	32	2	0	6	4	.600	0	0-4	12	4.36	3.86
2004	ATL	NL	69	0	0	10	50.2	217	54	22	16	2	1	0	0	23	4	24	5	0	3	2	.600	0	2-4	16	4.22	2.84
2005	2 Tms		42	0	0	9	31.0	154	41	25	19	1	4	2	3	20	5	10	2	0	1	1	.500	0	0-2	5	6.48	5.52
05	Atl	NL	31	0	0	7	21.1	99	24	10	7	0	3	2	2	12	3	8	1	0	0	0	-	0	0-2	2	4.78	2.95
05	Tex	AL	11	0	0	2	9.2	55	17	15	12	1	1	0	1	8	2	2	1	0	1	1	.500	0	0-0	3	10.60	11.17
	4 ML YEARS		232	0	0	38	177.2	800	189	89	74	12	10	2	10	103	20	99	11	0	12	8	.600	0	2-12	44	5.03	3.75

Eddie Guardado

Pitches: L **Bats:** R **Pos:** RP-58　　　　　　**Ht:** 6'0" **Wt:** 194 **Born:** 10/2/1970 **Age:** 35

			HOW MUCH HE PITCHED						WHAT HE GAVE UP												THE RESULTS					
Year	Team	Lg	G	GS	CG	GF	IP	BFP	H	R	ER	HR	SH	SF	HB	TBB	IBB	SO	WP	Bk	W	L	Pct	ShO	Sv-Op	Hld	ERC	ERA
1993	MIN	AL	19	16	0	2	94.2	426	123	68	65	13	1	3	1	36	2	46	0	0	3	8	.273	0	0-0	0	6.18	6.18
1994	MIN	AL	4	4	0	0	17.0	81	26	16	16	3	1	0	2	4	0	8	0	0	0	2	.000	0	0-0	0	7.01	8.47
1995	MIN	AL	51	5	0	10	91.1	410	99	54	52	13	6	5	0	45	2	71	5	1	4	9	.308	0	2-5	5	5.20	5.12
1996	MIN	AL	83	0	0	17	73.2	313	61	45	43	12	6	4	3	33	4	74	3	0	6	5	.545	0	4-7	18	3.81	5.25
1997	MIN	AL	69	0	0	20	46.0	201	45	23	20	7	2	1	2	17	2	54	2	0	0	4	.000	0	1-1	13	4.23	3.91
1998	MIN	AL	79	0	0	12	65.2	286	66	34	33	10	3	6	0	28	6	53	2	0	3	1	.750	0	0-4	16	4.42	4.52
1999	MIN	AL	63	0	0	13	48.0	197	37	25	25	6	2	1	2	25	4	50	0	0	2	5	.286	0	2-4	15	3.63	4.69
2000	MIN	AL	70	0	0	36	61.2	262	55	27	27	14	3	2	1	25	3	52	1	1	7	4	.636	0	9-11	8	4.34	3.94
2001	MIN	AL	67	0	0	26	66.2	270	47	27	26	5	5	3	1	23	4	67	4	0	7	1	.875	0	12-14	14	2.13	3.51
2002	MIN	AL	68	0	0	62	67.2	270	53	22	22	9	2	2	1	18	2	70	0	0	1	3	.250	0	45-51	0	2.66	2.93
2003	MIN	AL	66	0	0	60	65.1	260	50	22	21	7	3	2	0	14	2	60	5	0	3	5	.375	0	41-45	0	2.14	2.89
2004	SEA	AL	41	0	0	35	45.1	176	31	14	14	8	0	1	0	14	0	45	0	0	2	2	.500	0	18-25	0	2.69	2.78
2005	SEA	AL	58	0	0	55	56.1	238	52	23	17	7	3	2	0	15	3	48	1	0	2	3	.400	0	36-41	0	3.12	2.72
	13 ML YEARS		738	25	0	348	799.1	3390	745	400	381	114	37	34	12	297	34	698	23	2	40	52	.435	0	170-208	89	3.87	4.29

Vladimir Guerrero

Bats: R **Throws:** R **Pos:** RF-120; DH-19; PH-2 **Ht:** 6'3" **Wt:** 210 **Born:** 2/9/1976 **Age:** 30

								BATTING													BASERUNNING				AVERAGES		
Year	Team	Lg	G	AB	H	2B	3B	HR	(Hm	Rd)	TB	R	RBI	RC	TBB	IBB	SO	HBP	SH	SF	SB	CS	SB%	GDP	Avg	OBP	Slg
1996	MON	NL	9	27	5	0	0	1	(0	1)	8	2	1	1	0	0	3	0	0	0	0	0	-	1	.185	.185	.296
1997	MON	NL	90	325	98	22	2	11	(5	6)	157	44	40	51	19	2	39	7	0	3	3	4	.43	11	.302	.350	.483
1998	MON	NL	159	623	202	37	7	38	(19	19)	367	108	109	124	42	13	95	7	0	5	11	9	.55	15	.324	.371	.589
1999	MON	NL	160	610	193	37	5	42	(23	19)	366	102	131	127	55	14	62	7	0	2	14	7	.67	18	.316	.378	.600
2000	MON	NL	154	571	197	28	11	44	(25	19)	379	101	123	137	58	23	74	8	0	4	9	10	.47	15	.345	.410	.664
2001	MON	NL	159	599	184	45	4	34	(21	13)	339	107	108	116	60	24	88	9	0	3	37	16	.70	24	.307	.377	.566
2002	MON	NL	161	614	206	37	2	39	(20	19)	364	106	111	123	84	32	70	6	0	5	40	20	.67	20	.336	.417	.593
2003	MON	NL	112	394	130	20	3	25	(15	10)	231	71	79	83	63	21	53	6	0	4	9	5	.64	18	.330	.426	.586
2004	ANA	AL	156	612	206	39	2	39	(19	20)	366	124	126	122	52	14	74	8	0	8	15	3	.83	19	.337	.391	.598
2005	LAA	AL	141	520	165	29	2	32	(19	13)	294	95	108	108	61	26	48	8	0	5	13	1	.93	17	.317	.394	.565
	10 ML YEARS		1301	4895	1586	294	38	305	(166	139)	2871	860	936	992	494	169	606	66	0	39	151	75	.67	158	.324	.391	.587

Matt Guerrier

Pitches: R **Bats:** R **Pos:** RP-43 **Ht:** 6'3" **Wt:** 185 **Born:** 8/2/1978 **Age:** 27

			HOW MUCH HE PITCHED					WHAT HE GAVE UP										THE RESULTS					
Year	Team	Lg	G	GS	CG	GF	IP	BFP	H	R	ER	HR	SH	SF	HB	TBB	IBB	SO	WP	Bk	W	L	Pct	ShO	Sv-Op Hld	ERC	ERA
1999	Bristol	R+	21	0	0	19	25.2	109	18	9	2	1	0	2	1	14	2	37	1	1	5	0	1.000	0	10- - -	2.61	0.70
1999	WinSa	A+	4	0	0	4	3.1	15	3	2	2	0	0	0	1	0	0	5	2	0	0	0	-	0	2- - -	2.26	5.40
2000	WinSa	A+	30	0	0	28	34.2	147	25	13	5	0	2	1	3	12	0	35	2	0	0	3	.000	0	19- - -	2.01	1.30
2000	Brham	AA	23	0	0	19	23.1	95	17	9	7	1	0	0	1	12	1	19	3	0	3	1	.750	0	7- - -	2.87	2.70
2001	Brham	AA	15	15	1	0	98.2	402	85	42	34	8	5	0	5	32	1	75	5	0	11	3	.786	1	0- - -	3.17	3.10
2001	Charltt	AAA	12	12	3	0	81.1	328	75	33	32	7	4	2	4	18	0	43	2	0	7	1	.875	0	0- - -	3.14	3.54
2002	Nashv	AAA	27	26	2	0	157.0	676	154	88	80	20	7	4	10	47	3	130	7	0	7	12	.368	1	0- - -	3.93	4.59
2003	Nashv	AAA	20	19	0	1	105.1	442	108	56	53	15	4	3	4	18	1	78	5	0	4	6	.400	0	0- - -	3.69	4.53
2004	Roch	AAA	24	23	0	1	144.0	579	135	65	51	15	8	9	5	25	0	97	2	0	5	10	.333	0	0- - -	3.08	3.19
2004	MIN	AL	9	2	0	5	19.0	84	22	13	12	5	2	0	1	6	0	11	0	0	0	1	.000	0	0-0 - 0	6.10	5.68
2005	MIN	AL	43	0	0	14	71.2	306	71	29	27	6	4	1	3	24	5	46	3	0	3	0	.000	0	0-0 - 1	3.71	3.39
	2 ML YEARS		52	2	0	19	90.2	390	93	42	39	11	6	1	4	30	5	57	3	0	0	4	.000	0	0-0 - 1	4.19	3.87

Aaron Guiel

Bats: L **Throws:** R **Pos:** CF-24; RF-7; PH-6 **Ht:** 5'10" **Wt:** 190 **Born:** 10/5/1972 **Age:** 33

								BATTING													BASERUNNING				AVERAGES		
Year	Team	Lg	G	AB	H	2B	3B	HR	(Hm	Rd)	TB	R	RBI	RC	TBB	IBB	SO	HBP	SH	SF	SB	CS	SB%	GDP	Avg	OBP	Slg
2005	Omha*	AAA	128	496	137	32	4	30	(-	-)	267	94	95	101	64	4	103	15	0	7	6	3	.67	13	.276	.371	.538
2002	KC	AL	70	240	56	13	0	4	(4	0)	81	30	38	33	19	1	61	4	2	4	1	5	.17	3	.233	.296	.338
2003	KC	AL	99	354	98	30	0	15	(4	11)	173	63	52	59	27	0	63	13	2	5	3	5	.38	3	.277	.346	.489
2004	KC	AL	42	135	21	4	0	5	(2	3)	40	15	13	8	17	0	42	3	1	1	1	1	.50	3	.156	.263	.296
2005	KC	AL	33	109	32	5	0	4	(3	1)	49	18	7	14	6	1	21	5	0	1	1	0	1.00	3	.294	.355	.450
	4 ML YEARS		244	838	207	52	0	28	(13	15)	343	126	110	114	69	2	187	25	5	11	6	11	.35	12	.247	.319	.409

Carlos Guillen

Bats: B **Throws:** R **Pos:** SS-75; DH-10; PH-5 **Ht:** 6'1" **Wt:** 202 **Born:** 9/30/1975 **Age:** 30

								BATTING													BASERUNNING				AVERAGES		
Year	Team	Lg	G	AB	H	2B	3B	HR	(Hm	Rd)	TB	R	RBI	RC	TBB	IBB	SO	HBP	SH	SF	SB	CS	SB%	GDP	Avg	OBP	Slg
1998	SEA	AL	10	39	13	1	1	0	(0	0)	16	9	5	7	3	0	9	0	0	0	2	0	1.00	0	.333	.381	.410
1999	SEA	AL	5	19	3	0	0	1	(1	0)	6	2	3	1	1	0	6	0	1	0	0	0	-	1	.158	.200	.316
2000	SEA	AL	90	288	74	15	7	7	(3	4)	124	45	42	36	28	0	53	2	7	3	1	3	.25	6	.257	.324	.396
2001	SEA	AL	140	456	118	21	4	5	(2	3)	162	72	53	56	53	0	89	1	7	6	4	1	.80	9	.259	.333	.355
2002	SEA	AL	134	475	124	24	6	9	(4	5)	187	73	56	58	46	4	91	1	3	3	4	5	.44	8	.261	.326	.394
2003	SEA	AL	109	388	107	19	3	7	(4	3)	153	63	52	53	52	2	64	1	5	5	4	4	.50	12	.276	.359	.394
2004	DET	AL	136	522	166	37	10	20	(7	13)	283	97	97	98	52	3	87	2	4	3	12	5	.71	12	.318	.379	.542
2005	DET	AL	87	334	107	15	4	5	(3	2)	145	48	23	39	24	3	45	2	0	1	2	3	.40	9	.320	.368	.434
	8 ML YEARS		711	2521	712	132	30	54	(24	30)	1066	409	331	348	259	12	444	9	26	22	29	21	.58	57	.282	.349	.423

Jose Guillen

Bats: R **Throws:** R **Pos:** RF-140; PH-8; LF-2; DH-2 **Ht:** 5'11" **Wt:** 195 **Born:** 5/17/1976 **Age:** 30

								BATTING													BASERUNNING				AVERAGES		
Year	Team	Lg	G	AB	H	2B	3B	HR	(Hm	Rd)	TB	R	RBI	RC	TBB	IBB	SO	HBP	SH	SF	SB	CS	SB%	GDP	Avg	OBP	Slg
1997	PIT	NL	143	498	133	20	5	14	(5	9)	205	58	70	56	17	0	88	8	0	3	1	2	.33	16	.267	.300	.412
1998	PIT	NL	153	573	153	38	2	14	(10	4)	237	60	84	68	21	0	100	6	1	4	3	5	.38	7	.267	.298	.414
1999	2 Tms		87	288	73	16	0	3	(1	2)	98	42	31	28	20	2	57	7	1	2	1	0	1.00	16	.253	.315	.340
2000	TB	AL	105	316	80	16	5	10	(5	5)	136	40	41	43	18	1	65	13	2	0	3	1	.75	6	.253	.320	.430
2001	TB	AL	41	135	37	5	0	3	(3	0)	51	14	11	15	6	2	26	3	0	1	2	3	.40	2	.274	.317	.378
2002	2 Tms	NL	85	240	57	7	0	8	(5	3)	88	25	31	16	14	1	43	3	1	1	4	5	.44	13	.238	.287	.367
2003	2 Tms	NL	136	485	151	28	2	31	(14	17)	276	77	86	86	24	2	95	14	8	3	1	3	.25	16	.311	.359	.569
2004	ANA	AL	148	565	166	28	2	27	(13	14)	281	88	104	98	37	5	92	15	0	3	5	4	.56	14	.294	.352	.497
2005	WAS	NL	148	551	156	32	2	24	(3	21)	264	81	76	72	31	6	102	19	1	9	1	1	.50	14	.283	.338	.479
99	Pit	NL	40	120	32	6	0	1	(0	1)	41	18	18	12	10	1	21	0	1	1	1	0	1.00	7	.267	.321	.342
99	TB	NL	47	168	41	10	0	2	(1	1)	57	24	13	16	10	1	36	7	0	1	0	0	-	9	.244	.312	.339
02	Ari	NL	54	131	30	4	0	4	(3	1)	46	13	15	7	7	1	25	2	0	1	3	4	.43	7	.229	.277	.351
02	Cin	NL	31	109	27	3	0	4	(2	2)	42	12	16	9	7	0	18	1	1	0	1	1	.50	6	.248	.299	.385
03	Cin	NL	91	315	106	21	1	23	(10	13)	198	52	63	64	17	1	63	9	6	2	1	3	.25	8	.337	.385	.629
03	Oak	AL	45	170	45	7	1	8	(4	4)	78	25	23	22	7	1	32	5	2	1	0	0	-	8	.265	.311	.459
	9 ML YEARS		1046	3651	1006	190	19	134	(56	78)	1636	485	534	482	188	19	668	88	14	26	21	24	.47	104	.276	.324	.448

Jeremy Guthrie

Pitches: R **Bats:** R **Pos:** RP-1 **Ht:** 6'1" **Wt:** 200 **Born:** 4/8/1979 **Age:** 27

				HOW MUCH HE PITCHED					WHAT HE GAVE UP												THE RESULTS						
Year	Team	Lg	G	GS	CG	GF	IP	BFP	H	R	ER	HR	SH	SF	HB	TBB	IBB	SO	WP	Bk	W	L	Pct	ShO	Sv-Op	Hld	ERC	ERA
2003	Akron	AA	10	9	2	0	62.2	243	44	11	10	0	3	2	0	14	0	35	2	1	6	2	.750	2	0- --		1.47	1.44
2003	Buffalo	AAA	18	18	1	0	96.2	444	129	75	70	15	3	1	7	30	1	62	3	1	4	9	.308	0	0- --		6.43	6.52
2004	Akron	AA	23	21	1	1	130.1	587	145	76	61	16	6	5	16	42	0	94	5	0	8	8	.500	0	0- --		5.02	4.21
2004	Buffalo	AAA	4	4	0	0	19.1	99	23	19	17	0	0	1	4	18	0	10	2	1	1	2	.333	0	0- --		7.48	7.91
2005	Buffalo	AAA	25	25	1	0	136.1	610	152	88	77	15	7	6	12	49	0	100	4	2	12	10	.545	0	0- --		4.99	5.08
2004	CLE	AL	6	0	0	2	11.2	49	9	6	6	1	0	0	1	6	0	7	1	0	0	0	-	0	0-0	0	3.58	4.63
2005	CLE	AL	1	0	0	1	6.0	29	9	4	4	2	1	1	0	2	0	3	0	0	0	0	-	0	0-0	0	8.58	6.00
	2 ML YEARS		7	0	0	3	17.2	78	18	10	10	3	1	1	1	8	0	10	1	0	0	0	-	0	0-0	0	5.17	5.09

Franklin Gutierrez

Bats: R **Throws:** R **Pos:** PR-5; CF-2; DH-2; PH-1 **Ht:** 6'2" **Wt:** 180 **Born:** 2/21/1983 **Age:** 23

									BATTING												BASERUNNING				AVERAGES		
Year	Team	Lg	G	AB	H	2B	3B	HR	(Hm	Rd)	TB	R	RBI	RC	TBB	IBB	SO	HBP	SH	SF	SB	CS	SB%	GDP	Avg	OBP	Slg
2001	Ddgrs	R	56	234	63	16	0	4	(-	-)	91	38	30	31	16	0	39	4	2	2	9	3	.75	1	.269	.324	.389
2002	SoGA	A	92	362	102	18	4	12	(-	-)	164	61	45	59	31	1	88	6	4	5	13	4	.76	5	.282	.344	.453
2002	LsVgs	AAA	2	10	3	2	0	0	(-	-)	5	2	2	1	1	0	4	0	0	0	0	0	-	1	.300	.364	.500
2003	VeroB	A+	110	425	120	28	5	20	(-	-)	218	65	68	77	39	4	111	3	4	3	17	5	.77	9	.282	.345	.513
2003	Erie	AA	18	67	21	3	2	4	(-	-)	40	12	12	14	7	0	20	1	0	0	3	3	.50	1	.313	.387	.597
2004	Akron	AA	70	262	79	24	2	5	(-	-)	122	38	35	47	23	3	77	9	0	4	6	3	.67	4	.302	.372	.466
2004	Buffalo	AAA	7	27	4	1	0	1	(-	-)	8	4	3	1	1	0	11	0	0	0	0	0	-	0	.148	.179	.296
2005	Akron	AA	95	383	100	25	2	11	(-	-)	162	70	42	56	30	1	77	7	1	5	14	4	.78	7	.261	.322	.423
2005	Buffalo	AAA	19	67	17	6	2	0	(-	-)	27	10	7	8	6	1	13	1	0	1	2	2	.50	1	.254	.320	.403
2005	CLE	AL	7	1	0	0	0	0	(0	0)	0	2	0	0	1	0	0	0	0	0	0	0	-	0	.000	.500	.000

Cristian Guzman

Bats: B **Throws:** R **Pos:** SS-142; PH-3; PR-2 **Ht:** 6'0" **Wt:** 195 **Born:** 3/21/1978 **Age:** 28

									BATTING												BASERUNNING				AVERAGES		
Year	Team	Lg	G	AB	H	2B	3B	HR	(Hm	Rd)	TB	R	RBI	RC	TBB	IBB	SO	HBP	SH	SF	SB	CS	SB%	GDP	Avg	OBP	Slg
1999	MIN	AL	131	420	95	12	3	1	(1	0)	116	47	26	29	22	0	90	3	7	4	9	7	.56	5	.226	.267	.276
2000	MIN	AL	156	631	156	25	20	8	(3	5)	245	89	54	76	46	1	101	2	7	4	28	10	.74	5	.247	.299	.388
2001	MIN	AL	118	493	149	28	14	10	(7	3)	235	80	51	79	21	0	78	5	8	0	25	8	.76	6	.302	.337	.477
2002	MIN	AL	148	623	170	31	6	9	(6	3)	240	80	59	63	17	2	79	2	8	6	12	13	.48	12	.273	.292	.385
2003	MIN	AL	143	534	143	15	14	3	(1	2)	195	78	53	62	30	0	79	5	12	4	18	9	.67	4	.268	.311	.365
2004	MIN	AL	145	576	158	31	4	8	(5	3)	221	84	46	66	30	4	64	1	13	4	10	5	.67	15	.274	.309	.384
2005	WAS	NL	142	456	100	19	6	4	(0	4)	143	39	31	26	25	6	76	1	8	2	7	4	.64	12	.219	.260	.314
	7 ML YEARS		983	3733	971	161	67	43	(23	20)	1395	497	320	401	191	13	567	19	63	24	109	56	.66	59	.260	.298	.374

Freddy Guzman

Bats: B **Throws:** R **Pos:** OF **Ht:** 5'10" **Wt:** 165 **Born:** 1/20/1981 **Age:** 25

									BATTING												BASERUNNING				AVERAGES		
Year	Team	Lg	G	AB	H	2B	3B	HR	(Hm	Rd)	TB	R	RBI	RC	TBB	IBB	SO	HBP	SH	SF	SB	CS	SB%	GDP	Avg	OBP	Slg
2001	Idaho	A-	12	46	16	4	1	0	(-	-)	22	11	5	9	2	0	10	1	1	0	5	0	1.00	0	.348	.388	.478
2002	Lk Els	A+	21	81	21	3	0	1	(-	-)	27	13	6	10	8	0	12	0	0	0	14	4	.78	0	.259	.326	.333
2002	FtWyn	A	47	190	53	7	5	0	(-	-)	70	35	18	29	18	0	37	0	2	0	39	7	.85	0	.279	.341	.368
2002	Eugene	A-	21	80	18	2	1	0	(-	-)	22	14	8	9	7	0	15	2	1	3	16	1	.94	0	.225	.293	.275
2003	Lk Els	A+	70	281	80	12	3	2	(-	-)	104	64	22	47	40	1	60	2	1	2	49	10	.83	1	.285	.375	.370
2003	Mobile	AA	46	177	48	5	2	1	(-	-)	60	30	11	28	26	2	34	1	1	0	38	7	.84	0	.271	.359	.339
2003	Portlnd	AAA	2	10	3	0	0	0	(-	-)	3	1	0	1	0	0	1	0	0	0	3	0	1.00	0	.300	.300	.300
2004	Mobile	AA	35	138	39	5	2	1	(-	-)	51	21	7	20	16	1	28	1	1	1	17	5	.77	2	.283	.359	.370
2004	Portlnd	AAA	66	264	77	12	4	1	(-	-)	100	48	19	45	30	1	46	1	4	1	48	5	.91	1	.292	.365	.379
2004	SD	NL	20	76	16	3	0	0	(0	0)	19	8	5	4	3	0	13	1	0	0	5	2	.71	0	.211	.250	.250

Yamid Haad

Bats: R **Throws:** R **Pos:** C-16; PH-1 **Ht:** 6'2" **Wt:** 215 **Born:** 9/2/1977 **Age:** 28

									BATTING												BASERUNNING				AVERAGES		
Year	Team	Lg	G	AB	H	2B	3B	HR	(Hm	Rd)	TB	R	RBI	RC	TBB	IBB	SO	HBP	SH	SF	SB	CS	SB%	GDP	Avg	OBP	Slg
1997	Erie	A-	43	155	45	7	3	1	(-	-)	61	27	19	19	7	0	27	0	1	6	3	3	.50	5	.290	.310	.394
1998	Lynbrg	A+	88	299	76	8	2	5	(-	-)	103	32	34	28	13	0	54	3	4	4	1	7	.13	11	.254	.288	.344
1999	Lynbrg	A+	59	209	53	11	1	5	(-	-)	81	31	33	32	33	1	42	1	2	3	5	2	.71	8	.254	.354	.388
1999	Altna	AA	43	137	25	3	0	6	(-	-)	46	20	10	14	19	0	32	0	1	1	7	2	.78	4	.182	.280	.336
2000	Altna	AA	59	183	36	7	0	4	(-	-)	55	24	13	14	18	0	44	0	1	1	1	1	.50	4	.197	.267	.301
2000	Lynbrg	A+	25	91	23	8	0	3	(-	-)	40	14	9	14	11	0	16	0	0	1	2	0	1.00	4	.253	.330	.440
2001	Lynbrg	A+	3	11	2	1	0	0	(-	-)	3	1	0	0	0	0	3	0	0	0	1	0	1.00	0	.182	.182	.273
2001	Altna	AA	1	3	0	0	0	0	(-	-)	0	0	0	0	0	0	0	0	0	0	0	0	-	0	.000	.000	.000
2001	Nashv	AAA	51	194	37	5	0	2	(-	-)	48	14	10	7	7	0	27	0	2	0	0	3	.00	2	.191	.219	.247
2002	Mobile	AA	18	53	15	1	0	1	(-	-)	19	6	3	7	5	0	8	0	0	0	1	0	1.00	1	.283	.333	.358
2002	Orlndo	AA	29	108	20	2	0	3	(-	-)	31	12	15	6	6	1	23	0	1	3	2	1	.67	3	.185	.222	.287
2002	Drham	AAA	20	70	12	1	0	0	(-	-)	13	6	5	1	2	0	13	0	0	2	0	0	-	2	.171	.189	.186
2003	Mobile	AA	9	29	8	2	0	1	(-	-)	13	1	4	3	5	4	3	0	0	0	0	0	-	2	.276	.344	.448
2003	Portlnd	AAA	80	258	60	13	1	10	(-	-)	105	24	34	30	15	0	55	2	0	2	3	2	.60	1	.233	.278	.407
2004	Portlnd	AAA	80	295	89	21	0	9	(-	-)	137	47	35	46	16	1	41	0	1	0	3	0	1.00	3	.302	.338	.464
2005	Fresno	AAA	63	216	61	13	1	10	(-	-)	106	23	34	34	8	0	32	2	2	3	2	0	1.00	5	.282	.310	.491

							BATTING														BASERUNNING				AVERAGES		
Year	Team	Lg	G	AB	H	2B	3B	HR	(Hm	Rd)	TB	R	RBI	RC	TBB	IBB	SO	HBP	SH	SF	SB	CS	SB%	GDP	Avg	OBP	Slg
1999	PIT	NL	1	1	0	0	0	0	(	)	0	0	0	0	0	0	0	0	0	0	0	0	-	0	.000	.000	.000
2005	SF	NL	17	28	2	1	0	0	(0	0)	3	0	1	0	3	0	7	0	0	1	0	0	-	2	.071	.156	.107
	2 ML YEARS		18	29	2	1	0	0	(0	0)	3	0	1	0	3	0	7	0	0	1	0	0	-	2	.069	.152	.103

Travis Hafner

Bats: L **Throws:** R **Pos:** DH-129; PH-7; 1B-1   **Ht:** 6'3" **Wt:** 240 **Born:** 6/3/1977 **Age:** 29

							BATTING														BASERUNNING				AVERAGES		
Year	Team	Lg	G	AB	H	2B	3B	HR	(Hm	Rd)	TB	R	RBI	RC	TBB	IBB	SO	HBP	SH	SF	SB	CS	SB%	GDP	Avg	OBP	Slg
2005	Akron*	AA	3	9	0	0	0	0	(-	-)	0	0	0	0	1	0	1	1	0	0	0	0	-	0	.000	.182	.000
2002	TEX	AL	23	62	15	4	1	1	(0	1)	24	6	6	7	8	1	15	0	0	0	0	1	.00	0	.242	.329	.387
2003	CLE	AL	91	291	74	19	3	14	(7	7)	141	35	40	42	22	2	81	10	0	1	2	1	.67	7	.254	.327	.485
2004	CLE	AL	140	482	150	41	3	28	(7	21)	281	96	109	103	68	7	111	17	0	6	3	2	.60	11	.311	.410	.583
2005	CLE	AL	137	486	148	42	0	33	(14	19)	289	94	108	115	79	7	123	9	0	4	0	0	-	9	.305	.408	.595
	4 ML YEARS		391	1321	387	106	7	76	(28	48)	735	231	263	267	177	17	330	36	0	11	5	4	.56	27	.293	.388	.556

Jerry Hairston

Bats: R **Throws:** R **Pos:** CF-48; 2B-44; LF-20; PH-15; SS-1; RF-1; PR-1   **Ht:** 5'10" **Wt:** 175 **Born:** 5/29/1976 **Age:** 30

							BATTING														BASERUNNING				AVERAGES		
Year	Team	Lg	G	AB	H	2B	3B	HR	(Hm	Rd)	TB	R	RBI	RC	TBB	IBB	SO	HBP	SH	SF	SB	CS	SB%	GDP	Avg	OBP	Slg
2005	Iowa*	AAA	5	22	7	0	1	0	(-	-)	9	3	2	4	0	0	3	2	0	1	3	0	1.00	0	.318	.360	.409
1998	BAL	AL	6	7	0	0	0	0	(0	0)	0	2	0	0	0	0	1	0	0	0	0	0	-	0	.000	.000	.000
1999	BAL	AL	50	175	47	12	1	4	(1	3)	73	26	17	24	11	0	24	3	4	0	9	4	.69	2	.269	.323	.417
2000	BAL	AL	49	180	46	5	0	5	(2	3)	66	27	19	22	21	0	22	6	5	0	8	5	.62	8	.256	.353	.367
2001	BAL	AL	159	532	124	25	5	8	(5	3)	183	63	47	57	44	0	73	13	9	4	29	11	.73	12	.233	.305	.344
2002	BAL	AL	122	426	114	25	3	5	(2	3)	160	55	32	55	34	0	55	7	8	4	21	6	.78	5	.268	.329	.376
2003	BAL	AL	58	218	59	12	2	2	(1	1)	81	25	21	32	23	0	25	6	10	2	14	5	.74	8	.271	.353	.372
2004	BAL	AL	86	287	87	19	1	2	(0	2)	114	43	24	45	29	1	29	8	6	4	13	8	.62	3	.303	.378	.397
2005	CHN	NL	114	380	99	25	2	4	(3	1)	140	51	30	46	31	0	46	12	7	0	8	9	.47	5	.261	.336	.368
	8 ML YEARS		644	2205	576	123	14	30	(14	16)	817	292	190	281	193	1	275	55	49	14	102	48	.68	43	.261	.334	.371

Scott Hairston

Bats: R **Throws:** R **Pos:** PH-10; LF-4; DH-2; CF-1; PR-1   **Ht:** 6'0" **Wt:** 188 **Born:** 5/25/1980 **Age:** 26

							BATTING														BASERUNNING				AVERAGES		
Year	Team	Lg	G	AB	H	2B	3B	HR	(Hm	Rd)	TB	R	RBI	RC	TBB	IBB	SO	HBP	SH	SF	SB	CS	SB%	GDP	Avg	OBP	Slg
2001	Msoula	R+	74	291	101	16	6	14	(-	-)	171	81	65	69	38	2	50	7	0	2	2	2	.50	5	.347	.432	.588
2002	Sbend	A	109	394	131	35	4	16	(-	-)	222	79	72	89	58	3	74	10	1	5	9	3	.75	11	.332	.426	.563
2002	Lancst	A+	18	79	32	11	1	6	(-	-)	63	20	26	21	6	0	16	0	0	1	1	0	1.00	4	.405	.442	.797
2003	ElPaso	AA	88	337	93	21	7	10	(-	-)	158	53	47	51	30	1	80	6	0	1	6	2	.75	10	.276	.345	.469
2003	Tucsn	AAA	1	0	0	0	0	0	(-	-)	0	0	1	0	0	0	0	0	0	0	0	0	-	0	-	.000	-
2004	Tucsn	AAA	28	115	36	8	3	5	(-	-)	65	29	20	22	11	0	21	1	0	1	0	3	.00	1	.313	.375	.565
2005	Tucsn	AAA	58	209	65	8	3	16	(-	-)	127	45	40	48	21	0	40	5	0	2	3	0	1.00	4	.311	.384	.608
2004	ARI	NL	101	339	84	15	6	13	(6	7)	150	39	29	32	21	0	88	1	2	1	3	3	.50	4	.248	.293	.442
2005	ARI	NL	15	20	2	1	0	0	(0	0)	3	0	0	0	0	0	6	0	0	0	0	0	-	1	.100	.100	.150
	2 ML YEARS		116	359	86	16	6	13	(6	7)	153	39	29	32	21	0	94	1	2	1	3	3	.50	5	.240	.283	.426

John Halama

Pitches: L **Bats:** L **Pos:** RP-36; SP-4   **Ht:** 6'5" **Wt:** 210 **Born:** 2/22/1972 **Age:** 34

			HOW MUCH HE PITCHED						WHAT HE GAVE UP												THE RESULTS						
Year	Team	Lg	G	GS	CG	GF	IP	BFP	H	R	ER	HR	SH	SF	HB	TBB	IBB	SO	WP	Bk	W	L	Pct	ShO	Sv-Op	Hld	ERC	ERA
2005	NewOr*	AAA	2	2	0	0	8.0	30	6	2	1	0	1	0	0	0	0	1	0	0	1	0	1.000	0	0- -	-	1.13	1.13
1998	HOU	NL	6	6	0	0	32.1	147	37	21	21	0	3	4	2	13	0	21	2	1	1	1	.500	0	0-0	0	4.34	5.85
1999	SEA	AL	38	24	1	7	179.0	763	193	88	84	20	5	9	7	56	3	105	4	0	11	10	.524	1	0-0	1	4.47	4.22
2000	SEA	AL	30	30	1	0	166.2	736	206	108	94	19	4	6	2	56	0	87	4	1	14	9	.609	1	0-0	0	5.42	5.08
2001	SEA	AL	31	17	0	6	110.1	485	132	69	58	18	3	4	6	26	0	50	2	0	10	7	.588	0	0-0	1	5.21	4.73
2002	SEA	AL	31	10	0	12	101.0	435	112	45	40	9	3	2	1	33	5	70	2	1	6	5	.545	0	0-0	0	4.29	3.56
2003	OAK	AL	35	13	0	4	108.2	484	117	68	51	18	7	3	2	36	2	51	3	3	3	5	.375	0	0-0	3	4.61	4.22
2004	TB	AL	34	14	0	7	118.2	513	134	68	62	17	1	3	10	27	3	59	1	1	7	6	.538	0	0-0	0	4.76	4.70
2005	2 Tms		40	4	0	15	65.0	298	79	44	41	6	2	2	7	17	3	37	2	0	1	4	.200	0	0-0	0	4.93	5.68
05	Bos	AL	30	1	0	13	43.2	205	56	33	30	5	1	1	7	9	3	26	2	0	1	1	.500	0	0-0	0	5.38	6.18
05	Was	NL	10	3	0	2	21.1	93	23	11	11	1	1	1	0	8	0	11	0	0	0	3	.000	0	0-0	0	4.03	4.64
	8 ML YEARS		245	118	2	51	881.2	3864	1010	511	451	107	28	33	37	264	16	480	20	7	53	47	.530	2	0-0	5	4.81	4.60

Bill Hall

Bats: R **Throws:** R **Pos:** SS-66; 3B-59; 2B-23; PH-16   **Ht:** 6'0" **Wt:** 175 **Born:** 12/28/1979 **Age:** 26

							BATTING														BASERUNNING				AVERAGES		
Year	Team	Lg	G	AB	H	2B	3B	HR	(Hm	Rd)	TB	R	RBI	RC	TBB	IBB	SO	HBP	SH	SF	SB	CS	SB%	GDP	Avg	OBP	Slg
2002	MIL	NL	19	36	7	1	1	1	(0	1)	13	3	5	3	3	0	13	0	0	0	1	0	1.00	1	.194	.256	.361
2003	MIL	NL	52	142	37	9	2	5	(2	3)	65	23	20	18	7	0	28	1	4	1	1	2	.33	5	.261	.298	.458
2004	MIL	NL	126	390	93	20	3	9	(5	4)	146	43	53	41	20	1	119	1	2	2	12	6	.67	4	.238	.276	.374
2005	MIL	NL	146	501	146	39	6	17	(12	5)	248	69	62	73	39	2	103	1	2	3	18	6	.75	11	.291	.342	.495
	4 ML YEARS		343	1069	283	69	12	32	(19	13)	472	138	140	135	69	3	263	3	8	6	31	15	.67	21	.265	.310	.442

107

Toby Hall

Bats: R Throws: R Pos: C-135; PH-3; 1B-2   Ht: 6'3" Wt: 240 Born: 10/21/1975 Age: 30

								BATTING												BASERUNNING				AVERAGES		
Year	Team	Lg	G	AB	H	2B	3B	HR	(Hm | Rd)	TB	R	RBI	RC	TBB	IBB	SO	HBP	SH	SF	SB	CS	SB%	GDP	Avg	OBP	Slg
2000	TB	AL	4	12	2	0	0	1	(0 | 1)	5	1	1	1	1	0	0	0	0	0	0	0	-	0	.167	.231	.417
2001	TB	AL	49	188	56	16	0	4	(1 | 3)	84	28	30	25	4	0	16	3	0	1	2	2	.50	5	.298	.321	.447
2002	TB	AL	85	330	85	19	1	6	(2 | 4)	124	37	42	39	17	3	27	1	2	3	0	1	.00	14	.258	.293	.376
2003	TB	AL	130	463	117	23	0	12	(4 | 8)	176	50	47	45	23	4	40	7	0	5	0	1	.00	14	.253	.295	.380
2004	TB	AL	119	404	103	21	0	8	(6 | 2)	148	35	60	42	24	1	41	5	1	7	0	2	.00	20	.255	.300	.366
2005	TB	AL	135	432	124	20	0	5	(1 | 4)	159	28	48	46	16	1	39	5	3	7	0	0	-	15	.287	.315	.368
6 ML YEARS			522	1829	487	99	1	36	(14 | 22)	696	179	228	198	85	9	163	21	6	23	2	6	.25	68	.266	.303	.381

Roy Halladay

Pitches: R Bats: R Pos: SP-19   Ht: 6'6" Wt: 230 Born: 5/14/1977 Age: 29

			HOW MUCH HE PITCHED						WHAT HE GAVE UP										THE RESULTS							
Year	Team	Lg	G	GS	CG	GF	IP	BFP	H	R	ER	HR	SH	SF	HB	TBB	IBB	SO	WP	Bk	W	L	Pct	ShO	Sv-Op	Hld	ERC	ERA
1998	TOR	AL	2	2	1	0	14.0	53	9	4	3	2	0	0	0	2	0	13	0	0	1	0	1.000	0	0-0	0	1.61	1.93
1999	TOR	AL	36	18	1	2	149.1	668	156	76	65	19	3	4	4	79	1	82	6	0	8	7	.533	1	1-1	2	5.19	3.92
2000	TOR	AL	19	13	0	4	67.2	349	107	87	80	14	2	3	2	42	0	44	6	1	4	7	.364	0	0-0	0	9.70	10.64
2001	TOR	AL	17	16	1	0	105.1	432	97	41	37	3	3	1	1	25	0	96	4	1	5	3	.625	1	0-0	0	2.61	3.16
2002	TOR	AL	34	34	2	0	239.1	993	223	93	78	10	9	2	7	62	6	168	4	1	19	7	.731	1	0-0	0	2.85	2.93
2003	TOR	AL	36	36	9	0	266.0	1071	253	111	96	26	3	2	9	32	1	204	6	1	22	7	.759	2	0-0	0	2.86	3.25
2004	TOR	AL	21	21	1	0	133.0	561	140	66	62	13	4	3	1	39	1	95	2	2	8	8	.500	1	0-0	0	4.00	4.20
2005	TOR	AL	19	19	5	0	141.2	553	118	39	38	11	2	1	7	18	2	108	2	1	12	4	.750	2	0-0	0	2.26	2.41
8 ML YEARS			184	159	20	6	1116.1	4680	1103	517	459	98	26	16	31	299	11	810	30	7	79	43	.648	8	1-1	2	3.51	3.70

Brad Halsey

Pitches: L Bats: L Pos: SP-26; RP-2   Ht: 6'1" Wt: 180 Born: 2/14/1981 Age: 25

			HOW MUCH HE PITCHED						WHAT HE GAVE UP										THE RESULTS							
Year	Team	Lg	G	GS	CG	GF	IP	BFP	H	R	ER	HR	SH	SF	HB	TBB	IBB	SO	WP	Bk	W	L	Pct	ShO	Sv-Op	Hld	ERC	ERA
2002	StsInd	A-	11	10	0	0	56.0	223	39	15	12	0	1	1	4	17	0	53	0	0	6	1	.857	0	0--	-	1.83	1.93
2003	Tampa	A+	14	13	1	0	84.0	354	96	36	32	3	3	2	1	14	0	56	4	0	10	4	.714	0	0--	-	3.57	3.43
2003	Trentn	AA	15	15	0	0	91.1	410	123	51	50	4	0	4	5	22	0	78	3	0	7	5	.583	0	0--	-	5.29	4.93
2004	Clmbs	AAA	24	23	3	0	144.0	589	128	46	42	8	8	3	7	37	0	109	2	1	11	4	.733	2	0--	-	2.86	2.63
2004	NYA	AL	8	7	0	0	32.0	153	41	26	23	4	1	2	2	14	0	25	0	0	1	3	.250	0	0-0	0	6.20	6.47
2005	ARI	NL	28	26	0	1	160.0	700	191	101	82	20	11	5	9	39	3	82	2	1	8	12	.400	0	0-0	0	4.96	4.61
2 ML YEARS			36	33	0	1	192.0	853	232	127	105	24	12	7	11	53	3	107	2	1	9	15	.375	0	0-0	0	5.16	4.92

Chris Hammond

Pitches: L Bats: L Pos: RP-55   Ht: 6'1" Wt: 195 Born: 1/21/1966 Age: 40

			HOW MUCH HE PITCHED						WHAT HE GAVE UP										THE RESULTS							
Year	Team	Lg	G	GS	CG	GF	IP	BFP	H	R	ER	HR	SH	SF	HB	TBB	IBB	SO	WP	Bk	W	L	Pct	ShO	Sv-Op	Hld	ERC	ERA
1990	CIN	NL	3	3	0	0	11.1	56	13	9	8	2	1	0	0	12	1	4	1	3	0	2	.000	0	0-0	0	8.50	6.35
1991	CIN	NL	20	18	0	0	99.2	425	92	51	45	4	6	1	2	48	3	50	3	0	7	7	.500	0	0-0	0	3.63	4.06
1992	FLA	NL	28	26	0	1	147.1	627	149	75	69	13	5	3	3	55	6	79	6	0	7	10	.412	0	0-0	0	4.02	4.21
1993	FLA	NL	32	32	1	0	191.0	826	207	106	99	18	10	2	1	66	2	108	10	5	11	12	.478	0	0-0	0	4.31	4.66
1994	FLA	NL	13	13	1	0	73.1	312	79	30	25	5	5	2	1	23	1	40	3	0	4	4	.500	1	0-0	0	4.03	3.07
1995	FLA	NL	25	24	3	0	161.0	683	157	73	68	17	7	7	9	47	2	126	3	1	9	6	.600	2	0-0	0	3.75	3.80
1996	FLA	NL	38	9	0	5	88.0	368	104	65	59	14	3	4	4	27	3	50	1	0	5	8	.385	0	0-0	5	6.21	6.56
1997	BOS	AL	29	8	0	6	65.1	293	81	45	43	5	0	3	2	27	4	48	2	0	3	4	.429	0	1-2	4	5.47	5.92
1998	FLA	NL	3	3	0	0	13.2	67	20	11	10	3	2	0	1	8	0	8	0	0	0	2	.000	0	0-0	0	9.33	6.59
2002	ATL	NL	63	0	0	6	76.0	311	53	15	8	1	5	2	1	31	9	63	1	0	7	2	.778	0	0-2	17	1.85	0.95
2003	NYA	AL	62	0	0	16	63.0	262	65	23	20	5	5	3	2	11	0	45	1	0	3	2	.600	0	1-4	17	3.36	2.86
2004	OAK	AL	41	0	0	9	53.2	224	56	21	16	4	3	3	3	13	1	34	0	0	4	1	.800	0	1-3	3	3.79	2.68
2005	SD	NL	55	0	0	17	58.2	242	51	25	25	9	1	2	2	14	0	34	0	0	5	1	.833	0	0-3	6	3.17	3.84
13 ML YEARS			412	136	5	60	1095.0	4696	1127	549	495	100	53	32	31	382	32	689	31	9	65	61	.516	3	3-14	52	4.07	4.07

Jeffrey Hammonds

Bats: R Throws: R Pos: LF-10; PH-3; RF-1; DH-1   Ht: 6'0" Wt: 200 Born: 3/5/1971 Age: 35

								BATTING												BASERUNNING				AVERAGES		
Year	Team	Lg	G	AB	H	2B	3B	HR	(Hm	Rd)	TB	R	RBI	RC	TBB	IBB	SO	HBP	SH	SF	SB	CS	SB%	GDP	Avg	OBP	Slg
2005	Hrsbrg*	AA	2	6	1	1	0	0	(-	-)	2	1	1	0	1	0	1	1	0	0	0	0	-	0	.167	.375	.333
2005	NewOr*	AAA	19	60	15	5	1	2	(-	-)	28	10	9	10	7	1	5	2	0	1	1	0	1.00	2	.250	.343	.467
1993	BAL	AL	33	105	32	8	0	3	(2	1)	49	10	19	15	2	1	16	0	1	2	4	0	1.00	3	.305	.312	.467
1994	BAL	AL	68	250	74	18	2	8	(6	2)	120	45	31	42	17	1	39	2	0	5	5	0	1.00	3	.296	.339	.480
1995	BAL	AL	57	178	43	9	1	4	(2	2)	66	18	23	18	9	0	30	1	1	2	4	2	.67	3	.242	.279	.371
1996	BAL	AL	71	248	56	10	1	9	(6	3)	95	38	27	27	23	1	53	4	6	1	3	3	.50	7	.226	.301	.383
1997	BAL	AL	118	397	105	19	3	21	(9	12)	193	71	55	64	32	1	73	3	0	2	15	1	.94	6	.264	.323	.486
1998	2 Tms		89	257	72	16	2	6	(1	5)	110	50	39	45	39	1	56	3	3	4	8	3	.73	2	.280	.376	.428
1999	CIN	NL	123	262	73	13	0	17	(5	12)	137	43	41	45	27	0	64	1	2	3	6	3	.33	4	.279	.347	.523
2000	COL	NL	122	454	152	24	2	20	(14	6)	240	94	106	90	44	4	83	5	2	6	14	7	.67	11	.335	.395	.529
2001	MIL	NL	49	174	43	11	1	6	(3	3)	74	20	21	23	14	1	42	4	0	2	5	3	.63	2	.247	.314	.425
2002	MIL	NL	128	448	116	28	5	9	(2	7)	178	47	41	53	52	0	86	2	1	7	4	5	.44	13	.257	.332	.397
2003	2 Tms	NL	46	132	32	12	0	4	(3	1)	56	22	13	15	16	0	28	1	0	0	1	0	1.00	3	.242	.329	.424
2004	SF	NL	40	95	20	5	0	3	(2	1)	34	14	6	9	14	0	22	3	0	0	1	0	1.00	1	.211	.336	.358
2005	WAS	NL	13	32	7	0	0	0	(0	0)	8	3	1	2	2	1	4	1	2	0	0	0	-	0	.219	.286	.250
98	Bal	AL	63	171	46	12	1	6	(1	5)	78	36	28	31	26	1	38	3	0	3	7	2	.78	2	.269	.369	.456
98	Cin	NL	26	86	26	4	1	0	(0	0)	32	14	11	14	13	0	18	0	3	1	1	1	.50	0	.302	.390	.372

Year	Team	Lg	G	AB	H	2B	3B	HR	(Hm	Rd)	TB	R	RBI	RC	TBB	IBB	SO	HBP	SH	SF	SB	CS	SB%	GDP	Avg	OBP	Slg
									BATTING												**BASERUNNING**				**AVERAGES**		
03	Mil	NL	10	38	6	2	0	1	(1	0)	11	2	3	0	3	0	7	0	0	0	0	0	-	2	.158	.220	.289
03	SF	NL	36	94	26	10	0	3	(2	1)	45	20	10	15	13	0	21	1	0	0	1	0	1.00	1	.277	.370	.479
13 ML YEARS			957	3032	824	172	17	110	(52	58)	1360	475	423	448	292	11	596	30	18	32	67	30	.69	59	.272	.338	.449

Mike Hampton

Pitches: L **Bats:** R **Pos:** SP-12   **Ht:** 5'10" **Wt:** 180 **Born:** 9/9/1972 **Age:** 33

Year	Team	Lg	G	GS	CG	GF	IP	BFP	H	R	ER	HR	SH	SF	HB	TBB	IBB	SO	WP	Bk	W	L	Pct	ShO	Sv-Op	Hld	ERC	ERA
									WHAT HE GAVE UP												**THE RESULTS**							
2005	Braves*	R	1	1	0	0	5.0	21	6	0	0	0	0	0	0	0	0	4	0	0	0	0	-	0	0--		2.89	0.00
2005	Rchmd*	AAA	1	1	0	0	4.0	16	4	1	1	0	0	0	0	0	0	3	0	0	0	0	-	0	0--		1.95	2.25
1993	SEA	AL	13	3	0	2	17.0	95	28	20	18	3	1	1	0	17	3	8	1	1	1	3	.250	0	1-1	2	11.09	9.53
1994	HOU	NL	44	0	0	7	41.1	181	46	19	17	4	0	0	2	16	1	24	5	1	2	1	.667	0	0-1	10	4.88	3.70
1995	HOU	NL	24	24	0	0	150.2	641	141	73	56	13	11	5	4	49	3	115	3	1	9	8	.529	0	0-0	0	3.37	3.35
1996	HOU	NL	27	27	2	0	160.1	691	175	79	64	12	10	3	3	49	1	101	7	2	10	10	.500	1	0-0	0	4.11	3.59
1997	HOU	NL	34	34	7	0	223.0	941	217	105	95	16	11	7	2	77	2	139	6	1	15	10	.600	2	0-0	0	3.56	3.83
1998	HOU	NL	32	32	1	0	211.2	917	227	92	79	18	7	7	5	81	1	137	4	2	11	7	.611	1	0-0	0	4.45	3.36
1999	HOU	NL	34	34	3	0	239.0	979	206	86	77	12	10	9	5	101	2	177	9	0	22	4	.846	2	0-0	0	3.25	2.90
2000	NYN	NL	33	33	3	0	217.2	929	194	89	76	10	11	5	8	99	5	151	10	0	15	10	.600	1	0-0	0	3.44	3.14
2001	COL	NL	32	32	2	0	203.0	904	236	138	122	31	8	6	8	85	7	122	6	0	14	13	.519	1	0-0	0	5.69	5.41
2002	COL	NL	30	30	0	0	178.2	838	228	135	122	24	2	9	7	91	4	74	9	2	7	15	.318	0	0-0	0	6.61	6.15
2003	ATL	NL	31	31	1	0	190.0	823	186	91	81	14	10	5	1	78	4	110	10	1	14	8	.636	0	0-0	0	3.77	3.84
2004	ATL	NL	29	29	1	0	172.1	760	198	86	82	15	8	3	1	65	3	87	3	2	13	9	.591	0	0-0	0	4.76	4.28
2005	ATL	NL	12	12	1	0	69.1	284	74	28	27	5	2	1	0	18	0	27	1	0	5	3	.625	1	0-0	0	3.85	3.50
13 ML YEARS			375	321	21	9	2074.0	8983	2156	1041	916	177	91	61	46	826	36	1272	74	13	138	101	.577	9	1-2	12	4.28	3.97

Tim Hamulack

Pitches: L **Bats:** R **Pos:** RP-6   **Ht:** 6'4" **Wt:** 220 **Born:** 11/14/1976 **Age:** 29

Year	Team	Lg	G	GS	CG	GF	IP	BFP	H	R	ER	HR	SH	SF	HB	TBB	IBB	SO	WP	Bk	W	L	Pct	ShO	Sv-Op	Hld	ERC	ERA
									WHAT HE GAVE UP												**THE RESULTS**							
1996	Astros	R	22	0	0	9	27.0	117	23	9	7	1	0	2	0	13	1	24	1	0	4	1	.800	0	2--		3.33	2.33
1997	Astros	R	23	0	0	17	45.0	209	56	31	21	3	0	0	0	18	0	38	2	2	1	1	.500	0	9--		5.10	4.20
1998	QuadC	A	52	0	0	14	58.1	259	58	23	21	3	3	2	3	26	3	52	0	2	0	2	.000	0	2--		3.93	3.24
1999	Mich	A	25	0	0	12	26.2	114	23	9	9	0	1	2	0	11	0	32	2	1	3	0	1.000	0	0--		2.65	3.04
2000	Kissim	A+	41	0	0	20	56.0	256	67	37	31	3	2	1	1	21	1	54	0	0	3	1	.750	0	1--		4.69	4.98
2001	BrvdCt	A+	40	0	0	13	71.1	318	83	42	25	3	3	3	3	21	1	39	1	0	2	4	.333	0	1--		4.23	3.15
2002	Portlnd	AA	38	1	0	23	78.0	336	73	32	25	6	4	1	0	29	5	53	3	0	8	4	.667	0	6--		3.28	2.88
2003	SnAnt	AA	40	0	0	11	47.1	189	32	13	11	0	0	1	3	15	2	54	2	0	1	0	1.000	0	1--		1.69	2.09
2003	Tacom	AAA	10	0	0	5	14.0	66	16	6	6	1	1	0	0	8	0	12	0	0	1	1	.500	0	0--		5.24	3.86
2004	Portlnd	AA	7	0	0	2	15.1	69	16	6	6	0	0	0	0	7	0	16	1	0	2	0	1.000	0	0--		3.70	3.52
2004	Pwtckt	AAA	35	0	0	15	29.2	152	44	26	23	4	0	1	2	19	2	25	1	0	7	4	.636	0	2--		8.46	6.98
2005	Bnghtn	AA	21	0	0	14	28.2	112	20	7	4	0	1	0	0	6	1	27	0	0	2	2	.500	0	1--		1.37	1.26
2005	Norfolk	AAA	28	0	0	16	35.1	135	20	5	4	1	3	0	1	9	1	34	2	0	3	1	.750	0	6--		1.27	1.02
2005	NYN	NL	6	0	0	2	2.1	14	7	6	6	3	0	1	0	1	1	2	0	0	0	0	-	0	0-0	1	32.83	23.14

Josh Hancock

Pitches: R **Bats:** R **Pos:** RP-11   **Ht:** 6'3" **Wt:** 217 **Born:** 4/11/1978 **Age:** 28

Year	Team	Lg	G	GS	CG	GF	IP	BFP	H	R	ER	HR	SH	SF	HB	TBB	IBB	SO	WP	Bk	W	L	Pct	ShO	Sv-Op	Hld	ERC	ERA
									WHAT HE GAVE UP												**THE RESULTS**							
2005	Lsvlle*	AAA	11	8	0	1	44.0	208	59	33	29	5	3	0	3	17	0	38	3	0	1	2	.333	0	0--		6.38	5.93
2002	BOS	AL	3	1	0	2	7.1	28	5	3	3	1	1	0	0	2	0	6	0	0	0	1	.000	0	0-0	0	2.25	3.68
2003	PHI	NL	2	0	0	0	3.0	11	2	1	1	0	0	0	0	0	0	4	0	0	0	0	-	0	0-0	0	0.91	3.00
2004	2 Tms	NL	16	11	0	2	63.2	293	73	43	36	17	3	2	1	28	2	36	5	0	5	2	.714	0	0-0	0	6.24	5.09
2005	CIN	NL	11	0	0	5	14.0	54	11	4	3	1	0	0	0	1	0	5	0	0	1	0	1.000	0	0-0	0	1.64	1.93
04	Phi	NL	4	2	0	0	9.0	42	13	9	9	3	0	0	0	3	0	5	0	0	0	1	.000	0	0-0	0	8.40	9.00
04	Cin	NL	12	9	0	2	54.2	251	60	34	27	14	3	2	1	25	2	31	5	0	5	1	.833	0	0-0	0	5.91	4.45
4 ML YEARS			32	12	0	9	88.0	386	91	51	43	19	4	2	1	31	2	51	5	0	6	3	.667	0	0-0	0	4.81	4.40

Craig Hansen

Pitches: R **Bats:** R **Pos:** RP-4   **Ht:** 6'6" **Wt:** 210 **Born:** 11/15/1983 **Age:** 22

Year	Team	Lg	G	GS	CG	GF	IP	BFP	H	R	ER	HR	SH	SF	HB	TBB	IBB	SO	WP	Bk	W	L	Pct	ShO	Sv-Op	Hld	ERC	ERA
									WHAT HE GAVE UP												**THE RESULTS**							
2005	RedSx	R	2	1	0	0	3.0	11	2	0	0	0	0	0	0	0	0	4	0	0	1	0	1.000	0	0--		0.91	0.00
2005	Portlnd	AA	8	0	0	2	9.2	39	9	0	0	0	0	0	0	1	0	10	0	0	0	0	-	0	1--		1.97	0.00
2005	BOS	AL	4	0	0	1	3.0	16	6	2	2	1	0	1	0	1	0	3	0	0	0	0	-	0	0-1	0	12.18	6.00

Dave Hansen

Bats: L **Throws:** R **Pos:** PH-41; 1B-9; 3B-7; DH-5   **Ht:** 6'0" **Wt:** 195 **Born:** 11/24/1968 **Age:** 37

Year	Team	Lg	G	AB	H	2B	3B	HR	(Hm	Rd)	TB	R	RBI	RC	TBB	IBB	SO	HBP	SH	SF	SB	CS	SB%	GDP	Avg	OBP	Slg
									BATTING												**BASERUNNING**				**AVERAGES**		
2005	Tacom*	AAA	6	20	6	0	0	0	(-	-)	6	2	3	2	2	0	4	0	0	1	0	0	-	1	.300	.348	.300
1990	LA	NL	5	7	1	0	0	0	(0	0)	1	0	1	0	0	0	3	0	0	0	0	0	-	0	.143	.143	.143
1991	LA	NL	53	56	15	4	0	1	(0	1)	22	3	5	6	2	0	12	0	0	0	1	0	1.00	0	.268	.293	.393
1992	LA	NL	132	341	73	11	0	6	(1	5)	102	30	22	27	34	3	49	1	0	2	0	2	.00	9	.214	.286	.299
1993	LA	NL	84	105	38	3	0	4	(2	2)	53	13	30	25	21	3	13	0	1	0	0	1	.00	0	.362	.465	.505
1994	LA	NL	40	44	15	3	0	0	(0	0)	18	3	5	8	5	0	5	0	0	0	0	0	-	0	.341	.408	.409

BATTING / BASERUNNING / AVERAGES

Year	Team	Lg	G	AB	H	2B	3B	HR	(Hm	Rd)	TB	R	RBI	RC	TBB	IBB	SO	HBP	SH	SF	SB	CS	SB%	GDP	Avg	OBP	Slg
1995	LA	NL	100	181	52	10	0	1	(0	1)	65	19	14	26	28	4	28	1	0	1	0	0	-	4	.287	.384	.359
1996	LA	NL	80	104	23	1	0	0	(0	0)	24	7	6	6	11	1	22	0	0	1	0	0	-	4	.221	.293	.231
1997	CHN	NL	90	151	47	8	2	3	(1	2)	68	19	21	31	31	1	32	1	2	1	1	2	.33	0	.311	.429	.450
1999	LA	NL	100	107	27	8	1	2	(2	0)	43	14	17	19	26	0	20	2	0	1	0	0	-	2	.252	.404	.402
2000	LA	NL	102	121	35	6	2	8	(4	4)	69	18	26	27	26	0	32	0	0	0	0	1	.00	3	.289	.415	.570
2001	LA	NL	92	140	33	10	0	2	(1	1)	49	13	20	20	32	5	29	0	0	3	0	1	.00	3	.236	.371	.350
2002	LA	NL	96	120	35	6	0	2	(0	2)	47	15	17	17	14	3	22	0	0	1	1	0	1.00	3	.292	.363	.392
2003	SD	NL	110	135	33	4	1	2	(2	0)	45	13	15	18	23	3	25	1	0	0	1	0	1.00	5	.244	.358	.333
2004	2 Tms		86	106	26	5	0	2	(2	0)	37	15	12	14	21	3	21	0	0	1	0	0	-	6	.245	.367	.349
2005	SEA	AL	60	75	13	0	0	2	(2	0)	19	5	11	6	9	1	19	0	2	2	1	0	1.00	1	.173	.256	.253
04	Sea	AL	57	78	22	5	0	2	(2	0)	33	14	12	14	18	3	16	0	0	0	0	0	-	3	.282	.412	.423
04	SD	NL	29	28	4	0	0	0	(0	0)	4	1	0	0	3	0	5	0	0	0	0	0	-	3	.143	.226	.143
15 ML YEARS			1230	1793	466	79	6	35	(17	18)	662	187	222	250	283	27	332	6	4	14	5	7	.42	40	.260	.360	.369

Aaron Harang

Pitches: R **Bats:** R **Pos:** SP-32 **Ht:** 6'7" **Wt:** 240 **Born:** 5/9/1978 **Age:** 28

HOW MUCH HE PITCHED / WHAT HE GAVE UP / THE RESULTS

Year	Team	Lg	G	GS	CG	GF	IP	BFP	H	R	ER	HR	SH	SF	HB	TBB	IBB	SO	WP	Bk	W	L	Pct	ShO	Sv-Op	Hld	ERC	ERA
2002	OAK	AL	16	15	0	0	78.1	354	78	44	42	7	3	4	3	45	2	64	1	0	5	4	.556	0	0-0	0	4.76	4.83
2003	2 Tms		16	15	0	0	76.1	327	89	47	45	11	5	1	1	19	0	42	3	1	5	6	.455	0	0-0	0	4.84	5.31
2004	CIN	NL	28	28	1	0	161.0	711	177	90	87	26	13	6	5	53	5	125	7	0	10	9	.526	1	0-0	0	4.81	4.86
2005	CIN	NL	32	32	1	0	211.2	887	217	93	90	22	11	5	8	51	3	163	6	0	11	13	.458	0	0-0	0	3.77	3.83
03	Oak	AL	7	6	0	1	30.1	136	41	19	18	5	2	1	0	9	0	16	0	1	1	3	.250	0	0-0	0	6.32	5.34
03	Cin	NL	9	9	0	0	46.0	191	48	28	27	6	3	0	1	10	0	26	3	0	4	3	.571	0	0-0	0	3.94	5.28
4 ML YEARS			92	90	2	1	527.1	2279	561	274	264	66	32	16	17	168	10	394	17	1	31	32	.492	1	0-0	0	4.39	4.51

Rich Harden

Pitches: R **Bats:** L **Pos:** SP-19; RP-3 **Ht:** 6'1" **Wt:** 180 **Born:** 11/30/1981 **Age:** 24

HOW MUCH HE PITCHED / WHAT HE GAVE UP / THE RESULTS

Year	Team	Lg	G	GS	CG	GF	IP	BFP	H	R	ER	HR	SH	SF	HB	TBB	IBB	SO	WP	Bk	W	L	Pct	ShO	Sv-Op	Hld	ERC	ERA
2005	Scrmto*	AAA	1	1	0	0	3.0	10	1	0	0	0	0	0	0	0	0	7	0	0	0	0	-	0	0--	-	0.25	0.00
2003	OAK	AL	15	13	0	0	74.2	324	72	38	37	5	2	3	1	40	1	67	6	0	5	4	.556	0	0-0	0	4.28	4.46
2004	OAK	AL	31	31	0	0	189.2	803	171	90	84	16	5	6	3	81	6	167	4	1	11	7	.611	0	0-0	0	3.57	3.99
2005	OAK	AL	22	19	2	0	128.0	514	93	42	36	7	4	2	2	43	0	121	6	0	10	5	.667	0	0-0	1	2.20	2.53
3 ML YEARS			68	63	2	0	392.1	1641	336	170	157	28	11	11	6	164	7	355	16	1	26	16	.619	1	0-0	1	3.22	3.60

J.J. Hardy

Bats: R **Throws:** R **Pos:** SS-119; PH-6 **Ht:** 6'2" **Wt:** 181 **Born:** 8/19/1982 **Age:** 23

BATTING / BASERUNNING / AVERAGES

Year	Team	Lg	G	AB	H	2B	3B	HR	(Hm	Rd)	TB	R	RBI	RC	TBB	IBB	SO	HBP	SH	SF	SB	CS	SB%	GDP	Avg	OBP	Slg
2001	Ogden	R+	35	125	31	5	0	2	(-	-)	42	20	15	14	15	0	12	0	3	1	1	2	.33	2	.248	.326	.336
2001	Brewrs	R	5	20	5	2	1	0	(-	-)	9	6	1	2	1	0	2	0	1	0	0	0	-	0	.250	.286	.450
2002	Hi Dsrt	A+	84	335	98	19	1	6	(-	-)	137	53	48	47	19	0	38	1	3	6	9	3	.75	3	.293	.327	.409
2002	Huntsvl	AA	38	145	33	7	0	1	(-	-)	43	14	13	11	9	0	19	0	4	2	1	2	.33	4	.228	.269	.297
2003	Huntsvl	AA	114	416	116	26	0	12	(-	-)	178	67	62	70	58	4	54	3	4	4	6	4	.60	11	.279	.368	.428
2004	Indy	AAA	26	101	28	10	0	4	(-	-)	50	17	20	17	9	0	8	0	0	2	0	0	-	1	.277	.330	.495
2005	MIL	NL	124	372	92	22	1	9	(6	3)	143	46	50	49	44	7	48	1	8	2	0	0	-	10	.247	.327	.384

Danny Haren

Pitches: R **Bats:** R **Pos:** SP-34 **Ht:** 6'5" **Wt:** 220 **Born:** 9/17/1980 **Age:** 25

HOW MUCH HE PITCHED / WHAT HE GAVE UP / THE RESULTS

Year	Team	Lg	G	GS	CG	GF	IP	BFP	H	R	ER	HR	SH	SF	HB	TBB	IBB	SO	WP	Bk	W	L	Pct	ShO	Sv-Op	Hld	ERC	ERA
2003	STL	NL	14	14	0	0	72.2	320	84	44	41	9	4	2	5	22	0	43	3	0	3	7	.300	0	0-0	0	5.07	5.08
2004	STL	NL	14	5	0	2	46.0	195	45	23	23	4	4	2	2	17	2	32	1	0	3	3	.500	0	0-0	0	3.91	4.50
2005	OAK	AL	34	34	3	0	217.0	897	212	101	92	26	3	5	6	53	5	163	6	0	14	12	.538	0	0-0	0	3.58	3.73
3 ML YEARS			62	53	3	2	335.2	1412	341	168	154	39	11	9	13	92	7	238	10	0	20	22	.476	0	0-0	0	3.94	4.13

Tim Harikkala

Pitches: R **Bats:** R **Pos:** RP-8 **Ht:** 6'2" **Wt:** 185 **Born:** 7/15/1971 **Age:** 34

HOW MUCH HE PITCHED / WHAT HE GAVE UP / THE RESULTS

Year	Team	Lg	G	GS	CG	GF	IP	BFP	H	R	ER	HR	SH	SF	HB	TBB	IBB	SO	WP	Bk	W	L	Pct	ShO	Sv-Op	Hld	ERC	ERA
2005	Scrmto*	AAA	11	0	0	6	21.1	84	13	5	3	1	4	0	0	7	3	14	0	0	1	2	.333	0	3--	-	1.45	1.27
1995	SEA	AL	1	0	0	1	3.1	18	7	6	6	1	0	0	0	1	0	1	0	0	0	0	-	0	0-0	0	12.43	16.20
1996	SEA	AL	1	1	0	0	4.1	20	4	6	6	1	1	0	1	2	0	1	0	0	0	1	.000	0	0-0	0	5.68	12.46
1999	BOS	AL	7	0	0	2	13.0	58	15	9	9	0	2	0	1	6	1	7	1	0	1	1	.500	0	0-0	0	4.72	6.23
2004	COL	NL	55	0	0	11	62.2	262	55	34	33	10	2	2	1	23	5	30	0	1	6	6	.500	0	0-7	15	3.62	4.74
2005	OAK	AL	8	0	0	5	12.2	56	16	9	9	3	0	0	0	4	0	7	0	0	0	0	-	0	0-0	0	6.40	6.39
5 ML YEARS			72	1	0	19	96.0	414	97	64	63	15	5	2	3	36	6	46	1	1	7	8	.467	0	0-7	15	4.47	5.91

Travis Harper

Pitches: R Bats: R Pos: RP-52   Ht: 6'4" Wt: 192 Born: 5/21/1976 Age: 30

Year	Team	Lg	G	GS	CG	GF	IP	BFP	H	R	ER	HR	SH	SF	HB	TBB	IBB	SO	WP	Bk	W	L	Pct	ShO	Sv-Op	Hld	ERC	ERA
2000	TB	AL	6	5	1	0	32.0	141	30	17	17	5	1	1	1	15	0	14	1	0	1	2	.333	1	0-0	0	4.46	4.78
2001	TB	AL	2	2	0	0	7.0	36	15	11	6	5	0	0	0	3	0	2	1	0	0	2	.000	0	0-0	0	19.14	7.71
2002	TB	AL	37	7	0	16	85.2	394	101	54	52	14	5	4	9	27	3	60	2	0	5	9	.357	0	1-2	3	5.49	5.46
2003	TB	AL	61	0	0	14	93.0	387	86	45	39	9	7	3	6	31	8	64	6	0	4	8	.333	0	1-6	15	3.57	3.77
2004	TB	AL	52	0	0	11	78.2	330	69	37	34	8	3	2	7	23	3	59	3	0	6	2	.750	0	0-1	9	3.27	3.89
2005	TB	AL	52	0	0	13	73.1	322	88	57	55	14	5	2	1	24	9	40	2	0	4	6	.400	0	0-3	11	5.53	6.75
6 ML YEARS			210	14	1	54	369.2	1610	389	221	203	55	21	12	24	123	23	239	15	0	20	29	.408	1	2-12	38	4.61	4.94

Brendan Harris

Bats: R Throws: R Pos: 2B-2; 3B-1; PH-1; PR-1   Ht: 6'1" Wt: 200 Born: 8/26/1980 Age: 25

Year	Team	Lg	G	AB	H	2B	3B	HR	(Hm	Rd)	TB	R	RBI	RC	TBB	IBB	SO	HBP	SH	SF	SB	CS	SB%	GDP	Avg	OBP	Slg
2001	Lansng	A	32	113	31	5	1	4	(-	-)	50	25	22	19	17	0	26	2	1	3	5	1	.83	4	.274	.370	.442
2002	Dytona	A+	110	425	140	35	6	13	(-	-)	226	82	54	85	43	4	57	4	1	2	16	4	.80	7	.329	.395	.532
2002	WTenn	AA	13	53	17	4	1	2	(-	-)	29	8	11	9	2	0	5	0	0	0	1	1	.50	1	.321	.345	.547
2003	WTenn	AA	120	435	122	34	7	5	(-	-)	185	56	52	66	51	1	72	8	5	3	6	7	.46	10	.280	.364	.425
2004	Iowa	AAA	69	254	79	21	1	11	(-	-)	135	48	35	42	16	1	40	1	3	1	2	0	.00	8	.311	.353	.531
2004	Edmtn	AAA	33	123	35	6	0	6	(-	-)	59	20	24	19	10	2	21	3	1	3	0	1	.00	3	.285	.345	.480
2005	NewOr	AAA	127	470	127	22	4	13	(-	-)	196	67	81	67	40	3	77	3	1	4	9	5	.64	11	.270	.329	.417
2004	2 Tms	NL	23	59	10	3	0	1	(0	1)	16	4	3	2	3	0	12	1	0	0	0	0	-	0	.169	.222	.271
2005	WAS	NL	4	9	3	1	0	1	(0	1)	7	1	3	3	0	0	0	1	0	0	0	0	-	2	.333	.400	.778
04	ChC	NL	3	9	2	1	0	0	(0	0)	3	0	1	1	1	0	1	0	0	0	0	0	-	0	.222	.300	.333
04	Mon	NL	20	50	8	2	0	1	(0	1)	13	4	2	1	2	0	11	1	0	0	0	0	-	0	.160	.208	.260
2 ML YEARS			27	68	13	4	0	2	(0	2)	23	5	6	5	3	0	12	2	0	0	0	0	-	2	.191	.247	.338

Jeff Harris

Pitches: R Bats: R Pos: SP-8; RP-3   Ht: 6'1" Wt: 190 Born: 7/4/1974 Age: 31

Year	Team	Lg	G	GS	CG	GF	IP	BFP	H	R	ER	HR	SH	SF	HB	TBB	IBB	SO	WP	Bk	W	L	Pct	ShO	Sv-Op	Hld	ERC	ERA
1995	Elizab	R+	21	0	0	10	33.0	155	42	15	14	2	1	0	4	13	1	27	6	1	1	3	.250	0	0--	-	5.75	3.82
1996	FtWyn	A	42	0	0	15	89.2	393	90	35	31	4	3	8	4	33	1	85	10	1	8	3	.727	0	3--	-	3.67	3.11
1997	FtMyrs	A+	24	0	0	6	42.0	173	30	11	10	4	3	1	0	15	2	32	1	0	2	4	.333	0	1--	-	2.26	2.14
1997	NwBrit	AA	28	0	0	14	42.1	173	30	15	11	2	3	2	3	16	0	44	3	0	2	1	.667	0	3--	-	2.39	2.34
1998	NwBrit	AA	26	0	0	11	38.0	140	21	7	7	3	1	1	0	5	0	40	0	1	1	0	1.000	0	5--	-	1.11	1.66
1998	Salt Lk	AAA	25	0	0	18	32.0	157	38	24	21	4	3	0	0	19	4	24	3	0	8	0	1.000	0	3--	-	5.63	5.91
1999	Salt Lk	AAA	36	0	0	7	45.2	225	61	38	35	7	3	4	3	26	1	20	2	0	4	3	.571	0	0--	-	7.40	6.90
1999	NwBrit	AA	20	0	0	6	24.1	110	21	5	4	0	3	0	1	14	2	12	1	0	3	1	.750	0	0--	-	3.16	1.48
2000	NwBrit	AA	24	0	0	12	28.0	129	35	17	15	5	2	2	3	10	0	28	2	0	2	0	1.000	0	0--	-	6.45	4.82
2004	Tacom	AAA	26	8	1	4	74.2	310	60	37	36	6	1	2	4	26	0	53	4	0	5	3	.625	1	1--	-	2.89	4.34
2005	SnAnt	AA	11	2	0	4	34.1	136	25	9	8	4	2	1	3	8	1	31	0	0	5	0	1.000	0	0--	-	2.44	2.10
2005	Tacom	AAA	16	9	0	0	68.0	271	50	22	21	8	3	2	1	17	0	56	0	0	5	2	.714	0	1--	-	2.28	2.78
2005	SEA	AL	11	8	0	1	53.2	227	48	27	25	9	0	2	3	20	2	25	0	0	2	5	.286	0	0-0	0	4.02	4.19

Lenny Harris

Bats: L Throws: R Pos: PH-77; 3B-2; DH-2; 1B-1; LF-1; RF-1   Ht: 5'10" Wt: 220 Born: 10/28/1964 Age: 41

Year	Team	Lg	G	AB	H	2B	3B	HR	(Hm	Rd)	TB	R	RBI	RC	TBB	IBB	SO	HBP	SH	SF	SB	CS	SB%	GDP	Avg	OBP	Slg
1988	CIN	NL	16	43	16	1	0	0	(0	0)	17	7	8	8	5	0	4	0	1	2	4	1	.80	0	.372	.420	.395
1989	2 Tms	NL	115	335	79	10	1	3	(1	2)	100	36	26	23	20	0	33	2	1	0	14	9	.61	14	.236	.283	.299
1990	LA	NL	137	431	131	16	4	2	(0	2)	161	61	29	55	29	2	31	1	3	1	15	10	.60	8	.304	.348	.374
1991	LA	NL	145	429	123	16	1	3	(1	2)	150	59	38	52	37	5	32	5	12	4	12	3	.80	16	.287	.349	.350
1992	LA	NL	135	347	94	11	0	0	(0	0)	105	28	30	33	24	3	24	1	6	2	19	7	.73	10	.271	.318	.303
1993	LA	NL	107	160	38	6	1	2	(0	2)	52	20	11	15	15	4	15	0	1	0	3	1	.75	4	.238	.303	.325
1994	CIN	NL	66	100	31	3	1	0	(0	0)	36	13	14	13	5	0	13	0	0	0	7	2	.78	0	.310	.340	.360
1995	CIN	NL	101	197	41	8	3	2	(0	2)	61	32	16	15	14	0	20	0	3	1	10	1	.91	6	.208	.259	.310
1996	CIN	NL	125	302	86	17	2	5	(2	3)	122	33	32	41	21	1	31	1	6	3	14	6	.70	3	.285	.330	.404
1997	CIN	NL	120	238	65	13	1	3	(2	1)	89	32	28	27	18	1	18	2	3	2	3	5	.37	10	.273	.327	.374
1998	2 Tms	NL	132	290	75	15	0	6	(2	4)	108	30	27	29	17	3	21	2	4	4	6	5	.55	13	.259	.300	.372
1999	2 Tms	NL	110	187	58	13	0	1	(1	0)	74	17	20	23	6	0	7	0	0	1	2	1	.67	7	.310	.330	.396
2000	2 Tms	NL	112	223	58	7	4	4	(2	2)	85	31	26	28	20	2	22	0	0	2	13	1	.93	7	.260	.317	.381
2001	NYN	NL	110	135	30	5	1	0	(0	0)	37	12	9	9	8	0	9	0	0	0	3	2	.60	3	.222	.266	.274
2002	MIL	NL	122	197	60	8	2	3	(2	1)	81	23	17	26	14	1	17	2	1	1	4	1	.80	4	.305	.355	.411
2003	2 Tms	NL	88	145	28	3	0	1	(0	1)	34	14	8	9	16	3	21	0	1	0	1	0	1.00	2	.193	.272	.234
2004	FLA	NL	79	95	20	5	0	1	(1	0)	28	7	17	4	3	0	8	0	0	1	0	0	-	4	.211	.232	.295
2005	FLA	NL	83	70	22	4	0	1	(1	0)	29	5	13	13	7	1	11	1	0	0	1	0	1.00	3	.314	.385	.414
89	Cin	NL	61	188	42	4	0	2	(0	2)	52	17	11	11	9	0	20	1	1	0	10	6	.63	5	.223	.263	.277
89	LA	NL	54	147	37	6	1	1	(1	0)	48	19	15	12	11	0	13	1	0	0	4	3	.57	9	.252	.308	.327
98	Cin	NL	57	122	36	8	0	0	(0	0)	44	12	10	12	8	2	9	1	0	2	1	3	.25	8	.295	.338	.361
98	NYM	NL	75	168	39	7	0	6	(2	4)	64	18	17	17	9	1	12	1	4	2	5	2	.71	5	.232	.272	.381
99	Col	NL	91	158	47	12	0	0	(0	0)	59	15	13	17	6	0	6	0	0	0	1	1	.50	7	.297	.323	.373
99	Ari	NL	19	29	11	1	0	1	(1	0)	15	2	7	6	0	0	1	0	0	1	1	0	1.00	0	.379	.367	.517
00	Ari	NL	36	85	16	1	1	1	(1	0)	22	9	13	4	3	1	5	0	0	3	5	0	1.00	3	.188	.209	.259
00	NYM	NL	76	138	42	6	3	3	(1	2)	63	22	13	24	17	1	17	0	0	2	8	1	.89	4	.304	.381	.457
03	ChC	NL	75	131	24	3	0	1	(0	1)	30	11	7	7	13	3	20	0	1	0	1	0	1.00	1	.183	.255	.229
03	Fla	NL	13	14	4	0	0	0	(0	0)	4	3	1	2	3	0	1	0	0	0	0	0	-	1	.286	.412	.286
18 ML YEARS			1903	3924	1055	161	21	37	(15	22)	1369	460	369	423	279	26	337	17	44	25	131	54	.71	112	.269	.318	.349

Willie Harris

Bats: L **Throws:** R **Pos:** 2B-32; PH-12; PR-10; DH-8; SS-5   **Ht:** 5'9" **Wt:** 175 **Born:** 6/22/1978 **Age:** 28

Year	Team	Lg	G	AB	H	2B	3B	HR	(Hm	Rd)	TB	R	RBI	RC	TBB	IBB	SO	HBP	SH	SF	SB	CS	SB%	GDP	Avg	OBP	Slg
2005	Charltt*	AAA	28	109	29	11	1	1	(-	-)	45	21	10	18	16	0	27	0	4	0	10	2	.83	0	.266	.360	.413
2001	BAL	AL	9	24	3	1	0	0	(0	0)	4	3	0	0	0	0	7	0	1	0	0	0	-	0	.125	.125	.167
2002	CHA	AL	49	163	38	4	0	2	(2	0)	48	14	12	15	9	0	21	0	3	2	8	0	1.00	3	.233	.270	.294
2003	CHA	AL	79	137	28	3	1	0	(0	0)	33	19	5	11	10	0	28	0	3	0	12	2	.86	1	.204	.259	.241
2004	CHA	AL	129	409	107	15	2	2	(2	0)	132	68	27	53	51	0	79	1	7	3	19	7	.73	4	.262	.343	.323
2005	CHA	AL	56	121	31	2	1	1	(1	0)	38	17	8	15	13	0	25	1	4	0	10	3	.77	1	.256	.333	.314
	5 ML YEARS		322	854	207	25	4	5	(5	0)	255	121	52	94	83	0	160	2	18	5	49	12	.80	9	.242	.309	.299

Corey Hart

Bats: R **Throws:** R **Pos:** CF-11; RF-3; PH-3; LF-2; PR-2   **Ht:** 6'6" **Wt:** 200 **Born:** 3/24/1982 **Age:** 24

Year	Team	Lg	G	AB	H	2B	3B	HR	(Hm	Rd)	TB	R	RBI	RC	TBB	IBB	SO	HBP	SH	SF	SB	CS	SB%	GDP	Avg	OBP	Slg
2000	Ogden	R+	57	216	62	9	1	2	(-	-)	79	32	30	27	13	0	27	2	1	1	6	0	1.00	6	.287	.332	.366
2001	Ogden	R+	69	262	89	18	1	11	(-	-)	142	53	62	56	26	1	47	2	0	6	14	1	.93	4	.340	.395	.542
2002	Hi Dsrt	A+	100	393	113	26	10	22	(-	-)	225	76	84	75	37	2	101	5	1	1	24	11	.69	3	.288	.356	.573
2002	Huntsvl	AA	28	94	25	3	0	2	(-	-)	34	16	15	12	7	0	16	4	0	1	3	2	.60	1	.266	.340	.362
2003	Wichta	AA	93	334	92	9	0	4	(-	-)	113	40	47	47	49	4	69	2	3	3	12	4	.75	5	.275	.369	.338
2003	Huntsvl	AA	130	493	149	40	1	13	(-	-)	230	70	94	76	28	5	101	5	0	9	25	8	.76	7	.302	.340	.467
2004	Wichta	AA	75	240	55	13	0	1	(-	-)	71	37	29	26	42	0	52	3	1	5	0	6	.00	4	.229	.345	.296
2004	Indy	AAA	121	441	124	29	8	15	(-	-)	214	68	67	71	41	3	92	3	0	6	17	7	.71	7	.281	.342	.485
2004	Omha	AAA	21	65	17	3	0	1	(-	-)	23	8	2	6	3	0	15	0	2	0	0	0	-	2	.262	.294	.354
2005	Nashv	AAA	113	429	132	29	9	17	(-	-)	230	85	69	90	48	1	88	3	3	6	31	7	.82	11	.308	.377	.536
2004	MIL	NL	1	1	0	0	0	0	(0	0)	0	0	0	0	0	0	1	0	0	0	0	0	-	0	.000	.000	.000
2005	MIL	NL	21	57	11	2	1	2	(2	0)	21	9	7	4	6	0	11	0	0	0	2	0	1.00	6	.193	.270	.368
	2 ML YEARS		22	58	11	2	1	2	(2	0)	21	9	7	4	6	0	12	0	0	0	2	0	1.00	6	.190	.266	.362

Ken Harvey

Bats: R **Throws:** R **Pos:** DH-7; 1B-5   **Ht:** 6'2" **Wt:** 240 **Born:** 3/1/1978 **Age:** 28

Year	Team	Lg	G	AB	H	2B	3B	HR	(Hm	Rd)	TB	R	RBI	RC	TBB	IBB	SO	HBP	SH	SF	SB	CS	SB%	GDP	Avg	OBP	Slg
2005	Omha*	AAA	25	104	36	4	1	3	(-	-)	51	10	18	18	5	0	18	0	0	1	0	0	-	2	.346	.373	.490
2001	KC	AL	4	12	3	1	0	0	(0	0)	4	1	2	0	0	0	4	0	0	0	0	1	.00	1	.250	.250	.333
2003	KC	AL	135	485	129	30	0	13	(5	8)	198	50	64	58	29	4	94	5	3	2	2	3	.40	15	.266	.313	.408
2004	KC	AL	120	456	131	20	1	13	(6	7)	192	47	55	59	28	2	89	8	0	2	1	1	.50	14	.287	.338	.421
2005	KC	AL	12	45	10	3	0	1	(0	1)	16	4	5	4	3	0	13	0	0	0	0	0	-	0	.222	.271	.356
	4 ML YEARS		271	998	273	54	1	27	(11	16)	410	102	126	121	60	6	200	13	3	4	3	5	.38	30	.274	.322	.411

Chad Harville

Pitches: R **Bats:** R **Pos:** RP-45   **Ht:** 5'9" **Wt:** 185 **Born:** 9/16/1976 **Age:** 29

Year	Team	Lg	G	GS	CG	GF	IP	BFP	H	R	ER	HR	SH	SF	HB	TBB	IBB	SO	WP	Bk	W	L	Pct	ShO	Sv-Op	Hld	ERC	ERA
1999	OAK	AL	15	0	0	0	14.1	69	18	11	11	2	0	0	0	10	0	15	0	0	0	2	.000	0	0-0	0	7.23	6.91
2001	OAK	AL	3	0	0	0	3.0	11	2	0	0	0	0	0	0	0	0	2	0	0	0	0	-	0	0-0	0	0.91	0.00
2003	OAK	AL	21	0	0	5	21.2	104	25	15	14	3	0	1	1	17	1	18	3	0	1	0	1.000	0	1-1	0	7.13	5.82
2004	2 Tms		59	0	0	15	55.2	249	56	36	29	8	2	0	2	27	2	46	5	0	3	2	.600	0	0-4	4	4.81	4.69
2005	2 Tms		45	0	0	20	45.1	203	43	26	24	8	1	2	5	27	1	36	4	0	0	3	.000	0	0-1	2	5.67	4.76
04	Oak	AL	3	0	0	1	2.2	11	2	1	1	0	0	0	0	1	0	0	0	0	0	0	-	0	0-0	1	2.01	3.38
04	Hou	NL	56	0	0	14	53.0	238	54	35	28	8	2	0	2	26	2	46	5	0	3	2	.600	0	0-4	3	4.96	4.75
05	Hou	NL	37	0	0	16	38.1	173	36	21	19	7	1	2	4	24	1	33	4	0	0	2	.000	0	0-1	2	5.73	4.46
05	Bos	AL	8	0	0	4	7.0	30	7	5	5	1	0	0	1	3	0	3	0	0	0	1	.000	0	0-0	0	5.33	6.43
	5 ML YEARS		143	0	0	40	140.0	636	144	88	78	21	3	3	8	81	4	117	12	0	4	7	.364	0	1-6	6	5.56	5.01

Shigetoshi Hasegawa

Pitches: R **Bats:** R **Pos:** RP-46   **Ht:** 5'11" **Wt:** 178 **Born:** 8/1/1968 **Age:** 37

Year	Team	Lg	G	GS	CG	GF	IP	BFP	H	R	ER	HR	SH	SF	HB	TBB	IBB	SO	WP	Bk	W	L	Pct	ShO	Sv-Op	Hld	ERC	ERA
1997	ANA	AL	50	7	0	17	116.2	497	118	60	51	14	5	5	3	46	6	83	2	1	3	7	.300	0	0-1	3	4.37	3.93
1998	ANA	AL	61	0	0	20	97.1	401	86	37	34	14	4	6	2	32	2	73	5	2	8	3	.727	0	5-7	10	3.54	3.14
1999	ANA	AL	64	1	0	26	77.0	333	80	45	42	14	3	4	2	34	2	44	4	0	4	6	.400	0	2-5	6	5.25	4.91
2000	ANA	AL	66	0	0	26	95.2	415	100	43	38	11	2	3	2	38	6	59	2	1	10	6	.625	0	9-18	19	4.44	3.57
2001	ANA	AL	46	0	0	10	55.2	235	52	26	25	5	1	2	2	20	5	41	2	0	5	6	.455	0	0-6	12	3.50	4.04
2002	SEA	AL	53	0	0	20	70.1	288	60	26	25	4	3	1	2	30	8	39	0	1	8	3	.727	0	1-3	13	3.13	3.20
2003	SEA	AL	63	0	0	36	73.0	283	62	12	12	5	1	0	0	18	3	32	0	0	2	4	.333	0	16-17	12	2.57	1.48
2004	SEA	AL	68	0	0	19	68.0	300	67	42	39	5	5	4	2	31	4	46	1	1	4	6	.400	0	0-5	12	4.00	5.16
2005	SEA	AL	46	0	0	17	66.2	279	66	31	31	4	2	3	3	16	1	30	0	0	1	3	.250	0	0-1	3	3.29	4.19
	9 ML YEARS		517	8	0	191	720.1	3031	691	324	297	76	26	28	18	265	37	447	16	6	45	44	.506	0	33-65	85	3.84	3.71

Scott Hatteberg

Bats: L Throws: R Pos: DH-78; 1B-53; PH-11   Ht: 6'1" Wt: 210 Born: 12/14/1969 Age: 36

								BATTING												BASERUNNING				AVERAGES		
Year	Team	Lg	G	AB	H	2B	3B	HR	(Hm	Rd)	TB	R	RBI	RC	TBB	IBB	SO	HBP	SH	SF	SB	CS	SB%	GDP	Avg	OBP	Slg
1995	BOS	AL	2	2	1	0	0	0	(0	0)	1	1	0	0	0	0	0	0	0	0	0	0	-	1	.500	.500	.500
1996	BOS	AL	10	11	2	1	0	0	(0	0)	3	3	0	1	3	0	2	0	0	0	0	0	-	2	.182	.357	.273
1997	BOS	AL	114	350	97	23	1	10	(5	5)	152	46	44	52	40	2	70	2	2	1	0	1	.00	11	.277	.354	.434
1998	BOS	AL	112	359	99	23	1	12	(4	8)	160	46	43	56	43	3	58	5	0	3	0	0	-	11	.276	.359	.446
1999	BOS	AL	30	80	22	5	0	1	(1	0)	30	12	11	14	18	0	14	1	0	1	0	0	-	2	.275	.410	.375
2000	BOS	AL	92	230	61	15	0	8	(2	6)	100	21	36	36	38	3	39	0	1	2	0	1	.00	8	.265	.367	.435
2001	BOS	AL	94	278	68	19	0	3	(2	1)	96	34	25	32	33	0	26	4	0	1	1	1	.50	7	.245	.332	.345
2002	OAK	AL	136	492	138	22	4	15	(8	7)	213	58	61	77	68	1	56	6	1	0	0	0	-	8	.280	.374	.433
2003	OAK	AL	147	541	137	34	0	12	(6	6)	207	63	61	80	66	0	53	9	3	3	0	1	.00	14	.253	.342	.383
2004	OAK	AL	152	550	156	30	0	15	(8	7)	231	87	82	90	72	5	48	5	3	8	0	0	-	9	.284	.367	.420
2005	OAK	AL	134	464	119	19	0	7	(3	4)	159	52	59	60	51	4	54	4	2	2	0	1	.00	22	.256	.334	.343
11 ML YEARS			1023	3357	900	191	6	83	(40	43)	1352	423	422	498	432	18	420	36	12	22	1	5	.17	95	.268	.356	.403

LaTroy Hawkins

Pitches: R Bats: R Pos: RP-66   Ht: 6'5" Wt: 204 Born: 12/21/1972 Age: 33

			HOW MUCH HE PITCHED						WHAT HE GAVE UP											THE RESULTS						
Year	Team	Lg	G	GS	CG	GF	IP	BFP	H	R	ER	HR	SH	SF	HB	TBB	IBB	SO	WP	Bk	W	L	Pct	ShO	Sv-Op	Hld	ERC	ERA
2005	Fresno*	AAA	2	0	0	0	2.0	8	2	0	0	0	0	0	0	0	0	1	0	0	0	0	-	0	0- -	-	1.95	0.00
1995	MIN	AL	6	6	1	0	27.0	131	39	29	26	3	0	3	1	12	0	9	1	1	2	3	.400	0	0-0	0	7.14	8.67
1996	MIN	AL	7	6	0	1	26.1	124	42	24	24	8	1	1	0	9	0	24	1	1	1	1	.500	0	0-0	0	9.49	8.20
1997	MIN	AL	20	20	0	0	103.1	478	134	71	67	19	2	2	4	47	0	58	6	3	6	12	.333	0	0-0	0	7.01	5.84
1998	MIN	AL	33	33	0	0	190.1	840	227	126	111	27	4	10	5	61	1	105	10	2	7	14	.333	0	0-0	0	5.31	5.25
1999	MIN	AL	33	33	1	0	174.1	803	238	136	129	29	1	5	1	60	2	103	9	0	10	14	.417	0	0-0	0	6.55	6.66
2000	MIN	AL	66	0	0	38	87.2	370	85	34	33	7	4	1	1	32	1	59	6	0	2	5	.286	0	14-14	7	3.70	3.39
2001	MIN	AL	62	0	0	51	51.1	248	59	34	34	3	1	4	1	39	3	36	7	0	1	5	.167	0	28-37	1	6.02	5.96
2002	MIN	AL	65	0	0	15	80.1	310	63	23	19	5	2	3	0	15	1	63	5	0	6	0	1.000	0	0-3	13	1.99	2.13
2003	MIN	AL	74	0	0	12	77.1	310	69	20	16	4	4	1	1	15	1	75	5	0	9	3	.750	0	2-8	28	2.48	1.86
2004	CHN	NL	77	0	0	50	82.0	333	72	27	24	10	6	2	2	14	5	69	2	0	5	4	.556	0	25-34	4	2.66	2.63
2005	2 Tms	NL	66	0	0	21	56.1	247	58	27	24	7	3	1	0	24	3	43	1	0	2	8	.200	0	6-15	15	4.41	3.83
05	ChC	NL	21	0	0	12	19.0	80	18	9	7	4	1	0	0	7	0	13	0	0	1	4	.200	0	4-8	0	4.44	3.32
05	SF	NL	45	0	0	9	37.1	167	40	18	17	3	2	1	0	17	3	30	1	0	1	4	.200	0	2-7	15	4.36	4.10
11 ML YEARS			509	98	2	188	956.1	4194	1086	551	507	122	28	33	16	328	17	644	53	7	51	69	.425	0	75-111	68	4.88	4.77

Brad Hawpe

Bats: L Throws: L Pos: RF-89; PH-20   Ht: 6'3" Wt: 200 Born: 6/22/1979 Age: 27

								BATTING												BASERUNNING				AVERAGES		
Year	Team	Lg	G	AB	H	2B	3B	HR	(Hm	Rd)	TB	R	RBI	RC	TBB	IBB	SO	HBP	SH	SF	SB	CS	SB%	GDP	Avg	OBP	Slg
2000	Portlnd	A-	62	205	59	19	2	7	(-	-)	103	38	29	43	40	2	51	2	0	7	2	0	1.00	1	.288	.398	.502
2001	Ashvlle	A	111	393	105	22	3	22	(-	-)	199	78	72	71	59	3	113	6	0	10	7	4	.64	8	.267	.363	.506
2002	Salem	A+	122	450	156	38	2	22	(-	-)	264	87	97	109	81	23	84	2	0	2	1	1	.50	7	.347	.447	.587
2003	Tulsa	AA	93	346	96	27	0	17	(-	-)	174	52	68	54	31	2	84	1	0	1	3	3	.25	5	.277	.338	.503
2004	ColSpr	AAA	92	345	111	19	1	31	(-	-)	225	62	86	76	36	1	91	1	3	3	3	2	.60	10	.322	.384	.652
2005	ColSpr	AAA	7	28	13	3	0	3	(-	-)	25	7	11	11	6	0	7	0	0	0	0	0	-	2	.464	.559	.893
2004	COL	NL	42	105	26	3	2	3	(1	2)	42	12	9	11	11	3	34	1	0	1	1	1	.50	4	.248	.322	.400
2005	COL	NL	101	305	80	10	3	9	(5	4)	123	38	47	44	43	3	70	0	0	3	2	2	.50	5	.262	.350	.403
2 ML YEARS			143	410	106	13	5	12	(6	6)	165	50	56	55	54	6	104	1	0	4	3	3	.50	9	.259	.343	.402

Aaron Heilman

Pitches: R Bats: R Pos: RP-46; SP-7   Ht: 6'5" Wt: 220 Born: 11/12/1978 Age: 27

			HOW MUCH HE PITCHED						WHAT HE GAVE UP											THE RESULTS						
Year	Team	Lg	G	GS	CG	GF	IP	BFP	H	R	ER	HR	SH	SF	HB	TBB	IBB	SO	WP	Bk	W	L	Pct	ShO	Sv-Op	Hld	ERC	ERA
2003	NYN	NL	14	13	0	0	65.1	315	79	53	49	13	5	3	3	41	2	51	5	0	2	7	.222	0	0-0	0	7.16	6.75
2004	NYN	NL	5	5	0	0	28.0	119	27	17	17	4	1	0	0	13	0	22	0	0	1	3	.250	0	0-0	0	4.54	5.46
2005	NYN	NL	53	7	1	20	108.0	439	87	40	38	6	4	1	6	37	4	106	1	1	5	3	.625	1	5-6	5	2.74	3.17
3 ML YEARS			72	25	1	20	201.1	873	193	110	104	23	10	4	9	91	6	179	6	1	8	13	.381	1	5-6	5	4.31	4.65

Chris Heintz

Bats: R Throws: R Pos: C-8; PR-1   Ht: 6'1" Wt: 210 Born: 8/6/1974 Age: 31

								BATTING												BASERUNNING				AVERAGES		
Year	Team	Lg	G	AB	H	2B	3B	HR	(Hm	Rd)	TB	R	RBI	RC	TBB	IBB	SO	HBP	SH	SF	SB	CS	SB%	GDP	Avg	OBP	Slg
1996	Bristol	R+	8	29	10	7	0	2	(-	-)	23	7	8	8	4	0	2	0	0	0	1	1	.50	0	.345	.424	.793
1996	Sbend	A	64	230	61	12	1	1	(-	-)	78	25	22	28	23	0	46	3	1	1	1	1	.50	3	.265	.339	.339
1997	Hickory	A	107	388	110	28	1	2	(-	-)	146	57	54	52	28	0	57	9	2	5	1	3	.25	6	.284	.342	.376
1998	WinSa	A+	130	508	147	21	4	8	(-	-)	200	66	79	68	31	0	87	5	3	9	10	8	.56	17	.289	.331	.394
1999	WinSa	A+	118	417	122	33	2	7	(-	-)	180	55	60	67	40	1	72	4	3	7	6	3	.67	7	.293	.359	.432
2000	Brham	AA	73	239	64	15	1	2	(-	-)	87	27	34	30	21	0	33	0	1	6	4	1	.80	2	.268	.320	.364
2001	Brham	AA	37	119	28	8	0	2	(-	-)	42	14	8	12	10	0	23	2	2	1	0	2	.00	2	.235	.303	.353
2001	Charltt	AAA	5	10	1	1	0	0	(-	-)	2	1	1	0	0	0	3	0	0	0	0	0	-	0	.100	.091	.200
2002	NwHav	AA	105	373	117	29	1	7	(-	-)	169	40	45	46	19	3	61	2	2	1	1	0	1.00	13	.314	.349	.453
2003	Altna	AA	78	271	70	12	4	2	(-	-)	96	28	26	24	19	2	24	3	5	1	0	0	-	6	.258	.313	.354
2004	Roch	AAA	85	290	81	14	0	8	(-	-)	119	32	45	39	16	0	40	3	7	5	0	2	.00	6	.279	.318	.410
2005	Roch	AAA	89	329	100	18	2	8	(-	-)	146	38	58	51	22	0	61	0	4	5	0	0	-	16	.304	.343	.444
2005	MIN	AL	8	25	5	3	0	0	(0	0)	8	1	2	2	1	0	6	0	0	0	0	0	-	1	.200	.231	.320

Rick Helling

Pitches: R **Bats:** R **Pos:** RP-8; SP-7 **Ht:** 6'3" **Wt:** 220 **Born:** 12/15/1970 **Age:** 35

			HOW MUCH HE PITCHED							WHAT HE GAVE UP											THE RESULTS						
Year	Team	Lg	G	GS	CG	GF	IP	BFP	H	R	ER	HR	SH	SF	HB	TBB	IBB	SO	WP	Bk	W	L	Pct	ShO	Sv-Op	Hld	ERC	ERA
2005	Nashv*	AAA	21	21	0	0	130.2	570	128	74	60	12	8	5	7	50	1	105	5	1	9	3	.750	0	0- -	-	3.99	4.13
1994	TEX	AL	9	9	1	0	52.0	228	62	34	34	14	0	0	0	18	0	25	4	1	3	2	.600	1	0-0	0	6.33	5.88
1995	TEX	AL	3	3	0	0	12.1	62	17	11	9	2	0	2	2	8	0	5	0	0	0	2	.000	0	0-0	0	8.81	6.57
1996	2 Tms		11	6	0	2	48.0	198	37	23	23	9	1	1	0	16	0	42	1	1	3	3	.500	0	0-0	1	3.07	4.31
1997	2 Tms		41	16	0	9	131.0	550	108	67	65	17	3	9	6	69	2	99	3	0	5	9	.357	0	0-1	6	4.08	4.47
1998	TEX	AL	33	33	4	0	216.1	922	209	109	106	27	6	10	1	78	6	164	10	0	20	7	.741	2	0-0	0	3.86	4.41
1999	TEX	AL	35	35	3	0	219.1	943	228	127	118	41	5	10	6	85	5	131	8	0	13	11	.542	0	0-0	0	5.03	4.84
2000	TEX	AL	35	35	0	0	217.0	963	212	122	108	29	4	9	9	99	2	146	2	0	16	13	.552	0	0-0	0	4.50	4.48
2001	TEX	AL	34	34	2	0	215.2	941	256	134	124	38	3	4	9	63	2	154	6	0	12	11	.522	1	0-0	0	5.39	5.17
2002	ARI	NL	30	30	0	0	175.2	751	180	94	88	31	10	6	6	48	6	120	7	1	10	12	.455	0	0-0	0	4.29	4.51
2003	2 Tms		35	24	0	5	155.0	665	167	91	89	31	4	2	12	45	0	98	5	1	8	8	.500	0	0-0	1	5.19	5.17
2005	MIL	NL	15	7	0	0	49.0	199	39	13	13	2	0	1	2	18	1	42	1	0	3	1	.750	0	0-0	2	2.66	2.39
96	Tex	AL	6	2	0	2	20.1	92	23	17	17	7	0	1	0	9	0	16	1	0	1	2	.333	0	0-0	1	6.80	7.52
96	Fla	NL	5	4	0	0	27.2	106	14	6	6	2	1	0	0	7	0	26	0	1	2	1	.667	0	0-0	0	1.18	1.95
97	Fla	NL	31	8	0	8	76.0	324	61	38	37	12	2	7	4	48	2	53	0	0	2	6	.250	0	0-1	6	4.62	4.38
97	Tex	AL	10	8	0	1	55.0	226	47	29	28	5	1	2	2	21	0	46	3	0	3	3	.500	0	0-0	0	3.37	4.58
03	Bal	AL	24	24	0	0	138.2	603	156	90	88	30	4	2	12	40	0	86	4	1	7	8	.467	0	0-0	0	5.63	5.71
03	Fla	NL	11	0	0	5	16.1	62	11	1	1	1	0	0	0	5	0	12	1	0	1	0	1.000	0	0-0	1	1.93	0.55
	11 ML YEARS		281	232	10	18	1491.1	6422	1515	825	777	241	36	60	48	547	24	1026	47	4	93	79	.541	4	0-1	10	4.60	4.69

Wes Helms

Bats: R **Throws:** R **Pos:** PH-50; 3B-35; 1B-16; DH-3 **Ht:** 6'4" **Wt:** 230 **Born:** 5/12/1976 **Age:** 30

			BATTING																			BASERUNNING				AVERAGES		
Year	Team	Lg	G	AB	H	2B	3B	HR	(Hm	Rd)	TB	R	RBI	RC	TBB	IBB	SO	HBP	SH	SF	SB	CS	SB%	GDP	Avg	OBP	Slg
1998	ATL	NL	7	13	4	1	0	1	(0	1)	8	2	2	2	0	0	4	0	0	0	0	0	-	0	.308	.308	.615
2000	ATL	NL	6	5	1	0	0	0	(0	0)	1	0	0	0	0	0	2	0	0	0	0	0	-	0	.200	.200	.200
2001	ATL	NL	100	216	48	10	3	10	(6	4)	94	28	36	27	21	2	56	1	0	1	1	1	.50	3	.222	.293	.435
2002	ATL	NL	85	210	51	16	0	6	(4	2)	85	20	22	15	11	2	57	3	1	6	1	1	.50	5	.243	.283	.405
2003	MIL	NL	134	476	124	21	0	23	(16	7)	214	56	67	66	43	3	131	10	0	7	0	1	.00	10	.261	.330	.450
2004	MIL	NL	92	274	72	13	1	4	(3	1)	99	24	28	28	24	1	60	5	1	2	0	1	.00	10	.263	.331	.361
2005	MIL	NL	95	168	50	13	1	4	(2	2)	77	18	24	26	14	0	30	3	0	3	0	1	.00	7	.298	.356	.458
	7 ML YEARS		519	1362	350	74	5	48	(31	17)	578	148	179	164	113	8	340	22	2	19	2	5	.29	35	.257	.320	.424

Todd Helton

Bats: L **Throws:** L **Pos:** 1B-144; PH-1 **Ht:** 6'2" **Wt:** 204 **Born:** 8/20/1973 **Age:** 32

			BATTING																			BASERUNNING				AVERAGES		
Year	Team	Lg	G	AB	H	2B	3B	HR	(Hm	Rd)	TB	R	RBI	RC	TBB	IBB	SO	HBP	SH	SF	SB	CS	SB%	GDP	Avg	OBP	Slg
2005	ColSpr*	AAA	2	5	3	2	0	0	(-	-)	5	1	1	2	1	0	0	1	0	0	0	0	-	0	.600	.714	1.000
1997	COL	NL	35	93	26	2	1	5	(3	2)	45	13	11	15	8	0	11	0	0	0	0	1	.00	1	.280	.337	.484
1998	COL	NL	152	530	167	37	1	25	(13	12)	281	78	97	101	53	5	54	6	1	5	3	3	.50	15	.315	.380	.530
1999	COL	NL	159	578	185	39	5	35	(23	12)	339	114	113	124	68	6	77	6	0	4	7	6	.54	14	.320	.395	.587
2000	COL	NL	160	580	216	59	2	42	(27	15)	405	138	147	169	103	22	61	4	0	10	5	3	.63	12	.372	.463	.698
2001	COL	NL	159	587	197	54	2	49	(27	22)	402	132	146	157	98	15	104	5	1	5	7	5	.58	14	.336	.432	.685
2002	COL	NL	156	553	182	39	4	30	(18	12)	319	107	109	127	99	21	91	5	0	10	5	1	.83	10	.329	.429	.577
2003	COL	NL	160	583	209	49	5	33	(23	10)	367	135	117	160	111	21	72	2	0	7	0	4	.00	19	.358	.458	.630
2004	COL	NL	154	547	190	49	2	32	(21	11)	339	115	96	143	127	19	72	3	0	6	3	0	1.00	12	.347	.469	.620
2005	COL	NL	144	509	163	45	2	20	(13	7)	272	92	79	114	106	22	80	9	1	1	3	0	1.00	14	.320	.445	.534
	9 ML YEARS		1279	4560	1535	373	24	271	(168	103)	2769	924	915	1110	773	131	622	40	3	48	33	23	.59	111	.337	.433	.607

Mark Hendrickson

Pitches: L **Bats:** L **Pos:** SP-31 **Ht:** 6'9" **Wt:** 230 **Born:** 6/23/1974 **Age:** 32

			HOW MUCH HE PITCHED							WHAT HE GAVE UP											THE RESULTS						
Year	Team	Lg	G	GS	CG	GF	IP	BFP	H	R	ER	HR	SH	SF	HB	TBB	IBB	SO	WP	Bk	W	L	Pct	ShO	Sv-Op	Hld	ERC	ERA
2002	TOR	AL	16	4	0	0	36.2	142	25	11	10	1	2	2	1	12	3	21	0	0	3	0	1.000	0	0-1	1	1.90	2.45
2003	TOR	AL	30	30	1	0	158.1	703	207	111	97	24	1	8	0	40	3	76	4	0	9	9	.500	1	0-0	0	5.64	5.51
2004	TB	AL	32	30	2	1	183.1	803	211	113	98	21	4	5	7	46	5	87	5	2	10	15	.400	0	0-0	0	4.51	4.81
2005	TB	AL	31	31	1	0	178.1	796	227	126	117	24	8	7	2	49	1	89	4	1	11	8	.579	0	0-0	0	5.44	5.90
	4 ML YEARS		109	95	4	1	556.2	2444	670	361	322	70	15	22	11	147	12	273	13	3	33	32	.508	1	0-1	1	4.92	5.21

Sean Henn

Pitches: L **Bats:** R **Pos:** SP-3 **Ht:** 6'4" **Wt:** 215 **Born:** 4/23/1981 **Age:** 25

			HOW MUCH HE PITCHED							WHAT HE GAVE UP											THE RESULTS						
Year	Team	Lg	G	GS	CG	GF	IP	BFP	H	R	ER	HR	SH	SF	HB	TBB	IBB	SO	WP	Bk	W	L	Pct	ShO	Sv-Op	Hld	ERC	ERA
2001	StIsInd	A-	9	8	0	1	42.0	167	26	15	14	3	0	1	1	15	0	49	4	0	3	1	.750	0	1- -	-	1.88	3.00
2003	Yanks	R	2	1	0	0	8.0	32	5	3	2	1	0	0	1	3	0	10	1	0	1	1	.500	0	0- -	-	2.69	2.25
2003	Tampa	A+	16	16	0	0	72.1	323	69	31	29	3	0	1	0	37	0	52	7	0	4	3	.571	0	0- -	-	3.73	3.61
2004	Trentn	AA	27	27	0	0	163.1	726	173	94	80	11	10	8	6	63	2	118	12	1	6	8	.429	0	0- -	-	4.17	4.41
2005	Trent	AA	4	4	0	0	25.1	101	16	2	2	1	0	0	0	9	0	21	2	0	2	1	.667	0	0- -	-	1.67	0.71
2005	Clmbs	AAA	16	16	1	0	86.1	365	79	37	31	5	3	3	4	27	1	64	0	0	5	5	.500	1	0- -	-	3.12	3.23
2005	NYA	AL	3	3	0	0	11.1	61	18	16	14	3	0	0	1	11	0	3	0	0	0	3	.000	0	0-0	0	12.12	11.12

Brad Hennessey

Pitches: R **Bats:** R **Pos:** SP-21   **Ht:** 6'2" **Wt:** 185 **Born:** 2/7/1980 **Age:** 26

			HOW MUCH HE PITCHED							WHAT HE GAVE UP										THE RESULTS							
Year	Team	Lg	G	GS	CG	GF	IP	BFP	H	R	ER	HR	SH	SF	HB	TBB	IBB	SO	WP	Bk	W	L	Pct	ShO	Sv-Op	Hld	ERC	ERA
2001	SlmKzr	A-	9	9	0	0	34.0	140	28	9	9	1	0	0	4	11	0	22	2	0	1	0	1.000	0	0- -	-	2.86	2.38
2003	Hgrstn	A	15	15	1	0	79.1	346	81	49	37	6	3	4	5	27	0	44	4	0	3	9	.250	0	0- -	-	4.00	4.20
2004	Nrwich	AA	18	18	0	0	101.0	425	106	42	40	8	7	4	3	34	0	55	0	0	5	5	.500	0	0- -	-	4.20	3.56
2004	Fresno	AAA	5	5	0	0	35.2	141	26	8	8	2	2	0	0	15	0	16	1	0	4	1	.800	0	0- -	-	2.55	2.02
2005	Fresno	AAA	11	11	0	0	67.2	300	75	40	39	7	3	3	4	22	1	46	3	2	4	2	.667	0	0- -	-	4.58	5.19
2004	SF	NL	7	7	0	0	34.1	163	42	24	19	2	4	1	0	15	1	25	1	0	2	2	.500	0	0-0	0	4.91	4.98
2005	SF	NL	21	21	0	0	118.1	521	127	63	61	15	2	3	4	52	3	64	3	1	5	8	.385	0	0-0	0	5.00	4.64
	2 ML YEARS		28	28	0	0	152.2	684	169	87	80	17	6	4	4	67	4	89	4	1	7	10	.412	0	0-0	0	4.98	4.72

Clay Hensley

Pitches: R **Bats:** R **Pos:** RP-23; SP-1   **Ht:** 5'11" **Wt:** 190 **Born:** 8/31/1979 **Age:** 26

			HOW MUCH HE PITCHED							WHAT HE GAVE UP										THE RESULTS							
Year	Team	Lg	G	GS	CG	GF	IP	BFP	H	R	ER	HR	SH	SF	HB	TBB	IBB	SO	WP	Bk	W	L	Pct	ShO	Sv-Op	Hld	ERC	ERA
2002	SlmKzr	A-	15	15	1	0	81.2	342	72	31	23	3	2	1	3	25	0	84	6	1	7	0	1.000	0	0- -	-	2.77	2.53
2003	SnJos	A+	5	5	0	0	29.1	135	38	20	19	4	3	4	1	9	0	25	0	0	2	3	.400	0	0- -	-	5.75	5.83
2003	Lk Els	A+	8	8	0	0	44.1	198	51	24	17	0	0	0	0	14	0	40	3	0	3	4	.429	0	0- -	-	3.76	3.45
2003	Hgrstn	A	12	12	3	0	68.0	280	56	26	24	4	1	0	1	20	0	74	4	0	3	4	.571	2	0- -	-	2.50	3.18
2004	Mobile	AA	27	27	2	0	159.0	692	167	84	76	14	8	7	8	48	2	125	6	0	11	10	.524	1	0- -	-	4.02	4.30
2005	Portlnd	AAA	15	14	0	0	90.1	356	63	31	30	8	3	3	2	22	0	71	1	1	2	2	.500	0	0- -	-	1.96	2.99
2005	SD	NL	24	1	0	5	47.2	189	33	12	9	0	1	2	0	17	2	28	2	0	1	1	.500	0	0-0	2	1.70	1.70

Felix Heredia

Pitches: L **Bats:** L **Pos:** RP-3   **Ht:** 6'0" **Wt:** 190 **Born:** 6/20/1975 **Age:** 31

			HOW MUCH HE PITCHED							WHAT HE GAVE UP										THE RESULTS							
Year	Team	Lg	G	GS	CG	GF	IP	BFP	H	R	ER	HR	SH	SF	HB	TBB	IBB	SO	WP	Bk	W	L	Pct	ShO	Sv-Op	Hld	ERC	ERA
2005	StLuci*	A+	5	0	0	0	4.0	20	6	6	6	0	0	0	1	2	0	3	1	1	0	1	.000	0	0- -	-	7.93	13.50
1996	FLA	NL	21	0	0	5	16.2	78	21	8	8	1	0	1	0	10	1	10	2	0	1	1	.500	0	0-0	2	6.08	4.32
1997	FLA	NL	56	0	0	10	56.2	259	53	30	27	3	2	2	5	30	1	54	2	0	5	3	.625	0	0-1	7	4.06	4.29
1998	2 Tms	NL	71	2	0	18	58.2	268	57	33	33	2	1	2	1	38	3	54	6	1	3	3	.500	0	2-5	17	4.31	5.06
1999	CHN	NL	69	0	0	15	52.0	237	56	35	28	7	1	4	1	25	2	50	2	0	3	1	.750	0	1-7	12	5.01	4.85
2000	CHN	NL	74	0	0	24	58.2	250	46	31	31	6	4	2	2	33	4	52	5	0	7	3	.700	0	2-5	12	3.59	4.76
2001	CHN	NL	48	0	0	9	35.0	165	45	27	24	6	1	3	2	16	1	28	3	0	2	2	.500	0	0-3	8	6.75	6.17
2002	TOR	AL	53	0	0	15	52.1	232	51	29	21	5	3	2	2	26	3	31	5	0	1	2	.333	0	0-2	7	4.31	3.61
2003	2 Tms	NL	69	0	0	22	87.0	365	74	32	26	10	4	2	2	33	7	45	5	0	5	3	.625	0	1-5	8	3.23	2.69
2004	NYA	AL	47	0	0	9	38.2	182	44	28	27	5	1	1	2	20	0	25	1	0	1	1	.500	0	0-1	5	5.66	6.28
2005	NYN	NL	3	0	0	1	2.2	10	1	0	0	0	0	0	1	1	0	2	1	0	0	0	-	0	0-0	1	1.70	0.00
	98	Fla	NL	41	2	0	12	41.0	194	38	25	25	1	1	2	1	32	2	38	5	1	0	3	.000	0	2-3	9	4.44	5.49
	98	ChC	NL	30	0	0	6	17.2	74	19	8	8	1	0	0	0	6	1	16	1	0	3	0	1.000	0	0-2	8	3.99	4.08
	03	Cin	NL	57	0	0	18	72.0	303	61	27	24	9	4	2	2	28	5	41	5	0	5	2	.714	0	1-4	7	3.35	3.00
	03	NYY	AL	12	0	0	4	15.0	62	13	5	2	1	0	0	0	5	2	4	0	0	0	1	.000	0	0-1	1	2.69	1.20
	10 ML YEARS		511	2	0	128	458.1	2046	448	253	225	45	17	19	18	232	22	351	31	1	28	19	.596	0	6-29	78	4.38	4.42

Matt Herges

Pitches: R **Bats:** L **Pos:** RP-28   **Ht:** 6'0" **Wt:** 200 **Born:** 4/1/1970 **Age:** 36

			HOW MUCH HE PITCHED							WHAT HE GAVE UP										THE RESULTS							
Year	Team	Lg	G	GS	CG	GF	IP	BFP	H	R	ER	HR	SH	SF	HB	TBB	IBB	SO	WP	Bk	W	L	Pct	ShO	Sv-Op	Hld	ERC	ERA
2005	Tucsn*	AAA	26	0	0	2	29.0	138	40	15	12	3	1	0	1	11	0	29	1	0	1	2	.333	0	0- -	-	6.31	3.72
1999	LA	NL	17	0	0	9	24.1	104	24	13	11	5	1	0	1	8	0	18	0	0	0	2	.000	0	0-2	1	4.61	4.07
2000	LA	NL	59	4	0	17	110.2	461	100	43	39	7	9	4	6	40	5	75	4	0	11	3	.786	0	1-3	4	3.35	3.17
2001	LA	NL	75	0	0	22	99.1	435	97	39	38	8	4	3	8	46	12	76	2	0	9	8	.529	0	1-8	15	4.23	3.44
2002	MON	NL	62	0	0	25	64.2	298	80	33	29	10	6	1	0	26	8	50	3	0	2	5	.286	0	6-14	9	5.74	4.04
2003	2 Tms	NL	67	0	0	24	79.0	332	68	27	24	3	2	6	3	29	2	68	1	1	3	2	.600	0	3-6	9	2.87	2.62
2004	SF	NL	70	0	0	43	65.1	301	90	44	38	8	7	4	3	21	4	39	2	0	4	5	.444	0	23-31	5	6.29	5.23
2005	2 Tms	NL	28	0	0	7	29.0	132	35	23	23	6	2	2	1	12	1	9	0	0	1	1	.500	0	0-0	3	6.29	7.14
	03	SD	NL	40	0	0	21	44.0	192	40	16	14	2	1	5	2	20	2	40	1	0	2	2	.500	0	3-5	4	3.45	2.86
	03	SF	NL	27	0	0	3	35.0	140	28	11	9	1	1	1	1	9	0	28	0	1	1	0	1.000	0	0-1	5	2.18	2.31
	05	SF	NL	21	0	0	5	21.0	90	23	11	11	2	2	1	0	7	1	6	0	0	1	1	.500	0	0-0	3	4.29	4.71
	05	Ari	NL	7	0	0	2	8.0	42	12	12	12	4	0	1	1	5	0	3	0	0	0	0	-	0	0-0	0	12.23	13.50
	7 ML YEARS		378	4	0	147	472.1	2063	494	222	201	47	31	21	24	182	32	335	12	1	30	26	.536	0	34-64	46	4.38	3.83

Dustin Hermanson

Pitches: R **Bats:** R **Pos:** RP-57   **Ht:** 6'2" **Wt:** 200 **Born:** 12/21/1972 **Age:** 33

			HOW MUCH HE PITCHED							WHAT HE GAVE UP										THE RESULTS							
Year	Team	Lg	G	GS	CG	GF	IP	BFP	H	R	ER	HR	SH	SF	HB	TBB	IBB	SO	WP	Bk	W	L	Pct	ShO	Sv-Op	Hld	ERC	ERA
1995	SD	NL	26	0	0	6	31.2	151	35	26	24	8	3	0	1	22	1	19	3	0	3	1	.750	0	0-0	1	7.19	6.82
1996	SD	NL	8	0	0	4	13.2	62	18	15	13	3	2	3	0	4	0	11	0	1	1	0	1.000	0	0-0	0	6.37	8.56
1997	MON	NL	32	28	1	0	158.1	656	134	68	65	15	10	6	1	66	2	136	4	1	8	8	.500	1	0-0	0	3.32	3.69
1998	MON	NL	32	30	1	0	187.0	768	163	80	65	19	9	3	3	56	3	154	4	3	14	11	.560	0	0-0	1	3.12	3.13
1999	MON	NL	34	34	0	0	216.1	928	225	110	101	20	16	7	7	69	4	145	4	1	9	14	.391	0	0-0	0	4.03	4.20
2000	MON	NL	38	30	2	7	198.0	876	226	128	105	26	10	9	4	75	5	94	5	0	12	14	.462	1	4-7	1	5.10	4.77
2001	STL	NL	33	33	0	0	192.1	801	195	106	95	34	7	2	8	73	3	123	6	0	14	13	.519	0	0-0	0	4.80	4.45
2002	BOS	AL	12	1	0	4	22.0	107	35	19	19	3	0	1	0	7	0	13	2	0	1	1	.500	0	0-1	0	7.52	7.77
2003	2 Tms	NL	32	6	0	12	68.2	291	70	32	31	9	4	2	3	24	4	39	3	0	3	3	.500	0	1-6	1	4.38	4.06
2004	SF	NL	47	18	0	26	131.0	565	132	71	66	15	7	5	3	46	5	102	4	0	6	9	.400	0	17-20	1	4.03	4.53

Year	Team	Lg	G	GS	CG	GF	IP	BFP	H	R	ER	HR	SH	SF	HB	TBB	IBB	SO	WP	Bk	W	L	Pct	ShO	Sv-Op	Hld	ERC	ERA
					HOW MUCH HE PITCHED						WHAT HE GAVE UP												THE RESULTS				
2005	CHA	AL	57	0	0	45	57.1	228	46	17	13	4	3	0	1	17	4	33	3	0	2	4	.333	0	34-39	5	2.48	2.04
03	StL	NL	23	0	0	10	29.2	129	35	18	18	4	2	1	1	14	2	12	1	0	1	2	.333	0	1-6	1	6.04	5.46
03	SF	NL	9	6	0	2	39.0	162	35	14	13	5	2	1	2	10	2	27	2	0	1	2	.667	0	0-0	1	3.25	3.00
11 ML YEARS			351	180	4	104	1276.1	5462	1279	672	597	158	69	40	31	459	31	869	38	6	73	78	.483	2	56-73	12	4.17	4.21

Jeremy Hermida

Bats: L **Throws:** R **Pos:** RF-10; PH-10; LF-4   **Ht:** 6'4" **Wt:** 200 **Born:** 1/30/1984 **Age:** 22

									BATTING													BASERUNNING				AVERAGES		
Year	Team	Lg	G	AB	H	2B	3B	HR	(Hm	Rd)	TB	R	RBI	RC	TBB	IBB	SO	HBP	SH	SF	SB	CS	SB%	GDP	Avg	OBP	Slg
2002	Marlins	R	38	134	30	7	3	0	(-	-)	43	15	14	15	15	0	25	3	0	0	5	0	1.00	3	.224	.316	.321
2002	Jmstwn	A-	13	47	15	2	1	0	(-	-)	19	8	7	7	7	0	10	0	0	0	1	3	.25	0	.319	.407	.404
2003	Grnsbr	A	133	468	133	23	5	6	(-	-)	184	73	49	83	80	3	100	2	4	6	28	2	.93	3	.284	.387	.393
2003	Albq	AAA	1	3	0	0	0	0	(-	-)	0	0	0	0	0	0	3	0	0	0	0	0	-	0	.000	.000	.000
2004	Jupiter	A+	91	340	101	17	1	10	(-	-)	150	53	50	60	42	7	73	5	0	6	10	3	.77	3	.297	.377	.441
2005	Carlina	AA	118	386	113	29	2	18	(-	-)	200	77	63	102	111	5	89	7	1	2	23	2	.92	8	.293	.457	.518
2005	FLA	NL	23	41	12	2	0	4	(4	0)	26	9	11	10	6	1	12	0	0	0	2	0	1.00	1	.293	.383	.634

Anderson Hernandez

Bats: B **Throws:** R **Pos:** 2B-5; SS-2   **Ht:** 5'9" **Wt:** 168 **Born:** 10/30/1982 **Age:** 23

									BATTING													BASERUNNING				AVERAGES		
Year	Team	Lg	G	AB	H	2B	3B	HR	(Hm	Rd)	TB	R	RBI	RC	TBB	IBB	SO	HBP	SH	SF	SB	CS	SB%	GDP	Avg	OBP	Slg
2001	Tigers	R	55	216	57	5	11	0	(-	-)	84	37	18	29	13	0	38	0	3	2	34	8	.81	0	.264	.303	.389
2001	Lkland	A+	7	21	4	0	1	0	(-	-)	6	2	1	0	0	0	8	0	2	0	0	0	-	0	.190	.190	.286
2002	Lkland	A+	123	410	106	13	7	2	(-	-)	139	52	42	43	33	0	102	0	10	5	16	14	.53	2	.259	.310	.339
2003	Lkland	A+	106	380	87	11	4	2	(-	-)	112	47	28	32	27	0	69	0	14	3	15	7	.68	10	.229	.278	.295
2004	Lkland	A+	37	139	43	6	3	0	(-	-)	55	23	14	21	8	0	31	0	2	2	8	0	1.00	2	.309	.342	.396
2004	Erie	AA	101	394	108	19	3	5	(-	-)	148	65	29	51	26	0	89	5	13	2	17	6	.74	5	.274	.326	.376
2005	Bnghtn	AA	66	273	89	14	1	7	(-	-)	126	46	24	43	14	2	58	1	7	1	11	9	.55	0	.326	.360	.462
2005	Norfolk	AAA	66	261	79	6	4	2	(-	-)	99	34	30	38	22	1	46	1	4	4	24	9	.73	2	.303	.354	.379
2005	NYN	NL	6	18	1	0	0	0	(0	0)	1	1	0	0	1	0	4	0	0	0	0	1	.00	0	.056	.105	.056

Felix Hernandez

Pitches: R **Bats:** R **Pos:** SP-12   **Ht:** 6'3" **Wt:** 225 **Born:** 4/8/1986 **Age:** 20

					HOW MUCH HE PITCHED						WHAT HE GAVE UP												THE RESULTS				
Year	Team	Lg	G	GS	CG	GF	IP	BFP	H	R	ER	HR	SH	SF	HB	TBB	IBB	SO	WP	Bk	W	L	Pct	ShO	Sv-Op	Hld	ERC	ERA
2003	Everett	A-	11	7	0	0	55.0	232	43	17	14	2	5	5	8	24	0	73	7	0	7	2	.778	0	0--	-	3.19	2.29
2003	Wisc	A	2	2	0	0	14.0	54	9	4	3	1	6	6	0	3	0	18	0	0	0	0	-	0	0--	-	1.52	1.93
2004	InldEm	A+	16	15	0	1	92.0	387	85	31	28	5	6	2	8	26	0	114	6	0	9	3	.750	0	0--	-	3.24	2.74
2004	SnAnt	AA	10	10	1	0	57.1	240	47	23	21	3	6	0	4	21	0	58	2	0	5	1	.833	1	0--	-	2.92	3.30
2005	Tacom	AAA	19	14	1	0	88.0	374	62	24	22	3	1	2	3	48	0	100	2	2	9	4	.692	0	0--	-	2.69	2.25
2005	SEA	AL	12	12	0	0	84.1	328	61	26	25	5	1	2	2	23	0	77	3	0	4	4	.500	0	0-0	0	2.08	2.67

Jose Hernandez

Bats: R **Throws:** R **Pos:** 1B-45; 3B-21; PH-14; 2B-4; LF-3; RF-3; SS-1   **Ht:** 6'1" **Wt:** 188 **Born:** 7/14/1969 **Age:** 36

									BATTING													BASERUNNING				AVERAGES		
Year	Team	Lg	G	AB	H	2B	3B	HR	(Hm	Rd)	TB	R	RBI	RC	TBB	IBB	SO	HBP	SH	SF	SB	CS	SB%	GDP	Avg	OBP	Slg
1991	TEX	AL	45	98	18	2	1	0	(0	0)	22	8	4	2	3	0	31	0	6	0	0	1	.00	2	.184	.208	.224
1992	CLE	AL	3	4	0	0	0	0	(0	0)	0	0	0	0	0	0	2	0	0	0	0	0	-	0	.000	.000	.000
1994	CHN	NL	56	132	32	2	3	1	(0	1)	43	18	9	11	8	0	29	1	5	0	2	2	.50	4	.242	.291	.326
1995	CHN	NL	93	245	60	11	4	13	(6	7)	118	37	40	31	13	3	69	1	8	2	1	0	1.00	8	.245	.281	.482
1996	CHN	NL	131	331	80	14	1	10	(4	6)	126	52	41	35	24	4	97	1	5	2	4	0	1.00	10	.242	.293	.381
1997	CHN	NL	121	183	50	8	5	7	(4	3)	89	33	26	26	14	2	42	0	1	1	2	5	.29	5	.273	.323	.486
1998	CHN	NL	149	488	124	23	7	23	(11	12)	230	76	75	67	40	3	140	1	2	2	4	6	.40	12	.254	.311	.471
1999	2 Tms	NL	147	508	135	20	2	19	(6	13)	216	79	62	73	52	6	145	5	2	1	11	3	.79	10	.266	.339	.425
2000	MIL	NL	124	446	109	22	1	11	(8	3)	166	51	59	48	41	3	125	6	0	3	3	7	.30	12	.244	.315	.372
2001	MIL	NL	152	542	135	26	2	25	(9	16)	240	67	78	69	39	8	185	2	5	4	5	4	.56	9	.249	.300	.443
2002	MIL	NL	152	525	151	24	2	24	(13	11)	251	72	73	76	52	5	188	4	0	1	3	5	.38	19	.288	.356	.478
2003	3 Tms	NL	150	519	117	18	3	13	(7	6)	180	58	57	41	46	0	177	1	0	5	2	1	.67	16	.225	.287	.347
2004	LA	NL	95	211	61	12	1	13	(5	8)	114	32	29	33	26	6	61	1	0	0	3	1	.75	3	.289	.370	.540
2005	CLE	AL	84	234	54	7	0	6	(3	3)	79	28	31	20	26	2	60	2	3	3	1	3	.25	11	.231	.277	.338
99	ChC	NL	99	342	93	12	2	15	(5	10)	154	57	43	55	40	3	101	5	1	0	7	2	.78	5	.272	.357	.450
99	Atl	NL	48	166	42	8	0	4	(1	3)	62	22	19	18	12	3	44	0	1	1	4	1	.80	5	.253	.302	.373
03	Col	NL	69	257	61	6	1	8	(4	4)	93	33	27	23	27	0	95	0	0	2	1	1	.50	6	.237	.308	.362
03	ChC	NL	23	69	13	3	1	2	(1	1)	24	6	9	4	3	0	26	0	0	0	0	0	-	1	.188	.222	.348
03	Pit	NL	58	193	43	9	1	3	(2	1)	63	19	21	14	16	0	56	1	0	3	1	0	1.00	9	.223	.282	.326
14 ML YEARS			1502	4466	1126	189	32	165	(76	89)	1874	611	584	532	372	40	1351	24	37	24	41	38	.52	121	.252	.312	.420

Livan Hernandez

Pitches: R **Bats:** R **Pos:** SP-35   **Ht:** 6'2" **Wt:** 240 **Born:** 2/20/1975 **Age:** 31

					HOW MUCH HE PITCHED						WHAT HE GAVE UP												THE RESULTS				
Year	Team	Lg	G	GS	CG	GF	IP	BFP	H	R	ER	HR	SH	SF	HB	TBB	IBB	SO	WP	Bk	W	L	Pct	ShO	Sv-Op	Hld	ERC	ERA
1996	FLA	NL	1	0	0	0	3.0	13	3	0	0	0	0	0	0	2	0	2	0	0	0	0	-	0	0-0	0	4.60	0.00
1997	FLA	NL	17	17	0	0	96.1	405	81	39	34	5	4	7	3	38	1	72	0	0	9	3	.750	0	0-0	0	2.96	3.18
1998	FLA	NL	33	33	9	0	234.1	1040	265	133	123	37	8	5	6	104	3	162	4	3	10	12	.455	0	0-0	0	5.58	4.72
1999	2 Tms	NL	30	30	2	0	199.2	886	227	110	103	23	7	6	2	76	5	144	2	2	8	12	.400	0	0-0	0	4.88	4.64

Year	Team	Lg	G	GS	CG	GF	IP	BFP	H	R	ER	HR	SH	SF	HB	TBB	IBB	SO	WP	Bk	W	L	Pct	ShO	Sv-Op	Hld	ERC	ERA
			HOW MUCH HE PITCHED						**WHAT HE GAVE UP**												**THE RESULTS**							
2000	SF	NL	33	33	5	0	240.0	1030	254	114	100	22	12	9	4	73	3	165	3	0	17	11	.607	2	0-0	0	4.01	3.75
2001	SF	NL	34	34	2	0	226.2	1008	266	143	132	24	12	12	3	85	7	138	7	0	13	15	.464	0	0-0	0	5.03	5.24
2002	SF	NL	33	33	5	0	216.0	921	233	113	105	19	14	8	4	71	5	134	1	1	12	16	.429	3	0-0	0	4.26	4.38
2003	MON	NL	33	33	8	0	233.1	967	225	92	83	27	6	4	10	57	3	178	6	1	15	10	.600	0	0-0	0	3.55	3.20
2004	MON	NL	35	35	9	0	255.0	1053	234	105	102	26	11	4	10	83	9	186	1	0	11	15	.423	2	0-0	0	3.52	3.60
2005	WAS	NL	35	35	2	0	246.1	1065	268	116	109	25	15	9	13	84	14	147	3	2	15	10	.600	0	0-0	0	4.54	3.98
99	Fla	NL	20	20	2	0	136.0	612	161	78	72	17	3	4	2	55	3	97	2	1	5	9	.357	0	0-0	0	5.37	4.76
99	SF	NL	10	10	0	0	63.2	274	66	32	31	6	4	2	0	21	2	47	0	1	3	3	.500	0	0-0	0	3.88	4.38
10 ML YEARS			284	283	42	0	1950.2	8388	2056	965	891	208	89	64	55	673	55	1328	27	9	110	104	.514	7	0-0	0	4.31	4.11

Orlando Hernandez

Pitches: R **Bats:** R **Pos:** SP-22; RP-2 **Ht:** 6'2" **Wt:** 220 **Born:** 10/11/1969 **Age:** 36

Year	Team	Lg	G	GS	CG	GF	IP	BFP	H	R	ER	HR	SH	SF	HB	TBB	IBB	SO	WP	Bk	W	L	Pct	ShO	Sv-Op	Hld	ERC	ERA
			HOW MUCH HE PITCHED						**WHAT HE GAVE UP**												**THE RESULTS**							
2005	Charltt*	AAA	1	1	0	0	4.0	16	4	1	1	0	0	0	0	0	0	2	0	0	1	0	1.000	0	0--	-	1.95	2.25
1998	NYA	AL	21	21	3	0	141.0	574	113	53	49	11	3	5	6	52	1	131	5	2	12	4	.750	1	0-0	0	2.96	3.13
1999	NYA	AL	33	33	2	0	214.1	910	187	108	98	24	3	11	8	87	2	157	4	0	17	9	.654	1	0-0	0	3.60	4.12
2000	NYA	AL	29	29	3	0	195.2	820	186	104	98	34	4	5	6	51	2	141	1	0	12	13	.480	0	0-0	0	3.82	4.51
2001	NYA	AL	17	16	0	0	94.2	414	90	51	51	19	2	2	5	42	1	77	0	0	4	7	.364	0	0-0	0	4.87	4.85
2002	NYA	AL	24	22	0	1	146.0	606	131	63	59	17	1	5	8	36	2	113	8	0	8	5	.615	0	1-1	1	3.20	3.64
2004	NYA	AL	15	15	0	0	84.2	359	73	31	31	9	0	1	5	36	0	84	3	0	8	2	.800	0	0-0	0	3.71	3.30
2005	CHA	AL	24	22	0	1	128.1	568	137	77	73	18	3	5	12	50	1	91	3	2	9	9	.500	0	1-1	1	5.12	5.12
7 ML YEARS			163	158	8	2	1004.2	4251	917	487	459	132	16	34	50	354	9	794	24	4	70	49	.588	2	2-2	2	3.80	4.11

Ramon Hernandez

Bats: R **Throws:** R **Pos:** C-97; PH-3 **Ht:** 6'0" **Wt:** 210 **Born:** 5/20/1976 **Age:** 30

Year	Team	Lg	G	AB	H	2B	3B	HR	(Hm	Rd)	TB	R	RBI	RC	TBB	IBB	SO	HBP	SH	SF	SB	CS	SB%	GDP	Avg	OBP	Slg
			BATTING																		**BASERUNNING**				**AVERAGES**		
1999	OAK	AL	40	136	38	7	0	3	(1	2)	54	13	21	20	18	0	11	1	1	2	1	0	1.00	5	.279	.363	.397
2000	OAK	AL	143	419	101	19	0	14	(7	7)	162	52	62	49	38	1	64	7	10	5	1	0	1.00	14	.241	.311	.387
2001	OAK	AL	136	453	115	25	0	15	(5	10)	185	55	60	58	37	3	68	6	9	4	1	1	.50	10	.254	.316	.408
2002	OAK	AL	136	403	94	20	0	7	(3	4)	135	51	42	41	43	1	64	5	3	3	0	0	-	11	.233	.313	.335
2003	OAK	AL	140	483	132	24	1	21	(9	12)	221	70	78	69	33	2	79	12	2	6	0	0	-	14	.273	.331	.458
2004	SD	NL	111	384	106	23	0	18	(10	8)	183	45	63	50	35	0	45	5	4	4	1	0	1.00	16	.276	.341	.477
2005	SD	NL	99	369	107	19	2	12	(5	7)	166	36	58	44	18	0	40	1	1	3	1	0	1.00	14	.290	.322	.450
7 ML YEARS			805	2647	693	137	3	90	(40	50)	1106	322	384	331	222	7	371	37	30	27	5	1	.83	84	.262	.325	.418

Roberto Hernandez

Pitches: R **Bats:** R **Pos:** RP-67 **Ht:** 6'4" **Wt:** 250 **Born:** 11/11/1964 **Age:** 41

Year	Team	Lg	G	GS	CG	GF	IP	BFP	H	R	ER	HR	SH	SF	HB	TBB	IBB	SO	WP	Bk	W	L	Pct	ShO	Sv-Op	Hld	ERC	ERA
			HOW MUCH HE PITCHED						**WHAT HE GAVE UP**												**THE RESULTS**							
1991	CHA	AL	9	3	0	1	15.0	69	18	15	13	1	0	0	0	7	0	6	1	0	1	0	1.000	0	0-0	0	5.19	7.80
1992	CHA	AL	43	0	0	27	71.0	277	45	15	13	4	0	3	4	20	1	68	2	0	7	3	.700	0	12-16	6	1.74	1.65
1993	CHA	AL	70	0	0	67	78.2	314	66	21	20	6	2	2	0	20	1	71	2	0	3	4	.429	0	38-44	0	2.54	2.29
1994	CHA	AL	45	0	0	43	47.2	206	44	29	26	5	0	1	1	19	1	50	1	0	4	4	.500	0	14-20	0	3.66	4.91
1995	CHA	AL	60	0	0	57	59.2	272	63	30	26	9	4	0	3	28	4	84	1	0	3	7	.300	0	32-42	0	5.04	3.92
1996	CHA	AL	72	0	0	61	84.2	355	65	21	18	2	2	2	0	38	5	85	6	0	6	5	.545	0	38-46	0	2.40	1.91
1997	2 Tms		74	0	0	50	80.2	340	67	24	22	7	2	1	1	38	5	82	3	0	10	3	.769	0	31-39	9	3.30	2.45
1998	TB	AL	67	0	0	58	71.1	310	55	33	32	5	4	0	5	41	4	55	1	0	2	6	.250	0	26-35	0	3.43	4.04
1999	TB	AL	72	0	0	66	73.1	321	68	27	25	1	2	3	4	33	1	69	3	0	2	3	.400	0	43-47	0	3.40	3.07
2000	TB	AL	68	0	0	58	73.1	315	76	33	26	9	7	3	3	23	1	61	2	1	4	7	.364	0	32-40	1	4.24	3.19
2001	KC	AL	63	0	0	55	67.2	287	69	34	31	7	1	0	1	26	3	46	6	0	5	6	.455	0	28-34	0	4.23	4.12
2002	KC	AL	53	0	0	42	52.0	227	62	29	25	6	4	1	3	12	2	39	3	0	1	3	.250	0	26-33	0	4.79	4.33
2003	ATL	NL	66	0	0	12	60.0	282	61	36	29	10	4	0	3	43	7	45	0	0	5	3	.625	0	0-4	19	5.95	4.35
2004	PHI	NL	63	0	0	11	56.2	260	66	39	30	9	7	1	1	29	3	44	3	0	3	5	.375	0	0-4	9	5.94	4.76
2005	NYN	NL	67	0	0	20	69.2	291	57	20	20	5	9	2	2	28	4	61	4	0	8	6	.571	0	4-10	18	2.93	2.58
97	CWS	AL	46	0	0	43	48.0	203	38	15	13	5	1	1	1	24	4	47	2	0	5	1	.833	0	27-31	0	3.30	2.44
97	SF	NL	28	0	0	7	32.2	137	29	9	9	2	1	0	0	14	1	35	1	0	5	2	.714	0	4-8	9	3.29	2.48
15 ML YEARS			892	3	0	628	961.1	4126	882	406	356	86	48	19	31	405	42	866	38	1	64	65	.496	0	324-414	62	3.67	3.33

Runelvys Hernandez

Pitches: R **Bats:** R **Pos:** SP-29 **Ht:** 6'1" **Wt:** 205 **Born:** 4/27/1978 **Age:** 28

Year	Team	Lg	G	GS	CG	GF	IP	BFP	H	R	ER	HR	SH	SF	HB	TBB	IBB	SO	WP	Bk	W	L	Pct	ShO	Sv-Op	Hld	ERC	ERA
			HOW MUCH HE PITCHED						**WHAT HE GAVE UP**												**THE RESULTS**							
2002	KC	AL	12	12	0	0	74.1	316	79	36	36	8	1	3	1	22	0	45	2	0	4	4	.500	0	0-0	0	4.16	4.36
2003	KC	AL	16	16	0	0	91.2	397	87	51	47	9	1	4	6	37	0	48	2	1	7	5	.583	0	0-0	0	4.05	4.61
2005	KC	AL	29	29	0	0	159.2	706	172	101	98	18	1	6	7	70	0	88	4	0	8	14	.364	0	0-0	0	4.99	5.52
3 ML YEARS			57	57	0	0	325.2	1419	338	188	181	35	3	13	14	129	0	181	8	1	19	23	.452	0	0-0	0	4.53	5.00

Richard Hidalgo

Bats: R **Throws:** R **Pos:** RF-83; PH-4; CF-3; DH-1 **Ht:** 6'3" **Wt:** 220 **Born:** 6/28/1975 **Age:** 31

								BATTING												BASERUNNING				AVERAGES		
Year	Team	Lg	G	AB	H	2B	3B	HR	(Hm | Rd)	TB	R	RBI	RC	TBB	IBB	SO	HBP	SH	SF	SB	CS	SB%	GDP	Avg	OBP	Slg
1997	HOU	NL	19	62	19	5	0	2	(0 | 2)	30	8	6	11	4	0	18	1	0	0	1	0	1.00	0	.306	.358	.484
1998	HOU	NL	74	211	64	15	0	7	(3 | 4)	100	31	35	34	17	0	37	2	0	4	3	3	.50	5	.303	.355	.474
1999	HOU	NL	108	383	87	25	2	15	(5 | 10)	161	49	56	55	56	2	73	4	0	5	8	5	.62	5	.227	.328	.420
2000	HOU	NL	153	558	175	42	3	44	(16 | 28)	355	118	122	130	56	3	110	21	0	9	13	6	.68	13	.314	.391	.636
2001	HOU	NL	146	512	141	29	3	19	(13 | 6)	233	70	80	81	54	3	107	16	0	11	3	5	.38	15	.275	.356	.455
2002	HOU	NL	114	388	91	17	4	15	(4 | 11)	161	54	48	42	43	1	85	6	0	2	6	2	.75	13	.235	.319	.415
2003	HOU	NL	141	514	159	43	4	28	(11 | 17)	294	91	88	87	58	8	104	8	0	5	9	7	.56	10	.309	.385	.572
2004	2 Tms	NL	144	523	125	26	3	25	(13 | 12)	232	67	82	59	44	7	129	5	0	6	4	4	.50	19	.239	.301	.444
2005	TEX	AL	88	308	68	12	0	16	(9 | 7)	128	43	43	34	26	1	74	4	0	1	1	2	.33	8	.221	.289	.416
04	Hou	NL	58	199	51	15	2	4	(2 | 2)	82	21	30	22	17	4	53	0	0	4	1	2	.33	7	.256	.309	.412
04	NYM	NL	86	324	74	11	1	21	(11 | 10)	150	46	52	37	27	3	76	5	0	2	3	2	.60	12	.228	.296	.463
	9 ML YEARS		987	3459	929	214	19	171	(74 | 97)	1694	531	560	533	358	25	737	67	0	43	48	34	.59	88	.269	.345	.490

Bobby Higginson

Bats: L **Throws:** R **Pos:** RF-6; PH-3; LF-1; DH-1 **Ht:** 5'11" **Wt:** 202 **Born:** 8/18/1970 **Age:** 35

								BATTING												BASERUNNING				AVERAGES		
Year	Team	Lg	G	AB	H	2B	3B	HR	(Hm | Rd)	TB	R	RBI	RC	TBB	IBB	SO	HBP	SH	SF	SB	CS	SB%	GDP	Avg	OBP	Slg
1995	DET	AL	131	410	92	17	5	14	(10 | 4)	161	61	43	56	62	3	107	5	2	7	6	4	.60	5	.224	.329	.393
1996	DET	AL	130	440	141	35	0	26	(15 | 11)	254	75	81	99	65	7	66	1	3	6	6	3	.67	7	.320	.404	.577
1997	DET	AL	146	546	163	30	5	27	(16 | 11)	284	94	101	105	70	2	85	3	0	4	12	7	.63	10	.299	.379	.520
1998	DET	AL	157	612	174	37	4	25	(10 | 15)	294	92	85	100	63	2	101	6	0	4	3	3	.50	16	.284	.355	.480
1999	DET	AL	107	377	90	18	0	12	(8 | 4)	144	51	46	54	64	2	66	2	0	3	4	6	.40	2	.239	.351	.382
2000	DET	AL	154	597	179	44	4	30	(12 | 18)	321	104	102	121	74	6	99	2	2	3	15	3	.83	5	.300	.377	.538
2001	DET	AL	147	541	150	28	6	17	(7 | 10)	241	84	71	91	80	3	65	2	1	9	20	12	.63	8	.277	.367	.445
2002	DET	AL	119	444	125	24	3	10	(6 | 4)	185	50	63	72	41	3	45	6	1	7	12	5	.71	8	.282	.345	.417
2003	DET	AL	130	469	110	13	4	14	(6 | 8)	173	61	52	54	59	3	73	3	1	6	8	2	.80	12	.235	.320	.369
2004	DET	AL	131	448	110	24	2	12	(4 | 8)	174	63	64	72	70	5	84	7	2	4	5	2	.71	10	.246	.353	.388
2005	DET	AL	10	26	2	0	0	0	(0 | 0)	2	1	1	0	1	0	5	0	0	0	0	0	-	0	.077	.111	.077
	11 ML YEARS		1362	4910	1336	270	33	187	(94 | 93)	2233	736	709	824	649	36	796	37	12	52	91	53	.63	83	.272	.358	.455

Aaron Hill

Bats: R **Throws:** R **Pos:** 3B-35; DH-34; 2B-22; SS-16; PH-4; PR-2 **Ht:** 5'11" **Wt:** 195 **Born:** 3/21/1982 **Age:** 24

								BATTING												BASERUNNING				AVERAGES		
Year	Team	Lg	G	AB	H	2B	3B	HR	(Hm | Rd)	TB	R	RBI	RC	TBB	IBB	SO	HBP	SH	SF	SB	CS	SB%	GDP	Avg	OBP	Slg
2003	Auburn	A-	33	122	44	4	0	4	(- | -)	60	22	34	28	16	2	20	6	0	4	1	1	.50	2	.361	.446	.492
2003	Dnedin	A+	32	119	34	7	0	0	(- | -)	41	26	11	15	11	0	10	1	0	3	1	0	1.00	3	.286	.343	.345
2004	Ham	AA	135	480	134	26	2	11	(- | -)	197	78	80	79	63	2	61	11	0	11	3	2	.60	12	.279	.368	.410
2005	Syrcse	AAA	38	156	47	11	0	5	(- | -)	73	22	18	25	4	0	17	6	0	2	2	0	1.00	5	.301	.339	.468
2005	TOR	AL	105	361	99	25	3	3	(3 | 0)	139	49	40	50	34	0	41	5	3	4	2	1	.67	5	.274	.342	.385

Bobby Hill

Bats: B **Throws:** R **Pos:** PH-35; 3B-24; 2B-1 **Ht:** 5'10" **Wt:** 190 **Born:** 4/3/1978 **Age:** 28

								BATTING												BASERUNNING				AVERAGES		
Year	Team	Lg	G	AB	H	2B	3B	HR	(Hm | Rd)	TB	R	RBI	RC	TBB	IBB	SO	HBP	SH	SF	SB	CS	SB%	GDP	Avg	OBP	Slg
2005	Indy*	AAA	35	116	28	4	0	0	(- | -)	32	15	5	12	14	0	29	3	3	1	2	0	1.00	5	.241	.336	.276
2002	CHN	NL	59	190	48	7	2	4	(1 | 3)	71	26	20	24	17	4	42	4	4	0	6	1	.86	5	.253	.327	.374
2003	2 Tms	NL	6	7	2	0	0	0	(0 | 0)	2	1	0	2	2	0	2	0	0	0	0	0	-	1	.286	.444	.286
2004	PIT	NL	126	233	62	7	2	2	(1 | 1)	79	28	27	25	20	2	39	12	1	1	0	3	.00	12	.266	.353	.339
2005	PIT	NL	58	93	25	6	0	0	(0 | 0)	31	12	11	11	9	0	17	2	0	1	0	0	-	3	.269	.343	.333
03	ChC	NL	5	4	1	0	0	0	(0 | 0)	1	0	0	1	1	0	2	0	0	0	0	0	-	1	.250	.400	.250
03	Pit	NL	1	3	1	0	0	0	(0 | 0)	1	1	0	1	1	0	0	0	0	0	0	0	-	0	.333	.500	.333
	4 ML YEARS		249	523	137	20	4	6	(2 | 4)	183	67	58	62	48	6	100	18	5	2	6	4	.60	16	.262	.343	.350

Koyie Hill

Bats: B **Throws:** R **Pos:** C-32; PH-3 **Ht:** 6'0" **Wt:** 190 **Born:** 3/9/1979 **Age:** 27

								BATTING												BASERUNNING				AVERAGES		
Year	Team	Lg	G	AB	H	2B	3B	HR	(Hm | Rd)	TB	R	RBI	RC	TBB	IBB	SO	HBP	SH	SF	SB	CS	SB%	GDP	Avg	OBP	Slg
2005	Tucsn*	AAA	50	168	41	9	1	5	(- | -)	67	22	26	24	23	0	37	1	0	1	3	0	1.00	9	.244	.337	.399
2003	LA	NL	3	3	1	1	0	0	(0 | 0)	2	0	0	0	0	0	2	0	0	0	0	0	-	0	.333	.333	.667
2004	ARI	NL	13	36	9	1	0	1	(1 | 0)	13	3	6	5	2	1	6	0	0	0	1	0	1.00	1	.250	.289	.361
2005	ARI	NL	34	78	17	5	0	0	(0 | 0)	22	6	6	6	11	0	27	0	0	2	0	1	.00	0	.218	.308	.282
	3 ML YEARS		50	117	27	7	0	1	(1 | 0)	37	9	12	11	13	1	35	0	0	2	1	1	.50	1	.231	.303	.316

Rich Hill

Pitches: L **Bats:** L **Pos:** RP-6; SP-4 **Ht:** 6'5" **Wt:** 205 **Born:** 3/11/1980 **Age:** 26

				HOW MUCH HE PITCHED						WHAT HE GAVE UP										THE RESULTS						
Year	Team	Lg	G	GS	CG	GF	IP	BFP	H	R	ER	HR	SH	SF	HB	TBB	IBB	SO	WP	Bk	W	L	Pct	ShO	Sv-Op	Hld	ERC	ERA
2002	Boise	A-	6	5	0	1	14.0	71	15	19	13	0	0	0	1	14	0	12	4	0	0	2	.000	0	0- -	-	6.27	8.36
2003	Boise	A-	14	14	0	0	68.0	293	57	40	33	5	0	0	9	32	0	99	5	1	1	6	.143	0	0- -	-	3.82	4.37
2003	Lansng	A	15	4	0	0	29.1	138	14	12	9	0	3	1	3	36	0	50	9	0	1	0	1.000	0	0- -	-	3.86	2.76
2004	Dytona	A+	28	19	0	0	109.1	488	88	64	49	9	4	2	19	72	0	136	12	5	7	6	.538	0	0- -	-	4.61	4.03
2005	Peoria	A	1	1	0	0	8.0	29	5	2	1	0	0	0	0	0	0	12	0	0	1	0	1.000	0	0- -	-	0.81	1.13

			HOW MUCH HE PITCHED							WHAT HE GAVE UP												THE RESULTS						
Year	Team	Lg	G	GS	CG	GF	IP	BFP	H	R	ER	HR	SH	SF	HB	TBB	IBB	SO	WP	Bk	W	L	Pct	ShO	Sv-Op	Hld	ERC	ERA
2005	WTenn	AA	10	10	0	0	57.2	236	42	22	21	9	1	0	2	21	0	90	0	0	4	3	.571	0	0- -	-	2.96	3.28
2005	Iowa	AAA	11	10	1	0	65.0	262	53	28	26	11	0	1	4	14	0	92	2	0	6	1	.857	0	0- -	-	3.05	3.60
2005	CHN	NL	10	4	0	1	23.2	115	25	24	24	3	1	0	1	17	1	21	0	0	0	2	.000	0	0-0	-	5.81	9.13

Shea Hillenbrand

Bats: R **Throws:** R **Pos:** 1B-67; 3B-54; DH-33; PH-2   **Ht:** 6'1" **Wt:** 211 **Born:** 7/27/1975 **Age:** 30

			BATTING																	BASERUNNING				AVERAGES		
Year	Team	Lg	G	AB	H	2B	3B	HR	(Hm	Rd)	TB	R	RBI	RC	TBB	IBB	SO	HBP	SH	SF	SB	CS	SB%	GDP	Avg	OBP	Slg
2001	BOS	AL	139	468	123	20	2	12	(5	7)	183	52	49	49	13	3	61	7	1	4	3	4	.43	12	.263	.291	.391
2002	BOS	AL	156	634	186	43	4	18	(5	13)	291	94	83	88	25	4	95	12	0	5	4	2	.67	18	.293	.330	.459
2003	2 Tms		134	515	144	35	1	20	(11	9)	241	60	97	66	24	4	70	6	0	9	1	0	1.00	22	.280	.314	.468
2004	ARI	NL	148	562	174	36	3	15	(9	6)	261	68	80	82	24	2	49	12	0	6	2	0	1.00	18	.310	.348	.464
2005	TOR	AL	152	594	173	36	2	18	(13	5)	267	91	82	88	26	2	79	**22**	0	3	5	1	.83	21	.291	.343	.449
03	Bos	AL	49	185	56	17	0	3	(0	3)	82	20	38	27	7	1	26	4	0	4	1	0	1.00	9	.303	.335	.443
03	Ari	NL	85	330	88	18	1	17	(11	6)	159	40	59	39	17	3	44	2	0	5	0	0	-	13	.267	.302	.482
	5 ML YEARS		729	2773	800	170	12	83	(43	40)	1243	365	391	373	112	15	354	59	1	27	15	7	.68	91	.288	.327	.448

Eric Hinske

Bats: L **Throws:** R **Pos:** 1B-100; DH-42; PH-18; PR-1   **Ht:** 6'2" **Wt:** 225 **Born:** 8/5/1977 **Age:** 28

			BATTING																	BASERUNNING				AVERAGES		
Year	Team	Lg	G	AB	H	2B	3B	HR	(Hm	Rd)	TB	R	RBI	RC	TBB	IBB	SO	HBP	SH	SF	SB	CS	SB%	GDP	Avg	OBP	Slg
2002	TOR	AL	151	566	158	38	2	24	(15	9)	272	99	84	103	77	5	138	2	0	5	13	1	.93	12	.279	.365	.481
2003	TOR	AL	124	449	109	45	3	12	(4	8)	196	74	63	66	59	1	104	1	0	5	12	2	.86	11	.243	.329	.437
2004	TOR	AL	155	570	140	23	3	15	(6	9)	214	66	69	60	54	2	109	4	0	6	12	8	.60	14	.246	.312	.375
2005	TOR	AL	147	477	125	31	2	15	(7	8)	205	79	68	71	46	4	121	8	0	6	8	4	.67	8	.262	.333	.430
	4 ML YEARS		577	2062	532	137	10	66	(32	34)	887	318	284	300	236	12	472	15	0	22	45	15	.75	45	.258	.335	.430

Denny Hocking

Bats: B **Throws:** R **Pos:** 2B-13; PH-9; 3B-1; SS-1   **Ht:** 5'10" **Wt:** 183 **Born:** 4/2/1970 **Age:** 36

			BATTING																	BASERUNNING				AVERAGES		
Year	Team	Lg	G	AB	H	2B	3B	HR	(Hm	Rd)	TB	R	RBI	RC	TBB	IBB	SO	HBP	SH	SF	SB	CS	SB%	GDP	Avg	OBP	Slg
2005	Omha*	AAA	68	230	66	14	2	0	(-	-)	84	37	24	32	25	2	44	0	5	3	1	0	1.00	5	.287	.353	.365
1993	MIN	AL	15	36	5	1	0	0	(0	0)	6	7	0	1	6	0	8	0	0	0	1	0	1.00	1	.139	.262	.167
1994	MIN	AL	11	31	10	3	0	0	(0	0)	13	3	2	4	0	0	4	0	0	0	2	0	1.00	1	.323	.323	.419
1995	MIN	AL	9	25	5	0	2	0	(0	0)	9	4	3	2	2	1	2	0	1	0	1	0	1.00	1	.200	.259	.360
1996	MIN	AL	49	127	25	6	0	1	(0	1)	34	16	10	6	8	0	24	0	1	1	3	3	.50	3	.197	.243	.268
1997	MIN	AL	115	253	65	12	4	2	(0	2)	91	28	25	26	18	0	51	1	5	1	3	5	.38	6	.257	.308	.360
1998	MIN	AL	110	198	40	6	1	3	(1	2)	57	32	15	14	16	1	44	0	3	2	2	1	.67	2	.202	.259	.288
1999	MIN	AL	136	386	103	18	2	7	(2	5)	146	47	41	43	22	1	54	3	4	6	11	7	.61	10	.267	.307	.378
2000	MIN	AL	134	373	111	24	4	4	(1	3)	155	52	47	61	48	1	77	0	7	5	7	5	.58	2	.298	.373	.416
2001	MIN	AL	112	327	82	16	2	3	(1	2)	111	34	25	35	29	1	67	2	4	1	6	1	.86	7	.251	.315	.339
2002	MIN	AL	102	260	65	13	0	2	(1	1)	84	28	25	26	24	0	44	1	4	5	0	2	.00	3	.250	.310	.323
2003	MIN	AL	83	188	45	10	2	3	(0	3)	68	22	22	19	15	0	37	0	3	3	0	1	.00	3	.239	.291	.362
2004	COL	NL	55	94	19	2	0	0	(0	0)	21	7	4	5	7	0	20	0	5	0	0	1	.00	3	.202	.257	.223
2005	KC	AL	23	60	16	1	0	0	(0	0)	17	14	7	9	10	0	10	0	1	0	0	1	.00	1	.267	.371	.283
	13 ML YEARS		954	2358	591	112	17	25	(6	19)	812	294	226	251	205	5	442	7	38	24	36	27	.57	43	.251	.310	.344

Trevor Hoffman

Pitches: R **Bats:** R **Pos:** RP-60   **Ht:** 6'0" **Wt:** 205 **Born:** 10/13/1967 **Age:** 38

			HOW MUCH HE PITCHED							WHAT HE GAVE UP												THE RESULTS						
Year	Team	Lg	G	GS	CG	GF	IP	BFP	H	R	ER	HR	SH	SF	HB	TBB	IBB	SO	WP	Bk	W	L	Pct	ShO	Sv-Op	Hld	ERC	ERA
1993	2 Tms	NL	67	0	0	26	90.0	391	80	43	39	10	4	5	1	39	13	79	5	0	4	6	.400	0	5-8	15	3.40	3.90
1994	SD	NL	47	0	0	41	56.0	225	39	16	16	4	1	2	0	20	6	68	3	0	4	4	.500	0	20-23	1	2.02	2.57
1995	SD	NL	55	0	0	51	53.1	218	48	25	23	10	0	0	0	14	3	52	1	0	7	4	.636	0	31-38	0	3.48	3.88
1996	SD	NL	70	0	0	62	88.0	348	50	23	22	6	2	2	2	31	5	111	2	0	9	5	.643	0	42-49	0	1.58	2.25
1997	SD	NL	70	0	0	59	81.1	322	59	25	24	9	2	1	0	24	4	111	7	0	6	4	.600	0	37-44	0	2.27	2.66
1998	SD	NL	66	0	0	61	73.0	274	41	12	12	2	3	0	1	21	2	86	8	0	4	2	.667	0	53-54	1	1.32	1.48
1999	SD	NL	64	0	0	54	67.1	263	48	23	16	5	1	3	0	15	2	73	4	0	2	3	.400	0	40-43	0	1.78	2.14
2000	SD	NL	70	0	0	59	72.1	291	61	29	24	7	3	5	0	11	4	85	4	0	4	7	.364	0	43-50	0	2.18	2.99
2001	SD	NL	62	0	0	55	60.1	248	48	25	23	10	2	2	1	21	2	63	3	0	3	4	.429	0	43-46	0	3.20	3.43
2002	SD	NL	61	0	0	52	59.1	245	52	20	18	2	2	2	1	18	2	69	3	0	2	5	.286	0	38-41	0	2.63	2.73
2003	SD	NL	9	0	0	7	9.0	36	7	2	2	1	0	0	0	3	0	11	0	0	0	0	-	0	0-0	0	2.76	2.00
2004	SD	NL	55	0	0	51	54.2	209	42	14	14	5	2	0	0	8	1	53	2	0	3	3	.500	0	41-45	0	1.92	2.30
2005	SD	NL	60	0	0	54	57.2	240	52	23	19	3	2	3	1	12	1	54	1	0	1	6	.143	0	43-46	0	2.49	2.97
93	Fla	NL	28	0	0	13	35.2	152	24	13	13	5	2	1	0	19	7	26	3	0	2	2	.500	0	2-3	8	2.71	3.28
93	SD	NL	39	0	0	13	54.1	239	56	30	26	5	2	4	1	20	6	53	2	0	2	4	.333	0	3-5	7	3.88	4.31
	13 ML YEARS		756	0	0	632	822.1	3310	627	280	252	74	24	25	7	237	45	915	43	0	49	53	.480	0	436-487	16	2.30	2.76

Aaron Holbert

Bats: R **Throws:** R **Pos:** PH-14; 2B-4; 1B-2; 3B-2; PR-1   **Ht:** 6'0" **Wt:** 160 **Born:** 1/9/1973 **Age:** 33

			BATTING																	BASERUNNING				AVERAGES		
Year	Team	Lg	G	AB	H	2B	3B	HR	(Hm	Rd)	TB	R	RBI	RC	TBB	IBB	SO	HBP	SH	SF	SB	CS	SB%	GDP	Avg	OBP	Slg
1990	JhsCty	R+	54	174	30	4	1	1	(-	-)	39	27	18	11	24	1	31	3	1	1	4	5	.44	2	.172	.282	.224
1991	Sprgfld	A	59	215	48	5	1	1	(-	-)	58	22	24	16	15	0	28	6	1	2	5	8	.38	3	.223	.290	.270
1992	Savann	A	119	438	117	17	4	1	(-	-)	145	53	34	56	40	0	57	8	6	3	62	25	.71	4	.267	.337	.331

Year	Team	Lg	G	AB	H	2B	3B	HR	(Hm	Rd)	TB	R	RBI	RC	TBB	IBB	SO	HBP	SH	SF	SB	CS	SB%	GDP	Avg	OBP	Slg
1993	StPete	A+	121	457	121	18	3	2	(-	-)	151	60	31	50	28	2	61	4	15	1	45	22	.67	6	.265	.312	.330
1994	Cards	R	5	12	2	0	0	0	(-	-)	2	3	0	1	2	0	2	0	0	0	2	0	1.00	0	.167	.286	.167
1994	Ark	AA	59	233	69	10	6	2	(-	-)	97	41	19	33	14	0	25	2	4	1	9	7	.56	5	.296	.340	.416
1995	Lsvlle	AAA	112	401	103	16	4	9	(-	-)	154	57	40	48	20	1	60	5	3	5	14	6	.70	10	.257	.297	.384
1996	Lsvlle	AAA	112	401	103	16	4	9	(-	-)	154	57	40	48	20	1	60	5	3	5	14	6	.70	10	.257	.297	.384
1997	Lsvlle	AAA	93	314	80	14	3	4	(-	-)	112	32	32	33	15	1	56	2	3	4	9	5	.64	9	.255	.290	.357
1998	Orlndo	AA	68	251	72	13	5	3	(-	-)	104	46	34	35	22	0	41	5	4	1	10	14	.42	3	.287	.355	.414
1998	Tacom	AAA	56	229	72	12	0	9	(-	-)	111	38	31	38	12	0	40	3	2	1	6	6	.50	3	.314	.355	.485
1999	Drham	AAA	100	347	108	18	4	12	(-	-)	170	77	56	63	25	0	56	5	8	5	14	5	.74	4	.311	.361	.490
2000	Pwtckt	AAA	80	294	74	13	2	3	(-	-)	100	38	23	29	15	0	54	4	1	0	8	6	.57	4	.252	.297	.340
2000	Calgry	AAA	29	104	29	5	1	4	(-	-)	48	18	16	16	10	0	12	1	0	0	3	4	.43	2	.279	.348	.462
2001	Syrcse	AAA	55	212	52	10	2	2	(-	-)	72	25	19	22	8	1	33	2	5	3	9	0	1.00	4	.245	.276	.340
2002	Tacom	AAA	120	399	124	24	3	7	(-	-)	175	62	42	62	19	0	50	12	7	3	17	13	.57	12	.311	.358	.439
2003	Nashv	AAA	116	397	107	20	7	3	(-	-)	150	57	37	49	19	1	78	8	8	3	29	13	.69	5	.270	.314	.378
2004	Lsvlle	AAA	115	380	103	16	3	4	(-	-)	137	66	46	53	41	1	66	6	3	3	32	14	.70	9	.271	.349	.361
2005	Lsvlle	AAA	68	230	70	14	2	6	(-	-)	106	33	23	38	11	1	31	6	4	1	12	5	.71	5	.304	.351	.461
2005	CIN	NL	22	27	6	3	0	0	(0	0)	9	3	2	2	3	1	8	0	1	1	1	0	1.00	1	.222	.290	.333

Todd Hollandsworth

Bats: L **Throws:** L **Pos:** LF-98; PH-46; RF-9; 1B-2; PR-1   **Ht:** 6'2" **Wt:** 207 **Born:** 4/20/1973 **Age:** 33

Year	Team	Lg	G	AB	H	2B	3B	HR	(Hm	Rd)	TB	R	RBI	RC	TBB	IBB	SO	HBP	SH	SF	SB	CS	SB%	GDP	Avg	OBP	Slg
1995	LA	NL	41	103	24	2	0	5	(3	2)	41	16	13	13	10	2	29	1	0	1	2	1	.67	1	.233	.304	.398
1996	LA	NL	149	478	139	26	4	12	(2	10)	209	64	59	76	41	1	93	2	3	2	21	6	.78	2	.291	.348	.437
1997	LA	NL	106	296	73	20	2	4	(1	3)	109	39	31	28	17	2	60	0	2	2	5	5	.50	8	.247	.286	.368
1998	LA	NL	55	175	47	6	4	3	(1	2)	70	23	20	21	9	0	42	1	2	0	4	3	.57	2	.269	.308	.400
1999	LA	NL	92	261	74	12	2	9	(5	4)	117	39	32	41	24	1	61	1	0	1	5	2	.71	2	.284	.345	.448
2000	2 Tms	NL	137	428	115	20	0	19	(13	6)	192	81	47	63	41	3	99	1	0	1	18	7	.72	8	.269	.333	.449
2001	COL	NL	33	117	43	15	1	6	(3	3)	78	21	19	30	8	2	20	0	0	0	5	0	1.00	1	.368	.408	.667
2002	2 Tms	NL	134	430	122	27	1	16	(11	5)	199	55	67	67	40	4	98	1	3	3	8	8	.50	8	.284	.344	.463
2003	FLA	NL	93	228	58	23	3	3	(1	2)	96	32	20	26	22	4	55	0	2	2	2	3	.40	2	.254	.317	.421
2004	CHN	NL	57	148	47	6	2	8	(3	5)	81	28	22	27	17	3	26	1	1	0	1	1	.50	7	.318	.392	.547
2005	2 Tms	NL	131	303	74	17	2	6	(2	4)	113	26	36	28	23	1	66	1	1	2	4	5	.44	5	.244	.298	.373
00	LA	NL	81	261	61	12	0	8	(6	2)	97	42	24	31	30	2	61	1	0	1	11	4	.73	4	.234	.314	.372
00	Col	NL	56	167	54	8	0	11	(7	4)	95	39	23	32	11	1	38	0	0	0	7	3	.70	4	.323	.365	.569
02	Col	NL	95	298	88	21	1	11	(9	2)	144	39	48	45	26	4	71	1	1	2	7	8	.47	8	.295	.352	.483
02	Tex	AL	39	132	34	6	0	5	(2	3)	55	16	19	22	14	0	27	0	2	1	1	0	1.00	0	.258	.327	.417
05	ChC	NL	107	268	68	17	2	5	(2	3)	104	23	35	27	18	1	53	1	1	2	4	4	.50	4	.254	.301	.388
05	Atl	NL	24	35	6	0	0	1	(0	1)	9	3	1	1	5	0	13	0	0	0	0	1	.00	1	.171	.275	.257
11 ML YEARS			1028	2967	816	174	21	91	(45	46)	1305	424	366	420	252	23	649	9	14	14	75	41	.65	41	.275	.332	.440

Matt Holliday

Bats: R **Throws:** R **Pos:** LF-123; PH-2   **Ht:** 6'4" **Wt:** 235 **Born:** 1/15/1980 **Age:** 26

Year	Team	Lg	G	AB	H	2B	3B	HR	(Hm	Rd)	TB	R	RBI	RC	TBB	IBB	SO	HBP	SH	SF	SB	CS	SB%	GDP	Avg	OBP	Slg
1998	Rckies	R	32	117	40	4	1	5	(-	-)	61	20	23	26	15	2	21	2	0	4	2	1	.67	0	.342	.413	.521
1999	Ashvlle	A	121	444	117	28	0	16	(-	-)	193	76	64	68	53	0	116	9	0	5	10	3	.77	8	.264	.350	.435
2000	Salem	A+	123	460	126	28	2	7	(-	-)	179	64	72	59	43	1	74	2	0	5	11	5	.69	12	.274	.335	.389
2001	Salem	A+	72	255	121	16	1	11	(-	-)	172	36	52	79	33	3	42	3	0	5	11	3	.79	10	.475	.530	.675
2002	Carlina	AA	130	463	128	19	2	10	(-	-)	181	79	64	72	67	2	102	7	1	1	16	2	.89	14	.276	.375	.391
2003	Tulsa	AA	135	522	132	28	5	12	(-	-)	206	65	72	63	43	4	74	6	0	7	15	9	.63	9	.253	.313	.395
2004	ColSpr	AAA	6	22	8	5	0	2	(-	-)	19	8	4	7	5	0	6	0	0	0	2	0	1.00	1	.364	.481	.864
2005	Tulsa	AA	7	26	14	3	0	1	(-	-)	20	6	6	9	1	0	3	0	0	1	1	0	1.00	0	.538	.536	.769
2004	COL	NL	121	400	116	31	3	14	(10	4)	195	65	57	61	31	0	86	6	1	1	3	3	.50	10	.290	.349	.488
2005	COL	NL	125	479	147	24	7	19	(12	7)	242	68	87	88	36	1	79	7	0	4	14	3	.82	11	.307	.361	.505
2 ML YEARS			246	879	263	55	10	33	(22	11)	437	133	144	149	67	1	165	13	1	5	17	6	.74	21	.299	.356	.497

Damon Hollins

Bats: R **Throws:** L **Pos:** CF-80; RF-48; LF-8; PH-7; PR-4   **Ht:** 5'11" **Wt:** 180 **Born:** 6/12/1974 **Age:** 32

Year	Team	Lg	G	AB	H	2B	3B	HR	(Hm	Rd)	TB	R	RBI	RC	TBB	IBB	SO	HBP	SH	SF	SB	CS	SB%	GDP	Avg	OBP	Slg
2005	Drham*	AAA	22	81	24	5	0	2	(-	-)	35	11	17	15	15	0	17	2	0	1	3	2	.60	3	.296	.414	.432
1998	2 Tms	NL	8	15	3	0	0	0	(0	0)	3	1	2	0	0	0	3	0	0	0	0	1	.00	0	.200	.200	.200
2004	ATL	NL	7	22	8	2	0	0	(0	0)	10	3	5	2	0	0	4	0	1	0	0	0	-	0	.364	.364	.455
2005	TB	AL	120	342	85	17	1	13	(5	8)	143	44	46	41	23	0	63	1	1	2	8	1	.89	8	.249	.296	.418
98	LA	NL	5	9	2	0	0	0	(0	0)	2	1	2	0	0	0	2	0	0	0	0	1	.00	0	.222	.222	.222
98	Atl	NL	3	6	1	0	0	0	(0	0)	1	0	0	0	0	0	1	0	0	0	0	0	-	0	.167	.167	.167
3 ML YEARS			135	379	96	19	1	13	(5	8)	156	48	53	43	23	0	70	1	2	2	8	2	.80	8	.253	.296	.412

Kevin Hooper

Bats: R **Throws:** R **Pos:** LF-3; SS-2; 2B-1; PR-1   **Ht:** 5'10" **Wt:** 160 **Born:** 12/7/1976 **Age:** 29

Year	Team	Lg	G	AB	H	2B	3B	HR	(Hm	Rd)	TB	R	RBI	RC	TBB	IBB	SO	HBP	SH	SF	SB	CS	SB%	GDP	Avg	OBP	Slg
1999	Utica	A-	73	289	81	18	6	0	(-	-)	111	52	22	45	39	0	35	4	2	3	14	8	.64	2	.280	.370	.384
2000	Kane	A	123	457	114	25	6	3	(-	-)	160	73	38	67	73	2	83	6	9	1	17	2	.89	6	.249	.359	.350
2001	Kane	A	17	65	19	2	0	0	(-	-)	21	11	4	9	11	0	13	0	0	1	3	1	.75	0	.292	.390	.323
2001	Portlnd	AA	117	468	144	19	6	2	(-	-)	181	70	39	77	59	4	78	7	7	2	24	12	.67	8	.308	.392	.387

							BATTING																BASERUNNING				AVERAGES		
Year	Team	Lg	G	AB	H	2B	3B	HR	(Hm	Rd)	TB	R	RBI	RC	TBB	IBB	SO	HBP	SH	SF	SB	CS	SB%	GDP	Avg	OBP	Slg
2002	Calgry	AAA	117	452	130	21	3	2	(-	-)	163	70	38	58	34	0	51	4	6	2	17	10	.63	7	.288	.341	.361
2003	Albq	AAA	130	493	131	9	4	1	(-	-)	151	77	54	55	35	3	62	10	9	4	25	9	.74	5	.266	.325	.306
2004	Buffalo	AAA	29	87	17	1	0	0	(-	-)	18	6	4	3	5	0	11	0	3	0	1	1	.75	1	.195	.239	.207
2004	Omha	AAA	27	92	15	2	0	0	(-	-)	17	12	4	3	9	0	14	1	3	0	2	2	.50	1	.163	.245	.185
2004	Albq	AAA	39	155	43	3	2	0	(-	-)	50	21	17	17	14	0	24	0	5	1	6	5	.55	1	.277	.335	.323
2005	Toledo	AAA	85	313	75	13	2	1	(-	-)	95	41	27	31	22	1	37	2	10	3	16	4	.80	1	.240	.291	.304
2005	DET	AL	6	5	1	0	0	0	(0	0)	1	0	0	1	0	0	1	0	2	0	0	0	-	0	.200	.200	.200

Joe Horgan

Pitches: L **Bats:** L **Pos:** RP-8　　　　　　　　**Ht:** 6'1" **Wt:** 200 **Born:** 6/7/1977 **Age:** 29

			HOW MUCH HE PITCHED						WHAT HE GAVE UP										THE RESULTS						
Year	Team	Lg	G	GS	CG	GF	IP	BFP	H	R	ER	HR	SH	SF	HB	TBB	IBB	SO	WP	Bk	W	L	Pct	ShO	Sv-Op	Hld	ERC	ERA
1996	Burlgtn	R+	23	0	0	18	34.1	157	37	25	16	1	0	0	4	9	0	48	4	0	1	2	.333	0	7--	-	3.70	4.19
1997	Wtrtwn	A-	15	4	0	2	38.1	179	48	31	26	4	2	2	1	18	1	31	4	1	0	1	.000	0	0--	-	5.90	6.10
1997	Kinston	A	4	2	0	0	17.1	83	23	15	14	1	1	1	1	9	0	9	0	0	1	2	.333	0	0--	-	6.40	7.27
1998	Clmbs	A	22	1	0	9	34.0	134	19	9	9	3	0	0	0	21	0	27	7	0	2	1	.667	0	0--	-	2.63	2.38
1999	Bkrsfld	A+	25	19	1	1	117.1	520	129	76	68	18	2	2	10	43	0	101	5	2	6	10	.375	0	0--	-	5.29	5.22
2000	SnJos	A+	27	27	1	0	166.1	739	190	104	85	15	5	6	14	66	0	92	14	0	14	10	.583	0	0--	-	5.25	4.60
2000	Shreve	AA	1	0	0	1	5.1	20	2	2	2	0	0	0	0	2	1	3	0	0	0	0	-	0	0--	-	0.71	3.38
2001	Shreve	AA	31	14	0	3	103.2	438	97	51	42	10	6	7	4	27	1	61	2	0	3	5	.375	0	1--	-	3.23	3.65
2001	Fresno	AAA	3	1	0	0	7.2	36	11	5	5	1	0	0	0	3	0	5	0	0	0	0	-	0	0--	-	6.93	5.87
2002	Fresno	AAA	27	4	0	6	57.2	258	65	38	38	8	4	2	4	21	0	37	5	0	2	2	.500	0	0--	-	5.22	5.93
2002	Shreve	AA	10	10	1	0	56.0	257	69	35	27	5	4	4	3	20	1	35	0	0	4	3	.571	0	0--	-	5.29	4.34
2003	Fresno	AAA	55	0	0	23	74.2	333	80	51	47	9	4	4	5	30	1	65	7	1	7	7	.500	0	3--	-	4.87	5.67
2004	Memp	AAA	10	0	0	6	9.2	45	14	7	7	3	1	1	0	3	0	8	1	0	1	0	1.000	0	0--	-	8.11	6.52
2004	Edmtn	AAA	13	0	0	4	17.0	70	15	6	6	2	0	0	2	4	0	11	1	0	1	0	1.000	0	0--	-	3.41	3.18
2005	NewOr	AAA	46	2	0	15	63.1	288	68	35	29	9	8	0	5	30	3	48	1	0	4	3	.571	0	3--	-	5.33	4.12
2004	MON	NL	47	0	0	12	40.0	178	35	18	14	5	1	0	3	22	3	30	0	0	4	1	.800	0	2-3	12	4.27	3.15
2005	WAS	NL	8	0	0	1	6.0	44	19	15	14	0	1	1	1	4	0	5	1	0	0	0	-	0	0-0	0	19.09	21.00
	2 ML YEARS		55	0	0	13	46.0	222	54	33	28	5	2	1	4	26	3	35	1	0	4	1	.800	0	2-3	12	5.93	5.48

D.J. Houlton

Pitches: R **Bats:** R **Pos:** SP-19; RP-16　　　　　　**Ht:** 6'4" **Wt:** 220 **Born:** 8/12/1979 **Age:** 26

			HOW MUCH HE PITCHED						WHAT HE GAVE UP										THE RESULTS						
Year	Team	Lg	G	GS	CG	GF	IP	BFP	H	R	ER	HR	SH	SF	HB	TBB	IBB	SO	WP	Bk	W	L	Pct	ShO	Sv-Op	Hld	ERC	ERA
2001	Mrtnsvl	R+	13	13	1	0	72.0	290	67	24	20	7	1	2	3	7	0	71	2	0	5	4	.556	0	0--	-	2.68	2.50
2001	Mich	A	1	1	0	0	5.0	23	7	5	3	0	0	0	0	1	0	4	0	0	1	0	1.000	0	0--	-	4.69	5.40
2002	Mich	A	35	16	0	7	140.2	572	120	57	49	12	2	4	3	30	0	138	4	0	14	5	.737	0	2--	-	2.55	3.14
2003	RdRck	AA	18	18	1	0	109.0	448	93	45	42	11	4	4	3	28	1	101	2	0	5	4	.556	1	0--	-	2.81	3.47
2003	NewOrl	AAA	11	11	0	0	61.2	274	70	39	37	12	8	6	3	19	0	48	3	1	3	4	.429	0	0--	-	5.31	5.40
2004	RdRck	AA	28	28	3	0	159.0	665	141	59	52	14	7	2	12	47	2	159	4	0	12	5	.706	1	0--	-	3.25	2.94
2005	LAN	NL	35	19	0	4	129.0	578	145	79	74	21	11	5	8	52	3	90	2	0	6	9	.400	0	0-0	0	5.51	5.16

Ryan Howard

Bats: L **Throws:** L **Pos:** 1B-84; PH-8　　　　　　**Ht:** 6'4" **Wt:** 230 **Born:** 11/19/1979 **Age:** 26

							BATTING																BASERUNNING				AVERAGES		
Year	Team	Lg	G	AB	H	2B	3B	HR	(Hm	Rd)	TB	R	RBI	RC	TBB	IBB	SO	HBP	SH	SF	SB	CS	SB%	GDP	Avg	OBP	Slg
2001	Batvia	A-	48	169	46	7	3	6	(-	-)	77	26	35	31	30	5	55	2	0	2	0	0	-	1	.272	.384	.456
2002	Lakwd	A	135	493	138	20	6	19	(-	-)	227	56	87	82	66	13	145	5	1	5	5	4	.56	9	.280	.367	.460
2003	Clrwtr	A+	130	490	149	32	1	23	(-	-)	252	67	82	88	50	9	151	8	0	5	0	0	-	12	.304	.374	.514
2004	Rdng	AA	102	374	111	18	1	37	(-	-)	242	73	102	86	46	6	129	10	0	3	1	2	.33	2	.297	.386	.647
2004	S-WB	AAA	29	111	30	10	0	9	(-	-)	67	21	29	21	14	1	37	2	0	0	0	0	-	4	.270	.362	.604
2005	S-WB	AAA	61	210	78	19	0	16	(-	-)	145	38	54	63	39	6	66	3	0	5	0	0	-	3	.371	.467	.690
2004	PHI	NL	19	39	11	5	0	2	(1	1)	22	5	5	7	2	0	13	1	0	0	0	0	-	2	.282	.333	.564
2005	PHI	NL	88	312	90	17	2	22	(11	11)	177	52	63	50	33	8	100	1	0	2	0	1	.00	6	.288	.356	.567
	2 ML YEARS		107	351	101	22	2	24	(12	12)	199	57	68	57	35	8	113	2	0	2	0	1	.00	8	.288	.354	.567

J.P. Howell

Pitches: L **Bats:** L **Pos:** SP-15　　　　　　　　**Ht:** 6'0" **Wt:** 175 **Born:** 4/25/1983 **Age:** 23

			HOW MUCH HE PITCHED						WHAT HE GAVE UP										THE RESULTS						
Year	Team	Lg	G	GS	CG	GF	IP	BFP	H	R	ER	HR	SH	SF	HB	TBB	IBB	SO	WP	Bk	W	L	Pct	ShO	Sv-Op	Hld	ERC	ERA
2004	Idaho	R+	6	4	0	0	26.0	101	16	9	8	1	0	0	2	12	0	38	9	0	3	1	.750	0	0--	-	2.33	2.77
2005	Wichta	AA	3	3	0	0	18.0	71	12	5	5	2	0	0	1	5	0	23	2	0	2	0	1.000	0	0--	-	2.18	2.50
2005	Omha	AAA	7	7	0	0	37.2	172	40	19	17	1	2	0	1	19	0	29	3	0	3	1	.750	0	0--	-	4.30	4.06
2005	Hi Dsrt	A+	8	8	0	0	46.0	195	33	16	10	2	0	0	3	24	0	48	5	1	3	1	.750	0	0--	-	2.86	1.96
2005	KC	AL	15	15	0	0	72.2	328	73	55	50	9	3	3	6	39	0	54	7	0	3	5	.375	0	0-0	0	5.18	6.19

Bob Howry

Pitches: R **Bats:** L **Pos:** RP-79　　　　　　　　**Ht:** 6'5" **Wt:** 220 **Born:** 8/4/1973 **Age:** 32

			HOW MUCH HE PITCHED						WHAT HE GAVE UP										THE RESULTS						
Year	Team	Lg	G	GS	CG	GF	IP	BFP	H	R	ER	HR	SH	SF	HB	TBB	IBB	SO	WP	Bk	W	L	Pct	ShO	Sv-Op	Hld	ERC	ERA
1998	CHA	AL	44	0	0	15	54.1	217	37	20	19	7	2	3	2	19	2	51	2	0	0	3	.000	0	9-11	19	2.50	3.15
1999	CHA	AL	69	0	0	54	67.2	298	58	34	27	8	3	1	3	38	3	80	3	1	5	3	.625	0	28-34	1	4.11	3.59
2000	CHA	AL	65	0	0	29	71.0	289	54	26	25	6	2	4	4	29	2	60	2	0	2	4	.333	0	7-12	14	2.96	3.17
2001	CHA	AL	69	0	0	23	78.2	346	85	41	41	11	4	3	4	30	9	64	6	0	4	5	.444	0	5-11	21	4.78	4.69

Year	Team	Lg	G	GS	CG	GF	IP	BFP	H	R	ER	HR	SH	SF	HB	TBB	IBB	SO	WP	Bk	W	L	Pct	ShO	Sv-Op	Hld	ERC	ERA
2002	2 Tms	AL	67	0	0	26	68.2	292	67	37	32	9	4	6	5	21	4	45	2	0	3	5	.375	0	0-1	15	4.00	4.19
2003	BOS	AL	4	0	0	3	4.1	27	11	6	6	1	0	1	0	3	1	4	0	0	0	0	-	0	0-1	0	16.51	12.46
2004	CLE	AL	37	0	0	6	42.2	178	37	14	13	5	1	1	2	12	0	39	0	0	4	2	.667	0	0-2	8	3.15	2.74
2005	CLE	AL	79	0	0	24	73.0	277	49	23	20	4	3	2	0	16	1	48	0	0	7	4	.636	0	3-5	29	1.58	2.47
02	CWS	AL	47	0	0	17	50.2	209	45	22	22	7	1	4	3	17	2	31	1	0	2	2	.500	0	0-0	10	3.72	3.91
02	BOS	AL	20	0	0	9	18.0	83	22	15	10	2	3	2	2	4	2	14	1	0	1	3	.250	0	0-1	5	4.79	5.00
8 ML YEARS			434	0	0	180	460.1	1924	398	201	183	51	19	21	20	168	22	391	15	1	25	26	.490	0	52-77	107	3.38	3.58

Justin Huber

Bats: R **Throws:** R **Pos:** 1B-19; DH-4; PH-3   **Ht:** 6'5" **Wt:** 190 **Born:** 7/1/1982 **Age:** 23

Year	Team	Lg	G	AB	H	2B	3B	HR	(Hm	Rd)	TB	R	RBI	RC	TBB	IBB	SO	HBP	SH	SF	SB	CS	SB%	GDP	Avg	OBP	Slg
2001	Kngspt	R+	47	159	50	11	1	7	(-	-)	84	24	31	36	17	0	42	13	1	4	4	2	.67	4	.314	.415	.528
2001	StLuci	A+	2	6	0	0	0	0	(-	-)	0	0	0	0	0	0	4	0	0	0	0	0	-	0	.000	.000	.000
2001	Bklyn	A-	3	9	0	0	0	0	(-	-)	0	0	0	0	0	0	4	0	0	0	0	0	-	1	.000	.000	.000
2002	StLuci	A+	28	100	27	2	1	3	(-	-)	40	15	15	16	11	0	18	6	0	2	0	0	-	3	.270	.370	.400
2002	Bklyn	A-	95	330	96	22	2	11	(-	-)	155	49	78	67	45	10	81	23	0	4	1	2	.33	5	.291	.408	.470
2003	StLuci	A+	50	183	52	15	0	9	(-	-)	94	26	36	35	17	0	30	9	0	2	1	1	.50	9	.284	.370	.514
2003	Bnghtn	AA	55	193	51	13	0	6	(-	-)	82	16	36	29	19	0	54	7	3	1	0	2	.00	4	.264	.350	.425
2004	StLuci	A+	13	48	12	2	0	2	(-	-)	20	10	8	7	5	0	8	1	0	0	1	0	1.00	0	.250	.333	.417
2004	Bnghtn	AA	70	236	64	16	1	11	(-	-)	115	44	33	50	46	4	57	12	0	1	2	2	.50	5	.271	.414	.487
2004	Norfolk	AAA	5	16	5	2	0	0	(-	-)	7	3	3	3	3	0	3	0	0	0	0	0	-	0	.313	.421	.438
2005	Wichta	AA	88	335	115	22	3	16	(-	-)	191	68	74	82	51	2	70	5	0	5	7	3	.70	11	.343	.432	.570
2005	Omha	AAA	32	113	31	6	1	7	(-	-)	60	19	23	23	16	1	33	2	0	0	3	0	1.00	3	.274	.374	.531
2005	KC	AL	25	78	17	3	0	0	(0	0)	20	6	6	4	5	0	20	1	0	1	0	0	-	1	.218	.271	.256

Ken Huckaby

Bats: R **Throws:** R **Pos:** C-35; PH-1   **Ht:** 6'1" **Wt:** 205 **Born:** 1/27/1971 **Age:** 35

Year	Team	Lg	G	AB	H	2B	3B	HR	(Hm	Rd)	TB	R	RBI	RC	TBB	IBB	SO	HBP	SH	SF	SB	CS	SB%	GDP	Avg	OBP	Slg
2005	Syrcse*	AAA	15	56	15	1	0	1	(-	-)	19	3	3	5	1	0	13	0	1	0	0	0	-	1	.268	.281	.339
2001	ARI	NL	1	1	0	0	0	0	(0	0)	0	0	0	0	0	0	1	0	0	0	0	0	-	0	.000	.000	.000
2002	TOR	AL	88	273	67	6	1	3	(1	2)	84	29	22	19	9	1	44	0	1	0	0	0	-	10	.245	.270	.308
2003	TOR	AL	5	11	2	1	0	0	(0	0)	3	1	2	1	0	0	2	0	0	0	0	0	-	0	.182	.182	.273
2004	2 Tms	AL	24	50	7	3	0	0	(0	0)	10	4	0	4	5	0	12	0	0	0	0	0	-	1	.140	.218	.200
2005	TOR	AL	35	87	18	4	0	0	(0	0)	22	8	6	3	5	0	19	0	4	0	0	0	-	4	.207	.250	.253
04	Tex	AL	16	38	5	2	0	0	(0	0)	7	3	0	0	5	0	12	0	0	0	0	0	-	0	.132	.233	.184
04	Bal	AL	8	12	2	1	0	0	(0	0)	3	1	0	0	0	0	0	0	0	0	0	0	-	0	.167	.167	.250
5 ML YEARS			153	422	94	14	1	3	(1	2)	119	42	30	23	19	1	78	0	5	0	0	0	-	15	.223	.256	.282

Luke Hudson

Pitches: R **Bats:** R **Pos:** SP-16; RP-3   **Ht:** 6'3" **Wt:** 195 **Born:** 5/2/1977 **Age:** 29

Year	Team	Lg	G	GS	CG	GF	IP	BFP	H	R	ER	HR	SH	SF	HB	TBB	IBB	SO	WP	Bk	W	L	Pct	ShO	Sv-Op	Hld	ERC	ERA
2005	Chatt*	AA	1	1	0	0	6.2	27	6	4	4	2	0	0	1	1	0	7	0	0	0	1	.000	0	0--	-	4.52	5.40
2002	CIN	NL	3	0	0	0	6.0	28	5	5	3	1	0	0	0	6	0	7	2	0	0	0	-	0	0-0	1	6.15	4.50
2004	CIN	NL	9	9	0	0	48.1	204	36	16	13	3	2	2	2	25	1	38	5	0	4	2	.667	0	0-0	0	3.01	2.42
2005	CIN	NL	19	16	0	1	84.2	380	83	62	60	14	5	4	11	50	2	53	5	0	6	9	.400	0	0-0	0	5.88	6.38
3 ML YEARS			31	25	0	1	139.0	612	124	83	76	18	7	6	13	81	3	98	12	0	10	11	.476	0	0-0	1	4.82	4.92

Orlando Hudson

Bats: B **Throws:** R **Pos:** 2B-130; PH-8   **Ht:** 6'0" **Wt:** 185 **Born:** 12/12/1977 **Age:** 28

Year	Team	Lg	G	AB	H	2B	3B	HR	(Hm	Rd)	TB	R	RBI	RC	TBB	IBB	SO	HBP	SH	SF	SB	CS	SB%	GDP	Avg	OBP	Slg
2002	TOR	AL	54	192	53	10	5	4	(2	2)	85	20	23	30	11	0	27	2	0	2	0	1	.00	6	.276	.319	.443
2003	TOR	AL	142	474	127	21	6	9	(5	4)	187	54	57	64	39	1	87	5	0	3	5	4	.56	13	.268	.328	.395
2004	TOR	AL	135	489	132	32	7	12	(5	7)	214	73	58	71	51	0	98	4	3	4	7	3	.70	12	.270	.341	.438
2005	TOR	AL	131	461	125	25	5	10	(4	6)	190	62	63	59	30	1	65	3	0	7	7	1	.88	10	.271	.315	.412
4 ML YEARS			462	1616	437	88	23	35	(16	19)	676	209	201	224	131	2	277	14	3	16	19	9	.68	41	.270	.328	.418

Tim Hudson

Pitches: R **Bats:** R **Pos:** SP-29   **Ht:** 6'1" **Wt:** 164 **Born:** 7/14/1975 **Age:** 30

Year	Team	Lg	G	GS	CG	GF	IP	BFP	H	R	ER	HR	SH	SF	HB	TBB	IBB	SO	WP	Bk	W	L	Pct	ShO	Sv-Op	Hld	ERC	ERA
1999	OAK	AL	21	21	1	0	136.1	580	121	56	49	8	1	2	4	62	2	132	6	0	11	2	.846	0	0-0	0	3.50	3.23
2000	OAK	AL	32	32	2	0	202.1	847	169	100	93	24	5	7	7	82	5	169	7	0	20	6	.769	2	0-0	0	3.43	4.14
2001	OAK	AL	35	35	3	0	235.0	980	216	100	88	20	12	8	6	71	5	181	9	1	18	9	.667	0	0-0	0	3.22	3.37
2002	OAK	AL	34	34	4	0	238.1	983	237	87	79	19	6	5	8	62	9	152	7	1	15	9	.625	2	0-0	0	3.51	2.98
2003	OAK	AL	34	34	3	0	240.0	967	197	84	72	15	11	2	10	61	9	162	6	0	16	7	.696	2	0-0	0	2.47	2.70
2004	OAK	AL	27	27	3	0	188.2	793	194	82	74	8	7	4	12	44	3	103	4	1	12	6	.667	2	0-0	0	3.44	3.53
2005	ATL	NL	29	29	2	0	192.0	817	194	79	75	20	9	1	9	65	5	115	4	0	14	9	.609	0	0-0	0	4.12	3.52
7 ML YEARS			212	212	18	0	1432.2	5967	1328	588	530	114	51	29	56	447	38	1014	43	3	106	48	.688	8	0-0	0	3.34	3.33

Aubrey Huff

Bats: L **Throws:** R **Pos:** RF-97; DH-33; 1B-25; PH-6; 3B-4   **Ht:** 6'4" **Wt:** 231 **Born:** 12/20/1976 **Age:** 29

										BATTING										BASERUNNING				AVERAGES		
Year	Team	Lg	G	AB	H	2B	3B	HR	(Hm	Rd)	TB	R	RBI	RC	TBB	IBB	SO	HBP	SH	SF	SB	CS	SB%	GDP	Avg	OBP	Slg
2000	TB	AL	39	122	35	7	0	4	(3	1)	54	12	14	15	5	1	18	1	0	1	0	0	-	6	.287	.318	.443
2001	TB	AL	111	411	102	25	1	8	(5	3)	153	42	45	37	23	2	72	0	0	0	1	3	.25	18	.248	.288	.372
2002	TB	AL	113	454	142	25	0	23	(17	6)	236	67	59	66	37	7	55	1	0	2	4	1	.80	17	.313	.364	.520
2003	TB	AL	162	636	198	47	3	34	(15	19)	353	91	107	112	53	17	80	8	0	9	2	3	.40	19	.311	.367	.555
2004	TB	AL	157	600	178	27	2	29	(16	13)	296	92	104	96	56	6	74	6	0	5	5	1	.83	10	.297	.360	.493
2005	TB	AL	154	575	150	26	2	22	(9	13)	246	70	92	77	49	13	88	5	0	7	8	7	.53	12	.261	.321	.428
6 ML YEARS			736	2798	805	157	8	120	(65	55)	1338	374	421	403	223	46	387	21	0	24	20	15	.57	82	.288	.342	.478

Travis Hughes

Pitches: R **Bats:** R **Pos:** RP-14   **Ht:** 6'5" **Wt:** 240 **Born:** 5/25/1978 **Age:** 28

			HOW MUCH HE PITCHED					WHAT HE GAVE UP											THE RESULTS						
Year	Team	Lg	G	GS	CG	GF	IP	BFP	H	R	ER	HR	SH	SF	HB	TBB	IBB	SO	WP	Bk	W	L	Pct	ShO	Sv-Op	Hld	ERC	ERA
1998	Pulaski	R+	22	3	0	17	41.2	188	30	25	18	2	0	0	4	25	1	48	8	3	2	6	.250	0	2--	-	3.11	3.89
1999	Savann	A	30	23	1	5	157.0	646	127	60	49	9	3	3	11	54	0	150	9	2	11	7	.611	0	2--	-	2.85	2.81
2000	Charltt	A+	39	14	19	19	126.1	553	122	76	62	9	6	1	12	54	3	96	11	0	9	9	.500	0	9--	-	4.13	4.42
2001	Tulsa	AA	47	5	0	29	87.1	393	91	52	45	8	3	4	4	45	2	86	2	1	5	7	.417	0	8--	-	4.86	4.64
2002	Tulsa	AA	26	26	1	0	143.1	637	139	68	56	11	1	2	7	82	0	137	3	0	9	7	.563	1	0--	-	4.65	3.52
2003	Frisco	AA	24	10	1	3	74.0	330	81	47	41	6	2	5	5	26	1	58	0	0	4	8	.333	1	0--	-	4.47	4.99
2003	Okla	AAA	11	11	0	0	57.2	278	79	41	35	4	3	3	5	27	0	36	1	0	1	3	.250	0	0--	-	6.66	5.46
2004	Frisco	AA	40	0	0	19	62.2	282	63	34	26	4	0	1	1	33	5	66	6	1	3	6	.333	0	7--	-	4.20	3.73
2004	Okla	AAA	13	0	0	2	25.2	107	21	15	15	2	0	0	0	9	0	24	2	0	1	2	.333	0	0--	-	2.72	5.26
2005	NewOr	AAA	52	0	0	27	59.2	251	47	25	20	3	1	0	4	25	1	73	4	0	2	5	.286	0	13--	-	2.89	3.02
2004	TEX	AL	2	0	0	1	1.1	10	4	2	2	0	0	0	0	2	0	4	0	0	0	0	-	0	0-0	0	22.07	13.50
2005	WAS	NL	14	0	0	0	13.0	64	18	8	8	4	1	0	1	8	1	8	0	0	1	1	.500	0	0-1	0	9.47	5.54
2 ML YEARS			16	0	0	1	14.1	74	22	10	10	4	1	0	1	10	1	12	0	0	1	1	.500	0	0-1	0	10.63	6.28

Torii Hunter

Bats: R **Throws:** R **Pos:** CF-93; DH-5; PH-1   **Ht:** 6'2" **Wt:** 205 **Born:** 7/18/1975 **Age:** 30

										BATTING										BASERUNNING				AVERAGES		
Year	Team	Lg	G	AB	H	2B	3B	HR	(Hm	Rd)	TB	R	RBI	RC	TBB	IBB	SO	HBP	SH	SF	SB	CS	SB%	GDP	Avg	OBP	Slg
1997	MIN	AL	1	0	0	0	0	0	(0	0)	0	0	0	0	0	0	0	0	0	0	0	0	-	0	-	-	-
1998	MIN	AL	6	17	4	1	0	0	(0	0)	5	0	2	1	2	0	6	0	0	0	0	1	.00	1	.235	.316	.294
1999	MIN	AL	135	384	98	17	2	9	(2	7)	146	52	35	44	26	1	72	6	1	5	10	6	.63	9	.255	.309	.380
2000	MIN	AL	99	336	94	14	7	5	(4	1)	137	44	44	39	18	2	68	2	0	2	4	3	.57	13	.280	.318	.408
2001	MIN	AL	148	564	147	32	5	27	(13	14)	270	82	92	79	29	0	125	8	1	1	9	6	.60	12	.261	.306	.479
2002	MIN	AL	148	561	162	37	4	29	(13	16)	294	89	94	85	35	3	118	5	0	3	23	8	.74	17	.289	.334	.524
2003	MIN	AL	154	581	145	31	4	26	(12	14)	262	83	102	76	50	7	106	5	0	6	6	7	.46	15	.250	.312	.451
2004	MIN	AL	138	520	141	37	0	23	(14	9)	247	79	81	69	40	4	101	7	0	2	21	7	.75	23	.271	.330	.475
2005	MIN	AL	98	372	100	24	1	14	(6	8)	168	63	56	53	34	3	65	6	0	4	23	7	.77	8	.269	.337	.452
9 ML YEARS			927	3335	891	193	23	133	(59	74)	1529	492	506	446	234	20	661	39	2	23	96	45	.68	98	.267	.321	.458

Adam Hyzdu

Bats: R **Throws:** R **Pos:** LF-14; CF-8; PH-8; RF-5; PR-1   **Ht:** 6'2" **Wt:** 205 **Born:** 12/6/1971 **Age:** 34

										BATTING										BASERUNNING				AVERAGES		
Year	Team	Lg	G	AB	H	2B	3B	HR	(Hm	Rd)	TB	R	RBI	RC	TBB	IBB	SO	HBP	SH	SF	SB	CS	SB%	GDP	Avg	OBP	Slg
2005	Portlnd*	AAA	62	207	57	9	1	11	(-	-)	101	38	32	42	47	1	61	1	1	1	2	5	.29	5	.275	.410	.488
2005	Pwtckt*	AAA	31	118	30	7	0	4	(-	-)	49	17	25	17	16	0	32	0	0	0	0	1	.00	2	.254	.343	.415
2000	PIT	NL	12	18	7	2	0	1	(0	1)	12	2	4	4	0	0	4	0	0	0	0	0	-	0	.389	.389	.667
2001	PIT	NL	51	72	15	1	0	5	(0	5)	31	7	9	8	4	0	18	1	0	0	0	1	.00	1	.208	.260	.431
2002	PIT	NL	59	155	36	6	0	11	(6	5)	75	24	34	27	21	0	44	1	0	2	0	0	-	1	.232	.324	.484
2003	PIT	NL	51	63	13	5	0	1	(0	1)	21	16	8	6	10	0	21	1	0	1	0	0	-	2	.206	.320	.333
2004	BOS	AL	17	10	3	2	0	1	(0	1)	8	3	2	2	1	0	2	0	0	0	0	0	-	0	.300	.364	.800
2005	2 Tms		29	36	7	2	0	0	(0	0)	9	2	4	1	5	0	7	0	1	1	1	0	1.00	1	.194	.286	.250
05	SD	NL	17	20	3	1	0	0	(0	0)	4	1	4	1	3	0	4	0	1	1	1	0	1.00	1	.150	.250	.200
05	Bos	AL	12	16	4	1	0	0	(0	0)	5	1	0	0	2	0	3	0	0	0	0	0	-	0	.250	.333	.313
6 ML YEARS			219	354	81	18	0	19	(6	13)	156	54	61	48	41	0	96	3	1	4	1	1	.50	5	.229	.311	.441

Raul Ibanez

Bats: L **Throws:** R **Pos:** DH-101; LF-55; 1B-4; RF-3   **Ht:** 6'2" **Wt:** 200 **Born:** 6/2/1972 **Age:** 34

										BATTING										BASERUNNING				AVERAGES		
Year	Team	Lg	G	AB	H	2B	3B	HR	(Hm	Rd)	TB	R	RBI	RC	TBB	IBB	SO	HBP	SH	SF	SB	CS	SB%	GDP	Avg	OBP	Slg
1996	SEA	AL	4	5	0	0	0	0	(0	0)	0	0	0	0	0	0	1	1	0	0	0	0	-	0	.000	.167	.000
1997	SEA	AL	11	26	4	0	1	1	(1	0)	9	3	4	1	0	0	6	0	0	0	0	0	-	0	.154	.154	.346
1998	SEA	AL	37	98	25	7	1	2	(1	1)	40	12	12	10	5	0	22	0	0	0	0	0	-	4	.255	.291	.408
1999	SEA	AL	87	209	54	7	0	9	(3	6)	88	23	27	28	17	1	32	0	0	1	5	1	.83	4	.258	.313	.421
2000	SEA	AL	92	140	32	8	0	2	(2	0)	46	21	15	15	14	1	25	1	0	1	2	0	1.00	1	.229	.301	.329
2001	KC	AL	104	279	78	11	5	13	(5	8)	138	44	54	46	32	2	51	0	0	1	0	2	.00	6	.280	.353	.495
2002	KC	AL	137	497	146	37	6	24	(14	10)	267	70	103	90	40	5	76	2	1	4	5	3	.63	11	.294	.346	.537
2003	KC	AL	157	608	179	33	5	18	(8	10)	276	95	90	91	49	5	81	3	1	10	8	4	.67	10	.294	.345	.454
2004	SEA	AL	123	481	146	31	1	16	(9	7)	227	67	62	67	36	5	72	3	0	4	1	2	.33	10	.304	.353	.472
2005	SEA	AL	162	614	172	32	2	20	(9	11)	268	92	89	99	71	6	99	2	0	3	9	4	.69	12	.280	.355	.436
10 ML YEARS			914	2957	836	166	21	105	(52	53)	1359	427	456	446	264	25	465	12	2	24	30	16	.65	58	.283	.341	.460

Kei Igawa

Pitches: L **Bats:** L **Pos:** P   **Ht:** 6'1" **Wt:** 211 **Born:** 7/13/1979 **Age:** 26

							HOW MUCH HE PITCHED				WHAT HE GAVE UP											THE RESULTS						
Year	Team	Lg	G	GS	CG	GF	IP	BFP	H	R	ER	HR	SH	SF	HB	TBB	IBB	SO	WP	Bk	W	L	Pct	ShO	Sv-Op	Hld	ERC	ERA
1999	Hnshn	Jap	7	3	0	1	15.1	80	23	11	11	1	-	-	1	13	-	14	0	0	1	1	.500	0	0- -	-	9.03	6.46
2000	Hnshn	Jap	9	5	0	1	39.1	172	36	16	16	5	-	-	0	19	-	37	7	0	1	3	.250	0	0- -	-	3.96	3.66
2001	Hnshn	Jap	29	28	3	0	192.0	829	174	76	57	11	-	-	3	89	-	171	6	0	9	13	.409	2	0- -	-	3.42	2.67
2002	Hnshn	Jap	31	29	8	2	209.2	830	163	63	58	15	-	-	7	53	-	206	8	0	14	9	.609	4	0- -	-	2.30	2.49
2003	Hnshn	Jap	29	29	8	0	206.0	839	184	72	64	15	0	0	3	58	3	179	5	0	20	5	.800	2	0- -	-	2.94	2.80
2004	Hnshn	Jap	29	29	6	0	200.1	840	190	95	83	29	11	2	6	54	0	228	5	0	14	11	.560	3	0- -	-	3.67	3.73
2005	Hnshn	Jap	27	27	2	0	172.1	778	199	91	74	23	-	-	-	60	-	145	-	-	13	9	.591	1	0- -	-	4.84	3.86

Tadahito Iguchi

Bats: R **Throws:** R **Pos:** 2B-133; PH-5   **Ht:** 5'9" **Wt:** 185 **Born:** 12/4/1974 **Age:** 31

								BATTING													BASERUNNING				AVERAGES		
Year	Team	Lg	G	AB	H	2B	3B	HR	(Hm	Rd)	TB	R	RBI	RC	TBB	IBB	SO	HBP	SH	SF	SB	CS	SB%	GDP	Avg	OBP	Slg
1997	Fk Dai	Jap	76	217	44	6	3	8	(-	-)	80	31	23	25	24	-	67	8	2	1	3	3	.50	-	.203	.304	.369
1998	Fk Dai	Jap	135	421	93	18	4	21	(-	-)	182	58	66	53	28	-	121	8	15	4	12	6	.67	-	.221	.280	.432
1999	Fk Dai	Jap	116	370	83	15	1	14	(-	-)	142	38	47	47	38	-	113	9	4	3	14	7	.67	-	.224	.310	.384
2000	Fk Dai	Jap	54	162	40	9	2	7	(-	-)	74	21	23	24	15	-	29	2	5	1	5	2	.71	-	.247	.317	.457
2001	Fk Dai	Jap	140	552	144	26	1	30	(-	-)	262	104	97	99	61	-	117	12	9	2	44	9	.83	-	.261	.346	.475
2002	Fk Dai	Jap	114	428	111	14	1	18	(-	-)	181	64	53	60	27	-	84	10	5	2	21	7	.75	-	.259	.317	.423
2003	Fk Dai	Jap	135	515	175	37	1	27	(-	-)	295	112	109	134	81	-	81	14	1	6	42	6	.88	-	.340	.438	.573
2004	Fk Dai	Jap	124	510	170	34	2	24	(-	-)	280	96	89	110	47	-	90	9	0	8	18	5	.78	-	.333	.394	.549
2005	CHA	AL	135	511	142	25	6	15	(7	8)	224	74	71	74	47	0	114	6	11	6	15	5	.75	16	.278	.342	.438

Omar Infante

Bats: R **Throws:** R **Pos:** 2B-69; SS-50; PH-4; PR-3   **Ht:** 5'9" **Wt:** 150 **Born:** 12/26/1981 **Age:** 24

								BATTING													BASERUNNING				AVERAGES		
Year	Team	Lg	G	AB	H	2B	3B	HR	(Hm	Rd)	TB	R	RBI	RC	TBB	IBB	SO	HBP	SH	SF	SB	CS	SB%	GDP	Avg	OBP	Slg
2002	DET	AL	18	72	24	3	0	1	(0	1)	30	4	6	12	3	0	10	0	0	0	0	1	.00	0	.333	.360	.417
2003	DET	AL	69	221	49	6	1	0	(0	0)	57	24	8	16	18	0	37	0	3	2	6	3	.67	1	.222	.278	.258
2004	DET	AL	142	503	132	27	9	16	(9	7)	226	69	55	69	40	3	112	1	7	5	13	7	.65	4	.264	.317	.449
2005	DET	AL	121	406	90	28	2	9	(3	6)	149	36	43	38	16	0	73	2	8	2	8	0	1.00	5	.222	.254	.367
	4 ML YEARS		350	1202	296	64	12	26	(10	16)	462	133	112	135	77	3	232	3	18	9	27	11	.71	10	.246	.291	.384

Brandon Inge

Bats: R **Throws:** R **Pos:** 3B-160; LF-1; CF-1   **Ht:** 5'11" **Wt:** 189 **Born:** 5/19/1977 **Age:** 29

								BATTING													BASERUNNING				AVERAGES		
Year	Team	Lg	G	AB	H	2B	3B	HR	(Hm	Rd)	TB	R	RBI	RC	TBB	IBB	SO	HBP	SH	SF	SB	CS	SB%	GDP	Avg	OBP	Slg
2001	DET	AL	79	189	34	11	0	0	(0	0)	45	13	15	6	9	0	41	0	2	2	1	4	.20	2	.180	.215	.238
2002	DET	AL	95	321	65	15	3	7	(3	4)	107	27	24	24	24	0	101	4	1	1	1	3	.25	7	.202	.266	.333
2003	DET	AL	104	330	67	15	4	8	(4	4)	112	32	30	23	24	0	79	5	4	3	4	4	.50	9	.203	.265	.339
2004	DET	AL	131	408	117	15	7	13	(9	4)	185	43	64	63	32	0	72	4	8	6	5	4	.56	4	.287	.340	.453
2005	DET	AL	160	616	161	31	9	16	(10	6)	258	75	72	82	63	1	140	3	6	6	7	6	.54	14	.261	.330	.419
	5 ML YEARS		569	1864	444	87	22	44	(26	18)	707	190	205	198	152	1	433	16	21	18	18	21	.46	36	.238	.299	.379

Kazuhisa Ishii

Pitches: L **Bats:** L **Pos:** SP-16; RP-3   **Ht:** 6'0" **Wt:** 190 **Born:** 9/9/1973 **Age:** 32

							HOW MUCH HE PITCHED				WHAT HE GAVE UP											THE RESULTS						
Year	Team	Lg	G	GS	CG	GF	IP	BFP	H	R	ER	HR	SH	SF	HB	TBB	IBB	SO	WP	Bk	W	L	Pct	ShO	Sv-Op	Hld	ERC	ERA
2005	StLuci*	A+	1	1	0	0	4.0	13	0	0	0	0	0	0	0	1	0	3	0	0	0	0	-	0	0- -	-	0.07	0.00
2005	Norfolk*	AAA	5	2	0	1	15.1	70	16	4	3	3	0	0	3	8	0	18	2	0	2	2	.500	0	0- -	-	6.54	1.76
2002	LA	NL	28	28	0	0	154.0	692	137	82	73	20	6	5	4	106	3	143	7	0	14	10	.583	0	0-0	0	4.90	4.27
2003	LA	NL	27	27	0	0	147.0	656	129	72	63	16	6	2	0	101	4	140	10	2	9	7	.563	0	0-0	0	4.75	3.86
2004	LA	NL	31	31	2	0	172.0	749	155	97	90	21	10	7	4	98	2	99	3	0	13	8	.619	2	0-0	0	4.47	4.71
2005	NYN	NL	19	16	0	0	91.0	399	87	59	52	13	6	3	3	49	3	53	2	0	3	9	.250	0	0-0	0	4.83	5.14
	4 ML YEARS		105	102	2	0	564.0	2496	508	310	278	70	28	17	17	354	12	435	22	2	39	34	.534	2	0-0	0	4.72	4.44

Jason Isringhausen

Pitches: R **Bats:** R **Pos:** RP-63   **Ht:** 6'3" **Wt:** 230 **Born:** 9/7/1972 **Age:** 33

							HOW MUCH HE PITCHED				WHAT HE GAVE UP											THE RESULTS						
Year	Team	Lg	G	GS	CG	GF	IP	BFP	H	R	ER	HR	SH	SF	HB	TBB	IBB	SO	WP	Bk	W	L	Pct	ShO	Sv-Op	Hld	ERC	ERA
1995	NYN	NL	14	14	1	0	93.0	385	88	29	29	6	3	3	2	31	2	55	4	1	9	2	.818	0	0-0	0	3.40	2.81
1996	NYN	NL	27	27	2	0	171.2	766	190	103	91	13	7	9	8	73	5	114	14	0	6	14	.300	1	0-0	0	4.75	4.77
1997	NYN	NL	6	6	0	0	29.2	145	40	27	25	3	1	2	1	22	0	25	3	0	2	2	.500	0	0-0	0	7.99	7.58
1999	2 Tms		33	5	0	20	64.2	286	64	35	34	9	0	1	2	34	4	51	5	0	1	4	.200	0	9-9	0	4.86	4.73
2000	OAK	AL	66	0	0	57	69.0	304	67	34	29	6	2	1	3	32	5	57	5	1	6	4	.600	0	33-40	0	4.09	3.78
2001	OAK	AL	65	0	0	54	71.1	293	54	24	21	5	3	1	0	23	5	74	2	0	4	3	.571	0	34-43	0	2.18	2.65
2002	STL	NL	60	0	0	51	65.1	257	46	22	18	0	4	3	1	18	1	68	0	0	3	2	.600	0	32-37	1	1.61	2.48
2003	STL	NL	40	0	0	31	42.0	174	31	14	11	2	1	0	0	18	1	41	6	0	0	1	.000	0	22-25	1	2.40	2.36
2004	STL	NL	74	0	0	66	75.1	308	55	27	24	5	6	1	2	23	4	71	1	0	4	2	.667	0	47-54	0	2.09	2.87
2005	STL	NL	63	0	0	52	59.0	245	43	14	14	4	3	1	1	27	5	51	2	0	1	2	.333	0	39-43	1	2.56	2.14
99	NYM	NL	13	5	0	2	39.1	179	43	29	28	7	0	1	1	22	2	31	3	0	1	3	.250	0	1-1	0	5.93	6.41
99	Oak	AL	20	0	0	18	25.1	107	21	6	6	2	0	0	1	12	2	20	2	0	0	1	.000	0	8-8	0	3.33	2.13
	10 ML YEARS		448	52	3	331	741.0	3163	678	329	296	53	30	22	20	301	32	607	42	2	36	36	.500	1	216-251	2	3.46	3.60

Akinori Iwamura

Bats: L **Throws:** R **Pos:** 3B   **Ht:** 5'9" **Wt:** 176 **Born:** 2/9/1979 **Age:** 27

Year	Team	Lg	G	AB	H	2B	3B	HR	(Hm	Rd)	TB	R	RBI	RC	TBB	IBB	SO	HBP	SH	SF	SB	CS	SB%	GDP	Avg	OBP	Slg
1998	Yakult	Jap	1	3	0	0	0	0	(-	-)	0	0	0	0	0	-	2	0	0	0	0	0	-	-	.000	.000	.000
1999	Yakult	Jap	83	252	74	11	4	11	(1	1)	126	28	35	44	18	-	46	1	0	2	7	1	.88	-	.294	.341	.500
2000	Yakult	Jap	130	436	121	13	9	18	(-	-)	206	67	66	74	39	-	103	4	9	1	13	1	.93	-	.278	.342	.472
2001	Yakult	Jap	136	520	149	24	4	19	(-	-)	238	79	81	80	32	-	111	3	5	4	15	6	.71	-	.287	.329	.458
2002	Yakult	Jap	140	510	163	35	2	23	(-	-)	271	67	75	104	58	6	114	3	2	4	5	4	.56	-	.320	.390	.531
2003	Yakult	Jap	60	232	61	6	2	12	(-	-)	107	43	31	36	22	3	55	1	2	1	5	1	.83	-	.263	.328	.461
2004	Yakult	Jap	138	533	160	19	0	44	(-	-)	311	99	103	117	70	3	173	4	0	4	8	3	.73	-	.300	.383	.583
2005	Yakult	Jap	143	545	173	31	4	29	(-	-)	299	82	101	114	62	-	145	2	0	5	5	3	.63	-	.317	.386	.549

Cesar Izturis

Bats: B **Throws:** R **Pos:** SS-106   **Ht:** 5'9" **Wt:** 175 **Born:** 2/10/1980 **Age:** 26

Year	Team	Lg	G	AB	H	2B	3B	HR	(Hm	Rd)	TB	R	RBI	RC	TBB	IBB	SO	HBP	SH	SF	SB	CS	SB%	GDP	Avg	OBP	Slg
2001	TOR	AL	46	134	36	6	2	1	(1	1)	52	19	9	16	2	0	15	0	4	0	8	1	.89	0	.269	.279	.388
2002	LA	NL	135	439	102	24	2	1	(0	1)	133	43	31	26	14	1	39	0	10	5	7	7	.50	12	.232	.253	.303
2003	LA	NL	158	558	140	21	6	1	(0	1)	176	47	40	42	25	8	70	0	7	3	10	5	.67	9	.251	.282	.315
2004	LA	NL	159	670	193	32	9	4	(1	3)	255	90	62	95	43	2	70	0	12	3	25	9	.74	6	.288	.330	.381
2005	LAN	NL	106	444	114	19	2	2	(1	1)	143	48	31	37	25	1	51	4	4	1	8	8	.50	11	.257	.302	.322
5 ML YEARS			604	2245	585	102	21	10	(3	7)	759	247	173	216	109	12	245	4	37	12	58	30	.66	38	.261	.295	.338

Maicer Izturis

Bats: B **Throws:** R **Pos:** 3B-45; SS-29; PR-7; PH-2; 2B-1; CF-1   **Ht:** 5'8" **Wt:** 155 **Born:** 9/12/1980 **Age:** 25

Year	Team	Lg	G	AB	H	2B	3B	HR	(Hm	Rd)	TB	R	RBI	RC	TBB	IBB	SO	HBP	SH	SF	SB	CS	SB%	GDP	Avg	OBP	Slg
1998	Burlgtn	R+	55	217	63	8	2	2	(-	-)	81	33	33	28	17	0	32	0	2	0	16	6	.73	4	.290	.342	.373
1999	Clmbs	A	57	220	66	5	3	4	(-	-)	89	46	23	35	20	0	28	1	1	3	14	2	.88	2	.300	.357	.405
2000	Clmbs	A	10	29	8	1	0	0	(-	-)	9	4	1	3	3	0	3	0	0	0	0	0	-	1	.276	.344	.310
2001	Kinston	A+	114	433	104	16	6	1	(-	-)	135	47	39	43	31	1	81	8	10	4	32	9	.78	8	.240	.300	.312
2002	Kinston	A+	58	233	61	13	1	1	(-	-)	79	28	30	29	24	0	26	1	3	1	24	6	.80	2	.262	.332	.339
2002	Akron	AA	67	253	70	12	7	0	(-	-)	96	34	32	30	17	0	28	3	5	3	8	4	.67	10	.277	.326	.379
2003	Akron	AA	54	218	61	11	5	1	(-	-)	85	31	20	31	24	1	23	1	6	2	14	6	.70	4	.280	.351	.390
2003	Buffalo	AAA	85	301	79	16	4	2	(-	-)	109	43	29	32	24	0	28	1	9	2	14	6	.70	14	.262	.317	.362
2004	Edmtn	AAA	99	376	127	19	2	3	(-	-)	159	65	36	69	57	1	30	4	4	2	14	12	.54	12	.338	.428	.423
2005	Salt Lk	AAA	10	31	14	4	0	0	(-	-)	18	10	2	9	7	0	4	0	1	0	4	2	.67	2	.452	.553	.581
2004	MON	AL	32	107	22	5	2	1	(1	0)	34	10	4	8	10	1	20	2	2	0	4	0	1.00	1	.206	.286	.318
2005	LAA	AL	77	191	47	8	4	1	(0	1)	66	18	15	25	17	2	21	0	1	1	9	3	.75	5	.246	.306	.346
2 ML YEARS			109	298	69	13	6	2	(1	1)	100	28	19	33	27	3	41	2	3	1	13	3	.81	6	.232	.299	.336

Conor Jackson

Bats: R **Throws:** R **Pos:** 1B-20; PH-19; LF-1   **Ht:** 6'2" **Wt:** 225 **Born:** 5/7/1982 **Age:** 24

Year	Team	Lg	G	AB	H	2B	3B	HR	(Hm	Rd)	TB	R	RBI	RC	TBB	IBB	SO	HBP	SH	SF	SB	CS	SB%	GDP	Avg	OBP	Slg
2003	Yakima	A-	68	257	82	35	1	6	(-	-)	137	44	60	57	36	4	41	5	0	2	3	0	1.00	7	.319	.410	.533
2004	Lancst	A+	67	258	89	19	2	11	(-	-)	145	64	54	64	45	1	36	3	0	7	4	3	.57	3	.345	.438	.562
2004	ElPaso	AA	60	226	68	13	2	6	(-	-)	103	33	37	39	24	0	36	2	0	4	3	3	.50	4	.301	.367	.456
2005	Tucsn	AAA	93	333	118	38	2	8	(-	-)	184	66	73	85	69	1	32	0	0	7	3	2	.60	8	.354	.457	.553
2005	ARI	NL	40	85	17	3	0	2	(2	0)	26	8	8	6	12	0	11	1	0	1	0	0	-	6	.200	.303	.306

Damian Jackson

Bats: R **Throws:** R **Pos:** LF-37; 2B-35; SS-26; PR-16; CF-15; 3B-8; PH-8; RF-1   **Ht:** 5'11" **Wt:** 185 **Born:** 8/16/1973 **Age:** 32

Year	Team	Lg	G	AB	H	2B	3B	HR	(Hm	Rd)	TB	R	RBI	RC	TBB	IBB	SO	HBP	SH	SF	SB	CS	SB%	GDP	Avg	OBP	Slg
2005	Portlnd*	AAA	14	51	18	4	1	3	(-	-)	33	14	10	15	13	0	9	0	0	1	1	1	.50	0	.353	.477	.647
1996	CLE	AL	5	10	3	0	0	0	(0	0)	5	2	1	2	1	0	4	0	0	0	0	0	-	0	.300	.364	.500
1997	2 Tms		20	36	7	2	1	1	(0	1)	14	8	2	4	4	1	8	1	1	0	2	1	.67	0	.194	.293	.389
1998	CIN	NL	13	38	12	5	0	0	(0	0)	17	4	7	7	6	0	4	0	0	1	2	0	1.00	1	.316	.400	.447
1999	SD	NL	133	388	87	20	2	9	(6	3)	138	56	39	50	53	3	105	3	0	3	34	10	.77	2	.224	.320	.356
2000	SD	NL	138	470	120	27	6	6	(5	1)	177	68	37	66	62	2	108	3	4	2	28	6	.82	7	.255	.345	.377
2001	SD	NL	122	440	106	21	6	4	(1	3)	151	69	38	51	44	2	128	6	2	3	23	6	.79	6	.241	.316	.343
2002	DET	AL	81	245	63	20	1	1	(0	1)	88	31	25	32	21	0	36	3	2	1	12	3	.80	2	.257	.320	.359
2003	BOS	AL	109	161	42	7	0	1	(0	1)	52	34	13	12	8	0	28	0	2	1	16	8	.67	4	.261	.294	.323
2004	2 Tms		21	30	3	2	0	1	(1	0)	8	2	3	1	4	2	12	0	0	0	0	0	-	4	.100	.206	.267
2005	SD	NL	118	275	70	9	0	5	(3	2)	94	44	23	31	30	1	48	4	3	1	15	2	.88	4	.255	.335	.342
97	Cle	AL	8	9	1	0	0	0	(0	0)	1	2	0	0	0	0	1	1	0	0	1	0	1.00	0	.111	.200	.111
97	Cin	NL	12	27	6	2	1	1	(0	1)	13	6	2	4	4	1	7	0	1	0	1	1	.50	0	.222	.323	.481
04	ChC	NL	7	15	1	0	0	1	(1	0)	4	1	3	2	3	2	6	0	0	0	0	0	-	0	.067	.222	.267
04	KC	AL	14	15	2	2	0	0	(0	0)	4	1	2	1	1	0	6	0	0	0	0	0	-	4	.133	.188	.267
10 ML YEARS			760	2093	513	115	16	28	(16	12)	744	316	188	256	233	11	478	20	14	14	132	36	.79	27	.245	.325	.355

Edwin Jackson

Pitches: R **Bats:** R **Pos:** SP-6; RP-1   **Ht:** 6'3" **Wt:** 190 **Born:** 9/9/1983 **Age:** 22

Year	Team	Lg	G	GS	CG	GF	IP	BFP	H	R	ER	HR	SH	SF	HB	TBB	IBB	SO	WP	Bk	W	L	Pct	ShO	Sv-Op	Hld	ERC	ERA
2005	Jaxnvl*	AA	11	11	0	0	62.0	256	52	31	24	7	3	2	2	18	0	44	3	0	6	4	.600	0	0--	-	2.97	3.48
2005	LsVgs*	AAA	12	11	1	0	55.1	279	76	61	53	13	2	1	5	37	2	33	2	0	3	7	.300	0	0--	-	9.01	8.62
2003	LA	NL	4	3	0	0	22.0	91	17	6	6	2	1	1	1	11	1	19	3	0	2	1	.667	0	0-0	0	3.36	2.45
2004	LA	NL	8	5	0	1	24.2	113	31	20	20	7	1	0	0	11	1	16	0	0	2	1	.667	0	0-0	0	7.21	7.30
2005	LAN	NL	7	6	0	0	28.2	134	31	22	20	2	0	2	1	17	0	13	2	1	2	2	.500	0	0-0	0	5.13	6.28
	3 ML YEARS		19	14	0	1	75.1	338	79	48	46	11	2	3	2	39	2	48	5	1	6	4	.600	0	0-0	0	5.25	5.50

Mike Jacobs

Bats: L **Throws:** R **Pos:** 1B-28; PH-2   **Ht:** 6'2" **Wt:** 180 **Born:** 10/30/1980 **Age:** 25

Year	Team	Lg	G	AB	H	2B	3B	HR	(Hm	Rd)	TB	R	RBI	RC	TBB	IBB	SO	HBP	SH	SF	SB	CS	SB%	GDP	Avg	OBP	Slg
1999	Mets	R	44	147	49	12	0	4	(-	-)	73	18	30	29	14	2	30	1	0	5	2	0	1.00	3	.333	.383	.497
2000	Kngspt	R+	59	204	55	15	4	7	(-	-)	99	28	40	39	33	1	62	1	1	2	6	1	.86	3	.270	.371	.485
2000	CptCty	A	18	56	12	5	0	0	(-	-)	17	1	8	4	6	1	19	0	0	0	1	1	.50	2	.214	.290	.304
2001	Bklyn	A-	19	66	19	5	0	1	(-	-)	27	12	15	10	6	0	11	3	0	2	1	1	.50	1	.288	.364	.409
2001	CptCty	A	46	180	50	13	0	2	(-	-)	69	18	26	23	13	0	46	1	1	1	0	1	.00	4	.278	.328	.383
2002	StLuci	A+	118	467	117	26	1	11	(-	-)	178	62	64	53	25	5	95	4	0	5	2	3	.40	11	.251	.291	.381
2003	Bnghtn	AA	119	407	134	36	1	17	(-	-)	223	56	81	81	28	1	87	7	0	8	0	3	.00	11	.329	.376	.548
2004	Norfolk	AAA	27	96	17	3	0	2	(-	-)	26	8	6	6	9	2	30	0	0	1	0	0	-	1	.177	.245	.271
2005	Bnghtn	AA	117	433	139	37	2	25	(-	-)	255	66	93	93	35	6	94	7	1	6	1	2	.33	11	.321	.376	.589
2005	NYN	NL	30	100	31	7	0	11	(6	5)	71	19	23	21	10	0	22	1	0	1	0	0	-	5	.310	.375	.710

Chuck James

Pitches: L **Bats:** L **Pos:** RP-2   **Ht:** 6'0" **Wt:** 170 **Born:** 11/9/1981 **Age:** 24

Year	Team	Lg	G	GS	CG	GF	IP	BFP	H	R	ER	HR	SH	SF	HB	TBB	IBB	SO	WP	Bk	W	L	Pct	ShO	Sv-Op	Hld	ERC	ERA
2003	Danvle	R+	11	11	0	0	50.1	196	26	9	7	1	2	0	0	19	0	68	2	0	2	1	.667	0	0--	-	1.30	1.25
2004	Rome	A	26	22	1	2	132.0	536	92	41	33	6	9	9	7	48	1	156	3	0	10	5	.667	0	0--	-	2.20	2.25
2005	Missi	AA	16	16	0	0	86.0	338	62	25	20	4	6	0	2	18	0	104	4	0	9	1	.900	0	0--	-	1.73	2.09
2005	Rchmd	AAA	6	6	0	0	33.2	132	21	13	13	4	0	1	1	10	0	30	2	0	1	3	.250	0	0--	-	1.99	3.48
2005	MrtlBh	A+	7	7	0	0	41.2	153	20	6	5	1	0	0	0	8	0	59	2	0	3	3	.500	0	0--	-	0.87	1.08
2005	ATL	NL	2	0	0	0	5.2	23	4	1	1	0	0	0	0	3	0	5	1	0	0	0	-	0	0-0	0	2.41	1.59

Kevin Jarvis

Pitches: R **Bats:** L **Pos:** RP-4   **Ht:** 6'2" **Wt:** 200 **Born:** 8/1/1969 **Age:** 36

Year	Team	Lg	G	GS	CG	GF	IP	BFP	H	R	ER	HR	SH	SF	HB	TBB	IBB	SO	WP	Bk	W	L	Pct	ShO	Sv-Op	Hld	ERC	ERA
2005	Memp*	AAA	26	25	1	0	157.0	674	164	63	59	19	5	4	2	39	1	112	6	0	11	6	.647	0	0--	-	3.83	3.38
1994	CIN	NL	6	3	0	0	17.2	79	22	14	14	4	1	0	0	5	0	10	1	0	1	1	.500	0	0-0	0	5.91	7.13
1995	CIN	NL	19	11	1	2	79.0	354	91	56	50	13	2	5	3	32	2	33	2	0	3	4	.429	1	0-0	0	5.60	5.70
1996	CIN	NL	24	20	2	2	120.1	552	152	93	80	17	6	2	2	43	5	63	3	0	8	9	.471	1	0-0	0	5.68	5.98
1997	3 Tms		32	5	0	13	68.0	329	99	62	58	17	2	1	1	29	0	48	4	0	0	4	.000	0	1-1	0	7.21	7.68
1999	OAK	AL	4	1	0	0	14.0	75	28	19	18	6	0	1	4	6	0	11	0	0	0	1	.000	0	0-0	0	14.40	11.57
2000	COL	NL	24	19	0	0	115.0	505	138	83	76	26	6	2	4	33	3	60	2	0	3	4	.429	0	0-0	0	5.86	5.95
2001	SD	NL	32	32	1	0	193.1	809	189	107	103	37	7	4	5	49	4	133	1	0	12	11	.522	1	0-0	0	4.05	4.79
2002	SD	NL	7	7	0	0	35.0	146	36	19	17	5	0	1	1	10	1	24	2	0	2	4	.333	0	0-0	0	4.24	4.37
2003	SD	NL	16	16	0	0	92.0	413	113	65	60	15	2	5	2	32	5	49	2	0	4	8	.333	0	0-0	0	5.68	5.87
2004	2 Tms		10	0	0	2	15.0	78	26	18	18	5	1	0	0	9	2	7	2	0	1	0	1.000	0	0-0	0	11.60	10.80
2005	STL	NL	4	0	0	1	3.1	17	3	5	5	1	0	0	2	3	0	2	0	0	0	1	.000	0	0-1	0	10.36	13.50
97	Cin	NL	9	0	0	3	13.1	70	21	16	15	4	1	0	1	7	0	12	2	0	0	1	.000	0	1-1	0	9.98	10.13
97	Min	AL	6	2	0	1	13.0	70	23	18	18	4	0	0	0	8	0	9	2	0	0	0	-	0	0-0	0	11.69	12.46
97	Det	AL	17	3	0	9	41.2	189	55	28	25	9	1	1	0	14	0	27	0	0	0	3	.000	0	0-0	0	6.64	5.40
04	Sea	AL	8	0	0	2	13.0	63	20	12	12	4	0	0	0	5	0	7	2	0	1	0	1.000	0	0-0	0	9.03	8.31
04	Col	NL	2	0	0	0	2.0	15	6	6	6	1	1	0	0	4	2	0	0	0	0	0	-	0	0-0	0	30.23	27.00
	11 ML YEARS		178	114	4	20	752.2	3357	897	541	499	146	27	21	21	251	22	440	19	0	34	47	.420	3	1-2	0	5.68	5.97

Geoff Jenkins

Bats: L **Throws:** R **Pos:** RF-144; DH-2; PH-2   **Ht:** 6'1" **Wt:** 213 **Born:** 7/21/1974 **Age:** 31

Year	Team	Lg	G	AB	H	2B	3B	HR	(Hm	Rd)	TB	R	RBI	RC	TBB	IBB	SO	HBP	SH	SF	SB	CS	SB%	GDP	Avg	OBP	Slg
1998	MIL	NL	84	262	60	12	1	9	(4	5)	101	33	28	26	20	4	61	2	0	1	1	3	.25	7	.229	.288	.385
1999	MIL	NL	135	447	140	43	3	21	(10	11)	252	70	82	88	35	7	87	7	3	1	5	1	.83	10	.313	.371	.564
2000	MIL	NL	135	512	155	36	4	34	(15	19)	301	100	94	104	33	6	135	15	0	4	11	1	.92	9	.303	.360	.588
2001	MIL	NL	105	397	105	21	1	20	(11	9)	188	60	63	60	36	7	120	8	0	5	4	2	.67	11	.264	.334	.474
2002	MIL	NL	67	243	59	17	1	10	(4	6)	108	35	29	28	22	1	60	6	0	1	1	2	.33	8	.243	.320	.444
2003	MIL	NL	124	487	144	30	2	28	(14	14)	262	81	95	90	58	10	120	6	0	3	0	0	-	12	.296	.375	.538
2004	MIL	NL	157	617	163	36	6	27	(13	14)	292	88	93	76	46	10	152	12	0	6	3	1	.75	19	.264	.325	.473
2005	MIL	NL	148	538	157	42	1	25	(10	15)	276	87	86	87	56	9	138	**19**	0	5	0	0	-	13	.292	.375	.513
	8 ML YEARS		955	3503	983	237	19	174	(83	91)	1780	554	570	559	306	54	873	75	3	26	25	10	.71	89	.281	.349	.508

Bobby Jenks

Pitches: R Bats: R Pos: RP-32   Ht: 6'3" Wt: 270 Born: 3/14/1981 Age: 25

			HOW MUCH HE PITCHED						WHAT HE GAVE UP											THE RESULTS						
Year	Team	Lg	G	GS	CG	GF	IP	BFP	H	R	ER	HR	SH	SF	HB	TBB	IBB	SO	WP	Bk	W	L	Pct	ShO	Sv-Op	Hld	ERC	ERA
2000	Butte	R+	14	12	0	0	52.2	263	61	57	46	2	2	4	5	44	0	42	19	2	1	7	.125	0	0- -	-	6.62	7.86
2001	CRpds	A	21	21	0	0	99.0	451	90	74	58	10	2	4	12	64	0	98	13	1	3	7	.300	0	0- -	-	5.05	5.27
2001	Ark	AA	2	2	0	0	10.0	43	8	5	4	0	0	0	2	5	0	10	3	0	1	0	1.000	0	0- -	-	3.48	3.60
2002	RCuca	A+	11	10	1	0	65.1	292	50	42	35	4	4	5	4	46	0	64	11	2	3	5	.375	1	0- -	-	3.86	4.82
2002	Ark	AA	10	10	1	0	58.0	267	49	34	30	2	2	3	2	44	0	58	2	1	3	6	.333	0	0- -	-	4.15	4.66
2003	Angels	R	1	1	0	0	4.0	14	2	0	0	0	0	0	0	0	0	5	0	0	0	0	-	0	0- -	-	0.54	0.00
2003	Ark	AA	16	16	0	0	83.0	356	56	23	20	2	1	3	1	51	0	103	6	0	7	2	.778	0	0- -	-	2.62	2.17
2004	Angels	R	1	1	0	0	3.1	15	2	3	3	0	0	0	0	3	0	5	1	0	0	0	-	0	0- -	-	2.96	8.10
2004	RCuca	A+	1	1	0	0	3.2	23	5	8	8	0	0	2	1	7	0	3	0	0	0	1	.000	0	0- -	-	13.40	19.64
2004	Salt Lk	AAA	3	3	0	0	12.1	62	19	15	12	1	1	0	0	6	0	13	0	0	0	1	.000	0	0- -	-	7.88	8.76
2005	Brham	AA	35	0	0	32	41.0	177	34	17	13	1	1	2	4	20	1	48	6	0	1	2	.333	0	19- -	-	3.27	2.85
2005	CHA	AL	32	0	0	18	39.1	168	34	15	12	3	1	0	1	15	3	50	4	0	1	1	.500	0	6-8	3	3.02	2.75

Jason Jennings

Pitches: R Bats: L Pos: SP-20   Ht: 6'2" Wt: 242 Born: 7/17/1978 Age: 27

			HOW MUCH HE PITCHED						WHAT HE GAVE UP											THE RESULTS						
Year	Team	Lg	G	GS	CG	GF	IP	BFP	H	R	ER	HR	SH	SF	HB	TBB	IBB	SO	WP	Bk	W	L	Pct	ShO	Sv-Op	Hld	ERC	ERA
2001	COL	NL	7	7	1	0	39.1	174	42	21	20	2	1	1	1	19	0	26	1	0	4	1	.800	1	0-0	0	4.58	4.58
2002	COL	NL	32	32	0	0	185.1	808	201	102	93	26	9	3	8	70	2	127	10	0	16	8	.667	0	0-0	0	4.98	4.52
2003	COL	NL	32	32	1	0	181.1	820	212	115	103	20	11	6	5	88	7	119	6	0	12	13	.480	0	0-0	0	5.60	5.11
2004	COL	NL	33	33	0	0	201.0	925	241	125	123	27	9	3	7	101	14	133	6	1	11	12	.478	0	0-0	0	5.99	5.51
2005	COL	NL	20	20	1	0	122.0	551	130	73	68	11	6	3	5	62	4	75	8	0	6	9	.400	0	0-0	0	4.91	5.02
5 ML YEARS			124	124	3	0	729.0	3278	826	436	407	86	36	16	26	340	27	480	31	1	49	43	.533	1	0-0	0	5.38	5.02

Ryan Jensen

Pitches: R Bats: R Pos: RP-6; SP-3   Ht: 6'0" Wt: 205 Born: 9/17/1975 Age: 30

			HOW MUCH HE PITCHED						WHAT HE GAVE UP											THE RESULTS						
Year	Team	Lg	G	GS	CG	GF	IP	BFP	H	R	ER	HR	SH	SF	HB	TBB	IBB	SO	WP	Bk	W	L	Pct	ShO	Sv-Op	Hld	ERC	ERA
2005	Omha*	AAA	18	18	0	0	90.0	431	123	80	72	12	1	4	3	38	0	55	6	0	2	11	.154	0	0- -	-	6.66	7.20
2001	SF	NL	10	7	0	2	42.1	193	44	21	20	5	0	0	4	25	0	26	2	0	1	2	.333	0	0-0	0	5.68	4.25
2002	SF	NL	32	30	1	0	171.2	744	183	93	86	21	7	8	5	66	4	105	3	0	13	8	.619	0	0-0	0	4.69	4.51
2003	SF	NL	6	2	0	3	13.1	64	21	16	16	6	4	2	1	5	0	3	0	0	0	0	-	0	0-0	0	11.25	10.80
2005	KC	AL	9	3	0	3	25.1	115	31	20	20	4	0	2	2	7	1	18	0	0	3	2	.600	0	0-1	0	5.48	7.11
4 ML YEARS			57	42	1	8	252.2	1116	279	150	142	36	11	12	12	103	5	152	5	0	17	12	.586	0	0-1	0	5.24	5.06

Derek Jeter

Bats: R Throws: R Pos: SS-157; DH-1; PR-1   Ht: 6'3" Wt: 195 Born: 6/26/1974 Age: 32

			BATTING																			BASERUNNING				AVERAGES		
Year	Team	Lg	G	AB	H	2B	3B	HR	(Hm	Rd)	TB	R	RBI	RC	TBB	IBB	SO	HBP	SH	SF			SB	CS	SB%	GDP	Avg	OBP	Slg
1995	NYA	AL	15	48	12	4	1	0	(0	0)	18	5	7	5	3	0	11	0	0	0			0	0	-	0	.250	.294	.375
1996	NYA	AL	157	582	183	25	6	10	(3	7)	250	104	78	92	48	1	102	9	6	9			14	7	.67	13	.314	.370	.430
1997	NYA	AL	159	654	190	31	7	10	(5	5)	265	116	70	99	74	0	125	10	8	2			23	12	.66	14	.291	.370	.405
1998	NYA	AL	149	626	203	25	8	19	(9	10)	301	127	84	115	57	1	119	5	3	3			30	6	.83	13	.324	.384	.481
1999	NYA	AL	158	627	219	37	9	24	(15	9)	346	134	102	146	91	5	116	12	3	6			19	8	.70	12	.349	.438	.552
2000	NYA	AL	148	593	201	31	4	15	(8	7)	285	119	73	118	68	4	99	12	3	3			22	4	.85	14	.339	.416	.481
2001	NYA	AL	150	614	191	35	3	21	(13	8)	295	110	74	112	56	3	99	10	5	1			27	3	.90	13	.311	.377	.480
2002	NYA	AL	157	644	191	26	0	18	(10	8)	271	124	75	108	73	2	114	7	3	3			32	3	.91	14	.297	.373	.421
2003	NYA	AL	119	482	156	25	3	10	(7	3)	217	87	52	86	43	2	88	13	3	1			11	5	.69	10	.324	.393	.450
2004	NYA	AL	154	643	188	44	1	23	(11	12)	303	111	78	100	46	1	99	14	16	2			23	4	.85	19	.292	.352	.471
2005	NYA	AL	159	654	202	25	5	19	(12	7)	294	122	70	105	77	3	117	11	7	3			14	5	.74	15	.309	.389	.450
11 ML YEARS			1525	6167	1936	308	47	169	(91	78)	2845	1159	763	1086	636	22	1089	103	57	33			215	57	.79	137	.314	.386	.461

D'Angelo Jimenez

Bats: B Throws: R Pos: 2B-27; PH-9   Ht: 6'0" Wt: 194 Born: 12/21/1977 Age: 28

			BATTING																			BASERUNNING				AVERAGES		
Year	Team	Lg	G	AB	H	2B	3B	HR	(Hm	Rd)	TB	R	RBI	RC	TBB	IBB	SO	HBP	SH	SF			SB	CS	SB%	GDP	Avg	OBP	Slg
2005	Chatt*	AA	90	327	91	20	0	9	(-	-)	138	55	45	63	69	2	34	0	0	3			16	4	.80	4	.278	.401	.422
1999	NYA	AL	7	20	8	2	0	0	(0	0)	10	3	4	5	3	0	4	0	0	0			0	0	-	0	.400	.478	.500
2001	SD	NL	86	308	85	19	0	3	(2	1)	113	45	33	39	39	4	68	0	0	2			2	3	.40	9	.276	.355	.367
2002	2 Tms		114	429	108	15	7	4	(3	1)	149	61	44	54	50	1	73	1	0	0			6	3	.67	11	.252	.330	.347
2003	2 Tms		146	561	153	24	7	14	(6	8)	233	69	57	78	66	1	89	2	6	4			11	7	.61	7	.273	.349	.415
2004	CIN	NL	152	563	152	28	3	12	(6	6)	222	76	67	87	82	1	99	2	3	2			13	7	.65	15	.270	.364	.394
2005	CIN	NL	35	105	24	7	0	0	(0	0)	31	14	5	10	14	0	23	0	0	0			2	1	.67	1	.229	.319	.295
02	SD	NL	87	321	77	11	4	3	(2	1)	105	39	33	34	34	1	63	0	0	2			4	2	.67	10	.240	.311	.327
02	CWS	AL	27	108	31	4	3	1	(1	0)	44	22	11	20	16	0	10	1	0	0			2	1	.67	1	.287	.384	.407
03	CWS	AL	73	271	69	11	5	7	(3	4)	111	35	26	35	32	1	46	0	4	1			4	3	.57	3	.255	.332	.410
03	Cin	NL	73	290	84	13	2	7	(3	4)	122	34	31	43	34	0	43	2	2	3			7	4	.64	4	.290	.365	.421
6 ML YEARS			540	1986	530	95	17	33	(17	16)	758	268	210	273	254	7	356	5	9	10			34	21	.62	43	.267	.350	.382

Charlton Jimerson

Bats: R **Throws:** R **Pos:** CF-1   **Ht:** 6'3" **Wt:** 210 **Born:** 9/22/1979 **Age:** 26

								BATTING												BASERUNNING				AVERAGES		
Year	Team	Lg	G	AB	H	2B	3B	HR	(Hm | Rd)	TB	R	RBI	RC	TBB	IBB	SO	HBP	SH	SF	SB	CS	SB%	GDP	Avg	OBP	Slg
2001	Pittsfld	A-	51	197	46	12	1	9	(- | -)	87	35	31	28	18	1	79	2	1	0	15	4	.79	4	.234	.304	.442
2002	Lxngtn	A	125	439	100	22	4	14	(- | -)	172	65	57	55	36	0	168	7	2	2	34	9	.79	7	.228	.295	.392
2003	Salem	A+	97	336	89	19	3	12	(- | -)	150	53	55	52	25	1	109	2	1	3	27	4	.87	4	.265	.317	.446
2004	RdRck	AA	131	488	116	22	5	18	(- | -)	202	78	53	64	31	5	163	5	3	1	39	6	.87	8	.238	.290	.414
2005	CpChr	AA	115	425	110	24	3	16	(- | -)	188	67	44	62	29	4	145	8	3	2	27	10	.73	0	.259	.317	.442
2005	RdRck	AAA	7	23	7	1	0	0	(- | -)	8	1	1	3	0	0	7	0	1	1	3	0	1.00	0	.304	.292	.348
2005	HOU	NL	1	0	0	0	0	0	(0 | 0)	0	0	0	0	0	0	0	0	0	0	0	0	-	0	-	-	-

Ben Johnson

Bats: R **Throws:** R **Pos:** LF-13; RF-11; CF-9; PH-5   **Ht:** 6'1" **Wt:** 200 **Born:** 6/18/1981 **Age:** 25

								BATTING												BASERUNNING				AVERAGES		
Year	Team	Lg	G	AB	H	2B	3B	HR	(Hm | Rd)	TB	R	RBI	RC	TBB	IBB	SO	HBP	SH	SF	SB	CS	SB%	GDP	Avg	OBP	Slg
1999	JhsCty	R+	57	203	67	9	1	10	(- | -)	108	38	51	46	29	1	57	5	1	2	14	6	.70	0	.330	.423	.532
2000	FtWyn	A	29	109	21	6	2	3	(- | -)	40	11	13	9	7	1	25	3	2	0	0	3	.00	5	.193	.261	.367
2000	Peoria	A	93	330	80	22	1	13	(- | -)	143	58	46	55	53	0	78	5	0	3	17	6	.74	8	.242	.353	.433
2001	Lk Els	A+	136	503	139	35	6	12	(- | -)	222	79	63	84	54	1	141	11	1	2	22	7	.76	15	.276	.358	.441
2002	Mobile	AA	131	456	110	23	4	10	(- | -)	171	58	55	65	65	1	127	3	0	4	11	9	.55	9	.241	.337	.375
2003	Lk Els	A+	52	184	49	9	0	8	(- | -)	82	30	29	31	20	0	49	5	1	0	6	1	.86	5	.266	.354	.446
2003	Mobile	AA	44	127	23	5	0	1	(- | -)	31	8	7	7	10	0	36	2	1	0	0	1	.00	0	.181	.252	.244
2004	Mobile	AA	136	475	119	28	6	23	(- | -)	228	80	85	78	55	3	136	7	2	5	5	6	.45	0	.251	.334	.480
2005	Portlnd	AAA	107	414	129	27	0	25	(- | -)	231	79	83	90	51	0	88	6	0	1	6	1	.86	7	.312	.394	.558
2005	SD	NL	31	75	16	8	1	3	(1 | 2)	35	10	13	8	11	1	23	0	1	1	0	2	.00	4	.213	.310	.467

Charles Johnson

Bats: R **Throws:** R **Pos:** C-19   **Ht:** 6'3" **Wt:** 250 **Born:** 7/20/1971 **Age:** 34

								BATTING												BASERUNNING				AVERAGES		
Year	Team	Lg	G	AB	H	2B	3B	HR	(Hm | Rd)	TB	R	RBI	RC	TBB	IBB	SO	HBP	SH	SF	SB	CS	SB%	GDP	Avg	OBP	Slg
1994	FLA	NL	4	11	5	1	0	1	(1 | 0)	9	5	4	3	1	0	4	0	0	1	0	0	-	1	.455	.462	.818
1995	FLA	NL	97	315	79	15	1	11	(3 | 8)	129	40	39	44	46	2	71	4	4	2	0	2	.00	11	.251	.351	.410
1996	FLA	NL	120	386	84	13	1	13	(9 | 4)	138	34	37	35	40	6	91	2	2	4	1	0	1.00	20	.218	.292	.358
1997	FLA	NL	124	416	104	26	1	19	(7 | 12)	189	43	63	63	60	6	109	3	3	2	0	2	.00	13	.250	.347	.454
1998	2 Tms		133	459	100	18	0	19	(14 | 5)	175	44	58	48	45	1	129	1	1	0	0	2	.00	12	.218	.289	.381
1999	BAL	AL	135	426	107	19	1	16	(8 | 8)	176	58	54	59	55	2	107	4	4	3	0	0	-	13	.251	.340	.413
2000	2 Tms		128	421	128	24	0	31	(19 | 12)	245	76	91	89	52	0	106	1	1	3	2	0	1.00	8	.304	.379	.582
2001	FLA	NL	128	451	117	32	0	18	(5 | 13)	203	51	75	64	38	2	133	4	0	3	0	0	-	8	.259	.321	.450
2002	FLA	NL	83	244	53	19	0	6	(2 | 4)	90	18	36	22	31	7	61	0	1	4	0	0	-	10	.217	.301	.369
2003	COL	NL	108	356	82	20	0	20	(12 | 8)	162	49	61	46	49	2	84	1	1	7	1	3	.25	8	.230	.320	.455
2004	COL	NL	109	305	72	20	0	13	(7 | 6)	131	42	47	46	49	1	91	5	2	1	2	1	.67	6	.236	.350	.430
2005	TB	AL	19	46	9	4	0	0	(0 | 0)	13	5	5	4	9	0	11	0	0	0	0	0	-	2	.196	.327	.283
98	Fla	NL	31	113	25	5	0	7	(5 | 2)	51	13	23	16	16	0	30	0	0	1	0	1	.00	3	.221	.315	.451
98	LA	NL	102	346	75	13	0	12	(9 | 3)	124	31	35	32	29	1	99	1	1	0	0	1	.00	9	.217	.279	.358
00	Bal	AL	84	286	84	16	0	21	(12 | 9)	163	52	55	56	32	0	69	0	1	1	2	0	1.00	8	.294	.364	.570
00	CWS	AL	44	135	44	8	0	10	(7 | 3)	82	24	36	33	20	0	37	1	0	2	0	0	-	0	.326	.411	.607
12 ML YEARS			1188	3836	940	211	4	167	(87 | 80)	1660	465	570	523	475	29	997	25	18	31	6	10	.38	112	.245	.330	.433

Dan Johnson

Bats: L **Throws:** R **Pos:** 1B-101; PH-6; DH-5   **Ht:** 6'2" **Wt:** 220 **Born:** 8/10/1979 **Age:** 26

								BATTING												BASERUNNING				AVERAGES		
Year	Team	Lg	G	AB	H	2B	3B	HR	(Hm | Rd)	TB	R	RBI	RC	TBB	IBB	SO	HBP	SH	SF	SB	CS	SB%	GDP	Avg	OBP	Slg
2001	Vancvr	A-	69	247	70	15	2	11	(- | -)	122	36	41	44	27	2	63	2	0	4	0	0	-	6	.283	.354	.494
2002	Mdest	A+	126	426	125	23	1	21	(- | -)	213	56	85	82	57	4	87	0	1	8	4	1	.80	8	.293	.371	.500
2003	Mdland	AA	139	538	156	26	4	27	(- | -)	271	90	114	102	68	16	82	2	0	11	7	4	.64	14	.290	.365	.504
2003	Scrmto	AAA	4	4	1	1	0	0	(- | -)	2	0	0	0	0	0	0	0	0	0	0	0	-	0	.250	.250	.500
2004	Scrmto	AAA	142	536	160	29	5	29	(- | -)	286	95	111	118	89	2	93	9	0	6	0	1	.00	15	.299	.403	.534
2005	Scrmto	AAA	47	182	59	17	0	8	(- | -)	100	36	41	42	32	2	24	1	0	2	0	1	.00	1	.324	.424	.549
2005	OAK	AL	109	375	103	21	0	15	(2 | 13)	169	54	58	56	50	1	52	1	0	8	0	1	.00	11	.275	.355	.451

Jason Johnson

Pitches: R **Bats:** R **Pos:** SP-33   **Ht:** 6'6" **Wt:** 235 **Born:** 10/27/1973 **Age:** 32

			HOW MUCH HE PITCHED						WHAT HE GAVE UP												THE RESULTS						
Year	Team	Lg	G	GS	CG	GF	IP	BFP	H	R	ER	HR	SH	SF	HB	TBB	IBB	SO	WP	Bk	W	L	Pct	ShO	Sv-Op	Hld	ERC	ERA
1997	PIT	NL	3	0	0	0	6.0	27	10	4	4	2	0	1	0	1	0	3	0	0	0	0	-	0	0-0	0	9.59	6.00
1998	TB	AL	13	13	0	0	60.0	274	74	38	38	9	1	1	3	27	0	36	2	0	2	5	.286	0	0-0	0	6.35	5.70
1999	BAL	AL	22	21	0	0	115.1	515	120	74	70	16	2	4	3	55	0	71	5	1	8	7	.533	0	0-0	0	4.99	5.46
2000	BAL	AL	25	13	0	3	107.2	501	119	95	84	21	3	5	4	61	2	79	3	0	1	10	.091	0	0-0	2	6.18	7.02
2001	BAL	AL	32	32	2	0	196.0	856	194	109	89	28	6	6	13	77	3	114	4	0	10	12	.455	0	0-0	0	4.53	4.09
2002	BAL	AL	22	22	1	0	131.1	561	141	68	67	19	0	3	6	41	2	97	4	0	5	14	.263	0	0-0	0	4.70	4.59
2003	BAL	AL	32	32	0	0	189.2	858	216	100	88	22	3	1	10	80	8	118	7	0	10	10	.500	0	0-0	0	5.21	4.18
2004	DET	AL	33	33	2	0	196.2	859	222	121	112	22	1	10	5	60	3	125	7	1	8	15	.348	1	0-0	0	4.58	5.13
2005	DET	AL	33	33	1	0	210.0	888	233	117	106	23	9	7	6	49	4	93	17	0	8	13	.381	0	0-0	0	4.24	4.54
9 ML YEARS			215	199	6	3	1212.2	5339	1329	726	658	162	25	38	50	451	22	736	54	2	52	86	.377	1	0-0	2	4.91	4.88

Josh Johnson

Pitches: R Bats: L Pos: RP-3; SP-1　　　　　　　　　**Ht: 6'7" Wt: 240 Born: 1/31/1984 Age: 22**

Year	Team	Lg	G	GS	CG	GF	IP	BFP	H	R	ER	HR	SH	SF	HB	TBB	IBB	SO	WP	Bk	W	L	Pct	ShO	Sv-Op	Hld	ERC	ERA
2002	Marlins	R	4	3	0	0	15.0	58	8	3	1	0	0	0	2	3	0	11	0	0	2	0	1.000	0	0- -	-	1.18	0.60
2002	Jmstwn	A-	2	2	0	0	8.0	47	15	15	11	0	0	0	1	7	0	5	0	0	2	0	.000	0	0- -	-	11.13	12.38
2003	Grnsbr	A	17	17	0	0	82.1	354	69	44	33	5	6	3	9	29	0	59	2	0	4	7	.364	0	0- -	-	3.09	3.61
2004	Jupiter	A+	23	22	1	0	114.1	518	124	63	43	4	4	12	3	47	1	103	12	0	5	12	.294	0	0- -	-	4.09	3.38
2005	Carlina	AA	26	26	1	0	139.2	608	139	67	60	4	9	2	4	50	4	113	9	1	12	4	.750	0	0- -	-	3.39	3.87
2005	FLA	NL	4	1	0	0	12.1	55	11	5	5	0	1	0	1	10	0	10	0	0	0	0	-	0	0-0	0	4.82	3.65

| | | | **HOW MUCH HE PITCHED** | | | | | | **WHAT HE GAVE UP** | | | | | | | | | | | | **THE RESULTS** | | | | | | |

Kelly Johnson

Bats: L Throws: R Pos: LF-79; PH-5; PR-4; DH-1　　　　　　　**Ht: 6'1" Wt: 205 Born: 2/22/1982 Age: 24**

Year	Team	Lg	G	AB	H	2B	3B	HR	(Hm	Rd)	TB	R	RBI	RC	TBB	IBB	SO	HBP	SH	SF	SB	CS	SB%	GDP	Avg	OBP	Slg
2000	Braves	R	53	193	52	12	3	4	(-	-)	82	27	29	30	24	0	45	0	1	1	6	1	.86	4	.269	.349	.425
2001	Macon	A	124	415	120	22	1	23	(-	-)	213	75	66	91	71	7	111	10	1	1	25	6	.81	0	.289	.404	.513
2002	MrtlBh	A+	126	482	123	21	5	12	(-	-)	190	62	49	62	51	0	105	1	2	4	12	15	.44	5	.255	.325	.394
2003	Braves	R	6	26	10	1	1	1	(-	-)	16	10	3	6	3	1	4	1	0	0	1	1	.50	2	.385	.467	.615
2003	Grnville	AA	98	334	92	22	5	6	(-	-)	142	46	45	51	35	3	81	0	3	5	10	3	.77	4	.275	.340	.425
2004	Grnville	AA	135	479	135	35	3	16	(-	-)	224	70	50	78	49	2	102	3	0	3	9	9	.50	5	.282	.350	.468
2005	Rchmd	AAA	44	155	48	12	3	8	(-	-)	90	35	22	40	34	7	22	2	0	1	7	1	.88	5	.310	.438	.581
2005	ATL	NL	87	290	70	12	3	9	(2	7)	115	46	40	41	40	1	75	1	2	1	2	1	.67	11	.241	.334	.397

| | | | **BATTING** | | | | | | | | | | | | | | | | | **BASERUNNING** | | | | **AVERAGES** | | |

Nick Johnson

Bats: L Throws: L Pos: 1B-129; PH-3　　　　　　　　　　　**Ht: 6'3" Wt: 224 Born: 9/19/1978 Age: 27**

Year	Team	Lg	G	AB	H	2B	3B	HR	(Hm	Rd)	TB	R	RBI	RC	TBB	IBB	SO	HBP	SH	SF	SB	CS	SB%	GDP	Avg	OBP	Slg
2005	NewOr*	AAA	3	6	0	0	0	0	(-	-)	0	0	0	0	1	0	2	0	0	0	0	0	-	0	.000	.143	.000
2001	NYA	AL	23	67	13	2	0	2	(1	1)	21	6	8	6	7	0	15	4	0	0	0	0	-	3	.194	.308	.313
2002	NYA	AL	129	378	92	15	0	15	(7	8)	152	56	58	59	48	5	98	12	3	0	1	3	.25	11	.243	.347	.402
2003	NYA	AL	96	324	92	19	0	14	(8	6)	153	60	47	65	70	4	57	8	3	1	5	2	.71	9	.284	.422	.472
2004	MON	NL	73	251	63	16	0	7	(4	3)	100	35	33	36	40	2	58	3	0	1	6	3	.67	5	.251	.359	.398
2005	WAS	NL	131	453	131	35	3	15	(7	8)	217	66	74	83	80	8	87	12	0	2	3	8	.27	15	.289	.408	.479
	5 ML YEARS		452	1473	391	87	3	53	(27	26)	643	223	220	249	245	19	315	39	6	4	15	16	.48	43	.265	.383	.437

| | | | **BATTING** | | | | | | | | | | | | | | | | | **BASERUNNING** | | | | **AVERAGES** | | |

Randy Johnson

Pitches: L Bats: R Pos: SP-34　　　　　　　　　　　　　**Ht: 6'10" Wt: 232 Born: 9/10/1963 Age: 42**

Year	Team	Lg	G	GS	CG	GF	IP	BFP	H	R	ER	HR	SH	SF	HB	TBB	IBB	SO	WP	Bk	W	L	Pct	ShO	Sv-Op	Hld	ERC	ERA
1988	MON	NL	4	4	1	0	26.0	109	23	8	7	3	0	0	0	7	0	25	3	0	3	0	1.000	0	0-0	0	2.96	2.42
1989	2 Tms		29	28	2	1	160.2	715	147	100	86	13	10	13	3	96	2	130	7	7	7	13	.350	0	0-0	0	4.26	4.82
1990	SEA	AL	33	33	5	0	219.2	944	174	103	89	26	7	6	5	120	2	194	4	2	14	11	.560	2	0-0	0	3.68	3.65
1991	SEA	AL	33	33	2	0	201.1	889	151	96	89	15	9	8	12	152	0	228	12	2	13	10	.565	1	0-0	0	4.15	3.98
1992	SEA	AL	31	31	6	0	210.1	922	154	104	88	13	3	8	18	144	1	241	11	3	12	14	.462	2	0-0	0	3.75	3.77
1993	SEA	AL	35	34	10	0	255.1	1043	185	97	92	22	8	7	16	99	1	308	8	2	19	8	.704	3	1-1	0	2.73	3.24
1994	SEA	AL	23	23	9	0	172.0	694	132	65	61	14	3	1	6	72	2	204	5	0	13	6	.684	4	0-0	0	2.99	3.19
1995	SEA	AL	30	30	6	0	214.1	866	159	65	59	12	2	1	6	65	1	294	5	2	18	2	.900	3	0-0	0	2.18	2.48
1996	SEA	AL	14	8	0	2	61.1	256	48	27	25	8	1	0	2	25	0	85	3	1	5	0	1.000	0	1-2	0	3.24	3.67
1997	SEA	AL	30	29	5	0	213.0	850	147	60	54	20	4	1	10	77	2	291	4	0	20	4	.833	2	0-0	0	2.47	2.28
1998	2 Tms		34	34	10	0	244.1	1014	203	102	89	23	5	2	14	86	1	329	7	2	19	11	.633	6	0-0	0	3.16	3.28
1999	ARI	NL	35	35	12	0	271.2	1079	207	86	75	30	4	3	9	70	3	364	5	2	17	9	.654	2	0-0	0	2.49	2.48
2000	ARI	NL	35	35	8	0	248.2	1001	202	89	73	23	14	5	6	76	1	347	5	2	19	7	.731	3	0-0	0	2.80	2.64
2001	ARI	NL	35	34	3	1	249.2	994	181	74	69	19	10	5	18	71	2	372	8	1	21	6	.778	2	0-0	0	2.35	2.49
2002	ARI	NL	35	35	8	0	260.0	1035	197	78	67	26	4	2	13	71	4	334	3	2	24	5	.828	4	0-0	0	2.54	2.32
2003	ARI	NL	18	18	1	0	114.0	489	125	61	54	16	4	3	8	27	3	125	1	1	6	8	.429	1	0-0	0	4.52	4.26
2004	ARI	NL	35	35	4	0	245.2	964	177	88	71	18	7	5	10	44	1	290	3	1	16	14	.533	2	0-0	0	1.82	2.60
2005	NYA	AL	34	34	4	0	225.2	920	207	102	95	32	5	5	12	47	2	211	3	1	17	8	.680	0	0-0	0	3.38	3.79
89	Mon	NL	7	6	0	1	29.2	143	29	25	22	2	3	4	0	26	1	26	2	2	0	4	.000	0	0-0	0	5.42	6.67
89	Sea	AL	22	22	2	0	131.0	572	118	75	64	11	7	9	3	70	1	104	5	5	7	9	.438	0	0-0	0	4.01	4.40
98	Sea	AL	23	23	6	0	160.0	685	146	90	77	19	5	1	11	60	0	213	7	2	9	10	.474	2	0-0	0	3.88	4.33
98	Hou	NL	11	11	4	0	84.1	329	57	12	12	4	0	1	3	26	1	116	0	0	10	1	.909	4	0-0	0	1.93	1.28
	18 ML YEARS		523	513	96	5	3593.2	14784	2819	1405	1243	333	100	75	168	1349	25	4372	98	29	263	136	.659	37	2-3	0	2.96	3.11

| | | | **HOW MUCH HE PITCHED** | | | | | | **WHAT HE GAVE UP** | | | | | | | | | | | | **THE RESULTS** | | | | | | |

Reed Johnson

Bats: R Throws: R Pos: LF-118; RF-35; PH-22; CF-9; PR-3　　　　**Ht: 5'10" Wt: 180 Born: 12/8/1976 Age: 29**

Year	Team	Lg	G	AB	H	2B	3B	HR	(Hm	Rd)	TB	R	RBI	RC	TBB	IBB	SO	HBP	SH	SF	SB	CS	SB%	GDP	Avg	OBP	Slg
2003	TOR	AL	114	412	121	21	2	10	(6	4)	176	79	52	64	20	1	67	20	1	4	5	3	.63	10	.294	.353	.427
2004	TOR	AL	141	537	145	25	2	10	(8	2)	204	68	61	65	28	2	98	12	3	2	6	3	.67	17	.270	.320	.380
2005	TOR	AL	142	398	107	21	6	8	(4	4)	164	55	58	57	22	1	82	16	2	1	5	6	.45	8	.269	.332	.412
	3 ML YEARS		397	1347	373	67	10	28	(18	10)	544	202	171	186	70	4	247	48	6	7	16	12	.57	35	.277	.334	.404

| | | | **BATTING** | | | | | | | | | | | | | | | | | **BASERUNNING** | | | | **AVERAGES** | | |

Russ Johnson

Bats: R Throws: R Pos: 3B-8; 1B-7; PR-5; RF-3; PH-3; DH-2; 2B-1   **Ht:** 5'10" **Wt:** 198 **Born:** 2/22/1973 **Age:** 33

								BATTING													BASERUNNING				AVERAGES		
Year	Team	Lg	G	AB	H	2B	3B	HR	(Hm	Rd)	TB	R	RBI	RC	TBB	IBB	SO	HBP	SH	SF	SB	CS	SB%	GDP	Avg	OBP	Slg
2005	Clmbs*	AAA	73	281	82	26	0	9	(-	-)	135	43	40	51	39	0	50	1	1	3	5	5	.50	8	.292	.377	.480
1997	HOU	NL	21	60	18	1	0	2	(2	0)	25	7	9	8	6	0	14	0	1	0	1	1	.50	2	.300	.364	.417
1998	HOU	NL	8	13	3	1	0	0	(0	0)	4	2	0	1	1	0	5	1	0	0	1	0	1.00	1	.231	.333	.308
1999	HOU	NL	83	156	44	10	0	5	(2	3)	69	24	23	24	20	0	31	0	4	3	2	3	.40	3	.282	.358	.442
2000	2 Tms		100	230	55	8	0	2	(0	0)	69	32	20	23	27	0	40	1	4	1	5	2	.71	7	.239	.320	.300
2001	TB	AL	85	248	73	19	2	4	(1	3)	108	32	33	42	34	0	57	1	4	1	2	2	.50	2	.294	.380	.435
2002	TB	AL	45	111	24	5	0	1	(0	1)	32	15	12	13	16	1	22	1	2	0	5	2	.71	2	.216	.320	.288
2005	NYA	AL	22	18	4	2	0	0	(0	0)	6	5	0	2	1	0	4	1	0	0	0	0	-	0	.222	.300	.333
00	Hou	NL	26	45	8	0	0	0	(0	0)	8	4	3	0	2	0	10	0	1	0	1	1	.50	3	.178	.213	.178
00	TB	AL	74	185	47	8	0	2	(2	0)	61	28	17	23	25	0	30	1	3	1	4	1	.80	4	.254	.344	.330
	7 ML YEARS		364	836	221	46	2	14	(7	7)	313	117	97	113	105	1	173	5	15	5	16	10	.62	17	.264	.348	.374

Tyler Johnson

Pitches: L Bats: B Pos: RP-5   **Ht:** 6'2" **Wt:** 180 **Born:** 6/7/1981 **Age:** 25

					HOW MUCH HE PITCHED								WHAT HE GAVE UP									THE RESULTS					
Year	Team	Lg	G	GS	CG	GF	IP	BFP	H	R	ER	HR	SH	SF	HB	TBB	IBB	SO	WP	Bk	W	L	Pct	ShO	Sv-Op	Hld	ERC	ERA
2001	JhsCty	R+	9	9	0	0	41.0	170	26	17	12	1	0	0	3	21	0	58	9	5	1	1	.500	0	0--	-	2.34	2.63
2001	Peoria	A	3	3	0	0	14.0	66	14	9	6	1	0	0	0	10	0	15	2	1	0	1	.000	0	0--	-	4.98	3.86
2002	Peoria	A	22	18	0	1	121.1	502	96	35	27	7	4	0	4	42	1	132	8	4	15	3	.833	0	0--	-	2.58	2.00
2003	PlmBh	A+	22	10	0	3	79.0	354	79	29	27	2	10	2	1	38	2	81	8	0	5	5	.500	0	0--	-	3.76	3.08
2003	Tenn	AA	20	0	0	6	27.1	113	16	7	5	1	4	2	3	15	1	39	0	0	1	1	.500	0	0--	-	2.40	1.65
2004	Tenn	AA	53	0	0	21	56.1	254	48	32	30	4	0	0	3	37	1	77	8	0	2	2	.500	0	4--	-	4.16	4.79
2005	Memp	AA	57	0	0	15	59.0	254	51	31	28	6	1	0	3	26	2	77	2	0	2	1	.667	0	7--	-	3.61	4.27
2005	STL	NL	5	0	0	1	2.2	13	3	0	0	0	0	0	0	3	0	4	0	0	0	0	-	0	0-1	1	7.28	0.00

Mike Johnston

Pitches: L Bats: L Pos: RP-1   **Ht:** 6'2" **Wt:** 215 **Born:** 3/30/1979 **Age:** 27

					HOW MUCH HE PITCHED								WHAT HE GAVE UP									THE RESULTS					
Year	Team	Lg	G	GS	CG	GF	IP	BFP	H	R	ER	HR	SH	SF	HB	TBB	IBB	SO	WP	Bk	W	L	Pct	ShO	Sv-Op	Hld	ERC	ERA
1998	Pirates	R	13	3	0	3	29.2	127	28	17	11	0	1	2	2	10	0	17	5	1	1	2	.333	0	0--	-	3.01	3.34
1998	Erie	AA	2	0	0	2	2.0	11	4	4	1	0	0	0	0	1	0	2	0	0	0	0	-	0	0--	-	9.72	4.50
1999	Wmspt	A-	14	2	0	3	42.1	193	46	26	20	5	0	0	3	18	0	30	3	1	3	2	.600	0	2--	-	5.00	4.25
2000	Hickory	A	26	0	0	7	50.2	245	66	42	35	2	2	2	5	30	0	52	0	2	4	2	.667	0	2--	-	6.63	6.22
2001	Hickory	A	16	16	0	0	93.1	404	88	47	35	5	0	4	5	42	1	80	7	1	4	5	.444	0	0--	-	3.83	3.38
2001	Lynbrg	A+	11	10	1	0	62.0	276	66	27	23	2	4	2	3	24	0	44	4	2	4	4	.500	0	0--	-	4.02	3.34
2002	Lynbrg	A+	15	10	0	1	57.0	253	50	29	23	2	1	2	7	26	0	50	8	0	4	2	.667	0	0--	-	3.54	3.63
2003	Altna	AA	46	0	0	19	72.1	285	49	17	17	4	5	2	5	27	3	65	7	1	6	2	.750	0	7--	-	2.30	2.12
2004	Nashv	AAA	19	0	0	1	15.0	79	19	14	14	3	0	0	2	13	1	6	0	0	0	0	-	0	0--	-	8.84	8.40
2005	Indy	AAA	52	0	0	8	57.2	246	43	21	19	5	3	1	4	30	2	52	6	0	2	1	.667	0	0--	-	3.26	2.97
2004	PIT	NL	24	0	0	5	22.2	110	29	16	11	2	1	0	2	15	1	18	0	0	0	3	.000	0	0-1	4	7.12	4.37
2005	PIT	NL	1	0	0	1	1.0	7	4	4	4	2	0	0	0	0	0	2	0	0	0	0	-	0	0-0	0	47.55	36.00
	2 ML YEARS		25	0	0	6	23.2	117	33	20	15	4	1	0	2	15	1	20	0	0	0	3	.000	0	0-1	4	8.47	5.70

Kenji Jojima

Bats: R Throws: R Pos: C   **Ht:** 5'11" **Wt:** 198 **Born:** 6/8/1976 **Age:** 30

								BATTING													BASERUNNING				AVERAGES		
Year	Team	Lg	G	AB	H	2B	3B	HR	(Hm	Rd)	TB	R	RBI	RC	TBB	IBB	SO	HBP	SH	SF	SB	CS	SB%	GDP	Avg	OBP	Slg
1995	Fk Dai	Jap	12	12	2	0	0	0	(-	-)	2	2	1	0	1	-	4	0	0	0	0	0	-	-	.167	.231	.167
1996	Fk Dai	Jap	17	58	14	2	0	4	(-	-)	28	5	9	8	3	-	9	1	0	0	1	0	1.00	-	.241	.290	.483
1997	Fk Dai	Jap	120	432	133	24	2	15	(-	-)	206	49	68	72	22	-	62	5	4	7	6	2	.75	-	.308	.343	.477
1998	Fk Dai	Jap	122	395	99	19	0	16	(-	-)	166	53	58	54	27	-	67	8	6	4	5	2	.71	-	.251	.309	.420
1999	Fk Dai	Jap	135	493	151	33	1	17	(-	-)	237	65	77	85	31	-	61	8	6	1	6	2	.75	-	.306	.356	.481
2000	Fk Dai	Jap	84	303	94	22	2	9	(-	-)	147	38	50	57	27	-	48	6	5	1	10	2	.83	-	.310	.377	.485
2001	Fk Dai	Jap	140	534	138	18	0	31	(-	-)	249	63	95	78	31	-	55	6	5	2	9	4	.69	-	.258	.305	.466
2002	Fk Dai	Jap	115	416	122	18	0	25	(-	-)	215	60	74	75	30	5	41	8	3	6	8	7	.53	-	.293	.348	.517
2003	Fk Dai	Jap	140	551	182	39	2	34	(-	-)	327	101	119	128	53	10	50	15	2	7	9	4	.69	-	.330	.399	.593
2004	Fk Dai	Jap	116	426	144	25	1	36	(-	-)	279	91	91	113	49	5	45	22	0	1	6	5	.55	-	.338	.432	.655
2005	Sbank	Jap	116	411	127	22	4	24	(-	-)	229	70	57	86	33	-	32	17	0	3	3	4	.43	-	.309	.381	.557

Andruw Jones

Bats: R Throws: R Pos: CF-159; PH-1   **Ht:** 6'1" **Wt:** 210 **Born:** 4/23/1977 **Age:** 29

								BATTING													BASERUNNING				AVERAGES		
Year	Team	Lg	G	AB	H	2B	3B	HR	(Hm	Rd)	TB	R	RBI	RC	TBB	IBB	SO	HBP	SH	SF	SB	CS	SB%	GDP	Avg	OBP	Slg
1996	ATL	NL	31	106	23	7	1	5	(3	2)	47	11	13	13	7	0	29	0	0	0	3	0	1.00	1	.217	.265	.443
1997	ATL	NL	153	399	92	18	1	18	(5	13)	166	60	70	54	56	2	107	4	5	3	20	11	.65	11	.231	.329	.416
1998	ATL	NL	159	582	158	33	8	31	(16	15)	300	89	90	97	40	8	129	4	1	4	27	4	.87	10	.271	.321	.515
1999	ATL	NL	**162**	592	163	35	5	26	(10	16)	286	97	84	103	76	11	103	9	0	2	24	12	.67	12	.275	.365	.483
2000	ATL	NL	161	**656**	199	36	6	36	(15	21)	355	122	104	127	59	0	100	9	0	5	21	6	.78	12	.303	.366	.541
2001	ATL	NL	161	625	157	25	2	34	(16	18)	288	104	104	90	56	3	142	3	0	9	11	4	.73	10	.251	.312	.461
2002	ATL	NL	154	560	148	34	0	35	(18	17)	287	91	94	94	83	4	135	10	0	6	8	3	.73	14	.264	.366	.513
2003	ATL	NL	156	595	165	28	2	36	(16	20)	305	101	116	92	53	2	125	5	0	6	4	5	.57	18	.277	.338	.513
2004	ATL	NL	154	570	149	34	4	29	(13	16)	278	85	91	75	71	9	147	3	0	2	6	6	.50	24	.261	.345	.488
2005	ATL	NL	160	586	154	24	3	**51**	(21	30)	337	95	**128**	91	64	13	112	15	0	7	5	3	.63	19	.263	.347	.575
	10 ML YEARS		1451	5271	1408	274	32	301	(133	168)	2649	855	894	836	565	52	1129	62	6	44	129	52	.71	131	.267	.342	.503

Chipper Jones

Bats: B Throws: R Pos: 3B-101; PH-9   Ht: 6'4" Wt: 210 Born: 4/24/1972 Age: 34

									BATTING														BASERUNNING				AVERAGES		
Year	Team	Lg	G	AB	H	2B	3B	HR	(Hm	Rd)	TB	R	RBI	RC	TBB	IBB	SO	HBP	SH	SF	SB	CS	SB%	GDP	Avg	OBP	Slg
2005	Rome*	A	3	6	3	0	0	0	(-	-)	3	1	2	2	3	0	1	0	0	0	0	0	-	1	.500	.667	.500
1993	ATL	NL	8	3	2	1	0	0	(0	0)	3	2	0	2	1	0	1	0	0	0	0	0	-	0	.667	.750	1.000
1995	ATL	NL	140	524	139	22	3	23	(15	8)	236	87	86	84	73	1	99	0	1	4	8	4	.67	10	.265	.353	.450
1996	ATL	NL	157	598	185	32	5	30	(18	12)	317	114	110	123	87	0	88	0	1	7	14	1	.93	14	.309	.393	.530
1997	ATL	NL	157	597	176	41	3	21	(7	14)	286	100	111	104	76	8	88	0	0	6	20	5	.80	19	.295	.371	.479
1998	ATL	NL	160	601	188	29	5	34	(17	17)	329	123	107	129	96	1	93	1	1	8	16	6	.73	17	.313	.404	.547
1999	ATL	NL	157	567	181	41	1	45	(25	20)	359	116	110	150	126	18	94	2	0	6	25	3	.89	20	.319	.441	.633
2000	ATL	NL	156	579	180	38	1	36	(18	18)	328	118	111	128	95	10	64	2	0	10	14	7	.67	14	.311	.404	.566
2001	ATL	NL	159	572	189	33	5	38	(19	19)	346	113	102	136	98	20	82	2	0	5	9	10	.47	13	.330	.427	.605
2002	ATL	NL	158	548	179	35	1	26	(17	9)	294	90	100	119	107	23	89	2	0	5	8	2	.80	18	.327	.435	.536
2003	ATL	NL	153	555	169	33	2	27	(16	11)	287	103	106	110	94	13	83	1	0	6	2	2	.50	11	.305	.402	.517
2004	ATL	NL	137	472	117	20	1	30	(11	19)	229	69	96	82	84	8	96	4	0	7	2	0	1.00	15	.248	.362	.485
2005	ATL	NL	109	358	106	30	0	21	(9	12)	199	66	72	78	72	5	56	0	0	2	5	1	.83	9	.296	.412	.556
	12 ML YEARS		1651	5974	1811	355	27	331	(180	151)	3213	1101	1111	1245	1009	107	933	14	3	66	123	41	.75	159	.303	.401	.538

Greg Jones

Pitches: R Bats: R Pos: RP-6   Ht: 6'2" Wt: 195 Born: 11/15/1976 Age: 29

			HOW MUCH HE PITCHED						WHAT HE GAVE UP											THE RESULTS						
Year	Team	Lg	G	GS	CG	GF	IP	BFP	H	R	ER	HR	SH	SF	HB	TBB	IBB	SO	WP	Bk	W	L	Pct	ShO	Sv-Op	Hld	ERC	ERA
1997	Boise	A-	21	4	0	4	37.1	172	35	19	16	1	2	4	3	19	1	39	5	1	2	2	.500	0	2--	-	3.70	3.86
1998	Boise	A-	22	0	0	3	34.2	152	37	22	19	3	2	1	3	13	0	28	3	0	0	2	.000	0	1--	-	4.66	4.93
1999	CRpds	A	34	0	0	29	40.0	165	37	18	17	5	2	0	0	13	2	41	5	0	2	4	.333	0	13--	-	3.51	3.83
2000	Lk Els	A+	16	0	0	12	17.2	81	19	9	8	0	2	1	1	10	3	12	3	0	0	0	-	0	3--	-	4.29	4.08
2000	Erie	AA	11	0	0	8	15.0	66	19	9	9	1	0	0	0	4	0	7	0	0	0	2	.000	0	2--	-	4.86	5.40
2000	Edmtn	AAA	25	0	0	13	42.1	217	57	42	36	5	1	3	4	33	1	21	6	0	2	2	.500	0	1--	-	8.28	7.65
2001	RCuca	A+	6	6	0	0	27.2	118	25	15	13	2	1	1	0	11	0	27	3	0	1	3	.250	0	0--	-	3.31	4.23
2001	Angels	R	2	2	0	0	2.0	10	3	0	0	0	0	0	0	2	0	2	0	0	0	0	-	0	0--	-	9.50	0.00
2002	Salt Lk	AAA	39	0	0	9	62.2	274	68	35	30	5	0	2	1	22	0	55	3	0	7	4	.636	0	2--	-	4.26	4.31
2003	Salt Lk	AAA	33	0	0	14	47.0	184	36	24	23	4	0	1	0	9	0	56	2	0	2	3	.400	0	4--	-	2.02	4.40
2004	Salt Lk	AAA	36	0	0	11	53.1	244	63	38	34	11	0	0	2	19	0	43	2	0	1	4	.200	0	3--	-	5.77	5.74
2005	Ark	AA	3	0	0	3	3.1	13	2	1	1	0	0	0	0	1	0	2	0	0	1	0	1.000	0	0--	-	1.31	2.70
2005	Salt Lk	AAA	23	0	0	23	25.1	102	20	9	9	3	0	0	0	6	0	25	1	0	1	2	.333	0	10--	-	2.43	3.20
2003	ANA	AL	18	0	0	7	27.2	127	29	15	15	3	0	0	2	14	0	28	5	0	0	0	-	0	0-0	2	5.05	4.88
2005	LAA	AL	6	0	0	6	5.1	24	7	4	4	2	0	0	0	2	0	6	0	0	0	0	-	0	0-0	0	8.19	6.75
	2 ML YEARS		24	0	0	13	33.0	151	36	19	19	5	0	0	2	16	0	34	5	0	0	0	-	0	0-0	2	5.54	5.18

Jacque Jones

Bats: L Throws: L Pos: RF-123; CF-10; DH-9; PH-2; PR-1   Ht: 5'10" Wt: 176 Born: 4/25/1975 Age: 31

									BATTING														BASERUNNING				AVERAGES		
Year	Team	Lg	G	AB	H	2B	3B	HR	(Hm	Rd)	TB	R	RBI	RC	TBB	IBB	SO	HBP	SH	SF	SB	CS	SB%	GDP	Avg	OBP	Slg
1999	MIN	AL	95	322	93	24	2	9	(5	4)	148	54	44	46	17	1	63	4	1	3	3	4	.43	7	.289	.329	.460
2000	MIN	AL	154	523	149	26	5	19	(11	8)	242	66	76	70	26	4	111	0	1	0	7	5	.58	17	.285	.319	.463
2001	MIN	AL	149	475	131	25	0	14	(5	9)	198	57	49	63	39	2	92	3	2	0	12	9	.57	10	.276	.335	.417
2002	MIN	AL	149	577	173	37	2	27	(6	21)	295	96	85	100	37	2	129	2	4	6	6	7	.46	8	.300	.341	.511
2003	MIN	AL	136	517	157	33	1	16	(7	9)	240	76	69	73	21	2	105	4	1	5	13	1	.93	10	.304	.333	.464
2004	MIN	AL	151	555	141	22	1	24	(9	15)	237	69	80	73	40	2	117	10	2	1	13	10	.57	12	.254	.315	.427
2005	MIN	AL	142	523	130	22	4	23	(9	14)	229	74	73	72	51	12	120	5	2	4	13	4	.76	17	.249	.319	.438
	7 ML YEARS		976	3492	974	189	15	132	(52	80)	1589	492	476	497	231	25	737	28	13	19	67	40	.63	81	.279	.327	.455

Todd Jones

Pitches: R Bats: B Pos: RP-68   Ht: 6'3" Wt: 230 Born: 4/24/1968 Age: 38

			HOW MUCH HE PITCHED						WHAT HE GAVE UP											THE RESULTS						
Year	Team	Lg	G	GS	CG	GF	IP	BFP	H	R	ER	HR	SH	SF	HB	TBB	IBB	SO	WP	Bk	W	L	Pct	ShO	Sv-Op	Hld	ERC	ERA
1993	HOU	NL	27	0	0	8	37.1	150	28	14	13	4	2	1	1	15	2	25	1	1	1	2	.333	0	2-3	6	2.90	3.13
1994	HOU	NL	48	0	0	20	72.2	288	52	23	22	3	3	1	1	26	4	63	1	0	5	2	.714	0	5-9	8	2.10	2.72
1995	HOU	NL	68	0	0	40	99.2	442	89	38	34	8	5	4	6	52	17	96	5	0	6	5	.545	0	15-20	8	3.70	3.07
1996	HOU	NL	51	0	0	37	57.1	263	61	30	28	5	2	1	5	32	6	44	3	0	6	3	.667	0	17-23	1	5.16	4.40
1997	DET	AL	68	0	0	51	70.0	301	60	29	24	3	1	4	1	35	2	70	7	0	5	4	.556	0	31-36	5	3.27	3.09
1998	DET	AL	65	0	0	63	63.1	279	58	38	35	7	2	6	2	36	4	57	5	0	1	4	.200	0	28-32	0	4.37	4.97
1999	DET	AL	65	0	0	62	66.1	287	64	30	28	7	3	1	1	35	1	64	2	0	4	4	.500	0	30-35	0	4.55	3.80
2000	DET	AL	67	0	0	60	64.0	271	67	28	25	6	1	1	1	25	1	67	2	0	2	4	.333	0	42-46	0	4.43	3.52
2001	2 Tms	AL	69	0	0	36	68.0	314	87	39	32	9	3	3	0	29	1	54	3	0	5	5	.500	0	13-21	10	6.03	4.24
2002	COL	NL	79	0	0	20	82.1	352	84	43	43	10	6	3	3	28	3	73	1	0	1	4	.200	0	1-3	30	4.22	4.70
2003	2 Tms	AL	59	1	0	14	68.2	326	93	58	54	10	3	3	1	31	2	50	0	0	3	5	.375	0	0-5	4	6.73	7.08
2004	2 Tms	AL	78	0	0	16	82.1	358	84	39	38	7	5	6	6	33	5	59	2	0	11	5	.688	0	2-8	27	4.32	4.15
2005	FLA	NL	68	0	0	55	73.0	289	61	19	19	2	6	1	3	14	2	62	2	0	1	5	.167	0	40-45	1	2.15	2.10
01	Det	AL	45	0	0	28	48.2	225	60	31	25	6	2	3	0	22	1	39	3	0	4	5	.444	0	11-17	3	5.74	4.62
01	Min	AL	24	0	0	8	19.1	89	27	8	7	3	1	0	0	7	0	15	0	0	1	0	1.000	0	2-4	7	6.80	3.26
03	Col	NL	33	1	0	7	39.1	193	61	39	36	8	3	2	1	18	0	28	0	0	1	4	.200	0	0-5	3	8.77	8.24
03	Bos	NL	26	0	0	7	29.1	133	32	19	18	2	0	1	0	13	2	31	0	0	2	1	.667	0	0-0	1	4.30	5.52
04	Cin	NL	51	0	0	10	57.0	235	49	25	24	4	2	5	1	25	2	37	2	0	8	2	.800	0	1-6	22	3.37	3.79
04	Phi	NL	27	0	0	6	25.1	123	35	14	14	3	3	1	5	8	3	22	0	0	3	3	.500	0	1-2	5	6.65	4.97
	13 ML YEARS		812	1	0	472	905.0	3920	888	428	393	81	42	35	31	391	50	793	34	1	51	52	.495	0	226-286	100	4.09	3.91

131

Brian Jordan

Bats: R **Throws:** R **Pos:** LF-45; RF-17; PH-17　　　　　　**Ht:** 6'1" **Wt:** 205 **Born:** 3/29/1967 **Age:** 39

				BATTING																	**BASERUNNING**			**AVERAGES**		
Year	Team	Lg	G	AB	H	2B	3B	HR	(Hm | Rd)	TB	R	RBI	RC	TBB	IBB	SO	HBP	SH	SF	SB	CS	SB%	GDP	Avg	OBP	Slg
2005	Rome*	A	5	16	8	1	0	1	(- | -)	12	5	7	5	2	1	2	0	0	2	1	0	1.00	0	.500	.500	.750
1992	STL	NL	55	193	40	9	4	5	(3 | 2)	72	17	22	16	10	1	48	1	0	0	7	2	.78	6	.207	.250	.373
1993	STL	NL	67	223	69	10	6	10	(4 | 6)	121	33	44	39	12	0	35	4	0	3	6	6	.50	6	.309	.351	.543
1994	STL	NL	53	178	46	8	2	5	(4 | 1)	73	14	15	22	16	0	40	1	0	2	4	3	.57	6	.258	.320	.410
1995	STL	NL	131	490	145	20	4	22	(14 | 8)	239	83	81	80	22	4	79	11	0	2	24	9	.73	5	.296	.339	.488
1996	STL	NL	140	513	159	36	1	17	(3 | 14)	248	82	104	88	29	4	84	7	2	9	22	5	.81	6	.310	.349	.483
1997	STL	NL	47	145	34	5	0	0	(0 | 0)	39	17	10	13	10	1	21	6	0	0	1	6	.86	4	.234	.311	.269
1998	STL	NL	150	564	178	34	7	25	(9 | 16)	301	100	91	104	40	1	66	9	0	4	17	5	.77	18	.316	.368	.534
1999	ATL	NL	153	576	163	28	4	23	(11 | 12)	268	100	115	92	51	2	81	9	0	9	13	8	.62	9	.283	.346	.465
2000	ATL	NL	133	489	129	26	0	17	(10 | 7)	206	71	77	66	38	1	80	5	0	5	10	2	.83	12	.264	.320	.421
2001	ATL	NL	148	560	165	32	3	25	(14 | 11)	278	82	97	87	31	3	88	6	0	8	3	2	.60	18	.295	.334	.496
2002	LA	NL	128	471	134	27	3	18	(7 | 11)	221	65	80	72	34	3	86	6	0	4	2	2	.50	10	.285	.338	.469
2003	LA	NL	66	224	67	9	0	6	(3 | 3)	94	28	28	34	23	3	30	4	0	2	1	1	.50	3	.299	.372	.420
2004	TEX	AL	61	212	47	13	1	5	(4 | 1)	77	27	23	14	16	2	35	1	0	4	2	2	.50	7	.222	.275	.363
2005	ATL	NL	76	231	57	8	2	3	(2 | 1)	78	25	24	24	14	0	46	3	0	3	2	0	1.00	5	.247	.295	.338
	14 ML YEARS		1408	5069	1433	265	37	181	(85 | 96)	2315	744	811	751	346	25	819	73	2	55	119	48	.71	115	.283	.334	.457

Ryan Jorgensen

Bats: R **Throws:** R **Pos:** C-3; PH-1　　　　　　**Ht:** 6'2" **Wt:** 200 **Born:** 5/4/1979 **Age:** 27

				BATTING																	**BASERUNNING**			**AVERAGES**		
Year	Team	Lg	G	AB	H	2B	3B	HR	(Hm | Rd)	TB	R	RBI	RC	TBB	IBB	SO	HBP	SH	SF	SB	CS	SB%	GDP	Avg	OBP	Slg
2000	Eugene	A-	41	130	39	10	2	1	(- | -)	56	17	23	21	17	0	27	1	2	2	2	4	.33	1	.300	.380	.431
2001	Dytona	A+	54	188	53	12	1	8	(- | -)	91	24	29	33	23	0	39	2	0	0	1	3	.25	6	.282	.366	.484
2001	WTenn	AA	32	109	13	4	0	2	(- | -)	23	8	7	3	11	0	38	0	0	3	0	0	-	5	.119	.195	.211
2002	Jupiter	A+	60	223	58	16	0	3	(- | -)	83	26	35	30	24	0	38	1	3	0	4	1	.80	4	.260	.335	.372
2002	Portlnd	AA	41	144	32	4	0	2	(- | -)	42	15	14	12	12	0	33	1	0	0	3	1	.75	3	.222	.287	.292
2003	Carlina	AA	67	211	51	16	0	6	(- | -)	85	28	34	31	30	2	53	2	0	3	1	0	1.00	2	.242	.337	.403
2004	Albq	AAA	61	201	52	11	0	8	(- | -)	87	20	29	25	9	0	51	0	1	1	0	0	-	7	.259	.289	.433
2005	Albq	AAA	53	137	27	5	0	2	(- | -)	38	20	11	13	21	3	46	1	2	0	1	0	1.00	1	.197	.308	.277
2005	FLA	NL	4	4	0	0	0	0	(0 | 0)	0	0	0	0	0	0	3	0	0	0	0	0	-	0	.000	.000	.000

Jimmy Journell

Pitches: R **Bats:** R **Pos:** RP-5　　　　　　**Ht:** 6'4" **Wt:** 205 **Born:** 12/29/1977 **Age:** 28

			HOW MUCH HE PITCHED						**WHAT HE GAVE UP**											**THE RESULTS**					
Year	Team	Lg	G	GS	CG	GF	IP	BFP	H	R	ER	HR	SH	SF	HB	TBB	IBB	SO	WP	Bk	W	L	Pct	ShO	Sv-Op Hld	ERC	ERA
2000	NewJrs	A-	13	1	0	3	32.0	136	12	12	7	0	0	2	2	24	0	39	8	0	1	0	1.000	0	0- -	1.65	1.97
2001	Ptomc	A+	26	26	0	0	151.0	520	121	54	42	8	6	5	18	42	0	156	7	0	14	6	.700	0	0- -	3.35	2.50
2001	NwHav	AA	1	1	1	0	7.0	21	0	0	0	0	0	0	0	3	0	6	0	0	1	0	1.000	1	0- -	0.23	0.00
2002	NwHav	AA	10	10	2	0	66.2	269	50	22	20	3	2	0	6	18	0	66	2	0	3	3	.500	0	0- -	2.29	2.70
2002	Memp	AAA	7	7	0	0	36.2	166	38	16	15	3	1	1	2	18	0	32	3	0	2	4	.333	0	0- -	4.67	3.68
2003	Memp	AAA	40	7	0	16	78.0	343	80	38	34	3	5	1	6	32	2	70	5	0	6	6	.500	0	5- -	4.08	3.92
2004	Memp	AAA	4	0	0	2	2.2	13	4	0	0	0	0	0	0	1	0	5	0	0	0	0	-	0	1- -	5.97	0.00
2005	Memp	AAA	34	0	0	12	42.1	204	39	25	22	5	1	0	1	38	1	49	10	0	1	4	.200	0	1- -	5.70	4.68
2003	STL	NL	7	0	0	2	9.0	48	10	7	6	0	0	1	0	11	0	8	1	0	0	0	-	0	0-0	7.02	6.00
2005	STL	NL	5	0	0	3	4.1	23	6	6	5	1	0	0	0	5	0	5	0	0	0	1	.000	0	0-0 0	11.30	10.38
	2 ML YEARS		12	0	0	5	13.1	71	16	13	11	1	0	1	0	16	0	13	1	0	0	1	.000	0	0-0 0	8.35	7.43

Jorge Julio

Pitches: R **Bats:** R **Pos:** RP-67　　　　　　**Ht:** 6'1" **Wt:** 190 **Born:** 3/3/1979 **Age:** 27

			HOW MUCH HE PITCHED						**WHAT HE GAVE UP**											**THE RESULTS**					
Year	Team	Lg	G	GS	CG	GF	IP	BFP	H	R	ER	HR	SH	SF	HB	TBB	IBB	SO	WP	Bk	W	L	Pct	ShO	Sv-Op Hld	ERC	ERA
2001	BAL	AL	18	0	0	8	21.1	99	25	13	9	2	2	0	1	9	0	22	1	0	1	1	.500	0	0-1 3	5.17	3.80
2002	BAL	AL	67	0	0	61	68.0	289	55	22	15	5	1	1	2	27	3	55	8	0	5	6	.455	0	25-31 1	2.83	1.99
2003	BAL	AL	64	0	0	51	61.2	273	60	36	30	10	2	1	2	34	4	52	0	0	0	7	.000	0	36-44 2	5.05	4.38
2004	BAL	AL	65	0	0	50	69.0	306	59	35	35	11	2	3	3	39	4	70	7	0	2	5	.286	0	22-26 2	4.35	4.57
2005	BAL	AL	67	0	0	19	71.2	314	76	50	47	14	1	3	2	24	4	58	10	0	3	5	.375	0	0-2 12	4.80	5.90
	5 ML YEARS		281	0	0	189	291.2	1281	275	156	136	42	8	8	10	133	15	257	26	0	11	24	.314	0	83-104 20	4.29	4.20

Gabe Kapler

Bats: R **Throws:** R **Pos:** RF-22; CF-12; LF-8; PH-4; PR-3　　　　　　**Ht:** 6'2" **Wt:** 208 **Born:** 8/31/1975 **Age:** 30

				BATTING																	**BASERUNNING**			**AVERAGES**		
Year	Team	Lg	G	AB	H	2B	3B	HR	(Hm | Rd)	TB	R	RBI	RC	TBB	IBB	SO	HBP	SH	SF	SB	CS	SB%	GDP	Avg	OBP	Slg
2005	Lowell*	A-	2	8	1	0	0	0	(- | -)	1	1	0	0	1	0	3	0	0	0	0	0	-	0	.125	.222	.125
2005	Pwtckt*	AAA	6	22	14	3	1	2	(- | -)	25	7	6	10	0	0	3	0	0	0	0	0	-	0	.636	.636	1.136
1998	DET	AL	7	25	5	0	1	0	(0 | 0)	7	3	0	2	1	0	4	0	0	0	2	0	1.00	0	.200	.231	.280
1999	DET	AL	130	416	102	22	4	18	(12 | 6)	186	60	49	59	42	0	74	2	4	4	11	5	.69	7	.245	.315	.447
2000	TEX	AL	116	444	134	32	1	14	(11 | 3)	210	59	66	72	42	2	57	0	2	3	8	4	.67	12	.302	.360	.473
2001	TEX	AL	134	483	129	29	1	17	(11 | 6)	211	77	72	77	61	2	70	3	2	7	23	6	.79	10	.267	.348	.437
2002	2 Tms		112	315	88	16	4	2	(1 | 1)	118	37	34	44	16	0	53	1	7	3	11	4	.73	5	.279	.313	.375
2003	2 Tms		107	225	61	13	1	4	(2 | 2)	88	39	27	28	22	1	41	0	0	0	6	2	.75	8	.271	.336	.391
2004	BOS	AL	136	290	79	14	1	6	(3 | 3)	113	51	33	32	15	0	49	3	5	2	5	4	.56	5	.272	.311	.390
2005	BOS	AL	36	97	24	7	0	1	(0 | 1)	34	15	9	7	3	0	15	2	1	1	1	0	1.00	1	.247	.282	.351
	02 Tex	AL	72	196	51	12	1	0	(0 | 0)	65	25	17	20	8	0	30	0	7	3	5	2	.71	3	.260	.285	.332
	02 Col	NL	40	119	37	4	3	2	(1 | 1)	53	12	17	24	8	0	23	1	0	0	6	2	.75	2	.311	.359	.445

Year Team	Lg	G	AB	H	2B	3B	HR	(Hm Rd)	TB	R	RBI	RC	TBB	IBB	SO	HBP	SH	SF	SB	CS	SB%	GDP	Avg	OBP	Slg
								BATTING											BASERUNNING				AVERAGES		
03 Col	NL	39	67	15	2	0	0	(0 0)	17	10	4	5	8	1	18	0	0	0	2	0	1.00	3	.224	.307	.254
03 Bos	AL	68	158	46	11	1	4	(2 2)	71	29	23	23	14	0	23	0	0	0	4	2	.67	5	.291	.349	.449
8 ML YEARS		778	2295	622	133	13	62	(40 22)	967	341	290	321	202	5	363	10	17	20	67	25	.73	48	.271	.330	.421

Jason Karnuth

Pitches: R **Bats:** R **Pos:** RP-3   **Ht:** 6'2" **Wt:** 190 **Born:** 5/15/1976 **Age:** 30

Year	Team	Lg	G	GS	CG	GF	IP	BFP	H	R	ER	HR	SH	SF	HB	TBB	IBB	SO	WP	Bk	W	L	Pct	ShO	Sv-Op	Hld	ERC	ERA
1997	NewJrs	A-	7	7	0	0	38.2	158	33	8	8	0	1	1	1	9	0	23	2	0	4	1	.800	0	0- -	-	2.13	1.86
1997	Peoria	A	4	4	0	0	23.0	105	29	19	17	1	1	1	2	7	1	12	2	1	0	3	.000	0	0- -	-	5.01	6.65
1998	PrWill	A+	16	15	2	1	108.0	424	86	26	20	3	6	0	7	14	0	53	4	0	8	1	.889	2	0- -	-	1.86	1.67
1999	Ark	AA	26	26	2	0	160.1	711	175	105	93	16	5	7	11	55	0	71	2	0	7	11	.389	0	0- -	-	4.61	5.22
2000	Ark	AA	8	8	1	0	50.1	224	59	30	21	3	1	2	1	14	0	31	5	1	2	3	.400	0	0- -	-	4.26	3.75
2000	Memp	AA	16	13	0	1	78.0	350	89	47	35	7	4	2	5	27	0	28	3	0	5	4	.556	0	0- -	-	4.80	4.04
2001	Memp	AAA	55	0	0	17	73.2	327	82	37	35	7	3	2	6	24	0	42	2	0	4	4	.500	0	3- -	-	4.69	4.28
2002	NwHav	AA	58	0	0	20	70.0	307	74	34	28	7	3	1	2	23	2	46	3	0	3	4	.429	0	4- -	-	4.11	3.60
2002	Memp	AAA	1	0	0	1	1.0	4	1	0	0	0	0	0	0	0	0	0	0	0	0	0	-	0	0- -	-	1.95	0.00
2003	WTenn	AA	45	0	0	36	48.1	208	53	21	18	3	8	4	2	11	2	36	0	0	3	5	.375	0	13- -	-	3.73	3.35
2003	Iowa	AAA	13	0	0	4	19.0	88	23	12	10	4	2	0	0	12	0	7	0	0	0	1	.000	0	1- -	-	7.39	4.74
2004	Erie	AA	9	0	0	9	10.0	44	10	3	3	0	1	0	0	4	1	9	0	0	0	0	-	0	6- -	-	3.12	2.70
2004	Toledo	AAA	46	0	0	16	55.1	229	45	26	23	4	0	0	2	16	2	34	1	0	5	2	.714	0	2- -	-	2.53	3.74
2005	Toledo	AAA	63	0	0	51	67.2	285	65	19	16	1	6	0	1	17	4	36	0	0	7	2	.778	0	23- -	-	2.65	2.13
2005	DET	AL	3	0	0	2	1.2	7	2	1	1	0	0	0	0	0	0	0	0	0	0	0	-	0	0-0	0	2.89	5.40

Steve Karsay

Pitches: R **Bats:** R **Pos:** RP-20   **Ht:** 6'3" **Wt:** 215 **Born:** 3/24/1972 **Age:** 34

Year	Team	Lg	G	GS	CG	GF	IP	BFP	H	R	ER	HR	SH	SF	HB	TBB	IBB	SO	WP	Bk	W	L	Pct	ShO	Sv-Op	Hld	ERC	ERA
2005	Frisco*	AA	19	0	0	4	29.2	124	29	18	12	2	2	1	0	6	2	30	1	0	1	2	.333	0	0- -	-	2.82	3.64
2005	Okla*	AAA	4	0	0	0	4.0	24	11	9	6	0	0	0	0	1	0	5	1	0	0	1	.000	0	0- -	-	13.89	13.50
1993	OAK	AL	8	8	0	0	49.0	210	49	23	22	4	0	2	2	16	1	33	1	0	3	3	.500	0	0-0	0	3.78	4.04
1994	OAK	AL	4	4	1	0	28.0	115	26	8	8	1	2	1	1	8	0	15	0	0	1	1	.500	0	0-0	0	3.01	2.57
1997	OAK	AL	24	24	0	0	132.2	609	166	92	85	20	2	5	9	47	3	92	7	0	3	12	.200	0	0-0	0	5.97	5.77
1998	CLE	AL	11	1	0	4	24.1	111	31	16	16	3	1	2	2	6	1	13	2	0	0	2	.000	0	0-0	2	5.40	5.92
1999	CLE	AL	50	3	0	13	78.2	324	71	29	26	6	2	3	2	30	3	68	5	0	10	2	.833	0	1-3	9	3.45	2.97
2000	CLE	AL	72	0	0	46	76.2	329	79	33	32	5	2	2	3	25	4	66	0	0	5	9	.357	0	20-29	11	3.79	3.76
2001	2 Tms	AL	74	0	0	29	88.0	356	73	27	23	5	6	4	1	25	10	83	3	0	3	5	.375	0	8-12	12	2.36	2.35
2002	NYA	AL	78	0	0	38	88.1	379	87	33	32	7	7	3	2	30	14	65	3	0	6	4	.600	0	12-16	14	3.42	3.26
2004	NYA	AL	7	0	0	6	6.2	27	5	3	2	2	0	2	0	2	0	4	1	0	0	0	-	0	0-0	3	3.50	2.70
2005	2 Tms	AL	20	0	0	10	21.2	106	36	19	17	2	0	2	0	7	1	14	1	0	0	1	.000	0	0-0	2	7.61	7.06
01	Cle	AL	31	0	0	8	43.1	166	29	6	6	1	3	1	0	8	2	44	2	0	0	1	.000	0	1-1	8	1.33	1.25
01	Atl	NL	43	0	0	21	44.2	190	44	21	17	4	3	3	1	17	8	39	1	0	3	4	.429	0	7-11	4	3.68	3.43
05	NYY	AL	6	0	0	2	6.0	29	10	5	4	0	0	1	0	2	1	5	0	0	0	0	-	0	0-0	0	6.72	6.00
05	Tex	AL	14	0	0	8	15.2	77	26	14	13	2	0	1	0	5	0	9	1	0	0	1	.000	0	0-0	2	7.93	7.47
10 ML YEARS			348	40	1	146	594.0	2566	623	283	263	55	22	26	22	196	37	453	23	0	31	39	.443	0	41-60	50	4.07	3.98

Matt Kata

Bats: B **Throws:** R **Pos:** PH-26; 2B-10; PR-6; SS-1; RF-1; DH-1   **Ht:** 6'1" **Wt:** 185 **Born:** 3/14/1978 **Age:** 28

Year	Team	Lg	G	AB	H	2B	3B	HR	(Hm Rd)	TB	R	RBI	RC	TBB	IBB	SO	HBP	SH	SF	SB	CS	SB%	GDP	Avg	OBP	Slg
									BATTING											BASERUNNING				AVERAGES		
2005	Tucsn*	AAA	46	200	62	10	3	3	(- -)	87	25	28	29	6	0	25	1	4	3	5	1	.83	4	.310	.329	.435
2005	S-WB*	AAA	24	96	30	5	1	0	(- -)	37	10	4	12	4	0	14	0	2	0	2	1	.67	6	.313	.340	.385
2003	ARI	NL	78	288	74	16	5	7	(3 4)	121	42	29	40	25	0	53	1	5	3	3	2	.60	4	.257	.315	.420
2004	ARI	NL	42	162	40	9	2	2	(1 1)	59	17	13	19	13	2	29	0	1	1	4	1	.80	1	.247	.301	.364
2005	2 Tms	NL	40	37	7	2	1	0	(0 0)	11	7	0	2	5	0	6	0	2	0	0	1	.00	0	.189	.286	.297
05	Ari	NL	30	31	6	2	1	0	(0 0)	10	6	0	2	5	0	4	0	2	0	0	1	.00	0	.194	.306	.323
05	Phi	NL	10	6	1	0	0	0	(0 0)	1	1	0	0	0	0	2	0	0	0	0	0	-	0	.167	.167	.167
3 ML YEARS			160	487	121	27	8	9	(4 5)	191	66	42	61	43	2	88	1	8	4	7	4	.64	5	.248	.308	.392

Scott Kazmir

Pitches: L **Bats:** L **Pos:** SP-32   **Ht:** 6'0" **Wt:** 170 **Born:** 1/24/1984 **Age:** 22

Year	Team	Lg	G	GS	CG	GF	IP	BFP	H	R	ER	HR	SH	SF	HB	TBB	IBB	SO	WP	Bk	W	L	Pct	ShO	Sv-Op	Hld	ERC	ERA
2002	Bklyn	A-	5	5	0	0	18.0	65	5	2	1	0	0	0	0	7	0	34	0	0	0	1	.000	0	0- -	-	0.86	0.50
2003	CptCty	A	18	18	0	0	76.1	304	50	26	20	6	3	0	3	28	0	105	12	1	4	4	.500	0	0- -	-	2.20	2.36
2003	StLuci	A+	7	7	0	0	33.0	141	29	15	12	0	1	1	2	16	0	40	2	0	1	2	.333	0	0- -	-	3.30	3.27
2004	StLuci	A+	11	11	0	0	50.0	211	49	20	19	3	5	5	0	22	0	51	5	0	1	2	.333	0	0- -	-	3.95	3.42
2004	Mont	AA	4	4	0	0	25.0	96	14	7	4	0	3	2	1	11	0	24	1	0	1	2	.333	0	0- -	-	1.63	1.44
2004	Bnghtn	AA	4	4	0	0	26.0	100	16	6	5	0	3	2	3	9	0	29	1	0	2	1	.667	0	0- -	-	1.82	1.73
2004	TB	AL	8	7	0	0	33.1	152	33	22	21	4	0	0	2	21	0	41	3	0	2	3	.400	0	0-0	0	5.36	5.67
2005	TB	AL	32	32	0	0	186.0	818	172	90	78	12	6	9	10	100	3	174	7	1	10	9	.526	0	0-0	0	4.13	3.77
2 ML YEARS			40	39	0	0	219.1	970	205	112	99	16	6	9	12	121	3	215	10	1	12	12	.500	0	0-0	0	4.31	4.06

Austin Kearns

Bats: R **Throws:** R **Pos:** RF-107; PH-7; CF-2   **Ht:** 6'3" **Wt:** 220 **Born:** 5/20/1980 **Age:** 26

Year	Team	Lg	G	AB	H	2B	3B	HR	(Hm	Rd)	TB	R	RBI	RC	TBB	IBB	SO	HBP	SH	SF	SB	CS	SB%	GDP	Avg	OBP	Slg
2005	Lsvlle*	AAA	28	111	38	15	1	7	(-	-)	76	24	21	28	11	2	30	1	0	0	0	0	-	9	.342	.407	.685
2002	CIN	NL	107	372	117	24	3	13	(7	6)	186	66	56	70	54	3	81	6	0	3	6	3	.67	11	.315	.407	.500
2003	CIN	NL	82	292	77	11	0	15	(8	7)	133	39	58	52	41	1	68	5	0	0	5	2	.71	7	.264	.364	.455
2004	CIN	NL	64	217	50	10	2	9	(3	6)	91	28	32	26	28	0	71	1	0	0	2	1	.67	8	.230	.321	.419
2005	CIN	NL	112	387	93	26	1	18	(9	9)	175	62	67	55	48	2	107	8	0	5	0	0	-	8	.240	.333	.452
	4 ML YEARS		365	1268	337	71	6	55	(27	28)	585	195	213	203	171	6	327	20	0	8	13	6	.68	34	.266	.360	.461

Randy Keisler

Pitches: L **Bats:** L **Pos:** RP-20; SP-4   **Ht:** 6'3" **Wt:** 190 **Born:** 2/24/1976 **Age:** 30

Year	Team	Lg	G	GS	CG	GF	IP	BFP	H	R	ER	HR	SH	SF	HB	TBB	IBB	SO	WP	Bk	W	L	Pct	ShO	Sv-Op	Hld	ERC	ERA
2005	Lsvlle*	AAA	12	7	0	2	56.1	236	54	19	18	6	0	2	0	13	0	46	0	0	5	2	.714	0	2--	-	3.17	2.88
2000	NYA	AL	4	1	0	0	10.2	52	16	14	14	1	0	0	0	8	0	6	0	0	1	0	1.000	0	0-0	0	9.10	11.81
2001	NYA	AL	10	10	0	0	50.2	236	52	36	35	12	0	0	0	34	0	36	0	0	1	2	.333	0	0-0	0	6.33	6.22
2003	SD	NL	2	2	0	0	6.0	33	7	9	8	3	0	1	1	7	0	5	0	1	0	1	.000	0	0-0	0	12.82	12.00
2005	CIN	NL	24	4	0	7	56.0	262	64	45	39	10	1	1	1	28	2	43	2	0	2	1	.667	0	0-0	0	5.77	6.27
	4 ML YEARS		40	17	0	7	123.1	583	139	104	96	26	1	2	2	77	2	90	2	1	4	4	.500	0	0-0	0	6.59	7.01

The "HOW MUCH HE PITCHED" columns: G GS CG GF IP BFP. "WHAT HE GAVE UP" columns: H R ER HR SH SF HB TBB IBB SO WP Bk. "THE RESULTS" columns: W L Pct ShO Sv-Op Hld ERC ERA.

Kenny Kelly

Bats: R **Throws:** R **Pos:** PR-12; PH-9; RF-3; CF-2; LF-1   **Ht:** 6'3" **Wt:** 180 **Born:** 1/26/1979 **Age:** 27

Year	Team	Lg	G	AB	H	2B	3B	HR	(Hm	Rd)	TB	R	RBI	RC	TBB	IBB	SO	HBP	SH	SF	SB	CS	SB%	GDP	Avg	OBP	Slg
1997	DRays	R	27	99	21	2	1	2	(-	-)	31	21	7	10	11	0	24	2	0	0	6	3	.67	1	.212	.304	.313
1998	CtnSC	A	54	218	61	7	5	3	(-	-)	87	46	17	33	19	0	52	4	0	1	19	4	.83	1	.280	.347	.399
1999	StPtrb	A+	51	206	57	10	4	3	(-	-)	84	39	21	31	18	0	46	4	0	0	14	5	.74	1	.277	.346	.408
2000	Orlndo	AA	124	489	123	17	8	3	(-	-)	165	73	29	59	59	1	119	6	4	2	31	21	.60	9	.252	.338	.337
2001	SnAnt	AA	121	478	125	20	5	11	(-	-)	188	72	46	63	45	0	111	3	5	5	18	12	.60	9	.262	.326	.393
2002	Tacom	AAA	122	391	97	13	10	11	(-	-)	163	51	53	47	26	0	93	2	9	4	11	3	.79	11	.248	.296	.417
2003	Tacom	AAA	96	341	84	15	5	13	(-	-)	148	42	37	47	29	1	79	6	1	4	20	7	.74	4	.246	.313	.434
2003	Norfolk	AAA	30	92	24	6	2	4	(-	-)	46	15	8	14	6	0	25	0	1	0	5	0	1.00	1	.261	.306	.500
2004	Chatt	AA	51	191	68	15	3	5	(-	-)	104	33	28	43	26	4	46	4	5	1	13	7	.65	1	.356	.441	.545
2004	Lsvlle	AAA	78	268	68	15	4	9	(-	-)	118	44	43	37	24	0	71	3	4	2	7	4	.64	3	.254	.318	.440
2005	Srsota	A+	3	12	2	1	0	0	(-	-)	3	1	0	0	1	0	2	0	0	0	0	0	-	0	.167	.231	.250
2005	Hrsbrg	AA	12	47	10	3	1	2	(-	-)	21	5	6	6	5	0	10	0	0	0	2	1	.67	1	.213	.288	.447
2005	Lsvlle	AAA	61	233	76	9	4	3	(-	-)	102	43	17	41	20	0	49	1	6	0	18	4	.82	7	.326	.382	.438
2005	NewOr	AAA	20	82	19	3	1	0	(-	-)	24	11	6	7	9	0	15	0	0	0	3	2	.60	2	.232	.308	.293
2000	TB	AL	2	1	0	0	0	0	(0	0)	0	0	0	0	0	0	0	0	0	0	0	0	-	0	.000	.000	.000
2005	2 Tms	NL	24	13	4	1	0	0	(0	0)	5	5	2	1	1	0	6	0	0	0	1	2	.33	0	.308	.357	.385
05	Cin	NL	7	9	3	0	0	0	(0	0)	3	2	2	1	0	0	3	0	0	0	0	1	.00	0	.333	.333	.333
05	Was	NL	17	4	1	1	0	0	(0	0)	2	3	0	0	1	0	3	0	0	0	1	1	.50	0	.250	.400	.500
	2 ML YEARS		26	14	4	1	0	0	(0	0)	5	5	2	1	1	0	6	0	0	0	1	2	.33	0	.286	.333	.357

Jason Kendall

Bats: R **Throws:** R **Pos:** C-147; DH-3   **Ht:** 6'0" **Wt:** 195 **Born:** 6/26/1974 **Age:** 32

Year	Team	Lg	G	AB	H	2B	3B	HR	(Hm	Rd)	TB	R	RBI	RC	TBB	IBB	SO	HBP	SH	SF	SB	CS	SB%	GDP	Avg	OBP	Slg
1996	PIT	NL	130	414	124	23	5	3	(2	1)	166	54	42	63	35	11	30	15	3	4	5	2	.71	7	.300	.372	.401
1997	PIT	NL	144	486	143	36	4	8	(5	3)	211	71	49	86	49	2	53	31	1	5	18	6	.75	11	.294	.391	.434
1998	PIT	NL	149	535	175	36	3	12	(6	6)	253	95	75	110	51	3	51	31	2	8	26	5	.84	6	.327	.411	.473
1999	PIT	NL	78	280	93	25	8	8	(5	3)	143	61	41	63	38	3	32	12	0	4	22	3	.88	3	.332	.428	.511
2000	PIT	NL	152	579	185	33	6	14	(7	7)	272	112	58	112	79	3	79	15	1	4	22	12	.65	13	.320	.412	.470
2001	PIT	NL	157	606	161	22	2	10	(3	7)	217	84	53	68	44	4	48	20	0	2	13	14	.48	18	.266	.335	.358
2002	PIT	NL	145	545	154	25	3	3	(1	2)	194	59	44	66	49	1	29	9	0	2	15	8	.65	11	.283	.350	.356
2003	PIT	NL	150	587	191	29	3	6	(3	3)	244	84	58	97	49	3	40	25	1	3	8	7	.53	9	.325	.399	.416
2004	PIT	NL	147	574	183	32	0	3	(2	1)	224	86	51	95	60	2	41	19	1	4	11	8	.58	12	.319	.399	.390
2005	OAK	AL	150	601	163	28	1	0	(0	0)	193	70	53	79	50	0	39	20	0	5	8	3	.73	26	.271	.345	.321
	10 ML YEARS		1402	5207	1572	284	30	67	(34	33)	2117	776	524	839	504	32	442	197	9	41	148	68	.69	121	.302	.382	.407

Adam Kennedy

Bats: L **Throws:** R **Pos:** 2B-127; PH-2; PR-1   **Ht:** 6'1" **Wt:** 192 **Born:** 1/10/1976 **Age:** 30

Year	Team	Lg	G	AB	H	2B	3B	HR	(Hm	Rd)	TB	R	RBI	RC	TBB	IBB	SO	HBP	SH	SF	SB	CS	SB%	GDP	Avg	OBP	Slg
2005	RCuca*	A+	2	5	2	0	0	0	(-	-)	2	1	1	0	1	0	1	0	0	0	1	1	.50	0	.400	.500	.400
2005	Salt Lk*	AAA	4	17	7	1	0	0	(-	-)	8	4	4	4	2	0	2	0	0	2	2	0	1.00	0	.412	.429	.471
1999	STL	NL	33	102	26	10	1	1	(1	0)	41	12	16	12	3	0	8	2	1	2	0	1	.00	1	.255	.284	.402
2000	ANA	AL	156	598	159	33	11	9	(7	2)	241	82	72	72	28	5	73	3	8	4	22	8	.73	10	.266	.300	.403
2001	ANA	AL	137	478	129	25	3	6	(4	2)	178	48	40	57	27	3	71	11	7	9	12	7	.63	7	.270	.318	.372
2002	ANA	AL	144	474	148	32	6	7	(6	1)	213	65	52	70	19	1	80	7	5	4	17	4	.81	5	.312	.345	.449
2003	ANA	AL	143	449	121	17	1	13	(8	5)	179	71	49	61	45	4	73	9	2	5	22	9	.71	7	.269	.344	.399
2004	ANA	AL	144	468	130	20	5	10	(5	5)	190	70	48	60	41	7	92	13	9	2	15	5	.75	10	.278	.351	.406
2005	LAA	AL	129	416	125	23	0	2	(1	1)	154	49	37	62	29	1	64	7	5	3	19	4	.83	5	.300	.354	.370
	7 ML YEARS		886	2985	838	160	27	48	(32	16)	1196	397	314	394	192	21	461	52	37	29	107	38	.74	45	.281	.332	.401

Joe Kennedy

Pitches: L **Bats:** R **Pos:** SP-24; RP-11   **Ht:** 6'4" **Wt:** 237 **Born:** 5/24/1979 **Age:** 27

Year	Team	Lg	G	GS	CG	GF	IP	BFP	H	R	ER	HR	SH	SF	HB	TBB	IBB	SO	WP	Bk	W	L	Pct	ShO	Sv-Op	Hld	ERC	ERA
2001	TB	AL	20	20	0	0	117.2	498	122	63	58	16	2	5	3	34	0	78	5	1	7	8	.467	0	0-0	0	4.23	4.44
2002	TB	AL	30	30	5	0	196.2	840	204	114	99	23	2	9	16	55	0	109	4	0	8	11	.421	1	0-0	0	4.29	4.53
2003	TB	AL	32	22	1	7	133.2	619	167	101	91	19	1	8	11	47	1	77	3	1	3	12	.200	1	1-2	1	5.92	6.13
2004	COL	NL	27	27	1	0	162.1	705	163	68	66	17	9	6	8	67	12	117	5	0	9	7	.563	0	0-0	0	4.29	3.66
2005	2 Tms		35	24	0	3	152.2	704	192	114	102	20	4	6	7	64	6	97	8	1	8	13	.381	0	0-2	0	6.04	6.01
05	Col	NL	16	16	0	0	92.0	442	128	81	72	12	4	5	6	44	4	52	7	1	4	8	.333	0	0-0	0	7.24	7.04
05	Oak	AL	19	8	0	3	60.2	262	64	33	30	8	0	1	1	20	2	45	1	0	4	5	.444	0	0-2	0	4.33	4.45
	5 ML YEARS		144	123	7	10	763.0	3366	848	460	416	95	18	34	45	267	19	478	25	3	35	51	.407	2	1-4	1	4.90	4.91

Logan Kensing

Pitches: R **Bats:** R **Pos:** RP-3   **Ht:** 6'1" **Wt:** 185 **Born:** 7/3/1982 **Age:** 23

Year	Team	Lg	G	GS	CG	GF	IP	BFP	H	R	ER	HR	SH	SF	HB	TBB	IBB	SO	WP	Bk	W	L	Pct	ShO	Sv-Op	Hld	ERC	ERA
2003	Jmstwn	A-	8	6	0	0	33.0	155	48	23	21	1	0	2	3	6	0	20	2	0	2	4	.333	0	0- -	-	5.57	5.73
2003	Grnsbr	A	4	4	0	0	20.0	82	18	10	10	2	1	1	1	5	0	11	0	0	0	2	.000	0	0- -	-	3.17	4.50
2004	Jupiter	A+	23	23	1	0	127.2	525	120	53	42	5	7	8	8	35	1	100	8	1	6	7	.462	0	0- -	-	3.16	2.96
2005	Carlina	AA	7	7	0	0	39.2	168	35	16	14	4	2	1	5	14	1	33	3	0	4	1	.800	0	0- -	-	3.74	3.18
2004	FLA	NL	5	3	0	2	13.2	66	19	15	15	5	0	1	1	9	0	7	2	0	0	3	.000	0	0-0	0	10.74	9.88
2005	FLA	NL	3	0	0	0	5.2	31	11	7	7	2	0	1	0	3	0	4	0	0	0	0	-	0	0-0	1	12.96	11.12
	2 ML YEARS		8	3	0	2	19.1	97	30	22	22	7	0	2	1	12	0	11	2	0	0	3	.000	0	0-0	1	11.39	10.24

Jeff Kent

Bats: R **Throws:** R **Pos:** 2B-140; 1B-14; PH-1   **Ht:** 6'1" **Wt:** 220 **Born:** 3/7/1968 **Age:** 38

Year	Team	Lg	G	AB	H	2B	3B	HR	(Hm	Rd)	TB	R	RBI	RC	TBB	IBB	SO	HBP	SH	SF	SB	CS	SB%	GDP	Avg	OBP	Slg
1992	2 Tms		102	305	73	21	2	11	(4	7)	131	52	50	40	27	0	76	7	0	4	2	3	.40	5	.239	.312	.430
1993	NYN	NL	140	496	134	24	0	21	(9	12)	221	65	80	68	30	2	88	8	6	4	4	4	.50	11	.270	.320	.446
1994	NYN	NL	107	415	121	24	5	14	(10	4)	197	53	68	64	23	3	84	10	1	3	1	4	.20	7	.292	.341	.475
1995	NYN	NL	125	472	131	22	3	20	(11	9)	219	65	65	69	29	3	89	8	1	4	3	3	.50	9	.278	.327	.464
1996	2 Tms		128	437	124	27	1	12	(4	8)	189	61	55	61	31	1	78	2	1	6	6	4	.60	8	.284	.330	.432
1997	SF	NL	155	580	145	38	2	29	(13	16)	274	90	121	86	48	6	133	13	0	10	11	3	.79	14	.250	.316	.472
1998	SF	NL	137	526	156	37	3	31	(17	14)	292	94	128	100	48	4	110	9	1	10	9	4	.69	16	.297	.359	.555
1999	SF	NL	138	511	148	40	2	23	(11	12)	261	86	101	93	61	3	112	5	0	8	13	6	.68	12	.290	.366	.511
2000	SF	NL	159	587	196	41	7	33	(14	19)	350	114	125	138	90	6	107	9	0	9	12	9	.57	17	.334	.424	.596
2001	SF	NL	159	607	181	49	6	22	(8	14)	308	84	106	112	65	4	96	11	0	13	7	6	.54	11	.298	.369	.507
2002	SF	NL	152	623	195	42	2	37	(11	26)	352	102	108	105	52	3	101	4	0	3	5	1	.83	20	.313	.368	.565
2003	HOU	NL	130	505	150	39	1	22	(9	13)	257	77	93	92	39	2	85	5	0	3	6	2	.75	13	.297	.351	.509
2004	HOU	NL	145	540	156	34	8	27	(14	13)	287	96	107	87	49	3	96	6	0	11	7	3	.70	22	.289	.348	.531
2005	LAN	NL	149	553	160	36	0	29	(15	14)	283	100	105	105	72	8	85	8	0	4	6	2	.75	19	.289	.377	.512
92	Tor	AL	65	192	46	13	1	8	(2	6)	85	36	35	28	20	0	47	6	0	4	2	1	.67	3	.240	.324	.443
92	NYM	NL	37	113	27	8	1	3	(2	1)	46	16	15	12	7	0	29	1	0	0	0	2	.00	2	.239	.289	.407
96	NYM	NL	89	335	97	20	1	9	(2	7)	146	45	39	46	21	1	56	1	1	3	4	3	.57	7	.290	.331	.436
96	Cle	AL	39	102	27	7	0	3	(2	1)	43	16	16	15	10	0	22	1	0	3	2	1	.67	1	.265	.328	.422
	14 ML YEARS		1926	7157	2070	474	42	331	(150	181)	3621	1139	1312	1220	664	48	1340	105	10	92	92	54	.63	185	.289	.354	.506

Masao Kida

Pitches: R **Bats:** R **Pos:** RP-1   **Ht:** 6'3" **Wt:** 210 **Born:** 9/12/1968 **Age:** 37

Year	Team	Lg	G	GS	CG	GF	IP	BFP	H	R	ER	HR	SH	SF	HB	TBB	IBB	SO	WP	Bk	W	L	Pct	ShO	Sv-Op	Hld	ERC	ERA
2005	Tacom*	AAA	53	0	0	38	79.1	337	72	37	36	6	7	5	4	27	1	66	6	0	3	6	.333	0	22- -	-	3.32	4.08
1999	DET	AL	49	0	0	0	64.2	292	73	48	45	6	0	0	0	30	0	50	0	0	1	0	1.000	0	1-0	0	4.99	6.26
2000	DET	AL	2	0	0	0	2.2	13	5	3	3	1	0	0	0	0	0	0	0	0	0	0	-	0	0-0	0	9.86	10.13
2003	LA	NL	3	2	0	1	12.0	53	15	5	4	0	0	0	0	3	0	8	3	0	0	1	.000	0	0-0	0	4.14	3.00
2004	2 Tms		10	0	0	1	14.1	66	19	9	9	1	0	0	2	6	0	10	0	0	0	0	-	0	0-0	0	6.67	5.65
2005	SEA	AL	1	0	0	1	2.0	8	2	1	1	0	0	0	0	0	0	0	0	0	0	0	-	0	0-0	0	4.70	4.50
04	LA	NL	3	0	0	1	4.2	19	4	0	0	0	0	0	1	1	0	5	0	0	0	0	-	0	0-0	0	2.84	0.00
04	Sea	AL	7	0	0	0	9.2	47	15	9	9	1	0	0	1	5	0	5	0	0	0	0	-	0	0-0	0	8.82	8.38
	5 ML YEARS		65	2	0	3	95.2	432	114	66	62	9	0	0	2	39	0	68	3	0	1	1	.500	0	1-0	0	5.26	5.83

Bobby Kielty

Bats: B **Throws:** R **Pos:** LF-58; RF-42; DH-15; PH-14; PR-1   **Ht:** 6'1" **Wt:** 215 **Born:** 8/5/1976 **Age:** 29

Year	Team	Lg	G	AB	H	2B	3B	HR	(Hm	Rd)	TB	R	RBI	RC	TBB	IBB	SO	HBP	SH	SF	SB	CS	SB%	GDP	Avg	OBP	Slg
2001	MIN	AL	37	104	26	8	0	2	(1	1)	40	8	14	13	8	2	25	1	0	5	3	0	1.00	2	.250	.297	.385
2002	MIN	AL	112	289	84	14	3	12	(8	4)	140	49	46	59	52	4	66	5	0	2	4	1	.80	4	.291	.405	.484
2003	2 Tms		137	427	104	26	1	13	(6	7)	171	71	57	68	71	6	92	7	0	4	8	3	.73	11	.244	.358	.400
2004	OAK	AL	83	238	51	14	1	7	(6	1)	88	29	31	29	35	0	47	3	1	1	1	0	1.00	5	.214	.321	.370
2005	OAK	AL	116	377	99	20	0	10	(6	4)	149	55	57	53	50	3	67	2	2	2	3	2	.60	14	.263	.350	.395
03	Min	AL	75	238	60	13	0	9	(4	5)	100	40	32	41	42	2	56	3	0	1	6	2	.75	5	.252	.370	.420
03	Tor	AL	62	189	44	13	1	4	(2	2)	71	31	25	27	29	4	36	4	0	3	2	1	.67	6	.233	.342	.376
	5 ML YEARS		485	1435	364	82	5	44	(27	17)	588	212	205	222	216	15	297	18	3	14	19	6	.76	36	.254	.355	.410

Byung-Hyun Kim

Pitches: R **Bats:** R **Pos:** SP-22; RP-18   **Ht:** 5'11" **Wt:** 177 **Born:** 1/19/1979 **Age:** 27

Year	Team	Lg	G	GS	CG	GF	IP	BFP	H	R	ER	HR	SH	SF	HB	TBB	IBB	SO	WP	Bk	W	L	Pct	ShO	Sv-Op	Hld	ERC	ERA
1999	ARI	NL	25	0	0	10	27.1	121	20	15	14	2	1	0	5	20	2	31	4	1	1	2	.333	0	1-4	3	4.35	4.61
2000	ARI	NL	61	1	0	30	70.2	320	52	39	35	9	2	3	9	46	5	111	3	2	6	6	.500	0	14-20	5	4.04	4.46
2001	ARI	NL	78	0	0	44	98.0	392	58	32	32	10	5	0	8	44	3	113	5	1	5	6	.455	0	19-23	11	2.45	2.94
2002	ARI	NL	72	0	0	66	84.0	343	64	20	19	5	1	2	6	26	2	92	2	0	8	3	.727	0	36-42	0	2.45	2.04
2003	2 Tms		56	12	0	35	122.1	517	104	55	45	12	6	2	12	33	3	102	1	0	9	10	.474	0	16-19	1	3.02	3.31
2004	BOS	AL	7	3	0	2	17.1	77	17	15	12	1	0	2	2	7	1	6	1	0	2	1	.667	0	0-0	0	3.98	6.23
2005	COL	NL	40	22	0	3	148.0	668	156	82	80	17	8	7	14	71	8	115	11	1	5	12	.294	0	0-2	1	5.12	4.86
03	Ari	NL	7	7	0	0	43.0	181	34	17	17	6	3	0	4	15	0	33	0	0	1	5	.167	0	0-0	0	3.32	3.56
03	Bos	AL	49	5	0	35	79.1	336	70	38	28	6	3	2	8	18	3	69	1	0	8	5	.615	0	16-19	1	2.87	3.18
	7 ML YEARS		339	38	0	190	567.2	2438	471	258	237	56	23	16	56	247	24	570	27	5	36	40	.474	0	86-110	21	3.56	3.76

Sunny Kim

Pitches: R **Bats:** R **Pos:** RP-14; SP-10   **Ht:** 6'2" **Wt:** 188 **Born:** 9/4/1977 **Age:** 28

Year	Team	Lg	G	GS	CG	GF	IP	BFP	H	R	ER	HR	SH	SF	HB	TBB	IBB	SO	WP	Bk	W	L	Pct	ShO	Sv-Op	Hld	ERC	ERA
2005	NewOr*	AAA	9	9	0	0	49.0	208	46	23	15	4	2	0	2	15	0	38	2	0	4	2	.667	0	0- -		3.37	2.76
2001	BOS	AL	20	2	0	7	41.2	201	54	27	27	1	3	0	4	21	5	27	5	0	0	0	.000	0	0-0	1	5.72	5.83
2002	2 Tms		19	5	0	7	49.1	208	52	26	26	5	0	2	2	14	2	29	2	0	3	0	1.000	0	0-0	2	4.10	4.74
2003	MON	NL	4	3	0	1	14.0	72	24	13	13	6	0	1	4	8	0	5	0	0	1	0	1.000	0	0-0	0	14.93	8.36
2004	MON	NL	43	17	0	3	135.2	603	145	80	69	17	5	3	13	55	11	87	6	0	4	6	.400	0	0-0	1	4.96	4.58
2005	2 Tms		24	10	1	3	82.2	363	97	46	45	10	5	3	3	21	2	55	4	0	6	3	.667	1	0-0	0	4.71	4.90
02	Bos	AL	15	2	0	7	29.0	128	34	24	24	5	0	2	1	7	0	18	2	0	2	0	1.000	0	0-0	2	5.01	7.45
02	Mon	NL	4	3	0	0	20.1	80	18	2	2	0	0	0	1	7	2	11	0	0	1	0	1.000	0	0-0	0	2.82	0.89
05	Was	NL	12	2	0	3	29.1	135	41	20	20	3	1	2	2	8	2	17	1	0	1	2	.333	0	0-0	0	6.12	6.14
05	Col	NL	12	8	1	0	53.1	228	56	26	25	7	4	1	1	13	0	38	3	0	5	1	.833	1	0-0	0	3.97	4.22
	5 ML YEARS		110	37	1	21	323.1	1447	372	192	180	39	13	9	26	119	20	203	17	0	13	12	.520	1	0-0	5	5.22	5.01

Ray King

Pitches: L **Bats:** L **Pos:** RP-77   **Ht:** 6'1" **Wt:** 242 **Born:** 1/15/1974 **Age:** 32

Year	Team	Lg	G	GS	CG	GF	IP	BFP	H	R	ER	HR	SH	SF	HB	TBB	IBB	SO	WP	Bk	W	L	Pct	ShO	Sv-Op	Hld	ERC	ERA
1999	CHN	NL	10	0	0	0	10.2	50	11	8	7	2	1	0	1	10	0	5	1	0	0	0	—	0	0-0	2	8.10	5.91
2000	MIL	NL	36	0	0	8	28.2	111	18	7	4	1	0	1	0	10	1	19	1	0	3	2	.600	0	0-1	5	1.64	1.26
2001	MIL	NL	82	0	0	19	55.0	234	49	22	22	5	3	2	1	25	7	49	2	0	0	4	.000	0	1-4	18	3.51	3.60
2002	MIL	NL	76	0	0	15	65.0	273	61	24	22	5	5	2	3	24	6	50	0	1	3	2	.600	0	0-1	15	3.55	3.05
2003	ATL	NL	80	0	0	9	59.0	247	46	30	23	3	1	2	1	27	2	43	4	0	3	4	.429	0	0-1	18	2.79	3.51
2004	STL	NL	86	0	0	9	62.0	248	43	19	18	1	2	1	3	24	0	40	2	0	5	2	.714	0	0-1	31	2.13	2.61
2005	STL	NL	77	0	0	18	40.0	177	46	17	15	4	0	1	3	16	0	23	1	0	4	4	.500	0	0-6	16	5.37	3.38
	7 ML YEARS		447	0	0	78	320.1	1340	274	127	111	21	12	9	12	136	16	229	11	1	18	18	.500	0	1-14	105	3.26	3.12

Matt Kinney

Pitches: R **Bats:** R **Pos:** RP-4; SP-1   **Ht:** 6'5" **Wt:** 220 **Born:** 12/16/1976 **Age:** 29

Year	Team	Lg	G	GS	CG	GF	IP	BFP	H	R	ER	HR	SH	SF	HB	TBB	IBB	SO	WP	Bk	W	L	Pct	ShO	Sv-Op	Hld	ERC	ERA
2005	SnJos*	A+	5	5	0	0	30.0	127	23	8	7	3	0	1	0	14	0	34	0	0	3	0	1.000	0	0- -	-	3.01	2.10
2005	Fresno*	AAA	19	19	1	0	114.0	504	117	68	66	18	7	5	2	45	0	110	6	0	7	8	.467	0	0- -	-	4.60	5.21
2000	MIN	AL	8	8	0	0	42.1	186	41	26	24	7	0	4	0	25	1	24	4	0	2	2	.500	0	0-0	0	5.20	5.10
2002	MIN	AL	14	12	0	1	66.0	305	78	39	34	13	3	4	1	33	0	45	5	0	2	7	.222	0	0-0	0	6.35	4.64
2003	MIL	NL	33	31	1	1	190.2	847	201	121	110	27	10	11	6	80	4	152	10	2	10	13	.435	0	0-0	0	4.82	5.19
2004	2 Tms		43	6	0	14	78.2	370	104	55	53	11	2	4	4	30	2	73	7	0	3	5	.375	0	0-0	3	6.31	6.06
2005	SF	NL	5	1	0	1	12.0	55	18	8	8	2	1	0	1	6	0	3	0	0	2	0	1.000	0	0-1	0	9.30	6.00
04	Mil	NL	32	6	0	10	62.1	286	77	41	40	8	2	3	2	23	1	52	5	0	3	4	.429	0	0-0	3	5.57	5.78
04	KC	AL	11	0	0	4	16.1	84	27	14	13	3	0	1	2	7	1	21	2	0	0	1	.000	0	0-0	0	9.35	7.16
	5 ML YEARS		103	58	0	17	389.2	1763	442	249	229	60	16	23	12	174	7	297	26	2	19	27	.413	0	0-1	3	5.53	5.29

Ryan Klesko

Bats: L **Throws:** L **Pos:** LF-121; PH-13; DH-3; 1B-1   **Ht:** 6'3" **Wt:** 220 **Born:** 6/12/1971 **Age:** 35

Year	Team	Lg	G	AB	H	2B	3B	HR	(Hm	Rd)	TB	R	RBI	RC	TBB	IBB	SO	HBP	SH	SF	SB	CS	SB%	GDP	Avg	OBP	Slg
1992	ATL	NL	13	14	0	0	0	0	(0	0)	0	0	1	0	0	0	5	1	0	0	0	0	-	0	.000	.067	.000
1993	ATL	NL	22	17	6	1	0	2	(2	0)	13	3	5	5	3	1	4	0	0	0	0	0	-	0	.353	.450	.765
1994	ATL	NL	92	245	68	13	3	17	(7	10)	138	42	47	45	26	3	48	1	0	4	1	0	1.00	8	.278	.344	.563
1995	ATL	NL	107	329	102	25	2	23	(15	8)	200	48	70	73	47	10	72	2	0	3	5	4	.56	9	.310	.396	.608
1996	ATL	NL	153	528	149	21	4	34	(20	14)	280	90	93	99	68	10	129	2	0	4	6	3	.67	10	.282	.364	.530
1997	ATL	NL	143	467	122	21	4	24	(10	14)	229	67	84	73	48	5	130	4	1	2	4	4	.50	12	.261	.334	.490
1998	ATL	NL	129	427	117	29	1	18	(8	10)	202	69	70	72	56	5	66	3	0	4	5	3	.63	6	.274	.359	.473
1999	ATL	NL	133	404	120	28	2	21	(12	9)	215	55	80	80	53	8	69	2	0	7	5	2	.71	6	.297	.376	.532
2000	SD	NL	145	494	140	26	3	26	(9	17)	255	88	92	101	91	9	81	1	0	4	23	7	.77	10	.283	.393	.516
2001	SD	NL	146	538	154	34	6	30	(15	15)	290	105	113	111	88	7	89	3	0	9	23	4	.85	16	.286	.384	.539
2002	SD	NL	146	540	162	39	1	29	(11	18)	290	90	95	111	76	11	86	4	1	3	6	2	.75	7	.300	.388	.537
2003	SD	NL	121	397	100	18	0	21	(13	8)	181	47	67	59	65	5	83	3	0	9	2	5	.29	11	.252	.354	.456
2004	SD	NL	127	402	117	32	2	9	(3	6)	180	58	66	76	73	6	67	1	1	3	3	2	.60	8	.291	.399	.448
2005	SD	NL	137	443	110	19	1	18	(10	8)	185	61	58	64	75	2	80	1	0	1	3	4	.43	6	.248	.358	.418
	14 ML YEARS		1614	5245	1467	315	30	272	(130	142)	2658	823	941	969	769	82	1009	28	3	54	86	40	.68	111	.280	.371	.507

Steve Kline

Pitches: L Bats: B Pos: RP-67   Ht: 6'1" Wt: 215 Born: 8/22/1972 Age: 33

			HOW MUCH HE PITCHED						WHAT HE GAVE UP											THE RESULTS						
Year	Team	Lg	G	GS	CG	GF	IP	BFP	H	R	ER	HR	SH	SF	HB	TBB	IBB	SO	WP	Bk	W	L	Pct	ShO	Sv-Op	Hld	ERC	ERA
1997	2 Tms		46	1	0	7	52.2	248	73	37	35	10	4	2	2	23	4	37	4	1	4	4	.500	0	0-3	5	7.39	5.98
1998	MON	NL	78	0	0	18	71.2	319	62	25	22	4	1	2	3	41	7	76	5	0	3	6	.333	0	1-2	18	3.60	2.76
1999	MON	NL	82	0	0	18	69.2	297	56	32	29	8	3	1	3	33	6	69	2	0	7	4	.636	0	0-2	16	3.40	3.75
2000	MON	NL	83	0	0	42	82.1	349	88	36	32	8	2	1	3	27	2	64	4	0	1	5	.167	0	14-18	12	4.37	3.50
2001	STL	NL	89	0	0	26	75.0	303	53	16	15	3	4	5	4	29	7	54	1	0	3	3	.500	0	9-10	17	2.20	1.80
2002	STL	NL	66	0	0	17	58.1	241	54	23	22	3	2	2	1	21	2	41	1	0	2	1	.667	0	6-8	21	3.28	3.39
2003	STL	NL	78	0	0	22	63.2	274	56	29	27	5	3	2	3	30	5	31	2	0	5	5	.500	0	3-7	18	3.59	3.82
2004	STL	NL	67	0	0	22	50.1	202	37	12	10	3	3	1	4	17	4	35	1	0	2	2	.500	0	3-4	15	2.43	1.79
2005	BAL	AL	67	0	0	23	61.0	263	59	34	29	11	2	2	0	30	5	36	4	3	2	4	.333	0	0-3	9	4.77	4.28
97	Cle	AL	20	1	0	0	26.1	130	42	19	17	6	1	0	1	13	1	17	3	1	3	1	.750	0	0-2	4	9.58	5.81
97	Mon	NL	26	0	0	7	26.1	118	31	18	18	4	3	2	1	10	3	20	1	0	1	3	.250	0	0-1	1	5.39	6.15
	9 ML YEARS		656	1	0	195	584.2	2496	538	244	221	55	24	18	23	251	42	443	24	4	29	34	.460	0	36-57	131	3.77	3.40

Justin Knoedler

Bats: R Throws: R Pos: C-4; PH-4   Ht: 6'2" Wt: 210 Born: 7/17/1980 Age: 25

									BATTING												BASERUNNING				AVERAGES		
Year	Team	Lg	G	AB	H	2B	3B	HR	(Hm	Rd)	TB	R	RBI	RC	TBB	IBB	SO	HBP	SH	SF	SB	CS	SB%	GDP	Avg	OBP	Slg
2002	Hgrstn	A	86	280	72	16	2	5	(-	-)	107	32	33	37	37	0	56	4	2	3	6	5	.55	8	.257	.349	.382
2003	SnJos	A+	101	354	91	25	2	10	(-	-)	150	48	43	49	35	0	78	3	2	4	13	3	.81	5	.257	.326	.424
2004	Nrwich	AA	115	409	112	28	3	9	(-	-)	173	64	47	57	32	0	98	8	0	5	5	3	.63	7	.274	.335	.423
2005	Nrwich	AA	4	10	3	0	0	0	(-	-)	3	2	0	1	2	0	0	0	0	0	2	1	.67	0	.300	.417	.300
2005	Fresno	AAA	85	287	78	19	1	4	(-	-)	111	35	32	40	26	0	61	7	5	2	5	5	.50	2	.272	.345	.387
2004	SF	NL	1	1	0	0	0	0	(0	0)	0	0	0	0	0	0	0	0	0	0	0	0	-	0	.000	.000	.000
2005	SF	NL	8	10	1	0	0	0	(0	0)	1	0	0	0	0	0	1	1	0	0	0	0	-	0	.100	.182	.100
	2 ML YEARS		9	11	1	0	0	0	(0	0)	1	0	0	0	0	0	1	1	0	0	0	0	-	0	.091	.167	.091

Danny Kolb

Pitches: R Bats: R Pos: RP-65   Ht: 6'4" Wt: 215 Born: 3/29/1975 Age: 31

					HOW MUCH HE PITCHED						WHAT HE GAVE UP									THE RESULTS						
Year	Team	Lg	G	GS	CG	GF	IP	BFP	H	R	ER	HR	SH	SF	HB	TBB	IBB	SO	WP	Bk	W	L	Pct	ShO	Sv-Op	Hld	ERC	ERA
1999	TEX	AL	16	0	0	6	31.0	139	33	18	16	2	0	0	1	15	0	15	2	0	2	1	.667	0	0-0	0	4.63	4.65
2000	TEX	AL	1	0	0	0	0.2	9	5	5	5	0	0	1	0	2	0	0	0	0	0	0	-	0	0-0	0	69.84	67.50
2001	TEX	AL	17	0	0	1	15.1	70	15	8	8	2	1	1	0	10	1	15	3	0	0	0	-	0	0-0	7	5.03	4.70
2002	TEX	AL	34	0	0	14	32.0	145	27	17	15	1	1	2	1	22	2	20	6	0	3	6	.333	0	1-4	2	3.74	4.22
2003	MIL	NL	37	0	0	25	41.1	175	34	10	9	2	1	0	1	19	3	39	1	0	1	2	.333	0	21-23	4	2.96	1.96
2004	MIL	NL	64	0	0	48	57.1	236	50	22	19	3	3	1	3	15	1	21	2	0	0	4	.000	0	39-44	1	2.73	2.98
2005	ATL	NL	65	0	0	34	57.2	271	78	39	38	5	2	1	1	29	5	39	5	0	3	8	.273	0	11-18	6	6.49	5.93
	7 ML YEARS		234	0	0	128	235.1	1045	242	119	110	15	8	6	7	112	12	149	19	0	9	21	.300	0	72-89	20	4.29	4.21

Paul Konerko

Bats: R Throws: R Pos: 1B-146; DH-11; PH-2   Ht: 6'2" Wt: 215 Born: 3/5/1976 Age: 30

									BATTING												BASERUNNING				AVERAGES		
Year	Team	Lg	G	AB	H	2B	3B	HR	(Hm	Rd)	TB	R	RBI	RC	TBB	IBB	SO	HBP	SH	SF	SB	CS	SB%	GDP	Avg	OBP	Slg
1997	LA	NL	6	7	1	0	0	0	(0	0)	1	0	0	0	1	0	2	0	0	0	0	0	-	1	.143	.250	.143
1998	2 Tms	NL	75	217	47	4	0	7	(2	5)	72	21	29	17	16	0	40	3	0	3	0	1	.00	10	.217	.276	.332
1999	CHA	AL	142	513	151	31	4	24	(16	8)	262	71	81	86	45	0	68	2	1	3	1	0	1.00	19	.294	.352	.511
2000	CHA	AL	143	524	156	31	1	21	(10	11)	252	84	97	86	47	0	72	10	0	5	1	0	1.00	22	.298	.363	.481
2001	CHA	AL	156	582	164	35	2	32	(19	13)	295	92	99	99	54	6	89	9	0	5	1	0	1.00	17	.282	.349	.507
2002	CHA	AL	151	570	173	30	0	27	(13	14)	284	81	104	96	44	2	72	9	0	7	0	0	-	17	.304	.359	.498
2003	CHA	AL	137	444	104	19	0	18	(9	9)	177	49	65	42	43	7	50	4	0	4	0	0	-	28	.234	.305	.399
2004	CHA	AL	155	563	156	22	0	41	(29	12)	301	84	117	106	69	5	107	6	0	5	1	0	1.00	23	.277	.359	.535
2005	CHA	AL	158	575	163	24	0	40	(23	17)	307	98	100	106	81	10	109	5	0	3	0	0	-	9	.283	.375	.534
98	LA	NL	49	144	31	1	0	4	(2	2)	44	14	16	10	10	0	30	2	0	2	0	1	.00	5	.215	.272	.306
98	Cin	NL	26	73	16	3	0	3	(0	3)	28	7	13	7	6	0	10	1	0	1	0	0	-	5	.219	.284	.384
	9 ML YEARS		1123	3995	1115	196	5	210	(121	89)	1951	580	692	638	400	30	609	48	1	35	4	1	.80	146	.279	.349	.488

Dae-Sung Koo

Pitches: L Bats: L Pos: RP-33   Ht: 6'1" Wt: 187 Born: 8/2/1968 Age: 37

						HOW MUCH HE PITCHED						WHAT HE GAVE UP									THE RESULTS						
Year	Team	Lg	G	GS	CG	GF	IP	BFP	H	R	ER	HR	SH	SF	HB	TBB	IBB	SO	WP	Bk	W	L	Pct	ShO	Sv-Op	Hld	ERC	ERA
2001	Orix	Jap	51	8	1	32	126.1	549	96	58	57	14	11	2	4	71	3	143	3	0	7	9	.438	0	10--	-	3.47	4.06
2002	Orix	Jap	22	21	1	0	146.1	609	122	45	41	13	16	1	3	47	1	144	3	0	5	7	.417	0	0--	-	2.84	2.52
2003	Orix	Jap	19	19	0	0	113.2	523	131	72	63	23	8	3	7	51	0	118	2	0	6	8	.429	0	0--	-	6.16	4.99
2004	Orix	Jap	18	15	3	0	116.2	499	105	65	56	24	10	3	8	44	0	99	2	0	6	10	.375	0	0--	-	4.42	4.32
2005	Norfolk	AAA	2	1	0	0	4.0	16	4	0	0	0	0	0	0	0	0	0	0	0	0	0	-	0	0--	-	1.95	0.00
2005	NYN	NL	33	0	0	4	23.0	106	22	12	10	2	0	3	2	13	1	23	0	0	0	0	-	0	0-2	6	4.53	3.91

Mike Koplove

Pitches: R **Bats:** R **Pos:** RP-44   **Ht:** 6'0" **Wt:** 170 **Born:** 8/30/1976 **Age:** 29

			HOW MUCH HE PITCHED						WHAT HE GAVE UP										THE RESULTS						
Year	Team	Lg	G	GS	CG	GF	IP	BFP	H	R	ER	HR	SH	SF	HB	TBB	IBB	SO	WP	Bk	W	L	Pct	ShO	Sv-Op Hld	ERC	ERA
2005	Tucsn*	AAA	9	0	0	3	9.0	46	12	13	13	1	1	0	2	7	0	6	0	0	0	2	.000	0	0-0 -	8.98	13.00
2001	ARI	NL	9	0	0	1	10.0	50	8	7	4	1	1	0	2	9	1	14	1	0	0	1	.000	0	0-0 1	5.25	3.60
2002	ARI	NL	55	0	0	15	61.2	249	47	24	23	2	4	1	0	23	4	46	1	0	6	1	.857	0	0-0 10	2.23	3.36
2003	ARI	NL	31	0	0	5	37.2	157	31	11	9	3	2	2	5	10	1	27	1	0	3	0	1.000	0	0-1 5	2.93	2.15
2004	ARI	NL	76	0	0	24	87.0	371	86	42	39	7	8	1	5	37	10	55	4	0	4	4	.500	0	2-8 19	4.12	4.03
2005	ARI	NL	44	0	0	11	49.2	217	48	31	28	6	1	3	6	20	3	28	1	1	2	1	.667	0	0-2 9	4.45	5.07
	5 ML YEARS		215	0	0	56	246.0	1044	220	115	103	19	16	7	18	99	19	170	8	1	15	7	.682	0	2-11 44	3.54	3.77

John Koronka

Pitches: L **Bats:** L **Pos:** SP-3; RP-1   **Ht:** 6'1" **Wt:** 180 **Born:** 7/3/1980 **Age:** 25

			HOW MUCH HE PITCHED						WHAT HE GAVE UP										THE RESULTS						
Year	Team	Lg	G	GS	CG	GF	IP	BFP	H	R	ER	HR	SH	SF	HB	TBB	IBB	SO	WP	Bk	W	L	Pct	ShO	Sv-Op Hld	ERC	ERA
1998	Billings	R+	12	3	0	3	31.1	167	47	43	28	2	1	3	3	26	0	36	4	1	0	3	.000	0	0- -	9.06	8.04
1999	Billings	R+	7	7	0	0	40.1	179	41	26	25	1	2	2	2	17	0	34	1	0	2	3	.400	0	0- -	3.84	5.58
1999	Reds	R	7	7	0	0	37.1	151	25	11	7	1	1	1	3	14	0	27	1	1	3	3	.500	0	0- -	2.11	1.69
2000	Clinton	A	20	18	4	0	104.0	473	123	65	50	7	2	3	0	38	2	74	4	0	4	13	.235	0	0- -	4.58	4.33
2001	Mudvle	A+	12	12	0	0	71.0	330	78	44	39	10	1	1	2	39	0	66	3	3	5	2	.714	0	0- -	5.59	4.94
2001	Dayton	A	5	5	0	0	24.0	103	23	12	2	0	0	0	2	8	0	25	0	0	3	1	.750	0	0- -	3.20	0.75
2001	Chatt	AA	9	9	0	0	55.0	255	62	37	35	7	4	1	1	28	0	44	1	1	1	5	.167	0	0- -	5.43	5.73
2002	Stcktn	A+	12	12	0	0	73.1	314	59	36	25	4	0	2	3	35	0	69	3	1	11	0	1.000	0	0- -	3.12	3.07
2002	Chatt	AA	16	15	0	0	95.2	448	109	56	53	10	5	4	1	52	1	69	4	1	2	8	.200	0	0- -	5.40	4.99
2003	WTenn	AA	1	1	0	0	7.0	25	3	0	0	0	1	2	0	1	0	3	0	0	0	0	-	0	0- -	0.60	0.00
2003	Chatt	AA	25	25	0	0	155.2	704	177	88	76	8	0	3	5	60	1	115	7	5	7	13	.350	0	0- -	4.47	4.39
2004	Iowa	AAA	29	23	2	1	153.1	689	164	86	74	19	8	9	5	65	3	116	6	5	12	9	.571	2	0- -	4.76	4.34
2005	Iowa	AAA	23	21	0	0	136.0	591	135	65	64	12	9	2	3	48	0	96	6	3	9	11	.450	0	0- -	3.79	4.24
2005	CHN	NL	4	3	0	1	15.2	76	19	13	13	2	1	0	0	8	0	10	1	2	1	2	.333	0	0-0 0	5.68	7.47

Corey Koskie

Bats: L **Throws:** R **Pos:** 3B-76; DH-19; PH-3   **Ht:** 6'3" **Wt:** 217 **Born:** 6/28/1973 **Age:** 33

			BATTING																		BASERUNNING				AVERAGES		
Year	Team	Lg	G	AB	H	2B	3B	HR	(Hm	Rd)	TB	R	RBI	RC	TBB	IBB	SO	HBP	SH	SF	SB	CS	SB%	GDP	Avg	OBP	Slg
2005	Syrcse*	AAA	7	25	6	2	0	0	(-	-)	8	1	2	3	2	1	6	2	0	0	0	0	-	1	.240	.367	.320
1998	MIN	AL	11	29	4	0	0	1	(1	0)	7	2	2	1	2	0	10	0	0	0	0	0	-	0	.138	.194	.241
1999	MIN	AL	117	342	106	21	0	11	(4	7)	160	42	58	61	40	4	72	5	2	3	4	4	.50	6	.310	.387	.468
2000	MIN	AL	146	474	142	32	4	9	(1	8)	209	79	65	84	77	7	104	4	1	3	5	4	.56	11	.300	.400	.441
2001	MIN	AL	153	562	155	37	2	26	(11	15)	274	100	103	99	68	9	118	12	0	7	27	6	.82	16	.276	.362	.488
2002	MIN	AL	140	490	131	37	3	15	(6	9)	219	71	69	72	72	4	127	9	0	5	10	11	.48	14	.267	.368	.447
2003	MIN	AL	131	469	137	29	2	14	(8	6)	212	76	69	84	77	5	113	7	0	9	11	5	.69	5	.292	.393	.452
2004	MIN	AL	118	422	106	24	2	25	(16	9)	209	68	71	67	49	10	103	12	0	5	9	3	.75	6	.251	.342	.495
2005	TOR	AL	97	354	88	20	0	11	(5	6)	141	49	36	41	44	3	90	4	0	2	4	1	.80	10	.249	.337	.398
	8 ML YEARS		913	3142	869	200	13	112	(52	60)	1431	487	473	509	429	42	737	53	3	34	70	34	.67	68	.277	.369	.455

Casey Kotchman

Bats: L **Throws:** L **Pos:** 1B-20; DH-20; PH-11   **Ht:** 6'3" **Wt:** 210 **Born:** 2/22/1983 **Age:** 23

			BATTING																		BASERUNNING				AVERAGES		
Year	Team	Lg	G	AB	H	2B	3B	HR	(Hm	Rd)	TB	R	RBI	RC	TBB	IBB	SO	HBP	SH	SF	SB	CS	SB%	GDP	Avg	OBP	Slg
2001	Angels	R	4	15	9	1	0	1	(-	-)	13	5	5	6	3	1	2	0	0	1	0	0	-	0	.600	.632	.867
2001	Provo	R+	7	22	11	3	0	0	(-	-)	14	6	7	6	2	0	0	0	0	0	0	0	-	0	.500	.542	.636
2002	CRpds	A	81	288	81	30	1	5	(-	-)	128	42	50	50	48	2	37	6	1	4	2	1	.67	7	.281	.390	.444
2003	Angels	R	7	27	9	1	0	2	(-	-)	16	5	6	5	2	1	3	0	0	0	0	0	-	1	.333	.379	.593
2003	RCuca	A+	57	206	72	12	0	8	(-	-)	108	42	28	47	30	5	16	6	0	3	2	0	1.00	4	.350	.441	.524
2004	Ark	AA	28	114	42	11	0	3	(-	-)	62	19	18	24	10	0	7	5	0	1	0	0	-	6	.368	.438	.544
2004	Salt Lk	AAA	49	199	74	22	0	5	(-	-)	111	32	38	41	14	0	25	5	0	2	0	0	-	9	.372	.423	.558
2005	Salt Lk	AAA	94	363	105	23	1	10	(-	-)	160	62	58	62	43	2	40	7	0	4	0	2	.00	15	.289	.372	.441
2004	ANA	AL	38	116	26	6	0	0	(0	0)	32	7	15	14	7	3	11	4	0	1	3	0	1.00	3	.224	.289	.276
2005	LAA	AL	47	126	35	5	0	7	(5	2)	61	16	22	21	15	0	18	0	1	1	1	1	.50	3	.278	.352	.484
	2 ML YEARS		85	242	61	11	0	7	(5	2)	93	23	37	35	22	3	29	4	1	2	4	1	.80	6	.252	.322	.384

Mark Kotsay

Bats: L **Throws:** L **Pos:** CF-137; DH-2   **Ht:** 6'0" **Wt:** 201 **Born:** 12/2/1975 **Age:** 30

			BATTING																		BASERUNNING				AVERAGES		
Year	Team	Lg	G	AB	H	2B	3B	HR	(Hm	Rd)	TB	R	RBI	RC	TBB	IBB	SO	HBP	SH	SF	SB	CS	SB%	GDP	Avg	OBP	Slg
1997	FLA	NL	14	52	10	1	1	0	(0	0)	13	5	4	3	4	0	7	0	1	0	3	0	1.00	1	.192	.250	.250
1998	FLA	NL	154	578	161	25	7	11	(5	6)	233	72	68	70	34	2	61	1	7	3	10	5	.67	17	.279	.318	.403
1999	FLA	NL	148	495	134	23	9	8	(5	3)	199	57	50	58	29	5	50	0	2	9	7	6	.54	11	.271	.306	.402
2000	FLA	NL	152	530	158	31	5	12	(5	7)	235	87	57	78	42	2	46	0	2	4	19	9	.68	17	.298	.347	.443
2001	SD	NL	119	406	118	29	1	10	(3	7)	179	67	58	65	48	1	58	2	1	3	13	5	.72	11	.291	.366	.441
2002	SD	NL	153	569	169	27	7	17	(11	6)	261	82	61	92	59	0	89	3	2	4	11	9	.55	10	.292	.359	.459
2003	SD	NL	128	482	128	28	4	7	(1	6)	185	64	38	59	56	3	82	1	1	1	6	3	.67	8	.266	.343	.384
2004	OAK	AL	148	606	190	37	3	15	(9	6)	278	78	63	94	55	5	70	2	5	5	8	5	.62	6	.314	.370	.459
2005	OAK	AL	139	582	163	35	1	15	(4	11)	245	75	82	86	40	3	51	1	2	4	5	5	.50	13	.280	.325	.421
	9 ML YEARS		1155	4309	1231	236	38	95	(43	52)	1828	587	481	605	367	21	514	10	23	33	82	47	.64	94	.286	.341	.424

Dave Krynzel

Bats: L Throws: L Pos: PH-3; CF-1; PR-1   Ht: 6'1" Wt: 180 Born: 11/7/1981 Age: 24

Year	Team	Lg	G	AB	H	2B	3B	HR	(Hm	Rd)	TB	R	RBI	RC	TBB	IBB	SO	HBP	SH	SF	SB	CS	SB%	GDP	Avg	OBP	Slg
2000	Ogden	R+	34	131	47	8	3	1	(-	-)	64	25	29	29	16	3	23	5	1	2	8	4	.67	0	.359	.442	.489
2001	Beloit	A	35	141	43	1	1	1	(-	-)	49	22	19	19	9	2	28	4	0	0	11	5	.69	1	.305	.364	.348
2001	Hi Dsrt	A+	89	383	106	19	5	5	(-	-)	150	65	33	50	27	1	122	4	3	2	34	17	.67	0	.277	.329	.392
2002	Hi Dsrt	A+	97	365	98	13	12	11	(-	-)	168	76	45	68	64	3	100	11	1	3	29	17	.63	2	.268	.391	.460
2002	Huntsvl	AA	31	129	31	2	3	2	(-	-)	45	13	13	12	4	0	30	1	0	0	13	5	.72	0	.240	.269	.349
2003	Huntsvl	AA	124	457	122	13	11	2	(-	-)	163	72	34	64	60	4	119	6	5	3	43	21	.67	3	.267	.357	.357
2004	Brewrs	R	5	16	8	1	1	0	(-	-)	11	8	6	3	0	2	1	0	0	2	0	1.00	0	.500	.600	.688
2004	Indy	AAA	69	257	71	10	4	6	(-	-)	107	36	27	36	20	1	65	3	8	3	10	8	.56	0	.276	.332	.416
2005	Nashv	AAA	115	450	115	25	7	11	(-	-)	187	71	51	65	43	2	138	5	8	5	24	8	.75	3	.256	.324	.416
2004	MIL	NL	16	41	9	1	0	0	(0	0)	10	6	3	4	3	0	15	3	0	0	0	0	-	0	.220	.319	.244
2005	MIL	NL	5	7	0	0	0	0	(-	-)	0	0	0	0	0	0	3	0	0	0	0	0	-	0	.000	.000	.000
	2 ML YEARS		21	48	9	1	0	0	(0	0)	10	6	3	4	3	0	18	3	0	0	0	0	-	0	.188	.278	.208

Jason Kubel

Bats: L Throws: R Pos: OF   Ht: 5'11" Wt: 200 Born: 5/25/1982 Age: 24

Year	Team	Lg	G	AB	H	2B	3B	HR	(Hm	Rd)	TB	R	RBI	RC	TBB	IBB	SO	HBP	SH	SF	SB	CS	SB%	GDP	Avg	OBP	Slg
2000	Twins	R	23	78	22	3	2	0	(-	-)	29	17	13	11	10	0	9	1	1	1	0	0	-	1	.282	.367	.372
2001	Twins	R	37	124	41	10	4	1	(-	-)	62	14	30	25	19	3	14	2	0	2	3	2	.60	3	.331	.422	.500
2002	QuadA	A	115	424	136	26	4	17	(-	-)	221	60	69	77	41	2	48	1	2	3	3	5	.38	11	.321	.380	.521
2003	FtMyrs	A+	116	420	125	20	4	5	(-	-)	168	56	82	61	48	8	54	1	0	13	4	6	.40	11	.298	.361	.400
2004	NwBrit	AA	37	138	52	14	4	6	(-	-)	92	25	29	36	19	1	19	1	0	1	0	2	.00	3	.377	.453	.667
2004	Roch	AAA	90	350	120	28	0	16	(-	-)	196	71	71	76	34	2	40	1	1	4	16	3	.84	2	.343	.398	.560
2004	MIN	AL	23	60	18	2	0	2	(0	2)	26	10	7	13	6	0	9	0	0	1	1	1	.50	0	.300	.358	.433

Hong-Chih Kuo

Pitches: L Bats: L Pos: RP-9   Ht: 6'0" Wt: 200 Born: 7/23/1981 Age: 24

Year	Team	Lg	G	GS	CG	GF	IP	BFP	H	R	ER	HR	SH	SF	HB	TBB	IBB	SO	WP	Bk	W	L	Pct	ShO	Sv-Op	Hld	ERC	ERA
2000	SnBrn	A+	1	1	0	0	3.0	9	0	0	0	0	0	0	1	0	0	7	0	0	0	0	-	0	0--	-	0.14	0.00
2001	Ddgrs	R	7	6	0	0	19.1	75	13	5	5	0	0	0	2	4	0	21	0	0	0	0	-	0	0--	-	1.58	2.33
2002	Ddgrs	R	3	3	0	0	6.0	23	4	3	3	0	0	1	0	1	0	9	0	0	0	0	-	0	0--	-	1.23	4.50
2002	VeroB	A+	4	4	0	0	8.0	37	11	6	6	0	0	0	3	2	0	8	1	0	0	1	.000	0	0--	-	6.78	6.75
2004	Clmbs	A	3	0	0	1	6.0	30	8	3	3	0	0	0	1	4	0	10	1	0	1	0	1.000	0	0--	-	7.07	4.50
2005	Jaxnvl	AA	17	0	0	9	28.1	118	22	7	6	1	0	1	1	11	1	44	3	0	1	1	.500	0	3--	-	2.48	1.91
2005	VeroB	A+	11	3	0	0	26.0	107	19	7	6	2	0	1	2	10	0	42	1	0	1	1	.500	0	0--	-	2.73	2.08
2005	LAN	NL	9	0	0	0	5.1	26	5	4	4	1	0	0	0	5	1	10	0	1	0	1	.000	0	0-1	3	6.10	6.75

John Lackey

Pitches: R Bats: R Pos: SP-33   Ht: 6'6" Wt: 205 Born: 10/23/1978 Age: 27

Year	Team	Lg	G	GS	CG	GF	IP	BFP	H	R	ER	HR	SH	SF	HB	TBB	IBB	SO	WP	Bk	W	L	Pct	ShO	Sv-Op	Hld	ERC	ERA
2002	ANA	AL	18	18	1	0	108.1	465	113	52	44	10	0	4	4	33	0	69	7	2	9	4	.692	0	0-0	0	4.03	3.66
2003	ANA	AL	33	33	2	0	204.0	885	223	117	105	31	2	6	10	66	4	151	11	1	10	16	.385	2	0-0	0	4.88	4.63
2004	ANA	AL	33	32	1	0	198.1	855	215	108	103	22	9	4	8	60	4	144	11	1	14	13	.519	1	0-0	0	4.39	4.67
2005	LAA	AL	33	33	1	0	209.0	892	208	85	80	13	1	2	11	71	3	199	18	0	14	5	.737	0	0-0	0	3.76	3.44
	4 ML YEARS		117	116	5	0	719.2	3097	759	362	332	76	12	16	33	230	11	563	47	4	47	38	.553	3	0-0	0	4.29	4.15

Pete LaForest

Bats: L Throws: R Pos: C-21; DH-2; PH-2; 1B-1   Ht: 6'2" Wt: 208 Born: 1/17/1978 Age: 28

Year	Team	Lg	G	AB	H	2B	3B	HR	(Hm	Rd)	TB	R	RBI	RC	TBB	IBB	SO	HBP	SH	SF	SB	CS	SB%	GDP	Avg	OBP	Slg
1995	Expos	R	2	6	0	0	0	0	(-	-)	0	1	0	0	2	0	4	0	0	0	0	0	-	0	.000	.250	.000
1997	DRays	R	34	107	28	7	2	3	(-	-)	48	21	21	15	10	0	18	1	0	1	4	3	.57	1	.262	.328	.449
1998	Princtn	R+	25	91	25	7	1	2	(-	-)	40	18	14	15	12	1	18	1	1	0	4	1	.80	0	.275	.365	.440
1999	CtnSC	A	125	445	114	21	3	13	(-	-)	180	64	53	62	55	6	97	5	6	3	9	3	.75	11	.256	.343	.404
2000	StPete	A+	129	474	128	28	7	14	(-	-)	212	85	70	75	56	4	108	6	1	5	2	4	.33	4	.270	.351	.447
2001	Orlndo	AA	7	21	2	0	0	1	(-	-)	5	3	1	1	5	0	9	0	0	0	0	0	-	0	.095	.269	.238
2002	Orlndo	AA	106	359	97	18	1	20	(-	-)	177	57	64	66	60	3	94	2	0	4	9	6	.60	4	.270	.374	.493
2002	Drham	AAA	17	66	17	3	0	3	(-	-)	29	7	15	7	3	0	28	0	0	0	1	0	1.00	1	.258	.290	.439
2003	Orlndo	AA	21	72	18	8	0	3	(-	-)	35	9	15	13	16	1	17	1	0	2	0	0	-	1	.250	.385	.486
2003	Drham	AAA	61	201	54	14	2	14	(-	-)	114	40	38	42	36	2	56	2	0	2	2	1	.67	2	.269	.382	.567
2004	Drham	AAA	84	275	61	19	0	7	(-	-)	101	37	31	29	35	5	64	0	2	1	1	1	.50	0	.222	.309	.367
2005	Drham	AAA	70	270	73	18	1	21	(-	-)	156	41	52	50	17	3	98	3	1	2	2	0	1.00	1	.270	.318	.578
2003	TB	AL	19	48	8	2	0	0	(-	-)	10	0	6	1	1	0	14	1	0	1	0	0	-	1	.167	.196	.208
2005	TB	AL	25	64	11	3	0	1	(1	0)	17	5	4	2	6	1	23	0	0	0	0	1	.00	2	.172	.243	.266
	2 ML YEARS		44	112	19	5	0	1	(1	0)	27	5	10	3	7	1	37	1	0	1	0	1	.00	3	.170	.223	.241

Gerald Laird

Bats: R **Throws:** R **Pos:** C-13; RF-1; PR-1   **Ht:** 6'2" **Wt:** 195 **Born:** 11/3/1979 **Age:** 26

Year	Team	Lg	G	AB	H	2B	3B	HR	(Hm	Rd)	TB	R	RBI	RC	TBB	IBB	SO	HBP	SH	SF	SB	CS	SB%	GDP	Avg	OBP	Slg
2005	Rngrs*	R	8	26	5	2	2	0	(-	-)	11	4	3	3	2	0	2	1	0	0	1	0	1.00	1	.192	.276	.423
2005	Okla*	AAA	75	281	87	12	4	17	(-	-)	158	51	55	60	28	0	61	5	1	2	12	2	.86	5	.310	.380	.562
2003	TEX	AL	19	44	12	2	1	1	(0	1)	19	9	4	5	5	0	11	1	0	0	0	0	-	2	.273	.360	.432
2004	TEX	AL	49	147	33	6	0	1	(1	0)	42	20	16	11	12	0	35	2	4	3	0	1	.00	5	.224	.287	.286
2005	TEX	AL	13	40	9	2	0	1	(0	1)	14	7	4	4	2	0	7	0	0	0	0	0	-	1	.225	.262	.350
3 ML YEARS			81	231	54	10	1	3	(1	2)	75	36	24	20	19	0	53	3	4	3	0	1	.00	8	.234	.297	.325

Tim Laker

Bats: R **Throws:** R **Pos:** C-1; PH-1   **Ht:** 6'3" **Wt:** 225 **Born:** 11/27/1969 **Age:** 36

Year	Team	Lg	G	AB	H	2B	3B	HR	(Hm	Rd)	TB	R	RBI	RC	TBB	IBB	SO	HBP	SH	SF	SB	CS	SB%	GDP	Avg	OBP	Slg
2005	Drham*	AAA	89	327	74	19	0	11	(-	-)	126	48	44	41	37	1	80	2	0	4	0	0	-	12	.226	.305	.385
1992	MON	NL	28	46	10	3	0	0	(0	0)	13	8	4	2	2	0	14	0	0	0	1	1	.50	1	.217	.250	.283
1993	MON	NL	43	86	17	2	1	0	(0	0)	21	3	7	4	2	0	16	1	3	1	2	0	1.00	1	.198	.222	.244
1995	MON	NL	64	141	33	8	1	3	(1	2)	52	17	20	14	14	4	38	1	1	1	0	1	.00	5	.234	.306	.369
1997	BAL	AL	7	14	0	0	0	0	(0	0)	0	0	1	0	2	0	9	0	1	1	0	0	-	0	.000	.118	.000
1998	2 Tms		17	29	10	1	0	1	(0	1)	14	3	2	5	2	0	4	0	0	1	0	1	.00	1	.345	.375	.483
1999	PIT	NL	6	9	3	0	0	0	(0	0)	3	0	0	1	0	0	2	0	0	0	0	0	-	0	.333	.333	.333
2001	CLE	AL	16	33	6	0	0	1	(0	1)	9	5	5	3	6	0	8	0	1	0	0	0	-	1	.182	.308	.273
2003	CLE	AL	52	162	39	11	0	3	(1	2)	59	17	21	18	9	1	38	0	5	0	2	2	.50	4	.241	.281	.364
2004	CLE	AL	44	117	25	2	0	3	(0	3)	36	12	17	10	7	1	28	1	2	1	0	0	-	5	.214	.262	.308
2005	TB	AL	1	1	0	0	0	0	(0	0)	0	0	0	0	0	0	1	0	0	0	0	0	-	0	.000	.000	.000
98	TB	AL	3	5	1	0	0	0	(0	0)	1	1	0	0	1	0	1	0	0	0	0	1	.00	0	.200	.333	.200
98	Pit	NL	14	24	9	1	0	1	(0	1)	13	2	2	5	1	0	3	0	0	1	0	0	-	1	.375	.385	.542
10 ML YEARS			278	638	143	27	2	11	(2	9)	207	65	77	57	44	6	158	3	13	5	5	5	.50	19	.224	.275	.324

Mike Lamb

Bats: L **Throws:** R **Pos:** 1B-68; PH-40; 3B-15; LF-12; RF-1; DH-1; PR-1   **Ht:** 6'1" **Wt:** 195 **Born:** 8/9/1975 **Age:** 30

Year	Team	Lg	G	AB	H	2B	3B	HR	(Hm	Rd)	TB	R	RBI	RC	TBB	IBB	SO	HBP	SH	SF	SB	CS	SB%	GDP	Avg	OBP	Slg
2000	TEX	AL	138	493	137	25	2	6	(4	2)	184	65	47	59	34	6	60	4	5	2	0	2	.00	10	.278	.328	.373
2001	TEX	AL	76	284	87	18	0	4	(1	3)	117	42	35	40	14	1	27	5	1	2	2	1	.67	6	.306	.348	.412
2002	TEX	AL	115	314	89	13	0	9	(7	2)	129	54	33	46	33	5	48	3	2	3	0	0	-	7	.283	.354	.411
2003	TEX	AL	28	38	5	0	0	0	(0	0)	5	3	2	0	2	0	7	1	0	1	1	0	1.00	1	.132	.190	.132
2004	HOU	NL	112	278	80	14	3	14	(8	6)	142	38	58	51	31	3	63	0	0	3	1	1	.50	4	.288	.356	.511
2005	HOU	NL	125	322	76	13	5	12	(4	8)	135	41	53	38	22	1	65	1	0	4	1	1	.50	10	.236	.284	.419
6 ML YEARS			594	1729	474	83	10	45	(24	21)	712	243	228	234	136	16	270	14	8	15	5	5	.50	38	.274	.329	.412

Jason Lane

Bats: R **Throws:** L **Pos:** RF-137; CF-6; PH-5; LF-4   **Ht:** 6'2" **Wt:** 215 **Born:** 12/22/1976 **Age:** 29

Year	Team	Lg	G	AB	H	2B	3B	HR	(Hm	Rd)	TB	R	RBI	RC	TBB	IBB	SO	HBP	SH	SF	SB	CS	SB%	GDP	Avg	OBP	Slg
2002	HOU	NL	44	69	20	3	1	4	(2	2)	37	12	10	11	10	1	12	0	0	1	1	1	.50	0	.290	.375	.536
2003	HOU	NL	18	27	8	2	0	4	(4	0)	22	5	10	6	0	0	2	0	0	0	0	0	-	0	.296	.296	.815
2004	HOU	NL	107	136	37	10	2	4	(4	0)	63	21	19	23	16	0	33	1	1	2	1	0	1.00	2	.272	.348	.463
2005	HOU	NL	145	517	138	34	4	26	(14	12)	258	65	78	72	32	1	105	7	0	5	6	2	.75	10	.267	.316	.499
4 ML YEARS			314	749	203	49	7	38	(24	14)	380	103	117	112	58	2	152	8	1	* 8	8	3	.73	12	.271	.327	.507

Ryan Langerhans

Bats: L **Throws:** L **Pos:** LF-54; RF-48; CF-19; PH-16; PR-10   **Ht:** 6'3" **Wt:** 195 **Born:** 2/20/1980 **Age:** 26

Year	Team	Lg	G	AB	H	2B	3B	HR	(Hm	Rd)	TB	R	RBI	RC	TBB	IBB	SO	HBP	SH	SF	SB	CS	SB%	GDP	Avg	OBP	Slg
2002	ATL	NL	1	1	0	0	0	0	(0	0)	0	0	0	0	0	0	0	0	0	0	0	0	-	0	.000	.000	.000
2003	ATL	NL	16	15	4	0	0	0	(0	0)	4	2	0	1	0	0	6	0	0	0	0	0	-	1	.267	.267	.267
2005	ATL	NL	128	326	87	22	3	8	(3	5)	139	48	42	53	37	3	75	5	2	3	0	2	.00	2	.267	.348	.426
3 ML YEARS			145	342	91	22	3	8	(3	5)	143	50	42	54	37	3	81	5	2	3	0	2	.00	3	.266	.344	.418

Adam LaRoche

Bats: L **Throws:** L **Pos:** 1B-125; PH-19; PR-1   **Ht:** 6'3" **Wt:** 180 **Born:** 11/6/1979 **Age:** 26

Year	Team	Lg	G	AB	H	2B	3B	HR	(Hm	Rd)	TB	R	RBI	RC	TBB	IBB	SO	HBP	SH	SF	SB	CS	SB%	GDP	Avg	OBP	Slg
2000	Danvle	R+	56	201	62	13	3	7	(-	-)	102	38	45	39	24	2	46	2	1	4	4	1	.80	2	.308	.381	.507
2001	MrtlBh	A+	126	471	118	31	0	7	(-	-)	170	49	47	47	30	3	108	9	0	4	10	8	.56	13	.251	.305	.361
2002	MrtlBh	A+	69	250	84	17	0	9	(-	-)	128	30	53	50	27	4	37	4	2	2	0	2	.00	8	.336	.406	.512
2002	Grnville	AA	45	173	50	9	0	4	(-	-)	71	17	19	24	19	2	38	1	0	0	1	1	.50	6	.289	.363	.410
2003	Grnville	AA	61	219	62	12	1	12	(-	-)	112	42	37	40	34	3	53	3	0	4	1	2	.33	6	.283	.381	.511
2003	Rchmd	AAA	72	264	78	21	0	8	(-	-)	123	33	35	42	27	3	58	3	0	6	1	2	.33	6	.295	.360	.466
2004	Rchmd	AAA	4	11	2	0	0	1	(-	-)	5	1	2	0	1	0	0	0	0	0	0	0	-	2	.182	.250	.455
2004	ATL	NL	110	324	90	27	1	13	(7	6)	158	45	45	43	27	1	78	1	2	2	0	0	-	10	.278	.333	.488
2005	ATL	NL	141	451	117	28	0	20	(11	9)	205	53	78	63	39	7	87	4	2	6	0	2	.00	15	.259	.320	.455
2 ML YEARS			251	775	207	55	1	33	(18	15)	363	98	123	106	66	8	165	5	4	8	0	2	.00	25	.267	.326	.468

Jason LaRue

Bats: R Throws: R Pos: C-109; PH-3; RF-1   Ht: 5'11" Wt: 200 Born: 3/19/1974 Age: 32

Year	Team	Lg	G	AB	H	2B	3B	HR	(Hm	Rd)	TB	R	RBI	RC	TBB	IBB	SO	HBP	SH	SF	SB	CS	SB%	GDP	Avg	OBP	Slg
1999	CIN	NL	36	90	19	7	0	3	(1	2)	35	12	10	10	11	1	32	2	0	0	4	1	.80	4	.211	.311	.389
2000	CIN	NL	31	98	23	3	0	5	(1	4)	41	12	12	12	5	2	19	4	0	0	0	0	-	1	.235	.299	.418
2001	CIN	NL	121	364	86	21	2	12	(3	9)	147	39	43	42	27	4	106	9	1	2	3	3	.50	11	.236	.303	.404
2002	CIN	NL	113	353	88	17	1	12	(5	7)	143	42	52	44	27	6	117	13	2	2	1	2	.33	13	.249	.324	.405
2003	CIN	NL	118	379	87	23	1	16	(12	4)	160	52	50	47	33	4	111	20	1	4	3	3	.50	9	.230	.321	.422
2004	CIN	NL	114	390	98	24	2	14	(3	11)	168	46	55	53	26	5	108	24	2	3	0	2	.00	7	.251	.334	.431
2005	CIN	NL	110	361	94	27	0	14	(6	8)	163	38	60	60	41	7	101	13	5	2	0	0	-	8	.260	.355	.452
7 ML YEARS			643	2035	495	122	6	76	(31	45)	857	241	282	271	170	29	594	85	11	13	11	11	.50	53	.243	.326	.421

Brian Lawrence

Pitches: R Bats: R Pos: SP-33   Ht: 6'0" Wt: 195 Born: 5/14/1976 Age: 30

Year	Team	Lg	G	GS	CG	GF	IP	BFP	H	R	ER	HR	SH	SF	HB	TBB	IBB	SO	WP	Bk	W	L	Pct	ShO	Sv-Op	Hld	ERC	ERA
2001	SD	NL	27	15	1	5	114.2	484	107	53	44	10	4	3	5	34	5	84	1	0	5	5	.500	0	0-0	0	3.30	3.45
2002	SD	NL	35	31	2	0	210.0	894	230	97	86	16	8	4	11	52	6	149	2	1	12	12	.500	2	0-0	1	4.05	3.69
2003	SD	NL	33	33	1	0	210.2	884	206	106	98	27	11	6	11	57	8	116	4	0	10	15	.400	0	0-0	0	3.81	4.19
2004	SD	NL	34	34	2	0	203.0	870	226	101	93	26	11	9	7	55	7	121	2	0	15	14	.517	1	0-0	0	4.53	4.12
2005	SD	NL	33	33	1	0	195.2	852	211	106	105	18	3	7	11	57	7	109	3	1	7	15	.318	0	0-0	0	4.17	4.83
5 ML YEARS			162	146	7	5	934.0	3984	980	463	426	97	37	29	45	255	33	579	12	2	49	61	.445	3	0-0	1	4.03	4.10

Matt Lawton

Bats: L Throws: R Pos: RF-113; LF-26; PR-4; PH-3   Ht: 5'10" Wt: 186 Born: 11/3/1971 Age: 34

Year	Team	Lg	G	AB	H	2B	3B	HR	(Hm	Rd)	TB	R	RBI	RC	TBB	IBB	SO	HBP	SH	SF	SB	CS	SB%	GDP	Avg	OBP	Slg
1995	MIN	AL	21	60	19	4	1	1	(1	0)	28	11	12	11	7	0	11	3	0	0	1	1	.50	1	.317	.414	.467
1996	MIN	AL	79	252	65	7	1	6	(1	5)	92	34	42	31	28	1	28	4	0	2	4	4	.50	6	.258	.339	.365
1997	MIN	AL	142	460	114	29	3	14	(8	6)	191	74	60	73	76	3	81	10	1	1	7	4	.64	7	.248	.366	.415
1998	MIN	AL	152	557	155	36	6	21	(11	10)	266	91	77	105	86	6	64	15	0	4	16	8	.67	10	.278	.387	.478
1999	MIN	AL	118	406	105	18	0	7	(5	2)	144	58	54	57	57	7	42	6	0	7	26	4	.87	1	.259	.353	.355
2000	MIN	AL	156	561	171	44	2	13	(8	5)	258	84	88	109	91	8	63	7	0	5	23	7	.77	10	.305	.405	.460
2001	2 Tms	AL	151	559	155	36	1	13	(5	8)	232	95	64	92	85	6	80	11	0	2	29	8	.78	16	.277	.382	.415
2002	CLE	AL	114	416	98	19	2	15	(8	7)	166	71	57	59	59	0	34	8	1	0	8	9	.47	13	.236	.342	.399
2003	CLE	AL	99	374	93	19	0	15	(6	9)	157	57	53	57	47	0	47	7	0	1	10	3	.77	8	.249	.343	.420
2004	CLE	AL	150	591	164	25	0	20	(10	10)	249	109	70	86	74	3	84	11	0	4	23	9	.72	21	.277	.366	.421
2005	3 Tms	AL	141	500	127	30	1	13	(5	8)	198	67	53	69	69	0	77	12	0	4	18	9	.67	10	.254	.356	.396
01	Min	AL	103	376	110	25	0	10	(4	6)	165	71	51	66	63	6	46	3	0	2	19	6	.76	14	.293	.396	.439
01	NYM	AL	48	183	45	11	1	3	(1	2)	67	24	13	26	22	0	34	8	0	0	10	2	.83	2	.246	.352	.366
05	Pit	NL	101	374	102	28	1	10	(4	6)	162	53	44	61	58	0	61	9	0	4	16	9	.64	7	.273	.380	.433
05	ChC	NL	19	78	19	2	0	1	(1	0)	24	8	5	5	4	0	8	1	0	0	1	1	1.00	3	.244	.289	.308
05	NYY	AL	21	48	6	0	0	2	(1	1)	12	6	4	3	7	0	8	2	0	0	1	1	1.00	0	.125	.263	.250
11 ML YEARS			1323	4736	1266	267	17	138	(68	70)	1981	751	630	749	679	34	611	94	2	30	165	66	.71	113	.267	.368	.418

Brandon League

Pitches: R Bats: R Pos: RP-20   Ht: 6'3" Wt: 192 Born: 3/16/1983 Age: 23

Year	Team	Lg	G	GS	CG	GF	IP	BFP	H	R	ER	HR	SH	SF	HB	TBB	IBB	SO	WP	Bk	W	L	Pct	ShO	Sv-Op	Hld	ERC	ERA
2001	MdHat	R+	9	9	0	0	38.2	165	36	23	20	3	1	2	4	11	1	38	2	0	2	2	.500	0	0--	-	3.42	4.66
2002	Auburn	A-	16	19	0	0	85.2	357	80	42	30	2	2	1	8	23	0	72	6	0	7	2	.778	0	0--	-	3.09	3.15
2003	CtnWV	A	12	12	0	0	70.2	277	58	15	15	1	0	1	4	18	0	61	3	0	2	3	.400	0	0--	-	2.37	1.91
2003	Dnedin	A+	13	12	0	0	66.1	296	76	40	35	3	5	1	6	20	0	34	8	1	4	3	.571	0	0--	-	4.43	4.43
2004	Ham	AA	41	10	0	6	104.0	441	92	44	39	3	2	1	8	41	1	90	8	0	6	4	.600	0	2--	-	3.23	3.38
2005	Syrcse	AAA	19	10	0	1	63.0	285	78	44	40	7	2	3	4	18	0	35	5	0	4	4	.500	0	0--	-	5.28	5.71
2004	TOR	AL	3	0	0	0	4.2	18	3	0	0	0	0	0	0	1	0	2	0	0	1	0	1.000	0	0-0	1	1.26	0.00
2005	TOR	AL	20	0	0	4	35.2	162	42	27	26	8	0	1	2	20	1	17	5	0	1	0	1.000	0	0-0	1	7.24	6.56
2 ML YEARS			23	0	0	4	40.1	180	45	27	26	8	0	1	2	21	1	19	5	0	2	0	1.000	0	0-0	2	6.36	5.80

Matt LeCroy

Bats: R Throws: R Pos: DH-63; 1B-23; PH-17; C-1   Ht: 6'2" Wt: 225 Born: 12/13/1975 Age: 30

Year	Team	Lg	G	AB	H	2B	3B	HR	(Hm	Rd)	TB	R	RBI	RC	TBB	IBB	SO	HBP	SH	SF	SB	CS	SB%	GDP	Avg	OBP	Slg
2000	MIN	AL	56	167	29	10	0	5	(2	3)	54	18	17	12	17	2	38	2	1	3	0	0	-	6	.174	.254	.323
2001	MIN	AL	15	40	17	5	0	3	(0	3)	31	6	12	11	0	0	8	1	0	1	0	1	.00	0	.425	.429	.775
2002	MIN	AL	63	181	47	11	1	7	(2	5)	81	19	27	24	13	1	38	0	0	2	0	2	.00	5	.260	.306	.448
2003	MIN	AL	107	345	99	19	0	17	(9	8)	169	39	64	60	25	1	82	4	0	0	0	1	.00	8	.287	.342	.490
2004	MIN	AL	88	264	71	14	0	9	(5	4)	112	25	39	32	16	0	60	5	0	2	0	0	-	7	.269	.321	.424
2005	MIN	AL	101	304	79	5	0	17	(10	7)	135	33	50	48	41	2	85	4	0	1	0	0	-	7	.260	.354	.444
6 ML YEARS			430	1301	342	64	1	58	(28	30)	582	140	209	187	112	6	311	16	1	9	0	4	.00	33	.263	.327	.447

Ricky Ledee

Bats: L Throws: L Pos: LF-57; PH-43; RF-17   Ht: 6'1" Wt: 190 Born: 11/22/1973 Age: 32

									BATTING												BASERUNNING				AVERAGES		
Year	Team	Lg	G	AB	H	2B	3B	HR	(Hm	Rd)	TB	R	RBI	RC	TBB	IBB	SO	HBP	SH	SF	SB	CS	SB%	GDP	Avg	OBP	Slg
1998	NYA	AL	42	79	19	5	2	1	(0	1)	31	13	12	9	7	0	29	0	0	1	3	1	.75	1	.241	.299	.392
1999	NYA	AL	88	250	69	13	5	9	(4	5)	119	45	40	41	28	5	73	0	0	2	4	3	.57	2	.276	.346	.476
2000	3 Tms	AL	137	467	110	19	5	13	(6	7)	178	59	77	56	59	4	98	2	0	3	13	6	.68	17	.236	.322	.381
2001	TEX	AL	78	242	56	21	1	2	(1	1)	85	33	36	26	23	0	58	3	1	3	3	3	.50	3	.231	.303	.351
2002	PHI	NL	96	203	46	13	1	8	(4	4)	85	33	23	24	35	0	50	1	1	1	1	2	.33	3	.227	.342	.419
2003	PHI	NL	121	255	63	15	2	13	(6	7)	121	37	46	36	34	5	59	0	1	1	0	0	-	4	.247	.334	.475
2004	2 Tms	NL	104	176	41	9	0	7	(3	4)	71	25	30	24	27	2	47	1	0	1	3	0	1.00	6	.233	.337	.403
2005	LAN	NL	102	237	66	16	1	7	(5	2)	105	31	39	34	20	1	55	3	0	6	0	0	-	5	.278	.335	.443
00	NYY	AL	62	191	46	11	1	7	(2	5)	80	23	31	26	26	2	39	1	0	2	7	3	.70	7	.241	.332	.419
00	Cle	AL	17	63	14	2	1	2	(2	0)	24	13	8	7	8	0	9	0	0	0	0	0	-	3	.222	.310	.381
00	Tex	AL	58	213	50	6	3	4	(2	2)	74	23	38	23	25	2	50	1	0	1	6	3	.67	7	.235	.317	.347
04	Phi	NL	73	123	35	7	0	7	(3	4)	63	19	26	23	22	2	27	0	0	0	2	0	1.00	5	.285	.393	.512
04	SF	NL	31	53	6	2	0	0	(0	0)	8	6	4	1	5	0	20	1	0	1	1	0	1.00	1	.113	.200	.151
	8 ML YEARS		768	1909	470	111	17	60	(29	31)	795	276	303	250	233	17	469	10	3	18	27	15	.64	41	.246	.329	.416

Wil Ledezma

Pitches: L Bats: L Pos: SP-10   Ht: 6'3" Wt: 150 Born: 1/21/1981 Age: 25

			HOW MUCH HE PITCHED						WHAT HE GAVE UP												THE RESULTS						
Year	Team	Lg	G	GS	CG	GF	IP	BFP	H	R	ER	HR	SH	SF	HB	TBB	IBB	SO	WP	Bk	W	L	Pct	ShO	Sv-Op	Hld	ERC	ERA
2005	Toledo*	AAA	11	10	0	0	51.0	232	52	30	30	3	2	1	1	27	0	44	2	0	5	3	.625	0		4.37	5.29
2003	DET	AL	34	8	0	13	84.0	376	99	55	54	12	1	4	3	35	3	49	2	0	3	7	.300	0	0-1	1	5.67	5.79
2004	DET	AL	15	8	0	1	53.1	225	55	28	26	3	0	3	2	18	0	29	3	1	4	3	.571	0	0-1	0	3.94	4.39
2005	DET	AL	10	10	0	0	49.2	234	61	46	39	10	3	4	2	24	0	30	2	2	2	4	.333	0	0-0	0	6.66	7.07
	3 ML YEARS		59	26	0	14	187.0	835	215	129	119	25	4	11	7	77	3	108	7	3	9	14	.391	0	0-2	1	5.41	5.73

Carlos Lee

Bats: R Throws: R Pos: LF-162   Ht: 6'2" Wt: 235 Born: 6/20/1976 Age: 30

									BATTING												BASERUNNING				AVERAGES		
Year	Team	Lg	G	AB	H	2B	3B	HR	(Hm	Rd)	TB	R	RBI	RC	TBB	IBB	SO	HBP	SH	SF	SB	CS	SB%	GDP	Avg	OBP	Slg
1999	CHA	AL	127	492	144	32	2	16	(10	6)	228	66	84	68	13	0	72	4	1	7	4	2	.67	11	.293	.312	.463
2000	CHA	AL	152	572	172	29	2	24	(12	12)	277	107	92	91	38	1	94	3	1	5	13	4	.76	17	.301	.345	.484
2001	CHA	AL	150	558	150	33	3	24	(12	12)	261	75	84	81	38	2	85	6	1	2	17	7	.71	15	.269	.321	.468
2002	CHA	AL	140	492	130	26	2	26	(14	12)	238	82	80	86	75	4	73	2	0	7	1	4	.20	5	.264	.359	.484
2003	CHA	AL	158	623	181	35	1	31	(18	13)	311	100	113	105	37	2	91	4	0	7	18	4	.82	20	.291	.331	.499
2004	CHA	AL	153	591	180	37	0	31	(17	14)	310	103	99	112	54	3	86	7	0	6	11	5	.69	10	.305	.366	.525
2005	MIL	NL	162	618	164	41	0	32	(15	17)	301	85	114	98	57	7	87	2	0	11	13	4	.76	8	.265	.324	.487
	7 ML YEARS		1042	3946	1121	233	10	184	(98	86)	1926	618	666	641	312	19	588	28	3	45	77	30	.72	86	.284	.337	.488

Cliff Lee

Pitches: L Bats: L Pos: SP-32   Ht: 6'3" Wt: 190 Born: 8/30/1978 Age: 27

			HOW MUCH HE PITCHED						WHAT HE GAVE UP												THE RESULTS						
Year	Team	Lg	G	GS	CG	GF	IP	BFP	H	R	ER	HR	SH	SF	HB	TBB	IBB	SO	WP	Bk	W	L	Pct	ShO	Sv-Op	Hld	ERC	ERA
2002	CLE	AL	2	2	0	0	10.1	44	6	2	2	0	1	0	0	8	1	6	0	1	0	1	.000	0	0-0	0	2.38	1.74
2003	CLE	AL	9	9	0	0	52.1	230	41	28	21	7	1	1	2	20	1	44	3	0	3	3	.500	0	0-0	0	3.29	3.61
2004	CLE	AL	33	33	0	0	179.0	802	188	113	108	30	2	6	11	81	1	161	6	0	14	8	.636	0	0-0	0	5.31	5.43
2005	CLE	AL	32	32	1	0	202.0	838	194	91	85	22	5	7	0	52	1	143	4	0	18	5	.783	0	0-0	0	3.35	3.79
	4 ML YEARS		76	76	1	0	443.2	1894	429	234	216	59	9	14	13	161	4	354	13	1	35	17	.673	0	0-0	0	4.08	4.38

Derrek Lee

Bats: R Throws: R Pos: 1B-158   Ht: 6'5" Wt: 248 Born: 9/6/1975 Age: 30

									BATTING												BASERUNNING				AVERAGES		
Year	Team	Lg	G	AB	H	2B	3B	HR	(Hm	Rd)	TB	R	RBI	RC	TBB	IBB	SO	HBP	SH	SF	SB	CS	SB%	GDP	Avg	OBP	Slg
1997	SD	NL	22	54	14	3	0	1	(0	1)	20	9	4	8	9	0	24	0	0	0	0	0	-	1	.259	.365	.370
1998	FLA	NL	141	454	106	29	1	17	(4	13)	188	62	74	59	47	1	120	10	0	2	5	2	.71	12	.233	.318	.414
1999	FLA	NL	70	218	45	9	1	5	(0	5)	71	21	20	18	17	1	70	0	0	1	2	1	.67	3	.206	.263	.326
2000	FLA	NL	158	477	134	18	3	28	(9	19)	242	70	70	84	63	6	123	4	0	2	0	3	.00	14	.281	.368	.507
2001	FLA	NL	158	561	158	37	4	21	(8	13)	266	83	75	88	50	1	126	8	0	6	2	2	.67	18	.282	.346	.474
2002	FLA	NL	162	581	157	35	7	27	(9	18)	287	95	86	96	98	8	164	5	0	4	19	9	.68	14	.270	.378	.494
2003	FLA	NL	155	539	146	31	2	31	(11	20)	274	91	92	99	88	7	131	10	0	6	21	8	.72	9	.271	.379	.508
2004	CHN	NL	161	605	168	39	1	32	(18	14)	305	90	98	101	68	4	128	8	2	5	12	5	.71	14	.278	.356	.504
2005	CHN	NL	158	594	199	50	3	46	(24	22)	393	120	107	135	85	23	109	5	0	7	15	3	.83	12	.335	.418	.662
	9 ML YEARS		1185	4083	1127	251	22	208	(83	125)	2046	641	626	688	525	51	995	50	2	33	78	33	.70	97	.276	.363	.501

Travis Lee

Bats: L Throws: L Pos: 1B-124; PH-23   Ht: 6'3" Wt: 210 Born: 5/26/1975 Age: 31

									BATTING												BASERUNNING				AVERAGES		
Year	Team	Lg	G	AB	H	2B	3B	HR	(Hm	Rd)	TB	R	RBI	RC	TBB	IBB	SO	HBP	SH	SF	SB	CS	SB%	GDP	Avg	OBP	Slg
1998	ARI	NL	146	562	151	20	2	22	(12	10)	241	71	72	83	67	5	123	0	0	1	8	1	.89	13	.269	.346	.429
1999	ARI	NL	120	375	89	16	2	9	(7	2)	136	57	50	49	58	4	50	0	0	3	3	.85	10	.237	.337	.363
2000	2 Tms	NL	128	404	95	24	1	9	(2	7)	148	53	54	53	65	1	79	2	0	2	8	1	.89	12	.235	.342	.366
2001	PHI	NL	157	555	143	34	2	20	(11	9)	241	75	90	81	71	5	109	4	1	9	3	4	.43	15	.258	.341	.434
2002	PHI	NL	153	536	142	26	2	13	(8	5)	211	55	70	65	54	10	104	0	0	2	5	3	.63	12	.265	.331	.394

142

Year	Team	Lg	G	AB	H	2B	3B	HR	(Hm	Rd)	TB	R	RBI	RC	TBB	IBB	SO	HBP	SH	SF	SB	CS	SB%	GDP	Avg	OBP	Slg
																					BASERUNNING				**AVERAGES**		
						BATTING																					
2003	TB	AL	145	542	149	37	3	19	(9	10)	249	75	70	77	64	4	97	0	1	6	6	2	.75	13	.275	.348	.459
2004	NYA	AL	7	19	2	1	0	0	(0	0)	3	1	2	0	1	1	3	0	0	0	0	0	-	2	.105	.150	.158
2005	TB	AL	129	404	110	22	2	12	(5	7)	172	54	49	51	35	4	66	1	0	1	7	4	.64	7	.272	.331	.426
00	Ari	NL	72	224	52	13	0	8	(1	7)	89	34	40	27	25	1	46	0	0	1	5	1	.83	6	.232	.308	.397
00	Phi	NL	56	180	43	11	1	1	(1	0)	59	19	14	26	40	0	33	2	0	1	3	0	1.00	6	.239	.381	.328
8 ML YEARS			985	3397	881	180	14	104	(54	50)	1401	441	457	459	415	34	631	7	2	24	54	18	.75	84	.259	.339	.412

Justin Lehr

Pitches: R Bats: R Pos: RP-23   **Ht: 6'1" Wt: 200 Born: 8/3/1977 Age: 28**

Year	Team	Lg	G	GS	CG	GF	IP	BFP	H	R	ER	HR	SH	SF	HB	TBB	IBB	SO	WP	Bk	W	L	Pct	ShO	Sv-Op	Hld	ERC	ERA
			HOW MUCH HE PITCHED						**WHAT HE GAVE UP**												**THE RESULTS**							
1999	SoOre	A-	14	4	0	7	42.1	207	62	36	28	3	5	1	2	17	3	40	9	0	2	6	.250	0	0--	-	6.56	5.95
2000	Scrmto	AAA	1	1	0	0	4.0	21	7	5	5	1	0	0	0	3	0	3	0	0	0	0	-	0	0--	-	12.23	11.25
2000	Mdest	A+	29	25	0	1	175.0	709	161	71	62	10	8	4	5	46	1	138	15	5	13	6	.684	0	0--	-	3.01	3.19
2001	Mdland	AA	29	27	0	2	155.1	709	206	107	94	20	6	2	11	43	1	103	4	2	11	12	.478	0	0--	-	6.00	5.45
2002	Mdland	AA	58	0	0	21	80.0	348	88	39	36	7	7	4	3	31	10	59	3	0	8	3	.727	0	4--	-	4.52	4.05
2003	Scrmto	AAA	53	0	0	16	75.0	320	74	34	31	3	3	0	4	27	3	64	5	0	3	2	.600	0	4--	-	3.60	3.72
2004	Scrmto	AAA	32	0	0	28	37.1	159	37	14	11	1	0	1	1	10	0	40	6	0	4	2	.667	0	13--	-	3.07	2.65
2005	Nashv	AAA	27	11	0	5	88.0	398	102	49	39	8	4	2	2	32	2	68	3	0	7	7	.500	0	1--	-	4.73	3.99
2004	OAK	AL	27	0	0	11	32.2	144	35	19	19	3	1	2	2	14	2	16	2	0	1	1	.500	0	0-1	5	4.73	5.23
2005	MIL	NL	23	0	0	9	34.2	154	32	19	15	4	2	1	1	18	2	23	1	1	1	1	.500	0	0-1	3	4.17	3.89
2 ML YEARS			50	0	0	20	67.1	298	67	38	34	7	3	3	3	32	4	39	3	1	2	2	.500	0	0-2	8	4.44	4.54

Jon Leicester

Pitches: R Bats: R Pos: RP-5; SP-1   **Ht: 6'3" Wt: 230 Born: 2/7/1979 Age: 27**

Year	Team	Lg	G	GS	CG	GF	IP	BFP	H	R	ER	HR	SH	SF	HB	TBB	IBB	SO	WP	Bk	W	L	Pct	ShO	Sv-Op	Hld	ERC	ERA
			HOW MUCH HE PITCHED						**WHAT HE GAVE UP**												**THE RESULTS**							
2000	Eugene	A-	17	7	0	1	49.2	224	47	36	30	4	6	4	2	22	1	31	2	0	1	5	.167	0	0--	-	3.76	5.44
2001	Lansng	A	28	27	1	1	153.0	693	182	117	90	16	2	4	16	58	0	109	12	1	9	10	.474	0	0--	-	5.61	5.29
2002	Dytona	A+	20	14	0	0	81.2	371	77	43	36	2	2	2	8	48	1	57	8	1	2	3	.400	0	0--	-	4.25	3.97
2002	WTenn	AA	5	4	0	0	27.1	123	24	16	14	1	2	1	3	13	0	18	4	0	2	2	.500	0	0--	-	3.53	4.61
2003	WTenn	AA	45	9	1	13	106.1	455	89	54	46	7	5	1	4	53	0	106	4	1	6	7	.462	1	6--	-	3.47	3.89
2003	Iowa	AAA	1	1	0	0	5.0	23	6	4	4	0	0	2	0	2	0	4	0	0	0	0	-	0	0--	-	4.34	7.20
2004	Iowa	AAA	13	12	0	0	66.2	295	62	31	27	3	1	2	2	37	0	61	3	0	6	2	.750	0	0--	-	3.99	3.65
2005	Iowa	AAA	24	16	0	2	98.0	451	115	65	60	17	1	1	0	42	1	73	7	0	3	8	.273	0	1--	-	5.61	5.51
2004	CHN	NL	32	0	0	6	41.2	175	40	20	18	7	2	2	0	15	0	35	0	0	5	1	.833	0	0-2	5	4.20	3.89
2005	CHN	NL	6	1	0	2	9.0	46	11	10	9	2	1	0	2	9	0	7	1	0	0	2	.000	0	0-0	0	10.60	9.00
2 ML YEARS			38	1	0	8	50.2	221	51	30	27	9	3	2	2	24	0	42	1	0	5	3	.625	0	0-2	5	5.23	4.80

Al Leiter

Pitches: L Bats: L Pos: SP-26; RP-7   **Ht: 6'3" Wt: 220 Born: 10/23/1965 Age: 40**

Year	Team	Lg	G	GS	CG	GF	IP	BFP	H	R	ER	HR	SH	SF	HB	TBB	IBB	SO	WP	Bk	W	L	Pct	ShO	Sv-Op	Hld	ERC	ERA
			HOW MUCH HE PITCHED						**WHAT HE GAVE UP**												**THE RESULTS**							
1987	NYA	AL	4	4	0	0	22.2	104	24	16	16	2	1	0	0	15	0	28	4	0	2	2	.500	0	0-0	0	5.41	6.35
1988	NYA	AL	14	14	0	0	57.1	251	49	27	25	7	1	0	5	33	0	60	1	4	4	4	.500	0	0-0	0	4.51	3.92
1989	2 Tms	AL	5	5	0	0	33.1	154	32	23	21	2	1	1	2	23	0	26	2	1	1	2	.333	0	0-0	0	4.90	5.67
1990	TOR	AL	4	0	0	2	6.1	22	1	0	0	0	0	0	0	2	0	5	0	0	0	0	-	0	0-0	0	0.33	0.00
1991	TOR	AL	3	0	0	1	1.2	13	3	5	5	0	1	0	0	5	0	1	0	0	0	0	-	0	0-0	0	19.88	27.00
1992	TOR	AL	1	0	0	0	1.0	7	1	1	1	0	0	0	0	2	0	0	0	0	0	0	-	0	0-0	0	8.07	9.00
1993	TOR	AL	34	12	1	4	105.0	454	93	52	48	8	3	3	4	56	2	66	2	2	9	6	.600	1	2-3	3	3.94	4.11
1994	TOR	AL	20	20	1	0	111.2	516	125	68	63	6	3	8	2	65	3	100	7	5	6	7	.462	0	0-0	0	5.14	5.08
1995	TOR	AL	28	28	2	0	183.0	805	162	80	74	15	6	4	6	**108**	1	153	**14**	0	11	11	.500	1	0-0	0	4.18	3.64
1996	FLA	NL	33	33	2	0	215.1	896	153	74	70	14	7	3	11	**119**	3	200	5	0	16	12	.571	1	0-0	0	3.09	2.93
1997	FLA	NL	27	27	0	0	151.1	668	133	78	73	13	10	3	12	91	4	132	2	0	11	9	.550	0	0-0	0	4.39	4.34
1998	NYN	NL	28	28	4	0	193.0	789	151	55	53	8	6	2	11	71	2	174	4	1	17	6	.739	2	0-0	0	2.65	2.47
1999	NYN	NL	32	32	1	0	213.0	923	209	107	100	19	13	10	9	93	8	162	4	1	13	12	.520	0	0-0	0	4.17	4.23
2000	NYN	NL	31	31	2	0	208.0	874	176	84	74	19	10	6	11	76	1	200	4	1	16	8	.667	1	0-0	0	3.23	3.20
2001	NYN	NL	29	29	0	0	187.1	772	178	81	69	18	9	6	4	46	3	142	5	2	11	11	.500	0	0-0	0	3.26	3.31
2002	NYN	NL	33	33	2	0	204.1	868	194	99	79	23	12	2	8	69	5	172	1	1	13	13	.500	2	0-0	0	3.75	3.48
2003	NYN	NL	30	30	1	0	180.2	798	176	83	80	15	11	6	9	94	11	139	5	1	15	9	.625	1	0-0	0	4.40	3.99
2004	NYN	NL	30	30	0	0	173.2	750	138	65	62	16	8	2	11	97	8	117	1	1	10	8	.556	0	0-0	0	3.68	3.21
2005	2 Tms	NL	33	26	0	2	142.1	669	154	103	97	13	7	6	12	98	2	97	2	0	7	12	.368	0	0-0	0	6.03	6.13
89	NYY	AL	4	4	0	0	26.2	123	23	20	18	1	1	1	2	21	0	22	1	1	1	2	.333	0	0-0	0	4.62	6.08
89	Tor	AL	1	1	0	0	6.2	31	9	3	3	1	0	0	0	2	0	4	1	0	0	0	-	0	0-0	0	5.96	4.05
05	Fla	NL	17	16	0	0	80.0	376	88	61	59	9	7	3	6	60	2	52	0	0	3	7	.300	0	0-0	0	6.63	6.64
05	NYY	AL	16	10	0	2	62.1	293	66	42	38	4	0	3	6	38	0	45	2	0	4	5	.444	0	0-0	0	5.30	5.49
19 ML YEARS			419	382	16	9	2391.0	10333	2152	1101	1010	198	109	62	117	1163	53	1974	63	20	162	132	.551	10	2-3	3	3.91	3.80

Anthony Lerew

Pitches: R Bats: L Pos: RP-7   **Ht: 6'3" Wt: 220 Born: 10/28/1982 Age: 23**

Year	Team	Lg	G	GS	CG	GF	IP	BFP	H	R	ER	HR	SH	SF	HB	TBB	IBB	SO	WP	Bk	W	L	Pct	ShO	Sv-Op	Hld	ERC	ERA
			HOW MUCH HE PITCHED						**WHAT HE GAVE UP**												**THE RESULTS**							
2001	Braves	R	12	7	0	1	49.0	204	43	25	16	3	0	1	0	14	0	40	4	2	1	2	.333	0	0--	-	2.68	2.94
2002	Danvle	R+	14	14	0	0	83.0	334	60	23	16	2	3	2	5	25	0	75	0	0	8	3	.727	0	0--	-	2.03	1.73
2003	Rome	A	25	25	0	0	143.2	586	112	45	38	7	8	6	3	43	2	127	0	0	7	6	.538	0	0--	-	2.26	2.38
2004	MrtlBh	A+	27	27	0	0	144.0	623	145	75	60	12	7	5	3	46	0	125	0	0	8	9	.471	0	0--	-	3.70	3.75

Year	Team	Lg	G	GS	CG	GF	IP	BFP	H	R	ER	HR	SH	SF	HB	TBB	IBB	SO	WP	Bk	W	L	Pct	ShO	Sv-Op	Hld	ERC	ERA
2005	Missi	AA	14	14	1	0	75.2	329	70	34	33	6	4	1	2	32	1	64	0	0	6	2	.750	0	0--	-	3.63	3.93
2005	Rchmd	AAA	13	13	0	0	72.1	303	63	34	28	9	3	2	3	23	0	53	1	0	4	4	.500	0	0--	-	3.35	3.48
2005	ATL	NL	7	0	0	4	8.0	37	9	5	5	1	1	0	0	5	2	5	0	0	0	0	-	0	0-1	-	5.47	5.63

Al Levine

Pitches: R Bats: L Pos: RP-9   Ht: 6'3" Wt: 190 Born: 5/22/1968 Age: 38

Year	Team	Lg	G	GS	CG	GF	IP	BFP	H	R	ER	HR	SH	SF	HB	TBB	IBB	SO	WP	Bk	W	L	Pct	ShO	Sv-Op	Hld	ERC	ERA
2005	Fresno*	AAA	9	0	0	3	12.2	57	12	5	4	0	1	2	1	7	1	6	0	0	0	0	-	0	1--	-	3.76	2.84
1996	CHA	AL	16	0	0	5	18.1	85	22	14	11	1	0	1	1	7	1	12	0	0	0	1	.000	0	0-1	0	4.80	5.40
1997	CHA	AL	25	0	0	6	27.1	133	35	22	21	4	1	2	1	16	1	22	2	0	2	2	.500	0	0-1	3	7.10	6.91
1998	TEX	AL	30	0	0	11	58.0	251	68	30	29	6	1	3	0	16	1	19	5	0	1	1	.000	0	0-0	4	4.58	4.50
1999	ANA	AL	50	1	0	12	85.0	349	76	40	32	13	2	7	3	29	2	37	3	0	1	1	.500	0	0-1	3	3.81	3.39
2000	ANA	AL	51	5	0	12	95.1	426	98	44	41	10	3	3	2	49	5	42	1	0	3	4	.429	0	2-2	5	4.71	3.87
2001	ANA	AL	64	1	0	21	75.2	316	71	25	20	7	5	5	2	28	4	40	6	0	8	10	.444	0	2-6	17	2.86	2.38
2002	ANA	AL	52	0	0	21	63.2	286	61	35	30	8	2	7	2	34	3	40	6	0	4	4	.500	0	5-7	10	4.53	4.24
2003	2 Tms	AL	54	0	0	21	71.0	303	67	29	22	9	4	0	3	29	1	30	2	0	3	6	.333	0	1-4	10	4.17	2.79
2004	DET	AL	65	0	0	14	70.2	310	83	37	36	10	2	2	1	24	1	32	3	0	3	4	.429	0	0-1	16	5.23	4.58
2005	SF	NL	9	0	0	4	10.1	51	16	11	11	2	0	0	0	4	1	4	0	0	0	0	-	0	0-0	1	7.79	9.58
03	TB	AL	36	0	0	14	49.2	208	45	23	16	7	3	0	2	18	0	25	2	0	3	5	.375	0	0-2	8	3.89	2.90
03	KC	AL	18	0	0	7	21.1	95	22	6	6	2	1	0	1	11	1	5	0	0	0	1	.000	0	1-2	2	4.82	2.53
10 ML YEARS			416	7	0	127	575.1	2510	597	287	253	70	20	30	16	236	20	278	24	0	24	33	.421	0	10-23	64	4.56	3.96

Brad Lidge

Pitches: R Bats: R Pos: RP-70   Ht: 6'5" Wt: 200 Born: 12/23/1976 Age: 29

Year	Team	Lg	G	GS	CG	GF	IP	BFP	H	R	ER	HR	SH	SF	HB	TBB	IBB	SO	WP	Bk	W	L	Pct	ShO	Sv-Op	Hld	ERC	ERA
2002	HOU	NL	6	1	0	2	8.2	48	12	6	6	0	0	2	0	9	1	12	0	0	1	0	1.000	0	0-0	0	8.90	6.23
2003	HOU	NL	78	0	0	9	85.0	349	60	36	34	6	2	3	5	42	7	97	4	1	6	3	.667	0	1-6	28	2.82	3.60
2004	HOU	NL	80	0	0	44	94.2	369	57	21	20	8	3	2	6	30	5	157	3	1	6	5	.545	0	29-33	17	1.85	1.90
2005	HOU	NL	70	0	0	65	70.2	291	58	21	18	5	4	1	3	23	1	103	8	0	4	4	.500	0	42-46	0	2.79	2.29
4 ML YEARS			234	1	0	120	259.0	1057	187	84	78	19	10	6	16	104	14	369	15	2	17	12	.586	0	72-85	45	2.62	2.71

Cory Lidle

Pitches: R Bats: R Pos: SP-31   Ht: 5'11" Wt: 192 Born: 3/22/1972 Age: 34

Year	Team	Lg	G	GS	CG	GF	IP	BFP	H	R	ER	HR	SH	SF	HB	TBB	IBB	SO	WP	Bk	W	L	Pct	ShO	Sv-Op	Hld	ERC	ERA
1997	NYN	NL	54	2	0	20	81.2	345	86	38	32	7	4	4	3	20	4	54	2	0	7	2	.778	0	2-3	9	3.75	3.53
1999	TB	AL	5	1	0	1	5.0	24	8	4	4	0	0	0	0	2	0	4	0	0	1	0	1.000	0	0-0	0	6.98	7.20
2000	TB	AL	31	11	0	5	96.2	424	114	61	54	13	3	1	3	29	3	62	6	0	4	6	.400	0	0-0	2	5.06	5.03
2001	OAK	AL	29	29	1	0	188.0	762	170	84	75	23	2	1	10	47	7	118	5	0	13	6	.684	0	0-0	0	3.35	3.59
2002	OAK	AL	31	30	2	0	192.0	796	191	90	83	17	5	6	6	39	3	111	6	1	8	10	.444	2	0-0	0	3.31	3.89
2003	TOR	AL	31	31	2	0	192.2	840	216	133	123	24	5	5	5	60	3	112	9	0	12	15	.444	0	0-0	0	4.67	5.75
2004	2 Tms	NL	34	34	5	0	211.1	911	224	123	115	27	14	6	10	61	5	126	8	0	12	12	.500	3	0-0	0	4.31	4.90
2005	PHI	NL	31	31	1	0	184.2	792	210	105	93	18	11	8	6	40	5	121	6	0	13	11	.542	0	0-0	0	4.19	4.53
04	Cin	NL	24	24	3	0	149.0	656	170	95	88	24	12	4	5	44	4	93	8	0	7	10	.412	1	0-0	0	4.96	5.32
04	Phi	NL	10	10	2	0	62.1	255	54	28	27	3	2	2	5	17	1	33	0	0	5	2	.714	2	0-0	0	2.86	3.90
8 ML YEARS			246	169	11	26	1152.0	4894	1219	638	579	129	44	31	43	298	30	708	42	1	70	62	.530	5	2-3	11	4.05	4.52

Jon Lieber

Pitches: R Bats: L Pos: SP-35   Ht: 6'2" Wt: 230 Born: 4/2/1970 Age: 36

Year	Team	Lg	G	GS	CG	GF	IP	BFP	H	R	ER	HR	SH	SF	HB	TBB	IBB	SO	WP	Bk	W	L	Pct	ShO	Sv-Op	Hld	ERC	ERA
1994	PIT	NL	17	17	1	0	108.2	460	116	62	45	12	3	3	1	25	3	71	2	3	6	7	.462	0	0-0	0	3.83	3.73
1995	PIT	NL	21	12	0	3	72.2	327	103	56	51	7	5	6	4	14	0	45	3	0	4	7	.364	0	0-1	3	5.96	6.32
1996	PIT	NL	51	15	0	6	142.0	600	156	70	63	19	7	2	3	28	2	94	0	0	9	5	.643	0	1-4	9	4.12	3.99
1997	PIT	NL	33	32	1	0	188.1	799	193	102	94	23	6	7	1	51	8	160	3	1	11	14	.440	0	0-0	0	3.78	4.49
1998	PIT	NL	29	28	2	1	171.0	731	182	93	78	23	7	4	3	40	4	138	0	3	8	14	.364	0	1-1	0	4.00	4.11
1999	CHN	NL	31	31	3	0	203.1	875	226	107	92	28	7	11	3	46	6	186	2	2	10	11	.476	1	0-0	0	4.19	4.07
2000	CHN	NL	35	35	6	0	251.0	1047	248	130	123	36	9	7	10	54	3	192	2	2	12	11	.522	1	0-0	0	3.70	4.41
2001	CHN	NL	34	34	5	0	232.1	958	226	104	98	25	13	9	7	41	4	148	4	1	20	6	.769	1	0-0	0	3.19	3.80
2002	CHN	NL	21	21	3	0	141.0	582	153	64	58	15	10	6	1	12	2	87	0	0	6	8	.429	0	0-0	0	3.33	3.70
2004	NYA	AL	27	27	0	0	176.2	749	216	95	85	20	3	7	2	18	2	102	7	0	14	8	.636	0	0-0	0	4.26	4.33
2005	PHI	NL	35	35	1	0	218.1	912	223	107	102	33	13	5	1	41	6	149	3	0	17	13	.567	0	0-0	0	3.72	4.20
11 ML YEARS			334	287	22	10	1905.1	8040	2042	990	889	241	83	67	38	370	40	1372	26	12	117	104	.529	3	2-6	12	3.87	4.20

Mike Lieberthal

Bats: R Throws: R Pos: C-117; PH-1   Ht: 6'0" Wt: 190 Born: 1/18/1972 Age: 34

Year	Team	Lg	G	AB	H	2B	3B	HR	(Hm	Rd)	TB	R	RBI	RC	TBB	IBB	SO	HBP	SH	SF	SB	CS	SB%	GDP	Avg	OBP	Slg
1994	PHI	NL	24	79	21	3	1	1	(1	0)	29	6	5	8	3	0	5	1	1	0	0	0	-	4	.266	.301	.367
1995	PHI	NL	16	47	12	2	0	0	(0	0)	14	1	4	5	5	0	5	0	2	0	0	0	-	1	.255	.327	.298
1996	PHI	NL	50	166	42	8	0	7	(4	3)	71	21	23	21	10	0	30	2	0	4	0	0	-	4	.253	.297	.428
1997	PHI	NL	134	455	112	27	1	20	(11	9)	201	59	77	62	44	1	76	4	0	7	3	4	.43	10	.246	.314	.442
1998	PHI	NL	86	313	80	15	3	8	(5	3)	125	39	45	39	17	1	44	7	0	5	2	1	.67	4	.256	.304	.399

Year	Team	Lg	G	AB	H	2B	3B	HR	(Hm	Rd)	TB	R	RBI	RC	TBB	IBB	SO	HBP	SH	SF	SB	CS	SB%	GDP	Avg	OBP	Slg
						BATTING																BASERUNNING				AVERAGES	
1999	PHI	NL	145	510	153	33	1	31	(10	21)	281	84	96	96	44	7	86	11	1	8	0	0	-	15	.300	.363	.551
2000	PHI	NL	108	389	108	30	0	15	(8	7)	183	55	71	62	40	3	53	6	0	3	2	0	1.00	12	.278	.352	.470
2001	PHI	NL	34	121	28	8	0	2	(0	2)	42	21	11	13	12	2	21	3	0	0	0	0	-	2	.231	.316	.347
2002	PHI	NL	130	476	133	29	2	15	(7	8)	211	46	52	56	38	2	58	14	0	2	0	1	.00	16	.279	.349	.443
2003	PHI	NL	131	508	159	30	1	13	(6	7)	230	68	81	81	38	2	59	12	0	3	0	0	-	14	.313	.373	.453
2004	PHI	NL	131	476	129	31	1	17	(8	9)	213	58	61	49	37	2	69	11	1	4	1	1	.50	19	.271	.335	.447
2005	PHI	NL	118	392	103	25	0	12	(6	6)	164	48	47	49	35	14	35	11	0	5	0	0	-	6	.263	.336	.418
12 ML YEARS			1107	3932	1080	241	10	141	(66	75)	1764	506	573	541	323	34	541	82	5	41	8	7	.53	107	.275	.339	.449

Jeff Liefer

Bats: L Throws: R Pos: DH-8; PH-7; 1B-5; RF-3　　　　　　**Ht: 6'3" Wt: 210 Born: 8/17/1974 Age: 31**

Year	Team	Lg	G	AB	H	2B	3B	HR	(Hm	Rd)	TB	R	RBI	RC	TBB	IBB	SO	HBP	SH	SF	SB	CS	SB%	GDP	Avg	OBP	Slg
						BATTING																BASERUNNING				AVERAGES	
2005	Buffalo*	AAA	89	321	103	27	2	19	(-	-)	191	59	66	72	35	4	62	2	0	3	2	1	.67	8	.321	.388	.595
1999	CHA	AL	45	113	28	7	1	0	(0	0)	37	8	14	11	8	0	28	0	0	1	2	0	1.00	3	.248	.295	.327
2000	CHA	AL	5	11	2	0	0	0	(0	0)	2	0	0	0	0	0	4	0	0	0	0	0	-	0	.182	.182	.182
2001	CHA	AL	83	254	65	13	0	18	(10	8)	132	36	39	40	20	1	69	2	1	2	0	1	.00	6	.256	.313	.520
2002	CHA	AL	76	204	47	8	0	7	(4	3)	76	28	26	24	19	2	60	0	0	1	0	0	-	3	.230	.295	.373
2003	2 Tms		44	113	20	4	0	4	(0	4)	36	10	21	13	6	1	39	0	0	1	0	1	.00	2	.177	.217	.319
2004	MIL	NL	16	28	6	2	0	1	(0	1)	11	2	5	2	2	0	8	0	0	1	0	0	-	2	.214	.258	.393
2005	CLE	AL	19	56	11	2	0	1	(0	1)	16	5	8	4	1	0	15	0	0	0	0	0	-	1	.196	.211	.286
03	Mon	NL	35	88	17	3	0	3	(0	3)	29	6	18	11	3	0	26	0	0	1	0	1	.00	2	.193	.217	.330
03	TB	AL	9	25	3	1	0	1	(0	1)	7	4	3	2	3	1	13	0	0	0	0	0	-	0	.120	.214	.280
7 ML YEARS			288	779	179	36	1	31	(14	17)	310	89	113	94	56	4	223	2	1	6	2	2	.50	17	.230	.281	.398

Kerry Ligtenberg

Pitches: R Bats: R Pos: RP-7　　　　　　**Ht: 6'2" Wt: 215 Born: 5/11/1971 Age: 35**

Year	Team	Lg	G	GS	CG	GF	IP	BFP	H	R	ER	HR	SH	SF	HB	TBB	IBB	SO	WP	Bk	W	L	Pct	ShO	Sv-Op	Hld	ERC	ERA
			HOW MUCH HE PITCHED						WHAT HE GAVE UP												THE RESULTS						
2005	Tucsn*	AAA	38	0	0	11	50.0	208	51	18	18	4	1	1	1	7	1	50	0	0	4	3	.571	0	1- -	-	3.05	3.24
1997	ATL	NL	15	0	0	9	15.0	61	12	5	5	4	0	0	0	4	2	19	0	1	1	0	1.000	0	1-1	-	3.26	3.00
1998	ATL	NL	75	0	0	56	73.0	290	51	24	22	6	1	1	0	24	1	79	3	0	3	2	.600	0	30-34	11	2.13	2.71
2000	ATL	NL	59	0	0	19	52.1	217	43	21	21	7	2	1	0	24	5	51	0	0	2	3	.400	0	12-14	12	3.46	3.61
2001	ATL	NL	53	0	0	24	59.2	254	50	22	20	4	1	2	0	30	8	56	3	0	3	3	.500	0	1-2	5	3.14	3.02
2002	ATL	NL	52	0	0	25	66.2	281	52	23	22	6	3	1	0	33	3	51	1	1	3	4	.429	0	0-0	2	3.10	2.97
2003	BAL	AL	68	0	0	21	59.1	247	60	23	22	9	2	1	2	14	3	47	0	0	4	2	.667	0	1-4	14	3.93	3.34
2004	TOR	AL	57	0	0	20	55.0	263	73	40	39	6	3	0	2	25	7	49	5	0	1	6	.143	0	3-5	4	6.12	6.38
2005	ARI	NL	7	0	0	2	9.2	48	16	15	15	4	0	0	0	4	0	5	0	0	0	0	-	0	0-0	0	11.03	13.97
8 ML YEARS			386	0	0	176	390.2	1661	357	173	166	46	12	6	4	158	29	357	12	1	17	20	.459	0	48-60	43	3.66	3.82

Ted Lilly

Pitches: L Bats: L Pos: SP-25　　　　　　**Ht: 6'0" Wt: 185 Born: 1/4/1976 Age: 30**

Year	Team	Lg	G	GS	CG	GF	IP	BFP	H	R	ER	HR	SH	SF	HB	TBB	IBB	SO	WP	Bk	W	L	Pct	ShO	Sv-Op	Hld	ERC	ERA
			HOW MUCH HE PITCHED						WHAT HE GAVE UP												THE RESULTS						
2005	Syrcse*	AAA	2	2	0	0	8.2	36	5	4	3	1	0	1	3	5	0	9	0	0	0	1	.000	0	0- -	-	4.13	3.12
1999	MON	NL	9	3	0	1	23.2	110	30	20	20	7	0	1	3	9	0	28	1	0	0	1	.000	0	0-0	0	7.76	7.61
2000	NYA	AL	7	0	0	1	8.0	39	8	6	5	1	0	0	0	5	0	11	1	1	0	0	-	0	0-0	0	4.76	5.63
2001	NYA	AL	26	21	0	2	120.2	537	126	81	72	20	2	5	7	51	1	112	9	2	5	6	.455	0	0-0	0	5.10	5.37
2002	2 Tms		22	16	2	1	100.0	413	80	43	41	15	0	3	6	31	3	77	6	1	5	7	.417	1	0-0	0	3.14	3.69
2003	OAK	AL	32	31	0	0	178.1	773	179	92	86	24	3	4	5	58	3	147	5	4	12	10	.545	2	0-0	0	4.06	4.34
2004	TOR	AL	32	32	0	0	197.1	845	171	92	89	26	3	3	6	89	2	168	6	4	12	10	.545	1	0-0	0	3.84	4.06
2005	TOR	AL	25	25	0	0	126.1	566	135	79	78	23	3	5	3	58	1	96	2	2	10	11	.476	0	0-0	0	5.38	5.56
02	NYY	AL	16	11	2	1	76.2	314	57	31	29	10	0	3	5	24	3	59	6	0	3	6	.333	1	0-0	0	2.74	3.40
02	Oak	AL	6	5	0	0	23.1	99	23	12	12	5	0	0	1	7	0	18	0	1	2	1	.667	0	0-0	0	4.56	4.63
7 ML YEARS			153	128	4	5	754.1	3283	729	413	391	116	11	21	30	301	10	639	30	14	44	45	.494	2	0-0	0	4.36	4.67

Jose Lima

Pitches: R Bats: R Pos: SP-32　　　　　　**Ht: 6'2" Wt: 205 Born: 9/30/1972 Age: 33**

Year	Team	Lg	G	GS	CG	GF	IP	BFP	H	R	ER	HR	SH	SF	HB	TBB	IBB	SO	WP	Bk	W	L	Pct	ShO	Sv-Op	Hld	ERC	ERA
			HOW MUCH HE PITCHED						WHAT HE GAVE UP												THE RESULTS						
1994	DET	AL	3	1	0	1	6.2	34	11	10	10	2	0	0	0	3	1	7	1	0	0	1	.000	0	0-0	0	9.61	13.50
1995	DET	AL	15	15	0	0	73.2	320	85	52	50	10	2	1	4	18	4	37	5	0	3	9	.250	0	0-0	0	4.73	6.11
1996	DET	AL	39	4	0	15	72.2	329	87	48	46	13	5	3	5	22	4	59	3	0	5	6	.455	0	3-7	6	5.53	5.70
1997	HOU	NL	52	1	0	15	75.0	321	79	45	44	9	6	3	5	16	2	63	2	0	1	6	.143	0	2-2	3	3.96	5.28
1998	HOU	NL	33	33	3	0	233.1	950	229	100	96	34	11	5	7	32	1	169	4	0	16	8	.667	1	0-0	0	3.36	3.70
1999	HOU	NL	35	35	3	0	246.1	1024	256	108	98	30	5	7	2	44	3	187	8	0	21	10	.677	0	0-0	0	3.58	3.58
2000	HOU	NL	33	33	0	0	196.1	895	251	152	145	48	12	12	2	68	3	124	9	0	7	16	.304	0	0-0	0	6.59	6.65
2001	2 Tms		32	27	2	3	165.2	719	197	114	102	35	5	9	9	38	3	84	4	0	6	12	.333	0	0-0	0	5.53	5.54
2002	DET	AL	20	12	0	3	68.1	304	86	60	59	12	1	6	2	21	0	33	2	0	4	6	.400	0	0-0	0	5.97	7.77
2003	KC	AL	14	14	0	0	73.1	321	80	40	40	7	1	3	5	26	0	32	2	2	8	3	.727	0	0-0	0	4.69	4.91
2004	LA	NL	36	24	0	3	170.1	702	178	81	77	33	9	1	1	34	6	93	3	0	13	5	.722	0	0-0	1	4.18	4.07
2005	KC	AL	32	32	1	0	168.2	780	219	140	131	31	5	7	6	61	1	80	5	0	5	16	.238	0	0-0	0	6.54	6.99
01	Hou	NL	14	9	0	3	53.0	249	77	48	43	12	4	4	5	16	1	41	3	0	1	2	.333	0	0-0	0	7.90	7.30
01	Det	AL	18	18	2	0	112.2	470	120	66	59	23	1	5	4	22	2	43	1	0	5	10	.333	0	0-0	0	4.49	4.71
12 ML YEARS			344	231	9	40	1550.1	6699	1758	950	898	264	62	57	51	383	27	968	42	2	89	98	.476	1	5-9	10	4.83	5.21

Todd Linden

Bats: B Throws: R Pos: RF-40; LF-18; PH-11; PR-2   Ht: 6'3" Wt: 210 Born: 6/30/1980 Age: 26

									BATTING												BASERUNNING				AVERAGES		
Year	Team	Lg	G	AB	H	2B	3B	HR	(Hm	Rd)	TB	R	RBI	RC	TBB	IBB	SO	HBP	SH	SF	SB	CS	SB%	GDP	Avg	OBP	Slg
2005	Fresno*	AAA	95	340	109	25	4	30	(-	-)	232	81	80	97	62	5	97	10	1	2	6	2	.75	11	.321	.437	.682
2003	SF	NL	18	38	8	1	0	1	(0	1)	12	2	6	5	1	0	8	0	0	0	0	0	-	2	.211	.231	.316
2004	SF	NL	16	32	5	1	0	0	(0	0)	6	6	1	1	5	0	7	1	2	0	0	0	-	0	.156	.289	.188
2005	SF	NL	60	171	37	8	0	4	(2	2)	57	20	13	12	10	0	54	5	1	0	3	0	1.00	5	.216	.280	.333
	3 ML YEARS		94	241	50	10	0	5	(2	3)	75	28	20	18	16	0	69	6	3	0	3	0	1.00	7	.207	.274	.311

Scott Linebrink

Pitches: R Bats: R Pos: RP-73   Ht: 6'2" Wt: 200 Born: 8/4/1976 Age: 29

			HOW MUCH HE PITCHED						WHAT HE GAVE UP												THE RESULTS							
Year	Team	Lg	G	GS	CG	GF	IP	BFP	H	R	ER	HR	SH	SF	HB	TBB	IBB	SO	WP	Bk	W	L	Pct	ShO	Sv-Op	Hld	ERC	ERA
2000	2 Tms	NL	11	0	0	4	12.0	63	18	8	8	4	0	0	3	8	0	6	0	0	0	0	-	0	0-0	0	11.88	6.00
2001	HOU	NL	9	0	0	2	10.1	44	6	4	3	0	1	1	2	6	0	9	1	0	0	0	-	0	0-0	1	2.54	2.61
2002	HOU	NL	22	0	0	4	24.1	120	31	21	19	2	0	2	1	13	4	24	0	0	0	0	-	0	0-0	1	5.70	7.03
2003	2 Tms	NL	52	6	0	8	92.1	397	93	37	34	9	4	6	6	36	4	68	11	0	3	2	.600	0	0-0	6	4.32	3.31
2004	SD	NL	73	0	0	7	84.0	326	61	22	20	8	2	3	3	26	2	83	3	0	7	3	.700	0	0-5	28	2.48	2.14
2005	SD	NL	73	0	0	17	73.2	288	55	17	15	4	2	0	0	23	4	70	3	0	8	1	.889	0	1-6	26	2.15	1.83
00	SF	NL	3	0	0	1	2.1	16	7	3	3	1	0	0	0	2	0	0	0	0	0	0	-	0	0-0	0	24.13	11.57
00	Hou	NL	8	0	0	3	9.2	47	11	5	5	3	0	0	3	6	0	6	0	0	0	0	-	0	0-0	0	9.21	4.66
03	Hou	NL	9	6	0	2	31.2	140	38	15	15	4	2	1	3	14	1	17	5	0	1	1	.500	0	0-0	0	6.27	4.26
03	SD	NL	43	0	0	6	60.2	257	55	22	19	5	2	5	3	22	3	51	6	0	2	1	.667	0	0-0	6	3.41	2.82
	6 ML YEARS		240	6	0	42	296.2	1238	264	109	99	27	9	12	15	112	14	260	18	0	18	6	.750	0	1-11	61	3.50	3.00

Francisco Liriano

Pitches: L Bats: L Pos: SP-4; RP-2   Ht: 6'2" Wt: 185 Born: 10/26/1983 Age: 22

			HOW MUCH HE PITCHED						WHAT HE GAVE UP												THE RESULTS							
Year	Team	Lg	G	GS	CG	GF	IP	BFP	H	R	ER	HR	SH	SF	HB	TBB	IBB	SO	WP	Bk	W	L	Pct	ShO	Sv-Op	Hld	ERC	ERA
2001	Giants	R	13	12	0	0	62.0	261	51	26	25	3	1	0	1	24	0	67	6	3	5	4	.556	0	0- -	-	2.75	3.63
2001	SlmKzr	A-	2	2	0	0	9.0	35	7	5	5	2	0	0	0	1	0	12	0	0	0	0	-	0	0- -	-	2.47	5.00
2002	Hgrstn	A	16	16	0	0	80.0	332	61	45	31	6	4	3	0	31	0	85	4	0	3	6	.333	0	0- -	-	2.56	3.49
2003	Giants	R	4	4	0	0	8.1	36	5	4	4	1	0	0	0	6	0	9	1	1	1	0	1.000	0	0- -	-	3.20	4.32
2003	SnJos	A+	1	1	0	0	0.2	9	5	4	4	0	3	1	0	2	0	1	0	1	0	1	.000	0	0- -	-	69.84	54.00
2004	FtMyrs	A+	21	21	0	0	117.0	512	118	56	52	6	4	1	0	43	2	125	6	2	6	7	.462	0	0- -	-	3.54	4.00
2004	NwBrit	AA	7	7	0	0	39.2	181	45	14	14	4	3	1	2	17	0	49	3	0	3	2	.600	0	0- -	-	5.11	3.18
2005	NwBrit	AA	13	13	0	0	76.2	326	70	36	31	6	0	0	2	26	0	92	3	1	3	5	.375	0	0- -	-	3.27	3.64
2005	Roch	AAA	14	14	0	0	91.0	353	56	25	18	4	0	2	0	24	0	112	2	1	9	2	.818	0	0- -	-	1.44	1.78
2005	MIN	AL	6	4	0	2	23.2	93	19	15	15	4	0	0	0	7	0	33	0	0	1	2	.333	0	0-0	0	3.15	5.70

Pedro Liriano

Pitches: R Bats: R Pos: RP-5   Ht: 6'2" Wt: 170 Born: 10/23/1980 Age: 25

			HOW MUCH HE PITCHED						WHAT HE GAVE UP												THE RESULTS							
Year	Team	Lg	G	GS	CG	GF	IP	BFP	H	R	ER	HR	SH	SF	HB	TBB	IBB	SO	WP	Bk	W	L	Pct	ShO	Sv-Op	Hld	ERC	ERA
2001	Provo	R+	15	14	0	1	77.2	342	80	39	24	3	1	3	5	31	0	76	4	3	11	2	.846	0	0- -	-	4.03	2.78
2002	RCuca	A+	28	28	1	0	167.1	699	129	86	67	14	6	1	10	74	1	174	5	0	10	14	.417	1	0- -	-	3.12	3.60
2003	Huntsvl	AA	27	26	0	0	142.2	621	138	77	60	12	7	5	7	62	2	116	9	1	9	13	.409	0	0- -	-	4.09	3.79
2004	Indy	AAA	29	21	1	2	126.1	555	149	81	73	21	4	4	5	50	1	97	7	3	3	10	.231	0	1- -	-	5.93	5.20
2005	S-WB	AAA	22	17	1	3	99.1	436	90	49	43	11	4	4	8	48	1	79	2	0	4	9	.308	0	0- -	-	4.24	3.90
2004	MIL	NL	11	0	0	1	15.2	67	15	10	7	3	0	0	1	3	0	10	1	0	0	0	-	0	0-0	1	3.73	4.02
2005	PHI	NL	5	0	0	4	7.2	40	10	11	9	3	1	0	1	6	0	6	0	0	0	0	-	0	0-0	0	10.62	10.57
	2 ML YEARS		16	0	0	5	23.1	107	25	21	16	6	1	0	2	9	0	16	1	0	0	0	-	0	0-0	1	5.77	6.17

Paul Lo Duca

Bats: R Throws: R Pos: C-128; PH-12   Ht: 5'10" Wt: 185 Born: 4/12/1972 Age: 34

									BATTING												BASERUNNING				AVERAGES		
Year	Team	Lg	G	AB	H	2B	3B	HR	(Hm	Rd)	TB	R	RBI	RC	TBB	IBB	SO	HBP	SH	SF	SB	CS	SB%	GDP	Avg	OBP	Slg
1998	LA	NL	6	14	4	1	0	0	(0	0)	5	2	1	1	0	0	1	0	0	0	0	0	-	0	.286	.286	.357
1999	LA	NL	36	95	22	1	0	3	(1	2)	32	11	11	9	10	4	9	2	1	2	1	2	.33	3	.232	.312	.337
2000	LA	NL	34	65	16	2	0	2	(0	2)	24	6	8	6	6	0	8	0	2	2	0	2	.00	2	.246	.301	.369
2001	LA	NL	125	460	147	28	0	25	(11	14)	250	71	90	89	39	2	30	6	5	9	2	4	.33	11	.320	.374	.543
2002	LA	NL	149	580	163	38	1	10	(5	5)	233	74	64	73	34	2	31	10	4	4	3	1	.75	20	.281	.330	.402
2003	LA	NL	147	568	155	34	2	7	(4	3)	214	64	52	67	44	6	54	10	7	1	0	2	.00	21	.273	.335	.377
2004	2 Tms	NL	143	535	153	29	2	13	(8	5)	225	68	80	78	36	0	49	9	8	6	4	5	.44	22	.286	.338	.421
2005	FLA	NL	132	445	126	23	1	6	(2	4)	169	45	57	50	34	5	31	4	5	8	4	3	.57	16	.283	.334	.380
04	LA	NL	91	349	105	18	1	10	(6	4)	155	41	49	51	22	0	27	6	2	2	2	4	.33	15	.301	.351	.444
04	Fla	NL	52	186	48	11	1	3	(2	1)	70	27	31	27	14	0	22	3	6	4	2	1	.67	7	.258	.314	.376
	8 ML YEARS		772	2762	786	156	6	66	(31	35)	1152	341	363	373	203	19	213	41	32	32	14	19	.42	95	.285	.339	.417

Esteban Loaiza

Pitches: R **Bats:** R **Pos:** SP-34 **Ht:** 6'3" **Wt:** 205 **Born:** 12/31/1971 **Age:** 34

Year	Team	Lg	G	GS	CG	GF	IP	BFP	H	R	ER	HR	SH	SF	HB	TBB	IBB	SO	WP	Bk	W	L	Pct	ShO	Sv-Op	Hld	ERC	ERA
1995	PIT	NL	32	31	1	0	172.2	762	205	115	99	21	10	9	5	55	3	85	6	1	8	9	.471	0	0-0	0	5.10	5.16
1996	PIT	NL	10	10	1	0	52.2	236	65	32	29	11	3	1	2	19	2	32	0	0	2	3	.400	1	0-0	0	6.30	4.96
1997	PIT	NL	33	32	1	0	196.1	851	214	99	90	17	10	7	12	56	9	122	2	3	11	11	.500	1	0-0	0	4.20	4.13
1998	2 Tms		35	28	1	3	171.0	751	199	107	98	28	7	12	5	52	4	108	4	2	9	11	.450	0	0-1	0	5.19	5.16
1999	TEX	AL	30	15	0	4	120.1	517	128	65	61	10	7	4	0	40	2	77	2	0	9	5	.643	0	0-0	0	4.03	4.56
2000	2 Tms	AL	34	31	1	2	199.1	871	228	112	101	29	4	5	13	57	1	137	1	0	10	13	.435	1	1-1	0	5.07	4.56
2001	TOR	AL	36	30	1	1	190.0	837	239	113	106	27	6	4	9	40	1	110	1	1	11	11	.500	1	0-0	0	5.30	5.02
2002	TOR	AL	25	25	3	0	151.1	670	192	102	96	29	18	1	6	4	38	3	87	1	0	9	10	.474	1	0-0	0	5.26	5.71
2003	CHA	AL	34	34	1	0	226.1	922	196	75	73	17	7	6	10	56	2	207	3	1	21	9	.700	0	0-0	0	2.79	2.90
2004	2 Tms	AL	31	27	2	1	183.0	818	217	124	116	32	1	10	3	71	5	117	4	0	10	7	.588	1	0-0	0	5.72	5.70
2005	WAS	NL	34	34	0	0	217.0	912	227	93	91	18	9	3	5	55	3	173	6	0	12	10	.545	0	0-0	0	3.74	3.77
98	Pit	NL	21	14	0	3	91.2	394	96	50	46	13	5	7	3	30	1	53	1	2	6	5	.545	0	0-1	0	4.48	4.52
98	Tex	AL	14	14	1	0	79.1	357	103	57	52	15	2	5	2	22	3	55	3	0	3	6	.333	0	0-0	0	6.04	5.90
00	Tex	AL	20	17	0	2	107.1	480	133	67	64	21	2	4	3	31	1	75	1	0	5	6	.455	0	1-1	0	5.81	5.37
00	Tor	AL	14	14	1	0	92.0	391	95	45	37	8	2	1	10	26	0	62	0	0	5	7	.417	1	0-0	0	4.22	3.62
04	CWS	AL	21	21	2	0	140.2	604	156	81	76	23	1	5	1	45	3	83	2	0	9	5	.643	1	0-0	0	4.89	4.86
04	NYY	AL	10	6	0	1	42.1	214	61	43	40	9	0	5	2	26	2	34	2	0	1	2	.333	0	0-0	0	8.70	8.50
11 ML YEARS			334	297	12	11	1880.0	8147	2110	1037	960	228	65	67	68	539	35	1255	30	8	112	99	.531	5	1-2	0	4.60	4.60

Kameron Loe

Pitches: R **Bats:** R **Pos:** RP-40; SP-8 **Ht:** 6'8" **Wt:** 225 **Born:** 9/10/1981 **Age:** 24

Year	Team	Lg	G	GS	CG	GF	IP	BFP	H	R	ER	HR	SH	SF	HB	TBB	IBB	SO	WP	Bk	W	L	Pct	ShO	Sv-Op	Hld	ERC	ERA
2002	Pulaski	R+	14	11	0	2	58.1	263	64	34	29	3	3	1	6	17	0	55	6	1	4	4	.500	0	1--	-	4.12	4.47
2003	Clinton	A	23	11	0	5	97.0	388	78	34	21	3	5	1	4	19	0	94	1	0	4	3	.571	0	2--	-	2.03	1.95
2003	Stcktn	A+	9	4	0	2	37.2	152	26	7	4	1	0	1	3	6	0	31	3	0	3	0	1.000	0	1--	-	1.51	0.96
2004	Frisco	AA	19	19	0	0	112.2	478	122	42	39	5	6	4	6	29	3	97	5	1	7	7	.500	0	0--	-	3.81	3.12
2004	Okla	AAA	8	8	0	0	52.1	206	52	20	19	6	1	0	2	13	0	42	2	0	5	2	.714	0	0--	-	3.98	3.27
2005	Okla	AAA	5	5	0	0	28.1	127	32	17	16	5	0	0	0	10	1	23	0	0	2	1	.667	0	0--	-	5.01	5.08
2004	TEX	AL	2	1	0	0	6.2	29	6	5	4	0	0	0	1	6	0	3	0	0	0	0	-	0	0-0	0	5.87	5.40
2005	TEX	AL	48	8	0	13	92.0	392	89	43	35	7	5	1	2	31	6	45	2	0	9	6	.600	0	1-4	4	3.45	3.42
2 ML YEARS			50	9	0	13	98.2	421	95	48	39	7	5	1	3	37	6	48	2	0	9	6	.600	0	1-4	4	3.60	3.56

Kenny Lofton

Bats: L **Throws:** L **Pos:** CF-97; PH-15; PR-3; DH-1 **Ht:** 6'0" **Wt:** 180 **Born:** 5/31/1967 **Age:** 39

Year	Team	Lg	G	AB	H	2B	3B	HR	(Hm	Rd)	TB	R	RBI	RC	TBB	IBB	SO	HBP	SH	SF	SB	CS	SB%	GDP	Avg	OBP	Slg
1991	HOU	NL	20	74	15	1	0	0	(0	0)	16	9	0	4	5	0	19	0	0	0	2	1	.67	0	.203	.253	.216
1992	CLE	AL	148	576	164	15	8	5	(3	2)	210	96	42	88	68	3	54	2	4	1	66	12	.85	7	.285	.362	.365
1993	CLE	AL	148	569	185	28	8	1	(1	0)	232	116	42	107	81	6	83	1	2	4	70	14	.83	8	.325	.408	.408
1994	CLE	AL	112	459	160	32	9	12	(10	2)	246	105	57	105	52	5	56	2	4	6	60	12	.83	5	.349	.412	.536
1995	CLE	AL	118	481	149	22	13	7	(5	2)	218	93	53	83	40	6	49	1	4	3	54	15	.78	6	.310	.362	.453
1996	CLE	AL	154	662	210	35	4	14	(7	7)	295	132	67	118	61	3	82	0	7	6	75	17	.82	7	.317	.372	.446
1997	ATL	NL	122	493	164	20	6	5	(3	2)	211	90	48	84	64	5	83	2	2	3	27	20	.57	10	.333	.409	.428
1998	CLE	AL	154	600	169	31	6	12	(6	6)	248	101	64	103	87	1	80	2	6	6	54	10	.84	7	.282	.371	.413
1999	CLE	AL	120	465	140	28	6	7	(1	6)	201	110	39	89	79	2	84	6	5	5	25	6	.81	6	.301	.405	.432
2000	CLE	AL	137	543	151	23	5	15	(10	5)	229	107	73	91	79	3	72	4	6	8	30	7	.81	11	.278	.369	.422
2001	CLE	AL	133	517	135	21	4	14	(9	5)	206	91	66	67	47	1	69	2	5	5	16	8	.67	8	.261	.322	.398
2002	2 Tms		139	532	139	30	9	11	(3	8)	220	98	51	83	72	0	73	1	5	1	29	11	.73	1	.261	.350	.414
2003	2 Tms	NL	140	547	162	32	8	12	(5	7)	246	97	46	79	46	3	51	4	7	4	30	9	.77	6	.296	.352	.450
2004	NYA	AL	83	276	76	10	7	3	(2	1)	109	51	18	36	31	1	27	1	1	4	7	3	.70	4	.275	.346	.395
2005	PHI	NL	110	367	123	15	5	2	(1	1)	154	67	36	62	32	2	41	2	5	0	22	3	.88	3	.335	.392	.420
02	CWS	AL	93	352	91	20	6	8	(3	5)	147	68	42	57	49	0	51	0	4	1	22	8	.73	0	.259	.348	.418
02	SF	NL	46	180	48	10	3	3	(0	3)	73	30	9	26	23	0	22	1	1	0	7	3	.70	1	.267	.353	.406
03	Pit	NL	84	339	94	19	4	9	(4	5)	148	58	26	42	28	1	29	2	2	3	18	5	.78	2	.277	.333	.437
03	ChC	NL	56	208	68	13	4	3	(1	2)	98	39	20	37	18	2	22	2	5	3	12	4	.75	4	.327	.381	.471
15 ML YEARS			1838	7161	2142	343	98	120	(66	54)	3041	1363	702	1199	844	41	923	30	60	58	567	148	.79	89	.299	.373	.425

Nook Logan

Bats: B **Throws:** R **Pos:** CF-123; PR-15; PH-3; DH-2 **Ht:** 6'2" **Wt:** 180 **Born:** 11/28/1979 **Age:** 26

Year	Team	Lg	G	AB	H	2B	3B	HR	(Hm	Rd)	TB	R	RBI	RC	TBB	IBB	SO	HBP	SH	SF	SB	CS	SB%	GDP	Avg	OBP	Slg
2000	Tigers	R	43	136	38	2	2	0	(-	-)	44	29	14	25	31	0	36	1	1	2	20	3	.87	1	.279	.412	.324
2000	Lkland	A+	11	42	14	1	0	0	(-	-)	15	4	3	5	2	0	13	0	1	0	2	1	.67	0	.333	.364	.357
2001	W Mich	A	128	522	137	19	8	1	(-	-)	175	82	27	66	53	2	129	2	3	4	67	19	.78	3	.262	.330	.335
2002	Lkland	A+	124	506	136	14	7	2	(-	-)	170	75	26	62	40	0	111	0	6	2	55	16	.77	2	.269	.321	.336
2003	Erie	AA	136	514	129	16	7	4	(-	-)	171	71	38	59	51	3	103	1	12	6	37	13	.74	5	.251	.316	.333
2004	Toledo	AAA	105	427	112	14	9	2	(-	-)	150	67	27	49	23	0	95	3	7	2	38	11	.78	3	.262	.303	.351
2004	DET	AL	47	133	37	5	2	0	(0	0)	46	12	10	15	13	0	24	0	5	1	8	2	.80	1	.278	.340	.346
2005	DET	AL	129	322	83	12	5	1	(0	1)	108	47	17	33	21	3	52	1	12	0	23	6	.79	5	.258	.305	.335
2 ML YEARS			176	455	120	17	7	1	(0	1)	154	59	27	48	34	3	76	1	17	1	31	8	.79	6	.264	.316	.338

Kyle Lohse

Pitches: R Bats: R Pos: SP-30; RP-1   Ht: 6'2" Wt: 190 Born: 10/4/1978 Age: 27

			HOW MUCH HE PITCHED							WHAT HE GAVE UP											THE RESULTS							
Year	Team	Lg	G	GS	CG	GF	IP	BFP	H	R	ER	HR	SH	SF	HB	TBB	IBB	SO	WP	Bk	W	L	Pct	ShO	Sv-Op	Hld	ERC	ERA
2001	MIN	AL	19	16	0	2	90.1	402	102	60	57	16	1	5	8	29	0	64	5	0	4	7	.364	0	0-0	0	5.43	5.68
2002	MIN	AL	32	31	1	0	180.2	783	181	92	85	26	3	3	9	70	2	124	8	0	13	8	.619	1	0-1	0	4.55	4.23
2003	MIN	AL	33	33	2	0	201.0	850	211	107	103	28	8	5	5	45	1	130	10	1	14	11	.560	1	0-0	0	4.00	4.61
2004	MIN	AL	35	34	1	1	194.0	883	240	128	115	28	5	7	7	76	5	111	6	0	9	13	.409	1	0-0	0	5.89	5.34
2005	MIN	AL	31	30	0	1	178.2	769	211	85	83	22	3	7	9	44	5	86	4	1	9	13	.409	0	0-0	0	4.91	4.18
	5 ML YEARS		150	144	4	4	844.2	3687	945	472	443	120	20	27	38	264	13	515	33	2	49	52	.485	3	0-1	0	4.88	4.72

Terrence Long

Bats: L Throws: L Pos: LF-103; PH-19; RF-17; CF-6; DH-3; PR-1   Ht: 6'1" Wt: 202 Born: 2/29/1976 Age: 30

					BATTING																	BASERUNNING				AVERAGES		
Year	Team	Lg	G	AB	H	2B	3B	HR	(Hm	Rd)	TB	R	RBI	RC	TBB	IBB	SO	HBP	SH	SF	SB	CS	SB%	GDP	Avg	OBP	Slg
1999	NYN	NL	3	3	0	0	0	0	(0	0)	0	0	0	0	0	0	2	0	0	0	0	0	-	1	.000	.000	.000
2000	OAK	AL	138	584	168	34	4	18	(9	9)	264	104	80	85	43	1	77	1	0	3	5	0	1.00	18	.288	.336	.452
2001	OAK	AL	162	629	178	37	4	12	(6	6)	259	90	85	84	52	8	103	0	0	6	9	3	.75	17	.283	.335	.412
2002	OAK	AL	162	587	141	32	4	16	(9	7)	229	71	67	61	48	6	96	2	0	3	3	6	.33	17	.240	.298	.390
2003	OAK	AL	140	486	119	22	2	14	(8	6)	187	64	61	61	31	4	67	3	0	2	4	1	.80	9	.245	.293	.385
2004	SD	NL	136	288	85	19	4	3	(1	2)	121	31	28	30	19	4	51	1	0	5	3	2	.60	13	.295	.335	.420
2005	KC	AL	137	455	127	21	3	6	(2	4)	172	62	53	57	30	0	56	0	0	4	3	3	.50	15	.279	.321	.378
	7 ML YEARS		878	3032	818	165	21	69	(35	34)	1232	422	374	378	223	23	452	7	0	23	27	15	.64	90	.270	.319	.406

Braden Looper

Pitches: R Bats: R Pos: RP-60   Ht: 6'3" Wt: 220 Born: 10/28/1974 Age: 31

				HOW MUCH HE PITCHED						WHAT HE GAVE UP											THE RESULTS							
Year	Team	Lg	G	GS	CG	GF	IP	BFP	H	R	ER	HR	SH	SF	HB	TBB	IBB	SO	WP	Bk	W	L	Pct	ShO	Sv-Op	Hld	ERC	ERA
1998	STL	NL	4	0	0	3	3.1	16	5	4	2	1	0	1	0	1	0	4	1	0	0	1	.000	0	0-2	0	8.14	5.40
1999	FLA	NL	72	0	0	22	83.0	370	96	43	35	7	5	5	1	31	5	50	2	2	3	3	.500	0	0-4	8	4.67	3.80
2000	FLA	NL	73	0	0	23	67.1	311	71	41	33	3	3	2	5	36	6	29	5	0	5	1	.833	0	2-5	18	4.55	4.41
2001	FLA	NL	71	0	0	21	71.0	295	63	28	28	8	0	3	2	30	3	52	0	0	3	3	.500	0	3-6	16	3.77	3.55
2002	FLA	NL	78	0	0	40	86.0	349	73	31	30	8	3	0	1	28	3	55	1	0	2	5	.286	0	13-16	16	2.98	3.14
2003	FLA	NL	74	0	0	64	80.2	347	82	34	33	4	3	3	1	29	1	56	2	0	6	4	.600	0	28-34	3	3.67	3.68
2004	NYN	NL	71	0	0	60	83.1	346	86	28	25	5	2	2	3	16	3	60	1	0	2	5	.286	0	29-34	0	3.28	2.70
2005	NYN	NL	60	0	0	54	59.1	271	65	31	26	7	4	0	5	22	3	27	1	0	4	7	.364	0	28-36	0	4.75	3.94
	8 ML YEARS		503	0	0	287	534.0	2305	541	240	212	43	20	16	18	193	24	333	13	2	25	29	.463	0	103-137	58	3.92	3.57

Aquilino Lopez

Pitches: R Bats: R Pos: RP-11   Ht: 6'3" Wt: 165 Born: 4/21/1975 Age: 31

				HOW MUCH HE PITCHED						WHAT HE GAVE UP											THE RESULTS							
Year	Team	Lg	G	GS	CG	GF	IP	BFP	H	R	ER	HR	SH	SF	HB	TBB	IBB	SO	WP	Bk	W	L	Pct	ShO	Sv-Op	Hld	ERC	ERA
2005	LsVgs*	AAA	27	0	0	5	36.2	159	40	24	24	9	0	1	2	6	3	32	0	0	3	4	.429	0	5--	-	4.59	5.89
2005	ColSpr*	AAA	14	0	0	2	19.2	77	14	10	6	2	0	0	0	4	0	25	1	0	2	0	1.000	0	0--	-	1.88	2.75
2005	S-WB*	AAA	4	0	0	1	9.0	33	5	1	1	0	0	0	0	1	0	11	0	0	0	0	-	0	0--	-	0.84	1.00
2003	TOR	AL	72	0	0	34	73.2	316	58	31	28	5	2	2	5	34	5	64	2	1	1	3	.250	0	14-16	16	3.04	3.42
2004	TOR	AL	18	0	0	6	21.0	95	21	15	14	5	0	1	2	13	3	13	0	0	1	1	.500	0	0-0	3	6.32	6.00
2005	2 Tms	NL	11	0	0	5	16.2	72	16	5	4	2	1	0	0	7	1	22	1	0	0	1	.000	0	0-0	0	3.95	2.16
05	Col	NL	1	0	0	0	4.0	15	3	1	1	0	0	0	0	0	0	6	0	0	0	0	-	0	0-0	0	1.13	2.25
05	Phi	NL	10	0	0	5	12.2	57	13	4	3	2	1	0	0	7	1	16	1	0	0	1	.000	0	0-0	0	5.12	2.13
	3 ML YEARS		101	0	0	45	111.1	483	95	51	46	12	3	3	7	54	9	99	3	1	2	5	.286	0	14-16	19	3.74	3.72

Felipe Lopez

Bats: B Throws: R Pos: SS-140; 2B-7; PH-5; 3B-1; PR-1   Ht: 6'0" Wt: 185 Born: 5/12/1980 Age: 26

					BATTING																	BASERUNNING				AVERAGES		
Year	Team	Lg	G	AB	H	2B	3B	HR	(Hm	Rd)	TB	R	RBI	RC	TBB	IBB	SO	HBP	SH	SF	SB	CS	SB%	GDP	Avg	OBP	Slg
2001	TOR	AL	49	177	46	5	4	5	(3	2)	74	21	23	22	12	1	39	0	1	2	4	3	.57	2	.260	.304	.418
2002	TOR	AL	85	282	64	15	3	8	(5	3)	109	35	34	32	23	1	90	1	2	1	5	4	.56	4	.227	.287	.387
2003	CIN	NL	59	197	42	7	2	2	(0	2)	59	28	13	21	28	1	59	1	2	1	8	5	.62	2	.213	.313	.299
2004	CIN	NL	79	264	64	18	2	7	(3	4)	107	35	31	34	25	0	81	3	2	1	1	1	.50	1	.242	.314	.405
2005	CIN	NL	148	580	169	34	5	23	(16	7)	282	97	85	95	57	2	111	1	3	7	15	7	.68	8	.291	.352	.486
	5 ML YEARS		420	1500	385	79	16	45	(27	18)	631	216	186	204	145	5	380	6	10	12	33	20	.62	17	.257	.322	.421

Javier Lopez

Pitches: L Bats: L Pos: RP-32   Ht: 6'4" Wt: 200 Born: 7/11/1977 Age: 28

				HOW MUCH HE PITCHED						WHAT HE GAVE UP											THE RESULTS							
Year	Team	Lg	G	GS	CG	GF	IP	BFP	H	R	ER	HR	SH	SF	HB	TBB	IBB	SO	WP	Bk	W	L	Pct	ShO	Sv-Op	Hld	ERC	ERA
2005	Tucsn*	AAA	27	0	0	8	24.1	102	17	7	6	0	2	2	1	12	1	16	1	0	0	1	.000	0	2--	-	2.24	2.22
2003	COL	NL	75	0	0	11	58.1	242	58	25	24	5	1	0	4	12	2	40	1	3	4	1	.800	0	1-2	15	3.44	3.70
2004	COL	NL	64	0	0	10	40.2	187	45	34	34	1	1	0	3	26	4	20	3	0	1	2	.333	0	0-1	12	5.28	7.52
2005	2 Tms	NL	32	0	0	6	16.1	87	26	20	20	2	1	0	1	11	3	12	0	0	1	1	.500	0	2-4	6	8.82	11.02
05	Col	NL	3	0	0	1	2.0	13	7	5	5	0	0	0	0	0	0	1	0	0	0	0	-	0	0-1	0	18.39	22.50
05	Ari	NL	29	0	0	5	14.1	74	19	15	15	2	1	0	1	11	3	11	0	0	1	1	.500	0	2-3	6	7.63	9.42
	3 ML YEARS		171	0	0	27	115.1	516	129	79	78	8	3	0	8	49	9	72	4	3	6	4	.600	0	3-7	33	4.80	6.09

Javy Lopez

Bats: R **Throws:** R **Pos:** C-75; DH-28; 1B-1; PH-1　　　　**Ht:** 6'3" **Wt:** 225 **Born:** 11/5/1970 **Age:** 35

Year	Team	Lg	G	AB	H	2B	3B	HR	(Hm	Rd)	TB	R	RBI	RC	TBB	IBB	SO	HBP	SH	SF	SB	CS	SB%	GDP	Avg	OBP	Slg
2005	Bowie*	AA	4	15	6	1	0	0	(-	-)	7	1	3	2	0	0	3	0	0	1	0	0	-	0	.400	.375	.467
1992	ATL	NL	9	16	6	2	0	0	(0	0)	8	3	2	3	0	0	1	0	0	0	0	0	-	0	.375	.375	.500
1993	ATL	NL	8	16	6	1	1	1	(0	1)	12	1	2	4	0	0	2	1	0	0	0	0	-	0	.375	.412	.750
1994	ATL	NL	80	277	68	9	0	13	(4	9)	116	27	35	31	17	0	61	5	2	2	0	2	.00	12	.245	.299	.419
1995	ATL	NL	100	333	105	11	4	14	(8	6)	166	37	51	51	14	0	57	2	0	3	0	1	.00	13	.315	.344	.498
1996	ATL	NL	138	489	138	19	1	23	(10	13)	228	56	69	66	28	5	84	3	1	5	1	6	.14	17	.282	.322	.466
1997	ATL	NL	123	414	122	28	1	23	(11	12)	221	52	68	76	40	10	82	5	1	4	1	1	.50	9	.295	.361	.534
1998	ATL	NL	133	489	139	21	1	34	(18	16)	264	73	106	79	30	1	85	6	1	8	5	3	.63	22	.284	.328	.540
1999	ATL	NL	65	246	78	18	1	11	(1	10)	131	34	45	45	20	2	41	3	0	0	0	3	.00	6	.317	.375	.533
2000	ATL	NL	134	481	138	21	1	24	(12	12)	233	60	89	72	35	3	80	4	0	5	0	0	-	20	.287	.337	.484
2001	ATL	NL	128	438	117	16	1	17	(10	7)	186	45	66	58	28	3	82	10	1	5	1	0	1.00	12	.267	.322	.425
2002	ATL	NL	109	347	81	15	0	11	(1	10)	129	31	52	40	26	8	63	8	0	4	0	1	.00	15	.233	.299	.372
2003	ATL	NL	129	457	150	29	3	43	(26	17)	314	89	109	102	33	5	90	4	0	1	0	1	.00	10	.328	.378	.687
2004	BAL	AL	150	579	183	33	3	23	(14	9)	291	83	86	90	47	4	97	6	0	6	0	0	-	16	.316	.370	.503
2005	BAL	AL	103	395	110	24	1	15	(12	3)	181	47	49	56	19	2	68	7	0	2	0	1	.00	10	.278	.322	.458
	14 ML YEARS		1409	4977	1441	247	18	252	(127	125)	2480	638	829	773	337	43	893	64	6	45	8	19	.30	162	.290	.340	.498

Jose Lopez

Bats: R **Throws:** R **Pos:** 2B-51; PH-2; 3B-1　　　　**Ht:** 6'2" **Wt:** 170 **Born:** 11/24/1983 **Age:** 22

Year	Team	Lg	G	AB	H	2B	3B	HR	(Hm	Rd)	TB	R	RBI	RC	TBB	IBB	SO	HBP	SH	SF	SB	CS	SB%	GDP	Avg	OBP	Slg
2001	Everett	A-	70	289	74	15	0	2	(-	-)	95	42	20	30	13	0	44	10	1	2	13	6	.68	3	.256	.309	.329
2002	SnBrn	A+	123	522	169	39	5	8	(-	-)	242	82	60	84	27	2	45	5	4	4	31	13	.70	8	.324	.360	.464
2003	SnAnt	AA	132	538	139	35	2	13	(-	-)	217	82	69	63	27	3	56	10	7	6	18	8	.69	12	.258	.303	.403
2004	Ms	R	4	12	2	1	0	0	(-	-)	3	3	1	0	2	0	1	0	0	1	1	0	1.00	1	.167	.267	.250
2004	Tacom	AAA	74	275	81	19	0	13	(-	-)	139	40	39	47	16	0	30	6	2	4	5	2	.71	2	.295	.342	.505
2005	Tacom	AAA	44	182	58	19	0	5	(-	-)	92	29	31	31	8	1	25	2	2	0	2	3	.40	6	.319	.354	.505
2004	SEA	AL	57	207	48	13	0	5	(4	1)	76	28	22	20	8	0	31	1	1	1	0	1	.00	1	.232	.263	.367
2005	SEA	AL	54	190	47	19	0	2	(1	1)	72	18	25	24	6	0	25	4	1	2	4	2	.67	5	.247	.282	.379
	2 ML YEARS		111	397	95	32	0	7	(5	2)	148	46	47	44	14	0	56	5	2	3	4	3	.57	6	.239	.272	.373

Luis Lopez

Bats: B **Throws:** R **Pos:** PH-9; 3B-6; 2B-4; PR-1　　　　**Ht:** 5'11" **Wt:** 175 **Born:** 9/4/1970 **Age:** 35

Year	Team	Lg	G	AB	H	2B	3B	HR	(Hm	Rd)	TB	R	RBI	RC	TBB	IBB	SO	HBP	SH	SF	SB	CS	SB%	GDP	Avg	OBP	Slg
2005	Lsvlle*	AAA	29	87	23	8	0	1	(-	-)	34	10	9	11	8	0	18	3	0	0	0	2	.00	0	.264	.347	.391
1993	SD	NL	17	43	5	1	0	0	(0	0)	6	1	1	0	0	0	8	0	0	1	0	0	-	0	.116	.114	.140
1994	SD	NL	77	235	65	16	1	2	(2	0)	89	29	20	27	15	2	39	3	2	2	3	2	.60	7	.277	.325	.379
1996	SD	NL	63	139	25	3	0	2	(1	1)	34	10	11	5	9	1	35	1	1	1	0	0	-	7	.180	.233	.245
1997	NYN	NL	78	178	48	12	1	1	(1	0)	65	19	19	21	12	2	42	4	2	0	2	4	.33	2	.270	.330	.365
1998	NYN	NL	117	266	67	13	2	2	(1	1)	90	37	22	26	20	3	60	4	3	2	2	2	.50	10	.252	.312	.338
1999	NYN	NL	68	104	22	4	0	2	(1	1)	32	11	13	10	12	0	33	3	1	1	1	1	.50	1	.212	.308	.308
2000	MIL	NL	78	201	53	14	0	6	(3	3)	85	24	27	26	9	1	35	5	8	2	1	2	.33	2	.264	.309	.423
2001	MIL	NL	92	222	60	8	3	4	(2	2)	86	22	18	27	14	2	44	5	5	1	0	1	.00	6	.270	.326	.387
2002	2 Tms		58	117	23	6	0	2	(1	1)	35	11	10	7	5	0	21	0	0	0	1	0	1.00	3	.197	.230	.299
2004	BAL	AL	56	88	16	5	0	1	(0	1)	24	7	8	3	3	0	20	1	2	3	0	0	-	1	.182	.211	.273
2005	CIN	NL	17	27	6	3	0	0	(0	0)	9	0	2	2	1	0	6	0	0	0	0	0	-	1	.222	.250	.333
02	Mil	NL	6	8	0	0	0	0	(0	0)	0	1	1	0	2	0	1	0	0	0	0	0	-	0	.000	.200	.000
02	Bal	AL	52	109	23	6	0	2	(1	1)	35	10	9	7	3	0	20	0	0	0	1	0	1.00	3	.211	.232	.321
	11 ML YEARS		721	1620	390	85	7	22	(12	10)	555	171	151	154	100	11	343	26	24	13	10	12	.45	40	.241	.293	.343

Pedro Lopez

Bats: R **Throws:** R **Pos:** 2B-1; SS-1　　　　**Ht:** 6'1" **Wt:** 160 **Born:** 4/28/1984 **Age:** 22

Year	Team	Lg	G	AB	H	2B	3B	HR	(Hm	Rd)	TB	R	RBI	RC	TBB	IBB	SO	HBP	SH	SF	SB	CS	SB%	GDP	Avg	OBP	Slg
2001	WhSox	R	50	199	62	11	3	1	(-	-)	82	26	19	30	16	0	24	0	3	2	12	6	.67	4	.312	.359	.412
2002	Bristol	R+	63	260	83	11	0	0	(-	-)	94	42	35	38	20	0	17	1	17	0	22	8	.73	3	.319	.370	.362
2003	Knapol	A-	109	390	103	23	0	0	(-	-)	126	40	33	41	26	1	43	3	16	2	24	14	.63	8	.264	.314	.323
2003	WinSa	A+	4	13	3	0	0	0	(-	-)	3	1	0	0	1	0	0	0	0	0	0	0	-	0	.231	.286	.231
2004	WinSa	A+	111	430	124	13	0	4	(-	-)	149	62	35	51	23	0	35	4	16	3	12	9	.57	9	.288	.328	.347
2004	Brham	AA	7	23	5	0	1	0	(-	-)	7	3	0	3	5	0	2	1	2	0	2	0	1.00	0	.217	.379	.304
2005	Brham	AA	68	239	57	7	1	3	(-	-)	75	26	24	22	13	0	29	4	13	2	0	2	.00	9	.238	.287	.314
2005	Charltt	AAA	55	188	38	6	0	3	(-	-)	53	14	17	12	7	0	24	2	9	2	1	1	.50	4	.202	.236	.282
2005	CHA	AL	2	7	2	0	0	0	(0	0)	2	1	2	2	0	0	1	0	1	0	0	0	-	0	.286	.286	.286

Rodrigo Lopez

Pitches: R **Bats:** R **Pos:** SP-35　　　　**Ht:** 6'1" **Wt:** 180 **Born:** 12/14/1975 **Age:** 30

	HOW MUCH HE PITCHED								WHAT HE GAVE UP												THE RESULTS							
Year	Team	Lg	G	GS	CG	GF	IP	BFP	H	R	ER	HR	SH	SF	HB	TBB	IBB	SO	WP	Bk	W	L	Pct	ShO	Sv-Op	Hld	ERC	ERA
2000	SD	NL	6	6	0	0	24.2	120	40	24	24	5	0	1	0	13	0	17	0	0	0	3	.000	0	0-0	0	9.78	8.76
2002	BAL	AL	33	28	1	0	196.2	809	172	83	78	23	2	4	5	62	4	136	2	1	15	9	.625	0	0-0	0	3.27	3.57
2003	BAL	AL	26	26	3	0	147.0	663	188	101	95	24	3	7	10	43	6	103	2	1	7	10	.412	1	0-0	0	6.00	5.82

			HOW MUCH HE PITCHED						WHAT HE GAVE UP												THE RESULTS							
Year	Team	Lg	G	GS	CG	GF	IP	BFP	H	R	ER	HR	SH	SF	HB	TBB	IBB	SO	WP	Bk	W	L	Pct	ShO	Sv-Op	Hld	ERC	ERA
2004	BAL	AL	37	23	1	3	170.2	714	164	71	68	21	5	2	2	54	2	121	4	1	14	9	.609	1	0-1	4	3.74	3.59
2005	BAL	AL	35	35	0	0	209.1	918	232	126	114	28	3	5	7	63	1	118	5	1	15	12	.556	0	0-0	0	4.62	4.90
	5 ML YEARS		137	118	5	3	748.1	3224	796	405	379	101	13	19	24	235	13	495	13	4	51	43	.543	2	0-1	4	4.45	4.56

Mark Loretta

Bats: R **Throws:** R **Pos:** 2B-105; 3B-1   **Ht:** 6'0" **Wt:** 186 **Born:** 8/14/1971 **Age:** 34

			BATTING																		BASERUNNING				AVERAGES		
Year	Team	Lg	G	AB	H	2B	3B	HR	(Hm	Rd)	TB	R	RBI	RC	TBB	IBB	SO	HBP	SH	SF	SB	CS	SB%	GDP	Avg	OBP	Slg
2005	Portlnd*	AAA	3	10	1	0	0	0	(-	-)	1	0	0	0	2	0	1	0	0	0	0	0	-	1	.100	.250	.100
1995	MIL	AL	19	50	13	3	0	1	(0	1)	19	13	3	6	4	0	7	1	1	0	1	1	.50	1	.260	.327	.380
1996	MIL	AL	73	154	43	3	0	1	(0	1)	49	20	13	16	14	0	15	0	2	0	2	1	.67	7	.279	.339	.318
1997	MIL	AL	132	418	120	17	5	5	(2	3)	162	56	47	56	47	2	60	2	5	10	5	5	.50	15	.287	.354	.388
1998	MIL	NL	140	434	137	29	0	6	(3	3)	184	55	54	68	42	1	47	7	4	4	9	6	.60	14	.316	.382	.424
1999	MIL	NL	153	587	170	34	5	5	(2	3)	229	93	67	82	52	1	59	10	9	6	4	1	.80	14	.290	.354	.390
2000	MIL	NL	91	352	99	21	1	7	(3	4)	143	49	40	48	37	2	38	1	8	1	0	3	.00	9	.281	.350	.406
2001	MIL	NL	102	384	111	14	2	2	(0	2)	135	40	29	48	28	0	46	7	7	3	1	2	.33	6	.289	.346	.352
2002	2 Tms	NL	107	283	86	18	0	4	(2	2)	116	33	27	50	32	1	37	5	6	3	1	1	.50	7	.304	.381	.410
2003	SD	NL	154	589	185	28	4	13	(10	3)	260	74	72	93	54	2	62	3	3	4	5	4	.56	17	.314	.372	.441
2004	SD	NL	154	620	208	47	2	16	(11	5)	307	108	76	112	58	3	45	9	4	16	5	3	.63	10	.335	.391	.495
2005	SD	NL	105	404	113	16	1	3	(1	2)	140	54	38	53	45	4	34	8	2	4	8	4	.67	11	.280	.360	.347
02	Mil	NL	86	217	58	14	0	2	(1	1)	78	23	19	33	23	1	32	5	6	1	0	0	-	6	.267	.350	.359
02	Hou	NL	21	66	28	4	0	2	(1	1)	38	10	8	17	9	0	5	0	0	2	1	1	.50	1	.424	.481	.576
	11 ML YEARS		1230	4275	1285	230	20	63	(34	29)	1744	595	466	632	413	16	450	53	51	51	41	31	.57	111	.301	.365	.408

Derek Lowe

Pitches: R **Bats:** R **Pos:** SP-35   **Ht:** 6'6" **Wt:** 214 **Born:** 6/1/1973 **Age:** 33

			HOW MUCH HE PITCHED						WHAT HE GAVE UP												THE RESULTS							
Year	Team	Lg	G	GS	CG	GF	IP	BFP	H	R	ER	HR	SH	SF	HB	TBB	IBB	SO	WP	Bk	W	L	Pct	ShO	Sv-Op	Hld	ERC	ERA
1997	2 Tms	AL	20	9	0	1	69.0	298	74	49	47	11	4	2	4	23	3	52	2	0	2	6	.250	0	0-2	1	4.88	6.13
1998	BOS	AL	63	10	0	8	123.0	527	126	65	55	5	4	5	4	42	5	77	8	0	3	9	.250	0	4-9	12	3.64	4.02
1999	BOS	AL	74	0	0	32	109.1	436	84	35	32	7	1	2	4	25	1	80	1	0	6	3	.667	0	15-20	22	2.14	2.63
2000	BOS	AL	74	0	0	64	91.1	379	90	27	26	6	4	1	2	22	5	79	1	1	4	4	.500	0	42-47	0	3.17	2.56
2001	BOS	AL	67	3	0	50	91.2	404	103	39	36	7	5	1	5	29	9	82	4	0	5	10	.333	0	24-30	4	4.31	3.53
2002	BOS	AL	32	32	1	0	219.2	854	166	65	63	12	5	2	12	48	2	127	5	0	21	8	.724	1	0-0	0	2.13	2.58
2003	BOS	AL	33	33	1	0	203.1	886	216	113	101	17	3	5	11	72	4	110	3	0	17	7	.708	0	0-0	0	4.32	4.47
2004	BOS	AL	33	33	0	0	182.2	839	224	138	101	19	5	8	4	71	2	105	3	0	14	12	.538	0	0-0	0	5.31	5.42
2005	LAN	NL	35	35	2	0	222.0	934	223	113	89	28	12	5	5	55	1	146	3	2	12	15	.444	2	0-0	0	3.75	3.61
97	Sea	AL	12	9	0	1	53.0	234	59	43	41	11	2	1	2	20	2	39	2	0	2	4	.333	0	0-0	0	5.55	6.96
97	Bos	AL	8	0	0	0	16.0	64	15	6	6	0	2	1	2	3	1	13	0	0	0	2	.000	0	0-2	1	2.78	3.38
	9 ML YEARS		431	155	4	155	1312.0	5557	1306	644	559	108	46	27	55	387	30	858	30	3	84	74	.532	3	85-108	39	3.65	3.83

Mike Lowell

Bats: R **Throws:** R **Pos:** 3B-135; PH-10; 2B-9   **Ht:** 6'3" **Wt:** 217 **Born:** 2/24/1974 **Age:** 32

			BATTING																		BASERUNNING				AVERAGES		
Year	Team	Lg	G	AB	H	2B	3B	HR	(Hm	Rd)	TB	R	RBI	RC	TBB	IBB	SO	HBP	SH	SF	SB	CS	SB%	GDP	Avg	OBP	Slg
1998	NYA	AL	8	15	4	0	0	0	(0	0)	4	1	0	1	0	0	1	0	0	0	0	0	-	0	.267	.267	.267
1999	FLA	NL	97	308	78	15	0	12	(7	5)	129	32	47	40	26	1	69	5	0	5	0	0	-	8	.253	.317	.419
2000	FLA	NL	140	508	137	38	0	22	(11	11)	241	73	91	86	54	4	79	9	0	11	4	0	1.00	4	.270	.344	.474
2001	FLA	NL	146	551	156	37	0	18	(12	6)	247	65	100	84	43	3	79	10	0	10	1	2	.33	9	.283	.340	.448
2002	FLA	NL	160	597	165	44	0	24	(13	11)	281	88	92	84	65	5	92	4	0	11	4	3	.57	16	.276	.346	.471
2003	FLA	NL	130	492	136	27	1	32	(14	18)	261	78	105	88	56	6	78	3	0	6	3	1	.75	14	.276	.350	.530
2004	FLA	NL	158	598	175	44	1	27	(14	13)	302	87	85	96	64	8	77	6	0	3	5	1	.83	17	.293	.365	.505
2005	FLA	NL	150	500	118	36	1	8	(5	3)	180	56	58	46	46	1	58	2	1	9	4	0	1.00	14	.236	.298	.360
	8 ML YEARS		989	3569	969	241	3	143	(76	67)	1645	478	578	525	354	28	529	39	1	55	21	7	.75	82	.272	.339	.461

Noah Lowry

Pitches: L **Bats:** R **Pos:** SP-33   **Ht:** 6'2" **Wt:** 190 **Born:** 10/10/1980 **Age:** 25

			HOW MUCH HE PITCHED						WHAT HE GAVE UP												THE RESULTS							
Year	Team	Lg	G	GS	CG	GF	IP	BFP	H	R	ER	HR	SH	SF	HB	TBB	IBB	SO	WP	Bk	W	L	Pct	ShO	Sv-Op	Hld	ERC	ERA
2003	SF	NL	4	0	0	3	6.1	24	1	0	0	0	0	0	0	2	0	5	0	0	0	0	-	0	0-0	0	0.50	0.00
2004	SF	NL	16	14	2	0	92.0	383	91	41	39	10	2	1	0	28	1	72	2	0	6	0	1.000	1	0-0	0	3.73	3.82
2005	SF	NL	33	33	0	0	204.2	874	193	92	86	21	13	3	7	76	1	172	2	0	13	13	.500	0	0-0	0	3.78	3.78
	3 ML YEARS		53	47	2	3	303.0	1281	285	133	125	31	15	4	8	106	2	249	4	0	19	13	.594	1	0-0	0	3.67	3.71

Ryan Ludwick

Bats: R **Throws:** L **Pos:** LF-9; RF-6; DH-3; PR-1   **Ht:** 6'3" **Wt:** 203 **Born:** 7/13/1978 **Age:** 27

			BATTING																		BASERUNNING				AVERAGES		
Year	Team	Lg	G	AB	H	2B	3B	HR	(Hm	Rd)	TB	R	RBI	RC	TBB	IBB	SO	HBP	SH	SF	SB	CS	SB%	GDP	Avg	OBP	Slg
2005	Buffalo*	AAA	54	188	36	10	2	4	(-	-)	62	27	16	17	17	0	48	5	0	3	0	1	.00	9	.191	.272	.330
2002	TEX	AL	23	81	19	6	0	1	(1	0)	28	10	9	6	7	0	24	0	0	0	2	1	.67	4	.235	.295	.346
2003	2 Tms	AL	47	162	40	8	1	7	(2	5)	71	17	26	28	12	1	48	0	1	0	2	0	1.00	1	.247	.299	.438
2004	CLE	AL	15	50	11	2	0	2	(0	2)	19	3	4	4	2	0	14	2	0	0	0	0	-	0	.220	.278	.380
2005	CLE	AL	19	41	9	0	0	4	(3	1)	21	8	5	3	7	0	13	0	0	0	0	1	.00	0	.220	.333	.512

							BATTING																**BASERUNNING**				**AVERAGES**		
Year	Team	Lg	G	AB	H	2B	3B	HR	(Hm	Rd)	TB	R	RBI	RC	TBB	IBB	SO	HBP	SH	SF	SB	CS	SB%	GDP	Avg	OBP	Slg
03	Tex	AL	8	26	4	1	0	0	(0	0)	5	3	0	1	4	0	9	0	0	0	0	0	-	0	.154	.267	.192
03	Cle	AL	39	136	36	7	1	7	(2	5)	66	14	26	27	8	1	39	0	1	0	2	0	1.00	1	.265	.306	.485
4 ML YEARS			104	334	79	16	1	14	(6	8)	139	38	44	41	28	1	99	2	1	0	4	2	.67	6	.237	.299	.416

Julio Lugo

Bats: R **Throws:** R **Pos:** SS-156; PH-3 **Ht:** 6'1" **Wt:** 170 **Born:** 11/16/1975 **Age:** 30

							BATTING																**BASERUNNING**				**AVERAGES**		
Year	Team	Lg	G	AB	H	2B	3B	HR	(Hm	Rd)	TB	R	RBI	RC	TBB	IBB	SO	HBP	SH	SF	SB	CS	SB%	GDP	Avg	OBP	Slg
2000	HOU	NL	116	420	119	22	5	10	(6	4)	181	78	40	62	37	0	93	4	3	1	22	9	.71	9	.283	.346	.431
2001	HOU	NL	140	513	135	20	3	10	(6	4)	191	93	37	63	46	0	116	5	15	7	12	11	.52	7	.263	.326	.372
2002	HOU	NL	88	322	84	15	1	8	(6	2)	125	45	35	43	28	3	74	2	4	2	9	3	.75	6	.261	.322	.388
2003	2 Tms		139	498	135	16	4	15	(5	10)	204	64	55	68	44	1	100	4	7	3	12	4	.75	7	.271	.333	.410
2004	TB	AL	157	581	160	41	4	7	(3	4)	230	83	75	86	54	0	106	5	7	8	21	5	.81	5	.275	.338	.396
2005	TB	AL	158	616	182	36	6	6	(0	6)	248	89	57	94	61	0	72	6	3	4	39	11	.78	5	.295	.362	.403
03	Hou	NL	22	65	16	3	0	0	(0	0)	19	6	2	7	9	1	12	0	0	0	2	1	.67	2	.246	.338	.292
03	TB	AL	117	433	119	13	4	15	(5	10)	185	58	53	61	35	0	88	4	7	3	10	3	.77	5	.275	.333	.427
6 ML YEARS			798	2950	815	150	23	56	(26	30)	1179	452	299	416	270	4	561	26	39	25	115	43	.73	42	.276	.340	.400

Hector Luna

Bats: R **Throws:** R **Pos:** 2B-22; RF-21; PH-19; 3B-7; SS-6; PR-6; LF-3; CF-1 **Ht:** 6'1" **Wt:** 170 **Born:** 2/1/1980 **Age:** 26

							BATTING																**BASERUNNING**				**AVERAGES**		
Year	Team	Lg	G	AB	H	2B	3B	HR	(Hm	Rd)	TB	R	RBI	RC	TBB	IBB	SO	HBP	SH	SF	SB	CS	SB%	GDP	Avg	OBP	Slg
2000	Burlgtn	R+	55	201	41	5	0	1	(-	-)	49	25	15	18	27	0	35	3	0	1	19	4	.83	4	.204	.306	.244
2000	MhVlly	A-	5	19	6	2	0	0	(-	-)	8	2	4	2	1	0	3	0	1	0	0	0	-	0	.316	.350	.421
2001	Clmbs	A	66	241	64	8	3	3	(-	-)	87	36	23	33	23	0	48	5	3	2	15	4	.79	2	.266	.339	.361
2002	Kinston	A+	128	468	129	15	6	11	(-	-)	189	67	51	65	39	0	73	3	6	2	32	11	.74	7	.276	.334	.404
2003	Akron	AA	127	462	137	19	2	2	(-	-)	166	87	38	66	48	1	64	5	5	2	17	5	.77	10	.297	.368	.359
2005	Memp	AAA	57	223	50	13	1	3	(-	-)	74	24	21	23	20	0	38	2	2	0	11	4	.73	2	.224	.294	.332
2004	STL	NL	83	173	43	7	2	3	(1	2)	63	25	22	20	13	0	37	2	1	3	6	3	.67	2	.249	.304	.364
2005	STL	NL	64	137	39	10	2	1	(0	1)	56	26	18	19	9	0	25	4	2	1	10	2	.83	4	.285	.344	.409
2 ML YEARS			147	310	82	17	4	4	(1	3)	119	51	40	39	22	0	62	6	3	4	16	5	.76	6	.265	.322	.384

Brandon Lyon

Pitches: R **Bats:** R **Pos:** RP-32 **Ht:** 6'1" **Wt:** 185 **Born:** 8/10/1979 **Age:** 26

			HOW MUCH HE PITCHED					**WHAT HE GAVE UP**												**THE RESULTS**						
Year	Team	Lg	G	GS	CG	GF	IP	BFP	H	R	ER	HR	SH	SF	HB	TBB	IBB	SO	WP	Bk	W	L	Pct	ShO	Sv-Op	Hld	ERC	ERA
2005	Tucsn*	AAA	5	4	0	0	5.0	20	5	3	3	0	0	0	0	4	0	0	0	0	0	1	.000	0	0- -	-	1.95	5.40
2001	TOR	AL	11	11	0	0	63.0	261	63	31	30	6	2	6	1	15	0	35	0	1	5	4	.556	0	0-0	0	3.50	4.29
2002	TOR	AL	15	10	0	0	62.0	279	78	47	45	14	3	2	2	19	2	30	2	0	1	4	.200	0	0-1	0	6.24	6.53
2003	BOS	AL	49	0	0	31	59.0	273	73	33	27	6	1	4	2	19	5	50	0	0	4	6	.400	0	9-12	2	4.96	4.12
2005	ARI	NL	32	0	0	22	29.1	144	44	25	21	6	2	1	2	10	2	17	1	1	0	2	.000	0	14-15	1	7.72	6.44
4 ML YEARS			107	21	0	53	213.1	957	258	136	123	32	8	13	7	63	9	132	3	2	10	16	.385	0	23-28	3	5.23	5.19

John Mabry

Bats: L **Throws:** R **Pos:** RF-49; PH-39; LF-23; 3B-18; 1B-14 **Ht:** 6'4" **Wt:** 210 **Born:** 10/17/1970 **Age:** 35

							BATTING																**BASERUNNING**				**AVERAGES**		
Year	Team	Lg	G	AB	H	2B	3B	HR	(Hm	Rd)	TB	R	RBI	RC	TBB	IBB	SO	HBP	SH	SF	SB	CS	SB%	GDP	Avg	OBP	Slg
1994	STL	NL	6	23	7	3	0	0	(0	0)	10	2	3	4	2	0	4	0	0	0	0	0	-	0	.304	.360	.435
1995	STL	NL	129	388	119	21	1	5	(2	3)	157	35	41	53	24	5	45	2	0	4	0	3	.00	6	.307	.347	.405
1996	STL	NL	151	543	161	30	2	13	(3	10)	234	63	74	74	37	11	84	3	3	5	3	2	.60	21	.297	.342	.431
1997	STL	NL	116	388	110	19	0	5	(1	4)	144	40	36	49	39	9	77	3	2	2	0	1	.00	11	.284	.352	.371
1998	STL	NL	142	377	94	22	0	9	(4	5)	143	41	46	42	30	6	76	1	3	2	0	2	.00	6	.249	.305	.379
1999	SEA	AL	87	262	64	14	0	9	(5	4)	105	34	33	30	20	1	60	0	2	1	2	1	.67	6	.244	.297	.401
2000	2 Tms		95	226	53	13	0	8	(3	5)	90	35	32	25	15	0	69	2	0	1	0	1	.00	4	.235	.287	.398
2001	2 Tms	NL	87	154	32	7	0	6	(2	4)	57	14	20	16	13	1	44	5	0	2	1	0	1.00	6	.208	.287	.370
2002	2 Tms		110	214	59	13	1	11	(8	3)	107	28	43	34	15	2	42	1	0	4	1	1	.50	7	.276	.321	.500
2003	SEA	AL	64	104	22	6	0	3	(1	2)	37	12	16	11	15	2	21	3	0	0	0	0	-	3	.212	.328	.356
2004	STL	NL	87	240	71	11	0	13	(7	6)	121	32	40	37	26	5	63	1	5	3	0	1	.00	6	.296	.363	.504
2005	STL	NL	112	246	59	15	1	8	(2	6)	100	26	25	25	20	1	63	0	6	2	0	0	-	6	.240	.295	.407
00	Sea	AL	47	103	25	5	0	1	(0	1)	33	14	7	11	10	0	31	2	0	0	0	1	.00	1	.243	.322	.320
00	SD	NL	48	123	28	8	0	7	(3	4)	57	17	25	14	5	0	38	0	0	1	0	0	-	3	.228	.256	.463
01	StL	NL	5	7	0	0	0	0	(0	0)	0	0	0	0	0	0	2	0	0	0	0	0	-	0	.000	.000	.000
01	Fla	NL	82	147	32	7	0	6	(2	4)	57	14	20	16	13	1	44	5	0	2	1	0	1.00	6	.218	.299	.388
02	Phi	NL	21	21	6	0	0	0	(0	0)	6	1	3	3	1	1	5	0	0	1	0	0	-	0	.286	.304	.286
02	Oak	AL	89	193	53	13	1	11	(8	3)	101	27	40	31	14	1	37	1	0	3	1	1	.50	7	.275	.322	.523
12 ML YEARS			1186	3165	851	174	5	90	(42	48)	1305	362	416	400	256	43	650	21	21	26	7	12	.37	82	.269	.325	.412

Mike MacDougal

Pitches: R **Bats:** B **Pos:** RP-68 **Ht:** 6'4" **Wt:** 195 **Born:** 3/5/1977 **Age:** 29

			HOW MUCH HE PITCHED					**WHAT HE GAVE UP**												**THE RESULTS**						
Year	Team	Lg	G	GS	CG	GF	IP	BFP	H	R	ER	HR	SH	SF	HB	TBB	IBB	SO	WP	Bk	W	L	Pct	ShO	Sv-Op	Hld	ERC	ERA
2001	KC	AL	3	3	0	0	15.1	67	18	10	8	2	0	0	1	4	0	7	3	0	1	1	.500	0	0-0	0	5.04	4.70
2002	KC	AL	6	0	0	0	9.0	38	5	5	5	0	0	0	0	7	1	10	1	0	0	1	.000	0	0-0	0	2.26	5.00
2003	KC	AL	68	0	0	61	64.0	285	64	36	29	4	3	2	8	32	0	57	6	0	3	5	.375	0	27-35	1	4.76	4.08

	HOW MUCH HE PITCHED						WHAT HE GAVE UP												THE RESULTS							
Year Team Lg	G	GS	CG	GF	IP	BFP	H	R	ER	HR	SH	SF	HB	TBB	IBB	SO	WP	Bk	W	L	Pct	ShO	Sv-Op	Hld	ERC	ERA
2004 KC AL	13	0	0	8	11.1	61	16	8	7	2	0	0	1	9	0	14	2	0	1	1	.500	0	1-3	0	9.04	5.56
2005 KC AL	68	0	0	53	70.1	299	69	32	26	6	1	1	3	24	2	72	6	1	5	6	.455	0	21-25	0	3.78	3.33
5 ML YEARS	158	3	0	123	170.0	750	172	91	75	14	4	3	13	76	3	160	18	1	10	14	.417	0	49-63	1	4.50	3.97

Alejandro Machado

Bats: B Throws: R Pos: PR-4; 2B-3; CF-3; LF-2; SS-1; RF-1   Ht: 6'0" Wt: 184 Born: 4/26/1982 Age: 24

		BATTING																		BASERUNNING				AVERAGES		
Year Team	Lg	G	AB	H	2B	3B	HR	(Hm	Rd)	TB	R	RBI	RC	TBB	IBB	SO	HBP	SH	SF	SB	CS	SB%	GDP	Avg	OBP	Slg
1999 Braves	R	56	223	62	11	0	0	(-	-)	73	45	14	29	20	1	22	5	2	2	19	6	.76	3	.278	.348	.327
2000 Danvle	R+	61	217	74	6	2	0	(-	-)	84	45	16	49	53	0	29	6	2	3	30	12	.71	3	.341	.477	.387
2001 Macon	A	82	306	83	6	3	1	(-	-)	98	43	24	40	34	1	56	13	5	0	20	13	.61	1	.271	.368	.320
2001 Burlgtn	A	28	109	26	5	0	0	(-	-)	31	17	11	10	10	0	16	2	1	1	5	2	.71	2	.239	.311	.284
2002 Wilmg	A	101	325	102	9	1	2	(-	-)	119	53	29	52	27	1	43	12	12	6	20	6	.77	2	.314	.381	.366
2003 Huntsvl	AA	45	155	35	4	1	0	(-	-)	41	14	13	15	15	1	24	2	5	0	11	1	.92	0	.226	.302	.265
2003 Wichta	AA	78	289	83	13	5	1	(-	-)	109	59	31	44	34	2	45	4	5	2	19	9	.68	4	.287	.368	.377
2004 BrvdCt	A+	46	186	66	10	2	1	(-	-)	83	34	19	36	22	0	27	1	7	1	11	6	.65	2	.355	.424	.446
2004 Hrsbrg	AA	93	346	97	5	4	4	(-	-)	122	54	26	49	41	1	39	5	10	2	19	9	.68	8	.280	.363	.353
2005 Pwtckt	AAA	117	383	115	17	2	3	(-	-)	145	60	43	58	32	0	47	5	4	2	21	4	.84	11	.300	.360	.379
2005 BOS	AL	10	5	1	1	0	0	(0	0)	2	4	0	0	1	0	1	0	0	0	0	0	-	0	.200	.333	.400

Andy Machado

Bats: B Throws: R Pos: SS-4; PH-2   Ht: 5'11" Wt: 165 Born: 1/25/1981 Age: 25

		BATTING																		BASERUNNING				AVERAGES		
Year Team	Lg	G	AB	H	2B	3B	HR	(Hm	Rd)	TB	R	RBI	RC	TBB	IBB	SO	HBP	SH	SF	SB	CS	SB%	GDP	Avg	OBP	Slg
2005 Lsvlle*	AAA	21	80	11	2	1	0	(-	-)	15	9	6	3	12	0	23	0	0	1	1	2	.33	0	.138	.247	.188
2005 ColSpr*	AAA	25	63	10	3	1	0	(-	-)	15	6	8	6	16	0	17	0	1	1	0	1	.00	1	.159	.325	.238
2003 PHI	NL	1	0	0	0	0	0	(0	0)	0	0	0	0	0	0	0	0	0	0	1	0	1.00	0	-	-	-
2004 CIN	NL	17	56	15	5	1	0	(0	0)	22	6	4	8	10	2	26	0	0	0	3	1	.75	0	.268	.379	.393
2005 2 Tms	NL	6	12	0	0	0	0	(0	0)	0	1	2	0	2	0	6	0	0	1	0	0	-	0	.000	.133	.000
05 Cin	NL	2	2	0	0	0	0	(0	0)	0	0	0	0	0	0	1	0	0	0	0	0	-	0	.000	.000	.000
05 Col	NL	4	10	0	0	0	0	(0	0)	0	1	2	0	2	0	5	0	0	1	0	0	-	0	.000	.154	.000
3 ML YEARS		24	68	15	5	1	0	(0	0)	22	7	6	8	12	2	32	0	0	1	4	1	.80	0	.221	.333	.324

Jose Macias

Bats: B Throws: R Pos: PH-59; 3B-23; 2B-20; RF-8; CF-7; PR-6; LF-5   Ht: 5'10" Wt: 189 Born: 1/25/1972 Age: 34

		BATTING																		BASERUNNING				AVERAGES		
Year Team	Lg	G	AB	H	2B	3B	HR	(Hm	Rd)	TB	R	RBI	RC	TBB	IBB	SO	HBP	SH	SF	SB	CS	SB%	GDP	Avg	OBP	Slg
1999 DET	AL	5	4	1	0	0	1	(1	0)	4	2	2	1	0	0	1	0	0	0	0	0	-	0	.250	.250	1.000
2000 DET	AL	73	173	44	3	5	2	(2	0)	63	25	24	21	18	0	24	1	4	0	2	0	1.00	3	.254	.328	.364
2001 DET	AL	137	488	131	24	6	8	(7	1)	191	62	51	62	32	0	54	3	8	3	21	6	.78	7	.268	.316	.391
2002 2 Tms		123	338	84	21	1	7	(4	3)	128	43	39	40	21	0	57	2	8	4	8	8	.50	6	.249	.293	.379
2003 MON	NL	111	272	65	15	2	4	(3	1)	96	31	22	23	11	1	45	2	2	1	4	3	.57	5	.239	.273	.353
2004 CHN	NL	98	194	52	6	3	3	(2	1)	73	23	22	22	5	0	38	2	2	1	4	1	.80	2	.268	.292	.376
2005 CHN	NL	112	177	45	8	0	1	(1	0)	56	15	13	11	6	0	24	0	4	3	4	3	.57	6	.254	.274	.316
02 Det	AL	33	107	25	4	0	0	(0	0)	29	10	6	7	8	0	13	1	4	1	3	2	.60	4	.234	.291	.271
02 Mon	NL	90	231	59	17	1	7	(4	3)	99	33	33	33	13	0	44	1	4	3	5	6	.45	2	.255	.294	.429
7 ML YEARS		659	1646	422	77	17	26	(20	6)	611	201	173	180	93	1	243	10	28	12	43	21	.67	29	.256	.298	.371

Rob Mackowiak

Bats: L Throws: R Pos: 3B-65; CF-41; RF-23; PH-21; 2B-20; 1B-3; LF-1   Ht: 5'10" Wt: 190 Born: 6/20/1976 Age: 30

		BATTING																		BASERUNNING				AVERAGES		
Year Team	Lg	G	AB	H	2B	3B	HR	(Hm	Rd)	TB	R	RBI	RC	TBB	IBB	SO	HBP	SH	SF	SB	CS	SB%	GDP	Avg	OBP	Slg
2001 PIT	NL	83	214	57	15	2	4	(3	1)	88	30	21	28	15	5	52	3	2	3	4	3	.57	3	.266	.319	.411
2002 PIT	NL	136	385	94	22	0	16	(9	7)	164	57	48	57	42	5	120	7	3	2	9	3	.75	0	.244	.328	.426
2003 PIT	NL	77	174	47	4	4	6	(1	5)	77	20	19	27	15	2	53	4	0	0	6	0	1.00	1	.270	.342	.443
2004 PIT	NL	155	491	121	22	6	17	(11	6)	206	65	75	73	50	2	114	6	1	7	13	4	.76	3	.246	.319	.420
2005 PIT	NL	142	463	126	21	3	9	(7	2)	180	57	58	59	43	4	100	3	2	1	8	4	.67	7	.272	.337	.389
5 ML YEARS		593	1727	445	84	15	52	(31	21)	715	229	221	244	165	18	439	23	8	13	40	14	.74	14	.258	.328	.414

Greg Maddux

Pitches: R Bats: R Pos: SP-35   Ht: 6'0" Wt: 185 Born: 4/14/1966 Age: 40

		HOW MUCH HE PITCHED						WHAT HE GAVE UP												THE RESULTS							
Year Team	Lg	G	GS	CG	GF	IP	BFP	H	R	ER	HR	SH	SF	HB	TBB	IBB	SO	WP	Bk	W	L	Pct	ShO	Sv-Op	Hld	ERC	ERA
1986 CHN	NL	6	5	1	1	31.0	144	44	20	19	3	1	0	1	11	2	20	2	0	2	4	.333	0	0-0	0	6.45	5.52
1987 CHN	NL	30	27	1	2	155.2	701	181	111	97	17	7	1	4	74	13	101	4	7	6	14	.300	1	0-0	0	5.42	5.61
1988 CHN	NL	34	34	9	0	249.0	1047	230	97	88	13	11	2	9	81	16	140	3	6	18	8	.692	3	0-0	0	3.09	3.18
1989 CHN	NL	35	35	7	0	238.1	1002	222	90	78	13	18	6	6	82	13	135	5	3	19	12	.613	1	0-0	0	3.20	2.95
1990 CHN	NL	35	35	8	0	237.0	1011	242	116	91	11	18	5	6	71	10	144	3	3	15	15	.500	2	0-0	0	3.41	3.46
1991 CHN	NL	37	37	7	0	263.0	1070	232	113	98	18	16	3	6	66	9	198	6	3	15	11	.577	2	0-0	0	2.73	3.35
1992 CHN	NL	35	35	9	0	268.0	1061	201	68	65	7	15	3	14	70	7	199	5	0	20	11	.645	4	0-0	0	2.01	2.18
1993 ATL	NL	36	36	8	0	267.0	1064	228	85	70	14	15	7	6	52	7	197	5	1	20	10	.667	1	0-0	0	2.32	2.36
1994 ATL	NL	25	25	10	0	202.0	774	150	44	35	4	6	5	6	31	3	156	3	1	16	6	.727	3	0-0	0	1.59	1.56
1995 ATL	NL	28	28	10	0	209.2	785	147	39	38	8	9	1	4	23	3	181	1	0	19	2	.905	3	0-0	0	1.41	1.63
1996 ATL	NL	35	35	5	0	245.0	978	225	85	74	11	8	5	3	28	11	172	4	0	15	11	.577	1	0-0	0	2.22	2.72
1997 ATL	NL	33	33	5	0	232.2	893	200	58	57	9	11	7	6	20	6	177	0	0	19	4	.826	2	0-0	0	1.95	2.20

Year	Team	Lg	G	GS	CG	GF	IP	BFP	H	R	ER	HR	SH	SF	HB	TBB	IBB	SO	WP	Bk	W	L	Pct	ShO	Sv-Op	Hld	ERC	ERA
1998	ATL	NL	34	34	9	0	251.0	987	201	75	62	13	15	5	7	45	10	204	4	0	18	9	.667	5	0-0	0	2.01	2.22
1999	ATL	NL	33	33	4	0	219.1	940	258	103	87	16	15	5	4	37	8	136	1	0	19	9	.679	0	0-0	0	3.95	3.57
2000	ATL	NL	35	35	6	0	249.1	1012	225	91	83	19	8	5	10	42	12	190	1	2	19	9	.679	3	0-0	0	2.60	3.00
2001	ATL	NL	34	34	3	0	233.0	927	220	86	79	20	12	11	7	27	10	173	2	0	17	11	.607	3	0-0	0	2.70	3.05
2002	ATL	NL	34	34	0	0	199.1	820	194	67	58	14	13	4	4	45	7	118	1	0	16	6	.727	0	0-0	0	3.11	2.62
2003	ATL	NL	36	36	1	0	218.1	901	225	112	96	24	10	9	8	33	7	124	3	0	16	11	.593	0	0-0	0	3.44	3.96
2004	CHN	NL	33	33	2	0	212.2	872	218	103	95	35	12	8	9	33	4	151	2	0	16	11	.593	1	0-0	0	3.86	4.02
2005	CHN	NL	35	35	3	0	225.0	936	239	112	106	29	19	6	7	36	4	136	8	0	13	15	.464	0	0-0	0	3.77	4.24
20 ML YEARS			643	639	108	3	4406.1	17925	4082	1675	1476	298	239	98	125	907	162	3052	63	26	318	189	.627	35	0-0	0	2.81	3.01

Bobby Madritsch

Pitches: L **Bats:** L **Pos:** SP-1   **Ht:** 6'2" **Wt:** 190 **Born:** 2/28/1976 **Age:** 30

Year	Team	Lg	G	GS	CG	GF	IP	BFP	H	R	ER	HR	SH	SF	HB	TBB	IBB	SO	WP	Bk	W	L	Pct	ShO	Sv-Op	Hld	ERC	ERA
1998	Billings	R+	14	13	0	0	80.1	341	72	30	25	3	3	2	1	35	1	87	2	1	7	3	.700	0	0--	-	3.25	2.80
2000	Reds	R	6	4	0	0	22.1	90	15	5	5	0	1	0	2	9	0	27	0	0	1	1	.500	0	0--	-	2.11	2.01
2000	Dayton	A	2	2	0	0	10.0	44	8	1	1	0	0	1	0	7	0	7	1	0	0	0	-	0	0--	-	3.38	0.90
2003	SnAnt	AA	27	27	2	0	158.2	668	133	75	64	11	6	5	2	67	0	154	5	2	13	7	.650	1	0--	-	3.11	3.63
2004	Tacom	AAA	12	12	0	0	62.1	272	61	33	26	3	2	1	4	26	0	53	3	0	5	2	.714	0	0--	-	3.90	3.75
2004	SEA	AL	15	11	1	4	88.0	359	74	33	32	3	3	0	4	33	2	60	2	1	6	3	.667	0	0-0	0	2.91	3.27
2005	SEA	AL	1	1	0	0	4.1	17	4	3	3	1	0	0	0	1	0	1	0	0	0	1	.000	0	0-0	0	4.00	6.23
2 ML YEARS			16	12	1	4	92.1	376	78	36	35	4	3	0	4	34	2	61	2	1	6	4	.600	0	0-0	0	2.96	3.41

Ryan Madson

Pitches: R **Bats:** L **Pos:** RP-78   **Ht:** 6'6" **Wt:** 180 **Born:** 8/28/1980 **Age:** 25

Year	Team	Lg	G	GS	CG	GF	IP	BFP	H	R	ER	HR	SH	SF	HB	TBB	IBB	SO	WP	Bk	W	L	Pct	ShO	Sv-Op	Hld	ERC	ERA
2003	PHI	NL	1	0	0	0	2.0	6	0	0	0	0	0	0	0	0	0	0	0	0	0	0	-	0	0-0	0	0.00	0.00
2004	PHI	NL	52	1	0	14	77.0	312	68	23	20	6	1	1	5	19	4	55	7	0	9	3	.750	0	1-2	7	2.95	2.34
2005	PHI	NL	78	0	0	10	87.0	365	84	44	40	11	5	5	6	25	6	79	6	1	6	5	.545	0	0-7	32	3.83	4.14
3 ML YEARS			131	1	0	24	166.0	683	152	67	60	17	6	6	11	44	10	134	13	1	15	8	.652	0	1-9	39	3.33	3.25

Chris Magruder

Bats: B **Throws:** R **Pos:** PH-61; RF-31; CF-9; LF-5; PR-4   **Ht:** 5'11" **Wt:** 200 **Born:** 4/26/1977 **Age:** 29

Year	Team	Lg	G	AB	H	2B	3B	HR	(Hm	Rd)	TB	R	RBI	RC	TBB	IBB	SO	HBP	SH	SF	SB	CS	SB%	GDP	Avg	OBP	Slg
2001	TEX	AL	17	29	5	0	0	0	(0	0)	5	3	1	0	1	0	5	1	0	0	0	0	-	1	.172	.226	.172
2002	CLE	AL	87	258	56	15	1	6	(3	3)	91	34	29	20	15	2	55	1	2	2	2	0	1.00	7	.217	.261	.353
2003	CLE	AL	9	26	9	2	1	1	(1	0)	16	3	3	6	3	0	6	1	0	0	0	1	.00	0	.346	.433	.615
2004	MIL	NL	56	89	21	6	1	2	(1	1)	35	11	10	8	8	2	21	2	1	1	0	1	.00	3	.236	.310	.393
2005	MIL	NL	101	138	28	9	0	2	(2	0)	43	16	13	10	7	1	33	5	4	1	3	0	1.00	3	.203	.265	.312
5 ML YEARS			270	540	119	32	3	11	(7	4)	190	67	56	44	34	5	120	10	7	4	5	2	.71	14	.220	.277	.352

Ron Mahay

Pitches: L **Bats:** L **Pos:** RP-30   **Ht:** 6'2" **Wt:** 190 **Born:** 6/28/1971 **Age:** 35

Year	Team	Lg	G	GS	CG	GF	IP	BFP	H	R	ER	HR	SH	SF	HB	TBB	IBB	SO	WP	Bk	W	L	Pct	ShO	Sv-Op	Hld	ERC	ERA
2005	Frisco*	AA	5	5	0	0	19.2	92	24	19	17	3	0	1	2	9	0	20	1	0	1	3	.250	0	0--	-	6.46	7.78
2005	Okla*	AAA	3	0	0	1	3.2	14	2	0	0	0	0	0	0	1	0	5	0	0	0	0	-	0	0--	-	1.10	0.00
1997	BOS	AL	28	0	0	7	25.0	105	19	7	7	3	1	0	0	11	0	22	3	0	3	0	1.000	0	0-2	6	3.01	2.52
1998	BOS	AL	29	0	0	6	26.0	120	26	16	10	2	0	4	2	15	1	14	3	0	1	1	.500	0	1-2	7	4.76	3.46
1999	OAK	AL	6	1	0	2	19.1	68	8	4	4	2	0	0	0	3	0	15	0	0	2	0	1.000	0	1-1	0	0.88	1.86
2000	2 Tms		23	2	0	7	41.1	199	57	35	33	10	1	2	0	25	1	32	4	0	1	1	.500	0	0-0	2	8.55	7.19
2001	CHN	NL	17	0	0	4	20.2	86	14	6	6	4	0	0	0	15	1	24	1	0	0	0	-	0	0-0	2	4.32	2.61
2002	CHN	NL	11	0	0	1	14.2	65	13	14	14	6	0	0	0	8	0	14	0	0	2	0	1.000	0	0-0	0	6.11	8.59
2003	TEX	AL	35	0	0	5	45.1	189	33	19	16	3	0	0	0	20	7	38	4	0	3	3	.500	0	0-3	9	2.31	3.18
2004	TEX	AL	60	0	0	12	67.0	290	60	23	19	5	4	0	2	29	5	54	2	0	3	0	1.000	0	0-2	14	3.39	2.55
2005	TEX	AL	30	0	0	9	35.2	166	47	28	27	8	0	1	0	16	1	30	2	0	2	0	.000	0	1-1	6	7.14	6.81
00	Oak	AL	5	2	0	1	16.0	82	26	18	16	4	1	1	0	9	0	5	2	0	0	1	.000	0	0-0	0	9.97	9.00
00	Fla	NL	18	0	0	6	25.1	117	31	17	17	6	0	1	0	16	1	27	2	0	1	0	1.000	0	0-0	2	7.67	6.04
9 ML YEARS			239	3	0	53	295.0	1288	277	152	136	43	6	7	4	142	16	243	19	0	15	7	.682	0	3-11	46	4.32	4.15

Paul Maholm

Pitches: L **Bats:** L **Pos:** SP-6   **Ht:** 6'2" **Wt:** 225 **Born:** 6/25/1982 **Age:** 24

Year	Team	Lg	G	GS	CG	GF	IP	BFP	H	R	ER	HR	SH	SF	HB	TBB	IBB	SO	WP	Bk	W	L	Pct	ShO	Sv-Op	Hld	ERC	ERA
2003	Wmspt	A-	8	8	0	0	34.1	138	25	11	7	1	1	1	0	10	0	32	1	0	2	1	.667	0	0--	-	1.83	1.83
2004	Pirates	R	1	0	0	0	4.0	18	5	1	1	0	0	0	0	1	0	2	0	0	0	0	-	0	0--	-	4.05	2.25
2004	Lynbrg	A+	8	8	0	0	44.0	186	39	11	9	2	2	2	1	15	0	28	3	0	1	3	.250	0	0--	-	2.91	1.84
2004	Hickory	A	3	3	0	0	12.1	64	17	14	13	2	1	0	3	10	0	12	4	1	0	2	.000	0	0--	-	10.10	9.49
2005	Altna	AA	16	16	0	0	81.2	344	73	32	29	5	10	2	3	26	3	75	3	0	6	2	.750	0	0--	-	2.98	3.20
2005	Indy	AAA	6	6	0	0	35.2	159	40	19	14	2	0	0	1	12	0	21	1	0	1	1	.500	0	0--	-	4.22	3.53
2005	PIT	NL	6	6	0	0	41.1	168	31	10	10	2	0	0	3	17	0	26	0	0	3	1	.750	0	0-0	0	2.79	2.18

Mike Mahoney

Bats: R **Throws:** R **Pos:** C-25; PH-1; PR-1   **Ht:** 6'1" **Wt:** 200 **Born:** 12/5/1972 **Age:** 33

												BATTING										BASERUNNING					AVERAGES		
Year	Team	Lg	G	AB	H	2B	3B	HR	(Hm	Rd)	TB	R	RBI	RC	TBB	IBB	SO	HBP	SH	SF		SB	CS	SB%	GDP		Avg	OBP	Slg
2005	Memp*	AAA	71	230	61	19	1	5	(-	-)	97	30	27	33	14	3	40	7	2	2		2	0	1.00	9		.265	.324	.422
2000	CHN	NL	4	7	2	1	0	0	(0	0)	3	1	1	2	1	0	1	0	0	0		0	0	-	0		.286	.444	.429
2002	CHN	NL	16	29	6	3	0	0	(0	0)	9	2	3	0	1	1	10	0	1	0		0	0	-	1		.207	.233	.310
2005	STL	NL	26	64	10	1	0	1	(0	1)	14	5	6	1	4	1	10	1	6	0		0	0	-	3		.156	.217	.219
	3 ML YEARS		46	100	18	5	0	1	(0	1)	26	8	10	3	6	2	20	2	7	0		0	0	-	4		.180	.241	.260

John Maine

Pitches: R **Bats:** R **Pos:** SP-8; RP-2   **Ht:** 6'4" **Wt:** 193 **Born:** 5/8/1981 **Age:** 25

			HOW MUCH HE PITCHED						WHAT HE GAVE UP										THE RESULTS						
Year	Team	Lg	G	GS	CG	GF	IP	BFP	H	R	ER	HR	SH	SF	HB	TBB	IBB	SO	WP	Bk	W	L	Pct	ShO	Sv-Op Hld	ERC	ERA
2002	Abrdn	A-	4	2	0	1	10.1	42	6	2	2	0	0	0	0	3	0	21	2	0	1	1	.500	0	0-- -	1.17	1.74
2002	Dlmrva	A	6	5	0	0	33.0	128	21	8	5	0	3	1	2	4	0	39	2	1	1	1	.500	0	0-- -	1.16	1.36
2003	Dlmrva	A	14	14	1	0	76.1	283	43	16	13	1	2	0	2	18	0	108	1	1	7	3	.700	0	0-- -	1.21	1.53
2003	Frdrck	A+	12	12	1	0	70.1	276	48	27	24	5	2	1	1	20	0	77	0	0	6	1	.857	1	0-- -	1.92	3.07
2004	Bowie	AA	5	5	0	0	28.0	109	16	8	7	1	0	1	1	7	0	34	0	0	4	0	1.000	0	0-- -	1.32	2.25
2004	Ottawa	AAA	22	22	0	0	119.2	512	123	59	52	12	12	5	5	52	0	105	2	1	5	7	.417	0	0-- -	4.69	3.91
2005	Ottawa	AAA	23	23	1	0	128.1	555	128	72	65	13	5	3	6	42	1	111	3	2	6	11	.353	1	0-- -	3.91	4.56
2004	BAL	AL	1	1	0	0	3.2	19	7	4	4	1	0	0	0	3	0	1	1	0	1	0	1.000	0	0-0 0	14.87	9.82
2005	BAL	AL	10	8	0	1	40.0	184	39	30	28	8	0	2	1	24	0	24	0	1	2	3	.400	0	0-0 0	5.47	6.30
	2 ML YEARS		11	9	0	1	43.2	203	46	34	32	9	0	2	1	27	0	25	1	1	2	4	.333	0	0-0 0	6.13	6.60

Gary Majewski

Pitches: R **Bats:** R **Pos:** RP-79   **Ht:** 6'1" **Wt:** 215 **Born:** 2/26/1980 **Age:** 26

			HOW MUCH HE PITCHED						WHAT HE GAVE UP										THE RESULTS						
Year	Team	Lg	G	GS	CG	GF	IP	BFP	H	R	ER	HR	SH	SF	HB	TBB	IBB	SO	WP	Bk	W	L	Pct	ShO	Sv-Op Hld	ERC	ERA
1999	Bristol	R+	13	13	1	0	76.2	325	67	34	26	4	4	1	7	37	0	91	1	0	7	1	.875	1	0-- -	3.82	3.05
1999	Burlgtn	R+	3	0	0	0	3.1	28	11	14	14	3	1	0	2	4	0	1	0	0	0	0	-	0	0-- -	37.10	37.80
2000	Burlgtn	R+	22	22	3	0	134.2	546	83	53	46	8	3	6	12	68	0	137	2	0	6	7	.462	3	0-- -	2.57	3.07
2000	WinSa	A+	6	6	0	0	37.0	163	32	21	21	1	2	2	8	17	0	24	2	0	4	4	.333	0	0-- -	3.88	5.11
2001	VeroB	A+	23	13	0	5	75.0	351	103	57	52	9	3	4	5	36	0	41	3	1	4	5	.444	0	1-- -	7.32	6.24
2001	WinSa	A+	9	6	1	3	43.0	176	42	15	14	3	2	0	6	10	0	31	1	0	4	2	.667	0	0-- -	3.80	2.93
2002	Brham	AA	57	1	0	26	74.2	317	61	31	22	3	2	2	2	34	2	75	1	1	5	3	.625	0	3-- -	2.98	2.65
2003	Charltt	AAA	42	1	0	13	72.2	307	62	33	32	3	3	1	5	29	2	72	3	0	6	4	.600	0	4-- -	3.10	3.96
2004	Charltt	AAA	35	0	0	31	42.1	175	30	16	15	2	1	0	3	16	0	41	1	0	3	3	.500	0	14-- -	2.36	3.19
2004	Edmtn	AAA	14	0	0	10	15.1	72	18	8	7	0	0	0	0	8	1	17	1	0	1	2	.333	0	1-- -	4.53	4.11
2005	NewOr	AAA	3	0	0	0	6.1	28	7	3	3	0	0	0	0	2	0	2	0	0	0	0	-	0	0-- -	3.52	4.26
2004	MON	NL	16	0	0	7	21.0	95	28	15	9	2	1	1	2	5	1	12	0	0	0	1	.000	0	1-2 0	5.68	3.86
2005	WAS	NL	79	0	0	24	86.0	376	80	32	28	2	5	4	7	37	6	50	1	0	4	4	.500	0	1-5 24	3.43	2.93
	2 ML YEARS		95	0	0	31	107.0	471	108	47	37	4	6	5	9	42	7	62	1	0	4	5	.444	0	2-7 24	3.84	3.11

Matt Mantei

Pitches: R **Bats:** R **Pos:** RP-34   **Ht:** 6'1" **Wt:** 200 **Born:** 7/7/1973 **Age:** 32

			HOW MUCH HE PITCHED						WHAT HE GAVE UP										THE RESULTS						
Year	Team	Lg	G	GS	CG	GF	IP	BFP	H	R	ER	HR	SH	SF	HB	TBB	IBB	SO	WP	Bk	W	L	Pct	ShO	Sv-Op Hld	ERC	ERA
1995	FLA	NL	12	0	0	3	13.1	64	12	8	7	1	1	1	0	15	1	0	0	1	0	.554	0	0-0 0	5.54	4.73
1996	FLA	NL	14	0	0	1	18.1	89	13	13	13	2	1	0	1	21	1	25	2	0	1	0	1.000	0	0-1 0	5.46	6.38
1998	FLA	NL	42	0	0	23	54.2	224	38	19	18	1	3	4	7	23	3	63	0	0	3	4	.429	0	9-12 0	2.44	2.96
1999	2 Tms	NL	65	0	0	60	65.1	284	44	21	20	5	1	1	5	44	1	99	2	0	1	3	.250	0	32-37 0	3.42	2.76
2000	ARI	NL	47	0	0	38	45.1	200	31	24	23	4	2	0	2	35	1	53	5	0	1	1	.500	0	17-20 0	3.80	4.57
2001	ARI	NL	8	0	0	7	7.0	31	6	2	2	2	0	0	0	4	0	12	2	0	0	0	-	0	2-2 1	5.18	2.57
2002	ARI	NL	31	0	0	26	26.2	122	28	15	14	3	0	0	1	12	0	26	1	0	2	2	.500	0	0-1 2	4.64	4.73
2003	ARI	NL	50	0	0	44	55.0	220	37	17	16	6	4	2	2	18	1	68	1	0	5	4	.556	0	29-32 0	2.26	2.62
2004	ARI	NL	12	0	0	9	10.2	55	17	15	14	5	0	1	0	6	1	13	0	0	3	0	.000	0	4-7 0	11.44	11.81
2005	BOS	NL	34	0	0	16	26.1	125	23	20	19	1	0	0	5	24	1	22	5	0	1	0	1.000	0	0-0 8	5.67	6.49
99	Fla	NL	35	0	0	32	36.1	157	24	11	11	4	0	1	2	25	1	50	0	0	1	2	.333	0	10-12 0	3.55	2.72
99	Ari	NL	30	0	0	28	29.0	127	20	10	9	1	1	0	3	19	0	49	2	0	0	1	.000	0	22-25 0	3.25	2.79
	10 ML YEARS		315	0	0	196	322.2	1414	249	154	146	30	12	9	23	200	9	396	19	0	14	18	.438	0	93-112 13	3.83	4.07

Shaun Marcum

Pitches: R **Bats:** R **Pos:** RP-5   **Ht:** 6'0" **Wt:** 180 **Born:** 12/14/1981 **Age:** 24

			HOW MUCH HE PITCHED						WHAT HE GAVE UP										THE RESULTS						
Year	Team	Lg	G	GS	CG	GF	IP	BFP	H	R	ER	HR	SH	SF	HB	TBB	IBB	SO	WP	Bk	W	L	Pct	ShO	Sv-Op Hld	ERC	ERA
2003	Auburn	A-	21	0	0	13	34.0	125	15	6	5	1	1	1	7	0	47	2	0	1	0	1.000	0	8-- -	0.86	1.32
2004	Dnedin	A+	12	12	0	0	69.1	286	74	30	24	6	6	3	3	4	0	72	0	0	3	2	.600	0	0-- -	3.16	3.12
2004	CtnWV	A	13	13	1	0	79.0	317	64	32	28	7	6	3	0	16	0	83	1	0	7	4	.636	1	0-- -	2.24	3.19
2005	Ham	AA	9	9	1	0	53.1	214	44	15	15	5	2	2	2	10	0	40	1	0	7	1	.875	1	0-- -	2.45	2.53
2005	Syrcse	AAA	18	18	0	0	103.2	441	112	59	57	17	1	2	4	18	2	90	2	0	6	4	.600	0	0-- -	4.13	4.95
2005	TOR	AL	5	0	0	3	8.0	32	6	0	0	0	0	0	0	4	0	4	0	0	0	0	-	0	0-0 0	2.58	0.00

Mike Maroth

Pitches: L **Bats:** L **Pos:** SP-34   **Ht:** 6'0" **Wt:** 180 **Born:** 8/17/1977 **Age:** 28

			HOW MUCH HE PITCHED					WHAT HE GAVE UP										THE RESULTS						
Year	Team	Lg	G	GS	CG	GF	IP	BFP	H	R	ER	HR	SH	SF	HB	TBB	IBB	SO	WP	Bk	W	L	Pct	ShO	Sv-Op	Hld	ERC	ERA
2002	DET	AL	21	21	0	0	128.2	538	136	68	64	7	5	3	2	36	1	58	4	0	6	10	.375	0	0-0	0	3.73	4.48
2003	DET	AL	33	33	1	0	193.1	847	231	131	123	34	9	8	8	50	2	87	7	0	9	21	.300	0	0-0	0	5.36	5.73
2004	DET	AL	33	33	2	0	217.0	928	244	112	104	25	11	4	7	59	1	108	10	1	11	13	.458	1	0-0	0	4.57	4.31
2005	DET	AL	34	34	0	0	209.0	889	235	123	110	30	3	11	9	51	1	115	5	0	14	14	.500	0	0-0	0	4.71	4.74
4 ML YEARS			121	121	3	0	748.0	3202	846	434	401	96	28	26	26	196	5	368	26	1	40	58	.408	1	0-0	0	4.66	4.82

Jason Marquis

Pitches: R **Bats:** L **Pos:** SP-32; RP-1   **Ht:** 6'1" **Wt:** 210 **Born:** 8/21/1978 **Age:** 27

			HOW MUCH HE PITCHED					WHAT HE GAVE UP										THE RESULTS						
Year	Team	Lg	G	GS	CG	GF	IP	BFP	H	R	ER	HR	SH	SF	HB	TBB	IBB	SO	WP	Bk	W	L	Pct	ShO	Sv-Op	Hld	ERC	ERA
2000	ATL	NL	15	0	0	7	23.1	103	23	16	13	4	1	1	1	12	1	17	1	0	1	0	1.000	0	0-1	1	5.13	5.01
2001	ATL	NL	38	16	0	9	129.1	556	113	62	50	14	6	5	4	59	4	98	1	2	5	6	.455	0	0-2	2	3.70	3.48
2002	ATL	NL	22	22	0	0	114.1	507	127	66	64	19	4	3	3	49	3	84	4	0	8	9	.471	0	0-0	0	5.43	5.04
2003	ATL	NL	21	2	0	10	40.2	182	43	27	25	3	0	3	2	18	2	19	2	0	0	0	-	0	1-1	0	4.45	5.53
2004	STL	NL	32	32	0	0	201.1	874	215	90	83	26	5	6	10	70	1	138	6	0	15	7	.682	0	0-0	0	4.69	3.71
2005	STL	NL	33	32	3	0	207.0	868	206	110	95	29	4	3	5	69	2	100	10	3	13	14	.481	1	0-0	0	4.23	4.13
6 ML YEARS			161	104	3	26	716.0	3090	727	371	330	95	20	21	25	277	13	456	24	5	42	36	.538	1	1-4	3	4.49	4.15

Eli Marrero

Bats: R **Throws:** R **Pos:** LF-15; PH-14; RF-13; 1B-9; CF-8; DH-2; PR-2   **Ht:** 6'1" **Wt:** 180 **Born:** 11/17/1973 **Age:** 32

			BATTING																			BASERUNNING				AVERAGES		
Year	Team	Lg	G	AB	H	2B	3B	HR	(Hm	Rd)	TB	R	RBI	RC	TBB	IBB	SO	HBP	SH	SF	SB	CS	SB%	GDP	Avg	OBP	Slg
1997	STL	NL	17	45	11	2	0	2	(0	2)	19	4	7	6	2	1	13	0	0	1	4	0	1.00	1	.244	.271	.422
1998	STL	NL	83	254	62	18	1	4	(2	2)	94	28	20	30	28	5	42	0	1	1	6	2	.75	5	.244	.318	.370
1999	STL	NL	114	317	61	13	1	6	(3	3)	94	32	34	18	18	4	56	1	4	3	11	2	.85	14	.192	.236	.297
2000	STL	NL	53	102	23	3	1	5	(2	3)	43	21	17	14	9	0	16	3	0	2	5	0	1.00	3	.225	.302	.422
2001	STL	NL	86	203	54	11	3	6	(2	4)	89	37	23	27	15	2	36	0	3	3	3	6	.33	4	.266	.312	.438
2002	STL	NL	131	397	104	19	1	18	(9	9)	179	63	66	59	40	11	72	0	5	4	14	2	.88	5	.262	.327	.451
2003	STL	NL	41	107	24	4	2	2	(1	1)	38	10	20	15	7	0	18	0	0	2	0	1	.00	4	.224	.267	.355
2004	ATL	NL	90	250	80	18	1	10	(6	4)	130	37	40	50	23	1	50	1	2	4	4	1	.80	4	.320	.374	.520
2005	2 Tms		54	138	25	7	2	7	(2	5)	57	19	19	8	11	0	38	1	1	5	1	0	1.00	3	.181	.239	.413
05	KC	AL	32	88	14	4	0	4	(1	3)	30	11	9	2	7	0	18	1	1	3	1	0	1.00	2	.159	.222	.341
05	Bal	AL	22	50	11	3	2	3	(1	2)	27	8	10	6	4	0	20	0	0	2	0	0	-	1	.220	.268	.540
9 ML YEARS			669	1813	444	95	12	60	(27	33)	743	251	246	227	153	24	341	6	16	25	51	11	.82	39	.245	.302	.410

Andy Marte

Bats: R **Throws:** R **Pos:** 3B-17; PH-7; PR-1   **Ht:** 6'1" **Wt:** 185 **Born:** 10/21/1983 **Age:** 22

			BATTING																			BASERUNNING				AVERAGES		
Year	Team	Lg	G	AB	H	2B	3B	HR	(Hm	Rd)	TB	R	RBI	RC	TBB	IBB	SO	HBP	SH	SF	SB	CS	SB%	GDP	Avg	OBP	Slg
2001	Danvle	R+	37	125	25	6	0	1	(-	-)	34	12	12	12	20	0	45	0	1	2	3	0	1.00	3	.200	.306	.272
2002	Macon	A	126	488	137	32	4	21	(-	-)	240	69	105	83	41	3	114	6	0	7	2	1	.67	6	.281	.339	.492
2003	MrtlBh	A+	130	463	132	35	1	16	(-	-)	217	69	63	85	67	8	109	2	0	9	5	2	.71	13	.285	.372	.469
2004	Braves	R	3	15	7	4	0	1	(-	-)	14	4	6	5	2	0	2	0	0	0	0	0	-	0	.467	.529	.933
2004	Grnville	AA	107	387	104	28	1	23	(-	-)	203	52	68	75	58	4	105	2	0	3	1	1	.50	8	.269	.364	.525
2005	Rchmd	AAA	109	389	107	26	1	20	(-	-)	197	51	74	75	64	2	83	0	0	7	0	3	.00	8	.275	.372	.506
2005	ATL	NL	24	57	8	2	1	0	(0	0)	12	3	4	1	7	0	13	0	0	2	0	1	.00	2	.140	.227	.211

Damaso Marte

Pitches: L **Bats:** L **Pos:** RP-66   **Ht:** 6'2" **Wt:** 200 **Born:** 2/14/1975 **Age:** 31

			HOW MUCH HE PITCHED					WHAT HE GAVE UP										THE RESULTS						
Year	Team	Lg	G	GS	CG	GF	IP	BFP	H	R	ER	HR	SH	SF	HB	TBB	IBB	SO	WP	Bk	W	L	Pct	ShO	Sv-Op	Hld	ERC	ERA
2005	Charltt*	AAA	1	0	0	0	1.2	10	4	1	1	0	0	0	0	1	0	2	1	0	0	0	-	0	0--	-	13.02	5.40
1999	SEA	AL	5	0	0	2	8.2	47	16	9	9	3	0	0	0	6	0	3	0	0	0	1	.000	0	0-0	0	13.32	9.35
2001	PIT	NL	23	0	0	4	36.1	154	34	21	19	5	1	2	3	12	3	39	1	0	0	1	.000	0	0-0	0	3.93	4.71
2002	CHA	AL	68	0	0	22	60.1	240	44	19	19	5	1	1	4	18	2	72	3	1	1	1	.500	0	10-12	14	2.42	2.83
2003	CHA	AL	71	0	0	25	79.2	314	50	16	14	3	3	3	3	34	6	87	1	0	4	2	.667	0	11-18	14	1.96	1.58
2004	CHA	AL	74	0	0	24	73.2	303	56	28	28	10	2	6	3	34	4	68	3	0	6	5	.545	0	6-12	21	3.39	3.42
2005	CHA	AL	66	0	0	15	45.1	213	45	21	19	5	1	0	3	33	4	54	1	1	3	4	.429	0	4-8	22	5.51	3.77
6 ML YEARS			307	0	0	92	304.0	1271	245	114	108	31	8	12	16	137	19	323	9	2	14	14	.500	0	31-50	71	3.37	3.20

Tom Martin

Pitches: L **Bats:** L **Pos:** RP-4   **Ht:** 6'1" **Wt:** 206 **Born:** 5/21/1970 **Age:** 36

			HOW MUCH HE PITCHED					WHAT HE GAVE UP										THE RESULTS						
Year	Team	Lg	G	GS	CG	GF	IP	BFP	H	R	ER	HR	SH	SF	HB	TBB	IBB	SO	WP	Bk	W	L	Pct	ShO	Sv-Op	Hld	ERC	ERA
2005	RdRck*	AAA	20	0	0	12	27.1	128	33	11	11	4	2	1	1	13	2	13	0	0	0	0	-	0	5--	-	5.89	3.62
1997	HOU	NL	55	0	0	18	56.0	236	52	13	13	4	2	6	1	23	2	36	3	0	5	3	.625	0	2-3	7	3.34	2.09
1998	CLE	AL	14	0	0	1	14.2	85	29	21	21	3	1	1	0	12	0	9	2	0	1	1	.500	0	0-0	3	13.19	12.89
1999	CLE	AL	6	0	0	0	9.1	44	13	9	9	2	0	1	0	3	1	8	0	0	0	0	-	0	0-0	0	6.64	8.68
2000	CLE	AL	31	0	0	7	33.1	143	32	16	15	3	0	1	1	15	2	21	1	0	1	0	1.000	0	0-0	4	4.05	4.05
2001	NYN	NL	14	0	0	2	17.0	85	23	22	19	4	1	1	1	10	2	12	0	0	1	0	1.000	0	0-0	1	8.02	10.06
2002	TB	AL	2	0	0	2	1.2	11	5	3	3	0	0	0	0	1	0	1	0	0	0	0	-	0	0-0	0	17.54	16.20
2003	LA	NL	80	0	0	13	51.0	210	36	21	20	6	0	2	2	24	4	51	1	0	1	2	.333	0	0-1	28	2.94	3.53

Year	Team	Lg	G	GS	CG	GF	IP	BFP	H	R	ER	HR	SH	SF	HB	TBB	IBB	SO	WP	Bk	W	L	Pct	ShO	Sv-Op	Hld	ERC	ERA
2004	2 Tms	NL	76	0	0	11	45.1	204	49	20	20	7	5	4	3	19	3	30	1	0	0	2	.000	0	1-4	12	5.14	3.97
2005	ATL	NL	4	0	0	1	2.1	14	6	5	5	1	0	0	0	2	0	0	0	0	0	0	-	0	0-0	0	22.06	19.29
04	LA	NL	47	0	0	9	28.1	132	32	13	13	3	3	2	3	14	1	18	1	0	0	1	.000	0	1-1	5	5.58	4.13
04	Atl	NL	29	0	0	2	17.0	72	17	7	7	4	2	2	0	5	2	12	0	0	0	1	.000	0	0-3	7	4.36	3.71
	9 ML YEARS		282	0	0	55	230.2	1032	245	130	125	28	13	11	8	109	14	168	8	0	9	9	.500	0	3-8	51	4.91	4.88

Pedro Martinez

Pitches: R Bats: R Pos: SP-31   **Ht: 5'11" Wt: 180 Born: 10/25/1971 Age: 34**

			HOW MUCH HE PITCHED						WHAT HE GAVE UP												THE RESULTS							
Year	Team	Lg	G	GS	CG	GF	IP	BFP	H	R	ER	HR	SH	SF	HB	TBB	IBB	SO	WP	Bk	W	L	Pct	ShO	Sv-Op	Hld	ERC	ERA
1992	LA	NL	2	1	0	1	8.0	31	6	2	2	0	0	0	0	1	0	8	0	0	0	1	.000	0	0-0	0	1.38	2.25
1993	LA	NL	65	2	0	20	107.0	444	76	34	31	5	0	5	4	57	4	119	3	1	10	5	.667	0	2-3	14	2.79	2.61
1994	MON	NL	24	23	1	1	144.2	584	115	58	55	11	2	3	11	45	3	142	6	0	11	5	.688	1	1-1	0	2.81	3.42
1995	MON	NL	30	30	2	0	194.2	784	158	79	76	21	7	3	11	66	1	174	5	2	14	10	.583	2	0-0	0	3.19	3.51
1996	MON	NL	33	33	4	0	216.2	901	189	100	89	19	9	6	3	70	3	222	6	0	13	10	.565	1	0-0	0	3.02	3.70
1997	MON	NL	31	31	13	0	241.1	947	158	65	51	16	9	1	9	67	5	305	3	1	17	8	.680	4	0-0	0	1.79	1.90
1998	BOS	AL	33	33	3	0	233.2	951	188	82	75	26	4	7	8	67	3	251	9	0	19	7	.731	2	0-0	0	2.78	2.89
1999	BOS	AL	31	29	5	1	213.1	835	160	56	49	9	3	6	9	37	1	313	6	0	23	4	.852	1	0-0	0	1.79	2.07
2000	BOS	AL	29	29	7	0	217.0	817	128	44	42	17	2	1	14	32	0	284	1	0	18	6	.750	4	0-0	0	1.39	1.74
2001	BOS	AL	18	18	1	0	116.2	456	84	33	31	5	2	0	6	25	0	163	4	0	7	3	.700	0	0-0	0	1.84	2.39
2002	BOS	AL	30	30	2	0	199.1	787	144	62	50	13	2	4	15	40	1	239	3	0	20	4	.833	0	0-0	0	1.98	2.26
2003	BOS	AL	29	29	3	0	186.2	749	147	52	46	7	4	4	9	47	0	206	5	0	14	4	.778	0	0-0	0	2.22	2.22
2004	BOS	AL	33	33	1	0	217.0	903	193	99	94	26	5	9	16	61	0	227	2	0	16	9	.640	1	0-0	0	3.44	3.90
2005	NYN	NL	31	31	4	0	217.0	843	159	69	68	19	9	2	4	47	3	208	4	0	15	8	.652	1	0-0	0	2.03	2.82
	14 ML YEARS		419	352	46	23	2513.0	10032	1905	835	759	194	58	51	119	662	24	2861	57	4	197	84	.701	17	3-4	14	2.34	2.72

Ramon Martinez

Bats: R Throws: R Pos: PH-19; SS-15; 1B-12; 2B-5; 3B-4   **Ht: 6'1" Wt: 183 Born: 10/10/1972 Age: 33**

						BATTING														BASERUNNING				AVERAGES		
Year	Team	Lg	G	AB	H	2B	3B	HR	(Hm	Rd)	TB	R	RBI	RC	TBB	IBB	SO	HBP	SH	SF	SB	CS	SB%	GDP	Avg	OBP	Slg
2005	Toledo*	AAA	3	15	11	0	0	0	(-	-)	11	4	1	6	1	0	1	0	0	0	0	0	-	0	.733	.750	.733
1998	SF	NL	19	19	6	1	0	0	(0	0)	7	4	0	4	4	0	2	0	1	0	0	0	-	0	.316	.435	.368
1999	SF	NL	61	144	38	6	0	5	(3	2)	59	21	19	19	14	0	17	0	6	1	1	2	.33	2	.264	.327	.410
2000	SF	NL	88	189	57	13	2	6	(4	2)	92	30	25	31	15	1	22	1	4	1	3	2	.60	6	.302	.354	.487
2001	SF	NL	128	391	99	18	3	5	(1	4)	138	48	37	44	38	6	52	5	6	6	1	2	.33	11	.253	.323	.353
2002	SF	NL	72	181	49	10	2	4	(4	0)	75	26	25	33	14	2	26	4	0	1	2	0	1.00	1	.271	.335	.414
2003	CHN	NL	108	293	83	16	1	3	(3	0)	110	30	34	34	24	1	50	2	6	8	0	1	.00	8	.283	.333	.375
2004	CHN	NL	102	260	64	15	1	3	(1	2)	90	22	30	28	26	3	40	1	7	4	0	1	1.00	5	.246	.313	.346
2005	2 Tms	NL	52	112	31	3	0	1	(1	0)	37	11	14	14	6	0	11	1	4	4	0	0	-	2	.277	.309	.330
05	Det	AL	19	56	15	1	0	0	(0	0)	16	4	5	7	3	0	4	0	2	1	0	0	-	1	.268	.300	.286
05	Phi	NL	33	56	16	2	0	1	(1	0)	21	7	9	7	3	0	7	1	2	3	0	0	-	1	.286	.317	.375
	8 ML YEARS		630	1589	427	82	9	27	(17	10)	608	192	184	207	141	13	220	14	34	25	8	7	.53	35	.269	.329	.383

Tino Martinez

Bats: L Throws: R Pos: 1B-122; PH-11; PR-4   **Ht: 6'2" Wt: 210 Born: 12/7/1967 Age: 38**

						BATTING														BASERUNNING				AVERAGES		
Year	Team	Lg	G	AB	H	2B	3B	HR	(Hm	Rd)	TB	R	RBI	RC	TBB	IBB	SO	HBP	SH	SF	SB	CS	SB%	GDP	Avg	OBP	Slg
1990	SEA	AL	24	68	15	4	0	0	(0	0)	19	4	5	7	9	0	9	0	0	1	0	0	-	0	.221	.308	.279
1991	SEA	AL	36	112	23	2	0	4	(3	1)	37	11	9	10	11	0	24	0	0	2	0	0	-	2	.205	.272	.330
1992	SEA	AL	136	460	118	19	2	16	(10	6)	189	53	66	54	42	9	77	2	1	8	2	1	.67	24	.257	.316	.411
1993	SEA	AL	109	408	108	25	1	17	(9	8)	186	48	60	62	45	9	56	5	3	3	0	3	.00	7	.265	.343	.456
1994	SEA	AL	97	329	86	21	0	20	(8	12)	167	42	61	51	29	2	52	1	4	3	1	2	.33	9	.261	.320	.508
1995	SEA	AL	141	519	152	35	3	31	(14	17)	286	92	111	102	62	15	91	4	2	6	0	0	-	10	.293	.369	.551
1996	NYA	AL	155	595	174	28	0	25	(9	16)	277	82	117	97	68	4	85	2	1	5	2	1	.67	18	.292	.364	.466
1997	NYA	AL	158	594	176	31	2	44	(18	26)	343	96	141	122	75	14	75	3	0	13	3	1	.75	15	.296	.371	.577
1998	NYA	AL	142	531	149	33	1	28	(12	16)	268	92	123	92	61	3	83	6	0	10	2	1	.67	18	.281	.355	.505
1999	NYA	AL	159	589	155	27	2	28	(7	21)	270	95	105	90	69	7	86	3	0	4	3	4	.43	14	.263	.341	.458
2000	NYA	AL	155	569	147	37	4	16	(12	4)	240	69	91	76	52	9	74	8	0	3	4	1	.80	16	.258	.328	.422
2001	NYA	AL	154	589	165	24	2	34	(22	12)	295	89	113	93	42	2	89	2	0	2	1	2	.33	12	.280	.329	.501
2002	STL	NL	150	511	134	25	1	21	(12	9)	224	63	75	70	58	9	71	2	1	4	3	2	.60	12	.262	.337	.438
2003	STL	NL	138	476	130	25	2	15	(6	9)	204	66	69	64	53	7	71	9	2	7	1	1	.50	14	.273	.352	.429
2004	TB	AL	138	458	120	20	1	23	(9	14)	211	63	76	77	66	9	72	9	0	5	3	1	.75	10	.262	.362	.461
2005	NYA	AL	131	303	73	9	0	17	(9	8)	133	43	49	41	38	3	54	3	0	4	2	0	1.00	10	.241	.328	.439
	16 ML YEARS		2023	7111	1925	365	21	339	(160	179)	3349	1008	1271	1108	780	102	1069	59	14	80	27	20	.57	191	.271	.344	.471

Victor Martinez

Bats: B Throws: R Pos: C-142; PH-5; DH-2   **Ht: 6'2" Wt: 170 Born: 12/23/1978 Age: 27**

						BATTING														BASERUNNING				AVERAGES		
Year	Team	Lg	G	AB	H	2B	3B	HR	(Hm	Rd)	TB	R	RBI	RC	TBB	IBB	SO	HBP	SH	SF	SB	CS	SB%	GDP	Avg	OBP	Slg
2002	CLE	AL	12	32	9	1	0	1	(0	1)	13	2	5	5	3	0	2	0	0	1	0	0	-	1	.281	.333	.406
2003	CLE	AL	49	159	46	4	0	1	(0	1)	53	15	16	17	13	0	21	1	0	1	1	1	.50	8	.289	.345	.333
2004	CLE	AL	141	520	149	38	1	23	(8	15)	256	77	108	90	60	11	69	5	0	6	0	1	.00	16	.283	.359	.492
2005	CLE	AL	147	547	167	33	0	20	(10	10)	260	73	80	90	63	9	78	5	0	7	0	1	.00	16	.305	.378	.475
	4 ML YEARS		349	1258	369	76	1	45	(19	26)	582	167	209	202	139	20	170	11	0	15	1	3	.25	41	.293	.365	.463

Henry Mateo

Bats: B Throws: R Pos: 2B-1   Ht: 5'11" Wt: 170 Born: 10/14/1976 Age: 29

Year	Team	Lg	G	AB	H	2B	3B	HR	(Hm	Rd)	TB	R	RBI	RC	TBB	IBB	SO	HBP	SH	SF	SB	CS	SB%	GDP	Avg	OBP	Slg
2005	Ptomc*	A+	13	50	14	5	1	3	(-	-)	30	13	9	11	3	0	10	3	2	0	2	0	1.00	1	.280	.357	.600
2005	Hrsbrg*	AA	32	122	20	5	1	0	(-	-)	27	13	6	7	16	1	27	0	2	0	11	5	.69	3	.164	.261	.221
2005	NewOr*	AAA	9	31	9	0	0	0	(-	-)	9	2	3	3	3	0	7	0	0	0	3	1	.75	0	.290	.353	.290
2001	MON	NL	5	9	3	1	0	0	(0	0)	4	1	0	1	0	0	1	0	0	0	0	0	-	0	.333	.333	.444
2002	MON	NL	22	23	4	0	1	0	(0	0)	6	1	0	1	2	1	6	0	0	0	2	0	1.00	0	.174	.240	.261
2003	MON	NL	100	154	37	3	1	0	(0	0)	42	29	7	16	11	0	38	3	1	0	11	1	.92	0	.240	.304	.273
2004	MON	NL	40	44	12	2	0	0	(0	0)	14	3	0	1	1	0	9	0	1	0	2	3	.40	1	.273	.289	.318
2005	WAS	NL	1	1	0	0	0	0	(0	0)	0	0	0	0	1	0	0	0	0	0	0	0	-	0	.000	.500	.000
5 ML YEARS			168	231	56	6	2	0	(0	0)	66	34	7	19	15	1	54	3	2	0	15	4	.79	1	.242	.297	.286

Julio Mateo

Pitches: R Bats: R Pos: RP-54; SP-1   Ht: 6'0" Wt: 177 Born: 8/2/1977 Age: 28

Year	Team	Lg	G	GS	CG	GF	IP	BFP	H	R	ER	HR	SH	SF	HB	TBB	IBB	SO	WP	Bk	W	L	Pct	ShO	Sv-Op	Hld	ERC	ERA
2002	SEA	AL	12	0	0	7	21.0	94	20	10	10	2	0	0	1	12	0	15	1	0	0	0	-	0	0-0	2	4.63	4.29
2003	SEA	AL	50	0	0	17	85.2	338	69	32	30	14	2	4	5	13	1	71	1	1	4	0	1.000	0	1-1	2	2.71	3.15
2004	SEA	AL	45	0	0	9	57.2	248	56	30	30	11	0	4	5	16	3	43	2	0	1	2	.333	0	1-4	6	4.26	4.68
2005	SEA	AL	55	1	0	7	88.1	364	79	32	30	12	5	2	7	17	6	52	1	0	3	6	.333	0	0-2	8	3.12	3.06
4 ML YEARS			162	1	0	40	252.2	1044	224	104	100	39	7	10	18	58	10	181	5	1	8	8	.500	0	2-7	18	3.35	3.56

Mike Matheny

Bats: R Throws: R Pos: C-132; PH-3   Ht: 6'3" Wt: 205 Born: 9/22/1970 Age: 35

Year	Team	Lg	G	AB	H	2B	3B	HR	(Hm	Rd)	TB	R	RBI	RC	TBB	IBB	SO	HBP	SH	SF	SB	CS	SB%	GDP	Avg	OBP	Slg
1994	MIL	AL	28	53	12	3	0	1	(1	0)	18	3	2	5	3	0	13	2	1	0	0	1	.00	1	.226	.293	.340
1995	MIL	AL	80	166	41	9	1	0	(0	0)	52	13	21	16	12	0	28	2	1	0	2	1	.67	3	.247	.306	.313
1996	MIL	AL	106	313	64	15	2	8	(5	3)	107	31	46	23	14	0	80	3	7	4	3	2	.60	9	.204	.243	.342
1997	MIL	AL	123	320	78	16	1	4	(2	2)	108	29	32	30	17	0	68	7	9	3	0	1	.00	9	.244	.294	.338
1998	MIL	NL	108	320	76	13	0	6	(4	2)	107	24	27	28	11	0	63	7	3	0	1	0	1.00	6	.238	.278	.334
1999	TOR	AL	57	163	35	6	0	3	(1	2)	50	16	17	13	12	0	37	1	2	1	0	0	-	3	.215	.271	.307
2000	STL	NL	128	417	109	22	1	6	(2	4)	151	43	47	46	32	8	96	4	7	4	0	0	-	11	.261	.317	.362
2001	STL	NL	121	381	83	12	0	7	(4	3)	116	40	42	29	28	5	76	4	8	3	1	0	.00	11	.218	.276	.304
2002	STL	NL	110	315	77	12	1	3	(1	2)	100	31	35	36	32	6	49	2	8	6	1	3	.25	3	.244	.313	.317
2003	STL	NL	141	441	111	18	2	8	(4	4)	157	43	47	52	44	16	81	2	8	3	1	1	.50	11	.252	.320	.356
2004	STL	NL	122	385	95	22	1	5	(4	1)	134	28	50	32	23	7	83	3	5	3	0	2	.00	12	.247	.292	.348
2005	SF	NL	134	443	107	34	0	13	(8	5)	180	42	59	52	29	10	91	6	3	4	0	2	.00	11	.242	.295	.406
12 ML YEARS			1258	3717	888	182	9	64	(36	28)	1280	343	425	362	257	52	765	43	62	31	8	14	.36	90	.239	.293	.344

Jeff Mathis

Bats: R Throws: R Pos: C-3; DH-2; PH-1; PR-1   Ht: 6'0" Wt: 180 Born: 3/31/1983 Age: 23

Year	Team	Lg	G	AB	H	2B	3B	HR	(Hm	Rd)	TB	R	RBI	RC	TBB	IBB	SO	HBP	SH	SF	SB	CS	SB%	GDP	Avg	OBP	Slg
2001	Provo	R+	22	77	23	6	3	0	(-	-)	35	14	18	15	11	0	13	2	0	3	1	0	1.00	1	.299	.387	.455
2001	Angels	R	7	23	7	1	0	0	(-	-)	8	1	3	3	2	0	4	0	0	1	0	0	-	1	.304	.346	.348
2002	CRpds	A	128	491	141	41	3	10	(-	-)	218	75	73	78	40	3	75	8	2	8	7	4	.64	6	.287	.346	.444
2003	RCuca	A+	98	378	122	28	3	11	(-	-)	189	74	54	72	35	0	74	5	0	4	5	3	.63	4	.323	.384	.500
2003	Ark	AA	24	95	27	11	0	2	(-	-)	44	19	14	16	12	1	16	1	1	2	1	2	.33	2	.284	.364	.463
2004	Ark	AA	116	426	95	24	3	14	(-	-)	167	55	55	55	49	1	100	5	4	4	2	1	.67	5	.223	.308	.392
2005	Salt Lk	AAA	112	427	118	26	3	21	(-	-)	213	78	73	73	42	1	85	1	5	4	4	3	.57	7	.276	.340	.499
2005	LAA	AL	5	3	1	0	0	0	(0	0)	1	1	0	0	0	0	1	0	0	0	0	0	-	0	.333	.333	.333

Luis Matos

Bats: R Throws: R Pos: CF-120; PH-3; PR-2   Ht: 6'0" Wt: 179 Born: 10/30/1978 Age: 27

Year	Team	Lg	G	AB	H	2B	3B	HR	(Hm	Rd)	TB	R	RBI	RC	TBB	IBB	SO	HBP	SH	SF	SB	CS	SB%	GDP	Avg	OBP	Slg
2005	Bowie*	AA	5	20	5	0	0	1	(-	-)	8	4	2	2	1	0	4	1	0	0	1	1	.50	0	.250	.318	.400
2000	BAL	AL	72	182	41	6	3	1	(1	0)	56	21	17	15	12	0	30	3	2	2	13	4	.76	7	.225	.281	.308
2001	BAL	AL	31	98	21	7	0	4	(1	3)	40	16	12	14	11	0	30	1	2	0	7	0	1.00	1	.214	.300	.408
2002	BAL	AL	17	31	4	1	0	0	(0	0)	5	0	1	0	1	0	6	0	1	0	1	0	1.00	1	.129	.156	.161
2003	BAL	AL	109	439	133	23	3	13	(6	7)	201	70	45	66	28	0	90	7	10	2	15	7	.68	9	.303	.353	.458
2004	BAL	AL	89	330	74	18	0	6	(2	4)	110	36	28	27	19	2	60	5	3	2	12	4	.75	7	.224	.275	.333
2005	BAL	AL	121	389	109	20	2	4	(3	1)	145	53	32	51	27	0	58	10	3	4	17	9	.65	4	.280	.340	.373
6 ML YEARS			439	1469	382	75	8	28	(13	15)	557	196	135	173	98	2	274	26	21	10	65	24	.73	29	.260	.316	.379

Dave Matranga

Bats: R Throws: R Pos: 2B-1   Ht: 6'0" Wt: 170 Born: 1/8/1977 Age: 29

Year	Team	Lg	G	AB	H	2B	3B	HR	(Hm	Rd)	TB	R	RBI	RC	TBB	IBB	SO	HBP	SH	SF	SB	CS	SB%	GDP	Avg	OBP	Slg
1998	Auburn	A-	40	144	44	13	1	4	(-	-)	71	34	24	32	25	1	38	5	1	1	16	3	.84	0	.306	.423	.493
1999	Kissim	A+	124	472	109	20	4	6	(-	-)	155	70	48	59	68	0	118	12	9	2	17	10	.63	3	.231	.341	.328
2000	RdRck	AA	120	373	87	14	3	6	(-	-)	125	50	44	48	48	0	99	17	2	1	5	5	.50	1	.233	.346	.335
2001	RdRck	AA	103	387	117	34	2	10	(-	-)	185	78	60	73	45	1	91	14	7	4	17	7	.71	2	.302	.391	.478

Year	Team	Lg	G	AB	H	2B	3B	HR	(Hm	Rd)	TB	R	RBI	RC	TBB	IBB	SO	HBP	SH	SF	SB	CS	SB%	GDP	Avg	OBP	Slg
2001	NewOrl	AAA	4	16	5	1	0	1	(-	-)	9	3	3	3	0	0	5	1	0	1	1	0	1.00	0	.313	.333	.563
2002	NewOrl	AAA	101	300	82	15	3	7	(-	-)	124	47	40	44	27	0	79	6	5	3	7	2	.78	4	.273	.342	.413
2003	NewOrl	AAA	102	315	76	16	4	3	(-	-)	109	34	25	32	21	3	71	4	9	1	3	3	.50	3	.241	.296	.346
2004	RdRck	AA	112	392	95	20	2	7	(-	-)	140	61	48	48	34	1	81	17	4	4	14	4	.78	7	.242	.327	.357
2005	Angels	R	3	10	0	0	0	0	(-	-)	0	0	0	0	0	0	6	0	0	0	0	0	-	0	.000	.000	.000
2005	Ark	AA	9	26	5	2	0	1	(-	-)	10	4	2	1	1	0	6	0	0	1	0	1	.00	0	.192	.214	.385
2005	Salt Lk	AAA	56	176	42	12	2	3	(-	-)	67	31	19	27	31	0	39	3	5	2	6	3	.67	2	.239	.358	.381
2003	HOU	NL	6	5	1	0	0	1	(1	0)	4	1	1	1	0	0	2	0	0	0	0	0	-	0	.200	.200	.800
2005	LAA	AL	1	1	0	0	0	0	(0	0)	0	0	0	0	0	0	0	0	0	0	0	0	-	0	.000	.000	.000
2 ML YEARS			7	6	1	0	0	1	(1	0)	4	1	1	1	0	0	2	0	0	0	0	0	-	0	.167	.167	.667

Hideki Matsui

Bats: L **Throws:** R **Pos:** LF-115; CF-28; DH-19; RF-4; PH-1   **Ht:** 6'2" **Wt:** 210 **Born:** 6/12/1974 **Age:** 32

Year	Team	Lg	G	AB	H	2B	3B	HR	(Hm	Rd)	TB	R	RBI	RC	TBB	IBB	SO	HBP	SH	SF	SB	CS	SB%	GDP	Avg	OBP	Slg
2003	NYA	AL	163	623	179	42	1	16	(9	7)	271	82	106	96	63	5	86	3	0	6	2	2	.50	25	.287	.353	.435
2004	NYA	AL	162	584	174	34	2	31	(18	13)	305	109	108	117	88	2	103	3	0	5	3	0	1.00	11	.298	.390	.522
2005	NYA	AL	162	629	192	45	3	23	(15	8)	312	108	116	109	63	7	78	3	0	8	2	2	.50	16	.305	.367	.496
3 ML YEARS			487	1836	545	121	6	70	(42	28)	888	299	330	322	214	14	267	9	0	19	7	4	.64	52	.297	.370	.484

Kazuo Matsui

Bats: B **Throws:** R **Pos:** 2B-71; PH-19   **Ht:** 5'10" **Wt:** 183 **Born:** 10/23/1975 **Age:** 30

Year	Team	Lg	G	AB	H	2B	3B	HR	(Hm	Rd)	TB	R	RBI	RC	TBB	IBB	SO	HBP	SH	SF	SB	CS	SB%	GDP	Avg	OBP	Slg
1995	Seibu	Jap	69	204	45	9	1	2	(-	-)	62	25	15	18	7	-	26	0	7	1	21	1	.95	4	.221	.245	.304
1996	Seibu	Jap	130	473	134	22	5	1	(-	-)	169	51	29	59	14	-	93	3	26	2	50	9	.85	2	.283	.307	.357
1997	Seibu	Jap	135	576	178	23	13	7	(-	-)	248	91	63	98	44	-	89	5	18	2	62	15	.81	4	.309	.362	.431
1998	Seibu	Jap	135	575	179	38	5	9	(-	-)	254	92	58	99	55	-	89	1	6	4	43	14	.75	10	.311	.370	.442
1999	Seibu	Jap	135	539	178	29	4	15	(-	-)	260	87	67	106	56	-	75	0	8	6	32	7	.82	7	.330	.389	.482
2000	Seibu	Jap	135	550	177	40	11	23	(-	-)	308	99	90	117	46	-	60	2	6	7	26	3	.90	8	.322	.372	.560
2001	Seibu	Jap	140	552	170	28	2	24	(-	-)	274	94	76	106	46	-	83	6	4	5	26	0	1.00	13	.308	.365	.496
2002	Seibu	Jap	140	582	193	46	6	36	(-	-)	359	119	87	136	53	-	112	4	9	3	33	11	.75	3	.332	.389	.617
2003	Seibu	Jap	140	587	179	36	4	33	(-	-)	322	104	84	115	55	-	124	4	3	6	13	10	.57	4	.305	.365	.549
2005	Mets	R	3	9	4	0	0	1	(-	-)	7	3	3	3	1	0	3	1	0	0	0	0	-	0	.444	.545	.778
2005	Bnghtn	AA	3	9	4	1	0	0	(-	-)	5	4	0	2	1	0	1	0	0	0	2	0	1.00	0	.444	.500	.556
2005	Bklyn	A-	1	2	0	0	0	0	(-	-)	0	0	1	0	2	0	0	0	0	0	0	0	-	0	.000	.400	.000
2004	NYN	NL	114	460	125	32	2	7	(4	3)	182	65	44	63	40	4	97	2	5	2	14	3	.82	9	.272	.331	.396
2005	NYN	NL	87	267	68	9	4	3	(1	2)	94	31	24	27	14	1	43	5	5	4	6	1	.86	2	.255	.300	.352
2 ML YEARS			201	727	193	41	6	10	(5	5)	276	96	68	90	54	5	140	7	10	6	20	4	.83	5	.265	.320	.380

Daisuke Matsuzaka

Pitches: R **Bats:** R **Pos:** P   **Ht:** 5'11" **Wt:** 187 **Born:** 9/13/1980 **Age:** 25

	HOW MUCH HE PITCHED						WHAT HE GAVE UP												THE RESULTS							
Year Team Lg	G	GS	CG	GF	IP	BFP	H	R	ER	HR	SH	SF	HB	TBB	IBB	SO	WP	Bk	W	L	Pct	ShO	Sv-Op	Hld	ERC	ERA
1999 Seibu Jap	25	18	6	1	180.0	743	124	55	52	14	-	-	8	87	-	151	6	-	16	5	.762	2	0--	-	2.65	2.60
2000 Seibu Jap	27	18	6	2	167.2	727	132	85	74	12	-	-	4	95	-	144	2	-	14	7	.667	2	1--	-	3.27	3.97
2001 Seibu Jap	33	20	12	1	240.1	1004	184	104	96	27	-	-	8	117	-	214	9	-	15	15	.500	2	0--	-	3.26	3.60
2002 Seibu Jap	14	9	2	0	73.1	302	60	30	30	13	-	-	7	15	-	78	2	-	6	2	.750	0	0--	-	3.08	3.68
2003 Seibu Jap	29	19	8	1	194.0	801	165	71	61	13	-	-	9	63	3	215	4	0	16	7	.696	2	0--	-	2.88	2.83
2004 Seibu Jap	23	23	10	0	143.1	605	127	50	47	7	-	-	6	42	-	127	5	-	10	6	.625	0	0--	-	2.75	2.95
2005 Seibu Jap	28	28	15	0	215.0	974	172	63	55	13	-	-	-	49	-	226			14	13	.519	3	0--	-	1.91	2.30

Mike Matthews

Pitches: L **Bats:** L **Pos:** RP-6   **Ht:** 6'2" **Wt:** 175 **Born:** 10/24/1973 **Age:** 32

	HOW MUCH HE PITCHED						WHAT HE GAVE UP												THE RESULTS							
Year Team Lg	G	GS	CG	GF	IP	BFP	H	R	ER	HR	SH	SF	HB	TBB	IBB	SO	WP	Bk	W	L	Pct	ShO	Sv-Op	Hld	ERC	ERA
2005 Norfolk* AAA	5	3	0	0	9.2	51	14	13	13	1	0	1	0	8	0	6	0	0	0	1	.000	0	0--	-	8.50	12.10
2000 STL NL	14	0	0	4	9.1	54	15	12	12	2	0	0	1	10	2	8	0	0	0	0	-	0	0-0	2	11.83	11.57
2001 STL NL	51	10	0	7	89.0	368	74	32	32	11	4	1	4	33	4	72	4	1	3	4	.429	0	1-3	3	3.34	3.24
2002 2 Tms NL	47	0	0	10	45.2	205	43	23	20	5	2	4	2	29	3	34	5	1	2	1	.667	0	0-2	4	4.84	3.94
2003 SD NL	77	0	0	20	64.2	281	65	34	32	4	3	5	4	29	5	44	4	0	6	4	.600	0	0-3	16	4.20	4.45
2004 CIN NL	35	0	0	6	30.0	137	31	22	21	7	1	1	2	16	1	15	4	1	2	1	.667	0	0-0	5	6.01	6.30
2005 NYN NL	6	0	0	0	5.0	28	9	6	6	0	1	2	0	4	1	2	2	0	1	0	1.000	0	0-0	0	9.25	10.80
02 StL NL	43	0	0	10	41.2	184	40	21	18	5	2	4	2	22	2	32	5	0	2	1	.667	0	0-2	4	4.64	3.89
02 Mil NL	4	0	0	0	4.0	21	3	2	2	0	0	0	0	7	1	2	0	1	0	0	-	0	0-0	0	6.63	4.50
6 ML YEARS	230	10	0	47	243.2	1073	237	129	123	29	11	13	13	121	16	175	19	3	14	10	.583	0	1-8	30	4.57	4.54

Gary Matthews Jr.

Bats: B **Throws:** R **Pos:** CF-97; RF-22; LF-5; PH-4; PR-3; DH-1   **Ht:** 6'3" **Wt:** 210 **Born:** 8/25/1974 **Age:** 31

Year	Team	Lg	G	AB	H	2B	3B	HR	(Hm	Rd)	TB	R	RBI	RC	TBB	IBB	SO	HBP	SH	SF	SB	CS	SB%	GDP	Avg	OBP	Slg
2005	Frisco*	AA	1	5	2	0	0	0	(-	-)	2	0	1	0	0	0	1	0	0	0	0	0	-	0	.400	.400	.400
1999	Norfolk*	AA	23	36	8	0	0	0	(0	0)	8	4	7	4	9	0	9	0	0	0	2	0	1.00	1	.222	.378	.222
2000	CHN	NL	80	158	30	1	2	4	(2	2)	47	24	14	13	15	1	28	1	1	0	3	0	1.00	1	.190	.264	.297
2001	2 Tms	NL	152	405	92	15	2	14	(4	10)	153	63	44	51	60	2	100	1	5	1	8	5	.62	8	.227	.328	.378

Year	Team	Lg	G	AB	H	2B	3B	HR	(Hm	Rd)	TB	R	RBI	RC	TBB	IBB	SO	HBP	SH	SF	SB	CS	SB%	GDP	Avg	OBP	Slg
2002	2 Tms		111	345	95	25	3	7	(6	1)	147	54	38	55	43	1	69	1	5	4	15	5	.75	4	.275	.354	.426
2003	2 Tms		144	468	116	31	2	6	(3	3)	169	71	42	51	43	0	95	2	0	0	12	8	.60	8	.248	.314	.361
2004	TEX	AL	87	280	77	17	1	11	(7	4)	129	37	36	48	33	5	64	1	0	3	5	1	.83	1	.275	.350	.461
2005	TEX	AL	131	475	121	25	5	17	(8	9)	207	72	55	63	47	1	90	0	1	3	9	2	.82	11	.255	.320	.436
01	ChC	NL	106	258	56	9	1	9	(2	7)	94	41	30	31	38	2	55	1	5	0	5	3	.63	4	.217	.320	.364
01	Pit	NL	46	147	36	6	1	5	(2	3)	59	22	14	20	22	0	45	0	0	1	3	2	.60	4	.245	.341	.401
02	NYM	NL	2	1	0	0	0	0	(0	0)	0	0	0	0	0	0	0	0	0	0	0	0	-	0	.000	.000	.000
02	Bal	AL	109	344	95	25	3	7	(6	1)	147	54	38	55	43	1	69	1	5	4	15	5	.75	4	.276	.355	.427
03	Bal	AL	41	162	33	12	1	2	(2	0)	53	21	20	15	9	0	29	1	0	0	0	3	.00	4	.204	.250	.327
03	SD	NL	103	306	83	19	1	4	(1	3)	116	50	22	36	34	0	66	1	0	0	12	5	.71	4	.271	.346	.379
7 ML YEARS			728	2167	539	114	15	59	(30	29)	860	325	236	285	250	10	455	6	12	11	54	21	.72	35	.249	.327	.397

Joe Mauer

Bats: L **Throws:** R **Pos:** C-116; DH-13; PH-7 **Ht:** 6'4" **Wt:** 220 **Born:** 4/19/1983 **Age:** 23

Year	Team	Lg	G	AB	H	2B	3B	HR	(Hm	Rd)	TB	R	RBI	RC	TBB	IBB	SO	HBP	SH	SF	SB	CS	SB%	GDP	Avg	OBP	Slg
2001	Elizab	R+	32	110	44	6	2	0	(-	-)	54	14	14	26	19	0	10	1	0	0	4	0	1.00	5	.400	.492	.491
2002	QuadC	A	110	411	124	23	1	4	(-	-)	161	58	62	64	61	4	42	2	0	2	0	0	-	16	.302	.393	.392
2003	FtMyrs	A+	62	233	78	13	1	1	(-	-)	96	25	44	37	24	3	24	1	0	3	3	0	1.00	11	.335	.395	.412
2003	NwBrit	AA	73	276	94	17	1	4	(-	-)	125	48	41	48	25	4	25	5	0	4	0	0	-	10	.341	.400	.453
2004	FtMyrs	A+	2	6	4	0	0	0	(-	-)	4	0	2	2	2	1	2	0	0	0	0	0	-	1	.667	.750	.667
2004	Roch	AAA	5	19	6	3	0	0	(-	-)	9	1	2	2	1	0	4	0	0	1	0	0	-	1	.316	.333	.474
2004	MIN	AL	35	107	33	8	1	6	(4	2)	61	18	17	21	11	0	14	1	0	3	1	0	1.00	1	.308	.369	.570
2005	MIN	AL	131	489	144	26	2	9	(4	5)	201	61	55	78	61	12	64	1	0	9	13	1	.93	9	.294	.372	.411
2 ML YEARS			166	596	177	34	3	15	(8	7)	262	79	72	99	72	12	78	2	0	6	14	1	.93	10	.297	.371	.440

Darrell May

Pitches: L **Bats:** L **Pos:** RP-15; SP-9 **Ht:** 6'2" **Wt:** 184 **Born:** 6/13/1972 **Age:** 34

Year	Team	Lg	G	GS	CG	GF	IP	BFP	H	R	ER	HR	SH	SF	HB	TBB	IBB	SO	WP	Bk	W	L	Pct	ShO	Sv-Op	Hld	ERC	ERA
2005	Clmbs*	AAA	10	7	0	1	58.1	247	67	29	27	6	1	2	0	5	0	39	0	0	6	2	.750	0	0- -	-	3.59	4.17
1995	ATL	NL	2	0	0	1	4.0	21	10	5	5	0	0	1	0	0	0	1	0	0	0	0	-	0	0-0	1	11.41	11.25
1996	2 Tms		10	2	0	2	11.1	60	18	13	12	6	0	2	1	6	0	6	0	0	0	1	.000	0	0-0	1	12.24	9.53
1997	ANA	AL	29	2	0	7	51.2	234	56	31	30	6	3	4	0	25	2	42	2	0	2	1	.667	0	0-1	2	4.87	5.23
2002	KC	AL	30	21	2	3	131.1	579	144	83	78	28	3	5	1	50	3	95	2	0	4	10	.286	1	0-1	0	5.35	5.35
2003	KC	AL	35	32	2	1	210.0	868	197	98	88	31	5	6	2	53	1	115	5	0	10	8	.556	1	0-1	0	3.50	3.77
2004	KC	AL	31	31	3	0	186.0	832	234	130	116	38	1	9	2	55	4	120	2	0	9	19	.321	1	0-0	0	5.94	5.61
2005	2 Tms		24	9	0	9	66.1	302	87	51	50	14	1	2	0	23	1	35	0	0	1	4	.200	0	0-0	0	6.54	6.78
96	Pit	NL	5	2	0	0	8.2	47	15	10	9	5	0	0	1	4	0	5	0	0	0	1	.000	0	0-0	1	13.48	9.35
96	Cal	AL	5	0	0	2	2.2	13	3	3	3	1	0	2	0	2	0	1	0	0	0	0	-	0	0-0	0	8.41	10.13
05	SD	NL	22	8	0	9	59.1	264	73	38	37	10	1	2	0	20	1	32	0	0	1	3	.250	0	0-0	0	5.67	5.61
05	NYY	AL	2	1	0	0	7.0	38	14	13	13	4	0	0	0	3	0	3	0	0	0	1	.000	0	0-0	0	15.02	16.71
7 ML YEARS			161	97	7	23	660.2	2896	746	411	379	123	13	29	6	212	11	414	11	0	26	43	.377	3	0-3	3	5.11	5.16

Joe Mays

Pitches: R **Bats:** B **Pos:** SP-26; RP-5 **Ht:** 6'1" **Wt:** 185 **Born:** 12/10/1975 **Age:** 30

Year	Team	Lg	G	GS	CG	GF	IP	BFP	H	R	ER	HR	SH	SF	HB	TBB	IBB	SO	WP	Bk	W	L	Pct	ShO	Sv-Op	Hld	ERC	ERA
1999	MIN	AL	49	20	2	8	171.0	746	179	92	83	24	7	6	2	67	2	115	6	0	6	11	.353	1	0-0	2	4.62	4.37
2000	MIN	AL	31	28	2	1	160.1	723	193	105	99	20	3	5	2	67	1	102	11	0	7	15	.318	1	0-0	0	5.59	5.56
2001	MIN	AL	34	34	4	0	233.2	957	205	87	82	25	8	8	5	64	2	123	11	0	17	13	.567	2	0-0	0	3.05	3.16
2002	MIN	AL	17	17	1	0	95.1	418	113	60	57	14	2	2	2	25	0	38	6	0	4	8	.333	1	0-0	0	4.99	5.38
2003	MIN	AL	31	21	0	4	130.0	576	159	92	91	21	3	3	4	39	2	50	3	0	8	8	.500	0	0-1	1	5.55	6.30
2005	MIN	AL	31	26	1	1	156.0	690	203	109	98	23	5	3	3	41	1	59	4	0	6	10	.375	1	0-0	0	5.78	5.65
6 ML YEARS			193	146	10	14	946.1	4110	1052	545	510	127	28	27	18	303	8	487	41	0	48	65	.425	6	0-1	3	4.72	4.85

Paul McAnulty

Bats: L **Throws:** R **Pos:** PH-16; LF-6; 1B-1 **Ht:** 5'10" **Wt:** 220 **Born:** 2/24/1981 **Age:** 25

Year	Team	Lg	G	AB	H	2B	3B	HR	(Hm	Rd)	TB	R	RBI	RC	TBB	IBB	SO	HBP	SH	SF	SB	CS	SB%	GDP	Avg	OBP	Slg
2002	Idaho	R+	67	235	89	29	0	8	(-	-)	142	56	51	68	49	2	43	4	0	3	7	2	.78	5	.379	.488	.604
2003	FtWyn	A	133	455	124	27	0	7	(-	-)	172	48	73	71	67	2	82	9	2	9	5	3	.63	7	.273	.370	.378
2004	Lk Els	A+	133	495	147	36	3	23	(-	-)	258	98	87	107	88	3	106	4	0	4	3	1	.75	5	.297	.404	.521
2005	Mobile	AA	79	298	84	17	2	10	(-	-)	135	39	42	52	34	3	66	7	0	3	5	2	.71	3	.282	.365	.453
2005	Portlnd	AAA	38	151	52	15	0	6	(-	-)	85	27	27	33	16	0	29	0	0	1	0	0	-	3	.344	.405	.563
2005	SD	NL	22	24	5	0	0	0	(0	0)	5	4	0	1	3	1	7	1	1	0	1	0	1.00	0	.208	.321	.208

Macay McBride

Pitches: L **Bats:** L **Pos:** RP-23 **Ht:** 5'11" **Wt:** 210 **Born:** 10/24/1982 **Age:** 23

Year	Team	Lg	G	GS	CG	GF	IP	BFP	H	R	ER	HR	SH	SF	HB	TBB	IBB	SO	WP	Bk	W	L	Pct	ShO	Sv-Op	Hld	ERC	ERA
2001	Braves	R	13	11	0	0	55.0	239	51	30	23	0	2	2	4	23	1	67	8	0	4	4	.500	0	0- -	-	3.26	3.76
2002	Macon	A	25	25	2	0	157.1	639	119	49	37	6	2	3	1	48	1	138	13	1	12	8	.600	1	0- -	-	2.06	2.12
2003	MrtlBh	A+	27	27	1	0	164.2	707	164	63	54	5	0	0	4	49	0	139	4	0	9	8	.529	0	0- -	-	3.22	2.95
2004	Grnville	AA	38	12	0	5	103.1	469	113	59	51	9	5	5	0	46	0	102	5	0	1	7	.125	0	0- -	-	4.58	4.44

Year	Team	Lg	G	GS	CG	GF	IP	BFP	H	R	ER	HR	SH	SF	HB	TBB	IBB	SO	WP	Bk	W	L	Pct	ShO	Sv-Op	Hld	ERC	ERA
									HOW MUCH HE PITCHED				WHAT HE GAVE UP									THE RESULTS					
2005	Missi	AA	6	3	0	1	24.2	107	21	11	10	2	1	0	0	12	1	16	1	0	3	1	.750	0	0--	-	3.32	3.65
2005	Rchmd	AAA	25	1	0	6	43.2	202	49	27	21	5	7	1	2	22	2	47	0	0	1	5	.167	0	2--	-	5.34	4.33
2005	ATL	NL	23	0	0	4	14.0	68	18	11	9	0	1	1	0	7	0	22	2	0	1	0	1.000	0	1-1	6	5.12	5.79

Brian McCann

Bats: L **Throws:** R **Pos:** C-57; PH-2 **Ht:** 6'3" **Wt:** 210 **Born:** 2/20/1984 **Age:** 22

Year	Team	Lg	G	AB	H	2B	3B	HR	(Hm	Rd)	TB	R	RBI	RC	TBB	IBB	SO	HBP	SH	SF	SB	CS	SB%	GDP	Avg	OBP	Slg
2002	Braves	R	29	100	22	5	0	2	(-	-)	33	9	11	10	10	0	22	1	0	1	0	0	-	0	.220	.295	.330
2003	Rome	A	115	424	123	31	3	12	(-	-)	196	40	71	65	24	2	73	2	0	3	7	4	.64	5	.290	.329	.462
2004	MrtlBth	A+	110	382	106	35	0	15	(-	-)	186	44	65	63	31	4	54	4	0	1	2	2	.50	5	.277	.337	.487
2005	Missi	AA	48	166	44	13	2	6	(-	-)	79	27	26	29	25	3	26	2	0	5	2	3	.40	2	.265	.359	.476
2005	ATL	NL	59	180	50	7	0	5	(2	3)	72	20	23	25	18	5	26	1	4	1	1	1	.50	5	.278	.345	.400

Brandon McCarthy

Pitches: R **Bats:** R **Pos:** SP-10; RP-2 **Ht:** 6'5" **Wt:** 210 **Born:** 7/7/1983 **Age:** 22

Year	Team	Lg	G	GS	CG	GF	IP	BFP	H	R	ER	HR	SH	SF	HB	TBB	IBB	SO	WP	Bk	W	L	Pct	ShO	Sv-Op	Hld	ERC	ERA
2002	WhSox	R	14	14	0	0	78.1	328	78	40	24	6	2	1	2	15	1	79	5	3	4	4	.500	0	0--	-	3.13	2.76
2003	Gr Falls	R+	16	15	1	0	101.0	423	105	49	41	7	2	0	3	15	0	125	3	3	9	4	.692	0	0--	-	3.18	3.65
2004	WinSa	A+	8	8	0	0	52.0	190	31	12	12	3	2	1	1	3	0	60	1	2	6	0	1.000	0	0--	-	1.06	2.08
2004	Knapol	A-	15	15	3	0	94.0	383	80	41	38	10	1	2	7	21	0	113	3	2	8	5	.615	1	0--	-	2.94	3.64
2004	Brham	AA	4	4	0	0	26.0	107	23	10	10	2	0	1	2	6	1	29	1	0	3	1	.750	0	0--	-	2.90	3.46
2005	Charltt	AAA	20	19	1	1	119.1	494	104	53	52	16	3	1	2	32	0	130	5	1	7	7	.500	1	0--	-	3.11	3.92
2005	CHA	AL	12	10	0	0	67.0	277	62	30	30	13	1	1	2	17	0	48	1	1	3	2	.600	0	0-0	0	3.83	4.03

David McCarty

Bats: R **Throws:** L **Pos:** 1B-12; PR-3; PH-2; LF-1 **Ht:** 6'5" **Wt:** 215 **Born:** 11/23/1969 **Age:** 36

Year	Team	Lg	G	AB	H	2B	3B	HR	(Hm	Rd)	TB	R	RBI	RC	TBB	IBB	SO	HBP	SH	SF	SB	CS	SB%	GDP	Avg	OBP	Slg
1993	MIN	AL	98	350	75	15	2	2	(2	0)	100	36	21	18	19	0	80	1	1	0	2	6	.25	13	.214	.257	.286
1994	MIN	AL	44	131	34	8	2	1	(1	0)	49	21	12	15	7	1	32	5	0	0	2	1	.67	3	.260	.322	.374
1995	2 Tms		37	75	17	4	1	0	(0	0)	23	11	6	6	6	0	22	1	0	1	1	1	.50	1	.227	.289	.307
1996	SF	NL	91	175	38	3	0	6	(5	1)	59	16	24	17	18	0	43	2	0	2	2	1	.67	5	.217	.294	.337
1998	SEA	AL	8	18	5	0	0	1	(1	0)	8	1	2	4	5	0	4	0	0	0	1	0	1.00	0	.278	.435	.444
2000	KC	AL	103	270	75	14	2	12	(6	6)	129	34	53	41	22	1	68	0	0	3	0	0	-	6	.278	.329	.478
2001	KC	AL	98	200	50	10	0	7	(5	2)	81	26	26	26	24	1	45	1	1	4	0	0	-	8	.250	.328	.405
2002	2 Tms	AL	25	66	9	1	0	2	(0	2)	16	5	4	2	6	0	19	2	0	0	0	0	-	1	.136	.230	.242
2003	2 Tms	AL	24	53	18	5	0	1	(1	0)	26	6	8	10	3	0	14	0	0	1	0	0	-	0	.340	.368	.491
2004	BOS	AL	91	151	39	8	1	4	(2	2)	61	24	17	17	14	0	40	2	0	1	1	0	1.00	5	.258	.327	.404
2005	BOS	AL	13	4	2	0	0	0	(0	0)	2	2	2	2	2	0	0	0	0	0	0	0	-	0	.500	.667	.500
95	Min	AL	25	55	12	3	1	0	(0	0)	17	10	4	4	4	0	18	1	0	1	0	1	.00	1	.218	.279	.309
95	SF	NL	12	20	5	1	0	0	(0	0)	6	1	2	2	2	0	4	0	0	0	1	0	1.00	0	.250	.318	.300
02	KC	AL	13	32	3	1	0	1	(0	1)	7	3	2	0	2	0	10	0	0	0	0	0	-	1	.094	.147	.219
02	TB	AL	12	34	6	0	0	1	(0	1)	9	2	2	2	4	0	9	2	0	0	0	0	-	0	.176	.300	.265
03	Oak	AL	8	26	7	2	0	0	(0	0)	9	2	2	2	1	0	7	0	0	1	0	0	-	0	.269	.286	.346
03	Bos	AL	16	27	11	3	0	1	(1	0)	17	4	6	8	2	0	7	0	0	0	0	0	-	0	.407	.448	.630
	11 ML YEARS		632	1493	362	68	8	36	(23	13)	554	182	175	158	126	3	367	14	2	12	9	9	.50	42	.242	.305	.371

Scott McClain

Bats: R **Throws:** R **Pos:** PH-6; 1B-4; 3B-3 **Ht:** 6'4" **Wt:** 220 **Born:** 5/19/1972 **Age:** 34

Year	Team	Lg	G	AB	H	2B	3B	HR	(Hm	Rd)	TB	R	RBI	RC	TBB	IBB	SO	HBP	SH	SF	SB	CS	SB%	GDP	Avg	OBP	Slg
1990	Bluefld	R+	40	107	21	2	0	4	(-	-)	35	20	15	13	22	0	35	2	0	4	2	3	.40	1	.196	.333	.327
1991	Kane	A	45	81	18	0	0	0	(-	-)	18	9	4	8	17	0	25	0	1	0	1	1	.50	4	.222	.357	.222
1991	Bluefld	R+	41	149	39	5	0	0	(-	-)	44	16	24	16	14	0	39	3	0	1	5	3	.63	3	.262	.335	.295
1992	Kane	A	96	316	84	12	2	3	(-	-)	109	43	30	46	48	1	62	6	6	1	7	4	.64	5	.266	.372	.345
1993	Frdrck	A+	133	427	111	22	2	9	(-	-)	164	65	54	67	70	0	88	6	3	2	10	6	.63	6	.260	.370	.384
1994	Bowie	AA	133	427	103	29	1	11	(-	-)	167	71	58	64	72	2	89	1	2	7	6	3	.67	14	.241	.347	.391
1995	Roch	AAA	61	189	50	9	1	8	(-	-)	85	32	22	30	23	0	34	1	1	2	0	1	.00	5	.265	.344	.450
1995	Bowie	AA	70	259	72	14	1	13	(-	-)	127	41	61	45	25	1	44	3	0	4	2	1	.67	13	.278	.344	.490
1996	Roch	AAA	131	463	130	23	4	17	(-	-)	212	76	69	79	61	1	109	1	0	7	8	6	.57	6	.281	.361	.458
1997	Norfolk	AAA	127	429	120	29	2	21	(-	-)	216	71	64	82	64	5	93	2	1	8	1	3	.25	8	.280	.370	.503
1998	Drham	AAA	126	472	141	35	0	34	(-	-)	278	91	109	106	66	5	113	2	1	3	6	2	.75	9	.299	.385	.589
1999	Drham	AAA	137	533	134	33	1	28	(-	-)	253	106	104	90	73	1	156	3	0	6	4	2	.67	11	.251	.341	.475
2000	ColSpr	AAA	123	438	121	25	3	25	(-	-)	227	76	87	84	62	2	89	6	0	6	8	9	.47	11	.276	.369	.518
2005	Iowa	AAA	121	423	123	27	2	30	(-	-)	244	75	93	88	45	2	84	4	0	9	1	1	.50	17	.291	.358	.577
1998	TB	AL	9	20	2	0	0	0	(	)	2	2	0	0	2	0	6	1	0	0	0	0	-	0	.100	.217	.100
2005	CHN	NL	13	14	2	1	0	0	(0	0)	3	1	1	0	2	0	2	0	0	1	0	0	-	1	.143	.250	.214
	2 ML YEARS		22	34	4	1	0	0	(0	0)	5	3	1	0	4	0	8	1	0	1	0	0	-	1	.118	.231	.147

160

Seth McClung

Pitches: R **Bats:** R **Pos:** SP-17; RP-17 **Ht:** 6'6" **Wt:** 235 **Born:** 2/7/1981 **Age:** 25

Year	Team	Lg	G	GS	CG	GF	IP	BFP	H	R	ER	HR	SH	SF	HB	TBB	IBB	SO	WP	Bk	W	L	Pct	ShO	Sv-Op	Hld	ERC	ERA
1999	Princtn	R+	13	10	0	0	45.2	244	53	47	39	3	0	1	9	48	0	46	20	0	2	4	.333	0	0--	-	8.19	7.69
2000	HudVal	A-	8	8	0	0	43.2	186	37	18	9	0	1	2	3	17	0	38	6	1	2	2	.500	0	0--	-	2.76	1.85
2000	CtnSC	A	6	6	0	0	31.0	145	30	14	11	0	1	0	3	19	0	26	8	0	2	1	.667	0	0--	-	4.21	3.19
2001	CtnSC	A	28	28	2	0	164.1	683	142	72	51	6	4	1	11	53	1	165	3	2	10	11	.476	1	0--	-	2.88	2.79
2002	Bkrsfld	A+	7	7	0	0	37.0	158	35	16	12	1	1	0	2	11	0	48	0	1	3	2	.600	0	0--	-	3.05	2.92
2002	Orlndo	AA	20	19	0	1	114.0	533	138	74	68	12	2	7	9	53	0	64	7	1	5	7	.417	0	0--	-	5.90	5.37
2004	CtnSC	A	3	3	0	0	9.1	39	5	0	0	0	2	0	0	4	0	10	0	0	0	0	-	0	0--	-	1.31	0.00
2004	Mont	AA	3	3	0	0	13.1	55	10	7	7	3	1	1	1	4	0	8	0	0	1	1	.500	0	0--	-	3.36	4.73
2004	Drham	AAA	11	0	0	2	13.2	58	10	5	5	0	0	0	0	7	0	12	2	0	2	1	.667	0	0--	-	2.35	3.29
2005	Drham	AAA	6	3	0	0	18.1	84	23	12	8	1	0	0	1	6	1	19	5	0	2	0	1.000	0	0--	-	4.96	3.93
2003	TB	AL	12	5	0	2	38.2	167	33	23	23	6	1	1	3	25	1	25	2	0	4	1	.800	0	0-0	1	5.11	5.35
2005	TB	AL	34	17	0	3	109.1	501	106	85	80	20	0	5	7	62	1	92	6	0	7	11	.389	0	0-1	2	5.34	6.59
	2 ML YEARS		46	22	0	5	148.0	668	139	108	103	26	1	6	10	87	2	117	8	0	11	12	.478	0	0-1	3	5.28	6.26

Quinton McCracken

Bats: B **Throws:** R **Pos:** PH-80; CF-46; LF-11; RF-2; PR-2 **Ht:** 5'7" **Wt:** 173 **Born:** 8/16/1970 **Age:** 35

Year	Team	Lg	G	AB	H	2B	3B	HR	(Hm	Rd)	TB	R	RBI	RC	TBB	IBB	SO	HBP	SH	SF	SB	CS	SB%	GDP	Avg	OBP	Slg
1995	COL	NL	3	1	0	0	0	0	(0	0)	0	0	0	0	0	0	1	0	0	0	0	0		0	.000	.000	.000
1996	COL	NL	124	283	82	13	6	3	(2	1)	116	50	40	43	32	4	62	1	12	1	17	6	.74	5	.290	.363	.410
1997	COL	NL	147	325	95	11	1	3	(1	2)	117	69	36	47	42	0	62	1	6	1	28	11	.72	6	.292	.374	.360
1998	TB	AL	155	614	179	38	7	7	(5	2)	252	77	59	83	41	1	107	3	9	8	19	10	.66	12	.292	.335	.410
1999	TB	AL	40	148	37	6	1	1	(1	0)	48	20	18	13	14	0	23	1	1	1	6	5	.55	7	.250	.317	.324
2000	TB	AL	15	31	4	0	0	0	(0	0)	4	5	2	0	6	0	4	0	0	0	0	1	.00	3	.129	.270	.129
2001	MIN	AL	24	64	14	2	2	0	(0	0)	20	7	3	5	5	0	13	0	1	0	0	1	.00	2	.219	.275	.313
2002	ARI	NL	123	349	108	27	8	3	(1	2)	160	60	40	62	32	0	68	2	13	4	5	4	.56	3	.309	.367	.458
2003	ARI	NL	115	203	46	5	2	0	(0	0)	55	17	16	16	15	2	34	0	5	3	5	1	.83	4	.227	.276	.271
2004	2 Tms		74	176	48	11	1	2	(2	0)	67	26	13	20	15	0	27	0	3	1	3	5	.38	3	.273	.328	.381
2005	ARI	NL	134	215	51	4	3	1	(1	0)	64	23	13	20	23	4	35	1	6	1	4	0	1.00	3	.237	.313	.298
04	Sea	AL	19	20	3	0	0	0	(0	0)	3	6	0	0	2	0	4	0	1	0	1	1	.50	1	.150	.227	.150
04	Ari	NL	55	156	45	11	1	2	(2	0)	64	20	13	20	13	0	23	0	2	1	2	4	.33	2	.288	.341	.410
	11 ML YEARS		954	2409	664	117	31	20	(13	7)	903	354	242	309	225	11	436	9	56	20	87	44	.66	49	.276	.337	.375

John McDonald

Bats: R **Throws:** R **Pos:** SS-54; 2B-13; PH-9; 3B-1; PR-1 **Ht:** 5'11" **Wt:** 175 **Born:** 9/24/1974 **Age:** 31

Year	Team	Lg	G	AB	H	2B	3B	HR	(Hm	Rd)	TB	R	RBI	RC	TBB	IBB	SO	HBP	SH	SF	SB	CS	SB%	GDP	Avg	OBP	Slg
1999	CLE	AL	18	21	7	0	0	0	(0	0)	7	2	0	1	0	0	3	0	0	0	0	1	.00	1	.333	.333	.333
2000	CLE	AL	9	9	4	0	0	0	(0	0)	4	0	0	2	0	0	1	0	0	0	0	0	-	0	.444	.444	.444
2001	CLE	AL	17	22	2	1	0	0	(0	0)	3	1	0	0	1	0	7	1	1	0	0	0	-	0	.091	.167	.136
2002	CLE	AL	93	264	66	11	3	1	(0	1)	86	35	12	24	10	0	50	5	7	2	3	0	1.00	4	.250	.288	.326
2003	CLE	AL	82	214	46	9	1	1	(0	1)	60	21	14	18	11	0	31	2	4	2	3	3	.50	4	.215	.258	.280
2004	CLE	AL	66	93	19	5	1	2	(0	2)	32	17	7	6	4	0	11	0	3	0	0	0	-	2	.204	.237	.344
2005	2 Tms	AL	68	166	46	6	1	0	(0	0)	54	18	16	19	11	0	24	2	3	2	6	1	.86	4	.277	.326	.325
05	Tor	AL	37	93	27	3	0	0	(0	0)	30	8	12	13	6	0	12	2	3	2	5	0	1.00	3	.290	.340	.323
05	Det	AL	31	73	19	3	1	0	(0	0)	24	10	4	6	5	0	12	0	0	0	1	1	.50	3	.260	.308	.329
	7 ML YEARS		353	789	190	32	6	4	(0	4)	246	94	49	70	37	0	127	10	18	6	12	5	.71	18	.241	.281	.312

Marshall McDougall

Bats: R **Throws:** R **Pos:** 3B-5; PR-5; RF-3; PH-3; 2B-2; DH-2; SS-1 **Ht:** 6'1" **Wt:** 200 **Born:** 12/19/1978 **Age:** 27

Year	Team	Lg	G	AB	H	2B	3B	HR	(Hm	Rd)	TB	R	RBI	RC	TBB	IBB	SO	HBP	SH	SF	SB	CS	SB%	GDP	Avg	OBP	Slg
2000	Vancvr	A-	27	102	28	4	2	0	(-	-)	36	17	11	15	19	0	19	0	0	1	5	3	.63	1	.275	.385	.353
2001	Visalia	A+	134	534	137	43	7	12	(-	-)	230	79	84	79	46	2	110	7	7	4	14	2	.88	9	.257	.321	.431
2002	MhVlly	A-	2	5	1	0	0	0	(-	-)	1	0	0	0	1	0	1	0	0	0	0	0	-	0	.200	.333	.200
2002	Akron	AA	7	18	7	2	0	1	(-	-)	12	6	4	6	6	0	2	0	0	0	0	0	-	0	.389	.542	.667
2002	Mdland	AA	84	323	98	22	5	9	(-	-)	157	60	56	60	38	3	57	1	3	4	7	4	.64	5	.303	.374	.486
2003	Frisco	AA	110	418	108	16	3	13	(-	-)	169	61	69	61	43	0	68	2	0	4	18	3	.86	12	.258	.328	.404
2003	Okla	AAA	30	111	30	4	2	2	(-	-)	44	11	9	16	13	0	21	0	0	3	1	1	.50	2	.270	.341	.396
2004	Frisco	AA	18	73	23	7	0	2	(-	-)	36	17	14	13	8	0	12	0	0	0	0	0	-	3	.315	.383	.493
2004	Okla	AAA	94	354	100	23	0	19	(-	-)	180	48	69	63	35	0	80	1	2	0	2	1	.67	8	.282	.349	.508
2005	Okla	AAA	57	223	76	16	2	11	(-	-)	129	40	64	63	30	1	45	0	1	2	5	0	1.00		.341	.416	.578
2005	TEX	AL	18	18	3	1	0	0	(0	0)	4	3	0	0	0	0	10	0	0	0	0	0	-	1	.167	.167	.222

Joe McEwing

Bats: R **Throws:** R **Pos:** 3B-29; 1B-20; PH-17; 2B-11; PR-10; SS-6; DH-5; LF-3; CF-1; RF-1 **Ht:** 5'11" **Wt:** 170 **Born:** 10/19/72 **Age:** 33

Year	Team	Lg	G	AB	H	2B	3B	HR	(Hm	Rd)	TB	R	RBI	RC	TBB	IBB	SO	HBP	SH	SF	SB	CS	SB%	GDP	Avg	OBP	Slg
2005	Omha*	AAA	5	18	3	1	0	0	(-	-)	4	4	1	1	4	0	2	0	0	0	0	0		1	.167	.318	.222
1998	STL	NL	10	20	4	1	0	0	(0	0)	5	5	1	1	1	0	3	1	1	0	0	1	.00	0	.200	.273	.250
1999	STL	NL	152	513	141	28	4	9	(5	4)	204	65	44	70	41	8	87	6	9	5	7	4	.64	3	.275	.333	.398
2000	NYN	NL	87	153	34	14	1	2	(1	1)	56	20	19	14	5	0	29	1	8	2	3	1	.75	2	.222	.248	.366
2001	NYN	NL	116	283	80	17	3	8	(3	5)	127	41	30	44	17	0	57	10	6	3	8	5	.62	2	.283	.342	.449
2002	NYN	NL	105	196	39	8	1	3	(2	1)	58	22	26	14	9	0	50	3	3	3	4	4	.50	2	.199	.242	.296

Year	Team	Lg	G	AB	H	2B	3B	HR	(Hm	Rd)	TB	R	RBI	RC	TBB	IBB	SO	HBP	SH	SF	SB	CS	SB%	GDP	Avg	OBP	Slg
									BATTING												BASERUNNING				AVERAGES		
2003	NYN	NL	119	278	67	11	0	1	(0	1)	81	31	16	26	25	4	57	3	6	1	3	0	1.00	6	.241	.309	.291
2004	NYN	NL	75	138	35	3	1	1	(1	0)	43	17	16	17	9	4	32	0	6	1	4	1	.80	2	.254	.297	.312
2005	KC	AL	83	180	43	7	0	1	(0	1)	53	16	6	11	6	0	35	0	5	0	4	4	.50	5	.239	.263	.294
	8 ML YEARS		747	1761	443	89	10	25	(12	13)	627	217	158	197	113	16	350	24	44	15	33	20	.62	18	.252	.303	.356

Dustin McGowan

Pitches: R Bats: R Pos: SP-7; RP-6   **Ht: 6'3" Wt: 220 Born: 3/24/1982 Age: 24**

Year	Team	Lg	G	GS	CG	GF	IP	BFP	H	R	ER	HR	SH	SF	HB	TBB	IBB	SO	WP	Bk	W	L	Pct	ShO	Sv-Op	Hld	ERC	ERA
				HOW MUCH HE PITCHED						WHAT HE GAVE UP											THE RESULTS						
2000	MdHat	R+	8	8	0	0	25.0	126	26	21	18	2	1	5	3	25	0	19	8	0	0	3	.000	0	0- -	-	7.09	6.48
2001	Auburn	A-	15	14	0	0	67.0	307	57	33	28	1	1	2	4	49	0	80	16	0	3	6	.333	0	0- -	-	4.05	3.76
2003	Dnedin	A+	14	14	1	0	75.2	314	62	29	24	1	2	0	4	25	0	66	9	0	5	6	.455	1	0- -	-	2.47	2.85
2003	NwHav	AA	14	14	1	0	76.2	327	78	28	27	1	5	1	4	19	0	72	5	1	7	0	1.000	0	0- -	-	3.15	3.17
2004	Ham	AA	6	6	0	0	31.0	132	24	14	14	4	0	0	0	15	0	29	2	0	2	0	1.000	0	0- -	-	3.30	4.06
2005	Dnedin	A+	5	5	0	0	21.0	89	21	12	10	2	1	0	2	5	0	20	0	1	0	1	.000	0	0- -	-	3.79	4.29
2005	Ham	AA	6	6	0	0	35.0	150	35	16	13	6	1	3	1	10	0	33	1	0	0	2	.000	0	0- -	-	4.16	3.34
2005	TOR	AL	13	7	0	2	45.1	205	49	34	32	7	0	4	7	17	0	34	7	0	1	3	.250	0	0-0	1	5.47	6.35

Nate McLouth

Bats: L Throws: R Pos: CF-21; PH-14; RF-8   **Ht: 5'11" Wt: 185 Born: 10/28/1981 Age: 24**

Year	Team	Lg	G	AB	H	2B	3B	HR	(Hm	Rd)	TB	R	RBI	RC	TBB	IBB	SO	HBP	SH	SF	SB	CS	SB%	GDP	Avg	OBP	Slg
									BATTING												BASERUNNING				AVERAGES		
2001	Hickory	A	96	351	100	17	5	12	(-	-)	163	59	54	65	43	6	54	7	2	3	21	5	.81	5	.285	.371	.464
2002	Lynbrg	A+	114	393	96	23	4	9	(-	-)	154	58	46	55	41	3	48	8	6	5	20	7	.74	12	.244	.324	.392
2003	Lynbrg	A+	117	440	132	27	2	6	(-	-)	181	85	33	80	55	2	68	7	5	1	40	4	.91	4	.300	.386	.411
2004	Altna	AA	133	515	166	40	4	8	(-	-)	238	93	73	98	48	2	62	8	14	7	31	7	.82	8	.322	.384	.462
2005	Indy	AAA	110	397	118	20	3	5	(-	-)	159	64	39	66	39	1	58	7	5	7	34	8	.81	10	.297	.364	.401
2005	PIT	NL	41	109	28	6	0	5	(2	3)	49	20	12	9	3	0	20	5	2	1	2	0	1.00	3	.257	.305	.450

Dallas McPherson

Bats: L Throws: R Pos: 3B-60; PH-1   **Ht: 6'4" Wt: 230 Born: 7/23/1980 Age: 25**

Year	Team	Lg	G	AB	H	2B	3B	HR	(Hm	Rd)	TB	R	RBI	RC	TBB	IBB	SO	HBP	SH	SF	SB	CS	SB%	GDP	Avg	OBP	Slg
									BATTING												BASERUNNING				AVERAGES		
2001	Provo	R+	31	124	49	11	0	5	(-	-)	75	30	29	30	12	0	22	0	0	0	1	0	1.00	2	.395	.449	.605
2002	CRpds	A	132	499	138	24	3	15	(-	-)	213	71	88	86	78	3	128	7	0	2	30	6	.83	9	.277	.381	.427
2003	RCuca	A+	77	292	90	21	6	18	(-	-)	177	65	59	66	41	2	79	6	0	0	12	6	.67	4	.308	.404	.606
2003	Ark	AA	28	102	32	9	1	5	(-	-)	58	22	27	22	19	4	25	1	0	0	4	0	1.00	4	.314	.426	.569
2004	Ark	AA	68	262	84	17	6	20	(-	-)	173	53	69	63	34	5	74	4	0	2	6	5	.55	2	.321	.404	.660
2004	Salt Lk	AAA	67	259	81	19	8	20	(-	-)	176	54	57	57	23	4	95	1	0	1	6	3	.67	5	.313	.370	.680
2005	Angels	R	3	9	2	1	1	0	(-	-)	5	1	2	1	0	0	5	0	0	0	0	0	-	0	.222	.222	.556
2005	RCuca	A+	5	16	7	2	0	2	(-	-)	15	3	5	6	3	2	4	1	0	0	1	1	.50	0	.438	.550	.938
2005	Salt Lk	AAA	14	54	15	1	2	6	(-	-)	38	8	19	12	7	0	20	0	0	2	1	2	.33	1	.278	.349	.704
2004	ANA	AL	16	40	9	1	0	3	(2	1)	19	5	6	5	3	0	17	0	0	0	1	0	1.00	0	.225	.279	.475
2005	LAA	AL	61	205	50	14	2	8	(6	2)	92	29	26	28	14	0	64	1	0	0	3	3	.50	5	.244	.295	.449
	2 ML YEARS		77	245	59	15	2	11	(8	3)	111	34	32	33	17	0	81	1	0	0	4	3	.57	5	.241	.293	.453

Brian Meadows

Pitches: R Bats: R Pos: RP-65   **Ht: 6'4" Wt: 220 Born: 11/21/1975 Age: 30**

Year	Team	Lg	G	GS	CG	GF	IP	BFP	H	R	ER	HR	SH	SF	HB	TBB	IBB	SO	WP	Bk	W	L	Pct	ShO	Sv-Op	Hld	ERC	ERA
				HOW MUCH HE PITCHED						WHAT HE GAVE UP											THE RESULTS						
1998	FLA	NL	31	31	1	0	174.1	772	222	106	101	20	14	4	3	46	3	88	5	1	11	13	.458	0	0-0	0	5.29	5.21
1999	FLA	NL	31	31	0	0	178.1	795	214	117	111	31	16	8	5	57	5	72	4	1	11	15	.423	0	0-0	0	5.51	5.60
2000	2 Tms		33	32	2	0	196.1	869	234	119	112	32	7	5	8	64	6	79	3	0	13	10	.565	0	0-0	0	5.52	5.13
2001	KC	AL	10	10	0	0	50.1	224	73	41	39	12	1	2	1	12	2	21	1	0	1	6	.143	0	0-0	0	7.47	6.97
2002	PIT	NL	11	11	0	0	62.2	259	62	29	27	7	2	0	1	14	8	31	2	0	1	6	.143	0	0-0	0	3.29	3.88
2003	PIT	NL	34	7	0	11	76.1	329	91	45	40	8	2	1	1	11	2	38	4	0	2	1	.667	0	1-1	5	4.12	4.72
2004	PIT	NL	68	0	0	15	78.0	323	76	40	31	7	6	5	0	19	7	46	5	0	2	4	.333	0	1-2	13	3.13	3.58
2005	PIT	NL	65	0	0	9	74.2	326	84	42	38	8	3	9	0	21	7	44	3	0	3	1	.750	0	0-2	7	4.15	4.58
00	SD	NL	22	22	0	0	124.2	565	150	80	74	24	7	2	8	50	6	53	3	0	7	8	.467	0	0-0	0	6.23	5.34
00	KC	AL	11	10	2	0	71.2	304	84	39	38	8	0	3	0	14	0	26	0	0	6	2	.750	0	0-0	0	4.35	4.77
	8 ML YEARS		283	122	3	35	891.0	3897	1056	539	499	125	51	34	19	244	40	419	27	2	44	56	.440	0	2-5	25	4.94	5.04

Gil Meche

Pitches: R Bats: R Pos: SP-26; RP-3   **Ht: 6'3" Wt: 200 Born: 9/8/1978 Age: 27**

Year	Team	Lg	G	GS	CG	GF	IP	BFP	H	R	ER	HR	SH	SF	HB	TBB	IBB	SO	WP	Bk	W	L	Pct	ShO	Sv-Op	Hld	ERC	ERA
				HOW MUCH HE PITCHED						WHAT HE GAVE UP											THE RESULTS						
1999	SEA	AL	16	15	0	0	85.2	375	73	48	45	9	5	3	2	57	1	47	1	0	8	4	.667	0	0-0	0	4.47	4.73
2000	SEA	AL	15	15	1	0	85.2	363	75	37	36	7	5	4	1	40	0	60	2	0	4	4	.500	1	0-0	0	3.60	3.78
2003	SEA	AL	32	32	1	0	186.1	785	187	97	95	30	3	5	3	63	2	130	7	0	15	13	.536	0	0-0	0	4.39	4.59
2004	SEA	AL	23	23	1	0	127.2	565	139	73	71	21	1	3	5	47	0	99	4	0	7	7	.500	1	0-0	0	5.06	5.01
2005	SEA	AL	29	26	0	2	143.1	638	153	92	81	18	1	5	2	72	1	83	4	0	10	8	.556	0	0-0	0	5.15	5.09
	5 ML YEARS		115	111	3	2	628.2	2726	627	347	328	85	15	20	13	279	4	419	18	0	44	36	.550	2	0-0	0	4.60	4.70

Jim Mecir

Pitches: R **Bats:** B **Pos:** RP-52   **Ht:** 6'1" **Wt:** 230 **Born:** 5/16/1970 **Age:** 36

			HOW MUCH HE PITCHED						WHAT HE GAVE UP												THE RESULTS							
Year	Team	Lg	G	GS	CG	GF	IP	BFP	H	R	ER	HR	SH	SF	HB	TBB	IBB	SO	WP	Bk	W	L	Pct	ShO	Sv-Op	Hld	ERC	ERA
1995	SEA	AL	2	0	0	1	4.2	21	5	1	0	0	0	0	0	2	0	3	0	0	0	0	-	0	0-0	0	3.75	0.00
1996	NYA	AL	26	0	0	10	40.1	185	42	24	23	6	5	4	0	23	4	38	6	0	1	1	.500	0	0-0	0	5.10	5.13
1997	NYA	AL	25	0	0	11	33.2	142	36	23	22	5	0	1	2	10	1	25	1	0	0	4	.000	0	0-1	1	4.73	5.88
1998	TB	AL	68	0	0	23	84.0	343	68	30	29	6	3	2	3	33	5	77	2	0	7	2	.778	0	0-3	14	2.95	3.11
1999	TB	AL	17	0	0	3	20.2	91	15	7	6	0	0	2	1	14	0	15	0	0	0	1	.000	0	0-2	6	3.05	2.61
2000	2 Tms	AL	63	0	0	17	85.0	352	70	31	28	4	1	2	2	36	2	70	2	0	10	3	.769	0	5-13	21	2.95	2.96
2001	OAK	AL	54	0	0	14	63.0	264	54	25	24	4	3	0	1	26	7	61	2	0	2	8	.200	0	3-8	17	3.00	3.43
2002	OAK	AL	61	0	0	10	67.2	304	68	36	32	5	4	4	4	29	4	53	4	1	6	4	.600	0	1-6	20	4.05	4.26
2003	OAK	AL	41	0	0	7	37.0	165	40	25	23	4	3	2	1	16	1	25	1	0	2	3	.400	0	1-2	12	4.77	5.59
2004	OAK	AL	65	0	0	17	47.2	212	45	21	19	5	1	0	4	19	2	49	1	0	0	5	.000	0	2-7	21	3.94	3.59
2005	FLA	NL	52	0	0	13	43.1	184	39	17	15	2	3	2	5	17	2	34	0	0	1	4	.200	0	0-4	13	3.55	3.12
00	TB	AL	38	0	0	10	49.2	199	35	17	17	2	1	1	1	22	0	33	0	0	7	2	.778	0	1-4	11	2.44	3.08
00	Oak	AL	25	0	0	7	35.1	153	35	14	11	2	0	1	1	14	2	37	2	0	3	1	.750	0	4-9	10	3.71	2.80
11 ML YEARS			474	0	0	126	527.0	2263	482	240	221	41	23	19	23	225	28	450	19	1	29	35	.453	0	12-46	125	3.64	3.77

Brandon Medders

Pitches: R **Bats:** R **Pos:** RP-27   **Ht:** 6'1" **Wt:** 191 **Born:** 1/26/1980 **Age:** 26

			HOW MUCH HE PITCHED						WHAT HE GAVE UP												THE RESULTS							
Year	Team	Lg	G	GS	CG	GF	IP	BFP	H	R	ER	HR	SH	SF	HB	TBB	IBB	SO	WP	Bk	W	L	Pct	ShO	Sv-Op	Hld	ERC	ERA
2001	Lancst	A+	31	0	0	15	41.0	164	26	8	6	1	2	1	2	15	3	53	2	1	1	2	.333	0	3-	-	1.70	1.32
2002	Lancst	A+	43	12	0	25	98.2	443	111	73	59	9	2	3	8	36	1	104	10	3	4	8	.333	0	15-	-	4.87	5.38
2003	ElPaso	AA	56	0	0	37	69.1	299	65	37	34	3	10	5	0	26	6	72	3	1	5	3	.625	0	7-	-	3.04	4.41
2004	Tucsn	AAA	11	0	0	3	12.2	57	15	7	6	3	1	0	0	4	1	17	0	0	0	0	-	0	0-	-	5.54	4.26
2005	Tucsn	AAA	36	0	0	24	36.1	158	31	11	10	3	2	1	1	18	3	44	6	0	3	2	.600	0	8-	-	3.43	2.48
2005	ARI	NL	27	0	0	10	30.1	122	21	6	6	2	0	2	1	11	0	31	1	0	4	1	.800	0	0-0	2	2.25	1.78

Adam Melhuse

Bats: B **Throws:** R **Pos:** C-24; PH-14; DH-8   **Ht:** 6'2" **Wt:** 200 **Born:** 3/27/1972 **Age:** 34

			BATTING																			BASERUNNING				AVERAGES		
Year	Team	Lg	G	AB	H	2B	3B	HR	(Hm	Rd)	TB	R	RBI	RC	TBB	IBB	SO	HBP	SH	SF	SB	CS	SB%	GDP	Avg	OBP	Slg
2000	2 Tms	NL	24	24	4	0	1	0	(0	0)	6	3	4	2	3	0	6	0	0	0	0	0	-	1	.167	.259	.250
2001	COL	NL	40	71	13	2	0	1	(0	1)	18	5	8	4	6	0	18	0	0	2	1	0	1.00	1	.183	.241	.254
2003	OAK	AL	40	77	23	7	0	5	(2	3)	45	13	14	15	9	0	19	0	0	0	0	0	-	2	.299	.372	.584
2004	OAK	AL	69	214	55	11	0	11	(3	8)	99	23	31	21	16	1	47	0	1	0	0	1	.00	4	.257	.309	.463
2005	OAK	AL	39	97	24	7	0	2	(1	1)	37	11	12	12	5	0	28	0	0	0	0	0	-	2	.247	.284	.381
00	LA	NL	1	1	0	0	0	0	(0	0)	0	0	0	0	0	0	1	0	0	0	0	0	-	0	.000	.000	.000
00	Col	NL	23	23	4	0	1	0	(0	0)	6	3	4	2	3	0	5	0	0	0	0	0	-	0	.174	.269	.261
5 ML YEARS			212	483	119	27	1	19	(6	13)	205	55	69	54	39	1	118	0	1	2	1	1	.50	10	.246	.302	.424

Kevin Mench

Bats: R **Throws:** R **Pos:** LF-119; RF-41; PH-3; CF-1; DH-1   **Ht:** 6'0" **Wt:** 215 **Born:** 1/7/1978 **Age:** 28

			BATTING																			BASERUNNING				AVERAGES		
Year	Team	Lg	G	AB	H	2B	3B	HR	(Hm	Rd)	TB	R	RBI	RC	TBB	IBB	SO	HBP	SH	SF	SB	CS	SB%	GDP	Avg	OBP	Slg
2002	TEX	AL	110	366	95	20	2	15	(8	7)	164	52	60	59	31	0	83	8	2	5	1	1	.50	4	.260	.327	.448
2003	TEX	AL	38	125	40	12	0	2	(1	1)	58	15	11	23	10	0	17	3	0	1	1	1	.50	2	.320	.381	.464
2004	TEX	AL	125	438	122	30	3	26	(14	12)	236	69	71	72	33	2	63	6	0	4	0	0	-	6	.279	.335	.539
2005	TEX	AL	150	557	147	33	3	25	(13	12)	261	71	73	75	50	4	68	5	0	3	4	3	.57	6	.264	.328	.469
4 ML YEARS			423	1486	404	95	8	68	(36	32)	719	207	215	229	124	6	231	22	2	13	6	5	.55	18	.272	.334	.484

Ramiro Mendoza

Pitches: R **Bats:** R **Pos:** RP-1   **Ht:** 6'2" **Wt:** 195 **Born:** 6/15/1972 **Age:** 34

			HOW MUCH HE PITCHED						WHAT HE GAVE UP												THE RESULTS							
Year	Team	Lg	G	GS	CG	GF	IP	BFP	H	R	ER	HR	SH	SF	HB	TBB	IBB	SO	WP	Bk	W	L	Pct	ShO	Sv-Op	Hld	ERC	ERA
2005	Yanks*	R	2	2	0	0	5.0	19	3	1	0	0	0	0	0	1	0	3	0	0	0	0	-	0	0-	-	1.11	0.00
2005	Clmbs*	AAA	8	0	0	3	12.0	47	4	2	1	0	0	0	1	0	1	15	1	1	0	1	.000	0	1-	-	0.46	0.75
1996	NYA	AL	12	11	0	0	53.0	249	80	43	40	5	1	1	4	10	1	34	2	1	4	5	.444	0	0-0	0	6.42	6.79
1997	NYA	AL	39	15	0	9	133.2	578	157	67	63	15	3	5	5	28	2	82	2	1	8	6	.571	0	2-4	4	4.52	4.24
1998	NYA	AL	41	14	1	6	130.1	548	131	50	47	9	6	7	9	30	6	56	3	0	10	2	.833	1	1-4	5	3.44	3.25
1999	NYA	AL	53	6	0	15	123.2	536	141	68	59	13	6	4	3	27	3	80	2	0	9	9	.500	0	3-6	4	4.19	4.29
2000	NYA	AL	14	9	1	0	65.2	281	66	32	31	9	1	2	4	20	1	30	0	0	7	4	.636	1	0-1	0	4.21	4.25
2001	NYA	AL	56	2	0	11	100.2	401	89	44	42	9	4	3	2	23	3	70	2	0	8	4	.667	0	6-8	13	2.84	3.75
2002	NYA	AL	62	0	0	14	91.2	394	102	43	35	8	1	4	2	16	2	61	1	0	8	4	.667	0	4-8	12	3.70	3.44
2003	BOS	AL	37	5	0	8	66.2	311	98	51	50	10	1	4	5	20	4	36	1	0	3	5	.375	0	0-1	3	7.22	6.75
2004	BOS	AL	27	0	0	12	30.2	119	25	12	12	3	0	0	1	7	1	13	1	0	2	1	.667	0	0-0	3	2.63	3.52
2005	NYA	AL	1	0	0	1	1.0	5	2	2	2	1	0	0	0	0	0	1	0	0	0	0	-	0	0-0	0	16.28	18.00
10 ML YEARS			342	62	2	76	797.0	3422	891	412	381	82	23	30	35	181	23	463	14	3	59	40	.596	2	16-32	44	4.20	4.30

Frank Menechino

Bats: R Throws: R Pos: 2B-26; DH-24; PH-17; 3B-9; SS-1   Ht: 5'8" Wt: 198 Born: 1/7/1971 Age: 35

								BATTING													BASERUNNING				AVERAGES		
Year	Team	Lg	G	AB	H	2B	3B	HR	(Hm	Rd)	TB	R	RBI	RC	TBB	IBB	SO	HBP	SH	SF	SB	CS	SB%	GDP	Avg	OBP	Slg
1999	OAK	AL	9	9	2	0	0	0	(0	0)	2	0	0	0	0	0	4	0	0	0	0	0	-	0	.222	.222	.222
2000	OAK	AL	66	145	37	9	1	6	(3	3)	66	31	26	22	20	0	45	1	1	2	1	4	.20	1	.255	.345	.455
2001	OAK	AL	139	471	114	22	2	12	(4	8)	176	82	60	69	79	0	97	19	3	6	2	3	.40	13	.242	.369	.374
2002	OAK	AL	38	132	27	7	0	3	(2	1)	43	22	15	14	20	0	32	1	0	1	0	0	-	4	.205	.312	.326
2003	OAK	AL	43	83	16	0	0	2	(1	1)	22	10	9	11	19	1	16	4	2	1	0	0	-	2	.193	.364	.265
2004	2 Tms	AL	85	269	74	13	4	9	(6	3)	122	40	26	43	37	1	52	4	1	0	0	2	.00	5	.275	.371	.454
2005	TOR	AL	70	148	32	7	0	4	(4	0)	51	22	13	12	25	0	33	6	1	0	0	1	.00	3	.216	.352	.345
04	Oak	AL	13	33	3	0	0	0	(0	0)	3	0	1	0	1	0	8	1	0	0	0	0	-	2	.091	.143	.091
04	Tor	AL	72	236	71	13	4	9	(6	3)	119	40	25	43	36	1	44	3	1	0	0	2	.00	3	.301	.400	.504
	7 ML YEARS		450	1257	302	58	7	36	(20	16)	482	207	149	171	200	2	279	35	8	10	3	10	.23	28	.240	.358	.383

Kent Mercker

Pitches: L Bats: L Pos: RP-78   Ht: 6'2" Wt: 195 Born: 2/1/1968 Age: 38

			HOW MUCH HE PITCHED						WHAT HE GAVE UP											THE RESULTS						
Year	Team	Lg	G	GS	CG	GF	IP	BFP	H	R	ER	HR	SH	SF	HB	TBB	IBB	SO	WP	Bk	W	L	Pct	ShO	Sv-Op	Hld	ERC	ERA
1989	ATL	NL	2	1	0	1	4.1	26	8	6	6	0	0	0	0	6	0	4	0	0	0	0	-	0	0-0	0	13.19	12.46
1990	ATL	NL	36	0	0	28	48.1	211	43	22	17	6	1	2	2	24	3	39	2	0	4	7	.364	0	7-10	6	4.04	3.17
1991	ATL	NL	50	4	0	28	73.1	306	56	23	21	5	2	2	1	35	3	62	4	1	5	3	.625	0	6-8	3	2.88	2.58
1992	ATL	NL	53	0	0	18	68.1	289	51	27	26	4	4	1	3	35	1	49	6	0	3	2	.600	0	6-9	6	2.99	3.42
1993	ATL	NL	43	6	0	9	66.0	283	52	24	21	2	0	0	2	36	3	59	5	1	3	1	.750	0	0-3	4	3.02	2.86
1994	ATL	NL	20	17	2	0	112.1	461	90	46	43	16	4	3	0	45	3	111	4	1	9	4	.692	1	0-0	1	3.27	3.45
1995	ATL	NL	29	26	0	1	143.0	622	140	73	66	16	8	7	3	61	2	102	6	2	7	8	.467	0	0-0	4	4.19	4.15
1996	2 Tms	AL	24	12	0	2	69.2	329	83	60	54	13	3	6	3	38	2	29	3	1	4	6	.400	0	0-0	2	6.56	6.98
1997	CIN	NL	28	25	0	0	144.2	616	135	65	63	16	8	4	2	62	6	75	2	1	8	11	.421	0	0-0	0	3.91	3.92
1998	STL	NL	30	29	0	1	161.2	716	199	99	91	11	10	9	3	53	4	72	6	4	11	11	.500	0	0-0	0	4.96	5.07
1999	2 Tms	NL	30	23	0	2	129.1	589	148	85	69	16	8	4	3	64	3	81	3	1	8	5	.615	0	0-0	0	5.54	4.80
2000	ANA	AL	21	7	0	2	48.1	225	57	35	35	12	3	1	2	29	3	30	2	0	1	3	.250	0	0-0	1	7.35	6.52
2002	COL	NL	58	0	0	8	44.0	208	55	33	30	12	0	0	2	22	2	37	1	0	3	1	.750	0	0-3	9	7.45	6.14
2003	2 Tms	NL	67	0	0	15	55.1	242	46	16	12	6	6	1	0	32	4	48	4	1	0	2	.000	0	1-5	11	3.72	1.95
2004	CHN	NL	71	0	0	7	53.0	223	39	15	15	4	0	3	3	27	2	51	4	1	3	1	.750	0	0-3	16	3.07	2.55
2005	CHN	NL	78	0	0	23	61.2	265	64	27	25	8	4	2	3	19	4	45	1	0	3	1	.750	0	4-7	20	4.23	3.65
96	Bal	AL	14	12	0	0	58.0	283	73	56	50	12	3	4	3	35	1	22	3	1	3	6	.333	0	0-0	1	7.45	7.76
96	Cle	AL	10	0	0	2	11.2	46	10	4	4	1	0	2	0	3	1	7	0	0	1	0	1.000	0	0-0	2	2.65	3.09
99	StL	NL	25	18	0	2	103.2	476	125	73	59	16	8	3	2	51	3	64	3	1	6	5	.545	0	0-0	0	6.15	5.12
99	Bos	AL	5	5	0	0	25.2	113	23	12	10	0	0	1	1	13	0	17	0	0	2	0	1.000	0	0-0	0	3.29	3.51
03	Cin	NL	49	0	0	8	38.1	169	31	13	10	5	6	0	0	25	2	41	2	1	0	2	.000	0	0-3	10	4.09	2.35
03	Atl	NL	18	0	0	7	17.0	73	15	3	2	1	0	1	0	7	2	7	2	0	0	0	-	0	1-2	1	2.95	1.06
	16 ML YEARS		640	150	2	145	1283.1	5611	1266	656	594	147	61	45	32	588	45	894	53	14	72	66	.522	1	24-48	72	4.38	4.17

Cla Meredith

Pitches: R Bats: R Pos: RP-3   Ht: 6'0" Wt: 180 Born: 6/4/1983 Age: 23

			HOW MUCH HE PITCHED						WHAT HE GAVE UP											THE RESULTS						
Year	Team	Lg	G	GS	CG	GF	IP	BFP	H	R	ER	HR	SH	SF	HB	TBB	IBB	SO	WP	Bk	W	L	Pct	ShO	Sv-Op	Hld	ERC	ERA
2004	Srsota	A+	16	0	0	16	16.1	68	15	4	4	0	0	0	1	3	0	16	0	0	0	2	.000	0	12--	-	2.36	2.20
2004	Augsta	A	13	0	0	10	15.1	57	8	0	0	0	0	0	2	3	0	18	0	0	1	0	1.000	0	6--	-	1.18	0.00
2005	Portlnd	AA	12	0	0	11	15.0	53	5	0	0	0	1	0	1	3	1	12	0	0	1	0	1.000	0	9--	-	0.56	0.00
2005	Pwtckt	AAA	40	0	0	25	48.1	220	63	30	30	6	1	0	1	12	2	42	2	0	2	5	.286	0	10--	-	5.31	5.59
2005	Wilmg	A	1	0	0	0	1.0	4	1	0	0	0	0	0	0	0	0	2	0	0	0	0	-	0	0--	-	1.95	0.00
2005	BOS	AL	3	0	0	0	2.1	18	6	7	7	1	0	0	1	4	0	4	0	1	0	0	-	0	0-0	0	27.60	27.00

Lou Merloni

Bats: R Throws: R Pos: 3B-4; 1B-1   Ht: 5'10" Wt: 201 Born: 4/6/1971 Age: 35

								BATTING													BASERUNNING				AVERAGES		
Year	Team	Lg	G	AB	H	2B	3B	HR	(Hm	Rd)	TB	R	RBI	RC	TBB	IBB	SO	HBP	SH	SF	SB	CS	SB%	GDP	Avg	OBP	Slg
2005	Angels*	R	6	15	5	1	0	0	(-	-)	6	3	2	2	2	0	2	0	0	0	0	0	-	0	.333	.412	.400
2005	Salt Lk*	AAA	6	25	8	3	0	0	(-	-)	11	6	6	4	2	0	5	1	0	0	0	0	-	0	.320	.393	.440
1998	BOS	AL	39	96	27	6	0	1	(1	0)	36	10	15	13	7	1	20	2	1	0	1	0	1.00	1	.281	.343	.375
1999	BOS	AL	43	126	32	7	0	1	(0	1)	42	18	13	12	8	0	16	2	3	1	0	0	-	6	.254	.307	.333
2000	BOS	AL	40	128	41	11	2	0	(0	0)	56	10	18	17	4	1	22	1	4	2	1	0	1.00	6	.320	.341	.438
2001	BOS	AL	52	146	39	10	0	3	(0	3)	58	21	13	16	6	0	31	3	2	2	2	1	.67	6	.267	.306	.397
2002	BOS	AL	84	194	48	12	2	4	(1	3)	76	28	18	26	20	0	35	5	2	1	1	2	.33	4	.247	.332	.392
2003	2 Tms	AL	80	181	48	8	2	1	(1	0)	63	24	18	22	26	2	41	1	2	3	2	3	.40	1	.265	.355	.348
2004	CLE	AL	71	190	55	12	1	4	(1	3)	81	25	28	28	14	1	41	3	4	3	1	2	.33	9	.289	.343	.426
2005	LAA	AL	5	5	0	0	0	0	(0	0)	0	1	1	0	1	0	2	0	0	0	0	0	-	0	.000	.143	.000
03	SD	NL	65	151	41	7	2	1	(1	0)	55	20	17	19	22	2	33	1	2	3	2	3	.40	1	.272	.362	.364
03	Bos	AL	15	30	7	1	0	0	(0	0)	8	4	1	3	4	0	8	0	0	0	0	0	-	0	.233	.324	.267
	8 ML YEARS		414	1066	290	66	7	14	(4	10)	412	137	124	134	86	5	208	17	18	13	8	8	.50	37	.272	.332	.386

Jose Mesa

Pitches: R **Bats:** R **Pos:** RP-55   **Ht:** 6'3" **Wt:** 225 **Born:** 5/22/1966 **Age:** 40

			HOW MUCH HE PITCHED							WHAT HE GAVE UP												THE RESULTS						
Year	Team	Lg	G	GS	CG	GF	IP	BFP	H	R	ER	HR	SH	SF	HB	TBB	IBB	SO	WP	Bk	W	L	Pct	ShO	Sv-Op	Hld	ERC	ERA
1987	BAL	AL	6	5	0	0	31.1	143	38	23	21	7	0	0	0	15	0	17	4	0	1	3	.250	0	0-0	1	6.67	6.03
1990	BAL	AL	7	7	0	0	46.2	202	37	20	20	7	2	2	1	27	0	24	1	1	3	2	.600	0	0-0	0	3.21	3.86
1991	BAL	AL	23	23	2	0	123.2	566	151	86	82	11	5	4	3	62	2	64	3	0	6	11	.353	1	0-0	0	5.85	5.97
1992	2 Tms	AL	28	27	1	1	160.2	700	169	86	82	14	2	5	4	70	1	62	2	0	7	12	.368	1	0-0	0	4.57	4.59
1993	CLE	AL	34	33	3	0	208.2	897	232	122	114	21	9	9	7	62	2	118	8	2	10	12	.455	0	0-0	0	4.48	4.92
1994	CLE	AL	51	0	0	22	73.0	315	71	33	31	3	3	4	3	26	7	63	3	0	7	5	.583	0	2-6	8	3.31	3.82
1995	CLE	AL	62	0	0	57	64.0	250	49	9	8	3	4	2	0	17	2	58	5	0	3	0	1.000	0	46-48	0	2.06	1.13
1996	CLE	AL	69	0	0	60	72.1	304	69	32	30	6	2	2	3	28	4	64	4	0	2	7	.222	0	39-44	0	3.81	3.73
1997	CLE	AL	66	0	0	38	82.1	356	83	28	22	7	2	2	3	28	3	69	1	0	4	4	.500	0	16-21	9	3.83	2.40
1998	2 Tms		76	0	0	36	84.2	383	91	50	43	8	6	2	4	38	5	63	10	0	8	7	.533	0	1-4	13	4.68	4.57
1999	SEA	AL	68	0	0	60	68.2	325	84	42	38	11	2	4	4	40	4	42	7	0	3	6	.333	0	33-38	1	6.83	4.98
2000	SEA	AL	66	0	0	29	80.2	372	89	48	48	11	2	6	5	41	0	84	3	0	4	6	.400	0	1-3	11	5.60	5.36
2001	PHI	NL	71	0	0	59	69.1	291	65	26	18	4	2	3	2	20	2	59	2	1	3	3	.500	0	42-46	1	3.07	2.34
2002	PHI	NL	74	0	0	64	75.2	331	65	26	25	5	6	1	4	39	7	64	9	0	4	6	.400	0	45-54	0	3.51	2.97
2003	PHI	NL	61	0	0	47	58.0	273	71	44	42	7	1	0	1	31	2	45	3	0	5	7	.417	0	24-28	2	6.07	6.52
2004	PIT	NL	70	0	0	65	69.1	295	78	26	25	6	4	2	1	20	3	37	1	0	5	2	.714	0	43-48	0	4.31	3.25
2005	PIT	NL	55	0	0	48	56.2	257	61	30	30	7	8	6	3	26	3	37	2	0	2	8	.200	0	27-34	1	4.99	4.76
92	Bal	AL	13	12	0	1	67.2	300	77	41	39	9	0	3	2	27	1	22	2	0	3	8	.273	0	0-0	0	5.25	5.19
92	Cle	AL	15	15	1	0	93.0	400	92	45	43	5	2	2	2	43	0	40	0	0	4	4	.500	1	0-0	0	4.09	4.16
98	Cle	AL	44	0	0	18	54.0	244	61	36	31	7	2	2	4	20	3	35	2	0	3	4	.429	0	1-3	7	5.07	5.17
98	SF	NL	32	0	0	18	30.2	139	30	14	12	1	4	0	0	18	2	28	8	0	5	3	.625	0	0-1	6	3.99	3.52
	17 ML YEARS		887	95	6	586	1425.2	6260	1503	731	679	133	60	54	48	590	49	970	68	4	77	101	.433	2	319-374	47	4.48	4.29

Randy Messenger

Pitches: R **Bats:** R **Pos:** RP-29   **Ht:** 6'6" **Wt:** 247 **Born:** 8/13/1981 **Age:** 24

			HOW MUCH HE PITCHED							WHAT HE GAVE UP												THE RESULTS						
Year	Team	Lg	G	GS	CG	GF	IP	BFP	H	R	ER	HR	SH	SF	HB	TBB	IBB	SO	WP	Bk	W	L	Pct	ShO	Sv-Op	Hld	ERC	ERA
1999	Marlins	R	13	2	0	6	26.1	126	28	25	22	1	0	1	3	19	0	23	1	0	0	3	.000	0	2--	-	5.68	7.52
2000	Marlins	R	12	12	0	0	59.2	267	66	37	32	6	1	1	3	22	0	29	7	2	2	2	.500	0	0--	-	4.70	4.83
2001	BrvdCt	A+	18	18	0	0	92.2	412	99	55	42	3	1	3	5	35	0	42	3	0	7	4	.636	0	0--	-	4.04	4.08
2001	Kane	A	14	0	0	7	18.1	82	22	13	8	0	3	2	2	5	0	14	0	0	1	2	.667	0	0--	-	4.39	3.93
2002	Jupiter	A+	28	27	1	0	156.2	706	178	94	76	4	5	4	7	58	0	96	4	2	11	8	.579	0	0--	-	4.28	4.37
2003	Carlina	AA	29	23	0	3	113.2	529	137	83	69	7	2	0	3	51	1	78	9	0	5	7	.417	0	0--	-	5.15	5.46
2004	Carlina	AA	58	0	0	45	69.2	305	67	21	20	4	1	2	0	29	3	71	4	0	6	3	.667	0	21--	-	3.47	2.58
2005	Albq	AAA	39	0	0	15	48.2	209	46	25	21	5	1	1	2	17	1	35	1	0	4	2	.667	0	7--	-	3.68	3.88
2005	FLA	NL	29	0	0	8	37.0	178	39	22	22	5	2	3	0	30	7	29	1	0	0	0	-	0	0-0	2	5.91	5.35

Danny Miceli

Pitches: R **Bats:** R **Pos:** RP-19   **Ht:** 6'0" **Wt:** 216 **Born:** 9/9/1970 **Age:** 35

			HOW MUCH HE PITCHED							WHAT HE GAVE UP												THE RESULTS						
Year	Team	Lg	G	GS	CG	GF	IP	BFP	H	R	ER	HR	SH	SF	HB	TBB	IBB	SO	WP	Bk	W	L	Pct	ShO	Sv-Op	Hld	ERC	ERA
2005	ColSpr*	AAA	5	0	0	1	5.0	21	4	3	3	1	0	0	1	2	0	8	0	0	0	0	-	0	0--	-	4.59	5.40
1993	PIT	NL	9	0	0	1	5.1	25	6	3	3	0	0	0	0	3	0	4	0	1	0	0	-	0	0-0	0	4.53	5.06
1994	PIT	NL	28	0	0	9	27.1	121	28	19	18	5	1	2	2	11	2	27	2	0	2	1	.667	0	2-3	4	4.98	5.93
1995	PIT	NL	58	0	0	51	58.0	264	61	30	30	7	2	4	4	28	5	56	4	0	4	4	.500	0	21-27	2	4.93	4.66
1996	PIT	NL	44	9	0	17	85.2	398	99	65	55	15	3	7	3	45	5	66	9	0	2	10	.167	0	1-1	6	6.09	5.78
1997	DET	AL	71	0	0	24	82.2	357	77	49	46	13	5	3	1	38	4	79	3	0	3	2	.600	0	3-8	11	4.30	5.01
1998	SD	NL	67	0	0	18	72.2	302	64	28	26	6	3	2	1	27	4	70	5	1	10	5	.667	0	2-8	20	3.20	3.22
1999	SD	NL	66	0	0	28	68.2	296	67	39	34	7	4	2	2	36	5	59	2	0	4	5	.444	0	2-4	9	4.57	4.46
2000	FLA	NL	45	0	0	9	48.2	207	45	23	23	4	1	1	1	18	2	40	3	0	6	4	.600	0	0-3	11	3.42	4.25
2001	2 Tms	NL	51	0	0	15	45.0	199	47	29	24	7	2	2	0	16	2	48	4	0	2	5	.286	0	1-4	8	4.34	4.80
2002	TEX	AL	9	0	0	5	8.1	42	13	8	8	1	0	0	0	3	0	5	0	1	0	2	.000	0	0-1	0	7.11	8.64
2003	4 Tms	NL	57	0	0	16	70.1	294	59	27	25	13	3	0	2	25	3	58	4	1	2	4	.333	0	1-2	5	3.60	3.20
2004	HOU	NL	74	0	0	15	77.2	336	74	34	31	10	5	3	2	27	12	83	4	0	6	6	.500	0	2-8	24	3.58	3.59
2005	COL	NL	19	0	0	3	18.1	86	19	12	12	1	2	0	1	13	0	19	0	0	1	2	.333	0	0-2	5	5.37	5.89
01	Fla	NL	29	0	0	9	24.2	114	29	21	19	5	1	1	0	11	2	31	3	0	0	5	.000	0	0-3	8	5.80	6.93
01	Col	NL	22	0	0	6	20.1	85	18	8	5	2	1	1	0	5	0	17	1	0	2	0	1.000	0	1-1	0	2.77	2.21
03	Col	NL	14	0	0	1	20.2	95	24	13	13	7	1	0	1	9	1	18	1	0	0	2	.000	0	0-0	1	7.07	5.66
03	Cle	AL	13	0	0	4	15.0	61	9	4	2	1	0	0	0	6	1	19	1	0	1	1	.500	0	0-1	0	1.70	1.20
03	NYY	AL	7	0	0	3	4.2	22	4	3	3	2	0	0	0	3	0	1	0	0	0	0	-	0	1-1	1	6.21	5.79
03	Hou	NL	23	0	0	8	30.0	116	22	7	7	3	2	0	1	7	1	20	2	1	1	1	.500	0	0-0	3	2.22	2.10
	13 ML YEARS		598	9	0	211	668.2	2927	659	366	335	89	31	26	19	290	44	614	40	4	42	50	.457	0	35-71	103	4.34	4.51

Jason Michaels

Bats: R **Throws:** R **Pos:** CF-75; PH-32; LF-22; RF-13; PR-1   **Ht:** 6'0" **Wt:** 204 **Born:** 5/4/1976 **Age:** 30

			BATTING																	BASERUNNING				AVERAGES		
Year	Team	Lg	G	AB	H	2B	3B	HR	(Hm	Rd)	TB	R	RBI	RC	TBB	IBB	SO	HBP	SH	SF	SB	CS	SB%	GDP	Avg	OBP	Slg
2001	PHI	NL	6	6	1	0	0	0	(0	0)	1	0	1	0	0	0	2	0	0	0	0	0	-	0	.167	.167	.167
2002	PHI	NL	81	105	28	10	3	2	(0	2)	50	16	11	14	13	1	33	1	0	2	1	1	.50	1	.267	.347	.476
2003	PHI	NL	76	109	36	11	0	5	(1	4)	62	20	17	19	15	1	22	1	0	0	0	0	-	3	.330	.416	.569
2004	PHI	NL	115	299	82	12	0	10	(5	5)	124	44	40	47	42	1	80	2	0	3	2	2	.50	3	.274	.364	.415
2005	PHI	NL	105	289	88	16	2	4	(1	3)	120	54	31	47	44	1	45	4	2	4	3	3	.50	3	.304	.399	.415
	5 ML YEARS		383	808	235	49	5	21	(7	14)	357	134	100	127	114	4	182	8	2	9	6	6	.50	10	.291	.380	.442

Doug Mientkiewicz

Bats: L **Throws:** R **Pos:** 1B-83; PH-7   **Ht:** 6'2" **Wt:** 200 **Born:** 6/19/1974 **Age:** 32

Year	Team	Lg	G	AB	H	2B	3B	HR	(Hm	Rd)	TB	R	RBI	RC	TBB	IBB	SO	HBP	SH	SF	SB	CS	SB%	GDP	Avg	OBP	Slg
2005	Mets*	R	4	10	5	1	0	1	(-	-)	9	2	5	4	4	0	1	0	0	0	0	0	-	0	.500	.643	.900
2005	StLuci*	A+	8	27	7	4	0	0	(-	-)	11	3	2	5	7	0	7	0	0	0	0	0	-	0	.259	.412	.407
1998	MIN	AL	8	25	5	1	0	0	(0	0)	6	1	2	2	4	0	3	0	0	0	1	1	.50	0	.200	.310	.240
1999	MIN	AL	118	327	75	21	3	2	(0	2)	108	34	32	34	43	3	51	4	3	2	1	1	.50	13	.229	.324	.330
2000	MIN	AL	3	14	6	0	0	0	(0	0)	6	0	4	2	0	0	0	0	0	1	0	0	-	1	.429	.400	.429
2001	MIN	AL	151	543	166	39	1	15	(11	4)	252	77	74	96	67	6	92	9	0	7	2	6	.25	10	.306	.387	.464
2002	MIN	AL	143	467	122	29	1	10	(6	4)	183	60	64	76	74	8	69	6	0	7	1	2	.33	7	.261	.365	.392
2003	MIN	AL	142	487	146	38	1	11	(6	5)	219	67	65	89	74	4	55	5	2	6	4	1	.80	9	.300	.393	.450
2004	2 Tms	AL	127	391	93	24	1	6	(1	5)	137	47	35	46	48	2	56	4	2	2	2	3	.40	12	.238	.326	.350
2005	NYN	NL	87	275	66	13	0	11	(3	8)	112	36	29	28	32	7	39	2	2	2	0	1	.00	11	.240	.322	.407
04	Min	AL	78	284	70	18	0	5	(1	4)	103	34	25	34	38	2	38	3	2	1	2	2	.50	9	.246	.340	.363
04	Bos	AL	49	107	23	6	1	1	(0	1)	34	13	10	12	10	0	18	1	0	1	0	1	.00	3	.215	.286	.318
	8 ML YEARS		779	2529	679	165	7	55	(27	28)	1023	322	305	373	342	30	365	30	9	27	11	15	.42	63	.268	.359	.405

Aaron Miles

Bats: B **Throws:** R **Pos:** 2B-79; PH-24; SS-1; PR-1   **Ht:** 5'8" **Wt:** 170 **Born:** 12/15/1976 **Age:** 29

Year	Team	Lg	G	AB	H	2B	3B	HR	(Hm	Rd)	TB	R	RBI	RC	TBB	IBB	SO	HBP	SH	SF	SB	CS	SB%	GDP	Avg	OBP	Slg
2005	ColSpr*	AAA	8	32	7	0	1	0	(-	-)	9	6	1	2	0	0	3	1	1	0	1	0	1.00	0	.219	.242	.281
2003	CHA	AL	8	12	4	3	0	0	(0	0)	7	3	2	3	0	0	0	0	0	0	0	0	-	0	.333	.333	.583
2004	COL	NL	134	522	153	15	3	6	(4	2)	192	75	47	70	29	0	53	2	7	6	12	7	.63	12	.293	.329	.368
2005	COL	NL	99	324	91	12	3	2	(0	2)	115	37	28	42	8	1	38	4	10	1	4	2	.67	6	.281	.306	.355
	3 ML YEARS		241	858	248	30	6	8	(4	4)	314	115	77	115	37	1	91	6	17	7	16	9	.64	18	.289	.320	.366

Kevin Millar

Bats: R **Throws:** R **Pos:** 1B-110; LF-20; RF-14; PH-7   **Ht:** 6'0" **Wt:** 210 **Born:** 9/24/1971 **Age:** 34

Year	Team	Lg	G	AB	H	2B	3B	HR	(Hm	Rd)	TB	R	RBI	RC	TBB	IBB	SO	HBP	SH	SF	SB	CS	SB%	GDP	Avg	OBP	Slg
1998	FLA	NL	2	2	1	0	0	0	(0	0)	1	1	0	1	1	0	0	0	0	0	0	0	-	0	.500	.667	.500
1999	FLA	NL	105	351	100	17	4	9	(3	6)	152	48	67	57	40	2	64	7	1	8	1	0	1.00	7	.285	.362	.433
2000	FLA	NL	123	259	67	14	3	14	(6	8)	129	36	42	47	36	0	47	8	0	2	0	0	-	5	.259	.364	.498
2001	FLA	NL	144	449	141	39	5	20	(13	7)	250	62	85	89	39	2	70	5	0	2	0	0	-	8	.314	.374	.557
2002	FLA	NL	126	438	134	41	0	16	(11	5)	223	58	57	63	40	0	74	5	0	6	0	2	.00	15	.306	.366	.509
2003	BOS	AL	148	544	150	30	1	25	(10	15)	257	83	96	87	60	5	108	5	0	9	3	2	.60	14	.276	.348	.472
2004	BOS	AL	150	508	151	36	0	18	(12	6)	241	74	74	90	57	0	91	17	0	6	1	1	.50	16	.297	.383	.474
2005	BOS	AL	134	449	122	28	1	9	(8	1)	179	57	50	58	54	0	74	8	0	8	0	1	.00	12	.272	.355	.399
	8 ML YEARS		932	3000	866	205	14	111	(63	48)	1432	419	471	492	327	9	528	55	1	41	5	6	.45	77	.289	.365	.477

Corky Miller

Bats: R **Throws:** R **Pos:** C-4; DH-1; PH-1   **Ht:** 6'1" **Wt:** 225 **Born:** 3/18/1976 **Age:** 30

Year	Team	Lg	G	AB	H	2B	3B	HR	(Hm	Rd)	TB	R	RBI	RC	TBB	IBB	SO	HBP	SH	SF	SB	CS	SB%	GDP	Avg	OBP	Slg
2005	Roch*	AAA	59	170	39	7	0	11	(-	-)	79	35	25	32	27	1	30	14	8	0	0	2	.00	4	.229	.379	.465
2001	CIN	NL	17	49	9	2	0	3	(1	2)	20	5	7	6	4	0	16	2	0	2	1	0	1.00	1	.184	.263	.408
2002	CIN	NL	39	114	29	10	0	3	(2	1)	48	9	15	15	9	2	20	4	1	1	0	0	-	7	.254	.328	.421
2003	CIN	NL	14	30	8	0	0	0	(0	0)	8	4	1	5	5	0	7	2	0	1	0	0	-	1	.267	.395	.267
2004	CIN	NL	13	39	1	0	0	0	(0	0)	1	2	3	0	6	0	12	3	0	1	0	0	-	3	.026	.204	.026
2005	MIN	AL	5	12	0	0	0	0	(0	0)	0	0	0	0	0	0	2	0	0	0	0	0	-	0	.000	.000	.000
	5 ML YEARS		88	244	47	12	0	6	(3	3)	77	20	26	26	24	2	57	11	1	5	1	0	1.00	12	.193	.289	.316

Damian Miller

Bats: R **Throws:** R **Pos:** C-111; PH-5   **Ht:** 6'2" **Wt:** 218 **Born:** 10/13/1969 **Age:** 36

Year	Team	Lg	G	AB	H	2B	3B	HR	(Hm	Rd)	TB	R	RBI	RC	TBB	IBB	SO	HBP	SH	SF	SB	CS	SB%	GDP	Avg	OBP	Slg
1997	MIN	AL	25	66	18	1	0	2	(1	1)	25	5	13	7	2	0	12	0	0	3	0	0	-	2	.273	.282	.379
1998	ARI	NL	57	168	48	14	2	3	(2	1)	75	17	14	25	11	2	43	2	2	0	1	0	1.00	6	.286	.337	.446
1999	ARI	NL	86	296	80	19	0	11	(3	8)	132	35	47	40	19	3	78	2	4	0	0	0	-	6	.270	.316	.446
2000	ARI	NL	100	324	89	24	0	10	(6	4)	143	43	44	49	36	4	74	1	1	2	2	2	.50	6	.275	.347	.441
2001	ARI	NL	123	380	103	19	0	13	(9	4)	161	45	47	52	35	9	80	4	4	2	0	1	.00	9	.271	.337	.424
2002	ARI	NL	101	297	74	22	0	11	(4	7)	129	40	42	35	38	5	88	3	2	0	0	0	-	14	.249	.340	.434
2003	CHN	NL	114	352	82	19	1	9	(6	3)	130	34	36	36	39	6	91	1	7	1	1	0	1.00	15	.233	.310	.369
2004	OAK	AL	110	397	108	25	0	9	(5	4)	160	39	58	54	39	0	87	2	2	2	0	1	.00	19	.272	.339	.403
2005	MIL	NL	114	385	105	25	1	9	(3	6)	159	50	43	39	37	4	94	4	2	3	0	1	.00	16	.273	.340	.413
	9 ML YEARS		830	2665	707	168	4	77	(39	38)	1114	308	344	337	256	35	647	19	20	16	4	5	.44	89	.265	.332	.418

Justin Miller

Pitches: R **Bats:** R **Pos:** RP-1   **Ht:** 6'2" **Wt:** 195 **Born:** 8/27/1977 **Age:** 28

			HOW MUCH HE PITCHED						WHAT HE GAVE UP											THE RESULTS						
Year	Team	Lg	G	GS	CG	GF	IP	BFP	H	R	ER	HR	SH	SF	HB	TBB	IBB	SO	WP	Bk	W	L	Pct	ShO	Sv-Op	Hld	ERC	ERA
2005	Syrcse*	AAA	28	4	0	9	50.1	204	39	15	13	3	0	0	3	14	0	56	5	0	3	1	.750	0	2- -	-	2.41	2.32
2002	TOR	AL	25	18	0	2	102.1	469	103	70	63	12	1	6	11	66	2	68	6	0	9	5	.643	0	0-0	1	5.73	5.54

Year	Team	Lg	G	GS	CG	GF	IP	BFP	H	R	ER	HR	SH	SF	HB	TBB	IBB	SO	WP	Bk	W	L	Pct	ShO	Sv-Op	Hld	ERC	ERA
2004	TOR	AL	19	15	0	0	81.2	375	101	58	55	14	2	6	5	42	3	47	3	1	3	4	.429	0	0-0	0	6.91	6.06
2005	TOR	AL	1	0	0	0	2.1	12	5	4	4	3	0	0	0	0	0	2	0	0	0	0	-	0	0-0	0	20.19	15.43
	3 ML YEARS		45	33	0	2	186.1	856	209	132	122	29	3	12	16	108	5	117	9	1	12	9	.571	0	0-0	1	6.41	5.89

Matt Miller

Pitches: R **Bats:** R **Pos:** RP-23   **Ht:** 6'3" **Wt:** 215 **Born:** 11/23/1971 **Age:** 34

Year	Team	Lg	G	GS	CG	GF	IP	BFP	H	R	ER	HR	SH	SF	HB	TBB	IBB	SO	WP	Bk	W	L	Pct	ShO	Sv-Op	Hld	ERC	ERA
2005	MhVlly*	A-	1	1	0	0	0.2	7	5	4	4	0	0	0	1	0	0	1	0	0	0	0	-	0	0--	-	70.54	54.00
2005	Akron*	AA	1	0	0	0	1.0	3	0	0	0	0	0	0	0	0	0	0	0	0	0	0	-	0	0--	-	0.00	0.00
2005	Buffalo*	AAA	9	0	0	6	10.1	36	3	1	1	0	1	0	0	2	0	15	0	0	0	0	-	0	3--	-	0.41	0.87
2003	COL	NL	4	0	0	2	4.1	18	5	1	1	0	0	0	0	2	0	5	0	0	0	0	-	0	0-0	0	4.86	2.08
2004	CLE	AL	57	0	0	13	55.1	226	42	22	19	1	2	1	6	23	8	55	1	1	4	1	.800	0	1-2	7	2.56	3.09
2005	CLE	AL	23	0	0	4	29.2	118	22	6	6	1	0	1	3	10	3	23	1	1	1	0	1.000	0	1-2	4	2.37	1.82
	3 ML YEARS		84	0	0	19	89.1	362	69	29	26	2	2	2	9	35	11	83	2	2	5	1	.833	0	2-4	11	2.60	2.62

Trever Miller

Pitches: L **Bats:** R **Pos:** RP-61   **Ht:** 6'4" **Wt:** 195 **Born:** 5/29/1973 **Age:** 33

Year	Team	Lg	G	GS	CG	GF	IP	BFP	H	R	ER	HR	SH	SF	HB	TBB	IBB	SO	WP	Bk	W	L	Pct	ShO	Sv-Op	Hld	ERC	ERA
1996	DET	AL	5	4	0	0	16.2	88	28	17	17	3	2	2	2	9	0	8	0	0	0	4	.000	0	0-0	0	10.15	9.18
1998	HOU	NL	37	1	0	15	53.1	235	57	21	18	4	0	0	1	20	1	30	1	0	2	0	1.000	0	1-2	1	4.18	3.04
1999	HOU	NL	47	0	0	11	49.2	232	58	29	28	6	2	2	5	29	1	37	4	0	3	2	.600	0	1-1	4	6.48	5.07
2000	2 Tms	NL	16	0	0	2	16.1	90	27	22	19	3	1	1	2	12	1	11	1	0	0	0	-	0	0-0	0	10.68	10.47
2003	TOR	AL	79	0	0	18	52.2	233	46	30	27	7	1	0	5	28	3	44	2	0	2	2	.500	0	4-5	16	4.38	4.61
2004	TB	AL	60	0	0	15	49.0	208	48	21	17	3	3	0	3	15	4	43	2	0	1	1	.500	0	1-3	9	3.45	3.12
2005	TB	AL	61	0	0	13	44.1	206	45	23	20	4	3	5	7	29	6	35	2	0	2	2	.500	0	0-3	11	5.57	4.06
00	Phi	NL	14	0	0	2	14.0	72	19	16	13	3	1	1	1	9	1	10	1	0	0	0	-	0	0-0	0	8.14	8.36
00	LA	NL	2	0	0	0	2.1	18	8	6	6	0	0	0	1	3	0	1	0	0	0	0	-	0	0-0	0	28.18	23.14
	7 ML YEARS		305	5	0	74	282.0	1292	309	163	146	30	12	10	25	142	16	208	12	0	10	11	.476	0	7-14	41	5.35	4.66

Wade Miller

Pitches: R **Bats:** R **Pos:** SP-16   **Ht:** 6'2" **Wt:** 210 **Born:** 9/13/1976 **Age:** 29

Year	Team	Lg	G	GS	CG	GF	IP	BFP	H	R	ER	HR	SH	SF	HB	TBB	IBB	SO	WP	Bk	W	L	Pct	ShO	Sv-Op	Hld	ERC	ERA
2005	Wilmg*	A	1	1	0	0	5.0	21	6	1	1	1	0	0	0	0	0	6	0	0	0	0	-	0	0--	-	4.14	1.80
2005	Grnvlle*	A	1	1	0	0	4.2	19	4	2	2	1	0	0	0	1	0	4	2	0	0	0	-	0	0--	-	3.23	3.86
2005	Pwtckt*	AAA	2	2	0	0	10.2	48	10	4	3	1	0	0	0	6	0	10	0	0	0	0	-	0	0--	-	4.21	2.53
1999	HOU	NL	5	1	0	2	10.1	52	17	11	11	4	0	0	0	5	0	8	0	0	0	1	.000	0	0-0	0	11.07	9.58
2000	HOU	NL	16	16	2	0	105.0	453	104	66	60	14	3	1	3	42	1	89	1	0	6	6	.500	0	0-0	0	4.37	5.14
2001	HOU	NL	32	32	1	0	212.0	873	183	91	80	31	7	5	4	76	3	183	8	0	16	8	.667	0	0-0	0	3.57	3.40
2002	HOU	NL	26	26	1	0	164.2	688	151	63	60	14	8	5	6	62	9	144	4	0	15	4	.789	1	0-0	0	3.54	3.28
2003	HOU	NL	33	33	1	0	187.1	797	168	96	86	17	8	7	10	77	1	161	4	0	14	13	.519	0	0-0	0	3.70	4.13
2004	HOU	NL	15	15	0	0	88.2	383	76	35	33	11	5	1	0	44	0	74	1	0	7	7	.500	0	0-0	0	3.78	3.35
2005	BOS	AL	16	16	0	0	91.0	414	96	53	50	8	1	4	3	47	0	64	6	0	4	4	.500	0	0-0	0	4.84	4.95
	7 ML YEARS		143	139	5	2	859.0	3660	795	415	380	99	32	23	26	353	14	723	24	0	62	43	.590	1	0-0	0	3.92	3.98

Kevin Millwood

Pitches: R **Bats:** R **Pos:** SP-30   **Ht:** 6'4" **Wt:** 220 **Born:** 12/24/1974 **Age:** 31

Year	Team	Lg	G	GS	CG	GF	IP	BFP	H	R	ER	HR	SH	SF	HB	TBB	IBB	SO	WP	Bk	W	L	Pct	ShO	Sv-Op	Hld	ERC	ERA
1997	ATL	NL	12	8	0	2	51.1	227	55	26	23	1	3	5	2	21	1	42	1	0	5	3	.625	0	0-0	0	4.03	4.03
1998	ATL	NL	31	29	3	1	174.1	748	175	86	79	18	8	3	3	56	3	163	6	1	17	8	.680	1	0-0	1	3.81	4.08
1999	ATL	NL	33	33	2	0	228.0	906	168	80	68	24	9	3	4	59	2	205	5	0	18	7	.720	0	0-0	0	2.26	2.68
2000	ATL	NL	36	35	0	0	212.2	903	213	115	110	26	8	5	3	62	2	168	4	0	10	13	.435	0	0-0	0	3.83	4.66
2001	ATL	NL	21	21	0	0	121.0	515	121	66	58	20	7	2	1	40	6	84	5	1	7	7	.500	0	0-0	0	4.20	4.31
2002	ATL	NL	35	34	1	0	217.0	895	186	83	78	16	9	4	8	65	7	178	4	0	18	8	.692	1	0-0	0	2.85	3.24
2003	PHI	NL	35	35	5	0	222.0	930	210	103	99	19	12	5	4	68	6	169	2	0	14	12	.538	3	0-0	0	3.35	4.01
2004	PHI	NL	25	25	0	0	141.0	628	155	81	76	14	11	2	7	51	5	125	4	0	9	6	.600	0	0-0	0	4.57	4.85
2005	CLE	AL	30	30	1	0	192.0	799	182	72	61	20	6	4	4	52	0	146	2	0	9	11	.450	0	0-0	0	3.40	2.86
	9 ML YEARS		258	250	12	3	1559.1	6551	1465	712	652	158	73	33	36	474	32	1280	33	2	107	75	.588	5	0-0	1	3.42	3.76

Eric Milton

Pitches: L **Bats:** L **Pos:** SP-34   **Ht:** 6'3" **Wt:** 220 **Born:** 8/4/1975 **Age:** 30

Year	Team	Lg	G	GS	CG	GF	IP	BFP	H	R	ER	HR	SH	SF	HB	TBB	IBB	SO	WP	Bk	W	L	Pct	ShO	Sv-Op	Hld	ERC	ERA
1998	MIN	AL	32	32	1	0	172.1	772	195	113	108	25	2	6	2	70	0	107	1	0	8	14	.364	0	0-0	0	5.21	5.64
1999	MIN	AL	34	34	4	0	206.1	858	190	111	103	28	3	6	3	63	2	163	2	0	7	11	.389	2	0-0	0	3.56	4.49
2000	MIN	AL	33	33	0	0	200.0	849	205	123	108	35	4	6	7	44	0	160	5	0	13	10	.565	0	0-0	0	4.09	4.86
2001	MIN	AL	35	34	2	0	220.2	944	222	109	106	35	8	6	5	61	0	157	2	0	15	7	.682	1	0-0	0	4.05	4.32
2002	MIN	AL	29	29	2	0	171.0	707	173	96	92	24	0	4	3	30	0	121	4	0	13	9	.591	1	0-0	0	3.59	4.84
2003	MIN	AL	3	3	0	0	17.0	66	15	5	5	2	0	1	0	1	0	7	0	0	1	0	1.000	0	0-0	0	2.29	2.65
2004	PHI	NL	34	34	0	0	201.0	862	196	110	106	43	11	6	1	75	6	161	3	0	14	6	.700	0	0-0	0	4.57	4.75
2005	CIN	NL	34	34	0	0	186.1	855	237	141	134	40	6	6	7	52	2	123	8	0	8	15	.348	0	0-0	0	6.03	6.47
	8 ML YEARS		234	233	9	0	1374.2	5913	1433	808	762	232	34	41	28	396	10	999	25	0	79	72	.523	4	0-0	0	4.37	4.99

Doug Mirabelli

Bats: R **Throws:** R **Pos:** C-43; PH-7; DH-5   **Ht:** 6'1" **Wt:** 227 **Born:** 10/18/1970 **Age:** 35

									BATTING													BASERUNNING				AVERAGES		
Year	Team	Lg	G	AB	H	2B	3B	HR	(Hm	Rd)	TB	R	RBI	RC	TBB	IBB	SO	HBP	SH	SF	SB	CS	SB%	GDP	Avg	OBP	Slg
1996	SF	NL	9	18	4	1	0	0	(0	0)	5	2	1	2	3	0	4	0	0	0	0	0	-	0	.222	.333	.278
1997	SF	NL	6	7	1	0	0	0	(0	0)	1	0	0	0	1	0	3	0	0	0	0	0	-	0	.143	.250	.143
1998	SF	NL	10	17	4	2	0	1	(1	0)	9	2	4	3	2	0	6	0	0	0	0	0	-	0	.235	.316	.529
1999	SF	NL	33	87	22	6	0	1	(1	0)	31	10	10	10	9	1	25	1	0	1	0	0	-	1	.253	.327	.356
2000	SF	NL	82	230	53	10	2	6	(2	4)	85	23	28	30	36	2	57	2	3	2	1	0	1.00	6	.230	.337	.370
2001	2 Tms	AL	77	190	43	10	0	11	(5	6)	86	20	29	29	27	2	57	4	1	2	0	0	-	3	.226	.332	.453
2002	BOS	AL	57	151	34	7	0	7	(5	2)	62	17	25	19	17	0	33	3	0	2	0	0	-	6	.225	.312	.411
2003	BOS	AL	62	163	42	13	0	6	(3	3)	73	23	18	15	11	0	36	1	0	1	0	0	-	5	.258	.307	.448
2004	BOS	AL	59	160	45	12	0	9	(3	6)	84	27	32	32	19	0	46	3	0	0	0	0	-	5	.281	.368	.525
2005	BOS	AL	50	136	31	7	0	6	(4	2)	56	16	18	19	14	0	48	2	0	0	2	0	1.00	4	.228	.309	.412
01	Tex	AL	23	49	5	2	0	2	(1	1)	13	4	3	3	10	0	21	0	0	0	0	0	-	1	.102	.254	.265
01	Bos	AL	54	141	38	8	0	9	(4	5)	73	16	26	26	17	2	36	4	1	2	0	0	-	2	.270	.360	.518
	10 ML YEARS		445	1159	279	68	2	47	(24	23)	492	140	165	159	139	5	315	16	4	8	3	0	1.00	26	.241	.328	.425

Sergio Mitre

Pitches: R **Bats:** R **Pos:** RP-14; SP-7   **Ht:** 6'4" **Wt:** 210 **Born:** 2/16/1981 **Age:** 25

			HOW MUCH HE PITCHED						WHAT HE GAVE UP								THE RESULTS							
Year	Team	Lg	G	GS	CG	GF	IP	BFP	H	R	ER	HR	SH	SF	HB	TBB	IBB	SO	WP	Bk	W	L	Pct	ShO	Sv-Op	Hld	ERC	ERA
2005	Iowa*	AAA	13	13	1	0	70.2	306	72	34	34	5	2	2	1	22	0	55	4	2	5	6	.455	0	0- -	-	3.61	4.33
2003	CHN	NL	3	2	0	1	8.2	43	15	8	8	1	0	1	0	4	1	3	0	0	0	1	.000	0	0-0	0	9.02	8.31
2004	CHN	NL	12	9	0	2	51.2	244	71	38	38	6	3	0	4	20	1	37	5	1	2	4	.333	0	0-0	0	6.69	6.62
2005	CHN	NL	21	7	1	7	60.1	268	62	37	36	11	1	3	3	23	2	37	5	0	2	5	.286	1	0-0	0	4.81	5.37
	3 ML YEARS		36	18	1	10	120.2	555	148	83	82	18	4	4	7	47	4	77	10	1	4	10	.286	1	0-0	0	5.88	6.12

Brian Moehler

Pitches: R **Bats:** R **Pos:** SP-25; RP-12   **Ht:** 6'3" **Wt:** 235 **Born:** 12/31/1971 **Age:** 34

			HOW MUCH HE PITCHED						WHAT HE GAVE UP								THE RESULTS							
Year	Team	Lg	G	GS	CG	GF	IP	BFP	H	R	ER	HR	SH	SF	HB	TBB	IBB	SO	WP	Bk	W	L	Pct	ShO	Sv-Op	Hld	ERC	ERA
1996	DET	AL	2	2	0	0	10.1	51	11	10	5	1	1	0	0	8	1	2	1	0	0	1	.000	0	0-0	0	5.49	4.35
1997	DET	AL	31	31	2	0	175.1	770	198	97	91	22	1	8	5	61	1	97	3	0	11	12	.478	1	0-0	0	4.92	4.67
1998	DET	AL	33	33	4	0	221.1	912	220	103	96	30	3	3	2	56	1	123	4	0	14	13	.519	3	0-0	0	3.79	3.90
1999	DET	AL	32	32	2	0	196.1	859	229	116	110	22	8	5	7	59	5	106	4	0	10	16	.385	2	0-0	0	4.85	5.04
2000	DET	AL	29	29	2	0	178.0	776	222	99	89	20	3	4	2	40	0	103	2	1	12	9	.571	0	0-0	0	4.95	4.50
2001	DET	AL	1	1	0	0	8.0	30	6	3	3	0	0	0	0	1	0	2	0	0	0	0	-	0	0-0	0	1.43	3.38
2002	2 Tms		13	12	0	0	63.0	278	78	39	34	11	4	2	1	13	0	31	0	0	3	5	.375	0	0-0	0	5.20	4.86
2003	HOU	NL	3	3	0	0	13.2	66	22	12	12	4	1	1	0	6	0	5	0	0	0	0	-	0	0-0	0	9.97	7.90
2005	FLA	NL	37	25	0	4	158.1	696	198	82	80	16	13	4	5	42	9	95	1	0	6	12	.333	0	0-0	1	5.07	4.55
02	Det	AL	3	3	0	0	19.2	77	17	5	5	3	1	1	0	2	0	13	0	0	1	1	.500	0	0-0	0	2.54	2.29
02	Cin	NL	10	9	0	0	43.1	201	61	34	29	8	3	1	1	11	0	18	0	0	2	4	.333	0	0-0	0	6.56	6.02
	9 ML YEARS		181	168	10	4	1024.1	4438	1184	561	520	126	34	27	22	286	17	564	15	1	56	68	.452	6	0-0	1	4.74	4.57

Chad Moeller

Bats: R **Throws:** R **Pos:** C-65; PH-1; PR-1   **Ht:** 6'3" **Wt:** 210 **Born:** 2/18/1975 **Age:** 31

									BATTING													BASERUNNING				AVERAGES		
Year	Team	Lg	G	AB	H	2B	3B	HR	(Hm	Rd)	TB	R	RBI	RC	TBB	IBB	SO	HBP	SH	SF	SB	CS	SB%	GDP	Avg	OBP	Slg
2000	MIN	AL	48	128	27	3	1	1	(1	0)	35	13	9	8	9	0	33	0	1	1	1	0	1.00	4	.211	.261	.273
2001	ARI	NL	25	56	13	0	1	1	(1	0)	18	8	2	5	6	1	12	0	1	0	0	0	-	2	.232	.306	.321
2002	ARI	NL	37	105	30	11	1	2	(2	0)	49	10	16	17	17	3	23	0	1	0	0	1	.00	6	.286	.385	.467
2003	ARI	NL	78	239	64	17	1	7	(2	5)	104	29	29	28	23	11	59	2	3	2	1	2	.33	7	.268	.335	.435
2004	MIL	NL	101	317	66	13	1	5	(3	2)	96	25	27	14	21	1	74	4	6	1	0	1	.00	12	.208	.265	.303
2005	MIL	NL	66	199	41	9	1	7	(5	2)	73	23	23	14	13	1	48	1	2	1	0	0	-	9	.206	.257	.367
	6 ML YEARS		355	1044	241	53	6	23	(14	9)	375	108	106	86	89	17	249	7	14	5	2	4	.33	40	.231	.294	.359

Dustan Mohr

Bats: R **Throws:** R **Pos:** RF-55; PH-26; LF-17; CF-10   **Ht:** 6'0" **Wt:** 210 **Born:** 6/19/1976 **Age:** 30

									BATTING													BASERUNNING				AVERAGES		
Year	Team	Lg	G	AB	H	2B	3B	HR	(Hm	Rd)	TB	R	RBI	RC	TBB	IBB	SO	HBP	SH	SF	SB	CS	SB%	GDP	Avg	OBP	Slg
2005	ColSpr*	AAA	3	12	3	2	0	1	(-	-)	8	2	4	2	0	0	4	0	0	0	0	0	-	1	.250	.250	.667
2001	MIN	AL	20	51	12	2	0	0	(0	0)	14	6	4	4	5	0	17	0	0	1	1	1	.50	1	.235	.298	.275
2002	MIN	AL	120	383	103	23	2	12	(3	9)	166	55	45	51	31	3	86	1	2	0	6	3	.67	5	.269	.325	.433
2003	MIN	AL	121	348	87	22	0	10	(4	6)	139	50	36	37	33	0	106	4	1	3	5	2	.71	10	.250	.314	.399
2004	SF	NL	117	263	72	20	1	7	(3	4)	115	52	28	43	46	3	64	8	4	3	0	3	.00	5	.274	.394	.437
2005	COL	NL	98	266	57	10	3	17	(13	4)	124	34	38	27	23	2	94	2	0	2	1	2	.33	3	.214	.280	.466
	5 ML YEARS		476	1311	331	77	6	46	(23	23)	558	197	151	162	138	8	367	12	8	9	13	11	.54	23	.252	.327	.426

Bengie Molina

Bats: R **Throws:** R **Pos:** C-105; DH-11; PH-7   **Ht:** 5'11" **Wt:** 210 **Born:** 7/20/1974 **Age:** 31

									BATTING													BASERUNNING				AVERAGES		
Year	Team	Lg	G	AB	H	2B	3B	HR	(Hm	Rd)	TB	R	RBI	RC	TBB	IBB	SO	HBP	SH	SF	SB	CS	SB%	GDP	Avg	OBP	Slg
1998	ANA	AL	2	1	0	0	0	0	(0	0)	0	0	0	0	0	0	0	0	0	0	0	0	-	0	.000	.000	.000
1999	ANA	AL	31	101	26	5	0	1	(0	1)	34	8	10	9	6	0	6	2	0	0	0	1	.00	5	.257	.312	.337
2000	ANA	AL	130	473	133	20	2	14	(11	3)	199	59	71	60	23	0	33	6	4	7	1	0	1.00	17	.281	.318	.421

Year	Team	Lg	G	AB	H	2B	3B	HR	(Hm	Rd)	TB	R	RBI	RC	TBB	IBB	SO	HBP	SH	SF	SB	CS	SB%	GDP	Avg	OBP	Slg
2001	ANA	AL	96	325	85	11	0	6	(6	0)	114	31	40	34	16	3	51	8	2	4	0	1	.00	8	.262	.309	.351
2002	ANA	AL	122	428	105	18	0	5	(2	3)	138	34	47	33	15	3	34	4	6	6	0	0	-	15	.245	.274	.322
2003	ANA	AL	119	409	115	24	0	14	(7	7)	181	37	71	57	13	2	31	2	2	4	1	1	.50	17	.281	.304	.443
2004	ANA	AL	97	337	93	13	0	10	(5	5)	136	36	54	44	18	1	35	2	2	4	0	1	.00	18	.276	.313	.404
2005	LAA	AL	119	410	121	17	0	15	(8	7)	183	45	69	53	27	2	41	1	5	6	0	2	.00	14	.295	.336	.446
8 ML YEARS			716	2484	678	108	2	65	(39	26)	985	250	362	290	118	11	231	25	21	31	2	6	.25	94	.273	.309	.397

Jose Molina

Bats: R **Throws:** R **Pos:** C-65; PH-6; 1B-4; DH-4; PR-1   **Ht:** 6'1" **Wt:** 215 **Born:** 6/3/1975 **Age:** 31

Year	Team	Lg	G	AB	H	2B	3B	HR	(Hm	Rd)	TB	R	RBI	RC	TBB	IBB	SO	HBP	SH	SF	SB	CS	SB%	GDP	Avg	OBP	Slg
1999	CHN	NL	10	19	5	1	0	0	(0	0)	6	3	1	2	2	1	4	0	0	0	0	0	-	0	.263	.333	.316
2001	ANA	AL	15	37	10	3	0	2	(0	2)	19	8	4	6	3	0	8	0	2	0	0	0	-	2	.270	.325	.514
2002	ANA	AL	29	70	19	3	0	0	(0	0)	22	5	5	4	5	0	15	0	4	2	0	2	.00	2	.271	.312	.314
2003	ANA	AL	53	114	21	4	0	0	(0	0)	25	12	6	5	1	0	26	3	4	1	0	0	-	1	.184	.210	.219
2004	ANA	AL	73	203	53	10	2	3	(1	2)	76	26	25	19	10	0	52	0	5	0	4	1	.80	7	.261	.296	.374
2005	LAA	AL	75	184	42	4	0	6	(2	4)	64	14	25	19	13	0	41	2	4	0	2	0	1.00	5	.228	.286	.348
6 ML YEARS			255	627	150	25	2	11	(3	8)	212	68	66	55	34	1	146	5	19	3	6	3	.67	17	.239	.283	.338

Yadier Molina

Bats: R **Throws:** R **Pos:** C-114; 1B-1   **Ht:** 5'11" **Wt:** 225 **Born:** 7/13/1982 **Age:** 23

Year	Team	Lg	G	AB	H	2B	3B	HR	(Hm	Rd)	TB	R	RBI	RC	TBB	IBB	SO	HBP	SH	SF	SB	CS	SB%	GDP	Avg	OBP	Slg
2001	JhsCty	R+	44	158	41	11	0	4	(-	-)	64	18	18	19	12	1	23	3	0	2	1	1	.50	4	.259	.320	.405
2002	Peoria	A	112	393	110	20	7	7	(-	-)	165	39	50	49	21	0	36	10	4	2	2	7	.22	14	.280	.331	.420
2003	Tenn	AA	104	364	100	13	1	2	(-	-)	121	32	51	40	25	2	45	5	0	3	0	1	.00	11	.275	.327	.332
2004	Memp	AAA	37	129	39	6	0	1	(-	-)	48	19	14	20	17	0	14	2	0	2	0	0	-	2	.302	.387	.372
2004	STL	NL	51	135	36	6	0	2	(1	1)	48	12	15	15	13	3	20	0	2	1	0	1	.00	4	.267	.329	.356
2005	STL	NL	114	385	97	15	1	8	(6	2)	138	36	49	46	23	3	30	2	8	3	2	3	.40	10	.252	.295	.358
2 ML YEARS			165	520	133	21	1	10	(7	3)	186	48	64	61	36	6	50	2	10	4	2	4	.33	14	.256	.304	.358

Raul Mondesi

Bats: R **Throws:** R **Pos:** RF-40; PH-2   **Ht:** 5'11" **Wt:** 230 **Born:** 3/12/1971 **Age:** 35

Year	Team	Lg	G	AB	H	2B	3B	HR	(Hm	Rd)	TB	R	RBI	RC	TBB	IBB	SO	HBP	SH	SF	SB	CS	SB%	GDP	Avg	OBP	Slg
1993	LA	NL	42	86	25	3	1	4	(2	2)	42	13	10	14	4	0	16	0	1	0	4	1	.80	1	.291	.322	.488
1994	LA	NL	112	434	133	27	8	16	(10	6)	224	63	56	69	16	5	78	2	0	2	11	8	.58	9	.306	.333	.516
1995	LA	NL	139	536	153	23	6	26	(13	13)	266	91	88	89	33	4	96	4	0	7	27	4	.87	7	.285	.328	.496
1996	LA	NL	157	634	188	40	7	24	(11	13)	314	98	88	102	32	9	122	5	0	3	14	7	.67	6	.297	.334	.495
1997	LA	NL	159	616	191	42	5	30	(16	14)	333	95	87	114	44	7	105	6	1	3	32	15	.68	11	.310	.360	.541
1998	LA	NL	148	580	162	26	5	30	(13	17)	288	85	90	88	30	4	112	3	0	4	16	10	.62	8	.279	.316	.497
1999	LA	NL	159	601	152	29	5	33	(16	17)	290	98	99	102	71	6	134	3	0	5	36	9	.80	3	.253	.332	.483
2000	TOR	AL	96	388	105	22	2	24	(10	14)	203	78	67	67	32	0	73	3	0	3	22	6	.79	8	.271	.329	.523
2001	TOR	AL	149	572	144	26	4	27	(10	17)	259	84	84	89	73	3	128	6	0	2	30	11	.73	13	.252	.342	.453
2002	2 Tms	AL	146	569	132	34	1	26	(16	10)	246	90	88	73	59	3	103	5	0	4	15	6	.71	11	.232	.308	.432
2003	2 Tms		143	523	142	31	4	24	(14	10)	253	83	71	65	56	6	97	3	0	4	22	11	.67	9	.272	.343	.484
2004	2 Tms		34	133	32	9	0	3	(2	1)	50	10	15	16	13	0	31	1	0	0	0	3	.00	5	.241	.313	.376
2005	ATL	NL	41	142	30	7	1	4	(1	3)	51	17	17	10	12	3	35	0	0	1	0	1	.00	5	.211	.271	.359
02	Tor	AL	75	299	67	16	1	15	(10	5)	130	51	45	37	31	1	57	3	0	2	9	2	.82	8	.224	.301	.435
02	NYY	AL	71	270	65	18	0	11	(6	5)	116	39	43	36	28	2	46	2	0	2	6	4	.60	3	.241	.315	.430
03	NYY	AL	98	361	93	23	3	16	(9	7)	170	56	49	42	38	6	66	2	0	2	17	7	.71	6	.258	.330	.471
03	Ari	NL	45	162	49	8	1	8	(5	3)	83	27	22	23	18	0	31	1	0	2	5	4	.56	3	.302	.372	.512
04	Pit	NL	26	99	28	8	0	2	(1	1)	42	8	14	16	11	0	27	0	0	0	0	2	.00	1	.283	.355	.424
04	Ana	AL	8	34	4	1	0	1	(1	0)	8	2	1	0	2	0	4	1	0	0	0	1	.00	1	.118	.189	.235
13 ML YEARS			1525	5814	1589	319	49	271	(136	135)	2819	909	860	898	475	50	1130	41	2	37	229	92	.71	93	.273	.331	.485

Craig Monroe

Bats: R **Throws:** R **Pos:** RF-85; LF-69; CF-33; DH-1; PH-1; PR-1   **Ht:** 6'1" **Wt:** 195 **Born:** 2/27/1977 **Age:** 29

Year	Team	Lg	G	AB	H	2B	3B	HR	(Hm	Rd)	TB	R	RBI	RC	TBB	IBB	SO	HBP	SH	SF	SB	CS	SB%	GDP	Avg	OBP	Slg
2001	TEX	AL	27	52	11	1	0	2	(1	1)	18	8	5	6	6	0	18	0	0	0	2	0	1.00	1	.212	.293	.346
2002	DET	AL	13	25	3	1	0	1	(0	1)	7	3	1	0	0	0	5	1	0	0	0	2	.00	1	.120	.154	.280
2003	DET	AL	128	425	102	18	1	23	(10	13)	191	51	70	61	27	2	89	2	1	3	4	2	.67	10	.240	.287	.449
2004	DET	AL	128	447	131	27	3	18	(9	9)	218	65	72	66	29	1	79	2	0	3	3	4	.43	8	.293	.337	.488
2005	DET	AL	157	567	157	30	3	20	(9	11)	253	69	89	77	40	4	95	3	1	**12**	8	3	.73	16	.277	.322	.446
5 ML YEARS			453	1516	404	77	7	64	(29	35)	687	196	237	210	102	7	286	8	2	18	17	11	.61	36	.266	.313	.453

Melvin Mora

Bats: R **Throws:** R **Pos:** 3B-148; DH-1; PH-1   **Ht:** 5'10" **Wt:** 180 **Born:** 2/2/1972 **Age:** 34

Year	Team	Lg	G	AB	H	2B	3B	HR	(Hm	Rd)	TB	R	RBI	RC	TBB	IBB	SO	HBP	SH	SF	SB	CS	SB%	GDP	Avg	OBP	Slg
1999	NYN	NL	66	31	5	0	0	0	(0	0)	5	6	1	2	4	0	7	1	3	0	2	1	.67	0	.161	.278	.161
2000	2 Tms		132	414	114	22	5	8	(5	3)	170	60	47	56	35	3	80	6	4	5	12	11	.52	9	.275	.337	.411
2001	BAL	AL	128	436	109	28	0	7	(6	1)	158	49	48	55	41	2	91	14	5	7	11	4	.73	6	.250	.329	.362
2002	BAL	AL	149	557	130	30	4	19	(8	11)	225	86	64	78	70	2	108	20	1	4	16	10	.62	7	.233	.338	.404

Year	Team	Lg	G	AB	H	2B	3B	HR	(Hm	Rd)	TB	R	RBI	RC	TBB	IBB	SO	HBP	SH	SF	SB	CS	SB%	GDP	Avg	OBP	Slg
2003	BAL	AL	96	344	109	17	1	15	(8	7)	173	68	48	67	49	0	71	12	6	2	6	3	.67	3	.317	.418	.503
2004	BAL	AL	140	550	187	41	0	27	(15	12)	309	111	104	115	66	0	95	11	6	3	11	6	.65	10	.340	**.419**	.562
2005	BAL	AL	149	593	168	30	1	27	(13	14)	281	86	88	88	50	0	112	10	8	3	7	4	.64	9	.283	.348	.474
00	NYM	NL	79	215	56	13	2	6	(4	2)	91	35	30	29	18	3	48	2	2	5	7	3	.70	3	.260	.317	.423
00	Bal	AL	53	199	58	9	3	2	(1	1)	79	25	17	27	17	0	32	4	2	0	5	8	.38	2	.291	.359	.397
7 ML YEARS			860	2925	822	168	11	103	(55	48)	1321	466	400	461	315	7	564	74	33	24	65	39	.63	40	.281	.363	.452

Mike Mordecai

Bats: R **Throws:** R **Pos:** 2B-1; SS-1   **Ht:** 5'10" **Wt:** 185 **Born:** 12/13/1967 **Age:** 38

Year	Team	Lg	G	AB	H	2B	3B	HR	(Hm	Rd)	TB	R	RBI	RC	TBB	IBB	SO	HBP	SH	SF	SB	CS	SB%	GDP	Avg	OBP	Slg
1994	ATL	NL	4	4	1	0	0	1	(1	0)	4	1	3	1	1	0	0	0	0	0	0	0	-	0	.250	.400	1.000
1995	ATL	NL	69	75	21	6	0	3	(1	2)	36	10	11	13	9	0	16	0	2	1	0	0	-	0	.280	.353	.480
1996	ATL	NL	66	108	26	5	0	2	(0	2)	37	12	8	11	9	1	24	0	4	1	1	0	1.00	1	.241	.297	.343
1997	ATL	NL	61	81	14	2	1	0	(0	0)	18	8	3	2	6	0	16	0	1	1	0	1	.00	4	.173	.227	.222
1998	MON	NL	73	119	24	4	2	3	(1	2)	41	12	10	10	9	0	20	0	2	0	1	0	1.00	2	.202	.258	.345
1999	MON	NL	109	226	53	10	2	5	(4	1)	82	29	25	24	20	0	31	1	1	2	2	5	.29	1	.235	.297	.363
2000	MON	NL	86	169	48	16	0	4	(2	2)	76	20	16	25	12	0	34	1	1	0	2	2	.50	1	.284	.335	.450
2001	MON	NL	96	254	71	17	2	3	(1	2)	101	28	32	32	19	1	53	1	1	2	2	2	.50	6	.280	.330	.398
2002	2 Tms	NL	93	151	37	8	0	0	(0	0)	45	19	11	15	13	4	27	2	10	0	2	2	.50	3	.245	.313	.298
2003	FLA	NL	65	89	19	4	0	2	(1	1)	29	11	8	6	8	3	21	0	3	1	3	0	1.00	0	.213	.276	.326
2004	FLA	NL	69	84	19	3	0	1	(0	1)	25	7	5	9	6	0	18	0	1	1	0	1	.00	1	.226	.278	.298
2005	FLA	NL	2	2	0	0	0	0	(0	0)	0	0	0	0	0	0	1	0	0	0	0	0	-	0	.000	.000	.000
02	Mon	NL	55	74	15	4	0	0	(0	0)	19	9	4	6	8	3	14	1	7	0	1	1	.50	2	.203	.289	.257
02	Fla	NL	38	77	22	4	0	0	(0	0)	26	10	7	9	5	1	13	1	3	0	1	1	.50	1	.286	.337	.338
12 ML YEARS			793	1362	333	75	7	24	(11	13)	494	157	132	148	112	9	261	5	25	8	13	13	.50	19	.244	.303	.363

Orber Moreno

Pitches: R **Bats:** R **Pos:** P   **Ht:** 6'3" **Wt:** 200 **Born:** 4/27/1977 **Age:** 29

			HOW MUCH HE PITCHED						WHAT HE GAVE UP										THE RESULTS						
Year	Team	Lg	G	GS	CG	GF	IP	BFP	H	R	ER	HR	SH	SF	HB	TBB	IBB	SO	WP	Bk	W	L	Pct	ShO	Sv-Op	Hld	ERC	ERA
1999	KC	AL	7	0	0	0	8.0	34	4	5	5	1	0	0	0	6	0	7	0	0	0	0	-	0	0-1	2	2.84	5.63
2003	NYN	NL	7	0	0	4	8.0	36	10	7	7	1	1	0	0	3	0	5	0	0	0	0	-	0	0-0	0	5.65	7.88
2004	NYN	NL	33	0	0	8	34.2	146	29	17	13	0	1	0	3	11	0	29	2	1	3	1	.750	0	1-3	3	2.52	3.38
3 ML YEARS			47	0	0	12	50.2	216	43	29	25	2	2	0	3	20	0	41	2	1	3	1	.750	0	1-4	3	3.01	4.44

Justin Morneau

Bats: L **Throws:** R **Pos:** 1B-138; PH-4; PR-2; DH-1   **Ht:** 6'4" **Wt:** 225 **Born:** 5/15/1981 **Age:** 25

Year	Team	Lg	G	AB	H	2B	3B	HR	(Hm	Rd)	TB	R	RBI	RC	TBB	IBB	SO	HBP	SH	SF	SB	CS	SB%	GDP	Avg	OBP	Slg
2003	MIN	AL	40	106	24	4	0	4	(1	3)	40	14	16	11	9	1	30	0	0	0	0	0	-	4	.226	.287	.377
2004	MIN	AL	74	280	76	17	0	19	(9	10)	150	39	58	48	28	8	54	2	0	2	0	0	-	4	.271	.340	.536
2005	MIN	AL	141	490	117	23	4	22	(9	13)	214	62	79	58	44	8	94	4	0	5	0	2	.00	12	.239	.304	.437
3 ML YEARS			255	876	217	44	4	45	(19	26)	404	115	153	117	81	17	178	6	0	7	0	2	.00	20	.248	.313	.461

Matt Morris

Pitches: R **Bats:** R **Pos:** SP-31   **Ht:** 6'5" **Wt:** 210 **Born:** 8/9/1974 **Age:** 31

			HOW MUCH HE PITCHED						WHAT HE GAVE UP										THE RESULTS						
Year	Team	Lg	G	GS	CG	GF	IP	BFP	H	R	ER	HR	SH	SF	HB	TBB	IBB	SO	WP	Bk	W	L	Pct	ShO	Sv-Op	Hld	ERC	ERA
2005	PlmBh*	A+	2	2	0	0	9.2	43	12	7	7	0	0	0	0	2	0	15	0	0	0	1	.000	0	0--	-	3.84	6.52
1997	STL	NL	33	33	3	0	217.0	900	208	88	77	12	11	7	7	69	2	149	5	3	12	9	.571	0	0-0	0	3.41	3.19
1998	STL	NL	17	17	2	0	113.2	468	101	37	32	8	6	1	3	42	6	79	3	0	7	5	.583	1	0-0	0	3.25	2.53
2000	STL	NL	31	0	0	12	53.0	226	53	22	21	3	3	1	2	17	1	34	0	0	3	3	.500	0	4-7	7	3.58	3.57
2001	STL	NL	34	34	2	0	216.1	909	218	86	76	13	14	5	13	54	3	185	5	1	**22**	8	.733	1	0-0	0	3.50	3.16
2002	STL	NL	32	32	1	0	210.1	890	210	86	80	16	7	8	6	64	3	171	3	0	17	9	.654	1	0-0	0	3.63	3.42
2003	STL	NL	27	27	5	0	172.1	703	164	76	72	20	5	3	4	39	1	120	3	0	11	8	.579	**3**	0-0	0	3.37	3.76
2004	STL	NL	32	32	0	0	202.0	850	205	116	106	35	13	5	8	56	3	131	3	1	15	10	.600	0	0-0	0	4.30	4.72
2005	STL	NL	31	31	2	0	192.2	818	209	101	88	22	10	5	8	37	3	117	1	1	14	10	.583	0	0-0	0	3.95	4.11
8 ML YEARS			237	206	18	12	1377.1	5764	1368	612	552	129	69	35	49	378	22	986	23	6	101	62	.620	8	4-7	7	3.65	3.61

Mike Morse

Bats: R **Throws:** R **Pos:** SS-55; DH-9; LF-8; PH-4; PR-1   **Ht:** 6'4" **Wt:** 220 **Born:** 3/22/1982 **Age:** 24

Year	Team	Lg	G	AB	H	2B	3B	HR	(Hm	Rd)	TB	R	RBI	RC	TBB	IBB	SO	HBP	SH	SF	SB	CS	SB%	GDP	Avg	OBP	Slg
2000	WhSox	R	45	180	46	6	1	2	(-	-)	60	32	24	20	15	0	29	1	0	5	5	2	.71	6	.256	.308	.333
2001	Bristol	R+	57	181	41	7	3	4	(-	-)	66	23	27	23	17	1	57	9	0	0	6	2	.75	4	.227	.324	.365
2002	Knapol	A-	113	417	107	30	4	2	(-	-)	151	43	56	48	25	0	73	8	7	2	7	6	.54	16	.257	.310	.362
2003	WinSa	A+	122	432	106	30	2	10	(-	-)	170	45	55	51	25	0	91	7	2	2	4	4	.50	12	.245	.296	.394
2004	SnAnt	AA	41	157	43	10	1	6	(-	-)	73	18	33	23	9	0	27	4	1	1	0	2	.00	8	.274	.326	.465
2004	Brham	AA	54	209	60	9	5	11	(-	-)	112	30	38	36	15	1	46	1	0	1	0	3	.00	4	.287	.336	.536
2005	Tacom	AAA	49	182	46	12	2	4	(-	-)	74	20	23	24	16	1	36	2	1	2	1	0	1.00	6	.253	.317	.407
2005	SEA	AL	72	230	64	10	1	3	(3	0)	85	27	23	28	18	0	50	8	0	2	3	1	.75	9	.278	.349	.370

Julio Mosquera

Bats: R Throws: R Pos: PH-1   Ht: 6'0" Wt: 190 Born: 1/29/1972 Age: 34

								BATTING												BASERUNNING				AVERAGES		
Year	Team	Lg	G	AB	H	2B	3B	HR	(Hm	Rd)	TB	R	RBI	RC	TBB	IBB	SO	HBP	SH	SF	SB	CS	SB%	GDP	Avg	OBP	Slg
2005	Nashv*	AAA	64	240	62	18	0	4	(-	-)	92	32	30	27	10	0	34	1	1	1	4	1	.80	10	.258	.290	.383
1996	TOR	AL	8	22	5	2	0	0	(0	0)	7	2	2	1	0	0	3	1	0	0	0	1	.00	0	.227	.261	.318
1997	TOR	AL	3	8	2	1	0	0	(0	0)	3	0	0	0	0	0	2	0	0	0	0	0	-	0	.250	.250	.375
2005	MIL	NL	1	1	0	0	0	0	(0	0)	0	0	0	0	0	0	0	0	0	0	0	0	-	0	.000	.000	.000
	3 ML YEARS		12	31	7	3	0	0	(0	0)	10	2	2	1	0	0	5	1	0	0	0	1	.00	0	.226	.250	.323

Guillermo Mota

Pitches: R Bats: R Pos: RP-56   Ht: 6'4" Wt: 205 Born: 7/25/1973 Age: 32

			HOW MUCH HE PITCHED						WHAT HE GAVE UP											THE RESULTS						
Year	Team	Lg	G	GS	CG	GF	IP	BFP	H	R	ER	HR	SH	SF	HB	TBB	IBB	SO	WP	Bk	W	L	Pct	ShO	Sv-Op	Hld	ERC	ERA
2005	Jupiter*	A+	2	2	0	0	2.2	11	3	1	0	0	0	0	0	0	0	4	0	0	0	0	-	0	0--	-	2.52	0.00
1999	MON	NL	51	0	0	18	55.1	243	54	24	18	5	3	3	2	25	3	27	1	1	2	4	.333	0	0-1	3	4.10	2.93
2000	MON	NL	29	0	0	7	30.0	126	27	21	20	3	1	1	2	12	0	24	1	1	1	1	.500	0	0-0	5	3.86	6.00
2001	MON	NL	53	0	0	12	49.2	212	51	30	29	9	3	2	1	18	1	31	1	0	1	3	.250	0	0-3	12	4.77	5.26
2002	LA	NL	43	0	0	11	60.2	256	45	30	28	4	3	1	2	27	6	49	3	0	1	3	.250	0	0-1	4	2.57	4.15
2003	LA	NL	76	0	0	18	105.0	410	78	23	23	7	3	1	1	26	4	99	0	0	6	3	.667	0	1-3	13	2.01	1.97
2004	2 Tms	NL	78	0	0	18	96.2	393	75	33	33	8	5	3	4	37	6	85	5	0	9	8	.529	0	4-8	30	2.82	3.07
2005	FLA	NL	56	0	0	24	67.0	293	65	38	35	5	1	3	1	32	7	60	4	0	2	2	.500	0	2-4	14	3.90	4.70
04	LA	NL	52	0	0	11	63.0	259	51	15	15	4	4	2	2	27	5	52	5	0	8	4	.667	0	1-1	17	2.98	2.14
04	Fla	NL	26	0	0	7	33.2	134	24	18	18	4	1	1	2	10	1	33	0	0	1	4	.200	0	3-7	13	2.51	4.81
	7 ML YEARS		386	0	0	108	464.1	1933	395	199	186	41	19	14	13	177	27	375	15	2	22	24	.478	0	7-20	81	3.15	3.61

Jamie Moyer

Pitches: L Bats: L Pos: SP-32   Ht: 6'0" Wt: 175 Born: 11/18/1962 Age: 43

			HOW MUCH HE PITCHED						WHAT HE GAVE UP											THE RESULTS						
Year	Team	Lg	G	GS	CG	GF	IP	BFP	H	R	ER	HR	SH	SF	HB	TBB	IBB	SO	WP	Bk	W	L	Pct	ShO	Sv-Op	Hld	ERC	ERA
1986	CHN	NL	16	16	1	0	87.1	395	107	52	49	10	3	3	3	42	1	45	3	3	7	4	.636	0	0-0	0	6.13	5.05
1987	CHN	NL	35	33	1	1	201.0	899	210	127	114	28	14	7	5	97	9	147	11	2	12	15	.444	0	0-0	0	4.96	5.10
1988	CHN	NL	34	30	3	1	202.0	855	212	84	78	20	14	4	4	55	7	121	4	0	9	15	.375	1	0-2	0	3.89	3.48
1989	TEX	AL	15	15	1	0	76.0	337	84	51	41	10	1	4	4	33	0	44	1	0	4	9	.308	0	0-0	0	5.20	4.86
1990	TEX	AL	33	10	1	6	102.1	447	115	59	53	6	1	7	4	39	4	58	1	0	2	6	.250	0	0-0	1	4.57	4.66
1991	STL	NL	8	7	0	1	31.1	142	38	21	20	5	4	2	1	16	0	20	2	1	0	5	.000	0	0-0	0	6.58	5.74
1993	BAL	AL	25	25	3	0	152.0	630	154	63	58	11	3	1	6	38	2	90	1	1	12	9	.571	1	0-0	0	3.58	3.43
1994	BAL	AL	23	23	0	0	149.0	631	158	81	79	23	5	2	2	38	3	87	1	0	5	7	.417	0	0-0	0	4.24	4.77
1995	BAL	AL	27	18	0	3	115.2	483	117	70	67	18	5	3	3	30	0	65	0	0	8	6	.571	0	0-0	0	4.11	5.21
1996	2 Tms	AL	34	21	0	1	160.2	703	177	86	71	23	7	6	2	46	5	79	3	1	13	3	.813	0	0-0	1	4.42	3.98
1997	SEA	AL	30	30	2	0	188.2	787	187	82	81	21	6	1	7	43	2	113	3	0	17	5	.773	0	0-0	0	3.56	3.86
1998	SEA	AL	34	34	4	0	234.1	974	234	99	92	23	4	3	10	42	2	158	3	1	15	9	.625	3	0-0	0	3.34	3.53
1999	SEA	AL	32	32	4	0	228.0	945	235	108	98	23	6	2	9	48	1	137	3	0	14	8	.636	0	0-0	0	3.71	3.87
2000	SEA	AL	26	26	0	0	154.0	678	173	100	94	22	3	3	3	53	2	98	4	1	13	10	.565	0	0-0	0	4.91	5.49
2001	SEA	AL	33	33	1	0	209.2	851	187	84	80	24	5	11	10	44	4	119	1	0	20	6	.769	0	0-0	0	3.03	3.43
2002	SEA	AL	34	34	4	0	230.2	931	198	89	85	28	5	7	9	50	4	147	3	0	13	8	.619	2	0-0	0	2.89	3.32
2003	SEA	AL	33	33	1	0	215.0	897	199	83	78	19	7	6	8	66	3	129	0	0	21	7	.750	0	0-0	0	3.37	3.27
2004	SEA	AL	34	33	1	0	202.0	888	217	127	117	44	9	6	11	63	3	125	1	0	7	13	.350	0	0-0	0	5.13	5.21
2005	SEA	AL	32	32	1	0	200.0	868	225	99	95	23	6	6	8	52	2	102	3	0	13	7	.650	0	0-0	0	4.46	4.28
96	Bos	AL	23	10	0	1	90.0	405	111	50	45	14	4	3	1	27	2	50	2	1	7	1	.875	0	0-0	1	5.37	4.50
96	Sea	AL	11	11	0	0	70.2	298	66	36	26	9	3	3	1	19	3	29	1	0	6	2	.750	0	0-0	0	3.31	3.31
	19 ML YEARS		538	485	28	14	3139.2	13341	3227	1568	1450	381	108	84	107	895	54	1884	48	10	205	152	.574	8	0-2	2	4.04	4.16

Bill Mueller

Bats: B Throws: R Pos: 3B-142; 2B-5; PH-5   Ht: 5'10" Wt: 180 Born: 3/17/1971 Age: 35

								BATTING												BASERUNNING				AVERAGES		
Year	Team	Lg	G	AB	H	2B	3B	HR	(Hm	Rd)	TB	R	RBI	RC	TBB	IBB	SO	HBP	SH	SF	SB	CS	SB%	GDP	Avg	OBP	Slg
1996	SF	NL	55	200	66	15	1	0	(0	0)	83	31	19	35	24	0	26	1	1	2	0	0	-	1	.330	.401	.415
1997	SF	NL	128	390	114	26	3	7	(5	2)	167	51	44	62	48	1	71	3	6	6	4	3	.57	10	.292	.369	.428
1998	SF	NL	145	534	157	27	0	9	(8	1)	211	93	59	83	79	1	83	1	3	5	3	3	.50	12	.294	.383	.395
1999	SF	NL	116	414	120	24	0	2	(1	1)	150	61	36	62	65	1	52	3	8	2	4	2	.67	11	.290	.388	.362
2000	SF	NL	153	560	150	29	4	10	(3	7)	217	97	55	72	52	0	62	6	7	6	4	2	.67	16	.268	.333	.388
2001	CHN	NL	70	210	62	12	1	6	(3	3)	94	38	23	39	37	3	19	3	4	3	1	1	.50	4	.295	.403	.448
2002	2 Tms	NL	111	366	96	19	4	7	(4	3)	144	51	38	56	52	2	42	0	4	5	0	0	-	9	.262	.350	.393
2003	BOS	AL	146	524	171	45	5	19	(6	13)	283	85	85	102	59	2	77	7	4	6	1	4	.20	11	.326	.398	.540
2004	BOS	AL	110	399	113	27	1	12	(9	3)	178	75	57	61	51	1	56	4	0	6	2	2	.50	8	.283	.365	.446
2005	BOS	AL	150	519	153	34	3	10	(6	4)	223	69	62	82	59	3	74	6	0	6	0	0	-	22	.295	.369	.430
02	ChC	NL	103	353	94	19	4	7	(4	3)	142	51	37	56	52	2	41	0	4	5	0	0	-	8	.266	.355	.402
02	SF	NL	8	13	2	0	0	0	(0	0)	2	0	1	0	0	0	1	0	0	0	0	0	-	1	.154	.214	.154
	10 ML YEARS		1184	4116	1202	258	22	82	(38	44)	1750	651	478	654	526	14	562	34	37	47	19	17	.53	104	.292	.373	.425

Mark Mulder

Pitches: L Bats: L Pos: SP-32   Ht: 6'6" Wt: 215 Born: 8/5/1977 Age: 28

			HOW MUCH HE PITCHED						WHAT HE GAVE UP											THE RESULTS						
Year	Team	Lg	G	GS	CG	GF	IP	BFP	H	R	ER	HR	SH	SF	HB	TBB	IBB	SO	WP	Bk	W	L	Pct	ShO	Sv-Op	Hld	ERC	ERA
2000	OAK	AL	27	27	0	0	154.0	705	191	106	93	22	3	8	4	69	3	88	6	0	9	10	.474	0	0-0	0	6.14	5.44
2001	OAK	AL	34	34	6	0	229.1	927	214	92	88	16	8	3	5	51	4	153	4	0	21	8	.724	4	0-0	0	2.95	3.45
2002	OAK	AL	30	30	2	0	207.1	862	182	88	80	21	6	4	11	55	3	159	7	1	19	7	.731	1	0-0	0	3.06	3.47

			HOW MUCH HE PITCHED							WHAT HE GAVE UP									THE RESULTS							
Year	Team	Lg	G	GS	CG	GF	IP	BFP	H	R	ER	HR	SH	SF	HB	TBB	IBB	SO	WP	Bk	W	L	Pct	ShO	Sv-Op	Hld	ERC	ERA
2003	OAK	AL	26	26	9	0	186.2	747	180	66	65	15	7	2	2	40	2	128	7	0	15	9	.625	2	0-0	0	3.17	3.13
2004	OAK	AL	33	33	5	0	225.2	952	223	119	111	25	7	6	12	83	1	140	10	0	17	8	.680	1	0-0	0	4.27	4.43
2005	STL	NL	32	32	3	0	205.0	868	212	90	83	19	9	4	9	70	1	111	9	0	16	8	.667	2	0-0	0	4.25	3.64
	6 ML YEARS		182	182	25	0	1208.0	5061	1202	561	520	118	40	27	43	368	14	779	43	1	97	50	.660	10	0-0	0	3.84	3.87

Terry Mulholland

Pitches: L Bats: R Pos: RP-49　　　　　　　　**Ht: 6'3" Wt: 220 Born: 3/9/1963 Age: 43**

			HOW MUCH HE PITCHED							WHAT HE GAVE UP									THE RESULTS							
Year	Team	Lg	G	GS	CG	GF	IP	BFP	H	R	ER	HR	SH	SF	HB	TBB	IBB	SO	WP	Bk	W	L	Pct	ShO	Sv-Op	Hld	ERC	ERA
1986	SF	NL	15	10	0	1	54.2	245	51	33	30	3	5	1	1	35	2	27	6	0	1	7	.125	0	0-0	0	4.31	4.94
1988	SF	NL	9	6	2	1	46.0	191	50	20	19	3	5	0	1	7	0	18	1	0	2	1	.667	1	0-0	0	3.46	3.72
1989	2 Tms		25	18	2	4	115.1	513	137	66	63	8	7	1	1	36	3	66	3	0	4	7	.364	1	0-0	1	4.64	4.92
1990	PHI	NL	33	26	6	2	180.2	746	172	78	67	15	7	12	4	42	7	75	7	2	9	10	.474	1	0-1	0	3.04	3.34
1991	PHI	NL	34	34	8	0	232.0	956	231	100	93	15	11	6	3	49	2	142	3	0	16	13	.552	3	0-0	0	3.15	3.61
1992	PHI	NL	32	32	12	0	229.0	937	227	101	97	14	10	7	3	46	3	125	3	0	13	11	.542	2	0-0	0	3.07	3.81
1993	PHI	NL	29	28	7	0	191.0	786	177	80	69	20	5	4	3	40	2	116	5	0	12	9	.571	2	0-0	0	2.99	3.25
1994	NYA	AL	24	19	2	4	120.2	542	150	94	87	24	3	4	3	37	1	72	5	0	6	7	.462	0	0-0	0	5.92	6.49
1995	SF	NL	29	24	2	2	149.0	666	190	112	96	25	11	6	4	38	1	65	4	0	5	13	.278	1	0-0	0	5.67	5.80
1996	2 Tms		33	33	3	0	202.2	871	232	112	105	22	11	8	5	49	4	86	6	0	13	11	.542	0	0-0	0	4.41	4.66
1997	2 Tms	NL	40	27	1	5	186.2	794	190	100	88	24	17	4	11	51	3	99	3	0	6	13	.316	0	0-0	1	4.09	4.24
1998	CHN	NL	70	6	0	14	112.0	476	100	49	36	7	5	3	4	39	7	72	4	0	6	5	.545	0	3-5	19	3.04	2.89
1999	2 Tms	NL	42	24	0	7	170.1	736	201	95	83	21	9	4	1	45	6	83	3	0	10	8	.556	0	1-1	4	4.73	4.39
2000	ATL	NL	54	20	1	14	156.2	702	198	96	89	24	10	5	4	41	7	78	0	0	9	9	.500	0	1-3	2	5.43	5.11
2001	2 Tms	NL	41	4	0	8	65.2	285	78	35	34	12	1	1	2	17	1	42	1	0	1	1	.500	0	0-0	7	5.34	4.66
2002	2 Tms		37	3	0	17	79.0	357	101	56	50	15	2	6	6	21	3	38	1	0	3	2	.600	0	0-0	3	6.09	5.70
2003	CLE	AL	45	3	0	14	99.0	445	117	60	54	17	0	6	6	37	6	42	1	0	3	4	.429	0	0-2	5	5.75	4.91
2004	MIN	AL	39	15	0	9	123.1	549	163	76	71	17	7	5	5	33	3	60	2	0	5	9	.357	0	0-0	2	5.94	5.18
2005	MIN	AL	49	0	0	26	59.0	246	61	30	28	6	5	1	2	17	4	18	3	1	0	2	.000	0	0-1	3	3.96	4.27
89	SF	NL	5	1	0	2	11.0	51	15	5	5	0	0	0	0	4	0	6	0	0	0	0	-	0	0-0	1	5.23	4.09
89	Phi		20	17	2	2	104.1	462	122	61	58	8	7	1	4	32	3	60	3	0	4	7	.364	1	0-0	0	4.58	5.00
96	Phi	NL	21	21	3	0	133.1	571	157	74	69	17	6	5	3	21	1	52	5	0	8	7	.533	0	0-0	0	4.36	4.66
96	Sea	AL	12	12	0	0	69.1	300	75	38	36	5	5	3	2	28	3	34	1	0	5	4	.556	0	0-0	0	4.49	4.67
97	ChC	NL	25	25	1	0	157.0	668	162	79	71	20	13	3	9	45	2	74	2	0	6	12	.333	0	0-0	0	4.24	4.07
97	SF	NL	15	2	0	5	29.2	126	28	21	17	4	4	1	2	6	1	25	1	0	0	1	.000	0	0-0	1	3.34	5.16
99	ChC	NL	26	16	0	4	110.0	485	137	71	63	16	6	3	1	32	4	44	2	0	6	6	.500	0	0-0	1	5.42	5.15
99	Atl		16	8	0	3	60.1	251	64	24	20	5	3	1	0	13	2	39	1	0	4	2	.667	0	1-1	3	3.55	2.98
01	Pit	NL	22	1	0	3	36.1	150	38	15	15	5	1	1	1	10	1	17	1	0	0	0	-	0	0-0	3	4.32	3.72
01	LA	NL	19	3	0	5	29.1	135	40	20	19	7	0	0	1	7	0	25	0	0	1	1	.500	0	0-0	4	6.67	5.83
02	LA	NL	21	0	0	12	32.0	147	45	29	26	10	0	2	2	7	0	17	1	0	0	0	-	0	0-0	0	7.68	7.31
02	Cle	AL	16	3	0	5	47.0	210	56	27	24	5	2	4	4	14	3	21	0	0	3	2	.600	0	0-0	3	5.05	4.60
	19 ML YEARS		680	332	46	128	2572.2	11043	2826	1393	1259	292	131	84	70	680	65	1324	64	3	124	142	.466	10	5-13	44	4.26	4.40

Eric Munson

Bats: L Throws: R Pos: PH-7; DH-3; 3B-2; 1B-1; LF-1　　　　**Ht: 6'3" Wt: 228 Born: 10/3/1977 Age: 28**

			BATTING																				BASERUNNING				AVERAGES		
Year	Team	Lg	G	AB	H	2B	3B	HR	(Hm	Rd)	TB	R	RBI	RC	TBB	IBB	SO	HBP	SH	SF			SB	CS	SB%	GDP	Avg	OBP	Slg
2005	Drham*	AAA	100	382	109	22	0	25	(-	-)	206	67	71	72	38	4	81	2	1	2			1	1	.50	12	.285	.351	.539
2000	DET	AL	3	5	0	0	0	0	(0	0)	0	0	1	0	0	0	1	0	0	0			0	0	-	0	.000	.000	.000
2001	DET	AL	17	66	10	3	1	1	(1	0)	18	4	6	2	3	0	21	0	0	0			0	1	.00	2	.152	.188	.273
2002	DET	AL	18	59	11	0	0	2	(0	2)	17	3	5	3	6	0	11	1	0	1			0	0	-	1	.186	.269	.288
2003	DET	AL	99	313	75	9	0	18	(7	11)	138	28	50	45	35	1	61	1	1	7			3	0	1.00	4	.240	.312	.441
2004	DET	AL	109	321	68	14	2	19	(13	6)	143	36	49	48	29	3	90	6	1	0			1	1	.50	1	.212	.289	.445
2005	TB	AL	11	18	3	1	0	0	(0	0)	4	2	2	2	4	0	3	1	0	1			0	0	-	2	.167	.333	.222
	6 ML YEARS		257	782	167	27	3	40	(21	19)	320	73	113	100	77	4	187	9	2	9			4	2	.67	10	.214	.288	.409

Scott Munter

Pitches: R Bats: R Pos: RP-45　　　　　　　　**Ht: 6'6" Wt: 240 Born: 3/7/1980 Age: 26**

			HOW MUCH HE PITCHED							WHAT HE GAVE UP									THE RESULTS							
Year	Team	Lg	G	GS	CG	GF	IP	BFP	H	R	ER	HR	SH	SF	HB	TBB	IBB	SO	WP	Bk	W	L	Pct	ShO	Sv-Op	Hld	ERC	ERA
2001	SlmKzr	A-	15	0	0	1	35.0	159	42	26	23	3	0	1	1	12	0	28	3	0	1	2	.333	0	0--	-	4.91	5.91
2001	Hgrstn	A	1	1	0	0	5.0	25	5	3	2	0	1	1	0	1	0	2	0	0	1	0	1.000	0	0--	-	2.60	3.60
2002	SnJos	A+	3	0	0	0	4.1	29	12	5	5	0	0	1	0	4	0	2	0	0	0	0	-	0	0--	-	17.37	10.38
2002	SlmKzr	A-	10	4	0	1	29.2	142	33	24	23	0	1	3	2	20	0	20	3	1	1	1	.500	0	0--	-	5.22	6.98
2003	Hgrstn	A	40	0	0	18	68.2	296	62	28	23	3	3	0	2	28	0	47	7	1	3	5	.375	0	5--	-	3.24	3.01
2004	Nrwich	AA	42	0	0	19	65.0	280	63	19	17	4	1	0	2	22	5	30	9	0	2	4	.333	0	3--	-	3.35	2.35
2004	Fresno	AAA	13	0	0	6	15.2	71	20	8	6	1	0	0	0	4	0	5	1	0	1	1	.500	0	1--	-	4.69	3.45
2005	Fresno	AAA	12	0	0	5	12.1	58	17	8	7	0	1	2	0	4	0	5	1	0	1	3	.250	0	0--	-	5.05	5.11
2005	SF	NL	45	0	0	7	38.2	159	40	15	11	1	2	1	1	12	1	11	1	0	2	0	1.000	0	0-3	12	3.62	2.56

Donnie Murphy

Bats: R Throws: R Pos: 2B-29; PH-6; SS-2; DH-1　　　　**Ht: 5'10" Wt: 180 Born: 3/10/1983 Age: 23**

			BATTING																				BASERUNNING				AVERAGES		
Year	Team	Lg	G	AB	H	2B	3B	HR	(Hm	Rd)	TB	R	RBI	RC	TBB	IBB	SO	HBP	SH	SF			SB	CS	SB%	GDP	Avg	OBP	Slg
2002	Burlgtn	A	33	120	27	6	3	0	(-	-)	39	12	15	12	11	0	31	4	1	5			0	2	.00	1	.225	.300	.325
2002	Spkane	A-	28	109	33	10	2	0	(-	-)	47	20	15	16	6	0	17	3	0	0			0	0	-	2	.303	.356	.431
2003	Burlgtn	A	132	504	158	29	6	5	(-	-)	214	77	98	90	65	1	96	9	3	7			15	6	.71	8	.313	.397	.425
2004	Wilmg	A+	129	485	124	32	5	10	(-	-)	196	67	75	62	52	2	96	4	2	8			1	1	.50	16	.256	.328	.404

Year	Team	Lg	G	AB	H	2B	3B	HR	(Hm	Rd)	TB	R	RBI	RC	TBB	IBB	SO	HBP	SH	SF	SB	CS	SB%	GDP	Avg	OBP	Slg
2005	Wichta	AA	50	214	67	13	1	10	(-	-)	112	33	32	40	13	0	32	4	3	1	1	1	.50	6	.313	.362	.523
2004	KC	AL	7	27	5	3	0	0	(0	0)	8	1	3	2	0	0	7	0	0	0	1	0	1.00	1	.185	.185	.296
2005	KC	AL	32	77	12	5	0	1	(0	1)	20	4	8	1	9	0	23	0	1	1	0	1	.00	3	.156	.241	.260
	2 ML YEARS		39	104	17	8	0	1	(0	1)	28	5	11	3	9	0	30	0	1	1	1	1	.50	4	.163	.228	.269

Matt Murton

Bats: R Throws: R Pos: LF-43; PH-12

Ht: 6'1" Wt: 215 Born: 10/3/1981 Age: 24

Year	Team	Lg	G	AB	H	2B	3B	HR	(Hm	Rd)	TB	R	RBI	RC	TBB	IBB	SO	HBP	SH	SF	SB	CS	SB%	GDP	Avg	OBP	Slg
2003	Lowell	A-	53	189	54	11	2	2	(-	-)	75	30	29	32	27	0	39	4	0	7	9	3	.75	5	.286	.374	.397
2004	Dytona	A+	24	79	20	1	1	2	(-	-)	29	13	8	10	8	1	10	1	0	1	2	0	1.00	3	.253	.326	.367
2004	Srsota	A+	102	376	113	16	4	11	(-	-)	170	60	55	65	42	4	61	3	0	4	5	4	.56	7	.301	.372	.452
2005	WTenn	AA	78	313	107	17	4	8	(-	-)	156	46	46	64	29	3	42	4	3	1	18	5	.78	10	.342	.403	.498
2005	Iowa	AAA	9	34	12	2	0	1	(-	-)	17	4	3	7	4	0	8	0	0	0	0	0	-	2	.353	.421	.500
2005	CHN	NL	51	140	45	3	2	7	(2	5)	73	19	14	19	16	4	22	0	2	2	2	1	.67	4	.321	.386	.521

Mike Mussina

Pitches: R Bats: L Pos: SP-30

Ht: 6'2" Wt: 185 Born: 12/8/1968 Age: 37

Year	Team	Lg	G	GS	CG	GF	IP	BFP	H	R	ER	HR	SH	SF	HB	TBB	IBB	SO	WP	Bk	W	L	Pct	ShO	Sv-Op	Hld	ERC	ERA
1991	BAL	AL	12	12	2	0	87.2	349	77	31	28	7	3	2	1	21	0	52	3	1	4	5	.444	0	0-0	0	2.80	2.87
1992	BAL	AL	32	32	8	0	241.0	957	212	70	68	16	13	6	2	48	2	130	6	0	18	5	.783	4	0-0	0	2.54	2.54
1993	BAL	AL	25	25	3	0	167.2	693	163	84	80	20	6	4	3	44	2	117	5	0	14	6	.700	2	0-0	0	3.61	4.46
1994	BAL	AL	24	24	3	0	176.1	712	163	63	60	19	3	9	1	42	1	99	0	0	16	5	.762	0	0-0	0	3.16	3.06
1995	BAL	AL	32	32	7	0	221.2	882	187	86	81	24	2	2	1	50	4	158	2	0	19	9	.679	4	0-0	0	2.66	3.29
1996	BAL	AL	36	36	4	0	243.1	1039	264	137	130	31	4	4	3	69	0	204	3	0	19	11	.633	1	0-0	0	4.36	4.81
1997	BAL	AL	33	33	4	0	224.2	905	197	87	80	27	4	2	3	54	3	218	5	0	15	8	.652	1	0-0	0	3.00	3.20
1998	BAL	AL	29	29	4	0	206.1	835	189	85	80	22	6	3	4	41	3	175	10	0	13	10	.565	2	0-0	0	2.96	3.49
1999	BAL	AL	31	31	4	0	203.1	842	207	88	79	16	9	7	1	52	0	172	2	0	18	7	.720	0	0-0	0	3.54	3.50
2000	BAL	AL	34	34	6	0	237.2	987	236	105	100	28	8	6	3	46	0	210	3	0	11	15	.423	1	0-0	0	3.37	3.79
2001	NYA	AL	34	34	4	0	228.2	909	202	87	80	20	5	6	4	42	2	214	6	0	17	11	.607	3	0-0	0	2.65	3.15
2002	NYA	AL	33	33	2	0	215.2	886	208	103	97	27	5	5	5	48	1	182	7	0	18	10	.643	2	0-0	0	3.46	4.05
2003	NYA	AL	31	31	2	0	214.2	855	192	86	81	21	1	4	3	40	4	195	4	0	17	8	.680	1	0-0	0	2.75	3.40
2004	NYA	AL	27	27	1	0	164.2	697	178	91	84	22	5	4	2	40	1	132	5	0	12	9	.571	0	0-0	0	4.19	4.59
2005	NYA	AL	30	30	2	0	179.2	766	199	93	88	23	6	4	7	47	0	142	2	0	13	8	.619	2	0-0	0	4.55	4.41
	15 ML YEARS		443	443	56	0	3013.0	12314	2874	1296	1219	323	79	68	43	684	23	2400	63	1	224	127	.638	23	0-0	0	3.28	3.64

Brett Myers

Pitches: R Bats: R Pos: SP-34

Ht: 6'4" Wt: 215 Born: 8/17/1980 Age: 25

Year	Team	Lg	G	GS	CG	GF	IP	BFP	H	R	ER	HR	SH	SF	HB	TBB	IBB	SO	WP	Bk	W	L	Pct	ShO	Sv-Op	Hld	ERC	ERA
2002	PHI	NL	12	12	1	0	72.0	307	73	38	34	11	6	2	6	29	1	34	2	1	4	5	.444	0	0-0	0	5.04	4.25
2003	PHI	NL	32	32	1	0	193.0	848	205	99	95	20	6	3	9	76	8	143	9	0	14	9	.609	1	0-0	0	4.56	4.43
2004	PHI	NL	32	31	1	1	176.0	778	196	113	108	31	9	3	6	62	4	116	5	0	11	11	.500	1	0-0	0	5.17	5.52
2005	PHI	NL	34	34	2	0	215.1	905	193	94	89	31	9	3	11	68	2	208	4	4	13	8	.619	0	0-0	0	3.64	3.72
	4 ML YEARS		110	109	5	1	656.1	2838	667	344	326	93	30	11	32	235	15	501	20	5	42	33	.560	2	0-0	0	4.46	4.47

Greg Myers

Bats: L Throws: R Pos: C-4; PH-3

Ht: 6'2" Wt: 225 Born: 4/14/1966 Age: 40

Year	Team	Lg	G	AB	H	2B	3B	HR	(Hm	Rd)	TB	R	RBI	RC	TBB	IBB	SO	HBP	SH	SF	SB	CS	SB%	GDP	Avg	OBP	Slg
1987	TOR	AL	7	9	1	0	0	0	(0	0)	1	1	0	0	0	0	3	0	0	0	0	0	-	2	.111	.111	.111
1989	TOR	AL	17	44	5	2	0	0	(0	0)	7	0	1	0	2	0	9	0	0	0	0	1	.00	2	.114	.152	.159
1990	TOR	AL	87	250	59	7	1	5	(3	2)	83	33	22	21	22	0	33	0	1	4	0	1	.00	12	.236	.293	.332
1991	TOR	AL	107	309	81	22	0	8	(5	3)	127	25	36	35	21	4	45	0	0	3	0	0	-	13	.262	.306	.411
1992	2 Tms		30	78	18	7	0	1	(0	1)	28	4	13	7	5	0	11	0	1	2	0	0	-	2	.231	.271	.359
1993	CAL	AL	108	290	74	10	0	7	(4	3)	105	27	40	29	17	2	47	2	3	3	3	3	.50	8	.255	.298	.362
1994	CAL	AL	45	126	31	6	0	2	(1	1)	43	10	8	12	10	3	27	0	5	1	0	2	.00	4	.246	.299	.341
1995	CAL	AL	85	273	71	12	2	9	(6	3)	114	35	38	34	17	3	49	1	1	2	0	1	.00	4	.260	.304	.418
1996	MIN	AL	97	329	94	22	3	6	(3	3)	140	37	47	42	19	5	52	0	0	5	0	0	-	11	.286	.320	.426
1997	2 Tms		71	174	45	11	1	5	(3	2)	73	24	29	23	17	2	32	0	0	2	0	0	-	4	.259	.321	.420
1998	SD	NL	69	171	42	10	0	4	(1	3)	64	19	20	18	17	1	36	0	0	1	0	1	.00	6	.246	.312	.374
1999	2 Tms	NL	84	200	53	6	0	5	(3	2)	74	19	24	24	26	4	30	0	0	1	0	0	-	6	.265	.348	.370
2000	BAL	AL	43	125	28	6	0	3	(1	2)	43	9	12	9	8	0	29	0	1	0	0	0	-	7	.224	.271	.344
2001	2 Tms	AL	58	161	36	3	0	11	(5	6)	72	24	31	22	21	1	38	0	0	0	0	0	-	5	.224	.313	.447
2002	OAK	AL	65	144	32	5	0	6	(2	4)	55	15	21	17	26	3	36	0	0	0	0	0	-	6	.222	.341	.382
2003	TOR	AL	121	329	101	19	0	15	(8	7)	165	51	52	51	37	2	57	0	0	3	0	3	.00	14	.307	.374	.502
2004	TOR	AL	8	18	4	2	0	0	(0	0)	6	0	1	1	2	0	1	0	0	1	0	0	-	1	.222	.300	.333
2005	TOR	AL	6	12	1	0	0	0	(0	0)	1	0	1	0	1	0	1	0	0	0	0	0	-	1	.083	.154	.083
92	Tor	AL	22	61	14	6	0	1	(0	1)	23	4	13	6	5	0	5	0	0	2	0	0	-	2	.230	.279	.377
92	Cal	AL	8	17	4	1	0	0	(0	0)	5	0	0	1	0	0	6	0	1	0	0	0	-	0	.235	.235	.294
97	Min	AL	62	165	44	11	1	5	(3	2)	72	24	28	23	16	2	29	0	0	2	0	0	-	4	.267	.328	.436
97	Atl	NL	9	9	1	0	0	0	(0	0)	1	0	1	0	1	0	3	0	0	0	0	0	-	0	.111	.200	.111
99	SD	NL	50	128	37	4	0	3	(2	1)	50	9	15	17	13	2	14	0	0	0	0	0	-	5	.289	.355	.391
99	Atl	NL	34	72	16	2	0	2	(1	1)	24	10	9	7	13	2	16	0	0	1	0	0	-	0	.222	.337	.333

Year	Team	Lg	G	AB	H	2B	3B	HR	(Hm	Rd)	TB	R	RBI	RC	TBB	IBB	SO	HBP	SH	SF	SB	CS	SB%	GDP	Avg	OBP	Slg
																										BATTING → BASERUNNING → AVERAGES		
01	Bal	AL	25	74	20	2	0	4	(3	1)	34	11	18	11	8	0	17	0	0	0	0	0	-	3	.270	.341	.459
01	Oak	AL	33	87	16	1	0	7	(2	5)	38	13	13	11	13	1	21	0	0	0	0	0	-	2	.184	.290	.437
18 ML YEARS			1108	3042	776	150	7	87	(45	42)	1201	333	396	347	268	28	539	3	12	27	3	12	.20	106	.255	.313	.395

Mike Myers

Pitches: L Bats: L Pos: RP-65 **Ht: 6'4" Wt: 212 Born: 6/26/1969 Age: 37**

Year	Team	Lg	G	GS	CG	GF	IP	BFP	H	R	ER	HR	SH	SF	HB	TBB	IBB	SO	WP	Bk	W	L	Pct	ShO	Sv-Op	Hld	ERC	ERA
1995	2 Tms		13	0	0	5	8.1	42	11	7	7	1	0	1	2	7	0	4	0	0	1	0	1.000	0	0-1	1	9.61	7.56
1996	DET	AL	83	0	0	25	64.2	298	70	41	36	6	2	1	4	34	8	69	2	0	1	5	.167	0	6-8	17	4.97	5.01
1997	DET	AL	88	0	0	23	53.2	246	58	36	34	12	4	3	2	25	2	50	0	0	0	4	.000	0	2-5	18	5.70	5.70
1998	MIL	NL	70	0	0	14	50.0	211	44	19	15	5	4	2	6	22	1	40	2	1	2	2	.500	0	1-3	23	4.14	2.70
1999	MIL	NL	71	0	0	14	41.1	179	46	24	24	7	5	0	3	13	1	35	1	0	2	1	.667	0	0-3	14	5.24	5.23
2000	COL	NL	78	0	0	22	45.1	177	24	10	10	2	1	2	2	24	3	41	1	0	0	1	.000	0	1-2	15	1.94	1.99
2001	COL	NL	73	0	0	14	40.0	169	32	17	16	2	1	1	1	24	7	36	0	0	2	3	.400	0	0-2	10	3.29	3.60
2002	ARI	NL	69	0	0	15	37.0	171	39	18	18	2	3	1	8	17	0	31	0	0	4	3	.571	0	4-9	17	5.13	4.38
2003	ARI	NL	64	0	0	17	36.1	172	38	23	23	4	1	0	5	21	1	21	1	0	0	1	.000	0	0-3	6	5.54	5.70
2004	2 Tms	AL	75	0	0	15	42.2	192	45	22	22	5	2	1	2	23	5	32	2	0	5	1	.833	0	0-0	10	5.11	4.64
2005	BOS	AL	65	0	0	11	37.1	151	30	14	13	3	1	1	0	13	2	21	0	0	3	1	.750	0	0-1	9	2.90	3.13
95	Fla	NL	2	0	0	2	2.0	9	1	0	0	0	0	0	0	3	0	0	0	0	0	0	-	0	0-0	1	5.03	0.00
95	Det	AL	11	0	0	3	6.1	33	10	7	7	1	0	1	2	4	0	4	0	0	1	0	1.000	0	0-1	1	11.13	9.95
04	Sea	AL	50	0	0	10	27.2	126	29	15	15	3	2	1	2	17	4	23	1	0	4	1	.800	0	0-0	8	5.40	4.88
04	Bos	AL	25	0	0	5	15.0	66	16	7	7	2	0	0	0	6	1	9	1	0	1	0	1.000	0	0-0	2	4.55	4.20
11 ML YEARS			749	0	0	175	456.2	2008	437	231	218	49	24	11	37	223	30	380	9	1	20	22	.476	0	14-37	140	4.48	4.30

Brian Myrow

Bats: L Throws: R Pos: PH-15; 1B-5 **Ht: 5'11" Wt: 190 Born: 9/4/1976 Age: 29**

Year	Team	Lg	G	AB	H	2B	3B	HR	(Hm	Rd)	TB	R	RBI	RC	TBB	IBB	SO	HBP	SH	SF	SB	CS	SB%	GDP	Avg	OBP	Slg
2001	Tampa	A+	48	149	38	11	1	3	(-	-)	60	30	28	28	32	0	29	5	4	2	5	1	.83	4	.255	.399	.403
2002	Tampa	A+	61	225	63	12	1	5	(-	-)	92	29	40	42	42	2	45	9	0	3	0	0	-	4	.280	.409	.409
2002	Nrwich	AA	61	188	57	16	0	3	(-	-)	82	37	30	41	41	1	42	6	0	1	5	0	1.00	4	.303	.441	.436
2003	Trentn	AA	137	461	141	31	8	18	(-	-)	242	99	78	114	107	8	113	16	1	6	6	3	.67	3	.306	.447	.525
2004	Clmbs	AAA	47	164	44	12	3	3	(-	-)	71	28	15	26	23	2	37	2	2	0	3	4	.43	2	.268	.365	.433
2004	LsVgs	AAA	50	153	55	15	2	6	(-	-)	92	29	29	38	21	2	47	4	0	2	2	3	.40	2	.359	.444	.601
2005	LsVgs	AAA	121	393	111	28	5	22	(-	-)	215	83	73	90	74	3	83	10	0	5	4	2	.67	4	.282	.405	.547
2005	LAN	NL	19	20	4	1	0	0	(0	0)	5	2	0	3	5	0	8	0	0	0	0	0	-	0	.200	.360	.250

Xavier Nady

Bats: R Throws: R Pos: 1B-44; CF-30; LF-26; PH-17; RF-13; 3B-3; PR-3; DH-1 **Ht: 6'0" Wt: 180 Born: 11/14/1978 Age: 27**

Year	Team	Lg	G	AB	H	2B	3B	HR	(Hm	Rd)	TB	R	RBI	RC	TBB	IBB	SO	HBP	SH	SF	SB	CS	SB%	GDP	Avg	OBP	Slg
2000	SD	NL	1	1	1	0	0	0	(0	0)	1	1	0	1	0	0	0	0	0	0	0	0	-	0	1.000	1.000	1.000
2003	SD	NL	110	371	99	17	1	9	(5	4)	145	50	39	39	24	0	74	6	2	1	6	2	.75	14	.267	.321	.391
2004	SD	NL	34	77	19	4	0	3	(1	2)	32	7	9	8	5	0	13	1	1	0	0	0	-	2	.247	.301	.416
2005	SD	NL	124	326	85	15	2	13	(5	8)	143	40	43	37	22	1	67	7	1	0	2	1	.67	5	.261	.321	.439
4 ML YEARS			269	775	204	36	3	25	(11	14)	321	98	91	85	51	1	154	14	4	1	8	3	.73	23	.263	.320	.414

Clint Nageotte

Pitches: R Bats: R Pos: RP-3 **Ht: 6'3" Wt: 200 Born: 10/25/1980 Age: 25**

Year	Team	Lg	G	GS	CG	GF	IP	BFP	H	R	ER	HR	SH	SF	HB	TBB	IBB	SO	WP	Bk	W	L	Pct	ShO	Sv-Op	Hld	ERC	ERA
2000	Ms	R	12	7	0	1	50.0	207	29	15	12	0	0	2	3	28	0	59	2	0	4	1	.800	0	1--	-	2.04	2.16
2001	Wisc	A	28	26	0	0	152.1	648	141	65	53	10	10	1	11	50	1	187	6	4	11	8	.579	0	0--	-	3.41	3.13
2002	SnBrn	A+	29	29	1	0	164.2	723	153	101	83	10	3	4	12	68	0	214	11	2	9	6	.600	0	0--	-	3.67	4.54
2003	SnAnt	AA	27	27	2	0	154.0	653	127	60	53	6	2	3	14	67	1	157	8	1	11	7	.611	1	0--	-	3.19	3.10
2004	Tacom	AA	14	14	0	0	80.2	350	78	42	40	9	3	3	5	35	0	63	8	0	6	6	.500	0	0--	-	4.39	4.46
2005	Ms	R	1	1	0	0	3.0	9	0	0	0	0	0	0	0	0	0	6	0	0	0	0	-	0	0--	-	0.00	0.00
2005	Tacom	AAA	19	0	0	6	34.0	145	21	16	16	2	0	1	9	22	0	36	2	0	2	1	.667	0	2--	-	2.75	2.65
2004	SEA	AL	12	5	0	4	36.2	185	48	31	30	3	4	2	4	27	1	24	3	0	1	6	.143	0	0-0	0	7.59	7.36
2005	SEA	AL	3	0	0	0	4.0	19	6	3	3	0	0	0	1	1	0	1	0	0	0	0	-	0	0-0	0	6.85	6.75
2 ML YEARS			15	5	0	4	40.2	204	54	34	33	3	4	2	5	28	1	25	3	0	1	6	.143	0	0-0	0	7.52	7.30

Norihiro Nakamura

Bats: R Throws: R Pos: 3B-10; PH-7; 1B-4; SS-2; 2B-1 **Ht: 5'10" Wt: 203 Born: 7/24/1973 Age: 32**

Year	Team	Lg	G	AB	H	2B	3B	HR	(Hm	Rd)	TB	R	RBI	RC	TBB	IBB	SO	HBP	SH	SF	SB	CS	SB%	GDP	Avg	OBP	Slg
2005	LsVgs	AAA	101	357	89	17	1	22	(-	-)	174	54	67	60	45	0	70	1	0	5	0	0	-	19	.249	.331	.487
2005	LAN	NL	17	39	5	2	0	0	(0	0)	7	1	3	0	2	0	7	0	0	0	0	0	-	3	.128	.171	.179

Joe Nathan

Pitches: R **Bats:** R **Pos:** RP-69
Ht: 6'4" **Wt:** 195 **Born:** 11/22/1974 **Age:** 31

Year	Team	Lg	G	GS	CG	GF	IP	BFP	H	R	ER	HR	SH	SF	HB	TBB	IBB	SO	WP	Bk	W	L	Pct	ShO	Sv-Op	Hld	ERC	ERA
1999	SF	NL	19	14	0	2	90.1	395	84	45	42	17	2	0	1	46	0	54	2	0	7	4	.636	0	1-1	0	4.78	4.18
2000	SF	NL	20	15	0	3	93.1	426	89	63	54	12	5	5	4	63	4	61	5	0	5	2	.714	0	0-1	0	5.23	5.21
2002	SF	NL	4	0	0	3	3.2	12	1	0	0	0	0	0	0	0	0	2	0	0	0	0	—	0	0-0	0	0.17	0.00
2003	SF	NL	78	0	0	9	79.0	316	51	26	26	7	2	4	3	33	3	83	4	1	12	4	.750	0	0-3	20	2.34	2.96
2004	MIN	AL	73	0	0	63	72.1	284	48	14	13	3	2	0	2	23	3	89	5	0	1	2	.333	0	44-47	0	1.78	1.62
2005	MIN	AL	69	0	0	58	70.0	276	46	22	21	5	1	2	0	22	1	94	2	0	7	4	.636	0	43-48	0	1.83	2.70
	6 ML YEARS		263	29	0	135	408.2	1709	319	170	156	44	12	11	10	187	11	383	18	1	32	16	.667	0	88-100	20	3.22	3.44

Dioner Navarro

Bats: B **Throws:** R **Pos:** C-50
Ht: 5'10" **Wt:** 189 **Born:** 2/9/1984 **Age:** 22

Year	Team	Lg	G	AB	H	2B	3B	HR	(Hm	Rd)	TB	R	RBI	RC	TBB	IBB	SO	HBP	SH	SF	SB	CS	SB%	GDP	Avg	OBP	Slg
2001	Yanks	R	43	143	40	10	1	2	(-	-)	58	27	22	21	17	0	23	0	1	5	6	0	1.00	4	.280	.345	.406
2002	Grnsbr	A	92	328	78	12	2	8	(-	-)	118	41	36	38	39	0	61	5	0	2	1	2	.33	9	.238	.326	.360
2002	Tampa	A+	1	2	1	0	0	0	(-	-)	1	1	0	0	0	0	0	0	0	0	0	0	—	0	.500	.500	.500
2003	Tampa	A+	52	197	59	16	4	3	(-	-)	92	28	28	33	17	0	27	4	1	2	1	0	1.00	4	.299	.364	.467
2003	Trentn	AA	58	208	71	15	0	4	(-	-)	98	28	37	36	18	1	26	1	1	5	2	3	.40	6	.341	.388	.471
2004	Trentn	AA	70	255	69	14	1	3	(-	-)	94	32	29	34	33	3	44	1	1	2	1	0	1.00	6	.271	.354	.369
2004	Clmbs	AAA	40	136	34	8	2	1	(-	-)	49	18	16	16	14	0	17	1	0	4	1	0	1.00	4	.250	.316	.360
2005	LsVgs	AAA	75	241	64	12	0	6	(-	-)	94	31	29	38	38	2	24	2	2	3	2	2	.50	8	.266	.366	.390
2004	NYA	AL	5	7	3	0	0	0	(0	0)	3	2	1	1	0	0	0	0	0	0	0	0	—	1	.429	.429	.429
2005	LAN	NL	50	176	48	9	0	3	(3	0)	66	21	14	18	20	1	21	2	1	0	0	0	—	3	.273	.354	.375
	2 ML YEARS		55	183	51	9	0	3	(3	0)	69	23	15	19	20	1	21	2	1	0	0	0	—	4	.279	.356	.377

Blaine Neal

Pitches: R **Bats:** L **Pos:** RP-19
Ht: 6'5" **Wt:** 240 **Born:** 4/6/1978 **Age:** 28

Year	Team	Lg	G	GS	CG	GF	IP	BFP	H	R	ER	HR	SH	SF	HB	TBB	IBB	SO	WP	Bk	W	L	Pct	ShO	Sv-Op	Hld	ERC	ERA
2005	Tulsa*	AA	4	1	0	0	3.0	14	4	4	3	1	0	0	0	1	0	2	1	0	0	1	.000	0	0--	-	7.44	9.00
2005	ColSpr*	AAA	1	0	0	1	1.0	4	1	0	0	0	0	0	0	0	0	0	0	0	0	0	—	0	0--	-	1.95	0.00
2001	FLA	NL	4	0	0	0	5.1	28	7	4	4	0	0	0	0	5	0	3	1	0	0	0	—	0	0-0	0	7.12	6.75
2002	FLA	NL	32	0	0	6	33.0	144	32	12	10	1	1	0	0	14	2	33	4	0	3	0	1.000	0	0-0	0	3.35	2.73
2003	FLA	NL	18	0	0	6	21.0	108	38	20	19	2	1	5	1	9	1	10	1	0	0	0	—	0	0-0	2	9.42	8.14
2004	SD	NL	40	0	0	8	42.0	183	49	19	19	6	2	2	2	11	3	36	0	0	1	1	.500	0	0-2	3	4.88	4.07
2005	2 Tms		19	0	0	7	22.2	111	35	19	18	4	2	3	0	12	2	11	1	0	1	3	.250	0	0-2	0	8.60	7.15
05	Bos	AL	8	0	0	4	8.0	41	15	9	8	2	2	1	0	3	0	3	0	0	0	1	.000	0	0-0	0	10.96	9.00
05	Col	NL	11	0	0	3	14.2	70	20	10	10	2	0	2	0	9	2	8	1	0	1	2	.333	0	0-2	0	7.36	6.14
	5 ML YEARS		113	0	0	27	124.0	574	161	74	70	13	6	10	3	51	8	93	7	0	5	4	.556	0	0-4	7	5.89	5.08

Jeff Nelson

Pitches: R **Bats:** R **Pos:** RP-49
Ht: 6'8" **Wt:** 235 **Born:** 11/17/1966 **Age:** 39

Year	Team	Lg	G	GS	CG	GF	IP	BFP	H	R	ER	HR	SH	SF	HB	TBB	IBB	SO	WP	Bk	W	L	Pct	ShO	Sv-Op	Hld	ERC	ERA
1992	SEA	AL	66	0	0	27	81.0	352	71	34	31	7	9	3	6	44	12	46	2	0	1	7	.125	0	6-14	6	3.93	3.44
1993	SEA	AL	71	0	0	13	60.0	269	57	30	29	5	2	4	8	34	10	61	2	0	5	3	.625	0	1-11	17	4.62	4.35
1994	SEA	AL	28	0	0	7	42.1	185	35	18	13	3	1	1	8	20	4	44	2	0	0	0	—	0	0-2	2	3.77	2.76
1995	SEA	AL	62	0	0	24	78.2	318	58	21	19	4	5	3	6	27	5	96	1	0	7	3	.700	0	2-4	14	2.39	2.17
1996	NYA	AL	73	0	0	27	74.1	328	75	38	36	6	3	1	2	36	1	91	4	0	4	4	.500	0	2-4	10	4.41	4.36
1997	NYA	AL	77	0	0	22	78.2	327	53	32	25	7	7	2	4	37	12	81	4	0	3	7	.300	0	2-8	22	2.48	2.86
1998	NYA	AL	45	0	0	13	40.1	192	44	18	17	1	1	3	8	22	4	35	2	0	5	3	.625	0	3-6	10	5.13	3.79
1999	NYA	AL	39	0	0	8	30.1	139	27	14	14	2	2	2	3	22	2	35	2	1	2	1	.667	0	1-2	10	4.76	4.15
2000	SEA	AL	73	0	0	13	69.2	296	44	24	19	2	6	2	2	45	1	71	4	0	8	4	.667	0	0-4	15	2.61	2.45
2001	SEA	AL	69	0	0	16	65.1	273	30	21	20	3	2	0	6	44	1	88	2	0	4	3	.571	0	4-5	26	2.20	2.76
2002	SEA	AL	41	0	0	12	45.2	199	36	20	20	2	4	3	2	27	3	55	5	0	3	2	.600	0	2-4	12	3.70	3.94
2003	2 Tms		70	0	0	28	55.1	240	51	25	23	4	4	2	4	25	3	68	3	1	4	2	.667	0	8-14	14	3.76	3.74
2004	TEX	AL	29	0	0	9	23.2	103	17	16	14	3	1	1	0	19	0	22	2	0	1	2	.333	0	1-1	9	4.35	5.32
2005	SEA	AL	49	0	0	15	36.2	166	32	17	16	3	4	1	4	22	0	34	1	1	1	3	.250	0	1-4	9	4.38	3.93
03	Sea	AL	46	0	0	25	37.2	159	34	16	14	3	4	2	2	14	1	47	2	1	3	2	.600	0	7-11	6	3.48	3.35
03	NYY	AL	24	0	0	3	17.2	81	17	9	9	1	0	0	2	10	2	21	1	0	1	0	1.000	0	1-3	8	4.37	4.58
	14 ML YEARS		792	0	0	234	782.0	3387	630	328	296	54	49	29	64	423	58	827	36	3	48	44	.522	0	33-81	176	3.52	3.41

Phil Nevin

Bats: R **Throws:** R **Pos:** 1B-74; DH-25; PH-4; C-2; 3B-1
Ht: 6'2" **Wt:** 231 **Born:** 1/19/1971 **Age:** 35

Year	Team	Lg	G	AB	H	2B	3B	HR	(Hm	Rd)	TB	R	RBI	RC	TBB	IBB	SO	HBP	SH	SF	SB	CS	SB%	GDP	Avg	OBP	Slg
2005	PortInd*	AAA	2	7	1	0	0	0	(-	-)	1	0	1	0	0	0	2	0	0	0	0	0	—	0	.143	.143	.143
1995	2 Tms		47	156	28	4	1	2	(2	0)	40	13	13	10	18	1	40	4	1	0	0	1	1.00	5	.179	.281	.256
1996	DET	AL	38	120	35	5	0	8	(3	5)	64	15	19	21	8	0	39	1	0	1	1	0	1.00	1	.292	.338	.533
1997	DET	AL	93	251	59	16	1	9	(4	5)	104	32	35	31	25	1	68	1	0	1	0	1	.00	6	.235	.306	.414
1998	ANA	AL	75	237	54	8	1	8	(3	5)	88	27	27	25	17	0	67	5	0	2	0	0	—	6	.228	.291	.371
1999	SD	NL	128	383	103	27	0	24	(12	12)	202	52	85	71	51	1	82	1	1	5	0	1	1.00	7	.269	.352	.527
2000	SD	NL	143	538	163	34	1	31	(13	18)	292	87	107	102	59	9	121	4	0	4	2	0	1.00	17	.303	.374	.543
2001	SD	NL	149	546	167	31	0	41	(19	22)	321	97	126	116	71	7	147	4	0	3	4	4	.50	13	.306	.388	.588
2002	SD	NL	107	407	116	16	0	12	(5	7)	168	53	57	52	38	4	87	4	0	4	4	0	1.00	12	.285	.344	.413

175

Year	Team	Lg	G	AB	H	2B	3B	HR	(Hm	Rd)	TB	R	RBI	RC	TBB	IBB	SO	HBP	SH	SF	SB	CS	SB%	GDP	Avg	OBP	Slg
2003	SD	NL	59	226	63	8	0	13	(6	7)	110	30	46	37	21	1	44	0	0	1	2	0	1.00	9	.279	.339	.487
2004	SD	NL	147	547	158	31	1	26	(12	14)	269	78	105	97	66	5	121	5	0	5	0	0	-	16	.289	.368	.492
2005	2 Tms		102	380	90	16	1	12	(6	6)	144	46	55	37	27	0	97	2	0	5	3	0	1.00	6	.237	.287	.379
95	Hou	NL	18	60	7	1	0	0	(0	0)	8	4	1	0	7	1	13	1	1	0	1	0	1.00	2	.117	.221	.133
95	Det	AL	29	96	21	3	1	2	(2	0)	32	9	12	10	11	0	27	3	0	0	0	0	-	3	.219	.318	.333
05	SD	NL	73	281	72	11	1	9	(4	5)	112	31	47	34	19	0	67	1	0	5	1	0	1.00	0	.256	.301	.399
05	Tex	AL	29	99	18	5	0	3	(2	1)	32	15	8	3	8	0	30	1	0	0	2	0	1.00	6	.182	.250	.323
11 ML YEARS			1088	3791	1036	196	6	186	(85	101)	1802	530	675	599	401	29	913	28	2	31	18	5	.78	99	.273	.345	.475

David Newhan

Bats: L **Throws:** R **Pos:** CF-32; RF-30; LF-20; PR-16; PH-11; 3B-8; DH-5   **Ht:** 5'10" **Wt:** 180 **Born:** 9/7/1973 **Age:** 32

Year	Team	Lg	G	AB	H	2B	3B	HR	(Hm	Rd)	TB	R	RBI	RC	TBB	IBB	SO	HBP	SH	SF	SB	CS	SB%	GDP	Avg	OBP	Slg
2005	Ottawa*	AAA	11	41	15	4	0	1	(-	-)	22	11	8	9	2	0	6	1	0	1	2	0	1.00	0	.366	.400	.537
1999	SD	NL	32	43	6	1	0	2	(1	1)	13	7	6	1	1	0	11	0	0	0	2	1	.67	0	.140	.159	.302
2000	2 Tms	NL	24	37	6	1	0	1	(1	0)	10	8	2	2	8	1	13	0	0	0	0	0	-	2	.162	.311	.270
2001	PHI	NL	7	6	2	1	0	0	(0	0)	3	2	1	1	1	0	0	0	0	1	0	0	-	0	.333	.375	.500
2004	BAL	AL	95	373	116	15	7	8	(3	5)	169	66	54	70	27	0	72	4	5	3	11	1	.92	4	.311	.361	.453
2005	BAL	AL	96	218	44	9	0	5	(1	4)	68	31	21	19	22	1	45	2	5	2	9	2	.82	2	.202	.279	.312
00	SD	NL	14	20	3	1	0	1	(1	0)	7	5	2	2	6	1	7	0	0	0	0	0	-	0	.150	.346	.350
00	Phi	NL	10	17	3	0	0	0	(0	0)	3	3	0	0	2	0	6	0	0	0	0	0	-	2	.176	.263	.176
5 ML YEARS			254	677	174	27	7	16	(6	10)	263	114	84	93	59	2	141	6	10	6	22	4	.85	8	.257	.320	.388

Lance Niekro

Bats: R **Throws:** R **Pos:** 1B-74; PH-45; DH-1; PR-1   **Ht:** 6'3" **Wt:** 210 **Born:** 1/29/1979 **Age:** 27

Year	Team	Lg	G	AB	H	2B	3B	HR	(Hm	Rd)	TB	R	RBI	RC	TBB	IBB	SO	HBP	SH	SF	SB	CS	SB%	GDP	Avg	OBP	Slg
2000	SlmKzr	A-	49	196	71	14	4	5	(-	-)	108	27	44	40	11	2	25	4	0	2	2	0	1.00	6	.362	.404	.551
2001	SnJos	A+	42	163	47	11	0	3	(-	-)	67	18	34	19	4	0	14	0	0	4	4	2	.67	2	.288	.298	.411
2002	Shreve	AA	79	297	92	20	1	4	(-	-)	126	33	34	37	7	0	32	2	1	3	0	2	.00	11	.310	.327	.424
2003	Fresno	AAA	98	381	115	15	2	4	(-	-)	146	43	41	47	19	1	39	1	1	3	3	3	.50	12	.302	.334	.383
2004	SnJos	A+	15	61	19	7	1	1	(-	-)	31	13	14	7	2	0	5	0	0	1	0	0	-	5	.311	.328	.508
2004	Fresno	AAA	67	241	72	21	4	12	(-	-)	137	42	47	42	14	1	32	1	0	1	1	1	.50	5	.299	.339	.568
2005	Fresno	AAA	1	4	1	0	0	0	(-	-)	1	0	0	0	0	0	1	0	0	0	0	0	-	0	.250	.250	.250
2003	SF	NL	5	5	1	1	0	0	(0	0)	2	2	2	1	0	0	1	0	0	0	0	0	-	0	.200	.200	.400
2005	SF	NL	113	278	70	16	3	12	(5	7)	128	32	46	35	17	0	53	2	0	5	0	2	.00	11	.252	.295	.460
2 ML YEARS			118	283	71	17	3	12	(5	7)	130	34	48	36	17	0	54	2	0	5	0	2	.00	11	.251	.293	.459

Wil Nieves

Bats: R **Throws:** R **Pos:** C-3   **Ht:** 5'11" **Wt:** 190 **Born:** 9/25/1977 **Age:** 28

Year	Team	Lg	G	AB	H	2B	3B	HR	(Hm	Rd)	TB	R	RBI	RC	TBB	IBB	SO	HBP	SH	SF	SB	CS	SB%	GDP	Avg	OBP	Slg
1996	Padres	R	43	113	39	5	0	2	(-	-)	50	23	22	20	13	0	19	0	2	0	3	4	.43	1	.345	.413	.442
1997	Clinton	A	18	55	12	1	1	1	(-	-)	18	6	7	5	6	0	10	0	1	1	2	1	.67	0	.218	.290	.327
1997	Padres	R	8	27	8	2	0	0	(-	-)	10	2	2	4	5	0	5	0	1	0	1	0	1.00	0	.296	.406	.370
1998	Clinton	A	115	380	97	22	0	3	(-	-)	128	47	55	42	47	4	69	7	4	6	7	9	.44	16	.255	.343	.337
1999	RCuca	A+	120	427	140	26	2	7	(-	-)	191	58	61	71	40	1	54	5	1	4	2	7	.22	12	.328	.389	.447
2000	LsVgs	AAA	1	1	0	0	0	0	(-	-)	0	0	0	0	0	0	0	0	0	0	0	0	-	0	.000	.000	.000
2000	Mobile	AA	68	214	57	4	0	4	(-	-)	73	18	30	22	16	4	22	1	2	1	1	1	.50	9	.266	.319	.341
2000	RCuca	A+	31	101	26	5	0	0	(-	-)	31	16	9	12	15	0	17	0	2	0	2	0	1.00	3	.257	.350	.307
2001	Mobile	AA	95	330	99	24	0	3	(-	-)	132	28	41	43	18	2	40	2	2	4	1	0	1.00	8	.300	.336	.400
2002	Portlnd	AAA	70	237	73	20	2	7	(-	-)	118	24	29	34	5	0	40	0	2	1	0	0	-	7	.308	.321	.498
2003	Salt Lk	AAA	102	361	102	16	2	4	(-	-)	134	48	38	43	25	3	53	1	3	5	1	2	.33	8	.283	.327	.371
2004	Salt Lk	AAA	108	421	125	22	8	10	(-	-)	193	60	53	55	12	0	64	0	1	3	3	6	.33	11	.297	.316	.458
2005	Clmbs	AAA	102	380	110	22	3	4	(-	-)	150	45	37	48	13	1	38	2	3	5	1	1	.50	16	.289	.313	.395
2002	SD	NL	28	72	13	3	1	0	(0	0)	18	2	3	4	4	4	15	0	0	0	1	0	1.00	1	.181	.224	.250
2005	NYA	AL	3	4	0	0	0	0	(0	0)	0	0	0	0	0	0	1	0	0	0	0	0	-	0	.000	.000	.000
2 ML YEARS			31	76	13	3	1	0	(0	0)	18	2	3	4	4	4	16	0	0	0	1	0	1.00	1	.171	.213	.237

Dustin Nippert

Pitches: R **Bats:** R **Pos:** SP-3   **Ht:** 6'7" **Wt:** 217 **Born:** 5/6/1981 **Age:** 25

			HOW MUCH HE PITCHED						WHAT HE GAVE UP										THE RESULTS						
Year	Team	Lg	G	GS	CG	GF	IP	BFP	H	R	ER	HR	SH	SF	HB	TBB	IBB	SO	WP	Bk	W	L	Pct	ShO	Sv-Op Hld	ERC	ERA
2002	Msoula	R+	17	11	0	2	54.2	215	42	12	10	2	0	0	0	9	0	77	4	0	4	2	.667	0	0- - -	1.66	1.65
2004	ElPaso	AA	14	14	0	0	71.2	332	77	45	29	0	6	3	4	40	1	73	4	0	2	5	.286	0	0- - -	4.48	3.64
2005	Tenn	AA	18	18	3	0	117.1	489	95	33	31	4	6	2	7	42	1	97	4	0	8	3	.727	2	0- - -	2.66	2.38
2005	ARI	NL	3	3	0	0	14.2	68	10	9	9	1	0	0	1	13	0	11	1	0	1	0	1.000	0	0-0 -	4.09	5.52

C.J. Nitkowski

Pitches: L **Bats:** L **Pos:** RP-7   **Ht:** 6'3" **Wt:** 205 **Born:** 3/9/1973 **Age:** 33

			HOW MUCH HE PITCHED						WHAT HE GAVE UP										THE RESULTS						
Year	Team	Lg	G	GS	CG	GF	IP	BFP	H	R	ER	HR	SH	SF	HB	TBB	IBB	SO	WP	Bk	W	L	Pct	ShO	Sv-Op Hld	ERC	ERA
2005	NewOr*	AAA	27	0	0	8	32.1	140	36	15	13	3	2	2	5	7	0	24	0	0	2	2	.500	0	4- - -	4.62	3.62
2005	Indy*	AAA	18	0	0	5	21.2	80	6	5	2	0	1	1	0	9	0	18	1	0	2	0	1.000	0	2- - -	0.69	0.83
1995	2 Tms		20	18	0	0	71.2	338	94	57	53	11	2	4	5	35	3	31	2	2	2	7	.222	0	0-1 - 0	7.04	6.66

				HOW MUCH HE PITCHED						WHAT HE GAVE UP												THE RESULTS							
Year	Team	Lg	G	GS	CG	GF	IP	BFP	H	R	ER	HR	SH	SF	HB	TBB	IBB	SO	WP	Bk	W	L	Pct	ShO	Sv-Op	Hld	ERC	ERA
1996	DET	AL	11	8	0	0	45.2	234	62	44	41	7	0	2	7	38	1	36	2	0	2	3	.400	0	0-0	0	9.44	8.08
1998	HOU	NL	43	0	0	11	59.2	250	49	27	25	4	4	2	6	23	2	44	3	1	3	3	.500	0	3-5	8	3.19	3.77
1999	DET	AL	68	7	0	7	81.2	349	63	44	39	11	1	4	3	45	3	66	4	3	4	5	.444	0	0-0	11	3.73	4.30
2000	DET	AL	67	11	0	7	109.2	497	124	79	64	13	3	8	4	49	3	81	3	1	4	9	.308	0	0-2	15	5.23	5.25
2001	2 Tms	AL	61	0	0	14	51.0	241	54	30	28	7	3	1	5	34	8	42	1	0	1	3	.250	0	0-6	6	5.89	4.94
2002	TEX	AL	12	0	0	2	13.2	63	11	4	4	0	1	0	0	13	0	14	0	0	0	1	.000	0	0-0	1	4.35	2.63
2003	TEX	AL	6	0	0	0	9.2	52	17	8	8	0	1	2	0	8	1	5	0	0	0	0	-	0	0-0	1	9.69	7.45
2004	2 Tms	AL	41	0	0	14	33.0	160	40	22	21	4	1	2	6	16	0	26	5	0	2	1	.667	0	0-0	0	6.50	5.73
2005	WAS	NL	7	0	0	0	3.1	17	5	3	3	0	1	0	2	2	0	2	0	0	0	0	-	0	0-0	1	6.89	8.10
95	Cin	NL	9	7	0	0	32.1	154	41	25	22	4	2	1	2	15	1	18	1	2	1	3	.250	0	0-1	0	6.20	6.12
95	Det	AL	11	11	0	0	39.1	184	53	32	31	7	0	3	3	20	2	13	1	0	1	4	.200	0	0-0	0	7.76	7.09
01	Det	AL	56	0	0	12	45.1	220	51	30	28	7	3	1	5	31	7	38	1	0	0	3	.000	0	0-6	6	6.53	5.56
01	NYM	NL	5	0	0	2	5.2	21	3	0	0	0	0	0	0	3	1	4	0	0	1	0	1.000	0	0-0	0	1.52	0.00
04	Atl	NL	22	0	0	10	20.0	95	22	11	10	3	1	2	2	10	0	16	3	0	1	0	1.000	0	0-0	0	5.66	4.50
04	NYY	AL	19	0	0	4	13.0	65	18	11	11	1	0	0	4	6	0	10	2	0	1	1	.500	0	0-0	0	7.83	7.62
10 ML YEARS			336	44	0	55	479.0	2201	519	318	286	57	17	25	36	263	21	347	20	7	18	32	.360	0	3-14	43	5.55	5.37

Ramon Nivar

Bats: R Throws: R Pos: CF-4; PH-3; PR-1   Ht: 5'10" Wt: 170 Born: 2/22/1980 Age: 26

				BATTING																	BASERUNNING				AVERAGES		
Year	Team	Lg	G	AB	H	2B	3B	HR	(Hm	Rd)	TB	R	RBI	RC	TBB	IBB	SO	HBP	SH	SF	SB	CS	SB%	GDP	Avg	OBP	Slg
2005	Bowie*	AA	41	150	37	7	0	1	(-	-)	47	22	12	15	12	0	21	2	3	0	11	6	.65	4	.247	.311	.313
2005	Ottawa*	AAA	33	111	22	4	0	1	(-	-)	29	13	5	6	3	0	10	2	4	1	9	4	.69	4	.198	.231	.261
2003	TEX	AL	28	90	19	1	2	0	(0	0)	24	9	7	7	4	0	10	1	2	0	4	2	.67	1	.211	.253	.267
2004	TEX	AL	7	18	4	0	0	0	(0	0)	4	3	4	1	0	0	7	0	2	1	1	1	.50	0	.222	.211	.222
2005	BAL	AL	7	13	4	0	0	0	(0	0)	4	1	1	2	0	0	2	1	1	0	0	1	.00	0	.308	.357	.308
3 ML YEARS			42	121	27	1	2	0	(0	0)	32	13	12	10	4	0	19	2	5	1	5	4	.56	1	.223	.258	.264

Laynce Nix

Bats: L Throws: L Pos: CF-61; PH-1; PR-1   Ht: 6'0" Wt: 190 Born: 10/30/1980 Age: 25

				BATTING																	BASERUNNING				AVERAGES		
Year	Team	Lg	G	AB	H	2B	3B	HR	(Hm	Rd)	TB	R	RBI	RC	TBB	IBB	SO	HBP	SH	SF	SB	CS	SB%	GDP	Avg	OBP	Slg
2005	Okla*	AAA	10	36	12	1	1	3	(-	-)	24	8	6	10	9	2	6	0	1	1	0	1	.00	0	.333	.467	.667
2003	TEX	AL	53	184	47	10	0	8	(7	1)	81	25	30	25	9	0	53	0	1	1	3	0	1.00	7	.255	.289	.440
2004	TEX	AL	115	371	92	20	4	14	(9	5)	162	58	46	44	23	4	113	2	1	3	1	1	.50	6	.248	.293	.437
2005	TEX	AL	63	229	55	12	3	6	(3	3)	91	28	32	26	9	3	45	0	0	2	2	0	1.00	3	.240	.267	.397
3 ML YEARS			231	784	194	42	7	28	(19	9)	334	111	108	95	41	7	211	2	2	6	6	1	.86	10	.247	.285	.426

Trot Nixon

Bats: L Throws: L Pos: RF-118; PH-13; DH-2; PR-1   Ht: 6'2" Wt: 211 Born: 4/11/1974 Age: 32

				BATTING																	BASERUNNING				AVERAGES		
Year	Team	Lg	G	AB	H	2B	3B	HR	(Hm	Rd)	TB	R	RBI	RC	TBB	IBB	SO	HBP	SH	SF	SB	CS	SB%	GDP	Avg	OBP	Slg
2005	Pwtckt*	AAA	2	6	3	0	0	1	(-	-)	6	3	2	3	2	1	2	0	0	1	0	0	-	0	.500	.556	1.000
1996	BOS	AL	2	4	2	1	0	0	(0	0)	3	2	0	1	0	0	1	0	0	0	1	0	1.00	0	.500	.500	.750
1998	BOS	AL	13	27	7	1	0	0	(0	0)	8	3	0	2	1	0	3	0	0	0	0	0	-	0	.259	.286	.296
1999	BOS	AL	124	381	103	22	5	15	(3	12)	180	67	52	66	53	1	75	3	2	8	3	1	.75	7	.270	.357	.472
2000	BOS	AL	123	427	118	27	8	12	(4	8)	197	66	60	74	63	2	85	2	5	5	8	1	.89	11	.276	.368	.461
2001	BOS	AL	148	535	150	31	4	27	(14	13)	270	100	88	102	79	1	113	7	6	6	7	4	.64	8	.280	.376	.505
2002	BOS	AL	152	532	136	36	3	24	(8	16)	250	81	94	85	65	2	109	5	3	7	4	2	.67	7	.256	.338	.470
2003	BOS	AL	134	441	135	24	6	28	(10	18)	255	81	87	90	65	4	96	3	1	3	4	2	.67	3	.306	.396	.578
2004	BOS	AL	48	149	47	9	1	6	(3	3)	76	24	23	24	15	1	24	1	0	2	0	0	-	3	.315	.377	.510
2005	BOS	AL	124	408	112	29	1	13	(5	8)	182	64	67	70	53	3	59	3	0	6	2	1	.67	7	.275	.357	.446
9 ML YEARS			868	2904	810	180	28	125	(47	78)	1421	488	471	514	394	14	565	24	17	37	29	11	.73	46	.279	.366	.489

Hideo Nomo

Pitches: R Bats: R Pos: SP-19   Ht: 6'2" Wt: 210 Born: 8/31/1968 Age: 37

				HOW MUCH HE PITCHED						WHAT HE GAVE UP												THE RESULTS							
Year	Team	Lg	G	GS	CG	GF	IP	BFP	H	R	ER	HR	SH	SF	HB	TBB	IBB	SO	WP	Bk	W	L	Pct	ShO	Sv-Op	Hld	ERC	ERA
2005	Clmbs*	AAA	7	7	0	0	37.1	164	30	19	15	1	0	3	0	22	1	41	0	0	2	3	.400	0	0- -	-	3.09	3.62
1995	LA	NL	28	28	4	0	191.1	780	124	63	54	14	11	4	5	78	2	236	19	5	13	6	.684	3	0-0	0	2.16	2.54
1996	LA	NL	33	33	3	0	228.1	932	180	93	81	23	12	6	2	85	6	234	11	3	16	11	.593	2	0-0	0	2.86	3.19
1997	LA	NL	33	33	1	0	207.1	904	193	104	98	23	7	1	9	92	2	233	10	4	14	12	.538	2	0-0	0	4.06	4.25
1998	2 Tms	NL	29	28	3	0	157.1	687	130	88	86	19	8	5	4	94	2	167	13	4	6	12	.333	0	0-0	0	4.10	4.92
1999	MIL	NL	28	28	0	0	176.1	767	173	96	89	27	5	5	3	78	2	161	10	1	12	8	.600	0	0-0	0	4.57	4.54
2000	DET	AL	32	31	1	0	190.0	828	191	102	100	31	6	3	3	89	1	181	16	0	8	12	.400	0	0-0	0	4.95	4.74
2001	BOS	AL	33	33	2	0	198.0	849	171	105	99	26	4	7	3	96	1	220	6	0	13	10	.565	2	0-0	0	3.90	4.50
2002	LA	NL	34	34	0	0	220.1	926	189	92	83	26	17	4	2	101	5	193	6	0	16	6	.727	2	0-0	0	3.68	3.39
2003	LA	NL	33	33	2	0	218.1	897	175	82	75	24	11	3	1	98	6	177	11	0	16	13	.552	2	0-0	0	3.30	3.09
2004	LA	NL	18	18	0	0	84.0	393	105	77	77	19	7	3	4	42	1	54	3	0	4	11	.267	0	0-0	0	7.22	8.25
2005	TB	AL	19	19	0	0	100.2	471	127	82	81	16	6	8	2	51	2	59	3	0	5	8	.385	0	0-0	0	6.60	7.24
98	LA	NL	12	12	2	0	67.2	295	57	39	38	8	2	2	3	38	0	73	4	1	2	7	.222	0	0-0	0	4.13	5.05
98	NYM	NL	17	16	1	0	89.2	392	73	49	48	11	6	3	1	56	2	94	9	3	4	5	.444	0	0-0	0	4.07	4.82
11 ML YEARS			320	318	16	0	1972.0	8434	1758	984	923	248	94	49	38	904	31	1915	108	17	123	109	.530	9	0-0	0	3.94	4.21

Roberto Novoa

Pitches: R Bats: R Pos: RP-49   Ht: 6'5" Wt: 200 Born: 8/15/1979 Age: 26

			HOW MUCH HE PITCHED						WHAT HE GAVE UP										THE RESULTS						
Year	Team	Lg	G	GS	CG	GF	IP	BFP	H	R	ER	HR	SH	SF	HB	TBB	IBB	SO	WP	Bk	W	L	Pct	ShO	Sv-Op Hld	ERC	ERA
2001	Wmspt	A-	14	13	1	1	79.2	331	76	40	30	4	5	1	7	20	0	55	4	1	5	5	.500	0	0-- -	3.30	3.39
2002	Wmspt	A-	12	12	0	0	66.2	277	62	32	27	4	3	1	6	8	0	56	5	0	8	3	.727	0	0-- -	2.66	3.65
2002	Hickory	A	10	10	0	0	42.2	205	61	30	26	2	1	3	4	15	0	29	7	1	1	5	.167	0	0-- -	6.33	5.48
2003	Lkland	A+	19	15	2	1	99.0	414	93	45	41	8	1	0	5	25	0	71	2	2	4	5	.444	0	0-- -	3.23	3.73
2004	Erie	AA	41	0	0	11	79.0	317	63	32	26	7	2	2	1	18	1	59	4	1	7	0	1.000	0	4-- -	2.31	2.96
2005	Iowa	AAA	19	0	0	7	27.1	113	20	11	10	1	3	1	4	11	1	18	1	0	2	2	.500	0	4-- -	2.77	3.29
2004	DET	AL	16	0	0	2	21.0	94	25	15	13	4	1	4	2	6	0	15	1	0	1	1	.500	0	0-1 3	5.79	5.57
2005	CHN	NL	49	0	0	11	44.2	205	47	22	22	4	2	0	0	25	6	47	4	1	4	5	.444	0	0-5 14	4.60	4.43
	2 ML YEARS		65	0	0	13	65.2	299	72	37	35	8	3	4	2	31	6	62	5	1	5	6	.455	0	0-6 17	4.98	4.80

Abraham Nunez

Bats: B Throws: R Pos: 3B-98; PH-25; 2B-22; SS-21   Ht: 5'11" Wt: 185 Born: 3/16/1976 Age: 30

			BATTING																			BASERUNNING				AVERAGES		
Year	Team	Lg	G	AB	H	2B	3B	HR	(Hm	Rd)	TB	R	RBI	RC	TBB	IBB	SO	HBP	SH	SF	SB	CS	SB%	GDP	Avg	OBP	Slg
1997	PIT	NL	19	40	9	2	2	0	(0	0)	15	3	6	4	3	0	10	1	0	1	1	0	1.00	1	.225	.289	.375
1998	PIT	NL	24	52	10	2	0	1	(0	1)	15	6	2	6	12	0	14	0	3	0	4	2	.67	1	.192	.344	.288
1999	PIT	NL	90	259	57	8	0	0	(0	0)	65	25	17	22	28	0	54	1	13	0	9	1	.90	2	.220	.299	.251
2000	PIT	NL	40	91	20	1	0	1	(0	1)	24	10	8	6	8	1	14	0	0	0	0	0	-	3	.220	.283	.264
2001	PIT	NL	115	301	79	11	4	1	(0	1)	101	30	21	36	28	1	53	1	4	1	8	2	.80	5	.262	.326	.336
2002	PIT	NL	112	253	59	14	1	2	(2	0)	81	28	15	25	27	1	44	2	3	1	3	4	.43	2	.233	.311	.320
2003	PIT	NL	118	311	77	8	7	4	(2	2)	111	37	35	28	26	1	53	3	9	2	9	3	.75	8	.248	.310	.357
2004	PIT	NL	112	182	43	9	0	2	(1	1)	58	17	13	12	10	0	36	0	2	1	1	3	.25	8	.236	.275	.319
2005	STL	NL	139	421	120	13	2	5	(3	2)	152	64	44	54	37	4	63	0	9	0	0	1	.00	6	.285	.343	.361
	9 ML YEARS		769	1910	474	68	16	16	(8	8)	622	220	161	193	179	8	341	8	43	6	35	16	.69	31	.248	.314	.326

Franklin Nunez

Pitches: R Bats: R Pos: RP-5   Ht: 6'0" Wt: 175 Born: 1/18/1977 Age: 29

			HOW MUCH HE PITCHED						WHAT HE GAVE UP										THE RESULTS						
Year	Team	Lg	G	GS	CG	GF	IP	BFP	H	R	ER	HR	SH	SF	HB	TBB	IBB	SO	WP	Bk	W	L	Pct	ShO	Sv-Op Hld	ERC	ERA
1998	Mrtnsvl	R+	6	4	0	0	25.1	109	23	10	7	0	0	0	2	8	0	19	2	3	2	2	.500	0	0-- -	2.81	2.49
1999	Pmont	A	13	13	1	0	77.0	326	69	39	29	4	4	1	6	25	0	88	2	1	4	8	.333	0	0-- -	3.18	3.39
2000	Clrwtr	A+	23	14	1	6	112.0	492	112	54	45	4	1	3	7	57	0	81	9	1	10	4	.714	0	2-- -	4.35	3.62
2001	Rdng	AA	39	14	0	10	110.0	486	107	68	54	9	3	2	6	51	3	112	9	0	8	7	.533	0	3-- -	4.18	4.42
2002	Phillies	R	1	1	0	0	2.0	9	2	0	0	0	0	0	0	1	0	4	0	0	0	0	-	0	0-- -	3.63	0.00
2002	S-WB	AAA	4	4	0	0	17.0	69	9	6	6	2	0	0	0	12	0	16	1	0	2	1	.667	0	0-- -	2.93	3.18
2003	Bklyn	A-	7	0	0	3	5.1	26	5	4	3	0	0	1	1	4	0	8	1	0	0	1	.000	0	0-- -	0.72	0.84
2004	Mont	AA	6	0	0	0	10.2	38	4	3	1	0	0	0	0	3	0	19	1	0	1	0	1.000	0	0-- -	2.78	2.81
2004	Drham	AAA	40	0	0	21	51.1	227	36	21	16	1	0	0	0	34	0	70	5	0	4	2	.667	0	9-- -	2.78	2.81
2005	Drham	AAA	27	0	0	11	32.2	151	32	27	23	1	2	2	2	21	0	34	5	0	5	1	.833	0	3-- -	4.56	6.34
2004	TB	AL	8	0	0	0	10.2	54	11	8	7	1	1	2	3	7	0	14	2	0	1	3	.000	0	0-1 1	6.11	5.91
2005	TB	AL	5	0	0	0	5.0	22	5	6	6	0	0	0	0	4	0	2	0	0	0	0	1.000	0	0-0 1	5.20	10.80
	2 ML YEARS		13	0	0	0	15.2	76	16	14	13	1	1	2	3	11	0	16	2	0	1	3	.250	0	0-1 1	5.82	7.47

Leo Nunez

Pitches: R Bats: R Pos: RP-41   Ht: 6'1" Wt: 160 Born: 8/14/1983 Age: 22

			HOW MUCH HE PITCHED						WHAT HE GAVE UP										THE RESULTS						
Year	Team	Lg	G	GS	CG	GF	IP	BFP	H	R	ER	HR	SH	SF	HB	TBB	IBB	SO	WP	Bk	W	L	Pct	ShO	Sv-Op Hld	ERC	ERA
2001	Pirates	R	10	7	1	0	53.1	231	62	28	26	4	3	3	3	9	0	34	4	0	2	2	.500	1	0-- -	4.08	4.39
2002	Pirates	R	11	11	0	0	60.1	240	54	23	23	5	2	0	5	5	0	52	1	0	4	2	.667	0	0-- -	2.55	3.43
2002	Hickory	A	1	1	0	0	4.0	20	5	0	0	0	0	0	0	3	0	1	0	0	0	0	-	0	0-- -	5.98	0.00
2003	Wmspt	A-	8	8	0	0	38.1	158	31	14	13	0	0	1	0	12	0	41	0	0	4	3	.571	0	0-- -	2.08	3.05
2003	Hickory	A	13	7	0	4	48.1	218	59	34	30	6	8	6	5	14	0	37	4	2	2	1	.667	0	0-- -	5.52	5.59
2004	Hickory	A	27	20	3	3	144.0	599	121	53	49	16	4	6	9	46	0	140	5	1	10	4	.714	0	1-- -	3.21	3.06
2005	Hi Dsrt	A+	8	0	0	0	13.0	65	23	15	13	2	2	0	0	3	2	15	3	0	0	0	-	0	0-- -	8.06	9.00
2005	Wichta	AA	12	0	0	11	13.0	49	8	3	1	1	0	0	0	2	0	14	1	0	1	0	1.000	0	4-- -	1.32	0.69
2005	KC	AL	41	0	0	10	53.2	246	73	45	45	9	1	2	3	18	2	32	1	0	3	2	.600	0	0-1 2	6.76	7.55

Wes Obermueller

Pitches: R Bats: R Pos: RP-15; SP-8   Ht: 6'2" Wt: 195 Born: 12/22/1976 Age: 29

			HOW MUCH HE PITCHED						WHAT HE GAVE UP										THE RESULTS						
Year	Team	Lg	G	GS	CG	GF	IP	BFP	H	R	ER	HR	SH	SF	HB	TBB	IBB	SO	WP	Bk	W	L	Pct	ShO	Sv-Op Hld	ERC	ERA
2005	Nashv*	AAA	9	8	0	1	42.1	180	39	14	12	1	1	1	0	14	0	39	0	0	3	1	.750	0	1-- -	2.81	2.55
2002	KC	AL	2	2	0	0	7.2	39	14	10	10	3	0	0	0	2	0	5	0	0	0	2	.000	0	0-0 0	11.04	11.74
2003	MIL	NL	12	11	0	0	65.2	303	81	40	37	10	1	2	6	25	2	34	5	0	2	5	.286	0	0-0 0	6.08	5.07
2004	MIL	NL	25	20	1	1	118.0	529	138	80	76	15	4	5	3	42	0	59	4	0	6	8	.429	1	0-0 0	5.14	5.80
2005	MIL	NL	23	8	0	4	65.0	305	74	41	38	7	4	4	5	36	2	33	3	0	1	4	.200	0	0-0 0	5.79	5.26
	4 ML YEARS		62	41	1	5	256.1	1176	307	171	161	35	9	11	14	105	4	131	12	0	9	19	.321	1	0-0 0	5.71	5.65

Jose Offerman

Bats: B **Throws:** R **Pos:** PH-74; 1B-15; 2B-1   **Ht:** 6'0" **Wt:** 192 **Born:** 11/11/1968 **Age:** 37

Year	Team	Lg	G	AB	H	2B	3B	HR	(Hm	Rd)	TB	R	RBI	RC	TBB	IBB	SO	HBP	SH	SF	SB	CS	SB%	GDP	Avg	OBP	Slg
2005	Norfolk*	AAA	9	36	6	0	0	0	(-	-)	6	1	1	0	1	0	4	0	0	0	1	0	1.00	1	.167	.189	.167
1990	LA	NL	29	58	9	0	0	1	(1	0)	12	7	7	2	4	1	14	0	1	0	1	0	1.00	0	.155	.210	.207
1991	LA	NL	52	113	22	2	0	0	(0	0)	24	10	3	9	25	2	32	1	1	0	3	2	.60	5	.195	.345	.212
1992	LA	NL	149	534	139	20	8	1	(1	0)	178	67	30	60	57	4	98	0	5	2	23	16	.59	5	.260	.331	.333
1993	LA	NL	158	590	159	21	6	1	(1	0)	195	77	62	72	71	7	75	2	25	8	30	13	.70	12	.269	.346	.331
1994	LA	NL	72	243	51	8	4	1	(0	1)	70	27	25	23	38	4	38	0	6	2	2	1	.67	6	.210	.314	.288
1995	LA	NL	119	429	123	14	6	4	(2	2)	161	69	33	66	69	0	67	3	10	0	2	7	.22	5	.287	.389	.375
1996	KC	AL	151	561	170	33	8	5	(1	4)	234	85	47	93	74	3	98	1	7	2	24	10	.71	9	.303	.384	.417
1997	KC	AL	106	424	126	23	6	2	(2	0)	167	59	39	59	41	3	64	0	6	0	9	10	.47	5	.297	.359	.394
1998	KC	AL	158	607	191	28	13	7	(4	3)	266	102	66	116	89	1	96	5	2	6	45	12	.79	7	.315	.403	.438
1999	BOS	AL	149	586	172	37	11	8	(5	3)	255	107	69	101	96	5	79	2	2	7	18	12	.60	11	.294	.391	.435
2000	BOS	AL	116	451	115	14	3	9	(3	6)	162	73	41	58	70	0	70	1	2	3	0	8	.00	9	.255	.354	.359
2001	BOS	AL	128	524	140	23	3	9	(4	5)	196	76	49	69	61	2	97	1	3	5	5	2	.71	9	.267	.342	.374
2002	2 Tms		101	284	66	12	1	5	(1	0)	95	48	31	34	37	0	38	1	1	3	9	6	.60	12	.232	.320	.335
2004	MIN	AL	77	172	44	14	2	2	(0	2)	68	22	22	24	29	2	31	0	1	0	1	1	.50	1	.256	.363	.395
2005	2 Tms		86	105	24	3	1	2	(2	0)	35	11	13	13	11	0	17	1	1	0	0	0	-	4	.229	.308	.333
02	Bos	AL	72	237	55	10	4	4	(1	3)	77	39	27	31	33	0	29	1	1	3	8	5	.62	9	.232	.325	.325
02	Sea	AL	29	47	11	2	1	1	(1	0)	18	9	4	3	4	0	9	0	0	0	1	1	.50	3	.234	.294	.383
05	Phi	NL	33	33	6	1	1	1	(1	0)	12	6	3	3	5	0	6	0	0	0	0	0	-	1	.182	.289	.364
05	NYM	NL	53	72	18	2	0	1	(1	0)	23	5	10	10	6	0	11	1	1	0	0	0	-	3	.250	.316	.319
	15 ML YEARS		1651	5681	1551	252	72	57	(28	29)	2118	840	537	800	772	34	914	18	73	38	172	100	.63	100	.273	.360	.373

Tomo Ohka

Pitches: R **Bats:** R **Pos:** SP-29; RP-3   **Ht:** 6'1" **Wt:** 180 **Born:** 3/18/1976 **Age:** 30

Year	Team	Lg	G	GS	CG	GF	IP	BFP	H	R	ER	HR	SH	SF	HB	TBB	IBB	SO	WP	Bk	W	L	Pct	ShO	Sv-Op	Hld	ERC	ERA
1999	BOS	AL	8	2	0	3	13.0	65	21	12	9	2	0	1	0	6	0	8	0	0	1	2	.333	0	0-0	0	8.56	6.23
2000	BOS	AL	13	12	0	1	69.1	297	70	25	24	7	1	2	2	26	0	40	3	0	3	6	.333	0	0-0	0	4.19	3.12
2001	2 Tms		22	21	0	1	107.0	469	134	70	65	15	2	2	3	29	0	68	2	1	3	9	.250	0	0-0	0	5.52	5.47
2002	MON	NL	32	31	2	1	192.2	806	194	83	68	19	13	6	7	45	7	118	2	1	13	8	.619	0	0-0	0	3.55	3.18
2003	MON	NL	34	34	2	0	199.0	864	233	106	92	24	8	3	9	45	11	118	8	0	10	12	.455	0	0-0	0	4.59	4.16
2004	MON	NL	15	15	0	0	84.2	367	98	40	32	11	4	2	1	20	1	38	3	0	3	7	.300	0	0-0	0	4.53	3.40
2005	2 Tms		32	29	1	0	180.1	774	189	88	81	22	7	4	3	55	5	98	8	0	11	9	.550	1	0-0	1	4.13	4.04
01	Bos	AL	12	11	0	1	52.1	241	69	40	36	7	1	1	2	19	0	37	1	1	2	5	.286	0	0-0	0	6.24	6.19
01	Mon	NL	10	10	0	0	54.2	228	65	30	29	8	1	1	1	10	0	31	1	0	1	4	.200	0	0-0	0	4.83	4.77
05	Was	NL	10	9	0	0	54.0	231	44	23	20	6	1	1	2	27	1	17	3	0	4	3	.571	0	0-0	0	3.54	3.33
05	Mil	NL	22	20	1	0	126.1	543	145	65	61	16	1	3	2	28	4	81	5	0	7	6	.538	1	0-0	1	4.39	4.35
	7 ML YEARS		156	144	5	6	846.0	3642	939	424	371	100	35	20	25	226	24	488	26	2	44	53	.454	1	0-0	1	4.38	3.95

Will Ohman

Pitches: L **Bats:** L **Pos:** RP-69   **Ht:** 6'2" **Wt:** 205 **Born:** 8/13/1977 **Age:** 28

Year	Team	Lg	G	GS	CG	GF	IP	BFP	H	R	ER	HR	SH	SF	HB	TBB	IBB	SO	WP	Bk	W	L	Pct	ShO	Sv-Op	Hld	ERC	ERA
2005	Iowa*	AAA	8	0	0	6	8.2	32	4	4	4	2	0	0	0	2	0	12	0	0	1	0	1.000	0	1--	-	1.53	4.15
2000	CHN	NL	6	0	0	2	3.1	17	4	3	3	0	0	0	0	4	1	2	1	0	1	0	1.000	0	0-0	1	7.25	8.10
2001	CHN	NL	11	0	0	0	11.2	54	14	10	10	2	0	0	0	0	0	12	2	0	0	1	.000	0	0-0	1	3.54	7.71
2005	CHN	NL	69	0	0	13	43.1	187	32	14	14	6	1	0	3	24	3	45	6	1	2	2	.500	0	0-3	13	3.62	2.91
	3 ML YEARS		86	0	0	15	58.1	258	50	27	27	8	1	0	3	28	4	59	9	1	3	3	.500	0	0-3	15	3.82	4.17

Miguel Ojeda

Bats: R **Throws:** R **Pos:** C-41; PH-17; LF-3; RF-2; DH-1   **Ht:** 6'2" **Wt:** 190 **Born:** 1/29/1975 **Age:** 31

Year	Team	Lg	G	AB	H	2B	3B	HR	(Hm	Rd)	TB	R	RBI	RC	TBB	IBB	SO	HBP	SH	SF	SB	CS	SB%	GDP	Avg	OBP	Slg
2005	Portlnd*	AAA	17	57	11	1	0	3	(-	-)	21	8	5	6	7	0	16	1	0	0	0	0	-	0	.193	.292	.368
2005	Tacom*	AAA	9	33	11	1	0	3	(-	-)	21	7	11	13	1	0	5	1	0	0	0	0	-	0	.333	.371	.636
2003	SD	NL	61	141	33	6	0	4	(3	1)	51	13	22	20	18	2	26	3	0	1	1	1	.50	2	.234	.331	.362
2004	SD	NL	62	156	40	3	0	8	(1	7)	67	23	26	24	15	1	34	1	0	2	0	0	-	1	.256	.322	.429
2005	2 Tms		59	102	15	3	1	1	(1	0)	23	8	9	4	15	2	24	0	3	0	1	2	.33	2	.147	.256	.225
05	SD	NL	43	73	10	3	1	0	(1	0)	15	6	6	1	9	2	21	0	1	0	1	1	.50	2	.137	.232	.205
05	Sea	AL	16	29	5	0	0	1	(1	0)	8	2	3	3	6	0	3	0	2	0	0	1	.00	0	.172	.314	.276
	3 ML YEARS		182	399	88	12	1	13	(5	8)	141	44	57	48	48	5	84	4	3	3	2	3	.40	5	.221	.308	.353

John Olerud

Bats: L **Throws:** L **Pos:** 1B-80; PH-14   **Ht:** 6'5" **Wt:** 220 **Born:** 8/5/1968 **Age:** 37

Year	Team	Lg	G	AB	H	2B	3B	HR	(Hm	Rd)	TB	R	RBI	RC	TBB	IBB	SO	HBP	SH	SF	SB	CS	SB%	GDP	Avg	OBP	Slg
2005	Pwtckt*	AAA	3	10	3	0	0	1	(-	-)	6	2	2	2	2	0	1	0	0	0	0	0	-	2	.300	.417	.600
1989	TOR	AL	6	8	3	0	0	0	(0	0)	3	2	0	1	0	0	1	0	0	0	0	0	-	0	.375	.375	.375
1990	TOR	AL	111	358	95	15	1	14	(11	3)	154	43	48	57	57	6	75	1	1	4	0	2	.00	6	.265	.364	.430
1991	TOR	AL	139	454	116	30	1	17	(7	10)	199	64	68	71	68	9	84	6	3	10	0	2	.00	12	.256	.353	.438
1992	TOR	AL	138	458	130	28	0	16	(4	12)	206	68	66	76	70	11	61	1	1	7	1	0	1.00	15	.284	.375	.450
1993	TOR	AL	158	551	200	54	2	24	(9	15)	330	109	107	146	114	33	65	7	0	7	0	2	.00	12	.363	.473	.599
1994	TOR	AL	108	384	114	29	2	12	(6	6)	183	47	67	70	61	12	53	3	0	5	1	2	.33	11	.297	.393	.477
1995	TOR	AL	135	492	143	32	0	8	(1	7)	199	72	54	80	84	10	54	4	0	1	0	0	-	17	.291	.398	.404

Year	Team	Lg	G	AB	H	2B	3B	HR	(Hm	Rd)	TB	R	RBI	RC	TBB	IBB	SO	HBP	SH	SF	SB	CS	SB%	GDP	Avg	OBP	Slg
1996	TOR	AL	125	398	109	25	0	18	(9	9)	188	59	61	72	60	6	37	10	0	1	1	0	1.00	10	.274	.382	.472
1997	NYN	NL	154	524	154	34	1	22	(13	9)	256	90	102	101	85	5	67	13	0	8	0	0	-	19	.294	.400	.489
1998	NYN	NL	160	557	197	36	4	22	(13	9)	307	91	93	131	96	11	73	4	1	7	2	2	.50	15	.354	.447	.551
1999	NYN	NL	**162**	581	173	39	0	19	(11	8)	269	107	96	118	125	5	66	11	0	6	3	0	1.00	22	.298	.427	.463
2000	SEA	AL	159	565	161	45	0	14	(8	6)	248	84	103	98	102	11	96	4	2	10	0	2	.00	17	.285	.392	.439
2001	SEA	AL	159	572	173	32	1	21	(15	6)	270	91	95	106	94	19	70	5	1	7	3	1	.75	**21**	.302	.401	.472
2002	SEA	AL	154	553	166	39	0	22	(9	13)	271	85	102	108	98	6	66	5	0	**12**	0	0	-	19	.300	.403	.490
2003	SEA	AL	152	539	145	35	0	10	(8	2)	210	64	83	79	84	7	67	6	2	3	0	1	.00	20	.269	.372	.390
2004	2 Tms	AL	127	425	110	20	1	9	(5	4)	159	45	48	57	61	4	61	8	1	5	0	0	-	11	.259	.359	.374
2005	BOS	AL	87	173	50	7	0	7	(5	2)	78	18	37	31	16	2	20	0	0	3	0	0	-	6	.289	.344	.451
04	Sea	AL	78	261	64	13	1	5	(2	3)	94	29	22	30	40	3	41	6	1	4	0	0	-	6	.245	.354	.360
04	NYY	AL	49	164	46	7	0	4	(3	1)	65	16	26	27	21	1	20	2	0	1	0	0	-	5	.280	.367	.396
17 ML YEARS			2234	7592	2239	500	13	255	(134	121)	3530	1139	1230	1402	1275	157	1016	88	12	96	11	14	.44	232	.295	.398	.465

Miguel Olivo

Bats: R Throws: R Pos: C-91; PR-3; PH-2
Ht: 6'0" Wt: 180 Born: 7/15/1978 Age: 27

Year	Team	Lg	G	AB	H	2B	3B	HR	(Hm	Rd)	TB	R	RBI	RC	TBB	IBB	SO	HBP	SH	SF	SB	CS	SB%	GDP	Avg	OBP	Slg
2005	Tacom*	AAA	24	90	21	4	1	3	(-	-)	36	13	21	12	7	0	19	1	0	1	8	1	.89	1	.233	.293	.400
2002	CHA	AL	6	19	4	1	0	1	(0	1)	8	2	5	4	2	0	5	0	0	0	0	0	-	1	.211	.286	.421
2003	CHA	AL	114	317	75	19	1	6	(4	2)	114	37	27	32	19	0	80	4	4	2	6	4	.60	3	.237	.287	.360
2004	2 Tms	AL	96	301	70	15	4	13	(8	5)	132	46	40	33	20	2	84	3	4	1	7	6	.54	4	.233	.286	.439
2005	2 Tms	AL	91	267	58	11	1	9	(5	4)	98	30	34	23	8	2	80	3	1	2	7	2	.78	7	.217	.246	.367
04	CWS	AL	46	141	38	7	2	7	(4	3)	70	21	26	21	10	1	29	0	4	1	5	4	.56	2	.270	.316	.496
04	Sea	AL	50	160	32	8	2	6	(4	2)	62	25	14	12	10	1	55	3	0	0	2	2	.50	2	.200	.260	.388
05	Sea	AL	54	152	23	4	0	5	(4	1)	42	14	18	6	4	0	49	0	0	1	1	1	.50	3	.151	.172	.276
05	SD	NL	37	115	35	7	1	4	(1	3)	56	16	16	17	4	2	31	3	1	1	6	1	.86	4	.304	.341	.487
4 ML YEARS			307	904	207	46	6	29	(17	12)	352	115	106	92	49	4	249	10	9	5	20	12	.63	15	.229	.275	.389

Ray Olmedo

Bats: B Throws: R Pos: 2B-31; PH-21; SS-5; PR-4
Ht: 5'11" Wt: 155 Born: 5/31/1981 Age: 25

Year	Team	Lg	G	AB	H	2B	3B	HR	(Hm	Rd)	TB	R	RBI	RC	TBB	IBB	SO	HBP	SH	SF	SB	CS	SB%	GDP	Avg	OBP	Slg
2005	Lsvlle*	AAA	14	58	16	3	0	1	(-	-)	22	8	5	6	1	0	11	1	0	0	2	2	.50	0	.276	.300	.379
2003	CIN	NL	79	230	55	6	1	0	(0	0)	63	24	17	19	13	0	46	0	7	0	1	1	.50	4	.239	.280	.274
2004	CIN	NL	8	1	0	0	0	0	(0	0)	0	0	0	0	1	0	0	0	0	0	0	0	-	0	.000	.500	.000
2005	CIN	NL	54	77	17	4	1	1	(1	0)	26	10	4	6	6	0	22	1	3	1	4	0	1.00	1	.221	.282	.338
3 ML YEARS			141	308	72	10	2	1	(1	0)	89	34	21	25	20	0	68	1	10	1	5	1	.83	5	.234	.282	.289

Scott Olsen

Pitches: L Bats: L Pos: SP-4; RP-1
Ht: 6'4" Wt: 198 Born: 1/12/1984 Age: 22

Year	Team	Lg	G	GS	CG	GF	IP	BFP	H	R	ER	HR	SH	SF	HB	TBB	IBB	SO	WP	Bk	W	L	Pct	ShO	Sv-Op	Hld	ERC	ERA
2002	Marlins	R	13	11	0	0	51.2	211	39	18	17	0	1	1	5	17	0	50	5	2	2	3	.400	0	0--	-	2.25	2.96
2003	Grnsbr	A	25	24	0	1	128.1	545	101	51	40	4	1	7		59	0	129	7	0	7	9	.438	0	0--	-	2.87	2.81
2004	Jupiter	A+	25	25	1	0	136.1	589	127	57	45	8	5	4		53	0	158	7	0	7	6	.538	1	0--	-	3.43	2.97
2005	Carlina	AA	14	14	1	0	80.1	343	75	38	35	7	3	5		27	1	94	6	0	6	4	.600	1	0--	-	3.46	3.92
2005	FLA	NL	5	4	0	0	20.1	91	21	13	9	5	0	0		10	0	21	1	0	1	1	.500	0	0-0	0	5.66	3.98

Tim Olson

Bats: R Throws: R Pos: PH-2; DH-1; PR-1
Ht: 6'2" Wt: 200 Born: 8/1/1978 Age: 27

Year	Team	Lg	G	AB	H	2B	3B	HR	(Hm	Rd)	TB	R	RBI	RC	TBB	IBB	SO	HBP	SH	SF	SB	CS	SB%	GDP	Avg	OBP	Slg
2000	Sbend	A	68	261	57	14	2	2	(-	-)	81	37	26	23	15	0	49	8	0	1	15	3	.83	5	.218	.281	.310
2001	Lancst	A+	61	239	69	12	4	6	(-	-)	107	36	32	33	14	0	49	3	2	0	13	9	.59	4	.289	.336	.448
2001	ElPaso	AA	46	167	53	13	0	2	(-	-)	72	29	24	25	11	0	36	6	0	1	4	4	.50	4	.317	.378	.431
2002	ElPaso	AA	126	433	118	24	2	10	(-	-)	176	61	64	55	27	1	91	19	4	7	9	11	.45	13	.273	.337	.406
2003	ElPaso	AA	14	56	11	2	0	2	(-	-)	19	5	8	3	5	0	19	0	0	1	2	2	.00	1	.196	.258	.339
2003	Tucsn	AAA	115	397	104	22	0	6	(-	-)	144	59	40	45	31	2	77	6	3	2	11	2	.85	14	.262	.323	.363
2004	Tucsn	AAA	37	147	44	11	0	7	(-	-)	76	32	25	27	16	0	28	2	1	1	5	1	.83	2	.299	.373	.517
2005	ColSpr	AAA	89	322	96	26	2	12	(-	-)	162	53	51	58	28	2	70	5	5	4	9	7	.56	9	.298	.359	.503
2004	ARI	NL	48	97	18	7	0	2	(2	0)	31	8	5	8	16	0	18	0	1	0	1	0	1.00	4	.186	.301	.320
2005	COL	NL	3	2	0	0	0	0	(0	0)	0	0	0	0	1	0	2	0	0	0	0	0	-	0	.000	.333	.000
2 ML YEARS			51	99	18	7	0	2	(2	0)	31	8	5	8	17	0	20	0	1	0	1	0	1.00	4	.182	.302	.313

Magglio Ordonez

Bats: R Throws: R Pos: RF-81; PH-2; DH-1
Ht: 6'0" Wt: 210 Born: 1/28/1974 Age: 32

Year	Team	Lg	G	AB	H	2B	3B	HR	(Hm	Rd)	TB	R	RBI	RC	TBB	IBB	SO	HBP	SH	SF	SB	CS	SB%	GDP	Avg	OBP	Slg
2005	Toledo*	AAA	4	14	3	1	0	0	(-	-)	7	3	2	2	2	0	3	0	0	0	0	0	-	0	.214	.313	.500
1997	CHA	AL	21	69	22	6	0	4	(2	2)	40	12	11	12	2	0	8	0	1	0	1	2	.33	1	.319	.338	.580
1998	CHA	AL	145	535	151	25	2	14	(8	6)	222	70	65	67	28	1	53	9	2	4	9	7	.56	19	.282	.326	.415
1999	CHA	AL	157	624	188	34	3	30	(16	14)	318	100	117	102	47	4	64	1	0	5	13	6	.68	24	.301	.349	.510
2000	CHA	AL	153	588	185	34	3	32	(21	11)	321	102	126	112	60	3	64	2	0	15	18	4	.82	28	.315	.371	.546
2001	CHA	AL	160	593	181	40	1	31	(17	14)	316	97	113	117	70	7	70	5	0	3	25	7	.78	14	.305	.382	.533

Year	Team	Lg	G	AB	H	2B	3B	HR	(Hm	Rd)	TB	R	RBI	RC	TBB	IBB	SO	HBP	SH	SF	SB	CS	SB%	GDP	Avg	OBP	Slg
2002	CHA	AL	153	590	189	47	1	38	(24	14)	352	116	135	119	53	2	77	7	0	3	7	5	.58	21	.320	.381	.597
2003	CHA	AL	160	606	192	46	3	29	(17	12)	331	95	99	109	57	1	73	7	0	4	9	5	.64	20	.317	.380	.546
2004	CHA	AL	52	202	59	8	2	9	(4	5)	98	32	37	39	16	2	22	3	0	1	0	2	.00	4	.292	.351	.485
2005	DET	AL	82	305	92	17	0	8	(2	6)	133	38	46	51	30	1	35	1	0	7	0	0	-	8	.302	.359	.436
9 ML YEARS			1083	4112	1259	257	15	195	(111	84)	2131	662	749	728	363	21	466	35	3	42	82	38	.68	139	.306	.364	.518

Pete Orr

Bats: L **Throws:** R **Pos:** PH-54; 2B-25; PR-23; 3B-12; LF-3; SS-1; DH-1   **Ht:** 6'1" **Wt:** 185 **Born:** 6/8/1979 **Age:** 27

Year	Team	Lg	G	AB	H	2B	3B	HR	(Hm	Rd)	TB	R	RBI	RC	TBB	IBB	SO	HBP	SH	SF	SB	CS	SB%	GDP	Avg	OBP	Slg
2000	Jmstwn	A-	69	265	64	8	1	2	(-	-)	80	40	15	27	24	0	51	6	0	4	9	5	.64	4	.242	.314	.302
2001	MrtlBh	A+	92	317	74	10	1	4	(-	-)	98	38	23	31	19	0	70	11	3	1	17	6	.74	3	.233	.299	.309
2002	MrtlBh	A+	17	51	20	0	2	0	(-	-)	24	8	8	10	3	0	6	1	1	0	3	0	1.00	6	.392	.436	.471
2002	Grnville	AA	89	305	76	10	2	2	(-	-)	96	36	36	33	21	2	47	3	7	2	23	4	.85	8	.249	.302	.315
2003	Grnville	AA	98	257	58	10	2	2	(-	-)	78	22	31	26	25	3	48	3	4	3	14	5	.74	3	.226	.299	.304
2004	Rchmd	AAA	115	460	147	16	10	1	(-	-)	186	69	35	66	20	0	59	2	7	2	24	11	.69	7	.320	.349	.404
2005	ATL	NL	112	150	45	8	1	1	(0	1)	58	32	8	18	6	0	23	1	5	0	7	1	.88	2	.300	.331	.387

David Ortiz

Bats: L **Throws:** L **Pos:** DH-148; 1B-10; PH-3   **Ht:** 6'4" **Wt:** 230 **Born:** 11/18/1975 **Age:** 30

Year	Team	Lg	G	AB	H	2B	3B	HR	(Hm	Rd)	TB	R	RBI	RC	TBB	IBB	SO	HBP	SH	SF	SB	CS	SB%	GDP	Avg	OBP	Slg
1997	MIN	AL	15	49	16	3	0	1	(0	1)	22	10	6	7	2	0	19	0	0	0	0	0	-	1	.327	.353	.449
1998	MIN	AL	86	278	77	20	0	9	(2	7)	124	47	46	46	39	3	72	5	0	4	1	0	1.00	8	.277	.371	.446
1999	MIN	AL	10	20	0	0	0	0	(0	0)	0	1	0	0	5	0	12	0	0	0	0	0	-	2	.000	.200	.000
2000	MIN	AL	130	415	117	36	1	10	(7	3)	185	59	63	66	57	2	81	0	0	6	1	0	1.00	13	.282	.364	.446
2001	MIN	AL	89	303	71	17	1	18	(6	12)	144	46	48	46	40	8	68	1	1	2	1	0	1.00	6	.234	.324	.475
2002	MIN	AL	125	412	112	32	1	20	(5	15)	206	52	75	62	43	0	87	3	0	8	1	2	.33	8	.272	.339	.500
2003	BOS	AL	128	448	129	39	2	31	(17	14)	265	79	101	80	58	8	83	1	0	2	0	0	-	9	.288	.369	.592
2004	BOS	AL	150	582	175	47	3	41	(17	24)	351	94	139	127	75	8	133	4	0	8	0	0	-	12	.301	.380	.603
2005	BOS	AL	159	601	180	40	1	47	(20	27)	363	119	148	137	102	9	124	1	0	9	1	0	1.00	13	.300	.397	.604
9 ML YEARS			892	3108	877	234	9	177	(74	103)	1660	507	626	571	421	38	679	15	1	39	5	2	.71	69	.282	.366	.534

Ramon Ortiz

Pitches: R **Bats:** R **Pos:** SP-30   **Ht:** 6'0" **Wt:** 170 **Born:** 5/23/1973 **Age:** 33

Year	Team	Lg	G	GS	CG	GF	IP	BFP	H	R	ER	HR	SH	SF	HB	TBB	IBB	SO	WP	Bk	W	L	Pct	ShO	Sv-Op Hld	ERC	ERA
2005	Srsota	A+	1	1	0	0	3.0	16	7	4	3	1	0	0	0	0	0	3	0	0	0	1	.000	0	0- - -	12.91	9.00
1999	ANA	AL	9	9	0	0	48.1	218	50	35	35	7	0	2	2	25	0	44	2	2	2	3	.400	0	0-0 0	5.23	6.52
2000	ANA	AL	18	18	2	0	111.1	472	96	69	63	18	4	4	2	55	0	73	7	4	8	6	.571	0	0-0 0	4.24	5.09
2001	ANA	AL	32	32	2	0	208.2	916	223	114	101	25	9	6	12	76	6	135	7	0	13	11	.542	0	0-0 0	4.65	4.36
2002	ANA	AL	32	32	4	0	217.1	896	188	97	91	40	2	5	5	68	0	162	7	3	15	9	.625	1	0-0 0	3.64	3.77
2003	ANA	AL	32	32	1	0	180.0	814	209	121	104	28	3	7	12	63	0	94	4	0	16	13	.552	0	0-0 0	5.44	5.20
2004	ANA	AL	34	14	0	13	128.0	543	139	64	63	18	2	3	4	38	4	82	5	3	5	7	.417	0	0-0 0	4.61	4.43
2005	CIN	NL	30	30	1	0	171.1	755	206	110	102	34	7	8	7	51	1	96	4	1	9	11	.450	0	0-0 0	5.78	5.36
7 ML YEARS			187	167	10	13	1065.0	4614	1111	610	559	170	27	35	44	376	11	686	36	13	68	60	.531	1	0-0 0	4.73	4.72

Russ Ortiz

Pitches: R **Bats:** R **Pos:** SP-22   **Ht:** 6'1" **Wt:** 208 **Born:** 6/5/1974 **Age:** 32

Year	Team	Lg	G	GS	CG	GF	IP	BFP	H	R	ER	HR	SH	SF	HB	TBB	IBB	SO	WP	Bk	W	L	Pct	ShO	Sv-Op Hld	ERC	ERA
2005	Lancst*	A+	1	1	0	0	2.1	20	12	11	11	2	0	0	1	1	0	1	0	0	0	1	.000	0	0- - -	46.70	42.43
2005	Tucsn*	AAA	2	2	0	0	9.0	46	14	14	13	4	0	0	0	5	0	5	0	0	0	1	.000	0	0- - -	11.09	13.00
1998	SF	NL	22	13	0	3	88.1	394	90	51	49	11	5	4	4	46	1	75	3	0	4	4	.500	0	0-0 1	5.05	4.99
1999	SF	NL	33	33	3	0	207.2	922	189	109	88	24	11	6	6	125	5	164	13	0	18	9	.667	0	0-0 0	4.56	3.81
2000	SF	NL	33	32	0	0	195.2	871	192	117	109	28	10	6	7	112	1	167	8	0	14	12	.538	0	0-0 0	5.17	5.01
2001	SF	NL	33	33	1	0	218.2	911	187	90	80	13	10	4	0	91	3	169	8	1	17	9	.654	1	0-0 0	3.08	3.29
2002	SF	NL	33	33	2	0	214.1	911	191	89	86	15	15	6	4	94	5	137	5	0	14	10	.583	0	0-0 0	3.46	3.61
2003	ATL	NL	34	34	1	0	212.1	912	177	101	90	17	6	7	4	102	7	149	5	0	21	7	.750	1	0-0 0	3.32	3.81
2004	ATL	NL	34	34	2	0	204.2	896	197	98	94	23	10	7	3	112	7	143	4	1	15	9	.625	0	0-0 0	4.60	4.13
2005	ARI	NL	22	22	0	0	115.0	551	147	92	88	18	5	8	4	65	3	46	5	0	5	11	.313	0	0-0 0	6.96	6.89
8 ML YEARS			244	234	9	3	1456.2	6368	1370	747	684	149	72	48	32	747	32	1050	51	2	108	71	.603	3	0-0 1	4.26	4.23

Dan Ortmeier

Bats: B **Throws:** L **Pos:** PH-8; RF-7   **Ht:** 6'4" **Wt:** 220 **Born:** 5/11/1981 **Age:** 25

Year	Team	Lg	G	AB	H	2B	3B	HR	(Hm	Rd)	TB	R	RBI	RC	TBB	IBB	SO	HBP	SH	SF	SB	CS	SB%	GDP	Avg	OBP	Slg
2002	SlmKzr	A-	49	195	57	9	1	5	(-	-)	83	32	31	31	18	1	37	1	0	2	3	0	1.00	4	.292	.352	.426
2003	SnJos	A+	115	408	124	32	6	8	(-	-)	192	62	56	74	39	4	89	11	0	2	13	6	.68	13	.304	.378	.471
2004	Nrwich	AA	106	377	95	23	6	10	(-	-)	160	55	48	62	47	4	110	12	0	2	18	2	.90	5	.252	.352	.424
2005	Nrwich	AA	135	503	138	23	6	20	(-	-)	233	85	79	89	48	1	115	21	0	3	35	12	.74	4	.274	.360	.463
2005	SF	NL	15	22	3	0	0	0	(0	0)	3	1	1	1	3	0	5	1	0	0	1	0	1.00	2	.136	.269	.136

Chad Orvella

Pitches: R Bats: R Pos: RP-37   Ht: 5'11" Wt: 190 Born: 10/1/1980 Age: 25

			HOW MUCH HE PITCHED					WHAT HE GAVE UP											THE RESULTS						
Year	Team	Lg	G	GS	CG	GF	IP	BFP	H	R	ER	HR	SH	SF	HB	TBB	IBB	SO	WP	Bk	W	L	Pct	ShO	Sv-Op Hld	ERC	ERA
2003	HudVal	A-	10	0	0	9	12.1	44	6	0	0	0	1	2	0	1	0	15	0	0	0	0	-	0	8-- -	0.63	0.00
2004	Bkrsfld	A+	15	0	0	13	17.2	70	13	7	6	2	0	0	1	4	1	24	1	0	0	1	.000	0	4-- -	2.28	3.06
2004	Mont	AA	6	0	0	6	7.0	21	0	0	0	0	0	0	1	0	0	14	0	0	0	0	-	0	4-- -	0.03	0.00
2004	Drham	AAA	2	0	0	0	1.2	7	1	1	1	1	0	0	1	1	0	2	1	0	0	0	-	0	0-- -	10.27	5.40
2005	Mont	AA	16	0	0	15	25.0	96	15	1	1	0	1	0	0	6	0	29	1	0	0	0	-	0	9-- -	1.19	0.36
2005	TB	AL	37	0	0	9	50.0	219	47	26	20	4	1	4	1	23	2	43	0	0	3	3	.500	0	1-2 14	3.79	3.60

Keith Osik

Bats: R Throws: R Pos: C-5; PH-1   Ht: 6'0" Wt: 200 Born: 10/22/1968 Age: 37

			BATTING																		BASERUNNING				AVERAGES		
Year	Team	Lg	G	AB	H	2B	3B	HR	(Hm	Rd)	TB	R	RBI	RC	TBB	IBB	SO	HBP	SH	SF		SB	CS	SB%	GDP	Avg	OBP	Slg
2005	NewOr*	AAA	17	44	9	2	0	0	(-	-)	11	3	3	3	4	0	7	0	1	1		1	0	1.00	2	.205	.265	.250
1996	PIT	NL	48	140	41	14	1	1	(0	1)	60	18	14	21	14	1	22	1	1	0		1	0	1.00	3	.293	.361	.429
1997	PIT	NL	49	105	27	9	1	0	(0	0)	38	10	7	12	9	1	21	1	2	0		0	1	.00	1	.257	.322	.362
1998	PIT	NL	39	98	21	4	0	0	(0	0)	25	8	7	7	13	2	16	2	2	1		1	2	.33	4	.214	.316	.255
1999	PIT	NL	66	167	31	3	1	2	(1	1)	42	12	13	7	11	0	30	1	1	1		0	0	-	8	.186	.239	.251
2000	PIT	NL	46	123	36	6	1	4	(1	3)	56	11	22	23	14	0	11	5	1	0		3	0	1.00	1	.293	.387	.455
2001	PIT	NL	56	120	25	4	0	2	(0	2)	35	9	13	11	13	0	24	3	0	1		1	0	1.00	1	.208	.299	.292
2002	PIT	NL	55	100	16	3	0	2	(1	1)	25	6	11	4	6	0	25	1	2	2		0	0	-	2	.160	.211	.250
2003	MIL	NL	80	241	60	12	0	2	(1	1)	78	22	21	20	31	0	44	3	0	0		0	1	.00	7	.249	.342	.324
2004	BAL	AL	11	25	2	0	0	0	(0	0)	2	0	0	0	0	0	7	0	0	0		0	0	-	1	.080	.080	.080
2005	WAS	NL	6	4	0	0	0	0	(0	0)	0	0	0	0	0	0	2	0	0	0		0	0	-	0	.000	.000	.000
	10 ML YEARS		456	1123	259	55	4	13	(4	9)	361	96	108	105	111	4	202	17	9	5		6	4	.60	29	.231	.308	.321

Franquelis Osoria

Pitches: R Bats: R Pos: RP-24   Ht: 6'0" Wt: 165 Born: 9/12/1981 Age: 24

			HOW MUCH HE PITCHED					WHAT HE GAVE UP											THE RESULTS						
Year	Team	Lg	G	GS	CG	GF	IP	BFP	H	R	ER	HR	SH	SF	HB	TBB	IBB	SO	WP	Bk	W	L	Pct	ShO	Sv-Op Hld	ERC	ERA
2002	VeroB	A+	3	0	0	1	7.1	28	4	2	2	0	0	0	1	2	0	10	0	0	0	1	.000	0	0-- -	1.41	2.45
2002	SoGA	A	21	1	0	7	43.1	183	40	22	16	1	2	1	2	13	1	30	3	0	2	2	.500	0	1-- -	2.87	3.32
2003	VeroB	A+	33	3	0	20	75.0	313	69	34	25	4	5	5	5	19	5	53	5	1	3	6	.333	0	6-- -	2.92	3.00
2004	Jaxnvl	AA	51	0	0	24	81.0	332	71	36	33	2	2	0	5	18	4	73	3	0	8	5	.615	0	5-- -	2.42	3.67
2004	LsVgs	AAA	4	0	0	0	8.1	39	13	6	6	0	1	1	1	1	0	3	0	0	0	0	-	0	0-- -	5.94	6.48
2005	LsVgs	AAA	40	0	0	21	55.0	241	63	18	16	3	1	1	4	13	6	35	3	0	6	4	.600	0	9-- -	4.00	2.62
2005	LAN	NL	24	0	0	6	29.2	122	28	14	13	3	3	0	3	8	0	15	0	0	0	2	.000	0	0-2 3	3.78	3.94

Antonio Osuna

Pitches: R Bats: R Pos: RP-4   Ht: 5'11" Wt: 205 Born: 4/12/1973 Age: 33

			HOW MUCH HE PITCHED					WHAT HE GAVE UP											THE RESULTS						
Year	Team	Lg	G	GS	CG	GF	IP	BFP	H	R	ER	HR	SH	SF	HB	TBB	IBB	SO	WP	Bk	W	L	Pct	ShO	Sv-Op Hld	ERC	ERA
2005	NewOr*	AAA	2	0	0	0	3.0	10	1	0	0	0	0	0	0	1	0	1	0	0	0	0	-	0	0-- -	0.25	0.00
1995	LA	NL	39	0	0	8	44.2	186	39	22	22	5	2	1	1	20	2	46	1	0	2	4	.333	0	0-2 11	3.76	4.43
1996	LA	NL	73	0	0	21	84.0	342	65	33	28	6	7	5	2	32	12	85	3	2	9	6	.600	0	4-9 16	2.53	3.00
1997	LA	NL	48	0	0	18	61.2	245	46	15	15	6	4	1	1	19	2	68	2	0	3	4	.429	0	0-10 12	2.43	2.19
1998	LA	NL	54	0	0	25	64.2	272	50	26	22	8	2	2	2	32	0	72	1	0	7	1	.875	0	6-11 12	3.50	3.06
1999	LA	NL	5	0	0	1	4.2	22	4	5	4	0	0	0	1	3	0	5	1	0	0	0	-	0	0-0 2	4.14	7.71
2000	LA	NL	46	0	0	16	67.1	293	57	30	28	7	4	3	2	35	2	70	1	2	3	6	.333	0	0-3 4	3.74	3.74
2001	CHA	AL	4	0	0	0	4.1	23	8	10	10	3	0	1	0	2	1	6	0	0	0	0	-	0	0-1 0	16.71	20.77
2002	CHA	AL	59	0	0	28	67.2	296	64	32	29	1	5	3	4	28	4	66	0	1	8	2	.800	0	11-14 9	3.31	3.86
2003	NYA	AL	48	0	0	16	50.2	232	58	22	21	3	2	2	2	20	3	47	3	0	2	5	.286	0	0-1 9	4.51	3.73
2004	SD	NL	31	0	0	6	36.2	151	32	11	10	3	0	1	0	11	0	36	0	0	2	1	.667	0	0-2 3	3.00	2.45
2005	WAS	NL	4	0	0	1	2.1	23	9	11	11	2	0	1	0	7	1	0	0	0	0	0	-	0	0-0 0	48.54	42.43
	11 ML YEARS		411	0	0	140	488.2	2085	432	217	200	44	26	20	17	209	27	501	12	5	36	29	.554	0	21-43 75	3.52	3.68

Roy Oswalt

Pitches: R Bats: R Pos: SP-35   Ht: 6'0" Wt: 175 Born: 8/29/1977 Age: 28

			HOW MUCH HE PITCHED					WHAT HE GAVE UP											THE RESULTS						
Year	Team	Lg	G	GS	CG	GF	IP	BFP	H	R	ER	HR	SH	SF	HB	TBB	IBB	SO	WP	Bk	W	L	Pct	ShO	Sv-Op Hld	ERC	ERA
2001	HOU	NL	28	20	3	4	141.2	575	126	48	43	13	4	4	6	24	2	144	0	0	14	3	.824	1	0-0 0	2.68	2.73
2002	HOU	NL	35	34	0	0	233.0	956	215	86	78	17	12	7	5	62	4	208	3	0	19	9	.679	0	0-0 0	3.05	3.01
2003	HOU	NL	21	21	0	0	127.1	514	116	48	42	15	7	1	5	29	0	108	1	0	10	5	.667	0	0-0 0	3.26	2.97
2004	HOU	NL	36	35	2	0	237.0	983	233	100	92	17	11	4	11	62	5	206	5	1	20	10	.667	2	0-0 0	3.46	3.49
2005	HOU	NL	35	35	4	0	241.2	1002	243	85	79	18	12	7	8	48	3	184	5	1	20	12	.625	1	0-0 0	3.27	2.94
	5 ML YEARS		155	145	9	4	980.2	4030	933	367	334	80	46	23	35	225	14	850	14	2	83	39	.680	4	0-0 0	3.18	3.07

Akinori Otsuka

Pitches: R Bats: R Pos: RP-66   Ht: 6'0" Wt: 200 Born: 1/13/1972 Age: 34

			HOW MUCH HE PITCHED					WHAT HE GAVE UP											THE RESULTS						
Year	Team	Lg	G	GS	CG	GF	IP	BFP	H	R	ER	HR	SH	SF	HB	TBB	IBB	SO	WP	Bk	W	L	Pct	ShO	Sv-Op Hld	ERC	ERA
2004	SD	NL	73	0	0	18	77.1	312	56	16	15	6	4	0	0	26	6	87	0	0	7	2	.778	0	2-7 34	2.14	1.75
2005	SD	NL	66	0	0	17	62.2	276	55	28	25	3	5	0	2	34	8	60	1	0	2	8	.200	0	1-7 22	3.44	3.59
	2 ML YEARS		139	0	0	35	140.0	588	111	44	40	9	9	0	2	60	14	147	1	0	9	10	.474	0	3-14 56	2.71	2.57

Lyle Overbay

Bats: L **Throws:** L **Pos:** 1B-154; PH-6 **Ht:** 6'2" **Wt:** 215 **Born:** 1/28/1977 **Age:** 29

										BATTING													BASERUNNING				AVERAGES		
Year	Team	Lg	G	AB	H	2B	3B	HR	(Hm	Rd)	TB	R	RBI	RC	TBB	IBB	SO	HBP	SH	SF		SB	CS	SB%	GDP		Avg	OBP	Slg
2001	ARI	NL	2	2	1	0	0	0	(0	0)	1	0	0	0	0	0	1	0	0	0		0	0	-	0		.500	.500	.500
2002	ARI	NL	10	10	1	0	0	0	(0	0)	1	0	1	0	0	0	5	0	0	0		0	0	-	0		.100	.100	.100
2003	ARI	NL	86	254	70	20	0	4	(2	2)	102	23	28	34	35	7	67	2	0	2		1	0	1.00	8		.276	.365	.402
2004	MIL	NL	159	579	174	53	1	16	(6	10)	277	83	87	94	81	9	128	2	0	6		2	1	.67	11		.301	.385	.478
2005	MIL	NL	158	537	148	34	1	19	(10	9)	241	80	72	84	78	8	98	2	1	4		1	0	1.00	17		.276	.367	.449
5 ML YEARS			415	1382	394	107	2	39	(18	21)	622	186	188	212	194	24	299	6	1	12		4	1	.80	36		.285	.373	.450

Chris Oxspring

Pitches: R **Bats:** L **Pos:** RP-5 **Ht:** 6'0" **Wt:** 185 **Born:** 5/13/1977 **Age:** 29

							HOW MUCH HE PITCHED			WHAT HE GAVE UP												THE RESULTS						
Year	Team	Lg	G	GS	CG	GF	IP	BFP		H	R	ER	HR	SH	SF	HB	TBB	IBB	SO	WP	Bk		W	L	Pct	ShO	Sv-Op	Hld	ERC	ERA
2001	Lk Els	A+	7	0	0	2	14.0	58		10	2	1	1	0	0	0	6	2	17	0	0		0	0	-	0	0--	-	2.25	0.64
2001	FtWyn	A	41	2	0	8	56.1	259		66	29	26	5	3	3	3	25	5	54	2	2		4	1	.800	0	0--	-	5.17	4.15
2002	Lk Els	A+	15	1	0	3	26.1	111		24	16	14	2	0	2	2	8	0	30	3	0		0	1	.000	0	0--	-	3.34	4.78
2002	Mobile	AA	6	1	0	0	14.1	64		13	3	2	0	1	0	0	8	0	21	1	0		0	0	-	0	0--	-	3.35	1.26
2003	Mobile	AA	40	18	1	8	135.2	575		106	47	44	6	3	0	1	62	3	129	1	0		10	6	.625	0	0--	-	2.69	2.92
2004	Portlnd	AAA	17	17	0	0	85.2	383		82	45	38	7	7	3	2	44	1	81	5	0		6	4	.600	0	0--	-	4.14	3.99
2005	Portlnd	AAA	26	26	3	0	160.2	672		148	81	72	15	4	5	2	42	0	125	4	0		12	6	.667	2	0--	-	3.07	4.03
2005	SD	NL	5	0	0	0	12.0	49		9	8	5	2	1	2	0	6	0	11	0	0		0	0	-	0	0-0	0	3.64	3.75

Pablo Ozuna

Bats: R **Throws:** R **Pos:** 3B-32; SS-15; PH-10; LF-9; PR-7; 2B-6; DH-3; 1B-2; RF-1 **Ht:** 6'0" **Wt:** 160 **Born:** 8/25/1974 **Age:** 31

										BATTING													BASERUNNING				AVERAGES		
Year	Team	Lg	G	AB	H	2B	3B	HR	(Hm	Rd)	TB	R	RBI	RC	TBB	IBB	SO	HBP	SH	SF		SB	CS	SB%	GDP		Avg	OBP	Slg
2000	FLA	NL	14	24	8	1	0	0	(0	0)	9	2	0	3	0	0	2	0	2	0		1	0	1.00	0		.333	.333	.375
2002	FLA	NL	34	47	13	2	2	0	(0	0)	19	4	3	4	1	0	3	1	0	1		1	1	.50	2		.277	.300	.404
2003	COL	NL	17	40	8	1	0	0	(0	0)	9	5	2	4	2	0	6	2	1	0		3	0	1.00	1		.200	.273	.225
2005	CHA	AL	70	203	56	7	2	0	(0	0)	67	27	11	20	7	0	26	4	3	0		14	7	.67	5		.276	.313	.330
4 ML YEARS			135	314	85	11	4	0	(0	0)	104	38	16	31	10	0	37	7	6	1		19	8	.70	8		.271	.307	.331

Juan Padilla

Pitches: R **Bats:** R **Pos:** RP-24 **Ht:** 6'0" **Wt:** 200 **Born:** 2/17/1977 **Age:** 29

							HOW MUCH HE PITCHED			WHAT HE GAVE UP												THE RESULTS						
Year	Team	Lg	G	GS	CG	GF	IP	BFP		H	R	ER	HR	SH	SF	HB	TBB	IBB	SO	WP	Bk		W	L	Pct	ShO	Sv-Op	Hld	ERC	ERA
1998	Twins	R	17	0	0	14	25.2	100		19	4	4	1	1	0	2	1	0	27	1	0		1	1	.500	0	10--	-	1.47	1.40
1999	QuadC	A	14	0	0	4	15.0	69		18	8	4	0	0	1	0	6	2	16	4	1		0	2	.000	0	0--	-	4.10	2.40
1999	NwBrit	AA	11	0	0	3	19.0	92		31	15	14	3	2	1	1	7	0	12	2	0		1	1	.500	0	2--	-	8.76	6.63
1999	FtMyrs	A+	22	0	0	11	33.2	146		32	14	13	1	3	2	1	17	2	28	3	0		2	2	.500	0	0--	-	3.76	3.48
2000	QuadC	A	32	0	0	27	33.0	133		24	7	7	0	3	0	1	9	2	40	1	0		2	2	.500	0	16--	-	1.64	1.91
2000	NwBrit	AA	23	0	0	6	33.2	144		35	15	14	1	1	0	2	11	0	24	0	0		0	1	.000	0	0--	-	3.79	3.74
2001	FtMyrs	A+	56	0	0	49	69.1	306		72	35	23	2	1	1	3	25	6	77	1	0		6	4	.600	0	23--	-	3.58	2.99
2002	NwBrit	AA	54	0	0	48	65.1	283		69	30	24	2	1	2	4	18	6	52	2	0		3	5	.375	0	29--	-	3.47	3.31
2003	Roch	AAA	57	0	0	29	91.0	386		94	40	34	7	8	3	4	17	3	68	5	0		7	4	.636	0	6--	-	3.33	3.36
2004	Trentn	AA	3	0	0	1	4.0	19		4	4	4	1	0	0	1	3	0	4	0	0		0	0	-	0	0--	-	8.11	9.00
2004	Clmbs	AAA	45	0	0	11	58.0	228		49	20	13	1	0	0	2	6	2	52	4	1		2	1	.667	0	3--	-	1.79	2.02
2005	Norfolk	AAA	37	2	0	24	63.1	244		45	13	10	4	3	1	5	9	0	59	4	0		3	2	.600	0	11--	-	1.77	1.42
2004	2 Tms		18	0	0	3	25.2	124		39	22	22	7	1	0	1	12	0	17	0	0		1	0	1.000	0	0-0	0	9.43	7.71
2005	NYN	NL	24	0	0	5	36.1	149		24	7	6	0	1	0	2	13	2	17	0	0		3	1	.750	0	1-2	6	1.66	1.49
04	NYY	AL	6	0	0	1	11.1	50		16	5	5	1	0	0	0	4	0	5	0	0		0	0	-	0	0-0	0	6.60	3.97
04	Cin	NL	12	0	0	2	14.1	74		23	17	17	6	1	0	1	8	0	12	0	0		1	0	1.000	0	0-0	0	11.76	10.67
2 ML YEARS			42	0	0	8	62.0	273		63	29	28	7	2	0	3	25	2	34	0	0		4	1	.800	0	1-2	6	4.38	4.06

Vicente Padilla

Pitches: R **Bats:** R **Pos:** SP-27 **Ht:** 6'2" **Wt:** 200 **Born:** 9/27/1977 **Age:** 28

							HOW MUCH HE PITCHED			WHAT HE GAVE UP												THE RESULTS						
Year	Team	Lg	G	GS	CG	GF	IP	BFP		H	R	ER	HR	SH	SF	HB	TBB	IBB	SO	WP	Bk		W	L	Pct	ShO	Sv-Op	Hld	ERC	ERA
2005	Clrwtr*	A+	1	1	0	0	5.0	20		4	1	1	0	0	0	0	1	0	3	0	0		1	0	1.000	0	0--	-	1.70	1.80
2005	S-WB*	AAA	1	1	0	0	5.0	23		6	2	2	0	0	0	0	2	0	4	0	0		1	0	1.000	0	0--	-	4.34	3.60
1999	ARI	NL	5	0	0	2	2.2	19		7	5	5	1	1	0	0	3	0	0	1	0		0	0	.000	0	0-1	1	20.65	16.88
2000	2 Tms	NL	55	0	0	16	65.1	291		72	33	27	3	5	3	1	28	7	51	1	0		4	7	.364	0	2-7	15	4.22	3.72
2001	PHI	NL	23	0	0	5	34.0	144		36	18	16	1	0	0	0	12	0	29	1	0		3	1	.750	0	0-3	1	3.80	4.24
2002	PHI	NL	32	32	1	0	206.0	862		198	83	75	16	10	3	16	53	5	128	6	2		14	11	.560	1	0-0	0	3.42	3.28
2003	PHI	NL	32	32	1	0	208.2	876		196	94	84	22	11	7	16	62	4	133	3	2		14	12	.538	1	0-0	0	3.68	3.62
2004	PHI	NL	20	20	0	0	115.1	503		119	63	58	16	7	5	10	36	6	82	2	0		7	7	.500	1	0-0	0	4.42	4.53
2005	PHI	NL	27	27	0	0	147.0	654		146	79	77	22	7	3	8	74	9	103	1	0		9	12	.429	0	0-0	0	4.94	4.41
00	Ari	NL	27	0	0	12	35.0	143		32	10	9	0	0	0	0	10	2	30	0	0		2	1	.667	0	0-1	7	2.48	2.31
00	Phi	NL	28	0	0	4	30.1	148		40	23	18	3	5	2	1	18	5	21	1	0		2	6	.250	0	2-6	8	6.52	5.34
7 ML YEARS			194	111	2	23	779.0	3349		774	375	342	81	41	21	50	268	31	526	14	4		51	51	.500	2	2-11	17	4.05	3.95

Orlando Palmeiro

Bats: L **Throws:** L **Pos:** PH-64; LF-47; RF-26; CF-5; PR-1   **Ht:** 5'10" **Wt:** 182 **Born:** 1/19/1969 **Age:** 37

								BATTING													BASERUNNING				AVERAGES		
Year	Team	Lg	G	AB	H	2B	3B	HR	(Hm	Rd)	TB	R	RBI	RC	TBB	IBB	SO	HBP	SH	SF	SB	CS	SB%	GDP	Avg	OBP	Slg
1995	CAL	AL	15	20	7	0	0	0	(0	0)	7	3	1	3	1	0	1	0	0	0	0	0	-	0	.350	.381	.350
1996	CAL	AL	50	87	25	6	1	0	(0	0)	33	6	6	12	8	1	13	2	1	0	0	1	.00	1	.287	.361	.379
1997	ANA	AL	74	134	29	2	2	0	(0	0)	35	19	8	10	17	1	11	1	3	1	2	2	.50	4	.216	.307	.261
1998	ANA	AL	75	165	53	7	2	0	(0	0)	64	28	21	26	20	1	11	0	7	0	5	4	.56	2	.321	.395	.388
1999	ANA	AL	109	317	88	12	1	1	(0	1)	105	46	23	41	39	1	30	6	6	3	5	5	.50	4	.278	.364	.331
2000	ANA	AL	108	243	73	20	2	0	(0	0)	97	38	25	42	38	0	20	2	10	3	4	1	.80	4	.300	.395	.399
2001	ANA	AL	104	230	56	10	1	2	(0	2)	74	29	23	25	25	2	24	3	7	5	6	6	.50	3	.243	.319	.322
2002	ANA	AL	110	263	79	12	1	0	(0	0)	93	35	31	39	30	1	22	0	4	3	7	2	.78	7	.300	.368	.354
2003	STL	NL	141	317	86	13	1	3	(1	2)	110	37	33	37	32	3	31	2	7	6	3	3	.50	1	.271	.336	.347
2004	HOU	NL	102	133	32	5	0	3	(1	2)	46	19	12	18	18	1	19	3	2	0	2	1	.67	1	.241	.344	.346
2005	HOU	NL	114	204	58	17	2	3	(1	2)	88	22	20	29	15	1	23	4	5	3	3	1	.75	4	.284	.341	.431
	11 ML YEARS		1002	2113	586	104	13	12	(3	9)	752	282	203	282	243	12	205	23	52	24	37	26	.59	31	.277	.355	.356

Rafael Palmeiro

Bats: L **Throws:** L **Pos:** 1B-93; DH-15; PH-3   **Ht:** 6'0" **Wt:** 190 **Born:** 9/24/1964 **Age:** 41

								BATTING													BASERUNNING				AVERAGES		
Year	Team	Lg	G	AB	H	2B	3B	HR	(Hm	Rd)	TB	R	RBI	RC	TBB	IBB	SO	HBP	SH	SF	SB	CS	SB%	GDP	Avg	OBP	Slg
1986	CHN	NL	22	73	18	4	0	3	(2	1)	31	9	12	8	4	0	6	1	0	0	1	1	.50	4	.247	.295	.425
1987	CHN	NL	84	221	61	15	1	14	(5	9)	120	32	30	39	20	1	26	1	0	2	2	2	.50	4	.276	.336	.543
1988	CHN	NL	152	580	178	41	5	8	(8	0)	253	75	53	88	38	6	34	3	2	6	12	2	.86	11	.307	.349	.436
1989	TEX	AL	156	559	154	23	4	8	(4	4)	209	76	64	73	63	3	48	6	2	2	4	3	.57	18	.275	.354	.374
1990	TEX	AL	154	598	191	35	6	14	(9	5)	280	72	89	93	40	6	59	3	2	8	3	3	.50	24	.319	.361	.468
1991	TEX	AL	159	631	203	49	3	26	(12	14)	336	115	88	123	68	10	72	6	2	7	4	3	.57	17	.322	.389	.532
1992	TEX	AL	159	608	163	27	4	22	(8	14)	264	84	85	94	72	8	83	10	5	6	2	3	.40	10	.268	.352	.434
1993	TEX	AL	160	597	176	40	2	37	(22	15)	331	124	105	123	73	22	85	5	2	9	22	3	.88	8	.295	.371	.554
1994	BAL	AL	111	436	139	32	0	23	(11	12)	240	82	76	90	54	1	63	2	0	6	7	3	.70	11	.319	.392	.550
1995	BAL	AL	143	554	172	30	2	39	(21	18)	323	89	104	116	62	5	65	3	0	5	3	1	.75	12	.310	.380	.583
1996	BAL	AL	162	626	181	40	2	39	(21	18)	342	110	142	130	95	12	96	3	0	8	8	0	1.00	9	.289	.381	.546
1997	BAL	AL	158	614	156	24	2	38	(20	18)	298	95	110	97	67	7	109	5	0	6	5	2	.71	14	.254	.329	.485
1998	BAL	AL	162	619	183	36	1	43	(25	18)	350	98	121	126	79	8	91	7	0	4	11	7	.61	14	.296	.379	.565
1999	TEX	AL	158	565	183	30	1	47	(28	19)	356	96	148	139	97	14	69	3	0	9	2	4	.33	13	.324	.420	.630
2000	TEX	AL	158	565	163	29	3	39	(26	13)	315	102	120	121	103	17	77	3	0	7	2	1	.67	14	.288	.397	.558
2001	TEX	AL	160	600	164	33	0	47	(23	24)	338	98	123	128	101	8	90	7	0	6	1	1	.50	8	.273	.381	.563
2002	TEX	AL	155	546	149	34	0	43	(23	20)	312	99	105	104	104	16	94	6	0	7	2	0	1.00	10	.273	.391	.571
2003	TEX	AL	154	561	146	21	2	38	(21	17)	285	92	112	106	84	9	77	5	0	4	2	0	1.00	7	.260	.359	.508
2004	BAL	AL	154	550	142	29	0	23	(12	11)	240	68	88	81	86	15	61	6	0	9	2	1	.67	15	.258	.359	.436
2005	BAL	AL	110	369	98	13	0	18	(11	7)	165	47	60	54	43	4	43	2	0	8	2	0	1.00	9	.266	.339	.447
	20 ML YEARS		2831	10472	3020	585	38	569	(311	258)	5388	1663	1835	1933	1353	172	1348	87	15	119	97	40	.71	232	.288	.371	.515

Jonathan Papelbon

Pitches: R **Bats:** R **Pos:** RP-14; SP-3   **Ht:** 6'4" **Wt:** 230 **Born:** 11/23/1980 **Age:** 25

			HOW MUCH HE PITCHED						WHAT HE GAVE UP											THE RESULTS						
Year	Team	Lg	G	GS	CG	GF	IP	BFP	H	R	ER	HR	SH	SF	HB	TBB	IBB	SO	WP	Bk	W	L	Pct	ShO	Sv-Op	Hld	ERC	ERA
2003	Lowell	A-	13	6	0	1	32.2	154	43	23	23	2	2	1	4	43	9	36	3	0	1	2	.333	0	0- -	-	5.47	6.34
2004	Srsota	A+	24	24	2	0	129.2	529	97	43	38	6	6	3	7	43	2	153	3	0	12	7	.632	0	0- -	-	2.33	2.64
2005	Portlnd	AA	14	14	0	0	87.0	343	59	28	24	9	4	3	5	23	3	83	2	1	5	2	.714	0	0- -	-	2.11	2.48
2005	Pwtckt	AAA	7	4	0	3	27.2	107	21	9	9	2	2	0	1	3	0	27	0	0	1	2	.333	0	1- -	-	1.76	2.93
2005	BOS	AL	17	3	0	4	34.0	148	33	11	10	4	1	0	3	17	2	34	1	0	3	1	.750	0	0-1	4	4.82	2.65

Chan Ho Park

Pitches: R **Bats:** R **Pos:** SP-29; RP-1   **Ht:** 6'2" **Wt:** 204 **Born:** 6/30/1973 **Age:** 33

			HOW MUCH HE PITCHED						WHAT HE GAVE UP											THE RESULTS						
Year	Team	Lg	G	GS	CG	GF	IP	BFP	H	R	ER	HR	SH	SF	HB	TBB	IBB	SO	WP	Bk	W	L	Pct	ShO	Sv-Op	Hld	ERC	ERA
1994	LA	NL	2	0	0	1	4.0	23	5	5	5	1	0	0	1	5	0	6	0	0	0	0	-	0	0-0	0	11.69	11.25
1995	LA	NL	2	1	0	0	4.0	16	2	2	2	1	0	0	0	2	0	7	0	1	0	0	-	0	0-0	0	2.70	4.50
1996	LA	NL	48	10	0	7	108.2	477	82	48	44	7	8	1	4	71	3	119	4	3	5	5	.500	0	0-0	4	3.50	3.64
1997	LA	NL	32	29	2	1	192.0	792	149	79	72	24	9	5	8	70	1	166	4	1	14	8	.636	0	0-0	0	3.04	3.38
1998	LA	NL	34	34	2	0	220.2	946	199	101	91	16	11	10	11	97	1	191	6	2	15	9	.625	0	0-0	0	3.69	3.71
1999	LA	NL	33	33	0	0	194.1	883	208	120	113	31	10	5	14	100	4	174	11	1	13	11	.542	0	0-0	0	5.68	5.23
2000	LA	NL	34	34	3	0	226.0	963	173	92	82	21	12	5	12	124	4	217	13	0	18	10	.643	1	0-0	0	3.51	3.27
2001	LA	NL	36	35	2	0	234.0	981	183	98	91	23	16	7	20	91	1	218	3	3	15	11	.577	1	0-0	0	3.15	3.50
2002	TEX	AL	25	25	0	0	145.2	666	154	95	93	20	4	3	17	78	2	121	9	0	9	8	.529	0	0-0	0	5.75	5.75
2003	TEX	AL	7	7	0	0	29.2	146	34	26	25	5	1	3	6	21	0	16	1	1	1	3	.250	0	0-0	0	8.56	7.58
2004	TEX	AL	16	16	0	0	95.2	428	105	63	58	22	4	4	13	33	0	63	1	1	4	7	.364	0	0-0	0	5.97	5.46
2005	2 Tms		30	29	0	0	155.1	715	180	103	99	11	7	3	10	80	1	113	6	0	12	8	.600	0	0-0	0	5.52	5.74
05	Tex	AL	20	20	0	0	109.2	502	130	70	69	8	5	2	6	54	1	80	3	0	8	5	.615	0	0-0	0	5.58	5.66
05	SD	NL	10	9	0	0	45.2	213	50	33	30	3	2	1	4	26	0	33	3	0	4	3	.571	0	0-0	0	5.36	5.91
	12 ML YEARS		299	253	9	9	1610.0	7036	1474	833	775	182	82	46	116	776	17	1411	58	13	106	80	.570	2	0-0	4	4.29	4.33

John Parrish

Pitches: L Bats: L Pos: RP-14   Ht: 5'11" Wt: 181 Born: 11/26/1977 Age: 28

			HOW MUCH HE PITCHED							WHAT HE GAVE UP										THE RESULTS							
Year	Team	Lg	G	GS	CG	GF	IP	BFP	H	R	ER	HR	SH	SF	HB	TBB	IBB	SO	WP	Bk	W	L	Pct	ShO	Sv-Op	Hld	ERC	ERA
2005	Bowie*	AAA	5	0	0	0	9.1	41	7	3	3	1	0	2		6	0	13	2	0	0	0	-	0	0--	-	3.78	2.89
2000	BAL	AL	8	8	0	0	36.1	180	40	32	29	6	0	0	0	35	0	28	0	0	2	4	.333	0	0-0	0	7.59	7.18
2001	BAL	AL	16	1	0	0	22.0	107	22	17	15	5	0	0	0	17	0	20	0	0	1	2	.333	0	0-0	0	6.34	6.14
2003	BAL	AL	14	0	0	2	23.2	93	17	7	5	2	0	1	1	8	2	15	2	0	1	0	.000	0	0-2	1	2.39	1.90
2004	BAL	AL	56	1	0	17	78.0	353	68	39	30	4	3	6	3	55	6	71	6	0	6	3	.667	0	1-1	2	4.17	3.46
2005	BAL	AL	14	0	0	2	17.1	86	19	6	6	1	1	0	0	17	1	25	6	0	1	0	1.000	0	0-0	1	6.53	3.12
	5 ML YEARS		108	10	0	21	177.1	819	166	101	85	18	4	7	4	132	9	159	14	0	10	10	.500	0	1-3	4	5.06	4.31

Corey Patterson

Bats: L Throws: R Pos: CF-122; PH-9; PR-3   Ht: 5'9" Wt: 175 Born: 8/13/1979 Age: 26

						BATTING													BASERUNNING				AVERAGES		
Year	Team	Lg	G	AB	H	2B	3B	HR	(Hm	Rd)	TB	R	RBI	RC	TBB	IBB	SO	HBP	SH	SF	SB	CS	SB%	GDP	Avg	OBP	Slg
2005	Iowa*	AAA	24	91	27	4	0	5	(-	-)	46	16	12	17	8	1	19	2	1	0	6	1	.86	0	.297	.366	.505
2000	CHN	NL	11	42	7	1	0	2	(1	1)	14	9	2	3	3	0	14	1	1	0	1	1	.50	1	.167	.239	.333
2001	CHN	NL	59	131	29	3	0	4	(1	3)	44	26	14	13	6	0	33	3	2	3	4	0	1.00	1	.221	.266	.336
2002	CHN	NL	153	592	150	30	5	14	(7	7)	232	71	54	61	19	1	142	8	4	5	18	3	.86	8	.253	.284	.392
2003	CHN	NL	83	329	98	17	7	13	(7	6)	168	49	55	55	15	2	77	1	0	2	16	5	.76	5	.298	.329	.511
2004	CHN	NL	157	631	168	33	6	24	(14	10)	285	91	72	87	45	7	168	5	5	1	32	9	.78	7	.266	.320	.452
2005	CHN	NL	126	451	97	15	3	13	(9	4)	157	47	34	32	23	3	118	1	5	1	15	5	.75	5	.215	.254	.348
	6 ML YEARS		589	2176	549	99	21	70	(39	31)	900	293	231	251	111	13	552	19	17	12	86	23	.79	26	.252	.293	.414

John Patterson

Pitches: R Bats: R Pos: SP-31   Ht: 6'5" Wt: 183 Born: 1/30/1978 Age: 28

						HOW MUCH HE PITCHED						WHAT HE GAVE UP										THE RESULTS							
Year	Team	Lg	G	GS	CG	GF	IP	BFP	H	R	ER	HR	SH	SF	HB	TBB	IBB	SO	WP	Bk	W	L	Pct	ShO	Sv-Op	Hld	ERC	ERA
2002	ARI	NL	7	5	0	1	30.2	123	27	11	11	7	0	0	1	7	0	31	2	0	2	0	1.000	0	0-0	0	3.76	3.23
2003	ARI	NL	16	8	0	3	55.0	252	61	39	37	7	1	2	2	30	5	43	4	0	1	4	.200	0	1-1	0	5.50	6.05
2004	MON	NL	19	19	0	0	98.1	445	100	58	55	18	4	2	8	46	4	99	0	0	4	7	.364	0	0-0	0	5.26	5.03
2005	WAS	NL	31	31	2	0	198.1	817	172	71	69	19	5	4	5	65	11	185	9	1	9	7	.563	1	0-0	0	3.09	3.13
	4 ML YEARS		73	63	2	4	382.1	1637	360	179	172	51	10	8	16	148	20	358	15	1	16	18	.471	1	1-1	0	4.02	4.05

Josh Paul

Bats: R Throws: R Pos: C-29; PR-4; PH-3; LF-2   Ht: 6'1" Wt: 200 Born: 5/19/1975 Age: 31

						BATTING													BASERUNNING				AVERAGES		
Year	Team	Lg	G	AB	H	2B	3B	HR	(Hm	Rd)	TB	R	RBI	RC	TBB	IBB	SO	HBP	SH	SF	SB	CS	SB%	GDP	Avg	OBP	Slg
2005	Salt Lk*	AAA	9	33	9	4	0	0	(-	-)	13	6	6	5	6	1	7	0	0	0	1	0	1.00	0	.273	.385	.394
1999	CHA	AL	6	18	4	1	0	0	(0	0)	5	2	1	1	0	0	4	0	0	0	0	0	-	0	.222	.222	.278
2000	CHA	AL	36	71	20	3	2	1	(1	0)	30	15	8	9	5	0	17	1	2	0	1	0	1.00	3	.282	.338	.423
2001	CHA	AL	57	139	37	11	0	3	(0	3)	57	20	18	19	13	0	25	0	1	1	6	2	.75	3	.266	.327	.410
2002	CHA	AL	33	104	25	4	0	0	(0	0)	29	11	11	12	9	0	22	1	2	2	2	0	1.00	1	.240	.302	.279
2003	2 Tms		16	23	6	0	0	0	(0	0)	6	6	4	5	3	0	6	0	1	0	0	0	-	0	.261	.346	.261
2004	ANA	AL	46	70	17	3	0	2	(0	2)	26	11	10	9	7	0	17	0	3	1	2	1	.67	2	.243	.308	.371
2005	LAA	AL	34	37	7	1	0	2	(2	0)	14	4	4	3	2	0	9	0	1	0	0	0	-	1	.189	.231	.378
03	CWS	AL	13	17	6	0	0	0	(0	0)	6	6	4	5	3	0	3	0	0	0	0	0	-	0	.353	.450	.353
03	ChC	NL	3	6	0	0	0	0	(0	0)	0	0	0	0	0	0	3	0	1	0	0	0	-	0	.000	.000	.000
	7 ML YEARS		228	462	116	23	2	8	(3	5)	167	69	56	58	39	0	100	2	10	4	11	3	.79	10	.251	.310	.361

Ronny Paulino

Bats: R Throws: R Pos: C-2   Ht: 6'3" Wt: 235 Born: 4/21/1981 Age: 25

						BATTING													BASERUNNING				AVERAGES		
Year	Team	Lg	G	AB	H	2B	3B	HR	(Hm	Rd)	TB	R	RBI	RC	TBB	IBB	SO	HBP	SH	SF	SB	CS	SB%	GDP	Avg	OBP	Slg
1999	Bradtn	R	29	83	21	2	4	1	(-	-)	34	6	13	11	8	0	19	1	1	2	1	2	.33	0	.253	.319	.410
2000	Hickory	A	88	301	87	16	2	6	(-	-)	125	38	39	45	27	0	71	4	0	1	3	2	.60	9	.289	.354	.415
2001	Lynbrg	A+	103	352	102	16	1	6	(-	-)	138	30	51	52	36	0	76	2	3	7	4	1	.80	11	.290	.353	.392
2002	Lynbrg	A+	119	442	116	26	2	12	(-	-)	182	63	55	61	39	2	87	1	2	4	2	1	.67	15	.262	.321	.412
2003	Lynbrg	A+	23	81	19	3	0	1	(-	-)	25	8	12	8	8	0	8	1	0	1	1	0	1.00	6	.235	.308	.309
2003	Altna	AA	46	159	36	6	1	6	(-	-)	62	19	19	17	12	1	35	1	3	1	0	2	.00	4	.226	.283	.390
2004	Altna	AA	99	369	105	23	2	15	(-	-)	177	54	60	62	32	1	62	3	1	3	3	2	.60	7	.285	.344	.480
2005	Altna	AA	43	168	49	6	0	6	(-	-)	73	24	20	26	15	1	30	0	1	0	3	0	1.00	3	.292	.350	.435
2005	Indy	AAA	77	273	86	18	2	13	(-	-)	147	49	42	54	26	1	48	0	1	2	3	0	1.00	11	.315	.372	.538
2005	PIT	NL	2	4	2	0	0	0	(0	0)	2	1	0	1	1	0	0	0	0	0	0	0	-	0	.500	.600	.500

Carl Pavano

Pitches: R Bats: R Pos: SP-17   Ht: 6'5" Wt: 230 Born: 1/8/1976 Age: 30

						HOW MUCH HE PITCHED						WHAT HE GAVE UP										THE RESULTS							
Year	Team	Lg	G	GS	CG	GF	IP	BFP	H	R	ER	HR	SH	SF	HB	TBB	IBB	SO	WP	Bk	W	L	Pct	ShO	Sv-Op	Hld	ERC	ERA
2005	Yanks*	R	1	1	0	0	5.0	17	2	2	1	1	0	0	0	0	0	5	0	0	0	0	-	0	0--	-	0.74	1.80
2005	Tampa*	A+	1	1	0	0	6.0	24	6	3	3	1	0	0	0	0	0	3	0	0	0	1	.000	0	0--	-	2.87	4.50
1998	MON	NL	24	23	0	0	134.2	580	130	70	63	18	5	6	8	43	1	83	1	0	6	9	.400	0	0-0	0	3.97	4.21
1999	MON	NL	19	18	1	0	104.0	457	117	66	65	8	5	2	4	35	1	70	1	3	6	8	.429	1	0-0	0	4.51	5.63
2000	MON	NL	15	15	0	0	97.0	408	89	40	33	8	4	3	8	34	1	64	1	1	8	4	.667	0	0-0	0	3.67	3.06
2001	MON	NL	8	8	0	0	42.2	199	59	33	30	7	2	1	2	16	1	36	0	1	1	6	.143	0	0-0	0	6.99	6.33

			HOW MUCH HE PITCHED						WHAT HE GAVE UP										THE RESULTS						
Year	Team	Lg	G	GS	CG	GF	IP	BFP	H	R	ER	HR	SH	SF	HB	TBB	IBB	SO	WP	Bk	W	L	Pct	ShO	Sv-Op Hld	ERC	ERA
2002	2 Tms	NL	37	22	0	2	136.0	619	174	88	78	19	4	4	10	45	8	92	3	2	6	10	.375	0	0-0 3	5.98	5.16
2003	FLA	NL	33	32	2	1	201.0	846	204	99	96	19	9	10	7	49	10	133	3	2	12	13	.480	0	0-0 0	3.57	4.30
2004	FLA	NL	31	31	2	0	222.1	909	212	80	74	16	7	4	11	49	13	139	2	3	18	8	.692	2	0-0 0	3.10	3.00
2005	NYA	AL	17	17	1	0	100.0	442	129	66	53	17	4	3	8	18	1	56	2	1	4	6	.400	1	0-0 0	5.74	4.77
02	Mon	NL	15	14	0	0	74.1	350	98	55	52	14	2	2	7	31	5	51	2	1	3	8	.273	0	0-0 0	7.07	6.30
02	Fla	NL	22	8	0	2	61.2	269	76	33	26	5	2	2	3	14	3	41	1	1	3	2	.600	0	0-0 3	4.74	3.79
	8 ML YEARS		184	166	6	3	1037.2	4460	1114	542	492	112	40	33	58	289	36	673	13	13	61	64	.488	4	0-0 3	4.25	4.27

Jay Payton

Bats: R **Throws:** R **Pos:** LF-60; CF-41; RF-31; PH-11; PR-4   **Ht:** 5'10" **Wt:** 185 **Born:** 11/22/1972 **Age:** 33

								BATTING													BASERUNNING				AVERAGES		
Year	Team	Lg	G	AB	H	2B	3B	HR	(Hm	Rd)	TB	R	RBI	RC	TBB	IBB	SO	HBP	SH	SF	SB	CS	SB%	GDP	Avg	OBP	Slg
1998	NYN	NL	15	22	7	1	0	0	(0	0)	8	2	0	3	1	0	4	0	0	0	0	0	-	0	.318	.348	.364
1999	NYN	NL	13	8	2	1	0	0	(0	0)	3	1	1	0	0	0	2	1	0	0	1	2	.33	0	.250	.333	.375
2000	NYN	NL	149	488	142	23	1	17	(9	8)	218	63	62	68	30	0	60	3	0	8	5	11	.31	9	.291	.331	.447
2001	NYN	NL	104	361	92	16	1	8	(6	2)	134	44	34	37	18	1	52	5	0	2	4	3	.57	11	.255	.298	.371
2002	2 Tms	NL	134	445	135	20	7	16	(9	7)	217	69	59	71	29	0	54	4	2	1	7	4	.64	11	.303	.351	.488
2003	COL	NL	157	600	181	32	5	28	(13	15)	307	93	89	95	43	3	77	7	5	3	6	4	.60	27	.302	.354	.512
2004	SD	NL	143	458	119	17	4	8	(0	8)	168	57	55	61	43	2	56	4	2	4	2	0	1.00	12	.260	.326	.367
2005	2 Tms	NL	124	408	109	16	1	18	(11	7)	181	62	63	56	24	2	47	0	0	3	0	1	.00	8	.267	.306	.444
02	NYM	NL	87	275	78	6	3	8	(4	4)	114	33	31	38	21	0	34	1	2	1	4	1	.80	5	.284	.336	.415
02	Col	NL	47	170	57	14	4	8	(5	3)	103	36	28	33	8	0	20	3	0	0	3	3	.50	3	.335	.376	.606
05	Bos	AL	55	133	35	7	0	5	(2	3)	57	24	21	16	10	0	14	0	0	1	0	0	-	4	.263	.313	.429
05	Oak	AL	69	275	74	9	1	13	(9	4)	124	38	42	40	14	2	33	0	0	2	0	1	.00	4	.269	.302	.451
	8 ML YEARS		839	2790	787	126	19	95	(48	47)	1236	391	363	391	188	8	352	24	9	21	25	25	.50	78	.282	.330	.443

Jake Peavy

Pitches: R **Bats:** R **Pos:** SP-30   **Ht:** 6'1" **Wt:** 180 **Born:** 5/31/1981 **Age:** 25

			HOW MUCH HE PITCHED						WHAT HE GAVE UP												THE RESULTS						
Year	Team	Lg	G	GS	CG	GF	IP	BFP	H	R	ER	HR	SH	SF	HB	TBB	IBB	SO	WP	Bk	W	L	Pct	ShO	Sv-Op Hld	ERC	ERA
2002	SD	NL	17	17	0	0	97.2	430	106	54	49	11	5	2	3	33	4	90	4	1	6	7	.462	0	0-0 0	4.41	4.52
2003	SD	NL	32	32	0	0	194.2	827	173	94	89	33	7	5	6	82	3	156	2	0	12	11	.522	0	0-0 0	4.13	4.11
2004	SD	NL	27	27	0	0	166.1	694	146	49	42	13	5	6	11	53	4	173	1	1	15	6	.714	0	0-0 0	3.18	2.27
2005	SD	NL	30	30	3	0	203.0	812	162	70	65	18	4	5	7	50	3	216	3	1	13	7	.650	3	0-0 0	2.49	2.88
	4 ML YEARS		106	106	3	0	661.2	2763	587	267	245	75	21	18	27	218	14	635	10	3	46	31	.597	3	0-0 0	3.41	3.33

Brayan Pena

Bats: B **Throws:** R **Pos:** C-15; PH-6   **Ht:** 5'11" **Wt:** 220 **Born:** 1/7/1982 **Age:** 24

								BATTING													BASERUNNING				AVERAGES		
Year	Team	Lg	G	AB	H	2B	3B	HR	(Hm	Rd)	TB	R	RBI	RC	TBB	IBB	SO	HBP	SH	SF	SB	CS	SB%	GDP	Avg	OBP	Slg
2001	Danvle	R+	64	235	87	16	2	1	(-	-)	110	39	33	50	31	2	2	0	1	2	3	1	.75	5	.370	.440	.468
2002	MrtlBh	A+	6	19	4	1	0	0	(-	-)	5	3	1	1	3	0	4	0	0	0	0	0	-	0	.211	.318	.263
2002	Macon	A	81	271	62	10	0	3	(-	-)	81	26	25	23	22	1	37	2	3	2	0	3	.00	5	.229	.290	.299
2003	MrtlBh	A+	82	286	84	14	1	2	(-	-)	106	24	27	33	11	0	28	1	6	2	2	5	.29	8	.294	.320	.371
2004	Grnville	AA	77	277	87	10	4	2	(-	-)	111	30	30	39	15	2	29	1	4	2	3	4	.43	6	.314	.349	.401
2005	Rchmd	AAA	81	282	92	21	2	0	(-	-)	117	27	25	47	28	2	19	0	6	3	3	1	.75	15	.326	.383	.415
2005	ATL	NL	18	39	7	2	0	0	(0	0)	9	2	4	0	1	1	7	0	0	0	0	0	-	1	.179	.200	.231

Carlos Pena

Bats: L **Throws:** L **Pos:** 1B-51; DH-24; PH-5; PR-1   **Ht:** 6'2" **Wt:** 210 **Born:** 5/17/1978 **Age:** 28

								BATTING													BASERUNNING				AVERAGES		
Year	Team	Lg	G	AB	H	2B	3B	HR	(Hm	Rd)	TB	R	RBI	RC	TBB	IBB	SO	HBP	SH	SF	SB	CS	SB%	GDP	Avg	OBP	Slg
2005	Toledo*	AAA	71	257	80	17	1	12	(-	-)	135	43	45	57	45	5	65	6	0	1	3	4	.43	4	.311	.424	.525
2001	TEX	AL	22	62	16	4	1	3	(2	1)	31	6	12	11	10	0	17	0	0	0	0	0	-	1	.258	.361	.500
2002	2 Tms	AL	115	397	96	17	4	19	(10	9)	178	43	52	56	41	0	111	3	0	2	2	2	.50	7	.242	.316	.448
2003	DET	AL	131	452	112	21	6	18	(8	10)	199	51	50	61	53	1	123	6	1	4	4	5	.44	6	.248	.332	.440
2004	DET	AL	142	481	116	22	4	27	(10	17)	227	89	82	73	70	2	146	3	2	5	7	1	.88	11	.241	.338	.472
2005	DET	AL	79	260	61	9	0	18	(14	4)	124	37	44	40	31	2	95	4	0	0	1	0	.00	3	.235	.325	.477
02	Oak	AL	40	124	27	4	0	7	(5	2)	52	12	16	17	15	0	38	1	0	1	0	0	-	2	.218	.305	.419
02	Det	AL	75	273	69	13	4	12	(5	7)	126	31	36	39	26	0	73	2	0	1	2	2	.50	5	.253	.321	.462
	5 ML YEARS		489	1652	401	73	15	85	(44	41)	759	226	240	241	205	5	492	16	3	11	13	9	.59	28	.243	.330	.459

Wily Mo Pena

Bats: R **Throws:** R **Pos:** RF-50; CF-25; PH-18; LF-10   **Ht:** 6'3" **Wt:** 215 **Born:** 1/23/1982 **Age:** 24

								BATTING													BASERUNNING				AVERAGES		
Year	Team	Lg	G	AB	H	2B	3B	HR	(Hm	Rd)	TB	R	RBI	RC	TBB	IBB	SO	HBP	SH	SF	SB	CS	SB%	GDP	Avg	OBP	Slg
2005	Lsville*	AAA	7	24	7	1	0	1	(-	-)	11	1	4	3	1	0	10	0	0	0	0	0	-	0	.292	.320	.458
2002	CIN	NL	13	18	4	0	0	1	(1	0)	7	1	1	1	0	0	11	0	0	0	0	0	-	0	.222	.222	.389
2003	CIN	NL	80	165	36	6	1	5	(1	4)	59	20	16	14	12	2	53	3	1	0	3	2	.60	2	.218	.283	.358
2004	CIN	NL	110	336	87	10	1	26	(13	13)	177	45	66	54	22	1	108	6	0	0	5	2	.71	7	.259	.316	.527
2005	CIN	NL	99	311	79	17	0	19	(11	8)	153	42	51	40	20	0	116	3	0	1	2	1	.67	7	.254	.304	.492
	4 ML YEARS		302	830	206	33	2	51	(26	25)	396	108	134	109	54	3	288	12	1	1	10	5	.67	16	.248	.303	.477

Hayden Penn

Pitches: R Bats: R Pos: SP-8   Ht: 6'3" Wt: 185 Born: 10/13/1984 Age: 21

Year	Team	Lg	G	GS	CG	GF	IP	BFP	H	R	ER	HR	SH	SF	HB	TBB	IBB	SO	WP	Bk	W	L	Pct	ShO	Sv-Op	Hld	ERC	ERA
2003	Bluefld	R+	12	11	0	0	52.1	234	58	27	25	4	0	0	4	19	0	38	3	0	1	4	.200	0	0--	-	4.64	4.30
2003	Orioles	R	1	1	0	0	3.1	14	3	1	1	0	1	1	0	1	0	4	0	0	0	0	-	0	0--	-	2.46	2.70
2004	Frdrck	A+	13	13	0	0	73.1	299	59	33	31	7	1	1	2	20	0	61	1	0	6	5	.545	0	0--	-	2.61	3.80
2004	Dlmrva	A	13	6	0	2	43.1	179	30	18	16	4	2	1	3	19	1	41	4	0	4	1	.800	0	1--	-	2.76	3.32
2004	Bowie	AA	4	4	0	0	20.1	92	22	12	11	0	0	0	1	9	0	20	0	0	3	0	1.000	0	0--	-	4.09	4.87
2005	Bowie	AA	20	19	1	0	110.1	469	101	51	47	11	1	8	1	37	0	120	6	0	7	6	.538	0	0--	-	3.33	3.83
2005	BAL	AL	8	8	0	0	38.1	178	46	30	27	6	1	0	0	21	3	18	3	1	3	2	.600	0	0-0	0	6.17	6.34

Brad Penny

Pitches: R Bats: R Pos: SP-29   Ht: 6'4" Wt: 247 Born: 5/24/1978 Age: 28

Year	Team	Lg	G	GS	CG	GF	IP	BFP	H	R	ER	HR	SH	SF	HB	TBB	IBB	SO	WP	Bk	W	L	Pct	ShO	Sv-Op	Hld	ERC	ERA
2005	VeroB*	A+	1	1	0	0	5.0	18	2	1	1	0	0	0	0	1	0	3	0	0	1	0	1.000	0	0--	-	1.18	1.80
2005	LsVgs*	AAA	1	1	0	0	6.0	25	5	2	2	1	0	0	0	2	0	9	0	0	1	0	1.000	0	0--	-	3.28	3.00
2000	FLA	NL	23	22	0	0	119.2	529	120	70	64	13	6	2	5	60	4	80	4	1	8	7	.533	0	0-0	0	4.70	4.81
2001	FLA	NL	31	31	1	0	205.0	833	183	92	84	15	8	2	7	54	3	154	2	0	10	10	.500	1	0-0	0	2.96	3.69
2002	FLA	NL	24	24	1	0	129.1	574	148	76	67	18	6	4	1	50	7	93	4	0	8	7	.533	1	0-0	0	5.08	4.66
2003	FLA	NL	32	32	0	0	196.1	811	195	96	90	21	7	5	3	56	6	138	3	4	14	10	.583	0	0-0	0	3.73	4.13
2004	2 Tms	NL	24	24	0	0	143.0	590	130	55	50	12	3	3	3	45	6	111	5	0	9	10	.474	0	0-0	0	3.20	3.15
2005	LAN	NL	29	29	1	0	175.1	738	185	78	76	17	7	1	3	41	2	122	3	0	7	9	.438	0	0-0	0	3.77	3.90
04	Fla	NL	21	21	0	0	131.1	545	124	50	46	10	3	3	3	39	6	105	5	0	8	8	.500	0	0-0	0	3.26	3.15
04	LA	NL	3	3	0	0	11.2	45	6	5	4	2	0	0	0	6	0	6	0	0	1	2	.333	0	0-0	0	2.51	3.09
	6 ML YEARS		163	162	3	0	968.2	4075	961	467	431	96	37	17	22	306	28	698	21	5	56	53	.514	2	0-0	0	3.78	4.00

Jhonny Peralta

Bats: R Throws: R Pos: SS-141; PH-1   Ht: 6'1" Wt: 180 Born: 5/28/1982 Age: 24

Year	Team	Lg	G	AB	H	2B	3B	HR	(Hm	Rd)	TB	R	RBI	RC	TBB	IBB	SO	HBP	SH	SF	SB	CS	SB%	GDP	Avg	OBP	Slg
2003	CLE	AL	77	242	55	10	1	4	(3	1)	79	24	21	24	20	0	65	4	2	2	1	3	.25	5	.227	.295	.326
2004	CLE	AL	8	25	6	1	0	0	(0	0)	7	2	2	2	3	0	6	0	0	0	0	1	.00	0	.240	.321	.280
2005	CLE	AL	141	504	147	35	4	24	(14	10)	262	82	78	87	58	3	128	3	1	4	0	2	.00	12	.292	.366	.520
	3 ML YEARS		226	771	208	46	5	28	(17	11)	348	108	101	113	81	3	199	7	3	6	1	6	.14	17	.270	.342	.451

Joel Peralta

Pitches: R Bats: R Pos: RP-28   Ht: 5'11" Wt: 170 Born: 3/23/1976 Age: 30

Year	Team	Lg	G	GS	CG	GF	IP	BFP	H	R	ER	HR	SH	SF	HB	TBB	IBB	SO	WP	Bk	W	L	Pct	ShO	Sv-Op	Hld	ERC	ERA
2000	Butte	R+	10	1	0	8	19.0	91	24	15	14	2	1	2	2	10	1	17	2	1	2	1	.667	0	1--	-	6.53	6.63
2000	Boise	A-	4	0	0	1	8.1	42	12	6	6	0	0	1	1	5	0	9	0	0	0	0	-	0	0--	-	7.20	6.48
2001	CRpds	A	41	0	0	39	42.1	159	27	13	10	3	2	1	4	5	0	53	0	0	0	0	-	0	23--	-	1.54	2.13
2001	Ark	AA	9	0	0	9	10.0	50	15	10	7	2	0	1	2	5	0	14	0	1	0	1	.000	0	2--	-	9.56	6.30
2002	CRpds	A	41	0	0	39	47.1	181	28	7	5	2	0	0	2	11	3	53	6	1	5	0	1.000	0	21--	-	1.35	0.95
2002	Ark	AA	12	0	0	4	17.2	88	25	15	13	5	0	2	1	10	0	11	2	0	0	0	-	0	0--	-	9.09	6.62
2003	Ark	AA	47	0	0	43	52.1	208	39	13	13	5	2	2	5	12	2	48	3	0	5	4	.556	0	20--	-	2.19	2.24
2003	Salt Lk	AAA	1	0	0	0	0.0	1	0	0	0	0	0	2	0	1	0	0	0	0	0	0	-	0	0--	-	-	-
2004	Angels	R	2	0	0	0	4.1	14	1	1	1	0	0	0	0	0	0	9	0	0	0	0	-	0	0--	-	0.12	2.08
2004	RCuca	A+	1	0	0	1	2.0	12	5	2	2	1	0	0	0	1	0	1	0	0	0	0	-	0	0--	-	18.76	9.00
2004	Salt Lk	AAA	39	0	0	21	56.0	250	64	33	31	6	0	0	2	18	0	68	5	0	4	2	.667	0	1--	-	4.70	4.98
2005	Salt Lk	AAA	19	0	0	20	20.0	77	11	6	6	0	0	2	3	6	0	18	0	0	4	1	.800	0	10--	-	1.52	2.70
2005	LAA	AL	28	0	0	10	34.2	145	28	15	15	6	2	1	0	14	2	30	2	0	1	0	1.000	0	0-0	0	3.40	3.89

Troy Percival

Pitches: R Bats: R Pos: RP-26   Ht: 6'3" Wt: 235 Born: 8/9/1969 Age: 36

Year	Team	Lg	G	GS	CG	GF	IP	BFP	H	R	ER	HR	SH	SF	HB	TBB	IBB	SO	WP	Bk	W	L	Pct	ShO	Sv-Op	Hld	ERC	ERA
1995	CAL	AL	62	0	0	16	74.0	284	37	19	16	6	4	1	2	26	2	94	2	2	3	2	.600	0	3-6	29	1.44	1.95
1996	CAL	AL	62	0	0	52	74.0	291	38	20	19	8	2	1	2	31	4	100	2	0	0	2	.000	0	36-39	2	1.76	2.31
1997	ANA	AL	55	0	0	46	52.0	224	40	20	20	6	1	2	4	22	2	72	5	0	5	5	.500	0	27-31	0	3.15	3.46
1998	ANA	AL	67	0	0	60	66.2	287	45	31	27	5	3	2	3	37	4	87	3	0	2	7	.222	0	42-48	0	2.74	3.65
1999	ANA	AL	60	0	0	50	57.0	230	38	24	24	9	0	1	3	22	0	58	3	0	4	6	.400	0	31-39	0	2.83	3.79
2000	ANA	AL	54	0	0	45	50.0	221	42	27	25	7	3	2	2	30	4	49	1	0	5	5	.500	0	32-42	0	4.24	4.50
2001	ANA	AL	57	0	0	50	57.2	230	39	19	17	3	1	0	2	18	1	71	2	0	4	2	.667	0	39-42	0	1.90	2.65
2002	ANA	AL	58	0	0	50	56.1	228	38	12	12	5	0	1	0	25	1	68	5	0	4	1	.800	0	40-44	0	2.45	1.92
2003	ANA	AL	52	0	0	49	49.1	206	33	22	19	7	0	1	4	23	1	48	1	0	0	5	.000	0	33-37	0	2.99	3.47
2004	ANA	AL	52	0	0	48	49.2	211	43	19	16	7	0	2	3	19	3	33	2	0	2	3	.400	0	33-38	0	3.67	2.90
2005	DET	AL	26	0	0	23	25.0	107	19	16	16	7	1	1	2	11	3	20	0	0	1	3	.250	0	8-11	0	4.17	5.76
	11 ML YEARS		605	0	0	489	611.2	2519	412	229	211	70	15	14	25	264	25	700	26	2	30	41	.423	0	324-377	31	2.63	3.10

Antonio Perez

Bats: R **Throws:** R **Pos:** 3B-35; 2B-29; PH-27; SS-9; PR-3; LF-1; DH-1 **Ht:** 5'11" **Wt:** 175 **Born:** 1/26/1980 **Age:** 26

Year	Team	Lg	G	AB	H	2B	3B	HR	(Hm	Rd)	TB	R	RBI	RC	TBB	IBB	SO	HBP	SH	SF	SB	CS	SB%	GDP	Avg	OBP	Slg
2005	LsVgs*	AAA	16	56	13	3	0	2	(-	-)	22	8	6	6	3	0	20	1	1	1	2	1	.67	1	.232	.279	.393
2003	TB	AL	48	125	31	6	1	2	(0	2)	45	19	12	19	18	0	34	1	2	1	4	1	.80	1	.248	.345	.360
2004	LA	NL	13	13	3	1	0	0	(0	0)	4	5	0	1	0	0	5	1	0	0	1	0	1.00	0	.231	.286	.308
2005	LAN	NL	98	259	77	13	2	3	(1	2)	103	28	23	40	21	1	61	5	1	1	11	4	.73	4	.297	.360	.398
3 ML YEARS			159	397	111	20	3	5	(1	4)	152	52	35	60	39	1	100	7	3	2	16	5	.76	5	.280	.353	.383

Eddie Perez

Bats: R **Throws:** R **Pos:** C-13; PH-3 **Ht:** 6'1" **Wt:** 220 **Born:** 5/4/1968 **Age:** 38

Year	Team	Lg	G	AB	H	2B	3B	HR	(Hm	Rd)	TB	R	RBI	RC	TBB	IBB	SO	HBP	SH	SF	SB	CS	SB%	GDP	Avg	OBP	Slg
1995	ATL	NL	7	13	4	1	0	1	(0	1)	8	1	4	2	0	0	2	0	0	0	0	0	-	0	.308	.308	.615
1996	ATL	NL	68	156	40	9	1	4	(2	2)	63	19	17	17	8	0	19	1	0	2	0	0	-	6	.256	.293	.404
1997	ATL	NL	73	191	41	5	0	6	(4	2)	64	20	18	14	10	0	35	2	1	2	0	1	.00	8	.215	.259	.335
1998	ATL	NL	61	149	50	12	0	6	(3	3)	80	18	32	30	15	0	28	2	1	0	1	1	.50	3	.336	.404	.537
1999	ATL	NL	104	309	77	17	0	7	(0	7)	115	30	30	32	17	4	40	6	4	3	0	1	.00	9	.249	.299	.372
2000	ATL	NL	7	22	4	1	0	0	(0	0)	5	0	3	1	0	0	2	0	0	0	0	0	-	0	.182	.182	.227
2001	ATL	NL	5	10	3	0	0	0	(0	0)	3	0	0	1	0	0	2	0	0	0	0	0	-	0	.300	.300	.300
2002	CLE	AL	42	117	25	9	0	0	(0	0)	34	6	4	4	5	0	25	1	2	0	0	0	-	6	.214	.252	.291
2003	MIL	NL	107	350	95	17	1	11	(5	6)	147	26	45	38	17	3	47	0	6	2	0	1	.00	16	.271	.304	.420
2004	TB	AL	74	170	39	12	0	3	(1	2)	60	14	13	12	11	1	29	3	3	1	0	0	-	5	.229	.286	.353
2005	ATL	NL	16	38	8	2	0	2	(1	1)	16	3	6	5	1	0	5	0	0	0	0	0	-	1	.211	.231	.421
11 ML YEARS			564	1525	386	85	2	40	(16	24)	595	137	172	156	84	8	234	15	17	10	1	4	.20	54	.253	.297	.390

Eduardo Perez

Bats: R **Throws:** R **Pos:** 1B-49; PH-22; DH-7; 3B-3; LF-3; RF-1 **Ht:** 6'4" **Wt:** 215 **Born:** 9/11/1969 **Age:** 36

Year	Team	Lg	G	AB	H	2B	3B	HR	(Hm	Rd)	TB	R	RBI	RC	TBB	IBB	SO	HBP	SH	SF	SB	CS	SB%	GDP	Avg	OBP	Slg
2005	Ddgrs*	R	48	179	63	16	1	6	(-	-)	99	35	37	39	12	0	26	4	2	0	4	0	1.00	6	.352	.405	.553
2005	Clmbs*	A	10	33	7	2	0	0	(-	-)	9	0	4	2	1	0	10	1	0	0	0	0	-	2	.212	.257	.273
2005	Jaxnvl*	AA	2	4	0	0	0	0	(-	-)	0	0	0	0	0	0	2	0	0	0	0	0	-	0	.000	.000	.000
1993	CAL	AL	52	180	45	6	2	4	(2	2)	67	16	30	18	9	0	39	2	0	1	5	4	.56	4	.250	.292	.372
1994	CAL	AL	38	129	27	7	0	5	(3	2)	49	10	16	13	12	1	29	0	1	1	3	0	1.00	5	.209	.275	.380
1995	CAL	AL	29	71	12	4	1	1	(0	1)	21	9	7	6	12	0	9	2	0	1	0	2	.00	3	.169	.302	.296
1996	CIN	NL	18	36	8	0	0	3	(3	0)	17	8	5	5	5	1	9	0	0	0	0	0	-	2	.222	.317	.472
1997	CIN	NL	106	297	75	18	0	16	(7	9)	141	44	52	45	29	1	76	2	0	2	5	1	.83	6	.253	.321	.475
1998	CIN	NL	84	172	41	4	0	4	(1	3)	57	20	30	19	21	2	45	2	1	2	0	1	.00	2	.238	.325	.331
1999	STL	NL	21	32	11	2	0	1	(0	1)	16	6	9	8	7	0	6	0	0	0	0	0	-	0	.344	.462	.500
2000	STL	NL	35	91	27	4	0	3	(0	3)	40	9	10	14	5	0	19	3	2	1	1	0	1.00	2	.297	.350	.440
2002	STL	NL	96	154	31	9	0	10	(4	6)	70	22	26	17	17	0	36	3	1	2	0	0	-	7	.201	.290	.455
2003	STL	NL	105	253	72	16	0	11	(5	6)	121	47	41	38	29	1	53	4	1	2	5	2	.71	7	.285	.365	.478
2004	TB	AL	13	38	8	2	0	1	(1	0)	13	2	7	6	4	0	9	0	0	0	0	0	-	1	.211	.286	.342
2005	TB	AL	77	161	41	6	0	11	(5	6)	80	23	28	31	26	0	30	3	0	0	0	2	.00	6	.255	.368	.497
12 ML YEARS			674	1614	398	78	3	70	(31	39)	692	216	261	220	176	6	360	21	6	12	19	12	.61	45	.247	.326	.429

Miguel Perez

Bats: R **Throws:** R **Pos:** PH-2; C-1 **Ht:** 6'3" **Wt:** 190 **Born:** 9/25/1983 **Age:** 22

Year	Team	Lg	G	AB	H	2B	3B	HR	(Hm	Rd)	TB	R	RBI	RC	TBB	IBB	SO	HBP	SH	SF	SB	CS	SB%	GDP	Avg	OBP	Slg
2002	Reds	R	26	86	31	1	0	0	(-	-)	32	12	11	13	2	0	9	3	1	0	3	0	1.00	2	.360	.396	.372
2003	Billings	R+	60	227	77	11	2	1	(-	-)	95	46	25	40	18	1	27	10	1	1	1	1	.50	3	.339	.410	.419
2003	Dayton	A	20	58	10	0	0	0	(-	-)	10	3	3	3	4	0	19	4	2	0	1	0	1.00	4	.172	.273	.172
2004	Ptomc	A+	18	69	16	2	0	0	(-	-)	18	7	5	4	1	0	12	0	0	1	1	0	1.00	4	.232	.239	.261
2004	Dayton	A	74	249	59	7	0	1	(-	-)	69	22	22	22	16	0	62	11	0	2	2	2	.50	5	.237	.309	.277
2005	Srsota	A+	80	291	78	11	0	4	(-	-)	101	36	33	33	16	1	63	1	1	3	7	1	.88	3	.268	.305	.347
2005	Lsvlle	AAA	21	72	15	3	0	1	(-	-)	21	5	5	6	5	1	19	2	0	1	0	0	-	2	.208	.275	.292
2005	CIN	NL	2	3	0	0	0	0	(-	-)	0	0	0	0	0	0	1	0	0	0	0	0	-	0	.000	.000	.000

Neifi Perez

Bats: B **Throws:** R **Pos:** SS-130; 2B-26; PH-8; 3B-4; PR-1 **Ht:** 6'0" **Wt:** 175 **Born:** 6/2/1973 **Age:** 33

Year	Team	Lg	G	AB	H	2B	3B	HR	(Hm	Rd)	TB	R	RBI	RC	TBB	IBB	SO	HBP	SH	SF	SB	CS	SB%	GDP	Avg	OBP	Slg
1996	COL	NL	17	45	7	2	0	0	(0	0)	9	4	3	0	0	0	8	0	1	0	2	2	.50	2	.156	.156	.200
1997	COL	NL	83	313	91	13	10	5	(3	2)	139	46	31	46	21	4	43	1	5	4	4	3	.57	3	.291	.333	.444
1998	COL	NL	162	647	177	25	9	9	(6	3)	247	80	59	77	38	0	70	1	22	4	5	6	.45	8	.274	.313	.382
1999	COL	NL	157	690	193	27	11	12	(8	4)	278	108	70	87	28	0	54	1	9	4	13	5	.72	4	.280	.307	.403
2000	COL	NL	162	651	187	39	11	10	(7	3)	278	92	71	85	30	6	63	0	7	11	3	6	.33	9	.287	.314	.427
2001	2 Tms		136	581	162	26	9	8	(7	1)	230	83	59	69	26	1	68	1	11	4	9	6	.60	10	.279	.309	.396
2002	KC	AL	145	554	131	20	4	3	(1	2)	168	65	37	37	20	2	53	0	5	6	8	9	.47	11	.236	.260	.303
2003	SF	NL	120	328	84	19	4	1	(1	0)	114	27	31	29	14	3	23	0	9	2	3	2	.60	10	.256	.285	.348
2004	2 Tms	NL	126	381	97	17	1	4	(2	2)	128	40	39	39	24	3	41	0	11	4	1	1	.50	8	.255	.296	.336
2005	CHN	NL	154	572	157	33	1	9	(4	5)	219	59	54	58	18	3	47	3	12	4	8	4	.67	22	.274	.298	.383
01	Col	NL	87	382	114	19	8	7	(7	0)	170	65	47	53	16	1	49	0	4	1	6	2	.75	8	.298	.326	.445
01	KC	AL	49	199	48	7	1	1	(0	1)	60	18	12	16	10	0	19	1	7	3	3	4	.43	2	.241	.277	.302

Year	Team	Lg	G	AB	H	2B	3B	HR	(Hm	Rd)	TB	R	RBI	RC	TBB	IBB	SO	HBP	SH	SF	SB	CS	SB%	GDP	Avg	OBP	Slg
04	SF	NL	103	319	74	12	1	2	(0	2)	94	28	33	26	21	3	35	0	9	4	0	1	.00	7	.232	.276	.295
04	ChC	NL	23	62	23	5	0	2	(2	0)	34	12	6	13	3	0	6	0	2	0	1	0	1.00	1	.371	.400	.548
	10 ML YEARS		1262	4762	1286	221	60	61	(39	22)	1810	604	454	527	219	22	470	7	92	43	56	44	.56	87	.270	.301	.380

Odalis Perez

Pitches: L Bats: L Pos: SP-19   Ht: 6'0" Wt: 150 Born: 6/7/1977 Age: 29

Year	Team	Lg	G	GS	CG	GF	IP	BFP	H	R	ER	HR	SH	SF	HB	TBB	IBB	SO	WP	Bk	W	L	Pct	ShO	Sv-Op	Hld	ERC	ERA
2005	LsVgs*	AAA	4	4	0	0	14.2	62	14	7	7	1	1	0	0	4	0	11	0	0	1	0	1.000	0	0- -	-	3.06	4.30
1998	ATL	NL	10	0	0	0	10.2	45	10	5	5	1	0	0	0	4	0	5	0	0	0	1	.000	0	0-1	5	3.60	4.22
1999	ATL	NL	18	17	0	0	93.0	424	100	65	62	12	3	4	1	53	2	82	5	3	4	6	.400	0	0-0	0	5.42	6.00
2001	ATL	NL	24	16	0	1	95.1	418	108	55	52	7	3	3	1	39	0	71	2	3	7	8	.467	0	0-0	0	4.79	4.91
2002	LA	NL	32	32	4	0	222.1	869	182	76	74	21	13	7	4	38	5	155	2	3	15	10	.600	2	0-0	0	2.31	3.00
2003	LA	NL	30	30	0	0	185.1	772	191	98	93	28	5	3	3	46	4	141	2	1	12	12	.500	0	0-0	0	4.07	4.52
2004	LA	NL	31	31	0	0	196.1	787	180	76	71	26	16	3	3	44	4	128	2	2	7	6	.538	0	0-0	0	3.26	3.25
2005	LAN	NL	19	19	0	0	108.2	453	109	59	55	13	8	1	0	28	2	74	3	0	7	8	.467	0	0-0	0	3.65	4.56
	7 ML YEARS		164	145	4	1	911.2	3768	880	434	412	108	48	21	12	252	17	656	16	12	52	51	.505	2	0-1	5	3.59	4.07

Oliver Perez

Pitches: L Bats: L Pos: SP-20   Ht: 6'3" Wt: 160 Born: 8/15/1981 Age: 24

Year	Team	Lg	G	GS	CG	GF	IP	BFP	H	R	ER	HR	SH	SF	HB	TBB	IBB	SO	WP	Bk	W	L	Pct	ShO	Sv-Op	Hld	ERC	ERA
2005	Indy*	AAA	3	3	0	0	10.0	56	14	11	11	3	0	1	1	12	1	4	1	0	0	1	.000	0	0- -	-	12.32	9.90
2002	SD	NL	16	15	0	0	90.0	387	71	37	35	13	5	3	5	48	1	94	3	0	4	5	.444	0	0-0	0	3.93	3.50
2003	2 Tms	NL	24	24	0	0	126.2	579	129	80	77	22	5	2	4	77	3	141	7	1	4	10	.286	0	0-0	0	5.66	5.47
2004	PIT	NL	30	30	2	0	196.0	805	145	71	65	22	9	5	8	81	2	239	2	1	12	10	.545	1	0-0	0	2.99	2.98
2005	PIT	NL	20	20	0	0	103.0	471	102	68	67	23	5	4	6	70	1	97	3	0	7	5	.583	0	0-0	0	6.44	5.85
03	SD	NL	19	19	0	0	103.2	473	103	65	62	20	4	2	3	65	2	117	6	1	4	7	.364	0	0-0	0	5.74	5.38
03	Pit	NL	5	5	0	0	23.0	106	26	15	15	2	1	0	1	12	1	24	1	0	0	3	.000	0	0-0	0	5.29	5.87
	4 ML YEARS		90	89	2	0	515.2	2242	447	256	244	80	24	14	24	276	7	571	15	2	27	30	.474	1	0-0	0	4.43	4.26

Timo Perez

Bats: L Throws: L Pos: LF-27; PH-25; RF-21; DH-11; 1B-2; CF-2; PR-2   Ht: 5'9" Wt: 167 Born: 4/8/1975 Age: 31

Year	Team	Lg	G	AB	H	2B	3B	HR	(Hm	Rd)	TB	R	RBI	RC	TBB	IBB	SO	HBP	SH	SF	SB	CS	SB%	GDP	Avg	OBP	Slg
2000	NYN	NL	24	49	14	4	1	1	(0	1)	23	11	3	8	3	0	5	1	0	1	1	1	.50	0	.286	.333	.469
2001	NYN	NL	85	239	59	9	1	5	(2	3)	85	26	22	23	12	0	25	2	6	1	1	6	.14	1	.247	.287	.356
2002	NYN	NL	136	444	131	27	6	8	(3	5)	194	52	47	63	23	2	36	2	10	2	10	6	.63	10	.295	.331	.437
2003	NYN	NL	127	346	93	21	0	4	(1	3)	126	32	42	37	18	1	29	2	7	9	5	6	.45	5	.269	.301	.364
2004	CHA	AL	103	293	72	12	0	5	(2	3)	99	38	40	39	15	0	29	2	9	2	3	1	.75	9	.246	.285	.338
2005	CHA	AL	76	179	39	8	0	2	(1	1)	53	13	15	13	12	1	25	0	4	1	2	2	.50	3	.218	.266	.296
	6 ML YEARS		551	1550	408	81	8	25	(9	16)	580	172	169	183	83	4	149	9	36	16	22	22	.50	28	.263	.302	.374

Tomas Perez

Bats: B Throws: R Pos: PH-52; 1B-24; 3B-15; SS-14; PR-3   Ht: 5'11" Wt: 177 Born: 12/29/1973 Age: 32

Year	Team	Lg	G	AB	H	2B	3B	HR	(Hm	Rd)	TB	R	RBI	RC	TBB	IBB	SO	HBP	SH	SF	SB	CS	SB%	GDP	Avg	OBP	Slg
1995	TOR	AL	41	98	24	3	1	1	(1	0)	32	12	8	7	7	0	18	0	0	1	0	1	.00	6	.245	.292	.327
1996	TOR	AL	91	295	74	13	4	1	(1	0)	98	24	19	28	25	0	29	1	6	1	1	2	.33	10	.251	.311	.332
1997	TOR	AL	40	123	24	3	2	0	(0	0)	31	9	9	8	11	0	28	1	3	0	1	1	.50	2	.195	.267	.252
1998	TOR	AL	6	9	1	0	0	0	(0	0)	1	1	0	0	1	0	3	0	1	0	0	0	-	1	.111	.200	.111
2000	PHI	NL	45	140	31	7	1	1	(0	1)	43	17	13	11	11	2	30	0	1	0	1	1	.50	3	.221	.278	.307
2001	PHI	NL	62	135	41	7	1	3	(2	1)	59	11	19	20	7	1	22	2	1	0	0	1	.00	2	.304	.347	.437
2002	PHI	NL	92	212	53	13	1	5	(2	3)	83	22	20	20	21	6	40	1	2	1	1	0	1.00	5	.250	.319	.392
2003	PHI	NL	125	298	79	18	1	5	(2	3)	114	39	33	29	23	11	54	0	4	2	0	1	.00	7	.265	.316	.383
2004	PHI	NL	86	176	38	13	2	6	(4	2)	73	22	21	20	9	2	44	1	3	1	0	0	-	2	.216	.257	.415
2005	PHI	NL	94	159	37	7	0	0	(0	0)	44	17	22	14	11	2	27	2	3	1	1	0	1.00	6	.233	.289	.277
	10 ML YEARS		682	1645	402	84	13	22	(12	10)	578	174	164	157	126	24	295	8	24	7	5	7	.42	44	.244	.300	.351

Matt Perisho

Pitches: L Bats: L Pos: RP-25   Ht: 6'0" Wt: 205 Born: 6/8/1975 Age: 31

Year	Team	Lg	G	GS	CG	GF	IP	BFP	H	R	ER	HR	SH	SF	HB	TBB	IBB	SO	WP	Bk	W	L	Pct	ShO	Sv-Op	Hld	ERC	ERA
2005	Albq*	AAA	17	1	0	3	14.1	75	25	20	19	4	2	0	0	7	0	10	0	0	0	2	.000	0	1- -	-	10.59	11.93
2005	Pwtckt*	AAA	13	0	0	3	13.0	51	6	3	3	0	0	0	0	6	0	7	0	0	2	0	1.000	0	0- -	-	1.23	2.08
1997	ANA	AL	11	8	0	2	45.0	217	59	34	30	6	2	2	3	28	0	35	5	2	0	2	.000	0	0-0	0	7.56	6.00
1998	TEX	AL	2	2	0	0	5.0	40	15	17	15	2	0	0	2	8	0	2	0	0	0	2	.000	0	0-0	0	30.09	27.00
1999	TEX	AL	4	1	0	3	10.1	40	8	3	3	0	0	0	0	2	1	17	1	0	0	0	-	0	0-0	0	1.55	2.61
2000	TEX	AL	34	13	0	4	105.0	515	136	99	86	20	6	5	6	67	3	74	4	0	2	7	.222	0	0-1	0	7.79	7.37
2001	DET	AL	30	4	0	5	39.1	186	54	29	25	5	2	1	4	14	1	19	0	0	2	3	.400	0	0-2	4	6.71	5.72
2002	DET	AL	5	0	0	1	10.1	50	16	11	10	2	0	1	0	6	0	3	0	0	0	0	-	0	0-0	0	9.45	8.71
2004	FLA	NL	66	0	0	16	47.0	212	45	23	23	6	1	1	2	26	2	42	1	0	5	3	.625	0	0-2	10	4.68	4.40
2005	2 Tms		25	0	0	4	14.0	66	13	5	4	1	2	1	1	11	0	10	0	0	2	0	1.000	0	0-0	4	5.21	2.57

			HOW MUCH HE PITCHED						WHAT HE GAVE UP										THE RESULTS						
Year	Team	Lg	G	GS	CG	GF	IP	BFP	H	R	ER	HR	SH	SF	HB	TBB	IBB	SO	WP	Bk	W	L	Pct	ShO	Sv-Op Hld	ERC	ERA
05	Fla	NL	24	0	0	4	14.0	65	12	4	3	1	2	1	1	11	0	10	0	0	2	0	1.000	0	0-0 4	4.80	1.93
05	Bos	AL	1	0	0	0	0.0	1	1	1	1	0	0	0	0	0	0	0	0	0	0	0	-	0	0-0 0	-	-
	8 ML YEARS		177	28	0	35	276.0	1326	346	221	196	42	13	11	18	162	7	202	11	2	11	17	.393	0	0-5 18	7.02	6.39

Roberto Petagine

Bats: L **Throws:** L **Pos:** 1B-10; PH-7; LF-2; DH-2   **Ht:** 6'1" **Wt:** 172 **Born:** 6/7/1971 **Age:** 35

			BATTING																	BASERUNNING				AVERAGES		
Year	Team	Lg	G	AB	H	2B	3B	HR	(Hm | Rd)	TB	R	RBI	RC	TBB	IBB	SO	HBP	SH	SF	SB	CS	SB%	GDP	Avg	OBP	Slg
2005	Pwtckt*	AAA	74	266	87	18	2	20	(- | -)	169	54	69	75	63	5	46	2	0	5	0	1	.00	9	.327	.452	.635
1994	HOU	NL	8	7	0	0	0	0	(0 | 0)	0	0	0	0	1	0	3	0	0	0	0	0	-	0	.000	.125	.000
1995	SD	NL	89	124	29	8	0	3	(2 | 1)	46	15	17	18	26	2	41	0	2	0	0	0	-	2	.234	.367	.371
1996	NYN	NL	50	99	23	3	0	4	(2 | 2)	38	10	17	10	9	1	27	3	1	1	0	2	.00	4	.232	.313	.384
1997	NYN	NL	12	15	1	0	0	0	(0 | 0)	1	2	2	0	3	0	6	0	0	0	0	0	-	0	.067	.222	.067
1998	CIN	NL	34	62	16	2	1	3	(1 | 2)	29	14	7	12	16	0	11	0	0	2	1	0	1.00	2	.258	.400	.468
2005	BOS	AL	18	32	9	2	0	1	(1 | 0)	14	4	9	4	4	0	5	0	0	0	0	0	-	3	.281	.361	.438
	6 ML YEARS		211	339	78	15	1	11	(6 | 5)	128	45	52	44	59	3	93	3	3	3	1	2	.33	11	.230	.347	.378

Andy Pettitte

Pitches: L **Bats:** L **Pos:** SP-33   **Ht:** 6'5" **Wt:** 225 **Born:** 6/15/1972 **Age:** 34

			HOW MUCH HE PITCHED						WHAT HE GAVE UP											THE RESULTS						
Year	Team	Lg	G	GS	CG	GF	IP	BFP	H	R	ER	HR	SH	SF	HB	TBB	IBB	SO	WP	Bk	W	L	Pct	ShO	Sv-Op Hld	ERC	ERA
1995	NYA	AL	31	26	3	1	175.0	745	183	86	81	15	4	5	1	63	3	114	8	1	12	9	.571	0	0-0 0	4.13	4.17
1996	NYA	AL	35	34	2	1	221.0	929	229	105	95	23	7	3	3	72	2	162	6	1	21	8	.724	0	0-0 0	4.14	3.87
1997	NYA	AL	35	35	4	0	240.1	986	233	86	77	7	6	2	3	65	0	166	7	0	18	7	.720	1	0-0 0	3.05	2.88
1998	NYA	AL	33	32	5	0	216.1	932	226	110	102	20	6	7	6	87	1	146	5	0	16	11	.593	0	0-0 0	4.46	4.24
1999	NYA	AL	31	31	0	0	191.2	851	216	105	100	20	6	6	3	89	3	121	3	1	14	11	.560	0	0-0 0	5.22	4.70
2000	NYA	AL	32	32	3	0	204.2	903	219	111	99	17	7	4	4	80	4	125	2	3	19	9	.679	1	0-0 0	4.32	4.35
2001	NYA	AL	31	31	2	0	200.2	858	224	103	89	14	8	7	6	41	3	164	2	2	15	10	.600	0	0-0 0	3.82	3.99
2002	NYA	AL	22	22	3	0	134.2	570	144	58	49	6	3	2	4	32	2	97	2	1	13	5	.722	1	0-0 0	3.55	3.27
2003	NYA	AL	33	33	1	0	208.1	896	227	109	93	21	5	5	1	50	3	180	5	0	21	8	.724	0	0-0 0	3.89	4.02
2004	HOU	NL	15	15	0	0	83.0	346	71	37	36	8	1	0	0	31	2	79	4	0	6	4	.600	0	0-0 0	3.12	3.90
2005	HOU	NL	33	33	0	0	222.1	875	188	66	59	17	10	4	3	41	0	171	2	0	17	9	.654	0	0-0 0	2.40	2.39
	11 ML YEARS		331	324	23	2	2098.0	8891	2160	976	880	168	63	45	34	651	23	1525	46	9	172	91	.654	3	0-0 0	3.82	3.78

Josh Phelps

Bats: R **Throws:** R **Pos:** DH-42; PH-5; 1B-1   **Ht:** 6'3" **Wt:** 220 **Born:** 5/12/1978 **Age:** 28

			BATTING																	BASERUNNING				AVERAGES		
Year	Team	Lg	G	AB	H	2B	3B	HR	(Hm	Rd)	TB	R	RBI	RC	TBB	IBB	SO	HBP	SH	SF	SB	CS	SB%	GDP	Avg	OBP	Slg
2005	Drham*	AAA	59	222	60	14	3	14	(-	-)	122	35	33	40	15	1	53	5	0	1	0	1	.00	6	.270	.329	.550
2000	TOR	AL	1	1	0	0	0	0	(0	0)	0	0	0	0	0	0	1	0	0	0	0	0	-	0	.000	.000	.000
2001	TOR	AL	8	12	0	0	0	0	(0	0)	0	3	1	0	2	0	5	0	0	0	1	0	1.00	1	.000	.143	.000
2002	TOR	AL	74	265	82	20	1	15	(6	9)	149	41	58	52	19	0	82	3	0	0	0	0	-	7	.309	.362	.562
2003	TOR	AL	119	396	106	18	1	20	(11	9)	186	57	66	65	39	3	115	17	0	1	1	2	.33	12	.268	.358	.470
2005	TB	AL	47	158	42	10	0	5	(4	1)	67	21	26	23	12	1	48	4	0	3	0	0	-	3	.266	.328	.424
	04 Tor	AL	79	295	70	13	2	12	(7	5)	123	38	51	40	18	2	73	7	0	1	0	0	-	9	.237	.296	.417
	04 Cle	AL	24	76	23	6	0	5	(2	3)	44	13	10	10	4	0	20	0	0	0	0	0	-	4	.303	.338	.579
	6 ML YEARS		352	1203	323	67	4	57	(30	27)	569	173	212	190	94	6	344	31	0	5	2	2	.50	36	.268	.336	.473

Tommy Phelps

Pitches: L **Bats:** L **Pos:** RP-29   **Ht:** 6'3" **Wt:** 192 **Born:** 3/4/1974 **Age:** 32

			HOW MUCH HE PITCHED						WHAT HE GAVE UP											THE RESULTS						
Year	Team	Lg	G	GS	CG	GF	IP	BFP	H	R	ER	HR	SH	SF	HB	TBB	IBB	SO	WP	Bk	W	L	Pct	ShO	Sv-Op Hld	ERC	ERA
2005	Nashv*	AAA	5	4	0	0	16.0	63	13	3	2	0	0	0	0	2	0	14	0	0	1	0	1.000	0	0- -	1.57	1.13
2003	FLA	NL	27	7	0	8	63.0	276	70	32	28	3	1	2	2	23	1	43	1	0	3	2	.600	0	0-0 1	4.31	4.00
2004	FLA	NL	19	4	0	2	34.0	144	34	20	18	6	3	2	0	12	0	28	0	0	1	1	.500	0	0-0 4	4.46	4.76
2005	MIL	NL	29	0	0	8	23.1	106	25	12	12	2	0	0	2	12	4	14	2	0	0	2	.000	0	1-2 4	4.89	4.63
	3 ML YEARS		75	11	0	18	120.1	526	129	64	58	11	4	4	4	47	5	85	3	0	4	5	.444	0	1-2 9	4.47	4.34

Andy Phillips

Bats: R **Throws:** R **Pos:** 1B-19; DH-6; PH-3; PR-3; 3B-1; LF-1   **Ht:** 6'0" **Wt:** 205 **Born:** 4/6/1977 **Age:** 29

			BATTING																	BASERUNNING				AVERAGES		
Year	Team	Lg	G	AB	H	2B	3B	HR	(Hm	Rd)	TB	R	RBI	RC	TBB	IBB	SO	HBP	SH	SF	SB	CS	SB%	GDP	Avg	OBP	Slg
1999	StlsInd	A-	64	233	75	11	7	7	(-	-)	121	35	48	50	37	1	40	3	0	3	3	3	.50	4	.322	.417	.519
2000	Tampa	A+	127	478	137	33	2	13	(-	-)	213	66	58	73	46	0	98	2	0	8	2	0	1.00	9	.287	.346	.446
2000	Nrwich	AA	7	28	7	2	1	0	(-	-)	11	5	3	3	3	0	11	0	1	0	1	0	1.00	1	.250	.323	.393
2001	Nrwich	AA	51	183	49	9	2	6	(-	-)	80	23	25	26	21	2	54	0	1	2	1	0	1.00	6	.268	.340	.437
2001	Tampa	A+	75	288	87	17	4	11	(-	-)	145	43	50	49	25	1	55	3	1	10	3	3	.50	6	.302	.353	.503
2002	Nrwich	AA	73	272	83	24	2	19	(-	-)	168	58	51	58	33	2	56	3	0	4	4	3	.57	6	.305	.381	.618
2002	Clmbs	AAA	51	205	54	11	1	9	(-	-)	94	32	36	24	10	0	56	0	1	1	0	1	.00	8	.263	.296	.459
2003	Clmbs	AAA	17	67	14	4	0	2	(-	-)	24	7	5	4	5	0	17	0	0	0	0	0	-	4	.209	.264	.358
2004	Trentn	AA	10	42	15	2	1	4	(-	-)	31	8	16	11	3	0	6	0	0	0	3	0	1.00	0	.357	.383	.738
2004	Clmbs	AAA	115	434	138	19	6	26	(-	-)	247	83	85	87	51	5	60	2	1	5	2	1	.67	18	.318	.388	.569
2005	Clmbs	AAA	75	300	90	14	1	22	(-	-)	172	60	54	64	36	3	61	3	0	1	2	0	1.00	15	.300	.379	.573

Year	Team	Lg	G	AB	H	2B	3B	HR	(Hm	Rd)	TB	R	RBI	RC	TBB	IBB	SO	HBP	SH	SF	SB	CS	SB%	GDP	Avg	OBP	Slg
2004	NYA	AL	5	8	2	0	0	1	(0	1)	5	1	2	1	0	0	1	0	0	0	0	0	-	1	.250	.250	.625
2005	NYA	AL	27	40	6	4	0	1	(1	0)	13	7	4	2	1	0	13	0	0	0	0	0	-	1	.150	.171	.325
2 ML YEARS			32	48	8	4	0	2	(1	1)	18	8	6	3	1	0	14	0	0	0	0	0	-	2	.167	.184	.375

Brandon Phillips

Bats: R **Throws:** R **Pos:** PR-3; 2B-2; SS-1; DH-1   **Ht:** 5'11" **Wt:** 185 **Born:** 6/28/1981 **Age:** 25

Year	Team	Lg	G	AB	H	2B	3B	HR	(Hm	Rd)	TB	R	RBI	RC	TBB	IBB	SO	HBP	SH	SF	SB	CS	SB%	GDP	Avg	OBP	Slg
2005	Buffalo*	AAA	112	465	119	24	1	15	(-	-)	190	79	46	64	39	0	90	10	2	2	7	5	.58	11	.256	.326	.409
2002	CLE	AL	11	31	8	3	1	0	(0	0)	13	5	4	5	3	0	6	1	1	0	0	0	-	0	.258	.343	.419
2003	CLE	AL	112	370	77	18	1	6	(3	3)	115	36	33	22	14	0	77	3	5	1	4	5	.44	12	.208	.242	.311
2004	CLE	AL	6	22	4	2	0	0	(0	0)	6	1	1	0	2	0	5	0	0	0	0	2	.00	1	.182	.250	.273
2005	CLE	AL	6	9	0	0	0	0	(0	0)	0	1	0	0	0	0	4	0	0	0	0	0	-	0	.000	.000	.000
4 ML YEARS			135	432	89	23	2	6	(3	3)	134	43	38	27	19	0	92	4	6	1	4	7	.36	13	.206	.246	.310

Jason Phillips

Bats: R **Throws:** R **Pos:** C-93; 1B-21; PH-13   **Ht:** 6'1" **Wt:** 177 **Born:** 9/27/1976 **Age:** 29

Year	Team	Lg	G	AB	H	2B	3B	HR	(Hm	Rd)	TB	R	RBI	RC	TBB	IBB	SO	HBP	SH	SF	SB	CS	SB%	GDP	Avg	OBP	Slg
2001	NYN	NL	6	7	1	1	0	0	(0	0)	2	2	0	0	0	0	1	0	0	0	0	0	-	0	.143	.143	.286
2002	NYN	NL	11	19	7	0	0	1	(0	1)	10	4	3	3	1	0	1	1	0	1	0	0	-	1	.368	.409	.526
2003	NYN	NL	119	403	120	25	0	11	(7	4)	178	45	58	65	39	3	50	10	0	1	0	1	.00	21	.298	.373	.442
2004	NYN	NL	128	362	79	18	0	7	(2	5)	118	34	34	30	35	4	42	8	2	5	0	1	.00	11	.218	.298	.326
2005	LAN	NL	121	399	95	20	0	10	(6	4)	145	38	55	42	25	4	50	4	2	4	0	1	.00	16	.238	.287	.363
5 ML YEARS			385	1190	302	64	0	29	(15	14)	453	123	150	140	100	11	144	23	4	11	0	3	.00	49	.254	.321	.381

Paul Phillips

Bats: R **Throws:** R **Pos:** C-20; DH-2; PH-2; PR-2   **Ht:** 5'11" **Wt:** 185 **Born:** 4/15/1977 **Age:** 29

Year	Team	Lg	G	AB	H	2B	3B	HR	(Hm	Rd)	TB	R	RBI	RC	TBB	IBB	SO	HBP	SH	SF	SB	CS	SB%	GDP	Avg	OBP	Slg
1998	Spkane	A-	59	234	72	12	2	4	(-	-)	100	55	25	39	18	0	19	4	0	1	12	1	.92	2	.308	.366	.427
1998	Wilmg	A+	2	5	2	0	0	0	(-	-)	2	0	2	0	0	0	1	0	0	1	0	0	-	0	.400	.333	.400
1999	Wichta	AA	108	393	105	20	2	3	(-	-)	138	58	56	41	26	0	38	2	3	3	8	9	.47	8	.267	.314	.351
2000	Wichta	AA	82	291	85	11	5	4	(-	-)	118	49	30	37	21	1	22	1	1	4	4	5	.44	11	.292	.338	.405
2003	Royals	R	4	13	6	2	0	1	(-	-)	11	3	2	4	1	0	0	0	0	0	0	0	-	0	.462	.500	.846
2003	Wilmg	A+	13	46	11	1	0	0	(-	-)	12	1	6	2	1	0	6	1	0	0	0	1	.00	3	.239	.271	.261
2004	Omha	AAA	86	311	97	17	1	6	(-	-)	134	40	41	45	20	0	36	3	0	1	4	3	.57	10	.312	.358	.431
2005	Omha	AAA	87	332	89	21	1	7	(-	-)	133	45	42	42	21	0	44	4	2	2	1	4	.20	7	.268	.318	.401
2004	KC	AL	4	5	1	0	0	0	(0	0)	1	2	0	0	0	0	1	1	0	0	0	0	-	0	.200	.333	.200
2005	KC	AL	23	67	18	4	1	1	(0	1)	27	6	9	8	0	0	5	0	0	0	0	0	-	4	.269	.269	.403
2 ML YEARS			27	72	19	4	1	1	(0	1)	28	8	9	8	0	0	6	1	0	0	0	0	-	4	.264	.274	.389

Mike Piazza

Bats: R **Throws:** R **Pos:** C-101; PH-7; DH-5   **Ht:** 6'3" **Wt:** 215 **Born:** 9/4/1968 **Age:** 37

Year	Team	Lg	G	AB	H	2B	3B	HR	(Hm	Rd)	TB	R	RBI	RC	TBB	IBB	SO	HBP	SH	SF	SB	CS	SB%	GDP	Avg	OBP	Slg
1992	LA	NL	21	69	16	3	0	1	(1	0)	22	5	7	6	4	0	12	1	0	0	0	0	-	0	.232	.284	.319
1993	LA	NL	149	547	174	24	2	35	(21	14)	307	81	112	107	46	6	86	3	0	6	3	4	.43	10	.318	.370	.561
1994	LA	NL	107	405	129	18	0	24	(13	11)	219	64	92	74	33	10	65	1	0	2	1	3	.25	11	.319	.370	.541
1995	LA	NL	112	434	150	17	0	32	(9	23)	263	82	93	96	39	10	80	1	0	1	1	0	1.00	10	.346	.400	.606
1996	LA	NL	148	547	184	16	0	36	(14	22)	308	87	105	117	81	21	93	1	0	2	0	3	.00	21	.336	.422	.563
1997	LA	NL	152	556	201	32	1	40	(22	18)	355	104	124	137	69	11	77	3	0	5	5	1	.83	19	.362	.431	.638
1998	3 Tms	NL	151	561	184	38	1	32	(15	17)	320	88	111	116	58	14	80	2	0	5	1	0	1.00	16	.328	.390	.570
1999	NYN	NL	141	534	162	25	0	40	(18	22)	307	100	124	99	51	11	70	1	0	7	2	2	.50	27	.303	.361	.575
2000	NYN	NL	136	482	156	26	0	38	(17	21)	296	90	113	107	58	10	69	3	0	2	4	2	.67	15	.324	.398	.614
2001	NYN	NL	141	503	151	29	0	36	(16	20)	288	81	94	100	67	19	87	2	0	1	0	2	.00	15	.300	.384	.573
2002	NYN	NL	135	478	134	23	2	33	(12	21)	260	69	98	82	57	9	82	3	0	3	0	3	.00	26	.280	.359	.544
2003	NYN	NL	68	234	67	13	0	11	(4	7)	113	37	34	42	35	3	40	1	0	3	0	0	-	11	.286	.377	.483
2004	NYN	NL	129	455	121	21	0	20	(12	8)	202	47	54	63	68	14	78	2	0	3	0	0	-	14	.266	.362	.444
2005	NYN	NL	113	398	100	23	0	19	(9	10)	180	41	62	55	41	6	67	3	0	0	0	0	-	7	.251	.326	.452
98	LA	NL	37	149	42	5	0	9	(5	4)	74	20	30	23	11	4	27	0	0	1	0	0	-	3	.282	.329	.497
98	Fla	NL	5	18	5	0	1	0	(0	0)	7	1	5	2	0	0	0	0	0	1	0	0	-	0	.278	.263	.389
98	NYM	NL	109	394	137	33	0	23	(10	13)	239	67	76	91	47	10	53	2	0	3	1	0	1.00	12	.348	.417	.607
14 ML YEARS			1703	6203	1929	308	6	397	(183	214)	3440	976	1223	1201	707	144	986	27	0	40	17	20	.46	207	.311	.382	.555

Calvin Pickering

Bats: L **Throws:** L **Pos:** DH-7   **Ht:** 6'5" **Wt:** 267 **Born:** 9/29/1976 **Age:** 29

Year	Team	Lg	G	AB	H	2B	3B	HR	(Hm	Rd)	TB	R	RBI	RC	TBB	IBB	SO	HBP	SH	SF	SB	CS	SB%	GDP	Avg	OBP	Slg
2005	Omha*	AAA	92	335	92	16	0	23	(-	-)	177	56	67	69	56	2	130	4	0	1	1	0	1.00	4	.275	.384	.528
1998	BAL	AL	9	21	5	0	0	2	(1	1)	11	4	3	3	3	0	4	0	0	0	1	0	1.00	2	.238	.333	.524
1999	BAL	AL	23	40	5	1	0	1	(1	0)	9	4	5	3	11	0	16	0	0	0	0	0	-	4	.125	.314	.225
2001	2 Tms	AL	21	54	15	1	0	3	(1	2)	25	4	8	7	8	0	15	0	0	0	0	0	-	4	.278	.371	.463
2004	KC	AL	35	122	30	8	1	7	(4	3)	61	21	26	25	18	1	42	0	0	2	0	0	-	6	.246	.338	.500
2005	KC	AL	7	27	4	0	0	1	(0	1)	7	4	3	4	3	0	14	0	0	0	0	0	-	0	.148	.226	.259

Year	Team	Lg	G	AB	H	2B	3B	HR	(Hm	Rd)	TB	R	RBI	RC	TBB	IBB	SO	HBP	SH	SF	SB	CS	SB%	GDP	Avg	OBP	Slg
01	Cin	NL	4	4	1	0	0	0	(1	2)	1	0	1	0	0	0	2	0	0	0	0	0	-	0	.250	.250	.250
01	Bos	AL	17	50	14	1	0	3	(0	0)	24	4	7	7	8	0	13	0	0	0	0	0	-	4	.280	.379	.480
5 ML YEARS			95	264	59	10	1	14	(7	7)	113	37	45	39	43	1	91	0	0	3	1	0	1.00	13	.223	.329	.428

Jorge Piedra

Bats: L **Throws:** L **Pos:** PH-37; RF-17; LF-9; DH-1   **Ht:** 6'0" **Wt:** 190 **Born:** 4/17/1979 **Age:** 27

Year	Team	Lg	G	AB	H	2B	3B	HR	(Hm	Rd)	TB	R	RBI	RC	TBB	IBB	SO	HBP	SH	SF	SB	CS	SB%	GDP	Avg	OBP	Slg
1998	Gr Falls	R+	72	282	108	22	7	2	(-	-)	150	72	33	66	39	3	29	1	3	0	16	7	.70	4	.383	.460	.532
1999	SnBrn	A+	8	30	9	2	0	0	(-	-)	11	6	3	4	3	0	3	0	1	2	1	0	1.00	0	.300	.343	.367
1999	VeroB	A+	15	59	17	3	1	1	(-	-)	25	13	6	9	7	1	9	0	0	1	2	2	.50	0	.288	.358	.424
2000	VeroB	A+	92	360	102	11	6	6	(-	-)	143	59	52	52	29	1	57	5	3	7	21	5	.81	6	.283	.339	.397
2000	Dytona	A+	34	139	48	11	1	1	(-	-)	64	24	17	23	6	0	15	0	2	2	8	4	.67	0	.345	.367	.460
2001	WTenn	AA	124	441	108	26	6	8	(-	-)	170	55	54	53	37	2	80	8	2	7	12	5	.71	8	.245	.310	.385
2002	WTenn	AA	23	60	10	3	1	0	(-	-)	15	5	4	2	3	0	11	1	1	0	2	0	1.00	1	.167	.219	.250
2002	Salem	A+	104	392	118	37	12	13	(-	-)	218	64	64	77	37	3	55	8	3	8	10	2	.83	4	.301	.366	.556
2003	Tulsa	AA	96	357	98	17	7	18	(-	-)	183	56	53	61	31	4	50	8	0	5	5	2	.71	6	.275	.342	.513
2004	ColSpr	AAA	99	377	126	29	5	15	(-	-)	210	71	55	72	23	1	56	3	3	6	4	3	.57	7	.334	.372	.557
2005	ColSpr	AAA	47	186	58	20	1	6	(-	-)	98	35	45	36	18	0	23	1	0	2	4	2	.67	4	.312	.372	.527
2004	COL	NL	38	91	27	8	0	3	(1	2)	44	15	10	11	5	0	19	1	1	0	0	1	.00	1	.297	.340	.484
2005	COL	NL	61	112	35	8	1	6	(3	3)	63	19	16	19	10	0	15	1	0	1	2	1	.67	2	.313	.371	.563
2 ML YEARS			99	203	62	16	1	9	(4	5)	107	34	26	30	15	0	34	2	1	1	2	2	.50	3	.305	.357	.527

Juan Pierre

Bats: L **Throws:** L **Pos:** CF-160; PH-2; PR-2   **Ht:** 6'0" **Wt:** 180 **Born:** 8/14/1977 **Age:** 28

Year	Team	Lg	G	AB	H	2B	3B	HR	(Hm	Rd)	TB	R	RBI	RC	TBB	IBB	SO	HBP	SH	SF	SB	CS	SB%	GDP	Avg	OBP	Slg
2000	COL	NL	51	200	62	2	0	0	(0	0)	64	26	20	23	13	0	15	1	4	1	7	6	.54	2	.310	.353	.320
2001	COL	NL	156	617	202	26	11	2	(0	2)	256	108	55	91	41	1	29	10	14	1	46	17	.73	6	.327	.378	.415
2002	COL	NL	152	592	170	20	5	1	(0	1)	203	90	35	79	31	0	52	9	8	0	47	12	.80	7	.287	.332	.343
2003	FLA	NL	162	668	204	28	7	1	(1	0)	249	100	41	92	55	1	35	5	15	3	65	20	.76	9	.305	.361	.373
2004	FLA	NL	162	678	221	22	12	3	(1	2)	276	100	49	91	45	1	35	8	15	2	45	24	.65	9	.326	.374	.407
2005	FLA	NL	162	656	181	19	13	2	(1	1)	232	96	47	76	41	1	45	9	10	2	57	17	.77	10	.276	.326	.354
6 ML YEARS			845	3411	1040	117	48	9	(3	6)	1280	520	247	472	226	4	211	42	66	9	267	96	.74	43	.305	.355	.375

A.J. Pierzynski

Bats: L **Throws:** R **Pos:** C-128; PH-2   **Ht:** 6'3" **Wt:** 220 **Born:** 12/30/1976 **Age:** 29

Year	Team	Lg	G	AB	H	2B	3B	HR	(Hm	Rd)	TB	R	RBI	RC	TBB	IBB	SO	HBP	SH	SF	SB	CS	SB%	GDP	Avg	OBP	Slg
1998	MIN	AL	7	10	3	0	0	0	(0	0)	3	1	1	2	1	0	2	1	0	1	0	0	-	0	.300	.385	.300
1999	MIN	AL	9	22	6	2	0	0	(0	0)	8	3	3	3	1	0	4	1	0	0	0	0	-	0	.273	.333	.364
2000	MIN	AL	33	88	27	5	1	2	(1	1)	40	12	11	14	5	0	14	2	0	1	1	0	1.00	1	.307	.354	.455
2001	MIN	AL	114	381	110	33	2	7	(3	4)	168	51	55	50	16	4	57	4	1	3	1	7	.13	7	.289	.322	.441
2002	MIN	AL	130	440	132	31	6	6	(2	4)	193	54	49	60	13	1	61	11	2	3	1	2	.33	14	.300	.334	.439
2003	MIN	AL	137	487	152	35	3	11	(6	5)	226	63	74	80	24	12	55	15	2	5	3	1	.75	13	.312	.360	.464
2004	SF	NL	131	471	128	28	2	11	(3	8)	193	45	77	58	19	4	27	15	2	3	0	1	.00	28	.272	.319	.410
2005	CHA	AL	128	460	118	21	0	18	(12	6)	193	61	56	55	23	5	68	12	1	1	0	2	.00	13	.257	.308	.420
8 ML YEARS			689	2359	676	155	14	55	(27	28)	1024	290	326	322	102	26	288	61	8	17	6	13	.32	76	.287	.330	.434

Joel Pineiro

Pitches: R **Bats:** R **Pos:** SP-30   **Ht:** 6'1" **Wt:** 180 **Born:** 9/25/1978 **Age:** 27

Year	Team	Lg	G	GS	CG	GF	IP	BFP	H	R	ER	HR	SH	SF	HB	TBB	IBB	SO	WP	Bk	W	L	Pct	ShO	Sv-Op	Hld	ERC	ERA
2005	Tacom*	AAA	1	1	0	0	7.0	26	5	1	1	1	0	0	0	0	0	6	0	0	0	0	-	0	0--	-	1.49	1.29
2000	SEA	AL	8	1	0	5	19.1	94	25	13	12	3	0	2	0	13	0	10	0	0	1	0	1.000	0	0-0	0	7.44	5.59
2001	SEA	AL	17	11	0	1	75.1	289	50	24	17	2	1	2	3	21	0	56	2	0	6	2	.750	0	0-0	2	1.71	2.03
2002	SEA	AL	37	28	2	4	194.1	812	189	75	70	24	5	7	7	54	1	136	8	0	14	7	.667	1	0-0	3	3.77	3.24
2003	SEA	AL	32	32	3	0	211.2	890	192	94	89	19	3	9	6	76	3	151	5	0	16	11	.593	2	0-0	0	3.43	3.78
2004	SEA	AL	21	21	1	0	140.2	596	144	77	73	21	1	5	4	43	1	111	4	0	6	11	.353	0	0-0	0	4.32	4.67
2005	SEA	AL	30	30	2	0	189.0	822	224	118	118	23	5	7	6	56	4	107	7	1	7	11	.389	0	0-0	0	5.05	5.62
6 ML YEARS			145	123	8	10	830.1	3503	824	401	379	92	15	32	26	263	9	571	26	1	50	42	.543	3	0-0	5	3.92	4.11

Scott Podsednik

Bats: L **Throws:** L **Pos:** LF-124; CF-7; PH-3; PR-2   **Ht:** 6'0" **Wt:** 170 **Born:** 3/18/1976 **Age:** 30

Year	Team	Lg	G	AB	H	2B	3B	HR	(Hm	Rd)	TB	R	RBI	RC	TBB	IBB	SO	HBP	SH	SF	SB	CS	SB%	GDP	Avg	OBP	Slg
2005	Charltt*	AAA	2	9	2	2	0	0	(-	-)	4	2	1	0	0	0	2	0	0	0	0	0	-	0	.222	.222	.444
2001	SEA	AL	5	6	1	0	1	0	(0	0)	3	1	3	0	0	0	1	0	0	0	0	0	-	1	.167	.167	.500
2002	SEA	AL	14	20	4	0	0	1	(0	1)	7	2	5	3	4	0	6	0	0	1	0	0	-	1	.200	.320	.350
2003	MIL	NL	154	558	175	29	8	9	(7	2)	247	100	58	101	56	2	91	4	8	2	43	10	.81	11	.314	.379	.443
2004	MIL	NL	154	640	156	27	7	12	(3	9)	233	85	39	76	58	2	105	7	6	1	70	13	.84	7	.244	.313	.364
2005	CHA	AL	129	507	147	28	1	0	(0	0)	177	80	25	64	47	0	75	3	6	5	59	23	.72	7	.290	.351	.349
5 ML YEARS			456	1731	483	84	17	22	(10	12)	667	268	130	244	165	4	278	14	20	9	172	46	.79	27	.279	.345	.385

Placido Polanco

Bats: R **Throws:** R **Pos:** 2B-113; 3B-9; LF-5; PH-5; SS-1; PR-1   **Ht:** 5'10" **Wt:** 168 **Born:** 10/10/1975 **Age:** 30

											BATTING										BASERUNNING				AVERAGES		
Year	Team	Lg	G	AB	H	2B	3B	HR	(Hm	Rd)	TB	R	RBI	RC	TBB	IBB	SO	HBP	SH	SF	SB	CS	SB%	GDP	Avg	OBP	Slg
1998	STL	NL	45	114	29	3	2	1	(1	0)	39	10	11	12	5	0	9	1	2	0	2	0	1.00	1	.254	.292	.342
1999	STL	NL	88	220	61	9	3	1	(0	1)	79	24	19	23	15	1	24	0	3	2	1	3	.25	7	.277	.321	.359
2000	STL	NL	118	323	102	12	3	5	(2	3)	135	50	39	44	16	0	26	1	7	3	4	4	.50	8	.316	.347	.418
2001	STL	NL	144	564	173	26	4	3	(1	2)	216	87	38	70	25	0	43	6	14	1	12	3	.80	22	.307	.342	.383
2002	2 Tms	NL	147	548	158	32	2	9	(8	1)	221	75	49	64	26	1	41	8	13	0	5	3	.63	15	.288	.330	.403
2003	PHI	NL	122	492	142	30	3	14	(7	7)	220	87	63	74	42	1	38	8	8	4	14	2	.88	16	.289	.352	.447
2004	PHI	NL	126	503	150	21	0	17	(10	7)	222	74	55	71	27	0	39	12	7	6	7	4	.64	13	.298	.345	.441
2005	2 Tms	NL	129	501	166	27	2	9	(6	3)	224	84	56	86	33	0	25	11	2	4	4	3	.57	12	.331	.383	.447
02	StL	NL	94	342	97	19	1	5	(5	0)	133	47	27	38	12	1	27	4	9	0	3	1	.75	12	.284	.316	.389
02	Phi	NL	53	206	61	13	1	4	(3	1)	88	28	22	26	14	0	14	4	4	0	2	2	.50	3	.296	.353	.427
05	Phi	NL	43	158	50	7	0	3	(2	1)	66	26	20	26	12	0	9	3	0	0	0	0	-	3	.316	.376	.418
05	Det	AL	86	343	116	20	2	6	(4	2)	158	58	36	60	21	0	16	8	2	4	4	3	.57	9	.338	.386	.461
	8 ML YEARS		919	3265	981	160	19	59	(35	24)	1356	491	330	444	189	3	245	47	56	20	49	22	.69	94	.300	.346	.415

Cliff Politte

Pitches: R **Bats:** R **Pos:** RP-68   **Ht:** 5'11" **Wt:** 185 **Born:** 2/27/1974 **Age:** 32

			HOW MUCH HE PITCHED						WHAT HE GAVE UP											THE RESULTS						
Year	Team	Lg	G	GS	CG	GF	IP	BFP	H	R	ER	HR	SH	SF	HB	TBB	IBB	SO	WP	Bk	W	L	Pct	ShO	Sv-Op	Hld	ERC	ERA
1998	PHI	NL	8	8	0	0	37.0	172	45	32	26	6	3	1	1	18	0	22	2	1	2	3	.400	0	0-0	0	6.28	6.32
1999	PHI	NL	13	0	0	0	17.2	85	19	14	14	2	1	0	0	15	0	15	2	0	1	0	1.000	0	0-0	1	6.47	7.13
2000	PHI	NL	12	8	0	1	59.0	251	55	24	24	8	1	1	0	27	1	50	3	0	4	3	.571	0	0-0	0	4.20	3.66
2001	PHI	NL	23	0	0	7	26.0	109	24	8	7	2	1	3	1	8	3	23	1	0	2	3	.400	0	0-0	1	3.11	2.42
2002	2 Tms		68	0	0	20	73.2	304	57	33	30	5	3	1	2	28	2	72	2	0	3	3	.500	0	1-4	25	2.64	3.67
2003	TOR	AL	54	0	0	30	49.1	216	52	32	31	11	1	3	1	17	4	40	1	0	1	5	.167	0	12-18	8	4.93	5.66
2004	CHA	AL	54	0	0	9	51.1	225	52	26	25	6	0	2	2	22	5	48	2	0	0	3	.000	0	1-1	19	4.38	4.38
2005	CHA	AL	68	0	0	14	67.1	262	42	15	15	7	2	4	3	21	4	57	1	0	7	1	.875	0	1-2	23	1.97	2.00
02	Phi	NL	13	0	0	7	16.1	77	19	10	7	0	1	0	1	9	1	15	1	0	2	0	1.000	0	0-1	0	4.89	3.86
02	Tor	AL	55	0	0	13	57.1	227	38	23	23	5	2	1	1	19	1	57	1	0	1	3	.250	0	1-3	25	2.06	3.61
	8 ML YEARS		300	16	0	81	381.1	1624	346	184	172	47	12	15	10	156	19	327	14	1	20	21	.488	0	15-25	77	3.78	4.06

Sidney Ponson

Pitches: R **Bats:** R **Pos:** SP-23   **Ht:** 6'1" **Wt:** 225 **Born:** 11/2/1976 **Age:** 29

			HOW MUCH HE PITCHED						WHAT HE GAVE UP											THE RESULTS						
Year	Team	Lg	G	GS	CG	GF	IP	BFP	H	R	ER	HR	SH	SF	HB	TBB	IBB	SO	WP	Bk	W	L	Pct	ShO	Sv-Op	Hld	ERC	ERA
1998	BAL	AL	31	20	0	5	135.0	588	157	82	79	19	3	4	3	42	2	85	4	1	8	9	.471	0	1-2	0	5.07	5.27
1999	BAL	AL	32	32	6	0	210.0	897	227	118	110	35	4	7	1	80	2	112	4	0	12	12	.500	0	0-0	0	5.08	4.71
2000	BAL	AL	32	32	6	0	222.0	953	223	125	119	30	3	3	1	83	0	152	5	0	9	13	.409	1	0-0	0	4.26	4.82
2001	BAL	AL	23	23	3	0	138.1	605	161	83	76	21	3	2	6	37	0	84	2	0	5	10	.333	1	0-0	0	5.04	4.94
2002	BAL	AL	28	28	3	0	176.0	736	172	84	80	26	2	3	2	63	1	120	3	0	7	9	.438	0	0-0	0	4.24	4.09
2003	2 Tms		31	31	4	0	216.0	898	211	94	90	16	6	5	5	61	5	134	9	0	17	12	.586	0	0-0	0	3.41	3.75
2004	BAL	AL	33	33	5	0	215.2	954	265	136	127	23	6	3	8	69	3	115	8	2	11	15	.423	2	0-0	0	5.33	5.30
2005	BAL	AL	23	23	1	0	130.1	595	177	97	90	16	2	8	3	48	1	68	10	0	7	11	.389	0	0-0	0	6.45	6.21
03	Bal	AL	21	21	4	0	148.0	622	147	65	62	10	2	3	4	43	2	100	6	0	14	6	.700	0	0-0	0	3.50	3.77
03	SF	NL	10	10	0	0	68.0	276	64	29	28	6	4	2	1	18	3	34	3	0	3	6	.333	0	0-0	0	3.23	3.71
	8 ML YEARS		233	222	28	5	1443.1	6226	1593	819	771	186	29	35	29	483	14	870	45	3	76	91	.455	4	1-2	0	4.74	4.81

Jorge Posada

Bats: B **Throws:** R **Pos:** C-133; PH-16; DH-3   **Ht:** 6'2" **Wt:** 205 **Born:** 8/17/1971 **Age:** 34

											BATTING										BASERUNNING				AVERAGES		
Year	Team	Lg	G	AB	H	2B	3B	HR	(Hm	Rd)	TB	R	RBI	RC	TBB	IBB	SO	HBP	SH	SF	SB	CS	SB%	GDP	Avg	OBP	Slg
1995	NYA	AL	1	0	0	0	0	0	(0	0)	0	0	0	0	0	0	0	0	0	0	0	0	-	0	-	-	-
1996	NYA	AL	8	14	1	0	0	0	(0	0)	1	1	0	0	1	0	6	0	0	0	0	0	-	1	.071	.133	.071
1997	NYA	AL	60	188	47	12	0	6	(2	4)	77	29	25	29	30	2	33	3	1	2	1	2	.33	2	.250	.359	.410
1998	NYA	AL	111	358	96	23	0	17	(6	11)	170	56	63	56	47	7	92	0	0	4	0	1	.00	14	.268	.350	.475
1999	NYA	AL	112	379	93	19	2	12	(4	8)	152	50	57	52	53	2	91	3	0	2	1	0	1.00	9	.245	.341	.401
2000	NYA	AL	151	505	145	35	1	28	(18	10)	266	92	86	110	107	10	151	8	0	4	2	2	.50	11	.287	.417	.527
2001	NYA	AL	138	484	134	28	1	22	(14	8)	230	59	95	80	62	10	132	6	0	5	2	6	.25	10	.277	.363	.475
2002	NYA	AL	143	511	137	40	1	20	(12	8)	239	79	99	92	81	9	143	3	0	3	1	0	1.00	23	.268	.370	.468
2003	NYA	AL	142	481	135	24	0	30	(15	15)	249	83	101	98	93	6	110	10	0	4	2	4	.33	13	.281	.405	.518
2004	NYA	AL	137	449	122	31	0	21	(11	10)	216	72	81	78	88	5	92	9	0	1	1	3	.25	24	.272	.400	.481
2005	NYA	AL	142	474	124	23	0	19	(11	8)	204	67	71	71	66	5	94	2	0	4	1	0	1.00	8	.262	.352	.430
	11 ML YEARS		1145	3843	1034	235	5	175	(93	82)	1804	588	678	666	628	56	944	44	1	29	11	18	.38	115	.269	.375	.469

Jay Powell

Pitches: R **Bats:** R **Pos:** RP-5   **Ht:** 6'4" **Wt:** 225 **Born:** 1/9/1972 **Age:** 34

			HOW MUCH HE PITCHED						WHAT HE GAVE UP											THE RESULTS						
Year	Team	Lg	G	GS	CG	GF	IP	BFP	H	R	ER	HR	SH	SF	HB	TBB	IBB	SO	WP	Bk	W	L	Pct	ShO	Sv-Op	Hld	ERC	ERA
2005	Braves*	R	2	2	0	0	2.0	11	4	2	1	0	0	0	1	1	0	1	0	0	0	0	-	0	0--	-	13.16	4.50
2005	Missi*	AA	11	0	0	3	14.0	51	6	1	1	0	2	0	1	3	1	8	0	0	2	0	1.000	0	0--	-	0.79	0.64
1995	FLA	NL	9	0	0	1	8.1	38	7	2	1	0	1	0	2	6	1	4	0	0	0	0	-	0	0-0	2	4.44	1.08
1996	FLA	NL	67	0	0	16	71.1	321	71	41	36	5	2	1	4	36	1	52	3	0	4	3	.571	0	2-5	10	4.39	4.54
1997	FLA	NL	74	0	0	23	79.2	337	71	35	29	3	6	4	4	30	3	65	3	0	7	2	.778	0	2-4	24	3.10	3.28
1998	2 Tms	NL	62	0	0	35	70.1	302	58	28	26	6	3	1	3	37	9	62	1	0	7	7	.500	0	7-11	3	3.46	3.33
1999	HOU	NL	67	0	0	26	75.0	341	82	38	36	3	5	2	3	40	4	77	5	0	5	4	.556	0	4-7	16	4.75	4.32

			HOW MUCH HE PITCHED						WHAT HE GAVE UP												THE RESULTS							
Year	Team	Lg	G	GS	CG	GF	IP	BFP	H	R	ER	HR	SH	SF	HB	TBB	IBB	SO	WP	Bk	W	L	Pct	ShO	Sv-Op	Hld	ERC	ERA
2000	HOU	NL	29	0	0	10	27.0	127	29	18	17	1	1	0	0	19	1	16	0	0	1	1	.500	0	0-0	5	5.10	5.67
2001	2 Tms	NL	74	0	0	20	75.0	327	75	36	27	9	5	1	2	31	3	54	0	1	5	3	.625	0	7-13	8	4.30	3.24
2002	TEX	AL	51	0	0	5	49.2	224	50	28	19	5	1	0	1	24	4	35	2	0	3	2	.600	0	0-4	12	4.28	3.44
2003	TEX	AL	51	0	0	20	58.2	279	75	58	51	7	1	6	2	34	3	40	6	0	3	0	1.000	0	0-0	2	6.72	7.82
2004	TEX	AL	23	0	0	4	24.0	103	24	11	9	3	1	1	0	11	1	17	0	0	1	1	.500	0	0-0	4	4.50	3.38
2005	ATL	NL	5	0	0	1	3.1	15	1	0	0	0	0	0	0	4	0	1	0	0	0	0	-	0	0-0	1	2.46	0.00
98	Fla	NL	33	0	0	26	36.1	165	36	19	17	5	3	1	2	22	6	24	1	0	4	4	.500	0	3-6	6	5.07	4.21
98	Hou	NL	29	0	0	9	34.0	137	22	9	9	1	0	0	1	15	3	38	0	0	3	3	.500	0	4-5	3	1.96	2.38
01	Hou	NL	35	0	0	5	36.1	170	41	18	15	4	1	1	0	19	0	28	0	1	2	2	.500	0	0-5	5	5.23	3.72
01	Col	NL	39	0	0	15	38.2	157	34	18	12	5	4	0	2	12	3	26	0	0	3	1	.750	0	7-8	3	3.45	2.79
11 ML YEARS			512	0	0	161	542.1	2414	543	295	251	42	26	16	21	272	30	423	20	1	36	23	.610	0	22-44	87	4.36	4.17

Todd Pratt

Bats: R **Throws:** R **Pos:** C-57; PH-4   **Ht:** 6'3" **Wt:** 230 **Born:** 2/9/1967 **Age:** 39

			BATTING																		BASERUNNING				AVERAGES		
Year	Team	Lg	G	AB	H	2B	3B	HR	(Hm	Rd)	TB	R	RBI	RC	TBB	IBB	SO	HBP	SH	SF	SB	CS	SB%	GDP	Avg	OBP	Slg
1992	PHI	NL	16	46	13	1	0	2	(2	0)	20	6	10	6	4	0	12	0	0	0	0	0	-	2	.283	.340	.435
1993	PHI	NL	33	87	25	6	0	5	(4	1)	46	8	13	15	5	0	19	1	1	1	0	0	-	2	.287	.330	.529
1994	PHI	NL	28	102	20	6	1	2	(1	1)	34	10	9	9	12	0	29	0	0	0	0	1	.00	3	.196	.281	.333
1995	CHN	NL	25	60	8	2	0	0	(0	0)	10	3	4	1	6	1	21	0	0	1	0	0	-	1	.133	.209	.167
1997	NYN	NL	39	106	30	6	0	2	(1	1)	42	12	19	16	13	0	32	2	0	0	0	1	.00	1	.283	.372	.396
1998	NYN	NL	41	69	19	9	1	2	(1	1)	36	9	18	11	2	0	20	0	0	0	0	0	-	0	.275	.296	.522
1999	NYN	NL	71	140	41	4	0	3	(1	2)	54	18	21	22	15	0	32	3	0	2	2	0	1.00	1	.293	.369	.386
2000	NYN	NL	80	160	44	6	0	6	(2	6)	74	33	25	28	22	1	31	5	2	1	0	0	-	5	.275	.378	.463
2001	2 Tms	NL	80	173	32	8	0	4	(0	4)	52	18	11	18	34	3	61	3	1	1	1	0	1.00	6	.185	.327	.301
2002	PHI	NL	39	106	33	11	0	3	(2	1)	53	14	16	21	24	6	28	4	0	2	2	0	1.00	3	.311	.449	.500
2003	PHI	NL	43	125	34	10	1	4	(3	1)	58	16	20	25	22	0	38	6	1	2	0	0	-	3	.272	.400	.464
2004	PHI	NL	45	128	33	5	0	3	(2	1)	47	16	16	18	18	0	38	1	1	1	0	0	-	5	.258	.351	.367
2005	PHI	NL	60	175	44	4	0	7	(7	0)	69	17	23	22	19	5	50	2	0	0	0	0	-	3	.251	.332	.394
01	NYM	NL	45	80	13	5	0	2	(0	2)	24	6	4	7	15	1	36	2	0	1	1	0	1.00	4	.163	.306	.300
01	Phi	NL	35	93	19	3	0	2	(0	2)	28	12	7	11	19	2	25	1	1	0	0	0	-	2	.204	.345	.301
13 ML YEARS			600	1477	376	78	3	45	(26	19)	595	180	205	212	196	16	411	27	6	11	5	2	.71	35	.255	.350	.403

Curtis Pride

Bats: L **Throws:** R **Pos:** LF-4; DH-3; PH-3; PR-2   **Ht:** 6'0" **Wt:** 210 **Born:** 12/17/1968 **Age:** 37

			BATTING																		BASERUNNING				AVERAGES		
Year	Team	Lg	G	AB	H	2B	3B	HR	(Hm	Rd)	TB	R	RBI	RC	TBB	IBB	SO	HBP	SH	SF	SB	CS	SB%	GDP	Avg	OBP	Slg
2005	Salt Lk*	AAA	82	280	81	17	6	9	(-	-)	137	44	56	56	49	3	65	1	0	0	10	5	.67	6	.289	.397	.489
1993	MON	NL	10	9	4	1	1	1	(0	0)	10	3	5	5	0	0	3	0	0	0	1	0	1.00	1	.444	.444	1.111
1995	MON	NL	48	63	11	1	0	0	(0	0)	12	10	2	3	5	0	16	0	1	0	3	2	.60	2	.175	.235	.190
1996	DET	AL	95	267	80	17	5	10	(5	5)	137	52	31	52	31	1	63	0	3	0	11	6	.65	2	.300	.372	.513
1997	2 Tms	AL	81	164	35	4	4	3	(3	0)	56	22	20	19	24	1	46	1	2	1	6	4	.60	4	.213	.316	.341
1998	ATL	NL	70	107	27	6	1	3	(1	2)	44	19	9	15	9	0	29	3	1	1	4	0	1.00	2	.252	.325	.411
2000	BOS	AL	9	20	5	1	0	0	(0	0)	6	4	0	2	1	0	7	0	0	0	0	0	-	0	.250	.286	.300
2001	MON	NL	36	76	19	3	1	1	(0	1)	27	8	9	9	9	0	22	2	0	0	3	2	.60	4	.250	.345	.355
2003	NYA	AL	4	12	1	0	0	1	(1	0)	4	1	1	0	0	0	2	0	0	0	0	0	-	1	.083	.083	.333
2004	MON	NL	35	40	10	3	0	0	(0	0)	13	5	3	3	0	0	11	1	1	0	1	0	1.00	1	.250	.268	.325
2005	LAA	AL	11	11	1	1	0	0	(0	0)	2	2	0	0	0	0	4	0	0	0	0	0	-	0	.091	.091	.182
97	Det	AL	79	162	34	4	4	2	(2	0)	52	21	19	17	24	1	45	1	2	1	6	4	.60	4	.210	.314	.321
97	Bos	AL	2	2	1	0	0	1	(1	0)	4	1	1	2	0	0	1	0	0	0	0	0	-	0	.500	.500	2.000
10 ML YEARS			399	769	193	37	12	19	(10	8)	311	126	80	108	79	2	203	7	8	2	29	14	.67	16	.251	.326	.404

Chris Prieto

Bats: L **Throws:** L **Pos:** CF-2   **Ht:** 5'11" **Wt:** 185 **Born:** 8/24/1972 **Age:** 33

			BATTING																		BASERUNNING				AVERAGES		
Year	Team	Lg	G	AB	H	2B	3B	HR	(Hm	Rd)	TB	R	RBI	RC	TBB	IBB	SO	HBP	SH	SF	SB	CS	SB%	GDP	Avg	OBP	Slg
1993	Spkane	A-	73	280	81	17	5	1	(-	-)	111	64	28	55	47	0	30	5	0	3	36	3	.92	4	.289	.397	.396
1994	RCuca	A+	102	353	87	10	3	1	(-	-)	106	64	29	44	52	1	49	5	6	4	29	11	.73	3	.246	.348	.300
1995	RCuca	A+	114	366	100	12	6	2	(-	-)	130	80	35	60	64	2	55	5	8	5	39	14	.74	10	.273	.384	.355
1996	RCuca	A+	55	217	52	11	2	2	(-	-)	73	36	23	31	39	1	36	0	1	0	23	8	.74	2	.240	.355	.336
1996	Memp	AA	7	12	4	0	1	0	(-	-)	6	1	0	2	1	0	2	0	0	0	2	0	1.00	0	.333	.385	.500
1996	LsVgs	AAA	5	7	0	0	0	0	(-	-)	0	1	0	0	0	0	0	0	0	0	0	0	-	0	.000	.000	.000
1997	RCuca	A+	22	82	23	4	0	4	(-	-)	39	21	12	17	19	1	16	0	3	0	4	3	.57	0	.280	.416	.476
1997	Mobile	AA	109	388	124	22	9	2	(-	-)	170	80	58	79	59	0	55	10	1	5	26	6	.81	2	.320	.418	.438
1998	LsVgs	AAA	92	352	107	18	6	2	(-	-)	143	65	35	56	40	1	48	1	1	0	20	11	.65	4	.304	.377	.406
1999	LsVgs	AAA	108	348	84	14	6	6	(-	-)	128	66	29	49	46	0	51	6	2	2	21	6	.78	2	.241	.338	.368
2000	Albq	AAA	85	248	69	13	3	8	(-	-)	112	53	31	52	50	1	42	4	3	1	25	5	.83	3	.278	.406	.452
2001	LsVgs	AAA	118	446	130	27	6	19	(-	-)	226	98	58	99	67	3	79	13	2	1	25	7	.78	6	.291	.398	.507
2002	NewOrl	AAA	21	86	17	2	0	0	(-	-)	19	10	1	4	8	1	11	1	0	0	1	0	1.00	0	.198	.274	.221
2003	Scrmto	AAA	111	390	110	12	7	4	(-	-)	148	70	54	59	48	1	40	7	4	6	5	3	.63	7	.282	.366	.379
2004	LsVgs	AAA	130	451	128	21	6	6	(-	-)	166	73	41	69	51	0	56	9	6	2	28	8	.78	4	.284	.366	.368
2005	Salt Lk	AAA	97	363	115	18	12	3	(-	-)	166	71	45	75	60	1	41	5	12	3	26	10	.72	4	.317	.418	.457
2005	LAA	AL	2	2	0	0	0	0	(0	0)	0	0	0	0	0	0	0	0	1	0	0	0	-	0	.000	.000	.000

Bret Prinz

Pitches: R Bats: R Pos: RP-3   Ht: 6'3" Wt: 185 Born: 6/15/1977 Age: 29

Year	Team	Lg	G	GS	CG	GF	IP	BFP	H	R	ER	HR	SH	SF	HB	TBB	IBB	SO	WP	Bk	W	L	Pct	ShO	Sv-Op	Hld	ERC	ERA
2005	Angels*	R	2	0	0	0	3.0	16	5	5	4	1	0	0	0	2	0	6	1	0	0	1	.000	0	0--	-	11.45	12.00
2005	RCuca*	A+	2	0	0	0	5.0	20	2	1	1	0	0	1	1	3	0	6	0	0	0	0	-	0	0--	-	1.86	1.80
2005	Salt Lk*	AAA	5	0	0	1	9.2	47	12	7	6	1	0	0	0	6	0	8	0	0	0	0	-	0	1--	-	6.29	5.59
2001	ARI	NL	46	0	0	26	41.0	174	33	13	12	4	3	1	1	19	1	27	1	1	4	1	.800	0	9-12	6	3.27	2.63
2002	ARI	NL	20	0	0	5	13.1	71	23	14	14	1	2	1	1	10	1	10	3	0	0	2	.000	0	0-2	5	10.34	9.45
2003	2 Tms		3	0	0	2	3.0	20	7	4	4	1	0	0	0	4	2	3	0	0	0	0	-	0	0-0	0	18.22	12.00
2004	NYA	AL	26	0	0	10	28.1	124	28	17	16	5	0	1	1	14	0	22	2	0	1	0	1.000	0	0-0	1	5.16	5.08
2005	LAA	AL	3	0	0	2	3.0	14	4	1	1	1	0	0	0	1	0	1	0	0	0	1	.000	0	0-0	0	7.44	3.00
03	Ari	NL	1	0	0	0	1.0	5	1	0	0	0	0	0	0	1	1	1	0	0	0	0	-	0	0-0	0	3.46	0.00
03	NYY	AL	2	0	0	2	2.0	15	6	4	4	1	0	0	0	3	1	2	0	0	0	0	-	0	0-0	0	27.15	18.00
	5 ML YEARS		98	0	0	45	88.2	403	95	49	47	12	5	3	4	48	4	63	6	1	5	4	.556	0	9-14	12	5.39	4.77

Mark Prior

Pitches: R Bats: R Pos: SP-27   Ht: 6'5" Wt: 225 Born: 9/7/1980 Age: 25

Year	Team	Lg	G	GS	CG	GF	IP	BFP	H	R	ER	HR	SH	SF	HB	TBB	IBB	SO	WP	Bk	W	L	Pct	ShO	Sv-Op	Hld	ERC	ERA
2005	Iowa*	AAA	1	1	0	0	6.0	28	9	7	7	0	0	1	1	1	0	7	0	0	0	1	.000	0	0--	-	6.02	10.50
2002	CHN	NL	19	19	1	0	116.2	486	98	45	43	14	3	4	7	38	0	147	1	0	6	6	.500	0	0-0	0	3.27	3.32
2003	CHN	NL	30	30	3	0	211.1	863	183	67	57	15	9	2	9	50	4	245	9	0	18	6	.750	1	0-0	0	2.69	2.43
2004	CHN	NL	21	21	0	0	118.2	510	112	53	53	14	8	4	3	48	2	139	2	1	6	4	.600	0	0-0	0	3.97	4.02
2005	CHN	NL	27	27	1	0	166.2	701	143	73	68	25	5	3	4	59	2	188	4	1	11	7	.611	0	0-0	0	3.49	3.67
	4 ML YEARS		97	97	5	0	613.1	2560	536	238	221	68	25	13	23	195	8	719	16	2	41	23	.641	1	0-0	0	3.25	3.24

Scott Proctor

Pitches: R Bats: R Pos: RP-28; SP-1   Ht: 6'1" Wt: 198 Born: 1/2/1977 Age: 29

Year	Team	Lg	G	GS	CG	GF	IP	BFP	H	R	ER	HR	SH	SF	HB	TBB	IBB	SO	WP	Bk	W	L	Pct	ShO	Sv-Op	Hld	ERC	ERA
1998	Yakima	A-	3	1	0	2	5.0	26	9	8	6	1	0	1	0	1	0	4	1	2	0	1	.000	0	2--	-	8.48	10.80
1999	Yakima	A-	16	6	0	5	50.0	235	57	45	40	4	1	4	5	26	0	41	7	1	4	2	.667	0	0--	-	5.56	7.20
2000	VeroB	A+	35	5	0	15	89.0	413	93	65	51	13	2	4	6	54	1	70	6	1	3	7	.300	0	1--	-	5.76	5.16
2001	VeroB	A+	15	15	0	0	90.2	366	73	30	25	8	2	2	9	30	1	79	3	0	6	4	.600	0	0--	-	3.16	2.48
2001	Jaxnvl	AA	10	9	0	0	49.2	215	39	26	23	6	3	2	2	31	1	48	2	0	4	3	.571	0	0--	-	4.06	4.17
2002	Jaxnvl	AA	26	25	0	0	133.1	592	111	63	52	10	6	5	7	85	1	131	9	1	7	9	.438	0	0--	-	4.05	3.51
2003	Jaxnvl	AA	17	0	0	12	27.0	108	20	6	3	0	2	3	0	7	3	24	1	1	2	2	.333	0	0--	-	1.54	1.00
2003	LsVgs	AAA	24	0	0	8	39.1	160	35	17	16	2	4	1	0	13	3	35	0	0	4	2	.667	0	1--	-	2.84	3.66
2003	Clmbs	AAA	10	0	0	1	19.0	71	13	3	3	2	1	0	1	3	0	26	0	0	2	0	1.000	0	0--	-	1.90	1.42
2004	Clmbs	AAA	35	0	0	15	44.0	187	37	15	14	4	1	0	1	18	2	42	3	0	2	3	.400	0	4--	-	3.15	2.86
2005	Clmbs	AAA	35	1	0	29	42.2	186	47	20	20	8	2	1	3	11	0	54	5	0	6	1	.857	0	14--	-	4.97	4.22
2004	NYA	AL	26	0	0	12	25.0	118	29	18	15	5	0	2	0	14	0	21	1	1	2	1	.667	0	0-0	2	6.32	5.40
2005	NYA	AL	29	1	0	11	44.2	199	46	32	30	10	0	1	2	17	4	36	4	0	1	0	1.000	0	0-0	0	4.98	6.04
	2 ML YEARS		55	1	0	23	69.2	317	75	50	45	15	0	3	2	31	4	57	5	1	3	1	.750	0	0-0	2	5.45	5.81

Brandon Puffer

Pitches: R Bats: R Pos: RP-3   Ht: 6'3" Wt: 190 Born: 10/5/1975 Age: 30

Year	Team	Lg	G	GS	CG	GF	IP	BFP	H	R	ER	HR	SH	SF	HB	TBB	IBB	SO	WP	Bk	W	L	Pct	ShO	Sv-Op	Hld	ERC	ERA
2005	Fresno*	AAA	54	0	0	12	73.1	328	85	54	45	9	6	0	12	23	3	48	3	1	6	5	.545	0	0--	-	5.49	5.52
2002	HOU	NL	55	0	0	19	69.0	310	67	37	34	3	5	2	5	38	8	48	2	0	3	3	.500	0	0-0	2	4.15	4.43
2003	HOU	NL	13	0	0	4	21.0	99	24	13	12	2	2	0	1	16	3	10	1	0	0	0	-	0	0-1	1	6.46	5.14
2004	SD	NL	14	0	0	9	18.0	89	24	13	11	3	2	0	1	11	1	12	0	0	0	1	.000	0	0-0	0	7.59	5.50
2005	SF	NL	3	0	0	2	7.0	31	9	8	8	2	0	0	0	2	0	1	0	0	0	0	-	0	0-0	0	6.77	10.29
	4 ML YEARS		85	0	0	34	115.0	529	124	71	65	10	9	2	7	67	12	71	3	0	3	4	.429	0	0-1	3	5.23	5.09

Albert Pujols

Bats: R Throws: R Pos: 1B-158; PH-6   Ht: 6'3" Wt: 210 Born: 1/16/1980 Age: 26

Year	Team	Lg	G	AB	H	2B	3B	HR	(Hm	Rd)	TB	R	RBI	RC	TBB	IBB	SO	HBP	SH	SF	SB	CS	SB%	GDP	Avg	OBP	Slg
2001	STL	NL	161	590	194	47	4	37	(18	19)	360	112	130	132	69	6	93	9	1	7	1	3	.25	21	.329	.403	.610
2002	STL	NL	157	590	185	40	2	34	(14	20)	331	118	127	121	72	13	69	9	0	4	2	4	.33	20	.314	.394	.561
2003	STL	NL	157	591	212	51	1	43	(21	22)	394	137	124	160	79	12	65	10	0	5	5	1	.83	13	.359	.439	.667
2004	STL	NL	154	592	196	51	2	46	(18	28)	389	133	123	143	84	12	52	7	0	9	5	5	.50	21	.331	.415	.657
2005	STL	NL	161	591	195	38	2	41	(23	18)	360	129	117	139	97	27	65	9	0	3	16	2	.89	19	.330	.430	.609
	5 ML YEARS		790	2954	982	227	11	201	(94	107)	1834	629	621	695	401	70	344	44	1	28	29	15	.66	94	.332	.416	.621

Bill Pulsipher

Pitches: L Bats: L Pos: RP-5   Ht: 6'3" Wt: 200 Born: 10/9/1973 Age: 32

Year	Team	Lg	G	GS	CG	GF	IP	BFP	H	R	ER	HR	SH	SF	HB	TBB	IBB	SO	WP	Bk	W	L	Pct	ShO	Sv-Op	Hld	ERC	ERA
2005	Sprgfld*	AA	1	1	0	0	6.2	29	8	2	2	2	0	0	0	1	0	7	1	0	1	0	1.000	0	0--	-	5.47	2.70
2005	Memp*	AAA	25	18	0	1	124.1	554	152	72	62	17	6	2	2	29	2	96	3	0	7	7	.462	0	0--	-	4.88	4.49
1995	NYN	NL	17	17	2	0	126.2	530	122	58	56	11	0	0	1	45	0	81	2	1	5	7	.417	0	0-0	0	3.69	3.98
1998	2 Tms	NL	26	11	0	2	72.1	320	86	41	41	8	4	4	1	31	4	51	2	2	3	4	.429	0	0-1	2	5.46	5.10

Year	Team	Lg	G	GS	CG	GF	IP	BFP	H	R	ER	HR	SH	SF	HB	TBB	IBB	SO	WP	Bk	W	L	Pct	ShO	Sv-Op	Hld	ERC	ERA
			HOW MUCH HE PITCHED						**WHAT HE GAVE UP**												**THE RESULTS**							
1999	MIL	NL	19	16	0	0	87.1	398	100	65	58	19	6	4	2	36	2	42	2	0	5	6	.455	0	0-0	0	5.81	5.98
2000	NYN	NL	2	2	0	0	6.2	39	12	9	9	1	1	0	1	6	0	7	0	0	0	2	.000	0	0-0	0	12.44	12.15
2001	2 Tms	AL	37	0	0	8	30.0	146	36	23	20	5	0	2	3	21	0	20	1	0	0	0	-	0	0-0	6	7.56	6.00
2005	STL	NL	5	0	0	2	4.0	19	5	3	3	0	2	1	0	2	1	1	0	0	0	0	-	0	0-0	0	4.53	6.75
98	NYM	NL	15	1	0	1	14.1	68	23	11	11	2	1	0	0	5	1	13	0	0	0	0	-	0	0-1	2	7.92	6.91
98	Mil	NL	11	10	0	1	58.0	252	63	30	30	6	3	4	1	26	3	38	2	2	3	4	.429	0	0-0	0	4.90	4.66
01	CWS	AL	14	0	0	2	8.0	44	11	8	7	2	0	1	1	7	0	4	0	0	0	0	-	0	0-2	2	9.96	7.88
01	Bos	AL	23	0	0	6	22.0	102	25	15	13	3	0	1	2	14	0	16	1	0	0	0	-	0	0-0	4	6.71	5.32
6 ML YEARS			106	46	2	13	327.0	1452	361	199	187	44	13	11	8	141	7	202	7	3	13	19	.406	0	0-1	8	5.15	5.15

Nick Punto

Bats: B **Throws:** R **Pos:** 2B-73; SS-34; 3B-12; PR-8; DH-3; CF-2; PH-2; RF-1 **Ht:** 5'9" **Wt:** 170 **Born:** 11/8/1977 **Age:** 28

Year	Team	Lg	G	AB	H	2B	3B	HR	(Hm	Rd)	TB	R	RBI	RC	TBB	IBB	SO	HBP	SH	SF	SB	CS	SB%	GDP	Avg	OBP	Slg
			BATTING																		**BASERUNNING**				**AVERAGES**		
2005	Roch*	AAA	4	15	3	1	0	0	(-	-)	4	2	1	1	2	0	2	0	0	0	0	0	-	0	.200	.294	.267
2001	PHI	NL	4	5	2	0	0	0	(0	0)	2	0	0	1	0	0	0	0	0	0	0	0	-	0	.400	.400	.400
2002	PHI	NL	9	6	1	0	0	0	(0	0)	1	0	0	0	0	0	3	0	1	0	0	0	-	0	.167	.167	.167
2003	PHI	NL	64	92	20	2	0	1	(0	1)	25	14	4	7	7	1	22	0	0	0	2	1	.67	0	.217	.273	.272
2004	MIN	AL	38	91	23	0	0	2	(2	0)	29	17	12	15	12	0	19	0	0	0	6	0	1.00	2	.253	.340	.319
2005	MIN	AL	112	394	94	18	4	4	(3	1)	132	45	26	35	36	0	86	0	7	2	13	8	.62	9	.239	.301	.335
5 ML YEARS			227	588	140	20	4	7	(5	2)	189	76	42	58	55	1	130	0	8	2	21	9	.70	11	.238	.302	.321

J.J. Putz

Pitches: R **Bats:** R **Pos:** RP-64 **Ht:** 6'5" **Wt:** 220 **Born:** 2/22/1977 **Age:** 29

Year	Team	Lg	G	GS	CG	GF	IP	BFP	H	R	ER	HR	SH	SF	HB	TBB	IBB	SO	WP	Bk	W	L	Pct	ShO	Sv-Op	Hld	ERC	ERA
			HOW MUCH HE PITCHED						**WHAT HE GAVE UP**												**THE RESULTS**							
2003	SEA	AL	3	0	0	0	3.2	18	4	2	2	0	0	0	0	3	0	3	0	0	0	0	-	0	0-0	0	5.31	4.91
2004	SEA	AL	54	0	0	30	63.0	275	66	35	33	10	3	2	5	24	4	47	1	0	0	3	.000	0	9-13	3	4.97	4.71
2005	SEA	AL	64	0	0	20	60.0	259	58	27	24	8	3	3	2	23	2	45	2	0	6	5	.545	0	1-4	21	4.11	3.60
3 ML YEARS			121	0	0	50	126.2	552	128	64	59	18	6	5	7	50	6	95	3	0	6	8	.429	0	10-17	24	4.57	4.19

Chad Qualls

Pitches: R **Bats:** R **Pos:** RP-77 **Ht:** 6'5" **Wt:** 220 **Born:** 8/17/1978 **Age:** 27

Year	Team	Lg	G	GS	CG	GF	IP	BFP	H	R	ER	HR	SH	SF	HB	TBB	IBB	SO	WP	Bk	W	L	Pct	ShO	Sv-Op	Hld	ERC	ERA
			HOW MUCH HE PITCHED						**WHAT HE GAVE UP**												**THE RESULTS**							
2001	Mich	A	26	26	3	0	162.0	673	149	77	67	8	2	6	11	31	0	125	10	2	15	6	.714	2	0--	-	2.51	3.72
2002	RdRck	AA	29	29	0	0	163.0	722	174	92	79	3	3	6	9	67	3	142	3	4	6	13	.316	0	0--	-	4.08	4.36
2003	RdRck	AA	28	28	3	0	175.1	744	174	85	75	12	6	8	10	61	0	132	8	0	8	11	.421	2	0--	-	3.89	3.85
2004	NewOrl	AAA	32	14	1	8	106.2	483	134	69	66	8	7	8	7	30	3	72	2	0	3	6	.333	0	1--	-	5.06	5.57
2004	HOU	NL	25	0	0	4	33.0	141	34	13	13	3	0	1	4	8	1	24	0	0	4	0	1.000	0	1-2	9	4.02	3.55
2005	HOU	NL	77	0	0	19	79.2	329	73	33	29	7	4	3	6	23	2	60	1	0	6	4	.600	0	0-0	22	3.42	3.28
2 ML YEARS			102	0	0	23	112.2	470	107	46	42	10	4	4	10	31	3	84	1	0	10	4	.714	0	1-2	31	3.60	3.36

Paul Quantrill

Pitches: R **Bats:** L **Pos:** RP-50 **Ht:** 6'1" **Wt:** 195 **Born:** 11/3/1968 **Age:** 37

Year	Team	Lg	G	GS	CG	GF	IP	BFP	H	R	ER	HR	SH	SF	HB	TBB	IBB	SO	WP	Bk	W	L	Pct	ShO	Sv-Op	Hld	ERC	ERA
			HOW MUCH HE PITCHED						**WHAT HE GAVE UP**												**THE RESULTS**							
1992	BOS	AL	27	0	0	10	49.1	213	55	18	12	1	4	2	1	15	5	24	1	0	2	3	.400	0	1-5	3	3.70	2.19
1993	BOS	AL	49	14	1	8	138.0	594	151	73	60	13	4	2	2	44	14	66	0	1	6	12	.333	1	1-2	3	4.16	3.91
1994	2 Tms	AL	35	1	0	9	53.0	236	64	31	29	7	5	3	5	15	4	28	0	2	3	3	.500	0	1-4	3	5.34	4.92
1995	PHI	NL	33	29	0	1	179.1	784	212	102	93	20	9	6	6	44	3	103	0	3	11	12	.478	0	0-0	4	4.67	4.67
1996	TOR	AL	38	20	0	7	134.1	609	172	90	81	27	5	7	2	51	3	86	1	1	5	14	.263	0	0-2	1	6.52	5.43
1997	TOR	AL	77	0	0	29	88.0	373	103	25	19	5	5	3	1	17	3	56	1	0	6	7	.462	0	5-10	16	3.94	1.94
1998	TOR	AL	82	0	0	32	80.0	345	88	26	23	5	7	4	3	22	6	59	1	0	3	4	.429	0	7-14	27	3.90	2.59
1999	TOR	AL	41	0	0	13	48.2	212	53	19	18	5	1	2	4	17	1	28	0	0	3	2	.600	0	0-4	8	4.77	3.33
2000	TOR	AL	68	0	0	24	83.2	367	100	45	42	7	1	3	2	25	1	47	1	0	2	5	.286	0	1-3	13	4.78	4.52
2001	TOR	AL	80	0	0	20	83.0	341	86	29	28	6	7	2	6	12	7	58	0	0	11	2	.846	0	2-9	21	3.31	3.04
2002	LA	NL	86	0	0	22	76.2	330	80	27	23	1	1	1	3	25	7	53	0	0	5	4	.556	0	1-3	33	3.42	2.70
2003	LA	NL	89	0	0	21	77.1	291	61	18	15	2	4	0	3	15	2	44	0	0	2	5	.286	0	1-5	28	2.03	1.75
2004	NYA	AL	86	0	0	17	95.1	424	124	54	50	5	3	4	2	20	9	37	0	0	7	3	.700	0	1-5	22	4.68	4.72
2005	3 Tms		50	0	0	15	69.0	309	93	44	41	8	0	10	3	14	3	36	0	1	2	2	.500	0	0-1	1	5.53	5.35
94	Bos	AL	17	0	0	4	23.0	101	25	10	9	4	2	2	2	5	1	15	0	0	1	1	.500	0	0-2	2	4.53	3.52
94	Phi	NL	18	1	0	5	30.0	135	39	21	20	3	3	1	3	10	3	13	0	2	2	2	.500	0	1-2	1	5.97	6.00
05	NYY	AL	22	0	0	6	32.0	149	48	24	24	5	0	7	2	7	2	11	0	1	1	0	1.000	0	0-1	0	6.94	6.75
05	SD	NL	22	0	0	7	31.2	132	37	13	12	2	0	3	1	2	1	24	0	0	1	1	.500	0	0-0	1	3.52	3.41
05	Fla	NL	6	0	0	2	5.1	28	8	7	5	1	0	0	0	5	0	1	0	0	0	1	.000	0	0-0	0	10.55	8.44
14 ML YEARS			841	64	1	228	1255.2	5428	1442	601	534	112	56	49	45	336	68	725	5	8	68	78	.466	1	21-67	179	4.40	3.83

Robb Quinlan

Bats: R **Throws:** R **Pos:** 3B-33; PH-12; 1B-9; LF-6; PR-1 **Ht:** 6'1" **Wt:** 195 **Born:** 3/17/1977 **Age:** 29

Year	Team	Lg	G	AB	H	2B	3B	HR	(Hm	Rd)	TB	R	RBI	RC	TBB	IBB	SO	HBP	SH	SF	SB	CS	SB%	GDP	Avg	OBP	Slg
			BATTING																		**BASERUNNING**				**AVERAGES**		
2005	Angels*	R	4	12	3	2	0	0	(-	-)	5	3	3	2	2	0	3	0	0	1	1	0	1.00	0	.250	.333	.417
2005	Salt Lk*	AAA	15	60	23	6	0	1	(-	-)	32	13	4	12	2	0	8	0	0	0	0	0	-	4	.383	.403	.533
2003	ANA	AL	38	94	27	4	2	0	(0	0)	35	13	4	8	6	0	16	0	1	0	1	2	.33	3	.287	.330	.372

Year	Team	Lg	G	AB	H	2B	3B	HR	(Hm	Rd)	TB	R	RBI	RC	TBB	IBB	SO	HBP	SH	SF	SB	CS	SB%	GDP	Avg	OBP	Slg
2004	ANA	AL	56	160	55	14	0	5	(3	2)	84	23	23	33	14	0	26	2	0	1	3	1	.75	1	.344	.401	.525
2005	LAA	AL	54	134	31	8	0	5	(3	2)	54	17	14	11	7	0	26	1	0	1	0	1	.00	4	.231	.273	.403
	3 ML YEARS		148	388	113	26	2	10	(6	4)	173	53	41	52	27	0	68	3	1	2	4	4	.50	8	.291	.340	.446

Omar Quintanilla

Bats: L **Throws:** R **Pos:** SS-31; 2B-6; PR-2   **Ht:** 5'9" **Wt:** 190 **Born:** 10/24/1981 **Age:** 24

BATTING

Year	Team	Lg	G	AB	H	2B	3B	HR	(Hm	Rd)	TB	R	RBI	RC	TBB	IBB	SO	HBP	SH	SF	SB	CS	SB%	GDP	Avg	OBP	Slg
2003	Mdest	A+	8	36	15	3	0	2	(-	-)	24	9	6	9	3	0	6	0	0	0	0	0	-	0	.417	.462	.667
2003	Vancvr	A-	32	129	44	5	4	0	(-	-)	57	22	14	24	12	0	20	1	1	0	7	1	.88	3	.341	.401	.442
2004	Mdest	A+	108	452	142	32	5	11	(-	-)	217	75	72	80	37	1	54	1	6	3	1	3	.25	11	.314	.370	.480
2004	Mdland	AA	23	94	33	10	0	2	(-	-)	49	20	20	20	10	0	9	1	0	0	2	0	1.00	1	.351	.419	.521
2005	Mdland	AA	78	294	86	14	2	4	(-	-)	116	46	25	41	23	1	40	2	1	1	2	3	.40	5	.293	.347	.395
2005	ColSpr	AAA	13	52	18	3	2	1	(-	-)	28	14	7	10	3	0	8	0	1	1	0	0	-	1	.346	.375	.538
2005	COL	NL	39	128	28	1	1	0	(0	0)	31	16	7	9	9	0	15	0	6	0	2	1	.67	3	.219	.270	.242

Humberto Quintero

Bats: R **Throws:** R **Pos:** C-16; PH-3; 1B-1   **Ht:** 6'1" **Wt:** 190 **Born:** 8/8/1979 **Age:** 26

BATTING

Year	Team	Lg	G	AB	H	2B	3B	HR	(Hm	Rd)	TB	R	RBI	RC	TBB	IBB	SO	HBP	SH	SF	SB	CS	SB%	GDP	Avg	OBP	Slg
2005	CpChr*	AA	4	11	2	1	0	0	(-	-)	3	0	1	0	1	1	2	0	0	0	0	0	-	1	.182	.250	.273
2005	RdRck*	AAA	52	191	55	13	0	8	(-	-)	92	23	31	30	10	1	30	2	0	2	2	1	.67	2	.288	.327	.482
2003	SD	NL	12	23	5	0	0	0	(-	-)	5	1	2	2	1	1	6	0	0	0	0	0	-	0	.217	.250	.217
2004	SD	NL	23	72	18	3	0	2	(1	1)	27	7	10	6	5	0	16	0	0	1	0	2	.00	4	.250	.295	.375
2005	HOU	NL	18	54	10	1	0	1	(1	0)	14	6	8	2	1	1	10	0	2	0	0	0	-	3	.185	.200	.259
	3 ML YEARS		53	149	33	4	0	3	(2	1)	46	14	20	10	7	2	32	0	2	1	0	2	.00	8	.221	.255	.309

Guillermo Quiroz

Bats: R **Throws:** R **Pos:** C-10; DH-2   **Ht:** 6'1" **Wt:** 202 **Born:** 11/29/1981 **Age:** 24

BATTING

Year	Team	Lg	G	AB	H	2B	3B	HR	(Hm	Rd)	TB	R	RBI	RC	TBB	IBB	SO	HBP	SH	SF	SB	CS	SB%	GDP	Avg	OBP	Slg
1999	MdHat	R+	63	208	46	7	0	9	(-	-)	80	25	28	22	18	0	55	4	2	0	0	2	.00	4	.221	.296	.385
2000	Queens	A-	55	196	44	9	0	5	(-	-)	68	27	29	22	27	0	48	4	0	1	1	2	.33	4	.224	.329	.347
2000	Hgrstn	A	43	136	22	4	0	1	(-	-)	29	14	12	7	16	0	44	4	3	0	0	1	.00	3	.162	.269	.213
2001	CtnWV	A	82	261	52	12	0	7	(-	-)	85	25	25	25	29	0	67	6	7	0	5	1	.83	5	.199	.294	.326
2002	Dnedin	A+	111	411	107	28	1	12	(-	-)	173	50	68	52	35	2	91	9	2	3	1	0	1.00	18	.260	.330	.421
2002	Syrcse	AAA	13	45	10	4	0	1	(-	-)	17	7	6	4	3	0	14	0	1	0	0	0	-	1	.222	.271	.378
2003	NwHav	AA	108	369	104	27	0	20	(-	-)	191	63	79	67	45	1	83	12	1	7	0	0	-	13	.282	.372	.518
2004	Syrcse	AAA	76	255	58	19	1	8	(-	-)	103	32	32	29	28	1	54	3	0	2	0	0	-	8	.227	.309	.404
2005	Dnedin	A+	11	38	9	1	0	2	(-	-)	16	4	6	5	2	0	8	3	0	0	0	0	-	1	.237	.326	.421
2005	Syrcse	AAA	25	83	19	3	0	6	(-	-)	40	11	18	13	9	1	19	2	0	1	0	0	-	5	.229	.316	.482
2004	TOR	AL	17	52	11	2	0	0	(0	0)	13	2	6	4	2	0	8	2	0	1	1	0	1.00	1	.212	.263	.250
2005	TOR	AL	12	36	7	2	0	0	(0	0)	9	3	4	3	2	0	13	1	0	0	0	0	-	0	.194	.256	.250
	2 ML YEARS		29	88	18	4	0	0	(0	0)	22	5	10	7	4	0	21	3	0	1	1	0	1.00	1	.205	.260	.250

Brad Radke

Pitches: R **Bats:** R **Pos:** SP-31   **Ht:** 6'2" **Wt:** 188 **Born:** 10/27/1972 **Age:** 33

			HOW MUCH HE PITCHED						WHAT HE GAVE UP											THE RESULTS						
Year	Team	Lg	G	GS	CG	GF	IP	BFP	H	R	ER	HR	SH	SF	HB	TBB	IBB	SO	WP	Bk	W	L	Pct	ShO	Sv-Op Hld	ERC	ERA
1995	MIN	AL	29	28	2	0	181.0	772	195	112	107	32	2	9	4	47	0	75	4	0	11	14	.440	1	0-0 0	4.58	5.32
1996	MIN	AL	35	35	3	0	232.0	973	231	125	115	40	5	6	4	57	2	148	1	0	11	16	.407	0	0-0 0	3.97	4.46
1997	MIN	AL	35	35	4	0	239.2	989	238	114	103	28	9	3	9	48	1	174	1	1	20	10	.667	1	0-0 0	3.41	3.87
1998	MIN	AL	32	32	5	0	213.2	904	238	109	102	23	9	3	9	43	1	146	3	1	12	14	.462	1	0-0 0	4.18	4.30
1999	MIN	AL	33	33	4	0	218.2	910	239	97	91	28	5	5	1	44	0	121	4	0	12	14	.462	0	0-0 0	4.07	3.75
2000	MIN	AL	34	34	4	0	226.2	978	261	119	112	27	7	4	5	51	1	141	5	0	12	16	.429	1	0-0 0	4.44	4.45
2001	MIN	AL	33	33	6	0	226.0	919	235	105	99	24	10	6	10	26	0	137	4	1	15	11	.577	2	0-0 0	3.45	3.94
2002	MIN	AL	21	21	2	0	118.1	490	124	64	62	12	2	5	7	20	0	62	0	0	9	5	.643	1	0-0 0	3.73	4.72
2003	MIN	AL	33	33	3	0	212.1	888	242	111	106	32	12	4	5	28	2	120	0	0	14	10	.583	1	0-0 0	4.24	4.49
2004	MIN	AL	34	34	1	0	219.2	901	229	92	85	23	5	5	6	26	1	143	2	0	11	8	.579	1	0-0 0	3.35	3.48
2005	MIN	AL	31	31	3	0	200.2	831	214	98	90	33	4	10	7	23	1	117	2	0	9	12	.429	1	0-0 0	3.86	4.04
	11 ML YEARS		350	349	37	0	2288.2	9555	2446	1146	1072	302	63	66	61	413	9	1384	26	3	136	130	.511	10	0-0 0	3.92	4.22

Aaron Rakers

Pitches: R **Bats:** R **Pos:** RP-10   **Ht:** 6'3" **Wt:** 205 **Born:** 1/22/1977 **Age:** 29

			HOW MUCH HE PITCHED						WHAT HE GAVE UP											THE RESULTS						
Year	Team	Lg	G	GS	CG	GF	IP	BFP	H	R	ER	HR	SH	SF	HB	TBB	IBB	SO	WP	Bk	W	L	Pct	ShO	Sv-Op Hld	ERC	ERA
1999	Bluefld	R+	3	0	0	1	7.0	28	5	2	2	1	0	0	0	3	0	12	0	0	0	0	-	0	- -	3.01	2.57
1999	Dlmrva	A	18	0	0	16	25.1	97	9	6	4	0	0	1	0	13	0	38	1	1	4	1	.800	0	8- -	1.05	1.42
2000	Frdrck	A+	26	0	0	19	40.2	157	23	8	7	2	0	2	2	12	1	57	1	0	1	1	.500	0	8- -	1.48	1.55
2000	Bowie	AA	24	0	0	18	29.0	118	20	11	9	5	1	3	1	10	0	21	0	0	3	2	.600	0	8- -	2.76	2.79
2001	Bowie	AA	51	0	0	39	60.1	257	53	21	16	4	1	1	1	20	1	74	4	0	4	4	.500	0	14- -	3.38	2.39
2002	Bowie	AA	31	0	0	29	48.0	189	39	12	11	3	5	3	1	12	2	45	1	0	5	1	.833	0	10- -	2.38	2.06
2003	Bowie	AA	31	0	0	21	39.1	161	27	12	12	7	2	0	2	19	1	42	1	0	5	0	1.000	0	8- -	3.43	2.75
2003	Ottawa	AAA	21	0	0	8	26.1	111	19	18	15	1	0	2	1	11	2	26	3	0	2	4	.333	0	1- -	2.38	5.13
2004	Ottawa	AAA	54	1	0	18	78.2	326	65	27	24	8	0	1	2	25	4	80	2	0	4	5	.444	0	1- -	2.83	2.75

Year	Team	Lg	G	GS	CG	GF	IP	BFP	H	R	ER	HR	SH	SF	HB	TBB	IBB	SO	WP	Bk	W	L	Pct	ShO	Sv-Op	Hld	ERC	ERA
2005	Ottawa	AAA	57	0	0	34	77.0	321	69	26	22	9	6	0	1	21	5	92	2	0	6	5	.545	0	7--	-	3.04	2.57
2004	BAL	AL	3	0	0	1	4.1	19	5	2	2	0	0	0	0	1	0	3	0	0	0	0	-	0	0-0	0	3.47	4.15
2005	BAL	AL	10	0	0	1	13.2	55	11	5	5	3	0	2	0	3	0	11	0	0	1	0	1.000	0	0-0	1	3.01	3.29
	2 ML YEARS		13	0	0	2	18.0	74	16	7	7	3	0	2	0	4	0	14	0	0	1	0	1.000	0	0-0	1	3.15	3.50

Aramis Ramirez

Bats: R Throws: R Pos: 3B-119; PH-4   Ht: 6'1" Wt: 211 Born: 6/25/1978 Age: 28

								BATTING														BASERUNNING				AVERAGES		
Year	Team	Lg	G	AB	H	2B	3B	HR	(Hm	Rd)	TB	R	RBI	RC	TBB	IBB	SO	HBP	SH	SF	SB	CS	SB%	GDP	Avg	OBP	Slg
1998	PIT	NL	72	251	59	9	1	6	(3	3)	88	23	24	26	18	0	72	4	1	1	0	1	.00	3	.235	.296	.351
1999	PIT	NL	18	56	10	2	1	0	(0	0)	14	2	7	4	6	0	9	0	1	1	0	0	-	0	.179	.254	.250
2000	PIT	NL	73	254	65	15	2	6	(4	2)	102	19	35	28	10	0	36	5	1	4	0	0	-	9	.256	.293	.402
2001	PIT	NL	158	603	181	40	0	34	(16	18)	323	83	112	108	40	4	100	8	0	4	5	4	.56	9	.300	.350	.536
2002	PIT	NL	142	522	122	26	0	18	(7	11)	202	51	71	49	29	3	95	8	0	11	2	0	1.00	17	.234	.279	.387
2003	2 Tms	NL	159	607	165	32	2	27	(10	17)	282	75	106	88	42	3	99	10	0	11	2	2	.50	21	.272	.324	.465
2004	CHN	NL	145	547	174	32	1	36	(22	14)	316	99	103	100	49	6	62	3	0	7	0	2	.00	25	.318	.373	.578
2005	CHN	NL	123	463	140	30	0	31	(11	20)	263	72	92	79	35	4	60	6	0	2	0	1	.00	15	.302	.358	.568
03	Pit	NL	96	375	105	25	1	12	(6	6)	168	44	67	49	25	3	68	7	0	8	1	1	.50	17	.280	.330	.448
03	ChC	NL	63	232	60	7	1	15	(4	11)	114	31	39	39	17	0	31	3	0	3	1	1	.50	4	.259	.314	.491
	8 ML YEARS		890	3303	916	186	7	158	(73	85)	1590	424	550	482	229	20	533	44	3	41	9	10	.47	99	.277	.329	.481

Elizardo Ramirez

Pitches: R Bats: L Pos: SP-4; RP-2   Ht: 6'0" Wt: 180 Born: 1/28/1983 Age: 23

				HOW MUCH HE PITCHED						WHAT HE GAVE UP								THE RESULTS							
Year	Team	Lg	G	GS	CG	GF	IP	BFP	H	R	ER	HR	SH	SF	HB	TBB	IBB	SO	WP	Bk	W	L	Pct	ShO	Sv-Op	Hld	ERC	ERA
2002	Phillies	R	11	11	2	0	73.1	275	44	18	9	3	3	1	3	2	0	73	3	1	7	1	.875	1	0--	-	0.97	1.10
2003	Clrwtr	A+	27	25	1	0	157.1	668	181	85	66	4	4	2	4	33	0	101	4	2	13	9	.591	0	0--	-	3.78	3.78
2004	Clrwtr	A+	9	9	1	0	59.0	230	55	17	16	3	1	1	4	8	0	33	0	0	5	1	.833	0	0--	-	2.79	2.44
2004	Chatt	AA	5	5	1	0	31.0	129	35	11	11	6	1	1	2	4	1	23	0	0	1	0	1.000	1	0--	-	4.66	3.19
2004	Rdng	AA	8	8	1	0	33.2	162	51	34	25	4	2	4	1	14	1	20	1	1	2	5	.286	0	0--	-	7.56	6.68
2005	Lsvlle	AAA	21	21	0	0	131.1	562	150	63	55	14	3	2	3	18	1	82	3	5	7	7	.500	0	0--	-	3.88	3.77
2004	PHI	NL	7	0	0	5	15.0	67	17	8	8	3	0	1	1	5	1	9	1	0	0	0	-	0	0-0	0	5.44	4.80
2005	CIN	NL	6	4	0	1	22.1	110	33	22	21	5	2	0	2	10	2	9	2	0	0	3	.000	0	0-0	0	8.45	8.46
	2 ML YEARS		13	4	0	6	37.1	177	50	30	29	8	2	1	3	15	3	18	3	0	0	3	.000	0	0-0	0	7.20	6.99

Erasmo Ramirez

Pitches: L Bats: L Pos: RP-16   Ht: 6'0" Wt: 180 Born: 4/29/1976 Age: 30

				HOW MUCH HE PITCHED						WHAT HE GAVE UP								THE RESULTS							
Year	Team	Lg	G	GS	CG	GF	IP	BFP	H	R	ER	HR	SH	SF	HB	TBB	IBB	SO	WP	Bk	W	L	Pct	ShO	Sv-Op	Hld	ERC	ERA
2005	Okla*	AAA	16	0	0	8	19.0	81	19	10	8	3	0	1	3	5	0	11	0	0	0	0	-	0	1--	-	4.66	3.79
2003	TEX	AL	34	0	0	9	49.0	200	46	21	21	4	2	2	4	9	0	28	1	0	3	1	.750	0	0-1	2	3.15	3.86
2004	TEX	AL	34	0	0	6	35.2	148	34	19	17	5	2	1	3	7	1	21	1	0	5	3	.625	0	0-2	3	3.58	4.29
2005	TEX	AL	16	0	0	4	23.0	96	24	10	10	3	3	0	2	3	0	6	0	0	0	0	-	0	0-1	0	3.81	3.91
	3 ML YEARS		84	0	0	19	107.2	444	104	50	48	12	7	3	9	19	1	55	2	0	8	4	.667	0	0-4	5	3.43	4.01

Hanley Ramirez

Bats: R Throws: R Pos: SS-2; PH-1   Ht: 6'3" Wt: 195 Born: 12/23/1983 Age: 22

								BATTING														BASERUNNING				AVERAGES		
Year	Team	Lg	G	AB	H	2B	3B	HR	(Hm	Rd)	TB	R	RBI	RC	TBB	IBB	SO	HBP	SH	SF	SB	CS	SB%	GDP	Avg	OBP	Slg
2002	RedSx	R	45	164	56	11	3	6	(-	-)	91	29	26	35	16	1	15	2	0	2	8	6	.57	5	.341	.402	.555
2002	Lowell	A-	22	97	36	9	2	1	(-	-)	52	17	19	19	4	0	14	2	0	2	4	3	.57	2	.371	.400	.536
2003	Augsta	A	111	422	116	24	3	8	(-	-)	170	69	50	59	32	0	73	2	5	3	36	13	.73	12	.275	.327	.403
2004	RedSx	R	6	20	8	0	1	0	(-	-)	10	5	7	5	2	0	3	2	0	2	1	0	1.00	1	.400	.462	.500
2004	Srsota	A+	62	239	74	8	4	1	(-	-)	93	33	24	35	17	1	39	4	2	1	12	7	.63	2	.310	.364	.389
2004	Portlnd	AA	32	129	40	7	2	5	(-	-)	66	26	15	24	10	0	26	0	0	0	12	3	.80	5	.310	.360	.512
2005	Portlnd	AA	122	465	126	21	7	6	(-	-)	179	66	52	63	39	1	62	7	6	3	26	13	.67	12	.271	.335	.385
2005	BOS	AL	2	2	0	0	0	0	(0	0)	0	0	0	0	0	0	2	0	0	0	0	0	-	0	.000	.000	.000

Horacio Ramirez

Pitches: L Bats: L Pos: SP-32; RP-1   Ht: 6'1" Wt: 170 Born: 11/24/1979 Age: 26

				HOW MUCH HE PITCHED						WHAT HE GAVE UP								THE RESULTS							
Year	Team	Lg	G	GS	CG	GF	IP	BFP	H	R	ER	HR	SH	SF	HB	TBB	IBB	SO	WP	Bk	W	L	Pct	ShO	Sv-Op	Hld	ERC	ERA
2003	ATL	NL	29	29	1	0	182.1	781	181	91	81	21	12	3	6	72	10	100	5	1	12	4	.750	0	0-0	0	4.21	4.00
2004	ATL	NL	10	9	1	0	60.1	259	51	24	16	7	2	1	0	30	5	31	0	2	2	4	.333	0	0-0	0	3.55	2.39
2005	ATL	NL	33	32	1	0	202.1	847	214	108	104	31	13	5	2	67	4	80	4	1	11	9	.550	1	0-0	0	4.66	4.63
	3 ML YEARS		72	70	3	0	445.0	1887	446	223	201	59	27	9	8	169	19	211	9	4	25	17	.595	1	0-0	0	4.32	4.07

Julio Ramirez

Bats: R Throws: R Pos: PR-7; RF-4; CF-2; PH-2   Ht: 5'11" Wt: 170 Born: 8/10/1977 Age: 28

								BATTING												BASERUNNING				AVERAGES		
Year	Team	Lg	G	AB	H	2B	3B	HR	(Hm | Rd)	TB	R	RBI	RC	TBB	IBB	SO	HBP	SH	SF	SB	CS	SB%	GDP	Avg	OBP	Slg
2005	Fresno*	AAA	113	386	93	13	1	23	(- | -)	177	57	60	53	22	0	113	3	3	2	22	8	.73	10	.241	.286	.459
1999	FLA	NL	15	21	3	1	0	0	(0 | 0)	4	3	2	0	1	0	6	0	0	0	0	1	.00	0	.143	.182	.190
2001	CHA	AL	22	37	3	0	0	0	(0 | 0)	3	2	1	0	2	0	15	0	0	0	2	0	1.00	0	.081	.128	.081
2002	ANA	AL	29	32	9	0	1	1	(1 | 0)	14	6	7	5	2	0	14	1	0	0	0	2	.00	0	.281	.343	.438
2003	ANA	AL	6	2	0	0	0	0	(0 | 0)	0	1	0	0	0	0	0	0	1	0	0	0	-	0	.000	.000	.000
2005	SF	NL	12	4	1	0	0	0	(0 | 0)	1	3	1	1	0	0	1	0	0	0	0	0	-	0	.250	.250	.250
	5 ML YEARS		84	96	16	1	1	1	(1 | 0)	22	15	11	6	5	0	36	1	1	0	2	3	.40	0	.167	.216	.229

Manny Ramirez

Bats: R Throws: R Pos: LF-149; PH-3; DH-2   Ht: 6'0" Wt: 213 Born: 5/30/1972 Age: 34

								BATTING												BASERUNNING				AVERAGES		
Year	Team	Lg	G	AB	H	2B	3B	HR	(Hm | Rd)	TB	R	RBI	RC	TBB	IBB	SO	HBP	SH	SF	SB	CS	SB%	GDP	Avg	OBP	Slg
1993	CLE	AL	22	53	9	1	0	2	(0 | 2)	16	5	5	2	2	0	8	0	0	0	0	0	-	3	.170	.200	.302
1994	CLE	AL	91	290	78	22	0	17	(9 | 8)	151	51	60	53	42	4	72	0	0	4	4	2	.67	6	.269	.357	.521
1995	CLE	AL	137	484	149	26	1	31	(12 | 19)	270	85	107	103	75	6	112	5	2	5	6	6	.50	13	.308	.402	.558
1996	CLE	AL	152	550	170	45	3	33	(19 | 14)	320	94	112	120	85	8	104	3	0	9	8	5	.62	18	.309	.399	.582
1997	CLE	AL	150	561	184	40	0	26	(14 | 12)	302	99	88	117	79	5	115	7	0	4	2	3	.40	19	.328	.415	.538
1998	CLE	AL	150	571	168	35	2	45	(25 | 20)	342	108	145	121	76	6	121	6	0	10	5	3	.63	18	.294	.377	.599
1999	CLE	AL	147	522	174	34	3	44	(21 | 23)	346	131	165	141	96	9	131	13	0	9	2	4	.33	12	.333	.442	.663
2000	CLE	AL	118	439	154	34	2	38	(22 | 16)	306	92	122	127	86	9	117	3	0	4	1	1	.50	9	.351	.457	.697
2001	BOS	AL	142	529	162	33	2	41	(21 | 20)	322	93	125	122	81	25	147	8	0	2	0	1	-.00	9	.306	.405	.609
2002	BOS	AL	120	436	152	31	0	33	(18 | 15)	282	84	107	125	73	14	85	8	0	1	0	0	-	13	.349	.450	.647
2003	BOS	AL	154	569	185	36	1	37	(18 | 19)	334	117	104	128	97	28	94	8	0	5	3	1	.75	22	.325	.427	.587
2004	BOS	AL	152	568	175	44	0	43	(23 | 20)	348	108	130	124	82	15	124	6	0	7	2	4	.33	17	.308	.397	.613
2005	BOS	AL	152	554	162	30	1	45	(22 | 23)	329	112	144	134	80	9	119	10	0	6	1	0	1.00	20	.292	.388	.594
	13 ML YEARS		1687	6126	1922	411	15	435	(224 | 211)	3668	1179	1414	1417	954	138	1349	77	2	66	34	30	.53	179	.314	.409	.599

Joe Randa

Bats: R Throws: R Pos: 3B-142; PH-7; DH-2; PR-1   Ht: 5'11" Wt: 190 Born: 12/18/1969 Age: 36

								BATTING												BASERUNNING				AVERAGES		
Year	Team	Lg	G	AB	H	2B	3B	HR	(Hm | Rd)	TB	R	RBI	RC	TBB	IBB	SO	HBP	SH	SF	SB	CS	SB%	GDP	Avg	OBP	Slg
1995	KC	AL	34	70	12	2	0	1	(1 | 0)	17	6	5	3	6	0	17	0	0	0	0	1	.00	2	.171	.237	.243
1996	KC	AL	110	337	102	24	1	6	(2 | 4)	146	36	47	50	26	4	47	1	2	4	13	4	.76	10	.303	.351	.433
1997	PIT	NL	126	443	134	27	9	7	(5 | 2)	200	58	60	72	41	1	64	6	4	5	4	2	.67	10	.302	.366	.451
1998	DET	AL	138	460	117	21	2	9	(3 | 6)	169	56	50	54	41	1	70	7	3	3	8	7	.53	9	.254	.323	.367
1999	KC	AL	156	628	197	36	8	16	(7 | 9)	297	92	84	103	50	4	80	3	1	7	5	4	.56	15	.314	.363	.473
2000	KC	AL	158	612	186	29	4	15	(9 | 6)	268	88	106	88	36	3	66	6	1	10	6	3	.67	19	.304	.343	.438
2001	KC	AL	151	581	147	34	2	13	(8 | 5)	224	59	83	67	42	2	80	6	1	6	3	2	.60	15	.253	.307	.386
2002	KC	AL	151	549	155	36	5	11	(6 | 5)	234	63	80	77	46	1	69	9	2	11	2	1	.67	13	.282	.341	.426
2003	KC	AL	131	502	146	31	1	16	(9 | 7)	227	80	72	79	41	0	61	7	9	7	1	0	1.00	11	.291	.348	.452
2004	KC	AL	128	485	139	31	2	8	(1 | 7)	198	65	56	67	40	1	77	6	0	8	0	1	.00	11	.287	.343	.408
2005	2 Tms		150	555	153	43	2	17	(11 | 6)	251	71	68	71	47	3	81	4	0	3	0	1	.00	11	.276	.335	.452
05	Cin	NL	92	332	96	26	1	13	(9 | 4)	163	44	48	50	33	2	52	2	0	1	0	0	-	6	.289	.356	.491
05	SD	NL	58	223	57	17	1	4	(2 | 2)	88	27	20	21	14	1	29	2	0	2	0	1	.00	5	.256	.303	.395
	11 ML YEARS		1433	5222	1488	314	36	119	(62 | 57)	2231	674	711	731	416	20	712	55	23	64	42	26	.62	127	.285	.340	.427

Darrell Rasner

Pitches: R Bats: R Pos: RP-4; SP-1   Ht: 6'3" Wt: 210 Born: 1/13/1981 Age: 25

			HOW MUCH HE PITCHED						WHAT HE GAVE UP											THE RESULTS						
Year	Team	Lg	G	GS	CG	GF	IP	BFP	H	R	ER	HR	SH	SF	HB	TBB	IBB	SO	WP	Bk	W	L	Pct	ShO	Sv-Op Hld	ERC	ERA
2003	Savann	A	22	22	2	0	105.1	458	106	53	49	8	5	2	7	36	0	90	9	1	7	7	.500	0	0- - -	3.94	4.19
2004	BrvdCt	A+	22	21	0	0	119.1	522	133	55	42	6	10	4	8	31	0	88	1	1	6	5	.545	0	0- - -	4.04	3.17
2004	Hrsbrg	AA	5	5	0	0	29.2	119	21	4	4	1	3	2	2	9	1	15	0	0	1	1	.500	0	0- - -	2.01	1.21
2005	Hrsbrg	AA	27	26	1	0	150.1	630	150	66	60	10	7	5	10	29	2	96	2	0	6	7	.462	0	0- - -	3.26	3.59
2005	WAS	NL	5	1	0	1	7.1	31	5	3	3	0	1	0	2	2	1	4	0	0	0	1	.000	0	0-0 0	2.03	3.68

Jon Rauch

Pitches: R Bats: R Pos: RP-14; SP-1   Ht: 6'10" Wt: 230 Born: 9/27/1978 Age: 27

			HOW MUCH HE PITCHED						WHAT HE GAVE UP											THE RESULTS						
Year	Team	Lg	G	GS	CG	GF	IP	BFP	H	R	ER	HR	SH	SF	HB	TBB	IBB	SO	WP	Bk	W	L	Pct	ShO	Sv-Op Hld	ERC	ERA
2005	NewOr*	AAA	7	5	0	1	21.1	85	19	7	6	3	0	0	0	2	0	25	2	0	1	1	.500	0	0- - -	2.53	2.53
2002	CHA	AL	8	6	0	1	28.2	130	28	26	21	7	0	1	2	14	2	19	1	1	2	1	.667	0	0-0 0	5.41	6.59
2004	2 Tms		11	4	0	1	32.0	131	30	10	10	1	2	1	0	11	2	22	2	0	4	1	.800	0	0-0 0	3.05	2.81
2005	WAS	NL	15	1	0	4	30.0	124	24	12	12	3	1	1	1	11	2	23	2	0	2	4	.333	0	0-0 0	2.90	3.60
04	CWS	AL	2	2	0	0	8.2	43	16	6	6	0	1	1	0	4	0	4	1	0	1	1	.500	0	0-0 0	9.15	6.23
04	Mon	NL	9	2	0	1	23.1	88	14	4	4	1	1	0	0	7	2	18	1	0	3	0	1.000	0	0-0 0	1.44	1.54
	3 ML YEARS		34	11	0	6	90.2	385	82	48	43	11	3	3	3	36	6	64	5	1	8	6	.571	0	0-0 0	3.71	4.27

Chris Ray

Pitches: R Bats: R Pos: RP-41   Ht: 6'3" Wt: 200 Born: 1/12/1982 Age: 24

				HOW MUCH HE PITCHED						WHAT HE GAVE UP											THE RESULTS							
Year	Team	Lg	G	GS	CG	GF	IP	BFP	H	R	ER	HR	SH	SF	HB	TBB	IBB	SO	WP	Bk	W	L	Pct	ShO	Sv-Op	Hld	ERC	ERA
2003	Abrdn	A-	9	8	0	0	38.1	161	32	15	12	0	0	0	4	10	0	44	0	0	2	0	1.000	0	0--	-	2.36	2.82
2004	Frdrck	A+	14	14	1	0	73.1	322	82	31	31	6	5	2	1	20	0	74	3	0	6	3	.667	1	0--	-	4.07	3.80
2004	Dlmrva	A	10	9	0	0	50.0	210	43	21	19	3	3	4	5	17	0	46	1	1	2	3	.400	0	0--	-	3.21	3.42
2005	Bowie	AA	31	0	0	28	37.1	136	17	5	4	3	1	2	3	7	0	40	1	0	1	2	.333	0	18--	-	1.15	0.96
2005	BAL	AL	41	0	0	8	40.2	174	34	15	12	5	1	1	1	18	3	43	0	1	1	3	.250	0	0-4	8	3.43	2.66

Britt Reames

Pitches: R Bats: R Pos: RP-2   Ht: 5'11" Wt: 175 Born: 8/19/1973 Age: 32

				HOW MUCH HE PITCHED						WHAT HE GAVE UP											THE RESULTS							
Year	Team	Lg	G	GS	CG	GF	IP	BFP	H	R	ER	HR	SH	SF	HB	TBB	IBB	SO	WP	Bk	W	L	Pct	ShO	Sv-Op	Hld	ERC	ERA
2005	Scrmto*	AAA	42	7	0	16	92.1	403	91	46	34	3	5	3	6	35	3	85	7	0	6	6	.500	0	8--	-	3.60	3.31
2000	STL	NL	8	7	0	0	40.2	170	30	17	13	4	0	1	1	23	1	31	2	1	2	1	.667	0	0-0	0	3.39	2.88
2001	MON	NL	41	13	0	3	95.0	432	101	68	59	16	7	2	5	48	3	86	2	0	4	8	.333	0	0-1	6	5.52	5.59
2002	MON	NL	42	6	0	7	68.0	308	70	42	38	8	3	1	3	38	6	76	2	0	1	4	.200	0	0-1	6	5.04	5.03
2003	MON	NL	2	0	0	0	1.1	10	4	4	4	0	0	0	0	2	0	1	0	0	0	0	-	0	0-0	0	22.07	27.00
2005	OAK	AL	2	0	0	0	5.2	29	10	6	6	2	0	1	1	2	0	4	1	0	0	0	-	0	0-0	0	12.07	9.53
	5 ML YEARS		95	26	0	10	210.2	949	215	137	120	30	10	5	10	113	10	198	7	1	7	13	.350	0	0-2	12	5.17	5.13

Tim Redding

Pitches: R Bats: R Pos: SP-7; RP-3   Ht: 6'0" Wt: 195 Born: 2/12/1978 Age: 28

				HOW MUCH HE PITCHED						WHAT HE GAVE UP											THE RESULTS							
Year	Team	Lg	G	GS	CG	GF	IP	BFP	H	R	ER	HR	SH	SF	HB	TBB	IBB	SO	WP	Bk	W	L	Pct	ShO	Sv-Op	Hld	ERC	ERA
2005	Portlnd*	AAA	2	2	0	0	10.0	39	7	1	1	0	0	0	1	2	0	5	0	1	0	0	-	0	0--	-	1.64	0.90
2005	Clmbs*	AAA	10	10	0	0	51.1	229	62	29	29	5	1	1	2	13	0	47	0	0	3	4	.429	0	0--	-	4.74	5.08
2001	HOU	NL	13	9	0	1	55.2	249	62	38	34	11	2	3	3	24	0	55	2	0	3	1	.750	0	0-0	0	5.87	5.50
2002	HOU	NL	18	14	0	1	73.1	325	78	49	44	10	4	3	0	35	3	63	5	1	3	6	.333	0	0-0	0	4.96	5.40
2003	HOU	NL	33	32	0	0	176.0	769	179	85	72	16	7	3	7	65	4	116	3	0	10	14	.417	0	0-0	0	4.07	3.68
2004	HOU	NL	27	17	0	2	100.2	465	125	73	64	15	10	3	5	43	3	56	2	0	5	7	.417	0	0-0	0	6.14	5.72
2005	2 Tms		10	7	0	0	30.2	154	44	41	36	7	3	3	2	17	1	19	1	0	0	6	.000	0	0-0	0	8.60	10.57
05	SD	NL	9	6	0	0	29.2	143	40	35	30	7	3	3	2	13	1	17	1	0	0	5	.000	0	0-0	0	7.56	9.10
05	NYY	AL	1	1	0	0	1.0	11	4	6	6	0	0	0	0	4	0	2	0	0	0	1	.000	0	0-0	0	43.35	54.00
	5 ML YEARS		101	79	0	4	436.1	1962	488	286	250	59	26	15	17	184	11	309	13	1	21	34	.382	0	0-0	0	5.20	5.16

Mark Redman

Pitches: L Bats: L Pos: SP-30   Ht: 6'5" Wt: 245 Born: 1/5/1974 Age: 32

				HOW MUCH HE PITCHED						WHAT HE GAVE UP											THE RESULTS							
Year	Team	Lg	G	GS	CG	GF	IP	BFP	H	R	ER	HR	SH	SF	HB	TBB	IBB	SO	WP	Bk	W	L	Pct	ShO	Sv-Op	Hld	ERC	ERA
1999	MIN	AL	5	1	0	0	12.2	65	17	13	12	3	0	0	0	7	0	11	0	0	1	0	1.000	0	0-0	0	7.86	8.53
2000	MIN	AL	32	24	0	3	151.1	651	168	81	80	22	3	2	3	45	0	117	6	0	12	9	.571	0	0-0	0	4.73	4.76
2001	2 Tms	AL	11	11	0	0	58.0	261	68	32	29	7	2	0	1	23	0	33	6	0	2	6	.250	0	0-0	0	5.26	4.50
2002	DET	AL	30	30	3	0	203.0	858	211	107	95	15	5	8	6	51	2	109	11	1	8	15	.348	0	0-0	0	3.64	4.21
2003	FLA	NL	29	29	3	0	190.2	802	172	82	76	16	10	5	5	61	3	151	7	2	14	9	.609	0	0-0	0	3.17	3.59
2004	OAK	AL	32	32	2	0	191.0	832	218	110	100	28	5	7	6	68	6	102	6	1	11	12	.478	0	0-0	0	5.23	4.71
2005	PIT	NL	30	30	2	0	178.1	751	188	100	97	18	11	5	2	56	3	101	7	3	5	15	.250	1	0-0	0	4.15	4.90
01	Min	AL	9	9	0	0	49.0	219	57	26	23	6	1	0	0	19	0	29	6	0	2	4	.333	0	0-0	0	5.11	4.22
01	Det	AL	2	2	0	0	9.0	42	11	6	6	1	1	0	1	4	0	4	0	0	0	2	.000	0	0-0	0	6.12	6.00
	7 ML YEARS		169	157	10	3	985.0	4220	1042	525	489	109	36	27	24	311	14	624	43	7	53	66	.445	1	0-0	0	4.24	4.47

Tike Redman

Bats: L Throws: L Pos: CF-75; PH-59; RF-8; LF-2; PR-2   Ht: 5'11" Wt: 166 Born: 3/10/1977 Age: 29

									BATTING													BASERUNNING				AVERAGES		
Year	Team	Lg	G	AB	H	2B	3B	HR	(Hm	Rd)	TB	R	RBI	RC	TBB	IBB	SO	HBP	SH	SF	SB	CS	SB%	GDP	Avg	OBP	Slg
2000	PIT	NL	9	18	6	1	0	1	(1	0)	10	2	1	4	1	0	7	0	0	0	1	0	1.00	0	.333	.368	.556
2001	PIT	NL	37	125	28	4	1	1	(1	0)	37	8	4	8	4	0	25	0	0	1	3	5	.38	2	.224	.246	.296
2003	PIT	NL	56	230	76	16	5	3	(2	1)	111	36	19	41	14	0	18	2	2	0	7	3	.70	1	.330	.374	.483
2004	PIT	NL	155	546	153	19	4	8	(5	3)	204	65	51	61	23	2	52	3	4	5	18	6	.75	6	.280	.310	.374
2005	PIT	NL	135	319	80	12	4	2	(1	1)	106	33	26	31	19	0	27	1	2	3	4	1	.80	8	.251	.292	.332
	5 ML YEARS		392	1238	343	52	14	15	(9	6)	468	144	101	145	61	2	129	6	8	9	33	15	.69	17	.277	.312	.378

Mike Redmond

Bats: R Throws: R Pos: C-45   Ht: 5'11" Wt: 208 Born: 5/5/1971 Age: 35

									BATTING													BASERUNNING				AVERAGES		
Year	Team	Lg	G	AB	H	2B	3B	HR	(Hm	Rd)	TB	R	RBI	RC	TBB	IBB	SO	HBP	SH	SF	SB	CS	SB%	GDP	Avg	OBP	Slg
1998	FLA	NL	37	118	39	9	0	2	(1	1)	54	10	12	18	5	2	16	2	4	0	0	0	-	6	.331	.368	.458
1999	FLA	NL	84	242	73	9	0	1	(0	1)	85	22	27	33	26	2	34	5	5	0	0	0	-	8	.302	.381	.351
2000	FLA	NL	87	210	53	8	1	0	(0	0)	63	17	15	20	13	3	19	8	1	3	0	0	-	5	.252	.316	.300
2001	FLA	NL	48	141	44	4	0	4	(3	1)	60	19	14	21	13	4	13	2	1	1	0	0	-	6	.312	.376	.426
2002	FLA	NL	89	256	78	15	0	2	(1	1)	99	19	28	37	21	8	34	8	2	3	0	2	.00	4	.305	.372	.387
2003	FLA	NL	59	125	30	7	1	0	(0	0)	39	12	11	10	7	0	16	5	2	2	0	0	-	2	.240	.302	.312
2004	FLA	NL	81	246	63	15	0	2	(0	2)	84	19	25	27	14	0	28	3	3	2	1	0	1.00	10	.256	.315	.341
2005	MIN	AL	45	148	46	9	0	1	(0	1)	58	17	26	23	6	0	14	3	2	0	0	0	-	9	.311	.350	.392
	8 ML YEARS		530	1486	426	76	2	12	(5	7)	542	135	158	189	105	19	174	41	20	11	1	2	.33	50	.287	.348	.365

Jeremy Reed

Bats: L **Throws:** L **Pos:** CF-137; PH-9; PR-2   **Ht:** 6'0" **Wt:** 185 **Born:** 6/15/1981 **Age:** 25

Year	Team	Lg	G	AB	H	2B	3B	HR	(Hm	Rd)	TB	R	RBI	RC	TBB	IBB	SO	HBP	SH	SF	SB	CS	SB%	GDP	Avg	OBP	Slg
2002	Knapol	A-	57	210	67	15	0	4	(-	-)	94	37	31	35	11	1	24	11	3	4	17	5	.77	7	.319	.377	.448
2003	WinSa	A+	65	222	74	18	1	4	(-	-)	106	37	52	49	41	3	17	1	5	5	27	6	.82	5	.333	.431	.477
2003	Brham	AA	66	242	99	17	3	7	(-	-)	143	51	43	59	29	5	19	2	7	1	18	13	.58	7	.409	.474	.591
2004	Charltt	AAA	73	276	76	14	1	8	(-	-)	116	44	37	42	36	0	34	3	2	7	12	7	.63	7	.275	.357	.420
2004	Tacom	AAA	61	233	71	10	5	5	(-	-)	106	40	36	39	23	1	22	0	2	1	13	2	.87	6	.305	.366	.455
2004	SEA	AL	18	58	23	4	0	0	(0	0)	27	11	5	11	7	1	4	1	0	0	3	1	.75	2	.397	.470	.466
2005	SEA	AL	141	488	124	33	3	3	(0	3)	172	61	45	49	48	1	74	2	4	2	12	11	.52	10	.254	.322	.352
	2 ML YEARS		159	546	147	37	3	3	(0	3)	199	72	50	60	55	2	78	3	4	2	15	12	.56	12	.269	.338	.364

Keith Reed

Bats: R **Throws:** R **Pos:** RF-5; PR-3; CF-1   **Ht:** 6'4" **Wt:** 205 **Born:** 10/8/1978 **Age:** 27

Year	Team	Lg	G	AB	H	2B	3B	HR	(Hm	Rd)	TB	R	RBI	RC	TBB	IBB	SO	HBP	SH	SF	SB	CS	SB%	GDP	Avg	OBP	Slg
1999	Bluefld	R+	4	16	3	0	0	0	(-	-)	3	2	0	0	1	0	3	0	0	0	0	1	.00	0	.188	.235	.188
1999	Dlmrva	A	61	240	62	14	3	4	(-	-)	94	36	27	32	22	0	53	3	2	2	3	2	.60	4	.258	.326	.392
2000	Frdrck	A+	65	243	57	10	1	8	(-	-)	93	33	31	31	21	2	58	4	0	3	9	1	.90	4	.235	.303	.383
2000	Dlmrva	A	70	269	78	16	1	11	(-	-)	129	43	59	49	25	5	56	5	1	3	20	4	.83	3	.290	.358	.480
2001	Frdrck	A+	72	267	72	14	0	7	(-	-)	107	28	29	32	13	1	57	1	1	1	8	6	.57	7	.270	.305	.401
2001	Bowie	AA	18	67	17	3	0	1	(-	-)	23	7	8	7	6	0	10	0	0	0	2	2	.50	3	.254	.315	.343
2001	Roch	AAA	20	74	23	7	1	2	(-	-)	38	11	11	13	5	0	14	0	0	0	1	1	.50	1	.311	.354	.514
2002	Bowie	AA	137	488	120	20	1	15	(-	-)	187	57	64	58	40	0	107	10	2	3	3	10	.23	13	.246	.314	.383
2003	Bowie	AA	114	419	108	11	1	10	(-	-)	151	63	39	49	31	1	94	5	4	4	16	9	.64	7	.258	.314	.360
2004	Bowie	AA	121	464	137	32	0	16	(-	-)	217	62	65	74	31	2	101	6	1	3	3	6	.33	12	.295	.345	.468
2005	Abrdn	A-	16	62	16	2	0	4	(-	-)	30	10	11	10	7	1	18	0	0	0	2	0	1.00	0	.258	.333	.484
2005	Ottawa	AAA	80	271	79	19	1	8	(-	-)	124	39	37	38	10	0	55	1	1	3	1	3	.25	5	.292	.316	.458
2005	BAL	AL	6	5	1	0	0	0	(0	0)	1	1	1	1	1	0	2	0	0	0	0	0	-	0	.200	.333	.200

Steve Reed

Pitches: R **Bats:** R **Pos:** RP-30   **Ht:** 6'2" **Wt:** 212 **Born:** 3/11/1965 **Age:** 41

Year	Team	Lg	G	GS	CG	GF	IP	BFP	H	R	ER	HR	SH	SF	HB	TBB	IBB	SO	WP	Bk	W	L	Pct	ShO	Sv-Op	Hld	ERC	ERA
1992	SF	NL	18	0	0	2	15.2	63	13	5	4	2	0	0	1	3	0	11	0	0	1	0	1.000	0	0-0	1	2.80	2.30
1993	COL	NL	64	0	0	14	84.1	347	80	47	42	13	2	3	3	30	5	51	1	0	9	5	.643	0	3-6	9	4.19	4.48
1994	COL	NL	61	0	0	11	64.0	297	79	33	28	9	0	7	6	26	3	51	1	0	3	2	.600	0	3-10	14	6.09	3.94
1995	COL	NL	71	0	0	15	84.0	327	61	24	20	8	3	1	1	21	3	79	0	2	5	2	.714	0	3-6	11	2.11	2.14
1996	COL	NL	70	0	0	7	75.0	307	66	38	33	11	2	4	6	19	0	51	1	0	4	3	.571	0	0-6	22	3.52	3.96
1997	COL	NL	63	0	0	23	62.1	260	49	28	28	10	3	1	5	27	1	43	0	0	4	6	.400	0	6-13	10	3.78	4.04
1998	2 Tms		70	0	0	19	80.1	322	56	29	28	8	2	0	5	27	5	73	0	0	4	3	.571	0	1-6	21	2.42	3.14
1999	CLE	AL	63	0	0	15	61.2	274	69	33	29	10	4	5	3	20	5	44	2	0	3	2	.600	0	0-3	8	4.91	4.23
2000	CLE	AL	57	0	0	16	56.0	243	58	30	27	7	4	1	1	21	4	39	2	1	2	0	1.000	0	0-1	9	4.31	4.34
2001	2 Tms		70	0	0	14	58.1	250	52	25	23	6	3	1	3	23	5	46	0	0	3	3	.500	0	1-2	11	3.51	3.55
2002	2 Tms	NL	64	0	0	15	67.0	269	56	15	15	2	6	0	8	14	3	50	2	0	2	5	.286	0	1-4	17	2.48	2.01
2003	COL	NL	67	0	0	22	63.1	269	59	24	23	9	2	1	8	26	3	39	1	2	5	3	.625	0	0-2	14	4.61	3.27
2004	COL	NL	65	0	0	18	66.0	285	72	29	27	7	4	1	7	17	7	38	1	0	3	8	.273	0	0-4	15	4.36	3.68
2005	BAL	AL	30	0	0	6	32.2	149	41	24	24	5	0	1	4	11	2	15	0	0	1	2	.333	0	0-0	4	6.20	6.61
98	SF	NL	50	0	0	14	54.2	213	30	10	9	4	2	0	4	19	5	50	0	0	2	1	.667	0	1-5	13	1.64	1.48
98	Cle	AL	20	0	0	5	25.2	109	26	19	19	4	0	0	1	8	0	23	0	0	2	2	.500	0	0-1	8	4.38	6.66
01	Cle	AL	31	0	0	8	27.1	116	22	11	11	3	0	0	2	10	2	21	0	0	1	1	.500	0	0-1	6	3.06	3.62
01	Atl	NL	39	0	0	6	31.0	134	30	14	12	3	3	1	1	13	3	25	0	0	2	2	.500	0	1-1	5	3.92	3.48
02	SD	NL	40	0	0	11	41.0	166	33	9	9	2	5	0	6	10	2	36	1	0	2	4	.333	0	1-3	11	2.65	1.98
02	NYM	NL	24	0	0	4	26.0	103	23	6	6	0	1	0	2	4	1	14	1	0	0	1	.000	0	0-1	6	2.22	2.08
	14 ML YEARS		833	0	0	197	870.2	3662	811	384	351	107	35	26	61	285	46	630	11	5	49	44	.527	0	18-63	166	3.80	3.63

Kevin Reese

Bats: L **Throws:** L **Pos:** LF-1; CF-1; PR-1   **Ht:** 5'11" **Wt:** 195 **Born:** 3/11/1978 **Age:** 28

Year	Team	Lg	G	AB	H	2B	3B	HR	(Hm	Rd)	TB	R	RBI	RC	TBB	IBB	SO	HBP	SH	SF	SB	CS	SB%	GDP	Avg	OBP	Slg
2000	Idaho	R+	53	201	72	14	4	2	(-	-)	100	51	36	51	43	2	30	3	0	2	12	3	.80	5	.358	.474	.498
2001	FtWyn	A	125	459	151	30	6	13	(-	-)	232	84	73	96	54	3	62	5	2	4	30	10	.75	5	.329	.402	.505
2002	Nrwich	AA	138	514	149	24	6	4	(-	-)	197	80	45	82	77	1	87	4	5	2	22	14	.61	6	.290	.385	.383
2003	Trentn	AA	86	309	84	13	2	4	(-	-)	113	42	21	42	25	1	58	2	4	2	27	5	.84	4	.272	.328	.366
2003	Buffalo	AAA	15	55	12	1	0	1	(-	-)	16	11	3	5	6	0	8	0	2	0	1	0	1.00	0	.218	.295	.291
2004	Trentn	AA	78	329	98	37	4	6	(-	-)	161	57	40	57	23	1	48	3	2	1	13	5	.72	5	.298	.348	.489
2004	Buffalo	AAA	53	217	70	13	3	8	(-	-)	113	41	28	40	12	0	34	5	5	1	4	4	.50	5	.323	.370	.521
2005	Clmbs	AAA	133	540	149	38	7	14	(-	-)	243	92	69	93	63	5	86	10	2	5	16	5	.76	10	.276	.359	.450
2005	NYA	AL	2	1	0	0	0	0	(0	0)	0	0	0	0	1	0	1	0	0	0	0	0	-	0	.000	.500	.000

Pokey Reese

Bats: R **Throws:** R **Pos:** SS   **Ht:** 5'11" **Wt:** 188 **Born:** 6/10/1973 **Age:** 33

Year	Team	Lg	G	AB	H	2B	3B	HR	(Hm	Rd)	TB	R	RBI	RC	TBB	IBB	SO	HBP	SH	SF	SB	CS	SB%	GDP	Avg	OBP	Slg
2005	InldEm*	A+	3	12	3	2	0	0	(-	-)	5	2	3	1	2	0	1	0	1	0	0	0	-	0	.250	.357	.417
2005	SnAnt*	AA	2	8	1	0	0	0	(-	-)	1	1	0	0	2	0	1	0	0	0	1	0	1.00	0	.125	.300	.125
1997	CIN	NL	128	397	87	15	0	4	(3	1)	114	48	26	35	31	2	82	5	4	0	25	7	.78	1	.219	.284	.287

Year	Team	Lg	BATTING																						BASERUNNING				AVERAGES		
			G	AB	H	2B	3B	HR	(Hm	Rd)	TB	R	RBI	RC	TBB	IBB	SO	HBP	SH	SF					SB	CS	SB%	GDP	Avg	OBP	Slg
1998	CIN	NL	59	133	34	2	2	1	(0	1)	43	20	16	14	14	1	28	0	2	2					3	2	.60	3	.256	.322	.323
1999	CIN	NL	149	585	167	37	5	10	(5	5)	244	85	52	84	35	3	81	6	5	5					38	7	.84	9	.285	.330	.417
2000	CIN	NL	135	518	132	20	6	12	(3	9)	200	76	46	69	45	5	86	6	3	5					29	3	**.91**	8	.255	.319	.386
2001	CIN	NL	133	428	96	20	2	9	(4	5)	147	50	40	44	34	4	82	3	5	4					25	4	**.86**	7	.224	.284	.343
2002	PIT	NL	119	421	111	25	0	4	(3	1)	148	46	50	60	41	4	81	3	5	5					12	1	.92	4	.264	.330	.352
2003	PIT	NL	37	107	23	2	0	1	(0	1)	28	9	12	9	9	1	31	0	2	2					6	0	1.00	2	.215	.271	.262
2004	BOS	AL	96	244	54	7	2	3	(3	0)	74	32	29	20	17	1	60	0	6	1					6	2	.75	5	.221	.271	.303
8 ML YEARS			856	2833	704	128	17	44	(21	23)	998	366	271	335	226	21	531	23	32	24					144	26	.85	39	.248	.307	.352

Nick Regilio

Pitches: R **Bats:** R **Pos:** RP-18   **Ht:** 6'2" **Wt:** 205 **Born:** 9/4/1978 **Age:** 27

Year	Team	Lg	HOW MUCH HE PITCHED						WHAT HE GAVE UP												THE RESULTS							
			G	GS	CG	GF	IP	BFP	H	R	ER	HR	SH	SF	HB	TBB	IBB	SO	WP	Bk	W	L	Pct	ShO	Sv-Op	Hld	ERC	ERA
1999	Pulaski	R+	11	8	1	0	49.2	194	30	12	9	2	0	1	3	16	0	58	4	1	4	2	.667	1	0- -		1.68	1.63
2000	Charltt	A+	20	20	0	0	85.2	369	94	54	43	8	3	1	7	29	0	63	10	2	4	3	.571	0	0- -		4.80	4.52
2001	Charltt	A+	11	11	1	0	64.0	254	47	16	11	5	1	1	1	16	0	60	0	1	6	2	.750	1	0- -		2.07	1.55
2001	Tulsa	AA	10	10	0	0	52.0	236	62	34	32	2	2	1	4	20	0	40	2	0	1	3	.250	0	0- -		4.96	5.54
2002	Tulsa	AA	19	19	2	0	104.2	452	97	46	40	8	3	3	3	47	2	59	4	0	8	4	.429	1	0- -		3.77	3.44
2002	Okla	AAA	1	1	0	0	5.0	29	9	6	6	1	0	1	0	5	0	4	0	0	1	0	1.000	0	0- -		12.73	10.80
2003	Rngrs	R	2	2	0	0	5.0	19	4	2	0	0	0	0	1	1	0	7	0	0	0	0	-	0	0- -		2.62	0.00
2003	Frisco	AA	1	0	0	0	1.2	10	5	4	4	0	0	0	1	1	0	2	1	0	0	1	.000	0	0- -		19.35	21.60
2004	Okla	AAA	17	17	0	0	91.2	399	98	49	48	6	2	3	3	46	0	72	4	0	6	5	.545	0	0- -		4.92	4.71
2005	Rngrs	R	1	1	0	0	1.0	5	2	1	1	0	0	0	0	1	0	0	0	0	0	0	-	0	0- -		7.48	9.00
2005	Okla	AAA	1	0	0	0	2.0	8	1	0	0	0	0	0	0	1	0	2	1	0	0	0	-	0	0- -		1.41	0.00
2004	TEX	AL	6	4	0	1	19.1	91	20	16	13	3	1	1	2	15	1	12	1	0	0	4	.000	0	0-0	0	6.75	6.05
2005	TEX	AL	18	0	0	5	17.2	83	22	10	9	2	0	1	3	7	1	14	0	0	1	2	.333	0	0-2	2	5.59	4.58
2 ML YEARS			24	4	0	6	37.0	174	42	26	22	5	1	2	3	22	2	26	1	0	1	6	.143	0	0-2	2	6.18	5.35

Chris Reitsma

Pitches: R **Bats:** R **Pos:** RP-76   **Ht:** 6'5" **Wt:** 215 **Born:** 12/31/1977 **Age:** 28

Year	Team	Lg	HOW MUCH HE PITCHED						WHAT HE GAVE UP												THE RESULTS							
			G	GS	CG	GF	IP	BFP	H	R	ER	HR	SH	SF	HB	TBB	IBB	SO	WP	Bk	W	L	Pct	ShO	Sv-Op	Hld	ERC	ERA
2001	CIN	NL	36	29	0	1	182.0	800	209	121	107	23	13	8	5	49	6	96	5	0	7	15	.318	0	0-0	0	4.59	5.29
2002	CIN	NL	32	21	1	6	138.1	598	144	73	56	17	4	4	5	45	5	84	4	0	6	12	.333	1	0-0	0	4.24	3.64
2003	CIN	NL	57	3	0	36	84.0	351	92	41	40	14	4	1	0	19	6	53	2	0	9	5	.643	0	12-18	3	4.33	4.29
2004	ATL	NL	84	0	0	79	79.2	344	89	38	36	9	2	6	3	20	3	60	1	0	6	4	.600	0	2-9	31	4.32	4.07
2005	ATL	NL	76	0	0	37	73.1	307	79	32	32	3	1	2	0	14	3	42	2	0	3	6	.333	0	15-24	13	3.22	3.93
5 ML YEARS			285	53	1	92	557.1	2400	613	305	271	66	24	21	13	147	23	335	14	0	31	42	.425	1	29-51	48	4.24	4.38

Desi Relaford

Bats: B **Throws:** R **Pos:** SS-37; 3B-21; 2B-11; PH-8; RF-3; PR-2; CF-1   **Ht:** 5'9" **Wt:** 174 **Born:** 9/16/1973 **Age:** 32

Year	Team	Lg	BATTING																						BASERUNNING				AVERAGES		
			G	AB	H	2B	3B	HR	(Hm	Rd)	TB	R	RBI	RC	TBB	IBB	SO	HBP	SH	SF					SB	CS	SB%	GDP	Avg	OBP	Slg
2005	ColSpr*	AAA	3	12	4	1	0	0	(-	-)	5	4	0	3	3	0	3	1	0	0					1	0	1.00	0	.333	.500	.417
2005	Syrcse*	AAA	22	76	16	2	0	2	(-	-)	24	15	6	11	13	0	12	4	0	0					5	0	1.00	1	.211	.355	.316
1996	PHI	NL	15	40	7	2	0	0	(0	0)	9	2	1	2	3	0	9	0	1	0					1	0	1.00	1	.175	.233	.225
1997	PHI	NL	15	38	7	1	2	0	(0	0)	12	3	6	4	5	0	6	0	1	0					3	0	1.00	0	.184	.279	.316
1998	PHI	NL	142	494	121	25	3	5	(4	1)	167	45	41	48	33	4	87	3	10	6					9	5	.64	9	.245	.293	.338
1999	PHI	NL	65	211	51	11	2	1	(0	1)	69	31	26	22	19	2	34	6	6	0					4	3	.57	5	.242	.322	.327
2000	2 Tms	NL	128	410	88	14	3	5	(0	5)	123	55	46	51	75	7	71	12	3	2					13	0	1.00	10	.215	.351	.300
2001	NYN	NL	120	301	91	27	0	8	(4	4)	142	43	36	52	27	1	65	6	2	5					13	5	.72	4	.302	.364	.472
2002	SEA	AL	112	329	88	13	2	6	(1	5)	123	55	43	43	33	2	51	6	1	7					10	3	.77	6	.267	.339	.374
2003	KC	AL	141	500	127	27	5	8	(5	3)	188	70	59	68	40	1	70	6	8	3					20	4	.83	10	.254	.351	.376
2004	KC	AL	114	380	84	14	0	6	(2	4)	116	45	34	37	34	3	56	8	4	4					5	4	.56	10	.221	.296	.305
2005	COL	NL	73	210	47	13	2	1	(0	1)	67	24	16	19	22	2	42	4	1	1					3	3	.50	1	.224	.308	.319
00 Phi		NL	83	253	56	12	3	3	(0	3)	83	29	30	34	48	7	45	9	2	1					5	0	1.00	7	.221	.363	.328
00 SD		NL	45	157	32	2	0	2	(0	2)	40	26	16	17	27	0	26	3	1	1					8	0	1.00	3	.204	.330	.255
10 ML YEARS			925	2913	711	147	19	40	(16	24)	1016	373	308	346	291	22	491	50	37	28					81	27	.75	56	.244	.321	.349

Mike Remlinger

Pitches: L **Bats:** L **Pos:** RP-43   **Ht:** 6'1" **Wt:** 210 **Born:** 3/23/1966 **Age:** 40

Year	Team	Lg	HOW MUCH HE PITCHED						WHAT HE GAVE UP												THE RESULTS							
			G	GS	CG	GF	IP	BFP	H	R	ER	HR	SH	SF	HB	TBB	IBB	SO	WP	Bk	W	L	Pct	ShO	Sv-Op	Hld	ERC	ERA
1991	SF	NL	8	6	1	1	35.0	155	36	17	17	5	1	1	0	20	1	19	2	1	2	1	.667	1	0-0	0	5.30	4.37
1994	NYN	NL	10	9	0	0	54.2	252	55	30	28	9	2	3	1	35	4	33	3	0	1	5	.167	0	0-0	1	5.46	4.61
1995	2 Tms	NL	7	0	0	4	6.2	34	9	6	5	1	1	0	0	5	0	7	0	0	0	1	.000	0	0-1	0	7.94	6.75
1996	CIN	NL	19	4	0	2	27.1	125	24	17	17	4	3	1	3	19	2	19	2	2	0	1	.000	0	0-0	1	5.23	5.60
1997	CIN	NL	69	12	2	10	124.0	525	100	61	57	11	6	4	7	60	6	145	**12**	2	8	8	.500	0	2-5	14	3.43	4.14
1998	CIN	NL	35	28	1	0	164.1	727	164	96	88	23	12	7	5	87	1	144	11	1	8	15	.348	1	0-0	0	5.04	4.82
1999	ATL	NL	73	0	0	14	83.2	346	66	24	22	9	4	1	3	35	6	81	5	0	10	1	.909	0	1-3	21	3.03	2.37
2000	ATL	NL	71	0	0	18	72.2	311	55	29	26	6	3	2	3	37	1	72	3	0	5	3	.625	0	12-16	23	3.15	3.47
2001	ATL	NL	74	0	0	6	75.0	313	67	25	23	9	2	0	2	23	4	93	4	0	3	3	.500	0	1-5	31	3.27	2.76
2002	ATL	NL	73	0	0	7	68.0	275	48	17	15	3	4	0	1	28	3	69	2	0	7	3	.700	0	0-5	30	2.24	1.99
2003	CHN	NL	73	0	0	26	69.0	301	54	30	28	11	2	2	2	39	4	83	2	0	6	5	.545	0	0-1	17	3.88	3.65
2004	CHN	NL	48	0	0	6	36.2	156	33	16	14	3	1	4	1	16	3	35	1	0	1	2	.333	0	2-6	13	3.53	3.44
2005	2 Tms	NL	43	0	0	9	39.2	182	46	33	29	7	3	0	2	17	2	35	2	0	0	5	.000	0	0-1	5	5.76	6.58
95 NYM		NL	5	0	0	4	5.2	27	7	5	4	1	1	0	0	2	0	6	0	0	0	1	.000	0	0-1	0	5.47	6.35

		HOW MUCH HE PITCHED						WHAT HE GAVE UP												THE RESULTS							
Year	Team	Lg	G	GS	CG	GF	IP	BFP	H	R	ER	HR	SH	SF	HB	TBB	IBB	SO	WP	Bk	W	L	Pct	ShO	Sv-Op	Hld	ERC	ERA
95	Cin	NL	2	0	0	0	1.0	7	2	1	1	0	0	0	0	3	0	1	0	0	0	0		0	0-0	0	24.60	9.00
05	ChC	NL	35	0	0	7	33.0	141	31	19	18	5	3	0	2	12	2	30	0	0	0	3	.000	0	0-1	5	4.10	4.91
05	Bos	AL	8	0	0	2	6.2	41	15	14	11	2	0	0	0	5	0	5	2	0	0	0		0	0-0	0	15.53	14.85
13 ML YEARS			603	59	4	103	856.2	3702	757	401	371	101	42	25	28	421	36	835	47	6	51	51	.500	2	18-40	156	3.97	3.90

Edgar Renteria

Bats: R **Throws:** R **Pos:** SS-153; PH-3   **Ht:** 6'1" **Wt:** 180 **Born:** 8/7/1975 **Age:** 30

							BATTING														BASERUNNING				AVERAGES		
Year	Team	Lg	G	AB	H	2B	3B	HR	(Hm	Rd)	TB	R	RBI	RC	TBB	IBB	SO	HBP	SH	SF	SB	CS	SB%	GDP	Avg	OBP	Slg
1996	FLA	NL	106	431	133	18	3	5	(2	3)	172	68	31	62	33	0	68	2	2	3	16	2	.89	12	.309	.358	.399
1997	FLA	NL	154	617	171	21	3	4	(3	1)	210	90	52	68	45	1	108	4	19	6	32	15	.68	17	.277	.327	.340
1998	FLA	NL	133	517	146	18	2	3	(2	1)	177	79	31	61	48	1	78	4	9	2	41	22	.65	13	.282	.347	.342
1999	STL	NL	154	585	161	36	2	11	(6	5)	234	92	63	81	53	0	82	2	6	7	37	8	.82	16	.275	.334	.400
2000	STL	NL	150	562	156	32	1	16	(4	12)	238	94	76	80	63	3	77	1	8	9	21	13	.62	19	.278	.346	.423
2001	STL	NL	141	493	128	19	3	10	(3	7)	183	54	57	57	39	4	73	3	8	6	17	4	.81	15	.260	.314	.371
2002	STL	NL	152	544	166	36	2	11	(4	7)	239	77	83	94	49	7	57	4	7	5	22	7	.76	17	.305	.364	.439
2003	STL	NL	157	587	194	47	1	13	(4	9)	282	96	100	103	65	12	54	1	3	7	34	7	.83	21	.330	.394	.480
2004	STL	NL	149	586	168	37	0	10	(7	3)	235	84	72	74	39	5	78	1	6	10	17	11	.61	14	.287	.327	.401
2005	BOS	AL	153	623	172	36	4	8	(3	5)	240	100	70	82	55	0	100	3	6	5	9	4	.69	15	.276	.335	.385
10 ML YEARS			1449	5545	1595	300	21	91	(38	53)	2210	834	635	762	489	33	775	25	74	60	246	93	.73	159	.288	.345	.399

Jason Repko

Bats: R **Throws:** R **Pos:** CF-58; RF-42; LF-24; PR-13; PH-12; DH-1   **Ht:** 5'11" **Wt:** 175 **Born:** 12/27/1980 **Age:** 25

							BATTING														BASERUNNING				AVERAGES		
Year	Team	Lg	G	AB	H	2B	3B	HR	(Hm	Rd)	TB	R	RBI	RC	TBB	IBB	SO	HBP	SH	SF	SB	CS	SB%	GDP	Avg	OBP	Slg
1999	Gr Falls	R+	49	207	63	9	9	8	(-	-)	114	51	32	42	21	0	43	3	1	1	12	5	.71	1	.304	.375	.551
2000	Yakima	A-	8	17	5	2	0	0	(-	-)	7	3	1	2	1	0	7	0	0	0	0	0	-	0	.294	.333	.412
2001	Wilmg	A	88	337	74	17	4	4	(-	-)	111	36	32	29	15	0	68	3	6	3	17	8	.68	2	.220	.257	.329
2002	VeroB	A+	120	470	128	29	5	9	(-	-)	194	73	53	64	25	1	92	8	8	2	29	13	.69	3	.272	.319	.413
2003	Jaxnvl	AA	119	416	100	14	5	10	(-	-)	154	62	23	53	42	0	89	6	9	3	21	8	.72	1	.240	.317	.370
2004	Jaxnvl	AA	46	189	55	11	2	6	(-	-)	88	26	19	30	13	1	43	2	2	1	10	5	.67	1	.291	.341	.466
2004	LsVgs	AAA	75	302	94	26	4	7	(-	-)	149	55	41	53	18	2	57	3	2	1	13	5	.72	4	.311	.355	.493
2005	LsVgs	AAA	8	31	12	0	0	3	(-	-)	21	6	6	7	0	0	4	0	1	0	1	0	1.00	0	.387	.387	.677
2005	LAN	NL	129	276	61	15	3	8	(4	4)	106	43	30	28	16	1	80	7	2	0	5	0	1.00	7	.221	.281	.384

Chris Resop

Pitches: R **Bats:** R **Pos:** RP-15   **Ht:** 6'3" **Wt:** 222 **Born:** 11/4/1982 **Age:** 23

			HOW MUCH HE PITCHED						WHAT HE GAVE UP												THE RESULTS							
Year	Team	Lg	G	GS	CG	GF	IP	BFP	H	R	ER	HR	SH	SF	HB	TBB	IBB	SO	WP	Bk	W	L	Pct	ShO	Sv-Op	Hld	ERC	ERA
2003	Grnsbr	A	11	0	0	2	12.2	54	11	7	7	1	4	5	0	5	0	15	1	1	0	1	.000	0	0--	-	3.13	4.97
2004	Grnsbr	A	41	0	0	36	41.2	158	26	11	9	1	0	0	2	7	0	68	2	1	3	1	.750	0	13--	-	1.31	1.94
2005	Carlina	AA	43	0	0	40	49.0	210	47	15	14	2	1	1	0	16	1	56	4	0	3	2	.600	0	24--	-	3.06	2.57
2005	FLA	NL	15	0	0	6	17.0	80	22	16	16	1	0	2	1	9	0	15	3	0	2	0	1.000	0	0-0	0	6.35	8.47

Mike Restovich

Bats: R **Throws:** R **Pos:** PH-28; RF-27; LF-15; PR-3   **Ht:** 6'4" **Wt:** 233 **Born:** 1/3/1979 **Age:** 27

							BATTING														BASERUNNING				AVERAGES		
Year	Team	Lg	G	AB	H	2B	3B	HR	(Hm	Rd)	TB	R	RBI	RC	TBB	IBB	SO	HBP	SH	SF	SB	CS	SB%	GDP	Avg	OBP	Slg
2002	MIN	AL	8	13	4	0	0	1	(0	1)	7	3	1	0	1	0	4	0	0	0	1	0	1.00	0	.308	.357	.538
2003	MIN	AL	24	53	15	3	2	0	(0	0)	22	10	4	8	10	0	12	1	0	0	0	0	-	3	.283	.406	.415
2004	MIN	AL	29	47	12	3	0	2	(1	1)	21	9	6	6	4	0	10	0	0	0	0	0	-	0	.255	.314	.447
2005	2 Tms	NL	66	115	27	5	1	3	(1	2)	43	15	8	10	11	0	29	0	0	0	0	0	-	5	.235	.302	.374
05	Col	NL	14	31	9	2	0	1	(1	0)	14	5	3	5	3	0	5	0	0	0	0	0	-	2	.290	.353	.452
05	Pit	NL	52	84	18	3	1	2	(0	2)	29	10	5	5	8	0	24	0	0	0	0	0	-	3	.214	.283	.345
4 ML YEARS			127	228	58	11	3	6	(2	4)	93	37	19	24	26	0	55	1	0	0	1	0	1.00	10	.254	.333	.408

Al Reyes

Pitches: R **Bats:** R **Pos:** RP-65   **Ht:** 6'1" **Wt:** 206 **Born:** 4/10/1970 **Age:** 36

			HOW MUCH HE PITCHED						WHAT HE GAVE UP												THE RESULTS							
Year	Team	Lg	G	GS	CG	GF	IP	BFP	H	R	ER	HR	SH	SF	HB	TBB	IBB	SO	WP	Bk	W	L	Pct	ShO	Sv-Op	Hld	ERC	ERA
1995	MIL	AL	27	0	0	13	33.1	138	19	9	9	3	1	2	3	18	2	29	0	0	1	1	.500	0	1-1	4	2.51	2.43
1996	MIL	AL	5	0	0	2	5.2	27	8	5	5	1	0	0	0	2	0	2	2	0	1	0	1.000	0	0-0	0	6.79	7.94
1997	MIL	AL	19	0	0	7	29.2	131	32	19	18	4	2	0	3	9	0	28	1	0	1	2	.333	0	1-1	1	4.76	5.46
1998	MIL	NL	50	0	0	13	57.0	253	55	26	25	9	2	1	2	31	1	58	2	0	5	1	.833	0	0-1	10	5.01	3.95
1999	2 Tms		53	0	0	12	65.2	287	50	33	33	9	4	3	6	41	3	67	3	0	4	3	.571	0	0-4	6	4.19	4.52
2000	2 Tms		19	0	0	6	19.2	86	15	10	10	2	1	2	0	12	1	18	0	0	1	0	1.000	0	0-1	3	3.43	4.58
2001	LA	NL	19	0	0	9	25.2	120	28	13	11	3	0	2	1	13	1	23	0	1	2	1	.667	0	1-2	5	5.07	3.86
2002	PIT	NL	15	0	0	6	17.0	67	9	5	5	1	1	1	2	7	0	21	1	0	0	0	-	0	0-1	3	1.93	2.65
2003	NYA	AL	13	0	0	2	17.0	73	13	7	6	1	0	0	0	6	0	9	1	0	0	0	-	0	0-1	0	2.86	3.18
2004	STL	NL	12	2	0	4	12.0	41	3	1	1	0	2	0	0	2	0	11	0	0	0	0	-	0	0-0	0	0.31	0.75
2005	STL	NL	65	0	0	18	62.2	244	38	15	15	5	3	1	5	20	2	67	1	0	4	2	.667	0	3-3	16	1.94	2.15
99	Mil	NL	26	0	0	6	36.0	161	27	17	17	5	1	1	3	25	1	39	2	0	2	0	1.000	0	0-1	2	4.35	4.25
99	Bal	AL	27	0	0	6	29.2	126	23	16	16	4	3	2	3	16	2	28	1	0	2	3	.400	0	0-3	4	3.99	4.85

Year	Team	Lg	G	GS	CG	GF	IP	BFP	H	R	ER	HR	SH	SF	HB	TBB	IBB	SO	WP	Bk	W	L	Pct	ShO	Sv-Op	Hld	ERC	ERA
00	Bal	AL	13	0	0	2	13.0	62	13	10	10	2	1	2	0	11	1	10	0	0	1	0	1.000	0	0-1	2	6.14	6.92
00	LA	NL	6	0	0	4	6.2	24	2	0	0	0	0	0	0	1	0	8	0	0	0	0	-	0	-	-	0.35	0.00
11 ML YEARS			297	2	0	92	345.1	1467	270	143	138	38	16	12	22	164	11	333	11	1	19	10	.655	0	6-15	43	3.43	3.60

Anthony Reyes

Pitches: R **Bats:** R **Pos:** RP-3; SP-1   **Ht:** 6'2" **Wt:** 215 **Born:** 10/16/1981 **Age:** 24

Year	Team	Lg	G	GS	CG	GF	IP	BFP	H	R	ER	HR	SH	SF	HB	TBB	IBB	SO	WP	Bk	W	L	Pct	ShO	Sv-Op	Hld	ERC	ERA
2004	PlmBh	A+	7	7	0	0	36.2	159	41	21	19	5	0	0	1	7	0	38	3	1	3	0	1.000	0	0--	-	4.17	4.66
2004	Tenn	AA	12	12	0	0	74.1	298	62	27	24	3	6	1	5	13	1	102	3	1	6	2	.750	0	0--	-	2.24	2.91
2005	Memp	AAA	23	23	2	0	128.2	525	105	55	52	13	5	4	4	34	0	136	3	0	7	6	.538	1	0--	-	2.69	3.64
2005	STL	NL	4	1	0	0	13.1	51	6	4	4	2	1	0	0	4	1	12	2	0	1	1	.500	0	0-0	1	1.32	2.70

Dennys Reyes

Pitches: L **Bats:** R **Pos:** RP-35; SP-1   **Ht:** 6'3" **Wt:** 246 **Born:** 4/19/1977 **Age:** 29

Year	Team	Lg	G	GS	CG	GF	IP	BFP	H	R	ER	HR	SH	SF	HB	TBB	IBB	SO	WP	Bk	W	L	Pct	ShO	Sv-Op	Hld	ERC	ERA
1997	LA	NL	14	5	0	0	47.0	207	51	21	20	4	5	1	1	18	3	36	2	1	2	3	.400	0	0-0	0	4.34	3.83
1998	2 Tms	NL	19	10	0	4	67.1	300	62	36	34	3	7	2	1	47	5	77	6	1	3	5	.375	0	0-0	0	4.37	4.54
1999	CIN	NL	65	1	0	12	61.2	277	53	30	26	5	4	3	3	39	1	72	5	1	2	2	.500	0	2-3	14	4.16	3.79
2000	CIN	NL	62	0	0	15	43.2	200	43	31	22	5	3	3	1	29	0	36	6	0	2	1	.667	0	0-1	10	5.24	4.53
2001	CIN	NL	35	6	0	2	53.0	246	51	35	29	5	2	2	1	35	1	52	5	0	2	6	.250	0	0-0	6	4.77	4.92
2002	2 Tms	NL	58	5	0	15	82.2	378	98	52	49	10	3	2	0	45	4	59	10	1	4	4	.500	0	0-0	4	5.90	5.33
2003	2 Tms	NL	15	0	0	4	12.2	63	15	16	15	2	1	2	0	10	1	16	5	0	0	0	-	0	0-0	2	6.96	10.66
2004	KC	AL	40	12	0	5	108.0	483	114	64	57	12	7	5	4	50	3	91	6	2	4	8	.333	0	0-1	5	4.81	4.75
2005	SD	NL	36	1	0	9	43.2	215	57	30	25	3	1	0	1	32	2	35	3	1	3	2	.600	0	0-1	0	7.06	5.15
98	LA	NL	11	3	0	4	28.2	130	27	17	15	1	3	1	0	20	4	33	1	0	0	4	.000	0	0-0	0	4.16	4.71
98	Cin	NL	8	7	0	0	38.2	170	35	19	19	2	4	1	1	27	1	44	5	0	3	1	.750	0	0-0	0	4.54	4.42
02	Col	NL	43	0	0	13	40.1	182	43	19	19	1	2	2	0	24	3	30	4	0	0	1	.000	0	0-0	4	4.55	4.24
02	Tex	NL	15	5	0	2	42.1	196	55	33	30	9	1	0	0	21	1	29	6	1	4	3	.571	0	0-0	0	7.24	6.38
03	Pit	NL	12	0	0	4	10.1	50	10	13	12	1	1	2	0	9	1	11	5	0	0	0	-	0	0-0	2	5.43	10.45
03	Ari	NL	3	0	0	0	2.1	13	5	3	3	1	0	0	0	1	0	5	0	0	0	0	-	0	0-0	0	14.73	11.57
9 ML YEARS			344	40	0	66	519.2	2369	544	315	277	49	33	20	12	305	20	474	48	7	22	31	.415	0	2-6	41	5.07	4.80

Jose Reyes

Bats: B **Throws:** R **Pos:** SS-161; PH-1   **Ht:** 6'0" **Wt:** 160 **Born:** 6/11/1983 **Age:** 23

Year	Team	Lg	G	AB	H	2B	3B	HR	(Hm	Rd)	TB	R	RBI	RC	TBB	IBB	SO	HBP	SH	SF	SB	CS	SB%	GDP	Avg	OBP	Slg
2003	NYN	NL	69	274	84	12	4	5	(1	4)	119	47	32	64	13	0	36	0	2	3	13	3	.81	1	.307	.334	.434
2004	NYN	NL	53	220	56	16	2	2	(1	1)	82	33	14	25	5	0	31	0	4	0	19	2	.90	1	.255	.271	.373
2005	NYN	NL	161	696	190	24	17	7	(2	5)	269	99	58	84	27	0	78	2	4	4	60	15	.80	7	.273	.300	.386
3 ML YEARS			283	1190	330	52	23	14	(4	10)	470	179	104	155	45	0	145	2	10	7	92	20	.82	9	.277	.303	.395

Arthur Rhodes

Pitches: L **Bats:** L **Pos:** RP-47   **Ht:** 6'2" **Wt:** 205 **Born:** 10/24/1969 **Age:** 36

Year	Team	Lg	G	GS	CG	GF	IP	BFP	H	R	ER	HR	SH	SF	HB	TBB	IBB	SO	WP	Bk	W	L	Pct	ShO	Sv-Op	Hld	ERC	ERA
2005	Akron*	AA	1	1	0	0	1.0	3	0	0	0	0	0	0	0	0	0	0	0	0	0	0	-	0	0--	-	0.00	0.00
1991	BAL	AL	8	8	0	0	36.0	174	47	35	32	4	1	3	0	23	0	23	2	0	0	3	.000	0	0-0	0	7.00	8.00
1992	BAL	AL	15	15	2	0	94.1	394	87	39	38	6	5	1	1	38	2	77	2	1	7	5	.583	1	0-0	0	3.48	3.63
1993	BAL	AL	17	17	0	0	85.2	387	91	62	62	16	2	3	1	49	1	49	2	0	5	6	.455	0	0-0	0	5.88	6.51
1994	BAL	AL	10	10	3	0	52.2	238	51	34	34	8	2	3	2	30	1	47	3	0	3	5	.375	2	0-0	0	5.03	5.81
1995	BAL	AL	19	9	0	3	75.1	336	68	53	52	13	4	0	0	48	1	77	3	1	2	5	.286	0	0-1	0	4.97	6.21
1996	BAL	AL	28	2	0	5	53.0	224	48	28	24	6	1	1	0	23	3	62	0	0	9	1	.900	0	1-1	2	3.72	4.08
1997	BAL	AL	53	0	0	9	95.1	378	75	32	32	9	0	4	4	26	5	102	2	0	10	3	.769	0	1-2	9	2.58	3.02
1998	BAL	AL	45	0	0	10	77.0	321	65	30	30	8	2	5	1	34	2	83	1	1	4	4	.500	0	4-8	10	3.47	3.51
1999	BAL	AL	43	0	0	11	53.0	244	43	37	32	9	2	2	0	45	6	59	4	0	3	4	.429	0	3-5	5	5.07	5.43
2000	SEA	AL	72	0	0	9	69.1	281	51	34	33	6	1	2	0	29	3	77	4	0	5	8	.385	0	0-7	24	2.62	4.28
2001	SEA	AL	71	0	0	16	68.0	258	46	14	13	5	1	0	1	12	0	83	3	0	8	0	1.000	0	3-7	32	1.61	1.72
2002	SEA	AL	66	0	0	9	69.2	257	45	18	18	4	2	1	0	13	1	81	2	0	10	4	.714	0	2-7	27	1.46	2.33
2003	SEA	AL	67	0	0	14	54.0	228	53	25	25	4	2	0	1	18	2	48	2	0	3	3	.500	0	3-6	18	3.57	4.17
2004	OAK	AL	37	0	0	25	38.2	182	46	23	22	9	3	1	0	21	4	34	2	0	3	3	.500	0	9-14	3	6.54	5.12
2005	CLE	AL	47	0	0	8	43.1	175	33	13	10	2	0	2	1	12	2	43	0	0	3	1	.750	0	0-3	16	2.06	2.08
15 ML YEARS			598	61	5	116	965.1	4077	849	477	457	109	28	28	12	421	33	945	32	3	75	55	.577	3	26-61	146	3.66	4.26

John Riedling

Pitches: R **Bats:** R **Pos:** RP-29   **Ht:** 5'11" **Wt:** 190 **Born:** 8/29/1975 **Age:** 30

Year	Team	Lg	G	GS	CG	GF	IP	BFP	H	R	ER	HR	SH	SF	HB	TBB	IBB	SO	WP	Bk	W	L	Pct	ShO	Sv-Op	Hld	ERC	ERA
2005	Albq*	AAA	14	0	0	7	21.0	91	19	9	7	0	2	0	1	9	1	15	1	0	4	0	1.000	0	3--	-	3.03	3.00
2000	CIN	NL	13	0	0	5	15.1	63	11	7	4	1	1	0	1	8	0	18	1	0	3	1	.750	0	1-2	2	3.12	2.35
2001	CIN	NL	29	0	0	14	33.2	136	22	9	9	1	2	0	2	14	0	23	5	0	1	1	.500	0	1-3	5	2.13	2.41
2002	CIN	NL	33	0	0	7	46.2	203	39	16	14	2	6	1	3	26	6	30	1	0	2	4	.333	0	0-0	8	3.40	2.70
2003	CIN	NL	55	8	0	11	101.0	455	107	61	55	7	2	6	3	47	0	65	7	1	2	3	.400	0	1-4	6	4.50	4.90

Year	Team	Lg	G	GS	CG	GF	IP	BFP	H	R	ER	HR	SH	SF	HB	TBB	IBB	SO	WP	Bk	W	L	Pct	ShO	Sv-Op	Hld	ERC	ERA
2004	CIN	NL	70	0	0	15	77.2	365	90	54	44	10	3	3	4	40	5	46	6	0	5	3	.625	0	0-7	14	5.69	5.10
2005	FLA	NL	29	0	0	7	27.2	130	34	23	22	3	1	1	1	13	2	16	6	0	4	1	.800	0	0-0	2	5.69	7.16
	6 ML YEARS		229	8	0	59	302.0	1352	303	170	148	24	15	11	14	148	13	198	26	1	17	13	.567	0	3-16	37	4.37	4.41

Matt Riley

Pitches: L Bats: L Pos: RP-7

Ht: 6'1" Wt: 201 Born: 8/2/1979 Age: 26

Year	Team	Lg	G	GS	CG	GF	IP	BFP	H	R	ER	HR	SH	SF	HB	TBB	IBB	SO	WP	Bk	W	L	Pct	ShO	Sv-Op	Hld	ERC	ERA
2005	Rngrs*	R	1	0	0	0	0.2	2	0	0	0	0	0	0	0	0	0	2	0	0	0	0	-	0	0--	-	0.00	0.00
2005	Okla*	AAA	4	4	0	0	12.0	55	12	11	11	3	0	1	0	7	0	15	2	0	0	1	.000	0	0--	-	5.83	8.25
1999	BAL	AL	3	3	0	0	11.0	59	17	9	9	4	0	0	0	13	0	6	0	0	0	0	-	0	0-0	0	14.43	7.36
2003	BAL	AL	2	2	0	0	10.0	41	7	2	2	1	0	0	0	5	0	8	0	0	1	0	1.000	0	0-0	0	2.88	1.80
2004	BAL	AL	14	13	0	0	64.0	292	60	43	40	11	1	0	1	44	0	60	2	0	3	4	.429	0	0-0	0	5.46	5.63
2005	TEX	AL	7	0	0	0	12.2	62	16	14	14	2	0	1	1	10	0	4	1	1	1	0	1.000	0	0-0	0	8.39	9.95
	4 ML YEARS		26	18	0	0	97.2	454	100	68	65	18	1	1	2	72	0	78	3	1	5	4	.556	0	0-0	0	6.40	5.99

Juan Rincon

Pitches: R Bats: R Pos: RP-75

Ht: 5'11" Wt: 190 Born: 1/23/1979 Age: 27

Year	Team	Lg	G	GS	CG	GF	IP	BFP	H	R	ER	HR	SH	SF	HB	TBB	IBB	SO	WP	Bk	W	L	Pct	ShO	Sv-Op	Hld	ERC	ERA
2001	MIN	AL	4	0	0	1	5.2	28	7	5	4	1	1	0	0	5	0	4	0	0	0	0	-	0	0-0	0	8.33	6.35
2002	MIN	AL	10	3	0	0	28.2	135	44	23	20	5	0	1	0	9	0	21	2	0	0	2	.000	0	0-1	0	7.62	6.28
2003	MIN	AL	58	0	0	20	85.2	370	74	38	35	5	2	5	4	38	7	63	7	0	5	6	.455	0	0-1	5	3.21	3.68
2004	MIN	AL	77	0	0	18	82.0	327	52	27	24	5	3	3	2	32	1	106	2	0	11	6	.647	0	2-6	16	2.00	2.63
2005	MIN	AL	75	0	0	18	77.0	319	63	26	21	2	4	1	3	30	3	84	5	1	6	6	.500	0	0-5	25	2.68	2.45
	5 ML YEARS		224	3	0	57	279.0	1179	240	119	104	18	10	10	9	114	11	278	16	1	22	20	.524	0	2-13	46	3.16	3.35

Ricardo Rincon

Pitches: L Bats: L Pos: RP-67

Ht: 5'9" Wt: 187 Born: 4/13/1970 Age: 36

Year	Team	Lg	G	GS	CG	GF	IP	BFP	H	R	ER	HR	SH	SF	HB	TBB	IBB	SO	WP	Bk	W	L	Pct	ShO	Sv-Op	Hld	ERC	ERA
1997	PIT	NL	62	0	0	23	60.0	254	51	26	23	5	5	1	2	24	6	71	2	3	4	8	.333	0	4-6	18	3.10	3.45
1998	PIT	NL	60	0	0	27	65.0	272	50	31	21	6	1	2	0	29	2	64	2	0	0	2	.000	0	14-17	11	2.88	2.91
1999	CLE	AL	59	0	0	14	44.2	193	41	22	22	6	2	1	1	24	5	30	2	1	2	3	.400	0	0-2	11	4.38	4.43
2000	CLE	AL	35	0	0	4	20.0	90	17	7	6	1	0	1	0	13	1	20	1	0	2	0	1.000	0	0-0	10	3.89	2.70
2001	CLE	AL	67	0	0	19	54.0	223	44	18	17	3	2	3	0	21	5	50	1	0	2	1	.667	0	2-4	12	2.62	2.83
2002	2 Tms		71	0	0	9	56.0	222	47	28	26	4	2	4	1	11	1	49	0	0	1	4	.200	0	1-5	27	2.36	4.18
2003	OAK	AL	64	0	0	16	55.1	241	45	21	20	4	8	2	3	32	4	40	0	0	8	4	.667	0	0-3	13	3.62	3.25
2004	OAK	AL	67	0	0	10	44.0	201	45	22	18	3	1	1	1	22	4	40	4	0	1	1	.500	0	0-4	18	4.16	3.68
2005	OAK	AL	67	0	0	4	37.1	162	34	19	18	7	2	1	1	20	4	27	1	0	1	1	.500	0	0-2	16	4.73	4.34
02	Cle		46	0	0	6	35.2	150	36	21	19	3	2	2	1	8	1	30	0	0	1	4	.200	0	0-3	11	3.38	4.79
02	Oak		25	0	0	3	20.1	72	11	7	7	1	0	2	0	3	0	19	0	0	0	0	-	0	1-2	16	1.06	3.10
	9 ML YEARS		552	0	0	126	436.1	1858	374	194	171	39	23	15	10	196	32	391	13	4	21	24	.467	0	21-43	136	3.37	3.53

Royce Ring

Pitches: L Bats: L Pos: RP-15

Ht: 6'0" Wt: 220 Born: 12/21/1980 Age: 25

Year	Team	Lg	G	GS	CG	GF	IP	BFP	H	R	ER	HR	SH	SF	HB	TBB	IBB	SO	WP	Bk	W	L	Pct	ShO	Sv-Op	Hld	ERC	ERA
2002	WinSa	A+	21	0	0	13	23.0	100	20	11	10	2	2	2	0	11	2	22	1	0	2	0	1.000	0	5--	-	3.35	3.91
2003	Brham	AA	36	0	0	32	35.2	154	33	11	10	1	0	1	3	14	1	44	3	0	1	4	.200	0	19--	-	3.39	2.52
2003	Bnghtn	AA	18	0	0	15	21.2	89	13	4	4	2	2	1	0	11	0	18	1	0	3	1	.750	0	7--	-	2.49	1.66
2004	Bnghtn	AA	19	0	0	8	28.2	122	25	13	12	5	0	0	1	11	1	23	0	0	2	2	.500	0	2--	-	3.85	3.77
2004	Norfolk	AAA	29	0	0	10	34.2	153	37	15	14	5	0	0	0	12	1	22	1	0	3	1	.750	0	0--	-	4.40	3.63
2005	Norfolk	AAA	33	0	0	11	38.2	163	34	16	14	2	4	0	3	13	1	26	2	0	3	0	1.000	0	2--	-	3.10	3.26
2005	NYN	NL	15	0	0	2	10.2	51	10	6	6	0	1	0	0	10	1	8	0	0	0	2	.000	0	0-0	3	4.80	5.06

Alexis Rios

Bats: R Throws: R Pos: RF-138; PH-10; CF-5; PR-2

Ht: 6'5" Wt: 194 Born: 2/18/1981 Age: 25

Year	Team	Lg	G	AB	H	2B	3B	HR	(Hm	Rd)	TB	R	RBI	RC	TBB	IBB	SO	HBP	SH	SF	SB	CS	SB%	GDP	Avg	OBP	Slg
1999	MdHat	R+	67	234	63	7	3	0	(-	-)	76	35	13	24	17	0	31	1	0	0	8	4	.67	6	.269	.321	.325
2000	Queens	A-	50	206	55	9	2	1	(-	-)	71	22	25	21	11	2	22	4	1	2	5	5	.50	5	.267	.314	.345
2000	Hgrstn	A	22	74	17	3	1	0	(-	-)	22	5	5	4	2	0	14	1	0	1	2	3	.40	0	.230	.256	.297
2001	CtnWV	A	130	480	126	20	9	2	(-	-)	170	40	58	47	25	1	59	4	3	14	22	14	.61	16	.263	.296	.354
2002	Dnedin	A+	111	456	139	22	8	3	(-	-)	186	60	61	60	27	0	55	3	1	5	14	8	.64	19	.305	.344	.408
2003	NwHav	AA	127	514	181	32	11	11	(-	-)	268	86	82	98	39	4	85	6	1	3	11	3	.79	22	.352	.402	.521
2004	Syrcse	AAA	46	185	48	10	1	3	(-	-)	69	14	23	16	9	0	30	0	0	1	2	1	.67	10	.259	.292	.373
2004	TOR	AL	111	426	122	24	7	1	(0	1)	163	55	28	49	31	0	84	2	1	0	15	3	.83	14	.286	.338	.383
2005	TOR	AL	146	481	126	23	6	10	(5	5)	191	71	59	56	28	1	101	5	0	5	14	9	.61	14	.262	.306	.397
	2 ML YEARS		257	907	248	47	13	11	(5	6)	354	126	87	105	59	1	185	7	1	5	29	12	.71	28	.273	.321	.390

David Riske

Pitches: R **Bats:** R **Pos:** RP-58 **Ht:** 6'2" **Wt:** 175 **Born:** 10/23/1976 **Age:** 29

Year	Team	Lg	G	GS	CG	GF	IP	BFP	H	R	ER	HR	SH	SF	HB	TBB	IBB	SO	WP	Bk	W	L	Pct	ShO	Sv-Op	Hld	ERC	ERA
1999	CLE	AL	12	0	0	3	14.0	68	20	15	13	2	1	1	0	6	0	16	0	0	1	1	.500	0	0-1	0	6.96	8.36
2001	CLE	AL	26	0	0	6	27.1	118	20	7	6	3	0	1	2	18	3	29	1	0	2	0	1.000	0	1-1	3	3.81	1.98
2002	CLE	AL	51	0	0	17	51.1	237	49	32	30	8	4	3	4	35	4	65	1	0	2	2	.500	0	1-1	5	5.55	5.26
2003	CLE	AL	68	0	0	24	74.2	293	52	21	19	9	4	1	3	20	3	82	1	0	2	2	.500	0	8-13	17	2.26	2.29
2004	CLE	AL	72	0	0	27	77.1	336	69	32	32	11	3	2	2	41	4	78	3	0	7	3	.700	0	5-12	9	4.32	3.72
2005	CLE	AL	58	0	0	33	72.2	288	55	28	25	11	3	1	4	15	0	48	0	0	3	4	.429	0	1-1	0	2.59	3.10
6 ML YEARS			287	0	0	110	317.1	1340	265	135	125	44	15	9	15	135	14	318	6	0	17	12	.586	0	16-29	34	3.65	3.55

Luis Rivas

Bats: R **Throws:** R **Pos:** 2B-53; PR-8; SS-6; PH-1 **Ht:** 5'11" **Wt:** 175 **Born:** 8/30/1979 **Age:** 26

Year	Team	Lg	G	AB	H	2B	3B	HR	(Hm	Rd)	TB	R	RBI	RC	TBB	IBB	SO	HBP	SH	SF	SB	CS	SB%	GDP	Avg	OBP	Slg
2005	Roch*	AAA	43	145	36	14	0	2	(-	-)	56	17	22	16	8	1	18	0	2	4	2	2	.60	2	.248	.280	.386
2000	MIN	AL	16	58	18	4	1	0	(0	0)	24	8	6	8	2	0	4	0	2	2	2	0	1.00	2	.310	.323	.414
2001	MIN	AL	153	563	150	21	6	7	(3	4)	204	70	47	65	40	0	99	6	5	5	31	11	.74	15	.266	.319	.362
2002	MIN	AL	93	316	81	23	4	4	(2	2)	124	46	35	35	19	2	51	3	8	0	9	4	.69	12	.256	.305	.392
2003	MIN	AL	135	475	123	16	9	8	(4	4)	181	69	43	46	30	0	65	5	8	3	17	7	.71	20	.259	.308	.381
2004	MIN	AL	109	336	86	19	5	10	(4	6)	145	44	34	34	13	0	53	1	5	3	15	1	.94	8	.256	.283	.432
2005	MIN	AL	59	136	35	3	1	1	(0	1)	43	21	12	16	9	0	17	2	0	1	4	0	1.00	2	.257	.311	.316
6 ML YEARS			565	1884	493	86	26	30	(13	17)	721	258	177	204	113	2	289	17	28	14	78	23	.77	59	.262	.307	.383

Juan Rivera

Bats: R **Throws:** R **Pos:** RF-38; LF-33; DH-27; PH-13; CF-4 **Ht:** 6'2" **Wt:** 170 **Born:** 7/3/1978 **Age:** 27

Year	Team	Lg	G	AB	H	2B	3B	HR	(Hm	Rd)	TB	R	RBI	RC	TBB	IBB	SO	HBP	SH	SF	SB	CS	SB%	GDP	Avg	OBP	Slg
2005	Ogden*	R+	41	171	43	5	0	1	(-	-)	51	27	16	16	14	0	32	2	2	2	9	7	.56	2	.251	.312	.298
2001	NYA	AL	3	4	0	0	0	0	(0	0)	0	0	0	0	0	0	0	0	0	0	0	0	-	0	.000	.000	.000
2002	NYA	AL	28	83	22	5	0	1	(0	1)	30	9	6	8	6	0	10	0	1	1	1	1	.50	4	.265	.311	.361
2003	NYA	AL	57	173	46	14	0	7	(4	3)	81	22	26	23	10	1	27	0	1	1	0	0	-	8	.266	.304	.468
2004	MON	NL	134	391	120	24	1	12	(6	6)	182	48	49	60	34	7	45	1	0	0	6	2	.75	11	.307	.364	.465
2005	LAA	AL	106	350	95	17	1	15	(8	7)	159	46	59	49	23	0	44	0	2	1	1	9	.10	15	.271	.316	.454
5 ML YEARS			328	1001	283	60	2	35	(18	17)	452	125	140	140	73	8	126	1	4	3	8	12	.40	38	.283	.331	.452

Mariano Rivera

Pitches: R **Bats:** R **Pos:** RP-71 **Ht:** 6'2" **Wt:** 185 **Born:** 11/29/1969 **Age:** 36

Year	Team	Lg	G	GS	CG	GF	IP	BFP	H	R	ER	HR	SH	SF	HB	TBB	IBB	SO	WP	Bk	W	L	Pct	ShO	Sv-Op	Hld	ERC	ERA
1995	NYA	AL	19	10	0	2	67.0	301	71	43	41	11	0	2	2	30	0	51	0	1	5	3	.625	0	0-1	0	5.14	5.51
1996	NYA	AL	61	0	0	14	107.2	425	73	25	25	1	2	1	2	34	3	130	1	0	8	3	.727	0	5-8	27	1.65	2.09
1997	NYA	AL	66	0	0	56	71.2	301	65	17	15	5	3	4	0	20	6	68	2	0	6	4	.600	0	43-52	0	2.73	1.88
1998	NYA	AL	54	0	0	49	61.1	246	48	13	13	3	2	3	1	17	1	36	0	0	3	0	1.000	0	36-41	0	2.21	1.91
1999	NYA	AL	66	0	0	63	69.0	268	43	15	14	2	0	2	3	18	3	52	2	1	4	3	.571	0	45-49	0	1.47	1.83
2000	NYA	AL	66	0	0	61	75.2	311	58	26	24	4	5	2	2	25	3	58	2	0	7	4	.636	0	36-41	0	2.20	2.85
2001	NYA	AL	71	0	0	66	80.2	310	61	24	21	5	4	1	1	12	2	83	1	0	4	6	.400	0	50-57	0	1.74	2.34
2002	NYA	AL	45	0	0	37	46.0	187	35	16	14	3	2	0	2	11	2	41	1	1	1	4	.200	0	28-32	2	2.08	2.74
2003	NYA	AL	64	0	0	57	70.2	277	61	15	13	3	1	2	4	10	1	63	0	0	5	2	.714	0	40-46	0	2.29	1.66
2004	NYA	AL	74	0	0	67	78.2	316	65	17	17	3	2	0	5	20	3	66	0	0	4	2	.667	0	53-57	0	2.45	1.94
2005	NYA	AL	71	0	0	67	78.1	306	50	18	12	2	0	1	4	18	0	80	0	0	7	4	.636	0	43-47	0	1.48	1.38
11 ML YEARS			657	10	0	541	806.2	3248	630	229	209	42	21	18	24	215	24	728	9	3	54	35	.607	0	379-431	29	2.21	2.33

Rene Rivera

Bats: R **Throws:** R **Pos:** C-15; PH-2 **Ht:** 5'10" **Wt:** 190 **Born:** 7/31/1983 **Age:** 22

Year	Team	Lg	G	AB	H	2B	3B	HR	(Hm	Rd)	TB	R	RBI	RC	TBB	IBB	SO	HBP	SH	SF	SB	CS	SB%	GDP	Avg	OBP	Slg
2001	Ms	R	21	71	24	4	0	2	(-	-)	34	13	12	12	2	0	11	1	0	1	0	0	-	0	.338	.360	.479
2001	Everett	A-	15	45	4	1	0	2	(-	-)	11	3	3	0	1	0	19	0	1	1	0	0	-	1	.089	.106	.244
2002	Everett	A-	62	227	55	18	1	1	(-	-)	78	29	26	25	16	1	38	9	1	3	5	2	.71	3	.242	.314	.344
2003	Wisc	A	116	407	112	19	0	9	(-	-)	158	39	54	56	38	2	81	7	1	5	2	2	.50	6	.275	.344	.388
2004	InldEm	A+	107	379	89	22	1	6	(-	-)	131	43	53	35	28	1	70	9	4	4	0	1	.00	17	.235	.300	.346
2004	Tacom	AAA	4	15	6	1	0	1	(-	-)	10	3	1	3	0	0	3	0	0	0	0	0	-	0	.400	.400	.667
2005	SnAnt	AA	57	212	59	14	1	2	(-	-)	81	20	21	25	7	2	35	1	1	0	1	0	1.00	6	.278	.305	.382
2005	Tacom	AAA	14	49	10	3	0	1	(-	-)	16	3	6	3	2	0	12	0	0	0	0	1	.00	2	.204	.235	.327
2004	SEA	AL	2	3	0	0	0	0	(0	0)	0	0	0	0	0	0	1	0	0	0	0	0	-	0	.000	.000	.000
2005	SEA	AL	16	48	19	3	0	1	(0	1)	25	3	6	8	1	0	11	0	1	0	0	0	-	0	.396	.408	.521
2 ML YEARS			18	51	19	3	0	1	(0	1)	25	3	6	8	1	0	12	0	1	0	0	0	-	0	.373	.385	.490

Brian Roberts

Bats: B **Throws:** R **Pos:** 2B-141; PH-3; PR-1   **Ht:** 5'9" **Wt:** 170 **Born:** 10/9/1977 **Age:** 28

Year	Team	Lg	G	AB	H	2B	3B	HR	(Hm	Rd)	TB	R	RBI	RC	TBB	IBB	SO	HBP	SH	SF	SB	CS	SB%	GDP	Avg	OBP	Slg
2001	BAL	AL	75	273	69	12	3	2	(0	2)	93	42	17	27	13	0	36	0	3	3	12	3	.80	3	.253	.284	.341
2002	BAL	AL	38	128	29	6	0	1	(1	0)	38	18	11	12	15	0	21	1	3	2	9	2	.82	3	.227	.308	.297
2003	BAL	AL	112	460	124	22	4	5	(3	2)	169	65	41	62	46	1	58	1	4	1	23	6	.79	9	.270	.337	.367
2004	BAL	AL	159	641	175	50	2	4	(0	4)	241	107	53	91	71	1	95	1	15	6	29	12	.71	3	.273	.344	.376
2005	BAL	AL	143	561	176	45	7	18	(9	9)	289	92	73	106	67	5	83	3	5	4	27	10	.73	6	.314	.387	.515
5 ML YEARS			527	2063	573	135	16	30	(13	17)	830	324	195	298	212	7	293	6	30	16	100	33	.75	24	.278	.344	.402

Dave Roberts

Bats: L **Throws:** L **Pos:** CF-109; PR-7; PH-5   **Ht:** 5'10" **Wt:** 180 **Born:** 5/31/1972 **Age:** 34

Year	Team	Lg	G	AB	H	2B	3B	HR	(Hm	Rd)	TB	R	RBI	RC	TBB	IBB	SO	HBP	SH	SF	SB	CS	SB%	GDP	Avg	OBP	Slg
2005	Lk Els*	A+	3	10	2	1	0	0	(-	-)	3	2	0	1	3	0	1	0	0	0	0	1	.00	0	.200	.385	.300
1999	CLE	AL	41	143	34	4	0	2	(1	1)	44	26	12	14	9	0	16	0	3	1	11	3	.79	0	.238	.281	.308
2000	CLE	AL	19	10	2	0	0	0	(0	0)	2	1	0	1	2	0	2	0	1	0	1	1	.50	0	.200	.333	.200
2001	CLE	AL	15	12	4	1	0	0	(0	0)	5	3	2	2	1	0	2	0	0	0	0	1	.00	0	.333	.385	.417
2002	LA	NL	127	422	117	14	7	3	(0	3)	154	63	34	67	48	0	51	2	6	1	45	10	.82	1	.277	.353	.365
2003	LA	NL	107	388	97	6	5	2	(1	1)	119	56	16	43	43	1	39	4	5	0	40	14	.74	0	.250	.331	.307
2004	2 Tms		113	319	81	14	7	4	(2	2)	121	64	35	52	38	0	48	5	3	6	38	3	.93	4	.254	.337	.379
2005	SD	NL	115	411	113	19	10	8	(5	3)	176	65	38	59	53	3	59	1	11	4	23	12	.66	9	.275	.356	.428
04	LA	NL	68	233	59	4	7	2	(1	1)	83	45	21	41	28	0	31	4	2	3	33	1	.97	2	.253	.340	.356
04	Bos	AL	45	86	22	10	0	2	(1	1)	38	19	14	11	10	0	17	1	1	3	5	2	.71	2	.256	.330	.442
7 ML YEARS			537	1705	448	58	29	19	(9	10)	621	278	137	238	194	4	217	12	29	12	158	44	.78	14	.263	.340	.364

Nate Robertson

Pitches: L **Bats:** R **Pos:** SP-32   **Ht:** 6'2" **Wt:** 215 **Born:** 9/3/1977 **Age:** 28

			HOW MUCH HE PITCHED					WHAT HE GAVE UP										THE RESULTS						
Year	Team	Lg	G	GS	CG	GF	IP	BFP	H	R	ER	HR	SH	SF	HB	TBB	IBB	SO	WP	Bk	W	L	Pct	ShO	Sv-Op Hld	ERC	ERA
2002	FLA	NL	6	1	0	1	8.1	46	15	11	11	3	0	0	2	4	1	3	0	0	0	1	.000	0	0-0 0	12.69	11.88
2003	DET	AL	8	8	0	0	44.2	203	55	27	27	6	0	0	0	23	2	33	3	0	1	2	.333	0	0-0 0	6.24	5.44
2004	DET	AL	34	32	1	1	196.2	852	210	116	107	30	12	4	4	66	1	155	5	1	12	10	.545	0	1-1 0	4.65	4.90
2005	DET	AL	32	32	2	0	196.2	846	202	113	98	28	3	11	7	65	2	122	6	1	7	16	.304	0	0-0 0	4.38	4.48
4 ML YEARS			80	73	3	2	446.1	1947	482	267	243	67	15	15	13	158	6	313	14	2	20	29	.408	0	1-1 0	4.81	4.90

Oscar Robles

Bats: L **Throws:** R **Pos:** SS-54; 3B-40; PH-21; 2B-1; PR-1   **Ht:** 5'11" **Wt:** 155 **Born:** 4/9/1976 **Age:** 30

Year	Team	Lg	G	AB	H	2B	3B	HR	(Hm	Rd)	TB	R	RBI	RC	TBB	IBB	SO	HBP	SH	SF	SB	CS	SB%	GDP	Avg	OBP	Slg
1994	Astros	R	55	165	54	5	1	0	(-	-)	61	40	19	30	32	0	17	2	10	0	14	9	.61	5	.327	.442	.370
1995	Auburn	A-	58	216	62	9	1	0	(-	-)	73	49	19	34	39	1	15	0	1	1	8	2	.80	5	.287	.395	.338
1996	Kissim	A+	125	427	115	13	2	0	(-	-)	132	57	29	60	74	3	37	6	8	2	10	8	.56	13	.269	.383	.309
1997	NewOrl	AAA	2	3	1	0	0	0	(-	-)	1	0	0	0	1	0	1	0	0	0	0	0	-	0	.333	.500	.333
1997	Kissim	A+	66	236	53	4	0	0	(-	-)	57	39	21	24	43	0	28	1	8	2	0	1	.00	4	.225	.344	.242
1998	Jacksn	AA	4	5	1	0	0	0	(-	-)	1	0	0	0	1	1	1	0	0	0	0	0	-	0	.200	.333	.200
1998	Kissim	A+	66	207	56	7	1	0	(-	-)	65	31	24	31	38	0	14	3	2	1	6	2	.75	1	.271	.390	.314
2005	LAN	NL	110	364	99	18	1	5	(2	3)	134	44	34	41	31	0	33	2	1	1	0	8	.00	8	.272	.332	.368

Fernando Rodney

Pitches: R **Bats:** R **Pos:** RP-39   **Ht:** 5'11" **Wt:** 170 **Born:** 3/18/1977 **Age:** 29

			HOW MUCH HE PITCHED					WHAT HE GAVE UP										THE RESULTS						
Year	Team	Lg	G	GS	CG	GF	IP	BFP	H	R	ER	HR	SH	SF	HB	TBB	IBB	SO	WP	Bk	W	L	Pct	ShO	Sv-Op Hld	ERC	ERA
2005	Toledo*	AAA	3	0	0	1	3.0	12	2	1	1	0	0	0	2	1	0	4	1	0	0	0	-	0	0- -	4.33	3.00
2002	DET	AL	20	0	0	10	18.0	89	25	15	12	2	2	1	0	12	0	10	0	1	1	3	.250	0	0-4 0	6.77	6.00
2003	DET	AL	27	0	0	11	29.2	143	35	20	20	2	3	3	1	17	1	33	0	0	1	3	.250	0	3-6 3	5.46	6.07
2005	DET	AL	39	0	0	26	44.0	185	39	14	14	5	2	0	2	17	3	42	2	0	2	3	.400	0	9-15 3	3.59	2.86
3 ML YEARS			86	0	0	47	91.2	417	99	49	46	9	7	4	3	44	6	85	2	1	4	9	.308	0	12-25 6	4.79	4.52

Alex Rodriguez

Bats: R **Throws:** R **Pos:** 3B-161; SS-3; DH-1   **Ht:** 6'3" **Wt:** 210 **Born:** 7/27/1975 **Age:** 30

Year	Team	Lg	G	AB	H	2B	3B	HR	(Hm	Rd)	TB	R	RBI	RC	TBB	IBB	SO	HBP	SH	SF	SB	CS	SB%	GDP	Avg	OBP	Slg
1994	SEA	AL	17	54	11	0	0	0	(0	0)	11	4	2	3	3	0	20	0	1	1	3	0	1.00	0	.204	.241	.204
1995	SEA	AL	48	142	33	6	2	5	(1	4)	58	15	19	15	6	0	42	0	1	0	4	2	.67	0	.232	.264	.408
1996	SEA	AL	146	601	215	54	1	36	(18	18)	379	141	123	144	59	1	104	4	6	7	15	4	.79	15	.358	.414	.631
1997	SEA	AL	141	587	176	40	3	23	(16	7)	291	100	84	100	41	1	99	5	4	1	29	6	.83	14	.300	.350	.496
1998	SEA	AL	161	686	213	35	5	42	(18	24)	384	123	124	135	45	0	121	10	3	4	46	13	.78	12	.310	.360	.560
1999	SEA	AL	129	502	143	25	0	42	(20	22)	294	110	111	102	56	2	109	5	1	8	21	7	.75	12	.285	.357	.586
2000	SEA	AL	148	554	175	34	2	41	(13	28)	336	134	132	138	100	5	121	7	0	11	15	4	.79	14	.316	.420	.606
2001	TEX	AL	162	632	201	34	1	52	(26	26)	393	133	135	148	75	6	131	16	0	9	18	3	.86	17	.318	.399	.622
2002	TEX	AL	162	624	187	27	2	57	(34	23)	389	125	142	152	87	12	122	10	0	4	9	4	.69	17	.300	.392	.623
2003	TEX	AL	161	607	181	30	6	47	(26	21)	364	124	118	131	87	10	126	15	0	6	17	3	.85	16	.298	.396	.600

Year	Team	Lg		BATTING																			BASERUNNING				AVERAGES		
			G	AB	H	2B	3B	HR	(Hm	Rd)	TB	R	RBI	RC	TBB	IBB	SO	HBP	SH	SF				SB	CS	SB%	GDP	Avg	OBP	Slg
2004	NYA	AL	155	601	172	24	2	36	(17	19)	308	112	106	112	80	6	131	10	0	7				28	4	.88	18	.286	.375	.512
2005	NYA	AL	**162**	605	194	29	1	**48**	(26	22)	369	**124**	130	137	91	8	139	16	0	3				21	6	.78	8	.321	.421	**.610**
	12 ML YEARS		1592	6195	1901	338	25	429	(215	214)	3576	1245	1226	1317	730	51	1265	98	16	61				226	56	.80	136	.307	.385	.577

Felix Rodriguez

Pitches: R **Bats:** R **Pos:** RP-34

Ht: 6'1" **Wt:** 198 **Born:** 9/9/1972 **Age:** 33

Year	Team	Lg		HOW MUCH HE PITCHED						WHAT HE GAVE UP										THE RESULTS								
			G	GS	CG	GF	IP	BFP	H	R	ER	HR	SH	SF	HB	TBB	IBB	SO	WP	Bk	W	L	Pct	ShO	Sv-Op	Hld	ERC	ERA
2005	StlsInd*	A-	2	2	0	0	3.0	13	4	1	1	1	0	0	0	0	0	5	0	0	0	0	-	0	0- -	-	5.82	3.00
2005	Trent*	AA	2	2	0	0	3.0	13	1	0	0	0	0	0	0	3	0	3	0	0	0	0	-	0	0- -	-	2.02	0.00
1995	LA	NL	11	0	0	5	10.2	45	11	3	3	2	0	0	0	5	0	5	0	0	1	1	.500	0	0-1	0	5.43	2.53
1997	CIN	NL	26	1	0	13	46.0	212	48	23	22	2	0	1	6	28	2	34	4	1	0	0	-	0	0-0	0	5.22	4.30
1998	ARI	NL	43	0	0	23	44.0	207	44	31	30	5	4	3	1	29	1	36	5	2	0	2	.000	0	5-8	0	5.11	6.14
1999	SF	NL	47	0	0	26	66.1	292	67	32	28	6	2	3	2	29	2	55	2	0	2	3	.400	0	0-1	3	4.25	3.80
2000	SF	NL	76	0	0	19	81.2	346	65	29	24	5	2	3	3	42	2	95	3	1	4	2	.667	0	3-8	30	3.26	2.64
2001	SF	NL	80	0	0	13	80.1	314	53	16	15	5	1	3	1	27	2	91	1	0	9	1	.900	0	0-3	32	1.92	1.68
2002	SF	NL	71	0	0	12	69.0	288	53	33	32	5	2	3	4	29	1	58	4	0	8	6	.571	0	0-6	24	2.92	4.17
2003	SF	NL	68	0	0	24	61.0	265	59	21	21	5	3	1	4	29	2	46	5	1	8	2	.800	0	2-3	19	4.33	3.10
2004	2 Tms	NL	76	0	0	13	65.2	289	61	25	24	8	4	1	5	29	4	59	4	0	5	8	.385	0	1-4	20	4.15	3.29
2005	NYA	AL	34	0	0	10	32.1	147	33	18	18	2	0	0	2	20	0	18	3	0	0	0	-	0	0-0	3	5.07	5.01
04	SF	NL	53	0	0	8	44.2	199	43	18	17	7	3	1	4	19	2	31	4	0	3	5	.375	0	0-3	13	4.58	3.43
04	Phi	NL	23	0	0	5	21.0	90	18	7	7	1	1	0	1	10	2	28	0	0	2	3	.400	0	1-1	7	3.25	3.00
	10 ML YEARS		532	1	0	158	557.0	2405	494	231	217	45	18	18	28	267	16	497	31	5	37	25	.597	0	11-34	131	3.78	3.51

Francisco Rodriguez

Pitches: R **Bats:** R **Pos:** RP-66

Ht: 6'0" **Wt:** 175 **Born:** 1/7/1982 **Age:** 24

Year	Team	Lg		HOW MUCH HE PITCHED						WHAT HE GAVE UP										THE RESULTS								
			G	GS	CG	GF	IP	BFP	H	R	ER	HR	SH	SF	HB	TBB	IBB	SO	WP	Bk	W	L	Pct	ShO	Sv-Op	Hld	ERC	ERA
2002	ANA	AL	5	0	0	4	5.2	21	3	0	0	0	0	0	1	2	1	13	0	0	0	0	-	0	0-0	0	1.52	0.00
2003	ANA	AL	59	0	0	23	86.0	334	50	30	29	12	2	4	2	35	5	95	7	0	8	3	.727	0	2-6	7	2.25	3.03
2004	ANA	AL	69	0	0	29	84.0	335	51	21	17	2	2	1	1	33	1	123	5	0	4	1	.800	0	12-19	27	1.64	1.82
2005	LAA	AL	66	0	0	58	67.1	279	45	20	20	7	1	1	0	32	3	91	8	0	2	5	.286	0	**45-50**	0	2.52	2.67
	4 ML YEARS		199	0	0	114	243.0	969	149	71	66	21	5	6	4	102	10	322	20	0	14	9	.609	0	59-75	34	2.09	2.44

Ivan Rodriguez

Bats: R **Throws:** R **Pos:** C-123; PH-5; DH-3

Ht: 5'9" **Wt:** 205 **Born:** 11/30/1971 **Age:** 34

Year	Team	Lg		BATTING																			BASERUNNING				AVERAGES		
			G	AB	H	2B	3B	HR	(Hm	Rd)	TB	R	RBI	RC	TBB	IBB	SO	HBP	SH	SF				SB	CS	SB%	GDP	Avg	OBP	Slg
1991	TEX	AL	88	280	74	16	0	3	(3	0)	99	24	27	23	5	0	42	0	2	1				0	1	.00	10	.264	.276	.354
1992	TEX	AL	123	420	109	16	1	8	(4	4)	151	39	37	41	24	2	73	1	7	2				0	0	-	15	.260	.300	.360
1993	TEX	AL	137	473	129	28	4	10	(7	3)	195	56	66	57	29	3	70	4	5	8				8	7	.53	16	.273	.315	.412
1994	TEX	AL	99	363	108	19	1	16	(7	9)	177	56	57	61	31	5	42	7	0	4				6	3	.67	10	.298	.360	.488
1995	TEX	AL	130	492	149	32	2	12	(5	7)	221	56	67	68	16	2	48	4	0	5				0	2	.00	11	.303	.327	.449
1996	TEX	AL	153	639	192	47	3	19	(10	9)	302	116	86	99	38	7	55	4	0	4				5	0	1.00	15	.300	.342	.473
1997	TEX	AL	150	597	187	34	4	20	(12	8)	289	98	77	98	38	7	89	8	1	4				7	3	.70	18	.313	.360	.484
1998	TEX	AL	145	579	186	40	4	21	(12	9)	297	88	91	100	32	4	88	3	0	3				9	0	1.00	18	.321	.358	.513
1999	TEX	AL	144	600	199	29	1	35	(12	23)	335	116	113	104	24	2	64	1	0	5				25	12	.68	**31**	.332	.356	.558
2000	TEX	AL	91	363	126	27	4	27	(16	11)	242	66	83	78	19	5	48	1	0	6				5	5	.50	17	.347	.375	.667
2001	TEX	AL	111	442	136	24	2	25	(16	9)	239	70	65	77	23	3	73	4	0	1				10	3	.77	13	.308	.347	.541
2002	TEX	AL	108	408	128	32	2	19	(15	4)	221	67	60	63	25	2	71	2	1	4				5	4	.56	13	.314	.353	.542
2003	FLA	NL	144	511	152	36	3	16	(8	8)	242	90	85	91	55	6	92	6	1	5				10	6	.63	18	.297	.369	.474
2004	DET	AL	135	527	176	32	2	19	(7	12)	269	72	86	98	41	6	91	3	0	4				7	4	.64	16	.334	.383	.510
2005	DET	AL	129	504	139	33	5	14	(8	6)	224	71	50	44	11	2	93	2	1	7				7	3	.70	19	.276	.290	.444
	15 ML YEARS		1887	7198	2190	445	38	264	(142	122)	3503	1085	1050	1102	411	56	1039	50	18	63				104	53	.66	240	.304	.343	.487

John Rodriguez

Bats: L **Throws:** L **Pos:** LF-40; PH-14; RF-9

Ht: 6'0" **Wt:** 205 **Born:** 1/20/1978 **Age:** 28

Year	Team	Lg		BATTING																			BASERUNNING				AVERAGES		
			G	AB	H	2B	3B	HR	(Hm	Rd)	TB	R	RBI	RC	TBB	IBB	SO	HBP	SH	SF				SB	CS	SB%	GDP	Avg	OBP	Slg
1997	Yanks	R	46	157	47	10	2	3	(-	-)	70	31	23	32	30	1	32	0	0	3				7	0	1.00	3	.299	.405	.446
1998	Grnsbr	A	119	408	103	18	4	10	(-	-)	159	64	49	63	64	1	93	4	0	3				14	3	.82	7	.252	.357	.390
1999	Yanks	R	3	7	2	0	1	0	(-	-)	4	1	1	2	3	0	0	0	0	0				0	0	-	0	.286	.500	.571
1999	Tampa	A+	71	269	82	14	3	8	(-	-)	126	37	43	51	41	7	52	3	1	3				2	5	.29	5	.305	.399	.468
2000	Tampa	A+	105	362	97	14	2	16	(-	-)	163	59	44	59	40	5	81	8	1	0				3	2	.60	6	.268	.354	.450
2000	Nrwich	AA	17	56	11	4	0	1	(-	-)	18	4	10	6	8	0	22	1	0	0				0	0	-	1	.196	.308	.321
2001	Yanks	R	2	6	5	0	0	0	(-	-)	5	2	2	2	0	0	0	0	0	0				0	0	-	0	.833	.833	.833
2001	Nrwich	AA	103	393	112	31	1	22	(-	-)	211	64	66	72	26	2	117	11	3	2				2	3	.40	7	.285	.345	.537
2002	Nrwich	AA	103	354	76	18	3	15	(-	-)	145	51	63	48	35	2	94	11	1	4				13	3	.81	4	.215	.302	.410
2003	Clmbs	AAA	79	232	61	9	2	10	(-	-)	104	35	33	37	24	1	50	1	3	1				6	0	1.00	2	.263	.333	.448
2004	Clmbs	AAA	112	378	111	26	10	16	(-	-)	205	78	68	79	48	7	84	8	1	3				10	3	.77	7	.294	.382	.542
2005	Buffalo	AAA	46	170	42	13	3	5	(-	-)	76	25	23	27	15	1	40	1	2	1				5	0	1.00	1	.247	.323	.447
2005	Memp	AAA	34	120	41	5	0	17	(-	-)	97	24	47	36	13	3	28	3	1	0				1	1	.50	2	.342	.419	.808
2005	STL	NL	56	149	44	6	0	5	(2	3)	65	15	24	24	19	4	45	3	2	2				2	0	1.00	0	.295	.382	.436

Luis Rodriguez

Bats: B **Throws:** R **Pos:** 2B-40; 3B-27; SS-10; PR-7; PH-6; DH-2   **Ht:** 5'9" **Wt:** 180 **Born:** 6/27/1980 **Age:** 26

Year	Team	Lg	G	AB	H	2B	3B	HR	(Hm	Rd)	TB	R	RBI	RC	TBB	IBB	SO	HBP	SH	SF	SB	CS	SB%	GDP	Avg	OBP	Slg
1998	Twins	R	52	180	50	11	1	1	(-	-)	66	33	15	27	22	2	17	0	1	2	14	3	.82	4	.278	.353	.367
1999	QuadC	A	119	434	117	20	0	3	(-	-)	146	63	50	58	53	0	49	4	13	9	8	4	.67	10	.270	.348	.336
2000	QuadC	A	106	342	77	11	2	0	(-	-)	92	35	28	32	40	1	29	5	19	2	4	5	.44	10	.225	.314	.269
2001	FtMyrs	A+	125	463	127	21	3	4	(-	-)	166	71	64	74	82	2	42	6	14	5	11	8	.58	14	.274	.387	.359
2002	NwBrit	AA	129	455	117	18	2	8	(-	-)	163	60	40	64	61	1	44	5	32	4	3	2	.60	8	.257	.349	.358
2003	Roch	AAA	131	518	153	35	2	1	(-	-)	195	65	44	72	46	2	46	3	9	3	6	8	.43	15	.295	.354	.376
2004	Roch	AAA	126	482	138	33	1	5	(-	-)	188	72	51	71	53	1	49	1	18	6	3	3	.50	17	.286	.354	.390
2005	Roch	AAA	40	138	42	10	0	1	(-	-)	55	19	17	21	16	0	14	1	2	0	0	1	.00	3	.304	.381	.399
2005	MIN	AL	79	175	47	10	2	2	(1	1)	67	21	20	27	18	0	23	1	6	3	2	2	.50	4	.269	.335	.383

Ricardo Rodriguez

Pitches: R **Bats:** L **Pos:** SP-10; RP-2   **Ht:** 6'3" **Wt:** 165 **Born:** 5/21/1978 **Age:** 28

Year	Team	Lg	G	GS	CG	GF	IP	BFP	H	R	ER	HR	SH	SF	HB	TBB	IBB	SO	WP	Bk	W	L	Pct	ShO	Sv-Op	Hld	ERC	ERA
2005	Okla*	AAA	13	12	3	0	80.1	328	64	30	26	8	1	2	6	23	0	48	0	0	7	3	.700	2	0- -	-	2.85	2.91
2002	CLE	AL	7	7	0	0	41.1	183	40	27	26	5	0	0	8	18	3	24	1	0	2	2	.500	0	0-0	0	4.92	5.66
2003	CLE	AL	15	15	0	0	81.2	360	89	57	52	16	3	2	3	28	1	41	4	1	3	9	.250	0	0-0	0	5.14	5.73
2004	TEX	AL	5	4	1	0	26.2	119	28	10	6	1	0	0	0	12	0	15	1	1	3	1	.750	1	0-0	0	4.03	2.03
2005	TEX	AL	12	10	0	0	57.0	255	67	39	35	11	3	1	1	17	0	24	2	0	2	3	.400	0	0-0	0	5.32	5.53
	4 ML YEARS		39	36	1	0	206.2	917	224	133	119	33	6	3	12	75	4	104	8	2	10	15	.400	1	0-0	0	5.01	5.18

Wandy Rodriguez

Pitches: L **Bats:** B **Pos:** SP-22; RP-3   **Ht:** 5'11" **Wt:** 160 **Born:** 1/18/1979 **Age:** 27

Year	Team	Lg	G	GS	CG	GF	IP	BFP	H	R	ER	HR	SH	SF	HB	TBB	IBB	SO	WP	Bk	W	L	Pct	ShO	Sv-Op	Hld	ERC	ERA
2001	Mrtnsvl	R+	12	12	1	0	74.0	296	54	19	13	6	2	3	4	20	0	67	4	1	4	3	.571	0	0- -	-	2.27	1.58
2002	Lxngtn	A	28	28	0	0	159.1	689	167	74	67	12	8	5	13	44	0	137	8	2	11	4	.733	0	0- -	-	3.99	3.78
2003	Salem	A+	20	20	1	0	111.0	476	102	51	43	9	7	8	6	41	1	72	1	1	8	7	.533	1	0- -	-	3.54	3.49
2004	RdRck	AA	26	25	1	0	142.2	644	159	77	71	15	6	6	7	57	1	115	2	6	11	6	.647	0	0- -	-	4.89	4.48
2005	CpChr	AA	1	1	0	0	3.1	15	3	1	1	0	0	0	0	2	1	3	0	0	0	0	-	0	0- -	-	2.96	2.70
2005	RdRck	AAA	8	8	0	0	46.1	198	43	20	19	7	0	1	4	16	0	48	1	0	4	2	.667	0	0- -	-	4.16	3.69
2005	HOU	NL	25	22	0	0	128.2	560	135	82	79	19	3	3	8	53	2	80	3	3	10	10	.500	0	0-0	0	5.08	5.53

Eddie Rogers

Bats: R **Throws:** R **Pos:** PR-7; DH-2; SS-1   **Ht:** 6'1" **Wt:** 172 **Born:** 8/29/1978 **Age:** 27

Year	Team	Lg	G	AB	H	2B	3B	HR	(Hm	Rd)	TB	R	RBI	RC	TBB	IBB	SO	HBP	SH	SF	SB	CS	SB%	GDP	Avg	OBP	Slg
1999	Orioles	R	53	177	51	5	1	1	(-	-)	61	34	19	29	23	0	22	4	4	2	20	3	.87	2	.288	.379	.345
2000	Dlmrva	A	80	332	91	14	5	5	(-	-)	130	46	42	44	22	0	63	0	10	3	27	6	.82	3	.274	.317	.392
2000	Bowie	AA	13	49	14	3	0	1	(-	-)	20	4	8	6	3	0	15	0	0	1	1	1	.50	0	.286	.321	.408
2001	Bowie	AA	53	191	38	10	1	0	(-	-)	50	11	13	9	6	0	40	2	4	0	10	2	.83	4	.199	.231	.262
2001	Frdrck	A+	73	292	76	20	3	8	(-	-)	126	39	41	37	14	0	47	8	2	2	18	6	.75	8	.260	.310	.432
2002	Bowie	AA	112	422	110	26	2	11	(-	-)	173	59	57	50	16	1	70	10	5	6	14	4	.78	9	.261	.300	.410
2003	Bowie	AA	97	340	72	13	1	6	(-	-)	105	48	35	28	12	0	64	6	7	3	27	8	.77	7	.212	.249	.309
2003	Abrdn	A-	3	14	5	2	0	1	(-	-)	10	2	6	3	0	0	2	0	0	1	0	0	-	0	.357	.333	.714
2004	Bowie	AA	124	482	137	32	1	4	(-	-)	183	71	37	66	37	2	78	4	15	1	20	7	.74	4	.284	.340	.380
2005	Ottawa	AAA	125	431	113	21	3	7	(-	-)	161	52	48	48	17	0	66	1	5	1	14	6	.70	10	.262	.291	.374
2002	BAL	AL	5	3	0	0	0	0	(0	0)	0	0	0	0	0	0	0	0	0	1	0	0	-	1	.000	.000	.000
2005	BAL	AL	8	1	1	0	0	1	(1	0)	4	4	2	0	0	0	0	0	0	0	0	2	.00	0	1.000	1.000	4.000
	2 ML YEARS		13	4	1	0	0	1	(1	0)	4	4	2	0	0	0	0	0	0	1	0	2	.00	1	.250	.250	1.000

Kenny Rogers

Pitches: L **Bats:** L **Pos:** SP-30   **Ht:** 6'1" **Wt:** 217 **Born:** 11/10/1964 **Age:** 41

Year	Team	Lg	G	GS	CG	GF	IP	BFP	H	R	ER	HR	SH	SF	HB	TBB	IBB	SO	WP	Bk	W	L	Pct	ShO	Sv-Op	Hld	ERC	ERA
1989	TEX	AL	73	0	0	24	73.2	314	60	28	24	2	6	3	4	42	9	63	6	0	3	4	.429	0	2-5	15	3.26	2.93
1990	TEX	AL	69	3	0	46	97.2	428	93	40	34	6	7	4	1	42	5	74	5	0	10	6	.625	0	15-23	6	3.53	3.13
1991	TEX	AL	63	9	0	20	109.2	511	121	80	66	14	9	5	6	61	7	73	3	1	10	10	.500	0	5-6	11	5.57	5.42
1992	TEX	AL	81	0	0	38	78.2	337	80	32	27	7	4	1	0	26	8	70	4	1	3	6	.333	0	6-10	16	3.63	3.09
1993	TEX	AL	35	33	5	0	208.1	885	210	108	95	18	7	5	4	71	2	140	6	5	16	10	.615	0	0-0	1	3.88	4.10
1994	TEX	AL	24	24	6	0	167.1	714	169	93	83	24	3	6	3	52	1	120	3	1	11	8	.579	2	0-0	0	4.12	4.46
1995	TEX	AL	31	31	3	0	208.0	877	192	87	78	26	3	5	2	76	1	140	8	1	17	7	.708	1	0-0	0	3.72	3.38
1996	NYA	AL	30	30	2	0	179.0	786	179	97	93	16	6	3	8	83	2	92	5	0	12	8	.600	1	0-0	0	4.43	4.68
1997	NYA	AL	31	22	1	4	145.0	651	161	100	91	18	2	4	7	62	1	78	2	2	6	7	.462	0	0-0	1	5.18	5.65
1998	OAK	AL	34	34	7	0	238.2	970	215	96	84	19	4	6	7	67	0	138	5	2	16	8	.667	1	0-0	0	3.13	3.17
1999	2 Tms		31	31	5	0	195.1	845	206	101	91	16	7	7	13	69	1	126	4	1	10	4	.714	0	0-0	0	4.38	4.19
2000	TEX	AL	34	34	2	0	227.1	998	257	126	115	20	3	4	11	78	2	127	1	1	13	13	.500	0	0-0	0	4.72	4.55
2001	TEX	AL	20	20	0	0	120.2	552	150	88	83	18	1	6	8	49	2	74	4	1	5	7	.417	0	0-0	0	6.22	6.19
2002	TEX	AL	33	33	2	0	210.2	892	212	101	90	21	3	1	6	70	1	107	5	1	13	8	.619	2	0-0	0	3.99	3.84
2003	MIN	AL	33	31	0	0	195.0	851	227	108	99	22	9	3	11	50	5	116	6	4	13	8	.619	0	0-0	0	4.73	4.57
2004	TEX	AL	35	35	2	0	211.2	935	248	117	112	24	7	4	9	66	0	126	2	1	18	9	.667	0	0-0	0	4.99	4.76
2005	TEX	AL	30	30	1	0	195.1	828	205	86	75	15	5	6	8	53	1	87	0	0	14	8	.636	1	0-0	0	3.87	3.46

209

	HOW MUCH HE PITCHED					WHAT HE GAVE UP												THE RESULTS						
Year Team	Lg	G GS CG GF	IP	BFP	H	R	ER	HR	SH	SF	HB	TBB	IBB	SO	WP	Bk	W	L	Pct	ShO	Sv-Op	Hld	ERC	ERA
99 Oak	AL	19 19 3 0	119.1	528	135	66	57	8	4	6	9	41	1	68	3	1	5	3	.625	1	0-0	0	4.68	4.30
99 NYM	NL	12 12 2 0	76.0	317	71	35	34	8	4	9	1	28	1	58	1	0	5	1	.833	1	0-0	0	3.91	4.03
17 ML YEARS		687 400 36 132	2862.0	12374	2985	1488	1340	286	86	72	108	1017	48	1751	69	22	190	131	.592	9	28-44	50	4.28	4.21

Scott Rolen

Bats: R Throws: R Pos: 3B-56; PH-1 **Ht: 6'4" Wt: 226 Born: 4/4/1975 Age: 31**

			BATTING																BASERUNNING				AVERAGES		
Year Team	Lg	G	AB	H	2B	3B	HR	(Hm | Rd)	TB	R	RBI	RC	TBB	IBB	SO	HBP	SH	SF	SB	CS	SB%	GDP	Avg	OBP	Slg
1996 PHI	NL	37	130	33	7	0	4	(2 | 2)	52	10	18	16	13	0	27	1	0	2	0	2	.00	4	.254	.322	.400
1997 PHI	NL	156	561	159	35	3	21	(11 | 10)	263	93	92	103	76	4	138	13	0	7	16	6	.73	6	.283	.377	.469
1998 PHI	NL	160	601	174	45	4	31	(19 | 12)	320	120	110	124	93	6	141	11	0	6	14	7	.67	10	.290	.391	.532
1999 PHI	NL	112	421	113	28	1	26	(9 | 17)	221	74	77	83	67	2	114	3	0	6	12	2	.86	8	.268	.368	.525
2000 PHI	NL	128	483	144	32	6	26	(12 | 14)	266	88	89	97	51	9	99	5	0	2	8	1	.89	4	.298	.370	.551
2001 PHI	NL	151	554	160	39	1	25	(12 | 13)	276	96	107	108	74	6	127	13	0	12	16	5	.76	6	.289	.378	.498
2002 2 Tms	NL	155	580	154	29	4	31	(14 | 17)	292	89	110	98	72	4	102	12	0	3	8	4	.67	22	.266	.357	.503
2003 STL	NL	154	559	160	49	1	28	(12 | 16)	295	98	104	104	82	5	104	9	0	7	13	3	.81	19	.286	.382	.528
2004 STL	NL	142	500	157	32	4	34	(10 | 24)	299	109	124	124	72	5	92	13	1	7	4	3	.57	8	.314	.409	.598
2005 STL	NL	56	196	46	12	1	5	(2 | 3)	75	28	28	22	25	1	28	1	0	1	1	2	.33	3	.235	.323	.383
02 Phi	NL	100	375	97	21	4	17	(8 | 9)	177	52	66	60	52	2	68	8	0	3	5	2	.71	12	.259	.358	.472
02 StL	NL	55	205	57	8	4	14	(6 | 8)	115	37	44	38	20	2	34	4	0	0	3	2	.60	10	.278	.354	.561
10 ML YEARS		1251	4585	1300	308	29	231	(103 | 128)	2359	805	859	879	625	42	972	81	1	53	92	35	.72	90	.284	.375	.515

Jimmy Rollins

Bats: B Throws: R Pos: SS-157; PR-1 **Ht: 5'8" Wt: 165 Born: 11/27/1978 Age: 27**

			BATTING																BASERUNNING				AVERAGES		
Year Team	Lg	G	AB	H	2B	3B	HR	(Hm | Rd)	TB	R	RBI	RC	TBB	IBB	SO	HBP	SH	SF	SB	CS	SB%	GDP	Avg	OBP	Slg
2000 PHI	NL	14	53	17	1	1	0	(0 | 0)	20	5	5	8	2	0	7	0	0	5	3	0	1.00	5	.321	.345	.377
2001 PHI	NL	158	656	180	29	12	14	(8 | 6)	275	97	54	96	48	2	108	2	9	5	46	8	.85	5	.274	.323	.419
2002 PHI	NL	154	637	156	33	10	11	(3 | 8)	242	82	60	72	54	3	103	4	6	4	31	13	.70	14	.245	.306	.380
2003 PHI	NL	156	628	165	42	6	8	(5 | 3)	243	85	62	76	54	4	113	0	5	2	20	12	.63	9	.263	.320	.387
2004 PHI	NL	154	657	190	43	12	14	(8 | 6)	299	119	73	108	57	3	73	3	6	2	30	9	.77	4	.289	.348	.455
2005 PHI	NL	158	677	196	38	11	12	(5 | 7)	292	115	54	100	47	8	71	4	2	2	41	6	.87	9	.290	.338	.431
6 ML YEARS		794	3308	904	186	52	59	(29 | 30)	1371	503	308	460	262	20	475	13	28	15	171	48	.78	41	.273	.328	.414

Jason Romano

Bats: R Throws: R Pos: LF-7; PH-6; CF-5; RF-2; PR-2 **Ht: 6'0" Wt: 185 Born: 6/24/1979 Age: 27**

			BATTING																BASERUNNING				AVERAGES		
Year Team	Lg	G	AB	H	2B	3B	HR	(Hm | Rd)	TB	R	RBI	RC	TBB	IBB	SO	HBP	SH	SF	SB	CS	SB%	GDP	Avg	OBP	Slg
2005 Lsvlle*	AAA	56	224	69	17	2	4	(- | -)	102	34	32	36	14	0	36	1	2	2	5	1	.83	4	.308	.349	.455
2005 Albq*	AAA	1	1	0	0	0	0	(- | -)	0	0	0	0	1	0	0	0	0	0	0	0	-	0	.000	.500	.000
2002 2 Tms		47	91	23	4	1	0	(0 | 0)	29	17	5	10	7	0	24	0	2	1	6	1	.86	0	.253	.303	.319
2003 LA	NL	37	36	3	0	0	0	(0 | 0)	3	3	0	0	1	0	8	0	0	0	2	0	1.00	2	.083	.108	.083
2004 2 Tms		26	34	5	0	0	1	(1 | 0)	8	3	4	2	2	0	12	0	1	0	0	0	-	0	.147	.194	.235
2005 CIN	NL	19	30	8	2	0	1	(0 | 1)	13	3	3	5	3	0	9	1	0	0	0	0	-	0	.267	.353	.433
02 Tex	AL	29	54	11	4	0	0	(0 | 0)	15	8	4	5	4	0	13	0	1	1	2	0	1.00	0	.204	.254	.278
02 Col	NL	18	37	12	0	1	0	(0 | 0)	14	9	1	5	3	0	11	0	1	0	4	1	.80	0	.324	.375	.378
04 TB	AL	4	8	1	0	0	0	(0 | 0)	1	0	1	0	0	0	2	0	0	0	0	0	-	0	.125	.125	.125
04 Cin	NL	22	26	4	0	0	1	(1 | 0)	7	3	3	2	2	0	10	0	1	0	0	0	-	0	.154	.214	.269
4 ML YEARS		129	191	39	6	1	2	(1 | 1)	53	26	12	17	13	0	53	1	3	1	8	1	.89	2	.204	.257	.277

J.C. Romero

Pitches: L Bats: B Pos: RP-68 **Ht: 5'11" Wt: 195 Born: 6/4/1976 Age: 30**

	HOW MUCH HE PITCHED					WHAT HE GAVE UP												THE RESULTS						
Year Team	Lg	G GS CG GF	IP	BFP	H	R	ER	HR	SH	SF	HB	TBB	IBB	SO	WP	Bk	W	L	Pct	ShO	Sv-Op	Hld	ERC	ERA
1999 MIN	AL	5 0 0 3	9.2	39	13	4	4	0	0	0	0	0	0	4	0	0	0	0	-	0	0-0	0	3.95	3.72
2000 MIN	AL	12 11 0 0	57.2	268	72	51	45	8	4	2	1	30	0	50	2	1	2	7	.222	0	0-0	0	6.48	7.02
2001 MIN	AL	14 11 0 1	65.0	286	71	48	45	10	3	2	1	24	1	39	1	0	1	4	.200	0	0-0	0	4.89	6.23
2002 MIN	AL	81 0 0 15	81.0	332	62	17	17	3	1	0	4	36	4	76	9	0	9	2	.818	0	1-5	33	2.74	1.89
2003 MIN	AL	73 0 0 17	63.0	295	66	37	36	7	4	0	6	42	7	50	9	2	2	0	1.000	0	0-4	22	5.72	5.00
2004 MIN	AL	74 0 0 12	74.1	319	61	32	29	4	3	1	6	38	6	69	5	0	7	4	.636	0	1-8	16	3.33	3.51
2005 MIN	AL	68 0 0 11	57.0	264	50	26	22	6	5	1	6	39	8	48	1	1	4	3	.571	0	0-1	11	4.62	3.47
7 ML YEARS		327 22 0 59	407.2	1803	395	215	197	38	20	6	23	209	26	336	27	4	25	20	.556	0	2-18	82	4.43	4.35

Mike Rose

Bats: B Throws: R Pos: C-13; PH-2 **Ht: 6'1" Wt: 185 Born: 8/25/1976 Age: 29**

			BATTING																BASERUNNING				AVERAGES		
Year Team	Lg	G	AB	H	2B	3B	HR	(Hm | Rd)	TB	R	RBI	RC	TBB	IBB	SO	HBP	SH	SF	SB	CS	SB%	GDP	Avg	OBP	Slg
1995 Astros	R	35	89	23	2	1	1	(- | -)	30	13	9	12	11	0	18	3	0	0	2	1	.67	1	.258	.359	.337
1996 Kissim	A+	2	1	0	0	0	0	(- | -)	0	0	0	0	0	0	1	0	0	0	0	0	-	0	.000	.000	.000
1996 Auburn	A-	61	180	45	5	1	2	(- | -)	58	20	11	23	30	0	41	1	4	0	9	3	.75	5	.250	.360	.322
1997 QuadC	A	79	234	60	6	1	3	(- | -)	77	22	27	30	28	0	62	4	8	3	3	1	.75	1	.256	.342	.329
1998 QuadC	A	88	267	81	13	2	7	(- | -)	119	48	40	50	52	3	56	1	3	1	10	8	.56	5	.303	.417	.446
1998 Kissim	A+	18	62	14	4	0	3	(- | -)	27	9	9	8	8	0	14	0	1	1	0	1	1.00	2	.226	.314	.435
1999 Kissim	A+	95	303	84	16	2	11	(- | -)	137	61	32	56	59	0	64	3	0	2	12	6	.67	7	.277	.398	.452
1999 Jacksn	AA	15	45	11	0	0	3	(- | -)	20	8	8	8	13	1	10	0	1	0	0	2	.00	1	.244	.414	.444

Year	Team	Lg	G	AB	H	2B	3B	HR	Hm	Rd	TB	R	RBI	RC	TBB	IBB	SO	HBP	SH	SF	SB	CS	SB%	GDP	Avg	OBP	Slg
2000	ElPaso	AA	117	352	100	22	1	10	(-	-)	154	58	62	58	68	2	70	1	1	4	8	11	.42	16	.284	.398	.438
2001	Tucsn	AAA	20	55	10	1	2	0	(-	-)	15	9	8	5	12	1	16	0	1	1	0	0	-	3	.182	.324	.273
2001	ElPaso	AA	62	205	53	13	1	3	(-	-)	77	28	23	29	37	1	40	0	0	1	4	1	.80	8	.259	.370	.376
2001	Trentn	AA	9	24	4	0	0	1	(-	-)	7	3	2	1	6	1	10	0	0	0	0	4	.00	0	.167	.333	.292
2002	Trentn	AA	10	29	3	1	1	0	(-	-)	6	1	0	0	5	0	7	0	0	0	0	0	-	2	.103	.235	.207
2002	Omha	AAA	52	177	46	12	2	3	(-	-)	71	22	17	24	28	1	40	1	1	0	2	3	.40	7	.260	.364	.401
2002	Wichta	AAA	14	59	18	5	0	2	(-	-)	29	13	14	9	7	0	11	0	0	0	0	1	.00	3	.305	.379	.492
2003	Scrmto	AAA	70	221	58	10	1	8	(-	-)	94	44	30	38	44	4	50	4	2	3	2	1	.67	6	.262	.390	.425
2004	Scrmto	AAA	107	349	98	20	2	6	(-	-)	140	56	49	61	76	1	80	3	1	7	0	0	-	14	.281	.407	.401
2005	LsVgs	AAA	69	205	53	20	1	5	(-	-)	90	31	36	32	25	1	51	2	0	3	2	0	1.00	3	.259	.340	.439
2004	OAK	AL	2	2	0	0	0	0	(0	0)	0	1	0	0	0	0	2	0	0	0	0	0	-	0	.000	.000	.000
2005	LAN	NL	15	43	9	2	0	1	(0	1)	14	2	1	1	3	0	6	0	0	0	0	0	-	3	.209	.261	.326
2 ML YEARS			17	45	9	2	0	1	(0	1)	14	3	1	1	3	0	8	0	0	0	0	0	-	3	.200	.250	.311

Cody Ross

Bats: R Throws: L Pos: RF-9; PH-5   Ht: 5'11" Wt: 180 Born: 12/23/1980 Age: 25

Year	Team	Lg	G	AB	H	2B	3B	HR	Hm	Rd	TB	R	RBI	RC	TBB	IBB	SO	HBP	SH	SF	SB	CS	SB%	GDP	Avg	OBP	Slg
1999	Tigers	R	42	142	31	8	3	4	(-	-)	57	19	18	17	16	0	28	2	2	1	3	1	.75	3	.218	.304	.401
2000	W Mich	A	122	434	116	17	9	7	(-	-)	172	71	68	64	55	0	83	9	2	7	11	3	.79	14	.267	.356	.396
2001	Lkland	A+	127	482	133	34	5	15	(-	-)	222	84	80	76	44	0	96	5	6	9	28	5	.85	9	.276	.337	.461
2002	Erie	AA	105	400	112	28	3	19	(-	-)	203	73	72	69	44	1	86	3	2	5	16	2	.89	11	.280	.352	.508
2003	Toledo	AAA	124	470	135	35	6	20	(-	-)	242	74	61	76	32	0	86	5	4	9	15	6	.71	12	.287	.333	.515
2004	LsVgs	AAA	60	238	65	17	2	14	(-	-)	128	44	49	37	18	0	43	2	0	1	2	0	1.00	11	.273	.328	.538
2005	LsVgs	AAA	115	393	105	21	4	22	(-	-)	200	79	63	71	49	1	103	2	0	4	4	2	.67	8	.267	.348	.509
2003	DET	AL	6	19	4	1	0	1	(1	0)	8	1	5	4	1	0	3	1	1	0	0	0	-	0	.211	.286	.421
2005	LAN	NL	14	25	4	1	0	0	(0	0)	5	1	1	0	1	0	10	0	0	0	0	0	-	1	.160	.192	.200
2 ML YEARS			20	44	8	2	0	1	(1	0)	13	2	6	4	2	0	13	1	1	0	0	0	-	1	.182	.234	.295

Dave Ross

Bats: R Throws: R Pos: C-42; PH-11   Ht: 6'2" Wt: 205 Born: 3/19/1977 Age: 29

Year	Team	Lg	G	AB	H	2B	3B	HR	Hm	Rd	TB	R	RBI	RC	TBB	IBB	SO	HBP	SH	SF	SB	CS	SB%	GDP	Avg	OBP	Slg
2005	Portlnd*	AAA	6	21	3	1	0	0	(-	-)	4	3	1	0	2	0	4	0	0	0	0	0	-	0	.143	.217	.190
2005	Indy*	AAA	6	19	4	1	0	0	(-	-)	5	1	1	1	3	0	7	0	0	1	0	0	-	0	.211	.304	.263
2002	LA	NL	8	10	2	1	0	1	(0	1)	6	2	2	2	2	0	4	1	0	0	0	0	-	-	.200	.385	.600
2003	LA	NL	40	124	32	7	0	10	(5	5)	69	19	18	18	13	0	42	2	0	1	0	0	-	4	.258	.336	.556
2004	LA	NL	70	165	28	3	1	5	(2	3)	48	13	15	11	15	1	62	5	0	5	0	0	-	3	.170	.253	.291
2005	2 Tms	NL	51	125	30	8	1	3	(2	1)	49	11	15	13	6	0	28	2	2	3	0	0	-	3	.240	.279	.392
05	Pit	NL	40	108	24	8	0	3	(2	1)	41	9	15	9	6	0	24	1	1	3	0	0	-	3	.222	.263	.380
05	SD	NL	11	17	6	0	1	0	(0	0)	8	2	0	4	0	0	4	1	1	0	0	0	-	0	.353	.389	.471
4 ML YEARS			169	424	92	19	2	19	(9	10)	172	45	50	44	36	1	136	10	2	9	0	0	-	10	.217	.288	.406

Aaron Rowand

Bats: R Throws: R Pos: CF-157; PH-4   Ht: 6'1" Wt: 200 Born: 8/29/1977 Age: 28

Year	Team	Lg	G	AB	H	2B	3B	HR	Hm	Rd	TB	R	RBI	RC	TBB	IBB	SO	HBP	SH	SF	SB	CS	SB%	GDP	Avg	OBP	Slg
2001	CHA	AL	63	123	36	5	0	4	(3	1)	53	21	20	22	15	0	28	4	5	1	5	1	.83	2	.293	.385	.431
2002	CHA	AL	126	302	78	16	2	7	(5	2)	119	41	29	37	12	1	54	6	9	2	0	1	.00	8	.258	.298	.394
2003	CHA	AL	93	157	45	8	0	6	(5	1)	71	22	24	28	7	0	21	3	2	1	0	0	-	1	.287	.327	.452
2004	CHA	AL	140	487	151	38	2	24	(12	12)	265	94	69	92	30	1	91	10	5	2	17	5	.77	5	.310	.361	.544
2005	CHA	AL	157	578	156	30	5	13	(8	5)	235	77	69	78	32	3	116	21	5	4	16	5	.76	17	.270	.329	.407
5 ML YEARS			579	1647	466	97	9	54	(33	21)	743	255	211	257	96	5	310	44	26	10	38	12	.76	33	.283	.337	.451

Kirk Rueter

Pitches: L Bats: L Pos: SP-18; RP-2   Ht: 6'3" Wt: 212 Born: 12/1/1970 Age: 35

Year	Team	Lg	G	GS	CG	GF	IP	BFP	H	R	ER	HR	SH	SF	HB	TBB	IBB	SO	WP	Bk	W	L	Pct	ShO	Sv-Op	Hld	ERC	ERA
1993	MON	NL	14	14	1	0	85.2	341	85	33	26	5	1	0	0	18	1	31	0	0	8	0	1.000	0	0-0	0	3.14	2.73
1994	MON	NL	20	20	0	0	92.1	397	106	60	53	11	6	6	2	23	1	50	2	0	7	3	.700	0	0-0	0	4.54	5.17
1995	MON	NL	9	9	1	0	47.1	184	38	17	17	3	4	0	1	9	0	28	0	0	5	3	.625	1	0-0	0	2.19	3.23
1996	2 Tms	NL	20	19	0	0	102.0	430	109	50	45	12	4	1	2	27	0	46	2	0	6	8	.429	0	0-0	0	4.18	3.97
1997	SF	NL	32	32	0	0	190.2	802	194	83	73	17	10	6	1	51	8	115	3	0	13	6	.684	0	0-0	0	3.54	3.45
1998	SF	NL	33	33	1	0	187.2	806	193	100	91	27	5	8	7	57	3	102	6	0	16	9	.640	0	0-0	0	4.27	4.36
1999	SF	NL	33	33	1	0	184.2	804	219	118	111	28	6	4	2	55	2	94	2	0	15	10	.600	0	0-0	0	5.19	5.41
2000	SF	NL	32	31	0	0	184.0	799	205	92	81	23	**19**	9	2	62	5	71	1	0	11	9	.550	0	0-0	0	4.68	3.96
2001	SF	NL	34	34	0	0	195.1	840	213	105	96	25	11	6	4	66	4	83	1	0	14	12	.538	0	0-0	0	4.65	4.42
2002	SF	NL	33	33	0	0	203.2	846	200	83	74	22	6	6	1	54	7	76	3	0	14	8	.636	0	0-0	0	3.61	3.23
2003	SF	NL	27	27	0	0	147.0	632	170	77	74	14	9	2	1	47	2	41	0	0	10	5	.667	0	0-0	0	4.72	4.53
2004	SF	NL	33	33	0	0	190.1	840	225	108	100	21	9	4	1	66	5	56	1	0	9	12	.429	0	0-0	0	4.98	4.73
2005	SF	NL	20	18	0	1	107.1	489	131	78	71	12	3	8	1	47	3	25	3	0	5	7	.222	0	0-0	0	5.60	5.95
96	Mon	NL	16	16	0	0	78.2	338	91	44	40	12	4	1	2	22	0	30	0	0	6	5	.455	0	0-0	0	5.06	4.58
96	SF	NL	4	3	0	0	23.1	92	18	6	5	0	0	0	0	5	0	16	2	0	1	2	.333	0	0-0	0	1.66	1.93
13 ML YEARS			340	336	4	1	1918.0	8210	2092	1004	911	220	93	60	25	582	41	818	24	0	130	92	.586	1	0-0	0	4.36	4.27

Josh Rupe

Pitches: R Bats: R Pos: RP-3; SP-1　　　　　　　　**Ht: 6'2" Wt: 200 Born: 8/18/1982 Age: 23**

Year	Team	Lg	G	GS	CG	GF	IP	BFP	H	R	ER	HR	SH	SF	HB	TBB	IBB	SO	WP	Bk	W	L	Pct	ShO	Sv-Op	Hld	ERC	ERA
2002	Bristol	R+	17	2	0	3	40.2	185	41	23	22	4	1	0	4	22	1	41	6	1	4	3	.571	0	0--	-	5.02	4.87
2003	Knapol	A-	26	7	2	11	65.2	283	50	27	22	1	1	1	2	36	2	69	2	0	5	5	.500	0	6--	-	2.68	3.02
2003	Clinton	A	6	5	0	0	27.2	119	29	14	12	1	0	0	3	7	0	23	2	0	4	1	.800	0	0--	-	3.75	3.90
2004	Stcktn	A+	4	3	0	1	18.1	71	12	4	3	0	1	1	3	4	0	14	2	0	2	0	1.000	0	0--	-	1.72	1.47
2004	Spkane	A-	4	3	0	0	18.0	71	14	3	3	1	1	0	2	3	0	19	0	0	2	0	1.000	0	0--	-	2.23	1.50
2004	Frisco	AA	7	6	0	0	37.0	168	41	23	18	5	1	4	5	16	1	16	2	0	2	2	.500	0	0--	-	5.65	4.38
2005	Frisco	AA	11	10	0	0	65.0	285	64	29	27	7	1	1	3	26	0	55	2	0	4	3	.571	0	0--	-	4.18	3.74
2005	Okla	AAA	17	17	0	0	93.2	435	116	75	65	12	6	3	8	38	1	62	4	1	6	7	.462	0	0--	-	6.03	6.25
2005	TEX	AL	4	1	0	1	9.2	39	7	4	3	0	1	0	2	4	0	6	1	0	1	0	1.000	0	0-0	0	2.91	2.79

Glendon Rusch

Pitches: L Bats: L Pos: RP-27; SP-19　　　　　　　　**Ht: 6'1" Wt: 200 Born: 11/7/1974 Age: 31**

Year	Team	Lg	G	GS	CG	GF	IP	BFP	H	R	ER	HR	SH	SF	HB	TBB	IBB	SO	WP	Bk	W	L	Pct	ShO	Sv-Op	Hld	ERC	ERA
1997	KC	AL	30	27	1	0	170.1	758	206	111	104	28	8	7	7	52	0	116	0	1	6	9	.400	0	0-0	0	5.56	5.50
1998	KC	AL	29	24	1	2	154.2	686	191	104	101	22	1	2	4	50	0	94	1	0	6	15	.286	1	1-1	0	5.62	5.88
1999	2 Tms		4	0	0	2	5.0	26	8	7	7	1	0	0	1	3	0	4	0	0	0	1	.000	0	0-0	0	10.75	12.60
2000	NYN	NL	31	30	2	0	190.2	802	196	91	85	18	10	7	6	44	2	157	2	0	11	11	.500	0	0-0	0	3.64	4.01
2001	NYN	NL	33	33	1	0	179.0	785	216	101	92	23	11	5	7	43	2	156	3	2	8	12	.400	0	0-0	0	4.97	4.63
2002	MIL	NL	34	34	4	0	210.2	913	227	118	110	30	14	5	5	76	1	140	6	0	10	16	.385	1	0-0	0	4.80	4.70
2003	MIL	NL	32	19	1	1	123.1	573	171	93	88	11	5	2	4	45	3	93	3	0	1	12	.077	0	1-1	7	6.27	6.42
2004	CHN	NL	32	16	0	5	129.2	545	127	54	50	10	8	2	4	33	1	90	1	1	6	2	.750	0	2-3	3	3.33	3.47
2005	CHN	NL	46	19	1	6	145.1	655	175	79	73	14	13	9	1	53	8	111	1	1	9	8	.529	1	0-1	3	4.97	4.52
99	KC	AL	3	0	0	1	4.0	23	7	7	7	1	0	0	1	3	0	4	0	0	0	1	.000	0	0-0	0	12.89	15.75
99	NYM	NL	1	0	0	1	1.0	3	1	0	0	0	0	0	0	0	0	0	0	0	0	0	-	0	0-0	0	2.79	0.00
9 ML YEARS			271	202	11	16	1308.2	5743	1517	758	710	157	70	39	39	399	17	961	17	5	57	86	.399	3	4-5	13	4.86	4.88

B.J. Ryan

Pitches: L Bats: L Pos: RP-69　　　　　　　　**Ht: 6'6" Wt: 230 Born: 12/28/1975 Age: 30**

Year	Team	Lg	G	GS	CG	GF	IP	BFP	H	R	ER	HR	SH	SF	HB	TBB	IBB	SO	WP	Bk	W	L	Pct	ShO	Sv-Op	Hld	ERC	ERA
1999	2 Tms		14	0	0	3	20.1	82	13	7	7	0	0	1	0	13	1	29	1	0	1	0	1.000	0	0-0	0	2.42	3.10
2000	BAL	AL	42	0	0	9	42.2	193	36	29	28	7	1	1	0	31	1	41	2	1	2	3	.400	0	0-3	7	4.87	5.91
2001	BAL	AL	61	0	0	9	53.0	237	47	31	25	6	1	2	2	30	4	54	0	0	2	4	.333	0	2-4	14	4.13	4.25
2002	BAL	AL	67	0	0	13	57.2	251	51	31	30	7	3	0	4	33	4	56	4	0	2	1	.667	0	1-2	12	4.48	4.68
2003	BAL	AL	76	0	0	17	50.1	219	42	19	19	1	1	3	3	27	0	63	2	0	4	1	.800	0	0-2	19	3.33	3.40
2004	BAL	AL	76	0	0	19	87.0	361	64	24	22	4	3	2	1	35	9	122	0	0	4	6	.400	0	3-7	21	2.20	2.28
2005	BAL	AL	69	0	0	61	70.1	290	54	20	19	4	1	1	2	26	2	100	5	0	1	4	.200	0	36-41	0	2.50	2.43
99	Cin	NL	1	0	0	0	2.0	9	4	1	1	0	0	0	0	1	0	1	0	0	0	0	-	0	0-0	0	12.01	4.50
99	Bal	AL	13	0	0	3	18.1	73	9	6	6	0	0	1	0	12	1	28	1	0	1	0	1.000	0	0-0	0	1.73	2.95
7 ML YEARS			405	0	0	131	381.1	1634	307	161	150	29	10	10	12	195	21	465	14	1	16	19	.457	0	42-59	73	3.29	3.54

Mike Ryan

Bats: L Throws: R Pos: PH-25; LF-16; RF-10; DH-9; PR-2; 3B-1　　　　　　　　**Ht: 6'0" Wt: 185 Born: 7/6/1977 Age: 28**

Year	Team	Lg	G	AB	H	2B	3B	HR	(Hm	Rd)	TB	R	RBI	RC	TBB	IBB	SO	HBP	SH	SF	SB	CS	SB%	GDP	Avg	OBP	Slg
2005	Roch*	AAA	46	152	43	7	1	6	(-	-)	70	16	26	23	15	0	34	0	1	2	3	0	.00	4	.283	.343	.461
2002	MIN	AL	7	11	1	0	0	0	(0	0)	1	3	0	0	0	0	0	0	0	0	0	0	-	0	.091	.091	.091
2003	MIN	AL	27	61	24	7	0	5	(4	1)	46	13	13	15	6	0	12	0	0	1	2	1	.67	4	.393	.441	.754
2004	MIN	AL	36	71	17	2	1	0	(0	0)	21	9	7	5	4	1	16	0	0	0	1	1	.50	2	.239	.280	.296
2005	MIN	AL	57	117	27	5	0	2	(1	1)	38	7	13	10	9	1	22	0	4	1	1	2	.33	5	.231	.283	.325
4 ML YEARS			127	260	69	14	1	7	(5	2)	106	32	33	30	19	2	52	0	4	2	4	4	.50	11	.265	.313	.408

Kirk Saarloos

Pitches: R Bats: R Pos: SP-27; RP-2　　　　　　　　**Ht: 6'0" Wt: 185 Born: 5/23/1979 Age: 27**

Year	Team	Lg	G	GS	CG	GF	IP	BFP	H	R	ER	HR	SH	SF	HB	TBB	IBB	SO	WP	Bk	W	L	Pct	ShO	Sv-Op	Hld	ERC	ERA
2002	HOU	NL	17	17	1	0	85.1	372	100	59	57	12	5	2	6	27	5	54	1	0	6	7	.462	1	0-0	0	5.35	6.01
2003	HOU	NL	36	4	0	11	49.1	218	55	31	27	4	1		3	17	3	43	0	0	2	1	.667	0	0-0	4	4.51	4.93
2004	OAK	AL	6	5	0	1	24.1	112	27	13	12	4	2	1	2	12	0	10	0	0	2	1	.667	0	0-0	0	5.91	4.44
2005	OAK	AL	29	27	2	0	159.2	682	170	75	74	11	3	3	11	54	8	53	1	0	10	9	.526	1	0-0	0	4.27	4.17
4 ML YEARS			88	53	3	12	318.2	1384	352	178	170	31	11	7	22	110	16	160	2	0	20	18	.526	2	0-0	4	4.71	4.80

C.C. Sabathia

Pitches: L Bats: L Pos: SP-31　　　　　　　　**Ht: 6'7" Wt: 270 Born: 7/21/1980 Age: 25**

Year	Team	Lg	G	GS	CG	GF	IP	BFP	H	R	ER	HR	SH	SF	HB	TBB	IBB	SO	WP	Bk	W	L	Pct	ShO	Sv-Op	Hld	ERC	ERA
2005	Akron*	AA	2	2	0	0	9.0	33	4	3	1	0	1	0	1	2	0	9	1	0	1	0	1.000	0	0--	-	0.98	1.00
2001	CLE	AL	33	33	0	0	180.1	763	149	93	88	19	3	5	7	95	1	171	7	3	17	5	.773	0	0-0	0	3.86	4.39
2002	CLE	AL	33	33	2	0	210.0	891	198	109	102	17	5	10	1	88	2	149	6	3	13	11	.542	0	0-0	0	3.74	4.37
2003	CLE	AL	30	30	2	0	197.2	832	190	85	79	19	10	4	6	66	3	141	4	2	13	9	.591	1	0-0	0	3.70	3.60

Year	Team	Lg	G	GS	CG	GF	IP	BFP	H	R	ER	HR	SH	SF	HB	TBB	IBB	SO	WP	Bk	W	L	Pct	ShO	Sv-Op	Hld	ERC	ERA
			HOW MUCH HE PITCHED						WHAT HE GAVE UP												THE RESULTS						
2004	CLE	AL	30	30	1	0	188.0	787	176	90	86	20	3	6	7	72	3	139	1	1	11	10	.524	1	0-0	0	3.91	4.12
2005	CLE	AL	31	31	1	0	196.2	823	185	92	88	19	6	3	7	62	1	161	7	0	15	10	.600	0	0-0	0	3.55	4.03
5 ML YEARS			157	157	6	0	972.2	4096	898	469	443	94	27	28	28	383	10	761	25	9	69	45	.605	2	0-0	0	3.75	4.10

Ray Sadler

Bats: R **Throws:** R **Pos:** LF-3   **Ht:** 6'1" **Wt:** 200 **Born:** 9/19/1980 **Age:** 25

Year	Team	Lg	G	AB	H	2B	3B	HR	(Hm	Rd)	TB	R	RBI	RC	TBB	IBB	SO	HBP	SH	SF	SB	CS	SB%	GDP	Avg	OBP	Slg
2000	Cubs	R	42	165	56	5	5	1	(-	-)	74	32	27	29	16	1	27	1	0	3	4	3	.57	1	.339	.395	.448
2001	Lansng	A	94	378	129	27	3	10	(-	-)	192	74	50	72	22	3	58	3	1	4	18	7	.72	3	.341	.378	.508
2002	Dytona	A+	112	462	132	31	1	11	(-	-)	198	81	47	68	27	2	91	6	3	1	30	12	.71	7	.286	.333	.429
2002	WTenn	AA	10	30	2	1	0	0	(-	-)	3	4	1	1	5	0	5	3	0	0	2	0	1.00	3	.067	.263	.100
2003	WTenn	AA	110	412	120	31	5	6	(-	-)	179	56	42	65	33	4	81	7	2	3	17	7	.71	8	.291	.352	.434
2003	Altna	AA	14	53	14	5	0	1	(-	-)	22	8	7	7	3	0	16	1	0	1	0	0	-	0	.264	.310	.415
2004	Altna	AA	120	429	115	25	1	20	(-	-)	202	61	72	64	23	1	89	3	1	4	16	6	.73	6	.268	.307	.471
2005	Altna	AA	62	209	51	17	2	5	(-	-)	87	23	23	26	17	1	54	0	1	0	4	4	.50	4	.244	.301	.416
2005	Indy	AAA	69	251	65	9	1	10	(-	-)	106	28	30	33	15	1	57	5	1	3	8	6	.57	5	.259	.310	.422
2005	PIT	NL	3	8	2	0	0	1	(0	1)	5	1	1	1	0	0	1	0	0	0	0	0	-	0	.250	.250	.625

Olmedo Saenz

Bats: R **Throws:** R **Pos:** 1B-66; PH-32; 3B-17; DH-8   **Ht:** 5'11" **Wt:** 221 **Born:** 10/8/1970 **Age:** 35

Year	Team	Lg	G	AB	H	2B	3B	HR	(Hm	Rd)	TB	R	RBI	RC	TBB	IBB	SO	HBP	SH	SF	SB	CS	SB%	GDP	Avg	OBP	Slg
1994	CHA	AL	5	14	2	0	1	0	(0	0)	4	2	0	0	0	0	5	0	1	0	0	0	-	1	.143	.143	.286
1999	OAK	AL	97	255	70	18	0	11	(8	3)	121	41	41	44	22	1	47	15	0	3	1	1	.50	6	.275	.363	.475
2000	OAK	AL	76	214	67	12	2	9	(3	6)	110	40	33	42	25	2	40	7	0	1	1	0	1.00	6	.313	.401	.514
2001	OAK	AL	106	305	67	21	1	9	(6	3)	117	33	32	32	19	1	64	13	1	3	0	1	.00	9	.220	.291	.384
2002	OAK	AL	68	156	43	10	1	6	(3	3)	73	15	18	23	13	1	31	7	0	2	1	1	.50	2	.276	.354	.468
2004	LA	NL	77	111	31	1	0	8	(3	5)	56	17	22	18	12	1	33	2	0	3	0	0	-	4	.279	.352	.505
2005	LAN	NL	109	319	84	24	0	15	(9	6)	153	39	63	50	27	1	63	3	0	2	0	1	.00	12	.263	.325	.480
7 ML YEARS			538	1374	364	86	5	58	(32	26)	634	187	209	209	118	7	283	47	2	14	3	4	.43	40	.265	.341	.461

Alex Sanchez

Bats: L **Throws:** L **Pos:** CF-22; RF-20; PH-16; DH-8; PR-1   **Ht:** 5'10" **Wt:** 159 **Born:** 8/26/1976 **Age:** 29

Year	Team	Lg	G	AB	H	2B	3B	HR	(Hm	Rd)	TB	R	RBI	RC	TBB	IBB	SO	HBP	SH	SF	SB	CS	SB%	GDP	Avg	OBP	Slg
2005	Giants*	R	4	10	6	1	0	0	(-	-)	7	5	2	4	3	0	1	1	0	0	1	1	.50	0	.600	.714	.700
2005	Fresno*	AAA	2	9	1	0	0	0	(-	-)	1	0	1	0	0	0	0	0	0	0	0	1	.00	0	.111	.111	.111
2001	MIL	NL	30	68	14	3	2	0	(0	0)	21	7	4	6	5	0	13	0	0	0	6	2	.75	0	.206	.260	.309
2002	MIL	NL	112	394	114	10	7	1	(0	1)	141	55	33	54	31	0	62	2	6	2	37	14	.73	4	.289	.343	.358
2003	2 Tms		144	557	160	23	8	1	(0	1)	202	58	32	60	25	0	74	3	9	5	52	24	.68	5	.287	.319	.363
2004	DET	AL	79	332	107	9	3	2	(1	1)	128	41	26	40	7	0	50	0	12	1	19	13	.59	5	.322	.335	.386
2005	2 Tms		62	176	57	11	1	2	(2	0)	76	32	16	23	8	1	34	1	5	2	8	5	.62	3	.324	.353	.432
03	Mil	NL	43	163	46	10	3	0	(0	0)	62	15	10	17	7	0	28	2	2	2	8	6	.57	1	.282	.316	.380
03	Det	AL	101	394	114	13	5	1	(0	1)	140	43	22	43	18	0	46	1	7	3	44	18	.71	4	.289	.320	.355
05	TB	AL	43	133	46	8	1	2	(2	0)	62	28	13	19	7	1	25	0	3	2	6	3	.67	3	.346	.373	.466
05	SF	NL	19	43	11	3	0	0	(0	0)	14	4	3	4	1	0	9	1	2	0	2	2	.50	0	.256	.289	.326
5 ML YEARS			427	1527	452	56	21	6	(3	3)	568	193	111	183	76	1	233	6	32	10	122	58	.68	17	.296	.330	.372

Duaner Sanchez

Pitches: R **Bats:** R **Pos:** RP-79   **Ht:** 6'0" **Wt:** 190 **Born:** 10/14/1979 **Age:** 26

Year	Team	Lg	G	GS	CG	GF	IP	BFP	H	R	ER	HR	SH	SF	HB	TBB	IBB	SO	WP	Bk	W	L	Pct	ShO	Sv-Op	Hld	ERC	ERA
2002	2 Tms	NL	9	0	0	5	6.0	31	6	6	6	2	0	0	0	7	0	6	0	0	0	0	-	0	0-1	1	9.19	9.00
2003	PIT	NL	6	0	0	2	6.0	34	15	11	11	2	0	1	2	1	0	3	0	0	1	0	1.000	0	0-0	0	17.96	16.50
2004	LA	NL	67	0	0	27	80.0	342	81	34	30	9	2	3	6	27	2	44	6	0	3	1	.750	0	0-1	4	4.31	3.38
2005	LAN	NL	79	0	0	31	82.0	353	75	36	34	8	10	1	3	36	6	71	7	1	4	7	.364	0	8-12	13	3.76	3.73
02	Ari	NL	6	0	0	3	3.2	19	3	2	2	1	0	0	0	5	0	4	0	0	0	0	-	0	0-1	1	8.32	4.91
02	Pit	NL	3	0	0	2	2.1	12	3	4	4	1	0	0	0	2	0	2	0	0	0	0	-	0	0-0	0	10.55	15.43
4 ML YEARS			161	0	0	65	174.0	760	177	87	81	21	12	5	11	71	8	124	13	1	8	8	.500	0	8-14	18	4.56	4.19

Freddy Sanchez

Bats: R **Throws:** R **Pos:** 3B-65; 2B-58; PH-20; SS-11; PR-1   **Ht:** 5'11" **Wt:** 185 **Born:** 12/21/1977 **Age:** 28

Year	Team	Lg	G	AB	H	2B	3B	HR	(Hm	Rd)	TB	R	RBI	RC	TBB	IBB	SO	HBP	SH	SF	SB	CS	SB%	GDP	Avg	OBP	Slg
2002	BOS	AL	12	16	3	0	0	0	(0	0)	3	3	2	1	2	0	3	0	0	0	0	0	-	0	.188	.278	.188
2003	BOS	AL	20	34	8	2	0	0	(0	0)	10	6	2	1	0	0	8	0	0	0	0	0	-	0	.235	.235	.294
2004	PIT	NL	9	19	3	0	0	0	(0	0)	3	2	2	2	0	0	3	0	1	0	0	0	-	0	.158	.158	.158
2005	PIT	NL	132	453	132	26	4	5	(3	2)	181	54	35	57	27	1	36	5	4	3	2	2	.50	6	.291	.336	.400
4 ML YEARS			173	522	146	28	4	5	(3	2)	197	65	41	61	29	1	50	5	5	3	2	2	.50	6	.280	.322	.377

Rey Sanchez

Bats: R Throws: R Pos: SS-10; 2B-9; PH-5; PR-2; 3B-1; DH-1   Ht: 5'9" Wt: 175 Born: 10/5/1967 Age: 38

								BATTING													BASERUNNING				AVERAGES		
Year	Team	Lg	G	AB	H	2B	3B	HR	(Hm	Rd)	TB	R	RBI	RC	TBB	IBB	SO	HBP	SH	SF	SB	CS	SB%	GDP	Avg	OBP	Slg
1991	CHN	NL	13	23	6	0	0	0	(0	0)	6	1	2	3	4	0	3	0	0	0	0	0	-	0	.261	.370	.261
1992	CHN	NL	74	255	64	14	3	1	(0	0)	87	24	19	23	10	1	17	3	5	2	2	1	.67	7	.251	.285	.341
1993	CHN	NL	105	344	97	11	2	0	(0	0)	112	35	28	34	15	7	22	3	9	2	1	1	.50	8	.282	.316	.326
1994	CHN	NL	96	291	83	13	1	0	(0	0)	98	26	24	32	20	4	29	7	4	1	2	5	.29	9	.285	.345	.337
1995	CHN	NL	114	428	119	22	2	3	(0	3)	154	57	27	44	14	2	48	1	8	2	6	4	.60	9	.278	.301	.360
1996	CHN	NL	95	289	61	9	0	1	(1	0)	73	28	12	19	22	6	42	3	8	2	7	1	.88	6	.211	.272	.253
1997	2 Tms		135	343	94	21	0	2	(1	1)	121	35	27	34	16	2	47	1	9	1	4	6	.40	8	.274	.307	.353
1998	SF	NL	109	316	90	14	2	2	(0	2)	114	44	30	35	16	0	47	4	1	2	0	0	-	11	.285	.325	.361
1999	KC	AL	134	479	141	18	6	2	(1	1)	177	66	56	56	22	2	48	4	10	3	11	5	.69	14	.294	.329	.370
2000	KC	AL	143	509	139	18	2	1	(1	0)	164	68	38	49	28	0	55	4	11	3	7	3	.70	17	.273	.314	.322
2001	2 Tms		149	544	153	18	6	0	(0	0)	183	56	37	52	15	1	49	2	13	5	11	1	.92	20	.281	.300	.336
2002	BOS	AL	107	357	102	12	3	1	(1	0)	123	46	38	42	17	1	31	2	5	5	2	2	.50	9	.286	.318	.345
2003	2 Tms		102	344	86	8	2	0	(0	0)	98	33	23	25	16	3	39	2	4	3	2	1	.67	10	.250	.285	.285
2004	TB	AL	91	285	70	14	3	2	(2	0)	96	23	26	28	12	0	28	3	4	3	0	1	.00	6	.246	.281	.337
2005	NYA	AL	23	43	12	1	0	0	(0	0)	13	7	2	3	2	0	3	1	2	0	0	1	.00	2	.279	.326	.302
97	ChC	NL	97	205	51	9	0	1	(1	0)	63	14	12	16	11	2	26	0	4	0	4	2	.67	7	.249	.287	.307
97	NYY		38	138	43	12	0	1	(0	1)	58	21	15	18	5	0	21	1	5	1	0	4	.00	1	.312	.338	.420
01	KC	AL	100	390	118	14	5	0	(0	0)	142	46	28	45	11	0	34	2	9	4	9	1	.90	11	.303	.322	.364
01	Atl	NL	49	154	35	4	1	0	(0	0)	41	10	9	7	4	1	15	0	4	1	2	0	1.00	9	.227	.245	.266
03	NYM	NL	56	174	36	3	1	0	(0	0)	41	11	12	7	8	2	18	0	0	1	1	1	.50	7	.207	.240	.236
03	Sea	AL	46	170	50	5	1	0	(0	0)	57	22	11	18	8	1	21	2	4	2	1	0	1.00	3	.294	.330	.335
	15 ML YEARS		1490	4850	1317	193	32	15	(8	7)	1619	549	389	479	229	29	508	40	93	34	55	32	.63	136	.272	.308	.334

David Sanders

Pitches: L Bats: L Pos: RP-2   Ht: 6'0" Wt: 200 Born: 8/29/1979 Age: 26

				HOW MUCH HE PITCHED					WHAT HE GAVE UP											THE RESULTS						
Year	Team	Lg	G	GS	CG	GF	IP	BFP	H	R	ER	HR	SH	SF	HB	TBB	IBB	SO	WP	Bk	W	L	Pct	ShO	Sv-Op	Hld	ERC	ERA
1999	WhSox	R	7	1	0	2	16.1	66	12	3	2	0	1	0	1	6	3	26	1	0	1	0	1.000	0	1--	-	1.92	1.10
2000	WinSa	A+	51	0	0	20	48.1	228	39	35	28	4	2	4	4	39	1	50	12	1	3	2	.600	0	6--	-	4.59	5.21
2001	Brham	AA	36	0	0	12	34.0	150	27	12	10	1	1	2	3	25	1	25	2	0	3	0	1.000	0	0--	-	4.07	2.65
2002	Charltt	AA	47	0	0	10	63.2	272	56	17	13	3	1	1	3	28	7	61	4	0	3	1	.750	0	0--	-	3.21	1.84
2003	Charltt	AAA	19	0	0	10	22.0	97	23	9	9	3	0	0	4	6	0	25	1	0	1	1	.500	0	4--	-	4.81	3.68
2004	Lowell	A-	17	0	0	3	28.1	139	42	20	20	1	0	0	4	10	0	17	2	0	2	2	.500	0	0--	-	6.36	6.35
2004	Charltt	AAA	40	0	0	18	52.0	243	61	38	35	7	1	0	3	24	0	45	3	0	2	2	.500	0	2--	-	5.73	6.06
2005	Charltt	AAA	57	0	0	1	65.2	305	68	28	22	10	3	2	5	32	8	47	2	0	4	2	.667	0	1--	-	4.94	3.02
2003	CHA	AL	20	0	0	7	22.0	102	25	16	15	5	0	1	1	11	0	14	0	0	0	0	-	0	0-0	0	6.39	6.14
2005	CHA	AL	2	0	0	0	2.0	10	3	3	3	1	0	1	0	1	0	1	0	0	0	0	-	0	0-0	0	10.88	13.50
	2 ML YEARS		22	0	0	7	24.0	112	28	19	18	6	0	2	1	12	0	15	0	0	0	0	-	0	0-0	0	6.74	6.75

Reggie Sanders

Bats: R Throws: R Pos: LF-80; PH-13; RF-1; DH-1   Ht: 6'1" Wt: 205 Born: 12/1/1967 Age: 38

								BATTING													BASERUNNING				AVERAGES		
Year	Team	Lg	G	AB	H	2B	3B	HR	(Hm	Rd)	TB	R	RBI	RC	TBB	IBB	SO	HBP	SH	SF	SB	CS	SB%	GDP	Avg	OBP	Slg
1991	CIN	NL	9	40	8	0	0	1	(0	1)	11	6	3	1	0	0	9	0	0	0	1	1	.50	1	.200	.200	.275
1992	CIN	NL	116	385	104	26	6	12	(6	6)	178	62	36	64	48	2	98	4	0	1	16	7	.70	6	.270	.356	.462
1993	CIN	NL	138	496	136	16	4	20	(8	12)	220	90	83	76	51	7	118	5	3	8	27	10	.73	10	.274	.343	.444
1994	CIN	NL	107	400	105	20	8	17	(10	7)	192	66	62	65	41	1	114	2	1	3	21	9	.70	2	.263	.332	.480
1995	CIN	NL	133	484	148	36	6	28	(9	19)	280	91	99	109	69	4	122	8	0	6	36	12	.75	9	.306	.397	.579
1996	CIN	NL	81	287	72	17	1	14	(7	7)	133	49	33	47	44	4	86	2	0	1	24	8	.75	8	.251	.353	.463
1997	CIN	NL	86	312	79	19	2	19	(11	8)	159	52	56	53	42	3	93	3	1	0	13	7	.65	9	.253	.347	.510
1998	CIN	NL	135	481	129	18	6	14	(7	7)	201	83	59	69	51	2	137	7	4	2	20	9	.69	10	.268	.346	.418
1999	SD	NL	133	478	136	24	7	26	(11	15)	252	92	72	94	65	1	108	6	0	1	36	13	.73	10	.285	.376	.527
2000	ATL	NL	103	340	79	23	1	11	(4	7)	137	43	37	42	32	2	78	2	3	1	21	4	.84	9	.232	.302	.403
2001	ARI	NL	126	441	116	21	3	33	(19	14)	242	84	90	80	46	7	126	5	1	3	14	10	.58	2	.263	.337	.549
2002	SF	NL	140	505	126	23	6	23	(12	11)	230	75	85	65	47	3	121	12	0	7	18	6	.75	10	.250	.324	.455
2003	PIT	NL	130	453	129	27	4	31	(17	14)	257	74	87	78	38	4	110	5	0	2	15	5	.75	10	.285	.345	.567
2004	STL	NL	135	446	116	27	3	22	(8	14)	215	64	67	65	33	5	118	4	1	3	21	5	.81	5	.260	.315	.482
2005	STL	NL	93	295	80	14	2	21	(14	7)	161	49	54	49	28	1	75	4	0	2	14	1	.93	8	.271	.340	.546
	15 ML YEARS		1665	5843	1563	311	59	292	(143	149)	2868	980	923	957	635	46	1513	69	14	39	297	107	.74	109	.267	.344	.491

Danny Sandoval

Bats: B Throws: R Pos: PH-2; SS-1; PR-1   Ht: 5'11" Wt: 192 Born: 4/7/1979 Age: 27

								BATTING													BASERUNNING				AVERAGES		
Year	Team	Lg	G	AB	H	2B	3B	HR	(Hm	Rd)	TB	R	RBI	RC	TBB	IBB	SO	HBP	SH	SF	SB	CS	SB%	GDP	Avg	OBP	Slg
1998	Hickory	A	126	430	99	12	2	0	(-	-)	115	43	30	31	29	0	88	5	14	2	12	15	.44	10	.230	.285	.267
1999	Burlgtn	A	76	255	58	5	1	3	(-	-)	74	34	37	20	17	0	39	0	6	2	8	5	.62	7	.227	.274	.290
2000	WinSa	A+	52	199	53	11	2	2	(-	-)	74	29	17	25	18	1	21	1	7	0	11	7	.61	7	.266	.330	.372
2000	Burlgtn	A	75	269	87	9	3	0	(-	-)	102	34	34	39	18	1	22	2	8	1	37	18	.67	6	.323	.369	.379
2000	Charltt	AAA	2	8	1	0	0	0	(-	-)	1	0	1	0	1	0	1	0	0	0	0	0	-	0	.125	.222	.125
2001	WinSa	A+	48	176	48	11	0	3	(-	-)	68	25	14	24	11	1	31	3	6	2	11	2	.85	3	.273	.323	.386
2001	Brham	AA	58	203	57	7	1	0	(-	-)	66	24	29	26	17	1	26	1	6	3	7	4	.64	5	.281	.335	.325
2002	Brham	AA	135	504	133	30	2	5	(-	-)	182	86	45	62	45	1	56	5	10	3	39	24	.62	12	.264	.329	.361
2003	Brham	AA	130	478	137	30	2	3	(-	-)	180	62	49	67	43	2	67	3	14	9	21	11	.66	9	.287	.343	.377
2004	Tulsa	AA	133	530	169	37	4	8	(-	-)	238	73	66	80	37	3	64	2	10	1	23	8	.74	13	.319	.365	.449
2005	S-WB	AAA	104	390	129	20	0	7	(-	-)	170	53	48	64	31	7	49	2	10	4	11	11	.50	16	.331	.379	.436
2005	PHI	NL	3	2	0	0	0	0	(0	0)	0	1	0	0	0	0	1	0	0	0	0	0	-	0	.000	.000	.000

Ervin Santana

Pitches: R Bats: R Pos: SP-23　　　　　　　　　　　　　　Ht: 6'2" Wt: 160 Born: 1/10/1983 Age: 23

				HOW MUCH HE PITCHED				WHAT HE GAVE UP									THE RESULTS							
Year	Team	Lg	G	GS	CG	GF	IP	BFP	H	R	ER	HR	SH	SF	HB	TBB	IBB	SO	WP	Bk	W	L	Pct	ShO	Sv-Op Hld	ERC	ERA
2001	Angels	R	10	9	1	0	58.2	251	40	27	21	0	2	0	2	35	0	69	8	1	3	2	.600	0	0-- -	2.52	3.22
2001	Provo	R+	4	4	0	0	18.2	88	19	17	16	1	0	2	2	12	1	22	3	1	2	1	.667	0	0-- -	5.03	7.71
2002	CRpds	A	27	27	0	0	147.0	625	133	75	68	10	2	8	6	48	3	146	9	3	14	8	.636	0	0-- -	3.13	4.16
2003	RCuca	A+	20	20	1	0	124.2	508	98	44	35	9	0	0	7	36	0	130	14	0	10	2	.833	0	0-- -	2.56	2.53
2003	Ark	AA	6	6	0	0	29.2	124	23	15	13	4	1	1	3	12	0	23	1	0	1	1	.500	0	0-- -	3.52	3.94
2004	Ark	AA	8	8	0	0	43.2	190	41	19	16	3	3	0	4	18	0	48	5	0	2	1	.667	0	0-- -	3.91	3.30
2005	Ark	AA	7	7	0	0	39.0	166	34	12	10	2	0	0	2	15	0	32	1	0	5	1	.833	0	0-- -	3.15	2.31
2005	Salt Lk	AAA	3	3	0	0	19.1	79	19	11	9	2	0	1	2	2	0	17	0	0	1	0	1.000	0	0-- -	3.28	4.19
2005	LAA	AL	23	23	1	0	133.2	583	139	73	69	17	1	4	8	47	2	99	4	0	12	8	.600	1	0-0 0	4.51	4.65

Johan Santana

Pitches: L Bats: L Pos: SP-33　　　　　　　　　　　　　　Ht: 6'0" Wt: 195 Born: 3/13/1979 Age: 27

				HOW MUCH HE PITCHED				WHAT HE GAVE UP									THE RESULTS							
Year	Team	Lg	G	GS	CG	GF	IP	BFP	H	R	ER	HR	SH	SF	HB	TBB	IBB	SO	WP	Bk	W	L	Pct	ShO	Sv-Op Hld	ERC	ERA
2000	MIN	AL	30	5	0	9	86.0	398	102	64	62	11	1	3	2	54	0	64	5	2	2	3	.400	0	0-0 0	6.59	6.49
2001	MIN	AL	15	4	0	5	43.2	195	50	25	23	6	2	3	3	16	0	28	3	0	1	0	1.000	0	0-0 0	5.36	4.74
2002	MIN	AL	27	14	0	2	108.1	452	84	41	36	7	3	3	1	49	0	137	15	2	8	6	.571	0	1-1 3	2.86	2.99
2003	MIN	AL	45	18	0	7	158.1	644	127	56	54	17	2	4	3	47	1	169	6	2	12	3	.800	0	0-0 5	2.73	3.07
2004	MIN	AL	34	34	1	0	228.0	881	156	70	66	24	3	3	9	54	0	265	7	0	20	6	.769	1	0-0 0	2.07	2.61
2005	MIN	AL	33	33	3	0	231.2	910	180	77	74	22	6	2	1	45	1	238	6	0	16	7	.696	2	0-0 0	2.14	2.87
	6 ML YEARS		184	108	4	23	856.0	3480	699	333	315	87	17	18	19	265	2	901	44	6	59	25	.702	3	1-1 8	2.86	3.31

Julio Santana

Pitches: R Bats: R Pos: RP-41　　　　　　　　　　　　　　Ht: 6'0" Wt: 225 Born: 1/20/1974 Age: 32

				HOW MUCH HE PITCHED				WHAT HE GAVE UP									THE RESULTS							
Year	Team	Lg	G	GS	CG	GF	IP	BFP	H	R	ER	HR	SH	SF	HB	TBB	IBB	SO	WP	Bk	W	L	Pct	ShO	Sv-Op Hld	ERC	ERA
2005	Nashv*	AAA	8	0	0	4	12.0	48	8	2	2	0	0	0	0	4	0	15	0	0	2	0	1.000	0	1-- -	1.57	1.50
1997	TEX	AL	30	14	0	3	104.0	496	141	86	78	16	1	5	4	49	2	64	8	1	4	6	.400	0	0-1 1	7.06	6.75
1998	2 Tms		35	19	1	5	145.2	630	151	77	71	18	2	5	5	62	3	61	3	0	5	6	.455	0	0-0 0	4.75	4.39
1999	TB	AL	22	5	0	7	55.1	261	66	49	45	10	1	1	7	32	0	34	0	0	1	4	.200	0	0-0 0	7.29	7.32
2000	MON	NL	36	4	0	9	66.2	293	69	45	42	11	1	2	2	33	2	58	2	0	1	5	.167	0	0-2 1	5.31	5.67
2002	DET	AL	38	0	0	8	57.0	239	49	19	18	8	3	0	2	28	2	38	3	1	3	5	.375	0	0-0 0	4.13	2.84
2005	MIL	NL	41	0	0	12	42.0	177	34	21	21	6	1	3	0	19	4	49	5	0	3	5	.375	0	1-4 11	3.36	4.50
98	Tex	AL	3	0	0	0	5.1	27	7	5	5	0	0	0	0	4	1	1	0	0	0	0	-	0	0-0 0	5.97	8.44
98	TB	AL	32	19	1	5	140.1	603	144	72	66	18	2	5	5	58	2	60	3	0	5	6	.455	0	0-0 0	4.70	4.23
	6 ML YEARS		202	42	1	44	470.2	2096	510	297	275	69	9	16	20	223	13	304	21	2	17	31	.354	0	1-8 20	5.40	5.26

Benito Santiago

Bats: R Throws: R Pos: C-6　　　　　　　　　　　　　　Ht: 6'1" Wt: 200 Born: 3/9/1965 Age: 41

						BATTING															BASERUNNING				AVERAGES		
Year	Team	Lg	G	AB	H	2B	3B	HR	(Hm	Rd)	TB	R	RBI	RC	TBB	IBB	SO	HBP	SH	SF	SB	CS	SB%	GDP	Avg	OBP	Slg
2005	StLuci*	A+	3	9	3	1	0	0	(-	-)	4	1	1	1	1	0	0	0	0	0	0	0	-	2	.333	.400	.444
2005	Norfolk*	AAA	9	33	8	1	0	0	(-	-)	9	5	4	3	4	0	8	1	0	1	0	0	-	1	.242	.333	.273
1986	SD	NL	17	62	18	2	0	3	(2	1)	29	10	6	9	2	0	12	0	0	1	0	1	.00	0	.290	.308	.468
1987	SD	NL	146	546	164	33	2	18	(11	7)	255	64	79	77	16	2	112	5	1	4	21	12	.64	12	.300	.324	.467
1988	SD	NL	139	492	122	22	2	10	(3	7)	178	49	46	45	24	2	82	1	5	5	15	7	.68	18	.248	.282	.362
1989	SD	NL	129	462	109	16	3	16	(8	8)	179	50	62	47	26	6	89	1	3	2	11	6	.65	9	.236	.277	.387
1990	SD	NL	100	344	93	8	5	11	(5	6)	144	42	53	47	27	2	55	3	1	7	5	5	.50	4	.270	.323	.419
1991	SD	NL	152	580	155	22	3	17	(6	11)	234	60	87	61	23	5	114	4	0	7	8	10	.44	21	.267	.296	.403
1992	SD	NL	106	386	97	21	0	10	(8	2)	148	37	42	37	21	1	52	0	0	4	2	5	.29	14	.251	.287	.383
1993	FLA	NL	139	469	108	19	6	13	(6	7)	178	49	50	50	37	2	88	5	0	4	10	7	.59	7	.230	.291	.380
1994	FLA	NL	101	337	92	14	2	11	(4	7)	143	35	41	43	25	1	57	1	2	4	1	2	.33	11	.273	.322	.424
1995	CIN	NL	81	266	76	20	0	11	(7	4)	129	40	44	43	24	1	48	4	0	2	2	2	.50	7	.286	.351	.485
1996	PHI	NL	136	481	127	21	2	30	(8	22)	242	71	85	79	49	7	104	1	0	2	2	0	1.00	5	.264	.332	.503
1997	TOR	AL	97	341	83	10	0	13	(7	6)	132	31	42	35	17	1	80	2	1	5	1	0	1.00	10	.243	.279	.387
1998	TOR	AL	15	29	9	5	0	0	(0	0)	14	3	4	4	1	0	6	0	0	0	0	0	-	1	.310	.333	.483
1999	CHN	NL	109	350	87	18	3	7	(2	5)	132	28	36	39	32	6	71	2	0	2	1	1	.50	12	.249	.313	.377
2000	CIN	NL	89	252	66	11	1	8	(7	1)	103	22	45	30	19	8	45	1	0	5	2	2	.50	7	.262	.310	.409
2001	SF	NL	133	477	125	25	4	6	(3	3)	176	39	45	46	23	0	78	2	7	6	5	4	.56	19	.262	.295	.369
2002	SF	NL	126	478	133	24	5	16	(6	10)	215	56	74	57	27	3	73	2	3	7	4	2	.67	19	.278	.315	.450
2003	SF	NL	108	401	112	21	2	11	(2	9)	170	53	56	50	29	2	69	2	0	13	0	1	.00	13	.279	.329	.424
2004	KC	AL	49	175	48	10	0	6	(3	3)	76	15	23	19	8	0	32	2	3	1	1	2	.33	9	.274	.312	.434
2005	PIT	NL	6	23	6	1	1	0	(0	0)	9	1	0	1	0	0	3	0	0	0	0	0	-	1	.261	.261	.391
	20 ML YEARS		1978	6951	1830	323	41	217	(98	119)	2886	755	920	819	430	52	1270	38	26	70	91	69	.57	204	.263	.307	.415

Jose Santiago

Pitches: R Bats: R Pos: RP-4　　　　　　　　　　　　　　Ht: 6'3" Wt: 215 Born: 11/5/1974 Age: 31

				HOW MUCH HE PITCHED				WHAT HE GAVE UP									THE RESULTS							
Year	Team	Lg	G	GS	CG	GF	IP	BFP	H	R	ER	HR	SH	SF	HB	TBB	IBB	SO	WP	Bk	W	L	Pct	ShO	Sv-Op Hld	ERC	ERA
2005	Norfolk*	AAA	29	17	0	1	122.2	546	138	62	58	10	4	1	7	40	1	61	2	0	7	6	.538	0	0-- -	4.52	4.26
1997	KC	AL	4	0	0	3	4.2	24	7	2	1	0	0	0	1	2	1	1	0	0	0	0	-	0	0-0 0	6.62	1.93
1998	KC	AL	2	0	0	2	2.0	9	4	2	2	0	0	0	0	0	0	2	0	0	0	0	-	0	0-0 0	8.38	9.00
1999	KC	AL	34	0	0	15	47.1	203	46	23	18	7	1	3	2	14	2	15	2	1	3	4	.429	0	2-3 4	3.87	3.42
2000	KC	AL	45	0	0	20	69.0	302	70	33	30	7	1	3	3	26	3	44	0	0	8	6	.571	0	2-8 5	4.14	3.91

Year	Team	Lg	G	GS	CG	GF	IP	BFP	H	R	ER	HR	SH	SF	HB	TBB	IBB	SO	WP	Bk	W	L	Pct	ShO	Sv-Op	Hld	ERC	ERA
2001	2 Tms		73	0	0	11	91.2	397	106	47	47	5	4	5	3	22	2	43	1	0	4	6	.400	0	0-2	9	4.09	4.61
2002	PHI	NL	42	0	0	7	47.0	214	56	35	35	7	1	2	3	15	1	30	1	0	1	3	.250	0	0-1	9	5.34	6.70
2003	CLE	AL	25	0	0	4	31.2	138	37	11	10	2	0	0	0	14	3	15	0	0	1	3	.250	0	0-2	4	4.94	2.84
2005	NYN	NL	4	0	0	1	5.2	27	10	2	2	0	0	0	1	2	0	3	0	0	0	0	-	0	0-0	0	9.27	3.18
01	KC	AL	20	0	0	6	29.1	136	40	22	22	2	3	3	1	9	1	15	1	0	2	2	.500	0	0-1	0	5.60	6.75
01	Phi	NL	53	0	0	5	62.1	261	66	25	25	3	1	2	2	13	1	28	0	0	2	4	.333	0	0-1	9	3.42	3.61
8 ML YEARS			229	0	0	63	299.0	1314	336	155	145	28	7	13	13	95	12	153	4	1	17	22	.436	0	4-16	31	4.50	4.36

Ramon Santiago

Bats: B **Throws:** R **Pos:** PH-4; 2B-2; SS-2; PR-2 **Ht:** 5'11" **Wt:** 150 **Born:** 8/31/1979 **Age:** 26

Year	Team	Lg	G	AB	H	2B	3B	HR	(Hm	Rd)	TB	R	RBI	RC	TBB	IBB	SO	HBP	SH	SF	SB	CS	SB%	GDP	Avg	OBP	Slg
2005	Tacom*	AAA	129	441	111	22	3	10	(-	-)	169	68	50	61	38	0	62	15	17	6	18	7	.72	11	.252	.328	.383
2002	DET	AL	65	222	54	5	5	4	(3	1)	81	33	20	23	13	0	48	8	4	2	8	5	.62	2	.243	.306	.365
2003	DET	AL	141	444	100	18	1	2	(1	1)	126	41	29	38	33	0	66	10	18	2	10	4	.71	9	.225	.292	.284
2004	SEA	AL	19	39	7	1	0	0	(0	0)	8	8	2	1	3	0	3	1	2	0	0	0	-	1	.179	.256	.205
2005	SEA	AL	8	8	1	0	0	0	(0	0)	1	2	0	1	1	0	2	3	1	0	0	0	-	0	.125	.417	.125
4 ML YEARS			233	713	162	24	6	6	(4	2)	216	84	51	63	50	0	119	22	25	4	18	9	.67	12	.227	.297	.303

Victor Santos

Pitches: R **Bats:** R **Pos:** SP-24; RP-5 **Ht:** 6'3" **Wt:** 195 **Born:** 10/2/1976 **Age:** 29

Year	Team	Lg	G	GS	CG	GF	IP	BFP	H	R	ER	HR	SH	SF	HB	TBB	IBB	SO	WP	Bk	W	L	Pct	ShO	Sv-Op	Hld	ERC	ERA
2001	DET	AL	33	7	0	6	76.1	335	62	33	28	9	1	3	3	49	4	52	0	0	2	2	.500	0	0-0	2	4.18	3.30
2002	COL	NL	24	2	0	6	26.0	140	41	30	30	3	3	1	0	22	3	25	2	0	0	4	.000	0	0-0	1	9.37	10.38
2003	TEX	AL	8	4	0	2	25.2	117	29	21	20	5	1	1	1	16	1	15	0	0	2	2	.000	0	0-0	0	6.82	7.01
2004	MIL	NL	31	28	0	2	154.0	684	169	95	85	18	6	7	7	57	5	115	2	1	11	12	.478	0	0-0	0	4.73	4.97
2005	MIL	NL	29	24	1	2	141.0	639	153	87	72	20	5	1	5	60	8	89	7	0	4	13	.235	0	0-0	0	4.89	4.57
5 ML YEARS			125	65	1	18	423.2	1915	454	266	235	55	16	13	16	204	21	296	11	1	17	33	.340	0	0-0	3	5.07	4.99

Dane Sardinha

Bats: R **Throws:** R **Pos:** C-1 **Ht:** 6'0" **Wt:** 215 **Born:** 4/8/1979 **Age:** 27

Year	Team	Lg	G	AB	H	2B	3B	HR	(Hm	Rd)	TB	R	RBI	RC	TBB	IBB	SO	HBP	SH	SF	SB	CS	SB%	GDP	Avg	OBP	Slg
2001	Mudvle	A+	109	422	99	24	2	9	(-	-)	154	45	55	35	12	2	9	3	4	4	0	1	.00	12	.235	.259	.365
2002	Chatt	AA	106	394	81	20	0	4	(-	-)	113	0	40	23	14	0	114	0	0	0	2	2	.00	0	.206	.233	.287
2003	Chatt	AA	72	246	63	15	0	3	(-	-)	87	21	32	28	22	3	61	1	0	6	5	3	.63	1	.256	.313	.354
2004	Lsvlle	AAA	89	324	85	17	1	9	(-	-)	131	32	40	35	10	0	94	6	1	4	0	1	.00	9	.262	.294	.404
2005	Lsvlle	AAA	86	299	67	10	0	10	(-	-)	107	36	36	32	22	1	72	4	3	2	1	0	1.00	12	.224	.284	.358
2003	CIN	NL	1	2	0	0	0	0	(0	0)	0	0	0	0	0	0	1	0	0	0	0	0	-	0	.000	.000	.000
2005	CIN	NL	1	3	0	0	0	0	(0	0)	0	0	0	0	0	0	1	0	0	0	0	0	-	0	.000	.000	.000
2 ML YEARS			2	5	0	0	0	0	(0	0)	0	0	0	0	0	0	2	0	0	0	0	0	-	0	.000	.000	.000

Scott Sauerbeck

Pitches: L **Bats:** R **Pos:** RP-58 **Ht:** 6'3" **Wt:** 197 **Born:** 11/9/1971 **Age:** 34

Year	Team	Lg	G	GS	CG	GF	IP	BFP	H	R	ER	HR	SH	SF	HB	TBB	IBB	SO	WP	Bk	W	L	Pct	ShO	Sv-Op	Hld	ERC	ERA
1999	PIT	NL	65	0	0	16	67.2	287	53	19	15	6	4	0	4	38	5	55	3	0	4	1	.800	0	2-5	10	3.60	2.00
2000	PIT	NL	75	0	0	13	75.2	349	76	36	34	4	3	3	1	61	8	83	9	2	5	4	.556	0	1-4	13	5.31	4.04
2001	PIT	NL	70	0	0	14	62.2	281	61	41	39	4	2	0	2	40	6	79	3	0	2	2	.500	0	2-4	19	4.60	5.60
2002	PIT	NL	78	0	0	21	62.2	255	50	18	16	4	0	0	1	27	4	70	2	1	5	4	.556	0	0-0	28	2.91	2.30
2003	2 Tms		79	0	0	13	56.2	260	47	34	30	6	2	1	5	43	5	50	1	0	3	5	.375	0	0-5	18	4.73	4.76
2005	CLE	AL	58	0	0	10	35.2	157	35	18	16	4	1	1	4	16	2	35	2	0	1	0	1.000	0	0-2	14	4.65	4.04
03	Pit	NL	53	0	0	11	40.0	173	30	20	18	5	2	0	1	25	2	32	0	0	3	4	.429	0	0-4	16	3.75	4.05
03	Bos	AL	26	0	0	2	16.2	87	17	14	12	1	0	1	4	18	3	18	1	0	0	1	.000	0	0-1	2	7.20	6.48
6 ML YEARS			425	0	0	87	361.0	1589	322	166	150	28	12	5	17	225	30	372	20	3	20	16	.556	0	5-20	102	4.28	3.74

Joe Saunders

Pitches: L **Bats:** L **Pos:** SP-2 **Ht:** 6'3" **Wt:** 210 **Born:** 6/16/1981 **Age:** 25

Year	Team	Lg	G	GS	CG	GF	IP	BFP	H	R	ER	HR	SH	SF	HB	TBB	IBB	SO	WP	Bk	W	L	Pct	ShO	Sv-Op	Hld	ERC	ERA
2002	CRpds	A	5	5	0	0	28.2	111	16	7	6	2	1	0	2	9	0	27	2	0	3	1	.750	0	0--	-	1.66	1.88
2004	RCuca	A+	19	19	0	0	105.2	446	106	49	40	13	2	3	5	23	0	76	5	1	9	7	.563	0	0--	-	3.68	3.41
2004	Ark	AA	8	8	0	0	39.0	182	51	26	25	5	5	2	5	14	0	25	2	0	4	3	.571	0	0--	-	6.52	5.77
2005	Ark	AA	18	18	2	0	105.1	456	107	52	41	9	0	2	3	32	0	80	2	0	7	4	.636	1	0--	-	3.71	3.49
2005	Salt Lk	AAA	9	9	1	0	55.0	251	65	38	28	3	3	4	1	21	0	29	1	0	3	3	.500	1	0--	-	4.67	4.58
2005	LAA	AL	2	2	0	0	9.1	41	10	8	8	3	0	0	0	4	0	4	1	0	0	0	-	0	0-0	0	6.27	7.71

Curt Schilling

Pitches: R **Bats:** R **Pos:** RP-21; SP-11   **Ht:** 6'4" **Wt:** 231 **Born:** 11/14/1966 **Age:** 39

| | | | HOW MUCH HE PITCHED | | | | | | WHAT HE GAVE UP | | | | | | | | | | THE RESULTS | | | | | | | |
Year	Team	Lg	G	GS	CG	GF	IP	BFP	H	R	ER	HR	SH	SF	HB	TBB	IBB	SO	WP	Bk	W	L	Pct	ShO	Sv-Op	Hld	ERC	ERA
2005	Pwtckt*	AAA	6	3	0	2	19.0	87	27	15	14	3	0	0	3	0	0	21	0	0	0	2	.000	0	0--	-	5.84	6.63
1988	BAL	AL	4	4	0	0	14.2	76	22	19	16	3	0	3	1	10	1	4	2	0	0	3	.000	0	0-0	0	9.43	9.82
1989	BAL	AL	5	1	0	0	8.2	38	10	6	6	2	0	0	0	3	0	6	1	0	0	1	.000	0	0-0	0	5.74	6.23
1990	BAL	AL	35	0	0	16	46.0	191	38	13	13	1	2	4	0	19	0	32	0	0	1	2	.333	0	3-9	5	2.68	2.54
1991	HOU	NL	56	0	0	34	75.2	336	79	35	32	2	5	1	0	39	7	71	4	1	3	5	.375	0	8-11	5	4.08	3.81
1992	PHI	NL	42	26	10	10	226.1	895	165	67	59	11	7	8	1	59	4	147	4	0	14	11	.560	4	2-3	0	**1.86**	2.35
1993	PHI	NL	34	34	7	0	235.1	982	234	114	105	23	9	7	4	57	6	186	9	3	16	7	.696	2	0-0	0	3.44	4.02
1994	PHI	NL	13	13	1	0	82.1	360	87	42	41	10	6	1	3	28	3	58	3	1	2	8	.200	0	0-0	0	4.36	4.48
1995	PHI	NL	17	17	1	0	116.0	473	96	52	46	12	5	2	3	26	2	114	0	1	7	5	.583	0	0-0	0	2.55	3.57
1996	PHI	NL	26	26	8	0	183.1	732	149	69	65	16	6	4	3	50	5	182	5	0	9	10	.474	2	0-0	0	2.59	3.19
1997	PHI	NL	35	**35**	7	0	254.1	1009	208	96	84	25	8	8	5	58	3	**319**	5	1	17	11	.607	2	0-0	0	2.55	2.97
1998	PHI	NL	35	**35**	15	0	**268.2**	**1089**	236	101	97	23	14	7	6	61	3	**300**	12	0	15	14	.517	2	0-0	0	2.75	3.25
1999	PHI	NL	24	24	8	0	180.1	735	159	74	71	25	11	5	3	44	0	152	4	0	15	6	.714	1	0-0	0	3.20	3.54
2000	2 Tms	NL	29	29	8	0	210.1	862	204	90	89	27	11	4	1	45	4	168	4	0	11	12	.478	2	0-0	0	3.38	3.81
2001	ARI	NL	35	**35**	6	0	**256.2**	**1021**	237	86	85	**37**	8	5	1	39	0	293	4	0	**22**	6	.786	1	0-0	0	3.03	2.98
2002	ARI	NL	36	35	5	0	259.1	1017	218	95	93	29	4	3	3	33	1	316	6	0	23	7	.767	1	0-0	0	2.33	3.23
2003	ARI	NL	24	24	3	0	168.0	673	144	58	55	17	11	1	3	32	2	194	4	0	8	9	.471	2	0-0	0	2.59	2.95
2004	BOS	AL	32	32	3	0	226.2	910	206	84	82	23	3	6	5	35	0	203	3	0	**21**	6	**.778**	0	0-0	0	2.75	3.26
2005	BOS	AL	32	11	0	21	93.1	418	121	59	59	12	3	5	2	22	0	87	1	1	8	8	.500	0	9-11	9	5.45	5.69
00	Phi	NL	16	16	4	0	112.2	474	110	49	49	17	5	1	1	32	4	96	4	0	6	6	.500	1	0-0	0	3.79	3.91
00	Ari	NL	13	13	4	0	97.2	388	94	41	40	10	6	3	0	13	0	72	0	0	5	6	.455	1	0-0	0	2.91	3.69
	18 ML YEARS		514	381	82	81	2906.0	11817	2613	1160	1098	298	113	72	47	660	41	2832	71	8	192	131	.594	19	22-34	10	2.94	3.40

Jason Schmidt

Pitches: R **Bats:** R **Pos:** SP-29   **Ht:** 6'5" **Wt:** 205 **Born:** 1/29/1973 **Age:** 33

| | | | HOW MUCH HE PITCHED | | | | | | WHAT HE GAVE UP | | | | | | | | | | THE RESULTS | | | | | | | |
Year	Team	Lg	G	GS	CG	GF	IP	BFP	H	R	ER	HR	SH	SF	HB	TBB	IBB	SO	WP	Bk	W	L	Pct	ShO	Sv-Op	Hld	ERC	ERA
1995	ATL	NL	9	2	0	1	25.0	119	27	17	16	2	2	4	1	18	3	19	1	0	2	2	.500	0	0-1	0	5.56	5.76
1996	2 Tms	NL	19	17	1	0	96.1	445	108	67	61	10	4	9	2	53	0	74	8	1	5	6	.455	0	0-0	0	5.46	5.70
1997	PIT	NL	32	32	2	0	187.2	825	193	106	96	16	10	3	9	76	2	136	8	0	10	9	.526	0	0-0	0	4.31	4.60
1998	PIT	NL	33	33	0	0	214.1	916	228	106	97	24	10	3	4	71	3	158	**15**	1	11	14	.440	0	0-0	0	4.35	4.07
1999	PIT	NL	33	33	2	0	212.2	937	219	110	99	24	7	7	3	85	4	148	6	4	13	11	.542	0	0-0	0	4.30	4.19
2000	PIT	NL	11	11	0	0	63.1	295	71	39	38	6	1	2	1	41	2	51	1	0	2	5	.286	0	0-0	0	5.77	5.40
2001	2 Tms	NL	25	25	1	0	150.1	641	138	75	68	13	5	3	7	61	3	142	8	1	13	7	.650	0	0-0	0	3.72	4.07
2002	SF	NL	29	29	2	0	185.1	769	148	78	71	15	11	5	2	73	1	196	12	0	13	8	.619	2	0-0	0	2.87	3.45
2003	SF	NL	29	29	5	0	207.2	819	152	56	54	14	6	3	5	46	1	208	7	1	17	5	**.773**	**3**	0-0	0	**1.93**	**2.34**
2004	SF	NL	32	32	4	0	225.0	907	165	84	80	18	7	3	3	77	3	251	7	1	18	7	.720	3	0-0	0	2.37	3.20
2005	SF	NL	29	29	0	0	172.0	757	160	90	84	16	8	8	5	85	4	165	7	1	12	7	.632	0	0-0	0	4.04	4.40
96	Atl	NL	13	11	0	0	58.2	274	69	48	44	8	3	6	0	32	0	48	5	1	3	4	.429	0	0-0	0	5.92	6.75
96	Pit	NL	6	6	1	0	37.2	171	39	19	17	2	1	3	2	21	0	26	3	0	2	2	.500	0	0-0	0	4.75	4.06
01	Pit	NL	14	14	1	0	84.0	357	81	46	43	11	3	2	7	28	2	77	3	1	6	6	.500	0	0-0	0	4.17	4.61
01	SF	NL	11	11	0	0	66.1	284	57	29	25	2	2	1	0	33	1	65	5	0	7	1	.875	0	0-0	0	3.16	3.39
	11 ML YEARS		281	272	17	1	1739.2	7430	1609	832	764	158	71	50	42	686	26	1548	80	10	116	81	.589	8	0-1	0	3.63	3.95

Steve Schmoll

Pitches: R **Bats:** R **Pos:** RP-48   **Ht:** 6'2" **Wt:** 200 **Born:** 2/4/1980 **Age:** 26

| | | | HOW MUCH HE PITCHED | | | | | | WHAT HE GAVE UP | | | | | | | | | | THE RESULTS | | | | | | | |
Year	Team	Lg	G	GS	CG	GF	IP	BFP	H	R	ER	HR	SH	SF	HB	TBB	IBB	SO	WP	Bk	W	L	Pct	ShO	Sv-Op	Hld	ERC	ERA
2003	Ogden	R+	24	1	0	22	32.2	140	27	23	15	2	2	2	7	15	0	53	4	0	3	1	.750	0	7--	-	4.01	4.13
2004	VeroB	A+	37	0	0	23	65.0	270	57	18	13	0	0	0	5	18	3	58	1	0	3	3	.500	0	10--	-	2.51	1.80
2004	Jaxnvl	AA	11	0	0	7	19.2	80	14	7	4	0	0	0	3	7	1	18	2	0	0	2	.000	0	2--	-	2.28	1.83
2005	LsVgs	AAA	22	0	0	9	26.1	116	24	15	14	1	1	3	2	13	1	31	0	0	0	3	.000	0	5--	-	3.70	4.78
2005	LAN	NL	48	0	0	14	46.2	205	47	29	26	4	5	4	3	22	2	29	0	1	2	2	.500	0	3-4	9	4.53	5.01

Brian Schneider

Bats: L **Throws:** R **Pos:** C-113; PH-8   **Ht:** 6'1" **Wt:** 200 **Born:** 11/26/1976 **Age:** 29

| | | | BATTING | | | | | | | | | | | | | | | | | | | | | BASERUNNING | | | | AVERAGES | | |
Year	Team	Lg	G	AB	H	2B	3B	HR	(Hm	Rd)	TB	R	RBI	RC	TBB	IBB	SO	HBP	SH	SF	SB	CS	SB%	GDP	Avg	OBP	Slg
2000	MON	NL	45	115	27	6	0	0	(0	0)	33	6	11	8	7	2	24	0	0	1	0	1	.00	1	.235	.276	.287
2001	MON	NL	27	41	13	3	0	1	(1	0)	19	4	6	8	6	1	3	0	0	1	0	0	-	0	.317	.396	.463
2002	MON	NL	73	207	57	19	2	5	(3	2)	95	21	29	29	21	8	41	0	2	2	1	2	.33	7	.275	.339	.459
2003	MON	NL	108	335	77	26	1	9	(0	9)	132	34	46	36	37	8	75	2	1	2	0	2	.00	12	.230	.309	.394
2004	MON	NL	135	436	112	20	3	12	(5	7)	174	40	49	52	42	10	63	3	5	2	0	1	.00	9	.257	.325	.399
2005	WAS	NL	116	369	99	20	1	10	(5	5)	151	38	44	48	29	7	48	6	2	2	1	0	1.00	10	.268	.330	.409
	6 ML YEARS		504	1503	385	94	7	37	(23	14)	604	143	185	181	142	36	254	11	10	10	2	6	.25	39	.256	.323	.402

Scott Schoeneweis

Pitches: L **Bats:** L **Pos:** RP-80   **Ht:** 6'0" **Wt:** 185 **Born:** 10/2/1973 **Age:** 32

| | | | HOW MUCH HE PITCHED | | | | | | WHAT HE GAVE UP | | | | | | | | | | THE RESULTS | | | | | | | |
Year	Team	Lg	G	GS	CG	GF	IP	BFP	H	R	ER	HR	SH	SF	HB	TBB	IBB	SO	WP	Bk	W	L	Pct	ShO	Sv-Op	Hld	ERC	ERA
1999	ANA	AL	31	0	0	6	39.1	175	47	27	24	4	0	0	1	14	1	22	1	0	1	1	.500	0	0-0	3	4.99	5.49
2000	ANA	AL	27	27	1	0	170.0	742	183	112	103	21	2	5	6	67	2	78	4	3	7	10	.412	1	0-0	0	4.84	5.45
2001	ANA	AL	32	32	1	0	205.1	910	227	122	116	21	3	8	14	77	2	104	4	1	10	11	.476	0	0-0	0	4.87	5.08
2002	ANA	AL	54	15	0	4	118.0	510	119	68	64	17	1	5	5	49	4	65	1	1	9	8	.529	0	1-4	11	4.68	4.88

Year	Team	Lg	G	GS	CG	GF	IP	BFP	H	R	ER	HR	SH	SF	HB	TBB	IBB	SO	WP	Bk	W	L	Pct	ShO	Sv-Op	Hld	ERC	ERA
							HOW MUCH HE PITCHED					WHAT HE GAVE UP												THE RESULTS				
2003	2 Tms	AL	59	0	0	19	64.2	276	63	35	30	3	2	1	4	19	5	56	3	0	3	2	.600	0	0-2	4	3.25	4.18
2004	CHA	AL	20	19	0	0	112.2	500	129	74	70	17	3	2	3	49	0	69	3	0	6	9	.400	0	0-0	0	5.65	5.59
2005	TOR	AL	80	0	0	15	57.0	250	54	23	21	2	1	0	4	25	5	43	2	0	3	4	.429	0	1-4	21	3.56	3.32
03	Ana	AL	39	0	0	12	38.2	163	37	19	17	2	1	1	3	10	3	29	1	0	1	1	.500	0	0-1	4	3.14	3.96
03	CWS	AL	20	0	0	7	26.0	113	26	16	13	1	1	0	1	9	2	27	2	0	2	1	.667	0	0-1	0	3.41	4.50
	7 ML YEARS		303	93	2	44	767.0	3363	822	461	428	85	12	22	36	300	19	437	18	5	39	45	.464	1	2-10	39	4.71	5.02

Jared Schumaker

Bats: L **Throws:** R **Pos:** LF-14; PH-8; RF-7; PR-6; CF-4 **Ht:** 5'10" **Wt:** 175 **Born:** 2/3/1980 **Age:** 26

Year	Team	Lg	G	AB	H	2B	3B	HR	(Hm	Rd)	TB	R	RBI	RC	TBB	IBB	SO	HBP	SH	SF	SB	CS	SB%	GDP	Avg	OBP	Slg
2001	NewJrs	A-	49	162	41	10	1	0	(-	-)	53	22	14	22	29	1	33	1	2	1	1	2	.33	4	.253	.368	.327
2002	Ptomc	A+	136	551	158	22	4	2	(-	-)	194	71	44	69	45	3	84	2	6	2	26	16	.62	10	.287	.342	.352
2003	Tenn	AA	91	342	86	20	3	2	(-	-)	118	43	22	41	37	2	54	4	2	2	6	6	.50	4	.251	.330	.345
2004	Tenn	AA	138	516	163	29	6	4	(-	-)	216	78	43	86	60	3	61	2	4	1	19	14	.58	7	.316	.389	.419
2005	Memp	AAA	115	443	127	24	3	7	(-	-)	178	66	34	62	29	1	54	2	8	5	13	3	.81	15	.287	.330	.402
2005	STL	NL	27	24	6	1	0	0	(0	0)	7	9	1	2	2	0	2	0	0	0	1	0	1.00	0	.250	.308	.292

Luke Scott

Bats: L **Throws:** R **Pos:** LF-21; PH-11; RF-4; CF-1 **Ht:** 6'0" **Wt:** 210 **Born:** 6/25/1978 **Age:** 28

Year	Team	Lg	G	AB	H	2B	3B	HR	(Hm	Rd)	TB	R	RBI	RC	TBB	IBB	SO	HBP	SH	SF	SB	CS	SB%	GDP	Avg	OBP	Slg
2002	Clmbs	A	49	171	44	15	4	7	(-	-)	88	28	32	32	21	0	58	3	1	2	9	1	.90	3	.257	.345	.515
2002	Kinston	A+	48	163	39	7	1	8	(-	-)	72	22	30	24	16	0	47	5	2	0	2	1	.67	2	.239	.326	.442
2003	Kinston	A+	67	241	67	12	1	13	(-	-)	120	37	44	43	27	0	62	4	0	0	6	3	.67	0	.278	.360	.498
2003	Akron	AA	50	183	50	13	1	7	(-	-)	86	21	37	27	11	0	37	2	3	3	0	1	.00	2	.273	.317	.470
2004	Salem	A+	66	241	67	20	1	8	(-	-)	113	45	35	46	41	4	58	0	0	5	6	1	.86	5	.278	.376	.469
2004	RdRck	AA	63	208	62	17	0	19	(-	-)	136	45	62	53	33	1	43	6	1	5	0	2	.00	4	.298	.401	.654
2005	RdRck	AAA	103	398	114	25	4	31	(-	-)	240	69	87	85	43	1	96	6	0	2	2	2	.50	4	.286	.363	.603
2005	HOU	NL	34	80	15	4	2	0	(0	0)	23	6	4	6	9	1	23	0	0	0	1	1	.50	0	.188	.270	.288

Marco Scutaro

Bats: R **Throws:** R **Pos:** SS-81; 2B-30; 3B-5; PH-3; LF-2; PR-2 **Ht:** 5'10" **Wt:** 170 **Born:** 10/30/1975 **Age:** 30

Year	Team	Lg	G	AB	H	2B	3B	HR	(Hm	Rd)	TB	R	RBI	RC	TBB	IBB	SO	HBP	SH	SF	SB	CS	SB%	GDP	Avg	OBP	Slg
2002	NYN	NL	27	36	8	0	1	1	(-	-)	13	2	6	2	0	0	11	0	1	1	0	1	.00	1	.222	.216	.361
2003	NYN	NL	48	75	16	4	0	2	(0	2)	26	10	6	10	13	2	14	1	1	1	2	0	1.00	1	.213	.333	.347
2004	OAK	AL	137	455	124	32	1	7	(6	1)	179	50	43	48	16	1	58	0	5	1	0	0	-	9	.273	.297	.393
2005	OAK	AL	118	381	94	22	3	9	(5	4)	149	48	37	45	36	1	48	0	4	2	5	2	.71	6	.247	.310	.391
	4 ML YEARS		330	947	242	58	5	19	(12	7)	367	110	92	105	65	4	131	1	11	5	7	3	.70	17	.256	.303	.388

Scott Seabol

Bats: R **Throws:** R **Pos:** PH-29; 3B-20; 2B-8; 1B-5; DH-3; LF-2; RF-2; PR-2 **Ht:** 6'4" **Wt:** 200 **Born:** 5/17/1975 **Age:** 31

Year	Team	Lg	G	AB	H	2B	3B	HR	(Hm	Rd)	TB	R	RBI	RC	TBB	IBB	SO	HBP	SH	SF	SB	CS	SB%	GDP	Avg	OBP	Slg
1996	Oneont	A-	43	142	30	9	1	3	(-	-)	50	16	10	16	15	0	30	6	2	0	2	3	.40	1	.211	.313	.352
1997	Grnsbr	A	48	136	36	12	2	2	(-	-)	58	11	15	19	9	0	26	4	0	2	3	1	.75	1	.265	.325	.426
1998	Grnsbr	A	71	210	60	11	0	7	(-	-)	92	24	33	31	13	2	40	3	1	2	2	2	.50	2	.286	.333	.438
1999	Grnsbr	A	138	543	171	55	6	15	(-	-)	283	86	89	105	45	1	91	9	0	11	6	5	.55	9	.315	.370	.521
2000	Nrwich	AA	132	493	146	45	2	20	(-	-)	255	82	78	89	42	1	108	4	1	2	2	4	.33	11	.296	.355	.517
2001	Clmbs	AAA	78	282	75	19	1	10	(-	-)	126	32	42	38	14	1	56	4	2	2	3	4	.43	6	.266	.308	.447
2001	Nrwich	AA	31	128	32	7	0	4	(-	-)	51	16	19	15	5	0	30	3	0	2	1	1	.50	4	.250	.290	.398
2002	Clmbs	AAA	121	428	111	29	1	15	(-	-)	187	56	68	56	29	0	89	5	1	7	3	3	.50	5	.259	.309	.437
2003	Memp	AAA	88	307	92	22	1	16	(-	-)	164	40	58	59	32	1	64	8	0	4	2	0	1.00	5	.300	.376	.534
2003	Indy	AAA	25	81	19	1	2	0	(-	-)	24	6	9	5	4	0	18	0	1	0	0	1	.00	1	.235	.264	.296
2004	Memp	AAA	138	514	156	26	1	31	(-	-)	277	92	78	90	37	0	93	7	0	4	6	3	.67	17	.304	.356	.539
2005	Memp	AAA	54	203	54	18	2	9	(-	-)	103	34	33	34	20	0	40	0	0	1	0	0	-	5	.266	.330	.507
2001	NYA	AL	1	1	0	0	0	0	(0	0)	0	0	0	0	0	0	0	0	0	0	0	0	-	0	.000	.000	.000
2005	STL	NL	59	105	23	5	0	1	(1	0)	31	11	10	10	8	0	23	0	0	1	0	0	-	1	.219	.272	.295
	2 ML YEARS		60	106	23	5	0	1	(1	0)	31	11	10	10	8	0	23	0	0	1	0	0	-	1	.217	.270	.292

Rudy Seanez

Pitches: R **Bats:** R **Pos:** RP-57 **Ht:** 5'11" **Wt:** 205 **Born:** 10/20/1968 **Age:** 37

Year	Team	Lg	G	GS	CG	GF	IP	BFP	H	R	ER	HR	SH	SF	HB	TBB	IBB	SO	WP	Bk	W	L	Pct	ShO	Sv-Op	Hld	ERC	ERA
2005	Lk Els*	A+	1	0	0	0	1.0	7	3	4	4	2	0	0	0	1	0	0	0	0	0	1	.000	0	0- -	-	44.68	36.00
1989	CLE	AL	5	0	0	2	5.0	20	1	2	2	0	0	2	0	4	1	7	1	1	0	0	-	0	0-0	0	0.94	3.60
1990	CLE	AL	24	0	0	12	27.1	127	22	17	17	2	0	1	1	25	1	24	5	0	2	1	.667	0	0-0	3	4.85	5.60
1991	CLE	AL	5	0	0	0	5.0	33	10	12	9	2	0	0	0	7	0	7	2	0	0	0	-	0	0-1	0	17.96	16.20
1993	SD	NL	3	0	0	3	3.1	20	8	6	5	1	1	0	0	2	0	1	0	0	0	0	-	0	0-0	0	16.31	13.50
1994	LA	NL	17	0	0	6	23.2	104	24	7	7	2	4	2	1	9	1	18	3	0	1	1	.500	0	0-1	1	4.01	2.66
1995	LA	NL	37	0	0	12	34.2	159	39	27	26	5	3	0	1	18	3	29	0	0	1	3	.250	0	3-4	6	5.57	6.75
1998	ATL	NL	34	0	0	8	36.0	148	25	13	11	2	1	2	1	16	0	50	2	0	4	1	.800	0	2-4	8	2.44	2.75
1999	ATL	NL	56	0	0	13	53.2	225	47	21	20	3	0	2	1	21	1	41	3	0	6	1	.857	0	3-8	18	3.12	3.35
2000	ATL	NL	23	0	0	8	21.0	89	15	11	10	3	1	0	1	9	1	20	0	0	2	4	.333	0	2-3	6	2.95	4.29

			HOW MUCH HE PITCHED						WHAT HE GAVE UP												THE RESULTS							
Year	Team	Lg	G	GS	CG	GF	IP	BFP	H	R	ER	HR	SH	SF	HB	TBB	IBB	SO	WP	Bk	W	L	Pct	ShO	Sv-Op	Hld	ERC	ERA
2001	2 Tms	NL	38	0	0	8	36.0	150	23	12	11	4	0	1	1	19	0	41	4	0	0	2	.000	0	1-3	9	2.78	2.75
2002	TEX	AL	33	0	0	4	33.0	150	28	25	21	5	3	1	0	24	1	40	6	0	1	3	.250	0	0-4	10	4.77	5.73
2003	BOS	AL	9	0	0	4	8.2	44	11	7	6	2	0	1	0	6	1	9	3	0	0	1	.000	0	0-1	0	7.45	6.23
2004	2 Tms	AL	39	0	0	15	46.0	193	39	17	17	3	0	3	0	19	3	46	4	0	3	2	.600	0	0-2	4	2.96	3.33
2005	SD	NL	57	0	0	9	60.1	248	49	19	18	4	2	1	2	22	4	84	4	0	7	1	.875	0	0-2	11	2.76	2.69
01	SD	NL	26	0	0	8	24.0	102	15	8	7	3	0	1	1	15	0	24	1	0	0	2	.000	0	1-3	5	3.21	2.63
01	Atl	NL	12	0	0	0	12.0	48	8	4	4	1	0	0	0	4	0	17	3	0	0	0	-	0	0-0	4	1.99	3.00
04	KC	AL	16	0	0	7	23.0	100	21	10	10	0	0	3	0	11	2	21	3	0	0	1	.000	0	0-1	1		3.91
04	Fla	NL	23	0	0	8	23.0	93	18	7	7	3	0	0	0	8	1	25	1	0	3	1	.750	0	0-1	3	2.87	2.74
14 ML YEARS			380	0	0	104	393.2	1710	341	196	180	38	15	16	9	201	17	417	37	1	27	20	.574	0	11-33	76	3.73	4.12

Bobby Seay

Pitches: L **Bats:** L **Pos:** RP-17   **Ht:** 6'2" **Wt:** 235 **Born:** 6/20/1978 **Age:** 28

			HOW MUCH HE PITCHED						WHAT HE GAVE UP												THE RESULTS							
Year	Team	Lg	G	GS	CG	GF	IP	BFP	H	R	ER	HR	SH	SF	HB	TBB	IBB	SO	WP	Bk	W	L	Pct	ShO	Sv-Op	Hld	ERC	ERA
2005	Tulsa*	AA	4	0	0	2	5.0	18	3	1	1	0	0	0	1	0	0	3	0	0	1	0	1.000	0	1--	-	1.17	1.80
2005	ColSpr*	AAA	17	0	0	12	22.2	101	23	8	6	2	1	1	1	10	0	24	0	0	1	0	1.000	0	3--	-	4.35	2.38
2001	TB	AL	12	0	0	0	13.0	58	13	11	9	3	0	0	1	5	1	12	1	0	1	1	.500	0	0-0	0	5.03	6.23
2003	TB	AL	12	0	0	2	9.0	39	7	3	3	0	0	2	0	6	0	5	0	0	0	0	-	0	0-1	0	3.17	3.00
2004	TB	AL	21	0	0	6	22.2	95	21	6	6	2	0	0	2	5	1	17	1	0	0	0	-	0	0-0	0	3.15	2.38
2005	COL	NL	17	0	0	5	11.2	57	18	11	11	3	1	0	0	8	1	11	0	1	0	0	-	0	0-1	1	10.47	8.49
4 ML YEARS			62	0	0	13	56.1	249	59	31	29	8	1	2	3	24	3	45	2	1	1	1	.500	0	0-2	1	4.90	4.63

Aaron Sele

Pitches: R **Bats:** R **Pos:** SP-21   **Ht:** 6'5" **Wt:** 220 **Born:** 6/25/1970 **Age:** 36

			HOW MUCH HE PITCHED						WHAT HE GAVE UP												THE RESULTS							
Year	Team	Lg	G	GS	CG	GF	IP	BFP	H	R	ER	HR	SH	SF	HB	TBB	IBB	SO	WP	Bk	W	L	Pct	ShO	Sv-Op	Hld	ERC	ERA
2005	Okla*	AAA	2	2	0	0	12.1	61	22	12	11	2	0	1	0	2	0	6	0	0	1	1	.500	0	0--	-	8.22	8.03
1993	BOS	AL	18	18	0	0	111.2	484	100	42	34	5	2	5	7	48	2	93	5	0	7	2	.778	0	0-0	0	3.40	2.74
1994	BOS	AL	22	22	2	0	143.1	615	140	68	61	13	4	5	9	60	2	105	4	0	8	7	.533	0	0-0	0	4.26	3.83
1995	BOS	AL	6	6	0	0	32.1	146	32	14	11	3	1	1	3	14	0	21	3	0	3	1	.750	0	0-0	0	4.35	3.06
1996	BOS	AL	29	29	1	0	157.1	722	192	110	93	14	6	7	8	67	2	137	2	0	7	11	.389	0	0-0	0	5.56	5.32
1997	BOS	AL	33	33	1	0	177.1	810	196	115	106	25	5	7	15	80	4	122	7	0	13	12	.520	0	0-0	0	5.47	5.38
1998	TEX	AL	33	33	3	0	212.2	954	239	116	100	14	5	7	13	84	6	167	4	0	19	11	.633	2	0-0	0	4.69	4.23
1999	TEX	AL	33	33	2	0	205.0	920	244	115	109	21	1	3	12	70	3	186	4	0	18	9	.667	2	0-0	0	5.17	4.79
2000	SEA	AL	34	34	2	0	211.2	908	221	110	106	17	5	8	5	74	7	137	5	0	17	10	.630	2	0-0	0	4.06	4.51
2001	SEA	AL	34	33	2	0	215.0	899	216	93	86	25	5	9	7	51	2	114	1	0	15	5	.750	1	0-0	0	3.70	3.60
2002	ANA	AL	26	26	1	0	160.0	706	190	92	87	21	5	10	7	49	2	82	5	0	8	9	.471	0	0-0	0	5.20	4.89
2003	ANA	AL	25	25	0	0	121.2	553	135	82	78	17	2	5	12	58	1	53	5	0	7	11	.389	0	0-0	0	5.77	5.77
2004	ANA	AL	28	24	0	1	132.0	593	163	84	74	16	3	8	5	51	2	51	4	2	9	4	.692	0	0-0	0	5.77	5.05
2005	SEA	AL	21	21	1	0	116.0	523	147	76	73	18	1	9	5	41	2	53	2	0	6	12	.333	1	0-0	0	6.11	5.66
13 ML YEARS			342	337	15	1	1996.0	8833	2215	1117	1018	209	45	84	108	747	35	1321	51	2	137	104	.568	9	0-0	0	4.84	4.59

Todd Self

Bats: L **Throws:** R **Pos:** RF-10; LF-5; PH-5; PR-2; DH-1   **Ht:** 6'5" **Wt:** 215 **Born:** 11/9/1978 **Age:** 27

			BATTING														BASERUNNING				AVERAGES		
Year	Team	Lg	G	AB	H	2B	3B	HR	(Hm Rd)	TB	R	RBI	RC	TBB	IBB	SO	HBP	SH	SF	SB	CS	SB%	GDP	Avg	OBP	Slg
2000	Auburn	A-	52	160	31	3	1	1	(- -)	39	13	19	16	28	0	42	4	2	1	10	4	.71	1	.194	.326	.244
2000	SlmKzr	A-	59	176	38	6	3	4	(- -)	62	27	19	23	30	0	60	2	0	1	2	1	.67	4	.216	.335	.352
2001	Pittsfld	A-	73	261	79	13	4	3	(- -)	109	52	49	48	46	3	61	2	1	6	10	6	.63	2	.303	.403	.418
2002	Mich	A	136	491	152	36	5	12	(- -)	234	81	94	98	65	4	104	9	2	8	10	1	.91	8	.310	.394	.477
2003	Salem	A+	126	431	137	27	2	6	(- -)	186	84	57	89	87	5	93	5	2	6	2	1	.67	9	.318	.433	.432
2004	RdRck	AA	131	476	150	34	1	11	(- -)	219	86	81	99	89	6	95	1	0	5	8	0	1.00	8	.315	.420	.460
2005	RdRck	AAA	100	326	97	25	2	8	(- -)	150	42	47	65	58	6	91	4	0	3	4	1	.80	5	.298	.407	.460
2005	HOU	NL	21	45	9	2	0	1	(1 0)	14	7	4	5	3	0	9	0	1	0	0	0	-	2	.200	.250	.311

Jae Seo

Pitches: R **Bats:** R **Pos:** SP-14   **Ht:** 6'1" **Wt:** 215 **Born:** 5/24/1977 **Age:** 29

			HOW MUCH HE PITCHED						WHAT HE GAVE UP												THE RESULTS							
Year	Team	Lg	G	GS	CG	GF	IP	BFP	H	R	ER	HR	SH	SF	HB	TBB	IBB	SO	WP	Bk	W	L	Pct	ShO	Sv-Op	Hld	ERC	ERA
2005	Norfolk*	AAA	19	19	0	0	121.2	521	126	64	58	13	7	6	1	30	0	111	2	1	7	4	.636	0	0--	-	3.67	4.29
2002	NYN	NL	1	0	0	1	1.0	3	0	0	0	0	0	0	0	0	0	1	0	0	0	0	-	0	0-0	0	0.00	0.00
2003	NYN	NL	32	31	0	0	188.1	806	193	94	80	18	8	4	6	46	11	110	2	0	9	12	.429	0	0-0	0	3.54	3.82
2004	NYN	NL	24	21	0	1	117.2	512	133	67	64	17	12	3	2	50	7	54	0	1	5	10	.333	0	0-0	0	5.39	4.90
2005	NYN	NL	14	14	1	0	90.1	363	84	26	26	9	9	3	1	16	0	59	2	0	8	2	.800	0	0-0	0	2.91	2.59
4 ML YEARS			71	66	1	2	397.1	1684	410	187	170	44	29	10	9	112	18	224	4	1	22	24	.478	0	0-0	0	3.89	3.85

Richie Sexson

Bats: R **Throws:** R **Pos:** 1B-151; DH-5   **Ht:** 6'8" **Wt:** 227 **Born:** 12/29/1974 **Age:** 31

			BATTING														BASERUNNING				AVERAGES		
Year	Team	Lg	G	AB	H	2B	3B	HR	(Hm Rd)	TB	R	RBI	RC	TBB	IBB	SO	HBP	SH	SF	SB	CS	SB%	GDP	Avg	OBP	Slg
1997	CLE	AL	5	11	3	0	0	0	(0 0)	3	1	0	0	0	0	2	0	0	0	0	0	-	2	.273	.273	.273
1998	CLE	AL	49	174	54	14	1	11	(9 2)	103	28	35	33	6	0	42	3	0	0	1	1	.50	3	.310	.344	.592
1999	CLE	AL	134	479	122	17	7	31	(18 13)	246	72	116	70	34	0	117	4	0	8	3	3	.50	19	.255	.305	.514
2000	2 Tms	AL	148	537	146	30	1	30	(15 15)	268	89	91	91	59	2	159	7	0	4	2	0	1.00	11	.272	.349	.499

Year	Team	Lg	BATTING																			BASERUNNING				AVERAGES		
			G	AB	H	2B	3B	HR	(Hm	Rd)	TB	R	RBI	RC	TBB	IBB	SO	HBP	SH	SF		SB	CS	SB%	GDP	Avg	OBP	Slg
2001	MIL	NL	158	598	162	24	3	45	(28	17)	327	94	125	103	60	5	178	6	0	3		2	4	.33	20	.271	.342	.547
2002	MIL	NL	157	570	159	37	2	29	(13	16)	287	86	102	98	70	7	136	8	0	4		0	0	-	17	.279	.363	.504
2003	MIL	NL	162	606	165	28	2	45	(23	22)	332	97	124	116	98	7	151	9	0	5		2	3	.40	18	.272	.379	.548
2004	ARI	NL	23	90	21	4	0	9	(6	3)	52	20	23	18	14	0	21	0	0	0		0	0	-	2	.233	.337	.578
2005	SEA	AL	156	558	147	36	1	39	(21	18)	302	99	121	117	89	4	167	6	0	3		1	1	.50	14	.263	.369	.541
00	Cle	AL	91	324	83	16	1	16	(8	8)	149	45	44	45	25	0	96	4	0	3		1	0	1.00	8	.256	.315	.460
00	Mil	NL	57	213	63	14	0	14	(7	7)	119	44	47	46	34	2	63	3	0	1		1	0	1.00	3	.296	.398	.559
9 ML YEARS			992	3623	979	190	17	239	(133	106)	1920	586	737	646	430	25	973	43	0	27		11	12	.48	106	.270	.352	.530

Adam Shabala

Bats: L Throws: R Pos: LF-4; PH-2; RF-1   Ht: 6'1" Wt: 190 Born: 2/6/1978 Age: 28

Year	Team	Lg	BATTING																			BASERUNNING				AVERAGES		
			G	AB	H	2B	3B	HR	(Hm	Rd)	TB	R	RBI	RC	TBB	IBB	SO	HBP	SH	SF		SB	CS	SB%	GDP	Avg	OBP	Slg
2000	SlmKzr	A-	59	176	38	6	3	4	(-	-)	62	27	19	23	30	0	60	2	0	1		2	1	.67	4	.216	.335	.352
2001	SnJos	A+	3	7	1	0	0	0	(-	-)	1	1	0	0	2	0	4	0	0	0		0	0	-	0	.143	.333	.143
2001	Hgrstn	A	70	256	80	16	2	1	(-	-)	103	37	29	46	37	0	37	6	5	0		11	4	.73	9	.313	.411	.402
2001	Shreve	AA	12	35	12	0	0	1	(-	-)	15	9	4	7	7	0	10	0	1	0		2	0	1.00	1	.343	.452	.429
2002	SnJos	A+	73	244	80	18	2	7	(-	-)	123	42	45	51	36	0	64	1	5	3		11	7	.61	2	.328	.412	.504
2002	Shreve	AA	40	148	32	8	0	1	(-	-)	43	14	16	10	6	1	35	1	4	1		3	1	.75	3	.216	.250	.291
2003	Nrwich	AA	132	513	137	22	6	9	(-	-)	198	71	54	67	46	0	99	2	3	3		10	7	.59	11	.267	.328	.386
2004	Fresno	AAA	118	401	126	17	5	9	(-	-)	180	63	48	69	32	0	81	1	4	2		21	3	.88	5	.314	.365	.449
2005	Fresno	AAA	95	373	102	24	1	14	(-	-)	170	58	42	61	35	0	73	4	3	1		10	2	.83	4	.273	.341	.456
2005	SF	NL	6	15	3	0	0	0	(0	0)	3	1	4	0	1	0	5	0	1	1		0	0	-	1	.200	.235	.200

Brian Shackelford

Pitches: L Bats: L Pos: RP-37   Ht: 6'1" Wt: 195 Born: 8/30/1976 Age: 29

Year	Team	Lg	HOW MUCH HE PITCHED						WHAT HE GAVE UP												THE RESULTS						
			G	GS	CG	GF	IP	BFP	H	R	ER	HR	SH	SF	HB	TBB	IBB	SO	WP	Bk	W	L	Pct	ShO	Sv-Op	Hld	ERC	ERA
2001	Wichta	AA	1	0	0	0	1.0	7	3	2	2	0	4	6	0	1	0	0	0	0	0	0	-	0	0--	-	19.55	18.00
2002	Wichta	AA	22	0	0	7	25.2	126	23	12	10	1	2	0	3	26	2	15	6	1	3	1	.750	0	0--	-	5.70	3.51
2003	Ptomc	A+	18	0	0	5	27.1	111	17	6	6	1	0	2	4	8	0	20	1	0	1	0	1.000	0	1--	-	1.86	1.98
2003	Chatt	AA	13	1	0	0	20.0	102	26	18	14	3	14	9	5	14	2	19	2	1	3	2	.600	0	1--	-	8.55	6.30
2003	Lsvlle	AAA	12	0	0	4	15.2	70	15	4	4	0	1	1	1	7	0	10	0	0	1	0	1.000	0	0--	-	3.45	2.30
2004	Lsvlle	AAA	59	0	0	13	73.0	319	58	31	29	6	0	0	1	42	1	63	4	2	8	1	.889	0	0--	-	3.46	3.58
2005	Lsvlle	AAA	31	0	0	8	32.2	143	35	19	19	1	3	0	2	10	0	21	1	0	1	6	.143	0	1--	-	3.81	5.23
2005	CIN	NL	37	0	0	5	29.2	119	21	9	8	2	0	1	6	9	1	17	3	1	1	0	1.000	0	0-0	3	2.76	2.43

Ryan Shealy

Bats: R Throws: R Pos: 1B-19; PH-14; DH-5   Ht: 6'5" Wt: 240 Born: 8/29/1979 Age: 26

Year	Team	Lg	BATTING																			BASERUNNING				AVERAGES		
			G	AB	H	2B	3B	HR	(Hm	Rd)	TB	R	RBI	RC	TBB	IBB	SO	HBP	SH	SF		SB	CS	SB%	GDP	Avg	OBP	Slg
2002	Casper	R+	69	231	85	21	1	19	(-	-)	165	55	70	79	50	7	52	18	0	9		0	0	-	7	.368	.497	.714
2003	Visalia	A+	93	341	102	31	1	14	(-	-)	177	70	73	71	42	0	72	14	0	7		0	0	-	5	.299	.391	.519
2004	Tulsa	AA	132	469	149	32	3	29	(-	-)	274	88	99	111	61	7	123	16	2	4		1	1	.50	10	.318	.411	.584
2005	ColSpr	AAA	108	411	135	30	2	26	(-	-)	247	85	88	95	41	2	81	7	2	7		4	0	1.00	13	.328	.393	.601
2005	COL	NL	36	91	30	7	0	2	(0	2)	43	14	16	14	13	0	22	0	0	0		1	0	1.00	6	.330	.413	.473

Ben Sheets

Pitches: R Bats: R Pos: SP-22   Ht: 6'1" Wt: 203 Born: 7/18/1978 Age: 27

Year	Team	Lg	HOW MUCH HE PITCHED						WHAT HE GAVE UP												THE RESULTS						
			G	GS	CG	GF	IP	BFP	H	R	ER	HR	SH	SF	HB	TBB	IBB	SO	WP	Bk	W	L	Pct	ShO	Sv-Op	Hld	ERC	ERA
2001	MIL	NL	25	25	1	0	151.1	653	166	89	80	23	8	5	5	48	6	94	3	0	11	10	.524	1	0-0	0	4.78	4.76
2002	MIL	NL	34	34	1	0	216.2	934	237	105	100	21	10	0	10	70	10	170	9	0	11	16	.407	0	0-0	0	4.45	4.15
2003	MIL	NL	34	34	1	0	220.2	931	232	122	109	29	11	6	6	43	2	157	7	0	11	13	.458	0	0-0	0	3.83	4.45
2004	MIL	NL	34	34	5	0	237.0	937	201	85	71	25	6	4	4	32	1	264	8	1	12	14	.462	0	0-0	0	2.37	2.70
2005	MIL	NL	22	22	3	0	156.2	633	142	66	58	19	6	2	2	25	1	141	7	0	10	9	.526	0	0-0	0	2.81	3.33
5 ML YEARS			149	149	11	0	982.1	4088	978	467	418	117	41	17	27	218	20	826	34	1	55	62	.470	1	0-0	0	3.56	3.83

Gary Sheffield

Bats: R Throws: R Pos: RF-131; DH-23; PH-1   Ht: 6'0" Wt: 205 Born: 11/18/1968 Age: 37

Year	Team	Lg	BATTING																			BASERUNNING				AVERAGES		
			G	AB	H	2B	3B	HR	(Hm	Rd)	TB	R	RBI	RC	TBB	IBB	SO	HBP	SH	SF		SB	CS	SB%	GDP	Avg	OBP	Slg
1988	MIL	AL	24	80	19	1	0	4	(1	3)	32	12	12	8	7	0	7	0	1	1		3	1	.75	5	.238	.295	.400
1989	MIL	AL	95	368	91	18	0	5	(2	3)	124	34	32	38	27	0	33	4	3	3		10	6	.63	4	.247	.303	.337
1990	MIL	AL	125	487	143	30	1	10	(3	7)	205	67	67	73	44	1	41	3	4	9		25	10	.71	11	.294	.350	.421
1991	MIL	AL	50	175	34	12	2	2	(2	0)	56	25	22	15	19	1	15	3	1	5		5	5	.50	3	.194	.277	.320
1992	SD	NL	146	557	184	34	3	33	(23	10)	323	87	100	113	48	5	40	6	0	7		5	6	.45	19	.330	.385	.580
1993	2 Tms	NL	140	494	145	20	5	20	(10	10)	235	67	73	84	47	6	42	9	0	7		17	5	.77	11	.294	.361	.476
1994	FLA	NL	87	322	89	16	1	27	(15	12)	188	61	78	68	51	11	50	6	0	5		12	6	.67	10	.276	.380	.584
1995	FLA	NL	63	213	69	8	0	16	(4	12)	125	46	46	60	55	8	45	4	0	2		19	4	.83	3	.324	.467	.587
1996	FLA	NL	161	519	163	33	1	42	(19	23)	324	118	120	144	142	19	66	10	0	6		16	9	.64	16	.314	.465	.624
1997	FLA	NL	135	444	111	22	1	21	(13	8)	198	86	71	92	121	11	79	15	0	2		11	7	.61	7	.250	.424	.446
1998	2 Tms	NL	130	437	132	27	2	22	(11	11)	229	73	85	102	95	12	46	8	0	9		22	7	.76	7	.302	.428	.524
1999	LA	NL	152	549	165	20	3	34	(15	19)	287	103	101	118	101	4	64	4	0	9		11	5	.69	10	.301	.407	.523
2000	LA	NL	141	501	163	24	3	43	(23	20)	322	105	109	131	101	7	71	4	0	6		4	6	.40	13	.325	.438	.643

Year	Team	Lg	G	AB	H	2B	3B	HR	(Hm	Rd)	TB	R	RBI	RC	TBB	IBB	SO	HBP	SH	SF	SB	CS	SB%	GDP	Avg	OBP	Slg
2001	LA	NL	143	515	160	28	2	36	(16	20)	300	98	100	120	94	13	67	4	0	5	10	4	.71	12	.311	.417	.583
2002	ATL	NL	135	492	151	26	0	25	(10	15)	252	82	84	102	72	2	53	11	0	4	12	2	.86	16	.307	.404	.512
2003	ATL	NL	155	576	190	37	2	39	(20	19)	348	126	132	134	86	6	55	8	0	8	18	4	.82	16	.330	.419	.604
2004	NYA	AL	154	573	166	30	1	36	(19	17)	306	117	121	123	92	7	83	11	0	8	5	6	.45	16	.290	.393	.534
2005	NYA	AL	154	584	170	27	0	34	(19	15)	299	104	123	130	78	7	76	8	0	5	10	2	.83	11	.291	.379	.512
93	SD	NL	68	258	76	12	2	10	(6	4)	122	34	36	40	18	0	30	3	0	3	5	1	.83	9	.295	.344	.473
93	Fla	NL	72	236	69	8	3	10	(4	6)	113	33	37	44	29	6	34	6	0	4	12	4	.75	2	.292	.378	.479
98	Fla	NL	40	136	37	11	1	6	(6	0)	68	21	28	27	26	1	16	2	0	2	4	2	.67	3	.272	.392	.500
98	LA	NL	90	301	95	16	1	16	(5	11)	161	52	57	75	69	11	30	6	0	7	18	5	.78	4	.316	.444	.535
18 ML YEARS			2190	7886	2345	413	24	449	(225	224)	4153	1411	1476	1655	1280	120	955	118	9	101	215	95	.69	190	.297	.399	.527

Chris Shelton

Bats: R Throws: R Pos: 1B-84; DH-15; PH-10; LF-1   Ht: 6'0" Wt: 220 Born: 6/26/1980 Age: 26

Year	Team	Lg	G	AB	H	2B	3B	HR	(Hm	Rd)	TB	R	RBI	RC	TBB	IBB	SO	HBP	SH	SF	SB	CS	SB%	GDP	Avg	OBP	Slg
2001	Wmspt	A-	50	174	53	11	0	2	(-	-)	70	22	33	33	33	1	31	2	1	3	4	1	.80	1	.305	.415	.402
2002	Hickory	A	93	332	113	27	2	17	(-	-)	195	72	65	79	47	2	74	5	0	4	0	0	-	1	.340	.425	.587
2003	Lynbrg	A+	95	315	113	24	1	21	(-	-)	202	71	69	88	68	8	67	5	0	1	1	4	.20	5	.359	.478	.641
2003	Altna	AA	35	122	34	10	1	0	(-	-)	46	17	14	15	8	0	23	2	0	1	0	1	.00	1	.279	.331	.377
2004	Toledo	AAA	18	62	21	2	0	0	(-	-)	23	5	7	11	10	0	13	0	0	1	0	0	-	0	.339	.425	.371
2005	Toledo	AAA	48	181	60	19	0	8	(-	-)	103	34	39	41	25	0	33	3	0	2	0	2	.00	3	.331	.417	.569
2004	DET	AL	27	46	9	1	0	1	(1	0)	13	6	3	4	9	0	14	0	0	1	0	0	-	2	.196	.321	.283
2005	DET	AL	107	388	116	22	3	18	(10	8)	198	61	59	65	34	0	87	5	0	4	0	0	-	12	.299	.360	.510
2 ML YEARS			134	434	125	23	3	19	(11	8)	211	67	62	69	43	0	101	5	0	5	0	0	-	14	.288	.355	.486

George Sherrill

Pitches: L Bats: L Pos: RP-29   Ht: 6'0" Wt: 210 Born: 4/19/1977 Age: 29

Year	Team	Lg	G	GS	CG	GF	IP	BFP	H	R	ER	HR	SH	SF	HB	TBB	IBB	SO	WP	Bk	W	L	Pct	ShO	Sv-Op	Hld	ERC	ERA
2003	SnAnt	AA	16	0	0	6	27.1	111	19	2	1	1	2	1	0	12	1	31	0	0	3	0	1.000	0	0--	-	2.18	0.33
2004	Tacom	AAA	36	0	0	25	50.1	201	42	13	13	4	0	0	0	9	1	62	0	0	4	2	.667	0	13--	-	2.21	2.32
2005	Ms	R	3	2	0	0	4.0	12	0	0	0	0	0	0	0	0	0	5	0	0	0	0	-	0	0--	-	0.00	0.00
2005	Tacom	AAA	22	0	0	19	23.2	96	19	7	6	0	0	0	0	6	0	38	1	0	1	3	.250	0	7--	-	1.87	2.28
2004	SEA	AL	21	0	0	4	23.2	104	24	12	10	3	0	1	1	9	1	16	4	1	2	1	.667	0	0-0	3	4.31	3.80
2005	SEA	AL	29	0	0	2	19.0	77	13	12	11	3	1	1	1	7	2	24	0	0	4	3	.571	0	0-0	9	2.70	5.21
2 ML YEARS			50	0	0	6	42.2	181	37	24	21	6	1	2	2	16	3	40	4	1	6	4	.600	0	0-0	12	3.57	4.43

Scot Shields

Pitches: R Bats: R Pos: RP-78   Ht: 6'1" Wt: 175 Born: 7/22/1975 Age: 30

Year	Team	Lg	G	GS	CG	GF	IP	BFP	H	R	ER	HR	SH	SF	HB	TBB	IBB	SO	WP	Bk	W	L	Pct	ShO	Sv-Op	Hld	ERC	ERA
2001	ANA	AL	8	0	0	6	11.0	48	8	1	0	0	0	0	0	7	0	7	2	0	0	0	-	0	0-0	0	3.10	0.00
2002	ANA	AL	29	1	0	13	49.0	188	31	13	12	4	1	0	1	21	1	30	3	0	5	3	.625	0	0-0	3	2.35	2.20
2003	ANA	AL	44	13	0	5	148.1	609	138	56	47	12	3	4	5	38	6	111	4	0	5	6	.455	0	1-1	3	3.12	2.85
2004	ANA	AL	60	0	0	12	105.1	454	97	42	39	6	2	2	3	40	5	109	4	0	8	2	.800	0	4-7	17	3.24	3.33
2005	LAA	AL	78	0	0	21	91.2	375	66	33	28	5	4	3	2	37	2	98	12	0	10	11	.476	0	7-13	33	2.37	2.75
5 ML YEARS			219	14	0	57	405.1	1674	340	145	126	27	10	9	12	143	14	355	25	0	28	22	.560	0	12-21	56	2.88	2.80

Kelly Shoppach

Bats: R Throws: R Pos: C-7; DH-2; PH-2; PR-1   Ht: 6'1" Wt: 210 Born: 4/29/1980 Age: 26

Year	Team	Lg	G	AB	H	2B	3B	HR	(Hm	Rd)	TB	R	RBI	RC	TBB	IBB	SO	HBP	SH	SF	SB	CS	SB%	GDP	Avg	OBP	Slg
2002	Srsota	A+	116	414	112	35	1	10	(-	-)	179	54	66	69	59	2	112	6	0	1	2	1	.67	11	.271	.369	.432
2003	Portlnd	AA	92	340	96	30	2	12	(-	-)	166	45	60	60	35	2	83	5	0	5	0	0	-	10	.282	.353	.488
2004	Pwtckt	AAA	113	399	93	25	0	22	(-	-)	184	62	64	61	46	0	138	6	1	2	0	0	-	7	.233	.320	.461
2005	Pwtckt	AAA	102	371	94	16	0	26	(-	-)	188	60	75	68	46	2	116	12	0	3	0	0	-	9	.253	.352	.507
2005	BOS	AL	9	15	0	0	0	0	(0	0)	0	1	0	0	0	0	7	1	0	0	0	0	-	0	.000	.063	.000

Rick Short

Bats: R Throws: R Pos: 2B-6; PH-5; 1B-1   Ht: 6'0" Wt: 200 Born: 12/6/1972 Age: 33

Year	Team	Lg	G	AB	H	2B	3B	HR	(Hm	Rd)	TB	R	RBI	RC	TBB	IBB	SO	HBP	SH	SF	SB	CS	SB%	GDP	Avg	OBP	Slg
1994	Bluefld	R+	64	229	69	8	0	4	(-	-)	89	39	35	33	22	1	23	2	0	2	4	6	.40	3	.301	.365	.389
1995	Bluefld	R+	11	39	11	2	0	2	(-	-)	19	9	12	6	2	0	1	1	0	1	2	1	.67	2	.282	.326	.487
1995	Hi Dsrt	A+	29	98	41	3	0	4	(-	-)	56	14	12	24	10	0	5	2	0	0	1	2	.33	2	.418	.482	.571
1995	Frdrck	A+	5	13	1	0	0	0	(-	-)	1	1	2	0	1	0	2	0	0	0	1	0	1.00	0	.077	.143	.077
1996	Frdrck	A+	126	474	148	33	0	3	(-	-)	190	68	54	70	29	2	44	5	5	4	12	7	.63	14	.312	.355	.401
1997	Frdrck	A+	126	480	153	29	1	10	(-	-)	214	73	72	84	38	2	44	12	7	1	10	6	.63	20	.319	.382	.446
1998	Frdrck	A+	59	221	68	14	0	6	(-	-)	100	36	28	39	18	1	29	8	1	3	3	2	.60	12	.308	.376	.452
1998	Bowie	AA	34	87	20	4	0	2	(-	-)	30	12	18	11	13	0	18	0	1	4	0	0	-	2	.230	.317	.345
1998	Roch	AAA	13	34	6	1	0	1	(-	-)	10	3	4	3	4	0	4	1	0	1	0	0	-	0	.176	.275	.294
1999	Bowie	AA	112	392	123	19	0	16	(-	-)	190	60	62	77	43	2	48	9	0	5	1	1	.86	9	.314	.390	.485
2000	Bowie	AA	116	447	148	39	1	9	(-	-)	216	63	82	87	44	2	54	8	0	8	3	3	.50	14	.331	.394	.483
2000	Roch	AAA	13	37	9	1	0	1	(-	-)	13	3	3	5	4	0	4	2	0	0	0	0	-	0	.243	.349	.351
2001	WTenn	AA	8	19	5	0	0	0	(-	-)	5	5	0	2	5	0	1	1	0	0	0	1	.00	0	.263	.440	.263

Year	Team	Lg	G	AB	H	2B	3B	HR	(Hm	Rd)	TB	R	RBI	RC	TBB	IBB	SO	HBP	SH	SF	SB	CS	SB%	GDP	Avg	OBP	Slg
2001	Iowa	AAA	105	313	86	19	1	5	(-	-)	122	38	34	41	22	0	42	3	5	1	2	1	.67	13	.275	.327	.390
2002	Edmtn	AAA	105	410	146	29	2	7	(-	-)	200	71	68	79	23	1	43	9	0	4	3	2	.60	4	.356	.399	.488
2004	Omha	AAA	89	316	89	16	0	7	(-	-)	126	30	48	41	15	0	39	4	1	3	1	1	.50	15	.282	.320	.399
2004	Edmtn	AAA	40	152	51	13	0	2	(-	-)	70	13	19	26	10	0	7	1	0	1	1	1	.50	5	.336	.378	.461
2005	NewOr	AAA	108	376	144	35	1	11	(-	-)	214	72	70	94	46	6	27	7	1	3	5	4	.56	8	.383	.456	.569
2005	WAS	NL	11	15	6	2	0	2	(2	0)	14	4	4	6	1	0	1	1	0	0	0	0	-	0	.400	.471	.933

Brian Shouse

Pitches: L Bats: L Pos: RP-64   **Ht: 5'11" Wt: 180 Born: 9/26/1968 Age: 37**

Year	Team	Lg	G	GS	CG	GF	IP	BFP	H	R	ER	HR	SH	SF	HB	TBB	IBB	SO	WP	Bk	W	L	Pct	ShO	Sv-Op	Hld	ERC	ERA
1993	PIT	NL	6	0	0	1	4.0	22	7	4	4	1	0	1	0	2	0	3	1	0	0	0	-	0	0-0	1	9.92	9.00
1998	BOS	AL	7	0	0	4	8.0	36	9	5	5	2	0	0	1	4	0	5	0	0	0	1	.000	0	0-0	1	6.42	5.63
2002	KC	AL	23	0	0	7	14.2	71	15	10	10	3	1	1	2	9	1	11	2	0	0	0	-	0	0-0	2	6.11	6.14
2003	TEX	AL	62	0	0	14	61.0	253	62	24	21	1	3	0	4	14	6	40	2	0	0	1	.000	0	1-1	10	3.10	3.10
2004	TEX	AL	53	0	0	14	44.1	184	36	12	11	3	2	2	1	18	3	34	0	0	2	0	1.000	0	0-0	12	2.87	2.23
2005	TEX	AL	64	0	0	12	53.1	233	55	37	31	7	2	3	3	18	4	35	2	0	3	2	.600	0	0-2	11	4.29	5.23
6 ML YEARS			215	0	0	52	185.1	799	184	92	82	17	8	7	10	65	14	128	7	0	5	4	.556	0	1-3	36	3.87	3.98

Ruben Sierra

Bats: B Throws: R Pos: DH-28; PH-24; RF-10; LF-8; PR-1   **Ht: 6'1" Wt: 215 Born: 10/6/1965 Age: 40**

Year	Team	Lg	G	AB	H	2B	3B	HR	(Hm	Rd)	TB	R	RBI	RC	TBB	IBB	SO	HBP	SH	SF	SB	CS	SB%	GDP	Avg	OBP	Slg
2005	Clmbs*	AAA	3	11	2	0	0	1	(-	-)	5	2	1	1	2	1	3	0	0	0	0	0	-	0	.182	.308	.455
1986	TEX	AL	113	382	101	13	10	16	(8	8)	182	50	55	52	22	3	65	1	1	5	7	8	.47	8	.264	.302	.476
1987	TEX	AL	158	643	169	35	4	30	(15	15)	302	97	109	86	39	4	114	2	0	12	16	11	.59	18	.263	.302	.470
1988	TEX	AL	156	615	156	32	2	23	(15	8)	261	77	91	78	44	10	91	1	0	8	18	4	.82	15	.254	.301	.424
1989	TEX	AL	162	634	194	35	14	29	(21	8)	344	101	119	118	43	2	82	2	0	10	8	2	.80	7	.306	.347	.543
1990	TEX	AL	159	608	170	37	2	16	(10	6)	259	70	96	84	49	13	86	1	0	8	9	0	1.00	16	.280	.330	.426
1991	TEX	AL	161	661	203	44	5	25	(12	13)	332	110	116	114	56	7	91	0	0	9	16	4	.80	17	.307	.357	.502
1992	2 Tms		151	601	167	34	7	17	(10	7)	266	83	87	86	45	12	68	0	0	10	14	4	.78	11	.278	.323	.443
1993	OAK	AL	158	630	147	23	5	22	(9	13)	246	77	101	70	52	16	97	0	0	10	25	5	.83	17	.233	.288	.390
1994	OAK	AL	110	426	114	21	1	23	(11	12)	206	71	92	58	23	4	64	0	0	11	8	5	.62	15	.268	.298	.484
1995	2 Tms		126	479	126	32	0	19	(8	11)	215	73	86	69	46	4	76	0	0	8	5	4	.56	8	.263	.323	.449
1996	2 Tms		142	518	128	26	2	12	(4	8)	194	61	72	62	60	12	83	0	0	9	4	4	.50	12	.247	.320	.375
1997	2 Tms		39	138	32	5	3	3	(3	0)	52	10	12	14	9	2	34	0	0	1	0	0	-	1	.232	.277	.377
1998	CHA	AL	27	74	16	4	1	4	(0	4)	34	7	11	8	3	0	11	0	0	0	2	0	1.00	2	.216	.247	.459
2000	TEX	AL	20	60	14	0	0	1	(0	1)	17	5	7	5	4	0	9	0	0	0	1	0	1.00	1	.233	.281	.283
2001	TEX	AL	94	344	100	22	1	23	(13	10)	193	55	67	58	19	0	52	0	0	6	2	0	1.00	13	.291	.322	.561
2002	SEA	AL	122	419	113	23	0	13	(6	7)	175	47	60	47	31	5	66	0	0	2	4	0	1.00	17	.270	.319	.418
2003	2 Tms		106	307	83	17	1	9	(7	2)	129	33	43	35	27	3	47	0	0	2	2	1	.67	9	.270	.327	.420
2004	NYA	AL	107	307	75	12	1	17	(8	9)	140	40	65	46	25	4	55	0	0	6	1	0	1.00	5	.244	.296	.456
2005	NYA	AL	61	170	39	12	0	4	(3	1)	63	14	29	19	9	1	41	0	0	2	0	0	-	2	.229	.265	.371
92	Tex	AL	124	500	139	30	6	14	(8	6)	223	66	70	70	31	6	59	0	0	8	12	4	.75	9	.278	.315	.446
92	Oak	AL	27	101	28	4	1	3	(2	1)	43	17	17	16	14	6	9	0	0	2	2	0	1.00	2	.277	.359	.426
95	Oak	AL	70	264	70	17	0	12	(3	9)	123	40	42	40	24	2	42	0	0	3	4	4	.50	2	.265	.323	.466
95	NYY	AL	56	215	56	15	0	7	(5	2)	92	33	44	29	22	2	34	0	0	5	1	0	1.00	6	.260	.322	.428
96	NYY	AL	96	360	93	17	1	11	(4	7)	145	39	52	46	40	11	58	0	0	7	1	3	.25	10	.258	.327	.403
96	Det	AL	46	158	35	9	1	1	(0	1)	49	22	20	16	20	1	25	0	0	2	3	1	.75	2	.222	.306	.310
97	Cin	NL	25	90	22	5	1	2	(2	0)	35	6	7	10	6	1	21	0	0	0	0	0	-	1	.244	.292	.389
97	Tor	AL	14	48	10	0	2	1	(1	0)	17	4	5	4	3	1	13	0	0	1	0	0	-	0	.208	.250	.354
03	Tex	AL	43	133	35	9	0	3	(2	1)	53	14	12	15	14	1	27	0	0	0	1	1	.50	2	.263	.333	.398
03	Tor	AL	63	174	48	8	1	6	(5	1)	76	19	31	20	13	2	20	0	0	2	1	0	1.00	7	.276	.323	.437
19 ML YEARS			2172	8016	2147	427	59	306	(163	143)	3610	1081	1318	1109	606	102	1232	7	1	119	142	52	.73	193	.268	.316	.450

Carlos Silva

Pitches: R Bats: R Pos: SP-27   **Ht: 6'4" Wt: 225 Born: 4/23/1979 Age: 27**

Year	Team	Lg	G	GS	CG	GF	IP	BFP	H	R	ER	HR	SH	SF	HB	TBB	IBB	SO	WP	Bk	W	L	Pct	ShO	Sv-Op	Hld	ERC	ERA
2005	Beloit*	A	1	1	0	0	5.0	20	5	1	1	0	0	0	0	0	0	3	0	0	0	0	-	0	0--	-	3.05	1.80
2002	PHI	NL	68	0	0	21	84.0	350	88	34	30	4	9	3	4	22	6	41	3	0	5	0	1.000	0	1-5	8	3.60	3.21
2003	PHI	NL	62	1	0	15	87.1	381	92	43	43	7	6	1	8	37	5	48	12	1	3	1	.750	0	1-3	4	4.71	4.43
2004	MIN	AL	33	33	1	0	203.0	869	255	100	95	25	6	5	5	35	2	76	5	1	14	8	.636	1	0-0	0	4.89	4.21
2005	MIN	AL	27	27	2	0	188.1	749	212	83	72	25	2	5	3	9	2	71	0	0	9	8	.529	0	0-0	0	3.78	3.44
4 ML YEARS			190	61	3	36	562.2	2349	647	260	240	59	23	9	20	103	15	236	20	2	31	17	.646	1	2-8	12	4.30	3.84

Allan Simpson

Pitches: R Bats: R Pos: RP-11   **Ht: 6'4" Wt: 185 Born: 8/26/1977 Age: 28**

Year	Team	Lg	G	GS	CG	GF	IP	BFP	H	R	ER	HR	SH	SF	HB	TBB	IBB	SO	WP	Bk	W	L	Pct	ShO	Sv-Op	Hld	ERC	ERA
1997	Everett	A-	16	0	0	6	26.1	127	26	23	20	1	1	1	2	24	1	26	3	0	0	3	.000	0	0--	-	5.80	6.84
1998	Wisc	A	19	19	0	0	93.1	420	89	52	46	5	4	2	7	61	0	86	5	2	3	5	.375	0	0--	-	4.84	4.44
1998	Ms	R	3	0	0	1	9.1	37	8	2	1	0	0	0	0	3	0	12	0	0	1	0	1.000	0	1--	-	3.18	0.96
1999	Wisc	A	24	13	1	3	90.1	402	83	56	44	4	4	8	3	48	0	88	4	1	2	9	.182	0	0--	-	3.79	4.38
1999	Lancst	A+	9	0	0	0	21.1	96	17	16	15	4	0	2	2	14	0	25	2	0	0	0	-	0	0--	-	4.91	6.33
2000	Lancst	A+	46	0	0	20	52.0	217	34	17	12	1	4	0	2	27	1	67	2	0	3	2	.600	0	6--	-	2.26	2.08
2001	SnBrn	A+	16	0	0	5	30.0	121	19	7	6	1	1	0	1	12	1	40	2	0	1	0	1.000	0	1--	-	1.73	1.80

222

Year	Team	Lg	G	GS	CG	GF	IP	BFP	H	R	ER	HR	SH	SF	HB	TBB	IBB	SO	WP	Bk	W	L	Pct	ShO	Sv-Op	Hld	ERC	ERA
2001	SnAnt	AA	22	0	0	16	38.2	157	25	8	8	1	1	3	2	15	1	37	2	0	2	1	.667	0	9--	-	1.89	1.86
2002	SnAnt	AA	56	0	0	28	82.1	346	53	33	28	4	4	4	6	50	5	99	5	0	10	5	.667	0	7--	-	2.80	3.06
2003	Tacom	AAA	43	0	0	23	62.2	291	60	30	29	7	3	1	6	42	1	69	2	0	2	5	.286	0	1--	-	5.33	4.16
2004	ColSpr	AAA	27	0	0	19	35.1	154	30	14	11	1	1	0	7	10	0	43	4	1	2	1	.667	0	4--	-	2.97	2.80
2005	Lsvlle	AAA	50	0	0	13	64.1	282	51	30	29	5	0	3	8	38	1	89	11	0	4	4	.500	0	1--	-	3.98	4.06
2004	COL	NL	32	0	0	9	39.0	183	44	26	22	4	3	4	4	20	0	46	3	0	2	1	.667	0	0-1	1	5.64	5.08
2005	2 Tms	NL	11	0	0	2	7.1	36	6	10	10	1	0	1	1	8	0	6	2	0	0	1	.000	0	0-1	0	6.69	12.27
05	Col	NL	2	0	0	0	0.2	9	3	5	5	0	0	0	1	3	0	0	1	0	0	0	-	0	0-0	0	50.38	67.50
05	Cin	NL	9	0	0	2	6.2	28	3	5	5	1	0	0	1	5	0	6	1	0	0	1	.000	0	0-1	0	3.41	6.75
2 ML YEARS			43	0	0	11	46.1	219	50	36	32	5	3	5	5	28	0	52	5	0	2	2	.500	0	0-2	1	5.81	6.22

Chris Singleton

Bats: L **Throws:** L **Pos:** PH-12; RF-11; CF-6; DH-3; LF-2 **Ht:** 6'2" **Wt:** 210 **Born:** 8/15/1972 **Age:** 33

Year	Team	Lg	G	AB	H	2B	3B	HR	(Hm	Rd)	TB	R	RBI	RC	TBB	IBB	SO	HBP	SH	SF	SB	CS	SB%	GDP	Avg	OBP	Slg
2005	Drham*	AAA	1	3	1	0	0	0	(-	-)	1	0	0	0	0	0	1	0	0	0	0	0	-	0	.333	.333	.333
1999	CHA	AL	133	496	149	31	6	17	(5	12)	243	72	72	79	22	1	45	1	4	6	20	5	.80	10	.300	.328	.490
2000	CHA	AL	147	511	130	22	5	11	(5	6)	195	83	62	61	35	2	85	1	12	4	22	7	.76	6	.254	.301	.382
2001	CHA	AL	140	392	117	21	5	7	(4	3)	169	57	45	54	20	2	61	1	14	4	12	11	.52	5	.298	.331	.431
2002	BAL	AL	136	466	122	30	6	9	(4	5)	191	67	50	55	21	0	83	4	6	5	20	2	.91	8	.262	.296	.410
2003	OAK	AL	120	306	75	24	1	1	(0	1)	104	38	36	32	26	4	55	1	2	6	7	2	.78	2	.245	.301	.340
2005	TB	AL	28	59	16	5	0	0	(0	0)	21	9	11	9	6	0	14	1	1	0	0	0	-	1	.271	.348	.356
6 ML YEARS			704	2230	609	133	23	45	(18	27)	923	326	276	290	130	9	343	9	39	25	81	27	.75	32	.273	.312	.414

Andy Sisco

Pitches: L **Bats:** L **Pos:** RP-67 **Ht:** 6'10" **Wt:** 270 **Born:** 1/13/1983 **Age:** 23

Year	Team	Lg	G	GS	CG	GF	IP	BFP	H	R	ER	HR	SH	SF	HB	TBB	IBB	SO	WP	Bk	W	L	Pct	ShO	Sv-Op	Hld	ERC	ERA
2001	Cubs	R	10	7	0	0	34.0	148	36	28	20	1	1	0	6	10	0	31	2	1	1	0	1.000	0	0--	-	4.24	5.29
2002	Boise	A-	14	14	0	0	77.2	323	51	23	21	3	3	0	6	39	0	101	6	0	7	2	.778	0	0--	-	2.52	2.43
2003	Lansng	A	19	19	3	0	94.0	389	76	44	37	3	1	0	5	31	0	99	8	0	6	8	.429	0	0--	-	2.54	3.54
2004	Dytona	A+	26	25	0	0	126.0	561	118	64	59	11	8	6	7	65	1	134	9	1	4	10	.286	0	0--	-	4.24	4.21
2005	KC	AL	67	0	0	13	75.1	329	68	27	26	6	2	3	2	42	4	76	2	0	2	5	.286	0	0-5	14	4.04	3.11

Grady Sizemore

Bats: L **Throws:** L **Pos:** CF-155; PH-5 **Ht:** 6'2" **Wt:** 200 **Born:** 8/2/1982 **Age:** 23

Year	Team	Lg	G	AB	H	2B	3B	HR	(Hm	Rd)	TB	R	RBI	RC	TBB	IBB	SO	HBP	SH	SF	SB	CS	SB%	GDP	Avg	OBP	Slg
2000	Expos	R	55	205	60	8	3	1	(-	-)	77	31	14	34	23	0	24	6	2	0	16	2	.89	1	.293	.380	.376
2001	Clinton	A	123	451	121	16	4	2	(-	-)	151	64	61	68	81	4	92	4	0	5	32	11	.74	7	.268	.381	.335
2002	BrvdCt	A+	75	256	66	15	4	0	(-	-)	89	37	26	31	36	3	41	2	0	2	9	9	.50	6	.258	.351	.348
2002	Kinston	A+	47	172	59	9	3	3	(-	-)	83	31	20	38	33	2	30	1	1	0	14	7	.67	1	.343	.451	.483
2003	Akron	AA	128	496	151	26	11	13	(-	-)	238	96	78	88	46	1	73	11	1	5	10	9	.53	5	.304	.373	.480
2004	Buffalo	AAA	101	418	120	23	8	8	(-	-)	183	73	51	66	42	0	72	8	1	4	15	10	.60	6	.287	.360	.438
2004	CLE	AL	43	138	34	6	2	4	(2	2)	56	15	24	21	14	0	34	5	0	2	2	0	1.00	3	.246	.333	.406
2005	CLE	AL	158	640	185	37	11	22	(10	12)	310	111	81	101	52	1	132	7	5	2	22	10	.69	17	.289	.348	.484
2 ML YEARS			201	778	219	43	13	26	(12	14)	366	126	105	122	66	1	166	12	5	4	24	10	.71	17	.281	.345	.470

Terrmel Sledge

Bats: L **Throws:** L **Pos:** LF-12; PH-10; RF-1 **Ht:** 6'0" **Wt:** 185 **Born:** 3/18/1977 **Age:** 29

Year	Team	Lg	G	AB	H	2B	3B	HR	(Hm	Rd)	TB	R	RBI	RC	TBB	IBB	SO	HBP	SH	SF	SB	CS	SB%	GDP	Avg	OBP	Slg
1999	Everett	A	62	233	74	8	3	5	(-	-)	103	43	32	43	27	0	35	9	2	2	9	8	.53	2	.318	.406	.442
2000	Wisc	A	7	23	5	2	2	0	(-	-)	11	5	3	3	3	0	1	1	0	0	1	0	1.00	1	.217	.333	.478
2000	Lancst	A+	103	384	130	22	7	11	(-	-)	199	90	75	96	72	3	49	17	1	5	35	11	.76	4	.339	.458	.518
2001	Hrsbrg	AA	129	448	124	22	6	9	(-	-)	185	66	48	72	51	0	72	9	3	5	30	8	.79	5	.277	.359	.413
2002	Hrsbrg	AA	102	396	119	18	6	8	(-	-)	173	74	43	72	55	2	70	12	4	1	11	8	.58	4	.301	.401	.437
2002	Ottawa	AAA	24	80	21	5	2	1	(-	-)	33	12	11	11	11	0	15	1	0	0	1	1	.50	2	.263	.359	.413
2003	Edmtn	AAA	131	497	161	26	9	22	(-	-)	271	95	92	104	61	3	93	5	0	9	13	5	.72	10	.324	.397	.545
2004	MON	NL	133	398	107	20	6	15	(6	9)	184	45	62	66	40	4	66	1	6	1	3	3	.50	2	.269	.336	.462
2005	WAS	NL	20	37	9	0	1	1	(0	1)	14	7	8	4	7	1	8	0	0	2	2	1	.67	3	.243	.348	.378
2 ML YEARS			153	435	116	20	7	16	(6	10)	198	52	70	70	47	5	74	1	6	3	5	4	.56	5	.267	.337	.455

Aaron Small

Pitches: R **Bats:** R **Pos:** SP-9; RP-6 **Ht:** 6'5" **Wt:** 237 **Born:** 11/23/1971 **Age:** 34

Year	Team	Lg	G	GS	CG	GF	IP	BFP	H	R	ER	HR	SH	SF	HB	TBB	IBB	SO	WP	Bk	W	L	Pct	ShO	Sv-Op	Hld	ERC	ERA
2005	Trent*	AA	1	1	0	0	5.0	23	7	3	2	1	0	0	0	1	0	3	1	0	1	0	1.000	0	0--	-	6.22	3.60
2005	Clmbs*	AAA	11	10	0	0	49.0	217	62	30	27	5	2	1	1	8	0	21	2	0	1	4	.200	0	0--	-	4.64	4.96
1994	TOR	AL	1	0	0	0	2.0	13	5	2	2	1	0	1	0	2	0	0	0	0	0	0	-	0	0-0	0	21.61	9.00
1995	FLA	NL	7	0	0	0	6.1	32	7	2	1	1	0	0	0	6	0	5	0	0	1	0	1.000	0	0-0	0	7.30	1.42
1996	OAK	AL	12	3	0	4	28.2	144	37	28	26	3	0	1	1	22	1	17	2	0	1	3	.250	0	0-0	0	7.42	8.16
1997	OAK	AL	71	0	0	22	96.2	425	109	50	46	6	5	6	3	40	6	45	4	0	9	5	.643	0	4-6	8	4.67	4.28
1998	2 Tms	AL	47	0	0	13	67.2	304	83	48	42	8	5	1	4	22	4	33	4	0	4	2	.667	0	0-2	4	5.38	5.59
2002	ATL	NL	1	0	0	0	0.1	5	2	1	1	0	0	0	0	2	0	1	1	0	0	0	-	0	0-0	0	71.88	27.00

			HOW MUCH HE PITCHED						WHAT HE GAVE UP											THE RESULTS						
Year	Team	Lg	G	GS	CG	GF	IP	BFP	H	R	ER	HR	SH	SF	HB	TBB	IBB	SO	WP	Bk	W	L	Pct	ShO	Sv-Op	Hld	ERC	ERA
2004	FLA	NL	7	0	0	0	16.1	78	24	15	15	5	1	0	0	7	0	8	1	0	0	0		0	0-0	1	8.84	8.27
2005	NYA	AL	15	9	1	1	76.0	316	71	27	27	4	1	2	5	24	0	37	0	0	10	0	1.000	1	0-1	0	3.39	3.20
98	Oak	AL	24	0	0	4	36.0	174	51	34	29	3	3	1	3	14	3	19	4	0	1	1	.500	0	0-0	3	6.49	7.25
98	Ari	NL	23	0	0	9	31.2	130	32	14	13	5	2	0	1	8	1	14	0	0	3	1	.750	0	0-2	1	4.14	3.69
	8 ML YEARS		161	12	1	43	294.0	1317	338	173	160	28	12	11	13	125	11	158	12	0	25	10	.714	1	4-9	13	5.16	4.90

Jason Smith

Bats: L **Throws:** R **Pos:** SS-15; 2B-6; PH-5; 3B-3; PR-2; 1B-1; DH-1   **Ht:** 6'3" **Wt:** 199 **Born:** 7/24/1977 **Age:** 28

			BATTING																BASERUNNING				AVERAGES		
Year	Team	Lg	G	AB	H	2B	3B	HR	(Hm | Rd)	TB	R	RBI	RC	TBB	IBB	SO	HBP	SH	SF	SB	CS	SB%	GDP	Avg	OBP	Slg
2005	Toledo*	AAA	55	187	43	11	2	6	(- | -)	76	24	25	21	11	0	53	0	6	3	8	4	.67	1	.230	.269	.406
2001	CHN	NL	2	1	0	0	0	0	(0)	0)	0	0	0	0	0	0	1	0	0	0	0	0	-	0	.000	.000	.000
2002	TB	AL	26	65	13	1	2	1	(0 | 1)	21	9	6	5	2	0	24	0	2	0	3	0	1.00	0	.200	.224	.323
2003	TB	AL	1	4	1	0	0	0	(0 | 0)	1	0	0	0	0	0	0	0	0	0	0	0	-	0	.250	.250	.250
2004	DET	AL	61	155	37	7	4	5	(0 | 5)	67	20	19	13	8	0	37	1	5	0	1	2	.33	0	.239	.280	.432
2005	DET	AL	27	58	11	1	2	0	(0 | 16)	16	4	2	4	0	0	16	1	4	0	2	1	.67	0	.190	.203	.276
	5 ML YEARS		117	283	62	9	8	6	(0 | 6)	105	33	27	22	10	0	78	2	11	0	6	3	.67	0	.219	.251	.371

Travis Smith

Pitches: R **Bats:** R **Pos:** RP-12   **Ht:** 5'10" **Wt:** 165 **Born:** 11/7/1972 **Age:** 33

			HOW MUCH HE PITCHED						WHAT HE GAVE UP											THE RESULTS						
Year	Team	Lg	G	GS	CG	GF	IP	BFP	H	R	ER	HR	SH	SF	HB	TBB	IBB	SO	WP	Bk	W	L	Pct	ShO	Sv-Op	Hld	ERC	ERA
2005	Albq*	AAA	18	17	0	0	103.2	449	107	54	47	12	2	1	5	31	1	73	5	0	7	8	.467	0	0--	-	4.10	4.08
1998	MIL	NL	1	0	0	0	2	7	1	0	0	0	0	0	0	0	0	1	0	0	0	0		0	0-0	0	0.54	0.00
2002	STL	NL	12	10	0	0	54.0	244	69	44	43	10	7	0	3	20	0	32	2	0	4	2	.667	0	0-0	0	6.63	7.17
2004	ATL	NL	16	4	0	4	40.2	180	48	28	28	12	3	0	1	12	2	26	1	0	2	3	.400	0	0-0	1	6.12	6.20
2005	FLA	NL	12	0	0	4	10.2	52	17	8	8	1	0	1	0	5	1	9	0	0	0	0	-	0	0-0	0	7.89	6.75
	4 ML YEARS		41	14	0	8	107.1	483	135	80	79	23	10	1	4	37	3	68	3	0	6	5	.545	0	0-0	1	6.41	6.62

John Smoltz

Pitches: R **Bats:** R **Pos:** SP-33   **Ht:** 6'3" **Wt:** 220 **Born:** 5/15/1967 **Age:** 39

			HOW MUCH HE PITCHED						WHAT HE GAVE UP											THE RESULTS						
Year	Team	Lg	G	GS	CG	GF	IP	BFP	H	R	ER	HR	SH	SF	HB	TBB	IBB	SO	WP	Bk	W	L	Pct	ShO	Sv-Op	Hld	ERC	ERA
1988	ATL	NL	12	12	0	0	64.0	297	74	40	39	10	2	0	2	33	4	37	2	1	2	7	.222	0	0-0	0	5.86	5.48
1989	ATL	NL	29	29	5	0	208.0	847	160	79	68	15	10	7	2	72	2	168	8	3	12	11	.522	0	0-0	0	2.50	2.94
1990	ATL	NL	34	34	6	0	231.1	966	206	109	99	20	9	8	1	90	3	170	14	3	14	11	.560	2	0-0	0	3.37	3.85
1991	ATL	NL	36	36	5	0	229.2	947	206	101	97	16	9	9	3	77	1	148	20	2	14	13	.519	0	0-0	0	3.15	3.80
1992	ATL	NL	35	35	9	0	246.2	1021	206	90	78	17	7	8	5	80	5	215	17	1	15	12	.556	3	0-0	0	2.73	2.85
1993	ATL	NL	35	35	3	0	243.2	1028	208	104	98	23	13	4	6	100	12	208	13	1	15	11	.577	1	0-0	0	3.29	3.62
1994	ATL	NL	21	21	1	0	134.2	568	120	69	62	15	7	6	4	48	4	113	7	0	6	10	.375	0	0-0	0	3.44	4.14
1995	ATL	NL	29	29	2	0	192.2	808	166	76	68	15	13	5	4	72	8	193	13	0	12	7	.632	1	0-0	0	3.08	3.18
1996	ATL	NL	35	35	6	0	253.2	995	199	93	83	19	12	4	2	55	3	276	10	1	24	8	.750	2	0-0	0	2.17	2.94
1997	ATL	NL	35	35	7	0	256.0	1043	234	97	86	21	10	3	1	63	9	241	10	1	15	12	.556	2	0-0	0	2.89	3.02
1998	ATL	NL	26	26	2	0	167.2	681	145	58	54	10	4	2	4	44	2	173	3	1	17	3	.850	2	0-0	0	2.67	2.90
1999	ATL	NL	29	29	1	0	186.1	746	168	70	66	14	10	5	4	40	2	156	2	0	11	8	.579	1	0-0	0	2.81	3.19
2001	ATL	NL	36	5	0	20	59.0	238	53	24	22	7	1	2	2	10	2	57	0	0	3	3	.500	0	10-11	5	2.85	3.36
2002	ATL	NL	75	0	0	68	80.1	314	59	30	29	4	2	1	0	24	1	85	1	1	3	2	.600	0	55-59	0	2.06	3.25
2003	ATL	NL	62	0	0	55	64.1	244	48	9	8	2	0	1	0	8	1	73	2	0	0	2	.000	0	45-49	0	1.50	1.12
2004	ATL	NL	73	0	0	61	81.2	323	75	25	25	8	4	0	0	13	2	85	6	0	0	1	.000	0	44-49	0	2.73	2.76
2005	ATL	NL	33	33	3	0	229.2	931	210	83	78	18	10	3	1	53	7	169	2	1	14	7	.667	1	0-0	0	2.83	3.06
	17 ML YEARS		635	394	50	204	2929.1	11997	2537	1157	1060	234	123	68	41	882	68	2567	130	16	177	128	.580	15	154-168	5	2.88	3.26

Ian Snell

Pitches: R **Bats:** R **Pos:** RP-10; SP-5   **Ht:** 5'11" **Wt:** 170 **Born:** 10/30/1981 **Age:** 24

			HOW MUCH HE PITCHED						WHAT HE GAVE UP											THE RESULTS						
Year	Team	Lg	G	GS	CG	GF	IP	BFP	H	R	ER	HR	SH	SF	HB	TBB	IBB	SO	WP	Bk	W	L	Pct	ShO	Sv-Op	Hld	ERC	ERA
2000	Pirates	R	4	0	0	1	7.2	28	5	2	2	1	0	1	0	1	0	8	0	0	1	0	1.000	0	0--	-	2.12	2.35
2001	Pirates	R	3	3	0	0	19.0	74	12	2	1	0	1	0	1	5	0	13	0	0	3	0	1.000	0	0--	-	1.32	0.47
2001	Wmspt	A-	10	9	1	0	64.2	260	55	16	10	2	3	2	1	10	0	56	2	0	7	0	1.000	0	0--	-	2.00	1.39
2002	Hickory	A	24	22	0	0	139.2	591	127	49	42	8	5	3	0	45	0	149	13	2	11	6	.647	0	0--	-	2.94	2.71
2003	Lynbrg	A+	20	20	1	0	116.1	477	105	46	43	3	8	3	3	33	1	122	4	2	10	3	.769	1	0--	-	2.74	3.33
2003	Altna	AA	6	6	0	0	36.2	155	36	13	8	2	0	1	0	10	0	23	2	0	4	0	1.000	0	0--	-	3.25	1.96
2004	Altna	AA	26	26	3	0	151.0	624	147	54	53	16	9	6	5	40	2	142	6	0	11	7	.611	2	0--	-	3.61	3.16
2005	Indy	AAA	18	18	2	0	112.0	449	90	49	46	14	4	2	1	23	0	104	7	1	11	3	.786	1	0--	-	2.46	3.70
2004	PIT	NL	3	1	0	1	12.0	56	14	10	10	2	0	0	0	9	0	9	0	0	0	1	.000	0	0-0	0	7.31	7.50
2005	PIT	NL	15	5	0	2	42.0	189	43	25	24	5	2	1	1	24	3	34	4	0	1	2	.333	0	0-0	1	5.03	5.14
	2 ML YEARS		18	6	0	3	54.0	245	57	35	34	7	2	1	1	33	3	43	4	0	1	3	.250	0	0-0	1	5.51	5.67

Chris Snelling

Bats: L **Throws:** L **Pos:** LF-7; PH-5; RF-3   **Ht:** 5'10" **Wt:** 165 **Born:** 12/3/1981 **Age:** 24

			BATTING																BASERUNNING				AVERAGES		
Year	Team	Lg	G	AB	H	2B	3B	HR	(Hm | Rd)	TB	R	RBI	RC	TBB	IBB	SO	HBP	SH	SF	SB	CS	SB%	GDP	Avg	OBP	Slg
1999	Everett	A-	12	40	11	0	1	0	(- | -)	13	9	2	3	1	0	4	0	0	0	2	1	.67	1	.275	.293	.325
2000	Wisc	A	72	259	79	9	5	9	(- | -)	125	44	56	51	34	3	34	6	1	9	7	4	.64	2	.305	.386	.483
2001	SnBrn	A+	114	450	151	29	10	7	(- | -)	221	90	73	92	45	4	63	21	2	3	12	5	.71	7	.336	.418	.491

Year	Team	Lg	G	AB	H	2B	3B	HR	(Hm	Rd)	TB	R	RBI	RC	TBB	IBB	SO	HBP	SH	SF	SB	CS	SB%	GDP	Avg	OBP	Slg
2002	SnAnt	AA	23	89	29	9	2	1	(-	-)	45	10	12	19	12	3	11	4	3	0	5	1	.83	1	.326	.429	.506
2003	SnAnt	AA	47	186	62	12	2	3	(-	-)	87	24	25	30	8	0	30	5	0	3	1	7	.13	0	.333	.371	.468
2003	Tacom	AAA	18	67	18	2	0	3	(-	-)	29	11	10	10	5	0	12	2	0	1	1	0	1.00	0	.269	.333	.433
2004	Ms	R	10	32	10	4	1	0	(-	-)	16	8	9	7	7	0	3	3	0	0	1	0	1.00	2	.313	.476	.500
2005	Tacom	AAA	65	246	91	17	2	8	(-	-)	136	50	46	60	36	5	43	4	1	4	2	3	.40	2	.370	.452	.553
2002	SEA	AL	8	27	4	0	0	1	(0	1)	7	2	3	3	2	0	4	0	0	0	0	0	-	2	.148	.207	.259
2005	SEA	AL	15	29	8	2	0	1	(1	0)	13	4	1	3	5	0	2	0	1	0	0	2	.00	0	.276	.382	.448
	2 ML YEARS		23	56	12	2	0	2	(1	1)	20	6	4	6	7	0	6	0	1	0	0	2	.00	2	.214	.302	.357

J.T. Snow

Bats: L **Throws:** L **Pos:** 1B-108; PH-12   **Ht:** 6'2" **Wt:** 209 **Born:** 2/26/1968 **Age:** 38

Year	Team	Lg	G	AB	H	2B	3B	HR	(Hm	Rd)	TB	R	RBI	RC	TBB	IBB	SO	HBP	SH	SF	SB	CS	SB%	GDP	Avg	OBP	Slg
1992	NYA	AL	7	14	2	1	0	0	(0	0)	3	1	2	2	5	1	5	0	0	0	0	0	-	0	.143	.368	.214
1993	CAL	AL	129	419	101	18	2	16	(10	6)	171	60	57	57	55	4	88	2	7	6	3	0	1.00	10	.241	.328	.408
1994	CAL	AL	61	223	49	4	0	8	(7	1)	77	22	30	22	19	1	48	3	2	1	0	1	.00	2	.220	.289	.345
1995	CAL	AL	143	544	157	22	1	24	(14	10)	253	80	102	85	52	4	91	3	5	2	2	1	.67	16	.289	.353	.465
1996	CAL	AL	155	575	148	20	1	17	(8	9)	221	69	67	67	56	6	96	5	2	3	1	6	.14	19	.257	.327	.384
1997	SF	NL	157	531	149	36	1	28	(14	14)	271	81	104	105	96	13	124	1	2	7	6	4	.60	8	.281	.387	.510
1998	SF	NL	138	435	108	29	1	15	(9	6)	184	65	79	60	58	3	84	0	0	7	1	2	.33	12	.248	.332	.423
1999	SF	NL	161	570	156	25	2	24	(7	17)	257	93	98	93	86	7	121	5	1	6	0	4	.00	16	.274	.370	.451
2000	SF	NL	155	536	152	33	2	19	(10	9)	246	82	96	87	66	6	129	11	0	14	1	3	.25	20	.284	.365	.459
2001	SF	NL	101	285	70	12	1	8	(3	5)	108	43	34	44	55	10	81	4	0	4	0	0	-	2	.246	.371	.379
2002	SF	NL	143	422	104	26	2	6	(1	5)	152	47	53	54	59	5	90	7	0	6	0	0	-	11	.246	.344	.360
2003	SF	NL	103	330	90	18	3	8	(2	6)	138	48	51	59	55	0	55	8	1	2	1	2	.33	7	.273	.387	.418
2004	SF	NL	107	346	113	32	1	12	(5	7)	183	62	60	79	58	0	61	7	2	4	4	0	1.00	5	.327	.429	.529
2005	SF	NL	117	367	101	17	2	4	(1	3)	134	40	40	48	32	1	61	7	2	2	1	0	1.00	6	.275	.343	.365
	14 ML YEARS		1677	5597	1500	293	19	189	(91	98)	2398	793	873	862	752	61	1134	63	24	64	20	23	.47	134	.268	.357	.428

Chris Snyder

Bats: R **Throws:** R **Pos:** C-113; PH-2   **Ht:** 6'3" **Wt:** 220 **Born:** 2/12/1981 **Age:** 25

Year	Team	Lg	G	AB	H	2B	3B	HR	(Hm	Rd)	TB	R	RBI	RC	TBB	IBB	SO	HBP	SH	SF	SB	CS	SB%	GDP	Avg	OBP	Slg
2002	Lancst	A+	60	217	56	16	0	9	(-	-)	99	31	44	31	25	0	54	3	1	4	0	0	-	7	.258	.337	.456
2003	Lancst	A+	69	245	77	16	2	10	(-	-)	127	53	53	51	35	2	43	8	0	2	0	1	.00	4	.314	.414	.518
2003	ElPaso	AA	53	188	38	14	0	4	(-	-)	64	21	26	15	19	1	29	4	0	2	0	0	-	9	.202	.286	.340
2004	ElPaso	AA	99	346	104	31	0	15	(-	-)	180	66	57	67	46	1	57	6	0	3	3	1	.75	7	.301	.389	.520
2004	ARI	NL	29	96	23	6	0	5	(1	4)	44	10	15	11	13	1	25	0	0	1	0	0	-	1	.240	.327	.458
2005	ARI	NL	115	326	66	14	0	6	(2	4)	98	24	28	25	40	5	87	4	3	0	0	1	.00	6	.202	.297	.301
	2 ML YEARS		144	422	89	20	0	11	(3	8)	142	34	43	36	53	6	112	4	3	1	0	1	.00	7	.211	.304	.336

Kyle Snyder

Pitches: R **Bats:** B **Pos:** RP-10; SP-3   **Ht:** 6'8" **Wt:** 220 **Born:** 9/9/1977 **Age:** 28

Year	Team	Lg	G	GS	CG	GF	IP	BFP	H	R	ER	HR	SH	SF	HB	TBB	IBB	SO	WP	Bk	W	L	Pct	ShO	Sv-Op	Hld	ERC	ERA
1999	Spkane	A-	7	7	0	0	24.0	103	20	13	11	1	2	1	2	7	0	25	1	0	1	0	1.000	0	0--	-	2.59	4.13
2000	Royals	R	1	1	0	0	2.0	7	1	0	0	0	0	0	0	1	0	4	0	0	0	0	-	0	0--	-	0.54	0.00
2000	Wilmg	A+	1	1	0	0	0.0	1	0	1	0	0	0	0	0	1	0	0	0	0	0	0	-	0	0--	-	-	-
2002	Wilmg	A+	15	15	0	0	48.1	207	49	19	16	1	1	2	5	11	0	48	2	0	0	2	.000	0	0--	-	3.31	2.98
2002	Wichta	AA	6	6	0	0	25.2	101	21	12	12	4	0	0	1	7	1	18	3	0	2	2	.500	0	0--	-	3.18	4.21
2003	Royals	R	1	1	0	0	2.0	8	3	1	1	0	0	0	0	0	0	1	0	0	0	0	-	0	0--	-	5.09	4.50
2003	Wichta	AA	1	1	0	0	5.0	17	2	0	0	0	0	0	1	0	0	2	0	0	0	0	-	0	0--	-	0.67	0.00
2003	Omha	AAA	5	5	0	0	29.0	116	28	9	9	3	0	1	1	6	0	15	0	0	3	0	1.000	0	0--	-	3.42	2.79
2005	Wichta	AA	1	1	0	0	5.0	21	5	3	3	1	0	1	0	1	0	1	0	0	1	0	1.000	0	0--	-	3.86	5.40
2005	Omha	AAA	15	12	0	0	66.0	281	61	32	26	2	2	5	3	22	0	48	2	1	2	3	.400	0	0--	-	3.17	3.55
2003	KC	AL	15	15	0	0	85.1	364	94	52	49	11	0	9	2	21	3	39	4	0	1	6	.143	0	0-0	0	4.29	5.17
2005	KC	AL	13	3	0	4	36.0	169	55	29	27	3	0	2	1	10	1	19	1	0	1	3	.250	0	0-0	0	6.70	6.75
	2 ML YEARS		28	18	0	4	121.1	533	149	81	76	14	0	11	3	31	4	58	5	0	2	9	.182	0	0-0	0	4.98	5.64

Zach Sorensen

Bats: B **Throws:** R **Pos:** PR-7; 2B-5; 3B-1; DH-1; PH-1   **Ht:** 6'0" **Wt:** 190 **Born:** 1/3/1977 **Age:** 29

Year	Team	Lg	G	AB	H	2B	3B	HR	(Hm	Rd)	TB	R	RBI	RC	TBB	IBB	SO	HBP	SH	SF	SB	CS	SB%	GDP	Avg	OBP	Slg
1998	Wtrtwn	A-	53	200	60	7	8	4	(-	-)	95	38	26	41	35	0	35	0	2	0	14	4	.78	2	.300	.404	.475
1999	Kinston	R	130	508	121	16	7	7	(-	-)	172	79	59	59	62	1	126	2	8	7	24	12	.67	6	.238	.322	.339
2000	Akron	AA	96	382	99	17	4	6	(-	-)	142	62	38	49	42	0	62	2	4	3	16	6	.73	6	.259	.333	.372
2000	Buffalo	AAA	12	38	10	1	1	0	(-	-)	13	5	2	3	3	0	9	0	0	1	1	0	1.00	2	.263	.310	.342
2001	Akron	AA	46	194	45	6	1	5	(-	-)	68	24	16	16	11	1	30	0	3	0	10	8	.56	3	.232	.273	.351
2001	MhVlly	A-	14	53	13	0	1	1	(-	-)	18	10	11	4	2	0	8	0	1	2	2	0	1.00	0	.245	.263	.340
2001	Buffalo	AAA	2	7	2	0	0	0	(-	-)	2	2	1	0	0	0	0	0	0	0	0	0	-	0	.286	.286	.286
2002	Buffalo	AAA	120	455	120	12	12	7	(-	-)	177	55	54	53	24	1	72	1	15	4	13	6	.68	9	.264	.300	.389
2003	Buffalo	AAA	61	238	57	12	3	3	(-	-)	84	39	29	26	22	0	42	0	5	4	12	5	.71	3	.239	.299	.353
2004	Akron	AA	26	93	24	2	1	1	(-	-)	31	12	9	15	17	0	19	0	1	2	9	1	.90	3	.258	.366	.333
2004	Salt Lk	AAA	95	359	111	16	4	3	(-	-)	144	73	37	60	45	0	58	0	6	6	22	5	.81	6	.309	.380	.401
2004	Buffalo	AAA	4	8	0	0	0	0	(-	-)	0	0	0	0	1	1	3	0	0	0	0	0	-	0	.000	.111	.000
2005	Salt Lk	AAA	78	287	87	11	3	2	(-	-)	110	47	41	45	34	0	55	1	10	6	21	9	.70	5	.303	.372	.383

Year	Team	Lg	G	AB	H	2B	3B	HR	(Hm	Rd)	TB	R	RBI	RC	TBB	IBB	SO	HBP	SH	SF	SB	CS	SB%	GDP	Avg	OBP	Slg
2003	CLE	AL	36	37	5	1	0	1	(0	1)	9	2	2	1	7	0	13	0	0	0	0	3	.00	0	.135	.273	.243
2005	LAA	AL	12	12	2	1	0	0	(0	0)	3	3	0	0	0	0	2	0	1	0	0	0	-	0	.167	.167	.250
2 ML YEARS			48	49	7	2	0	1	(0	1)	12	5	2	1	7	0	15	0	1	0	0	3	.00	0	.143	.250	.245

Alfonso Soriano

Bats: R **Throws:** R **Pos:** 2B-153; DH-2; PH-1   **Ht:** 6'1" **Wt:** 180 **Born:** 1/7/1976 **Age:** 30

Year	Team	Lg	G	AB	H	2B	3B	HR	(Hm	Rd)	TB	R	RBI	RC	TBB	IBB	SO	HBP	SH	SF	SB	CS	SB%	GDP	Avg	OBP	Slg
1999	NYA	AL	9	8	1	0	0	1	(1	0)	4	2	1	0	0	0	3	0	0	0	0	1	.00	0	.125	.125	.500
2000	NYA	AL	22	50	9	3	0	2	(0	2)	18	5	3	4	1	0	15	0	2	0	2	0	1.00	0	.180	.196	.360
2001	NYA	AL	158	574	154	34	3	18	(8	10)	248	77	73	77	29	0	125	3	3	5	43	14	.75	7	.268	.304	.432
2002	NYA	AL	156	696	209	51	2	39	(17	22)	381	128	102	121	23	1	157	14	1	7	41	13	.76	8	.300	.332	.547
2003	NYA	AL	156	682	198	36	5	38	(15	23)	358	114	91	110	38	7	130	12	0	2	35	8	.81	8	.290	.338	.525
2004	TEX	AL	145	608	170	32	4	28	(12	16)	294	77	91	90	33	4	121	10	0	7	18	5	.78	7	.280	.324	.484
2005	TEX	AL	156	637	171	43	2	36	(25	11)	326	102	104	93	33	3	125	7	0	5	30	2	.94	6	.268	.309	.512
7 ML YEARS			802	3255	912	199	16	162	(78	84)	1629	505	465	495	157	15	676	46	6	26	169	43	.80	36	.280	.320	.500

Rafael Soriano

Pitches: R **Bats:** R **Pos:** RP-7   **Ht:** 6'1" **Wt:** 175 **Born:** 12/19/1979 **Age:** 26

	HOW MUCH HE PITCHED						WHAT HE GAVE UP												THE RESULTS						
Year	Team	Lg	G	GS	CG	GF	IP	BFP	H	R	ER	HR	SH	SF	HB	TBB	IBB	SO	WP	Bk	W	L	Pct	ShO	Sv-Op	Hld	ERC	ERA
2005	InldEm*	A+	3	3	0	0	4.0	14	2	0	0	0	0	0	0	0	0	5	0	0	0	0	-	0	0--	-	0.54	0.00
2005	Everett*	A-	4	4	0	0	6.0	26	6	3	2	0	0	0	1	2	0	8	0	1	0	0	-	0	0--	-	3.79	3.00
2005	SnAnt*	AA	1	1	0	0	1.0	3	0	0	0	0	0	0	0	0	0	0	0	0	0	0	-	0	0--	-	1.26	0.00
2005	Tacom*	AAA	5	0	0	0	5.1	20	3	0	0	0	0	0	0	1	0	11	0	0	1	0	1.000	0	0--	-	0.99	0.00
2002	SEA	AL	10	8	0	1	47.1	202	45	25	24	8	1	0	0	16	1	32	2	0	0	3	.000	0	1-1	0	3.93	4.56
2003	SEA	AL	40	0	0	12	53.0	201	30	9	9	2	0	1	3	12	1	68	0	0	3	0	1.000	0	1-2	5	1.32	1.53
2004	SEA	AL	6	0	0	0	3.1	23	9	6	5	0	0	0	0	3	0	3	0	0	0	3	.000	0	0-1	0	15.97	13.50
2005	SEA	AL	7	0	0	4	7.1	30	6	2	2	0	0	1	1	1	0	9	0	0	0	0	-	0	0-0	1	2.00	2.45
4 ML YEARS			63	8	0	17	111.0	456	90	42	40	10	1	2	4	32	2	112	2	0	3	6	.333	0	2-4	6	2.67	3.24

Jorge Sosa

Pitches: R **Bats:** R **Pos:** RP-24; SP-20   **Ht:** 6'2" **Wt:** 177 **Born:** 4/28/1977 **Age:** 29

	HOW MUCH HE PITCHED						WHAT HE GAVE UP												THE RESULTS						
Year	Team	Lg	G	GS	CG	GF	IP	BFP	H	R	ER	HR	SH	SF	HB	TBB	IBB	SO	WP	Bk	W	L	Pct	ShO	Sv-Op	Hld	ERC	ERA
2002	TB	AL	31	14	0	10	99.1	434	88	63	61	16	0	5	2	54	0	48	5	0	2	7	.222	0	0-0	1	4.51	5.53
2003	TB	AL	29	19	1	4	128.2	566	137	71	66	14	4	5	4	60	4	72	8	1	5	12	.294	1	0-0	0	4.93	4.62
2004	TB	AL	43	8	0	6	99.1	447	100	67	61	17	2	4	1	54	3	94	2	0	4	7	.364	0	1-1	6	5.17	5.53
2005	ATL	NL	44	20	0	5	134.0	577	122	42	38	12	5	2	0	64	8	85	3	0	13	3	.813	0	0-0	4	3.70	2.55
4 ML YEARS			147	61	1	25	461.1	2024	447	243	226	59	11	16	7	232	15	299	18	1	24	29	.453	1	1-1	11	4.52	4.41

Sammy Sosa

Bats: R **Throws:** R **Pos:** RF-66; DH-35; PH-1   **Ht:** 6'0" **Wt:** 220 **Born:** 11/12/1968 **Age:** 37

Year	Team	Lg	G	AB	H	2B	3B	HR	(Hm	Rd)	TB	R	RBI	RC	TBB	IBB	SO	HBP	SH	SF	SB	CS	SB%	GDP	Avg	OBP	Slg
1989	2 Tms	AL	58	183	47	8	0	4	(1	3)	67	27	13	18	11	2	47	2	5	2	7	5	.58	6	.257	.303	.366
1990	CHA	AL	153	532	124	26	10	15	(10	5)	215	72	70	59	33	4	150	6	2	6	32	16	.67	10	.233	.282	.404
1991	CHA	AL	116	316	64	10	1	10	(3	7)	106	39	33	23	14	2	98	2	5	1	13	6	.68	5	.203	.240	.335
1992	CHN	NL	67	262	68	7	2	8	(4	4)	103	41	25	33	19	1	63	4	4	2	15	7	.68	4	.260	.317	.393
1993	CHN	NL	159	598	156	25	5	33	(23	10)	290	92	93	88	38	6	135	4	0	1	36	11	.77	14	.261	.309	.485
1994	CHN	NL	105	426	128	17	6	25	(11	14)	232	59	70	75	25	1	92	2	1	4	22	13	.63	7	.300	.339	.545
1995	CHN	NL	144	564	151	17	3	36	(19	17)	282	89	119	98	58	11	134	5	0	2	34	7	.83	8	.268	.340	.500
1996	CHN	NL	124	498	136	21	2	40	(26	14)	281	84	100	87	34	6	134	5	0	4	18	5	.78	14	.273	.323	.564
1997	CHN	NL	162	642	161	31	4	36	(25	11)	308	90	119	88	45	9	174	2	0	5	22	12	.65	16	.251	.300	.480
1998	CHN	NL	159	643	198	20	0	66	(35	31)	416	134	158	142	73	14	171	1	0	5	18	9	.67	20	.308	.377	.647
1999	CHN	NL	162	625	180	24	2	63	(33	30)	397	114	141	134	78	8	171	3	0	6	7	8	.47	17	.288	.367	.635
2000	CHN	NL	156	604	193	38	1	50	(22	28)	383	106	138	144	91	19	168	2	0	8	7	4	.64	12	.320	.406	.634
2001	CHN	NL	160	577	189	34	5	64	(34	30)	425	146	160	170	116	37	153	6	0	12	0	2	.00	6	.328	.437	.737
2002	CHN	NL	150	556	160	19	2	49	(24	25)	330	122	108	121	103	15	144	3	0	4	2	0	1.00	14	.288	.399	.594
2003	CHN	NL	137	517	144	22	0	40	(19	21)	286	99	103	94	62	9	143	5	0	5	0	1	.00	14	.279	.358	.553
2004	CHN	NL	126	478	121	21	0	35	(18	17)	247	69	80	68	56	4	133	2	0	3	0	0	-	9	.253	.332	.517
2005	BAL	AL	102	380	84	15	1	14	(4	10)	143	39	45	36	39	3	84	2	0	3	1	1	.50	15	.221	.295	.376
89	Tex	AL	25	84	20	3	0	1	(0	1)	26	8	3	4	0	0	20	0	4	0	0	2	.00	3	.238	.238	.310
89	CWS	AL	33	99	27	5	0	3	(1	2)	41	19	10	14	11	2	27	2	1	2	7	3	.70	3	.273	.351	.414
17 ML YEARS			2240	8401	2304	355	44	588	(311	277)	4511	1422	1575	1478	895	151	2194	56	17	73	234	107	.69	191	.274	.345	.537

Geovany Soto

Bats: R **Throws:** R **Pos:** PH-1   **Ht:** 6'1" **Wt:** 230 **Born:** 1/20/1983 **Age:** 23

Year	Team	Lg	G	AB	H	2B	3B	HR	(Hm	Rd)	TB	R	RBI	RC	TBB	IBB	SO	HBP	SH	SF	SB	CS	SB%	GDP	Avg	OBP	Slg
2001	Cubs	R	41	150	39	16	0	1	(-	-)	58	18	20	21	15	1	33	3	1	0	1	0	1.00	3	.260	.339	.387
2002	Cubs	R	44	156	42	10	2	3	(-	-)	65	24	24	22	13	1	35	3	1	2	0	2	.00	2	.269	.333	.417
2002	Boise	A-	1	5	2	0	0	0	(-	-)	2	1	0	0	0	0	1	0	0	0	0	0	-	0	.400	.400	.400
2003	Dytona	A+	89	297	72	12	2	2	(-	-)	94	26	38	32	31	0	58	2	4	6	0	0	-	10	.242	.313	.316

Year	Team	Lg	G	AB	H	2B	3B	HR	(Hm	Rd)	TB	R	RBI	RC	TBB	IBB	SO	HBP	SH	SF	SB	CS	SB%	GDP	Avg	OBP	Slg
2004	WTenn	AA	104	332	90	16	0	9	(-	-)	133	47	48	50	40	1	71	5	1	3	1	2	.33	10	.271	.355	.401
2005	Iowa	AAA	91	292	74	14	0	4	(-	-)	100	30	39	39	48	0	77	0	3	2	0	1	.00	15	.253	.357	.342
2005	CHN	NL	1	1	0	0	0	0	(0	0)	0	0	0	0	0	0	0	0	0	0	0	0	-	0	.000	.000	.000

Justin Speier

Pitches: R Bats: R Pos: RP-65　　　　　　　　**Ht: 6'4" Wt: 205 Born: 11/6/1973 Age: 32**

Year	Team	Lg	G	GS	CG	GF	IP	BFP	H	R	ER	HR	SH	SF	HB	TBB	IBB	SO	WP	Bk	W	L	Pct	ShO	Sv-Op	Hld	ERC	ERA
1998	2 Tms	NL	19	0	0	10	20.2	99	27	20	20	7	2	1	0	13	1	17	3	0	0	3	.000	0	0-1	5	8.94	8.71
1999	ATL	NL	19	0	0	8	28.2	127	28	18	18	8	0	1	0	13	1	22	0	0	0	0	-	0	0-0	0	5.27	5.65
2000	CLE	AL	47	0	0	12	68.1	290	57	27	25	9	2	4	4	28	3	69	7	1	5	2	.714	0	0-1	6	3.56	3.29
2001	2 Tms	NL	54	0	0	10	76.2	324	71	40	39	13	2	7	8	20	3	62	6	1	6	3	.667	0	0-1	4	3.93	4.58
2002	COL	NL	63	0	0	7	62.1	259	51	31	30	9	0	1	3	19	4	47	1	2	5	1	.833	0	1-4	18	3.06	4.33
2003	COL	NL	72	0	0	31	73.1	319	73	37	33	11	1	4	7	23	6	66	0	0	3	1	.750	0	9-12	12	4.27	4.05
2004	TOR	AL	62	0	0	32	69.0	294	61	32	30	8	6	3	5	25	6	52	4	0	3	8	.273	0	7-11	7	3.52	3.91
2005	TOR	AL	65	0	0	36	66.2	264	48	20	19	10	4	0	3	15	2	56	1	1	3	2	.600	0	0-4	11	2.38	2.57
98	ChC	NL	1	0	0	0	1.1	7	2	2	2	0	0	0	0	1	0	2	1	0	0	0	-	0	0-0	0	7.52	13.50
98	Fla	NL	18	0	0	10	19.1	92	25	18	18	7	2	1	0	12	1	15	2	0	0	3	.000	0	0-1	1	9.02	8.38
01	Cle	AL	12	0	0	2	20.2	96	24	16	16	5	0	3	3	8	0	15	2	0	2	0	1.000	0	0-0	0	6.61	6.97
01	Col	AL	42	0	0	8	56.0	228	47	24	23	8	2	4	5	12	3	47	4	1	4	3	.571	0	0-1	4	3.04	3.70
	8 ML YEARS		401	0	0	146	465.2	1976	416	225	214	75	17	21	30	156	26	391	22	5	25	20	.556	0	17-34	59	3.78	4.14

Ryan Speier

Pitches: R Bats: R Pos: RP-22　　　　　　　　**Ht: 6'7" Wt: 200 Born: 7/24/1979 Age: 26**

Year	Team	Lg	G	GS	CG	GF	IP	BFP	H	R	ER	HR	SH	SF	HB	TBB	IBB	SO	WP	Bk	W	L	Pct	ShO	Sv-Op	Hld	ERC	ERA
2001	Casper	R+	17	0	0	8	26.0	106	19	12	9	2	1	0	2	9	4	24	2	0	1	2	.333	0	1- -	-	2.38	3.12
2002	Salem	A+	24	0	0	14	32.0	142	35	21	14	0	6	0	2	11	2	33	2	0	2	2	.500	0	4- -	-	3.74	3.94
2002	Ashvlle	A	28	0	0	6	36.2	155	32	21	16	3	2	1	1	13	1	39	5	0	3	1	.750	0	1- -	-	3.11	3.93
2003	Visalia	A+	56	0	0	43	58.2	243	50	14	10	2	5	7	6	17	2	73	2	0	4	2	.667	0	18- -	-	2.78	1.53
2004	Tulsa	AA	62	0	0	59	62.1	246	33	14	14	3	0	0	3	26	1	71	4	1	3	1	.750	0	37- -	-	1.63	2.02
2005	ColSpr	AAA	45	0	0	22	52.1	245	70	30	29	2	4	0	8	18	0	45	6	0	2	2	.500	0	6- -	-	6.02	4.99
2005	COL	NL	22	0	0	10	24.2	111	26	12	10	0	2	1	1	13	0	10	2	0	2	1	.667	0	0-1	2	4.29	3.65

Scott Spiezio

Bats: B Throws: R Pos: PH-15; 3B-6; DH-5; 1B-4; 2B-1; PR-1　　　**Ht: 6'2" Wt: 225 Born: 9/21/1972 Age: 33**

Year	Team	Lg	G	AB	H	2B	3B	HR	(Hm	Rd)	TB	R	RBI	RC	TBB	IBB	SO	HBP	SH	SF	SB	CS	SB%	GDP	Avg	OBP	Slg
2005	Tacom*	AAA	14	58	19	3	1	2	(-	-)	30	11	9	10	1	0	9	1	0	3	0	0	-	2	.328	.333	.517
1996	OAK	AL	9	29	9	2	0	2	(1	1)	17	6	8	6	4	1	4	0	0	2	0	1	.00	1	.310	.394	.586
1997	OAK	AL	147	538	131	28	4	14	(6	8)	209	58	65	61	44	2	75	1	3	4	9	3	.75	13	.243	.300	.388
1998	OAK	AL	114	406	105	19	1	9	(6	3)	153	54	50	50	44	3	56	2	7	2	1	3	.25	10	.259	.333	.377
1999	OAK	AL	89	247	60	24	0	8	(3	5)	108	31	33	35	29	3	36	2	1	3	0	0	-	5	.243	.324	.437
2000	ANA	AL	123	297	72	11	2	17	(10	7)	138	47	49	47	40	2	56	3	1	4	1	2	.33	5	.242	.334	.465
2001	ANA	AL	139	457	124	29	4	13	(8	5)	200	57	54	65	34	4	65	5	3	4	5	2	.71	6	.271	.326	.438
2002	ANA	AL	153	491	140	34	2	12	(7	5)	214	80	82	86	67	7	52	4	3	6	6	7	.46	12	.285	.371	.436
2003	ANA	AL	158	521	138	36	7	16	(7	9)	236	69	83	72	46	8	66	5	2	7	6	3	.67	12	.265	.326	.453
2004	SEA	AL	112	367	79	12	3	10	(5	5)	127	38	41	31	36	2	60	4	2	6	4	1	.80	7	.215	.288	.346
2005	SEA	AL	29	47	3	1	0	1	(0	1)	7	2	1	0	4	0	18	0	0	0	0	0	-	1	.064	.137	.149
	10 ML YEARS		1073	3400	861	196	23	102	(53	49)	1409	442	466	453	348	32	488	26	24	36	32	22	.59	71	.253	.324	.414

Ryan Spilborghs

Bats: R Throws: R Pos: RF-1　　　　　　　　**Ht: 6'1" Wt: 190 Born: 9/5/1979 Age: 26**

Year	Team	Lg	G	AB	H	2B	3B	HR	(Hm	Rd)	TB	R	RBI	RC	TBB	IBB	SO	HBP	SH	SF	SB	CS	SB%	GDP	Avg	OBP	Slg
2002	Tri-Cit	A-	71	261	60	11	1	4	(-	-)	85	34	34	28	29	1	61	3	1	1	11	7	.61	5	.230	.313	.326
2003	Ashvlle	A	119	434	122	22	2	15	(-	-)	193	78	61	75	63	0	96	8	1	4	10	11	.48	4	.281	.379	.445
2004	Visalia	A+	125	444	115	26	3	8	(-	-)	171	59	57	66	64	0	98	6	2	4	8	6	.57	13	.259	.357	.385
2005	Tulsa	AA	71	255	87	23	3	6	(-	-)	134	52	54	59	42	2	49	2	0	2	10	3	.77	7	.341	.435	.525
2005	ColSpr	AAA	60	227	77	23	5	5	(-	-)	125	49	30	49	22	0	53	3	1	0	7	3	.70	5	.339	.405	.551
2005	COL	NL	1	4	2	0	0	0	(0	0)	2	0	1	1	0	0	1	0	0	0	0	0	-	0	.500	.500	.500

Junior Spivey

Bats: R Throws: R Pos: 2B-70; PR-6; PH-4　　　　　　**Ht: 6'0" Wt: 185 Born: 1/28/1975 Age: 31**

Year	Team	Lg	G	AB	H	2B	3B	HR	(Hm	Rd)	TB	R	RBI	RC	TBB	IBB	SO	HBP	SH	SF	SB	CS	SB%	GDP	Avg	OBP	Slg
2001	ARI	NL	72	163	42	6	3	5	(4	1)	69	33	21	26	23	0	47	2	6	1	3	0	1.00	3	.258	.354	.423
2002	ARI	NL	143	538	162	34	6	16	(9	7)	256	103	78	94	65	5	100	16	1	6	11	6	.65	10	.301	.389	.476
2003	ARI	NL	106	365	93	22	2	13	(10	3)	158	52	50	47	33	1	95	7	0	3	4	3	.57	7	.255	.326	.433
2004	MIL	NL	59	228	62	13	0	7	(4	3)	96	33	28	28	25	0	48	7	1	2	5	3	.63	7	.272	.359	.421
2005	2 Tms	NL	77	259	60	15	1	7	(4	3)	98	37	24	28	29	2	83	3	1	1	9	3	.75	3	.232	.315	.378
05	Mil	NL	49	182	43	8	1	5	(2	3)	68	22	17	16	18	1	57	1	1	0	7	3	.70	3	.236	.308	.374
05	Was	NL	28	77	17	7	0	2	(2	0)	30	15	7	12	11	1	26	2	0	1	2	0	1.00	0	.221	.330	.390
	5 ML YEARS		457	1553	419	90	12	48	(31	17)	677	258	201	223	175	8	373	35	9	13	32	15	.68	30	.270	.354	.436

Russ Springer

Pitches: R **Bats:** R **Pos:** RP-62 **Ht:** 6'4" **Wt:** 211 **Born:** 11/7/1968 **Age:** 37

				HOW MUCH HE PITCHED					WHAT HE GAVE UP												THE RESULTS							
Year	Team	Lg	G	GS	CG	GF	IP	BFP	H	R	ER	HR	SH	SF	HB	TBB	IBB	SO	WP	Bk	W	L	Pct	ShO	Sv-Op	Hld	ERC	ERA
1992	NYA	AL	14	0	0	5	16.0	75	18	11	11	0	0	0	1	10	0	12	0	0	0	0	-	0	0-0	2	5.15	6.19
1993	CAL	AL	14	9	1	3	60.0	278	73	48	48	11	1	1	3	32	1	31	6	0	1	6	.143	0	0-0	0	6.87	7.20
1994	CAL	AL	18	5	0	6	45.2	198	53	28	28	9	1	1	0	14	0	28	2	0	2	2	.500	0	2-3	1	5.38	5.52
1995	2 Tms		33	6	0	6	78.1	350	82	48	46	16	2	2	7	35	4	70	2	0	1	2	.333	0	1-2	0	5.63	5.29
1996	PHI	NL	51	7	0	12	96.2	437	106	60	50	12	5	3	1	38	6	94	5	0	3	10	.231	0	0-3	6	4.57	4.66
1997	HOU	NL	54	0	0	13	55.1	241	48	28	26	4	1	2	4	27	2	74	4	0	3	3	.500	0	3-7	9	3.69	4.23
1998	HOU	NL	48	0	0	14	52.2	232	51	26	24	4	2	1	1	30	4	56	5	0	5	4	.556	0	0-4	7	4.38	4.10
1999	ATL	NL	49	0	0	8	47.1	194	31	20	18	5	0	2	2	22	2	49	0	0	2	1	.667	0	1-1	8	2.63	3.42
2000	ARI	NL	52	0	0	10	62.0	282	63	36	35	11	2	3	2	34	6	59	3	0	2	4	.333	0	0-2	3	5.25	5.08
2001	ARI	NL	18	0	0	9	17.2	79	20	16	14	5	1	1	0	4	0	12	2	0	0	0	-	0	1-1	2	5.13	7.13
2003	STL	NL	17	0	0	4	17.1	77	19	16	16	8	0	0	1	6	0	11	1	0	1	1	.500	0	0-1	5	7.27	8.31
2004	HOU	NL	16	0	0	3	13.2	62	15	4	4	1	0	1	1	6	0	9	2	0	0	1	.000	0	0-0	5	4.84	2.63
2005	HOU	NL	62	0	0	11	59.0	246	49	34	31	9	1	0	3	21	3	54	2	0	4	4	.500	0	0-3	10	3.45	4.73
95	Cal	AL	19	6	0	3	51.2	238	60	37	35	11	1	0	5	25	1	38	1	0	1	2	.333	0	1-2	0	6.69	6.10
95	Phi	NL	14	0	0	3	26.2	112	22	11	11	5	1	2	2	10	3	32	1	0	0	0	-	0	0-0	0	3.73	3.71
98	Altna	AA	26	0	0	13	32.2	140	29	16	15	4	0	0	1	14	1	37	3	0	4	3	.571	0	0-3	1	3.77	4.13
98	Atl	NL	22	0	0	1	20.0	92	22	10	9	0	2	1	0	16	3	19	2	0	1	1	.500	0	0-1	6	5.36	4.05
13 ML YEARS			446	27	1	104	621.2	2751	628	375	351	95	16	17	26	279	28	559	34	0	24	38	.387	0	8-27	58	4.79	5.08

Chris Spurling

Pitches: R **Bats:** R **Pos:** RP-56 **Ht:** 6'6" **Wt:** 240 **Born:** 6/28/1977 **Age:** 29

				HOW MUCH HE PITCHED					WHAT HE GAVE UP												THE RESULTS							
Year	Team	Lg	G	GS	CG	GF	IP	BFP	H	R	ER	HR	SH	SF	HB	TBB	IBB	SO	WP	Bk	W	L	Pct	ShO	Sv-Op	Hld	ERC	ERA
1998	Yanks	R	13	6	0	2	51.1	219	57	21	13	3	0	2	2	11	0	44	2	0	2	1	.667	0	1--	-	3.83	2.28
1998	Grnsbr	A	1	1	0	0	6.0	25	7	2	2	1	0	0	0	1	0	5	0	0	1	0	1.000	0	0--	-	4.63	3.00
1999	Grnsbr	A	49	0	0	26	76.1	332	78	34	31	8	4	9	2	23	3	68	7	0	4	6	.400	0	4--	-	3.79	3.66
2000	Tampa	A+	34	0	0	15	57.0	239	50	27	24	1	2	3	1	22	5	55	3	0	4	6	.400	0	1--	-	2.74	3.79
2000	Lynbrg	A+	9	0	0	6	18.1	66	8	2	2	1	0	1	0	3	0	17	0	0	1	0	1.000	0	5--	-	0.80	0.98
2001	Altna	AA	34	15	0	11	121.2	512	133	48	42	9	1	3	4	28	1	63	2	0	5	7	.417	0	1--	-	3.92	3.11
2002	Altna	AA	51	0	0	45	70.0	275	54	18	17	8	2	1	2	12	1	60	1	0	4	3	.571	0	20--	-	2.21	2.19
2005	Toledo	AAA	12	0	0	4	19.2	80	18	10	9	2	1	0	0	3	0	15	0	0	2	1	.667	0	1--	-	2.64	4.12
2003	DET	AL	66	0	0	18	77.0	326	78	42	40	9	3	5	3	22	1	38	2	1	1	3	.250	0	3-6	5	3.97	4.68
2005	DET	AL	56	0	0	8	70.2	284	58	30	27	8	3	5	2	22	6	26	4	0	3	4	.429	0	0-1	11	2.91	3.44
2 ML YEARS			122	0	0	26	147.2	610	136	72	67	17	6	10	5	44	7	64	6	1	4	7	.364	0	3-7	16	3.45	4.08

Matt Stairs

Bats: L **Throws:** R **Pos:** 1B-64; DH-40; PH-14; RF-13; LF-2 **Ht:** 5'9" **Wt:** 215 **Born:** 2/27/1968 **Age:** 38

									BATTING												BASERUNNING				AVERAGES		
Year	Team	Lg	G	AB	H	2B	3B	HR	(Hm	Rd)	TB	R	RBI	RC	TBB	IBB	SO	HBP	SH	SF	SB	CS	SB%	GDP	Avg	OBP	Slg
1992	MON	NL	13	30	5	2	0	0	(0	0)	7	2	5	3	7	0	7	0	0	1	0	0	-	0	.167	.316	.233
1993	MON	NL	6	8	3	1	0	0	(0	0)	4	1	2	1	0	0	1	0	0	0	0	0	-	1	.375	.375	.500
1995	BOS	AL	39	88	23	7	1	1	(0	1)	35	8	17	9	4	0	14	1	1	1	0	1	.00	4	.261	.298	.398
1996	OAK	AL	61	137	38	5	1	10	(5	5)	75	21	23	27	19	2	23	1	0	1	1	1	.50	2	.277	.367	.547
1997	OAK	AL	133	352	105	19	0	27	(20	7)	205	62	73	77	50	1	60	3	1	4	3	2	.60	4	.298	.386	.582
1998	OAK	AL	149	523	154	33	1	26	(16	10)	267	88	106	96	59	4	93	6	1	4	8	3	.73	13	.294	.370	.511
1999	OAK	AL	146	531	137	26	3	38	(15	23)	283	94	102	101	89	6	124	2	0	1	2	7	.22	8	.258	.366	.533
2000	OAK	AL	143	476	108	26	0	21	(9	12)	197	74	81	69	78	4	122	1	1	6	5	2	.71	7	.227	.333	.414
2001	CHN	NL	128	340	85	21	0	17	(5	12)	157	48	61	57	52	7	76	7	1	3	2	3	.40	4	.250	.358	.462
2002	MIL	NL	107	270	66	15	0	16	(6	10)	129	41	41	38	36	4	50	8	0	1	2	0	1.00	7	.244	.349	.478
2003	PIT	NL	121	305	89	20	1	20	(13	7)	171	49	57	58	45	3	64	5	0	2	0	1	.00	7	.292	.389	.561
2004	KC	AL	126	439	117	21	3	18	(6	12)	198	48	66	65	49	2	92	5	0	3	1	0	1.00	15	.267	.345	.451
2005	KC	AL	127	396	109	26	1	13	(5	8)	176	55	66	70	60	4	69	5	0	5	1	2	.33	9	.275	.373	.444
13 ML YEARS			1299	3895	1039	222	11	207	(100	107)	1904	591	700	671	548	37	795	44	5	32	25	22	.53	83	.267	.361	.489

Jason Standridge

Pitches: R **Bats:** R **Pos:** RP-34 **Ht:** 6'4" **Wt:** 230 **Born:** 11/9/1978 **Age:** 27

				HOW MUCH HE PITCHED					WHAT HE GAVE UP												THE RESULTS							
Year	Team	Lg	G	GS	CG	GF	IP	BFP	H	R	ER	HR	SH	SF	HB	TBB	IBB	SO	WP	Bk	W	L	Pct	ShO	Sv-Op	Hld	ERC	ERA
2005	Okla*	AAA	15	10	0	0	76.0	347	83	41	38	3	2	2	2	36	0	47	3	0	5	3	.625	0	0--	-	4.45	4.50
2005	Lsvlle*	AAA	2	0	0	0	1.2	9	3	3	3	0	0	0	0	1	0	4	0	0	0	0	-	0	0--	-	8.83	16.20
2001	TB	AL	9	1	0	6	19.1	87	19	10	10	5	0	0	0	14	1	9	0	0	0	0	-	0	0-0	0	6.63	4.66
2002	TB	AL	1	0	0	0	3.0	18	7	3	3	1	0	0	0	4	0	1	0	0	0	0	-	0	0-0	0	22.36	9.00
2003	TB	AL	8	7	1	1	35.1	157	38	25	25	7	1	1	1	16	0	20	4	0	0	5	.000	0	0-0	0	5.60	6.37
2004	TB	AL	3	1	0	1	10.0	48	14	10	10	5	0	1	0	4	0	7	1	0	0	0	-	0	0-0	0	9.60	9.00
2005	2 Tms		34	0	0	6	33.1	156	45	17	17	3	2	0	1	17	8	19	2	0	2	2	.500	0	0-0	5	6.33	4.59
05	Tex	AL	2	0	0	0	2.1	16	7	3	3	0	0	0	0	1	1	2	1	0	0	0	-	0	0-0	0	14.52	11.57
05	Cin	NL	32	0	0	6	31.0	140	38	14	14	3	2	0	1	16	7	17	1	0	2	2	.500	0	0-0	5	5.76	4.06
5 ML YEARS			55	9	1	14	101.0	466	123	65	65	21	3	2	2	55	9	56	7	0	2	7	.222	0	0-0	5	6.86	5.79

Mike Stanton

Pitches: L **Bats:** L **Pos:** RP-59   **Ht:** 6'1" **Wt:** 215 **Born:** 6/2/1967 **Age:** 39

Year	Team	Lg	G	GS	CG	GF	IP	BFP	H	R	ER	HR	SH	SF	HB	TBB	IBB	SO	WP	Bk	W	L	Pct	ShO	Sv-Op	Hld	ERC	ERA
1989	ATL	NL	20	0	0	10	24.0	94	17	4	4	0	4	0	0	8	1	27	1	0	0	1	.000	0	7-8	5	1.72	1.50
1990	ATL	NL	7	0	0	4	7.0	42	16	16	14	1	1	0	1	4	2	7	1	0	0	3	.000	0	2-3	0	13.58	18.00
1991	ATL	NL	74	0	0	20	78.0	314	62	27	25	6	6	0	1	21	6	54	0	0	5	5	.500	0	7-10	15	2.31	2.88
1992	ATL	NL	65	0	0	23	63.2	264	59	32	29	6	1	2	2	20	2	44	3	0	5	4	.556	0	8-11	15	3.42	4.10
1993	ATL	NL	63	0	0	41	52.0	236	51	35	27	4	5	2	0	29	7	43	1	0	4	6	.400	0	27-33	5	4.08	4.67
1994	ATL	NL	49	0	0	15	45.2	197	41	18	18	2	2	1	3	26	3	35	1	0	3	1	.750	0	3-4	10	4.01	3.55
1995	2 Tms		48	0	0	22	40.1	178	48	23	19	6	2	1	1	14	2	23	2	1	2	1	.667	0	1-3	5	5.41	4.24
1996	2 Tms	AL	81	0	0	28	78.2	327	78	32	32	11	4	2	0	27	5	60	3	2	4	4	.500	0	1-6	22	4.08	3.66
1997	NYA	AL	64	0	0	15	66.2	283	50	19	19	3	2	0	3	34	2	70	3	2	6	1	.857	0	3-5	26	2.88	2.57
1998	NYA	AL	67	0	0	26	79.0	330	71	51	48	13	1	2	4	26	1	69	0	0	4	1	.800	0	6-10	18	3.88	5.47
1999	NYA	AL	73	1	0	10	62.1	271	71	30	30	5	4	2	1	18	4	59	2	0	2	2	.500	0	0-5	21	4.23	4.33
2000	NYA	AL	69	0	0	20	68.0	291	68	32	31	5	2	4	2	24	2	75	1	0	2	3	.400	0	0-4	15	3.78	4.10
2001	NYA	AL	76	0	0	16	80.1	342	80	25	23	4	2	3	4	29	9	78	3	1	9	4	.692	0	0-1	23	3.61	2.58
2002	NYA	AL	79	0	0	25	78.0	324	73	29	26	4	4	7	0	28	3	44	4	0	7	1	.875	0	6-9	17	3.23	3.00
2003	NYN	NL	50	0	0	24	45.1	194	37	25	23	6	1	3	2	19	4	34	2	1	2	7	.222	0	5-7	10	3.33	4.57
2004	NYN	NL	83	0	0	19	77.0	337	70	32	27	6	6	1	2	33	6	58	1	0	2	6	.250	0	0-6	25	3.41	3.16
2005	3 Tms		59	0	0	12	42.2	185	49	24	22	3	3	1	0	15	4	27	1	1	3	3	.500	0	0-1	9	4.42	4.64
95	Atl	NL	26	0	0	10	19.1	94	31	14	12	3	2	1	1	6	2	13	1	1	1	1	.500	0	1-2	4	7.86	5.59
95	Bos	AL	22	0	0	12	21.0	84	17	9	7	3	0	0	0	8	0	10	1	0	1	0	1.000	0	0-1	4	3.37	3.00
96	Bos	AL	59	0	0	19	56.1	239	58	24	24	9	3	2	0	23	4	46	3	2	4	3	.571	0	1-5	15	4.71	3.83
96	Tex	AL	22	0	0	9	22.1	88	20	8	8	2	1	0	0	4	1	14	0	0	0	1	.000	0	0-1	7	2.62	3.22
05	NYY	AL	28	0	0	6	14.0	64	17	11	11	1	0	1	0	6	0	12	1	0	1	2	.333	0	0-0	4	5.17	7.07
05	Was	NL	30	0	0	6	27.2	118	31	13	11	2	3	0	0	9	4	14	0	1	2	1	.667	0	0-1	5	4.11	3.58
05	Bos	AL	1	0	0	0	1.0	3	1	0	0	0	0	0	0	0	0	1	0	0	0	0	-	0	0-0	0	2.79	0.00
17 ML YEARS			1027	1	0	330	988.2	4209	941	454	417	85	50	31	26	375	63	807	29	8	60	53	.531	0	76-126	241	3.64	3.80

Tim Stauffer

Pitches: R **Bats:** R **Pos:** SP-14; RP-1   **Ht:** 6'1" **Wt:** 214 **Born:** 6/2/1982 **Age:** 24

Year	Team	Lg	G	GS	CG	GF	IP	BFP	H	R	ER	HR	SH	SF	HB	TBB	IBB	SO	WP	Bk	W	L	Pct	ShO	Sv-Op	Hld	ERC	ERA
2004	Lk Els	A+	6	6	0	0	35.1	139	28	10	7	0	1	2	1	9	0	30	0	0	2	0	1.000	0	0- -	-	2.01	1.78
2004	Mobile	AA	8	8	1	0	51.1	223	56	17	15	3	0	0	0	13	1	33	2	0	3	2	.600	0	0- -	-	3.60	2.63
2004	Portlnd	AAA	14	14	0	0	81.1	353	83	46	32	15	4	3	3	26	1	50	1	1	6	3	.667	0	0- -	-	4.53	3.54
2005	Portlnd	AAA	13	13	1	0	75.1	333	90	48	43	5	3	3	5	17	0	64	3	0	3	5	.375	1	0- -	-	4.47	5.14
2005	SD	NL	15	14	0	0	81.0	355	92	50	48	10	2	0	2	29	0	49	0	0	3	6	.333	0	0-0	0	5.00	5.33

Steve Stemle

Pitches: R **Bats:** R **Pos:** RP-7   **Ht:** 6'4" **Wt:** 200 **Born:** 5/20/1977 **Age:** 29

Year	Team	Lg	G	GS	CG	GF	IP	BFP	H	R	ER	HR	SH	SF	HB	TBB	IBB	SO	WP	Bk	W	L	Pct	ShO	Sv-Op	Hld	ERC	ERA
1998	NewJrs	A-	9	9	0	0	44.1	184	37	17	9	1	0	1	4	14	0	47	4	1	3	3	.500	0	0- -	-	2.43	1.83
1999	Peoria	A	28	28	0	0	148.0	688	177	104	90	11	3	5	6	67	0	113	12	0	7	10	.412	0	0- -	-	5.31	5.47
2000	Ptomc	AA	26	26	1	0	150.0	678	169	89	80	15	2	4	12	59	1	84	16	0	9	10	.474	0	0- -	-	5.06	4.80
2001	NwHav	AA	26	25	0	0	134.0	604	159	76	71	12	4	3	10	43	2	75	4	0	7	10	.412	0	0- -	-	4.99	4.77
2002	NwHav	AA	8	7	0	0	43.1	190	45	24	21	3	2	2	3	15	1	26	0	0	5	2	.714	0	0- -	-	4.06	4.36
2002	Memp	AAA	20	11	0	1	93.2	401	97	41	38	8	3	1	4	23	1	55	5	1	7	4	.636	0	0- -	-	3.67	3.65
2003	Memp	AAA	26	26	1	0	156.0	659	155	71	60	12	2	1	5	36	4	89	3	0	6	11	.353	0	0- -	-	3.27	3.46
2004	PlmBh	A+	3	1	0	0	6.0	23	5	1	1	0	0	0	3	0	2	2	0	0	2	0	1.000	0	0- -	-	2.65	1.50
2004	Memp	AAA	54	0	0	11	76.1	326	85	28	28	7	1	0	0	12	0	42	1	0	6	3	.667	0	3- -	-	3.61	3.30
2005	Omha	AAA	14	0	0	5	20.0	76	13	3	1	0	1	2	0	3	0	12	0	0	1	1	.500	0	3- -	-	1.15	0.45
2005	KC	AL	7	0	0	1	10.2	43	10	6	6	0	0	0	0	4	0	9	0	0	0	0	-	0	0-0	1	3.12	5.06

Adam Stern

Bats: L **Throws:** R **Pos:** PR-18; RF-13; CF-6; LF-2; PH-1   **Ht:** 5'11" **Wt:** 180 **Born:** 2/12/1980 **Age:** 26

Year	Team	Lg	G	AB	H	2B	3B	HR	(Hm	Rd)	TB	R	RBI	RC	TBB	IBB	SO	HBP	SH	SF	SB	CS	SB%	GDP	Avg	OBP	Slg
2001	Jmstwn	A-	21	75	23	4	2	0	(-	-)	31	20	11	14	15	0	11	0	0	2	9	4	.69	0	.307	.413	.413
2002	MrtlBh	A+	119	462	117	22	10	3	(-	-)	168	65	47	56	27	2	89	3	10	1	40	8	.83	3	.253	.298	.364
2003	Braves	R	7	29	10	1	0	1	(-	-)	14	6	6	6	6	0	3	0	0	0	2	2	.50	1	.345	.457	.483
2003	MrtlBh	A+	28	103	20	2	0	0	(-	-)	22	11	6	7	13	0	21	0	4	1	7	3	.70	1	.194	.282	.214
2004	Grnville	AA	102	394	127	26	6	8	(-	-)	189	64	47	73	35	2	58	2	1	3	27	10	.73	2	.322	.378	.480
2005	Pwtckt	AAA	20	81	26	8	0	2	(-	-)	40	16	14	15	8	1	10	1	1	1	3	1	.75	2	.321	.385	.494
2005	BOS	AL	36	15	2	0	0	1	(0	1)	5	4	2	1	0	0	4	1	0	0	1	1	.50	0	.133	.188	.333

Shannon Stewart

Bats: R **Throws:** R **Pos:** LF-125; DH-5; PH-2   **Ht:** 6'1" **Wt:** 210 **Born:** 2/25/1974 **Age:** 32

Year	Team	Lg	G	AB	H	2B	3B	HR	(Hm	Rd)	TB	R	RBI	RC	TBB	IBB	SO	HBP	SH	SF	SB	CS	SB%	GDP	Avg	OBP	Slg
1995	TOR	AL	12	38	8	0	0	0	(0	0)	8	2	1	3	5	0	5	1	0	0	2	0	1.00	0	.211	.318	.211
1996	TOR	AL	7	17	3	1	0	0	(0	0)	4	2	2	1	1	0	4	0	0	0	1	0	1.00	1	.176	.222	.235
1997	TOR	AL	44	168	48	13	7	0	(0	0)	75	25	22	29	19	1	24	4	0	2	10	3	.77	3	.286	.368	.446
1998	TOR	AL	144	516	144	29	3	12	(6	6)	215	90	55	88	67	1	77	15	6	1	51	18	.74	5	.279	.377	.417
1999	TOR	AL	145	608	185	28	2	11	(4	7)	250	102	67	95	59	0	83	8	3	4	37	14	.73	12	.304	.371	.411
2000	TOR	AL	136	583	186	43	5	21	(12	9)	302	107	69	106	37	1	79	6	1	4	20	5	.80	12	.319	.363	.518

Year	Team	Lg	BATTING																					BASERUNNING				AVERAGES		
			G	AB	H	2B	3B	HR	(Hm	Rd)	TB	R	RBI	RC	TBB	IBB	SO	HBP	SH	SF				SB	CS	SB%	GDP	Avg	OBP	Slg
2001	TOR	AL	155	640	202	44	7	12	(6	6)	296	103	60	109	46	1	72	11	0	1				27	10	.73	9	.316	.371	.463
2002	TOR	AL	141	577	175	38	6	10	(4	6)	255	103	45	92	54	2	60	9	0	1				14	2	.88	17	.303	.371	.442
2003	2 Tms	AL	136	573	176	44	2	13	(7	6)	263	90	73	93	52	3	66	6	2	11				4	6	.40	10	.307	.364	.459
2004	MIN	AL	92	378	115	17	2	11	(5	6)	169	46	47	68	47	4	44	1	1	3				6	3	.67	5	.304	.380	.447
2005	MIN	AL	132	551	151	27	3	10	(4	6)	214	69	56	68	34	2	73	8	1	5				7	5	.58	11	.274	.323	.388
03	Tor	AL	71	303	89	22	2	7	(3	4)	136	47	35	51	27	2	30	2	0	8				1	2	.33	6	.294	.347	.449
03	Min	AL	65	270	87	22	0	6	(4	2)	127	43	38	42	25	1	36	4	2	3				3	4	.43	4	.322	.384	.470
11 ML YEARS			1144	4649	1393	284	37	100	(48	52)	2051	739	497	752	421	15	587	69	14	32				179	66	.73	85	.300	.364	.441

Kelly Stinnett

Bats: R **Throws:** R **Pos:** C-56; PH-6; PR-1   **Ht:** 5'11" **Wt:** 225 **Born:** 2/4/1970 **Age:** 36

Year	Team	Lg	BATTING																					BASERUNNING				AVERAGES		
			G	AB	H	2B	3B	HR	(Hm	Rd)	TB	R	RBI	RC	TBB	IBB	SO	HBP	SH	SF				SB	CS	SB%	GDP	Avg	OBP	Slg
2005	Lancst*	A+	3	11	3	1	0	1	(-	-)	7	4	5	2	2	1	1	0	0	0				0	0	-	0	.273	.385	.636
2005	Tucsn*	AAA	11	35	8	2	0	1	(-	-)	13	4	2	4	3	0	12	2	0	0				0	0	-	0	.229	.325	.371
1994	NYN	NL	47	150	38	6	2	2	(0	2)	54	20	14	18	11	1	28	5	0	1				2	0	1.00	3	.253	.323	.360
1995	NYN	NL	77	196	43	8	1	4	(1	3)	65	23	18	24	29	3	65	6	0	0				2	0	1.00	3	.219	.338	.332
1996	MIL	AL	14	26	2	0	0	0	(0	0)	2	1	0	0	2	0	11	1	0	0				0	0	-	0	.077	.172	.077
1997	MIL	AL	30	36	9	4	0	0	(0	0)	13	2	3	4	3	0	9	0	0	0				0	0	-	0	.250	.308	.361
1998	ARI	NL	92	274	71	14	1	11	(5	6)	120	35	34	41	35	3	74	6	1	2				0	1	.00	9	.259	.353	.438
1999	ARI	NL	88	284	66	13	0	14	(3	11)	121	36	38	37	24	2	83	5	2	2				2	1	.67	4	.232	.302	.426
2000	ARI	NL	76	240	52	7	0	8	(2	6)	83	22	33	23	19	4	56	6	0	0				0	1	.00	5	.217	.291	.346
2001	CIN	NL	63	187	48	11	0	9	(6	3)	86	27	25	27	17	3	61	5	1	1				2	2	.50	5	.257	.333	.460
2002	CIN	NL	34	93	21	5	0	3	(1	2)	35	10	13	13	15	1	25	0	0	0				0	0	-	1	.226	.333	.376
2003	2 Tms	NL	67	186	44	13	0	3	(2	1)	66	14	19	20	14	3	52	4	2	1				0	0	-	3	.237	.302	.355
2004	KC	AL	20	59	18	0	0	3	(0	3)	27	10	7	9	5	0	16	2	3	0				0	0	-	0	.305	.379	.458
2005	ARI	NL	59	129	32	4	0	6	(2	4)	54	15	12	9	12	3	32	1	1	0				0	0	-	4	.248	.317	.419
03	Cin	NL	60	179	41	13	0	3	(2	1)	63	14	19	18	13	3	51	4	2	1				0	0	-	3	.229	.294	.352
03	Phi	NL	7	7	3	0	0	0	(0	0)	3	0	0	2	1	0	1	0	0	0				0	0	-	0	.429	.500	.429
12 ML YEARS			667	1860	444	85	4	63	(22	41)	726	215	216	225	186	23	512	41	10	7				10	5	.67	37	.239	.320	.390

Ricky Stone

Pitches: R **Bats:** R **Pos:** RP-23   **Ht:** 6'1" **Wt:** 190 **Born:** 2/28/1975 **Age:** 31

Year	Team	Lg	HOW MUCH HE PITCHED						WHAT HE GAVE UP												THE RESULTS							
			G	GS	CG	GF	IP	BFP	H	R	ER	HR	SH	SF	HB	TBB	IBB	SO	WP	Bk	W	L	Pct	ShO	Sv-Op	Hld	ERC	ERA
2005	Memp*	AAA	14	0	0	12	16.1	67	12	5	3	0	0	0	1	2	0	16	0	0	1	1	.500	0	6--	-	1.48	1.65
2005	Lsvlle*	AAA	9	0	0	7	14.0	55	10	4	4	0	0	0	1	3	0	15	0	0	2	1	.667	0	3--	-	1.65	2.57
2001	HOU	NL	6	0	0	3	7.2	33	8	3	2	1	0	0	0	2	1	4	0	0	0	0	-	0	0-0	0	3.69	2.35
2002	HOU	NL	78	0	0	16	77.1	335	78	36	31	9	5	2	1	34	3	63	1	0	3	3	.500	0	1-2	12	4.43	3.61
2003	HOU	NL	65	0	0	20	83.0	350	76	36	34	11	4	1	6	31	4	47	1	0	6	4	.600	0	1-1	7	4.00	3.69
2004	2 Tms	NL	43	0	0	17	51.2	238	66	39	37	11	0	1	6	16	3	38	2	0	2	2	.500	0	0-0	1	6.60	6.45
2005	CIN	NL	23	0	0	4	30.2	143	48	24	23	8	0	2	2	7	2	15	2	0	0	0	-	0	0-0	2	8.46	6.75
04	Hou	NL	16	0	0	7	19.0	92	26	12	12	5	0	0	3	7	3	16	1	0	1	1	.500	0	0-0	1	7.81	5.68
04	SD	NL	27	0	0	10	32.2	146	40	27	25	6	0	1	3	9	0	22	1	0	1	1	.500	0	0-0	0	5.92	6.89
5 ML YEARS			215	0	0	60	250.1	1099	276	138	127	40	9	6	15	90	13	167	6	0	11	9	.550	0	2-3	22	5.14	4.57

Huston Street

Pitches: R **Bats:** R **Pos:** RP-67   **Ht:** 6'0" **Wt:** 185 **Born:** 8/2/1983 **Age:** 22

Year	Team	Lg	HOW MUCH HE PITCHED						WHAT HE GAVE UP												THE RESULTS							
			G	GS	CG	GF	IP	BFP	H	R	ER	HR	SH	SF	HB	TBB	IBB	SO	WP	Bk	W	L	Pct	ShO	Sv-Op	Hld	ERC	ERA
2004	Kane	A	9	0	0	7	10.2	46	9	2	2	0	0	0	0	5	1	14	1	0	0	1	.000	0	4--	-	2.60	1.69
2004	Mdland	AA	10	0	0	8	13.1	53	10	2	2	0	0	0	1	3	0	14	1	0	0	1	1.000	0	3--	-	1.83	1.35
2004	Scrmto	AAA	2	0	0	1	2.0	8	2	0	0	0	0	0	0	0	0	2	0	0	0	0	-	0	1--	-	1.95	0.00
2005	OAK	AL	67	0	0	47	78.1	306	53	17	15	3	3	2	2	26	4	72	1	0	5	1	.833	0	23-27	0	1.87	1.72

Scott Strickland

Pitches: R **Bats:** R **Pos:** RP-5   **Ht:** 5'11" **Wt:** 180 **Born:** 4/26/1976 **Age:** 30

Year	Team	Lg	HOW MUCH HE PITCHED						WHAT HE GAVE UP												THE RESULTS							
			G	GS	CG	GF	IP	BFP	H	R	ER	HR	SH	SF	HB	TBB	IBB	SO	WP	Bk	W	L	Pct	ShO	Sv-Op	Hld	ERC	ERA
2005	StLuci*	A+	1	0	0	0	1.2	9	4	2	2	0	0	0	0	0	0	2	0	0	0	0	-	0	0--	-	16.03	10.80
2005	Norfolk*	AAA	13	0	0	11	11.2	54	14	9	7	1	0	0	0	5	1	9	0	0	0	3	.000	0	5--	-	4.96	5.40
2005	RdRck*	AAA	15	0	0	9	19.0	72	11	5	5	2	0	1	1	4	0	20	0	0	2	0	1.000	0	5--	-	1.58	2.37
1999	MON	NL	17	0	0	5	18.0	78	15	10	9	3	2	0	0	11	0	23	0	0	0	1	.000	0	0-0	2	4.48	4.50
2000	MON	NL	49	0	0	20	48.0	200	38	18	16	3	3	3	1	16	2	48	2	0	4	3	.571	0	9-13	6	2.44	3.00
2001	MON	NL	77	0	0	31	81.1	351	67	36	29	9	3	1	4	41	5	85	4	0	2	6	.250	0	9-12	12	3.65	3.21
2002	2 Tms	NL	69	0	0	21	68.2	299	61	29	27	7	1	2	2	33	9	69	3	0	6	9	.400	0	2-6	15	3.64	3.54
2003	NYN	NL	19	0	0	3	20.0	84	16	6	5	1	0	0	1	10	1	16	1	0	0	2	.000	0	0-1	4	3.19	2.25
2005	HOU	NL	5	0	0	0	4.0	16	4	3	3	2	0	0	0	0	0	2	0	0	0	0	-	0	0-0	0	4.70	6.75
02	Mon	NL	1	0	0	0	1.0	3	0	0	0	0	0	0	0	0	0	0	0	0	0	0	-	0	0-0	0	0.00	0.00
02	NYM	NL	68	0	0	21	67.2	296	61	29	27	7	1	2	2	33	9	67	3	0	6	9	.400	0	2-6	15	3.74	3.59
6 ML YEARS			236	0	0	80	240.0	1028	201	102	89	25	9	6	8	111	17	243	10	0	12	21	.364	0	20-32	39	3.44	3.34

Jamal Strong

Bats: R Throws: R Pos: LF-7; PR-5; CF-4; DH-3; PH-3; RF-1   Ht: 5'10" Wt: 175 Born: 8/5/1978 Age: 27

												BATTING									BASERUNNING				AVERAGES		
Year	Team	Lg	G	AB	H	2B	3B	HR	(Hm	Rd)	TB	R	RBI	RC	TBB	IBB	SO	HBP	SH	SF	SB	CS	SB%	GDP	Avg	OBP	Slg
2000	Everett	A-	75	296	93	7	3	1	(-	-)	109	63	28	59	52	1	29	4	5	1	60	14	.81	0	.314	.422	.368
2001	Wisc	A	51	184	65	12	1	0	(-	-)	79	41	19	46	40	2	27	5	1	1	35	4	.90	2	.353	.478	.429
2001	SnBrn	A+	81	331	103	11	2	0	(-	-)	118	74	32	60	51	2	60	5	6	0	47	8	.85	4	.311	.411	.356
2002	SnAnt	AA	127	503	140	16	5	1	(-	-)	169	63	31	71	62	1	87	10	2	5	46	16	.74	7	.278	.366	.336
2003	Ms	R	2	7	5	0	1	0	(-	-)	7	5	4	5	3	0	1	1	0	2	3	0	1.00	0	.714	.692	1.000
2003	Tacom	AAA	56	210	64	6	1	2	(-	-)	78	38	19	33	25	0	38	5	3	1	26	11	.70	3	.305	.390	.371
2004	Tacom	AAA	64	238	77	11	2	3	(-	-)	101	46	24	47	38	0	28	3	6	1	19	6	.76	3	.324	.421	.424
2005	Tacom	AAA	93	382	112	16	5	4	(-	-)	150	57	36	62	43	0	67	5	6	1	25	6	.81	4	.293	.371	.393
2003	SEA	AL	12	2	0	0	0	0	(0	0)	0	2	0	0	0	0	0	0	0	0	0	0	-	0	.000	.000	.000
2005	SEA	AL	16	20	5	0	1	0	(0	0)	7	6	2	3	2	0	6	1	0	1	0	0	-	0	.250	.333	.350
	2 ML YEARS		28	22	5	0	1	0	(0	0)	7	8	2	3	2	0	6	1	0	1	0	0	-	0	.227	.308	.318

Tanyon Sturtze

Pitches: R Bats: R Pos: RP-63; SP-1   Ht: 6'5" Wt: 221 Born: 10/12/1970 Age: 35

			HOW MUCH HE PITCHED						WHAT HE GAVE UP											THE RESULTS						
Year	Team	Lg	G	GS	CG	GF	IP	BFP	H	R	ER	HR	SH	SF	HB	TBB	IBB	SO	WP	Bk	W	L	Pct	ShO	Sv-Op	Hld	ERC	ERA
2005	Tampa*	A+	2	2	0	0	3.0	13	4	2	2	0	0	0	0	4	0	0	0	0	0	1	.000	0	0--	-	3.56	6.00
1995	CHN	NL	2	0	0	0	2.0	9	2	2	2	1	0	0	0	1	0	0	0	0	0	0	-	0	0-0	0	7.30	9.00
1996	CHN	NL	6	0	0	3	16	11	11	3	0	0	0	5	0	7	0	0	0	1.000	0	0-0	0	8.87	9.00				
1997	TEX	AL	9	5	0	1	32.2	155	45	30	30	6	0	4	0	18	0	18	1	1	1	1	.500	0	0-0	0	7.84	8.27
1999	CHA	AL	1	1	0	0	6.0	22	4	0	0	0	0	0	0	2	0	2	0	0	0	0	-	0	0-0	0	1.73	0.00
2000	2 Tms	AL	29	6	0	9	68.1	300	72	39	36	8	1	2	3	29	1	44	1	0	5	2	.714	0	0-0	4	4.80	4.74
2001	TB	AL	39	27	0	6	195.1	837	200	98	96	23	2	10	9	79	0	110	11	0	11	12	.478	0	1-3	3	4.65	4.42
2002	TB	AL	33	33	4	0	224.0	1008	271	141	129	33	7	6	9	89	2	137	7	2	4	18	.182	0	0-0	0	5.87	5.18
2003	TOR	AL	40	8	0	7	89.1	415	107	67	59	14	2	2	7	43	3	54	6	0	7	6	.538	0	0-0	1	6.30	5.94
2004	NYA	AL	28	3	0	7	77.1	337	75	49	47	9	2	1	6	33	2	56	2	1	6	2	.750	0	1-1	4	4.42	5.47
2005	NYA	AL	64	1	0	12	78.0	332	76	43	41	10	1	2	6	27	1	45	3	0	5	3	.625	0	1-6	16	4.26	4.73
00	CWS	AL	10	1	0	2	15.2	85	25	23	21	4	0	2	2	15	0	6	0	0	1	2	.333	0	0-0	0	12.84	12.06
00	TB	AL	19	5	0	7	52.2	215	47	16	15	4	1	0	1	14	1	38	1	0	4	0	1.000	0	0-0	4	2.89	2.56
	10 ML YEARS		251	84	4	45	784.0	3466	868	480	451	107	15	27	40	326	9	473	31	4	40	44	.476	0	3-10	21	5.29	5.18

Chris Stynes

Bats: R Throws: R Pos: 3B   Ht: 5'10" Wt: 205 Born: 1/19/1973 Age: 33

												BATTING									BASERUNNING				AVERAGES		
Year	Team	Lg	G	AB	H	2B	3B	HR	(Hm	Rd)	TB	R	RBI	RC	TBB	IBB	SO	HBP	SH	SF	SB	CS	SB%	GDP	Avg	OBP	Slg
1995	KC	AL	22	35	6	1	0	0	(0	0)	7	7	2	1	4	0	3	0	0	0	0	0	-	3	.171	.256	.200
1996	KC	AL	36	92	27	6	0	0	(0	0)	33	8	6	10	2	0	5	0	1	0	5	2	.71	1	.293	.309	.359
1997	CIN	NL	49	198	69	7	1	6	(2	4)	96	31	28	37	11	1	13	4	2	0	11	2	.85	5	.348	.394	.485
1998	CIN	NL	123	347	88	10	1	6	(3	3)	118	52	27	42	32	1	36	4	4	1	15	1	.94	5	.254	.323	.340
1999	CIN	NL	73	113	27	1	0	2	(1	1)	34	18	14	11	12	1	13	0	3	1	5	2	.71	2	.239	.310	.301
2000	CIN	NL	119	380	127	24	1	12	(8	4)	189	71	40	71	32	2	54	2	3	3	5	2	.71	5	.334	.386	.497
2001	BOS	AL	96	361	101	19	2	8	(3	5)	148	52	33	43	20	0	56	3	1	1	4	5	.44	12	.280	.322	.410
2002	BOS	AL	98	195	47	9	1	5	(1	4)	73	25	26	27	21	1	29	1	5	3	1	1	.50	5	.241	.314	.374
2003	COL	NL	138	443	113	31	3	11	(10	1)	183	71	73	65	48	1	76	6	3	2	3	1	.75	8	.255	.335	.413
2004	PIT	NL	74	162	35	10	0	1	(1	0)	48	16	16	10	9	2	23	2	1	0	0	0	-	3	.216	.266	.296
	10 ML YEARS		828	2326	640	118	9	51	(29	22)	929	351	265	317	191	9	308	22	23	11	49	16	.75	49	.275	.335	.399

Cory Sullivan

Bats: L Throws: L Pos: CF-83; PH-35; LF-24; RF-8; PR-2   Ht: 6'0" Wt: 180 Born: 8/20/1979 Age: 26

												BATTING									BASERUNNING				AVERAGES		
Year	Team	Lg	G	AB	H	2B	3B	HR	(Hm	Rd)	TB	R	RBI	RC	TBB	IBB	SO	HBP	SH	SF	SB	CS	SB%	GDP	Avg	OBP	Slg
2001	Ashvlle	A	67	258	71	12	1	5	(-	-)	100	36	22	35	25	0	56	2	0	0	13	9	.59	2	.275	.344	.388
2002	Salem	A+	138	560	161	42	6	12	(-	-)	251	90	67	91	36	3	70	12	7	7	26	5	.84	8	.288	.340	.448
2003	Tulsa	AA	135	557	167	34	8	5	(-	-)	232	81	61	81	39	3	83	4	5	5	17	13	.57	4	.300	.347	.417
2005	COL	NL	139	378	111	15	4	4	(1	3)	146	64	30	54	28	0	83	3	10	5	12	3	.80	6	.294	.343	.386

Jeff Suppan

Pitches: R Bats: R Pos: SP-32   Ht: 6'2" Wt: 210 Born: 1/2/1975 Age: 31

			HOW MUCH HE PITCHED						WHAT HE GAVE UP											THE RESULTS						
Year	Team	Lg	G	GS	CG	GF	IP	BFP	H	R	ER	HR	SH	SF	HB	TBB	IBB	SO	WP	Bk	W	L	Pct	ShO	Sv-Op	Hld	ERC	ERA
1995	BOS	AL	8	3	0	1	22.2	100	29	15	15	4	1	1	0	5	1	19	0	0	1	2	.333	0	0-0	1	5.43	5.96
1996	BOS	AL	8	4	0	2	22.2	107	29	19	19	3	1	4	1	13	0	13	3	0	1	1	.500	0	0-0	0	7.03	7.54
1997	BOS	AL	23	22	0	1	112.1	503	140	75	71	12	0	4	4	36	1	67	5	0	7	3	.700	0	0-0	0	5.39	5.69
1998	2 Tms		17	14	1	2	78.2	345	91	56	50	13	3	2	1	22	1	51	2	0	1	7	.125	0	0-0	0	4.95	5.72
1999	KC	AL	32	32	4	0	208.2	887	222	110	105	28	7	5	3	62	4	103	5	1	10	12	.455	1	0-0	0	4.33	4.53
2000	KC	AL	35	33	3	0	217.0	948	240	121	119	36	5	6	7	84	3	128	7	1	10	9	.526	1	0-0	0	5.31	4.94
2001	KC	AL	34	34	1	0	218.1	946	227	120	106	26	5	6	12	74	3	120	6	0	10	14	.417	0	0-0	0	4.40	4.37
2002	KC	AL	33	33	3	0	208.0	912	229	134	123	32	4	11	7	68	3	109	10	1	9	16	.360	1	0-0	0	4.84	5.32
2003	2 Tms		32	31	3	0	204.0	873	217	99	95	23	11	6	8	51	5	110	7	0	13	11	.542	2	0-0	0	4.03	4.19
2004	STL	NL	31	31	0	0	188.0	811	192	98	87	25	8	5	8	65	1	110	4	1	16	9	.640	0	0-0	0	4.38	4.16
2005	STL	NL	32	32	0	0	194.1	834	206	93	77	24	11	5	7	63	1	114	6	1	16	10	.615	0	0-0	0	4.46	3.57
98	Ari	NL	13	13	1	0	66.0	299	82	55	49	12	3	2	1	21	1	39	2	0	1	7	.125	0	0-0	0	5.73	6.68
98	KC	AL	4	1	0	2	12.2	46	9	1	1	1	0	0	0	1	0	12	0	0	0	0	-	0	0-0	0	1.51	0.71

			HOW MUCH HE PITCHED						WHAT HE GAVE UP											THE RESULTS							
Year	Team	Lg	G	GS	CG	GF	IP	BFP	H	R	ER	HR	SH	SF	HB	TBB	IBB	SO	WP	Bk	W	L	Pct	ShO	Sv-Op	Hld	ERC	ERA
03	Pit	NL	21	21	3	0	141.0	597	147	57	56	11	10	2	6	31	5	78	3	0	10	7	.588	2	0-0	0	3.55	3.57
03	Bos	AL	11	10	0	0	63.0	276	70	41	39	12	1	4	2	20	0	32	4	0	3	4	.429	0	0-0	0	5.15	5.57
11 ML YEARS			285	269	15	6	1674.2	7266	1822	942	867	226	56	55	58	543	23	944	55	5	94	94	.500	5	0-0	1	4.66	4.66

B.J. Surhoff

Bats: L **Throws:** R **Pos:** LF-46; 1B-18; RF-16; PH-12; DH-7   **Ht:** 6'1" **Wt:** 200 **Born:** 8/4/1964 **Age:** 41

									BATTING											BASERUNNING				AVERAGES		
Year	Team	Lg	G	AB	H	2B	3B	HR	(Hm	Rd)	TB	R	RBI	RC	TBB	IBB	SO	HBP	SH	SF	SB	CS	SB%	GDP	Avg	OBP	Slg
1987	MIL	AL	115	395	242	22	3	7	(5	2)	167	50	68	56	36	1	30	0	5	9	11	10	.52	13	.299	.350	.423
1988	MIL	AL	139	493	121	21	0	5	(2	3)	157	47	38	45	31	9	49	3	11	3	21	6	.78	12	.245	.292	.318
1989	MIL	AL	126	436	108	17	4	5	(3	2)	148	42	55	41	25	1	29	3	3	10	14	12	.54	8	.248	.287	.339
1990	MIL	AL	135	474	131	21	4	6	(4	2)	178	55	59	61	41	5	37	1	7	7	18	7	.72	8	.276	.331	.376
1991	MIL	AL	143	505	146	19	4	5	(3	2)	188	57	68	53	26	2	33	0	13	9	5	8	.38	21	.289	.319	.372
1992	MIL	AL	139	480	121	19	1	4	(3	1)	154	63	62	50	46	8	41	2	5	10	14	8	.64	9	.252	.314	.321
1993	MIL	AL	148	552	151	38	3	7	(4	3)	216	66	79	67	36	5	47	2	4	5	12	9	.57	9	.274	.318	.391
1994	MIL	AL	40	134	35	11	2	5	(2	3)	65	20	22	21	16	0	14	0	2	2	0	1	.00	5	.261	.336	.485
1995	MIL	AL	117	415	133	26	3	13	(7	6)	204	72	73	75	37	4	43	4	2	4	7	3	.70	7	.320	.378	.492
1996	BAL	AL	143	537	157	27	6	21	(12	9)	259	74	82	89	47	8	79	3	2	1	0	1	.00	7	.292	.352	.482
1997	BAL	AL	147	528	150	30	4	18	(10	8)	242	80	88	84	49	14	60	5	3	10	1	1	.50	7	.284	.345	.458
1998	BAL	AL	162	573	160	34	1	22	(9	13)	262	79	92	84	49	9	81	1	1	10	9	7	.56	13	.279	.332	.457
1999	BAL	AL	162	673	207	38	1	28	(9	19)	331	104	107	111	43	1	78	2	1	8	5	1	.83	15	.308	.347	.492
2000	2 Tms		147	539	157	36	2	14	(7	7)	239	69	68	81	41	3	58	3	2	2	10	2	.83	10	.291	.344	.443
2001	ATL	NL	141	484	131	33	1	10	(5	5)	196	68	58	65	38	5	48	1	1	7	9	3	.75	5	.271	.321	.405
2002	ATL	NL	25	75	22	5	0	0	(0	0)	27	5	9	10	9	0	5	0	1	0	1	3	.25	1	.293	.369	.360
2003	BAL	AL	93	319	94	20	0	5	(4	1)	129	32	41	51	29	3	29	1	3	2	2	2	.50	4	.295	.353	.404
2004	BAL	AL	100	343	106	12	1	8	(4	4)	144	49	50	56	30	2	46	1	3	1	2	0	1.00	9	.309	.365	.420
2005	BAL	AL	91	303	78	11	2	5	(1	4)	108	30	34	28	11	1	32	1	2	4	0	0	-	6	.257	.282	.356
00	Bal	AL	103	411	120	27	0	13	(6	7)	186	56	57	63	29	3	46	2	1	1	7	2	.78	5	.292	.341	.453
00	Atl	NL	44	128	37	9	2	1	(1	0)	53	13	11	18	12	0	12	1	1	1	3	0	1.00	5	.289	.352	.414
19 ML YEARS			2313	8258	2326	440	42	188	(94	94)	3414	1062	1153	1128	640	81	839	33	71	104	141	84	.63	169	.282	.332	.413

Ichiro Suzuki

Bats: L **Throws:** R **Pos:** RF-158; DH-3; PH-1   **Ht:** 5'9" **Wt:** 160 **Born:** 10/22/1973 **Age:** 32

									BATTING											BASERUNNING				AVERAGES		
Year	Team	Lg	G	AB	H	2B	3B	HR	(Hm	Rd)	TB	R	RBI	RC	TBB	IBB	SO	HBP	SH	SF	SB	CS	SB%	GDP	Avg	OBP	Slg
2001	SEA	AL	157	692	242	34	8	8	(5	3)	316	127	69	124	30	10	53	8	4	4	56	14	.80	3	.350	.381	.457
2002	SEA	AL	157	647	208	27	8	8	(4	4)	275	111	51	110	68	27	62	5	3	5	31	15	.67	8	.321	.388	.425
2003	SEA	AL	159	679	212	29	8	13	(8	5)	296	111	62	107	36	7	69	6	3	1	34	8	.81	3	.312	.352	.436
2004	SEA	AL	161	704	262	24	5	8	(4	4)	320	101	60	125	49	19	63	4	2	3	36	11	.77	6	.372	.414	.455
2005	SEA	AL	162	679	206	21	12	15	(8	7)	296	111	68	109	48	23	66	4	2	6	33	8	.80	5	.303	.350	.436
5 ML YEARS			796	3401	1130	135	41	52	(29	23)	1503	561	310	575	231	86	313	27	14	19	190	56	.77	25	.332	.377	.442

Mark Sweeney

Bats: L **Throws:** L **Pos:** PH-82; 1B-53; DH-5; RF-4; LF-1; CF-1   **Ht:** 6'1" **Wt:** 215 **Born:** 10/26/1969 **Age:** 36

									BATTING											BASERUNNING				AVERAGES		
Year	Team	Lg	G	AB	H	2B	3B	HR	(Hm	Rd)	TB	R	RBI	RC	TBB	IBB	SO	HBP	SH	SF	SB	CS	SB%	GDP	Avg	OBP	Slg
1995	STL	NL	37	77	21	2	0	2	(0	2)	29	5	13	10	10	0	15	0	1	2	1	1	.50	3	.273	.348	.377
1996	STL	NL	98	170	45	9	0	3	(0	3)	63	32	22	27	33	2	29	1	5	0	3	0	1.00	4	.265	.387	.371
1997	2 Tms	NL	115	164	46	7	0	2	(2	0)	59	16	23	22	20	1	32	1	1	2	2	3	.40	3	.280	.358	.360
1998	SD	NL	122	192	45	8	3	2	(1	1)	65	17	15	21	26	0	37	1	0	3	1	2	.33	5	.234	.324	.339
1999	CIN	NL	37	31	11	3	0	2	(1	1)	20	6	7	7	4	1	9	0	0	0	0	0	-	2	.355	.429	.645
2000	MIL	NL	71	73	16	6	0	1	(0	1)	25	9	6	9	12	1	18	1	1	0	0	0	-	1	.219	.337	.342
2001	MIL	NL	48	89	23	3	1	3	(1	2)	37	9	11	14	12	0	23	0	2	0	2	1	.67	0	.258	.347	.416
2002	SD	NL	48	65	11	3	0	1	(0	1)	17	3	4	1	4	0	19	0	0	-	1	0	-	1	.169	.217	.262
2003	COL	NL	67	97	25	9	0	2	(1	1)	40	13	14	15	9	1	27	0	0	0	0	1	.00	2	.258	.321	.412
2004	COL	NL	122	177	47	12	2	9	(6	3)	90	25	40	36	32	2	51	2	0	4	1	0	1.00	5	.266	.377	.508
2005	SD	NL	135	221	65	12	1	8	(5	3)	103	31	40	37	40	3	58	0	1	5	4	0	1.00	6	.294	.395	.466
97	StL	NL	44	61	13	3	0	0	(0	0)	16	5	4	5	9	1	14	1	1	1	0	1	.00	2	.213	.319	.262
97	SD	NL	71	103	33	4	0	2	(2	0)	43	11	19	17	11	0	18	0	0	1	2	2	.50	1	.320	.383	.417
11 ML YEARS			900	1356	355	74	7	35	(15	20)	548	166	195	199	202	11	318	6	11	16	14	8	.64	29	.262	.356	.404

Mike Sweeney

Bats: R **Throws:** R **Pos:** DH-73; 1B-49   **Ht:** 6'3" **Wt:** 225 **Born:** 7/22/1973 **Age:** 32

									BATTING											BASERUNNING				AVERAGES		
Year	Team	Lg	G	AB	H	2B	3B	HR	(Hm	Rd)	TB	R	RBI	RC	TBB	IBB	SO	HBP	SH	SF	SB	CS	SB%	GDP	Avg	OBP	Slg
1995	KC	AL	4	4	1	0	0	0	(0	0)	1	1	0	0	0	0	0	0	0	0	0	0	-	0	.250	.250	.250
1996	KC	AL	50	165	46	10	0	4	(1	3)	68	23	24	23	18	0	21	4	0	3	1	2	.33	7	.279	.358	.412
1997	KC	AL	84	240	58	8	0	7	(5	2)	87	30	31	25	17	0	33	6	1	2	3	2	.60	8	.242	.306	.363
1998	KC	AL	92	282	73	18	0	8	(6	2)	115	32	35	35	24	1	38	2	2	1	2	3	.40	7	.259	.320	.408
1999	KC	AL	150	575	185	44	2	22	(10	12)	299	101	102	109	54	0	48	10	0	4	6	1	.86	21	.322	.387	.520
2000	KC	AL	159	618	206	30	0	29	(17	12)	323	105	144	128	71	5	67	15	0	13	8	3	.73	15	.333	.407	.523
2001	KC	AL	147	559	170	46	0	29	(14	15)	303	97	99	106	64	13	64	2	1	6	10	3	.77	13	.304	.374	.542
2002	KC	AL	126	471	160	31	1	24	(14	10)	265	81	86	112	61	10	46	6	0	7	9	7	.56	9	.340	.417	.563
2003	KC	AL	108	392	115	18	1	16	(7	9)	183	62	83	83	64	5	56	2	0	5	3	2	.60	13	.293	.391	.467
2004	KC	AL	106	411	118	23	0	22	(8	14)	207	56	79	75	33	9	44	6	0	2	3	2	.60	7	.287	.347	.504
2005	KC	AL	122	470	141	39	0	21	(7	14)	243	63	83	80	33	7	61	4	1	6	3	0	1.00	16	.300	.347	.517
11 ML YEARS			1148	4187	1273	267	4	182	(89	93)	2094	651	766	779	439	50	478	57	5	49	48	25	.66	116	.304	.374	.500

Nick Swisher

Bats: B Throws: L Pos: RF-121; 1B-21; PH-3

Ht: 6'0" Wt: 194 Born: 11/25/1980 Age: 25

										BATTING										BASERUNNING				AVERAGES		
Year	Team	Lg	G	AB	H	2B	3B	HR	(Hm	Rd)	TB	R	RBI	RC	TBB	IBB	SO	HBP	SH	SF	SB	CS	SB%	GDP	Avg	OBP	Slg
2002	Vancvr	A-	13	44	11	3	0	2	(-	-)	20	10	12	10	13	0	11	2	0	1	3	0	1.00	0	.250	.433	.455
2002	Visalia	A+	49	183	44	13	2	4	(-	-)	73	22	23	24	26	1	48	2	2	1	3	1	.75	6	.240	.340	.399
2003	Mdest	A+	51	189	56	14	2	10	(-	-)	104	38	43	42	41	1	49	2	0	5	0	2	.00	4	.296	.418	.550
2003	Mdland	AA	76	287	66	24	2	5	(-	-)	109	36	43	34	37	1	76	6	0	6	0	1	.00	8	.230	.324	.380
2004	Scrmto	AAA	125	443	119	28	2	29	(-	-)	238	109	92	93	103	1	109	3	0	5	3	3	.50	16	.269	.406	.537
2005	Scrmto	AAA	6	23	9	3	0	0	(-	-)	12	4	1	4	2	0	7	1	0	0	0	1	.00	0	.391	.462	.522
2004	OAK	AL	20	60	15	4	0	2	(1	1)	25	11	8	8	8	0	11	2	0	1	0	0	-	2	.250	.352	.417
2005	OAK	AL	131	462	109	32	1	21	(11	10)	206	66	74	62	55	3	110	4	0	1	0	1	.00	9	.236	.322	.446
	2 ML YEARS		151	522	124	36	1	23	(12	11)	231	77	82	70	63	3	121	6	0	2	0	1	.00	11	.238	.325	.443

Jon Switzer

Pitches: L Bats: L Pos: RP-2

Ht: 6'3" Wt: 191 Born: 8/13/1979 Age: 26

			HOW MUCH HE PITCHED					WHAT HE GAVE UP												THE RESULTS					
Year	Team	Lg	G	GS	CG	GF	IP	BFP	H	R	ER	HR	SH	SF	HB	TBB	IBB	SO	WP	Bk	W	L	Pct	ShO	Sv-Op Hld	ERC	ERA
2001	HudVal	A-	5	0	0	2	14.1	57	9	3	1	0	1	0	2	2	0	20	2	0	2	0	1.000	0	0- -	1.32	0.63
2002	Bkrsfld	A+	20	20	0	0	103.1	441	108	55	49	8	4	1	8	26	0	129	4	0	7	5	.583	0	0- -	3.91	4.27
2003	Orlndo	AA	22	22	2	0	126.0	522	117	63	48	10	5	4	5	32	1	100	9	1	8	8	.500	0	0- -	3.13	3.43
2003	Drham	AAA	1	1	0	0	5.0	19	6	1	1	1	0	0	0	0	0	3	0	0	1	0	1.000	0	0- -	4.64	1.80
2005	Mont	AA	6	6	0	0	31.1	132	33	14	12	2	0	2	5	5	0	20	0	1	3	1	.750	0	0- -	3.87	3.45
2005	Drham	AAA	17	8	0	2	44.1	219	64	38	35	6	1	2	7	22	1	28	3	0	0	5	.000	0	0- -	8.22	7.11
2003	TB	AL	5	0	0	1	9.2	46	13	8	8	2	0	1	4	3	0	7	1	0	0	0	-	0	0-0 0	8.88	7.45
2005	TB	AL	2	0	0	0	4.0	25	5	4	3	0	0	0	0	7	0	5	0	0	0	0	-	0	0-0 0	9.71	6.75
	2 ML YEARS		7	0	0	1	13.2	71	18	12	11	2	0	1	4	10	0	12	1	0	0	0	-	0	0-0 0	9.18	7.24

Kazuhito Tadano

Pitches: R Bats: R Pos: RP-1

Ht: 6'0" Wt: 180 Born: 4/25/1980 Age: 26

			HOW MUCH HE PITCHED					WHAT HE GAVE UP												THE RESULTS					
Year	Team	Lg	G	GS	CG	GF	IP	BFP	H	R	ER	HR	SH	SF	HB	TBB	IBB	SO	WP	Bk	W	L	Pct	ShO	Sv-Op Hld	ERC	ERA
2003	Kinston	A	7	1	0	2	19.0	73	13	5	4	0	1	0	1	3	0	28	2	0	2	1	.667	0	0- -	1.39	1.89
2003	Akron	AA	31	0	0	9	72.2	294	62	15	10	4	2	1	2	15	2	78	4	0	4	1	.800	0	3- -	2.35	1.24
2003	Buffalo	AAA	2	0	0	2	7.0	31	6	3	3	0	0	1	0	4	1	6	0	1	0	0	-	0	0- -	2.92	3.86
2004	Buffalo	AAA	12	8	0	2	44.2	195	49	28	27	9	1	3	2	14	0	39	3	1	2	4	.333	0	0- -	5.19	5.44
2005	Buffalo	AAA	32	8	0	11	96.1	416	105	54	47	16	3	6	1	22	3	86	3	0	5	5	.500	0	5- -	4.26	4.39
2004	CLE	AL	14	4	0	1	50.1	225	55	30	26	6	2	0	3	18	0	39	2	0	1	1	.500	0	0-0 0	4.75	4.65
2005	CLE	AL	1	0	0	1	4.0	16	4	1	1	0	0	0	0	0	0	1	0	0	0	0	-	0	0-0 0	1.95	2.25
	2 ML YEARS		15	4	0	2	54.1	241	59	31	27	6	2	0	3	18	0	40	2	0	1	1	.500	0	0-0 0	4.52	4.47

So Taguchi

Bats: R Throws: R Pos: RF-57; LF-52; CF-50; PH-23; PR-3

Ht: 5'10" Wt: 163 Born: 7/2/1969 Age: 36

										BATTING										BASERUNNING				AVERAGES		
Year	Team	Lg	G	AB	H	2B	3B	HR	(Hm	Rd)	TB	R	RBI	RC	TBB	IBB	SO	HBP	SH	SF	SB	CS	SB%	GDP	Avg	OBP	Slg
2002	STL	NL	19	15	6	0	0	0	(0	0)	6	4	2	4	2	0	1	0	2	0	1	0	1.00	0	.400	.471	.400
2003	STL	NL	43	54	14	3	1	3	(1	2)	28	9	13	11	4	1	11	0	1	0	0	0	-	2	.259	.310	.519
2004	STL	NL	109	179	52	10	2	3	(1	2)	75	26	25	27	12	1	23	2	10	3	6	3	.67	6	.291	.337	.419
2005	STL	NL	143	396	114	21	2	8	(5	3)	163	45	53	59	20	2	62	2	2	4	11	2	.85	11	.288	.322	.412
	4 ML YEARS		314	644	186	34	5	14	(7	7)	272	84	93	101	38	4	97	4	15	7	18	5	.78	19	.289	.329	.422

Shingo Takatsu

Pitches: R Bats: R Pos: RP-40

Ht: 6'0" Wt: 180 Born: 11/25/1968 Age: 37

			HOW MUCH HE PITCHED					WHAT HE GAVE UP												THE RESULTS					
Year	Team	Lg	G	GS	CG	GF	IP	BFP	H	R	ER	HR	SH	SF	HB	TBB	IBB	SO	WP	Bk	W	L	Pct	ShO	Sv-Op Hld	ERC	ERA
2005	Norfolk	AAA	7	1	0	2	8.0	31	6	3	3	3	0	0	0	1	0	10	0	0	0	1	.000	0	0- -	3.15	3.38
2004	CHA	AL	59	0	0	45	62.1	245	40	17	16	6	2	0	2	21	3	50	1	0	6	4	.600	0	19-20 4	2.06	2.31
2005	2 Tms		40	0	0	24	36.1	168	41	21	21	11	2	1	0	19	2	38	1	0	2	2	.500	0	8-11 4	6.71	5.20
	05 CWS	AL	31	0	0	20	28.2	130	30	19	19	9	2	1	0	16	1	32	1	0	1	2	.333	0	8-9 3	6.54	5.97
	05 NYM	NL	9	0	0	4	7.2	38	11	2	2	2	0	0	0	3	1	6	0	0	1	0	1.000	0	0-2 1	7.35	2.35
	2 ML YEARS		99	0	0	69	98.2	413	81	38	37	17	4	1	2	40	5	88	2	0	8	6	.571	0	27-31 8	3.59	3.38

Brian Tallet

Pitches: L Bats: L Pos: RP-2

Ht: 6'7" Wt: 208 Born: 9/21/1977 Age: 28

			HOW MUCH HE PITCHED					WHAT HE GAVE UP												THE RESULTS					
Year	Team	Lg	G	GS	CG	GF	IP	BFP	H	R	ER	HR	SH	SF	HB	TBB	IBB	SO	WP	Bk	W	L	Pct	ShO	Sv-Op Hld	ERC	ERA
2005	Buffalo*	AAA	22	17	0	2	97.2	416	98	51	44	17	4	4	3	25	0	61	4	1	6	5	.545	0	0- -	4.09	4.05
2002	CLE	AL	2	2	0	0	12.0	47	9	3	2	0	0	0	1	4	0	5	0	0	1	0	1.000	0	0-0 0	2.31	1.50
2003	CLE	AL	5	3	0	1	19.0	87	23	14	10	2	2	0	1	8	0	9	0	0	0	2	.000	0	0-0 0	5.65	4.74
2005	CLE	AL	2	0	0	0	4.2	24	6	4	4	2	0	0	1	3	0	2	0	0	0	0	-	0	0-0 0	10.55	7.71
	3 ML YEARS		9	5	0	1	35.2	158	38	21	16	4	2	0	3	15	0	16	0	0	1	2	.333	0	0-0 0	5.01	4.04

Jack Taschner

Pitches: L Bats: L Pos: RP-24   Ht: 6'3" Wt: 207 Born: 4/21/1978 Age: 28

				HOW MUCH HE PITCHED						WHAT HE GAVE UP									THE RESULTS							
Year	Team	Lg	G	GS	CG	GF	IP	BFP	H	R	ER	HR	SH	SF	HB	TBB	IBB	SO	WP	Bk	W	L	Pct	ShO	Sv-Op	Hld	ERC	ERA
2003	Nrwich	AA	34	12	0	10	75.2	347	78	53	48	7	0	2	5	45	0	46	6	0	0	6	.000	0	0- -	-	5.24	5.71
2004	Nrwich	AA	14	10	0	1	58.0	237	47	17	16	5	2	1	0	16	0	55	3	0	3	1	.750	0	0- -	-	2.48	2.48
2004	Fresno	AAA	18	9	0	4	53.1	263	71	59	55	14	1	2	3	32	1	44	3	0	4	7	.364	0	0- -	-	8.45	9.28
2005	Fresno	AAA	44	0	0	26	49.1	202	30	9	9	3	1	1	1	24	0	62	3	0	3	0	1.000	0	10- -	-	2.16	1.64
2005	SF	NL	24	0	0	7	22.2	95	15	5	4	0	0	1	0	13	0	19	0	0	2	0	1.000	0	0-1	3	2.25	1.59

Julian Tavarez

Pitches: R Bats: L Pos: RP-74   Ht: 6'2" Wt: 195 Born: 5/22/1973 Age: 33

				HOW MUCH HE PITCHED						WHAT HE GAVE UP									THE RESULTS							
Year	Team	Lg	G	GS	CG	GF	IP	BFP	H	R	ER	HR	SH	SF	HB	TBB	IBB	SO	WP	Bk	W	L	Pct	ShO	Sv-Op	Hld	ERC	ERA
1993	CLE	AL	8	7	0	0	37.0	172	53	29	27	7	0	1	2	13	2	19	3	1	2	2	.500	0	0-0	0	7.48	6.57
1994	CLE	AL	1	1	0	0	1.2	14	6	8	4	1	0	1	0	1	1	0	0	0	0	1	.000	0	0-0	0	24.13	21.60
1995	CLE	AL	57	0	0	15	85.0	350	76	36	23	7	0	2	3	21	0	68	3	2	10	2	.833	0	0-4	19	2.93	2.44
1996	CLE	AL	51	4	0	13	80.2	353	101	49	48	9	5	4	1	22	5	46	1	0	4	7	.364	0	0-0	13	5.12	5.36
1997	SF	NL	89	0	0	13	88.1	378	91	43	38	6	3	8	4	34	5	38	4	0	6	4	.600	0	0-3	26	4.13	3.87
1998	SF	NL	60	0	0	12	85.1	374	96	41	36	5	5	3	8	36	11	52	1	1	5	3	.625	0	1-6	10	4.89	3.80
1999	SF	NL	47	0	0	12	54.2	258	65	38	36	7	3	2	8	25	3	33	4	1	2	0	1.000	0	0-2	5	6.10	5.93
2000	COL	NL	51	12	1	8	120.0	530	124	68	59	11	3	4	7	53	9	62	2	1	11	5	.688	0	1-1	6	4.49	4.43
2001	CHN	NL	34	28	0	1	161.1	712	172	98	81	13	8	4	11	69	4	107	2	1	10	9	.526	0	0-0	2	4.70	4.52
2002	FLA	NL	29	27	0	1	153.2	714	188	100	92	9	13	2	15	74	7	67	7	2	10	12	.455	0	0-1	0	5.75	5.39
2003	PIT	NL	64	0	0	29	83.2	350	75	37	34	1	9	1	5	27	8	39	3	0	3	3	.500	0	11-14	9	2.72	3.66
2004	STL	NL	77	0	0	27	64.1	268	57	21	17	1	3	1	6	19	0	48	2	1	7	4	.636	0	4-6	19	2.87	2.38
2005	STL	NL	74	0	0	16	65.2	278	68	28	25	6	3	3	8	19	4	47	1	0	2	3	.400	0	4-6	32	4.29	3.43
	13 ML YEARS		642	79	1	147	1081.1	4751	1172	596	520	83	55	36	78	413	59	626	33	10	72	55	.567	0	21-43	141	4.55	4.33

Willy Taveras

Bats: R Throws: R Pos: CF-148; PR-4; PH-1   Ht: 6'0" Wt: 160 Born: 12/25/1981 Age: 24

							BATTING													BASERUNNING				AVERAGES		
Year	Team	Lg	G	AB	H	2B	3B	HR	(Hm	Rd)	TB	R	RBI	RC	TBB	IBB	SO	HBP	SH	SF	SB	CS	SB%	GDP	Avg	OBP	Slg
2000	Burlgtn	R+	50	190	50	4	3	1	(-	-)	63	46	16	29	23	0	44	6	1	3	36	9	.80	0	.263	.356	.332
2001	Clmbs	A	97	395	107	15	7	3	(-	-)	145	55	32	48	22	0	73	6	4	3	29	9	.76	7	.271	.317	.367
2002	Clmbs	A	85	313	83	14	1	4	(-	-)	111	68	27	53	45	0	68	18	2	3	54	12	.82	3	.265	.385	.355
2003	Kinston	A+	113	397	112	9	6	2	(-	-)	139	64	35	66	52	1	68	12	6	1	57	12	.83	3	.282	.381	.350
2004	RdRck	AA	103	409	137	13	1	2	(-	-)	158	76	27	75	38	2	76	9	6	2	55	11	.83	2	.335	.402	.386
2004	HOU	NL	10	1	0	0	0	0	(0	0)	0	2	0	0	0	0	1	0	1	0	1	0	1.00	0	.000	.000	.000
2005	HOU	NL	152	592	172	13	4	3	(2	1)	202	82	29	61	25	1	103	7	7	4	34	11	.76	4	.291	.325	.341
	2 ML YEARS		162	593	172	13	4	3	(2	1)	202	84	29	61	25	1	104	7	8	4	35	11	.76	4	.290	.324	.341

Reggie Taylor

Bats: L Throws: R Pos: CF-9; PH-3; RF-1   Ht: 6'1" Wt: 178 Born: 1/12/1977 Age: 29

							BATTING													BASERUNNING				AVERAGES		
Year	Team	Lg	G	AB	H	2B	3B	HR	(Hm	Rd)	TB	R	RBI	RC	TBB	IBB	SO	HBP	SH	SF	SB	CS	SB%	GDP	Avg	OBP	Slg
2005	ColSpr*	AAA	1	4	1	1	0	0	(-	-)	2	0	1	0	0	0	0	0	0	0	0	0	-	0	.250	.250	.500
2005	Drham*	AAA	67	253	66	10	3	7	(-	-)	103	30	35	34	24	1	55	3	3	0	12	10	.55	5	.261	.332	.407
2005	Memp*	AAA	34	107	25	5	2	1	(-	-)	37	18	11	9	5	1	21	1	2	1	1	5	.17	1	.234	.272	.346
2000	PHI	NL	9	11	1	0	0	0	(0	0)	1	1	0	0	0	0	8	0	0	0	1	0	1.00	0	.091	.091	.091
2001	PHI	NL	5	7	0	0	0	0	(0	0)	0	1	0	0	1	0	1	0	0	0	0	0	-	0	.000	.125	.000
2002	CIN	NL	135	287	73	15	4	9	(6	3)	123	41	38	33	14	3	79	2	5	3	11	8	.58	6	.254	.291	.429
2003	CIN	NL	100	180	39	5	2	5	(3	2)	63	17	19	12	11	0	68	1	2	0	7	0	1.00	4	.217	.266	.350
2005	TB	AL	11	22	4	2	0	0	(0	0)	6	2	1	1	2	0	7	0	0	0	2	0	1.00	0	.182	.250	.273
	5 ML YEARS		260	507	117	22	6	14	(9	5)	193	62	58	46	28	3	163	3	7	3	21	8	.72	10	.231	.274	.381

Mark Teahen

Bats: L Throws: R Pos: 3B-128; PH-5   Ht: 6'3" Wt: 210 Born: 9/6/1981 Age: 24

							BATTING													BASERUNNING				AVERAGES		
Year	Team	Lg	G	AB	H	2B	3B	HR	(Hm	Rd)	TB	R	RBI	RC	TBB	IBB	SO	HBP	SH	SF	SB	CS	SB%	GDP	Avg	OBP	Slg
2002	Mdest	A+	59	234	56	9	1	1	(-	-)	70	25	26	22	21	1	53	2	0	0	1	2	.33	4	.239	.307	.299
2002	Vancvr	A-	13	57	23	5	1	0	(-	-)	30	10	6	13	5	0	9	0	0	1	4	1	.80	0	.404	.444	.526
2003	Mdest	A+	121	453	128	27	4	3	(-	-)	172	68	71	72	66	1	113	6	0	5	4	0	1.00	19	.283	.377	.380
2004	Mdland	AA	53	197	66	15	4	6	(-	-)	107	31	36	44	29	3	44	1	0	2	0	0	-	12	.335	.419	.543
2004	Scrmto	AAA	20	69	19	8	0	0	(-	-)	27	9	10	10	11	0	22	1	0	0	0	1	.00	1	.275	.383	.391
2004	Omha	AAA	66	246	69	15	1	8	(-	-)	110	33	31	39	21	0	69	4	1	2	0	0	-	4	.280	.344	.447
2005	Omha	AAA	8	27	7	2	0	0	(-	-)	9	4	4	4	7	0	9	0	0	0	0	0	-	1	.259	.412	.333
2005	KC	AL	130	447	110	29	4	7	(3	4)	168	60	55	52	40	2	107	1	2	1	7	2	.78	13	.246	.309	.376

Mark Teixeira

Bats: B Throws: R Pos: 1B-155; DH-8   Ht: 6'2" Wt: 215 Born: 4/11/1980 Age: 26

							BATTING													BASERUNNING				AVERAGES		
Year	Team	Lg	G	AB	H	2B	3B	HR	(Hm	Rd)	TB	R	RBI	RC	TBB	IBB	SO	HBP	SH	SF	SB	CS	SB%	GDP	Avg	OBP	Slg
2003	TEX	AL	146	529	137	29	5	26	(19	7)	254	66	84	78	44	5	120	14	0	2	1	2	.33	14	.259	.331	.480

Year	Team	Lg	G	AB	H	2B	3B	HR	(Hm	Rd)	TB	R	RBI	RC	TBB	IBB	SO	HBP	SH	SF	SB	CS	SB%	GDP	Avg	OBP	Slg
2004	TEX	AL	145	545	153	34	2	38	(18	20)	305	101	112	120	68	12	117	10	0	2	4	1	.80	6	.281	.370	.560
2005	TEX	AL	162	644	194	41	8	43	(30	13)	370	112	144	148	72	5	124	11	0	3	4	0	1.00	18	.301	.379	.575
3 ML YEARS			453	1718	484	104	10	107	(67	40)	929	279	340	346	184	22	361	35	0	7	9	3	.75	38	.282	.362	.541

Miguel Tejada

Bats: R **Throws:** R **Pos:** SS-160; DH-2 **Ht:** 5'9" **Wt:** 200 **Born:** 5/25/1976 **Age:** 30

Year	Team	Lg	G	AB	H	2B	3B	HR	(Hm	Rd)	TB	R	RBI	RC	TBB	IBB	SO	HBP	SH	SF	SB	CS	SB%	GDP	Avg	OBP	Slg
1997	OAK	AL	26	99	20	3	2	2	(1	1)	33	10	10	7	2	0	22	3	0	0	2	0	1.00	3	.202	.240	.333
1998	OAK	AL	105	365	85	20	1	11	(5	6)	140	53	45	40	28	0	86	7	4	3	5	6	.45	8	.233	.298	.384
1999	OAK	AL	159	593	149	33	4	21	(12	9)	253	93	84	82	57	3	94	10	9	5	8	7	.53	11	.251	.325	.427
2000	OAK	AL	160	607	167	32	1	30	(16	14)	291	105	115	99	66	6	102	4	2	2	6	0	1.00	15	.275	.349	.479
2001	OAK	AL	162	622	166	31	3	31	(17	14)	296	107	113	94	43	5	89	13	1	4	11	5	.69	14	.267	.326	.476
2002	OAK	AL	162	662	204	30	0	34	(17	17)	336	108	131	123	38	3	84	11	0	4	7	2	.78	21	.308	.354	.508
2003	OAK	AL	162	636	177	42	0	27	(15	12)	300	98	106	103	53	7	65	6	0	8	10	0	1.00	12	.278	.336	.472
2004	BAL	AL	162	653	203	40	2	34	(17	17)	349	107	150	124	48	6	73	10	0	14	4	1	.80	24	.311	.360	.534
2005	BAL	AL	162	654	199	50	5	26	(16	10)	337	89	98	102	40	9	83	7	0	3	5	1	.83	26	.304	.349	.515
9 ML YEARS			1260	4891	1370	281	18	216	(116	100)	2335	770	852	774	375	39	698	71	16	43	58	22	.73	134	.280	.338	.477

Robinson Tejeda

Pitches: R **Bats:** R **Pos:** SP-13; RP-13 **Ht:** 6'3" **Wt:** 188 **Born:** 3/24/1982 **Age:** 24

Year	Team	Lg	G	GS	CG	GF	IP	BFP	H	R	ER	HR	SH	SF	HB	TBB	IBB	SO	WP	Bk	W	L	Pct	ShO	Sv-Op	Hld	ERC	ERA
1999	Phillies	R	12	9	0	2	46.1	213	47	27	22	5	3	1	2	27	0	39	1	1	1	3	.250	0	0--	-	5.05	4.27
2000	Phillies	R	10	6	1	1	39.0	173	44	30	24	3	1	2	2	12	0	22	5	1	2	5	.286	1	0--	-	4.42	5.54
2001	Lakwd	A	26	24	1	0	150.2	638	128	74	57	10	6	5	8	58	1	152	11	2	8	9	.471	1	0--	-	3.14	3.40
2002	Clrwtr	A+	17	17	1	0	99.2	420	73	48	44	14	2	4	5	48	0	87	3	1	4	8	.333	0	0--	-	3.38	3.97
2003	Clrwtr	A+	11	11	1	0	64.2	270	53	25	23	4	4	1	2	23	0	42	3	0	2	4	.333	0	0--	-	2.78	3.20
2003	Lakwd	A	5	4	0	0	18.2	89	17	11	11	4	3	4	1	16	0	20	1	0	0	3	.000	0	0--	-	6.49	5.30
2004	Rdng	AA	27	26	0	0	150.1	658	148	93	86	29	6	8	6	59	0	133	6	1	8	14	.364	0	0--	-	4.72	5.15
2005	S-WB	AAA	5	5	0	0	28.1	119	21	8	7	0	0	3	0	13	0	28	0	0	2	0	1.000	0	0--	-	2.23	2.22
2005	PHI	NL	26	13	0	5	85.2	371	67	36	34	5	3	2	8	51	4	72	3	1	4	3	.571	0	0-0	1	3.64	3.57

Michael Tejera

Pitches: L **Bats:** L **Pos:** RP-3 **Ht:** 5'9" **Wt:** 175 **Born:** 10/18/1976 **Age:** 29

Year	Team	Lg	G	GS	CG	GF	IP	BFP	H	R	ER	HR	SH	SF	HB	TBB	IBB	SO	WP	Bk	W	L	Pct	ShO	Sv-Op	Hld	ERC	ERA
2005	Okla*	AAA	43	2	0	11	59.1	259	52	28	25	5	3	2	8	29	5	52	4	0	3	2	.600	0	2--	-	4.04	3.79
1999	FLA	NL	3	1	0	1	6.1	31	10	8	8	1	0	0	0	6	0	7	0	0	0	0	-	0	0-0	0	10.73	11.37
2002	FLA	NL	47	18	0	2	139.2	611	144	71	69	17	5	4	6	60	3	95	3	0	8	8	.500	0	1-3	6	4.70	4.45
2003	FLA	NL	50	6	0	10	81.0	353	82	44	42	6	8	1	1	36	3	58	0	0	3	4	.429	0	2-2	5	4.13	4.67
2004	2 Tms		8	2	0	1	9.1	52	15	14	14	1	0	0	2	9	0	10	0	0	0	1	.000	0	0-0	0	11.67	13.50
2005	TEX	AL	3	0	0	1	2.0	13	5	3	3	1	0	0	1	1	0	2	1	0	0	0	-	0	0-0	0	21.61	13.50
04	Fla	NL	2	2	0	0	4.0	23	6	8	8	0	0	0	1	6	0	3	0	0	0	1	.000	0	0-0	0	12.95	18.00
04	Tex	AL	6	0	0	1	5.1	29	9	6	6	1	0	0	1	3	0	7	0	0	0	0	-	0	0-0	0	10.59	10.13
5 ML YEARS			111	27	0	15	238.1	1060	256	140	136	26	13	5	10	111	6	172	4	0	11	13	.458	0	3-5	13	5.00	5.14

Amaury Telemaco

Pitches: R **Bats:** R **Pos:** RP-7 **Ht:** 6'3" **Wt:** 222 **Born:** 1/19/1974 **Age:** 32

Year	Team	Lg	G	GS	CG	GF	IP	BFP	H	R	ER	HR	SH	SF	HB	TBB	IBB	SO	WP	Bk	W	L	Pct	ShO	Sv-Op	Hld	ERC	ERA
2005	S-WB*	AAA	9	3	0	1	22.0	98	24	11	10	1	0	2	0	8	0	14	0	0	0	1	.000	0	0--	-	3.95	4.09
1996	CHN	NL	25	17	0	0	97.1	427	108	67	59	20	5	3	3	31	2	64	3	0	5	7	.417	0	0-0	0	5.20	5.46
1997	CHN	NL	10	5	0	0	38.0	169	47	26	26	4	2	1	0	11	0	29	1	0	0	3	.000	0	0-0	0	5.00	6.16
1998	2 Tms	NL	41	18	0	0	148.2	637	150	75	65	18	8	6	4	46	2	78	7	0	7	10	.412	0	0-0	0	3.97	3.93
1999	2 Tms	NL	49	0	0	0	53.0	234	52	34	34	10	4	1	2	26	4	43	5	0	4	0	1.000	0	0-1	0	5.01	5.77
2000	PHI	NL	13	2	0	0	24.1	107	25	22	18	6	0	2	0	14	0	22	1	0	1	3	.250	0	0-1	0	6.24	6.66
2001	PHI	NL	24	14	1	0	89.1	388	93	59	55	15	5	2	9	32	3	59	3	0	5	5	.500	0	0-0	0	5.07	5.54
2003	PHI	NL	8	8	0	0	45.1	194	41	22	20	5	3	1	7	11	2	29	3	0	1	4	.200	0	0-0	0	3.48	3.97
2004	PHI	NL	42	0	0	9	54.1	225	51	27	26	12	1	0	4	19	2	32	2	1	2	0	1.000	0	0-0	5	4.38	4.31
2005	PHI	NL	7	0	0	4	10.2	41	5	5	5	2	0	1	0	4	0	8	0	0	0	1	.000	0	0-0	0	1.79	4.22
98	ChC	NL	14	0	0	0	27.2	118	23	12	12	5	0	0	0	13	0	18	3	0	1	1	.500	0	0-0	0	3.92	3.90
98	Ari	NL	27	18	0	0	121.0	519	127	63	53	13	8	6	4	33	2	60	4	0	6	9	.400	0	0-0	0	3.98	3.94
99	Ari	NL	5	0	0	0	6.0	28	7	5	5	2	1	0	0	6	1	2	0	0	1	0	1.000	0	0-0	0	10.24	7.50
99	Phi	NL	44	0	0	0	47.0	206	45	29	29	8	3	1	2	20	3	41	5	0	3	0	1.000	0	0-1	0	4.45	5.55
9 ML YEARS			219	64	1	13	561.0	2422	572	337	308	92	28	17	25	194	15	364	25	1	23	35	.397	0	0-2	5	4.56	4.94

Luis Terrero

Bats: R **Throws:** R **Pos:** CF-74; PR-16; PH-7; RF-2; LF-1 **Ht:** 6'2" **Wt:** 206 **Born:** 5/18/1980 **Age:** 26

Year	Team	Lg	G	AB	H	2B	3B	HR	(Hm	Rd)	TB	R	RBI	RC	TBB	IBB	SO	HBP	SH	SF	SB	CS	SB%	GDP	Avg	OBP	Slg
2005	Tucsn*	AAA	7	30	8	1	0	0	(-	-)	9	4	1	3	1	0	9	1	1	0	1	0	1.00	2	.267	.313	.300
2003	ARI	NL	5	4	1	0	0	0	(0	0)	1	0	0	1	0	0	1	1	0	0	0	0	-	0	.250	.400	.250

Year	Team	Lg	G	AB	H	2B	3B	HR	(Hm	Rd)	TB	R	RBI	RC	TBB	IBB	SO	HBP	SH	SF	SB	CS	SB%	GDP	Avg	OBP	Slg
2004	ARI	NL	62	229	56	14	0	4	(2	2)	82	21	14	25	20	2	78	5	1	0	10	2	.83	5	.245	.319	.358
2005	ARI	NL	88	161	37	6	1	4	(2	2)	57	23	20	17	14	0	40	6	2	1	3	2	.60	5	.230	.313	.354
3 ML YEARS			155	394	94	20	1	8	(4	4)	140	44	34	43	34	2	119	12	3	1	13	4	.76	10	.239	.317	.355

Marcus Thames

Bats: R **Throws:** R **Pos:** LF-21; RF-10; DH-4; PH-4; PR-1   **Ht:** 6'2" **Wt:** 205 **Born:** 3/6/1977 **Age:** 29

Year	Team	Lg	G	AB	H	2B	3B	HR	(Hm	Rd)	TB	R	RBI	RC	TBB	IBB	SO	HBP	SH	SF	SB	CS	SB%	GDP	Avg	OBP	Slg
2005	Toledo*	AAA	73	265	90	18	3	22	(-	-)	180	53	56	73	41	3	59	3	0	5	4	1	.80	5	.340	.427	.679
2002	NYA	AL	7	13	3	1	0	1	(1	0)	7	2	2	2	0	0	4	0	0	0	0	0	-	0	.231	.231	.538
2003	TEX	AL	30	73	15	2	0	1	(0	1)	20	12	4	5	8	0	18	2	0	1	0	1	.00	2	.205	.298	.274
2004	DET	AL	61	165	42	12	0	10	(5	5)	84	24	33	30	16	0	42	2	0	1	0	1	.00	3	.255	.326	.509
2005	DET	AL	38	107	21	2	0	7	(3	4)	44	11	16	10	9	1	38	1	0	1	0	0	-	1	.196	.263	.411
4 ML YEARS			136	358	81	17	0	19	(9	10)	155	49	55	47	33	1	102	5	0	3	0	2	.00	6	.226	.298	.433

Ryan Theriot

Bats: R **Throws:** R **Pos:** PH-5; 2B-3; PR-2   **Ht:** 5'11" **Wt:** 175 **Born:** 12/7/1979 **Age:** 26

Year	Team	Lg	G	AB	H	2B	3B	HR	(Hm	Rd)	TB	R	RBI	RC	TBB	IBB	SO	HBP	SH	SF	SB	CS	SB%	GDP	Avg	OBP	Slg
2001	Dytona	A+	30	103	21	5	0	0	(-	-)	26	20	9	10	21	0	17	1	3	1	2	4	.33	2	.204	.341	.252
2002	Lansng	A	130	489	123	19	4	1	(-	-)	153	75	37	60	59	1	77	4	3	3	32	8	.80	3	.252	.335	.313
2003	Lansng	A	58	220	57	8	1	1	(-	-)	70	29	17	30	31	1	34	1	5	0	21	5	.81	4	.259	.353	.318
2003	WTenn	AA	53	178	42	3	0	1	(-	-)	48	20	9	19	29	1	21	3	4	1	9	8	.53	6	.236	.351	.270
2004	Dytona	A+	103	330	90	14	3	1	(-	-)	113	47	34	45	48	0	43	3	6	3	13	11	.54	4	.273	.367	.342
2005	WTenn	AA	120	448	136	28	4	1	(-	-)	175	52	53	69	45	2	38	1	4	5	24	10	.71	8	.304	.365	.391
2005	CHN	NL	9	13	2	1	0	0	(0	0)	3	3	0	0	1	0	2	0	0	0	0	0	-	0	.154	.214	.231

Charles Thomas

Bats: L **Throws:** L **Pos:** LF-13; CF-9; RF-8; PR-5; PH-2   **Ht:** 6'0" **Wt:** 190 **Born:** 12/26/1978 **Age:** 27

Year	Team	Lg	G	AB	H	2B	3B	HR	(Hm	Rd)	TB	R	RBI	RC	TBB	IBB	SO	HBP	SH	SF	SB	CS	SB%	GDP	Avg	OBP	Slg
2000	Jmstwn	A-	68	264	80	20	8	1	(-	-)	119	39	25	40	19	0	58	1	0	1	10	2	.83	7	.303	.351	.451
2001	MrtlBh	A+	12	44	7	1	0	0	(-	-)	8	4	6	0	3	1	8	0	0	1	1	0	1.00	3	.159	.208	.182
2001	Macon	A	108	408	102	19	5	11	(-	-)	164	59	59	50	32	3	87	3	0	3	17	7	.71	6	.250	.307	.402
2002	MrtlBh	A+	2	7	2	0	0	0	(-	-)	2	0	0	0	0	0	2	0	0	0	0	0	-	0	.286	.286	.286
2002	Grnville	AA	71	229	53	8	0	2	(-	-)	67	40	18	23	28	1	43	4	3	3	5	3	.63	5	.231	.322	.293
2003	VeroB	A+	108	338	80	19	0	4	(-	-)	111	53	37	45	61	0	84	6	5	5	30	15	.67	5	.237	.359	.328
2003	MrtlBh	A+	66	207	50	8	1	2	(-	-)	66	30	15	26	29	2	54	8	4	0	6	2	.75	5	.242	.357	.319
2003	Grnville	AA	47	176	57	14	4	0	(-	-)	79	29	23	31	18	0	25	3	0	0	5	4	.56	1	.324	.396	.449
2004	Rchmd	AAA	61	215	77	18	4	4	(-	-)	115	31	32	44	16	0	40	6	2	1	7	5	.58	4	.358	.416	.535
2005	Scrmto	AAA	75	277	63	16	3	5	(-	-)	100	43	33	36	35	0	56	3	3	2	16	4	.80	7	.227	.319	.361
2004	ATL	NL	83	236	68	8	4	7	(2	5)	105	35	31	37	21	9	45	9	1	0	3	1	.75	3	.288	.368	.445
2005	OAK	AL	30	46	5	0	0	0	(0	0)	5	4	1	1	5	0	8	4	0	0	0	1	.00	0	.109	.255	.109
2 ML YEARS			113	282	73	8	4	7	(2	5)	110	39	32	38	26	9	53	13	1	0	3	2	.60	3	.259	.349	.390

Frank Thomas

Bats: R **Throws:** R **Pos:** DH-28; PH-6   **Ht:** 6'5" **Wt:** 275 **Born:** 5/27/1968 **Age:** 38

Year	Team	Lg	G	AB	H	2B	3B	HR	(Hm	Rd)	TB	R	RBI	RC	TBB	IBB	SO	HBP	SH	SF	SB	CS	SB%	GDP	Avg	OBP	Slg
2005	Charltt*	AAA	11	42	8	1	0	1	(-	-)	12	3	4	3	4	0	9	0	0	0	0	0	-	2	.190	.261	.286
1990	CHA	AL	60	191	63	11	3	7	(2	5)	101	39	31	46	44	0	54	2	0	3	0	1	.00	3	.330	.454	.529
1991	CHA	AL	158	559	178	31	2	32	(24	8)	309	104	109	134	138	13	112	1	0	2	1	2	.33	20	.318	.453	.553
1992	CHA	AL	160	573	185	46	2	24	(10	14)	307	108	115	132	122	6	88	5	0	11	6	3	.67	19	.323	.439	.536
1993	CHA	AL	153	549	174	36	0	41	(26	15)	333	106	128	137	112	23	54	2	0	13	4	2	.67	10	.317	.426	.607
1994	CHA	AL	113	399	141	34	1	38	(22	16)	291	106	101	127	109	12	61	2	0	7	2	3	.40	5	.353	.487	.729
1995	CHA	AL	145	493	152	27	0	40	(15	25)	299	102	111	132	136	29	74	6	0	12	3	2	.60	14	.308	.454	.606
1996	CHA	AL	141	527	184	26	0	40	(16	24)	330	110	134	137	109	26	70	5	0	8	1	1	.50	25	.349	.459	.626
1997	CHA	AL	146	530	184	35	0	35	(16	19)	324	110	125	139	109	9	69	3	0	7	1	1	.50	17	.347	.456	.611
1998	CHA	AL	160	585	155	35	2	29	(15	14)	281	109	109	111	110	2	93	6	0	11	7	0	1.00	14	.265	.381	.480
1999	CHA	AL	135	486	148	36	0	15	(9	6)	229	74	77	95	87	13	66	9	0	8	3	3	.50	15	.305	.414	.471
2000	CHA	AL	159	582	191	44	0	43	(30	13)	364	115	143	148	112	18	94	5	0	8	1	3	.25	13	.328	.436	.625
2001	CHA	AL	20	68	15	3	0	4	(2	2)	30	8	10	10	10	2	12	0	0	1	0	0	-	0	.221	.316	.441
2002	CHA	AL	148	523	132	29	1	28	(24	4)	247	77	92	96	88	2	115	7	0	10	3	0	1.00	10	.252	.361	.472
2003	CHA	AL	153	546	146	35	0	42	(29	13)	307	87	105	115	100	4	115	12	0	4	0	0	-	11	.267	.390	.562
2004	CHA	AL	74	240	65	16	0	18	(14	4)	135	53	49	59	64	3	57	0	0	1	0	2	.00	2	.271	.434	.563
2005	CHA	AL	34	105	23	3	0	12	(9	3)	62	19	26	18	16	0	31	0	0	3	0	0	-	2	.219	.315	.590
16 ML YEARS			1959	6956	2136	447	11	448	(263	185)	3949	1327	1465	1636	1466	162	1165	71	0	109	32	23	.58	190	.307	.427	.568

Jim Thome

Bats: L **Throws:** R **Pos:** 1B-52; DH-5; PH-2   **Ht:** 6'4" **Wt:** 220 **Born:** 8/27/1970 **Age:** 35

Year	Team	Lg	G	AB	H	2B	3B	HR	(Hm	Rd)	TB	R	RBI	RC	TBB	IBB	SO	HBP	SH	SF	SB	CS	SB%	GDP	Avg	OBP	Slg
2005	Clrwtr*	A+	5	12	4	0	0	1	(-	-)	7	2	3	4	6	0	1	0	0	0	0	0	-	0	.333	.556	.583
1991	CLE	AL	27	98	25	4	2	1	(0	1)	36	7	9	9	5	1	16	1	0	0	1	1	.50	4	.255	.298	.367
1992	CLE	AL	40	117	24	3	1	2	(1	1)	35	8	12	9	10	2	34	2	0	2	2	0	1.00	3	.205	.275	.299

			BATTING																						BASERUNNING				AVERAGES		
Year	Team	Lg	G	AB	H	2B	3B	HR	(Hm	Rd)	TB	R	RBI	RC	TBB	IBB	SO	HBP	SH	SF		SB	CS	SB%	GDP		Avg	OBP	Slg
1993	CLE	AL	47	154	41	11	0	7	(5	2)	73	28	22	30	29	1	36	4	0	5		2	1	.67	3		.266	.385	.474
1994	CLE	AL	98	321	86	20	1	20	(10	10)	168	58	52	56	46	5	84	0	1	1		3	3	.50	11		.268	.359	.523
1995	CLE	AL	137	452	142	29	3	25	(13	12)	252	92	73	109	97	3	113	5	0	3		4	3	.57	8		.314	.438	.558
1996	CLE	AL	151	505	157	28	5	38	(18	20)	309	122	116	132	123	8	141	6	0	2		2	2	.50	13		.311	.450	.612
1997	CLE	AL	147	496	142	25	0	40	(17	23)	287	104	102	120	120	9	146	3	0	8		1	1	.50	9		.286	.423	.579
1998	CLE	AL	123	440	129	34	2	30	(18	12)	257	89	85	104	89	8	141	4	0	4		1	0	1.00	7		.293	.413	.584
1999	CLE	AL	146	494	137	27	2	33	(19	14)	267	101	108	116	127	13	171	4	0	4		0	0	-	6		.277	.426	.540
2000	CLE	AL	158	557	150	33	1	37	(21	16)	296	106	106	119	118	4	171	4	0	5		1	0	1.00	8		.269	.398	.531
2001	CLE	AL	156	526	153	26	1	49	(30	19)	328	101	124	130	111	14	185	4	0	3		0	1	.00	9		.291	.416	.624
2002	CLE	AL	147	480	146	19	2	52	(30	22)	325	101	118	139	122	18	139	5	0	6		1	2	.33	5		.304	.445	.677
2003	PHI	NL	159	578	154	30	3	47	(28	19)	331	111	131	125	111	11	182	4	0	5		0	3	.00	5		.266	.385	.573
2004	PHI	NL	143	508	139	28	1	42	(19	23)	295	97	105	97	104	26	144	2	0	4		0	2	.00	10		.274	.396	.581
2005	PHI	NL	59	193	40	7	0	7	(6	1)	68	26	30	25	45	4	59	2	0	2		0	0	-	5		.207	.360	.352
	15 ML YEARS		1738	5919	1665	324	24	430	(235	195)	3327	1151	1193	1320	1257	127	1762	50	1	54		18	19	.49	106		.281	.408	.562

Brad Thompson

Pitches: R Bats: R Pos: RP-40   Ht: 6'1" Wt: 190 Born: 1/31/1982 Age: 24

			HOW MUCH HE PITCHED						WHAT HE GAVE UP												THE RESULTS							
Year	Team	Lg	G	GS	CG	GF	IP	BFP	H	R	ER	HR	SH	SF	HB	TBB	IBB	SO	WP	Bk	W	L	Pct	ShO	Sv-Op	Hld	ERC	ERA
2003	PlmBh	A+	2	1	0	0	6.0	21	3	0	0	0	4	1	0	0	0	4	0	0	1	1	.500	0	0--	-	0.54	0.00
2003	Peoria	A	30	4	0	7	65.0	275	70	23	21	2	2	0	6	10	2	43	4	2	5	3	.625	0	0--	-	3.38	2.91
2004	Tenn	AA	13	12	2	0	72.1	284	56	19	19	6	4	3	9	11	0	57	1	0	8	2	.800	2	0--	-	2.38	2.36
2004	Memp	AAA	3	3	0	0	14.2	67	20	10	9	3	0	0	0	3	0	10	0	0	1	0	1.000	0	0--	-	6.04	5.52
2005	Memp	AAA	9	0	0	4	13.2	60	12	5	5	1	2	0	1	7	5	11	0	1	2	1	.667	0	0--	-	3.29	3.29
2005	STL	NL	40	0	0	8	55.0	225	46	22	18	5	3	0	4	15	2	29	0	0	4	0	1.000	0	1-1	7	2.90	2.95

Derek Thompson

Pitches: L Bats: L Pos: SP-3; RP-1   Ht: 6'2" Wt: 180 Born: 1/8/1981 Age: 25

			HOW MUCH HE PITCHED						WHAT HE GAVE UP												THE RESULTS							
Year	Team	Lg	G	GS	CG	GF	IP	BFP	H	R	ER	HR	SH	SF	HB	TBB	IBB	SO	WP	Bk	W	L	Pct	ShO	Sv-Op	Hld	ERC	ERA
2000	Burlgtn	R+	12	12	0	0	43.1	194	50	38	28	2	0	2	2	14	0	40	4	0	0	4	.000	0	0--	-	4.36	5.82
2001	Clmbs	A	2	2	0	0	12.0	55	16	13	13	2	0	1	0	3	0	5	1	0	0	2	.000	0	0--	-	5.77	9.75
2002	Kinston	A+	13	13	0	0	74.1	327	72	36	32	1	2	2	11	32	1	41	8	0	2	3	.400	0	0--	-	3.97	3.87
2002	Clmbs	A	14	14	0	0	73.2	319	71	39	28	3	1	2	3	27	0	50	2	0	3	4	.429	0	0--	-	3.44	3.42
2004	Jaxnvl	AA	22	22	0	0	118.2	539	132	59	49	3	7	5	5	51	2	100	5	0	5	7	.417	0	0--	-	4.33	3.72
2005	Jaxnvl	AA	8	8	0	0	41.2	189	45	20	18	3	3	1	3	19	0	43	3	0	2	0	.000	0	0--	-	4.79	3.89
2005	LsVgs	AAA	4	3	0	1	21.0	95	21	11	8	1	1	2	0	11	0	17	1	0	1	2	.333	0	0--	-	4.07	3.43
2005	LAN	NL	4	3	0	0	18.0	74	16	7	7	0	1	1	0	10	1	13	0	0	0	0	-	0	0-0	0	3.46	3.50

Justin Thompson

Pitches: L Bats: L Pos: RP-2   Ht: 6'4" Wt: 215 Born: 3/8/1973 Age: 33

			HOW MUCH HE PITCHED						WHAT HE GAVE UP												THE RESULTS							
Year	Team	Lg	G	GS	CG	GF	IP	BFP	H	R	ER	HR	SH	SF	HB	TBB	IBB	SO	WP	Bk	W	L	Pct	ShO	Sv-Op	Hld	ERC	ERA
2005	Frisco	AA	12	0	0	8	12.2	54	14	5	4	1	0	1	0	2	0	11	0	0	2	0	1.000	0	2--	-	3.48	2.84
2005	Okla	AAA	25	1	0	3	44.0	186	47	24	23	3	1	2	1	7	3	29	1	0	2	2	.500	0	0--	-	3.23	4.70
1996	DET	AL	11	11	0	0	59.0	267	62	35	30	7	0	2	2	31	2	44	1	0	1	6	.143	0	0-0	0	5.07	4.58
1997	DET	AL	32	32	4	0	223.1	891	188	82	75	20	5	10	2	66	1	151	4	0	15	11	.577	0	0-0	0	2.87	3.02
1998	DET	AL	34	34	5	0	222.0	946	227	114	100	20	10	6	2	79	4	149	4	0	11	15	.423	0	0-0	0	4.00	4.05
1999	DET	AL	24	24	0	0	142.2	626	152	85	81	24	1	7	4	59	1	83	2	0	9	11	.450	0	0-0	0	5.14	5.11
2005	TEX	AL	2	0	0	2	1.2	9	4	4	4	2	0	0	0	0	0	1	0	0	0	0	-	0	0-0	0	21.89	21.60
	5 ML YEARS		103	101	9	2	648.2	2739	633	320	290	73	16	25	10	235	8	428	11	0	36	43	.456	0	0-0	0	3.97	4.02

John Thomson

Pitches: R Bats: R Pos: SP-17   Ht: 6'3" Wt: 190 Born: 10/1/1973 Age: 32

			HOW MUCH HE PITCHED						WHAT HE GAVE UP												THE RESULTS							
Year	Team	Lg	G	GS	CG	GF	IP	BFP	H	R	ER	HR	SH	SF	HB	TBB	IBB	SO	WP	Bk	W	L	Pct	ShO	Sv-Op	Hld	ERC	ERA
2005	Rome*	A	1	1	0	0	4.0	15	2	0	0	0	0	0	0	1	0	1	0	0	0	0	-	0	0--	-	0.94	0.00
2005	Missi*	AA	1	1	0	0	6.0	22	4	1	1	0	0	0	0	1	0	4	1	0	1	0	1.000	0	0--	-	0.91	1.50
2005	Rchmd*	AAA	1	1	0	0	3.2	17	5	2	2	0	0	0	1	1	0	2	0	0	0	0	-	0	0--	-	6.22	4.91
1997	COL	NL	27	27	2	0	166.1	721	193	94	87	15	10	3	5	51	0	106	2	0	7	9	.438	1	0-0	0	4.74	4.71
1998	COL	NL	26	26	2	0	161.0	680	174	86	86	21	8	5	0	49	0	106	4	2	8	11	.421	0	0-0	0	4.45	4.81
1999	COL	NL	14	13	1	1	62.2	305	85	62	56	11	4	2	1	36	1	34	2	0	1	10	.091	0	0-0	0	7.60	8.04
2001	COL	NL	14	14	1	0	93.2	386	84	46	42	15	3	3	4	25	3	68	1	0	4	5	.444	1	0-0	0	3.52	4.04
2002	2 Tms	NL	30	30	0	0	181.2	800	201	116	95	28	13	10	2	44	9	107	2	0	9	14	.391	0	0-0	0	4.24	4.71
2003	TEX	AL	35	35	3	0	217.0	910	234	125	117	27	2	7	4	49	2	136	5	0	13	14	.481	1	0-0	0	4.10	4.85
2004	ATL	NL	33	33	0	0	198.1	834	210	93	82	20	11	4	6	52	5	133	3	0	14	8	.636	0	0-0	0	4.01	3.72
2005	ATL	NL	17	17	1	0	98.2	427	111	52	49	6	2	4	2	28	2	61	3	0	4	6	.400	0	0-0	0	4.09	4.47
02	Col	NL	21	21	0	0	127.1	550	136	77	69	21	7	7	2	27	6	76	2	0	7	8	.467	0	0-0	0	4.02	4.88
02	NYM	NL	9	9	0	0	54.1	250	65	39	26	7	6	3	0	17	3	31	0	0	2	6	.250	0	0-0	0	4.74	4.31
	8 ML YEARS		196	195	10	1	1179.1	5063	1292	674	614	143	53	38	24	334	22	751	22	2	60	77	.438	3	0-0	0	4.37	4.69

Matt Thornton

Pitches: L Bats: L Pos: RP-55
Ht: 6'6" Wt: 220 Born: 9/15/1976 Age: 29

				HOW MUCH HE PITCHED						WHAT HE GAVE UP										THE RESULTS						
Year	Team	Lg	G	GS	CG	GF	IP	BFP	H	R	ER	HR	SH	SF	HB	TBB	IBB	SO	WP	Bk	W	L	Pct	ShO	Sv-Op	Hld	ERC	ERA
1998	Everett	A-	2	0	0	0	1.1	8	1	4	4	0	0	0	0	3	0	0	0	0	0	0	-	0	0- -		8.88	27.00
1999	Wisc	A	25	1	0	3	29.1	154	39	19	16	1	4	1	0	25	0	34	5	0	0	0	-	0	1- -		7.09	4.91
2000	Wisc	A	26	17	0	3	103.1	465	94	59	46	2	3	0	6	72	1	88	12	2	6	9	.400	0	0- -		4.37	4.01
2001	SnBrn	A+	27	27	0	0	157.0	650	126	56	44	9	2	5	11	60	0	192	12	0	14	7	.667	0	0- -		2.96	2.52
2002	SnAnt	AA	12	12	0	0	62.0	258	52	31	25	3	1	4	5	29	0	44	8	0	1	5	.167	0	0- -		3.53	3.63
2003	InldEm	A+	2	2	0	0	9.0	40	9	4	4	2	0	1	1	4	0	14	0	0	0	0	-	0	0- -		5.65	4.00
2003	SnAnt	AA	4	4	0	0	25.1	87	8	3	1	0	0	1	0	9	0	18	0	0	3	0	1.000	0	0- -		0.73	0.36
2003	Tacom	AAA	2	2	0	0	9.0	44	14	11	8	2	0	2	0	3	0	5	1	0	2	0	.000	0	0- -		8.02	8.00
2004	Tacom	AAA	16	15	1	0	83.0	393	85	58	48	4	4	9	6	63	1	74	10	0	7	5	.583	0	0- -		5.51	5.20
2004	SEA	AL	19	1	0	8	32.2	148	30	15	15	2	2	1	0	25	1	30	2	0	1	2	.333	0	0-0	4	4.75	4.13
2005	SEA	AL	55	0	0	15	57.0	262	54	33	33	13	1	1	0	42	2	57	7	0	0	4	.000	0	0-1	5	6.06	5.21
	2 ML YEARS		74	1	0	23	89.2	410	84	48	48	15	3	2	0	67	3	87	9	0	1	6	.143	0	0-1	5	5.59	4.82

Terry Tiffee

Bats: B Throws: R Pos: 3B-24; PH-16; 1B-13; DH-10; PR-1
Ht: 6'3" Wt: 210 Born: 4/21/1979 Age: 27

					BATTING																BASERUNNING				AVERAGES		
Year	Team	Lg	G	AB	H	2B	3B	HR	(Hm	Rd)	TB	R	RBI	RC	TBB	IBB	SO	HBP	SH	SF	SB	CS	SB%	GDP	Avg	OBP	Slg
2000	QuadC	A	129	493	125	25	0	7	(-	-)	171	59	60	47	29	0	73	0	0	5	2	0	1.00	14	.254	.292	.347
2001	QuadC	A	128	495	153	32	1	11	(-	-)	220	65	86	74	32	4	48	1	0	8	3	1	.75	13	.309	.347	.444
2002	FtMyrs	A+	126	473	133	31	0	8	(-	-)	188	47	64	56	25	3	49	2	3	6	0	3	.00	12	.281	.316	.397
2003	NwBrit	AA	139	530	167	31	3	14	(-	-)	246	77	93	83	31	5	49	2	0	7	4	1	.80	13	.315	.351	.464
2004	Roch	AAA	82	316	97	26	3	12	(-	-)	165	42	68	54	21	2	26	4	0	1	0	0	-	9	.307	.357	.522
2005	Roch	AAA	58	229	61	11	1	10	(-	-)	104	33	39	33	15	2	24	3	0	5	0	1	.00	9	.266	.313	.454
2004	MIN	AL	17	44	12	4	0	2	(1	1)	22	7	8	5	3	0	3	1	0	0	0	0	-	2	.273	.333	.500
2005	MIN	AL	54	150	31	8	1	1	(1	0)	44	9	15	8	8	1	15	0	0	1	1	0	1.00	10	.207	.245	.293
	2 ML YEARS		71	194	43	12	1	3	(2	1)	66	16	23	13	11	1	18	1	0	1	1	0	1.00	12	.222	.266	.340

Mike Timlin

Pitches: R Bats: R Pos: RP-81
Ht: 6'4" Wt: 210 Born: 3/10/1966 Age: 40

				HOW MUCH HE PITCHED						WHAT HE GAVE UP										THE RESULTS						
Year	Team	Lg	G	GS	CG	GF	IP	BFP	H	R	ER	HR	SH	SF	HB	TBB	IBB	SO	WP	Bk	W	L	Pct	ShO	Sv-Op	Hld	ERC	ERA
1991	TOR	AL	63	3	0	17	108.1	463	94	43	38	6	6	2	1	50	11	85	5	0	11	6	.647	0	3-8	9	3.14	3.16
1992	TOR	AL	26	0	0	14	43.2	190	45	23	20	8	2	1	1	20	5	35	0	0	0	2	.000	0	1-1	5	3.68	4.12
1993	TOR	AL	54	0	0	27	55.2	254	63	32	29	7	1	3	1	27	3	49	1	0	4	2	.667	0	1-4	9	5.32	4.69
1994	TOR	AL	34	0	0	16	40.0	179	41	25	23	5	0	0	2	20	0	38	3	0	0	1	.000	0	2-4	5	5.01	5.18
1995	TOR	AL	31	0	0	19	42.0	179	38	13	10	1	3	0	2	17	5	36	3	1	4	3	.571	0	5-9	4	3.04	2.14
1996	TOR	AL	59	0	0	56	56.2	230	47	25	23	4	2	3	2	18	4	52	3	0	1	6	.143	0	31-38	2	2.74	3.65
1997	2 Tms	AL	64	0	0	31	72.2	297	69	30	26	8	6	1	1	20	5	45	1	1	6	4	.600	0	10-18	9	3.40	3.22
1998	SEA	AL	70	0	0	40	79.1	321	78	26	26	5	4	2	3	16	2	60	0	0	3	3	.500	0	19-24	6	3.17	2.95
1999	BAL	AL	62	0	0	52	63.0	261	51	30	25	9	1	1	5	23	3	50	1	0	3	9	.250	0	27-36	6	3.46	3.57
2000	2 Tms	AL	62	0	0	40	64.2	295	67	33	30	8	7	2	4	35	6	52	0	0	5	4	.556	0	12-18	6	5.08	4.18
2001	STL	NL	67	0	0	19	72.2	307	78	35	33	6	1	2	3	19	4	47	3	1	4	5	.444	0	3-7	12	3.95	4.09
2002	2 Tms	NL	72	1	0	17	96.2	376	75	35	32	15	2	1	5	14	2	50	3	0	4	6	.400	0	0-4	20	2.46	2.98
2003	BOS	AL	72	0	0	13	83.2	340	77	37	33	11	4	1	4	9	3	65	0	0	6	4	.600	0	2-6	17	2.81	3.55
2004	BOS	AL	76	0	0	12	76.1	320	75	35	35	8	3	1	5	19	3	56	1	0	5	4	.556	0	1-4	20	3.64	4.13
2005	BOS	AL	81	0	0	27	80.1	342	86	23	20	2	3	6	2	20	5	59	3	0	7	3	.700	0	13-20	24	3.35	2.24
97	Tor	AL	38	0	0	26	47.0	190	41	17	15	6	4	1	1	15	4	36	1	1	3	2	.600	0	9-13	2	3.30	2.87
97	Sea	AL	26	0	0	5	25.2	107	28	13	11	2	2	0	0	5	1	9	0	0	3	2	.600	0	1-5	7	3.59	3.86
00	Bal	AL	37	0	0	31	35.0	157	37	22	19	6	5	1	2	15	3	26	0	0	2	3	.400	0	11-15	1	5.08	4.89
00	StL	NL	25	0	0	9	29.2	138	30	11	11	2	2	1	2	20	3	26	0	0	3	1	.750	0	1-3	5	5.05	3.34
02	StL	NL	42	1	0	10	61.0	236	48	19	17	9	2	0	4	7	2	35	1	0	1	3	.250	0	0-2	12	2.41	2.51
02	Phi	NL	30	0	0	7	35.2	140	27	16	15	6	0	1	1	7	0	15	2	0	3	3	.500	0	0-2	8	2.55	3.79
	15 ML YEARS		893	4	0	400	1035.2	4354	984	445	403	95	45	26	41	327	61	779	27	3	63	62	.504	0	130-201	144	3.50	3.50

Brett Tomko

Pitches: R Bats: R Pos: SP-30; RP-3
Ht: 6'4" Wt: 215 Born: 4/7/1973 Age: 33

				HOW MUCH HE PITCHED						WHAT HE GAVE UP										THE RESULTS						
Year	Team	Lg	G	GS	CG	GF	IP	BFP	H	R	ER	HR	SH	SF	HB	TBB	IBB	SO	WP	Bk	W	L	Pct	ShO	Sv-Op	Hld	ERC	ERA
1997	CIN	NL	22	19	0	1	126.0	519	106	50	48	14	5	9	4	47	4	95	5	0	11	7	.611	0	0-0	0	3.31	3.43
1998	CIN	NL	34	34	1	0	210.2	887	198	111	104	22	12	2	7	64	3	162	9	1	13	12	.520	0	0-0	0	3.50	4.44
1999	CIN	NL	33	26	1	1	172.0	744	175	103	94	31	9	5	4	60	10	132	8	0	5	7	.417	0	0-0	1	4.51	4.92
2000	SEA	AL	32	8	0	10	92.1	401	92	53	48	12	5	5	3	40	4	59	1	1	7	5	.583	0	1-2	3	4.49	4.68
2001	SEA	AL	11	4	0	1	34.2	164	42	24	20	9	1	2	0	15	2	22	1	0	3	1	.750	0	0-1	0	6.31	5.19
2002	SD	NL	32	32	3	0	204.1	871	212	107	102	31	6	8	2	60	9	126	3	0	10	10	.500	0	0-0	0	4.18	4.49
2003	STL	NL	33	32	2	0	202.2	903	252	126	119	35	12	13	3	57	2	114	6	0	13	9	.591	0	0-0	0	5.63	5.28
2004	SF	NL	32	31	2	1	194.0	825	196	98	87	19	7	1	0	64	3	108	10	0	11	7	.611	1	0-0	0	3.82	4.04
2005	SF	NL	33	30	3	1	190.2	823	205	99	95	20	6	5	7	57	11	114	5	0	8	15	.348	0	1-1	1	4.18	4.48
	9 ML YEARS		262	216	12	15	1427.1	6137	1478	771	717	193	63	40	32	464	48	932	48	2	81	73	.526	1	2-4	5	4.25	4.52

Tony Torcato

Bats: L **Throws:** R **Pos:** PH-10; RF-1   **Ht:** 6'1" **Wt:** 195 **Born:** 10/25/1979 **Age:** 26

Year	Team	Lg	G	AB	H	2B	3B	HR	(Hm	Rd)	TB	R	RBI	RC	TBB	IBB	SO	HBP	SH	SF	SB	CS	SB%	GDP	Avg	OBP	Slg
2005	Fresno*	AAA	105	376	101	15	5	10	(-	-)	156	41	57	49	21	4	43	4	1	5	3	4	.43	7	.269	.310	.415
2002	SF	NL	5	11	3	1	0	0	(0	0)	4	0	0	0	0	0	2	0	0	0	0	0	-	0	.273	.273	.364
2003	SF	NL	14	16	3	1	0	0	(0	0)	4	0	1	1	0	0	4	1	1	0	0	0	-	0	.188	.235	.250
2004	SF	NL	13	9	5	0	0	0	(0	0)	5	1	2	3	1	0	0	1	0	1	0	0	-	0	.556	.583	.556
2005	SF	NL	11	11	3	0	0	0	(0	0)	3	1	0	1	1	0	2	0	0	0	0	0	-	2	.273	.333	.273
	4 ML YEARS		43	47	14	2	0	0	(0	0)	16	2	3	5	2	0	8	2	1	1	0	0	-	2	.298	.346	.340

Yorvit Torrealba

Bats: R **Throws:** R **Pos:** C-68; PR-5; PH-4; DH-1   **Ht:** 5'11" **Wt:** 180 **Born:** 7/19/1978 **Age:** 27

Year	Team	Lg	G	AB	H	2B	3B	HR	(Hm	Rd)	TB	R	RBI	RC	TBB	IBB	SO	HBP	SH	SF	SB	CS	SB%	GDP	Avg	OBP	Slg
2001	SF	NL	3	4	2	0	1	0	(0	0)	4	0	2	2	0	0	0	0	0	0	0	0	-	0	.500	.500	1.000
2002	SF	NL	53	136	38	10	0	2	(0	2)	54	17	14	16	14	2	20	2	3	0	0	0	-	11	.279	.355	.397
2003	SF	NL	66	200	52	10	2	4	(3	1)	78	22	29	25	14	1	39	2	3	2	1	0	1.00	7	.260	.312	.390
2004	SF	NL	64	172	39	7	3	6	(3	3)	70	19	23	18	17	3	31	2	4	1	2	0	1.00	7	.227	.302	.407
2005	2 Tms		76	201	47	12	0	3	(2	1)	68	32	15	14	16	1	50	2	5	0	1	0	1.00	8	.234	.297	.338
05	SF	NL	34	93	21	8	0	1	(1	0)	32	18	7	7	9	1	25	1	2	0	1	0	1.00	3	.226	.301	.344
05	Sea	AL	42	108	26	4	0	2	(1	1)	36	14	8	7	7	0	25	1	3	0	0	0	-	5	.241	.293	.333
	5 ML YEARS		262	713	178	39	6	15	(8	7)	274	90	83	75	61	7	140	8	15	3	4	0	1.00	29	.250	.315	.384

Andres Torres

Bats: B **Throws:** R **Pos:** CF-4; PH-3; RF-2   **Ht:** 5'10" **Wt:** 175 **Born:** 1/26/1978 **Age:** 28

Year	Team	Lg	G	AB	H	2B	3B	HR	(Hm	Rd)	TB	R	RBI	RC	TBB	IBB	SO	HBP	SH	SF	SB	CS	SB%	GDP	Avg	OBP	Slg
2005	Okla*	AAA	15	63	19	3	1	0	(-	-)	24	12	1	9	6	0	17	0	0	0	6	1	.86	0	.302	.362	.381
2002	DET	AL	19	70	14	1	1	0	(0	0)	17	7	3	2	6	0	16	1	0	2	2	2	.50	2	.200	.266	.243
2003	DET	AL	59	168	37	4	3	1	(1	0)	50	23	9	9	10	0	35	0	6	1	5	5	.50	5	.220	.263	.298
2004	DET	AL	3	0	0	0	0	0	(0	0)	0	1	0	0	0	0	0	0	0	0	1	0	1.00	0	-	-	-
2005	TEX	AL	8	19	3	1	0	0	(0	0)	4	2	1	1	1	0	6	0	0	1	1	0	1.00	0	.158	.190	.211
	4 ML YEARS		89	257	54	6	4	1	(1	0)	71	33	13	12	17	0	57	1	6	4	9	7	.56	7	.210	.258	.276

Salomon Torres

Pitches: R **Bats:** R **Pos:** RP-78   **Ht:** 5'11" **Wt:** 165 **Born:** 3/11/1972 **Age:** 34

Year	Team	Lg	G	GS	CG	GF	IP	BFP	H	R	ER	HR	SH	SF	HB	TBB	IBB	SO	WP	Bk	W	L	Pct	ShO	Sv-Op	Hld	ERC	ERA
1993	SF	NL	8	8	0	0	44.2	196	37	21	20	5	7	1	1	27	3	23	3	1	3	5	.375	0	0-0	0	3.95	4.03
1994	SF	NL	16	14	1	2	84.1	378	95	55	51	10	4	8	7	34	2	42	4	1	2	8	.200	0	0-0	0	5.29	5.44
1995	2 Tms		20	14	1	4	80.0	384	100	61	56	16	1	0	2	49	3	47	1	2	3	9	.250	0	0-0	0	7.30	6.30
1996	SEA	AL	10	7	1	1	49.0	212	44	27	25	5	3	1	3	23	2	36	1	0	3	3	.500	1	0-0	0	3.98	4.59
1997	2 Tms		14	0	0	4	25.2	127	32	29	28	2	3	1	3	15	0	11	3	0	0	0	-	0	0-0	0	6.44	9.82
2002	PIT	NL	5	5	0	0	30.0	127	28	10	9	2	2	0	3	13	1	12	0	0	2	1	.667	0	0-0	0	4.07	2.70
2003	PIT	NL	41	16	0	7	121.0	518	128	65	64	19	4	1	7	42	5	84	3	0	7	5	.583	0	2-3	6	4.88	4.76
2004	PIT	NL	84	0	0	20	92.0	380	87	33	27	6	9	3	6	22	6	62	5	0	7	7	.500	0	0-4	30	3.12	2.64
2005	PIT	NL	78	0	0	32	94.2	388	76	34	29	7	3	2	5	36	7	55	5	0	5	5	.500	0	3-3	6	2.91	2.76
95	SF	NL	4	1	0	2	8.0	40	13	8	8	4	0	0	0	7	0	2	0	0	0	1	.000	0	0-0	0	15.31	9.00
95	Sea	AL	16	13	1	2	72.0	344	87	53	48	12	1	0	2	42	3	45	1	2	3	8	.273	0	0-0	0	6.55	6.00
97	Sea	AL	2	0	0	1	3.1	21	7	10	10	0	0	0	1	3	0	0	0	0	0	0	-	0	0-0	0	13.67	27.00
97	Mon	NL	12	0	0	3	22.1	106	25	19	18	2	3	1	2	12	0	11	3	0	0	0	-	0	0-0	0	5.47	7.25
	9 ML YEARS		276	64	3	70	621.1	2710	627	335	309	72	36	17	37	261	29	372	25	4	32	43	.427	1	5-10	44	4.52	4.48

Josh Towers

Pitches: R **Bats:** R **Pos:** SP-33   **Ht:** 6'1" **Wt:** 165 **Born:** 2/26/1977 **Age:** 29

Year	Team	Lg	G	GS	CG	GF	IP	BFP	H	R	ER	HR	SH	SF	HB	TBB	IBB	SO	WP	Bk	W	L	Pct	ShO	Sv-Op	Hld	ERC	ERA
2001	BAL	AL	24	20	1	2	140.1	586	165	74	70	21	3	4	6	16	0	58	1	0	8	10	.444	1	0-0	0	4.51	4.49
2002	BAL	AL	5	3	0	1	27.1	124	42	24	24	11	1	2	0	5	0	13	1	0	0	3	.000	0	0-0	0	9.00	7.90
2003	TOR	AL	14	8	1	2	64.1	265	67	34	32	15	0	2	4	7	1	42	1	0	8	1	.889	0	1-1	0	4.26	4.48
2004	TOR	AL	21	21	0	0	116.1	518	148	70	66	16	2	4	9	26	4	51	0	1	9	9	.500	0	0-0	0	5.50	5.11
2005	TOR	AL	33	33	2	0	208.2	876	237	101	86	24	3	7	6	29	2	112	1	1	13	12	.520	1	0-0	0	4.02	3.71
	5 ML YEARS		97	85	4	5	557.0	2369	659	303	278	87	9	19	25	83	7	276	4	2	38	35	.521	2	1-1	0	4.70	4.49

Steve Trachsel

Pitches: R **Bats:** R **Pos:** SP-6   **Ht:** 6'4" **Wt:** 205 **Born:** 10/31/1970 **Age:** 35

Year	Team	Lg	G	GS	CG	GF	IP	BFP	H	R	ER	HR	SH	SF	HB	TBB	IBB	SO	WP	Bk	W	L	Pct	ShO	Sv-Op	Hld	ERC	ERA
2005	StLuci*	A+	2	2	0	0	6.2	26	5	2	1	0	0	0	1	1	0	5	1	0	0	1	.000	0	0--	-	1.88	1.35
2005	Bnghtn*	AA	2	2	1	0	12.0	48	8	4	4	2	1	0	0	4	0	7	0	0	1	0	1.000	0	0--	-	2.45	3.00
2005	Norfolk*	AAA	2	2	0	0	14.0	54	10	4	4	2	0	0	2	2	0	12	0	0	1	1	.500	0	0--	-	1.89	2.57
1993	CHN	NL	3	3	0	0	19.2	78	16	10	10	4	1	1	0	3	0	14	1	0	0	2	.000	0	0-0	0	2.71	4.58
1994	CHN	NL	22	22	1	0	146.0	612	133	57	52	19	3	3	3	54	4	108	6	0	9	7	.563	0	0-0	0	3.74	3.21
1995	CHN	NL	30	29	2	0	160.2	722	174	104	92	25	12	5	0	76	8	117	2	1	7	13	.350	0	0-0	0	5.13	5.15
1996	CHN	NL	31	31	3	0	205.0	845	181	82	69	30	3	3	6	62	3	132	5	2	13	9	.591	2	0-0	0	3.52	3.03

HOW MUCH HE PITCHED								WHAT HE GAVE UP													THE RESULTS							
Year	Team	Lg	G	GS	CG	GF	IP	BFP	H	R	ER	HR	SH	SF	HB	TBB	IBB	SO	WP	Bk	W	L	Pct	ShO	Sv-Op	Hld	ERC	ERA
1997	CHN	NL	34	34	0	0	201.1	878	225	110	101	32	8	11	5	69	6	160	4	1	8	12	.400	0	0-0	0	5.04	4.51
1998	CHN	NL	33	33	1	0	208.0	894	204	107	103	27	9	7	8	84	5	149	3	2	15	8	.652	0	0-0	0	4.35	4.46
1999	CHN	NL	34	34	4	0	205.2	894	226	133	127	32	6	14	3	64	4	149	8	3	8	18	.308	0	0-0	0	4.69	5.56
2000	2 Tms	AL	34	34	3	0	200.2	882	232	116	107	26	6	6	6	74	2	110	4	0	8	15	.348	1	0-0	0	5.25	4.80
2001	NYN	NL	28	28	1	0	173.2	726	168	90	86	28	8	7	3	47	7	144	4	0	11	13	.458	1	0-0	0	3.80	4.46
2002	NYN	NL	30	30	1	0	173.2	741	170	80	65	16	9	3	0	69	4	105	4	0	11	11	.500	1	0-0	0	3.88	3.37
2003	NYN	NL	33	33	2	0	204.2	857	204	90	86	26	8	8	3	65	9	111	5	2	16	10	.615	2	0-0	0	3.97	3.78
2004	NYN	NL	33	33	0	0	202.2	881	203	104	90	25	11	8	5	83	9	117	4	2	12	13	.480	0	0-0	0	4.31	4.00
2005	NYN	NL	6	6	0	0	37.0	157	37	20	17	6	2	2	1	12	0	24	1	0	1	4	.200	0	0-0	0	4.34	4.14
00	TB	AL	23	23	3	0	137.2	606	160	76	70	16	2	5	6	49	1	78	3	0	6	10	.375	1	0-0	0	5.19	4.58
00	Tor	AL	11	11	0	0	63.0	276	72	40	37	10	4	1	0	25	1	32	1	0	2	5	.286	0	0-0	0	5.38	5.29
13 ML YEARS			351	350	18	0	2138.2	9167	2173	1103	1005	296	86	78	45	762	61	1440	51	13	119	135	.469	7	0-0	0	4.32	4.23

Chad Tracy

Bats: L Throws: R Pos: 1B-80; RF-47; PH-20; LF-6; DH-1 Ht: 6'2" Wt: 200 Born: 5/22/1980 Age: 26

			BATTING																	BASERUNNING				AVERAGES		
Year	Team	Lg	G	AB	H	2B	3B	HR	(Hm	Rd)	TB	R	RBI	RC	TBB	IBB	SO	HBP	SH	SF	SB	CS	SB%	GDP	Avg	OBP	Slg
2001	Yakima	A-	10	36	10	1	0	0	(-	-)	11	2	5	4	3	0	5	1	0	0	1	0	1.00	1	.278	.350	.306
2001	Sbend	A	54	215	73	11	0	4	(-	-)	96	43	36	38	19	2	19	2	0	3	3	0	1.00	4	.340	.393	.447
2002	ElPaso	AA	129	514	177	39	5	8	(-	-)	250	80	74	93	39	7	51	4	1	7	2	3	.40	10	.344	.390	.486
2003	Tucsn	AAA	133	522	169	31	4	10	(-	-)	238	91	80	89	41	3	52	4	0	9	0	2	.00	7	.324	.372	.456
2004	Tucsn	AAA	11	40	16	4	0	2	(-	-)	26	7	11	12	8	1	5	0	0	1	2	0	1.00	0	.400	.490	.650
2004	ARI	NL	143	481	137	29	3	8	(6	2)	196	45	53	63	45	3	60	0	1	5	2	3	.40	11	.285	.343	.407
2005	ARI	NL	145	503	155	34	4	27	(9	18)	278	73	72	82	35	4	78	8	1	6	3	1	.75	9	.308	.359	.553
2 ML YEARS			288	984	292	63	7	35	(15	20)	474	118	125	145	80	7	138	8	2	11	5	4	.56	21	.297	.351	.482

Matt Treanor

Bats: R Throws: R Pos: C-55; PH-3 Ht: 6'2" Wt: 220 Born: 3/3/1976 Age: 30

			BATTING																	BASERUNNING				AVERAGES		
Year	Team	Lg	G	AB	H	2B	3B	HR	(Hm	Rd)	TB	R	RBI	RC	TBB	IBB	SO	HBP	SH	SF	SB	CS	SB%	GDP	Avg	OBP	Slg
1994	Royals	R	46	99	18	5	0	1	(-	-)	26	17	12	8	14	1	23	3	1	1	1	1	.50	2	.182	.299	.263
1995	Sprgfld	A	75	211	39	6	2	3	(-	-)	58	17	19	16	21	0	59	4	2	2	1	1	.50	1	.185	.269	.275
1996	Lansng	A	119	384	100	18	2	6	(-	-)	140	56	33	49	35	1	63	13	6	1	5	3	.63	9	.260	.342	.365
1997	Wilmg	A+	80	257	51	6	1	5	(-	-)	74	22	25	18	25	0	59	2	6	0	1	6	.14	4	.198	.275	.288
1997	BrvdCt	A+	23	70	15	4	1	0	(-	-)	21	11	3	8	12	0	14	2	1	0	0	0	-	1	.214	.345	.300
1998	BrvdCt	A+	80	243	57	8	0	3	(-	-)	74	24	28	29	38	0	45	5	1	3	3	2	.60	4	.235	.346	.305
1999	Kane	A	86	308	88	21	1	10	(-	-)	141	56	53	54	36	0	65	15	2	2	4	1	.80	9	.286	.385	.458
2000	Kane	A+	109	350	86	17	0	3	(-	-)	112	51	37	45	48	0	65	14	4	3	3	3	.50	6	.246	.357	.320
2001	Portlnd	AA	35	89	14	2	0	2	(-	-)	22	7	8	8	13	0	18	9	2	0	1	1	.50	2	.157	.324	.247
2001	Marlins	R	11	34	14	4	0	1	(-	-)	21	10	4	10	7	0	7	0	0	0	3	0	1.00	1	.412	.512	.618
2001	Kane	A	1	1	1	0	0	0	(-	-)	1	2	0	1	3	0	0	0	0	0	0	0	-	0	1.000	1.000	1.000
2002	Portlnd	AA	50	156	39	5	1	9	(-	-)	73	24	28	29	28	0	33	7	1	0	3	0	1.00	4	.250	.387	.468
2002	Calgry	AAA	36	95	27	8	0	1	(-	-)	38	10	18	14	12	0	13	5	0	0	1	1	.50	4	.284	.393	.400
2003	Albq	AAA	98	315	86	18	1	11	(-	-)	139	45	40	54	39	1	44	17	1	3	9	4	.69	8	.273	.380	.441
2004	Albq	AAA	62	198	51	8	0	8	(-	-)	83	32	38	35	34	1	44	10	2	3	2	0	1.00	5	.258	.388	.419
2004	FLA	NL	29	55	13	2	0	0	(0	0)	15	7	1	4	4	0	13	2	0	0	0	0	-	3	.236	.311	.273
2005	FLA	NL	58	134	27	8	0	0	(0	0)	35	10	13	13	16	1	28	3	1	0	0	0	-	5	.201	.301	.261
2 ML YEARS			87	189	40	10	0	0	(0	0)	50	17	14	17	20	1	41	5	1	0	0	0	-	8	.212	.304	.265

Chin-hui Tsao

Pitches: R Bats: R Pos: RP-10 Ht: 6'2" Wt: 177 Born: 6/2/1981 Age: 25

HOW MUCH HE PITCHED								WHAT HE GAVE UP													THE RESULTS							
Year	Team	Lg	G	GS	CG	GF	IP	BFP	H	R	ER	HR	SH	SF	HB	TBB	IBB	SO	WP	Bk	W	L	Pct	ShO	Sv-Op	Hld	ERC	ERA
2005	Mdest*	A+	1	0	0	1	1.0	3	0	0	0	0	0	0	0	0	0	1	0	0	0	0	-	0	0--	-	0.00	0.00
2005	ColSpr*	AAA	1	1	0	0	1.0	4	1	0	0	0	0	0	0	0	0	1	0	0	0	0	-	0	0--	-	1.95	0.00
2003	COL	NL	9	8	0	1	43.1	196	48	30	29	11	3	0	4	20	1	29	0	0	3	3	.500	0	0-0	0	6.56	6.02
2004	COL	NL	10	0	0	5	9.1	37	7	4	4	2	1	0	0	1	0	11	0	0	0	0	-	0	1-2	1	2.21	3.86
2005	COL	NL	10	0	0	9	11.0	56	16	8	8	3	1	1	1	5	1	4	1	0	1	0	1.000	0	3-4	0	8.44	6.55
3 ML YEARS			29	8	0	15	63.2	289	71	42	41	16	5	1	5	26	2	44	1	0	4	3	.571	0	4-6	1	6.16	5.80

Michael Tucker

Bats: L Throws: R Pos: RF-64; PH-57; CF-8; LF-4; DH-4; PR-2 Ht: 6'2" Wt: 195 Born: 6/25/1971 Age: 35

			BATTING																	BASERUNNING				AVERAGES		
Year	Team	Lg	G	AB	H	2B	3B	HR	(Hm	Rd)	TB	R	RBI	RC	TBB	IBB	SO	HBP	SH	SF	SB	CS	SB%	GDP	Avg	OBP	Slg
1995	KC	AL	62	177	46	10	0	4	(1	3)	68	23	17	22	18	2	51	1	2	0	2	3	.40	3	.260	.332	.384
1996	KC	AL	108	339	88	18	4	12	(2	10)	150	55	53	53	40	1	69	7	3	4	10	4	.71	7	.260	.346	.442
1997	ATL	NL	138	499	141	25	7	14	(5	9)	222	80	56	76	44	0	116	6	4	1	12	7	.63	7	.283	.347	.445
1998	ATL	NL	130	414	101	27	3	13	(10	3)	173	54	46	58	49	10	112	3	1	2	8	3	.73	4	.244	.327	.418
1999	CIN	NL	133	296	75	8	5	11	(5	6)	126	55	44	44	37	3	81	3	0	4	11	4	.73	5	.253	.338	.426
2000	CIN	NL	148	270	72	13	4	15	(7	8)	138	55	36	53	44	7	64	7	0	2	13	6	.68	6	.267	.381	.511
2001	2 Tms	NL	149	436	110	19	8	12	(4	8)	181	62	61	59	44	4	102	2	10	6	16	8	.67	8	.252	.322	.415
2002	KC	AL	144	475	118	27	6	12	(7	5)	193	65	56	64	56	1	105	3	7	2	23	9	.72	5	.248	.330	.406
2003	KC	AL	104	389	102	20	5	13	(8	5)	171	61	55	60	39	3	88	2	6	2	8	10	.44	8	.262	.331	.440
2004	SF	NL	140	464	119	21	6	13	(4	9)	191	77	62	68	70	3	106	2	6	5	5	2	.71	9	.256	.353	.412
2005	2 Tms	NL	126	268	64	16	1	5	(4	1)	97	35	36	36	31	3	52	2	2	4	4	0	1.00	7	.239	.318	.362
01	Cin	NL	86	231	56	10	1	7	(1	6)	89	31	30	28	23	1	55	1	5	5	12	5	.71	4	.242	.308	.385
01	ChC	NL	63	205	54	9	7	5	(3	2)	92	31	31	31	23	3	47	1	5	1	4	3	.57	4	.263	.339	.449

Year	Team	Lg	G	AB	H	2B	3B	HR	(Hm	Rd)	TB	R	RBI	RC	TBB	IBB	SO	HBP	SH	SF	SB	CS	SB%	GDP	Avg	OBP	Slg
05	SF	NL	104	250	60	16	1	5	(1	4)	93	32	33	33	28	3	48	2	2	4	4	0	1.00	6	.240	.317	.372
05	Phi	NL	22	18	4	0	0	0	(0	0)	4	3	3	3	3	0	4	0	0	0	0	0	-	1	.222	.333	.222
11 ML YEARS			1382	4027	1036	204	49	124	(57	67)	1710	622	522	593	474	31	946	38	41	32	112	56	.67	65	.257	.339	.425

T.J. Tucker

Pitches: R **Bats:** R **Pos:** RP-13   **Ht:** 6'3" **Wt:** 245 **Born:** 8/20/1978 **Age:** 27

Year	Team	Lg	G	GS	CG	GF	IP	BFP	H	R	ER	HR	SH	SF	HB	TBB	IBB	SO	WP	Bk	W	L	Pct	ShO	Sv-Op	Hld	ERC	ERA
2005	NewOr*	AAA	2	2	0	0	4.0	14	2	0	0	0	0	0	0	0	0	2	0	0	0	0	-	0	0--	-	0.54	0.00
2000	MON	NL	2	2	0	0	7.0	35	11	9	9	5	0	0	0	3	0	2	1	0	0	1	.000	0	0-0	0	12.90	11.57
2002	MON	NL	57	0	0	19	61.1	276	69	32	28	5	5	2	0	31	9	42	4	0	6	3	.667	0	4-7	17	4.84	4.11
2003	MON	NL	45	7	0	7	80.0	349	90	49	42	8	0	1	4	20	1	47	1	0	2	3	.400	0	0-2	3	4.33	4.73
2004	MON	NL	54	1	0	15	67.2	291	73	28	28	5	3	2	4	17	6	44	1	1	4	2	.667	0	0-2	3	3.83	3.72
2005	WAS	NL	13	0	0	1	12.2	58	20	9	9	4	1	1	0	2	0	5	1	0	1	0	1.000	0	0-0	0	8.40	6.39
5 ML YEARS			171	10	0	42	228.2	1009	263	127	116	27	9	6	8	73	16	140	8	1	13	9	.591	0	4-11	23	4.76	4.57

Derrick Turnbow

Pitches: R **Bats:** R **Pos:** RP-69   **Ht:** 6'3" **Wt:** 200 **Born:** 1/25/1978 **Age:** 28

Year	Team	Lg	G	GS	CG	GF	IP	BFP	H	R	ER	HR	SH	SF	HB	TBB	IBB	SO	WP	Bk	W	L	Pct	ShO	Sv-Op	Hld	ERC	ERA
2000	ANA	AL	24	1	0	0	38.0	181	36	21	20	7	0	0	0	36	0	25	0	0	0	0	-	0	0-0	0	6.74	4.74
2003	ANA	AL	11	0	0	7	15.1	53	7	1	1	0	0	0	0	3	0	15	0	0	2	0	1.000	0	0-0	0	0.79	0.59
2004	ANA	AL	4	0	0	4	6.1	26	2	0	0	0	0	0	0	7	0	3	0	0	0	0	-	0	0-0	0	2.47	0.00
2005	MIL	NL	69	0	0	62	67.1	271	49	15	13	5	0	0	1	24	2	64	9	0	7	1	.875	0	39-43	2	2.35	1.74
4 ML YEARS			108	1	0	73	127.0	531	94	37	34	12	0	0	1	70	2	107	9	0	9	1	.900	0	39-43	2	3.25	2.41

Jason Tyner

Bats: L **Throws:** L **Pos:** LF-12; DH-3; CF-2; RF-2; PR-1   **Ht:** 6'1" **Wt:** 168 **Born:** 4/23/1977 **Age:** 29

Year	Team	Lg	G	AB	H	2B	3B	HR	(Hm	Rd)	TB	R	RBI	RC	TBB	IBB	SO	HBP	SH	SF	SB	CS	SB%	GDP	Avg	OBP	Slg
2005	Roch*	AAA	133	524	150	18	2	1	(-	-)	175	81	36	68	48	0	57	5	13	1	18	6	.75	9	.286	.351	.334
2000	2 Tms		50	124	28	4	0	0	(0	0)	32	9	13	9	5	0	16	2	8	3	7	2	.78	2	.226	.261	.258
2001	TB	AL	105	396	111	8	5	0	(0	0)	129	51	21	43	15	0	42	3	1	1	31	6	.84	6	.280	.311	.326
2002	TB	AL	44	168	36	2	1	0	(0	0)	40	17	9	8	7	0	19	1	3	1	7	1	.88	1	.214	.249	.238
2003	TB	AL	46	90	25	7	0	0	(0	0)	32	12	6	12	10	0	12	0	2	0	2	1	.67	1	.278	.350	.356
2005	MIN	AL	18	56	18	1	1	0	(0	0)	21	8	5	8	4	0	4	0	1	0	2	0	1.00	2	.321	.367	.375
00	NYM	NL	13	41	8	2	0	0	(0	0)	10	3	5	2	1	0	4	1	3	2	1	1	.50	1	.195	.222	.244
00	TB	NL	37	83	20	2	0	0	(0	0)	22	6	8	7	4	0	12	1	5	1	6	1	.86	1	.241	.281	.265
5 ML YEARS			263	834	218	22	7	0	(0	0)	254	97	54	80	41	0	93	6	18	5	49	10	.83	12	.261	.299	.305

Ugueth Urbina

Pitches: R **Bats:** R **Pos:** RP-81   **Ht:** 6'0" **Wt:** 205 **Born:** 2/15/1974 **Age:** 32

Year	Team	Lg	G	GS	CG	GF	IP	BFP	H	R	ER	HR	SH	SF	HB	TBB	IBB	SO	WP	Bk	W	L	Pct	ShO	Sv-Op	Hld	ERC	ERA
1995	MON	NL	7	4	0	0	23.1	109	26	17	16	6	2	0	0	14	1	15	2	0	2	2	.500	0	0-0	0	6.66	6.17
1996	MON	NL	33	17	0	2	114.0	484	102	54	47	18	1	3	1	44	4	108	3	1	10	5	.667	0	0-1	6	3.78	3.71
1997	MON	NL	63	0	0	50	64.1	276	52	29	27	9	3	0	1	29	2	84	2	0	5	8	.385	0	27-32	1	3.42	3.78
1998	MON	NL	64	0	0	59	69.1	272	37	11	10	2	2	1	0	33	2	94	3	2	6	3	.667	0	34-38	0	1.59	1.30
1999	MON	NL	71	0	0	62	75.2	323	59	35	31	6	1	2	0	36	6	100	6	0	6	6	.500	0	41-50	0	2.85	3.69
2000	MON	NL	13	0	0	11	13.1	54	11	6	6	1	0	0	0	5	0	22	1	0	0	1	.000	0	8-10	0	2.95	4.05
2001	2 Tms		64	0	0	53	66.2	278	58	29	27	9	2	1	0	24	1	89	2	1	2	2	.500	0	24-28	3	3.41	3.65
2002	BOS	AL	61	0	0	55	60.0	242	44	21	20	8	1	3	0	20	5	71	3	1	1	6	.143	0	40-46	0	2.50	3.00
2003	2 Tms		72	0	0	48	77.0	316	56	25	24	8	6	5	0	31	2	78	4	1	3	4	.429	0	32-38	11	2.60	2.81
2004	DET	AL	54	0	0	46	54.0	234	38	28	27	7	1	2	3	32	3	56	2	0	4	6	.400	0	21-24	0	3.47	4.50
2005	2 Tms		81	0	0	22	79.2	330	56	34	32	12	0	1	1	39	4	97	1	0	5	6	.455	0	10-18	21	3.12	3.62
01	Mon	NL	45	0	0	40	46.2	201	42	24	22	8	1	1	0	21	1	57	2	1	2	1	.667	0	15-18	1	4.13	4.24
01	Bos	AL	19	0	0	13	20.0	77	16	5	5	1	1	0	0	3	0	32	0	0	0	1	.000	0	9-10	2	1.88	2.25
03	Tex	AL	39	0	0	37	38.2	167	33	19	18	6	4	3	0	18	2	41	2	1	0	4	.000	0	26-30	0	3.74	4.19
03	Fla	NL	33	0	0	11	38.1	149	23	6	6	2	2	2	0	13	0	37	2	0	3	0	1.000	0	6-8	11	1.61	1.41
05	Det	AL	25	0	0	14	27.1	116	21	9	8	4	0	0	1	14	2	31	1	0	1	3	.250	0	9-11	3	3.58	2.63
05	Phi	NL	56	0	0	8	52.1	214	35	25	24	8	0	1	0	25	2	66	0	0	4	3	.571	0	1-7	18	2.89	4.13
11 ML YEARS			583	21	0	408	697.1	2918	539	289	267	86	19	18	6	307	30	814	29	6	44	49	.473	0	237-285	42	3.10	3.45

Juan Uribe

Bats: R **Throws:** R **Pos:** SS-146; PR-2   **Ht:** 5'11" **Wt:** 173 **Born:** 7/22/1979 **Age:** 26

Year	Team	Lg	G	AB	H	2B	3B	HR	(Hm	Rd)	TB	R	RBI	RC	TBB	IBB	SO	HBP	SH	SF	SB	CS	SB%	GDP	Avg	OBP	Slg
2001	COL	NL	72	273	82	15	11	8	(3	5)	143	32	53	44	8	1	55	2	0	0	3	0	1.00	6	.300	.325	.524
2002	COL	NL	155	566	136	25	7	6	(4	4)	193	69	49	53	34	1	120	5	7	6	9	2	.82	17	.240	.286	.341
2003	COL	NL	87	316	80	19	3	10	(6	4)	135	45	33	45	17	0	60	3	6	1	7	2	.78	3	.253	.297	.427
2004	CHA	AL	134	502	142	31	6	23	(16	7)	254	82	74	81	32	1	96	3	11	5	9	11	.45	10	.283	.327	.506
2005	CHA	AL	146	481	121	23	3	16	(10	6)	198	58	71	59	34	0	77	4	11	10	4	6	.40	7	.252	.301	.412
5 ML YEARS			594	2138	561	113	30	63	(39	24)	923	286	280	282	125	3	408	17	35	22	32	21	.60	43	.262	.305	.432

Chase Utley

Bats: L Throws: R Pos: 2B-135; 1B-8; PH-6   Ht: 6'1" Wt: 170 Born: 12/17/1978 Age: 27

									BATTING											BASERUNNING				AVERAGES		
Year	Team	Lg	G	AB	H	2B	3B	HR	(Hm	Rd)	TB	R	RBI	RC	TBB	IBB	SO	HBP	SH	SF	SB	CS	SB%	GDP	Avg	OBP	Slg
2003	PHI	NL	43	134	32	10	1	2	(1	1)	50	13	21	19	11	0	22	6	0	1	2	0	1.00	3	.239	.322	.373
2004	PHI	NL	94	267	71	11	2	13	(8	5)	125	36	57	37	15	1	40	2	1	2	4	1	.80	5	.266	.308	.468
2005	PHI	NL	147	543	158	39	6	28	(12	16)	293	93	105	102	69	5	109	9	0	7	16	3	.84	10	.291	.376	.540
	3 ML YEARS		284	944	261	60	9	43	(21	22)	468	142	183	158	95	6	171	17	1	10	22	4	.85	18	.276	.350	.496

Ismael Valdez

Pitches: R Bats: R Pos: SP-7; RP-7   Ht: 6'4" Wt: 225 Born: 8/21/1973 Age: 32

			HOW MUCH HE PITCHED						WHAT HE GAVE UP												THE RESULTS							
Year	Team	Lg	G	GS	CG	GF	IP	BFP	H	R	ER	HR	SH	SF	HB	TBB	IBB	SO	WP	Bk	W	L	Pct	ShO	Sv-Op	Hld	ERC	ERA
2005	Jupiter*	A+	2	2	0	0	8.0	33	7	7	7	1	0	0	0	2	0	5	1	0	1	1	.500	0	0- -	-	2.93	7.88
2005	Albq*	AAA	1	1	0	0	6.0	25	3	0	0	0	0	0	0	4	0	4	0	0	1	0	1.000	0	0- -	-	1.79	0.00
1994	LA	NL	21	1	0	7	28.1	115	21	10	10	2	3	0	0	10	2	28	1	2	3	1	.750	0	0-0	4	2.25	3.18
1995	LA	NL	33	27	6	1	197.2	804	168	76	67	17	10	5	1	51	5	150	1	3	13	11	.542	2	1-1	2	2.62	3.05
1996	LA	NL	33	33	0	0	225.0	945	219	94	83	20	7	7	3	54	10	173	1	5	15	7	.682	0	0-0	0	3.18	3.32
1997	LA	NL	30	30	0	0	196.2	795	171	68	58	16	11	3	3	47	1	140	3	2	10	11	.476	0	0-0	0	2.72	2.65
1998	LA	NL	27	27	2	0	174.0	745	171	82	77	17	5	3	2	66	4	122	4	2	11	10	.524	2	0-0	0	3.89	3.98
1999	LA	NL	32	32	2	0	203.1	871	213	97	90	32	9	8	6	58	2	143	6	0	9	14	.391	1	0-0	0	4.38	3.98
2000	2 Tms	NL	21	20	0	1	107.0	469	124	69	67	22	0	4	3	40	2	74	0	0	2	7	.222	0	0-0	0	5.89	5.64
2001	ANA	AL	27	27	1	0	163.2	699	177	82	81	20	3	0	8	50	3	100	3	0	9	13	.409	0	0-0	0	4.57	4.45
2002	2 Tms	AL	31	31	1	0	196.0	818	194	94	91	26	2	4	9	47	1	102	0	2	8	12	.400	0	0-0	0	3.80	4.18
2003	TEX	AL	22	22	0	0	115.0	511	148	83	78	23	4	7	5	29	0	47	2	0	8	8	.500	0	0-0	0	6.14	6.10
2004	2 Tms	NL	34	31	1	2	170.0	751	202	105	98	33	10	4	2	49	3	67	1	0	14	9	.609	1	0-0	0	5.38	5.19
2005	FLA	NL	14	7	0	1	50.2	237	64	32	30	6	4	2	5	22	6	27	1	2	2	2	.500	0	0-0	0	6.12	5.33
00	ChC	NL	12	12	0	0	67.0	291	71	40	40	17	0	2	2	27	2	45	0	0	2	4	.333	0	0-0	0	5.72	5.37
00	LA	NL	9	8	0	1	40.0	178	53	29	27	5	0	2	1	13	0	29	0	0	0	3	.000	0	0-0	0	6.15	6.08
02	Tex	AL	23	23	0	0	146.2	608	135	65	64	19	2	2	9	36	1	75	0	2	6	9	.400	0	0-0	0	3.47	3.93
02	Sea	AL	8	8	1	0	49.1	210	59	29	27	7	0	2	0	11	0	27	0	0	2	3	.400	0	0-0	0	4.86	4.93
04	SD	NL	23	20	1	2	114.0	509	141	75	70	21	8	2	2	31	1	37	1	0	9	6	.600	1	0-0	0	5.56	5.53
04	Fla	NL	11	11	0	0	56.0	242	61	30	28	12	2	2	0	18	2	30	0	0	5	3	.625	0	0-0	0	5.02	4.50
	12 ML YEARS		325	288	13	12	1827.1	7760	1872	892	830	234	68	47	47	523	39	1173	23	18	104	105	.498	6	1-1	6	4.03	4.09

Wilson Valdez

Bats: R Throws: R Pos: SS-50; PH-1   Ht: 5'11" Wt: 160 Born: 5/20/1978 Age: 28

									BATTING											BASERUNNING				AVERAGES		
Year	Team	Lg	G	AB	H	2B	3B	HR	(Hm	Rd)	TB	R	RBI	RC	TBB	IBB	SO	HBP	SH	SF	SB	CS	SB%	GDP	Avg	OBP	Slg
1999	Expos	R	22	82	24	2	0	0	(-	-)	26	12	7	11	5	0	7	0	2	1	10	0	1.00	1	.293	.330	.317
1999	Vrmnt	A-	36	130	32	7	0	1	(-	-)	42	19	10	10	7	0	21	0	0	1	4	3	.57	3	.246	.283	.323
2000	Vrmnt	A-	65	248	66	8	1	1	(-	-)	79	32	30	25	17	0	32	1	3	3	16	9	.64	3	.266	.312	.319
2001	Clinton	A	59	214	54	8	1	0	(-	-)	64	31	11	16	9	0	22	2	5	2	6	7	.46	5	.252	.286	.299
2001	Jupiter	A+	64	233	58	13	2	2	(-	-)	81	34	19	22	10	0	33	2	10	0	7	3	.70	4	.249	.286	.348
2002	Portlnd	AA	114	375	98	19	5	1	(-	-)	130	51	30	36	15	1	47	4	3	4	18	6	.75	12	.261	.294	.347
2003	Carlina	AA	37	144	45	6	2	0	(-	-)	55	28	14	23	15	1	17	0	7	2	16	5	.76	2	.313	.373	.382
2003	Albq	AAA	90	338	97	12	4	0	(-	-)	117	45	18	39	19	2	37	1	12	1	33	9	.79	10	.287	.326	.346
2004	Charltt	AAA	70	281	85	7	2	2	(-	-)	102	37	15	35	12	0	40	3	15	0	13	5	.72	6	.302	.338	.363
2004	Albq	AAA	66	285	91	11	3	2	(-	-)	114	36	25	39	16	0	35	2	6	2	19	12	.61	8	.319	.357	.400
2005	Tacom	AAA	1	4	0	0	0	0	(-	-)	0	0	1	0	0	0	1	0	0	0	0	0	-	0	.000	.000	.000
2005	Portlnd	AAA	50	155	38	5	3	1	(-	-)	52	14	15	18	15	0	27	0	4	1	8	0	1.00	4	.245	.310	.335
2004	CHA	AL	19	43	10	1	0	1	(1	0)	14	8	4	2	2	0	5	0	1	0	1	2	.33	1	.233	.267	.326
2005	2 Tms	AL	51	139	28	7	1	0	(0	0)	37	9	9	8	8	0	26	0	1	0	2	2	.50	2	.201	.245	.266
05	Sea	AL	42	126	25	5	1	0	(0	0)	32	9	8	6	6	0	25	0	1	0	2	2	.50	1	.198	.235	.254
05	SD	NL	9	13	3	2	0	0	(0	0)	5	0	1	2	2	0	1	0	0	0	0	0	-	1	.231	.333	.385
	2 ML YEARS		70	182	38	8	1	1	(1	0)	51	17	13	10	10	0	31	0	2	0	3	4	.43	3	.209	.250	.280

Eric Valent

Bats: L Throws: L Pos: PH-18; RF-8; LF-2; CF-2   Ht: 6'0" Wt: 191 Born: 4/4/1977 Age: 29

									BATTING											BASERUNNING				AVERAGES		
Year	Team	Lg	G	AB	H	2B	3B	HR	(Hm	Rd)	TB	R	RBI	RC	TBB	IBB	SO	HBP	SH	SF	SB	CS	SB%	GDP	Avg	OBP	Slg
2005	Norfolk*	AAA	79	275	70	13	1	9	(-	-)	112	44	38	47	55	4	58	1	1	1	1	1	.50	6	.255	.380	.407
2001	PHI	NL	22	41	4	2	0	0	(0	0)	6	3	1	0	4	0	11	1	0	0	0	0	-	0	.098	.196	.146
2002	PHI	NL	7	10	2	0	0	0	(0	0)	2	1	0	0	0	0	3	0	0	0	0	0	-	1	.200	.200	.200
2003	CIN	NL	18	42	9	0	0	0	(0	0)	9	3	1	2	2	0	9	0	0	0	0	0	-	0	.214	.250	.214
2004	NYN	NL	130	270	72	15	2	13	(5	8)	130	39	34	36	28	4	61	1	0	1	0	1	.00	10	.267	.337	.481
2005	NYN	NL	28	43	8	3	0	0	(0	0)	11	4	1	3	7	3	17	0	0	0	0	0	-	0	.186	.300	.256
	5 ML YEARS		205	406	95	20	2	13	(5	8)	158	50	37	41	41	7	101	2	0	1	0	1	.00	11	.234	.307	.389

Javier Valentin

Bats: B Throws: R Pos: C-62; PH-13; 1B-2   Ht: 5'10" Wt: 192 Born: 9/19/1975 Age: 30

									BATTING											BASERUNNING				AVERAGES		
Year	Team	Lg	G	AB	H	2B	3B	HR	(Hm	Rd)	TB	R	RBI	RC	TBB	IBB	SO	HBP	SH	SF	SB	CS	SB%	GDP	Avg	OBP	Slg
1997	MIN	AL	4	7	2	0	0	0	(0	0)	2	1	0	1	0	0	3	0	0	0	0	0	-	0	.286	.286	.286
1998	MIN	AL	55	162	32	7	1	3	(1	2)	50	11	18	10	11	1	30	0	3	1	0	0	-	7	.198	.247	.309
1999	MIN	AL	78	218	54	12	1	5	(2	3)	83	22	28	27	22	0	39	1	1	5	0	0	-	2	.248	.313	.381
2002	MIN	AL	4	4	2	0	0	0	(0	0)	2	0	0	0	0	0	0	0	0	0	0	0	-	0	.500	.500	.500
2003	TB	AL	49	135	30	7	1	3	(2	1)	48	13	15	11	5	0	31	1	0	1	0	0	-	7	.222	.254	.356

Year	Team	Lg	G	AB	H	2B	3B	HR	(Hm	Rd)	TB	R	RBI	RC	TBB	IBB	SO	HBP	SH	SF	SB	CS	SB%	GDP	Avg	OBP	Slg
																	BATTING					**BASERUNNING**			**AVERAGES**		
2004	CIN	NL	82	202	47	10	1	6	(2	4)	77	18	20	20	17	3	36	1	0	2	0	0	-	4	.233	.293	.381
2005	CIN	NL	76	221	62	11	0	14	(7	7)	115	36	50	41	30	3	37	0	0	3	0	0	-	5	.281	.362	.520
7 ML YEARS			348	949	229	47	4	31	(14	17)	377	101	131	110	85	7	176	3	4	12	0	0	-	25	.241	.302	.397

Jose Valentin

Bats: L **Throws:** R **Pos:** 3B-29; LF-22; PH-11; SS-1   **Ht:** 5'10" **Wt:** 185 **Born:** 10/12/1969 **Age:** 36

Year	Team	Lg	G	AB	H	2B	3B	HR	(Hm	Rd)	TB	R	RBI	RC	TBB	IBB	SO	HBP	SH	SF	SB	CS	SB%	GDP	Avg	OBP	Slg
2005	LsVgs*	AAA	12	35	14	3	0	2	(-	-)	23	8	5	11	7	1	6	1	0	0	1	0	1.00	0	.400	.512	.657
1992	MIL	AL	4	3	0	0	0	0	(0	0)	0	1	1	0	0	0	0	0	0	1	0	0	-	0	.000	.000	.000
1993	MIL	AL	19	53	13	1	2	1	(1	0)	21	10	7	8	7	1	16	1	2	0	1	0	1.00	1	.245	.344	.396
1994	MIL	AL	97	285	68	19	0	11	(8	3)	120	47	46	43	38	1	75	2	4	2	12	3	.80	1	.239	.330	.421
1995	MIL	AL	112	338	74	23	3	11	(3	8)	136	62	49	42	37	0	83	0	7	4	16	8	.67	0	.219	.293	.402
1996	MIL	AL	154	552	143	33	7	24	(10	14)	262	90	95	91	66	9	145	0	6	4	17	4	.81	4	.259	.336	.475
1997	MIL	AL	136	494	125	23	1	17	(4	13)	201	58	58	64	39	4	109	4	4	5	19	8	.70	5	.253	.310	.407
1998	MIL	NL	151	428	96	24	0	16	(7	9)	168	65	49	57	63	8	105	1	2	3	10	7	.59	2	.224	.323	.393
1999	MIL	NL	89	259	58	9	5	10	(3	7)	107	45	38	40	48	7	52	2	2	5	3	2	.60	3	.227	.347	.418
2000	CHA	AL	144	568	155	37	6	25	(16	9)	279	107	92	97	59	1	106	4	13	4	19	2	.90	11	.273	.343	.491
2001	CHA	AL	124	438	113	22	2	28	(14	14)	223	74	68	74	50	2	114	3	8	3	9	6	.60	7	.258	.336	.509
2002	CHA	AL	135	474	118	26	4	25	(15	10)	227	70	75	75	43	2	99	2	3	5	3	3	.50	9	.249	.311	.479
2003	CHA	AL	144	503	119	26	2	28	(14	14)	233	79	74	72	54	4	114	3	7	2	8	3	.73	6	.237	.313	.463
2004	CHA	AL	125	450	97	20	3	30	(16	14)	213	73	70	64	43	4	139	3	6	2	8	6	.57	5	.216	.287	.473
2005	LAN	NL	56	147	25	4	2	2	(0	2)	39	17	14	15	31	2	38	4	0	2	3	1	.75	2	.170	.326	.265
14 ML YEARS			1490	4989	1204	267	37	228	(111	117)	2229	798	736	742	578	45	1195	29	64	42	128	53	.71	56	.241	.321	.447

Joe Valentine

Pitches: R **Bats:** R **Pos:** RP-16   **Ht:** 6'2" **Wt:** 195 **Born:** 12/24/1979 **Age:** 26

Year	Team	Lg	G	GS	CG	GF	IP	BFP	H	R	ER	HR	SH	SF	HB	TBB	IBB	SO	WP	Bk	W	L	Pct	ShO	Sv-Op	Hld	ERC	ERA
2005	Lsvlle*	AAA	49	0	0	22	53.2	256	56	36	34	4	2	1	2	39	4	44	7	0	0	7	.000	0	3-	-	5.35	5.70
2003	CIN	NL	2	0	0	1	2.0	12	5	4	4	1	0	0	0	1	0	1	0	0	0	0	-	0	0-0	0	18.76	18.00
2004	CIN	NL	24	1	0	13	29.1	136	23	18	17	4	0	0	2	25	1	29	2	0	2	3	.400	0	4-4	5	5.08	5.22
2005	CIN	NL	16	0	0	5	14.1	76	18	15	13	4	1	1	2	11	0	9	1	0	1	0	.000	0	0-1	2	8.96	8.16
3 ML YEARS			42	1	0	19	45.2	224	46	37	34	9	1	1	4	37	1	39	3	0	2	4	.333	0	4-5	7	6.77	6.70

Jose Valverde

Pitches: R **Bats:** R **Pos:** RP-61   **Ht:** 6'4" **Wt:** 254 **Born:** 7/24/1979 **Age:** 26

Year	Team	Lg	G	GS	CG	GF	IP	BFP	H	R	ER	HR	SH	SF	HB	TBB	IBB	SO	WP	Bk	W	L	Pct	ShO	Sv-Op	Hld	ERC	ERA
2005	Tucsn*	AAA	2	0	0	0	2.0	8	1	0	0	0	0	0	0	1	0	3	0	0	0	0	-	0	0-	-	1.41	0.00
2003	ARI	NL	54	0	0	33	50.1	204	24	16	12	4	0	1	2	26	2	71	2	0	2	1	.667	0	10-11	8	1.77	2.15
2004	ARI	NL	29	0	0	20	29.2	131	23	17	14	7	3	2	1	17	4	38	4	0	1	2	.333	0	8-10	5	4.25	4.25
2005	ARI	NL	61	0	0	34	66.1	268	51	19	18	5	3	1	2	20	1	75	3	0	3	4	.429	0	15-17	7	2.43	2.44
3 ML YEARS			144	0	0	87	146.1	603	98	52	44	16	6	4	5	63	7	184	9	0	6	7	.462	0	33-38	20	2.53	2.71

John Van Benschoten

Pitches: R **Bats:** R **Pos:** P   **Ht:** 6'4" **Wt:** 217 **Born:** 4/14/1980 **Age:** 26

Year	Team	Lg	G	GS	CG	GF	IP	BFP	H	R	ER	HR	SH	SF	HB	TBB	IBB	SO	WP	Bk	W	L	Pct	ShO	Sv-Op	Hld	ERC	ERA
2001	Wmspt	A-	9	9	0	0	25.2	104	23	11	10	0	0	0	1	10	0	19	5	0	0	2	.000	0	0-	-	3.09	3.51
2002	Hickory	A	27	27	0	0	148.0	620	119	57	46	6	4	2	7	62	1	145	7	0	11	4	.733	0	0-	-	2.86	2.80
2003	Lynbrg	A+	9	9	0	0	48.2	192	33	14	12	1	1	0	1	18	0	61	4	0	6	0	1.000	0	0-	-	1.94	2.22
2003	Altna	AA	17	17	1	0	90.1	399	95	46	37	5	4	1	6	34	1	78	2	2	7	6	.538	0	0-	-	4.16	3.69
2004	Nashv	AAA	23	23	0	0	131.2	574	135	75	69	16	2	3	9	49	1	101	4	1	4	11	.267	0	0-	-	4.54	4.72
2004	PIT	NL	6	5	0	0	28.2	135	33	27	22	3	2	2	2	19	0	18	1	0	1	3	.250	0	0-0	0	6.47	6.91

Jermaine Van Buren

Pitches: R **Bats:** R **Pos:** RP-6   **Ht:** 6'1" **Wt:** 220 **Born:** 7/2/1980 **Age:** 25

Year	Team	Lg	G	GS	CG	GF	IP	BFP	H	R	ER	HR	SH	SF	HB	TBB	IBB	SO	WP	Bk	W	L	Pct	ShO	Sv-Op	Hld	ERC	ERA
1998	Rckies	R	12	11	1	0	65.0	259	42	20	16	2	0	0	3	22	0	92	3	2	7	2	.778	1	0-	-	1.80	2.22
1998	Portlnd	A-	2	2	0	0	10.0	44	7	4	4	0	0	2	1	7	0	9	1	1	0	0	-	0	0-	-	3.21	3.60
1999	Ashvlle	A	28	28	0	0	143.0	642	143	87	78	16	1	13	19	70	0	133	19	2	7	10	.412	0	0-	-	5.10	4.91
2000	Portlnd	A-	13	13	0	0	69.0	291	54	27	20	1	4	2	3	30	0	41	3	2	4	5	.444	0	0-	-	2.61	2.61
2001	Casper	R+	6	3	1	0	23.2	106	25	15	14	2	1	1	0	20	0	25	1	0	3	0	1.000	0	0-	-	4.26	5.32
2001	Tri-Cit	A-	1	1	0	0	5.0	25	7	4	4	0	0	0	0	3	0	2	1	0	0	0	-	0	0-	-	6.28	7.20
2002	Ashvlle	A	30	17	0	4	107.0	480	115	71	59	13	4	10	14	44	1	88	6	5	6	9	.400	0	0-	-	5.26	4.96
2004	Lansng	A	3	0	0	1	5.0	26	6	1	1	0	0	1	0	5	0	7	2	0	0	1	.000	0	0-	-	7.80	1.80
2004	WTenn	A	51	0	0	46	53.0	206	23	11	11	2	0	0	1	24	0	64	4	0	3	2	.600	0	21-	-	1.32	1.87
2004	Iowa	AAA	3	0	0	2	4.1	16	3	1	1	1	0	0	0	0	0	5	0	0	0	0	-	0	1-	-	1.70	2.08
2005	Iowa	AAA	52	0	0	42	54.2	219	33	13	12	5	5	1	3	22	2	65	1	0	2	3	.400	0	25-	-	2.14	1.98
2005	CHN	NL	6	0	0	1	6.0	27	2	2	1	0	0	0	2	9	2	3	0	0	0	2	.000	0	0-0	0	3.20	3.00

Claudio Vargas

Pitches: R **Bats:** R **Pos:** SP-23; RP-2   **Ht:** 6'3" **Wt:** 225 **Born:** 6/19/1978 **Age:** 28

Year	Team	Lg	G	GS	CG	GF	IP	BFP	H	R	ER	HR	SH	SF	HB	TBB	IBB	SO	WP	Bk	W	L	Pct	ShO	Sv-Op	Hld	ERC	ERA
2005	NewOr*	AAA	5	5	0	0	28.0	120	24	13	13	4	2	2	0	12	0	35	2	0	2	2	.500	0	0- -	-	3.62	4.18
2003	MON	NL	23	20	0	0	114.0	492	111	59	55	16	5	4	7	41	5	62	1	0	6	8	.429	0	0-0	0	4.21	4.34
2004	MON	NL	45	14	0	6	118.1	530	120	75	69	26	4	4	7	64	7	89	8	0	5	5	.500	0	0-0	3	5.84	5.25
2005	2 Tms	NL	25	23	0	0	132.1	586	146	81	77	25	6	1	7	47	5	95	6	0	9	9	.500	0	0-0	0	5.28	5.24
05	Was	NL	4	4	0	0	12.2	66	22	15	13	4	0	0	0	7	2	5	0	0	0	3	.000	0	0-0	0	11.04	9.24
05	Ari	NL	21	19	0	0	119.2	520	124	66	64	21	6	1	7	40	3	90	6	0	9	6	.600	0	0-0	0	4.74	4.81
	3 ML YEARS		93	57	0	6	364.2	1608	377	215	201	67	15	9	21	152	17	246	16	0	20	22	.476	0	0-0	3	5.11	4.96

Jason Vargas

Pitches: L **Bats:** L **Pos:** SP-13; RP-4   **Ht:** 6'0" **Wt:** 215 **Born:** 2/2/1983 **Age:** 23

Year	Team	Lg	G	GS	CG	GF	IP	BFP	H	R	ER	HR	SH	SF	HB	TBB	IBB	SO	WP	Bk	W	L	Pct	ShO	Sv-Op	Hld	ERC	ERA
2004	Jmstwn	A-	8	8	0	0	41.1	168	35	17	9	2	0	0	3	13	0	41	3	0	3	1	.750	0	0- -	-	2.94	1.96
2004	Grnsbr	A	3	3	0	0	19.0	68	9	5	5	1	2	0	0	2	0	17	0	0	2	1	.667	0	0- -	-	0.78	2.37
2005	Carlina	AA	3	3	0	0	19.0	77	13	6	6	3	2	0	0	7	0	25	0	0	1	0	1.000	0	0- -	-	2.61	2.84
2005	Jupiter	A+	9	9	0	0	55.1	227	47	24	21	6	0	0	0	14	0	60	0	0	2	3	.400	0	0- -	-	2.72	3.42
2005	Grnsbr	A	5	5	0	0	33.2	127	16	4	3	1	0	0	2	10	0	33	1	0	4	1	.800	0	0- -	-	1.20	0.80
2005	FLA	NL	17	13	1	0	73.2	325	71	34	33	4	4	1	4	31	4	59	0	0	5	5	.500	0	0-0	0	3.68	4.03

Jason Varitek

Bats: B **Throws:** R **Pos:** C-130; PH-6   **Ht:** 6'2" **Wt:** 237 **Born:** 4/11/1972 **Age:** 34

Year	Team	Lg	G	AB	H	2B	3B	HR	(Hm	Rd)	TB	R	RBI	RC	TBB	IBB	SO	HBP	SH	SF	SB	CS	SB%	GDP	Avg	OBP	Slg
1997	BOS	AL	1	1	1	0	0	0	(0	0)	1	0	0	1	0	0	0	0	0	0	0	0	-	0	1.000	1.000	1.000
1998	BOS	AL	86	221	56	13	0	7	(1	6)	90	31	33	26	17	1	45	2	4	3	2	2	.50	8	.253	.309	.407
1999	BOS	AL	144	483	130	39	2	20	(12	8)	233	70	76	75	46	2	85	2	5	8	1	2	.33	13	.269	.330	.482
2000	BOS	AL	139	448	111	31	1	10	(8)	174	55	65	59	60	3	84	6	1	4	1	1	.50	16	.248	.342	.388
2001	BOS	AL	51	174	51	11	1	7	(2	5)	85	19	25	30	21	3	35	1	1	1	0	0	-	6	.293	.371	.489
2002	BOS	AL	132	467	124	27	1	10	(4	6)	183	58	61	52	41	3	95	7	1	3	4	3	.57	13	.266	.332	.392
2003	BOS	AL	142	451	123	31	1	25	(13	12)	231	63	85	79	51	8	106	7	5	7	3	2	.60	10	.273	.351	.512
2004	BOS	AL	137	463	137	30	1	18	(8	10)	223	67	73	79	62	9	126	10	0	1	10	3	.77	11	.296	.390	.482
2005	BOS	AL	133	470	132	30	1	22	(7	15)	230	70	70	78	62	3	117	3	1	3	2	0	1.00	10	.281	.366	.489
	9 ML YEARS		965	3178	865	212	8	119	(51	68)	1450	433	488	479	360	32	693	38	18	30	23	13	.64	87	.272	.350	.456

Jorge Vasquez

Pitches: R **Bats:** R **Pos:** RP-7   **Ht:** 6'1" **Wt:** 165 **Born:** 7/16/1978 **Age:** 27

Year	Team	Lg	G	GS	CG	GF	IP	BFP	H	R	ER	HR	SH	SF	HB	TBB	IBB	SO	WP	Bk	W	L	Pct	ShO	Sv-Op	Hld	ERC	ERA
2001	Royals	R	4	2	0	1	16.0	63	10	2	2	0	0	0	2	1	0	19	0	0	0	1	.000	0	0- -	-	1.12	1.13
2001	Spkane	A-	10	8	0	0	50.1	214	50	33	28	3	1	2	5	13	0	67	3	10	1	6	.143	0	0- -	-	3.60	5.01
2002	Wilmg	A+	10	0	0	5	11.0	50	12	6	6	1	0	0	0	3	0	17	1	0	0	0	-	0	0- -	-	3.74	4.91
2002	Burlgtn	A	22	0	0	14	46.0	176	22	8	8	3	3	1	1	15	0	55	4	3	2	1	.667	0	6- -	-	1.29	1.57
2003	Wilmg	A+	17	0	0	12	23.0	102	19	7	5	1	3	0	0	14	3	31	1	0	1	2	.333	0	7- -	-	3.22	1.96
2003	Wichta	AA	36	0	0	32	51.2	211	39	12	11	3	2	2	5	18	2	52	8	1	3	1	.750	0	22- -	-	2.65	1.92
2004	Wichta	AA	49	0	0	41	59.2	263	52	34	31	3	0	0	5	27	1	71	8	0	4	5	.444	0	18- -	-	3.43	4.68
2005	Missi	AA	29	0	0	24	40.1	154	22	7	5	1	3	3	3	11	2	45	4	0	2	1	.667	0	10- -	-	1.32	1.12
2005	Rchmd	AAA	14	0	0	8	14.0	67	16	17	17	1	2	1	1	9	1	20	1	0	0	1	.000	0	2- -	-	5.77	10.93
2004	KC	AL	2	0	0	1	3.1	17	4	4	3	1	0	0	1	1	0	4	1	0	0	0	-	0	0-0	0	7.09	8.10
2005	ATL	NL	7	0	0	2	9.0	42	11	4	3	2	0	0	0	5	0	9	1	1	1	0	1.000	0	0-0	0	7.05	3.00
	2 ML YEARS		9	0	0	3	12.1	59	15	8	6	3	0	0	1	6	0	13	2	1	1	0	1.000	0	0-0	0	7.06	4.38

Javier Vazquez

Pitches: R **Bats:** R **Pos:** SP-33   **Ht:** 6'2" **Wt:** 195 **Born:** 7/25/1976 **Age:** 29

Year	Team	Lg	G	GS	CG	GF	IP	BFP	H	R	ER	HR	SH	SF	HB	TBB	IBB	SO	WP	Bk	W	L	Pct	ShO	Sv-Op	Hld	ERC	ERA
1998	MON	NL	33	32	0	1	172.1	764	196	121	116	31	9	4	11	68	2	139	2	0	5	15	.250	0	0-0	0	5.79	6.06
1999	MON	NL	26	26	3	0	154.2	667	154	98	86	20	3	3	4	52	4	113	2	0	9	8	.529	1	0-0	0	4.02	5.00
2000	MON	NL	33	33	2	0	217.2	945	247	104	98	24	11	3	5	61	10	196	3	0	11	9	.550	1	0-0	0	4.45	4.05
2001	MON	NL	32	32	5	0	223.2	898	197	92	85	24	9	2	3	44	4	208	3	1	16	11	.593	3	0-0	0	2.75	3.42
2002	MON	NL	34	34	2	0	230.1	971	243	111	100	28	15	7	4	49	6	179	3	0	10	13	.435	0	0-0	0	3.80	3.91
2003	MON	NL	34	34	4	0	230.2	938	198	93	83	28	6	6	4	57	5	241	11	1	13	12	.520	1	0-0	0	2.90	3.24
2004	NYA	AL	32	32	0	0	198.0	849	195	114	108	33	4	8	10	60	3	150	12	2	14	10	.583	0	0-0	0	4.23	4.91
2005	ARI	NL	33	33	3	0	215.2	904	223	112	106	35	13	3	5	46	4	192	7	0	11	15	.423	1	0-0	0	4.00	4.42
	8 ML YEARS		257	256	19	1	1643.0	6936	1653	845	782	223	70	36	47	437	38	1418	43	4	89	93	.489	7	0-0	0	3.90	4.28

Ramon Vazquez

Bats: L **Throws:** R **Pos:** SS-14; 2B-12; 3B-8; PH-7; PR-5; DH-1   **Ht:** 5'11" **Wt:** 170 **Born:** 8/21/1976 **Age:** 29

Year	Team	Lg	G	AB	H	2B	3B	HR	(Hm	Rd)	TB	R	RBI	RC	TBB	IBB	SO	HBP	SH	SF	SB	CS	SB%	GDP	Avg	OBP	Slg
2005	Buffalo*	AAA	21	84	18	3	1	0	(-	-)	23	13	4	6	7	0	16	0	1	0	1	1	.50	2	.214	.275	.274
2001	SEA	AL	17	35	8	0	0	0	(0	0)	8	5	4	2	0	0	3	0	1	1	0	0	-	0	.229	.222	.229
2002	SD	NL	128	423	116	21	5	2	(0	2)	153	50	32	55	45	3	79	1	3	2	7	2	.78	6	.274	.344	.362

Year	Team	Lg	G	AB	H	2B	3B	HR	(Hm	Rd)	TB	R	RBI	RC	TBB	IBB	SO	HBP	SH	SF	SB	CS	SB%	GDP	Avg	OBP	Slg

BATTING / **BASERUNNING** / **AVERAGES**

Year	Team	Lg	G	AB	H	2B	3B	HR	(Hm	Rd)	TB	R	RBI	RC	TBB	IBB	SO	HBP	SH	SF	SB	CS	SB%	GDP	Avg	OBP	Slg
2003	SD	NL	116	422	110	17	4	3	(1	2)	144	56	30	49	52	2	88	2	5	3	10	3	.77	4	.261	.342	.341
2004	SD	NL	52	115	27	3	2	1	(1	0)	37	12	13	9	11	2	24	0	4	2	1	1	.50	2	.235	.297	.322
2005	2 Tms	AL	39	85	18	5	0	0	(0	0)	23	7	5	5	5	0	17	0	2	0	0	0	-	0	.212	.256	.271
05	Bos	AL	27	61	12	2	0	0	(0	0)	14	6	4	3	3	0	14	0	2	0	0	0	-	0	.197	.234	.230
05	Cle	AL	12	24	6	3	0	0	(0	0)	9	1	1	2	2	0	3	0	0	0	0	0	-	0	.250	.308	.375
5 ML YEARS			352	1080	279	46	11	6	(2	4)	365	130	84	120	113	7	211	3	15	8	18	6	.75	12	.258	.328	.338

Mike Vento

Bats: R **Throws:** R **Pos:** RF-2; PR-1   **Ht:** 6'0" **Wt:** 195 **Born:** 5/25/1978 **Age:** 28

BATTING / **BASERUNNING** / **AVERAGES**

Year	Team	Lg	G	AB	H	2B	3B	HR	(Hm	Rd)	TB	R	RBI	RC	TBB	IBB	SO	HBP	SH	SF	SB	CS	SB%	GDP	Avg	OBP	Slg
1998	Oneont	A-	43	148	45	9	3	1	(-	-)	63	25	23	25	14	0	28	5	0	2	8	3	.73	1	.304	.379	.426
1999	Tampa	A+	70	255	66	10	1	7	(-	-)	99	37	28	31	17	1	69	3	0	2	2	3	.40	1	.259	.310	.388
1999	Grnsbr	A	40	148	37	11	1	3	(-	-)	59	20	16	20	14	1	46	2	0	1	3	1	.75	1	.250	.321	.399
2000	Tampa	A+	10	30	5	0	0	1	(-	-)	8	1	4	2	4	0	12	1	1	1	1	0	1.00	0	.167	.278	.267
2000	Grnsbr	A	84	318	83	15	2	6	(-	-)	120	49	52	49	47	0	66	11	2	3	13	8	.62	11	.261	.372	.377
2001	Tampa	A+	130	457	137	20	10	20	(-	-)	237	71	87	87	45	1	88	9	0	3	13	10	.57	9	.300	.372	.519
2002	Nrwich	AA	64	227	54	16	2	4	(-	-)	86	29	26	28	25	1	49	1	2	2	3	3	.50	6	.238	.314	.379
2003	Trentn	AA	81	314	95	19	3	9	(-	-)	147	46	56	52	22	1	52	5	0	4	4	4	.50	6	.303	.354	.468
2003	Buffalo	AAA	51	184	56	14	1	5	(-	-)	87	28	31	31	14	0	36	3	0	0	1	2	.33	6	.304	.363	.473
2004	Buffalo	AAA	122	451	124	28	1	15	(-	-)	199	64	72	68	34	3	77	9	0	7	2	3	.40	8	.275	.333	.441
2005	Clmbs	AAA	130	501	146	37	2	12	(-	-)	223	62	84	84	49	1	96	13	1	7	1	4	.20	13	.291	.365	.445
2005	NYA	AL	2	2	0	0	0	0	(0	0)	0	0	0	0	0	0	1	0	0	0	0	0	-	0	.000	.000	.000

Justin Verlander

Pitches: R **Bats:** R **Pos:** SP-2   **Ht:** 6'5" **Wt:** 200 **Born:** 2/20/1983 **Age:** 23

			HOW MUCH HE PITCHED						WHAT HE GAVE UP									THE RESULTS							
Year	Team	Lg	G	GS	CG	GF	IP	BFP	H	R	ER	HR	SH	SF	HB	TBB	IBB	SO	WP	Bk	W	L	Pct	ShO	Sv-Op	Hld	ERC	ERA
2005	Lkland	A+	13	13	2	0	86.0	347	70	19	16	3	4	2	7	19	0	104	8	2	9	2	.818	0	0--	-	2.34	1.67
2005	Erie	AA	7	7	0	0	32.2	116	11	1	1	1	1	0	1	7	0	32	0	1	2	0	1.000	0	0--	-	0.65	0.28
2005	DET	AL	2	2	0	0	11.1	54	15	9	9	1	0	0	1	5	0	7	1	0	0	2	.000	0	0-0	0	6.41	7.15

Shane Victorino

Bats: B **Throws:** R **Pos:** PH-14; CF-5; PR-5; LF-4; RF-3   **Ht:** 5'9" **Wt:** 160 **Born:** 11/30/1980 **Age:** 25

BATTING / **BASERUNNING** / **AVERAGES**

Year	Team	Lg	G	AB	H	2B	3B	HR	(Hm	Rd)	TB	R	RBI	RC	TBB	IBB	SO	HBP	SH	SF	SB	CS	SB%	GDP	Avg	OBP	Slg
1999	Gr Falls	R+	55	225	63	7	6	2	(-	-)	88	53	25	32	20	0	31	0	6	3	20	5	.80	3	.280	.335	.391
2000	Yakima	A-	61	236	58	7	2	2	(-	-)	75	32	20	25	20	1	44	3	12	2	21	9	.70	3	.246	.310	.318
2001	Wilmg	A+	112	435	123	21	9	4	(-	-)	174	71	32	65	36	0	61	5	13	1	47	13	.78	3	.283	.344	.400
2001	VeroB	A+	2	6	1	0	0	0	(-	-)	1	2	0	1	3	0	1	0	0	0	0	0	-	0	.167	.444	.167
2002	Jaxnvl	AA	122	481	124	15	1	4	(-	-)	153	61	34	56	47	0	49	4	16	2	45	16	.74	6	.258	.328	.318
2003	Jaxnvl	AA	66	266	75	9	4	2	(-	-)	98	37	15	35	21	1	41	3	2	1	16	7	.70	3	.282	.340	.368
2003	LsVgs	AAA	11	41	16	1	2	1	(-	-)	24	6	9	8	1	0	5	0	2	1	0	1	.00	1	.390	.395	.585
2004	Jaxnvl	AA	75	293	96	13	7	16	(-	-)	171	70	43	61	20	0	64	5	5	5	9	7	.56	2	.328	.375	.584
2004	LsVgs	AAA	55	200	47	9	1	3	(-	-)	67	28	20	18	11	0	37	1	4	0	7	2	.78	3	.235	.278	.335
2005	S-WB	AAA	126	494	153	25	16	18	(-	-)	264	93	70	99	51	2	74	5	5	4	17	9	.65	4	.310	.377	.534
2003	SD	NL	36	73	11	2	0	0	(0	0)	13	8	4	1	7	0	17	1	1	1	7	2	.78	5	.151	.232	.178
2005	PHI	NL	21	17	5	0	0	2	(1	1)	11	5	8	4	0	0	3	0	0	2	0	0	-	0	.294	.263	.647
2 ML YEARS			57	90	16	2	0	2	(1	1)	24	13	12	5	7	0	20	1	1	3	7	2	.78	5	.178	.238	.267

Jose Vidro

Bats: B **Throws:** R **Pos:** 2B-79; PH-8   **Ht:** 5'11" **Wt:** 195 **Born:** 8/27/1974 **Age:** 31

BATTING / **BASERUNNING** / **AVERAGES**

Year	Team	Lg	G	AB	H	2B	3B	HR	(Hm	Rd)	TB	R	RBI	RC	TBB	IBB	SO	HBP	SH	SF	SB	CS	SB%	GDP	Avg	OBP	Slg
2005	Ptomc*	A+	5	13	2	1	0	0	(-	-)	3	3	3	1	4	0	2	0	0	0	0	0	-	0	.154	.353	.231
1997	MON	NL	67	169	42	12	1	2	(0	2)	62	19	17	19	11	0	20	2	0	3	1	0	1.00	1	.249	.297	.367
1998	MON	NL	83	205	45	12	0	0	(0	0)	57	24	18	19	27	0	33	4	6	3	2	2	.50	5	.220	.318	.278
1999	MON	NL	140	494	150	45	2	12	(5	7)	235	67	59	76	29	2	51	4	2	2	0	4	.00	12	.304	.346	.476
2000	MON	NL	153	606	200	51	2	24	(11	13)	327	101	97	115	49	4	69	2	0	6	5	4	.56	17	.330	.379	.540
2001	MON	NL	124	486	155	34	1	15	(6	9)	236	82	59	81	31	2	49	10	2	2	4	1	.80	18	.319	.371	.486
2002	MON	NL	152	604	190	43	3	19	(11	8)	296	103	96	112	60	1	70	3	11	3	2	1	.67	12	.315	.378	.490
2003	MON	NL	144	509	158	36	0	15	(7	8)	239	77	65	89	69	6	50	7	2	5	3	2	.60	16	.310	.397	.470
2004	MON	NL	110	412	121	24	0	14	(6	8)	187	51	60	59	49	7	43	0	4	2	3	1	.75	14	.294	.367	.454
2005	WAS	NL	87	309	85	21	2	7	(2	5)	131	38	32	41	31	3	30	1	2	4	0	0	-	8	.275	.339	.424
9 ML YEARS			1060	3794	1146	278	11	108	(48	60)	1770	562	503	611	356	25	415	33	29	30	20	15	.57	103	.302	.364	.467

Oscar Villarreal

Pitches: R **Bats:** L **Pos:** RP-11   **Ht:** 6'0" **Wt:** 205 **Born:** 11/22/1981 **Age:** 24

			HOW MUCH HE PITCHED						WHAT HE GAVE UP									THE RESULTS							
Year	Team	Lg	G	GS	CG	GF	IP	BFP	H	R	ER	HR	SH	SF	HB	TBB	IBB	SO	WP	Bk	W	L	Pct	ShO	Sv-Op	Hld	ERC	ERA
2005	Tucsn*	AAA	12	8	0	0	17.1	75	19	12	10	1	0	3	0	4	0	8	1	0	0	3	.000	0	0--	-	3.56	5.19
2003	ARI	NL	86	1	0	14	98.0	422	80	40	28	6	9	3	3	46	10	80	3	2	10	7	.588	0	0-4	10	2.97	2.57
2004	ARI	NL	17	0	0	4	18.0	84	25	14	14	3	3	0	1	7	1	17	5	0	0	2	.000	0	0-0	2	7.13	7.00
2005	ARI	NL	11	0	0	0	13.2	57	11	8	8	2	2	1	1	6	2	5	0	0	2	0	1.000	0	0-2	2	3.59	5.27
3 ML YEARS			114	1	0	18	129.2	563	116	62	50	11	14	4	5	59	13	102	8	2	12	9	.571	0	0-6	14	3.55	3.47

Ron Villone

Pitches: L Bats: L Pos: RP-79   Ht: 6'4" Wt: 235 Born: 1/16/1970 Age: 36

			HOW MUCH HE PITCHED						WHAT HE GAVE UP										THE RESULTS							
Year	Team	Lg	G	GS	CG	GF	IP	BFP	H	R	ER	HR	SH	SF	HB	TBB	IBB	SO	WP	Bk	W	L	Pct	ShO	Sv-Op	Hld	ERC	ERA
1995	2 Tms		38	0	0	15	45.0	212	44	31	29	11	3	1	1	34	0	63	3	0	2	3	.400	0	1-5	6	6.57	5.80
1996	2 Tms		44	0	0	19	43.0	182	31	15	15	6	0	2	5	25	0	38	2	0	1	1	.500	0	2-3	9	4.08	3.14
1997	MIL	AL	50	0	0	15	52.2	238	54	23	20	4	2	0	1	36	2	40	3	0	1	0	1.000	0	0-2	8	5.30	3.42
1998	CLE	AL	25	0	0	6	27.0	129	30	18	18	3	2	2	2	22	0	15	0	0	0	0	-	0	0-0	1	7.01	6.00
1999	CIN	NL	29	22	0	2	142.2	610	114	70	67	8	9	3	5	73	2	97	6	0	9	7	.563	0	2-2	0	3.20	4.23
2000	CIN	NL	35	23	2	5	141.0	643	154	95	85	22	10	8	9	78	3	77	7	0	10	10	.500	0	0-0	1	5.97	5.43
2001	2 Tms		53	12	0	12	114.2	523	133	81	75	18	1	1	5	53	5	113	4	1	6	10	.375	0	0-0	6	5.81	5.89
2002	PIT	NL	45	7	0	6	93.0	399	95	63	60	8	5	3	5	34	3	55	1	0	4	6	.400	0	0-1	0	4.18	5.81
2003	HOU	NL	19	19	0	0	106.2	449	91	51	49	16	3	3	5	48	1	91	1	0	6	6	.500	0	0-0	0	4.04	4.13
2004	SEA	AL	56	10	0	14	117.0	523	102	64	53	12	4	4	12	64	3	86	6	0	8	6	.571	0	0-1	7	4.26	4.08
2005	2 Tms		79	0	0	24	64.0	287	57	34	29	4	3	5	7	35	2	70	3	1	5	5	.500	0	1-9	21	4.09	4.08
95	Sea	AL	19	0	0	7	19.1	101	20	19	17	6	3	0	1	23	0	26	1	0	0	2	.000	0	0-3	3	9.67	7.91
95	SD	NL	19	0	0	8	25.2	111	24	12	12	5	0	1	0	11	0	37	2	0	2	1	.667	0	1-2	3	4.44	4.21
96	SD	NL	21	0	0	9	18.1	78	17	6	6	2	0	0	1	7	0	19	0	0	1	1	.500	0	0-1	4	3.90	2.95
96	Mil	AL	23	0	0	10	24.2	104	14	9	9	4	0	2	4	18	0	19	2	0	0	0	-	0	2-2	5	4.21	3.28
01	Col	NL	22	6	0	6	46.2	222	56	35	33	6	1	1	1	29	4	48	2	0	1	3	.250	0	0-0	2	6.30	6.36
01	Hou	NL	31	6	0	6	68.0	301	77	46	42	12	0	0	4	24	1	65	2	1	5	7	.417	0	0-0	4	5.46	5.56
05	Sea	AL	52	0	0	14	40.1	178	33	14	11	2	1	3	5	23	1	41	2	1	2	3	.400	0	1-6	17	3.79	2.45
05	Fla	NL	27	0	0	10	23.2	109	24	20	18	2	2	2	2	12	1	29	1	0	3	2	.600	0	0-3	4	4.61	6.85
11 ML YEARS			473	93	2	118	946.2	4195	905	545	500	112	42	32	57	502	21	745	36	2	52	54	.491	0	6-23	59	4.70	4.75

Jose Vizcaino

Bats: B Throws: R Pos: PH-56; 2B-23; SS-17; 1B-13; 3B-8   Ht: 6'1" Wt: 185 Born: 3/26/1968 Age: 38

						BATTING															BASERUNNING				AVERAGES		
Year	Team	Lg	G	AB	H	2B	3B	HR	(Hm	Rd)	TB	R	RBI	RC	TBB	IBB	SO	HBP	SH	SF	SB	CS	SB%	GDP	Avg	OBP	Slg
1989	LA	NL	7	10	2	0	0	0	(0	0)	2	2	0	0	0	0	1	0	1	0	0	0	-	0	.200	.200	.200
1990	LA	NL	37	51	14	1	1	0	(0	0)	17	3	2	5	4	1	8	0	0	0	1	1	.50	1	.275	.327	.333
1991	CHN	NL	93	145	38	5	0	0	(0	0)	43	7	10	12	5	0	18	0	2	2	2	1	.67	1	.262	.283	.297
1992	CHN	NL	86	285	64	10	4	1	(0	1)	85	25	17	21	14	2	35	0	5	1	3	0	1.00	4	.225	.260	.298
1993	CHN	NL	151	551	158	19	4	4	(1	3)	197	74	54	68	46	2	71	3	8	9	12	9	.57	9	.287	.340	.358
1994	NYN	NL	103	410	105	13	3	3	(1	2)	133	47	33	39	33	3	62	2	5	6	1	11	.08	5	.256	.310	.324
1995	NYN	NL	135	509	146	21	5	3	(2	1)	186	66	56	60	35	4	76	1	13	3	8	3	.73	14	.287	.332	.365
1996	2 Tms		144	542	161	17	8	1	(1	0)	197	70	45	68	35	0	82	3	10	3	15	7	.68	8	.297	.341	.363
1997	SF	NL	151	568	151	19	7	5	(1	4)	199	77	50	62	48	1	87	0	13	1	8	8	.50	13	.266	.323	.350
1998	LA	NL	67	237	62	9	0	3	(0	3)	80	30	29	25	17	0	35	1	10	2	7	3	.70	4	.262	.311	.338
1999	LA	NL	94	266	67	9	0	1	(1	0)	79	27	29	23	20	0	23	1	9	2	2	1	.67	5	.252	.304	.297
2000	2 Tms		113	267	67	10	2	0	(0	0)	81	32	14	23	22	3	43	1	5	2	6	7	.46	6	.251	.308	.303
2001	HOU	NL	107	256	71	8	3	1	(1	0)	88	38	14	28	15	0	33	2	9	0	3	2	.60	5	.277	.322	.344
2002	HOU	NL	125	406	123	19	2	5	(4	1)	161	53	37	53	24	2	40	1	5	2	3	5	.38	5	.303	.342	.397
2003	HOU	NL	91	189	47	7	3	3	(2	1)	69	14	26	24	8	3	22	1	4	1	0	1	.00	5	.249	.281	.365
2004	HOU	NL	138	358	98	21	3	3	(1	2)	134	34	33	40	20	5	39	0	5	2	1	1	.50	8	.274	.311	.374
2005	HOU	NL	98	187	46	10	2	1	(1	0)	63	15	23	22	15	4	40	0	1	2	2	0	1.00	2	.246	.299	.337
96	NYM	NL	96	363	110	12	6	1	(1	0)	137	47	32	49	28	0	58	3	6	2	9	5	.64	6	.303	.356	.377
96	Cle	AL	48	179	51	5	2	0	(0	0)	60	23	13	19	7	0	24	0	4	1	6	2	.75	2	.285	.310	.335
00	LA	NL	40	93	19	2	1	0	(0	0)	23	9	4	6	10	3	15	1	2	0	1	0	1.00	3	.204	.288	.247
00	NYY	AL	73	174	48	8	1	0	(0	0)	58	23	10	17	12	0	28	0	3	2	5	7	.42	3	.276	.319	.333
17 ML YEARS			1740	5237	1420	198	47	34	(16	18)	1814	614	472	573	361	30	715	16	105	38	74	60	.55	100	.271	.318	.346

Luis Vizcaino

Pitches: R Bats: R Pos: RP-65   Ht: 5'11" Wt: 174 Born: 8/6/1974 Age: 31

			HOW MUCH HE PITCHED						WHAT HE GAVE UP										THE RESULTS							
Year	Team	Lg	G	GS	CG	GF	IP	BFP	H	R	ER	HR	SH	SF	HB	TBB	IBB	SO	WP	Bk	W	L	Pct	ShO	Sv-Op	Hld	ERC	ERA
1999	OAK	AL	1	0	0	1	3.1	16	3	2	2	1	0	0	0	3	0	2	1	0	0	0	-	0	0-0	0	7.01	5.40
2000	OAK	AL	12	0	0	1	19.1	96	25	17	16	2	0	1	2	11	0	18	1	0	0	1	.000	0	0-0	0	6.83	7.45
2001	OAK	AL	36	0	0	15	36.2	156	38	19	19	8	0	1	0	12	1	31	3	0	2	1	.667	0	1-1	3	4.80	4.66
2002	MIL	NL	76	0	0	30	81.1	326	55	27	27	6	3	3	3	30	4	79	3	2	5	3	.625	0	5-6	19	2.20	2.99
2003	MIL	NL	75	0	0	21	62.0	272	64	45	44	16	2	1	1	25	3	61	3	0	4	3	.571	0	0-6	9	5.37	6.39
2004	MIL	NL	73	0	0	21	72.0	298	61	35	30	12	1	5	1	24	3	63	9	0	4	4	.500	0	1-5	21	3.40	3.75
2005	CHA	AL	65	0	0	20	70.0	305	74	30	29	8	4	1	2	29	6	43	3	0	6	5	.545	0	0-3	9	4.58	3.73
7 ML YEARS			338	0	0	109	344.2	1469	320	175	167	53	10	12	9	134	17	297	23	2	21	17	.553	0	7-21	61	4.03	4.36

Omar Vizquel

Bats: B Throws: R Pos: SS-150; PH-3   Ht: 5'9" Wt: 175 Born: 4/24/1967 Age: 39

						BATTING															BASERUNNING				AVERAGES		
Year	Team	Lg	G	AB	H	2B	3B	HR	(Hm	Rd)	TB	R	RBI	RC	TBB	IBB	SO	HBP	SH	SF	SB	CS	SB%	GDP	Avg	OBP	Slg
1989	SEA	AL	143	387	85	7	3	1	(1	0)	101	45	20	25	28	0	40	1	13	2	1	4	.20	6	.220	.273	.261
1990	SEA	AL	81	255	63	3	2	2	(0	2)	76	19	18	22	18	0	22	0	10	2	4	1	.80	7	.247	.295	.298
1991	SEA	AL	142	426	98	16	4	1	(1	0)	125	42	41	39	45	0	37	0	8	3	7	2	.78	8	.230	.302	.293
1992	SEA	AL	136	483	142	20	4	0	(0	0)	170	49	21	54	32	0	38	2	9	1	15	13	.54	14	.294	.340	.352
1993	SEA	AL	158	560	143	14	2	2	(1	1)	167	68	31	53	50	2	71	4	13	3	12	14	.46	7	.255	.319	.298
1994	CLE	AL	69	286	78	10	1	1	(0	1)	93	39	33	32	23	0	23	0	11	2	13	4	.76	4	.273	.325	.325
1995	CLE	AL	136	542	144	28	0	6	(3	3)	190	87	56	70	59	0	59	1	10	10	29	11	.73	4	.266	.333	.351
1996	CLE	AL	151	542	161	36	1	9	(2	7)	226	98	64	87	56	0	42	4	12	9	35	9	.80	10	.297	.362	.417
1997	CLE	AL	153	565	158	23	6	5	(3	2)	208	89	49	75	57	1	58	2	16	2	43	12	.78	16	.280	.347	.368
1998	CLE	AL	151	576	166	30	6	2	(0	2)	214	86	50	82	62	1	64	4	12	6	37	12	.76	10	.288	.358	.372
1999	CLE	AL	144	574	191	36	4	5	(3	2)	250	112	66	106	65	0	50	1	17	7	42	9	.82	8	.333	.397	.436

246

(Batting — continued)

Year	Team	Lg	G	AB	H	2B	3B	HR	(Hm	Rd)	TB	R	RBI	RC	TBB	IBB	SO	HBP	SH	SF	SB	CS	SB%	GDP	Avg	OBP	Slg
2000	CLE	AL	156	613	176	27	3	7	(1	6)	230	101	66	92	87	0	72	5	7	5	22	10	.69	13	.287	.377	.375
2001	CLE	AL	155	611	156	26	8	2	(2	0)	204	84	50	66	61	0	72	2	15	4	13	9	.59	14	.255	.323	.334
2002	CLE	AL	151	582	160	31	5	14	(9	5)	243	85	72	91	56	3	64	8	7	10	18	10	.64	7	.275	.341	.418
2003	CLE	AL	64	250	61	13	2	2	(2	0)	84	43	19	25	29	0	20	0	5	1	8	3	.73	11	.244	.321	.336
2004	CLE	AL	148	567	165	28	3	7	(2	5)	220	82	59	86	57	0	62	1	20	6	19	6	.76	12	.291	.353	.388
2005	SF	NL	152	568	154	28	4	3	(0	3)	199	66	45	76	56	0	58	5	20	2	24	10	.71	10	.271	.341	.350
17 ML YEARS			2290	8387	2301	376	58	69	(30	39)	3000	1195	760	1081	841	7	852	40	205	75	342	139	.71	161	.274	.341	.358

Ryan Vogelsong

Pitches: R Bats: R Pos: RP-44   Ht: 6'3" Wt: 205 Born: 7/22/1977 Age: 28

	HOW MUCH HE PITCHED						WHAT HE GAVE UP												THE RESULTS							
Year Team	Lg	G	GS	CG	GF	IP	BFP	H	R	ER	HR	SH	SF	HB	TBB	IBB	SO	WP	Bk	W	L	Pct	ShO	Sv-Op	Hld	ERC	ERA
2000 SF	NL	4	0	0	0	6.0	24	4	0	0	0	0	0	0	2	0	6	0	0	0	0	-	0	0-0	0	1.57	0.00
2001 2 Tms	R	15	2	0	0	34.2	164	39	31	26	6	0	0	0	20	0	24	0	0	0	5	.000	0	0-0	0	5.92	6.75
2003 PIT	NL	6	5	0	0	22.0	108	30	19	16	1	3	1	2	9	3	15	1	0	2	2	.500	0	0-0	0	5.72	6.55
2004 PIT	NL	31	26	0	4	133.0	610	148	97	96	22	8	6	10	67	7	92	3	0	6	13	.316	0	0-0	0	5.89	6.50
2005 PIT	NL	44	0	0	19	81.1	369	82	43	40	5	1	4	8	40	1	52	7	0	2	2	.500	0	0-1	4	4.51	4.43
01 SF	NL	13	0	0	0	28.2	130	29	21	18	5	0	0	0	14	0	17	0	0	0	3	.000	0	0-0	0	4.89	5.65
01 Pit	NL	2	2	0	0	6.0	34	10	10	8	1	0	0	0	6	0	7	0	0	0	2	.000	0	0-0	0	11.42	12.00
5 ML YEARS		100	33	0	23	277.0	1275	303	190	178	34	12	11	20	138	11	189	11	0	10	22	.313	0	0-1	5	5.36	5.78

Edison Volquez

Pitches: R Bats: R Pos: SP-3; RP-3   Ht: 6'1" Wt: 190 Born: 7/3/1983 Age: 22

	HOW MUCH HE PITCHED						WHAT HE GAVE UP												THE RESULTS							
Year Team	Lg	G	GS	CG	GF	IP	BFP	H	R	ER	HR	SH	SF	HB	TBB	IBB	SO	WP	Bk	W	L	Pct	ShO	Sv-Op	Hld	ERC	ERA
2003 Rngrs	R	10	4	0	1	27.0	116	24	14	12	1	0	0	2	11	0	28	4	0	2	1	.667	0	1--	-	3.32	4.00
2004 Stcktn	A+	8	8	0	0	39.2	164	31	16	13	6	3	3	2	14	0	34	2	0	4	1	.800	0	0--	-	3.23	2.95
2004 Clinton	A	21	15	0	3	87.2	372	82	49	41	8	2	3	3	27	1	74	4	0	4	4	.500	0	3--	-	3.38	4.21
2005 Rngrs	R	1	1	0	0	2.0	8	2	0	0	0	0	0	0	0	0	2	1	0	0	0	-	0	0--	-	1.95	0.00
2005 Frisco	AA	10	10	1	0	58.2	251	58	29	27	6	1	1	1	17	0	49	1	0	1	5	.167	1	0--	-	3.60	4.14
2005 Bkrsfld	A+	11	11	1	1	66.2	276	64	34	31	9	0	0	7	12	0	77	3	0	5	4	.556	0	0--	-	3.67	4.19
2005 TEX	AL	6	3	0	0	12.2	75	25	22	20	3	0	1	2	10	0	11	0	0	0	4	.000	0	0-0	0	14.15	14.21

Doug Waechter

Pitches: R Bats: R Pos: SP-25; RP-4   Ht: 6'4" Wt: 209 Born: 1/28/1981 Age: 25

	HOW MUCH HE PITCHED						WHAT HE GAVE UP												THE RESULTS							
Year Team	Lg	G	GS	CG	GF	IP	BFP	H	R	ER	HR	SH	SF	HB	TBB	IBB	SO	WP	Bk	W	L	Pct	ShO	Sv-Op	Hld	ERC	ERA
2005 Drham*	AAA	3	3	0	0	13.2	63	17	14	14	3	0	0	1	5	0	16	0	1	0	2	.000	0	0--	-	6.57	9.22
2003 TB	AL	6	5	1	0	35.1	145	29	13	13	4	0	0	1	15	0	29	0	0	3	2	.600	1	0-0	0	3.48	3.31
2004 TB	AL	14	14	0	0	70.1	309	68	54	47	20	0	2	4	33	1	36	1	1	5	7	.417	0	0-0	0	5.74	6.01
2005 TB	AL	29	25	0	3	157.0	692	191	109	98	29	4	4	3	38	5	87	4	2	5	12	.294	0	0-0	0	5.29	5.62
3 ML YEARS		49	44	1	3	262.2	1146	288	176	158	53	4	6	8	86	6	152	5	3	13	21	.382	1	0-0	0	5.16	5.41

Billy Wagner

Pitches: L Bats: L Pos: RP-75   Ht: 5'11" Wt: 195 Born: 7/25/1971 Age: 34

	HOW MUCH HE PITCHED						WHAT HE GAVE UP												THE RESULTS							
Year Team	Lg	G	GS	CG	GF	IP	BFP	H	R	ER	HR	SH	SF	HB	TBB	IBB	SO	WP	Bk	W	L	Pct	ShO	Sv-Op	Hld	ERC	ERA
1995 HOU	NL	1	0	0	0	0.1	1	0	0	0	0	0	0	0	0	0	0	0	0	0	0	-	0	0-0	0	0.00	0.00
1996 HOU	NL	37	0	0	20	51.2	212	28	16	14	6	7	2	3	30	2	67	1	0	2	2	.500	0	9-13	3	2.61	2.44
1997 HOU	NL	62	0	0	49	66.1	277	49	23	21	5	3	1	3	30	1	106	3	0	7	8	.467	0	23-29	1	2.85	2.85
1998 HOU	NL	58	0	0	50	60.0	247	46	19	18	6	4	0	0	25	1	97	2	0	4	3	.571	0	30-35	1	2.87	2.70
1999 HOU	NL	66	0	0	55	74.2	286	35	14	13	5	2	1	1	23	0	124	2	0	4	1	.800	0	39-42	1	1.20	1.57
2000 HOU	NL	28	0	0	19	27.2	129	28	19	19	6	0	0	1	18	0	28	7	0	2	4	.333	0	6-15	0	6.15	6.18
2001 HOU	NL	64	0	0	58	62.2	251	44	19	19	5	3	1	5	20	0	79	3	0	2	5	.286	0	39-41	0	2.42	2.73
2002 HOU	NL	70	0	0	61	75.0	289	51	21	21	7	2	3	2	22	5	88	6	0	4	2	.667	0	35-41	0	2.08	2.52
2003 HOU	NL	78	0	0	67	86.0	335	52	18	17	8	1	0	3	23	5	105	4	0	1	4	.200	0	44-47	0	1.63	1.78
2004 PHI	NL	45	0	0	38	48.1	182	31	16	13	5	3	0	2	6	1	59	1	0	4	0	1.000	0	21-25	1	1.52	2.42
2005 PHI	NL	75	0	0	70	77.2	297	45	17	13	6	0	2	3	20	2	87	3	1	4	3	.571	0	38-41	0	1.53	1.51
11 ML YEARS		584	0	0	487	630.1	2506	409	182	168	59	25	10	23	217	18	840	32	1	34	32	.515	0	284-329	7	2.12	2.40

Ryan Wagner

Pitches: R Bats: R Pos: RP-42   Ht: 6'4" Wt: 210 Born: 7/15/1982 Age: 23

	HOW MUCH HE PITCHED						WHAT HE GAVE UP												THE RESULTS							
Year Team	Lg	G	GS	CG	GF	IP	BFP	H	R	ER	HR	SH	SF	HB	TBB	IBB	SO	WP	Bk	W	L	Pct	ShO	Sv-Op	Hld	ERC	ERA
2003 CIN	NL	17	0	0	3	21.2	88	13	4	4	2	0	1	0	12	1	25	4	0	2	0	1.000	0	0-1	6	2.46	1.66
2004 CIN	NL	49	0	0	5	51.2	242	59	31	27	7	2	3	2	27	2	37	5	0	3	2	.600	0	0-3	8	5.66	4.70
2005 CIN	NL	42	0	0	8	45.2	210	56	33	31	4	1	3	4	17	1	39	2	0	3	2	.600	0	0-1	12	5.48	6.11
3 ML YEARS		108	0	0	16	119.0	540	128	68	62	13	3	7	6	56	4	101	11	0	8	4	.667	0	0-5	26	4.95	4.69

Adam Wainwright

Pitches: R Bats: R Pos: RP-2   **Ht: 6'7" Wt: 205 Born: 8/30/1981 Age: 24**

Year	Team	Lg	G	GS	CG	GF	IP	BFP	H	R	ER	HR	SH	SF	HB	TBB	IBB	SO	WP	Bk	W	L	Pct	ShO	Sv-Op	Hld	ERC	ERA
2000	Danvle	R+	6	6	0	0	29.1	118	28	13	12	3	1	0	1	2	0	39	1	0	2	2	.500	0	0- -	-	2.69	3.68
2000	Braves	R	7	5	0	1	32.0	121	15	5	4	1	0	0	0	10	0	42	1	1	4	0	1.000	0	0- -	-	1.08	1.13
2001	Macon	A	28	28	1	0	164.2	686	144	89	69	9	7	2	8	48	1	184	9	2	10	10	.500	0	0- -	-	2.84	3.77
2002	MrtlBh	A+	28	28	1	0	163.1	705	149	67	60	7	1	2	10	66	0	167	11	3	9	6	.600	0	0- -	-	3.42	3.31
2003	Grnville	AA	27	27	1	0	149.2	619	133	59	56	9	2	3	7	37	0	128	4	2	10	8	.556	0	0- -	-	2.80	3.37
2004	Memp	AAA	12	12	0	0	63.2	287	68	47	38	12	7	1	3	28	0	64	2	1	4	4	.500	0	0- -	-	5.42	5.37
2005	Memp	AAA	29	29	0	0	182.0	801	204	98	89	18	7	6	5	51	6	147	11	1	10	10	.500	0	0- -	-	4.25	4.40
2005	STL	NL	2	0	0	1	2.0	9	2	3	3	1	0	0	0	1	0	0	0	0	0	0	-	0	0-0	0	7.30	13.50

Tim Wakefield

Pitches: R Bats: R Pos: SP-33   **Ht: 6'2" Wt: 214 Born: 8/2/1966 Age: 39**

Year	Team	Lg	G	GS	CG	GF	IP	BFP	H	R	ER	HR	SH	SF	HB	TBB	IBB	SO	WP	Bk	W	L	Pct	ShO	Sv-Op	Hld	ERC	ERA
1992	PIT	NL	13	13	4	0	92.0	373	76	26	22	3	6	4	1	35	1	51	3	1	8	1	.889	1	0-0	0	2.72	2.15
1993	PIT	NL	24	20	3	1	128.1	595	145	83	80	14	7	5	9	75	2	59	6	0	6	11	.353	2	0-0	0	5.97	5.61
1995	BOS	AL	27	27	6	0	195.1	804	163	76	64	22	3	7	9	68	0	119	11	0	16	8	.667	1	0-0	0	3.28	2.95
1996	BOS	AL	32	32	6	0	211.2	963	238	151	121	38	1	9	12	90	0	140	4	1	14	13	.519	0	0-0	0	5.68	5.14
1997	BOS	AL	35	29	4	2	201.1	866	193	109	95	24	3	7	16	87	5	151	6	0	12	15	.444	2	0-0	1	4.47	4.25
1998	BOS	AL	36	33	2	1	216.0	939	211	123	110	30	1	8	14	79	1	146	6	1	17	8	.680	0	0-0	0	4.30	4.58
1999	BOS	AL	49	17	0	28	140.0	635	146	93	79	19	1	8	5	72	2	104	1	0	6	11	.353	0	15-18	5	5.12	5.08
2000	BOS	AL	51	17	0	13	159.1	706	170	107	97	31	4	8	4	65	3	102	4	0	6	10	.375	0	0-1	3	5.23	5.48
2001	BOS	AL	45	17	0	5	168.2	732	156	84	73	13	3	9	18	73	5	148	5	1	9	12	.429	0	3-5	3	4.02	3.90
2002	BOS	AL	45	15	0	10	163.1	657	121	57	51	15	1	4	9	51	2	134	5	2	11	5	.688	0	3-5	5	2.54	2.81
2003	BOS	AL	35	33	0	2	202.1	872	193	106	92	23	2	4	12	71	0	169	8	0	11	7	.611	0	1-1	0	3.92	4.09
2004	BOS	AL	32	30	0	0	188.1	831	197	121	102	29	2	4	16	63	3	116	9	0	12	10	.545	0	0-0	1	4.73	4.87
2005	BOS	AL	33	33	3	0	225.1	943	210	113	104	35	1	6	11	68	4	151	8	0	16	12	.571	0	0-0	0	3.87	4.15
	13 ML YEARS		457	316	28	62	2292.0	9916	2219	1249	1090	296	35	83	136	897	28	1590	76	6	144	123	.539	6	22-30	13	4.29	4.28

Jamie Walker

Pitches: L Bats: L Pos: RP-66   **Ht: 6'2" Wt: 190 Born: 7/1/1971 Age: 34**

Year	Team	Lg	G	GS	CG	GF	IP	BFP	H	R	ER	HR	SH	SF	HB	TBB	IBB	SO	WP	Bk	W	L	Pct	ShO	Sv-Op	Hld	ERC	ERA
1997	KC	AL	50	0	0	15	43.0	197	46	28	26	6	2	2	3	20	3	24	2	0	3	3	.500	0	0-1	3	5.10	5.44
1998	KC	AL	6	2	0	2	17.1	86	30	20	19	5	1	1	2	3	0	15	0	0	0	1	.000	0	0-0	1	9.69	9.87
2002	DET	AL	57	0	0	16	43.2	175	32	19	18	9	0	1	4	9	1	40	1	1	1	1	.500	0	1-4	5	2.86	3.71
2003	DET	AL	78	0	0	19	65.0	273	61	30	24	9	5	2	2	17	1	45	1	0	4	3	.571	0	3-7	12	3.51	3.32
2004	DET	AL	70	0	0	18	64.2	277	69	28	23	8	1	1	1	12	3	53	4	0	3	4	.429	0	1-7	18	3.65	3.20
2005	DET	AL	66	0	0	11	48.2	208	49	22	20	5	1	1	2	13	3	30	0	0	4	3	.571	0	0-2	14	3.63	3.70
	6 ML YEARS		327	2	0	81	282.1	1216	287	147	130	42	10	8	14	74	11	207	8	1	15	15	.500	0	5-21	53	4.02	4.14

Kevin Walker

Pitches: L Bats: L Pos: RP-9   **Ht: 6'4" Wt: 190 Born: 9/20/1976 Age: 29**

Year	Team	Lg	G	GS	CG	GF	IP	BFP	H	R	ER	HR	SH	SF	HB	TBB	IBB	SO	WP	Bk	W	L	Pct	ShO	Sv-Op	Hld	ERC	ERA
2005	Charltt*	AAA	51	0	0	19	46.0	208	49	35	27	7	5	1	6	21	3	52	2	0	1	2	.333	0	5- -	-	5.54	5.28
2000	SD	NL	70	0	0	14	66.2	287	49	35	31	5	4	2	5	38	6	56	2	1	7	1	.875	0	0-0	19	3.23	4.19
2001	SD	NL	16	0	0	5	12.0	49	5	4	4	0	0	0	0	8	2	17	0	1	0	0	-	0	0-1	4	1.33	3.00
2002	SD	NL	11	0	0	1	8.0	42	12	6	5	2	1	0	0	5	1	11	1	0	0	1	.000	0	0-1	1	8.79	5.63
2003	SD	NL	11	0	0	2	6.2	30	5	4	4	1	0	0	0	5	0	5	0	0	0	0	-	0	0-0	0	4.31	5.40
2004	SF	NL	5	0	0	0	1.2	10	3	3	3	1	0	0	1	2	0	1	0	0	0	0	-	0	0-0	1	23.66	16.20
2005	CHA	AL	9	0	0	3	7.0	35	10	7	7	1	0	0	0	5	1	5	0	0	0	1	.000	0	0-1	0	8.18	9.00
	6 ML YEARS		122	0	0	25	102.0	453	84	59	54	10	5	2	6	63	10	95	3	2	7	3	.700	0	0-3	25	3.95	4.76

Larry Walker

Bats: L Throws: R Pos: RF-83; PH-13; DH-6; CF-1   **Ht: 6'3" Wt: 233 Born: 12/1/1966 Age: 39**

Year	Team	Lg	G	AB	H	2B	3B	HR	(Hm	Rd)	TB	R	RBI	RC	TBB	IBB	SO	HBP	SH	SF	SB	CS	SB%	GDP	Avg	OBP	Slg
1989	MON	NL	20	47	8	0	0	0	(0	0)	8	4	4	2	5	0	13	1	3	0	1	1	.50	0	.170	.264	.170
1990	MON	NL	133	419	101	18	3	19	(9	10)	182	59	51	60	49	5	112	5	3	2	21	7	.75	8	.241	.326	.434
1991	MON	NL	137	487	141	30	2	16	(5	11)	223	59	64	77	42	2	102	5	1	4	14	9	.61	7	.290	.349	.458
1992	MON	NL	143	528	159	31	4	23	(13	10)	267	85	93	93	41	10	97	6	0	8	18	6	.75	9	.301	.353	.506
1993	MON	NL	138	490	130	24	5	22	(13	9)	230	85	86	89	80	20	76	6	0	6	29	7	.81	8	.265	.371	.469
1994	MON	NL	103	395	127	44	2	19	(7	12)	232	76	86	88	47	5	74	4	0	6	15	5	.75	8	.322	.394	.587
1995	COL	NL	131	494	151	31	5	36	(24	12)	300	96	101	108	49	13	72	14	0	5	16	3	.84	13	.306	.381	.607
1996	COL	NL	83	272	75	18	4	18	(12	6)	155	58	58	53	20	2	58	9	0	3	18	2	.90	7	.276	.342	.570
1997	COL	NL	153	568	208	46	4	49	(20	29)	409	143	130	166	78	14	90	14	0	4	33	8	.80	15	.366	.452	.720
1998	COL	NL	130	454	165	46	3	23	(17	6)	286	113	67	117	64	2	61	4	0	2	14	4	.78	11	.363	.445	.630
1999	COL	NL	127	438	166	26	4	37	(26	11)	311	108	115	127	57	8	52	12	0	6	11	4	.73	12	.379	.458	.710
2000	COL	NL	87	314	97	21	7	9	(7	2)	159	64	51	61	46	4	40	9	0	3	5	5	.50	12	.309	.409	.506
2001	COL	NL	142	497	174	35	3	38	(20	18)	329	107	123	138	82	6	103	14	0	8	14	5	.74	9	.350	.449	.662
2002	COL	NL	136	477	161	40	4	26	(18	8)	287	95	104	112	65	6	73	7	0	4	6	5	.55	8	.338	.421	.602
2003	COL	NL	143	454	129	25	7	16	(8	8)	216	86	79	98	98	14	87	11	0	1	7	4	.64	9	.284	.422	.476
2004	2 Tms	NL	82	258	77	16	4	17	(7	10)	152	51	47	54	49	3	57	8	0	1	6	0	1.00	8	.298	.424	.589
2005	STL	NL	100	315	91	20	1	15	(9	6)	158	66	52	56	41	3	64	9	0	2	2	1	.67	9	.289	.384	.502

Year	Team	Lg	G	AB	H	2B	3B	HR	(Hm	Rd)	TB	R	RBI	RC	TBB	IBB	SO	HBP	SH	SF	SB	CS	SB%	GDP	Avg	OBP	Slg
04	Col	NL	38	108	35	9	3	6	(2	4)	68	22	20	25	25	2	23	4	0	1	2	0	1.00	2	.324	.464	.630
04	StL	NL	44	150	42	7	1	11	(5	6)	84	29	27	29	24	1	34	4	0	1	4	0	1.00	6	.280	.393	.560
17 ML YEARS			1988	6907	2160	471	62	383	(215	168)	3904	1355	1311	1499	913	117	1231	138	7	65	230	76	.75	153	.313	.400	.565

Pete Walker

Pitches: R Bats: R Pos: RP-37; SP-4　　　　　　**Ht: 6'2" Wt: 195 Born: 4/8/1969 Age: 37**

Year	Team	Lg	G	GS	CG	GF	IP	BFP	H	R	ER	HR	SH	SF	HB	TBB	IBB	SO	WP	Bk	W	L	Pct	ShO	Sv-Op	Hld	ERC	ERA
1995	NYN	NL	13	0	0	10	17.2	79	24	9	9	3	0	1	0	5	0	5	0	0	1	0	1.000	0	0-0	1	6.35	4.58
1996	SD	NL	1	0	0	0	0.2	5	0	0	0	0	0	0	0	3	0	1	0	0	0	0	-	0	0-0	0	13.05	0.00
2000	COL	NL	3	0	0	1	4.2	27	10	9	9	1	0	0	0	4	0	2	0	0	0	0	-	0	0-0	0	15.29	17.36
2001	NYN	NL	2	0	0	1	6.2	25	6	2	2	0	0	0	0	0	0	4	0	0	0	0	-	0	0-0	0	1.63	2.70
2002	2 Tms		38	20	0	4	140.1	599	145	73	68	18	4	6	3	51	5	80	2	1	10	5	.667	0	1-1	3	4.41	4.36
2003	TOR	AL	23	7	0	2	55.1	242	59	31	30	11	2	1	2	24	2	29	2	0	2	2	.500	0	0-0	2	5.51	4.88
2005	TOR	AL	41	4	0	8	84.0	358	81	33	33	10	0	4	2	33	0	43	2	0	6	6	.500	0	2-5	4	4.11	3.54
02	NYM	NL	1	0	0	0	1.0	5	2	1	1	0	0	0	0	0	0	0	0	0	0	0	-	0	0-0	0	7.48	9.00
02	Tor	AL	37	20	0	4	139.1	594	143	72	67	18	4	6	3	51	5	80	2	1	10	5	.667	0	1-1	3	4.39	4.33
7 ML YEARS			121	31	0	26	309.1	1335	325	157	151	43	6	12	7	120	7	164	6	1	19	13	.594	0	3-6	10	4.71	4.39

Todd Walker

Bats: L Throws: R Pos: 2B-97; PH-9; 1B-4; DH-2　　　　　　**Ht: 6'0" Wt: 190 Born: 5/25/1973 Age: 33**

Year	Team	Lg	G	AB	H	2B	3B	HR	(Hm	Rd)	TB	R	RBI	RC	TBB	IBB	SO	HBP	SH	SF	SB	CS	SB%	GDP	Avg	OBP	Slg
2005	Iowa*	AAA	9	37	8	3	0	0	(-	-)	11	3	3	2	1	0	4	0	0	0	0	0	-	4	.216	.237	.297
1996	MIN	AL	25	82	21	6	0	0	(0	0)	27	8	6	7	4	0	13	0	0	3	2	0	1.00	4	.256	.281	.329
1997	MIN	AL	52	156	37	7	1	3	(1	2)	55	15	16	16	11	1	30	1	1	2	7	0	1.00	5	.237	.288	.353
1998	MIN	AL	143	528	167	41	3	12	(7	5)	250	85	62	90	47	9	65	2	0	4	19	7	.73	13	.316	.372	.473
1999	MIN	AL	143	531	148	37	4	6	(4	2)	211	62	46	70	52	5	83	1	0	2	18	10	.64	15	.279	.343	.397
2000	2 Tms		80	248	72	11	4	9	(5	4)	118	42	44	43	27	0	29	1	1	6	7	1	.88	5	.290	.355	.476
2001	2 Tms	NL	151	551	163	35	2	17	(13	4)	253	93	75	84	51	1	82	1	4	3	1	8	.11	14	.296	.355	.459
2002	CIN	NL	155	612	183	42	3	11	(7	4)	264	79	64	90	50	7	81	3	7	3	8	5	.62	9	.299	.353	.431
2003	BOS	AL	144	587	166	38	4	13	(6	7)	251	92	85	84	48	0	54	1	1	10	1	1	.50	17	.283	.333	.428
2004	CHN	NL	129	372	102	19	4	15	(6	9)	174	60	50	61	43	8	52	4	1	4	0	3	.00	2	.274	.352	.468
2005	CHN	NL	110	397	121	25	3	12	(5	7)	188	50	40	56	31	1	40	1	2	2	1	1	.50	7	.305	.355	.474
00	Min	AL	23	77	18	1	0	2	(0	2)	25	14	8	7	7	0	10	0	0	3	3	0	1.00	3	.234	.287	.325
00	Col	NL	57	171	54	10	4	7	(5	2)	93	28	36	36	20	0	19	1	1	3	4	1	.80	2	.316	.385	.544
01	Col	NL	85	290	86	18	2	12	(10	2)	144	52	43	47	25	1	40	0	3	3	1	3	.25	8	.297	.349	.497
01	Cin	NL	66	261	77	17	0	5	(3	2)	109	41	32	37	26	0	42	1	1	0	0	5	.00	6	.295	.361	.418
10 ML YEARS			1132	4064	1180	261	28	98	(54	44)	1791	586	488	601	364	32	529	15	17	39	64	36	.64	92	.290	.348	.441

Tyler Walker

Pitches: R Bats: R Pos: RP-67　　　　　　**Ht: 6'3" Wt: 255 Born: 5/15/1976 Age: 30**

Year	Team	Lg	G	GS	CG	GF	IP	BFP	H	R	ER	HR	SH	SF	HB	TBB	IBB	SO	WP	Bk	W	L	Pct	ShO	Sv-Op	Hld	ERC	ERA
2002	NYN	NL	5	1	0	3	10.2	49	11	7	7	3	0	0	0	5	1	7	0	0	1	0	1.000	0	0-0	5	5.46	5.91
2004	SF	NL	52	0	0	13	63.2	275	69	31	30	8	3	7	1	24	1	48	1	0	5	1	.833	0	1-1	5	4.76	4.24
2005	SF	NL	67	0	0	39	61.2	279	68	31	29	9	5	1	3	27	6	54	4	0	6	4	.600	0	23-28	2	5.15	4.23
3 ML YEARS			124	1	0	55	136.0	603	148	69	66	20	8	8	4	56	8	109	5	0	12	5	.706	0	24-29	7	4.99	4.37

Chien-Ming Wang

Pitches: R Bats: R Pos: SP-17; RP-1　　　　　　**Ht: 6'3" Wt: 200 Born: 3/31/1980 Age: 26**

Year	Team	Lg	G	GS	CG	GF	IP	BFP	H	R	ER	HR	SH	SF	HB	TBB	IBB	SO	WP	Bk	W	L	Pct	ShO	Sv-Op	Hld	ERC	ERA
2000	StlsInd	A-	14	14	2	0	87.0	359	77	34	24	2	3	2		21	1	75	7	1	4	4	.500	1	0- -		2.41	2.48
2002	StlsInd	A-	13	13	0	0	78.1	312	63	23	15	2	3	3	0	14	0	64	1	2	6	1	.857		0- -		1.80	1.72
2003	Yanks	R	1	1	0	0	3.0	11	2	0	0	0	0	0	0	0	0	2	0	0	0	0	-		0- -		0.91	0.00
2003	Trentn	AA	21	21	2	0	122.0	541	143	71	63	7	0	0	2	32	2	84	3	1	7	6	.538	1	0- -		4.14	4.65
2004	Trentn	AA	18	18	0	0	109.0	465	112	53	49	6	6	5	3	26	0	90	2	0	6	5	.545	0	0- -		3.35	4.05
2004	Clmbs	AAA	6	5	2	1	40.1	160	31	9	9	3	1	0	1	8	0	35	0	0	5	1	.833	0	0- -		2.06	2.01
2005	Clmbs	AAA	6	6	0	0	34.0	148	40	16	16	4	1	2	0	6	0	21	1	0	2	1	.667	0	0- -		4.20	4.24
2005	NYA	AL	18	17	0	0	116.1	486	113	58	52	9	3	4	6	32	3	47	3	0	8	5	.615	0	0-0	0	3.47	4.02

Daryle Ward

Bats: L Throws: L Pos: 1B-109; PH-26　　　　　　**Ht: 6'2" Wt: 240 Born: 6/27/1975 Age: 31**

Year	Team	Lg	G	AB	H	2B	3B	HR	(Hm	Rd)	TB	R	RBI	RC	TBB	IBB	SO	HBP	SH	SF	SB	CS	SB%	GDP	Avg	OBP	Slg
1998	HOU	NL	4	3	1	0	0	0	(0	0)	1	1	0	1	1	0	2	0	0	0	0	0	-	3	.333	.500	.333
1999	HOU	NL	64	150	41	6	0	8	(2	6)	71	11	30	21	9	0	31	0	0	2	0	0	-	3	.273	.311	.473
2000	HOU	NL	119	264	68	10	2	20	(13	7)	142	36	47	40	15	4	61	0	0	2	0	0	-	6	.258	.295	.538
2001	HOU	NL	95	213	56	15	0	9	(5	4)	98	21	39	31	19	4	48	1	0	2	0	0	-	3	.263	.323	.460
2002	HOU	NL	136	453	125	31	0	12	(9	3)	192	41	72	61	33	5	82	1	0	4	1	3	.25	9	.276	.324	.424
2003	LA	NL	52	109	20	1	0	0	(0	0)	21	6	9	1	3	0	19	1	0	1	0	0	-	4	.183	.211	.193
2004	PIT	NL	79	293	73	17	2	15	(8	7)	139	39	57	40	22	3	45	3	0	3	0	0	-	8	.249	.305	.474
2005	PIT	NL	133	407	106	21	1	12	(7	5)	165	46	63	49	37	10	60	1	0	8	0	2	.00	18	.260	.318	.405
8 ML YEARS			682	1892	490	101	5	76	(44	32)	829	201	317	244	139	24	348	7	0	22	1	5	.17	51	.259	.309	.438

John Wasdin

Pitches: R Bats: R Pos: RP-25; SP-6   Ht: 6'2" Wt: 196 Born: 8/5/1972 Age: 33

				HOW MUCH HE PITCHED			WHAT HE GAVE UP												THE RESULTS						
Year	Team	Lg	G	GS	CG	GF	IP	BFP	H	R	ER	HR	SH	SF	HB	TBB	IBB	SO	WP	Bk	W	L	Pct	ShO	Sv-Op	Hld	ERC	ERA
2005	Okla*	AAA	13	11	0	0	73.0	327	84	43	40	11	0	2	2	24	1	57	2	0	9	2	.818	0	0- -	-	5.03	4.93
1995	OAK	AL	5	2	0	0	17.1	69	14	9	9	4	0	0	0	3	0	6	0	0	1	1	.500	0	0-0	0	2.91	4.67
1996	OAK	AL	25	21	1	0	131.1	575	145	96	87	24	0	0	0	50	0	75	0	0	8	7	.533	0	0-0	0	5.22	5.96
1997	BOS	AL	53	7	0	0	124.2	534	121	68	61	18	0	0	0	38	0	84	0	0	4	6	.400	0	0-0	0	3.75	4.40
1998	BOS	AL	47	8	0	0	96.0	424	111	57	56	14	0	0	0	27	0	59	0	0	6	4	.600	0	0-0	0	4.73	5.25
1999	BOS	AL	45	0	0	0	74.1	302	66	38	34	14	0	0	0	18	0	57	0	0	8	3	.727	0	2-0	0	3.41	4.12
2000	2 Tms		39	4	1	0	80.1	352	90	48	48	14	0	0	0	24	0	71	0	0	1	6	.143	0	1-0	0	4.82	5.38
2001	2 Tms		44	0	0	0	74.0	330	86	44	42	11	0	0	0	24	0	64	0	0	3	2	.600	0	0-0	0	4.97	5.11
2003	TOR	AL	3	2	0	0	5.0	35	16	13	13	2	0	1	0	4	0	5	0	0	0	1	.000	0	0-0	0	25.15	23.40
2004	TEX	AL	15	10	0	0	65.0	301	83	52	49	18	1	2	3	23	2	36	0	0	2	4	.333	0	0-0	0	6.97	6.78
2005	TEX	AL	31	6	0	7	75.2	319	77	37	36	9	1	2	1	20	2	44	2	0	3	2	.600	0	4-6	4	3.77	4.28
00	Bos	AL	25	1	0	0	44.2	198	48	25	25	8	0	0	0	15	0	36	0	0	1	3	.250	0	1-0	0	4.67	5.04
00	Col	NL	14	3	1	0	35.2	154	42	23	23	6	0	0	0	9	0	35	0	0	0	3	.000	0	0-0	0	5.01	5.80
01	Col	NL	18	0	0	0	24.1	110	32	19	19	7	0	0	0	8	0	17	0	0	2	1	.667	0	0-0	0	7.15	7.03
01	Bal	AL	26	0	0	0	49.2	220	54	25	23	4	0	0	0	16	0	47	0	0	1	1	.500	0	0-0	0	4.00	4.17
	10 ML YEARS		307	60	2	7	743.2	3241	809	462	435	128	2	5	4	231	4	501	2	0	36	36	.500	0	7-6	4	4.69	5.26

Jarrod Washburn

Pitches: L Bats: L Pos: SP-29   Ht: 6'1" Wt: 187 Born: 8/13/1974 Age: 31

				HOW MUCH HE PITCHED			WHAT HE GAVE UP												THE RESULTS						
Year	Team	Lg	G	GS	CG	GF	IP	BFP	H	R	ER	HR	SH	SF	HB	TBB	IBB	SO	WP	Bk	W	L	Pct	ShO	Sv-Op	Hld	ERC	ERA
1998	ANA	AL	15	11	0	0	74.0	317	70	40	38	11	2	3	3	27	1	48	0	0	6	3	.667	0	0-0	1	4.09	4.62
1999	ANA	AL	16	10	0	3	61.2	264	61	36	36	6	1	2	1	26	0	39	2	0	4	5	.444	0	0-0	1	4.20	5.25
2000	ANA	AL	14	14	0	0	84.1	340	64	38	35	16	1	3	1	37	0	49	1	0	7	2	.778	0	0-0	0	3.66	3.74
2001	ANA	AL	30	31	1	0	193.1	813	196	89	81	25	4	4	7	54	4	126	3	0	11	10	.524	0	0-0	0	4.03	3.77
2002	ANA	AL	32	32	1	0	206.0	852	183	75	72	19	4	7	3	59	1	139	5	1	18	6	.750	0	0-0	0	3.02	3.15
2003	ANA	AL	32	32	2	0	207.1	876	205	106	102	34	5	6	11	54	4	118	4	1	10	15	.400	0	0-0	0	4.07	4.43
2004	ANA	AL	25	25	1	0	149.1	640	159	81	77	20	2	4	4	40	1	86	5	0	11	8	.579	1	0-0	0	4.23	4.64
2005	LAA	AL	29	29	1	0	177.1	740	184	66	63	19	4	6	8	51	0	94	2	0	8	8	.500	1	0-0	0	4.19	3.20
	8 ML YEARS		193	183	6	3	1153.1	4842	1122	531	504	150	23	35	38	348	11	699	22	2	75	57	.568	2	0-0	2	3.89	3.93

Brandon Watson

Bats: L Throws: R Pos: LF-12; PH-12; PR-2; CF-1   Ht: 6'1" Wt: 170 Born: 9/30/1981 Age: 24

									BATTING											BASERUNNING				AVERAGES		
Year	Team	Lg	G	AB	H	2B	3B	HR	(Hm	Rd)	TB	R	RBI	RC	TBB	IBB	SO	HBP	SH	SF	SB	CS	SB%	GDP	Avg	OBP	Slg
1999	Expos	R	33	119	36	2	0	0	(-	-)	38	15	12	12	1	1	11	1	2	2	4	2	.67	0	.303	.309	.319
2000	Vrmnt	A-	69	278	81	9	1	0	(-	-)	92	53	30	37	25	0	38	3	4	2	26	9	.74	4	.291	.354	.331
2001	Clinton	A	117	489	160	16	9	2	(-	-)	200	74	38	73	29	0	65	1	3	3	33	20	.62	6	.327	.364	.409
2002	BrvdCt	A+	111	424	113	16	2	0	(-	-)	133	57	24	43	27	0	53	3	11	2	22	13	.63	5	.267	.314	.314
2002	Hrsbrg	AA	2	6	2	0	0	0	(-	-)	2	2	0	1	1	0	0	0	0	0	0	0	-	0	.333	.429	.333
2003	Hrsbrg	AA	139	565	180	17	6	1	(-	-)	212	86	39	78	38	2	60	3	11	4	18	17	.51	7	.319	.362	.375
2004	Edmtn	AAA	139	526	154	17	3	2	(-	-)	183	74	41	64	31	2	68	1	6	2	22	10	.69	3	.293	.332	.348
2005	Hrsbrg	AA	34	146	36	1	0	0	(-	-)	37	13	6	10	7	0	21	2	1	0	7	5	.58	2	.247	.290	.253
2005	NewOr	AAA	88	372	132	15	3	1	(-	-)	156	69	25	65	28	0	33	1	5	2	31	13	.70	5	.355	.400	.419
2005	WAS	NL	25	40	7	1	1	1	(0	1)	13	8	5	3	4	0	8	0	4	0	0	2	.00	1	.175	.250	.325

Matt Watson

Bats: L Throws: R Pos: LF-14; PH-6; RF-3   Ht: 5'9" Wt: 200 Born: 9/5/1978 Age: 27

									BATTING											BASERUNNING				AVERAGES		
Year	Team	Lg	G	AB	H	2B	3B	HR	(Hm	Rd)	TB	R	RBI	RC	TBB	IBB	SO	HBP	SH	SF	SB	CS	SB%	GDP	Avg	OBP	Slg
1999	Vrmnt	A-	70	284	108	12	3	7	(-	-)	147	55	47	63	30	1	27	3	2	4	17	7	.71	6	.380	.439	.518
2000	Jupiter	A+	40	137	24	5	2	0	(-	-)	33	10	8	7	18	2	23	1	0	0	4	3	.57	6	.175	.276	.241
2001	Jupiter	A+	124	446	147	33	4	5	(-	-)	203	70	74	85	63	4	45	6	0	3	17	9	.65	11	.330	.417	.455
2002	Bnghtn	AA	127	437	122	26	2	10	(-	-)	182	55	67	58	39	4	52	3	2	5	12	8	.60	14	.279	.339	.416
2002	Hrsbrg	AA	1	4	1	0	0	0	(-	-)	1	1	0	0	0	0	0	0	0	0	0	0	-	0	.250	.250	.250
2003	Bklyn	A-	4	14	2	1	0	0	(-	-)	3	0	0	0	2	0	3	1	0	0	2	1	.67	0	.143	.294	.214
2003	StLuci	A+	2	7	2	0	1	0	(-	-)	4	2	2	1	1	0	2	0	0	1	1	0	1.00	0	.286	.333	.571
2003	Bnghtn	AA	8	28	11	3	0	1	(-	-)	17	6	1	6	2	0	2	1	0	0	1	1	.50	0	.393	.452	.607
2003	Norfolk	AAA	74	254	75	18	1	11	(-	-)	128	40	55	45	23	1	23	8	1	5	2	2	.50	4	.295	.366	.504
2004	Scrmto	AAA	125	476	145	37	3	19	(-	-)	245	79	96	86	54	2	75	4	2	5	3	4	.43	12	.305	.377	.515
2005	Scrmto	AAA	113	419	132	27	3	17	(-	-)	216	82	81	92	67	0	57	2	2	10	12	1	.92	7	.315	.404	.516
2003	NYN	NL	15	23	4	2	0	0	(0	0)	6	0	2	0	1	0	5	0	1	0	0	0	-	1	.174	.208	.261
2005	OAK	AL	19	48	9	3	0	0	(0	0)	12	4	5	3	2	0	4	0	0	1	0	0	-	1	.188	.220	.250
	2 ML YEARS		34	71	13	5	0	0	(0	0)	18	4	7	3	3	0	9	0	1	1	0	0	-	2	.183	.216	.254

David Weathers

Pitches: R Bats: R Pos: RP-73   Ht: 6'3" Wt: 230 Born: 9/25/1969 Age: 36

				HOW MUCH HE PITCHED			WHAT HE GAVE UP												THE RESULTS						
Year	Team	Lg	G	GS	CG	GF	IP	BFP	H	R	ER	HR	SH	SF	HB	TBB	IBB	SO	WP	Bk	W	L	Pct	ShO	Sv-Op	Hld	ERC	ERA
1991	TOR	AL	15	0	0	4	14.2	79	15	9	8	1	2	1	2	17	3	13	0	0	1	0	1.000	0	0-0	1	6.88	4.91
1992	TOR	AL	2	0	0	0	3.1	15	5	3	3	1	0	0	0	2	0	3	0	0	0	0	-	0	0-0	0	10.97	8.10
1993	FLA	NL	14	6	0	2	45.2	202	57	26	26	3	2	0	1	13	1	34	6	0	2	3	.400	0	0-0	0	4.86	5.12
1994	FLA	NL	24	24	0	0	135.0	621	166	87	79	13	12	4	4	59	9	72	7	1	8	12	.400	0	0-0	0	5.52	5.27
1995	FLA	NL	28	15	0	0	90.1	419	104	68	60	8	7	3	5	52	3	60	3	0	4	5	.444	0	0-0	1	5.79	5.98

Year	Team	Lg	G	GS	CG	GF	IP	BFP	H	R	ER	HR	SH	SF	HB	TBB	IBB	SO	WP	Bk	W	L	Pct	ShO	Sv-Op	Hld	ERC	ERA
1996	2 Tms		42	12	0	9	88.2	409	108	60	54	8	5	2	6	42	5	53	3	0	2	4	.333	0	0-0	3	5.80	5.48
1997	2 Tms	AL	19	1	0	5	25.2	126	38	24	24	3	2	1	1	15	0	18	3	0	1	3	.250	0	0-1	0	8.27	8.42
1998	2 Tms	NL	44	9	0	9	110.0	492	130	69	60	6	6	2	3	41	3	94	7	2	6	5	.545	0	0-1	3	4.73	4.91
1999	MIL	NL	63	0	0	14	93.0	414	102	49	48	14	4	4	2	38	3	74	1	1	7	4	.636	0	2-6	9	5.04	4.65
2000	MIL	NL	69	0	0	23	76.1	320	73	29	26	7	4	1	2	32	8	50	0	0	3	5	.375	0	1-7	14	3.90	3.07
2001	2 Tms	NL	80	0	0	25	86.0	351	65	24	23	6	10	3	3	34	8	66	0	0	4	5	.444	0	4-10	16	2.59	2.41
2002	NYN	NL	71	0	0	12	77.1	331	69	30	25	6	6	4	3	36	7	61	2	0	6	3	.667	0	0-5	18	3.60	2.91
2003	NYN	NL	77	0	0	20	87.2	384	87	33	30	6	8	0	6	40	6	75	1	0	1	6	.143	0	7-9	26	4.21	3.08
2004	3 Tms	NL	66	2	0	20	82.1	357	85	44	38	12	5	2	5	35	2	61	1	1	7	7	.500	0	0-4	12	5.01	4.15
2005	CIN	NL	73	0	0	41	77.2	331	71	36	34	7	4	2	2	29	2	61	4	0	7	4	.636	0	15-19	8	3.46	3.94
96	Fla	NL	31	8	0	8	71.1	319	85	41	36	7	5	1	4	28	4	40	2	0	2	2	.500	0	0-0	3	5.35	4.54
96	NYY	AL	11	4	0	1	17.1	90	23	19	18	1	0	1	2	14	1	13	1	0	0	2	.000	0	0-0	0	7.66	9.35
97	NYY	AL	10	0	0	3	9.0	47	15	10	10	1	0	0	0	7	0	4	2	0	0	1	.000	0	0-1	0	10.26	10.00
97	Cle	AL	9	1	0	2	16.2	79	23	14	14	2	2	1	1	8	0	14	1	0	1	2	.333	0	0-0	0	7.23	7.56
98	Cin	NL	16	9	0	0	62.1	294	86	47	43	3	4	1	1	27	2	51	5	1	2	4	.333	0	0-0	0	6.04	6.21
98	Mil	NL	28	0	0	9	47.2	198	44	22	17	3	2	1	2	14	1	43	2	1	4	1	.800	0	0-1	3	3.15	3.21
01	Mil	NL	52	0	0	21	57.2	233	37	14	13	3	8	1	2	25	7	46	0	0	3	4	.429	0	4-7	10	2.01	2.03
01	ChC	NL	28	0	0	4	28.1	118	28	10	10	3	2	2	1	9	1	20	0	0	1	1	.500	0	0-3	6	3.90	3.18
04	NYM	NL	32	0	0	10	33.2	156	41	19	16	5	2	2	2	15	0	25	1	1	5	3	.625	0	0-1	6	6.15	4.28
04	Hou	NL	26	0	0	9	32.0	137	31	20	17	5	2	0	3	13	1	26	0	0	1	4	.200	0	0-3	5	4.77	4.78
04	Fla	NL	8	2	0	1	16.2	64	13	5	5	2	1	0	0	7	1	10	0	0	1	0	1.000	0	0-0	1	3.28	2.70
15 ML YEARS			687	69	0	184	1093.2	4851	1175	591	538	101	77	29	45	485	60	795	38	5	59	66	.472	0	29-62	111	4.71	4.43

Jeff Weaver

Pitches: R Bats: R Pos: SP-34 Ht: 6'5" Wt: 200 Born: 8/22/1976 Age: 29

Year	Team	Lg	G	GS	CG	GF	IP	BFP	H	R	ER	HR	SH	SF	HB	TBB	IBB	SO	WP	Bk	W	L	Pct	ShO	Sv-Op	Hld	ERC	ERA
1999	DET	AL	30	29	0	1	163.2	717	176	104	101	27	5	5	17	56	2	114	0	0	9	12	.429	0	0-0	0	5.21	5.55
2000	DET	AL	31	30	2	0	200.0	849	205	102	96	26	3	9	15	52	2	136	3	2	11	15	.423	0	0-0	0	4.18	4.32
2001	DET	AL	33	33	5	0	229.1	985	235	116	104	19	12	7	14	68	4	152	3	0	13	16	.448	0	0-0	0	3.89	4.08
2002	2 Tms	AL	32	25	3	3	199.2	840	193	88	78	16	6	3	11	48	4	132	6	0	11	11	.500	3	2-2	0	3.30	3.52
2003	NYA	AL	32	24	0	3	159.1	735	211	113	106	16	9	9	11	47	2	93	2	0	7	9	.438	0	0-0	1	5.77	5.99
2004	LA	NL	34	34	0	0	220.0	935	219	103	98	19	5	7	14	67	9	153	9	0	13	13	.500	0	0-0	0	3.79	4.01
2005	LAN	NL	34	34	3	0	224.0	930	220	111	105	35	8	3	18	43	1	157	2	0	14	11	.560	2	0-0	0	3.87	4.22
02	Det	AL	17	17	3	0	121.2	509	112	50	43	4	5	2	8	33	1	75	4	0	6	8	.429	3	0-0	0	2.94	3.18
02	NYY	AL	15	8	0	3	78.0	331	81	38	35	12	1	1	3	15	3	57	2	0	5	3	.625	0	2-2	0	3.86	4.04
7 ML YEARS			226	209	13	7	1396.0	5991	1459	737	688	158	48	43	100	381	24	937	25	2	78	87	.473	5	2-2	1	4.18	4.44

Brandon Webb

Pitches: R Bats: R Pos: SP-33 Ht: 6'2" Wt: 228 Born: 5/9/1979 Age: 27

Year	Team	Lg	G	GS	CG	GF	IP	BFP	H	R	ER	HR	SH	SF	HB	TBB	IBB	SO	WP	Bk	W	L	Pct	ShO	Sv-Op	Hld	ERC	ERA
2003	ARI	NL	29	28	1	1	180.2	750	140	65	57	12	9	1	13	68	4	172	9	1	10	9	.526	1	0-0	0	2.80	2.84
2004	ARI	NL	35	35	1	0	208.0	933	194	111	83	17	14	6	11	119	11	164	17	1	7	16	.304	0	0-0	0	4.32	3.59
2005	ARI	NL	33	33	1	0	229.0	943	229	98	90	21	10	7	2	59	4	172	14	1	14	12	.538	0	0-0	0	3.54	3.54
3 ML YEARS			97	96	3	1	617.2	2626	563	274	230	50	33	14	26	246	19	508	40	3	31	37	.456	1	0-0	0	3.58	3.35

John Webb

Pitches: R Bats: R Pos: SP-1 Ht: 6'3" Wt: 220 Born: 5/23/1979 Age: 27

Year	Team	Lg	G	GS	CG	GF	IP	BFP	H	R	ER	HR	SH	SF	HB	TBB	IBB	SO	WP	Bk	W	L	Pct	ShO	Sv-Op	Hld	ERC	ERA
1999	Cubs	R	18	0	0	14	32.2	147	33	20	13	0	1	1	3	8	0	39	2	2	0	0	-	0	3--	-	2.99	3.58
1999	Eugene	A-	2	0	0	2	4.0	14	1	0	0	0	0	0	0	1	0	3	0	0	1	0	1.000	0	1--	-	0.40	0.00
2000	Lansng	A	21	21	1	0	134.2	559	125	53	37	4	3	6	8	40	0	108	9	1	7	6	.538	1	0--	-	3.09	2.47
2000	Dytona	A+	4	2	0	1	17.0	71	17	11	9	1	0	0	0	3	0	18	2	0	1	1	.500	0	1--	-	2.89	4.76
2001	Dytona	A+	5	4	0	0	20.0	91	23	13	12	0	0	0	2	7	1	20	2	1	1	1	.500	0	0--	-	4.21	5.40
2002	Dytona	A+	10	10	1	0	57.2	240	43	23	22	3	1	3	5	23	0	65	4	1	5	3	.625	1	0--	-	2.72	3.43
2002	WTenn	AA	11	11	0	0	61.2		52	33	31	5	1	2	5	22	0	45	3	1	4	5	.444	0	0--	-		4.52
2003	WTenn	AA	30	22	0	5	132.0	573	135	74	66	11	6	5	10	52	1	85	4	1	5	8	.385	0	1--	-	4.41	4.50
2004	Mont	AA	9	3	0	2	26.1	113	26	12	12	3	0	2	3	8	0	12	1	0	2	1	.667	0	0--	-	4.20	4.10
2004	Drham	AAA	6	6	0	0	33.0	142	31	19	12	5	1	3	4	14	0	22	3	0	1	3	.250	0	0--	-	4.80	3.27
2005	Drham	AAA	28	27	1	1	163.1	726	175	103	88	23	7	2	13	61	2	86	7	0	10	6	.625	0	0--	-	4.96	4.85
2004	TB	AL	4	0	0	1	9.0	45	12	7	7	2	0	0	1	7	0	9	1	0	0	0	-	0	0-0	0	9.56	7.00
2005	TB	AL	1	1	0	0	4.0	23	6	8	8	1	0	0	1	4	0	2	0	0	0	1	.000	0	0-0	0	12.29	18.00
2 ML YEARS			5	1	0	1	13.0	68	18	15	15	3	0	0	2	11	0	11	1	0	0	1	.000	0	0-0	0	10.40	10.38

Ben Weber

Pitches: R Bats: R Pos: RP-10 Ht: 6'4" Wt: 210 Born: 11/17/1969 Age: 36

Year	Team	Lg	G	GS	CG	GF	IP	BFP	H	R	ER	HR	SH	SF	HB	TBB	IBB	SO	WP	Bk	W	L	Pct	ShO	Sv-Op	Hld	ERC	ERA
2005	Dayton*	A	2	0	0	0	3.0	10	1	0	0	0	0	0	0	0	0	4	0	0	0	0	-	0	0--	-	0.25	0.00
2005	Chatt*	A	9	0	0	0	11.2	47	9	3	3	2	1	0	1	3	0	5	2	0	1	1	.500	0	0--	-	3.11	2.31
2005	Lsvlle*	AAA	7	0	0	2	7.0	35	8	5	5	0	0	0	2	6	0	5	0	0	0	1	.000	0	0--	-	7.33	6.43
2000	2 Tms	AL	19	0	0	3	22.2	103	28	19	16	0	0	1	0	6	1	14	2	0	1	1	.500	0	0-2	2	3.91	6.35
2001	ANA	AL	56	0	0	19	68.1	299	66	28	26	4	0	0	5	31	8	40	0	1	6	2	.750	0	0-1	6	3.90	3.42
2002	ANA	AL	63	0	0	16	78.0	312	70	25	22	4	4	2	3	22	3	43	2	0	7	2	.778	0	7-11	18	2.96	2.54
2003	ANA	AL	62	0	0	20	80.1	332	84	26	24	7	4	1	0	22	7	46	4	0	5	1	.833	0	0-2	11	3.71	2.69

			HOW MUCH HE PITCHED						WHAT HE GAVE UP													THE RESULTS							
Year	Team	Lg	G	GS	CG	GF	IP	BFP	H	R	ER	HR	SH	SF	HB	TBB	IBB	SO	WP	Bk	W	L	Pct	ShO	Sv-Op	Hld	ERC	ERA
2004	ANA	AL	18	0	0	5	22.1	117	37	24	20	4	0	0	0	15	0	11	0	0	0	2	.000	0	0-1	2	10.10	8.06
2005	CIN	NL	10	0	0	3	12.1	66	20	11	11	0	0	1	1	9	1	8	0	0	0	0	-	0	0-0	0	8.52	8.03
00	SF	NL	9	0	0	2	8.0	44	16	13	13	0	0	0	0	4	0	6	1	0	0	1	.000	0	0-2	1	9.72	14.63
00	Ana	AL	10	0	0	1	14.2	59	12	6	3	0	0	1	0	2	1	8	1	0	1	0	1.000	0	0-0	1	1.52	1.84
6 ML YEARS			228	0	0	66	284.0	1229	305	133	119	19	8	5	9	105	20	162	8	1	19	8	.704	0	7-17	39	4.19	3.77

Rickie Weeks

Bats: R **Throws:** R **Pos:** 2B-95; PH-1   **Ht:** 6'0" **Wt:** 195 **Born:** 9/13/1982 **Age:** 23

			BATTING																BASERUNNING				AVERAGES		
Year	Team	Lg	G	AB	H	2B	3B	HR	(Hm | Rd)	TB	R	RBI	RC	TBB	IBB	SO	HBP	SH	SF	SB	CS	SB%	GDP	Avg	OBP	Slg
2003	Brewrs	R	1	4	2	0	0	0	(- | -)	2	0	4	1	0	0	2	1	0	0	1	0	1.00	0	.500	.600	.500
2003	Beloit	A	20	63	22	8	1	1	(- | -)	35	13	16	18	15	0	9	6	0	0	2	0	1.00	1	.349	.494	.556
2004	Huntsvl	AA	133	479	124	35	6	8	(- | -)	195	67	42	73	55	1	107	28	3	3	11	12	.48	5	.259	.366	.407
2005	Nashv	AAA	55	203	65	14	9	12	(- | -)	133	43	48	57	28	0	51	14	3	1	10	1	.91	4	.320	.435	.655
2003	MIL	NL	7	12	2	1	0	0	(0 | 0)	3	1	0	0	1	0	6	1	0	0	0	0	-	0	.167	.286	.250
2005	MIL	NL	96	360	86	13	2	13	(8 | 5)	142	56	42	49	40	2	96	11	2	1	15	2	.88	11	.239	.333	.394
2 ML YEARS			103	372	88	14	2	13	(8 | 5)	145	57	42	49	41	2	102	12	2	1	15	2	.88	11	.237	.331	.390

Todd Wellemeyer

Pitches: R **Bats:** R **Pos:** RP-22   **Ht:** 6'3" **Wt:** 205 **Born:** 8/30/1978 **Age:** 27

			HOW MUCH HE PITCHED						WHAT HE GAVE UP													THE RESULTS							
Year	Team	Lg	G	GS	CG	GF	IP	BFP	H	R	ER	HR	SH	SF	HB	TBB	IBB	SO	WP	Bk	W	L	Pct	ShO	Sv-Op	Hld	ERC	ERA
2005	Iowa*	AAA	12	12	0	0	53.2	233	47	21	18	2	2	0	2	25	0	48	2	0	3	2	.600	0	0--	-	3.30	3.02
2003	CHN	NL	15	0	0	8	27.2	122	25	22	20	5	1	0	0	19	1	30	0	0	1	1	.500	0	1-1	1	5.33	6.51
2004	CHN	NL	20	0	0	7	24.1	119	27	16	16	1	3	2	0	20	2	30	0	1	2	1	.667	0	0-0	0	5.67	5.92
2005	CHN	NL	22	0	0	6	32.1	146	32	23	22	7	2	1	0	22	1	32	3	0	2	1	.667	0	1-1	3	6.09	6.12
3 ML YEARS			57	0	0	21	84.1	387	84	61	58	13	6	3	0	61	4	92	3	1	5	3	.625	0	2-2	4	5.74	6.19

David Wells

Pitches: L **Bats:** L **Pos:** SP-30   **Ht:** 6'4" **Wt:** 240 **Born:** 5/20/1963 **Age:** 43

			HOW MUCH HE PITCHED						WHAT HE GAVE UP													THE RESULTS							
Year	Team	Lg	G	GS	CG	GF	IP	BFP	H	R	ER	HR	SH	SF	HB	TBB	IBB	SO	WP	Bk	W	L	Pct	ShO	Sv-Op	Hld	ERC	ERA
1987	TOR	AL	18	2	0	6	29.1	132	37	14	13	0	1	0	0	12	0	32	4	0	4	3	.571	0	1-2	2	4.91	3.99
1988	TOR	AL	41	0	0	15	64.1	279	65	36	33	12	2	2	2	31	9	56	6	2	3	5	.375	0	4-6	8	5.11	4.62
1989	TOR	AL	54	0	0	19	86.1	352	66	25	23	5	3	2	0	28	7	78	6	3	7	4	.636	0	2-9	8	2.16	2.40
1990	TOR	AL	43	25	0	8	189.0	759	165	72	66	14	9	2	2	45	3	115	7	1	11	6	.647	0	3-3	3	2.67	3.14
1991	TOR	AL	40	28	2	3	198.1	811	188	88	82	24	6	6	2	49	1	106	10	3	15	10	.600	0	1-2	3	3.41	3.72
1992	TOR	AL	41	14	0	14	120.0	529	138	84	72	16	3	4	8	36	6	62	3	1	7	9	.438	0	2-4	3	4.98	5.40
1993	DET	AL	32	30	0	0	187.0	776	183	93	87	26	3	3	7	42	6	139	13	0	11	9	.550	0	0-0	1	3.64	4.19
1994	DET	AL	16	16	5	0	111.1	464	113	54	49	13	3	1	2	24	6	71	5	0	5	7	.417	1	0-0	0	3.54	3.96
1995	2 Tms		29	29	6	0	203.0	839	194	88	73	23	7	3	2	53	9	133	7	2	16	8	.667	0	0-0	0	3.37	3.24
1996	BAL	AL	34	34	3	0	224.1	946	247	132	128	32	8	14	7	51	7	130	4	2	11	14	.440	0	0-0	0	4.39	5.14
1997	NYA	AL	32	32	5	0	218.0	922	239	109	102	24	7	3	6	45	0	156	8	0	16	10	.615	2	0-0	0	4.04	4.21
1998	NYA	AL	30	30	8	0	214.1	851	195	86	83	29	2	2	1	29	0	163	2	0	18	4	.818	5	0-0	0	2.83	3.49
1999	TOR	AL	34	34	7	0	231.2	987	246	132	124	32	6	6	6	62	2	169	1	0	17	10	.630	1	0-0	0	4.26	4.82
2000	TOR	AL	35	35	9	0	229.2	972	266	115	105	23	6	7	8	31	0	166	9	1	20	8	.714	0	0-0	0	4.05	4.11
2001	CHA	AL	16	16	1	0	100.2	432	120	55	50	12	2	2	3	21	1	59	2	0	5	7	.417	0	0-0	0	4.69	4.47
2002	NYA	AL	31	31	2	0	206.1	873	210	100	86	21	6	5	5	45	2	137	4	0	19	7	.731	1	0-0	0	3.50	3.75
2003	NYA	AL	31	30	4	0	213.0	887	242	101	98	24	6	7	8	20	0	101	3	0	15	7	.682	0	0-0	0	3.87	4.14
2004	SD	NL	31	31	0	0	195.2	804	203	85	81	23	14	4	2	20	1	101	2	1	12	8	.600	0	0-0	0	3.23	3.73
2005	BOS	AL	30	30	2	0	184.0	780	220	95	91	21	1	6	9	21	0	107	4	1	15	7	.682	0	0-0	0	4.36	4.45
95	Det	AL	18	18	3	0	130.1	539	120	54	44	17	3	2	2	37	5	83	6	1	10	3	.769	0	0-0	0	3.40	3.04
95	Cin	NL	11	11	3	0	72.2	300	74	34	29	6	4	1	0	16	4	50	1	1	6	5	.545	0	0-0	0	3.31	3.59
19 ML YEARS			618	447	54	65	3206.1	13395	3337	1564	1446	374	95	79	80	665	60	2081	100	17	227	143	.614	12	13-26	28	3.74	4.06

Kip Wells

Pitches: R **Bats:** R **Pos:** SP-33   **Ht:** 6'3" **Wt:** 205 **Born:** 4/21/1977 **Age:** 29

			HOW MUCH HE PITCHED						WHAT HE GAVE UP													THE RESULTS							
Year	Team	Lg	G	GS	CG	GF	IP	BFP	H	R	ER	HR	SH	SF	HB	TBB	IBB	SO	WP	Bk	W	L	Pct	ShO	Sv-Op	Hld	ERC	ERA
1999	CHA	AL	7	7	0	0	35.2	153	33	17	16	2	0	2	3	15	0	29	1	2	4	1	.800	0	0-0	0	3.80	4.04
2000	CHA	AL	20	20	0	0	98.2	468	126	76	66	15	1	3	2	58	4	71	7	0	6	9	.400	0	0-0	0	7.01	6.02
2001	CHA	AL	40	20	0	3	133.1	603	145	80	71	14	8	6	12	61	5	99	14	0	10	11	.476	0	0-2	6	5.16	4.79
2002	PIT	NL	33	33	1	0	198.1	845	197	92	79	21	7	5	7	71	11	134	7	0	12	14	.462	1	0-0	0	4.00	3.58
2003	PIT	NL	31	31	1	0	197.1	835	171	77	72	24	15	2	7	76	7	147	6	0	10	9	.526	0	0-0	0	3.49	3.28
2004	PIT	NL	24	24	0	0	138.1	621	145	71	70	14	5	6	6	66	4	116	3	0	5	7	.417	0	0-0	0	4.77	4.55
2005	PIT	NL	33	33	1	0	182.0	828	186	116	103	23	9	10	12	99	8	132	8	0	8	18	.308	1	0-0	0	5.14	5.09
7 ML YEARS			188	168	3	3	983.2	4353	1003	529	477	113	45	34	49	446	39	728	46	2	55	69	.444	2	0-2	6	4.64	4.36

Vernon Wells

Bats: R **Throws:** R **Pos:** CF-155; DH-2   **Ht:** 6'1" **Wt:** 225 **Born:** 12/8/1978 **Age:** 27

			BATTING																BASERUNNING				AVERAGES		
Year	Team	Lg	G	AB	H	2B	3B	HR	(Hm	Rd)	TB	R	RBI	RC	TBB	IBB	SO	HBP	SH	SF	SB	CS	SB%	GDP	Avg	OBP	Slg
1999	TOR	AL	24	88	23	5	0	1	(1	0)	31	8	8	7	4	0	18	0	0	0	1	1	.50	6	.261	.293	.352
2000	TOR	AL	3	2	0	0	0	0	(0	0)	0	0	0	0	0	0	0	0	0	0	0	0	-	0	.000	.000	.000
2001	TOR	AL	30	96	30	8	0	1	(1	0)	41	14	6	16	5	0	15	1	0	1	5	0	1.00	0	.313	.350	.427

Year	Team	Lg	G	AB	H	2B	3B	HR	(Hm	Rd)	TB	R	RBI	RC	TBB	IBB	SO	HBP	SH	SF	SB	CS	SB%	GDP	Avg	OBP	Slg
																									BASERUNNING			AVERAGES	
2002	TOR	AL	159	608	167	34	4	23	(10	13)	278	87	100	88	27	0	85	3	2	8	9	4	.69	15	.275	.305	.457
2003	TOR	AL	161	678	215	49	5	33	(13	20)	373	118	117	124	42	2	80	7	0	8	4	1	.80	21	.317	.359	.550
2004	TOR	AL	134	536	146	34	2	23	(14	9)	253	82	67	72	51	2	83	2	0	1	9	2	.82	17	.272	.337	.472
2005	TOR	AL	156	620	167	30	3	28	(14	14)	287	78	97	96	47	3	86	3	0	8	8	3	.73	13	.269	.320	.463
7 ML YEARS			667	2628	748	160	14	109	(53	56)	1263	387	395	403	176	7	367	16	2	26	36	11	.77	72	.285	.330	.481

Jayson Werth

Bats: R **Throws:** R **Pos:** LF-64; RF-43; CF-30; PH-2 **Ht:** 6'5" **Wt:** 190 **Born:** 5/20/1979 **Age:** 27

Year	Team	Lg	G	AB	H	2B	3B	HR	(Hm	Rd)	TB	R	RBI	RC	TBB	IBB	SO	HBP	SH	SF	SB	CS	SB%	GDP	Avg	OBP	Slg
										BATTING											BASERUNNING				AVERAGES	
2005	LsVgs*	AAA	15	49	18	0	0	3	(-	-)	27	9	10	15	13	0	17	2	0	0	6	1	.86	0	.367	.516	.551
2002	TOR	AL	15	46	12	2	1	0	(0	0)	16	4	6	5	6	0	11	0	0	1	1	0	1.00	4	.261	.340	.348
2003	TOR	AL	26	48	10	4	0	2	(0	2)	20	7	10	6	3	0	22	0	0	0	1	0	1.00	0	.208	.255	.417
2004	LA	NL	89	290	76	11	3	16	(11	5)	141	56	47	47	30	0	85	4	1	1	4	1	.80	1	.262	.338	.486
2005	LAN	NL	102	337	79	22	2	7	(1	6)	126	46	43	44	48	2	114	6	1	3	11	2	.85	10	.234	.338	.374
4 ML YEARS			232	721	177	39	6	25	(12	13)	303	113	106	102	87	2	232	10	2	5	17	3	.85	15	.245	.333	.420

Jake Westbrook

Pitches: R **Bats:** R **Pos:** SP-34 **Ht:** 6'3" **Wt:** 185 **Born:** 9/29/1977 **Age:** 28

Year	Team	Lg	G	GS	CG	GF	IP	BFP	H	R	ER	HR	SH	SF	HB	TBB	IBB	SO	WP	Bk	W	L	Pct	ShO	Sv-Op	Hld	ERC	ERA
			HOW MUCH HE PITCHED						WHAT HE GAVE UP												THE RESULTS							
2000	NYA	AL	3	2	0	1	6.2	38	15	10	10	1	0	2	0	4	1	1	0	0	0	2	.000	0	0-0	0	13.53	13.50
2001	CLE	AL	23	6	0	3	64.2	290	79	43	42	6	1	5	4	22	4	48	4	0	4	4	.500	0	0-0	5	5.25	5.85
2002	CLE	AL	11	4	0	1	41.2	185	50	30	27	6	2	1	1	12	1	20	1	0	1	3	.250	0	0-2	1	5.12	5.83
2003	CLE	AL	34	22	1	4	133.0	580	142	70	64	9	4	3	12	56	1	58	3	0	7	10	.412	0	0-0	1	4.78	4.33
2004	CLE	AL	33	30	5	2	215.2	895	208	95	81	19	6	6	5	61	3	116	4	1	14	9	.609	1	0-0	0	3.45	3.38
2005	CLE	AL	34	34	2	0	210.2	895	218	121	105	19	5	4	7	56	3	119	3	0	15	15	.500	0	0-0	0	3.78	4.49
6 ML YEARS			138	98	8	11	672.1	2883	712	369	329	60	18	21	29	211	13	362	15	1	41	43	.488	1	0-2	7	4.17	4.40

Dan Wheeler

Pitches: R **Bats:** R **Pos:** RP-71 **Ht:** 6'3" **Wt:** 222 **Born:** 12/10/1977 **Age:** 28

Year	Team	Lg	G	GS	CG	GF	IP	BFP	H	R	ER	HR	SH	SF	HB	TBB	IBB	SO	WP	Bk	W	L	Pct	ShO	Sv-Op	Hld	ERC	ERA
			HOW MUCH HE PITCHED						WHAT HE GAVE UP												THE RESULTS							
1999	TB	AL	6	6	0	0	30.2	136	35	20	20	7	0	0	0	13	0	32	0	0	0	4	.000	0	0-0	0	6.01	5.87
2000	TB	AL	11	2	0	0	23.0	111	29	14	14	2	0	0	0	11	0	17	0	0	1	1	.500	0	0-0	0	5.57	5.48
2001	TB	AL	13	0	0	0	17.2	87	30	17	17	3	0	0	0	5	0	12	0	0	1	0	1.000	0	0-0	0	8.38	8.66
2003	NYN	NL	35	0	0	10	51.0	215	49	23	21	6	0	3	1	17	4	35	1	0	1	3	.250	0	2-3	5	3.69	3.71
2004	2 Tms	NL	46	1	0	11	65.0	287	76	33	31	10	2	1	1	20	2	55	4	1	3	1	.750	0	0-0	5	5.05	4.29
2005	HOU	NL	71	0	0	20	73.1	288	53	18	18	7	5	1	3	19	3	69	0	0	2	3	.400	0	3-5	17	2.22	2.21
04	NYM	NL	32	1	0	7	50.2	232	65	29	27	9	2	1	0	17	2	46	4	1	3	1	.750	0	0-0	3	5.91	4.80
04	Hou	NL	14	0	0	4	14.1	55	11	4	4	1	0	0	1	3	0	9	0	0	0	0	-	0	0-0	2	2.35	2.51
6 ML YEARS			182	9	0	41	260.2	1124	272	125	121	35	7	5	5	85	9	220	5	1	8	12	.400	0	5-8	22	4.27	4.18

Gabe White

Pitches: L **Bats:** L **Pos:** RP-6 **Ht:** 6'2" **Wt:** 204 **Born:** 11/20/1971 **Age:** 34

Year	Team	Lg	G	GS	CG	GF	IP	BFP	H	R	ER	HR	SH	SF	HB	TBB	IBB	SO	WP	Bk	W	L	Pct	ShO	Sv-Op	Hld	ERC	ERA
			HOW MUCH HE PITCHED						WHAT HE GAVE UP												THE RESULTS							
2005	Memp*	AAA	8	0	0	5	7.1	27	4	0	0	0	0	0	0	1	0	8	0	0	0	0	-	0	1- -	-	0.86	0.00
1994	MON	NL	7	5	0	2	23.2	106	24	16	16	4	1	1	1	11	0	17	0	0	1	1	.500	0	1-1	0	5.03	6.08
1995	MON	NL	19	1	0	8	25.2	115	26	21	20	7	2	3	1	9	0	25	0	0	1	2	.333	0	0-0	0	5.12	7.01
1997	CIN	NL	12	6	0	2	41.0	168	39	20	20	6	3	2	1	8	1	25	0	0	2	2	.500	0	1-1	3	3.37	4.39
1998	CIN	NL	69	3	0	29	98.2	404	86	46	44	17	2	2	1	27	6	83	3	0	5	5	.500	0	9-13	6	3.30	4.01
1999	CIN	NL	50	0	0	18	61.0	261	68	31	30	13	2	1	2	14	1	61	0	0	1	2	.333	0	0-1	3	4.95	4.43
2000	2 Tms	NL	68	0	0	17	84.0	329	64	23	22	6	2	6	3	15	2	84	1	0	11	2	.846	0	5-9	19	1.98	2.36
2001	COL	NL	69	0	0	16	67.2	290	70	47	47	18	2	2	1	26	5	47	1	0	1	7	.125	0	0-2	8	5.42	6.25
2002	CIN	NL	62	0	0	7	54.1	219	49	19	18	3	1	0	2	10	2	41	0	0	6	1	.857	0	0-11	19	2.56	2.98
2003	2 Tms	NL	46	0	0	5	46.2	190	44	22	21	7	2	3	2	8	4	29	0	0	5	1	.833	0	0-2	12	3.26	4.05
2004	2 Tms	NL	64	0	0	15	59.2	265	72	46	46	14	3	3	2	12	4	41	1	0	1	3	.250	0	1-5	12	5.33	6.94
2005	STL	NL	6	0	0	3	8.1	38	14	2	2	1	0	0	0	1	1	1	0	0	0	0	-	0	0-0	0	7.15	2.16
00	Cin	NL	1	0	0	0	1.0	6	2	2	2	1	0	0	0	1	0	2	0	0	0	0	-	0	0-0	0	23.01	18.00
00	Col	NL	67	0	0	17	83.0	323	62	21	20	5	2	6	3	14	2	82	1	0	11	2	.846	0	5-9	19	1.82	2.17
03	Cin	NL	34	0	0	4	34.1	141	36	15	15	5	1	2	1	6	3	23	0	0	3	0	1.000	0	0-1	6	3.81	3.93
03	NYY	AL	12	0	0	1	12.1	49	8	7	6	2	1	1	1	2	1	6	0	0	2	1	.667	0	0-1	6	1.89	4.38
04	NYY	AL	24	0	0	6	20.2	104	33	19	19	2	1	1	2	7	4	8	0	0	0	1	.000	0	0-2	3	7.27	8.27
04	NYN	NL	40	0	0	9	39.0	161	39	27	27	12	2	2	0	5	0	33	1	0	1	2	.333	0	1-3	9	4.21	6.23
11 ML YEARS			472	15	0	122	570.2	2385	556	293	286	96	20	23	16	141	26	454	6	0	34	26	.567	0	17-35	82	3.82	4.51

Matt White

Pitches: L **Bats:** R **Pos:** SP-1 **Ht:** 6'5" **Wt:** 234 **Born:** 8/19/1977 **Age:** 28

Year	Team	Lg	G	GS	CG	GF	IP	BFP	H	R	ER	HR	SH	SF	HB	TBB	IBB	SO	WP	Bk	W	L	Pct	ShO	Sv-Op	Hld	ERC	ERA
			HOW MUCH HE PITCHED						WHAT HE GAVE UP												THE RESULTS							
1998	Burlgtn	R+	8	8	0	0	46.1	190	34	14	10	1	0	2	0	24	0	47	4	4	4	1	.800	0	0- -	-	2.49	1.94
1998	Wtrtwn	A-	6	6	0	0	27.1	120	31	19	13	4	0	2	2	11	1	24	1	2	3	2	.600	0	0- -	-	5.61	4.28
1999	Clmbs	A	19	18	1	0	95.1	414	99	67	56	12	3	3	5	31	0	75	7	1	3	10	.231	0	0- -	-	4.37	5.29
2000	Kinston	A+	28	26	2	1	143.2	616	136	76	65	14	7	7	10	63	0	115	7	1	11	9	.550	0	0- -	-	4.26	4.07

HOW MUCH HE PITCHED / WHAT HE GAVE UP / THE RESULTS

Year	Team	Lg	G	GS	CG	GF	IP	BFP	H	R	ER	HR	SH	SF	HB	TBB	IBB	SO	WP	Bk	W	L	Pct	ShO	Sv-Op	Hld	ERC	ERA
2001	Akron	AA	25	25	0	0	144.0	618	151	84	77	18	6	3	3	60	1	72	7	2	8	10	.444	0	0- -	-	4.79	4.81
2002	Akron	AA	27	11	0	5	89.1	392	97	42	39	9	6	0	0	39	0	63	3	0	6	2	.750	0	1- -	-	4.76	3.93
2002	Buffalo	AAA	7	1	0	2	17.0	81	23	13	9	1	0	1	2	6	0	12	0	0	0	0	-	0	0- -	-	6.05	4.76
2003	Pwtckt	AAA	2	0	0	0	3.1	12	1	1	0	0	0	0	0	0	0	5	0	0	0	0	-	0	0- -	-	0.19	0.00
2003	Buffalo	AAA	19	1	0	7	42.1	177	36	12	10	3	4	1	0	16	0	34	2	0	2	3	.400	0	0- -	-	2.97	2.13
2003	Srsota	A+	2	2	0	0	5.0	22	6	1	0	0	0	0	0	1	0	2	0	0	0	0	-	0	0- -	-	3.60	0.00
2003	Portlnd	AA	2	1	0	1	3.0	13	1	1	0	0	1	0	1	2	0	3	1	0	0	0	-	0	0- -	-	2.02	0.00
2004	Buffalo	AAA	13	4	0	2	31.2	155	45	25	21	1	3	1	0	19	3	24	0	0	2	2	.500	0	0- -	-	6.68	5.97
2004	Omha	AAA	23	4	0	8	55.1	266	71	45	38	12	3	1	1	34	2	43	2	3	2	2	.500	0	1- -	-	7.68	6.18
2005	NewOr	AAA	35	16	0	3	125.2	544	122	62	52	7	4	3	2	45	0	102	9	2	8	6	.571	0	0- -	-	3.44	3.72
2003	2 Tms		6	0	0	3	5.2	33	13	14	14	3	0	1	0	5	0	0	0	0	0	1	.000	0	0-0	0	20.79	22.24
2005	WAS	NL	1	1	0	0	4.0	20	4	4	4	0	0	1	1	3	0	3	1	0	0	0	.000	0	0-0	0	5.48	9.00
03	Bos	AL	3	0	0	1	3.2	23	10	11	11	1	0	1	0	3	0	0	0	0	0	1	.000	0	0-0	0	20.66	27.00
03	Sea	AL	3	0	0	2	2.0	10	3	3	3	2	0	0	0	2	0	0	0	0	0	0	-	0	0-0	0	20.49	13.50
	2 ML YEARS		7	1	0	3	9.2	53	17	18	18	3	0	2	1	8	0	3	1	0	0	2	.000	0	0-0	0	13.76	16.76

Rick White

Pitches: R **Bats:** R **Pos:** RP-71 **Ht:** 6'4" **Wt:** 230 **Born:** 12/23/1968 **Age:** 37

Year	Team	Lg	G	GS	CG	GF	IP	BFP	H	R	ER	HR	SH	SF	HB	TBB	IBB	SO	WP	Bk	W	L	Pct	ShO	Sv-Op	Hld	ERC	ERA
1994	PIT	NL	43	5	0	23	75.1	317	79	35	32	9	7	5	6	17	3	38	2	2	4	5	.444	0	6-9	3	4.11	3.82
1995	PIT	NL	15	9	0	2	55.0	247	66	33	29	3	3	3	2	18	0	29	2	0	2	3	.400	0	0-0	0	4.70	4.75
1998	TB	AL	38	3	0	12	68.2	289	66	32	29	8	0	3	2	23	2	39	3	0	2	6	.250	0	0-0	2	3.82	3.80
1999	TB	AL	63	1	0	11	108.0	480	132	56	49	8	2	5	1	38	5	81	3	0	5	3	.625	0	0-2	4	4.96	4.08
2000	2 Tms	NL	66	0	0	14	99.2	420	83	44	39	9	1	3	7	38	5	67	3	0	5	9	.357	0	3-7	4	3.21	3.52
2001	NYN	NL	55	0	0	15	69.2	299	71	38	30	7	2	2	2	17	4	51	1	0	4	5	.444	0	2-4	10	3.52	3.88
2002	2 Tms	NL	61	0	0	10	62.2	264	62	33	30	4	3	4	1	21	5	41	3	0	5	7	.417	0	0-1	16	3.49	4.31
2003	2 Tms		49	0	0	15	67.0	293	74	48	43	13	2	2	4	21	2	54	2	0	1	2	.333	0	1-1	4	5.22	5.78
2004	CLE	AL	59	0	0	20	78.1	340	88	52	46	15	6	3	2	29	7	44	2	0	5	5	.500	0	1-3	2	5.41	5.29
2005	PIT	NL	71	0	0	23	75.0	338	90	39	31	3	9	4	4	29	10	40	4	0	4	7	.364	0	2-3	12	4.71	3.72
00	TB	AL	44	0	0	8	71.1	293	57	30	27	7	1	2	5	26	3	47	3	0	3	6	.333	0	2-5	2	3.09	3.41
00	NYM	NL	22	0	0	6	28.1	127	26	14	12	2	0	1	2	12	2	20	0	0	2	3	.400	0	1-2	2	3.51	3.81
02	Col	NL	41	0	0	8	40.2	182	49	30	28	4	1	4	1	18	4	27	3	0	2	6	.250	0	0-1	9	5.47	6.20
02	StL	NL	20	0	0	2	22.0	82	13	3	2	0	2	0	0	3	1	14	0	0	3	1	.750	0	0-0	7	0.94	0.82
03	CWS	AL	34	0	0	12	47.2	207	56	39	35	11	1	2	1	13	2	37	0	0	1	2	.333	0	1-1	3	5.58	6.61
03	Hou	NL	15	0	0	3	19.1	86	18	9	8	2	1	0	3	8	0	17	2	0	0	0	-	0	0-0	1	4.33	3.72
	10 ML YEARS		520	18	0	145	759.1	3287	811	410	358	79	35	34	31	251	43	484	25	2	37	52	.416	0	15-30	57	4.30	4.24

Rondell White

Bats: R **Throws:** R **Pos:** LF-65; DH-30; PH-2 **Ht:** 6'1" **Wt:** 225 **Born:** 2/23/1972 **Age:** 34

									BATTING												BASERUNNING				AVERAGES		
Year	Team	Lg	G	AB	H	2B	3B	HR	(Hm	Rd)	TB	R	RBI	RC	TBB	IBB	SO	HBP	SH	SF	SB	CS	SB%	GDP	Avg	OBP	Slg
1993	MON	NL	23	73	19	3	1	2	(1	1)	30	9	15	9	7	0	16	0	2	1	1	2	.33	2	.260	.321	.411
1994	MON	NL	40	97	27	10	1	2	(1	1)	45	16	13	16	9	0	18	3	0	0	1	1	.50	1	.278	.358	.464
1995	MON	NL	130	474	140	33	4	13	(6	7)	220	87	57	79	41	1	87	6	0	4	25	5	.83	11	.295	.356	.464
1996	MON	NL	88	334	98	19	4	6	(2	4)	143	35	41	46	22	0	53	2	0	1	14	6	.70	11	.293	.340	.428
1997	MON	NL	151	592	160	29	5	28	(9	19)	283	84	82	84	31	3	111	10	1	4	16	8	.67	18	.270	.316	.478
1998	MON	NL	97	357	107	21	2	17	(9	8)	183	54	58	65	30	2	57	7	0	3	16	7	.70	7	.300	.363	.513
1999	MON	NL	138	539	168	26	6	22	(10	12)	272	83	64	91	32	2	85	11	0	6	10	6	.63	17	.312	.359	.505
2000	MON	NL	94	357	111	26	0	13	(3	10)	176	59	61	64	33	0	79	4	0	2	5	3	.63	4	.311	.374	.493
2001	CHN	NL	95	323	99	19	1	17	(7	10)	171	43	50	57	26	4	56	7	1	0	1	0	1.00	14	.307	.371	.529
2002	NYA	AL	126	455	109	21	0	14	(5	9)	172	59	49	62	25	1	86	8	1	5	1	2	.33	11	.240	.288	.378
2003	2 Tms	NL	137	488	141	23	4	22	(5	14)	238	62	87	72	31	2	79	10	0	5	1	4	.20	13	.289	.341	.488
2004	DET	AL	121	448	121	21	2	19	(5	14)	203	76	67	69	39	4	77	8	0	3	1	2	.33	13	.270	.337	.453
2005	DET	AL	97	374	117	24	3	12	(7	5)	183	49	53	61	17	0	48	5	0	4	1	0	1.00	8	.313	.348	.489
00	Mon	NL	75	290	89	24	0	11	(3	8)	146	52	54	53	28	0	67	2	0	2	5	1	.83	4	.307	.370	.503
00	ChC	NL	19	67	22	2	0	2	(0	2)	30	7	7	11	5	0	12	2	0	0	0	2	.00	0	.328	.392	.448
03	SD	NL	115	413	115	17	3	18	(4	14)	192	49	66	54	25	2	71	8	0	3	1	4	.20	11	.278	.330	.465
03	KC	AL	22	75	26	6	1	4	(1	3)	46	13	21	18	6	0	8	2	0	2	0	0	-	2	.347	.400	.613
	13 ML YEARS		1337	4911	1417	275	33	187	(70	117)	2319	716	710	756	343	19	852	81	5	38	93	46	.67	130	.289	.343	.472

Eli Whiteside

Bats: R **Throws:** R **Pos:** C-9 **Ht:** 6'2" **Wt:** 208 **Born:** 10/22/1979 **Age:** 26

									BATTING												BASERUNNING				AVERAGES		
Year	Team	Lg	G	AB	H	2B	3B	HR	(Hm	Rd)	TB	R	RBI	RC	TBB	IBB	SO	HBP	SH	SF	SB	CS	SB%	GDP	Avg	OBP	Slg
2001	Dlmrva	A	61	212	53	11	0	7	(-	-)	85	30	28	26	9	1	45	7	0	2	1	1	.50	11	.250	.300	.401
2002	Frdrck	A+	80	313	81	19	0	8	(-	-)	124	34	42	38	14	0	57	4	0	4	0	0	-	8	.259	.296	.396
2002	Bowie	AA	27	99	26	5	0	2	(-	-)	37	11	11	11	4	0	18	3	1	0	0	1	.00	4	.263	.311	.374
2003	Orioles	R	1	3	1	1	0	0	(-	-)	2	0	0	0	0	0	1	0	0	0	0	0	-	0	.333	.500	.667
2003	Abrdn	A-	2	10	7	3	0	0	(-	-)	10	0	4	4	0	0	1	0	0	0	1	0	1.00	0	.700	.700	1.000
2003	Bowie	AA	81	265	54	13	1	1	(-	-)	72	21	23	14	5	0	44	4	1	0	0	0	-	7	.204	.230	.272
2004	Bowie	AA	90	297	75	18	0	18	(-	-)	147	41	60	46	25	0	65	1	0	3	2	2	.50	3	.253	.310	.495
2005	Ottawa	AAA	95	317	74	22	1	4	(-	-)	110	28	27	31	21	1	65	2	1	3	1	3	.25	7	.233	.283	.347
2005	BAL	AL	9	12	3	0	0	0	(0	0)	3	1	1	0	0	0	2	0	0	0	0	0	-	1	.250	.250	.250

Matt Whiteside

Pitches: R Bats: R Pos: RP-2   Ht: 6'0" Wt: 200 Born: 8/8/1967 Age: 38

			HOW MUCH HE PITCHED						WHAT HE GAVE UP												THE RESULTS							
Year	Team	Lg	G	GS	CG	GF	IP	BFP	H	R	ER	HR	SH	SF	HB	TBB	IBB	SO	WP	Bk	W	L	Pct	ShO	Sv-Op	Hld	ERC	ERA
2005	Syrcse*	AAA	40	0	0	36	41.2	165	35	14	12	4	0	4	1	5	1	39	2	0	0	4	.500	0	27--	-	2.21	2.59
1992	TEX	AL	20	0	0	8	28.0	118	26	8	6	1	0	1	0	11	2	13	2	0	1	1	.500	0	4-4	0	3.12	1.93
1993	TEX	AL	60	0	0	10	73.0	305	78	37	35	7	2	1	1	23	6	39	0	2	2	1	.667	0	1-5	14	4.15	4.32
1994	TEX	AL	47	0	0	16	61.0	272	68	40	34	6	3	2	1	28	3	37	1	0	2	2	.500	0	1-3	7	4.97	5.02
1995	TEX	AL	40	0	0	18	53.0	223	48	24	24	5	2	3	1	19	2	46	4	0	5	4	.556	0	3-4	7	3.37	4.08
1996	TEX	AL	14	0	0	7	32.1	148	43	24	24	8	1	2	0	11	1	15	1	0	0	1	.000	0	0-0	1	6.87	6.68
1997	TEX	AL	42	1	0	8	72.2	382	85	45	41	4	2	5	3	26	3	44	3	2	4	1	.800	0	0-4	2	4.65	5.08
1998	PHI	NL	10	0	0	4	18.0	85	27	18	17	6	0	0	0	5	0	14	0	1	1	1	.500	0	0-0	0	8.40	8.50
1999	SD	NL	10	0	0	4	11.0	55	19	17	17	1	1	1	0	5	0	9	1	0	1	0	1.000	0	0-0	0	8.89	13.91
2000	SD	NL	28	0	0	9	37.0	159	32	21	17	6	2	1	1	17	3	27	2	1	2	3	.400	0	0-0	6	3.94	4.14
2001	ATL	NL	13	0	0	8	16.1	81	23	14	13	5	0	1	1	7	1	10	2	0	1	0	.000	0	0-0	1	8.26	7.16
2005	TOR	AL	2	0	0	0	3.2	23	6	8	8	3	0	0	1	5	0	5	0	0	0	0	-	0	0-0	0	21.71	19.64
11 ML YEARS			286	1	0	89	406.0	1792	455	256	236	52	13	17	9	157	21	259	16	6	18	15	.545	0	9-20	38	4.94	5.23

Bob Wickman

Pitches: R Bats: R Pos: RP-64   Ht: 6'1" Wt: 240 Born: 2/6/1969 Age: 37

			HOW MUCH HE PITCHED						WHAT HE GAVE UP												THE RESULTS							
Year	Team	Lg	G	GS	CG	GF	IP	BFP	H	R	ER	HR	SH	SF	HB	TBB	IBB	SO	WP	Bk	W	L	Pct	ShO	Sv-Op	Hld	ERC	ERA
1992	NYA	AL	8	1	0	4	50.1	213	51	25	23	2	1	3	2	20	0	21	3	0	6	1	.857	0	0-0	0	3.99	4.11
1993	NYA	AL	41	19	1	9	140.0	629	156	82	72	13	4	1	5	69	7	70	2	0	14	4	.778	1	4-8	2	5.16	4.63
1994	NYA	AL	53	0	0	19	70.0	286	54	26	24	3	0	5	1	27	3	56	2	0	5	4	.556	0	6-10	11	2.45	3.09
1995	NYA	AL	63	1	0	14	80.0	347	77	38	36	6	4	1	5	33	3	51	2	0	2	4	.333	0	1-10	21	3.92	4.05
1996	2 Tms		70	0	0	14	95.2	429	106	50	47	10	2	4	5	44	3	75	4	0	7	1	.875	0	0-4	10	5.17	4.42
1997	MIL	AL	74	0	0	20	95.2	405	89	32	29	8	6	2	3	41	7	78	8	0	7	6	.538	0	1-5	28	3.76	2.73
1998	MIL	NL	72	0	0	51	82.1	357	79	38	34	5	10	3	4	39	2	71	1	0	6	9	.400	0	25-32	9	4.05	3.72
1999	MIL	NL	71	0	0	63	74.1	331	75	31	28	6	3	2	2	38	6	60	2	0	3	8	.273	0	37-45	0	4.38	3.39
2000	2 Tms		69	0	0	60	72.2	309	64	30	25	1	3	1	1	32	5	55	2	0	3	5	.375	0	30-37	0	2.92	3.10
2001	CLE	AL	70	0	0	56	67.2	270	61	18	18	4	0	0	2	14	2	66	2	0	5	0	1.000	0	32-35	4	2.69	2.39
2002	CLE	AL	36	0	0	30	34.1	159	42	22	17	3	0	0	1	10	0	36	0	0	1	3	.250	0	20-22	0	4.72	4.46
2004	CLE	AL	30	0	0	21	29.2	129	33	14	14	4	0	0	2	10	0	26	0	0	0	2	.000	0	13-14	4	5.09	4.25
2005	CLE	AL	64	0	0	55	62.0	257	57	17	17	9	2	2	1	21	3	41	0	1	0	4	.000	0	45-50	0	3.74	2.47
96	NYY	AL	58	0	0	14	79.0	358	94	41	41	7	1	4	5	34	1	61	3	0	4	1	.800	0	0-3	6	5.51	4.67
96	Mil	AL	12	0	0	4	16.2	71	12	9	6	3	1	0	0	10	2	14	1	0	3	0	1.000	0	0-1	4	3.66	3.24
00	Mil	NL	43	0	0	36	46.0	194	37	18	15	1	0	1	1	20	2	44	2	0	2	2	.500	0	16-20	0	2.62	2.93
00	Cle	AL	26	0	0	24	26.2	115	27	12	10	0	3	0	0	12	3	11	0	0	1	3	.250	0	14-17	0	3.47	3.38
13 ML YEARS			721	28	1	416	954.2	4121	944	423	384	74	35	24	34	398	41	706	28	1	59	51	.536	1	214-272	89	4.02	3.62

Chris Widger

Bats: R Throws: R Pos: C-42; 1B-1; 3B-1; DH-1; PH-1   Ht: 6'3" Wt: 215 Born: 5/21/1971 Age: 35

			BATTING																		BASERUNNING				AVERAGES		
Year	Team	Lg	G	AB	H	2B	3B	HR	(Hm	Rd)	TB	R	RBI	RC	TBB	IBB	SO	HBP	SH	SF	SB	CS	SB%	GDP	Avg	OBP	Slg
1995	SEA	AL	23	45	9	0	0	1	(1	0)	12	2	2	3	3	0	11	0	0	1	0	0	-	0	.200	.245	.267
1996	SEA	AL	8	11	2	0	0	0	(0	0)	2	1	0	0	0	0	5	1	0	0	0	0	-	0	.182	.250	.182
1997	MON	NL	91	278	65	20	3	7	(4	3)	112	30	37	32	22	1	59	1	2	2	2	0	1.00	7	.234	.290	.403
1998	MON	NL	125	417	97	18	1	15	(6	9)	162	36	53	46	29	2	85	0	0	2	6	1	.86	5	.233	.281	.388
1999	MON	NL	124	383	101	24	1	14	(11	3)	169	42	56	53	28	0	86	7	0	1	1	4	.20	5	.264	.325	.441
2000	2 Tms		96	292	68	17	2	13	(6	7)	128	32	35	39	30	3	63	1	0	1	1	2	.33	5	.233	.306	.438
2002	NYA	AL	21	64	19	5	0	0	(0	0)	24	4	5	8	2	0	9	2	0	0	0	0	-	0	.297	.338	.375
2003	STL	NL	44	102	24	9	0	0	(0	0)	33	9	14	10	6	1	20	1	1	2	0	0	-	5	.235	.279	.324
2005	CHA	AL	45	141	34	8	0	4	(2	2)	54	18	11	12	10	0	22	1	2	0	0	2	.00	5	.241	.296	.383
00	Mon	NL	86	281	67	17	2	12	(6	6)	124	31	34	38	29	3	61	1	0	1	1	2	.33	5	.238	.311	.441
00	Sea	AL	10	11	1	0	0	1	(0	1)	4	1	1	1	1	0	2	0	0	0	0	0	-	0	.091	.167	.364
9 ML YEARS			577	1733	419	101	7	54	(30	24)	696	174	213	203	130	7	360	14	5	9	10	9	.53	32	.242	.299	.402

Ty Wigginton

Bats: R Throws: R Pos: 3B-40; PH-16; 1B-3; 2B-1   Ht: 6'0" Wt: 200 Born: 10/11/1977 Age: 28

			BATTING																		BASERUNNING				AVERAGES		
Year	Team	Lg	G	AB	H	2B	3B	HR	(Hm	Rd)	TB	R	RBI	RC	TBB	IBB	SO	HBP	SH	SF	SB	CS	SB%	GDP	Avg	OBP	Slg
2005	Indy*	AAA	72	280	82	18	0	14	(-	-)	142	53	52	56	45	4	56	1	0	2	8	5	.62	4	.293	.390	.507
2002	NYN	NL	46	116	35	8	0	6	(4	2)	61	18	18	15	8	0	19	2	0	1	2	1	.67	4	.302	.354	.526
2003	NYN	NL	156	573	146	36	6	11	(4	7)	227	73	71	76	46	2	124	9	1	4	12	2	.86	15	.255	.318	.396
2004	2 Tms		144	494	129	30	2	17	(6	11)	214	63	66	59	45	6	82	2	1	3	7	1	.88	15	.261	.324	.433
2005	PIT	NL	57	155	40	9	1	7	(1	6)	72	20	25	22	14	0	30	1	1	0	0	1	.00	3	.258	.324	.465
04	NYM	NL	86	312	89	23	2	12	(5	7)	152	46	42	38	23	4	48	1	1	2	6	1	.86	11	.285	.334	.487
04	Pit	NL	58	182	40	7	0	5	(1	4)	62	17	24	21	22	2	34	1	0	1	1	0	1.00	4	.220	.306	.341
4 ML YEARS			403	1338	350	83	9	41	(15	26)	574	174	180	172	113	8	255	14	3	8	21	5	.81	37	.262	.324	.429

Brad Wilkerson

Bats: L Throws: L Pos: CF-92; LF-38; 1B-25; RF-6; PH-3   Ht: 6'0" Wt: 200 Born: 6/1/1977 Age: 29

			BATTING																		BASERUNNING				AVERAGES		
Year	Team	Lg	G	AB	H	2B	3B	HR	(Hm	Rd)	TB	R	RBI	RC	TBB	IBB	SO	HBP	SH	SF	SB	CS	SB%	GDP	Avg	OBP	Slg
2001	MON	NL	47	117	24	7	2	1	(1	0)	38	11	5	12	17	1	41	0	1	1	2	1	.67	2	.205	.304	.325
2002	MON	NL	153	507	135	27	8	20	(12	8)	238	92	59	83	81	7	161	5	6	4	7	8	.47	5	.266	.370	.469
2003	MON	NL	146	504	135	34	4	19	(9	10)	234	78	77	90	89	0	155	4	2	3	13	10	.57	5	.268	.380	.464

(continued)

Year	Team	Lg	G	AB	H	2B	3B	HR	(Hm	Rd)	TB	R	RBI	RC	TBB	IBB	SO	HBP	SH	SF	SB	CS	SB%	GDP	Avg	OBP	Slg
2004	MON	NL	160	572	146	39	2	32	(15	17)	285	112	67	95	106	8	152	4	3	3	13	6	.68	6	.255	.374	.498
2005	WAS	NL	148	565	140	42	7	11	(6	5)	229	76	57	83	84	9	147	7	3	2	8	10	.44	6	.248	.351	.405
5 ML YEARS			654	2265	580	149	23	83	(43	40)	1024	369	265	363	377	25	656	20	15	13	43	35	.55	24	.256	.365	.452

Bernie Williams

Bats: B Throws: R Pos: CF-112; DH-23; PH-16; PR-1　　　　**Ht: 6'2" Wt: 205 Born: 9/13/1968 Age: 37**

Year	Team	Lg	G	AB	H	2B	3B	HR	(Hm	Rd)	TB	R	RBI	RC	TBB	IBB	SO	HBP	SH	SF	SB	CS	SB%	GDP	Avg	OBP	Slg
1991	NYA	AL	85	320	76	19	4	3	(1	2)	112	43	34	41	48	0	57	1	2	3	10	5	.67	4	.238	.336	.350
1992	NYA	AL	62	261	73	14	2	5	(3	2)	106	39	26	37	29	1	36	1	2	0	7	6	.54	5	.280	.354	.406
1993	NYA	AL	139	567	152	31	4	12	(5	7)	227	67	68	71	53	4	106	4	1	3	9	9	.50	17	.268	.333	.400
1994	NYA	AL	108	408	118	29	1	12	(4	8)	185	80	57	70	61	2	54	3	1	2	16	9	.64	11	.289	.384	.453
1995	NYA	AL	144	563	173	29	9	18	(7	11)	274	93	82	105	75	1	98	5	2	3	8	6	.57	12	.307	.392	.487
1996	NYA	AL	143	551	168	26	7	29	(12	17)	295	108	102	113	82	8	72	0	1	7	17	4	.81	15	.305	.391	.535
1997	NYA	AL	129	509	167	35	6	21	(13	8)	277	107	100	109	73	7	80	1	0	8	15	8	.65	10	.328	.408	.544
1998	NYA	AL	128	499	169	30	5	26	(14	12)	287	101	97	110	74	9	81	1	0	4	15	9	.63	19	**.339**	.422	.575
1999	NYA	AL	158	591	202	28	6	25	(11	14)	317	116	115	131	100	**17**	95	1	0	5	9	10	.47	11	.342	.435	.536
2000	NYA	AL	141	537	165	37	6	30	(15	15)	304	108	121	112	71	11	84	5	0	3	13	5	.72	15	.307	.391	.566
2001	NYA	AL	146	540	166	38	0	26	(14	12)	282	102	94	108	78	11	67	6	0	9	11	5	.69	15	.307	.395	.522
2002	NYA	AL	154	612	204	37	2	19	(13	6)	302	102	102	124	83	7	97	3	0	1	8	4	.67	19	.333	.415	.493
2003	NYA	AL	119	445	117	19	1	15	(5	10)	183	77	64	66	71	8	61	3	0	2	5	0	1.00	19	.263	.367	.411
2004	NYA	AL	148	561	147	29	1	22	(13	9)	244	105	70	82	85	5	96	2	1	2	1	5	.17	19	.262	.360	.435
2005	NYA	AL	141	485	121	19	1	12	(7	5)	178	53	64	62	53	1	75	1	1	6	1	2	.33	16	.249	.321	.367
15 ML YEARS			1945	7449	2218	420	55	275	(137	138)	3573	1301	1196	1341	1036	92	1159	37	11	58	145	87	.63	209	.298	.384	.480

Dave Williams

Pitches: L Bats: L Pos: SP-25　　　　**Ht: 6'2" Wt: 213 Born: 3/12/1979 Age: 27**

Year	Team	Lg	G	GS	CG	GF	IP	BFP	H	R	ER	HR	SH	SF	HB	TBB	IBB	SO	WP	Bk	W	L	Pct	ShO	Sv-Op	Hld	ERC	ERA
2001	PIT	NL	22	18	0	1	114.0	472	100	53	47	15	3	8	7	45	4	57	0	0	3	7	.300	0	0-0	0	3.89	3.71
2002	PIT	NL	9	9	0	0	43.1	195	38	26	24	9	2	1	4	24	2	33	2	2	2	5	.286	0	0-0	0	4.99	4.98
2004	PIT	NL	10	6	0	0	38.2	162	31	21	19	4	1	1	3	13	2	33	0	0	2	3	.400	0	0-0	0	2.97	4.42
2005	PIT	NL	25	25	1	0	138.2	600	137	74	68	20	7	2	8	58	5	88	3	0	10	11	.476	1	0-0	0	4.62	4.41
4 ML YEARS			66	58	1	1	334.2	1429	306	174	158	48	13	12	22	140	13	211	5	2	17	26	.395	1	0-0	1	4.22	4.25

Gerald Williams

Bats: R Throws: R Pos: LF-10; CF-10; PR-9; RF-7; PH-7　　　　**Ht: 6'2" Wt: 187 Born: 8/10/1966 Age: 39**

Year	Team	Lg	G	AB	H	2B	3B	HR	(Hm	Rd)	TB	R	RBI	RC	TBB	IBB	SO	HBP	SH	SF	SB	CS	SB%	GDP	Avg	OBP	Slg
2005	Norfolk*	AAA	47	139	32	10	2	4	(-	-)	58	24	16	16	9	0	21	1	1	1	1	2	.33	1	.230	.280	.417
1992	NYA	AL	15	27	8	2	0	3	(2	1)	19	7	6	6	0	0	3	0	0	0	2	0	1.00	0	.296	.296	.704
1993	NYA	AL	42	67	10	2	3	0	(0	0)	18	11	6	2	1	0	14	2	0	1	2	0	1.00	4	.149	.183	.269
1994	NYA	AL	57	86	25	8	0	4	(2	2)	45	19	13	11	4	0	17	0	0	1	1	3	.25	6	.291	.319	.523
1995	NYA	AL	100	182	45	18	2	6	(4	2)	85	33	28	28	22	1	34	1	0	3	4	2	.67	4	.247	.327	.467
1996	2 Tms	AL	125	325	82	19	4	5	(3	2)	124	43	34	34	19	3	57	3	5	5	10	9	.53	8	.252	.299	.382
1997	MIL	AL	155	566	143	32	2	10	(3	7)	209	73	41	58	19	1	90	6	5	5	23	9	.72	9	.253	.282	.369
1998	ATL	NL	129	266	81	19	2	10	(5	5)	134	46	44	45	17	1	48	3	2	1	11	5	.69	5	.305	.352	.504
1999	ATL	NL	143	422	116	24	1	17	(7	10)	193	76	68	63	33	1	67	6	4	2	19	11	.63	8	.275	.335	.457
2000	TB	AL	146	632	173	30	2	21	(6	15)	270	87	89	83	34	0	103	3	9	4	12	12	.50	15	.274	.312	.427
2001	2 Tms	AL	100	279	56	18	0	4	(3	1)	86	42	19	20	18	0	55	5	4	0	13	5	.72	9	.201	.262	.308
2002	NYA	AL	33	17	0	0	0	0	(0	0)	0	6	0	0	2	0	4	0	0	0	2	0	1.00	1	.000	.105	.000
2003	FLA	NL	27	31	4	1	0	0	(0	0)	5	5	3	1	2	0	5	0	2	0	3	0	1.00	0	.129	.182	.161
2004	NYN	NL	57	129	30	8	2	4	(0	4)	54	17	11	13	8	1	26	0	1	0	2	1	.67	2	.233	.277	.419
2005	NYN	NL	39	30	7	2	0	1	(0	1)	12	9	3	4	1	0	7	0	1	0	2	0	1.00	0	.233	.258	.400
96	NYY	AL	99	233	63	15	4	5	(3	2)	101	37	30	29	15	2	39	4	1	5	7	8	.47	7	.270	.319	.433
96	Mil	AL	26	92	19	4	0	0	(0	0)	23	6	4	5	4	1	18	1	2	0	3	1	.75	1	.207	.247	.250
01	TB	AL	62	232	48	17	0	4	(3	1)	77	30	17	18	13	0	42	4	3	0	10	4	.71	8	.207	.261	.332
01	NYY	AL	38	47	8	1	0	0	(0	0)	9	12	2	2	5	0	13	1	1	0	3	1	.75	1	.170	.264	.191
14 ML YEARS			1168	3059	780	183	18	85	(35	50)	1254	474	365	368	180	8	530	31	31	22	106	57	.65	59	.255	.301	.410

Glenn Williams

Bats: B Throws: R Pos: 3B-12; PH-2　　　　**Ht: 6'2" Wt: 195 Born: 7/18/1977 Age: 28**

Year	Team	Lg	G	AB	H	2B	3B	HR	(Hm	Rd)	TB	R	RBI	RC	TBB	IBB	SO	HBP	SH	SF	SB	CS	SB%	GDP	Avg	OBP	Slg
1994	Danvle	R+	24	79	20	2	0	1	(-	-)	25	11	9	8	8	0	20	3	0	0	2	4	.33	4	.253	.344	.316
1994	Braves	R	24	89	18	2	0	2	(-	-)	26	8	7	7	9	0	32	0	0	1	4	1	.80	0	.202	.273	.292
1995	Eugene	A-	71	268	60	11	4	7	(-	-)	100	39	36	30	21	1	71	5	0	2	7	4	.64	4	.224	.291	.373
1995	Macon	A	38	120	21	4	0	0	(-	-)	25	13	14	7	16	0	42	1	1	3	2	1	.67	3	.175	.271	.208
1996	Macon	A	51	181	35	7	3	3	(-	-)	57	14	18	16	18	2	47	2	1	2	4	2	.67	3	.193	.271	.315
1997	Macon	A	77	297	79	18	2	14	(-	-)	143	52	52	47	24	1	105	5	1	4	9	6	.60	4	.266	.327	.481
1998	Danvle	A+	134	470	101	26	1	9	(-	-)	156	40	44	44	37	3	132	6	3	3	1	3	.25	5	.215	.279	.332
1999	Grnville	AA	57	204	46	11	0	4	(-	-)	69	19	15	16	7	1	58	4	1	1	1	4	.20	2	.225	.264	.338
2000	Dnedin	A+	107	391	102	26	4	13	(-	-)	175	53	77	59	33	1	91	6	0	6	4	2	.67	11	.261	.323	.448
2001	Tenn	AA	130	487	124	28	0	11	(-	-)	185	63	65	61	45	4	120	5	2	5	1	5	.17	8	.255	.321	.380
2002	Syrcse	AAA	94	339	93	18	3	15	(-	-)	162	49	47	52	20	0	80	2	1	0	2	0	1.00	7	.274	.319	.478
2003	Syrcse	AAA	59	210	49	10	3	3	(-	-)	74	27	24	20	12	2	56	1	2	1	2	1	.67	6	.233	.277	.352

								BATTING												BASERUNNING				AVERAGES		
Year	Team	Lg	G	AB	H	2B	3B	HR	(Hm Rd)	TB	R	RBI	RC	TBB	IBB	SO	HBP	SH	SF	SB	CS	SB%	GDP	Avg	OBP	Slg
2004	Syrcse	AAA	117	432	114	23	4	23	(- -)	214	65	79	71	34	1	79	8	4	8	2	4	.33	9	.264	.324	.495
2005	Roch	AAA	48	175	53	12	1	5	(- -)	82	21	22	28	7	1	35	3	2	0	2	0	1.00	3	.303	.341	.469
2005	MIN	AL	13	40	17	1	0	0	(0 0)	18	3	3	9	2	0	7	0	1	0	1	2	.33	0	.425	.452	.450

Jerome Williams

Pitches: R **Bats:** R **Pos:** SP-20; RP-2 **Ht:** 6'1" **Wt:** 189 **Born:** 12/4/1981 **Age:** 24

			HOW MUCH HE PITCHED						WHAT HE GAVE UP										THE RESULTS						
Year	Team	Lg	G	GS	CG	GF	IP	BFP	H	R	ER	HR	SH	SF	HB	TBB	IBB	SO	WP	Bk	W	L	Pct	ShO	Sv-Op	Hld	ERC	ERA
2005	Fresno*	AAA	6	6	0	0	30.2	156	47	34	32	3	2	3	3	17	0	15	2	1	1	4	.200	0	0- -	-	8.39	9.39
2005	Iowa*	AAA	4	4	0	0	24.1	106	27	10	6	2	1	1	2	6	0	17	5	0	1	1	.500	0	0- -	-	4.27	2.22
2003	SF	NL	21	21	2	0	131.0	545	116	54	48	10	6	3	7	49	3	88	2	1	7	5	.583	1	0-0	0	3.42	3.30
2004	SF	NL	22	22	0	0	129.1	559	123	69	61	14	4	9	17	44	1	80	2	1	10	7	.588	0	0-0	0	4.14	4.24
2005	2 Tms	NL	22	20	0	0	122.2	532	119	62	58	14	11	8	10	49	1	70	2	0	6	10	.375	0	0-0	1	4.34	4.26
05	SF	NL	4	3	0	0	16.2	73	21	12	12	2	1	0	1	4	1	11	0	0	0	2	.000	0	0-0	0	5.32	6.48
05	ChC	NL	18	17	0	0	106.0	459	98	50	46	12	10	8	9	45	0	59	2	0	6	8	.429	0	0-0	1	4.19	3.91
	3 ML YEARS		65	63	2	0	383.0	1636	358	185	167	38	21	20	34	142	5	238	6	2	23	22	.511	1	0-0	1	3.95	3.92

Randy Williams

Pitches: L **Bats:** L **Pos:** RP-32 **Ht:** 6'3" **Wt:** 195 **Born:** 9/18/1975 **Age:** 30

			HOW MUCH HE PITCHED						WHAT HE GAVE UP										THE RESULTS						
Year	Team	Lg	G	GS	CG	GF	IP	BFP	H	R	ER	HR	SH	SF	HB	TBB	IBB	SO	WP	Bk	W	L	Pct	ShO	Sv-Op	Hld	ERC	ERA
1998	R		2	1	0	0	3.0	11	0	0	0	0	0	0	0	2	0	6	0	0	1	0	1.000	0	0- -	-	0.46	0.00
1999	Dytona	A+	14	9	0	3	53.0	243	55	36	28	5	4	1	1	30	0	47	3	0	3	4	.429	0	1- -	-	4.91	4.75
2003	SnAnt	AA	29	0	0	11	41.2	165	33	9	8	2	2	1	0	7	0	38	0	0	4	1	.800	0	2- -	-	1.83	1.73
2003	Tacom	AAA	18	0	0	4	25.2	112	25	17	15	3	0	1	1	11	0	19	1	0	2	2	.500	0	1- -	-	4.30	5.26
2004	Tacom	AAA	50	0	0	16	79.1	355	68	37	32	6	0	1	3	46	0	64	4	0	7	2	.778	0	8- -	-	3.85	3.63
2005	Portlnd	AAA	12	0	0	1	12.2	60	13	10	9	1	0	0	0	9	0	7	1	1	1	1	.500	0	0- -	-	5.17	6.39
2005	ColSpr	AAA	26	0	0	9	28.1	173	18	14	11	1	2	1	2	10	0	36	1	0	2	2	.500	0	4- -	-	1.21	3.49
2004	SEA	AL	6	0	0	1	4.2	22	3	3	3	0	0	0	0	6	0	4	0	0	0	0	-	0	0-0	1	4.73	5.79
2005	2 Tms	NL	32	0	0	6	26.1	125	33	21	20	5	0	1	1	13	3	21	0	0	3	1	.750	0	0-2	4	6.54	6.84
05	SD	NL	2	0	0	0	4.1	25	7	6	6	1	0	0	0	4	0	2	0	0	1	0	1.000	0	0-0	0	12.46	12.46
05	Col	NL	30	0	0	6	22.0	100	26	15	14	4	0	1	1	9	3	19	0	0	2	1	.667	0	0-2	4	5.48	5.73
	2 ML YEARS		38	0	0	7	31.0	147	36	24	23	5	0	1	1	19	3	25	0	0	3	1	.750	0	0-2	5	6.29	6.68

Todd Williams

Pitches: R **Bats:** R **Pos:** RP-72 **Ht:** 6'3" **Wt:** 210 **Born:** 2/13/1971 **Age:** 35

			HOW MUCH HE PITCHED						WHAT HE GAVE UP										THE RESULTS						
Year	Team	Lg	G	GS	CG	GF	IP	BFP	H	R	ER	HR	SH	SF	HB	TBB	IBB	SO	WP	Bk	W	L	Pct	ShO	Sv-Op	Hld	ERC	ERA
1995	LA	NL	16	0	0	5	19.1	83	19	11	11	3	3	1	0	7	2	8	0	0	2	2	.500	0	0-1	0	4.01	5.12
1998	CIN	NL	6	0	0	2	9.1	50	15	8	8	1	0	0	0	6	0	4	0	0	0	1	.000	0	0-0	0	8.58	7.71
1999	SEA	AL	13	0	0	7	9.2	47	11	5	5	1	1	0	1	7	0	7	0	0	0	0	-	0	0-0	0	6.67	4.66
2001	NYA	AL	15	0	0	6	15.1	82	22	9	8	1	0	3	2	9	2	13	0	0	1	0	1.000	0	0-0	1	7.01	4.70
2004	BAL	AL	29	0	0	7	31.1	126	26	10	10	2	0	0	5	9	0	13	1	0	2	0	1.000	0	0-0	3	3.25	2.87
2005	BAL	AL	72	0	0	12	76.1	321	72	34	28	5	2	4	3	26	4	38	4	1	5	5	.500	0	1-3	18	3.40	3.30
	6 ML YEARS		151	0	0	39	161.1	709	165	77	70	13	6	8	11	64	8	83	5	1	10	8	.556	0	1-4	22	4.23	3.90

Woody Williams

Pitches: R **Bats:** R **Pos:** SP-28 **Ht:** 6'0" **Wt:** 195 **Born:** 8/19/1966 **Age:** 39

			HOW MUCH HE PITCHED						WHAT HE GAVE UP										THE RESULTS						
Year	Team	Lg	G	GS	CG	GF	IP	BFP	H	R	ER	HR	SH	SF	HB	TBB	IBB	SO	WP	Bk	W	L	Pct	ShO	Sv-Op	Hld	ERC	ERA
1993	TOR	AL	30	0	0	9	37.0	172	40	18	18	2	2	1	1	22	3	24	2	1	3	1	.750	0	0-2	4	4.85	4.38
1994	TOR	AL	38	0	0	14	59.1	253	44	24	24	5	1	2	2	33	1	56	4	0	1	3	.250	0	0-0	5	3.25	3.64
1995	TOR	AL	23	3	0	10	53.2	232	44	23	22	6	2	0	2	28	1	41	0	0	1	2	.333	0	0-1	1	3.72	3.69
1996	TOR	AL	12	10	1	0	59.0	255	64	33	31	8	2	1	1	21	1	43	2	0	4	5	.444	0	0-0	0	4.73	4.73
1997	TOR	AL	31	31	0	0	194.2	833	201	98	94	31	6	8	5	66	3	124	7	0	9	14	.391	0	0-0	0	4.55	4.35
1998	TOR	AL	32	32	1	0	209.2	894	196	112	104	36	5	6	2	81	3	151	2	1	10	9	.526	1	0-0	0	4.15	4.46
1999	SD	NL	33	33	0	0	208.1	887	213	106	102	33	9	9	2	73	5	137	9	0	12	12	.500	0	0-0	0	4.46	4.41
2000	SD	NL	23	23	4	0	168.0	700	152	74	70	23	4	3	3	54	2	111	4	0	10	8	.556	0	0-0	0	3.55	3.75
2001	2 Tms	NL	34	34	3	0	220.0	922	224	110	99	35	13	8	8	56	5	154	5	0	15	9	.625	1	0-0	0	4.15	4.05
2002	STL	NL	17	17	1	0	103.1	412	84	30	29	10	3	1	4	25	2	76	2	0	9	4	.692	0	0-0	0	2.63	2.53
2003	STL	NL	34	33	0	1	220.2	944	220	101	95	20	11	6	11	55	2	153	3	0	18	9	.667	0	0-1	0	3.52	3.87
2004	STL	NL	31	31	0	0	189.2	817	193	93	88	20	9	5	9	58	3	131	12	1	11	8	.579	0	0-0	0	3.97	4.18
2005	SD	NL	28	28	0	0	159.2	697	174	92	86	24	6	5	3	51	1	106	1	0	9	12	.429	0	0-0	0	4.65	4.85
01	SD	NL	23	23	0	0	145.0	632	170	88	80	28	8	8	5	37	4	102	4	0	8	8	.500	0	0-0	0	5.26	4.97
01	StL	NL	11	11	3	0	75.0	290	54	22	19	7	5	0	3	19	1	52	1	0	7	1	.875	1	0-0	0	2.24	2.28
	13 ML YEARS		366	275	10	34	1883.0	8018	1849	914	862	253	73	55	53	623	32	1307	53	3	112	96	.538	2	0-4	10	4.02	4.12

Scott Williamson

Pitches: R **Bats:** R **Pos:** RP-17 **Ht:** 6'0" **Wt:** 185 **Born:** 2/17/1976 **Age:** 30

			HOW MUCH HE PITCHED						WHAT HE GAVE UP										THE RESULTS						
Year	Team	Lg	G	GS	CG	GF	IP	BFP	H	R	ER	HR	SH	SF	HB	TBB	IBB	SO	WP	Bk	W	L	Pct	ShO	Sv-Op	Hld	ERC	ERA
2005	Cubs*	R	4	1	0	0	7.1	31	7	8	2	0	0	0	2	9	0	9	0	0	0	2	.000	0	0- -	-	3.82	2.45
2005	Iowa*	AAA	6	0	0	2	7.0	28	4	3	3	1	0	0	0	3	0	10	0	0	1	0	1.000	0	0- -	-	2.20	3.86
1999	CIN	NL	62	0	0	40	93.1	366	54	29	25	8	5	2	1	43	6	107	13	0	12	7	.632	0	19-26	5	2.05	2.41
2000	CIN	NL	48	10	0	13	112.0	495	92	45	41	7	4	2	3	75	7	136	21	1	5	8	.385	0	6-8	6	3.85	3.29

Year	Team	Lg	G	GS	CG	GF	IP	BFP	H	R	ER	HR	SH	SF	HB	TBB	IBB	SO	WP	Bk	W	L	Pct	ShO	Sv-Op	Hld	ERC	ERA
2001	CIN	NL	2	0	0	0	0.2	6	1	0	0	0	0	0	1	2	0	0	1	0	0	0	-	0	0-0	1	24.61	0.00
2002	CIN	NL	63	0	0	23	74.0	299	46	27	24	5	5	2	2	36	5	84	8	1	3	4	.429	0	8-12	8	2.24	2.92
2003	2 Tms	NL	66	0	0	40	62.2	276	54	30	29	7	2	1	1	34	6	74	11	0	5	4	.556	0	21-28	5	3.78	4.16
2004	BOS	AL	28	0	0	5	28.2	120	11	6	4	0	0	3	3	18	1	28	4	0	0	0	1.000	0	1-2	3	1.27	1.26
2005	CHN	NL	17	0	0	4	14.1	65	15	9	9	3	2	0	2	6	0	23	4	1	0	0	-	0	0-0	1	5.79	5.65
03	Cin	NL	42	0	0	34	42.1	187	34	15	15	6	2	0	1	25	4	53	7	0	5	3	.625	0	21-26	0	3.87	3.19
03	Bos	AL	24	0	0	6	20.1	89	20	15	14	1	0	1	0	9	2	21	4	0	0	1	.000	0	0-2	5	3.58	6.20
7 ML YEARS			286	10	0	125	385.2	1627	273	146	132	30	18	10	13	214	25	452	62	3	25	24	.510	0	55-76	31	2.96	3.08

Josh Willingham

Bats: R **Throws:** R **Pos:** PH-9; C-8; LF-1; DH-1 **Ht:** 6'1" **Wt:** 200 **Born:** 2/17/1979 **Age:** 27

Year	Team	Lg	G	AB	H	2B	3B	HR	(Hm	Rd)	TB	R	RBI	RC	TBB	IBB	SO	HBP	SH	SF	SB	CS	SB%	GDP	Avg	OBP	Slg
2000	Utica	A-	65	205	54	16	0	6	(-	-)	88	37	29	37	39	1	55	9	1	2	9	5	.64	2	.263	.400	.429
2001	Kane	A	97	320	83	20	2	7	(-	-)	128	57	36	55	53	0	85	13	0	4	24	2	.92	7	.259	.382	.400
2002	Jupiter	A+	107	376	103	21	4	17	(-	-)	183	72	69	74	63	0	88	13	0	2	18	5	.78	7	.274	.394	.487
2003	Marlins	R	2	7	3	1	0	1	(-	-)	7	3	3	2	1	0	2	0	0	0	0	0	-	0	.429	.500	1.000
2003	Jupiter	A+	59	193	51	17	1	12	(-	-)	106	46	34	45	46	3	42	9	0	3	9	2	.82	3	.264	.422	.549
2003	Carlina	AA	22	67	20	2	1	5	(-	-)	39	15	14	16	13	2	20	3	0	0	0	0	-	0	.299	.434	.582
2004	Carlina	AA	112	338	95	24	0	24	(-	-)	191	81	76	86	91	8	87	18	1	7	6	3	.67	7	.281	.449	.565
2005	Jupiter	A+	2	9	2	1	0	0	(-	-)	3	1	1	0	0	0	2	1	0	0	0	0	-	0	.222	.300	.333
2005	Albq	AAA	66	219	71	14	3	19	(-	-)	148	56	54	66	47	1	54	9	0	4	5	1	.83	5	.324	.455	.676
2004	FLA	NL	12	25	5	0	0	1	(0	1)	8	2	1	1	4	0	8	0	0	0	0	0	-	1	.200	.310	.320
2005	FLA	NL	16	23	7	1	0	0	(0	0)	8	3	4	3	2	0	5	2	1	0	0	0	-	1	.304	.407	.348
2 ML YEARS			28	48	12	1	0	1	(0	1)	16	5	5	4	6	0	13	2	1	0	0	0	-	2	.250	.357	.333

Dontrelle Willis

Pitches: L **Bats:** L **Pos:** SP-34 **Ht:** 6'4" **Wt:** 200 **Born:** 1/12/1982 **Age:** 24

Year	Team	Lg	G	GS	CG	GF	IP	BFP	H	R	ER	HR	SH	SF	HB	TBB	IBB	SO	WP	Bk	W	L	Pct	ShO	Sv-Op	Hld	ERC	ERA
2003	FLA	NL	27	27	2	0	160.2	668	148	61	59	13	3	1	3	58	0	142	7	1	14	6	.700	2	0-0	0	3.49	3.30
2004	FLA	NL	32	32	2	0	197.0	848	210	99	88	20	8	2	8	61	8	139	2	0	11	11	.476	0	0-0	0	4.21	4.02
2005	FLA	NL	34	34	7	0	236.1	960	213	79	69	11	14	5	8	55	3	170	2	1	22	10	.688	5	0-0	0	2.71	2.63
3 ML YEARS			93	93	11	0	594.0	2476	571	239	216	44	25	8	19	174	11	451	11	2	46	27	.630	7	0-0	0	3.40	3.27

C.J. Wilson

Pitches: L **Bats:** L **Pos:** RP-18; SP-6 **Ht:** 6'2" **Wt:** 200 **Born:** 11/18/1980 **Age:** 25

Year	Team	Lg	G	GS	CG	GF	IP	BFP	H	R	ER	HR	SH	SF	HB	TBB	IBB	SO	WP	Bk	W	L	Pct	ShO	Sv-Op	Hld	ERC	ERA
2001	Pulaski	R+	8	8	0	0	37.2	149	24	6	4	2	0	0	4	9	0	49	0	0	1	0	1.000	0	0--	-	1.75	0.96
2001	Savann	A	5	5	2	0	34.0	141	30	13	12	2	2	1	1	9	0	26	3	2	1	2	.333	0	0--	-	2.74	3.18
2002	Charltt	A+	26	15	0	2	106.0	445	86	48	36	4	2	0	6	41	1	76	7	0	10	2	.833	0	1--	-	2.78	3.06
2002	Tulsa	AA	5	5	0	0	30.0	125	23	6	6	0	1	0	1	12	0	17	1	0	1	0	1.000	0	0--	-	2.29	1.80
2003	Frisco	AA	22	21	0	0	123.0	542	135	79	69	11	1	1	8	38	3	89	6	0	6	9	.400	0	0--	-	4.37	5.05
2005	Frisco	AA	12	12	0	0	44.2	199	51	32	22	7	1	2	3	14	0	43	0	0	0	4	.000	0	0--	-	5.20	4.43
2005	Bkrsfld	A+	4	4	0	0	13.2	55	10	5	5	2	0	0	3	4	0	14	0	0	0	1	.000	0	0--	-	2.51	3.29
2005	TEX	AL	24	6	0	5	48.0	220	63	39	37	5	1	2	2	18	1	30	4	1	1	7	.125	0	1-1	4	6.03	6.94

Craig Wilson

Bats: R **Throws:** R **Pos:** RF-30; LF-19; 1B-15; PH-3 **Ht:** 6'2" **Wt:** 225 **Born:** 11/30/1976 **Age:** 29

Year	Team	Lg	G	AB	H	2B	3B	HR	(Hm	Rd)	TB	R	RBI	RC	TBB	IBB	SO	HBP	SH	SF	SB	CS	SB%	GDP	Avg	OBP	Slg
2005	Indy*	AAA	7	21	8	1	0	3	(-	-)	18	4	11	7	3	0	6	1	0	0	1	0	1.00	1	.381	.480	.857
2001	PIT	NL	88	158	49	3	1	13	(8	5)	93	27	32	34	15	1	53	7	1	2	3	1	.75	3	.310	.390	.589
2002	PIT	NL	131	368	97	16	1	16	(3	13)	163	48	57	55	32	0	116	21	1	2	2	3	.40	10	.264	.355	.443
2003	PIT	NL	116	309	81	15	4	18	(9	9)	158	49	48	49	35	4	89	13	0	1	3	1	.75	6	.262	.360	.511
2004	PIT	NL	155	561	148	35	5	29	(16	13)	280	97	82	84	50	3	169	30	0	3	2	2	.50	10	.264	.354	.499
2005	PIT	NL	59	197	52	14	1	5	(3	2)	83	23	22	28	30	2	69	10	0	1	3	0	1.00	6	.264	.387	.421
5 ML YEARS			549	1593	427	83	12	81	(39	42)	777	244	241	250	162	10	496	81	2	9	13	7	.65	36	.268	.363	.488

Dan Wilson

Bats: R **Throws:** R **Pos:** C-11 **Ht:** 6'3" **Wt:** 214 **Born:** 3/25/1969 **Age:** 37

Year	Team	Lg	G	AB	H	2B	3B	HR	(Hm	Rd)	TB	R	RBI	RC	TBB	IBB	SO	HBP	SH	SF	SB	CS	SB%	GDP	Avg	OBP	Slg
1992	CIN	NL	12	25	9	1	0	0	(0	0)	10	2	3	4	3	0	8	0	0	0	0	0	-	2	.360	.429	.400
1993	CIN	NL	36	76	17	3	0	0	(0	0)	20	6	8	6	9	4	16	0	2	1	0	0	-	2	.224	.302	.263
1994	SEA	AL	91	282	61	14	2	3	(1	2)	88	24	27	17	10	0	57	1	8	2	1	2	.33	11	.216	.244	.312
1995	SEA	AL	119	399	111	23	3	9	(5	4)	166	40	51	53	33	1	63	2	5	1	2	1	.67	12	.278	.336	.416
1996	SEA	AL	138	491	140	24	0	18	(7	11)	218	51	83	68	32	2	88	3	9	5	1	2	.33	15	.285	.330	.444
1997	SEA	AL	146	508	137	31	1	15	(9	6)	215	66	74	69	39	1	72	5	6	3	7	2	.78	12	.270	.326	.423
1998	SEA	AL	96	325	82	17	1	9	(6	3)	128	39	44	40	24	0	56	5	4	6	2	1	.67	6	.252	.308	.394
1999	SEA	AL	123	414	110	23	2	7	(3	4)	158	46	38	49	29	4	83	2	10	2	5	0	1.00	10	.266	.315	.382
2000	SEA	AL	90	268	63	12	0	9	(2	3)	90	31	27	24	22	0	51	0	11	2	1	2	.33	6	.235	.291	.336
2001	SEA	AL	123	377	100	20	1	10	(4	6)	152	44	42	45	20	0	69	2	8	1	3	2	.60	6	.265	.305	.403
2002	SEA	AL	115	359	106	16	1	4	(3	3)	142	35	44	42	18	1	81	2	7	8	1	0	1.00	5	.295	.326	.396

Year	Team	Lg	G	AB	H	2B	3B	HR	(Hm	Rd)	TB	R	RBI	RC	TBB	IBB	SO	HBP	SH	SF	SB	CS	SB%	GDP	Avg	OBP	Slg
2003	SEA	AL	96	316	76	15	2	4	(1	3)	107	32	43	28	15	0	52	0	3	3	0	0	-	8	.241	.272	.339
2004	SEA	AL	103	319	80	13	0	2	(1	1)	99	23	33	28	26	0	57	1	8	5	0	1	.00	8	.251	.305	.310
2005	SEA	AL	11	27	5	0	0	0	(0	0)	5	2	2	0	0	0	10	1	0	0	0	1	.00	1	.185	.214	.185
14 ML YEARS			1299	4186	1097	211	13	88	(42	46)	1598	441	519	473	280	13	763	24	87	39	23	14	.62	109	.262	.309	.382

Enrique Wilson

Bats: B Throws: R Pos: PH-6; 2B-5; 1B-3; SS-3; 3B-1   Ht: 5'11" Wt: 195 Born: 7/27/1973 Age: 32

Year	Team	Lg	G	AB	H	2B	3B	HR	(Hm	Rd)	TB	R	RBI	RC	TBB	IBB	SO	HBP	SH	SF	SB	CS	SB%	GDP	Avg	OBP	Slg
2005	Ottawa*	AAA	20	61	17	4	0	3	(-	-)	30	7	8	11	8	0	5	0	2	0	1	0	1.00	1	.279	.362	.492
1997	CLE	AL	5	15	5	0	0	0	(0	0)	5	2	1	2	0	0	2	0	0	0	0	0	-	0	.333	.333	.333
1998	CLE	AL	32	90	29	6	0	2	(1	1)	41	13	12	13	4	0	8	1	1	1	2	4	.33	1	.322	.354	.456
1999	CLE	AL	113	332	87	22	1	2	(1	1)	117	41	24	34	25	1	41	1	4	6	5	4	.56	12	.262	.310	.352
2000	2 Tms		80	239	70	15	1	5	(3	2)	102	27	27	34	18	2	24	0	4	2	2	2	.50	6	.293	.340	.427
2001	2 Tms		94	228	48	8	1	2	(1	1)	64	17	20	9	9	0	37	0	2	2	0	5	.00	10	.211	.238	.281
2002	NYA	AL	60	105	19	2	2	2	(2	0)	31	17	11	9	8	0	22	0	6	0	1	1	.50	2	.181	.239	.295
2003	NYA	AL	63	135	31	9	0	3	(1	2)	49	18	15	13	7	0	14	2	2	1	3	1	.75	3	.230	.276	.363
2004	NYA	AL	93	240	51	9	0	6	(2	4)	78	19	31	24	15	0	20	0	2	5	1	2	.33	5	.213	.254	.325
2005	CHN	NL	15	22	3	2	0	0	(0	0)	5	1	0	1	3	0	1	0	0	0	0	0	-	0	.136	.240	.227
00	Cle	AL	40	117	38	9	0	2	(2	0)	53	16	12	19	7	0	11	0	2	1	2	1	.67	2	.325	.360	.453
00	Pit	NL	40	122	32	6	1	3	(1	2)	49	11	15	15	11	2	13	0	2	1	0	1	.00	4	.262	.321	.402
01	Pit	NL	46	129	24	3	0	1	(0	1)	30	7	8	1	3	0	23	0	0	1	0	3	.00	7	.186	.203	.233
01	NYY	AL	48	99	24	5	1	1	(1	0)	34	10	12	8	6	0	14	0	2	1	0	2	.00	3	.242	.283	.343
9 ML YEARS			555	1406	343	73	5	22	(11	11)	492	155	141	139	89	3	169	4	21	17	14	19	.42	39	.244	.288	.350

Jack Wilson

Bats: R Throws: R Pos: SS-157; PH-2   Ht: 6'0" Wt: 195 Born: 12/29/1977 Age: 28

Year	Team	Lg	G	AB	H	2B	3B	HR	(Hm	Rd)	TB	R	RBI	RC	TBB	IBB	SO	HBP	SH	SF	SB	CS	SB%	GDP	Avg	OBP	Slg
2001	PIT	NL	108	390	87	17	1	3	(0	3)	115	44	25	27	16	2	70	1	17	1	3	3	.25	4	.223	.255	.295
2002	PIT	NL	147	527	133	22	4	4	(2	2)	175	77	47	60	37	2	74	4	17	1	5	2	.71	7	.252	.306	.332
2003	PIT	NL	150	558	143	21	3	9	(2	7)	197	58	62	62	36	3	74	4	11	6	5	5	.50	11	.256	.303	.353
2004	PIT	NL	157	652	201	41	12	11	(7	4)	299	82	59	84	26	0	71	3	7	5	8	4	.67	15	.308	.335	.459
2005	PIT	NL	158	587	151	24	7	8	(3	5)	213	60	52	60	31	6	58	6	11	4	7	3	.70	11	.257	.299	.363
5 ML YEARS			720	2714	715	125	27	35	(14	21)	999	321	245	293	146	13	347	18	63	17	26	17	.60	48	.263	.304	.368

Josh Wilson

Bats: R Throws: R Pos: SS-6; 2B-4; PR-3; PH-1   Ht: 6'1" Wt: 178 Born: 3/26/1981 Age: 25

Year	Team	Lg	G	AB	H	2B	3B	HR	(Hm	Rd)	TB	R	RBI	RC	TBB	IBB	SO	HBP	SH	SF	SB	CS	SB%	GDP	Avg	OBP	Slg
1999	Marlins	R	53	203	54	9	4	0	(-	-)	71	29	27	30	24	0	36	5	1	4	14	2	.88	4	.266	.352	.350
2000	Utica	A-	66	259	89	13	6	3	(-	-)	123	43	43	51	29	3	47	5	1	1	9	8	.53	6	.344	.418	.475
2000	Kane	A	13	52	14	3	1	1	(-	-)	22	2	6	7	3	0	14	1	0	1	0	0	-	2	.269	.316	.423
2001	Kane	A	97	320	83	20	2	7	(-	-)	128	57	36	58	53	0	85	13	0	4	24	2	.92	7	.259	.382	.400
2002	Jupiter	A+	111	398	102	17	1	11	(-	-)	154	51	50	49	28	0	67	10	3	4	7	10	.41	6	.256	.318	.387
2002	Portlnd	AA	12	41	14	3	0	2	(-	-)	23	5	5	7	2	0	6	0	1	0	0	1	.00	0	.341	.372	.561
2003	Carlina	AA	118	434	110	30	6	3	(-	-)	161	53	58	49	27	0	70	2	2	10	6	5	.55	9	.253	.294	.371
2004	Carlina	AA	81	311	98	21	1	10	(-	-)	151	63	41	61	42	1	50	1	2	2	8	4	.67	4	.315	.396	.486
2005	Albq	AAA	56	240	67	12	2	5	(-	-)	98	32	23	34	19	0	51	2	2	0	6	1	.86	5	.279	.337	.408
2005	Albq	AAA	143	526	135	31	6	17	(-	-)	229	88	82	79	48	2	114	9	2	12	17	7	.71	8	.257	.323	.435
2005	FLA	NL	11	10	1	1	0	0	(0	0)	2	2	0	0	0	0	4	1	0	0	0	0	-	0	.100	.182	.200

Paul Wilson

Pitches: R Bats: R Pos: SP-9   Ht: 6'5" Wt: 214 Born: 3/28/1973 Age: 33

Year	Team	Lg	G	GS	CG	GF	IP	BFP	H	R	ER	SH	SF	HB	TBB	IBB	SO	WP	Bk	W	L	Pct	ShO	Sv-Op	Hld	ERC	ERA
1996	NYN	NL	26	26	1	0	149.0	677	157	102	89	15	7	3	10	71	11	109	3	3	5	12	.294	0	0-0	0	4.77	5.38
2000	TB	AL	11	7	0	0	51.0	206	38	20	19	1	2	2	4	16	2	40	1	0	1	4	.200	0	0-0	1	2.17	3.35
2001	TB	AL	37	24	0	0	151.1	674	165	94	82	21	3	12	13	52	2	119	7	0	8	9	.471	0	0-1	0	4.94	4.88
2002	TB	AL	30	30	1	0	193.2	851	219	113	104	29	2	16	13	67	2	111	4	1	6	12	.333	0	0-0	0	5.30	4.83
2003	CIN	NL	28	28	0	0	166.2	730	190	97	86	24	7	0	7	50	5	93	1	0	8	10	.444	0	0-0	0	4.92	4.64
2004	CIN	NL	29	29	1	0	183.2	798	192	93	89	26	10	8	8	63	5	117	7	0	11	6	.647	0	0-0	0	4.53	4.36
2005	CIN	NL	9	9	0	0	46.1	224	68	41	40	10	2	3	4	17	1	30	2	0	1	5	.167	0	0-0	0	8.05	7.77
7 ML YEARS			170	153	3	6	941.2	4160	1029	560	509	126	33	34	59	336	28	619	25	4	40	58	.408	0	0-1	1	4.88	4.86

Preston Wilson

Bats: R Throws: R Pos: CF-124; LF-11; PH-4; RF-2   Ht: 6'2" Wt: 213 Born: 7/19/1974 Age: 31

Year	Team	Lg	G	AB	H	2B	3B	HR	(Hm	Rd)	TB	R	RBI	RC	TBB	IBB	SO	HBP	SH	SF	SB	CS	SB%	GDP	Avg	OBP	Slg
1998	2 Tms	NL	22	51	8	2	0	1	(1	0)	13	7	3	3	6	0	21	1	2	0	1	1	.50	0	.157	.259	.255
1999	FLA	NL	149	482	135	21	4	26	(8	18)	242	67	71	81	46	3	156	9	0	6	11	4	.73	15	.280	.350	.502
2000	FLA	NL	161	605	160	35	3	31	(12	19)	294	94	121	97	55	1	187	8	0	6	36	14	.72	11	.264	.331	.486
2001	FLA	NL	123	468	128	30	2	23	(9	14)	231	70	71	73	36	2	107	6	0	3	20	8	.71	14	.274	.331	.494
2002	FLA	NL	141	510	124	22	2	23	(8	15)	219	80	65	58	58	3	140	9	2	3	20	11	.65	17	.243	.329	.429
2003	COL	NL	155	600	169	43	1	36	(21	15)	322	94	141	111	54	1	139	4	0	3	14	7	.67	23	.282	.343	.537

						BATTING																BASERUNNING				AVERAGES		
Year	Team	Lg	G	AB	H	2B	3B	HR	(Hm	Rd)	TB	R	RBI	RC	TBB	IBB	SO	HBP	SH	SF	SB	CS	SB%	GDP	Avg	OBP	Slg
2004	COL	NL	58	202	50	11	0	6	(3	3)	79	24	29	19	17	2	49	3	0	0	2	1	.67	9	.248	.315	.391
2005	2 Tms	NL	139	520	135	29	2	25	(13	12)	243	73	90	72	45	0	148	7	1	3	6	6	.50	18	.260	.325	.467
98	NYM	NL	8	20	6	2	0	0	(0	0)	8	3	2	3	2	0	8	0	0	0	1	1	.50	0	.300	.364	.400
98	Fla	NL	14	31	2	0	0	1	(1	0)	5	4	1	0	4	0	13	1	2	0	0	0	-	0	.065	.194	.161
05	Col	NL	71	267	69	15	1	15	(10	5)	131	39	47	33	25	0	77	1	1	2	3	2	.60	8	.258	.322	.491
05	Was	NL	68	253	66	14	1	10	(3	7)	112	34	43	39	20	0	71	6	0	1	3	4	.43	10	.261	.329	.443
	8 ML YEARS		948	3438	909	193	14	171	(75	96)	1643	509	591	514	317	12	947	47	5	24	110	52	.68	107	.264	.333	.478

Vance Wilson

Bats: R **Throws:** R **Pos:** C-60; PH-6   **Ht:** 5'11" **Wt:** 190 **Born:** 3/17/1973 **Age:** 33

						BATTING																BASERUNNING				AVERAGES		
Year	Team	Lg	G	AB	H	2B	3B	HR	(Hm	Rd)	TB	R	RBI	RC	TBB	IBB	SO	HBP	SH	SF	SB	CS	SB%	GDP	Avg	OBP	Slg
1999	NYN	NL	1	0	0	0	0	0	(0	0)	0	0	0	0	0	0	0	0	0	0	0	0	-	0	-	-	-
2000	NYN	NL	4	4	0	0	0	0	(0	0)	0	0	0	0	0	0	2	0	0	0	0	0	-	0	.000	.000	.000
2001	NYN	NL	32	57	17	3	0	0	(0	0)	20	3	6	6	2	0	16	2	0	1	0	1	.00	1	.298	.339	.351
2002	NYN	NL	74	163	40	7	0	5	(3	2)	62	19	26	21	5	0	32	8	2	0	0	1	.00	4	.245	.301	.380
2003	NYN	NL	96	268	65	9	1	8	(3	5)	100	28	39	31	15	1	56	5	2	2	1	2	.33	6	.243	.293	.373
2004	NYN	NL	79	157	43	10	1	4	(1	3)	67	18	21	23	11	2	24	5	1	3	1	0	1.00	5	.274	.335	.427
2005	DET	AL	61	152	30	4	0	3	(1	2)	43	18	19	13	11	0	26	6	2	2	0	0	-	6	.197	.275	.283
	7 ML YEARS		347	801	195	33	2	20	(8	12)	292	86	111	94	44	3	156	26	7	8	2	4	.33	22	.243	.301	.365

Randy Winn

Bats: B **Throws:** R **Pos:** LF-92; CF-61; PH-7; DH-2   **Ht:** 6'2" **Wt:** 197 **Born:** 6/9/1974 **Age:** 32

						BATTING																BASERUNNING				AVERAGES		
Year	Team	Lg	G	AB	H	2B	3B	HR	(Hm	Rd)	TB	R	RBI	RC	TBB	IBB	SO	HBP	SH	SF	SB	CS	SB%	GDP	Avg	OBP	Slg
1998	TB	AL	109	338	94	9	9	1	(0	1)	124	51	17	44	29	0	69	1	11	0	26	12	.68	2	.278	.337	.367
1999	TB	AL	79	303	81	16	4	2	(2	0)	111	44	24	32	17	0	63	1	1	2	9	9	.50	3	.267	.307	.366
2000	TB	AL	51	159	40	5	0	1	(1	0)	48	28	16	18	26	0	25	2	2	1	6	7	.46	2	.252	.362	.302
2001	TB	AL	128	429	117	25	6	6	(3	3)	172	54	50	56	38	0	81	6	5	2	12	10	.55	10	.273	.339	.401
2002	TB	AL	152	607	181	39	9	14	(9	5)	280	87	75	104	55	3	109	6	1	5	27	8	.77	9	.298	.360	.461
2003	SEA	AL	157	600	177	37	4	11	(6	5)	255	103	75	96	41	0	108	8	6	5	23	5	.82	9	.295	.346	.425
2004	SEA	AL	157	626	179	34	6	14	(6	8)	267	84	81	91	53	1	98	8	9	7	21	7	.75	16	.286	.346	.427
2005	2 Tms		160	617	189	47	6	20	(9	11)	308	85	63	95	48	4	91	5	10	3	19	11	.63	11	.306	.360	.499
05	Sea	AL	102	386	106	25	1	6	(2	4)	151	46	37	52	37	3	53	4	6	3	12	6	.67	7	.275	.342	.391
05	SF	NL	58	231	83	22	5	14	(7	7)	157	39	26	43	11	1	38	1	4	0	7	5	.58	4	.359	.391	.680
	8 ML YEARS		993	3679	1058	212	44	69	(36	33)	1565	536	401	536	307	8	644	37	45	25	143	69	.67	62	.288	.346	.425

Matt Wise

Pitches: R **Bats:** R **Pos:** RP-49   **Ht:** 6'4" **Wt:** 195 **Born:** 11/18/1975 **Age:** 30

			HOW MUCH HE PITCHED					WHAT HE GAVE UP										THE RESULTS							
Year	Team	Lg	G	GS	CG	GF	IP	BFP	H	R	ER	HR	SH	SF	HB	TBB	IBB	SO	WP	Bk	W	L	Pct	ShO	Sv-Op Hld	ERC	ERA
2000	ANA	AL	8	6	0	0	37.1	163	40	23	23	7	0	2	1	13	1	20	1	0	3	3	.500	0	0-0 0	4.96	5.54
2001	ANA	AL	11	9	0	2	49.1	211	47	27	24	11	2	1	2	18	1	50	0	0	1	4	.200	0	0-0 0	4.65	4.38
2002	ANA	AL	7	0	0	6	8.1	33	7	3	3	0	1	0	1	1	0	6	0	0	0	0	-	0	0-0 0	2.07	3.24
2004	MIL	NL	30	3	0	5	52.2	222	51	27	26	3	1	2	2	15	1	30	2	0	1	2	.333	0	0-0 3	3.27	4.44
2005	MIL	NL	49	0	0	11	64.1	262	37	25	24	6	1	2	3	25	5	62	1	1	4	4	.500	0	1-3 10	1.83	3.36
	5 ML YEARS		105	18	0	24	212.0	891	182	105	100	27	5	7	9	72	8	168	4	1	9	13	.409	0	1-3 13	3.33	4.25

Jay Witasick

Pitches: R **Bats:** R **Pos:** RP-60   **Ht:** 6'4" **Wt:** 235 **Born:** 8/28/1972 **Age:** 33

			HOW MUCH HE PITCHED					WHAT HE GAVE UP										THE RESULTS							
Year	Team	Lg	G	GS	CG	GF	IP	BFP	H	R	ER	HR	SH	SF	HB	TBB	IBB	SO	WP	Bk	W	L	Pct	ShO	Sv-Op Hld	ERC	ERA
2005	ColSpr*	AAA	8	0	0	2	10.0	45	10	5	4	0	0	1	0	5	0	14	2	0	0	0	-	0	0- - -	3.63	3.60
1996	OAK	AL	12	0	0	6	13.0	55	12	9	9	5	0	1	0	5	0	12	2	0	1	1	.500	0	0-1 0	5.52	6.23
1997	OAK	AL	8	0	0	1	11.0	53	14	7	7	2	1	0	0	6	0	8	0	0	0	0	-	0	0-0 1	6.81	5.73
1998	OAK	AL	7	3	0	1	27.0	131	36	24	19	9	0	0	0	15	1	29	2	0	1	3	.250	0	0-0 0	8.53	6.33
1999	KC	AL	32	28	1	2	158.1	732	191	108	98	23	4	8	8	83	1	102	4	2	9	12	.429	1	0-0 0	6.45	5.57
2000	2 Tms		33	25	2	2	150.0	697	178	107	97	24	8	4	7	73	5	121	5	1	6	10	.375	0	0-0 0	6.09	5.82
2001	2 Tms		63	0	0	17	79.0	352	78	41	29	8	3	2	6	33	4	106	4	0	8	2	.800	0	1-4 10	4.22	3.30
2002	SF	NL	44	0	0	9	68.1	276	58	19	18	3	2	1	4	21	3	54	3	0	1	0	1.000	0	0-0 4	2.78	2.37
2003	SD	NL	46	0	0	14	45.2	202	42	24	23	6	3	1	1	25	4	42	5	0	3	7	.300	0	2-7 12	4.34	4.53
2004	SD	NL	44	0	0	20	61.2	266	57	28	22	8	3	2	1	26	2	57	4	0	0	1	.000	0	1-3 2	3.92	3.21
2005	2 Tms		60	0	0	11	63.1	277	53	26	20	4	4	0	6	29	5	73	5	0	1	5	.167	0	1-4 17	3.31	2.84
00	KC	AL	22	14	2	2	89.1	410	109	65	59	15	3	3	4	38	0	67	3	0	3	8	.273	0	0-0 0	6.19	5.94
00	SD	NL	11	11	0	0	60.2	287	69	42	38	9	5	1	3	35	5	54	2	1	3	2	.600	0	0-0 0	5.94	5.64
01	KC	AL	31	0	0	9	38.2	164	31	14	8	3	3	0	4	15	3	53	3	0	5	2	.714	0	1-3 5	3.05	1.86
01	NYY	AL	32	0	0	8	40.1	188	47	27	21	5	0	2	2	18	1	53	1	0	3	0	1.000	0	0-1 5	5.43	4.69
05	Col	NL	32	0	0	7	35.2	148	27	11	10	2	4	0	3	12	3	40	2	0	1	4	.000	0	0-1 11	2.43	2.52
05	Oak	AL	28	0	0	4	27.2	129	26	15	10	2	0	0	3	17	2	33	3	0	0	1	.500	0	1-3 6	4.54	3.25
	10 ML YEARS		349	56	3	83	677.1	3041	719	393	342	92	28	19	33	316	25	604	34	3	30	41	.423	1	5-19 46	5.08	4.54

Randy Wolf

Pitches: L **Bats:** L **Pos:** SP-13   **Ht:** 6'0" **Wt:** 194 **Born:** 8/22/1976 **Age:** 29

			HOW MUCH HE PITCHED						WHAT HE GAVE UP											THE RESULTS							
Year	Team	Lg	G	GS	CG	GF	IP	BFP	H	R	ER	HR	SH	SF	HB	TBB	IBB	SO	WP	Bk	W	L	Pct	ShO	Sv-Op	Hld	ERC	ERA
1999	PHI	NL	22	21	0	0	121.2	552	126	78	75	20	5	1	5	67	0	116	4	0	6	9	.400	0	0-0	0	5.54	5.55
2000	PHI	NL	32	32	1	0	206.1	889	210	107	100	25	10	8	8	83	2	160	1	0	11	9	.550	0	0-0	0	4.54	4.36
2001	PHI	NL	28	25	4	1	163.0	684	150	74	67	15	11	7	10	51	4	152	1	0	10	11	.476	2	0-0	0	3.46	3.70
2002	PHI	NL	31	31	3	0	210.2	855	172	77	75	23	7	6	7	63	5	172	4	0	11	9	.550	2	0-0	0	2.88	3.20
2003	PHI	NL	33	33	2	0	200.0	850	176	101	94	27	8	4	6	78	4	177	6	0	16	10	.615	2	0-0	0	3.67	4.23
2004	PHI	NL	23	23	1	0	136.2	585	145	73	65	20	6	3	5	36	4	89	2	0	5	8	.385	1	0-0	0	4.29	4.28
2005	PHI	NL	13	13	0	0	80.0	346	87	40	39	14	4	1	6	26	2	61	1	0	6	4	.600	0	0-0	0	5.17	4.39
7 ML YEARS			182	178	11	1	1118.1	4761	1066	550	515	144	51	30	47	404	21	927	19	0	65	60	.520	7	0-0	0	4.01	4.14

Tony Womack

Bats: L **Throws:** R **Pos:** LF-40; 2B-24; CF-22; PR-21; DH-11; RF-4; PH-4   **Ht:** 5'9" **Wt:** 170 **Born:** 9/25/1969 **Age:** 36

									BATTING													BASERUNNING				AVERAGES		
Year	Team	Lg	G	AB	H	2B	3B	HR	(Hm	Rd)	TB	R	RBI	RC	TBB	IBB	SO	HBP	SH	SF	SB	CS	SB%	GDP	Avg	OBP	Slg
1993	PIT	NL	15	24	2	0	0	0	(0	0)	2	5	0	0	3	0	3	0	1	0	2	0	1.00	0	.083	.185	.083
1994	PIT	NL	5	12	4	0	0	0	(0	0)	4	4	1	2	2	0	3	0	0	0	0	0	-	0	.333	.429	.333
1996	PIT	NL	17	30	10	3	1	0	(0	0)	15	11	7	8	6	0	1	1	3	0	2	0	1.00	0	.333	.459	.500
1997	PIT	NL	155	641	178	26	9	6	(5	1)	240	85	50	87	43	2	109	3	2	0	60	7	.90	6	.278	.326	.374
1998	PIT	NL	159	655	185	26	7	3	(2	1)	234	85	45	84	38	1	94	0	6	5	58	8	.88	4	.282	.319	.357
1999	ARI	NL	144	614	170	25	10	4	(1	3)	227	111	41	88	52	0	68	2	9	7	72	13	.85	4	.277	.332	.370
2000	ARI	NL	146	617	167	21	**14**	7	(4	3)	237	95	57	78	30	0	74	5	2	5	45	11	.80	5	.271	.307	.384
2001	ARI	NL	125	481	128	19	5	3	(2	1)	166	66	30	54	23	2	54	6	7	1	28	7	.80	4	.266	.307	.345
2002	ARI	NL	153	590	160	23	5	5	(4	1)	208	90	57	76	46	2	80	4	6	6	29	12	.71	9	.271	.325	.353
2003	3 Tms	NL	103	349	79	14	4	2	(2	0)	107	43	22	23	9	0	47	3	2	1	13	5	.72	7	.226	.251	.307
2004	STL	NL	145	553	170	22	3	5	(3	2)	213	91	38	77	36	1	60	3	8	6	26	5	.84	6	.307	.349	.385
2005	NYA	AL	108	329	82	8	1	0	(0	0)	92	46	15	27	12	0	49	1	7	2	27	5	.84	7	.249	.276	.280
03	Ari	NL	61	219	52	10	3	2	(2	0)	74	30	15	16	8	0	27	2	1	1	8	3	.73	6	.237	.270	.338
03	Col	NL	21	79	15	2	0	0	(0	0)	17	9	5	3	0	0	9	1	1	0	3	1	.75	1	.190	.200	.215
03	ChC	NL	21	51	12	2	1	0	(0	0)	16	4	2	4	1	0	11	0	0	0	2	1	.67	0	.235	.250	.314
12 ML YEARS			1275	4895	1335	187	59	35	(23	12)	1745	732	363	604	300	8	642	28	53	33	362	73	.83	53	.273	.316	.356

Kerry Wood

Pitches: R **Bats:** R **Pos:** RP-11; SP-10   **Ht:** 6'5" **Wt:** 230 **Born:** 6/16/1977 **Age:** 29

							HOW MUCH HE PITCHED						WHAT HE GAVE UP											THE RESULTS						
Year	Team	Lg	G	GS	CG	GF	IP	BFP	H	R	ER	HR	SH	SF	HB	TBB	IBB	SO	WP	Bk	W	L	Pct	ShO	Sv-Op	Hld	ERC	ERA
2005	Peoria*	A	2	0	0	0	2.1	8	1	0	0	0	0	0	0	0	0	5	0	0	0	0	-	0	0--	-	0.40	0.00
2005	Iowa*	AAA	3	3	0	0	12.2	55	11	4	4	1	0	1	1	6	0	18	0	0	0	0	-	0	0--	-	3.78	2.84
1998	CHN	NL	26	26	1	0	166.2	699	117	69	63	14	2	4	11	85	1	233	6	3	13	6	.684	1	0-0	0	3.03	3.40
2000	CHN	NL	23	23	1	0	137.0	603	112	77	73	17	7	5	9	87	0	132	5	1	8	7	.533	0	0-0	0	4.43	4.80
2001	CHN	NL	28	28	1	0	174.1	740	127	70	65	16	4	5	10	92	3	217	9	0	12	6	.667	1	0-0	0	3.22	3.36
2002	CHN	NL	33	33	4	0	213.2	895	169	92	87	22	13	5	**16**	97	5	217	8	1	12	11	.522	1	0-0	0	3.46	3.66
2003	CHN	NL	32	32	4	0	211.0	887	152	77	75	24	11	6	**21**	100	2	**266**	10	0	14	11	.560	2	0-0	0	3.31	3.20
2004	CHN	NL	22	22	0	0	140.1	595	127	62	58	16	6	6	11	51	0	144	7	0	8	9	.471	0	0-0	0	3.83	3.72
2005	CHN	NL	21	10	0	4	66.0	273	52	32	31	14	2	1	2	26	0	77	0	0	3	4	.429	0	0-0	4	3.75	4.23
7 ML YEARS			185	174	11	4	1109.0	4692	856	479	452	123	45	32	80	538	11	1286	45	5	70	54	.565	5	0-0	4	3.51	3.67

Mike Wood

Pitches: R **Bats:** R **Pos:** RP-37; SP-10   **Ht:** 6'3" **Wt:** 180 **Born:** 4/26/1980 **Age:** 26

							HOW MUCH HE PITCHED						WHAT HE GAVE UP											THE RESULTS						
Year	Team	Lg	G	GS	CG	GF	IP	BFP	H	R	ER	HR	SH	SF	HB	TBB	IBB	SO	WP	Bk	W	L	Pct	ShO	Sv-Op	Hld	ERC	ERA
2005	Omha*	AAA	2	2	0	0	9.0	39	10	2	2	0	0	0	0	2	0	8	0	0	0	0	-	0	0--	-	3.22	2.00
2003	OAK	AL	7	1	0	2	13.2	72	24	17	16	1	1	0	2	7	2	15	2	0	2	1	.667	0	0-0	0	9.45	10.54
2004	KC	AL	17	17	0	0	100.0	432	112	67	66	16	5	2	6	28	3	54	6	1	3	8	.273	0	0-0	0	4.96	5.94
2005	KC	AL	47	10	0	10	115.0	520	129	66	57	18	5	5	8	52	5	60	7	0	5	8	.385	0	2-2	7	5.67	4.46
3 ML YEARS			71	28	0	12	228.2	1024	265	150	139	35	11	7	16	87	10	129	15	1	10	17	.370	0	2-2	7	5.57	5.47

Jake Woods

Pitches: L **Bats:** L **Pos:** RP-28   **Ht:** 6'1" **Wt:** 190 **Born:** 9/3/1981 **Age:** 24

							HOW MUCH HE PITCHED						WHAT HE GAVE UP											THE RESULTS						
Year	Team	Lg	G	GS	CG	GF	IP	BFP	H	R	ER	HR	SH	SF	HB	TBB	IBB	SO	WP	Bk	W	L	Pct	ShO	Sv-Op	Hld	ERC	ERA
2001	Provo	R+	15	14	1	1	65.0	294	70	41	38	6	2	3	2	29	0	84	2	2	4	3	.571	1	0--	-	4.68	5.26
2002	CRpds	A	27	27	1	0	153.1	642	128	66	52	12	4	3	11	54	0	121	5	0	10	5	.667	0	0--	-	3.12	3.05
2003	RCuca	A+	28	28	2	0	171.1	746	178	90	77	9	3	1	8	54	0	109	2	2	12	7	.632	1	0--	-	3.76	4.04
2004	Ark	AA	14	14	1	0	90.0	374	85	29	26	5	7	4	4	19	0	60	5	0	9	2	.818	0	0--	-	2.91	2.60
2004	Salt Lk	AAA	15	14	1	1	83.0	398	107	67	56	13	2	3	4	42	0	60	2	1	6	4	.600	0	0--	-	6.82	6.07
2005	Salt Lk	AAA	15	5	0	2	36.2	177	50	27	24	7	0	1	2	17	2	36	1	0	3	1	.750	0	0--	-	7.33	5.89
2005	LAA	AL	28	0	0	10	27.2	122	30	18	14	7	1	0	2	8	0	20	2	1	1	1	.500	0	0-0	2	5.44	4.55

Chris Woodward

Bats: R **Throws:** R **Pos:** 1B-34; PH-18; LF-13; SS-7; 3B-6; RF-6; 2B-5; CF-5   **Ht:** 6'0" **Wt:** 185 **Born:** 6/27/1976 **Age:** 30

Year	Team	Lg	G	AB	H	2B	3B	HR	(Hm	Rd)	TB	R	RBI	RC	TBB	IBB	SO	HBP	SH	SF	SB	CS	SB%	GDP	Avg	OBP	Slg
1999	TOR	AL	14	26	6	1	0	0	(0	0)	7	1	2	2	2	0	6	0	0	1	0	0	-	1	.231	.276	.269
2000	TOR	AL	37	104	19	7	0	3	(1	2)	35	16	14	9	10	3	28	0	1	0	1	0	1.00	1	.183	.254	.337
2001	TOR	AL	37	63	12	3	2	2	(2	0)	25	9	5	4	1	0	14	0	2	0	0	1	.00	1	.190	.203	.397
2002	TOR	AL	90	312	86	13	4	13	(9	4)	146	48	45	45	26	0	72	3	1	8	3	0	1.00	8	.276	.330	.468
2003	TOR	AL	104	349	91	22	2	7	(4	3)	138	49	45	42	28	0	72	3	0	6	1	2	.33	6	.261	.316	.395
2004	TOR	AL	69	213	50	13	4	1	(0	1)	74	21	24	24	14	0	46	1	2	2	1	2	.33	3	.235	.283	.347
2005	NYN	NL	81	173	49	10	0	3	(2	1)	68	16	18	20	13	0	46	2	2	2	0	0	-	2	.283	.337	.393
	7 ML YEARS		432	1240	313	69	12	29	(18	11)	493	160	153	146	94	3	284	9	8	19	6	5	.55	22	.252	.305	.398

Mark Woodyard

Pitches: R **Bats:** R **Pos:** RP-3   **Ht:** 6'2" **Wt:** 195 **Born:** 12/19/1978 **Age:** 27

Year	Team	Lg	G	GS	CG	GF	IP	BFP	H	R	ER	HR	SH	SF	HB	TBB	IBB	SO	WP	Bk	W	L	Pct	ShO	Sv-Op	Hld	ERC	ERA
2000	Oneont	A-	11	9	0	1	51.0	240	48	32	26	0	1	0	6	39	0	38	8	0	1	5	.167	0	0- -	-	4.83	4.59
2001	W Mich	A	25	25	2	0	143.2	647	147	81	72	5	1	6	9	69	2	84	13	0	7	12	.368	1	0- -	-	4.21	4.51
2002	Lkland	A+	17	7	0	3	66.0	311	81	62	56	10	0	4	6	32	0	22	6	0	2	8	.200	0	2- -	-	6.55	7.64
2003	Lkland	A+	23	23	1	0	117.1	538	133	69	59	7	1	4	4	53	2	84	10	0	4	8	.333	0	0- -	-	4.76	4.53
2003	Erie	AA	2	2	0	0	11.1	53	14	7	7	1	3	2	0	5	0	6	1	0	1	1	.500	0	0- -	-	5.38	5.56
2004	Erie	AA	43	9	0	14	102.1	446	102	53	40	5	5	5	9	37	3	55	5	0	6	4	.600	0	0- -	-	3.82	3.52
2005	Toledo	AAA	45	0	0	11	70.1	310	67	34	30	7	1	1	2	32	2	62	6	0	5	2	.714	0	1- -	-	4.02	3.84
2005	DET	AL	3	0	0	0	6.0	22	4	1	1	1	0	0	0	0	0	3	0	0	0	0	-	0	0-0	0	1.41	1.50

Shawn Wooten

Bats: R **Throws:** R **Pos:** C-1   **Ht:** 5'10" **Wt:** 225 **Born:** 7/24/1972 **Age:** 33

Year	Team	Lg	G	AB	H	2B	3B	HR	(Hm	Rd)	TB	R	RBI	RC	TBB	IBB	SO	HBP	SH	SF	SB	CS	SB%	GDP	Avg	OBP	Slg
2005	Pwtckt*	AAA	114	427	114	20	0	17	(-	-)	185	45	60	64	35	2	72	8	0	9	0	0	-	16	.267	.328	.433
2000	ANA	AL	7	9	5	1	0	0	(0	0)	6	2	1	3	0	0	0	0	0	0	0	0	-	0	.556	.556	.667
2001	ANA	AL	79	221	69	8	1	8	(3	5)	103	24	32	33	5	0	42	3	0	3	2	0	1.00	5	.312	.332	.466
2002	ANA	AL	49	113	33	8	0	3	(2	1)	50	13	19	17	6	1	24	1	0	1	2	0	1.00	3	.292	.331	.442
2003	ANA	AL	98	272	66	8	0	7	(5	2)	95	25	32	22	24	5	45	1	0	3	0	4	.00	7	.243	.303	.349
2004	PHI	NL	33	53	9	3	0	0	(0	0)	12	2	2	0	2	0	9	2	0	0	0	0	-	4	.170	.228	.226
2005	BOS	AL	1	1	0	0	0	0	(0	0)	0	0	0	0	0	0	0	0	0	0	0	0	-	0	.000	.000	.000
	6 ML YEARS		267	669	182	28	1	18	(10	8)	266	66	86	75	37	6	120	7	0	7	4	4	.50	19	.272	.314	.398

Tim Worrell

Pitches: R **Bats:** R **Pos:** RP-51   **Ht:** 6'4" **Wt:** 230 **Born:** 7/5/1967 **Age:** 38

Year	Team	Lg	G	GS	CG	GF	IP	BFP	H	R	ER	HR	SH	SF	HB	TBB	IBB	SO	WP	Bk	W	L	Pct	ShO	Sv-Op	Hld	ERC	ERA
2005	Lakwd*	A	3	3	0	0	4.1	20	7	3	1	0	0	0	0	0	0	6	0	0	0	0	-	0	0- -	-	5.12	2.08
2005	Rdng*	AA	2	1	0	0	3.0	9	0	0	0	0	0	0	1	0	0	3	0	0	0	0	-	0	0- -	-	0.14	0.00
1993	SD	NL	21	16	0	1	100.2	443	104	63	55	11	8	5	0	43	5	52	3	0	2	7	.222	0	0-0	1	4.31	4.92
1994	SD	NL	3	3	0	0	14.2	59	9	7	6	0	0	1	0	5	0	14	0	0	0	1	.000	0	0-0	0	1.40	3.68
1995	SD	NL	9	0	0	4	13.1	63	16	7	7	2	1	0	1	6	0	13	1	0	1	0	1.000	0	0-0	0	6.01	4.73
1996	SD	NL	50	11	0	8	121.0	510	109	45	41	9	3	1	6	39	1	99	0	0	9	7	.563	0	1-2	10	3.22	3.05
1997	SD	NL	60	10	0	14	106.1	483	116	67	61	14	6	6	7	50	2	81	2	1	4	8	.333	0	3-7	16	5.34	5.16
1998	3 Tms		43	9	0	5	103.0	440	106	62	60	16	2	3	1	29	3	82	2	0	2	7	.222	0	0-3	6	4.10	5.24
1999	OAK	AL	53	0	0	17	69.1	309	69	38	32	6	1	1	3	34	1	62	1	0	2	2	.500	0	0-5	5	4.42	4.15
2000	2 Tms		59	0	0	29	69.1	307	72	26	23	10	4	1	1	29	11	57	1	0	5	6	.455	0	3-6	12	4.42	2.99
2001	SF	NL	73	0	0	12	78.1	339	71	33	30	4	3	4	3	33	4	63	2	0	2	5	.286	0	0-3	13	3.32	3.45
2002	SF	NL	80	0	0	23	72.0	296	55	21	18	3	3	4	0	30	2	55	0	0	8	2	.800	0	0-1	23	2.47	2.25
2003	SF	NL	76	0	0	64	78.1	335	74	35	25	5	3	3	0	28	6	65	5	0	4	4	.500	0	38-45	1	3.19	2.87
2004	PHI	NL	77	0	0	36	78.1	327	75	36	32	10	4	5	2	21	4	64	0	0	5	6	.455	0	19-27	20	3.53	3.68
2005	2 Tms	NL	51	0	0	17	48.2	220	59	30	22	8	4	5	2	12	2	39	0	1	1	2	.333	0	1-4	12	5.10	4.07
98	Det	AL	15	9	0	0	61.2	265	66	42	41	11	0	1	1	19	2	47	0	0	2	6	.250	0	0-1	0	4.68	5.98
98	Cle	AL	3	0	0	1	5.1	24	6	3	3	0	0	2	0	2	0	2	0	0	0	0	-	0	0-0	0	3.84	5.06
98	Oak	AL	25	0	0	4	36.0	151	34	17	16	5	2	0	0	8	1	33	2	0	0	1	.000	0	0-2	6	3.20	4.00
00	Bal	AL	5	0	0	2	7.1	39	12	6	6	3	0	0	0	5	3	5	0	0	2	2	.500	0	0-0	0	11.13	7.36
00	ChC	NL	54	0	0	27	62.0	268	60	20	17	7	4	1	1	24	8	52	1	0	3	4	.429	0	3-6	12	3.75	2.47
05	Phi	NL	19	0	0	9	17.0	83	29	17	14	4	1	1	1	3	0	17	0	1	0	1	.000	0	1-3	3	8.79	7.41
05	Ari	NL	32	0	0	8	31.2	137	30	13	8	4	3	4	1	9	2	22	0	0	1	1	.500	0	0-1	9	3.40	2.27
	13 ML YEARS		655	49	0	230	953.1	4131	935	470	412	98	42	39	26	359	41	746	17	2	45	57	.441	0	65-103	119	3.89	3.89

David Wright

Bats: R **Throws:** R **Pos:** 3B-160   **Ht:** 6'0" **Wt:** 200 **Born:** 12/20/1982 **Age:** 23

Year	Team	Lg	G	AB	H	2B	3B	HR	(Hm	Rd)	TB	R	RBI	RC	TBB	IBB	SO	HBP	SH	SF	SB	CS	SB%	GDP	Avg	OBP	Slg
2001	Kngspt	R+	36	120	36	7	0	4	(-	-)	55	27	17	22	16	0	30	1	0	1	9	1	.90	3	.300	.391	.458
2002	CptCty	A	135	496	132	30	2	11	(-	-)	199	85	93	79	76	2	114	5	1	4	21	5	.81	4	.266	.367	.401
2003	StLuci	A+	133	466	126	39	2	15	(-	-)	214	69	75	80	72	5	98	4	1	6	19	5	.79	8	.270	.369	.459
2004	Bnghtn	AA	60	223	81	27	0	10	(-	-)	138	44	40	60	39	3	41	7	0	3	20	6	.77	6	.363	.467	.619
2004	Norfolk	AAA	31	114	34	8	0	8	(-	-)	66	18	17	22	16	1	19	2	0	2	4	4	.33	3	.298	.388	.579

Year	Team	Lg	G	AB	H	2B	3B	HR	BATTING (Hm Rd)	TB	R	RBI	RC	TBB	IBB	SO	HBP	SH	SF	BASERUNNING SB	CS	SB%	GDP	AVERAGES Avg	OBP	Slg
2004	NYN	NL	69	263	77	17	1	14	(8 6)	138	41	40	42	14	0	40	3	0	3	6	0	1.00	7	.293	.332	.525
2005	NYN	NL	160	575	176	42	1	27	(12 15)	301	99	102	105	72	2	113	7	0	3	17	7	.71	16	.306	.388	.523
2 ML YEARS			229	838	253	59	2	41	(20 21)	439	140	142	147	86	2	153	10	0	6	23	7	.77	23	.302	.371	.524

Jamey Wright

Pitches: R Bats: R Pos: SP-27; RP-7   **Ht: 6'5" Wt: 234 Born: 12/24/1974 Age: 31**

Year	Team	Lg	HOW MUCH HE PITCHED G	GS	CG	GF	IP	BFP	WHAT HE GAVE UP H	R	ER	HR	SH	SF	HB	TBB	IBB	SO	WP	Bk	THE RESULTS W	L	Pct	ShO	Sv-Op	Hld	ERC	ERA
1996	COL	NL	16	15	0	0	91.1	406	105	60	50	8	4	2	7	41	1	45	1	2	4	4	.500	0	0-0	1	5.50	4.93
1997	COL	NL	26	26	1	0	149.2	698	198	113	104	19	8	3	11	71	3	59	6	2	8	12	.400	0	0-0	0	6.96	6.25
1998	COL	NL	34	34	1	0	206.1	919	235	143	130	24	8	6	11	95	3	86	6	3	9	14	.391	0	0-0	0	5.57	5.67
1999	COL	NL	16	16	0	0	94.1	423	110	52	51	10	3	4	4	54	3	49	3	0	4	3	.571	0	0-0	0	6.19	4.87
2000	MIL	NL	26	25	0	1	164.2	718	157	81	75	12	4	6	18	88	5	96	9	2	7	9	.438	0	0-0	0	4.67	4.10
2001	MIL	NL	33	33	1	0	194.2	868	201	115	106	26	7	5	20	98	10	129	6	1	11	12	.478	1	0-0	0	5.36	4.90
2002	2 Tms	NL	23	22	1	0	129.1	585	130	80	76	17	9	6	11	75	9	77	9	0	7	13	.350	1	0-0	0	5.35	5.29
2003	KC	AL	4	4	2	0	25.1	106	23	14	12	1	0	0	1	11	0	19	0	0	1	2	.333	1	0-0	0	3.53	4.26
2004	COL	NL	14	14	0	0	78.2	361	82	39	36	8	1	1	6	45	3	41	3	0	2	3	.400	0	0-0	0	5.26	4.12
2005	COL	NL	34	27	0	1	171.1	782	201	119	104	22	4	3	15	81	4	101	2	2	8	16	.333	0	0-0	1	6.02	5.46
02	Mil	NL	19	19	1	0	114.1	515	115	72	68	15	9	6	11	63	8	69	8	0	5	13	.278	1	0-0	0	5.28	5.35
02	StL	NL	4	3	0	0	15.0	70	15	8	8	2	0	0	0	12	1	8	1	0	2	0	1.000	0	0-0	0	5.87	4.80
10 ML YEARS			226	216	6	2	1305.2	5866	1442	816	744	147	48	36	104	659	41	702	45	12	61	88	.409	3	0-0	2	5.59	5.13

Jaret Wright

Pitches: R Bats: R Pos: SP-13   **Ht: 6'2" Wt: 230 Born: 12/29/1975 Age: 30**

Year	Team	Lg	HOW MUCH HE PITCHED G	GS	CG	GF	IP	BFP	WHAT HE GAVE UP H	R	ER	HR	SH	SF	HB	TBB	IBB	SO	WP	Bk	THE RESULTS W	L	Pct	ShO	Sv-Op	Hld	ERC	ERA
2005	Yanks*	R	1	1	0	0	2.1	13	4	2	2	0	0	0	0	2	0	3	0	0	0	1	.000	0	0--	-	9.39	7.71
2005	Tampa*	A+	2	2	0	0	12.0	48	9	2	2	0	0	3	0	3	0	12	0	0	1	0	1.000	0	0--	-	2.58	1.50
1997	CLE	AL	16	16	0	0	90.1	388	81	45	44	9	3	4	5	35	0	63	1	0	8	3	.727	0	0-0	0	3.63	4.38
1998	CLE	AL	32	32	1	0	192.2	855	207	109	101	22	4	6	11	87	4	140	6	0	12	10	.545	1	0-0	0	5.07	4.72
1999	CLE	AL	26	26	0	0	133.2	609	144	99	90	18	3	3	7	77	1	91	4	0	8	10	.444	0	0-0	0	5.77	6.06
2000	CLE	AL	9	9	1	0	51.2	217	44	27	27	6	0	1	1	28	0	36	2	0	3	4	.429	1	0-0	0	4.13	4.70
2001	CLE	AL	7	7	0	0	29.0	140	36	23	21	2	2	1	0	22	0	18	1	1	2	2	.500	0	0-0	0	6.82	6.52
2002	CLE	AL	8	6	0	1	18.1	116	40	34	32	3	1	2	2	19	0	12	1	0	2	3	.400	0	0-0	0	15.90	15.71
2003	2 Tms	NL	50	0	0	17	56.1	269	76	46	46	9	2	4	3	31	2	50	12	0	2	5	.286	0	2-5	4	7.59	7.35
2004	ATL	NL	32	32	0	0	186.1	781	168	79	68	11	8	6	3	70	5	159	3	0	15	8	.652	0	0-0	0	3.20	3.28
2005	NYA	AL	13	13	0	0	63.2	302	81	51	43	8	0	5	6	32	1	34	4	0	5	5	.500	0	0-0	0	6.72	6.08
03	SD	NL	39	0	0	14	47.1	233	69	44	44	9	1	4	2	28	2	41	10	0	1	5	.167	0	2-4	1	8.71	8.37
03	Atl	NL	11	0	0	3	9.0	36	7	2	2	0	1	0	1	3	0	9	2	0	1	0	1.000	0	0-1	3	2.51	2.00
9 ML YEARS			193	141	2	18	822.0	3677	877	513	472	88	22	33	38	401	13	603	34	1	57	50	.533	2	2-5	4	5.06	5.17

Mike Wuertz

Pitches: R Bats: R Pos: RP-75   **Ht: 6'3" Wt: 205 Born: 12/15/1978 Age: 27**

Year	Team	Lg	HOW MUCH HE PITCHED G	GS	CG	GF	IP	BFP	WHAT HE GAVE UP H	R	ER	HR	SH	SF	HB	TBB	IBB	SO	WP	Bk	THE RESULTS W	L	Pct	ShO	Sv-Op	Hld	ERC	ERA
1998	Wmspt	A-	14	14	1	0	86.1	359	79	36	33	4	3	2	0	19	0	59	1	2	7	5	.583	0	0--	-	2.53	3.44
1999	Lansng	A	28	28	1	0	161.1	716	191	104	86	11	2	10	1	44	0	127	11	0	11	12	.478	0	0--	-	4.32	4.80
2000	Dytona	A+	28	28	3	0	171.1	732	166	79	72	15	6	4	3	64	1	142	7	1	12	7	.632	2	0--	-	3.77	3.78
2001	WTenn	AA	27	27	1	0	160.0	694	160	80	71	20	9	6	6	58	2	135	10	0	4	9	.308	1	0--	-	4.20	3.99
2002	Iowa	AAA	28	27	0	1	154.0	712	154	109	95	24	8	3	4	69	3	131	11	0	9	5	.643	0	0--	-	4.47	5.55
2003	Iowa	AAA	43	16	0	4	124.0	536	140	70	63	16	5	5	5	35	8	92	0	1	3	9	.250	0	1--	-	4.64	4.57
2004	Iowa	AAA	37	0	0	35	44.2	179	30	13	12	4	0	0	0	15	2	59	0	0	1	1	.500	0	19--	-	2.00	2.42
2004	CHN	NL	31	0	0	11	29.0	124	22	14	14	4	4	2	0	17	1	30	2	1	1	0	1.000	0	1-1	5	3.67	4.34
2005	CHN	NL	75	0	0	12	75.2	319	60	36	32	6	3	2	0	40	7	89	7	0	6	2	.750	0	0-3	18	3.17	3.81
2 ML YEARS			106	0	0	23	104.2	443	82	50	46	10	7	4	0	57	8	119	9	1	7	2	.778	0	1-4	19	3.31	3.96

Kelly Wunsch

Pitches: L Bats: L Pos: RP-46   **Ht: 6'5" Wt: 225 Born: 7/12/1972 Age: 33**

Year	Team	Lg	HOW MUCH HE PITCHED G	GS	CG	GF	IP	BFP	WHAT HE GAVE UP H	R	ER	HR	SH	SF	HB	TBB	IBB	SO	WP	Bk	THE RESULTS W	L	Pct	ShO	Sv-Op	Hld	ERC	ERA
2000	CHA	AL	83	0	0	12	61.1	259	50	22	20	4	0	2	2	29	1	51	0	0	6	3	.667	0	1-5	25	3.22	2.93
2001	CHA	AL	33	0	0	2	22.1	105	21	19	19	4	3	2	6	9	1	16	0	0	2	1	.667	0	0-2	3	5.11	7.66
2002	CHA	AL	50	0	0	9	31.2	138	26	12	12	3	1	0	5	19	1	22	1	0	2	1	.667	0	0-1	9	4.51	3.41
2003	CHA	AL	43	0	0	6	36.0	160	17	13	11	1	1	5	7	25	4	33	1	0	0	0	-	0	0-0	5	2.28	2.75
2004	CHA	AL	3	0	0	1	2.0	8	2	0	0	0	0	0	0	1	0	1	0	0	0	0	-	0	0-0	0	4.15	0.00
2005	LAN	NL	46	0	0	6	23.2	105	20	12	12	2	1	0	2	14	2	22	2	0	1	1	.500	0	0-1	15	4.01	4.56
6 ML YEARS			258	0	0	36	177.0	775	136	78	74	14	6	9	22	97	9	145	4	0	11	6	.647	0	1-9	57	3.58	3.76

Keiichi Yabu

Pitches: R Bats: R Pos: RP-40   **Ht: 6'1" Wt: 201 Born: 9/28/1968 Age: 37**

Year	Team	Lg	HOW MUCH HE PITCHED G	GS	CG	GF	IP	BFP	WHAT HE GAVE UP H	R	ER	HR	SH	SF	HB	TBB	IBB	SO	WP	Bk	THE RESULTS W	L	Pct	ShO	Sv-Op	Hld	ERC	ERA
1994	Hnshn	Jap	26	25	8		181.1	762	174	67	64	12	-	-	2	42	-	110	2	1	9	9	.500	1	0--	-	2.92	3.18
1995	Hnshn	Jap	27	27	7		196.0	833	185	73	65	19	-	-	10	50	-	118	4	1	7	13	.350	2	0--	-	3.24	2.98
1996	Hnshn	Jap	30	30	6		195.1	852	204	97	87	14	-	-	11	51	-	145	1	1	11	14	.440	1	0--	-	3.64	4.01

Year	Team	Lg	G	GS	CG	GF	IP	BFP	H	R	ER	HR	SH	SF	HB	TBB	IBB	SO	WP	Bk	W	L	Pct	ShO	Sv-Op	Hld	ERC	ERA
1997	Hnshn	Jap	29	22	4		183.0	794	172	79	73	23	-	-	11	62	-	111	9	0	10	12	.455	1	0--	-	3.73	3.59
1998	Hnshn	Jap	24	24	3		164.0	710	159	74	64	11	-	-	8	51	-	90	4	2	11	10	.524	2	0--	-	3.36	3.51
1999	Hnshn	Jap	28	27	4		173.1	763	175	80	76	16	-	-	11	57	-	95	4	0	6	16	.273	2	0--	-	3.86	3.95
2000	Hnshn	Jap	25	24	1		151.0	649	162	76	70	19	-	-	4	30	-	95	7	0	6	10	.375	1	0--	-	3.82	4.17
2001	Hnshn	Jap	17	8	0		55.0	258	55	32	25	2	-	-	5	33	-	26	5	0	0	4	.000	0	0--	-	4.42	4.09
2002	Hnshn	Jap	20	15	5		131.2	549	118	48	46	14	-	-	6	30	-	97	3	0	10	6	.625	2	0--	-	2.96	3.14
2003	Hnshn	Jap	23	15	0		97.2	419	97	50	43	13	-	-	2	27	-	67	4	0	8	3	.727	0	0--	-	3.72	3.96
2004	Hnshn	Jap	19	19	1		116.1	499	108	44	33	8	-	-	6	36	-	75	5	0	6	9	.400	1	0--	-	3.17	2.55
2005	OAK	AL	40	0	0	15	58.0	262	64	34	29	6	2	3	8	26	3	44	2	0	4	0	1.000	0	1-2	1	5.45	4.50

Esteban Yan

Pitches: R Bats: R Pos: RP-49   Ht: 6'4" Wt: 255 Born: 6/22/1975 Age: 31

			HOW MUCH HE PITCHED						WHAT HE GAVE UP												THE RESULTS							
Year	Team	Lg	G	GS	CG	GF	IP	BFP	H	R	ER	HR	SH	SF	HB	TBB	IBB	SO	WP	Bk	W	L	Pct	ShO	Sv-Op	Hld	ERC	ERA
1996	BAL	AL	4	0	0	0	9.1	42	13	7	6	3	0	0	0	3	1	7	0	0	0	0	-	0	0-0	0	7.88	5.79
1997	BAL	AL	3	2	0	0	9.2	58	20	18	17	3	0	1	2	7	0	4	1	0	0	1	.000	0	0-0	0	15.60	15.83
1998	TB	AL	64	0	0	18	88.2	381	78	41	38	11	1	3	5	41	2	77	6	0	5	4	.556	0	1-5	8	4.02	3.86
1999	TB	AL	50	1	0	15	61.0	286	77	41	40	8	6	3	9	32	4	46	2	0	3	4	.429	0	0-3	7	7.13	5.90
2000	TB	AL	43	20	0	8	137.2	618	158	98	95	26	4	6	11	42	0	111	7	1	7	8	.467	0	0-2	3	5.46	6.21
2001	TB	AL	54	0	0	51	62.1	264	64	34	27	7	3	1	5	11	1	64	5	0	4	6	.400	0	22-31	0	3.68	3.90
2002	TB	AL	55	0	0	47	69.0	305	70	35	33	10	2	1	3	29	1	53	5	1	7	8	.467	0	19-27	0	4.67	4.30
2003	2 Tms		54	0	0	23	66.2	309	84	48	47	13	2	4	7	23	5	53	9	0	2	1	.667	0	1-1	4	6.39	6.35
2004	DET	AL	69	0	0	27	87.0	379	92	43	37	8	4	3	4	32	5	69	7	0	3	6	.333	0	7-17	11	4.32	3.83
2005	LAA	AL	49	0	0	21	66.2	293	66	36	34	8	3	4	0	30	4	45	5	0	1	1	.500	0	0-0	1	4.21	4.59
03	Tex	AL	15	0	0	6	23.1	110	31	19	18	5	0	0	2	7	1	25	5	0	0	1	.000	0	0-0	1	6.64	6.94
03	StL	NL	39	0	0	17	43.1	199	53	29	29	8	2	4	5	16	4	28	4	0	2	0	1.000	0	1-1	3	6.26	6.02
10 ML YEARS			445	23	0	212	658.0	2935	722	401	374	97	25	26	46	250	23	529	47	2	32	39	.451	0	50-86	34	5.12	5.12

Kevin Youkilis

Bats: R Throws: R Pos: 3B-24; PH-10; 1B-9; PR-3; 2B-2   Ht: 6'1" Wt: 220 Born: 3/15/1979 Age: 27

			BATTING																			BASERUNNING				AVERAGES		
Year	Team	Lg	G	AB	H	2B	3B	HR	(Hm	Rd)	TB	R	RBI	RC	TBB	IBB	SO	HBP	SH	SF		SB	CS	SB%	GDP	Avg	OBP	Slg
2001	Lowell	A-	59	183	58	14	2	3	(-	-)	85	52	28	52	70	0	28	5	0	2		4	3	.57	0	.317	.512	.464
2001	Augsta	A	5	12	2	0	0	0	(-	-)	2	0	0	1	3	0	3	1	0	0		0	0	-	0	.167	.375	.167
2002	Augsta	A	15	53	15	5	0	0	(-	-)	20	5	6	10	13	1	8	1	0	0		0	0	-	0	.283	.433	.377
2002	Srsota	A+	76	268	79	16	0	3	(-	-)	104	45	48	50	49	2	37	15	0	7		0	2	.00	5	.295	.422	.388
2002	Trentn	AA	44	160	55	10	0	5	(-	-)	80	34	26	38	31	1	18	5	0	1		5	4	.56	1	.344	.462	.500
2003	Portlnd	AA	94	312	102	23	1	6	(-	-)	145	74	37	80	86	2	40	15	0	4		7	0	1.00	7	.327	.487	.465
2003	Pwtckt	AAA	32	109	18	3	0	2	(-	-)	27	9	15	8	18	2	21	3	0	2		0	1	.00	2	.165	.295	.248
2004	Lowell	A-	2	4	3	1	1	0	(-	-)	6	1	0	3	2	0	0	1	0	0		0	0	-	0	.750	.857	1.500
2004	Pwtckt	AAA	38	154	41	12	0	3	(-	-)	62	25	18	23	19	1	28	2	1	2		2	0	1.00	1	.266	.350	.403
2005	Pwtckt	AAA	43	152	49	15	1	8	(-	-)	90	30	27	41	35	0	29	5	0	2		1	2	.33	0	.322	.459	.592
2004	BOS	AL	72	208	54	11	0	7	(2	5)	86	38	35	36	33	0	45	4	0	3		0	1	.00	1	.260	.367	.413
2005	BOS	AL	44	79	22	7	0	1	(0	1)	32	11	9	13	14	0	19	2	0	0		0	1	.00	0	.278	.400	.405
2 ML YEARS			116	287	76	18	0	8	(2	6)	118	49	44	49	47	0	64	6	0	3		0	2	.00	1	.265	.376	.411

Chris Young

Pitches: R Bats: R Pos: SP-31   Ht: 6'10" Wt: 260 Born: 5/25/1979 Age: 27

			HOW MUCH HE PITCHED						WHAT HE GAVE UP												THE RESULTS							
Year	Team	Lg	G	GS	CG	GF	IP	BFP	H	R	ER	HR	SH	SF	HB	TBB	IBB	SO	WP	Bk	W	L	Pct	ShO	Sv-Op	Hld	ERC	ERA
2001	Hickory	A	12	12	2	0	74.1	320	79	39	34	6	2	1	3	20	0	72	0	0	5	3	.625	0	0--	-	3.91	4.12
2002	Hickory	A	26	26	1	0	144.2	587	127	57	50	11	4	4	4	34	1	136	3	1	11	9	.550	0	0--	-	2.75	3.11
2003	BrvdCt	A+	8	8	0	0	50.0	180	26	9	9	3	1	0	1	5	0	39	0	0	5	2	.714	0	0--	-	0.95	1.62
2003	Hrsbrg	AA	15	15	0	0	83.0	354	83	39	37	9	4	4	5	22	0	64	5	2	4	4	.500	0	0--	-	3.81	4.01
2004	Frisco	AA	18	18	0	0	88.1	383	94	48	44	9	5	4	5	31	1	75	4	0	6	5	.545	0	0--	-	4.51	4.48
2004	Okla	AAA	5	5	1	0	30.1	116	20	7	5	2	1	0	0	9	0	34	0	0	3	0	1.000	0	0--	-	1.83	1.48
2004	TEX	AL	7	7	0	0	36.1	158	36	21	19	7	1	0	2	10	0	27	1	0	3	2	.600	0	0-0	-	4.26	4.71
2005	TEX	AL	31	31	0	0	164.2	700	162	84	78	19	2	4	7	45	2	137	3	0	12	7	.632	0	0-0	0	3.71	4.26
2 ML YEARS			38	38	0	0	201.0	858	198	105	97	26	3	4	9	55	2	164	4	0	15	9	.625	0	0-0	0	3.81	4.34

Dmitri Young

Bats: B Throws: R Pos: DH-71; 1B-30; LF-19; PH-7; RF-1   Ht: 6'2" Wt: 235 Born: 10/11/1973 Age: 32

			BATTING																			BASERUNNING				AVERAGES		
Year	Team	Lg	G	AB	H	2B	3B	HR	(Hm	Rd)	TB	R	RBI	RC	TBB	IBB	SO	HBP	SH	SF		SB	CS	SB%	GDP	Avg	OBP	Slg
1996	STL	NL	16	29	7	0	0	0	(0	0)	7	3	2	2	4	0	5	1	0	0		0	1	.00	1	.241	.353	.241
1997	STL	NL	110	333	86	14	3	5	(2	3)	121	38	34	40	38	3	63	2	1	3		6	5	.55	8	.258	.335	.363
1998	CIN	NL	144	536	166	48	1	14	(3	11)	258	81	83	88	47	4	94	2	0	5		2	4	.33	16	.310	.364	.481
1999	CIN	NL	127	373	112	30	2	14	(9	5)	188	63	56	63	30	1	71	2	0	4		3	1	.75	11	.300	.352	.504
2000	CIN	NL	152	548	166	37	6	18	(6	12)	269	68	88	86	36	6	80	3	1	5		9	3	.00	16	.303	.346	.491
2001	CIN	NL	142	540	163	28	3	21	(8	13)	260	68	69	83	37	10	77	5	1	3		8	5	.62	22	.302	.350	.481
2002	DET	AL	54	201	57	14	0	7	(5	2)	92	25	27	27	12	5	39	2	0	1		2	0	1.00	12	.284	.329	.458
2003	DET	AL	155	562	167	34	7	29	(10	19)	302	78	85	101	58	16	130	11	0	4		1	1	.67	16	.297	.372	.537
2004	DET	AL	104	389	106	23	2	18	(8	10)	187	72	60	57	33	4	71	6	0	4		0	1	.00	8	.272	.336	.481
2005	DET	AL	126	469	127	25	3	21	(10	11)	221	61	72	60	29	7	100	9	0	1		1	0	1.00	16	.271	.325	.471
10 ML YEARS			1130	3980	1157	253	27	147	(61	86)	1905	557	576	607	324	56	730	43	3	30		24	21	.53	126	.291	.348	.479

Eric Young

Bats: R **Throws:** R **Pos:** PH-23; LF-21; 2B-14; CF-4   **Ht:** 5'8" **Wt:** 180 **Born:** 5/18/1967 **Age:** 39

Year	Team	Lg	G	AB	H	2B	3B	HR	(Hm	Rd)	TB	R	RBI	RC	TBB	IBB	SO	HBP	SH	SF	SB	CS	SB%	GDP	Avg	OBP	Slg
2005	PortInd*	AAA	5	16	0	0	0	0	(-	-)	0	3	0	0	6	0	2	0	0	0	0	0	-	0	.000	.273	.000
1992	LA	NL	49	132	34	1	0	1	(0	1)	38	9	11	12	8	0	9	0	4	0	6	1	.86	3	.258	.300	.288
1993	COL	NL	144	490	132	16	8	3	(3	0)	173	82	42	66	63	3	41	4	4	4	42	19	.69	9	.269	.355	.353
1994	COL	NL	90	228	62	13	1	7	(6	1)	98	37	30	40	38	1	17	2	5	2	18	7	.72	3	.272	.378	.430
1995	COL	NL	120	366	116	21	9	6	(5	1)	173	68	36	73	49	3	29	5	3	1	35	12	.74	4	.317	.404	.473
1996	COL	NL	141	568	184	23	4	8	(7	1)	239	113	74	99	47	1	31	21	2	5	53	19	.74	9	.324	.393	.421
1997	2 Tms	NL	155	622	174	33	8	8	(2	6)	247	106	61	93	71	1	54	9	10	6	45	14	.76	18	.280	.359	.397
1998	LA	NL	117	452	129	24	1	8	(7	1)	179	78	43	70	45	0	32	5	9	2	42	13	.76	4	.285	.355	.396
1999	LA	NL	119	456	128	24	2	2	(2	0)	162	73	41	65	63	0	26	5	6	4	51	22	.70	12	.281	.371	.355
2000	CHN	NL	153	607	180	40	2	6	(5	1)	242	98	47	99	63	1	39	8	7	5	54	7	.89	12	.297	.367	.399
2001	CHN	NL	149	603	168	43	4	6	(4	2)	237	98	42	78	42	1	45	9	15	3	31	14	.69	15	.279	.333	.393
2002	MIL	NL	138	496	139	29	3	3	(2	1)	183	57	28	53	39	0	38	6	8	4	31	11	.74	14	.280	.338	.369
2003	2 Tms	NL	135	475	119	20	1	15	(7	8)	186	80	34	54	57	2	44	5	2	2	28	12	.70	12	.251	.336	.392
2004	TEX	AL	104	344	99	25	2	1	(1	0)	131	55	27	54	43	0	28	8	4	3	14	9	.61	9	.288	.377	.381
2005	SD	NL	56	142	39	9	0	2	(0	2)	54	22	12	17	18	0	12	0	3	0	7	6	.54	4	.275	.356	.380
97	Col	NL	118	468	132	29	6	6	(2	4)	191	78	45	71	57	0	37	5	8	5	32	12	.73	16	.282	.363	.408
97	LA	NL	37	154	42	4	2	2	(0	2)	56	28	16	22	14	1	17	4	2	1	13	2	.87	2	.273	.347	.364
03	Mil	NL	109	404	105	18	1	15	(7	8)	170	71	31	51	48	2	34	4	2	1	25	7	.78	9	.260	.344	.421
03	SF	NL	26	71	14	2	0	0	(0	0)	16	9	3	3	9	0	10	1	0	1	3	5	.38	3	.197	.293	.225
	14 ML YEARS		1670	5981	1703	321	45	76	(51	25)	2342	976	528	873	646	13	445	87	82	41	457	166	.73	128	.285	.361	.392

Michael Young

Bats: R **Throws:** R **Pos:** SS-155; DH-4   **Ht:** 6'1" **Wt:** 190 **Born:** 10/19/1976 **Age:** 29

Year	Team	Lg	G	AB	H	2B	3B	HR	(Hm	Rd)	TB	R	RBI	RC	TBB	IBB	SO	HBP	SH	SF	SB	CS	SB%	GDP	Avg	OBP	Slg
2000	TEX	AL	2	2	0	0	0	0	(0	0)	0	0	0	0	0	0	1	0	0	0	0	0	-	0	.000	.000	.000
2001	TEX	AL	106	386	96	18	4	11	(7	4)	155	57	49	45	26	0	91	3	9	5	3	1	.75	9	.249	.298	.402
2002	TEX	AL	156	573	150	26	8	9	(3	6)	219	77	62	64	41	1	112	0	13	6	6	7	.46	14	.262	.308	.382
2003	TEX	AL	160	666	204	33	9	14	(9	5)	297	106	72	106	36	1	103	1	3	7	13	2	.87	14	.306	.339	.446
2004	TEX	AL	160	690	216	33	9	22	(9	13)	333	114	99	124	44	1	89	1	0	4	12	3	.80	11	.313	.353	.483
2005	TEX	AL	159	668	221	40	5	24	(12	12)	343	114	91	131	58	0	91	3	0	3	5	2	.71	20	.331	.385	.513
	6 ML YEARS		743	2985	887	150	35	80	(40	40)	1347	468	373	470	205	3	487	8	25	25	39	15	.72	68	.297	.341	.451

Walter Young

Bats: L **Throws:** R **Pos:** 1B-10; PH-4; DH-3   **Ht:** 6'5" **Wt:** 322 **Born:** 2/18/1980 **Age:** 26

Year	Team	Lg	G	AB	H	2B	3B	HR	(Hm	Rd)	TB	R	RBI	RC	TBB	IBB	SO	HBP	SH	SF	SB	CS	SB%	GDP	Avg	OBP	Slg
1999	Pirates	R	37	130	30	6	2	0	(-	-)	40	9	15	10	4	1	34	3	1	0	2	2	.50	4	.231	.270	.308
2000	Pirates	R	45	162	48	11	1	10	(-	-)	91	32	34	32	8	1	29	9	0	3	3	2	.60	2	.296	.357	.562
2000	Wmspt	A-	24	92	17	4	0	2	(-	-)	27	5	12	4	1	0	26	1	0	1	0	0	-	1	.185	.200	.293
2001	Wmspt	A-	66	232	67	10	1	13	(-	-)	118	40	47	42	19	5	43	5	0	2	1	1	.50	6	.289	.353	.509
2002	Hickory	A	132	492	164	34	2	25	(-	-)	277	84	103	104	36	6	102	15	0	8	2	6	.25	11	.333	.390	.563
2003	Lynbrg	A+	117	431	120	15	2	20	(-	-)	199	76	87	70	35	3	88	12	0	2	2	4	.33	10	.278	.348	.462
2004	Bowie	AA	133	486	133	28	1	33	(-	-)	262	88	98	90	47	3	145	8	0	7	2	3	.40	11	.274	.343	.539
2005	Ottawa	AAA	123	466	134	29	1	13	(-	-)	204	48	81	69	30	4	91	5	0	5	1	1	.50	14	.288	.334	.438
2005	BAL	AL	14	33	10	1	0	1	(0	1)	14	2	3	5	4	1	7	0	0	0	0	0	-	1	.303	.378	.424

Carlos Zambrano

Pitches: R **Bats:** B **Pos:** SP-33   **Ht:** 6'5" **Wt:** 250 **Born:** 6/1/1981 **Age:** 25

Year	Team	Lg	G	GS	CG	GF	IP	BFP	H	R	ER	HR	SH	SF	HB	TBB	IBB	SO	WP	Bk	W	L	Pct	ShO	Sv-Op	Hld	ERC	ERA
2001	CHN	NL	6	1	0	1	7.2	42	11	13	13	2	1	1	1	8	0	4	1	0	1	2	.333	0	0-1	0	11.86	15.26
2002	CHN	NL	32	16	0	3	108.1	477	94	53	44	9	9	1	4	63	2	93	6	0	4	8	.333	0	0-0	0	4.02	3.66
2003	CHN	NL	32	32	3	0	214.0	907	188	88	74	9	11	6	10	94	12	168	6	1	13	11	.542	1	0-0	0	3.28	3.11
2004	CHN	NL	31	31	1	0	209.2	887	174	73	64	14	10	3	20	81	4	188	6	2	16	8	.667	1	0-0	0	3.20	2.75
2005	CHN	NL	33	33	2	0	223.1	909	170	88	81	21	9	5	8	86	3	202	7	0	14	6	.700	0	0-0	0	2.86	3.26
	5 ML YEARS		134	113	6	4	763.0	3222	637	315	276	55	40	16	43	332	21	655	26	3	48	35	.578	2	0-1	0	3.31	3.26

Victor Zambrano

Pitches: R **Bats:** B **Pos:** SP-27; RP-4   **Ht:** 6'0" **Wt:** 203 **Born:** 8/6/1975 **Age:** 30

Year	Team	Lg	G	GS	CG	GF	IP	BFP	H	R	ER	HR	SH	SF	HB	TBB	IBB	SO	WP	Bk	W	L	Pct	ShO	Sv-Op	Hld	ERC	ERA
2001	TB	AL	36	0	0	19	51.1	212	38	21	18	6	2	0	3	18	0	58	4	0	6	2	.750	0	2-6	5	2.80	3.16
2002	TB	AL	42	11	0	11	114.0	519	120	77	70	15	7	8	4	68	5	73	10	0	8	8	.500	0	1-3	6	5.52	5.53
2003	TB	AL	34	28	1	2	188.1	836	165	97	88	21	3	10	20	106	2	132	15	3	12	10	.545	0	0-0	2	4.51	4.21
2004	2 Tms		26	25	0	2	142.0	650	119	77	69	13	1	10	16	102	2	123	6	1	11	7	.611	0	0-0	1	4.75	4.37
2005	NYN	NL	31	27	0	2	166.1	748	170	85	77	12	6	6	15	77	2	112	8	2	7	12	.368	0	0-0	0	4.55	4.17
04	TB	AL	23	22	0	0	128.0	588	107	68	63	13	0	10	16	96	2	109	5	0	9	7	.563	0	0-0	1	5.01	4.43
04	NYM	NL	3	3	0	0	14.0	62	12	9	6	0	1	0	0	6	0	14	1	0	2	0	1.000	0	0-0	0	2.57	3.86
	5 ML YEARS		169	91	1	34	662.0	2965	612	357	322	67	19	34	58	371	11	498	43	5	44	39	.530	0	3-9	14	4.60	4.38

Gregg Zaun

Bats: B **Throws:** R **Pos:** C-132; PH-11   **Ht:** 5'10" **Wt:** 190 **Born:** 4/14/1971 **Age:** 35

Year	Team	Lg	G	AB	H	2B	3B	HR	(Hm	Rd)	TB	R	RBI	RC	TBB	IBB	SO	HBP	SH	SF	SB	CS	SB%	GDP	Avg	OBP	Slg
2005	Ham*	AA	2	6	2	1	0	0	(-	-)	3	1	0	1	2	0	2	0	0	0	0	0	-	0	.333	.500	.500
1995	BAL	AL	40	104	27	5	0	3	(1	2)	41	18	14	15	16	0	14	0	2	0	1	1	.50	2	.260	.358	.394
1996	2 Tms		60	139	34	9	1	2	(1	1)	51	20	15	16	14	3	20	2	1	2	1	0	1.00	5	.245	.318	.367
1997	FLA	NL	58	143	43	10	2	2	(0	2)	63	21	20	27	26	4	18	2	1	0	1	0	1.00	3	.301	.415	.441
1998	FLA	NL	106	298	56	12	2	5	(2	3)	87	19	29	23	35	2	52	1	2	2	5	2	.71	7	.188	.274	.292
1999	TEX	AL	43	93	23	2	1	1	(0	1)	30	12	12	10	10	0	7	0	1	2	1	0	1.00	2	.247	.314	.323
2000	KC	AL	83	234	64	11	0	7	(2	5)	96	36	33	40	43	3	34	3	0	2	7	3	.70	4	.274	.390	.410
2001	KC	AL	39	125	40	9	0	6	(1	5)	67	15	18	24	12	0	16	0	0	1	1	2	.33	2	.320	.377	.536
2002	HOU	NL	76	185	41	7	1	3	(3	0)	59	18	24	17	12	1	36	2	2	1	1	0	1.00	4	.222	.275	.319
2003	2 Tms		74	166	38	8	0	4	(1	3)	58	15	21	20	19	0	21	1	1	2	1	1	.50	5	.229	.309	.349
2004	TOR	AL	107	338	91	24	0	6	(2	4)	133	46	36	50	47	3	61	6	0	1	0	2	.00	7	.269	.367	.393
2005	TOR	AL	133	434	109	18	1	11	(7	4)	162	61	61	65	73	2	70	0	0	5	2	3	.40	11	.251	.355	.373
96	Bal	AL	50	108	25	8	1	1	(1	0)	38	16	13	12	11	2	15	2	0	2	0	0	-	3	.231	.309	.352
96	Fla	NL	10	31	9	1	0	1	(0	1)	13	4	2	4	3	1	5	0	1	0	1	0	1.00	2	.290	.353	.419
03	Hou	NL	59	120	26	7	0	1	(1	0)	36	9	13	12	14	0	14	1	1	2	1	0	1.00	5	.217	.299	.300
03	Col	NL	15	46	12	1	0	3	(0	3)	22	6	8	8	5	0	7	0	0	0	0	1	.00	0	.261	.333	.478
	11 ML YEARS		819	2259	566	115	8	50	(20	30)	847	281	283	307	307	18	349	17	10	18	21	14	.60	52	.251	.342	.375

Ryan Zimmerman

Bats: R **Throws:** R **Pos:** 3B-14; PH-5; SS-1   **Ht:** 6'3" **Wt:** 210 **Born:** 9/28/1984 **Age:** 21

Year	Team	Lg	G	AB	H	2B	3B	HR	(Hm	Rd)	TB	R	RBI	RC	TBB	IBB	SO	HBP	SH	SF	SB	CS	SB%	GDP	Avg	OBP	Slg
2005	Savann	A	4	17	8	2	1	2	(-	-)	18	5	6	6	0	0	3	0	0	0	0	1	.00	0	.471	.471	1.059
2005	Hrsbrg	AA	63	233	76	20	0	9	(-	-)	123	40	32	43	15	3	34	2	1	1	1	5	.17	3	.326	.371	.528
2005	WAS	NL	20	58	23	10	0	0	(0	0)	33	6	6	9	3	0	12	0	0	1	0	0	-	1	.397	.419	.569

Barry Zito

Pitches: L **Bats:** L **Pos:** SP-35   **Ht:** 6'4" **Wt:** 215 **Born:** 5/13/1978 **Age:** 28

Year	Team	Lg	HOW MUCH HE PITCHED						WHAT HE GAVE UP										THE RESULTS							
			G	GS	CG	GF	IP	BFP	H	R	ER	HR	SH	SF	HB	TBB	IBB	SO	WP	Bk	W	L	Pct	ShO	Sv-Op	Hld	ERC	ERA
2000	OAK	AL	14	14	1	0	92.2	376	64	30	28	6	1	0	2	45	2	78	2	0	7	4	.636	1	0-0	0	2.63	2.72
2001	OAK	AL	35	35	3	0	214.1	902	184	92	83	18	5	4	13	80	0	205	6	1	17	8	.680	2	0-0	0	3.33	3.49
2002	OAK	AL	35	35	1	0	229.1	939	182	79	70	24	9	7	9	78	2	182	2	1	23	5	.821	0	0-0	0	2.92	2.75
2003	OAK	AL	35	35	4	0	231.2	957	186	98	85	19	7	7	6	88	3	146	4	0	14	12	.538	1	0-0	0	2.91	3.30
2004	OAK	AL	34	34	0	0	213.0	926	216	116	106	28	7	9	9	81	2	163	4	1	11	11	.500	0	0-0	0	4.45	4.48
2005	OAK	AL	35	35	0	0	228.1	953	185	106	98	26	8	7	13	89	0	171	4	0	14	13	.519	0	0-0	0	3.32	3.86
	6 ML YEARS		188	188	9	0	1209.1	5053	1017	521	470	121	37	34	52	461	9	945	22	3	86	53	.619	4	0-0	0	3.30	3.50

2005 Fielding Statistics

In this section you will find all of the traditional fielding statistics for the 2005 season. However, these fielding stats are not official. You will certainly find some differences when the official Major League Baseball numbers arrive later this year. We hope you'll agree that having an unofficial statistical fielding record in this November book is better than holding up the entire process for the official totals. Even though our statistics are unofficial, they are no less accurate.

You'll notice that each position is broken down into "The Regulars" and "The Rest" so you can get a truer sense of how the starters compare to each other without having to sort through the September call-ups. Of course, if you are really interested in knowing how many putouts Ryan Spilborghs had, then we have that too.

The last column for the non-catchers is range factor labeled "Rng". Range Factor is the number of successful chances (Putouts plus Assists) times nine, divided by the number of Defensive Innings played.

Be sure to check out our "Catchers Special" section for our catcher ERA and stolen base numbers. If you look hard enough you may be able to figure out why your team's catcher is still behind the dish even though he hovers around the Mendoza Line at the plate.

Just to clarify, PCS is the number of Total Caught Stealing attributed to the pitcher, not the catcher in question. So, CS% is the percentage of runners caught stealing not including PCS.

First Basemen - Regulars

Player	Tm	G	GS	Inn	PO	A	E	DP	Pct.	Rng
Casey,Sean	Cin	134	132	1138.2	1153	55	5	91	.998	
Teixeira,Mark	Tex	155	154	1358.0	1377	101	3	127	.998	
Choi,Hee Seop	LAD	83	78	664.2	698	62	2	59	.997	
Clark,Tony	Ari	83	70	642.2	663	45	2	59	.997	
Erstad,Darin	LAA	147	144	1279.1	1218	79	4	109	.997	
Snow,J.T.	SF	108	96	825.2	813	56	3	62	.997	
Konerko,Paul	CWS	146	145	1272.2	1320	82	5	135	.996	
Helton,Todd	Col	144	142	1229.2	1236	118	5	136	.996	
Tracy,Chad	Ari	80	72	652.2	706	47	3	75	.996	
Lee,Derrek	ChC	158	158	1386.0	1323	122	6	118	.996	
Lee,Travis	TB	124	101	918.1	874	67	4	87	.996	
Johnson,Nick	Was	129	126	1098.2	1017	95	5	109	.996	
Palmeiro,Rafael	Bal	93	82	748.1	748	58	4	68	.995	
Mientkiewicz,D	NYM	83	79	675.0	690	42	4	59	.995	
Sexson,Richie	Sea	151	151	1302.0	1147	119	7	121	.995	
Berkman,Lance	Hou	96	84	737.2	772	49	5	77	.994	
LaRoche,Adam	Atl	125	117	1019.1	1070	77	7	105	.994	
Morneau,Justin	Min	138	128	1166.1	1191	91	8	123	.994	
Johnson,Dan	Oak	101	98	883.2	898	57	6	94	.994	
Nevin,Phil	TOT	74	71	620.0	592	38	4	52	.994	
Ward,Daryle	Pit	109	101	891.2	863	76	6	114	.994	
Howard,Ryan	Phi	84	79	706.1	707	40	5	53	.993	
Shelton,Chris	Det	84	83	738.1	778	60	6	88	.993	
Hinske,Eric	Tor	100	97	859.2	868	69	7	77	.993	
Broussard,Ben	Cle	138	114	1050.2	1082	60	9	112	.992	
Millar,Kevin	Bos	110	102	796.1	799	85	7	67	.992	
Overbay,Lyle	Mil	154	143	1265.0	1134	96	10	104	.992	
Pujols,Albert	StL	158	155	1358.2	1596	97	14	175	.992	
Martinez,Tino	NYY	122	78	770.2	797	49	8	73	.991	
Delgado,Carlos	Fla	141	140	1206.0	1147	83	14	132	.989	

First Basemen - The Rest

Player	Tm	G	GS	Inn	PO	A	E	DP	Pct.	Rng
Alexander,Manny	SD	1	0	0.0	0	0	0	0	-	
Anderson,Marlon	NYM	23	16	155.1	173	16	2	18	.990	
Baerga,Carlos	Was	11	9	86.2	65	2	1	2	.985	
Bagwell,Jeff	Hou	24	24	202.2	211	14	0	13	1.000	
Barajas,Rod	Tex	1	0	1.0	1	0	0	0	1.000	
Blake,Casey	Cle	4	4	30.0	28	5	1	4	.971	
Blanco,Tony	Was	3	1	14.0	11	1	2	2	.857	
Bloomquist,Wil	Sea	1	0	1.2	0	1	0	0	1.000	
Blum,Geoff	SD	2	0	3.0	1	0	0	0	1.000	
Blum,Geoff	CWS	12	9	89.0	92	6	0	7	1.000	
Branyan,Russell	Mil	5	2	24.0	29	2	0	0	1.000	
Bruntlett,Eric	Hou	1	1	1.0	1	0	0	0	1.000	
Burke,Jamie	CWS	1	0	1.0	0	0	0	0	-	
Cairo,Miguel	NYM	8	6	50.2	48	2	1	6	.980	
Cirillo,Jeff	Mil	1	0	0.2	0	0	0	0	-	
Conine,Jeff	Fla	45	22	231.1	247	17	4	27	.985	
Cordero,Wil	Was	12	7	68.2	66	2	0	5	1.000	
Cruz,Jacob	Cin	5	2	20.0	15	1	0	2	1.000	
Cuddyer,Mike	Min	8	3	33.0	36	1	0	8	1.000	
Daubach,Brian	NYM	6	4	43.0	39	3	1	3	.977	
DeRosa,Mark	Tex	1	0	1.0	2	0	0	1	1.000	
Diaz,Einar	StL	3	0	8.0	9	0	0	2	1.000	
Dillon,Joe	Fla	1	0	2.0	2	0	0	0	1.000	
Dobbs,Greg	Sea	5	4	37.0	32	8	0	0	1.000	
Duncan,Chris	StL	2	0	2.0	1	0	0	0	1.000	
Dunn,Adam	Cin	33	27	251.1	244	11	4	31	.985	
Durazo,Erubiel	Oak	1	1	8.0	8	0	0	2	1.000	
Dye,Jermaine	CWS	1	1	9.0	7	1	0	0	1.000	
Eldred,Brad	Pit	50	46	406.0	435	15	7	46	.985	
Ellis,Mark	Oak	2	0	3.0	3	0	0	0	1.000	
Escalona,Felix	NYY	1	0	1.0	2	0	0	1	1.000	
Fasano,Sal	Bal	1	0	2.0	0	0	0	0	-	
Feliz,Pedro	SF	15	9	89.2	76	7	1	7	.988	
Fick,Robert	SD	29	22	199.1	224	12	2	23	.992	
Fielder,Prince	Mil	7	3	34.0	26	4	0	2	1.000	
Flaherty,John	NYY	1	0	3.0	1	0	0	0	1.000	
Franco,Julio	Atl	62	45	423.1	450	37	5	46	.990	
Freire,Alejan	Bal	16	13	103.0	101	5	1	10	.991	
Giambi,Jason	NYY	78	77	560.0	581	19	7	50	.988	
Gibbons,Jay	Bal	22	19	164.1	171	8	1	10	.994	
Gload,Ross	CWS	24	6	89.0	72	4	1	9	.987	
Gomez,Chris	Bal	42	27	241.0	252	15	2	29	.993	
Gonzalez,Adrian	Tex	10	7	71.0	85	6	2	7	.978	
Gonzalez,Luis A	Col	10	3	36.1	37	3	0	4	1.000	
Grabowski,Jason	LAD	3	1	8.0	11	0	0	1	1.000	
Graffanino,Tony	KC	22	14	134.0	137	7	1	19	.993	
Hafner,Travis	Cle	1	1	7.0	6	2	0	0	1.000	
Hall,Toby	TB	2	0	5.0	5	2	0	0	1.000	
Hansen,Dave	Sea	9	0	27.0	18	2	0	3	1.000	
Harris,Lenny	Fla	1	0	3.0	3	0	0	2	1.000	
Harvey,Ken	KC	5	5	37.0	41	0	0	2	1.000	
Hatteberg,Scott	Oak	53	50	436.2	423	38	7	47	.985	
Helms,Wes	Mil	16	14	114.1	103	9	1	9	.991	
Hernandez,Jose	Cle	45	41	339.0	337	27	2	28	.995	
Hillenbrand,Shea	Tor	67	65	587.1	627	48	6	69	.991	
Holbert,Aaron	Cin	2	0	5.0	4	0	0	0	1.000	
Hollandsworth,T	ChC	1	0	1.0	3	0	0	0	1.000	
Hollandsworth,T	Atl	1	0	1.0	0	0	0	0	-	
Huber,Justin	KC	19	17	142.1	123	8	3	16	.978	
Huff,Aubrey	TB	25	18	161.1	134	5	0	15	1.000	
Ibanez,Raul	Sea	4	4	34.0	26	3	0	0	1.000	
Jackson,Conor	Ari	20	20	161.0	171	11	5	19	.973	
Jacobs,Mike	NYM	28	28	236.0	237	10	4	24	.984	
Johnson,Russ	NYY	7	2	29.0	30	0	0	5	1.000	
Kent,Jeff	LAD	14	10	81.1	92	6	2	9	.980	
Klesko,Ryan	SD	1	0	1.0	2	0	0	0	1.000	
Kotchman,Casey	LAA	20	13	131.0	111	7	0	10	1.000	
LaForest,Pete	TB	1	1	8.0	4	0	0	0	1.000	
Lamb,Mike	Hou	68	47	428.0	429	28	5	39	.989	
LeCroy,Matt	Min	23	21	179.0	203	8	3	18	.986	
Liefer,Jeff	Cle	5	4	26.0	17	2	1	2	.950	
Lopez,Javy	Bal	1	0	2.0	1	0	0	1	1.000	
Mabry,John	StL	14	5	53.0	55	8	0	8	1.000	
Mackowiak,Rob	Pit	3	1	16.0	18	1	0	4	1.000	
Marrero,Eli	KC	9	8	73.2	72	3	1	7	.987	
Martinez,Ramon	Det	2	0	3.0	3	0	0	0	1.000	
Martinez,Ramon	Phi	10	9	76.0	75	6	0	8	1.000	
McAnulty,Paul	SD	1	0	4.0	4	0	0	1	1.000	
McCarty,David	Bos	12	0	23.0	19	3	0	3	1.000	
McClain,Scott	ChC	4	1	16.0	15	0	0	1	1.000	
McEwing,Joe	KC	20	8	97.1	101	11	0	15	1.000	
Merloni,Lou	LAA	1	0	2.0	0	0	0	0	-	
Molina,Jose	LAA	4	1	10.0	10	0	0	2	1.000	
Molina,Yadier	StL	1	0	1.0	0	0	0	0	-	
Munson,Eric	TB	1	0	3.0	3	0	0	0	1.000	
Myrow,Brian	LAD	5	2	26.2	20	0	0	2	1.000	
Nady,Xavier	SD	44	34	299.1	261	27	4	27	.986	
Nakamura,Nor	LAD	4	1	15.0	18	0	1	2	.947	
Nevin,Phil	SD	71	70	611.0	579	37	4	51	.994	
Nevin,Phil	Tex	3	1	9.0	13	1	0	1	1.000	
Niekro,Lance	SF	74	57	529.0	543	38	5	56	.991	
Offerman,Jose	Phi	4	1	16.0	15	0	1	1	.938	
Offerman,Jose	NYM	11	8	76.2	81	4	1	9	.988	
Olerud,John	Bos	80	38	431.0	416	40	1	41	.998	
Ortiz,David	Bos	10	10	78.0	69	11	2	8	.976	
Ozuna,Pablo	CWS	2	0	3.0	2	1	0	0	1.000	
Pena,Carlos	Det	51	49	429.1	418	35	3	46	.993	
Perez,Eduardo	TB	49	42	320.0	264	17	2	22	.993	
Perez,Timo	CWS	2	1	11.0	13	1	1	1	.933	
Perez,Tomas	Phi	24	15	146.0	148	10	0	17	1.000	
Petagine,Rob	Bos	10	7	53.2	51	6	1	4	.983	
Phelps,Josh	TB	1	0	6.0	5	0	0	2	1.000	
Phillips,Andy	NYY	19	5	67.0	75	2	1	7	.987	
Phillips,Jason	LAD	21	18	156.2	143	12	0	16	1.000	
Quinlan,Robb	LAA	9	4	42.0	38	1	0	5	1.000	
Quintero,Humb	Hou	1	0	1.0	0	1	0	0	1.000	
Saenz,Olmedo	LAD	66	52	475.0	460	19	1	36	.998	
Seabol,Scott	StL	5	2	23.0	33	3	0	4	1.000	
Shealy,Ryan	Col	19	17	152.2	155	8	0	8	1.000	
Short,Rick	Was	1	0	4.2	4	1	0	0	1.000	
Smith,Jason	Det	1	0	8.0	10	1	0	0	1.000	
Spiezio,Scott	Sea	4	3	26.0	30	0	0	1	1.000	
Stairs,Matt	KC	64	61	509.2	500	37	4	60	.993	
Surhoff,B.J.	Bal	18	14	113.0	116	8	1	14	.992	
Sweeney,Mark	SD	53	36	337.2	314	21	4	26	.988	
Sweeney,Mike	KC	49	49	419.1	441	29	1	28	.998	
Swisher,Nick	Oak	21	13	119.0	109	10	0	10	1.000	
Thome,Jim	Phi	52	52	436.0	404	30	0	36	1.000	
Tiffee,Terry	Min	13	10	86.0	92	7	1	6	.990	

Player	Tm	G	GS	Inn	PO	A	E	DP	Pct.	Rng
Utley,Chase	Phi	8	6	54.2	45	9	1	7	.982	-
Valentin,Javier	Cin	2	2	18.0	21	0	0	2	1.000	-
Vizcaino,Jose	Hou	13	8	72.2	63	4	2	7	.971	-
Walker,Todd	ChC	4	3	31.0	26	4	0	4	1.000	-
Widger,Chris	CWS	1	0	1.0	0	0	0	0		-
Wigginton,Ty	Pit	3	3	23.0	22	2	0	1	1.000	-
Wilkerson,Brad	Was	25	19	185.1	172	14	1	20	.995	-
Wilson,Craig	Pit	15	11	99.1	86	6	1	10	.989	-
Wilson,Enrique	ChC	3	0	6.0	7	0	0	1	1.000	-
Woodward,Chris	NYM	34	21	199.0	206	10	2	16	.991	-
Youkilis,Kevin	Bos	9	5	47.0	48	0	0	4	1.000	-
Young,Dmitri	Det	30	30	257.0	265	22	3	25	.990	-
Young,Walter	Bal	10	7	54.0	55	6	0	9	1.000	-

Second Basemen - Regulars

Player	Tm	G	GS	Inn	PO	A	E	DP	Pct.	Rng
Hudson,Orlando	Tor	130	120	1067.2	302	390	6	80	.991	5.83
Castillo,Jose	Pit	100	99	840.1	237	279	12	92	.977	5.53
Counsell,Craig	Ari	143	140	1244.1	304	458	8	97	.990	5.51
Miles,Aaron	Col	79	69	602.0	154	207	6	48	.984	5.40
Polanco,Placido	TOT	113	109	945.2	244	322	3	95	.995	5.39
Grudzielanek,M	StL	137	132	1158.1	245	442	7	108	.990	5.34
Castillo,Luis	Fla	120	116	1012.1	245	352	7	87	.988	5.31
Kent,Jeff	LAD	140	138	1209.2	284	424	16	88	.978	5.27
Gotay,Ruben	KC	81	74	666.0	156	231	8	51	.980	5.23
Giles,Marcus	Atl	149	147	1276.0	266	468	12	96	.984	5.18
Bellhorn,Mark	TOT	85	84	728.0	152	264	7	56	.983	5.14
Cano,Robinson	NYY	131	130	1142.2	258	391	17	77	.974	5.11
Utley,Chase	Phi	135	135	1195.1	296	376	15	72	.978	5.06
Ellis,Mark	Oak	115	109	972.0	204	333	6	83	.989	4.97
Cairo,Miguel	NYM	82	74	657.1	151	212	6	58	.984	4.97
Biggio,Craig	Hou	141	141	1172.1	249	395	16	81	.976	4.94
Soriano,Alfonso	Tex	153	153	1351.0	284	447	21	101	.972	4.87
Belliard,Ronnie	Cle	141	139	1243.2	259	413	13	95	.981	4.86
Roberts,Brian	Bal	141	138	1208.0	238	413	8	93	.988	4.85
Iguchi,Tadahito	CWS	133	129	1171.1	234	375	14	84	.978	4.68
Boone,Bret	TOT	88	88	768.2	170	229	9	54	.978	4.67
Durham,Ray	SF	133	131	1143.0	250	341	11	81	.982	4.65
Kennedy,Adam	LAA	127	123	1107.2	212	352	5	71	.991	4.58
Walker,Todd	ChC	97	93	797.2	164	242	6	44	.985	4.58
Loretta,Mark	SD	105	105	910.1	201	261	6	61	.987	4.57
Weeks,Rickie	Mil	95	94	837.1	178	233	21	60	.951	4.42
Vidro,Jose	Was	79	79	665.1	134	191	5	39	.985	4.40
Green,Nick	TB	91	83	731.0	141	195	4	45	.988	4.14
Cantu,Jorge	TB	80	76	667.2	119	181	9	39	.971	4.04

Second Basemen - The Rest

Player	Tm	G	GS	Inn	PO	A	E	DP	Pct.	Rng
Abernathy,Brent	Min	17	14	124.0	24	37	2	9	.968	4.43
Alexander,Manny	SD	5	1	20.0	1	4	0	0	1.000	2.25
Alfonzo,Edgardo	SF	2	2	12.1	4	4	0	2	1.000	5.84
Anderson,Marlon	NYM	20	16	141.1	35	47	1	9	.988	5.22
Aurilia,Rich	Cin	68	64	547.1	128	175	6	38	.981	4.98
Ausmus,Brad	Hou	1	0	1.0	0	0	0	0	-	.00
Aybar,Willy	LAD	6	2	23.1	2	6	0	1	1.000	3.09
Baerga,Carlos	Was	7	5	46.0	15	19	3	3	.919	6.65
Bellhorn,Mark	Bos	83	82	712.0	148	253	6	54	.985	5.07
Bellhorn,Mark	NYY	2	2	16.0	4	11	1	2	.938	8.44
Bergolla,Will	Cin	9	6	62.0	11	29	0	6	1.000	5.81
Betancourt,Yun	Sea	9	6	63.0	23	21	0	5	1.000	6.29
Betemit,Wilson	Atl	1	1	8.0	1	3	0	0	1.000	4.50
Blanco,Andres	KC	24	22	184.0	57	68	3	23	.977	6.11
Bloomquist,Wil	Sea	32	29	254.0	60	83	2	22	.986	5.07
Blum,Geoff	SD	19	18	162.0	28	48	0	10	1.000	4.22
Blum,Geoff	CWS	2	2	18.0	3	4	0	2	1.000	3.50
Boone,Bret	Sea	74	74	646.2	131	192	7	43	.979	4.50
Boone,Bret	Min	14	14	122.0	39	37	2	11	.974	5.61
Bruntlett,Eric	Hou	28	5	79.2	10	16	2	3	.929	2.94
Burke,Chris	Hou	18	7	80.1	15	24	0	5	1.000	4.37
Bynum,Freddie	Oak	3	0	5.0	0	0	0	0	-	.00
Carroll,Jamey	Was	63	44	427.2	96	145	5	33	.980	5.07
Castro,Bernie	Bal	11	11	96.0	17	31	3	7	.941	4.50
Castro,Juan	Min	5	3	23.0	4	9	0	3	1.000	5.09

Player	Tm	G	GS	Inn	PO	A	E	DP	Pct.	Rng
Cedeno,Ronny	ChC	1	0	1.0	0	1	0	0	1.000	9.00
Chavez,Angel	SF	5	1	19.2	3	4	0	0	1.000	3.20
Cintron,Alex	Ari	23	15	144.2	31	39	1	12	.986	4.35
Cirillo,Jeff	Mil	3	1	11.2	4	2	0	1	1.000	4.63
Clark,Jermaine	Oak	2	0	2.0	0	0	0	0		.00
Cora,Alex	Cle	15	14	119.0	24	45	0	11	1.000	5.22
Cora,Alex	Bos	35	21	209.1	52	62	2	18	.983	4.90
Cortez,Fernando	TB	3	3	23.0	0	3	0	0	1.000	1.17
Cruz,Deivi	SF	33	27	258.2	54	76	2	22	.985	4.52
Cruz,Deivi	Was	16	8	79.2	27	25	0	10	1.000	5.87
Cuddyer,Mike	Min	11	6	55.0	12	18	0	7	1.000	4.91
Dallimore,Brian	SF	2	1	10.2	0	6	0	3	1.000	5.06
DeRosa,Mark	Tex	17	8	78.0	13	20	1	3	.971	3.81
Dillon,Joe	Fla	4	2	26.0	5	7	1	2	.923	4.15
Easley,Damion	Fla	46	34	324.0	80	98	4	26	.978	4.94
Escalona,Felix	NYY	1	1	9.0	4	1	0	1	1.000	5.00
Figgins,Chone	LAA	42	36	322.1	67	101	5	20	.971	4.69
Freel,Ryan	Cin	48	48	382.2	91	127	6	24	.973	5.13
Furmaniak,J.J.	Pit	9	6	53.0	14	10	1	1	.960	4.08
Garabito,Eddy	Col	18	16	132.1	33	37	1	12	.986	4.76
Garcia,Jesse	SD	2	0	7.0	2	3	0	1	1.000	6.43
German,Esteban	Tex	1	1	9.0	3	8	1	2	.917	11.00
Ginter,Keith	Oak	25	24	203.2	49	69	3	17	.975	5.21
Gomez,Chris	Bal	18	13	123.2	31	40	1	12	.986	5.17
Gonzalez,Luis A	Col	83	66	579.1	121	196	0	40	1.000	4.92
Graffanino,Tony	KC	22	21	163.1	31	46	1	8	.987	4.24
Graffanino,Tony	Bos	51	50	424.2	90	140	3	29	.987	4.87
Green,Andy	Ari	5	4	39.1	10	11	0	4	1.000	4.81
Hairston,Jerry	ChC	44	36	331.2	69	111	5	23	.973	4.88
Hall,Bill	Mil	23	21	185.0	44	53	4	5	.960	4.72
Harris,Brendan	Was	2	1	13.1	2	5	0	1	1.000	4.73
Harris,Willie	CWS	32	28	248.1	58	78	2	20	.986	4.93
Hernandez,An	NYM	5	5	45.0	9	18	0	1	1.000	5.40
Hernandez,Jose	Cle	4	3	27.0	6	9	0	6	1.000	5.00
Hill,Aaron	Tor	22	19	177.2	33	77	1	15	.991	5.57
Hill,Bobby	Pit	1	0	0.2	0	0	1	0	.000	.00
Hocking,Denny	KC	13	12	119.0	33	48	2	13	.976	6.13
Holbert,Aaron	Cin	4	3	28.0	11	8	1	3	.950	6.11
Hooper,Kevin	Det	1	1	9.0	2	1	0	1	1.000	3.00
Infante,Omar	Det	69	65	591.2	153	186	4	51	.988	5.16
Izturis,Maicer	LAA	1	1	8.0	4	4	0	0	1.000	9.00
Jackson,Damian	SD	35	28	265.0	53	93	1	21	.993	4.96
Jimenez,D'Ang	Cin	27	23	211.2	56	63	2	17	.983	5.06
Johnson,Russ	NYY	1	0	1.0	0	0	0	0		.00
Kata,Matt	Ari	7	3	28.0	8	12	0	6	1.000	6.43
Kata,Matt	Phi	3	0	5.0	0	0	0	0	-	.00
Lopez,Felipe	Cin	7	5	48.0	15	11	0	4	1.000	4.88
Lopez,Jose	Sea	51	50	439.0	123	159	6	32	.979	5.78
Lopez,Luis	Cin	4	2	16.0	3	5	0	0	1.000	4.50
Lopez,Pedro	CWS	1	1	9.0	3	5	0	2	1.000	8.00
Lowell,Mike	Fla	9	9	67.0	18	13	1	3	.969	4.16
Luna,Hector	StL	22	15	143.0	41	52	2	14	.979	5.85
Machado,Alej	Bos	3	0	8.0	0	0	0	0	-	.00
Macias,Jose	ChC	20	11	112.1	27	34	0	8	1.000	4.89
Mackowiak,Rob	Pit	20	17	146.1	37	43	2	10	.976	4.92
Martinez,Ramon	Det	4	4	34.0	10	12	2	3	.917	5.82
Martinez,Ramon	Phi	1	1	5.0	1	2	1	0	.750	5.40
Mateo,Henry	Was	1	1	6.0	1	2	0	1	1.000	4.50
Matranga,Dave	LAA	1	0	2.0	2	1	0	1	1.000	13.50
Matsui,Kazuo	NYM	71	64	560.0	107	187	9	32	.970	4.73
McDonald,John	Tor	5	2	23.1	9	7	0	3	1.000	6.17
McDonald,John	Det	8	3	34.0	6	9	0	3	1.000	3.97
McDougall,Mar	Tex	2	0	2.0	0	0	0	0	-	.00
McEwing,Joe	KC	11	10	76.1	15	25	0	6	1.000	4.72
Menechino,Frank	Tor	26	21	178.1	37	70	1	18	.991	5.40
Mordecai,Mike	Fla	1	1	6.0	2	2	0	0	1.000	6.00
Mueller,Bill	Bos	5	5	43.0	10	13	1	1	.958	4.81
Murphy,Donald	KC	29	23	204.2	42	61	3	14	.972	4.53
Nakamura,Nor	LAD	1	0	2.0	1	0	0	0	1.000	4.50
Nunez,Abraham	StL	22	15	132.0	26	38	2	15	.970	4.36
Offerman,Jose	NYM	1	0	2.0	0	0	0	0	-	.00
Olmedo,Ray	Cin	12	3	137.1	38	40	2	8	.975	5.11
Orr,Pete	Atl	25	14	159.2	35	57	5	11	.948	5.19
Ozuna,Pablo	CWS	6	2	29.0	6	6	1	0	.923	3.72
Perez,Antonio	LAD	21	14	184.1	40	58	3	10	.970	4.78
Perez,Neifi	ChC	26	18	160.0	32	47	2	10	.975	4.44
Phillips,Brand	Cle	2	2	18.0	5	4	0	2	1.000	4.50
Polanco,Placido	Phi	29	26	229.2	57	74	0	26	1.000	5.13
Polanco,Placido	Det	84	83	716.0	187	248	3	69	.993	5.47

Player	Tm	G	GS	Inn	PO	A	E	DP	Pct.	Rng
Punto,Nick	Min	73	63	564.1	131	193	7	44	.979	5.17
Quintanilla,Om	Col	6	3	31.1	10	10	0	5	1.000	5.74
Relaford,Desi	Col	11	8	73.2	10	31	2	4	.953	5.01
Rivas,Luis	Min	53	40	360.0	77	112	1	26	.995	4.73
Robles,Oscar	LAD	1	1	8.0	0	1	1	1	.500	1.13
Rodriguez,Luis	Min	40	22	216.0	53	73	0	22	1.000	5.25
Sanchez,Freddy	Pit	58	39	387.1	108	117	2	40	.991	5.23
Sanchez,Rey	NYY	9	7	63.0	18	24	1	5	.977	6.00
Santiago,Ramon	Sea	2	2	17.0	0	4	0	1	1.000	2.12
Scutaro,Marco	Oak	30	29	267.2	56	92	1	18	.993	4.98
Seabol,Scott	StL	8	0	12.1	1	5	0	0	1.000	4.38
Short,Rick	Was	6	3	30.0	7	8	1	2	.938	4.50
Smith,Jason	Det	6	6	51.0	8	16	1	4	.960	4.24
Sorensen,Zach	LAA	5	2	24.1	3	5	0	1	1.000	2.96
Spiezio,Scott	Sea	1	1	8.0	1	1	0	0	1.000	2.25
Spivey,Junior	Mil	48	46	404.0	93	117	7	27	.968	4.68
Spivey,Junior	Was	22	21	190.0	34	62	0	14	1.000	4.55
Theriot,Ryan	ChC	3	2	18.2	3	9	0	0	1.000	5.79
Vazquez,Ramon	Bos	4	3	25.0	3	6	2	1	.818	3.24
Vazquez,Ramon	Cle	8	4	45.0	17	10	0	5	1.000	5.40
Vizcaino,Jose	Hou	23	10	109.2	30	39	0	14	1.000	5.66
Wigginton,Ty	Pit	1	1	8.1	3	2	0	0	1.000	5.40
Wilson,Enrique	ChC	5	2	18.2	4	9	1	5	.929	6.27
Wilson,Josh	Fla	4	0	7.0	1	1	0	0	1.000	2.57
Womack,Tony	NYY	24	22	199.0	42	89	1	22	.992	5.92
Woodward,Chris	NYM	5	3	30.0	4	7	2	1	.846	3.30
Youkilis,Kevin	Bos	2	1	7.0	0	2	0	0	1.000	2.57
Young,Eric	SD	14	10	91.0	25	26	3	8	.944	5.04

Third Basemen - Regulars

Player	Tm	G	GS	Inn	PO	A	E	DP	Pct.	Rng
Inge,Brandon	Det	160	159	1399.2	128	378	23	41	.957	3.25
Nunez,Abraham	StL	98	77	720.2	54	203	10	19	.963	3.21
Glaus,Troy	Ari	145	144	1264.0	113	310	24	25	.946	3.01
Teahen,Mark	KC	128	122	1068.1	113	244	20	22	.947	3.01
Bell,David	Phi	150	148	1296.2	105	304	21	22	.951	2.84
Chavez,Eric	Oak	153	153	1348.1	121	301	15	27	.966	2.82
Wright,David	NYM	160	160	1404.1	101	337	24	23	.948	2.81
Koskie,Corey	Tor	76	74	674.1	52	158	7	19	.968	2.80
Burroughs,Sean	SD	78	70	656.2	59	145	6	15	.962	2.80
Lowell,Mike	Fla	135	126	1126.2	107	243	6	34	.983	2.80
Beltre,Adrian	Sea	155	155	1325.2	140	271	14	25	.967	2.79
Mora,Melvin	Bal	148	148	1289.2	96	301	18	23	.957	2.77
Ensberg,Morgan	Hou	148	147	1286.1	100	295	15	31	.963	2.76
Gonzalez,Alex S	TB	98	90	779.2	65	173	14	10	.944	2.75
Boone,Aaron	Cle	142	139	1249.2	81	298	18	20	.955	2.73
Crede,Joe	CWS	130	122	1120.1	95	243	10	27	.971	2.72
Cuddyer,Mike	Min	95	92	816.0	57	188	15	14	.942	2.70
Jones,Chipper	Atl	101	100	830.1	80	169	5	18	.980	2.70
Castilla,Vinny	Was	138	135	1171.1	142	209	11	23	.970	2.70
Atkins,Garrett	Col	136	136	1161.2	78	262	18	23	.950	2.63
Blalock,Hank	Tex	158	156	1374.0	96	304	11	23	.973	2.62
Mueller,Bill	Bos	142	140	1209.1	87	265	10	20	.972	2.62
Rodriguez,Alex	NYY	161	161	1384.2	115	288	12	26	.971	2.62
Randa,Joe	TOT	142	140	1209.2	126	225	12	21	.967	2.61
Alfonzo,Edgardo	SF	97	92	813.0	76	157	8	10	.967	2.58
Ramirez,Aramis	ChC	119	119	1020.1	70	218	16	13	.947	2.54

Third Basemen - The Rest

Player	Tm	G	GS	Inn	PO	A	E	DP	Pct.	Rng
Alexander,Manny	SD	1	0	1.0	0	0	0	0	-	.00
Amezaga,Alfredo	Col	1	0	3.0	0	0	0	0	-	.00
Aurilia,Rich	Cin	18	14	129.1	12	33	1	4	.978	3.13
Aybar,Willy	LAD	20	20	174.0	16	35	2	3	.962	2.64
Baerga,Carlos	Was	20	10	100.2	7	16	2	1	.920	2.06
Baker,Jeff	Col	10	10	79.0	3	20	1	1	.958	2.62
Bautista,Jose	Pit	8	7	58.2	6	14	1	2	.952	3.07
Bellhorn,Mark	NYY	4	1	18.0	1	3	0	0	1.000	2.00
Betemit,Wilson	Atl	63	46	431.0	26	94	6	6	.952	2.51
Blake,Casey	Cle	6	6	40.0	4	9	1	1	.929	2.93
Blanco,Tony	Was	5	0	13.0	0	3	0	0	1.000	2.08
Bloomquist,Wil	Sea	6	1	25.0	1	4	0	0	1.000	1.80
Blum,Geoff	SD	34	26	230.2	20	62	6	7	.965	3.20

Player	Tm	G	GS	Inn	PO	A	E	DP	Pct.	Rng
Blum,Geoff	CWS	12	9	86.0	4	29	3	2	.917	3.45
Bocachica,Hiram	Oak	2	2	18.0	2	3	0	1	1.000	2.50
Branyan,Russell	Mil	59	56	456.2	40	82	7	10	.946	2.40
Bruntlett,Eric	Hou	8	0	13.0	1	1	0	0	1.000	1.38
Cabrera,Miguel	Fla	30	29	238.0	21	46	2	5	.971	2.53
Cairo,Miguel	NYM	2	0	6.0	0	2	0	0	1.000	3.00
Cantu,Jorge	TB	62	58	496.0	31	93	12	7	.912	2.25
Carroll,Jamey	Was	12	5	54.0	1	8	0	0	1.000	1.50
Castro,Juan	Min	22	13	123.0	14	22	4	1	.900	2.63
Chavez,Angel	SF	1	0	2.0	0	0	0	0	-	.00
Cintron,Alex	Ari	32	18	192.1	15	41	2	9	.966	2.62
Cirillo,Jeff	Mil	53	40	365.1	28	70	5	8	.951	2.41
Cora,Alex	Bos	5	2	24.2	2	7	3	0	.750	3.28
Cortez,Fernando	TB	1	0	1.0	0	0	0	0	-	.00
Cruz,Deivi	SF	5	3	37.2	1	11	0	1	1.000	2.87
DeRosa,Mark	Tex	5	4	36.0	2	5	1	1	.875	1.75
Dillon,Joe	Fla	2	0	9.0	2	1	0	0	1.000	3.00
Dobbs,Greg	Sea	2	1	11.0	4	5	0	1	1.000	7.36
Durrington,Tr	Mil	1	0	2.0	0	0	3	0	.000	.00
Easley,Damion	Fla	10	7	66.1	9	16	1	1	.962	3.39
Edwards,Mike	LAD	39	33	294.2	22	56	7	6	.918	2.38
Encarnacion,Ed	Cin	56	55	478.0	54	116	10	9	.944	3.20
Escalona,Felix	NYY	3	0	6.0	0	1	0	0	1.000	1.50
Feliz,Pedro	SF	79	67	591.2	47	144	6	16	.970	2.91
Fick,Robert	SD	1	0	2.0	0	0	0	0	-	.00
Figgins,Chone	LAA	56	48	437.2	34	95	3	8	.977	2.65
Freel,Ryan	Cin	10	8	69.0	5	25	2	1	.938	3.91
Garciaparra,N	ChC	34	34	295.2	20	65	6	1	.934	2.59
German,Esteban	Tex	1	0	3.0	0	0	0	0	-	.00
Giles,Marcus	Atl	1	0	6.0	0	6	0	0	1.000	9.00
Ginter,Keith	Oak	12	5	63.0	12	11	3	0	.885	3.29
Gomez,Chris	Bal	17	13	120.0	11	23	1	1	.971	2.55
Gonzalez,Luis A	Col	12	4	51.0	6	7	0	1	1.000	2.29
Graffanino,Tony	KC	17	14	134.1	7	31	5	3	.884	2.55
Green,Nick	TB	13	11	104.0	4	21	3	2	.893	2.16
Hall,Bill	Mil	59	49	435.1	39	84	6	11	.953	2.54
Hansen,Dave	Sea	7	4	43.0	5	7	0	0	1.000	2.51
Harris,Brendan	Was	1	1	8.0	1	4	0	0	1.000	5.63
Harris,Lenny	Fla	2	0	2.1	0	0	0	0	-	.00
Helms,Wes	Mil	35	17	178.2	12	41	2	4	.964	2.67
Hernandez,Jose	Cle	17	17	163.0	16	35	0	2	1.000	2.82
Hill,Aaron	Tor	35	32	286.2	21	73	5	8	.949	2.95
Hill,Bobby	Pit	24	14	147.2	10	32	1	4	.977	2.56
Hillenbrand,Shea	Tor	54	52	451.0	31	94	6	8	.954	2.49
Hocking,Denny	KC	2	0	2.0	0	0	0	0	-	.00
Holbert,Aaron	Cin	2	1	10.0	0	5	0	0	1.000	4.50
Huff,Aubrey	TB	4	2	21.0	2	2	0	1	1.000	1.71
Izturis,Maicer	LAA	45	24	275.2	20	62	8	5	.911	2.68
Jackson,Damian	SD	8	7	53.0	2	6	1	1	.889	1.36
Johnson,Russ	NYY	8	0	18.0	1	2	0	0	1.000	1.50
Lamb,Mike	Hou	15	12	103.1	16	34	1	0	.980	4.35
Lopez,Felipe	Cin	1	0	1.0	0	1	0	0	1.000	9.00
Lopez,Jose	Sea	1	1	9.0	2	2	1	0	.800	4.00
Lopez,Luis	Cin	6	2	29.0	5	4	1	0	.900	2.79
Loretta,Mark	SD	1	0	1.0	0	0	0	0	-	.00
Luna,Hector	StL	7	4	29.1	4	7	0	2	1.000	3.38
Mabry,John	StL	18	12	106.2	12	19	1	2	.969	2.62
Macias,Jose	ChC	23	7	98.2	6	15	2	1	.913	1.92
Mackowiak,Rob	Pit	65	50	447.0	38	123	8	15	.953	3.24
Marte,Andy	Atl	17	13	130.2	4	14	3	1	.857	1.24
Martinez,Ramon	Det	1	0	1.0	0	0	0	0	-	.00
Martinez,Ramon	Phi	3	2	17.0	1	3	0	0	1.000	2.12
McClain,Scott	ChC	3	1	10.1	1	1	0	0	1.000	1.74
McDonald,John	Det	1	1	9.0	2	0	0	0	1.000	2.00
McDougall,Mar	Tex	5	2	26.0	3	4	0	0	1.000	2.42
McEwing,Joe	KC	29	26	208.2	18	57	3	2	.962	3.23
McPherson,D	LAA	60	55	483.1	32	86	7	14	.944	2.20
Menechino,Frank	Tor	9	4	35.0	2	9	0	2	1.000	2.83
Merloni,Lou	LAA	4	2	16.2	1	8	0	0	1.000	4.86
Munson,Eric	TB	2	1	13.0	1	1	0	0	1.000	1.38
Nady,Xavier	SD	3	2	18.0	0	6	0	0	1.000	3.00
Nakamura,Nor	LAD	10	6	57.0	3	16	0	2	1.000	3.00
Nevin,Phil	Tex	1	0	1.0	0	1	0	0	1.000	9.00
Newhan,David	Bal	8	1	18.0	1	3	0	1	1.000	2.00
Orr,Pete	Atl	12	3	45.2	2	14	1	2	.941	3.15
Ozuna,Pablo	CWS	32	30	261.0	29	67	6	4	.941	3.31
Perez,Antonio	LAD	35	33	273.0	18	70	5	5	.946	2.90
Perez,Eduardo	TB	3	0	7.0	2	0	0	0	1.000	2.57
Perez,Neifi	ChC	4	0	6.0	0	1	0	0	1.000	1.50

Player	Tm	G	GS	Inn	PO	A	E	DP	Pct.	Rng
Perez,Tomas	Phi	15	7	73.0	11	17	0	2	1.000	3.45
Phillips,Andy	NYY	1	0	3.0	0	0	0	0	-	.00
Polanco,Placido	Phi	8	5	48.1	6	17	0	2	1.000	4.28
Polanco,Placido	Det	1	1	9.0	1	3	0	0	1.000	4.00
Punto,Nick	Min	12	7	69.0	6	22	0	3	1.000	3.65
Quinlan,Robb	LAA	33	30	243.0	22	51	7	4	.913	2.70
Randa,Joe	Cin	84	83	716.2	76	148	6	13	.974	2.81
Randa,Joe	SD	58	57	493.0	50	77	6	8	.955	2.32
Relaford,Desi	Col	21	12	124.0	9	22	2	2	.939	2.25
Robles,Oscar	LAD	40	31	292.1	24	70	2	5	.939	2.89
Rodriguez,Luis	Min	27	21	198.0	14	43	3	4	.950	2.59
Rolen,Scott	StL	56	55	486.0	22	151	6	17	.966	3.20
Ryan,Mike	Min	1	0	1.0	0	0	0	0	-	.00
Saenz,Olmedo	LAD	17	15	120.0	17	22	2	3	.951	2.93
Sanchez,Freddy	Pit	65	55	477.2	39	130	4	19	.977	3.18
Sanchez,Rey	NYY	1	0	1.0	0	0	0	0	-	.00
Scutaro,Marco	Oak	5	2	21.0	4	6	0	1	1.000	4.29
Seabol,Scott	StL	20	14	103.0	9	30	3	5	.929	3.41
Smith,Jason	Det	3	1	17.0	5	6	0	2	1.000	5.82
Sorensen,Zach	LAA	1	1	8.0	2	3	1	0	.833	5.63
Spiezio,Scott	Sea	6	0	14.0	1	1	0	1	1.000	1.29
Tiffee,Terry	Min	24	20	176.1	18	34	5	6	.912	2.65
Valentin,Jose	LAD	29	24	216.1	19	54	7	4	.913	3.04
Vazquez,Ramon	Bos	8	6	56.0	6	11	0	3	1.000	2.73
Vizcaino,Jose	Hou	8	4	40.1	2	9	3	2	.786	2.45
Widger,Chris	CWS	1	1	8.1	1	1	0	0	1.000	2.16
Wigginton,Ty	Pit	40	36	305.0	19	57	9	5	.894	2.24
Williams,Glenn	Min	12	9	81.0	7	19	2	2	.929	2.89
Wilson,Enrique	ChC	1	1	9.0	0	0	0	0	-	.00
Woodward,Chris	NYM	6	2	25.1	1	11	0	0	1.000	4.26
Youkilis,Kevin	Bos	24	14	139.0	10	29	0	3	1.000	2.53
Zimmerman,Ryan	Was	14	11	111.0	6	26	0	5	1.000	2.59

Shortstops - Regulars

Player	Tm	G	GS	Inn	PO	A	E	DP	Pct.	Rng
Furcal,Rafael	Atl	152	152	1306.1	255	504	15	118	.981	5.23
Eckstein,David	StL	156	154	1340.2	244	516	15	122	.981	5.10
Barmes,Clint	Col	80	78	681.2	139	247	17	62	.958	5.10
Wilson,Jack	Pit	157	155	1360.0	246	522	14	126	.982	5.08
Lugo,Julio	TB	156	155	1338.2	311	424	24	94	.968	4.94
Gonzalez,Alex	Fla	124	124	1087.1	221	367	16	102	.974	4.87
Jeter,Derek	NYY	157	157	1352.2	262	454	15	96	.979	4.76
Perez,Neifi	ChC	130	118	1063.1	175	385	10	81	.982	4.74
Tejada,Miguel	Bal	160	160	1394.2	252	480	22	105	.971	4.72
Uribe,Juan	CWS	146	143	1293.1	250	422	16	99	.977	4.68
Izturis,Cesar	LAD	106	105	918.0	146	325	11	62	.977	4.62
Berroa,Angel	KC	159	159	1360.1	254	442	25	107	.965	4.60
Vizquel,Omar	SF	150	144	1292.1	234	426	8	80	.988	4.60
Peralta,Jhonny	Cle	141	138	1232.1	207	412	19	104	.970	4.52
Guillen,Carlos	Det	75	74	625.0	85	227	7	44	.978	4.49
Clayton,Royce	Ari	141	131	1177.1	180	404	11	90	.982	4.46
Crosby,Bobby	Oak	84	84	743.1	117	251	7	59	.981	4.46
Scutaro,Marco	Oak	81	73	663.0	115	213	6	50	.976	4.45
Young,Michael	Tex	155	155	1356.0	239	426	18	95	.974	4.41
Everett,Adam	Hou	150	147	1291.2	209	420	14	96	.978	4.38
Renteria,Edgar	Bos	153	150	1293.0	227	398	30	90	.954	4.35
Reyes,Jose	NYM	161	159	1398.1	237	427	18	105	.974	4.27
Adams,Russ	Tor	132	122	1100.0	194	326	26	69	.952	4.24
Guzman,Cristian	Was	142	133	1161.0	217	327	15	85	.973	4.22
Cabrera,Orlando	LAA	141	140	1240.2	229	347	7	81	.988	4.18
Lopez,Felipe	Cin	158	153	1175.1	186	357	17	71	.970	4.16
Greene,Khalil	SD	121	120	1028.2	161	312	14	64	.971	4.14
Rollins,Jimmy	Phi	157	156	1356.0	208	411	12	80	.981	4.11
Hardy,J.J.	Mil	119	104	937.2	133	259	10	52	.975	3.76

Shortstops - The Rest

Player	Tm	G	GS	Inn	PO	A	E	DP	Pct.	Rng
Alexander,Manny	SD	4	3	31.0	4	10	1	1	.933	4.06
Amezaga,Alfredo	Pit	1	0	4.0	1	2	0	1	1.000	6.75
Andino,Robert	Fla	17	13	120.0	19	25	2	7	.957	3.30
Aurilia,Rich	Cin	30	29	237.2	29	86	3	14	.975	4.35
Ausmus,Brad	Hou	1	0	1.0	1	1	0	1	1.000	18.00
Bartlett,Jason	Min	68	65	585.2	95	227	7	45	.979	4.95

Player	Tm	G	GS	Inn	PO	A	E	DP	Pct.	Rng
Bellhorn,Mark	Bos	1	1	9.0	1	3	1	0	.800	4.00
Bellhorn,Mark	NYY	2	0	5.0	2	2	0	0	1.000	7.20
Bergolla,Will	Cin	1	0	1.0	0	1	0	0	1.000	9.00
Betancourt,Yun	Sea	53	52	454.0	82	136	5	34	.978	4.32
Betemit,Wilson	Atl	25	10	136.1	24	40	1	10	.985	4.22
Blanco,Andres	KC	7	2	24.0	7	7	0	2	1.000	5.25
Bloomquist,Wil	Sea	24	21	180.0	34	49	3	6	.965	4.15
Blum,Geoff	SD	14	9	81.1	12	25	0	6	1.000	4.09
Blum,Geoff	SD	6	4	41.0	6	10	0	2	1.000	3.51
Bruntlett,Eric	Hou	10	4	49.0	9	21	0	4	1.000	5.51
Burroughs,Sean	SD	1	0	2.0	0	0	0	0	-	.00
Carroll,Jamey	Was	41	23	241.0	53	65	0	18	1.000	4.41
Castro,Juan	Min	73	66	568.2	98	231	5	49	.985	5.21
Cedeno,Ronny	ChC	29	18	158.2	30	39	1	8	.986	3.91
Chavez,Angel	SF	4	3	27.1	6	5	1	2	.917	3.62
Cintron,Alex	Ari	29	21	271.0	44	99	5	19	.966	4.75
Cora,Alex	Cle	24	22	197.1	28	83	3	11	.974	5.06
Cora,Alex	Bos	11	5	48.1	9	24	0	5	1.000	6.14
Cortez,Fernando	TB	2	0	3.0	1	2	0	0	1.000	9.00
Counsell,Craig	Ari	1	0	1.0	0	0	0	0	-	.00
Crede,Joe	CWS	1	1	8.0	1	3	0	2	1.000	4.50
Cruz,Deivi	SF	16	15	123.2	23	48	1	13	.986	5.17
Cruz,Deivi	Was	8	5	47.0	4	13	1	2	.944	3.26
Dallimore,Brian	SF	1	0	1.0	0	0	0	0	-	.00
DeRosa,Mark	Tex	16	7	83.0	17	38	1	5	.982	5.96
Dye,Jermaine	CWS	1	0	0.1	0	0	0	0	-	.00
Easley,Damion	Fla	30	24	215.2	43	77	4	13	.968	5.01
Edwards,Mike	LAD	1	0	2.0	0	2	0	0	1.000	9.00
Ellis,Mark	Oak	7	5	44.0	6	15	0	4	1.000	4.30
Escalona,Felix	NYY	5	2	29.0	8	8	0	3	1.000	4.97
Figgins,Chone	LAA	4	1	11.0	2	4	0	1	1.000	4.91
Furmaniak,J.J.	Pit	2	1	8.0	1	4	0	0	1.000	5.63
Garabito,Eddy	Col	2	2	18.0	3	5	0	0	1.000	4.00
Garcia,Jesse	SD	13	7	82.0	15	19	0	4	1.000	3.73
Garciaparra,N	ChC	26	25	206.0	41	51	6	16	.939	4.02
Giarratano,Tony	Det	13	12	110.0	16	40	3	5	.949	4.58
Gomez,Chris	Bal	12	2	31.0	5	8	1	3	.929	3.77
Gonzalez,Alex S	TB	12	7	80.0	12	18	2	0	.938	3.38
Gonzalez,Luis A	Col	17	16	132.0	28	34	4	13	.939	4.23
Graffanino,Tony	KC	1	0	1.0	1	0	0	0	1.000	9.00
Green,Andy	Ari	2	0	7.0	1	4	0	0	1.000	6.43
Hairston,Jerry	ChC	1	0	2.0	1	1	0	1	1.000	9.00
Hall,Bill	Mil	66	58	500.1	87	158	6	31	.976	4.41
Harris,Willie	CWS	5	2	25.0	1	9	0	1	1.000	3.60
Hernandez,An	NYM	2	0	4.0	0	0	1	0	.000	.00
Hernandez,Jose	Cle	1	0	3.0	1	1	0	0	1.000	6.00
Hill,Aaron	Tor	16	15	121.0	18	48	0	9	1.000	4.91
Hocking,Denny	KC	1	0	2.0	1	3	0	2	1.000	18.00
Hooper,Kevin	Det	2	0	5.0	2	3	1	0	.833	9.00
Infante,Omar	Det	50	43	389.1	82	149	6	35	.975	5.34
Izturis,Maicer	LAA	29	21	212.2	44	55	2	8	.980	4.19
Jackson,Damian	SD	26	18	189.1	34	52	7	14	.925	4.09
Kata,Matt	Phi	1	0	1.0	0	0	0	0	-	.00
Lopez,Pedro	CWS	1	1	9.0	0	2	0	0	1.000	2.00
Luna,Hector	StL	6	0	14.0	3	3	1	0	.857	3.86
Machado,Alej	Bos	1	0	2.2	1	1	0	0	1.000	6.75
Machado,Andy	Col	4	4	34.0	7	6	1	1	.929	3.44
Martinez,Ramon	Det	12	11	92.1	13	29	2	4	.955	4.09
Martinez,Ramon	Phi	3	0	8.0	2	0	0	0	1.000	2.25
McDonald,John	Tor	32	25	224.0	38	88	3	19	.977	5.06
McDonald,John	Det	22	17	151.1	29	69	5	16	.951	5.83
McDougall,Mar	Tex	1	0	1.0	1	1	0	1	1.000	18.00
McEwing,Joe	KC	6	1	24.0	7	10	1	4	.944	6.38
Menechino,Frank	Tor	1	0	2.0	1	1	0	1	1.000	9.00
Miles,Aaron	Col	1	0	3.0	0	0	1	0	.000	.00
Mordecai,Mike	Fla	1	0	1.1	0	0	0	0	-	.00
Morse,Mike	Sea	55	50	450.0	91	120	12	33	.946	4.22
Murphy,Donald	KC	2	0	2.0	0	0	1	0	.000	.00
Nakamura,Nor	LAD	2	0	3.0	0	1	0	1	1.000	3.00
Nunez,Abraham	StL	21	8	91.0	14	30	2	9	.957	4.35
Olmedo,Ray	Cin	5	1	19.0	4	6	0	2	1.000	4.74
Orr,Pete	Atl	1	0	1.0	0	0	0	0	-	.00
Ozuna,Pablo	CWS	15	11	99.0	19	35	2	12	.964	4.91
Perez,Antonio	LAD	9	8	65.0	10	25	1	6	.972	4.85
Perez,Tomas	Phi	14	5	61.0	8	12	0	2	1.000	2.95
Phillips,Brand	Cle	3	0	3.0	1	2	1	1	.750	9.00
Polanco,Placido	Phi	1	1	8.0	3	2	0	1	1.000	5.63
Punto,Nick	Min	34	26	244.0	47	76	2	16	.984	4.54
Quintanilla,Om	Col	31	30	268.2	41	89	1	16	.992	4.35

Player	Tm	G	GS	Inn	PO	A	E	DP	Pct.	Rng
Ramirez,Hanley	Bos	2	0	6.0	0	1	0	0	1.000	1.50
Relaford,Desi	Col	37	32	281.1	45	100	6	16	.960	4.64
Rivas,Luis	Min	6	2	22.0	3	5	1	1	.889	3.27
Robles,Oscar	LAD	54	49	437.1	76	132	4	28	.981	4.28
Rodriguez,Alex	NYY	3	0	6.0	1	2	0	0	1.000	4.50
Rodriguez,Luis	Min	10	3	44.0	8	14	0	4	1.000	4.50
Rogers,Eddie	Bal	1	0	2.0	0	0	0	0	-	.00
Sanchez,Freddy	Pit	11	6	64.0	11	25	0	3	1.000	5.06
Sanchez,Rey	NYY	10	3	38.0	7	14	1	4	.955	4.97
Sandoval,Danny	Phi	1	0	1.0	1	0	0	0	1.000	9.00
Santiago,Ramon	Sea	2	0	2.0	0	1	0	0	.500	4.50
Smith,Jason	Det	15	5	62.2	14	27	0	6	1.000	5.89
Valdez,Wilson	Sea	42	39	341.2	67	111	5	22	.973	4.69
Valdez,Wilson	SD	8	5	41.0	9	8	1	2	.944	3.73
Valentin,Jose	LAD	1	0	2.0	0	2	0	1	1.000	9.00
Vazquez,Ramon	Bos	12	6	70.0	16	15	1	3	.969	3.99
Vazquez,Ramon	Cle	2	2	17.0	2	5	0	1	1.000	3.71
Vizcaino,Jose	Hou	17	12	101.1	9	34	0	1	1.000	3.82
Wilson,Enrique	ChC	3	1	10.0	2	6	0	1	1.000	7.20
Wilson,Josh	Fla	6	1	18.0	3	6	0	2	1.000	4.50
Woodward,Chris	NYM	7	3	33.1	5	7	1	1	.923	3.24
Zimmerman,Ryan	Was	1	1	9.0	3	4	2	0	.778	7.00

Left Fielders - Regulars

Player	Tm	G	GS	Inn	PO	A	E	DP	Pct.	Rng
Winn,Randy	TOT	92	90	795.2	226	2	0	0	1.000	2.58
Crawford,Carl	TB	147	142	1246.2	341	3	2	1	.994	2.48
Byrnes,Eric	TOT	106	90	803.0	209	5	4	1	.982	2.40
Johnson,Kelly	Atl	79	73	648.1	166	6	0	1	1.000	2.39
Podsednik,Scott	CWS	124	118	1061.2	260	3	3	1	.989	2.23
Crisp,Coco	Cle	138	133	1200.0	294	3	4	0	.987	2.23
Mench,Kevin	Tex	119	108	978.1	230	8	2	3	.992	2.19
Floyd,Cliff	NYM	150	147	1263.2	283	15	2	0	.993	2.12
Stewart,Shannon	Min	125	125	1107.0	249	7	4	2	.985	2.08
Matsui,Hideki	NYY	115	110	977.1	219	7	3	1	.987	2.08
Dunn,Adam	Cin	133	126	1090.2	246	6	5	0	.981	2.08
Holliday,Matt	Col	123	121	1049.2	236	5	7	2	.972	2.07
Klesko,Ryan	SD	121	120	927.0	204	7	4	1	.981	2.05
Bay,Jason	Pit	146	133	1185.2	264	3	1	1	.996	2.03
Lee,Carlos	Mil	162	161	1404.0	307	8	6	3	.981	2.02
Feliz,Pedro	SF	75	70	615.2	138	0	3	0	.979	2.02
Anderson,Garret	LAA	106	106	920.0	201	4	5	1	.976	2.01
Long,Terrence	KC	103	94	794.0	166	9	2	1	.989	1.98
Catalanotto,Fr	Tor	111	99	761.0	163	4	0	0	1.000	1.98
Ramirez,Manny	Bos	149	147	1225.0	243	17	7	0	.974	1.91
Gonzalez,Luis	Ari	152	149	1318.1	270	7	3	1	.989	1.89
Burke,Chris	Hou	83	74	634.0	120	3	1	1	.992	1.75
Burrell,Pat	Phi	153	153	1296.2	236	10	7	2	.972	1.71
Cabrera,Miguel	Fla	134	128	1105.2	188	12	5	3	.976	1.63
Sanders,Reggie	StL	80	78	636.0	108	5	2	0	.983	1.60

Left Fielders - The Rest

Player	Tm	G	GS	Inn	PO	A	E	DP	Pct.	Rng
Abernathy,Brent	Min	5	3	31.1	5	0	0	0	1.000	1.44
Aguila,Chris	Fla	27	2	53.1	13	0	0	0	1.000	2.19
Allen,Chad	Tex	1	0	3.0	0	0	0	0	-	.00
Alou,Moises	SF	74	66	576.0	132	1	4	0	.971	2.08
Ambres,Chip	KC	23	18	170.0	36	0	1	0	.973	1.91
Anderson,Brian	CWS	9	3	42.0	10	1	0	1	1.000	2.36
Anderson,Marlon	NYM	9	4	45.0	9	1	0	1	1.000	2.00
Berkman,Lance	Hou	39	35	284.2	50	2	3	1	.945	1.64
Bigbie,Larry	Bal	57	54	480.1	98	3	0	0	1.000	1.89
Blanco,Tony	Was	9	4	42.0	9	1	0	1	1.000	2.14
Bloomquist,Wil	Sea	1	0	2.0	0	0	0	0	-	.00
Bonds,Barry	SF	13	13	95.0	18	0	0	0	1.000	1.71
Botts,Jason	Tex	7	5	40.0	8	1	1	1	.900	2.03
Branyan,Russell	Mil	3	0	7.0	1	0	0	0	1.000	1.29
Brown,Emil	KC	11	9	82.1	21	2	1	0	.958	2.51
Bruntlett,Eric	Hou	11	2	28.2	11	0	0	0	1.000	3.45
Bubela,Jaime	Sea	1	0	1.1	0	0	0	0	-	.00
Bynum,Freddie	Oak	1	0	2.0	1	0	0	0	1.000	4.50
Byrd,Marlon	Was	54	41	386.0	100	5	2	2	.981	2.45
Byrnes,Eric	Oak	51	44	388.0	109	3	1	1	.991	2.60

Player	Tm	G	GS	Inn	PO	A	E	DP	Pct.	Rng
Byrnes,Eric	Col	4	4	33.0	9	0	0	0	1.000	2.45
Byrnes,Eric	Bal	51	42	382.0	91	2	3	0	.969	2.19
Cairo,Miguel	NYM	2	0	3.0	0	0	0	0	-	.00
Calzado,Nap	Bal	1	1	8.0	2	0	0	0	1.000	2.25
Castro,Bernie	Bal	1	1	7.0	1	0	1	0	.500	1.29
Cedeno,Roger	StL	6	4	33.1	2	0	0	0	1.000	.54
Cepicky,Matt	Was	5	5	35.2	13	0	0	0	1.000	3.28
Chavez,Endy	Phi	20	3	59.0	15	1	0	0	1.000	2.44
Chen,Chin-Feng	LAD	3	1	11.0	2	0	0	0	1.000	1.64
Church,Ryan	Was	51	37	334.2	77	2	0	0	1.000	2.12
Clark,Jermaine	Oak	1	0	1.0	0	0	0	0	-	.00
Conine,Jeff	Fla	37	30	257.2	54	2	0	0	1.000	1.96
Cora,Alex	Cle	1	0	1.0	0	0	0	0	-	.00
Costa,Shane	KC	20	18	162.0	30	1	0	0	1.000	1.72
Crosby,Bubba	NYY	4	2	20.0	2	0	0	0	1.000	.90
Cruz,Jacob	Cin	8	5	48.0	5	1	0	1	1.000	1.13
Cruz,Jose	Ari	3	2	17.2	3	0	0	0	1.000	1.53
Cruz,Jose	LAD	1	0	1.0	0	0	0	0	-	.00
Cruz,Nelson	Mil	2	0	2.0	0	0	0	0	-	.00
Cummings,Midre	Bal	1	0	2.0	0	0	0	0	-	.00
DaVanon,Jeff	LAA	17	9	88.2	30	1	0	0	1.000	3.15
Davis,J.J.	Was	9	7	54.0	15	1	0	0	1.000	2.67
Dellucci,David	Tex	47	44	378.2	84	4	2	1	.978	2.09
Denorfia,Chris	Cin	2	1	9.1	3	0	0	0	1.000	2.89
Diaz,Matt	KC	19	16	136.0	34	0	2	0	.944	2.25
Diaz,Victor	NYM	3	3	26.0	3	1	0	0	1.000	1.38
Dillon,Joe	Fla	3	0	6.0	2	0	0	0	1.000	3.00
Dobbs,Greg	Sea	4	2	26.0	4	0	0	0	1.000	1.38
Dubois,Jason	ChC	38	35	285.1	47	2	1	0	.980	1.55
Dubois,Jason	Cle	3	3	26.0	6	0	0	0	1.000	2.08
Edwards,Mike	LAD	32	27	223.1	51	0	0	0	1.000	2.06
Ellison,Jason	SF	15	0	23.1	3	0	1	0	.750	1.16
Everett,Carl	CWS	14	14	117.1	16	1	0	1	1.000	1.30
Fick,Robert	SD	4	2	18.0	1	0	0	0	1.000	.50
Figgins,Chone	LAA	15	13	130.0	27	1	0	1	1.000	1.94
Ford,Lew	Min	18	14	134.0	32	2	1	0	.971	2.28
Freel,Ryan	Cin	25	17	164.1	45	6	0	0	1.000	2.79
Freire,Alejan	Bal	1	0	1.0	0	0	0	0	-	.00
Gall,John	StL	10	6	48.2	7	1	0	0	1.000	1.48
Gerut,Jody	Cle	17	15	143.2	24	1	0	0	1.000	1.57
Gerut,Jody	ChC	4	1	12.1	6	0	0	0	1.000	4.38
Giles,Brian	SD	1	0	1.0	2	0	0	0	1.000	18.00
Ginter,Keith	Oak	2	0	6.0	0	0	0	0	-	.00
Gipson,Charles	Hou	7	2	23.0	3	0	0	0	1.000	1.17
Gload,Ross	CWS	2	2	14.0	3	0	0	0	1.000	1.93
Gomes,Jonny	TB	14	14	110.0	30	1	0	0	1.000	2.54
Gomez,Alexis	Det	6	3	28.0	7	0	0	0	1.000	2.25
Gonzalez,Luis A	Col	1	1	8.0	2	0	0	0	1.000	2.25
Grabowski,Jason	LAD	28	20	170.0	31	1	1	0	.970	1.69
Granderson,C	Det	20	3	54.2	10	0	0	0	1.000	1.65
Green,Andy	Ari	2	2	17.0	3	0	0	0	1.000	1.59
Grieve,Ben	ChC	1	1	7.0	0	0	0	0	-	.00
Grissom,Marquis	SF	1	1	9.0	1	0	0	0	1.000	1.00
Gross,Gabe	Tor	19	8	95.1	19	1	0	1	1.000	1.89
Guillen,Jose	Was	2	2	17.0	2	0	0	0	1.000	1.06
Hairston,Jerry	ChC	20	10	92.2	22	1	0	0	1.000	2.23
Hairston,Scott	Ari	4	1	13.1	3	0	0	0	1.000	2.03
Hammonds,Jeff	Was	10	8	58.0	16	0	0	0	1.000	2.48
Harris,Lenny	Fla	1	0	1.2	0	0	0	0	-	.00
Hart,Corey	Mil	2	0	6.0	1	0	0	0	1.000	1.50
Hermida,Jeremy	Fla	4	2	17.0	3	0	0	0	1.000	1.59
Hernandez,Jose	Cle	3	3	23.0	3	0	0	0	1.000	1.17
Higginson,Bobby	Det	1	1	9.0	2	1	0	0	1.000	3.00
Hollandsworth,T	ChC	92	60	566.1	95	2	1	0	.990	1.54
Hollandsworth,T	Atl	6	3	32.2	8	0	0	0	1.000	2.25
Hollins,Damon	TB	8	3	38.0	14	1	2	1	.882	3.55
Hooper,Kevin	Det	3	0	4.1	1	0	0	0	1.000	2.08
Hyzdu,Adam	SD	11	1	30.2	11	1	0	1	1.000	3.52
Hyzdu,Adam	Bos	3	0	3.1	0	0	0	0	.000	.00
Ibanez,Raul	Sea	55	54	463.2	105	6	2	3	.982	2.15
Inge,Brandon	Det	1	0	6.0	2	0	0	0	1.000	3.00
Jackson,Conor	Ari	1	1	9.0	0	0	0	0	-	.00
Jackson,Damian	SD	37	2	97.0	25	2	0	0	1.000	2.51
Johnson,Ben	SD	13	6	56.0	10	0	0	0	1.000	1.61
Johnson,Reed	Tor	118	55	590.2	134	4	1	1	.993	2.10
Jordan,Brian	Atl	45	42	358.1	74	5	0	1	1.000	1.98
Kapler,Gabe	Bos	8	0	15.0	1	0	0	0	1.000	.60
Kelly,Kenny	Cin	1	1	8.0	2	0	0	0	1.000	2.25
Kielty,Bobby	Oak	58	52	457.0	99	3	1	0	.990	2.01

272

Player	Tm	G	GS	Inn	PO	A	E	DP	Pct.	Rng
Lamb,Mike	Hou	12	11	90.0	11	0	0	0	1.000	1.10
Lane,Jason	Hou	4	3	24.0	3	0	0	0	1.000	1.13
Langerhans,Ryan	Atl	54	41	379.1	91	0	0	0	1.000	2.16
Lawton,Matt	ChC	18	17	140.0	29	0	1	0	.967	1.86
Lawton,Matt	NYY	8	5	44.1	11	0	0	0	1.000	2.23
Ledee,Ricky	LAD	57	46	390.1	57	1	2	1	.967	1.34
Linden,Todd	SF	18	7	77.0	22	0	1	0	.957	2.57
Ludwick,Ryan	Cle	9	8	59.0	16	0	1	0	.941	2.44
Luna,Hector	StL	3	1	13.0	3	1	0	0	1.000	2.77
Mabry,John	StL	23	12	117.2	19	0	2	0	.905	1.45
Machado,Alej	Bos	2	0	4.0	1	0	0	0	1.000	2.25
Macias,Jose	ChC	5	0	7.1	3	0	1	0	.750	3.68
Mackowiak,Rob	Pit	1	0	2.0	0	0	0	0	-	.00
Magruder,Chris	Mil	5	1	19.0	3	0	0	0	1.000	1.42
Marrero,Eli	KC	8	7	59.0	15	1	0	0	1.000	2.44
Marrero,Eli	Bal	7	6	48.0	10	0	1	0	.909	1.88
Matthews Jr.,G	Tex	5	5	40.0	8	0	0	0	1.000	1.80
McAnulty,Paul	SD	6	2	29.0	5	0	0	0	1.000	1.55
McCarty,David	Bos	1	0	2.0	0	0	0	0	-	.00
McCracken,Q	Ari	11	3	38.1	8	0	0	0	1.000	1.88
McEwing,Joe	KC	3	0	4.0	1	0	0	0	1.000	2.25
Michaels,Jason	Phi	22	2	46.1	11	1	0	1	1.000	2.33
Millar,Kevin	Bos	20	12	119.0	19	0	0	0	1.000	1.44
Mohr,Dustan	Col	17	13	122.1	25	3	0	1	1.000	2.06
Monroe,Craig	Det	69	56	501.2	99	6	1	4	.991	1.88
Morse,Mike	Sea	8	7	55.0	10	1	0	1	1.000	1.80
Munson,Eric	TB	1	0	1.0	1	0	0	0	1.000	9.00
Murton,Matt	ChC	43	38	329.0	62	1	2	1	.969	1.72
Nady,Xavier	SD	26	6	100.0	18	0	1	0	.947	1.62
Newhan,David	Bal	20	16	132.0	18	1	0	0	1.000	1.30
Ojeda,Miguel	SD	3	3	24.0	6	0	0	0	1.000	2.25
Orr,Pete	Atl	3	3	25.0	5	0	0	0	1.000	1.80
Ozuna,Pablo	CWS	9	8	65.0	10	0	0	0	1.000	1.38
Palmeiro,Orl	Hou	47	16	187.1	27	0	0	0	1.000	1.30
Paul,Josh	LAA	2	0	3.0	0	0	0	0	-	.00
Payton,Jay	Bos	13	3	51.0	8	1	0	0	1.000	1.59
Payton,Jay	Oak	47	47	414.1	99	0	0	0	1.000	2.15
Pena,Wily Mo	Cin	10	9	73.2	12	0	2	0	.857	1.47
Perez,Antonio	LAD	1	0	1.0	0	0	0	0	-	.00
Perez,Eduardo	TB	3	2	16.0	2	0	0	0	1.000	1.13
Perez,Timo	CWS	27	17	175.2	33	3	1	0	.973	1.84
Petagine,Rob	Bos	2	0	5.2	0	0	0	0	-	.00
Phillips,Andy	NYY	1	0	2.0	0	0	0	0	-	.00
Piedra,Jorge	Col	9	6	47.1	5	1	0	0	1.000	1.14
Polanco,Placido	Phi	5	4	29.0	10	0	0	0	1.000	3.10
Pride,Curtis	LAA	4	0	5.0	2	0	0	0	1.000	3.60
Quinlan,Robb	LAA	6	2	20.0	3	0	0	0	1.000	1.35
Redman,Tike	Pit	2	0	9.0	4	0	0	0	1.000	4.00
Reese,Kevin	NYY	1	1	7.0	1	0	0	0	1.000	1.29
Repko,Jason	LAD	24	13	127.0	26	0	1	0	.963	1.84
Restovich,Mike	Col	1	1	9.0	4	0	0	0	1.000	4.00
Restovich,Mike	Pit	14	8	80.0	22	1	1	0	.958	2.59
Rivera,Juan	LAA	33	32	297.2	72	3	0	0	1.000	2.27
Rodriguez,John	StL	40	32	283.1	60	2	1	0	.984	1.97
Romano,Jason	Cin	7	4	39.0	5	1	0	0	1.000	1.38
Ryan,Mike	Min	16	9	99.0	13	1	0	0	1.000	1.27
Sadler,Ray	Pit	3	3	21.0	4	0	0	0	1.000	1.71
Schumaker,Jared	StL	14	0	22.1	6	0	0	0	1.000	2.42
Scott,Luke	Hou	21	18	151.1	22	2	1	0	.960	1.43
Scutaro,Marco	Oak	2	1	16.0	5	0	0	0	1.000	2.81
Seabol,Scott	StL	2	2	11.0	5	0	0	0	1.000	4.09
Self,Todd	Hou	5	2	20.0	3	0	0	0	1.000	1.35
Shabala,Adam	SF	4	3	27.1	5	0	1	0	.833	1.65
Shelton,Chris	Det	1	0	2.0	0	0	0	0	-	.00
Sierra,Ruben	NYY	8	6	54.0	10	0	0	0	1.000	1.67
Singleton,Chris	TB	2	1	10.0	0	1	0	0	1.000	.90
Sledge,Terrmel	Was	12	9	79.1	21	1	0	0	1.000	2.50
Snelling,Chris	Sea	7	7	66.0	17	2	0	1	1.000	2.59
Stairs,Matt	KC	2	0	6.0	1	0	0	0	1.000	1.50
Stern,Adam	Bos	2	0	4.0	0	0	0	0	-	.00
Strong,Jamal	Sea	7	2	18.0	4	1	0	0	1.000	2.50
Sullivan,Cory	Col	24	16	149.1	32	2	1	0	.971	2.05
Surhoff,B.J.	Bal	46	42	367.1	76	3	0	0	1.000	1.94
Sweeney,Mark	SD	1	1	5.0	0	0	0	0	-	.00
Taguchi,So	StL	52	28	280.1	50	2	0	1	1.000	1.67
Terrero,Luis	Ari	1	0	2.0	0	0	0	0	-	.00
Thames,Marcus	Det	21	16	153.0	31	0	0	0	1.000	1.82
Thomas,Charles	Oak	13	8	77.2	17	1	1	0	.947	2.09
Tracy,Chad	Ari	6	4	40.2	7	0	0	0	1.000	1.55

Player	Tm	G	GS	Inn	PO	A	E	DP	Pct.	Rng
Tucker,Michael	SF	4	2	21.0	6	0	0	0	1.000	2.57
Tyner,Jason	Min	12	11	93.0	19	0	0	0	1.000	1.84
Valent,Eric	NYM	2	1	12.0	6	0	0	0	1.000	4.50
Valentin,Jose	LAD	22	19	158.1	35	0	1	0	.972	1.99
Victorino,Shane	Phi	4	0	4.0	0	0	0	0	-	.00
Watson,Brandon	Was	12	7	69.0	11	1	1	0	.923	1.57
Watson,Matt	Oak	14	10	88.1	26	0	0	0	1.000	2.65
Werth,Jayson	LAD	64	36	345.1	84	3	0	0	1.000	2.27
White,Rondell	Det	65	65	534.2	119	0	0	0	1.000	2.00
Wilkerson,Brad	Was	38	31	288.1	67	0	1	0	.985	2.09
Williams,Gerald	NYM	10	0	17.0	3	0	0	0	1.000	1.59
Willingham,Josh	Fla	1	0	1.0	0	0	0	0	-	.00
Wilson,Craig	Pit	19	18	138.1	27	3	0	1	1.000	1.95
Wilson,Preston	Was	11	11	94.0	20	0	0	0	1.000	1.91
Womack,Tony	NYY	40	38	326.0	72	2	2	0	.974	2.04
Woodward,Chris	NYM	13	7	69.0	17	2	1	1	.950	2.48
Young,Dmitri	Det	19	18	142.1	35	1	0	0	1.000	2.28
Young,Eric	SD	21	19	167.2	47	0	0	0	1.000	2.52

Center Fielders - Regulars

Player	Tm	G	GS	Inn	PO	A	E	DP	Pct.	Rng
Reed,Jeremy	Sea	137	129	1149.2	383	7	3	1	.992	3.05
Hollins,Damon	TB	80	72	619.0	199	4	3	2	.985	2.95
Logan,Nook	Det	123	93	874.1	282	3	6	2	.979	2.93
Damon,Johnny	Bos	147	144	1225.0	394	5	6	0	.985	2.93
Clark,Brady	Mil	145	145	1275.1	399	5	2	4	.995	2.85
Wilkerson,Brad	Was	92	88	758.2	233	6	3	1	.988	2.84
DeJesus,David	KC	119	118	1005.1	306	7	4	3	.987	2.80
Matthews Jr.,G	Tex	97	95	846.0	257	5	5	2	.981	2.79
Matos,Luis	Bal	120	110	990.0	298	7	5	2	.984	2.77
Finley,Steve	LAA	104	100	895.2	266	5	4	2	.985	2.72
Bradley,Milton	LAD	73	73	628.0	181	6	2	0	.989	2.68
Beltran,Carlos	NYM	150	149	1289.1	378	5	4	1	.990	2.67
Rowand,Aaron	CWS	157	151	1367.2	388	3	3	1	.992	2.57
Sullivan,Cory	Col	83	67	617.2	172	4	2	2	.989	2.56
Lofton,Kenny	Phi	97	88	741.0	201	7	4	1	.981	2.53
Edmonds,Jim	StL	139	132	1153.1	318	5	2	1	.994	2.52
Hunter,Torii	Min	93	92	813.1	218	9	3	4	.987	2.51
Jones,Andruw	Atl	159	158	1366.1	365	11	2	1	.995	2.48
Sizemore,Grady	Cle	155	152	1370.0	373	3	3	1	.992	2.47
Griffey Jr.,Ken	Cin	124	124	1065.2	285	6	3	1	.990	2.46
Taveras,Willy	Hou	148	144	1254.0	332	10	3	2	.991	2.45
Williams,Bernie	NYY	112	99	862.2	226	6	2	1	.991	2.42
Wells,Vernon	Tor	155	153	1358.0	351	12	0	4	1.000	2.41
Roberts,Dave	SD	109	101	900.2	235	4	2	1	.992	2.39
Kotsay,Mark	Oak	137	137	1184.1	298	7	4	3	.987	2.32
Wilson,Preston	TOT	124	122	1068.2	265	5	3	0	.989	2.27
Patterson,Corey	ChC	122	111	986.2	239	6	5	2	.980	2.23
Pierre,Juan	Fla	160	155	1383.0	332	7	4	3	.988	2.21

Center Fielders - The Rest

Player	Tm	G	GS	Inn	PO	A	E	DP	Pct.	Rng
Aguila,Chris	Fla	2	1	7.0	3	0	0	0	1.000	3.86
Ambres,Chip	KC	24	16	157.0	47	2	0	0	1.000	2.81
Anderson,Brian	CWS	3	3	36.0	7	0	0	0	1.000	1.75
Bay,Jason	Pit	30	29	217.0	57	1	3	0	.951	2.41
Bigbie,Larry	Bal	6	6	45.0	10	0	0	0	1.000	2.00
Bigbie,Larry	Col	11	11	91.0	28	1	0	1	1.000	2.87
Bloomquist,Wil	Sea	15	13	117.0	25	1	1	1	.963	2.00
Bocachica,Hiram	Oak	1	0	3.0	3	0	0	0	1.000	9.00
Bruntlett,Eric	Hou	14	10	95.0	34	2	0	1	1.000	3.41
Bubela,Jaime	Sea	6	5	45.0	17	0	0	0	1.000	3.40
Burke,Chris	Hou	6	1	13.0	1	0	0	0	1.000	.69
Burnitz,Jeromy	ChC	3	2	19.2	8	1	0	0	1.000	4.12
Bynum,Freddie	Oak	1	1	9.0	4	0	0	0	1.000	4.00
Byrd,Marlon	Phi	5	4	34.0	6	0	0	0	1.000	1.59
Byrd,Marlon	Was	11	6	61.0	14	0	0	0	1.000	2.07
Byrnes,Eric	Oak	2	2	15.0	3	1	0	1	1.000	2.40
Byrnes,Eric	Col	4	3	25.0	11	0	0	0	1.000	3.96
Byrnes,Eric	Bal	1	0	2.0	0	0	0	0	-	.00
Cabrera,Melky	NYY	6	6	49.0	9	0	0	0	1.000	1.65
Calzado,Nap	Bal	1	0	1.0	0	0	0	0	-	.00
Cameron,Mike	NYM	10	9	79.0	15	1	0	0	1.000	1.82

273

Player	Tm	G	GS	Inn	PO	A	E	DP	Pct.	Rng
Chavez,Endy	Was	6	2	21.0	4	0	0	0	1.000	1.71
Chavez,Endy	Phi	28	8	116.0	28	3	1	1	.969	2.41
Choo,Shin-Soo	Sea	5	5	39.0	16	0	0	0	1.000	3.69
Church,Ryan	Was	20	12	125.2	49	0	0	0	1.000	3.51
Crawford,Carl	TB	8	8	65.0	20	0	0	0	1.000	2.77
Crisp,Coco	Cle	10	10	79.2	21	0	1	0	.955	2.37
Crosby,Bubba	NYY	41	12	144.2	57	1	0	1	1.000	3.61
Cruz,Jose	Ari	53	50	415.0	87	1	2	0	.978	1.91
DaVanon,Jeff	LAA	24	12	130.2	45	0	1	0	.978	3.10
Dellucci,David	Tex	3	2	19.0	3	0	0	0	1.000	1.42
Denorfia,Chris	Cin	10	4	43.0	13	0	1	0	.929	2.72
Drew,J.D.	LAD	30	28	241.2	64	0	0	0	1.000	2.38
Duffy,Chris	Pit	33	27	248.0	80	1	1	0	.988	2.94
Durham,Ray	SF	1	0	1.0	0	0	0	0	-	.00
Ellison,Jason	SF	78	64	591.2	196	4	6	0	.971	3.04
Encarnacion,Ju	Fla	11	6	52.1	10	0	0	0	1.000	1.72
Figgins,Chone	LAA	50	45	398.1	131	1	2	0	.985	2.98
Fiorentino,Jeff	Bal	12	10	96.0	29	0	0	0	1.000	2.72
Ford,Lew	Min	63	60	548.0	140	7	4	1	.974	2.41
Freel,Ryan	Cin	18	10	101.1	41	1	0	0	1.000	3.73
Freeman,Choo	Col	6	5	41.0	12	2	0	1	1.000	3.07
Gathright,Joey	TB	70	56	505.2	180	3	3	2	.984	3.26
Giles,Brian	SD	17	15	133.0	32	0	0	0	1.000	2.17
Gipson,Charles	Hou	5	0	12.0	3	0	0	0	1.000	2.25
Gomez,Alexis	Det	3	1	11.0	2	0	0	0	1.000	1.64
Granderson,C	Det	41	39	320.0	119	2	0	0	1.000	3.40
Green,Shawn	Ari	41	40	315.0	80	2	0	1	1.000	2.34
Grissom,Marquis	SF	34	34	284.2	68	0	1	0	.986	2.15
Guiel,Aaron	KC	24	21	185.0	54	1	1	0	.982	2.68
Gutierrez,Franklin	Cle	2	0	3.0	1	0	0	0	1.000	3.00
Hairston,Jerry	ChC	48	44	386.0	90	2	2	0	.979	2.15
Hairston,Scott	Ari	1	0	0.2	0	0	0	0	-	.00
Hart,Corey	Mil	11	11	96.0	19	0	0	0	1.000	1.78
Hidalgo,Richard	Tex	3	2	18.0	5	0	0	0	1.000	2.50
Hyzdu,Adam	SD	3	1	16.0	3	0	0	0	1.000	1.69
Hyzdu,Adam	Bos	5	1	18.2	8	0	0	0	1.000	3.86
Inge,Brandon	Det	1	0	1.0	0	0	0	0	-	.00
Izturis,Maicer	LAA	1	0	0.2	1	1	0	1	1.000	27.00
Jackson,Damian	SD	15	8	79.2	23	0	0	0	1.000	2.60
Jimerson,Char	Hou	1	0	1.0	0	0	0	0	-	.00
Johnson,Ben	SD	9	6	60.0	14	0	1	0	.933	2.10
Johnson,Reed	Tor	9	5	53.0	11	0	0	0	1.000	1.87
Jones,Jacque	Min	10	9	86.0	17	1	0	0	1.000	1.88
Kapler,Gabe	Bos	12	9	80.0	19	0	0	0	1.000	2.14
Kearns,Austin	Cin	2	0	2.0	1	0	0	0	1.000	4.50
Kelly,Kenny	Cin	2	0	2.1	2	0	0	0	1.000	7.71
Krynzel,Dave	Mil	1	1	8.1	2	0	0	0	1.000	2.16
Lane,Jason	Hou	6	4	37.0	11	0	0	0	1.000	2.68
Langerhans,Ryan	Atl	19	4	77.1	28	0	0	0	1.000	3.26
Long,Terrence	KC	6	4	35.0	5	0	0	0	1.000	1.29
Luna,Hector	StL	1	0	1.0	1	0	0	0	1.000	9.00
Machado,Alej	Bos	3	0	7.1	2	0	0	0	1.000	2.45
Macias,Jose	ChC	7	5	47.2	20	1	1	0	.955	3.97
Mackowiak,Rob	Pit	41	31	281.2	68	2	1	0	.986	2.24
Magruder,Chris	Mil	9	5	58.1	19	0	2	0	.905	2.93
Marrero,Eli	KC	5	3	30.0	5	0	0	0	1.000	1.50
Marrero,Eli	Bal	3	3	26.0	10	0	0	0	1.000	3.46
Matsui,Hideki	NYY	28	28	222.1	54	0	0	0	1.000	2.19
McCracken,Q	Ari	46	30	306.0	66	2	2	0	.971	2.00
McEwing,Joe	KC	1	0	1.0	0	0	0	0	-	.00
McLouth,Nate	Pit	21	19	166.0	36	0	0	0	1.000	1.95
Mench,Kevin	Tex	1	0	1.0	0	0	0	0	-	.00
Michaels,Jason	Phi	75	62	536.0	161	5	2	1	.988	2.79
Mohr,Dustan	Col	10	8	63.0	19	1	0	0	1.000	2.86
Monroe,Craig	Det	33	29	229.1	63	0	1	0	.984	2.47
Nady,Xavier	SD	30	28	244.1	54	0	1	0	.982	1.99
Newhan,David	Bal	32	29	234.2	61	0	0	0	1.000	2.34
Nivar,Ramon	Bal	4	3	25.0	10	0	0	0	1.000	3.60
Nix,Laynce	Tex	61	60	526.0	160	3	2	1	.988	2.79
Palmeiro,Orl	Hou	5	4	30.0	6	0	0	0	1.000	1.80
Payton,Jay	Bos	16	7	80.0	20	0	0	0	1.000	2.25
Payton,Jay	Oak	25	21	210.0	54	2	0	0	1.000	2.40
Pena,Wily Mo	Cin	25	22	192.2	57	0	1	0	.983	2.66
Perez,Timo	CWS	2	2	17.0	7	0	0	0	1.000	3.71
Podsednik,Scott	CWS	7	6	55.0	14	0	0	0	1.000	2.29
Prieto,Chris	LAA	2	1	9.0	5	0	0	0	1.000	5.00
Punto,Nick	Min	2	1	11.0	0	0	0	0	-	.00
Ramirez,Julio	SF	2	0	5.1	3	0	0	0	1.000	5.06
Redman,Tike	Pit	75	56	523.1	158	5	7	0	.959	2.80

Player	Tm	G	GS	Inn	PO	A	E	DP	Pct.	Rng
Reed,Keith	Bal	1	1	8.0	0	0	0	0	-	.00
Reese,Kevin	NYY	1	0	2.0	1	0	0	0	1.000	4.50
Relaford,Desi	Col	1	0	1.0	0	0	0	0	-	.00
Repko,Jason	LAD	58	38	363.0	97	5	1	1	.990	2.53
Rios,Alexis	Tor	5	4	36.0	12	0	0	0	1.000	3.00
Rivera,Juan	LAA	4	4	30.0	10	0	0	0	1.000	3.00
Romano,Jason	Cin	5	3	26.0	10	0	1	0	.909	3.46
Sanchez,Alex	TB	18	17	144.0	50	1	3	0	.944	3.19
Sanchez,Alex	SF	4	4	31.0	9	0	1	0	.900	2.61
Schumaker,Jared	StL	4	1	12.1	4	0	0	0	1.000	2.92
Scott,Luke	Hou	1	0	1.0	0	0	0	0	-	.00
Singleton,Chris	TB	6	4	39.1	15	0	0	0	1.000	3.43
Stern,Adam	Bos	6	1	18.0	3	0	0	0	1.000	1.50
Strong,Jamal	Sea	4	4	30.0	8	0	0	0	1.000	2.40
Sweeney,Mark	SD	1	0	1.2	0	0	0	0	-	.00
Taguchi,So	StL	50	28	274.0	58	0	0	0	1.000	1.91
Taylor,Reggie	TB	9	5	48.2	17	0	0	0	1.000	3.14
Terrero,Luis	Ari	74	42	419.2	121	1	2	0	.984	2.62
Thomas,Charles	Oak	9	1	29.0	14	0	0	0	1.000	4.34
Torres,Andres	Tex	4	3	30.0	11	0	0	0	1.000	3.30
Tucker,Michael	SF	7	5	45.0	13	1	1	0	.933	2.80
Tucker,Michael	Phi	1	0	1.0	0	0	0	0	-	.00
Tyner,Jason	Min	2	0	6.0	3	0	0	0	1.000	4.50
Valent,Eric	NYM	2	0	4.0	2	0	0	0	1.000	4.50
Victorino,Shane	Phi	5	0	7.0	0	0	0	0	-	.00
Walker,Larry	StL	1	1	5.0	1	0	0	0	1.000	1.80
Watson,Brandon	Was	1	0	3.0	2	0	0	0	1.000	6.00
Werth,Jayson	LAD	30	23	194.2	63	1	3	0	.955	2.96
Williams,Gerald	NYM	10	4	51.0	12	0	0	0	1.000	2.12
Wilson,Preston	Col	69	68	580.0	140	2	3	0	.979	2.20
Wilson,Preston	Was	55	54	488.2	125	3	0	0	1.000	2.36
Winn,Randy	Sea	6	6	47.0	19	1	0	0	1.000	3.83
Winn,Randy	SF	55	55	485.2	165	1	1	1	.994	3.08
Womack,Tony	NYY	22	17	150.0	36	0	0	0	1.000	2.16
Woodward,Chris	NYM	5	0	12.1	4	0	0	0	1.000	2.92
Young,Eric	SD	4	3	20.0	6	0	0	0	1.000	2.70

Right Fielders - Regulars

Player	Tm	G	GS	Inn	PO	A	E	DP	Pct.	Rng
Suzuki,Ichiro	Sea	158	158	1388.1	381	9	2	2	.995	2.53
Kearns,Austin	Cin	107	103	890.0	237	8	3	3	.988	2.48
Huff,Aubrey	TB	97	95	786.2	204	6	3	2	.986	2.40
Nixon,Trot	Bos	118	107	935.1	240	8	1	3	.996	2.39
Guillen,Jose	Was	140	135	1189.2	299	10	7	4	.978	2.34
Jenkins,Geoff	Mil	144	144	1241.1	307	10	5	7	.984	2.30
Hidalgo,Richard	Tex	83	78	699.2	174	3	2	0	.989	2.28
Jones,Jacque	Min	123	121	1080.1	261	9	4	2	.985	2.25
Giles,Brian	SD	143	140	1220.0	295	6	4	1	.987	2.22
Lawton,Matt	TOT	113	109	953.0	230	4	2	1	.992	2.21
Blake,Casey	Cle	138	132	1188.2	287	3	8	0	.973	2.20
Guerrero,Vladimir	LAA	120	120	1040.0	242	8	3	2	.988	2.16
Rios,Alexis	Tor	138	116	1056.2	245	7	2	1	.992	2.15
Diaz,Victor	NYM	78	74	651.2	153	2	3	1	.981	2.14
Hawpe,Brad	Col	89	79	693.0	148	10	3	2	.981	2.05
Brown,Emil	KC	129	126	1097.1	243	7	11	0	.958	2.05
Green,Shawn	Ari	135	109	1031.1	232	2	0	0	1.000	2.04
Burnitz,Jeromy	ChC	158	153	1359.2	303	5	5	1	.984	2.04
Sheffield,Gary	NYY	131	130	1099.1	239	5	3	0	.988	2.00
Dye,Jermaine	CWS	140	137	1235.1	259	9	8	2	.971	1.95
Monroe,Craig	Det	85	69	632.1	132	4	4	0	.971	1.94
Ordonez,Magglio	Det	81	79	672.1	139	5	1	0	.993	1.93
Lane,Jason	Hou	137	126	1115.2	225	4	6	0	.974	1.85
Abreu,Bobby	Phi	158	158	1364.0	266	7	4	0	.986	1.80
Encarnacion,Ju	Fla	135	126	1112.2	216	4	4	0	.982	1.78
Swisher,Nick	Oak	121	115	1027.1	196	6	2	2	.990	1.77
Walker,Larry	StL	83	78	648.2	107	5	2	0	.982	1.55

Right Fielders - The Rest

Player	Tm	G	GS	Inn	PO	A	E	DP	Pct.	Rng
Aguila,Chris	Fla	14	9	84.0	24	1	0	0	1.000	2.68
Allen,Chad	Tex	1	1	6.0	1	0	0	0	1.000	1.50
Alou,Moises	SF	53	51	412.2	90	4	4	3	.959	2.05
Anderson,Brian	CWS	1	1	7.0	2	0	0	0	1.000	2.57

Player	Tm	G	GS	Inn	PO	A	E	DP	Pct.	Rng
Anderson,Marlon	NYM	14	9	73.0	13	1	0	0	1.000	1.73
Berkman,Lance	Hou	11	10	78.0	16	0	0	0	1.000	1.85
Bigbie,Larry	Col	5	4	38.0	8	0	0	0	1.000	1.89
Blanco,Tony	Was	2	1	9.0	1	0	0	0	1.000	1.00
Bocachica,Hiram	Oak	5	3	25.0	3	0	0	0	1.000	1.08
Borchard,Joe	CWS	2	0	7.0	3	0	0	0	1.000	3.86
Bruntlett,Eric	Hou	1	0	2.0	1	1	0	1	1.000	9.00
Byrd,Marlon	Was	4	3	34.0	10	0	0	0	1.000	2.65
Byrnes,Eric	Oak	5	3	27.0	5	0	1	0	.833	1.67
Byrnes,Eric	Col	8	7	59.0	19	1	1	1	.952	3.05
Byrnes,Eric	Bal	1	0	1.0	0	0	0	0	-	.00
Cairo,Miguel	NYM	1	1	7.0	1	0	0	0	1.000	1.29
Cameron,Mike	NYM	68	67	593.0	136	2	6	1	.958	2.09
Cedeno,Roger	StL	10	5	42.0	7	0	2	0	.778	1.50
Cepicky,Matt	Was	1	1	9.0	5	0	0	0	1.000	5.00
Chavez,Endy	Phi	5	0	10.0	2	0	0	0	1.000	1.80
Church,Ryan	Was	21	14	135.2	43	0	0	0	1.000	2.85
Conine,Jeff	Fla	28	21	186.2	51	0	3	0	.944	2.46
Crosby,Bubba	NYY	23	9	100.0	24	1	0	0	1.000	2.25
Cruz,Jacob	Cin	12	5	48.1	7	0	0	0	1.000	1.30
Cruz,Jose	Ari	6	5	35.2	8	1	0	0	1.000	2.27
Cruz,Jose	Bos	4	4	31.0	2	0	0	0	1.000	.58
Cruz,Jose	LAD	45	42	366.1	100	3	5	0	.954	2.53
Cruz,Nelson	Mil	6	1	16.0	4	0	0	0	1.000	2.25
Cuddyer,Mike	Min	20	18	159.0	35	0	0	0	1.000	1.98
DaVanon,Jeff	LAA	26	12	133.2	30	0	0	0	1.000	2.02
Davis,J.J.	Was	1	0	3.0	1	0	0	0	1.000	3.00
Dellucci,David	Tex	3	3	26.0	6	0	1	0	.857	2.08
Denorfia,Chris	Cin	2	2	16.1	9	0	0	0	1.000	4.96
DeRosa,Mark	Tex	25	21	185.0	46	1	0	0	1.000	2.29
Diaz,Matt	KC	2	1	11.0	4	0	0	0	1.000	3.27
Doumit,Ryan	Pit	3	3	23.0	0	0	0	0	-	.00
Drew,J.D.	LAD	44	44	382.0	83	3	2	0	.977	2.03
Dubois,Jason	Cle	4	4	30.0	8	0	0	0	1.000	2.40
Duffy,Chris	Pit	1	0	1.0	0	0	0	0	-	.00
Duncan,Chris	StL	1	0	1.0	0	0	0	0	-	.00
Edwards,Mike	LAD	1	1	11.0	2	0	0	0	1.000	1.64
Ellison,Jason	SF	32	18	166.1	36	1	1	1	.974	2.31
Everett,Carl	CWS	8	8	70.0	18	0	0	0	1.000	2.31
Fick,Robert	SD	9	6	57.0	16	1	0	0	1.000	2.68
Figgins,Chone	LAA	8	7	53.0	12	1	0	0	1.000	2.21
Ford,Lew	Min	16	14	133.0	26	0	1	0	.963	1.76
Francoeur,Jeff	Atl	67	65	589.0	131	13	5	3	.966	2.20
Freel,Ryan	Cin	13	6	69.2	23	0	0	0	1.000	2.97
Gerut,Jody	Cle	21	20	176.0	34	0	0	0	1.000	1.74
Gerut,Jody	ChC	1	1	8.0	3	0	0	0	1.000	3.38
Gerut,Jody	Pit	4	4	33.1	3	0	0	0	1.000	.81
Gibbons,Jay	Bal	71	69	558.2	133	6	2	1	.986	2.24
Gipson,Charles	Hou	1	0	1.0	0	0	0	0	-	.00
Gload,Ross	CWS	1	0	2.0	2	0	0	0	1.000	9.00
Gomes,Jonny	TB	36	34	291.0	68	6	4	1	.949	2.29
Gonzalez,Adrian	Tex	1	1	8.0	3	0	1	0	.750	3.38
Gonzalez,Juan	Cle	1	1	0.0	0	0	0	0	-	
Gonzalez,Luis A	Col	7	5	43.1	14	0	0	0	1.000	2.91
Grabowski,Jason	LAD	4	2	23.1	5	0	0	0	1.000	1.93
Green,Nick	TB	1	0	1.0	0	0	0	0	-	.00
Grissom,Marquis	SF	1	1	8.0	0	0	0	0	-	.00
Gross,Gabe	Tor	20	16	143.1	32	1	1	0	.971	2.07
Guiel,Aaron	KC	7	5	47.2	10	0	0	0	1.000	1.89
Hairston,Jerry	ChC	1	1	7.0	2	0	0	0	1.000	2.57
Hammonds,Jeff	Was	1	1	9.0	2	0	0	0	1.000	2.00
Harris,Lenny	Fla	1	0	0.1	0	0	0	0	-	.00
Hart,Corey	Mil	3	3	27.0	8	1	1	0	.900	3.00
Hermida,Jeremy	Fla	10	6	58.2	17	0	0	0	1.000	2.61
Hernandez,Jose	Cle	1	1	8.0	1	0	0	0	1.000	1.13
Higginson,Bobby	Det	6	5	48.0	6	0	0	0	1.000	1.13
Hollandsworth,T	ChC	6	2	19.1	1	0	1	0	.500	.47
Hollandsworth,T	Atl	3	2	18.0	2	0	0	0	1.000	1.00
Hollins,Damon	TB	48	15	170.0	38	3	1	2	.976	2.17
Hyzdu,Adam	Bos	5	2	22.0	2	0	0	0	1.000	.82
Ibanez,Raul	Sea	3	3	24.1	0	0	0	0	-	.00
Jackson,Damian	SD	1	0	1.0	0	0	0	0	-	.00
Johnson,Ben	SD	11	8	73.1	27	0	1	0	.964	3.31
Johnson,Reed	Tor	35	30	247.0	51	1	1	0	.981	1.89
Johnson,Russ	NYY	3	0	6.1	1	0	0	0	1.000	1.42
Jordan,Brian	Atl	17	17	141.2	38	1	0	0	1.000	2.48
Kapler,Gabe	Bos	22	16	144.2	45	0	0	0	1.000	2.80
Kata,Matt	Phi	1	0	3.0	0	0	0	0	-	.00
Kelly,Kenny	Cin	1	0	3.0	0	0	0	0	-	.00
Kelly,Kenny	Was	2	0	4.0	0	0	0	0	-	.00
Kielty,Bobby	Oak	42	37	324.0	67	2	2	1	.972	1.92
Laird,Gerald	Tex	1	0	1.0	0	0	0	0	-	.00
Lamb,Mike	Hou	1	1	7.0	1	0	0	0	1.000	1.29
Langerhans,Ryan	Atl	48	39	356.0	75	3	1	1	.987	1.97
LaRue,Jason	Cin	1	0	1.0	1	0	0	0	1.000	9.00
Lawton,Matt	Pit	98	98	841.2	206	4	1	1	.995	2.25
Lawton,Matt	ChC	3	2	18.2	4	0	0	0	1.000	1.93
Lawton,Matt	NYY	12	9	92.2	20	0	1	0	.952	1.94
Ledee,Ricky	LAD	17	9	87.2	19	1	0	0	1.000	2.05
Liefer,Jeff	Cle	3	1	16.0	4	0	0	0	1.000	2.25
Linden,Todd	SF	40	36	318.2	92	0	1	0	.989	2.60
Long,Terrence	KC	17	15	128.0	32	3	1	0	.972	2.46
Ludwick,Ryan	Cle	6	3	34.0	6	0	0	0	1.000	1.59
Luna,Hector	StL	21	12	113.2	29	2	2	0	.939	2.45
Mabry,John	StL	49	25	252.0	35	1	0	0	1.000	1.29
Machado,Alej	Bos	1	0	1.0	0	0	0	0	-	.00
Macias,Jose	ChC	8	3	27.1	3	1	0	0	1.000	1.32
Mackowiak,Rob	Pit	23	13	127.1	34	2	1	2	.973	2.54
Magruder,Chris	Mil	31	14	153.2	32	0	0	0	1.000	1.87
Marrero,Eli	KC	7	3	34.0	7	1	1	0	.889	2.12
Marrero,Eli	Bal	6	6	46.0	8	0	0	0	1.000	1.57
Matsui,Hideki	NYY	4	4	29.2	6	0	0	0	1.000	1.82
Matthews Jr.,G	Tex	22	21	189.2	51	2	1	2	.981	2.51
McCracken,Q	Ari	2	0	3.0	1	0	0	0	1.000	3.00
McDougall,Mar	Tex	3	1	10.0	0	0	0	0	-	.00
McEwing,Joe	KC	1	0	1.0	0	0	0	0	-	.00
McLouth,Nate	Pit	8	5	52.2	10	0	2	0	.833	1.71
Mench,Kevin	Tex	41	36	311.1	60	0	2	0	.968	1.73
Michaels,Jason	Phi	14	4	53.0	13	2	0	0	1.000	2.55
Millar,Kevin	Bos	14	12	87.0	22	1	0	0	1.000	2.38
Mohr,Dustan	Col	55	43	382.2	103	0	2	0	.981	2.42
Mondesi,Raul	Atl	40	39	339.0	67	2	1	0	.986	1.83
Nady,Xavier	SD	13	7	82.0	11	0	0	0	1.000	1.21
Newhan,David	Bal	30	9	116.0	20	0	1	0	.952	1.55
Ojeda,Miguel	SD	2	1	10.0	4	0	0	0	1.000	3.60
Ortmeier,Dan	SF	7	5	46.2	13	0	0	0	1.000	2.51
Ozuna,Pablo	CWS	1	0	2.0	0	0	0	0	-	.00
Palmeiro,Orl	Hou	26	15	149.1	35	2	1	2	.974	2.23
Payton,Jay	Bos	31	20	181.0	54	2	0	0	1.000	2.78
Pena,Wily Mo	Cin	50	47	401.2	92	2	1	0	.989	2.11
Perez,Eduardo	TB	1	0	5.0	3	0	0	0	1.000	5.40
Perez,Timo	CWS	21	16	152.1	35	2	2	1	.949	2.19
Piedra,Jorge	Col	17	16	121.2	22	0	0	0	1.000	1.63
Punto,Nick	Min	1	0	2.0	1	0	0	0	1.000	4.50
Ramirez,Julio	SF	4	0	5.1	0	0	0	0	-	.00
Redman,Tike	Pit	8	3	37.1	8	0	0	0	1.000	1.93
Reed,Keith	Bal	5	0	11.0	3	0	0	0	1.000	2.45
Relaford,Desi	Col	3	0	4.0	0	1	0	0	1.000	2.25
Repko,Jason	LAD	42	22	213.2	50	2	4	2	.929	2.19
Restovich,Mike	Col	7	7	53.0	14	0	0	0	1.000	2.38
Restovich,Mike	Pit	20	9	83.2	17	0	0	0	1.000	1.83
Rivera,Juan	LAA	38	23	237.2	45	2	1	1	.979	1.78
Rodriguez,John	StL	9	4	38.1	9	1	1	0	.909	2.35
Romano,Jason	Cin	2	0	3.0	0	0	0	0	-	.00
Ross,Cody	LAD	9	5	52.1	12	2	1	1	.933	2.41
Ryan,Mike	Min	10	7	76.0	17	1	0	0	1.000	2.13
Sanchez,Alex	TB	14	12	104.1	15	0	0	0	1.000	1.29
Sanchez,Alex	SF	6	5	41.0	10	1	2	0	.846	2.41
Sanders,Reggie	StL	1	1	6.0	0	0	0	0	-	.00
Schumaker,Jared	StL	7	0	11.1	3	0	0	0	1.000	2.38
Scott,Luke	Hou	4	2	18.0	2	0	0	0	1.000	1.00
Seabol,Scott	StL	2	2	14.0	1	0	0	0	1.000	.64
Self,Todd	Hou	10	9	72.0	20	0	0	0	1.000	2.50
Shabala,Adam	SF	1	0	3.0	2	0	0	0	1.000	6.00
Sierra,Ruben	NYY	10	7	64.0	13	0	1	0	.929	1.83
Singleton,Chris	TB	11	6	62.0	20	0	1	0	.952	2.90
Sledge,Terrmel	Was	1	0	2.0	0	0	0	0	-	.00
Snelling,Chris	Sea	3	1	12.0	3	0	0	0	1.000	2.25
Sosa,Sammy	Bal	66	66	577.0	121	3	3	1	.976	1.93
Spilborghs,Ryan	Col	1	1	8.0	6	1	0	1	1.000	7.88
Stairs,Matt	KC	13	12	94.1	17	0	0	0	1.000	1.62
Stern,Adam	Bos	13	1	27.0	7	0	0	0	1.000	2.33
Strong,Jamal	Sea	1	0	3.0	0	0	0	0	-	.00
Sullivan,Cory	Col	8	0	16.0	7	0	0	0	1.000	3.94
Surhoff,B.J.	Bal	16	12	118.0	33	0	1	0	.971	2.52
Sweeney,Mark	SD	4	0	12.0	5	0	1	0	.833	3.75
Taguchi,So	StL	57	35	318.2	75	3	2	0	.975	2.20
Taylor,Reggie	TB	1	0	1.2	0	0	0	0	-	.00

Player	Tm	G	GS	Inn	PO	A	E	DP	Pct.	Rng
Terrero,Luis	Ari	2	1	10.1	3	0	0	0	1.000	2.61
Thames,Marcus	Det	10	9	82.0	14	0	1	0	.933	1.54
Thomas,Charles	Oak	8	3	30.0	7	0	1	0	.875	2.10
Torcato,Tony	SF	1	0	3.0	1	0	0	0	1.000	3.00
Torres,Andres	Tex	2	0	3.1	1	0	0	0	1.000	2.70
Tracy,Chad	Ari	47	47	376.0	86	2	2	0	.978	2.11
Tucker,Michael	SF	64	46	439.2	90	5	1	1	.990	1.94
Tyner,Jason	Min	2	2	14.0	8	0	0	0	1.000	5.14
Valent,Eric	NYM	8	7	63.0	13	0	1	0	.929	1.86
Vento,Mike	NYY	2	0	7.0	2	1	0	1	1.000	3.86
Victorino,Shane	Phi	3	0	5.0	0	0	0	0	-	.00
Watson,Matt	Oak	3	2	17.0	4	0	0	0	1.000	2.12
Werth,Jayson	LAD	43	37	291.0	71	3	0	2	1.000	2.29
Wilkerson,Brad	Was	6	5	45.2	12	0	1	0	.923	2.36
Williams,Gerald	NYM	7	0	10.0	1	1	0	0	1.000	1.80
Wilson,Craig	Pit	30	27	236.0	50	0	1	0	.980	1.91
Wilson,Preston	Was	2	2	17.0	4	0	0	0	1.000	2.12
Womack,Tony	NYY	4	3	31.2	5	0	0	0	1.000	1.42
Woodward,Chris	NYM	6	4	38.0	6	1	0	0	1.000	1.66
Young,Dmitri	Det	1	0	1.0	0	0	0	0	-	.00

Catchers - Regulars

Player	Tm	G	GS	Inn	PO	A	E	DP	PB	Pct.
Ausmus,Brad	Hou	134	118	1065.2	884	65	1	6	5	.999
Matheny,Mike	SF	132	127	1122.0	784	77	1	12	4	.999
Pierzynski,A.J.	CWS	128	124	1117.2	803	48	1	8	7	.999
Snyder,Chris	Ari	113	105	915.2	679	44	2	0	7	.997
Piazza,Mike	NYM	101	100	809.1	618	39	2	5	3	.997
Estrada,Johnny	Atl	104	97	826.1	574	51	2	6	2	.997
Posada,Jorge	NYY	133	123	1076.2	718	76	3	6	8	.996
Miller,Damian	Mil	111	104	917.1	723	50	3	10	4	.996
Buck,John	KC	117	112	976.2	638	57	3	4	3	.996
Molina,Bengie	LAA	105	100	873.1	641	48	3	5	10	.996
Martinez,Victor	Cle	142	139	1233.0	904	58	5	6	3	.995
Rodriguez,Ivan	Det	123	121	1032.2	702	60	4	4	4	.995
Lopez,Javy	Bal	75	75	628.2	500	27	3	4	4	.994
Barrett,Michael	ChC	122	114	1017.2	870	51	6	7	4	.994
Kendall,Jason	Oak	147	146	1286.0	985	52	7	6	4	.993
Mauer,Joe	Min	116	110	999.2	692	46	5	6	6	.993
Lieberthal,Mike	Phi	117	113	998.2	808	44	6	5	7	.993
Schneider,Brian	Was	113	105	926.2	654	52	5	10	3	.993
LaRue,Jason	Cin	109	104	914.2	646	52	5	2	6	.993
Cota,Humberto	Pit	87	77	681.2	476	38	4	4	8	.992
Phillips,Jason	LAD	93	88	774.0	562	36	5	6	4	.992
Lo Duca,Paul	Fla	128	118	1033.1	817	61	8	7	4	.991
Molina,Yadier	StL	114	111	959.1	684	66	7	4	8	.991
Varitek,Jason	Bos	130	127	1089.0	783	33	8	4	7	.990
Zaun,Gregg	Tor	132	121	1088.0	761	49	8	3	5	.990
Hall,Toby	TB	135	122	1061.2	759	51	9	6	8	.989
Hernandez,Ram	SD	97	94	806.0	640	36	8	4	6	.988
Barajas,Rod	Tex	119	117	1025.1	689	41	9	5	7	.988
Olivo,Miguel	TOT	91	77	690.0	505	29	9	3	7	.983

Catchers - The Rest

Player	Tm	G	GS	Inn	PO	A	E	DP	PB	Pct.
Alomar Jr.,Sandy	Tex	46	34	315.2	232	5	2	0	3	.992
Ardoin,Danny	Col	80	66	591.0	452	48	6	5	6	.988
Bako,Paul	LAD	13	13	107.0	61	6	1	0	1	.985
Bard,Josh	Cle	31	23	219.2	164	10	3	2	3	.983
Bennett,Gary	Was	64	57	523.1	384	25	6	1	4	.986
Blanco,Henry	ChC	54	48	422.1	407	31	1	2	2	.998
Borders,Pat	Sea	39	37	313.0	175	15	2	2	3	.990
Casanova,Raul	CWS	6	0	14.0	9	0	0	0	0	1.000
Cash,Kevin	TB	13	10	89.0	56	8	0	1	4	1.000
Castillo,Alb	KC	34	32	277.0	235	10	2	3	0	.992
Castillo,Alb	Oak	1	0	3.0	2	0	0	0	0	1.000
Castro,Ramon	NYM	99	57	576.1	402	22	3	3	2	.993
Chavez,Raul	Hou	36	30	253.1	213	19	2	2	1	.991
Closser,JD	Col	80	64	565.2	410	25	8	1	5	.982
Diaz,Einar	StL	50	30	299.0	189	21	1	1	4	.995
DiFelice,Mike	NYM	11	5	50.0	39	2	1	1	0	.976
Dominique,Andy	Tor	1	1	6.0	4	0	0	0	0	1.000
Doumit,Ryan	Pit	50	48	422.0	286	29	8	1	4	.975

Player	Tm	G	GS	Inn	PO	A	E	DP	PB	Pct.
Fasano,Sal	Bal	60	47	417.0	284	25	4	1	6	.987
Fick,Robert	SD	28	20	189.2	167	10	4	0	2	.978
Flaherty,John	NYY	45	39	345.0	291	19	2	3	3	.994
Gil,Geronimo	Bal	62	37	349.1	264	26	2	5	3	.993
Gonzalez,Wiki	Sea	14	13	115.0	78	8	0	2	1	1.000
Greene,Todd	Col	33	32	262.0	151	7	4	0	3	.975
Haad,Yamid	SF	16	10	89.2	61	6	3	1	0	.957
Heintz,Chris	Min	8	6	60.0	48	1	0	0	0	1.000
Hill,Koyie	Ari	32	23	211.1	144	13	0	1	3	1.000
Huckaby,Ken	Tor	35	27	243.0	144	11	2	1	1	.987
Johnson,Charles	TB	19	16	136.0	90	3	4	0	1	.959
Jorgensen,Ryan	Fla	3	1	10.2	7	0	0	0	0	1.000
Knoedler,Justin	SF	4	1	15.1	8	1	0	0	0	1.000
LaForest,Pete	TB	21	14	133.0	74	3	0	1	0	1.000
Laird,Gerald	Tex	13	11	99.0	61	5	3	2	1	.957
Laker,Tim	TB	1	0	2.0	1	0	0	0	0	1.000
LeCroy,Matt	Min	1	0	1.0	0	0	0	0	0	-
Mahoney,Mike	StL	25	21	187.1	110	11	2	2	0	.984
Mathis,Jeff	LAA	3	0	5.0	4	0	0	0	0	1.000
McCann,Brian	Atl	57	49	449.1	310	21	3	1	5	.991
Melhuse,Adam	Oak	24	16	161.1	115	7	0	0	1	1.000
Miller,Corky	Min	4	3	27.1	24	2	0	0	2	1.000
Mirabelli,Doug	Bos	33	33	309.0	224	17	3	0	6	.988
Moeller,Chad	Mil	65	58	520.2	454	32	3	6	4	.994
Molina,Jose	LAA	65	53	480.1	409	40	3	6	3	.993
Myers,Greg	Tor	4	3	25.0	20	1	0	0	0	1.000
Navarro,Dioner	LAD	50	49	435.2	336	29	2	1	3	.995
Nevin,Phil	SD	2	2	17.1	11	1	0	0	0	1.000
Nieves,Wil	NYY	3	0	9.0	11	0	0	0	0	1.000
Ojeda,Miguel	SD	25	12	124.0	100	7	0	0	2	1.000
Ojeda,Miguel	Sea	16	10	94.2	69	3	1	2	2	.986
Olivo,Miguel	Sea	54	45	402.2	281	15	4	1	5	.987
Olivo,Miguel	SD	37	32	287.1	224	14	5	2	2	.979
Osik,Keith	Was	5	0	8.0	8	0	0	0	0	1.000
Paul,Josh	LAA	29	9	105.2	84	4	1	0	0	.989
Paulino,Ronny	Pit	2	1	11.0	10	0	0	0	0	1.000
Pena,Brayan	Atl	15	7	81.0	46	5	0	0	0	1.000
Perez,Eddie	Atl	13	9	87.0	38	4	0	1	1	1.000
Perez,Miguel	Cin	1	0	2.0	2	0	0	0	0	1.000
Phillips,Paul	KC	20	18	159.2	91	10	1	1	2	.990
Pratt,Todd	Phi	57	49	436.1	377	18	1	4	5	.997
Quintero,Humb	Hou	16	15	124.0	86	5	1	0	0	.989
Quiroz,Guill	Tor	10	10	85.0	56	5	0	1	0	1.000
Redmond,Mike	Min	45	43	376.1	230	13	0	2	1	1.000
Rivera,Rene	Sea	15	12	111.0	69	4	3	2	3	.961
Rose,Mike	LAD	13	12	110.2	83	5	2	3	1	.978
Ross,Dave	Pit	35	31	273.0	183	23	3	4	4	.986
Ross,Dave	SD	7	2	31.0	28	0	0	1	0	1.000
Santiago,Benito	Pit	6	5	48.1	43	0	0	0	0	1.000
Sardinha,Dane	Cin	1	1	8.0	7	0	0	0	0	1.000
Shoppach,Kelly	Bos	7	2	29.0	14	0	0	0	0	1.000
Stinnett,Kelly	Ari	56	34	329.1	237	15	6	1	1	.977
Torrealba,Yorv	SF	27	24	217.1	147	16	0	1	1	1.000
Torrealba,Yorv	Sea	41	36	319.1	225	18	0	1	0	1.000
Treanor,Matt	Fla	55	41	366.2	309	14	5	4	4	.985
Valentin,Javier	Cin	62	58	508.1	341	28	3	2	3	.992
Whiteside,Eli	Bal	9	3	32.2	21	4	2	1	0	.926
Widger,Chris	CWS	42	38	344.0	252	12	5	2	2	.981
Willingham,Josh	Fla	8	2	31.2	22	0	0	0	1	1.000
Wilson,Dan	Sea	11	9	72.0	36	3	1	1	0	.975
Wilson,Vance	Det	60	41	403.0	234	29	3	4	0	.989
Wooten,Shawn	Bos	1	0	2.0	0	0	0	0	0	-

Catchers Special - Regulars

Player	Tm	G	GS	Inn	SBA	CS	PCS	CS%	ER	CERA
Ausmus,Brad	Hou	134	118	1065.2	57	18	4	.26	374	3.16
Molina,Yadier	StL	114	111	959.1	39	25	8	.55	361	3.39
Molina,Bengie	LAA	105	100	873.1	64	20	2	.29	344	3.55
Martinez,Victor	Cle	142	139	1233.0	125	29	3	.21	504	3.68
Mauer,Joe	Min	116	110	999.2	54	23	4	.38	410	3.69
Pierzynski,A.J.	CWS	128	124	1117.2	102	23	3	.20	464	3.74
Zaun,Gregg	Tor	132	121	1088.0	93	21	4	.19	458	3.79
Kendall,Jason	Oak	147	146	1286.0	123	22	4	.15	542	3.79
Lo Duca,Paul	Fla	128	118	1033.1	118	29	5	.21	436	3.80
Schneider,Brian	Was	113	105	926.2	80	32	3	.38	400	3.88
Piazza,Mike	NYM	101	100	809.1	95	13	3	.11	350	3.89

Player	Tm	G	GS	Inn	SBA	CS	PCS	CS%	ER	CERA
Estrada,Johnny	Atl	104	97	826.1	84	26	5	.27	366	3.99
Miller,Damian	Mil	111	104	917.1	76	24	9	.22	410	4.02
Hernandez,Ram	SD	97	94	806.0	70	18	0	.26	362	4.04
Olivo,Miguel	TOT	91	77	690.0	46	14	2	.27	326	4.25
Phillips,Jason	LAD	93	88	774.0	97	19	4	.16	373	4.34
Cota,Humberto	Pit	87	77	681.2	47	13	2	.24	330	4.36
Barrett,Michael	ChC	122	114	1017.2	91	21	1	.22	503	4.45
Rodriguez,Ivan	Det	123	121	1032.2	68	35	8	.45	511	4.45
Matheny,Mike	SF	132	127	1122.0	102	39	9	.32	557	4.47
Lieberthal,Mike	Phi	117	113	998.2	80	17	2	.19	501	4.52
Snyder,Chris	Ari	113	105	915.2	63	17	5	.21	462	4.54
Posada,Jorge	NYY	133	123	1076.2	129	39	4	.28	559	4.67
Lopez,Javy	Bal	75	75	628.2	68	16	5	.17	329	4.71
Barajas,Rod	Tex	119	117	1025.1	67	23	2	.32	567	4.98
Varitek,Jason	Bos	130	127	1089.0	86	21	5	.20	609	5.03
Hall,Toby	TB	135	122	1061.2	79	33	5	.38	608	5.15
LaRue,Jason	Cin	109	104	914.2	76	25	3	.30	539	5.30
Buck,John	KC	117	112	976.2	91	31	4	.31	615	5.67

Catchers Special - The Rest

Player	Tm	G	GS	Inn	SBA	CS	PCS	CS%	ER	CERA
Alomar Jr.,Sandy	Tex	46	34	315.2	17	0	0	.00	173	4.93
Ardoin,Danny	Col	80	66	591.0	45	22	4	.44	322	4.90
Bako,Paul	LAD	13	13	107.0	4	3	1	.67	64	5.38
Bard,Josh	Cle	31	23	219.2	11	4	2	.22	78	3.20
Bennett,Gary	Was	64	57	523.1	34	9	3	.19	225	3.87
Blanco,Henry	ChC	54	48	422.1	39	19	0	.49	168	3.58
Borders,Pat	Sea	39	37	313.0	35	10	0	.29	142	4.08
Casanova,Raul	CWS	6	0	14.0	0	0	0	-	2	1.29
Cash,Kevin	TB	13	10	89.0	6	3	0	.50	69	6.98
Castillo,Alb	KC	34	32	277.0	12	6	0	.50	157	5.10
Castillo,Alb	Oak	1	0	3.0	0	0	0	-	0	0.00
Castro,Ramon	NYM	99	57	576.1	35	11	2	.27	230	3.59
Chavez,Raul	Hou	36	30	253.1	18	11	0	.61	136	4.83
Closser,JD	Col	80	64	565.2	64	11	4	.12	336	5.35
Diaz,Einar	StL	50	30	299.0	19	8	1	.39	125	3.76
DiFelice,Mike	NYM	11	5	50.0	2	1	0	.50	22	3.96
Dominique,Andy	Tor	1	1	6.0	2	0	0	.00	3	4.50
Doumit,Ryan	Pit	50	48	422.0	35	14	4	.32	217	4.63
Fasano,Sal	Bal	60	47	417.0	44	7	2	.12	236	5.09
Fick,Robert	SD	28	20	189.2	24	3	1	.09	97	4.60
Flaherty,John	NYY	45	39	345.0	46	11	2	.20	158	4.12
Gil,Geronimo	Bal	62	37	349.1	33	10	1	.28	145	3.74
Gonzalez,Wiki	Sea	14	13	115.0	6	3	0	.50	70	5.48
Greene,Todd	Col	33	32	262.0	30	4	3	.04	152	5.22
Haad,Yamid	SF	16	10	89.2	10	5	0	.50	25	2.51
Heintz,Chris	Min	8	6	60.0	4	1	0	.25	26	3.90
Hill,Koyie	Ari	32	23	211.1	16	4	2	.14	128	5.45
Huckaby,Ken	Tor	35	27	243.0	22	10	2	.40	131	4.85
Johnson,Charles	TB	19	16	136.0	18	5	3	.13	95	6.29
Jorgensen,Ryan	Fla	3	1	10.2	2	0	0	.00	6	5.06
Knoedler,Justin	SF	4	1	15.1	0	0	0	-	2	1.17
LaForest,Pete	TB	21	14	133.0	10	4	2	.25	80	5.41
Laird,Gerald	Tex	13	11	99.0	11	3	0	.27	55	5.00
Laker,Tim	TB	1	0	2.0	0	0	0	-	1	4.50
LeCroy,Matt	Min	1	0	1.0	0	0	0	-	0	0.00
Mahoney,Mike	StL	25	21	187.1	7	0	0	.00	74	3.56
Mathis,Jeff	LAA	3	0	5.0	0	0	0	-	0	0.00
McCann,Brian	Atl	57	49	449.1	27	5	0	.19	195	3.91
Melhuse,Adam	Oak	24	16	161.1	11	3	0	.27	54	3.01
Miller,Corky	Min	4	3	27.1	3	2	0	.67	8	2.63
Mirabelli,Doug	Bos	43	33	309.0	28	8	3	.20	128	3.73
Moeller,Chad	Mil	65	58	520.2	44	10	4	.15	226	3.91
Molina,Jose	LAA	65	53	480.1	39	20	2	.49	195	3.65
Myers,Greg	Tor	4	3	25.0	4	1	0	.25	14	5.04
Navarro,Dioner	LAD	50	49	435.2	42	9	1	.20	210	4.34
Nevin,Phil	SD	2	2	17.1	0	0	0	-	15	7.79
Nieves,Wil	NYY	3	0	9.0	0	0	0	-	4	4.00
Ojeda,Miguel	SD	25	12	124.0	9	0	0	.00	60	4.35
Ojeda,Miguel	Sea	16	10	94.2	11	5	1	.40	49	4.66
Olivo,Miguel	Sea	54	45	402.0	31	10	1	.30	210	4.69
Olivo,Miguel	SD	37	32	287.1	15	4	1	.21	116	3.63
Osik,Keith	Was	5	0	8.0	3	0	0	.00	2	2.25
Paul,Josh	LAA	29	9	105.2	7	2	0	.29	59	5.03
Paulino,Ronny	Pit	2	1	11.0	1	0	0	.00	2	1.64
Pena,Brayan	Atl	15	7	81.0	10	2	1	.11	57	6.33

Player	Tm	G	GS	Inn	SBA	CS	PCS	CS%	ER	CERA
Perez,Eddie	Atl	13	9	87.0	4	3	0	.75	21	2.17
Perez,Miguel	Cin	1	0	2.0	0	0	0	-	0	0.00
Phillips,Paul	KC	20	18	159.2	11	7	1	.60	101	5.69
Pratt,Todd	Phi	57	49	436.1	28	9	0	.32	171	3.53
Quintero,Humb	Hou	16	15	124.0	9	2	1	.13	54	3.92
Quiroz,Guill	Tor	10	10	85.0	14	3	1	.15	47	4.98
Redmond,Mike	Min	45	43	376.1	19	10	1	.50	162	3.87
Rivera,Rene	Sea	15	12	111.0	6	2	1	.20	54	4.38
Rose,Mike	LAD	13	12	110.2	21	3	0	.14	48	3.90
Ross,Dave	Pit	35	31	273.0	14	9	2	.58	122	4.02
Ross,Dave	SD	7	2	31.0	1	0	0	.00	18	5.23
Santiago,Benito	Pit	6	5	48.1	3	0	0	.00	37	6.89
Sardinha,Dane	Cin	1	1	8.0	0	0	0	-	7	7.88
Shoppach,Kelly	Bos	7	2	29.0	2	0	0	.00	16	4.97
Stinnett,Kelly	Ari	56	34	329.1	27	7	3	.17	198	5.41
Torrealba,Yorv	SF	27	24	217.1	20	10	3	.41	114	4.72
Torrealba,Yorv	Cin	41	36	319.1	36	10	2	.24	157	4.42
Treanor,Matt	Fla	55	41	366.2	33	9	0	.27	195	4.79
Valentin,Javier	Cin	62	58	508.1	35	10	1	.26	278	4.92
Whiteside,Eli	Bal	9	3	32.2	4	1	0	.25	14	3.86
Widger,Chris	CWS	42	38	344.0	26	2	0	.08	126	3.30
Willingham,Josh	Fla	8	2	31.2	3	0	0	.00	34	9.66
Wilson,Dan	Sea	11	9	72.0	7	3	1	.33	30	3.75
Wilson,Vance	Det	60	41	403.0	41	14	5	.25	210	4.69
Wooten,Shawn	Bos	1	0	2.0	0	0	0	-	0	0.00

Baserunning

Bill James

On April 14, 2002, Matt LeCroy hit a triple off of Steve Sparks of Detroit. Have you ever seen Matt LeCroy run? Neither has anybody else.

Matt LeCroy is a fun player. He is built like a catcher, only more so. Later in the game, David Ortiz pinch hit for LeCroy, and he also hit a triple. Must have been something in the air conditioning.

David can't run, either, but David once hit two triples in a game. LeCroy has never hit two in a career. He has never stolen a base, either, despite several tries. He hits 17 homers a year, but last year that was accompanied by 5 doubles and 0 triples. He was the first player in history to have 17 homers with 22 (or fewer) extra base hits, although Art Shamsky once hit 5 doubles, 0 triples and 21 homers. My kind of player.

Last year, Matt LeCroy was on first base when a single was hit 14 times. He was 0-for-14 on making it to third. He was on second when a single was hit 3 times, and was 0-for-3 at scoring on those, and he was on first base when a double was hit six times, and he was 0-for-6 on those. Altogether, he was 0-for-23 on opportunities to take an extra base on a teammate's hit.

This doesn't make LeCroy the worst baserunner in the majors. LeCroy was 0-for-23, but at least he wasn't thrown out. Frank Thomas was 0-for-7, and he was thrown out. Calvin Pickering of Kansas City, who sort of looks as if he might have eaten Frank Thomas for breakfast with peanut butter and pancakes, was one-for-three with an out, which is also certainly worse than LeCroy.

On the other hand, Aaron Guiel of Kansas City—who is fast but not terribly fast—was 3-for-3 going first to third, 2-for-2 scoring from second on a single and 3-for-3 scoring from first on a double—overall, 8 for 8. Among regular players, Aaron Boone had the highest percentage of advances to opportunities (31 for 44, 70%), based mostly on an unusual number of opportunities to score from second on a single, which is the highest percentage situation of the three.

Carlos Beltran—who I think is actually the best baserunner in the majors—was 32-for-47, 68%, and also with only one time thrown out.

Are these differences meaningful? Certainly. Let's suppose that a regular player has 40 chances a year to advance on a teammate's hit, and that the range of performance is from 15% to 70%. That's a difference of 22 bases between the players. If you figure that a run is four bases, that's five runs. That's a very meaningful difference.

In addition, Rookie Rickie Weeks (say that three times quickly) was thrown out trying to advance five times. J.J. Hardy, who was on base more times than Weeks and who was more successful than Weeks at picking up extra bases (60% vs. 50%), was not thrown out at all. If you figure that the team is going to lose a little more than half a run for each runner thrown out, that's another three runs. That's certainly significant.

There are a great many other things that one could do to measure baserunning, and we will do more of those over the years; we are in the business of improving the statistical record of the game. We hope that this chart will serve as a fun and instructive introduction for the subject.

Note: Chart includes all players who have been on base ten or more times during the 2005 season.

2005 Baserunning

Player, Team	Score Percent (excl. HRs) Times On Base	Score Percentage	Extra Bases Taken on Base Hits — First to Third Extra Bases Per Opp	Percent	Second to Home Extra Bases Per Opp	Percent	First to Home Extra Bases Per Opp	Percent	Thrown Out	Overall Percent
Abernathy, Brent, Min	25	16%	1-4	25%	0-2	0%	0-0	-	0	17%
Abreu, Bobby, Phi	290	28%	6-22	27%	24-36	67%	2-8	25%	2	48%
Adams, Russ, Tor	195	31%	10-25	40%	12-21	57%	1-4	25%	1	46%
Aguila, Chris, Fla	37	30%	1-3	33%	4-6	67%	0-0	-	0	56%
Alexander, Manny, SD	10	0%	0-0	-	0-0	-	0-0	-	0	-
Alfonzo, Edgardo, SF	141	24%	3-14	21%	5-14	36%	2-5	40%	1	30%
Allen, Chad, Tex	21	24%	0-2	0%	2-3	67%	0-1	0%	0	33%
Alomar Jr., Sandy, Tex	47	23%	0-2	0%	1-5	20%	0-1	0%	0	13%
Alou, Moises, SF	200	24%	7-24	29%	7-14	50%	1-4	25%	1	36%
Ambres, Chip, KC	62	34%	5-15	33%	1-3	33%	0-0	-	0	33%
Anderson, Garret, LAA	182	28%	3-22	14%	11-19	58%	0-4	0%	1	31%
Anderson, Marlon, NYM	85	28%	4-13	31%	2-7	29%	0-1	0%	0	29%
Andino, Robert, Fla	15	27%	0-0	-	1-1	100%	1-1	100%	0	100%
Ardoin, Danny, Col	80	28%	2-8	25%	4-7	57%	1-2	50%	0	41%
Atkins, Garrett, Col	216	23%	9-29	31%	11-20	55%	3-7	43%	0	41%
Aurilia, Rich, Cin	158	30%	7-21	33%	8-14	57%	1-4	25%	4	41%
Ausmus, Brad, Hou	178	18%	8-14	57%	6-15	40%	1-9	11%	3	39%
Aybar, Willy, LAD	46	24%	3-9	33%	1-3	33%	0-0	-	0	33%
Backe, Brandon, Hou	16	31%	0-4	0%	2-3	67%	1-1	100%	0	38%
Baerga, Carlos, Was	57	28%	2-5	40%	2-3	67%	2-5	40%	0	46%
Bagwell, Jeff, Hou	46	17%	0-2	0%	1-6	17%	0-3	0%	1	9%
Baker, Jeff, Col	15	33%	0-1	0%	1-2	50%	0-1	0%	0	25%
Bako, Paul, LAD	20	5%	0-0	-	0-1	0%	0-0	-	0	0%
Barajas, Rod, Tex	126	25%	5-14	36%	5-11	45%	0-3	0%	1	36%
Bard, Josh, Cle	26	19%	0-5	0%	1-2	50%	0-0	-	1	14%
Barmes, Clint, Col	127	35%	8-20	40%	11-13	85%	4-5	80%	0	61%
Barrett, Michael, ChC	173	18%	5-10	50%	7-14	50%	1-3	33%	1	48%
Bartlett, Jason, Min	93	32%	1-9	11%	4-7	57%	1-4	25%	0	30%
Bay, Jason, Pit	282	28%	8-24	33%	14-25	56%	6-13	46%	0	45%
Beckett, Josh, Fla	19	21%	1-3	33%	0-3	0%	0-0	-	0	17%
Bell, David, Phi	195	22%	5-20	25%	8-16	50%	3-10	30%	4	35%
Bellhorn, Mark, Bos-NYY	115	30%	3-13	23%	5-13	38%	0-1	0%	1	30%
Belliard, Ronnie, Cle	196	28%	7-20	35%	7-11	64%	2-4	50%	1	46%
Beltran, Carlos, NYM	222	30%	17-28	61%	12-15	80%	3-4	75%	1	68%
Beltre, Adrian, Sea	203	25%	6-18	33%	6-16	38%	3-6	50%	0	38%
Bennett, Gary, Was	73	14%	0-5	0%	2-4	50%	0-0	-	0	22%
Benson, Kris, NYM	16	25%	1-3	33%	0-1	0%	0-1	0%	0	20%
Bergolla, William, Cin	10	30%	1-2	50%	1-1	100%	1-1	100%	0	75%
Berkman, Lance, Hou	221	24%	1-19	5%	3-16	19%	2-6	33%	2	15%
Berroa, Angel, KC	221	25%	9-26	35%	13-16	81%	1-1	100%	0	53%
Betancourt, Yuniesky, Sea	75	31%	1-4	25%	5-7	71%	1-2	50%	0	54%
Betemit, Wilson, Atl	114	28%	2-12	17%	7-8	88%	0-3	0%	0	39%
Bigbie, Larry, Bal-Col	96	23%	1-9	11%	7-9	78%	0-1	0%	0	42%
Biggio, Craig, Hou	216	31%	0-12	0%	12-19	63%	7-11	64%	1	45%
Blake, Casey, Cle	173	28%	5-21	24%	12-14	86%	3-4	75%	0	51%
Blalock, Hank, Tex	222	25%	1-17	6%	6-12	50%	0-5	0%	1	21%
Blanco, Andres, KC	27	22%	2-4	50%	1-2	50%	0-0	-	0	50%
Blanco, Henry, ChC	53	19%	1-3	33%	1-4	25%	1-1	100%	0	38%
Blanco, Tony, Was	28	21%	1-2	50%	0-1	0%	0-1	0%	0	25%
Bloomquist, Willie, Sea	95	28%	6-13	46%	5-10	50%	1-2	50%	0	48%
Blum, Geoff, SD-CWS	107	24%	2-12	17%	6-9	67%	2-4	50%	0	40%
Bonds, Barry, SF	16	19%	0-2	0%	1-1	100%	1-1	100%	0	50%
Boone, Aaron, Cle	179	25%	8-16	50%	20-23	87%	3-5	60%	2	70%
Boone, Bret, Sea-Min	109	24%	3-13	23%	5-10	50%	3-6	50%	1	38%
Borders, Pat, Sea	34	32%	0-0	-	4-7	57%	1-1	100%	0	63%
Botts, Jason, Tex	12	33%	0-1	0%	0-0	-	0-1	0%	0	0%
Bradley, Milton, LAD	104	35%	3-9	33%	6-14	43%	1-3	33%	4	38%
Branyan, Russell, Mil	80	14%	2-5	40%	2-4	50%	0-1	0%	0	40%
Broussard, Ben, Cle	154	26%	2-14	14%	7-11	64%	1-7	14%	1	31%
Brown, Emil, KC	221	26%	6-18	33%	17-27	63%	2-8	25%	0	47%
Bruntlett, Eric, Hou	57	26%	1-5	20%	4-6	67%	0-0	-	0	45%
Buck, John, KC	126	22%	3-14	21%	6-12	50%	2-6	33%	0	34%
Burke, Chris, Hou	117	38%	8-17	47%	8-16	50%	2-4	50%	0	49%
Burnett, A.J., Fla	15	13%	0-1	0%	0-0	-	0-0	-	0	0%
Burnitz, Jeromy, ChC	219	27%	10-41	24%	9-16	56%	3-6	50%	1	35%
Burrell, Pat, Phi	237	19%	6-15	40%	6-16	38%	0-8	0%	5	31%
Burroughs, Sean, SD	119	16%	1-11	9%	4-6	67%	2-3	67%	1	35%
Byrd, Marlon, Phi-Was	90	20%	1-9	11%	4-8	50%	1-2	50%	1	32%
Byrnes, Eric, Oak-Col-Bal	141	28%	6-15	40%	9-10	90%	2-3	67%	0	61%
Cabrera, Miguel, Fla	253	28%	7-34	21%	13-25	52%	2-6	33%	1	34%

2005 Baserunning

Player, Team	Times On Base	Score Percentage	First to Third Extra Bases Per Opp	Percent	Second to Home Extra Bases Per Opp	Percent	First to Home Extra Bases Per Opp	Percent	Thrown Out	Overall Percent
Cabrera, Orlando, LAA	191	32%	7-23	30%	13-20	65%	4-5	80%	0	50%
Cairo, Miguel, NYM	116	25%	1-7	14%	2-10	20%	2-5	40%	0	23%
Cameron, Mike, NYM	117	30%	6-11	55%	4-6	67%	4-5	80%	0	64%
Cano, Robinson, NYY	189	34%	9-28	32%	21-24	88%	3-5	60%	1	58%
Cantu, Jorge, TB	200	23%	7-23	30%	9-14	64%	4-6	67%	2	47%
Capuano, Chris, Mil	16	31%	0-2	0%	1-1	100%	0-0	-	0	33%
Carpenter, Chris, StL	18	39%	1-4	25%	1-2	50%	0-0	-	0	33%
Carroll, Jamey, Was	141	31%	7-22	32%	8-13	62%	5-8	63%	0	47%
Casey, Sean, Cin	224	29%	4-23	17%	8-17	47%	2-9	22%	0	29%
Castilla, Vinny, Was	181	23%	4-22	18%	8-17	47%	1-1	100%	0	33%
Castillo, Alberto, KC-Oak	35	34%	0-3	0%	3-4	75%	1-3	33%	0	40%
Castillo, Jose, Pit	134	28%	5-19	26%	11-17	65%	1-3	33%	0	44%
Castillo, Luis, Fla	214	32%	16-36	44%	14-19	74%	5-9	56%	2	55%
Castro, Bernie, Bal	36	39%	2-3	67%	2-3	67%	2-2	100%	0	75%
Castro, Juan, Min	89	25%	3-12	25%	4-9	44%	0-2	0%	0	30%
Castro, Ramon, NYM	76	24%	0-3	0%	5-8	63%	1-2	50%	0	46%
Catalanotto, Frank, Tor	179	26%	7-18	39%	7-11	64%	0-6	0%	2	40%
Cedeno, Roger, StL	17	24%	0-4	0%	0-1	0%	0-1	0%	0	0%
Cedeno, Ronny, ChC	33	36%	1-3	33%	4-7	57%	0-2	0%	0	42%
Chavez, Endy, Was-Phi	61	31%	1-4	25%	4-6	67%	1-2	50%	0	50%
Chavez, Eric, Oak	218	30%	8-30	27%	16-24	67%	5-7	71%	0	48%
Chavez, Raul, Hou	22	18%	1-3	33%	0-3	0%	0-0	-	0	17%
Choi, Hee Seop, LAD	118	21%	3-12	25%	5-10	50%	2-3	67%	0	40%
Church, Ryan, Was	107	30%	1-11	9%	9-14	64%	1-3	33%	0	39%
Cintron, Alex, Ari	109	26%	3-9	33%	4-8	50%	1-1	100%	0	44%
Cirillo, Jeff, Mil	87	29%	4-8	50%	5-5	100%	0-2	0%	0	60%
Clark, Brady, Mil	250	32%	9-29	31%	11-20	55%	3-7	43%	2	41%
Clark, Tony, Ari	125	14%	1-15	7%	2-9	22%	0-2	0%	0	12%
Clayton, Royce, Ari	208	27%	9-22	41%	7-14	50%	3-4	75%	0	48%
Clemens, Roger, Hou	20	10%	0-4	0%	0-3	0%	0-0	-	0	0%
Closser, JD, Col	89	27%	3-10	30%	9-11	82%	1-1	100%	0	59%
Conine, Jeff, Fla	152	26%	4-10	40%	5-10	50%	0-2	0%	3	41%
Cora, Alex, Cle-Bos	88	25%	2-5	40%	3-7	43%	2-3	67%	0	47%
Cordero, Wil, Was	10	20%	0-1	0%	0-0	-	0-0	-	0	0%
Costa, Shane, KC	27	41%	2-4	50%	1-1	100%	0-0	-	0	60%
Cota, Humberto, Pit	93	24%	1-8	13%	3-6	50%	1-3	33%	0	29%
Counsell, Craig, Ari	243	31%	8-25	32%	17-24	71%	4-7	57%	0	52%
Crawford, Carl, TB	231	37%	8-18	44%	15-28	54%	5-7	71%	2	53%
Crede, Joe, CWS	133	24%	5-16	31%	9-12	75%	0-2	0%	1	47%
Crisp, Coco, Cle	226	31%	8-20	40%	13-19	68%	8-10	80%	0	59%
Crosby, Bobby, Oak	144	40%	4-14	29%	13-15	87%	4-7	57%	0	58%
Crosby, Bubba, NYY	54	26%	2-7	29%	2-5	40%	0-1	0%	0	31%
Cruz, Deivi, SF-Was	91	25%	4-10	40%	6-7	86%	2-3	67%	1	60%
Cruz, Jacob, Cin	45	18%	0-3	0%	1-2	50%	1-1	100%	0	33%
Cruz, Jose, Ari-Bos-LAD	149	19%	4-14	29%	7-14	50%	2-3	67%	0	42%
Cuddyer, Mike, Min	161	27%	6-28	21%	12-18	67%	2-3	67%	2	41%
Damon, Johnny, Bos	276	38%	6-31	19%	22-34	65%	7-10	70%	2	47%
Daubach, Brian, NYM	11	27%	0-0	-	1-1	100%	0-0	-	0	100%
DaVanon, Jeff, LAA	110	36%	2-15	13%	7-12	58%	6-6	100%	1	45%
Davis, Doug, Mil	14	14%	0-2	0%	1-1	100%	0-0	-	0	33%
Davis, J.J., Was	11	0%	0-1	0%	0-0	-	0-0	-	0	0%
DeJesus, David, KC	194	31%	14-31	45%	10-15	67%	4-5	80%	0	55%
Delgado, Carlos, Fla	220	22%	3-26	12%	9-20	45%	1-9	11%	0	24%
Dellucci, David, Tex	171	40%	8-23	35%	12-22	55%	2-7	29%	0	42%
Denorfia, Chris, Cin	17	41%	0-0	-	3-4	75%	0-0	-	0	75%
DeRosa, Mark, Tex	53	34%	2-6	33%	4-5	80%	1-2	50%	1	54%
Diaz, Einar, StL	43	30%	0-4	0%	4-5	80%	0-0	-	0	44%
Diaz, Matt, KC	37	16%	0-2	0%	0-1	0%	0-1	0%	0	0%
Diaz, Victor, NYM	105	28%	4-11	36%	9-12	75%	1-1	100%	0	58%
Dobbs, Greg, Sea	50	14%	1-8	13%	3-5	60%	1-2	50%	1	33%
Doumit, Ryan, Pit	84	23%	2-9	22%	4-10	40%	1-3	33%	0	32%
Drew, J.D., LAD	120	28%	4-14	29%	4-6	67%	0-4	0%	1	33%
Dubois, Jason, ChC-Cle	55	22%	2-6	33%	3-7	43%	0-2	0%	0	33%
Duffy, Chris, Pit	57	37%	3-9	33%	8-11	73%	2-3	67%	1	57%
Dunn, Adam, Cin	231	29%	6-29	21%	8-13	62%	4-9	44%	0	35%
Durazo, Erubiel, Oak	55	20%	1-7	14%	5-8	63%	0-1	0%	0	38%
Durham, Ray, SF	200	28%	8-29	28%	13-15	87%	0-4	0%	0	44%
Durrington, Trent, Mil	15	20%	0-1	0%	0-0	-	0-0	-	0	0%
Dye, Jermaine, CWS	181	24%	3-21	14%	7-14	50%	2-4	50%	2	31%
Easley, Damion, Fla	98	29%	3-11	27%	7-11	64%	1-1	100%	0	48%
Eaton, Adam, SD	12	17%	0-1	0%	0-0	-	0-0	-	0	0%
Eckstein, David, StL	268	31%	11-39	28%	10-17	59%	3-9	33%	1	37%
Edmonds, Jim, StL	195	30%	6-13	46%	10-23	43%	4-5	80%	0	49%

2005 Baserunning

Player, Team	Times On Base	Score Percentage	Extra Bases Per Opp (First to Third)	Percent	Extra Bases Per Opp (Second to Home)	Percent	Extra Bases Per Opp (First to Home)	Percent	Thrown Out	Overall Percent
Edwards, Mike, LAD	84	24%	0-8	0%	2-6	33%	4-5	80%	1	32%
Eldred, Brad, Pit	54	20%	0-6	0%	3-4	75%	1-1	100%	0	36%
Ellis, Mark, Oak	189	33%	2-22	9%	12-24	50%	7-12	58%	1	36%
Ellison, Jason, SF	145	31%	7-21	33%	6-9	67%	2-3	67%	1	45%
Encarnacion, Edwin, Cin	72	22%	2-7	29%	2-5	40%	1-2	50%	2	36%
Encarnacion, Juan, Fla	196	22%	2-18	11%	8-15	53%	1-3	33%	2	31%
Ensberg, Morgan, Hou	221	23%	4-18	22%	12-16	75%	2-3	67%	0	49%
Erstad, Darin, LAA	231	34%	11-33	33%	18-26	69%	4-6	67%	0	51%
Estrada, Johnny, Atl	122	22%	2-13	15%	3-11	27%	1-6	17%	1	20%
Everett, Adam, Hou	189	25%	12-23	52%	7-14	50%	4-5	80%	1	55%
Everett, Carl, CWS	165	21%	5-11	45%	10-11	91%	4-9	44%	2	61%
Fasano, Sal, Bal	46	30%	4-6	67%	4-7	57%	0-1	0%	0	57%
Feliz, Pedro, SF	193	25%	5-19	26%	12-21	57%	5-7	71%	0	47%
Fick, Robert, SD	89	25%	8-13	62%	3-5	60%	2-2	100%	0	65%
Fielder, Prince, Mil	18	0%	0-1	0%	0-2	0%	0-0	-	0	0%
Figgins, Chone, LAA	268	39%	15-22	68%	19-31	61%	4-8	50%	3	62%
Finley, Steve, LAA	126	23%	6-13	46%	10-13	77%	1-5	20%	0	55%
Fiorentino, Jeff, Bal	16	38%	2-4	50%	1-2	50%	2-2	100%	0	63%
Flaherty, John, NYY	34	24%	1-5	20%	2-6	33%	0-1	0%	0	25%
Floyd, Cliff, NYM	209	24%	8-28	29%	7-14	50%	1-4	25%	1	35%
Fogg, Josh, Pit	11	27%	0-4	0%	1-2	50%	0-0	-	0	17%
Ford, Lew, Min	226	28%	4-12	33%	17-21	81%	4-9	44%	0	60%
Francis, Jeff, Col	17	41%	0-2	0%	0-1	0%	0-1	0%	0	0%
Franco, Julio, Atl	96	22%	0-7	0%	3-4	75%	1-2	50%	0	31%
Francoeur, Jeff, Atl	88	31%	3-11	27%	5-7	71%	1-2	50%	0	45%
Freel, Ryan, Cin	166	39%	5-10	50%	12-17	71%	4-5	80%	0	66%
Freeman, Choo, Col	16	38%	1-3	33%	0-0	-	0-0	-	0	33%
Freire, Alejandro, Bal	23	26%	0-0	-	3-5	60%	0-0	-	0	60%
Furcal, Rafael, Atl	253	35%	8-26	31%	17-26	65%	1-3	33%	0	47%
Furmaniak, J.J., Pit	12	25%	1-2	50%	2-2	100%	0-0	-	0	75%
Gall, John, StL	16	19%	0-4	0%	1-2	50%	0-0	-	0	17%
Garabito, Eddy, Col	44	32%	2-6	33%	1-5	20%	0-0	-	1	27%
Garciaparra, Nomar, ChC	87	22%	0-7	0%	4-8	50%	1-2	50%	0	29%
Gathright, Joey, TB	88	33%	2-7	29%	4-5	80%	1-1	100%	0	54%
Gerut, Jody, Cle-ChC-Pit	69	20%	0-4	0%	3-5	60%	0-1	0%	0	30%
Giambi, Jason, NYY	215	20%	14-30	47%	4-7	57%	1-5	20%	0	45%
Giarratano, Tony, Det	11	27%	0-1	0%	1-1	100%	0-0	-	0	50%
Gibbons, Jay, Bal	154	30%	3-14	21%	7-16	44%	1-3	33%	1	33%
Gil, Geronimo, Bal	31	10%	0-2	0%	0-1	0%	0-1	0%	0	0%
Giles, Brian, SD	288	26%	6-27	22%	13-28	46%	5-9	56%	2	38%
Giles, Marcus, Atl	240	37%	8-16	50%	14-20	70%	4-9	44%	0	58%
Ginter, Keith, Oak	37	24%	0-5	0%	2-3	67%	1-2	50%	1	30%
Gipson, Charles, Hou	11	18%	0-0	-	0-0	-	0-2	0%	1	0%
Glaus, Troy, Ari	215	19%	8-29	28%	10-15	67%	0-2	0%	0	39%
Glavine, Tom, NYM	18	11%	0-1	0%	2-2	100%	0-0	-	0	67%
Gload, Ross, CWS	15	13%	0-4	0%	0-0	-	0-0	-	0	0%
Gomes, Jonny, TB	138	29%	5-16	31%	7-11	64%	2-2	100%	1	48%
Gomez, Chris, Bal	100	26%	4-10	40%	6-10	60%	3-3	100%	2	57%
Gonzalez, Adrian, Tex	41	27%	2-5	40%	1-2	50%	0-2	0%	0	33%
Gonzalez, Alex S, TB	135	28%	4-20	20%	10-16	63%	4-6	67%	0	43%
Gonzalez, Alex, Fla	161	25%	1-9	11%	10-19	53%	3-4	75%	2	44%
Gonzalez, Luis A, Col	155	27%	4-18	22%	9-12	75%	2-3	67%	0	45%
Gonzalez, Luis, Ari	235	28%	4-25	16%	7-15	47%	1-8	13%	4	25%
Gonzalez, Wiki, Sea	16	44%	0-2	0%	1-4	25%	0-1	0%	0	14%
Gotay, Ruben, KC	95	28%	3-8	38%	8-11	73%	4-4	100%	0	65%
Grabowski, Jason, LAD	29	34%	0-1	0%	2-4	50%	0-1	0%	1	33%
Graffanino, Tony, KC-Bos	168	36%	4-13	31%	12-17	71%	6-10	60%	1	55%
Granderson, Curtis, Det	48	21%	1-7	14%	2-5	40%	1-1	100%	1	31%
Green, Andy, Ari	15	33%	1-2	50%	1-1	100%	0-0	-	0	67%
Green, Nick, TB	130	37%	4-15	27%	12-15	80%	5-8	63%	0	55%
Green, Shawn, Ari	233	28%	5-21	24%	13-20	65%	5-8	63%	0	47%
Greene, Khalil, SD	135	27%	4-10	40%	4-12	33%	1-1	100%	0	39%
Greene, Todd, Col	38	8%	0-3	0%	0-1	0%	2-2	100%	0	33%
Grieve, Ben, ChC	11	9%	0-0	-	0-1	0%	0-0	-	0	0%
Griffey Jr., Ken, Cin	184	27%	6-21	29%	6-15	40%	1-5	20%	1	32%
Grissom, Marquis, SF	40	15%	3-5	60%	0-1	0%	1-1	100%	0	57%
Gross, Gabe, Tor	33	30%	0-4	0%	1-2	50%	1-2	50%	0	25%
Grudzielanek, Mark, StL	201	28%	5-16	31%	14-18	78%	3-3	100%	0	59%
Guerrero, Vladimir, LAA	221	29%	10-32	31%	9-16	56%	6-8	75%	1	45%
Guiel, Aaron, KC	39	36%	3-3	100%	2-2	100%	3-3	100%	0	100%
Guillen, Carlos, Det	144	30%	7-18	39%	6-11	55%	2-7	29%	2	42%
Guillen, Jose, Was	202	28%	6-21	29%	14-16	88%	0-3	0%	2	50%
Guzman, Cristian, Was	153	23%	3-9	33%	6-11	55%	0-0	-	0	45%

283

2005 Baserunning

Player, Team	Score Percent (excl. HRs)		Extra Bases Taken on Base Hits						Thrown Out	Overall Percent
	Times On Base	Score Percentage	First to Third		Second to Home		First to Home			
			Extra Bases Per Opp	Percent	Extra Bases Per Opp	Percent	Extra Bases Per Opp	Percent		
Hafner, Travis, Cle	210	29%	7-30	23%	15-25	60%	2-6	33%	0	39%
Hairston Jr., Jerry, ChC	150	31%	14-24	58%	4-9	44%	2-2	100%	0	57%
Hall, Bill, Mil	190	27%	7-13	54%	9-12	75%	3-6	50%	1	61%
Hall, Toby, TB	149	15%	5-20	25%	6-11	55%	1-2	50%	2	36%
Halsey, Brad, Ari	13	15%	0-1	0%	0-1	0%	0-1	0%	0	0%
Hammonds, Jeffrey, Was	12	25%	1-1	100%	0-1	0%	0-0	-	0	50%
Hansen, Dave, Sea	22	14%	0-3	0%	1-1	100%	1-1	100%	0	40%
Hardy, J.J., Mil	146	25%	6-16	38%	11-12	92%	1-2	50%	0	60%
Harris, Lenny, Fla	32	13%	0-4	0%	0-1	0%	1-1	100%	0	17%
Harris, Willie, CWS	58	28%	2-9	22%	4-5	80%	1-1	100%	0	47%
Hart, Corey, Mil	18	39%	1-3	33%	2-3	67%	0-1	0%	0	43%
Harvey, Ken, KC	15	20%	0-1	0%	1-4	25%	0-0	-	1	20%
Hatteberg, Scott, Oak	183	25%	4-16	25%	10-14	71%	3-8	38%	0	45%
Hawpe, Brad, Col	122	24%	1-11	9%	6-10	60%	1-1	100%	0	36%
Helms, Wes, Mil	69	20%	3-7	43%	3-4	75%	0-0	-	0	55%
Helton, Todd, Col	267	27%	3-16	19%	15-22	68%	4-11	36%	1	45%
Hermida, Jeremy, Fla	17	29%	2-2	100%	1-1	100%	0-0	-	0	100%
Hernandez, Jose, Cle	75	29%	0-8	0%	4-5	80%	0-2	0%	0	27%
Hernandez, Livan, Was	23	22%	0-5	0%	0-1	0%	0-1	0%	0	0%
Hernandez, Ramon, SD	129	19%	2-13	15%	2-10	20%	2-8	25%	1	19%
Hidalgo, Richard, Tex	91	30%	0-7	0%	6-8	75%	1-3	33%	0	39%
Hill, Aaron, Tor	150	31%	3-17	18%	9-13	69%	0-2	0%	0	38%
Hill, Bobby, Pit	43	28%	4-7	57%	2-3	67%	0-1	0%	0	55%
Hill, Koyie, Ari	30	20%	0-1	0%	0-0	-	0-0	-	0	0%
Hillenbrand, Shea, Tor	233	31%	8-24	33%	11-17	65%	6-9	67%	0	50%
Hinske, Eric, Tor	172	37%	11-22	50%	12-15	80%	1-2	50%	1	62%
Hocking, Denny, KC	30	47%	0-5	0%	5-7	71%	1-2	50%	0	43%
Holbert, Aaron, Cin	11	27%	0-1	0%	1-1	100%	0-1	0%	0	33%
Hollandsworth, Todd, ChC-Atl	104	19%	2-5	40%	6-8	75%	1-4	25%	0	53%
Holliday, Matt, Col	193	25%	5-19	26%	10-13	77%	1-3	33%	1	46%
Hollins, Damon, TB	109	28%	3-11	27%	6-9	67%	2-5	40%	0	44%
Howard, Ryan, Phi	114	26%	2-14	14%	6-11	55%	2-4	50%	0	34%
Huber, Justin, KC	26	23%	0-3	0%	0-2	0%	0-1	0%	0	0%
Huckaby, Ken, Tor	29	24%	0-4	0%	2-3	67%	0-1	0%	0	25%
Hudson, Luke, Cin	15	47%	0-1	0%	0-3	0%	0-1	0%	0	0%
Hudson, Orlando, Tor	163	32%	6-27	22%	12-18	67%	1-1	100%	1	41%
Hudson, Tim, Atl	15	13%	1-2	50%	1-2	50%	0-0	-	0	50%
Huff, Aubrey, TB	194	25%	9-24	38%	11-18	61%	2-3	67%	0	49%
Hunter, Torii, Min	142	35%	6-12	50%	10-25	40%	0-3	0%	2	40%
Hyzdu, Adam, SD-Bos	15	13%	1-3	33%	2-2	100%	0-0	-	0	60%
Ibanez, Raul, Sea	239	30%	0-18	0%	19-29	66%	6-8	75%	1	45%
Iguchi, Tadahito, CWS	194	30%	11-25	44%	10-12	83%	3-6	50%	0	56%
Infante, Omar, Det	117	23%	5-14	36%	6-16	38%	0-2	0%	0	34%
Inge, Brandon, Det	225	26%	6-28	21%	11-19	58%	1-2	50%	0	37%
Izturis, Cesar, LAD	160	29%	9-21	43%	5-11	45%	1-5	20%	0	41%
Izturis, Maicer, LAA	82	21%	3-6	50%	4-5	80%	0-1	0%	0	58%
Jackson, Conor, Ari	29	21%	2-4	50%	1-1	100%	1-2	50%	0	57%
Jackson, Damian, SD	126	31%	4-15	27%	12-17	71%	3-5	60%	1	51%
Jacobs, Mike, NYM	35	23%	0-2	0%	1-2	50%	0-0	-	0	25%
Jenkins, Geoff, Mil	217	29%	4-21	19%	12-22	55%	2-7	29%	2	36%
Jeter, Derek, NYY	306	34%	18-43	42%	15-21	71%	5-10	50%	3	51%
Jimenez, D'Angelo, Cin	40	35%	1-4	25%	3-6	50%	1-2	50%	1	42%
Johnson, Ben, SD	29	24%	1-2	50%	0-1	0%	0-0	-	0	33%
Johnson, Charles, TB	20	25%	0-2	0%	0-2	0%	0-0	-	0	0%
Johnson, Dan, Oak	149	26%	1-12	8%	8-12	67%	4-9	44%	0	39%
Johnson, Kelly, Atl	117	32%	6-17	35%	6-11	55%	3-5	60%	0	45%
Johnson, Nick, Was	220	23%	9-20	45%	9-11	82%	1-3	33%	2	56%
Johnson, Reed, Tor	154	31%	5-15	33%	10-14	71%	5-7	71%	1	56%
Johnson, Russ, NYY	11	45%	1-2	50%	0-1	0%	0-0	-	0	33%
Jones, Andruw, Atl	214	21%	5-19	26%	8-12	67%	3-6	50%	0	43%
Jones, Chipper, Atl	171	26%	4-15	27%	8-13	62%	3-8	38%	1	42%
Jones, Jacque, Min	183	28%	7-32	22%	6-13	46%	2-7	29%	0	29%
Jordan, Brian, Atl	85	26%	0-2	0%	4-4	100%	6-7	86%	0	77%
Kapler, Gabe, Bos	43	33%	1-6	17%	2-3	67%	0-1	0%	0	30%
Kata, Matt, Ari-Phi	18	39%	1-1	100%	2-4	50%	0-1	0%	0	50%
Kearns, Austin, Cin	152	29%	3-10	30%	9-11	82%	3-5	60%	0	58%
Kelly, Kenny, Cin-Was	17	29%	1-1	100%	3-3	100%	0-0	-	0	100%
Kendall, Jason, Oak	268	26%	13-27	48%	11-18	61%	6-9	67%	1	56%
Kennedy, Adam, LAA	172	27%	5-18	28%	12-22	55%	0-1	0%	2	41%
Kent, Jeff, LAD	235	30%	6-27	22%	13-22	59%	0-6	0%	3	35%
Kielty, Bobby, Oak	154	29%	6-11	55%	8-13	62%	5-6	83%	0	63%
Klesko, Ryan, SD	180	24%	4-14	29%	8-13	62%	2-5	40%	1	44%
Koskie, Corey, Tor	131	29%	0-13	0%	7-12	58%	1-9	11%	0	24%

284

2005 Baserunning

Player, Team	Times On Base	Score Percentage	First to Third Extra Bases Per Opp	Percent	Second to Home Extra Bases Per Opp	Percent	First to Home Extra Bases Per Opp	Percent	Thrown Out	Overall Percent
Kotchman, Casey, LAA	47	19%	2-7	29%	1-2	50%	0-1	0%	0	30%
Kotsay, Mark, Oak	208	29%	10-22	45%	12-21	57%	1-5	20%	0	48%
LaForest, Pete, TB	19	21%	0-2	0%	1-4	25%	0-1	0%	0	14%
Laird, Gerald, Tex	13	46%	0-1	0%	2-3	67%	0-1	0%	0	40%
Lamb, Mike, Hou	102	28%	3-12	25%	3-6	50%	2-4	50%	1	36%
Lane, Jason, Hou	171	23%	5-13	38%	8-18	44%	0-2	0%	3	39%
Langerhans, Ryan, Atl	143	28%	7-20	35%	4-7	57%	3-3	100%	0	47%
LaRoche, Adam, Atl	159	21%	3-14	21%	3-9	33%	2-6	33%	2	28%
LaRue, Jason, Cin	144	17%	2-7	29%	4-7	57%	1-4	25%	0	39%
Lawton, Matt, Pit-ChC-NYY	215	25%	4-23	17%	9-18	50%	1-12	8%	3	26%
LeCroy, Matt, Min	112	14%	0-14	0%	0-3	0%	0-6	0%	0	0%
Ledee, Ricky, LAD	88	27%	3-11	27%	5-9	56%	1-2	50%	0	41%
Lee, Carlos, Mil	215	25%	3-17	18%	5-10	50%	1-6	17%	1	27%
Lee, Derrek, ChC	262	28%	5-25	20%	20-31	65%	5-9	56%	1	46%
Lee, Travis, TB	145	29%	8-20	40%	7-11	64%	1-3	33%	0	47%
Lidle, Cory, Phi	10	20%	1-2	50%	0-1	0%	0-0	-	0	33%
Lieber, Jon, Phi	15	47%	0-1	0%	1-3	33%	0-1	0%	0	20%
Lieberthal, Mike, Phi	155	23%	1-8	13%	10-23	43%	0-0	-	1	35%
Liefer, Jeff, Cle	12	33%	0-1	0%	1-1	100%	0-0	-	0	50%
Linden, Todd, SF	55	29%	3-5	60%	5-7	71%	1-1	100%	2	69%
Lo Duca, Paul, Fla	175	22%	6-20	30%	5-10	50%	0-5	0%	0	31%
Loaiza, Esteban, Was	14	21%	1-5	20%	0-2	0%	0-0	-	1	14%
Lofton, Kenny, Phi	179	36%	7-19	37%	11-16	69%	3-5	60%	1	53%
Logan, Nook, Det	136	32%	12-19	63%	6-9	67%	3-3	100%	0	68%
Long, Terrence, KC	171	33%	8-19	42%	8-13	62%	5-8	63%	1	53%
Lopez, Felipe, Cin	241	31%	9-33	27%	13-17	76%	3-3	100%	1	47%
Lopez, Javy, Bal	147	22%	1-13	8%	6-13	46%	4-4	100%	0	37%
Lopez, Jose, Sea	64	25%	0-2	0%	4-7	57%	1-1	100%	1	50%
Loretta, Mark, SD	175	29%	3-23	13%	10-21	48%	2-6	33%	5	30%
Lowe, Derek, Bos-LAD	19	16%	0-0	-	1-1	100%	0-1	0%	0	50%
Lowell, Mike, Fla	179	27%	3-15	20%	9-21	43%	4-7	57%	1	37%
Lowry, Noah, SF	23	26%	0-1	0%	0-2	0%	0-2	0%	0	0%
Ludwick, Ryan, Cle	13	31%	0-2	0%	0-1	0%	0-2	0%	0	0%
Lugo, Julio, TB	277	30%	13-30	43%	12-21	57%	3-9	33%	0	47%
Luna, Hector, StL	64	39%	2-5	40%	9-12	75%	0-0	-	0	65%
Mabry, John, StL	76	24%	0-3	0%	6-8	75%	0-0	-	0	55%
Macias, Jose, ChC	62	23%	2-6	33%	4-5	80%	1-2	50%	0	54%
Mackowiak, Rob, Pit	187	26%	4-16	25%	11-19	58%	2-8	25%	1	40%
Maddux, Greg, ChC	19	16%	1-2	50%	0-0	-	0-0	-	0	50%
Magruder, Chris, Mil	50	28%	2-8	25%	4-6	67%	0-0	-	1	43%
Mahoney, Mike, StL	22	18%	1-2	50%	0-2	0%	0-2	0%	0	17%
Marquis, Jason, StL	33	27%	1-2	50%	2-3	67%	0-0	-	0	60%
Marrero, Eli, KC-Bal	36	33%	0-1	0%	2-2	100%	0-0	-	0	67%
Marte, Andy, Atl	20	15%	0-1	0%	0-1	0%	0-1	0%	0	0%
Martinez, Pedro, NYM	13	15%	2-5	40%	0-1	0%	0-0	-	0	33%
Martinez, Ramon, Det-Phi	42	24%	2-3	67%	0-1	0%	1-1	100%	0	60%
Martinez, Tino, NYY	113	23%	2-14	14%	4-16	25%	0-4	0%	2	18%
Martinez, Victor, Cle	231	23%	2-25	8%	6-18	33%	3-11	27%	0	20%
Matheny, Mike, SF	142	20%	1-9	11%	4-14	29%	1-2	50%	1	24%
Matos, Luis, Bal	160	31%	5-15	33%	8-12	67%	3-5	60%	0	50%
Matsui, Hideki, NYY	260	33%	10-25	40%	16-24	67%	1-3	33%	1	52%
Matsui, Kazuo, NYM	98	29%	2-9	22%	4-7	57%	1-2	50%	0	39%
Matthews Jr., Gary, Tex	181	30%	11-19	58%	10-14	71%	2-6	33%	1	59%
Mauer, Joe, Min	217	24%	9-24	38%	10-15	67%	1-3	33%	0	48%
McCann, Brian, Atl	71	21%	2-5	40%	2-6	33%	0-1	0%	1	33%
McCracken, Quinton, Ari	87	25%	2-10	20%	4-6	67%	2-5	40%	0	38%
McDonald, John, Tor-Det	69	26%	3-8	38%	3-6	50%	0-1	0%	1	40%
McEwing, Joe, KC	67	22%	0-7	0%	3-4	75%	2-3	67%	1	36%
McLouth, Nate, Pit	37	41%	2-5	40%	6-6	100%	2-2	100%	0	77%
McPherson, Dallas, LAA	61	34%	3-7	43%	3-7	43%	0-0	-	2	43%
Melhuse, Adam, Oak	33	27%	1-4	25%	4-5	80%	0-1	0%	0	50%
Mench, Kevin, Tex	196	23%	6-17	35%	5-7	71%	3-5	60%	0	48%
Menechino, Frank, Tor	69	26%	1-8	13%	5-7	71%	0-2	0%	0	35%
Michaels, Jason, Phi	140	36%	6-23	26%	6-10	60%	2-4	50%	2	38%
Mientkiewicz, Doug, NYM	102	25%	2-8	25%	6-9	67%	0-1	0%	1	44%
Miles, Aaron, Col	119	29%	4-14	29%	8-9	89%	7-7	100%	0	63%
Millar, Kevin, Bos	191	25%	6-27	22%	4-17	24%	1-7	14%	1	22%
Miller, Damian, Mil	148	27%	1-17	6%	8-17	47%	5-8	63%	0	33%
Milton, Eric, Cin	13	38%	0-1	0%	0-3	0%	0-0	-	0	0%
Mirabelli, Doug, Bos	46	22%	2-6	33%	0-4	0%	0-1	0%	0	18%
Moeller, Chad, Mil	54	30%	0-5	0%	2-4	50%	1-3	33%	0	25%
Mohr, Dustan, Col	73	23%	2-3	67%	5-7	71%	1-1	100%	0	73%
Molina, Bengie, LAA	149	20%	1-19	5%	2-16	13%	0-2	0%	0	8%

2005 Baserunning

Player, Team	Score Percent (excl. HRs) Times On Base	Score Percentage	First to Third Extra Bases Per Opp	Percent	Second to Home Extra Bases Per Opp	Percent	First to Home Extra Bases Per Opp	Percent	Thrown Out	Overall Percent
Molina, Jose, LAA	59	14%	1-5	20%	4-5	80%	0-3	0%	0	38%
Molina, Yadier, StL	130	22%	0-10	0%	6-18	33%	1-1	100%	2	24%
Mondesi, Raul, Atl	46	28%	2-4	50%	1-1	100%	1-1	100%	0	67%
Monroe, Craig, Det	209	23%	3-17	18%	7-14	50%	0-0	-	0	32%
Mora, Melvin, Bal	211	28%	6-28	21%	12-16	75%	3-11	27%	3	38%
Morneau, Justin, Min	161	25%	2-10	20%	7-9	78%	1-2	50%	0	48%
Morris, Matt, StL	11	36%	0-2	0%	0-0	-	0-0	-	0	0%
Morse, Mike, Sea	93	26%	2-8	25%	8-11	73%	2-4	50%	0	52%
Mueller, Bill, Bos	234	25%	5-27	19%	6-22	27%	4-11	36%	0	25%
Mulder, Mark, StL	15	20%	1-2	50%	1-3	33%	1-1	100%	0	50%
Murphy, Donald, KC	22	14%	0-1	0%	0-1	0%	0-0	-	0	0%
Murton, Matt, ChC	64	19%	4-6	67%	4-5	80%	0-0	-	0	73%
Myers, Brett, Phi	15	7%	1-1	100%	1-1	100%	0-1	0%	0	67%
Myrow, Brian, LAD	10	20%	1-2	50%	1-1	100%	0-0	-	0	67%
Nady, Xavier, SD	115	23%	2-7	29%	6-12	50%	2-5	40%	0	42%
Navarro, Dioner, LAD	73	25%	1-3	33%	6-14	43%	0-3	0%	1	35%
Nevin, Phil, SD-Tex	121	28%	4-14	29%	6-14	43%	1-3	33%	3	35%
Newhan, David, Bal	93	28%	3-9	33%	6-9	67%	1-3	33%	2	48%
Niekro, Lance, SF	90	22%	0-9	0%	5-10	50%	1-2	50%	0	29%
Nix, Laynce, Tex	70	31%	4-8	50%	5-7	71%	4-4	100%	0	68%
Nixon, Trot, Bos	170	30%	5-17	29%	5-15	33%	4-9	44%	0	34%
Nunez, Abraham O, StL	174	34%	3-20	15%	12-16	75%	5-7	71%	0	47%
Offerman, Jose, Phi-NYM	37	24%	3-6	50%	0-0	-	0-1	0%	0	43%
Ohka, Tomo, Was-Mil	11	18%	0-0	-	1-2	50%	0-0	-	0	50%
Ojeda, Miguel, SD-Sea	35	20%	0-4	0%	1-2	50%	1-1	100%	0	29%
Olerud, John, Bos	62	18%	1-5	20%	1-4	25%	0-2	0%	0	18%
Olivo, Miguel, Sea-SD	80	26%	2-7	29%	3-8	38%	0-2	0%	0	29%
Olmedo, Ray, Cin	29	31%	2-3	67%	2-2	100%	2-3	67%	0	75%
Ordonez, Magglio, Det	120	25%	1-14	7%	4-12	33%	3-6	50%	0	25%
Orr, Pete, Atl	78	40%	6-10	60%	5-7	71%	1-3	33%	0	60%
Ortiz, David, Bos	249	29%	4-22	18%	3-16	19%	1-5	20%	1	19%
Ortiz, Russ, Ari	12	8%	0-1	0%	0-1	0%	0-0	-	0	0%
Oswalt, Roy, Hou	21	5%	1-5	20%	1-3	33%	0-0	-	0	25%
Overbay, Lyle, Mil	226	27%	8-24	33%	12-21	57%	6-9	67%	0	48%
Ozuna, Pablo, CWS	88	31%	6-10	60%	2-3	67%	3-4	75%	0	65%
Padilla, Vicente, Phi	12	17%	1-3	33%	0-2	0%	0-0	-	0	20%
Palmeiro, Orlando, Hou	79	24%	4-9	44%	4-11	36%	0-0	-	0	40%
Palmeiro, Rafael, Bal	135	21%	2-12	17%	4-5	80%	1-7	14%	1	29%
Patterson, Corey, ChC	131	25%	2-7	29%	8-11	73%	0-1	0%	1	53%
Paul, Josh, LAA	14	14%	1-1	100%	0-0	-	0-0	-	0	100%
Payton, Jay, Bos-Oak	144	31%	6-18	33%	7-14	50%	4-4	100%	0	47%
Peavy, Jake, SD	15	33%	0-2	0%	2-3	67%	0-0	-	0	40%
Pena, Brayan, Atl	10	20%	0-0	-	0-1	0%	0-0	-	0	0%
Pena, Carlos, Det	81	23%	1-7	14%	3-5	60%	1-3	33%	1	33%
Pena, Wily Mo, Cin	91	25%	1-4	25%	3-4	75%	0-0	-	0	50%
Penny, Brad, LAD	14	7%	0-1	0%	0-0	-	0-0	-	0	0%
Peralta, Jhonny, Cle	208	28%	4-12	33%	10-16	63%	4-10	40%	0	47%
Perez, Antonio, LAD	113	22%	4-12	33%	5-7	71%	2-2	100%	0	52%
Perez, Eduardo, TB	64	19%	2-7	29%	1-2	50%	1-1	100%	0	40%
Perez, Neifi, ChC	193	26%	7-26	27%	11-15	73%	3-5	60%	1	46%
Perez, Oliver, Pit	10	10%	1-2	50%	0-1	0%	0-0	-	0	33%
Perez, Timo, CWS	57	19%	1-4	25%	2-4	50%	0-1	0%	0	33%
Perez, Tomas, Phi	54	31%	3-7	43%	4-5	80%	1-2	50%	0	57%
Petagine, Roberto, Bos	12	25%	0-0	-	0-1	0%	0-0	-	0	0%
Pettitte, Andy, Hou	10	10%	0-2	0%	0-2	0%	0-0	-	1	0%
Phelps, Josh, TB	58	28%	3-7	43%	1-2	50%	0-2	0%	0	36%
Phillips, Andy, NYY	13	46%	3-3	100%	1-3	33%	0-0	-	0	67%
Phillips, Jason, LAD	127	22%	3-18	17%	6-12	50%	0-3	0%	2	27%
Phillips, Paul, KC	20	25%	1-6	17%	1-1	100%	0-1	0%	1	25%
Piazza, Mike, NYM	145	15%	3-13	23%	2-9	22%	2-4	50%	0	27%
Piedra, Jorge, Col	43	30%	1-3	33%	3-5	60%	2-3	67%	0	55%
Pierre, Juan, Fla	268	35%	16-37	43%	8-21	38%	2-3	67%	0	43%
Pierzynski, A.J., CWS	150	29%	5-22	23%	6-11	55%	4-6	67%	2	38%
Podsednik, Scott, CWS	219	37%	8-18	44%	15-24	63%	4-7	57%	0	55%
Polanco, Placido, Phi-Det	220	34%	8-33	24%	13-25	52%	4-9	44%	0	37%
Posada, Jorge, NYY	192	25%	8-27	30%	5-14	36%	0-5	0%	0	28%
Pratt, Todd, Phi	62	16%	0-4	0%	0-7	0%	0-1	0%	0	0%
Prior, Mark, ChC	16	31%	0-0	-	1-2	50%	0-2	0%	0	25%
Pujols, Albert, StL	283	31%	11-28	39%	16-20	80%	4-11	36%	2	53%
Punto, Nick, Min	145	28%	4-14	29%	11-15	73%	3-5	60%	0	53%
Quinlan, Robb, LAA	45	27%	3-6	50%	5-6	83%	0-0	-	0	67%
Quintanilla, Omar, Col	45	36%	3-6	50%	0-1	0%	1-1	100%	0	50%
Quintero, Humberto, Hou	10	50%	1-2	50%	0-0	-	0-0	-	0	50%

2005 Baserunning

Player, Team	Score Percent (excl. HRs)		Extra Bases Taken on Base Hits							
	Times On Base	Score Percentage	First to Third Extra Bases Per Opp	Percent	Second to Home Extra Bases Per Opp	Percent	First to Home Extra Bases Per Opp	Percent	Thrown Out	Overall Percent
Quiroz, Guillermo, Tor	10	30%	0-0	-	0-0	-	0-0	-	0	-
Ramirez, Aramis, ChC	166	25%	5-24	21%	7-15	47%	2-9	22%	2	29%
Ramirez, Horacio, Atl	23	17%	0-2	0%	1-1	100%	0-1	0%	0	25%
Ramirez, Manny, Bos	233	29%	7-29	24%	12-23	52%	5-10	50%	1	39%
Randa, Joe, Cin-SD	213	25%	5-19	26%	10-14	71%	1-5	20%	0	42%
Redman, Mark, Pit	11	9%	0-1	0%	0-0	-	0-3	0%	0	0%
Redman, Tike, Pit	120	26%	6-19	32%	6-10	60%	2-4	50%	1	42%
Redmond, Mike, Min	58	28%	1-10	10%	4-11	36%	0-3	0%	0	21%
Reed, Jeremy, Sea	188	31%	4-10	40%	11-16	69%	3-8	38%	0	53%
Relaford, Desi, Col	86	27%	1-10	10%	5-6	83%	1-2	50%	0	39%
Renteria, Edgar, Bos	253	36%	12-24	50%	15-24	63%	5-6	83%	0	59%
Repko, Jason, LAD	110	32%	3-8	38%	12-15	80%	0-1	0%	0	63%
Restovich, Mike, Col-Pit	44	27%	0-6	0%	1-1	100%	1-1	100%	0	25%
Reyes, Jose, NYM	245	38%	11-24	46%	12-20	60%	4-6	67%	1	54%
Rios, Alexis, Tor	182	34%	6-20	30%	11-18	61%	2-5	40%	1	44%
Rivas, Luis, Min	59	34%	2-6	33%	6-9	67%	0-1	0%	0	50%
Rivera, Juan, LAA	114	27%	0-12	0%	8-12	67%	2-3	67%	0	37%
Rivera, Rene, Sea	23	9%	1-5	20%	0-1	0%	0-0	-	1	17%
Roberts, Brian, Bal	242	31%	7-33	21%	9-20	45%	2-7	29%	2	30%
Roberts, Dave, SD	174	33%	4-18	22%	10-15	67%	3-6	50%	0	44%
Robles, Oscar, LAD	146	27%	5-18	28%	0-4	0%	2-5	40%	0	26%
Rodriguez, Alex, NYY	284	27%	7-26	27%	16-23	70%	0-4	0%	1	43%
Rodriguez, Ivan, Det	165	35%	7-21	33%	11-16	69%	3-7	43%	2	48%
Rodriguez, John, StL	66	15%	2-7	29%	1-3	33%	0-1	0%	0	27%
Rodriguez, Luis, Min	77	25%	2-6	33%	2-3	67%	2-4	50%	1	46%
Rolen, Scott, StL	77	30%	1-8	13%	7-12	58%	0-0	-	0	40%
Rollins, Jimmy, Phi	256	40%	11-33	33%	23-31	74%	3-8	38%	2	51%
Romano, Jason, Cin	15	13%	0-1	0%	0-1	0%	0-0	-	0	0%
Rose, Mike, LAD	11	9%	0-0	-	0-1	0%	0-0	-	0	0%
Ross, Dave, Pit-SD	40	20%	0-1	0%	2-2	100%	0-1	0%	0	50%
Rowand, Aaron, CWS	227	28%	10-27	37%	12-19	63%	4-6	67%	1	50%
Ryan, Mike, Min	40	13%	1-6	17%	1-3	33%	0-0	-	1	22%
Saenz, Olmedo, LAD	111	22%	3-10	30%	3-8	38%	0-7	0%	1	24%
Sanchez, Alex, TB-SF	71	42%	6-12	50%	5-10	50%	0-0	-	0	50%
Sanchez, Freddy, Pit	186	26%	4-18	22%	16-21	76%	3-8	38%	2	49%
Sanchez, Rey, NYY	20	35%	0-3	0%	3-3	100%	0-0	-	0	50%
Sanders, Reggie, StL	101	28%	1-7	14%	5-9	56%	1-1	100%	2	41%
Schneider, Brian, Was	136	21%	2-9	22%	6-9	67%	2-3	67%	0	48%
Schumaker, Jared, StL	18	50%	1-4	25%	0-4	0%	1-1	100%	0	22%
Scott, Luke, Hou	27	22%	0-2	0%	1-2	50%	2-2	100%	0	50%
Scutaro, Marco, Oak	145	27%	6-23	26%	14-22	64%	2-4	50%	0	45%
Seabol, Scott, StL	34	29%	0-2	0%	3-4	75%	0-1	0%	0	43%
Self, Todd, Hou	15	40%	0-4	0%	1-1	100%	1-2	50%	0	29%
Sexson, Richie, Sea	221	27%	3-19	16%	8-13	62%	2-7	29%	0	33%
Shealy, Ryan, Col	44	27%	1-3	33%	2-7	29%	0-1	0%	0	27%
Sheffield, Gary, NYY	252	28%	8-28	29%	15-22	68%	2-2	100%	0	48%
Shelton, Chris, Det	149	29%	7-28	25%	10-14	71%	2-4	50%	0	41%
Sierra, Ruben, NYY	59	17%	1-5	20%	1-2	50%	0-0	-	0	29%
Singleton, Chris, TB	27	33%	2-3	67%	3-5	60%	1-1	100%	0	67%
Sizemore, Grady, Cle	248	36%	5-26	19%	18-26	69%	4-7	57%	0	46%
Sledge, Terrmel, Was	15	40%	0-2	0%	1-1	100%	0-0	-	0	33%
Smith, Jason, Det	15	27%	0-2	0%	0-0	-	0-0	-	0	0%
Smoltz, John, Atl	17	6%	0-1	0%	0-0	-	1-1	100%	0	50%
Snelling, Chris, Sea	13	23%	1-2	50%	0-0	-	0-0	-	0	50%
Snow, J.T., SF	146	25%	3-21	14%	12-16	75%	2-4	50%	0	41%
Snyder, Chris, Ari	122	15%	0-11	0%	2-8	25%	0-4	0%	1	9%
Sorensen, Zach, LAA	10	30%	1-2	50%	2-2	100%	0-0	-	0	75%
Soriano, Alfonso, Tex	211	31%	5-17	29%	12-18	67%	4-10	40%	0	47%
Sosa, Sammy, Bal	131	19%	2-16	13%	4-8	50%	1-3	33%	2	26%
Spivey, Junior, Mil-Was	100	30%	4-11	36%	5-6	83%	3-4	75%	0	57%
Stairs, Matt, KC	172	24%	4-19	21%	6-18	33%	1-6	17%	0	26%
Stern, Adam, Bos	22	14%	2-4	50%	1-1	100%	0-0	-	0	60%
Stewart, Shannon, Min	212	28%	7-27	26%	13-25	52%	2-5	40%	1	39%
Stinnett, Kelly, Ari	45	20%	1-3	33%	3-5	60%	0-0	-	1	50%
Strong, Jamal, Sea	15	40%	0-1	0%	1-1	100%	0-0	-	0	50%
Sullivan, Cory, Col	158	38%	6-15	40%	20-23	87%	2-5	40%	2	65%
Suppan, Jeff, StL	17	24%	0-2	0%	2-4	50%	0-0	-	0	33%
Surhoff, B.J., Bal	100	25%	1-14	7%	1-3	33%	1-5	20%	0	14%
Suzuki, Ichiro, Sea	278	35%	12-36	33%	16-22	73%	5-9	56%	1	49%
Sweeney, Mark, SD	103	22%	1-9	11%	7-10	70%	1-1	100%	1	45%
Sweeney, Mike, KC	165	25%	3-22	14%	10-14	71%	1-5	20%	1	34%
Swisher, Nick, Oak	162	28%	4-15	27%	9-15	60%	0-2	0%	1	41%
Taguchi, So, StL	147	25%	3-15	20%	7-10	70%	0-1	0%	0	38%

2005 Baserunning

Player, Team	Times On Base	Score Percentage	First to Third Extra Bases Per Opp	Percent	Second to Home Extra Bases Per Opp	Percent	First to Home Extra Bases Per Opp	Percent	Thrown Out	Overall Percent
Taveras, Willy, Hou	238	33%	9-23	39%	14-20	70%	7-9	78%	0	58%
Teahen, Mark, KC	166	31%	6-16	38%	15-19	79%	2-3	67%	0	61%
Teixeira, Mark, Tex	261	26%	8-28	29%	14-21	67%	6-10	60%	1	47%
Tejada, Miguel, Bal	251	25%	12-35	34%	18-27	67%	1-5	20%	1	46%
Terrero, Luis, Ari	78	24%	2-7	29%	4-7	57%	0-1	0%	1	40%
Thames, Marcus, Det	27	15%	1-4	25%	0-1	0%	1-1	100%	0	33%
Thomas, Charles, Oak	24	17%	3-4	75%	0-1	0%	0-0	-	0	60%
Thomas, Frank, CWS	27	26%	0-4	0%	0-2	0%	0-1	0%	1	0%
Thome, Jim, Phi	89	21%	1-11	9%	4-10	40%	0-4	0%	2	20%
Tiffee, Terry, Min	44	18%	0-3	0%	2-5	40%	0-1	0%	1	22%
Tomko, Brett, SF	13	23%	0-1	0%	0-0	-	0-1	0%	0	0%
Torrealba, Yorvit, SF-Sea	78	37%	2-4	50%	8-10	80%	1-1	100%	0	73%
Tracy, Chad, Ari	182	25%	8-21	38%	15-18	83%	0-1	0%	0	58%
Treanor, Matt, Fla	55	18%	1-4	25%	2-4	50%	0-0	-	0	38%
Tucker, Michael, SF-Phi	104	29%	2-14	14%	8-12	67%	0-1	0%	0	37%
Tyner, Jason, Min	28	29%	2-7	29%	0-1	0%	0-0	-	0	25%
Uribe, Juan, CWS	157	27%	7-21	33%	11-14	79%	0-3	0%	0	47%
Utley, Chase, Phi	232	28%	6-21	29%	14-21	67%	0-3	0%	0	44%
Valdez, Wilson, Sea-SD	42	21%	2-3	67%	1-3	33%	1-1	100%	0	57%
Valent, Eric, NYM	17	24%	0-2	0%	0-2	0%	0-0	-	0	0%
Valentin, Javier, Cin	82	27%	0-3	0%	5-8	63%	1-1	100%	0	50%
Valentin, Jose, LAD	63	24%	2-6	33%	2-5	40%	0-0	-	0	36%
Vargas, Jason, Fla	10	30%	0-1	0%	0-0	-	0-1	0%	0	0%
Varitek, Jason, Bos	198	24%	3-21	14%	10-23	43%	2-6	33%	2	30%
Vazquez, Javier, Ari	17	6%	1-1	100%	0-0	-	0-1	0%	0	50%
Vazquez, Ramon, Bos-Cle	32	22%	2-4	50%	2-5	40%	0-1	0%	0	40%
Victorino, Shane, Phi	10	30%	0-0	-	0-0	-	0-0	-	0	-
Vidro, Jose, Was	110	28%	2-16	13%	4-7	57%	1-5	20%	0	25%
Vizcaino, Jose, Hou	73	19%	2-3	67%	4-8	50%	0-1	0%	0	50%
Vizquel, Omar, SF	235	27%	8-31	26%	14-23	61%	1-8	13%	2	37%
Walker, Larry, StL	146	35%	8-22	36%	8-17	47%	5-7	71%	0	46%
Walker, Todd, ChC	156	24%	5-14	36%	3-7	43%	3-8	38%	0	38%
Ward, Daryle, Pit	141	24%	1-18	6%	5-12	42%	1-2	50%	1	22%
Watson, Brandon, Was	15	47%	1-2	50%	0-0	-	2-2	100%	0	75%
Watson, Matt, Oak	13	31%	1-3	33%	2-2	100%	0-1	0%	0	50%
Weaver, Jeff, LAD	23	26%	0-5	0%	1-3	33%	0-0	-	0	13%
Webb, Brandon, Ari	10	0%	0-2	0%	0-0	-	0-0	-	0	0%
Weeks, Rickie, Mil	138	31%	5-16	31%	11-16	69%	2-4	50%	5	50%
Wells, Kip, Pit	11	27%	2-3	67%	0-0	-	0-0	-	0	67%
Wells, Vernon, Tor	211	24%	9-25	36%	5-12	42%	2-4	50%	0	39%
Werth, Jayson, LAD	139	28%	3-13	23%	6-12	50%	1-2	50%	0	37%
White, Rondell, Det	152	24%	4-17	24%	6-18	33%	2-4	50%	0	31%
Widger, Chris, CWS	49	29%	5-8	63%	4-6	67%	0-0	-	2	64%
Wigginton, Ty, Pit	53	25%	0-6	0%	3-8	38%	0-1	0%	1	20%
Wilkerson, Brad, Was	227	29%	8-21	38%	16-26	62%	0-2	0%	1	49%
Williams, Bernie, NYY	184	22%	6-15	40%	13-22	59%	3-4	75%	0	54%
Williams, Gerald, NYM	17	47%	0-2	0%	1-2	50%	1-1	100%	0	40%
Williams, Glenn, Min	20	15%	1-4	25%	0-0	-	0-2	0%	0	17%
Willingham, Josh, Fla	12	25%	0-2	0%	2-3	67%	0-0	-	0	40%
Willis, Dontrelle, Fla	35	37%	1-4	25%	3-5	60%	0-2	0%	0	36%
Wilson, Craig, Pit	89	20%	3-5	60%	1-3	33%	0-1	0%	0	44%
Wilson, Jack, Pit	219	24%	9-20	45%	13-25	52%	2-4	50%	2	49%
Wilson, Preston, Col-Was	184	26%	6-24	25%	6-17	35%	6-6	100%	0	38%
Wilson, Vance, Det	49	31%	0-6	0%	2-5	40%	1-2	50%	0	23%
Winn, Randy, Sea-SF	246	26%	9-25	36%	10-18	56%	5-6	83%	0	49%
Womack, Tony, NYY	140	33%	5-15	33%	6-10	60%	3-6	50%	2	45%
Woodward, Chris, NYM	69	19%	1-7	14%	1-2	50%	1-2	50%	0	27%
Wright, David, NYM	253	28%	11-20	55%	12-18	67%	3-6	50%	0	59%
Wright, Jamey, Col	13	15%	0-0	-	1-2	50%	1-2	50%	0	50%
Youkilis, Kevin, Bos	42	24%	0-0	-	2-4	50%	1-1	100%	0	60%
Young, Dmitri, Det	157	25%	1-13	8%	8-9	89%	2-4	50%	0	42%
Young, Eric, SD	62	32%	1-4	25%	4-6	67%	1-3	33%	0	46%
Young, Michael, Tex	292	31%	5-31	16%	13-15	87%	6-10	60%	0	43%
Young, Walter, Bal	15	7%	0-0	-	0-0	-	0-0	-	0	-
Zambrano, Carlos, ChC	26	27%	1-5	20%	1-2	50%	1-1	100%	0	38%
Zaun, Gregg, Tor	183	27%	6-27	22%	5-12	42%	0-6	0%	0	24%
Zimmerman, Ryan, Was	30	20%	1-3	33%	1-1	100%	2-2	100%	0	67%

Pitchers Hitting, Fielding & Holding Runners,

and Hitters Pitching

Pitchers Hitting, Fielding and Holding Runners

Pitcher	2005 Hitting						Career Hitting										2005 Fielding and Holding Runners											
	Avg	AB	H	HR	RBI	SH	Avg	AB	H	2B	3B	HR	RBI	BB	SO	SH	G	Inn	PO	A	E	DP	Pct	SBA	CS	PCS	PPO	CS%
Accardo,Jeremy, SF	.500	2	1	0	0	0	.500	2	1	0	0	0	0	0	0	0	28	29.2	1	4	1		.833	2	0	0	0	.00
Acevedo,Jose, Col	.125	8	1	0	0	1	.079	101	8	2	0	0	4	5	61	12	36	64.0	8	7	0	1	1.000	3	3	1	0	1.00
Adams,Mike, Mil	-	0	0	0	0	0	-	0	0	0	0	0	0	0	0	0	13	13.1	1	0	0	0	1.000	1	0	0	0	.00
Adams,Terry, Phi	-	0	0	0	0	0	.051	78	4	1	0	0	2	7	41	12	16	13.1	0	2	0	0	1.000	1	0	0	0	.00
Adkins,Jon, CWS	-	0	0	0	0	0	-	0	0	0	0	0	0	0	0	0	8	5.1	0	2	0	0	1.000	0	0	0	0	-
Affeldt,Jeremy, KC	-	0	0	0	0	0	.333	6	2	0	0	0	2	1	1	0	49	49.2	1	6	1	0	.875	3	0	0	0	.00
Alfonseca,Ant, Fla	-	0	0	0	0	0	.154	13	2	0	0	0	2	0	8	1	33	27.1	3	4	0	2	1.000	3	1	0	0	.33
Almanza,Armando, Ari	-	0	0	0	0	0	.000	4	0	0	0	0	0	0	2	2	6	4.0	1	1	0	1	1.000	0	0	0	0	-
Almanzar,Carlos, Tex	-	0	0	0	0	0	.000	4	0	0	0	0	0	0	3	0	6	5.0	0	0	0	0	-	0	0	0	0	-
Alvarez,Abe, Bos	-	0	0	0	0	0	-	0	0	0	0	0	0	0	0	0	2	2.1	0	1	0	0	1.000	0	0	0	0	-
Alvarez,Wilson, LAD	.000	2	0	0	0	1	.133	98	13	0	0	0	1	4	35	5	21	24.0	0	2	0	0	1.000	2	0	0	0	.00
Anderson,Brian J, KC	-	0	0	0	0	0	.137	255	35	5	3	1	10	7	57	22	6	30.2	2	4	0	0	1.000	2	1	1	0	.50
Anderson,Jason, NYY	-	0	0	0	0	0	-	0	0	0	0	0	0	0	0	0	3	5.2	0	0	0	0	-	0	0	0	0	-
Anderson,Matt, Col	-	0	0	0	0	0	-	0	0	0	0	0	0	0	0	0	12	10.0	1	0	0	0	1.000	1	1	0	0	1.00
Aquino,Greg, Ari	-	0	0	0	0	0	.000	1	0	0	0	0	0	0	0	0	35	31.1	4	7	0	0	1.000	2	1	1	1	.50
Armas Jr.,Tony, Was	.125	32	4	0	0	1	.106	189	20	1	1	0	7	3	66	20	19	101.1	7	14	2	1	.913	7	4	1	0	.57
Arroyo,Bronson, Bos	.000	1	0	0	0	0	.073	55	4	2	0	0	1	1	33	3	35	205.1	21	21	2	1	.955	7	3	0	1	.43
Astacio,Ezeq, Hou	.143	21	3	0	0	2	.143	21	3	0	0	0	0	0	12	2	22	81.0	5	6	1	1	.917	4	1	0	1	.25
Astacio,Pedro, Tex-SD	.059	17	1	0	1	5	.131	651	85	7	1	0	28	5	248	82	22	126.2	6	20	0	0	1.000	12	4	1	0	.33
Atchison,Scott, Sea	-	0	0	0	0	0	-	0	0	0	0	0	0	0	0	0	6	6.2	1	0	0	0	1.000	2	1	0	0	.50
Ayala,Luis, Was	.333	3	1	0	0	1	.308	13	4	1	0	0	0	0	3	2	68	71.0	7	15	0	1	1.000	2	0	0	0	.00
Aybar,Manny, NYM	-	0	0	0	0	0	.186	70	13	0	0	1	5	2	28	4	22	25.1	1	1	0	0	1.000	3	0	0	0	.00
Backe,Brandon, Hou	.222	45	10	0	6	5	.246	61	15	2	2	1	12	4	20	8	26	149.1	8	19	0	1	1.000	8	4	0	0	.50
Baez,Danys, TB	-	0	0	0	0	0	.000	3	0	0	0	0	0	0	0	0	67	72.1	11	11	0	1	1.000	4	0	0	0	.00
Bajenaru,Jeff, CWS	-	0	0	0	0	0	-	0	0	0	0	0	0	0	0	0	4	4.1	0	0	0	0	-	0	0	0	0	-
Baker,Scott, Min	-	0	0	0	0	0	-	0	0	0	0	0	0	0	0	0	10	53.2	8	3	0	1	1.000	3	3	0	1	1.00
Baldwin,James, Bal-Tex	.000	1	0	0	0	0	.091	44	4	1	1	0	2	0	20	3	28	56.2	4	4	0	1	1.000	2	0	0	0	.00
Bartosh,Cliff, ChC	1.000	1	1	0	0	0	1.000	1	1	0	0	0	0	0	0	0	19	19.2	1	0	0	1	1.000	1	0	0	0	.00
Batista,Miguel, Tor	-	0	0	0	0	0	.094	224	21	4	0	2	5	9	129	14	71	74.2	2	6	1	0	.889	2	0	0	0	.00
Bauer,Rick, Bal	-	0	0	0	0	0	-	0	0	0	0	0	0	0	0	0	5	8.1	0	0	0	0	-	0	0	0	0	-
Bautista,Denny, KC	-	0	0	0	0	0	-	0	0	0	0	0	0	0	0	0	7	35.2	3	9	0	0	1.000	2	0	0	0	.00
Bayliss,Jonah, KC	-	0	0	0	0	0	-	0	0	0	0	0	0	0	0	0	11	11.2	0	0	0	0	-	1	0	0	0	.00
Bazardo,Yorman, Fla	.000	1	0	0	0	0	.000	1	0	0	0	0	0	0	1	0	1	1.2	0	0	0	0	-	1	0	0	0	.00
Bean,Colter, NYY	-	0	0	0	0	0	-	0	0	0	0	0	0	0	0	0	1	2.0	0	1	0	0	1.000	0	0	0	0	-
Beckett,Josh, Fla	.153	59	9	1	6	4	.139	187	26	8	0	1	11	10	71	25	29	178.2	6	31	1	1	.974	13	7	1	0	.54
Bedard,Erik, Bal	-	0	0	0	0	0	.000	4	0	0	0	0	0	0	1	3	24	141.2	6	22	1	3	.966	12	4	2	0	.33
Beimel,Joe, TB	-	0	0	0	0	0	.244	41	10	1	0	0	1	2	15	6	7	11.0	1	2	0	0	1.000	0	0	0	0	.00
Belisle,Matt, Cin	.143	7	1	0	0	1	.125	8	1	0	0	0	0	0	4	1	60	85.2	6	10	2	1	.889	9	2	0	0	.22
Bell,Heath, NYM	.000	3	0	0	0	0	.000	4	0	0	0	0	0	0	1	0	42	46.2	2	8	0	2	1.000	4	0	0	0	.00
Bell,Rob, TB	-	0	0	0	0	0	.083	60	5	2	0	0	0	3	34	5	8	25.0	5	1	1	0	.857	3	0	0	0	.00
Benitez,Armando, SF	-	0	0	0	0	0	.000	8	0	0	0	0	0	2	4	0	30	30.0	2	2	1	0	.800	3	2	0	0	.67
Benoit,Joaquin, Tex	.000	1	0	0	0	0	.000	9	0	0	0	0	0	0	4	0	32	87.0	2	7	0	0	1.000	7	2	0	0	.29
Benson,Kris, NYM	.184	49	9	0	6	6	.130	307	40	7	0	0	20	15	123	46	28	174.1	7	29	0	2	1.000	14	0	0	0	.00
Bentz,Chad, Fla	-	0	0	0	0	0	.500	2	1	0	0	0	0	0	0	0	4	2.0	0	0	0	0	-	0	0	0	0	-
Bergmann,Jason, Was	.333	3	1	0	0	0	.333	3	1	0	0	0	0	1	0	0	15	19.2	1	2	0	0	1.000	4	1	0	0	.25
Bernero,Adam, Atl	1.000	1	1	0	0	1	.063	16	1	0	0	0	0	0	9	3	36	47.0	3	4	1	0	.875	5	0	0	0	.00
Betancourt,Raf, Cle	-	0	0	0	0	0	-	0	0	0	0	0	0	0	0	0	54	67.2	3	3	0	0	1.000	7	4	0	0	.57
Blanton,Joe, Oak	.333	3	1	0	0	1	.333	3	1	0	0	0	0	0	0	1	33	201.1	13	20	1	1	.971	9	1	1	1	.11
Bonderman,Jer, Det	.000	6	0	0	0	0	.000	15	0	0	0	0	0	0	8	0	29	189.0	18	11	5	2	.853	9	5	0	0	.56
Booker,Chris, Cin	-	0	0	0	0	0	-	0	0	0	0	0	0	0	0	0	3	2.0	0	0	0	0	-	1	0	0	0	.00
Bootcheck,Chris, LAA	-	0	0	0	0	0	-	0	0	0	0	0	0	0	0	0	5	18.2	1	3	1	0	.800	2	1	0	0	.50
Borowski,Joe, ChC-TB	-	0	0	0	0	0	.222	9	2	0	0	0	0	0	7	1	43	46.1	5	3	0	0	1.000	8	4	0	0	.50
Bottalico,Ricky, Mil	-	0	0	0	0	0	.118	17	2	2	0	0	1	0	8	1	40	41.2	2	6	1	1	.889	3	2	0	0	.67
Bowyer,Travis, Min	-	0	0	0	0	0	-	0	0	0	0	0	0	0	0	0	8	9.2	1	0	0	1	1.000	2	0	0	0	.00
Boyer,Blaine, Atl	-	0	0	0	0	0	-	0	0	0	0	0	0	0	0	0	43	37.2	1	3	0	0	1.000	2	1	0	0	.50
Bradford,Chad, Bos	-	0	0	0	0	0	-	0	0	0	0	0	0	0	0	0	31	23.1	1	6	0	0	1.000	5	0	0	0	.00
Brazelton,Dewon, TB	-	0	0	0	0	0	.000	2	0	0	0	0	0	0	0	0	20	71.0	3	14	2	1	.895	14	5	3	0	.36
Brazoban,Yhency, LAD	.000	2	0	0	0	0	.000	3	0	0	0	0	0	0	2	0	74	72.2	4	10	0	0	1.000	10	2	0	0	.20
Breslow,Craig, SD	.000	1	0	0	0	0	.000	1	0	0	0	0	0	0	1	0	14	16.1	0	0	1	0	.000	0	0	0	0	-
Brito,Eude, Phi	.143	7	1	0	0	0	.143	7	1	0	0	0	0	0	2	0	6	22.0	1	7	0	0	1.000	0	0	0	0	-
Brocail,Doug, Tex	-	0	0	0	0	0	-	0	0	0	0	0	0	0	0	0	61	71.1	9	13	2	1	.917	4	0	0	0	.00
Brooks,Frank, Atl	-	0	0	0	0	0	.000	1	0	0	0	0	0	0	0	0	1	0.1	0	0	0	0	-	1	1	0	0	1.00
Brower,Jim, SF-Atl	.000	2	0	0	0	0	.203	59	12	1	0	0	4	1	20	4	69	60.1	4	8	0	0	1.000	5	2	0	0	.40
Brown,Kevin, NYY	.500	2	1	0	0	0	.129	495	64	10	0	2	29	19	187	54	13	73.1	4	8	1	1	.923	5	0	0	0	.09
Broxton,Jon, LAD	-	0	0	0	0	0	-	0	0	0	0	0	0	0	0	0	14	13.2	0	0	0	0	-	5	0	0	0	.00
Bruney,Brian, Ari	.000	1	0	0	0	0	.000	1	0	0	0	0	0	0	0	0	47	46.0	1	7	0	1	1.000	2	0	0	0	.00
Buehrle,Mark, CWS	.000	3	0	0	0	0	.095	21	2	0	0	0	1	1	12	2	33	236.2	13	45	2	2	.967	11	3	2	3	.27
Bukvich,Ryan, Tex	-	0	0	0	0	0	-	0	0	0	0	0	0	0	0	0	4	4.0	0	1	0	0	1.000	0	0	0	0	-
Bulger,Jason, Ari	-	0	0	0	0	0	-	0	0	0	0	0	0	0	0	0	9	10.0	1	2	0	0	1.000	0	0	0	0	-
Bullington,Bryan, Pit	-	0	0	0	0	0	-	0	0	0	0	0	0	0	0	0	1	1.1	0	0	0	0	-	0	0	0	0	-
Bump,Nate, Fla	.200	5	1	0	0	1	.100	10	1	0	0	0	0	0	6	2	31	38.0	3	8	1	1	.917	3	1	0	1	.33
Burgos,Ambiorix, KC	-	0	0	0	0	0	-	0	0	0	0	0	0	0	0	0	59	63.1	1	1	0	0	1.000	5	3	0	0	.60

Pitchers Hitting, Fielding and Holding Runners

Pitcher	2005 Hitting						Career Hitting										2005 Fielding and Holding Runners											
	Avg	AB	H	HR	RBI	SH	Avg	AB	H	2B	3B	HR	RBI	BB	SO	SH	G	Inn	PO	A	E	DP	Pct	SBA	CS	PCS	PPO	CS%
Burnett,A.J., Fla	.147	68	10	1	2	9	.134	253	34	6	3	3	9	12	123	33	32	209.0	11	18	2	1	.935	30	6	0	1	.20
Burns,Mike, Hou	-	0	0	0	0	0	-	0	0	0	0	0	0	0	0	0	27	31.0	7	3	0	0	1.000	0	0	0	0	-
Bush,Dave, Tor	-	0	0	0	0	0	.000	2	0	0	0	0	0	0	0	0	25	136.1	18	20	0	1	1.000	20	4	0	0	.20
Byrd,Paul, LAA	.250	4	1	0	0	0	.159	145	23	0	0	0	10	12	37	25	31	204.1	16	20	2	0	.947	19	6	0	0	.32
Byrdak,Tim, Bal	-	0	0	0	0	0	-	0	0	0	0	0	0	0	0	0	41	26.2	0	4	0	0	1.000	1	0	0	0	.00
Cabrera,Daniel, Bal	.000	1	0	0	0	0	.000	5	0	0	0	0	0	0	5	0	29	161.1	11	12	1	0	.958	23	7	0	0	.30
Cabrera,Fern, Cle	-	0	0	0	0	0	-	0	0	0	0	0	0	0	0	0	15	30.2	1	1	0	0	1.000	3	0	0	0	.00
Cain,Matt, SF	.067	15	1	0	0	1	.067	15	1	1	0	0	0	0	6	1	7	46.1	1	2	1	0	.750	2	1	0	0	.50
Calero,Kiko, Oak	.000	1	0	0	0	0	.167	6	1	0	0	0	1	2	2	0	58	55.2	2	5	0	1.000	7	0	0	0	.00
Cali,Carmen, StL	-	0	0	0	0	0	-	0	0	0	0	0	0	0	0	0	6	6.0	0	0	0	-	0	0	0	0	-
Camp,Shawn, KC	-	0	0	0	0	0	-	0	0	0	0	0	0	0	0	0	29	49.0	3	7	0	0	1.000	6	3	0	1	.50
Campillo,Jorge, Sea	-	0	0	0	0	0	-	0	0	0	0	0	0	0	0	0	2	2.0	0	0	0	-	0	0	0	0	-
Capellan,Jose, Mil	-	0	0	0	0	0	.000	2	0	0	0	0	0	0	0	1	0	17	15.2	1	0	0	1.000	3	1	0	0	.33
Capps,Matt, Pit	-	0	0	0	0	0	-	0	0	0	0	0	0	0	0	0	4	4.0	0	2	0	0	1.000	2	0	0	1	.00
Capuano,Chris, Mil	.169	71	12	0	9	5	.165	109	18	5	0	0	11	3	48	5	35	219.0	7	37	4	1	.917	11	9	6	6	.82
Carlyle,Buddy, LAD	-	0	0	0	0	0	-	0	0	0	0	0	0	0	0	0	10	14.0	1	1	0	0	1.000	0	0	0	0	-
Carpenter,Chris, StL	.065	77	5	0	2	10	.080	150	12	2	0	0	3	7	49	16	33	241.2	15	40	1	2	.982	6	5	1	1	.83
Carrara,Giov, LAD	.000	1	0	0	0	0	.097	31	3	0	0	0	1	11	4	72	75.2	4	20	2	3	.923	5	1	0	1	.20
Carrasco,D.J., KC	.000	7	0	0	0	1	.000	9	0	0	0	0	0	0	2	1	35	114.2	16	16	0	0	1.000	8	6	0	0	.75
Carrasco,Hector, Was	.000	8	0	0	0	2	.038	26	1	0	0	0	0	19	2	64	88.1	5	10	0	0	1.000	4	0	0	2	.00
Carter,Lance, TB	-	0	0	0	0	0	-	0	0	0	0	0	0	0	0	0	39	57.0	1	7	0	1	1.000	2	2	0	1	1.00
Carvajal,Marcos, Col	.250	4	1	0	2	0	.250	4	1	0	0	0	2	0	3	0	39	53.0	5	8	0	0	1.000	4	0	0	0	.00
Cassidy,Scott, Bos-SD	.000	1	0	0	0	0	.000	1	0	0	0	0	0	1	1	0	11	13.0	1	5	0	1	1.000	2	2	0	1	1.00
Castillo,Frank, Fla	.000	1	0	0	0	0	.109	338	37	0	0	0	13	13	111	42	1	4.1	0	0	0	-	2	0	0	0	.00
Cerda,Jaime, KC	-	0	0	0	0	0	.000	2	0	0	0	0	0	0	0	0	20	19.0	0	1	0	0	1.000	0	0	0	0	-
Chacin,Gustavo, Tor	.000	7	0	0	0	1	.000	7	0	0	0	0	0	0	2	1	34	203.0	10	25	2	0	.946	18	10	4	1	.56
Chacon,Shawn, Col-NYY	.150	20	3	0	1	3	.155	148	23	3	0	1	9	2	60	14	27	151.2	9	20	1	2	.967	10	3	1	2	.30
Chen,Bruce, Bal	.333	3	1	0	0	0	.123	114	14	1	0	0	3	2	53	17	34	197.1	10	25	2	1	.946	25	8	4	0	.32
Childers,Matt, Atl	-	0	0	0	0	0	.000	1	0	0	0	0	0	0	0	0	3	4.0	1	0	0	0	1.000	0	0	0	0	-
Choate,Randy, Ari	-	0	0	0	0	0	.000	5	0	0	0	0	0	0	3	0	8	7.0	1	2	1	0	.750	1	0	0	0	.00
Christiansen,J, SF-LAA	-	0	0	0	0	0	.100	10	1	0	0	0	1	0	7	1	68	45.2	3	5	2	0	.800	3	3	0	1	1.00
Chulk,Vinnie, Tor	-	0	0	0	0	0	-	0	0	0	0	0	0	0	0	0	62	72.0	4	13	2	2	.895	4	0	0	1	.00
Claussen,Bran, Cin	.091	55	5	0	0	6	.103	78	8	0	0	1	4	29	8	29	166.2	5	19	1	1	.960	13	1	0	1	.08
Clemens,Roger, Hou	.207	58	12	0	4	5	.187	150	28	5	0	12	10	50	11	32	211.1	8	36	1	1	.978	12	4	1	1	.33
Clement,Matt, Bos	.000	3	0	0	0	0	.093	345	32	5	1	0	12	14	172	43	32	191.0	22	20	1	4	.977	8	2	0	0	.25
Coffey,Todd, Cin	.000	3	0	0	0	0	.000	3	0	0	0	0	0	0	3	0	57	58.0	1	7	0	0	1.000	5	2	0	0	.40
Colome,Jesus, TB	-	0	0	0	0	0	.000	1	0	0	0	0	0	0	1	0	36	45.1	5	5	1	0	.909	6	1	0	0	.17
Colon,Bartolo, LAA	.333	3	1	0	1	0	.127	79	10	0	0	0	5	0	46	4	33	222.2	8	16	0	0	1.000	6	4	0	0	.67
Colon,Roman, Atl-Det	.000	7	0	0	0	1	.000	7	0	0	0	0	0	0	5	1	35	69.1	5	3	0	0	1.000	7	1	0	0	.14
Contreras,Jose, CWS	.000	3	0	0	0	0	.000	14	0	0	0	0	0	1	9	0	32	204.2	11	25	2	1	.947	30	2	0	2	.07
Cook,Aaron, Col	.167	30	5	0	0	5	.144	104	15	0	1	0	5	4	32	14	13	83.1	6	13	2	1	.905	3	0	0	0	.00
Cooper,Brian, SF	.500	2	1	0	0	0	.111	9	1	0	0	0	0	0	4	0	8	17.2	0	0	0	-	0	0	0	0	-
Corcoran,Tim, TB	-	0	0	0	0	0	-	0	0	0	0	0	0	0	0	0	10	22.2	1	1	0	0	1.000	1	0	0	0	.00
Cordero,Chad, Was	-	0	0	0	0	0	.000	2	0	0	0	0	0	0	2	2	74	74.1	2	4	2	0	.750	3	2	0	0	.67
Cordero,Franc, Tex	-	0	0	0	0	0	.000	1	0	0	0	0	0	0	0	1	0	69	69.0	2	10	0	1	1.000	4	0	0	0	.00
Cormier,Lance, Ari	.333	6	2	0	1	1	.286	14	4	1	0	0	2	1	3	2	67	79.1	3	11	1	1	.933	7	3	1	3	.43
Cormier,Rheal, Phi	.000	1	0	0	0	2	.188	192	36	4	1	0	12	5	45	30	57	47.1	4	10	0	1	1.000	2	0	0	0	.00
Correia,Kevin, SF	.071	14	1	0	0	0	.133	30	4	1	0	0	2	4	12	2	16	58.1	1	3	0	0	1.000	6	2	0	0	.33
Cortes,David, Col	.000	2	0	0	0	0	.000	2	0	0	0	0	0	0	0	0	50	52.2	8	6	0	1	1.000	6	1	0	0	.17
Cotts,Neal, CWS	-	0	0	0	0	0	1.000	1	1	1	0	0	0	0	0	0	69	60.1	2	14	0	2	1.000	3	1	1	0	.33
Crain,Jesse, Min	-	0	0	0	0	0	-	0	0	0	0	0	0	0	0	0	75	79.2	11	17	1	3	.966	3	0	0	0	.00
Creek,Doug, Det	-	0	0	0	0	0	.200	5	1	0	0	0	0	0	3	3	20	22.1	2	2	1	0	.800	1	1	1	0	1.00
Crowell,Jim, Fla	-	0	0	0	0	0	-	0	0	0	0	0	0	0	0	0	4	3.1	0	0	0	-	0	0	0	0	-
Cruz,Juan, Oak	-	0	0	0	0	0	.170	47	8	1	1	0	2	1	17	5	28	32.2	2	1	0	0	1.000	5	1	0	0	.20
Darensbourg,Vic, Det	-	0	0	0	0	0	.111	18	2	0	0	0	0	2	6	1	22	22.1	4	4	1	1	.889	1	0	0	0	.00
Davies,Kyle, Atl	.200	15	3	0	4	10	.200	15	3	0	0	0	4	2	3	10	21	87.2	7	9	1	2	.941	4	4	2	0	1.00
Davis,Doug, Mil	.137	73	10	0	3	2	.081	161	13	3	1	0	3	2	89	10	35	222.2	14	30	2	0	.957	18	7	4	1	.39
Davis,Jason, Cle	.000	2	0	0	0	1	.111	9	1	0	0	1	1	0	5	2	11	40.1	3	1	0	1	1.000	8	1	0	0	.13
Davis,Kane, Mil	-	0	0	0	0	0	.000	6	0	0	0	0	0	0	6	0	15	16.2	0	4	0	0	1.000	2	1	0	0	.50
Day,Zach, Was-Col	.182	11	2	0	0	1	.065	93	6	0	0	1	3	2	46	7	17	47.1	6	8	0	1	1.000	3	1	0	0	.33
de la Rosa,Jor, Mil	-	0	0	0	0	0	.000	6	0	0	0	0	0	0	6	1	38	42.1	1	6	1	0	.875	4	0	0	0	.00
de los Santos,V, Fla	-	0	0	0	0	0	.000	9	0	0	0	0	0	1	6	2	27	22.0	0	2	0	0	1.000	2	0	0	0	.00
DeJean,Mike, NYM-Col	-	0	0	0	0	0	.059	17	1	1	0	0	0	0	10	1	66	62.1	5	11	1	0	.941	4	0	0	0	.00
Delcarmen,Manny, Bos	-	0	0	0	0	0	-	0	0	0	0	0	0	0	0	0	10	9.0	1	1	0	0	1.000	0	0	0	0	-
Demaria,Chris, KC	-	0	0	0	0	0	-	0	0	0	0	0	0	0	0	0	8	9.0	0	1	0	1	1.000	0	0	0	0	-
Dempster,Ryan, ChC	.071	14	1	0	0	0	.077	311	24	5	1	0	7	6	133	32	63	92.0	3	17	0	1	1.000	8	2	0	0	.25
DePaula,Jorge, NYY	-	0	0	0	0	0	-	0	0	0	0	0	0	0	0	0	3	6.2	0	1	0	0	1.000	0	0	0	0	-
Dessens,Elmer, LAD	.000	10	0	0	0	0	.167	233	39	4	1	0	16	20	63	37	28	65.2	5	12	0	2	1.000	6	1	0	0	.17
Devine,Joey, Atl	.000	1	0	0	0	0	.000	1	0	0	0	0	0	0	1	0	5	5.0	0	1	0	0	1.000	1	0	0	0	.00
Dickey,R.A., Tex	-	0	0	0	0	0	1.000	1	1	0	0	0	0	0	0	0	9	29.2	1	9	0	1	1.000	3	0	0	0	.00
DiNardo,Lenny, Bos	-	0	0	0	0	0	-	0	0	0	0	0	0	0	0	0	8	14.2	0	1	0	0	1.000	1	0	0	0	.00
Dingman,Craig, Det	-	0	0	0	0	0	-	0	0	0	0	0	0	0	0	0	34	32.0	1	1	1	0	.667	3	0	0	0	.00
Dohmann,Scott, Col	.000	1	0	0	0	0	.000	2	0	0	0	0	0	0	1	1	32	31.0	3	0	1	0	.750	4	0	0	0	.00
Dominguez,Juan, Tex	-	0	0	0	0	0	-	0	0	0	0	0	0	0	0	0	22	70.1	4	3	0	0	1.000	8	1	0	0	.13
Donnelly,Brend, LAA	.000	1	0	0	0	0	.000	1	0	0	0	0	0	0	0	0	66	65.1	3	4	1	0	.875	6	3	0	0	.50

291

Pitchers Hitting, Fielding and Holding Runners

Pitcher	2005 Hitting						Career Hitting										2005 Fielding and Holding Runners											
	Avg	AB	H	HR	RBI	SH	Avg	AB	H	2B	3B	HR	RBI	BB	SO	SH	G	Inn	PO	A	E	DP	Pct	SBA	CS	PCS	PPO	CS%
Dotel,Octavio, Oak	-	0	0	0	0	0	.068	74	5	0	0	0	1	5	42	9	15	15.1	0	1	1	0	.500	4	0	0	0	.00
Douglass,Sean, Det	.000	2	0	0	0	0	.000	2	0	0	0	0	0	0	0	0	18	87.1	8	7	0	1	1.000	6	4	1	0	.67
Downs,Scott, Tor	-	0	0	0	0	0	.068	44	3	0	0	0	1	3	17	10	26	94.0	9	14	1	2	.958	2	2	0	0	1.00
Drese,Ryan, Tex-Was	.067	15	1	0	0	5	.136	22	3	1	0	0	0	1	13	6	23	129.1	13	14	3	1	.900	13	9	2	0	.69
Driskill,Travis, Hou	-	0	0	0	0	0	.000	5	0	0	0	0	0	1	4	0	1	1.0	0	0	0	0	-	0	0	0	0	-
DuBose,Eric, Bal	-	0	0	0	0	0	.000	2	0	0	0	0	0	0	2	0	15	29.1	1	4	0	0	1.000	2	1	0	0	.50
Duchscherer,J, Oak	-	0	0	0	0	0	-	0	0	0	0	0	0	0	0	0	65	85.2	1	14	3	3	.833	8	2	0	1	.25
Duckworth,Br, Hou	.667	3	2	0	0	0	.211	109	23	3	0	0	8	10	22	9	7	16.1	0	0	1	0	1.000	1	1	0	0	1.00
Duke,Zach, Pit	.143	28	4	0	1	0	.143	28	4	0	0	0	1	2	10	0	14	84.2	4	15	0	2	1.000	4	3	2	0	.75
Eaton,Adam, SD	.174	46	8	0	2	3	.191	251	48	13	1	2	19	24	85	17	24	128.2	7	16	1	1	.958	9	1	0	0	.11
Eischen,Joey, Was	.333	3	1	0	0	1	.192	26	5	1	0	0	0	1	10	2	57	36.1	2	6	1	0	.889	2	0	0	0	.00
Elarton,Scott, Cle	.000	2	0	0	0	0	.137	161	22	2	0	0	3	5	52	27	31	181.2	7	11	2	2	.900	8	4	0	1	.50
Eldred,Cal, StL	.000	2	0	0	0	0	.111	72	8	2	0	0	4	6	39	11	31	37.0	2	6	0	0	1.000	1	1	0	0	.50
Embree,Alan, Bos-NYY	-	0	0	0	0	0	.000	2	0	0	0	0	0	1	1	0	67	52.0	2	8	1	0	.909	7	1	0	0	.14
Erickson,Scott, LAD	.154	13	2	0	0	1	.114	35	4	1	0	0	1	4	15	5	19	55.1	4	15	0	1	1.000	1	0	0	0	.00
Escobar,Kelvim, LAA	.000	1	0	0	0	1	.059	17	1	0	0	0	1	0	8	1	16	59.2	5	4	1	0	.900	8	3	0	0	.38
Esposito,Mike, Col	.200	5	1	0	0	0	.200	5	1	0	0	0	0	0	0	1	3	14.2	1	2	0	0	1.000	1	1	0	0	1.00
Estes,Shawn, Ari	.069	29	2	0	0	2	.158	488	77	14	2	4	28	14	163	73	21	123.2	15	25	2	1	.952	5	1	1	0	.20
Etherton,Seth, Oak	-	0	0	0	0	0	.111	9	1	0	0	0	0	1	2	3	3	17.2	1	0	0	0	1.000	1	0	0	0	.00
Eveland,Dana, Mil	.000	1	0	0	0	0	.000	1	0	0	0	0	0	0	0	1	27	31.2	3	2	1	1	.833	0	0	0	0	
Eyre,Scott, SF	.000	2	0	0	0	0	.182	11	2	0	0	0	0	1	6	0	86	68.1	0	6	1	1	.857	3	2	1	0	.67
Falkenborg,Br, SD	-	0	0	0	0	0	.000	2	0	0	0	0	0	1	2	0	10	11.0	0	0	0	0	-	0	0	0	0	
Farnsworth,Kyle, Det-Atl	-	0	0	0	0	0	.074	54	4	1	0	0	3	2	18	8	72	70.0	4	7	1	1	.917	10	2	0	0	.20
Fassero,Jeff, SF	.000	13	0	0	0	1	.081	272	22	2	1	0	6	18	150	44	48	91.0	7	24	0	2	1.000	14	8	5	0	.57
Feldman,Scott, Tex	-	0	0	0	0	0	-	0	0	0	0	0	0	0	0	0	8	9.1	0	2	0	0	1.000	1	1	0	0	1.00
Field,Nate, KC	-	0	0	0	0	0	-	0	0	0	0	0	0	0	0	0	7	6.2	1	0	0	0	1.000	1	1	0	0	1.00
Flores,Randy, StL	.000	1	0	0	0	0	.000	7	0	0	0	0	0	0	4	0	50	41.2	2	2	1	0	.800	3	1	1	0	.33
Flores,Ron, Oak	-	0	0	0	0	0	-	0	0	0	0	0	0	0	0	0	11	8.2	1	0	0	0	1.000	0	0	0	0	
Floyd,Gavin, Phi	.111	9	1	0	0	0	.053	19	1	0	0	0	0	0	10	0	7	26.0	3	2	0	0	1.000	2	0	0	0	.00
Fogg,Josh, Pit	.106	47	5	0	3	6	.120	200	24	2	0	0	8	7	64	26	34	169.1	11	26	3	1	.925	16	7	1	0	.44
Foppert,Jesse, SF	-	0	0	0	0	0	.081	37	3	1	1	0	1	0	19	0	3	10.1	1	1	0	0	1.000	3	0	0	0	.00
Fossum,Casey, TB	.000	2	0	0	0	0	.091	44	4	0	0	0	0	1	16	4	36	162.2	11	16	1	2	.964	14	4	1	0	.29
Foster,John, Atl	-	0	0	0	0	0	-	0	0	0	0	0	0	0	0	0	62	34.2	1	7	0	0	1.000	3	0	0	0	.00
Foulke,Keith, Bos	-	0	0	0	0	0	.125	16	2	0	0	0	0	0	5	2	43	45.2	0	3	0	0	1.000	3	0	0	0	.00
Fox,Chad, ChC	-	0	0	0	0	0	.000	7	0	0	0	0	0	0	3	1	11	8.0	1	0	0	0	1.000	0	0	0	0	-
Francis,Jeff, Col	.103	58	6	0	4	6	.088	68	6	2	0	0	4	7	31	10	33	183.2	5	20	0	1	1.000	30	11	5	0	.37
Franco,John, Hou	-	0	0	0	0	0	.088	34	3	0	0	0	1	0	14	3	31	15.0	0	0	0	0	-	1	1	0	0	.50
Franklin,Ryan, Sea	.000	4	0	0	0	0	.091	11	1	0	0	0	0	2	3	2	32	190.2	14	13	0	0	1.000	12	5	0	2	.42
Franklin,Wayne, NYY	-	0	0	0	0	0	.157	70	11	1	0	0	5	3	22	12	13	12.2	0	1	0	0	1.000	1	0	0	0	.00
Frasor,Jason, Tor	-	0	0	0	0	0	-	0	0	0	0	0	0	0	0	0	67	74.2	6	7	1	1	.929	8	3	0	0	.38
Fuentes,Brian, Col	-	0	0	0	0	0	.000	1	0	0	0	0	0	0	0	0	78	74.1	0	8	0	0	1.000	3	1	1	0	.33
Fultz,Aaron, Phi	.333	3	1	0	0	0	.333	15	5	0	0	0	0	0	3	1	62	72.1	7	12	0	2	1.000	3	2	0	0	.67
Gagne,Eric, LAD	-	0	0	0	0	0	.140	86	12	2	1	0	3	1	25	12	14	13.1	2	4	0	0	1.000	2	0	0	0	.00
Gallo,Mike, Hou	-	0	0	0	0	0	.000	3	0	0	0	0	0	0	0	0	36	20.1	0	4	0	1	1.000	3	0	0	0	.00
Garcia,Freddy, CWS	.000	7	0	0	0	2	.194	36	7	1	0	0	2	0	10	10	33	228.0	18	29	0	4	1.000	24	5	0	1	.21
Garcia,Jairo, Oak	-	0	0	0	0	0	-	0	0	0	0	0	0	0	0	0	3	3.0	0	0	0	0	-	0	0	0	0	
Gardner,Lee, TB	-	0	0	0	0	0	-	0	0	0	0	0	0	0	0	0	5	7.1	0	1	0	0	1.000	0	0	0	0	-
Garland,Jon, CWS	.500	2	1	0	1	0	.167	12	2	0	0	0	1	1	2	3	32	221.0	12	35	1	1	.979	9	6	0	0	.67
Gassner,Dave, Min	-	0	0	0	0	0	-	0	0	0	0	0	0	0	0	0	2	7.2	0	1	1	0	.500	1	1	1	0	1.00
Gaudin,Chad, Tor	-	0	0	0	0	0	.000	1	0	0	0	0	0	0	0	0	5	13.0	0	4	0	0	1.000	2	0	0	1	.00
Geary,Geoff, Phi	.167	6	1	0	0	0	.143	7	1	0	0	0	0	0	4	0	40	58.0	3	9	1	0	.923	5	0	0	0	.00
German,Franklyn, Det	-	0	0	0	0	0	.000	1	0	0	0	0	0	0	1	0	58	59.0	4	3	0	0	1.000	6	0	0	0	.00
Ginter,Matt, Det	-	0	0	0	0	0	.214	14	3	1	0	0	1	2	5	3	14	35.0	4	4	0	0	1.000	6	4	1	0	.67
Glavine,Tom, NYM	.203	64	13	0	3	5	.187	1195	223	23	2	1	83	85	301	191	33	211.1	12	43	0	5	1.000	9	5	2	0	.56
Glover,Gary, Mil	.100	20	2	0	0	3	.071	28	2	0	0	0	1	2	14	3	15	64.2	3	4	1	0	.875	12	5	1	0	.42
Glynn,Ryan, Oak	.000	1	0	0	0	0	.000	1	0	0	0	0	0	0	1	0	5	17.0	0	4	0	0	1.000	1	0	0	0	.00
Gobble,Jimmy, KC	-	0	0	0	0	0	.000	2	0	0	0	0	0	0	1	1	28	53.2	2	4	2	1	.750	6	1	0	0	.17
Gonzalez,Edgar, Ari	-	0	0	0	0	0	.176	17	3	0	0	0	0	0	2	2	1	0.1	0	0	0	0	-	0	0	0	0	
Gonzalez,Jeremi, Bos	-	0	0	0	0	0	.128	78	10	1	0	0	3	3	26	16	28	56.0	2	6	0	0	1.000	9	0	0	1	.00
Gonzalez,Mike, Pit	-	0	0	0	0	0	1.000	1	1	1	0	0	2	0	0	0	51	50.0	1	6	0	1	1.000	3	1	0	0	.33
Good,Andy, Det	-	0	0	0	0	0	.095	21	2	0	0	0	2	0	7	4	2	5.0	0	0	0	0	-	0	0	0	0	
Gordon,Tom, NYY	-	0	0	0	0	0	.000	2	0	0	0	0	0	0	0	0	79	80.2	7	13	1	0	.952	4	1	0	0	.25
Gorzelanny,Tom, Pit	.000	1	0	0	0	1	.000	1	0	0	0	0	0	0	1	1	3	6.0	2	1	0	0	1.000	0	0	0	0	
Gosling,Mike, Ari	.000	6	0	0	0	0	.000	12	0	0	0	0	0	1	8	2	13	32.1	1	4	2	2	.714	2	1	0	0	.50
Grabow,John, Pit	-	0	0	0	0	0	.000	1	0	0	0	0	0	0	0	0	63	52.0	0	7	1	1	.875	3	1	1	0	.33
Graman,Alex, NYY	-	0	0	0	0	0	-	0	0	0	0	0	0	0	0	0	2	1.1	0	0	0	0	-	0	0	0	0	
Graves,Danny, Cin-NYM	-	0	0	0	0	0	.105	76	8	0	0	2	3	1	25	5	40	38.2	1	7	2	0	.800	6	0	0	0	
Gregg,Kevin, LAA	-	0	0	0	0	0	-	0	0	0	0	0	0	0	0	0	33	64.1	4	6	0	0	1.000	5	0	0	0	.00
Greinke,Zack, KC	.500	2	1	1	1	0	.250	4	1	0	0	1	1	0	1	0	33	183.0	19	24	1	2	.977	8	3	0	1	.38
Greisinger,Seth, Atl	.000	2	0	0	0	0	.167	6	1	0	0	0	1	0	1	0	1	5.0	0	0	0	0	-	0	0	0	0	
Grilli,Jason, Det	-	0	0	0	0	0	-	0	0	0	0	0	0	0	0	0	3	16.0	2	3	0	0	1.000	2	1	0	0	.50
Grimsley,Jason, Bal	-	0	0	0	0	0	.103	39	4	0	0	0	2	5	11	5	22	22.0	0	2	0	0	1.000	3	1	0	0	.33
Groom,Buddy, NYY-Ari	-	0	0	0	0	0	-	0	0	0	0	0	0	0	0	0	47	41.0	1	3	1	0	.800	3	1	1	0	.33
Gryboski,Kevin, Atl-Tex	-	0	0	0	0	0	.000	1	0	0	0	0	0	0	0	1	42	31.0	5	2	0	0	1.000	0	0	0	0	
Guardado,Eddie, Sea	-	0	0	0	0	0	.000	1	0	0	0	0	0	0	0	0	58	56.1	2	4	1	0	.857	5	1	0	0	.20

Pitchers Hitting, Fielding and Holding Runners

Pitcher	2005 Hitting Avg	AB	H	HR	RBI	SH	Career Avg	AB	H	2B	3B	HR	RBI	BB	SO	SH	G	Inn	PO	A	E	DP	Pct	SBA	CS	PCS	PPO	CS%
Guerrier,Matt, Min	.000	1	0	0	0	0	.000	2	0	0	0	0	0	0	1	0	43	71.2	9	15	0	0	1.000	5	3	0	1	.60
Guthrie,Jeremy, Cle		0	0	0	0	0		0	0	0	0	0	0	0	0	0	1	6.0	2	1	0	1	1.000	0	0	0	0	-
Halama,John, Bos-Was	.200	5	1	0	0	0	.115	26	3	1	0	0	0	3	12	3	40	65.0	3	11	1	1	.933	3	1	1	0	.33
Halladay,Roy, Tor	.000	2	0	0	0	0	.038	26	1	0	0	0	0	0	10	2	19	141.2	9	24	1	1	.971	18	2	0	0	.11
Halsey,Brad, Ari	.063	48	3	0	2	6	.080	50	4	0	0	0	2	6	19	6	28	160.0	5	25	3	2	.909	19	4	4	0	.21
Hammond,Chris, SD	.000	3	0	0	0	0	.202	238	48	7	1	4	14	28	96	19	55	58.2	1	8	0	0	1.000	1	0	0	0	.00
Hampton,Mike, Atl	.320	25	8	1	1	3	.242	664	161	19	5	15	68	43	176	59	12	69.1	2	11	2	1	.867	5	2	0	0	.40
Hamulack,Tim, NYM	-	0	0	0	0	0	-	0	0	0	0	0	0	0	0	0	6	2.1	0	0	0	0	-	0	0	0	0	-
Hancock,Josh, Cin	-	0	0	0	0	0	.118	17	2	0	0	0	1	3	12	1	11	14.0	0	2	0		1.000	0	0	0	1	
Hansen,Craig, Bos	-	0	0	0	0	0	-	0	0	0	0	0	0	0	0	0	4	3.0	0	0	0		-	0	0	0	0	
Harang,Aaron, Cin	.027	74	2	0	3	4	.046	152	7	1	0	0	3	0	87	8	32	211.2	6	24	0	2	1.000	18	9	0	0	.50
Harden,Rich, Oak	-	0	0	0	0	0	.000	5	0	0	0	0	0	0	0	0	22	128.0	12	8	1	2	.952	8	4	0	0	.50
Haren,Danny, Oak	.400	5	2	0	2	0	.095	42	4	3	0	0	3	1	16	3	34	217.0	22	18	2	4	.952	24	5	1	0	.21
Harikkala,Tim, Oak	-	0	0	0	0	0	.000	3	0	0	0	0	0	0	3	1	8	12.2	1	1	0		1.000	0	0	0	0	-
Harper,Travis, TB	.000	1	0	0	0	0	.000	1	0	0	0	0	0	0	1	0	52	73.1	1	6	1	0	.875	2	1	0	0	.50
Harris,Jeff, Sea	-	0	0	0	0	0	-	0	0	0	0	0	0	0	0	0	11	53.2	3	6	1	0	.900	9	4	1	0	.44
Harville,Chad, Hou-Bos	.000	1	0	0	0	0	.000	2	0	0	0	0	0	0	2	0	45	45.1	0	7	0	1	1.000	6	3	0	0	.50
Hasegawa,Shige, Sea	-	0	0	0	0	0	.000	1	0	0	0	0	0	0	0	0	46	66.2	7	12	0	1	1.000	2	2	0	1	1.00
Hawkins,LaTroy, ChC-SF	-	0	0	0	0	0	.000	5	0	0	0	0	0	0	4	1	66	56.1	3	8	2	1	.846	1	0	0	0	.00
Heilman,Aaron, NYM	.000	14	0	0	0	2	.023	43	1	0	0	0	1	2	23	5	53	108.0	5	19	0	3	1.000	12	3	0	0	.25
Helling,Rick, Mil	.000	13	0	0	0	1	.063	112	7	1	0	0	1	8	46	10	15	49.0	4	3	0		1.000	7	1	0	0	.14
Hendrickson,Ma, TB	.143	7	1	0	0	0	.188	16	3	0	0	1	1	1	8	0	31	178.1	16	23	1	1	.975	9	6	5	0	.67
Henn,Sean, NYY	-	0	0	0	0	0	-	0	0	0	0	0	0	0	0	0	3	11.1	0	3	0		1.000	3	0	0	0	-
Hennessey,Brad, SF	.231	39	9	2	5	2	.231	52	12	1	0	2	7	1	16	2	21	118.1	14	14	0	2	1.000	13	4	0	1	.31
Hensley,Clay, SD	.167	6	1	0	0	0	.167	6	1	1	0	0	0	0	3	0	24	47.2	0	11	1	0	.917	1	0	0	0	.00
Heredia,Felix, NYM	-	0	0	0	0	0	.267	15	4	0	0	0	1	0	4	1	3	2.2	0	0	0	0	-	0	0	0	0	-
Herges,Matt, SF-Ari	-	0	0	0	0	0	.222	27	6	0	0	0	1	1	14	2	28	29.0	0	3	0		1.000	1	1	0	0	1.00
Hermanson,Dustin, CWS	-	0	0	0	0	0	.093	322	30	5	0	2	10	20	161	40	57	57.1	0	6	1	1	.857	0	0	0	0	-
Hernandez,Fel, Sea	-	0	0	0	0	0		0	0	0	0	0	0	0	0	0	12	84.1	11	16	0	1	1.000	5	2	1	1	.40
Hernandez,Liv, Was	.244	82	20	2	7	14	.237	646	153	28	2	7	62	5	93	69	35	246.1	16	45	1	7	.984	25	11	1	1	.44
Hernandez,Orl, CWS	.333	3	1	0	0	0	.091	22	2	0	0	0	0	0	13	2	24	128.1	7	21	2	4	.933	21	2	0	1	.10
Hernandez,Rob, NYM	-	0	0	0	0	0	.500	2	1	0	0	0	0	0	1	0	67	69.2	1	16	0	1	1.000	10	1	0	0	.10
Hernandez,Run, KC	.000	5	0	0	0	0	.000	5	0	0	0	0	0	0	1	0	29	159.2	9	17	4	3	.867	21	6	0	1	.29
Hill,Rich, ChC	.333	6	2	0	0	0	.333	6	2	0	0	0	0	0	2	0	10	23.2	1	1	0		1.000	0	0	0	0	.00
Hoffman,Trevor, SD	-	0	0	0	0	0	.121	33	4	0	0	0	5	0	10	2	60	57.2	3	5	1	0	.889	2	1	0	0	.50
Horgan,Joe, Was	-	0	0	0	0	0	.250	4	1	0	0	0	1	0	1	0	8	6.0	1	0	0		1.000	0	0	0	0	-
Houlton,D.J., LAD	.100	30	3	0	1	2	.100	30	3	1	0	0	1	3	18	2	35	129.0	3	18	0	1	1.000	18	4	1	0	.22
Howell,J.P., KC	.000	3	0	0	0	0	.000	3	0	0	0	0	0	0	1	0	15	72.2	2	8	0		1.000	9	3	1	0	.33
Howry,Bob, Cle	.000	1	0	0	0	0	.000	1	0	0	0	0	0	0	0	0	79	73.0	6	6	1	2	.923	5	1	1	0	.20
Hudson,Luke, Cin	.320	25	8	0	3	2	.244	41	10	2	0	0	5	3	12	3	19	84.2	2	8	0	1	1.000	16	6	1	0	.38
Hudson,Tim, Atl	.138	65	9	0	6	4	.132	91	12	3	1	0	7	5	35	4	29	192.0	27	36	1	4	.984	17	7	1	1	.41
Hughes,Travis, Was	-	0	0	0	0	0	-	0	0	0	0	0	0	0	0	0	14	13.0	1	1	0		1.000	1	1	0	0	1.00
Ishii,Kazuhisa, NYM	.200	25	5	0	2	4	.110	164	18	0	1	1	10	4	73	23	19	91.0	4	9	0	1	1.000	12	4	3	0	.33
Isringhausen,Jason, StL	-	0	0	0	0	0	.206	102	21	4	1	2	16	5	35	8	63	59.0	4	10	1	1	.933	4	1	0	0	.25
Jackson,Edwin, LAD	.200	10	2	0	1	0	.150	20	3	0	0	0	2	2	5	3	7	28.2	0	2	0		1.000	3	1	0	0	.33
James,Chuck, Atl	1.000	1	1	0	1	0	1.000	1	1	0	0	0	1	0	0	0	2	5.2	0	0	0		-	0	0	0	0	-
Jarvis,Kevin, StL	-	0	0	0	0	0	.160	188	30	6	0	1	14	13	62	23	4	3.1	1	0	0		1.000	1	0	0	0	-
Jenks,Bobby, CWS	-	0	0	0	0	0	-	0	0	0	0	0	0	0	0	0	32	39.1	2	3	1	0	.833	7	0	0	0	.00
Jennings,Jason, Col	.158	38	6	0	1	4	.242	240	58	13	0	2	23	13	60	17	20	122.0	14	17	2	2	.939	9	1	1	0	.11
Jensen,Ryan, KC	.000	1	0	0	0	0	.135	74	10	2	0	0	6	1	22	9	9	25.1	0	2	0		.500	2	1	0	0	.50
Johnson,Jason, Det	.500	2	1	1	1	0	.125	24	3	0	0	1	1	2	15	3	33	210.0	10	32	4	2	.913	19	8	0	0	.42
Johnson,Josh, Fla	.250	4	1	0	0	0	.250	4	1	0	0	0	0	0	2	0	4	12.1	3	2	0	1	1.000	6	1	0	0	.17
Johnson,Randy, NYY	.000	5	0	0	0	0	.127	528	67	13	0	1	35	13	243	35	34	225.2	2	26	2	1	.933	37	14	4	0	.38
Johnson,Tyler, StL	-	0	0	0	0	0	-	0	0	0	0	0	0	0	0	0	25	2.2	0	0	0		-	0	0	0	0	-
Johnston,Mike, Pit	-	0	0	0	0	0	-	0	0	0	0	0	0	0	0	0	1	1.0	0	0	0		-	0	0	0	0	-
Jones,Greg, LAA	-	0	0	0	0	0	-	0	0	0	0	0	0	0	0	0	6	5.1	1	1	0		1.000	0	0	0	0	-
Jones,Todd, Fla	.333	3	1	0	0	0	.211	19	4	1	0	0	1		6	0	68	73.0	5	13	1	0	.947	4	1	0	0	.25
Journell,Jimmy, StL	-	0	0	0	0	0	-	0	0	0	0	0	0	0	0	0	5	4.1	0	0	0		-	0	0	0	0	-
Julio,Jorge, Bal	-	0	0	0	0	0	-	0	0	0	0	0	0	0	0	0	67	71.2	2	2	1	0	.800	9	0	0	0	.00
Karnuth,Jason, Det	-	0	0	0	0	0	-	0	0	0	0	0	0	0	0	0	3	1.2	0	0	0		-	0	0	0	0	-
Karsay,Steve, NYY-Tex	-	0	0	0	0	0	.000	4	0	0	0	0	0	0	2	0	20	21.2	2	3	0		1.000	2	1	0	0	.50
Kazmir,Scott, TB	.000	1	0	0	0	0	.000	1	0	0	0	0	0	0	2	0	32	186.0	7	17	3	0	.889	16	9	1	1	.56
Keisler,Randy, Cin	.267	15	4	1	2	0	.211	19	4	2	0	1	2	0	5	0	24	56.0	1	9	0		1.000	2	0	0	0	.00
Kennedy,Joe, Col-Oak	.172	29	5	0	1	5	.170	88	15	1	1	0	6	3	25	9	35	152.2	5	17	2	0	.917	7	1	1	1	.14
Kensing,Logan, Fla	-	0	0	0	0	0	.000	2	0	0	0	0	0	0	1	1	3	5.2	0	0	0		-	1	0	0	0	.00
Kida,Masao, Sea	-	0	0	0	0	0	.250	4	1	0	0	0	0	0	2	0	1	2.0	0	0	0		-	0	0	0	0	-
Kim,Byung-Hyun, Col	.079	38	3	0	2	4	.129	70	9	1	0	0	5	3	12	6	40	148.0	9	22	2	2	.939	17	5	1	0	.29
Kim,Sunny, Was-Col	.105	19	2	0	3	6	.172	58	10	2	0	0	8	0	17	10	24	82.2	3	8	2	0	.846	3	1	0	0	.33
King,Ray, StL	-	0	0	0	0	0	.000	5	0	0	0	0	0	0	2	0	77	40.0	2	3	2	1	.714	3	0	0	0	.00
Kinney,Matt, SF	.333	3	1	0	0	0	.072	69	5	0	0	0	1	2	30	6	5	12.0	0	2	0		1.000	1	1	1	1	1.00
Kline,Steve, Bal	-	0	0	0	0	0	.154	13	2	1	0	0	2	0	5	4	67	61.0	2	14	1	1	.941	4	2	0	0	.50
Kolb,Danny, Atl	.000	1	0	0	0	0	.000	1	0	0	0	0	0	0	0	0	65	57.2	2	4	1	0	.857	3	0	0	0	.00
Koo,Dae-Sung, NYM	.500	2	1	0	0	0	.500	2	1	1	0	0	0	0	1	0	33	23.0	1	6	0		1.000	1	1	0	0	1.00
Koplove,Mike, Ari	.000	2	0	0	0	0	.000	4	0	0	0	0	0	0	2	0	44	49.2	2	7	0		1.000	3	1	0	0	.33
Koronka,John, ChC	.000	4	0	0	0	0	.000	4	0	0	0	0	0	1	3	0	4	15.2	1	2	0		1.000	3	0	0	0	.00

Pitchers Hitting, Fielding and Holding Runners

Pitcher	2005 Hitting						Career Hitting										2005 Fielding and Holding Runners											
	Avg	AB	H	HR	RBI	SH	Avg	AB	H	2B	3B	HR	RBI	BB	SO	SH	G	Inn	PO	A	E	DP	Pct	SBA	CS	PCS	PPO	CS%
Kuo,Hong-Chih, LAD	-	0	0	0	0	0	-	0	0	0	0	0	0	0	0	0	9	5.1	0	0	0	0	-	0	0	0	0	-
Lackey,John, LAA	.000	6	0	0	0	0	.000	11	0	0	0	0	0	0	4	0	33	209.0	5	25	3	0	.909	19	8	1	1	.42
Lawrence,Brian, SD	.085	59	5	0	1	7	.126	277	35	7	0	1	17	13	93	22	33	195.2	12	31	2	4	.956	16	3	0	0	.19
League,Brandon, Tor	-	0	0	0	0	0	-	0	0	0	0	0	0	0	0	0	20	35.2	3	4	1	0	.875	0	0	0	0	-
Ledezma,Wil, Det	-	0	0	0	0	0	-	0	0	0	0	0	0	0	0	0	10	49.2	2	7	2	0	.818	7	4	1	0	.57
Lee,Cliff, Cle	.000	8	0	0	0	0	.091	11	1	0	0	0	0	0	2	0	32	202.0	5	10	3	0	.833	11	4	0	0	.36
Lehr,Justin, Mil	.000	3	0	0	0	0	.000	3	0	0	0	0	0	0	2	0	23	34.2	4	10	0	1	1.000	5	1	1	2	.20
Leicester,Jon, ChC	-	0	0	0	0	1	.000	1	0	0	0	0	0	0	0	1	6	9.0	0	1	0	0	1.000	0	0	0	0	-
Leiter,Al, Fla-NYY	.000	18	0	0	0	4	.085	530	45	7	1	0	16	35	290	48	33	142.1	3	18	1	2	.955	18	3	0	0	.17
Lerew,Anthony, Atl	-	0	0	0	0	0	-	0	0	0	0	0	0	0	0	0	7	8.0	0	3	0	0	1.000	1	0	0	0	.00
Levine,Al, SF	.000	2	0	0	0	0	.000	2	0	0	0	0	0	0	0	0	9	10.1	1	3	0	0	1.000	2	0	0	0	.00
Lidge,Brad, Hou	-	0	0	0	0	0	.286	7	2	1	0	0	2	0	4	0	70	70.2	2	4	1	0	.857	7	2	0	1	.29
Lidle,Cory, Phi	.138	58	8	0	2	8	.140	136	19	4	0	1	8	7	73	17	31	184.2	16	28	1	1	.978	25	6	0	0	.24
Lieber,Jon, Phi	.096	73	7	0	4	3	.147	537	79	17	0	0	24	22	194	47	35	218.1	12	28	4	0	.909	16	5	0	0	.31
Ligtenberg,K, Ari	.000	1	0	0	0	0	.000	1	0	0	0	0	0	0	1	0	7	9.2	1	1	0	0	1.000	1	1	0	1	1.00
Lilly,Ted, Tor	.000	3	0	0	0	0	.050	20	1	0	0	0	0	0	9	4	25	126.1	2	13	0	0	1.000	11	1	1	0	.09
Lima,Jose, KC	.333	3	1	0	0	1	.132	287	38	4	0	0	10	7	98	43	32	168.2	6	22	0	2	1.000	14	4	0	1	.29
Linebrink,Scott, SD	.000	1	0	0	0	0	.188	16	3	1	0	0	0	0	9	2	73	73.2	1	3	1	2	.800	9	1	0	0	.11
Liriano,Francisco, Min	-	0	0	0	0	0	-	0	0	0	0	0	0	0	0	0	6	23.2	2	3	0	1	1.000	4	1	1	0	.25
Liriano,Pedro, Phi	-	0	0	0	0	1	.000	1	0	0	0	0	0	0	0	1	5	7.2	0	2	0	0	1.000	1	0	0	0	.00
Loaiza,Esteban, Was	.162	74	12	0	4	6	.170	253	43	4	1	0	15	3	63	30	34	217.0	13	30	1	3	.977	6	2	0	0	.33
Loe,Kameron, Tex	-	0	0	0	0	0	-	0	0	0	0	0	0	0	0	0	48	92.0	9	17	4	0	.867	11	2	0	0	.18
Lohse,Kyle, Min	.000	5	0	0	0	0	.200	20	4	1	0	0	1	0	8	4	31	178.2	13	27	0	1	1.000	9	6	2	1	.67
Looper,Braden, NYM	-	0	0	0	0	0	.125	8	1	0	0	0	0	0	5	1	60	59.1	0	8	1	0	.889	3	1	0	0	.33
Lopez,Aquilino, Col-Phi	.000	1	0	0	0	0	.000	1	0	0	0	0	0	0	0	0	11	16.2	0	2	0	0	1.000	0	0	0	0	-
Lopez,Javier, Col-Ari	-	0	0	0	0	0	.143	7	1	0	0	0	1	0	3	1	32	16.1	2	2	0	0	1.000	1	0	0	0	.00
Lopez,Rodrigo, Bal	.000	4	0	0	0	0	.056	18	1	0	0	0	0	0	10	0	35	209.1	19	30	3	2	.942	28	6	2	0	.21
Lowe,Derek, Bos-LAD	.154	65	10	0	4	9	.141	85	12	3	0	0	5	4	25	12	35	222.0	21	48	1	5	.986	25	6	0	0	.24
Lowry,Noah, SF	.271	59	16	0	7	12	.245	94	23	8	0	0	7	3	23	15	33	204.2	10	25	0	1	1.000	17	8	1	0	.47
Lyon,Brandon, Ari	-	0	0	0	0	0	-	0	0	0	0	0	0	0	0	0	32	29.1	2	4	0	0	1.000	3	0	0	0	.00
MacDougal,Mike, KC	-	0	0	0	0	0	-	0	0	0	0	0	0	0	0	0	68	70.1	2	11	2	0	.867	7	2	0	0	.29
Maddux,Greg, ChC	.171	76	13	1	5	7	.176	1406	248	31	2	5	74	30	363	159	35	225.0	19	49	3	6	.958	40	8	0	0	.20
Madritsch,Bobby, Sea	-	0	0	0	0	0	-	0	0	0	0	0	0	0	0	0	2	4.1	0	2	0	0	1.000	0	0	0	0	-
Madson,Ryan, Phi	.000	6	0	0	0	1	.000	9	0	0	0	0	0	1	2	2	78	87.0	2	10	0	0	1.000	8	2	0	0	.25
Mahay,Ron, Tex	-	0	0	0	0	0	.286	7	2	1	0	0	0	0	2	0	30	35.2	2	3	1	0	.833	2	1	0	0	.50
Maholm,Paul, Pit	.133	15	2	0	0	1	.133	15	2	0	0	0	0	1	6	1	6	41.1	1	6	0	0	1.000	4	2	0	0	.50
Maine,John, Bal	-	0	0	0	0	0	-	0	0	0	0	0	0	0	0	0	10	40.0	3	4	1	0	.875	5	0	0	0	.00
Majewski,Gary, Was	.000	6	0	0	0	1	.000	8	0	0	0	0	0	0	5	1	79	86.0	3	8	0	0	1.000	2	0	0	0	.00
Mantei,Matt, Bos	-	0	0	0	0	0	.200	5	1	0	0	0	0	0	2	0	34	26.1	1	3	0	0	1.000	3	1	0	0	.33
Marcum,Shaun, Tor	-	0	0	0	0	0	-	0	0	0	0	0	0	0	0	0	5	8.0	0	0	0	0	-	0	0	0	0	-
Maroth,Mike, Det	.500	4	2	0	1	1	.250	16	4	0	0	0	2	2	10	3	34	209.0	6	30	0	1	1.000	16	12	8	2	.75
Marquis,Jason, StL	.310	87	27	1	10	2	.237	232	55	15	1	2	21	5	54	11	33	207.0	18	23	2	3	.953	9	6	0	0	.67
Marte,Damaso, CWS	-	0	0	0	0	0	.000	4	0	0	0	0	0	0	1	0	66	45.1	2	5	0	0	1.000	5	1	0	1	.20
Martin,Tom, Atl	-	0	0	0	0	0	.000	7	0	0	0	0	0	0	3	0	4	2.1	1	1	0	0	1.000	1	0	0	0	.00
Martinez,Pedro, NYM	.087	69	6	0	1	6	.093	334	31	3	2	0	12	12	147	44	31	217.0	6	19	0	0	1.000	18	4	0	0	.22
Mateo,Julio, Sea	-	0	0	0	0	0	-	0	0	0	0	0	0	0	0	0	55	88.1	1	10	0	0	1.000	6	4	0	0	.67
Matthews,Mike, NYM	-	0	0	0	0	0	.120	25	3	0	0	1	1	0	9	3	6	5.0	0	2	0	0	1.000	1	0	0	0	.00
May,Darrell, SD-NYY	.111	9	1	0	0	1	.077	26	2	0	0	1	0	1	13	2	24	66.1	5	7	1	0	.923	10	3	1	0	.30
Mays,Joe, Min	.333	3	1	0	0	0	.267	15	4	1	0	0	0	3	5	3	31	156.0	19	17	1	2	.973	7	5	0	0	.71
McBride,Macay, Atl	-	0	0	0	0	0	-	0	0	0	0	0	0	0	0	0	23	14.0	0	2	0	0	1.000	0	0	0	0	-
McCarthy,Bran, CWS	.000	2	0	0	0	0	.000	2	0	0	0	0	0	0	2	0	12	67.0	3	4	0	1	1.000	2	0	0	0	.00
McClung,Seth, TB	-	0	0	0	0	0	-	0	0	0	0	0	0	0	0	0	34	109.1	4	9	0	2	1.000	10	4	0	0	.40
McGowan,Dustin, Tor	-	0	0	0	0	0	-	0	0	0	0	0	0	0	0	0	13	45.1	2	5	1	0	.875	10	3	1	0	.30
Meadows,Brian, Pit	.000	1	0	0	0	0	.117	180	21	3	0	0	8	8	76	19	65	74.2	3	13	1	2	.941	2	0	0	0	.00
Meche,Gil, Sea	.250	4	1	0	1	0	.222	9	2	0	0	0	1	0	2	0	29	143.1	8	22	1	1	.968	16	8	0	2	.50
Mecir,Jim, Fla	-	0	0	0	0	0	.000	1	0	0	0	0	0	0	0	0	52	43.1	4	5	1	0	.900	4	1	0	1	.25
Medders,Brandon, Ari	.000	1	0	0	0	0	.000	1	0	0	0	0	0	0	0	0	27	30.1	1	1	0	0	1.000	2	1	0	0	.50
Mendoza,Ramiro, NYY	-	0	0	0	0	0	.000	3	0	0	0	0	0	0	3	1	1	2.1	0	0	0	0	-	0	0	0	0	-
Mercker,Kent, Cin	-	0	0	0	0	0	.113	248	28	5	2	1	18	11	115	22	78	61.2	0	11	2	0	.846	3	1	1	0	.33
Meredith,Cla, Bos	-	0	0	0	0	0	-	0	0	0	0	0	0	0	0	0	3	2.1	0	1	0	0	1.000	0	0	0	0	-
Mesa,Jose, Pit	.000	1	0	0	0	1	.000	1	0	0	0	0	0	1	1	1	55	56.2	2	13	1	1	.938	6	2	0	0	.33
Messenger,Randy, Fla	.333	3	1	0	0	0	.333	3	1	0	0	0	0	1	1	0	29	37.0	2	5	0	0	1.000	6	0	0	0	.00
Miceli,Danny, Col	-	0	0	0	0	0	.091	22	2	0	0	0	0	0	10	0	19	18.1	1	2	0	0	1.000	3	1	0	0	.33
Miller,Justin, Tor	-	0	0	0	0	0	.000	2	0	0	0	0	0	0	1	0	1	2.1	0	0	0	0	-	0	0	0	0	-
Miller,Matt, Cle	-	0	0	0	0	0	-	0	0	0	0	0	0	0	0	0	23	29.2	5	6	0	0	1.000	4	0	0	1	.00
Miller,Trever, TB	-	0	0	0	0	0	.167	6	1	1	0	0	0	0	1	2	61	44.1	2	5	1	2	.875	4	2	0	0	.50
Miller,Wade, Bos	.667	3	2	0	0	0	.172	262	45	9	0	0	17	4	81	30	16	91.0	8	10	1	0	.947	12	3	2	0	.25
Millwood,Kevin, Cle	.000	2	0	0	0	0	.124	428	53	14	0	2	24	19	193	50	30	192.0	8	17	0	2	1.000	39	6	0	0	.15
Milton,Eric, Cin	.143	56	8	2	4	5	.170	141	24	2	0	2	11	8	61	10	34	186.1	3	17	0	0	1.000	14	3	0	0	.21
Mitre,Sergio, ChC	.364	11	4	0	1	1	.214	28	6	2	0	0	1	1	10	4	21	60.1	7	12	0	1	1.000	9	1	0	0	.11
Moehler,Brian, Fla	.075	40	3	0	3	5	.043	70	3	1	0	0	3	3	27	6	37	158.1	21	26	1	2	.979	21	5	1	0	.24
Morris,Matt, StL	.088	57	5	0	2	8	.155	419	65	11	0	1	28	25	174	56	31	192.2	6	27	1	2	.971	6	1	0	0	.17
Mota,Guillermo, Fla	.000	3	0	0	0	0	.212	33	7	1	0	2	6	0	17	0	56	67.0	1	6	0	0	1.000	13	3	0	0	.23
Moyer,Jamie, Sea	.000	1	0	0	0	0	.155	174	27	2	0	0	6	15	57	23	32	200.0	18	28	0	2	1.000	34	7	2	0	.21
Mulder,Mark, StL	.145	62	9	0	3	1	.119	84	10	0	0	0	4	4	36	2	32	205.0	5	52	2	3	.966	10	8	5	0	.80

Pitchers Hitting, Fielding and Holding Runners

Pitcher	2005 Hitting Avg	AB	H	HR	RBI	SH	Career Hitting Avg	AB	H	2B	3B	HR	RBI	BB	SO	SH	2005 Fielding and Holding Runners G	Inn	PO	A	E	DP	Pct	SBA	CS	PCS	PPO	CS%
Mulholland,T, Min	-	0	0	0	0	0	.111	619	69	13	1	2	23	13	281	53	49	59.0	3	9	0	0	1.000	2	1	0	0	.50
Munter,Scott, SF	-	0	0	0	0	1	-	0	0	0	0	0	0	0	0	0	45	38.2	3	12	0	2	1.000	5	3	0	0	.60
Mussina,Mike, NYY	.000	3	0	0	0	0	.195	41	8	1	0	0	5	0	8	1	30	179.2	9	24	4	5	.892	22	7	0	0	.32
Myers,Brett, Phi	.154	65	10	0	5	11	.159	201	32	7	0	0	8	8	63	27	34	215.1	12	36	2	0	.960	19	4	0	1	.21
Myers,Mike, Bos	-	0	0	0	0	0	.000	1	0	0	0	0	0	0	1	0	65	37.1	3	10	0	2	1.000	4	0	0	0	.00
Nageotte,Clint, Sea	-	0	0	0	0	0	.000	2	0	0	0	0	0	0	2	0	3	4.0	0	2	0	0	1.000	0	0	0	0	-
Nathan,Joe, Min	-	0	0	0	0	0	.161	62	10	3	0	2	4	3	16	10	69	70.0	2	6	1	0	.889	3	1	0	0	.33
Neal,Blaine, Bos-Col	.000	1	0	0	0	0	.000	1	0	0	0	0	0	0	1	0	19	22.2	1	4	0	0	1.000	2	0	0	0	.00
Nelson,Jeff, Sea	-	0	0	0	0	0	.000	2	0	0	0	0	0	0	0	1	49	36.2	1	7	0	0	1.000	7	2	1	0	.29
Nippert,Dustin, Ari	.250	4	1	0	0	0	.250	4	1	0	0	0	0	1	3	0	3	14.2	1	4	0	0	1.000	3	0	0	0	.00
Nitkowski,C.J., Was	-	0	0	0	0	0	.133	15	2	0	0	0	1	0	10	1	7	3.1	0	2	0	0	1.000	0	0	0	0	-
Nomo,Hideo, TB	.000	4	0	0	0	0	.134	485	65	14	1	4	26	13	222	44	19	100.2	2	16	0	1	1.000	10	3	0	0	.30
Novoa,Roberto, ChC	.000	1	0	0	0	0	.000	1	0	0	0	0	0	0	0	0	49	44.2	1	2	0	0	1.000	0	0	0	0	-
Nunez,Franklin, TB	-	0	0	0	0	0	-	0	0	0	0	0	0	0	0	0	5	5.0	0	0	0	0	-	0	0	0	0	-
Nunez,Leo, KC	-	0	0	0	0	0	-	0	0	0	0	0	0	0	0	0	41	53.2	5	6	0	2	1.000	5	3	1	0	.60
Obermueller,Wes, Mil	.200	15	3	0	0	1	.273	77	21	4	1	0	6	1	22	5	23	65.0	4	10	1	0	.933	8	1	0	0	.13
Ohka,Tomo, Was-Mil	.111	54	6	0	3	3	.135	207	28	1	0	0	9	9	79	21	32	180.1	8	27	1	2	.972	10	5	1	1	.50
Ohman,Will, ChC	-	0	0	0	0	0	-	0	0	0	0	0	0	0	0	0	69	43.1	3	3	0	0	1.000	4	0	0	0	.00
Olsen,Scott, Fla	.000	3	0	0	0	1	.000	3	0	0	0	0	0	0	1	1	5	20.1	0	3	1	0	.750	4	2	1	0	.50
Ortiz,Ramon, Cin	.074	54	4	0	0	6	.053	76	4	2	0	0	1	1	30	7	30	171.1	10	28	7	2	.844	12	6	1	2	.50
Ortiz,Russ, Ari	.206	34	7	0	1	6	.206	456	94	22	0	6	42	32	121	55	22	115.0	7	17	0	2	1.000	7	5	0	0	.71
Orvella,Chad, TB	-	0	0	0	0	0	-	0	0	0	0	0	0	0	0	0	37	50.0	6	2	1	0	.889	3	0	0	0	.00
Osoria,Franq, LAD	.000	3	0	0	0	0	.000	3	0	0	0	0	0	0	2	0	24	29.2	6	4	0	0	1.000	2	1	0	0	.50
Osuna,Antonio, Was	-	0	0	0	0	0	.111	9	1	0	0	0	1	1	1	0	4	2.1	0	1	0	0	1.000	0	0	0	0	-
Oswalt,Roy, Hou	.178	73	13	0	2	7	.160	307	49	5	0	0	15	12	88	37	35	241.2	19	31	0	2	1.000	7	4	0	1	.57
Otsuka,Akinori, SD	.000	1	0	0	0	0	.000	2	0	0	0	0	0	0	1	0	66	62.2	5	7	1	1	.923	4	0	0	0	.00
Oxspring,Chris, SD	.000	2	0	0	0	0	.000	2	0	0	0	0	0	0	0	0	5	12.0	0	1	0	0	1.000	0	0	0	0	-
Padilla,Juan, NYM	.500	2	1	0	0	0	.500	2	1	0	0	0	0	0	1	0	24	36.1	1	6	0	1	1.000	0	0	0	0	-
Padilla,Vicente, Phi	.146	41	6	0	4	5	.093	205	19	3	1	0	13	14	108	19	27	147.0	4	23	1	2	.964	3	1	0	1	.33
Papelbon,Jonat, Bos	-	0	0	0	0	0	-	0	0	0	0	0	0	0	0	0	17	34.0	3	2	0	0	1.000	5	4	0	0	.80
Park,Chan Ho, Tex-SD	.263	19	5	0	2	4	.173	364	63	15	1	2	25	17	132	43	30	155.1	11	37	1	2	.980	5	2	0	0	.40
Parrish,John, Bal	-	0	0	0	0	0	.000	1	0	0	0	0	0	0	0	0	14	17.1	0	4	0	0	1.000	2	1	0	0	.50
Patterson,John, Was	.102	59	6	0	0	8	.105	114	12	3	0	0	2	2	48	15	31	198.1	12	16	1	2	.966	37	11	2	0	.30
Pavano,Carl, NYY	.000	7	0	0	0	0	.139	295	41	8	2	2	14	4	116	34	17	100.0	4	9	0	1	1.000	15	4	0	0	.27
Peavy,Jake, SD	.189	53	10	0	2	5	.155	200	31	5	0	0	8	11	67	20	30	203.0	10	24	1	1	.971	24	5	0	1	.21
Penn,Hayden, Bal	.000	1	0	0	0	0	.000	1	0	0	0	0	0	0	1	0	6	38.1	9	9	0	1	1.000	3	0	0	0	.00
Penny,Brad, LAD	.160	50	8	0	3	9	.133	324	43	7	2	2	16	2	109	20	29	175.1	11	25	0	3	1.000	22	5	1	0	.23
Peralta,Joel, LAA	-	0	0	0	0	0	-	0	0	0	0	0	0	0	0	0	28	34.2	1	6	0	0	1.000	3	2	1	1	.67
Percival,Troy, Det	-	0	0	0	0	0	.000	1	0	0	0	0	0	0	0	0	26	25.0	2	1	0	0	1.000	1	0	0	0	.00
Perez,Odalis, LAD	.121	33	4	0	0	8	.131	267	35	8	0	1	10	5	70	40	19	108.2	4	13	0	1	1.000	16	2	2	0	.13
Perez,Oliver, Pit	.182	33	6	0	3	7	.175	160	28	0	0	0	7	6	55	23	20	103.0	2	10	1	0	.923	8	5	2	0	.63
Perisho,Matt, Fla-Bos	-	0	0	0	0	0	.000	5	0	0	0	0	0	0	5	0	25	14.0	2	2	0	0	1.000	1	1	1	0	1.00
Pettitte,Andy, Hou	.081	62	5	0	3	15	.106	113	12	2	0	0	7	5	35	21	33	222.1	12	40	1	3	.981	9	4	2	0	.44
Phelps,Tommy, Mil	-	0	0	0	0	0	.059	17	1	0	0	0	0	2	5	1	29	23.1	2	3	0	1	1.000	1	0	0	0	.00
Pineiro,Joel, Sea	.000	4	0	0	0	1	.100	20	2	1	0	0	2	0	7	2	30	189.0	23	18	1	5	.976	9	2	0	0	.22
Politte,Cliff, CWS	1.000	1	1	0	1	0	.121	33	4	1	0	0	3	3	14	3	68	67.1	1	6	1	0	.875	8	2	0	0	.25
Ponson,Sidney, Bal	.250	4	1	0	0	0	.120	50	6	3	0	0	0	0	14	6	23	130.1	10	18	2	1	.933	10	1	0	0	.10
Powell,Jay, Atl	-	0	0	0	0	0	.167	12	2	0	0	0	1	0	8	1	5	3.1	0	0	0	0	-	0	0	0	0	-
Prinz,Bret, LAA	-	0	0	0	0	0	-	0	0	0	0	0	0	0	0	0	3	3.0	0	0	0	0	-	1	0	0	0	.00
Prior,Mark, ChC	.229	48	11	0	3	6	.209	191	40	10	0	1	13	8	76	21	27	166.2	9	9	1	0	.947	11	6	0	0	.55
Proctor,Scott, NYY	-	0	0	0	0	0	-	0	0	0	0	0	0	0	0	0	29	44.2	3	5	0	0	1.000	8	0	0	0	.00
Puffer,Brandon, SF	-	0	0	0	0	0	.000	9	0	0	0	0	0	1	7	1	3	7.0	1	2	0	0	1.000	0	0	0	0	-
Pulsipher,Bill, StL	-	0	0	0	0	0	-	0	0	0	0	0	0	0	0	0	2	1.0	0	0	0	0	-	0	0	0	0	-
Putz,J.J., Sea	-	0	0	0	0	0	-	0	0	0	0	0	0	0	0	0	64	60.0	4	13	0	2	1.000	4	3	0	0	.13
Qualls,Chad, Hou	.000	1	0	0	0	0	.000	2	0	0	0	0	0	0	2	0	77	79.2	7	12	0	0	1.000	6	2	0	0	.33
Quantrill,Paul, NYY-SD-Fla	.000	1	0	0	0	0	.104	67	7	0	0	0	4	4	29	7	50	69.0	5	5	0	0	1.000	6	1	0	0	.17
Radke,Brad, Min	.000	5	0	0	0	2	.107	28	3	0	0	0	0	0	9	4	33	200.2	20	26	2	1	.958	11	3	0	0	.27
Rakers,Aaron, Bal	-	0	0	0	0	0	-	0	0	0	0	0	0	0	0	0	10	13.2	0	1	0	0	1.000	0	0	0	0	-
Ramirez,Eliz, Cin	.000	8	0	0	0	0	.000	8	0	0	0	0	0	1	3	0	6	22.1	1	1	1	0	.667	1	0	0	0	.00
Ramirez,Erasmo, Tex	-	0	0	0	0	0	-	0	0	0	0	0	0	0	0	0	16	23.0	1	4	0	0	1.000	0	0	0	0	-
Ramirez,Horacio, Atl	.219	73	16	0	2	3	.155	155	24	3	1	0	5	1	34	10	33	202.1	7	43	2	8	.962	18	6	2	1	.33
Rasner,Darrell, Was	-	0	0	0	0	0	-	0	0	0	0	0	0	0	0	0	5	7.1	0	0	0	0	-	0	0	0	0	-
Rauch,Jon, Was	.143	7	1	0	1	1	.154	13	2	0	0	1	3	0	9	1	15	30.0	4	1	0	0	1.000	4	0	0	0	.00
Ray,Chris, Bal	-	0	0	0	0	0	-	0	0	0	0	0	0	0	0	0	41	40.2	4	3	1	0	.875	2	1	0	0	.50
Reames,Britt, Oak	-	0	0	0	0	0	.128	39	5	0	0	1	3	4	11	6	2	5.2	1	0	0	0	1.000	0	0	0	0	-
Redding,Tim, SD-NYY	.000	8	0	0	0	1	.157	121	19	3	0	0	5	2	60	13	10	30.2	3	4	1	0	.875	1	0	0	0	.00
Redman,Mark, Pit	.113	53	6	0	2	4	.062	129	8	0	0	0	3	4	59	9	30	178.1	15	34	1	5	.980	10	4	1	1	.40
Reed,Steve, Bal	-	0	0	0	0	0	.179	28	5	0	0	0	1	0	9	2	30	32.2	2	5	0	1	1.000	1	0	0	0	.00
Regilio,Nick, Tex	-	0	0	0	0	0	-	0	0	0	0	0	0	0	0	0	18	17.2	0	4	1	0	.800	0	0	0	0	-
Reitsma,Chris, Atl	.000	1	0	0	0	0	.103	87	9	1	0	0	5	3	42	14	76	73.1	5	12	0	0	1.000	5	0	0	0	.00
Remlinger,Mike, ChC-Bos	-	0	0	0	0	0	.073	110	8	3	0	0	8	8	37	19	43	39.2	1	6	0	0	1.000	2	2	0	1	1.00
Resop,Chris, Fla	.000	1	0	0	0	0	.000	1	0	0	0	0	0	0	0	0	15	17.0	1	1	0	0	1.000	2	1	0	0	.50
Reyes,Al, StL	.000	1	0	0	0	1	.250	12	3	0	0	0	0	1	6	2	65	62.2	3	7	0	2	1.000	2	2	0	0	1.00
Reyes,Anthony, StL	.000	4	0	0	0	0	.000	4	0	0	0	0	0	0	1	0	4	13.1	1	0	0	0	1.000	2	0	0	0	.00
Reyes,Dennys, SD	.200	5	1	0	0	0	.074	54	4	1	0	0	0	2	25	2	36	43.2	2	8	1	1	.909	8	1	0	1	.13

Pitchers Hitting, Fielding and Holding Runners

Pitcher	2005 Hitting						Career Hitting										2005 Fielding and Holding Runners											
	Avg	AB	H	HR	RBI	SH	Avg	AB	H	2B	3B	HR	RBI	BB	SO	SH	G	Inn	PO	A	E	DP	Pct	SBA	CS	PCS	PPO	CS%
Rhodes,Arthur, Cle	-	0	0	0	0	0	.250	4	1	0	0	0	0	0	3	0	47	43.1	3	4	1	1	.875	0	0	0	0	-
Riedling,John, Fla	.000	2	0	0	0	0	.148	27	4	0	0	0	2	0	16	1	29	27.2	2	6	0	0	1.000	3	0	0	0	.00
Riley,Matt, Tex	-	0	0	0	0	0	.000	2	0	0	0	0	0	0	2	0	7	12.2	1	1	0	0	1.000	1	1	0	0	1.00
Rincon,Juan, Min	-	0	0	0	0	0	.500	2	1	0	0	0	0	0	1	0	75	77.0	5	12	1	0	.944	4	2	1	1	.50
Rincon,Ricardo, Oak	-	0	0	0	0	0	.000	4	0	0	0	0	0	0	1	1	67	37.1	3	3	2	0	.750	0	0	0	0	-
Ring,Royce, NYM	-	0	0	0	0	0	-	0	0	0	0	0	0	0	0	0	15	10.2	0	3	0	0	1.000	1	0	0	0	.00
Riske,David, Cle	-	0	0	0	0	0	-	0	0	0	0	0	0	0	0	0	58	72.2	2	7	0	1	1.000	3	1	0	0	.33
Rivera,Mariano, NYY	-	0	0	0	0	0	-	0	0	0	0	0	0	0	0	0	71	78.1	7	22	0	1	1.000	9	3	0	0	.33
Robertson,Nate, Det	.000	3	0	0	0	1	.000	8	0	0	0	0	0	0	3	1	32	196.2	8	24	3	3	.914	13	5	1	0	.38
Rodney,Fernando, Det	-	0	0	0	0	0	-	0	0	0	0	0	0	0	0	0	39	44.0	3	3	1	0	.857	3	1	0	0	.33
Rodriguez,Felix, NYY	-	0	0	0	0	0	.250	16	4	1	0	1	3	0	5	2	34	32.1	2	2	0	0	1.000	9	2	0	0	.22
Rodriguez,Fran, LAA	-	0	0	0	0	0	-	0	0	0	0	0	0	0	0	0	66	67.1	7	4	1	0	.917	2	0	0	0	.00
Rodriguez,Ric, Tex	.333	3	1	0	1	0	.125	8	1	0	0	0	1	0	4	0	12	57.0	4	8	1	2	.923	0	0	0	0	-
Rodriguez,Wandy, Hou	.150	40	6	0	1	1	.150	40	6	0	0	0	1	2	16	1	25	128.2	10	19	2	4	.935	11	6	2	0	.55
Rogers,Kenny, Tex	.333	3	1	0	1	0	.143	56	8	0	1	0	4	4	21	4	30	195.1	18	47	1	7	.985	3	0	0	0	.00
Romero,J.C., Min	-	0	0	0	0	0	.333	3	1	1	0	0	0	0	1	0	68	57.0	7	10	3	0	.850	6	1	0	0	.17
Rueter,Kirk, SF	.167	30	5	0	1	6	.153	622	95	9	0	0	40	27	105	86	20	107.1	13	33	1	4	.979	5	4	3	0	.80
Rupe,Josh, Tex	-	0	0	0	0	0	-	0	0	0	0	0	0	0	0	0	4	9.2	2	1	1	0	.750	2	1	0	0	.50
Rusch,Glendon, ChC	.146	41	6	0	0	0	.152	290	44	3	0	3	19	9	95	35	46	145.1	4	17	2	2	.913	5	2	0	1	.40
Ryan,B.J., Bal	-	0	0	0	0	0	.000	2	0	0	0	0	0	0	0	0	69	70.1	1	4	2	1	.714	9	1	0	0	.11
Saarloos,Kirk, Oak	.000	1	0	0	0	0	.056	36	2	1	0	0	3	1	11	8	29	159.2	22	33	2	2	.965	19	5	0	0	.26
Sabathia,C.C., Cle	.333	6	2	1	4	0	.280	25	7	1	0	1	4	1	5	1	31	196.2	2	17	2	0	.905	18	7	2	0	.39
Sanchez,Duaner, LAD	.000	4	0	0	0	0	.125	8	1	1	0	0	2	0	1	1	79	82.0	4	9	0	0	1.000	9	1	0	1	.11
Sanders,David, CWS	-	0	0	0	0	0	-	0	0	0	0	0	0	0	0	0	2	2.0	0	0	0	0	-	0	0	0	0	-
Santana,Ervin, LAA	-	0	0	0	0	0	-	0	0	0	0	0	0	0	0	0	23	133.2	10	10	0	2	1.000	13	5	1	0	.38
Santana,Johan, Min	.167	6	1	0	0	0	.273	22	6	0	0	0	2	0	2	0	33	231.2	12	25	2	0	.949	9	5	0	0	.56
Santana,Julio, Mil	.000	1	0	0	0	0	.105	19	2	0	0	0	1	0	10	0	41	42.0	2	3	1	0	.833	2	0	1	0	.00
Santiago,Jose, NYM	-	0	0	0	0	0	.000	5	0	0	0	0	0	2	4	0	4	5.2	0	2	0	1	1.000	1	1	0	0	1.00
Santos,Victor, Mil	.075	40	3	0	0	3	.072	83	6	1	0	0	1	2	34	10	29	141.2	14	17	0	0	1.000	11	2	0	1	.18
Sauerbeck,Scott, Cle	-	0	0	0	0	0	.000	7	0	0	0	0	0	0	4	1	58	35.2	6	3	0	0	1.000	1	1	1	0	1.00
Saunders,Joe, LAA	-	0	0	0	0	0	-	0	0	0	0	0	0	0	0	0	2	9.1	0	0	0	0	-	1	0	0	0	.00
Schilling,Curt, Bos	-	0	0	0	0	0	.150	769	115	13	1	0	29	25	268	102	32	93.1	7	7	2	1	.875	4	0	0	1	.00
Schmidt,Jason, SF	.094	53	5	1	2	6	.100	518	52	6	0	5	19	22	252	82	29	172.0	11	9	1	0	.952	32	8	0	0	.25
Schmoll,Steve, LAD	.000	1	0	0	0	0	.000	1	0	0	0	0	0	0	0	0	48	46.2	4	4	1	0	.889	2	0	0	0	.00
Schoeneweis,S, Tor	-	0	0	0	0	0	.286	7	2	1	0	0	1	2	2	0	80	57.0	5	17	1	2	.957	9	1	1	0	.11
Seanez,Rudy, SD	-	0	0	0	0	0	.000	4	0	0	0	0	0	1	4	0	57	60.1	4	5	0	0	1.000	10	2	0	0	.20
Seay,Bobby, Col	-	0	0	0	0	0	-	0	0	0	0	0	0	0	0	0	17	11.2	0	2	1	0	.667	1	0	0	0	.00
Sele,Aaron, Sea	.000	3	0	0	0	1	.143	28	4	1	0	0	1	1	5	5	21	116.0	14	6	0	0	1.000	9	3	1	0	.33
Seo,Jae, NYM	.103	29	3	0	4	2	.116	112	13	3	0	0	5	8	39	9	14	90.1	5	11	0	1	1.000	8	1	0	0	.13
Shackelford,Br, Cin	.000	1	0	0	0	0	.000	1	0	0	0	0	0	0	0	0	37	29.2	0	2	0	0	1.000	2	1	1	1	.50
Sheets,Ben, Mil	.022	45	1	0	0	7	.083	288	24	1	0	0	7	15	142	27	22	156.2	7	63	3	0	.813	16	2	0	0	.13
Sherrill,George, Sea	-	0	0	0	0	0	-	0	0	0	0	0	0	0	0	0	29	19.0	1	3	0	0	1.000	0	0	0	0	-
Shields,Scot, LAA	.000	1	0	0	0	0	.000	2	0	0	0	0	0	0	2	0	78	91.2	8	14	2	2	.917	8	2	0	0	.25
Shouse,Brian, Tex	-	0	0	0	0	0	-	0	0	0	0	0	0	0	0	0	64	53.1	6	18	2	2	.923	4	2	1	0	.50
Silva,Carlos, Min	.000	2	0	0	0	0	.125	16	2	1	0	0	1	1	6	1	27	188.1	14	26	0	3	1.000	11	4	0	0	.36
Simpson,Allan, Col-Cin	-	0	0	0	0	0	.000	1	0	0	0	0	0	0	0	0	11	7.1	0	1	0	0	1.000	0	0	0	0	-
Sisco,Andy, KC	.000	1	0	0	0	0	.000	1	0	0	0	0	0	0	1	0	67	75.1	1	3	1	0	.800	5	2	1	0	.40
Small,Aaron, NYY	-	0	0	0	0	0	.000	3	0	0	0	0	0	0	0	0	15	76.0	1	7	0	0	1.000	4	2	0	0	.50
Smith,Travis, Fla	-	0	0	0	0	0	.148	27	4	0	0	0	2	0	7	2	12	10.2	1	0	0	0	1.000	1	0	0	0	.00
Smoltz,John, Atl	.147	68	10	0	3	12	.170	807	137	22	2	5	54	73	310	104	33	229.2	22	31	0	4	1.000	16	6	0	0	.38
Snell,Ian, Pit	.000	8	0	0	0	0	.000	10	0	0	0	0	0	0	5	1	15	42.0	2	2	0	0	1.000	2	1	0	0	.50
Snyder,Kyle, KC	-	0	0	0	0	0	.000	2	0	0	0	0	0	0	0	0	13	36.0	2	4	0	0	1.000	4	1	0	0	.25
Soriano,Rafael, Sea	-	0	0	0	0	0	.000	4	0	0	0	0	0	0	1	0	7	7.1	0	0	0	0	-	0	0	0	0	-
Sosa,Jorge, Atl	.097	31	3	0	0	3	.097	31	3	0	0	0	0	1	15	3	44	134.0	6	5	3	0	.786	21	1	0	0	.05
Speier,Justin, Tor	-	0	0	0	0	0	.176	17	3	0	0	0	0	0	8	0	65	66.2	0	7	0	0	1.000	4	2	0	0	.50
Speier,Ryan, Col	.000	2	0	0	0	0	.000	2	0	0	0	0	0	0	0	0	22	24.2	1	7	0	0	1.000	4	3	1	0	.75
Springer,Russ, Hou	-	0	0	0	0	0	.077	26	2	0	0	0	0	0	16	4	62	59.0	1	7	0	0	1.000	3	0	0	0	.00
Spurling,Chris, Det	-	0	0	0	0	0	-	0	0	0	0	0	0	0	0	0	56	70.2	4	8	0	2	1.000	3	1	0	0	.33
Standridge,Jas, Tex-Cin	-	0	0	0	0	0	-	0	0	0	0	0	0	1	0	0	34	33.1	0	4	0	1	1.000	2	0	0	0	.00
Stanton,Mike, NYY-Was-Bos	.000	1	0	0	0	0	.400	20	8	1	0	0	3	1	3	1	59	42.2	2	13	0	1	1.000	4	1	1	1	.25
Stauffer,Tim, SD	.125	24	3	0	1	3	.125	24	3	1	0	0	1	0	10	3	15	81.0	5	11	0	0	1.000	3	2	0	0	.67
Stemle,Steve, KC	-	0	0	0	0	0	-	0	0	0	0	0	0	0	0	0	7	10.2	1	0	0	0	1.000	1	1	0	0	1.00
Stone,Ricky, Cin	.000	2	0	0	0	0	.000	10	0	0	0	0	0	0	4	1	23	30.2	2	2	0	0	1.000	0	0	0	0	-
Street,Huston, Oak	-	0	0	0	0	0	-	0	0	0	0	0	0	0	0	0	67	78.1	7	12	0	2	1.000	9	2	0	1	.22
Strickland,Scott, Hou	-	0	0	0	0	0	.000	6	0	0	0	0	0	0	1	0	5	4.0	0	1	0	0	1.000	1	0	0	0	.00
Sturtze,Tanyon, NYY	-	0	0	0	0	0	.063	16	1	0	0	0	0	0	5	2	64	78.0	2	16	0	1	1.000	12	4	0	0	.33
Suppan,Jeff, StL	.207	58	12	1	5	6	.190	195	37	3	0	1	9	7	42	27	32	194.1	12	28	1	3	.976	10	5	1	0	.50
Switzer,Jon, TB	-	0	0	0	0	0	-	0	0	0	0	0	0	0	0	0	2	4.0	0	0	0	0	-	0	0	0	0	-
Tadano,Kazuhito, Cle	-	0	0	0	0	0	.333	3	1	0	0	0	0	0	1	0	1	4.0	0	0	0	0	-	1	0	0	0	.00
Takatsu,Shingo, CWS-NYM	-	0	0	0	0	0	-	0	0	0	0	0	0	0	0	0	40	36.1	3	4	0	1	1.000	3	1	0	0	.33
Tallet,Brian, Cle	-	0	0	0	0	0	.000	2	0	0	0	0	0	0	0	0	2	4.2	0	0	0	0	-	0	0	0	0	-
Taschner,Jack, SF	-	0	0	0	0	0	-	0	0	0	0	0	0	0	0	0	24	22.2	1	3	0	0	1.000	3	1	1	0	.33
Tavarez,Julian, StL	-	0	0	0	0	1	.111	135	15	0	0	0	8	6	57	21	74	65.2	3	7	0	0	1.000	3	1	0	0	.33
Tejeda,Robinson, Phi	.100	20	2	0	0	5	.100	20	2	0	1	0	0	0	9	5	26	85.2	5	6	0	0	1.000	3	2	1	0	.67
Tejera,Michael, Tex	-	0	0	0	0	0	.157	51	8	0	0	1	5	1	6	3	3	2.0	0	0	0	0	-	0	0	0	0	-

296

Pitchers Hitting, Fielding and Holding Runners

Pitcher	2005 Hitting						Career Hitting										2005 Fielding and Holding Runners											
	Avg	AB	H	HR	RBI	SH	Avg	AB	H	2B	3B	HR	RBI	BB	SO	SH	G	Inn	PO	A	E	DP	Pct	SBA	CS	PCS	PPO	CS%
Telemaco,Amaury, Phi	-	0	0	0	0	0	.121	116	14	4	1	0	3	6	51	8	7	10.2	2	1	0	0	1.000	0	0	0	0	
Thompson,Brad, StL	.167	6	1	0	0	1	.167	6	1	0	0	0	0	0	2	0	40	55.0	3	12	0	1	1.000	2	1	0	0	.50
Thompson,Derek, LAD	.000	4	0	0	0	1	.000	4	0	0	0	0	0	0	2	1	4	18.0	1	4	0	1	1.000	7	3	1	0	.43
Thompson,Justin, Tex	-	0	0	0	0	0	-	0	0	0	0	0	0	0	0	0	2	1.2	0	0	0	-		1	0	0	0	.00
Thomson,John, Atl	.200	25	5	0	2	9	.191	288	55	4	1	0	18	12	123	46	17	98.2	6	14	0	2	1.000	15	6	1	0	.40
Thornton,Matt, Sea	-	0	0	0	0	0	-	0	0	0	0	0	0	0	0	0	55	57.0	0	6	0	1	1.000	6	0	0	0	.00
Timlin,Mike, Bos	-	0	0	0	0	0	.000	7	0	0	0	0	0	0	4	0	81	80.1	6	12	1	0	.947	7	1	0	1	.14
Tomko,Brett, SF	.164	55	9	0	5	10	.173	394	68	9	0	0	28	17	144	61	33	190.2	13	19	1	3	.970	8	3	0	0	.38
Torres,Salomon, Pit	.500	4	2	0	0	0	.144	97	14	1	1	0	1	2	43	12	78	94.2	4	14	1	0	.947	4	2	0	0	.50
Towers,Josh, Tor	.000	6	0	0	0	0	.000	10	0	0	0	0	0	0	2	2	33	208.2	29	31	0	4	1.000	19	5	0	1	.26
Trachsel,Steve, NYM	.067	15	1	0	0	0	.166	589	98	16	1	2	38	22	183	83	6	37.0	2	8	1	1	.909	4	0	0	0	.00
Tsao,Chin-hui, Col	-	0	0	0	0	0	.154	13	2	1	0	0	0	0	1	2	10	11.0	0	2	1	0	.667	3	0	0	0	.00
Tucker,T.J., Was	-	0	0	0	0	0	.278	36	10	1	0	0	0	0	10	1	13	12.2	1	2	0	0	1.000	1	0	0	0	.00
Turnbow,Derrick, Mil	-	0	0	0	0	0	.000	1	0	0	0	0	0	0	0	0	69	67.1	6	4	0	0	1.000	0	0	0	0	-
Urbina,Ugueth, Det-Phi	-	0	0	0	0	0	.094	53	5	0	0	0	1	3	32	4	81	79.2	2	4	0	0	1.000	7	0	0	0	.00
Valdez,Ismael, Fla	.154	13	2	0	0	3	.130	399	52	9	0	1	17	13	122	61	14	50.2	5	7	0	1	1.000	6	1	0	0	.17
Valentine,Joe, Cin	-	0	0	0	0	0	.000	1	0	0	0	0	0	0	0	0	16	14.1	0	2	1	0	.667	2	0	0	0	.00
Valverde,Jose, Ari	-	0	0	0	0	0	1.000	1	1	1	0	0	0	0	0	0	61	66.1	3	7	0	0	1.000	2	1	1	0	.50
Van Buren,Jermaine, ChC	-	0	0	0	0	0	-	0	0	0	0	0	0	0	0	0	6	6.0	0	0	1	0	.000	1	1	0	0	1.00
Vargas,Claudio, Was-Ari	.111	36	4	0	3	7	.057	88	5	0	0	0	3	3	30	18	25	132.1	7	10	0	1	1.000	9	3	0	0	.33
Vargas,Jason, Fla	.308	26	8	0	2	0	.308	26	8	2	0	0	2	1	7	0	17	73.2	2	13	0	1	1.000	11	0	0	1	.00
Vasquez,Jorge, Atl	.000	1	0	0	0	0	.000	1	0	0	0	0	0	0	0	0	7	9.0	1	0	0	0	1.000	1	0	0	0	.00
Vazquez,Javier, Ari	.238	63	15	1	2	6	.214	426	91	10	2	1	24	17	68	72	33	215.2	8	34	3	2	.933	8	2	1	0	.25
Verlander,Just, Det	-	0	0	0	0	0	-	0	0	0	0	0	0	0	0	0	2	11.1	2	2	1	0	.800	1	0	0	0	.00
Villarreal,Osc, Ari	-	0	0	0	0	0	.000	3	0	0	0	0	0	0	2	0	11	13.2	1	1	0	0	1.000	1	0	0	0	.00
Villone,Ron, Sea-Fla	.000	1	0	0	0	0	.130	169	22	3	1	1	7	1	50	12	79	64.0	8	10	1	0	.947	2	1	0	1	.50
Vizcaino,Luis, CWS	-	0	0	0	0	0	.000	2	0	0	0	0	0	0	2	0	65	70.0	6	7	0	1	1.000	5	2	0	0	.40
Vogelsong,Ryan, Pit	.111	9	1	0	0	0	.179	56	10	4	0	0	3	2	22	12	44	81.1	7	6	0	0	1.000	4	1	0	0	.25
Volquez,Edison, Tex	-	0	0	0	0	0	-	0	0	0	0	0	0	0	0	0	6	12.2	1	0	0	0	1.000	1	0	0	0	.00
Waechter,Doug, TB	.000	2	0	0	0	1	.000	2	0	0	0	0	0	0	0	1	29	157.0	11	8	3	1	.864	9	4	0	0	.44
Wagner,Billy, Phi	.333	3	1	0	0	0	.100	20	2	0	0	0	0	1	1	12	0	75	77.2	4	6	0	1	1.000	11	2	0	0	.18
Wagner,Ryan, Cin	.000	1	0	0	0	0	.000	1	0	0	0	0	0	0	0	1	1	42	45.2	2	6	0	0	1.000	2	1	0	0	.50
Wainwright,Adam, StL	-	0	0	0	0	0	-	0	0	0	0	0	0	0	0	0	2	2.0	0	0	0	0	-	2	0	0	0	.00
Wakefield,Tim, Bos	.250	8	2	0	1	1	.130	92	12	2	0	1	4	2	32	13	33	225.1	30	20	2	2	.962	25	7	1	0	.28
Walker,Jamie, Det	-	0	0	0	0	0	-	0	0	0	0	0	0	0	0	0	66	48.2	2	7	1	0	.900	3	1	0	0	.33
Walker,Kevin, CWS	-	0	0	0	0	0	.250	4	1	0	0	0	0	0	1	0	9	7.0	0	1	0	0	1.000	0	0	0	0	-
Walker,Pete, Tor	-	0	0	0	0	0	.000	1	0	0	0	0	0	0	0	1	1	41	84.0	6	10	1	0	.941	6	2	0	2	.33
Walker,Tyler, SF	.000	1	0	0	0	0	.000	10	0	0	0	0	0	0	0	6	0	67	61.2	2	7	1	1	.900	4	1	0	0	.25
Wang,Chien-Ming, NYY	.000	1	0	0	0	0	.000	1	0	0	0	0	0	0	0	0	18	116.1	4	38	1	3	.977	13	4	0	0	.31
Wasdin,John, Tex	.000	1	0	0	0	0	.200	15	3	1	0	0	1	1	5	0	31	75.2	0	5	0	0	1.000	3	0	0	0	.00
Washburn,Jarrod, LAA	.000	4	0	0	0	0	.286	28	8	0	0	0	3	3	7	6	29	177.1	6	15	4	3	.840	6	6	1	0	1.00
Weathers,David, Cin	-	0	0	0	0	0	.101	138	14	0	0	2	4	7	84	16	73	77.2	2	4	0	0	1.000	7	3	0	0	.43
Weaver,Jeff, LAD	.229	70	16	0	7	6	.220	159	35	5	1	0	10	3	52	15	34	224.0	11	26	2	1	.949	26	6	0	1	.23
Webb,Brandon, Ari	.097	62	6	0	2	13	.097	176	17	1	0	0	6	6	87	24	33	229.0	18	44	2	7	.969	30	4	1	0	.13
Webb,John, TB	-	0	0	0	0	0	-	0	0	0	0	0	0	0	0	0	1	4.0	0	0	0	0	-	0	0	0	0	
Weber,Ben, Cin	-	0	0	0	0	0	-	0	0	0	0	0	0	0	0	0	10	12.1	3	3	0	0	1.000	3	0	0	0	.00
Wellemeyer,Todd, ChC	.250	4	1	0	0	0	.200	5	1	0	0	0	0	1	2	0	22	32.1	2	0	0	0	1.000	1	0	0	0	.00
Wells,David, Bos	.143	7	1	0	1	0	.117	120	14	1	0	0	4	3	39	11	30	184.0	3	19	3	2	.880	13	5	4	0	.38
Wells,Kip, Pit	.158	57	9	1	2	3	.180	239	43	9	1	3	12	4	104	24	33	182.0	6	33	2	4	.951	18	3	0	0	.17
Westbrook,Jake, Cle	.000	2	0	0	0	0	.000	6	0	0	0	0	0	1	5	2	34	210.2	31	49	2	2	.976	17	4	1	1	.24
Wheeler,Dan, Hou	-	0	0	0	0	0	.143	7	1	0	0	0	0	0	1	1	71	73.1	3	11	0	0	1.000	6	0	0	0	.00
White,Gabe, StL	-	0	0	0	0	0	.105	38	4	0	0	1	3	1	26	10	6	8.1	0	1	0	0	1.000	1	1	1	0	1.00
White,Matt, Was	.000	1	0	0	0	0	.000	1	0	0	0	0	0	0	0	0	4	4.0	0	0	0	0	-	0	0	0	0	-
White,Rick, Pit	.000	2	0	0	0	0	.095	42	4	1	0	0	1	0	12	2	71	75.0	2	16	1	0	.947	11	3	0	0	.27
Whiteside,Matt, Tor	-	0	0	0	0	0	-	0	0	0	0	0	0	0	0	0	2	3.2	0	0	0	0	-	2	0	0	0	.00
Wickman,Bob, Cle	-	0	0	0	0	0	.000	2	0	0	0	0	0	0	0	0	64	62.0	7	5	2	1	.857	11	0	0	0	.00
Williams,Dave, Pit	.119	42	5	0	4	6	.119	101	12	3	0	1	9	1	55	9	33	138.2	6	23	2	5	.935	3	1	1	1	.33
Williams,Jerome, SF-ChC	.088	34	3	0	0	6	.112	107	12	2	0	1	1	1	49	18	22	122.2	8	25	1	3	.971	9	2	1	3	.22
Williams,Randy, SD-Col	.000	1	0	0	0	0	.000	1	0	0	0	0	0	0	0	0	32	26.1	3	3	0	1	1.000	2	0	0	0	.00
Williams,Todd, Bal	-	0	0	0	0	0	-	0	0	0	0	0	0	0	0	0	72	76.1	5	7	1	0	.923	7	1	0	0	.14
Williams,Woody, SD	.152	46	7	0	3	8	.206	427	88	24	1	3	37	15	145	34	28	159.2	11	18	0	1	1.000	10	1	0	0	.10
Williamson,Sc, ChC	-	0	0	0	0	0	.043	23	1	0	0	0	0	3	14	7	17	14.1	0	1	0	0	1.000	1	0	0	0	.00
Willis,Dontrelle, Fla	.261	92	24	1	11	4	.237	224	53	8	1	3	18	10	38	12	34	236.1	9	36	3	3	.938	6	5	1	0	.83
Wilson,C.J., Tex	-	0	0	0	0	0	-	0	0	0	0	0	0	0	0	0	24	48.0	2	10	1	1	.923	1	0	0	0	.00
Wilson,Paul, Cin	.176	17	3	0	1	2	.103	184	19	3	0	1	8	5	113	18	9	46.1	1	6	1	0	.875	1	0	0	0	.00
Wise,Matt, Mil	1.000	1	1	0	1	0	.200	5	1	0	0	0	1	0	1	1	49	64.1	3	4	0	0	1.000	10	0	0	0	.00
Witasick,Jay, Col-Oak	-	0	0	0	0	0	.071	42	3	0	0	3	1	2	22	2	60	63.1	2	5	0	2	1.000	10	1	0	0	.10
Wolf,Randy, Phi	.154	26	4	0	1	1	.193	332	64	17	0	4	30	19	104	49	13	80.0	3	8	0	2	1.000	2	1	1	0	.50
Wood,Kerry, ChC	.111	18	2	0	2	2	.166	338	56	5	0	7	30	11	112	46	21	66.0	3	3	2	0	.750	7	4	1	0	.57
Wood,Mike, KC	-	0	0	0	0	0	.000	2	0	0	0	0	0	0	1	0	47	115.0	9	16	0	1	1.000	4	3	0	2	.75
Woods,Jake, LAA	-	0	0	0	0	0	-	0	0	0	0	0	0	0	0	0	28	27.2	0	2	0	0	1.000	3	0	0	0	.00
Woodyard,Mark, Det	-	0	0	0	0	0	-	0	0	0	0	0	0	0	0	0	3	6.0	1	2	0	0	1.000	1	0	0	0	.00
Worrell,Tim, Phi-Ari	.000	1	0	0	0	0	.100	80	8	1	0	0	4	4	43	10	51	48.2	2	4	0	0	1.000	2	1	0	0	.50
Wright,Jamey, Col	.145	55	8	0	3	3	.134	388	52	13	1	1	16	12	163	45	34	171.1	11	24	2	1	.946	32	7	0	6	.22
Wright,Jaret, NYY	-	0	0	0	0	0	.147	75	11	2	0	1	5	2	41	9	13	63.2	9	2	1	0	.846	6	1	0	0	.17

297

Pitchers Hitting, Fielding and Holding Runners

Pitcher	2005 Hitting						Career Hitting										2005 Fielding and Holding Runners										
	Avg	AB	H	HR	RBI	SH	Avg	AB	H	2B	3B	HR	RBI	BB	SO	SH	G	Inn	PO	A	E	DP	Pct	SBA	CS	PCS	PPO	CS%
Wuertz,Mike, ChC	.000	2	0	0	0	0	.000	3	0	0	0	0	0	0	3	0	75	75.2	2	7	0	2	1.000	11	4	0	0	.36
Wunsch,Kelly, LAD	.000	1	0	0	0	0	.000	1	0	0	0	0	0	0	1	0	46	23.2	2	6	0	1	1.000	3	1	1	1	.33
Yabu,Keiichi, Oak	.000	1	0	0	0	0	.000	1	0	0	0	0	0	0	0	0	40	58.0	5	5	0	0	1.000	4	1	0	0	.25
Yan,Esteban, LAA	-	0	0	0	0	0	1.000	2	2	0	0	1	1	0	0	1	49	66.2	7	10	0	0	1.000	7	2	0	0	.29
Young,Chris, Tex	.000	5	0	0	0	0	.000	5	0	0	0	0	0	0	3	0	31	164.2	8	12	0	1	1.000	19	6	0	0	.32
Zambrano,Carlos, ChC	.300	80	24	1	6	4	.230	257	59	13	2	4	17	4	95	18	33	223.1	21	34	2	4	.965	10	9	0	3	.90
Zambrano,Victor, NYM	.132	53	7	0	2	5	.132	68	9	1	1	0	3	0	27	8	31	166.1	20	20	3	2	.930	29	4	0	0	.14
Zito,Barry, Oak	.143	7	1	0	0	0	.038	26	1	0	0	0	0	0	13	2	35	228.1	12	34	0	1	1.000	26	4	2	0	.15

Hitters Pitching

Player	2005 Pitching											Career Pitching									
	G	W	L	Sv	IP	H	R	ER	BB	SO	ERA	G	W	L	Sv	IP	H	R	ER	BB	SO	ERA
Burroughs,Sean, SD	1	0	0	0	1.0	4	3	3	0	0	27.00	1	0	0	0	1.0	4	3	3	0	0	27.00
Durrington,Tr, Mil	0	0	0	0	0.0	0	0	0	0	0	-	1	0	0	0	0.1	0	0	0	0	0	0.00
Finley,Steve, LAA	0	0	0	0	0.0	0	0	0	0	0	-	1	0	0	0	1.0	0	0	0	1	0	0.00
Gonzalez,Wiki, Sea	0	0	0	0	0.0	0	0	0	0	0	-	1	0	0	0	1.0	0	0	0	1	0	0.00
Harris,Lenny, Fla	0	0	0	0	0.0	0	0	0	0	0	-	1	0	0	0	1.0	0	0	0	0	1	0.00
Jimenez,D'Ang, Cin	0	0	0	0	0.0	0	0	0	0	0	-	1	0	0	0	1.1	0	0	0	0	0	0.00
Laker,Tim, TB	0	0	0	0	0.0	0	0	0	0	0	-	2	0	0	0	2.0	2	0	0	2	1	0.00
Loretta,Mark, SD	0	0	0	0	0.0	0	0	0	0	0	-	1	0	0	0	1.0	1	0	0	1	2	0.00
Mabry,John, StL	0	0	0	0	0.0	0	0	0	0	0	-	2	0	0	0	1.0	6	7	7	4	0	63.00
McCarty,David, Bos	0	0	0	0	0.0	0	0	0	0	0	-	3	0	0	0	3.2	2	1	1	1	4	2.45
Menechino,Frank, Tor	0	0	0	0	0.0	0	0	0	0	0	-	2	0	0	0	1.1	8	4	4	0	0	27.00
Nunez,Abraham , StL	0	0	0	0	0.0	0	0	0	0	0	-	1	0	0	0	0.1	0	0	0	0	0	0.00
Osik,Keith, Was	0	0	0	0	0.0	0	0	0	0	0	-	2	0	0	0	2.0	7	9	9	2	2	40.50
Perez,Tomas, Phi	0	0	0	0	0.0	0	0	0	0	0	-	1	0	0	0	0.1	0	0	0	0	0	0.00
Relaford,Desi, Col	0	0	0	0	0.0	0	0	0	0	0	-	1	0	0	0	1.0	0	0	0	0	1	0.00

The Manager's Record

Fans know a lot about the abilities of players. They can answer questions concerning any two players, such as "Who has speed?" or "Who has more power?" The average fan, however, would not be able to make similar comparisons between managers. Who is quicker to the bullpen: Ozzie Guillen or Eric Wedge? Who platoons more: Bobby Cox or Tony LaRussa? Who uses the intentional walk more often: Terry Francona or Joe Torre?

You can also use this record to determine if a manager adjusts to the personnel on his team, or sticks with a strategy regardless. For example, Lou Piniella in 2002, managing the Mariners with Edgar Martinez, John Olerud, and Dan Wilson in the lineup, used 96 pinch runners. In 2003, managing the Devil Rays, he used only 29 pinch runners.

Brand new for 2006 is a new, updated version of the traditional Quick Hooks and Slow Hooks categories directly from Bill James. For Quick Hooks and Slow Hooks a score is calculated by adding the number of Pitches to 10 times the number of Runs Allowed for the starting pitcher. The bottom 25% of scores in the league are considered to be Quick Hooks. The top 25% of scores in the league are considered to be Slow Hooks.

Here is a description of the other categories:

Lineups
LUp is different Lineups Used. This looks at batting order, not fielding positions. For games in which a DH is used, lineup slots 1-9 are compared. For games in which the pitcher bats, lineup slots 1-8 are compared.

PL% is the Platoon Percentage of the starting lineup. For example, in 2005 Jack McKeon had a 43% platoon percentage, a low figure. This means that, on average, McKeon only had 43% of his starting-lineup hitters with a platoon advantage (i.e. batting lefty against right-handed starters or batting right-handed against lefty starters).

Substitutions
PH is Pinch Hitters used. PR is Pinch Runners used. DS is Defensive Substitutions

Pitcher Usage
Quick and Slow Hooks are mentioned above. LO is Long Outings, number of games in which the starter threw more than 120 pitches. Rel is Relief Appearances.

Tactics
SBA is Stolen Base Attempts. SacA is Sacrifice bunt Attempts. IBB is Intentional Walks issued. PO is Pitch Outs called

Results
Headings are self-explanatory.

Felipe Alou

Year	Team	Lg	G	LINEUPS		SUBSTITUTIONS			PITCHER USAGE				TACTICS				RESULTS		
				LUp	PL%	PH	PR	DS	Quick	Slow	LO	Rel	SBA	SacA	IBB	PO	W	L	Pct
1994	Expos	NL	114	72	.48	143	33	7	51	18	0	259	173	72	24	20	74	40	.649
1995	Expos	NL	144	116	.49	200	36	10	48	28	7	396	169	74	20	22	66	78	.458
1996	Expos	NL	162	113	.49	240	31	30	60	27	13	433	142	97	25	25	88	74	.543
1997	Expos	NL	162	138	.58	205	22	40	52	41	15	390	121	91	33	30	78	84	.481
1998	Expos	NL	162	133	.50	235	26	37	56	26	2	443	137	111	30	18	65	97	.401
1999	Expos	NL	162	143	.49	247	33	55	45	36	5	432	121	84	28	26	68	94	.420
2000	Expos	NL	162	120	.61	211	24	32	51	36	5	452	106	103	29	18	67	95	.414
2001	Expos	NL	53	40	.58	84	4	5	18	12	1	171	39	28	10	7	21	32	.396
2003	Giants	NL	161	127	.56	202	32	42	49	30	8	461	90	93	34	9	100	61	.621
2004	Giants	NL	162	138	.67	265	63	60	25	49	13	521	66	104	35	2	91	71	.562
2005	Giants	NL	162	139	.62	242	33	49	28	47	7	511	106	109	42	12	75	87	.463
	162-Game Average			129	.55	229	34	37	49	35	8	451	128	97	31	19	80	82	.494

Dusty Baker

Year	Team	Lg	G	LINEUPS		SUBSTITUTIONS			PITCHER USAGE				TACTICS				RESULTS		
				LUp	PL%	PH	PR	DS	Quick	Slow	LO	Rel	SBA	SacA	IBB	PO	W	L	Pct
1994	Giants	NL	115	76	.53	177	16	9	29	25	2	288	154	88	24	78	55	60	.478
1995	Giants	NL	144	96	.41	230	36	13	32	50	8	381	184	101	33	77	67	77	.465
1996	Giants	NL	162	129	.51	250	17	15	24	58	15	425	166	103	45	96	68	94	.420
1997	Giants	NL	162	114	.71	212	17	22	46	25	17	481	170	85	37	93	90	72	.556
1998	Giants	NL	163	130	.62	224	20	12	43	38	8	433	153	111	51	41	89	74	.546
1999	Giants	NL	162	120	.62	233	16	16	30	51	27	450	165	113	28	40	86	76	.531
2000	Giants	NL	162	82	.56	233	26	22	38	50	25	384	118	86	16	37	97	65	.599
2001	Giants	NL	162	122	.48	261	22	19	40	48	10	439	99	95	32	45	90	72	.556
2002	Giants	NL	162	118	.43	226	34	37	28	56	21	417	95	88	44	40	95	66	.590
2003	Cubs	NL	162	114	.49	274	25	43	24	59	26	420	104	93	36	24	88	74	.543
2004	Cubs	NL	162	113	.44	294	27	19	37	37	13	460	94	106	33	56	89	73	.549
2005	Cubs	NL	162	121	.59	240	21	29	40	46	10	457	104	87	48	70	79	83	.488
	162-Game Average			115	.53	246	24	22	35	47	16	434	138	100	37	60	86	76	.528

Buddy Bell

Year	Team	Lg	G	LINEUPS		SUBSTITUTIONS			PITCHER USAGE				TACTICS				RESULTS		
				LUp	PL%	PH	PR	DS	Quick	Slow	LO	Rel	SBA	SacA	IBB	PO	W	L	Pct
1996	Tigers	AL	162	128	.50	123	29	17	17	27	26	426	137	63	40	13	53	109	.327
1997	Tigers	AL	162	116	.61	163	19	22	24	7	12	417	233	44	24	32	79	83	.488
1998	Tigers	AL	137	88	.58	102	25	7	15	15	10	362	143	24	29	38	52	85	.380
2000	Rockies	NL	162	106	.64	285	21	8	12	18	10	480	192	100	53	40	82	80	.506
2001	Rockies	NL	162	116	.61	314	27	14	18	30	8	476	186	108	43	43	73	89	.451
2002	Rockies	NL	22	15	.55	48	1	5	5	11	2	69	17	9	11	5	6	16	.273
2005	Royals	AL	112	93	.61	97	18	8	31	25	0	310	48	38	17	25	43	69	.384
	162-Game Average			117	.59	200	25	14	22	23	12	448	169	68	38	35	68	94	.422

Bruce Bochy

Year	Team	Lg	G	LINEUPS		SUBSTITUTIONS			PITCHER USAGE				TACTICS				RESULTS		
				LUp	PL%	PH	PR	DS	Quick	Slow	LO	Rel	SBA	SacA	IBB	PO	W	L	Pct
1995	Padres	NL	144	96	.59	262	30	23	44	41	17	337	170	68	26	38	70	74	.486
1996	Padres	NL	162	114	.52	289	29	15	51	33	10	411	164	73	42	65	91	71	.562
1997	Padres	NL	162	111	.60	291	26	9	45	45	3	426	200	84	24	58	76	86	.469
1998	Padres	NL	162	110	.65	280	62	44	44	45	9	369	116	84	30	27	98	64	.605
1999	Padres	NL	162	137	.60	298	51	21	44	36	4	403	241	60	39	29	74	88	.457
2000	Padres	NL	162	134	.52	285	44	14	41	47	14	443	184	52	40	27	76	86	.469
2001	Padres	NL	162	116	.60	255	54	27	32	47	6	422	173	43	40	23	79	83	.488
2002	Padres	NL	162	123	.66	273	46	56	41	40	2	459	115	63	61	12	66	96	.407
2003	Padres	NL	162	134	.58	340	20	29	34	41	3	473	115	63	52	6	64	98	.395
2004	Padres	NL	162	96	.54	285	38	47	46	32	1	437	77	75	39	14	87	75	.537
2005	Padres	NL	162	128	.58	285	31	49	46	36	2	456	143	89	45	16	82	80	.506
	162-Game Average			119	.59	289	40	31	43	41	7	426	156	69	40	29	79	83	.489

Bobby Cox

Year	Team	Lg	G	LINEUPS		SUBSTITUTIONS			PITCHER USAGE				TACTICS				RESULTS		
				LUp	PL%	PH	PR	DS	Quick	Slow	LO	Rel	SBA	SacA	IBB	PO	W	L	Pct
1994	Braves	NL	114	64	.60	163	30	25	22	31	5	244	79	83	39	44	68	46	.596
1995	Braves	NL	144	59	.56	224	48	40	41	34	13	339	116	77	38	41	90	54	.625
1996	Braves	NL	162	162	.62	254	32	27	48	43	19	408	126	90	48	34	96	66	.593
1997	Braves	NL	162	87	.64	276	58	29	40	37	23	374	166	112	46	13	101	62	.620

Year Team	Lg	G	LUp	PL%	PH	PR	DS	Quick	Slow	LO	Rel	SBA	SacA	IBB	PO	W	L	Pct
1998 Braves	NL	162	80	.64	245	28	25	44	33	14	354	141	97	26	40	106	56	.654
1999 Braves	NL	162	76	.58	272	51	34	44	39	13	394	214	89	37	54	103	59	.636
2000 Braves	NL	162	103	.59	252	72	11	52	41	6	376	204	109	34	59	95	67	.586
2001 Braves	NL	162	113	.57	278	50	23	49	40	4	412	131	84	55	90	88	74	.543
2002 Braves	NL	161	105	.48	289	38	44	57	30	5	469	115	84	63	46	101	59	.631
2003 Braves	NL	162	69	.52	262	49	45	40	44	5	489	90	85	69	49	101	61	.623
2004 Braves	NL	162	105	.70	263	80	28	50	33	4	483	118	104	50	22	96	66	.593
2005 Braves	NL	162	110	.69	247	54	35	46	28	1	484	124	104	52	11	90	72	.556
162-Game Average			98	.60	261	51	32	46	37	10	417	140	96	48	43	98	64	.605

Terry Francona

Year Team	Lg	G	LUp	PL%	PH	PR	DS	Quick	Slow	LO	Rel	SBA	SacA	IBB	PO	W	L	Pct
1997 Phillies	NL	162	98	.66	288	19	28	28	54	22	409	148	91	31	30	68	94	.420
1998 Phillies	NL	162	84	.53	256	20	19	34	57	20	385	142	85	23	16	75	87	.463
1999 Phillies	NL	162	85	.51	239	13	31	29	41	16	441	160	81	17	27	77	85	.475
2000 Phillies	NL	162	108	.53	278	17	14	38	43	25	414	132	89	17	16	65	97	.401
2004 Red Sox	AL	162	141	.65	139	87	60	37	48	2	437	98	18	28	27	98	64	.605
2005 Red Sox	AL	162	104	.67	110	46	37	25	55	3	442	57	21	28	11	95	67	.586
162-Game Average			103	.59	218	34	32	32	50	15	421	123	64	24	21	80	82	.492

Ron Gardenhire

Year Team	Lg	G	LUp	PL%	PH	PR	DS	Quick	Slow	LO	Rel	SBA	SacA	IBB	PO	W	L	Pct
2002 Twins	AL	161	111	.69	157	42	42	53	22	4	435	141	45	24	11	94	67	.584
2003 Twins	AL	162	126	.63	144	50	26	50	33	2	399	138	59	35	14	90	72	.556
2004 Twins	AL	162	131	.59	148	55	29	54	21	1	435	162	66	27	19	92	70	.568
2005 Twins	AL	162	135	.58	104	45	26	51	22	0	396	146	58	38	16	83	79	.512
162-Game Average			126	.62	138	48	31	52	25	2	417	147	57	31	15	90	72	.555

Phil Garner

Year Team	Lg	G	LUp	PL%	PH	PR	DS	Quick	Slow	LO	Rel	SBA	SacA	IBB	PO	W	L	Pct
1994 Brewers	AL	115	94	.53	53	33	24	31	35	0	252	96	46	16	23	53	62	.461
1995 Brewers	AL	144	120	.58	83	67	52	42	42	10	321	145	64	23	52	65	79	.451
1996 Brewers	AL	162	114	.58	115	48	46	50	36	13	385	149	72	20	82	80	82	.494
1997 Brewers	AL	161	128	.59	190	42	36	51	34	6	367	158	65	21	55	78	83	.484
1998 Brewers	NL	162	125	.59	265	54	46	52	43	6	416	140	85	21	59	74	88	.457
1999 Brewers	NL	112	69	.57	182	15	5	28	26	4	294	75	85	19	57	52	60	.464
2000 Tigers	AL	162	128	.53	126	30	25	35	38	8	429	121	58	13	26	79	83	.488
2001 Tigers	AL	162	116	.64	93	40	14	25	51	9	391	194	58	29	36	66	96	.407
2002 Tigers	AL	6	3	.63	1	1	0	1	3	2	15	4	0	2	0	0	6	.000
2004 Astros	NL	74	31	.54	163	28	35	27	15	3	241	78	40	24	7	48	26	.649
2005 Astros	NL	163	101	.48	251	40	63	57	34	5	434	159	99	29	10	89	73	.549
162-Game Average			117	.57	173	45	39	45	41	8	404	150	77	25	46	78	84	.481

John Gibbons

Year Team	Lg	G	LUp	PL%	PH	PR	DS	Quick	Slow	LO	Rel	SBA	SacA	IBB	PO	W	L	Pct
2004 Blue Jays	AL	51	36	.68	55	3	2	14	8	2	130	34	2	11	21	20	30	.400
2005 Blue Jays	AL	162	124	.66	148	11	37	55	18	1	432	107	28	29	45	80	82	.494
162-Game Average			122	.67	154	11	30	52	20	2	427	107	23	30	50	76	85	.472

Ozzie Guillen

Year Team	Lg	G	LUp	PL%	PH	PR	DS	Quick	Slow	LO	Rel	SBA	SacA	IBB	PO	W	L	Pct
2004 White Sox	AL	162	134	.58	160	46	15	27	65	5	399	129	79	36	17	83	79	.512
2005 White Sox	AL	162	112	.51	100	32	21	31	55	3	412	204	68	42	15	99	63	.611
162-Game Average			123	.54	130	39	18	29	60	4	406	167	74	39	16	91	71	.562

Mike Hargrove

Year Team	Lg	G	LUp	PL%	PH	PR	DS	Quick	Slow	LO	Rel	SBA	SacA	IBB	PO	W	L	Pct
1994 Indians	AL	113	53	.67	79	18	31	23	31	3	222	179	43	22	40	66	47	.584
1995 Indians	AL	144	64	.66	101	34	21	36	23	12	335	185	40	12	22	100	44	.694
1996 Indians	AL	161	96	.56	115	20	25	39	31	14	382	210	58	31	41	99	62	.615
1997 Indians	AL	162	109	.58	86	17	14	34	46	14	429	177	60	30	37	86	75	.534
1998 Indians	AL	162	108	.62	88	21	32	29	39	19	423	203	53	39	47	89	73	.549
1999 Indians	AL	162	123	.66	99	25	22	41	44	15	466	197	82	36	28	97	65	.599
2000 Orioles	AL	162	107	.54	77	42	19	25	55	24	396	191	36	21	31	74	88	.457
2001 Orioles	AL	162	139	.53	82	27	20	39	42	3	392	186	57	17	71	63	98	.391
2002 Orioles	AL	162	125	.52	129	24	22	31	44	7	407	158	54	34	39	67	95	.414
2003 Orioles	AL	163	120	.52	78	37	22	30	52	11	425	125	67	43	16	71	91	.438
2005 Mariners	AL	162	97	.52	125	24	18	30	45	1	433	149	61	32	36	69	93	.426
162-Game Average			108	.58	100	27	23	34	43	12	407	185	58	30	39	83	78	.515

Clint Hurdle

Year Team	Lg	G	LUp	PL%	PH	PR	DS	Quick	Slow	LO	Rel	SBA	SacA	IBB	PO	W	L	Pct
2002 Rockies	NL	140	100	.52	283	30	41	31	44	3	437	139	44	38	13	67	73	.479
2003 Rockies	NL	162	108	.47	317	17	32	35	40	0	500	100	82	51	16	74	88	.457
2004 Rockies	NL	162	131	.57	330	24	36	35	62	3	473	77	126	84	11	68	94	.420
2005 Rockies	NL	162	135	.60	273	21	40	43	60	1	459	97	114	54	22	67	95	.414
162-Game Average			123	.54	311	24	39	37	53	2	484	107	95	59	16	71	91	.441

Tony LaRussa

Year Team	Lg	G	LUp	PL%	PH	PR	DS	Quick	Slow	LO	Rel	SBA	SacA	IBB	PO	W	L	Pct
1994 Athletics	AL	114	97	.62	89	28	14	43	21	5	308	130	31	23	32	51	63	.447
1995 Athletics	AL	144	120	.54	113	38	24	33	38	19	358	158	42	17	42	67	77	.465
1996 Cardinals	NL	162	120	.52	246	25	13	32	48	24	413	207	117	38	41	88	74	.543
1997 Cardinals	NL	162	146	.54	307	17	18	34	42	16	399	224	77	26	79	73	89	.451
1998 Cardinals	NL	162	146	.52	259	7	18	62	31	13	429	174	85	32	34	83	79	.512
1999 Cardinals	NL	161	138	.47	264	32	28	50	41	13	454	182	103	31	30	75	86	.466
2000 Cardinals	NL	162	137	.53	240	35	25	40	31	11	386	138	107	21	34	95	67	.586
2001 Cardinals	NL	162	117	.47	256	26	13	46	36	7	485	126	102	31	25	93	69	.574
2002 Cardinals	NL	162	117	.52	352	35	41	57	33	6	472	128	105	39	13	97	65	.599
2003 Cardinals	NL	162	126	.50	352	28	51	38	49	10	460	114	108	36	9	85	77	.525
2004 Cardinals	NL	162	119	.53	321	33	75	29	44	6	469	158	87	24	7	105	57	.648
2005 Cardinals	NL	162	138	.55	270	25	48	41	39	1	436	119	92	27	9	100	62	.617
162-Game Average			131	.52	265	28	32	44	39	11	437	160	91	30	31	87	75	.539

Ken Macha

Year Team	Lg	G	LUp	PL%	PH	PR	DS	Quick	Slow	LO	Rel	SBA	SacA	IBB	PO	W	L	Pct
2003 Athletics	AL	162	111	.57	140	29	23	45	37	4	364	62	31	42	9	96	66	.593
2004 Athletics	AL	162	119	.60	141	16	14	36	47	9	414	69	30	49	2	91	71	.562
2005 Athletics	AL	162	127	.62	83	17	11	45	36	4	410	53	29	42	13	88	74	.543
162-Game Average			119	.59	121	21	16	42	40	6	396	61	30	44	8	92	70	.566

Pete Mackanin

Year Team	Lg	G	LUp	PL%	PH	PR	DS	Quick	Slow	LO	Rel	SBA	SacA	IBB	PO	W	L	Pct
2005 Pirates	NL	26	24	.52	54	1	5	11	4	0	94	19	19	5	2	12	14	.462
162-Game Average			150	.52	336	6	31	69	25	0	586	118	118	31	12	75	87	.462

Charlie Manuel

Year Team	Lg	G	LUp	PL%	PH	PR	DS	Quick	Slow	LO	Rel	SBA	SacA	IBB	PO	W	L	Pct
2000 Indians	AL	162	102	.64	73	40	26	21	12	20	462	147	59	38	30	90	72	.556
2001 Indians	AL	162	114	.61	105	30	49	28	17	10	484	120	67	34	43	91	71	.562
2002 Indians	AL	87	68	.61	60	10	19	13	17	4	225	57	19	21	3	39	48	.448
2005 Phillies	NL	162	80	.64	265	36	19	43	28	3	442	143	86	51	11	88	74	.543
162-Game Average			103	.63	142	33	32	30	21	10	456	132	65	41	25	87	75	.538

Lee Mazzilli

Year	Team	Lg	G	LUp	PL%	PH	PR	DS	Quick	Slow	LO	Rel	SBA	SacA	IBB	PO	W	L	Pct
				LINEUPS		SUBSTITUTIONS			PITCHER USAGE				TACTICS				RESULTS		
2004	Orioles	AL	162	105	.60	106	52	19	45	35	2	452	142	57	43	32	78	84	.481
2005	Orioles	AL	107	81	.57	57	18	30	21	26	3	294	79	31	29	24	51	56	.477
	162-Game Average			112	.59	98	42	30	40	37	3	449	133	53	43	34	78	84	.480

Lloyd McClendon

Year	Team	Lg	G	LUp	PL%	PH	PR	DS	Quick	Slow	LO	Rel	SBA	SacA	IBB	PO	W	L	Pct
				LINEUPS		SUBSTITUTIONS			PITCHER USAGE				TACTICS				RESULTS		
2001	Pirates	NL	162	131	.51	255	17	32	45	38	2	410	166	83	49	52	62	100	.383
2002	Pirates	NL	161	121	.45	266	45	66	61	30	0	458	135	90	93	65	72	89	.447
2003	Pirates	NL	162	114	.57	315	27	59	48	34	4	457	123	99	58	73	75	87	.463
2004	Pirates	NL	162	114	.50	311	17	58	49	38	4	464	103	100	64	56	72	89	.447
2005	Pirates	NL	136	123	.53	218	8	19	36	34	2	357	84	62	60	37	55	81	.404
	162-Game Average			125	.51	282	24	48	49	36	2	444	126	90	67	59	70	92	.430

Jack McKeon

Year	Team	Lg	G	LUp	PL%	PH	PR	DS	Quick	Slow	LO	Rel	SBA	SacA	IBB	PO	W	L	Pct
				LINEUPS		SUBSTITUTIONS			PITCHER USAGE				TACTICS				RESULTS		
1997	Reds	NL	63	50	.46	102	18	7	23	11	5	154	79	42	12	18	33	30	.524
1998	Reds	NL	162	132	.55	288	30	25	49	25	10	366	137	98	31	7	77	85	.475
1999	Reds	NL	163	95	.50	251	30	38	58	23	9	381	218	88	43	14	96	67	.589
2000	Reds	NL	163	117	.51	270	31	41	52	27	10	387	137	82	43	24	85	77	.525
2003	Marlins	NL	124	57	.43	171	26	21	30	35	7	280	150	92	28	17	75	49	.605
2004	Marlins	NL	162	90	.48	240	38	34	42	37	2	404	139	103	61	19	83	79	.512
2005	Marlins	NL	162	82	.43	246	24	36	43	34	4	449	134	106	57	16	83	79	.512
	162-Game Average			101	.49	254	32	33	48	31	8	393	161	99	45	19	86	76	.533

Bob Melvin

Year	Team	Lg	G	LUp	PL%	PH	PR	DS	Quick	Slow	LO	Rel	SBA	SacA	IBB	PO	W	L	Pct
				LINEUPS		SUBSTITUTIONS			PITCHER USAGE				TACTICS				RESULTS		
2003	Mariners	AL	162	111	.62	81	62	33	25	45	7	366	145	44	24	5	93	69	.574
2004	Mariners	AL	162	151	.59	127	86	26	22	62	12	414	152	56	32	24	63	99	.389
2005	Diamondbacks	NL	162	120	.68	310	26	38	26	55	3	458	93	93	43	30	77	85	.475
	162-Game Average			127	.63	173	58	32	24	54	7	413	130	64	33	20	78	84	.479

Dave Miley

Year	Team	Lg	G	LUp	PL%	PH	PR	DS	Quick	Slow	LO	Rel	SBA	SacA	IBB	PO	W	L	Pct
				LINEUPS		SUBSTITUTIONS			PITCHER USAGE				TACTICS				RESULTS		
2003	Reds	NL	57	52	.61	98	12	18	22	10	0	168	27	25	21	7	22	35	.386
2004	Reds	NL	162	132	.61	284	33	52	42	44	2	497	102	78	55	9	76	86	.469
2005	Reds	NL	70	55	.61	104	10	7	14	20	1	204	45	19	22	5	27	43	.386
	162-Game Average			134	.61	272	31	43	44	41	2	487	98	68	55	12	70	92	.433

Jerry Narron

Year	Team	Lg	G	LUp	PL%	PH	PR	DS	Quick	Slow	LO	Rel	SBA	SacA	IBB	PO	W	L	Pct
				LINEUPS		SUBSTITUTIONS			PITCHER USAGE				TACTICS				RESULTS		
2001	Rangers	AL	134	94	.66	92	14	19	9	18	6	340	106	29	16	5	62	72	.463
2002	Rangers	AL	162	128	.52	159	63	38	29	50	9	487	96	58	32	6	72	90	.444
2005	Reds	NL	93	73	.61	156	9	14	13	22	1	287	50	44	25	7	46	46	.500
	162-Game Average			123	.59	169	36	30	21	37	7	464	105	55	30	7	75	87	.464

Tony Pena

Year	Team	Lg	G	LUp	PL%	PH	PR	DS	Quick	Slow	LO	Rel	SBA	SacA	IBB	PO	W	L	Pct
				LINEUPS		SUBSTITUTIONS			PITCHER USAGE				TACTICS				RESULTS		
2002	Royals	AL	126	102	.66	94	31	13	27	34	8	339	160	57	43	7	49	77	.389
2003	Royals	AL	162	125	.60	92	31	16	52	41	1	407	162	79	33	8	83	79	.512
2004	Royals	AL	162	141	.57	57	31	14	36	46	3	409	115	55	49	6	58	104	.358
2005	Royals	AL	33	33	.60	23	4	1	10	12	0	88	27	15	13	2	8	25	.242
	162-Game Average			134	.61	89	33	15	42	45	4	417	156	69	46	8	66	96	.410

Sam Perlozzo

Year Team	Lg	G	LINEUPS LUp	PL%	SUBSTITUTIONS PH	PR	DS	PITCHER USAGE Quick	Slow	LO	Rel	TACTICS SBA	SacA	IBB	PO	RESULTS W	L	Pct
2005 Orioles	AL	55	47	.61	28	23	26	16	11	0	180	41	24	3	8	23	32	.418
162-Game Average			138	.61	82	68	77	47	32	0	530	121	71	9	24	68	94	.418

Lou Piniella

Year Team	Lg	G	LINEUPS LUp	PL%	SUBSTITUTIONS PH	PR	DS	PITCHER USAGE Quick	Slow	LO	Rel	TACTICS SBA	SacA	IBB	PO	RESULTS W	L	Pct
1994 Mariners	AL	112	98	.49	113	24	6	30	35	4	252	69	54	28	37	49	63	.438
1995 Mariners	AL	145	98	.56	137	41	22	37	39	30	324	151	66	32	40	79	66	.545
1996 Mariners	AL	161	99	.55	190	28	14	56	21	15	403	129	65	40	40	85	76	.528
1997 Mariners	AL	162	84	.57	147	35	27	38	47	25	392	129	61	30	32	90	72	.556
1998 Mariners	AL	161	111	.53	99	38	43	38	54	32	368	154	58	18	20	76	85	.472
1999 Mariners	AL	162	130	.46	122	38	30	31	40	21	346	175	49	27	31	79	83	.488
2000 Mariners	AL	162	130	.50	109	43	52	51	37	1	383	178	73	32	22	91	71	.562
2001 Mariners	AL	162	115	.64	121	44	64	55	33	5	392	216	62	23	33	116	46	.716
2002 Mariners	AL	162	129	.64	98	135	50	47	37	8	343	195	59	34	25	93	69	.574
2003 Devil Rays	AL	162	124	.60	188	43	26	39	42	9	372	184	53	37	23	63	99	.389
2004 Devil Rays	AL	162	137	.63	121	30	37	50	34	8	401	174	44	35	16	70	91	.435
2005 Devil Rays	AL	162	135	.54	127	18	52	37	54	9	401	200	53	41	16	67	95	.414
162-Game Average			120	.56	136	45	37	44	41	14	378	169	60	33	29	83	79	.511

Willie Randolph

Year Team	Lg	G	LINEUPS LUp	PL%	SUBSTITUTIONS PH	PR	DS	PITCHER USAGE Quick	Slow	LO	Rel	TACTICS SBA	SacA	IBB	PO	RESULTS W	L	Pct
2005 Mets	NL	162	105	.64	222	10	51	46	34	4	392	193	89	43	18	83	79	.512
162-Game Average			105	.64	222	10	51	46	34	4	392	193	89	43	18	83	79	.512

Frank Robinson

Year Team	Lg	G	LINEUPS LUp	PL%	SUBSTITUTIONS PH	PR	DS	PITCHER USAGE Quick	Slow	LO	Rel	TACTICS SBA	SacA	IBB	PO	RESULTS W	L	Pct
2002 Expos	NL	162	121	.60	266	51	40	46	39	9	437	182	120	80	23	83	79	.512
2003 Expos	NL	162	134	.63	248	55	31	49	44	23	462	139	85	51	8	83	79	.512
2004 Expos	NL	162	131	.67	279	20	27	45	38	13	462	147	120	78	1	67	95	.414
2005 Nationals	NL	162	121	.63	266	48	35	45	47	16	470	90	115	77	4	81	81	.500
162-Game Average			127	.63	265	44	33	46	42	15	452	140	110	72	9	79	84	.485

Bob Schaefer

Year Team	Lg	G	LINEUPS LUp	PL%	SUBSTITUTIONS PH	PR	DS	PITCHER USAGE Quick	Slow	LO	Rel	TACTICS SBA	SacA	IBB	PO	RESULTS W	L	Pct
2005 Royals	AL	17	15	.57	13	3	2	4	5	0	46	11	3	3	3	5	12	.294
162-Game Average			143	.57	124	29	19	38	48	0	438	105	29	29	29	48	114	.294

Mike Scioscia

Year Team	Lg	G	LINEUPS LUp	PL%	SUBSTITUTIONS PH	PR	DS	PITCHER USAGE Quick	Slow	LO	Rel	TACTICS SBA	SacA	IBB	PO	RESULTS W	L	Pct
2000 Angels	AL	162	75	.62	110	41	4	56	42	6	441	145	63	32	40	82	80	.506
2001 Angels	AL	162	130	.62	118	30	8	29	41	5	384	168	66	33	50	75	87	.463
2002 Angels	AL	162	102	.64	170	60	24	32	32	5	400	168	61	24	29	99	63	.611
2003 Angels	AL	162	130	.64	134	54	40	50	47	1	375	190	64	38	25	77	85	.475
2004 Angels	AL	162	126	.57	115	43	46	35	40	3	343	189	69	27	32	92	70	.568
2005 Angels	AL	162	124	.65	92	37	37	47	37	1	379	218	58	24	43	95	67	.586
162-Game Average			115	.62	123	44	27	42	40	4	387	180	64	30	37	87	75	.535

Buck Showalter

Year Team	Lg	G	LINEUPS LUp	PL%	SUBSTITUTIONS PH	PR	DS	PITCHER USAGE Quick	Slow	LO	Rel	TACTICS SBA	SacA	IBB	PO	RESULTS W	L	Pct
1994 Yankees	AL	113	79	.59	95	31	3	24	30	0	241	95	34	18	22	70	43	.619
1995 Yankees	AL	145	107	.68	124	30	20	29	42	37	302	80	27	15	29	79	65	.549
1998 Diamondbacks	NL	162	124	.62	252	17	15	34	40	7	368	111	68	18	13	65	97	.401
1999 Diamondbacks	NL	162	97	.63	220	20	17	37	48	25	382	176	75	34	15	100	62	.617
2000 Diamondbacks	NL	162	99	.60	250	32	11	46	26	18	390	141	89	36	10	85	77	.525
2003 Rangers	AL	162	133	.61	88	51	41	34	33	4	494	90	35	45	12	71	91	.438

Year	Team	Lg	G	LINEUPS		SUBSTITUTIONS			PITCHER USAGE				TACTICS				RESULTS		
				LUp	PL%	PH	PR	DS	Quick	Slow	LO	Rel	SBA	SacA	IBB	PO	W	L	Pct
2004	Rangers	AL	162	120	.64	98	18	24	46	30	3	468	105	29	29	5	89	73	.549
2005	Rangers	AL	162	98	.59	57	22	11	42	39	2	454	82	11	31	5	79	83	.488
	162-Game Average			113	.62	156	29	19	38	38	13	408	116	48	30	15	84	78	.519

Joe Torre

Year	Team	Lg	G	LINEUPS		SUBSTITUTIONS			PITCHER USAGE				TACTICS				RESULTS		
				LUp	PL%	PH	PR	DS	Quick	Slow	LO	Rel	SBA	SacA	IBB	PO	W	L	Pct
1994	Cardinals	NL	115	79	.68	192	9	0	36	29	6	330	122	57	13	33	53	61	.465
1995	Cardinals	NL	47	36	.51	99	6	4	17	11	1	146	42	26	11	14	20	27	.426
1996	Yankees	AL	162	131	.57	92	62	55	59	23	22	411	142	53	27	19	92	70	.568
1997	Yankees	AL	162	118	.61	75	70	23	35	41	19	368	157	54	29	14	96	66	.593
1998	Yankees	AL	162	96	.62	94	36	28	43	38	27	334	216	44	18	9	114	48	.704
1999	Yankees	AL	162	76	.63	103	57	10	29	51	26	276	129	31	15	12	98	64	.605
2000	Yankees	AL	161	112	.63	86	49	27	43	53	27	382	147	22	16	8	87	74	.540
2001	Yankees	AL	161	94	.56	76	33	14	37	45	10	362	214	41	22	21	95	65	.594
2002	Yankees	AL	161	108	.62	92	60	31	37	49	10	334	138	34	44	17	103	58	.640
2003	Yankees	AL	163	104	.65	118	48	18	27	52	13	367	131	39	36	33	101	61	.623
2004	Yankees	AL	162	116	.65	99	42	47	48	35	3	436	117	48	32	33	101	61	.623
2005	Yankees	AL	162	117	.64	94	65	47	43	44	8	418	111	40	25	50	95	67	.586
	162-Game Average			108	.62	111	49	28	41	43	16	379	152	45	26	24	96	66	.594

Jim Tracy

Year	Team	Lg	G	LINEUPS		SUBSTITUTIONS			PITCHER USAGE				TACTICS				RESULTS		
				LUp	PL%	PH	PR	DS	Quick	Slow	LO	Rel	SBA	SacA	IBB	PO	W	L	Pct
2001	Dodgers	NL	162	111	.50	264	34	20	46	42	8	409	131	81	25	10	86	76	.531
2002	Dodgers	NL	162	102	.52	331	44	37	48	36	3	423	133	80	45	18	92	70	.568
2003	Dodgers	NL	162	103	.64	269	22	64	50	28	6	438	116	97	35	10	85	77	.525
2004	Dodgers	NL	162	94	.70	336	34	19	48	32	4	459	143	79	47	7	93	69	.574
2005	Dodgers	NL	162	129	.64	303	31	37	44	40	6	459	93	76	34	17	71	91	.438
	162-Game Average			108	.60	301	33	35	47	36	5	438	123	83	37	12	85	77	.527

Alan Trammell

Year	Team	Lg	G	LINEUPS		SUBSTITUTIONS			PITCHER USAGE				TACTICS				RESULTS		
				LUp	PL%	PH	PR	DS	Quick	Slow	LO	Rel	SBA	SacA	IBB	PO	W	L	Pct
2003	Tigers	AL	162	129	.72	138	29	14	47	39	2	451	161	92	35	28	43	119	.265
2004	Tigers	AL	162	131	.67	137	31	19	44	36	3	432	136	62	33	8	72	90	.444
2005	Tigers	AL	162	119	.49	75	26	16	35	39	0	425	94	56	33	11	71	91	.438
	162-Game Average			126	.63	117	29	16	42	38	2	436	130	70	34	16	62	100	.383

Eric Wedge

Year	Team	Lg	G	LINEUPS		SUBSTITUTIONS			PITCHER USAGE				TACTICS				RESULTS		
				LUp	PL%	PH	PR	DS	Quick	Slow	LO	Rel	SBA	SacA	IBB	PO	W	L	Pct
2003	Indians	AL	162	145	.67	117	43	27	48	33	1	428	147	67	37	12	68	94	.420
2004	Indians	AL	162	114	.72	110	41	20	42	38	2	479	149	56	47	25	80	82	.494
2005	Indians	AL	162	111	.66	88	18	16	44	44	0	409	98	52	20	9	93	69	.574
	162-Game Average			123	.69	105	34	21	45	38	1	439	131	58	35	15	80	82	.496

Ned Yost

Year	Team	Lg	G	LINEUPS		SUBSTITUTIONS			PITCHER USAGE				TACTICS				RESULTS		
				LUp	PL%	PH	PR	DS	Quick	Slow	LO	Rel	SBA	SacA	IBB	PO	W	L	Pct
2003	Brewers	NL	162	97	.44	304	22	39	23	59	5	460	138	85	43	23	68	94	.420
2004	Brewers	NL	162	131	.60	317	28	20	38	39	9	423	178	79	27	7	67	94	.416
2005	Brewers	NL	162	99	.46	259	18	35	26	40	4	395	113	89	52	50	81	81	.500
	162-Game Average			109	.50	293	23	31	29	46	6	426	143	84	41	27	72	90	.445

2005 American League Managers

Manager	G	LINEUPS		SUBSTITUTIONS			PITCHER USAGE				TACTICS				RESULTS		
		LUp	PL%	PH	PR	DS	Quick	Slow	LO	Rel	SBA	SacA	IBB	PO	W	L	Pct
Buddy Bell, KC	112	93	.61	97	18	8	31	25	0	310	48	38	17	25	43	69	.384
Terry Francona, Bos	162	104	.67	110	46	37	25	55	3	442	57	21	28	11	95	67	.586
Ron Gardenhire, Min	162	135	.58	104	45	26	51	22	0	396	146	58	38	16	83	79	.512
John Gibbons, Tor	162	124	.66	148	11	37	55	18	1	432	107	28	29	45	80	82	.494
Ozzie Guillen, CWS	162	112	.51	100	32	21	31	55	3	412	204	68	42	15	99	63	.611
Mike Hargrove, Sea	162	97	.52	125	24	18	30	45	1	433	149	61	32	36	69	93	.426
Ken Macha, Oak	162	127	.62	83	17	11	45	36	4	410	53	29	42	13	88	74	.543
Lee Mazzilli, Bal	107	81	.57	57	18	30	21	26	3	294	79	31	29	24	51	56	.477
Tony Pena, KC	33	33	.60	23	4	1	10	12	0	88	27	15	13	2	8	25	.242
Sam Perlozzo, Bal	55	47	.61	28	23	26	16	11	0	180	41	24	3	8	23	32	.418
Lou Piniella, TB	162	135	.54	127	18	52	37	54	9	401	200	53	41	16	67	95	.414
Bob Schaefer, KC	17	15	.57	13	3	2	4	5	0	46	11	3	3	3	5	12	.294
Mike Scioscia, LAA	162	124	.65	92	37	37	47	37	1	379	218	58	24	43	95	67	.586
Buck Showalter, Tex	162	98	.59	57	22	11	42	39	2	454	82	11	31	5	79	83	.488
Joe Torre, NYY	162	117	.64	94	65	47	43	44	8	418	111	40	25	50	95	67	.586
Alan Trammell, Det	162	119	.49	75	26	16	35	39	0	425	94	56	33	11	71	91	.438
Eric Wedge, Cle	162	111	.66	88	18	16	44	44	0	409	98	52	20	9	93	69	.574

2005 National League Managers

Manager	G	LINEUPS		SUBSTITUTIONS			PITCHER USAGE				TACTICS				RESULTS		
		LUp	PL%	PH	PR	DS	Quick	Slow	LO	Rel	SBA	SacA	IBB	PO	W	L	Pct
Felipe Alou, SF	162	139	.62	242	33	49	28	47	7	511	106	109	42	12	75	87	.463
Dusty Baker, ChC	162	121	.59	240	21	29	40	46	10	457	104	87	48	70	79	83	.488
Bruce Bochy, SD	162	128	.58	285	31	49	46	36	2	456	143	89	45	16	82	80	.506
Bobby Cox, Atl	162	110	.69	247	54	35	46	28	1	484	124	104	52	11	90	72	.556
Phil Garner, Hou	163	101	.48	251	40	63	57	34	5	434	159	99	29	10	89	73	.549
Clint Hurdle, Col	162	135	.60	273	21	40	43	60	1	459	97	114	54	22	67	95	.414
Tony LaRussa, StL	162	138	.55	270	25	48	41	39	1	436	119	92	27	9	100	62	.617
Pete Mackanin, Pit	26	24	.52	54	1	5	11	4	0	94	19	19	5	2	12	14	.462
Charlie Manuel, Phi	162	80	.64	265	36	19	43	28	3	442	143	86	51	11	88	74	.543
Lloyd McClendon, Pit	136	123	.53	218	8	19	36	34	2	357	84	62	60	37	55	81	.404
Jack McKeon, Fla	162	82	.43	246	24	36	43	34	4	449	134	106	57	16	83	79	.512
Bob Melvin, Ari	162	120	.68	310	26	38	26	55	3	458	93	93	43	30	77	85	.475
Dave Miley, Cin	70	55	.61	104	10	7	14	20	1	204	45	19	22	5	27	43	.386
Jerry Narron, Cin	93	73	.61	156	9	14	13	22	1	287	50	44	25	7	46	46	.500
Willie Randolph, NYM	162	105	.64	222	10	51	46	34	4	392	193	89	43	18	83	79	.512
Frank Robinson, Was	162	121	.63	266	48	35	45	47	16	470	90	115	77	4	81	81	.500
Jim Tracy, LAD	162	129	.64	303	31	37	44	40	6	459	93	76	34	17	71	91	.438
Ned Yost, Mil	162	99	.46	259	18	35	26	40	4	395	113	89	52	50	81	81	.500

2005 Park Indices

Park Indices are calculated in a way that neutralizes the effect of a team's makeup and isolates the effects of the park. This isolation is figured by comparing what both the team and its opponents accomplished at home, and comparing that to what the same team and its opponents accomplished on the road.

To calculate the Park Index for Home Runs in a given ballpark we take the total Home Runs of both the home team and its opponents at the ballpark and compare it to the total Home Runs of the home team and its opponents in other games. We then divide each of those totals by the At Bats in the equivalent situations so that if there are more at bats in either situation the index is not skewed. The result is then multiplied by 100 to yield the familiar form.

The park indices for Doubles, Triples, Walks, Strikeouts and Home Runs by Lefties and Righties are determined like Home Runs, above – relative to At Bats. Indices of At Bats, Runs, Hits, Errors and Infield Fielding Errors (E-Infield) are calculated relative to Games. The three Batting Average Indices are calculated as-is, as these are already relative to At Bats.

A park with an index of exactly 100 is neutral and can be said to have had no effect on that particular stat. An index above 100 means the ballpark favors that statistic. For example, if a park has a Home Run Index of 120, it was 20% easier to hit Home Runs in that park then the rest of the parks in that team's league.

Interleague games are not included in the underlying Park Index data, both because the interleague schedules are significantly imbalanced, and because the Designated Hitter rule, only used in American League parks, would artificially skew all AL parks towards appearing to be Hitters' Parks and all NL parks towards appearing to be Pitcher' Parks.

In addition to the 2005 Park Indices, we have included 2003-2005 park data as well. You will notice that only 2004-2005 data is included in the case of the two-year old PETCO Park and Citizens Bank Park, and for the ballparks in Kansas City and Detroit, due to their 2004 dimensions changes. For the Nationals, we have listed 2003-2004 Olympic Stadium data as a comparison.

Arizona Diamondbacks - Chase Field

| | 2005 Season | | | | | | | 2003-2005 | | | | | | |
| | Home Games | | | Away Games | | | | Home Games | | | Away Games | | | |
	D'Backs	Opp	Total	D'Backs	Opp	Total	Index	D'Backs	Opp	Total	D'Backs	Opp	Total	Index
G	72	72	144	72	72	144		219	219	438	216	216	432	
Avg	.252	.281	.267	.254	.275	.264	101	.264	.265	.264	.247	.264	.255	104
AB	2398	2582	4980	2509	2448	4957	100	7355	7727	15082	7515	7236	14751	101
R	284	410	694	318	342	660	105	952	1155	2107	823	1029	1852	112
H	605	725	1330	638	672	1310	102	1939	2047	3986	1859	1907	3766	104
2B	115	178	293	141	127	268	109	405	461	866	375	349	724	117
3B	16	19	35	7	15	22	158	59	51	110	38	38	76	142
HR	81	89	170	82	81	163	104	226	266	492	203	223	426	113
BB	268	259	527	280	226	506	104	750	802	1552	692	768	1460	104
SO	462	467	929	508	452	960	96	1330	1623	2953	1483	1519	3002	96
E	33	31	64	45	46	91	70	133	110	243	159	119	278	86
E-Infield	15	17	32	16	18	34	94	59	53	112	65	52	117	94
LHB-Avg	.258	.289	.272	.269	.263	.267	102	.274	.281	.277	.257	.271	.263	105
LHB-HR	46	36	82	57	34	91	89	119	113	232	117	92	209	108
RHB-Avg	.245	.275	.263	.234	.282	.262	100	.253	.254	.253	.237	.259	.249	102
RHB-HR	35	53	88	25	47	72	122	107	153	260	86	131	217	118

Atlanta Braves - Turner Field

| | 2005 Season | | | | | | | 2003-2005 | | | | | | |
| | Home Games | | | Away Games | | | | Home Games | | | Away Games | | | |
	Braves	Opp	Total	Braves	Opp	Total	Index	Braves	Opp	Total	Braves	Opp	Total	Index
G	72	72	144	75	75	150		219	219	438	219	219	438	
Avg	.284	.261	.272	.247	.271	.259	105	.279	.256	.267	.269	.268	.269	100
AB	2405	2520	4925	2584	2498	5082	101	7353	7613	14966	7757	7361	15118	99
R	379	286	665	320	312	632	110	1132	917	2049	1123	942	2065	99
H	684	658	1342	639	677	1316	106	2055	1948	4003	2090	1973	4063	99
2B	155	126	281	126	125	251	116	418	354	772	427	384	811	96
3B	20	10	30	13	9	22	141	52	26	78	46	30	76	104
HR	78	56	134	92	72	164	84	260	195	455	283	208	491	94
BB	257	217	474	236	247	483	101	784	717	1501	741	718	1459	104
SO	455	435	890	525	410	935	98	1397	1376	2773	1465	1279	2744	102
E	40	45	85	39	44	83	107	149	138	287	142	137	279	103
E-Infield	22	18	40	18	15	33	126	79	57	136	74	56	130	105
LHB-Avg	.299	.252	.276	.250	.276	.262	106	.286	.257	.271	.271	.266	.269	101
LHB-HR	32	23	55	40	30	70	80	95	76	171	102	80	182	94
RHB-Avg	.270	.268	.269	.245	.267	.257	105	.275	.255	.265	.268	.269	.269	99
RHB-HR	46	33	79	52	42	94	88	165	119	284	181	128	309	94

Baltimore Orioles - Oriole Park at Camden Yards

| | 2005 Season | | | | | | | 2003-2005 | | | | | | |
| | Home Games | | | Away Games | | | | Home Games | | | Away Games | | | |
	Orioles	Opp	Total	Orioles	Opp	Total	Index	Orioles	Opp	Total	Orioles	Opp	Total	Index
G	72	72	144	72	72	144		216	216	432	217	217	434	
Avg	.258	.261	.259	.277	.266	.271	96	.272	.265	.268	.274	.270	.272	99
AB	2395	2512	4907	2552	2423	4975	99	7291	7626	14917	7731	7328	15059	100
R	287	356	643	368	357	725	89	987	1097	2084	1097	1059	2156	97
H	618	655	1273	706	644	1350	94	1984	2021	4005	2119	1976	4095	98
2B	110	108	218	149	123	272	81	383	345	728	414	372	786	94
3B	12	5	17	11	14	25	69	22	25	47	34	43	77	62
HR	83	78	161	82	80	162	101	225	247	472	223	230	453	105
BB	233	273	506	165	251	416	123	649	824	1473	607	770	1377	108
SO	350	473	823	443	465	908	92	1089	1384	2473	1313	1381	2694	93
E	47	34	81	53	52	105	77	138	143	281	141	157	298	95
E-Infield	16	13	29	22	24	46	63	59	58	117	61	71	132	89
LHB-Avg	.239	.271	.257	.300	.288	.294	87	.258	.277	.268	.287	.272	.279	96
LHB-HR	31	34	65	34	35	69	93	82	116	198	93	105	198	100
RHB-Avg	.269	.252	.261	.262	.250	.256	102	.282	.255	.269	.265	.268	.267	101
RHB-HR	52	44	96	48	45	93	107	143	131	274	130	125	255	110

Boston Red Sox - Fenway Park

	2005 Season							2003-2005						
	Home Games			Away Games				Home Games			Away Games			
	Red Sox	Opp	Total	Red Sox	Opp	Total	Index	Red Sox	Opp	Total	Red Sox	Opp	Total	Index
G	72	72	144	72	72	144		216	216	432	216	216	432	
Avg	.277	.278	.277	.279	.282	.280	99	.297	.264	.280	.265	.267	.266	105
AB	2411	2584	4995	2577	2448	5025	99	7425	7667	15092	7721	7385	15106	100
R	429	366	795	376	369	745	107	1343	1059	2402	1122	1060	2182	110
H	667	718	1385	719	690	1409	98	2208	2024	4232	2048	1972	4020	105
2B	166	188	354	128	135	263	135	537	498	1035	404	408	812	128
3B	5	16	21	9	20	29	73	30	45	75	31	56	87	86
HR	85	78	163	88	77	165	99	282	208	490	294	212	506	97
BB	301	206	507	286	195	481	106	880	593	1473	813	628	1441	102
SO	457	422	879	470	416	886	100	1331	1421	2752	1484	1432	2916	94
E	49	49	98	51	48	99	99	156	146	302	143	124	267	113
E-Infield	24	21	45	15	24	39	115	79	69	148	47	56	103	144
LHB-Avg	.277	.284	.281	.285	.269	.278	101	.296	.265	.280	.262	.259	.261	107
LHB-HR	42	34	76	53	36	89	84	127	90	217	153	104	257	82
RHB-Avg	.276	.272	.274	.273	.293	.283	97	.299	.263	.281	.268	.275	.271	103
RHB-HR	43	44	87	35	41	76	118	155	118	273	141	108	249	113

Chicago Cubs - Wrigley Field

	2005 Season							2003-2005						
	Home Games			Away Games				Home Games			Away Games			
	Cubs	Opp	Total	Cubs	Opp	Total	Index	Cubs	Opp	Total	Cubs	Opp	Total	Index
G	72	72	144	75	75	150		220	220	440	221	221	442	
Avg	.270	.245	.258	.271	.251	.261	99	.266	.244	.255	.265	.244	.255	100
AB	2441	2494	4935	2647	2425	5072	101	7455	7629	15084	7753	7223	14976	101
R	317	316	633	329	318	647	102	1027	960	1987	1003	898	1901	105
H	659	612	1271	718	608	1326	100	1984	1861	3845	2053	1765	3818	101
2B	136	126	262	158	109	267	101	400	353	753	448	329	777	96
3B	12	7	19	9	10	19	103	32	30	62	33	33	66	93
HR	90	80	170	89	82	171	102	300	234	534	259	211	470	113
BB	189	263	452	203	264	467	99	664	801	1465	630	775	1405	104
SO	401	583	984	436	563	999	101	1430	1879	3309	1466	1768	3234	102
E	50	39	89	40	59	99	94	144	152	296	126	155	281	106
E-Infield	22	18	40	18	27	45	93	64	62	126	50	73	123	103
LHB-Avg	.264	.245	.255	.256	.259	.257	99	.260	.244	.251	.257	.258	.258	98
LHB-HR	33	32	65	21	37	58	119	74	103	177	66	106	172	104
RHB-Avg	.274	.246	.259	.284	.246	.265	98	.269	.244	.257	.269	.235	.253	101
RHB-HR	57	48	105	68	45	113	93	226	131	357	193	105	298	118

Chicago White Sox - U.S. Cellular Field

	2005 Season							2003-2005						
	Home Games			Away Games				Home Games			Away Games			
	White Sox	Opp	Total	White Sox	Opp	Total	Index	White Sox	Opp	Total	White Sox	Opp	Total	Index
G	72	72	144	72	72	144		216	216	432	216	216	432	
Avg	.261	.256	.258	.264	.247	.256	101	.265	.261	.263	.263	.255	.259	102
AB	2375	2531	4906	2548	2456	5004	98	7154	7527	14681	7575	7164	14739	100
R	321	302	623	322	276	598	104	1073	973	2046	1027	963	1990	103
H	620	647	1267	672	607	1279	99	1898	1966	3864	1994	1827	3821	101
2B	113	120	233	114	134	248	96	359	366	725	383	379	762	96
3B	10	10	20	12	13	25	82	28	31	59	30	34	64	93
HR	99	84	183	72	62	134	139	335	273	608	244	209	453	135
BB	201	211	412	189	199	388	108	651	649	1300	617	696	1313	99
SO	427	471	898	447	446	893	103	1227	1461	2688	1337	1302	2639	102
E	35	31	66	51	41	92	72	107	119	226	150	133	283	80
E-Infield	15	14	29	27	17	44	66	42	51	93	74	56	130	72
LHB-Avg	.257	.277	.269	.256	.239	.246	109	.250	.273	.265	.257	.257	.257	103
LHB-HR	23	44	67	11	29	40	163	73	132	205	61	97	158	131
RHB-Avg	.263	.237	.251	.267	.254	.261	96	.271	.251	.262	.266	.253	.261	101
RHB-HR	76	40	116	61	33	94	130	262	141	403	183	112	295	137

Cincinnati Reds - Great American Ballpark

	2005 Season							2003-2005						
	Home Games			Away Games			Index	Home Games			Away Games			Index
	Reds	Opp	Total	Reds	Opp	Total		Reds	Opp	Total	Reds	Opp	Total	
G	73	73	146	75	75	150		223	223	446	225	225	450	
Avg	.264	.299	.282	.256	.281	.268	105	.250	.278	.265	.252	.287	.269	98
AB	2433	2674	5107	2620	2514	5134	102	7386	8007	15393	7884	7689	15573	100
R	386	413	799	351	386	737	111	1016	1211	2227	1060	1229	2289	98
H	643	799	1442	671	706	1377	108	1847	2226	4073	1990	2206	4196	98
2B	157	191	348	155	135	290	121	393	505	898	404	468	872	104
3B	5	12	17	9	25	34	50	21	27	48	42	74	116	42
HR	106	109	215	88	90	178	121	282	335	617	261	276	537	116
BB	273	220	493	298	223	521	95	773	721	1494	824	777	1601	94
SO	537	454	991	636	407	1043	96	1709	1394	3103	1938	1236	3174	99
E	42	35	77	55	40	95	83	163	122	285	170	131	301	96
E-Infield	16	16	32	23	15	38	87	64	60	124	55	48	103	121
LHB-Avg	.280	.313	.295	.272	.260	.267	111	.265	.277	.271	.267	.279	.273	99
LHB-HR	56	44	100	48	30	78	127	153	130	283	138	109	247	117
RHB-Avg	.251	.291	.274	.243	.291	.269	102	.239	.279	.261	.241	.292	.267	98
RHB-HR	50	65	115	40	60	100	117	129	205	334	123	167	290	116

Cleveland Indians - Jacobs Field

	2005 Season							2003-2005						
	Home Games			Away Games			Index	Home Games			Away Games			Index
	Indians	Opp	Total	Indians	Opp	Total		Indians	Opp	Total	Indians	Opp	Total	
G	72	72	144	72	72	144		216	216	432	216	216	432	
Avg	.260	.238	.249	.276	.258	.268	93	.259	.255	.257	.273	.269	.271	95
AB	2389	2447	4836	2595	2455	5050	96	7209	7551	14760	7746	7382	15128	98
R	308	267	575	376	319	695	83	962	962	1924	1110	1089	2199	87
H	622	582	1204	717	634	1351	89	1869	1922	3791	2111	1984	4095	93
2B	146	119	265	146	122	268	103	434	399	833	415	405	820	104
3B	7	5	12	18	9	27	46	26	28	54	49	37	86	64
HR	76	67	143	107	72	179	83	201	214	415	298	264	562	76
BB	237	169	406	216	205	421	101	731	647	1378	666	684	1350	105
SO	464	459	923	512	447	959	101	1358	1427	2785	1445	1287	2732	104
E	49	50	99	47	43	90	110	143	178	321	151	122	273	118
E-Infield	24	21	45	19	20	39	115	76	70	146	75	49	124	118
LHB-Avg	.268	.244	.258	.296	.270	.285	90	.266	.254	.261	.281	.272	.277	94
LHB-HR	41	21	62	53	28	81	82	121	85	206	158	107	265	79
RHB-Avg	.253	.234	.243	.257	.251	.254	95	.252	.255	.253	.263	.267	.265	96
RHB-HR	35	46	81	54	44	98	85	80	129	209	140	157	297	72

Colorado Rockies - Coors Field

	2005 Season							2003-2005						
	Home Games			Away Games			Index	Home Games			Away Games			Index
	Rockies	Opp	Total	Rockies	Opp	Total		Rockies	Opp	Total	Rockies	Opp	Total	
G	72	72	144	75	75	150		216	216	432	222	222	444	
Avg	.305	.295	.300	.232	.276	.254	118	.300	.297	.298	.237	.277	.257	116
AB	2536	2602	5138	2509	2453	4962	108	7476	7813	15289	7527	7305	14832	106
R	404	402	806	273	383	656	128	1297	1276	2573	873	1122	1995	133
H	773	768	1541	581	677	1258	128	2245	2318	4563	1786	2022	3808	123
2B	142	171	313	112	155	267	113	477	476	953	376	432	808	114
3B	19	19	38	14	11	25	147	60	60	120	31	38	69	169
HR	79	79	158	60	84	144	106	283	283	566	216	238	454	121
BB	236	271	507	221	292	513	95	799	818	1617	727	865	1592	99
SO	426	438	864	554	427	981	85	1332	1279	2611	1738	1208	2946	86
E	48	60	108	56	56	112	100	140	180	320	146	139	285	115
E-Infield	16	26	42	19	26	45	97	49	81	130	55	62	117	114
LHB-Avg	.302	.307	.305	.242	.281	.262	116	.318	.305	.311	.250	.287	.269	115
LHB-HR	21	29	50	22	36	58	85	107	112	219	80	91	171	126
RHB-Avg	.307	.287	.297	.224	.272	.247	120	.290	.291	.290	.229	.269	.249	117
RHB-HR	58	50	108	38	48	86	120	176	171	347	136	147	283	118

Detroit Tigers - Comerica Park

| | 2005 Season | | | | | | | 2004-2005 | | | | | | |
| | Home Games | | | Away Games | | | | Home Games | | | Away Games | | | |
	Tigers	Opp	Total	Tigers	Opp	Total	Index	Tigers	Opp	Total	Tigers	Opp	Total	Index
G	72	72	144	72	72	144		144	144	288	144	144	288	
Avg	.279	.273	.276	.269	.274	.272	102	.275	.275	.275	.270	.276	.273	101
AB	2461	2552	5013	2529	2376	4905	102	4905	5130	10035	5080	4801	9881	102
R	321	346	667	325	370	695	96	656	728	1384	724	739	1463	95
H	687	697	1384	680	652	1332	104	1350	1412	2762	1371	1323	2694	103
2B	107	112	219	142	118	260	82	206	242	448	288	246	534	83
3B	26	19	45	12	13	25	176	59	40	99	24	24	48	203
HR	81	82	163	73	95	168	95	157	170	327	178	180	358	90
BB	171	209	380	172	197	369	101	401	443	844	401	426	827	100
SO	424	426	850	485	374	859	97	886	875	1761	1036	795	1831	95
E	48	49	97	47	34	81	120	106	80	186	118	81	199	93
E-Infield	16	25	41	20	13	33	124	37	43	80	45	30	75	107
LHB-Avg	.279	.293	.288	.257	.273	.267	108	.268	.276	.273	.258	.267	.263	104
LHB-HR	32	29	61	14	38	52	118	67	63	130	63	67	130	99
RHB-Avg	.279	.260	.271	.273	.275	.274	99	.279	.275	.277	.276	.281	.279	99
RHB-HR	49	53	102	59	57	116	85	90	107	197	115	113	228	85

Florida Marlins - Dolphins Stadium

| | 2005 Season | | | | | | | 2003-2005 | | | | | | |
| | Home Games | | | Away Games | | | | Home Games | | | Away Games | | | |
	Marlins	Opp	Total	Marlins	Opp	Total	Index	Marlins	Opp	Total	Marlins	Opp	Total	Index
G	72	72	144	75	75	150		213	213	426	223	223	446	
Avg	.266	.253	.259	.278	.278	.278	93	.268	.246	.257	.267	.271	.269	95
AB	2382	2448	4830	2619	2516	5135	98	7038	7313	14351	7753	7390	15143	99
R	297	292	589	349	378	727	84	930	835	1765	1018	1045	2063	90
H	634	619	1253	727	700	1427	91	1884	1800	3684	2073	2001	4074	95
2B	115	125	240	159	153	312	82	350	355	705	432	434	866	86
3B	18	20	38	11	23	34	119	54	56	110	40	50	90	129
HR	50	44	94	69	59	128	78	172	161	333	214	203	417	84
BB	246	255	501	203	264	467	114	700	731	1431	659	722	1381	109
SO	434	561	995	403	470	873	121	1267	1654	2921	1332	1388	2720	113
E	35	44	79	61	49	110	75	96	143	239	151	162	313	80
E-Infield	14	21	35	26	16	42	87	34	53	87	67	65	132	69
LHB-Avg	.272	.256	.263	.281	.276	.278	95	.285	.246	.263	.277	.268	.272	97
LHB-HR	20	21	41	19	19	38	114	34	72	106	31	72	103	104
RHB-Avg	.264	.251	.257	.276	.280	.278	93	.260	.246	.253	.263	.273	.267	95
RHB-HR	30	23	53	50	40	90	63	138	89	227	183	131	314	78

Houston Astros - Minute Maid Park

| | 2005 Season | | | | | | | 2003-2005 | | | | | | |
| | Home Games | | | Away Games | | | | Home Games | | | Away Games | | | |
	Astros	Opp	Total	Astros	Opp	Total	Index	Astros	Opp	Total	Astros	Opp	Total	Index
G	75	75	150	73	73	146		222	222	444	220	220	440	
Avg	.270	.237	.253	.246	.251	.249	102	.271	.242	.257	.254	.258	.256	100
AB	2451	2532	4983	2514	2399	4913	99	7313	7528	14841	7676	7309	14985	98
R	333	256	589	306	281	587	98	1071	866	1937	1022	915	1937	99
H	662	600	1262	619	602	1221	101	1984	1824	3808	1947	1883	3830	99
2B	116	111	227	142	124	266	84	375	337	712	425	387	812	89
3B	17	10	27	14	15	29	92	56	47	103	34	34	68	153
HR	84	72	156	61	62	123	125	256	229	485	232	207	439	112
BB	238	184	422	198	210	408	102	761	620	1381	720	754	1474	95
SO	451	551	1002	507	516	1023	97	1298	1701	2999	1498	1566	3064	99
E	51	46	97	33	46	79	120	138	141	279	118	142	260	106
E-Infield	24	13	37	15	30	45	80	62	51	113	54	80	134	84
LHB-Avg	.232	.242	.239	.253	.247	.249	96	.258	.251	.253	.262	.268	.266	95
LHB-HR	16	26	42	20	23	43	97	51	76	127	79	87	166	77
RHB-Avg	.281	.234	.260	.244	.254	.248	105	.275	.236	.258	.251	.250	.251	103
RHB-HR	68	46	114	41	39	80	140	205	153	358	153	120	273	133

Kansas City Royals - Ewing M. Kauffman Stadium

	2005 Season							2004-2005						
	Home Games			Away Games				Home Games			Away Games			
	Royals	Opp	Total	Royals	Opp	Total	Index	Royals	Opp	Total	Royals	Opp	Total	Index
G	72	72	144	72	72	144		143	143	286	145	145	290	
Avg	.266	.292	.279	.249	.296	.272	103	.265	.288	.277	.253	.296	.274	101
AB	2403	2601	5004	2450	2404	4854	103	4759	5131	9890	5022	4908	9930	101
R	313	411	724	287	428	715	101	626	789	1415	623	861	1484	97
H	639	759	1398	610	711	1321	106	1263	1476	2739	1272	1452	2724	102
2B	137	172	309	119	140	259	116	242	335	577	250	299	549	106
3B	15	20	35	11	19	30	113	28	38	66	21	32	53	125
HR	45	73	118	70	87	157	73	96	157	253	153	193	346	73
BB	199	251	450	173	258	431	101	414	460	874	374	493	867	101
SO	397	420	817	498	391	889	89	810	838	1648	1030	761	1791	92
E	46	43	89	62	45	107	83	89	82	171	129	103	232	75
E-Infield	20	18	38	28	16	44	86	39	39	78	52	42	94	84
LHB-Avg	.260	.301	.282	.260	.296	.278	101	.259	.295	.278	.254	.309	.281	99
LHB-HR	18	30	48	23	39	62	72	39	58	97	53	79	132	73
RHB-Avg	.270	.285	.277	.241	.295	.268	104	.269	.283	.276	.253	.287	.270	102
RHB-HR	27	43	70	47	48	95	74	57	99	156	100	114	214	74

Los Angeles Angels - Angel Stadium of Anaheim

	2005 Season							2003-2005						
	Home Games			Away Games				Home Games			Away Games			
	Angels	Opp	Total	Angels	Opp	Total	Index	Angels	Opp	Total	Angels	Opp	Total	Index
G	72	72	144	72	72	144		217	217	434	215	215	430	
Avg	.265	.250	.257	.273	.264	.269	96	.274	.261	.267	.274	.265	.269	99
AB	2408	2540	4948	2589	2448	5037	98	7235	7661	14896	7628	7211	14839	99
R	321	289	610	353	306	659	93	998	932	1930	1080	985	2065	93
H	638	636	1274	706	647	1353	94	1979	1999	3978	2088	1911	3999	99
2B	117	138	255	134	118	252	103	350	398	748	396	369	765	97
3B	14	13	27	11	16	27	102	37	29	66	46	46	92	71
HR	63	67	130	69	78	147	90	195	226	421	206	235	441	95
BB	201	189	390	190	209	399	100	591	634	1225	628	651	1279	95
SO	375	501	876	393	493	886	101	1128	1497	2625	1206	1398	2604	100
E	44	52	96	33	54	87	110	133	124	257	114	153	267	95
E-Infield	14	23	37	10	22	32	116	50	46	96	41	59	100	95
LHB-Avg	.254	.263	.258	.276	.268	.272	95	.269	.263	.266	.284	.267	.275	97
LHB-HR	22	32	54	32	35	67	85	69	114	183	86	108	194	93
RHB-Avg	.277	.240	.257	.268	.261	.264	97	.277	.259	.268	.265	.264	.264	101
RHB-HR	41	35	76	37	43	80	93	126	112	238	120	127	247	97

Los Angeles Dodgers - Dodger Stadium

	2005 Season							2003-2005						
	Home Games			Away Games				Home Games			Away Games			
	Dodgers	Opp	Total	Dodgers	Opp	Total	Index	Dodgers	Opp	Total	Dodgers	Opp	Total	Index
G	72	72	144	72	72	144		216	216	432	216	216	432	
Avg	.248	.250	.249	.262	.280	.271	92	.249	.240	.244	.260	.264	.262	93
AB	2326	2464	4790	2525	2411	4936	97	7035	7304	14339	7627	7180	14807	97
R	311	303	614	323	368	691	89	874	805	1679	960	971	1931	87
H	576	617	1193	661	675	1336	89	1752	1750	3502	1981	1892	3873	90
2B	130	129	259	136	134	270	99	332	298	630	368	377	745	87
3B	6	5	11	13	24	37	31	24	17	41	46	59	105	40
HR	65	80	145	62	85	147	102	214	221	435	207	215	422	106
BB	277	200	477	219	228	447	110	673	643	1316	680	732	1412	96
SO	466	497	963	511	403	914	109	1358	1602	2960	1474	1398	2872	106
E	42	43	85	51	44	95	89	133	134	267	136	149	285	94
E-Infield	21	18	39	23	24	47	83	47	53	100	50	65	115	87
LHB-Avg	.255	.263	.259	.258	.309	.283	91	.251	.253	.252	.251	.276	.262	96
LHB-HR	28	39	67	24	40	64	110	96	91	187	90	87	177	107
RHB-Avg	.242	.240	.241	.265	.254	.260	93	.247	.230	.238	.269	.255	.262	91
RHB-HR	37	41	78	38	45	83	95	118	130	248	117	128	245	106

Milwaukee Brewers - Miller Park

	2005 Season							2003-2005						
	Home Games			Away Games				Home Games			Away Games			
	Brewers	Opp	Total	Brewers	Opp	Total	Index	Brewers	Opp	Total	Brewers	Opp	Total	Index
G	75	75	150	72	72	144		225	225	450	221	221	442	
Avg	.259	.233	.246	.260	.263	.262	94	.254	.253	.253	.252	.273	.263	97
AB	2416	2536	4952	2523	2452	4975	96	7488	7949	15437	7617	7476	15093	100
R	354	305	659	313	325	638	99	987	1089	2076	904	1075	1979	103
H	626	592	1218	657	646	1303	90	1899	2014	3913	1922	2042	3964	97
2B	141	130	271	157	137	294	93	413	437	850	405	420	825	101
3B	13	10	23	5	18	23	100	38	47	85	32	52	84	99
HR	83	79	162	75	71	146	111	242	265	507	222	237	459	108
BB	256	256	512	236	250	486	106	800	761	1561	712	725	1437	106
SO	516	588	1104	537	486	1023	108	1688	1642	3330	1698	1415	3113	105
E	56	40	96	51	36	87	106	164	140	304	157	142	299	100
E-Infield	25	22	47	24	15	39	116	80	67	147	75	66	141	102
LHB-Avg	.245	.239	.242	.289	.253	.269	90	.263	.257	.259	.267	.263	.265	98
LHB-HR	25	24	49	31	27	58	86	87	92	179	94	79	173	101
RHB-Avg	.264	.230	.248	.248	.270	.258	96	.248	.251	.250	.243	.279	.261	96
RHB-HR	58	55	113	44	44	88	128	155	173	328	128	158	286	112

Minnesota Twins - Hubert H. Humphrey Metrodome Surface: AstroTurf

	2005 Season							2003-2005						
	Home Games			Away Games				Home Games			Away Games			
	Twins	Opp	Total	Twins	Opp	Total	Index	Twins	Opp	Total	Twins	Opp	Total	Index
G	72	72	144	72	72	144		216	216	432	216	216	432	
Avg	.264	.246	.255	.251	.270	.260	98	.269	.260	.265	.264	.267	.266	100
AB	2388	2482	4870	2546	2470	5016	97	7273	7706	14979	7664	7356	15020	100
R	312	281	593	291	291	582	102	1038	942	1980	977	935	1912	104
H	631	611	1242	639	666	1305	95	1959	2006	3965	2023	1967	3990	99
2B	113	106	219	120	122	242	93	389	354	743	400	360	760	98
3B	16	8	24	13	16	29	85	49	30	79	40	33	73	109
HR	59	74	133	52	72	124	110	213	233	446	210	227	437	102
BB	213	129	342	220	175	395	89	698	481	1179	654	572	1226	96
SO	431	451	882	428	396	824	110	1303	1473	2776	1304	1230	2534	110
E	42	59	101	47	48	95	106	120	153	273	138	152	290	94
E-Infield	25	18	43	19	19	38	113	52	53	105	59	62	121	87
LHB-Avg	.257	.250	.253	.260	.258	.259	98	.274	.258	.266	.270	.265	.268	99
LHB-HR	27	31	58	29	33	62	100	100	109	209	95	105	200	104
RHB-Avg	.269	.243	.257	.244	.278	.261	98	.266	.262	.264	.259	.269	.264	100
RHB-HR	32	43	75	23	39	62	122	113	124	237	115	122	237	101

New York Mets - Shea Stadium

	2005 Season							2003-2005						
	Home Games			Away Games				Home Games			Away Games			
	Mets	Opp	Total	Mets	Opp	Total	Index	Mets	Opp	Total	Mets	Opp	Total	Index
G	75	75	150	72	72	144		221	221	442	216	216	432	
Avg	.262	.254	.258	.259	.251	.255	101	.256	.260	.258	.247	.263	.255	101
AB	2497	2590	5087	2501	2347	4848	101	7335	7704	15039	7398	7119	14517	101
R	341	282	623	322	290	612	98	920	939	1859	913	950	1863	98
H	653	659	1312	648	589	1237	102	1879	2004	3883	1824	1875	3699	103
2B	120	132	252	129	123	252	95	376	412	788	370	384	754	101
3B	12	8	20	18	11	29	66	28	27	55	43	53	96	55
HR	79	60	139	84	64	148	90	198	193	391	233	218	451	84
BB	238	212	450	204	223	427	100	690	744	1434	663	738	1401	99
SO	467	483	950	520	449	969	93	1408	1394	2802	1552	1225	2777	97
E	54	59	113	39	45	84	129	177	153	330	136	131	267	121
E-Infield	19	22	41	23	21	44	89	88	61	149	60	56	116	126
LHB-Avg	.262	.267	.264	.259	.244	.253	104	.264	.263	.264	.253	.252	.253	104
LHB-HR	38	27	65	41	28	69	94	80	77	157	90	74	164	94
RHB-Avg	.261	.246	.253	.259	.256	.257	98	.251	.258	.255	.242	.270	.256	99
RHB-HR	41	33	74	43	36	79	86	118	116	234	143	144	287	78

New York Yankees - Yankee Stadium

	2005 Season							2003-2005						
	Home Games			Away Games				Home Games			Away Games			
	Yankees	Opp	Total	Yankees	Opp	Total	Index	Yankees	Opp	Total	Yankees	Opp	Total	Index
G	72	72	144	72	72	144		217	217	434	216	216	432	
Avg	.287	.276	.281	.267	.268	.267	105	.274	.268	.271	.270	.272	.271	100
AB	2446	2567	5013	2552	2389	4941	101	7242	7710	14952	7664	7355	15019	99
R	420	345	765	373	373	746	103	1163	1010	2173	1207	1066	2273	95
H	701	708	1409	681	640	1321	107	1981	2066	4047	2070	1997	4067	99
2B	109	119	228	119	141	260	86	343	388	731	408	439	847	87
3B	8	16	24	8	13	21	113	20	35	55	27	44	71	78
HR	116	70	186	98	76	174	105	321	215	536	309	211	520	104
BB	264	186	450	281	234	515	86	825	558	1383	914	610	1524	91
SO	444	467	911	437	405	842	107	1308	1481	2789	1364	1306	2670	105
E	43	56	99	39	48	87	114	138	156	294	127	134	261	112
E-Infield	24	32	56	16	24	40	140	68	73	141	57	61	118	119
LHB-Avg	.275	.276	.275	.266	.265	.266	104	.263	.272	.268	.267	.270	.268	100
LHB-HR	53	30	83	53	25	78	106	151	104	255	159	91	250	107
RHB-Avg	.301	.276	.287	.268	.270	.269	107	.284	.265	.274	.274	.273	.273	100
RHB-HR	63	40	103	45	51	96	104	170	111	281	150	120	270	101

Oakland Athletics - McAfee Coliseum

	2005 Season							2003-2005						
	Home Games			Away Games				Home Games			Away Games			
	Athletics	Opp	Total	Athletics	Opp	Total	Index	Athletics	Opp	Total	Athletics	Opp	Total	Index
G	72	72	144	72	72	144		216	216	432	216	216	432	
Avg	.264	.243	.254	.257	.242	.249	102	.260	.241	.251	.260	.254	.257	97
AB	2454	2495	4949	2570	2380	4950	100	7278	7480	14758	7719	7197	14916	99
R	343	319	662	344	276	620	107	996	871	1867	1051	919	1970	95
H	649	607	1256	660	575	1235	102	1892	1805	3697	2004	1830	3834	96
2B	147	116	263	124	114	238	111	412	369	781	430	336	766	103
3B	10	8	18	8	13	21	86	23	23	46	26	34	60	77
HR	62	69	131	77	68	145	90	221	196	417	243	196	439	96
BB	229	240	469	249	208	457	103	733	691	1424	781	676	1457	99
SO	337	485	822	419	485	904	91	1155	1421	2576	1334	1375	2709	96
E	38	41	79	36	53	89	89	113	146	259	135	129	264	98
E-Infield	19	18	37	18	26	44	84	48	60	108	55	70	125	86
LHB-Avg	.269	.252	.261	.250	.245	.248	105	.268	.248	.259	.262	.260	.261	99
LHB-HR	37	26	63	49	29	78	81	116	59	175	141	79	220	82
RHB-Avg	.260	.236	.247	.264	.239	.251	98	.251	.237	.243	.257	.250	.254	96
RHB-HR	25	43	68	28	39	67	101	105	137	242	102	117	219	109

Philadelphia Phillies - Citizens Bank Park

	2005 Season							2004-2005						
	Home Games			Away Games				Home Games			Away Games			
	Phillies	Opp	Total	Phillies	Opp	Total	Index	Phillies	Opp	Total	Phillies	Opp	Total	Index
G	75	75	150	72	72	144		147	147	294	144	144	288	
Avg	.281	.264	.272	.260	.238	.250	109	.275	.262	.268	.262	.249	.256	105
AB	2516	2625	5141	2508	2312	4820	102	4954	5165	10119	5069	4725	9794	101
R	398	355	753	350	301	651	111	775	705	1480	707	614	1321	110
H	706	693	1399	653	550	1203	112	1362	1351	2713	1328	1175	2503	106
2B	137	158	295	125	131	256	108	266	286	552	267	274	541	99
3B	20	15	35	13	11	24	137	33	30	63	23	25	48	127
HR	87	93	180	69	73	142	119	187	195	382	154	152	306	121
BB	309	196	505	286	242	528	90	584	412	996	573	468	1041	93
SO	430	551	981	550	513	1063	87	892	1046	1938	1074	961	2035	92
E	38	49	87	42	43	85	98	73	89	162	80	89	169	94
E-Infield	15	27	42	15	17	32	126	31	43	74	31	40	71	102
LHB-Avg	.277	.270	.274	.268	.260	.265	103	.275	.275	.275	.271	.264	.268	103
LHB-HR	47	46	93	42	31	73	117	93	83	176	88	53	141	121
RHB-Avg	.284	.260	.270	.252	.221	.236	115	.275	.252	.263	.254	.238	.246	107
RHB-HR	40	47	87	27	42	69	121	94	112	206	66	99	165	120

Pittsburgh Pirates - PNC Park

	2005 Season							2003-2005						
	Home Games			Away Games				Home Games			Away Games			
	Pirates	Opp	Total	Pirates	Opp	Total	Index	Pirates	Opp	Total	Pirates	Opp	Total	Index
G	75	75	150	75	75	150		224	224	448	225	225	450	
Avg	.262	.268	.265	.258	.260	.259	102	.268	.267	.268	.257	.265	.261	103
AB	2526	2627	5153	2631	2414	5045	102	7509	7833	15342	7848	7361	15209	101
R	299	369	668	323	343	666	100	950	1049	1999	985	1040	2025	99
H	661	705	1366	678	628	1306	105	2015	2089	4104	2020	1947	3967	104
2B	146	150	296	124	143	267	109	406	437	843	363	404	767	109
3B	21	11	32	12	11	23	136	58	33	91	53	44	97	93
HR	54	73	127	77	75	152	82	195	202	397	211	241	452	87
BB	230	280	510	206	292	498	100	646	762	1408	663	797	1460	96
SO	498	482	980	513	412	925	104	1399	1407	2806	1577	1334	2911	96
E	64	50	114	43	57	100	114	170	138	308	141	149	290	107
E-Infield	30	23	53	18	27	45	118	86	64	150	57	66	123	122
LHB-Avg	.264	.295	.279	.247	.261	.253	110	.272	.293	.283	.255	.269	.262	108
LHB-HR	24	27	51	18	28	46	107	79	76	155	67	83	150	103
RHB-Avg	.260	.255	.257	.265	.260	.262	98	.266	.251	.258	.259	.262	.260	99
RHB-HR	30	46	76	59	47	106	71	116	126	242	144	158	302	79

San Diego Padres - PETCO Park

	2005 Season							2004-2005						
	Home Games			Away Games				Home Games			Away Games			
	Padres	Opp	Total	Padres	Opp	Total	Index	Padres	Opp	Total	Padres	Opp	Total	Index
G	72	72	144	72	72	144		144	144	288	144	144	288	
Avg	.257	.237	.247	.263	.281	.272	91	.256	.250	.253	.278	.275	.277	91
AB	2357	2504	4861	2541	2488	5029	97	4710	5003	9713	5139	4926	10065	97
R	277	272	549	344	370	714	77	573	578	1151	744	701	1445	80
H	606	594	1200	669	699	1368	88	1204	1250	2454	1429	1354	2783	88
2B	106	132	238	140	152	292	84	223	274	497	294	293	587	88
3B	21	19	40	14	15	29	143	40	34	74	25	30	55	139
HR	41	51	92	71	74	145	66	89	116	205	148	174	322	66
BB	265	235	500	292	233	525	99	544	420	964	526	430	956	104
SO	435	546	981	438	455	893	114	827	1038	1865	847	927	1774	109
E	54	35	89	49	50	99	90	90	78	168	108	103	211	80
E-Infield	24	11	35	19	25	44	80	37	24	61	47	48	95	64
LHB-Avg	.258	.245	.251	.289	.279	.284	88	.267	.253	.259	.288	.276	.282	92
LHB-HR	21	27	48	25	29	54	90	34	58	92	48	74	122	78
RHB-Avg	.256	.231	.244	.246	.282	.263	93	.248	.247	.248	.271	.274	.272	91
RHB-HR	20	24	44	46	45	91	51	55	58	113	100	100	200	59

San Francisco Giants - Pacific Bell Park

	2005 Season							2003-2005						
	Home Games			Away Games				Home Games			Away Games			
	Giants	Opp	Total	Giants	Opp	Total	Index	Giants	Opp	Total	Giants	Opp	Total	Index
G	72	72	144	72	72	144		216	216	432	214	214	428	
Avg	.261	.255	.258	.262	.262	.262	99	.274	.257	.265	.256	.257	.256	104
AB	2347	2495	4842	2504	2397	4901	99	7144	7507	14651	7419	7095	14514	100
R	281	319	600	291	315	606	99	1015	934	1949	961	933	1894	102
H	613	636	1249	655	628	1283	97	1960	1928	3888	1899	1820	3719	104
2B	127	117	244	140	125	265	93	398	379	777	401	364	765	101
3B	11	15	26	14	16	30	88	50	46	96	27	48	75	127
HR	59	65	124	57	68	125	100	205	188	393	226	205	431	90
BB	188	257	445	195	275	470	96	778	721	1499	753	766	1519	98
SO	354	454	808	454	425	879	93	1127	1394	2521	1340	1258	2598	96
E	38	39	77	41	34	75	103	125	141	266	113	107	220	120
E-Infield	15	13	28	21	11	32	88	57	55	112	51	43	94	118
LHB-Avg	.258	.265	.262	.281	.261	.270	97	.272	.258	.265	.270	.265	.267	99
LHB-HR	16	21	37	23	26	49	75	82	66	148	103	78	181	82
RHB-Avg	.263	.248	.255	.251	.263	.257	100	.276	.256	.266	.247	.251	.249	107
RHB-HR	43	44	87	34	42	76	118	123	122	245	123	127	250	96

Seattle Mariners - Safeco Field

	2005 Season							2003-2005						
	Home Games			Away Games				Home Games			Away Games			
	Mariners	Opp	Total	Mariners	Opp	Total	Index	Mariners	Opp	Total	Mariners	Opp	Total	Index
G	72	72	144	72	72	144		217	217	434	215	215	430	
Avg	.257	.270	.263	.248	.278	.263	100	.260	.254	.257	.272	.276	.274	94
AB	2420	2571	4991	2455	2388	4843	103	7280	7631	14911	7698	7255	14953	99
R	313	341	654	300	350	650	101	969	984	1953	1014	1059	2073	93
H	621	693	1314	608	664	1272	103	1893	1938	3831	2097	2000	4097	93
2B	124	126	250	125	126	251	97	352	377	729	410	368	778	94
3B	11	5	16	17	11	28	55	33	20	53	44	30	74	72
HR	53	76	129	60	91	151	83	182	262	444	185	261	446	100
BB	205	230	435	216	196	412	102	710	699	1409	669	655	1324	107
SO	458	431	889	409	365	774	111	1373	1395	2768	1313	1206	2519	110
E	39	46	85	41	50	91	93	120	141	261	115	132	247	105
E-Infield	15	13	28	22	21	43	65	45	58	103	57	58	115	89
LHB-Avg	.276	.278	.277	.266	.270	.268	103	.277	.256	.266	.289	.275	.282	94
LHB-HR	17	36	53	23	34	57	91	67	136	203	60	112	172	119
RHB-Avg	.242	.263	.253	.233	.285	.258	98	.247	.252	.250	.260	.276	.268	93
RHB-HR	36	40	76	37	57	94	78	115	126	241	125	149	274	88

St Louis Cardinals - Busch Stadium

	2005 Season							2003-2005						
	Home Games			Away Games				Home Games			Away Games			
	Cardinals	Opp	Total	Cardinals	Opp	Total	Index	Cardinals	Opp	Total	Cardinals	Opp	Total	Index
G	75	75	150	72	72	144		222	222	444	219	219	438	
Avg	.272	.260	.266	.268	.256	.262	102	.279	.254	.266	.268	.265	.267	100
AB	2518	2612	5130	2517	2332	4849	102	7452	7720	15172	7718	7316	15034	100
R	379	307	686	353	271	624	106	1121	925	2046	1136	946	2082	97
H	685	680	1365	674	597	1271	103	2077	1964	4041	2071	1940	4011	99
2B	143	125	268	126	111	237	107	454	395	849	408	395	803	105
3B	10	7	17	15	13	28	57	29	30	59	45	33	78	75
HR	88	78	166	70	64	134	117	252	228	480	277	252	529	90
BB	252	204	456	239	204	443	97	760	641	1401	753	638	1391	100
SO	399	488	887	463	401	864	97	1253	1452	2705	1448	1277	2725	98
E	54	64	118	35	58	93	122	126	158	284	116	165	281	100
E-Infield	23	26	49	18	20	38	124	58	60	118	52	64	116	100
LHB-Avg	.265	.246	.254	.261	.254	.257	99	.273	.246	.258	.266	.265	.266	97
LHB-HR	30	32	62	27	28	55	103	100	92	192	101	104	205	92
RHB-Avg	.275	.270	.273	.271	.257	.265	103	.282	.260	.271	.269	.265	.268	101
RHB-HR	58	46	104	43	36	79	127	152	136	288	176	148	324	88

Tampa Bay Devil Rays - Tropicana Field Surface: NexTurf

	2005 Season							2003-2005						
	Home Games			Away Games				Home Games			Away Games			
	Devil Rays	Opp	Total	Devil Rays	Opp	Total	Index	Devil Rays	Opp	Total	Devil Rays	Opp	Total	Index
G	72	72	144	72	72	144		213	213	426	216	216	432	
Avg	.285	.272	.278	.266	.284	.275	101	.269	.260	.265	.264	.280	.272	97
AB	2429	2570	4999	2504	2390	4894	102	7214	7519	14733	7575	7184	14759	101
R	366	400	766	311	410	721	106	986	1093	2079	950	1239	2189	96
H	692	699	1391	667	679	1346	103	1942	1956	3898	1999	2013	4012	99
2B	126	130	256	126	149	275	91	369	395	764	383	452	835	92
3B	23	18	41	13	18	31	129	62	41	103	41	42	83	124
HR	64	90	154	76	84	160	94	181	260	441	216	268	484	91
BB	200	261	461	169	285	454	99	598	767	1365	531	852	1383	99
SO	424	471	895	461	372	833	105	1262	1313	2575	1359	1124	2483	104
E	61	42	103	49	38	87	118	161	142	303	149	121	270	114
E-Infield	26	15	41	19	10	29	141	69	55	124	57	47	104	121
LHB-Avg	.289	.268	.278	.275	.279	.277	100	.275	.259	.267	.265	.276	.270	99
LHB-HR	21	39	60	27	35	62	96	97	120	217	104	117	221	97
RHB-Avg	.283	.275	.279	.261	.288	.274	102	.264	.261	.262	.263	.284	.273	96
RHB-HR	43	51	94	49	49	98	93	84	140	224	112	151	263	86

Texas Rangers - The Ballpark in Arlington

	2005 Season							2003-2005						
	Home Games			Away Games				Home Games			Away Games			
	Rangers	Opp	Total	Rangers	Opp	Total	Index	Rangers	Opp	Total	Rangers	Opp	Total	Index
G	72	72	144	72	72	144		216	216	432	216	216	432	
Avg	.273	.278	.276	.261	.278	.269	102	.282	.279	.281	.250	.279	.264	106
AB	2477	2608	5085	2618	2473	5091	100	7412	7784	15196	7682	7317	14999	101
R	407	390	797	357	381	738	108	1289	1189	2478	966	1123	2089	119
H	675	726	1401	683	687	1370	102	2090	2175	4265	1919	2045	3964	108
2B	131	152	283	143	139	282	100	410	456	866	406	399	805	106
3B	15	18	33	11	6	17	194	57	52	109	33	32	65	166
HR	130	71	201	93	67	160	126	361	250	611	271	235	506	119
BB	222	230	452	214	247	461	98	683	736	1419	627	776	1403	100
SO	447	414	861	520	402	922	93	1342	1341	2683	1523	1253	2776	95
E	49	40	89	49	41	90	99	138	128	266	147	124	271	98
E-Infield	20	26	46	21	26	47	98	59	69	128	64	63	127	101
LHB-Avg	.266	.280	.274	.268	.259	.263	104	.278	.274	.276	.245	.271	.259	107
LHB-HR	58	45	103	34	23	57	172	171	129	300	110	100	210	137
RHB-Avg	.277	.277	.277	.256	.293	.273	101	.284	.284	.284	.253	.286	.268	106
RHB-HR	72	26	98	59	44	103	99	190	121	311	161	135	296	106

Toronto Blue Jays - Rogers Centre Surface: AstroTurf

	2005 Season							2003-2005						
	Home Games			Away Games				Home Games			Away Games			
	Blue Jays	Opp	Total	Blue Jays	Opp	Total	Index	Blue Jays	Opp	Total	Blue Jays	Opp	Total	Index
G	72	72	144	72	72	144		216	216	432	215	215	430	
Avg	.276	.264	.270	.262	.266	.264	102	.274	.276	.275	.264	.266	.265	104
AB	2468	2556	5024	2531	2424	4955	101	7345	7721	15066	7613	7210	14823	101
R	364	318	682	348	319	667	102	1113	1118	2231	1037	997	2034	109
H	680	674	1354	664	644	1308	104	2011	2134	4145	2010	1916	3926	105
2B	149	114	263	131	114	245	106	460	412	872	409	348	757	113
3B	20	8	28	15	11	26	106	54	37	91	39	40	79	113
HR	65	94	159	56	72	128	123	212	277	489	198	225	423	114
BB	204	178	382	222	221	443	85	708	681	1389	674	694	1368	100
SO	415	462	877	431	393	824	105	1339	1402	2741	1460	1171	2631	103
E	48	48	96	35	43	78	123	135	149	284	127	132	259	109
E-Infield	24	20	44	21	20	41	107	66	60	126	60	70	130	96
LHB-Avg	.275	.244	.260	.265	.268	.266	98	.272	.271	.271	.265	.265	.265	102
LHB-HR	25	33	58	29	28	57	104	103	119	222	100	102	202	109
RHB-Avg	.276	.277	.277	.260	.264	.262	106	.275	.281	.278	.263	.267	.265	105
RHB-HR	40	61	101	27	44	71	137	109	158	267	98	123	221	118

Washington Nationals - RFK Stadium

	2005 Season							2002-2004 (Olympic Stadium on NexTurf)						
	Home Games			Away Games				Home Games			Away Games			
	Nationals	Opp	Total	Nationals	Opp	Total	Index	Expos	Opp	Total	Expos	Opp	Total	Index
G	72	72	144	72	72	144		181	181	362	217	217	434	
Avg	.234	.248	.241	.270	.274	.272	89	.267	.260	.264	.247	.271	.259	102
AB	2299	2495	4794	2548	2442	4990	96	5985	6320	12305	7489	7291	14780	100
R	249	297	546	319	306	625	87	859	787	1646	864	996	1860	106
H	538	618	1156	687	670	1357	85	1599	1644	3243	1853	1973	3826	102
2B	128	124	252	155	130	285	92	388	369	757	346	374	720	126
3B	16	6	22	12	10	22	104	39	29	68	36	42	78	105
HR	39	62	101	64	59	123	85	182	189	371	201	232	433	103
BB	210	229	439	222	259	481	95	621	546	1167	701	735	1436	98
SO	465	495	960	518	407	925	108	1030	1205	2235	1472	1367	2839	95
E	45	39	84	38	37	75	112	122	125	247	155	148	303	98
E-Infield	24	22	46	17	18	35	131	42	51	93	73	65	138	81
LHB-Avg	.248	.257	.252	.276	.272	.274	92	.272	.263	.268	.247	.280	.262	102
LHB-HR	20	28	48	24	27	51	99	85	71	156	89	97	186	104
RHB-Avg	.223	.239	.231	.264	.277	.270	86	.263	.258	.261	.248	.264	.256	102
RHB-HR	19	34	53	40	32	72	76	97	118	215	112	135	247	102

2005 American League Ballpark Index Rankings - Runs

Team	Avg	AB	R	H	2B	3B	HR	BB	SO	E	E-Inf	LHB Avg	LHB HR	RHB Avg	RHB HR
Texas - The Ballpark in Arlington	102	100	108	102	100	194	126	98	93	99	98	104	172	101	99
Oakland - McAfee Coliseum	102	100	107	102	111	86	90	103	91	89	84	105	81	98	101
Boston - Fenway Park	99	99	107	98	135	73	99	106	100	99	115	101	84	97	118
Tampa Bay - Tropicana Field	101	102	106	103	91	129	94	99	105	118	141	100	96	102	93
Chicago - U.S. Cellular Field	101	98	104	99	96	82	139	108	103	72	66	109	163	96	130
New York - Yankee Stadium	105	101	103	107	86	113	105	86	107	114	140	104	106	107	104
Toronto - Rogers Centre	102	101	102	104	106	106	123	85	105	123	107	98	104	106	137
Minnesota - Hubert H. Humphrey Metrodome	98	97	102	95	93	85	110	89	110	106	113	98	100	98	122
Kansas City - Ewing M. Kauffman Stadium	103	103	101	106	116	113	73	101	89	83	86	101	72	104	74
Seattle - Safeco Field	100	103	101	103	97	55	83	102	111	93	65	103	91	98	78
Detroit - Comerica Park	102	102	96	104	82	176	95	101	97	120	124	108	118	99	85
Los Angeles - Angel Stadium of Anaheim	96	98	93	94	103	102	90	100	101	110	116	95	85	97	93
Baltimore - Oriole Park at Camden Yards	96	99	89	94	81	69	101	123	92	77	63	87	93	102	107
Cleveland - Jacobs Field	93	96	83	89	103	46	83	101	101	110	115	90	82	95	85

2005 American League Ballpark Index Rankings - Home Runs

Team	Avg	AB	R	H	2B	3B	HR	BB	SO	E	E-Inf	LHB Avg	LHB HR	RHB Avg	RHB HR
Chicago - U.S. Cellular Field	101	98	104	99	96	82	139	108	103	72	66	109	163	96	130
Texas - The Ballpark in Arlington	102	100	108	102	100	194	126	98	93	99	98	104	172	101	99
Toronto - Rogers Centre	102	101	102	104	106	106	123	85	105	123	107	98	104	106	137
Minnesota - Hubert H. Humphrey Metrodome	98	97	102	95	93	85	110	89	110	106	113	98	100	98	122
New York - Yankee Stadium	105	101	103	107	86	113	105	86	107	114	140	104	106	107	104
Baltimore - Oriole Park at Camden Yards	96	99	89	94	81	69	101	123	92	77	63	87	93	102	107
Boston - Fenway Park	99	99	107	98	135	73	99	106	100	99	115	101	84	97	118
Detroit - Comerica Park	102	102	96	104	82	176	95	101	97	120	124	108	118	99	85
Tampa Bay - Tropicana Field	101	102	106	103	91	129	94	99	105	118	141	100	96	102	93
Oakland - McAfee Coliseum	102	100	107	102	111	86	90	103	91	89	84	105	81	98	101
Los Angeles - Angel Stadium of Anaheim	96	98	93	94	103	102	90	100	101	110	116	95	85	97	93
Cleveland - Jacobs Field	93	96	83	89	103	46	83	101	101	110	115	90	82	95	85
Seattle - Safeco Field	100	103	101	103	97	55	83	102	111	93	65	103	91	98	78
Kansas City - Ewing M. Kauffman Stadium	103	103	101	106	116	113	73	101	89	83	86	101	72	104	74

2005 National League Ballpark Index Rankings - Runs

Team	Avg	AB	R	H	2B	3B	HR	BB	SO	E	E-Inf	LHB Avg	LHB HR	RHB Avg	RHB HR
Colorado - Coors Field	118	108	128	128	113	147	106	95	85	100	97	116	85	120	120
Cincinnati - Great American Ballpark	105	102	111	108	121	50	121	95	96	83	87	111	127	102	117
Philadelphia - Citizens Bank Park	109	102	111	112	108	137	119	90	87	98	126	103	117	115	121
Atlanta - Turner Field	105	101	110	106	116	141	84	101	98	107	126	106	80	105	88
St Louis - Busch Stadium	102	102	106	103	107	57	117	97	97	122	124	99	103	103	127
Arizona - Chase Field	101	100	105	102	109	158	104	104	96	70	94	102	89	100	122
Chicago - Wrigley Field	99	101	102	100	101	103	102	99	101	94	93	99	119	98	93
Pittsburgh - PNC Park	102	102	100	105	109	136	82	100	104	114	118	110	107	98	71
Milwaukee - Miller Park	94	96	99	90	93	100	111	106	108	106	116	90	86	96	128
San Francisco - Pacific Bell Park	99	99	99	97	93	88	100	96	93	103	88	97	75	100	118
New York - Shea Stadium	101	101	98	102	95	66	90	100	93	129	89	104	94	98	86
Houston - Minute Maid Park	102	99	98	101	84	92	125	102	97	120	80	96	97	105	140
Los Angeles - Dodger Stadium	92	97	89	89	99	31	102	110	109	89	83	91	110	93	95
Washington - RFK Stadium	89	96	87	85	92	104	85	95	108	112	131	92	99	86	76
Florida - Dolphins Stadium	93	98	84	91	82	119	78	114	121	75	87	95	114	93	63
San Diego - PETCO Park	91	97	77	88	84	143	66	99	114	90	80	88	90	93	51

2005 National League Ballpark Index Rankings - Home Runs

Team	Avg	AB	R	H	2B	3B	HR	BB	SO	E	E-Inf	LHB Avg	LHB HR	RHB Avg	RHB HR
Houston - Minute Maid Park	102	99	98	101	84	92	125	102	97	120	80	96	97	105	140
Cincinnati - Great American Ballpark	105	102	111	108	121	50	121	95	96	83	87	111	127	102	117
Philadelphia - Citizens Bank Park	109	102	111	112	108	137	119	90	87	98	126	103	117	115	121
St Louis - Busch Stadium	102	102	106	103	107	57	117	97	97	122	124	99	103	103	127
Milwaukee - Miller Park	94	96	99	90	93	100	111	106	108	106	116	90	86	96	128
Colorado - Coors Field	118	108	128	128	113	147	106	95	85	100	97	116	85	120	120
Arizona - Chase Field	101	100	105	102	109	158	104	104	96	70	94	102	89	100	122
Chicago - Wrigley Field	99	101	102	100	101	103	102	99	101	94	93	99	119	98	93
Los Angeles - Dodger Stadium	92	97	89	89	99	31	102	110	109	89	83	91	110	93	95
San Francisco - Pacific Bell Park	99	99	99	97	93	88	100	96	93	103	88	97	75	100	118
New York - Shea Stadium	101	101	98	102	95	66	90	100	93	129	89	104	94	98	86
Washington - RFK Stadium	89	96	87	85	92	104	85	95	108	112	131	92	99	86	76
Atlanta - Turner Field	105	101	110	106	116	141	84	101	98	107	126	106	80	105	88
Pittsburgh - PNC Park	102	102	100	105	109	136	82	100	104	114	118	110	107	98	71
Florida - Dolphins Stadium	93	98	84	91	82	119	78	114	121	75	87	95	114	93	63
San Diego - PETCO Park	91	97	77	88	84	143	66	99	114	90	80	88	90	93	51

2003-2005 American League Ballpark Index Rankings - Runs

Team	Avg	AB	R	H	2B	3B	HR	BB	SO	E	E-Inf	LHB Avg	LHB HR	RHB Avg	RHB HR
Texas - The Ballpark in Arlington	106	101	119	108	106	166	119	100	95	98	101	107	137	106	106
Boston - Fenway Park	105	100	110	105	128	86	97	102	94	113	144	107	82	103	113
Toronto - Rogers Centre	104	101	109	105	113	113	114	100	103	109	96	102	109	105	118
Minnesota - Hubert H. Humphrey Metrodome	100	100	104	99	98	109	102	96	110	94	87	99	104	100	101
Chicago - U.S. Cellular Field	102	100	103	101	96	93	135	99	102	80	72	103	131	101	137
Baltimore - Oriole Park at Camden Yards	99	100	97	98	94	62	105	108	93	95	89	96	100	101	110
Kansas City - Ewing M. Kauffman Stadium *	101	101	97	102	106	125	73	101	92	75	84	99	73	102	74
Tampa Bay - Tropicana Field	97	101	96	99	92	124	91	99	104	114	121	99	97	96	86
New York - Yankee Stadium	100	99	95	99	87	78	104	91	105	112	119	100	107	100	101
Oakland - McAfee Coliseum	97	99	95	96	103	77	96	99	96	98	86	99	82	96	109
Detroit - Comerica Park *	101	102	95	103	83	203	90	100	95	93	107	104	99	99	85
Seattle - Safeco Field	94	99	93	93	94	72	100	107	110	105	89	94	119	93	88
Anaheim - Angel Stadium of Anaheim	101	100	93	101	95	59	98	93	100	88	86	98	97	103	99
Los Angeles - Angel Stadium of Anaheim	96	98	93	94	103	102	90	100	101	110	116	95	85	97	93
Cleveland - Jacobs Field	95	98	87	93	104	64	76	105	104	118	118	94	79	96	72

2003-2005 American League Ballpark Index Rankings - Home Runs

Team	Avg	AB	R	H	2B	3B	HR	BB	SO	E	E-Inf	LHB Avg	LHB HR	RHB Avg	RHB HR
Chicago - U.S. Cellular Field	102	100	103	101	96	93	135	99	102	80	72	103	131	101	137
Texas - The Ballpark in Arlington	106	101	119	108	106	166	119	100	95	98	101	107	137	106	106
Toronto - Rogers Centre	104	101	109	105	113	113	114	100	103	109	96	102	109	105	118
Baltimore - Oriole Park at Camden Yards	99	100	97	98	94	62	105	108	93	95	89	96	100	101	110
New York - Yankee Stadium	100	99	95	99	87	78	104	91	105	112	119	100	107	100	101
Minnesota - Hubert H. Humphrey Metrodome	100	100	104	99	98	109	102	96	110	94	87	99	104	100	101
Seattle - Safeco Field	94	99	93	93	94	72	100	107	110	105	89	94	119	93	88
Anaheim - Angel Stadium of Anaheim	101	100	93	101	95	59	98	93	100	88	86	98	97	103	99
Boston - Fenway Park	105	100	110	105	128	86	97	102	94	113	144	107	82	103	113
Oakland - McAfee Coliseum	97	99	95	96	103	77	96	99	96	98	86	99	82	96	109
Tampa Bay - Tropicana Field	97	101	96	99	92	124	91	99	104	114	121	99	97	96	86
Los Angeles - Angel Stadium of Anaheim	96	98	93	94	103	102	90	100	101	110	116	95	85	97	93
Detroit - Comerica Park *	101	102	95	103	83	203	90	100	95	93	107	104	99	99	85
Cleveland - Jacobs Field	95	98	87	93	104	64	76	105	104	118	118	94	79	96	72
Kansas City - Ewing M. Kauffman Stadium *	101	101	97	102	106	125	73	101	92	75	84	99	73	102	74

2003-2005 National League Ballpark Index Rankings - Runs

Team	Avg	AB	R	H	2B	3B	HR	BB	SO	E	E-Inf	LHB Avg	LHB HR	RHB Avg	RHB HR
Colorado - Coors Field	116	106	133	123	114	169	121	99	86	115	114	115	126	117	118
Arizona - Chase Field	104	101	112	104	117	142	113	104	96	86	94	105	108	102	118
Philadelphia - Citizens Bank Park *	105	101	110	106	99	127	121	93	92	94	102	103	121	107	120
Chicago - Wrigley Field	100	101	105	101	96	93	113	104	102	106	103	98	104	101	118
Milwaukee - Miller Park	97	100	103	97	101	99	108	106	105	100	102	98	101	96	112
San Francisco - Pacific Bell Park	104	100	102	104	101	127	90	98	96	120	118	99	82	107	96
Atlanta - Turner Field	100	99	99	99	96	104	94	104	102	103	105	101	94	99	94
Pittsburgh - PNC Park	103	101	99	104	109	93	87	96	96	107	122	108	103	99	79
Houston - Minute Maid Park	100	98	99	99	89	153	112	95	99	106	84	95	77	103	133
Cincinnati - Great American Ballpark	98	100	98	98	104	42	116	94	99	96	121	99	117	98	116
New York - Shea Stadium	101	101	98	103	101	55	84	99	97	121	126	104	94	99	78
St Louis - Busch Stadium	100	100	97	99	105	75	90	100	98	100	100	97	92	101	88
Florida - Dolphins Stadium	95	99	90	95	86	129	84	109	113	80	69	97	104	95	78
Washington - RFK Stadium	89	96	87	85	92	104	85	95	108	112	131	92	99	86	76
Los Angeles - Dodger Stadium	93	97	87	90	87	40	106	96	106	94	87	96	107	91	106
San Diego - PETCO Park *	91	97	80	88	88	139	66	104	109	80	64	92	78	91	59

2003-2005 National League Ballpark Index Rankings - Home Runs

Team	Avg	AB	R	H	2B	3B	HR	BB	SO	E	E-Inf	LHB Avg	LHB HR	RHB Avg	RHB HR
Colorado - Coors Field	116	106	133	123	114	169	121	99	86	115	114	115	126	117	118
Philadelphia - Citizens Bank Park *	105	101	110	106	99	127	121	93	92	94	102	103	121	107	120
Cincinnati - Great American Ballpark	98	100	98	98	104	42	116	94	99	96	121	99	117	98	116
Arizona - Chase Field	104	101	112	104	117	142	113	104	96	86	94	105	108	102	118
Chicago - Wrigley Field	100	101	105	101	96	93	113	104	102	106	103	98	104	101	118
Houston - Minute Maid Park	100	98	99	99	89	153	112	95	99	106	84	95	77	103	133
Milwaukee - Miller Park	97	100	103	97	101	99	108	106	105	100	102	98	101	96	112
Los Angeles - Dodger Stadium	93	97	87	90	87	40	106	96	106	94	87	96	107	91	106
Atlanta - Turner Field	100	99	99	99	96	104	94	104	102	103	105	101	94	99	94
San Francisco - Pacific Bell Park	104	100	102	104	101	127	90	98	96	120	118	99	82	107	96
St Louis - Busch Stadium	100	100	97	99	105	75	90	100	98	100	100	97	92	101	88
Pittsburgh - PNC Park	103	101	99	104	109	93	87	96	96	107	122	108	103	99	79
Washington - RFK Stadium	89	96	87	85	92	104	85	95	108	112	131	92	99	86	76
Florida - Dolphins Stadium	95	99	90	95	86	129	84	109	113	80	69	97	104	95	78
New York - Shea Stadium	101	101	98	103	101	55	84	99	97	121	126	104	94	99	78
San Diego - PETCO Park *	91	97	80	88	88	139	66	104	109	80	64	92	78	91	59

* - Data since 2004

2005 Lefty/Righty Statistics

Batters vs. Left-Handed and Right-Handed Pitchers

Batter	vs	Avg	AB	H	2B	3B	HR	RBI	BB	SO	OBP	Slg
Abernathy,Brent	L	.227	22	5	1	0	0	1	3	5	.346	.273
Bats Right	R	.244	45	11	0	0	1	5	4	4	.300	.311
Abreu,Bobby	L	.275	207	57	12	0	5	28	23	45	.353	.406
Bats Left	R	.291	381	111	25	1	19	74	94	89	.430	.512
Adams,Russ	L	.193	88	17	5	1	1	8	13	18	.304	.307
Bats Left	R	.270	393	106	22	4	7	55	37	39	.330	.399
Aguila,Chris	L	.240	25	6	1	0	0	1	1	5	.269	.280
Bats Right	R	.245	53	13	2	0	0	3	2	14	.273	.283
Alexander,Manny	L	.250	4	1	0	0	0	0	0	1	.250	.250
Bats Right	R	.071	14	1	1	0	0	0	2	4	.235	.143
Alfonzo,Edgardo	L	.267	90	24	3	0	1	10	6	8	.313	.333
Bats Right	R	.281	278	78	14	1	1	33	21	26	.331	.349
Allen,Chad	L	.351	37	13	0	1	0	4	1	6	.368	.405
Bats Right	R	.125	16	2	1	0	0	1	1	7	.176	.188
Alomar Jr.,Sandy	L	.385	26	10	4	0	0	5	0	2	.407	.538
Bats Right	R	.245	102	25	3	0	0	9	5	10	.280	.275
Alou,Moises	L	.372	94	35	8	1	7	21	15	7	.455	.702
Bats Right	R	.306	333	102	13	2	12	42	41	36	.384	.465
Ambres,Chip	L	.239	88	21	6	0	3	6	7	14	.295	.409
Bats Right	R	.246	57	14	2	0	1	3	9	18	.362	.333
Amezaga,Alfredo	L	.000	4	0	0	0	0	0	1	0	.200	.000
Bats Both	R	.500	2	1	0	0	0	0	0	0	.500	.500
Anderson,Brian	L	.083	12	1	0	0	0	0	0	5	.083	.083
Bats Right	R	.227	22	5	1	0	2	3	0	7	.227	.545
Anderson,Garret	L	.330	188	62	7	0	5	37	6	32	.347	.447
Bats Left	R	.261	387	101	27	1	12	59	17	52	.290	.429
Anderson,Marlon	L	.267	15	4	1	0	0	2	0	4	.313	.333
Bats Left	R	.264	220	58	8	0	7	17	18	41	.317	.395
Andino,Robert	L	.111	9	1	1	0	0	0	0	4	.111	.222
Bats Right	R	.171	35	6	3	0	0	1	5	4	.275	.257
Ardoin,Danny	L	.277	47	13	3	0	1	5	6	12	.370	.404
Bats Right	R	.215	163	35	7	0	5	17	14	57	.305	.350
Atkins,Garrett	L	.291	110	32	7	0	3	17	11	11	.358	.436
Bats Right	R	.286	409	117	24	1	10	72	34	61	.344	.423
Aurilia,Rich	L	.272	125	34	6	0	4	18	15	16	.350	.416
Bats Right	R	.286	301	86	17	2	10	50	22	51	.333	.455
Ausmus,Brad	L	.293	92	27	6	0	2	19	18	3	.409	.424
Bats Right	R	.247	295	73	13	0	1	28	33	45	.332	.302
Aybar,Willy	L	.241	29	7	4	0	0	3	4	3	.353	.379
Bats Both	R	.368	57	21	4	0	1	7	14	8	.493	.491
Baerga,Carlos	L	.261	23	6	1	0	1	3	4	1	.414	.435
Bats Both	R	.252	135	34	6	0	1	16	3	16	.299	.319
Bagwell,Jeff	L	.300	20	6	0	0	1	4	5	7	.423	.450
Bats Right	R	.238	80	19	4	0	2	15	13	14	.340	.363
Baker,Jeff	L	.278	18	5	3	0	0	2	4	6	.409	.444
Bats Right	R	.150	20	3	1	0	1	2	1	6	.190	.350
Bako,Paul	L	.250	4	1	0	0	0	1	0	1	.250	.250
Bats Left	R	.250	36	9	2	0	0	3	7	11	.372	.306
Barajas,Rod	L	.272	92	25	5	0	5	12	4	14	.309	.489
Bats Right	R	.248	318	79	19	0	16	48	22	56	.305	.459
Bard,Josh	L	.148	27	4	1	0	1	2	3	4	.233	.296
Bats Both	R	.214	56	12	3	0	0	7	6	7	.281	.268
Barmes,Clint	L	.289	90	26	3	0	4	10	2	10	.312	.456
Bats Right	R	.288	260	75	16	1	6	36	14	26	.336	.427
Barrett,Michael	L	.320	125	40	13	2	7	24	20	12	.415	.624
Bats Right	R	.258	299	77	19	1	9	37	20	49	.314	.418
Bartlett,Jason	L	.277	65	18	3	0	3	8	3	9	.304	.462
Bats Right	R	.226	159	36	7	1	0	8	18	28	.320	.283
Bautista,Jose	L	.273	11	3	1	0	0	1	2	2	.385	.364
Bats Right	R	.059	17	1	0	0	0	0	1	5	.111	.059
Bay,Jason	L	.347	150	52	14	3	7	26	27	28	.444	.620
Bats Right	R	.292	449	131	30	3	25	75	68	114	.388	.539
Bell,David	L	.400	135	54	14	0	4	27	16	16	.461	.593
Bats Right	R	.199	422	84	17	1	6	34	51	53	.260	.287
Bellhorn,Mark	L	.228	101	23	9	0	3	7	15	41	.325	.406
Bats Both	R	.201	199	40	11	0	5	23	37	71	.324	.332
Belliard,Ronnie	L	.287	150	43	13	0	4	22	14	29	.345	.453
Bats Right	R	.282	386	109	23	1	13	56	21	43	.316	.448
Beltran,Carlos	L	.308	130	40	9	0	2	14	12	26	.364	.423
Bats Both	R	.254	452	115	25	2	14	64	44	70	.320	.412
Beltre,Adrian	L	.275	149	41	9	0	7	24	8	19	.325	.477
Bats Right	R	.249	454	113	27	1	12	63	30	89	.296	.392
Bennett,Gary	L	.198	81	16	3	0	1	7	8	10	.261	.272
Bats Right	R	.237	118	28	4	0	0	14	13	27	.323	.271
Bergolla,William	L	.214	14	3	0	0	0	0	0	4	.214	.214
Bats Right	R	.083	24	2	0	0	0	1	0	6	.083	.083
Berkman,Lance	L	.294	126	37	8	0	3	16	26	16	.416	.429
Bats Both	R	.292	342	100	26	1	21	66	65	56	.409	.558
Berroa,Angel	L	.278	176	49	6	1	5	11	7	32	.308	.409
Bats Right	R	.266	432	115	15	4	6	44	11	76	.304	.361
Betancourt,Yuniesky	L	.286	49	14	5	2	0	3	4	6	.340	.449
Bats Right	R	.247	162	40	6	3	1	12	7	18	.283	.340
Betemit,Wilson	L	.256	78	20	4	1	1	6	4	16	.289	.372
Bats Right	R	.327	168	55	8	3	3	14	18	39	.390	.464
Bigbie,Larry	L	.247	73	18	2	0	0	9	5	22	.295	.274
Bats Left	R	.236	199	47	8	2	5	14	19	45	.303	.372
Biggio,Craig	L	.243	148	36	8	1	6	16	11	18	.307	.432
Bats Right	R	.271	442	120	32	0	20	53	26	72	.331	.480
Blake,Casey	L	.241	137	33	6	0	11	17	11	34	.302	.526
Bats Right	R	.241	386	93	26	1	12	41	32	82	.310	.407
Blalock,Hank	L	.196	194	38	7	0	8	19	7	53	.228	.356
Bats Left	R	.291	453	132	27	0	17	73	44	79	.354	.464
Blanco,Andres	L	.111	27	3	0	0	0	1	0	0	.138	.111
Bats Both	R	.269	52	14	0	1	0	4	0	5	.264	.308
Blanco,Henry	L	.194	31	6	3	0	2	4	3	4	.265	.484
Bats Right	R	.254	130	33	3	0	4	21	8	20	.293	.369
Blanco,Tony	L	.172	29	5	2	0	0	1	1	11	.200	.241
Bats Right	R	.182	33	6	1	0	1	6	1	8	.229	.303
Bloomquist,Willie	L	.247	77	19	3	0	0	4	3	5	.280	.286
Bats Right	R	.262	172	45	12	2	0	18	8	33	.293	.355
Blum,Geoff	L	.213	94	20	2	0	3	6	6	15	.260	.330
Bats Both	R	.236	225	53	13	2	3	19	22	28	.311	.351
Bocachica,Hiram	L	.286	7	2	0	0	0	0	0	2	.286	.286
Bats Right	R	.000	12	0	0	0	0	0	0	5	.000	.000
Bonds,Barry	L	.600	5	3	0	0	1	2	2	0	.600	1.200
Bats Left	R	.243	37	9	1	0	4	8	9	6	.383	.595
Boone,Aaron	L	.229	118	27	4	0	7	14	17	22	.336	.441
Bats Right	R	.247	393	97	15	1	9	46	18	70	.288	.359
Boone,Bret	L	.203	79	16	4	1	2	8	11	15	.300	.354
Bats Right	R	.227	247	56	11	2	5	29	17	50	.286	.348
Borchard,Joe	L	1.000	1	1	0	0	0	0	0	0	1.000	1.000
Bats Both	R	.364	11	4	2	0	0	0	0	4	.364	.545
Borders,Pat	L	.324	37	12	3	0	1	4	2	6	.359	.486
Bats Right	R	.138	80	11	2	0	0	3	2	16	.167	.163
Botts,Jason	L	.000	1	0	0	0	0	0	1	0	.500	.000
Bats Both	R	.308	26	8	0	0	0	3	2	13	.357	.308
Bradley,Milton	L	.278	79	22	4	0	4	7	1	12	.293	.481
Bats Both	R	.294	204	60	10	1	9	31	24	35	.371	.485
Branyan,Russell	L	.050	20	1	0	0	0	1	1	13	.095	.050
Bats Left	R	.280	182	51	11	0	12	30	38	67	.405	.538
Broussard,Ben	L	.225	80	18	4	1	3	11	2	26	.250	.413
Bats Left	R	.262	386	101	26	4	16	57	30	72	.318	.474
Brown,Emil	L	.313	182	57	10	2	9	32	17	32	.368	.538
Bats Right	R	.273	363	99	21	3	8	54	31	76	.339	.413
Bruntlett,Eric	L	.295	61	18	4	2	2	8	7	14	.377	.525
Bats Right	R	.125	48	6	1	0	2	6	3	11	.176	.271
Bubela,Jaime	L	.167	6	1	0	0	0	0	0	2	.167	.167
Bats Left	R	.077	13	1	0	0	0	0	1	2	.143	.077
Buck,John	L	.310	116	36	7	0	2	11	12	27	.372	.422
Bats Right	R	.214	285	61	14	1	10	36	11	67	.250	.375
Burke,Chris	L	.265	117	31	7	1	2	8	8	18	.310	.393
Bats Right	R	.239	201	48	12	1	3	18	15	44	.308	.353
Burke,Jamie	L	.000	1	0	0	0	0	0	0	0	.000	.000
Bats Right	R	-	0	0	0	0	0	0	0	0	-	
Burnitz,Jeromy	L	.236	182	43	9	1	9	35	7	39	.268	.445
Bats Left	R	.267	423	113	22	1	15	52	50	70	.345	.430
Burrell,Pat	L	.318	154	49	6	0	10	29	35	38	.442	.552
Bats Right	R	.267	408	109	21	1	22	88	64	122	.367	.485
Burroughs,Sean	L	.172	58	10	0	0	1	5	1	9	.222	.224
Bats Left	R	.270	226	61	7	2	0	12	23	32	.343	.319
Bynum,Freddie	L	.000	1	0	0	0	0	0	0	1	.000	.000
Bats Left	R	.333	6	2	1	0	0	1	0	2	.333	.500
Byrd,Marlon	L	.323	93	30	8	1	1	15	8	19	.369	.462
Bats Right	R	.228	136	31	7	1	1	11	11	31	.291	.316
Byrnes,Eric	L	.263	156	41	10	2	5	20	15	20	.335	.449
Bats Right	R	.203	256	52	14	1	5	20	17	51	.268	.324
Cabrera,Melky	L	.333	6	2	0	0	0	0	0	0	.333	.333
Bats Both	R	.154	13	2	0	0	0	0	0	2	.154	.154
Cabrera,Miguel	L	.299	117	35	9	1	6	27	23	24	.408	.547
Bats Right	R	.329	496	163	34	1	27	89	41	101	.379	.565
Cabrera,Orlando	L	.242	157	38	8	2	1	19	16	11	.314	.338
Bats Right	R	.264	383	101	20	1	7	38	22	39	.306	.376

Batters vs. Left-Handed and Right-Handed Pitchers

Batter	vs	Avg	AB	H	2B	3B	HR	RBI	BB	SO	OBP	Slg
Cairo,Miguel	L	.191	89	17	4	0	1	4	4	8	.234	.270
Bats Right	R	.273	238	65	14	0	1	15	15	23	.318	.345
Calzado,Napoleon	L	.200	5	1	0	0	0	0	0	1	.200	.200
Bats Right	R	-	0	0	0	0	0	0	0	0	-	-
Cameron,Mike	L	.311	74	23	4	0	6	14	6	15	.370	.608
Bats Right	R	.261	234	61	19	2	6	25	23	70	.333	.436
Cano,Robinson	L	.270	148	40	7	0	2	17	7	25	.304	.358
Bats Left	R	.307	374	115	27	4	12	45	9	43	.326	.497
Cantu,Jorge	L	.253	158	40	11	1	6	26	4	30	.279	.449
Bats Right	R	.298	440	131	29	0	22	91	15	53	.323	.514
Carroll,Jamey	L	.293	82	24	3	0	0	7	10	11	.362	.329
Bats Right	R	.235	221	52	5	1	0	15	24	44	.323	.267
Casanova,Raul	L	.000	2	0	0	0	0	0	0	0	.000	.000
Bats Both	R	.333	3	1	0	0	0	0	0	0	.333	.333
Casey,Sean	L	.335	191	64	13	0	2	21	16	20	.389	.431
Bats Left	R	.298	332	99	19	0	7	37	32	28	.361	.419
Cash,Kevin	L	.250	8	2	0	0	1	1	1	4	.333	.625
Bats Right	R	.130	23	3	1	0	1	1	0	9	.167	.304
Castilla,Vinny	L	.314	118	37	11	0	1	15	18	14	.401	.432
Bats Right	R	.234	376	88	25	1	11	51	25	68	.292	.394
Castillo,Alberto	L	.139	36	5	0	1	1	4	2	9	.179	.278
Bats Right	R	.246	65	16	5	0	0	10	10	13	.347	.323
Castillo,Jose	L	.258	97	25	3	2	2	16	7	19	.308	.392
Bats Right	R	.271	273	74	13	1	9	37	16	40	.307	.425
Castillo,Luis	L	.423	111	47	9	2	4	14	8	8	.467	.649
Bats Both	R	.259	328	85	3	2	0	16	57	24	.368	.280
Castro,Bernie	L	.200	15	3	0	0	0	0	2	3	.294	.200
Bats Both	R	.308	65	20	3	1	0	7	7	7	.375	.385
Castro,Juan	L	.247	89	22	5	0	2	14	3	10	.272	.371
Bats Right	R	.262	183	48	13	1	3	19	6	29	.283	.393
Castro,Ramon	L	.290	31	9	3	0	1	2	8	4	.436	.484
Bats Right	R	.236	178	42	13	0	7	39	17	54	.298	.427
Catalanotto,Frank	L	.290	31	9	3	0	1	4	2		.371	.484
Bats Left	R	.302	388	117	26	5	7	55	35	51	.367	.448
Cedeno,Roger	L	.333	12	4	0	0	0	3	0	3	.333	.333
Bats Both	R	.111	45	5	1	0	0	5	2	3	.163	.133
Cedeno,Ronny	L	.256	39	10	3	0	0	2	1	4	.275	.333
Bats Right	R	.341	41	14	0	0	1	4	4	7	.426	.415
Cepicky,Matt	L	.000	2	0	0	0	0	0	0	2	.000	.000
Bats Left	R	.261	23	6	3	0	0	3	1	6	.292	.391
Chavez,Angel	L	.000	2	0	0	0	0	0	0	2	.000	.000
Bats Right	R	.294	17	5	1	0	0	1	0	1	.294	.353
Chavez,Endy	L	.381	21	8	2	2	0	4	0	1	.381	.667
Bats Left	R	.179	95	17	2	1	0	7	7	13	.235	.221
Chavez,Eric	L	.264	216	57	16	0	6	41	20	61	.328	.421
Bats Left	R	.271	409	111	24	1	21	60	38	68	.329	.449
Chavez,Raul	L	.133	30	4	0	0	0	0	4	5	.257	.133
Bats Right	R	.188	69	13	3	0	2	6	0	13	.186	.319
Chen,Chin-Feng	L	.400	5	2	0	0	0	2	0	2	.400	.400
Bats Right	R	.000	3	0	0	0	0	0	0	0	.000	.000
Choi,Hee Seop	L	.207	29	6	2	0	1	2	3	12	.343	.379
Bats Left	R	.258	291	75	13	2	14	40	31	68	.335	.460
Choo,Shin-Soo	L	.000	7	0	0	0	0	0	0	2	.000	.000
Bats Left	R	.091	11	1	0	0	0	1	3	2	.286	.091
Church,Ryan	L	.367	30	11	1	2	1	10	3	8	.441	.633
Bats Left	R	.277	238	66	14	1	8	32	21	62	.342	.445
Cintron,Alex	L	.301	83	25	4	0	2	9	3	6	.326	.422
Bats Both	R	.263	247	65	15	2	6	39	9	27	.288	.413
Cirillo,Jeff	L	.400	55	22	7	0	2	10	8	5	.484	.636
Bats Right	R	.231	130	30	8	0	2	13	15	17	.324	.338
Clark,Brady	L	.308	133	41	9	1	4	9	17	8	.403	.481
Bats Right	R	.305	466	142	22	0	9	44	30	47	.363	.410
Clark,Doug	L	-	0	0	0	0	0	0	0	0	-	-
Bats Left	R	.000	5	0	0	0	0	0	1	2	.167	.000
Clark,Jermaine	L	-	0	0	0	0	0	0	0	0	-	-
Bats Left	R	-	0	0	0	0	0	0	1	0	1.000	-
Clark,Tony	L	.313	115	36	8	0	6	27	16	15	.394	.539
Bats Both	R	.299	234	70	14	2	24	60	21	73	.352	.684
Clayton,Royce	L	.296	152	45	11	0	1	12	15	34	.361	.388
Bats Right	R	.259	370	96	17	4	1	32	23	71	.302	.335
Closser,JD	L	.270	37	10	2	0	2	8	5	7	.357	.486
Bats Both	R	.210	200	42	10	2	5	19	27	41	.306	.355
Conine,Jeff	L	.280	75	21	5	0	0	7	9	10	.353	.347
Bats Right	R	.312	260	81	15	2	3	26	29	48	.380	.419
Cora,Alex	L	.273	33	9	1	1	0	5	3	8	.324	.364
Bats Left	R	.226	217	49	7	3	3	19	18	22	.267	.327
Cordero,Wil	L	.105	19	2	0	0	0	0	1	7	.150	.105
Bats Right	R	.125	32	4	2	0	0	2	2	7	.167	.188
Cortez,Fernando	L	-	0	0	0	0	0	0	0	0	-	-
Bats Left	R	.077	13	1	0	0	0	1	1	3	.143	.077
Costa,Shane	L	.000	10	0	0	0	0	1	2	2	.167	.000
Bats Left	R	.268	71	19	2	0	2	6	3	9	.307	.380
Cota,Humberto	L	.294	85	25	5	1	3	20	3	21	.315	.482
Bats Right	R	.222	212	47	15	0	4	23	14	59	.274	.349
Counsell,Craig	L	.269	119	32	6	1	2	13	18	20	.362	.387
Bats Left	R	.253	459	116	28	3	7	29	60	49	.347	.373
Crawford,Carl	L	.247	194	48	4	3	2	17	12	41	.297	.330
Bats Left	R	.324	450	146	29	12	13	64	15	43	.347	.529
Crede,Joe	L	.277	83	23	4	0	4	13	8	9	.344	.470
Bats Right	R	.246	349	86	17	0	18	49	17	57	.292	.450
Crisp,Coco	L	.252	202	51	13	0	5	20	16	34	.305	.391
Bats Both	R	.324	392	127	29	4	11	49	28	47	.366	.503
Crosby,Bobby	L	.314	102	32	8	2	4	11	13	15	.391	.549
Bats Right	R	.260	231	60	17	2	5	27	22	39	.325	.416
Crosby,Bubba	L	.273	22	6	0	0	1	2	1	4	.304	.409
Bats Left	R	.276	76	21	0	1	0	4	3	10	.304	.303
Cruz,Deivi	L	.311	103	32	8	1	2	12	5	10	.343	.466
Bats Right	R	.236	157	37	3	0	3	8	6	24	.268	.312
Cruz,Jacob	L	.400	10	4	2	0	0	4	1	5	.455	.600
Bats Left	R	.222	117	26	8	0	4	14	15	41	.313	.393
Cruz,Jose	L	.325	80	26	7	0	3	11	14	16	.426	.525
Bats Both	R	.231	290	67	17	2	15	39	52	85	.347	.459
Cruz,Nelson	L	.000	2	0	0	0	0	0	1	0	.333	.000
Bats Right	R	.333	3	1	1	0	0	0	1	0	.500	.667
Cuddyer,Mike	L	.273	121	33	7	0	2	9	22	24	.382	.380
Bats Right	R	.259	301	78	18	3	10	33	19	69	.308	.439
Cummings,Midre	L	-	0	0	0	0	0	0	0	0	-	-
Bats Left	R	.000	2	0	0	0	0	0	0	1	.000	.000
Dallimore,Brian	L	.167	6	1	1	0	0	0	0	0	.167	.333
Bats Right	R	.000	1	0	0	0	0	0	0	0	.000	.000
Damon,Johnny	L	.327	208	68	13	2	2	30	19	32	.377	.438
Bats Left	R	.310	416	129	22	4	8	45	34	37	.361	.440
Daubach,Brian	L	.250	4	1	0	0	0	0	0	0	.250	.500
Bats Left	R	.095	21	2	1	0	1	3	7	5	.333	.286
DaVanon,Jeff	L	.393	28	11	1	0	1	3	6	7	.514	.536
Bats Both	R	.208	197	41	9	1	1	12	33	37	.322	.279
Davis,J.J.	L	.158	19	3	0	0	0	1	1	5	.200	.158
Bats Right	R	.429	7	3	0	0	0	1	1	2	.500	.429
DeJesus,David	L	.270	141	38	7	2	2	13	14	25	.350	.390
Bats Left	R	.303	320	97	24	4	7	43	28	51	.363	.469
Delgado,Carlos	L	.234	141	33	9	1	7	27	9	37	.308	.461
Bats Left	R	.326	380	124	32	2	26	88	63	84	.431	.626
Dellucci,David	L	.242	33	8	1	0	1	3	5	15	.342	.364
Bats Left	R	.251	402	101	16	5	28	62	71	106	.369	.525
Denorfia,Chris	L	.273	11	3	1	0	1	1	3	3	.429	.636
Bats Right	R	.259	27	7	2	0	0	1	3	6	.333	.333
DeRosa,Mark	L	.322	59	19	3	0	5	12	9	12	.412	.627
Bats Right	R	.191	89	17	2	0	3	8	7	23	.265	.315
Diaz,Einar	L	.229	35	8	1	0	0	6	1	3	.270	.257
Bats Right	R	.200	95	19	5	0	1	11	4	9	.240	.284
Diaz,Matt	L	.370	54	20	2	0	1	8	3	4	.407	.463
Bats Right	R	.143	35	5	2	2	0	1	1	11	.189	.314
Diaz,Victor	L	.259	54	14	2	0	1	4	7	12	.344	.352
Bats Right	R	.257	226	58	15	3	11	34	23	70	.325	.496
DiFelice,Mike	L	.000	3	0	0	0	0	0	0	0	.000	.000
Bats Right	R	.143	14	2	0	0	0	0	2	5	.250	.143
Dillon,Joe	L	.222	9	2	0	0	0	0	0	0	.222	.222
Bats Right	R	.148	27	4	1	0	1	1	1	7	.207	.296
Dobbs,Greg	L	.300	10	3	1	0	0	1	0	5	.300	.400
Bats Left	R	.242	132	32	6	1	1	19	9	20	.287	.326
Dominique,Andy	L	-	0	0	0	0	0	0	0	0	-	-
Bats Right	R	.000	2	0	0	0	0	0	0	0	.333	.000
Doumit,Ryan	L	.296	54	16	4	0	1	10	1	6	.361	.426
Bats Both	R	.243	177	43	9	1	5	29	10	38	.313	.390
Drew,J.D.	L	.235	68	16	3	0	0	6	17	15	.416	.279
Bats Left	R	.304	184	56	9	1	15	30	34	35	.410	.609
Dubois,Jason	L	.225	71	16	5	0	3	10	9	28	.321	.423
Bats Right	R	.241	116	28	7	0	6	14	3	46	.273	.457
Duffy,Chris	L	.355	31	11	0	0	0	2	1	4	.394	.355
Bats Left	R	.337	95	32	4	2	1	7	6	18	.382	.453
Duncan,Chris	L	1.000	2	2	1	0	1	3	0	0	1.000	3.000
Bats Left	R	.000	8	0	0	0	0	0	0	5	.000	.000

Batters vs. Left-Handed and Right-Handed Pitchers

Batter	vs	Avg	AB	H	2B	3B	HR	RBI	BB	SO	OBP	Slg
Dunn,Adam	L	.197	188	37	9	1	13	35	31	62	.321	.463
Bats Left	R	.273	355	97	26	1	27	66	83	106	.421	.580
Durazo,Erubiel	L	.350	40	14	2	1	2	8	2	5	.381	.600
Bats Left	R	.196	112	22	4	0	2	8	12	19	.280	.286
Durham,Ray	L	.290	93	27	7	0	3	12	9	10	.350	.462
Bats Both	R	.290	404	117	26	0	9	50	39	49	.357	.421
Durrington,Trent	L	.333	6	2	0	0	0	2	0	1	.333	.333
Bats Right	R	.125	8	1	1	0	0	0	1	2	.222	.250
Dye,Jermaine	L	.252	131	33	7	1	8	20	18	34	.353	.504
Bats Right	R	.281	398	112	22	1	23	66	21	65	.326	.515
Easley,Damion	L	.333	51	17	3	1	5	11	5	7	.390	.725
Bats Right	R	.218	216	47	16	0	4	19	21	40	.293	.347
Eckstein,David	L	.257	167	43	6	2	4	12	19	10	.346	.389
Bats Right	R	.307	463	142	20	5	4	49	39	34	.370	.397
Edmonds,Jim	L	.296	125	37	10	1	8	29	15	38	.385	.584
Bats Left	R	.251	342	86	27	0	21	60	76	101	.385	.515
Edwards,Mike	L	.253	75	19	2	1	0	5	5	13	.309	.307
Bats Right	R	.244	164	40	7	1	3	10	11	21	.295	.354
Eldred,Brad	L	.260	50	13	2	0	2	4	5	22	.321	.420
Bats Right	R	.207	140	29	7	0	10	23	8	55	.263	.471
Ellis,Mark	L	.313	112	35	7	3	3	15	15	10	.403	.509
Bats Right	R	.317	322	102	14	2	10	37	29	41	.377	.466
Ellison,Jason	L	.328	119	39	7	1	2	8	9	16	.375	.454
Bats Right	R	.232	233	54	11	1	2	16	15	28	.286	.313
Encarnacion,Edwin	L	.246	65	16	6	0	3	8	9	12	.338	.477
Bats Right	R	.226	146	33	10	0	6	23	11	48	.294	.418
Encarnacion,Juan	L	.309	94	29	6	0	3	14	14	18	.398	.468
Bats Right	R	.282	412	116	21	3	13	62	27	86	.337	.442
Ensberg,Morgan	L	.299	134	40	10	0	9	20	24	25	.411	.575
Bats Right	R	.278	392	109	20	3	27	81	61	94	.380	.551
Erstad,Darin	L	.232	190	44	5	1	3	20	17	39	.298	.316
Bats Left	R	.291	419	122	28	2	4	46	30	70	.337	.396
Escalona,Felix	L	.222	9	2	0	0	0	1	0	3	.300	.222
Bats Right	R	.400	5	2	1	0	0	1	1	1	.500	.600
Estrada,Johnny	L	.214	103	22	5	0	1	5	4	10	.257	.291
Bats Both	R	.280	254	71	21	0	3	34	16	28	.321	.398
Everett,Adam	L	.227	154	35	5	1	0	9	8	24	.265	.273
Bats Right	R	.256	395	101	22	1	11	45	18	79	.299	.400
Everett,Carl	L	.265	136	36	6	0	5	28	7	21	.295	.419
Bats Both	R	.246	354	87	11	2	18	59	35	78	.317	.441
Fasano,Sal	L	.310	42	13	1	0	6	6	4	7	.383	.762
Bats Right	R	.229	118	27	2	0	5	14	5	34	.283	.373
Feliz,Pedro	L	.271	133	36	8	1	6	17	14	18	.340	.481
Bats Right	R	.243	436	106	22	3	14	64	24	84	.281	.404
Fick,Robert	L	.297	37	11	0	1	0	4	6	7	.409	.351
Bats Left	R	.259	193	50	10	1	3	26	20	26	.326	.368
Fielder,Prince	L	.500	2	1	0	0	0	1	0	1	.500	.500
Bats Left	R	.281	57	16	4	0	2	9	2	16	.300	.456
Figgins,Chone	L	.244	217	53	7	2	2	16	27	38	.328	.323
Bats Both	R	.313	425	133	18	8	6	41	37	63	.364	.435
Finley,Steve	L	.271	118	32	7	2	3	21	6	16	.317	.441
Bats Left	R	.201	288	58	13	1	9	33	20	55	.252	.347
Fiorentino,Jeff	L	.176	17	3	1	0	1	2	0	3	.176	.412
Bats Left	R	.296	27	8	1	0	0	3	2	7	.333	.333
Flaherty,John	L	.161	31	5	0	0	0	0	4	6	.278	.161
Bats Right	R	.167	96	16	5	0	2	11	2	20	.180	.281
Floyd,Cliff	L	.224	143	32	2	0	9	25	10	37	.284	.427
Bats Left	R	.290	407	118	20	2	25	73	53	61	.382	.533
Fontenot,Mike	L	-	0	0	0	0	0	0	1	0	1.000	-
Bats Left	R	.000	2	0	0	0	0	0	1	0	.500	.000
Ford,Lew	L	.233	150	35	10	0	1	9	13	24	.308	.320
Bats Right	R	.277	372	103	20	4	6	44	32	61	.351	.401
Franco,Julio	L	.271	107	29	4	0	5	21	16	27	.365	.449
Bats Right	R	.278	126	35	8	1	4	21	11	30	.333	.452
Francoeur,Jeff	L	.379	66	25	8	1	6	17	2	15	.408	.803
Bats Right	R	.272	191	52	12	0	8	28	9	43	.310	.461
Freel,Ryan	L	.299	107	32	6	1	2	10	21	21	.419	.430
Bats Right	R	.260	262	68	13	2	2	11	30	38	.351	.347
Freeman,Choo	L	.231	13	3	0	1	0	0	0	2	.231	.385
Bats Right	R	.333	9	3	1	0	0	0	0	3	.333	.444
Freire,Alejandro	L	.200	45	9	1	0	1	4	5	13	.294	.289
Bats Right	R	.350	20	7	2	0	0	0	1	4	.381	.450
Furcal,Rafael	L	.294	163	48	9	4	4	20	12	17	.339	.472
Bats Both	R	.280	453	127	22	7	8	38	50	61	.351	.413
Furmaniak,J.J.	L	-	0	0	0	0	0	0	1	0	1.000	-
Bats Right	R	.192	26	5	1	1	0	1	3	4	.276	.308

Batter	vs	Avg	AB	H	2B	3B	HR	RBI	BB	SO	OBP	Slg
Gall,John	L	.313	16	5	1	0	2	8	1	4	.353	.750
Bats Right	R	.238	21	5	2	0	0	2	0	4	.227	.333
Garabito,Eddy	L	.192	26	5	2	0	0	0	0	9	.192	.269
Bats Both	R	.355	62	22	3	0	1	8	8	3	.452	.452
Garcia,Jesse	L	.357	14	5	0	0	1	3	3	2	.471	.571
Bats Right	R	.045	22	1	0	0	1	1	0	9	.045	.182
Garciaparra,Nomar	L	.281	89	25	4	0	2	11	3	9	.301	.393
Bats Right	R	.284	141	40	8	0	7	19	9	15	.331	.489
Garko,Ryan	L	-	0	0	0	0	0	0	0	0	-	-
Bats Right	R	.000	1	0	0	0	0	0	0	1	.000	.000
Gathright,Joey	L	.389	18	7	1	0	0	0	1	4	.421	.444
Bats Left	R	.265	185	49	6	3	0	13	9	35	.306	.330
German,Esteban	L	-	0	0	0	0	0	0	0	0	-	-
Bats Right	R	.750	4	3	1	0	0	1	0	1	.750	1.000
Gerut,Jody	L	.103	29	3	1	0	0	1	3	6	.188	.138
Bats Left	R	.284	141	40	10	1	1	13	17	14	.358	.390
Giambi,Jason	L	.261	138	36	4	0	8	28	25	42	.418	.464
Bats Left	R	.276	279	77	10	0	24	59	83	67	.451	.570
Giarratano,Tony	L	.000	5	0	0	0	0	0	1	2	.167	.000
Bats Both	R	.162	37	6	0	0	1	4	4	5	.244	.243
Gibbons,Jay	L	.250	132	33	8	0	7	24	5	17	.277	.470
Bats Left	R	.287	356	102	25	3	19	55	23	39	.331	.534
Gil,Geronimo	L	.200	50	10	2	0	2	9	2	12	.231	.360
Bats Right	R	.187	75	14	1	0	2	8	3	11	.213	.280
Giles,Brian	L	.289	166	48	11	4	2	23	32	25	.403	.440
Bats Left	R	.306	379	116	27	4	13	60	87	39	.431	.501
Giles,Marcus	L	.298	141	42	10	0	4	12	13	13	.357	.454
Bats Right	R	.289	436	126	35	4	11	51	51	95	.367	.463
Ginter,Keith	L	.164	61	10	3	0	0	14	4	11	.206	.213
Bats Right	R	.158	76	12	2	0	3	11	9	14	.256	.303
Gipson,Charles	L	.000	7	0	0	0	0	0	0	3	.000	.000
Bats Right	R	.500	4	2	1	0	0	1	1	0	.600	.750
Glaus,Troy	L	.244	131	32	6	0	10	27	32	30	.389	.519
Bats Right	R	.263	407	107	23	1	27	70	52	115	.353	.523
Gload,Ross	L	.000	5	0	0	0	0	0	0	2	.000	.000
Bats Left	R	.189	37	7	2	0	0	5	2	7	.231	.243
Godwin,Tyrell	L	-	0	0	0	0	0	0	0	0	-	-
Bats Left	R	.000	3	0	0	0	0	0	0	1	.000	.000
Gomes,Jonny	L	.288	104	30	4	0	6	11	12	37	.388	.500
Bats Right	R	.279	244	68	9	6	15	43	27	76	.365	.549
Gomez,Alexis	L	.000	2	0	0	0	0	0	0	0	.000	.000
Bats Left	R	.214	14	3	0	0	0	1	2	2	.313	.214
Gomez,Chris	L	.317	104	33	5	0	1	11	15	10	.400	.394
Bats Right	R	.243	115	28	6	0	0	7	12	7	.320	.296
Gonzalez,Adrian	L	.071	14	1	0	0	0	1	1	4	.133	.071
Bats Left	R	.243	136	33	7	1	6	16	9	33	.286	.441
Gonzalez,Alex	L	.216	88	19	5	0	1	3	8	20	.278	.307
Bats Right	R	.277	347	96	25	0	4	42	23	61	.329	.383
Gonzalez,Alex S	L	.280	118	33	6	0	1	10	8	25	.328	.356
Bats Right	R	.264	231	61	14	1	8	28	18	49	.320	.437
Gonzalez,Juan	L	-	0	0	0	0	0	0	0	0	-	-
Bats Right	R	.000	1	0	0	0	0	0	0	0	.000	.000
Gonzalez,Luis	L	.269	167	45	11	0	3	18	18	26	.359	.389
Bats Left	R	.272	412	112	26	0	21	61	60	64	.369	.488
Gonzalez,Luis A	L	.380	142	54	15	0	3	10	8	21	.413	.549
Bats Right	R	.244	262	64	10	0	6	34	12	42	.290	.351
Gonzalez,Wiki	L	.444	9	4	2	0	0	1	0	2	.444	.667
Bats Right	R	.222	36	8	3	0	0	1	2	1	.263	.306
Gotay,Ruben	L	.212	52	11	2	0	0	3	9	12	.323	.250
Bats Both	R	.230	230	53	12	2	5	26	13	39	.279	.365
Grabowski,Jason	L	.111	9	1	0	0	0	1	2	1	.273	.111
Bats Left	R	.165	103	17	0	0	4	11	8	28	.223	.282
Graffanino,Tony	L	.297	148	44	6	2	2	7	13	21	.358	.405
Bats Right	R	.316	231	73	11	1	5	31	18	30	.372	.437
Granderson,Curtis	L	.320	25	8	1	1	2	5	3	8	.393	.680
Bats Left	R	.263	137	36	5	2	6	15	7	35	.299	.460
Green,Andy	L	.385	13	5	1	0	0	2	1	0	.400	.462
Bats Right	R	.111	18	2	0	0	0	0	6	3	.333	.111
Green,Nick	L	.292	96	28	7	0	2	7	12	26	.373	.427
Bats Right	R	.216	222	48	8	2	3	22	21	60	.310	.311
Green,Shawn	L	.226	146	33	4	1	5	14	15	25	.299	.370
Bats Left	R	.306	435	133	33	3	17	59	47	70	.374	.513
Greenberg,Adam	L	-	0	0	0	0	0	0	0	0	1.000	-
Bats Left	R	-	0	0	0	0	0	0	0	0	-	-
Greene,Khalil	L	.200	105	21	9	0	4	18	5	23	.234	.400
Bats Right	R	.266	331	88	21	2	11	52	20	70	.315	.441

Batters vs. Left-Handed and Right-Handed Pitchers

Batter	vs	Avg	AB	H	2B	3B	HR	RBI	BB	SO	OBP	Slg
Greene,Todd	L	.294	51	15	2	0	3	8	5	5	.357	.510
Bats Right	R	.227	75	17	2	0	4	15	2	16	.256	.413
Grieve,Ben	L	.000	2	0	0	0	0	0	0	1	.000	.000
Bats Left	R	.278	18	5	0	0	0	1	5	6	.435	.278
Griffey Jr.,Ken	L	.278	169	47	11	0	11	31	20	35	.352	.538
Bats Left	R	.314	322	101	19	0	24	61	34	58	.378	.596
Griffin,John-Ford	L	1.000	1	1	0	0	1	1	0	0	1.000	4.000
Bats Left	R	.250	12	3	2	0	0	5	0	4	.250	.417
Grissom,Marquis	L	.217	46	10	2	0	0	6	2	6	.245	.261
Bats Right	R	.209	91	19	2	0	2	9	5	12	.250	.297
Gross,Gabe	L	.091	11	1	1	0	0	1	2	4	.231	.182
Bats Left	R	.272	81	22	3	1	1	6	8	17	.337	.370
Grudzielanek,Mark	L	.303	155	47	7	2	2	17	13	20	.357	.413
Bats Right	R	.290	373	108	23	1	6	42	13	61	.324	.405
Guerrero,Vladimir	L	.313	150	47	12	0	9	27	16	9	.382	.573
Bats Right	R	.319	370	118	17	2	23	81	45	39	.399	.562
Guiel,Aaron	L	.200	20	4	2	0	0	1	0	3	.292	.300
Bats Left	R	.315	89	28	3	0	4	6	6	18	.371	.483
Guillen,Carlos	L	.368	76	28	3	2	1	7	2	7	.385	.500
Bats Both	R	.306	258	79	12	2	4	16	22	38	.364	.415
Guillen,Jose	L	.215	135	29	10	0	4	13	10	26	.282	.378
Bats Right	R	.305	416	127	22	2	20	63	21	76	.356	.512
Gutierrez,Franklin	L	-	0	0	0	0	0	0	1	0	1.000	-
Bats Right	R	.000	1	0	0	0	0	0	0	0	.000	.000
Guzman,Cristian	L	.160	125	20	8	0	2	7	6	24	.198	.272
Bats Both	R	.242	331	80	11	6	2	24	19	52	.283	.329
Haad,Yamid	L	.000	1	0	0	0	0	0	0	0	.000	.000
Bats Right	R	.074	27	2	1	0	0	1	3	7	.161	.111
Hafner,Travis	L	.269	156	42	15	0	7	36	23	52	.378	.500
Bats Left	R	.321	330	106	27	0	26	72	56	71	.423	.639
Hairston,Jerry	L	.255	137	35	8	1	2	11	10	19	.306	.372
Bats Right	R	.263	243	64	17	1	2	19	21	27	.351	.366
Hairston,Scott	L	.182	11	2	1	0	0	0	0	2	.182	.273
Bats Right	R	.000	9	0	0	0	0	0	0	4	.000	.000
Hall,Bill	L	.336	125	42	17	1	3	13	14	25	.407	.560
Bats Right	R	.277	376	104	22	5	14	49	25	78	.319	.473
Hall,Toby	L	.300	130	39	4	0	3	15	6	10	.329	.400
Bats Right	R	.281	302	85	16	0	2	33	10	29	.309	.354
Hammonds,Jeffrey	L	.211	19	4	0	0	0	0	1	2	.286	.211
Bats Right	R	.231	13	3	1	0	0	1	1	2	.286	.308
Hansen,Dave	L	.000	2	0	0	0	0	0	0	2	.000	.000
Bats Left	R	.178	73	13	0	0	2	11	9	17	.262	.260
Hardy,J.J.	L	.268	97	26	10	1	4	13	10	13	.336	.515
Bats Right	R	.240	275	66	12	0	5	37	34	35	.324	.338
Harris,Brendan	L	.500	2	1	0	0	1	2	0	0	.500	2.000
Bats Right	R	.286	7	2	1	0	0	1	0	0	.375	.429
Harris,Lenny	L	.333	3	1	1	0	0	1	0	0	.333	.667
Bats Left	R	.313	67	21	3	0	1	12	7	11	.387	.403
Harris,Willie	L	.286	14	4	1	0	0	0	1	3	.333	.357
Bats Left	R	.252	107	27	1	1	1	8	12	22	.333	.308
Hart,Corey	L	.211	19	4	0	0	1	4	2	2	.286	.368
Bats Right	R	.184	38	7	2	1	1	3	4	9	.262	.368
Harvey,Ken	L	.263	19	5	2	0	1	4	1	5	.300	.526
Bats Right	R	.192	26	5	1	0	0	1	2	8	.250	.231
Hatteberg,Scott	L	.214	117	25	4	0	2	17	15	23	.311	.299
Bats Left	R	.271	347	94	15	0	5	42	36	31	.342	.357
Hawpe,Brad	L	.250	28	7	1	0	1	5	4	8	.344	.393
Bats Left	R	.264	277	73	9	3	8	42	39	62	.351	.404
Heintz,Chris	L	.231	13	3	2	0	0	0	0	4	.231	.385
Bats Right	R	.167	12	2	1	0	0	2	1	2	.231	.250
Helms,Wes	L	.301	83	25	6	1	3	15	10	19	.375	.506
Bats Right	R	.294	85	25	7	0	1	9	4	11	.337	.412
Helton,Todd	L	.245	155	38	6	1	1	17	24	33	.361	.316
Bats Left	R	.353	354	125	39	1	19	62	82	47	.480	.630
Hermida,Jeremy	L	.200	5	1	0	0	0	0	2	2	.429	.200
Bats Left	R	.306	36	11	2	0	4	11	4	10	.375	.694
Hernandez,Anderson	L	-	0	0	0	0	0	0	0	0	-	-
Bats Both	R	.056	18	1	0	0	0	0	1	4	.105	.056
Hernandez,Jose	L	.269	145	39	6	0	6	23	5	30	.288	.434
Bats Right	R	.169	89	15	1	0	0	8	9	30	.260	.180
Hernandez,Ramon	L	.238	80	19	2	1	3	18	6	10	.284	.400
Bats Right	R	.304	289	88	17	1	9	40	12	30	.333	.464
Hidalgo,Richard	L	.157	83	13	3	0	3	6	6	21	.231	.301
Bats Right	R	.244	225	55	9	0	13	37	20	53	.310	.458
Higginson,Bobby	L	.000	2	0	0	0	0	0	1	1	.333	.000
Bats Left	R	.083	24	2	0	0	0	1	0	4	.083	.083

Batter	vs	Avg	AB	H	2B	3B	HR	RBI	BB	SO	OBP	Slg
Hill,Aaron	L	.298	104	31	9	1	1	10	15	13	.387	.433
Bats Right	R	.265	257	68	16	2	2	30	19	28	.323	.366
Hill,Bobby	L	.357	14	5	0	0	0	2	4	4	.500	.357
Bats Both	R	.253	79	20	6	0	0	9	5	13	.310	.329
Hill,Koyie	L	.261	23	6	2	0	0	2	3	6	.333	.348
Bats Both	R	.200	55	11	3	0	0	4	8	21	.297	.255
Hillenbrand,Shea	L	.325	160	52	11	0	7	22	6	18	.361	.525
Bats Right	R	.279	434	121	25	2	11	60	20	61	.336	.422
Hinske,Eric	L	.170	88	15	2	0	4	13	4	32	.215	.330
Bats Left	R	.283	389	110	29	2	11	55	42	89	.358	.452
Hocking,Denny	L	.375	8	3	1	0	0	0	4	2	.583	.500
Bats Both	R	.250	52	13	0	0	0	7	6	8	.328	.250
Holbert,Aaron	L	.273	11	3	2	0	0	0	1	3	.333	.455
Bats Right	R	.188	16	3	1	0	0	2	2	5	.263	.250
Hollandsworth,Todd	L	.293	41	12	5	0	0	6	4	7	.356	.415
Bats Left	R	.237	262	62	12	2	6	30	19	59	.289	.366
Holliday,Matt	L	.324	105	34	3	1	3	16	10	15	.393	.457
Bats Right	R	.302	374	113	21	6	16	71	26	64	.352	.519
Hollins,Damon	L	.250	112	28	4	0	6	19	8	19	.298	.446
Bats Right	R	.248	230	57	13	1	7	27	15	44	.296	.404
Hooper,Kevin	L	.333	3	1	0	0	0	0	0	0	.333	.333
Bats Right	R	.000	2	0	0	0	0	0	0	1	.000	.000
Howard,Ryan	L	.148	61	9	1	1	1	6	2	26	.175	.246
Bats Left	R	.323	251	81	16	1	21	57	31	74	.396	.645
Huber,Justin	L	.179	39	7	1	0	0	2	3	10	.256	.205
Bats Right	R	.256	39	10	2	0	0	4	2	10	.286	.308
Huckaby,Ken	L	.267	30	8	2	0	0	1	4	9	.353	.333
Bats Right	R	.175	57	10	2	0	0	5	1	10	.190	.211
Hudson,Orlando	L	.227	128	29	4	1	2	9	10	19	.286	.320
Bats Both	R	.288	333	96	21	4	8	54	20	46	.327	.447
Huff,Aubrey	L	.255	208	53	8	2	6	30	11	35	.299	.399
Bats Left	R	.264	367	97	18	0	16	62	38	53	.333	.444
Hunter,Torii	L	.283	106	30	11	0	6	24	12	19	.355	.557
Bats Right	R	.263	266	70	13	1	8	32	22	46	.329	.410
Hyzdu,Adam	L	.167	18	3	1	0	0	3	5	5	.348	.222
Bats Right	R	.222	18	4	1	0	0	1	0	2	.211	.278
Ibanez,Raul	L	.275	189	52	7	0	7	38	19	39	.346	.423
Bats Left	R	.282	425	120	25	2	13	51	52	60	.359	.442
Iguchi,Tadahito	L	.274	146	40	7	1	6	27	18	34	.353	.459
Bats Right	R	.279	365	102	18	5	9	44	29	80	.337	.430
Infante,Omar	L	.174	92	16	4	0	2	9	3	16	.200	.283
Bats Right	R	.236	314	74	24	2	7	34	13	57	.269	.392
Inge,Brandon	L	.281	128	36	8	0	5	18	22	27	.382	.461
Bats Right	R	.256	488	125	23	9	11	54	41	113	.315	.408
Izturis,Cesar	L	.303	109	33	7	1	1	11	5	8	.333	.413
Bats Both	R	.242	335	81	12	1	1	20	20	43	.292	.293
Izturis,Maicer	L	.191	47	9	1	0	1	5	6	6	.278	.277
Bats Both	R	.264	144	38	7	4	0	10	11	15	.316	.368
Jackson,Conor	L	.258	31	8	2	0	2	4	4	3	.351	.516
Bats Right	R	.167	54	9	1	0	0	4	8	8	.274	.185
Jackson,Damian	L	.289	83	24	6	0	0	5	9	12	.366	.361
Bats Right	R	.240	192	46	3	0	5	18	21	33	.323	.333
Jacobs,Mike	L	.400	5	2	1	0	0	1	0	2	.400	.600
Bats Left	R	.305	95	29	6	0	11	22	10	20	.374	.716
Jenkins,Geoff	L	.255	157	40	16	0	5	21	13	48	.354	.452
Bats Left	R	.307	381	117	26	1	20	65	43	90	.384	.538
Jeter,Derek	L	.317	186	59	6	2	9	24	17	24	.382	.516
Bats Right	R	.306	468	143	19	3	10	46	60	93	.392	.423
Jimenez,D'Angelo	L	.355	31	11	2	0	0	3	4	3	.429	.419
Bats Both	R	.176	74	13	5	0	0	2	10	20	.274	.243
Jimerson,Charlton	L	-	0	0	0	0	0	0	0	0	-	-
Bats Right	R	-	0	0	0	0	0	0	0	0	-	-
Johnson,Ben	L	.185	27	5	4	0	1	6	4	10	.281	.444
Bats Right	R	.229	48	11	4	1	2	7	7	13	.327	.479
Johnson,Charles	L	.222	9	2	1	0	0	1	1	3	.300	.333
Bats Right	R	.189	37	7	3	0	0	4	8	8	.333	.270
Johnson,Dan	L	.283	99	28	6	0	2	22	20	19	.395	.404
Bats Left	R	.272	276	75	15	0	13	36	30	33	.339	.467
Johnson,Kelly	L	.257	74	19	3	1	2	12	8	23	.325	.405
Bats Left	R	.236	216	51	9	2	7	28	32	52	.337	.394
Johnson,Nick	L	.328	125	41	7	1	3	20	21	24	.444	.472
Bats Left	R	.274	328	90	28	2	12	54	59	63	.394	.482
Johnson,Reed	L	.279	165	46	10	2	3	22	7	31	.335	.418
Bats Right	R	.262	233	61	11	4	5	36	15	51	.329	.408
Johnson,Russ	L	.182	11	2	1	0	0	0	0	2	.250	.273
Bats Right	R	.286	7	2	1	0	0	0	1	2	.375	.429

Batters vs. Left-Handed and Right-Handed Pitchers

Batter	vs	Avg	AB	H	2B	3B	HR	RBI	BB	SO	OBP	Slg
Jones,Andruw	L	.256	125	32	7	0	9	23	16	22	.349	.528
Bats Right	R	.265	461	122	17	3	42	105	48	90	.346	.588
Jones,Chipper	L	.270	74	20	6	0	3	13	12	12	.372	.473
Bats Both	R	.303	284	86	24	0	18	59	60	44	.422	.577
Jones,Jacque	L	.201	154	31	2	3	6	24	9	36	.247	.370
Bats Left	R	.268	369	99	20	1	17	49	42	84	.348	.466
Jordan,Brian	L	.263	76	20	3	1	2	8	6	11	.329	.408
Bats Right	R	.239	155	37	5	1	1	16	8	35	.277	.303
Jorgensen,Ryan	L	-	0	0	0	0	0	0	0	0	-	
Bats Right	R	.000	4	0	0	0	0	0	0	3	.000	.000
Kapler,Gabe	L	.314	35	11	6	0	1	5	0	4	.306	.571
Bats Right	R	.210	62	13	1	0	0	4	3	11	.269	.226
Kata,Matt	L	.214	14	3	1	0	0	0	2	2	.313	.286
Bats Both	R	.174	23	4	1	1	0	0	3	4	.269	.304
Kearns,Austin	L	.233	103	24	4	0	4	13	22	28	.372	.388
Bats Right	R	.243	284	69	22	1	14	54	26	79	.317	.475
Kelly,Kenny	L	.333	9	3	1	0	0	0	0	3	.333	.444
Bats Right	R	.250	4	1	0	0	0	2	1	3	.400	.250
Kendall,Jason	L	.293	164	48	7	0	0	13	18	10	.366	.335
Bats Left	R	.263	437	115	21	1	0	40	32	29	.337	.316
Kennedy,Adam	L	.296	125	37	5	0	0	11	6	19	.348	.336
Bats Left	R	.302	291	88	18	0	2	26	23	45	.356	.385
Kent,Jeff	L	.306	121	37	7	0	4	23	16	12	.384	.463
Bats Right	R	.285	432	123	29	0	25	82	56	73	.375	.525
Kielty,Bobby	L	.322	143	46	9	0	4	23	18	22	.398	.469
Bats Both	R	.226	234	53	11	0	6	34	32	45	.322	.350
Klesko,Ryan	L	.200	100	20	4	1	0	8	15	27	.304	.260
Bats Left	R	.262	343	90	15	0	18	50	60	53	.373	.464
Knoedler,Justin	L	.000	1	0	0	0	0	0	0	0	.500	.000
Bats Right	R	.111	9	1	0	0	0	0	0	1	.111	.111
Konerko,Paul	L	.261	134	35	6	0	12	24	25	27	.381	.575
Bats Right	R	.290	441	128	18	0	28	76	56	82	.373	.522
Koskie,Corey	L	.211	109	23	5	0	2	8	8	32	.269	.312
Bats Left	R	.265	245	65	15	0	9	28	36	58	.365	.437
Kotchman,Casey	L	.250	28	7	0	0	0	2	4	7	.344	.250
Bats Left	R	.286	98	28	5	0	7	20	11	11	.355	.551
Kotsay,Mark	L	.324	179	58	15	0	3	24	10	20	.359	.458
Bats Left	R	.261	403	105	20	1	12	58	30	31	.310	.404
Krynzel,Dave	L	-	0	0	0	0	0	0	0	0	-	
Bats Left	R	.000	7	0	0	0	0	0	0	3	.000	.000
LaForest,Pete	L	.000	4	0	0	0	0	0	0	2	.000	.000
Bats Left	R	.183	60	11	3	0	1	4	6	21	.258	.283
Laird,Gerald	L	.222	9	2	1	0	0	0	0	3	.222	.333
Bats Right	R	.226	31	7	1	0	1	4	2	4	.273	.355
Laker,Tim	L	.000	1	0	0	0	0	0	0	1	.000	.000
Bats Right	R	-	0	0	0	0	0	0	0	0	-	
Lamb,Mike	L	.179	56	10	2	2	1	8	2	16	.217	.339
Bats Left	R	.248	266	66	11	3	11	45	20	49	.298	.436
Lane,Jason	L	.237	156	37	9	0	8	25	11	36	.300	.449
Bats Right	R	.280	361	101	25	4	18	53	21	69	.322	.521
Langerhans,Ryan	L	.293	58	17	3	1	1	5	5	15	.369	.431
Bats Left	R	.261	268	70	19	2	7	37	32	60	.343	.425
LaRoche,Adam	L	.188	48	9	2	0	1	5	1	9	.235	.292
Bats Left	R	.268	403	108	26	0	19	73	38	78	.330	.474
LaRue,Jason	L	.257	113	29	6	0	6	15	18	29	.368	.469
Bats Right	R	.262	248	65	21	0	8	45	23	72	.349	.444
Lawton,Matt	L	.207	145	30	4	0	4	14	18	23	.301	.317
Bats Left	R	.273	355	97	26	1	9	39	51	54	.377	.428
LeCroy,Matt	L	.306	124	38	0	0	13	24	20	32	.404	.621
Bats Right	R	.228	180	41	5	0	4	26	21	53	.319	.322
Ledee,Ricky	L	.200	20	4	1	0	1	4	2	9	.273	.400
Bats Left	R	.286	217	62	15	1	6	35	18	46	.340	.447
Lee,Carlos	L	.263	156	41	10	0	7	30	21	20	.348	.462
Bats Right	R	.266	462	123	31	0	25	84	36	67	.316	.496
Lee,Derrek	L	.333	147	49	12	1	12	28	28	27	.439	.673
Bats Right	R	.336	447	150	38	2	34	79	57	82	.411	.658
Lee,Travis	L	.250	56	14	3	0	0	3	2	16	.276	.304
Bats Left	R	.276	348	96	19	2	12	46	33	50	.339	.445
Lieberthal,Mike	L	.276	87	24	11	0	2	13	11	5	.354	.471
Bats Right	R	.259	305	79	14	0	10	34	24	30	.331	.403
Liefer,Jeff	L	.000	6	0	0	0	0	0	0	0	.000	.000
Bats Left	R	.220	50	11	2	0	1	8	1	12	.235	.320
Linden,Todd	L	.300	30	9	2	0	1	2	3	6	.364	.467
Bats Both	R	.199	141	28	6	0	3	11	7	48	.261	.305
Lo Duca,Paul	L	.314	86	27	8	1	1	9	5	2	.359	.465
Bats Right	R	.276	359	99	15	0	5	48	29	29	.328	.359
Lofton,Kenny	L	.348	46	16	2	0	0	6	1	6	.375	.391
Bats Left	R	.333	321	107	13	5	2	30	31	35	.394	.424
Logan,Nook	L	.281	89	25	5	2	1	3	6	15	.326	.416
Bats Both	R	.249	233	58	7	3	0	14	15	37	.297	.305
Long,Terrence	L	.291	103	30	1	1	0	14	3	19	.306	.320
Bats Left	R	.276	352	97	20	2	6	39	27	37	.325	.395
Lopez,Felipe	L	.243	173	42	4	0	5	22	12	37	.291	.353
Bats Both	R	.312	407	127	30	5	18	63	45	74	.377	.543
Lopez,Javy	L	.284	102	29	9	0	2	7	12	17	.362	.431
Bats Right	R	.276	293	81	15	1	13	42	7	51	.306	.468
Lopez,Jose	L	.276	58	16	4	0	1	10	2	5	.306	.397
Bats Right	R	.235	132	31	15	0	1	15	4	20	.271	.371
Lopez,Luis	L	.000	4	0	0	0	0	0	1	2	.200	.000
Bats Both	R	.261	23	6	3	0	0	2	0	4	.261	.391
Lopez,Pedro	L	.333	6	2	0	0	0	2	0	1	.333	.333
Bats Right	R	.000	1	0	0	0	0	0	0	0	.000	.000
Loretta,Mark	L	.309	94	29	2	0	1	8	20	8	.426	.362
Bats Right	R	.271	310	84	14	1	2	30	25	26	.338	.342
Lowell,Mike	L	.304	92	28	10	0	2	22	10	8	.362	.478
Bats Right	R	.221	408	90	26	1	6	36	36	50	.283	.333
Ludwick,Ryan	L	.200	25	5	0	0	3	4	6	10	.355	.560
Bats Right	R	.250	16	4	0	0	1	1	1	3	.294	.438
Lugo,Julio	L	.308	185	57	13	1	1	17	17	13	.363	.405
Bats Right	R	.290	431	125	23	5	5	40	44	59	.362	.401
Luna,Hector	L	.310	58	18	5	1	1	8	3	10	.385	.483
Bats Right	R	.266	79	21	5	1	0	10	6	15	.314	.354
Mabry,John	L	.226	31	7	1	0	0	1	1	12	.250	.258
Bats Left	R	.242	215	52	14	1	8	32	19	51	.301	.428
Machado,Alejandro	L	-	0	0	0	0	0	0	0	0	-	
Bats Both	R	.200	5	1	1	0	0	0	1	1	.333	.400
Machado,Andy	L	.000	7	0	0	0	0	2	2	3	.200	.000
Bats Both	R	.000	5	0	0	0	0	0	0	3	.000	.000
Macias,Jose	L	.277	47	13	3	0	1	3	4	5	.333	.404
Bats Both	R	.246	130	32	5	0	0	10	2	19	.252	.285
Mackowiak,Rob	L	.275	69	19	3	1	0	10	6	18	.342	.348
Bats Left	R	.272	394	107	18	2	9	48	37	82	.336	.396
Magruder,Chris	L	.256	39	10	3	0	0	2	0	6	.293	.333
Bats Both	R	.182	99	18	6	0	2	11	7	27	.255	.303
Mahoney,Mike	L	.100	10	1	0	0	0	2	2	2	.308	.100
Bats Right	R	.167	54	9	1	0	1	4	2	8	.196	.241
Marrero,Eli	L	.247	89	22	5	2	7	16	6	25	.293	.584
Bats Right	R	.061	49	3	2	0	0	3	5	13	.143	.102
Marte,Andy	L	.174	23	4	2	1	0	2	4	6	.286	.348
Bats Right	R	.118	34	4	0	0	0	2	3	7	.184	.118
Martinez,Ramon	L	.255	47	12	2	0	1	9	3	6	.296	.362
Bats Right	R	.292	65	19			0	0	5	3	5	.319	.308
Martinez,Tino	L	.217	83	18	1	0	3	12	15	19	.340	.337
Bats Left	R	.250	220	55	8	0	14	37	23	35	.323	.477
Martinez,Victor	L	.274	168	46	9	0	3	19	22	31	.362	.381
Bats Both	R	.319	379	121	24	0	17	61	41	47	.385	.517
Mateo,Henry	L	.000	1	0	0	0	0	0	1	0	.500	.000
Bats Both	R	-	0	0	0	0	0	0	0	0	-	
Matheny,Mike	L	.269	104	28	9	0	3	14	6	18	.306	.442
Bats Right	R	.233	339	79	25	0	10	45	23	73	.291	.395
Mathis,Jeff	L	-	0	0	0	0	0	0	0	0	-	
Bats Right	R	.333	3	1	0	0	0	0	0	1	.333	.333
Matos,Luis	L	.297	118	35	9	1	3	12	12	20	.368	.466
Bats Right	R	.273	271	74	11	1	1	20	15	38	.327	.332
Matranga,Dave	L	-	0	0	0	0	0	0	0	0	-	
Bats Right	R	.000	1	0	0	0	0	0	0	0	.000	.000
Matsui,Hideki	L	.354	209	74	19	2	8	49	16	33	.393	.579
Bats Left	R	.281	420	118	26	1	15	67	47	45	.354	.455
Matsui,Kazuo	L	.279	68	19	1	1	0	7	3	9	.315	.324
Bats Both	R	.246	199	49	8	3	3	17	11	34	.295	.362
Matthews Jr.,Gary	L	.241	133	32	6	2	9	18	10	29	.294	.519
Bats Both	R	.260	342	89	19	3	8	37	37	61	.330	.404
Mauer,Joe	L	.225	142	32	3	0	0	12	9	29	.268	.246
Bats Left	R	.323	347	112	23	2	9	43	52	35	.411	.478
McAnulty,Paul	L	.500	2	1	0	0	0	0	1	0	.667	.500
Bats Left	R	.182	22	4	0	0	0	2	2	7	.280	.182
McCann,Brian	L	.333	36	12	2	0	2	5	2	10	.385	.556
Bats Left	R	.264	144	38	5	0	3	18	16	16	.335	.361
McCarty,David	L	-	0	0	0	0	0	0	0	1	0	1.000	-
Bats Right	R	.500	4	2	0	0	0	2	1	0	.600	.500
McClain,Scott	L	.000	3	0	0	0	0	0	1	0	.250	.000
Bats Right	R	.182	11	2	0	0	0	1	1	2	.250	.273

Batters vs. Left-Handed and Right-Handed Pitchers

Batter	vs	Avg	AB	H	2B	3B	HR	RBI	BB	SO	OBP	Slg
McCracken,Quinton	L	.261	46	12	1	0	1	5	6	8	.340	.348
Bats Both	R	.231	169	39	3	3	0	8	17	27	.305	.284
McDonald,John	L	.291	86	25	3	0	0	11	6	16	.340	.326
Bats Right	R	.263	80	21	3	1	0	5	5	8	.310	.325
McDougall,Marshall	L	.200	10	2	1	0	0	0	0	6	.200	.300
Bats Right	R	.125	8	1	0	0	0	0	0	4	.125	.125
McEwing,Joe	L	.237	97	23	3	0	1	4	3	18	.260	.299
Bats Right	R	.241	83	20	4	0	0	2	3	17	.267	.289
McLouth,Nate	L	.100	20	2	0	0	1	2	1	4	.250	.250
Bats Left	R	.292	89	26	6	0	4	10	2	16	.319	.494
McPherson,Dallas	L	.196	46	9	1	1	0	3	1	17	.213	.261
Bats Left	R	.258	159	41	13	1	8	23	13	47	.318	.503
Melhuse,Adam	L	.077	13	1	0	0	0	1	3	4	.250	.077
Bats Both	R	.274	84	23	7	0	2	11	2	24	.291	.429
Mench,Kevin	L	.296	125	37	10	2	8	19	17	7	.380	.600
Bats Right	R	.255	432	110	23	1	17	54	33	61	.313	.431
Menechino,Frank	L	.191	94	18	4	0	3	9	17	21	.339	.330
Bats Right	R	.259	54	14	3	0	1	4	8	12	.375	.370
Merloni,Lou	L	.000	3	0	0	0	0	1	0	1	.000	.000
Bats Right	R	.000	2	0	0	0	0	0	1	1	.333	.000
Michaels,Jason	L	.323	130	42	10	1	0	10	29	20	.438	.415
Bats Right	R	.289	159	46	6	1	4	21	15	25	.363	.415
Mientkiewicz,Doug	L	.214	42	9	2	0	3	8	6	7	.306	.476
Bats Left	R	.245	233	57	11	0	8	21	26	32	.324	.395
Miles,Aaron	L	.234	64	15	2	0	1	8	2	11	.258	.313
Bats Both	R	.292	260	76	10	3	1	20	6	27	.317	.365
Millar,Kevin	L	.246	142	35	8	0	2	8	18	22	.341	.345
Bats Right	R	.283	307	87	20	1	7	42	36	52	.361	.423
Miller,Corky	L	.000	6	0	0	0	0	0	0	2	.000	.000
Bats Right	R	.000	6	0	0	0	0	0	0	0	.000	.000
Miller,Damian	L	.231	91	21	5	0	0	6	10	25	.307	.286
Bats Right	R	.286	294	84	20	1	9	37	27	69	.351	.452
Mirabelli,Doug	L	.240	50	12	3	0	2	8	9	20	.356	.420
Bats Right	R	.221	86	19	4	0	4	10	5	28	.280	.407
Moeller,Chad	L	.180	50	9	1	1	2	6	2	11	.212	.360
Bats Right	R	.215	149	32	8	0	5	17	11	37	.272	.369
Mohr,Dustan	L	.274	113	31	7	2	7	15	12	36	.349	.558
Bats Right	R	.170	153	26	3	1	10	23	11	58	.228	.399
Molina,Bengie	L	.393	122	48	10	0	7	28	10	10	.430	.648
Bats Right	R	.253	288	73	7	0	8	41	15	31	.294	.361
Molina,Jose	L	.306	62	19	0	0	5	13	4	17	.368	.548
Bats Right	R	.189	122	23	4	0	1	12	9	24	.244	.246
Molina,Yadier	L	.309	110	34	5	0	2	17	6	7	.339	.409
Bats Right	R	.229	275	63	10	1	6	32	17	23	.278	.338
Mondesi,Raul	L	.269	26	7	0	0	2	5	6	5	.406	.500
Bats Right	R	.198	116	23	7	1	2	12	6	30	.236	.328
Monroe,Craig	L	.303	122	37	7	1	7	23	12	25	.360	.549
Bats Right	R	.270	445	120	23	2	13	66	28	70	.311	.418
Mora,Melvin	L	.232	168	39	8	0	10	22	14	35	.293	.458
Bats Right	R	.304	425	129	22	1	17	66	36	77	.369	.480
Mordecai,Mike	L	-	0	0	0	0	0	0	0	0	-	-
Bats Right	R	.000	2	0	0	0	0	0	0	1	.000	.000
Morneau,Justin	L	.201	154	31	8	0	4	24	8	32	.255	.331
Bats Left	R	.256	336	86	15	4	18	55	36	62	.325	.485
Morse,Mike	L	.272	81	22	5	1	1	6	8	10	.352	.395
Bats Right	R	.282	149	42	5	0	2	17	10	40	.347	.356
Mosquera,Julio	L	-	0	0	0	0	0	0	0	0	-	-
Bats Right	R	.000	1	0	0	0	0	0	0	0	.000	.000
Mueller,Bill	L	.275	142	39	8	0	2	20	14	21	.346	.373
Bats Both	R	.302	377	114	26	3	8	42	45	53	.378	.451
Munson,Eric	L	.000	4	0	0	0	0	0	1	0	.000	.000
Bats Left	R	.214	14	3	1	0	0	2	4	2	.400	.286
Murphy,Donald	L	.146	41	6	2	0	1	5	5	13	.234	.268
Bats Right	R	.167	36	6	3	0	0	3	4	10	.250	.250
Murton,Matt	L	.380	71	27	2	1	3	8	8	8	.443	.563
Bats Right	R	.261	69	18	1	1	4	6	8	14	.329	.478
Myers,Greg	L	-	0	0	0	0	0	0	0	0	-	-
Bats Left	R	.083	12	1	0	0	0	1	1	1	.154	.083
Myrow,Brian	L	-	0	0	0	0	0	0	0	0	-	-
Bats Left	R	.200	20	4	1	0	0	6	5	8	.360	.250
Nady,Xavier	L	.323	124	40	7	0	3	16	13	22	.400	.452
Bats Right	R	.223	202	45	8	2	10	27	9	45	.270	.431
Nakamura,Norihiro	L	.118	17	2	1	0	0	0	1	5	.167	.176
Bats Right	R	.136	22	3	1	0	0	3	1	2	.174	.182
Navarro,Dioner	L	.435	23	10	1	0	1	2	9	2	.594	.609
Bats Both	R	.248	153	38	8	0	2	12	11	19	.307	.340

Batter	vs	Avg	AB	H	2B	3B	HR	RBI	BB	SO	OBP	Slg
Nevin,Phil	L	.205	127	26	8	0	4	13	16	34	.292	.362
Bats Right	R	.253	253	64	8	1	8	42	11	63	.285	.387
Newhan,David	L	.250	28	7	1	0	1	6	2	8	.333	.393
Bats Left	R	.195	190	37	8	0	4	15	20	37	.270	.300
Niekro,Lance	L	.324	108	35	7	1	9	26	7	17	.361	.657
Bats Right	R	.206	170	35	9	2	3	20	10	36	.251	.335
Nieves,Wil	L	.000	1	0	0	0	0	0	0	1	.000	.000
Bats Right	R	.000	3	0	0	0	0	0	0	0	.000	.000
Nivar,Ramon	L	.364	11	4	0	0	0	1	0	1	.364	.364
Bats Right	R	.000	2	0	0	0	0	0	0	1	.333	.000
Nix,Laynce	L	.333	18	6	0	0	0	3	0	1	.333	.333
Bats Left	R	.232	211	49	12	3	6	29	9	44	.261	.403
Nixon,Trot	L	.224	85	19	2	1	1	9	12	18	.333	.306
Bats Left	R	.288	323	93	27	0	12	58	41	41	.364	.483
Nunez,Abraham	L	.324	74	24	2	0	1	8	9	9	.398	.392
Bats Both	R	.277	347	96	11	2	4	36	28	54	.331	.354
Offerman,Jose	L	.111	27	3	0	0	0	1	4	4	.226	.111
Bats Both	R	.269	78	21	3	1	2	12	7	13	.337	.410
Ojeda,Miguel	L	.108	37	4	2	0	0	2	4	8	.195	.162
Bats Right	R	.169	65	11	1	1	1	7	11	16	.289	.262
Olerud,John	L	.300	40	12	2	0	2	12	3	8	.341	.500
Bats Left	R	.286	133	38	5	0	5	25	13	12	.345	.436
Olivo,Miguel	L	.284	74	21	3	1	6	9	1	17	.299	.595
Bats Right	R	.192	193	37	8	0	3	25	7	63	.227	.280
Olmedo,Ray	L	.111	9	1	1	0	0	0	1	2	.200	.222
Bats Both	R	.235	68	16	3	1	1	4	5	20	.293	.353
Olson,Tim	L	.000	1	0	0	0	0	0	0	1	.500	.000
Bats Right	R	.000	1	0	0	0	0	0	0	1	.000	.000
Ordonez,Magglio	L	.308	78	24	5	0	2	11	6	7	.357	.449
Bats Right	R	.300	227	68	12	0	6	35	24	28	.359	.432
Orr,Pete	L	.391	23	9	2	0	0	1	1	5	.440	.478
Bats Left	R	.283	127	36	6	1	1	7	5	18	.311	.370
Ortiz,David	L	.302	205	62	14	0	11	46	20	38	.362	.532
Bats Left	R	.298	396	118	26	1	36	102	82	86	.413	.641
Ortmeier,Dan	L	-	0	0	0	0	0	0	0	0	-	-
Bats Both	R	.136	22	3	0	0	0	1	3	5	.269	.136
Osik,Keith	L	.000	2	0	0	0	0	0	0	0	.000	.000
Bats Right	R	.000	2	0	0	0	0	0	0	1	.000	.000
Overbay,Lyle	L	.269	145	39	6	1	6	25	5	36	.299	.448
Bats Left	R	.278	392	109	28	0	13	47	73	62	.390	.449
Ozuna,Pablo	L	.306	98	30	5	0	0	3	2	11	.340	.357
Bats Right	R	.248	105	26	2	2	0	8	5	15	.288	.305
Palmeiro,Orlando	L	.136	22	3	0	0	0	2	3	5	.296	.136
Bats Left	R	.302	182	55	17	2	3	18	12	18	.347	.467
Palmeiro,Rafael	L	.221	95	21	1	0	3	20	5	12	.257	.326
Bats Left	R	.281	274	77	12	0	15	40	38	31	.366	.489
Patterson,Corey	L	.169	118	20	5	1	3	6	5	36	.203	.305
Bats Left	R	.231	333	77	11	0	10	28	18	82	.272	.363
Paul,Josh	L	.143	7	1	0	0	1	2	0	0	.143	.571
Bats Right	R	.200	30	6	1	0	1	2	2	9	.250	.333
Paulino,Ronny	L	.500	2	1	0	0	0	0	1	0	.667	.500
Bats Right	R	.500	2	1	0	0	0	0	0	0	.500	.500
Payton,Jay	L	.283	152	43	7	0	5	22	11	13	.329	.428
Bats Right	R	.258	256	66	9	1	13	41	13	34	.292	.453
Pena,Brayan	L	.273	11	3	0	0	0	0	0	0	.273	.364
Bats Both	R	.143	28	4	1	0	0	4	1	6	.172	.179
Pena,Carlos	L	.157	51	8	1	0	4	8	1	26	.189	.412
Bats Left	R	.254	209	53	8	0	14	36	30	69	.355	.493
Pena,Wily Mo	L	.291	110	32	6	0	7	18	8	41	.345	.536
Bats Right	R	.234	201	47	11	0	12	33	12	75	.282	.468
Peralta,Jhonny	L	.305	154	47	11	1	11	26	23	40	.394	.597
Bats Right	R	.286	350	100	25	3	13	52	35	88	.352	.486
Perez,Antonio	L	.312	77	24	3	0	2	10	8	16	.386	.429
Bats Right	R	.291	182	53	10	2	1	13	13	45	.348	.385
Perez,Eddie	L	.333	12	4	0	0	1	3	1	1	.385	.583
Bats Right	R	.154	26	4	2	0	1	3	0	4	.154	.346
Perez,Eduardo	L	.255	137	35	6	0	10	24	21	26	.366	.518
Bats Right	R	.250	24	6	0	0	1	4	5	4	.379	.375
Perez,Miguel	L	.000	1	0	0	0	0	0	0	0	.000	.000
Bats Right	R	.000	2	0	0	0	0	0	0	0	.000	.000
Perez,Neifi	L	.267	150	40	12	0	5	16	4	21	.290	.447
Bats Both	R	.277	422	117	21	1	4	38	14	26	.301	.360
Perez,Timo	L	.105	19	2	1	0	0	3	1	6	.143	.158
Bats Left	R	.231	160	37	7	0	2	12	11	19	.281	.313
Perez,Tomas	L	.283	46	13	3	0	0	6	3	4	.340	.348
Bats Both	R	.212	113	24	0	0	16	8	23	.268	.248

327

Batters vs. Left-Handed and Right-Handed Pitchers

Batter	vs	Avg	AB	H	2B	3B	HR	RBI	BB	SO	OBP	Slg
Petagine,Roberto	L	.333	3	1	0	0	0	1	0	1	.333	.333
Bats Left	R	.276	29	8	2	0	1	8	4	4	.364	.448
Phelps,Josh	L	.229	48	11	3	0	1	5	3	14	.302	.354
Bats Right	R	.282	110	31	7	0	4	21	9	34	.339	.455
Phillips,Andy	L	.150	20	3	1	0	1	3	1	7	.190	.350
Bats Right	R	.150	20	3	3	0	0	1	0	6	.150	.300
Phillips,Brandon	L	.000	3	0	0	0	0	0	0	1	.000	.000
Bats Right	R	.000	6	0	0	0	0	0	0	3	.000	.000
Phillips,Jason	L	.270	89	24	6	0	4	16	12	7	.353	.472
Bats Right	R	.229	310	71	14	0	6	39	13	43	.267	.332
Phillips,Paul	L	.227	22	5	2	1	1	4	0	2	.227	.545
Bats Right	R	.289	45	13	2	0	0	5	0	3	.289	.333
Piazza,Mike	L	.269	93	25	6	0	3	11	16	11	.376	.430
Bats Right	R	.246	305	75	17	0	16	51	25	56	.309	.459
Pickering,Calvin	L	.000	7	0	0	0	0	0	0	3	.000	.000
Bats Left	R	.200	20	4	0	0	1	3	3	11	.292	.350
Piedra,Jorge	L	.500	2	1	0	0	0	0	0	0	.500	.500
Bats Left	R	.309	110	34	8	1	6	16	10	15	.369	.564
Pierre,Juan	L	.299	144	43	3	0	0	4	7	11	.338	.319
Bats Left	R	.270	512	138	16	13	2	43	34	34	.323	.363
Pierzynski,A.J.	L	.230	87	20	1	0	4	9	0	16	.247	.379
Bats Left	R	.263	373	98	20	0	14	47	23	52	.322	.429
Podsednik,Scott	L	.330	100	33	2	0	0	8	11	17	.404	.350
Bats Left	R	.280	407	114	26	1	0	17	36	58	.337	.349
Polanco,Placido	L	.348	161	56	9	1	4	15	9	8	.387	.491
Bats Right	R	.324	340	110	18	1	5	41	24	17	.380	.426
Posada,Jorge	L	.281	171	48	9	0	7	25	21	34	.354	.456
Bats Both	R	.251	303	76	14	0	12	46	45	60	.350	.416
Pratt,Todd	L	.300	40	12	1	0	5	13	6	9	.404	.700
Bats Right	R	.237	135	32	3	0	2	31	13	41	.309	.304
Pride,Curtis	L	.000	1	0	0	0	0	0	0	1	.000	.000
Bats Left	R	.100	10	1	1	0	0	0	0	3	.100	.200
Prieto,Chris	L	.000	1	0	0	0	0	0	0	0	.000	.000
Bats Left	R	.000	1	0	0	0	0	0	0	0	.000	.000
Pujols,Albert	L	.300	150	45	10	1	8	26	33	17	.424	.540
Bats Right	R	.340	441	150	28	1	33	91	64	48	.432	.633
Punto,Nick	L	.210	81	17	5	0	0	2	8	17	.278	.272
Bats Both	R	.246	313	77	13	4	4	24	28	69	.307	.351
Quinlan,Robb	L	.289	83	24	6	0	5	13	3	10	.318	.542
Bats Right	R	.137	51	7	2	0	0	1	4	16	.200	.176
Quintanilla,Omar	L	.067	15	1	0	0	0	0	0	3	.067	.067
Bats Left	R	.239	113	27	1	1	0	7	9	12	.295	.265
Quintero,Humberto	L	.200	15	3	1	0	0	4	0	2	.200	.267
Bats Right	R	.179	39	7	0	0	1	4	1	8	.200	.256
Quiroz,Guillermo	L	.095	21	2	1	0	0	2	1	7	.174	.143
Bats Right	R	.333	15	5	1	0	0	2	1	6	.375	.400
Ramirez,Aramis	L	.355	121	43	11	0	10	24	10	19	.418	.694
Bats Right	R	.284	342	97	19	0	21	68	25	41	.336	.523
Ramirez,Hanley	L	-	0	0	0	0	0	0	0	0	-	-
Bats Right	R	.000	2	0	0	0	0	0	0	2	.000	.000
Ramirez,Julio	L	1.000	1	1	0	0	0	0	0	0	1.000	1.000
Bats Right	R	.000	3	0	0	0	0	0	0	1	.000	.000
Ramirez,Manny	L	.236	165	39	9	0	13	36	30	29	.358	.527
Bats Right	R	.316	389	123	21	1	32	108	50	90	.401	.622
Randa,Joe	L	.306	157	48	14	0	3	22	15	18	.368	.452
Bats Right	R	.264	398	105	29	2	14	46	32	63	.322	.452
Redman,Tike	L	.260	73	19	2	2	2	7	6	4	.316	.425
Bats Left	R	.248	246	61	10	2	0	19	13	23	.285	.305
Redmond,Mike	L	.345	58	20	4	0	0	9	3	2	.387	.414
Bats Right	R	.289	90	26	5	0	1	17	3	12	.326	.378
Reed,Jeremy	L	.200	105	21	3	2	0	12	10	16	.276	.267
Bats Right	R	.269	383	103	30	1	3	33	38	58	.335	.376
Reed,Keith	L	.000	3	0	0	0	0	0	1	1	.250	.000
Bats Right	R	.500	2	1	0	0	0	1	0	1	.500	.500
Reese,Kevin	L	-	0	0	0	0	0	0	0	0	-	-
Bats Left	R	.000	1	0	0	0	0	0	1	1	.500	.000
Relaford,Desi	L	.240	50	12	6	0	0	1	5	8	.309	.360
Bats Right	R	.219	160	35	7	2	1	15	17	34	.308	.306
Renteria,Edgar	L	.326	193	63	15	0	5	30	18	28	.384	.482
Bats Right	R	.253	430	109	21	4	3	40	37	72	.313	.342
Repko,Jason	L	.235	102	24	6	0	3	8	8	20	.278	.382
Bats Right	R	.213	174	37	9	3	5	22	13	58	.283	.385
Restovich,Mike	L	.250	88	22	5	1	3	6	8	20	.313	.432
Bats Right	R	.185	27	5	0	0	0	2	3	9	.267	.185
Reyes,Jose	L	.288	153	44	6	2	1	18	6	16	.313	.373
Bats Both	R	.269	543	146	18	15	6	40	21	62	.297	.390

Batter	vs	Avg	AB	H	2B	3B	HR	RBI	BB	SO	OBP	Slg
Rios,Alexis	L	.247	178	44	7	4	3	14	9	39	.289	.382
Bats Right	R	.271	303	82	16	2	7	45	19	62	.316	.406
Rivas,Luis	L	.283	53	15	3	0	1	8	3	5	.316	.396
Bats Right	R	.241	83	20	0	1	0	4	6	12	.308	.265
Rivera,Juan	L	.252	139	35	7	0	4	21	10	12	.300	.388
Bats Right	R	.284	211	60	10	1	11	38	13	32	.326	.498
Rivera,Rene	L	.364	11	4	1	0	0	1	0	3	.364	.455
Bats Right	R	.405	37	15	2	0	1	5	1	8	.421	.541
Roberts,Brian	L	.273	176	48	10	3	5	25	20	33	.352	.449
Bats Both	R	.332	385	128	35	4	13	48	47	50	.404	.545
Roberts,Dave	L	.258	66	17	1	1	1	3	10	13	.364	.348
Bats Left	R	.278	345	96	18	9	7	35	43	46	.355	.443
Robles,Oscar	L	.267	75	20	3	0	1	7	6	10	.329	.347
Bats Left	R	.273	289	79	15	1	4	27	25	23	.332	.374
Rodriguez,Alex	L	.300	150	45	8	0	11	30	30	32	.414	.573
Bats Right	R	.327	455	149	21	1	37	100	61	107	.423	.622
Rodriguez,Ivan	L	.294	109	32	7	2	4	15	5	18	.316	.505
Bats Right	R	.271	395	107	26	3	10	35	6	75	.283	.428
Rodriguez,John	L	.296	27	8	0	0	0	3	6	12	.441	.704
Bats Left	R	.295	122	36	6	0	5	21	13	33	.367	.467
Rodriguez,Luis	L	.233	30	7	2	0	0	2	4	5	.324	.300
Bats Both	R	.276	145	40	8	2	2	18	14	18	.337	.400
Rogers,Eddie	L	1.000	1	1	0	0	1	2	0	0	1.000	4.000
Bats Right	R	-	0	0	0	0	0	0	0	0	-	-
Rolen,Scott	L	.237	59	14	4	0	2	11	9	10	.333	.407
Bats Right	R	.234	137	32	8	1	3	17	16	18	.318	.372
Rollins,Jimmy	L	.278	187	52	9	3	3	15	8	9	.311	.406
Bats Both	R	.294	490	144	29	8	9	39	39	62	.348	.441
Romano,Jason	L	.294	17	5	2	0	0	0	3	5	.429	.412
Bats Right	R	.231	13	3	0	0	1	3	0	4	.231	.462
Rose,Mike	L	.125	16	2	0	0	0	0	0	1	.125	.125
Bats Both	R	.259	27	7	2	0	1	1	3	5	.333	.444
Ross,Cody	L	.333	9	3	1	0	0	1	1	5	.400	.444
Bats Right	R	.063	16	1	0	0	0	0	0	5	.063	.063
Ross,Dave	L	.200	30	6	1	1	0	2	1	2	.242	.300
Bats Right	R	.253	95	24	7	0	3	13	5	26	.291	.421
Rowand,Aaron	L	.303	152	46	9	4	3	20	9	42	.354	.474
Bats Right	R	.258	426	110	21	1	10	49	23	74	.321	.383
Ryan,Mike	L	.167	6	1	0	0	0	0	1	3	.286	.167
Bats Left	R	.234	111	26	5	0	2	13	8	19	.283	.423
Sadler,Ray	L	.167	6	1	0	0	1	1	0	0	.167	.667
Bats Right	R	.500	2	1	0	0	0	0	0	1	.500	.500
Saenz,Olmedo	L	.261	115	30	9	0	8	26	13	16	.338	.548
Bats Both	R	.265	204	54	15	0	7	37	14	47	.317	.441
Sanchez,Alex	L	.304	23	7	2	0	1	6	0	6	.304	.522
Bats Left	R	.327	153	50	9	1	1	10	5	28	.360	.418
Sanchez,Freddy	L	.326	135	44	9	3	1	11	10	5	.369	.459
Bats Right	R	.277	318	88	17	1	4	24	17	31	.322	.374
Sanchez,Rey	L	.364	22	8	1	0	0	1	1	1	.417	.409
Bats Right	R	.190	21	4	0	0	0	2	1	2	.227	.190
Sanders,Reggie	L	.257	109	28	4	1	8	17	11	21	.328	.532
Bats Right	R	.280	186	52	10	1	13	37	17	54	.348	.554
Sandoval,Danny	L	-	0	0	0	0	0	0	0	0	-	-
Bats Both	R	.000	2	0	0	0	0	0	0	1	.000	.000
Santiago,Benito	L	.125	8	1	0	0	0	0	0	0	.125	.125
Bats Right	R	.333	15	5	1	1	0	0	0	3	.333	.533
Santiago,Ramon	L	.000	1	0	0	0	0	0	1	0	.667	.000
Bats Both	R	.143	7	1	0	0	0	0	0	2	.333	.143
Sardinha,Dane	L	.000	2	0	0	0	0	0	0	0	.000	.000
Bats Right	R	.000	1	0	0	0	0	0	0	1	.000	.000
Schneider,Brian	L	.265	68	18	2	0	1	9	5	8	.324	.294
Bats Left	R	.269	301	81	18	1	10	42	25	37	.331	.435
Schumaker,Jared	L	.500	2	1	0	0	0	0	0	1	.500	.500
Bats Left	R	.227	22	5	1	0	0	1	2	1	.292	.273
Scott,Luke	L	.286	7	2	0	0	0	0	0	3	.286	.286
Bats Left	R	.178	73	13	4	2	0	4	9	20	.268	.288
Scutaro,Marco	L	.171	76	13	2	1	1	7	12	7	.284	.263
Bats Right	R	.266	305	81	20	2	8	30	24	41	.317	.423
Seabol,Scott	L	.224	49	11	4	0	0	5	5	9	.291	.306
Bats Right	R	.214	56	12	1	0	1	5	3	14	.254	.286
Self,Todd	L	.167	6	1	0	0	0	0	1	3	.167	.333
Bats Left	R	.205	39	8	1	0	1	4	3	8	.262	.308
Sexson,Richie	L	.333	123	41	11	1	9	31	28	34	.458	.659
Bats Right	R	.244	435	106	25	0	30	90	61	133	.342	.508
Shabala,Adam	L	.333	3	1	0	0	0	2	0	0	.333	.333
Bats Left	R	.167	12	2	0	0	0	0	1	5	.214	.167

Batters vs. Left-Handed and Right-Handed Pitchers

Batter	vs	Avg	AB	H	2B	3B	HR	RBI	BB	SO	OBP	Slg
Shealy,Ryan	L	.125	16	2	1	0	0	3	3	5	.263	.188
Bats Right	R	.373	75	28	6	0	2	13	10	17	.447	.533
Sheffield,Gary	L	.359	156	56	7	0	14	50	20	23	.436	.673
Bats Right	R	.266	428	114	20	0	20	73	58	53	.359	.453
Shelton,Chris	L	.278	97	27	3	0	4	14	10	20	.345	.433
Bats Right	R	.306	291	89	19	3	14	45	24	67	.364	.536
Shoppach,Kelly	L	.000	3	0	0	0	0	0	0	1	.250	.000
Bats Right	R	.000	12	0	0	0	0	0	0	6	.000	.000
Short,Rick	L	1.000	2	2	0	0	1	1	0	0	1.000	2.500
Bats Right	R	.308	13	4	2	0	1	3	1	1	.357	.692
Sierra,Ruben	L	.221	77	17	7	0	2	11	6	13	.277	.390
Bats Both	R	.237	93	22	5	0	2	18	3	28	.255	.355
Singleton,Chris	L	.000	3	0	0	0	0	0	0	2	.000	.000
Bats Left	R	.286	56	16	5	0	0	11	6	12	.365	.375
Sizemore,Grady	L	.245	184	45	9	2	3	17	12	49	.296	.364
Bats Left	R	.307	456	140	28	9	19	64	40	83	.369	.533
Sledge,Terrmel	L	.000	1	0	0	0	0	0	1	0	.000	.000
Bats Left	R	.250	36	9	0	1	1	7	7	8	.364	.389
Smith,Jason	L	.143	7	1	0	0	0	0	0	3	.143	.143
Bats Left	R	.196	51	10	1	2	0	2	0	13	.212	.294
Snelling,Chris	L	.333	3	1	0	0	0	0	0	0	.333	.333
Bats Left	R	.269	26	7	2	0	1	1	5	2	.387	.462
Snow,J.T.	L	.243	37	9	1	0	0	4	1	8	.282	.270
Bats Left	R	.279	330	92	16	2	4	36	31	53	.350	.376
Snyder,Chris	L	.260	77	20	3	0	2	11	15	17	.380	.377
Bats Both	R	.185	249	46	11	0	4	17	25	70	.270	.277
Sorensen,Zach	L	.167	6	1	1	0	0	0	0	1	.167	.333
Bats Both	R	.167	6	1	0	0	0	0	0	1	.167	.167
Soriano,Alfonso	L	.257	140	36	7	1	4	10	14	29	.327	.407
Bats Both	R	.272	497	135	36	1	32	94	19	96	.304	.541
Sosa,Sammy	L	.288	104	30	5	1	4	10	14	22	.370	.471
Bats Right	R	.196	276	54	10	0	10	35	25	62	.266	.341
Soto,Geovany	L	-	0	0	0	0	0	0	0	0	-	-
Bats Right	R	.000	1	0	0	0	0	0	0	0	.000	.000
Spiezio,Scott	L	.000	17	0	0	0	0	0	1	8	.056	.000
Bats Both	R	.100	30	3	1	0	1	1	3	10	.182	.233
Spilborghs,Ryan	L	.000	2	0	0	0	0	0	0	1	.000	.000
Bats Right	R	1.000	2	2	0	0	0	1	0	0	1.000	1.000
Spivey,Junior	L	.306	72	22	8	1	4	9	10	20	.390	.611
Bats Both	R	.203	187	38	7	0	3	15	19	63	.286	.289
Stairs,Matt	L	.259	54	14	4	0	1	15	12	11	.400	.389
Bats Left	R	.278	342	95	22	1	12	51	48	58	.369	.453
Stern,Adam	L	.000	6	0	0	0	0	0	0	1	.000	.000
Bats Left	R	.222	9	2	0	0	1	2	0	3	.300	.556
Stewart,Shannon	L	.244	131	32	3	2	2	7	9	24	.310	.344
Bats Right	R	.283	420	119	24	1	8	49	25	49	.327	.402
Stinnett,Kelly	L	.214	28	6	1	0	1	2	5	7	.333	.357
Bats Right	R	.257	101	26	3	0	5	10	7	25	.312	.436
Strong,Jamal	L	.273	11	3	0	0	0	2	1	4	.357	.273
Bats Right	R	.222	9	2	0	1	0	0	1	2	.300	.444
Sullivan,Cory	L	.250	44	11	1	1	0	2	3	11	.292	.318
Bats Left	R	.299	334	100	14	3	4	28	25	72	.350	.395
Surhoff,B.J.	L	.255	98	25	3	1	2	17	1	12	.260	.367
Bats Left	R	.259	205	53	8	1	3	17	10	20	.293	.351
Suzuki,Ichiro	L	.352	196	69	5	5	5	17	14	19	.394	.505
Bats Left	R	.284	483	137	16	7	10	51	34	47	.332	.408
Sweeney,Mark	L	.200	20	4	0	0	0	3	4	6	.320	.200
Bats Left	R	.303	201	61	12	1	8	37	36	52	.402	.493
Sweeney,Mike	L	.279	129	36	13	0	6	29	17	14	.358	.519
Bats Right	R	.308	341	105	26	0	15	54	16	47	.342	.516
Swisher,Nick	L	.203	123	25	6	0	3	18	16	21	.310	.325
Bats Both	R	.248	339	84	26	1	18	56	39	89	.326	.490
Taguchi,So	L	.276	156	43	5	2	4	25	7	28	.307	.410
Bats Right	R	.296	240	71	16	0	4	28	13	34	.332	.413
Taveras,Willy	L	.233	159	37	6	2	1	6	8	29	.272	.314
Bats Right	R	.312	433	135	7	2	2	23	17	74	.344	.351
Taylor,Reggie	L	.000	2	0	0	0	0	0	1	1	.333	.000
Bats Left	R	.200	20	4	2	0	0	1	1	6	.238	.300
Teahen,Mark	L	.200	120	24	7	2	2	14	9	32	.256	.342
Bats Left	R	.263	327	86	22	2	5	41	31	75	.328	.388
Teixeira,Mark	L	.292	171	50	13	2	6	29	17	33	.361	.497
Bats Both	R	.304	473	144	28	1	37	115	55	91	.386	.603
Tejada,Miguel	L	.293	164	48	8	2	5	21	20	19	.371	.457
Bats Right	R	.308	490	151	42	3	21	77	20	64	.342	.535
Terrero,Luis	L	.247	85	21	3	0	1	12	9	17	.323	.318
Bats Right	R	.211	76	16	3	1	3	8	5	23	.302	.395

Batter	vs	Avg	AB	H	2B	3B	HR	RBI	BB	SO	OBP	Slg
Thames,Marcus	L	.222	36	8	1	0	2	5	5	10	.317	.417
Bats Right	R	.183	71	13	1	0	5	11	4	28	.234	.408
Theriot,Ryan	L	.250	8	2	1	0	0	0	1	0	.333	.375
Bats Right	R	.000	5	0	0	0	0	0	0	2	.000	.000
Thomas,Charles	L	.143	7	1	0	0	0	1	0	0	.250	.143
Bats Left	R	.103	39	4	0	0	0	0	5	8	.255	.103
Thomas,Frank	L	.281	32	9	1	0	4	8	6	8	.385	.688
Bats Right	R	.192	73	14	2	0	8	18	10	23	.282	.548
Thome,Jim	L	.164	73	12	3	0	2	11	10	22	.271	.288
Bats Right	R	.233	120	28	4	0	5	19	35	37	.408	.392
Tiffee,Terry	L	.194	36	7	3	0	0	0	5	3	.293	.278
Bats Both	R	.211	114	24	5	1	1	15	3	12	.229	.298
Torcato,Tony	L	.000	1	0	0	0	0	0	0	1	.000	.000
Bats Left	R	.300	10	3	0	0	0	0	1	1	.364	.300
Torrealba,Yorvit	L	.302	53	16	8	0	1	4	4	8	.351	.509
Bats Right	R	.209	148	31	4	0	2	11	12	42	.278	.277
Torres,Andres	L	.167	12	2	1	0	0	1	1	3	.214	.250
Bats Both	R	.143	7	1	0	0	0	0	0	3	.143	.143
Tracy,Chad	L	.236	89	21	4	0	4	10	9	16	.307	.416
Bats Left	R	.324	414	134	30	4	23	62	26	62	.370	.582
Treanor,Matt	L	.148	27	4	2	0	0	0	6	8	.303	.222
Bats Right	R	.215	107	23	6	0	0	13	10	20	.300	.271
Tucker,Michael	L	.152	33	5	1	0	0	3	1	7	.189	.182
Bats Left	R	.251	235	59	15	1	5	33	30	45	.336	.387
Tyner,Jason	L	.333	12	4	0	0	0	2	1	2	.385	.333
Bats Left	R	.318	44	14	1	1	0	3	3	2	.362	.386
Uribe,Juan	L	.311	122	38	8	1	5	19	9	25	.351	.516
Bats Right	R	.231	359	83	15	2	11	52	25	52	.284	.376
Utley,Chase	L	.219	128	28	5	3	7	24	25	34	.348	.469
Bats Left	R	.313	415	130	34	3	21	81	44	75	.385	.561
Valdez,Wilson	L	.143	42	6	3	0	0	1	3	11	.200	.214
Bats Right	R	.227	97	22	4	1	0	8	5	15	.265	.289
Valent,Eric	L	.000	3	0	0	0	0	0	1	0	.250	.000
Bats Left	R	.200	40	8	3	0	0	1	6	17	.304	.275
Valentin,Javier	L	.184	38	7	0	0	2	10	10	7	.354	.342
Bats Both	R	.301	183	55	11	0	12	40	20	30	.364	.557
Valentin,Jose	L	.316	19	6	0	0	1	4	3	3	.417	.474
Bats Left	R	.148	128	19	4	2	1	10	28	35	.313	.234
Varitek,Jason	L	.320	122	39	5	0	9	27	22	24	.418	.582
Bats Both	R	.267	348	93	25	1	13	43	40	93	.347	.457
Vazquez,Ramon	L	.250	16	4	0	0	0	1	1	1	.294	.250
Bats Left	R	.203	69	14	5	0	0	4	4	16	.247	.275
Vento,Mike	L	-	0	0	0	0	0	0	0	0	-	-
Bats Right	R	.000	2	0	0	0	0	0	0	1	.000	.000
Victorino,Shane	L	1.000	1	1	0	0	1	3	0	0	.500	4.000
Bats Both	R	.250	16	4	0	0	1	5	0	3	.235	.438
Vidro,Jose	L	.258	66	17	3	0	5	15	11	7	.354	.530
Bats Both	R	.280	243	68	18	2	2	17	20	23	.335	.395
Vizcaino,Jose	L	.295	61	18	5	1	1	5	5	13	.348	.459
Bats Both	R	.222	126	28	5	1	0	18	10	27	.275	.278
Vizquel,Omar	L	.253	146	37	11	0	1	14	9	13	.302	.349
Bats Both	R	.277	422	117	17	4	2	31	47	45	.354	.351
Walker,Larry	L	.214	56	12	1	1	3	10	7	15	.338	.429
Bats Left	R	.305	259	79	19	0	12	42	34	49	.395	.517
Walker,Todd	L	.352	91	32	6	0	5	13	6	10	.398	.582
Bats Left	R	.291	306	89	19	3	7	27	25	30	.342	.441
Ward,Daryle	L	.200	105	21	5	1	0	14	7	17	.243	.267
Bats Left	R	.281	302	85	16	0	12	49	30	43	.343	.454
Watson,Brandon	L	.091	11	1	0	0	0	2	0	3	.091	.091
Bats Left	R	.207	29	6	1	1	1	3	4	5	.303	.414
Watson,Matt	L	.000	7	0	0	0	0	0	0	1	.000	.000
Bats Left	R	.220	41	9	3	0	0	5	2	3	.256	.293
Weeks,Rickie	L	.222	72	16	3	1	3	10	12	19	.364	.417
Bats Right	R	.243	288	70	10	1	10	32	28	77	.324	.389
Wells,Vernon	L	.347	147	51	8	2	12	34	16	17	.409	.673
Bats Right	R	.245	473	116	22	1	16	63	31	69	.292	.397
Werth,Jayson	L	.239	67	16	5	0	0	11	11	23	.342	.313
Bats Right	R	.233	270	63	17	3	12	32	37	91	.337	.389
White,Rondell	L	.325	83	27	4	1	4	12	5	12	.363	.542
Bats Right	R	.309	291	90	20	2	8	41	12	36	.343	.474
Whiteside,Eli	L	.400	5	2	0	0	0	0	0	1	.400	.400
Bats Right	R	.143	7	1	0	0	0	1	0	1	.143	.143
Widger,Chris	L	.237	76	18	6	0	4	9	4	13	.284	.474
Bats Right	R	.246	65	16	2	0	0	2	6	9	.310	.277
Wigginton,Ty	L	.247	73	18	3	0	5	14	8	14	.321	.493
Bats Right	R	.268	82	22	6	1	2	11	6	16	.326	.439

Batters vs. Left-Handed and Right-Handed Pitchers

Batter	vs	Avg	AB	H	2B	3B	HR	RBI	BB	SO	OBP	Slg
Wilkerson,Brad	L	.296	162	48	11	1	2	22	20	38	.390	.414
Bats Left	R	.228	403	92	31	6	9	35	64	109	.335	.402
Williams,Bernie	L	.231	182	42	7	0	1	12	20	27	.305	.286
Bats Both	R	.261	303	79	12	1	11	52	33	48	.330	.416
Williams,Gerald	L	.222	9	2	0	0	0	1	0	2	.222	.222
Bats Right	R	.238	21	5	2	0	1	2	1	5	.273	.476
Williams,Glenn	L	.533	15	8	0	0	0	2	1	4	.563	.533
Bats Both	R	.360	25	9	1	0	0	1	1	3	.385	.400
Willingham,Josh	L	.429	7	3	1	0	0	1	1	2	.600	.571
Bats Right	R	.250	16	4	0	0	0	3	1	3	.294	.250
Wilson,Craig	L	.283	53	15	4	0	1	5	12	18	.449	.415
Bats Right	R	.257	144	37	10	1	4	17	18	51	.361	.424
Wilson,Dan	L	.000	9	0	0	0	0	0	0	4	.000	.000
Bats Right	R	.278	18	5	0	0	0	2	0	6	.316	.278
Wilson,Enrique	L	.333	3	1	1	0	0	0	1	0	.500	.667
Bats Both	R	.105	19	2	1	0	0	0	2	1	.190	.158
Wilson,Jack	L	.257	140	36	5	3	2	11	14	12	.325	.379
Bats Right	R	.257	447	115	19	4	6	41	17	46	.291	.358
Wilson,Josh	L	-	0	0	0	0	0	0	0	0	-	-
Bats Right	R	.100	10	1	1	0	0	0	0	4	.182	.200
Wilson,Preston	L	.262	126	33	9	0	10	23	13	34	.336	.571
Bats Right	R	.259	394	102	20	2	15	67	32	114	.322	.434
Wilson,Vance	L	.214	42	9	0	0	3	6	5	8	.298	.429
Bats Right	R	.191	110	21	4	0	0	13	6	18	.266	.227
Winn,Randy	L	.269	156	42	13	2	2	14	11	21	.315	.417
Bats Both	R	.319	461	147	34	4	18	49	37	70	.374	.527
Womack,Tony	L	.254	67	17	0	0	0	2	3	15	.286	.254
Bats Left	R	.248	262	65	8	1	0	13	9	34	.274	.286
Woodward,Chris	L	.260	96	25	5	0	2	6	9	22	.330	.375
Bats Right	R	.312	77	24	5	0	1	12	4	24	.345	.416
Wooten,Shawn	L	-	0	0	0	0	0	0	0	0	-	-
Bats Right	R	.000	1	0	0	0	0	0	0	0	.000	.000
Wright,David	L	.336	128	43	7	0	9	21	15	17	.415	.602
Bats Right	R	.298	447	133	35	1	18	81	57	96	.380	.501
Youkilis,Kevin	L	.300	30	9	2	0	1	3	7	6	.432	.467
Bats Right	R	.265	49	13	5	0	0	6	7	13	.379	.367
Young,Dmitri	L	.277	119	33	8	1	4	18	2	24	.295	.462
Bats Both	R	.269	350	94	17	2	17	54	27	76	.334	.474
Young,Eric	L	.318	66	21	5	0	1	6	12	3	.423	.439
Bats Right	R	.237	76	18	4	0	1	6	6	9	.293	.329
Young,Michael	L	.340	153	52	14	1	3	16	15	15	.396	.503
Bats Right	R	.328	515	169	26	4	21	75	43	76	.382	.517
Young,Walter	L	.667	3	2	0	0	0	0	0	1	.667	.667
Bats Left	R	.267	30	8	1	0	1	3	4	6	.353	.400
Zaun,Gregg	L	.278	115	32	6	1	2	20	18	15	.370	.400
Bats Both	R	.241	319	77	12	0	9	41	55	55	.350	.364
Zimmerman,Ryan	L	.400	15	6	4	0	0	1	0	3	.400	.667
Bats Right	R	.395	43	17	6	0	0	5	3	9	.426	.535

Pitchers vs. Left-Handed and Right-Handed Batters

Pitcher	vs	Avg	AB	H	2B	3B	HR	RBI	BB	SO	OBP	Slg
Accardo,Jeremy	L	.182	44	8	0	0	0	2	3	8	.245	.182
Throws Right	R	.265	68	18	2	0	2	7	6	8	.324	.382
Acevedo,Jose	L	.346	136	47	11	3	7	28	11	10	.387	.625
Throws Right	R	.295	132	39	8	0	6	18	5	21	.321	.492
Adams,Mike	L	.200	20	4	1	0	0	1	4	7	.333	.250
Throws Right	R	.258	31	8	0	0	2	4	6	7	.378	.452
Adams,Terry	L	.385	26	10	1	0	2	5	7	2	.529	.654
Throws Right	R	.417	36	15	7	0	1	10	3	2	.500	.694
Adkins,Jon	L	.389	18	7	3	0	0	4	2	0	.476	.556
Throws Right	R	.316	19	6	1	0	0	5	2	1	.381	.368
Affeldt,Jeremy	L	.263	57	15	1	0	0	7	13	14	.400	.281
Throws Left	R	.283	145	41	8	2	3	20	16	25	.352	.428
Alfonseca,Antonio	L	.244	45	11	3	1	0	8	5	3	.308	.356
Throws Right	R	.346	52	18	2	0	2	11	9	13	.460	.500
Almanza,Armando	L	.286	7	2	0	0	1	3	1	2	.375	.714
Throws Left	R	.333	9	3	2	0	0	0	2	0	.455	.556
Almanzar,Carlos	L	.556	9	5	1	0	1	6	5	0	.667	1.000
Throws Right	R	.357	14	5	1	0	1	4	2	3	.444	.643
Alvarez,Abe	L	.750	4	3	0	0	0	2	0	1	.750	.750
Throws Left	R	.333	9	3	1	0	1	1	0	0	.333	.778
Alvarez,Wilson	L	.387	31	12	3	0	1	5	1	4	.406	.581
Throws Left	R	.284	67	19	3	0	6	16	6	12	.333	.597
Anderson,Brian J	L	.080	25	2	0	0	0	1	1	5	.115	.080
Throws Left	R	.359	103	37	7	2	7	21	3	12	.374	.670
Anderson,Jason	L	.125	8	1	0	0	0	0	3	1	.364	.125
Throws Right	R	.250	12	3	2	1	0	3	4	1	.438	.583
Anderson,Matt	L	.611	18	11	1	0	2	5	5	1	.696	1.000
Throws Right	R	.276	29	8	0	0	1	8	6	3	.421	.379
Aquino,Greg	L	.304	56	17	4	0	1	9	7	13	.391	.429
Throws Right	R	.329	76	25	8	0	6	19	10	21	.422	.671
Armas Jr.,Tony	L	.276	185	51	9	1	10	28	32	24	.385	.497
Throws Right	R	.241	203	49	11	2	6	25	22	35	.326	.404
Arroyo,Bronson	L	.288	469	135	35	4	17	58	30	50	.343	.488
Throws Right	R	.234	333	78	21	4	5	35	24	50	.291	.366
Astacio,Ezequiel	L	.313	163	51	10	2	12	32	14	30	.363	.620
Throws Right	R	.290	169	49	11	0	11	21	11	36	.330	.550
Astacio,Pedro	L	.244	270	66	18	1	11	32	25	50	.309	.441
Throws Right	R	.305	220	67	11	2	6	34	12	28	.340	.455
Atchison,Scott	L	.091	11	1	0	0	1	2	0	4	.091	.364
Throws Right	R	.400	15	6	2	0	0	2	1	5	.438	.533
Ayala,Luis	L	.352	122	43	12	0	5	19	7	17	.382	.574
Throws Right	R	.229	140	32	3	0	2	10	7	23	.292	.293
Aybar,Manny	L	.270	37	10	3	1	3	8	5	10	.349	.649
Throws Right	R	.318	66	21	7	1	1	10	2	17	.343	.500
Backe,Brandon	L	.260	273	71	13	0	8	34	31	45	.334	.396
Throws Right	R	.266	301	80	21	3	11	37	36	52	.352	.465
Baez,Danys	L	.268	149	40	6	1	4	21	17	26	.341	.403
Throws Right	R	.215	121	26	1	0	3	11	13	25	.299	.298
Bajenaru,Jeff	L	.300	10	3	0	0	2	3	0	2	.300	.900
Throws Right	R	.125	8	1	0	0	0	0	0	1	.125	.125
Baker,Scott	L	.221	86	19	2	0	2	5	7	16	.274	.314
Throws Right	R	.257	113	29	7	0	3	13	7	16	.300	.398
Baldwin,James	L	.209	110	23	8	1	2	14	13	17	.299	.355
Throws Right	R	.301	103	31	2	1	6	18	3	12	.318	.515
Bartosh,Cliff	L	.269	26	7	0	0	1	4	7	3	.412	.385
Throws Left	R	.327	49	16	5	0	6	9	4	12	.400	.796
Batista,Miguel	L	.256	156	40	6	0	3	19	15	29	.326	.353
Throws Right	R	.282	142	40	6	0	6	29	12	25	.338	.451
Bauer,Rick	L	.412	17	7	3	0	2	4	2	1	.474	.941
Throws Right	R	.316	19	6	1	0	0	7	2	4	.381	.368
Bautista,Denny	L	.288	80	23	6	0	1	11	10	11	.363	.400
Throws Right	R	.220	59	13	2	0	1	9	7	12	.324	.305
Bayliss,Jonah	L	.200	20	4	0	0	2	5	2	5	.304	.500
Throws Right	R	.136	22	3	1	0	0	2	2	5	.240	.182
Bazardo,Yorman	L	.250	4	1	1	0	0	2	1	0	.400	.500
Throws Right	R	.667	6	4	1	0	0	4	1	2	.714	.833
Bean,Colter	L	.500	2	1	0	0	0	1	1	0	.667	.500
Throws Right	R	.000	5	0	0	0	0	0	1	2	.167	.000
Beckett,Josh	L	.217	332	72	17	3	7	26	40	87	.303	.349
Throws Right	R	.252	322	81	17	3	7	37	18	79	.302	.388
Bedard,Erik	L	.252	135	34	3	0	2	12	11	36	.318	.319
Throws Left	R	.263	400	105	20	1	8	43	46	89	.338	.378
Beimel,Joe	L	.429	21	9	0	1	0	1	2	2	.478	.524
Throws Left	R	.231	26	6	1	2	1	4	2	1	.286	.538
Belisle,Matt	L	.331	127	42	7	0	4	16	14	21	.414	.480
Throws Right	R	.273	216	59	10	1	7	35	12	38	.315	.426

Pitcher	vs	Avg	AB	H	2B	3B	HR	RBI	BB	SO	OBP	Slg
Bell,Heath	L	.312	77	24	2	0	1	7	7	13	.369	.377
Throws Right	R	.288	111	32	5	0	2	17	6	30	.331	.387
Bell,Rob	L	.383	60	23	3	1	2	8	7	7	.448	.567
Throws Right	R	.333	54	18	4	0	5	20	5	6	.403	.685
Benitez,Armando	L	.212	52	11	2	0	4	9	10	8	.339	.481
Throws Right	R	.246	57	14	5	0	1	7	6	15	.308	.386
Benoit,Joaquin	L	.227	163	37	3	0	7	17	24	39	.326	.374
Throws Right	R	.196	163	32	6	1	2	17	14	39	.267	.282
Benson,Kris	L	.268	313	84	20	1	12	39	31	35	.334	.454
Throws Right	R	.240	363	87	13	0	12	37	18	60	.281	.375
Bentz,Chad	L	.333	6	2	0	0	0	0	0	0	.333	.333
Throws Left	R	.750	8	6	1	1	2	7	0	0	.750	1.875
Bergmann,Jason	L	.355	31	11	4	0	0	4	6	7	.447	.484
Throws Right	R	.077	39	3	0	0	1	2	5	14	.217	.154
Bernero,Adam	L	.263	99	26	4	1	4	14	6	18	.327	.444
Throws Right	R	.365	96	35	4	0	1	19	6	19	.394	.438
Betancourt,Rafael	L	.264	87	23	4	0	2	9	11	15	.347	.379
Throws Right	R	.204	167	34	10	0	3	19	6	58	.231	.317
Blanton,Joe	L	.228	404	92	24	2	8	33	33	56	.286	.356
Throws Right	R	.246	350	86	18	2	15	47	34	60	.316	.437
Bonderman,Jeremy	L	.287	425	122	34	5	12	53	32	83	.338	.475
Throws Right	R	.249	309	77	10	2	9	39	25	62	.310	.382
Booker,Chris	L	.667	3	2	0	0	1	2	2	0	.800	1.667
Throws Right	R	.500	8	4	1	0	1	5	2	2	.600	1.000
Bootcheck,Chris	L	.273	33	9	3	1	1	4	3	2	.324	.515
Throws Right	R	.244	41	10	1	0	0	2	1	6	.262	.268
Borowski,Joe	L	.198	81	16	2	1	2	13	7	14	.261	.321
Throws Right	R	.244	90	22	5	0	6	17	5	13	.284	.500
Bottalico,Ricky	L	.260	77	20	1	0	5	19	10	13	.341	.468
Throws Right	R	.271	85	23	3	0	2	11	9	16	.357	.376
Bowyer,Travis	L	.286	21	6	0	0	1	2	1	7	.318	.429
Throws Right	R	.250	16	4	0	0	2	6	2	5	.350	.625
Boyer,Blaine	L	.298	47	14	3	0	0	3	9	9	.411	.362
Throws Right	R	.200	90	18	4	0	1	7	8	24	.277	.278
Bradford,Chad	L	.409	22	9	0	0	1	8	2	1	.480	.545
Throws Right	R	.282	71	20	2	0	0	14	2	9	.316	.310
Brazelton,Dewon	L	.303	142	43	10	2	5	30	28	26	.423	.507
Throws Right	R	.312	141	44	8	0	7	27	32	17	.440	.518
Brazoban,Yhency	L	.267	135	36	7	1	9	30	22	29	.377	.533
Throws Right	R	.250	136	34	15	1	2	20	10	32	.311	.419
Breslow,Craig	L	.063	16	1	1	0	0	0	5	5	.286	.125
Throws Left	R	.298	47	14	1	0	1	3	8	9	.404	.383
Brito,Eude	L	.231	13	3	0	0	1	2	2	1	.375	.462
Throws Left	R	.254	67	17	6	1	1	6	9	14	.346	.418
Brocail,Doug	L	.346	127	44	11	2	1	20	19	16	.430	.488
Throws Right	R	.267	172	46	9	1	1	24	15	45	.333	.349
Brooks,Frank	L	1.000	1	1	0	0	0	1	0	0	1.000	1.000
Throws Left	R	-	0	0	0	0	0	0	0	0	-	-
Brower,Jim	L	.303	99	30	6	1	4	13	11	15	.375	.505
Throws Right	R	.301	143	43	5	0	7	25	21	38	.405	.483
Brown,Kevin	L	.335	167	56	12	1	0	21	11	24	.383	.419
Throws Right	R	.347	147	51	7	0	5	28	8	26	.394	.497
Broxton,Jonathan	L	.304	23	7	1	0	0	4	10	5	.486	.348
Throws Right	R	.200	30	6	2	0	0	4	2	17	.273	.267
Bruney,Brian	L	.280	82	23	4	1	3	18	19	22	.422	.463
Throws Right	R	.314	105	33	6	2	3	20	16	29	.421	.495
Buehrle,Mark	L	.271	207	56	12	1	4	25	4	35	.290	.396
Throws Left	R	.260	709	184	32	1	16	60	36	114	.296	.375
Bukvich,Ryan	L	.500	4	2	0	0	0	0	3	1	.714	.500
Throws Right	R	.000	8	0	0	0	0	0	3	3	.273	.000
Bulger,Jason	L	.294	17	5	1	2	0	4	4	2	.429	.588
Throws Right	R	.360	25	9	2	0	1	2	1	7	.385	.560
Bullington,Bryan	L	1.000	1	1	1	0	0	0	0	0	1.000	2.000
Throws Right	R	.000	3	0	0	0	0	2	1	1	.333	.000
Bump,Nate	L	.265	68	18	4	0	3	9	8	10	.342	.456
Throws Right	R	.309	81	25	1	0	2	8	4	8	.356	.395
Burgos,Ambiorix	L	.300	100	30	6	0	2	16	17	35	.403	.420
Throws Right	R	.216	139	30	5	1	4	13	14	30	.306	.353
Burnett,A.J.	L	.226	402	91	13	3	6	31	44	107	.305	.318
Throws Right	R	.249	373	93	14	3	6	45	35	91	.319	.351
Burns,Mike	L	.328	58	19	4	1	1	5	1	8	.361	.483
Throws Right	R	.156	64	10	3	0	5	11	7	12	.270	.438
Bush,Dave	L	.269	268	72	16	0	12	32	15	36	.312	.463
Throws Right	R	.269	260	70	21	2	8	34	14	39	.331	.458
Byrd,Paul	L	.306	421	129	23	4	13	40	21	33	.339	.473
Throws Right	R	.234	372	87	24	2	9	48	7	69	.257	.382

Pitchers vs. Left-Handed and Right-Handed Batters

Pitcher	vs	Avg	AB	H	2B	3B	HR	RBI	BB	SO	OBP	Slg
Byrdak,Tim	L	.214	56	12	4	0	0	6	9	16	.323	.286
Throws Left	R	.300	50	15	0	0	1	8	12	15	.438	.360
Cabrera,Daniel	L	.285	337	96	22	4	12	55	60	77	.400	.481
Throws Right	R	.174	276	48	7	0	2	25	27	80	.257	.221
Cabrera,Fernando	L	.196	46	9	2	1	0	5	7	7	.302	.283
Throws Right	R	.224	67	15	4	0	1	2	4	22	.268	.328
Cain,Matt	L	.160	75	12	0	1	2	7	12	10	.276	.267
Throws Right	R	.143	84	12	0	0	2	3	7	20	.207	.214
Calero,Kiko	L	.319	72	23	2	0	4	9	10	14	.398	.514
Throws Right	R	.162	136	22	3	0	2	13	8	38	.214	.228
Cali,Carmen	L	.333	9	3	0	0	2	3	2	2	.417	1.000
Throws Left	R	.412	17	7	3	0	1	4	4	3	.524	.765
Camp,Shawn	L	.407	91	37	9	0	0	21	7	12	.446	.505
Throws Right	R	.274	117	32	6	1	4	21	6	16	.323	.444
Campillo,Jorge	L	.000	4	0	0	0	0	0	0	1	.000	.000
Throws Right	R	.250	4	1	1	0	0	0	1	0	.400	.500
Capellan,Jose	L	.235	17	4	0	0	0	4	4	2	.348	.235
Throws Right	R	.317	41	13	3	1	1	4	1	12	.333	.512
Capps,Matt	L	.250	4	1	1	0	0	1	0	1	.250	.500
Throws Right	R	.364	11	4	0	0	0	2	0	2	.417	.364
Capuano,Chris	L	.202	163	33	4	0	4	14	14	36	.284	.301
Throws Left	R	.270	664	179	45	2	27	82	77	140	.350	.465
Carlyle,Buddy	L	.296	27	8	2	0	2	9	2	7	.345	.593
Throws Right	R	.286	28	8	2	0	2	8	2	6	.355	.571
Carpenter,Chris	L	.264	432	114	30	2	14	45	31	95	.313	.440
Throws Right	R	.199	452	90	16	1	4	31	20	118	.234	.265
Carrara,Giovanni	L	.234	111	26	7	2	2	12	20	22	.351	.387
Throws Right	R	.248	157	39	9	1	4	24	18	34	.339	.395
Carrasco,D.J.	L	.286	227	65	10	2	6	25	36	23	.387	.427
Throws Right	R	.292	219	64	12	0	5	31	15	26	.343	.416
Carrasco,Hector	L	.208	149	31	7	0	3	14	19	33	.306	.315
Throws Right	R	.178	157	28	5	0	3	18	19	42	.276	.268
Carter,Lance	L	.309	110	34	8	2	3	27	2	12	.327	.500
Throws Right	R	.248	109	27	2	1	6	17	13	10	.320	.450
Carvajal,Marcos	L	.233	86	20	6	0	2	9	9	24	.305	.372
Throws Right	R	.278	115	32	7	0	6	25	12	23	.356	.496
Cassidy,Scott	L	.364	22	8	1	2	1	3	1	6	.391	.727
Throws Right	R	.333	33	11	3	0	2	10	2	6	.371	.606
Castillo,Frank	L	.125	8	1	0	1	0	2	2	2	.300	.375
Throws Right	R	.333	9	3	0	0	0	1	3	2	.500	.333
Cerda,Jaime	L	.231	39	9	1	0	2	9	2	10	.262	.410
Throws Left	R	.343	35	12	4	0	1	5	9	8	.477	.543
Chacin,Gustavo	L	.225	169	38	10	0	2	18	15	33	.289	.320
Throws Left	R	.288	607	175	31	4	18	68	55	88	.350	.442
Chacon,Shawn	L	.232	284	66	16	1	4	15	35	42	.326	.338
Throws Right	R	.252	274	69	19	1	10	38	31	37	.343	.438
Chen,Bruce	L	.324	182	59	8	1	8	24	25	22	.406	.511
Throws Left	R	.224	572	128	24	1	25	63	38	111	.280	.400
Childers,Matt	L	.125	8	1	1	0	0	0	3	1	.364	.250
Throws Right	R	.444	9	4	0	0	1	4	0	1	.500	.778
Choate,Randy	L	.278	18	5	1	0	0	3	1	3	.350	.333
Throws Left	R	.273	11	3	2	0	0	5	4	1	.467	.455
Christiansen,Jason	L	.290	93	27	5	1	1	21	10	12	.349	.398
Throws Left	R	.301	93	28	4	0	3	12	7	9	.347	.441
Chulk,Vinnie	L	.283	120	34	5	0	6	16	15	12	.358	.475
Throws Right	R	.231	147	34	3	0	3	14	11	27	.286	.313
Claussen,Brandon	L	.242	132	32	6	0	8	19	9	31	.299	.470
Throws Left	R	.280	521	146	34	2	16	60	48	90	.344	.445
Clemens,Roger	L	.195	364	71	12	1	3	14	28	83	.256	.258
Throws Right	R	.202	397	80	14	2	8	31	34	102	.265	.307
Clement,Matt	L	.275	389	107	24	2	13	58	48	73	.354	.447
Throws Right	R	.244	349	85	20	0	5	29	20	73	.309	.344
Coffey,Todd	L	.337	86	29	9	0	1	16	3	6	.363	.477
Throws Right	R	.348	158	55	9	2	4	22	8	20	.392	.506
Colome,Jesus	L	.291	86	25	5	0	4	17	10	12	.365	.488
Throws Right	R	.276	105	29	9	0	3	11	8	16	.339	.448
Colon,Bartolo	L	.250	420	105	23	2	15	44	30	86	.300	.421
Throws Right	R	.258	427	110	19	3	11	42	13	71	.282	.393
Colon,Roman	L	.307	137	42	9	0	8	21	12	18	.358	.547
Throws Right	R	.280	143	40	5	1	9	23	9	29	.320	.517
Contreras,Jose	L	.231	386	89	10	3	12	40	48	74	.319	.365
Throws Right	R	.233	377	88	22	0	11	36	27	80	.295	.379
Cook,Aaron	L	.317	189	60	16	0	4	17	8	13	.347	.466
Throws Right	R	.281	146	41	7	0	4	14	8	11	.318	.411
Cooper,Brian	L	.190	21	4	1	0	0	2	5	1	.346	.238
Throws Right	R	.256	43	11	2	0	0	4	3	6	.304	.302

Pitcher	vs	Avg	AB	H	2B	3B	HR	RBI	BB	SO	OBP	Slg
Corcoran,Tim	L	.311	45	14	1	0	0	5	7	5	.404	.333
Throws Right	R	.128	39	5	0	0	1	4	5	8	.244	.205
Cordero,Chad	L	.192	146	28	2	0	3	11	13	31	.265	.267
Throws Right	R	.205	132	27	1	0	6	12	4	30	.228	.348
Cordero,Francisco	L	.250	144	36	11	0	2	19	20	40	.347	.368
Throws Right	R	.214	117	25	4	1	3	18	10	39	.282	.342
Cormier,Lance	L	.300	130	39	7	1	3	19	22	29	.410	.438
Throws Right	R	.273	172	47	14	1	4	27	21	34	.359	.436
Cormier,Rheal	L	.260	77	20	3	1	3	6	6	15	.329	.442
Throws Left	R	.321	112	36	11	0	6	22	10	19	.371	.580
Correia,Kevin	L	.311	103	32	8	2	4	8	23	16	.433	.544
Throws Right	R	.242	120	29	5	0	8	23	8	28	.311	.483
Cortes,David	L	.278	90	25	4	0	4	13	5	13	.313	.456
Throws Right	R	.229	109	25	3	1	5	14	5	23	.267	.413
Cotts,Neal	L	.206	102	21	7	0	0	14	9	33	.284	.275
Throws Left	R	.155	110	17	3	0	1	5	20	25	.288	.209
Crain,Jesse	L	.209	110	23	4	0	2	11	15	10	.307	.300
Throws Right	R	.225	169	38	2	0	4	18	14	15	.296	.308
Creek,Doug	L	.282	39	11	1	1	3	8	2	5	.317	.590
Throws Left	R	.302	53	16	2	1	4	10	5	13	.356	.604
Crowell,Jim	L	.500	4	2	1	0	0	2	0	1	.500	.750
Throws Left	R	.533	15	8	4	0	1	8	0	1	.563	1.000
Cruz,Juan	L	.283	60	17	3	2	1	6	14	12	.423	.450
Throws Right	R	.296	71	21	2	1	4	15	8	22	.383	.521
Darensbourg,Vic	L	.231	39	9	1	0	1	5	2	6	.262	.333
Throws Left	R	.326	46	15	4	0	1	4	5	3	.385	.478
Davies,Kyle	L	.264	174	46	11	0	4	15	27	32	.363	.397
Throws Right	R	.295	176	52	15	1	4	26	22	30	.377	.460
Davis,Doug	L	.259	174	45	8	2	7	22	7	41	.299	.448
Throws Left	R	.228	661	151	41	2	19	71	86	167	.317	.383
Davis,Jason	L	.193	57	11	0	1	0	6	9	11	.319	.228
Throws Right	R	.333	99	33	7	0	4	19	11	21	.398	.525
Davis,Kane	L	.158	19	3	0	0	1	3	4	3	.304	.316
Throws Right	R	.171	41	7	1	0	1	3	6	8	.277	.268
Day,Zach	L	.330	94	31	6	2	2	15	22	8	.457	.500
Throws Right	R	.300	100	30	4	0	4	19	10	15	.366	.460
de la Rosa,Jorge	L	.316	57	18	2	0	0	8	11	15	.420	.351
Throws Left	R	.275	109	30	12	1	1	16	27	27	.416	.431
de los Santos,Valerio	L	.324	37	12	3	1	1	10	3	8	.405	.541
Throws Left	R	.250	52	13	3	0	3	10	9	8	.361	.481
DeJean,Mike	L	.252	107	27	5	0	1	13	14	15	.347	.327
Throws Right	R	.257	136	35	9	1	2	18	16	37	.335	.382
Delcarmen,Manny	L	.267	15	4	0	0	0	0	4	3	.421	.267
Throws Right	R	.222	18	4	1	0	0	2	3	6	.364	.278
Demaria,Chris	L	.588	17	10	2	1	3	8	4	3	.667	1.353
Throws Right	R	.182	22	4	2	0	0	2	1	8	.217	.273
Dempster,Ryan	L	.278	144	40	7	0	2	19	29	39	.399	.368
Throws Right	R	.216	199	43	7	1	2	20	20	50	.300	.291
DePaula,Jorge	L	.313	16	5	3	0	1	4	1	1	.353	.688
Throws Right	R	.273	11	3	0	0	1	2	2	2	.385	.545
Dessens,Elmer	L	.243	111	27	6	0	4	14	11	17	.309	.405
Throws Right	R	.254	142	36	9	0	2	13	8	20	.294	.359
Devine,Joey	L	.429	7	3	0	0	1	4	1	0	.500	.857
Throws Right	R	.214	14	3	1	0	1	4	4	3	.389	.500
Dickey,R.A.	L	.192	52	10	1	2	2	9	8	7	.295	.404
Throws Right	R	.306	62	19	5	0	2	15	9	8	.411	.484
DiNardo,Lenny	L	.263	19	5	1	0	0	3	1	4	.300	.316
Throws Left	R	.222	36	8	1	0	1	5	4	11	.293	.333
Dingman,Craig	L	.208	48	10	1	0	2	6	4	13	.269	.354
Throws Right	R	.294	68	20	4	0	3	8	5	11	.351	.485
Dohmann,Scott	L	.328	58	19	1	3	2	13	11	10	.435	.552
Throws Right	R	.212	66	14	1	0	4	12	8	25	.297	.409
Dominguez,Juan	L	.241	137	33	6	1	6	17	16	21	.318	.431
Throws Right	R	.310	145	45	5	0	5	15	9	24	.357	.448
Donnelly,Brendan	L	.213	122	26	6	0	2	16	10	26	.278	.311
Throws Right	R	.274	124	34	4	0	7	12	9	27	.326	.476
Dotel,Octavio	L	.269	26	7	3	0	1	4	9	6	.457	.500
Throws Right	R	.107	28	3	1	0	1	4	2	10	.167	.250
Douglass,Sean	L	.315	178	56	10	3	9	35	18	24	.375	.556
Throws Right	R	.232	155	36	5	1	4	20	15	31	.301	.355
Downs,Scott	L	.234	107	25	1	0	3	10	9	28	.291	.327
Throws Left	R	.262	260	68	15	3	9	29	25	47	.338	.446
Drese,Ryan	L	.301	239	72	17	1	3	29	30	16	.385	.418
Throws Right	R	.320	281	90	24	1	5	45	16	30	.362	.466
Driskill,Travis	L	.000	1	0	0	0	0	0	0	1	.000	.000
Throws Right	R	.333	3	1	0	0	0	0	0	1	.333	.333

Pitchers vs. Left-Handed and Right-Handed Batters

Pitcher	vs	Avg	AB	H	2B	3B	HR	RBI	BB	SO	OBP	Slg
DuBose,Eric	L	.146	48	7	1	0	2	2	6	9	.241	.292
Throws Left	R	.313	67	21	3	0	2	12	13	8	.432	.448
Duchscherer,Justin	L	.225	138	31	5	0	4	16	7	42	.260	.348
Throws Right	R	.208	173	36	4	1	3	21	12	43	.266	.295
Duckworth,Brandon	L	.258	31	8	1	0	1	3	2	6	.314	.387
Throws Right	R	.421	38	16	4	0	3	16	5	4	.532	.763
Duke,Zach	L	.146	48	7	0	0	0	2	6	21	.241	.146
Throws Left	R	.273	264	72	17	1	3	17	17	37	.320	.379
Eaton,Adam	L	.297	246	73	20	2	8	32	26	41	.366	.492
Throws Right	R	.255	263	67	18	0	6	29	18	59	.305	.392
Eischen,Joey	L	.250	72	18	2	2	1	8	6	20	.325	.375
Throws Left	R	.254	63	16	1	0	0	3	13	10	.405	.270
Elarton,Scott	L	.275	327	90	17	2	14	44	21	56	.315	.468
Throws Right	R	.261	380	99	16	1	18	47	27	47	.315	.450
Eldred,Cal	L	.230	61	14	0	0	2	5	11	16	.347	.328
Throws Right	R	.284	74	21	4	0	1	7	7	13	.357	.378
Embree,Alan	L	.317	101	32	9	0	4	20	7	20	.360	.525
Throws Left	R	.278	108	30	12	1	6	23	7	18	.325	.574
Erickson,Scott	L	.295	112	33	4	1	4	18	13	6	.375	.455
Throws Right	R	.282	103	29	2	0	8	18	12	9	.364	.534
Escobar,Kelvim	L	.278	108	30	7	4	3	16	12	31	.355	.500
Throws Right	R	.138	109	15	5	0	1	1	9	32	.210	.211
Esposito,Mike	L	.432	37	16	2	2	1	8	6	4	.512	.676
Throws Right	R	.192	26	5	0	0	2	3	3	1	.276	.423
Estes,Shawn	L	.259	81	21	7	1	1	7	7	12	.333	.407
Throws Left	R	.284	391	111	23	2	14	51	38	51	.347	.460
Etherton,Seth	L	.289	38	11	3	1	3	6	4	6	.357	.658
Throws Right	R	.167	30	5	1	0	1	5	1	4	.188	.300
Eveland,Dana	L	.324	34	11	2	1	0	5	5	9	.410	.441
Throws Left	R	.315	92	29	3	3	2	15	13	14	.402	.478
Eyre,Scott	L	.182	99	18	6	0	0	5	11	30	.277	.242
Throws Left	R	.213	141	30	6	0	3	17	15	35	.292	.319
Falkenborg,Brian	L	.316	19	6	2	1	1	2	3	2	.409	.684
Throws Right	R	.367	30	11	1	0	1	8	2	8	.406	.500
Farnsworth,Kyle	L	.197	117	23	5	1	3	9	17	43	.301	.333
Throws Right	R	.165	127	21	1	0	2	14	10	44	.237	.220
Fassero,Jeff	L	.194	93	18	1	0	0	9	15	18	.300	.204
Throws Left	R	.296	250	74	16	2	7	43	16	42	.337	.460
Feldman,Scott	L	.308	13	4	0	0	0	0	1	0	.357	.308
Throws Right	R	.227	22	5	1	0	0	4	1	4	.261	.273
Field,Nate	L	.250	8	2	0	0	0	2	4	0	.500	.250
Throws Right	R	.500	22	11	1	1	1	9	1	4	.522	.773
Flores,Randy	L	.176	74	13	4	1	2	10	7	25	.253	.338
Throws Left	R	.300	80	24	2	0	3	13	6	18	.356	.438
Flores,Ron	L	.154	13	2	0	0	0	1	0	4	.154	.154
Throws Left	R	.286	21	6	0	0	1	1	0	2	.286	.429
Floyd,Gavin	L	.283	46	13	3	1	3	10	9	5	.393	.587
Throws Right	R	.283	60	17	7	0	2	18	7	12	.386	.500
Fogg,Josh	L	.340	315	107	18	3	15	45	30	34	.396	.559
Throws Right	R	.249	358	89	22	0	12	46	23	51	.301	.411
Foppert,Jesse	L	.200	15	3	0	0	0	1	4	2	.350	.200
Throws Right	R	.364	22	8	0	0	2	3	9	4	.545	.636
Fossum,Casey	L	.234	167	39	5	0	5	22	12	31	.283	.353
Throws Left	R	.278	472	131	19	4	16	68	48	97	.363	.436
Foster,John	L	.219	73	16	3	1	2	21	13	24	.345	.370
Throws Left	R	.204	54	11	1	0	1	4	6	8	.295	.278
Foulke,Keith	L	.255	106	27	6	0	3	17	12	25	.339	.396
Throws Right	R	.333	78	26	5	2	5	15	6	9	.402	.641
Fox,Chad	L	.308	13	4	2	0	1	6	2	4	.400	.692
Throws Right	R	.250	16	4	1	0	1	4	6	7	.435	.500
Francis,Jeff	L	.285	130	37	5	1	3	21	12	23	.342	.408
Throws Left	R	.317	603	191	45	4	23	92	58	105	.379	.519
Franco,John	L	.310	42	13	1	0	0	9	2	11	.356	.333
Throws Left	R	.400	25	10	3	0	0	4	7	5	.531	.520
Franklin,Ryan	L	.266	387	103	23	1	13	43	42	44	.338	.432
Throws Right	R	.295	370	109	14	3	15	53	20	49	.340	.470
Franklin,Wayne	L	.286	21	6	1	1	1	6	3	3	.385	.571
Throws Left	R	.200	25	5	1	0	0	2	5	7	.333	.240
Frasor,Jason	L	.236	123	29	3	0	1	10	9	32	.293	.285
Throws Right	R	.257	148	38	4	3	7	18	19	30	.347	.466
Fuentes,Brian	L	.164	73	12	3	0	0	4	8	35	.282	.205
Throws Left	R	.237	198	47	9	4	6	20	26	56	.342	.414
Fultz,Aaron	L	.220	82	18	6	1	1	8	7	13	.312	.354
Throws Left	R	.170	171	29	4	0	5	16	16	41	.243	.281
Gagne,Eric	L	.217	23	5	2	0	1	3	1	11	.250	.435
Throws Right	R	.185	27	5	1	0	1	1	2	11	.241	.333

Pitcher	vs	Avg	AB	H	2B	3B	HR	RBI	BB	SO	OBP	Slg
Gallo,Mike	L	.268	41	11	2	1	1	5	4	5	.340	.439
Throws Left	R	.226	31	7	1	0	0	1	6	7	.368	.258
Garcia,Freddy	L	.268	440	118	17	2	17	42	41	54	.330	.432
Throws Right	R	.249	430	107	25	3	9	42	19	92	.283	.384
Garcia,Jairo	L	.222	9	2	1	0	0	1	0	1	.222	.333
Throws Right	R	.000	2	0	0	0	0	0	1	0	.333	.000
Gardner,Lee	L	.500	16	8	2	1	2	8	1	1	.500	1.125
Throws Right	R	.222	18	4	0	0	0	1	1	3	.263	.222
Garland,Jon	L	.267	446	119	17	1	19	52	28	57	.308	.437
Throws Right	R	.242	384	93	20	1	7	37	19	58	.287	.354
Gassner,Dave	L	.250	8	2	0	1	0	0	0	2	.250	.500
Throws Left	R	.292	24	7	0	0	1	6	1	0	.308	.417
Gaudin,Chad	L	.481	27	13	1	0	3	8	3	4	.516	.852
Throws Right	R	.462	39	18	5	0	3	10	3	8	.512	.821
Geary,Geoff	L	.192	99	19	6	1	2	8	12	18	.279	.333
Throws Right	R	.294	119	35	5	1	3	25	9	24	.338	.429
German,Franklyn	L	.267	86	23	5	1	5	17	18	15	.413	.523
Throws Right	R	.294	136	40	3	1	2	12	16	23	.371	.375
Ginter,Matt	L	.349	63	22	4	0	4	13	5	9	.391	.603
Throws Right	R	.333	81	27	4	1	2	12	4	6	.379	.481
Glavine,Tom	L	.323	167	54	8	1	1	21	15	25	.383	.401
Throws Left	R	.267	648	173	35	4	11	65	46	80	.316	.384
Glover,Gary	L	.256	125	32	7	1	5	16	11	32	.321	.448
Throws Right	R	.318	132	42	11	2	5	20	9	26	.361	.545
Glynn,Ryan	L	.385	39	15	2	0	4	11	5	5	.455	.744
Throws Right	R	.250	36	9	0	0	1	8	2	10	.289	.333
Gobble,Jimmy	L	.310	71	22	3	0	5	11	6	17	.364	.563
Throws Left	R	.294	143	42	9	1	4	24	24	21	.396	.455
Gonzalez,Edgar	L	.667	3	2	1	0	1	2	1	1	.750	2.000
Throws Right	R	-	0	0	0	0	0	0	1	0	1.000	-
Gonzalez,Jeremi	L	.340	100	34	5	1	3	15	6	13	.377	.500
Throws Right	R	.246	122	30	8	3	4	22	10	15	.304	.459
Gonzalez,Mike	L	.152	66	10	1	0	0	5	10	27	.260	.167
Throws Left	R	.223	112	25	9	0	2	13	21	31	.348	.357
Good,Andy	L	.167	6	1	0	0	0	0	0	4	.167	.167
Throws Right	R	.231	13	3	0	0	1	3	1	3	.286	.462
Gordon,Tom	L	.187	134	25	4	1	2	14	18	39	.279	.276
Throws Right	R	.217	157	34	7	0	6	25	11	30	.266	.376
Gorzelanny,Tom	L	.000	6	0	0	0	0	0	0	2	.000	.000
Throws Left	R	.455	22	10	3	0	1	5	3	1	.520	.727
Gosling,Mike	L	.225	40	9	5	0	0	1	4	5	.295	.350
Throws Left	R	.333	93	31	12	1	2	15	15	9	.426	.548
Grabow,John	L	.219	73	16	2	0	4	10	8	18	.313	.411
Throws Left	R	.250	120	30	7	0	2	11	17	24	.343	.358
Graman,Alex	L	.750	4	3	1	0	1	4	0	0	.750	1.750
Throws Left	R	.000	3	0	0	0	0	0	2	0	.400	.000
Graves,Danny	L	.408	71	29	4	1	4	20	12	7	.500	.662
Throws Right	R	.303	99	30	8	0	5	24	8	13	.364	.535
Gregg,Kevin	L	.267	120	32	4	1	4	13	18	27	.362	.417
Throws Right	R	.279	136	38	6	0	4	21	11	25	.344	.412
Greinke,Zack	L	.340	377	128	29	5	13	71	31	42	.395	.546
Throws Right	R	.279	377	105	19	2	10	41	22	72	.331	.419
Greisinger,Seth	L	.556	9	5	1	0	1	1	0	1	.556	1.000
Throws Right	R	.182	11	2	1	0	0	1	1	1	.250	.273
Grilli,Jason	L	.222	27	6	2	1	0	3	1	2	.241	.370
Throws Right	R	.286	28	8	1	0	1	3	5	3	.394	.429
Grimsley,Jason	L	.324	34	11	2	0	2	6	5	1	.400	.559
Throws Right	R	.265	49	13	2	1	3	11	4	9	.321	.531
Groom,Buddy	L	.244	78	19	2	1	2	10	4	9	.280	.372
Throws Left	R	.356	90	32	7	2	3	14	8	11	.417	.578
Gryboski,Kevin	L	.227	44	10	0	1	0	7	10	6	.370	.273
Throws Right	R	.383	81	31	5	2	1	25	10	4	.458	.531
Guardado,Eddie	L	.231	65	15	5	0	2	10	0	14	.231	.400
Throws Left	R	.242	153	37	8	0	5	15	15	34	.306	.392
Guerrier,Matt	L	.279	104	29	5	1	1	6	15	23	.375	.375
Throws Right	R	.247	170	42	8	1	5	22	9	23	.291	.394
Guthrie,Jeremy	L	.375	16	6	1	0	0	1	0	2	.375	.438
Throws Right	R	.333	9	3	1	0	2	3	2	1	.417	1.111
Halama,John	L	.329	82	27	5	2	1	17	4	18	.404	.476
Throws Left	R	.277	188	52	14	3	5	28	13	19	.322	.463
Halladay,Roy	L	.217	277	60	8	0	4	16	13	50	.254	.289
Throws Right	R	.235	247	58	10	1	7	21	5	58	.266	.368
Halsey,Brad	L	.267	135	36	8	0	3	18	6	22	.308	.393
Throws Left	R	.309	501	155	33	3	17	66	33	60	.357	.489
Hammond,Chris	L	.167	72	12	3	0	2	13	4	14	.205	.292
Throws Left	R	.258	151	39	11	0	7	22	10	20	.313	.470

Pitchers vs. Left-Handed and Right-Handed Batters

Pitcher	vs	Avg	AB	H	2B	3B	HR	RBI	BB	SO	OBP	Slg
Hampton,Mike	L	.338	65	22	4	0	3	10	5	9	.380	.538
Throws Left	R	.263	198	52	13	0	2	14	13	18	.308	.359
Hamulack,Tim	L	.429	7	3	1	0	0	3	0	1	.429	.571
Throws Left	R	.800	5	4	0	0	3	6	1	1	.714	2.600
Hancock,Josh	L	.111	18	2	0	0	0	1	0	3	.111	.111
Throws Right	R	.257	35	9	3	0	1	4	1	2	.278	.429
Hansen,Craig	L	.600	5	3	0	0	0	1	0	0	.500	.600
Throws Right	R	.333	9	3	1	0	1	2	1	3	.400	.778
Harang,Aaron	L	.253	371	94	27	3	8	44	20	73	.291	.407
Throws Right	R	.279	441	123	25	5	14	46	31	90	.335	.454
Harden,Rich	L	.179	223	40	10	1	2	10	29	67	.276	.260
Throws Right	R	.221	240	53	10	0	5	22	14	54	.266	.325
Haren,Danny	L	.252	416	105	17	2	13	52	34	84	.305	.397
Throws Right	R	.258	414	107	23	2	13	38	19	79	.301	.418
Harikkala,Tim	L	.370	27	10	3	0	2	7	2	4	.414	.704
Throws Right	R	.240	25	6	3	0	1	6	2	3	.296	.480
Harper,Travis	L	.292	113	33	5	2	8	27	14	16	.364	.584
Throws Right	R	.313	176	55	10	2	6	27	10	24	.353	.494
Harris,Jeff	L	.180	100	18	5	0	2	13	13	15	.276	.290
Throws Right	R	.294	102	30	2	0	7	16	7	10	.351	.520
Harville,Chad	L	.244	82	20	4	0	4	17	13	18	.347	.439
Throws Right	R	.267	86	23	5	0	4	11	14	18	.394	.465
Hasegawa,Shigetoshi	L	.281	121	34	5	1	0	16	3	12	.302	.339
Throws Right	R	.239	134	32	5	0	4	15	13	18	.311	.366
Hawkins,LaTroy	L	.228	101	23	6	1	2	16	10	24	.295	.366
Throws Right	R	.297	118	35	5	0	5	14	14	19	.371	.466
Heilman,Aaron	L	.209	182	38	6	0	3	17	25	46	.314	.291
Throws Right	R	.234	209	49	4	1	3	20	12	60	.284	.306
Helling,Rick	L	.219	73	16	2	0	1	9	10	12	.310	.288
Throws Right	R	.219	105	23	5	0	1	6	8	30	.287	.295
Hendrickson,Mark	L	.258	178	46	11	1	3	22	10	28	.302	.382
Throws Left	R	.328	552	181	45	5	21	88	39	61	.369	.542
Henn,Sean	L	.429	14	6	0	0	2	5	1	1	.467	.857
Throws Left	R	.333	36	12	5	0	1	7	10	2	.478	.556
Hennessey,Brad	L	.320	194	62	15	2	7	35	26	28	.395	.526
Throws Right	R	.244	266	65	12	1	8	22	26	36	.321	.387
Hensley,Clay	L	.275	91	25	4	0	0	8	12	13	.359	.319
Throws Right	R	.103	78	8	1	1	0	6	5	15	.153	.141
Heredia,Felix	L	.000	2	0	0	0	0	0	1	2	.500	.000
Throws Left	R	.167	6	1	0	0	0	0	0	0	.167	.167
Herges,Matt	L	.256	43	11	5	2	1	10	6	5	.333	.535
Throws Right	R	.333	72	24	6	1	5	18	6	4	.392	.653
Hermanson,Dustin	L	.240	100	24	8	1	2	9	12	16	.321	.400
Throws Right	R	.206	107	22	3	1	2	10	5	17	.248	.308
Hernandez,Felix	L	.182	148	27	6	0	1	7	14	40	.255	.243
Throws Right	R	.224	152	34	3	0	4	17	9	37	.272	.322
Hernandez,Livan	L	.290	490	142	17	1	16	57	47	73	.358	.427
Throws Right	R	.278	454	126	31	5	9	54	37	74	.336	.427
Hernandez,Orlando	L	.291	268	78	18	4	9	39	28	33	.371	.489
Throws Right	R	.257	230	59	12	1	9	31	22	58	.329	.435
Hernandez,Roberto	L	.244	123	30	6	0	4	16	15	32	.321	.390
Throws Right	R	.213	127	27	4	0	1	9	13	29	.296	.268
Hernandez,Runelvys	L	.261	287	75	21	3	8	41	45	36	.362	.439
Throws Right	R	.290	335	97	19	3	10	53	25	52	.345	.454
Hill,Rich	L	.227	22	5	1	0	0	7	7	4	.414	.273
Throws Left	R	.270	74	20	5	0	3	12	10	17	.365	.459
Hoffman,Trevor	L	.298	104	31	6	1	0	8	7	25	.342	.375
Throws Right	R	.179	117	21	5	1	3	14	5	29	.214	.316
Horgan,Joe	L	.231	13	3	1	0	0	2	2	3	.375	.308
Throws Left	R	.667	24	16	7	0	0	12	2	2	.667	.958
Houlton,D.J.	L	.314	210	66	16	2	8	31	25	36	.387	.524
Throws Right	R	.271	292	79	20	1	13	43	27	54	.343	.479
Howell,J.P.	L	.213	47	10	2	0	1	7	7	10	.309	.319
Throws Left	R	.274	230	63	17	0	8	37	32	44	.374	.452
Howry,Bob	L	.180	89	16	4	0	1	3	6	21	.232	.258
Throws Right	R	.198	167	33	4	1	3	14	10	27	.240	.287
Hudson,Luke	L	.255	141	36	7	1	5	21	24	27	.372	.426
Throws Right	R	.278	169	47	16	1	9	34	26	26	.394	.544
Hudson,Tim	L	.285	396	113	23	3	9	35	43	54	.365	.427
Throws Right	R	.240	337	81	14	1	11	40	22	61	.291	.386
Hughes,Travis	L	.313	16	5	0	0	2	3	3	3	.421	.688
Throws Right	R	.342	38	13	0	0	2	6	5	5	.432	.500
Ishii,Kazuhisa	L	.208	72	15	2	0	5	16	10	16	.305	.444
Throws Left	R	.271	266	72	21	1	8	39	39	37	.367	.447
Isringhausen,Jason	L	.168	95	16	1	0	1	7	14	27	.279	.211
Throws Right	R	.229	118	27	4	1	3	6	13	24	.305	.356

Pitcher	vs	Avg	AB	H	2B	3B	HR	RBI	BB	SO	OBP	Slg
Jackson,Edwin	L	.333	42	14	4	1	0	10	6	3	.400	.476
Throws Right	R	.236	72	17	3	0	2	9	11	10	.345	.361
James,Chuck	L	.250	4	1	1	0	0	0	3	1	.571	.500
Throws Left	R	.188	16	3	0	0	0	1	0	4	.188	.188
Jarvis,Kevin	L	.333	6	2	0	0	1	5	3	0	.600	.833
Throws Right	R	.167	6	1	0	0	0	0	0	2	.286	.167
Jenks,Bobby	L	.105	57	6	3	0	1	6	7	21	.203	.211
Throws Right	R	.298	94	28	7	0	2	11	8	29	.359	.436
Jennings,Jason	L	.269	242	65	15	1	7	32	44	36	.380	.426
Throws Right	R	.279	233	65	17	0	4	34	18	39	.341	.403
Jensen,Ryan	L	.269	52	14	3	1	3	11	5	12	.328	.538
Throws Right	R	.327	52	17	1	1	1	7	2	6	.368	.442
Johnson,Jason	L	.310	426	132	26	3	13	54	34	55	.362	.477
Throws Right	R	.258	391	101	11	1	10	47	15	38	.288	.368
Johnson,Josh	L	.407	27	11	1	0	0	1	7	6	.529	.444
Throws Right	R	.000	16	0	0	0	0	0	3	4	.200	.000
Johnson,Randy	L	.185	162	30	6	1	1	11	7	45	.244	.253
Throws Left	R	.257	689	177	32	2	31	82	40	166	.302	.444
Johnson,Tyler	L	.400	5	2	0	0	0	0	2	2	.571	.400
Throws Left	R	.200	5	1	0	0	0	1	1	2	.333	.200
Johnston,Mike	L	.500	2	1	0	0	1	2	0	1	.500	2.000
Throws Left	R	.600	5	3	0	0	1	2	0	1	.600	1.200
Jones,Greg	L	.444	9	4	1	0	1	3	1	2	.500	.889
Throws Right	R	.231	13	3	0	0	1	1	1	4	.286	.462
Jones,Todd	L	.231	134	31	3	1	1	10	7	30	.273	.291
Throws Right	R	.229	131	30	3	0	1	8	7	32	.279	.275
Journell,Jimmy	L	1.000	3	3	0	0	0	2	2	0	1.000	1.000
Throws Right	R	.200	15	3	1	0	1	4	3	5	.333	.467
Julio,Jorge	L	.281	135	38	6	0	9	22	11	26	.331	.526
Throws Right	R	.257	148	38	4	0	5	17	13	32	.323	.385
Karnuth,Jason	L	.000	4	0	0	0	0	0	0	0	.000	.000
Throws Right	R	.667	3	2	1	0	0	2	0	0	.667	1.000
Karsay,Steve	L	.333	45	15	1	0	1	9	4	8	.380	.422
Throws Right	R	.404	52	21	2	1	1	11	3	6	.429	.538
Kazmir,Scott	L	.174	149	26	1	0	1	12	17	49	.256	.201
Throws Left	R	.268	544	146	40	5	11	67	83	125	.371	.421
Keisler,Randy	L	.309	68	21	2	0	5	20	8	9	.385	.559
Throws Left	R	.264	163	43	5	2	5	22	20	34	.344	.411
Kennedy,Joe	L	.265	132	35	6	0	4	24	11	27	.329	.402
Throws Left	R	.320	491	157	35	2	16	79	53	70	.388	.497
Kensing,Logan	L	.636	11	7	3	0	1	1	1	0	.667	1.182
Throws Right	R	.250	16	4	1	0	1	8	2	4	.316	.500
Kida,Masao	L	.500	2	1	0	0	0	0	0	0	.500	.500
Throws Right	R	.167	6	1	0	0	1	1	0	0	.167	.667
Kim,Byung-Hyun	L	.308	276	85	19	2	8	43	37	43	.406	.478
Throws Right	R	.244	291	71	21	2	9	38	34	72	.326	.423
Kim,Sunny	L	.279	147	41	4	1	2	18	6	21	.308	.361
Throws Right	R	.304	184	56	13	0	8	29	15	34	.361	.505
King,Ray	L	.244	86	21	2	1	2	19	6	16	.313	.360
Throws Left	R	.352	71	25	4	2	2	9	10	7	.432	.549
Kinney,Matt	L	.471	17	8	2	0	0	2	3	1	.550	.588
Throws Right	R	.333	30	10	1	0	2	6	3	2	.412	.567
Kline,Steve	L	.317	101	32	5	0	5	14	8	22	.364	.515
Throws Left	R	.209	129	27	3	0	6	19	22	14	.322	.372
Kolb,Danny	L	.336	110	37	8	1	2	17	18	22	.431	.482
Throws Right	R	.323	127	41	4	0	3	25	11	17	.377	.425
Koo,Dae-Sung	L	.239	46	11	2	0	1	12	9	14	.379	.348
Throws Left	R	.262	42	11	4	0	1	8	4	9	.313	.429
Koplove,Mike	L	.256	78	20	4	1	4	15	15	15	.385	.487
Throws Right	R	.257	109	28	4	1	2	28	5	13	.308	.367
Koronka,John	L	.385	13	5	1	0	0	2	0	3	.385	.462
Throws Left	R	.259	54	14	1	0	2	8	8	7	.355	.389
Kuo,Hong-Chih	L	.385	13	5	3	0	1	2	3	5	.500	.846
Throws Left	R	.000	8	0	0	0	0	0	2	5	.200	.000
Lackey,John	L	.274	401	110	19	0	6	43	35	86	.338	.367
Throws Right	R	.241	406	98	24	1	7	38	36	113	.313	.357
Lawrence,Brian	L	.300	360	108	29	2	10	37	31	36	.366	.475
Throws Right	R	.249	414	103	21	3	8	54	26	73	.295	.372
League,Brandon	L	.333	72	24	4	0	5	20	4	7	.377	.597
Throws Right	R	.269	67	18	3	0	3	10	16	10	.412	.448
Ledezma,Wil	L	.352	54	19	1	2	2	17	3	6	.379	.556
Throws Left	R	.286	147	42	8	0	8	24	21	24	.376	.503
Lee,Cliff	L	.293	188	55	13	2	6	20	8	35	.321	.479
Throws Left	R	.237	586	139	33	1	16	64	44	108	.287	.379
Lehr,Justin	L	.207	58	12	2	0	0	1	10	9	.324	.241
Throws Right	R	.270	74	20	10	0	4	15	8	14	.345	.568

Pitchers vs. Left-Handed and Right-Handed Batters

Pitcher	vs	Avg	AB	H	2B	3B	HR	RBI	BB	SO	OBP	Slg
Leicester,Jon	L	.462	13	6	1	0	1	1	5	3	.611	.769
Throws Right	R	.238	21	5	1	0	1	7	4	4	.407	.429
Leiter,Al	L	.250	156	39	8	0	3	31	12	31	.312	.359
Throws Left	R	.295	390	115	25	3	10	61	86	66	.429	.451
Lerew,Anthony	L	.267	15	4	2	0	1	3	2	1	.353	.600
Throws Right	R	.313	16	5	2	0	0	4	3	4	.421	.438
Levine,Al	L	.417	24	10	3	0	1	8	2	0	.462	.667
Throws Right	R	.261	23	6	0	0	1	4	2	4	.320	.391
Lidge,Brad	L	.244	131	32	7	0	1	13	11	38	.313	.321
Throws Right	R	.202	129	26	4	0	4	13	12	65	.273	.326
Lidle,Cory	L	.289	339	98	23	5	6	40	21	58	.329	.440
Throws Right	R	.289	388	112	24	2	12	52	19	63	.327	.454
Lieber,Jon	L	.301	429	129	25	4	17	57	26	62	.341	.497
Throws Right	R	.224	419	94	14	1	16	45	15	87	.255	.377
Ligtenberg,Kerry	L	.250	16	4	2	0	1	7	1	1	.294	.563
Throws Right	R	.429	28	12	4	0	3	9	3	4	.484	.893
Lilly,Ted	L	.336	134	45	8	2	4	18	10	26	.381	.515
Throws Left	R	.248	363	90	16	0	19	56	48	70	.337	.449
Lima,Jose	L	.302	324	98	28	3	17	65	37	29	.379	.565
Throws Right	R	.324	374	121	30	2	14	66	24	51	.367	.527
Linebrink,Scott	L	.195	133	26	5	2	2	13	10	38	.252	.308
Throws Right	R	.223	130	29	4	1	2	11	13	32	.294	.315
Liriano,Francisco	L	.222	18	4	1	0	1	3	2	10	.300	.444
Throws Left	R	.221	68	15	1	1	3	10	5	23	.274	.397
Liriano,Pedro	L	.400	15	6	3	1	1	6	0	0	.400	.933
Throws Right	R	.235	17	4	1	0	2	7	6	6	.458	.647
Loaiza,Esteban	L	.285	425	121	26	2	7	34	38	88	.346	.405
Throws Right	R	.255	415	106	16	0	11	48	17	85	.287	.373
Loe,Kameron	L	.284	169	48	9	1	5	21	18	12	.354	.438
Throws Right	R	.223	184	41	13	0	2	17	13	33	.278	.326
Lohse,Kyle	L	.291	323	94	18	5	10	36	23	44	.343	.471
Throws Right	R	.305	383	117	14	1	12	45	21	42	.346	.441
Looper,Braden	L	.336	116	39	8	1	6	24	13	8	.408	.578
Throws Right	R	.210	124	26	4	0	1	5	9	19	.285	.266
Lopez,Aquilino	L	.346	26	9	3	0	1	3	4	7	.433	.577
Throws Right	R	.184	38	7	1	0	1	4	3	15	.244	.289
Lopez,Javier	L	.278	36	10	3	0	1	10	5	7	.366	.444
Throws Left	R	.421	38	16	8	0	1	16	6	5	.511	.711
Lopez,Rodrigo	L	.288	459	132	28	2	13	57	30	59	.335	.442
Throws Right	R	.262	381	100	24	4	15	58	33	59	.325	.465
Lowe,Derek	L	.296	460	136	25	1	17	64	36	68	.349	.465
Throws Right	R	.219	397	87	16	0	11	37	19	78	.257	.343
Lowry,Noah	L	.213	178	38	8	0	3	13	22	43	.309	.309
Throws Left	R	.259	598	155	22	5	18	64	54	129	.324	.403
Lyon,Brandon	L	.317	63	20	4	0	3	10	4	7	.362	.524
Throws Right	R	.364	66	24	5	0	3	18	6	10	.425	.576
MacDougal,Mike	L	.240	121	29	8	1	3	14	14	29	.328	.397
Throws Right	R	.270	148	40	8	0	3	17	10	43	.319	.385
Maddux,Greg	L	.283	364	103	25	0	11	48	19	57	.324	.442
Throws Right	R	.270	504	136	25	2	18	56	17	79	.295	.435
Madritsch,Bobby	L	.250	4	1	0	0	0	0	0	1	.250	.250
Throws Left	R	.231	13	3	1	0	1	3	1	0	.286	.538
Madson,Ryan	L	.292	144	42	11	1	7	23	16	35	.364	.528
Throws Right	R	.233	180	42	8	0	4	25	9	44	.282	.344
Mahay,Ron	L	.302	63	19	2	0	5	14	4	13	.338	.571
Throws Left	R	.322	87	28	3	0	3	11	12	17	.404	.460
Maholm,Paul	L	.087	23	2	0	0	0	0	0	5	.125	.087
Throws Left	R	.232	125	29	8	0	2	8	17	21	.333	.344
Maine,John	L	.227	88	20	3	0	5	19	20	14	.364	.432
Throws Right	R	.275	69	19	3	0	3	8	4	10	.324	.449
Majewski,Gary	L	.236	157	37	11	1	2	23	27	29	.353	.357
Throws Right	R	.259	166	43	6	1	0	13	10	21	.315	.307
Mantei,Matt	L	.293	41	12	1	0	1	7	11	8	.473	.390
Throws Right	R	.200	55	11	6	0	0	5	13	14	.371	.309
Marcum,Shaun	L	.176	17	3	1	0	0	0	0	2	.176	.235
Throws Right	R	.273	11	3	1	0	0	0	4	2	.467	.364
Maroth,Mike	L	.278	209	58	11	2	3	22	9	43	.306	.392
Throws Left	R	.292	606	177	22	2	27	92	42	72	.342	.469
Marquis,Jason	L	.238	340	81	9	0	11	36	41	43	.321	.362
Throws Right	R	.280	447	125	28	3	18	58	28	57	.326	.477
Marte,Damaso	L	.267	90	24	7	0	1	11	15	32	.389	.378
Throws Left	R	.244	86	21	5	0	4	8	18	22	.375	.442
Martin,Tom	L	.800	5	4	2	0	1	1	2	0	.857	1.800
Throws Left	R	.286	7	2	1	0	0	0	0	0	.286	.429
Martinez,Pedro	L	.215	391	84	23	1	9	33	35	93	.281	.348
Throws Right	R	.192	390	75	14	3	10	35	12	115	.221	.321

Pitcher	vs	Avg	AB	H	2B	3B	HR	RBI	BB	SO	OBP	Slg
Mateo,Julio	L	.209	153	32	4	4	3	12	11	20	.261	.346
Throws Right	R	.261	180	47	10	0	9	20	6	32	.309	.467
Matthews,Mike	L	.400	10	4	0	0	0	1	1	1	.417	.400
Throws Left	R	.455	11	5	3	0	0	4	3	1	.533	.727
May,Darrell	L	.226	62	14	5	1	1	11	3	11	.258	.387
Throws Left	R	.341	214	73	16	3	13	41	20	24	.396	.626
Mays,Joe	L	.273	319	87	18	3	12	48	20	29	.317	.461
Throws Right	R	.364	319	116	26	1	11	52	21	30	.404	.555
McBride,Macay	L	.172	29	5	1	0	0	2	2	15	.226	.207
Throws Left	R	.433	30	13	1	0	0	5	5	7	.500	.467
McCarthy,Brandon	L	.205	122	25	8	0	3	13	9	28	.258	.344
Throws Right	R	.276	134	37	5	1	10	14	8	20	.326	.552
McClung,Seth	L	.294	228	67	15	3	15	51	31	49	.379	.583
Throws Right	R	.197	198	39	9	0	5	23	31	43	.318	.318
McGowan,Dustin	L	.243	74	18	4	1	5	10	10	12	.345	.527
Throws Right	R	.301	103	31	6	0	2	18	7	22	.364	.417
Meadows,Brian	L	.301	103	31	9	0	2	16	7	14	.333	.447
Throws Right	R	.279	190	53	15	2	6	31	14	30	.321	.474
Meche,Gil	L	.266	308	82	12	0	12	42	36	56	.339	.422
Throws Right	R	.285	249	71	17	2	6	36	36	27	.378	.442
Mecir,Jim	L	.226	62	14	2	0	1	12	10	19	.364	.306
Throws Right	R	.263	95	25	3	0	1	7	7	15	.317	.326
Medders,Brandon	L	.239	46	11	0	0	0	0	5	14	.314	.239
Throws Right	R	.161	62	10	2	0	2	8	6	17	.239	.290
Mendoza,Ramiro	L	.000	1	0	0	0	0	0	0	0	.000	.000
Throws Right	R	.500	4	2	1	0	1	3	0	1	.500	1.500
Mercker,Kent	L	.225	102	23	3	2	2	12	6	26	.286	.353
Throws Left	R	.304	135	41	13	1	6	24	13	19	.362	.548
Meredith,Cla	L	.500	8	4	1	1	0	3	2	0	.600	.875
Throws Right	R	.400	5	2	1	0	1	5	2	0	.625	1.200
Mesa,Jose	L	.309	97	30	5	0	4	18	15	13	.397	.485
Throws Right	R	.265	117	31	6	0	3	17	11	24	.331	.393
Messenger,Randy	L	.271	59	16	2	1	1	9	16	11	.421	.390
Throws Right	R	.274	84	23	7	0	4	23	14	18	.370	.500
Miceli,Danny	L	.303	33	10	2	0	0	4	5	8	.395	.364
Throws Right	R	.243	37	9	2	0	1	7	8	11	.391	.378
Miller,Justin	L	.333	3	1	0	0	1	2	0	2	.333	1.333
Throws Right	R	.444	9	4	0	0	2	4	0	0	.444	1.111
Miller,Matt	L	.194	36	7	1	0	0	1	6	4	.326	.222
Throws Right	R	.221	68	15	3	0	1	7	4	19	.280	.309
Miller,Trever	L	.267	86	23	7	0	2	29	15	20	.393	.419
Throws Left	R	.289	76	22	2	0	2	9	14	15	.407	.395
Miller,Wade	L	.255	196	50	13	2	3	28	23	43	.336	.388
Throws Right	R	.282	163	46	10	3	5	21	24	21	.374	.472
Millwood,Kevin	L	.269	368	99	21	1	10	36	32	83	.325	.413
Throws Right	R	.227	365	83	15	2	10	31	20	63	.274	.362
Milton,Eric	L	.284	155	44	10	1	5	19	8	30	.329	.458
Throws Left	R	.307	629	193	45	6	35	111	44	93	.353	.564
Mitre,Sergio	L	.294	102	30	2	1	5	12	13	8	.381	.480
Throws Right	R	.235	136	32	5	0	6	21	10	29	.289	.404
Moehler,Brian	L	.319	332	106	19	2	9	43	22	53	.366	.470
Throws Right	R	.307	300	92	25	0	7	30	20	42	.351	.460
Morris,Matt	L	.279	351	98	20	3	11	49	20	58	.320	.447
Throws Right	R	.273	406	111	24	0	11	42	17	59	.310	.414
Mota,Guillermo	L	.243	111	27	7	3	4	26	20	23	.356	.468
Throws Right	R	.262	145	38	17	2	1	23	12	37	.318	.428
Moyer,Jamie	L	.297	219	65	18	0	4	27	8	33	.332	.434
Throws Left	R	.277	577	160	29	5	19	68	44	69	.330	.444
Mulder,Mark	L	.201	139	28	7	0	3	8	15	30	.288	.317
Throws Left	R	.289	637	184	40	1	16	76	55	81	.350	.430
Mulholland,Terry	L	.202	84	17	3	1	1	8	4	12	.239	.298
Throws Left	R	.321	137	44	11	1	5	23	13	6	.386	.526
Munter,Scott	L	.353	51	18	2	1	0	3	6	5	.431	.431
Throws Right	R	.239	92	22	1	1	1	9	6	6	.283	.304
Mussina,Mike	L	.282	362	102	17	0	13	48	26	84	.334	.436
Throws Right	R	.286	339	97	19	1	10	41	21	58	.332	.437
Myers,Brett	L	.241	427	103	18	2	16	44	44	106	.317	.405
Throws Right	R	.233	387	90	26	0	15	46	24	102	.288	.416
Myers,Mike	L	.158	95	15	2	0	1	9	5	18	.198	.211
Throws Left	R	.385	39	15	4	0	2	9	8	3	.510	.641
Nageotte,Clint	L	.500	6	3	1	0	0	1	1	0	.571	.667
Throws Right	R	.273	11	3	1	0	0	4	0	1	.333	.364
Nathan,Joe	L	.158	120	19	3	0	4	12	15	49	.248	.283
Throws Right	R	.206	131	27	8	0	1	7	7	45	.246	.290
Neal,Blaine	L	.447	38	17	2	0	2	13	3	1	.465	.658
Throws Right	R	.321	56	18	1	0	2	9	9	10	.409	.446

Pitchers vs. Left-Handed and Right-Handed Batters

Pitcher	vs	Avg	AB	H	2B	3B	HR	RBI	BB	SO	OBP	Slg
Nelson,Jeff	L	.342	38	13	3	0	2	8	6	7	.457	.579
Throws Right	R	.196	97	19	2	0	1	8	16	27	.319	.247
Nippert,Dustin	L	.182	22	4	2	0	0	1	9	6	.419	.273
Throws Right	R	.188	32	6	2	0	1	6	4	5	.297	.344
Nitkowski,C.J.	L	.571	7	4	1	0	0	1	2	2	.667	.714
Throws Left	R	.143	7	1	1	0	0	1	0	0	.143	.286
Nomo,Hideo	L	.272	202	55	9	1	5	29	29	32	.366	.401
Throws Right	R	.355	203	72	16	2	11	46	22	27	.407	.616
Novoa,Roberto	L	.221	68	15	3	0	2	8	12	24	.338	.353
Throws Right	R	.291	110	32	7	3	2	15	13	23	.366	.464
Nunez,Franklin	L	.333	6	2	0	0	0	2	2	0	.500	.333
Throws Right	R	.250	12	3	0	0	0	1	2	2	.357	.250
Nunez,Leo	L	.374	91	34	7	2	4	29	10	9	.431	.626
Throws Right	R	.298	131	39	8	0	5	24	8	23	.350	.473
Obermueller,Wes	L	.262	103	27	1	0	3	15	19	11	.381	.359
Throws Right	R	.307	153	47	11	1	4	21	17	22	.383	.471
Ohka,Tomo	L	.258	333	86	16	2	7	32	28	40	.314	.381
Throws Right	R	.277	372	103	26	3	15	42	27	58	.329	.484
Ohman,Will	L	.173	81	14	0	0	4	8	10	26	.272	.321
Throws Left	R	.231	78	18	2	0	2	11	14	19	.362	.333
Olsen,Scott	L	.333	18	6	0	0	2	4	1	3	.368	.667
Throws Left	R	.238	63	15	2	0	3	5	9	18	.333	.413
Ortiz,Ramon	L	.288	320	92	11	4	19	54	28	41	.346	.525
Throws Right	R	.315	362	114	30	2	15	52	23	55	.359	.533
Ortiz,Russ	L	.329	246	81	12	8	6	30	31	17	.403	.516
Throws Right	R	.296	223	66	19	0	12	52	34	29	.388	.543
Orvella,Chad	L	.218	78	17	6	0	1	4	15	14	.344	.333
Throws Right	R	.265	113	30	9	0	3	23	8	29	.310	.425
Osoria,Franquelis	L	.392	51	20	1	1	2	15	3	4	.426	.569
Throws Right	R	.140	57	8	0	0	1	3	5	11	.246	.193
Osuna,Antonio	L	.000	1	0	0	0	0	1	5	0	.714	.000
Throws Right	R	.643	14	9	1	0	2	9	2	0	.688	1.143
Oswalt,Roy	L	.280	440	123	23	6	9	46	19	80	.313	.420
Throws Right	R	.246	487	120	25	2	9	33	29	104	.293	.361
Otsuka,Akinori	L	.207	121	25	4	0	2	10	20	35	.329	.289
Throws Right	R	.263	114	30	7	1	1	12	14	25	.344	.368
Oxspring,Chris	L	.222	18	4	1	0	1	4	4	6	.364	.444
Throws Right	R	.227	22	5	0	0	1	5	2	5	.269	.364
Padilla,Juan	L	.153	59	9	2	0	0	4	8	9	.254	.186
Throws Right	R	.203	74	15	2	1	0	3	5	8	.272	.257
Padilla,Vicente	L	.297	283	84	25	0	18	51	43	37	.395	.576
Throws Right	R	.222	279	62	19	0	4	24	31	66	.308	.333
Papelbon,Jonathan	L	.190	58	11	2	0	2	4	12	14	.338	.328
Throws Right	R	.319	69	22	6	0	2	7	5	20	.382	.493
Park,Chan Ho	L	.305	328	100	23	1	9	51	45	61	.395	.463
Throws Right	R	.279	287	80	17	2	2	35	35	52	.366	.373
Parrish,John	L	.200	30	6	1	0	1	4	5	10	.314	.333
Throws Left	R	.342	38	13	3	0	0	6	12	15	.500	.421
Patterson,John	L	.231	373	86	15	0	9	29	34	86	.298	.343
Throws Right	R	.236	365	86	18	1	10	34	31	99	.299	.373
Pavano,Carl	L	.335	215	72	14	2	9	27	13	19	.380	.544
Throws Right	R	.294	194	57	6	3	8	29	5	37	.324	.479
Peavy,Jake	L	.223	359	80	23	5	9	28	28	100	.284	.390
Throws Right	R	.212	387	82	18	2	9	33	22	116	.258	.339
Penn,Hayden	L	.289	83	24	6	2	0	14	11	9	.372	.410
Throws Right	R	.301	73	22	5	0	6	11	10	9	.386	.616
Penny,Brad	L	.263	334	88	15	5	5	24	24	44	.315	.383
Throws Right	R	.276	352	97	21	2	12	46	17	78	.312	.449
Peralta,Joel	L	.273	55	15	4	0	4	14	9	7	.369	.564
Throws Right	R	.178	73	13	3	0	2	4	5	23	.231	.301
Percival,Troy	L	.173	52	9	1	0	4	9	9	10	.306	.423
Throws Right	R	.250	40	10	2	0	3	7	2	10	.295	.525
Perez,Odalis	L	.256	86	22	0	1	2	12	6	23	.304	.349
Throws Left	R	.264	330	87	20	3	11	40	22	51	.309	.442
Perez,Oliver	L	.313	64	20	3	1	6	11	12	18	.443	.672
Throws Left	R	.255	322	82	14	0	17	50	58	79	.370	.457
Perisho,Matt	L	.346	26	9	4	0	1	8	9	4	.500	.615
Throws Left	R	.167	24	4	2	0	0	1	2	6	.259	.250
Pettitte,Andy	L	.200	180	36	7	1	2	11	6	38	.230	.283
Throws Left	R	.239	637	152	30	3	15	51	35	133	.279	.366
Phelps,Tommy	L	.300	40	12	4	0	1	7	4	7	.364	.475
Throws Left	R	.250	52	13	4	0	1	6	8	7	.371	.385
Pineiro,Joel	L	.295	400	118	21	2	7	47	32	61	.344	.410
Throws Right	R	.305	347	106	22	1	16	65	24	46	.358	.513
Politte,Cliff	L	.182	77	14	1	0	3	6	8	18	.267	.312
Throws Right	R	.181	155	28	9	1	4	17	13	39	.247	.329

Pitcher	vs	Avg	AB	H	2B	3B	HR	RBI	BB	SO	OBP	Slg
Ponson,Sidney	L	.360	283	102	19	0	8	43	33	33	.422	.512
Throws Right	R	.299	251	75	13	0	8	45	15	35	.339	.446
Powell,Jay	L	.000	4	0	0	0	0	0	2	0	.333	.000
Throws Right	R	.143	7	1	0	0	0	1	2	1	.333	.143
Prinz,Bret	L	.500	6	3	0	0	0	1	1	0	.571	.500
Throws Right	R	.143	7	1	0	0	1	1	0	1	.143	.571
Prior,Mark	L	.216	278	60	16	0	10	28	28	82	.291	.381
Throws Right	R	.236	352	83	14	0	15	41	31	106	.300	.403
Proctor,Scott	L	.315	73	23	3	1	6	15	10	9	.405	.630
Throws Right	R	.217	106	23	3	0	4	15	7	27	.270	.358
Puffer,Brandon	L	.250	12	3	1	0	1	4	2	1	.357	.583
Throws Right	R	.353	17	6	3	0	1	5	0	0	.353	.706
Pulsipher,Bill	L	.167	6	1	0	0	0	1	0	1	.167	.167
Throws Left	R	.500	8	4	0	0	0	2	2	0	.545	.500
Putz,J.J.	L	.321	106	34	4	0	6	22	9	26	.368	.528
Throws Right	R	.197	122	24	2	0	2	12	14	19	.288	.262
Qualls,Chad	L	.218	133	29	2	1	2	10	12	21	.284	.293
Throws Right	R	.275	160	44	7	0	5	20	11	39	.339	.413
Quantrill,Paul	L	.336	125	42	5	1	4	27	9	19	.373	.488
Throws Right	R	.325	157	51	12	0	4	29	5	17	.341	.478
Radke,Brad	L	.291	402	117	23	1	22	55	14	61	.315	.517
Throws Right	R	.252	385	97	15	4	11	37	9	56	.274	.397
Rakers,Aaron	L	.227	22	5	1	1	0	1	3	2	.308	.364
Throws Right	R	.214	28	6	1	0	3	6	0	9	.207	.571
Ramirez,Elizardo	L	.386	57	22	6	0	5	14	4	4	.435	.754
Throws Right	R	.282	39	11	4	0	0	5	6	5	.391	.385
Ramirez,Erasmo	L	.350	40	14	2	0	1	7	1	2	.381	.475
Throws Left	R	.208	48	10	1	0	2	7	2	4	.255	.354
Ramirez,Horacio	L	.267	180	48	5	1	4	21	12	27	.320	.372
Throws Left	R	.286	580	166	27	0	27	79	55	53	.345	.472
Rasner,Darrell	L	.143	14	2	1	0	0	2	2	2	.294	.214
Throws Right	R	.250	12	3	2	0	0	1	0	2	.308	.417
Rauch,Jon	L	.250	52	13	3	1	1	4	8	10	.344	.404
Throws Right	R	.190	58	11	4	0	2	8	3	13	.242	.362
Ray,Chris	L	.284	67	19	2	1	3	10	7	16	.347	.478
Throws Right	R	.174	86	15	4	0	2	13	11	27	.276	.291
Reames,Britt	L	.250	8	2	0	0	1	4	1	2	.300	.625
Throws Right	R	.471	17	8	2	0	1	4	1	2	.526	.765
Redding,Tim	L	.299	67	20	5	0	2	11	9	11	.385	.463
Throws Right	R	.387	62	24	4	1	5	20	8	8	.452	.726
Redman,Mark	L	.256	133	34	9	2	4	17	14	30	.327	.444
Throws Left	R	.283	544	154	33	2	14	73	42	71	.334	.428
Reed,Steve	L	.349	63	22	4	1	2	13	6	3	.400	.540
Throws Right	R	.271	70	19	4	0	3	13	5	12	.354	.457
Regilio,Nick	L	.214	28	6	1	0	1	6	3	5	.303	.357
Throws Right	R	.348	46	16	4	0	1	4	4	9	.400	.500
Reitsma,Chris	L	.252	159	40	9	0	1	15	12	25	.301	.327
Throws Right	R	.298	131	39	4	0	2	19	2	17	.308	.374
Remlinger,Mike	L	.296	54	16	5	0	1	9	6	14	.367	.444
Throws Left	R	.283	106	30	7	1	6	22	11	21	.361	.538
Resop,Chris	L	.316	38	12	4	0	0	5	5	5	.395	.421
Throws Right	R	.333	30	10	3	1	1	11	4	10	.405	.600
Reyes,Al	L	.184	87	16	3	0	2	8	8	28	.276	.287
Throws Right	R	.172	128	22	6	0	3	13	12	39	.252	.289
Reyes,Anthony	L	.111	18	2	2	0	0	0	1	6	.158	.222
Throws Right	R	.148	27	4	0	0	2	4	3	6	.226	.370
Reyes,Dennys	L	.222	54	12	3	0	0	6	8	11	.323	.278
Throws Left	R	.354	127	45	6	2	3	18	24	24	.461	.504
Rhodes,Arthur	L	.286	63	18	0	0	1	10	4	19	.328	.333
Throws Left	R	.155	97	15	4	0	1	6	8	24	.222	.227
Riedling,John	L	.306	62	19	2	1	2	8	6	5	.371	.468
Throws Right	R	.288	52	15	6	0	1	11	7	11	.373	.462
Riley,Matt	L	.200	20	4	1	0	0	4	6	2	.407	.250
Throws Left	R	.400	30	12	2	0	2	8	4	2	.457	.667
Rincon,Juan	L	.218	119	26	3	0	1	12	16	38	.311	.269
Throws Right	R	.228	162	37	3	1	1	11	14	46	.300	.278
Rincon,Ricardo	L	.250	88	22	2	1	3	16	8	20	.316	.398
Throws Left	R	.240	50	12	2	0	4	6	12	7	.387	.520
Ring,Royce	L	.250	24	6	0	0	0	3	7	6	.419	.250
Throws Left	R	.250	16	4	1	0	0	2	3	2	.368	.313
Riske,David	L	.213	108	23	5	0	6	11	8	23	.274	.426
Throws Right	R	.204	157	32	4	1	5	19	7	25	.250	.338
Rivera,Mariano	L	.177	141	25	2	1	1	5	5	36	.205	.227
Throws Right	R	.176	142	25	3	1	1	12	13	44	.263	.232
Robertson,Nate	L	.244	156	38	2	2	1	17	15	30	.316	.301
Throws Left	R	.272	604	164	32	5	27	82	50	92	.327	.475

Pitchers vs. Left-Handed and Right-Handed Batters

Pitcher	vs	Avg	AB	H	2B	3B	HR	RBI	BB	SO	OBP	Slg
Rodney,Fernando	L	.265	68	18	7	0	3	10	8	16	.359	.500
Throws Right	R	.219	96	21	3	0	2	10	9	26	.286	.313
Rodriguez,Felix	L	.239	46	11	2	0	1	5	10	11	.375	.348
Throws Right	R	.278	79	22	8	0	1	15	10	7	.374	.418
Rodriguez,Francisco	L	.213	127	27	4	2	4	14	15	48	.294	.370
Throws Right	R	.153	118	18	3	0	3	10	17	43	.259	.254
Rodriguez,Ricardo	L	.279	111	31	7	1	7	18	10	12	.339	.550
Throws Right	R	.298	121	36	6	0	4	16	7	12	.338	.446
Rodriguez,Wandy	L	.275	138	38	5	3	7	23	14	25	.359	.507
Throws Left	R	.273	355	97	22	0	12	44	39	55	.349	.437
Rogers,Kenny	L	.201	169	34	7	1	2	13	18	33	.292	.290
Throws Left	R	.291	587	171	35	4	13	68	35	54	.333	.431
Romero,J.C.	L	.198	101	20	1	0	2	19	10	28	.308	.267
Throws Left	R	.268	112	30	6	1	4	13	29	20	.415	.446
Rueter,Kirk	L	.286	112	32	8	1	1	10	15	9	.367	.402
Throws Left	R	.311	318	99	21	3	11	58	32	16	.369	.500
Rupe,Josh	L	.333	18	6	1	0	0	1	4	3	.478	.389
Throws Right	R	.071	14	1	0	0	0	2	0	3	.133	.071
Rusch,Glendon	L	.333	117	39	12	1	5	20	3	20	.341	.581
Throws Left	R	.294	462	136	21	4	9	49	50	91	.360	.416
Ryan,B.J.	L	.211	71	15	2	1	2	11	6	27	.288	.352
Throws Left	R	.206	189	39	5	0	2	11	20	73	.282	.265
Saarloos,Kirk	L	.304	322	98	14	2	4	25	34	27	.377	.398
Throws Right	R	.249	289	72	16	1	7	38	20	26	.311	.384
Sabathia,C.C.	L	.248	109	27	5	0	4	16	13	34	.325	.404
Throws Left	R	.248	636	158	31	0	15	68	49	127	.308	.368
Sanchez,Duaner	L	.310	155	48	10	1	5	28	18	29	.383	.484
Throws Right	R	.182	148	27	5	3	3	16	18	42	.280	.318
Sanders,David	L	.500	4	2	2	0	0	1	0	1	.500	1.000
Throws Left	R	.250	4	1	0	0	1	2	1	0	.333	1.000
Santana,Ervin	L	.261	268	70	19	4	7	35	26	47	.331	.440
Throws Right	R	.271	255	69	15	1	10	31	21	52	.336	.455
Santana,Johan	L	.256	156	40	8	2	6	15	7	43	.288	.449
Throws Left	R	.200	700	140	34	2	16	59	38	195	.242	.323
Santana,Julio	L	.247	73	18	4	0	3	12	8	20	.321	.425
Throws Right	R	.198	81	16	3	1	3	10	11	29	.284	.370
Santiago,Jose	L	.500	8	4	0	0	0	0	2	2	.600	.500
Throws Right	R	.375	16	6	4	0	0	2	0	1	.412	.625
Santos,Victor	L	.259	259	67	14	2	9	31	29	41	.336	.432
Throws Right	R	.277	310	86	22	1	11	47	31	48	.350	.461
Sauerbeck,Scott	L	.162	74	12	3	0	3	10	10	25	.284	.324
Throws Left	R	.377	61	23	5	0	1	6	6	10	.441	.508
Saunders,Joe	L	.417	12	5	1	0	1	5	2	1	.500	.750
Throws Left	R	.200	25	5	1	0	2	3	2	3	.259	.480
Schilling,Curt	L	.290	207	60	16	2	4	29	15	51	.338	.444
Throws Right	R	.343	178	61	14	2	8	30	7	36	.368	.579
Schmidt,Jason	L	.264	364	96	24	2	7	48	46	93	.342	.398
Throws Right	R	.223	287	64	13	3	9	37	39	72	.323	.383
Schmoll,Steve	L	.303	89	27	7	2	2	14	10	9	.376	.494
Throws Right	R	.244	82	20	4	0	2	15	12	20	.343	.366
Schoeneweis,Scott	L	.188	112	21	1	1	1	13	10	24	.260	.241
Throws Left	R	.306	108	33	6	0	1	12	15	19	.405	.389
Seanez,Rudy	L	.231	108	25	5	2	3	10	13	39	.320	.398
Throws Right	R	.212	113	24	4	0	1	11	9	45	.274	.274
Seay,Bobby	L	.421	19	8	1	0	1	3	4	4	.522	.632
Throws Left	R	.333	30	10	3	0	2	10	4	7	.412	.633
Sele,Aaron	L	.325	252	82	15	2	12	42	23	22	.377	.544
Throws Right	R	.302	215	65	10	1	6	26	18	31	.361	.442
Seo,Jae	L	.233	176	41	6	0	5	11	11	35	.275	.352
Throws Right	R	.272	158	43	11	0	4	14	5	24	.297	.418
Shackelford,Brian	L	.205	39	8	0	1	1	1	2	11	.295	.333
Throws Left	R	.203	64	13	3	0	1	5	7	6	.307	.297
Sheets,Ben	L	.234	303	71	17	2	10	28	15	84	.269	.403
Throws Right	R	.241	295	71	8	1	9	34	10	57	.270	.366
Sherrill,George	L	.156	45	7	2	0	2	8	0	18	.170	.333
Throws Left	R	.273	22	6	0	0	1	3	7	6	.448	.409
Shields,Scot	L	.199	171	34	10	0	2	19	21	60	.289	.292
Throws Right	R	.203	158	32	0	1	3	15	16	38	.276	.272
Shouse,Brian	L	.209	115	24	5	0	4	23	8	27	.271	.357
Throws Left	R	.337	92	31	8	0	3	19	10	8	.402	.522
Silva,Carlos	L	.302	394	119	21	1	14	40	8	42	.315	.467
Throws Right	R	.277	336	93	12	0	11	33	1	29	.282	.411
Simpson,Allan	L	.143	7	1	0	0	1	2	3	2	.364	.571
Throws Right	R	.263	19	5	2	0	0	3	5	4	.440	.368
Sisco,Andy	L	.216	88	19	1	1	2	9	10	22	.297	.318
Throws Left	R	.255	192	49	7	1	4	29	32	54	.363	.365

Pitcher	vs	Avg	AB	H	2B	3B	HR	RBI	BB	SO	OBP	Slg
Small,Aaron	L	.252	135	34	7	2	0	13	16	17	.331	.333
Throws Right	R	.248	149	37	9	1	4	16	8	20	.304	.403
Smith,Travis	L	.500	24	12	5	1	0	3	3	3	.556	.792
Throws Right	R	.227	22	5	0	0	1	6	2	6	.280	.364
Smoltz,John	L	.252	473	119	29	2	10	48	34	82	.301	.385
Throws Right	R	.233	391	91	15	1	8	31	19	87	.268	.338
Snell,Ian	L	.304	69	21	6	0	3	12	15	14	.429	.522
Throws Right	R	.239	92	22	6	1	2	12	9	20	.311	.391
Snyder,Kyle	L	.333	63	21	4	2	1	9	6	8	.400	.508
Throws Right	R	.366	93	34	12	0	2	14	4	11	.384	.559
Soriano,Rafael	L	.571	7	4	1	0	0	0	1	2	.625	.714
Throws Right	R	.100	20	2	1	0	0	2	0	7	.136	.150
Sosa,Jorge	L	.247	251	62	16	3	8	25	40	33	.351	.430
Throws Right	R	.235	255	60	9	0	4	14	24	52	.299	.318
Speier,Justin	L	.167	96	16	2	0	4	8	6	22	.216	.313
Throws Right	R	.219	146	32	7	0	6	17	9	34	.278	.390
Speier,Ryan	L	.289	38	11	4	0	0	5	9	5	.426	.395
Throws Right	R	.268	56	15	1	0	0	10	4	5	.323	.286
Springer,Russ	L	.209	91	19	4	1	4	10	10	23	.287	.407
Throws Right	R	.231	130	30	4	0	5	22	11	31	.306	.377
Spurling,Chris	L	.223	94	21	3	0	4	10	13	10	.312	.383
Throws Right	R	.234	158	37	8	0	4	20	9	16	.279	.361
Standridge,Jason	L	.356	45	16	4	0	1	8	4	7	.420	.511
Throws Right	R	.319	91	29	5	1	2	13	13	12	.404	.462
Stanton,Mike	L	.235	85	20	2	0	0	8	4	15	.270	.259
Throws Left	R	.358	81	29	9	1	3	14	11	12	.430	.605
Stauffer,Tim	L	.289	149	43	14	1	5	21	15	18	.358	.497
Throws Right	R	.283	173	49	13	0	5	23	14	31	.340	.445
Stemle,Steve	L	.211	19	4	1	0	0	1	1	6	.250	.263
Throws Right	R	.300	20	6	0	0	0	3	3	3	.391	.300
Stone,Ricky	L	.333	57	19	4	0	3	15	4	7	.387	.561
Throws Right	R	.387	75	29	7	0	5	16	3	8	.407	.680
Street,Huston	L	.224	116	26	8	0	2	14	17	29	.321	.345
Throws Right	R	.172	157	27	3	0	1	9	9	43	.225	.210
Strickland,Scott	L	.400	5	2	0	0	1	2	0	0	.400	1.000
Throws Right	R	.182	11	2	0	0	1	2	0	2	.182	.455
Sturtze,Tanyon	L	.233	120	28	7	0	3	13	12	15	.308	.367
Throws Right	R	.273	176	48	10	0	7	32	15	30	.343	.449
Suppan,Jeff	L	.271	350	95	15	1	10	40	27	43	.325	.406
Throws Right	R	.279	398	111	19	3	14	42	36	71	.344	.447
Switzer,Jon	L	.167	6	1	0	0	0	0	1	3	.286	.167
Throws Left	R	.333	12	4	1	0	0	5	6	2	.556	.417
Tadano,Kazuhito	L	.250	8	2	1	0	0	1	0	1	.250	.375
Throws Right	R	.250	8	2	1	0	0	0	0	0	.250	.375
Takatsu,Shingo	L	.254	59	15	1	1	6	11	11	18	.371	.610
Throws Right	R	.299	87	26	6	0	5	16	8	20	.354	.540
Tallet,Brian	L	.400	5	2	0	0	1	2	1	0	.500	1.000
Throws Left	R	.267	15	4	0	0	1	2	2	2	.389	.467
Taschner,Jack	L	.265	34	9	3	1	0	4	3	8	.316	.412
Throws Left	R	.128	47	6	2	0	0	1	10	11	.281	.170
Tavarez,Julian	L	.294	68	20	5	1	2	8	5	17	.347	.485
Throws Right	R	.271	177	48	8	0	4	19	14	30	.345	.384
Tejeda,Robinson	L	.210	143	30	5	0	4	14	29	25	.360	.329
Throws Right	R	.226	164	37	10	2	1	15	22	47	.326	.329
Tejera,Michael	L	.333	6	2	0	0	0	0	1	2	.500	.333
Throws Left	R	.600	5	3	0	0	1	3	0	0	.600	1.200
Telemaco,Amaury	L	.150	20	3	0	0	1	3	2	4	.217	.300
Throws Right	R	.125	16	2	0	0	1	3	2	4	.222	.313
Thompson,Brad	L	.224	76	17	2	0	3	7	4	6	.263	.368
Throws Right	R	.228	127	29	5	1	2	7	11	23	.310	.331
Thompson,Derek	L	.231	13	3	1	0	0	0	4	3	.412	.308
Throws Left	R	.265	49	13	1	0	0	6	6	10	.339	.286
Thompson,Justin	L	.400	5	2	0	0	1	4	0	0	.400	1.000
Throws Left	R	.500	4	2	0	0	1	3	0	1	.500	1.250
Thomson,John	L	.276	196	54	8	2	4	30	19	28	.341	.398
Throws Right	R	.292	195	57	17	1	2	18	9	33	.322	.421
Thornton,Matt	L	.262	103	27	2	0	7	21	18	29	.372	.485
Throws Left	R	.235	115	27	3	0	6	19	24	28	.364	.417
Timlin,Mike	L	.299	144	43	13	0	0	14	12	28	.348	.389
Throws Right	R	.257	167	43	11	2	2	24	8	31	.293	.383
Tomko,Brett	L	.282	411	116	28	6	12	49	33	53	.340	.467
Throws Right	R	.264	337	89	19	4	8	49	24	61	.316	.415
Torres,Salomon	L	.272	136	37	9	2	1	14	14	27	.346	.390
Throws Right	R	.189	206	39	6	1	6	21	22	28	.276	.316
Towers,Josh	L	.274	413	113	20	2	8	43	17	60	.305	.390
Throws Right	R	.297	418	124	24	0	16	52	12	52	.318	.469

Pitchers vs. Left-Handed and Right-Handed Batters

Pitcher	vs	Avg	AB	H	2B	3B	HR	RBI	BB	SO	OBP	Slg
Trachsel,Steve	L	.288	66	19	1	1	4	14	9	9	.377	.515
Throws Right	R	.243	74	18	6	0	2	4	3	15	.269	.405
Tsao,Chin-hui	L	.462	26	12	2	0	3	5	4	0	.548	.885
Throws Right	R	.182	22	4	2	0	0	3	1	4	.208	.273
Tucker,T.J.	L	.364	22	8	1	0	0	0	1	2	.391	.409
Throws Right	R	.375	32	12	1	0	4	9	1	3	.382	.781
Turnbow,Derrick	L	.233	120	28	4	1	1	6	12	25	.303	.308
Throws Right	R	.167	126	21	6	0	4	9	12	39	.245	.310
Urbina,Ugueth	L	.223	139	31	7	0	6	11	21	41	.325	.403
Throws Right	R	.167	150	25	11	0	6	21	18	56	.259	.360
Valdez,Ismael	L	.341	91	31	11	2	2	18	9	12	.408	.571
Throws Right	R	.292	113	33	6	1	4	15	13	15	.377	.469
Valentine,Joe	L	.350	20	7	1	0	2	5	6	3	.481	.700
Throws Right	R	.268	41	11	2	1	2	7	5	6	.375	.512
Valverde,Jose	L	.168	101	17	3	0	2	9	10	23	.248	.257
Throws Right	R	.241	141	34	3	0	3	14	10	52	.296	.326
Van Buren,Jermaine	L	.000	1	0	0	0	0	0	3	0	.750	.000
Throws Right	R	.125	16	2	0	0	0	0	6	3	.364	.125
Vargas,Claudio	L	.268	254	68	17	2	14	31	27	44	.345	.516
Throws Right	R	.288	271	78	19	3	11	41	20	51	.345	.502
Vargas,Jason	L	.192	73	14	3	2	0	7	5	14	.263	.288
Throws Left	R	.269	212	57	14	3	4	23	26	45	.353	.420
Vasquez,Jorge	L	.333	15	5	1	1	1	2	3	4	.444	.733
Throws Right	R	.273	22	6	2	0	1	1	2	5	.333	.500
Vazquez,Javier	L	.244	377	92	20	2	13	37	22	78	.287	.411
Throws Right	R	.285	460	131	20	5	22	65	24	114	.324	.493
Verlander,Justin	L	.333	30	10	5	0	1	5	4	4	.429	.600
Throws Right	R	.278	18	5	0	0	0	3	1	3	.316	.278
Villarreal,Oscar	L	.207	29	6	1	0	1	4	3	2	.294	.345
Throws Right	R	.278	18	5	1	0	1	3	3	3	.381	.500
Villone,Ron	L	.222	117	26	2	1	0	14	13	29	.326	.256
Throws Left	R	.258	120	31	6	0	4	25	22	41	.370	.408
Vizcaino,Luis	L	.321	112	36	6	0	3	12	15	16	.402	.455
Throws Right	R	.242	157	38	7	0	5	28	14	27	.310	.382
Vogelsong,Ryan	L	.275	120	33	5	2	1	18	20	22	.376	.375
Throws Right	R	.250	196	49	12	2	4	29	20	30	.339	.393
Volquez,Edison	L	.481	27	13	5	0	0	9	8	5	.583	.667
Throws Right	R	.343	35	12	2	0	3	10	2	6	.410	.657
Waechter,Doug	L	.310	342	106	22	3	18	59	23	38	.352	.550
Throws Right	R	.283	300	85	17	1	11	40	15	49	.321	.457
Wagner,Billy	L	.128	47	6	0	1	0	2	2	15	.192	.170
Throws Left	R	.173	225	39	7	0	6	19	18	72	.237	.284
Wagner,Ryan	L	.311	74	23	7	0	1	11	14	15	.422	.446
Throws Right	R	.297	111	33	6	0	3	18	3	24	.328	.432
Wainwright,Adam	L	.500	2	1	0	0	0	0	1	0	.667	.500
Throws Right	R	.167	6	1	0	0	1	3	0	0	.167	.667
Wakefield,Tim	L	.209	393	82	16	1	16	45	30	63	.269	.377
Throws Right	R	.276	464	128	31	1	19	54	38	88	.339	.470
Walker,Jamie	L	.245	106	26	4	0	2	18	4	23	.286	.340
Throws Left	R	.271	85	23	3	0	3	8	9	7	.337	.412
Walker,Kevin	L	.421	19	8	2	0	1	5	1	2	.450	.684
Throws Left	R	.182	11	2	0	1	0	2	4	3	.400	.364
Walker,Pete	L	.254	142	36	5	0	3	18	18	19	.333	.352
Throws Right	R	.254	177	45	8	1	7	20	15	24	.316	.429
Walker,Tyler	L	.284	116	33	5	1	3	17	14	25	.366	.422
Throws Right	R	.278	126	35	7	0	6	23	13	29	.352	.476
Wang,Chien-Ming	L	.258	213	55	8	2	6	27	19	21	.318	.399
Throws Right	R	.254	228	58	9	1	3	21	16	20	.308	.342
Wasdin,John	L	.229	140	32	8	0	3	19	13	17	.290	.350
Throws Right	R	.290	155	45	10	0	6	21	7	27	.325	.471
Washburn,Jarrod	L	.266	139	37	3	1	4	11	4	27	.299	.388
Throws Left	R	.276	532	147	28	4	15	47	47	67	.338	.429
Weathers,David	L	.265	117	31	4	0	3	16	16	22	.358	.376
Throws Right	R	.226	177	40	8	1	4	21	13	39	.280	.350
Weaver,Jeff	L	.297	464	138	27	3	22	62	13	73	.356	.511
Throws Right	R	.208	394	82	13	1	13	40	13	84	.241	.345
Webb,Brandon	L	.298	449	134	23	3	18	58	35	67	.347	.483
Throws Right	R	.228	416	95	18	1	3	32	24	105	.271	.298
Webb,John	L	.375	8	3	1	0	0	2	2	1	.545	.500
Throws Right	R	.300	10	3	1	0	1	4	2	0	.417	.700
Weber,Ben	L	.375	16	6	2	0	0	3	3	1	.474	.500
Throws Right	R	.359	39	14	4	0	0	6	7	7	.447	.462
Wellemeyer,Todd	L	.234	47	11	1	0	2	10	11	13	.373	.383
Throws Right	R	.284	74	21	4	0	5	13	11	19	.376	.541
Wells,David	L	.343	169	58	6	0	5	22	7	21	.383	.467
Throws Left	R	.282	574	162	35	3	16	65	14	86	.302	.437
Wells,Kip	L	.288	316	91	21	1	11	54	61	62	.395	.465
Throws Right	R	.249	382	95	25	1	12	50	38	70	.334	.414
Westbrook,Jake	L	.275	411	113	28	1	8	44	32	59	.330	.406
Throws Right	R	.255	411	105	18	1	11	66	24	60	.302	.384
Wheeler,Dan	L	.204	108	22	4	0	3	10	7	21	.259	.324
Throws Right	R	.204	152	31	9	0	4	14	12	48	.269	.342
White,Gabe	L	.250	12	3	1	0	0	1	0	0	.250	.333
Throws Left	R	.440	25	11	2	0	1	3	1	1	.462	.640
White,Matt	L	.000	0	0	0	0	0	0	0	3	.143	.000
Throws Left	R	.444	9	4	1	0	0	3	0	0	.538	.556
White,Rick	L	.314	102	32	8	0	1	16	14	15	.397	.422
Throws Right	R	.305	190	58	8	2	2	33	15	25	.362	.400
Whiteside,Matt	L	.333	6	2	0	0	1	4	3	1	.600	.833
Throws Right	R	.364	11	4	2	0	2	4	2	4	.462	1.091
Wickman,Bob	L	.243	107	26	2	0	4	6	14	20	.331	.374
Throws Right	R	.250	124	31	6	0	5	12	7	21	.291	.419
Williams,Dave	L	.281	96	27	4	1	7	23	11	21	.373	.563
Throws Left	R	.256	429	110	29	3	13	42	47	67	.335	.429
Williams,Jerome	L	.299	187	56	15	3	4	20	31	35	.408	.476
Throws Right	R	.236	267	63	9	0	10	37	18	45	.292	.382
Williams,Randy	L	.283	53	15	3	0	4	7	3	14	.333	.566
Throws Left	R	.316	57	18	5	0	1	16	10	7	.412	.456
Williams,Todd	L	.263	114	30	2	0	1	10	9	10	.312	.307
Throws Right	R	.244	172	42	6	1	4	24	17	28	.320	.360
Williams,Woody	L	.259	274	71	18	1	9	35	31	45	.336	.431
Throws Right	R	.288	358	103	17	5	15	50	20	61	.326	.489
Williamson,Scott	L	.333	15	5	0	0	1	4	1	4	.412	.533
Throws Right	R	.250	40	10	1	0	2	2	5	19	.348	.425
Willis,Dontrelle	L	.222	158	35	5	2	1	14	1	51	.236	.297
Throws Left	R	.247	720	178	40	7	10	52	54	119	.303	.364
Wilson,C.J.	L	.290	69	20	2	0	1	11	4	14	.329	.362
Throws Left	R	.339	127	43	10	0	4	22	14	16	.408	.512
Wilson,Paul	L	.417	84	35	7	1	5	20	9	13	.469	.702
Throws Right	R	.289	114	33	13	0	5	17	8	17	.347	.535
Wise,Matt	L	.130	108	14	1	0	1	8	13	32	.230	.167
Throws Right	R	.187	123	23	7	1	5	22	12	30	.266	.382
Witasick,Jay	L	.213	108	23	7	0	2	12	20	35	.341	.333
Throws Right	R	.231	130	30	12	0	2	13	9	38	.306	.369
Wolf,Randy	L	.238	63	15	5	0	2	5	1	19	.273	.413
Throws Left	R	.293	246	72	17	0	12	32	25	42	.366	.508
Wood,Kerry	L	.220	109	24	3	2	10	18	16	35	.317	.560
Throws Right	R	.211	133	28	7	0	4	13	10	42	.276	.353
Wood,Mike	L	.295	210	62	13	3	8	32	25	27	.370	.500
Throws Right	R	.279	240	67	14	1	10	36	27	33	.365	.471
Woods,Jake	L	.229	48	11	0	0	2	8	3	9	.288	.354
Throws Left	R	.302	63	19	4	0	5	7	5	11	.362	.603
Woodyard,Mark	L	.222	9	2	0	0	0	0	0	1	.222	.222
Throws Right	R	.154	13	2	0	0	1	1	0	2	.154	.385
Worrell,Tim	L	.295	88	26	5	2	2	13	4	15	.330	.466
Throws Right	R	.303	109	33	8	1	6	25	8	24	.344	.560
Wright,Jamey	L	.314	331	104	25	1	15	60	59	54	.419	.532
Throws Right	R	.279	348	97	26	2	7	43	22	47	.344	.425
Wright,Jaret	L	.273	139	38	6	0	6	23	21	19	.364	.446
Throws Right	R	.358	120	43	10	1	2	19	11	15	.431	.508
Wuertz,Mike	L	.260	96	25	4	1	2	13	18	26	.377	.385
Throws Right	R	.197	178	35	4	0	4	23	22	63	.282	.287
Wunsch,Kelly	L	.190	63	12	2	0	1	6	10	18	.311	.270
Throws Left	R	.320	25	8	2	0	1	2	4	4	.433	.520
Yabu,Keiichi	L	.294	102	30	6	0	2	16	14	13	.375	.412
Throws Right	R	.281	121	34	6	2	4	20	12	31	.379	.463
Yan,Esteban	L	.252	127	32	10	0	4	16	18	19	.340	.425
Throws Right	R	.264	129	34	9	0	4	18	12	26	.322	.426
Young,Chris	L	.281	338	95	22	2	8	36	26	77	.335	.429
Throws Right	R	.220	304	67	14	1	11	39	19	60	.275	.382
Zambrano,Carlos	L	.212	358	76	14	0	14	43	51	75	.313	.369
Throws Right	R	.212	443	94	22	1	7	41	35	127	.276	.314
Zambrano,Victor	L	.260	331	86	18	2	5	30	48	51	.354	.372
Throws Right	R	.268	313	84	20	2	7	39	29	65	.352	.412
Zito,Barry	L	.215	191	41	8	3	3	21	20	37	.296	.335
Throws Left	R	.223	645	144	25	0	23	72	69	134	.306	.369

2005 Leader Boards

We have added several new and interesting leader boards to this year's *Handbook* as we continue to improve upon the most complete leader board list you can find in print. On the following pages, we are sure you will find everything you have come to expect from our leader boards and more.

Many of our leader boards are derived from the complex pitch data that we collect. Our pitch charting data is the best in the business and the information found in these leader boards cannot be found anywhere else. We have everything from the pitchers who blow away hitters with the fastest fastballs, to the hitters who hammer curveballs.

And speaking of hammering pitches, we have a leader board of the longest Home Runs hit this year. Check it out and see who is stretching the limits of the tape measure.

Here are some definitions to help clarify some of the leader boards:

BPS stands for "Batting Average plus Slugging Percentage." We feel that BPS makes more sense than OPS for some leader boards because we wanted to know who was having success putting those balls in play, not just drawing walks.

OutZ is "Pitches Outside the Strike Zone."

HBP/BB Ratio is a measure of pitchers who aggressively pitch inside. It highlights those pitchers who walk few batters but still manage to hit them.

Holds Adjusted Saves Percentage is calculated by dividing Holds plus Saves by Holds plus Saves Opportunities.

2005 American League Batting Leaders

Batting Average (minimum 502 PA)		On Base Percentage (minimum 502 PA)		Slugging Average (minimum 502 PA)		Home Runs	
Young,Michael, Tex	.331	Giambi,Jason, NYY	.440	Rodriguez,Alex, NYY	.610	Rodriguez,Alex, NYY	48
Rodriguez,Alex, NYY	.321	Rodriguez,Alex, NYY	.421	Ortiz,David, Bos	.604	Ortiz,David, Bos	47
Guerrero,Vladimir, LAA	.317	Hafner,Travis, Cle	.408	Hafner,Travis, Cle	.595	Ramirez,Manny, Bos	45
Damon,Johnny, Bos	.316	Ortiz,David, Bos	.397	Ramirez,Manny, Bos	.594	Teixeira,Mark, Tex	43
Roberts,Brian, Bal	.314	Guerrero,Vladimir, LAA	.394	Teixeira,Mark, Tex	.575	Konerko,Paul, CWS	40
Jeter,Derek, NYY	.309	Jeter,Derek, NYY	.389	Guerrero,Vladimir, LAA	.565	Sexson,Richie, Sea	39
Martinez,Victor, Cle	.305	Ramirez,Manny, Bos	.388	Sexson,Richie, Sea	.541	Soriano,Alfonso, Tex	36
Matsui,Hideki, NYY	.305	Roberts,Brian, Bal	.387	Giambi,Jason, NYY	.535	Sheffield,Gary, NYY	34
Hafner,Travis, Cle	.305	Young,Michael, Tex	.385	Konerko,Paul, CWS	.534	Hafner,Travis, Cle	33
Tejada,Miguel, Bal	.304	Teixeira,Mark, Tex	.379	Peralta,Jhonny, Cle	.520	2 tied with	32

Games		Plate Appearances		At Bats		Hits	
Ibanez,Raul, Sea	162	Jeter,Derek, NYY	752	Suzuki,Ichiro, Sea	679	Young,Michael, Tex	221
Matsui,Hideki, NYY	162	Suzuki,Ichiro, Sea	739	Young,Michael, Tex	668	Suzuki,Ichiro, Sea	206
Rodriguez,Alex, NYY	162	Young,Michael, Tex	732	Jeter,Derek, NYY	654	Jeter,Derek, NYY	202
Suzuki,Ichiro, Sea	162	Teixeira,Mark, Tex	730	Tejada,Miguel, Bal	654	Tejada,Miguel, Bal	199
Teixeira,Mark, Tex	162	Figgins,Chone, LAA	720	Blalock,Hank, Tex	647	Damon,Johnny, Bos	197
Tejada,Miguel, Bal	162	Rodriguez,Alex, NYY	715	Crawford,Carl, TB	644	Crawford,Carl, TB	194
Blalock,Hank, Tex	161	Ortiz,David, Bos	713	Teixeira,Mark, Tex	644	Rodriguez,Alex, NYY	194
Chavez,Eric, Oak	160	Sizemore,Grady, Cle	706	Figgins,Chone, LAA	642	Teixeira,Mark, Tex	194
Inge,Brandon, Det	160	Blalock,Hank, Tex	705	Sizemore,Grady, Cle	640	Matsui,Hideki, NYY	192
4 tied with	159	2 tied with	704	Soriano,Alfonso, Tex	637	Figgins,Chone, LAA	186

Singles		Doubles		Triples		Total Bases	
Suzuki,Ichiro, Sea	158	Tejada,Miguel, Bal	50	Crawford,Carl, TB	15	Teixeira,Mark, Tex	370
Jeter,Derek, NYY	153	Matsui,Hideki, NYY	45	Suzuki,Ichiro, Sea	12	Rodriguez,Alex, NYY	369
Young,Michael, Tex	152	Roberts,Brian, Bal	45	Sizemore,Grady, Cle	11	Ortiz,David, Bos	363
Damon,Johnny, Bos	146	Soriano,Alfonso, Tex	43	Figgins,Chone, LAA	10	Young,Michael, Tex	343
Figgins,Chone, LAA	143	Crisp,Coco, Cle	42	Inge,Brandon, Det	9	Tejada,Miguel, Bal	337
Kendall,Jason, Oak	134	Hafner,Travis, Cle	42	Roberts,Brian, Bal	7	Ramirez,Manny, Bos	329
Lugo,Julio, TB	134	Teixeira,Mark, Tex	41	7 tied with	6	Soriano,Alfonso, Tex	326
Crawford,Carl, TB	131	4 tied with	40			Matsui,Hideki, NYY	312
Berroa,Angel, KC	127					Sizemore,Grady, Cle	310
Renteria,Edgar, Bos	124					Konerko,Paul, CWS	307

Runs Scored		RBI		Walks		Strikeouts	
Rodriguez,Alex, NYY	124	Ortiz,David, Bos	148	Giambi,Jason, NYY	108	Sexson,Richie, Sea	167
Jeter,Derek, NYY	122	Ramirez,Manny, Bos	144	Ortiz,David, Bos	102	Inge,Brandon, Det	140
Ortiz,David, Bos	119	Teixeira,Mark, Tex	144	Rodriguez,Alex, NYY	91	Rodriguez,Alex, NYY	139
Damon,Johnny, Bos	117	Rodriguez,Alex, NYY	130	Sexson,Richie, Sea	89	Blalock,Hank, Tex	132
Young,Michael, Tex	114	Sheffield,Gary, NYY	123	Konerko,Paul, CWS	81	Sizemore,Grady, Cle	132
Figgins,Chone, LAA	113	Sexson,Richie, Sea	121	Ramirez,Manny, Bos	80	Chavez,Eric, Oak	129
Ramirez,Manny, Bos	112	Cantu,Jorge, TB	117	Hafner,Travis, Cle	79	Peralta,Jhonny, Cle	128
Teixeira,Mark, Tex	112	Matsui,Hideki, NYY	116	Sheffield,Gary, NYY	78	Soriano,Alfonso, Tex	125
Sizemore,Grady, Cle	111	Guerrero,Vladimir, LAA	108	Jeter,Derek, NYY	77	Ortiz,David, Bos	124
Suzuki,Ichiro, Sea	111	Hafner,Travis, Cle	108	Dellucci,David, Tex	76	Teixeira,Mark, Tex	124

2005 American League Batting Leaders

Sacrifice Hits		Sacrifice Flies		Stolen Bases		Caught Stealing	
Crisp,Coco, Cle	13	Monroe,Craig, Det	12	Figgins,Chone, LAA	62	Podsednik,Scott, CWS	23
Logan,Nook, Det	12	Everett,Carl, CWS	10	Podsednik,Scott, CWS	59	Figgins,Chone, LAA	17
Iguchi,Tadahito, CWS	11	Uribe,Juan, CWS	10	Crawford,Carl, TB	46	Lugo,Julio, TB	11
Uribe,Juan, CWS	11	Chavez,Eric, Oak	9	Lugo,Julio, TB	39	Reed,Jeremy, Sea	11
Berroa,Angel, KC	10	Damon,Johnny, Bos	9	Suzuki,Ichiro, Sea	33	Roberts,Brian, Bal	10
Green,Nick, TB	10	Ortiz,David, Bos	9	Soriano,Alfonso, Tex	30	Sizemore,Grady, Cle	10
Castro,Juan, Min	9	6 tied with	8	Roberts,Brian, Bal	27	Matos,Luis, Bal	9
Figgins,Chone, LAA	9			Womack,Tony, NYY	27	Rios,Alexis, Tor	9
3 tied with	8			Hunter,Torii, Min	23	Rivera,Juan, LAA	9
				Logan,Nook, Det	23	3 tied with	8

Intentional Walks		Hit By Pitch		Grounded Into DP		Grounded Into DP Pct	
						(minimum 50 GIDP Ops)	
Guerrero,Vladimir, LAA	26	Hillenbrand,Shea, Tor	22	Kendall,Jason, Oak	26	Broussard,Ben, Cle	3.81
Suzuki,Ichiro, Sea	23	Rowand,Aaron, CWS	21	Tejada,Miguel, Bal	26	Damon,Johnny, Bos	4.50
Huff,Aubrey, TB	13	Kendall,Jason, Oak	20	Cantu,Jorge, TB	24	Adams,Russ, Tor	4.55
Jones,Jacque, Min	12	Giambi,Jason, NYY	19	Hatteberg,Scott, Oak	22	Bellhorn,M, Bos-NYY	4.60
Mauer,Joe, Min	12	Ford,Lew, Min	16	Mueller,Bill, Bos	22	Suzuki,Ichiro, Sea	4.76
Konerko,Paul, CWS	10	Johnson,Reed, Tor	16	Hillenbrand,Shea, Tor	21	Lugo,Julio, TB	4.81
Martinez,Victor, Cle	9	Rodriguez,Alex, NYY	16	Ramirez,Manny, Bos	20	Mench,Kevin, Tex	4.88
Ortiz,David, Bos	9	Berroa,Angel, KC	14	Young,Michael, Tex	20	Soriano,Alfonso, Tex	4.96
Ramirez,Manny, Bos	9	Gomes,Jonny, TB	14	Cuddyer,Mike, Min	19	Gotay,Ruben, KC	5.08
Tejada,Miguel, Bal	9	Pierzynski,A.J., CWS	12	Rodriguez,Ivan, Det	19	Rodriguez,Alex, NYY	5.30

Leadoff Hitters OBP		Cleanup Hitters SLG		BA vs. LHP		BA vs. RHP	
(minimum 150 PA)		(minimum 150 PA)		(minimum 125 PA)		(minimum 377 PA)	
Jeter,Derek, NYY	.391	Ramirez,Manny, Bos	.612	Molina,Bengie, LAA	.393	Roberts,Brian, Bal	.332
Roberts,Brian, Bal	.384	Guerrero,Vladimir, LAA	.597	Sheffield,Gary, NYY	.359	Young,Michael, Tex	.328
Polanco,Placido, Det	.383	Hafner,Travis, Cle	.589	Matsui,Hideki, NYY	.354	Rodriguez,Alex, NYY	.327
Inge,Brandon, Det	.371	Konerko,Paul, CWS	.554	Suzuki,Ichiro, Sea	.352	Crawford,Carl, TB	.324
Damon,Johnny, Bos	.367	Rodriguez,Alex, NYY	.553	Wells,Vernon, Tor	.347	Crisp,Coco, Cle	.324
Lugo,Julio, TB	.366	Sexson,Richie, Sea	.542	Young,Michael, Tex	.340	Mauer,Joe, Min	.323
Johnson,Reed, Tor	.366	Chavez,Eric, Oak	.531	Sexson,Richie, Sea	.333	Hafner,Travis, Cle	.321
Figgins,Chone, LAA	.356	Martinez,Victor, Cle	.503	Anderson,Garret, LAA	.330	Martinez,Victor, Cle	.319
Sizemore,Grady, Cle	.353	Tejada,Miguel, Bal	.479	Damon,Johnny, Bos	.327	Guerrero,Vladimir, LAA	.319
DeJesus,David, KC	.352	White,Rondell, Det	.472	Renteria,Edgar, Bos	.326	Ramirez,Manny, Bos	.316

Home BA		Away BA		OBP vs. LHP		OBP vs. RHP	
(minimum 251 PA)		(minimum 251 PA)		(minimum 125 PA)		(minimum 377 PA)	
Jeter,Derek, NYY	.354	Ellis,Mark, Oak	.335	Sexson,Richie, Sea	.458	Rodriguez,Alex, NYY	.423
Rodriguez,Alex, NYY	.351	Cano,Robinson, NYY	.335	Sheffield,Gary, NYY	.436	Hafner,Travis, Cle	.423
Damon,Johnny, Bos	.334	Young,Michael, Tex	.330	Molina,Bengie, LAA	.430	Ortiz,David, Bos	.413
Teixeira,Mark, Tex	.334	Roberts,Brian, Bal	.325	Giambi,Jason, NYY	.418	Mauer,Joe, Min	.411
Young,Michael, Tex	.331	Sizemore,Grady, Cle	.324	Varitek,Jason, Bos	.418	Roberts,Brian, Bal	.404
Ortiz,David, Bos	.322	Crisp,Coco, Cle	.323	Rodriguez,Alex, NYY	.414	Ramirez,Manny, Bos	.401
Matsui,Hideki, NYY	.321	Guerrero,Vladimir, LAA	.317	Wells,Vernon, Tor	.409	Guerrero,Vladimir, LAA	.399
Guerrero,Vladimir, LAA	.318	Crawford,Carl, TB	.314	LeCroy,Matt, Min	.404	Jeter,Derek, NYY	.392
Soriano,Alfonso, Tex	.315	Varitek,Jason, Bos	.312	Ellis,Mark, Oak	.403	Teixeira,Mark, Tex	.386
Tejada,Miguel, Bal	.313	Anderson,Garret, LAA	.307	Kielty,Bobby, Oak	.398	Martinez,Victor, Cle	.385

2005 American League Batting Leaders

BA Close & Late	
(minimum 50 PA)	
Guerrero,Vladimir, LAA	.408
Martinez,Victor, Cle	.372
Kotsay,Mark, Oak	.360
Kennedy,Adam, LAA	.351
Guillen,Carlos, Det	.346
Ortiz,David, Bos	.346
Matos,Luis, Bal	.345
Molina,Bengie, LAA	.344
Ibanez,Raul, Sea	.343
Pierzynski,A.J., CWS	.342

BA Bases Loaded	
(minimum 10 PA)	
Johnson,Reed, Tor	.625
Adams,Russ, Tor	.600
Mueller,Bill, Bos	.526
Sexson,Richie, Sea	.500
Matsui,Hideki, NYY	.474
Monroe,Craig, Det	.467
Young,Michael, Tex	.455
Boone,Bret, Sea-Min	.444
Hudson,Orlando, Tor	.444
Kielty,Bobby, Oak	.444

SLG vs. LHP	
(minimum 125 PA)	
Wells,Vernon, Tor	.673
Sheffield,Gary, NYY	.673
Sexson,Richie, Sea	.659
Molina,Bengie, LAA	.648
LeCroy,Matt, Min	.621
Mench,Kevin, Tex	.600
Peralta,Jhonny, Cle	.597
Varitek,Jason, Bos	.582
Matsui,Hideki, NYY	.579
Konerko,Paul, CWS	.575

SLG vs. RHP	
(minimum 377 PA)	
Ortiz,David, Bos	.641
Hafner,Travis, Cle	.639
Ramirez,Manny, Bos	.622
Rodriguez,Alex, NYY	.622
Teixeira,Mark, Tex	.603
Guerrero,Vladimir, LAA	.562
Roberts,Brian, Bal	.545
Soriano,Alfonso, Tex	.541
Tejada,Miguel, Bal	.535
Gibbons,Jay, Bal	.534

Batting Average w/ RISP	
(minimum 100 PA)	
Catalanotto,Fr, Tor	.409
Young,Michael, Tex	.368
Teixeira,Mark, Tex	.366
Sheffield,Gary, NYY	.364
White,Rondell, Det	.364
Ramirez,Manny, Bos	.358
Ortiz,David, Bos	.354
Kotsay,Mark, Oak	.346
Kendall,Jason, Oak	.344
Guerrero,Vladimir, LAA	.338

At Bats Per Home Run	
(minimum 502 PA)	
Ramirez,Manny, Bos	12.3
Rodriguez,Alex, NYY	12.6
Ortiz,David, Bos	12.8
Giambi,Jason, NYY	13.0
Sexson,Richie, Sea	14.3
Konerko,Paul, CWS	14.4
Hafner,Travis, Cle	14.7
Teixeira,Mark, Tex	15.0
Dellucci,David, Tex	15.0
Guerrero,Vladimir, LAA	16.3

Pitches Seen	
Jeter,Derek, NYY	2883
Ortiz,David, Bos	2852
Figgins,Chone, LAA	2814
Rodriguez,Alex, NYY	2797
Inge,Brandon, Det	2781
Konerko,Paul, CWS	2768
Ibanez,Raul, Sea	2733
Chavez,Eric, Oak	2732
Young,Michael, Tex	2731
Teixeira,Mark, Tex	2716

Pitches Per Plate App	
(minimum 502 PA)	
Blake,Casey, Cle	4.28
Zaun,Gregg, Tor	4.25
Dellucci,David, Tex	4.22
Giambi,Jason, NYY	4.21
Konerko,Paul, CWS	4.17
Hafner,Travis, Cle	4.17
Varitek,Jason, Bos	4.14
Swisher,Nick, Oak	4.14
Ramirez,Manny, Bos	4.06
Inge,Brandon, Det	4.01

Pct Pitches Taken	
(minimum 1500 Pitches)	
Giambi,Jason, NYY	64.9
Hatteberg,Scott, Oak	62.8
Kendall,Jason, Oak	62.7
Podsednik,Scott, CWS	62.0
Johnson,Dan, Oak	61.6
Dellucci,David, Tex	61.4
DeJesus,David, KC	60.9
Crosby,Bobby, Oak	60.8
Sheffield,Gary, NYY	60.6
Mauer,Joe, Min	60.3

Highest GB/FB Ratio	
(minimum 502 PA)	
Jeter,Derek, NYY	2.93
Podsednik,Scott, CWS	2.36
Jones,Jacque, Min	2.24
Suzuki,Ichiro, Sea	2.20
Mauer,Joe, Min	2.11
Kendall,Jason, Oak	1.93
Rowand,Aaron, CWS	1.84
Ford,Lew, Min	1.82
Cano,Robinson, NYY	1.71
Iguchi,Tadahito, CWS	1.66

Lowest GB/FB Ratio	
(minimum 502 PA)	
Ortiz,David, Bos	0.68
Giambi,Jason, NYY	0.69
Soriano,Alfonso, Tex	0.72
Millar,Kevin, Bos	0.73
Sweeney,Mike, KC	0.75
Konerko,Paul, CWS	0.79
Gibbons,Jay, Bal	0.79
Mora,Melvin, Bal	0.80
Mench,Kevin, Tex	0.82
Blake,Casey, Cle	0.87

Highest SB Success Pct	
(minimum 20 SBA)	
Soriano,Alfonso, Tex	93.8
Cabrera,Orlando, LAA	91.3
Crawford,Carl, TB	85.2
Womack,Tony, NYY	84.4
Kennedy,Adam, LAA	82.6
Suzuki,Ichiro, Sea	80.5
Gathright,Joey, TB	80.0
Logan,Nook, Det	79.3
Figgins,Chone, LAA	78.5
Lugo,Julio, TB	78.0

Steals of Third	
Podsednik,Scott, CWS	17
Lugo,Julio, TB	12
Jeter,Derek, NYY	9
Roberts,Brian, Bal	9
Crawford,Carl, TB	7
Hunter,Torii, Min	6
Soriano,Alfonso, Tex	6
Jones,Jacque, Min	5
4 tied with	4

Longest Home Run	
Rodriguez,A, NYY, 8/13	485
Hafner,Travis, Cle, 6/25	477
Hafner,Travis, Cle, 6/14	474
Hafner,Travis, Cle, 7/4	471
Perez,Eduardo,TB, 4/22	470
Gomes,Jonny, TB, 8/13	461
Pena,Carlos, Det, 9/25	461
Everett,Carl, CWS, 8/3	460
Rodriguez,A, NYY, 7/17	460
Thomas,F, CWS, 7/3	460

Best BPS on OutZ	
(minimum 502 PA)	
Sweeney,Mike, KC	.635
Suzuki,Ichiro, Sea	.629
Guerrero,Vladimir, LAA	.599
Ramirez,Manny, Bos	.594
Williams,Bernie, NYY	.562
Ibanez,Raul, Sea	.536
Young,Michael, Tex	.533
Roberts,Brian, Bal	.532
Dye,Jermaine, CWS	.527
Hillenbrand,Shea, Tor	.504

Worst BPS on OutZ	
(minimum 502 PA)	
Dellucci,David, Tex	.033
Hafner,Travis, Cle	.111
Swisher,Nick, Oak	.120
DeJesus,David, KC	.140
Crisp,Coco, Cle	.151
Zaun,Gregg, Tor	.185
Broussard,Ben, Cle	.187
Adams,Russ, Tor	.189
Matthews Jr.,G, Tex	.191
Hinske,Eric, Tor	.200

2005 American League Batting Leaders

Best BPS vs Fastballs
(minimum 251 PA)

Ortiz,David, Bos	1.077
Soriano,Alfonso, Tex	1.075
Hafner,Travis, Cle	1.055
Rodriguez,Alex, NYY	1.043
Peralta,Jhonny, Cle	.984
Ramirez,Manny, Bos	.983
Iguchi,Tadahito, CWS	.959
Tejada,Miguel, Bal	.955
Young,Michael, Tex	.942
Dye,Jermaine, CWS	.939

Best BPS vs Curveballs
(minimum 50 PA)

Suzuki,Ichiro, Sea	.887
Ortiz,David, Bos	.880
Morneau,Justin, Min	.868
Sheffield,Gary, NYY	.800
Hafner,Travis, Cle	.771
Sizemore,Grady, Cle	.741
Matsui,Hideki, NYY	.725
Rodriguez,Alex, NYY	.711
Crawford,Carl, TB	.688
Soriano,Alfonso, Tex	.647

Best BPS vs Changeups
(minimum 50 PA)

Monroe,Craig, Det	1.130
Sexson,Richie, Sea	1.043
Jones,Jacque, Min	1.017
Guerrero,Vladimir, LAA	1.000
Wells,Vernon, Tor	1.000
Hillenbrand,Shea, Tor	.980
Rodriguez,Ivan, Det	.965
Crawford,Carl, TB	.933
Teixeira,Mark, Tex	.925
Beltre,Adrian, Sea	.912

Best BPS vs Sliders
(minimum 32 PA)

Giambi,Jason, NYY	1.365
Gomes,Jonny, TB	1.000
Hidalgo,Richard, Tex	1.000
Hollins,Damon, TB	.980
Hafner,Travis, Cle	.954
Cantu,Jorge, TB	.885
Konerko,Paul, CWS	.871
Guerrero,Vladimir, LAA	.850
Young,Dmitri, Det	.840
Winn,Randy, Sea	.839

OPS
(minimum 502 PA)

Rodriguez,Alex, NYY	1.031
Hafner,Travis, Cle	1.003
Ortiz,David, Bos	1.001
Ramirez,Manny, Bos	.982
Giambi,Jason, NYY	.975
Guerrero,Vladimir, LAA	.959
Teixeira,Mark, Tex	.954
Sexson,Richie, Sea	.910
Konerko,Paul, CWS	.909
Roberts,Brian, Bal	.902

OPS First Half
(minimum 251 PA)

Hafner,Travis, Cle	1.020
Roberts,Brian, Bal	1.007
Rodriguez,Alex, NYY	.998
Ortiz,David, Bos	.981
Tejada,Miguel, Bal	.977
Guerrero,Vladimir, LAA	.972
Dellucci,David, Tex	.939
Teixeira,Mark, Tex	.930
Sheffield,Gary, NYY	.920
Matsui,Hideki, NYY	.914

OPS Second Half
(minimum 251 PA)

Ramirez,Manny, Bos	1.069
Rodriguez,Alex, NYY	1.069
Giambi,Jason, NYY	1.057
Martinez,Victor, Cle	1.027
Ortiz,David, Bos	1.024
Konerko,Paul, CWS	1.003
Ellis,Mark, Oak	.982
Teixeira,Mark, Tex	.981
Sexson,Richie, Sea	.962
Guerrero,Vladimir, LAA	.946

OPS by Catchers
(minimum 251 PA)

Martinez,Victor, Cle	.855
Varitek,Jason, Bos	.855
Lopez,Javy, Bal	.824
Mauer,Joe, Min	.791
Posada,Jorge, NYY	.780
Barajas,Rod, Tex	.772
Molina,Bengie, LAA	.751
Rodriguez,Ivan, Det	.732
Zaun,Gregg, Tor	.729
Pierzynski,A.J., CWS	.728

OPS by First Basemen
(minimum 251 PA)

Giambi,Jason, NYY	1.135
Teixeira,Mark, Tex	.955
Sexson,Richie, Sea	.918
Konerko,Paul, CWS	.897
Shelton,Chris, Det	.884
Palmeiro,Rafael, Bal	.839
Stairs,Matt, KC	.826
Hillenbrand,Shea, Tor	.810
Johnson,Dan, Oak	.801
Broussard,Ben, Cle	.780

OPS by Second Basemen
(minimum 251 PA)

Roberts,Brian, Bal	.902
Ellis,Mark, Oak	.859
Graffanino,T, KC-Bos	.854
Polanco,Placido, Det	.839
Cantu,Jorge, TB	.828
Soriano,Alfonso, Tex	.822
Belliard,Ronnie, Cle	.778
Cano,Robinson, NYY	.771
Iguchi,Tadahito, CWS	.766
Punto,Nick, Min	.744

OPS by Third Basemen
(minimum 251 PA)

Rodriguez,Alex, NYY	1.023
Mora,Melvin, Bal	.823
Mueller,Bill, Bos	.802
Chavez,Eric, Oak	.795
Koskie,Corey, Tor	.792
Crede,Joe, CWS	.764
Blalock,Hank, Tex	.750
Inge,Brandon, Det	.749
Cuddyer,Mike, Min	.746
Beltre,Adrian, Sea	.712

OPS by Shortstops
(minimum 251 PA)

Young,Michael, Tex	.905
Peralta,Jhonny, Cle	.887
Tejada,Miguel, Bal	.874
Jeter,Derek, NYY	.842
Crosby,Bobby, Oak	.802
Guillen,Carlos, Det	.790
Lugo,Julio, TB	.766
Scutaro,Marco, Oak	.724
Renteria,Edgar, Bos	.718
Uribe,Juan, CWS	.713

OPS by Left Fielders
(minimum 251 PA)

Ramirez,Manny, Bos	.989
White,Rondell, Det	.901
Matsui,Hideki, NYY	.867
Mench,Kevin, Tex	.850
Anderson,Garret, LAA	.830
Crawford,Carl, TB	.821
Crisp,Coco, Cle	.820
Johnson,Reed, Tor	.778
Catalanotto,Fr, Tor	.776
Stewart,Shannon, Min	.716

OPS by Center Fielders
(minimum 251 PA)

Sizemore,Grady, Cle	.834
Hunter,Torii, Min	.815
Damon,Johnny, Bos	.811
DeJesus,David, KC	.805
Wells,Vernon, Tor	.783
Kotsay,Mark, Oak	.745
Hollins,Damon, TB	.739
Rowand,Aaron, CWS	.738
Matthews Jr.,G, Tex	.729
Matos,Luis, Bal	.722

OPS by Right Fielders
(minimum 251 PA)

Guerrero,Vladimir, LAA	.976
Gibbons,Jay, Bal	.967
Sheffield,Gary, NYY	.881
Dye,Jermaine, CWS	.854
Nixon,Trot, Bos	.818
Brown,Emil, KC	.809
Ordonez,Magglio, Det	.808
Swisher,Nick, Oak	.798
Suzuki,Ichiro, Sea	.783
Jones,Jacque, Min	.774

OPS by Designated Hitters
(minimum 251 PA)

Ortiz,David, Bos	1.003
Hafner,Travis, Cle	1.001
Gomes,Jonny, TB	.920
Huff,Aubrey, TB	.904
Sweeney,Mike, KC	.883
Dellucci,David, Tex	.877
Hillenbrand,Shea, Tor	.821
Stairs,Matt, KC	.821
LeCroy,Matt, Min	.806
Ibanez,Raul, Sea	.792

2005 American League Batting Leaders

OPS Batting Left vs. LHP
(minimum 125 PA)

Matsui,Hideki, NYY	.972
Suzuki,Ichiro, Sea	.899
Ortiz,David, Bos	.894
Giambi,Jason, NYY	.879
Hafner,Travis, Cle	.878
Kotsay,Mark, Oak	.817
Damon,Johnny, Bos	.815
Anderson,Garret, LAA	.794
Ibanez,Raul, Sea	.769
Finley,Steve, LAA	.758

OPS Batting Left vs. RHP
(minimum 377 PA)

Hafner,Travis, Cle	1.062
Ortiz,David, Bos	1.054
Teixeira,Mark, Tex	.993
Roberts,Brian, Bal	.949
Martinez,Victor, Cle	.902
Sizemore,Grady, Cle	.902
Dellucci,David, Tex	.894
Mauer,Joe, Min	.889
Crawford,Carl, TB	.876
Crisp,Coco, Cle	.869

OPS Batting Right vs. LHP
(minimum 125 PA)

Sexson,Richie, Sea	1.117
Sheffield,Gary, NYY	1.109
Wells,Vernon, Tor	1.082
Molina,Bengie, LAA	1.078
LeCroy,Matt, Min	1.025
Varitek,Jason, Bos	1.000
Peralta,Jhonny, Cle	.991
Rodriguez,Alex, NYY	.987
Mench,Kevin, Tex	.980
Konerko,Paul, CWS	.956

OPS Batting Right vs. RHP
(minimum 377 PA)

Rodriguez,Alex, NYY	1.045
Ramirez,Manny, Bos	1.023
Guerrero,Vladimir, LAA	.961
Young,Michael, Tex	.899
Konerko,Paul, CWS	.895
Tejada,Miguel, Bal	.877
Sexson,Richie, Sea	.850
Mora,Melvin, Bal	.849
Soriano,Alfonso, Tex	.845
Dye,Jermaine, CWS	.841

OPS vs. LHP
(minimum 125 PA)

Sexson,Richie, Sea	1.117
Sheffield,Gary, NYY	1.109
Wells,Vernon, Tor	1.082
Molina,Bengie, LAA	1.078
LeCroy,Matt, Min	1.025
Varitek,Jason, Bos	1.000
Peralta,Jhonny, Cle	.991
Rodriguez,Alex, NYY	.987
Mench,Kevin, Tex	.980
Matsui,Hideki, NYY	.972

OPS vs. RHP
(minimum 377 PA)

Hafner,Travis, Cle	1.062
Ortiz,David, Bos	1.054
Rodriguez,Alex, NYY	1.045
Ramirez,Manny, Bos	1.023
Teixeira,Mark, Tex	.989
Guerrero,Vladimir, LAA	.961
Roberts,Brian, Bal	.949
Martinez,Victor, Cle	.902
Sizemore,Grady, Cle	.902
Young,Michael, Tex	.899

RC Per 27 Outs vs. LHP
(minimum 125 PA)

Sheffield,Gary, NYY	13.0
Sexson,Richie, Sea	10.7
Wells,Vernon, Tor	10.1
Molina,Bengie, LAA	9.1
LeCroy,Matt, Min	9.1
Varitek,Jason, Bos	9.1
Rodriguez,Alex, NYY	9.0
Matsui,Hideki, NYY	8.6
Peralta,Jhonny, Cle	8.2
Kielty,Bobby, Oak	7.7

RC Per 27 Outs vs. RHP
(minimum 377 PA)

Hafner,Travis, Cle	9.7
Ramirez,Manny, Bos	9.4
Teixeira,Mark, Tex	9.2
Ortiz,David, Bos	8.8
Rodriguez,Alex, NYY	8.4
Guerrero,Vladimir, LAA	7.7
Mauer,Joe, Min	7.4
Young,Michael, Tex	7.4
Roberts,Brian, Bal	7.3
Catalanotto,Fr, Tor	7.0

Highest RBI %
(minimum 502 PA)

Ramirez,Manny, Bos	12.58
Ortiz,David, Bos	12.07
Teixeira,Mark, Tex	11.80
Hafner,Travis, Cle	11.10
Guerrero,Vladimir, LAA	11.02
Cantu,Jorge, TB	11.01
Sexson,Richie, Sea	11.00
Sheffield,Gary, NYY	10.71
Rodriguez,Alex, NYY	10.60
Sweeney,Mike, KC	9.89

Lowest RBI %
(minimum 502 PA)

Podsednik,Scott, CWS	3.11
Kendall,Jason, Oak	4.90
Figgins,Chone, LAA	5.15
Reed,Jeremy, Sea	5.21
Lugo,Julio, TB	5.30
Berroa,Angel, KC	5.32
Ford,Lew, Min	5.47
Millar,Kevin, Bos	5.77
Rodriguez,Ivan, Det	5.88
Renteria,Edgar, Bos	5.97

Highest Strikeout per PA
(minimum 502 PA)

Sexson,Richie, Sea	.255
Dellucci,David, Tex	.234
Hinske,Eric, Tor	.225
Peralta,Jhonny, Cle	.225
Varitek,Jason, Bos	.217
Hafner,Travis, Cle	.213
Swisher,Nick, Oak	.211
Jones,Jacque, Min	.205
Inge,Brandon, Det	.202
Giambi,Jason, NYY	.200

Lowest Strikeout per PA
(minimum 502 PA)

Kendall,Jason, Oak	.058
Guerrero,Vladimir, LAA	.081
Kotsay,Mark, Oak	.081
Cabrera,Orlando, LAA	.085
Suzuki,Ichiro, Sea	.089
Damon,Johnny, Bos	.100
Hatteberg,Scott, Oak	.103
Lugo,Julio, TB	.104
Adams,Russ, Tor	.105
Gibbons,Jay, Bal	.108

Home Runs At Home

Teixeira,Mark, Tex	30
Rodriguez,Alex, NYY	26
Soriano,Alfonso, Tex	25
Konerko,Paul, CWS	23
Ramirez,Manny, Bos	22
Sexson,Richie, Sea	21
Blalock,Hank, Tex	20
Ortiz,David, Bos	20
Guerrero,Vladimir, LAA	19
Sheffield,Gary, NYY	19

Home Runs Away

Ortiz,David, Bos	27
Ramirez,Manny, Bos	23
Rodriguez,Alex, NYY	22
Hafner,Travis, Cle	19
Sexson,Richie, Sea	18
Konerko,Paul, CWS	17
Blake,Casey, Cle	16
Dye,Jermaine, CWS	16
Giambi,Jason, NYY	16
3 tied with	15

Longest Avg Home Run
(min 10 over the wall)

Hafner,Travis, Cle	407
Morneau,Justin, Min	405
Ortiz,David, Bos	404
Gomes,Jonny, TB	402
Rodriguez,Alex, NYY	402
Brown,Emil, KC	402
Sexson,Richie, Sea	401
Jones,Jacque, Min	401
Crawford,Carl, TB	400
Ramirez,Manny, Bos	400

Shortest Avg Home Run
(min 10 over the wall)

Roberts,Brian, Bal	358
Martinez,Tino, NYY	363
Palmeiro,Rafael, Bal	367
Kotsay,Mark, Oak	370
Lopez,Javy, Bal	370
Zaun,Gregg, Tor	370
Hollins,Damon, TB	372
Iguchi,Tadahito, CWS	376
Mueller,Bill, Bos	376
Belliard,Ronnie, Cle	376

2005 American League Batting Leaders

Under Age 25: AB Per HR
(minimum 502 PA)

Teixeira,Mark, Tex	15.0
Peralta,Jhonny, Cle	21.0
Cantu,Jorge, TB	21.4
Swisher,Nick, Oak	22.0
Morneau,Justin, Min	22.3
Blalock,Hank, Tex	25.9
Sizemore,Grady, Cle	29.1
Crisp,Coco, Cle	37.1
Cano,Robinson, NYY	37.3
Crawford,Carl, TB	42.9

Under Age 25: OPS
(minimum 502 PA)

Teixeira,Mark, Tex	.954
Peralta,Jhonny, Cle	.885
Sizemore,Grady, Cle	.832
Crisp,Coco, Cle	.810
Cantu,Jorge, TB	.808
DeJesus,David, KC	.804
Crawford,Carl, TB	.800
Mauer,Joe, Min	.783
Cano,Robinson, NYY	.778
Swisher,Nick, Oak	.768

Under Age 25: RC/27 Outs
(minimum 502 PA)

Teixeira,Mark, Tex	8.4
Peralta,Jhonny, Cle	6.2
DeJesus,David, KC	5.9
Mauer,Joe, Min	5.8
Crawford,Carl, TB	5.7
Sizemore,Grady, Cle	5.5
Crisp,Coco, Cle	5.5
Cantu,Jorge, TB	5.1
Adams,Russ, Tor	4.7
Blalock,Hank, Tex	4.6

Lowest SB Success Pct
(minimum 20 SBA)

Reed,Jeremy, Sea	52.2
Rios,Alexis, Tor	60.9
Punto,Nick, Min	61.9
Matos,Luis, Bal	65.4
Ozuna,Pablo, CWS	66.7
Sizemore,Grady, Cle	68.8
Crisp,Coco, Cle	71.4
Podsednik,Scott, CWS	72.0
Roberts,Brian, Bal	73.0
Iguchi,Tadahito, CWS	75.0

Home RC Per 27 Outs
(minimum 251 PA)

Teixeira,Mark, Tex	11.3
Ramirez,Manny, Bos	10.4
Rodriguez,Alex, NYY	10.2
Ortiz,David, Bos	9.8
Sheffield,Gary, NYY	9.2
Soriano,Alfonso, Tex	8.3
Hafner,Travis, Cle	8.2
Giambi,Jason, NYY	8.2
Guerrero,Vladimir, LAA	7.9
Peralta,Jhonny, Cle	7.8

Road RC Per 27 Outs
(minimum 251 PA)

Hafner,Travis, Cle	9.3
Giambi,Jason, NYY	9.2
Sexson,Richie, Sea	8.1
Roberts,Brian, Bal	7.8
Sizemore,Grady, Cle	7.6
Guerrero,Vladimir, LAA	7.4
Young,Michael, Tex	7.1
Rodriguez,Alex, NYY	7.1
Ramirez,Manny, Bos	7.1
Ellis,Mark, Oak	6.8

Swing and Miss %
(minimum 1500 Pitches Seen)

Sexson,Richie, Sea	24.4
Sosa,Sammy, Bal	23.0
Gomes,Jonny, TB	22.5
Jones,Jacque, Min	20.2
Rodriguez,Alex, NYY	19.1
Hafner,Travis, Cle	18.9
Koskie,Corey, Tor	18.7
Hinske,Eric, Tor	17.9
Dellucci,David, Tex	17.7
Everett,Carl, CWS	17.0

2005 National League Batting Leaders

Batting Average (minimum 502 PA)		On Base Percentage (minimum 502 PA)		Slugging Average (minimum 502 PA)		Home Runs	
Lee,Derrek, ChC	.335	Helton,Todd, Col	.445	Lee,Derrek, ChC	.662	Jones,Andruw, Atl	51
Pujols,Albert, StL	.330	Pujols,Albert, StL	.430	Pujols,Albert, StL	.609	Lee,Derrek, ChC	46
Cabrera,Miguel, Fla	.323	Giles,Brian, SD	.423	Delgado,Carlos, Fla	.582	Pujols,Albert, StL	41
Helton,Todd, Col	.320	Lee,Derrek, ChC	.418	Griffey Jr.,Ken, Cin	.576	Dunn,Adam, Cin	40
Casey,Sean, Cin	.312	Berkman,Lance, Hou	.411	Jones,Andruw, Atl	.575	Glaus,Troy, Ari	37
Tracy,Chad, Ari	.308	Johnson,Nick, Was	.408	Ramirez,Aramis, ChC	.568	Ensberg,Morgan, Hou	36
Holliday,Matt, Col	.307	Abreu,Bobby, Phi	.405	Cabrera,Miguel, Fla	.561	Griffey Jr.,Ken, Cin	35
Wright,David, NYM	.306	Bay,Jason, Pit	.402	Bay,Jason, Pit	.559	Floyd,Cliff, NYM	34
Bay,Jason, Pit	.306	Delgado,Carlos, Fla	.399	Ensberg,Morgan, Hou	.557	Cabrera,Miguel, Fla	33
Clark,Brady, Mil	.306	Castillo,Luis, Fla	.391	Tracy,Chad, Ari	.553	Delgado,Carlos, Fla	33

Games		Plate Appearances		At Bats		Hits	
Abreu,Bobby, Phi	162	Reyes,Jose, NYM	733	Reyes,Jose, NYM	696	Lee,Derrek, ChC	199
Bay,Jason, Pit	162	Rollins,Jimmy, Phi	732	Rollins,Jimmy, Phi	677	Cabrera,Miguel, Fla	198
Lee,Carlos, Mil	162	Abreu,Bobby, Phi	719	Pierre,Juan, Fla	656	Rollins,Jimmy, Phi	196
Pierre,Juan, Fla	162	Pierre,Juan, Fla	719	Eckstein,David, StL	630	Pujols,Albert, StL	195
Pujols,Albert, StL	161	Eckstein,David, StL	713	Lee,Carlos, Mil	618	Reyes,Jose, NYM	190
Reyes,Jose, NYM	161	Bay,Jason, Pit	707	Furcal,Rafael, Atl	616	Eckstein,David, StL	185
Burnitz,Jeromy, ChC	160	Pujols,Albert, StL	700	Cabrera,Miguel, Fla	613	Bay,Jason, Pit	183
Dunn,Adam, Cin	160	Lee,Derrek, ChC	691	Burnitz,Jeromy, ChC	605	Clark,Brady, Mil	183
Jones,Andruw, Atl	160	Furcal,Rafael, Atl	689	Bay,Jason, Pit	599	Pierre,Juan, Fla	181
Wright,David, NYM	160	Lee,Carlos, Mil	688	Clark,Brady, Mil	599	Wright,David, NYM	176

Singles		Doubles		Triples		Total Bases	
Taveras,Willy, Hou	152	Lee,Derrek, ChC	50	Reyes,Jose, NYM	17	Lee,Derrek, ChC	393
Pierre,Juan, Fla	147	Giles,Marcus, Atl	45	Pierre,Juan, Fla	13	Pujols,Albert, StL	360
Eckstein,David, StL	144	Helton,Todd, Col	45	Furcal,Rafael, Atl	11	Cabrera,Miguel, Fla	344
Reyes,Jose, NYM	142	Bay,Jason, Pit	44	Rollins,Jimmy, Phi	11	Jones,Andruw, Atl	337
Clark,Brady, Mil	138	Cabrera,Miguel, Fla	43	Roberts,Dave, SD	10	Bay,Jason, Pit	335
Rollins,Jimmy, Phi	135	Randa,Joe, Cin-SD	43	Giles,Brian, SD	8	Delgado,Carlos, Fla	303
Casey,Sean, Cin	124	Jenkins,Geoff, Mil	42	Eckstein,David, StL	7	Lee,Carlos, Mil	301
Furcal,Rafael, Atl	121	Wilkerson,Brad, Was	42	Holliday,Matt, Col	7	Wright,David, NYM	301
Cabrera,Miguel, Fla	120	Wright,David, NYM	42	Wilkerson,Brad, Was	7	3 tied with	293
Vizquel,Omar, SF	119	2 tied with	41	Wilson,Jack, Pit	7		

Runs Scored		RBI		Walks		Strikeouts	
Pujols,Albert, StL	129	Jones,Andruw, Atl	128	Giles,Brian, SD	119	Dunn,Adam, Cin	168
Lee,Derrek, ChC	120	Burrell,Pat, Phi	117	Abreu,Bobby, Phi	117	Burrell,Pat, Phi	160
Rollins,Jimmy, Phi	115	Pujols,Albert, StL	117	Dunn,Adam, Cin	114	Wilson,Pr, Col-Was	148
Bay,Jason, Pit	110	Cabrera,Miguel, Fla	116	Helton,Todd, Col	106	Wilkerson,Brad, Was	147
Dunn,Adam, Cin	107	Delgado,Carlos, Fla	115	Burrell,Pat, Phi	99	Glaus,Troy, Ari	145
Cabrera,Miguel, Fla	106	Lee,Carlos, Mil	114	Pujols,Albert, StL	97	Bay,Jason, Pit	142
Abreu,Bobby, Phi	104	Lee,Derrek, ChC	107	Bay,Jason, Pit	95	Edmonds,Jim, StL	139
Giles,Marcus, Atl	104	Kent,Jeff, LAD	105	Berkman,Lance, Hou	91	Jenkins,Geoff, Mil	138
Furcal,Rafael, Atl	100	Utley,Chase, Phi	105	Edmonds,Jim, StL	91	Abreu,Bobby, Phi	134
Kent,Jeff, LAD	100	2 tied with	102	2 tied with	85	Cabrera,Miguel, Fla	125

2005 National League Batting Leaders

Sacrifice Hits		Sacrifice Flies		Stolen Bases		Caught Stealing	
Vizquel,Omar, SF	20	Lee,Carlos, Mil	11	Reyes,Jose, NYM	60	Pierre,Juan, Fla	17
Castillo,Luis, Fla	18	Guillen,Jose, Was	9	Pierre,Juan, Fla	57	Reyes,Jose, NYM	15
Pettitte,Andy, Hou	15	Lowell,Mike, Fla	9	Furcal,Rafael, Atl	46	Clark,Brady, Mil	13
Hernandez,Liv, Was	14	Abreu,Bobby, Phi	8	Rollins,Jimmy, Phi	41	Roberts,Dave, SD	12
Carroll,Jamey, Was	13	Giles,Brian, SD	8	Freel,Ryan, Cin	36	Taveras,Willy, Hou	11
Webb,Brandon, Ari	13	Green,Shawn, Ari	8	Taveras,Willy, Hou	34	Freel,Ryan, Cin	10
Cairo,Miguel, NYM	12	Lo Duca,Paul, Fla	8	Abreu,Bobby, Phi	31	Furcal,Rafael, Atl	10
Lowry,Noah, SF	12	Ward,Daryle, Pit	8	Counsell,Craig, Ari	26	Vizquel,Omar, SF	10
Perez,Neifi, ChC	12	7 tied with	7	Vizquel,Omar, SF	24	Wilkerson,Brad, Was	10
Smoltz,John, Atl	12			Roberts,Dave, SD	23	3 tied with	9

Intentional Walks		Hit By Pitch		Grounded Into DP		Grounded Into DP Pct (minimum 50 GIDP Ops)	
Pujols,Albert, StL	27	Guillen,Jose, Was	19	Casey,Sean, Cin	27	Nevin,Phil, SD	3.39
Lee,Derrek, ChC	23	Jenkins,Geoff, Mil	19	Bell,David, Phi	24	Langerhans,Ryan, Atl	3.57
Helton,Todd, Col	22	Clark,Brady, Mil	18	Perez,Neifi, ChC	22	Carroll,Jamey, Was	3.85
Delgado,Carlos, Fla	20	Biggio,Craig, Hou	17	Cabrera,Miguel, Fla	20	Lofton,Kenny, Phi	4.17
Abreu,Bobby, Phi	15	Delgado,Carlos, Fla	17	Feliz,Pedro, SF	20	Dunn,Adam, Cin	4.48
Dunn,Adam, Cin	14	Jones,Andruw, Atl	15	Clayton,Royce, Ari	19	Mohr,Dustan, Col	4.48
Lieberthal,Mike, Phi	14	Doumit,Ryan, Pit	13	Durham,Ray, SF	19	Floyd,Cliff, NYM	4.63
Floyd,Cliff, NYM	13	Eckstein,David, StL	13	Jones,Andruw, Atl	19	Abreu,Bobby, Phi	4.70
Jones,Andruw, Atl	13	LaRue,Jason, Cin	13	Kent,Jeff, LAD	19	Drew,J.D., LAD	4.92
3 tied with	12	3 tied with	12	Pujols,Albert, StL	19	Everett,Adam, Hou	4.95

Leadoff Hitters OBP (minimum 150 PA)		Cleanup Hitters SLG (minimum 150 PA)		BA vs. LHP (minimum 125 PA)		BA vs. RHP (minimum 377 PA)	
Sanchez,Freddy, Pit	.390	Clark,Tony, Ari	.693	Bell,David, Phi	.400	Helton,Todd, Col	.353
Winn,Randy, SF	.382	Cabrera,Miguel, Fla	.649	Gonzalez,Luis A, Col	.380	Pujols,Albert, StL	.340
Clark,Brady, Mil	.372	Ensberg,Morgan, Hou	.600	Ramirez,Aramis, ChC	.355	Lee,Derrek, ChC	.336
Freel,Ryan, Cin	.371	Griffey Jr.,Ken, Cin	.595	Bay,Jason, Pit	.347	Cabrera,Miguel, Fla	.329
Lawton,Matt, Pit-ChC	.366	Jones,Andruw, Atl	.585	Hall,Bill, Mil	.336	Delgado,Carlos, Fla	.326
Eckstein,David, StL	.364	Delgado,Carlos, Fla	.573	Wright,David, NYM	.336	Tracy,Chad, Ari	.324
Wilkerson,Brad, Was	.353	Ramirez,Aramis, ChC	.569	Casey,Sean, Cin	.335	Utley,Chase, Phi	.313
Roberts,Dave, SD	.352	Guillen,Jose, Was	.560	Lee,Derrek, ChC	.333	Lopez,Felipe, Cin	.312
Counsell,Craig, Ari	.351	Holliday,Matt, Col	.533	Johnson,Nick, Was	.328	Taveras,Willy, Hou	.312
Furcal,Rafael, Atl	.348	Johnson,Nick, Was	.518	Ellison,Jason, SF	.328	Jenkins,Geoff, Mil	.307

Home BA (minimum 251 PA)		Away BA (minimum 251 PA)		OBP vs. LHP (minimum 125 PA)		OBP vs. RHP (minimum 377 PA)	
Holliday,Matt, Col	.357	Pujols,Albert, StL	.349	Bell,David, Phi	.461	Helton,Todd, Col	.480
Helton,Todd, Col	.353	Lee,Derrek, ChC	.342	Bay,Jason, Pit	.444	Pujols,Albert, StL	.432
Atkins,Garrett, Col	.339	Cabrera,Miguel, Fla	.341	Johnson,Nick, Was	.444	Giles,Brian, SD	.431
Taveras,Willy, Hou	.330	Bay,Jason, Pit	.337	Burrell,Pat, Phi	.442	Delgado,Carlos, Fla	.431
Lee,Derrek, ChC	.328	Giles,Brian, SD	.333	Lee,Derrek, ChC	.439	Abreu,Bobby, Phi	.430
Griffey Jr.,Ken, Cin	.325	Casey,Sean, Cin	.330	Michaels,Jason, Phi	.438	Dunn,Adam, Cin	.421
Clark,Brady, Mil	.324	Alou,Moises, SF	.323	Pujols,Albert, StL	.424	Lee,Derrek, ChC	.411
Grudzielanek,M, StL	.322	Guillen,Jose, Was	.320	Freel,Ryan, Cin	.419	Berkman,Lance, Hou	.409
Furcal,Rafael, Atl	.321	Kent,Jeff, LAD	.319	Ramirez,Aramis, ChC	.418	Johnson,Nick, Was	.394
Wilson,Jack, Pit	.311	Ramirez,Aramis, ChC	.318	Berkman,Lance, Hou	.416	Overbay,Lyle, Mil	.390

2005 National League Batting Leaders

BA Close & Late	
(minimum 50 PA)	
Hernandez,Ram, SD	.448
Lee,Derrek, ChC	.414
Clark,Tony, Ari	.397
Jones,Chipper, Atl	.397
Robles,Oscar, LAD	.384
Conine,Jeff, Fla	.379
Snow,J.T., SF	.371
Berkman,Lance, Hou	.370
Nunez,Abraham , StL	.369
Helton,Todd, Col	.353

BA Bases Loaded	
(minimum 10 PA)	
Pierre,Juan, Fla	.625
Lopez,Felipe, Cin	.600
Nunez,Abraham , StL	.600
Church,Ryan, Was	.571
Guillen,Jose, Was	.556
Taguchi,So, StL	.545
Wright,David, NYM	.538
Kent,Jeff, LAD	.533
5 tied with	.500

SLG vs. LHP	
(minimum 125 PA)	
Ramirez,Aramis, ChC	.694
Lee,Derrek, ChC	.673
Barrett,Michael, ChC	.624
Bay,Jason, Pit	.620
Wright,David, NYM	.602
Bell,David, Phi	.593
Edmonds,Jim, StL	.584
Ensberg,Morgan, Hou	.575
Wilson,Pr, Col-Was	.571
Hall,Bill, Mil	.560

SLG vs. RHP	
(minimum 377 PA)	
Lee,Derrek, ChC	.658
Pujols,Albert, StL	.633
Helton,Todd, Col	.630
Delgado,Carlos, Fla	.626
Jones,Andruw, Atl	.588
Tracy,Chad, Ari	.582
Dunn,Adam, Cin	.580
Cabrera,Miguel, Fla	.565
Utley,Chase, Phi	.561
Berkman,Lance, Hou	.558

Batting Average w/ RISP	
(minimum 100 PA)	
Taguchi,So, StL	.407
Eckstein,David, StL	.373
Kent,Jeff, LAD	.366
Giles,Brian, SD	.360
Bay,Jason, Pit	.346
Aurilia,Rich, Cin	.343
Saenz,Olmedo, LAD	.333
Encarnacion,Ju, Fla	.331
Lee,Derrek, ChC	.331
Vizquel,Omar, SF	.331

At Bats Per Home Run	
(minimum 502 PA)	
Jones,Andruw, Atl	11.5
Lee,Derrek, ChC	12.9
Dunn,Adam, Cin	13.6
Griffey Jr.,Ken, Cin	14.0
Pujols,Albert, StL	14.4
Glaus,Troy, Ari	14.5
Ensberg,Morgan, Hou	14.6
Ramirez,Aramis, ChC	14.9
Delgado,Carlos, Fla	15.8
Edmonds,Jim, StL	16.1

Pitches Seen	
Abreu,Bobby, Phi	3164
Burrell,Pat, Phi	2859
Eckstein,David, StL	2859
Dunn,Adam, Cin	2848
Lee,Derrek, ChC	2787
Wilkerson,Brad, Was	2787
Counsell,Craig, Ari	2735
Bay,Jason, Pit	2734
Pujols,Albert, StL	2720
Pierre,Juan, Fla	2663

Pitches Per Plate App	
(minimum 502 PA)	
Abreu,Bobby, Phi	4.40
Burrell,Pat, Phi	4.27
Dunn,Adam, Cin	4.24
Wilkerson,Brad, Was	4.22
Edmonds,Jim, StL	4.18
Hall,Bill, Mil	4.17
Helton,Todd, Col	4.13
Glaus,Troy, Ari	4.12
Johnson,Nick, Was	4.11
Counsell,Craig, Ari	4.08

Pct Pitches Taken	
(minimum 1500 Pitches)	
Abreu,Bobby, Phi	66.6
Giles,Brian, SD	65.9
Robles,Oscar, LAD	64.9
Roberts,Dave, SD	64.3
Counsell,Craig, Ari	63.7
Freel,Ryan, Cin	63.5
Castillo,Luis, Fla	63.4
Jones,Chipper, Atl	63.3
Lopez,Felipe, Cin	61.8
Johnson,Nick, Was	61.5

Highest GB/FB Ratio	
(minimum 502 PA)	
Castillo,Luis, Fla	4.13
Pierre,Juan, Fla	2.81
Clayton,Royce, Ari	2.63
Taveras,Willy, Hou	2.06
Lopez,Felipe, Cin	1.99
Lawton,Matt, Pit-ChC	1.94
Wilson,Pr, Col-Was	1.89
Overbay,Lyle, Mil	1.88
Casey,Sean, Cin	1.76
Green,Shawn, Ari	1.66

Lowest GB/FB Ratio	
(minimum 502 PA)	
Lane,Jason, Hou	0.57
Kent,Jeff, LAD	0.65
Lowell,Mike, Fla	0.67
Wilkerson,Brad, Was	0.69
Burrell,Pat, Phi	0.69
Lee,Carlos, Mil	0.71
Edmonds,Jim, StL	0.74
Dunn,Adam, Cin	0.75
Griffey Jr.,Ken, Cin	0.77
Tracy,Chad, Ari	0.77

Highest SB Success Pct	
(minimum 20 SBA)	
Bay,Jason, Pit	95.5
Lofton,Kenny, Phi	88.0
Rollins,Jimmy, Phi	87.2
Furcal,Rafael, Atl	82.1
Reyes,Jose, NYM	80.0
Counsell,Craig, Ari	78.8
Freel,Ryan, Cin	78.3
Abreu,Bobby, Phi	77.5
Pierre,Juan, Fla	77.0
Taveras,Willy, Hou	75.6

Steals of Third	
Rollins,Jimmy, Phi	13
Reyes,Jose, NYM	11
Freel,Ryan, Cin	8
Pierre,Juan, Fla	8
Biggio,Craig, Hou	6
Giles,Marcus, Atl	6
Lee,Carlos, Mil	6
Bay,Jason, Pit	5
Hall,Bill, Mil	5
Sanders,Reggie, StL	5

Longest Home Run		
Pena,Wily Mo, Cin, 6/29		492
Pena,Wily Mo, Cin, 4/17		490
Lee,Derrek, ChC, 4/18		482
Dunn,Adam, Cin, 5/4		470
Branyan,R, Mil, 4/11		465
Dunn,Adam, Cin, 7/22		464
6 tied with		460

Best BPS on OutZ	
(minimum 502 PA)	
Giles,Brian, SD	.738
Castillo,Luis, Fla	.614
Helton,Todd, Col	.591
Furcal,Rafael, Atl	.582
Johnson,Nick, Was	.564
Casey,Sean, Cin	.537
Lee,Derrek, ChC	.516
Rollins,Jimmy, Phi	.516
Counsell,Craig, Ari	.500
Ramirez,Aramis, ChC	.485

Worst BPS on OutZ	
(minimum 502 PA)	
Bay,Jason, Pit	.117
Dunn,Adam, Cin	.162
Castilla,Vinny, Was	.181
Kent,Jeff, LAD	.194
Gonzalez,Luis, Ari	.198
Clayton,Royce, Ari	.200
Wilkerson,Brad, Was	.206
Green,Shawn, Ari	.209
Wilson,Pr, Col-Was	.233
Berkman,Lance, Hou	.245

2005 National League Batting Leaders

Best BPS vs Fastballs		Best BPS vs Curveballs		Best BPS vs Changeups		Best BPS vs Sliders	
(minimum 251 PA)		(minimum 50 PA)		(minimum 50 PA)		(minimum 32 PA)	
Lee,Derrek, ChC	1.098	Cabrera,Miguel, Fla	.932	Alou,Moises, SF	1.358	Reyes,Jose, NYM	1.076
Griffey Jr.,Ken, Cin	1.040	Gonzalez,Alex, Fla	.926	Tracy,Chad, Ari	1.115	Sanders,Reggie, StL	1.065
Jones,Andruw, Atl	1.023	Floyd,Cliff, NYM	.750	Francoeur,Jeff, Atl	1.084	Lopez,Felipe, Cin	1.019
Glaus,Troy, Ari	1.007	Biggio,Craig, Hou	.722	Atkins,Garrett, Col	1.081	Pujols,Albert, StL	1.012
Pujols,Albert, StL	.976	Casey,Sean, Cin	.709	Encarnacion,Ju, Fla	1.052	Jones,Chipper, Atl	1.000
Cabrera,Miguel, Fla	.954	Wright,David, NYM	.674	Utley,Chase, Phi	1.030	Clark,Tony, Ari	.974
Delgado,Carlos, Fla	.947	Rollins,Jimmy, Phi	.673	Randa,Joe, Cin-SD	1.021	Walker,Larry, StL	.967
Abreu,Bobby, Phi	.938	Reyes,Jose, NYM	.644	Lamb,Mike, Hou	1.020	Lee,Derrek, ChC	.942
Utley,Chase, Phi	.922	Beltran,Carlos, NYM	.638	Dunn,Adam, Cin	1.014	Delgado,Carlos, Fla	.929
2 tied with	.921	Eckstein,David, StL	.627	Wright,David, NYM	1.000	Cabrera,Miguel, Fla	.895

OPS		OPS First Half		OPS Second Half		OPS by Catchers	
(minimum 502 PA)		(minimum 251 PA)		(minimum 251 PA)		(minimum 251 PA)	
Lee,Derrek, ChC	1.080	Lee,Derrek, ChC	1.185	Helton,Todd, Col	1.111	Barrett,Michael, ChC	.836
Pujols,Albert, StL	1.039	Pujols,Albert, StL	1.017	Pujols,Albert, StL	1.068	LaRue,Jason, Cin	.789
Delgado,Carlos, Fla	.981	Ensberg,Morgan, Hou	.983	Jenkins,Geoff, Mil	1.024	Piazza,Mike, NYM	.785
Helton,Todd, Col	.979	Cabrera,Miguel, Fla	.959	Bay,Jason, Pit	.998	Hernandez,Ram, SD	.779
Bay,Jason, Pit	.961	Abreu,Bobby, Phi	.954	Berkman,Lance, Hou	.994	Lieberthal,Mike, Phi	.756
Cabrera,Miguel, Fla	.946	Johnson,Nick, Was	.952	Wright,David, NYM	.991	Miller,Damian, Mil	.750
Ensberg,Morgan, Hou	.945	Edmonds,Jim, StL	.942	Tracy,Chad, Ari	.982	Schneider,Brian, Was	.738
Griffey Jr.,Ken, Cin	.945	Giles,Brian, SD	.942	Howard,Ryan, Phi	.968	Lo Duca,Paul, Fla	.715
Berkman,Lance, Hou	.935	Dunn,Adam, Cin	.934	Lee,Derrek, ChC	.961	Matheny,Mike, SF	.705
Dunn,Adam, Cin	.927	Drew,J.D., LAD	.932	Utley,Chase, Phi	.934	Ausmus,Brad, Hou	.684

OPS by First Basemen		OPS by Second Basemen		OPS by Third Basemen		OPS by Shortstops	
(minimum 251 PA)		(minimum 251 PA)		(minimum 251 PA)		(minimum 251 PA)	
Lee,Derrek, ChC	1.080	Utley,Chase, Phi	.933	Jones,Chipper, Atl	.986	Lopez,Felipe, Cin	.821
Clark,Tony, Ari	1.042	Kent,Jeff, LAD	.878	Ensberg,Morgan, Hou	.942	Furcal,Rafael, Atl	.777
Pujols,Albert, StL	1.042	Aurilia,Rich, Cin	.827	Ramirez,Aramis, ChC	.930	Rollins,Jimmy, Phi	.769
Berkman,Lance, Hou	1.007	Walker,Todd, ChC	.827	Wright,David, NYM	.911	Barmes,Clint, Col	.767
Helton,Todd, Col	.978	Giles,Marcus, Atl	.826	Glaus,Troy, Ari	.890	Eckstein,David, StL	.760
Delgado,Carlos, Fla	.973	Biggio,Craig, Hou	.816	Randa,Joe, Cin-SD	.774	Greene,Khalil, SD	.727
Howard,Ryan, Phi	.927	Durham,Ray, SF	.777	Atkins,Garrett, Col	.773	Hardy,J.J., Mil	.712
Johnson,Nick, Was	.889	Castillo,Luis, Fla	.768	Nunez,Abraham , StL	.736	Vizquel,Omar, SF	.694
Tracy,Chad, Ari	.879	Vidro,Jose, Was	.765	Castilla,Vinny, Was	.728	Gonzalez,Alex, Fla	.688
Choi,Hee Seop, LAD	.821	Gonzalez,Luis A, Col	.742	Feliz,Pedro, SF	.706	Reyes,Jose, NYM	.685

OPS by Left Fielders		OPS by Center Fielders		OPS by Right Fielders		OPS by Pitchers	
(minimum 251 PA)		(minimum 251 PA)		(minimum 251 PA)		(minimum 66 PA)	
Bay,Jason, Pit	1.005	Griffey Jr.,Ken, Cin	.960	Giles,Brian, SD	.904	Marquis,Jason, StL	.799
Cabrera,Miguel, Fla	.959	Jones,Andruw, Atl	.923	Francoeur,Jeff, Atl	.886	Zambrano,Carlos, ChC	.763
Dunn,Adam, Cin	.957	Edmonds,Jim, StL	.920	Jenkins,Geoff, Mil	.882	Lowry,Noah, SF	.685
Sanders,Reggie, StL	.914	Michaels,Jason, Phi	.886	Abreu,Bobby, Phi	.876	Willis,Dontrelle, Fla	.646
Burrell,Pat, Phi	.891	Bradley,Milton, LAD	.836	Walker,Larry, StL	.862	Hernandez,Liv, Was	.619
Alou,Moises, SF	.870	Wilkerson,Brad, Was	.818	Diaz,Victor, NYM	.820	Vazquez,Javier, Ari	.575
Holliday,Matt, Col	.870	Lofton,Kenny, Phi	.811	Guillen,Jose, Was	.818	Suppan,Jeff, StL	.539
Floyd,Cliff, NYM	.866	Wilson,Pr, Col-Was	.804	Green,Shawn, Ari	.809	Clemens,Roger, Hou	.522
Gonzalez,Luis, Ari	.824	Clark,Brady, Mil	.798	Lawton,Matt, Pit-ChC	.806	Weaver,Jeff, LAD	.515
Lee,Carlos, Mil	.811	Roberts,Dave, SD	.784	Encarnacion,Ju, Fla	.797	Ramirez,Horacio, Atl	.497

2005 National League Batting Leaders

OPS Batting Left vs. LHP
(minimum 125 PA)

Edmonds,Jim, StL	.969
Johnson,Nick, Was	.916
Griffey Jr.,Ken, Cin	.890
Giles,Brian, SD	.840
Casey,Sean, Cin	.820
Utley,Chase, Phi	.817
Jenkins,Geoff, Mil	.806
Wilkerson,Brad, Was	.804
Dunn,Adam, Cin	.784
Delgado,Carlos, Fla	.769

OPS Batting Left vs. RHP
(minimum 377 PA)

Helton,Todd, Col	1.110
Delgado,Carlos, Fla	1.057
Dunn,Adam, Cin	1.001
Berkman,Lance, Hou	.967
Tracy,Chad, Ari	.952
Utley,Chase, Phi	.946
Abreu,Bobby, Phi	.942
Giles,Brian, SD	.933
Jenkins,Geoff, Mil	.922
Lopez,Felipe, Cin	.920

OPS Batting Right vs. LHP
(minimum 125 PA)

Lee,Derrek, ChC	1.112
Ramirez,Aramis, ChC	1.112
Bay,Jason, Pit	1.064
Bell,David, Phi	1.054
Barrett,Michael, ChC	1.039
Wright,David, NYM	1.017
Burrell,Pat, Phi	.994
Ensberg,Morgan, Hou	.986
Hall,Bill, Mil	.967
Pujols,Albert, StL	.964

OPS Batting Right vs. RHP
(minimum 377 PA)

Lee,Derrek, ChC	1.069
Pujols,Albert, StL	1.065
Cabrera,Miguel, Fla	.944
Jones,Andruw, Atl	.934
Ensberg,Morgan, Hou	.931
Bay,Jason, Pit	.927
Kent,Jeff, LAD	.900
Wright,David, NYM	.881
Glaus,Troy, Ari	.876
Holliday,Matt, Col	.871

OPS vs. LHP
(minimum 125 PA)

Lee,Derrek, ChC	1.112
Ramirez,Aramis, ChC	1.112
Bay,Jason, Pit	1.064
Bell,David, Phi	1.054
Barrett,Michael, ChC	1.039
Wright,David, NYM	1.017
Burrell,Pat, Phi	.994
Ensberg,Morgan, Hou	.986
Edmonds,Jim, StL	.969
Hall,Bill, Mil	.967

OPS vs. RHP
(minimum 377 PA)

Helton,Todd, Col	1.110
Lee,Derrek, ChC	1.069
Pujols,Albert, StL	1.065
Delgado,Carlos, Fla	1.057
Dunn,Adam, Cin	1.001
Berkman,Lance, Hou	.967
Tracy,Chad, Ari	.952
Utley,Chase, Phi	.946
Cabrera,Miguel, Fla	.944
Abreu,Bobby, Phi	.942

RC Per 27 Outs vs. LHP
(minimum 125 PA)

Bell,David, Phi	10.3
Burrell,Pat, Phi	10.0
Bay,Jason, Pit	9.1
Barrett,Michael, ChC	8.9
Lee,Derrek, ChC	8.5
Ramirez,Aramis, ChC	8.5
Edmonds,Jim, StL	7.7
Gonzalez,Luis A, Col	7.6
Pujols,Albert, StL	7.1
Cabrera,Miguel, Fla	7.1

RC Per 27 Outs vs. RHP
(minimum 377 PA)

Helton,Todd, Col	10.2
Delgado,Carlos, Fla	9.5
Pujols,Albert, StL	9.4
Lee,Derrek, ChC	8.6
Dunn,Adam, Cin	8.4
Abreu,Bobby, Phi	8.0
Giles,Brian, SD	7.6
Ensberg,Morgan, Hou	7.4
Bay,Jason, Pit	7.4
Lopez,Felipe, Cin	7.3

Highest RBI %
(minimum 502 PA)

Delgado,Carlos, Fla	11.01
Jones,Andruw, Atl	10.83
Ramirez,Aramis, ChC	10.77
Griffey Jr.,Ken, Cin	10.19
Pujols,Albert, StL	9.96
Lee,Derrek, ChC	9.94
Burrell,Pat, Phi	9.91
Ensberg,Morgan, Hou	9.81
Cabrera,Miguel, Fla	9.78
Kent,Jeff, LAD	9.75

Lowest RBI %
(minimum 502 PA)

Taveras,Willy, Hou	3.07
Castillo,Luis, Fla	3.77
Counsell,Craig, Ari	4.29
Pierre,Juan, Fla	4.40
Vizquel,Omar, SF	4.54
Clayton,Royce, Ari	4.85
Rollins,Jimmy, Phi	4.98
Wilson,Jack, Pit	5.14
Reyes,Jose, NYM	5.45
Clark,Brady, Mil	5.55

Highest Strikeout per PA
(minimum 502 PA)

Wilson,Pr, Col-Was	.257
Dunn,Adam, Cin	.250
Edmonds,Jim, StL	.245
Burrell,Pat, Phi	.239
Glaus,Troy, Ari	.229
Jenkins,Geoff, Mil	.223
Wilkerson,Brad, Was	.222
Bay,Jason, Pit	.201
Delgado,Carlos, Fla	.196
Mackowiak,Rob, Pit	.195

Lowest Strikeout per PA
(minimum 502 PA)

Castillo,Luis, Fla	.061
Eckstein,David, StL	.062
Pierre,Juan, Fla	.063
Perez,Neifi, ChC	.077
Casey,Sean, Cin	.082
Clark,Brady, Mil	.082
Vizquel,Omar, SF	.089
Wilson,Jack, Pit	.091
Pujols,Albert, StL	.093
Giles,Brian, SD	.095

Home Runs At Home

Dunn,Adam, Cin	26
Lee,Derrek, ChC	24
Pujols,Albert, StL	23
Floyd,Cliff, NYM	21
Jones,Andruw, Atl	21
Burrell,Pat, Phi	20
Ensberg,Morgan, Hou	20
Glaus,Troy, Ari	20
Biggio,Craig, Hou	19
Clark,Tony, Ari	19

Home Runs Away

Jones,Andruw, Atl	30
Bay,Jason, Pit	23
Cabrera,Miguel, Fla	22
Lee,Derrek, ChC	22
Guillen,Jose, Was	21
Griffey Jr.,Ken, Cin	20
Ramirez,Aramis, ChC	20
Pujols,Albert, StL	18
Tracy,Chad, Ari	18
3 tied with	17

Longest Avg Home Run
(min 10 over the wall)

Pena,Wily Mo, Cin	415
Walker,Larry, StL	413
Drew,J.D., LAD	407
Bradley,Milton, LAD	407
Weeks,Rickie, Mil	407
Clark,Tony, Ari	405
Piazza,Mike, NYM	405
Cameron,Mike, NYM	404
Branyan,Russell, Mil	403
Nady,Xavier, SD	402

Shortest Avg Home Run
(min 10 over the wall)

Lieberthal,Mike, Phi	360
Everett,Adam, Hou	360
Biggio,Craig, Hou	361
Hernandez,Ram, SD	366
Clark,Brady, Mil	368
Rollins,Jimmy, Phi	368
Barmes,Clint, Col	369
Durham,Ray, SF	371
Schneider,Brian, Was	371
Mientkiewicz,D, NYM	371

2005 National League Batting Leaders

Under Age 25: AB Per HR
(minimum 502 PA)

Dunn,Adam, Cin	13.6
Pujols,Albert, StL	14.4
Cabrera,Miguel, Fla	18.6
Tracy,Chad, Ari	18.6
Wright,David, NYM	21.3
LaRoche,Adam, Atl	22.6
Holliday,Matt, Col	25.2
Lopez,Felipe, Cin	25.2
Hall,Bill, Mil	29.5
Atkins,Garrett, Col	39.9

Under Age 25: OPS
(minimum 502 PA)

Pujols,Albert, StL	1.039
Cabrera,Miguel, Fla	.947
Dunn,Adam, Cin	.927
Wright,David, NYM	.912
Tracy,Chad, Ari	.911
Holliday,Matt, Col	.866
Lopez,Felipe, Cin	.838
Hall,Bill, Mil	.837
LaRoche,Adam, Atl	.775
Atkins,Garrett, Col	.773

Under Age 25: RC/27 Outs
(minimum 502 PA)

Pujols,Albert, StL	8.8
Dunn,Adam, Cin	7.1
Holliday,Matt, Col	6.7
Wright,David, NYM	6.6
Cabrera,Miguel, Fla	6.5
Tracy,Chad, Ari	6.0
Lopez,Felipe, Cin	5.8
Hall,Bill, Mil	5.2
Atkins,Garrett, Col	5.0
LaRoche,Adam, Atl	4.7

Lowest SB Success Pct
(minimum 20 SBA)

Clark,Brady, Mil	43.5
Lawton,Matt, Pit-ChC	65.4
Roberts,Dave, SD	65.7
Lopez,Felipe, Cin	68.2
Ellison,Jason, SF	70.0
Vizquel,Omar, SF	70.6
Wright,David, NYM	70.8
Beltran,Carlos, NYM	73.9
3 tied with	75.0

Home RC Per 27 Outs
(minimum 251 PA)

Helton,Todd, Col	10.3
Holliday,Matt, Col	9.1
Dunn,Adam, Cin	8.4
Lee,Derrek, ChC	8.4
Griffey Jr.,Ken, Cin	8.4
Pujols,Albert, StL	8.3
Abreu,Bobby, Phi	7.8
Furcal,Rafael, Atl	7.8
Delgado,Carlos, Fla	7.6
Burrell,Pat, Phi	7.4

Road RC Per 27 Outs
(minimum 251 PA)

Giles,Brian, SD	10.1
Bay,Jason, Pit	9.4
Pujols,Albert, StL	9.3
Lee,Derrek, ChC	8.8
Kent,Jeff, LAD	8.0
Delgado,Carlos, Fla	7.6
Cabrera,Miguel, Fla	7.5
Edmonds,Jim, StL	7.5
Berkman,Lance, Hou	7.4
Utley,Chase, Phi	7.1

Swing and Miss %
(minimum 1500 Pitches Seen)

LaRue,Jason, Cin	24.0
Glaus,Troy, Ari	23.3
Cruz,Jose, Ari-LAD	22.6
Jones,Andruw, Atl	21.1
Delgado,Carlos, Fla	20.3
Clark,Tony, Ari	19.9
Jenkins,Geoff, Mil	19.5
Wilson,Pr, Col-Was	19.3
Dunn,Adam, Cin	18.5
Patterson,Corey, ChC	18.5

2005 American League Pitching Leaders

Earned Run Average
(minimum 162 IP)

Millwood,Kevin, Cle	2.86
Santana,Johan, Min	2.87
Buehrle,Mark, CWS	3.12
Washburn,Jarrod, LAA	3.20
Silva,Carlos, Min	3.44
Lackey,John, LAA	3.44
Rogers,Kenny, Tex	3.46
Colon,Bartolo, LAA	3.48
Garland,Jon, CWS	3.50
Blanton,Joe, Oak	3.53

Winning Percentage
(minimum 15 Decisions)

Lee,Cliff, Cle	.783
Halladay,Roy, Tor	.750
Lackey,John, LAA	.737
Colon,Bartolo, LAA	.724
Crain,Jesse, Min	.706
Santana,Johan, Min	.696
Clement,Matt, Bos	.684
Contreras,Jose, CWS	.682
Wells,David, Bos	.682
Johnson,Randy, NYY	.680

Opponent Batting Average
(minimum 162 IP)

Santana,Johan, Min	.210
Zito,Barry, Oak	.221
Contreras,Jose, CWS	.232
Blanton,Joe, Oak	.236
Johnson,Randy, NYY	.243
Wakefield,Tim, Bos	.245
Chen,Bruce, Bal	.248
Kazmir,Scott, TB	.248
Millwood,Kevin, Cle	.248
Sabathia,C.C., Cle	.248

Baserunners Per 9 IP
(minimum 162 IP)

Santana,Johan, Min	8.78
Colon,Bartolo, LAA	10.55
Johnson,Randy, NYY	10.61
Silva,Carlos, Min	10.70
Buehrle,Mark, CWS	10.80
Garland,Jon, CWS	10.83
Radke,Brad, Min	10.94
Lee,Cliff, Cle	10.96
Byrd,Paul, LAA	11.06
Millwood,Kevin, Cle	11.16

Most Pitches in a Game

Pavano,Carl, NYY, 5/17	133
Mussina,Mike, NYY, 5/7	131
Ponson,S, Bal, 4/24	131
Chacon,S, NYY, 8/20	127
Saarloos,Kirk, Oak, 6/23	127
Bedard,Erik, Bal, 5/4	126
Fossum,C, TB, 8/15	126
Moyer,Jamie, Sea, 6/5	126
Fossum,C, TB, 7/6	125
Leiter,Al, NYY, 8/12	125

Games Started

Lopez,Rodrigo, Bal	35
Zito,Barry, Oak	35
Chacin,Gustavo, Tor	34
Haren,Danny, Oak	34
Johnson,Randy, NYY	34
Maroth,Mike, Det	34
Westbrook,Jake, Cle	34
10 tied with	33

Complete Games

Halladay,Roy, Tor	5
Bonderman,Jer, Det	4
Johnson,Randy, NYY	4
Buehrle,Mark, CWS	3
Garland,Jon, CWS	3
Haren,Danny, Oak	3
Radke,Brad, Min	3
Santana,Johan, Min	3
Wakefield,Tim, Bos	3
16 tied with	2

Shutouts

Garland,Jon, CWS	3
Halladay,Roy, Tor	2
Mussina,Mike, NYY	2
Santana,Johan, Min	2
14 tied with	1

Wins

Colon,Bartolo, LAA	21
Garland,Jon, CWS	18
Lee,Cliff, Cle	18
Johnson,Randy, NYY	17
Buehrle,Mark, CWS	16
Santana,Johan, Min	16
Wakefield,Tim, Bos	16
5 tied with	15

Losses

Greinke,Zack, KC	17
Lima,Jose, KC	16
Robertson,Nate, Det	16
Franklin,Ryan, Sea	15
Westbrook,Jake, Cle	15
Hernandez,Run, KC	14
Maroth,Mike, Det	14
5 tied with	13

Innings Pitched

Buehrle,Mark, CWS	236.2
Santana,Johan, Min	231.2
Zito,Barry, Oak	228.1
Garcia,Freddy, CWS	228.0
Johnson,Randy, NYY	225.2
Wakefield,Tim, Bos	225.1
Colon,Bartolo, LAA	222.2
Garland,Jon, CWS	221.0
Haren,Danny, Oak	217.0
Westbrook,Jake, Cle	210.2

Batters Faced

Buehrle,Mark, CWS	971
Zito,Barry, Oak	953
Garcia,Freddy, CWS	943
Wakefield,Tim, Bos	943
Johnson,Randy, NYY	920
Lopez,Rodrigo, Bal	918
Santana,Johan, Min	910
Colon,Bartolo, LAA	906
Garland,Jon, CWS	901
Haren,Danny, Oak	897

Strikeouts

Santana,Johan, Min	238
Johnson,Randy, NYY	211
Lackey,John, LAA	199
Kazmir,Scott, TB	174
Zito,Barry, Oak	171
Haren,Danny, Oak	163
Sabathia,C.C., Cle	161
Cabrera,Daniel, Bal	157
Colon,Bartolo, LAA	157
Contreras,Jose, CWS	154

Walks Allowed

Kazmir,Scott, TB	100
Zito,Barry, Oak	89
Cabrera,Daniel, Bal	87
Contreras,Jose, CWS	75
Meche,Gil, Sea	72
Lackey,John, LAA	71
Chacin,Gustavo, Tor	70
Hernandez,Run, KC	70
Clement,Matt, Bos	68
Wakefield,Tim, Bos	68

Hit Batters

Fossum,Casey, TB	18
Clement,Matt, Bos	16
Arroyo,Bronson, Bos	14
Bush,Dave, Tor	13
Greinke,Zack, KC	13
Zito,Barry, Oak	13
Hernandez,Orl, CWS	12
Johnson,Randy, NYY	12
4 tied with	11

Wild Pitches

Contreras,Jose, CWS	20
Garcia,Freddy, CWS	20
Lackey,John, LAA	18
Johnson,Jason, Det	17
Clement,Matt, Bos	13
Shields,Scot, LAA	12
Julio,Jorge, Bal	10
Ponson,Sidney, Bal	10
Cabrera,Daniel, Bal	9
5 tied with	8

2005 American League Pitching Leaders

Runs Allowed		Hits Allowed		Doubles Allowed		Home Runs Allowed	
Lima,Jose, KC	140	Buehrle,Mark, CWS	240	Lima,Jose, KC	58	Wakefield,Tim, Bos	35
Hendrickson,Ma, TB	126	Towers,Josh, Tor	237	Arroyo,Bronson, Bos	56	Chen,Bruce, Bal	33
Lopez,Rodrigo, Bal	126	Maroth,Mike, Det	235	Hendrickson,Ma, TB	56	Radke,Brad, Min	33
Greinke,Zack, KC	125	Greinke,Zack, KC	233	Lopez,Rodrigo, Bal	52	Elarton,Scott, Cle	32
Maroth,Mike, Det	123	Johnson,Jason, Det	233	Greinke,Zack, KC	48	Johnson,Randy, NYY	32
Westbrook,Jake, Cle	121	Lopez,Rodrigo, Bal	232	Byrd,Paul, LAA	47	Lima,Jose, KC	31
Pineiro,Joel, Sea	118	Hendrickson,Ma, TB	227	Moyer,Jamie, Sea	47	Maroth,Mike, Det	30
Johnson,Jason, Det	117	Garcia,Freddy, CWS	225	Wakefield,Tim, Bos	47	Waechter,Doug, TB	29
Arroyo,Bronson, Bos	116	Moyer,Jamie, Sea	225	Lee,Cliff, Cle	46	3 tied with	28
2 tied with	113	Pineiro,Joel, Sea	224	Westbrook,Jake, Cle	46		

Run Support Per Nine IP (minimum 162 IP)		% Pitches In Strike Zone (minimum 162 IP)		Pitches Per Start (minimum 30 GS)		Pitches Per Batter (minimum 162 IP)	
Wells,David, Bos	7.97	Silva,Carlos, Min	65.2	Zito,Barry, Oak	108.7	Silva,Carlos, Min	3.06
Young,Chris, Tex	7.32	Colon,Bartolo, LAA	60.8	Lackey,John, LAA	105.7	Towers,Josh, Tor	3.37
Clement,Matt, Bos	6.88	Byrd,Paul, LAA	59.8	Buehrle,Mark, CWS	105.4	Johnson,Jason, Det	3.38
Lee,Cliff, Cle	6.46	Wells,David, Bos	59.2	Garland,Jon, CWS	103.6	Robertson,Nate, Det	3.46
Chacin,Gustavo, Tor	6.21	Towers,Josh, Tor	58.8	Kazmir,Scott, TB	103.0	Byrd,Paul, LAA	3.47
Rogers,Kenny, Tex	6.17	Buehrle,Mark, CWS	58.8	Garcia,Freddy, CWS	102.9	Franklin,Ryan, Sea	3.52
Colon,Bartolo, LAA	6.02	Elarton,Scott, Cle	57.8	Wakefield,Tim, Bos	102.8	Radke,Brad, Min	3.53
Garcia,Freddy, CWS	5.96	Lee,Cliff, Cle	57.4	Moyer,Jamie, Sea	102.0	Hendrickson,Ma, TB	3.55
Hendrickson,Ma, TB	5.96	Young,Chris, Tex	57.3	Sabathia,C.C., Cle	101.7	Wells,David, Bos	3.56
Haren,Danny, Oak	5.93	Millwood,Kevin, Cle	57.2	Santana,Johan, Min	101.1	Pineiro,Joel, Sea	3.56

Quality Starts		Easy Saves		Regular Saves		Tough Saves	
Santana,Johan, Min	24	Nathan,Joe, Min	30	Rodriguez,Fran, LAA	19	Batista,Miguel, Tor	6
Blanton,Joe, Oak	22	Wickman,Bob, Cle	28	Baez,Danys, TB	18	Rivera,Mariano, NYY	5
Byrd,Paul, LAA	22	Cordero,Franc, Tex	24	Wickman,Bob, Cle	17	Baez,Danys, TB	4
Garland,Jon, CWS	22	Rodriguez,Fran, LAA	24	Guardado,Eddie, Sea	16	Hermanson,D, CWS	4
Haren,Danny, Oak	22	Rivera,Mariano, NYY	23	Rivera,Mariano, NYY	15	Ryan,B.J., Bal	4
Johnson,Randy, NYY	22	Ryan,B.J., Bal	22	Hermanson,D, CWS	13	MacDougal,Mike, KC	3
Rogers,Kenny, Tex	22	Guardado,Eddie, Sea	20	Nathan,Joe, Min	13	5 tied with	2
4 tied with	21	Baez,Danys, TB	19	Cordero,Franc, Tex	12		
		Hermanson,D, CWS	17	3 tied with	10		
		Batista,Miguel, Tor	15				

Stolen Bases Allowed		Caught Stealing Off		Stolen Base Pct Allowed (minimum 162 IP)		Pickoffs	
Millwood,Kevin, Cle	33	Johnson,Randy, NYY	14	Washburn,Jarrod, LAA	0.0	Maroth,Mike, Det	10
Contreras,Jose, CWS	28	Maroth,Mike, Det	12	Maroth,Mike, Det	25.0	Buehrle,Mark, CWS	5
Moyer,Jamie, Sea	27	Chacin,Gustavo, Tor	10	Colon,Bartolo, LAA	33.3	Chacin,Gustavo, Tor	5
Johnson,Randy, NYY	23	Kazmir,Scott, TB	9	Garland,Jon, CWS	33.3	Hendrickson,Ma, TB	5
Lopez,Rodrigo, Bal	22	Chen,Bruce, Bal	8	Hendrickson,Ma, TB	33.3	Chen,Bruce, Bal	4
Zito,Barry, Oak	22	Johnson,Jason, Det	8	Lohse,Kyle, Min	33.3	Johnson,Randy, NYY	4
Garcia,Freddy, CWS	19	Lackey,John, LAA	8	Kazmir,Scott, TB	43.8	Wells,David, Bos	4
Haren,Danny, Oak	19	Meche,Gil, Sea	8	Bonderman,Jer, Det	44.4	Brazelton,Dewon, TB	3
Hernandez,Orl, CWS	19	5 tied with	7	Chacin,Gustavo, Tor	44.4	Lohse,Kyle, Min	3
Wakefield,Tim, Bos	18			Santana,Johan, Min	44.4	18 tied with	2

2005 American League Pitching Leaders

Strikeouts Per 9 IP
(minimum 162 IP)

Santana,Johan, Min	9.25
Lackey,John, LAA	8.57
Kazmir,Scott, TB	8.42
Johnson,Randy, NYY	8.42
Young,Chris, Tex	7.49
Sabathia,C.C., Cle	7.37
Mussina,Mike, NYY	7.11
Fossum,Casey, TB	7.08
Bonderman,Jer, Det	6.90
Clement,Matt, Bos	6.88

Opp On-Base Percentage
(minimum 162 IP)

Santana,Johan, Min	.250
Johnson,Randy, NYY	.291
Colon,Bartolo, LAA	.291
Buehrle,Mark, CWS	.295
Radke,Brad, Min	.295
Lee,Cliff, Cle	.295
Garland,Jon, CWS	.298
Silva,Carlos, Min	.300
Blanton,Joe, Oak	.300
Millwood,Kevin, Cle	.300

Opp Slugging Average
(minimum 162 IP)

Santana,Johan, Min	.346
Zito,Barry, Oak	.361
Lackey,John, LAA	.362
Contreras,Jose, CWS	.372
Sabathia,C.C., Cle	.373
Kazmir,Scott, TB	.374
Buehrle,Mark, CWS	.380
Millwood,Kevin, Cle	.387
Blanton,Joe, Oak	.394
Westbrook,Jake, Cle	.395

Hits Per Nine Innings
(minimum 162 IP)

Santana,Johan, Min	6.99
Zito,Barry, Oak	7.29
Contreras,Jose, CWS	7.78
Blanton,Joe, Oak	7.96
Johnson,Randy, NYY	8.26
Kazmir,Scott, TB	8.32
Wakefield,Tim, Bos	8.39
Sabathia,C.C., Cle	8.47
Chen,Bruce, Bal	8.53
Millwood,Kevin, Cle	8.53

Home Runs Per Nine IP
(minimum 162 IP)

Lackey,John, LAA	0.56
Kazmir,Scott, TB	0.58
Rogers,Kenny, Tex	0.69
Buehrle,Mark, CWS	0.76
Westbrook,Jake, Cle	0.81
Clement,Matt, Bos	0.85
Santana,Johan, Min	0.85
Sabathia,C.C., Cle	0.87
Chacin,Gustavo, Tor	0.89
Millwood,Kevin, Cle	0.94

Batting Average vs. LHB
(minimum 125 BF)

Nathan,Joe, Min	.158
Kazmir,Scott, TB	.174
Rivera,Mariano, NYY	.177
Harden,Rich, Oak	.179
Hernandez,Fel, Sea	.182
Johnson,Randy, NYY	.185
Gordon,Tom, NYY	.187
Shields,Scot, LAA	.199
Rogers,Kenny, Tex	.201
McCarthy,Bran, CWS	.205

Batting Average vs. RHB
(minimum 225 BF)

Cabrera,Daniel, Bal	.174
McClung,Seth, TB	.197
Santana,Johan, Min	.200
Young,Chris, Tex	.220
Harden,Rich, Oak	.221
Zito,Barry, Oak	.223
Chen,Bruce, Bal	.224
Millwood,Kevin, Cle	.227
Contreras,Jose, CWS	.233
Byrd,Paul, LAA	.234

Opp BA w/ RISP
(minimum 125 BF)

Millwood,Kevin, Cle	.194
Garcia,Freddy, CWS	.197
Wood,Mike, KC	.214
Zito,Barry, Oak	.222
Contreras,Jose, CWS	.222
Blanton,Joe, Oak	.223
Hernandez,Orl, CWS	.228
Buehrle,Mark, CWS	.230
Radke,Brad, Min	.232
Lee,Cliff, Cle	.235

OBP vs. Leadoff Hitter
(minimum 150 BF)

Santana,Johan, Min	.237
Blanton,Joe, Oak	.246
Wakefield,Tim, Bos	.252
Sabathia,C.C., Cle	.270
Lackey,John, LAA	.278
Mussina,Mike, NYY	.280
Colon,Bartolo, LAA	.281
Wells,David, Bos	.281
Towers,Josh, Tor	.290
Johnson,Randy, NYY	.291

Strikeouts / Walks Ratio
(minimum 162 IP)

Silva,Carlos, Min	7.89
Santana,Johan, Min	5.29
Wells,David, Bos	5.10
Radke,Brad, Min	5.09
Johnson,Randy, NYY	4.49
Towers,Josh, Tor	3.86
Buehrle,Mark, CWS	3.73
Colon,Bartolo, LAA	3.65
Byrd,Paul, LAA	3.64
Haren,Danny, Oak	3.08

Highest GB/FB Ratio
(minimum 162 IP)

Westbrook,Jake, Cle	3.40
Johnson,Jason, Det	1.68
Robertson,Nate, Det	1.63
Sabathia,C.C., Cle	1.61
Wells,David, Bos	1.60
Garcia,Freddy, CWS	1.59
Silva,Carlos, Min	1.58
Garland,Jon, CWS	1.48
Haren,Danny, Oak	1.46
Bonderman,Jer, Det	1.43

Lowest GB/FB Ratio
(minimum 162 IP)

Young,Chris, Tex	0.66
Elarton,Scott, Cle	0.72
Lee,Cliff, Cle	0.81
Arroyo,Bronson, Bos	0.87
Byrd,Paul, LAA	0.89
Lima,Jose, KC	0.90
Moyer,Jamie, Sea	0.90
Santana,Johan, Min	0.91
Chen,Bruce, Bal	0.95
Franklin,Ryan, Sea	0.97

Rel Opp BA w/ Runners On
(minimum 50 IP)

Politte,Cliff, CWS	.165
Mateo,Julio, Sea	.185
Gordon,Tom, NYY	.194
Rivera,Mariano, NYY	.194
Street,Huston, Oak	.197
Thornton,Matt, Sea	.213
Sisco,Andy, KC	.217
Rincon,Juan, Min	.219
Crain,Jesse, Min	.219
Riske,David, Cle	.220

Relief Opp BA w/ RISP
(minimum 50 IP)

Mateo,Julio, Sea	.188
Street,Huston, Oak	.194
Shields,Scot, LAA	.202
Williams,Todd, Bal	.204
Crain,Jesse, Min	.208
Sisco,Andy, KC	.235
Sturtze,Tanyon, NYY	.239
Walker,Pete, Tor	.246
Vizcaino,Luis, CWS	.250
Timlin,Mike, Bos	.258

GIDP Induced

Silva,Carlos, Min	35
Buehrle,Mark, CWS	29
Haren,Danny, Oak	26
Garcia,Freddy, CWS	25
Johnson,Jason, Det	25
Pineiro,Joel, Sea	25
Rogers,Kenny, Tex	25
Westbrook,Jake, Cle	25
Garland,Jon, CWS	24
Washburn,Jarrod, LAA	24

GIDP Per Nine IP
(minimum 162 IP)

Silva,Carlos, Min	1.67
Washburn,Jarrod, LAA	1.22
Pineiro,Joel, Sea	1.19
Lohse,Kyle, Min	1.16
Rogers,Kenny, Tex	1.15
Buehrle,Mark, CWS	1.10
Haren,Danny, Oak	1.08
Wells,David, Bos	1.08
Johnson,Jason, Det	1.07
Westbrook,Jake, Cle	1.07

2005 American League Pitching Leaders

Saves

Rodriguez,Fran, LAA	45
Wickman,Bob, Cle	45
Nathan,Joe, Min	43
Rivera,Mariano, NYY	43
Baez,Danys, TB	41
Cordero,Franc, Tex	37
Guardado,Eddie, Sea	36
Ryan,B.J., Bal	36
Hermanson,D, CWS	34
Batista,Miguel, Tor	31

Blown Saves

Baez,Danys, TB	8
Batista,Miguel, Tor	8
Cordero,Franc, Tex	8
Gordon,Tom, NYY	7
Timlin,Mike, Bos	7
Rodney,Fernando, Det	6
Shields,Scot, LAA	6
11 tied with	5

Save Pct
(minimum 20 Save Ops)

Rivera,Mariano, NYY	91.5
Rodriguez,Fran, LAA	90.0
Wickman,Bob, Cle	90.0
Nathan,Joe, Min	89.6
Guardado,Eddie, Sea	87.8
Ryan,B.J., Bal	87.8
Hermanson,D, CWS	87.2
Street,Huston, Oak	85.2
MacDougal,Mike, KC	84.0
Baez,Danys, TB	83.7

Relief Earned Run Average
(minimum 50 IP)

Rivera,Mariano, NYY	1.38
Street,Huston, Oak	1.72
Cotts,Neal, CWS	1.94
Politte,Cliff, CWS	2.00
Hermanson,D, CWS	2.04
Duchscherer,J, Oak	2.21
Timlin,Mike, Bos	2.24
Ryan,B.J., Bal	2.43
Rincon,Juan, Min	2.45
Howry,Bob, Cle	2.47

Relief Wins

Crain,Jesse, Min	12
Shields,Scot, LAA	10
Donnelly,Brend, LAA	9
Duchscherer,J, Oak	7
Howry,Bob, Cle	7
Nathan,Joe, Min	7
Politte,Cliff, CWS	7
Rivera,Mariano, NYY	7
Timlin,Mike, Bos	7
3 tied with	6

Relief Losses

Shields,Scot, LAA	11
Batista,Miguel, Tor	8
Harper,Travis, TB	6
MacDougal,Mike, KC	6
Rincon,Juan, Min	6
13 tied with	5

Holds

Gordon,Tom, NYY	33
Shields,Scot, LAA	33
Howry,Bob, Cle	29
Rincon,Juan, Min	25
Timlin,Mike, Bos	24
Politte,Cliff, CWS	23
Marte,Damaso, CWS	22
Putz,J.J., Sea	21
Schoeneweis,S, Tor	21
Borowski,Joe, TB	19

Relief Games

Timlin,Mike, Bos	81
Schoeneweis,S, Tor	80
Gordon,Tom, NYY	79
Howry,Bob, Cle	79
Shields,Scot, LAA	78
Crain,Jesse, Min	75
Rincon,Juan, Min	75
Williams,Todd, Bal	72
Batista,Miguel, Tor	71
Rivera,Mariano, NYY	71

Relief Innings

Shields,Scot, LAA	91.2
Duchscherer,J, Oak	85.2
Mateo,Julio, Sea	83.1
Gordon,Tom, NYY	80.2
Timlin,Mike, Bos	80.1
Crain,Jesse, Min	79.2
Rivera,Mariano, NYY	78.1
Street,Huston, Oak	78.1
Rincon,Juan, Min	77.0
Williams,Todd, Bal	76.1

Relief Opp Batting Average
(minimum 50 IP)

Rivera,Mariano, NYY	.177
Cotts,Neal, CWS	.179
Politte,Cliff, CWS	.181
Nathan,Joe, Min	.183
Rodriguez,Fran, LAA	.184
Howry,Bob, Cle	.191
Street,Huston, Oak	.194
Speier,Justin, Tor	.198
Shields,Scot, LAA	.201
Gordon,Tom, NYY	.203

Relief Opp On Base Pct
(minimum 50 IP)

Rivera,Mariano, NYY	.235
Howry,Bob, Cle	.237
Nathan,Joe, Min	.247
Politte,Cliff, CWS	.254
Speier,Justin, Tor	.254
Riske,David, Cle	.260
Duchscherer,J, Oak	.263
Street,Huston, Oak	.267
Gordon,Tom, NYY	.272
Betancourt,Raf, Cle	.273

Relief Opp Slugging Avg
(minimum 50 IP)

Rivera,Mariano, NYY	.230
Cotts,Neal, CWS	.241
Street,Huston, Oak	.267
Rincon,Juan, Min	.274
Howry,Bob, Cle	.277
Shields,Scot, LAA	.283
Nathan,Joe, Min	.287
Ryan,B.J., Bal	.288
Crain,Jesse, Min	.305
Schoeneweis,S, Tor	.314

Inherited Runners Scrd %
(minimum 30 IR)

Chulk,Vinnie, Tor	10.8
Rincon,Ricardo, Oak	13.9
Frasor,Jason, Tor	15.0
Sauerbeck,Scott, Cle	15.6
Donnelly,Brend, LAA	18.2
Howry,Bob, Cle	18.2
Baez,Danys, TB	19.4
Nelson,Jeff, Sea	19.4
Shields,Scot, LAA	20.0
Politte,Cliff, CWS	21.6

Rel OBP 1st Batter Faced
(minimum 40 BF)

Rivera,Mariano, NYY	.169
Riske,David, Cle	.190
Betancourt,Raf, Cle	.204
Cotts,Neal, CWS	.217
Putz,J.J., Sea	.219
Shouse,Brian, Tex	.222
Spurling,Chris, Det	.232
Farnsworth,Kyle, Det	.239
Rincon,Juan, Min	.240
Calero,Kiko, Oak	.241

Relief Opp BA Vs LHB
(minimum 50 AB)

Nathan,Joe, Min	.158
Speier,Justin, Tor	.167
Rivera,Mariano, NYY	.177
Howry,Bob, Cle	.180
Politte,Cliff, CWS	.182
Gordon,Tom, NYY	.187
Schoeneweis,S, Tor	.188
Mateo,Julio, Sea	.194
Romero,J.C., Min	.198
Shields,Scot, LAA	.199

Relief Opp BA Vs RHB
(minimum 50 AB)

Rodriguez,Fran, LAA	.153
Cotts,Neal, CWS	.155
Calero,Kiko, Oak	.162
Street,Huston, Oak	.172
Rivera,Mariano, NYY	.176
Politte,Cliff, CWS	.181
Putz,J.J., Sea	.197
Howry,Bob, Cle	.198
Shields,Scot, LAA	.203
Betancourt,Raf, Cle	.204

2005 American League Pitching Leaders

Fastest Average Fastball
(minimum 162 IP)

Sabathia,C.C., Cle	94.7
Bonderman,Jer, Det	93.2
Contreras,Jose, CWS	92.9
Johnson,Randy, NYY	92.7
Colon,Bartolo, LAA	92.7
Kazmir,Scott, TB	92.6
Santana,Johan, Min	92.4
Millwood,Kevin, Cle	92.4
Silva,Carlos, Min	92.1
Haren,Danny, Oak	91.9

Slowest Average Fastball
(minimum 162 IP)

Wakefield,Tim, Bos	76.1
Moyer,Jamie, Sea	81.8
Maroth,Mike, Det	85.2
Rogers,Kenny, Tex	85.6
Chen,Bruce, Bal	85.9
Buehrle,Mark, CWS	86.8
Byrd,Paul, LAA	87.2
Zito,Barry, Oak	87.3
Hendrickson,Ma, TB	87.5
Wells,David, Bos	87.6

Pitches 100+ Velocity

Cabrera,Daniel, Bal	37
Farnsworth,Kyle, Det	14
McClung,Seth, TB	11
Jenks,Bobby, CWS	10
Harden,Rich, Oak	4
Sabathia,C.C., Cle	4
Cordero,Franc, Tex	2
7 tied with	1

Pitches 95+ Velocity

Cabrera,Daniel, Bal	1015
Sabathia,C.C., Cle	776
Hernandez,Fel, Sea	522
Colon,Bartolo, LAA	463
Cordero,Franc, Tex	450
Burgos,Ambiorix, KC	423
Harden,Rich, Oak	395
Putz,J.J., Sea	366
Nathan,Joe, Min	361
Julio,Jorge, Bal	323

Pitches Less Than 80 MPH

Wakefield,Tim, Bos	2305
Zito,Barry, Oak	1205
Moyer,Jamie, Sea	1169
Chen,Bruce, Bal	1152
Arroyo,Bronson, Bos	1023
Maroth,Mike, Det	907
Rogers,Kenny, Tex	845
Wells,David, Bos	595
Hernandez,Orl, CWS	585
Elarton,Scott, Cle	576

Lowest % Fastballs
(minimum 162 IP)

Wakefield,Tim, Bos	11.9
Moyer,Jamie, Sea	40.1
Rogers,Kenny, Tex	43.5
Maroth,Mike, Det	44.8
Mussina,Mike, NYY	44.9
Clement,Matt, Bos	44.9
Chen,Bruce, Bal	46.2
Buehrle,Mark, CWS	47.4
Arroyo,Bronson, Bos	47.8
Robertson,Nate, Det	50.5

Highest % Fastballs
(minimum 162 IP)

Silva,Carlos, Min	83.0
Colon,Bartolo, LAA	81.3
Lee,Cliff, Cle	74.5
Westbrook,Jake, Cle	68.8
Garland,Jon, CWS	68.0
Millwood,Kevin, Cle	67.1
Sabathia,C.C., Cle	65.0
Kazmir,Scott, TB	64.5
Radke,Brad, Min	63.6
Greinke,Zack, KC	62.1

Highest % Curveballs
(minimum 162 IP)

Wells,David, Bos	29.0
Zito,Barry, Oak	25.6
Mussina,Mike, NYY	23.7
Johnson,Jason, Det	21.6
Lackey,John, LAA	19.8
Elarton,Scott, Cle	19.1
Arroyo,Bronson, Bos	18.6
Blanton,Joe, Oak	16.8
Chen,Bruce, Bal	16.7
Greinke,Zack, KC	15.1

Highest % Changeups
(minimum 162 IP)

Rogers,Kenny, Tex	32.9
Moyer,Jamie, Sea	27.3
Robertson,Nate, Det	24.0
Santana,Johan, Min	23.7
Chen,Bruce, Bal	23.4
Maroth,Mike, Det	23.4
Lopez,Rodrigo, Bal	19.3
Radke,Brad, Min	17.0
Buehrle,Mark, CWS	16.6
Sabathia,C.C., Cle	16.1

Highest % Sliders
(minimum 162 IP)

Johnson,Randy, NYY	36.8
Bonderman,Jer, Det	29.3
Clement,Matt, Bos	29.2
Towers,Josh, Tor	27.4
Arroyo,Bronson, Bos	24.9
Robertson,Nate, Det	22.6
Garcia,Freddy, CWS	22.3
Kazmir,Scott, TB	22.0
Millwood,Kevin, Cle	19.3
Byrd,Paul, LAA	19.2

Balks

Carrasco,D.J., KC	3
Kline,Steve, Bal	3
9 tied with	2

Earned Runs

Lima,Jose, KC	131
Greinke,Zack, KC	118
Pineiro,Joel, Sea	118
Hendrickson,Ma, TB	117
Lopez,Rodrigo, Bal	114
Maroth,Mike, Det	110
Franklin,Ryan, Sea	108
Johnson,Jason, Det	106
Westbrook,Jake, Cle	105
Wakefield,Tim, Bos	104

Opp BPS vs Fastballs
(minimum 251 BF)

Shields,Scot, LAA	.487
Harden,Rich, Oak	.576
Santana,Johan, Min	.581
Halladay,Roy, Tor	.588
Williams,Todd, Bal	.588
Wang,Chien-Ming, NYY	.612
Zito,Barry, Oak	.618
Garland,Jon, CWS	.627
Loe,Kameron, Tex	.639
Colon,Bartolo, LAA	.645

Opp BPS vs Curveballs
(minimum 100 BF)

Halladay,Roy, Tor	.260
Lackey,John, LAA	.424
Johnson,Jason, Det	.462
Fossum,Casey, TB	.466
Zito,Barry, Oak	.475
Pineiro,Joel, Sea	.491
Elarton,Scott, Cle	.495
Chen,Bruce, Bal	.547
Mussina,Mike, NYY	.550
Blanton,Joe, Oak	.602

Opp BPS vs Changeups
(minimum 100 BF)

Santana,Johan, Min	.346
Lee,Cliff, Cle	.537
Moyer,Jamie, Sea	.575
Hernandez,Run, KC	.579
Elarton,Scott, Cle	.590
Kazmir,Scott, TB	.594
Mays,Joe, Min	.631
Blanton,Joe, Oak	.637
Sabathia,C.C., Cle	.639
Lima,Jose, KC	.653

Opp BPS vs Sliders
(minimum 64 BF)

Politte,Cliff, CWS	.279
Nathan,Joe, Min	.288
Wickman,Bob, Cle	.325
Rodriguez,Fran, LAA	.328
Sabathia,C.C., Cle	.336
Calero,Kiko, Oak	.383
Julio,Jorge, Bal	.397
Millwood,Kevin, Cle	.398
Radke,Brad, Min	.400
Street,Huston, Oak	.402

2005 American League Pitching Leaders

Fastest Avg Fastball-Relief
(minimum 50 Rel IP)

Burgos,Ambiorix, KC	96.3
Cordero,Franc, Tex	95.9
MacDougal,Mike, KC	95.2
Nathan,Joe, Min	94.9
Putz,J.J., Sea	94.8
Julio,Jorge, Bal	94.5
Rincon,Juan, Min	94.1
Rivera,Mariano, NYY	93.5
Frasor,Jason, Tor	93.4
Thornton,Matt, Sea	93.3

Save Opportunities

Rodriguez,Fran, LAA	50
Wickman,Bob, Cle	50
Baez,Danys, TB	49
Nathan,Joe, Min	48
Rivera,Mariano, NYY	47
Cordero,Franc, Tex	45
Guardado,Eddie, Sea	41
Ryan,B.J., Bal	41
Batista,Miguel, Tor	39
Hermanson,D, CWS	39

Holds Adjusted Saves %
(minimum 20 Save Ops)

Rivera,Mariano, NYY	91.5
Rodriguez,Fran, LAA	90.0
Wickman,Bob, Cle	90.0
Nathan,Joe, Min	89.6
Hermanson,D, CWS	88.6
Guardado,Eddie, Sea	87.8
Ryan,B.J., Bal	87.8
Street,Huston, Oak	85.2
Timlin,Mike, Bos	84.1
MacDougal,Mike, KC	84.0

Highest HBP/BB Ratio
(minimum 50 IP)

Bush,Dave, Tor	.448
Pavano,Carl, NYY	.444
Wells,David, Bos	.429
Mateo,Julio, Sea	.412
Halladay,Roy, Tor	.389
Brown,Kevin, NYY	.368
Silva,Carlos, Min	.333
Yabu,Keiichi, Oak	.308
Radke,Brad, Min	.304
Fossum,Casey, TB	.300

Sacrifice Flies Allowed

Maroth,Mike, Det	11
Robertson,Nate, Det	11
Chacin,Gustavo, Tor	10
Elarton,Scott, Cle	10
Radke,Brad, Min	10
Kazmir,Scott, TB	9
Sele,Aaron, Sea	9
Garland,Jon, CWS	8
Nomo,Hideo, TB	8
Ponson,Sidney, Bal	8

Sacrifice Hits Allowed

Colon,Bartolo, LAA	9
Crain,Jesse, Min	9
Garland,Jon, CWS	9
Johnson,Jason, Det	9
Chacin,Gustavo, Tor	8
Hendrickson,Ma, TB	8
Zito,Barry, Oak	8
Buehrle,Mark, CWS	7
Byrd,Paul, LAA	7
Contreras,Jose, CWS	7

No Decisions

Lackey,John, LAA	14
Clement,Matt, Bos	13
Kazmir,Scott, TB	13
Washburn,Jarrod, LAA	13
Chacin,Gustavo, Tor	12
Hendrickson,Ma, TB	12
Johnson,Jason, Det	12
Moyer,Jamie, Sea	12
Pineiro,Joel, Sea	12
Young,Chris, Tex	12

Intentional Walks Allowed

Harper,Travis, TB	9
Romero,J.C., Min	8
Saarloos,Kirk, Oak	8
Crain,Jesse, Min	7
Loe,Kameron, Tex	6
Mateo,Julio, Sea	6
Miller,Trever, TB	6
Spurling,Chris, Det	6
Vizcaino,Luis, CWS	6
10 tied with	5

Strikeout/Hit Ratio
(minimum 50 IP)

Nathan,Joe, Min	2.04
Rodriguez,Fran, LAA	2.02
Ryan,B.J., Bal	1.85
Rivera,Mariano, NYY	1.60
Cotts,Neal, CWS	1.53
Shields,Scot, LAA	1.49
Escobar,Kelvim, LAA	1.40
Street,Huston, Oak	1.36
Politte,Cliff, CWS	1.36
Rincon,Juan, Min	1.33

2005 National League Pitching Leaders

Earned Run Average
(minimum 162 IP)

Clemens,Roger, Hou	1.87
Pettitte,Andy, Hou	2.39
Willis,Dontrelle, Fla	2.63
Martinez,Pedro, NYM	2.82
Carpenter,Chris, StL	2.83
Peavy,Jake, SD	2.88
Oswalt,Roy, Hou	2.94
Smoltz,John, Atl	3.06
Patterson,John, Was	3.13
Zambrano,Carlos, ChC	3.26

Winning Percentage
(minimum 15 Decisions)

Sosa,Jorge, Atl	.813
Carpenter,Chris, StL	.808
Zambrano,Carlos, ChC	.700
Eaton,Adam, SD	.688
Willis,Dontrelle, Fla	.688
Mulder,Mark, StL	.667
Smoltz,John, Atl	.667
Pettitte,Andy, Hou	.654
Beckett,Josh, Fla	.652
Martinez,Pedro, NYM	.652

Opponent Batting Average
(minimum 162 IP)

Clemens,Roger, Hou	.198
Martinez,Pedro, NYM	.204
Zambrano,Carlos, ChC	.212
Peavy,Jake, SD	.217
Prior,Mark, ChC	.227
Pettitte,Andy, Hou	.230
Carpenter,Chris, StL	.231
Patterson,John, Was	.233
Beckett,Josh, Fla	.234
Davis,Doug, Mil	.235

Baserunners Per 9 IP
(minimum 162 IP)

Martinez,Pedro, NYM	8.71
Clemens,Roger, Hou	9.20
Pettitte,Andy, Hou	9.39
Carpenter,Chris, StL	9.61
Peavy,Jake, SD	9.71
Smoltz,John, Atl	10.35
Willis,Dontrelle, Fla	10.51
Zambrano,Carlos, ChC	10.64
Beckett,Josh, Fla	10.98
Patterson,John, Was	10.98

Most Pitches in a Game

Hernandez,L, Was, 6/3	150
Hernandez,L, Was, 7/31	145
Hernandez,L, Was, 7/15	136
Zambrano,C, ChC, 5/8	136
Marquis,J, StL, 7/27	132
Harang,Aaron, Cin, 9/6	131
Hernandez,L, Was, 5/4	131
Prior,Mark, ChC, 8/24	131
Schmidt,Jason, SF, 4/26	131
3 tied with	130

Games Started

Capuano,Chris, Mil	35
Davis,Doug, Mil	35
Hernandez,Liv, Was	35
Lieber,Jon, Phi	35
Lowe,Derek, LAD	35
Maddux,Greg, ChC	35
Oswalt,Roy, Hou	35
5 tied with	34

Complete Games

Carpenter,Chris, StL	7
Willis,Dontrelle, Fla	7
Burnett,A.J., Fla	4
Martinez,Pedro, NYM	4
Oswalt,Roy, Hou	4
9 tied with	3

Shutouts

Willis,Dontrelle, Fla	5
Carpenter,Chris, StL	4
Peavy,Jake, SD	3
Burnett,A.J., Fla	2
Lowe,Derek, LAD	2
Mulder,Mark, StL	2
Weaver,Jeff, LAD	2
20 tied with	1

Wins

Willis,Dontrelle, Fla	22
Carpenter,Chris, StL	21
Oswalt,Roy, Hou	20
Capuano,Chris, Mil	18
Lieber,Jon, Phi	17
Pettitte,Andy, Hou	17
Mulder,Mark, StL	16
Suppan,Jeff, StL	16
3 tied with	15

Losses

Wells,Kip, Pit	18
Wright,Jamey, Col	16
Lawrence,Brian, SD	15
Lowe,Derek, LAD	15
Maddux,Greg, ChC	15
Milton,Eric, Cin	15
Redman,Mark, Pit	15
Tomko,Brett, SF	15
Vazquez,Javier, Ari	15
Marquis,Jason, StL	14

Innings Pitched

Hernandez,Liv, Was	246.1
Carpenter,Chris, StL	241.2
Oswalt,Roy, Hou	241.2
Willis,Dontrelle, Fla	236.1
Smoltz,John, Atl	229.2
Webb,Brandon, Ari	229.0
Maddux,Greg, ChC	225.0
Weaver,Jeff, LAD	224.0
Zambrano,Carlos, ChC	223.1
Davis,Doug, Mil	222.2

Batters Faced

Hernandez,Liv, Was	1065
Oswalt,Roy, Hou	1002
Willis,Dontrelle, Fla	960
Carpenter,Chris, StL	953
Capuano,Chris, Mil	949
Davis,Doug, Mil	946
Webb,Brandon, Ari	943
Maddux,Greg, ChC	936
Lowe,Derek, LAD	934
Smoltz,John, Atl	931

Strikeouts

Peavy,Jake, SD	216
Carpenter,Chris, StL	213
Davis,Doug, Mil	208
Martinez,Pedro, NYM	208
Myers,Brett, Phi	208
Zambrano,Carlos, ChC	202
Burnett,A.J., Fla	198
Vazquez,Javier, Ari	192
Prior,Mark, ChC	188
2 tied with	185

Walks Allowed

Wells,Kip, Pit	99
Davis,Doug, Mil	93
Capuano,Chris, Mil	91
Zambrano,Carlos, ChC	86
Schmidt,Jason, SF	85
Hernandez,Liv, Was	84
Wright,Jamey, Col	81
Burnett,A.J., Fla	79
Zambrano,Victor, NYM	77
Lowry,Noah, SF	76

Hit Batters

Weaver,Jeff, LAD	18
Wright,Jamey, Col	15
Zambrano,Victor, NYM	15
Kim,Byung-Hyun, Col	14
Hernandez,Liv, Was	13
Capuano,Chris, Mil	12
Wells,Kip, Pit	12
Hudson,Luke, Cin	11
Lawrence,Brian, SD	11
Myers,Brett, Phi	11

Wild Pitches

Webb,Brandon, Ari	14
Burnett,A.J., Fla	12
Kim,Byung-Hyun, Col	11
Marquis,Jason, StL	10
Mulder,Mark, StL	9
Patterson,John, Was	9
Turnbow,Derrick, Mil	9
8 tied with	8

2005 National League Pitching Leaders

Runs Allowed			Hits Allowed			Doubles Allowed			Home Runs Allowed	
Milton,Eric, Cin	141		Hernandez,Liv, Was	268		Milton,Eric, Cin	55		Milton,Eric, Cin	40
Francis,Jeff, Col	119		Oswalt,Roy, Hou	243		Harang,Aaron, Cin	52		Vazquez,Javier, Ari	35
Wright,Jamey, Col	119		Maddux,Greg, ChC	239		Wright,Jamey, Col	51		Weaver,Jeff, LAD	35
Hernandez,Liv, Was	116		Milton,Eric, Cin	237		Francis,Jeff, Col	50		Ortiz,Ramon, Cin	34
Wells,Kip, Pit	116		Webb,Brandon, Ari	229		Lawrence,Brian, SD	50		Lieber,Jon, Phi	33
Lowe,Derek, LAD	113		Francis,Jeff, Col	228		Maddux,Greg, ChC	50		Capuano,Chris, Mil	31
Maddux,Greg, ChC	112		Glavine,Tom, NYM	227		Capuano,Chris, Mil	49		Myers,Brett, Phi	31
Vazquez,Javier, Ari	112		Loaiza,Esteban, Was	227		Davis,Doug, Mil	49		Ramirez,Horacio, Atl	31
Weaver,Jeff, LAD	111		3 tied with	223		Hernandez,Liv, Was	48		Maddux,Greg, ChC	29
2 tied with	110					Oswalt,Roy, Hou	48		Marquis,Jason, StL	29

Run Support Per Nine IP			% Pitches In Strike Zone			Pitches Per Start			Pitches Per Batter	
(minimum 162 IP)			(minimum 162 IP)			(minimum 30 GS)			(minimum 162 IP)	
Francis,Jeff, Col	6.37		Loaiza,Esteban, Was	59.4		Hernandez,Liv, Was	114.5		Maddux,Greg, ChC	3.31
Morris,Matt, StL	6.26		Maddux,Greg, ChC	58.7		Zambrano,Carlos, ChC	107.9		Lieber,Jon, Phi	3.43
Beckett,Josh, Fla	5.89		Harang,Aaron, Cin	58.5		Lowry,Noah, SF	107.5		Lawrence,Brian, SD	3.45
Claussen,Bran, Cin	5.62		Martinez,Pedro, NYM	58.3		Harang,Aaron, Cin	106.7		Mulder,Mark, StL	3.47
Benson,Kris, NYM	5.58		Penny,Brad, LAD	57.5		Davis,Doug, Mil	106.5		Wright,Jamey, Col	3.49
Suppan,Jeff, StL	5.56		Willis,Dontrelle, Fla	57.4		Peavy,Jake, SD	105.2		Ortiz,Ramon, Cin	3.49
Lidle,Cory, Phi	5.56		Oswalt,Roy, Hou	57.3		Willis,Dontrelle, Fla	104.6		Morris,Matt, StL	3.51
Myers,Brett, Phi	5.52		Weaver,Jeff, LAD	57.3		Capuano,Chris, Mil	104.0		Lidle,Cory, Phi	3.53
Carpenter,Chris, StL	5.51		Ohka,Tomo, Was-Mil	56.5		Burnett,A.J., Fla	103.0		Hudson,Tim, Atl	3.54
Capuano,Chris, Mil	5.47		Milton,Eric, Cin	56.4		Carpenter,Chris, StL	102.9		Smoltz,John, Atl	3.54

Quality Starts			Easy Saves			Regular Saves			Tough Saves	
Carpenter,Chris, StL	27		Turnbow,Derrick, Mil	30		Hoffman,Trevor, SD	17		Jones,Todd, Fla	6
Pettitte,Andy, Hou	27		Cordero,Chad, Was	29		Cordero,Chad, Was	16		Wagner,Billy, Phi	4
Clemens,Roger, Hou	26		Lidge,Brad, Hou	29		Fuentes,Brian, Col	16		Weathers,David, Cin	4
Oswalt,Roy, Hou	25		Hoffman,Trevor, SD	26		Isringhausen,Jason, StL	13		Lyon,Brandon, Ari	3
Willis,Dontrelle, Fla	25		Isringhausen,Jason, StL	25		Jones,Todd, Fla	12		Walker,Tyler, SF	3
Loaiza,Esteban, Was	24		Jones,Todd, Fla	22		Wagner,Billy, Phi	12		8 tied with	2
6 tied with	23		Wagner,Billy, Phi	22		Dempster,Ryan, ChC	11			
			Dempster,Ryan, ChC	20		Lidge,Brad, Hou	11			
			Mesa,Jose, Pit	19		3 tied with	9			
			Looper,Braden, NYM	17						

Stolen Bases Allowed			Caught Stealing Off			Stolen Base Pct Allowed			Pickoffs	
						(minimum 162 IP)				
Maddux,Greg, ChC	32		Francis,Jeff, Col	11		Zambrano,Carlos, ChC	10.0		Capuano,Chris, Mil	12
Patterson,John, Was	26		Hernandez,Liv, Was	11		Carpenter,Chris, StL	16.7		Wright,Jamey, Col	6
Webb,Brandon, Ari	26		Patterson,John, Was	11		Willis,Dontrelle, Fla	16.7		Davis,Doug, Mil	5
Wright,Jamey, Col	25		Capuano,Chris, Mil	9		Capuano,Chris, Mil	18.2		Fassero,Jeff, SF	5
Zambrano,Victor, NYM	25		Harang,Aaron, Cin	9		Mulder,Mark, StL	20.0		Francis,Jeff, Col	5
Burnett,A.J., Fla	24		Zambrano,Carlos, ChC	9		Marquis,Jason, StL	33.3		Mulder,Mark, StL	5
Schmidt,Jason, SF	24		5 tied with	8		Oswalt,Roy, Hou	42.9		Cormier,Lance, Ari	4
Sosa,Jorge, Atl	20					Glavine,Tom, NYM	44.4		Halsey,Brad, Ari	4
Weaver,Jeff, LAD	20					Prior,Mark, ChC	45.5		Williams,Jer, SF-ChC	4
4 tied with	19					Beckett,Josh, Fla	46.2		6 tied with	3

2005 National League Pitching Leaders

Strikeouts Per 9 IP
(minimum 162 IP)

Prior,Mark, ChC	10.15
Peavy,Jake, SD	9.58
Myers,Brett, Phi	8.69
Schmidt,Jason, SF	8.63
Martinez,Pedro, NYM	8.63
Burnett,A.J., Fla	8.53
Davis,Doug, Mil	8.41
Patterson,John, Was	8.39
Beckett,Josh, Fla	8.36
Zambrano,Carlos, ChC	8.14

Opp On-Base Percentage
(minimum 162 IP)

Martinez,Pedro, NYM	.252
Clemens,Roger, Hou	.261
Pettitte,Andy, Hou	.268
Peavy,Jake, SD	.271
Carpenter,Chris, StL	.273
Smoltz,John, Atl	.287
Willis,Dontrelle, Fla	.292
Zambrano,Carlos, ChC	.293
Prior,Mark, ChC	.296
Patterson,John, Was	.298

Opp Slugging Average
(minimum 162 IP)

Clemens,Roger, Hou	.284
Martinez,Pedro, NYM	.334
Burnett,A.J., Fla	.334
Zambrano,Carlos, ChC	.338
Pettitte,Andy, Hou	.348
Carpenter,Chris, StL	.351
Willis,Dontrelle, Fla	.352
Patterson,John, Was	.358
Peavy,Jake, SD	.363
Smoltz,John, Atl	.363

Hits Per Nine Innings
(minimum 162 IP)

Clemens,Roger, Hou	6.43
Martinez,Pedro, NYM	6.59
Zambrano,Carlos, ChC	6.85
Peavy,Jake, SD	7.18
Carpenter,Chris, StL	7.60
Pettitte,Andy, Hou	7.61
Beckett,Josh, Fla	7.71
Prior,Mark, ChC	7.72
Patterson,John, Was	7.81
Davis,Doug, Mil	7.92

Home Runs Per Nine IP
(minimum 162 IP)

Willis,Dontrelle, Fla	0.42
Clemens,Roger, Hou	0.47
Glavine,Tom, NYM	0.51
Burnett,A.J., Fla	0.52
Zambrano,Victor, NYM	0.65
Carpenter,Chris, StL	0.67
Oswalt,Roy, Hou	0.67
Pettitte,Andy, Hou	0.69
Beckett,Josh, Fla	0.71
Smoltz,John, Atl	0.71

Batting Average vs. LHB
(minimum 125 BF)

Cordero,Chad, Was	.192
Clemens,Roger, Hou	.195
Linebrink,Scott, SD	.195
Pettitte,Andy, Hou	.200
Mulder,Mark, StL	.201
Capuano,Chris, Mil	.202
Otsuka,Akinori, SD	.207
Carrasco,Hector, Was	.208
Heilman,Aaron, NYM	.209
Tejeda,Robinson, Phi	.210

Batting Average vs. RHB
(minimum 225 BF)

Wagner,Billy, Phi	.173
Torres,Salomon, Pit	.189
Martinez,Pedro, NYM	.192
Carpenter,Chris, StL	.199
Clemens,Roger, Hou	.202
Weaver,Jeff, LAD	.208
Peavy,Jake, SD	.212
Zambrano,Carlos, ChC	.212
Dempster,Ryan, ChC	.216
Lowe,Derek, LAD	.219

Opp BA w/ RISP
(minimum 125 BF)

Clemens,Roger, Hou	.138
Sosa,Jorge, Atl	.194
Pettitte,Andy, Hou	.203
Padilla,Vicente, Phi	.205
Martinez,Pedro, NYM	.209
Hudson,Tim, Atl	.215
Sanchez,Duaner, LAD	.216
Vogelsong,Ryan, Pit	.216
Davis,Doug, Mil	.224
Peavy,Jake, SD	.229

OBP vs. Leadoff Hitter
(minimum 150 BF)

Carpenter,Chris, StL	.239
Clemens,Roger, Hou	.242
Martinez,Pedro, NYM	.253
Benson,Kris, NYM	.254
Pettitte,Andy, Hou	.258
Sheets,Ben, Mil	.259
Peavy,Jake, SD	.262
Vazquez,Javier, Ari	.262
Redman,Mark, Pit	.270
Tomko,Brett, SF	.272

Strikeouts / Walks Ratio
(minimum 162 IP)

Martinez,Pedro, NYM	4.43
Peavy,Jake, SD	4.32
Carpenter,Chris, StL	4.18
Vazquez,Javier, Ari	4.17
Pettitte,Andy, Hou	4.17
Oswalt,Roy, Hou	3.83
Maddux,Greg, ChC	3.78
Weaver,Jeff, LAD	3.65
Lieber,Jon, Phi	3.63
Harang,Aaron, Cin	3.20

Highest GB/FB Ratio
(minimum 162 IP)

Webb,Brandon, Ari	4.00
Lowe,Derek, LAD	3.01
Mulder,Mark, StL	2.88
Hudson,Tim, Atl	2.83
Burnett,A.J., Fla	2.63
Carpenter,Chris, StL	2.09
Wright,Jamey, Col	1.95
Lidle,Cory, Phi	1.95
Maddux,Greg, ChC	1.94
Pettitte,Andy, Hou	1.87

Lowest GB/FB Ratio
(minimum 162 IP)

Patterson,John, Was	0.65
Milton,Eric, Cin	0.70
Claussen,Bran, Cin	0.79
Martinez,Pedro, NYM	0.84
Prior,Mark, ChC	0.91
Capuano,Chris, Mil	0.92
Schmidt,Jason, SF	0.95
Francis,Jeff, Col	0.98
Harang,Aaron, Cin	1.00
Fogg,Josh, Pit	1.03

Rel Opp BA w/ Runners On
(minimum 50 IP)

Eyre,Scott, SF	.167
Wise,Matt, Mil	.170
Fuentes,Brian, Col	.171
Carrasco,Hector, Was	.175
Linebrink,Scott, SD	.186
Valverde,Jose, Ari	.200
Wheeler,Dan, Hou	.202
Lidge,Brad, Hou	.205
Torres,Salomon, Pit	.208
Heilman,Aaron, NYM	.216

Relief Opp BA w/ RISP
(minimum 50 IP)

Hernandez,Rob, NYM	.171
Majewski,Gary, Was	.212
Qualls,Chad, Hou	.212
Torres,Salomon, Pit	.212
Sanchez,Duaner, LAD	.216
Vogelsong,Ryan, Pit	.216
Madson,Ryan, Phi	.237
Ayala,Luis, Was	.247
Cormier,Lance, Ari	.265
Fassero,Jeff, SF	.282

GIDP Induced

Mulder,Mark, StL	32
Ramirez,Horacio, Atl	32
Webb,Brandon, Ari	30
Marquis,Jason, StL	29
Suppan,Jeff, StL	29
Burnett,A.J., Fla	26
Loaiza,Esteban, Was	25
Hernandez,Liv, Was	24
Redman,Mark, Pit	24
Willis,Dontrelle, Fla	23

GIDP Per Nine IP
(minimum 162 IP)

Ramirez,Horacio, Atl	1.42
Mulder,Mark, StL	1.40
Suppan,Jeff, StL	1.34
Marquis,Jason, StL	1.26
Redman,Mark, Pit	1.21
Webb,Brandon, Ari	1.18
Wright,Jamey, Col	1.16
Burnett,A.J., Fla	1.12
Loaiza,Esteban, Was	1.04
Lidle,Cory, Phi	1.02

2005 National League Pitching Leaders

Saves		Blown Saves		Save Pct		Relief Earned Run Average	
				(minimum 20 Save Ops)		(minimum 50 IP)	
Cordero,Chad, Was	47	Hawkins,L, ChC-SF	9	Dempster,Ryan, ChC	94.3	Wagner,Billy, Phi	1.51
Hoffman,Trevor, SD	43	Reitsma,Chris, Atl	9	Hoffman,Trevor, SD	93.5	Turnbow,Derrick, Mil	1.74
Lidge,Brad, Hou	42	Looper,Braden, NYM	8	Wagner,Billy, Phi	92.7	Cordero,Chad, Was	1.82
Jones,Todd, Fla	40	Cordero,Chad, Was	7	Lidge,Brad, Hou	91.3	Linebrink,Scott, SD	1.83
Isringhausen,Jason, StL	39	Kolb,Danny, Atl	7	Fuentes,Brian, Col	91.2	Dempster,Ryan, ChC	1.85
Turnbow,Derrick, Mil	39	Madson,Ryan, Phi	7	Isringhausen,Jason, StL	90.7	Carrasco,Hector, Was	2.04
Wagner,Billy, Phi	38	Mesa,Jose, Pit	7	Turnbow,Derrick, Mil	90.7	Jones,Todd, Fla	2.10
Dempster,Ryan, ChC	33	5 tied with	6	Jones,Todd, Fla	88.9	Isringhausen,Jason, StL	2.14
Fuentes,Brian, Col	31			Cordero,Chad, Was	87.0	Reyes,Al, StL	2.15
Looper,Braden, NYM	28			Benitez,Armando, SF	82.6	Heilman,Aaron, NYM	2.18

Relief Wins		Relief Losses		Holds		Relief Games	
Ayala,Luis, Was	8	Brazoban,Yhency, LAD	10	Eyre,Scott, SF	32	Eyre,Scott, SF	86
Hernandez,Rob, NYM	8	Hawkins,L, ChC-SF	8	Madson,Ryan, Phi	32	Majewski,Gary, Was	79
Linebrink,Scott, SD	8	Kolb,Danny, Atl	8	Tavarez,Julian, StL	32	Sanchez,Duaner, LAD	79
Carrara,Giov, LAD	7	Mesa,Jose, Pit	8	Linebrink,Scott, SD	26	Fuentes,Brian, Col	78
Cormier,Lance, Ari	7	Otsuka,Akinori, SD	8	Majewski,Gary, Was	24	Madson,Ryan, Phi	78
Seanez,Rudy, SD	7	Ayala,Luis, Was	7	Ayala,Luis, Was	22	Mercker,Kent, Cin	78
Turnbow,Derrick, Mil	7	Looper,Braden, NYM	7	Otsuka,Akinori, SD	22	Torres,Salomon, Pit	78
Weathers,David, Cin	7	Sanchez,Duaner, LAD	7	Qualls,Chad, Hou	22	King,Ray, StL	77
5 tied with	6	White,Rick, Pit	7	DeJean,Mike, NYM-Col	20	Qualls,Chad, Hou	77
		4 tied with	6	Mercker,Kent, Cin	20	Reitsma,Chris, Atl	76

Relief Innings		Relief Opp Batting Average		Relief Opp On Base Pct		Relief Opp Slugging Avg	
		(minimum 50 IP)		(minimum 50 IP)		(minimum 50 IP)	
Torres,Salomon, Pit	94.2	Wise,Matt, Mil	.160	Wagner,Billy, Phi	.229	Heilman,Aaron, NYM	.249
Madson,Ryan, Phi	87.0	Wagner,Billy, Phi	.165	Cordero,Chad, Was	.248	Wagner,Billy, Phi	.265
Majewski,Gary, Was	86.0	Reyes,Al, StL	.177	Wise,Matt, Mil	.249	Dempster,Ryan, ChC	.265
Sanchez,Duaner, LAD	82.0	Fultz,Aaron, Phi	.186	Reyes,Al, StL	.261	Wise,Matt, Mil	.281
Vogelsong,Ryan, Pit	81.1	Urbina,Ugueth, Phi	.186	Wheeler,Dan, Hou	.265	Jones,Todd, Fla	.283
Qualls,Chad, Hou	79.2	Gonzalez,Mike, Pit	.197	Fultz,Aaron, Phi	.266	Gonzalez,Mike, Pit	.287
Cormier,Lance, Ari	79.1	Cordero,Chad, Was	.198	Linebrink,Scott, SD	.273	Eyre,Scott, SF	.288
Wagner,Billy, Phi	77.2	Turnbow,Derrick, Mil	.199	Turnbow,Derrick, Mil	.273	Reyes,Al, StL	.288
Weathers,David, Cin	77.2	Carrasco,Hector, Was	.200	Hoffman,Trevor, SD	.274	Isringhausen,Jason, StL	.291
2 tied with	75.2	Eyre,Scott, SF	.200	Valverde,Jose, Ari	.275	Valverde,Jose, Ari	.298

Inherited Runners Scrd %		Rel OBP 1st Batter Faced		Relief Opp BA Vs LHB		Relief Opp BA Vs RHB	
(minimum 30 IR)		(minimum 40 BF)		(minimum 50 AB)		(minimum 50 AB)	
Grabow,John, Pit	10.3	Wagner,Billy, Phi	.187	Wise,Matt, Mil	.130	Turnbow,Derrick, Mil	.167
Eyre,Scott, SF	15.6	Eyre,Scott, SF	.190	Fassero,Jeff, SF	.149	Fultz,Aaron, Phi	.170
Cormier,Rheal, Phi	15.6	Heilman,Aaron, NYM	.196	Fuentes,Brian, Col	.164	Reyes,Al, StL	.172
Wunsch,Kelly, LAD	16.2	Urbina,Ugueth, Phi	.196	Hammond,Chris, SD	.167	Wagner,Billy, Phi	.173
Eischen,Joey, Was	17.0	Jones,Todd, Fla	.206	Valverde,Jose, Ari	.168	Hoffman,Trevor, SD	.179
Weathers,David, Cin	20.0	Weathers,David, Cin	.219	Isringhausen,Jason, StL	.168	Sanchez,Duaner, LAD	.182
Santana,Julio, Mil	20.5	Thompson,Brad, StL	.225	Eyre,Scott, SF	.182	Wise,Matt, Mil	.187
Flores,Randy, StL	20.6	Majewski,Gary, Was	.231	Reyes,Al, StL	.184	Torres,Salomon, Pit	.189
Gonzalez,Mike, Pit	21.2	Hoffman,Trevor, SD	.237	Heilman,Aaron, NYM	.185	Dempster,Ryan, ChC	.197
Reyes,Al, StL	22.9	Santana,Julio, Mil	.244	Cordero,Chad, Was	.192	Wuertz,Mike, ChC	.197

2005 National League Pitching Leaders

Fastest Average Fastball
(minimum 162 IP)

Burnett,A.J., Fla	95.6
Beckett,Josh, Fla	93.5
Tomko,Brett, SF	93.3
Oswalt,Roy, Hou	93.1
Zambrano,Carlos, ChC	92.8
Penny,Brad, LAD	92.7
Smoltz,John, Atl	92.3
Prior,Mark, ChC	92.2
Clemens,Roger, Hou	91.9
Schmidt,Jason, SF	91.8

Slowest Average Fastball
(minimum 162 IP)

Lawrence,Brian, SD	83.3
Maddux,Greg, ChC	84.3
Redman,Mark, Pit	84.4
Glavine,Tom, NYM	85.2
Hernandez,Liv, Was	86.0
Capuano,Chris, Mil	86.4
Davis,Doug, Mil	87.3
Claussen,Bran, Cin	87.3
Ohka,Tomo, Was-Mil	87.4
Webb,Brandon, Ari	87.6

Pitches 100+ Velocity

Wagner,Billy, Phi	18
Burnett,A.J., Fla	17
Beckett,Josh, Fla	3
Looper,Braden, NYM	2
Wood,Kerry, ChC	2
Farnsworth,Kyle, Atl	1
Lidge,Brad, Hou	1
Turnbow,Derrick, Mil	1
Zambrano,Carlos, ChC	1

Pitches 95+ Velocity

Burnett,A.J., Fla	1170
Zambrano,Carlos, ChC	489
Turnbow,Derrick, Mil	453
Beckett,Josh, Fla	442
Brazoban,Yhency, LAD	427
Lidge,Brad, Hou	409
Wagner,Billy, Phi	402
Tomko,Brett, SF	401
Oswalt,Roy, Hou	334
Penny,Brad, LAD	323

Pitches Less Than 80 MPH

Lowry,Noah, SF	1145
Weaver,Jeff, LAD	879
Capuano,Chris, Mil	876
Lawrence,Brian, SD	869
Glavine,Tom, NYM	866
Martinez,Pedro, NYM	697
Redman,Mark, Pit	634
Hernandez,Liv, Was	625
Lidle,Cory, Phi	615
Morris,Matt, StL	605

Lowest % Fastballs
(minimum 162 IP)

Morris,Matt, StL	43.7
Weaver,Jeff, LAD	46.2
Davis,Doug, Mil	50.3
Pettitte,Andy, Hou	50.8
Zambrano,Victor, NYM	51.6
Carpenter,Chris, StL	51.9
Martinez,Pedro, NYM	52.8
Lawrence,Brian, SD	53.3
Lowry,Noah, SF	53.7
Wright,Jamey, Col	54.8

Highest % Fastballs
(minimum 162 IP)

Webb,Brandon, Ari	76.2
Penny,Brad, LAD	73.2
Zambrano,Carlos, ChC	71.4
Marquis,Jason, StL	69.2
Hudson,Tim, Atl	68.9
Oswalt,Roy, Hou	68.5
Beckett,Josh, Fla	68.3
Prior,Mark, ChC	67.4
Harang,Aaron, Cin	67.3
Lowe,Derek, LAD	66.4

Highest % Curveballs
(minimum 162 IP)

Burnett,A.J., Fla	25.9
Morris,Matt, StL	23.3
Carpenter,Chris, StL	22.0
Myers,Brett, Phi	20.4
Lidle,Cory, Phi	18.8
Penny,Brad, LAD	18.4
Weaver,Jeff, LAD	17.9
Beckett,Josh, Fla	16.5
Martinez,Pedro, NYM	16.0
Patterson,John, Was	15.3

Highest % Changeups
(minimum 162 IP)

Glavine,Tom, NYM	36.1
Zambrano,Victor, NYM	26.6
Lowry,Noah, SF	26.5
Maddux,Greg, ChC	24.7
Schmidt,Jason, SF	22.7
Capuano,Chris, Mil	21.4
Vazquez,Javier, Ari	18.5
Martinez,Pedro, NYM	17.6
Lowe,Derek, LAD	15.9
Peavy,Jake, SD	15.0

Highest % Sliders
(minimum 162 IP)

Lieber,Jon, Phi	34.4
Lawrence,Brian, SD	31.0
Morris,Matt, StL	26.4
Benson,Kris, NYM	24.6
Smoltz,John, Atl	22.3
Hernandez,Liv, Was	21.2
Zambrano,Victor, NYM	19.4
Weaver,Jeff, LAD	17.9
Harang,Aaron, Cin	17.3
Willis,Dontrelle, Fla	17.0

Balks

Capuano,Chris, Mil	4
Myers,Brett, Phi	4
Marquis,Jason, StL	3
Redman,Mark, Pit	3
Rodriguez,Wandy, Hou	3
9 tied with	2

Earned Runs

Milton,Eric, Cin	134
Francis,Jeff, Col	116
Hernandez,Liv, Was	109
Maddux,Greg, ChC	106
Vazquez,Javier, Ari	106
Lawrence,Brian, SD	105
Weaver,Jeff, LAD	105
Ramirez,Horacio, Atl	104
Wright,Jamey, Col	104
Wells,Kip, Pit	103

Opp BPS vs Fastballs
(minimum 251 BF)

Majewski,Gary, Was	.515
Clemens,Roger, Hou	.526
Pettitte,Andy, Hou	.536
Zambrano,Carlos, ChC	.542
Willis,Dontrelle, Fla	.567
Peavy,Jake, SD	.601
Sosa,Jorge, Atl	.629
Martinez,Pedro, NYM	.635
Webb,Brandon, Ari	.640
Davis,Doug, Mil	.645

Opp BPS vs Curveballs
(minimum 100 BF)

Beckett,Josh, Fla	.211
Burnett,A.J., Fla	.263
Patterson,John, Was	.266
Davis,Doug, Mil	.352
Myers,Brett, Phi	.364
Carpenter,Chris, StL	.380
Martinez,Pedro, NYM	.404
Sheets,Ben, Mil	.404
Marquis,Jason, StL	.448
Prior,Mark, ChC	.492

Opp BPS vs Changeups
(minimum 100 BF)

Wise,Matt, Mil	.429
Martinez,Pedro, NYM	.443
Heilman,Aaron, NYM	.477
Lowry,Noah, SF	.515
Vazquez,Javier, Ari	.535
Perez,Odalis, LAD	.544
Beckett,Josh, Fla	.565
Redman,Mark, Pit	.573
Zambrano,Victor, NYM	.575
Madson,Ryan, Phi	.577

Opp BPS vs Sliders
(minimum 64 BF)

Wheeler,Dan, Hou	.167
Fultz,Aaron, Phi	.271
Lidge,Brad, Hou	.290
Carpenter,Chris, StL	.331
Wagner,Billy, Phi	.353
Wood,Kerry, ChC	.362
Ohman,Will, ChC	.393
Witasick,Jay, Col	.414
Perez,Oliver, Pit	.418
Weaver,Jeff, LAD	.427

2005 National League Pitching Leaders

Fastest Avg Fastball-Relief
(minimum 50 Rel IP)

Wagner,Billy, Phi	96.9
Lidge,Brad, Hou	96.0
Turnbow,Derrick, Mil	95.6
Brazoban,Yhency, LAD	95.1
Mota,Guillermo, Fla	94.1
Hawkins,L, ChC-SF	93.6
Mesa,Jose, Pit	93.3
Sanchez,Duaner, LAD	93.3
Dempster,Ryan, ChC	93.2
Valverde,Jose, Ari	93.2

Save Opportunities

Cordero,Chad, Was	54
Hoffman,Trevor, SD	46
Lidge,Brad, Hou	46
Jones,Todd, Fla	45
Isringhausen,Jason, StL	43
Turnbow,Derrick, Mil	43
Wagner,Billy, Phi	41
Looper,Braden, NYM	36
Dempster,Ryan, ChC	35
2 tied with	34

Holds Adjusted Saves %
(minimum 20 Save Ops)

Dempster,Ryan, ChC	94.3
Hoffman,Trevor, SD	93.5
Wagner,Billy, Phi	92.7
Fuentes,Brian, Col	92.5
Lidge,Brad, Hou	91.3
Turnbow,Derrick, Mil	91.1
Isringhausen,Jason, StL	90.9
Jones,Todd, Fla	89.1
Cordero,Chad, Was	87.0
Walker,Tyler, SF	83.3

Highest HBP/BB Ratio
(minimum 50 IP)

Coffey,Todd, Cin	.455
Ayala,Luis, Was	.429
Tavarez,Julian, StL	.421
Weaver,Jeff, LAD	.419
Fuentes,Brian, Col	.294
Thompson,Brad, StL	.267
Qualls,Chad, Hou	.261
Reyes,Al, StL	.250
Madson,Ryan, Phi	.240
3 tied with	.231

Sacrifice Flies Allowed

Francis,Jeff, Col	10
Wells,Kip, Pit	10
Hernandez,Liv, Was	9
Meadows,Brian, Pit	9
Rusch,Glendon, ChC	9
6 tied with	8

Sacrifice Hits Allowed

Glavine,Tom, NYM	19
Maddux,Greg, ChC	19
Hernandez,Liv, Was	15
Capuano,Chris, Mil	14
Willis,Dontrelle, Fla	14
6 tied with	13

No Decisions

Patterson,John, Was	15
Davis,Doug, Mil	13
Myers,Brett, Phi	13
Penny,Brad, LAD	13
Zambrano,Carlos, ChC	13
Fogg,Josh, Pit	12
Loaiza,Esteban, Was	12
Ramirez,Horacio, Atl	12
Smoltz,John, Atl	12
3 tied with	11

Intentional Walks Allowed

Hernandez,Liv, Was	14
Fogg,Josh, Pit	11
Patterson,John, Was	11
Tomko,Brett, SF	11
White,Rick, Pit	10
Moehler,Brian, Fla	9
Padilla,Vicente, Phi	9
6 tied with	8

Strikeout/Hit Ratio
(minimum 50 IP)

Wagner,Billy, Phi	1.93
Urbina,Ugueth, Phi	1.89
Lidge,Brad, Hou	1.78
Reyes,Al, StL	1.76
Seanez,Rudy, SD	1.71
Wise,Matt, Mil	1.68
Gonzalez,Mike, Pit	1.66
Fuentes,Brian, Col	1.54
Wuertz,Mike, ChC	1.48
Wood,Kerry, ChC	1.48

2005 American League Fielding Leaders

2B Double Play %
(minimum 98 G)

Belliard,Ronnie, Cle	0.579
Ellis,Mark, Oak	0.551
Kennedy,Adam, LAA	0.551
Hudson,Orlando, Tor	0.524
Iguchi,Tadahito, CWS	0.523
Roberts,Brian, Bal	0.522
Soriano,Alfonso, Tex	0.439
Cano,Robinson, NYY	0.435

3B Double Play %
(minimum 98 G)

Crede,Joe, CWS	0.435
Mueller,Bill, Bos	0.422
Inge,Brandon, Det	0.413
Rodriguez,Alex, NYY	0.379
Beltre,Adrian, Sea	0.379
Teahen,Mark, KC	0.368
Mora,Melvin, Bal	0.324
Chavez,Eric, Oak	0.313
Blalock,Hank, Tex	0.304
Boone,Aaron, Cle	0.250

SS Double Play %
(minimum 98 G)

Peralta,Jhonny, Cle	0.642
Berroa,Angel, KC	0.600
Uribe,Juan, CWS	0.573
Cabrera,Orlando, LAA	0.556
Adams,Russ, Tor	0.551
Tejada,Miguel, Bal	0.534
Lugo,Julio, TB	0.532
Young,Michael, Tex	0.518
Renteria,Edgar, Bos	0.506
Jeter,Derek, NYY	0.506

Lowest Pct CS by Catchers
(minimum 50 SBA)

Kendall,Jason, Oak	15.1
Lopez,Javy, Bal	17.5
Zaun,Gregg, Tor	19.1
Varitek,Jason, Bos	19.8
Pierzynski,A.J., CWS	20.2
Martinez,Victor, Cle	21.3
Posada,Jorge, NYY	28.0
Molina,Bengie, LAA	29.0
Buck,John, KC	31.0
Barajas,Rod, Tex	32.3

2B Pivot %
(minimum 98 G)

Iguchi,Tadahito, CWS	0.681
Roberts,Brian, Bal	0.675
Hudson,Orlando, Tor	0.662
Kennedy,Adam, LAA	0.657
Belliard,Ronnie, Cle	0.647
Ellis,Mark, Oak	0.597
Soriano,Alfonso, Tex	0.589
Cano,Robinson, NYY	0.558

SS Pivot %
(minimum 98 G)

Peralta,Jhonny, Cle	0.791
Uribe,Juan, CWS	0.670
Berroa,Angel, KC	0.659
Lugo,Julio, TB	0.600
Tejada,Miguel, Bal	0.600
Jeter,Derek, NYY	0.589
Renteria,Edgar, Bos	0.582
Adams,Russ, Tor	0.568
Young,Michael, Tex	0.548
Cabrera,Orlando, LAA	0.535

Highest Pct CS by Catchers
(minimum 50 SBA)

Rodriguez,Ivan, Det	45.0
Mauer,Joe, Min	38.0
Hall,Toby, TB	37.8
Barajas,Rod, Tex	32.3
Buck,John, KC	31.0
Molina,Bengie, LAA	29.0
Posada,Jorge, NYY	28.0
Martinez,Victor, Cle	21.3
Pierzynski,A.J., CWS	20.2
Varitek,Jason, Bos	19.8

Errors

Renteria,Edgar, Bos	30
Adams,Russ, Tor	26
Berroa,Angel, KC	25
Lugo,Julio, TB	24
Inge,Brandon, Det	23
Tejada,Miguel, Bal	22
Cantu,Jorge, TB	21
Soriano,Alfonso, Tex	21
Teahen,Mark, KC	20
Peralta,Jhonny, Cle	19

Fielding Errors

Adams,Russ, Tor	13
Renteria,Edgar, Bos	13
Lugo,Julio, TB	12
Inge,Brandon, Det	11
Mora,Melvin, Bal	10
Peralta,Jhonny, Cle	10
6 tied with	9

Throwing Errors

Berroa,Angel, KC	19
Renteria,Edgar, Bos	17
Soriano,Alfonso, Tex	15
Adams,Russ, Tor	13
Belliard,Ronnie, Cle	13
Tejada,Miguel, Bal	13
Cantu,Jorge, TB	12
Gonzalez,Alex S, TB	12
Inge,Brandon, Det	12
Lugo,Julio, TB	12

Range Factor for 2B
(minimum 98 games)

Hudson,Orlando, Tor	5.83
Cano,Robinson, NYY	5.11
Ellis,Mark, Oak	4.97
Soriano,Alfonso, Tex	4.87
Belliard,Ronnie, Cle	4.86
Roberts,Brian, Bal	4.85
Iguchi,Tadahito, CWS	4.68
Kennedy,Adam, LAA	4.58

Range Factor for 3B
(minimum 98 games)

Inge,Brandon, Det	3.25
Teahen,Mark, KC	3.01
Chavez,Eric, Oak	2.82
Beltre,Adrian, Sea	2.79
Mora,Melvin, Bal	2.77
Gonzalez,Alex S, TB	2.75
Boone,Aaron, Cle	2.73
Crede,Joe, CWS	2.72
3 tied with	2.62

Range Factor for SS
(minimum 98 games)

Lugo,Julio, TB	4.94
Jeter,Derek, NYY	4.76
Tejada,Miguel, Bal	4.72
Uribe,Juan, CWS	4.68
Berroa,Angel, KC	4.60
Peralta,Jhonny, Cle	4.52
Young,Michael, Tex	4.41
Renteria,Edgar, Bos	4.35
Adams,Russ, Tor	4.25
Cabrera,Orlando, LAA	4.18

2005 National League Fielding Leaders

2B Double Play %
(minimum 98 G)

Grudzielanek,M, StL	0.598
Castillo,Jose, Pit	0.593
Counsell,Craig, Ari	0.495
Loretta,Mark, SD	0.467
Giles,Marcus, Atl	0.462
Castillo,Luis, Fla	0.450
Biggio,Craig, Hou	0.442
Durham,Ray, SF	0.439
Kent,Jeff, LAD	0.426
Utley,Chase, Phi	0.408

3B Double Play %
(minimum 98 G)

Nunez,Abraham , StL	0.447
Lowell,Mike, Fla	0.431
Ensberg,Morgan, Hou	0.409
Randa,Joe, Cin-SD	0.404
Bell,David, Phi	0.375
Castilla,Vinny, Was	0.357
Jones,Chipper, Atl	0.350
Glaus,Troy, Ari	0.333
Ramirez,Aramis, ChC	0.318
Wright,David, NYM	0.302

SS Double Play %
(minimum 98 G)

Gonzalez,Alex, Fla	0.644
Wilson,Jack, Pit	0.638
Reyes,Jose, NYM	0.621
Furcal,Rafael, Atl	0.619
Guzman,Cristian, Was	0.605
Eckstein,David, StL	0.603
Hardy,J.J., Mil	0.590
Everett,Adam, Hou	0.572
Clayton,Royce, Ari	0.571
Rollins,Jimmy, Phi	0.563

Lowest Pct CS by Catchers
(minimum 50 SBA)

Piazza,Mike, NYM	10.9
Closser,JD, Col	11.7
Phillips,Jason, LAD	16.1
Lieberthal,Mike, Phi	19.2
Snyder,Chris, Ari	20.7
Lo Duca,Paul, Fla	21.2
Barrett,Michael, ChC	22.2
Miller,Damian, Mil	22.4
Hernandez,Ram, SD	25.7
Ausmus,Brad, Hou	26.4

2B Pivot %
(minimum 98 G)

Castillo,Jose, Pit	0.750
Giles,Marcus, Atl	0.740
Grudzielanek,M, StL	0.738
Castillo,Luis, Fla	0.732
Counsell,Craig, Ari	0.711
Loretta,Mark, SD	0.707
Kent,Jeff, LAD	0.690
Durham,Ray, SF	0.662
Utley,Chase, Phi	0.638
Biggio,Craig, Hou	0.634

SS Pivot %
(minimum 98 G)

Reyes,Jose, NYM	0.724
Guzman,Cristian, Was	0.679
Wilson,Jack, Pit	0.660
Rollins,Jimmy, Phi	0.653
Eckstein,David, StL	0.626
Gonzalez,Alex, Fla	0.609
Furcal,Rafael, Atl	0.607
Everett,Adam, Hou	0.598
Perez,Neifi, ChC	0.589
Clayton,Royce, Ari	0.582

Highest Pct CS by Catchers
(minimum 50 SBA)

Schneider,Brian, Was	37.7
Matheny,Mike, SF	32.3
LaRue,Jason, Cin	30.1
Estrada,Johnny, Atl	26.6
Ausmus,Brad, Hou	26.4
Hernandez,Ram, SD	25.7
Miller,Damian, Mil	22.4
Barrett,Michael, ChC	22.2
Lo Duca,Paul, Fla	21.2
Snyder,Chris, Ari	20.7

Errors

Glaus,Troy, Ari	24
Wright,David, NYM	24
Bell,David, Phi	21
Weeks,Rickie, Mil	21
Atkins,Garrett, Col	18
Kent,Jeff, LAD	18
Reyes,Jose, NYM	18
Barmes,Clint, Col	17
Lopez,Felipe, Cin	17
5 tied with	16

Fielding Errors

Glaus,Troy, Ari	15
Wright,David, NYM	12
Lopez,Felipe, Cin	11
Atkins,Garrett, Col	10
Eckstein,David, StL	10
Weeks,Rickie, Mil	10
Wilson,Jack, Pit	10
Everett,Adam, Hou	9
Hall,Bill, Mil	9
Rollins,Jimmy, Phi	9

Throwing Errors

Bell,David, Phi	14
Biggio,Craig, Hou	14
Kent,Jeff, LAD	14
Wright,David, NYM	12
Durham,Ray, SF	11
Reyes,Jose, NYM	11
Weeks,Rickie, Mil	11
Delgado,Carlos, Fla	10
Nunez,Abraham , StL	10
Ramirez,Aramis, ChC	10

Range Factor for 2B
(minimum 98 games)

Castillo,Jose, Pit	5.53
Counsell,Craig, Ari	5.51
Grudzielanek,M, StL	5.34
Castillo,Luis, Fla	5.31
Kent,Jeff, LAD	5.27
Giles,Marcus, Atl	5.18
Utley,Chase, Phi	5.06
Biggio,Craig, Hou	4.94
Durham,Ray, SF	4.65
Loretta,Mark, SD	4.57

Range Factor for 3B
(minimum 98 games)

Nunez,Abraham , StL	3.21
Glaus,Troy, Ari	3.01
Bell,David, Phi	2.84
Wright,David, NYM	2.81
Lowell,Mike, Fla	2.80
Ensberg,Morgan, Hou	2.76
Castilla,Vinny, Was	2.70
Jones,Chipper, Atl	2.70
Atkins,Garrett, Col	2.63
Randa,Joe, Cin-SD	2.61

Range Factor for SS
(minimum 98 games)

Furcal,Rafael, Atl	5.23
Eckstein,David, StL	5.10
Wilson,Jack, Pit	5.08
Gonzalez,Alex, Fla	4.87
Perez,Neifi, ChC	4.74
Izturis,Cesar, LAD	4.62
Vizquel,Omar, SF	4.60
Clayton,Royce, Ari	4.46
Everett,Adam, Hou	4.38
Reyes,Jose, NYM	4.27

2005 Active Career Batting Leaders

Batting Average		On Base Percentage		Slugging Average		Home Runs	
(minimum 1000 PA)		(minimum 1000 PA)		(minimum 1000 PA)			
Helton,Todd	.337	Bonds,Barry	.442	Pujols,Albert	.621	Bonds,Barry	708
Pujols,Albert	.332	Helton,Todd	.433	Bonds,Barry	.611	Sosa,Sammy	588
Suzuki,Ichiro	.332	Thomas,Frank	.427	Helton,Todd	.607	Palmeiro,Rafael	569
Guerrero,Vladimir	.324	Pujols,Albert	.416	Ramirez,Manny	.599	Griffey Jr.,Ken	536
Garciaparra,N	.320	Berkman,Lance	.416	Guerrero,Vladimir	.587	Bagwell,Jeff	449
Jeter,Derek	.314	Giambi,Jason	.413	Rodriguez,Alex	.577	Sheffield,Gary	449
Ramirez,Manny	.314	Giles,Brian	.413	Thomas,Frank	.568	Thomas,Frank	448
Walker,Larry	.313	Abreu,Bobby	.411	Walker,Larry	.565	Ramirez,Manny	435
Piazza,Mike	.311	Ramirez,Manny	.409	Thome,Jim	.562	Gonzalez,Juan	434
Thomas,Frank	.307	Thome,Jim	.408	Griffey Jr.,Ken	.561	Thome,Jim	430

Games		At Bats		Hits		Total Bases	
Palmeiro,Rafael	2831	Palmeiro,Rafael	10472	Palmeiro,Rafael	3020	Bonds,Barry	5584
Bonds,Barry	2730	Biggio,Craig	9811	Biggio,Craig	2795	Palmeiro,Rafael	5388
Biggio,Craig	2564	Bonds,Barry	9140	Bonds,Barry	2742	Sosa,Sammy	4511
Finley,Steve	2401	Finley,Steve	8877	Franco,Julio	2521	Griffey Jr.,Ken	4414
Franco,Julio	2377	Franco,Julio	8422	Finley,Steve	2426	Biggio,Craig	4283
Surhoff,B.J.	2313	Sosa,Sammy	8401	Sheffield,Gary	2345	Bagwell,Jeff	4213
Vizquel,Omar	2290	Vizquel,Omar	8387	Surhoff,B.J.	2326	Sheffield,Gary	4153
Sosa,Sammy	2240	Grissom,Marquis	8275	Bagwell,Jeff	2314	Finley,Steve	3966
Olerud,John	2234	Surhoff,B.J.	8258	Griffey Jr.,Ken	2304	Thomas,Frank	3949
Sheffield,Gary	2190	Sierra,Ruben	8016	Sosa,Sammy	2304	Walker,Larry	3904

Doubles		Triples		Runs Scored		RBI	
Biggio,Craig	604	Finley,Steve	112	Bonds,Barry	2078	Bonds,Barry	1853
Palmeiro,Rafael	585	Lofton,Kenny	98	Biggio,Craig	1697	Palmeiro,Rafael	1835
Bonds,Barry	564	Damon,Johnny	80	Palmeiro,Rafael	1663	Sosa,Sammy	1575
Olerud,John	500	Bonds,Barry	77	Bagwell,Jeff	1517	Griffey Jr.,Ken	1536
Gonzalez,Luis	495	Offerman,Jose	72	Sosa,Sammy	1422	Bagwell,Jeff	1529
Bagwell,Jeff	488	Durham,Ray	70	Sheffield,Gary	1411	Sheffield,Gary	1476
Kent,Jeff	474	Guzman,Cristian	67	Griffey Jr.,Ken	1405	Thomas,Frank	1465
Walker,Larry	471	Gonzalez,Luis	63	Finley,Steve	1368	Ramirez,Manny	1414
Thomas,Frank	447	Walker,Larry	62	Lofton,Kenny	1363	Gonzalez,Juan	1404
Rodriguez,Ivan	445	Perez,Neifi	60	Walker,Larry	1355	Sierra,Ruben	1318

Walks		Intentional Walks		Hit By Pitch		Strikeouts	
Bonds,Barry	2311	Bonds,Barry	607	Biggio,Craig	273	Sosa,Sammy	2194
Thomas,Frank	1466	Griffey Jr.,Ken	210	Kendall,Jason	197	Thome,Jim	1762
Bagwell,Jeff	1401	Palmeiro,Rafael	172	Delgado,Carlos	139	Bagwell,Jeff	1558
Palmeiro,Rafael	1353	Guerrero,Vladimir	169	Walker,Larry	138	Biggio,Craig	1557
Sheffield,Gary	1280	Thomas,Frank	162	Bagwell,Jeff	128	Sanders,Reggie	1513
Olerud,John	1275	Olerud,John	157	Sheffield,Gary	118	Bonds,Barry	1434
Thome,Jim	1257	Bagwell,Jeff	155	Easley,Damion	115	Griffey Jr.,Ken	1416
Biggio,Craig	1097	Sosa,Sammy	151	Giambi,Jason	111	Edmonds,Jim	1411
Griffey Jr.,Ken	1038	Delgado,Carlos	148	Kent,Jeff	105	Delgado,Carlos	1363
Williams,Bernie	1036	Piazza,Mike	144	Jeter,Derek	103	Hernandez,Jose	1351

2005 Active Career Batting Leaders

Sacrifice Hits	
Vizquel,Omar	205
Glavine,Tom	191
Maddux,Greg	159
Vizcaino,Jose	105
Smoltz,John	104
Clayton,Royce	103
Schilling,Curt	102
Sanchez,Rey	93
Perez,Neifi	92
Biggio,Craig	89

Sacrifice Flies	
Palmeiro,Rafael	119
Sierra,Ruben	119
Thomas,Frank	109
Surhoff,B.J.	104
Bagwell,Jeff	102
Sheffield,Gary	101
Olerud,John	96
Kent,Jeff	92
Conine,Jeff	91
Bonds,Barry	88

Stolen Bases	
Lofton,Kenny	567
Bonds,Barry	506
Young,Eric	457
Grissom,Marquis	429
Biggio,Craig	407
Womack,Tony	362
Vizquel,Omar	342
Finley,Steve	313
Sanders,Reggie	297
2 tied with	281

Seasons Played	
Clemens,Roger	22
Franco,John	21
Franco,Julio	21
Bonds,Barry	20
Maddux,Greg	20
Palmeiro,Rafael	20
Santiago,Benito	20
8 tied with	19

At Bats Per Home Run (minimum 1000 AB)	
Bonds,Barry	12.9
Thome,Jim	13.8
Ramirez,Manny	14.1
Sosa,Sammy	14.3
Dunn,Adam	14.4
Rodriguez,Alex	14.4
Griffey Jr.,Ken	14.7
Pujols,Albert	14.7
Delgado,Carlos	15.0
Gonzalez,Juan	15.1

Grounded Into DP	
Franco,Julio	299
Rodriguez,Ivan	240
Olerud,John	232
Palmeiro,Rafael	232
Bagwell,Jeff	221
Castilla,Vinny	217
Williams,Bernie	209
Piazza,Mike	207
Santiago,Benito	204
Clayton,Royce	197

Highest SB Success Pct (minimum 100 SBA)	
Beltran,Carlos	87.8
Womack,Tony	83.2
Reyes,Jose	82.1
Crawford,Carl	81.6
Rodriguez,Alex	80.1
Boone,Aaron	80.0
Soriano,Alfonso	79.7
Lofton,Kenny	79.3
Cameron,Mike	79.2
Jeter,Derek	79.0

At Bats Per RBI (minimum 1000 AB)	
Ramirez,Manny	4.3
Gonzalez,Juan	4.7
Delgado,Carlos	4.7
Thomas,Frank	4.7
Pujols,Albert	4.8
Sexson,Richie	4.9
Bonds,Barry	4.9
Thome,Jim	5.0
Ortiz,David	5.0
Helton,Todd	5.0

Strikeouts / Walks Ratio (minimum 1000 AB)	
Bonds,Barry	.621
Young,Eric	.689
Giles,Brian	.700
Sheffield,Gary	.746
Thomas,Frank	.795
Olerud,John	.797
Helton,Todd	.805
Palmeiro,Orl	.844
Pujols,Albert	.858
Kendall,Jason	.877

At Bats Per GIDP (minimum 1000 AB)	
Suzuki,Ichiro	136.0
Reyes,Jose	132.2
Mackowiak,Rob	123.4
Roberts,Dave	121.8
Infante,Omar	120.2
Crawford,Carl	119.9
Maddux,Greg	117.2
Branyan,Russell	104.6
Damon,Johnny	99.6
Glavine,Tom	99.6

OPS (minimum 1000 PA)	
Bonds,Barry	1.053
Helton,Todd	1.040
Pujols,Albert	1.037
Ramirez,Manny	1.008
Thomas,Frank	.995
Guerrero,Vladimir	.978
Berkman,Lance	.973
Thome,Jim	.970
Walker,Larry	.965
Rodriguez,Alex	.962

Secondary Average (minimum 1000 PA)	
Bonds,Barry	.619
Thome,Jim	.496
Dunn,Adam	.491
Thomas,Frank	.476
Berkman,Lance	.457
Giles,Brian	.456
Bagwell,Jeff	.449
Helton,Todd	.447
Ramirez,Manny	.446
Abreu,Bobby	.446

Highest Strikeout per PA (minimum 1000 PA)	
Branyan,Russell	.353
Bellhorn,Mark	.287
Hernandez,Jose	.274
Wilson,Craig	.269
Dunn,Adam	.263
Pena,Carlos	.261
Phelps,Josh	.258
LaRue,Jason	.257
Burrell,Pat	.248
Mohr,Dustan	.248

Lowest Strikeout per PA (minimum 1000 PA)	
Pierre,Juan	.056
Young,Eric	.065
Polanco,Placido	.068
Lo Duca,Paul	.069
Kendall,Jason	.074
Eckstein,David	.075
Harris,Lenny	.079
Hall,Toby	.083
Cabrera,Orlando	.084
Palmeiro,Orl	.084

Lowest SB Success Pct (minimum 100 SBA)	
Vizcaino,Jose	55.2
Perez,Neifi	56.0
Burnitz,Jeromy	56.2
Edmonds,Jim	56.2
Santiago,Benito	56.9
Gonzalez,Luis	59.6
Anderson,Garret	61.6
Mora,Melvin	62.5
Williams,Bernie	62.5
Jones,Jacque	62.6

2005 Active Career Pitching Leaders

Earned Run Average (minimum 750 IP)		Winning Percentage (minimum 100 Decisions)		Opponent Batting Average (minimum 750 IP)		Baserunners Per 9 IP (minimum 750 IP)	
Rivera,Mariano	2.33	Martinez,Pedro	.701	Hoffman,Trevor	.208	Hoffman,Trevor	9.53
Martinez,Pedro	2.72	Hudson,Tim	.688	Martinez,Pedro	.208	Martinez,Pedro	9.62
Hoffman,Trevor	2.76	Oswalt,Roy	.680	Rivera,Mariano	.212	Rivera,Mariano	9.70
Franco,John	2.89	Clemens,Roger	.665	Wood,Kerry	.214	Schilling,Curt	10.28
Maddux,Greg	3.01	Mulder,Mark	.660	Johnson,Randy	.215	Santana,Johan	10.34
Oswalt,Roy	3.07	Johnson,Randy	.659	Santana,Johan	.221	Maddux,Greg	10.45
Johnson,Randy	3.11	Pettitte,Andy	.654	Nelson,Jeff	.223	Smoltz,John	10.63
Clemens,Roger	3.12	Halladay,Roy	.648	Zito,Barry	.228	Mussina,Mike	10.76
Zambrano,Carlos	3.26	Mussina,Mike	.638	Zambrano,Carlos	.228	Clemens,Roger	10.84
Smoltz,John	3.26	Colon,Bartolo	.629	Clemens,Roger	.229	Johnson,Randy	10.86

Games		Games Started		Complete Games		Shutouts	
Franco,John	1119	Clemens,Roger	671	Clemens,Roger	118	Clemens,Roger	46
Stanton,Mike	1027	Maddux,Greg	639	Maddux,Greg	108	Johnson,Randy	37
Timlin,Mike	893	Glavine,Tom	603	Johnson,Randy	96	Maddux,Greg	35
Hernandez,Rob	892	Johnson,Randy	513	Schilling,Curt	82	Glavine,Tom	24
Mesa,Jose	887	Moyer,Jamie	485	Brown,Kevin	72	Mussina,Mike	23
Quantrill,Paul	841	Brown,Kevin	476	Mussina,Mike	56	Schilling,Curt	19
Reed,Steve	833	Wells,David	447	Glavine,Tom	55	Brown,Kevin	17
Jones,Todd	812	Mussina,Mike	443	Wells,David	54	Erickson,Scott	17
Nelson,Jeff	792	Rogers,Kenny	400	Erickson,Scott	51	Martinez,Pedro	17
Groom,Buddy	786	Smoltz,John	394	Smoltz,John	50	Smoltz,John	15

Wins		Losses		Innings Pitched		Batters Faced	
Clemens,Roger	341	Maddux,Greg	189	Clemens,Roger	4704.1	Clemens,Roger	19369
Maddux,Greg	318	Glavine,Tom	184	Maddux,Greg	4406.1	Maddux,Greg	17925
Glavine,Tom	275	Clemens,Roger	172	Glavine,Tom	3951.2	Glavine,Tom	16626
Johnson,Randy	263	Moyer,Jamie	152	Johnson,Randy	3593.2	Johnson,Randy	14784
Wells,David	227	Brown,Kevin	144	Brown,Kevin	3256.1	Brown,Kevin	13542
Mussina,Mike	224	Wells,David	143	Wells,David	3206.1	Wells,David	13395
Brown,Kevin	211	Mulholland,T	142	Moyer,Jamie	3139.2	Moyer,Jamie	13341
Moyer,Jamie	205	Erickson,Scott	136	Mussina,Mike	3013.0	Rogers,Kenny	12374
Martinez,Pedro	197	Johnson,Randy	136	Smoltz,John	2929.1	Mussina,Mike	12314
Schilling,Curt	192	Trachsel,Steve	135	Schilling,Curt	2906.0	Smoltz,John	11997

Strikeouts		Walks Allowed		Hit Batters		Wild Pitches	
Clemens,Roger	4502	Clemens,Roger	1520	Johnson,Randy	168	Clemens,Roger	133
Johnson,Randy	4372	Johnson,Randy	1349	Clemens,Roger	150	Smoltz,John	130
Maddux,Greg	3052	Glavine,Tom	1337	Brown,Kevin	139	Brown,Kevin	108
Martinez,Pedro	2861	Leiter,Al	1163	Wakefield,Tim	136	Nomo,Hideo	108
Schilling,Curt	2832	Rogers,Kenny	1017	Maddux,Greg	125	Gordon,Tom	102
Smoltz,John	2567	Gordon,Tom	922	Martinez,Pedro	119	Wells,David	100
Mussina,Mike	2400	Maddux,Greg	907	Leiter,Al	117	Clement,Matt	98
Brown,Kevin	2397	Nomo,Hideo	904	Park,Chan Ho	116	Johnson,Randy	98
Glavine,Tom	2350	Brown,Kevin	901	Astacio,Pedro	110	Grimsley,Jason	95
Wells,David	2081	Wakefield,Tim	897	2 tied with	108	Fassero,Jeff	84

2005 Active Career Pitching Leaders

Saves			Save Pct			Home Runs Allowed			Strikeouts Per 9 IP	
			(minimum 50 Save Ops)						(minimum 750 IP)	
Hoffman, Trevor	436		Gagne, Eric	96.4		Moyer, Jamie	381		Johnson, Randy	10.95
Franco, John	424		Smoltz, John	91.7		Wells, David	374		Wood, Kerry	10.44
Rivera, Mariano	379		Hoffman, Trevor	89.5		Clemens, Roger	347		Martinez, Pedro	10.25
Hernandez, Rob	324		Nathan, Joe	88.0		Johnson, Randy	333		Hoffman, Trevor	10.01
Percival, Troy	324		Rivera, Mariano	87.9		Mussina, Mike	323		Nelson, Jeff	9.52
Mesa, Jose	319		Wagner, Billy	86.3		Radke, Brad	302		Santana, Johan	9.47
Wagner, Billy	284		Isringhausen, Jason	86.1		Glavine, Tom	300		Rhodes, Arthur	8.81
Benitez, Armando	263		Benitez, Armando	85.9		Maddux, Greg	298		Remlinger, Mike	8.77
Urbina, Ugueth	237		Percival, Troy	85.9		Schilling, Curt	298		Schilling, Curt	8.77
Jones, Todd	226		Mesa, Jose	85.3		2 tied with	296		Nomo, Hideo	8.74

Opp On-Base Percentage			Opp Slugging Average			Hits Per Nine Innings			Home Runs Per Nine IP	
(minimum 750 IP)			(minimum 750 IP)			(minimum 750 IP)			(minimum 750 IP)	
Hoffman, Trevor	.265		Rivera, Mariano	.290		Martinez, Pedro	6.82		Rivera, Mariano	0.47
Rivera, Mariano	.269		Martinez, Pedro	.324		Hoffman, Trevor	6.86		Brown, Kevin	0.57
Martinez, Pedro	.269		Nelson, Jeff	.330		Wood, Kerry	6.95		Franco, John	0.59
Schilling, Curt	.284		Hoffman, Trevor	.337		Rivera, Mariano	7.03		Maddux, Greg	0.61
Santana, Johan	.284		Clemens, Roger	.341		Johnson, Randy	7.06		Nelson, Jeff	0.62
Maddux, Greg	.289		Johnson, Randy	.341		Nelson, Jeff	7.25		Zambrano, Carlos	0.65
Smoltz, John	.291		Zambrano, Carlos	.341		Santana, Johan	7.35		Adams, Terry	0.65
Clemens, Roger	.294		Franco, John	.343		Zambrano, Carlos	7.51		Clemens, Roger	0.66
Mussina, Mike	.294		Brown, Kevin	.349		Zito, Barry	7.57		Glavine, Tom	0.68
Johnson, Randy	.295		Burnett, A.J.	.350		Burnett, A.J.	7.58		Tavarez, Julian	0.69

Strikeouts / Walks Ratio			Stolen Base Pct Allowed			GIDP Induced			GIDP Per Nine IP	
(minimum 750 IP)			(minimum 750 IP)						(minimum 750 IP)	
Martinez, Pedro	4.32		Rueter, Kirk	34.3		Maddux, Greg	375		Estes, Shawn	1.29
Schilling, Curt	4.29		Carpenter, Chris	39.3		Glavine, Tom	374		Tavarez, Julian	1.22
Hoffman, Trevor	3.86		Mulholland, T	41.2		Brown, Kevin	328		Wickman, Bob	1.19
Sheets, Ben	3.79		Buehrle, Mark	42.4		Clemens, Roger	310		Erickson, Scott	1.18
Oswalt, Roy	3.78		Rogers, Kenny	43.1		Erickson, Scott	308		Wright, Jamey	1.17
Lieber, Jon	3.71		Zambrano, Carlos	45.2		Rogers, Kenny	292		Hampton, Mike	1.14
Mussina, Mike	3.51		Santana, Johan	48.6		Mulholland, T	266		Schoeneweis, S	1.13
Santana, Johan	3.40		Anderson, Brian J	49.1		Hampton, Mike	262		Garland, Jon	1.09
Rivera, Mariano	3.39		Ohka, Tomo	50.0		Moyer, Jamie	253		Mulder, Mark	1.09
Maddux, Greg	3.36		Oswalt, Roy	50.0		Wells, David	244		Graves, Danny	1.09

Complete Game %			Quality Start Pct			Walks Per 9 IP			Games Finished	
(minimum 100 GS)			(minimum 100 GS)			(minimum 750 IP)				
Schilling, Curt	0.22		Martinez, Pedro	70.7		Radke, Brad	1.62		Franco, John	774
Johnson, Randy	0.19		Johnson, Randy	70.0		Lieber, Jon	1.75		Hoffman, Trevor	632
Clemens, Roger	0.18		Oswalt, Roy	69.0		Maddux, Greg	1.85		Hernandez, Rob	628
Maddux, Greg	0.17		Maddux, Greg	67.0		Wells, David	1.87		Mesa, Jose	586
Brown, Kevin	0.15		Schilling, Curt	66.9		Anderson, Brian J	1.96		Rivera, Mariano	541
Hernandez, Liv	0.15		Zambrano, Carlos	66.4		Sheets, Ben	2.00		Percival, Troy	489
Erickson, Scott	0.14		Clemens, Roger	66.0		Mussina, Mike	2.04		Wagner, Billy	487
Mulholland, T	0.14		Brown, Kevin	66.0		Mendoza, Ramiro	2.04		Jones, Todd	472
Mulder, Mark	0.14		Hudson, Tim	65.6		Schilling, Curt	2.04		Benitez, Armando	468
Martinez, Pedro	0.13		Zito, Barry	64.9		Buehrle, Mark	2.06		Wickman, Bob	416

2005 American League Bill James Leaders

Top Game Scores

Pitcher	Date	Opp	IP	H	R	ER	BB	SO	GS
Halladay,Roy, Tor	5/29	Min	9.0	2	0	0	0	10	93
Harden,Rich, Oak	7/14	Tex	9.0	2	0	0	0	8	91
Halladay,Roy, Tor	4/29	NYY	9.0	3	0	0	1	9	89
Johnson,Randy, NYY	7/26	Min	8.0	2	0	0	0	11	89
Radke,Brad, Min	5/5	Cle	9.0	3	0	0	0	8	89
Santana,Johan, Min	8/12	Oak	9.0	3	0	0	1	9	89
Buehrle,Mark, CWS	4/16	Sea	9.0	3	1	1	1	12	88
Millwood,Kevin, Cle	5/9	LAA	8.0	1	0	0	0	8	88
Santana,Johan, Min	6/8	Ari	9.0	4	0	0	0	9	88
Byrd,Paul, LAA	7/1	KC	9.0	2	0	0	1	5	87

Worst Game Scores

Pitcher	Date	Opp	IP	H	R	ER	BB	SO	GS
Greinke,Zack, KC	6/10	Ari	4.1	15	11	11	2	2	-11
Bell,Rob, TB	4/18	NYY	1.1	9	10	10	1	0	-5
Park,Chan Ho, Tex	6/21	LAA	1.0	10	8	8	1	0	0
McGowan,Dustin, Tor	8/21	Det	4.1	9	12	10	2	2	1
Sele,Aaron, Sea	7/29	Cle	4.0	12	9	9	2	3	3
Westbrook,Jake, Cle	4/27	Det	2.1	8	9	9	2	0	3
Blanton,Joe, Oak	5/14	NYY	2.2	7	9	9	3	0	5
Lopez,Rodrigo, Bal	7/31	CWS	1.1	7	8	8	3	0	5
Zito,Barry, Oak	4/9	TB	3.1	7	11	8	3	0	5
4 tied with									6

Runs Created

Teixeira,Mark, Tex	148
Ortiz,David, Bos	137
Rodriguez,Alex, NYY	137
Ramirez,Manny, Bos	134
Young,Michael, Tex	131
Sheffield,Gary, NYY	130
Sexson,Richie, Sea	117
Hafner,Travis, Cle	115
Matsui,Hideki, NYY	109
Suzuki,Ichiro, Sea	109

Runs Created Per 27 Outs

Hafner,Travis, Cle	8.8
Giambi,Jason, NYY	8.7
Ramirez,Manny, Bos	8.6
Rodriguez,Alex, NYY	8.5
Teixeira,Mark, Tex	8.4
Ortiz,David, Bos	8.3
Sheffield,Gary, NYY	8.0
Guerrero,Vladimir, LAA	7.6
Young,Michael, Tex	7.4
Sexson,Richie, Sea	7.3

Offensive Winning %

Hafner,Travis, Cle	.795
Giambi,Jason, NYY	.771
Rodriguez,Alex, NYY	.763
Ramirez,Manny, Bos	.753
Teixeira,Mark, Tex	.744
Sheffield,Gary, NYY	.740
Ortiz,David, Bos	.739
Guerrero,Vladimir, LAA	.732
Sexson,Richie, Sea	.707
Roberts,Brian, Bal	.700

Secondary Average

(minimum 502 PA)

Giambi,Jason, NYY	.523
Ortiz,David, Bos	.476
Rodriguez,Alex, NYY	.474
Hafner,Travis, Cle	.453
Dellucci,David, Tex	.448
Ramirez,Manny, Bos	.448
Sexson,Richie, Sea	.439
Konerko,Paul, CWS	.391
Teixeira,Mark, Tex	.391
Guerrero,Vladimir, LAA	.390

Isolated Power

(minimum 502 PA)

Ortiz,David, Bos	.304
Ramirez,Manny, Bos	.301
Hafner,Travis, Cle	.290
Rodriguez,Alex, NYY	.289
Sexson,Richie, Sea	.278
Teixeira,Mark, Tex	.273
Giambi,Jason, NYY	.264
Dellucci,David, Tex	.262
Konerko,Paul, CWS	.250
Guerrero,Vladimir, LAA	.248

Power / Speed Number

Soriano,Alfonso, Tex	32.7
Rodriguez,Alex, NYY	29.2
Crawford,Carl, TB	22.6
Sizemore,Grady, Cle	22.0
Roberts,Brian, Bal	21.6
Suzuki,Ichiro, Sea	20.6
Guerrero,Vladimir, LAA	18.5
Jones,Jacque, Min	16.6
Dye,Jermaine, CWS	16.2
Jeter,Derek, NYY	16.1

Speed Scores (2004-2005)

Crawford,Carl, TB	8.73
Figgins,Chone, LAA	8.12
Damon,Johnny, Bos	7.62
Suzuki,Ichiro, Sea	7.39
Lugo,Julio, TB	7.13
Soriano,Alfonso, Tex	6.96
Roberts,Brian, Bal	6.88
DeJesus,David, KC	6.73
Infante,Omar, Det	6.67
Rios,Alexis, Tor	6.53

Cheap Wins

Hendrickson,Ma, TB	6
Lee,Cliff, Cle	5
Maroth,Mike, Det	5
Bonderman,Jer, Det	4
Garland,Jon, CWS	4
Johnson,Randy, NYY	4
Lohse,Kyle, Min	4
Meche,Gil, Sea	4
Silva,Carlos, Min	4
Small,Aaron, NYY	4

Tough Losses

Blanton,Joe, Oak	6
Haren,Danny, Oak	6
Millwood,Kevin, Cle	6
Zito,Barry, Oak	6
Bush,Dave, Tor	5
Johnson,Jason, Det	5
Radke,Brad, Min	5
Westbrook,Jake, Cle	5
Cabrera,Daniel, Bal	4
Robertson,Nate, Det	4

2005 National League Bill James Leaders

Top Game Scores

Pitcher	Date	Opp	IP	H	R	ER	BB	SO	GS
Carpenter,Chris, StL	6/14	Tor	9.0	1	0	0	1	10	94
Glavine,Tom, NYM	9/29	Col	9.0	2	0	0	2	11	92
Patterson,John, Was	8/4	LA	9.0	4	0	0	0	13	92
Carpenter,Chris, StL	6/25	Pit	9.0	4	0	0	0	11	90
Carpenter,Chris, StL	7/17	Hou	9.0	3	0	0	0	9	90
Lowe,Derek, LAD	8/31	ChC	9.0	1	0	0	2	7	90
Martinez,Pedro, NYM	6/7	Hou	9.0	2	1	1	1	12	90
Peavy,Jake, SD	6/20	LA	8.0	2	0	0	1	13	90
3 tied with									89

Worst Game Scores

Pitcher	Date	Opp	IP	H	R	ER	BB	SO	GS
Astacio,Ezeq, Hou	5/21	Tex	1.2	9	9	9	2	1	0
Francis,Jeff, Col	8/11	Pit	3.1	13	9	8	1	1	0
Acevedo,Jose, Col	8/9	Pit	3.1	12	9	9	1	2	1
Williams,Woody, SD	9/20	Col	1.0	9	9	8	0	0	1
Weaver,Jeff, LAD	4/22	Col	4.0	13	8	8	1	0	3
Wright,Jamey, Col	7/27	NYM	4.0	11	9	9	2	3	5
Wright,Jamey, Col	4/15	SF	4.0	9	9	9	4	1	5
Rodriguez,Wandy, Hou	6/4	StL	2.2	9	9	9	2	4	6
Vazquez,Javier, Ari	8/14	Atl	2.0	8	9	9	1	3	6
Weaver,Jeff, LAD	4/12	SF	3.0	11	8	8	0	1	6

Runs Created

Pujols,Albert, StL	139
Lee,Derek, ChC	135
Bay,Jason, Pit	128
Abreu,Bobby, Phi	116
Helton,Todd, Col	114
Dunn,Adam, Cin	112
Giles,Brian, SD	112
Delgado,Carlos, Fla	110
Burrell,Pat, Phi	109
Cabrera,Miguel, Fla	108

Runs Created Per 27 Outs

Pujols,Albert, StL	8.8
Lee,Derek, ChC	8.6
Helton,Todd, Col	8.4
Bay,Jason, Pit	7.8
Delgado,Carlos, Fla	7.6
Giles,Brian, SD	7.3
Dunn,Adam, Cin	7.1
Ensberg,Morgan, Hou	7.1
Edmonds,Jim, StL	7.0
Abreu,Bobby, Phi	7.0

Offensive Winning %

Pujols,Albert, StL	.790
Lee,Derek, ChC	.788
Delgado,Carlos, Fla	.768
Giles,Brian, SD	.766
Bay,Jason, Pit	.757
Helton,Todd, Col	.749
Ensberg,Morgan, Hou	.719
Cabrera,Miguel, Fla	.709
Kent,Jeff, LAD	.709
Edmonds,Jim, StL	.705

Secondary Average
(minimum 502 PA)

Dunn,Adam, Cin	.510
Lee,Derek, ChC	.495
Edmonds,Jim, StL	.475
Pujols,Albert, StL	.470
Bay,Jason, Pit	.447
Ensberg,Morgan, Hou	.447
Abreu,Bobby, Phi	.440
Berkman,Lance, Hou	.434
Jones,Andruw, Atl	.430
Helton,Todd, Col	.428

Isolated Power
(minimum 502 PA)

Lee,Derek, ChC	.327
Jones,Andruw, Atl	.312
Dunn,Adam, Cin	.293
Delgado,Carlos, Fla	.280
Pujols,Albert, StL	.279
Griffey Jr.,Ken, Cin	.275
Ensberg,Morgan, Hou	.274
Edmonds,Jim, StL	.270
Ramirez,Aramis, ChC	.266
Glaus,Troy, Ari	.264

Power / Speed Number

Abreu,Bobby, Phi	27.1
Bay,Jason, Pit	25.4
Pujols,Albert, StL	23.0
Lee,Derek, ChC	22.6
Wright,David, NYM	20.9
Utley,Chase, Phi	20.4
Furcal,Rafael, Atl	19.0
Rollins,Jimmy, Phi	18.6
Lee,Carlos, Mil	18.5
Lopez,Felipe, Cin	18.2

Speed Scores (2004-2005)

Reyes,Jose, NYM	9.08
Rollins,Jimmy, Phi	8.23
Pierre,Juan, Fla	7.79
Furcal,Rafael, Atl	7.72
Beltran,Carlos, NYM	7.29
Freel,Ryan, Cin	7.16
Everett,Adam, Hou	7.00
Patterson,Corey, ChC	6.86
Cameron,Mike, NYM	6.86
Abreu,Bobby, Phi	6.71

Cheap Wins

Capuano,Chris, Mil	6
Lidle,Cory, Phi	5
Glavine,Tom, NYM	4
Lieber,Jon, Phi	4
Lowry,Noah, SF	4
Moehler,Brian, Fla	4
Morris,Matt, StL	4
Ortiz,Ramon, Cin	4
Rodriguez,Wandy, Hou	4
Vargas,Claudio, Was-Ari	4

Tough Losses

Weaver,Jeff, LAD	6
Clemens,Roger, Hou	5
Davis,Doug, Mil	5
Glavine,Tom, NYM	5
Lieber,Jon, Phi	5
Maddux,Greg, ChC	5
Oswalt,Roy, Hou	5
Pettitte,Andy, Hou	5
Santos,Victor,	5
Sheets,Ben, Mil	5
Williams,Jerome, SF-ChC	5

Additional Bill James Leaders

AL Batters Win Shares
(2005)

Rodriguez,Alex, NYY	34
Ramirez,Manny, Bos	33
Teixeira,Mark, Tex	33
Sheffield,Gary, NYY	31
Ortiz,David, Bos	30
Young,Michael, Tex	29
Roberts,Brian, Bal	28
Guerrero,Vladimir, LAA	27
3 tied with	26

NL Batters Win Shares
(2005)

Pujols,Albert, StL	34
Lee,Derrek, ChC	33
Giles,Brian, SD	32
Bay,Jason, Pit	30
Delgado,Carlos, Fla	29
Kent,Jeff, LAD	28
Cabrera,Miguel, Fla	27
Eckstein,David, StL	27
Ensberg,Morgan, Hou	27
2 tied with	26

AL Pitchers Win Shares
(2005)

Santana,Johan, Min	23
Buehrle,Mark, CWS	22
Garland,Jon, CWS	20
Rivera,Mariano, NYY	19
Colon,Bartolo, LAA	18
Contreras,Jose, CWS	17
Garcia,Freddy, CWS	17
Nathan,Joe, Min	17
Lackey,John, LAA	16
Street,Huston, Oak	16

NL Pitchers Win Shares
(2005)

Clemens,Roger, Hou	24
Willis,Dontrelle, Fla	22
Oswalt,Roy, Hou	21
Pettitte,Andy, Hou	21
Carpenter,Chris, StL	20
Martinez,Pedro, NYM	19
Smoltz,John, Atl	19
Wagner,Billy, Phi	18
Zambrano,Carlos, ChC	18
2 tied with	17

Batters Win Shares
(Career)

Bonds,Barry	661
Biggio,Craig	411
Sheffield,Gary	398
Palmeiro,Rafael	394
Bagwell,Jeff	387
Thomas,Frank	362
Griffey Jr.,Ken	358
Rodriguez,Alex	315
Sosa,Sammy	311
Piazza,Mike	309

Pitchers Win Shares
(Career)

Clemens,Roger	421
Maddux,Greg	371
Johnson,Randy	297
Glavine,Tom	290
Smoltz,John	257
Martinez,Pedro	243
Brown,Kevin	241
Mussina,Mike	234
Schilling,Curt	227
Wells,David	203

2005 AL Component ERA
(minimum 162 IP)

Santana,Johan, Min	2.14
Buehrle,Mark, CWS	3.21
Colon,Bartolo, LAA	3.28
Zito,Barry, Oak	3.32
Lee,Cliff, Cle	3.35
Blanton,Joe, Oak	3.37
Johnson,Randy, NYY	3.38
Garland,Jon, CWS	3.39
Millwood,Kevin, Cle	3.40
Contreras,Jose, CWS	3.46

2005 NL Component ERA
(minimum 162 IP)

Clemens,Roger, Hou	1.96
Martinez,Pedro, NYM	2.03
Pettitte,Andy, Hou	2.40
Carpenter,Chris, StL	2.49
Peavy,Jake, SD	2.49
Willis,Dontrelle, Fla	2.71
Smoltz,John, Atl	2.83
Zambrano,Carlos, ChC	2.86
Beckett,Josh, Fla	3.06
Patterson,John, Was	3.09

Highest Avg Game Score
(AL - minimum 30 GS)

Santana,Johan, Min	62.79
Johnson,Randy, NYY	56.26
Millwood,Kevin, Cle	56.07
Buehrle,Mark, CWS	55.36
Colon,Bartolo, LAA	55.15
Zito,Barry, Oak	54.66
Lackey,John, LAA	54.45
Contreras,Jose, CWS	54.22
Garland,Jon, CWS	53.91
Haren,Danny, Oak	53.32

Lowest Avg Game Score
(AL - minimum 30 GS)

Lima,Jose, KC	38.22
Hendrickson,Ma, TB	41.84
Greinke,Zack, KC	42.48
Pineiro,Joel, Sea	44.20
Franklin,Ryan, Sea	45.53
Lopez,Rodrigo, Bal	46.49
Maroth,Mike, Det	46.91
Johnson,Jason, Det	47.58
Lohse,Kyle, Min	47.80
Arroyo,Bronson, Bos	48.06

Lowest Offensive Win %
(AL)

Rodriguez,Ivan, Det	.294
Reed,Jeremy, Sea	.337
Boone,Aaron, Cle	.360
Blake,Casey, Cle	.367
Berroa,Angel, KC	.399
Morneau,Justin, Min	.400
Uribe,Juan, CWS	.402
Rios,Alexis, Tor	.402
Cano,Robinson, NYY	.411
Cabrera,Orlando, LAA	.415

Highest Avg Game Score
(NL - minimum 30 GS)

Clemens,Roger, Hou	63.47
Martinez,Pedro, NYM	63.10
Carpenter,Chris, StL	61.42
Peavy,Jake, SD	61.37
Pettitte,Andy, Hou	60.45
Willis,Dontrelle, Fla	58.82
Zambrano,Carlos, ChC	58.79
Smoltz,John, Atl	57.79
Patterson,John, Was	57.58
Oswalt,Roy, Hou	56.94

Lowest Avg Game Score
(NL - minimum 30 GS)

Milton,Eric, Cin	41.47
Francis,Jeff, Col	43.24
Ortiz,Ramon, Cin	44.50
Wells,Kip, Pit	46.52
Ramirez,Horacio, Atl	47.63
Redman,Mark, Pit	47.67
Lidle,Cory, Phi	47.84
Lawrence,Brian, SD	47.85
Tomko,Brett, SF	48.57
Marquis,Jason, StL	49.47

Lowest Offensive Win %
(NL)

Bell,David, Phi	.328
Lowell,Mike, Fla	.343
Perez,Neifi, ChC	.363
Feliz,Pedro, SF	.365
Clayton,Royce, Ari	.374
Wilson,Jack, Pit	.376
Taveras,Willy, Hou	.402
Castilla,Vinny, Was	.406
Everett,Adam, Hou	.412
Pierre,Juan, Fla	.471

Win Shares

With three Astros having an excellent chance of passing the 400 Win Shares mark for their career, the 2005 season saw us just miss out on some Win Shares history. While Roger Clemens and Craig Biggio easily passed the milestone, Jeff Bagwell's injury plagued season left him just shy. If all three Houston players return in 2006, look for the Astros to become only the second team in history to feature a trio of players with 400+ Win Shares. The only other team—the 1928 Philadelphia Athletics with Ty Cobb, Tris Speaker, and Eddie Collins.

Bill James initially devised Win Shares as a way of relating a player's individual statistics to the number of wins he contributed to his team. As a single number Win Shares allow us to easily compare the accomplishments of each player.

The following pages contain the sum of a player's Win Shares prior to 1996, then individual season totals from 1996 through 2005. Career numbers are also included for each player.

We credit a team with three Win Shares for each win. If a team wins 100 games, the players on the team will be created with 300 Win Shares—or 300 thirds of a win. If a team wins 70 games, the players on the team will be credited with 210 Win Shares, and so on and so forth.

Additionally, the quality of the team does not affect an individual player's Win Shares. A great player on a bad team will rate just as well as a great player on a good team. For example, Alex Rodriguez had 31 win shares for the AL East Champion New York Yankees, while Jason Bay had 30 for a Pirates team that only won 67 games.

Win Shares are also a great tool for evaluating award voting and Hall of Fame credentials. Take a look and see if this year's Most Valuable Player, Cy Young, and Rookie of the Year award winners match up with the Win Shares leaders.

Win Shares can also be used to assess the value of trades. Take a look to see if your favorite team had a net gain or loss from their transactions.

WIN SHARES BY YEAR

Player	<96	96	97	98	99	00	01	02	03	04	05	Career
Abernathy,Brent							10	7	0		1	18
Abreu,Bobby		0	6	26	26	23	26	29	28	33	25	222
Accardo,Jeremy											2	2
Acevedo,Jose							2	0	2	1	1	6
Adams,Mike										5	1	6
Adams,Russ										2	10	12
Adams,Terry	0	9	5	5	9	6	8	5	7	5	0	59
Adkins,Jon									0	3	0	3
Affeldt,Jeremy							5	12	4	1		22
Aguila,Chris										0	0	0
Ainsworth,Kurt							0	2	3	0		5
Alexander,Manny	3	1	6	3	4	3				1	0	21
Alfonseca,Ant			0	3	11	10	9	7	1	8	1	50
Alfonzo,Edgardo	8	6	28	22	29	36	15	26	17	15	9	211
Allen,Chad					7	1	2	0	0	0	1	11
Almanza,Armando				2	3	2	3	0	0	0		10
Almanzar,Carlos			0	1	0	3	1	1		8	0	14
Alomar Jr.,Sandy	52	8	18	6	4	8	4	5	4	1	2	112
Alou,Moises	69	20	23	29		17	21	9	20	23	18	249
Alvarez,Abe										0	0	0
Alvarez,Wilson	42	13	15	7	10			2	10	6	0	105
Ambres,Chip											1	1
Amezaga,Alfredo							2	1	1	0		4
Anderson,Brian N	10	3	2	9	7	14	2	5	12	2	0	66
Anderson,Brian										0		0
Anderson,Garret	11	6	16	18	16	15	17	23	25	14	16	177
Anderson,Jason								1	0	0		1
Anderson,Marlon				2	8	2	16	10	12	3	4	57
Anderson,Matt				5	1	4	8	0	1		0	19
Andino,Robert											0	0
Aquino,Greg										6	0	6
Ardoin,Danny					0				0	3		3
Armas Jr.,Tony				0	5	12	7	4	2	2		32
Arroyo,Bronson					0	3	2	2	1	11	11	29
Astacio,Ezeq											0	0
Astacio,Pedro	23	13	10	6	19	11	7	5	0	0	5	99
Atchison,Scott									2	0		2
Atkins,Garrett									0	2	13	15
Aurilia,Rich	2	5	5	13	18	20	33	15	13	7	16	147
Ausmus,Brad	21	8	13	14	17	16	10	10	12	7	15	143
Ayala,Luis								11	10	8		29
Aybar,Manny			3	1	4	5	1	1	0			15
Aybar,Willy											6	6
Backe,Brandon							0	1	5	7		13
Baerga,Carlos	118	6	11	10	2			2	7	1	3	160
Baez,Danys							6	11	9	10	10	46
Bagwell,Jeff	124	41	32	29	37	25	30	22	22	22	3	387
Bajenaru,Jeff								0	0			0
Baker,Jeff											1	1
Baker,Scott											4	4
Bako,Paul				5	5	5	3	3	5	2	1	29
Baldelli,Rocco									14	14		28
Baldwin,James	0	10	6	6	9	11	8	3	0	0	3	56
Balfour,Grant							0		2	3		5
Barajas,Rod				1	0	1	3	5	9	11	30
Bard,Josh							1	7	2	2		12
Barmes,Clint								1	3	9		13
Barrett,Michael				1	11	1	2	12	7	14	18	66
Bartlett,Jason										0	6	6
Bartosh,Cliff										1	0	1
Batista,Miguel	0	0	0	6	6	0	11	9	14	11	8	65
Bauer,Rick							0	5	2	3	0	10
Bautista,Denny									0	1		1
Bautista,Jose									0	0		0
Bay,Jason									5	15	30	50
Bayliss,Jonah											0	0
Bazardo,Yorman											0	0
Bean,Colter											0	0
Beckett,Josh							3	5	11	9	12	40
Bedard,Erik								0		6	8	14
Beimel,Joe							4	3	2	0	1	10
Belisle,Matt											4	4
Bell,David	2	1	2	10	16	8	14	18	5	20	9	105
Bell,Heath										2	0	2
Bell,Rob							5	1	2	3	6	0	17
Bellhorn,Mark			5	0		0	1	18	4	20	5	53
Belliard,Ronnie				0	0	17	13	1	11	18	18	78
Beltran,Carlos					2	18	5	27	20	28	29	21	150

WIN SHARES BY YEAR

Player	<96	96	97	98	99	00	01	02	03	04	05	Career
Beltran,Francis								0		2		2
Beltre,Adrian				4	15	22	12	16	15	33	13	130
Benitez,Armando	2	3	11	10	19	17	14	12	10	18	4	120
Bennett,Gary	0	0		1	2	3	1	4	6	2	5	24
Benoit,Joaquin						0	3	5	4	6	18
Benson,Kris			12	14		5	2	10	10	53
Bentz,Chad										0	0	0
Bergmann,Jason											2	2
Bergolla,Will											0	0
Berkman,Lance					1	10	32	29	25	30	20	147
Bernero,Adam						2	0	1	1	1	1	6
Berroa,Angel							1	1	16	12	12	42
Betancourt,Raf								4	5	7	16
Betancourt,Yun										3	3
Betemit,Wilson						0			1	7	8
Bigbie,Larry						2	0	9	10	5	26
Biggio,Craig	170	32	38	35	31	11	25	15	20	16	18	411
Blackley,Travis									0			0
Blake,Casey					1	0	1	0	11	17	9	39
Blalock,Hank						1	17	24	14	56
Blanco,Andres									3	1	4
Blanco,Henry			0		6	9	6	4	2	5	6	38
Blanco,Tony										1	1
Blanton,Joe									0	13	13
Bloomquist,Wil								3	3	2	4	12
Blum,Geoff				3	10	8	15	5	3	7	51
Bocachica,Hiram							0	3	1	0	1	5
Bonderman,Jer									2	8	9	19
Bonds,Barry	309	39	36	34	19	32	54	49	39	48	2	661
Booker,Chris										0		0
Boone,Aaron			0	6	15	10	13	19	23		9	95
Boone,Bret	39	10	8	18	17	15	32	25	30	9	5	208
Bootcheck,Chris										2		2
Borchard,Joe							1	0	1	0	2
Borders,Pat	51	4	3	1	1		0	0	1	2	2	65
Borowski,Joe	1	1	2	0		0	8	14	0	3	29
Bottalico,Ricky	11	13	10	0	0	8	6	0	0	5	2	55
Botts,Jason										0	0
Bowyer,Travis											0	0
Boyer,Blaine											4	4
Bradford,Chad				3	0	2	3	9	9	5	2	33
Bradley,Milton					3	3	6	18	16	10	56
Branyan,Russell				0	1	5	10	8	6	5	9	44
Brazelton,Dewon							1	0	5	0	6
Brazoban,Yhency									4	4	8
Breslow,Craig											1	1
Brito,Eude											1	1
Brocail,Doug	7	1	7	8	12	5			4	3	47
Brooks,Frank										1	0	1
Broussard,Ben								0	9	16	10	35
Brower,Jim					2	1	8	5	7	8	1	32
Brown,Emil			1	0	0	1	2				18	22
Brown,Kevin	86	26	23	26	19	20	11	1	20	9	0	241
Broxton,Jon											0	0
Bruney,Brian									2	0	2
Bruntlett,Eric									1	2	3	6
Bubela,Jaime										0	0
Buck,John									4	10	14
Buehrle,Mark						4	18	17	13	17	22	91
Bukvich,Ryan							1	0	1	0	2
Bulger,Jason										1	1
Bullington,Bryan										0	0
Bump,Nate								2	1	1	4
Burgos,Ambiorix										4	4
Burke,Chris									0	6	6
Burke,Jamie						0		1	5	0	6
Burnett,A.J.					3	5	9	14	0	7	11	49
Burnett,Sean									2		2
Burnitz,Jeromy	11	6	20	19	19	16	18	7	12	17	16	161
Burns,Mike										1	1
Burrell,Pat						12	17	25	9	14	24	101
Burroughs,Sean								3	16	16	6	41
Bush,Dave									7	6	13
Bynum,Freddie										0	0
Byrd,Marlon							0	16	5	6	27
Byrd,Paul	3	2	1	7	10	0	6	19		7	13	68
Byrdak,Tim			0	0	0					1	1
Byrnes,Eric						0	1	2	16	17	9	45

WIN SHARES BY YEAR

Player	<96	96	97	98	99	00	01	02	03	04	05	Career
Cabrera,Daniel										8	7	15
Cabrera,Fern										0	4	4
Cabrera,Melky											0	0
Cabrera,Miguel									12	19	27	58
Cabrera,Orlando			0	6	8	9	26	14	20	11	14	108
Cain,Matt											5	5
Cairo,Miguel		0	0	10	10	10	4	3	3	14	5	59
Calero,Kiko									3	6	5	14
Cali,Carmen										0	0	0
Calzado,Nap											0	0
Cameron,Mike	0	0	17	6	19	19	29	18	21	15	11	155
Camp,Shawn										4	0	4
Campillo,Jorge											0	0
Cano,Robinson											12	12
Cantu,Jorge										4	18	22
Capellan,Jose										0	1	1
Capps,Matt											0	0
Capuano,Chris									1	4	13	18
Carlyle,Buddy					0	0						0
Carpenter,Chris			2	11	9	5	13	3		12	20	75
Carrara,Giov	0	0	0			0	8	7	0	7	5	27
Carrasco,D.J.									6	1	4	11
Carrasco,Hector	12	5	4	5	3	6	4		2		10	51
Carroll,Jamey								3	3	6	9	21
Carter,Lance				0				4	10	6	2	22
Carvajal,Marcos											2	2
Casanova,Raul							1				0	1
Casey,Sean			0	10	23	17	18	6	17	28	13	132
Cash,Kevin								0	0	3	0	3
Cassidy,Scott								2			0	2
Castilla,Vinny	22	23	21	21	11	3	13	1	14	12	10	151
Castillo,Alb	0	1	1	3	7	4	3	0	1	2	4	26
Castillo,Frank	32	3	6	0		12	8	4		0	0	65
Castillo,Jose										9	9	18
Castillo,Luis		3	3	3	14	18	14	20	22	22	18	137
Castro,Bernie											3	3
Castro,Juan	0	2	1	3	0	3	1	2	8	5	7	32
Castro,Ramon					1	3	0	4	2	1	7	18
Catalanotto,Fr			1	4	5	8	17	7	15	5	16	78
Cedeno,Roger	1	7	9	3	17	5	14	10	8	6	0	80
Cedeno,Ronny											2	2
Cepicky,Matt								1	0	0	0	1
Cerda,Jaime								2	0	4	0	6
Chacin,Gustavo										1	14	15
Chacon,Shawn							7	4	9	2	11	33
Chavez,Angel											0	0
Chavez,Endy							0	3	10	10	1	24
Chavez,Eric				2	9	16	26	24	25	18	20	140
Chavez,Raul			0	0	0	0		0	1	3	2	6
Chen,Bruce				1	1	11	4	1	0	4	13	35
Chen,Chin-Feng								0	0	0	0	0
Childers,Matt								0			0	0
Choate,Randy							1	4	0	0	3	8
Choi,Hee Seop								0	6	13	7	26
Choo,Shin-soo											0	0
Christiansen,J	4	0	4	9	4	4	4	0	1	3	2	35
Chulk,Vinnie									0	4	5	9
Church,Ryan										1	8	9
Cintron,Alex							0	1	14	8	7	30
Cirillo,Jeff	12	20	24	26	22	19	14	9	3	1	6	156
Clark,Brady						0	4	1	7	12	22	46
Clark,Doug											0	0
Clark,Jermaine							0		1	0	0	1
Clark,Tony	2	8	24	15	19	6	16	1	4	7	18	120
Claussen,Bran									1	0	7	8
Clayton,Royce	41	12	13	12	15	8	10	8	7	11	11	148
Clemens,Roger	230	20	32	25	10	16	19	11	15	19	24	421
Clement,Matt				1	6	5	4	11	10	12	11	60
Closser,JD										2	2	4
Coffey,Todd											3	3
Colome,Jesus							4	0	4	5	2	15
Colon,Bartolo			2	16	16	15	14	22	17	10	18	130
Colon,Roman										2	1	3
Conine,Jeff	53	17	9	6	10	9	24	9	16	17	10	180
Contreras,Jose									7	6	17	30
Cook,Aaron								2	3	6	6	17
Cooper,Brian				2	2	1	0			0	1	6
Cora,Alex				1	0	6	6	13	13	17	5	61

WIN SHARES BY YEAR

Player	<96	96	97	98	99	00	01	02	03	04	05	Career
Corcoran,Tim										0		0
Cordero,Chad									2	12	15	29
Cordero,Franc					2	3	0	8	12	17	11	53
Cordero,Wil	46	5	11	8	5	10	1	6	11	0	0	103
Cormier,Lance										0	4	4
Cormier,Rheal	25	8	0		5	4	4	1	14	7	1	69
Correia,Kevin									3	0	2	5
Cortes,David			0				0				5	5
Cortez,Fernando											0	0
Costa,Shane											0	0
Cota,Humberto							0	0	0	2	6	8
Cotts,Neal									0	2	9	11
Counsell,Craig	0		8	13	2	5	14	15	5	10	22	94
Crain,Jesse										4	10	14
Crawford,Carl								6	13	20	22	61
Crede,Joe						0	1	6	13	8	15	43
Creek,Doug	1	0	0		0	4	3	2	1		0	11
Crisp,Coco								3	7	14	20	44
Crosby,Bobby									0	14	12	26
Crosby,Bubba									0	1	2	3
Crowell,Jim			0							0	0	0
Cruz,Deivi			7	7	13	15	8	7	10	12	5	84
Cruz,Jacob		2	0	0	3	1	1	2		4	3	16
Cruz,Jose			11	12	11	15	16	13	17	14	11	120
Cruz,Juan							4	3	0	7	0	14
Cruz,Nelson											0	0
Cuddyer,Mike							0	3	1	10	7	21
Cummings,Midre	4	1	9	3	1	1	0			3	0	22
Dallimore,Brian										1	0	1
Damon,Johnny	6	9	11	17	18	26	17	22	18	26	25	195
Darensbourg,Vic				3	0	5	3	0	0	0	2	13
Daubach,Brian				0	14	10	13	14	4	2	0	57
DaVanon,Jeff			0				1	1	12	9	4	27
Davies,Kyle											4	4
Davis,Doug					0	5	8	3	7	16	12	51
Davis,J.J.								0	0	0	0	0
Davis,Jason								2	5	2	2	11
Davis,Kane								0			2	2
Day,Zach								3	8	6	0	17
de la Rosa,Jor										0	2	2
de los Santos,V			2	0	3	4	4	0	0			13
DeJean,Mike			7	9	0	4	8	8	6	2	5	49
DeJesus,David									0	9	16	25
Delcarmen,Manny											1	1
Delgado,Carlos	3	12	18	24	21	36	23	26	32	16	29	240
Dellucci,David			1	10	5	1	7	4	4	10	15	57
Demaria,Chris										0		0
Dempster,Ryan				0	6	17	7	4	0	2	14	50
Denorfia,Chris											0	0
DePaula,Jorge									2	0	0	2
DeRosa,Mark				0	0	1	6	7	5	2	4	25
Dessens,Elmer			1	1	1	10	10	15	7	5	4	54
Devine,Joey											0	0
Diaz,Einar	0	0	1	8	6	15	4	5	2	2		43
Diaz,Matt									0	0	2	2
Diaz,Victor										1	7	8
Dickey,R.A.							0		6	4	0	10
DiFelice,Mike		0	6	5	8	2	1	4	6	0	0	32
Dillon,Joe											0	0
Dinardo,Lenny										1	1	2
Dingman,Craig										0	3	3
Dobbs,Greg										1	2	3
Dohmann,Scott										3	1	4
Dominguez,Juan									0	2	4	6
Dominique,Andy									0		0	0
Donnelly,Brend								6	12	5	6	29
Dotel,Octavio					3	7	12	17	12	14	2	67
Douglass,Sean							1	0	0	1	2	4
Doumit,Ryan											6	6
Downs,Scott						3			0	0	5	8
Drese,Ryan							3	2	0	15	2	22
Drew,J.D.				3	10	18	22	15	13	31	12	124
Driskill,Travis								5	1	0	0	6
Dubois,Jason										1	3	4
DuBose,Eric								1	5	1	0	7
Duchscherer,J								0	1	9	11	21
Duckworth,Br							5	2	2	0	0	9
Duffy,Chris											5	5

WIN SHARES BY YEAR

Player	<96	96	97	98	99	00	01	02	03	04	05	Career
Duke,Zach											10	10
Duncan,Chris											0	0
Dunn,Adam							10	20	13	29	25	97
Durazo,Erubiel				9	5	7	10	17	20	1		69
Durham,Ray	8	17	13	25	20	19	21	20	16	19	14	192
Durrington,Tr					1	0			0	1	0	2
Dye,Jermaine		5	2	2	16	21	18	13	2	12	17	108
Easley,Damion	18	3	18	23	13	14	15	5	0	8	9	126
Eaton,Adam						9	5	0	7	6	5	32
Eckstein,David							12	21	11	10	27	81
Edmonds,Jim	29	18	19	24	5	29	30	29	22	33	25	263
Edwards,Mike											3	3
Eischen,Joey	1	3	0				1	9	5	1	3	23
Elarton,Scott				5	10	11	0		0	5	7	38
Eldred,Brad											1	1
Eldred,Cal	41	5	9	3	0	7	0		6	4	4	79
Ellis,Mark								14	18		21	53
Ellison,Jason									0	1	6	7
Embree,Alan	1	0	6	3	6	3	2	7	5	4	0	37
Encarnacion,Ed											4	4
Encarnacion,Ju			1	4	8	14	5	14	15	12	18	91
Ensberg,Morgan						0		2	15	11	27	55
Erickson,Scott	65	10	16	15	12	0		2		0	0	120
Erstad,Darin		3	19	21	9	30	14	17	3	15	15	146
Escalona,Felix								1	1	0	1	3
Escobar,Alex						1			1	3		5
Escobar,Kelvim			6	7	7	8	11	9	12	14	5	79
Esposito,Michael											0	0
Estes,Shawn	0	4	16	3	6	10	7	4	0	9	5	64
Estrada,Johnny							5	0	0	18	9	32
Etherton,Seth					3			0		0		3
Eveland,Dana											0	0
Everett,Adam						0	1	11	12	14		38
Everett,Carl	8	2	13	16	25	24	11	10	21	5	11	146
Eyre,Scott			2	2	0	0	2	4	5	4	9	28
Falkenborg,Br					0				0	0		0
Farnsworth,Kyle					5	0	9	0	7	3	14	38
Fasano,Sal								0			3	3
Fassero,Jeff	47	18	17	14	1	8	10	2	0	4	5	126
Feldman,Scott											1	1
Feliz,Pedro						0	0	2	8	9	9	28
Fick,Robert				2	2	4	10	12	14	2	6	52
Field,Nate								0	2	3	0	5
Fielder,Prince											2	2
Figgins,Chone								0	8	20	22	50
Finley,Steve	101	27	19	15	24	21	15	24	18	16	6	286
Fiorentino,Jeff											0	0
Flaherty,John	8	10	11	5	12	8	4	7	3	3	3	74
Flores,Randy							1			2	3	6
Flores,Ron											1	1
Floyd,Cliff	11	6	5	18	9	19	26	22	15	13	24	168
Floyd,Gavin										2	0	2
Fogg,Josh							2	10	4	7	3	26
Fontenot,Mike											0	0
Foppert,Jesse									2	0		2
Ford,Lew									4	21	12	37
Fossum,Casey							2	6	3	0	5	16
Foster,John							0	1			3	4
Foulke,Keith			4	5	16	16	17	9	21	18	3	109
Fox,Chad			2	4	0		9	0	5	0	0	20
Francis,Jeff										2	6	8
Francisco,Frank										6		6
Franco,John	131	10	12	8	6	7	5		3	1	0	183
Franco,Julio	219	13	9		0		3	6	6	12	7	275
Francoeur,Jeff											12	12
Franklin,Ryan				1			5	6	13	6	6	37
Franklin,Wayne					1	0	2	4	1	0		8
Frasor,Jason										9	6	15
Freel,Ryan							0		3	19	11	33
Freeman,Choo										1	0	1
Freire,Alejan											0	0
Fuentes,Brian							1	2	10	2	14	29
Fultz,Aaron						3	3	1	3	3	7	20
Furcal,Rafael						17	9	20	25	20	26	117
Furmaniak,J.J.											0	0
Gagne,Eric					3	2	4	20	25	19	3	76
Gall,John											1	1
Gallo,Mike									3	2	2	7

WIN SHARES BY YEAR

Player	<96	96	97	98	99	00	01	02	03	04	05	Career
Garabito,Eddy											3	3
Garcia,Freddy					16	8	18	11	8	15	17	93
Garcia,Jairo										0	0	0
Garcia,Jesse						0	0	1	1	2	0	4
Garciaparra,N		2	26	27	32	29	3	26	25	11	5	186
Gardner,Lee							0					0
Garko,Ryan											0	0
Garland,Jon						1	8	8	10	11	20	58
Gassner,Dave											0	0
Gathright,Joey										0	4	4
Gaudin,Chad									3	1	0	4
Geary,Geoff									0	1	3	4
German,Esteban								0	0	2	1	3
German,Franklyn									2	0	4	6
Gerut,Jody									14	10	3	27
Giambi,Jason	5	15	18	23	30	38	38	34	28	8	24	261
Giarratano,Tony											1	1
Gibbons,Jay							4	12	18	4	15	53
Gil,Geronimo							2	7	3	1	1	14
Giles,Brian	1	6	13	14	27	27	29	31	25	23	32	228
Giles,Marcus							9	5	28	17	23	82
Ginter,Keith						0	0	2	9	11	2	24
Ginter,Matt						0	2	2	0	2	0	6
Gipson,Charles				1	1	1	1	1	0	1	0	6
Glaus,Troy				3	16	25	21	22	9	8	23	127
Glavine,Tom	119	22	21	23	14	21	16	19	7	14	14	290
Gload,Ross						0		0		7	0	7
Glover,Gary						0	4	5	3	1	1	14
Glynn,Ryan					0	0	0			2	0	2
Gobble,Jimmy									3	5	1	9
Godwin,Tyrell										0		0
Gomes,Jonny									0	0	14	14
Gomez,Alexis							0		0	0		0
Gomez,Chris	16	11	7	15	6	1	8	11	2	8	4	89
Gonzalez,Adrian										1	1	2
Gonzalez,Alex			1	11	3	10	3	20	15	14		77
Gonzalez,Alex S	8	14	10	9	6	11	16	13	16	5	7	115
Gonzalez,Edgar							1	0	0			1
Gonzalez,Jeremi			9	2					8	0	1	20
Gonzalez,Juan	94	21	19	25	24	9	23	6	10	3	0	234
Gonzalez,Luis	74	17	12	12	26	27	37	27	24	10	19	285
Gonzalez,Luis A										7	9	16
Gonzalez,Mike								0	8	6		14
Gonzalez,Wiki				1	6	7	5	1			1	21
Good,Andy									2	1	0	3
Gordon,Tom	72	10	15	17	2		8	3	11	15	10	163
Gorzelanny,Tom											0	0
Gosling,Mike										1	1	2
Gotay,Ruben										3	5	8
Grabow,John									0	1	2	3
Grabowski,Jason								1	0	3	0	4
Graffanino,Tony		1	6	4	7	6	3	7	9	7	13	63
Graman,Alex										0	0	0
Granderson,C										0	6	6
Graves,Danny		2	0	8	16	18	11	17	3	6	0	81
Green,Andy										1	1	2
Green,Nick										8	6	14
Green,Shawn	10	8	14	21	24	22	34	29	20	15	17	214
Greenberg,Adam											0	0
Greene,Khalil									1	20	16	37
Greene,Todd		1	4	1	3	0	0	1	1	3	3	17
Gregg,Kevin									2	6	2	10
Greinke,Zack										9	3	12
Greisinger,Seth			6				1			0	0	7
Grieve,Ben		4	22	16	17	17	12	2	6	0		96
Griffey Jr.,Ken	151	28	36	29	31	24	14	5	6	15	19	358
Griffin,John-Ford											0	0
Grilli,Jason						0	1			0	1	2
Grimsley,Jason	10	1			6	5	8	7	4	4	0	45
Grissom,Marquis	121	24	14	11	13	8	6	14	22	14	1	248
Groom,Buddy	3	7	3	4	3	6	8	10	1	3	2	50
Gross,Gabe										2	2	4
Grudzielanek,M	3	17	14	13	13	15	17	12	18	8	18	148
Gryboski,Kevin								4	3	5	1	13
Guardado,Eddie	5	6	3	5	4	8	12	14	15	8	10	90
Guerrero,Vladimir		0	10	29	28	29	23	28	18	27	27	219
Guerrier,Matt										0	5	5
Guiel,Aaron								4	12	0	2	18

Player	<96	96	97	98	99	00	01	02	03	04	05	Career
Guillen,Carlos				2	0	8	14	12	12	22	8	78
Guillen,Jose			7	11	3	6	2	2	20	20	15	86
Guthrie,Jeremy										1	0	1
Gutierrez,Franklin											0	0
Guzman,Cristian					5	12	18	14	13	16	6	84
Guzman,Freddy										1		1
Haad,Yamid											1	1
Hafner,Travis								1	7	21	26	55
Hairston,Scott										3	0	3
Hairston Jr.,Jerry				0	5	4	10	12	7	8	9	55
Halama,John				0	13	6	4	6	4	6	0	39
Hall,Bill								1	4	7	17	29
Hall,Toby					0	6	7	10	8	11		42
Halladay,Roy				2	10	0	9	21	23	9	15	89
Halsey,Brad										0	6	6
Hammond,Chris	35	0	2	0				13	7	6	4	67
Hammonds,Jeff	14	3	14	9	8	14	5	8	4	1	0	80
Hampton,Mike	11	11	11	15	26	19	11	5	11	10	6	136
Hamulack,Tim											0	0
Hancock,Josh							0	0	2	1		3
Hansen,Craig											0	0
Hansen,Dave	19	0	6		3	6	4	4	3	3	0	48
Harang,Aaron								4	2	5	11	22
Harden,Rich								4	14	12		30
Hardy,J.J.											11	11
Haren,Danny									1	2	13	16
Harikkala,Tim	0	0		0						5	0	5
Harper,Travis						2	0	3	6	6	1	18
Harris,Brendan										0	1	1
Harris,Jeff											3	3
Harris,Lenny	52	10	3	3	4	5	0	5	1	0	3	86
Harris,Willie							0	2	2	10	4	18
Hart,Corey										0	0	0
Harvey,Ken						0		7	9	0		16
Harville,Chad					0		1		0	2	1	4
Hasegawa,Shige			7	11	5	11	5	6	13	2	4	64
Hatteberg,Scott	0	0	6	11	4	5	5	16	14	17	8	86
Hawkins,LaTroy	0	0	0	2	6	3	12	3	11	13	5	71
Hawpe,Brad										1	8	9
Heilman,Aaron								0	0	10		10
Heintz,Chris											1	1
Helling,Rick	2	3	6	15	12	15	7	8	6		5	79
Helms,Wes				1		0	5	1	12	4	5	28
Helton,Todd			2	17	19	29	26	27	34	30	25	209
Hendrickson,Ma							4	4	7	4		19
Henn,Sean											0	0
Hennessey,Brad										1	6	7
Hensley,Clay											5	5
Heredia,Felix		1	3	3	3	4	0	3	9	0	0	26
Herges,Matt					1	10	9	4	7	3	1	35
Hermanson,Dustin	0	0	10	13	12	9	8	0	4	9	14	79
Hermida,Jeremy											3	3
Hernandez,Anderson											0	0
Hernandez,Fel											8	8
Hernandez,Jose	8	6	4	16	16	9	13	19	6	9	2	108
Hernandez,Liv		1	8	6	9	14	5	7	22	19	13	104
Hernandez,Orl			13	14	12	4	11			8	5	67
Hernandez,Ram				6	10	13	12	19	13	10		83
Hernandez,Rob	40	17	15	10	14	12	9	7	3	1	10	138
Hernandez,Run							5	6			4	15
Hidalgo,Richard			2	6	9	21	17	7	20	10	4	96
Higginson,Bobby	8	21	25	16	9	26	18	15	6	12	0	156
Hill,Aaron											9	9
Hill,Bobby							5	0	4	2		11
Hill,Koyie							0	1	1		2
Hill,Rich											0	0
Hillenbrand,Shea						5	17	11	13	15		61
Hinske,Eric							22	12	6	11	51
Hocking,Denny	1	1	6	2	8	11	5	5	4	1	2	46
Hoffman,Trevor	27	20	11	20	14	13	9	8	1	11	10	144
Holbert,Aaron											0	0
Hollandsworth,T	2	19	7	6	7	8	4	12	5	6	4	80
Holliday,Matt										9	17	26
Hollins,Damon				0						0	7	7
Hooper,Kevin											0	0
Horgan,Joe										5	0	5
Houlton,D.J.											2	2
Howard,Ryan										1	10	11

Player	<96	96	97	98	99	00	01	02	03	04	05	Career
Howell,J.P.											1	1
Howry,Bob			7	10	9	5	3	0	4	11		49
Huber,Justin											0	0
Huckaby,Ken					0	2	0	0		1		3
Hudson,Luke							0		4	1		5
Hudson,Orlando							7	18	16	15		56
Hudson,Tim				12	15	17	23	23	16	14		120
Huff,Aubrey					3	5	12	21	20	14		75
Hughes,Travis										0	0	0
Hunter,Torii			0	0	5	8	19	20	15	13	11	91
Hyzdu,Adam						1	1	6	1	0	0	9
Ibanez,Raul	0	0	1	4	1	9	12	15	12	17		71
Iguchi,Tadahito											18	18
Infante,Omar							3	3	12	7		25
Inge,Brandon				3	4	5	13	17		42
Ishii,Kazuhisa							6	6	6	1		19
Isringhausen,Jason	8	6	0		4	10	14	13	7	15	12	89
Izturis,Cesar							4	4	11	25	6	50
Izturis,Maicer										1	6	7
Jackson,Conor											0	0
Jackson,Damian		1	1	2	11	15	11	6	2	0	8	57
Jackson,Edwin								2	0	0		2
Jacobs,Mike											5	5
James,Chuck											1	1
Jarvis,Kevin	0	0	1		0	4	7	1	0	0		13
Jenkins,Geoff			1	18	20	11	4	20	12	20		106
Jenks,Bobby											6	6
Jennings,Jason					3	14	9	9	5		40
Jensen,Ryan					2	5	0		0		7
Jeter,Derek	1	18	19	27	35	23	28	24	18	26	26	245
Jimenez,D'Ang			1		8	13	17	23	1		63
Jimerson,Charlton											0	0
Johnson,Ben										1	1	1
Johnson,Charles	13	10	21	15	12	20	17	6	10	6	0	130
Johnson,Dan											10	10
Johnson,Jason			0	2	4	0	9	5	10	6	8	44
Johnson,Josh											1	1
Johnson,Kelly											9	9
Johnson,Nick						0	11	14	6	20	51
Johnson,Randy	101	5	23	19	26	26	26	29	6	21	15	297
Johnson,Reed									11	9	10	30
Johnson,Russ							2			0		2
Johnson,Tyler											0	0
Johnston,Mike								0	0			0
Jones,Andruw		3	13	26	28	30	22	27	23	17	21	210
Jones,Chipper	20	26	23	29	32	27	29	31	26	18	18	279
Jones,Greg							1	0		1
Jones,Jacque				9	11	10	25	14	13	13	95
Jones,Todd	21	5	13	7	10	10	5	6	1	6	15	99
Jordan,Brian	31	27	1	21	22	14	19	18	7	2	4	166
Jorgensen,Ryan										0	0	0
Journell,Jimmy								0	0		0
Julio,Jorge						1	13	6	8	1	29
Kapler,Gabe			0	8	10	13	7	4	5	1	48
Karnuth,Jason									0	0	0
Karsay,Steve	6		3	0	9	11	11	11		1	0	52
Kata,Matt								8	3	0		11
Kazmir,Scott										1	10	11
Kearns,Austin								16	12	5	10	43
Keisler,Randy					0	0		0		0		0
Kelly,Kenny											0	0
Kendall,Jason		12	22	26	13	24	9	14	20	25	14	179
Kennedy,Adam				2	11	8	17	14	13	17	82
Kennedy,Joe						6	9	0	13	3	31
Kensing,Logan										0	0	0
Kent,Jeff	52	11	22	25	23	37	27	28	20	22	28	295
Kida,Masao				2	0			1	1	0		4
Kielty,Bobby						1	15	12	4	10	42
Kim,Byung-Hyun				2	8	16	20	14	0	6	66
Kim,Sunny					1	3	0	5	4	13
King,Ray			0	4	5	5	5	8	3	30
Kinney,Matt					1		2	3	4		10
Klesko,Ryan	27	20	16	13	18	23	29	30	13	18	15	222
Kline,Steve		1	6	7	9	12	6	5	7	3	56
Knoedler,Justin										0	0	0
Kolb,Danny				2	0	1	2	9	11	0	25
Konerko,Paul		0	1	14	15	17	17	4	20	24	112
Koo,Dae-Sung										1	1

Player	<96	96	97	98	99	00	01	02	03	04	05	Career
Koplove,Mike							0	7	5	6	2	20
Koronka,John											0	0
Koskie,Corey				0	13	17	24	18	21	13	6	112
Kotchman,Casey										2	4	6
Kotsay,Mark			1	13	6	12	16	22	14	21	18	123
Krynzel,Dave										1	0	1
Kubel,Jason										3		3
Kuo,Hong-Chih											0	0
Lackey,John								7	8	10	16	41
LaForest,Pete									0	0		0
Laird,Gerald									1	3	1	5
Laker,Tim	4		0	1	0		1		4	2	0	12
Lamb,Mike					6	8	7	0	12	6		39
Lane,Jason								3	1	5	14	23
Langerhans,Ryan								0	0		12	12
LaRoche,Adam										7	11	18
LaRue,Jason				2	3	9	11	10	15	17		67
Lawrence,Brian							6	8	8	8	4	34
Lawton,Matt	4	7	14	21	8	20	20	9	10	15	13	141
League,Brandon											1	1
LeCroy,Matt					2	3	4	12	4	8		33
Ledee,Ricky				2	9	10	4	4	7	5	7	48
Ledezma,Wil									2	3	0	5
Lee,Carlos					10	14	15	17	20	22	21	119
Lee,Cliff								1	3	6	13	23
Lee,Derek			2	10	1	16	16	22	25	19	33	144
Lee,Travis				13	8	6	15	13	13	0	10	78
Lehr,Justin										2	2	4
Leicester,Jon										3	0	3
Leiter,Al	31	19	7	21	11	17	14	11	9	12	1	153
Lerew,Anthony											0	0
Levine,Al			0	0	3	7	7	10	4	7	4	42
Lidge,Brad								1	8	22	15	46
Lidle,Cory			6		0	4	13	13	5	7	7	55
Lieber,Jon	6	9	9	8	13	12	16	7		10	12	102
Lieberthal,Mike	1	3	15	8	20	14	3	15	16	9	11	115
Liefer,Jeff				1	0	6	3	1	0	0		11
Ligtenberg,K			2	15		8	5	6	6	1	0	43
Lilly,Ted				0	0	3	6	10	15	4		38
Lima,Jose	2	3	1	14	18	2	4	0	5	9	0	58
Linden,Todd									1	0	1	2
Linebrink,Scott						1	1	0	5	10	11	28
Liriano,Francisco											0	0
Liriano,Pedro										1	0	1
Lo Duca,Paul				0	2	2	28	19	19	20	11	101
Loaiza,Esteban	5	2	11	6	8	12	8	4	23	7	12	98
Loe,Kameron										0	8	8
Lofton,Kenny	91	23	21	21	16	17	13	19	18	7	15	261
Logan,Nook										3	5	8
Lohse,Kyle							3	11	11	6	10	41
Long,Terrence				0	18	17	12	11	5	9		72
Looper,Braden				0	5	5	7	11	12	13	6	59
Lopez,Aquilino									10	1	1	12
Lopez,Felipe							5	6	3	9	21	44
Lopez,Javy	19	15	19	25	11	16	13	10	30	19	12	189
Lopez,Jose										3	5	8
Lopez,Luis M	5	1	5	5	3	4	4	1		0	0	28
Lopez,Pedro											1	1
Lopez,Rodrigo						0		15	2	14	8	39
Loretta,Mark	1	2	12	16	14	12	9	10	24	32	15	147
Lowe,Derek			1	7	19	19	11	22	12	6	11	108
Lowell,Mike				0	8	20	20	19	23	22	8	120
Lowry,Noah									1	6	15	22
Ludwick,Ryan								0	6	0		6
Lugo,Julio						9	9	9	14	20	24	85
Luna,Hector										4	5	9
Lyon,Brandon							4	0	5		0	9
Mabry,John	10	13	8	5	3	3	1	8	2	8	3	64
MacDougal,Mike							1	0	9	0	8	18
Machado,Alejandro											0	0
Machado,Andy									0	2		2
Macias,Jose					0	5	12	8	2	3	1	31
Mackowiak,Rob							4	12	6	14	12	48
Maddux,Greg	182	23	26	25	17	24	20	19	11	13	11	371
Madritsch,Bobby										7	0	7
Madson,Ryan									0	9	6	15
Magruder,Chris							0	1	1	1	1	4

Player	<96	96	97	98	99	00	01	02	03	04	05	Career
Mahay,Ron	0	3	2	3	1	2	0	5	8		0	24
Maholm,Paul											4	4
Mahoney,Mike								0			1	1
Maine,John										0	0	0
Majewski,Gary										1	8	9
Mantei,Matt	0	0		5	12	6	1	1	14	0	0	39
Marcum,Shaun											1	1
Maroth,Mike								6	4	11	8	29
Marquis,Jason						1	8	3	1	14	12	39
Marrero,Eli			1	6	5	5	7	14	3	12	1	54
Marte,Andy											0	0
Marte,Damaso					0		1	9	15	9	4	38
Martin,Tom			7		0	0	2	0	0	5	2	16
Martinez,Pedro	38	14	26	21	27	29	12	21	20	16	19	243
Martinez,Ramon				0	5	7	9	9	7	6	2	45
Martinez,Tino	47	21	27	21	19	12	21	15	11	16	6	216
Martinez,Victor								1	3	20	22	46
Mateo,Henry						0	0	2	0	0		2
Mateo,Julio								1	7	3	7	18
Matheny,Mike	3	4	8	4	3	14	8	9	13	11	11	94
Mathis,Jeff											0	0
Matos,Luis						2	3	0	14	3	12	34
Matranga,Dave									0	0		0
Matsui,Hideki									19	28	24	71
Matsui,Kazuo										13	5	18
Matthews,Mike					0	7	2	3	0	0		12
Matthews Jr.,G						1	1	10	10	9	11	53
Mauer,Joe										6	22	28
May,Darrell	0	0	2					6	17	3	0	28
Mays,Joe					10	6	22	2	2		2	44
McAnulty,Paul											0	0
McBride,Macay											0	0
McCann,Brian											6	6
McCarthy,Bran											5	5
McCarty,Dave	5	2		1		7	2	0	2	2	1	22
McClain,Scott			0							0	0	0
McClung,Seth									2		1	3
McCracken,Q	0	7	8	12	2	0	0	14	1	2	2	48
McDonald,John					0	0	0	5	2	1	4	12
McDougall,Mar										0		0
McEwing,Joe				0	11	2	8	2	5	4	1	33
McGowan,Dustin											0	0
McLouth,Nate											1	1
McPherson,D										1	6	7
Meadows,Brian			4	4	7	0	3	3	5	3		29
Meche,Gil				6	6				8	5	5	30
Mecir,Jim	1	2	0	9	2	12	6	6	1	5	3	47
Medders,Brandon											5	5
Melhuse,Adam						0	0		4	5	2	11
Mench,Kevin								10	4	13	12	39
Mendoza,Ramiro		1	7	12	8	5	10	8	0	0		54
Menechino,Frank					0	6	18	3	2	9	2	40
Mercker,Kent	42	1	9	5	6	1		1	6	7	5	83
Meredith,Cla											0	0
Merloni,Lou				4	2	3	2	6	5	5	0	27
Mesa,Jose	38	12	11	5	5	3	14	13	0	12	5	118
Messenger,Randy											1	1
Miceli,Danny	7	0	5	8	4	5	3	0	6	7	1	46
Michaels,Jason							0	3	5	10	12	30
Mientkiewicz,D				0	3	0	18	17	20	6	4	68
Miles,Aaron									1	12	8	21
Millar,Kevin				0	12	10	20	14	16	17	11	100
Miller,Corky							2	5	1	0		8
Miller,Damian			2	6	10	11	10	10	10	14	8	81
Miller,Justin									3		2	5
Miller,Matt									1	5	4	10
Miller,Trever		0		4	2	0			4	4	2	16
Miller,Wade					0	4	17	13	9	7	4	54
Millwood,Kevin			3	10	22	10	5	19	11	5	14	99
Milton,Eric				6	12	11	15	9	2	9	0	64
Mirabelli,Doug	1	0	1	3	6	7	4	2	7	4		35
Mitre,Sergio									0	0	2	2
Moehler,Brian		0	9	17	10	10	1	2	0		5	54
Moeller,Chad						2	0	6	6	5	3	22
Mohr,Dustan							1	11	6	9	3	30
Molina,Bengie					0	3	13	7	10	16	11	75
Molina,Jose			0				1	2	2	6	7	18
Molina,Yadier										5	14	19

WIN SHARES BY YEAR

Player	<96	96	97	98	99	00	01	02	03	04	05	Career
Mondesi,Raul	40	25	24	20	21	11	15	11	11	3	1	182
Monroe,Craig							1	0	10	11	13	35
Mora,Melvin					0	12	11	16	16	24	20	99
Mordecai,Mike	5	1	0	1	4	3	6	3	1	2	0	26
Moreno,Orber				0						0	3	3
Morneau,Justin									1	9	7	17
Morris,Matt			16	10		6	17	14	10	7	9	89
Morse,Mike											5	5
Mosquera,Julio		0	0									0
Mota,Guillermo					5	1	2	2	14	12	3	39
Moyer,Jamie	52	11	14	18	18	5	15	16	18	5	12	184
Mueller,Bill		9	14	18	12	10	8	12	23	12	19	137
Mulder,Mark						5	18	19	17	15	13	87
Mulholland,T	51	9	8	12	11	7	3	3	3	4	3	114
Munson,Eric						0	0	0	7	9	0	16
Munter,Scott											4	4
Murphy,Donald										0	0	0
Murton,Matt											4	4
Mussina,Mike	79	13	19	15	17	18	20	15	19	9	10	234
Myers,Brett								3	9	4	14	30
Myers,Greg	21	6	3	4	6	1	6	4	8	0	0	59
Myers,Mike	0	3	1	6	2	7	4	3	1	3	4	34
Myrow,Brian											1	1
Nady,Xavier					0				7	1	8	16
Nageotte,Clint										0	0	0
Nakamura,Nor											0	0
Nathan,Joe				5	2			1	11	19	17	55
Navarro,Dioner										0	4	4
Neal,Blaine							0	3	0	2	0	5
Nelson,Jeff	22	6	8	4	2	9	8	3	6	2	2	72
Nevin,Phil	2	5	6	2	19	22	31	12	9	21	7	136
Newhan,David						1	0	0		13	2	16
Niekro,Lance											6	6
Nieves,Wil								1			0	1
Nippert,Dustin											1	1
Nitkowski,C.J.	0	0		4	6	3	2	1	0	1	0	17
Nivar,Ramon									1	0	0	1
Nix,Laynce									4	7	4	15
Nixon,Trot		0		0	10	14	20	16	19	4	15	98
Nomo,Hideo	17	16	9	3	10	10	11	14	17	0	0	107
Novoa,Roberto										1	3	4
Nunez,Abraham			1	1	4	1	6	5	4	2	12	36
Nunez,Franklin										0	0	0
Nunez,Leo											0	0
Obermueller,Wes								0	2	4	1	7
Offerman,Jose	47	18	9	29	0	9	14	4		3	2	135
Ohka,Tomo					0	6	2	14	12	5	10	49
Ohman,Will						0	0				4	4
Ojeda,Miguel									4	6	1	11
Olerud,John	102	10	27	34	26	22	21	27	15	10	7	301
Olivo,Miguel								1	8	7	7	23
Olmedo,Ray									2	0	1	3
Olsen,Scott											1	1
Olson,Tim										1	0	1
Ordonez,Magglio			3	13	20	22	25	25	23	8	10	149
Orr,Pete											3	3
Ortiz,David			2	9	0	8	7	11	15	24	30	106
Ortiz,Ramon					1	6	12	14	5	7	3	48
Ortiz,Russ				3	12	7	15	13	16	12	0	78
Ortmeier,Dan											0	0
Orvella,Chad											3	3
Osik,Keith		4	3	1	3	5	1	1	4	0	0	22
Osoria,Franq											1	1
Osuna,Antonio	2	10	7	8	0	4	0	8	4	3	0	46
Oswalt,Roy							15	20	10	18	21	84
Otsuka,Akinori										11	4	15
Overbay,Lyle							0	0	6	17	17	40
Oxspring,Chris											0	0
Ozuna,Pablo					1			1	1		4	7
Padilla,Juan										1	6	7
Padilla,Vicente					0	6	3	14	13	5	6	47
Palmeiro,Orl	1	2	1	5	6	7	4	8	6	3	6	49
Palmeiro,Rafael	183	30	18	24	31	23	25	18	19	12	11	394
Papelbon,Jonat											4	4
Park,Chan Ho	0	7	13	13	6	18	16	5	0	4	5	87
Parrish,John						0	0		2	6	2	10
Patterson,Corey						0	3	8	13	17	4	45
Patterson,John								3	0	2	14	19

WIN SHARES BY YEAR

Player	<96	96	97	98	99	00	01	02	03	04	05	Career
Paul,Josh					0	3	4	2	1	2	1	13
Paulino,Ronny											0	0
Pavano,Carl				6	3	8	0	3	9	19	3	51
Payton,Jay				0	0	14	3	15	15	15	12	74
Peavy,Jake								3	7	15	16	41
Pena,Brayan											0	0
Pena,Carlos							3	11	9	11	7	41
Pena,Wily Mo								0	1	14	6	21
Penn,Hayden											0	0
Penny,Brad						5	12	4	10	10	9	50
Peralta,Jhonny									4	0	25	29
Peralta,Joel											2	2
Percival,Troy	12	16	10	12	11	8	14	13	8	9	2	115
Perez,Antonio									3	0	10	13
Perez,Eddie	1	5	2	10	8	0	0	2	7	2	2	39
Perez,Eduardo	5	1	0	4	2	1		3	7	1	7	31
Perez,Miguel											0	0
Perez,Neifi		0	9	12	14	15	11	6	8	7	12	94
Perez,Odalis					1	1	3	17	6	13	4	45
Perez,Oliver								4	1	16	2	23
Perez,Timo						2	4	14	5	6	1	32
Perez,Tomas	1	3	2	0		1	5	4	5	4	1	26
Perisho,Matt			0	0	1	0	1	0		3	2	7
Petagine,Rob	3	1	0	2						1		7
Pettitte,Andy	11	18	20	13	10	14	13	11	15	5	21	151
Phelps,Josh						0	0	10	10	5	4	29
Phelps,Tommy									3	1	1	5
Phillips,Andy										0	0	0
Phillips,Brand							1	4	0	0		5
Phillips,Jason							0	1	13	5	7	26
Phillips,Paul										0	2	2
Piazza,Mike	80	33	39	33	21	28	21	19	11	12	12	309
Pickering,Cal			0	0			1			5	0	6
Piedra,Jorge										2	3	5
Pierre,Juan						3	17	15	20	22	14	91
Pierzynski,A.J.				1	0	3	15	18	22	12	11	82
Pineiro,Joel						0	7	14	13	5	3	42
Podsednik,Scott							0	1	22	13	12	48
Polanco,Placido				2	3	11	14	16	18	17	22	103
Politte,Cliff				0	0	5	3	7	3	4	12	34
Ponson,Sidney				5	10	11	4	10	15	8	0	63
Posada,Jorge	0	0	6	15	10	29	23	22	28	21	19	173
Powell,Jay	1	4	9	7	6	1	9	4	0	2	1	44
Pratt,Todd		9	5	2	5	5	2	7	5	4	6	50
Pride,Curtis	2	9	2	2		0	1		0	0	0	16
Prieto,Chris											0	0
Prinz,Bret							7	0	0	1	0	8
Prior,Mark								8	22	7	12	49
Proctor,Scott										1	0	1
Puffer,Brandon								3	0	0	0	3
Pujols,Albert							29	32	41	37	34	173
Pulsipher,Bill	6			3	1	0	1					11
Punto,Nick							0	0	1	4	6	11
Putz,J.J.									0	3	5	8
Qualls,Chad										4	7	11
Quantrill,Paul	22	4	12	11	5	6	11	8	11	6	2	98
Quinlan,Robb									0	8	2	10
Quintanilla,Om										1		1
Quintero,Humb									0	1	1	2
Quiroz,Guill										0	0	0
Radke,Brad	7	14	16	14	17	15	17	6	12	18	11	147
Rakers,Aaron										0	1	1
Ramirez,Aramis					2	0	3	27	6	19	18	94
Ramirez,Eliz										1	0	1
Ramirez,Erasmo									4	3	1	8
Ramirez,Hanley											0	0
Ramirez,Horacio									9	5	8	22
Ramirez,Julio							0	1	1	0		2
Ramirez,Manny	36	23	21	25	35	27	25	29	28	25	33	307
Randa,Joe	1	9	16	9	17	18	11	10	14	13	15	133
Rasner,Darrell											0	0
Rauch,Jon									0	4	2	6
Ray,Chris											4	4
Reames,Britt						3	2	1	0		0	6
Redding,Tim							2	1	10	1	0	14
Redman,Mark					0	10	3	10	11	10	4	48
Redman,Tike							1	1	9	10	5	26
Redmond,Mike				4	12	5	6	13	1	6	7	54

Player	<96	96	97	98	99	00	01	02	03	04	05	Career
Reed,Jeremy										3	9	12
Reed,Keith											0	0
Reed,Steve	27	8	7	8	4	4	5	7	7	6	0	83
Reese,Kevin											0	0
Reese,Pokey			0	3	18	11	7	15	2	4		60
Regilio,Nick										0	1	1
Reitsma,Chris							3	7	8	7	9	34
Relaford,Desi		0	1	5	4	12	13	9	11	5	2	62
Remlinger,Mike	2	0	9	5	12	12	9	11	6	4	1	71
Renteria,Edgar		15	15	11	13	15	13	26	25	16	15	164
Repko,Jason											5	5
Resop,Chris											0	0
Restovich,Mike							0	2	1	1		4
Reyes,Al	4	0	1	4	5	1	2	2	1	2	9	31
Reyes,Anthony											1	1
Reyes,Dennys			2	2	5	2	1	4	0	4	1	21
Reyes,Jose									12	4	16	32
Rhodes,Arthur	11	5	10	7	2	6	12	11	4	2	6	76
Riedling,John						2	4	5	4	2	0	17
Riley,Matt					0			1	2	0		3
Rincon,Juan							0	0	7	12	10	29
Rincon,Ricardo			7	9	3	3	6	6	6	4	2	46
Ring,Royce											0	0
Rios,Alexis										7	9	16
Riske,David					0		3	2	10	7	5	27
Rivas,Luis						1	8	6	6	9	4	34
Rivera,Juan							0	1	4	12	9	26
Rivera,Mariano	2	18	15	14	17	16	19	9	18	18	19	165
Rivera,Rene										0	2	2
Roberts,Brian							3	2	13	16	28	62
Roberts,Dave				2	0	0	19	8	12	14		55
Robertson,Nate							0	1	8	7		16
Robles,Oscar											9	9
Rodney,Fernando							0	1		6		7
Rodriguez,Alex	2	34	22	30	23	37	37	35	32	29	34	315
Rodriguez,Felix	1		2	1	4	9	12	5	8	7	1	50
Rodriguez,Fran							1	9	17	14		41
Rodriguez,Ivan	65	23	26	27	28	19	18	11	23	22	10	272
Rodriguez,John											5	5
Rodriguez,Luis											6	6
Rodriguez,Ric							1	1	3	2		7
Rodriguez,Wandy											2	2
Rogers,Eddie							0			0		0
Rogers,Kenny	69	11	2	19	12	15	2	15	11	14	15	185
Rolen,Scott			2	29	30	15	18	29	26	25	35	5	214
Rollins,Jimmy						1	20	17	19	24	21	102
Romano,Jason							2	0	0	1		3
Romero,J.C.					1	0	1	14	3	8	5	32
Rose,Mike							0	0	0			0
Ross,Cody								1		0		1
Ross,Dave							1	4	2	3		10
Rowand,Aaron							5	7	6	20	18	56
Rueter,Kirk	14	5	12	8	5	9	7	12	6	7	0	85
Rupe,Josh											1	1
Rusch,Glendon			5	5	0	11	6	7	0	10	6	50
Ryan,B.J.				2	2	3	3	6	11	14		41
Ryan,Mike							0	4	0	1		5
Saarloos,Kirk							1	2	2	9		14
Sabathia,C.C.							12	13	13	11	12	61
Sadler,Ray											0	0
Saenz,Olmedo	0				7	8	1	5		4	11	36
Sanchez,Alex							0	11	9	5	4	29
Sanchez,Duaner							0	0	6	7		13
Sanchez,Freddy							0	0	0	12		12
Sanchez,Rey	29	5	7	8	12	9	13	9	6	5	1	104
Sanders,Dave							0	0	0			0
Sanders,Reggie	71	7	13	14	19	6	14	14	18	14	11	201
Sandoval,Danny											0	0
Santana,Ervin											6	6
Santana,Johan						2	2	10	16	26	23	79
Santana,Julio									5		3	8
Santiago,Benito	107	19	9	1	7	6	10	15	13	3	0	190
Santiago,Jose			0	0	4	7	5	0	2			18
Santiago,Ramon								4	5	0	0	9
Santos,Victor						5	0	0	5	3		13
Sardinha,Dane										0		0
Sauerbeck,Scott					9	6	3	9	3		2	32
Saunders,Joe											0	0

Player	<96	96	97	98	99	00	01	02	03	04	05	Career
Schilling,Curt	50	14	22	22	15	16	24	24	15	21	4	227
Schmidt,Jason	0	2	8	11	13	1	9	10	22	19	9	104
Schmoll,Steve											2	2
Schneider,Brian				1	2	7	13	17	16			56
Schoeneweis,S				1	6	9	5	3	4	6		34
Schumaker,Jared										0		0
Scott,Luke										0		0
Scutaro,Marco							0	2	11	11		24
Seabol,Scott							0			2		2
Seanez,Rudy	3		5	7	2	3	1	0	4	7		32
Seay,Bobby						0	1	2	0			3
Sele,Aaron	25	6	7	14	13	12	14	5	2	5	2	105
Self,Todd										1	1	4
Seo,Jae							0	9	3	9		21
Sexson,Richie			0	5	10	16	19	21	26	3	24	124
Shabala,Adam										0		0
Shackelford,Br										3		3
Shealy,Ryan										2		2
Sheets,Ben						6	8	9	21	11		55
Sheffield,Gary	105	34	22	30	24	31	30	26	35	30	31	398
Shelton,Chris									0	13		13
Sherrill,George									1	2		3
Shields,Scot						2	6	12	11	13		44
Shoppach,Kelly										0		0
Short,Rick										2		2
Shouse,Brian	0		0			0	6	6	2			14
Sierra,Ruben	185	6	1	1		1	6	7	5	8	2	222
Silva,Carlos							7	5	14	14		40
Simpson,Allan								2	0			2
Singleton,Chris					0	11	12	9	6		2	40
Sisco,Andrew										5		5
Sizemore,Grady										5	24	29
Sledge,Terrmel									13	1		14
Small,Aaron	1	0	7	2			0		0	7		17
Smith,Jason						0	0	0	2	1		3
Smith,Travis			0			0	0	0	0			0
Smoltz,John	99	27	21	16	18		8	17	16	16	19	257
Snell,Ian										0	1	1
Snelling,Chris							0			1		1
Snow,J.T.	27	7	28	13	18	16	6	11	14	19	10	169
Snyder,Chris									2	4		6
Snyder,Kyle								4		0		4
Sorensen,Zach								0		0		0
Soriano,Alfonso					0	0	16	28	27	16	16	103
Soriano,Rafael							1	7	0	1		9
Sosa,Jorge							2	5	3	14		24
Sosa,Sammy	81	18	14	35	26	30	42	27	22	12	4	311
Soto,Geovany										0	0	0
Speier,Justin				0	1	7	5	7	8	7	7	42
Speier,Ryan										2		2
Spiezio,Scott		2	10	10	6	9	17	12	4	0		76
Spilborghs,Ryan										0		0
Spivey,Junior						6	23	10	4	5		48
Springer,Russ	6	3	3	3	5	3	0		0	1	3	27
Spurling,Chris								4	5			9
Stairs,Matt	2	4	15	20	20	10	11	7	13	11	14	127
Standridge,Jas							1	0	0	0	2	3
Stanton,Mike	32	9	9	4	4	6	10	10	3	7	2	96
Stauffer,Tim										0		0
Stemle,Steve										0		0
Stern,Adam										0		0
Stewart,Shannon	0	0	7	18	17	17	18	17	19	13	11	137
Stinnett,Kelly	8	0	1	10	6	5	5	4	4	2	1	46
Stone,Ricky						1	5	6	0	0		12
Street,Huston											16	16
Strickland,Scott					0	8	10	5	2	0		25
Strong,Jamal								0		1		1
Sturtze,Tanyon	0	0	0		1	6	11	6	2	3	4	33
Stynes,Chris	1	1	10	5	2	13	8	5	10	1		56
Sullivan,Cory											10	10
Suppan,Jeff	1	0	4	2	12	12	12	9	14	9	13	88
Surhoff,B.J.	114	17	19	13	17	14	12	3	9	9		231
Suzuki,Ichiro							36	26	23	27	22	134
Sweeney,Mark	1	7	5	3	0	0	1	0	2	6	9	34
Sweeney,Mike	0	4	5	8	16	26	18	18	15	14	16	140
Swisher,Nick										1	12	13
Switzer,Jon									0	0		0
Tadano,Kazuhito										2	0	2

Player	<96	96	97	98	99	00	01	02	03	04	05	Career
Taguchi,So								1	3	6	12	22
Takatsu,Shingo									14	2	0	16
Tallet,Brian						2	0				0	2
Taschner,Jack											3	3
Tavarez,Julian	10	4	6	5	1	10	6	2	10	9	6	69
Taveras,Willy										0	13	13
Taylor,Reggie							0	0	5	1	0	6
Teahen,Mark											9	9
Teixeira,Mark									13	24	33	70
Tejada,Miguel			1	7	20	23	25	32	25	28	26	187
Tejeda,Robinson											5	5
Tejera,Michael				0			7	3	0		0	10
Telemaco,Amaury		1	0	8	2	0	2		2	2	0	17
Terrero,Luis									0	3	3	6
Thames,Marcus								0	0	6	1	7
Theriot,Ryan											0	0
Thomas,Charles										9	1	10
Thomas,Frank	165	28	39	25	16	34	1	16	23	12	3	362
Thome,Jim	42	28	26	19	26	20	31	33	30	20	4	279
Thompson,Brad											5	5
Thompson,Derek											1	1
Thompson,Justin		2	21	14	7						0	44
Thomson,John			10	9	0		7	7	11	13	4	61
Thornton,Matt										2	1	3
Tiffee,Terry										1	0	1
Timlin,Mike	24	10	9	12	9	6	5	8	8	7	14	112
Tomko,Brett			10	9	6	5	1	6	6	10	8	61
Torcato,Tony								0	0	1	0	1
Torrealba,Yorv							1	4	7	4	4	20
Torres,Andres							0	1	0	0	1	2
Torres,Salomon	3	3	0					3	5	11	10	35
Towers,Josh							6	0	5	6	13	30
Trachsel,Steve	15	15	9	13	6	11	8	10	13	10	1	111
Tracy,Chad										11	19	30
Treanor,Matt										1	2	3
Tsao,Chin-hui									1	1	0	2
Tucker,Michael	3	9	15	11	10	7	10	8	9	14	7	103
Tucker,T.J.					0			5	4	5	0	14
Turnbow,Derrick						2			2	1	17	22
Tyner,Jason						1	6	1	2		2	12
Urbina,Ugueth	0	8	10	17	14	2	11	11	15	7	9	104
Uribe,Juan							7	10	9	18	17	61
Utley,Chase									5	8	25	38
Valdez,Ismael	18	16	15	9	10	2	10	11	3	5	1	100
Valdez,Wilson										1	2	3
Valent,Eric							1	0	0	6	0	7
Valentin,Javier			0	2	5			0	2	4	11	24
Valentin,Jose	22	20	13	15	8	24	15	16	18	14	2	167
Valentine,Joe									0	1	0	1
Valverde,Jose									11	3	13	27
Van Benschoten,J										0		0
Van Buren,Jermaine											0	0
Vargas,Claudio									6	3	6	15
Vargas,Jason											4	4
Varitek,Jason			0	5	12	7	8	12	17	18	18	97
Vasquez,Jorge										0	1	1
Vazquez,Javier				0	8	14	21	13	21	9	12	98
Vazquez,Ramon							0	14	10	1	1	26
Vento,Mike											0	0
Verlander,Just											0	0
Victorino,Shane									0		1	1
Vidro,Jose			3	2	11	25	18	29	19	11	10	128
Villarreal,Osc									11	0	1	12
Villone,Ron	2	5	4	1	8	5	3	2	5	6	5	46
Vizcaino,Jose	45	14	17	8	4	3	4	11	4	8	4	122
Vizcaino,Luis				0	0	2	8	1	6	6		23
Vizquel,Omar	68	16	14	18	22	16	12	21	5	18	20	230
Vogelsong,Ryan						1	0		0	0	3	4
Volquez,Edison										0	0	0
Waechter,Doug									3	1	3	7
Wagner,Billy	0	8	11	11	20	1	13	16	19	10	18	127
Wagner,Ryan									3	2	1	6
Wainwright,Adam											0	0
Wakefield,Tim	29	10	12	11	8	5	11	15	12	8	15	136
Walker,Jamie			2	0				4	7	6	4	23
Walker,Kevin						5	1	0	0	0	0	6
Walker,Larry	121	10	32	17	24	11	25	25	18	12	12	307
Walker,Pete	1	0					0	1	9	3	7	21

Player	<96	96	97	98	99	00	01	02	03	04	05	Career
Walker,Todd		1	2	19	9	5	12	22	15	13	13	111
Walker,Tyler									0	4	7	11
Wang,Chien-Ming											7	7
Ward,Daryle				0	3	3	5	10	0	7	7	35
Wasdin,John	1	4	7	4	7	3	3		0	1	6	36
Washburn,Jarrod				4	3	7	15	18	10	8	14	79
Watson,Brandon										0		0
Watson,Matt										1		1
Weathers,David	5	3	0	4	6	7	10	7	8	5	8	63
Weaver,Jeff					7	12	13	14	2	11	13	72
Webb,Brandon									17	11	17	45
Webb,John										0	0	0
Weber,Ben						2	7	11	8	0	0	28
Weeks,Rickie											9	9
Wellemeyer,Todd									0	1	0	1
Wells,David	77	10	12	18	13	18	5	15	14	10	11	203
Wells,Kip					3	2	6	13	16	6	3	49
Wells,Vernon					1	0	3	18	26	13	20	81
Werth,Jayson								1	1	11	9	22
Westbrook,Jake						0	2	1	6	15	8	32
Wheeler,Dan					1	1	0		3	3	10	18
White,Gabe	0		3	8	3	15	2	7	4	1	1	44
White,Matt									0	0		0
White,Rick	9			5	7	9	5	5	1	3	5	49
White,Rondell	21	10	17	16	15	14	12	6	15	11	12	149
Whiteside,Eli										0		0
Whiteside,Matt	17	1	3	0	0	2	0					23
Wickman,Bob	25	7	11	11	11	12	14	4		3	10	108
Widger,Chris	0	0	5	10	8	4		2	2		2	33
Wigginton,Ty								3	15	10	4	32
Wilkerson,Brad							1	17	18	19	19	74
Williams,Bernie	73	26	24	27	33	26	24	30	13	16	11	303
Williams,Dave							7	1		2	6	16
Williams,Gerald	8	5	9	12	13	14	2	0	0	2	1	66
Williams,Glenn											2	2
Williams,Jerome									9	7	6	22
Williams,Randy										0	1	1
Williams,Todd	1			0		1		1		3	7	13
Williams,Woody	11	3	11	12	10	12	11	10	13	8	3	104
Williamson,Sc					17	11	0	10	7	4	0	49
Willingham,Josh										0	0	0
Willis,Dontrelle									14	9	22	45
Wilson,C.J.											0	0
Wilson,Craig							8	11	10	16	5	50
Wilson,Dan	22	15	21	7	9	4	14	13	7	7	0	119
Wilson,Enrique			1	3	3	5	3	2	2	5	0	24
Wilson,Jack							5	12	11	22	14	64
Wilson,Josh										0	0	0
Wilson,Paul		1				4	6	7	5	7	0	30
Wilson,Preston				1	13	20	10	10	20	2	14	90
Wilson,Vance					0	0	1	5	7	5	3	21
Winn,Randy				5	4	2	10	23	21	17	22	104
Wise,Matt						2	2	1		3	7	15
Witasick,Jay		0	0	0	5	3	6	2	3		6	31
Wolf,Randy					4	13	11	15	12	6	4	65
Womack,Tony	1	2	18	17	14	16	10	15	3	18	3	117
Wood,Kerry				14		7	13	12	18	9	4	77
Wood,Mike									0	2	5	7
Woods,Jake											1	1
Woodward,Chris					0	2	1	10	9	4	4	30
Woodyard,Mark										1		1
Wooten,Shawn						0	6	3	2	0	0	11
Worrell,Tim	4	10	3	3	4	7	5	9	13	10	4	72
Wright,David										9	26	35
Wright,Jamey		5	3	8	7	9	7	2	2	5	4	52
Wright,Jaret			6	11	3	3	0	0	1	14	1	39
Wuertz,Mike										2	6	8
Wunsch,Kelly						8	0	3	4	0	2	17
Yabu,Keiichi											3	3
Yan,Esteban		0	0	7	2	4	8	7	1	7	2	38
Youkilis,Kevin										8	3	11
Young,Chris										2	10	12
Young,Dmitri		0	5	16	10	14	13	5	19	8	9	99
Young,Eric	32	17	17	17	14	18	16	9	9	9	4	162
Young,Michael					0	7	11	21	25	29		93
Young,Walter											1	1
Zambrano,Carlos							0	5	18	20	18	61
Zambrano,Victor							6	4	10	8	7	35

Player	WIN SHARES BY YEAR											Career
	<96	96	97	98	99	00	01	02	03	04	05	
Zaun,Gregg	3	3	9	3	3	9	4	2	2	11	14	63
Zimmerman,Ryan											2	2
Zito,Barry						9	15	25	18	12	13	92

Hitter Projections

Bill James

Hello, and welcome to the second annual Baseball Info Solutions Player Projections. We would tell you how we did last year, except that frankly we don't have any idea. There are probably five or ten players who did exactly what we said they should do, just in the nature of luck, and at least an equal number who didn't.

Let's compare the batting, on base and slugging percentages projected and delivered for the Philadelphia Phillies:

		Avg.	OBA	Slg	OPS
C Lieberthal	Projected	.279	.334	.448	.782
	Delivered	.263	.336	.481	.754
1B Thome	Projected	.272	.399	.566	.965
	Delivered	.207	.360	.352	.712
1B R Howard	Projected	.267	.335	.561	.896
	Delivered	.288	.356	.567	.923
2B C Utley	Projected	.275	.333	.478	.811
	Delivered	.291	.376	.540	.916
3B D Bell	Projected	.257	.325	.402	.727
	Delivered	.248	.310	.361	.671
SS Rollins	Projected	.276	.335	.429	.764
	Delivered	.290	.338	.431	.769
LF Burrell	Projected	.249	.354	.470	.824
	Delivered	.281	.389	.504	.893
CF Lofton	Projected	.273	.348	.390	.738
	Delivered	.335	.392	.420	.812
RF Abreu	Projected	.305	.420	.527	.947
	Delivered	.286	.405	.474	.879

We'll have to let that stand for self-evaluation for now. We are certainly obligated at some point to do a serious study of how well our system works and where and when it fails, but our first season's worth of projections just ended a few days ago. There hasn't been time yet to do a serious study.

We're not claiming to be able to foresee the future. Next year some guys who are 34 years old will drive their batting averages off a cliff, and others will carry on as if they were 24. We have no way of knowing which is which. It's a simple process: what a player has done in the past, we predict he will do in the future, modified slightly by age, playing time and park effects, as much as we can foresee those things for 2006 in October, 2005.

2006 Hitter Projections

Hitter	Team	Age	Inj	G	AB	H	2B	3B	HR	R	RBI	RC	BB	SO	SB	CS	SB%	Avg	OBP	Slg	OPS
Abernathy,Brent	Min	28	low	47	103	27	5	0	1	12	10	11	8	10	3	1	.75	.262	.321	.340	.661
Abreu,Bobby	Phi	32	high	161	598	176	43	2	25	109	99	124	119	134	29	11	.73	.294	.415	.498	.913
Adams,Russ	Tor	25	low	139	511	135	27	5	10	74	65	68	53	56	11	4	.73	.264	.336	.395	.731
Aguila,Chris	Fla	27	low	72	153	44	9	1	4	22	17	23	12	31	4	2	.67	.288	.339	.438	.777
Alfonzo,Edgardo	SF	32	high	130	445	126	24	1	10	58	60	64	47	43	3	1	.75	.283	.357	.409	.766
Alomar Jr.,Sandy	Tex	40	high	76	208	53	10	0	3	20	23	21	9	21	0	0	.00	.255	.289	.346	.635
Alou,Moises	SF	39	high	148	558	164	29	1	26	82	92	100	65	67	4	2	.67	.294	.371	.489	.860
Ambres,Chip	KC	26	low	133	376	97	28	4	10	57	45	58	54	88	17	7	.71	.258	.353	.434	.786
Anderson,Garret	LAA	34	high	139	524	151	34	1	19	63	86	78	25	79	2	1	.67	.288	.321	.466	.786
Anderson,Marlon	NYM	32	med	90	183	47	10	1	4	22	20	22	13	29	4	2	.67	.257	.313	.388	.701
Ardoin,Danny	Col	31	med	77	227	55	12	1	6	29	26	27	22	62	2	1	.67	.242	.320	.383	.703
Atkins,Garrett	Col	26	med	142	537	154	33	1	15	72	83	81	47	68	1	0	.00	.287	.346	.436	.782
Aurilia,Rich	Cin	34	high	119	371	99	20	1	11	49	48	50	31	63	1	1	.50	.267	.327	.415	.742
Ausmus,Brad	Hou	37	high	129	390	95	16	1	4	40	38	40	41	56	4	2	.67	.244	.322	.321	.642
Aybar,Willy	LAD	23	low	98	237	63	15	1	2	22	25	28	23	34	3	3	.50	.266	.333	.363	.696
Bagwell,Jeff	Hou	38	high	110	367	99	20	1	19	66	63	68	65	83	4	2	.67	.270	.388	.485	.873
Bako,Paul	LAD	34	med	61	159	35	8	1	1	14	13	15	19	41	0	0	.00	.220	.307	.302	.609
Barajas,Rod	Tex	30	med	119	385	95	25	0	17	48	59	49	22	61	0	0	.00	.247	.293	.444	.737
Bard,Josh	Cle	28	med	58	152	41	10	0	4	15	21	21	13	20	0	0	.00	.270	.327	.414	.742
Barmes,Clint	Col	27	high	147	577	163	35	2	15	85	70	77	26	62	9	5	.64	.282	.317	.428	.745
Barrett,Michael	ChC	29	med	130	446	118	31	2	16	52	57	63	38	64	1	1	.50	.265	.328	.437	.765
Bartlett,Jason	Min	26	low	141	461	126	23	4	7	71	42	61	47	67	11	6	.65	.273	.343	.386	.729
Bay,Jason	Pit	27	high	156	571	174	38	5	33	102	104	128	86	133	18	5	.78	.305	.400	.562	.962
Bell,David	Phi	33	high	124	402	101	22	1	10	46	49	49	38	55	0	0	.00	.251	.324	.386	.709
Bellhorn,Mark	NYY	31	high	95	269	64	19	1	8	44	34	38	46	93	3	2	.60	.238	.353	.405	.759
Belliard,Ronnie	Cle	31	high	150	581	160	41	2	14	81	71	83	54	86	3	2	.60	.275	.339	.425	.764
Beltran,Carlos	NYM	29	high	156	596	167	33	6	25	103	96	104	70	102	24	6	.80	.280	.359	.482	.840
Beltre,Adrian	Sea	27	high	149	532	146	30	2	25	70	85	83	41	90	4	2	.67	.274	.331	.479	.810
Bennett,Gary	Was	34	med	66	163	37	6	0	2	11	15	14	15	26	0	0	.00	.227	.300	.301	.601
Berkman,Lance	Hou	30	high	152	547	166	41	2	30	101	106	125	109	98	5	4	.56	.303	.424	.550	.975
Berroa,Angel	KC	28	med	155	589	160	27	5	12	78	59	70	24	96	10	5	.67	.272	.313	.396	.708
Betancourt,Yuniesky	Sea	24	low	60	209	57	11	3	3	21	21	24	9	17	7	5	.58	.273	.309	.397	.706
Betemit,Wilson	Atl	25	low	115	334	91	16	4	6	43	35	44	30	73	1	1	.50	.272	.332	.398	.731
Bigbie,Larry	Col	28	high	118	373	98	19	1	9	46	38	48	38	88	6	3	.67	.263	.333	.391	.724
Biggio,Craig	Hou	40	high	158	628	161	39	1	19	92	63	81	52	106	10	4	.71	.256	.331	.412	.743
Blake,Casey	Cle	32	high	145	511	129	30	1	21	72	61	70	47	116	5	4	.56	.252	.324	.438	.762
Blalock,Hank	Tex	25	high	159	631	175	39	1	29	95	102	103	60	129	1	1	.50	.277	.343	.480	.823
Blanco,Andres	KC	22	low	59	133	31	3	2	1	13	10	11	7	18	1	1	.50	.233	.277	.308	.585
Blanco,Henry	ChC	34	med	85	227	48	12	1	6	22	25	22	19	41	0	0	.00	.211	.275	.352	.628
Bloomquist,Willie	Sea	28	med	90	205	53	11	1	1	27	20	22	13	33	11	3	.79	.259	.306	.337	.643
Blum,Geoff	CWS	33	med	88	197	46	11	1	4	21	20	21	18	32	1	1	.50	.234	.304	.360	.665
Bonds,Barry	SF	41	high	120	367	115	22	1	36	92	84	127	148	54	6	2	.75	.313	.515	.673	1.188
Boone,Aaron	Cle	33	med	142	509	129	27	1	18	66	71	65	39	94	11	4	.73	.253	.318	.417	.734
Boone,Bret	Min	37		105	362	89	17	1	14	46	51	47	35	79	5	3	.62	.246	.321	.414	.735
Bradley,Milton	LAD	28	high	126	476	133	30	2	17	72	63	78	59	95	12	7	.63	.279	.362	.458	.820
Branyan,Russell	Mil	30	high	107	334	78	19	1	20	44	53	53	51	138	1	1	.50	.234	.337	.476	.813
Broussard,Ben	Cle	29	med	132	407	107	24	3	17	54	62	61	37	80	2	1	.67	.263	.333	.462	.795
Brown,Emil	KC	31	high	148	536	152	30	3	16	72	80	80	44	99	10	3	.77	.284	.344	.440	.784
Bruntlett,Eric	Hou	28	low	95	206	49	9	1	4	32	20	22	20	36	12	5	.71	.238	.305	.350	.655
Buck,John	KC	25	med	118	389	98	22	1	13	46	56	47	23	87	2	1	.67	.252	.295	.414	.709
Burke,Chris	Hou	26	med	140	436	112	21	6	5	61	32	50	33	66	22	10	.69	.257	.314	.367	.681
Burnitz,Jeromy	ChC	37	high	152	557	139	27	1	28	80	89	81	62	123	4	4	.50	.250	.331	.452	.784
Burrell,Pat	Phi	29	high	149	527	137	30	1	28	72	97	92	87	152	0	0	.00	.260	.368	.480	.848
Burroughs,Sean	SD	25	med	112	363	102	17	2	3	44	33	44	28	43	4	2	.67	.281	.344	.364	.708
Byrd,Marlon	Was	28	med	102	309	87	16	2	7	47	32	43	25	55	7	2	.78	.282	.343	.414	.757
Byrnes,Eric	Bal	30	med	120	379	96	25	4	11	55	43	50	31	72	7	3	.70	.253	.320	.427	.747
Cabrera,Miguel	Fla	23	med	153	585	188	42	3	33	103	120	131	65	117	3	1	.75	.321	.392	.573	.965
Cabrera,Orlando	LAA	31	high	156	602	159	39	2	11	75	68	75	43	56	19	6	.76	.264	.315	.390	.706
Cairo,Miguel	NYM	32	med	112	325	86	16	2	3	40	30	35	19	37	11	5	.69	.265	.317	.354	.671
Cameron,Mike	NYM	33	high	119	444	109	26	2	19	67	64	65	55	128	18	6	.75	.245	.337	.441	.778
Cano,Robinson	NYY	23	low	157	612	182	41	6	17	92	79	92	22	72	1	1	.50	.297	.324	.467	.791
Cantu,Jorge	TB	24	med	150	570	158	42	1	21	71	92	81	22	79	1	0	1.00	.277	.308	.465	.772
Carroll,Jamey	Was	31	med	104	248	65	9	1	1	32	17	26	27	37	3	2	.60	.262	.342	.319	.660
Casey,Sean	Cin	31	high	148	570	174	36	1	15	81	82	94	53	54	2	1	.67	.305	.370	.451	.821
Cash,Kevin	TB	28	med	60	163	37	11	0	5	19	19	18	12	46	0	0	.00	.227	.288	.387	.675
Castilla,Vinny	Was	38	high	147	527	131	23	1	15	54	70	60	38	96	2	2	.50	.249	.305	.381	.687
Castillo,Alberto	Oak	36		52	120	28	5	0	1	13	13	11	12	20	1	0	1.00	.233	.303	.300	.603
Castillo,Jose	Pit	25	high	129	467	129	23	3	12	63	63	62	31	76	5	3	.62	.276	.321	.413	.735
Castillo,Luis	Fla	30	med	147	560	170	17	4	4	91	38	80	73	59	20	10	.67	.304	.385	.370	.755
Castro,Bernie	Bal	26		89	218	62	8	1	0	30	14	26	18	23	19	5	.79	.284	.339	.330	.669
Castro,Juan	Min	34	high	125	386	93	21	1	7	38	38	38	19	64	0	0	.00	.241	.277	.355	.631
Castro,Ramon	NYM	30	med	80	179	42	11	0	7	22	26	24	22	44	1	0	1.00	.235	.318	.413	.732
Catalanotto,Frank	Tor	32	med	128	442	130	30	3	9	64	54	67	37	58	2	2	.50	.294	.358	.437	.795
Cedeno,Ronny	ChC	23	low	116	335	104	18	1	8	50	38	54	23	43	16	4	.80	.310	.358	.442	.800
Chavez,Endy	Phi	28	low	77	166	44	7	1	1	19	11	18	11	15	7	3	.70	.265	.311	.337	.648
Chavez,Eric	Oak	28	high	153	592	162	37	2	30	94	103	104	72	116	6	2	.75	.274	.354	.495	.849
Choi,Hee Seop	LAD	27	med	130	357	92	20	1	17	53	52	58	53	88	1	1	.50	.258	.361	.462	.824
Choo,Shin-soo	Sea	23	low	87	292	76	14	2	7	45	33	40	40	65	15	7	.68	.260	.349	.394	.743
Church,Ryan	Was	27	med	110	339	90	14	2	9	40	42	43	27	77	2	1	.67	.265	.323	.398	.722
Cintron,Alex	Ari	27	med	105	298	85	19	3	5	36	33	40	16	26	1	1	.50	.285	.324	.419	.743

2006 Hitter Projections

Hitter	Team	Age	Inj	G	AB	H	2B	3B	HR	R	RBI	RC	BB	SO	SB	CS	SB%	Avg	OBP	Slg	OPS
Cirillo,Jeff	Mil	36	med	71	160	43	9	0	3	21	20	20	15	22	2	1	.67	.269	.346	.381	.728
Clark,Brady	Mil	33	high	136	452	130	24	1	9	60	49	63	42	48	8	6	.57	.288	.361	.405	.766
Clark,Tony	Ari	34	high	136	381	97	22	1	23	49	71	62	42	107	0	0	.00	.255	.330	.499	.829
Clayton,Royce	Ari	36	high	144	519	131	25	2	6	65	47	55	41	109	9	5	.64	.252	.310	.343	.653
Closser,JD	Col	26	med	92	297	80	20	2	10	39	40	46	33	55	1	0	1.00	.269	.344	.451	.796
Colbrunn,Greg	Ari	36		92	176	48	10	1	6	21	24	25	14	31	0	0	.00	.273	.330	.443	.773
Conine,Jeff	Fla	40	high	124	312	86	17	1	7	36	42	42	29	50	2	1	.67	.276	.343	.404	.747
Cora,Alex	Bos	30	med	115	320	77	12	3	5	31	28	32	23	41	5	3	.62	.241	.308	.344	.651
Cota,Humberto	Pit	27	med	86	249	61	16	1	7	27	34	29	16	63	0	0	.00	.245	.293	.402	.695
Counsell,Craig	Ari	35	high	148	549	137	26	3	6	75	41	63	70	78	18	8	.69	.250	.339	.341	.679
Crawford,Carl	TB	24	low	151	590	176	27	13	12	93	67	90	28	78	45	12	.79	.298	.333	.449	.782
Crede,Joe	CWS	28	med	142	475	122	26	0	23	63	72	65	30	74	1	1	.50	.257	.309	.457	.766
Crisp,Coco	Cle	26	med	144	557	165	34	4	13	86	64	85	44	69	18	9	.67	.296	.348	.442	.789
Crosby,Bobby	Oak	26	high	145	541	145	37	3	20	87	72	84	58	103	7	3	.70	.268	.342	.458	.801
Crosby,Bubba	NYY	29	high	55	163	41	7	1	4	19	18	18	9	27	3	1	.75	.252	.291	.380	.671
Cruz,Deivi	Was	33	high	103	271	71	14	1	4	28	29	29	10	30	0	0	.00	.262	.293	.365	.659
Cruz,Jacob	Cin	33	high	77	105	26	6	0	3	14	16	13	12	29	0	0	.00	.248	.336	.390	.727
Cruz,Jose	LAD	32	high	119	392	102	27	4	17	66	60	68	63	92	4	2	.67	.260	.364	.480	.844
Cuddyer,Mike	Min	27	med	129	438	118	25	4	16	63	51	67	46	88	5	3	.62	.269	.342	.454	.796
Damon,Johnny	Bos	32	med	154	633	185	35	5	13	112	73	98	65	73	19	6	.76	.292	.361	.425	.786
DaVanon,Jeff	LAA	32	med	97	217	57	10	1	5	35	23	31	34	39	10	5	.67	.263	.365	.387	.752
Davis,Ben	CWS	29		50	115	28	6	0	3	13	16	13	11	25	0	0	.00	.243	.315	.374	.689
DeJesus,David	KC	26	med	147	541	158	34	6	12	88	64	85	54	78	8	6	.57	.292	.365	.444	.808
Delgado,Carlos	Fla	34	high	150	551	155	38	1	36	94	118	117	93	136	0	0	.00	.281	.399	.550	.949
Dellucci,David	Tex	32	high	125	400	97	18	3	20	72	59	61	59	111	5	3	.62	.243	.346	.453	.798
Denorfia,Chris	Cin	25		90	249	75	15	4	8	41	37	45	26	45	6	3	.67	.301	.367	.490	.857
DeRosa,Mark	Tex	31	med	67	167	43	8	0	4	24	18	19	13	29	1	1	.50	.257	.322	.377	.700
Diaz,Einar	StL	33	med	64	145	35	8	0	1	14	14	13	7	14	1	0	1.00	.241	.304	.317	.621
Diaz,Matt	KC	28	med	69	205	63	15	2	6	27	30	34	11	35	7	3	.70	.307	.346	.488	.833
Diaz,Victor	NYM	24	med	89	324	89	19	1	14	48	50	50	27	82	7	3	.70	.275	.332	.469	.802
DiFelice,Mike	NYM	37	low	48	111	24	6	0	3	11	13	11	10	29	0	0	.00	.216	.287	.351	.638
Doumit,Ryan	Pit	25	low	127	388	111	24	1	16	59	65	60	24	78	3	3	.50	.286	.350	.477	.827
Drew,J.D.	LAD	30	high	125	444	130	22	3	25	90	70	94	82	94	6	3	.67	.293	.409	.525	.933
Duffy,Chris	Pit	26	low	148	569	164	25	7	7	91	46	73	33	96	28	14	.67	.288	.328	.394	.722
Dunn,Adam	Cin	26	high	157	557	140	34	1	44	110	101	118	120	177	6	3	.67	.251	.392	.553	.945
Durazo,Erubiel	Oak	32	high	122	467	132	26	1	20	74	76	82	68	94	2	1	.67	.283	.377	.471	.848
Durham,Ray	SF	34	high	142	538	151	33	4	14	89	60	83	60	80	10	5	.67	.281	.359	.435	.794
Dye,Jermaine	CWS	32	high	133	499	132	27	1	24	75	82	76	46	102	7	4	.64	.265	.334	.467	.801
Easley,Damion	Fla	36	high	108	292	68	16	1	8	36	34	32	26	53	4	2	.67	.233	.311	.377	.687
Eckstein,David	StL	31	med	152	595	169	26	3	6	90	50	74	50	47	13	7	.65	.284	.356	.368	.724
Edmonds,Jim	StL	36	high	152	524	144	37	1	34	98	98	110	96	161	5	4	.56	.275	.391	.544	.935
Eldred,Brad	Pit	25	low	144	529	138	32	1	38	81	107	87	35	170	7	3	.70	.261	.310	.541	.851
Ellis,Mark	Oak	29	low	131	467	136	25	4	12	78	52	73	49	56	2	1	.67	.291	.365	.439	.804
Ellison,Jason	SF	28	med	92	238	63	12	1	3	32	16	27	17	29	9	4	.69	.265	.316	.361	.678
Encarnacion,Edwin	Cin	23	low	123	488	129	26	2	22	65	75	76	46	102	10	4	.71	.264	.330	.473	.804
Encarnacion,Juan	Fla	30	high	140	491	130	27	3	16	62	69	66	35	94	8	5	.62	.265	.323	.430	.752
Ensberg,Morgan	Hou	30	med	149	512	144	26	2	27	81	88	94	72	90	6	4	.60	.281	.375	.498	.873
Erstad,Darin	LAA	32	high	110	359	99	19	1	6	52	40	46	28	60	8	3	.73	.276	.333	.384	.718
Escobar,Alex	Cle	27		42	135	34	5	1	6	18	19	18	11	37	2	1	.67	.252	.308	.437	.745
Estrada,Johnny	Atl	30	med	116	405	116	29	0	7	41	58	55	27	42	0	0	.00	.286	.339	.410	.749
Everett,Adam	Hou	29	med	142	499	129	24	3	10	69	49	57	28	81	17	6	.74	.259	.307	.379	.686
Everett,Carl	CWS	35	high	107	330	87	17	1	14	44	55	47	28	67	3	2	.60	.264	.336	.448	.785
Feliz,Pedro	SF	29	med	143	465	120	26	2	19	59	71	62	27	85	1	1	.50	.258	.300	.445	.745
Fick,Robert	SD	32	med	85	198	51	10	1	5	22	28	26	22	29	0	0	.00	.258	.338	.394	.732
Fielder,Prince	Mil	22	low	152	539	146	30	0	33	72	101	93	58	138	9	6	.60	.271	.342	.510	.852
Figgins,Chone	LAA	28	low	149	580	170	25	11	6	95	56	86	55	84	47	16	.75	.293	.354	.405	.760
Finley,Steve	LAA	41	high	102	345	84	16	2	13	42	45	44	32	58	6	3	.67	.243	.313	.414	.728
Flaherty,John	NYY	38	high	56	123	28	6	0	3	11	13	11	6	23	0	0	.00	.228	.269	.350	.619
Floyd,Cliff	NYM	33	high	143	524	145	34	1	28	82	92	94	64	106	11	4	.73	.277	.365	.506	.871
Ford,Lew	Min	29	high	142	512	147	33	3	10	77	60	75	48	70	14	6	.70	.287	.360	.422	.782
Franco,Julio	Atl	47	high	101	191	51	9	1	4	22	27	25	22	46	2	1	.67	.267	.346	.387	.733
Francoeur,Jeff	Atl	22	low	137	532	152	44	2	25	74	97	88	28	115	14	6	.70	.286	.326	.517	.843
Freel,Ryan	Cin	30	high	128	469	126	24	3	6	74	31	61	56	69	37	14	.73	.269	.355	.365	.720
Furcal,Rafael	Atl	28	med	155	627	179	32	6	13	109	58	95	64	82	37	11	.77	.285	.354	.418	.771
Garciaparra,Nomar	ChC	32	high	115	462	142	32	3	18	75	74	82	32	46	4	2	.67	.307	.359	.506	.865
Gathright,Joey	TB	25	low	113	368	102	13	5	1	58	22	45	27	73	46	13	.78	.277	.330	.348	.678
Gerut,Jody	Pit	28	high	118	414	109	27	2	10	55	49	57	47	55	6	4	.60	.263	.343	.411	.753
Giambi,Jason	NYY	35	high	153	527	141	27	0	34	91	105	109	118	132	1	0	1.00	.268	.414	.512	.927
Gibbons,Jay	Bal	29	high	147	526	140	32	2	25	71	83	80	40	71	0	0	.00	.266	.320	.477	.798
Gil,Geronimo	Bal	30	med	65	157	40	6	0	4	14	19	17	9	27	0	0	.00	.255	.299	.369	.669
Giles,Brian	SD	35	high	157	587	171	38	4	24	99	97	118	116	77	10	5	.67	.291	.412	.492	.904
Giles,Marcus	Atl	28	high	145	556	163	42	3	16	96	66	95	63	100	15	5	.75	.293	.371	.466	.837
Ginter,Keith	Oak	30	med	81	239	61	15	1	9	31	36	34	25	49	1	1	.50	.255	.336	.439	.775
Glaus,Troy	Ari	29	high	135	502	127	28	1	33	85	90	91	81	134	5	3	.62	.253	.362	.510	.872
Gload,Ross	CWS	30	med	95	291	89	21	1	12	39	43	51	18	43	0	0	.00	.306	.346	.509	.855
Gomes,Jonny	TB	25	low	146	499	139	28	5	29	86	82	94	59	150	18	7	.72	.279	.364	.529	.893
Gomez,Chris	Bal	35	high	80	183	49	10	1	2	20	18	21	15	20	1	1	.50	.268	.330	.366	.696
Gonzalez,Alex	Fla	29	high	151	542	135	34	2	13	59	65	61	33	109	4	3	.57	.249	.299	.391	.691
Gonzalez,Alex S	TB	33	high	109	339	83	19	1	10	42	37	40	26	77	3	2	.60	.245	.306	.395	.702
Gonzalez,Luis	Ari	38	high	148	557	154	34	2	26	88	86	100	82	85	4	2	.67	.276	.376	.485	.861
Gonzalez,Luis A	Col	27	med	124	431	129	24	2	11	63	54	64	26	61	2	2	.50	.299	.345	.441	.786

2006 Hitter Projections

Hitter	Team	Age	Inj	G	AB	H	2B	3B	HR	R	RBI	RC	BB	SO	SB	CS	SB%	Avg	OBP	Slg	OPS
Gonzalez,Wiki	Sea	32	low	43	103	27	6	0	2	10	13	13	9	9	0	0	.00	.262	.327	.379	.706
Gotay,Ruben	KC	23	low	73	195	48	11	2	4	25	22	23	16	31	1	1	.50	.246	.313	.385	.698
Graffanino,Tony	Bos	34	med	118	405	112	18	2	7	67	42	52	37	55	7	3	.70	.277	.342	.383	.724
Granderson,Curtis	Det	25	low	144	502	144	27	14	18	77	67	88	46	134	20	7	.74	.287	.347	.504	.851
Green,Nick	TB	27	med	108	311	78	17	2	7	45	35	37	26	72	3	2	.60	.251	.321	.386	.707
Green,Shawn	Ari	33	high	160	607	167	37	2	28	95	93	103	73	112	8	4	.67	.275	.359	.481	.840
Greene,Khalil	SD	26	high	151	562	149	39	3	19	70	82	79	43	107	6	3	.67	.265	.324	.447	.771
Greene,Todd	Col	35	high	89	295	79	15	0	16	32	47	42	12	49	0	0	.00	.268	.299	.481	.780
Grieve,Ben	ChC	30	med	71	146	38	10	0	5	20	21	22	20	33	0	0	.00	.260	.365	.432	.796
Griffey Jr.,Ken	Cin	36	high	125	469	126	25	1	30	75	86	86	61	99	2	1	.67	.269	.358	.518	.876
Grissom,Marquis	SF	39	high	55	159	41	7	0	5	20	21	19	9	26	2	1	.67	.258	.302	.396	.698
Gross,Gabe	Tor	26	high	62	150	39	10	1	3	19	17	21	19	32	4	1	.80	.260	.343	.400	.743
Grudzielanek,Mark	StL	36	high	134	511	145	26	2	7	64	48	62	27	78	6	4	.60	.284	.328	.384	.712
Guerrero,Vladimir	LAA	30	high	150	567	187	35	3	36	104	114	133	64	63	15	7	.68	.330	.405	.593	.998
Guiel,Aaron	KC	33	med	73	216	55	12	0	8	33	31	29	21	43	2	1	.67	.255	.337	.421	.759
Guillen,Carlos	Det	30	med	129	492	146	27	4	11	79	64	77	49	78	5	3	.62	.297	.363	.435	.798
Guillen,Jose	Was	30	high	152	572	161	26	2	20	72	79	80	33	108	2	2	.50	.281	.335	.439	.774
Guzman,Cristian	Was	28	med	136	459	117	17	5	4	52	34	46	25	71	9	5	.64	.255	.296	.340	.636
Guzman,Freddy	SD	25		99	330	81	11	2	1	44	19	34	31	56	49	15	.77	.245	.310	.300	.610
Guzman,Joel	LAD	21		72	282	74	18	1	10	35	42	39	23	84	4	3	.57	.262	.318	.440	.758
Hafner,Travis	Cle	29	high	154	557	169	43	2	34	102	113	126	87	125	1	1	.50	.303	.407	.571	.978
Hairston Jr.,Jerry	ChC	30	med	119	413	110	24	2	5	54	35	49	36	50	14	8	.64	.266	.338	.370	.709
Hairston,Scott	Ari	26	med	124	416	109	21	7	18	56	48	61	28	90	6	3	.67	.262	.309	.476	.785
Hall,Bill	Mil	26	med	129	436	118	29	3	13	58	52	60	30	92	14	7	.67	.271	.319	.440	.759
Hall,Toby	TB	30	high	133	459	123	25	0	8	40	56	52	21	42	0	0	.00	.268	.306	.375	.681
Hammock,Robby	Ari	29		67	203	52	12	2	5	23	23	25	15	36	1	1	.50	.256	.307	.409	.716
Hardy,J.J.	Mil	23	low	124	411	104	25	1	11	55	56	55	50	49	0	0	.00	.253	.335	.399	.735
Harris,Willie	CWS	28	med	106	288	75	12	2	3	44	21	35	32	56	21	8	.72	.260	.336	.347	.684
Hart,Corey	Mil	24	low	130	415	115	28	4	13	63	62	65	35	85	29	8	.78	.277	.333	.458	.791
Harvey,Ken	KC	28	high	78	237	66	13	0	7	25	31	32	15	43	0	0	.00	.278	.329	.422	.751
Hatteberg,Scott	Oak	36	high	97	292	75	15	0	6	34	35	37	36	33	0	0	.00	.257	.348	.370	.718
Hawpe,Brad	Col	27	med	130	442	123	24	3	18	61	76	74	55	98	2	1	.67	.278	.358	.468	.826
Helms,Wes	Mil	30	med	107	294	78	17	1	9	31	39	40	23	65	0	0	.00	.265	.327	.422	.749
Helton,Todd	Col	32	med	155	569	189	48	2	30	112	108	146	111	85	3	2	.60	.332	.446	.582	1.028
Hermida,Jeremy	Fla	22	low	145	521	145	36	3	27	103	90	121	141	126	33	5	.87	.278	.432	.514	.946
Hernandez,Anderson	NYM	23		127	356	105	12	3	5	47	31	45	22	69	25	14	.64	.295	.336	.388	.724
Hernandez,Jose	Cle	36	med	81	191	47	8	0	7	23	24	23	16	60	1	1	.50	.246	.311	.398	.709
Hernandez,Ramon	SD	30	high	124	454	123	25	1	16	53	69	64	35	58	1	1	.50	.271	.330	.436	.766
Hidalgo,Richard	Tex	31	high	114	372	95	23	1	19	55	59	57	37	86	3	2	.60	.255	.334	.476	.810
Higginson,Bobby	Det	35	high	66	177	44	9	1	5	23	22	23	23	30	3	2	.60	.249	.345	.395	.740
Hill,Aaron	Tor	24	low	105	352	97	24	2	5	46	38	46	26	37	3	1	.75	.276	.334	.398	.732
Hill,Koyie	Ari	27	low	53	128	31	7	0	2	14	13	14	13	27	1	1	.50	.242	.312	.344	.656
Hillenbrand,Shea	Tor	30	med	152	582	170	37	2	17	77	84	84	25	73	4	2	.67	.292	.337	.450	.787
Hinske,Eric	Tor	28	high	127	398	101	27	2	13	60	55	56	45	93	7	3	.70	.254	.337	.430	.767
Hocking,Denny	KC	36	high	56	107	26	5	0	1	13	9	10	10	22	0	0	.00	.243	.308	.318	.625
Hollandsworth,Todd	Atl	33	high	91	197	52	12	1	6	26	25	27	17	45	3	2	.60	.264	.326	.426	.752
Holliday,Matt	Col	26	high	154	548	163	32	5	20	84	89	92	44	87	13	6	.68	.297	.355	.484	.839
Hollins,Damon	TB	32	low	98	311	81	19	1	10	38	42	41	23	54	6	3	.67	.260	.311	.424	.736
Howard,Ryan	Phi	26	low	158	584	188	43	2	44	98	127	145	72	173	0	0	.00	.322	.397	.628	1.026
Huber,Justin	KC	23	low	91	281	80	16	1	9	38	46	45	31	65	5	2	.71	.285	.358	.445	.803
Hudson,Orlando	Tor	28	med	145	526	146	31	5	12	71	64	74	43	77	7	3	.70	.278	.336	.424	.760
Huff,Aubrey	TB	29	high	155	580	165	33	1	25	77	91	93	49	83	6	4	.60	.284	.345	.474	.820
Hunter,Torii	Min	30	high	137	525	141	33	2	22	80	83	78	41	99	21	10	.68	.269	.329	.465	.793
Hyzdu,Adam	Bos	34	low	82	237	57	14	0	9	32	35	32	33	61	1	1	.50	.241	.333	.414	.747
Ibanez,Raul	Sea	34	high	149	559	156	31	2	19	79	83	85	55	90	6	3	.67	.279	.346	.444	.789
Iguchi,Tadahito	CWS	31	low	133	513	145	25	4	15	75	72	77	48	104	14	6	.70	.283	.351	.435	.786
Infante,Omar	Det	24	med	111	334	83	18	3	7	39	34	38	21	56	10	4	.71	.249	.295	.383	.678
Inge,Brandon	Det	29	med	152	574	144	29	6	15	62	67	72	53	126	5	4	.56	.251	.317	.401	.718
Izturis,Cesar	LAD	26	high	135	502	135	24	4	2	58	40	53	28	55	11	7	.61	.269	.310	.345	.655
Izturis,Maicer	LAA	25	low	65	147	38	8	2	1	19	13	17	13	16	8	3	.73	.259	.319	.361	.679
Jackson,Conor	Ari	24	low	140	421	123	42	1	9	59	64	75	67	42	3	2	.60	.292	.391	.461	.851
Jackson,Damian	SD	32	med	96	297	74	15	1	5	47	28	35	34	60	13	5	.72	.249	.330	.357	.687
Jacobs,Mike	NYM	25	low	125	422	128	34	1	23	57	80	81	29	90	1	1	.50	.303	.350	.552	.902
Jenkins,Geoff	Mil	31	high	153	591	163	41	2	28	90	94	99	56	152	1	1	.50	.276	.351	.494	.845
Jeter,Derek	NYY	32	high	155	632	193	32	2	19	116	74	108	67	112	16	5	.76	.305	.382	.453	.834
Jimenez,D'Angelo'	Cin	28	med	119	441	115	23	2	8	60	49	59	64	71	12	6	.67	.261	.356	.376	.732
Johnson,Ben	SD	25	low	145	551	139	32	2	21	78	81	78	62	132	5	3	.62	.252	.328	.432	.760
Johnson,Dan	Oak	26	low	156	548	151	34	1	23	80	93	92	72	73	0	0	.00	.276	.361	.467	.828
Johnson,Kelly	Atl	24	low	102	341	92	20	4	12	59	48	58	52	70	8	3	.73	.270	.368	.457	.825
Johnson,Nick	Was	27	med	138	474	131	26	1	14	64	66	77	86	90	4	4	.50	.276	.397	.424	.821
Johnson,Reed	Tor	29	med	131	415	114	22	3	8	61	53	51	23	72	5	4	.56	.275	.334	.400	.734
Jones,Andruw	Atl	29	high	159	602	162	32	3	42	102	113	112	69	126	7	4	.64	.269	.353	.542	.894
Jones,Chipper	Atl	34	high	140	506	147	31	1	29	88	93	107	95	86	6	3	.67	.291	.404	.528	.931
Jones,Jacque	Min	31	high	144	512	138	28	2	21	72	71	74	39	113	10	6	.62	.270	.327	.455	.782
Jordan,Brian	Atl	39	high	61	141	36	7	0	4	19	17	17	10	26	1	1	.50	.255	.323	.390	.713
Kapler,Gabe	Bos	30	med	105	264	71	15	1	6	39	32	34	20	44	5	3	.62	.269	.323	.402	.724
Kata,Matt	Phi	28	low	79	231	64	15	3	3	28	20	30	13	32	4	2	.67	.277	.316	.407	.723
Kearns,Austin	Cin	26	high	114	392	106	27	1	20	65	71	69	51	99	1	1	.50	.270	.363	.497	.860
Kendall,Jason	Oak	32	high	146	569	168	29	1	4	78	53	75	53	41	9	6	.60	.295	.374	.371	.745
Kennedy,Adam	LAA	30	high	147	500	143	27	3	7	66	52	66	36	82	18	7	.72	.286	.344	.394	.738
Kent,Jeff	LAD	38	high	152	579	168	39	2	27	93	106	104	62	100	5	3	.62	.290	.366	.504	.870

386

2006 Hitter Projections

PLAYER				BATTING											BASERUNNING			AVERAGES			
Hitter	Team	Age	Inj	G	AB	H	2B	3B	HR	R	RBI	RC	BB	SO	SB	CS	SB%	Avg	OBP	Slg	OPS
Keppinger,Jeff	NYM	26		61	185	58	9	1	2	23	18	26	10	9	4	2	.67	.314	.349	.405	.754
Kielty,Bobby	Oak	29	high	108	310	80	18	1	9	46	46	45	46	54	3	2	.60	.258	.359	.410	.769
Klesko,Ryan	SD	35	high	141	471	125	28	1	19	67	76	78	77	88	4	3	.57	.265	.371	.450	.821
Konerko,Paul	CWS	30	high	154	541	148	27	0	32	81	97	95	63	94	0	0	.00	.274	.356	.501	.857
Koskie,Corey	Tor	33	high	126	444	116	28	1	16	65	63	68	60	112	7	4	.64	.261	.358	.437	.795
Kotchman,Casey	LAA	23	low	142	491	126	27	1	14	60	69	63	47	56	2	1	.67	.257	.323	.401	.724
Kotsay,Mark	Oak	30	high	149	596	174	35	3	14	81	70	89	52	65	7	5	.58	.292	.350	.431	.781
Laird,Gerald	Tex	26	low	63	181	47	9	2	6	27	24	25	15	37	5	2	.71	.260	.320	.431	.751
Lamb,Mike	Hou	30	low	104	243	64	12	1	8	34	36	33	22	47	1	0	1.00	.263	.330	.420	.749
Lane,Jason	Hou	29	med	142	519	143	38	3	24	73	86	84	39	94	6	3	.67	.276	.330	.499	.829
Langerhans,Ryan	Atl	26	low	128	373	97	25	3	9	50	46	52	45	80	2	2	.50	.260	.344	.416	.760
LaRoche,Adam	Atl	26	med	142	509	141	36	1	24	70	85	85	49	97	0	0	.00	.277	.343	.493	.836
LaRue,Jason	Cin	32	high	126	441	108	28	1	16	51	63	57	40	128	1	1	.50	.245	.327	.422	.749
Lawton,Matt	NYY	34	high	144	541	143	32	1	14	83	67	77	74	73	16	8	.67	.264	.363	.405	.768
LeCroy,Matt	Min	30	high	109	324	88	15	0	16	36	55	51	32	76	0	0	.00	.272	.343	.466	.809
Ledee,Ricky	LAD	32	high	121	292	73	18	1	9	40	46	39	35	72	1	1	.50	.250	.334	.411	.745
Lee,Carlos	Mil	30	high	160	622	176	39	1	31	98	110	105	55	91	12	6	.67	.283	.345	.498	.843
Lee,Derrek	ChC	30	high	160	598	176	41	2	36	102	100	125	82	126	13	6	.68	.294	.385	.550	.935
Lee,Travis	TB	31	med	90	259	69	15	1	8	33	35	37	29	45	4	2	.67	.266	.343	.425	.767
Lieberthal,Mike	Phi	34	high	133	494	135	31	1	16	61	68	71	42	59	0	0	.00	.273	.342	.437	.780
Linden,Todd	SF	26	low	121	401	105	22	2	16	61	50	60	43	108	7	3	.70	.262	.336	.446	.783
Lo Duca,Paul	Fla	34	high	141	528	147	30	1	10	60	67	68	39	43	3	2	.60	.278	.335	.396	.731
Lofton,Kenny	Phi	39	med	106	343	97	16	3	5	59	32	48	37	41	14	5	.74	.283	.356	.391	.747
Logan,Nook	Det	26	low	89	214	55	7	3	1	27	13	23	17	35	15	5	.75	.257	.315	.332	.646
Long,Terrence	KC	30	med	125	351	96	19	2	7	47	42	45	25	49	2	2	.50	.274	.324	.399	.722
Lopez,Felipe	Cin	26	med	148	550	155	32	5	20	91	78	89	56	112	13	7	.65	.282	.349	.467	.817
Lopez,Javy	Bal	35	high	132	502	143	26	1	22	63	81	78	33	92	0	0	.00	.285	.336	.472	.809
Lopez,Jose	Sea	22	low	104	337	89	31	0	7	42	45	40	12	44	5	3	.62	.264	.295	.418	.714
Loretta,Mark	SD	34	high	142	558	167	30	1	8	75	60	80	55	52	6	4	.60	.299	.369	.400	.769
Lowell,Mike	Fla	32	high	138	465	125	32	0	16	60	72	69	47	62	3	2	.60	.269	.341	.441	.782
Lugo,Julio	TB	30	high	158	597	171	32	3	9	88	61	83	57	92	28	12	.70	.286	.354	.395	.749
Luna,Hector	StL	26	low	81	185	47	10	1	2	28	18	21	15	30	11	4	.73	.254	.320	.351	.672
Mabry,John	StL	35	high	88	201	49	11	0	7	23	28	25	18	53	0	0	.00	.244	.309	.403	.712
Mackowiak,Rob	Pit	30	med	138	418	108	21	3	11	52	53	54	40	98	8	4	.67	.258	.329	.402	.731
Markakis,Nicholas	Bal	22		89	298	94	28	2	8	46	75	61	46	66	0	0	.00	.315	.407	.503	.910
Marrero,Eli	Bal	32	high	62	128	33	8	2	5	20	20	19	11	28	2	1	.67	.258	.321	.469	.790
Marte,Andy	Atl	22	low	46	159	40	10	1	7	19	28	26	25	33	0	0	.00	.252	.353	.459	.812
Martinez,Ramon	Phi	33	med	65	138	37	7	0	2	14	14	16	12	19	0	0	.00	.268	.336	.362	.698
Martinez,Tino	NYY	38	high	135	408	102	18	1	18	54	65	58	47	68	2	1	.67	.250	.335	.431	.766
Martinez,Victor	Cle	27	high	141	526	160	37	0	20	75	89	97	61	67	0	0	.00	.304	.381	.489	.869
Matheny,Mike	SF	35	high	132	426	100	22	0	8	37	49	42	31	91	0	0	.00	.235	.293	.343	.636
Matos,Luis	Bal	27	high	116	386	105	22	2	7	53	39	49	28	61	16	7	.70	.272	.331	.394	.725
Matsui,Hideki	NYY	32	high	162	621	187	42	1	24	103	114	113	72	78	2	1	.67	.301	.376	.488	.864
Matsui,Kazuo	NYM	30	med	96	302	83	17	2	4	41	28	38	22	50	8	3	.73	.275	.332	.384	.716
Matthews Jr.,Gary	Tex	31	med	133	458	116	25	2	14	68	51	61	50	94	9	4	.69	.253	.328	.408	.736
Mauer,Joe	Min	23	med	131	494	151	30	2	11	70	62	84	60	57	12	3	.80	.306	.382	.441	.823
McCann,Brian	Atl	22	low	89	311	85	19	1	10	41	44	48	38	45	3	2	.60	.273	.354	.437	.792
McCracken,Quinton	Ari	36	med	111	201	51	9	2	1	24	17	21	18	35	3	2	.60	.254	.318	.333	.652
McDonald,John	Det	31	med	90	211	53	11	1	1	29	16	20	13	29	5	2	.71	.251	.301	.327	.628
McPherson,Dallas	LAA	25	med	143	486	126	32	5	26	73	87	77	43	145	9	6	.60	.259	.321	.506	.827
Melhuse,Adam	Oak	34	med	84	255	67	17	0	9	31	35	36	22	57	0	0	.00	.263	.321	.435	.757
Mench,Kevin	Tex	28	high	146	541	150	36	2	27	77	82	91	50	66	3	2	.60	.277	.344	.501	.845
Menechino,Frank	Tor	35	med	97	268	63	11	1	7	39	30	32	40	52	0	0	.00	.235	.345	.362	.707
Michaels,Jason	Phi	30	med	127	370	114	23	2	9	63	47	67	55	65	3	2	.60	.308	.400	.454	.854
Mientkiewicz,Doug	NYM	32	med	99	276	72	18	0	7	36	33	38	37	39	1	1	.50	.261	.356	.402	.759
Miles,Aaron	Col	29	high	113	380	114	20	2	5	51	38	50	18	36	7	5	.58	.300	.335	.403	.738
Millar,Kevin	Bos	34	high	127	421	117	28	1	13	55	60	65	46	77	0	0	.00	.278	.360	.442	.802
Miller,Damian	Mil	36	high	125	439	111	27	0	11	47	52	55	43	111	0	0	.00	.253	.324	.390	.713
Mirabelli,Doug	Bos	35	med	51	135	33	8	0	6	17	20	19	15	37	1	1	.50	.244	.329	.437	.766
Moeller,Chad	Mil	31	med	82	221	53	11	1	6	24	26	25	18	48	0	0	.00	.240	.300	.380	.680
Mohr,Dustan	Col	30	med	115	308	77	19	1	14	48	39	45	33	87	2	1	.67	.250	.328	.455	.783
Molina,Bengie	LAA	31	high	125	452	124	20	0	13	45	69	57	24	45	0	0	.00	.274	.315	.405	.720
Molina,Jose	LAA	31	med	81	196	49	8	0	4	20	24	20	11	41	2	1	.67	.250	.293	.352	.645
Molina,Yadier	StL	23	high	128	418	110	17	1	8	39	56	48	29	36	2	1	.67	.263	.313	.366	.679
Monroe,Craig	Det	29	high	147	516	146	29	2	21	69	82	80	38	83	6	3	.67	.283	.335	.469	.804
Mora,Melvin	Bal	34	high	147	572	162	32	1	23	91	82	93	61	112	8	5	.62	.283	.363	.463	.827
Morneau,Justin	Min	25	med	135	474	125	25	3	25	66	83	75	44	86	0	0	.00	.264	.329	.487	.816
Morse,Mike	Sea	24	low	72	248	65	12	1	4	28	27	29	20	50	3	1	.75	.262	.337	.367	.704
Mueller,Bill	Bos	35	high	146	537	152	34	2	12	80	64	81	65	78	1	1	.50	.283	.365	.421	.786
Munson,Eric	TB	28	high	55	118	28	5	0	6	14	19	16	12	26	0	0	.00	.237	.318	.432	.750
Murton,Matt	ChC	24	low	132	422	134	20	5	13	58	59	78	41	59	18	6	.75	.318	.378	.481	.859
Nady,Xavier	SD	27	med	113	352	94	16	1	13	45	45	47	24	65	2	1	.67	.267	.321	.429	.750
Navarro,Dioner	LAD	22	low	119	361	95	18	0	7	40	35	45	38	39	2	1	.67	.263	.335	.371	.706
Nevin,Phil	Tex	35	high	100	299	73	14	0	10	32	44	37	32	80	2	1	.67	.244	.321	.391	.713
Newhan,David	Bal	32	med	95	274	77	14	2	6	46	34	38	22	48	9	4	.69	.281	.339	.412	.751
Niekro,Lance	SF	27	low	99	336	88	18	2	10	36	44	42	17	51	0	0	.00	.262	.299	.417	.716
Nix,Laynce	Tex	25	high	104	343	91	20	3	14	52	53	49	23	74	3	2	.60	.265	.313	.464	.777
Nixon,Trot	Bos	32	high	125	438	124	28	2	19	72	72	78	60	77	3	2	.60	.283	.373	.486	.860
Nunez,Abraham O	StL	30	med	114	270	70	10	2	3	34	24	30	24	44	1	1	.50	.259	.322	.344	.666
Ojeda,Miguel	Sea	31	med	76	177	39	5	0	6	20	25	18	20	37	1	1	.50	.220	.303	.350	.653
Olerud,John	Bos	37	med	121	373	100	19	0	13	47	56	58	57	51	0	0	.00	.268	.371	.424	.795

2006 Hitter Projections

Hitter	Team	Age	Inj	G	AB	H	2B	3B	HR	R	RBI	RC	BB	SO	SB	CS	SB%	Avg	OBP	Slg	OPS
Olivo,Miguel	SD	27	med	100	283	67	15	2	10	37	38	32	17	72	11	5	.69	.237	.287	.410	.697
Ordonez,Magglio	Det	32	high	145	520	157	34	1	23	80	93	95	50	62	4	2	.67	.302	.368	.504	.871
Ortiz,David	Bos	30	high	155	589	170	46	1	40	102	132	129	87	125	1	0	1.00	.289	.382	.574	.956
Overbay,Lyle	Mil	29	high	151	531	157	41	1	17	76	78	96	74	96	1	1	.50	.296	.384	.473	.857
Ozuna,Pablo	CWS	31	low	72	195	53	9	1	1	23	13	19	7	22	10	6	.62	.272	.307	.344	.651
Palmeiro,Orlando	Hou	37	med	102	185	49	10	1	2	23	18	22	19	21	3	2	.60	.265	.343	.362	.705
Palmeiro,Rafael	Bal	41	high	102	360	92	16	0	18	46	61	57	54	48	1	1	.50	.256	.359	.450	.809
Patterson,Corey	ChC	26	high	123	424	106	20	4	15	57	46	53	24	108	17	5	.77	.250	.295	.422	.717
Paul,Josh	LAA	31	low	61	123	30	6	0	2	15	13	12	10	26	1	1	.50	.244	.301	.341	.642
Payton,Jay	Oak	33	high	128	413	118	20	2	14	61	57	61	29	51	2	1	.67	.286	.337	.446	.783
Pena,Carlos	Det	28	high	126	431	110	21	3	23	64	68	71	59	120	3	2	.60	.255	.350	.478	.828
Pena,Wily Mo	Cin	24	high	117	340	88	16	1	21	46	57	51	23	111	3	2	.60	.259	.311	.497	.809
Peralta,Jhonny	Cle	24	med	148	541	151	34	4	19	80	75	89	57	122	0	0	.00	.279	.350	.473	.823
Perez,Antonio	LAD	26	med	120	328	93	18	3	6	46	33	46	28	81	12	5	.71	.284	.345	.412	.757
Perez,Eddie	Atl	38	high	72	197	47	11	0	5	15	21	20	10	31	0	0	.00	.239	.279	.371	.649
Perez,Eduardo	TB	36	high	79	186	46	9	0	10	27	31	29	24	39	1	0	1.00	.247	.340	.457	.797
Perez,Neifi	ChC	33	med	144	469	124	23	3	6	53	44	50	20	43	5	4	.56	.264	.296	.365	.661
Perez,Timo	CWS	31	med	63	118	30	6	0	2	12	13	12	7	13	1	1	.50	.254	.302	.356	.658
Petagine,Roberto	Bos	35	low	76	177	48	10	0	6	20	48	27	22	25	0	0	.00	.271	.352	.429	.781
Phelps,Josh	TB	28	med	79	223	60	14	1	11	32	38	35	17	57	0	0	.00	.269	.337	.489	.826
Phillips,Andy	NYY	29	low	58	145	39	9	0	9	25	22	25	12	31	1	0	1.00	.269	.325	.517	.842
Phillips,Jason	LAD	29	med	68	226	58	14	0	5	23	32	27	17	24	0	0	.00	.257	.323	.385	.708
Piazza,Mike	NYM	37	high	124	456	122	23	0	24	58	75	75	55	80	0	0	.00	.268	.349	.476	.825
Pie,Felix	ChC	21		127	476	140	34	8	22	76	48	82	30	103	27	16	.63	.294	.336	.538	.874
Piedra,Jorge	Col	27	low	90	287	83	22	3	12	43	43	49	21	36	4	3	.57	.289	.340	.512	.852
Pierre,Juan	Fla	28	low	156	609	184	22	7	2	91	44	81	42	38	48	18	.73	.302	.355	.371	.726
Pierzynski,A.J.	CWS	29	high	136	503	140	33	2	15	62	71	69	24	61	0	0	.00	.278	.325	.441	.767
Podsednik,Scott	CWS	30	med	150	536	150	29	3	5	80	41	71	51	76	51	19	.73	.280	.346	.373	.719
Polanco,Placido	Det	30	med	141	553	174	32	2	16	95	65	92	35	37	6	3	.67	.315	.364	.467	.831
Posada,Jorge	NYY	34	high	142	499	133	29	0	22	72	86	84	80	114	1	1	.50	.267	.373	.457	.830
Pratt,Todd	Phi	39	high	71	140	34	6	0	4	16	18	17	19	42	0	0	.00	.243	.346	.371	.717
Pujols,Albert	StL	26	med	160	608	205	49	2	46	140	135	168	92	64	11	5	.69	.337	.432	.651	1.083
Punto,Nick	Min	28	high	92	236	59	9	2	2	32	16	26	26	45	9	4	.69	.250	.324	.331	.655
Quinlan,Robb	LAA	29	med	90	262	78	15	2	7	36	35	40	16	41	3	1	.75	.298	.341	.450	.791
Quintanilla,Omar	Col	24	low	39	124	30	5	1	1	14	7	11	8	17	1	1	.50	.242	.288	.323	.610
Quintero,Humberto	Hou	26	med	88	280	67	16	0	5	22	33	27	13	43	2	1	.67	.239	.273	.350	.623
Quiroz,Guillermo	Tor	24	low	123	320	78	20	0	14	40	55	42	26	74	0	0	.00	.244	.303	.438	.740
Ramirez,Aramis	ChC	28	high	147	562	163	34	1	33	81	104	102	43	78	1	0	1.00	.290	.347	.530	.877
Ramirez,Manny	Bos	34	high	156	587	179	38	1	45	114	141	141	93	101	1	1	.50	.305	.407	.603	1.010
Randa,Joe	SD	36	high	148	550	149	34	1	18	72	73	76	40	80	1	1	.50	.271	.327	.435	.762
Redman,Tike	Pit	29	low	122	357	99	14	3	4	44	28	42	21	29	11	4	.73	.277	.319	.367	.686
Redmond,Mike	Min	35	med	88	262	73	14	0	2	23	29	30	16	30	0	0	.00	.279	.332	.355	.687
Reed,Jeremy	Sea	25	med	135	449	132	32	3	5	66	50	66	48	58	14	11	.56	.294	.363	.412	.775
Reese,Pokey	Bos	33		75	197	43	8	1	3	22	17	18	18	45	7	2	.78	.218	.287	.315	.602
Relaford,Desi	Col	32	med	59	168	39	9	1	2	22	17	17	17	30	4	2	.67	.232	.325	.333	.658
Renteria,Edgar	Bos	30	high	156	613	175	38	2	10	91	77	85	55	88	15	7	.68	.285	.346	.403	.749
Repko,Jason	LAD	25	low	65	112	26	5	1	4	17	10	13	8	27	3	1	.75	.232	.312	.402	.714
Reyes,Jose	NYM	23	low	161	653	183	29	14	7	101	57	84	28	72	59	15	.80	.280	.311	.400	.711
Rios,Alexis	Tor	25	med	116	374	109	21	5	6	55	43	53	25	69	11	6	.65	.291	.341	.422	.763
Rivas,Luis	Min	26	med	103	308	79	16	3	5	42	31	35	18	44	10	4	.71	.256	.304	.377	.681
Rivera,Juan	LAA	27	med	129	437	128	29	1	16	58	64	70	32	50	2	2	.50	.293	.341	.474	.815
Roberts,Brian	Bal	28	med	151	602	170	40	4	11	98	60	91	71	86	28	10	.74	.282	.360	.417	.777
Roberts,Dave	SD	34	med	127	419	107	15	5	6	67	33	52	51	60	27	11	.71	.255	.339	.358	.697
Robles,Oscar	LAD	30	low	118	328	94	19	2	4	42	33	44	29	26	0	0	.00	.287	.348	.393	.741
Rodriguez,Alex	NYY	30	high	160	615	186	31	2	46	124	127	140	87	136	19	7	.73	.302	.400	.584	.984
Rodriguez,Ivan	Det	34	high	138	529	157	34	2	19	76	75	83	29	97	7	4	.64	.297	.337	.476	.813
Rodriguez,John	StL	28	low	54	117	29	6	0	6	15	20	16	11	30	2	1	.67	.248	.323	.453	.776
Rodriguez,Luis	Min	26	low	79	246	67	15	1	2	30	23	30	25	25	1	1	.50	.272	.342	.366	.708
Rolen,Scott	StL	31	high	146	503	144	35	2	26	90	98	97	70	93	6	3	.67	.286	.381	.519	.900
Rollins,Jimmy	Phi	27	med	159	655	184	40	9	12	105	62	95	53	80	34	10	.77	.281	.338	.424	.762
Ross,Dave	SD	29	med	65	151	37	8	1	6	17	20	19	11	36	0	0	.00	.245	.309	.430	.740
Rowand,Aaron	CWS	28	med	153	528	147	32	2	16	79	67	74	32	101	12	5	.71	.278	.334	.438	.771
Saenz,Olmedo	LAD	35	med	100	259	67	16	0	11	32	42	37	22	56	0	0	.00	.259	.329	.448	.777
Sanchez,Alex	SF	29	med	91	295	88	11	3	2	37	21	36	13	41	17	10	.63	.298	.330	.376	.706
Sanchez,Freddy	Pit	28	low	137	492	148	32	2	6	69	46	71	36	44	5	2	.71	.301	.351	.411	.762
Sanchez,Rey	NYY	38	high	70	205	53	7	1	1	22	16	19	9	21	1	1	.50	.259	.296	.317	.613
Sanders,Reggie	StL	38	med	109	380	96	19	2	21	58	59	57	35	102	13	5	.72	.253	.324	.479	.803
Schneider,Brian	Was	29	med	131	444	114	23	2	10	38	49	54	41	69	1	1	.50	.257	.324	.385	.709
Scutaro,Marco	Oak	30	low	132	442	120	28	2	10	55	43	59	36	54	6	4	.60	.271	.326	.412	.738
Sexson,Richie	Sea	31	high	145	549	143	30	1	37	89	112	100	77	158	1	1	.50	.260	.357	.521	.878
Shealy,Ryan	Col	26	low	97	296	89	21	1	14	43	46	55	25	57	3	1	.75	.301	.355	.520	.875
Sheffield,Gary	NYY	37	high	157	597	174	29	1	35	107	115	120	92	80	9	4	.69	.291	.383	.519	.912
Shelton,Chris	Det	26	med	107	365	111	26	2	16	61	61	70	38	72	0	0	.00	.304	.374	.518	.892
Shoppach,Kelly	Bos	26	low	115	326	79	20	1	17	43	55	47	31	96	0	0	.00	.242	.310	.466	.776
Sierra,Ruben	NYY	40	high	67	143	33	7	0	5	14	21	15	10	29	0	0	.00	.231	.281	.385	.666
Sizemore,Grady	Cle	23	low	158	617	180	36	10	21	109	88	103	54	114	20	10	.67	.292	.354	.485	.838
Sledge,Terrmel	Was	29	med	112	432	119	17	4	11	55	55	61	48	76	9	5	.64	.275	.348	.410	.758
Smith,Jason	Det	28	low	71	186	46	8	3	5	23	22	20	7	47	6	3	.67	.247	.278	.403	.682
Snelling,Chris	Sea	24	low	116	394	125	26	2	10	61	56	71	45	66	2	2	.50	.317	.387	.470	.857
Snow,J.T.	SF	38	med	116	352	95	19	1	7	46	49	48	46	67	1	1	.50	.270	.364	.389	.753
Snyder,Chris	Ari	25	med	76	194	40	10	0	5	16	20	19	24	45	0	0	.00	.206	.300	.335	.635

2006 Hitter Projections

PLAYER				BATTING												BASERUNNING			AVERAGES			
Hitter	Team	Age	Inj	G	AB	H	2B	3B	HR	R	RBI	RC	BB	SO	SB	CS	SB%	Avg	OBP	Slg	OPS
Soriano,Alfonso	Tex	28	high	156	648	182	42	3	35	102	99	107	34	129	29	8	.78	.281	.325	.517	.842
Sosa,Sammy	Bal	37	high	115	388	103	16	1	27	62	70	71	51	103	1	1	.50	.265	.355	.521	.876
Spiezio,Scott	Sea	33	high	55	119	28	7	1	3	15	15	14	12	21	1	1	.50	.235	.321	.387	.707
Spivey,Junior	Was	31	high	106	377	98	21	2	11	57	46	52	43	97	9	5	.64	.260	.345	.414	.759
Stairs,Matt	KC	38	med	139	458	118	25	1	19	61	74	70	64	94	1	1	.50	.258	.355	.441	.796
Stewart,Shannon	Min	32	high	133	539	158	33	2	11	79	57	79	46	69	10	5	.67	.293	.356	.423	.779
Stinnett,Kelly	Ari	36	high	85	269	63	12	0	10	29	30	31	24	77	0	0	.00	.234	.302	.390	.692
Sullivan,Cory	Col	26	low	138	382	113	20	5	4	60	35	53	27	70	11	5	.69	.296	.345	.406	.751
Surhoff,B.J.	Bal	41	high	96	281	75	14	0	5	30	34	32	19	33	1	1	.50	.267	.316	.370	.686
Suzuki,Ichiro	Sea	32	med	153	642	209	25	5	11	102	59	104	45	63	29	10	.74	.326	.374	.431	.806
Sweeney,Mark	SD	36	med	84	242	62	14	1	8	30	38	37	39	66	2	1	.67	.256	.359	.421	.781
Sweeney,Mike	KC	32	high	133	512	153	35	0	24	75	96	94	52	64	4	2	.67	.299	.369	.508	.877
Swisher,Nick	Oak	26	med	147	496	120	38	1	21	73	79	72	59	111	0	0	.00	.242	.326	.450	.776
Taguchi,So	StL	36	med	123	300	80	15	1	5	35	36	34	17	42	7	3	.70	.267	.308	.373	.682
Taveras,Willy	Hou	24	med	151	590	176	14	4	3	87	30	69	26	94	34	13	.72	.298	.333	.351	.684
Teahen,Mark	KC	24	low	145	502	128	35	4	8	71	66	63	50	112	8	3	.73	.255	.324	.388	.712
Teixeira,Mark	Tex	26	high	157	600	179	39	4	42	108	131	130	70	111	3	2	.60	.298	.381	.587	.968
Tejada,Miguel	Bal	30	high	158	630	185	40	2	28	97	113	107	46	80	5	2	.71	.294	.349	.497	.846
Terrero,Luis	Ari	26	med	80	192	50	9	3	3	26	19	23	14	47	6	3	.67	.260	.324	.385	.709
Thames,Marcus	Det	29	med	82	238	60	13	1	12	35	36	36	27	56	2	1	.67	.252	.331	.466	.797
Thomas,Frank	CWS	38	high	90	283	71	16	0	18	45	52	52	52	66	0	0	.00	.251	.375	.498	.873
Thome,Jim	Phi	35	high	123	440	115	22	1	32	78	89	92	95	141	0	0	.00	.261	.396	.534	.930
Tiffee,Terry	Min	27	low	62	154	40	9	1	4	18	22	19	9	15	0	0	.00	.260	.301	.409	.710
Torrealba,Yorvit	Sea	27	med	92	272	71	17	3	6	37	31	35	22	51	1	1	.50	.261	.321	.412	.733
Tracy,Chad	Ari	26	med	145	503	153	34	4	18	70	69	88	38	63	2	1	.67	.304	.358	.495	.853
Tucker,Michael	Phi	35	high	75	199	49	10	2	4	27	24	25	24	45	4	2	.67	.246	.333	.377	.710
Upton,B.J.	TB	21		139	511	138	31	4	13	69	54	76	57	125	43	15	.74	.270	.343	.423	.766
Uribe,Juan	CWS	26	med	144	528	140	29	6	19	75	76	73	35	92	6	4	.60	.265	.316	.451	.766
Utley,Chase	Phi	27	med	152	539	153	38	3	25	87	100	96	58	94	13	5	.72	.284	.360	.505	.865
Valent,Eric	NYM	29	low	63	111	26	6	0	3	14	13	13	14	24	0	0	.00	.234	.320	.369	.689
Valentin,Javier	Cin	30	med	96	277	72	16	1	12	35	44	41	27	46	0	0	.00	.260	.326	.455	.781
Valentin,Jose	LAD	36	high	97	291	65	14	1	13	43	39	37	35	77	4	2	.67	.223	.313	.412	.725
Varitek,Jason	Bos	34	high	140	492	131	32	1	20	66	75	78	61	124	3	2	.60	.266	.353	.457	.810
Vazquez,Ramon	Cle	29	med	56	126	32	6	1	1	16	10	14	12	22	2	1	.67	.254	.319	.341	.660
Victorino,Shane	Phi	25	low	81	237	64	9	4	6	34	24	32	19	34	11	5	.69	.270	.324	.418	.742
Vidro,Jose	Was	31	high	127	471	139	27	1	11	59	55	72	49	51	1	1	.50	.295	.365	.427	.792
Vizcaino,Jose	Hou	38	high	72	116	29	5	1	1	11	10	11	7	18	1	1	.50	.250	.298	.336	.635
Vizquel,Omar	SF	39	high	146	560	150	26	2	5	76	50	66	58	61	18	9	.67	.268	.340	.348	.688
Walker,Larry	StL	39	high	102	350	105	22	2	17	68	62	72	55	71	4	2	.67	.300	.408	.520	.928
Walker,Todd	ChC	33	high	138	505	146	32	2	14	71	61	77	45	60	2	2	.50	.289	.350	.444	.793
Ward,Daryle	Pit	31	med	94	245	64	14	0	8	26	40	32	19	39	0	0	.00	.261	.317	.416	.733
Watson,Matt	Oak	27	low	47	103	27	7	0	3	14	15	14	11	13	2	1	.67	.262	.333	.417	.751
Weeks,Rickie	Mil	23	med	155	574	153	28	8	26	98	86	97	67	144	27	5	.84	.267	.351	.479	.830
Wells,Vernon	Tor	27	high	154	624	176	39	3	28	92	97	101	47	87	8	3	.73	.282	.335	.489	.824
Werth,Jayson	LAD	27	high	97	275	70	17	1	10	42	42	41	35	83	10	3	.77	.255	.347	.433	.780
White,Rondell	Det	34	high	132	497	141	27	2	19	68	72	75	33	79	2	1	.67	.284	.337	.461	.798
Widger,Chris	CWS	35	low	50	114	27	7	0	3	11	13	12	8	21	0	0	.00	.237	.293	.377	.670
Wigginton,Ty	Pit	28	med	74	176	47	11	1	6	24	25	26	18	31	3	1	.75	.267	.345	.443	.788
Wilkerson,Brad	Was	29	med	156	574	147	32	4	16	82	59	85	100	162	9	7	.56	.256	.371	.409	.781
Williams,Bernie	NYY	37	high	118	414	113	21	1	14	64	61	64	56	68	2	2	.50	.273	.362	.430	.792
Willingham,Josh	Fla	27	med	82	226	63	12	2	13	41	41	45	37	59	5	2	.71	.279	.383	.522	.905
Wilson,Craig	Pit	29	high	136	488	129	28	3	23	73	72	78	54	157	5	3	.62	.264	.357	.475	.832
Wilson,Jack	Pit	28	med	158	614	167	29	5	9	71	57	72	34	68	6	4	.60	.272	.314	.379	.694
Wilson,Preston	Was	31	high	131	495	136	27	1	26	79	95	81	45	128	8	5	.62	.275	.342	.491	.833
Wilson,Vance	Det	33	med	81	195	47	8	0	5	21	27	20	12	32	0	0	.00	.241	.302	.359	.661
Winn,Randy	SF	32	high	160	615	170	37	3	17	87	67	88	56	107	19	10	.66	.276	.343	.429	.772
Womack,Tony	NYY	36	med	77	206	54	7	1	1	29	13	20	11	28	12	4	.75	.262	.309	.320	.629
Woodward,Chris	NYM	30	med	75	176	47	11	1	4	22	22	23	13	38	0	0	.00	.267	.325	.409	.734
Wright,David	NYM	23	med	160	579	179	44	1	30	104	106	120	68	100	17	7	.71	.309	.387	.544	.931
Youkilis,Kevin	Bos	27	low	149	500	139	38	1	14	86	68	87	95	91	4	3	.57	.278	.395	.442	.837
Young,Delmon	TB	20		120	401	114	17	4	16	56	61	59	18	73	24	8	.75	.284	.315	.466	.781
Young,Dmitri	Det	32	high	132	467	130	29	2	20	65	69	73	36	97	1	1	.50	.278	.339	.478	.817
Young,Michael	Tex	29	med	160	664	206	36	6	20	108	87	112	50	97	6	3	.67	.309	.359	.471	.830
Young,Walter	Bal	26	low	128	404	113	24	1	11	37	64	55	26	75	1	1	.50	.280	.323	.426	.749
Zaun,Gregg	Tor	35	high	110	355	87	17	0	8	43	44	44	52	61	1	1	.50	.245	.345	.361	.705
Zimmerman,Ryan	Was	21	low	157	588	185	55	0	16	83	68	100	34	96	2	3	.40	.315	.352	.490	.842

Projected Career Totals for Active Players
Note: These projections assume that the player will be healthy.

PLAYER	BATTING												BASERUNNING			AVERAGES			
Hitter	G	AB	H	2B	3B	HR	R	RBI	RC	RC27	BB	SO	SB	CS	SB%	Avg	OBP	Slg	OPS
Abernathy,Brent	1062	3189	808	141	5	37	360	295	328	3.53	239	315	68	36	.65	.253	.309	.336	.645
Abreu,Bobby	2520	9057	2637	634	52	357	1588	1460	1833	7.26	1739	2087	397	146	.73	.291	.404	.491	.895
Alfonzo,Edgardo	2218	7725	2183	404	20	197	1068	1053	1151	5.38	843	862	65	23	.74	.283	.355	.417	.771
Alomar Jr.,Sandy	1513	4887	1325	262	10	118	555	623	599	4.34	230	533	25	24	.51	.271	.308	.401	.709
Alou,Moises	2257	8128	2410	467	40	371	1242	1433	1502	6.78	889	1055	111	40	.74	.297	.366	.501	.866
Anderson,Garret	2249	8638	2540	538	33	299	1081	1396	1311	5.55	405	1230	78	48	.62	.294	.323	.468	.791
Anderson,Marlon	1019	2983	785	161	17	53	351	328	360	4.22	206	424	67	19	.78	.263	.312	.382	.694
Aurilia,Rich	1911	6590	1779	345	22	206	872	850	909	4.89	534	1069	24	20	.55	.270	.325	.423	.748
Ausmus,Brad	1966	6219	1571	267	32	82	726	612	693	3.83	629	975	101	55	.65	.253	.326	.345	.671
Bagwell,Jeff	2586	9153	2666	557	33	516	1744	1748	1951	7.72	1635	1877	215	86	.71	.291	.403	.528	.931
Bako,Paul	698	1882	441	98	9	17	167	166	189	3.40	207	477	4	5	.44	.234	.311	.323	.634
Barajas,Rod	1351	4307	1015	268	1	167	497	626	495	3.91	240	777	1	1	.50	.236	.280	.415	.694
Barrett,Michael	2078	7127	1834	467	32	205	785	867	938	4.59	600	1056	16	19	.46	.257	.318	.418	.736
Bay,Jason	2166	7991	2309	514	42	426	1321	1377	1604	7.24	1203	2049	179	76	.70	.289	.385	.524	.909
Bell,David	1747	5804	1469	320	15	148	693	704	713	4.26	518	831	16	19	.46	.253	.318	.390	.708
Bellhorn,Mark	1112	3211	735	183	15	99	497	375	429	4.47	539	1144	42	21	.67	.229	.342	.388	.730
Belliard,Ronnie	2039	7394	1979	498	27	159	1007	853	1002	4.78	726	1158	48	33	.59	.268	.333	.407	.740
Beltran,Carlos	2536	9681	2650	511	86	391	1620	1509	1609	5.87	1098	1777	396	94	.81	.274	.348	.465	.813
Beltre,Adrian	2858	10359	2779	567	31	448	1306	1571	1535	5.23	818	1824	106	50	.68	.268	.324	.459	.783
Bennett,Gary	646	1799	432	81	3	19	148	195	172	3.26	157	297	5	4	.56	.240	.306	.320	.626
Berkman,Lance	2345	8368	2449	603	30	446	1487	1569	1814	7.90	1645	1645	83	53	.61	.293	.413	.532	.945
Berroa,Angel	2086	7707	2030	357	49	151	982	745	863	3.91	331	1395	129	65	.66	.263	.309	.381	.690
Bigbie,Larry	1676	5509	1474	291	13	132	720	619	732	4.67	536	1334	76	37	.67	.268	.332	.397	.729
Biggio,Craig	3093	11757	3278	721	55	314	1964	1248	1801	5.44	1256	1896	434	130	.77	.279	.364	.430	.793
Blake,Casey	1144	3841	957	227	7	149	534	457	505	4.49	346	885	39	38	.51	.249	.320	.428	.748
Blanco,Henry	873	2412	520	132	9	61	238	264	238	3.25	224	455	4	10	.29	.216	.283	.354	.636
Bloomquist,Willie	1079	2633	677	138	10	15	345	252	275	3.58	178	447	117	40	.75	.257	.305	.334	.640
Blum,Geoff	940	2696	674	144	11	70	320	312	326	4.16	234	451	20	16	.56	.250	.313	.389	.702
Bonds,Barry	3415	11422	3418	693	82	900	2586	2316	3248	10.35	3267	1794	533	155	.77	.299	.457	.611	1.067
Boone,Aaron	1445	4858	1254	264	19	168	642	694	650	4.64	373	892	135	40	.77	.258	.322	.424	.746
Boone,Bret	2297	8360	2190	448	32	313	1140	1262	1170	4.88	702	1664	114	64	.64	.262	.323	.436	.758
Bradley,Milton	2059	7593	2031	466	21	243	1087	961	1140	5.24	956	1626	161	95	.63	.267	.352	.430	.783
Branyan,Russell	1371	4142	921	217	10	242	523	634	607	4.88	610	1784	14	10	.58	.222	.323	.455	.778
Broussard,Ben	1293	3879	987	229	25	152	497	580	543	4.86	356	836	22	13	.63	.254	.326	.444	.770
Burnitz,Jeromy	2118	7193	1810	370	32	385	1132	1208	1135	5.41	914	1717	85	68	.56	.252	.342	.473	.814
Burrell,Pat	2054	7333	1848	401	16	370	977	1295	1208	5.73	1174	2192	6	1	.86	.252	.356	.462	.818
Byrd,Marlon	1233	3772	1026	217	19	66	534	373	483	4.53	299	719	63	28	.69	.272	.323	.392	.724
Byrnes,Eric	1164	3383	858	212	27	102	503	388	451	4.61	281	622	73	20	.78	.254	.322	.423	.745
Cabrera,Orlando	2226	8137	2125	513	35	150	984	911	994	4.25	575	781	214	70	.75	.261	.310	.388	.698
Cairo,Miguel	1555	4389	1165	212	28	44	546	405	487	3.86	263	511	144	53	.73	.265	.316	.357	.672
Cameron,Mike	1856	6329	1554	353	47	255	980	905	934	5.00	807	1804	297	86	.78	.246	.337	.437	.774
Carroll,Jamey	994	2442	641	107	12	8	354	175	269	3.85	265	365	29	17	.63	.262	.339	.326	.665
Casey,Sean	2007	7386	2222	460	15	201	1047	1071	1204	6.05	696	808	25	11	.69	.301	.366	.449	.815
Castilla,Vinny	2178	7899	2151	412	30	360	1024	1273	1174	5.27	509	1262	37	47	.44	.272	.319	.469	.788
Castillo,Alberto	459	1113	247	42	2	12	105	110	96	2.86	112	231	4	6	.40	.222	.294	.296	.590
Castillo,Luis	2302	8639	2518	250	62	45	1330	553	1147	4.73	1088	1127	403	183	.69	.291	.371	.350	.721
Castro,Juan	1311	3365	783	172	13	57	327	304	316	3.17	179	599	4	6	.40	.233	.270	.342	.612
Castro,Ramon	1221	3364	772	191	0	124	387	462	422	4.23	416	835	7	0	1.00	.229	.312	.397	.709
Catalanotto,Frank	1662	5294	1544	354	42	113	776	636	802	5.51	441	730	51	31	.62	.292	.355	.438	.794
Chavez,Endy	577	1588	413	72	22	13	212	128	174	3.76	95	163	67	28	.71	.260	.301	.358	.659
Chavez,Eric	2598	9620	2568	574	25	470	1469	1618	1591	5.83	1155	1937	82	39	.68	.267	.345	.478	.823
Choi,Hee Seop	1829	5504	1351	318	12	250	779	773	849	5.30	864	1457	12	12	.50	.245	.354	.444	.798
Cintron,Alex	1244	3432	959	207	29	59	409	366	445	4.66	192	331	12	12	.50	.279	.317	.408	.725
Cirillo,Jeff	1705	5581	1633	349	19	118	823	756	862	5.62	582	732	67	40	.63	.293	.364	.425	.789
Clark,Brady	1437	4381	1221	226	5	86	566	475	584	4.72	422	509	87	59	.60	.279	.355	.391	.746
Clark,Tony	1760	5414	1420	294	13	304	745	985	896	5.82	607	1456	6	9	.40	.262	.336	.490	.826
Clayton,Royce	2500	8736	2232	411	61	131	1104	846	982	3.86	620	1715	243	109	.69	.255	.311	.361	.672
Colbrunn,Greg	1084	2944	848	166	13	104	357	445	447	5.49	185	475	29	21	.58	.288	.338	.459	.797
Conine,Jeff	2072	6947	1983	386	33	214	871	1065	1071	5.58	672	1185	52	30	.63	.285	.347	.443	.790
Cora,Alex	1499	4035	981	164	36	56	407	359	408	3.44	293	526	47	28	.63	.243	.313	.343	.656
Counsell,Craig	1472	4816	1227	224	30	43	665	378	562	4.01	608	680	124	55	.69	.255	.342	.341	.682
Crede,Joe	1856	6324	1596	340	3	290	803	932	832	4.56	401	1030	11	11	.50	.252	.303	.444	.747
Crisp,Coco	2133	8066	2316	484	43	177	1164	884	1151	5.10	634	1109	220	123	.64	.287	.337	.424	.760
Crosby,Bobby	2343	8826	2245	609	30	311	1328	1116	1268	4.97	979	1842	88	47	.65	.254	.332	.436	.768
Cruz,Deivi	1755	5454	1451	325	19	94	578	608	601	3.88	179	579	17	28	.38	.266	.291	.384	.676
Cruz,Jacob	486	834	202	44	2	22	109	121	101	4.10	97	236	4	8	.33	.242	.331	.379	.710
Cruz,Jose	1882	6392	1568	341	41	283	937	870	962	5.13	901	1586	125	51	.71	.245	.337	.444	.781
Cuddyer,Mike	1922	6633	1732	386	34	226	902	746	948	4.99	709	1424	59	40	.60	.261	.334	.432	.766
Damon,Johnny	2572	10071	2888	534	101	205	1733	1129	1523	5.43	997	1184	378	113	.77	.287	.351	.421	.772
DaVanon,Jeff	719	1623	416	72	11	43	254	177	230	4.83	241	317	74	32	.70	.256	.350	.394	.744
Davis,Ben	1137	3242	750	166	2	84	347	439	349	3.63	311	814	15	10	.60	.231	.299	.360	.660
DeJesus,David	2160	8034	2272	496	48	162	1227	897	1164	5.19	828	1240	90	73	.55	.283	.358	.417	.775
Delgado,Carlos	2479	8815	2455	600	18	565	1492	1837	1829	7.47	1446	2228	9	7	.56	.279	.391	.543	.934
Dellucci,David	1266	3464	860	155	35	140	566	495	509	5.03	458	930	54	30	.64	.249	.343	.436	.778
DeRosa,Mark	813	1923	495	91	2	44	272	203	222	4.01	145	328	11	10	.52	.257	.317	.375	.692
Diaz,Einar	904	2545	636	142	6	25	268	248	249	3.37	118	247	24	10	.71	.250	.301	.340	.641
DiFelice,Mike	560	1585	374	85	8	31	151	170	163	3.49	102	339	3	2	.60	.236	.287	.358	.645
Drew,J.D.	2043	7148	1982	338	45	369	1340	1061	1369	6.82	1265	1629	117	50	.70	.277	.390	.492	.882

390

Projected Career Totals for Active Players
Note: These projections assume that the player will be healthy.

PLAYER	BATTING												BASERUNNING			AVERAGES			
Hitter	G	AB	H	2B	3B	HR	R	RBI	RC	RC27	BB	SO	SB	CS	SB%	Avg	OBP	Slg	OPS
Dunn,Adam	2601	9394	2244	549	14	662	1707	1576	1802	6.51	2025	3176	103	51	.67	.239	.383	.512	.894
Durazo,Erubiel	1287	4117	1135	230	8	183	659	669	720	6.26	625	894	14	10	.58	.276	.374	.469	.843
Durham,Ray	2430	9160	2528	535	84	224	1528	993	1369	5.27	1006	1484	295	116	.72	.276	.351	.426	.777
Dye,Jermaine	2027	7267	1925	397	24	324	1052	1157	1097	5.31	656	1507	63	34	.65	.265	.330	.460	.790
Easley,Damion	1852	5870	1447	324	27	166	781	707	728	4.22	551	1032	125	61	.67	.247	.324	.396	.720
Eckstein,David	1975	7459	2057	313	31	66	1088	598	873	4.14	610	643	172	82	.68	.276	.349	.353	.701
Edmonds,Jim	2476	8641	2410	566	26	512	1588	1531	1724	7.12	1391	2419	80	61	.57	.279	.380	.528	.908
Ellis,Mark	1757	6261	1741	323	38	141	980	660	889	5.09	658	878	28	17	.62	.278	.352	.409	.761
Encarnacion,Juan	1914	6672	1761	353	53	217	845	932	885	4.61	447	1282	162	78	.68	.264	.317	.430	.748
Ensberg,Morgan	1750	5993	1608	292	21	290	870	970	1001	5.88	817	1148	58	39	.60	.268	.360	.469	.830
Erstad,Darin	1695	6363	1811	333	32	132	980	751	902	5.08	505	981	194	60	.76	.285	.339	.409	.748
Estrada,Johnny	1487	5169	1420	355	0	90	495	713	657	4.56	348	598	0	0	.00	.275	.327	.396	.723
Everett,Adam	1715	5837	1461	273	21	104	761	554	614	3.60	339	1037	157	60	.72	.250	.302	.358	.659
Everett,Carl	1649	5447	1478	297	29	230	793	912	843	5.44	493	1161	114	57	.67	.271	.341	.463	.804
Feliz,Pedro	1600	4924	1244	265	23	195	605	732	622	4.38	271	940	16	12	.57	.253	.290	.435	.725
Fick,Robert	891	2525	661	131	12	77	302	366	341	4.72	258	392	5	7	.42	.259	.330	.412	.742
Figgins,Chone	1780	6677	1911	276	96	66	1056	626	914	4.81	632	1066	432	171	.72	.286	.346	.386	.732
Finley,Steve	2717	9855	2662	468	116	332	1483	1252	1455	5.17	882	1406	329	127	.72	.270	.331	.442	.774
Flaherty,John	1103	3495	877	182	3	83	330	408	377	3.72	181	537	10	19	.34	.251	.289	.376	.665
Floyd,Cliff	2182	7442	2041	479	25	349	1148	1229	1280	6.09	868	1546	189	66	.74	.274	.358	.486	.844
Ford,Lew	1655	5916	1642	365	26	116	854	677	829	4.98	575	865	135	57	.70	.278	.352	.407	.759
Franco,Julio	2550	8773	2614	410	55	177	1302	1200	1357	5.63	930	1354	276	107	.72	.298	.365	.418	.782
Freel,Ryan	1393	4848	1281	234	28	51	744	307	607	4.27	583	755	318	128	.71	.264	.354	.356	.710
Furcal,Rafael	2500	9724	2684	480	75	179	1595	860	1342	4.85	968	1409	453	161	.74	.276	.341	.396	.737
Garciaparra,Nomar	1986	7799	2397	527	64	312	1276	1244	1413	6.75	543	815	112	44	.72	.307	.356	.511	.867
Gerut,Jody	1531	5354	1420	350	22	139	715	641	744	4.86	568	682	69	47	.59	.265	.339	.417	.756
Giambi,Jason	2272	7794	2194	435	8	473	1352	1522	1647	7.63	1567	1712	15	10	.60	.281	.411	.521	.932
Gibbons,Jay	1799	6297	1635	374	15	288	811	961	904	5.04	483	909	2	6	.25	.260	.314	.461	.775
Gil,Geronimo	845	2195	531	85	0	50	182	247	217	3.39	126	393	2	2	.50	.242	.286	.349	.635
Giles,Brian	2280	7978	2322	500	65	372	1391	1371	1666	7.58	1551	1093	137	57	.71	.291	.406	.510	.916
Giles,Marcus	2269	8523	2423	616	27	241	1390	988	1367	5.75	961	1594	173	77	.69	.284	.362	.448	.809
Ginter,Keith	1278	3940	956	228	10	143	479	557	518	4.50	418	875	23	10	.69	.243	.324	.414	.738
Glaus,Troy	2333	8436	2063	461	14	516	1367	1453	1434	5.81	1357	2350	91	49	.65	.245	.353	.486	.839
Gomez,Chris	1424	4391	1131	224	18	60	491	461	497	3.93	404	719	35	31	.53	.258	.324	.358	.682
Gonzalez,Alex	2220	7856	1901	468	34	192	842	921	850	3.69	453	1668	48	34	.59	.242	.292	.384	.676
Gonzalez,Alex S	1800	6100	1480	339	30	170	758	661	711	3.96	479	1431	106	53	.67	.243	.302	.392	.694
Gonzalez,Luis	2762	9877	2775	619	68	405	1527	1562	1737	6.28	1305	1393	133	89	.60	.281	.369	.480	.850
Gonzalez,Luis A	2025	7178	2088	405	18	183	978	869	1015	5.16	436	1071	24	25	.49	.291	.336	.429	.765
Gonzalez,Wiki	817	2340	575	124	5	45	219	288	264	3.88	220	246	3	2	.60	.246	.314	.361	.674
Graffanino,Tony	1442	4340	1164	207	27	79	683	429	556	4.50	409	722	82	36	.69	.268	.335	.383	.718
Green,Nick	1510	4646	1135	252	16	88	633	485	507	3.73	378	1091	30	21	.59	.244	.311	.363	.674
Green,Shawn	2576	9345	2583	572	37	441	1467	1425	1604	6.11	1046	1809	183	66	.73	.276	.353	.487	.840
Greene,Khalil	2256	8341	2117	567	27	258	973	1145	1081	4.49	663	1714	62	35	.64	.254	.314	.421	.735
Greene,Todd	1030	3218	808	157	1	157	348	468	401	4.32	127	632	5	4	.56	.251	.282	.447	.729
Grieve,Ben	1426	4164	1098	248	5	150	594	622	648	5.49	609	1030	28	5	.85	.264	.365	.434	.798
Griffey Jr.,Ken	2833	10462	2967	561	38	686	1783	1970	2092	7.19	1374	1999	186	72	.72	.284	.369	.541	.910
Grissom,Marquis	2328	8708	2360	404	56	240	1239	1023	1170	4.70	577	1313	434	119	.78	.271	.316	.413	.729
Grudzielanek,Mark	2042	7715	2191	409	34	103	1000	689	955	4.45	398	1110	143	60	.70	.284	.328	.386	.714
Guerrero,Vladimir	2866	10800	3430	602	52	649	1806	2056	2343	8.11	1173	1336	266	137	.66	.318	.390	.567	.957
Guiel,Aaron	816	2618	651	148	1	92	385	356	334	4.37	241	535	18	20	.47	.249	.325	.411	.736
Guillen,Carlos	2037	7496	2097	391	55	156	1144	933	1060	5.06	759	1329	66	45	.59	.280	.346	.409	.755
Guillen,Jose	2252	8043	2212	425	28	324	1085	1195	1145	5.08	446	1522	35	35	.50	.275	.328	.456	.784
Guzman,Cristian	2335	8144	2076	364	105	91	1037	678	851	3.59	428	1247	181	102	.64	.255	.294	.359	.653
Hafner,Travis	1877	6743	1937	517	16	372	1143	1295	1372	7.41	1014	1689	13	8	.62	.287	.390	.534	.924
Hairston Jr.,Jerry	1557	5059	1317	291	24	60	652	424	587	3.97	447	639	183	99	.65	.260	.335	.363	.698
Hall,Bill	2250	7886	2039	519	37	207	964	906	988	4.32	544	1846	175	106	.62	.259	.307	.413	.719
Hall,Toby	1436	4774	1251	251	1	86	426	582	519	3.82	224	452	2	6	.25	.262	.300	.369	.669
Harris,Willie	1445	4095	1029	169	16	40	599	280	448	3.69	452	808	224	92	.71	.251	.326	.327	.654
Harvey,Ken	925	2767	762	154	1	77	284	357	364	4.71	174	524	3	5	.38	.275	.325	.415	.741
Hatteberg,Scott	1252	3986	1061	223	6	95	496	497	553	4.91	510	492	1	5	.17	.266	.354	.397	.751
Helms,Wes	968	2429	629	114	9	82	260	320	322	4.64	196	583	2	5	.29	.259	.321	.423	.744
Helton,Todd	2536	9157	2978	746	34	489	1758	1718	2261	9.46	1674	1376	49	34	.59	.325	.430	.574	1.005
Hernandez,Jose	1642	4770	1200	202	32	176	647	622	615	4.43	398	1447	43	39	.52	.252	.311	.418	.729
Hernandez,Ramon	1951	6807	1779	355	4	231	785	993	898	4.64	547	952	11	2	.85	.261	.322	.416	.738
Hidalgo,Richard	1873	6250	1610	376	25	302	917	978	963	5.34	637	1422	66	47	.58	.258	.335	.471	.806
Higginson,Bobby	1535	5332	1439	291	34	199	790	761	856	5.63	703	868	97	57	.63	.270	.356	.449	.805
Hillenbrand,Shea	1646	5962	1704	369	19	174	771	839	829	5.04	250	775	31	16	.66	.286	.330	.442	.771
Hinske,Eric	1481	4621	1168	309	17	143	693	629	643	4.79	526	1090	84	36	.70	.253	.332	.420	.752
Hocking,Denny	1010	2465	617	117	17	26	307	235	263	3.65	215	464	36	27	.57	.250	.309	.343	.652
Hollandsworth,Todd	1333	3576	976	212	24	109	500	440	517	5.08	307	789	83	47	.64	.273	.331	.437	.768
Holliday,Matt	2152	7887	2275	480	49	277	1149	1244	1259	5.76	653	1353	132	70	.65	.288	.348	.467	.815
Hudson,Orlando	1897	6785	1806	386	53	144	858	793	877	4.54	556	1138	69	39	.64	.266	.324	.402	.726
Huff,Aubrey	2047	7538	2105	415	15	316	973	1135	1170	5.56	630	1106	54	38	.59	.279	.337	.464	.801
Hunter,Torii	2033	7365	1922	438	33	293	1065	1113	1024	4.80	548	1491	208	106	.66	.261	.318	.449	.767
Hyzdu,Adam	709	1768	419	96	0	71	240	270	237	4.55	234	438	6	6	.50	.237	.326	.412	.737
Ibanez,Raul	1454	4775	1336	268	27	164	676	720	732	5.49	437	768	46	26	.64	.280	.340	.450	.790
Inge,Brandon	1560	5068	1230	245	45	125	526	567	589	3.95	446	1168	43	41	.51	.243	.307	.383	.690
Izturis,Cesar	2339	8667	2252	414	53	42	953	676	864	3.45	479	982	170	102	.62	.260	.299	.334	.634
Jackson,Damian	1001	2700	662	145	19	37	409	243	320	3.99	301	604	158	47	.77	.245	.325	.354	.679

Projected Career Totals for Active Players
Note: These projections assume that the player will be healthy.

PLAYER	BATTING												BASERUNNING			AVERAGES			
Hitter	G	AB	H	2B	3B	HR	R	RBI	RC	RC27	BB	SO	SB	CS	SB%	Avg	OBP	Slg	OPS
Jenkins,Geoff	2003	7319	1984	488	28	342	1098	1148	1185	5.76	669	1931	31	15	.67	.271	.344	.486	.830
Jeter,Derek	2836	11301	3413	556	57	307	2013	1322	1866	6.08	1164	2078	310	98	.76	.302	.377	.443	.820
Jimenez,D'Angelo'	1826	6562	1675	323	31	115	853	692	833	4.37	907	1161	118	71	.62	.255	.346	.367	.712
Johnson,Nick	2006	6995	1857	448	11	241	1027	1056	1146	5.75	1256	1453	51	44	.54	.265	.388	.436	.824
Johnson,Reed	1197	3579	967	183	21	71	515	443	428	4.22	193	667	37	28	.57	.270	.333	.393	.726
Jones,Andruw	3046	11183	2919	574	45	677	1770	1944	1879	5.85	1244	2485	177	83	.68	.261	.341	.502	.843
Jones,Chipper	2634	9478	2773	558	31	510	1655	1721	1974	7.59	1649	1576	152	56	.73	.293	.395	.519	.914
Jones,Jacque	1853	6377	1726	339	22	244	874	862	897	4.94	446	1403	114	70	.62	.271	.323	.446	.769
Jordan,Brian	1469	5210	1469	272	37	185	762	830	784	5.38	356	845	120	49	.71	.282	.334	.455	.788
Kapler,Gabe	1444	4033	1090	236	18	98	595	500	541	4.71	333	662	97	42	.70	.270	.327	.411	.738
Kearns,Austin	2189	7908	2057	531	19	379	1238	1381	1316	5.83	1083	2101	34	19	.64	.260	.355	.476	.831
Kendall,Jason	2449	9064	2667	469	35	91	1268	863	1247	4.99	863	741	196	101	.66	.294	.376	.384	.760
Kennedy,Adam	2074	7043	1958	371	40	103	911	717	887	4.45	489	1172	221	93	.70	.278	.334	.386	.720
Kent,Jeff	2670	9864	2812	645	48	446	1536	1768	1700	6.21	949	1832	112	65	.63	.285	.352	.496	.848
Kielty,Bobby	1299	3783	949	217	9	111	546	540	534	4.87	571	754	37	18	.67	.251	.353	.401	.754
Klesko,Ryan	2256	7290	1994	433	34	351	1103	1258	1314	6.39	1102	1404	104	51	.67	.274	.369	.487	.855
Konerko,Paul	2321	8194	2233	395	5	449	1180	1426	1374	5.99	890	1372	4	1	.80	.273	.349	.486	.835
Koskie,Corey	1643	5611	1486	351	17	196	831	809	868	5.40	761	1395	103	52	.66	.265	.359	.438	.797
Kotsay,Mark	2337	8834	2497	495	51	198	1165	981	1251	5.07	772	1064	124	77	.62	.283	.339	.417	.757
Lamb,Mike	1116	2899	776	142	16	83	401	396	390	4.77	244	501	7	5	.58	.268	.327	.414	.740
Lane,Jason	1568	5036	1339	355	20	223	668	803	762	5.32	391	979	47	26	.64	.266	.321	.477	.799
LaRoche,Adam	1951	6720	1800	485	4	296	870	1080	1059	5.59	662	1377	0	2	.00	.268	.334	.473	.807
LaRue,Jason	1518	4978	1176	301	10	175	556	680	601	4.10	433	1511	16	13	.55	.236	.323	.406	.729
Lawton,Matt	1924	6709	1758	371	18	191	1037	862	979	5.05	947	911	217	94	.70	.262	.363	.408	.772
LeCroy,Matt	1073	3070	801	142	1	140	323	446	443	5.07	285	760	0	4	.00	.261	.330	.445	.774
Ledee,Ricky	1230	2948	718	173	20	92	413	462	392	4.53	358	736	31	18	.63	.244	.326	.409	.736
Lee,Carlos	2258	8430	2346	507	13	398	1283	1431	1359	5.75	712	1282	143	66	.68	.278	.335	.483	.818
Lee,Derrek	2501	8924	2477	567	33	474	1404	1384	1653	6.59	1193	2120	157	76	.67	.278	.367	.508	.875
Lee,Travis	1463	4612	1197	250	17	139	591	617	645	4.87	550	854	69	27	.72	.260	.338	.412	.749
Lieberthal,Mike	1922	6836	1846	415	11	227	839	945	968	5.04	560	917	8	7	.53	.270	.337	.434	.770
Lo Duca,Paul	1573	5554	1540	307	9	117	645	703	721	4.64	405	452	26	28	.48	.277	.332	.399	.731
Lofton,Kenny	2270	8516	2512	402	108	138	1585	821	1366	5.76	987	1092	613	167	.79	.295	.368	.416	.784
Long,Terrence	1467	4535	1219	247	27	98	617	552	578	4.50	332	673	36	21	.63	.269	.317	.400	.717
Lopez,Felipe	2550	9543	2503	563	52	316	1429	1253	1363	4.97	1000	2244	156	96	.62	.262	.332	.432	.764
Lopez,Javy	2183	7835	2218	389	23	368	969	1252	1237	5.71	524	1451	8	19	.30	.283	.334	.480	.814
Loretta,Mark	2080	7434	2194	392	25	108	998	786	1058	5.20	720	766	66	48	.58	.295	.361	.398	.759
Lowell,Mike	1866	6386	1699	430	3	239	828	999	956	5.29	642	933	36	15	.71	.266	.335	.447	.781
Lugo,Julio	2129	7900	2151	407	40	129	1130	783	1021	4.52	742	1419	274	121	.69	.272	.338	.383	.721
Mabry,John	1428	3704	980	202	5	109	422	491	486	4.62	304	796	7	12	.37	.265	.322	.410	.732
Mackowiak,Rob	1469	4293	1088	209	27	117	539	537	542	4.35	413	1075	83	37	.69	.253	.325	.396	.722
Marrero,Eli	791	2065	505	108	14	70	286	282	267	4.41	175	398	55	13	.81	.245	.302	.412	.714
Martinez,Ramon	750	1828	491	94	9	30	218	210	227	4.39	162	254	8	7	.53	.269	.329	.379	.708
Martinez,Tino	2390	8084	2163	406	22	380	1131	1419	1280	5.60	890	1234	31	22	.58	.268	.342	.464	.807
Martinez,Victor	2131	8001	2320	535	1	277	1051	1305	1343	6.14	922	1111	1	3	.25	.290	.365	.461	.826
Matheny,Mike	1712	5036	1191	248	9	88	454	573	489	3.29	354	1053	8	14	.36	.236	.292	.342	.634
Matos,Luis	1802	6094	1593	332	20	111	798	588	717	4.05	440	1100	200	98	.67	.261	.320	.377	.697
Matsui,Hideki	1558	5752	1676	374	12	213	908	1017	992	6.31	671	829	16	10	.62	.291	.365	.472	.836
Matsui,Kazuo	1085	3570	946	196	17	45	461	325	416	4.07	263	617	80	32	.71	.265	.320	.367	.688
Matthews Jr.,Gary	1559	4876	1199	262	24	134	703	525	618	4.32	548	1048	96	43	.69	.246	.322	.392	.714
McCracken,Quinton	1065	2610	715	126	33	21	378	259	330	4.42	243	471	90	46	.66	.274	.336	.372	.707
McDonald,John	835	1894	454	78	11	10	222	122	162	2.89	96	281	31	15	.67	.240	.283	.308	.591
Melhuse,Adam	864	2578	660	156	1	86	297	346	342	4.63	220	560	1	1	.50	.256	.314	.417	.732
Mench,Kevin	1904	6887	1844	458	21	321	936	1009	1084	5.57	631	973	26	18	.59	.268	.334	.480	.815
Menechino,Frank	877	2394	559	104	10	64	367	271	290	4.09	369	521	3	10	.23	.234	.348	.365	.714
Michaels,Jason	1660	5035	1445	300	14	114	806	601	803	5.78	744	1049	29	22	.57	.287	.380	.420	.800
Mientkiewicz,Doug	1200	3606	955	234	7	82	457	432	509	4.96	487	525	14	17	.45	.265	.356	.402	.758
Miles,Aaron	1427	4906	1421	229	20	60	635	462	598	4.40	238	489	72	49	.60	.290	.324	.381	.706
Millar,Kevin	1515	4778	1348	321	16	165	644	717	774	5.86	520	865	5	6	.45	.282	.360	.460	.819
Miller,Damian	1374	4465	1145	271	4	118	492	549	572	4.47	434	1122	4	5	.44	.256	.326	.398	.724
Mirabelli,Doug	869	2479	585	143	2	100	292	347	326	4.47	283	690	8	4	.67	.236	.320	.416	.736
Moeller,Chad	918	2565	589	128	11	63	265	279	269	3.53	216	596	2	4	.33	.230	.293	.362	.655
Mohr,Dustan	1281	3455	842	208	12	134	509	405	465	4.60	372	1020	24	18	.57	.244	.322	.427	.749
Molina,Bengie	1614	5605	1505	239	2	150	543	823	667	4.22	280	562	2	6	.25	.269	.305	.392	.697
Molina,Jose	798	1968	480	77	2	37	199	221	192	3.33	105	427	17	9	.65	.244	.286	.341	.627
Monroe,Craig	1684	5851	1582	321	19	230	745	897	834	5.04	419	1056	52	33	.61	.270	.318	.450	.768
Mora,Melvin	1741	6169	1704	346	15	222	949	843	952	5.47	658	1241	102	63	.62	.276	.358	.445	.804
Mueller,Bill	1930	6684	1909	416	29	118	1019	777	1019	5.53	835	952	22	19	.54	.286	.366	.418	.784
Munson,Eric	685	1642	370	65	3	83	172	242	205	4.18	165	371	4	2	.67	.225	.301	.420	.721
Nady,Xavier	1287	3607	947	168	9	129	450	450	471	4.58	248	678	23	11	.68	.263	.320	.421	.741
Nevin,Phil	1396	4644	1258	238	6	221	638	820	751	5.75	486	1130	22	7	.76	.271	.341	.467	.809
Newhan,David	974	2749	738	128	16	57	442	329	349	4.45	221	503	74	30	.71	.268	.326	.389	.715
Nixon,Trot	1823	6184	1694	381	39	256	994	993	1057	6.09	838	1200	44	19	.70	.274	.361	.472	.833
Nunez,Abraham O	1320	3151	792	113	22	30	372	271	328	3.58	288	551	43	21	.67	.251	.316	.330	.645
Olerud,John	2618	8682	2532	560	13	284	1274	1396	1565	6.60	1443	1167	11	14	.44	.292	.394	.457	.852
Olivo,Miguel	1470	4501	1034	238	22	137	554	555	466	3.43	277	1195	121	70	.63	.230	.280	.384	.663
Ordonez,Magglio	2101	7807	2338	488	21	349	1199	1387	1403	6.61	718	947	108	53	.67	.299	.360	.501	.861
Ortiz,David	2174	7843	2175	586	15	476	1261	1631	1556	7.14	1113	1768	8	2	.80	.277	.365	.538	.903
Overbay,Lyle	1750	6067	1713	470	3	179	812	850	1009	6.02	843	1246	11	5	.69	.282	.370	.449	.819
Palmeiro,Orlando	1177	2408	664	119	14	15	318	231	299	4.38	274	239	41	29	.59	.276	.353	.355	.708

Projected Career Totals for Active Players
Note: These projections assume that the player will be healthy.

PLAYER	BATTING												BASERUNNING			AVERAGES			
Hitter	G	AB	H	2B	3B	HR	R	RBI	RC	RC27	BB	SO	SB	CS	SB%	Avg	OBP	Slg	OPS
Palmeiro,Rafael	3149	11476	3270	629	38	617	1788	2000	2159	6.81	1506	1486	100	42	.70	.285	.369	.508	.876
Patterson,Corey	2066	7168	1760	334	46	239	924	750	837	3.96	402	1887	234	89	.72	.246	.290	.405	.695
Paul,Josh	688	1445	354	67	2	21	182	157	147	3.47	118	286	20	9	.69	.245	.301	.338	.639
Payton,Jay	1333	4230	1173	189	24	144	585	547	591	4.98	288	541	31	29	.52	.277	.327	.435	.762
Pena,Carlos	1660	5676	1384	268	32	291	793	844	860	5.18	760	1713	37	26	.59	.244	.337	.456	.793
Perez,Eddie	748	1981	493	110	2	51	170	218	219	3.82	107	307	1	4	.20	.249	.292	.384	.675
Perez,Eduardo	952	2242	550	108	3	102	303	360	314	4.79	256	497	22	12	.65	.245	.328	.433	.761
Perez,Neifi	2008	7084	1880	333	69	87	853	662	772	3.81	318	696	75	58	.56	.265	.295	.369	.664
Perez,Timo	614	1668	438	87	8	27	184	182	183	3.80	90	162	23	23	.50	.263	.301	.373	.674
Phelps,Josh	1270	3898	1021	226	11	186	539	660	579	5.23	302	1090	2	2	.50	.262	.328	.469	.797
Phillips,Jason	1295	4132	1016	226	0	99	401	536	469	3.91	338	493	0	3	.00	.246	.312	.372	.684
Piazza,Mike	2337	8441	2497	413	6	500	1228	1556	1643	7.16	980	1400	17	20	.46	.296	.370	.524	.894
Pierre,Juan	2268	8633	2572	299	87	25	1272	602	1088	4.49	586	559	578	240	.71	.298	.351	.361	.712
Pierzynski,A.J.	2017	7212	1984	463	25	187	851	986	936	4.64	328	916	9	13	.41	.275	.323	.424	.747
Podsednik,Scott	1178	3979	1099	203	27	46	597	302	527	4.57	379	626	357	120	.75	.276	.343	.375	.718
Polanco,Placido	2202	8137	2418	405	27	156	1202	826	1128	5.09	491	597	89	46	.66	.297	.334	.411	.757
Posada,Jorge	2043	6968	1816	407	5	298	1006	1184	1139	5.72	1134	1719	16	22	.42	.261	.368	.449	.817
Pratt,Todd	891	2257	557	112	3	66	262	296	298	4.55	307	655	5	2	.71	.247	.345	.387	.732
Pujols,Albert	3111	11847	3845	941	26	830	2508	2507	3025	9.74	1787	1376	125	70	.64	.325	.418	.619	1.037
Punto,Nick	1049	2781	678	103	14	26	365	190	283	3.42	296	556	91	46	.66	.244	.315	.319	.634
Ramirez,Aramis	2580	9653	2693	568	10	503	1288	1687	1585	5.91	722	1485	15	12	.56	.279	.333	.496	.830
Ramirez,Manny	2735	10000	3036	648	17	696	1857	2257	2308	8.58	1552	2279	41	34	.55	.304	.401	.581	.981
Randa,Joe	1970	7041	1969	422	41	159	894	938	984	5.02	560	990	44	27	.62	.280	.336	.419	.755
Redman,Tike	1296	3648	994	147	29	40	429	287	413	3.97	204	347	101	48	.68	.272	.312	.362	.673
Redmond,Mike	989	2843	790	146	2	22	249	303	327	4.14	188	338	1	2	.33	.278	.336	.354	.690
Reese,Pokey	1178	3573	874	160	18	54	451	344	389	3.70	288	696	167	36	.82	.245	.303	.345	.648
Relaford,Desi	1455	4362	1038	216	24	59	553	447	464	3.58	438	760	111	43	.72	.238	.317	.339	.656
Renteria,Edgar	2829	10736	3010	613	29	171	1551	1272	1440	4.76	956	1572	343	145	.70	.280	.338	.391	.728
Rivas,Luis	1974	6348	1604	322	53	105	836	609	697	3.76	383	978	188	78	.71	.253	.299	.370	.669
Rivera,Juan	1874	6450	1825	413	7	217	801	911	959	5.36	473	801	27	28	.49	.283	.331	.450	.781
Roberts,Brian	2097	8062	2207	533	39	127	1238	767	1124	4.88	912	1216	308	133	.70	.274	.347	.397	.744
Roberts,Dave	1037	3226	831	111	44	39	513	252	403	4.23	376	442	248	82	.75	.258	.337	.356	.692
Rodriguez,Alex	3116	11933	3517	603	33	816	2280	2312	2522	7.69	1549	2663	346	111	.76	.295	.384	.556	.940
Rodriguez,Ivan	2720	10321	3073	635	47	365	1502	1463	1646	5.85	588	1649	136	73	.65	.298	.337	.474	.811
Rolen,Scott	2454	8736	2417	584	40	427	1485	1626	1595	6.50	1202	1809	131	58	.69	.277	.371	.499	.870
Rollins,Jimmy	2645	10581	2861	618	108	186	1596	958	1402	4.63	863	1459	431	157	.73	.270	.327	.402	.729
Rowand,Aaron	2056	6916	1874	418	22	208	995	851	926	4.72	417	1388	128	59	.68	.271	.328	.428	.756
Saenz,Olmedo	881	2224	576	137	5	94	288	339	322	5.07	190	475	3	4	.43	.259	.333	.452	.785
Sanchez,Alex	813	2566	763	97	29	12	326	187	312	4.28	124	391	180	93	.66	.297	.330	.372	.702
Sanchez,Rey	1686	5382	1453	201	35	16	605	430	539	3.54	252	564	58	34	.63	.270	.306	.331	.637
Sanders,Reggie	2019	6960	1837	365	64	349	1138	1092	1141	5.66	736	1819	331	121	.73	.264	.340	.485	.825
Schneider,Brian	1672	5531	1389	341	15	138	514	668	688	4.31	522	915	6	7	.46	.251	.319	.393	.712
Scutaro,Marco	1549	5129	1320	314	16	105	595	477	615	4.17	401	698	45	29	.61	.257	.310	.386	.697
Sexson,Richie	1915	6945	1803	367	22	447	1092	1374	1223	6.17	901	1985	16	15	.52	.260	.349	.512	.861
Sheffield,Gary	2943	10626	3112	543	25	594	1864	1973	2161	7.37	1696	1338	247	112	.69	.293	.394	.516	.911
Sierra,Ruben	2239	8159	2180	434	59	311	1095	1339	1176	5.07	616	1261	142	52	.73	.267	.315	.449	.764
Snow,J.T.	2013	6513	1744	343	21	208	910	996	976	5.29	874	1315	22	24	.48	.268	.358	.423	.781
Soriano,Alfonso	2536	10023	2730	628	31	506	1493	1448	1530	5.36	516	2130	386	126	.75	.272	.316	.493	.809
Sosa,Sammy	2773	10103	2730	425	45	694	1672	1851	1851	6.43	1122	2666	237	109	.68	.270	.344	.527	.871
Spiezio,Scott	1128	3519	889	203	24	105	457	481	469	4.60	360	509	33	23	.59	.253	.324	.413	.737
Spivey,Junior	1372	4699	1200	271	21	136	719	571	638	4.68	531	1233	88	49	.64	.255	.340	.409	.749
Stairs,Matt	1713	5167	1359	290	13	258	754	897	865	5.87	725	1064	28	24	.54	.263	.358	.474	.832
Stewart,Shannon	1887	7307	2152	442	46	154	1111	768	1117	5.54	648	940	218	88	.71	.295	.358	.431	.789
Stinnett,Kelly	1030	2895	677	129	4	98	320	326	336	3.93	279	824	10	5	.67	.234	.312	.383	.695
Surhoff,B.J.	2471	8697	2442	462	42	196	1108	1205	1191	4.88	670	891	143	85	.63	.281	.331	.411	.742
Suzuki,Ichiro	1799	7265	2342	277	63	113	1141	641	1150	5.94	498	715	327	112	.74	.322	.369	.425	.794
Sweeney,Mark	1160	1970	511	109	9	55	241	292	290	5.13	300	490	19	11	.63	.259	.356	.408	.763
Sweeney,Mike	2003	7296	2172	467	4	317	1083	1326	1311	6.60	755	891	69	37	.65	.298	.367	.493	.860
Taguchi,So	619	1361	376	68	7	26	167	179	171	4.45	79	197	34	13	.72	.276	.316	.394	.710
Teixeira,Mark	2547	9742	2751	629	36	641	1620	2008	1926	7.14	1152	2014	39	23	.63	.282	.369	.552	.921
Tejada,Miguel	2858	11090	3109	662	27	472	1644	1925	1740	5.64	827	1546	97	42	.70	.280	.337	.473	.810
Thomas,Frank	2327	8021	2395	505	11	512	1487	1653	1881	8.66	1661	1423	32	23	.58	.299	.419	.556	.975
Thome,Jim	2383	8028	2183	421	25	571	1496	1587	1752	7.77	1706	2474	18	19	.49	.272	.401	.544	.945
Torrealba,Yorvit	1456	4590	1110	260	19	96	582	510	519	3.87	415	915	21	10	.68	.242	.308	.369	.678
Tracy,Chad	2184	7796	2307	528	36	263	1000	1026	1283	6.06	620	1028	25	16	.61	.296	.350	.474	.824
Tucker,Michael	1528	4381	1123	221	52	133	673	566	619	4.85	517	1027	119	60	.66	.256	.338	.422	.759
Uribe,Juan	2542	9282	2365	510	70	296	1214	1226	1167	4.35	608	1775	91	63	.59	.255	.303	.420	.723
Utley,Chase	2140	7779	2111	524	31	334	1153	1384	1261	5.72	829	1466	130	61	.68	.271	.347	.476	.822
Valent,Eric	268	517	121	26	2	16	64	50	62	4.06	55	125	0	1	.00	.234	.310	.385	.694
Valentin,Javier	1308	4109	1008	217	7	158	462	601	534	4.48	385	760	0	0	.00	.245	.308	.411	.725
Valentin,Jose	1786	5772	1374	303	40	264	910	840	810	4.73	670	1407	138	59	.70	.238	.319	.442	.761
Varitek,Jason	1865	6307	1659	404	11	232	821	935	946	5.27	737	1540	40	22	.65	.263	.345	.441	.786
Vazquez,Ramon	807	2033	511	88	17	11	238	152	215	3.64	207	391	29	13	.69	.251	.321	.328	.648
Vidro,Jose	2233	8085	2364	565	16	222	1127	1039	1293	5.85	806	910	29	22	.57	.292	.359	.449	.807
Vizcaino,Jose	1812	5353	1449	203	48	35	625	482	583	3.82	368	733	75	61	.55	.271	.317	.346	.664
Vizquel,Omar	2832	10340	2805	463	64	84	1443	928	1263	4.26	1042	1074	394	166	.70	.271	.338	.353	.691
Walker,Larry	2512	8670	2650	576	70	456	1649	1599	1880	8.01	1193	1603	246	86	.74	.306	.398	.546	.944
Walker,Todd	2084	7380	2094	460	39	182	1024	870	1087	5.30	655	955	74	44	.63	.284	.342	.431	.772
Ward,Daryle	1084	2866	738	155	5	108	303	473	378	4.61	214	511	1	5	.17	.258	.308	.428	.736

Projected Career Totals for Active Players

Note: These projections assume that the player will be healthy.

PLAYER	BATTING												BASERUNNING			AVERAGES			
Hitter	G	AB	H	2B	3B	HR	R	RBI	RC	RC27	BB	SO	SB	CS	SB%	Avg	OBP	Slg	OPS
Wells,Vernon	2420	9405	2589	576	31	395	1320	1408	1436	5.44	694	1383	95	42	.69	.275	.326	.469	.795
Werth,Jayson	1458	4639	1144	277	18	163	694	697	649	4.76	590	1409	130	53	.71	.247	.336	.419	.756
White,Rondell	1941	7002	1993	383	38	263	990	1007	1069	5.49	479	1206	98	50	.66	.285	.339	.463	.802
Widger,Chris	807	2299	548	135	7	68	227	276	260	3.84	169	468	10	9	.53	.238	.294	.392	.686
Wigginton,Ty	1523	4976	1279	307	17	151	627	660	668	4.66	471	950	65	30	.68	.257	.325	.417	.742
Wilkerson,Brad	2107	7558	1877	513	49	257	1174	852	1159	5.22	1289	2209	111	87	.56	.248	.362	.431	.793
Williams,Bernie	2516	9347	2712	510	58	332	1576	1455	1643	6.35	1293	1481	153	93	.62	.290	.376	.464	.840
Wilson,Craig	1690	5661	1444	309	26	259	810	813	844	5.17	611	1887	41	24	.63	.255	.352	.456	.808
Wilson,Jack	2211	8271	2173	385	57	110	935	742	903	3.82	452	1018	68	46	.60	.263	.304	.363	.667
Wilson,Preston	1900	6776	1725	381	19	319	949	1136	980	4.96	623	1930	157	82	.66	.255	.324	.458	.782
Wilson,Vance	717	1671	401	67	2	40	178	229	168	3.43	96	304	2	4	.33	.240	.298	.354	.653
Winn,Randy	2065	7658	2177	456	63	160	1074	840	1094	5.08	635	1338	236	122	.66	.284	.344	.423	.767
Womack,Tony	1411	5243	1426	199	61	37	781	385	623	4.16	319	689	381	79	.83	.272	.316	.354	.670
Woodward,Chris	782	1967	502	113	16	46	249	242	242	4.28	149	451	6	5	.55	.255	.309	.399	.708
Young,Dmitri	1745	5970	1695	370	35	229	819	858	947	5.73	477	1159	29	24	.55	.284	.343	.473	.816
Young,Michael	2405	9529	2802	484	67	257	1438	1167	1438	5.52	687	1543	86	43	.67	.294	.341	.440	.781
Zaun,Gregg	1381	4041	992	200	8	87	492	496	499	4.23	562	671	26	18	.59	.245	.339	.364	.703

How We Project Pitcher Performance

A Q and A

Q. How do you guys project what a pitcher will do next year?

A. We're very wise. Trust us.

Q. How accurate are your projections?

A. We'll be able to answer that in a few years. For now, we make no claims whatsoever to accuracy. These are our projections. Take them for what they are worth.

Q. What's the point of doing them, then?

A. What's the point of baseball? What's the point of going to a baseball game? It's fun. It's an entertainment. We like it.

Q. Is there no serious sabermetric purpose to this, then?

A. No, there is. First of all, we're going to have **some** level of accuracy.   If we establish a certain level of accuracy, then we can investigate ways to improve those projections.   One could identify all of the pitchers who achieved much *more* (or much less) than we had projected, and we could ask "why did these projections go wrong?   Was their something about this group of pitchers which should have given us a clue that their careers were about ready to make a left turn?"   By doing this, we'll eventually learn things that we don't know now. Which is the essential goal of sabermetrics—to build up our stock of knowledge about baseball.

Q. Can we talk about the specifics of the projections?

A. Certainly.

Q. Who did the work?

A. John Dewan and Pat Quinn, assisted by Steve Moyer and Damon Lichtenwalner.

Q. Bill James?

A. Wasn't involved. He doesn't believe it can be done.

Q. What a jerk.

A. Yeah, well . . . it was nice of him to stay out of the way.

Q. So what are the projections based on?

A. The players are projected based on their stats over the last eight years, with the heaviest weights on the last three years.

Q. Playing time?

A. The primary element in assigning playing time is the pitcher's workload and role on the team over the last two months of the season. If a pitcher finishes the season as a closer for his team, we project him as a closer. If he finishes the season in the rotation over the last two months of the season, we project him as a rotation starter. What he has done earlier in the season is of not too much relevance in assigning playing time.

Q. What other kinds of research did you do?

A. The first thing we reviewed was the Voros McCracken theory that hits per balls hit into play is a constant for all pitchers. We discovered that over a short period of time (e.g. looking at a pitcher's season from one season to the next) there is some correlation between a pitcher's hits per balls in play from one season

396

to the next. However, as you look at longer periods of time (multiple years for each pitcher), the correlation strengthens. Looking at one-year, three-year, and five-year periods along with a pitcher's career, the strongest (and positive) correlation comes in when looking at career data.

Nevertheless the correlation is not completely unrelated to team performance. By mixing the team numbers with the individual pitcher numbers, we get a stronger correlation. As a result, to determine hits allowed for pitchers we used their career rate of hits allowed per innings pitched less strikeouts, along with the team rate from the previous season. Innings pitched less strikeouts (IP-K) are used to estimate balls hit into play from basic stats.

Q. Does the pitcher's age matter?

A. Our previous research had suggested that it didn't matter at all, for a pitcher . . . the sort of statement which borders on the insane, but is true in a very limited perspective. If you take a 25-year-old pitcher and a 35-year-old pitcher with the same record and the same strikeout rate, their future expectations are essentially the same.

Anyway, for this project we revisited that area. After extensive analysis, we found that while for the most part the theory remained valid, we did find a pattern in three statistics: strikeouts, wild pitches and balks. Strikeouts per IP increased until age 25, stayed level through age 27, then dropped by about 1% per year beginning at age 28. Wild pitches increased until age 24, remained level until about age 30, then dropped about 5% per year after age 30. Balks decreased steadily by 10% per age-year. For all other statistics (e.g. hits, walks, home runs), no discernable pattern was detected by pitcher age. So we project those changes in the pitcher, as he ages.

Q. What else did you do?

A. We wasted a whole lot of time trying to find non-traditional ways to predict certain statistics using the in-depth Baseball Info Solutions data. For example, could the distance of all flyballs and line drives (over 250 feet) be used to predict home run frequency? We didn't find anything.

Could home runs per hit be more predictive for pitchers than home runs per inning? No, they weren't.

Could home runs per batter faced be a better predictor than home runs per inning? No, no better.

Could other stats (like walks and strikeouts) be made more predictable by using batters faced rather than innings pitched?. For the most part, the predictability was similar using either, and we chose to use innings because the number is more readily available.

Could the Ground Ball/Fly Ball ratio be used to predict home runs allowed? No. Well . . . maybe. While the correlation was slightly better using the ground ball ratio, it was not enough of an improvement to be significant.

If you include line drives with flyballs, would it improve the ability to predict home runs? It doesn't.

When all was said and done, we stayed with the traditional statistics for predicting key statistics: walks per inning, strikeouts per inning, home runs per inning, hit batsmen per inning. And, of course, the ex-Cub factor.

We also looked for the importance of recent seasons in the various statistics. For example, is a pitcher's strikeout ratio in more recent years more predictive than older years? For each statistic we found and used weightings that varied from each other. As an example, recent performance in strikeout ratio was much more important than recent performance of walk ratio.

Q. Did you use minor league numbers?

A. We did.

Q. How?

A. Ron Shandler has a pitcher MLE system which is time-tested and proven, and we begged and pleaded to use it. Ron was kind enough to provide us with his, which we used as underlying data in the projections. But we didn't use MLEs older than three years.

Q. How do you estimate ERA?

A. We used Component ERA for each pitcher once all other statistics have been developed. However, we discovered that Component ERA seems to under-estimate ERA for pitchers with very good ERAs, so we modified the ERA upward by 25 points for each 100 points under 4.00. For example, a Component ERA calculation of 2.00 adjusts to 2.50.

Q. Do you make any subjective adjustments?

A. Sure. You can't tell the computer everything you know. Well, you can, but it takes forever. It's a lot easier, when the computer makes a prediction that looks stupid, just to kick the computer until it stops doing that.

Q. Do you think the system will work?

A. We've done everything we can to back it up to previous seasons and test-drive it. It works a lot of times. The system won't tell us whether Chris Carpenter will be hurt or healthy next year. It won't tell us when a pitcher is going to do what Doug Davis has done, for example . . . make a transition to become a power pitcher.

I would answer it this way. We are serious researchers who have done serious research. Predictions by their nature are quixotic and treacherous, but you learn things from the process of trying to make them. We thought it was time to step into the harness and try to pull this plow.

2006 Pitcher Projections

Pitcher	Team	Age	Inj	G	GS	IP	H	HR	BB	SO	HB	W	L	Pct	Sv	BR/9	ERA
Acevedo,Jose	Col	29	med	44	7	84	97	15	25	58	3	4	6	.400	0	13.4	5.21
Affeldt,Jeremy	KC	27	med	64	0	67	73	6	29	51	2	3	4	.429	0	14.0	4.61
Alfonseca,Antonio	Fla	34	low	51	0	40	42	3	16	27	1	2	2	.500	0	13.4	4.30
Aquino,Greg	Ari	28	low	43	0	38	42	4	16	30	2	2	3	.400	0	14.5	4.95
Armas Jr.,Tony	Was	28	high	22	22	120	111	16	60	88	6	6	8	.429	0	13.2	4.37
Arroyo,Bronson	Bos	29	med	37	32	206	218	19	58	135	14	12	11	.522	0	12.7	4.09
Astacio,Ezequiel	Hou	27		30	18	106	109	14	30	85	5	5	6	.455	0	12.3	4.16
Astacio,Pedro	SD	37	med	22	22	131	140	21	45	103	8	6	9	.400	0	13.2	4.78
Ayala,Luis	Was	28	med	52	0	54	55	5	10	34	4	3	3	.500	0	11.4	3.59
Backe,Brandon	Hou	28	med	26	26	157	161	20	70	115	6	7	10	.412	0	13.5	4.60
Baez,Danys	TB	29	med	74	0	74	68	7	31	59	4	4	4	.500	42	12.7	3.88
Baker,Scott	Min	25		29	29	182	182	15	40	128	3	11	9	.550	0	11.2	3.50
Baldwin,James	Bal	35	low	32	0	72	83	11	22	38	2	3	5	.375	0	13.4	4.98
Batista,Miguel	Tor	35		73	0	74	75	7	31	47	2	4	5	.444	28	13.2	4.22
Beckett,Josh	Fla	26	high	31	31	194	171	17	69	192	6	14	8	.636	0	11.4	3.42
Bedard,Erik	Bal	27	med	30	30	167	169	14	75	147	7	9	10	.474	0	13.5	4.24
Belisle,Matt	Cin	26		66	2	76	96	7	23	46	4	3	5	.375	0	14.5	5.25
Bell,Heath	NYM	29	low	28	0	34	35	3	11	31	1	2	2	.500	0	12.4	3.96
Benitez,Armando	SF	34	med	48	0	46	32	5	22	51	0	4	2	.667	46	10.6	3.04
Benoit,Joaquin	Tex	29	med	43	14	112	111	17	50	94	5	6	7	.462	0	13.3	4.66
Benson,Kris	NYM	32	high	30	30	186	191	21	64	121	6	10	10	.500	0	12.6	4.13
Betancourt,Rafael	Cle	31	low	58	0	72	64	6	21	78	1	5	3	.625	4	10.8	3.21
Blanton,Joe	Oak	26	med	34	34	212	209	19	58	134	6	14	10	.583	0	11.6	3.62
Bonderman,Jeremy	Det	24	high	31	31	198	204	25	68	158	7	11	11	.500	0	12.6	4.24
Borowski,Joe	TB	35	med	56	0	64	59	8	21	54	0	4	3	.571	0	11.4	3.62
Bradford,Chad	Bos	32	med	53	0	39	39	3	11	26	3	3	2	.600	0	12.2	3.73
Brazelton,Dewon	TB	26	med	16	4	46	52	5	25	27	3	2	3	.400	0	15.7	5.56
Brazoban,Yhency	LAD	26	med	78	0	79	72	9	33	71	3	5	4	.556	2	12.2	3.79
Brito,Eude	Phi	28		14	14	93	102	12	41	60	6	5	6	.455	0	14.4	5.11
Brocail,Doug	Tex	39	med	59	0	70	75	3	26	59	4	4	4	.500	0	13.5	4.08
Brower,Jim	Atl	34	low	60	0	52	52	6	23	36	2	3	3	.500	0	13.4	4.42
Bruney,Brian	Ari	24	high	32	0	35	31	2	22	36	4	2	2	.500	2	14.0	3.99
Buehrle,Mark	CWS	27	high	34	34	241	245	25	53	145	6	14	12	.538	0	11.3	3.66
Burnett,A.J.	Fla	29	high	32	32	210	181	15	89	188	8	15	8	.652	0	11.9	3.46
Burns,Mike	Hou	28		32	0	35	39	4	8	26	2	2	2	.500	0	12.7	4.43
Bush,Dave	Tor	27	med	32	30	170	188	19	37	112	12	8	11	.421	0	12.5	4.23
Byrd,Paul	LAA	36	high	30	30	201	211	28	43	112	7	11	11	.500	0	11.7	3.98
Cabrera,Daniel	Bal	25	med	30	30	179	170	16	101	158	8	9	11	.450	0	14.0	4.37
Cabrera,Fernando	Cle	25	low	55	0	65	55	5	24	66	1	5	2	.714	5	11.2	3.27
Cain,Matt	SF	22		30	30	184	142	17	74	181	6	14	7	.667	0	10.9	3.16
Calero,Kiko	Oak	31	med	70	0	65	49	7	22	68	1	5	2	.714	0	10.0	2.99
Camp,Shawn	KC	31	low	40	0	82	104	9	25	52	5	3	6	.333	0	14.8	5.50
Capuano,Chris	Mil	28	high	36	36	220	219	29	85	170	13	12	13	.480	0	12.9	4.34
Carpenter,Chris	StL	31	high	34	34	252	245	28	74	197	9	17	11	.607	0	11.7	3.74
Carrara,Giovanni	LAD	38	low	70	0	80	76	9	33	58	4	4	5	.444	0	12.8	4.01
Carrasco,D.J.	KC	29	low	21	19	106	123	10	46	60	7	4	8	.333	0	14.9	5.22
Carrasco,Hector	Was	37		34	12	86	77	7	39	71	4	5	5	.500	0	12.5	3.73
Carter,Lance	TB	32	low	26	0	46	49	7	13	23	1	2	3	.400	0	12.3	4.41
Chacin,Gustavo	Tor	26	med	35	35	212	223	20	75	135	8	11	13	.458	0	13.0	4.21
Chacon,Shawn	NYY	29	high	33	28	185	180	24	93	120	15	10	11	.476	0	14.0	4.71
Chen,Bruce	Bal	29	med	35	34	210	211	36	75	165	7	11	13	.458	0	12.5	4.49
Christiansen,Jason	LAA	37	high	62	0	38	37	3	18	28	1	2	2	.500	0	13.4	4.20
Chulk,Vinnie	Tor	28		64	0	70	74	9	28	45	2	3	5	.375	0	13.4	4.63
Claussen,Brandon	Cin	27	med	32	32	196	213	25	74	144	8	10	12	.455	0	13.6	4.76
Clemens,Roger	Hou	44	high	32	32	210	178	18	73	199	6	14	9	.609	0	12.3	3.24
Clement,Matt	Bos	32	med	32	32	190	175	20	83	166	13	12	10	.545	0	12.9	3.98
Coffey,Todd	Cin	26		68	0	62	75	5	10	40	3	3	3	.500	0	12.7	4.30
Colome,Jesus	TB	29	high	46	0	60	61	7	32	45	3	3	4	.429	0	14.3	4.78
Colon,Bartolo	LAA	33	med	34	34	231	222	29	75	176	4	14	12	.538	0	11.7	3.80
Colon,Roman	Det	27	low	36	8	72	82	9	23	45	1	3	5	.375	2	13.3	4.77
Contreras,Jose	CWS	35	med	32	32	221	197	29	91	182	11	12	12	.500	0	12.2	3.88
Cook,Aaron	Col	27	med	24	24	160	191	11	51	58	8	8	10	.444	0	14.1	4.75
Cooper,Brian	SF	32	low	16	2	35	42	5	12	17	1	1	3	.250	0	14.3	5.45
Cordero,Chad	Was	24	high	67	0	65	52	7	23	60	1	4	3	.571	43	10.6	3.19
Cordero,Francisco	Tex	31	high	66	0	66	59	4	31	67	2	4	3	.571	43	12.7	3.62
Cormier,Lance	Ari	26	low	68	0	75	89	7	32	51	3	3	5	.375	0	14.9	5.19
Cormier,Rheal	Phi	39	med	50	0	38	35	4	13	26	2	3	2	.600	0	11.8	3.63
Correia,Kevin	SF	26		22	16	80	85	9	31	55	3	4	5	.444	0	13.5	4.56
Cotts,Neal	CWS	26	low	70	0	55	45	4	30	54	3	3	3	.500	0	12.7	3.60
Crain,Jesse	Min	25	low	76	0	89	73	5	32	65	3	6	3	.667	0	10.9	3.06
Cruz,Juan	Oak	28	low	24	0	30	26	3	13	28	2	2	1	.667	0	12.5	3.72
Darensbourg,Vic	Det	36	low	40	0	39	40	3	16	28	1	2	2	.500	0	13.0	4.02
Davies,Kyle	Atl	23		24	10	79	76	9	37	65	3	4	4	.500	0	13.2	4.22
Davis,Doug	Mil	31	med	36	36	226	230	23	92	166	5	12	13	.480	0	13.0	4.20
Davis,Kane	Mil	31		30	0	33	32	5	19	25	1	2	2	.500	0	14.1	4.95
Day,Zach	Col	28	high	25	15	97	111	10	43	47	5	4	6	.400	0	14.8	5.17
de la Rosa,Jorge	Mil	25	low	37	0	38	40	2	20	31	4	2	2	.500	0	14.8	4.72
DeJean,Mike	Col	36		72	0	71	74	6	34	56	4	4	4	.500	0	14.3	4.69
Dempster,Ryan	ChC	29	high	64	0	62	63	7	33	51	3	3	4	.429	44	14.3	4.75

401

2006 Pitcher Projections

Pitcher	Team	Age	Inj	G	GS	IP	H	HR	BB	SO	HB	W	L	Pct	Sv	BR/9	ERA
Dessens,Elmer	LAD	34	high	40	6	80	88	10	24	48	2	4	5	.444	0	12.8	4.43
Dickey,R.A.	Tex	32	high	10	8	49	62	7	17	29	3	2	4	.333	0	15.1	5.89
Dingman,Craig	Det	32	low	56	0	51	51	5	19	44	4	3	3	.500	13	13.1	4.18
Dohmann,Scott	Col	28	low	50	0	52	58	10	22	52	2	2	4	.333	0	14.3	5.59
Dominguez,Juan	Tex	26	med	26	26	156	158	19	51	108	5	9	8	.529	0	12.3	4.07
Donnelly,Brendan	LAA	35	low	68	0	62	51	5	20	63	2	5	2	.714	0	10.7	3.14
Dotel,Octavio	Oak	33	low	57	0	70	52	8	30	85	3	5	3	.625	1	10.9	3.25
Douglass,Sean	Det	27	med	17	11	73	78	8	32	54	3	4	5	.444	0	13.9	4.69
Downs,Scott	Tor	30	med	30	23	139	162	19	41	76	4	6	10	.375	0	13.5	4.93
Drese,Ryan	Was	30	high	16	16	88	110	8	32	43	5	3	7	.300	0	15.0	5.37
DuBose,Eric	Bal	30	high	30	6	59	68	8	22	39	2	3	4	.429	0	14.2	5.17
Duchscherer,Justin	Oak	29	low	68	0	88	83	9	19	65	3	6	4	.600	0	10.7	3.33
Duke,Zach	Pit	23		32	32	202	199	11	44	123	4	14	8	.636	0	11.0	3.28
Eaton,Adam	SD	29	high	27	23	135	136	17	47	105	6	7	8	.467	0	12.5	4.15
Eischen,Joey	Was	36	high	56	0	40	38	3	16	33	3	2	2	.500	0	12.9	3.88
Elarton,Scott	Cle	30	high	34	34	188	211	36	67	120	7	8	13	.381	0	13.6	5.32
Eldred,Cal	StL	39	high	40	2	47	47	6	21	38	2	2	3	.400	0	13.6	4.66
Embree,Alan	NYY	36	low	66	0	47	46	7	15	41	1	3	2	.600	0	12.0	3.97
Escobar,Kelvim	LAA	30	high	30	30	191	182	18	81	172	7	11	11	.500	0	12.7	3.94
Estes,Shawn	Ari	33	high	16	16	90	97	10	45	58	3	4	6	.400	0	14.6	5.04
Eyre,Scott	SF	34	low	88	0	69	64	6	34	56	2	4	4	.500	0	13.0	3.96
Farnsworth,Kyle	Atl	30	high	75	0	76	66	9	34	82	2	5	4	.556	38	12.2	3.80
Fassero,Jeff	SF	43	low	44	3	86	96	11	33	61	2	4	6	.400	0	13.7	4.82
Flores,Randy	StL	31		54	0	40	46	5	16	27	2	2	3	.400	0	14.6	5.34
Floyd,Gavin	Phi	23	med	8	5	31	32	2	14	21	3	2	2	.500	0	14.1	4.49
Fogg,Josh	Pit	30	high	36	24	152	168	21	50	78	7	7	10	.412	0	13.3	4.75
Fossum,Casey	TB	28	high	34	29	170	185	25	66	137	14	7	12	.368	0	14.0	5.10
Foster,John	Atl	28		68	0	39	40	6	18	32	2	2	2	.500	0	13.9	4.90
Foulke,Keith	Bos	34	med	60	66	33	27	4	8	31	2	3	1	.750	33	10.2	3.09
Francis,Jeff	Col	25	med	33	33	176	187	24	55	150	7	10	10	.500	0	12.7	4.41
Franklin,Ryan	Sea	33	med	31	30	182	191	28	54	93	8	9	11	.450	0	12.5	4.45
Frasor,Jason	Tor	29	low	68	0	79	76	6	35	67	3	4	5	.444	0	12.9	3.92
Fuentes,Brian	Col	31	med	78	0	75	66	7	35	86	8	5	4	.556	33	13.0	3.93
Fultz,Aaron	Phi	33	low	67	0	77	72	8	29	61	3	5	3	.625	0	12.2	3.81
Gagne,Eric	LAD	30	high	68	0	57	42	5	18	69	3	4	2	.667	43	10.1	2.91
Garcia,Freddy	CWS	30	high	33	33	226	216	26	73	166	7	13	12	.520	0	11.8	3.77
Garland,Jon	CWS	27		34	34	232	231	32	80	126	6	12	14	.462	0	12.3	4.13
Geary,Geoff	Phi	30	low	46	0	62	63	5	18	44	2	4	3	.571	0	12.2	3.80
German,Franklyn	Det	26	low	58	0	60	62	8	39	48	5	2	4	.333	0	15.7	5.54
Ginter,Matt	Det	29	low	13	2	33	38	4	9	19	2	2	2	.500	0	13.2	4.57
Glavine,Tom	NYM	40	med	33	33	231	234	20	77	123	3	14	12	.538	0	12.2	3.84
Glover,Gary	Mil	30	low	12	8	55	64	8	19	33	2	2	4	.333	0	13.8	5.09
Gobble,Jimmy	KC	25	med	36	8	78	91	11	27	42	2	3	6	.333	0	13.9	5.16
Gonzalez,Jeremi	Bos	31	med	38	2	64	68	8	21	39	4	3	4	.429	0	13.1	4.53
Gonzalez,Mike	Pit	28	med	56	0	58	44	4	26	67	1	4	2	.667	36	11.2	3.12
Gordon,Tom	NYY	39	med	80	0	82	62	6	29	88	2	7	2	.778	2	10.1	2.84
Grabow,John	Pit	28	low	70	0	59	67	6	22	51	1	3	4	.429	0	13.8	4.77
Graves,Danny	NYM	33	low	32	0	30	34	4	10	15	1	1	2	.333	0	13.3	4.85
Gregg,Kevin	LAA	28	low	42	1	79	82	7	25	62	3	4	4	.500	0	12.5	3.98
Greinke,Zack	KC	23	high	33	33	188	218	27	44	122	12	8	13	.381	0	13.1	4.81
Grilli,Jason	Det	30	low	6	4	32	38	5	13	17	2	1	2	.333	0	14.8	5.74
Grimsley,Jason	Bal	39	high	34	0	32	33	3	15	22	1	2	2	.500	0	13.8	4.44
Groom,Buddy	Ari	41	low	58	0	44	49	4	12	30	2	2	3	.400	0	12.9	4.33
Guardado,Eddie	Sea	36	high	62	0	59	48	8	19	55	1	4	2	.667	39	10.4	3.29
Guerrier,Matt	Min	28	low	47	0	82	90	10	19	49	3	4	5	.444	0	12.3	4.20
Halama,John	Was	34	low	35	6	64	73	8	19	34	3	3	4	.429	0	13.3	4.75
Halladay,Roy	Tor	29	high	34	34	231	224	19	57	168	7	15	11	.577	0	11.2	3.46
Halsey,Brad	Ari	25	med	24	22	132	157	12	34	81	6	6	9	.400	0	13.4	4.62
Hammond,Chris	SD	40	high	54	0	49	47	4	14	33	2	3	2	.600	0	11.4	3.53
Harang,Aaron	Cin	28	med	32	32	214	230	26	63	159	7	12	12	.500	0	12.6	4.30
Harden,Rich	Oak	25		33	33	210	174	14	82	192	4	15	8	.652	0	11.1	3.18
Haren,Danny	Oak	26	med	35	35	226	229	27	55	179	7	14	11	.560	0	11.6	3.80
Harper,Travis	TB	30	low	48	0	70	74	10	23	45	4	3	5	.375	0	13.0	4.59
Harville,Chad	Bos	30	med	46	0	49	48	7	26	40	3	2	3	.400	0	14.1	4.80
Hasegawa,Shigetoshi	Sea	38	low	44	0	67	64	5	24	38	2	4	3	.571	0	12.0	3.67
Hawkins,LaTroy	SF	34	low	74	0	62	62	6	20	46	1	4	3	.571	0	12.1	3.84
Heilman,Aaron	NYM	28	low	58	4	104	110	11	44	80	5	5	6	.455	4	13.8	4.58
Helling,Rick	Mil	36		28	14	96	107	15	34	64	4	4	6	.400	0	13.6	5.07
Hendrickson,Mark	TB	32	med	32	32	197	240	25	52	95	4	8	14	.364	0	13.5	4.98
Hennessey,Brad	SF	26	med	28	28	163	179	14	61	85	5	8	10	.444	0	13.5	4.43
Hermanson,Dustin	CWS	34	high	57	0	55	56	7	19	35	2	3	3	.500	13	12.4	4.10
Hernandez,Felix	Sea	20		24	24	169	124	7	61	191	5	14	5	.737	0	10.1	2.67
Hernandez,Livan	Was	31	med	36	36	245	254	26	83	163	9	12	15	.444	0	12.7	4.12
Hernandez,Orlando	CWS	37	high	27	23	135	128	18	48	105	8	7	8	.467	1	12.3	4.02
Hernandez,Roberto	NYM	42	low	65	0	70	69	8	31	55	4	4	4	.500	0	13.3	4.34
Hernandez,Runelvys	KC	28		26	26	130	141	14	53	71	6	6	9	.400	0	13.8	4.70
Hoffman,Trevor	SD	39	med	63	0	61	51	5	14	64	1	4	3	.571	39	9.7	2.83
Houlton,D.J.	LAD	27		36	24	152	169	26	54	107	7	6	11	.353	0	13.7	5.16
Howry,Bob	Cle	33	med	84	0	82	71	8	28	65	3	6	3	.667	2	11.2	3.40
Hudson,Luke	Cin	29	high	24	18	110	112	15	53	77	8	5	7	.417	0	14.1	4.91
Hudson,Tim	Atl	31	high	32	32	227	214	17	70	151	10	16	9	.640	0	11.7	3.52

2006 Pitcher Projections

Pitcher	Team	Age	Inj	G	GS	IP	H	HR	BB	SO	HB	W	L	Pct	Sv	BR/9	ERA
Ishii,Kazuhisa	NYM	33	med	14	8	48	44	6	30	35	1	2	3	.400	0	14.0	4.56
Isringhausen,Jason	StL	34	high	66	0	62	49	4	24	57	1	4	3	.571	36	10.8	2.99
Jackson,Edwin	LAD	23	high	14	12	57	56	6	25	42	2	3	3	.500	0	13.0	4.09
Jenks,Bobby	CWS	25		54	0	66	55	3	34	72	4	4	3	.571	28	12.7	3.44
Jennings,Jason	Col	28	high	31	31	174	199	20	82	113	6	8	12	.400	0	14.9	5.33
Johnson,Jason	Det	33	high	34	34	219	241	27	76	128	8	11	14	.440	0	13.4	4.67
Johnson,Randy	NYY	43	high	34	34	218	178	23	55	263	11	18	7	.720	0	10.1	3.05
Jones,Todd	Fla	38	low	70	0	76	79	7	29	64	3	4	4	.500	43	13.1	4.24
Julio,Jorge	Bal	27		64	0	68	65	11	30	60	2	3	4	.429	0	12.9	4.41
Karsay,Steve	Tex	34	high	31	0	34	38	3	11	27	1	2	2	.500	0	13.0	4.18
Kazmir,Scott	TB	22	med	32	32	189	169	11	99	187	9	11	10	.524	0	13.2	3.78
Keisler,Randy	Cin	30		30	8	74	92	11	31	46	2	3	5	.375	0	15.2	5.91
Kennedy,Joe	Oak	27	high	38	24	151	168	19	55	95	9	7	10	.412	0	13.8	4.87
Kim,Byung-Hyun	Col	27	med	36	28	170	161	17	70	151	15	10	9	.526	0	13.0	4.05
Kim,Sunny	Col	29		30	17	121	140	15	43	72	8	6	8	.429	0	14.2	5.15
King,Ray	StL	32	low	76	0	37	33	2	16	26	2	3	1	.750	0	12.1	3.48
Kline,Steve	Bal	34	med	62	0	65	58	6	28	45	2	4	3	.571	0	12.2	3.70
Kolb,Danny	Atl	31	med	62	0	54	56	3	25	34	2	3	3	.500	0	13.9	4.31
Koplove,Mike	Ari	30	med	26	0	30	29	3	12	20	2	2	2	.500	0	13.1	4.01
Lackey,John	LAA	28	med	34	34	221	231	23	71	175	10	12	13	.480	0	12.7	4.14
Lawrence,Brian	SD	30		33	33	181	192	19	50	109	9	9	11	.450	0	12.4	4.08
League,Brandon	Tor	23	low	30	0	52	59	5	21	33	3	2	4	.333	0	14.4	5.00
Lee,Cliff	Cle	28	high	32	32	212	209	27	77	166	7	12	11	.522	0	12.4	4.07
Lehr,Justin	Mil	29	low	40	0	62	69	5	24	41	3	3	4	.429	0	13.9	4.59
Leiter,Al	NYY	41	high	45	6	86	81	8	39	66	5	5	4	.556	0	13.0	3.98
Lidge,Brad	Hou	30	med	74	0	75	53	6	29	107	4	5	3	.625	40	10.3	2.84
Lidle,Cory	Phi	34	med	29	29	169	181	19	43	102	6	10	8	.556	0	12.3	4.10
Lieber,Jon	Phi	36	high	36	36	231	246	30	41	157	5	15	11	.577	0	11.3	3.85
Lilly,Ted	Tor	30	high	20	20	96	92	14	39	79	3	5	6	.455	0	12.6	4.29
Lima,Jose	KC	34	high	31	31	163	189	29	42	91	5	7	12	.368	0	13.1	5.08
Linebrink,Scott	SD	30	low	77	0	81	71	7	29	71	3	5	4	.556	1	11.5	3.44
Liriano,Francisco	Min	23		20	20	120	102	9	38	140	4	8	5	.615	0	10.8	3.15
Loaiza,Esteban	Was	35	high	36	36	236	257	27	66	168	7	11	15	.423	0	12.6	4.26
Loe,Kameron	Tex	25	low	48	16	132	150	11	41	83	3	7	8	.467	0	13.2	4.39
Lohse,Kyle	Min	28	med	32	32	186	209	26	57	109	8	8	13	.381	0	13.3	4.78
Looper,Braden	NYM	32	med	58	0	58	59	5	20	36	2	3	3	.500	35	12.6	3.91
Lopez,Rodrigo	Bal	31	high	36	36	213	228	29	66	138	7	11	13	.458	0	12.7	4.43
Lowe,Derek	LAD	33	med	36	36	228	234	20	66	143	9	13	12	.520	0	12.2	3.86
Lowry,Noah	SF	26	med	33	33	215	216	18	74	166	6	13	11	.542	0	12.4	3.84
Lyon,Brandon	Ari	27		37	0	31	38	5	9	20	1	1	2	.333	4	14.0	5.40
MacDougal,Mike	KC	29	low	66	0	68	71	5	33	60	5	4	4	.500	27	14.5	4.63
Maddux,Greg	ChC	40	med	34	34	210	213	24	34	137	7	14	9	.609	0	10.9	3.56
Madson,Ryan	Phi	26	med	82	0	85	86	7	24	68	4	6	4	.600	0	12.1	3.78
Maine,John	Bal	25	low	6	6	33	36	4	13	25	1	2	2	.500	0	13.5	4.67
Majewski,Gary	Was	26		73	0	79	78	3	32	58	6	4	4	.500	2	13.2	3.82
Maroth,Mike	Det	29	med	35	35	220	249	29	57	109	8	11	14	.440	0	12.9	4.59
Marquis,Jason	StL	28	med	34	32	217	226	27	81	133	8	12	12	.500	0	13.1	4.43
Marte,Damaso	CWS	31	low	68	0	42	33	4	20	44	2	3	2	.600	0	11.9	3.48
Martinez,Pedro	NYM	35	med	30	30	209	160	16	47	235	11	18	5	.783	0	9.4	2.68
Mateo,Julio	Sea	29	high	58	0	84	78	13	19	59	6	5	4	.556	0	11.0	3.68
Mays,Joe	Min	31		32	24	140	161	20	43	66	3	6	10	.375	0	13.3	4.86
McCarthy,Brandon	CWS	23		27	27	174	162	29	45	154	5	10	9	.526	0	10.9	3.72
Meadows,Brian	Pit	31	low	66	0	82	91	10	21	41	1	4	5	.444	0	12.4	4.24
Meche,Gil	Sea	28	high	26	20	109	113	16	49	73	3	5	7	.417	0	13.6	4.80
Mecir,Jim	Fla	36	low	40	0	33	31	2	14	28	2	2	2	.500	0	12.8	3.82
Mercker,Kent	Cin	38	med	76	0	58	60	8	25	42	2	3	4	.429	0	13.5	4.65
Mesa,Jose	Pit	40	med	54	0	55	55	6	25	40	2	3	4	.429	10	13.9	4.65
Miller,Trever	TB	33	low	62	0	48	49	5	25	38	5	2	3	.400	0	14.7	4.87
Miller,Wade	Bos	30	high	17	17	101	95	11	43	83	3	6	5	.545	0	12.5	3.91
Millwood,Kevin	Cle	32	high	32	32	210	200	21	63	168	5	14	9	.609	0	11.5	3.60
Milton,Eric	Cin	31	high	34	34	180	194	33	52	129	4	9	11	.450	0	12.5	4.69
Mitre,Sergio	ChC	25	med	18	4	37	42	3	13	27	1	2	2	.500	0	13.7	4.65
Moehler,Brian	Fla	35		36	7	76	96	9	20	40	2	4	5	.444	0	14.0	5.17
Morris,Matt	StL	32	high	34	34	201	203	23	51	140	7	13	9	.591	0	11.7	3.82
Mota,Guillermo	Fla	33	high	54	0	68	59	6	26	57	2	5	3	.625	2	11.5	3.41
Moyer,Jamie	Sea	44		32	32	210	212	28	54	123	9	12	11	.522	0	11.8	3.92
Mulder,Mark	StL	29	high	31	31	200	198	19	62	126	8	13	9	.591	0	12.0	3.79
Mulholland,Terry	Min	43	high	33	0	38	45	6	11	18	2	1	3	.250	0	13.7	5.15
Mussina,Mike	NYY	38	high	27	27	150	150	17	33	127	3	10	6	.625	0	11.1	3.62
Myers,Brett	Phi	26	med	35	35	221	222	31	77	173	10	13	12	.520	0	12.6	4.31
Myers,Mike	Bos	37	low	68	0	39	37	4	18	29	3	2	2	.500	0	13.6	4.20
Nathan,Joe	Min	32	med	72	0	74	55	6	32	77	2	4	4	.500	44	10.8	3.05
Novoa,Roberto	ChC	27	low	62	0	54	55	6	20	40	1	3	3	.500	0	12.7	4.14
Obermueller,Wes	Mil	30	med	19	7	54	62	6	22	28	3	2	4	.333	0	14.4	5.10
Ohka,Tomo	Mil	30	med	36	32	200	221	24	54	112	6	11	12	.478	0	12.6	4.33
Ohman,Will	ChC	29		76	0	51	45	6	28	57	3	3	3	.500	0	13.5	4.31
Ortiz,Ramon	Cin	33	med	33	33	195	212	32	67	121	8	9	12	.429	0	13.3	4.90
Ortiz,Russ	Ari	32	med	23	23	113	109	12	58	77	2	6	7	.462	0	13.5	4.30
Osoria,Franquelis	LAD	25		32	0	41	42	2	9	25	2	3	2	.600	0	11.6	3.57
Oswalt,Roy	Hou	29	high	36	36	236	227	19	53	199	9	15	11	.577	0	11.0	3.37
Otsuka,Akinori	SD	34	low	66	0	58	48	4	26	60	1	4	3	.571	0	11.7	3.31

403

2006 Pitcher Projections

Pitcher	Team	Age	Inj	G	GS	IP	H	HR	BB	SO	HB	W	L	Pct	Sv	BR/9	ERA
Padilla,Juan	NYM	29	low	39	0	59	62	4	14	37	3	4	3	.571	0	12.0	3.73
Padilla,Vicente	Phi	29	high	30	30	175	174	20	63	117	12	11	9	.550	0	12.8	4.15
Park,Chan Ho	SD	33	high	30	28	146	150	19	70	118	13	6	10	.375	0	14.3	4.96
Patterson,John	Was	28	med	34	34	220	210	25	82	189	9	12	13	.480	0	12.3	3.92
Pavano,Carl	NYY	30	high	30	30	185	200	20	49	118	10	11	10	.524	0	12.6	4.17
Peavy,Jake	SD	25	high	30	30	208	182	23	65	202	9	13	10	.565	0	11.1	3.43
Penny,Brad	LAD	28	high	30	30	175	175	17	53	125	4	10	9	.526	0	11.9	3.78
Perez,Odalis	LAD	29	high	30	30	184	178	23	49	129	2	11	9	.550	0	11.2	3.66
Perez,Oliver	Pit	25	high	32	32	209	182	32	109	227	9	11	13	.458	0	12.9	4.26
Pettitte,Andy	Hou	34	high	34	34	235	235	19	68	179	3	14	12	.538	0	11.7	3.64
Pineiro,Joel	Sea	28	high	32	32	202	206	23	63	136	6	11	11	.500	0	12.3	4.00
Politte,Cliff	CWS	32	med	72	0	69	60	9	27	60	2	4	4	.500	0	11.6	3.64
Ponson,Sidney	Bal	30	high	14	14	77	87	9	26	45	2	4	5	.444	0	13.4	4.68
Prior,Mark	ChC	26	high	30	30	180	156	20	59	210	6	13	7	.650	0	11.1	3.42
Proctor,Scott	NYY	29	low	38	2	65	70	10	24	53	2	3	4	.429	0	13.2	4.71
Putz,J.J.	Sea	29	low	66	0	56	56	6	22	39	3	3	3	.500	6	13.0	4.20
Qualls,Chad	Hou	28	low	79	0	84	99	7	27	52	6	4	6	.400	0	14.1	4.86
Quantrill,Paul	Fla	38	low	49	0	64	72	4	15	35	3	4	3	.571	0	12.7	4.01
Radke,Brad	Min	34	high	29	29	182	196	24	28	108	6	10	10	.500	0	11.4	3.87
Ramirez,Erasmo	Tex	30	med	24	0	37	42	3	6	18	2	2	2	.500	0	12.0	3.96
Ramirez,Horacio	Atl	27	high	34	32	207	212	28	77	96	3	12	11	.522	0	12.7	4.32
Rauch,Jon	Was	28	high	31	18	135	138	21	44	91	4	6	9	.400	0	12.4	4.34
Redman,Mark	Pit	32	high	27	27	146	153	16	46	90	3	8	8	.500	0	12.5	4.11
Reitsma,Chris	Atl	29	med	77	0	70	77	8	18	42	1	4	4	.500	0	12.3	4.14
Remlinger,Mike	Bos	40	med	35	0	30	27	4	14	30	1	2	1	.667	0	12.4	3.89
Reyes,Al	StL	35	med	64	0	62	49	6	26	60	3	5	2	.714	0	11.4	3.30
Rincon,Juan	Min	27	low	81	0	82	68	5	33	84	3	6	3	.667	0	11.4	3.18
Rincon,Ricardo	Oak	36	med	66	0	37	33	4	17	30	1	2	2	.500	0	12.4	3.72
Riske,David	Cle	30	low	55	0	50	41	7	20	48	2	3	2	.600	1	11.3	3.57
Rivera,Mariano	NYY	37	med	79	0	87	69	4	20	77	4	7	3	.700	42	9.6	2.62
Robertson,Nate	Det	29	med	32	32	204	221	28	69	134	6	10	13	.435	0	13.0	4.57
Rodney,Fernando	Det	29		54	0	58	53	4	24	58	4	4	3	.571	26	12.3	3.62
Rodriguez,Felix	NYY	34	med	42	0	40	36	3	19	35	2	3	2	.600	0	12.8	3.80
Rodriguez,Francisco	LAA	24	high	74	0	71	46	6	30	95	1	5	3	.625	44	9.7	2.66
Rodriguez,Ricardo	Tex	28	high	9	8	40	44	6	13	19	2	2	2	.500	0	13.2	4.75
Rodriguez,Wandy	Hou	27		32	26	154	180	23	64	98	9	5	12	.294	0	14.8	5.60
Rogers,Kenny	Tex	42	high	30	30	191	212	19	59	104	9	10	11	.476	0	13.2	4.44
Romero,J.C.	Min	30	med	66	0	54	50	5	29	45	4	3	3	.500	0	13.8	4.25
Rusch,Glendon	ChC	32	high	37	25	163	187	17	51	120	4	8	10	.444	0	13.3	4.60
Ryan,B.J.	Bal	31	med	69	0	72	58	5	35	90	2	4	4	.500	39	11.9	3.32
Saarloos,Kirk	Oak	27	med	28	27	156	168	14	51	73	9	8	9	.471	0	13.2	4.28
Sabathia,C.C.	Cle	26	med	32	32	213	198	21	81	166	7	14	10	.583	0	12.1	3.72
Sanchez,Duaner	LAD	27	med	76	0	76	79	8	31	51	4	4	5	.444	2	13.7	4.50
Santana,Ervin	LAA	23		30	30	179	177	19	61	137	9	10	10	.500	0	12.4	3.96
Santana,Johan	Min	27	high	34	34	248	195	25	70	265	5	19	9	.679	0	9.8	2.91
Santana,Julio	Mil	32		31	0	30	29	4	14	23	1	2	2	.500	0	13.2	4.53
Santos,Victor	Mil	30	med	26	18	108	121	13	48	70	4	5	7	.417	0	14.4	5.09
Sauerbeck,Scott	Cle	35		58	0	32	28	3	19	33	2	2	2	.500	0	13.9	4.16
Schilling,Curt	Bos	40	high	31	31	190	179	22	35	193	3	14	7	.667	0	10.3	3.31
Schmidt,Jason	SF	33	high	28	28	164	139	14	63	158	4	11	7	.611	0	11.3	3.32
Schoeneweis,Scott	Tor	33	high	72	0	50	53	5	20	30	2	2	3	.400	0	13.6	4.58
Seanez,Rudy	SD	38	high	57	0	62	53	6	28	68	2	4	3	.571	0	12.0	3.62
Seo,Jae	NYM	29	med	24	24	154	166	18	42	92	3	9	9	.500	0	12.3	4.12
Sheets,Ben	Mil	28	high	34	34	224	218	26	47	192	5	15	10	.600	0	10.9	3.54
Sherrill,George	Sea	29	low	55	0	34	30	4	9	34	1	2	1	.667	0	10.8	3.36
Shields,Scot	LAA	31	low	76	0	85	73	6	31	76	2	6	3	.667	2	11.3	3.24
Shouse,Brian	Tex	38	med	65	0	52	53	4	18	36	3	3	3	.500	0	12.7	3.94
Silva,Carlos	Min	27	med	26	26	170	195	19	27	70	6	9	10	.474	0	12.0	4.11
Small,Aaron	NYY	35	low	26	15	132	169	15	34	67	4	6	8	.429	0	14.1	5.24
Smoltz,John	Atl	39	med	32	32	216	191	16	48	190	1	18	6	.750	0	10.0	2.96
Snell,Ian	Pit	25	low	34	17	121	119	14	34	94	3	7	6	.538	0	11.6	3.76
Snyder,Kyle	KC	29		14	3	39	47	4	11	19	1	2	3	.400	0	13.9	4.87
Sosa,Jorge	Atl	29	med	32	30	185	182	23	92	121	3	10	11	.476	0	13.5	4.49
Speier,Justin	Tor	33	med	66	0	69	61	10	22	57	5	4	4	.500	0	11.4	3.73
Speier,Ryan	Col	27		29	0	38	42	2	16	27	3	2	2	.500	0	14.5	4.59
Springer,Russ	Hou	38	high	62	0	62	59	10	27	54	3	3	4	.429	0	12.9	4.52
Spurling,Chris	Det	29		70	0	85	85	10	26	36	3	5	4	.556	0	12.1	3.91
Stanton,Mike	Bos	39	med	66	0	59	57	5	22	46	1	4	3	.571	0	12.3	3.74
Stauffer,Tim	SD	24		8	7	40	46	4	12	25	2	2	3	.400	0	13.5	4.71
Sturtze,Tanyon	NYY	36	low	66	0	71	76	9	28	43	4	4	4	.500	0	13.7	4.77
Suppan,Jeff	StL	31	high	32	32	203	215	27	66	113	8	11	11	.500	0	12.8	4.40
Takatsu,Shingo	NYM	38	low	34	0	30	26	5	13	27	1	2	2	.500	0	11.7	3.95
Taschner,Jack	SF	28		34	0	32	34	3	16	23	1	1	2	.333	0	14.4	4.81
Tavarez,Julian	StL	33	low	76	0	61	63	4	24	35	5	4	3	.571	7	13.7	4.18
Tejeda,Robinson	Phi	24		25	14	89	85	12	43	72	6	5	5	.500	0	13.5	4.51
Thomson,John	Atl	33	high	22	22	122	132	14	34	77	3	7	6	.538	0	12.4	4.15
Thornton,Matt	Sea	30	low	56	0	56	56	6	41	46	2	2	4	.333	0	15.9	5.39
Timlin,Mike	Bos	40	low	76	0	74	73	7	18	52	4	5	3	.625	4	11.5	3.63
Tomko,Brett	SF	33	med	33	30	188	203	25	60	114	4	10	11	.476	0	12.7	4.42
Torres,Salomon	Pit	34	low	79	0	90	87	9	30	56	5	5	5	.500	2	12.2	3.82
Towers,Josh	Tor	29	med	34	34	235	276	33	36	118	9	11	15	.423	0	12.3	4.46

2006 Pitcher Projections

Pitcher	Team	Age	Inj	G	GS	IP	H	HR	BB	SO	HB	W	L	Pct	Sv	BR/9	ERA
Trachsel,Steve	NYM	36	med	32	32	199	201	26	71	124	4	11	11	.500	0	12.5	4.15
Turnbow,Derrick	Mil	28	med	70	0	68	65	5	33	55	2	4	4	.500	42	13.2	3.98
Urbina,Ugueth	Phi	32	med	88	0	84	62	10	38	99	1	7	3	.700	0	10.8	3.25
Valdez,Ismael	Fla	33	high	25	12	94	107	15	29	50	4	5	6	.455	0	13.3	5.01
Valverde,Jose	Ari	27	high	66	0	73	54	8	29	91	2	5	3	.625	37	10.6	3.13
Vargas,Claudio	Ari	28	high	29	28	170	179	32	70	115	10	7	12	.368	0	13.7	5.18
Vazquez,Javier	Ari	30	med	33	33	211	209	29	55	182	6	12	11	.522	0	13.7	3.85
Villone,Ron	Fla	36	low	80	0	68	65	7	34	52	5	4	4	.500	0	13.7	4.40
Vizcaino,Luis	CWS	32	low	66	0	64	59	10	25	53	2	3	4	.429	0	12.1	4.04
Vogelsong,Ryan	Pit	29	med	49	0	87	95	9	40	62	6	4	6	.400	0	14.6	5.05
Waechter,Doug	TB	25	med	31	29	174	197	32	51	98	5	7	12	.368	0	13.1	5.05
Wagner,Billy	Phi	35	high	78	0	80	52	7	23	98	3	6	3	.667	42	8.8	2.47
Wakefield,Tim	Bos	40	med	34	34	241	232	32	86	173	15	14	13	.519	0	12.8	4.11
Walker,Jamie	Det	35	low	66	0	44	43	6	10	33	2	3	2	.600	0	11.3	3.75
Walker,Pete	Tor	37		44	2	70	72	10	27	37	2	3	5	.375	0	13.0	4.50
Walker,Tyler	SF	30	med	64	0	55	62	7	22	42	2	2	4	.333	5	14.1	5.05
Wang,Chien-Ming	NYY	26		32	32	209	238	16	52	116	8	13	11	.542	0	12.8	4.16
Wasdin,John	Tex	34	low	42	6	92	108	13	25	64	2	4	6	.400	1	13.2	4.88
Washburn,Jarrod	LAA	32	high	30	30	183	183	24	54	108	7	10	10	.500	0	12.0	3.96
Weathers,David	Cin	37	low	72	0	76	74	7	31	59	3	4	4	.500	3	12.9	4.05
Weaver,Jeff	LAD	30	med	35	35	239	250	27	63	159	17	13	14	.481	0	12.4	4.10
Webb,Brandon	Ari	27	med	33	33	234	219	19	88	190	9	14	12	.538	0	12.2	3.68
Wells,David	Bos	43	med	32	32	192	212	22	29	114	6	12	9	.571	0	11.5	3.88
Wells,Kip	Pit	29	med	33	33	170	171	20	79	125	8	8	11	.421	0	13.7	4.54
Westbrook,Jake	Cle	29	high	34	34	211	218	18	64	112	9	13	11	.542	0	12.4	3.91
Wheeler,Dan	Hou	29	low	73	0	75	74	9	24	63	2	4	4	.500	0	12.1	3.91
White,Rick	Pit	38	low	74	0	70	76	8	24	45	3	3	4	.429	0	13.2	4.53
Wickman,Bob	Cle	37	high	66	0	64	62	6	24	52	2	4	3	.571	39	12.3	3.85
Williams,Dave	Pit	27	med	22	22	119	118	16	49	76	7	6	7	.462	0	13.2	4.46
Williams,Jerome	ChC	25	high	28	26	160	161	15	59	97	12	9	9	.500	0	13.1	4.14
Williams,Todd	Bal	35	low	78	0	76	82	4	22	33	4	4	4	.500	0	12.8	3.91
Williams,Woody	SD	40	high	30	30	167	169	21	51	114	6	9	10	.474	0	12.1	3.99
Willis,Dontrelle	Fla	24	high	35	35	248	237	18	69	189	8	18	10	.643	0	11.4	3.44
Wise,Matt	Mil	31	low	41	0	48	41	5	17	38	2	3	2	.600	2	11.2	3.40
Witasick,Jay	Oak	34	med	62	0	63	61	7	29	58	3	3	4	.429	0	13.4	4.31
Wolf,Randy	Phi	30	high	6	6	40	38	5	14	32	2	3	2	.600	0	12.2	3.98
Wood,Kerry	ChC	29	high	28	28	168	133	20	80	190	13	11	8	.579	0	12.1	3.66
Wood,Mike	KC	26	med	33	28	174	194	21	59	99	9	8	12	.400	0	13.5	4.73
Worrell,Tim	Ari	39	low	68	0	67	66	7	23	54	1	4	4	.500	0	12.2	3.88
Wright,Jamey	Col	32	high	38	24	166	194	22	83	96	12	6	12	.333	0	15.7	5.86
Wright,Jaret	NYY	31	high	20	20	98	107	10	48	73	4	5	6	.455	0	14.6	4.95
Wuertz,Mike	ChC	28	low	75	0	85	81	9	35	80	2	5	4	.556	0	12.5	3.96
Yan,Esteban	LAA	31	low	50	0	65	69	9	25	51	4	3	4	.429	0	13.5	4.78
Young,Chris	Tex	27	med	30	30	157	169	21	46	120	7	8	9	.471	0	12.7	4.40
Zambrano,Carlos	ChC	25	high	34	34	238	200	17	101	206	14	17	10	.630	0	11.9	3.41
Zambrano,Victor	NYM	31	high	34	26	158	147	15	87	116	15	8	9	.471	0	14.2	4.46
Zito,Barry	Oak	28	med	35	35	226	194	24	86	172	10	15	10	.600	0	11.5	3.50

Injury Projections

"The effects of karma are inevitable and we must eventually undergo their effects."
-Dalai Lama

I have to thank the *Handbook* reader who shared with me the dangers of injury projections. I was emailed a link to a Buddhist text describing the 10 negative actions of body, speech and mind that generate bad karma. The 10th and final one is "wishing harm on others." Admittedly, I was wishing harm on others this past year. With *The Bill James Handbook* publishing my projections, I was indeed wishing for a Randy Wolf elbow injury and an Eddie Perez or a Wade Miller shoulder injury. I was hoping that Javy Lopez would break a finger and that Frank Thomas would hurt his ankle. Further, I learned that this behavior was guaranteed to increase my chances of being reborn in "one of the three lower realms." Really, I had no idea.

Undeterred, I am publishing my selections again.

Compared to the "success" of the 2004 injury projections, the 2005 prognostications were a disappointment. An early indication of my karma problems? I successfully predicted 8 major injuries this past year, while the 2004 numbers came in with 16 "hits." While this was disappointing, it is not hugely concerning. Over the years, the top 10 lists generate about 12 hits a year. 16 in 2004 and then 8 in 2005 isn't too far off that average.

The injury projections were created through an analysis of a database put together by David Neft and published in his The *Sports Encyclopedia: Baseball*. The good news about this database is that it covers a time span much longer than any other injury database that I have seen (I only use the more recent 35 years of injury data). The bad news is that the resolution of the "ruler" used to measure the injuries is not ideal. Injuries are categorized only if they cause the player to miss 30 consecutive days of work. This is unsatisfying at times. For instance, Griffey missed the last 28 days this season because of his injury, and Santiago was out for 23 days before he was released. Neither of these is categorized as a Neft injury. Despite these shortcomings, there is still much that can be teased out of the data. For instance, one can begin to understand how age, body-mass-index, past injuries, defensive position, career games, and high pitch outings all effect (or don't effect) the likelihood of impending injuries. Karma concerns aside, this is exactly what I have done with the database. Below are my 2006 projections of the various Neft injury categories.

Sig Mejdal (sig@baseballinfosolutions.com)
October, 2005

Hitter Injury Chances

Any Injury	chances	Back Injury	chances
Griffey Jr.,Ken	.382	Rodriguez,Ivan	.103
Jordan,Brian	.373	Sweeney,Mike	.093
Floyd,Cliff	.364	Catalanotto,Frank	.073
Sheffield,Gary	.362	Sosa,Sammy	.061
White,Rondell	.358	Anderson,Garret	.056
Sosa,Sammy	.356	Guerrero,Vladimir	.054
Sanders,Reggie	.333	Bell,David	.053
Valentin,Jose	.326	Nixon,Trot	.051
Alomar Jr.,Sandy	.317	Gonzalez,Juan	.051
Jenkins,Geoff	.314	Johnson,Nick	.048

Knee Injury	chances	Broken Finger	chances
Alomar Jr.,Sandy	.147	Rodriguez,Ivan	.033
Vizquel,Omar	.134	Matos,Luis	.028
Jordan,Brian	.109	Piazza,Mike	.027
Valentin,Jose	.108	Kendall,Jason	.027
Cordero,Wil	.096	Ausmus,Brad	.026
Matsui,Hideki	.092	Koskie,Corey	.026
Walker,Todd	.089	Holliday,Matt	.024
Williams,Bernie	.088	Branyan,Russell	.024
Berkman,Lance	.087	Lopez,Javy	.023
Palmeiro,Rafael	.087	Podsednik,Scott	.022

Leg Injury	chances	Ankle Injury	chances
Gonzalez,Juan	.111	Jenkins,Geoff	.024
Jordan,Brian	.098	Thomas,Frank	.021
White,Rondell	.089	Floyd,Cliff	.021
Grissom,Marquis	.089	Giles,Marcus	.020
Floyd,Cliff	.089	Spivey,Junior	.020
Griffey Jr.,Ken	.087	Griffey Jr.,Ken	.020
Conine,Jeff	.083	Sanders,Reggie	.019
Sheffield,Gary	.082	Dunn,Adam	.019
Sierra,Ruben	.081	Dellucci,David	.018
Alfonzo,Edgardo	.080	Cruz,Jose	.018

Shoulder Injury	chances	Elbow Injury	chances
Gonzalez,Alex	.079	Perez,Eddie	.032
Burroughs,Sean	.064	Rodriguez,Ivan	.030
Glaus,Troy	.063	Myers,Greg	.029
Everett,Carl	.062	Piazza,Mike	.028
Spivey,Junior	.059	Ausmus,Brad	.027
Sexson,Richie	.056	Stinnett,Kelly	.025
Griffey Jr.,Ken	.056	Alomar Jr.,Sandy	.025
White,Rondell	.056	Young,Eric	.025
LaRoche,Adam	.051	Cash,Kevin	.024
Bay,Jason	.049	Quinlan,Robb	.024

Pitcher Injury Chances

Any Injury chances		**Elbow Injury**	chances
Wood,Kerry	.363	Wolf,Randy	.151
Hernandez,Orlando	.343	Soriano,Rafael	.141
Miller,Wade	.336	Dempster,Ryan	.140
Pavano,Carl	.333	Escobar,Kelvim	.134
Wright,Jaret	.324	Burnett,A.J.	.132
Villarreal,Oscar	.304	Vargas,Claudio	.130
Wolf,Randy	.287	Mota,Guillermo	.125
Mantei,Matt	.283	Parrish,John	.118
Seanez,Rudy	.270	Wickman,Bob	.117
Penny,Brad	.268	Kensing,Logan	.117

Note: "Any" pitching injury is an elbow, shoulder or arm injury

Shoulder Injury	chances	**Arm Injury**	chances
Miller,Wade	.258	Witasick,Jay	.063
Hernandez,Orlando	.235	Valverde,Jose	.040
Wood,Kerry	.204	Eldred,Cal	.039
Wright,Jaret	.201	Miller,Matt	.033
Hernandez,Livan	.178	Dickey,R.A.	.031
Wagner,Ryan	.177	Lilly,Ted	.030
Pavano,Carl	.177	Nelson,Jeff	.029
Villarreal,Oscar	.177	Brown,Kevin	.028
Tsao,Chin-hui	.176	Pavano,Carl	.027
Rauch,Jon	.175	Pettitte,Andy	.026

Note: Pitching injury projections exclude pitchers 30 years or older who pitched 25 innings or less in 2005.

Sig Mejdal (sig@baseballinfosolutions.com)
San Francisco, California
October 9, 2005

Career Assessments

This section is designed to give probabilities on players achieving important career milestones. The method was developed by Bill James (formerly under the name of "The Favorite Toy") and takes into account a player's age and performance level in predicting the possibility that he will accumulate certain career stats. A detailed explanation of how the system works can be found in the glossary.

The 2005 season was quite slow in terms of milestone accomplishments with only a controversial 3,000th hit from Rafael Palmeiro making the list. The much anticipated chase for Hank Aaron's record 755 Home Runs was put on hold as Barry Bonds struggled to rehab a knee injury all season long. Bonds should resume his march toward the Home Run record in 2006 – with some controversy of his own.

Other than the run toward Aaron's record, 2006 looks like it will also be a slow year for milestone achievements. However, 2007 is shaping up to be an interesting year for milestone watchers with Alex Rodriguez, Gary Sheffield and Manny Ramirez all pushing closer to 500 Home Runs. In addition, Craig Biggio looks like he will be the next member of the 3,000 hit club. He currently has a 71% chance of reaching the plateau.

Career Assessments

Player	Age	HOME RUN GOALS						HIT GOALS				RBI GOALS		
		Current	500	600	700	756	800	Current	3000	4000	4257	Current	2000	2298
Barry Bonds	40	708	4/17/01	8/9/02	9/17/04	28%		2742				1853	5%	
Sammy Sosa	36	588	4/4/03	99%	18%			2304				1575		
Ken Griffey Jr.	35	536	6/20/04	93%	6%			2304	6%			1536	3%	
Rafael Palmeiro	40	569	5/11/03	61%				3020	7/15/05			1835	21%	
Gary Sheffield	36	449	96%	21%				2345	29%			1476	21%	
Manny Ramirez	33	435	96%	67%	23%	10%	3%	1922	21%			1414	52%	18%
Alex Rodriguez	29	429	95%	89%	55%	37%	27%	1901	59%	7%	1%	1226	51%	23%
Jim Thome	34	430	92%	10%				1665				1193		
Andruw Jones	28	301	86%	46%	22%	13%	8%	1408	18%			894	22%	7%
Albert Pujols	25	201	72%	42%	23%	16%	11%	982	33%	6%	1%	621	24%	11%
Carlos Delgado	33	369	67%	17%				1570				1173	12%	
Vladimir Guerrero	29	305	61%	23%	5%			1586	29%			936	17%	2%
Adam Dunn	25	158	49%	27%	12%	7%	3%	564				374		
Frank Thomas	37	448	41%					2136				1465		
Derrek Lee	29	208	36%	14%	1%			1127	12%			626		
David Ortiz	29	177	35%	15%	3%			877	2%			626	15%	3%
Jeff Bagwell	37	449	33%					2314				1529		
Mark Teixeira	25	107	33%	16%	5%	0%		484	8%			340	13%	4%
Paul Konerko	29	210	32%	11%				1115	2%			692		
Jim Edmonds	35	331	22%					1619				998		
Adrian Beltre	26	166	20%	4%				1103	20%			597	5%	
Aramis Ramirez	27	158	20%	4%				916	6%			550	1%	
Miguel Cabrera	22	78	20%	7%				459	18%			290	12%	3%
Troy Glaus	28	219	19%	1%				887				612		
Richie Sexson	30	239	19%					979				737		
Eric Chavez	27	190	18%	1%				1026	9%			644	1%	
Chipper Jones	33	331	17%					1811				1111		
Miguel Tejada	29	216	16%					1370	28%			852	16%	2%
Carlos Lee	29	184	15%					1121	10%			666	3%	
Alfonso Soriano	29	162	15%					912	5%			465		
Todd Helton	31	271	13%					1535	17%			915		
Hank Blalock	24	89	11%					543	13%			309	2%	
Shawn Green	32	303	10%					1726	14%			958		
Jason Giambi	34	313	7%					1526				1031		
Pat Burrell	28	159	6%					792				549		
Vernon Wells	26	109	6%					748	10%			395		
Lance Berkman	29	180	3%					951				617		
Carlos Beltran	28	162	2%					1140	9%			647		
Craig Biggio	39	260						2795	71%			1063		
Derek Jeter	31	169						1936	48%	1%		763		
Johnny Damon	31	130						1789	36%			700		
Edgar Renteria	29	91						1595	31%			635		
Juan Pierre	27	9						1040	26%	0%		247		
Carl Crawford	23	33						623	25%	3%		220		
Jimmy Rollins	26	59						904	22%			308		
Michael Young	28	80						887	22%			373		
Garret Anderson	33	224						1929	17%			1043		
Ichiro Suzuki	31	52						1130	16%			310		
Rafael Furcal	27	57						924	12%			292		
Mark Kotsay	29	95						1231	11%			481		
Bobby Abreu	31	190						1432	10%			776		
Ivan Rodriguez	33	264						2190	10%			1050		
Sean Casey	30	118						1225	8%			605		
Luis Castillo	29	20						1273	7%			271		
Jack Wilson	27	35						715	5%			245		
Jose Reyes	22	14						330	3%			104		
Aubrey Huff	28	120						805	3%			421		
Coco Crisp	25	35						467	2%			176		
Randy Winn	31	69						1058	2%			401		
Darin Erstad	31	114						1484	2%			620		
Jose Guillen	29	134						1006	2%			534		
Brian Roberts	27	30						573	2%			195		
Cesar Izturis	25	10						585	1%			173		

300-Win Candidates

Bill James

Almost ten years ago, I developed a system to estimate the chance that a given pitcher will win 300 games in his career. I have never explained this system anywhere, and, for reasons of space, I'm not going to explain it here, either. But I will say:

1) That it is not really an outgrowth of or similar to The Favorite Toy.

2) Each pitcher's chance of winning 300 games is based on two numbers: how many years the pitcher is away from 300 wins, and the per-season chance that he will continue to move forward.

If a pitcher is four years away from 300 wins and his per-season chance of continuing to move forward is 75%, his chance of winning 300 games would be .75 to the fourth power. Which would be 32%.

In the process of doing this, we look at a fairly wide range of material—the pitcher's age, his strikeout rate, his ERA, the consistency with which he has pitched 200 innings a year, etc. The process is complicated, and I don't know if this would be the right place to explain it even if we had the space, which we clearly don't. But the chart (below) estimates the 300-win chances for all active pitchers who have some reasonable chance to win 300 games.

Name	2005 Age	R/L	W	L	EWL	Momentum	Chance
Clemens, Roger	42	R	341	172	13.4	0.744	1.00
Maddux, Greg	39	R	318	189	12.2	0.782	1.00
Johnson, Randy	41	L	263	136	15.4	0.811	0.61
Glavine, Tom	39	L	275	184	10.7	0.711	0.45
Martinez, Pedro	33	R	197	84	14.7	0.853	0.33
Colon, Bartolo	32	R	139	82	16.6	0.829	0.16
Buehrle, Mark	26	L	85	53	13.9	0.873	0.12
Oswalt, Roy	27	R	83	39	16.7	0.840	0.10
Wells, David	42	L	227	143	12.1	0.685	0.10
Mussina, Mike	36	R	224	127	11.9	0.682	0.09
Hernandez, Livan	30	R	110	104	12.4	0.851	0.09
Moyer, Jamie	42	L	205	152	10.4	0.739	0.06
Pettitte, Andy	33	L	172	91	13.5	0.744	0.06
Zito, Barry	27	L	86	53	12.9	0.839	0.05
Rogers, Kenny	40	L	190	131	11.7	0.704	0.04
Vazquez, Javier	28	R	89	93	11.8	0.821	0.03
Garcia, Freddy	29	R	99	62	12.3	0.796	0.02
Wakefield, Tim	38	R	144	123	12.9	0.728	0.02
Mulder, Mark	27	L	97	50	13.3	0.758	0.01
Carpenter, Chris	30	R	85	60	16.0	0.727	0.01
Smoltz, John	38	R	177	128	9.9	0.704	0.01
Loaiza, Esteban	33	R	112	99	11.6	0.746	0.01
Weaver, Jeff	28	R	78	87	12.0	0.773	0.01
Lowe, Derek	32	R	84	74	12.0	0.764	0.01
Lieber, Jon	35	R	117	104	12.8	0.672	0.00
Radke, Brad	32	R	136	130	8.9	0.727	0.00
Leiter, Al	39	L	162	132	7.7	0.607	0.00

Note: EWL = Expected Win Level

Baseball Glossary

% Inherited Scored
The percentage of inherited baserunners a relief pitcher allows to score.

% Pitches Taken
The percentage of pitches that a batter does not swing at out of the total number of pitches thrown to him.

1st Batter Average
The Batting Average that a relief pitcher allows to the first batter he faces when he enters a game.

1st Batter OBP
The On-Base Percentage that a relief pitcher allows to the first batter he faces when he enters a game.

Active Career Batting Leaders
A list of batting leaders among active (appearing in the most recent season) players. An active player is eligible when he meets the minimum requirements for the following categories:

1,000 At Bats—Batting Average, On-Base Percentage, Slugging Average, At Bats Per HR, At Bats Per GDP, At Bats Per RBI, Strikeout to Walk Ratio
100 Stolen Base Attempts—Stolen Base Success Percentage

Active Career Pitching Leaders
A list of pitching leaders among active (appearing in the most recent season) players. An active player is eligible when he meets the minimum requirements for the following categories:

750 Innings Pitched—Earned Run Average, Opponent Batting Average, all "Per 9 Innings" categories, Strikeout to Walk Ratio
250 Games Started—Complete Game Frequency
100 Decisions—Win-Loss Percentage

AVG Allowed ScPos
The Batting Average allowed by a pitcher while pitching with runners in scoring position.

AVG Bases Loaded
The Batting Average of a hitter while batting with the bases loaded.

Batting Average
Hits divided by at bats.

Blown Save
When a relief pitcher enters a game in a Save Situation (see definition for Save Situation) and allows the other team to score the tying or go-ahead run.

Career Assessments
This method, once called the Favorite Toy, is a way to estimate the probability that a player will achieve a specific career goal. In this example, 3,000 hits will be used. The four components of the formula are Needed Hits, Years Remaining, Established Hit Level and Projected Remaining Hits.

Needed Hits. This is the number of Hits (or any statistic) that a player needs to reach a desired goal.

Years Remaining. This is the estimated number of years remaining in the player's career. It is determined using the player's age (on June 30th of the previous year; use 2003 when making the calculation after the 2003 season is complete). The formula is (42 - age) divided by two. This means a player who is 20 years old will have 11 remaining seasons, a player who is 25 years old will have 8.5 remaining seasons and a player who is 35 years old will have 3.5 remaining seasons. If the player is a catcher, then multiply his remaining seasons by .7. If a player is older than 39 (the Years Remaining calculation yields less than 1.5), consult the player's statistics for the most recent year. If the player either had 100 Hits or an Offensive Winning Percentage of .500 or greater, then the player will have 1.0 remaining seasons. If the player has both, he has 1.5 remaining seasons. If he has neither, he has .5 remaining seasons.

Established Hit Level. The Established Hit Level is a weighted average of the player's hits over the past three seasons. To calculate the Established Hit Level after the 2003 season is complete, add 2001 Hits, (2002 Hits multiplied by two) and (2003 Hits multiplied by three), then divide by six. If the Established Hit Level is less than 75% of the most recent performance (2003 Hits in this case), then the Established Hit Level is equal to .75 times the most recent performance.

Projected Remaining Hits. This is calculated by multiplying Years Remaining by the Established Hit Level.

The probability of achieving the specified goal is found by dividing Projected Remaining Hits by Need Hits, then subtracting .5. The maximum chance that any player has of achieving a goal is .97 raised to the power of (Need Hits / Established Hit Level). This prevents the possibility of a player reaching a goal from being higher than 100 percent, which is impossible.

Catcher's ERA
The ERA for a catcher is equal to the ERA of pitchers pitching while the catcher is playing behind the plate. It is calculated exactly like ERA for pitchers. Take the number of earned runs allowed while the catcher is playing, multiply it by 9 and then divide it by the total number of defensive innings that the catcher was behind the plate.

Cheap Win

A starting pitcher who wins the game with a game score under 50 gets credit for a cheap win. See Game Score.

Cleanup Slugging Average

The Slugging Average of a batter when he bats in the cleanup spot, or fourth, in the batting order.

Component ERA (ERC)

A statistic that estimates what a pitcher's ERA should have been, based on his pitching performance. The ERC formula is calculated as follows:

1. Subtract the pitcher's Home Runs Allowed from his Hits Allowed.
2. Multiply Step 1 by 1.255.
3. Multiply his Home Runs Allowed by four.
4. Add Steps 2 and 3 together.
5. Multiply Step 4 by .89.
6. Add his Walks and Hit Batsmen.
7. Multiply Step 6 by .475.
8. Add Steps 5 and 7 together.

This yields the pitcher's total base estimate (PTB), which is:

$$PTB = 0.89 \times (1.255 \times (H - HR) + 4 \times HR) + 0.475 \times (BB + HB)$$

For those pitchers for whom there is intentional walk data, use this formula instead:

$$PTB = 0.89 \times (1.255 \times (H - HR) + 4 \times HR) + 0.56 \times (BB + HB - IBB)$$

9. Add Hits and Walks and Hit Batsmen.
10. Multiply Step 9 by PTB.
11. Divide Step 10 by Batters Facing Pitcher. If BFP data is unavailable, approximate it by multiplying Innings Pitched by 2.9, then adding Step 9.
12. Multiply Step 11 by 9.
13. Divide Step 12 by Innings Pitched.
14. Subtract .56 from Step 13.

This is the pitcher's ERC, which is:

$$\frac{(H + BB + HB) \times PTB}{BFP \times IP} \times 9 - 0.56$$

If the result after Step 13 is less than 2.24, adjust the formula as follows:

$$\frac{(H + BB + HB) \times PTB}{BFP \times IP} \times 9 \times 0.75$$

Double Play %
Successful Double Plays divided by the number of Double Play opportunities. This statistic includes both the fielder who started the play and the pivot man.

Double Play Opportunity
A fielder is considered to have a double play opportunity when a ground ball is hit with a runner on first base and less than 2 outs and that fielder is involved in the play. This is used to calculate Double Play % and Pivot %.

Earned Run Average
The number of earned runs that a pitcher surrenders per nine innings that he pitches. It is calculated by multiplying the total earned runs allowed by nine and dividing by the total number of innings pitched.

Easy Save
This label is used to separate Saves by difficulty level (Easy or Tough). A Save is considered Easy if the relief pitcher enters the game, pitches one inning or less, and the first batter he faces does not at least represent the tying run.

Fielding Percentage
The percentage of plays a player makes in the field without making an error out of the total number of opportunities. It is calculated by adding (Putouts plus Assists) and dividing by (Putouts plus Assists plus Errors).

Games Finished
The relief pitcher who is in the game for each team when the game ends is credited with a Game Finished.

Game Score
To determine the starting pitcher's Game Score:
Start with 50.
Add 1 point for each out recorded by the starting pitcher.
Add 2 points for each inning the pitcher completes after the fourth inning.
Add 1 point for each strikeout.
Subtract 2 points for each hit allowed.
Subtract 4 points for each earned run allowed.
Subtract 2 points for an unearned run.
Subtract 1 point for each walk.

GDP
Grounded into Double Play

GDP Opportunity
This is a situation where the batter has a chance to ground into a double play. It occurs with at least a runner on first base and less than two outs.

Ground / Fly Ratio (Grd/Fly, GB/FB)

Calculated for both batters and pitchers. For batters, it is the number of groundballs hit divided by the number of flyballs hit. For pitchers, it is exactly the same but uses the number of groundballs and flyballs allowed. Every fair batted ball is included except for bunts and line drives.

Hold

A relief pitcher is given a Hold anytime he enters a game in a Save Situation (see definition for Save Situation), records one out or more, and exits the game without giving up the lead. If the pitcher finishes the game, then he will only earn credit for a Save. He cannot receive credit for both a Hold and a Save.

Holds Adjusted Saves Percentage

Holds plus Saves divided by Holds plus Saves Opportunities.

Inherited Runner

When a relief pitcher enters the game, any runner who is on base at the time is considered an Inherited Runner.

Isolated Power

Slugging Average minus Batting Average.

K/BB Ratio

Strikeouts divided by Walks.

Late & Close

A situation in a game that is very similar to a Save Situation. The following requirements are necessary for a Late & Close game:
1. The game is in the seventh inning or later AND
2. The batting team is either leading by one run or tied OR
3. The tying run is on base, at bat, or on deck.

Leadoff On-Base Percentage

The On-Base Percentage of a batter when he bats leadoff, or first, in the batting order.

Offensive Winning Percentage (OWP)

A player's Offensive Winning Percentage is the winning percentage of a hypothetical team which has an offense consisting of nine of that player, and pitching and defense which is average for the player's league. It is calculated by taking the square of RC/27 (see the definition for Runs Created per 27 Outs), dividing it by the sum of RC/27 and the square of the average runs scored per game in the league.

On-Base Percentage

(Hits plus Walks plus Hit by Pitcher) divided by (At Bats plus Walks plus Hit by Pitcher plus Sacrifice Flies).

$$\frac{H + BB + HBP}{AB + BB + HBP + SF}$$

Opponent Batting Average

Hits Allowed divided by (Batters Faced minus Walks minus Hit Batsmen minus Sacrifice Hits minus Sacrifice Flies minus Catcher's Interference).

$$\frac{H}{BFP - BB - HBP - SH - SF - CI}$$

PA*

Used in the denominator for the calculation of On-Base Percentage. It is calculated by subtracting (Sacrifice Hits plus Times Reached Base on Defensive Interference) from Plate Appearances (see definition for Plate Appearances).

Park Index

The Park Index of a given ballpark is the amount that the ballpark influences a given statistic. The following is a calculation of a park index using runs as the statistic:

1. Add Runs and Opponent Runs in home games.
2. Add At Bats and Opponent At Bats in home games. (If At Bats are unavailable, use home games.)
3. Divide Step 1 by Step 2.
4. Add Runs and Opponent Runs in road games.
5. Add At Bats and Opponent At Bats in road games. (If At Bats are unavailable, use road games.)
6. Divide Step 4 by Step 5.
7. Divide Step 3 by Step 6.
8. Multiply Step 7 by 100.

An index of 100 means the park is completely neutral and does not influence the particular statistic at all. A park index of 112 for runs indicates that teams score 12 percent more runs in this ballpark than a neutral park. A park index of 92 for runs means that teams tend to score 8 percent fewer runs in this ballpark than a neutral park.

PCS (Pitchers' Caught Stealing)

The number of runners officially scored as Caught Stealing where the pitcher initiated the play. The normal Caught Stealing is when a runner is out attempting to steal a base but the play was initiated by the catcher. PCS plays are often referred to as pickoffs, but differ when the runner breaks towards the next base as opposed to returning to the base he was currently on. Pickoffs occur when the pitcher throws to a base that a runner is leading from, and the runner is out attempting to return to that base. Pickoffs are not an official statistic.

Pitches per PA

The total number of pitches a hitter sees divided by his total Plate Appearances.

Pivot %

Successful Double Plays turned by pivot man divided by the number of Double Play opportunities with that pivot man involved.

Plate Appearances

At Bats plus Total Walks plus Hit By Pitcher plus Sacrifice Hits plus Sacrifice Flies plus Times Reached on Defensive Interference.

Power/Speed Number

A single number that reflects a combination of power and speed. To achieve a high Power/Speed Number, a player must score high in both power and speed. To calculate the Power/Speed Number, multiply Home Runs by Stolen Bases by two, and divide by the sum of Home Runs and Stolen Bases.

$$\frac{2 \times HR \times SB}{HR + SB}$$

PPO (Pitcher Pickoff)

The number of baserunners thrown out when a pitcher throws to a base with a leading baserunner, and the runner is tagged out attempting to return to the base. PPO is not an official statistic and does not count toward Caught Stealing totals.

Quality Start

A game where the starting pitcher pitches for at least six innings and allows no more than three earned runs.

Quality Start Percentage

Quality Starts divided by Games Started (see the definition for Quality Start).

Quick Hooks

Used in the Manager's Record. For Quick Hooks and Slow Hooks a score is calculated by adding the number of Pitches to 10 times the number of Runs Allowed for the starting pitcher. The bottom 25% of scores in the league are considered to be Quick Hooks.

Range Factor

The number of Successful Chances (Putouts plus Assists) times nine divided by the number of Defensive Innings Played. The average for a Regular Player at each position in 2005:
Second Base: 4.97
Third Base: 2.76
Shortstop: 4.55
Left Field: 2.02
Center Field: 2.59
Right Field: 2.11

Run Support Per 9 IP

The total number of runs scored by a pitcher's team while he is in the game multiplied by nine and divided by total Innings Pitched.

Runs Created

"Runs Created" is an estimate of the number of a team's runs which are created by each individual hitter. The Cincinnati Reds scored 820 runs last year, let us say. How many of those were created by Adam Dunn? How many by Ken Griffey Jr.? How many by Jason LaRue?

There are many different formulas for estimating runs created. . .did you want the one that involves swinging a dead cat in the cemetery under a full moon? Yeah, I don't blame you. . .worm-eaten persimmons are so hard to find in the modern world.

This is the one we use now; it is complicated enough. First, there is an "A" Factor in the formula, a "B" Factor, and a "C" factor. The "A" Factor, which represents the number of times the hitter is on base, is Hits, Plus Walks, Plus Hit Batsmen, Minus Caught Stealing, Minus Grounded Into Double Play. The "B" Factor, which represents the hitter's ability to advance other runners, is 1.125 times the player's Singles, plus 1.69 times his Doubles, plus 3.02 times his Triples, plus 3.73 times his Home Runs, plus .29 times his Walks and Hit Batsmen, not counting intentional walks, plus .492 times Sacrifice Hits, Sacrifice Flies and Stolen Bases, minus .04 times Strikeouts. The "C" Factor, which represents opportunities, is At Bats, Plus Walks, Plus Hit By Pitch, Plus Sacrifice Hits, Plus Sacrifice Flies.

Having made these initial calculations of the A, B and C factors, we then change the "A" factor to "A plus 2.4 times C".

We change the "B" factor to "B plus 3 times C".

We chance the "C" factor to "9 times C".

Multiply A times B, divide by C, and subtract .90 times C.

This is our first, temporary estimate of the player's runs created. We what we have done here is to ask these questions:
    1. How many runs would a team probably score that consisted of eight "ordinary" type of hitters, plus this particular hitter?
    2. How many of those runs would be created by the eight ordinary type of hitters?
    3. What is the difference-and thus, how many runs did our player create?

To estimate this, we have placed our player in the context of eight hitters with a .300 on base percentage (2.4 divided by 8) and a .375 advancement percentage (3 divided by 8). For each trip through the batting order, the eight ordinary-type hitters would produce 9/10 of a run (2.4 times 3, divided by 8). The "9" in the denominator is eight ordinary hitters plus our man. The "-.9" being subtracted at the end is the runs created by the "ordinary" hitters. In essence, we have placed the hitter in a neutral solution, measured the neutral solution without our hitter, measured it with our hitter, and then estimated the contribution of this hitter as being the difference between the two.

We're not quite done. After that, we adjust the player's runs created estimate for his performance in two "run-sensitive" situations. Suppose that a player whose overall batting average is .250 has batted 100 times with runners in scoring position, and has gone 30-for-100. That's five hits better than expected, 30 hits where we would have expected 25. His team will score an extra five runs because he has done that, and so we increase the player's runs created estimate by five runs. If the player has hit poorly with runners in scoring position, we decrease it by the shortfall in the same way.

Suppose that a player has batted 250 times with runners on base, 250 times with the bases empty, and that he has hit 20 home runs overall. We would expect him to have hit 10 with men on base, 10 with the bases empty, right?

Suppose that he didn't. Suppose that he hit 12 with the bases empty, 8 with men on base. His team would score two runs less than expected because he did this, and we would thus penalize him two runs for the shortfall.
This is our second runs created estimate-the player's runs created, adjusted for his batting performance in run-sensitive situations.

Suppose, however, that we figure the runs created for all of the individuals on a team, and we add them up, and it doesn't match the runs actually scored by the team? What if the formulas say that the team should have scored 800 runs, but they actually scored 820?

Then obviously, the formulas missed. We're trying to measure the runs ACTUALLY created by each hitter as best we can, in the real world, not the theoretical impact of some combination of singles, doubles, triples and walks. If the actual number is different than the estimates, we have to adjust the estimates to fit the facts. In this case-820 runs scored with only 800 runs created-we would multiply each runs created estimate by 820/800, or 1.025. Then we round it off to an integer, and that's the player's estimated runs created.

Let go of that cat, Arthur. Heck, the moon isn't full for three weeks, anyway.

Runs Created per 27 Outs (RC/27)
This statistic estimates the number of runs per game that a team made up of nine of the same player would score. To calculate RC/27, multiply Runs Created by league outs per team game, divide the result by outs made by the player (the sum of at bats plus sacrifice hits plus sacrifice flies plus caught stealing plus grounded into double plays, minus hits). The formula written out is:

$$\frac{\frac{RC \times 3 \times LgIP}{2 \times LgG}}{AB - H + SH + SF + CS + GDP}$$

Save Percentage
A pitcher's Saves divided by the total number of Save Situations he faces (see definition for Save Situation).

Save Situation

A relief pitcher is in a Save Situation when he enters the game with his team in the lead, has the opportunity to finish the game, is not the winning pitcher of record at the time, and meets any one of the three following conditions:

   1. The pitcher's team is leading by no more than three runs and the pitcher has the chance to pitch for at least one inning,
OR
   2. The pitcher enters the game with the potential tying run on base, at bat, or on deck,
OR
   3. The pitcher pitches three or more effective innings regardless of the lead. The determination of a save in this situation is made by the official scorer.

It is not possible to have more than one save credited to a single team in a game.

SB Success Percentage

Stolen Bases divided by the number of Stolen Base attempts (Stolen Bases plus Caught Stealing).

$$\frac{SB}{SB + CS}$$

Secondary Average

A number meant to reflect everything else except for batting average. A player will have a high Secondary Average if he hits for power, takes walks and steals bases. It is calculated with the following formula:

$$\frac{TB - H + BB + SB}{AB}$$

Similarity Score

A number which reflects the similarity between two different statistical lines, either for a player or for a team. A score of 1,000 means that the statistical lines are identical.

Slow Hooks

Used in the Manager's Record. For Quick Hooks and Slow Hooks a score is calculated by adding the number of Pitches to 10 times the number of Runs Allowed. The top 25% of scores in the league are considered to be Slow Hooks.

Slugging Average

Total Bases divided by At Bats.

$$\frac{TB}{AB}$$

Speed Score

Speed Score is a number which evaluates how fast a player is. To calculate the Speed Score, start with the player's statistics over the last two seasons combined. A value will be found for each of the following six categories and will be combined for a final score at the end:

1. Stolen Base Percentage. The value of this category is:

$$\left(\frac{SB + 3}{SB + CS + 7} - 0.4 \right) \times 20$$

2. Frequency of Stolen Base Attempts. The value of this category is:

$$\frac{\sqrt{\dfrac{SB + CS}{Singles + BB + HBP}}}{0.07}$$

3. Percentage of Triples. This is calculated by taking the percentage of triples out of the number of balls put in play. To get the percentage, use this formula:

$$\frac{3B}{AB - HR - SO}$$

From this assign an integer from 0 to 10, based on the following chart:

Less than .001	0
.001 - .0023	1
.0023 - .0039	2
.0039 - .0058	3
.0058 - .0080	4
.0080 - .0105	5
.0105 - .013	6
.013 - .0158	7
.0158 - .0189	8
.0189 - .0223	9
.0223 or more	10

4. Runs Scored Percentage. This is calculated by taking the percentage of times the player scores a run out of the number of times the player is on base. To get the percentage, use this formula:

$$\frac{\left(\dfrac{R - HR}{H + HBP + BB - HR} - 0.1 \right)}{0.04}$$

5. Grounded Into Double Play Frequency. To get the frequency, use this formula:

$$\frac{0.055 - \left(\dfrac{GIDP}{AB - HR - SO} \right)}{0.005}$$

6. Range Factor. The value of this category depends on the players position:

Catcher—1
First Baseman—2
Designated Hitter—1.5
Second Baseman—1.25 x Range Factor
Third Baseman—1.51 x Range Factor
Shortstop—1.52 x Range Factor
Outfield—3 x Range Factor

For an explanation on Range Factor, consult the definition in this glossary. Remember to figure range factors over a two-year period.

If any category value is greater than 10, then reduce it to 10. If any value is less than zero, then increase the value to zero. All category values must fall within the zero to 10 range. The Speed Score is then calculated by discarding the lowest of the six values, and taking the average of the remaining five.

Total Bases
Hits plus Doubles plus (2 times Triples) plus (3 times Home Runs).

$$H + 2B + (2 \times 3B) + (3 \times HR)$$

Tough Loss
A starting pitcher who loses the game with a game score over 50 gets credit for a tough loss. See Game Score.

Tough Save
This label is used to separate Saves by difficulty level (Easy or Tough). A Save is considered Tough if the relief pitcher enters the game with the tying run on base.

Winning Percentage
Wins divided by (Wins plus Losses).

Baseball Info Solutions

With roots that run deep within the industry, BIS has been providing high quality, innovative baseball data to its customers for four straight seasons.

John Dewan, the principal owner of BIS, has been on the cutting edge of baseball analysis for over 20 years. His experience goes all the way back to his days as Executive Director of Project Scoresheet, the Bill James led effort that pioneered the new wave of baseball statistics that are now common baseball terminology.

President Steve Moyer brings almost 15 years of baseball industry experience to BIS. His hands-on, can-do business demeanor helps set BIS apart from its competition.

The rest of the BIS team includes former professional and collegiate baseball players as well as programming and database management experts. Over the last three seasons, BIS has more than tripled its full-time staff.

BIS collects a statistical snapshot of every important moment of every Major League Baseball game with the most advanced technology, resulting in a database that includes traditional data, pitch-by-pitch data, and spray-chart hit location data. The company also has the highest quality pitch charting data available anywhere, including pitch type, location, and velocity.

With a commitment to top-notch customer service BIS is equipped to meet the statistical needs of any customer. No request is too large or small, as BIS provides comprehensive service to eight MLB teams, as well as many sports agents, media, fantasy services, game companies, and private individuals.

BIS continues to grow within the industry while emphasizing personal attention to its customers.

Contact BIS today for your baseball data needs:

Baseball Info Solutions
528 North New Street
Bethlehem, PA 18018-5752
610-814-0108
www.baseballinfosolutions.com
info@baseballinfosolutions.com

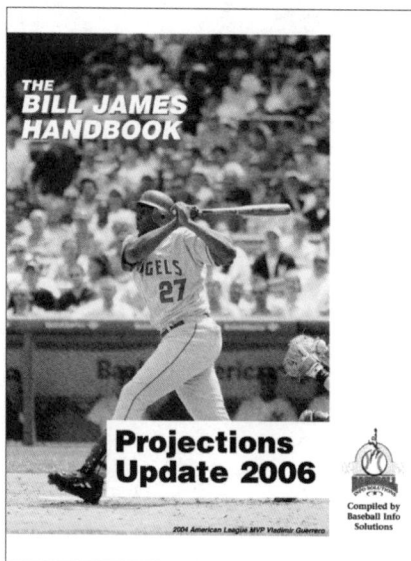

THE FIELDING BIBLE

JOHN DEWAN & BASEBALL INFO SOLUTIONS
Foreword by BILL JAMES

An exclusive insiders' guide, now available to the public for the first time ever!

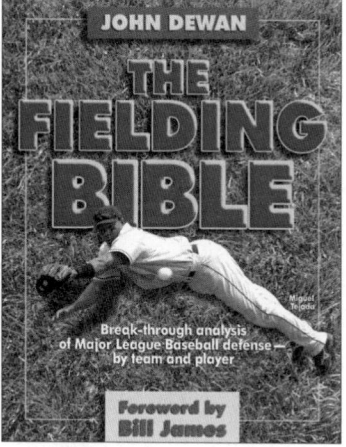

It's easy to understand why fans love big hitters like Barry Bonds and Albert Pujols. It's also relatively easy to measure their success as hitters. A comprehensive fielding analysis, by comparison, has never been available to the average fan. For the first time ever, that information is now contained in *The Fielding Bible* — the most comprehensive analysis of fielding statistics ever compiled for major league baseball players.

The Fielding Bible includes:

- <u>In-Depth Analysis by Position</u> – How do MLB players really stack up against each other defensively? A revolutionary new plus-minus system analyzes players position by position and provides top-to-bottom rankings.

The Fielding Bible also contains:

- <u>Where Hits Landed</u> – This allows a team to compare their defense point-by-point against other MLB teams.
- <u>Double Plays</u> – An analysis of double plays for every major league second baseman and shortstop, including double play percentage and pivot percentage.

JOHN DEWAN has consistently broken new ground in the area of sports statistical analysis, first as one of the founders and former CEO of STATS, Inc. and now as the owner of Baseball Info Solutions. He is also currently the co-publisher of ACTA Publications. As a noted sports expert, he is heard weekly on WSCR, "The Score," an all-sports radio station in Chicago, where he lives with his wife and two children.

BASEBALL INFO SOLUTIONS is an innovator in the collection, interpretation, commercialization and dissemination of in-depth baseball statistics.

BILL JAMES has been writing about baseball and compiling reference books about baseball since 1975. He is currently the Senior Baseball Operations Advisor for the Boston Red Sox.

224 pages, paperback
ISBN: 0-87946-297-3, $19.95

www.actasports.com

BEHIND-THE-SCENES BASEBALL
Real-Life Applications of Statistical Analysis
Actually Used by Major League Teams… and Other Stories
DOUG DECATUR

DOUG DECATUR lives in Williamsburg, Ohio, with his wife Caitlin and their two sons, Stephen and Joseph. Decatur has worked as a statistical consultant for the Cincinnati Reds, Milwaukee Brewers, Chicago Cubs, Manager Phil Garner of the Houston Astros, and player agent Myles Shoda. He has an MBA from Xavier University.

For the baseball fan wondering why, when and how analytical managers and GMs make key decisions in a game and over a season, this insider's book explains the practical applications of statistics in baseball. Written in three parts, *Behind-the-Scenes Baseball* begins with stories from Doug Decatur's long career as a statistical consultant. He details how teams have successfully used statistical analyses when building a team, making key decisions in a game, and preparing for the postseason. He also details the ignominious failures of teams that have ignored what the numbers have told them.

Part two is the GM IQ Test—what every major league manager and GM should know… but doesn't. Match your wits against some of the smartest baseball gurus out there. There's one manager who will be tough to beat — Houston Astros' manager Phil Garner only missed one question! Questions are multiple choice, true/false, and essay format.

The third part is a concise look at the Houston Astros 2004 run for the pennant, Decatur's relationship with Manager Phil Garner, and the Astro's amazing 36-10 run and their first-ever postseason series win.

While many baseball fans may have ambiguous feelings about the role statistical analysis plays in the game, this book shows how statistics and "sabermetrics" don't detract from the passion of the game, but rather contribute to an understanding of and love for baseball.

Sample GM IQ Test questions:

1) The correlation between winning a division title and leading the league in which category is the weakest:

    (A) home runs   (C) stolen bases

    (B) batting average   (D) walks

2) True or False — No team last in the league in walks has ever won a World Championship.

ANSWERS: 1) C; 2) True

www.actasports.com

256 pages, paperback

ISBN: 0-87946-300-7, $14.95

Other New Products from ACTA Sports

February 2006

THE BALLGAME OF LIFE

Lessons for Parents and Coaches of Young Baseball Players

DAVID ALLEN SMITH and JOSEPH AVERSA

Good coaches and good parents both try to teach kids the same things: persistence, hard work, how to handle pressure, and how to be a good winner. Baseball can help young players learn these lessons, but only if the coaches and parents stay focused on them.

112 pages, paperback, $9.95

THE LIFE OF LOU GEHRIG

Told by a Fan

SARA KADEN BRUNSVOLD

A new biography of the great Yankees' first baseman that covers his life from start to finish, while always being careful to highlight the human stories from his life that fill in the gaps between the facts, such as his cures for hitting slumps, his favorite foods, and even his attempt at comedy.

288 pages, paperback, $14.95

February 2006

STRAT-O-MATIC FANATICS

The Unlikely Success Story of a Game That Became an American Passion

GLENN GUZZO

Available Now!

This is the true story behind the creation—and re-creation—of America's most popular sports board game ever: Strat-O-Matic. *Strat-O-Matic Fanatics* looks at the hobby from every angle: the personal demons that Hal Richman overcame to bring his dream to life, the crises that nearly engulfed the small company, and fascinating anecdotes from real players of the game.

320 pages, paperback, $14.95

DIAMOND PRESENCE

Twelve Stories of Finding God at the Old Ball Park

Edited by GREGORY F. AUGUSTINE PIERCE

Foreword by JOHN DEWAN

Available Now!

*There are two things that one can never say often enough: one, that the game exists only to be enjoyed; and two, that there is no limit to the number of ways that it can be enjoyed. **Diamond Presence** shines a light upon these two truths.*
– Bill James, author of the ***The Bill James Handbook***

A touching collection of twelve true, short stories in which the authors relate how they came to feel the presence of God while enjoying the great American pastime of baseball as players, coaches, parents, children or just plain fans.

176 pages, hardcover, $17.95